THE
PULPIT COMMENTARY

THE
PULPIT COMMENTARY

Edited by

H. D. M. Spence

and

Joseph S. Exell

———

Volume 1
GENESIS
EXODUS

Wm. B. Eerdmans Publishing Company, Grand Rapids, Michigan

THE PULPIT COMMENTARY

Edited by

H. D. M. Spence *and* Joseph S. Exell

This large-type edition republished
from new plates by

WM. B. EERDMANS PUBLISHING COMPANY
Grand Rapids, Michigan

ISBN 0-8028-8058

Reprinted, February 1980

PHOTOLITHOPRINTED BY EERDMANS PRINTING COMPANY
GRAND RAPIDS, MICHIGAN, UNITED STATES OF AMERICA

GENESIS

INTRODUCTIONS BY

F. W. FARRAR   H. COTTERILL

T. WHITELAW

EXPOSITION AND HOMILETICS BY

THOMAS WHITELAW

HOMILIES BY VARIOUS AUTHORS

J. F. MONTGOMERY   R. A. REDFORD

W. ROBERTS   F. HASTINGS

GENERAL INTRODUCTION

TO

THE OLD TESTAMENT

BY THE

REV. CANON F. W. FARRAR, D.D., F.R.S.

IT is clear that it would be impossible to use to any good purpose the small space at my command without the most rigid limitation of the object in view. If it were my duty to enter into the masses of literary and critical questions which affect the date and authorship, the unity and special difficulties, of the books of the Old Testament, it would require a much larger space to furnish an adequate introduction to any one of them. In these few pages it would, for instance, be difficult to treat fully of the single question which meets us as soon as we begin to study even the Book of Genesis, namely, what are the true inferences to be drawn from the use of the different names of God—now Jehovah, now Elohim, and now both together, or interchangeably—which we find in the first chapters of the Bible.[1] For the discussion of all such questions the reader must turn to the Introductions to the several books, or to other sources. My present task is directly limited by the character of this Commentary as essentially HOMILETIC. I am required to furnish some suggestions respecting the use to be made of the Old Testament, the methods to be followed, and the principles to be kept in view, in dealing with it for purposes of religious instruction.

Now exegesis is one thing, and pulpit exhortation is another. A man may be a most useful preacher—he may have great powers of oratory, and may be enabled to enforce many practical and religious lessons with fervour and acceptance—without any pretence to the learning which is essential to a profound and thorough knowledge of Scripture. And such men are sometimes misled into the supposition that they can speak with authority on the meaning and interpretation of particular passages. The supposition is entirely baseless. Any man may gather for his own use, and that of others, the manna which lies everywhere upon the surface of the ground; but no man can without labour become master of all the hidden treasures which lie beneath. Holy Scripture contains all things necessary to salvation. A Christian child, an ignorant peasant, may have a deeper and more spiritual appreciation of all that is most necessary for the inner life of the regenerate soul than is possessed by the greatest master in Israel. But this saving knowledge, though infinitely more

---

[1] Jehovah, for instance, occurs in twelve consecutive passages in Gen. i.—ix., and Elohim in fifteen consecutive passages. For a brief examination of the subject, see 'Quarry on Genesis,' *passim*, and the 'Speaker's Commentary,' i. pp. 21—30.

important than any other kind of knowledge, does not entitle any one to an opinion of the smallest value on the removal of exegetical difficulties, or on difficult and dubious questions of fact or doctrine. The remark of St. Jerome, that in his day there was no old woman so ignorant and so stupid as not to hold herself entitled to lay down the law on matters of theology, is true in this day; and it applies also to Biblical interpretation. But he who would aspire not only to found upon Scripture texts a moral and spiritual exhortation, but to ascertain and unfold the actual meaning of Scripture,—to decipher the oracles of God as the inspiring light gleams over the letters of the jewelled Urim,—must have at his command a multifarious knowledge. Without this he may be at home in the shallows which the child can ford, but not in the depths where the elephant must swim. Piety and charity are far more important than learning for the sympathetic appreciation of Divine revelation; and prayer is most important of all. Without these a man may know the Bible by heart, and yet possess no effectual, no spiritual knowledge of a single line; but even *with* these there are many passages which, without study and learning, can never be rightly understood. On such passages no unlearned and untrained person should profess the ability to form an opinion of any value. The discovery of the true meaning of many pages of Scripture, the power of looking at it in its right perspective, is only rendered possible by an acquaintance with the original languages, and with the historic and other conditions under which the Scriptures were written. But, in the last few years especially, the results of accumulated study on all questions connected with sacred literature have been placed within the reach of even the humblest students. To neglect these sources of information is inexcusable in any who really reverence the word of God. Without holiness and sincerity their thoughts on Scripture may be useless for the amelioration of mankind; but even if they possess these spiritual gifts, their teaching, not only on minor matters, but even in matters of extreme importance, will be liable (unless it be very humble and very careful) to be defaced by incessant errors of ignorant misinterpretation, which will be all the more dangerous in proportion as it is more dogmatic. The duty of study, in order to ascertain the true rendering and the original sense of Scripture, cannot be impressed too earnestly on all who are to profit by a Homiletic Commentary. It is study alone which has in any degree rescued the Bible from masses of untenable exegesis, traditionally repeated in dull *catenæ* and biassed commentaries. It is study alone which can keep alive and increase the light which has been kindled in recent years.

There are, says Coleridge, some truths so true that they lie in the lumber-room of the memory side by side with the most exploded errors. Now there are two considerations, which are often overlooked from their very obviousness, which are yet of primary importance to the understanding of Scripture. One is, that in reading the Old Testament we must always bear in mind that it is not a *single* book, but a *collection of books*, written by authors very differently situated during a period of nearly 1000 years; that in fact we are dealing not with a book, but with a library and a literature. The other is, that the divisions which we call texts and chapters are entirely modern. There are some readers who may perhaps regard these suggestions as almost impertinently superfluous; but they are made not only under the strong conviction that their steady realisation would save us from multitudes of difficulties, but also with the proof historically before us that it is the neglect of these very considerations which has caused many of the worst errors which the misuse and misinterpretation of Scripture has ever inflicted, and still continues to inflict, upon mankind.

I. In the first place, then, the Old Testament is not "a talisman sent straight down from heaven, equipollent in all its parts," but contains the remnants of a library, the inspired fragments of a national literature, preserved for us by God's providence out of much that has passed away. To see that this is the case we need go no further than the Bible itself, which quotes passages from many books now lost, and in some instances directly refers to them as authorities for the facts which it narrates.[1] But the extant books of Scripture, in which has been preserved all that is essential for the salvation and enlightenment of mankind, are the diversified record of a progressive revelation, which during 4000 years gave, first to mankind, and then to the chosen people—by slow degrees, and as they were able to bear it—a gradually clearer vision and insight into the eternal relations between God and man.[2]

a. The *diversity* of this record is a very important element. St. Paul calls special attention to it when he speaks of "the *manifold* wisdom" of God. The word which he uses is extremely picturesque; it is ἡ πολυποίκιλος σοφία—literally, "the *richly-variegated wisdom* of God."[3] The soul of man is as little capable of grasping abstract truth as the eye is capable of gazing on the sun. The sunlight gives its glory and beauty to the world by being reflected in a thousand different colours from the objects around us. And because we should be only wearied and dazzled by a continuance of the intolerable blaze of noon, God's care for us is shown by the manner in which the clouds and the sunset refresh us with the softer glow of reflected and refracted light. Indeed this light is never more beautiful than when its sevenfold perfection and colourless indifference is divided by falling showers, and flung in the colours of the rainbow upon the clouds. It is even so in the spiritual world. God is light. When that light passes in one direct, unbroken ray we have, in his Son, "the brightness of his glory, and the express image of his person; "[4] but even *this* revelation of the Father passes in part through the medium of human language, and so reaches us in sweet gradations, and softened by gracious shadows of mystery which only faith can pierce. Much more is this the case in the Old Testament revelation. According to the wise saying of the Rabbis—in which lies the germ of all right Biblical interpretation, and which, had it been duly attended to, might have saved the Rabbis themselves, as well as generations of Christians, from grievous mistakes—"*the Law speaks in the tongue of the sons of men.*" Scripture ought always to have been interpreted with direct primary reference to what must have been the original meaning and intention of those who wrote, and of those who received it. It *has* been for centuries interpreted with reference to dogmatic bias and traditional conceptions. Ignorance of the laws which govern all the highest utterances of human thought and passion; ignorance alike of the "syllogism of grammar" and of the "syllogism of emotion; " neglect of th original languages in which Scripture was written; neglect of the circumstances by which its writers were surrounded; neglect of it as a whole, and of its books as separate wholes, and even of the context which alone gives the due meaning to its isolated expressions—these, and many other forms of theological carelessness, have led sometimes to an unintelligent literalism, sometimes to a spiritualising extravagance, which, while it could not indeed wholly frustrate the purpose of God by robbing

---

[1] As, for instance, the Book of Jasher, Josh. x. 13 ; the Book of the Acts of Solomon, 1 Kings xi. 41 ; the Book of the Wars of the Lord, Numb. xxi. 14 ; and others, 1 Chron. xxix. 29 ; 2 Chron. ix. 29 ; xii. 15 ; xx. 34, &c.

[2] The very name Bible implies that it is a library, for it is derived from the plural Biblia, and means "the books." In Early English literature it is called Biblioþece, as being the great treasure-house of books. St. Jerome, following 2 Macc. ii. 13, speaks of the Bible as "the Sacred Library." It is said that the collective term Biblia is first found in the writings of St. Chrysostom.

[3] Ephes. iii. 10.   [4] Heb. i. 3.   Haupt on 1 John iv. 8.

mankind of the broad, main truths of his revelation, has yet inflicted a twofold injury. This injury consists partly in the perpetuation of the virulent prejudices and hard errors of a loveless religionism, partly in the reduction of large portions of the Bible to the condition of a seven-sealed book, to be opened and misinterpreted at random by the most incompetent of mankind. Now, by bearing in mind the rich *diversity* of Scripture we not only gain elements of the deepest interest, but we are proceeding on the right path for its due comprehension. We are in a better position for understanding the truth of God when we have studied the peculiarities of the language in which it is embodied, and know something of the individuality with which the expression of it is tinged. To the variety of sources from which the revelation comes is due both the inexhaustible interest of the Bible and its Divine universality. In this it is wholly unlike the sacred books of other religions. It has something for all nations. In reading the Koran we can think only of Arabia; in reading Confucius only of China; in reading the Zend Avesta only of Persia; in reading the Vedas only of Hindostan. But in the Bible we meet with all races, from Arabian troglodytes to Greek poets, from Galilean fishermen to Roman consuls. From Nineveh to Babylon, from Babylon to Damascus, from Damascus to Jerusalem, from Jerusalem to Tyre, and the isles of the Gentiles, and Athens, and Corinth, and Rome, we see the light of revelation ever streaming westwards through the pages of the Bible, and

> "The giant forms of empires on their way
> To ruin"

fling their colossal shadows across its pages. The Bible is at once a sacred Iliad and a sacred Odyssey. Now its pages ring with the battles of the warrior, with their confused noise and garments rolled in blood; now the sea is dashing in our faces as we traverse it in the ship of Jonah, or toss a night and day among its breakers with St. Paul. It has indeed deep speculations for the philosophic mind, but for the most part it is intensely concrete. There is in it no stifling system, no chilling gloom, no self-centred absorption, no frozen sea of abstractions. The sanctimonious and heresy-hunting formalism of the Pharisee, the selfish asceticism of the Buddhist, the chill uncertainty of the Confucian, find no sanction here; nor are we placed at the mercy of the systematising refinements of the Schoolman, and the arbitrary tyranny of the Priest. The Bible shows us that religion may be as exquisite as music, as glowing as art, as rich as a gifted nature, as broad as a noble life. It is as universal as our race, as individual as ourselves.

β. Hence, to the Homilist and the Preacher, dulness is an inexcusable fault, and one which should be most earnestly avoided. If the preacher is dull—dull to *all* his hearers—he cannot possibly rouse their consciences or touch their hearts. Dulness might be pardonable if we had no better text-book than the Koran or the Tripitaka, but it is hardly pardonable when our sacred Book is so intensely and widely humanitarian. Where the human, the concrete, and the individual element is introduced, there hearers *must* find something to interest and instruct them; for the experience of one heart is more or less the experience of all hearts, and there is no one who does not sympathise with the multitude in the Roman theatre who rose to shout their delighted applause on hearing the line of the dramatist—

> "Homo sum; humani nihil a me alienum puto."

To the Buddhist the incidents, whether real or legendary, in the life of the Buddha Sakya Mouni furnish a theme of endless interest; the Chinese is never tired of even the dry and uneventful records of the biography of Kung foo tze; but the Bible furnishes us with thousands of thrilling incidents, and with human experiences under the most varied conditions. Not only so, but it comprises the writings of at least fifty different writers who lived in the most widely separated spheres. The voice which speaks to us is now that of a Gentile sorcerer, now that of a suffering prisoner, now that of a conquering king. Lawgivers like Moses, autocrats like Solomon, warriors like Joshua, historians like Samuel, prophets like Isaiah, priests like Ezra and Jeremiah and Ezekiel, poets like David, governors like Nehemiah, exiles like Daniel, peasants like Amos, fishermen like Peter and John, tax gatherers like Matthew, rabbis like Paul, have all contributed their quota to the sacred page. We may truly say that it is like the great tree of northern fable, whose leaves were the lives of men. It is for this very reason that nations, like birds of the air, shelter themselves under the shadow of it. It is a vine of God's planting, which

> " Reacheth to every corner under heaven
> Deep-rooted in the living soil of truth ;
> So that men's hopes and fears take refuge in
> The fragrance of its complicated glooms,
> And cool impleached twilights."

γ. St. Paul, in the expression to which we have referred, is not the only sacred writer who bids us notice this diversity and progressiveness of Scripture. The author of the Epistle to the Hebrews calls most marked attention to it in the elaborately beautiful introduction to his Epistle. " God," he says, " who *at sundry times and in divers manners* spake in time past unto the fathers by the prophets, hath in these last days spoken unto us by his Son." Here we have a striking allusion to the difference between the Old Testament and the New. In the New Testament also there is diversity ; but whereas there are only *nine* authors for the twenty-seven books of the New Testament, and the great bulk of it is the work of three, on the other hand, for the thirty-nine books of the Old Testament there are at the very least twenty-seven chief authors, and a very much larger number of minor contributors. The two words rendered " at sundry times and in divers manners " are πολυμερῶς καὶ πολυτρόπως, which might perhaps be rendered "*fragmentarily and multifariously.*" As regards the latter adverb, we have already seen that it is illustrated by the singular differences of station and circumstances among those to whom God sent his message of inspiration ; but it is yet further illustrated by the different ways in which that message came to them, and in which it is delivered to us. It came sometimes in the facts of history, sometimes in isolated promises, sometimes by Urim, sometimes by dreams and voices and similitudes, sometimes by types and sacrifices, sometimes by prophets specially commissioned. It takes the form now of annals, now of philosophic meditation, now of a sermon, now of an idyl, now of a lyric song. Sometimes it expands, through chapter after chapter, the details of a single day in an individual life ; sometimes it crushes into one single clause the sweeping summary of the records of twenty generations. At one time it will give the minutest incidents of one event in a single reign ; at another it will heap the dust of oblivion over dynasties of a hundred kings. We may compare its course to that of a stream which sometimes dwindles into a tiny rivulet, and sometimes broadens into an almost shoreless sea. But it is a stream whose fountains lie deep in the everlasting hills. Its sources are hidden in the depths of a past Eternity, and its issues in the depths of a future Eternity. It begins with the chaos of Genesis, " vast and void ; " it ends with a book which has been called " the majestic image of a high and stately tragedy, shutting up and intermingling her solemn scenes and acts with a sevenfold chorus of hallelujahs and harping symphonies." [1]

[1] Milton.

But in this diversity, so important and so precious, we are led also to re-cognise another point of the extremest value for a right estimate of the Old Testa-ment revelations—namely, its fragmentariness, or *progressiveness*. It was given to us πολυμερῶς—"*in many parts.*" The revelation was not given all at once ; it was not perfect and final ; but God revealed himself to man part by part ; he lifted the veil fold by fold. It is grievous to recall how many a blood-stained page of history might have been redeemed from its agony and desolation if men had only remembered that the law of the Old Testament was as yet an imperfect law, and the morality of the Old Testament a not yet fully enlightened morality. When the sanguinary maintainers of shibboleths defended their outrages by the injunctions of the Pentateuch ; when the treacherous and infamous assassinations of kings by a Jacques Clement or a Ravaillac were justified by the examples of Ehud and Jael ; when the Crusaders thought that they did God service by wading bridle-deep in the blood of "infidels," because they could refer to the exterminating wars of the Book of Judges ; when the examples of Samuel and Elijah were quoted to sanction the hideous cruel-ties of the Inquisition ; when the ruinous institutions of polygamy and slavery were supported by the records of the early patriarchs ; when texts extravagantly strained were made the chief buttress of immoral despotism ; when thousands of poor inno-cent women were burned as witches on the authority of a text in Leviticus ; when atrocious crimes like the massacre of St. Bartholomew were hailed by Popes with acclamation, and paralleled by the zeal for God of olden heroes ; when many another error of darkness was defended by "the devil quoting Scripture for his purpose,"—all these follies and iniquities (of which many find their pale reflex and faint analogy even in the present day) could never have occurred if men had studied the Bible in the light of the truths which we have just been considering. And those truths were quite distinctly enunciated not only by St. Paul, the greatest and wisest of the Apostles,[1] but by our blessed Lord himself. In many distinct passages—not to dwell on the spirit and the allusions of many more—he pointed out that the revelation of God was progressive ; that even the moral conceptions of the great saints and heroes of the Old Testament were but as the starlight compared to the glory of the risen day.[2] At the very period when the religious authorities of the Jews were more and more degrading into a dead fetish the letter of their law, and that in its most unessential particulars, our Lord drew the most marked contrast between that which had been "said to them of old time" and that which he said to them then.[3] At a period when the distinction between clean and unclean meats was becoming the main badge of the Jew, and an impassable barrier between the Jew and the Gentile, he drew the distinction between real and unreal defilement, and "this he said, . . . making all meats clean."[4] When the washings of Levitic scrupulosity were looked on, not only as a pious and conscientious, but as an absolutely binding development of the laws of ceremonial uncleanness, he openly neglected them, even at the table of a Pharisee.[5] Though the Levitical ordinances came under the direct sanction of inspired authority, he gave his direct approval to the terms in which the great prophets had treated them—not only as essentially transitory, and already in part obsolete, but as having always been of an importance absolutely infinitesimal compared with the weightier matters of the Law.[6] He declined to give any personal sanction to the Mosaic law about the stoning of the adulteress.[7] He said in express terms

---

[1] As in Gal. iv. 9, and *passim*.
[2] Matt. v. 21—43 ; Luke ix. 55.
[3] Matt. v. 21, &c., where the true rendering is "to," not "by," them of old time.
[4] Mark vii. 19 (in the true rendering).
[5] Matt. xv. 1 ; Mark vii. 2.
[6] Matt. xxiii. 23.
[7] John viii. 11.

that the Mosaic concession of polygamy was not in itself good, and had merely been granted to the Jews—as a boon evil indeed, but necessary—because of the hardness of their hearts.[1] Although the sabbath had become to the Jews the very badge of nationality, and was being more and more identified by them with the essence of all religious observances, he markedly and repeatedly discouraged the tendency to strain its sacredness into a burden or a bondage.[2] Lastly, when his own nearest disciples, in the very region where Elijah had called down fire from heaven, appealed to the example of that splendid prophet to justify them in their appeal to him to .call down fire from heaven upon those who had insulted his authority, he told them with stern rebuke that the Elijah spirit is not the Christ spirit, and that he had come not to destroy men's lives, but to save.[3] If this teaching of Christ be not reverently borne in mind we shall be constantly tempted to that treatment of the Old Testament which runs through whole modern commentaries, and which, by the straining of words and the invention of hypotheses, aims at concealing all semblance of difference between the tone of a Moses and of a St. John, or between the degree of enlightenment in the moral conduct of a Jael or a Mary of Bethany. Nothing but confusion, dishonesty, and retrogression can come of the attempt to elevate the mixed and imperfect conceptions of early Judaism to the dignity of gospel morality. To act thus is to assert that the stars yield as much light whereby to guide our footsteps as we receive from the Sun of righteousness when it has dawned into boundless day. Scripture has itself made clear to us, in words as plain as it is possible to utter, that the degree both of religion and morality which was vouchsafed to the patriarchs was altogether inferior to that which has been granted to us. "By what law would you justify the atrocity you would commit?" asks the young soldier in a great work of fiction. "If thou art ignorant of it," replied Burley, "thy companion is well aware of the law which gave the men of Jericho to the sword of Joshua, the son of Nun." "Yes; but we," answered the divine, "live under a better dispensation, which instructeth us to return good for evil, and to pray for those who despitefully use us and persecute us."[4]

δ. It will be hardly necessary to warn the Christian homilist that he must beware of recoiling into the opposite extreme. He is not indeed likely to fall into the error of Marcion, whose famous 'Antitheses' dwelt upon and exaggerated the supposed contradictions between the Old and New Testament with the express object of supporting his heresy—that the old dipensation was the work not of God, but of an inferior and imperfect Demiurgus;—but he *may* be led to underrate the unspeakable value of the Old Testament Scriptures. The unity of the Old and New Testaments is found in the person and work of Christ. *Thus* it is that "the Old Testament is not contrary to the New; for both in the Old and the New Testament everlasting life is offered to mankind by Christ, who is the only Mediator between God and man, being both God and man."[5] Nothing is more remarkable in the Old Testament, nothing is a more distinct and irrefragable proof of its inspired authority, than this interdependence of the two dispensations— "the Old Testament containing the germ and nucleus of the New, the New containing the realisation and fulfilment of the Old, not as a matter of contrivance, but as a matter of broad and patent history, so that the two parts correspond like a cloven tally."[6] We must avoid alike the heresy of those Gnostics who saw *nothing* of the New Testament in the Old, and the error of unwise controversialists who see *everything* of the New Testament in the Old. But the old rule is true,

---

[1] Mark x. 4.   [2] Mark ii. 27 ; Luke xiii. 15, &c.   [3] Luke ix. 55.
[4] Scott, 'Old Mortality.'   [5] Article.   [6] Professor Leathes.

that " In Vetere Testamento Novum latet ; in Novo Testamento Vetus patet." The fact that, from the days of Origen onwards, allegory and typology have been exaggerated to a most artificial extent, and that many events and allusions and customs have been made prophetic of Christ in which nothing of prophecy was intended,[1] must not blind us to the fact that the Old Testament is full of Christ ; for the very heart and essence of the Old Dispensation, as its features are exhibited in the writings of historians, lawgivers, and prophets, was the great and unquenchable Messianic hope. In the Old Testament Christ is prefigured ; in the New he is revealed. In his teaching we see in all their fulness those constant elements which all religion strives more and more clearly to express—the holiness and love of God, the dignity and brotherhood of man. And so he stands at the centre of all history as the fulfilment of all the yearnings of the past, the justification of all the hopes of the future. Apart from him all the deepest elements of the Old Testament become unintelligible. The Law is but the slave which leads us to his school.[2] He is the bruiser of the serpent's head in Genesis,[3] and the Lamb as it had been slain in the midst of the throne in Revelation ;[4] he is the Paschal Lamb of Moses ;[5] the true star and sceptre of Balaam's vision ;[6] the promised Son of David ;[7] Isaiah's rod of the stem of Jesse ;[8] him whose testimony is the spirit of prophecy,[9] and of whom bear all the prophets witness, as many as have spoken from Samuel and those that follow after.[10] The due comprehension of this vast hope, and the power of unfolding it, will be one of the highest results which can reward the study of the preacher who desires to fulfil the duty of a wise scribe by drawing from his treasures things old as well as new.[11] By studying the Bible in this spirit we shall make the New Testament an inspired Targum of the Old ; the Old Testament will become to us as the New, and the New as the Old.

II. But, to turn to the second point which I mentioned as one of primary importance, every preacher is certain to be led into constant errors who makes a habit of using texts without a faithful study of the context from which they are taken. Thousands of readers attach an entirely erroneous meaning to isolated expressions from forgetting that their true bearing can often only be understood in connection with the train of thought to which they belong. The sacred writers never contemplated the splitting up of their writings into these multitudinous and often arbitrary divisions. Those divisions are mere conveniences for purposes of reference, and owe their origin to the exigencies of the concordance.[12] No one who has not looked into the subject can be at all aware of the multitudes of "texts" which are habitually employed in senses which they never originally bore ; or of the absolute recklessness with which they are constantly misapplied, even by professed divines. Sometimes this misuse is so far harmless that the truth into the service of which the text is impressed finds abundant support from other passages ; but even in that case the habit springs up of the preacher using the words of prophet or evangelist, not in their proper sense, but as a sort of mask through which more authoritatively to utter thoughts which are not those of the sacred writer, but are his own.[13] I cannot more directly illustrate this fact than by showing that even the very texts which are

---

[1] The writings of the Fathers—notably of Origen, of St. Hilary of Poictiers, and even of St. Jerome and St. Augustine—are full of the most strained and untenable allegories.

[2] Gal. iii. 21.   [3] Gen. iii. 15.   [4] Rev. v. 6.
[5] Exod. xii.   [6] Numb. xxiv. 17.   [7] Mark x. 48, &c.
[8] Isa. xi. 1.   [9] Rev. xix. 10.   [10] Acts x. 43.

[11] But useful for this line of study we may recommend the beautiful treatise of Davison, ' On Prophecy.'

[12] See on this subject the article Bible in Smith's ' Dictionary of the Bible.'

[13] I have illustrated this danger in two papers on ' Wresting the Scriptures ' in the ' Expositor ' for July and August, 1880.

often used to enforce rules of sound Biblical interpretation are in several instances misinterpreted or misapplied. We should attend, it is said, to the spirit, not to the letter, for "*the letter killeth.*" We should interpret "*according to the proportion of faith.*" We should imitate the Divine method by teaching "*precept upon precept, precept upon precept; line upon line, line upon line;* here a little, and there a little." We should remember that "all scripture is given by inspiration of God." Now these remarks and suggestions may be true and wise, but in every one of these instances the text is misapplied, and a glance at the context will show that it is so. The expression "the letter killeth"[1] applies primarily to the sentence of death passed upon transgressors by the Mosaic law. The use of the expression "according to the proportion" (or analogy) "of faith" as a rule for the exposition of the Scriptures, is only a secondary and incorrect application of it; for "the faith" spoken of is not faith in the sense of the system of religion, but is subjective faith, and St. Paul is speaking of preaching within the limits of the spiritual gifts which we have received.[2] "Line upon line, precept upon precept," is so far from being an inspired description of the method of God's revelations, that it is a taunting mimicry of Isaiah's manner,[3] used to ridicule him by the drunken priests of Judah. Lastly, "all scripture is given by inspiration of God" is a translation which is so far from certain that it has been regarded as untenable by a very large number of orthodox and learned commentators from the days of Origen down to our own, and both the Syriac, St. Jerome, and Luther render it "all inspired scripture is useful also for doctrine," &c.[4] The misuse of this little group of texts, all referring to one subject—and that the very subject of the right method of Scriptural interpretation, which should surely not be formulated in terms of Scriptural misinterpretation—will at least serve to show the need for carefulness. For indeed the necessity for such carefulness is much greater when important doctrines are made to rest their main support on such texts as, "the whole head is sick, and the whole heart is faint;"[5] or, "which of us shall dwell with everlasting burnings?"[6] or, "in the place where the tree falleth there it shall be;" or, "cursed be Canaan;"[7] or indeed in a multitude of other texts which, as is proved by the context, have not, and could never have been intended to have, the controversial significance which has been attached to them. It has indeed been an unauthorised superstition, and one which has been prolific of error, to assert that "every passage of the Bible looks backward and forward and every way, like lights from the sun." It is a dogma which does not find in Scripture itself the faintest shadow of authorisation; it is due to that irreverent reverence which ends in superseding in favour of its own arbitrary fancies the professed object of its devotion; its final result is to hand over the Bible to the autocratic manipulation of prejudice and fancy, instead of demanding the toilsome and unbiassed discovery of its true meaning. Texts have been compared to those flints which, when struck open by the hammer, reveal a Drusic cavity full of crystals of the colour of amethyst, "purple with a dawn such as never was on land and sea." The comparison is as true as it is beautiful; but such rich contents will never be found—though they may be invented and imagined—by any student who does not study each text in its due place and under its proper relations.

III. After having endeavoured to show the importance of these broad principles of interpretation—and I have signalled them out as the most neglected and the most

---

[1] 2 Cor. iii. 6. [2] Rom. xii. 6. [3] Isa. xxviii. 10.
[4] 2 Tim. iii. 16. It was so taken by Origen, Clement Alexandrinus, Tertullian, and most of the Fathers · and by the Peshito, Arabic, and Vulgate; by Luther, &c.
[5] Isa. i. 5. [6] Isa. xxxiii. 14. [7] Gen. ix. 25.

important on which I could touch—it may now be useful to give a brief glance, from a homiletic point of view, at the great divisions of the Old Testament Scriptures.

The earliest trace of a classification of the Old Testament books is found in the Prologue to the Book of Ecclesiasticus, where we are told that Jesus, the son of Sirac, "had much given himself to the reading of the law, and the prophets, and other books of our fathers." In 2 Macc. ii. 13 we are told how Nehemiah, "founding a library, gathered together the acts of the kings, and the prophets, and of David." This is clearly analogous to the division referred to by our Lord in Luke xxiv. 44, "in the law of Moses, and in the prophets, and in the Psalms." More frequently, however, the Jews, when speaking generally, comprised the Old Testament Scriptures under the head of the Law and the Prophets (Matt. v. 17; Luke xxiv. 25). When entering more into detail they added "the writings" (Cethubim or Hagiographa). The Law (*Torah*) comprised the five books of the Pentateuch. The Prophets were divided into two classes—earlier and later. Under the head of Earlier Prophets the Jews placed the Books of Joshua, Judges, 1 and 2 Samuel, and 1 and 2 Kings. Under the Later Prophets they placed the three major prophets—Isaiah, Jeremiah, and Ezekiel—and the twelve minor prophets. The Cethubim, again, were ranged under three divisions, of which the first, called *Emeth* ("truth"), from the initial letters of the three books, comprised Psalms, Proverbs, and Job; the second, the Canticles, Ruth, Lamentations, Ecclesiastes, and Esther, which were called the five Megilloth, from being written on separate "Rolls" for use at particular festivals; the third division contained Daniel, Ezra, Nehemiah, and 1 and 2 Chronicles.

If we were entering on a critical introduction to the books of the Old Testament, this division — especially the position occupied in it by the Books of Daniel and Chronicles—would be found very important and suggestive. But for our present homiletic purpose it will be more convenient roughly to divide the books of Scripture into—(1) the Law, (2) the historic books, (3) the poetic books, (4) the prophetic books, and (5) the philosophic books. The division is only meant to be a general one for purposes of convenience; for some of the historic books contain prophetic passages, and some of the prophets contain historical sections; and, again, some of the poetic books are also prophetic, and large portions of the prophets are written in strains of the loftiest poetry, as also are parts of the books which we may term philosophic. The *general* divisions are, however, well marked and easily discernible.

1. The five books of the Pentateuch are partly composed of a history—first of the world, and then of the chosen family—up to the time of the entrance into Canaan, and partly of the system of Mosaic legislation.

a. We no sooner open the Book of Genesis than we are met by whole volumes of controversy as to the relations between science and religion, and the supposed contradictions between the results of the one and the declarations of the other. Do such controversies lie within the ordinary sphere of homiletics? We should say decidedly not, and that for many reasons. In the first place, few are competent really to deal with the question, and nothing is more irritating to men of science than to see obvious ignorance assuming the airs of infallibility, and demonstrating the impiousness of proved conclusions, the very elements of which it does not understand. The clergy in so many thousands of instances, in age after age, have so conclusively proved their entire incompetence to decide upon points of science,—they have been so repeatedly forced to modify their interpretations of Scripture in accordance with finally demonstrated and universally accepted truths,—that it is best to rest on the certainty that though exegesis may be erroneous, the scientific *results* which have rewarded centuries of labour have not in a single instance clashed with any truth of religion. How can they clash, seeing that truth must be truth, and that God reveals himself in the facts of nature no less surely than he reveals himself in his word? If the clergy desire to enter into scientific controversies, first let them acquire the requisite knowledge, and then let them urge their views in the press, or in places where they can be fairly met and criticised. The pulpit is not meant to be a place for doubtful disputations, but for the furtherance of the ends of revelation, which is "profitable for doctrine, for reproof, for correction, for instruction in righteousness; that the man of God may be perfect, throughly furnished unto all good works."[1] The first nine chapters of Genesis are singularly rich in moral and spiritual lessons. They summarise the history of at least 2000 years in the progress of mankind. In the pulpit, at any rate, we search them not for earthly wisdom, but for heavenly knowledge. Of the physical truths which the finger of God has written on the stars of heaven or carved upon the rocky tablets of the world; of the bands of Jupiter, or the ring of Saturn, or the snowy poles of Mars; of the extinct monsters which once trampled the forests or tempested the seas—a child may now know more than was dreamt by the wisest man of old. But, on the other hand, the nations of the world might have been saved from millenniums of error—not only from Fetish-worship and Devil-worship, but from Pantheism, and Atheism, and Polytheism, and Manicheism, and Materialism, and forms of error compatible with the most advanced culture—by that single verse of Genesis, speaking calmly as a voice out of the depths of eternity: "In the beginning God created the heavens and the earth."

β. In the story of the Creation the same truths are prominent, and the truths on which *all* may fix their thoughts are those of a loving Omnipotence and a glorious world. Similarly, in the story of the Fall of Man, while it would be possible to raise any number of perplexities which are incapable of present solution, it would argue a singular blindness if we missed the truth that the fall of Adam and Eve points the lesson of the fall of every man and woman brought into a sinful world. Be it a history or be it an allegory, we are in any case intended to read in it the causes of the loss of innocence, the certain consequences of retribution, and the Divine remedy for sin. And in the promise to Eve of that seed of the woman who should break the serpent's head we hear the first utterance of prophecy, and catch the first gleam of that light and hope which was to brighten into the perfect day. Have we not here the great elements which run through the whole Bible—"law and prophecy; the denunciation of sin and the promise of pardon; the flame which consumes and the light which comforts;" and is not this the whole of the covenant?

γ. We find the same truths repeated, with striking variations, in the story of Cain; and then we see the origin, on the one hand, of polygamy and a godless civilisation in the family of Lamech, and, on the other hand, of religious worship in the family of Seth. This salt of goodness was not, however, sufficient to save the world from moral corruption; and in the narrative of the Deluge we read the great moral truth that there is a point at which nations can fill no fuller the cup of their iniquity—at which God's wrath against corruption must express itself in retributive justice. Yet here again we find the beautiful symbols of mercy and of safety—the saving ark, the dove with the branch of olive plucked off in her mouth, the promise that God will no more smite every living thing; above all, the bow in the cloud as a pledge of mercy. With the family of Noah the story of man begins afresh, and begins with an awful warning against the curse of drunkenness; but the rainbow, which was made to him the sign of a new covenant, flashes and fades throughout

---

[1] 2 Tim. iii. 16, 17.

the whole of Scripture, and even amid the often terrible visions of the last book of the Bible we catch our last glimpse of it, spanning the throne of God, and "in sight like unto an emerald."[1]

δ. After the remarkable genealogy of nations in the tenth chapter of Genesis, and one glance at the first colossal empires of the East, we are told of the ruin of an attempt to establish an universal dominion. That story of Babel is the Divine sanction of nationality. From that point, through forty chapters, the sacred historian leaves the history of the world to dwell on the records of three biographies. For not only is the individual life sacred to God, but those three patriarchs—Abraham, Isaac, and Jacob—were the fathers of the chosen people. They lived peaceful and, for the most part, uneventful lives in their pastoral tents; they were but men; they were not sinless; they sometimes fell into acts of cruelty, meanness, and deceit. But even with all their human weaknesses they were men eminently good, and their one great distinguishing feature was faith in God. It is this which, more than anything else, differentiates one life from another. We are helped to grasp the lesson by the striking way in which each one of them is silently contrasted with another who has his good things in this life—Abraham with Lot, Isaac with Ishmael, Jacob with Esau. Few lessons are more instructive than those which spring from drawing out this contrast in its details and in its results. But the author of the Epistle to the Hebrews points out to us the great lesson that it was faith which lit up their characters with every virtue and every grace; it was like one sunbeam brightening jewels of many colours.

ε. It is needless to dwell on the rich symbolism of the historic narrative which runs through the remaining books of the Pentateuch. The burning bush, the plagues of Egypt, the drowning of Pharaoh and his host in the Red Sea, Marah and Elim and Kibroth Hattaavah, the darkness and splendour of Sinai, the pillar of cloud and fire, the smitten rock, the brazen serpent, the grand episode of Balaam, the zeal of Phinehas, the death of Moses, the doom to forty years of wandering in the wilderness, the conquest of Canaan—these are events which arrest our attention, and we can hardly miss their lessons. It is different with the judicial, ceremonial, and political law of the Jews, which occupy so many chapters in these books, and are too much neglected. They were intended to train Israel, and through Israel to train the world, in the knowledge of God as one God, as a Spirit, as eternal, as ever near us, as a God of holiness and justice, and above all as a God of love. The one utterance round which the entire law of Moses may be said to cluster is that in Exod. xxxiv. 5—7, which is the great proclamation of the name of God after the shameful apostasy of the people. The *moral* law—on the unequalled majesty and Divine originality of which we need not now dwell—was meant to reveal his will, and the aim of the *ceremonial* law was to habituate the people to the conception that they must be holy as God is holy, and pure as he is pure. This is the one main object of all the laws about clean and unclean meats, intended to keep Israel as a separate people; and of the long chapters about ceremonial uncleanness, which was meant to be a type of moral, mental, and spiritual uncleanness. This too was the meaning of all the ordinances of worship, which, like the laws of the fringes and the phylacteries, were meant to teach Israel that God was among them, and that therefore they must be pure in heart and obedient in life. If the student will carefully consider the thirteen long chapters of the Book of Exodus which are occupied with details

[1] Rev. iv. 3.

about the tabernacle and the dress of the priests, he will see that there is hardly one of those details, whether of substance, material, or colour, which is not demonstrably symbolical, and which did not tend to the one purpose of witnessing to the presence and holiness of God.[1] This is still more the case with the whole system of sacrifices, of which the meat offerings were eucharistic, the sin offerings propitiatory, and the burnt offerings typical of self-dedication. Although Moses makes no mention of prayer as a part of public worship, yet these sacrifices were preparations for prayer, and were themselves "prayers without words." They said to the Israelite, Show thy thankfulness to God; make thy peace with God; dedicate thy life to God. In the chapter which gives the method of declaring the purification of the leper (Levit. xiv.), and the magnificent ceremonial of the day of atonement, the student will see in its highest development the rich significance of the Levitic law as symbolising man's relationship to God, and God's restoration of fallen man.[2]

ζ. But, further than this, we see in many regulations that in the Old Testament, as in the New, love is the fulfilling of the law. In spite of concessions to rude times and hard hearts, there is a singular tenderness in the spirit of the Mosaic code. There is tenderness to slaves, whom in every way it sheltered from oppression;[3] to the accidental homicide, for whom it provided the cities of refuge;[4] to the poor, whom it protected from cruel usury;[5] to the depressed toilers, whose lands it restored in the Sabbatic year;[6] to the destitute, in whose interest it forbad the hard stripping of the fields, the mean exhaustion of the gleaned vineyards, or the niggardly beating of the topmost olive boughs.[7] There is even tenderness to the dumb animals. To show that God cared even for the falling sparrow and the dumb cattle, the great legislator was bidden to lay down a rule that the heedless boy should not take the mother-bird when he took from the nest her callow young;[8] that the oxen were not to be muzzled when they trod out the corn;[9] and that the ox and ass were not to be yoked together at the plough, that the burden might not fall on the smaller and weaker beast.[10] Even the thrice repeated rule, "Thou shalt not seethe the kid in its mother's milk,"[11] besides the deep warning which it conveys of the horrible sin of destroying human beings by means of their best affections, was rightly interpreted as a reprobation of unfeeling cruelty, because it looks like a hard mockery, an offence against the mercifulness of nature, to seethe the youngling in the very milk which nature had designed for its sustenance;—for "God's tender mercies are over all his works."[12]

2. Turning from the Law to the historical books of the Bible, how rich in all moral lessons is the great narrative which unfolds before us the story of the chosen people. One grand lesson runs through it all—that neither for men nor for nations is there any true life apart from God. There, as in no other books, shall we find the true statesman's manual and the true philosophy of history. It is related that when King Frederic William I. of Prussia asked one of his chaplains to give him in one sentence a proof of Christianity, the chaplain replied, "The Jews, your Majesty." An entire system of evidences of religion lies in that answer. The whole history of Israel may well be called the history of a prodigal—of a prodigal terribly punished yet freely forgiven. "When Israel was a child God loved him, and out of Egypt he called his son. The son grew up. In the days of prosperity he did not choose

---

[1] See on this subject Bähr's 'Symbolik,' and Kalisch on Exodus.   [2] Levit. xvi.
[3] Deut. v. 15 ; xii. 18, &c.   [4] Numb. xxxv. 13.   [5] Deut. xxiii. 19 ; xxiv. 6, &c.
[6] Levit. xxv. 4, &c.   [7] Deut. xxiv. 20.   [8] Deut. xxii. 6.
[9] Deut. xxv. 4.   [10] Deut. xxii. 10.   [11] Exod. xxiii. 19.   [12] Ps. cxlv. 9.

to keep God in his remembrance. The days of sorrow came, and he flung himself with sincere repentance into his Father's arms." [1] But even over his repentance crept the insincerity of formalism. In the days of his idolatry Israel murdered the prophets ; in the days of his Pharisaism he crucified the .Christ. Yet through all that long dark tragedy, in which Jehovah and his people were the actors, God's will was being accomplished. The vineyard had been given to the husbandmen for the blessing of the world. They proved unworthy, and were cast out ; [2] but "if the casting away of Israel was the reconciling of the world, what shall their receiving be but life from the dead ? " [3]

a. No lessons could be more instructive for the homilist than those which he may find abundantly in the scenes and characters of the historic books ; but among them the lesson of the history as a whole should not be overlooked. What conceivable explanation is there of the history of the Jews, with their inextinguishable vitality, and the fulfilment again and again of their unquenchable hopes, except the truth that God had chosen them, and that God was with them ? They had no righteousness, but were a stiff-necked people. They had no splendid territory, but a strip of barren, narrow, ill-watered land. They had no grand genealogy—a Syrian ready to perish was their father. They were not powerful enough of themselves even to conquer their own small land. They were not united ; Ephraim envied Judah, and Judah vexed Ephraim. They were not free, but became the prey of nation after nation. They were not a maritime people, for their strip of sea-coast was mostly harbourless, and not their own. They had no commercial industry like Venice or Holland ; no art like Greece ; no arms like Rome ; no colonies like England ; no philosophy like Germany. They were constantly starting aside like a broken bow. Yet no power has ever been able to crush, no persecution to destroy them. They have influenced, taught, pervaded mankind. Their sacred book is the sacred book of humanity, their religious ideas are becoming more and more the religious ideas of the race. What explains it all, and alone explains it ? Nothing but the truth that "God showed his word unto Jacob, his statutes and ordinances unto Israel. He hath not dealt so with any nation, neither have the heathen knowledge of his law."

β. The period of desert wanderings was to the Jews a special training for their future history. It was meant to transform them from a nation of full-fed slaves into a nation of warriors. With the entrance into Canaan their proper national history begins. In the Old Testament it falls into three epochs—that of the Judges, that of the Kings, and that of the Exile and return. The epoch of the Judges, so rich in heroic incidents, was a period of apparent anarchy, but of secret growth. The lesson which it was designed to teach them was that apart from God the Israelites were helpless and contemptible, but that with God they were happy and strong. Amid wild stories of crime and repentance, of raids and reprisals, of barbarity and generosity, we see, and not least in the exquisite story of Ruth, that the nation was gradually learning its appointed lesson. Then arose one of the greatest men in Jewish annals, the Prophet Samuel. The time for political unity had come, and, acting under God's permission, he reluctantly gave them a king. After the first tentative, which was a failure owing to the character of the passionate and unstable Saul, began the splendid career of David, the true hero of the monarchy and the darling of the people, whose personal ascendancy stamped a type of character on the nation's history. He gave them an army, he gave them a temple, he gave them a psalter, he gave them a capital. The reign of his son Solomon was but the gorgeous com-

---

[1] Munk.   [2] Matt. xxi. 39   [3] Rom. xi. 15.

mencement of a real decadence. It produced the revolt in the reign of Rehoboam. Israel and Judah split asunder for ever. The ten tribes apostatised into calf worship and Baal worship, and for 250 years, through a list of six unhappy dynasties and nineteen unhappy kings, of whom not one was good, their story dragged itself on, through revolts and assassinations, through foreign defeats and civil tumults, with little beyond the grand missions of Elijah, Elisha, and other prophets to shed a gleam on that long agony.[1] Then Assyria carried them away captive, and they disappear among the nations. Judah had twenty-one kings, but they were all of David's house, and some of them, like Hezekiah and Josiah, were conspicuously faithful. But their reformation came too late. The Jews murdered the prophets, and slew those that were sent unto them, and were carried captive to Babylon. Then came the Exile. In Chaldæa they were cured for ever of the temptation to apostasy, and nothing but their hopes, their promises, and their religion could have preserved them from final obliteration. Babylon fell; Persia prevailed. The Jews returned to a land desolated by war, famine, and disease; but they returned settled in the faith, and so " with the unresistible might of weakness they shook the world."[2] The history of Israel has four main heroes -Moses, Sa uel, David, Ezra. Moses gave them their freedom and their law. Samuel their order and unity; David their poetry and their power; Ezra gave them a collected literature and a religious education. If David was the founder of Israel as a monarchy, Ezra is the founder of Israel as a Church. But the lesson of the Old Testament history is mainly this—that, whether as a Kingdom or as a Church, the true Israel had but two sources of power and permanence—the law of a Divine holiness, the grasp of a Messianic hope.

3. Poetry is found throughout the Bible, from the song of Lamech in Gen. iv. to the Apocalypse. All who wish really to understand it must of course make themselves acquainted with the general features of that parallelism or " balance,"—the rapid stro e as of alternate wings, "the heaving and sinking as of the human heart,"[3] —of which there are three main forms—cognate, contrasted, or synthetic.[4] It is the rhythm both of thoughts and words. Thought corresponds to thought in repetition, amplification, contrast, or response; like wave answering to wave, each wave different, yet each swayed by the same setting tide of emotion. It is not easy to define the epochs of Hebrew poetry, because of the still unsettled date of certain books, like the Book of Job and the Song of Solomon. We can see that there was a great poetic outburst both at the Exodus and during the period of the Judges, which produced in the song of Deborah one of the most splendid and impassioned poems in the world. But David was pre-eminently the sweet psalmist of Israel. He found Hebrew poetry a wild flower, but " he planted it on Mount Zion, and nurtured it with kingly care." It never quite died away, and even the Exile and return produced some psalms of remarkable sweetness. The Bible contains poems of nearly all kinds. In the Book of Job we have its single drama of unequalled sublimity; in the songs of Moses and of Deborah the grandest pæans to liberty which were ever sung; in Proverbs and Ecclesiastes didactic and philosophic poems of great beauty and wisdom; in the Song of Solomon an exquisite pastoral; in the Lamentations a most pathetic elegy. Epic indeed there is none; but Hebrew history is itself a Divine epic, and in the intense utterances of the prophets and the sweet songs of the

[1] Hosea ii. 4—17 ; Amos ix. 7.   [2] Milton.   [3] Ewald.
[4] On this subject see Lowth ' De Sacri poesi Hebræorum,' and Kerdu, ' Geist der Hebr. Poesie.' A good sketch of Hebrew poetry by Mr. Wright may be found in Smith's ' Bible Dict.'

psalmists we have as it were the ivy and the passion-flowers which twine around its bole. But it is in lyric poetry that the Hebrew genius most characteristically displayed itself, and in its songs we have, as Luther said, " a garden in which the fairest flowers bloom, but over which there blow tempestuous winds." And of all the characteristics of Hebrew poetry, its fresh simplicity, its stainless purity, its lofty purpose, its genial cheerfulness, its free universality of tone, none is more remarkable than the fact that it is intensely religious, that it is full of God. What the son of Sirac says of David is true of all the Hebrew poets : " In all his works he praised the Holy One most high with words of glory ; with his whole heart he sung songs, and loved him that made him." [1]

4. In turning to the sixteen directly prophetical books of the Bible we are dealing with its most distinctive element. They do not fall into isolated masses, but interpenetrate one another, and form one organic whole. Prophecy—by which is mainly intended impassioned moral teaching, which insists on the certain vindication of great principles by the issue of events overruled by God—runs all through the Bible. " As we watch the weaving of the web (of Hebrew life) we endeavour to trace through it the more conspicuous threads. Long time the eye follows the crimson : it disappears at length ; but the golden thread of sacred prophecy stretches to the end." [2] The constant references to the prophets in the New Testament,[3] the marked approval of their teaching by our Lord,[4] his express statement that they prophesied of him,[5] give the Books of the Prophets an immense importance.

To foretell was one of the functions, but was not the main function, of the Prophets. A mere glance at their writings is sufficient to show that they were the moral and spiritual teachers of the people, the interpreters of God's will, the forth-tellers of Divine truth, far more than the foretellers of future circumstances. The horizon of their vision indeed, and especially its Messianic hope, extended even to the distant future ; but it was not like the view of a plain outstretched before them, but like that of a mountain chain, towering range after range and peak beyond peak to the crowning glory of one eternal summit—the view of æon after æon, all tending to the one far-off Divine event—the kingdom of God and of his Christ. The Hebrew Prophets were patriots, statesmen, reformers, leaders of the people.

> " In them is plainest taught and easiest learnt
> What makes a nation happy and keeps it so,
> What ruins kingdoms and lays cities flat." [6]

Their great characteristics — those which give them such an eternal value — are their heroic faith, their unquenchable hope, their inflexible righteousness, the manner in which they rose superior to the petty ritualisms of sacerdotal formalism, and made holiness the test of sincerity in worship.[7] All who would escape the average—all who would feel the sacredness of enthusiasm and self-sacrifice—must learn of them. In them, as in the moral truths which they enunciated, they were the true forerunners of him of whom they prophesied ; and he has given his eternal sanction to the truths which they have taught us : " to live and to struggle ; to believe with immovable firmness ; to hope even when all is dark around us ; to trust the voice of God in our inmost consciousness ; to speak with boldness and with power." [8]

5. It only remains to touch for one moment on what may be called the philosophic

---

[1] Ecclus. xlvii. 8.   [2] Kuenen, ' The Prophets.'   [3] Especially in Matthew's Gospel.
[4] Matt. ix. 13, &c.   [5] Luke xxiv. 45.   [6] Milton, ' Paradise Regained.'
[7] Hosea vi. 6, &c.   [8] Kuenen, ' The Prophets,' *ad fin.*

books of Scripture. It has been a subject of much discussion whether the Jews could be said to have possessed a philosophy or not, and it has been differently decided by different inquirers. But we may venture to give the name of philosophic books to those which specially discuss the perplexed problems of human existence. Of these the three chief are the Books of Job, Proverbs, and Ecclesiastes. All three might be also classed under the poetic books of Scripture, and the problems with which they deal are also touched on in several of the Psalms;[1] but they belong more directly to that practical wisdom which the Hebrews called *chokmah*.

a. The Book of Proverbs contains many of the most valuable results of human experience put into a terse, striking, and often antithetic form. Its earlier and more consecutive chapters (i.—ix.) are strikingly beautiful, and are aglow with the enthusiasm of lofty thought. In the two next sections (chs. x.—xxiv., and xxv.—xxix.) the form is more apothegmatic, and the maxims, especially in the earlier division, move at times on the lower level of prudential advice. The thirtieth chapter is ascribed to the unknown Agur, son of Jakeh, and the thirty-first to King Lemuel, respecting whom we have nothing but conjecture. The book concludes with the famous eulogy on the virtuous woman, which, like some of the later Psalms,[2] is written in the form of an acrostic—a sure sign that, however beautiful, it belongs to the less spontaneous and impassioned order of poetry. But the whole book in its diversified elements is a noble product of Hebrew thought, and furnishes us with a mine of instructive teaching for all classes, but especially for the young.

β. The Book of Ecclesiastes is one of the most singular books of the canon, and one which presents us with problems which have not yet been finally solved. It is invaluable as the faithful record and confession of a life which had been taught by evil that good is best; of a career which had struggled through luxury, sensuality, cynicism, and speculative despair into a firm conviction that to fear God and keep his commandments was the whole duty of man.

γ. Lastly, in the Book of Job, whatever may be the ultimate conclusion as to its date, authorship, and unity, we have a drama of inexhaustible interest, and one which has attracted the attention of many of the greatest thinkers, ancient and modern. The problem of the sufferings of the good does not indeed find in this book its final solution, for many of the best and noblest of mankind have not een restored, as Job was, to their old prosperity, but have died in anguish, loneliness, and apparent failure. But to the Book of Job we owe, among many other lessons, the most splendid vindication ever written of innocence against the uncharitable suspicion of those who see it overwhelmed with suffering, and the most majestic description of that power and majesty and love of God which are displayed in the works of his hands, and which make us involuntarily exclaim that "though he slay us, yet will we trust in him."

In the celebrated chapel of King's College, Cambridge, the huge windows of stained glass are filled on one side with subjects from the Old Testament, and on the other with subjects from the New; and often on summer days the student who walks on one side may see the windows nearest to him blazing with sunlight which stream through them from the other side. "Whenever," says an ingenious writer, "I thus saw the gospel story shining through the Old Testament story, I thought that it was a figure of what we see in the Bible." And so in truth it is. Both in the Old and the New Testament we have type and symbol, narrative and precept, parable and

[1] Ps. lxxiii. 3, &c.   [2] *E. g.* Ps. xxv., xxxiv., xxxvii., cxi., cxii., cxv., cxlv.

miracle ; but the sunlight, which can alone interpret and glorify their highest meaning, must come from him who is the Light of the world and the Sun of righteousness. It can only come from God in Christ ; and he who would understand and interpret Scripture duly to the enlightenment and salvation of men must often breathe the prayer of one of the greatest of earthly thinkers: "To God the Father, God the Word, God the Spirit we pour forth most humble and hearty supplications that he, remembering the calamities of mankind, and the pilgrimage of this our life, in which we wear out days few and evil, would please to open to us new refreshments out of the fountain of his goodness for the alleviating of our miseries. *This also we humbly and earnestly beg, that human things may not prejudice such as are Divine ; neither that from the unlocking of the gates of sense and the kindling of a greater natural light anything of incredulity or intellectual might may arise in our minds towards Divine mysteries ; but rather that by our minds thoroughly cleansed and purged from fancy and vanities, and yet subject and perfectly given-up to the Divine oracles, there may be given unto faith such things as are faith's.*" [1]

[1] Lord Bacon, 'The Student's Prayer.'

THE LEADING PRINCIPLES OF THE

𝔇𝔦𝔳𝔦𝔫𝔢 𝔏𝔞𝔴 𝔞𝔰 𝔪𝔞𝔫𝔦𝔣𝔢𝔰𝔱𝔢𝔡 𝔦𝔫 𝔱𝔥𝔢 𝔓𝔢𝔫𝔱𝔞𝔱𝔢𝔲𝔠𝔥

BY THE

RIGHT REV. H. COTTERILL, D.D., BISHOP OF EDINBURGH.

---

1. THE PENTATEUCH, or "Fivefold Book," is the name, derived from the Greek (ἡ πεντάτευχος, sc. βίβλος), of that collection of the writings of Moses which forms the first part of the Scriptures of the Old Testament. The titles of the several books are also of Greek origin, and were given them by the LXX. translators. In the Hebrew the Pentateuch forms one volume, known to the Jews of all ages as "the Law," (*Torah*); the separate books being divisions or parts of "the *Torah*," merely distinguished by the first or some important word in the opening sentence of each division. At the close of the Pentateuch are the words, "Here end the five fifth-parts of the Law" (*chamishah chomeshe Torah*). It is to be regretted that in our versions of the Bible this unity of "The Law" is somewhat obscured, by all notice of that significant name, common to all the five parts, being omitted. If it were retained, a very interesting and instructive parallelism in the structure of the two Testaments would be more obvious than it now is. It would be apparent that the Book of "the Law" holds the same relation to the Old Testament Scriptures as the four Gospels bear to the New. In each case the first portion of the sacred volume is a part complete in itself, the basis of the covenant or Divine economy, and bearing its characteristic name: "the Law" being the exponent of the relations between God and man by nature, "the Gospel" of those which are constituted in the incarnate Son. Similarly, the historical books of the Old Testament, describing the history of the chosen people from the giving of the law till the spirit of prophecy ceased, have their parallel in the brief history of the Church of Christ in the Acts of the Apostles; while the prophetical books of the Old Testament, being not merely predictions of future events, but also inspired expositions of the moral and spiritual principles of the Law, correspond to the Apostolic Epistles and the Apocalypse, which are in both cases a revelation of God by his Spirit in the spirit of man.

2. The purpose of this Introduction is to investigate the distinctive character of the Pentateuch as containing what, throughout the Scriptures both of the Old and of the New Testament, is called "the law," or the "law of Jehovah." The profound importance not only to Christian theology, but to all true religion, of a definite and comprehensive knowledge of this subject must be admitted by every one who receives Holy Scripture as the word of God and the rule of faith and practice. The

Psalm[1] with which the Book of Psalms commences, and which appears to be, as Jerome says, "the preface of the Holy Spirit" to the whole book, represents the man on whom God pronounces blessings as one whose "delight is in the law of Jehovah, and in his law doth he meditate day and night." In other psalms the writers describe the *Torah*—the word being varied by nearly equivalent expressions, rendered "commandments," "statutes," "judgments," "testimonies," and the like, in our English version—as the source of all righteousness, truth, and peace. We are so accustomed to read the Psalms in the light of our own Christian knowledge, that we are apt to forget that, to the pious Israelite, the law meant that which had been revealed through Moses and was contained in the Pentateuch. It is of this also that the Apostle Paul is speaking when he says[2] that "the law is holy, and the commandment holy, and just, and good;" and again (in almost the very words of the Psalmist), "I delight in the law of God after the inward man." [3]

3. That in this view of "the law," as the revelation to man of the mind of God, there is no difference between the Christian and the Israelite, except that the former possesses a key to its interpretation which the other had not, is sufficiently evident from Christ's own teaching. The force of our Lord's words in the Sermon on the Mount [4] is hardly appreciated as it ought to be in much of the popular theology of the present day. "Think not," he says, "that I am come to destroy the law, and the prophets; I am not come to destroy, but to fulfil. For verily I say unto you, Till heaven and earth pass, one jot or one tittle" (as we might say "one dotting of an *i* or crossing of a *t*") "shall in no wise pass from the law, until all be fulfilled." [5] That the meaning of this cannot be merely, as some suppose, that Christ came to fulfil the law in his own person by his life and death; and that he was not speaking, as others erroneously imagine, only of the moral law of the ten commandments, but that the words comprehend all that is included in the *Torah*, and that the fulfilment of the law is a fulfilment in the kingdom of Christ, and by his disciples, as well as by our Lord himself, is evident from the words that follow: "Whosoever therefore shall break one of these least commandments" (such as may seem, in comparison with "the weightier matters of the law, justice, mercy, and faith," [6] but as ἰῶτα ἓν ἢ μία κεραία) "and shall teach men so, he shall be called least[7] in the kingdom of heaven: but whosoever shall do and teach them, the same shall be called great in the kingdom of heaven." Our Lord clearly indicates by this language that there would be a danger in his Church of Christians neglecting, and teaching others to neglect, the secondary and subordinate parts of the law. It is of course certain, from his own exposition of the law, that this fulfilment is not, as scribes and Pharisees supposed, in the letter, the punctilious observance of which, even in the dispensation in which that letter was law, often indicated an ignorance of the real substance of the law. The exact fulfilment required must be one in spirit and in truth, such as sometimes under the law, and much more under the gospel, would supersede[8] the letter. But these words of our Divine Master, so solemnly and emphatically enunciated at the commencement of his ministry, undoubtedly ought to warn us all, and especially those whose office it is to "teach" in the kingdom of

---

[1] Ps. i. 2.   [2] Rom. vii. 12.   [3] *Ibid.* ver. 22.   [4] Matt. v. 17—19.

[5] The words ἕως ἂν πάντα γένηται are strictly parallel to the previous clause, ἕως ἂν παρέλθῃ ὁ οὐρανὸς καὶ ἡ γῆ, and have the same meaning; but the age which terminates in heaven and earth passing away is also that in which all things written in the law shall be fulfilled, as is implied by the English version.

[6] Matt. xxiii. 23. Observe, as illustrating Christ's words in the Sermon on the Mount, the concluding words of this verse: ταῦτα ἔδει ποιῆσαι κἀκεῖνα μὴ ἀφιέναι.

[7] Hardly *the* least, as in the English version; rather one in the class of the least

[8] Matt. xii. 1—7.

Christ, that very serious errors, even among those who are zealous for the "great things of God's law," may arise from the habit of treating the law given by Moses cursorily and superficially, as hardly necessary to us in the clearer light of the gospel. They remind us that much, which to the careless student seems utterly insignificant, may be found, if studied reverently as part of a Divine revelation, and so as to discern the underlying spirit, to be profitable to make the man of God perfect, thoroughly furnished unto all good works. Is it not possible that many of our theological and ecclesiastical differences might disappear, if the law of the Lord were more generally studied among Christians in such a spirit, and if its teachings in lesser matters were not set aside, as they are too often, by the feeling that they must be unsuitable for Christian thought and for the gospel dispensation? St. Paul, we know, drew an inference as to the will of God in respect to the support of the ministry in Christ's Church from the spirit of " one of these least commandments:" "Thou shalt not muzzle the mouth of the ox that treadeth out the corn."[1] Might not the careful investigation of other commandments and ordinances[2] of the law—if only we believed, as our Lord taught, that the spirit and animating principle of all these without exception is for all ages and circumstances to the end of time—lead to the solution of many controverted questions, and thus direct Christians to the fulfilment of that great intercessory prayer of our Redeemer for all that should believe on him : " That they all may be one ; as thou, Father, art in me, and I in thee, that they also may be one in us : that the world may believe that thou hast sent me."[3] In the examination of the *Torah* in this introduction it will of course be impossible to do more than illustrate the principles of interpretation, to which our Lord's words point, in some of the more obvious instances. But the necessity for reverence, patience, and spiritual understanding which his warning implies may well suggest the prayer of the Psalmist: "Open thou mine eyes, that I may behold wondrous things out of thy law."[4]

4. Besides the express teaching of the Divine Founder of our faith, there is one very significant fact in the history of Christianity which of itself is sufficient to prove the paramount importance, to a complete apprehension of the principles of Christ's kingdom, of exact and definite knowledge on the subject of "the law." In addition to the twelve apostles, who were associated with Jesus Christ during his earthly ministry, and whose office it was to give testimony as eye-witnesses to those facts which are the objects of our faith and the substance of his gospel,[5] and who are thus, next to Christ himself, the very foundation-stones of the Church, another apostle was subsequently raised up, and specially commissioned and endowed for an office supplementary to theirs. The man selected for this work was one who from his youth up had been trained in the knowledge of the *Torah,* and of all the traditions of his nation. He says of himself that he had made progress in this learning above many of those of his own age ; he was exceeding zealous for the law, and "touching the righteousness which is in the law," so far as its letter was concerned, he was "blameless." It may, however, seem strange that such training should be any preparation for that peculiar sphere of thought and action to which the Apostle Paul was called, namely, to expound to Jews and Gentiles those spiritual truths which, under the guidance of the Holy Ghost, he derived from the life and death and resurrection of the Son of God in our nature. St. Paul, in fact, held somewhat the same relation to the twelve as in the Old Testament "the prophets" held to Moses and "the law." But we are able to understand the value and meaning of St. Paul's preparation for his special work when we find that his reasonings on these spiritual

---

[1] 1 Cor. ix. 9, 10 ; 1 Tim. v. 18.   [2] Cf. 1 Cor. ix. 13.   [3] John xvii. 21.
[4] Ps. cxix. 18.   [5] Cf. in proof of this 1 Cor. xv. 1—7.

truths are all based on those profound relations between the law and the gospel, which he discusses so fully and exactly in his Epistles to the Galatians and the Romans. And it must be remembered that while no one so clearly exhibits the law, in its aspect of law, as the opposite pole to the gospel, yet it is St. Paul, the assertor of Christian liberty against the bondage of law, who says, as his Divine Master said in other words, " Do we then make void the law through faith ? God forbid : yea, we establish the law."[1] St. Peter says of the epistles of his brother apostle, that in them there are many things " hard to be understood, which they that are unlearned (ἀμαθεῖς) and unstable wrest to their own destruction."[2] And undoubtedly much of the mis-understanding and imperfect apprehension of these epistles, which has been prevalent in all ages of the Church, has been due to vague and inexact notions as to the Divine law. Certainly, without distinct conceptions and definite knowledge on this important subject, the foundations not only of Christian ethics, but of Christian doctrine, can be very insufficiently laid.

5. As the argument in this Introduction is purely theological, or, more strictly, theosophical,—if a much-abused term may be used in its true and proper sense of that which treats of the philosophy of religion,—it is neither necessary nor expedient to encumber it with any critical questions, except those which may be required for illustration of the argument. That the Pentateuch is what it claims to be, that is, of Mosaic origin,[3] and given by inspiration of God, is therefore assumed. It is sufficient for our purpose that it is recognised as such in other writings of the Old Testament, and was so received by Christ himself and his apostles, and is therefore so accepted by his Church. The book was, according to the account it gives of itself, in the first instance compiled and written out by Moses for the use of that nation of Israel, which, as is recorded in this Book of the Law, God had chosen out of all nations of the earth to be in covenant with himself. It was committed to the charge of the priesthood, as the " book of the covenant," to be preserved by the side of the ark of the covenant; and portions of it were to be read publicly to the people every seventh year, at one of their most solemn festivals, as a testimony of the covenant between God and the nation.[4] This was the primary purpose of the *Torah*, to be the Divine standard of a national religion; but, as we have already concluded from our Lord's teaching and from the office of St. Paul, it was written not for one nation only, but for mankind. Indeed we might draw the same conclusion from the book itself, in which the history of the chosen nation is but an episode in the history of man, all whose families were ultimately to receive the blessings of the seed of Abraham. How far particular laws given to the nation of Israel were given as suitable to their circumstances and for that age, and how far they are of universal obligation, can only be ascertained when the principles on which they were founded are determined. And, further, in what sense any of these, which were law in the fullest sense under the covenant of law, are law under a higher and better covenant, can only be determined through that knowledge of the second covenant, with which the New Testament supplies us.

6. For it must be observed here that there is an ambiguity in the use of the term " law " which causes much confusion at times, and which it will be necessary to preclude in our present argument. The definitions of law which are sometimes given are far too general and comprehensive to be of any value for this investi-

---

[1] Rom. iii. 31.   [2] 2 Pet. iii. 16.

[3] Of course this does not imply either that Moses did not make use of more ancient documents, or that the book was not revised by Ezra or others who had authority.

[4] Deut. xxxi. 9—13.

gation. For example, Hooker,[1] in opening his argument on law, defines it thus: "That which doth assign unto each thing the kind, that which doth moderate the force and power, that which doth appoint the form and measure, of working, the same we term a law." And he distinguishes four kinds of law: (1) "The law which God from before the beginning hath set for himself;" (2) "the law which natural agents have given them to observe;" (3) "the law which angels do work by;" (4) "the law whereby man is in his actions directed to the imitation of God." There are objections both to the definition and to the distinctions which it is unnecessary to discuss; but for our argument, the chief objection is that the one most important distinction is not sufficiently marked, viz. the difference between such laws as those which we call laws of nature—by which is meant the order in which certain physical events succeed one another as sequences of cause and effect—and such laws as those of the State, which originate in the authority of the lawgiver and are enforced by the punishment of the transgressor. The latter are laws in the strict sense of the word, as ordinarily understood in human language. The Hebrew word *Torah* in Holy Scripture seems hardly ever to be used in any other sense than as a *direction* to a rational being,[2] this involving a prohibition of the contrary.[3] The Greek word νόμος is sometimes used in a wider sense, as the English "law" is; e. g. St. Paul speaks of the "law of the spirit of life," and the "law of sin," where he means not any external direction, but a principle of causation; but these are exceptions both to the Scriptural usage of the word (which is ordinarily the equivalent of *Torah*), and to the classical usage, in which νόμος, when not law in its strict sense, is the opposite of φύσις. As, however, the argument of this introduction will be analytical and not synthetical, it is unnecessary to discuss further at present the exact force of the term, because its complete meaning must be gathered from that portion of Holy Scripture which is emphatically and distinctively "the LAW."

LAW BEFORE THE FALL.

7. For the origin of Divine law, both as regards those fundamental principles of the religious and moral duty of man of which "the law" is the formal exponent, and in respect of the reasons which make law, in its strict sense, necessary for man as man, we must look to that history of creation and of man's original state which is contained in the first three chapters of the Book of Genesis. That these principles and reasons are to be found there, or must be concluded from the history, will very clearly appear when we examine it. Indeed, the fact that the *Torah* begins with this history sufficiently indicates that the law given by God to man has its origin in and with man's own origin. In the law itself, the fourth of the Sinaitic commandments points expressly to that beginning of man's history as its own source and reason. That the connection of Divine law with man's creation is generally assumed, instead of being expressly enunciated, in the law given by Moses, is accounted for when we consider (1) that this law was primarily a national covenant, and therefore in it the relations of God with his chosen people have special prominence; and (2) that law as law is based on authority, not on reasons, and all that would be needed as the basis of the law was the assertion of the authority of Jehovah as God of the whole earth, which truth was kept continually before the mind of the nation in all the

---

[1] 'Eccles. Pol.,' I. ii. 2.

[2] The expression in Prov. xxxi. 26, "In her tongue is the law of kindness," is probably no exception, as its meaning is that her commands to her household are given with kindness, even as God's law is the law of love.

[3] In reference to inanimate nature the word *choq* is used (cf. Job xxviii. 26; Ps. cxlviii. 6; Prov viii 29; Jer. v. 22).

Mosaic teaching. When we pass to the New Testament we find that Christ more than once refers expressly to the primal state of man as supplying the standard by which the law itself must be interpreted. These cases we shall examine hereafter. St. Paul and other apostolic writers not unfrequently base duties which man owes, both to God and in the mutual relations of human life, not on any positive law or on responsibilities formed by redemption, but on those principles, antecedent to all law, which are involved in creation and its teachings.[1] But even without such authority it would be impossible not to conclude that a true history of man's origin must include and involve the fundamental principles of his duty both to God and to his neighbour. For these duties must be founded on the relations between God and man, and between man and man. And whatever relations might be formed, and responsibilities arise out of these relations, during the subsequent history of mankind, those which are involved in his origin must be primary, and all that are subsequently developed must have their basis in them.

8. (I.) It is evident, for example, that the first element in God's relation to us, the foundation of his universal and absolute authority, is that which the very first sentence of the book of the law expresses : "In the beginning God created the heavens and the earth." The eternity of God, his almighty power, his infinite superiority to all things created, are all revealed in those few words. In the rest of the first chapter of Genesis the process of the creation by the will and word and spirit of God is described in language which is necessarily symbolical and ideal, because no other language could represent the operations of the eternal and infinite God. It was not, we are there taught, by a solitary and immediate exercise of power that the universe assumed the form which we now behold. Through successive periods of the creative energy of God, and of the expression of the Divine mind, gradually from the dark and formless void, in due order and in connected sequences, all the manifold existences of the universe, the forms of dead matter, living organisms, vegetable and animal, are evolved after their several kinds. All the truths as to the being of God on which his law is founded, are implied in this work of creation. Nothing in heaven or earth is self-existent and eternal but God only. All being and all personality are derived from God and subsist in God. Nature is but the effect of which he is the cause. His unity is manifested in the unity and continuity of creation from its beginning to its consummation ; his reason in its order and in the harmony and mutual adaptations of its infinitely varied parts ; his Divine power and energy in the causation through which this universal order has been developed. Another general conclusion from creation is specially indicated by St. Paul as antecedent to all law, being manifested (he says) to man in God's visible works *ever since creation*,[2] viz. that he, being eternal and of infinite power, must be one who cannot be represented by any material form, so that idolatry, no less than polytheism, is a contradiction of his being.

9. (II.) But no less essential to the foundation of man's duty both to God and to his neighbour,—essential indeed as being the reason why there can be any such thing as religion and morality,—is that relation of man to God which was established in the origin of the human race. Of all this marvellous work, the creation of man is the climax and consummation. In the sublime representation given in the sacred record, we ascend from a state of chaos, through the successive stages of the development of the universe, to man, for whom this earth had been prepared as his habitation.[3] As

---

[1] Cf. *e. g.* Acts xiv. 15, xvii. 24, 25 ; Rom. i. 19, 20 ; 1 Cor. xi. 7—9 ; 1 Tim. ii. 12—14, iv. 3, 4 ; James iii. 9.

[2] ἀπὸ κτίσεως κόσμου, Rom. i. 20.   [3] Isa. xlv. 18.

marking distinctly that man, in his bodily nature, is related to the rest of created being, which has in him its completion, the creation of man has not a day to itself;[1] it is not separated from the creation of the lower animals even so widely as that is from the creation of the vegetable kingdom. Man is reminded that he has, in common with other animals, a material frame composed of the same constituents as theirs; that his body is but the perfection of animal organisation; indeed, that in some respects the very beasts of the field are his superiors, if he does not realise his own true position as man. On this side of man's nature lie those dangers and temptations which are of all the most common, and to mankind in general the most powerful. But in the complete revelation of man's origin, his physical relation to the animal and material world is far less distinctly marked than his relation to God. In his creation it is no longer, "God said; and it was so;" or, "God said, Let the earth bring forth; and it was so;" but "God said, Let us make man in our image, after our likeness." "So God created man in his image; in the image of God created he him." The creation of man therefore as one who, though possessing an animal nature, is yet in his entire being allied to the infinite and eternal God, is an act of a different order from that of calling into existence the phenomena of the visible universe, and the varied forms of organic life. He who is ushered on the stage of created being by so solemn a preparation is the son of God, the representative upon the earth of the Creator himself, who commits to him charge and authority over all his works.

10. That these remarkable words, "the image of God," do not mean only a state of spiritual and moral purity,—although without doubt such must be the initial and normal state of one thus created,—we must certainly infer from the fact that the same words are used of man, after his fall from this state of purity, both in the Old Testament and in the New.[2] They undoubtedly imply that man is not like the rest of creation, formed and determined by his environments. He has reason to judge, spirit to enlighten him, will to determine him, and is therefore responsible to God for his actions. He has a personality which gives every individual man personal rights; he is an end in himself, and cannot, like other creatures, be used merely as means to an end; his life has a sacredness almost Divine, and he has a dignity and authority resembling that of him whose offspring he is.[3] But all these results and consequences of man's state by creation have been more or less obscured, if not interrupted, by his fall. It is important, therefore, that we should look beyond all the indications of the image of God in man, whether in his reason or his conscience, to the fact itself of that mysterious relation between man and his infinitely holy and glorious Creator, which was constituted by his creation in the image and likeness of God. This relation is evidently the source—(a) Of all the duties which man owes to God of love, of belief, of obedience, and of the imitation of God,[4] his heavenly Father. (b) Of duties which he owes to his brother man as being equally with himself, by his origin, a son of God. Those rights of man which are called natural, as belonging equally to the whole human race, and which are sometimes represented as a discovery of modern philosophy, have no rational basis whatever except in that relation to God which all men of all nations and classes possess alike by their

[1] Augustin. 'De Genesi Imp. Lib.' § 55. Hic animadvertenda quædam et conjunctio, et discretio animalium. Nam eodem die factum hominem dicit quo bestias.
[2] Gen. ix. 6; 1 Cor. xi. 7; cf. James iii. 9.
[3] Compare Ps. lxxxii. 6; "I have said, Ye are gods; and all of you are children of the Most High," and our Lord's comment on this, John x. 34—36.
[4] Cf. 'Hooker's Fourth Class of Laws,' § 6, supra.

nature, a relation which "the law" given by God through Moses first expressly revealed.

11. (III.) But the history of creation supplies the foundation not only of the relations between God and man, and of each man with every other individual of the human race, but also of the social relations of the various members of the human family. For there is another peculiarity in the account of man's creation which we might have overlooked, had not Christ himself in his teaching specially directed attention to its force and meaning.[1] When a question was asked him on the subject of marriage, he answered, "Have ye not read, that he who made them at the beginning made them male and female?"[2] This expression is not used, it must be observed, in describing the creation of animals. The force of the words is explained in that full description of some parts of the work of creation which is given in the second chapter of Genesis.[3] From this we learn that "Adam was first formed, then Eve"; that "the man is not of the woman; but the woman of the man: neither was the man created for the woman; but the woman for the man":[4] from which the apostle Paul infers the authority of man over woman. The description given in Genesis,—whatever the process may have been which is represented by woman having been formed by God out of man,—explains to us why the words quoted by our Lord have such profound significance. The reality and the force of that relation between the sexes, of which marriage is the expression, could not be taught by volumes of commandments and precepts as they are by this mystical but simple history of the creation of man and woman. Christ confirms the teaching of that history, asserting that this original unity is the basis of the true unity of those whom "God joins together" in marriage, so that they two are one flesh. Marriage, it will be observed, is not the sexual union merely, but is represented by God *bringing the woman to the man*.[5] And our Lord quotes as the word of God himself the conclusion drawn, "Therefore shall a man leave his father and mother, and shall cleave unto his wife." It follows from all this argument that marriage, the normal type of which is the indissoluble union of one man with one woman, is the exponent of a relation between the sexes involved in their very origin, and that this ordinance, being antecedent to law, is the basis of all those rights and responsibilities which the Divine law maintains and defines. And it must be further observed, that this ordinance is the source not merely of human life, as indicated by the name given to the first woman,[6] but of human society. Without it there might have been a race of men, as of beasts, birds, and fishes; but the family, the unit of the social system, and thus of national life, could not have been formed. There could have been no civilisation and no progress. To the development of man as a social being marriage is essential, and the more nearly that the primal type of marriage is preserved in any nation, the stronger are all the social ties, and the more progressive is its social system. For from it all the duties, not only of the marriage relation itself, but of all other social relations, are derived. The fact that God ordained that mankind should increase and multiply on the earth through a holy union, which he appointed and blessed, determines also the mutual duties and responsibilities of parents and children, which are only limited, as the language of the sacred history indicates, by those which the husband and wife mutually owe to one another, and those which all owe alike to God.

12. (IV.) Thus far in the brief history of man's creation and original state, we

---

[1] Matt xix. 4—6; Mark x. 6.   [2] Gen. i. 27; v. 2.
[3] Gen. ii. 18, 20—24.   [4] 1 Cor. xi. 8, 9; 1 Tim. ii. 13.
[5] Gen. ii. 22. It must be remembered, however, that in one sense the language of Genesis applies even to unholy unions; 1 Cor. vi. 16.
[6] *Chavvîh*.

have found a basis for all those fundamental principles of religion and morality which the universal conscience of man cannot but recognise. We trace distinctly the lines of a Divine order, to which the nature of man, created as he is in God's image and likeness, itself bears witness. But it is certain, not only from the experience of man in his fallen condition, but from considerations that would equally apply if sin had never entered the world, that, for the maintenance of the religious life in man, more is required than all these principles which may be inferred from his natural relations to God and to the rest of mankind. The very charge committed to man by his Maker, of subduing the earth and exercising dominion therein, in fulfilling which man imitates the Creator so far as his limited powers enable him, would have itself interfered with the development of his spiritual life, even in his state of innocence, unless there had been some provision for the culture and sustenance of that life. This was made by the revelation of God as an example to man in his resting, as well as in his working. Of course it is not to be supposed that by the words, " God rested on the seventh day from all his work that he had made," the idea is meant to be conveyed to our minds, either that God needed repose as we need it, or that with him " who inhabiteth eternity " there is succession of days and times. He is indeed in one sense ever working,[1] and in another ever resting. But during the six days of creation his work had gradually proceeded to its consummation, and all being now completed and set in order and pronounced to be very good, that exercise of the Divine Will and Reason which distinguished the operation of God's power in creating the heavens and the earth and all that are therein, from his providential government of them, ceased.[1] The Genesis was accomplished ; nature, which itself subsists in God,—for in him all things live and move and have their being,—and which is the effect of a series of causations which all centre in him,—had attained a determined form and order which bore the same relation to those that preceded as the newborn infant bears to the embryo. This is the first and most obvious meaning of the rest of God. It also seems, as Augustine suggests,[3] that God's resting *from* the work of creation is intended to imply that these created things were not such as he could rest *in*.[4] However, the rest of God is not merely negative. In the Epistle to the Hebrews,[5] the apostle reminds those who were familiar with the teaching of the Old Testament, that this rest of God, of which the law speaks as succeeding to the work of creation, is the very rest promised to all that believe, of which the rest of the Israelites in the land into which Joshua brought them was a figure, of which David speaks in the Psalms as yet in prospect, into which we must still labour to enter by faith in God's promises, for the enjoyment of that rest[6] is reserved for the people of God when they shall have ceased from their earthly labours. From this argument of the apostle we must conclude that the seventh day of God's rest, which followed the six days of his work of creation, is not yet completed. It must be noticed indeed that after the mention of the seventh day the words do not recur, which are used of all the preceding days, and which, whatever be their exact meaning, imply that each had its beginning and its close. This rest of God, therefore, while it precludes the continued exercise of

---

[1] John v. 17 ; cf. Isa. xl. 28.

[2] Cf. Thom. Aq. ' Summæ Prim. Quæst.' LXXIII. iii. : " Dicendum quod requies Dei in die septima dupliciter accipitur : primo quidem quantum ad hoc quod cessavit a novis operibus condendis ; ita tamen quod creaturam conditam conservat et administrat. Alio modo secundum quod post opera requievit in seipso."

[3] ' De Genesi ad Literam,' IV. xv.

[4] Cf. the beautiful idea in Zeph. iii. 17, " He will rest in his love." But the word there is not *shabath*, rest from labour, but *charash*, be at peace or silent.

[5] Chap. iii. 11 to iv. 11.   [6] σαββατισμός.

creative power, includes the whole of the work of redemption, a work in a higher sphere of spiritual power, and more truly Divine, and one which, except in the eternal counsels of the Almighty, in which it was ordained before the foundations of the earth were laid, could not begin until the first Adam had been created as the τύπος, the form in outliue as it were, of that Divine man who should be hereafter revealed.

13. These considerations fully explain, so far as it can be explained, the mystery of the seventh day and its sanctification. What the days of God's working and God's rest mean in relation to his eternal being is beyond our knowledge; but in our imitation of God we must regard them as represented by the days of our short life on earth. Man being the son of God is to follow God's example alike in his working and his resting. The seventh day is sanctified for resting *from* those labours that belong to things seen and temporal, *in* those pursuits that pertain to things unseen and eternal. Both the works of man and the rest of man in his earthly life are intended to prepare him for the rest of God. As a fundamental principle in the natural constitution of man, this sanctification of the seventh day implies that those powers of body and mind, which he exercises in subduing the earth and having dominion over it, require for their refreshment and perfection not only that cessation from labour which is provided by the succession of evening and morning, of night and day, but periodical rest of a different kind. As a religious principle it is also as obviously that, for the invigoration and development of the spiritual life in man, a definite portion of time should be periodically set apart and consecrated to God as the Lord of our spirits, and devoted to those things tnat belong to a spiritual world. It is hardly necessary to point out that this interpretation of the sanctification of the seventh day is altogether different from the idea that, from the creation, a *particular* day, a certain time of the earth's revolution on its axis, was holier than others; this is to make of an ordinance antecedent to all law what St. Paul calls a "carnal commandment." On the other hand, if it be thought that the determining of one day in seven for a day of rest must be, from its very nature, an artificial and arbitrary appointment, and therefore inconsistent with a Divine and universal order, it must be remembered, not only that the fact of a sevenfold division occurring so frequently in Holy Scripture seems to indicate some corresponding reality in the Divine order beyond the range of our understanding, but also that he who created man must know, as we cannot know, what proportions of man's life are required for physical rest and spiritual activity, in order to preserve the true *equilibrium* of that life. Experience has abundantly proved of how great value this primeval ordinance is for the physical, moral, and religious welfare of man, and how full of profound truth are those words of our Blessed Lord, when in regard to this question, as on another occasion in reference to marriage, he directed those who were zealous for the law to the original ordinance as the true interpretationof the law: "The Sabbath was made for man, not man for the Sabbath." [1]

As our argument here is simply that the law (in the sense of a Divine order) of *rest* on the seventh day, after God's example, is involved in the history of creation, even as the true law of marriage is in the union of the first man and the first woman, it is unnecessary to enter into the question whether the Sabbath was observed in

---

[1] St. Mark ii. 27. That Christ here referred to the ordinance from the beginning, and not to the Mosaical law, is obvious from the word ἐγένετο which is used both of the Sabbath and of man. Οὐχ ὁ ἄνθρωπος [ἐγένετο], cannot mean anything else than "man was not *created*" for the Sabbath, and would be no reason at all in reference to a Jewish ordinance.

patriarchal times before the giving of the Mosaic law. It is sufficient to say, on the one hand, that both in the Scriptural history of man during that period, and in many nations of the Gentile world even to the present day, indications are found of a hebdomadal division of time,[1] which cannot easily be accounted for unless it were the result of some primeval tradition; on the other, that there is no intimation in the sacred history that this ordinance was given to man as a law, in the proper sense of the word, and, therefore, we need not be surprised that it was obscured and almost forgotten, even as other fundamental principles of religion were, when there was nothing to give it a definite and permanent form.

14. The history of the creation of man contains then, we find, all the elementary principles of his religious and moral duty, and (what we may call) the elementary provision for the order of his own life. It is indeed an internal evidence of no small weight to the Divine origin of the sacred history, that in this brief and so to speak condensed record, in which events of the largest import and the most profound significance are described in a few simple sentences, without any attempt to expound the mysterious truths hidden in the story, or to extract moral and religious instruction from it, much less to build up some system of religion upon the facts recorded—yet there are involved all the rudimentary truths both of religion and of morality. But it is necessary to observe, that in man's original state none of these were or could be laws in the strict sense of the word, that is, commands or prohibitions with promises attached to obedience, and threats of punishment for transgresssion. This Divine order, to which man's own nature belonged, required no law to enforce it on man. Created in God's image and likeness, good and pure in body, soul, and spirit, there was no temptation to him to depart from that order, nor any need for commands and prohibitions to restrain him from the sins to which we are liable. Not only had sin not entered into the world, but there was no concupiscence or tendency to sin.[2] The lamb requires no chain to prevent it from ravening as the wolf.

15. Yet if this had been all; if man had been left simply in a state of innocence, with no temptation, no trial of his submission to the will of God, merely living according to his own pure nature, without any necessity to deny himself and exercise self-control, how could he have rendered reasonable and willing obedience, the true service of the spirit, to God his Father? how could he ever have become what God certainly purposed that he should become, when he created him in his own likeness? We may affirm without any hesitation, since this was the method actually adopted in the wisdom and goodness of God, that it was essential to the spiritual development of man that he should be subject to some law by which he might be educated as a son of God, and might render spiritual obedience. And, as far as we can judge, the law suitable for one in such a condition, that is, for one in the infancy of his moral and spiritual life, must take the form of a prohibition of some act, not in itself evil,—for that would be contrary to his nature and therefore no trial of obedience,—but indifferent in itself, yet such as his own nature might incline him to, with a penalty attached to the transgression of the law. And further, if we consider this law of paradise, as we must in order to understand its reason and its force, in the light of the subsequent history of mankind, and of the teaching of St. Paul as to the purposes and the effect of the law given by Moses, it seems impossible not to conclude that the law given to man in his state of innocency was necessary, not only for the development

---

[1] I am informed by a learned Chinese friend, that although amongst them the hebdomadal division is not retained, yet, according to one of their sacred books, the I-King, or 'Book of Changes,' "the revolution of the order of the universe is completed in seven days."
[2] Cf. Gen. ii. 25.

of his spiritual life, but also in order that man, having a body by nature mortal, might have life in that body. There is nothing to indicate that man's body, though free from concupiscence and sin, would naturally, without that righteousness which is the result of obedience to a law, be exempt from the decay and dissolution to which all material creation is naturally subject. Indeed the sacred history itself intimates as much by the "tree of life" being planted in the midst of the garden as the "sacrament" of man's preservation from natural death, of which tree he might eat so long as he obeyed the command not to eat of the "tree of knowledge of good and evil."[1] We know indeed that the effect of the transgression was that man became like the rest of the animal creation in this respect, losing his right to "the tree of life;" and the converse, viz. that the obedience was required in order to entitle him to that right, seems to follow of necessity. On the other hand, we might infer from St. Paul's arguments, that while this law was necessary for man, in order that by obedience he might attain righteousness and life,[2] yet its effect on human nature, even though pure from sin, must have been somewhat the same as the law produced on sinful man; that is, that the command being a prohibition of that which was naturally desired, would of itself provoke transgression, even as the strength of the current is felt only when it is resisted. So that man in his natural state, though free from sinful passion, yet being destitute of that wisdom which experience alone can give, and of that supernatural grace which Christ's redemption alone can supply,— being also spiritually in a state of *unstable equilibrium*, in which the least deviation would create the tendency to decline further, while there was no power of recovery,—sooner or later could not but fall. Infidelity raises superficial objections against the sacred history, as if it were inconsistent with God's wisdom and justice that man should have been subjected to temptation, and again that the consequences of an act apparently so insignificant should have been so serious. But on the contrary, the difficulty really is to conceive it possible that the original history of man, a reasonable and spiritual being with a material nature, could have been, consistently with the goodness and wisdom of an Almighty Creator, other than that which Holy Scripture describes. Such a being *not* created with a pure and sinless nature; one with moral and spiritual faculties to be developed, *not* under some law; one with an animal nature *not* subject to the natural laws of decay and death, unless freedom from them should be gained as the reward of obedience; and one, thus constituted, *not* liable to fall and lose the reward, we may even say not certain to fall sooner or later;—all such hypotheses present difficulties to human thought far more serious than any that can be raised out of the sacred history.

And, it must be observed, these questions which we have discussed are not some curious, but unprofitable, speculations. They touch most nearly, and practically, the whole subject of the law, and illustrate very forcibly the necessity, on which the Apostle Paul so much insists, of an economy not of law but of grace, in order that man, even in his best state, may obtain righteousness and life.

LAW FROM ADAM TO MOSES.

16. No reverent reader of Holy Scripture can fail to recognise the profound insight into the moral and spiritual nature of man which is revealed in the history of

---

[1] S. August. 'De Gen. ad Lit.' vi. 36: "Denique non ait Apostolus, Corpus quidem mortale propter peccatum; sed *corpus mortuum propter peccatum.* Illud quippe, ante peccatum, et mortale secundum aliam et immortale secundum aliam causam dici poterat: id est mortale, quia poterat mori, immortale quia poterat non mori ... quod ei præstabatur de ligno vitæ, non de constitutione naturæ; a quo ligno separatus est cum peccasset," *etc.*

[2] Cf. Gal. iii. 21.

the Fall. We need not dwell on this further than as it affects our argument. The necessity for some external and positive law in paradise we have concluded from general considerations, as well as from some to which the teachings of the New Testament direct us. The force and meaning of the particular prohibition are apparent from the story itself. While there is no sufficient reason for questioning its literal truth, and supposing that it is only a myth or allegory, yet we must ever bear in mind that in Holy Scripture it is not the letter but " the spirit that profiteth," though the letter is the vase that holds the precious ointment. We must observe, then, in this case, that the prohibition was to eat of the " tree of *knowledge of good and evil.*" The temptation, though acting through the fleshly appetite, was addressed to the spirit;[1] " Ye shall be as gods, knowing good and evil." And such was the result. Their eyes *were* opened, though first of all to their own shame, through the sense of evil in themselves and the consciousness of their own alienation from God by transgression. But it must be remembered that in itself the knowledge of good and evil is a higher spiritual state than one of ignorance of the difference between them. This knowledge is indeed an essential condition to all spiritual wisdom.[2] " The man is become as one of us, to know good and evil," are the words of God himself, and to suppose that this is irony is to misapprehend the whole philosophy of the fall of man. And it might be supposed that now man, possessing the power to distinguish between good and evil, the principles also of all religious and moral duty having been established in his creation, would henceforth need no external law ; for he must be a law to himself. But that very knowledge, as the sacred record indicates, and as the subsequent history of the world abundantly proves, was his fall. And the effect of this inward law was the same as that of the law given by Moses, namely, that sin multiplied and abounded. The sin of eating the forbidden tree filled the earth with sin and guilt and death, not only by " the fault and corruption of the nature " of man which was transmitted from Adam by natural generation,[3] but through the necessary consequences of the knowledge of evil. Separated from God by transgression, and conscious of the evil desire in his fleshly nature, man was now out of harmony with the Divine order to which his own nature, as a whole, belonged ; and having no inherent ability to restore himself, the knowledge which he possessed gave him no spiritual power, but on the contrary increased his tendency to evil. It was equally true of this inward law, as of the law from Mount Sinai, that because by it was the knowledge of sin,[4] therefore by it man could not obtain righteousness and life. Therefore, as St. Paul says,[5] " *death reigned* from Adam to Moses, even over them that had not sinned after the similitude of Adam's transgression," that is, who had not, like our first parents, transgressed any positive command of God, but who sinned against " the law written in their hearts,"[6] and justly incurred the condemnation of God. The exceptional cases of men who served God and walked with him and pleased him[7] were the result of a supernatural principle superior to this natural law in man, even of that faith which was in them, as it is in all ages, " the substance of things hoped for, the evidence of things not seen." In such men the hopes were founded on the tokens of God's goodness and mercy to fallen man, and specially on the promises of redemption and deliverance from evil, which began in the assurance given immediately after the fall, that " the seed of the woman " should after a severe conflict crush the serpent's head.

17. During the antediluvian age, as described in the sacred history, although there are indications of God's manifesting himself to man, yet there are no traces whatever of any law, in the true sense of the word, either human or Divine. The sacrifices

---

[1] Gen. iii. 4—6. [2] Heb. v. 14. [3] Gen. v. 3. [4] Rom. iii. 20.
[5] Rom. v. 14. [6] Rom. ii. 15. [7] See Heb. xi. 1—7, &c.

that were offered do not appear to have originated in any express command of God, though he may have intimated to Adam himself, as to Abel, his acceptance of such offerings. Abel's offering was accepted as the expression of his faith; but there is nothing to prove that the offering of Cain, though rejected in consequence of his want of faith, was contrary to any law. The murder of Abel by his brother's hand was not punished by death, and the very language of the murderer, in which he complains of the severity of his punishment, points to a general state of lawlessness beyond the immediate "presence of the Lord." Indeed the general description of the world from the Fall to Noah represents a scene of unrestrained disorder and violence. The brief but very significant history of one of the most eminent descendants of Cain is representative of the period. The primeval ordinance of marriage was by him first forsaken. The personal right of the strongest and most powerful to avenge himself to the utmost for every injury is asserted as the only law.[1] The industry and ingenuity and skill of man were highly developed; woman was famous for her beauty; "there were giants in the earth in those days," and "mighty men, men of renown;" but man without law bęcame utterly and hopelessly corrupt, "the wickedness of man was great on the earth," and the disorganised, godless world was destroyed. It was the age of all but universal dominion of the flesh, ending in dissolution and death. At the same time it must be noticed that while ungodliness and irreligion reigned supreme, yet there are no evidences either of idolatry, or of those sins against nature, to which, as the Apostle Paul teaches, God subsequently gave men over as the punishment of idolatry.

18. The world after the Flood began with, what we may call, a new dispensation. Noah, on coming out of the ark, offered burnt sacrifices of every clean beast and every clean fowl—the distinction was probably natural and not ceremonial—his offerings were accepted, a covenant of mercy was established between God and man, and now for the first time in the history of mankind we have some express indication of Divine law revealed for the direction of man. There was first of all a prohibition of eating flesh "with the life thereof, which is the blood thereof," which prohibition (evidently, we may say, when the language is compared with that of the Mosaical law [2]) had reference to the use of the blood in those sacrifices, which had now received express and emphatic sanction from God as an acceptable method of worshipping him.[3] A second law was also given, which springs from the very first duty of man to his brother man—"Whoso sheddeth man's blood by man shall his blood be shed: for in the image of God made he man." But although these two commandments had in many respects the character of law, we do not find the word *torah* used of them; they were rather isolated commands,[4] the first elements and germs of a system of Divine law in which the whole duty of man to God and his neighbour should be comprehended.

19. Yet this beginning of Divine law on earth was, without doubt, of no small value for that which, the sacred history informs us, soon succeeded in this post-diluvian world; namely, the development of national life, of which in the long and dreary age of lawlessness before the Flood there are no signs whatever. The due protection of the person from violence is the first and most important object of that civil law, which is the bond of national order; and it may be well supposed that the consciousness of the necessity of such law, which the Divine command awakened, and of which the past history of the antediluvian world must have supplied abundant evidence,

---

[1] Gen. iv. 19—24. The interpretation here given to the language of Lamech is certainly the most probable.
[2] Cf. Levit. xvii. 11.   [3] Gen. viii. 21.
[4] Θέμιστες. Cf. Maine's 'Ancient Law,' p. 4.

gave that strong and general impulse in the direction of national organisation which we find described in the tenth chapter of the Book of Genesis. Of this remarkable movement, so characteristic of this period of the world's history, the ambitious and godless attempt to build a mighty capital of a universal empire, which was frustrated and turned to confusion by Divine interposition, is a signal and instructive instance. If the hypothesis suggested is correct—and certainly it has much appearance of probability—it is also a proof how soon a law given by God for man's benefit may be perverted and turned to evil by the sinful heart of man. And the same may be said of the other law, of a ceremonial nature, given to Noah and his sons. For if it referred to the law of sacrifice, as can hardly be doubted, it must have been the first element of a definite and orderly system of religious worship among the nations that were descended from Noah. And among them religion soon became perverted, and the worship of other gods, and idolatrous practices, of which before there had been no mention, appeared in a few generations after the Flood.[1] And this new development of man's life and man's ungodliness was also followed by those sins which brought God's judgments on Sodom and Gomorrah. It became sufficiently evident, therefore, that although even the first beginnings of law were a benefit to man as regards his present life, yet, to restrain transgressions, a merely rudimentary law was of no avail whatever.

20. The calling of Abram out of this world of idolatry and sin to be the father of a chosen nation, with the promise that in him and his seed all the families of the earth should be blessed, was the most important epoch in the spiritual history of man between Adam and Moses. The covenant made with Abram, however, as St. Paul has pointed out,[2] was a covenant not of law but of promise, and was established four or five centuries before the giving of the law. And although circumcision, the seal of that covenant, was an ordinance anticipating the law, and so distinctly embodying its spirit that it became ultimately the most significant emblem of the law; yet, as the apostle reminds the Romans,[3] the father of the faithful received the promises, while yet in uncircumcision, through faith only. However, speaking generally, we may say that with the rite of circumcision, which was in all respects a law, and with the restriction of the covenant to the seed of Abraham in the line of Isaac, the dispensation of the law, properly so called, began. And so far as our argument relates to that dispensation, we might pass over the intervening period between Abraham and Moses, and proceed at once to the consideration of that which is in the fullest and strictest sense the *Torah*, the law of God given by his chosen servant to the nation of Israel.

DEVELOPMENT OF HUMAN LAW WITHOUT REVELATION.

21. But, before we enter on any discussion of this important subject, it will be well first to examine briefly how far, independently of any express revelation from God either to man or through man,—at all events any known to us,—the Divine order, which man being created in God's image to some extent recognises, and against the transgression of which his knowledge of good and evil bears witness, has in different ages of the world been asserted by him in the form of external and positive law. He discovers indeed by his own experience that this order, so far as it affects relations between man and man, is essential to social and national life; and further that the order cannot be maintained, and the rights of these relations cannot be protected, except by law. We need only investigate this subject sufficiently to understand

---

[1] Josh. xxiv. 2, 14, 15.   [2] Gal. iii. 17.   [3] Rom. iv. 10—12.

more distinctly on the one hand the value, and indeed the absolute necessity to man's truest and highest life, of a complete revelation of Divine law, and on the other the form which all law must assume in order to be law indeed, and to effect the purposes for which the Divine law itself is given.

22. Not only the sacred history, but also the evidence afforded by the science of comparative jurisprudence [1] indicates that the original constitution of human society was that which is known as the Patriarchal, in which the father of the family possessed absolute authority over its persons and its property. In this condition of society the word of the parent was the only human law, he being the representative of God to the family in religion as well as in secular matters. Traces of this primeval government have survived even to the present day in some nations, in the form known to Roman law as the "Patria Potestas." But as the family life developed itself into the various forms of natural life,—a process which, as we have already observed, began and indeed was in active operation soon after the Deluge,—we find at all events wherever the nation became large and powerful, the national sovereign, succeeding to and superseding the more archaic government. His authority, however, like the paternal, was not that of a mere individual but of the representative of Divinity, and his judgments were regarded as not those of his own personal will but as emanating from above: indeed in the mythical history of ancient nations the original kings are with hardly an exception represented as gods or demi-gods. In regard to Egypt, the only great nation of the period preceding the giving of the law by Moses of which we have any description in the sacred history, we fortunately possess in the present day, in addition to the notices in the Holy Scripture, sufficient information from other contemporaneous records, or from subsequent history, to enable us to trace with some certainty the development of national law there.[2] The Egyptians believed that the origin of law was Divine, the god *Thoth* (or *Hermes* as he was called by the Greeks), who represented the Divine Reason, having first promulgated it for the benefit of man, and their complete code of law being gradually formed by the wisdom of early monarchs and sages, and interpreted from the precedents of the decisions of learned judges in noted cases, which corresponded somewhat to the *Responsa prudentium* of the Romans, and yet more nearly to the "case made" law of later times. This code was called the "Eight Books of Thoth." The study of that code was the special duty of those high priests who were called "prophets," and of the king who also held that office. To the king it belonged to legislate, as well as to administer the law, but in all matters of state he was assisted by the counsel of the wisest and most distinguished members of the priestly order.[3] "We are acquainted with few of the laws of the ancient Egyptians, but the superiority of their legislation has always been acknowledged as the cause of the duration of an empire which lasted with the same form of government for a much longer period than the generality of ancient states. Indeed the wisdom of these people was proverbial, and was held in such consideration by other nations that we find it taken by the Jews as the standard to which superior learning [4] in their own country was willingly compared; and Moses had prepared himself for the duties of a legislator by becoming versed in all the wisdom of the Egyptians" (Wilkinson).

---

[1] See Maine's 'Ancient Law,' p. 122.

[2] As the facts to which I shall allude are such as are mentioned in many modern works on Egypt, I do not consider it necessary to give references; but I have taken the statements chiefly, and in some cases verbatim, from Sir J. G. Wilkinson's well-known work.

[3] See in illustration Gen. xli. 28, 37, 38; l. 7; and Isa. xix. 11, 12.

[4] Cf. Solomon; 1 Kings iv. 30.

23. The characteristics of Egyptian law, so far as they are known to us, are well worth noticing. The object of the laws was to preserve life and reclaim the offender ; and therefore capital punishment was not inflicted except in cases of murder, and of some few other crimes specially injurious to the community. But the crime of murder was considered so heinous, " that to be the accidental witness of an attempt to murder without endeavouring to prevent it was a capital offence which could only be palliated by bringing proof of inability to act." In the same spirit, the witness of any injury to the person of another, or of a robbery, was bound, under the same penalty as the offender himself, to interfere, or, if that was impossible, to be a prosecutor. The only exception to the punishment of death for murder, at least when the royal prerogative was not exercised, was in the case of infanticide by a father, in which, on the principle of the *patria potestas*, a lesser punishment was inflicted. Of other crimes, adultery was severely punished in both the offenders. Truth or justice (personified in the goddess *Thmei*, who possessed both these attributes, and was often represented as a double form), was regarded as the highest of all virtues, " *inasmuch as it related more particularly to others*," while the other virtues immediately benefit him who possesses them. Whenever therefore a falsehood injured another it was punished, as in the Jewish law, according to the *lex talionis*, and when a falsehood against another was maintained by an oath, it became one of the extreme crimes which were punished by death. " For they considered that it involved two distinct crimes—a contempt for the gods and a violation of faith towards man ; the former the direct promoter of every sin, the latter destructive of all those ties which are most essential for the welfare of society."

24. The history and character of Egyptian law have been more particularly noticed, both because Egypt was more nearly connected than any other nation with the early history of the people to whom the God of heaven and earth revealed his law, and also because they supply interesting illustrations of our preceding argument, both in regard to the recognition by man of the Divine order, and also as to the need of law, in its true and proper sense, for national life. The subject of man's natural recognition of this order has been largely discussed by modern writers : there is indeed no nation under heaven, civilised or savage, a nomadic tribe or a vast empire like India, from whose traditions or literature illustrations of this truth might not be drawn. But there is one ancient nation of the world, which has been of all the furthest removed, in past ages, from the influences of the religious enlightenment and progressive civilisation of more favoured regions, whose witness to the Divine order, and to its recognition by the spirit of man, specially illustrates our argument, because among them that inward witness is expressly made the basis of national law. According to Bunsen,[1] " the actual aboriginal tribe of the primeval home has settled itself in the extreme east of Asia, and maintained itself there up to the present day ; forming the most numerous nation of the world, the oldest in history." The Chinese " language forms an irrefragable testimony to the autochthonous character of the unique position which it occupies. Hence whatever may prove to be an indigenous product of its religious consciousness, is both relatively and intrinsically of high import to universal history. It is the undivided main stream of history as it issues from its parent source, not a mere lagoon." Without accepting Bunsen's theory, it is at all events certain that at a period of very remote antiquity, anterior to the time of Abraham, China had its own language, literature, and polity. Confucius, who lived at the close of the fifth century before Christ, was but the collector of the ancient records and reminiscences of his nation. And in these we find a quite

---

[1] ' God in History,' Book III. chap. v.

independent confirmation of that which in this argument has been derived simply from the Scripture history of man, viz. that human law, in order to be the basis of national life, must be the assertion of principles of the Divine order which man's nature, as a whole, recognises. I prefer to use the language of another as an independent testimony to this truth:

Following Bunsen, as our latest and probably most trustworthy guide, "let us listen to one or two of the utterances of these sacred books which bear most closely on the point which concerns us. This is from the Shi-King:

"'The opinion and judgment of Heaven is learned (reveals itself) through the opinion and judgment of our people. Heaven's approval and disapproval (is recognised) through the approval and disapproval of our people. An intimate relation subsists between the upper and lower world. Oh, how careful should those be who govern countries!'"

Apropos of this remarkable specimen of antediluvian (?) politics, Bunsen relates an interesting anecdote of our own day. Gutzlaff told him, he says, that "when, after the peace of Nankin, in 1845, the Emperor of China felt himself impelled to refuse his assent to the execution of that treaty by which the Tartar city of Canton was to be opened to foreigners, he justified his repudiation by this great maxim of the sacred books. And 'the voice of the people is the voice of God' resounded once more through the whole empire. When the emperor's edict was published, and everywhere formed the subject of discussion, it was said to Gutzlaff by patriotic Chinese: 'That maxim of our sacred books is well known to us, it is our watchword;' but this was a new thing to us, that the Mandshee emperor should publicly appeal to this sacred text of the Scriptures, which testifies against himself." By what qualifications our primeval ancestors—if such they were—guarded this profound but perilous maxim against the false interpretations which it has received, and still receives, amongst ourselves, we are not informed. But it surely is a *striking* instance of the *consensus* of mankind in their anthropological conceptions, that a maxim which embodies so much, both of the truth and all the falsehood of modern politics, should have been familiar to the ears of what there is reason to believe was the oldest civilised community. * * * * In a subsequent passage he thus sums up their wisdom: "If we sum up the whole, we find one thought continually recurring in the works of all those sages, as the root-idea of the ancient system, and we may express it thus:—There is a law which governs the All in nature and in man, and this one law is reasonable. Thus, indeed, it had been said by Meng-Zo, the renowned successor of Confucius, in the fourth century before our era, 'He who knows *his own nature*, and that of all things, knows what heaven is; for heaven is, indeed, the inward essence and the vital energy of all things.' This thought is the dowry of the Chinese intellect in the general history of man; the conception of a Kosmos *in*, not *above*, the various objects, which, however, attains personality only in the human mind. Man's life is to be orderly, like that of nature; the sphere of this life in which the Chinese recognise something Divine, is that of the family; the bond between parents and children is to him the most sacred of all bonds." In these two conceptions—of the dignity of the person on the one hand, and the sacredness of paternal authority and filial obedience on the other—we have the secret of that marvellous length of days which, notwithstanding all their faults, has been granted to this strange people. * * * * Lest it should be supposed that the view which I have here presented rests on a single authority, it may be proper that I should mention that to whatever extent Baron Bunsen's view of the autochthonous character of the Chinese may be peculiar, his opinion on the point with which we are concerned is the common opinion. All are agreed that the history of Confucius is the most faithful expression of the national mind, and that that teaching was based on the revelations of our common nature. "I teach you nothing," he says, "but what you might learn yourselves, viz. the observance of the three fundamental laws of relation between sovereign and subject, father and child, husband and wife; and the five capital virtues, universal charity, impartial justice, conformity to ceremonies and established usages, rectitude of heart and mind, and pure sincerity."[1]

---

[1] Lorimer's 'Institutes of Law,' pp. 90, 91.

25. There is, however, another part of the world with the history of which we are more familiar than with those of Egypt, or China, or even of India, and in this history the actual process of the development of law may be more exactly traced from its elementary principles to its matured forms. Maine, in his well-known work on Ancient Law, has pointed out that " the earliest notions connected with the conception, now so fully developed, of a law or rule of life, are those contained in the Homeric words, Themis or Themistes." In the Greek Pantheon Themis is the goddess of justice in the abstract sense, and, according to Hesiod,[1] the mother by Zeus of Dike, the goddess of administrative justice. There can be little doubt that the name is derived from the Egyptian *Thmei* (see § 23, *supra*), and the idea conveyed by the mythology is not really different[2] from that expressed in Homer, with whom Themis is the personification of the order established by custom and equity, and the assessor of Zeus. As such Themis suggested judicial awards both to kings and to gods, the greatest of all kings; and the judgments themselves were called Themistes (the plural of Themis). It is evident that the personification was intended to represent the authority of kings as the representatives of God on earth, and thus the original basis of the idea is the truth, which Revelation supplies, of man being made in the image and likeness of God. From these divinely-directed judgments of kings there grew up in course of time, as the heroic age passed away, a body of unwritten " customary law," which was in the keeping of an aristocracy, civil or religious, invested with judicial authority and privileges. " From the period of customary law we come to another sharply-defined epoch in the history of jurisprudence. We arrive at the era of *Codes*, those ancient codes of which the Twelve Tables of Rome were the most famous specimen. In Greece, in Italy, in the Hellenised sea-board of Western Asia, these codes made their appearance at periods much the same everywhere, not, I mean, at periods identical in point of time, but similar in point of the relative progress of each community. Everywhere, in the countries I have named, laws engraved on tablets and published to the people take the place of usages deposited with the recollection of a privileged obligarchy." * * * "Quite enough too remains of these collections, both in the East and West, to show that they mingled up religious, civil, and merely moral ordinances, without any regard to differences in their essential character; and this is consistent with all we know of early thought from other sources, the severance of law from morality, and of religion from law, belonging very distinctly to the *later* stages of mental progress."[3] The real value to the nation of these codes of law depended much on circumstances. When, as in India, they were compiled at a comparatively late period by a religious oligarchy and remained in their charge, they only tended to perpetuate corruptions and check further development. In Rome, being the result of the struggles of the plebeians against the exclusive privileges of the patricians, and embodying the usages of a more primitive and simple age, their effect was in the highest degree beneficial, both as regards the liberty and the progress of the commonwealth.

26. Of the period in the history of jurisprudence subsequent to this, during which, in the great commonwealth of Rome, human law attained a maturity and perfection such that Roman law has formed a very large and powerful element in the progress and consolidation of the civilisation of modern Europe, it is unnecessary to speak; because the exact and complete provisions for the protection and security of person

[1] At least to the author of the Theogony.

[2] Maine supposes (p. 4) that the mythological notion is "a modern and more developed idea," but the parallel with the Egyptian deity seems to contradict this. The personification of an attribute soon became a deity.

[3] ' Ancient Law,' pp. 14—16, etc.

and property, which are the precious results of fully-developed human law, lie outside the purposes for which the Divine law was necessary. But it must be remembered that Divine law had to fulfil these purposes, as St. Paul teaches us, by its being truly law, and not merely a code of moral and religious precepts. It is therefore of importance to observe what conclusions as to the definite meaning and force of law have been drawn by the human mind with the aid of the experience gained in the development of law. By none in any age has the philosophy of law been more carefully studied, or its terms more exactly defined, than by the ancient Romans. The Roman mind, above all others, was a legal mind. The iron power of the Roman state, to which the modern nations of Europe have succeeded in proportion as they have accepted and assimilated the principles which constituted its strength, was the power of the sovereign authority of law. What, then, is the exact idea of law which presented itself to the Roman mind? The Romans used two words in somewhat the same sense, but by no means as perfectly synonymous, *lex* and *jus; jus* having the wider sense of the two, including often that which is right according to the general principles of justice, while *lex* is law in its strict and proper sense. Cicero ('De Leg.' i. 6) defines *lex* thus: "Quæ scripto sancit quod vult aut jubendo aut vetando." It has been thus defined by a modern scholar: "A law is a rule or command of the sovereign power in a state, published in writing, and addressed to and enforced upon the members of such state; and this is the proper sense of law in Roman writers."[1] This definition is singularly exact and complete. It includes all the elements into which writers[2] on the subject of jurisprudence have resolved every law; viz. "a *command* of the lawgiver, an *obligation* imposed thereby on the citizen, and a *sanction* (or punishment) threatened in the event of disobedience;" the command, which is the first element in law, being a rule which prescribes or forbids, not a single act merely, but all acts of the same kind. There are obviously three ideas, correlative to these three elements, involved in the complete idea of law, and necessary to its perfectness: the supreme *authority* of the lawgiver; his *right* to claim obedience; and his *power* to punish transgression. Only where these are absolute, can law have all its force; *so that it follows, that no law can be law in the fullest and most exact sense of the word except Divine law.*

It is important to bear these conclusions in mind in examining the subject of the giving of the law by Moses, and also in reference to St. Paul's argument respecting Divine law in his Epistle to the Romans. For there can be no doubt that much of that argument derives its force from the true meaning of "law" as understood by the Roman mind. The character of that mind gave a special direction to this exposition of the gospel, which the apostle adapted to the intellectual education of those to whom he was writing; a direction which we find in no other epistle except in that to the Galatians. In that epistle, however, the question of "law" is treated far less generally and philosophically, and rather in reference to a particular question, and to the teaching of the Old Testament Scriptures.

Necessity for the Revelation of Divine Law.

27. It is of course impossible to doubt that the development of human law has been, both in its process and in its results, of inestimable value for the education of man as a reasonable being, and specially as enabling him to realise the

---

[1] The late George Long in article *Lex* in Smith's 'Dictionary of Antiquities.'
[2] Bentham in the 'Fragment on Government,' and Austin in his 'Province of Jurisprudence Determined' (Maine's 'Ancient Law,' p. 7).

mutual duties and responsibilities of all human relations. It is also certain, as has been already intimated, that human aw has indirectly aided religion, by enabling man to understand more clearly, and appreciate more fully, the relations between the Divine law and the gospel of Christ. But it has been only too obvious in the history of the world, that of itself human law has been wholly insufficient— wo may oven say worse than useless—for the direction of man in his responsibilities to God his Creator, or for preserving among men the true knowledge of God. The history of all the nations of antiquity proves, that the knowledge of God was much sooner, and much more generally, obscured among them than that knowledge of good and evil, which is the basis of human law ; while the law, on the other hand, often promoted, or at least sanctioned, superstition and idolatry rather than true religion. In Egypt, for example, the fundamental and original idea was that of one God, not represented by any form ; but his attributes were personified under various names, each of which had its own significant form or representation, to which Divine honour and worship were paid. A kind of pantheism became polytheism, and this, recognised by the law, filled the land with the grossest idolatry. Whatever may have been the process in each nation through which the belief in one God became corrupted, it is notorious both that the corruption was universal, and that human law, even when it did not foster the tendency, nowhere prevented the downward movement. St. Paul, in the beginning of his great argument in the Epistle to the Romans, describes how, even among the most civilised and progressive nations of the whole world, such as the Greeks, the knowledge of God, which man possesses through the mani-festation of God's eternal power and Divinity in the visible works of creation, was suppressed and perverted. Through their alienation of heart from the living God, "though they knew God they glorified him not as God, neither were thankful ; but they became vain in their imaginations, and their foolish heart was darkened ; and they changed the truth of God into a lie, and worshipped and served the creature more than the Creator."[1] And the result of this apostasy from the worship of the one true God was that he "gave them over to a reprobate mind," a mind incapable of using aright that knowledge of good and evil which it naturally pos-sessed ; so that although they knew, of their own selves, without any revelation, what was the judgment of God upon evil in all its varied forms, and that those who did such things were worthy of death, yet they not only committed these evils themselves through the force of temptation, but even lost their consciousness of the distinctions between right and wrong, and approved of those who did evil ; a fact of which Greek and Roman literature supplies only too abundant confirmation. Such, St. Paul argues, was the necessity for God's law being given, or (as he expresses it) for the anger of God being "revealed from heaven against all ungodliness and un-righteousness of men who hold down the truth in unrighteousness." That "wrath of God" has indeed to be yet further revealed against all impenitent sinners, whether they have sinned without law or under the law, who reject the mercy and goodness of God. But in the first instance, the revelation of God's wrath against sin, and of his condemnation of it, was made in his law. This was the first and special purpose of the law, to convince man of sin, and compel him to recognise his own transgressions as offences, not only against the order of human society, but against the authority of God, and against the obligations under which we lie to our Creator, these offences rendering us therefore subject to the penalty of death, spiritual and eternal. To produce this effect, however, it was necessary that this revelation should be made in the form, not of religious and moral precepts merely, however holy and good, but of law in its strictest and fullest sense, as commanded by an authority which man could not question, imposing obligations of all the strongest, and enforced by the sanctions of a power which none could resist.

28. It is important that this definite idea of law should be present to our mind in considering the history of the revelation of Divine law in the *Torah*. We cannot fail to notice that in some of the characters of that history there is a strong resemblance to those of the development of human law. God in his revelations of himself to man before the time of Moses first of all spoke to his chosen people by separate commands and special directions. Religious usages, such as those of the burnt offering and other "sacrifices for God,"[1] the giving of tithes,[2] the erection of altars and of consecrated pillars,[3] and perhaps many other customs not mentioned in the history, which were afterwards embodied in the law, together with the rite of circumcision which had been expressly commanded, no doubt formed an unwritten "customary law," at all events from the time of Abraham; though probably, during the sojourning of the people in the land of Egypt, this traditionary law became corrupted through the admixture of heathen rites and superstitions. At the close of this period God first of all made himself known to them by Moses as the God of Abraham their father, the Eternal and Self-Existent; and, by his judgments upon Egypt, and his deliverance of his people out of the land of their bondage, he established his supreme authority and his special claim on their obedience. And, immediately before they left the scene of their captivity, another step was taken towards the revelation of his law, by the institution of the Passover, and of the various rites and ordinances connected with it.[4] And now the word *Torah*, which before had only once been used in a general way with reference to the obedience of Abraham,[5] is introduced as suitable for the directions given, for the economy of law was beginning. The time had arrived for forming the seed of Abraham into a nation; God, their King and Governor, was to deal with them no longer as individuals, or merely as a family united among themselves by the patriarchal ties, but as his own chosen *nation*. This nation, insignificant as it might appear in comparison with the great kingdoms of this world,[6] was to be mighty, not by the extent of its territory or the number of its population, but as the depositary of God's revelation and of his promises to man, and as the witness on earth to the one living and true God, and to his righteousness. And for this purpose it was necessary that their national life should be based on his law,—a law embodying all those principles of the Divine order which human law represented but partially and imperfectly,—a law with the most absolute authority, the strongest obligations, and the most tremendous sanctions. Of this law the nation was to be in its constitution and organisation the representative to the world.

29. But while this law must be in its fundamental principles the expression of that universal Divine order which is necessary to man as man, yet it was not less essential to the development of the national life of the chosen people, that in its details the law should be suitable for the actual circumstances and condition of that people at the time at which it was given, with such provision for their future condition as the Divine wisdom might see to be required and sufficient. Such considerations point to the conclusion, that to fulfil the several purposes of the law, both as to mankind generally and to the particular nation to whom it was given, that law must be twofold, the *primary* law embodying all the elements of that Divine order which is the immediate result of man's creation and original state; the *secondary*

---

[1] Exod. xviii. 12.   [2] Gen. xiv. 20; xxviii. 22.   [3] Gen. xxviii. 22; xxxi. 45.
[4] Exod. xii., xiii.   [5] Gen. xxvi. 5.   [6] Deut. vii. 7.

law applying the principles of that order to the religious, moral, political, and social life of the nation in such manner as should be best calculated for the true development of that life. That such a distinction as is here indicated is actually found in the law given by God to Israel cannot be questioned ; and the very distinction indicates, when the reasons for it are considered, that the laws of the first class are universal and permanent, those of the second special and, except in their spirit, variable. It is, however, very important to observe not only the broad line of distinction which by the mode of their promulgation is drawn between the primary law and the secondary, but also that which is not less apparent on further examination, the relation between the two, with its limitations.

THE PRIMARY LAW OF THE TWO TABLES.

30. The promulgation of the Divine law from Mount Sinai is described twice in the *Torah*, first as part of the history in the nineteenth and twentieth chapters of Exodus, and a second time, with some slight modifications, in the addresses made by Moses to the people before his death.[1] The event was one, as Moses reminded the Israelites,[2] unparalleled in the history of man ever since the creation of the world. No nation, whatever its traditions and legends may be, has ever even conceived the idea of the God of heaven and earth proclaiming his law to themselves " out of the midst of the fire,"—the light unapproachable, which hid his awful presence from the eyes of man,—with his own voice. At the creation " he spake and it was done ; he commanded and it stood fast." That was his decree (*Choq*) operative in nature ; he now speaks words of law (*Torah*) to man made in his image, demanding the obedience of a reasonable creature. He was afterwards to speak to man in his only begotten Son ; a yet more perfect and Divine utterance. But as regards the outward manifestations and visible signs of the majesty, authority, and power of God, the giving of the law from Mount Sinai is an event, so far as we may conclude from Holy Scripture, such as will not again be witnessed until that great day " when the Lord Jesus shall be revealed from heaven with the angels of his power in flaming fire taking vengeance on them that know not God, and obey not the gospel of our Lord Jesus Christ."[3] Of that terrible day Mount Sinai, as we inferred from the language of the Apostle Paul,[4] was the anticipation and precursor. It is impossible for us to conceive a more solemn expression of the awful holiness of Almighty God, and of the certain and terrible consequences of disobedience to his law, than is contained in the simple but sublime description of the whole scene. The great mountain, before which the hosts of Israel were encamped, itself inspiring awe by its desolate grandeur and the mysterious silence of nature there,[5] after a solemn warning to the people from Jehovah to prepare themselves for this Divine revelation, on the morning of the third day was covered with a thick cloud, out of which proceeded thunderings and lightnings, and the voice of a trumpet exceeding loud,—such as that which at the second coming of the Lord shall awake the dead,—and Israel, trembling with fear, was brought by Moses to the foot of the mountain, which itself quaked at the presence of the Lord, its smoke going up to heaven like the smoke of a furnace. And Moses spake, and God answered him " out of the midst of the fire and the cloud and the darkness,"—the very light was blackness to the eyes of man,[6]—with a great voice. And the voice uttered the ten *words*, the ten brief commandments of the law, which were afterwards written on two tables of stone by no human agency,

---

[1] Deut. v. [2] Deut. iv. 32, 33. [3] 2 Thess. i. 7, 8.
[4] Rom. i. 18 (see § 27, *supra*).
[5] Cf. Stanley's ' Syria and Palestine,' p. 13, 14. [6] See Deut. v. 23.

but by the very finger of God. It is emphatically said by Moses of the law thus given, "And he added no more."

31. What then were these ten solemn *words* proclaimed to the chosen nation by the voice of God with such awful testimonies of his dreadful presence and almighty power? Simple enough they seem to men now. They are indeed nothing else than those elementary principles of religious and moral duty,—which, as we have seen, are involved in man's origin, and which man, awakened to the knowledge of good and evil, ought of himself to recognise,—but now for the first time in man's history asserted as the law of God for man. Though given to one chosen nation in the first instance, and addressed to them by "the Lord their God, who brought them out of the land of Egypt from the house of bondage," yet, as the whole scene testifies, the commands are those of the God of all the earth, the Lord of all nations, the one living and true "God of the spirits of all flesh." And being his law, these commandments, simple as they may seem, cannot be understood aright unless their spirit, and not merely their letter, is recognised. To the outward ear, as to the Scribes and Pharisees of old, they sound merely as prohibitions of some great sins, which the natural conscience of man itself condemns. "All these have I kept from my youth up," is the natural feeling of many now, as of the young ruler in the gospel. It is only when, like St. Paul,[1] we are startled out of our self-righteousness by discovering the spiritual force and infinite comprehensiveness of this Divine law, that each commandment, however often reiterated, suggests the prayer, "Lord, have mercy upon us, and incline our hearts to keep this law."

32. The spiritual character of the Divine law, as condemning not only outward offences, but the first beginnings of sin within the heart, sufficiently appears from the last of the commandments, to which St. Paul refers as proof of this truth. But there is another principle, applicable to all law in some sense, and to the Divine law emphatically and to the fullest extent, of which it is necessary to have a clear apprehension in order to understand the scope and purport of this law of God. This is, that a law, when it is the expression of a duty, embraces the whole sphere of duties and responsibilities to any part of which it refers; in other words, not only that every command includes the prohibition of that which is opposed to it, which none would deny; but also that every prohibition involves a command to do that which is the opposite. This principle, which even in the science of human law is of no small importance,[2] is absolutely essential to the right interpretation of Divine law, of which the Psalmist truly says, "Thy commandment is *exceeding broad*." It means that justice covers the whole domain of man's responsibility, there being no distinction, such as some imagine, between perfect and imperfect obligations, but that whatever it is right to do it is wrong to leave undone: there is no middle ground between good and evil; and consequently the principles of justice and of charity or love are identical, requiring of us the same actions, having the same extent and the same limits. This view of the Divine law was obscured in mediæval and later Roman theology by the doctrine of "works of supererogation," works which transcend the sphere of absolute duty and therefore of law, a notion founded on an erroneous conception of justice. Yet even by such theologians it was allowed in theory, that "every human action proceeding from deliberative reason must be either good or bad."[3] Whatever, therefore, it is right to do, it cannot be right, and must be evil, to leave undone. If it be wrong to do any injury to our neighbour, it is right to

---

[1] Rom. vii. 7—10.

[2] Some thoughts are borrowed from a very interesting discussion of the question in a work to which reference has been already made—Lorimer's 'Institutes of Law,' Book I. xi., xii.

[3] Thom. Aquinas, 'Summæ Theol. Prima Sec. Quæst.' xviii. art. iv. 3.

love him, since this is the principle which alone will prevent us from doing him any injury ; and if it is right to love him, it is wrong not to love him. And thus it follows that every commandment of God's law reveals to us all that in that sphere we are either commanded or forbidden to do.[1] But there is indeed no place for theological disputation on this question, though, to make it more clear, its connection with the general subject of law has been noticed. For not only do our Lord and his apostles teach that love is the fulfilling of the law, and the only true fulfilment in other words, that love and righteousness or justice are in principle identical—but this teaching is that of the Old Testament itself. The words of Moses in the *Torah* are expressly quoted both by Christ and by St. James.[3] It was not, therefore, merely that the fuller light thrown upon the law by the gospel gave it this spiritual character; though no doubt Christ's own teaching, as in the Sermon on the Mount, asserted and expounded this aspect of the law in opposition to the false glosses and unspiritual doctrines of Scribes and Pharisees ; but the character was inherent in the law from the first, and was that which made it a living power to man's conscience, "perfect, converting the soul," the source of all truth and all wisdom.

33. It may be asked, however, why, if this be true of the law that every one of its commandments covers so wide a field of responsibility, in so many of them the offence only, and that in its extreme form, is prohibited, while we are left to infer from the prohibition all the positive duties ; for example, from the command not to take God's name in vain, the duty of honouring him with our lips ; from the prohibition of murder, the duty of caring for our neighbour, and aiding him in sickness and suffering? The sufficient answer to this is, that although the Divine law can only be fulfilled by love, yet it is nevertheless law, and must speak in the proper language of law, in order to fulfil its own stern and terrible functions. Its purpose is to detect, expose, and condemn all sin ; and, therefore, those sins are expressly condemned the evil of which is most distinctly recognised by the conscience, in order that we may learn what is the true character of all sins of this class, even of omissions of the duty which we owe to God and our neighbour under this head. We are reminded that if we do not honour God we do not love him, and if we do not love him it is because of the carnal mind which is enmity against God. On the other hand, we learn that "he that loveth not his brother abideth in death" as surely as he that hateth him ; and that "he that hateth his brother is a murderer, and ye know" from the law "that no murderer hath eternal life abiding in him."[4]

34. Another general remark as to the Divine law is important. It must be observed that while love to God first of all, and secondly to our neighbour as representing God to us—is the one principle from which all the duties of man are derived, nevertheless law is absolutely essential for man's direction in his earthly life, in order that this principle of spiritual life may not be the vague abstract sentiment of the mystic,

---

[1] Calvin, 'Instit. Christianæ Religionis,' lib. ii. c. viii. 9: Ita videre est ut semper nobis finis præcepti reseret quidquid illic facere aut jubemur aut vetamur. Calvin, in the passage which concludes with these words, expounds with singular clearness the positive character of the Divine law.

[2] Matt. xxii. 37—40 ; Mark xii. 29—34 ; Luke x. 25—28 ; Rom. xiii. 8—10 ; James ii. 8.

[3] Deut. vi. 5, and Levit. xix. 18.

[4] 1 John iii. 14, 15. Calvin's exposition of this is characteristic, but very true. "Quia peccatorum fœditatem, nisi ubi palpabilis est, diluere et speciosis prætextibus inducere semper caro molitur, (ergo) quod erat in unoquoque transgressionis genere deterrimum et scelestissimum exemplaris loco proposuit, cujus ad auditum sensus quoque exhorresceret, quo majorem peccati cujuslibet detestationem animis nostris imprimeret. Hoc nobis imponit sæpius in æstimandis vitiis, quod si tectiora sunt, elevamus. Has præstigias Dominus discutit quum nos assuefacit universam vitiorum multitudinem ad hæc capita referre quæ optime quantum sit in uno quoque genere abominationis repræsentant." ('Institut.' II. viii. 10.)

but may have a concrete form and substantial reality, through the definite lines of thought, feeling, and action, which law marks out. Or, as that Apostle said, who of all men spoke most fully and most profoundly of love both to God and to man: "By this we know that we love the children of God, when we love God and keep his commandments. · For this is the love of God, that we keep his commandments."[1] And so the Lord himself said : "He that hath my commandments and keepeth them, he it is that loveth me."[2] For sublime ideas as to the being and perfections of the Infinite and Eternal, even as to his love, are in themselves too often unfruitful, indeed unreal ; the finite mind, not directed by God's commandments, soon loses its hold of these ideas, before their shadowy forms can assume any substance ; and perhaps at last *nirvăna* or absorption into deity,—an escape from individual human existence into indefinite, impersonal being,—is the highest hope of the bewildered soul. From all these profitless and dangerous dreams the law is sent to awaken man to realities, that is, to his own duties and responsibilities which he owes to God, the God of love, his Creator and his Father.

35. The purpose of our argument being to mark out the leading principles of the Divine law as revealed in the Pentateuch, rather than to discuss details, it will be unnecessary to enter at length on that which belongs to the office of the commentator or expositor, the interpretation of the several commandments. It will be sufficient to explain briefly the scope of each, and its connection with our previous investigations. That these commandments were *ten* in number is certain from Scripture itself,[3] and it is also certain that the division must be such that in each commandment one distinct principle of law is enunciated, and one only. The question as to the distribution of the ten commandments between the two tables is more difficult to decide and of less practical importance. There is nothing in the history to indicate that there was any distinction between the laws on each table ; nor do the words of our Lord which distinguish the first and great commandment as that of love to God, and the second, "like unto it," as love to our neighbour, decide the question. For the two classes of duties so interpenetrate one another, and the whole law so hangs on that which man owes to God, that the attempt to draw any broad line between the commandments that belong to our duty to God, and those that teach our duty to our neighbour, can never be quite satisfactory. For example, the law as to the seventh day is in express words connected with our duty to man as well as with that which we owe to God. The law of filial obedience is, as has often been remarked, a kind of link between our duties to God and to man, for it is as representing God to us that honour is due to parents and others in authority. The prohibition of adultery again cannot but be interpreted to include many sins which are directly offences against God's holiness, but which affect only remotely and indirectly the welfare of our neighbour. Indeed, all those interpretations of the several commandments which are suggested by the general principle of the last of them, οὐκ ἐπιθυμήσεις,[4] introduces the element of our duty to God as that which is primary and most essential. For in ἐπιθυμία the first evil is, that it is a desire for that which is not given us by God, or which is not in our path of duty to him ;[5] the second evil, which is not always present, that it belongs to our neighbour. Without then attempting to classify the commandments under those which refer to our duty to God and those which contain our

---

[1] 1 John v. 2, 3.   [2] John xiv. 21. Cf. also vers. 15, 23, 24 ; xv. 10.
[3] Exod. xxxiv. 28 ; Deut. iv. 13 ; x. 4.
[4] Cf. Rom. vii. 7. It may be observed that the argument of St. Paul itself is sufficient to prove that the law against ἐπιθυμία cannot be divided into two.
[5] Compare our Lord's temptation to turn stones into bread, and again to throw himself from the pinnacle of the temple, as illustrations of this.

duty to our neighbour, we will examine them in order, so as to determine the distinct principle which each embodies.

36. (I.) The first commandment, as expressing the most fundamental of all principles, viz. the unity of God, is, in a certain sense, the basis and root of the whole law. In it he who was in covenant with his people Israel, the seed of Abraham his servant, asserts his own eternal and infinite Being, and that he is the only true and living God. The law proper is the prohibition, "Thou shalt have no other gods before me."[1] The unity of God is exclusive: he is one, and there is no other: first, and there is no second: alone to be loved, honoured, obeyed, and served, as God.

37. (II.) A second principle, distinct from this of unity, is embodied in the second commandment. God must be worshipped, not as man imagines him, but as he is. Ever since the fall, whenever man has not either denied the existence of God, or forgotten him altogether in fleshly lusts, he has been prone, being incapable of apprehending the idea of the personality of Infinite Spirit, to represent God to himself by those things which are outward and visible; which sin against the very being of God— in its grossest form, the worship of graven images—is prohibited in this law. The language of the commandment, in which those who transgress it are spoken of as "those who *hate* Me," reminds us that this tendency in man is the result of "the carnal mind which is enmity against God; for it is not subject to the law of God, neither indeed can be."[2] This sin, though closely allied to that of serving other gods, so that both are often classed together in Holy Scripture, is undoubtedly not the same. St. Paul, in the passage from the Romans which has already been discussed (§ 25), declares that, of all sins committed by man, this is the most direct insult to the majesty of the Creator, and has most entirely debased man and brought on him that most terrible of all judgments, his being given over by God to his own lusts; and the law itself threatens that this sin must of necessity, in God's government of the world, bring an inheritance of evil for several generations. When we regard this commandment from the other aspect, and consider not only what it forbids but what it commands,—that is, the worship of him who is a Spirit in spirit and in truth,—we find that this subject is necessarily connected, through this law, with the incarnation of the eternal Son of God. He being "the brightness of the glory" of God, and "the express image of his person," was and is, though in the likeness of man, to be worshipped as God, because "in him dwelleth the fulness of the Godhead bodily." In him God, though the Infinite Spirit, is fully represented to man; and Jesus Christ, the God-man, alone satisfies those cravings of the human soul which otherwise turn to idolatry. Thus we see that while the negative pole (so to speak) of this law is idolatry, the positive is the worship of God in Christ.

38. (III.) But God demands of man, not merely spiritual service and worship, but also that he should honour God with all that he is, and specially by that which distinguishes man as a reasonable being from all other creatures, and by which his reason expresses itself, that is, by language. The tongue, as we are frequently reminded by the psalmist and others in the Old Testament, and by our Lord and his apostles in the New, is the glory of man when it is used in the service of God, the condemnation of man when language, the overflowing of the heart, is a stream of purposeless or evil words. The third commandment prohibits the highest offence of this class, taking God's name in vain, of which the grossest form is "swearing falsely" And man is so little able to realise the profound and mysterious relation between our words, the expressions of our will and reason, and the mind

---

[1] Literally "before my face;" that is, *beside* or *in addition to,* not *but* or *instead of* me.
[2] Cf. Rom. viii. 7 and Rom. i. 28, with § 30.

of God, that he specially needs to be reminded that "God will not hold him guiltless that taketh his name in vain." On the other hand, regarding the law in its positive aspect, we must observe that the whole force and scope of the duty which man owes to God under this head can only be completely expounded from the truth, that not only has the Word of God taken our nature, but also the Spirit of God, who when he first came down on the Church, enabled men to speak in other tongues the high praises of God, has made our bodies and all their members the temples of God. Here the negative pole is "false swearing," the positive "praying in the Holy Ghost."

It seems, therefore, not without reason that S. Augustine and others have regarded the first three commandments of the law, not only as specially representing man's duty to God, but also as related to the three persons of the Godhead.

39. (IV.) In the preceding commandments all the fundamental principles of the service of God are indicated and asserted. But this service, as rendered by man on earth, must want definiteness and form unless Divine law should determine some order and proportion in respect of *time*. The fourth commandment expresses in the form of law the principles in regard to man's use of time which are involved in God's creation of man, and which have been already discussed under that head.[1] It must be noticed that, in this law, the duty of fulfilling during six days the original precept to replenish the earth and subdue it, which involves a very large and important class of practical duties and responsibilities which we owe to God, and not to man only,[2] is as distinctly asserted as the duty of resting from such labours, after the example of our Creator, on the seventh day. The interpretation and application of this law which was suited for the Mosaic dispensation we need not consider, here at least, except to observe that the secondary laws on this subject, by increasing the proportion of days which should be given to religious worship and observed as "Sabbaths," themselves prove that this commandment, as well as all others, though given for the instruction and direction of the conscience, is to be observed by man in the spirit and not in the letter.

Regarding it in this light, we must consider the fourth commandment, in its positive aspect, as indicating the duty of man to devote a sufficient portion of his time to the worship of God and to those pursuits which belong to a spiritual world. What the proportion should be must be determined by the enlightened spirit of the Christian, directed by the law itself, but not interpreting it in the literal and servile spirit of Scribes and Pharisees, which, by drawing a hard and fast line between day and day, would contradict the law itself. On the other hand, in its negative aspect, this law includes duties to our fellow-men, and even to the beasts of the field which labour in the service of man; and the mention of these last proves that the physical value of a periodical day of rest is a principle of this law. It is in this aspect of the Sabbath, as a day of rest for our fellow-men who serve us, that Moses, in reminding the Israelites of this commandment in his last addresses to them,[3] connects it with their deliverance from the land of their bondage, where their Egyptian taskmasters allowed them no rest; and, in reference to this, the particular day fixed for the Sabbath under the Mosaic law, was the day which began with the evening when they came out of Egypt.[4]

40. (V.) Man's duty to God leads to that which he owes to his neighbour, and, as has been already observed, the fifth commandment belongs as much to one class of

---

[1] See § 12.
[2] Cf. Rom. xii. 11 and Coloss. iii. 23. "Whatsoever ye do, do it heartily, as to the Lord and not unto men."
[3] Deut. v. 14, 15.   [4] Cf. Exod. xvi.

duties as to the other. For the authority of parents is to be respected and their persons are to be honoured, because they represent God to us, from whom the parental relation is derived and in whom it is constituted.[1] And certainly we may adapt to this case the argument which St. John uses more generally: "He that honoureth not his earthly parents whom he hath seen, how can he honour God, his heavenly Father, whom he hath not seen?" And the family, being a Divine ordinance involved in that of marriage,[2] is, so to speak, God's nursery in which man may be trained from his infancy in those habits of self-control, and in that respect and reverence for authority, without which all the bonds both of social and of natural life are of no avail. The duties which man owes to duly constituted authority in all these spheres are therefore included in this commandment; and it is certain, as indicated in its language, that, in what we understand by God's providential government of the world, the welfare of mankind depends on nothing so much as on that due respect for human authority,[3] as acting for God, and that obedience to law, which are first taught by the parental relation, the ties of which are of all the tenderest, the strongest, and the most sacred.

41. (VI.) The next four commandments of the law are nearly related together, for they all refer to those natural rights of man, which either directly or by necessary inference are derived from his creation. Of these the first of all is man's right to his own existence, as a being created by God in his image, whose life therefore cannot be used merely as means to other ends, for he must be an end in himself. The sixth commandment asserts in the form of law, as had been asserted after the Deluge many centuries before, the intrinsic sacredness of the life of man. In its negative aspect, the prohibition, "Thou shalt do no murder," forbids all those feelings which, if uncontrolled and matured, would end, as Cain's jealousy and anger ended, in murder, and which, even if checked in their course, would tend to the injury of another in some degree. Even the Talmud and other Jewish traditions recognise the truth that minor injuries to our neighbour are, in the eye of God's law, equivalent to murder.[4] On the positive side, this commandment requires that active and practical and loving concern for the lives of our brethren, above all for their spiritual being, the true and eternal life, which must proceed from the full belief of the truth that man is made in the image of God.[5] At the same time it must be remembered that all the rights of man as regards this present life, must from the very nature of the case be limited by the rights of other men; in other words, by those of human society. The principle of the sacredness of man's life is asserted as the basis for all law; the application of the principle, wherever it is not determined (as it was for Israel under special circumstances) by Divine direction, is left to that authority which is "God's minister" for human society.[6]

42. (VII.) The seventh commandment guards man's rights under the ordinance of marriage, the mutual duties and responsibilities of which, as we have already found, the history of man's creation plainly declares. And marriage being ordained for the following reasons,[7]—to take them in the order which its institution in man's state of

---

[1] Cf. Ephes. iii. 15, Ἐξ οὗ πᾶσα πατριὰ ἐν οὐρανοῖς καὶ ἐπὶ γῆς ὀνομάζεται, and vi. 1.
[2] See § 11.   [3] Rom. xiii. 1—7.
[4] "He who makes the face of his neighbour pale with shame is like a man that sheds blood." "He who makes his fellow-creature sin commits a greater crime than the murderer." Quoted by Kalisch on Exod. xx. 13: but the modern, rationalistic Jewish commentator, in a spirit similar to that of the Scribes and Pharisees in our Lord's time, refuses to recognise anything but the letter in the law itself.
[5] Cf. in illustration the remarkable passage, Prov. xxiv. 11, 12, and our Saviour's words, Matt. xvi. 25, 26.
[6] Rom. xiii. 4, "He beareth not the sword in vain."   [7] English Marriage Service.

innocence indicates,—first, " for the mutual society, help, and comfort which one ought to have of the other ; " secondly, " for the procreation of children, to be brought up in the fear and nurture of the Lord, and to the praise of his holy name ; " and thirdly, to preserve the purity of human life against the lusts of the flesh ;—the prohibition of the breach of this ordinance by adultery must involve, on its negative side, the prohibition of all things inconsistent with these reasons, and on its positive side, the command to fulfil all the duties and responsibilities which those reasons imply.

43. (VIII.) The eighth commandment deals with another natural right of man, that of property : not, like the two preceding, directly derived from his creation, yet the immediate consequence of his own personal right to existence, and of the rights of the family relation.[1] From these rights of man we conclude his right to acquire and possess such things as pertain to the maintenance and development of life, and to use and dispose of these for the benefit of himself and of those dependent on him. This natural right of man, and the duties involved in it, the commandment recognises and asserts. The whole sphere of these duties, both negative and positive, is included in one of those comprehensive and profoundly philosophical precepts of the Apostle Paul, which we find in his expositions of relative duties. " Let him that stole steal no more, but rather let him labour, working with his hands the thing which is good, that he may have to give to him that needeth."[2] The question of the limitation of the individual right of property by the rights of the society is one that specially belongs to the authority of human law, which is ordained by God for the protection of such rights.[3] The secondary laws on this subject, given to the nation of Israel as suitable for their peculiar circumstances, contain some important and suggestive illustrations of the extent of these rights and of the corresponding duties.

44. (IX.) The right of man to receive the truth from his neighbour, and the correlative duty of man to speak the truth of his neighbour and to his neighbour, arise, so far as human interests are concerned, from the order and constitution of society, the mutual relations and responsibilities of which could not be otherwise maintained.[4] St. Paul, while he describes the old man as corrupt according to the *lusts of deceit,* and the new man as created after God in righteousness and *holiness of truth,* yet expressly bases the duty on the ground of our mutual relation. " Wherefore " (he says), " putting away lying, let every man speak truth one with another ; for we are members one of another."[5] This consideration must necessarily to some extent govern the interpretation and application of the ninth commandment ; for the same principle that forbids us to bear false witness against our neighbour, would equally require us to bear true witness, even though it be to his personal injury, if the interests of man as a member of society, and the interests of social order, should be thereby benefited. This conclusion is obvious enough. But the question, which has been often discussed both in ancient and modern times, whether veracity is, under all circumstances and to all men, a duty *in itself,* and if not, what are the limitations which the ground of the duty, indicated by St. Paul, might suggest, is one of much greater difficulty, into which we need not enter here.[6] It must, however, be borne in mind with regard to all the four commandments that have reference to the natural rights of man, that while those rights mark out the corresponding duties, there is for the

---

[1] See Lorimer's ' Constitution of Law,' chap. vii. 3, c—h.
[2] Ephes. iv. 28.   [3] Cf. *e. g.* Rom. xiii. 6, 7.
[4] In this aspect of "truth" it is so closely allied to "justice" that it is difficult to separate them. See § 23 as to the personification of *Thmei.*
[5] Ephes. iv. 22, 25.
[6] See Mozley's ' Ruling Ideas in Early Ages,' pp. 155, &c. and Notes 4—7.

conscience a yet deeper foundation of these duties than any which human interests can supply. For the ethical virtues of love, purity, honesty, and truth are in man the counterpart of God's own perfections, and all that is contrary to these perfections must be, in the nature of things, sinful, because it is the contradiction of his image and likeness.

45. (X.) To all these commandments which relate to the natural rights and duties of man, one, the tenth and last, is added, which enlarges their scope beyond that of all human laws, and marks them as truly Divine ; laws in which he who is the Lord of the spirit and the conscience must be regarded. Even in human legislation, indeed, the intention of an act is taken into account, and sometimes even the absence of a due sense of the right and of its corresponding duty—as, for example, in the case of manslaughter, the absence of a sense of the value of human life, and of the duty of caring for it—may make an act criminal even though there is no positive intention to commit a crime. But human law can take no cognisance whatever of the inward thought before it is expressed either in word or in deed. To no one but God himself, the Judge of our spirits, can we be accountable for the angry or malicious feeling, the impure desire, the covetous wish, the deceitful thought and purpose, all which, as St. Paul discovered when the law came home to his conscience, are included under the general prohibition, "Thou shalt not covet." [1] The desire is manifestly unlawful when that which is desired belongs to another, because by this it is certain that it is contrary to the will of God that we should possess it ; but also, and no less truly, whenever the desire is not regulated by the Divine order, and subordinate to God's will. Such a desire, like that of Eve before she yielded to the tempter, "hath of itself the nature of sin," and is the harlot mother, as the apostle James reminds us, of all sin and death. [2]

46. The proclamation from Sinai of this law of the ten commandments is one of those events, the vast moral importance of which, as compared with all events in secular history, and indeed with all in sacred history from the Fall to the Incarnation, is, like a great mountain mass the comparative height of which is best distinguished at a distance, realised now that we look back on it through the ages of the past, as it could not be understood at the time when it was first delivered. How little, notwithstanding the awful manifestations of the Divine presence and authority, this law affected the minds of the Israelites at the time, is apparent from the fact that at the foot of Mount Sinai they made and worshipped the golden calf, committing, no doubt unwittingly through the darkness and blindness of their hearts, the very sin of which the voice of God had pronounced the most express and solemn condemnation. And of the spiritual force and meaning of these commandments,[3] although their general conviction that God who gave this law was to be feared is commended by him as in itself good, they evidently had no conception ; they had indeed to learn this through the teaching of God's prophets, and his dealings with them as a nation, for many generations ; and even to the last they were a foolish people, having eyes that could not see, and ears that could not understand. Now, looking back on the majestic scene from the distance of some thirty-four centuries, and interpreting those Divine

---

[1] Both the English words *covet* and *lust* have, unfortunately, special meanings. In Greek the words οὐκ ἐπιθυμήσεις forbid every class of evil desire. In the Hebrew a different word is used in Deuteronomy for desiring the neighbour's wife from that employed for coveting his property. According to Kalisch, the Rabbinical distinction between the two words was that *āvāh* (the word rendered *covet* in Deuteronomy) means the first motion of the evil desire, and *chāmād* that which is fully developed, and produces the sinful deed. But from the use of the words in Deuteronomy we should rather infer the opposite.

[2] See Alford's note on James i. 14, 15.   [3] Cf. Deut. v. 28, 29.

sentences by the light of the knowledge and experience that God has vouchsafed to man during the intervening period, we find in them a profound significance, a completeness, a harmony, and a due proportion of moral and spiritual truth, such as afford proofs of their Divine power and authority, far clearer and more convincing to the enlightened spirit of man, than any that could be given by the most overwhelming outward manifestations of the Divine presence. Who but the living and true God, he to whom is known all that is in the nature of man, and who foresees the end from the beginning—all that would be developed out of that nature in the history of the world—could thus in "ten words" have set forth the fundamental laws of the whole religious and moral order of human life, comprehending the principles necessary for every sphere of man's rights and man's duties, reaching at the same time not only to the outward act, but to the first germs of evil within the heart? Well might Moses, in his recapitulation of the Divine law, while he reminded the people of the privileges which the nation possessed above all other nations in the tokens of the Divine favour which they had received, urge on them, that true national greatness could only be maintained through obedience to the law of their God, especially that which was given "the day that thou stoodest before the Lord thy God in Horeb."

47. But is there not an important question here? We have examined the extent of the *commands* of this law of God; we recognise without difficulty the *obligations* imposed thereby; but one thing more is necessary in order that it may be law indeed; there must be "a *sanction*[1] threatened in the event of disobedience." What is the punishment which follows the transgression of the law of God? There can be no difficulty in answering this question. The *sanction* of the law of Paradise was, "In the day thou eatest thereof, thou shalt surely die;" the sentence being carried out, as we have seen (§ 15), by the body of man becoming not only mortal, but "dead because of sin," and his spirit being separated and alienated from God, "dead in sin." Those terrible curses denounced on Israel as a nation,[2] if they did not hearken to the voice of the Lord their God, which Moses called "*the curses of the covenant*,"[3] were the expression of that which no human language can fully express or human thought conceive, the wrath of the Infinitely Holy God against sin. But did the Israelites know and believe that this condemnation of God was not for this life only, but for a life after the death of the body? It is impossible to doubt this. The belief is inherent in the very nature of man, and only obscured in proportion as the belief in the existence of God is obscured. The Egyptians themselves, among whom the Israelites had lived for some centuries, fully believed in judgment after death; and it has been supposed, with some reason, that the silence of Moses on the subject of a future world and of the punishment of sin hereafter may be explained by the danger of the false and superstitious notions as to the future judgment, which formed so large a part of Egyptian religion, being confirmed in the minds of those who had been long familiarised with these errors. This explanation does, at all events, point to the true solution of the difficulty, namely, that the time had not yet come for a clear revelation of the realities of a future world, and therefore, under the dispensation of law, that world was hidden in a mysterious and awful darkness, which was only dispelled very gradually, until our Saviour Jesus Christ abolished

---

[1] See § 26, *supra*. The particular force of this word, which is a term from Roman law, will be explained by the following passages from Forcellini : "Sanctio legum quæ *certam pœnam* irrogat iis qui," &c. *Papinian*. "Plus valet sanctio permissione *h. e.* lex quæ cogit quam quæ permittit." It implies the solemn confirmation of a law by the penalty or punishment attached to it. Thus Cicero ('De Leg.' lib. iii. c. 20) says : "Noxiæ pœna par esto, ut in suo vitio quisque plectatur, vis capite, avaritia mulcta, honoris cupiditas ignominia sanciatur."

[2] Deut. xxviii. 15, &c.

[3] Deut. xxix. 21 ; and cf. Deut. xxvii. 26 and Gal. iii. 10.

death, and "brought life and immortality to light through the gospel."[1] At the same time it must be remembered that Christ himself teaches us that the language of the *Torah* itself implies both the immortality of the soul, and even the resurrection of the body.[2]

THE SECONDARY LAWS.

48. If the law given to Israel had consisted only of the ten commandments spoken by the voice of Jehovah from Mount Sinai, this alone would have been an inestimable blessing to the nation. Regarded also as a necessary step in Divine revelation and a preparation for the gospel of Christ, these primary laws of religious and moral duty, proclaimed with the fullest sanctions of Divine authority, and with the curse and condemnation of Almighty God denounced against the sinner, of themselves were sufficient, as is proved by St. Paul's reference to the last of these commandments, to convince man of sin, if only he would understand and apply them to himself, and thus to lead him to Christ "that he might be justified by faith." Why then was it necessary that to this grand and simple law, which was the covenant between God and the nation, there should be superadded other "statutes" and "judgments," which, both from the method in which they were delivered, and from their very nature, are obviously secondary and subordinate? Might not Israel have been now left, as other nations were, to develop for themselves, with the immeasurable advantage of having these commandments to direct them, the laws that might be necessary for their national life? One reply to this question has been given already (§ 29, *supra*). But further it must be answered, that for the complete development of the economy of law, so as to teach God's chosen people, and all nations through them, the real meaning and tremendous force of Divine law, and the impossibility of attaining life through any law, however fully it might provide for all the conditions of man on earth,—very much more was required than this one solemn and authoritative promulgation of its eternal principles. God therefore in his wisdom and goodness gave to Israel not only, directly from himself, these primary laws, but also, through his servant Moses, as a mediator between himself and the nation, a very large body of secondary laws, which were the application and adaptation of the principles of the primary law to the condition and circumstances of Israel at that time. It was necessary, in order to educate them in God's truth, and gradually prepare them for a better and more perfect and enduring covenant, that through these secondary laws the whole religious, social, and domestic life of the nation should be thoroughly permeated by Divine law ; that at every step law should meet them with its imperative demands, its warnings, its threatenings, and its promises ; that thus the law should never be out of their sight, and never be wanting in that distinctness and definiteness, which, as we well know in human legislation, is of all things most essential to its force. And further, the primary laws being laws for the conscience of man, the penalty of transgressing them is the wrath of God, which, even if it should never be manifested in this life, the awakened conscience recognises. But to bring the force of this home to the mind of man, it was necessary that there should be laws, the transgressions of which should be visited by such punishments as all must feel and fear even in this world. How this principle affected the character of the secondary laws we shall see hereafter. These laws may be divided, for the purpose of examining them, into two great classes, those that directly concern man's relations to God, and those that belong to his duty to his neighbour. But it must be remem-

---

[1] 2 Tim. i. 10.

[2] See Matt. xxii. 30 ; Mark xii. 25 ; and Luke xx. 38, where the remarkable words are added, πάντες γὰρ αὐτῷ ζῶσιν.

bered that no such distinction was made by Moses in delivering them ; and, for reasons before explained (§ 35, *supra*), no division of this kind can be completely or scientifically exact.

RELIGIOUS LAWS.

49. Those secondary laws which concern man's relations to God include all that are ritual or ceremonial, or are in any sense religious. In regard to these we must first of all recall to mind some general principles, affecting and governing the whole ritual and ceremonial system, which explain, what otherwise would be unintelligible, the great difference between the outward service of God under the law and that under the gospel, although the fundamental principles of the service of God must be the same in all ages.

(1) The first purpose of these religious laws was, without doubt, that the chosen nation should bear witness in its religion to the one living and true God against the polytheism, idolatry, and superstitions of the other nations of the world, from whom they were to be kept separate as a holy and peculiar people, dedicated to the service of him who had called and chosen the seed of Abraham his servant.

(2) Their outward service of God was not, however, to be something altogether new, as if Jehovah were now for the first time revealed ; but in its main elements such as the true worship of God had been from the beginning. He who had chosen them was the Creator of all men, the God of all who, ever since man had been on the earth, had served him by faith. Ever since the Fall, partly from the teachings of man's own conscience, and partly from the express monitions of God's Spirit, certain religious customs had grown up,[1] and one office of the Mosaic legislation was undoubtedly to confirm these usages, so far as they were suitable for that economy, by positive laws, and both to develop them yet further and to guard them against abuses and perversions.

(3) After the Fall, a new element in the relations between God and man of pre-eminent importance had been revealed ; first, in the promise of the final victory of the seed of the woman in the conflict with the enemy of God and man ; and afterwards, more definitely, in the promises given to Abraham and his seed. These were to be ultimately fulfilled in the redemption of the world by our Lord Jesus Christ, "born of a woman," "of the seed of Abraham," and "born under the law." This element in the faith of God's people could not but affect in the highest degree the relation to God of his chosen nation, and therefore must enter very largely into the laws which governed the service and worship of God. To be a step forward in God's revelation, these laws must point onwards to the work and offices of the promised Saviour. But at the same time, even more distinctly than they could teach the future realities, they must indicate that the victory not being as yet won, the redemption had not yet come, and the laws must therefore bear distinct witness to their own imperfection and insufficiency.

(4) And lastly, as St. Paul argues in his Epistle to the Galatians, the dispensation of the law being one of discipline and education, corresponding with the training of a child before he comes to the discretion and the rights of manhood,—the children of God, until the time should come for their adoption in Christ, and for that gift of the Spirit which is in the spiritual life what the age of discretion is in the natural life, needed to be taught by "elements of this world," outward and visible ordinances, and disciplined through restraints and the fear of punishment, before the reasons for obedience could be fully understood or explained.

[1] Cf. § 28, *supra*.

These principles are specially exemplified in the sacrificial system, which was the centre of the ceremonial law, and the key to all its observances and requirements. The question of the typical meaning of these, that is, the aspect of the Mosaical rites and ceremonies, when viewed in the full knowledge of the realities of the gospel, as figures of the work of Christ, lies outside our present argument, the object of which is to examine the system simply in its character of law, and, therefore, in the aspect in which it presented itself to those who were under the law. It is, however, important to observe, that in studying the question of the typical and allegorical meaning of Holy Scripture, the only safeguard against fanciful and unprofitable speculations is to be found in the spirit which underlies the letter; for example, in the typical interpretation of the law, by observing first of all the spiritual meaning of the observance *for those to whom it was commanded.*

50. In sacrifice, the primary idea, as represented by the word *minchah*,—originally applied in Scripture [1] to all offerings to God, though limited under the law to vegetable offerings, is that of a *gift* expressive of the faith and gratitude of the offerer. Yet the truth,—first indicated by God's acceptance of Abel's offering of "the first-fruits of his flock and the fat thereof," then confirmed in the covenant of mercy made with Noah, and afterwards, yet more expressly, by the Divine command given to Abram in the ratification of God's covenant with him, [2]—that the most suitable offering to God was that of a life, not merely to be dedicated to his service, but to be poured out at his altar, certainly involves, and cannot but have conveyed to the mind of the worshipper, the idea of propitiation for sin, and of the forgiveness of sin, through shedding of blood. [3] This mystery of the offering of life as the means of holding communion with a holy God was, no doubt, at first dimly apprehended; yet it could not fail to be associated with the knowledge, which St. Paul [4] says that man has by nature, that sin deserves death. There was, however, one event in the history of the chosen family that must have greatly intensified the mysterious awe with which the burnt offering was regarded; I mean the command given to Abraham to offer up as a burnt sacrifice his own son Isaac in whom the promises were given, followed by the substitution for Isaac of a ram divinely provided. It could not but be felt, hereafter, whenever a sacrifice was offered, that the victim did in some mysterious way represent the promised seed. There is also another idea connected with sacrifice, that of fellowship through eating the flesh of the victim, which it would seem was recognised before the giving of the law, [5] and which certainly was general in the later heathen world. The passover, instituted before the giving of the law, though anticipatory of it and afterwards embodied in it, was specially such a feast of fellowship with God and his people. Thus the ideas associated with sacrifice gradually grew in the minds of God's servants, until the time came when the law should exhibit them more distinctly and definitely, and should not merely through these figures direct the minds of the worshippers to better things to come, but also assert, by Divine authority, the necessity of the principles of worship thus expressed, to the service of the one true God. We need but touch on the several points in which the law affected the worship of God through sacrifice.

51. (1) First, it determined the minister of sacrifice and of all religious offices.

---

[1] Gen. iv. 3—5.   [2] Gen. xv. 8, &c.
[3] See Job i. 5; xlii. 8 as an evidence of the idea of atonement for sin being involved in burnt offerings, independently of the law of Moses.
[4] Rom i. 32.
[5] Cf. Exod. xviii. 12. The word *lechem* which is translated "bread" is simply "food," and the flesh of the sacrifice is frequently called God's *lechem.* Levit. xxii. 30, and *passim;* Mal. i. 7.

In patriarchal times, sacrifices were offered by the head of the family, though the case of Melchizedec and probably also that of Jethro [1] are instances of a priesthood among the servants of the true God; while in heathen lands, as in Egypt, the priests had long held the position of a privileged class. At the time of the giving of the law from Mount Sinai priests are mentioned, before the Levitical priesthood was established, but these were probably, as Jewish interpreters and the Talmud assert, the first-born of the nation, and the same as the "young men of the children of Israel" (Exod. xxiv.) who were appointed by Moses to offer those burnt-offerings and peace-offerings by the blood of which the Sinaitic covenant was ratified. But under the law, while the whole nation of Israel, if they kept God's covenant, was to be "a kingdom of priests," [2] the sacerdotal functions were restricted henceforth to one family, that of Aaron, the elder brother of Moses; the tribe of Levi, to which Aaron himself belonged, being given to him and his descendants as a substitute for the first-born of the nation, to assist the priests in the service of the tabernacle. [3] Thus the tribe was representative of the whole priestly nation. But it was not only that a priesthood was established; the duties of the priestly office were now strictly defined and their prerogatives jealously guarded by Divine law. We know, from the teaching of the New Testament, that this represented the imperative necessity of a mediator in order that sinful man might draw near to God, and that no man could take that office upon himself but one called of God, as Aaron was; [4] and no devout Israelite could fail to apprehend the general force of that teaching of the law. On the other hand, the selection, by Divine authority, of one tribe,—whether or not it was selected for its zeal against the worshippers of the golden calf, [5]—and of a particular family out of that tribe, was to the nation a test of obedience to law. There were those who were unwilling to submit to this law, because they did not fully understand the reason of the appointment. [6] They said to Moses and Aaron, "Ye take too much upon you, seeing all the congregation is holy, every one of them, and the Lord is among them." But Israel was taught by terrible proofs that the law of Jehovah was law indeed, and that death was the certain consequence of wilful transgression.

Other limitations made by the law in regard to sacrifices were those of place and time. It was provided that when Israel should have entered into the possession of the promised land, offerings of every kind should be made only "in the place which the Lord thy God shall choose to put his name in." [7] The practical purpose in this was obviously to secure both purity of worship and the unity of God's covenant people. This kind of limitation, indeed, as well as that of times and seasons as specially holy, was a principle that entered largely into the religious provisions of the law; but it is unnecessary to our argument to consider these limitations beyond observing, that important as they were, as educating the chosen nation both in the knowledge of God's relation to themselves, and as a test of their obedience to his law, they were indications of an imperfect, and, to the same extent, unspiritual economy, one that could only be a preparation for an enduring and universal covenant. [8]

---

[1] Exod. iii. 1; xviii. 1, 12. The original meaning of the word *cohen* is "chief" or "prince," and is sometimes used in this sense (see 2 Sam. viii. 18; xx. 26), but in the Epistle to the Hebrews it is translated ἱερεύς.

[2] Exod. xix. 6. [3] Num. viii. 6, &c. [4] Heb. v. 1—4.

[5] Exod. xxxii. 25—29; and cf. ver. 29 with Deut. xxxiii. 9.

[6] Num. xvi. It must be observed that Korah was the son of the second-born of Kohath, and Dathan and Abiram were sons of Eliab, a member of one of the leading families of the tribe of Reuben, cf. Num. xxvi. 8, 9. It is evident that they considered the selection of the priesthood arbitrary.

[7] Deut. xii. 5—11, &c.   [8] Cf. St. John iv. 21—27; Gal. iv. 3, 9, 10

52. (2) Again, the law, while adopting generally sacrifice as a suitable method of worshipping God, made very complete and elaborate provisions both as to the ritual of sacrifice, and as to the different kinds of offerings. These regulations, besides guarding against abuses of the rite, were obviously intended, and were calculated in a high degree, to educate the minds of the Israelites through outward symbols, and direct them, as far as was possible, till the redemption should be accomplished, to the true principles of spiritual worship. Among the heathen, the fundamental idea of sacrifice was perverted into the notion that the deity required these gifts; the offering up of a victim into the belief that he delighted in the suffering and death of his creatures; and while sacrifice implied that for communion of sinful man with God more was required than his own obedience, it was easily forgotten that, in themselves, sacrifices were only of value as expressing the faith and love of the offerer. These misapprehensions are so natural to the human mind that, even under the provisions of the law, men were liable to them, although the prophetical writings of the Old Testament contain distinct protests against them.[1] But the law gave no encouragement to such errors,[2] and by its elaborate distinctions directed the mind of the worshipper to truths inconsistent with them.

The animal sacrifices ordained by the law may be divided into three classes, in each of which one distinctive idea was prominent. 1. The burnt sacrifice (generally *'olah*, "that which goes up"), in which the blood was poured out "round about upon the altar," and the whole of the body of the victim with all the fat was burnt on the altar. The prominent idea in this was the free-will offering to God of spiritual worship, of prayer, praise, and adoration. 2. The peace offering (*shelem*, "peace"), in which the blood was used as in the burnt offering and the internal fat (*cheleb*, which was considered the sign of animal perfection and, as well as the blood, forbidden to be eaten) was burnt on the altar; the flesh was eaten partly by the offerer and partly by the priests and their families. The idea here was peace with a reconciled God, and communion with him and his Church. The passover may be considered as belonging to this class. 3. The sin-offering (*chattath*, "sin"), which was the special characteristic, as it was the creation, of the law. In this not only was the blood poured out as in the other sacrifices, but first of all some was put on the horns of the altar, and (when the offering was for the high priest or the whole congregation) also taken into the sanctuary and sprinkled on the vail and the altar of incense; and once in the year, on the great day of atonement, was taken into the holy of holies and sprinkled on (or before) the mercy-seat. The *cheleb* was burnt on the altar of burnt-offering, the flesh was generally eaten by the priests in the holy place, to bear the iniquity of the congregation, and make atonement for them before the Lord.[3] But whenever the blood was taken into the sanctuary, the body was burnt without the camp as utterly unclean and accursed. The idea in offerings of this class was evidently atonement for sin. But it must be observed that in all sacrifices of each of the three classes, atonement was represented by the pouring out of the blood, and the worship of God by burning the fat on the altar.

53. Into further details either of the sacrificial system or of the ceremonial law generally it is unnecessary to enter in this introduction, because that which we have noticed is sufficient to explain distinctly how this branch of the secondary law is connected with the fundamental principles of Divine law, and with the purposes for

---

[1] Such as Ps. l. 7—15; li. 16, 17; Micah vi. 6—9.
[2] *E. g.* The offerings by fire might be a bullock, sheep, or fowl, or even a handful of flour with oil and frankincense, and yet each was an offering "*of a sweet savour to the Lord.*"
[3] Levit. x. 17.

which it was given to man. Of this ceremonial law it is true that every "jot and tittle" must be fulfilled, not only *by* Christ himself "as born under the law," or *in* Christ as the antitype and substance of these shadows and figures, but, in their spirit, by the disciples of Christ. For the principles of the worship of God, which the ordinances of the ceremonial law embodied and demanded of the Israelites, were the very same as those which are necessary for ourselves. First of all this law, by its minute and strict provisions, required of man that he should recognise and acknowledge himself as a sinner, both in his nature from his birth to his death, and in his daily life. It was not only as an inference from the Sinaitic law that there was "by the law the knowledge of sin," but in the ceremonial system, the perpetual and ever-present exponent of God's law to Israel, sin and death stared man in the face, haunted him day and night, forced their presence upon him even in his holiest hours, compelled him to feel that all real and acceptable worship of a God of holiness and truth must begin with a consciousness that we have transgressed his commandments, and thus, in the emphatic language of St. Paul, "the Scripture," that is the *Torah,* "*shut up* all things under sin." [1] This law again, with equal clearness, continually and definitely required of man that he should worship God through faith in an atonement for sin. The author of the Epistle to the Hebrews reminds those to whom he writes [2] that the first covenant (that of the law) was inaugurated in blood; [3] and, he adds, "we may almost say that in blood all things are purified according to the law. and without shedding of blood there is no remission." The pouring out of the blood in every sacrifice was the "outward and visible sign" not of sin merely, but of atonement for sin. And to make it more apparent, through these "elements of the world," what kind of atonement it is on which sinful man can rely, the great sin offerings made once a year on the day of atonement had their blood taken within the Holy of Holies to the very mercy-seat of God, on which the *Shechinah*, the manifested Presence of Jehovah, rested. And yet, the annual repetition of this most significant rite —the most solemn by far of all the ordinances of the law—indicated emphatically that the atonement signified was not thus accomplished, that the blood of the true sacrifice, which would take away sin and satisfy the conscience, had not yet been taken before the true mercy-seat in the heavens, of which that in the tabernacle was but an image and pattern. The law therefore demanded by its ordinances faith in an atonement for sin by a real sacrifice, yet to be revealed, the blood of which must be, when offered, taken into the true Holy of Holies where God is in his glory. That which is required of us is the very same in every respect, save that now the true sacrifice has been finished, and the blood of Christ has been taken by our true High Priest within the veil. The very least of the commandments, which indicated to Israel these principles of acceptable worship to God, embodies that which cannot be neglected by the Christian without spiritual loss. Lastly, through these ordinances, Israel was assured of peace with a reconciled God, and of communion with him and with their brethren through sacrifice. Even the stern economy of law, the direct purpose of which was to make man's sin and guilt more distinctly seen and more keenly felt, yet was no reign of terror, or house of bondage. The son, though under restraints in his childhood, is nevertheless a son; none the less assured of his Father's love; assured that his own offences, though they are severely chastised, do not alienate his Father's heart from him, if only he approach God through the blood of the covenant. Perhaps there is no aspect of the law which is overlooked, or at least not sufficiently appreciated, by Christians so frequently, and with so much loss to their own enjoyment of the blessings of Christ's kingdom, as that which the peace offerings represented to Israel.

[1] Gal. iii. 22.   [2] Heb. x. 18—22.   [3] See Exod. xxiv. 6—8.

The Civil Laws of the Mosaic Code.

54. Those secondary laws, given by Moses, which were the development and application of the fundamental principles of man's duty to his neighbour, are, as before observed, intermingled in the *Torah* with those of a religious and cere-monial character. The reasons for this we have already considered ; and it has been noticed (§ 25) that in the development even of human law, the mingling together of "religious, civil, and merely moral ordinances without any regard to differences in their essential character," is invariably found in the early forms of written law. In the Divine law this was, we may say, necessary ; for its authority, being that of God, extended to all these spheres of human life and conduct. It must be observed, also, that even among those which we must consider as the civil laws of the Mosaic code, there are many directed against offences that are far more directly and clearly sins against God and his image in us, than against our neighbour. Under this head fall the most abominable of all crimes,[1] and others which might be considered very trivial offences if our duty to man only were regarded. It is remarkable that drunk-enness, a sin of this class, the evil consequences of which to a man himself are ex-emplified in the sacred history by two most emphatic instances, while its evil results to society are only too well known in the present day, was not the subject of any law, except as connected with other sins,[2] or in reference to sacerdotal duties.[3] Perhaps the abstinence from wine and strong drink required of the priests, "that ye may put difference between holy and unholy and between clean and unclean," was considered sufficient warning of the dangers of excess in those days, and under the circumstances of Oriental life.[4] It is evident, however, both that drunkenness was accounted as a sin,[5] and that, at all events in the times of the kings, it was a sin common both among priests and people. We must, however, restrict ourselves in this examination of the civil laws of Moses to those which distinctly belong to man's duty to his neighbour, and illustrate the leading principles which govern them by some of the most luminous instances.

55. (1) And first, regarding these laws in reference to the one purpose, which, St. Paul teaches us, was paramount in the whole revelation of Divine law, that is, to con-vince man of sin, not by mere counsels and precepts, but by commands which demanded obedience, and which had the sanction of severe punishment,—we must observe that this purpose itself explains the severity with which offences against the rights of others and the order of society were visited in this code. For example, under the head of honouring parents, the law affixed the punishment of death to smiting, or even cursing, either father or mother. In regard to homicide, wilful murder was punished with death, which could not be commuted into any other penalty ; against what would now be called manslaughter the sentence of death was recorded, but in some cases blood-money might be paid as a satisfaction ; for accidental homicide the cities of refuge were provided, where the slayer must remain till the death of the high priest. There is some difficulty in reconciling the laws, but it seems most pro-bable that in all cases of homicide, whether wilful, or the result of carelessness, or purely accidental, the Goel, or nearest kinsman, to whom it belonged to execute the sentence, had the right to kill the man-slayer if he found him outside the city ; and

---

[1] Levit. xviii. 22—30.   [2] Deut. xxi. 20.   [3] Levit. x. 8—10.
[4] It is certain that the Israelites would not learn temperance in Egypt, in which country there was a large consumption of wine, with the usual results among all classes, which are satirically represented in the sculptures.
[5] Cf. 1 Sam. i. 13—16.

that the judges, representing the congregation, determined respecting one who had taken refuge, according to the evidence of witnesses,[1] what the punishment should be. Adultery, even when the woman was only betrothed, was punished by the death of both offenders. Since the most precious possession of man is his own personal liberty, death was the punishment for stealing a man and either selling him or keeping him in bondage. Thefts generally were punished by restitution of either four or five times the value of the thing stolen; but a burglar breaking into a house at night might be slain with impunity. False witness was punished according to the *lex talionis*, the principle of which was also laid down in the law as that on which all cases of personal injury should be punished: " life for life, eye for eye, tooth for tooth, hand for hand, foot for foot, burning for burning, wound for wound, stripe for stripe." [2] This to us now may seem a rude and barbarous principle of justice; but it must be borne in mind that it is the natural and original idea of justice between man and man. The *lex talionis* was recognised in the twelve tables of Rome, and it was expressed in later Roman law in almost the same terms as in the law of Moses. Cicero accepts the general principle as the true basis of penal law; " Noxiæ pœna par esto." [3]

Of the necessity for the adaptation of these secondary laws to the actual moral condition of the people to whom they were given we shall speak presently; but there is another consideration which, from a religious point of view, has yet greater weight; namely, that it was essential to the purpose for which Divine law was given, that the severity, exactness, and inflexible impartiality of the justice of God should be exhibited in that law, and that, under this economy, his people should be taught this lesson, as children are, by a discipline suited to their age. We may ask, however, can a law of this nature be part of that law of which love is the fulfilment? Did not Christ expressly reject this law of retaliation as unsuitable for his disciples, and bid them, on the contrary, return good for evil? Yet he came " not to destroy but to fulfil the law," and we have seen (§ 32) that justice and charity are nothing else than opposite poles of the same principle, and Divine law necessarily involves both. The Scribes and Pharisees, whose false interpretations of God's law Christ condemned, altogether forgot, as many Christians do to the present day, that the " sanction " or penalty of a law is not for the guidance of our conduct and feeling towards others, but to direct those who are the representatives of God's justice on earth. To the personal conscience it is nothing more than a warning of the evil and guilt of the sin. In this particular case, that which the law *commands* us is that we should do unto others as we would that they should do unto us; the *penalty* for disobedience, which it belongs not to us to execute, but to God by those to whom he commits this office, exactly corresponds with the command; that is, it requires that whatever injury we do to others shall be " measured " out with perfect exactness " to us again." Our Lord, while he rejects the false interpretation of the law, asserts the principle of equal-handed justice on which it is founded, as a necessary and inviolable principle in God's government.[4] And without the distinct recognition of God's justice, charity is a barren sentiment. The soul that has not a deep conviction of the exact and inviolable justice of God, can have no real, or at least no profound sense of his love; and, therefore, no sufficient foundation for that love to his neighbour which alone fulfils the law. In fact, these severe penal laws are nothing else than the expression of God's righteous condemnation of him who does not love his neighbour as himself.

---

[1] Cf. Numb. xxxv. 12.
[3] See note, § 47, *supra*.
[2] Exod. xxi. 23—25; Levit. xxiv. 20; Deut. xix. 21.
[4] Cf. Matt. vii. 2 with ver. 7.

56. (2) But to realise this it is important that we should look at these civil laws of Moses from a different aspect from that of their "sanctions." Few Christians, even though reverent students of the Bible, sufficiently appreciate the fact that these laws do embody, and sometimes express in the very words, those principles of law which our Lord taught in the Sermon on the Mount and elsewhere, and which are the Christian rule of life, though not enforced on us by particular commandments (for we are not under an economy of law), but to be fulfilled in the freedom of the spirit. It will be sufficient to notice a few emphatic instances of this.

(*a*) The following general precept is identical with the teaching of the gospel: "Thou shalt not hate thy brother in thine heart: thou shalt in any wise rebuke thy neighbour, and not suffer sin upon him (*or*, not bear sin for him).[1] Thou shalt not avenge, nor bear any grudge against the children of thy people, but thou shalt love thy neighbour as thyself: I am the Lord" (Levit. xix. 17, 18).

(*b*) The Scribes and Pharisees misinterpreted and perverted certain directions of the law, given for the guidance of the nation in their relations with other surrounding nations (such as Deut. xxiii. 6) into the maxim, "Thou shalt love thy neighbour, and hate thine enemy." But the language of the law itself is the same as that of the gospel. "If thou meet thine enemy's ass or ox going astray, thou shalt surely bring it back to him again. If thou see the ass of him that hateth thee lying under its burden, and wouldest forbear to help him, thou shalt surely help with him" (Exod. xxiii. 4, 5). What is this but the very law of Christ, "Love your enemies, do good to them that hate you"?[2] And it is the more emphatic because elsewhere,[3] when the commandment is expanded, it is "thy brother" whom it is an offence against the law not to help. "Thine enemy" is in the eye of God's law as certainly "thy brother," as "thy friend" is.

(*c*) The lawyer who asked our Lord, "Who is my neighbour?" and to whom our Lord replied by the parable of the good Samaritan, had certainly no excuse from the law for his ignorance. The provisions for the "strangers in the land" are very numerous, and though they did not enjoy the same civil rights and privileges as those who belonged to the nation, the principle on which they were to be treated was the same. The language of the law is express (Levit. xix. 34): "The stranger that dwelleth with you shall be unto you as one born in the land, and thou shalt love him as thyself; for ye were strangers in the land of Egypt. I am the Lord thy God." The "stranger" then is a "neighbour," to be loved as oneself no less than the Israelite. And there is a special touch of compassion in the reason given: "Ye shall not oppress a stranger, for *ye know the heart of a stranger*, seeing ye were strangers in the land of Egypt."

(*d*) But, especially, the provisions made for the poor under these laws breathe the same spirit as the teaching of Christ and his apostles as to their peculiar claim on the people of God. Not only was it a purpose in the primary law of weekly Sabbaths, "that thy man-servant and thy maid-servant may rest as well as thou,"[4] "that the son of thine handmaid and the stranger may be refreshed;" but in the secondary laws every seventh year was made a year of rest from tillage and harvest expressly for this purpose. "Six years shalt thou sow thy land, and gather in the fruits thereof. But the seventh year thou shalt let it rest and lie still; that the poor of thy people may eat: and what they leave, the beasts of the field shall eat. In like manner shalt thou do with thy vineyard and with thy oliveyard."[5] In every

---

[1] The English version is probably not exactly accurate; but it expresses the general sense sufficiently.

[2] Cf. Gal. vi. 2.   [3] Deut. xxii. 1—4.   [4] Deut. v. 14.

[5] Exod. xxiii. 10, 11; Levit. xxv. 2—7.

year, indeed, the law required that, for the benefit of the poor and the stranger, the whole field should not be reaped, and the gleanings should be left ; and the same rule applied to the oliveyard and the vineyard—indeed, this law as to the yearly harvest alone could make the Sabbatical year of any value to the poor ; for a carefully-harvested field could have no natural crop. This Sabbatical year also was a year of release from debts,[1] in the case of loans made to a brother Israelite in his distress. " For " (Moses says) "the poor shall never cease out of the land ; therefore, I command thee, saying, Thou shalt open thy hand wide unto thy brother, to thy poor, and to thy needy, in the land." The principle in all this legislation in regard to property is, " The land is God's, and it belongs to you only as stewards under God." The rights of personal property are limited by God's rights. The poor of God's nation are both " thy poor " and also " God's poor." We in these days have learnt, indeed, that other methods of relieving the poor are more effectual than indiscriminate giving. But it was no purpose of the Divine law, any more than it was of Christ, when he said to his disciples " Sell that ye have, and give alms,"[2] to teach lessons of political and social economy ; the command simply was that they should deny themselves, and trust God as regards earthly things, in order to benefit the poor. The spirit of the law (as well as that of Christ's teaching) is equally binding on us at the present day, and, because it is binding, it is also our duty to use the methods which experience has proved to be most effectual and most beneficial, and therefore the truest charity.[3] But undoubtedly of such laws as these of the Mosaic code, interpreted not in their letter but in their spirit, it is emphatically true that "whosoever shall do and teach them, the same shall be called great in the kingdom of heaven."

The Imperfection of the Secondary Laws.

57. In our rapid survey of the secondary laws of the *Torah*, we have found no difficulty in proving,—for indeed the evidence lies (we may almost say) on the surface of the record,—that the principles embodied in the religious and ceremonial laws are none other than those which are necessary to the Christian under a better covenant ; and that the laws which relate to the duties between man and man are based on that truly Divine and eternal principle, one aspect of which is exact and absolute justice, and the other perfect love. These conclusions are themselves sufficient to explain the words of Christ in the Sermon on the Mount, for they prove both the complete identity of the spirit which underlies the commandments of the law with that of his own teaching, and further that, when he contrasts that which was said to them of old time with that which he himself says to his disciples, he was contrasting, not the law of Moses with a new law that he himself gave, but the righteousness of the letter with the righteousness of the spirit, which is the essence of the law, and necessary for the kingdom of heaven. But does this mean that the law of the Pentateuch was, perfect ? In the sense in which the Psalmist says, " The law of the Lord is perfect, converting the soul," in which our Lord declares that it must be obeyed and taught, in which St. Paul describes it as holy and spiritual, and St. James speaks of it as the " perfect law of liberty," that is in its spirit and essence, undoubtedly it is perfect. And yet, in another sense, it was as certainly very imperfect. Not only as regards the shadows and figures of the ceremonial law as compared with the

---

[1] Deut. xv. 1—11.   [2] St. Luke xii. 33.

[3] It should be observed also, that the law discouraged that merely sentimental feeling of compassion for the poor which is often practical injustice to others. It forbad them (Exod. xxiii. 3) to " countenance (*hadar*, be partial to) a poor man in his cause." The LXX. version is οὐκ ἐλεήσεις.

reality which is Christ, what St. Paul calls "the weakness and unprofitableness" of its commandments is apparent, so that when Christ had accomplished his work, the letter disappeared before the brightness of the spirit, it disannulled itself that it might be fulfilled in the spirit; but for the same reason, that is on account of the essential imperfection of law as law, and its utter inadequacy to be *of itself* a guide for the conscience of man, the same result followed with regard to all the secondary laws without exception.

58. This truth, which is fully exemplified in the history of human law,[1] may be thus explained.[2]

"Without definite and permanent law natural life cannot make progress, and law is law indeed in proportion to its definiteness, its certainty, its rigidity. And yet these very qualities in law, without which it cannot attain its perfectness as law,—because otherwise its results must in part depend on its interpretation by a judge, as is the case with most human laws,—are also the inherent defect of law itself, giving occasion for the saying, *Summum jus summa injuria*. For it is impossible that any fixed rules should be at all times suited to all the varying circumstances and conditions of human life, in which the self-same acts may at different times be wholly different in their true character. And laws may therefore both allow some things and command others, necessary or expedient in one stage of human life, yet in another injurious or very inexpedient; so that human laws made in one age often fall into desuetude in another, and their enforcement would lead to great injustice, and they need to be from time to time reformed and adapted to the altered circumstances of men. It is therefore impossible, in the nature of things, that institutions which are the expression of positive and fixed law, although that law be given by God himself, should be perfectly adapted for man, or be permanent. And those who live under such institutions are in an imperfect state for two reasons—first, because their own judgment is not exercised in their obedience, but they obey merely because it is commanded, which is the condition of an infant or a slave; and then also because of the imperfections which are necessarily inherent in law, because it is law."

These considerations do not affect the primary law for two very obvious reasons : first, because its commandments express nothing more than the religious and moral principles which are coeval with man's origin, and the necessary results of man's original and fundamental relations to God and his fellow-man, which therefore cannot be altered by any changes in his circumstances and condition; secondly, because being a law for the conscience of man, it entirely differs from human laws by the absence from it of all fixed rules, for it leaves to the enlightened and informed conscience the office of applying its principles to the varying conditions of human life. But with the secondary laws the case is totally different. These laws contain elaborate regulations in regard to the whole sphere of human life, the very purpose of them being, as we have seen, to bring law into all its relations, and to leave as little as possible to the judgment and conscience of the individual. They were made for a nation whose moral knowledge and moral development were totally different from ours, and who had to be educated, like children, gradually to apprehend truths which cannot be learned suddenly or *per saltum*, although to us, in our state of knowledge and development, they seem self-evident. We need not be surprised therefore if we find in them not only prohibitions which are utterly unsuited to our moral condition, but also many things allowed and sanctioned, or even commanded, which *to us* would be inconsistent with morality. This subject, which, as is well known, has given rise to many attacks upon the morality of the Pentateuch, has been discussed at length in some of its aspects, in a work by the late Canon

---

[1] See Maine's 'Ancient Law,' chap. 11.
[2] I quote from my 'Genesis of the Church,' pp. 36—38.

Mozley.[1] In regard to some questions in the Mosaic law with which he deals, particularly those of the law of retaliation and of the Goël, he does not appear to distinguish sufficiently between the law as representing God's justice, and the law as a guide to man's conscience, or indeed to give due weight to considerations that arise from the peculiar characteristics of law. But the general principle which he maintains, namely, that all legislation, intended to raise men from a lower standard of morality to a higher, must begin on the basis of the imperfect and crude notions of right and wrong which they already possess, and, by giving these ideas a right direction and wholesome limitation, elevate them gradually into a higher sphere, is beyond all question the true solution of the difficulty, and it is a method not only consistent with the wisdom and the goodness of God, but suggesting important lessons to the Christian as to the true mode of dealing with those who are "ignorant and out of the way."

59. The real proof, however, of the law given through Moses being consistent with the character of him whose relations with man are the foundation of all religious and moral duty, is to be found in the answer to the question, whether taken as a whole, and as part of a Divine dispensation, the law fulfilled ends worthy of God, by training man to live for the purposes for which he was created. There is no question as to this in regard to the ceremonial law. In other words, there is no doubt that, notwithstanding its weakness, and imperfection, and unspirituality in itself, the law was a necessary preparation for Christ and his gospel; "our schoolmaster to lead us to Christ, that we might be justified by faith." But is it equally true of that part of the secondary law which deals with what we understand by moral duties, that its tendency and its result was to elevate the people to whom it was given, up towards a perfect standard of morality, through the moral education which it supplied? This has been discussed by Canon Mozley in one of his Lectures (Lect. x.), and the answer is complete. Indeed, one fact is of itself sufficient proof of this, namely, that the moral standard of Christianity is nothing else than the legitimate development of those moral principles of which the Mosaical law was, from the circumstances under which it was given, an imperfect expression.

60. But it is probable that many feel a difficulty here which lies yet deeper, and which this argument will not remove. They may ask, Can the end, however good, justify the means? Can we suppose that God would have commanded or even sanctioned that which the true standard of morality condemns, in order that this true standard might be ultimately attained by others? This can only be answered by another question, viz. what is moral good and moral evil? Are they objective or subjective? or do both these elements enter into the determination of their character? And is evil only a defect of good, or a reality in itself? These questions have occupied the minds of moralists and theologians for many ages, and a brief answer cannot be a complete one. But the argument of this Introduction may at all events supply an answer sufficient for our present purpose. We have seen, in our previous investigations, that sin began with the knowledge of good and evil, without which the distinctions of good and evil in man himself did not exist; there could be no moral good and no moral evil. And in man's present condition morality, in the abstract, considered apart from all positive laws, must consist in a man's regulating his nature in accordance with the Divine order constituted in his creation in God's image, and doing unto other men, created equally in the Divine image, as he himself would be done by; the whole circumstances and condition of these other men as also belonging to the Divine order being taken into account. Moral good consists in man's recognising that order, and

---

[1] 'Ruling Ideas in Early Ages, and their Relation to Old Testament Faith.' 1877.

of his own will submitting to it; moral evil, in his departing from that order, whether by omission or by positive action, through the ἐπιθυμία (or desire for that which he has not) in a nature not regulated in accordance with that order. It necessarily follows from these considerations, that moral good and evil in man in its essence must be subjective; that the true moral character of an act, in the sight of him who judges the hearts of men, must be determined by the state of mind of him who commits it, his knowledge, his intentions, his motives. "To him that knoweth to do good and doeth it not, to him it is sin."[1] The fact therefore that God gave laws suited to the state of moral knowledge in which those were to whom they were given, with the view of cultivating that knowledge, and restraining the evils which might be caused from ἐπιθυμία, does not imply that God sanctioned or even allowed man's doing that which was immoral.

61. There are two questions to which this argument specially applies, and which will sufficiently illustrate it: namely, the law of marriage, and the sanction of slavery.

(1) Our Lord's own words as to divorce apply with equal force to the whole question of the Mosaic law of marriage. "He saith unto them, Moses, because of the hardness of your hearts, suffered you to put away your wives: but from the beginning it was not so."[2] That is, a deviation from the standard of the original institution was allowed under certain restrictions, because the absolute prohibition of the customs then prevalent in the world would, through the hardness of men's hearts, which makes them incapable of at once recognising some moral principles without previous education, prevent instead of promoting the ends for which marriage was ordained. But the law of Moses, by requiring a writing of divorce to be given, and by its other enactments, protected the law of marriage as then understood, and restrained transgressions, and thus gradually trained the mind of the people for a higher standard and for the true ideal of marriage. Indeed, we find in the prophetical writings[3] the true idea of the law of marriage asserted as if it were the law itself, being indeed the real spirit of the Divine law.

(2) The parallel case of the sanction of slavery was in all respects similar in principle. It is indeed a striking proof of the shock given to man's moral being by the Fall, that he so far lost the consciousness of God's image in every individual of the human race as to consider his brother man a mere chattel. It has been remarked[4] that "there seems to be somewhat in the institution of slavery which has at all times either shocked or perplexed mankind, however little habituated to reflection, and however slightly advanced in the cultivation of its moral instincts. The compunction which ancient communities, almost unconsciously experienced, appears to have always resulted in some imaginary principle upon which a defence, or at least a rationale, of slavery could be plausibly founded." One of these was the inferiority of certain races and their natural aptitude for the servile condition. Another, which historically was the cause of much of the slavery of the ancient world, was the supposed right of conquerors over a vanquished foe. But its more legitimate origin is to be found in the patriarchal system, and in the rights of the head of the family over all its members, among whom the servant was classed, as indicated both in the Roman term "familia," and by one of the Greek words for slave, "οἰκέτης," "one of the household."[5] However, whatever be the history of slavery, it is certain that it was universal in the ancient world, and that the conscience

---

[1] James iv. 17; cf. Rom. xiv. 14, 20; Tit. i. 15.
[2] St. Matt. xix. 8.　　　　　[3] Cf. Ps. cxxviii.; Prov. v. 18; Mal. ii. 14, 15.
[4] Maine's 'Ancient Law,' p. 162, &c.
[5] Cf. also Heb. iii. 2—6 and Gal. iv. 1—7, where the son during his minority is supposed to be on the same level as a δοῦλος in the house.

of man was not at that period prepared for its abolition, nor would human society have benefited by such interference. The Mosaic legislation recognised it, while, as in the case of the law of marriage, it greatly ameliorated the condition of the bondsman and bondswoman, especially of those of the Hebrew nation, who could not, except by their own will, be retained in perpetual servitude. How slowly the human mind could be educated in the apprehension of the true rights of humanity is evident from the fact, that even after the revelation of the full meaning of these rights in the incarnation of the Son of God, and of the truth that all, bond or free, are one in Christ Jesus, and when Christian masters were directed to give to "their slaves that which is just and *equal*," [1] a principle inconsistent with that power over the person which is implied by slavery; yet the principle was left to work out its true results, and slaves are cautioned not to presume on their equality, as brethren in Christ, with their master, while masters are not expressly commanded to set their slaves at liberty. The gospel recognised the fact of slavery being in the world as the law also had done; the law by its regulations modified the character of slavery and lessened its evils, until the gospel should reveal the truth, before the light of which not only the system itself but its spirit must disappear from the world.

62. In this Introduction the *Torah* has been examined only in that character of *law* which, as its name implies, distinguishes it from all the rest of Holy Scripture But it must be remembered that Moses was not only a lawgiver, but also a *prophet*, as is proved by his teaching in the Book of Deuteronomy, in which he expounds the inner spirit of the law, while he foresees and describes some of the future history of the chosen nation.[2] He was, indeed,[3] the first of that line of prophets which Jehovah promised to raise up as a perpetual witness for him to Israel, until the office in which they testified for God should have its complete fulfilment and realisation in that Divine Prophet who, raised up from the midst of Israel, of the seed of Abraham, is a Mediator between God and man in a sense that Moses could not be, and has revealed the whole will of God to man, and given his Spirit to abide with us for ever. How "the prophets," by their inspired teaching, and the authority they received from God, corrected the defects inherent in law as law,[4] awakening the consciences of men to the justice and the love of God by arguments independent of the law, and thus placing obedience to God upon a higher and surer foundation than that of mere submission to authority; and how they gradually taught the people of God that his service was in the spirit, not in the letter; freedom, and not bondage; that he would "have mercy and not sacrifice"; and thus prepared for that dispensation of the Spirit in which the veil over the face of Moses should be done away in Christ, and "the knowledge of good and evil," which to man under the dominion of ἐπιθυμία is death, should become, through the presence of God's Spirit in man, a higher law, the law of the spirit of life in Christ Jesus, which sets us free from the law of sin and death—all this is expounded in the other books of the Old Testament Scriptures. But to appreciate that part of the old economy, it is first of all necessary to have a clear and definite conception of the true character and force of the law itself; and to this end the whole of the present argument has been directed.

[1] τὴν ἰσότητα, Col. iv. 1; but it probably means "equity," as the τὰ αὐτά in Ephes. vi. 9, rather than "equality."

[2] *e. g.*, Deut. xxxii. and xxxiii.

[3] Cf. Deut. xviii. 15—19. The view of this passage given above seems the only one that at all connects it with the context.

[4] 'Genesis of the Church,' p. 38.

THE AUTHORSHIP OF THE PENTATEUCH.

BY THE

REV. THOMAS WHITELAW, M.A.

Is the Pentateuch the work of Moses? or is it the production of a later age? If anything were needed to attest the supreme importance attaching to this inquiry, it might be found in the voluminous literature which, on this subject alone, since the middle of last century, has issued from the English, but more especially from the Continental, press. Prior to that date, the claim of Moses to be regarded as the author of the Pentateuch may be said to have been supported by the almost unanimous consent of both Hebrew and Christian antiquity. In the second century, it is true, sentiments impugning the Mosaic authorship, either in whole or in part, began to be broached, but chiefly by writers of otherwise heretical tendencies. According to the testimony of Epiphanius (Hær. xviii.) and Johannes Damascenus (de Hæresibus, ch. xix.), an obscure party among the Nazarenes regarded the present Pentateuch as spurious. Ptolemæus, a Gnostic writer belonging to the same period, in an epistle (ad Florum) preserved by Epiphanius (Hæres. xxxiii. 4), ascribed only a portion of the work to Moses. The author of the Clementine Homilies (ii. 38, 40; iii. 47) considered the account of Moses' death (Deut. xxxiv. 5) conclusive evidence that the Pentateuch did not proceed from his pen, and entertained the belief that the Pentateuch had been often lost and re-written, each time with additions. Jerome is sometimes quoted as having been suspicious of the Mosaic authorship of the Pentateuch (Perowne, Smith's 'Dict.,' art. Pentateuch), but his language, *Sive Mosen dicere volueris auctorem Pentateuchi, sive Esdram ejusdem instauratorem operis non recuso*, only bears that he detected no insuperable barrier in the way of believing that the original composition of the Hebrew law-giver may have been revised by the post-Exilian reformer. Aben Ezra likewise, though claimed as an opponent of the orthodox opinion, merely expresses doubt of the Mosaic authorship of certain passages which he regarded as subsequent interpolations (*vide* Bleek's 'Introd.,' vol. i. § 68). With the exception of that offered by the second century heretics, it is problematical if the genuineness of the Mosaic writings encountered serious opposition until towards the close of the seventeenth century, when in rapid succession it was assailed by Hobbes in his 'Leviathan' (1651), Isaak Peyrerius in his 'Systema Theologicum ex præ-Adamitorum Hypothesi' (1655), Spinoza in his 'Tractatus Theologico-Politicus' (1670), Richard Simon in his 'Critical History of the Old Testament' (1678), and Clericus in his 'Sentimens' (1685), the opinions of which, however, he subsequently retracted.

lxv

Yet it was not until the publication by Astruc (1753) of what has since become known as the hypothesis of documents that the contrary belief of the post-Mosaic origin of the Pentateuch was able to make progress; but since then it has advanced with gigantic and rapid strides, more particularly in Germany, where it has enlisted in its propagation and defence a brilliant array of talent—gifted and able writers, who have expended on its demonstration and elucidation research the most minute and painstaking, ratiocination the most elaborate and careful, critical acumen the most penetrating and dexterous, eloquence the most attractive and engaging, not to speak of imagination the most wonderful and imposing. Among its advocates must be reckoned many of the most distinguished scholars of the present century. Nor can it be alleged that it is absolutely devoid of at least seemingly weighty considerations to advance in its support. That an opinion which has secured the allegiance of authorities so eminent as Tuch, Knobel, Hupfeld, De Wette, Bohlen, Bleek, Delitzsch, Ewald, Graf, Kuenen, Wellhausen, and others, should have nothing in the shape of evidence to produce in its behalf is simply incredible. Accordingly, it will be the aim of this investigation in the first place to examine the more important of those arguments which are commonly advanced in proof of the post-Mosaic or late authorship of the Pentateuch, and in the second place to review the principal of those considerations which by the advocates of the popular belief are still regarded as sufficient to establish the claim of Moses to the honour of having composed the first five books of the Old Testament Scriptures.

I. Considerations which are commonly regarded as supporting the post-Mosaic or late authorship of the Pentateuch.

1. THE SEEMING COMPOSITE STRUCTURE OF THE NARRATIVE. While the unity of the Pentateuch regarded as a whole is too palpable to be either denied or ignored, by critics of a certain school that is usually ascribed not to the circumstance of its having issued from one mind, which one would have imagined to be the natural and obvious inference, but to the literary genius of a late writer in the time of Saul (Stähelin) or of Josiah (De Wette, Knobel, Bleek), about the end of the seventh century B. C. (Kuenen), or at all events before the destruction of Jerusalem (Ewald), or even posterior to the Exile (Hartmann, Bohlen, Wellhausen), who, having found certain ancient records that had descended from primitive times, worked them up into the present Pentateuch. The original hypothesis of Astruc related solely to Genesis, which he conjectured had been put together from two principal documents, with the assistance of ten smaller memoirs—a speculation in which he had been forestalled by Vitringa, Clericus, and Richard Simon, who all assumed written sources for the first book of Moses; but with greater boldness the theory which he adopted with regard to Genesis has since been applied to the entire Pentateuch, and the process of disintegration and dismemberment carried forward with such zeal by the rationalistic criticism of Germany, that the pre-existing documents have now become so numerous and fragmentary, that it is fairly open to consideration whether a greater miracle is not involved in the compilation of the present Pentateuch out of such *disjecta membra* than in its original composition by the hand of Moses. Amid the manifold conflicting theories which have been propounded by successive advocates of this hypothesis, one point can be detected in which all are pretty generally agreed, and indeed it is the kernel of the hypothesis, viz., that of the ancient records, or source writings, the principal were a narrative of primitive history from the pen of an unknown composer who has been styled the Elohist, from his exclusive employment, at least in the earlier portion of his work, of that name for the Deity, and a

Jehovistic document, but whether an independent writing or only of a supplementary character may be said to be as yet undetermined, touching on many of the same points as the former narration, but, unlike it, using the name Jehovah for the Deity, not altogether to the exclusion of the term Elohim, but apparently as synonymous with it.

As to the grounds on which this, in some respects fascinating, theory rests, attention is directed to the circumstance that in the earlier portion of the Pentateuch, extending from Gen. i. 1 to Exod. vi. 3, the names Elohim and Jehovah appear to have been introduced into the narrative from two distinct sources, the first name occurring in sections from which the second is distinguished by its absence, and the second finding a place in paragraphs or subdivisions, if not to the complete excision, at least to the equal companionship, of the first. Indeed so palpable is this phenomenon, that attempts have been made, though with indifferent success, to reconstruct the two documents by bringing together the different chapters and verses, clauses and words, that belong to each respectively. Of this an example will be found, so far as relates to Genesis, in the Special Introduction to that Book (*vide* pp. iii, iv). Then it is confidently alleged that the two writers can be traced throughout almost the entire course of the Pentateuch, and even up to the end of Joshua, which by most critics of this school is included in the original Elohistic writing, or, as Ewald designates it, the Great Book of Origins. When they refer to the same subjects, not only do they employ different names for the Deity, but they either give what are alleged to be quite irreconcilable accounts, as in the narratives of the Creation (cf. Gen. i. 1—ii. 3 with ii. 4—25) and the Flood (cf. Gen. vi. 9—22 with vii. 1—5), the mission of Moses (cf. Exod. iv. 31 with vi. 9) and the story of the Exodus (cf. Exod. iii. 18; v. 1, 3; vii. 16 with vi. 11; vii. 2; ix. 35; xi. 10), the redemption of the firstborn (cf. Exod. xiii. 13; xxxiv. 20 with Levit. xxvii. 27; Numb. xviii. 16) and the number of the feasts (cf. Levit. xxiii.; Numb. xxviii., xxix. with Exod. xxiii. 14—16; xxxiv. 18—23; Deut. xvi. 1—7); or they present legendary variations, as witness the stories of the abduction of Sarah (cf. Gen. xii. 10—19 with xx. 1—18) and the flight of Hagar (cf. Gen. xvi. 4—16 with xxi. 9—21), the sending of the quails (cf. Exod. xvi. 11 with Numb. xi. 31) and the murmuring for water (cf. Exod. xvii. 1—7 with Numb. xx. 1—13); or they content themselves with simple repetitions, of which the precepts relating to the three great national festivals (cf. Exod. xxiii. 17—19 with xxxiv. 23—26) and the penal statutes for violations of the marriage law (cf. Levit. xviii. with xx.) may be taken as examples. Then they have their different circles of ideas in which they respectively move, the Elohist generally giving simpler and less artificial representations of primeval times, and the Jehovist not only throwing back the Mosaic cultus into the pre-Mosaic era, but ascribing the origin of arts and handicrafts to the first generations of the human race. They are distinguished likewise by peculiarities of language and modes of expression, each having his own favourite words and phrases—the Elohist showing a predilection for the phrases הֵקִים בְּרִית or נָתַן, to give or establish a covenant; זָכָר וּנְקֵבָה, male and female; פַּדַּן אֲרָם, the plain of Aram; for which the Jehovist has כָּרַת בְּרִית, to cut a covenant; אִישׁ וְאִשְׁתּוֹ, a male and his female; אֲרָם נַהֲרַיִם, Aram of the two rivers; and for the words בָּרָא, to create, שָׁחַת, to destroy, הִתְפַּלֵּל, to pray, in preference to the Jehovistic terms יָצַר, מָחָה, and עָתַר, besides employing words and phrases for which the Jehovist is alleged to have no corresponding equivalents, such as אֲחֻזָּה, possession; מִין, kind or sort; עֶצֶם הַיּוֹם הַזֶּה, the self-same day, literally, the bone of this day; אֶרֶץ מְגוּרִים, land of sojournings; הָעַרְבַּיִם בֵּין, between the two evenings, &c.; and the Jehovist, on the other hand, being

characterised, in addition to the above idiosyncrasies, by the use of the infinitive absolute for the sake of emphasis, the poetical suffix מוֹ, the Divine name אֱלֹיִן, and so on.
And lastly, as if to establish this remarkable hypothesis beyond the possibility of
challenge, the author of the Elohistic writing, by affirming that the name Jehovah
was not revealed until the time of Moses (Exod. vi. 2), seems to say that he could
not have written those delineations of patriarchal history in which the name Jehovah
is employed.

Now it must be admitted that, if this were in all respects an accurate representation
of the literary structure of the Pentateuch, the documentary hypothesis might be
said to be established; but in point of fact it is a representation which in almost
every particular is assailable. In the first place, it is not possible without the most
arbitrary suppositions and the most inexplicable lacunæ to reconstruct even the
Elohistic writing, as is partly indicated in the Special Introduction to Genesis (*vide*
pp. iv, v); and even if it were, its accomplishment may be regarded as well-nigh
hopeless, almost every critic having his own particular views as to what sections and
clauses of the narrative have been written by the Elohist, and what by the Jehovist,
and what by the third narrator, and so on. In the second place, the so-called contradictions are without exception capable of easy resolution by the application of a
little cultured common sense, not to mention critical acumen; and the recurrence of
similar events in times when manners were comparatively stereotyped ought not to
occasion perplexity to minds of ordinary penetration; while, if repetitions in a narrative are fatal to its literary unity, many writings, amongst which it might not be
impossible to detect some belonging to the higher criticism, whose authorship can be
accurately determined, will be open to suspicion as being the production of several
pens. In the third place, "when we examine the alleged instances more closely,"
i. e. instances of linguistic peculiarities, "we everywhere discover a difference in the
conception which is demanded by the sense and context of the individual passages, or
else the peculiar words ascribed to the one author are really not unknown to the other,
or they occur in a few solitary places, and therefore are not entitled to be considered
characteristic" (*vide* Keil, 'Introduction,' vol. i. pp. 129—136, Clark's Foreign Theological Library). And, in the last place, with reference to the supposed ignorance of
the term Jehovah in patriarchal times, it is now admitted by competent authorities that
this cannot be successfully maintained, since in the records relating to those times it
occurs not alone in the historian's account, but in language used by the patriarchs and
others' of the period (*vide* Gen. xiv. 22; xv. 2; xvi. 2;.xviii. 30; xx. 4; xxiv. 31, &c.),
as well as by persons of the pre-patriarchal age (*vide* Gen. iv. 1; v. 29; ix. 26); since
the way in which it is referred to by God himself in speaking to Moses, "my name,"
may be held as presupposing its previous revelation; and since the words in Exod.
vi. 2 need not imply more than that now for the first time was the full significance
of the name to be made known, that though the term was in use among the patriarchs,
it was not understood by them as it was thenceforth to be revealed to their descendants, or even as they themselves had comprehended the other familiar appellation of
the Deity, El-Shaddai. Consequently it is impossible to allow that the theory of the
composite structure of the Pentateuch has been made good.

2. THE ALLEGED UNHISTORICAL CHARACTER OF ITS CONTENTS. These are of such a
nature, it is averred, relate so many miraculous occurrences, include so many legendary and purely mythical compositions, perpetrate so many historical inaccuracies,
and commit so many geographical and other mistakes, that it is simply incredible
that they can have been the work of Moses. Without dwelling on what appears to
be here tacitly acknowledged, that if Moses could be proved the author of the

Pentateuch, its authenticity would be thereby established, it may be urged that the first objection largely insisted on by Kuenen ('The Religion of Israel,' vol. i. ch. ii. p. 109) and others is *ex hypothesi* out of court, for the obvious reason that it assumes what is not admitted by the other side in this contention, and what has never been demonstrated by those who advance it, viz., that it is impossible for the Supreme Intelligence who has made the world and established the laws of nature to interfere with the order of the first, or modify the operation of the second, whenever to his infinite mind an adequate occasion for such interposition shall appear to have arisen. The second objection, which sees in the Biblical cosmogony (Gen. i.), the narrative of the Flood (Gen. vi.—ix.), the story of the Exodus, &c., &c., only Hebrew counterparts of Babylonian, Persian, Indian, and other national legends, has little difficulty in ascribing them to the same source, viz., the mythologic spirit, which among all primeval peoples has antedated the age of written documents and historical research, and by adorning and handing down through oral tradition the popular tales of the country, has everywhere given to the literatures of the nations a similar commencement. But leaving out of view meanwhile the story of the Exodus, which will fall to be afterwards considered, there are three things to be said in favour of the credibility of the Pentateuchal Cosmogony and Noachic Deluge : viz., (1) that while the resemblances between the Mosaic narratives and those of the popular legends of antiquity are so great as to show that they rest upon a common basis of fact, the dissimilarities are so apparent as to prove that they belong to widely different categories of composition; (2) that so far from the Biblical cosmogony being hopelessly unscientific, there is already established a gratifying amount of harmony between it and the best ascertained results of geological research, which warrants the belief that when modern investigation shall have announced its last finding, it will be seen to completely corroborate the sublime utterances of the old Hebrew record, while, with regard to the Deluge, it is manifest that, as Scripture does not necessitate the belief in a universal flood, *i. e.* geographically viewed, but only in a flood destructive of the totality of the human race, there is no irreconcilable conflict between science and religion such as demands either the negation of the incontrovertible facts of science, or the relegation of the Mosaic story to the limbo of popular fable ; and (3) that the Chaldean monuments, one of the most valuable of recent archæological discoveries, have, by their marvellous correspondence with the Biblical narratives of the Creation and the Flood, not only completely disposed of the allegation that these narratives were entirely mythical, but likewise triumphantly vindicated their claim to be the composition of Moses by showing that they may have existed in a written form as early as the time of Abraham, and were probably among the ancient records which Moses consulted in the preparation of his great work. Then the third objection, which charges the Pentateuchal writing with historical inaccuracies, is supposed to have received, or rather, for the argument is now exactly reversed, was supposed to receive, a striking exemplification in the blunders which its unknown author had committed with reference to Egypt. The time was when Bohlen (*vide* ' Introduction to the Book of Genesis,' vol. i. ch. vi. p. 63) was believed to have annihilated the last shred of historic truth which had previously been lingering about the Egyptology of the Pentateuch. "The blunders and inaccuracies" with reference to this country of which it had been guilty were of such a character, that not only was historic criticism obliged to assign a later date than that of Moses to its origin, "but also to infer that its author was an absolute stranger to Egypt, and must have been indebted for his information to hearsay instead of observation." This literary person, who must have lived somewhere between the reign of Solomon and the time of the

Captivity, and who had never visited the land of the Pharaohs, but who was yet so well acquainted with the country, its manners and customs, its laws and religion, that in at least twenty-five different instances mentioned by Bohlen his information was correct, had committed the unpardonable error of making the Egyptians in the time of Moses build with brick, like the Babylonians, instead of stone; use "asses and camels" in the days f Abraham, like the Arabians; "bring the produce of Arabia in Ishmaelite caravans from Palestine to Egypt" in the era of Jacob; and in the time of Joseph cultivate the vine, "which was not adopted in Egypt till the reign of Psammetichus;" and had proved himself "so grossly ignorant of the climate of the country, that he transferred to it without a scruple the parching east wind of Palestine, and subsequently employed its agency to bring about the ebbing of the sea;" of the social and religious habits of the community, that he represented Joseph "as slaying animals to supply his entertainments—in glaring opposition to the sacred character they are known to have enjoyed;" and of the language of the people, "that many Aramean words were cited at random as Egyptian." So far, however, have these formidable charges been from being substantiated on closer investigation, that in every single instance they have received a triumphant refutation, proving that not the sacred writer, but the confident critic, is in the wrong. As it were, a dead and buried Egypt of which neither Psammetichus nor Herodotus was aware has risen up to deliver witness on this momentous theme. Uncovering her sepulchres and laying bare her sculptures, the Egypt of the times of Abraham and Joseph and Moses has added her testimony to what was already known of the Egypt of a later date in attestation of the authenticity of Pentateuchal history. In the department of Exposition in the various books, the light reflected upon the Mosaic writings by the decipherment of Egyptian hieroglyphics and the study of the monumental representations has been carefully collected, with the general result "that in the entire Mosaic description of ancient Egypt there is not a single feature which is out of harmony with what we know of the Egypt of this remote period from other sources," nay, more, that "almost every point in it is confirmed either by the classical writers, by the monuments, or by both" (vide Rawlinson's 'Historical Illustrations of the Old Testament,' pp. 39—52). And now the fourth objection to the historic credibility, and therefore by implication to the Mosaic authorship, of the Pentateuch is the geographical and other mistakes which have been allowed to slip into the narrative, but which, if that narrative had been composed by a contemporaneous author, would as certainly have been excluded. In the catalogue of blunders, which has been drawn up in support of the thesis that they never could have been committed by Moses, there are chronological and arithmetical as well as geographical inaccuracies—inaccuracies relating to the very times, circumstances, and events in which Moses lived, as well as belonging to a long antecedent period; and inasmuch as those mistakes will bear the heaviest against the Mosaic authorship which occur in connection with the age or epoch of the reputed author, the illustrations to be now given will be taken from the history of the Exodus, in which Moses himself was a prominent actor. Bleek quotes as a chronological inaccuracy Numb. i. 1 and ix. 1, but this assumes what will be difficult to establish—that in all minute details the Pentateuch was intended to adhere to strict chronological arrangement. A more hopeful instance (Vater, Hartmann) refers to the age of the Levites in entering on service, which in Numb. iv. 3 is mentioned as thirty, and in Numb. viii. 24 is fixed at twenty-five; but even this may be disposed of by remembering that the latter passage speaks of the age for entering on the duties of the tabernacle generally, which was to be from twenty-five to fifty, while the former refers to the transportation of the ark and tabernacle, for which work, as requiring the strength of a full-grown man, all males between the ages of thirty and fifty were to be enrolled (Hengstenberg, Keil). Among arithmetical blunders, the exact agreement of the census of the male heads of the people taken in the second year of the Exodus (Numb. i. 45) with that executed half a year earlier (Exod. xxxviii. 25, 26), for the purpose of imposing a poll tax, viz., 603,550, has long been regarded as inexplicable on any ground of historical truthfulness (Colenso); but a sufficient explanation is that the second census was not really a fresh enumeration of the people, which was not necessary, but simply a registration, according to thousands, hundreds, fifties, and tens, of those who had been previously entered on the public records (Keil). Geographical mistakes have been detected somewhat plentifully in the story of the Exodus, and in particular in the list of camping stations preserved in Numb. xxxiii. (Bohlen, 'Introd.,' vol. i. ch. viii. p. 88, London, 1855); but it is the less needful to offer refutation of what are mostly imaginary faults, that critics generally have felt themselves constrained to recognise the chapter in which they occur as one of the indubitable fragments of Mosaic composition contained in the Pentateuch (Hävernick, 'Introd.,' p. 335). Thus, so far as this second ground or reason for accepting the non-Mosaic authorship of the Pentateuch is concerned, it is far from being as conclusive as its advocates suppose.

3. THE ADMITTED RESEMBLANCE OF ITS LANGUAGE TO THAT OF THE LATER BOOKS. This objection applies with special force to the Book of Deuteronomy, between which and the other parts of the Pentateuch the dissimilarity is so palpable as to demand a diversity of authorship, while its correspondence in both thought and expression to the prophetic writings of Jeremiah is so great as to indicate, if not that it proceeded from that prophet's pen, at least that it had its origin in his time. Without attempting to discuss every minute point of criticism connected with the fifth book of Moses, which will doubtless be done in the special introduction to that portion of the Pentateuch, the two allegations that have just been referred to appear to call for notice on the ground that they bear more immediately on the larger question of the literary unity and Mosaic authorship of the Pentateuch. As to the first, the non-resemblance of the fifth book to the preceding four, it is alleged that not only are its contents different from theirs, promulgating as it does a legislation containing many important variations from, contradictions of, and even additions to, that contained in the preceding books, as, e. g., the law of the kingdom (Deut. xvii. 14), the law of the one high place (Deut. xii. 5), the law about the prophetic office (Deut. xviii. 15), &c., of all which the earlier legislation was completely ignorant, but its style of composition is characterised by a copiousness of diction altogether foreign to the other books of the Pentateuch, and by many forms of expression which are peculiarly its own. The so-called new legislation to be found in Deuteronomy we dismiss with the remark that only the exigencies of a pre-conceived theory can discover in it anything at variance with the earlier Sinaitic legislation recorded in Exodus. At present we confine our remarks to the charge of diversity of language supposed to be discernible between it and the preceding books. Colenso mentions forty-five expressions which he avers are of frequent occurrence in Deuteronomy, but are never found so much as once in the Pentateuch; but a careful examination of the examples quoted shows how much of accuracy this assertion really contains. The phrase, e. g., "cleave to Jehovah," דָּבַק בַּיהוָה (ch. iv. 4; x. 20; xi. 22; xiii. 4; xxx. 20), is claimed as being exclusively Deuteronomistic; but the same verb, דָּבַק, occurs in Gen. ii. 24; xix. 19; xxxiv. 3, and with precisely the same sense of attaching oneself to a person or thing. "Work of the hands" (ch. ii. 7; xiv. 29; xvi. 15, &c.) is only a rhetorical expression

such as might naturally be adopted in a hortatory discourse (it occurs frequently in the Psalms) instead of מַעֲשֶׂיךָ (Exod. xxiii. 12), the form more suitable for didactic composition; and indeed this explanation accounts for the larger number of the peculiar phrases cited, such as "with all the heart and with all the soul" (ch. iv. 29; vi. 5; x. 12, &c.), "that they may learn to fear Jehovah" (ch. iv. 10; xiv. 23; xvii. 19; xxxi. 12, 13), "which thou knewest not" (ch. viii. 3), "which thy fathers knew not" (ch. viii. 16), "be strong and of a good courage" (ch. iii. 28), and so on. The admonition, "take good heed" (ch. ii. 4; xxiv. 8), "take heed to thyself," הִשָּׁמֶר לְךָ (ch. iv. 9; vi. 12), is certainly not peculiar to the Deuteronomist, the stronger form being found in Gen. xxiv. 6; xxxi. 24, 29; Exod. x. 28; xix. 12; xxxiv. 12; nor is the frequent combination of law, or laws and statutes, or testimonies, or commandments, or judgments (ch. v. 28; vi. 1, 17, 20; vii. 11; viii. 11; xi. 1; xxvi. 17; xxx. 16), foreign to the earlier books (cf. Gen. xxvi. 5; Levit. xxvi. 15), while the injunction to "walk in the ways of Jehovah" (ch. v. 33; viii. 6; x. 12; xi. 22; xix. 9, &c.) is only an echo of Gen. xviii. 19. But even though every one of the cited instances could be made good, it would not amount to a necessary proof of diversity of authorship. It is too large a demand upon the credulity of the human mind to expect instantaneous assent to the proposition that no one can compose in two different styles (say an argumentative or didactic, and a rhetorical or hortatory), and much more that it was impossible for the great Hebrew lawgiver, "a prophet in whom we must acknowledge one of the most marvellous of minds of original power" (Ewald), to strike another key, and with a flood of impassioned eloquence, rendered all the more powerful and impressive because of his nearness to the better country, even an heavenly, ere he closed his earthly career to enforce upon the people's hearts the statutes and commandments he had been honoured, in the name of their covenant Jehovah, to prescribe for their obedience. Then, as to the second part of this objection, viz., the linguistic resemblance of Deuteronomy to the prophetical writings of Jeremiah, it is easy enough to show, as Bohlen has elaborately done, that a number of "words, favourite terms of expression, and peculiar phrases" are common to both, such as "the iron furnace," referring to the bondage in Egypt (Deut. iv. 20; Jer. xi. 4. The phrase also occurs in 1 Kings viii. 51, and in all the three places it unquestionably looks back to the "smoking furnace" of Gen. xv. 17); "to scatter among the people," or "among the heathen," in speaking of the Babylonish exile (Deut. iv. 27; Jer. ix. 16); "to circumcise the heart," or "the foreskin of the heart" (Deut. x. 16; xxx. 6; Jer. iv. 4; ix. 26); "to pollute the land" by means of divorce (Deut. xxiv. 4; Jer. iii. 1). Both writers pronounce "a curse" upon disobedience (Deut. xxvii. 26; Jer. xi. 3), threaten Israel, if rebellious, with becoming "a proverb and a byword" among the nations (Deut. xxviii. 37; Jer. xxiv. 9), describe their destroyers as "a nation from afar, whose tongue thou shalt not understand" (Deut. xxviii. 49; Jer. v. 15), and whose "horses are swifter than eagles" (Deut. xxviii. 49; Jer. iv. 13), and refer in like terms to the miseries they should endure while besieged (Deut. xxviii. 53; Jer. xix. 9), while both predict a subsequent restoration from captivity (Deut. xxx. 3; Jer. xxix. 14). Both denounce the worship of the sun and moon (Deut. xvii. 3; Jer. viii. 2), deliver warnings against false prophets (Deut. xiii. 1; xviii. 20; Jer. xiv. 13; xxiii. 16, 17), and forbid the practice of cutting the body as a sign of mourning for the dead (Deut. xiv. 1; Jer. xvi. 6; xli. 5). But while these resemblances are undeniable, and while it is scarcely likely that they can have been the result of pure chance, it is not quite "evident that father and son must have laboured in common on this compendium of the law" (Bohlen), or that Jeremiah, or Hilkiah, or some member of the Mosaic party, must have fabricated "this book of the law" as a legislative programme (Kuenen, 'The Religion of Israel,' vol. ii. pp. 18, 19). For (1) there are not a few resemblances between the other Pentateuchal books and Jeremiah, of which the appended list, collected by Bohlen, may be studied (cf. Gen. i. 22; xxxv. 11 with Jer. iii. 16; xxiii. 3; Gen. xxii. 15, 18 with Jer. iv. 2; Gen. xxviii. 3 with Jer. l. 9; Levit. xix. 28 with Jer. xvi. 6; Numb. xxi. 28, 29 with Jer. xlviii. 45, 46); so that Jeremiah may be as aptly spoken of as the author, or the contemporary of the author, of these earlier compositions. (2) The partial resemblance in respect of language between the Books of Deuteronomy and Jeremiah is more than counter-balanced by a thorough-going diversity between the two, not alone in their contents, but also in their literary style, as has been shown by König and others (cf. Keil, 'Introd.,' vol. i. p. 146). (3) In so far as Jeremiah corresponds with Deuteronomy, it admits of easy explanation if the book of the law found by Hilkiah, the priest in the house of the Lord (2 Kings xxii. 8), was either the present Pentateuch or a portion of it, viz., the Book of Deuteronomy. Nothing can be more natural than that Jeremiah, who had only five years before been installed into the prophetic office (Jer. i. 1), no less than Josiah, Hilkiah, and others of the reformers of the period, should have been profoundly stirred by the remarkable discovery of the lost Penta-teuch, and that in particular his earnest spirit should have drunk deeply into the soul-stirring words of the venerable Hebrew law-giver in his last great oration to the people. And (4) monumental evidence attests that the languages of antiquity were possessed of much greater fixity than modern tongues, as witness the Babylonian language, which was the same in the days of Khammurabi, who lived B. C. 1600, i. e. before Moses, as it was a thousand years later, in the time of Nebuchadnezzar (vide 'Records of the Past,' vol. i. p. 6).

4. THE SO-CALLED TRACES OF A LATER DATE. These, which may be called uncon-scious and unintentional indications of the age in which the author or authors lived, may be grouped under the following heads :—(1) *Passages which seem to presuppose the occupation of the land.* Of these the most remarkable are—(*a*) Gen. xii. 6 and xiii. 7, which appear to intimate that when these words were penned the conquest of the land had been completed, and the Canaanites expelled, whereas they are (or may have been) introduced into the narrative to inform the patriarch that the promised land was not any desolate moorland or unoccupied territory, which might have been comparatively easy for God to bestow, but a populated and populous region, which made the promise both on God's part hard to perform, and on Abraham's part hard to believe; and, on the other hand, to explain the reason why Lot and Abraham found it difficult to obtain pasture for their flocks. (*b*) Gen. xxxvi. 31, which is believed to be inexplicable, unless the writer lived under the monarchy; but, notwithstanding Bleek's confident assertion, there is nothing "in the highest degree unnatural" in the assumption that Moses meant by these words to contrast the promise made to Abraham and Jacob (ch. xvii. 6, 16; xxxv. 11), that kings should descend from their loins, which promise was at the time referred to unfulfilled, with the political greatness to which Esau, the disinherited son of Jacob, but distinguished ancestor of Edom, had so early attained. (*c*) Gen. xl. 15, from which the inference appears inevitable that at the time of Joseph's sale the land of Canaan was possessed by the Hebrews, which indeed is correct to this extent, and more is not required by the narrative (*vide* Exposition *in loco*), that the southern part of Palestine, *i. e.* the district round Hebron, was even then recognised as the land where the *Ibrim* lived. (*d*) Exod. xvi. 35, which implies, according to this hypothesis, that the Israelites had reached the land of their habitation, and were settled within its borders, before this

was written; but in point of fact Moses only states that they ate manna until they arrived upon the borders of Canaan, without saying when the manna ceased—in other words, Moses writes nothing here which was not quite within his own personal knowledge and observation. (e) Numb. xv. 32—36, which presupposes that the children of Israel were by this time no longer in the wilderness, i.e. were established in Canaan; but from the introductory words, "And the children of Israel were in the wilderness," all that can be gathered is that the historian, who consciously wrote for after times, wished it to be understood that the occurrence happened while the people were wandering in the desert. (f) Deut. ii. 12, which "also pretty plainly presupposes a time when the Israelites were settled in the possession of the land" (Bleek); but "the land of his possession" in this case was the land to the east of the Jordan (Gilead and Bashan), which was conquered by the Israelites under Moses, and divided among the two tribes and a half, and which is also described in ch. iii. 20 as "the possession" which Jehovah had given to these tribes (Keil). (2) *Passages which appear to imply the Palestinian standpoint of the author;* as, e. g., (a) Gen. xii. 8; xiii. 14; xxviii. 14; Exod. x. 19; xxvi. 22; Numb. ii. 18; iii. 23; Deut. i. 7; iii. 27, &c., in which the term "sea" is used for the west, a form of expression which "it is evident neither Moses nor one of his age could have invented either while wandering in the wilderness or even when, in the last year, according to the story, they had reached the borders of the promised land, *and the Mediterranean lay then actually to the west of their position*" (Colenso); but how, with the Mediterranean on the west, it should be impossible to speak of "a wind of the sea" for a west wind, or to use the phrase "towards the sea" for in a westward direction, passes comprehension. The expressions might even be employed by a writer in the Arabian desert, or in Northern Egypt, the more especially as the term *west* includes all points of the compass between west and north-west (cf. Keil, 'Introd.,' vol. i. p. 189). (β) Gen. l. 10, 11; Numb. xxii. 1; xxxii. 19; Deut. i. 1, &c., in which the phrase בְּעֵבֶר הַיַּרְדֵּן, or the similar expression מֵעֵבֶר לַיַּרְדֵּן, represents the writer's standpoint as being on the west of the Jordan, with reference to which the Moabitish plains were the parts beyond Jordan, or "the other side Jordan." But (1) it is certain that the term עֵבֶר may mean either that side or this: *vide* Numb. xxxii. 19, in which it must of necessity signify first the other side, from the speaker's standpoint (i. e. the west of Jordan), and second this side (i. e. the east of Jordan), on which the speaker at the time was; and Deut. iii. 8, in which it as clearly denotes the east of Jordan, which to the speaker Moses was "this side." Or (2) it is probable that Moses, who was consciously writing for posterity, may have occasionally assumed an ideal position, in which he proleptically represented matters as they would appear to the sons of Israel after they had entered Canaan (cf. 'Hengstenberg on the Genuineness of the Pentateuch,' vol. ii. p. 256; Keil's 'Introd.,' vol. i. p. 189). (3) *Passages which explain archaic usages and terms by those of a later origin.* (a) Names of places: Gen. xiv. 2, 8—"Bela, which is Zoar;" ch. xiv. 7—"En-mishpat, which is Kadesh;" ch. xiv. 17—"the valley of Shaveh, which is the king's dale;" ch. xxiii. 2— "Kirjath-arba, the same is Hebron;" ch. xxxv. 19—"Ephrath, which is Bethlehem." "But all these names in later use had either originated long before Moses, or did so in his time" (Keil, 'Introd.,' vol. i. p. 188; cf. 'Commentary on Genesis' *in locis*). (β) Names of measures: Exod. xvi. 36, "Now an omer is a tenth part of an ephah," which proves, it is argued, that the measure here called an omer (it occurs nowhere else in Scripture) had long fallen into disuse, and required to be explained; but (1) it is doubtful, as Michaelis (' Suppl.,' p. 1929) and Hengstenberg ('On the

Genuineness of the Pentateuch,' vol. i. p. 172) have shown, whether it really was a measure, and, (2) on the assumption that it was, it still requires proof that it was an old and not a new one, the words *omer* and *ephah* both being Egyptian ('Speaker's Commentary'). (4) *Passages which make citations from documents of recognised antiquity.* In Numb. xxi. 13—15, *e. g.*, the Book of the Wars of Jehovah is introduced in such a way as to convey the impression that in the days of the author of this portion of the Pentateuch it was a writing that had descended from ancient times; and yet " it certainly could not have been composed before the last period of the journeyings of the Israelites through the wilderness, and probably it was written at a still later time," so that " at all events this citation points to an author considerably later who wrote the history of the Israelites during the Mosaic time from either written or oral tradition" (Bleek, 'Introd.,' vol. i. § 82). But it is at the best an assumption that this Book of the Wars of Jehovah was composed many centuries previous to the other parts of the Pentateuch. Even Bleek admits (*vide supra*) that it might have been written during the last year of the wanderings; and no valid reason can be adduced why it might not have been a collection of odes made by Moses himself before beginning with the story of the wanderings. "That such a book should arise in the last days of Moses . . . is so far from being a surprising fact, that we can scarcely imagine a more suitable time for its commencement" (Baumgarten); and if this was the case, "the allusion to this collection of odes cannot be adduced as an argument against the Mosaic authorship of the Pentateuch" (Keil; cf. 'Hengstenberg on the Genuineness of the Pentateuch,' vol. i. p. 182). (5) *Passages which contain the formula,* "unto this day." These occur principally in Genesis (ch. xix. 37, 38 ; xxvi. 33 ; xxxii. 33 ; xxxv. 20 ; xlvii. 26) and Deuteronomy (ch. ii. 22 ; iii. 14 ; x. 8 ; xi. 4 ; xxix. 4 ; xxxiv. 6) ; but in Genesis the formula is used of events removed by centuries from the time of Moses, while in Deuteronomy a detailed examination of the passages discovers that only one is attended with any measure of difficulty. In what appears to be the last year of the desert march, Jair the son of Manasseh is represented as calling the cities of Bashan after his own name, Bashan-havoth-jair, unto this day (Deut. iii. 14). The similarity of the account preserved in Judges (ch. x. 3, 4) concerning Jair, a Gileadite judge, who had thirty sons who had thirty cities called "Havoth-jair unto this day," has led to the suggestion that the words "unto this day" in Deuteronomy may be an interpolation; but this is not really necessary, as Hengstenberg has shown that a considerable period may have intervened between the naming of the towns and the writing of the record, and that frequently, as employed in the Mosaic compositions, the phrase partakes of the nature of a proverbial expression which is designed to represent an event or transaction as of a permanent rather than of a transitory character and duration.

It appears then from this somewhat lengthened survey of the arguments commonly adduced in support of the non-Mosaic authorship of the Pentateuch, that there is really not one of them that can be fairly said to have fully established itself beyond the reach of cavil, but that, on the contrary, all of them are capable of vigorous disputation, and most of them of thorough-going refutation, so that, to say the least of it, it is premature to claim it as " one of the best ascertained results of modern criticism " that the Pentateuch is not the production either of Moses or of the Mosaic age, while a candid and ingenuous inquirer, sincerely desirous of arriving at the truth on this keenly agitated question, may warrantably deliver as his verdict concerning the non-Mosaic authorship, so far at least as he has yet been conducted by this investigation, *Non probatum est.* And this being so, the way seems cleared for advancing to the second branch of this inquiry.

II. Considerations which are generally believed to favour the Mosaic authorship of the Pentateuch.

1. IT WAS NOT IMPOSSIBLE FOR MOSES TO PRODUCE SUCH A BOOK AS THE PRESENT PENTATEUCH. In the first place, he had the means of doing so, inasmuch as it is capable of almost perfect demonstration that he was acquainted with the art of writing. So long of course as the assertion was allowed to pass current as an ascertained fact that " the earliest date which can be assigned to Semitic writing scarcely reaches to the tenth century B. C., and even this is not sufficiently accredited " (Bohlen, ' Introd.,' vol. i. p. 35), a fatal barrier existed to the claims of Moses to be regarded as the author of the present Pentateuch. But that assertion has been long since abandoned by the most eminent palæographists. Gesenius (' Heb. Gram.,' p. 8) admits that " the point of time at which we are to date the commencement of Hebrew literature in general is certainly as early as that of Moses, even if the Pentateuch, in its present shape and compass, be considered a work remodelled at a later period." Ewald (' History of Israel,' vol. i. p. 49), while doubting if written documents existed in patriarchal times, acknowledges " the two tables of the law" to be " an incontrovertible proof that there was writing in the age of Moses." Bleek (' Introd.,' vol. i. p. 82) states that " the pre-Mosaic use, among the Hebrews, of the art of writing is now generally acknowledged," and considers that " written records in the primitive times are proved by such passages as Gen. xiv. ; Numb. xiii. 22 ; Exod. v. 6 ; Josh. xv. 15." Prof. Smith (' Encyclopedia Britannica,' art. Hebrew Language and Literature, ninth edition) writes that " the Semitic peoples possessed the art of writing and an alphabetical character from a date so remote as to be lost in the mists of antiquity." Indeed the monumental records of antiquity have completely disposed of the allegation that the art of writing was a comparatively recent invention. The cuneiform inscriptions from Chaldea reach as far back at least as the days of Abraham. "Bricks and stone tablets, with inscriptions of the early Babylonian monarchs, have been found at most of the sites," and the inscription of Khammurabi (now in the Museum at Paris), written in the Babylonian language, according to George Smith cannot be placed later than the sixteenth century B. C. (vide ' Records of the Past,' vol. i. p. 6, and vol. iii. p. 5). In Egypt hieroglyphics are found as early as the second Egyptian dynasty (' Records of the Past,' vol. ii. p. vi) ; and recent excavations at Carchemish, Hamath, Aleppo, and Lycaonia show that the Hittites, a branch of which were settled in Canaan during the patriarchal period, were a literary people (possessing a peculiar system of hieroglyphic writing, which has not yet been deciphered) ; of which perhaps there was a hint in Kirjath-sepher, or " Book Town," the early name of their capital, Debir, the city of the oracle near Hebron (Josh. xv. 15). Then, in the second place, it is obvious that the materials could not be wanting in Moses' time for the composition of such a work as the Pentateuch. If, as is apparent, the art of writing was both known and practised in patriarchal times, it should not be difficult to credit the existence of ancient records in the patriarchal families. If the Chaldean monuments show that at a date as early as that of Abraham legendary accounts of the Creation, the Deluge, the building of the tower of Babel, closely resembling the narrations in Genesis, were preserved in Babylonia, the inference is irresistible that the true account of the primitive history of mankind might in the same manner, i. e. by written tablets, have been handed down at least from the days of Abraham, if not indeed from a much earlier period (vide supra), till they came into the hands of Moses in Egypt. Then, as Moses was himself the prominent figure in all that related to the Exodus, " quorum magna pars fui," the requisite material for constructing a history of that great national

emancipation and resuscitation could not be far to seek. Still further, in the third place, Moses enjoyed the leisure which was indispensable for the composition of such a work as the Pentateuch. The forty years' retirement to the land of Midian, carrying with him probably the ancient records of his people, must have afforded him, if he desired it, ample opportunity for the commencement of his literary enterprise by the composition of Genesis ; while the forty years of wandering in the same Arabian desert with which his career closed would enable him to carry forward at stated intervals the work he had begun, leaving, perhaps, the account of his last hours and death (Deut. xxxiv.) to be added by the hand of Joshua. And lastly, in the fourth place, Moses could not want a motive for undertaking even so arduous a task as the composition of the Pentateuch supposes. Bleek ('Introd.,' vol. i. § 92) deems it highly improbable that Moses should have left behind him an historical work of such extent and purport. While admitting that he might have bequeathed to his countrymen "a complete series of legal precepts, full of minute details, since he wished them to be minutely observed by his people," the German critic cannot understand why he should have wished to compose an elaborate history of events with which his people were as well acquainted, and were as little likely to forget, as himself. But not even Bleek, we imagine, supposes this to be conclusive reasoning. What might have been a pertinent observation, had Moses written solely for the information of his contemporaries, is totally deprived of force when it is remembered that he wrote for posterity. Besides, since it is acknowledged that Moses gave his people written laws, and conferred on them a nationality, "is it not highly probable that he should have tried to call out their national spirit by giving them a history of their ancestry, and of their own assertion of their national independence ? " ('Speaker's Commentary,' Introduction to the Pentateuch, p. 4). Altogether different from Bleek, we regard it as extremely likely that a wise and patriotic leader such as Moses should have wished, if it was in his power, to compose such a book as the Pentateuch.

2. An examination of the Pentateuch discovers at least a presumption that it was composed by Moses. In the first place, it is certain that Moses was commanded to prepare a book or historical writing of some sort (*vide* Exod. xvii. 14). Now, whether we read בַּסֵּפֶר, in the book, *i. e.* which thou hast, or which thou shalt prepare, or בְּסֵפֶר, in a book, it is clearly implied that Moses was expected to prepare a writing in which the account of Amalek's opposition to Israel and of Jehovah's determination concerning Amalek should be recorded for the benefit of after generations, and it is scarcely likely that this would be the only communication which such a writing would contain. In the second place, it is admitted that Moses did prepare a book or writing while in the wilderness. Even Professor Smith, though regarding it as doubtful whether anything has proceeded from the pen of Moses except the commandments on the tables of stone ('Ency. Brit.,' art. Hebrew Language and Literature), is constrained to recognise that these did ; but the majority of critics are considerably more liberal towards the Hebrew law-giver in this respect, Bleek, for instance, ascribing to Mosaic authorship the laws in Leviticus and the songs in the Pentateuch, with perhaps the list of camping stations in Numbers. The Pentateuch itself, however, distinctly assigns to Moses the authorship of certain well-defined portions : as, *e. g.*, the Book of the Covenant mentioned in Exod. xxiv. 3—7, the contents of which were Exod. xx. 2—14 ; xxi.—xxiii. ; the list of camping stations already referred to in Numb. xxxiii. 2—49 ; and the Deuteronomic law contained in the book of that name (Deut. xxxi. 9—11). Now even should we reject the contention of Hävernick, that the Book of the Covenant and the book containing the list of stations were not separate

documents, but the existing Pentateuch as far as it could be composed (*vide* 'Intro-duction,' § 4), and hold with Bleek that it cannot be certainly established that either the book which Moses was instructed to compose, or the law which Moses finished or made an end of writing, and committed to the Levites to be deposited in the side of the ark of the covenant, was "the connected historical work" of the Pentateuch "as we have it" ('Introduction,' vol. i. § 128); that is to say, if from each of the passages taken separately it might be perilous to infer the Mosaic authorship of the Pentateuch, it is yet observable that the cumulative weight of all four distinctly points towards this conclusion. When it is considered that almost on entering the wilderness the Hebrew Lawgiver received a Divine order to write in the (or a) book, that on reach-ing Sinai he is discovered again writing in a Book of the Covenant, that as the wander-ings are drawing to a termination he is again stated to have prepared a written record of the halting-places on the desert march, and that just before he dies he is once more exhibited as writing "this book of the law," the deduction seems obvious and natural that here at least is a *primâ facie* case in favour of the book in question being the present Pentateuch. In the third place, this presumption is strengthened when on examination it is further discovered that the contents of the present Pentateuch are of such a nature as to call for an author possessed of most, if not all, of the qualifications that are seen to meet in Moses. The singular accuracy of the Egyptology of the Pentateuch, which is constantly receiving confirmation from every fresh decipherment of the monumental remains of that ancient land, has already been commented on. The minute acquaintance which it displays with the social and religious customs of the people, and with the officials and etiquette of the Egyptian Court, is so remarkable that only an Egyptian could have written it. Sir Gardiner Wilkinson testifies ('Ancient Egyptians,' vol. i. ch. iv. p. 328, ed. 1878) that, like the Chinese, the ancient inhabitants of the Nile valley were proverbially jealous of foreigners, whom they prevented, if possible, from penetrating into the interior of the country, and to whom they imparted as little information as possible concerning the institutions of their country. Herodotus, it is true, contrived to collect a large amount of information concerning Egypt; but no one can compare the pages of Herodotus with those of Moses without discovering that the Egyptology of the Greek historian is that of a foreigner, as distinguished from that of a native, which is the Egyptology of the Hebrew law-giver. And a similar remark will hold good concerning the desert life depicted in the Books of Exodus and Numbers, which Bohlen, Colenso, and others have attempted to discredit, but which travellers have frequently and fully authenticated as, even in circumstantial detail, so accurate that it could only have proceeded from a writer who had an intimate acquaintance with the Sinaitic peninsula. "It is not merely that the length of each division of the journey, the numerous halting-places, are distinctly marked,—for although such notices could not possibly have been invented, or procured at any later period by a dweller in Palestine, the fact might be accounted for by the supposition gratuitously made, but hard to be rebutted, that some ancient records of the journey had been preserved by written or oral tradition,—but the chapters which belong either to the early sojourn of Moses, or to the wanderings of the Israelites, are pervaded by a peculiar tone, a local colouring, an atmosphere so to speak of the desert, which has made itself felt by all those who have explored the country, to whatever school of religious thought they may have belonged" ('Speaker's Com-mentary,' Introduction to the Book of Exodus, p. 244). Hence, if in Moses are found, as confessedly they can nowhere else be discovered, such intimate acquaintance with the Arabian desert and such familiarity with Egypt as are manifestly required for the production of the Pentateuch, the rational conclusion seems to be that he, and he alone, is its author; and the more so as, in the fourth place, there are certain water-marks, as it were, in the book itself which not only vouch for its antiquity, but appear to require it to have been composed about the time of Moses. It is doubtful if the existence of archaisms in the language of the Pentateuch is a certain index of the antiquity of the writing, since these might partake of the nature of survivals from early times; but it is not a little remarkable that a larger number of these archaic forms of expression are to be found in the Pentateuch than in compositions of a later date than Moses. Then perhaps the explanatory clauses in Gen. xxiii. 2; xxxv. 6, &c., &c., should not be pressed as indications of the non-Palestinian standpoint of the author, since exception has already been taken to Gen. xii. 6 and similar passages as establishing the author's Palestinian standpoint; but the one set of clauses may be fairly regarded as neutralising the other. A surer mark of high antiquity is found in the blessing of Jacob upon Levi (Gen. xlix. 5, 6) as compared with the Mosaic benediction of the tribe (Deut. xxxiii. 8). It is apparent that between these two prophetic utterances Levi's elevation to the priesthood has taken place. Is it likely that a late author, writing, say in the eighth or seventh century B. C., would have been careful to say nothing in the earlier benediction about Levi's promotion, and nothing in the second about Levi's sin? But if Moses wrote both, the difficulty disappears.

3. THE EXISTENCE OF THE PRESENT PENTATEUCH CAN BE TRACED BACKWARDS WITH CONSIDERABLE CLEARNESS FROM THE DAYS OF CHRIST TO THOSE OF MOSES. That the volume which we now possess was recognised in Christ's day as one book does not require demonstration. Even the interval between the birth of Christ and the return from captivity in Babylon may be overleaped at a bound, since critics of the most advanced type (Bohlen, Kuenen) are prepared to grant that at least it dates from the restoration under Ezra and Nehemiah. It is when we pass this limit on our backward journey that we encounter opposition in attempting to identify the Pentateuch. In Josiah's time, for instance, which was in the seventh century B. C., the Book of the Law of the Lord which Hilkiah found in the temple, and which there is *primâ facie* ground for believing was the whole Pentateuch, is affirmed by modern theorists to have been only the Book of Deuteronomy, which was first fabricated by the Mosaic party and then put (perhaps by Hilkiah himself) where Hilkiah could find it (Kuenen, 'The Religion of Israel,' vol. ii. ch. vi. pp. 18, 19). The arguments on which this conjecture is based are mainly three : the difficulty of understanding how, if ever the Pentateuch existed, it should have been lost; the impossibility of reading through the entire Pentateuch to the king in one day, as is represented to have been done; and the apparent fortuitousness (which it is believed was a designed fortuitousness) of finding the lost Pentateuch exactly at the moment when it was needed to assist the plans of the Reformers. As to the first, the deplorable idolatry that prevailed throughout the land during the preceding reigns of Manasseh and Amon, which extended over up-wards of half a century, might well enough occasion the Pentateuch, or Book of the Law of Jehovah, to be neglected and in a manner lost. As to the second, it is one assumption that the whole of what was found was read in one day either to the king or to the people, and another that what was read was the Book of Deuteronomy. The writer of the account in 2 Kings xxii.—xxiii. certainly states that Shaphan "read" the book first to himself, and then before the king, and then that the king read it in the ears of the people; but the chronicler (2 Chron. xxxiv. 18) informs us more exactly that this only signifies that Shaphan and the king read in the book. As to what they read, it is styled the Book of the Law, and the Book of the Covenant; but if the former of these expressions may appear to refer more particularly to Deute-ronomy, the latter just as certainly alludes to Exodus; whence the probability is that

both were in the book which Hilkiah found and Shaphan and the king read. Then, as to the discovery of the roll just at the moment when it was needed, it is not at all surprising that the wave of religious enthusiasm which had set in upon Judah with Josiah's coming to the throne should have caused the forgotten Pentateuch to be inquired after, and if so, it is less surprising still that Hilkiah should have found it. It may therefore be held as certain, in default of satisfactory evidence to the contrary, that the Pentateuch existed in the seventh century B.C. That the prophets who laboured among the Israelites in the eighth century B.C., *i. e.* Isaiah, Micah, Amos, and Hosea, appealed to the early history of the people as it is contained in the Pentateuch might be verified by numerous citations from their writings containing allusions to every one of the five books of the law ; but this is not required, inasmuch as that is conceded by the advocates of the post-Mosaic origin, only that to which they appealed, it is alleged, was not a formal history like the Pentateuch, but simply a traditional history which had not yet been reduced to writing (*vide* Kuenen, 'The Religion of Israel,' vol. i. ch. ii. p. 101), which, however, is begging the question in dispute. Then, passing to the times of David, it is comparatively easy, in spite of what Bleek asserts to the contrary, to detect the existence and influence of the Mosaic Pentateuch. In that "Law of the Lord" the entire poetical literature of the Davidic age may be said to have had its roots. Accepting only those Psalms which are confessedly the work of the shepherd king, it would not be difficult to show that they not only presuppose the entire Levitical system (*vide* Ps. xx., xxvii., xl., l., li.), but also allude to the story of the Exodus and the Sinaitic legislation (cf. Ps. iv. 6 with Numb. vi. 26 ; Ps. xv. 5 with Exod. xxii. 25 ; xxiii. 8 ; Levit. xxv. 36 ; Deut. xvi. 19 ; Ps. xvi. 4 with Exod. xxiii. 13 ; Ps. xvi. 5, 6 with Deut. xxxii. 9 ; Ps. xvii. 8 with Deut. xxxii. 10 ; Ps. xxiv. 1 with Exod. xix. 5 : Deut. x. 14 ; Ps. xxvi. 6 with Exod. xxx. 19, 20 ; Ps. xxx. (title) with Deut. xxx. 5 ; Ps. xxxix. 12 with Levit. xxv. 23 ; Ps. ciii. 17, 18 with Exod. xx. 6 : Deut. vii. 9), and even refer to the incidents of early patriarchal history (*e. g.* Ps. i. 3 to Gen. xxxix. 3, 23 ; Ps. viii. 6, 7, 8 to Gen. i. 26, 28 ; Ps. ix. 12 to Gen. ix. 5 ; Ps. cx. 4 to Gen. xiv. 18). Indeed the entire Hebrew Psalter, whensoever it was compiled, is a precious fruit of the religious life of Israel under the law, and everywhere requires for its full understanding just such a national history and just such an ecclesiastical system as are presented in the Pentateuchal books. Nor when we reach the ages of Samuel and the Judges does this Book of the Law cease to arrest our attention. 1 Sam. viii. 7 and Judges viii. 23 are indeed quoted as conclusive evidence that the Deuteronomic law of the kingdom (Deut. xvii. 14) was not at that time known. The toleration of several high places at one time, as in Shiloh (1 Sam. i. 3 ; iv. 3), Mizpah (Judges xi. 11 ; xx. 1, 18 ; xxi. 1 ; 1 Sam. vii. 5), Bethel (1 Sam. x. 3), Ramah (1 Sam. vii. 17), in opposition to the Mosaic ordinance (Deut. xii. 5) commanding worship to be offered at only one high place, is advanced as implying that the people were not acquainted with any such legislation as that contained in the last book of the Pentateuch ; whence the inference is meant to be deduced that the Pentateuchal books had not been at that time composed. Bleek, however, is candid enough to recognise ('Introduction,' vol. i. § 124) that the mere fact that the Mosaic laws were not observed is not sufficient proof that they did not exist, or were not known, and Keil ('Introduction,' vol. i. § 34) has satisfactorily shown that not only were Gideon's refusal of the crown of Israel and Samuel's unwillingness to elect a king in perfect harmony with the Mosaic law upon the subject of their future monarch, but that it is doubtful if even during those troublous and unsettled times between Joshua and David there ever was more than one national sanctuary, viz., at Shiloh, the other instances specified being places at which exceptional acts of worship were performed, and for perfectly adequate reasons, while abundant evidence exists that, notwithstanding all the turbulent disorder of the period, "the law of Moses formed the basis of the religious, civil, and political life of the nation." And thus we are conducted to the days of Joshua, in the history of which, as it lies recorded in the Book of Joshua, the references to the Pentateuch, which besides it often styles "the Book of the Law of Moses" (ch. i. 7, 8; viii. 31, 04, xxiii. 0, xxiv. 0), are so numerous that the opponents of the Mosaic authorship of the Pentateuch have only been able to escape from its overpowering testimony by the ingenious device of first adding it to the five books of Moses, so as to form not a Pentateuch, but a Hexateuch, and then relegating it for an author to the days immediately before or after the Babylonish exile.

4. THE MOSAIC AUTHORSHIP OF THE PENTATEUCH IS EXPRESSLY CERTIFIED BY CHRIST AND HIS APOSTLES. The force of this remark it has been usual to turn aside by observing that Christ and his disciples only shared in the popular belief of their age, and not only made no pretensions to instruct their countrymen in Biblical criticism, but were themselves wholly unacquainted with even the first principles of the science. But it is simply incredible that Christ should have spoken as he did (Matt. xix. 7; Mark xii. 19; Luke xvi. 31; John v. 46, 47), or allowed his apostles to speak and write as they did (John i. 45; Acts xv. 25; Rom. x. 5; Heb. xiii. 12, 13), if he knew that the Pentateuch was only a literary fiction, the production of a late age, that had been floated into public acceptance by being falsely imputed to the Hebrew lawgiver; while if he did not understand this, though in reality it was so, then it is clear he was not so wise as many learned critics of the nineteenth century, and it will come to be a question whether one who could be imposed upon by so impudent a forgery was entitled to claim the homage of mankind, saying, "I am the Light of the world: he that followeth me shall not walk in darkness;" "I am the Truth;" "Take my yoke upon you, and learn of me."

5. A VARIETY OF SUBORDINATE CONSIDERATIONS MAY HERE BE GROUPED TOGETHER WHICH TEND TO CORROBORATE, OR ARE SUPPOSED TO CORROBORATE, THE MOSAIC AUTHORSHIP OF THE PENTATEUCH. First, the Samaritan Pentateuch, which was known to Cyril of Alexandria, Eusebius, Jerome, and other early Christian writers, and which, after having been lost to the Christian Church for upwards of 1000 years, was in 1616 obtained from the Samaritans in Damascus by Pietro della Valle, accords in almost every point except dates with the Jewish Pentateuch; and since the Samaritans accepted no other books of the Hebrew Scriptures except this, and since their hostility to the Jews was so great that it is almost certain they would not have accepted this unless they had regarded it as the work of Moses, and since, moreover, it is written in the ancient Hebrew character, which is older than the Samaritan square character introduced by the Jews at the time of the Captivity, or at the latest by Ezra, it has been argued that it must have been in existence prior to the division of the kingdom, i. e. as early as the time of Solomon. But these arguments do not now appear to the defenders of the genuineness of the Pentateuch to be possessed of the weight they were once believed to have, and Hengstenberg accordingly ('On the Genuineness of the Pentateuch,' vol. i. p. 106) has given them up. The uncertainty, therefore, of the date when this copy of the Pentateuch was adopted by the Samaritans, whether about 409 B. C., when the Jewish priest Manasseh betook himself to the Samaritans (Neh. xiii. 28), or in the time of Josiah, whose reformation extended beyond Judah (2 Chron. xxxiv. 9), or earlier yet, in the days of Hoshea, when the king of Assyria sent an Israelitish priest to instruct the colonists whom he had settled in Samaria (2 Kings xvii. 28), renders it comparatively useless as an argument either on one side

or the other.   Secondly, of much greater value is the sufficiently accredited statement that all the Jewish sects and parties—Pharisees, Sadducees, and Essenes, Palestinian and Alexandrian Jews—have been unanimous in accepting the Hebrew Pentateuch as the work of Moses, while the chief opposition to its genuineness has arisen within the bosom of the Christian Church.   Then, thirdly, the difficulty of explaining the uprise, development, and consummation of Mosaism as a religious system without the initial impulse that is implied in the Mosaic composition of the Pentateuch must not be overlooked.   The modern theory of evolution as applied to religion will not account for ancient Judaism any more than for modern Christianity.   As the New Testament Church is inconceivable without the incarnation and the apostolic Gospels, so neither was the Old Testament Church possible without a Sinaitic revelation and a Mosaic Pentateuch.   And lastly, the advocates of the Mosaic authorship may fairly appeal to the hopeless confusion into which the supporters of the opposite theory are thrown whenever they are asked to condescend upon the individual, or even upon the age, to which it should be assigned—one thinking it should be given to the period immediately after the Conquest, and another to the age of Solomon, a third to the times of Josiah, and a fourth to the era after the Captivity.

The conclusion then to which we are conducted is that though the Pentateuch may have been partly compiled from written sources, and subsequently revised by Ezra, there is not sufficient ground for challenging its substantial Mosaic authorship, and still less for the tone of confident assertion which is assumed by the so-called higher criticism in proclaiming its late origin ; while there is good cause for such as belong to the conservative side in this important controversy adopting a somewhat less apologetic style than they have hitherto done in maintaining the ancient faith of both the Jewish and Christian Churches, that the Pentateuchal books proceeded from the pen of Moses, the man of God.

THE BOOK OF GENESIS.

---◇---

INTRODUCTION

---

§ 1. Its Title and Contents.

1. *Its title.* Like the other four divisions of the Pentateuch, the First Book of Moses derives its title in the Hebrew Scriptures from its initial word, Bereshith; in the LXX., which is followed by the A. V., it is designated by a term which defines its contents, Γενεσις (Genesis). Γενεσις referring to the source or primal cause of either thing or person, the work to which it has been assigned as a descriptive appellation has been styled the Book of Origins or Beginnings (Ewald); but since the LXX. employ Γενεσις as the Greek equivalent of the Hebrew Tôl'dôth, which signifies not the causes, but the effects, not the antecedents, but the consequents of either thing or person (*vid.* ii. 4 : Exp.), the writing might be more exactly characterised as the Book of Evolutions or Developments.

2. *Its contents.* As a Book of Origins or Beginnings, it describes the creation or absolute origination of the universe, the formation or cosmical arrangement of this terrestrial sphere, the origin of man and the commencement of the human race, while it narrates the primeval histories of mankind in the three initial ages of the world—the Antediluvian, the Postdiluvian, and the Patriarchal. Subsidiary to this, it depicts the pristine innocence of man in his first or Edenic state; recites the story of his fall through the temptation of an unseen adversary, with the revelation of Divine mercy which was made to him in the promise of the woman's seed, and the consequent establishment on earth of a Church of believing sinners, looking forward to the consummation of that glorious promise ; traces the onward course of the divided human family, in the deepening impiety of the wicked, and the decaying godliness of the righteous, till, ripe for destruction, the entire race, with the exception of one pious household, is wiped out or washed off from the face of the ground by the waters of a flood; then, resuming the thread of human history, after first sketching the principal features of that appalling catastrophe, pursues the fortunes of this family in its three sons, till it sees their descendants dividing off into nations, and spreading far and wide across the surface of the globe ; when, returning once more to the original centre of distribution, it takes up the story of one of these collateral branches into which the race has already separated, and carries it forward through successive stages till it connects itself with the later history of Israel. Or, regarding the work in the other mentioned aspect, as a Book of Evolutions or Developments, by which the standpoint of the writer is changed and brought round from the historical to the prophetic, from the *à posteriori* to the *à priori*, after sketching in a preliminary section the original creation of the universe and the arrangement of the present terrestrial cosmos, in ten successive sections it relates the Tôl'dôth or generations, *i. e.* the subsequent evolutions or onward developments of the cosmos which lead down to the point of departure for the history of Israel narrated in the ensuing books. The main divisions of the Book, according to the principle just stated, are indicated by the formula : "These are the generations of . . . ." The following tabular view of these successive sections will afford an idea of the wide range of topics comprehended in the First Book of Moses :—

Section 1.	The beginning	...	...	...	...	...	ch. i. 1—ch. ii. 3.
„ 2.	The generations of	the heavens and the earth					ch. ii. 4—ch. iv. 26.
„ 3.	„	„	„	Adam	...	...	...	ch. v. 1—ch. vi. 8.
„ 4.	„	„	„	Noah	...	...	...	ch. vi. 9—ch. ix. 29.
„ 5.	„	„	„	the sons of Noah	...	ch. x. 1—ch. xi. 9.
„ 6.	„	„	„	Shem	...	...	...	ch. xi. 10—26.
„ 7.	„	„	„	Terah	...	...	...	ch. xi. 27—ch. xxv. 11.
„ 8.	„	„	„	Ishmael	...	...	...	ch. xxv. 12—18.
„ 9.	„	„	„	Isaac	...	...	...	ch. xxv. 19—ch. xxxv. 29.
„ 10.	„	„	„	Esau	...	...	...	ch. xxxvi. 1—ch. xxxvii. 1.
„ 11.	„	„	„	Jacob	...	...	...	ch. xxxvii. 2—ch. l. 26.

§ 2. Its Sources and Authorship.

1. *Its sources of information.* That writings of an earlier period may have been employed in the compilation of the present narrative, however alarming the idea was when first propounded, and notwithstanding the fact that it is still frequently advanced in a hostile spirit, is now seen to be a comparatively innocuous hypothesis, at least when considered in itself. That the author of the Book of Origins should have availed himself of pre-existing materials in the composition of his great historical work seems no more an unreasonable suggestion than that the four evangelists should have drawn upon already circulating memoirs of our Lord's life and work in the construction of their respective Gospels. Nor does any sober critic or intelligent student of the Bible now believe that such a supposition is fatal to the claims either of the Pentateuch and the Gospels to be received as canonical Scriptures, or of their writers to be regarded as inspired teachers. Accordingly, the documentary hypothesis, as it is now familiarly styled, counts among its supporters not a few of those who maintain the Mosaic authorship of the Pentateuch, and therefore of Genesis, as well as the vast majority, if not all, of those by whom that authorship is assailed. The germ of the theory appears to have suggested itself so early as the seventeenth century to Hobbes, who wrote in his 'Leviathan' "that the Pentateuch

seems to have been written rather about than by Moses " ("Videtur Pentateuchus potius de Mose quam a Mose scriptus "), though doubtless it was based upon originals from his hand. About the beginning of the eighteenth century Vitringa, in his 'Observationes Sacræ,' propounded the view that Moses had employed sketches written by the patriarchs : "Schedas et scrinia Patrum (or ὑπομνήματα Patriarcharum) apud Israelitas conservata Mosen opinamur, collegisse, digessisse, ornasse, et ubi deficiebant compilasse, et ex iis priorem librorum suorum confecisse." Plausible and probable as this conjecture was, it seems to have attracted little attention to the subject of the composition of the Book of Genesis beyond causing written sources to be assumed by one or two subsequent writers, such as Clericus and Richard Simon. In 1753 the well-known theory of two principal documents, an Elohistic and a Jehovistic, was broached by Astruc, a Parisian doctor and professor of medicine, who believed ten additional but smaller memoirs to have been also employed by Moses. A few years later (1780) substantially the same view was espoused and recommended to public favour by the German scholar Eichhorn. In the hands of Ilgen (1798) and his follower Hupfeld (1853) the two original or primary documents were subdivided into three, a first Elohist, a second Elohist, and a Jehovist, all of which were manipulated and pieced together by an editor or redactor. In 1815 Vater, and in 1818 Hartmann, adopted the idea that the Pentateuch, and in particular Genesis, was composed of a number of disconnected fragments ; but this was so obviously erroneous that in due time (1830) it was followed by the supplementary hypothesis of De Wette, Bleek, Stähelin, Tuch, Lengerke, Knobel, Bunsen, Delitzsch, and others, which recognised two documents, of which the older and the principal, that of the Elohist, was a continuous narrative, extending from the creation to the close of the conquest as recorded in the Book of Joshua ; while the other, that of the Jehovist, was the work of a later writer, who made use of the earlier as the foundation of his composition. The latest form of the theory is that of Ewald, who claims for the Great Book of Origins at least seven different authors (thus reducing the Pentateuch, as Keil observes, into atoms), and assigns the Book of Genesis, in its present state, to an author whom he designates as " the fourth or fifth narrator of original history," who must have lived in the eighth century in the kingdom of Judah.

The supposed basis of this hypothesis of supplements is—1. The alternate use of the Divine names Elohim and Jehovah: e. g. Gen. i. 1—ii. 3 ; v. 1— 29a, 30—32 ; vi. 9—22 ; vii. 11—viii. 16a, 17—19 ; ix. 1—17, 28, 29 ; x. ; xi. 10—32 ; xii. 5, 6, 8a; xiii. 18 ; xvii. ; xix. 29 ; xx. 1—17 ; xxi. 2—32 ; xxii. 1—13, 19—24 ; xxiii. ; xxv. 1—20, 24—34 ; xxvi. 34, 35 ; xxvii. 46 ; xxviii. 1—12, 17—21a, 22 ; xxix. ; xxx. 1—13, 17—24a; xxxi. 4—48, 50—54 ; xxxii. 1—12, •14, 33 ; xxxiii. ; xxxvi. ; xxxvii. 2—36 ; xxxix. 6—20 ; xl.—l., are distinguished by the employment of the first of these Divine names, and are supposed to belong to the Elohistic document ; while ii. 3—iv. 26 ; v. 29b; vi. 1—8 ; vii. 1—10, 16b; viii. 20—22 ; ix.

18—27 ; xi. 1—9 ; xii. 1—4, 7, 8*b*, 9—20 ; xiii. 1—17 ; xiv.—xvi. ; xviii.
1—xix. 28, 30—38 ; xx. 18 ; xxi. 1, 33, 34 ; xxii. 14—18 ; xxiv. ; xxv. 21—
23 ; xxvi. 1—33 ; xxvii. 1—45 ; xxviii. 13—16, 21*b* ; xxx. 14—16, 24*b*—
43 ; xxxi. 1—3, 49 ; xxxii. 13, 15—32 (?) ; xxxvii. 1 (?) ; xxxviii. ; xxxix.
1—5, 21—23, are constituent parts of the supplementary or Jehovistic document, being characterised by the use of that particular name for the Deity. 2.
Contradictory accounts of the same event : as, *e. g.*, the narratives of (1) the
Creation (cf. i., ii. 4—25) ; (2) the Flood (cf. vi. 9—22 with vii. 1—10, and
in particular note the apparent discrepancy between the numbers of the animals
to be taken into the ark ; (3) the boundaries of the promised land (cf. xv. 18
with Num. xxxiv. 1—12). 3. Variations in the same legend or story : as, *e. g.*, (1)
the Abrahamic covenant (cf. xv. with xvii., xviii.) ; (2) the taking of Sarah
(cf. xii. 10—19 with xx. 1 and xxvi. 1—11) ; (3) the story of Hagar and
Ishmael (cf. xvi. 9—21 with xxi. 9—21) ; (4) the covenant with Abimelech
(cf. xxi. 22—34 with xxvi. 26—33) ; (5) the successive consecrations of Bethel
(cf. xxviii. 18, 19 ; xxxv. 14, 15) ; (6) the story of Esau and his birthright (cf.
xxv. 27—33 ; xxvii. 1—40). 4. Diversity of language and ideas in the two
documents—the Elohist generally depicting the simple and inartificial manners
of primeval times, and the Supplementer or Jehovist moving in a circle of ideas
that belong to the era of Mosaic laws and Levitical institutions. Cf. for Elohistic
ideas, the longevity of the patriarchs, v. ; the consecration of pillars, xxviii.
18*f* ; xxxv. 14*f* ; the giving or setting up of a covenant, vi. 18 ; ix. 9, 11,
instead of the cutting of a covenant, as in Exod. xxiv. 8 ; and for Elohistic
words and phrases—" possession, property," xvii. 8 ; xlviii. 4 ; " kind, sort," i.
11, 12, 21, 24, 25 ; vi. 20 ; vii. 14 ; " in the self-same day," vii. 13 ; xvii. 23 ;
" the land of wanderings," xvii. 8 ; xxviii. 4 ;—for Jehovistic ideas, iv. 17—24
(the arts and handicrafts of civilisation) ; iii. 8—24 ; xviii. 1 (Theophanies) ;
iv. 3, 4 ; viii. 20 ; xv. 9 (sacrificial worship) ; xii. 7 ; xiii. 4 ; xxi. 33 (the
erection of altars) ; vii. 2, 8 ; viii. 20 (the distinction between clean and unclean
animals) ; v. 29 ; ix. 25—27 (the prophetic element) ; and Jehovistic words
and phrases—יָעַר ii. 7, instead of בָּרָא i. 1 ; אִישׁ וְאִשְׁתּוֹ vii. 2, instead of וּנְקֵבָה
זָכָר i. 27 ; the inf. absol. for emphasis, ii. 16, 17 ; iii. 4, 16 ; xvi. 10 ; xxx.
16 ; the suffix מוֹ ix. 26, 27 ; the Divine name עֶלְיוֹן xiv. 18—20, 22. But, without
replying to these so-called arguments *seriatim*, it may be answered, as against
the entire hypothesis, that it is—1. *Unnecessary*, not being required for a perfectly
satisfactory elucidation of either the use of the Divine names, or the so-called
contradictions, variations, and peculiarities that have been detected by the
microscopic criticism to which the Book has been subjected (*vid.* the exposition
of the text in the body of the work). 2. *Unproved*. (1) As to the existence of
the documents,—though admitted to be probable, the use of such writings by
the author of Genesis is at the best inferential and problematical. (2) As to
the supposed evidence in support of this conjecture,—it is impossible to appor-

tion the narrative into Elohistic and Jehovistic sections, so that even the former shall compose one continuous narrative, without the expenditure of a vast amount of ingenuity, and the exercise of a high degree of arbitrariness in first disintegrating the body of the Book, and then recombining the pieces, with the assistance of sundry self-invented supplements—the so-called contradictions in event and legend existing solely in the imagination of the critic, not in the work of the author, and the alleged peculiarities in thought and diction of each document having parallels in the other, except in cases which admit of easy explanation. 3. *Incomplete;* that is to say, not accounting for all the facts of the case that require to be explained, as, *e. g.*—(1) The employment of the name Jehovah Elohim in ii. 4; iii. 24. (2) The omission in the fundamental or Elohistic document of sections that are indispensable not only to the continuity of the narrative, but to the right apprehension of its meaning, as, *e. g.*, between ii. 3 and v. 1, the incident of the Fall, thus rendering vi. 9—13 an enigma; between v. 32 and vi. 9, the corruption of the human race, without which the Deluge remains inexplicable; between vi. 22 and vii. 11, the Divine communication which advertised Noah of the exact moment when the Flood should commence; between xvii. 27 and xix. 29, the story of the destruction of the cities of the plain, which alone renders the latter verse intelligible. (3) Allusions in the fundamental document to events and incidents recorded in the Supplementer, as, *e. g.*, v. 3 to iv. 25; v. 29 to iii. 17; xvii. 20 to xvi. 10; xix. 29 to xiii. 10—13; xviii. 17—32, and xix. 1—25; xxi. 9 to xvi. 5. If these difficulties are not sufficient in themselves to discredit the hypothesis of documents altogether, they are at least of weight enough to show that, while the original conjecture of Vitringa may be true, the modern critical theory of an Elohistic and a Jehovistic author of the Book of Genesis has not yet been placed beyond the region of debate.

2. *Its authorship.* Principally on the ground of certain traces of a later age (1. The formula " unto this day "—xix. 37, 38; xxvi. 33; xxxii. 32; xxxv. 20; xlvii. 26. 2. Statements that seem to presuppose the occupation of the land— xii. 6; xiii. 7; xxxvi. 31; xl. 15. 3. The Palestinian standpoint of the writer —xii. 8; l. 11. 4. The explanation of ancient names of cities by the introduction of names of a later origin—xiv. 2, 8, 7, 17; xxiii. 2; xxxv. 19. 5. The mention of usages and customs that are alleged to belong to a later period— iv. 3, 4, 14; vii. 8; viii. 20; xvii. 26; xxiv. 22, 30; xxv. 22; xxxvii. 3, 23), the claims of Moses to be regarded as the author of the Book of Genesis, and indeed of the Pentateuch generally, have since the Reformation been vigorously assailed. Prior to that profound theological and religious awakening, it is but fair to acknowledge that certain grave doubts had been expressed as to whether the great Book of the Law should be attributed, either in whole or in part, to the Hebrew lawgiver. Ptolemæus, the Valentinian, in the second century, ascribed only a portion of the work to Moses; the Nazarenes, an ascetic sect spoken of by John Damascenus (' De Heræsibus,' ch. xix.), rejected the entire composition

as spurious; while, according to the Clementine Homilies (iii. 47), the present Pentateuch was written after Moses' death. There does not appear, however, to have been any serious questioning on the subject of the Mosaic authorship of the Pentateuch as a whole, or of Genesis as a part of that larger work, until the sixteenth century, when it began to be insinuated by Masius (1574), Spinoza (1670), and Anton Van Dale (1696), that not Moses, the Hebrew lawgiver, but Ezra, the priest-prophet of the Restoration, was the first composer of those parts of sacred Scripture. The publication of Astruc's views in 1753 gave a decided impulse to the science of historic criticism, which in course of time resulted in the widespread acceptance by Biblical scholars of the opinion that, while containing a slight substratum of Mosaic legislation, the present Pentateuch is not the work of the Hebrew lawgiver, but of an unknown writer belonging to a later period who made use of pre-existing documents, of which the principal were the Elohistic and Jehovistic memoirs already referred to. At the present moment this view extensively prevails in both England and Germany. At the same time, consistency requires it to be stated that, in the minds of those who have rejected the Mosaic authorship of the Book of Origins, the most hopeless perplexity reigns as to the person to whom that honour should be assigned. It is vain to look for anything like unanimity of sentiment among modern students of the higher historic criticism concerning the authorship and date of composition of the two principal documents or source writings (Quellenschriften), as Bleek designates them, out of which the first fifth of the Pentateuch was manufactured. In the judgment of Astruc and Eichhorn, the documents referred to were pre-Mosaic, and the Book of Genesis was the handiwork of Moses; but so safe and reasonable a solution of the authorship of Genesis has long been left behind by their scholars, the composition of the earliest or fundamental document being assigned by Stähelin to an unknown writer in the times of the Judges (Colenso suggests Samuel as the anonymous Elohist), by Bleek to a historian who flourished in the time of Saul, by Killisch to a contemporary of David, by Ewald to a brilliant Levite in the age of Solomon, by De Wette to an author in the time of the Kings, and by Bohlen to a literary artist who wrote as late as the captivity, or even later—the Jehovist or Supplementer in each case writing at a period considerably posterior. Accordingly, where such diversity of sentiment exists, the Biblical student may fairly hesitate to reject the pre-Reformation doctrine of the Mosaic authorship of Genesis, and all the more that it is still supported by such excellent names as those of Sack, Hengstenberg, Hävernick, Ranke, Dreschler, Baumgarten, Kurtz, Keil, and others, and is not so entirely destitute of evidence as is sometimes alleged. 1. Without attaching that importance to the direct testimony of the Pentateuch to its Mosaic authorship which it seems to possess in the eyes of some apologists (Exod. xvii. 14, xxiv. 3, 4, and Num. xxxiii. 2 can scarcely be pressed to mean more than that Moses composed the different writings of which they speak; while Deut. xvii. 18, 19; xxviii. 58, 61; xxix. 19, 20, 27; xxx. 10; xxxi. 9—11, 24—26 do not appear so conclusively to assert the composition by Moses of the entire law, as understood by Jewish tradition, as to preclude the opinion that the passages in question only refer to the Mosaic legislation proper), it may be maintained that the number and character of the direct references in the subsequent Hebrew Scriptures to the Pentateuch as the work of Moses are such as to involve the truth of his claim to be regarded as its author (cf. Josh. i. 7, 8; viii. 31; xxiii. 6; xxiv. 26; 1 Kings ii. 3; viii. 9, 53; 2 Kings x. 31; xi. 12; 1 Chron. xvi. 40; 2 Chron. xii. 1; Ezra iii. 2; vi. ·18; Neh. i. 7; viii. 1; Dan. ix. 11, 13 for the historical books; and *vid.* the poetical and prophetic writings *passim*). In every one of these Scriptures there is a clear recognition of the Pentateuch as having been in existence at a time prior to their composition, *i. e.* from the days of Joshua onward; in which case its only conceivable author was the celebrated lawgiver of the Hebrews. 2. It is allied to this to say that the historical development of the theocratic nation is inconceivable except upon the hypothesis of the Mosaic authorship of the Pentateuch, and therefore of Genesis. To imagine that the complicated system of the Mosaic institute gradually took shape, and perpetuated itself through several centuries, working itself in, by slow degrees, to the national life and conscience, without any accredited historical documents, in such a way that when at length the history of the nation came to be written, it should by every separate writer be judged necessary to misrepresent the facts of the case, by promulgating the belief that their great national institutions were the outcome of a previously-recorded writing from the hand of Moses, rather than that that writing (so-called by Moses) was the free historic product of their institutions—to accept this as the true solution of the inter-relation between Hebrew literature and Hebrew life is to make a far greater demand upon the historic faculty than to believe that the Pentateuch came first from Moses, and the national character and life were framed and moulded by the Pentateuch. 3. Then there is the fact that the Mosaic authorship of the Pentateuch, and therefore of Genesis, was universally recognised by Jewish sects and parties—by Pharisees, and Sadducees, and Essenes; by Alexandrian as well as by Palestinian Jews; and by the Samaritans as well as by the inhabitants of Judæa. 4. The testimony of Christ and his apostles lends its weight to this conclusion (cf. Matt. xix. 7; Mark xii. 19; Luke xxiv. 27, 44; John i. 45; v. 46, 47; Acts xv. 21; Rom. x. 5). Even Bleek with sufficient candour admits that this was the view entertained at the time of Christ and his apostles, as Philo and Josephus expressly testify; and the force of this admission is not rendered nugatory by the oft-quoted dicta that neither Christ nor his apostles came into the world to teach criticism (Clericus), and that faith in Christ cannot set limits to critical inquiries (De Wette); for, as Hermann Witsius justly observes, it is quite true that neither Christ nor his apostles were critical scholars (*critici doctores*) in the modern acceptation of the term; but they were certainly teachers of the truth (*doctores veritatis*) who did not come into the world to fortify popular errors by their authority. 5. An additional argument may be derived from the internal unity of the Pentateuch, and in particular of the Book of Genesis. It is true that in one sense this is the very question in dispute, whether Genesis is the work of one or more authors; but, as its (alleged) composite character is always paraded as an argument for its non-Mosaic authorship, it seems both reasonable and fair to claim any traces of internal unity which the writing may possess as supporting the opposite conclusion. Now one obvious mark of unity which belongs to Genesis is the exact chronological thread running through it from the beginning to the end; and another is the interdependence of all its parts, of which no section of any length can be removed without introducing into the narrative an inexplicable lacuna; while a third is the similarity of language which pervades it throughout, no one, as Keil observes, having been able clearly to establish a twofold *usus loquendi* in its pages. And this being the case, it is only a legitimate inference that such internal unity is more likely to have been impressed upon it by the hand of Moses than by that of a late redactor. And, 6. in proof of the Mosaic authorship of Genesis there is the insufficiency of evidence in support of every other hypothesis.

§ 3. Its Method and Purpose.

1. *Its method.* On this point, after what already has been written (*vid.* p. i.), a few words will suffice. The most cursory reader of the Book of Genesis cannot fail to discern that, so far from its being open to the charge of incoherency and want of arrangement which has been brought against it by some of its less scrupulous assailants, it is all through constructed on a simple, perfectly intelligible, and well-sustained plan. After the initial section, in which the sublime programme of the Divine cosmogony is unfolded, it divides itself into ten successive books, in each of which the story of human history is advanced a stage, till the period of the first captivity is reached. While possessing to each other the very closest of relations as parts of the same connected composition, it is observable that these successive subdivisions have the appearance of being each in itself a complete piece or monograph on the subject to which it relates. The cause of this, however, is not that each has been a separate document prepared without relation to the others, possibly at a different time and by a different hand, as is so commonly suggested; it rather seems attributable to the peculiar genius of Hebrew composition, which, being governed less by logic than by dramatic interest, advances more by sketching tableaux of events and scenes than by presenting a detailed narration of each historical incident exactly in its proper time and place. A remembrance of this will go far to account for the appearance of repetition and prolixity which in some parts the narrative exhibits. Then it is deserving of attention that, while treating of the fortunes of the human race, the record, almost instantly on starting, confines its regards, in the earlier portion, to one particular section (the line of Seth), and, in the later, to one particular family (the children of Abraham, in

the line of Isaac and Jacob), and deals with the other branches of the human family only in so far as they are needful to elucidate the story of the chosen seed. And still further it is noticeable that, in the elaboration of his plan, the author is always careful to keep the reader's eye fixed upon the special line whose fortunes he has set himself to trace, by dismissing at the outset of each section with a brief notice those collateral branches, that nothing may afterwards arise to divide the interest with the holy seed, and the narrative may flow on uninterruptedly in the recital of their story. "The materials of the history," writes Keil, "are arranged and distributed according to the law of Divine selection; the families which branched off from the main line are noticed first of all; and when they have been removed from the general scope of the history, the course of the main line is more elaborately described, and the history itself is carried forward. According to this plan, which is strictly adhered to, the history of Cain and his family precedes that of Seth and his posterity; the genealogies of Japhet and Ham stand before that of Shem; the histories of Ishmael and Esau before those of Isaac and Jacob; and the death of Terah before the call and migration of Abraham to Canaan;" and "in this regularity of composition," he further adds, "the Book of Genesis may be clearly seen to be the careful production of one single author, who looked at the historical development of the human race in the light of Divine revelation, and thus exhibited it as a complete and well-arranged introduction to the history of the Old Testament kingdom of God."

2. *Its purpose.* Consideration of the plan naturally leads to an examination of the purpose of the Book. And here it is at once obvious that Genesis was not designed to be a universal history of mankind. But just as little was it written (by a post-Mosaic author) with the special view of glorifying Judaism by tracing back the roots of its institutions to a hoary antiquity. It had indeed an aim which may be said to have been Jewish, but it had also a design which was cosmopolitan. As an integral part of the Pentateuch, it was intended to unfold the necessity and nature of the new economy which was about to be established; to show how the theocratic institutions of salvation had been rendered indispensable in consequence of the fall and the entire corruption of the race so signally punished by the Deluge, and again so strikingly displayed by the tower-builders of Babel; and to make it clear that they were not a new departure on the part of God in his efforts at redemption, but only a further development of the line he had pursued from the beginning. As the opening volume of revelation in which the history of salvation was to be recorded, it was designed to exhibit the primeval condition of the human race, with its melancholy lapse into sin which first of all rendered salvation necessary, and to disclose the initial movements of that Divine grace which ever since had been working for man's restoration, and of which the theocracy in Israel was only a specific manifestation. Thus while the Book of Genesis could not fail to be possessed of undying interest to every member of the Hebrew Church and

nation, it is likewise a writing of transcendent value and paramount importance to every scion of the human race, containing as it does the only authentic information which has ever yet reached the world of the original dignity of mankind, and of the conditions under which it commenced its career on earth ; the only satisfactory explanation which has ever yet been given of the estate of sin and misery in which, alas, it all too plainly finds itself to-day, and the only sufficient gospel of salvation that has ever yet been recommended to its attention and acceptance.

LITERATURE OF GENESIS.

Of the exceptionally rich and varied literature on Genesis, the principal works may be classified as under :—

I. INTRODUCTIONS. 1. *Foreign.* Bleek : Introduction to the Old Testament, Berlin, 1865 ; London, 1875. Bohlen : Introduction to Genesis, Königsberg, 1835 ; London, 1855. De Wette : Introduction to the Old Testament, Berlin, 1817 ; Boston, 1844. Ewald : History of Israel, vol. i., Tübingen, 1843 ; London, 1869. Hävernick : Introduction to the Pentateuch, Erlangen, 1837 ; Edinburgh, 1850. Hengstenberg : The Genuineness of the Pentateuch, Berlin, 1831—1839 ; Edinburgh, 1847. Keil : Introduction to the Old Testament, Dorpat, 1868 ; Edinburgh, 1869. Kurtz : History of the Old Covenant, Berlin, 1853 ; Edinburgh, 1859. Oehler : Theology of the Old Testament, Tübingen, 1873 ; Edinburgh, 1874.

2. *English.* Colenso : The Pentateuch and the Book of Joshua critically examined, London, 1862—1871. Davidson : Introduction to the Old Testament, London, 1862. Horne : Introduction to the Critical Study of the Scriptures, London, 1856 (tenth edition). Hamilton : The Pentateuch and its Assailants, Edinburgh, 1852. Macdonald · Introduction to the Pentateuch, Edinburgh, 1861. Quarry : Genesis and its Authorship, London, 1873.

II. COMMENTARIES. 1. *Patristic.* The writings of Irenæus, Origen, Eusebius, Theodoret, Jerome, Chrysostom, and Augustine.

2. *Rabbinical.* The works of Jarchi, Aben Ezra, and David Kimchi.

3. *Reformation.* Luther : Enarrationes in Primum librum Mose, Wittemberg, 1544 ; republished by Hengstenberg, Berlin, 1831. Calvin : Commentarii in Genesin, Geneva, 1563. Mercerus : Commentarius in Genesin, Geneva, 1598. Drusius : Ad loca difficiliora Pentateuchi, Franeker, 1617. Grotius : Annotationes ad Vetus Testamentum, Paris, 1641. Clericus : Translatio librorum V. T. cum paraphrasi perpetua, Comment. philol., dissertt. critt., &c., Amsterdam, 1693—1731. Venema : Dissertationes ad Genesin, 1747. Dathius : Pentateuchus ex recensione Textus Hebræi, Leipsic, 1791. Amongst Roman Catholic writers should be mentioned Pererius : Commentarii et disputationes in Genesin, Lugduni, 1594. Amongst English works, Willet's Hexapla, London, 1632 ; the Critici Sacri, London, 1690 ; and M. Poli, Synopsis Criticorum, London, 1699, in which the opinions of the Reformers and their successors are collected.

4. *Modern.* (1) Foreign. *Exegetical :*—Delitzsch : Commentary on Genesis, third edition, Leipsic, 1860. Keil and Delitzsch : Commentary on the Pentateuch, Leipsic, 1861 ; Edinburgh, 1864. Lange : Commentary on Genesis, Bohn, 1864 ; Edinburgh, 1868. Rosenmüller : Scholia in Genesin, Leipsic, 1821. *Theological :*— Baumgarten : Commentary on the Old Testament, Keil, 1843. *Popular :*—Von Gerlach : Commentary on the Pentateuch, 1801—1849. (2) English :—Ainsworth : Annotations on the Pentateuch, Edinburgh, 1843. Alford : Genesis, and Part of Exodus, for English Readers, London, 1877. Browne (Bishop of Ely) : Vol. i. of Speaker's Commentary, London, 1871. Inglis : Notes on Genesis, Edinburgh, 1877. Jamieson : Vol. i. of the Critical and Experimental Commentary, Edinburgh, 1863. Kalisch : Historical and Critical Commentary on the Old Testament, London, 1858. Macdonald : Creation and the Fall : a Defence and Exposition, London and Edinburgh, 1856. Murphy : Commentary on Genesis, Edinburgh, 1863. Patrick (Bishop of Ely) : A Commentary upon the Historical Books of the Old Testament : London, 1727.

Wordsworth: The Holy Bible, with Notes, London, 1864. Wright: The Book of Genesis, London, 1859. (3) American:—Bush: Notes on Genesis, New York, 1838. Jacobus: Notes, Critical and Explanatory, on Genesis, New York, 1865. Turner: Exegetical Commentary on Genesis, New York, 1846.

III. HOMILETICAL AND PRACTICAL EXPOSITIONS. In addition to the well-known Commentaries of A. Clarke, M. Henry, and Thomas Scott, to this department may be assigned:—Bonar: Earth's Morning, or Thoughts on the First Six Chapters of Genesis, London, 1875. Candlish: The Book of Genesis expounded in a Series of Discourses, Edinburgh, 1868. Exell: A Homiletical Commentary on Genesis, London, 1875 (*incomplete*). Fuller: Expository Discourses on the Book of Genesis London, 1836. Gray: The Biblical Museum, London, 1876. Hughes: An Analytical Exposition of the First Book of Moses, 1672. Ness: History and Mystery, London, 1690—1696. Robertson, F. W.: Notes on Genesis, London, 1877. White: A. Commentary upon the First Three Chapters of Genesis, London, 1656.

IV. GENERAL LITERATURE. Blunt: The History of Abraham, London, 1842. Bonnet: The Exile from Eden; Meditations on the Third Chapter, London, 1839. Bouchier: The History of Isaac, London, 1864. Dawson: The Origin of the World, London, 1877. Dykes: Abraham the Friend of God, London, 1877. Grant: The Bible Record true in every Age, London, 1877. Hengstenberg: Egypt and the Books of Moses, Edinburgh, 1845. Kitto: Bible Illustrations, Edinburgh, 1855. Lawson: Lectures on Joseph, Edinburgh, 1807; new edition, 1878. Overton: The Life of Joseph, London, 1866. Rawlinson: Ancient Monarchies, vol. i., London, 1871. Roberts: Oriental Illustrations of the Sacred Scriptures, London, 1835. Records of the Past: Biblical Archæological Society, London, 1875 (*publishing*). Robinson: Biblical Researches in Palestine, London, 1841. Sandys: In the Beginning, London, 1879. Smith: Assyrian Discoveries, London, 1875. Smith: Chaldean Account of Genesis, London, 1876. Smith (Thornley): The Life of Joseph, Edinburgh, 1875. Stanley: Sinai and Palestine, London, 1856; Lectures on Jewish Church, London, 1866. Tristram: The Land of Israel, London, 1865; The Land of Moab, London, 1873. Thomson: The Land and the Book, London, 1870. Wilkinson: Manners of the Ancient Egyptians, London, 1847.

For a more detailed account of the literature of Genesis, the works of Kurtz, Lange, and Rosenmüller may be consulted.

ANALYSIS OF CONTENTS.

§ 1. THE BEGINNING. i. 1—ii. 3.
1. The creation of the universe. i. 1, 2.
2. The six days' work. i. 3—31.
3. The institution of the sabbath. ii. 1—3.

§ 2. THE GENERATIONS OF THE HEAVENS AND THE EARTH. ii. 4—iv. 26.
1. The paradisaical state of man. ii. 4—25.
2. The history of the fall. iii. 1—24.
3. The story of Cain and Abel. iv. 1—15.
4. The development of the race. iv. 16—26.

§ 3. THE GENERATIONS OF ADAM. v. 1—vi. 8.
1. The first genealogical table. v. 1—32.
2. The degeneracy of the antediluvians. vi. 1—8.

§ 4. THE GENERATIONS OF NOAH. vi. 9—ix. 29.
1. The building of the ark. vi. 9—22.
2. The narrative of the Flood. vii. 1—viii. 14.
3. The Noachic covenant. viii. 15—ix. 17.
4. The destinies of Noah's sons. ix. 18—29.

§ 5. THE GENERATIONS OF THE SONS OF NOAH. x. 1—xi. 9.
1. The ethnological register. x. 1—32.
2. The confusion of tongues at Babel. xi. 1—9.

§ 6. THE GENERATIONS OF SHEM. xi. 10—26.

§ 7. THE GENERATIONS OF TERAH. xi. 27—xxv. 11.
1. The migration of the Terachites. xi. 27—32.
2. The history of Abraham, the son of Terah. xii. 1—xxv. 11.

(1) Abram is called, xii. 1—3; (2) enters Canaan, xii. 4—9; descends to Egypt, xii. 10—20; returns to Canaan, xiii. 1—4; separates from Lot, xiii. 5—18; pursues the kings, xiv. 1—16; meets with Melchisedeck, xiv. 17—24; is justified, xv. 1—6; and taken into covenant with God, xv. 7—21; marries Hagar, xvi. 1—16; receives the sign of circumcision, xvii. 1—27; is visited by Jehovah at Mamre, xviii. 1—8; and obtains the promise of Isaac, xviii. 9—15; intercedes for Sodom, xviii. 16—33; which is soon thereafter destroyed, xix. 1—38; sojourns in Gerar, xx. 1—18; rejoices in Isaac's birth, xxi. 1—8; casts out Ishmael, xxi. 9—21; covenants with Abimelech at Beersheba, xxi. 22—34; offers up Isaac on Moriah, xxii. 1—24; is bereaved of Sarah, whom he buries in Machpelah, xxiii. 1—20; commissions Eliezer to find a bride for Isaac, xxiv. 1—67; enters into a second marriage with Keturah, xxv. 1—6; and ultimately dies, xxv. 7—11.

§ 8. THE GENERATIONS OF ISHMAEL. xxv. 12—18.

§ 9. THE GENERATIONS OF ISAAC. xxv. 19—xxxv. 29.
1. The birth and early history of Isaac's sons. xxv. 19—34.
2. The subsequent career of Isaac. xxvi. 1—35.
3. The blessing of Jacob by Isaac. xxvii. 1—46.
4. The fortunes of Isaac's heir. xxviii. 1—xxxv. 26. Jacob departs to Padan-aram, xxviii. 1—xxxv. 26; sees God at Bethel, xxviii. 10—22; arrives at Haran, xxix. 1—14; marries Leah and Rachel, xxix. 15—35; serves with Laban, xxx. 1—43; flees from Laban, xxxi. 1—55; is met by angels at Mahanaim, xxxii. 1—12; sends a message to Esau, xxxii. 13—23; wrestles with an angel, xxxii. 24—32; is reconciled to Esau, xxxiii. 1—20; hears of his daughter's defilement, xxxiv. 1—31; revisits Bethel, xxxv. 1—15; is bereaved of Rachel, xxxv. 16—20; returns to Isaac at Mamre, xxxv. 27.
5. The death of Isaac. xxxv. 27—29.

§ 10. THE GENERATIONS OF ESAU. xxxvi. 1—xxxvii. 1.

§ 11. THE GENERATIONS OF JACOB. xxxvii. 2—l. 26.
1. The wickedness of Jacob's sons. xxxvii. 2—xxxviii. 30.
   (1) Joseph hated by his brethren. xxxvii. 2—36.
   (2) The sins of Judah and Onan. xxxviii. 1—30.
2. The fortunes of Joseph in Egypt. xxxix. 1—xli. 57.
   (1) His imprisonment by Potiphar. xxxix. 1—23.
   (2) His advancement by Pharaoh. xl. 1—xli. 57.
3. The famine in the land of Canaan. xlii. 1—xlv. 28.
   (1) The descent of Jacob's sons to Egypt without Benjamin. xlii. 1—38.
   (2) The second journey to Egypt with Benjamin. xliii. 1—34.
   (3) The stratagem of Joseph to detain Benjamin. xliv. 1—34.
   (4) Joseph's discovery of himself to his brethren, and invitation of his father to visit Egypt. xlv. 1—28.
4. The descent of Jacob to Egypt. xlvi. 1—xlvii. 10.
   (1) The departure from Beersheba. xlvi. 1—27.
   (2) The arrival at Goshen. xlvi. 28—34.
   (3) The presentation to Pharaoh. xlvii. 1—10.
5. The settlement of Jacob and his family in Egypt. xlvii. 11—26.
6. The last days of Jacob in Egypt. xlvii. 27—xlix. 32.
   (1) The charge given to Joseph. xlvii. 27—31.
   (2) The blessing of Joseph's sons. xlviii. 1—22.
   (3) The last prophetic utterance. xlix. 1—28.
   (4) The charge concerning his burial. xlix. 29—32.
7. The death of Jacob in Egypt. xlix. 33—l. 14.
   (1) The mourning for Jacob. l. 1—7.
   (2) The funeral of Jacob. l. 7—14.
8. The last of Jacob's sons. l. 15—26.
   (1) The fear of Joseph's brethren. l. 15—21.
   (2) The death of Joseph. l. 22—26.

THE
BOOK OF GENESIS

THE PRIMEVAL AGE OF THE WORLD (CHS. I.—IX.).

FROM THE CREATION TO THE DELUGE.

§ 1. THE BEGINNING (CH. I. 1—II. 3).

EXPOSITION.

CHAPTER I.

I. THAT this initial section is not *history* is apparent from the circumstance that the occurrences it describes belong to a period of time which antedates the dawn of history. That it is not *science* is evinced by the fact that, in some, at least, of its particulars, it refers to a condition of our globe concerning which even modern research has attained to no definite conclusions, while in all of them it claims to be regarded not as uttering the findings of reason, but as declaring the course of nature. That still less can it be *myth* must be obvious to any who will carefully contrast it with those heathen cosmogonies which it is said to resemble. Only the most absolute devotion to preconceived opinion can render one oblivious of its immense superiority to them in respect of both simplicity of construction and sublimity of conception. The absurdities, puerilities, and monstrosities that abound in them are conspicuously absent from it. It alone ascends to the idea of a creation *ex nihilo*, and of a supreme Intelligence by whom that creation is effected. Unlike

them, it is destitute of either local colouring or national peculiarity, being no more Jewish than it is Assyrian or Indian, Persian or Egyptian. The inspired original, of which heathen creation-stories are the corrupted traditions, it may be ; impartial reason and honest criticism alike forbid its relegation to a common category with them. Since, then, it is neither history, nor science, nor mythology, it must be REVELATION ; unless indeed it be regarded as either "the recorded intuition of the first man, handed down by tradition," a theory successfully demonstrated by Kurtz to be altogether inadequate, or the inductive speculation of some primitive cosmogonist, a solution of its genesis scarcely less satisfactory. To characterise it as *a pious fraud*, of post-Mosaic origin, written to uphold the Jewish week cycle and the institution of the Jewish sabbath, is not only to negative its inspiration, but to invalidate the Divine authority of the whole book, to which it serves as an introduction. Happily its *inspiration* is a much less violent supposition than its *invention*, and one which is susceptible of almost perfect demonstration. Rightly viewed, its inspiration is involved in the simpler question of its truthfulness. If the Mosaic cosmogony is true, it can only have been given by inspiration ; and that it is true may be said to be, with rapidly augmenting emphasis, the verdict of science.

II. As to the precise manner in which it was imparted to its author, THE VISION THEORY of Kurtz, though declared by Kalisch to be "a complicated tissue of conjectures and assumptions *utterly destitute of every, the faintest and remotest, Biblical foundation*," is perhaps, with certain modifications, the best. Rejecting the idea of a series of creative tableaux without any solid substratum of actual fact, there is clearly nothing in the nature of the case to discredit the hypothesis that the far past may have been disclosed to the writer of this ancient document in the same fashion as we know the remote future was discovered to the later prophets. On the contrary, there is much in Scripture to warrant the assumption that, as Daniel heard " the speaking between the banks of the Ulai," and received dream-revelations of the four great world monarchies, and as John beheld visions and heard voices concerning the things which were shortly to come to pass, so the Jewish lawgiver, or the primitive *Nabi* to whom this revelation was imparted, may have beheld in sublime panorama the evolution of the light, the uplifting of the atmosphere, the parting of the waters, the placing of the orbs, the filling of the land, sea, and sky with life, while he listened with awestruck silence to the voices of Elohim, as they were uttered at the opening of each creative day. Something like this, Professor Lewis aptly remarks, appears necessary to explain the reception by the prophet's mind of those ineffable ideas of which previously he had no types or conceptions.

III. Though not *poetical* in the sense of being composed in ornate and figurative language, the present section may be truthfully described as *rhythmical* in structure, possessing an artificial and orderly arrangement, much obscured by its division in the English version into chapters and verses, which almost justifies its designation as The Primeval Song, or Hymn of Creation, with which may be compared the lyric poem in Ps. civ., and the post-Exilian ode in Ps.

cxxxvi., in both of which a Hebrew bard recites the story of creation.

Ver. 1.—**In the beginning**, *Bereshith*, is neither "from eternity," as in John i. 1 ; nor "in wisdom" (Chaldee paraphrase), as if parallel with Prov. iii. 19 and Ps. civ. 24 ; nor "by Christ," who, in Col. i. 18, is denominated ἀρχή ; but "at the commencement of time." Without indicating *when* the beginning was, the expression intimates *that* the beginning was. Exod. xx. 11 seems to imply that this was the initiation of the first day's work. The formula, "And God said," with which each day opens, rather points to ver. 3 as its proper *terminus a quo*, which the beginning absolute may have antedated by an indefinite period. **God.** *Elohim* (either *the highest Being to be feared*, from *alah*, to fear,—Hengstenberg, Delitzsch, Keil, Oehler, &c., — or, more probably, *the strong and mighty One*, from *aūl*, to be strong—Gesenius, Lange, Tayler Lewis, Macdonald, Murphy, &c.) is the most frequent designation of the Supreme Being in the Old Testament, occurring upwards of 2000 times, and is exclusively employed in the present section. Its plural form is to be explained neither as a remnant of polytheism (Gesenius), nor as indicating a plurality of beings through whom the Deity reveals himself (Baumgarten, Lange), nor as a plural of majesty (Aben Ezra, Kalisch, Alford), like the royal "we" of earthly potentates, a usage which the best Hebraists affirm to have no existence in the Scriptures (Macdonald), nor as a cumulative plural, answering the same purpose as a repetition of the Divine name (Hengstenberg, Dreschler, and others); but either (1) as a *pluralis intensitatis*, expressive of the fulness of the Divine nature, and the multiplicity of the Divine powers (Delitzsch, Murphy, Macdonald) ; or, (2) notwithstanding Calvin's dread of Sabellianism, as a *pluralis trinitatis*, intended to foreshadow the threefold personality of the Godhead (Luther, Cocceius, Peter Lombard, Murphy, Candlish, &c.) ; or (3) both. The suggestion of Tayler Lewis, that the term may be a contraction for El-Elohim, the God of all superhuman powers, is inconsistent with neither of the above interpretations. That the Divine name should adjust itself without difficulty to all subsequent discoveries of the fulness of the Divine personality and nature is only what we should expect in a God-given revelation. Unless where it refers to the angels (Ps. viii. 5), or to heathen deities (Gen. xxxi. 32 ; Exod. xx. 3 ; Jer. xvi. 20), or to earthly rulers (Exod. xxii. 8, 9), *Elohim* is conjoined with verbs and adjectives in the singular, an anomaly in language which has been explained as suggesting the unity of the Godhead. **Created.** *Bara*, one of three terms employed in this section, and in Scripture generally, to describe the Divine activity ; the other two being *yatzar*, " formed," and *asah*, " made "—both signifying to construct out of pre-existing materials (cf. for *yatzar*, ch. ii. 7 ; viii. 19 ; Ps. xxxiii. 15 ; Isa. xliv. 9 ; for *asah*, ch. viii. 6 ; Exod. v. 16, Deut. iv. 10), and predicable equally of God and man. *Bara* is used exclusively of God. Though not necessarily involved in its significance, the idea of creation *ex nihilo* is acknowledged by the best expositors to be here intended. Its employment in vers. 21, 26, though seemingly against, is really in favour of a distinctively creative act ; in both of these instances something that did not previously exist, *i. e.* animal life and the human spirit, having been called into being. In the sense of producing what is new it frequently occurs in Scripture (cf. Ps. li. 12 ; Jer. xxxi. 12 ; Isa. lxv. 18). Thus, according to the teaching of this venerable document, the visible universe neither existed from eternity, nor was fashioned out of pre-existing materials, nor proceeded forth as an emanation from the Absolute, but was summoned into being by an express creative fiat. The New Testament boldly claims this as a doctrine peculiar to revelation (Heb. xi. 3). Modern science explicitly disavows it as a discovery of reason. The continuity of force admits of neither creation nor annihilation, but demands an unseen universe, out of which the visible has been produced " by an intelligent agency residing in the unseen," and into which it must eventually return ('The Unseen Universe,' pp. 167, 170). Whether the language of the writer to the Hebrews homologates the dogma of an "unseen universe" (μὴ φαινομένον), out of which τὸ βλεπόμενον γεγονέναι, the last result of science, as expressed by the authors of the above-named work, is practically an admission of the Biblical doctrine of creation. **The heavens and the earth** (i. e. *mundus universus*—Gesenius, Kalisch, &c. Cf. ch. ii. 1 ; xiv. 19, 22 ; Ps. cxv. 15 ; Jer. xxiii. 24. The earth and the heavens always mean the terrestrial globe with its aerial firmament. Cf. ch. ii. 4 ; Ps. cxlviii. 13 ; Zech. v. 9). The earth here alluded to is manifestly not the dry land (ver. 10), which was not separated from the waters till the third day, but the entire mass of which our planet is composed, including the superincumbent atmosphere, which was not uplifted from the chaotic deep until the second day. The heavens are the rest of the universe. The Hebrews were aware of other heavens than the " firmament " or gaseous expanse which over-arches the earth. " Tres regiones," says Poole, " ubi aves, ubi nubes, ubi sidera." But,

beyond these, the Shemitic mind conceived of the heaven where the angels dwell (1 Kings xxii. 19 ; Matt. xviii. 10), and where God specially resides (Deut. xxvi. 15 ; 1 Kings viii. 30 ; Ps. ii. 4), if, indeed, this latter was not distinguished as a more exalted region than that occupied by any creature—as " the heaven of heavens," the pre-eminently sacred abode of the Supreme (Deut. x. 14 ; 1 Kings viii. 27 ; Ps. cv. 16). The fundamental idea associated with the term was that of height (*shamayim*, literally, " the heights"—Gesenius, Fürst). To the Greek mind heaven meant " the boundary" (οὐρανος, from ὁρος—Arist.), or, " the raised up" (from ὁρ to be prominent—Liddell and Scott). The Latin spoke of " the concavity" (*cælum*, allied to κοῖλος, hollow), or " the engraved" (from *cælo*, to engrave). The Saxon thought of " the heaved-up arch." The Hebrew imagined great spaces rising tier upon tier above the earth (which, in contradistinction, was named " the flats"), just as with regard to time he spoke of *olamim* (Gr. αἰῶνες). Though not anticipating modern astronomical discovery, he had yet enlarged conceptions of the dimensions of the stellar world (Gen. xv. 5 ; Isa. xl. 26 ; Jer. xxxi. 37 ; Amos ix. 6) ; and, though unacquainted with our present geographical ideas of the earth's configuration, he was able to represent it as a globe, and as suspended upon nothing (Isa. xl. 11 ; Job xxvi. 7—10 ; Prov. viii. 27). The connection of the present verse with those which follow has been much debated. The proposal of Aben Ezra, adopted by Calvin, to read, " In the beginning when God created the heavens and the earth, the earth was . . . .," is grammatically inadmissible. Equally objectionable on the ground of grammar is the suggestion of Bunsen and Ewald, to connect the first verse with the third, and make the second parenthetical ; while it is opposed to that simplicity of construction which pervades the chapter. The device of Drs. Buckland and Chalmers, so favourably regarded by some harmonists of Scripture and geology, to read the first verse as a heading to the whole section, is exploded by the fact that no historical narration can begin with "and." To this Exod. i. 1 is no exception, the second book of Moses being in reality a continuation of the first. Honest exegesis requires that ver. 1 shall be viewed as descriptive of the first of the series of Divine acts detailed in the chapter, and that ver. 2, while admitting of an interval, shall be held as coming in immediate succession—an interpretation, it may be said, which is fatal to the theory which discovers the geologic ages between the creative beginning and primeval chaos.

Ver. 2.—**And the earth.** Clearly the earth

referred to in the preceding verse, the present terrestrial globe with its atmospheric firmament, and not simply "the land" as opposed to "the skies" (Murphy); certainly not "the heavens" of ver. 1 as well as the earth (Delitzsch); and least of all "a section of the dry land in Central Asia" (Buckland, Pye Smith). It is a sound principle of exegesis that a word shall retain the meaning it at first possesses till either intimation is made by the writer of a change in its significance, or such change is imperatively demanded by the necessities of the context, neither of which is the case here. **Was.** Not "had become." **Without form and void.** Literally, wasteness and emptiness, *tohu vabohu.* The words are employed in Isa. xxxiv. 11 and Jer. iv. 23 to depict the desolation and desertion of a ruined and depopulated land, and by many have been pressed into service to support the idea of a preceding cosmos, of which the chaotic condition of our planet was the wreck (Murphy, Wordsworth, Bush, &c.). Delitzsch argues, on the ground that *tohu vabohu* implies the ruin of a previous cosmos, that ver. 2 does not state specifically that God created the earth in this desolate and waste condition; and that death, which is inconceivable out of connection with sin, was in the world prior to the fall; that ver. 2 presupposes the fall of the angels, and adduces in support of his view Job xxxviii. 4—7 ('Bib. Psychology,' sect. i. p. 76; Clark's 'For. Theol. Lib.')—a notion which Kalisch contemptuously classes among "the aberrations of profound minds," and "the endless reveries" of "far-sighted thinkers." Bush is confident that Isa. xlv. 18, in which Jehovah declares that he created not the earth *tohu,* is conclusive against a primeval chaos. The parallel clause, however, shows that not the original state, but the ultimate design of the globe, was contemplated in Jehovah's language: "He created it not *tohu,* he formed it to be inhabited;" *i. e.* the Creator did not intend the earth to be a desolate region, but an inhabited planet. There can scarcely be a doubt, then, that the expression portrays the condition in which the new-created earth was, not innumerable ages, but very shortly, after it was summoned into existence. It was formless and lifeless; a huge, shapeless, objectless, tenantless mass of matter, the gaseous and solid elements commingled, in which neither organised structure, nor animated form, nor even distinctly-traced outline of any kind appeared. **And darkness (was) upon the face of the deep.** The "deep," from a root signifying to disturb, is frequently applied to the sea (Ps. xlii. 8), and here probably intimates that the primordial matter of our globe existed in a fluid, or liquid, or molten form. Dawson

distinguishes between "the deep" and the "waters," making the latter refer to the liquid condition of the globe, and the former apply to "the atmospheric waters," *i. e.* the vaporous or aeriform mass mantling the surface of our nascent planet, and containing the materials out of which the atmosphere was afterwards elaborated ('Origin of the World,' p. 105). As yet the whole was shrouded in the thick folds of Cimmerian gloom, giving not the slightest promise of that fair world of light, order, and life into which it was about to be transformed. Only one spark of hope might have been detected in the circumstance that **the Spirit of God moved** (literally, brooding) **upon the face of the waters.** That the *Ruach Elohim,* or breath of God, was not "a great wind," or "a wind of God," is determined by the non-existence of the air at this particular stage in the earth's development. In accordance with Biblical usage generally, it must be regarded as a designation not simply "of the Divine power, which, like the wind and the breath, cannot be perceived" (Gesenius), but of the Holy Spirit, who is uniformly represented as the source or formative cause of all life and order in the world, whether physical, intellectual, or spiritual (cf. Job xxvi. 13; xxvii. 3; Ps. xxxiii. 6; civ. 29; cxliii. 10; Isa. xxxiv. 16; lxi. 1; lxiii. 11). As it were, the mention of the *Ruach Elohim* is the first out-blossoming of the latent fulness of the Divine personality, the initial movement in that sublime revelation of the nature of the Godhead, which, advancing slowly, and at the best but indistinctly, throughout Old Testament times, culminated in the clear and ample disclosures of the gospel. The special form of this Divine agent's activity is described as that of "brooding" (*merachepheth,* from *rachaph,* to be tremulous, as with love; hence, in Piel, to cherish young—Deut. xxxii. 11) or fluttering over the liquid elements of the shapeless and tenantless globe, communicating to them, doubtless, those formative powers of life and order which were to burst forth into operation in answer to the six words of the six ensuing days. As might have been anticipated, traces of this primeval chaos are to be detected in various heathen cosmogonies, as the following brief extracts will show:—1. The *Chaldean* legend, deciphered from the creation tablet discovered in the palace of Assurbanipal, King of Assyria, B.C. 885, depicts the desolate and void condition of the earth thus :—

"When above were not raised the heavens,
   And below on the earth a plant had not grown up;
   The abyss also had not broken up their boundaries;

The chaos (or water) tiamat (the sea) was the producing-mother of the whole of them," &c.

('Chaldean Genesis,' p. 62.)

2. The *Babylonian* cosmogony, according to Berosus (B.C. 330—260), commences with a time "in which there existed nothing but darkness and an abyss of waters, wherein resided most hideous beings, which were produced of a twofold principle. . . . . The person who presided over them was a woman named Omoroca, which in the Chaldean language is Thalatth, in Greek Thalassa, the sea, but which might equally be interpreted the moon" ('Chaldean Genesis,' pp. 40, 41). 3. The *Egyptian* account of the origin of the universe, as given by Diodorus Siculus, represents the heaven and earth as blended together, till afterwards the elements began to separate and the air to move. According to another idea, there was a vast abyss enveloped in boundless darkness, with a subtle spirit, intellectual in power, existing in the chaos (Macdonald, 'Creation and the Fall,' p. 49). 4. The *Phœnician* cosmogony says, "The first principle of the universe was a dark windy air and an eternal dark chaos. Through the love of the Spirit to its own principles a mixture arose, and a connection called desire, the beginning of all things. From this connection of the Spirit was begotten *mot*, which, according to some, signifies *mud*, according to others, a corruption of a watery mixture, but is probably a feminine form of *mo*, water. From this were developed creatures in the shape of an egg, called zophasemin" (Macdonald, p. 50). 5. The *Indian* mythology is very striking in its resemblance to the Mosaic narrative. The institutes of Menu affirm·that at first all was dark, the world still resting in the purpose of the Eternal, whose first thought created water, and in it the seed of life. This became an egg, from which issued Brahma, the creative power, who divided his own substance and became male and female. The waters were called *nárá*, as being the production of Nara, or the Spirit of God, who, on acccunt of these being his first *ayana*, or place of motion, is named Náráyana, or *moving on the waters*. A remarkable hymn from the Rig Veda, translated by Dr. Max Müller, also closely approximates to the Scriptural account : —

"Nor aught nor nought existed ; yon bright sky
Was not, nor heaven's broad woof outstretched above.
The only one breathed breathless by itself ;
Other than it there nothing since hath been.
Darkness there was, and all at first was veiled

In gloom profound — an ocean without light."

(*Vid.* Macdonald's 'Creation,' &c., p. 51.)

6. The description of chaos given by Ovid is too appropriate to be overlooked :—

"Ante mare et tellus, et, quod tegit omnia, cœlum,
Unus erat toto naturæ vultus in orbe,
Quem dixêre chaos ; rudis indigestaque moles

. . . . quia corpore in uno
Frigida pugnabant calidis, humentia siccis,
Mollia cum duris, sine pondere habentia pondus" ('Metamor.,' lib. i. 1).

Yet not more remarkable are these indirect confirmations of the truthfulness of the Biblical cosmogony than the direct corroborations it derives from the discoveries of modern science. (1) The *nebular hypothesis* of Laplace, which, though only a hypothesis, must yet be admitted to possess a high degree of probability, strikingly attests its authenticity. That eminent astronomer demonstrated that a huge chaotic mass of nebulous matter, revolving in space on its own axis with a sufficient velocity, and gradually condensing from a high degree of heat, would eventually, by throwing off successive rings from the parent body, develop all the celestial orbs that presently compose our planetary system. Though for a long time regarded with suspicion by Biblical scholars, and at the first only tentatively thrown out by its author, Kant, yet so exactly does it account for the phenomena of our solar system as disclosed by the telescope, that it may now be said to have vindicated its claim to be accepted as the best solution science has to give of the formation of the universe ; while further and more dispassionate reflection has convinced theologians generally, that so far from conflicting with the utterances of inspiration, it rather surprisingly endorses them. (2) The researches of *physical philosophy* in connection with hydrodynamics have successfully established that the present form of our earth, that of (the solid of revolution called) an oblate spheroid, is such as it must necessarily have assumed had its original condition been that of a liquid mass revolving round its own axis. (3) *Geological science* likewise contributes its quota to the constantly accumulating weight of evidence in support of the Mosaic narrative, by announcing, as the result of its investigations in connection with the earth's crust, that below a certain point, called "the stratum of invariable temperature," the heat of the interior mass becomes greater in proportion to the depth beneath the surface, thus leading not unnaturally to the inference that "the earth has assumed its present state by cooling down from an intensely heated, or gaseous, or fluid state" (Green's 'Geology,' p. 487).

HOMILETICS.

Ver. 1.—*The visible universe.* I. ONE, yet NOT SIMPLE. 1. *One.* In age, origin, and nature one, "the heavens and the earth" also constitute one vast system. Cohering physically through the force of gravitation, which, in its ultimate analysis, is simply an expression of the Divine power, they are unified spiritually by Christ, who is the impersonation of the Divine wisdom and love (John i. 3, 9; Col. i. 15, 17). Hence, as constituting one stupendous system, they are not independent, but mutually influential—*physically* according to science, *spiritually* according to Scripture (Luke xv. 7, 10; Ephes. iii. 10; 1 Pet. i. 12, &c.). Yet—2. *Not simple,* but complex, consisting of two parts—of this mundane sphere, with its diversified contents of men, animals, and plants; and of those shining heavens, with their starry hosts and angelic races. Hence the histories of those two realms may be widely divergent—an inference which astronomy warrants as to their physical developments, and revelation endorses with regard to their spiritual experiences. Hence to argue from the one to the other is to reason hypothetically; as, *e. g.,* to conclude that the planets must be inhabited because the earth is, or to affirm that the Divine treatment of the human and angelic races must of necessity be alike.

II. VAST, yet NOT INFINITE. 1. *Vast.* Enlarged as were Shemitic notions of the dimensions of God's universe, modern astronomy, by the grandeur and sublimity of its revelations, gives definite shape to what were then only vague and shadowy conceptions. Imagination becomes bewildered in the attempt to comprehend the circle of the universe. Commencing with the sun, the central body of our planetary system, with a diameter about three times our distance from the moon, and passing, on her outward journey, no fewer than seven worlds in addition to our own, most of them immensely larger, she only reaches the outskirts of the first department of creation at a distance of 2,853,800,000 miles. Then, when to this is added that the nearest fixed star is so remote that three years are required for its light to reach the earth; that from some of the more distant nebulæ the light has been travelling for millions of years; that the number of the stars is practically infinite; and that each of them may be the centre of a system more resplendent than our own,—even then it is but a faint conception which she reaches of the dimensions of the universe (Job xxvi. 14). Yet—2. It is *not infinite.* Immeasurable by man, it has already been measured by God (Isa. xl. 12). Undiscoverable by science, its limits are known to its Creator (Acts xv. 18). The stars which man is unable to compute God calls by their names (Ps. cxlvii. 4; Isa. xl. 26). That the universe must have a boundary is involved in its creation. Two finites cannot make an infinite. Hence the *measured* earth (Hab. iii. 6) and the *bounded* heavens (Job xxii. 14) cannot compose an illimitable universe. Still less can there be two infinites, one filling all space, and another outside of it. But Elohim is such an infinite (Isa. lvii. 15; Jer. xxiii. 24); hence the universe is not such another.

III. OLD, yet NOT ETERNAL. 1. *Old.* How old God has not revealed and man has not discovered; geology and astronomy both say millions of years; one hundred millions at least, Sir W. Thomson alleges the sun to have been burning. Genesis gives ample scope to physicists in their researches by saying they may go as far back as "the beginning;" only that beginning they must find. For—2. The universe is *not eternal,* though its antiquity be vast. The frequency and certainty with which Scripture enunciates the non-eternity of the material universe is one of its most distinguishing characteristics (Ps. xc. 1; cii. 25, 26; Heb. i. 10). This may also now be regarded as the last word of science: "We have thus reached the beginning as well as the end of the present visible universe, and have come to the conclusion that it began in time, and will in time come to an end" ('The Unseen Universe,' p. 93).

IV. EXISTENT, yet NOT SELF-EXISTENT. 1. *Existent;* i. e. standing out as an entity in the infinite realm of space; standing out from eternity in the sphere of time; and also standing out from God, as essentially distinct from his personality. Yet—2. *Not self-existent*, not standing there in virtue of its own inherent energy, being neither self-produced nor self-sustained; but standing solely and always in obedience to the creative fiat of Elohim, the almighty and self-existent God.

Ver. 2.—*Chaos an emblem of the unrenewed soul.* I. WITHOUT ORDER: existing in a state of spiritual ruin, and requiring a special process of rearrangement to evolve symmetry and beauty from its confusion (2 Cor. v. 16).

II. WITHOUT LIFE: being dead in trespasses and sins (Ephes. ii. 1); absolutely "void" in the sense of being untenanted by lofty thoughts, pure emotions, holy volitions, spiritual imaginations, such as are the inmates of sinless and, in great part also, of renewed souls.

III. WITHOUT LIGHT: shrouded in darkness (Ephes. iv. 18); walking, perhaps, in the sparks that its own fire has kindled (Isa. l. 11), but devoid of that true light which is from heaven (John i. 9).

IV. Yet NOT WITHOUT GOD. As the Spirit brooded over chaos, so does God's Holy Spirit hover over fallen souls, waiting, as it were, for the forthcoming and insounding of the commanding word to introduce light, order, life.

HOMILIES BY VARIOUS AUTHORS.

Ver. 1.—"Beginning" is a word familiarly on our lips; but, for the most part, we mean only rearrangement, or the commencement of one link in the chain of events. But who can conceive the beginning of creation? Who can travel back in thought to the first moment of its existence, and look into the eternity beyond? The Bible carries us back to that beginning, the first moment when the universe existed. How far back was the starting-point of time we know not, nor in what form the universe came into being, whether completed, or in germs to be developed in the course of ages. Only we are taught that before that "beginning" the universe was not, and that "the worlds were framed by the word of God" (Heb. xi. 3)—their substance, and the laws by which they are governed. With this the conclusions of science agree. They point out that the forces of nature tend to extinction, and hence must have had a beginning. To the question what was that beginning, the Bible gives the answer. 1. *What was before the "beginning"?* God was; he created all (Ps. xc. 2); and if it surpass our power to conceive an eternal self-existent Being, still less can we realise life, power, law coming into existence without a cause. And "in the beginning was the Word;" and the Holy Ghost, through whom Christ offered himself (Heb. ix. 14). But further, before the beginning the Lamb was slain (Rev. xiii. 8)—*i. e.* the necessity for redemption was foreseen and the plan provided—and we were chosen (Ephes. i. 4), and a kingdom prepared for us (Matt. xxv. 34). Thus, redemption was no afterthought, no repairing of failure; but God's purpose from eternity, and therefore that which is best. 2. *What was the "beginning"?* The creation of a field on which God's plans were to be carried out and his perfections manifested. And in the course of his work the creation of beings to whom and in whom he might make himself known, who might glorify him here and enjoy him for ever. 3. *We mark then*—At the beginning God brought forth what had been ordained in eternity—his plan complete to the end—our salvation—redemption as well as creation. "Very good" (Gen. i. 31) went far beyond the things then existing on the earth. And if it be urged, How is "very good" consistent with sin?—An enemy has sown tares and marred the Creator's work—the world is a ruin. Oh, faithless! why fearful? If God could give life to dry bones (Ezek. xxxvii. 6), if he could of stones raise up children to Abraham, can he not out of seeming ruin raise up a more glorious temple? But thou sayest, How can this be? Canst thou solve one of the least mysteries of creation? And is it strange thou canst not solve that mystery into which angels desire to look? Enough to know "where sin abounded," &c. (Rom. v. 20); to remember, "we see not yet," &c. (Heb. ii. 8); and humbly to wait our Father's time and way. 4. *For personal encouragement.* Our state foreseen and provided for from the beginning. Thus our right to trust God's promises depends not on anything in us, but is part of his original plan. Our Lord's call to sinners is in closest agreement with what was ordained "in the beginning." "Whosoever will" (Rev. xxii. 17) but echoes the word which called the universe into being.—M.

Vers. 1—5.—A true and firm foundation of revelation and faith must be laid in a Divine doctrine of "Genesis," the *beginnings* out of which have come both the world of nature and the world of grace. In this book we are taught what is the *order* by which all things must be tried. Coming forth from Elohim, from the Infinite Personality; flowing in his appointed course. The genesis of *heaven and earth* becomes the genesis of *the human family*. Out of the *natural chaos* is brought forth the *Eden* of rest and beauty. Out of the *moral waste* of a fallen humanity is formed, by the gracious work of a Divine Spirit, through a covenant of infinite wisdom and love, a seed of redeemed and sanctified human beings, a *family of God*. The genesis of the *material creation* leads on to the genesis of the *invisible creation*. The lower is the type and symbol of the higher. The *first day* is the true beginning of days. See what is placed by the sacred writer between that evening and morning.

I. THE COMING FORTH OF THE EVERLASTING, UNSEARCHABLE SECRET OF THE DIVINE NATURE INTO MANIFESTATION. "*God created.*" The word employed denotes more than the bare summoning of existence out of nothingness. The analogy of human workmanship ("cutting," "carving," "framing") suggests the relation between creation and the God of creation. The heaven and the earth reflect their Maker. Works embody the mind, the spirit, the will, the nature of the workman. Although the name *Elohim*, in the plural form, cannot be taken as an equivalent of the Trinity, it points to the great fundamental fact of all revelation, the Divine Unity coming forth out of the infinite solitude of eternity, and declaring, in the manifold revelations of the visible and invisible worlds, all that the creature can know of his fathomless mystery.

II. HERE IS A GLIMPSE INTO GOD'S ORDER AND METHOD. "*In the beginning*," the immeasurable fulness of creative power and goodness. Formless void, darkness on the face of the deep, apparent confusion and emptiness, within a limited sphere, the earth; at a certain epoch, in preparation for an appointed future. *Chaos* is not the first beginning of things; it is a stage in their history. The evening of the first day preceded the morning in the recorded annals of the earth. That evening was itself a veiling of the light. Science itself leads back the thoughts from all chaotic periods to previous developments of power. *Order precedes disorder.* Disorder is itself permitted only as a temporary state. It is itself part of the *genesis* of that which shall be ultimately "*very good.*"

III. THE GREAT VITAL FACT OF THE WORLD'S ORDER IS THE INTIMATE UNION BETWEEN THE SPIRIT OF GOD AND THAT WHICH IS COVERED WITH DARKNESS UNTIL HE MAKES IT LIGHT. The moving of the Spirit upon the face of the waters represents the brooding, cherishing, vitalising presence of God in his creatures, over them, around them, at once the source and protection of their life. "*Breath;*" "*wind*," the word literally means, perhaps as a symbol at once of *life*, or living energy, and *freedom*, and with an immediate reference to the *creative word*, which is henceforth the breath of God in the world. Surely no candid mind can fail to feel the force of such a witness in the opening sentences of revelation to *the triune God*.

IV. TO US THE BEGINNING OF ALL THINGS IS LIGHT. The word of God "commands the light to shine out of darkness." "God *said*, Let there be light," or, Let light be. The going forth of *God's word* upon the universe very well represents the twofold fact, (1) that it is the *outcome* of his *will* and *nature;* and (2) that it is his *language*—the expression of *himself*. Hence all through this Mosaic cosmogony God is represented as speaking *to* creation, that we may understand that he speaks *in* creation, as he is also said to look at that which comes forth from himself to behold it, to approve it, to name it, to appoint its order and use. Such intimate blending of the *personal* with the *impersonal* is the teaching of Scripture as distinguished from all mere human wisdom. God is *in* creation and yet *above* it. Man is thus invited to seek the *personal presence* as that which is higher than nature, which his *own* personal life requires, that it may not be oppressed with nature's greatness, that it may be light, and not darkness. There is darkness in *creation*, darkness in the deep waters of *the world's history*, darkness in the *human soul* itself, until God speaks and man hears. *Light* is not, physically, the first thing created; but it is the first *fact* of the *Divine days*—that is, the beginning of the *new order*. For what we have to do with is not the infinite secret of creation, but the *manifestation of the visible world*, "*God manifest*." The first day in the history of the earth, *as man can read it*, must be the day when God removes the covering of darkness and says, "Let there be light." The word uplifted is itself a commencement. *God said that it was good*. His own appointment confirmed the abiding distinction between light and darkness, between day and night; in other words, the unfolding, progressive inter-change of work and rest, of revelation and concealment, the true beginning of the world's *week of labour*, which leads on to the everlasting *sabbath*. How appro-priately this first day of the week of creation stands at the threshold of God's word of grace! The light which he makes to shine in our hearts, which divides our exist-ence into the true order, the good and the evil separated from one another, which commences our life; and the Spirit is *the light of his own word*, the light which shines from the face of him who was "*the Word*," "*in the beginning with God*," "*without whom nothing was made that was made*."—R.

EXPOSITION.

Vers. 3—5.—The evolution of the cosmos was accomplished by a series of Divine forma-tive works which extended over a period of six successive days. In the character of those cosmic labours a progression is distinctly visible, though not continuous throughout. Unless, with Aristotle, the celestial lumin-aries are regarded as ζῶα λογικά, and so classed in the category of organised and living beings, it is impossible to find in their production an advance upon the pre-ceding vegetation. Arbitrary transpositions of the days, as of the third and fourth, in order to make the first half of the creative week an inorganic, and the second half an organic, era, are inadmissible. The arrange-ment of the days that accords most exactly with the requirements of the case, and most successfully preserves the order and con-nection of the record, is that which divides them into two triads (Lange, Kalisch, Dana, &c.), as exhibited underneath:—

1. Light.   4. Lights.
2. { Air,   5. { Fowl,
     { Water.   { Fish.
3. Dry Land and Plants. 6. Animals and Man,

—each triad beginning with the making of light, and ending with a double creation, and the works performed on the second having each a definite relation to the labours executed on the first. On the first creative day the formative energy of the Divine word, operating through the agency of the

Ruach Elohim, eliminates the light from the dark chaotic mass of earth, on the second uplifts the atmosphere above the waters, and on the third distinguishes the dry land from the sea—at a later period in this same day clothing the dry land with vegetation, as if to prophesy some correspondingly higher advance in the creation work at the close of the second series. At this stage, instead of pressing forward with its operations, the demiurgic potency of the invisible Artificer appears to pause, and, reverting to the point from which it started, enters on its second course of labours. On the fourth day the light developed on the first is concentrated and permanently fixed in the celestial lumin-aries; on the fifth the air and waters, which were separated on the second, are filled with fowl and fish, their respective inhabitants; and on the sixth the dry land of the third day is occupied by animals, the mute pre-diction of the third day's vegetation being fulfilled by the creation of man.

Ver. 3.—*Day one.* **And God said.** This phrase, which is ten times repeated in the narrative of the six days' work, is commonly regarded as an instance of anthropomorphism, a peculiarity of revelation, and of this chapter in particular, at which rationalism affects to be offended. But any other mode of repre-senting the Deity would have failed to convey to finite minds an intelligent idea of his nature. "Touching the Almighty, who can find him out?" The most that God himself could do in communicating to his creature man a conception of his ineffable and un-approachable Godhead was to supply him with an anthropomorphic image of himself—"the Word made flesh." Deeper insight, however, into this sublime statement discerns that "anthropomorphism" does not exhaust its significance. God spoke ; but to whom ? "This was an omnipotent word," says Luther, "spoken in the Divine essence. No one heard this word uttered but God himself. . . . . . The Father spoke within." It is observable too that every time the word goes forth from Elohim it is followed by instant-aneous movement in the chaos, as if the word itself were inherently creative. Re-membering, then, that the doctrine of a personal Logos was not unknown to the later theology of the Old Testament (cf. Ps. xxxiii. 6 ; cxlviii. 5), and is clearly revealed in the New (John i. 1 ; Heb. xi. 3), it is difficult to resist the inference that here we have its roots, and that a correct exegesis should find in the creative word of Elohim an adum-bration of the *Devar Jehovah* of the He-brew Psalter, the *Logos* of John's Gospel, and the *Rema Theou* of the writer to the Hebrews. **Let there be light : and there was light.** The sublimity of these words, which arrested the attention of the heathen Longinus (' De Sublimitate,' ix.), and which Milton (' Para-dise Lost,' vii.) and Du Bartas, an elder poet (*vid.* Kitto *in loco*), have tried to repro-duce, is in great measure lost in our English version. Γενηθήτω φῶς καὶ ἐγένετω φῶς (LXX.) and *sit lux et fuit lux* (Vulg.) are superior translations of וַיְהִי־אוֹר יְהִי־אוֹר which might be rendered, "Light be, and light was." With reference to their import, the least satisfactory explanation, notwith-standing the eminent names that have lent it their support (Bush, Kitto, Murphy, Wordsworth), is that which understands the sun to have been created a perfectly finished luminous body from the first, though hitherto its light had been intercepted by the earth's vapours, which were now dis-persed by Divine command. But the lan-guage of Elohim is too exalted to be applied to so familiar a phenomenon as the dis-sipation of terrestrial mists, and, besides, expressly negatives the hypothesis in ques-tion by affirming that the light was sum-moned into *being*, and not simply into *appearance*. The historian, too, explicitly asserts that the light was, *i. e.* began to be, and not merely to be visible. A modification of this view, viz., that the sun and moon were now created, but did not become visible until the fourth day (Inglis), must likewise be rejected, as according neither with ver. 1, which says that the heavenly bodies were created in the beginning, nor with vers. 16, 17, which declare that not until the fourth day were they constituted sources of light

for the earth. The exigencies of the text, as well as the ascertained facts of physical science, require the first day's work to be the original production of light throughout the universe, and in particular throughout our planetary system (Kalisch, Lange, Delitzsch, Dawson). Calvin, though much more deeply concerned about the refutation of Servetus, who maintained that the Word only began to be with the creation of light, was able to perceive that this light was independent of the sun and moon ; in this agreeing with Augustine, who, however, conjectured it to be not material, but spiritual in its nature (' De Genesi ad Literam,' lib. i. c. 3). Nor does it in the slightest conflict with ver. 1 to suppose that light was now for the first time produced, light being a *mode* or *condition* of matter, and not a distinct *element* or *sub-stance*, as was at one time believed. Lumin-osity is simply the result of incandescence, although what specific change is effected on the constitutions or adjustments of the mole-cules of a body by the process of heating which renders it luminous science is unable to explain. Any solid body can be rendered incandescent by being heated up to between 700° and 800° Fahrenheit. Any liquid that can absorb as great a quantity of heat like-wise emits light. Gases do not appear to be capable of incandescence, though the phe-nomena attending their sudden condensation discover light-producing properties in their composition. As to how the light of incan-descent bodies is transmitted to the eye, the Pythagorean and Newtonian theory of small, impalpable particles of luminous matter being constantly emitted from their surfaces towards the eye may be said to have been successfully displaced by that of Descartes, Huygens, and Euler, which accounts for the phenomena of vision by the existence throughout space, and in the interstitial spaces of bodies, of an infinitely attenuated *ether*, which is thrown into undulations by luminous bodies precisely as the atmosphere is made to vibrate by bodies which are sonorous. But whichever theory be adopted to solve the mystery of its transmission, that of *emanation* or of *undulation*, it is im-possible to resist the conclusion that the creation of light, which formed the *opus operatum* of the first day, was in reality the evolution from the dark-robed, seething mass of our condensing planet (and probably from the other bodies in our solar system) of that luminous matter which supplies the light. It seems unnecessary to add that it could not have been either the subterranean fire which produced the igneous rocks of geology (Tayler) or caloric (Clarke) ; though, as *aor* is used in Scripture for heat (Isa. xliv. 16), fire (Isa. xxxi. 9 ; Ezek. v. 2), the sun (Job xxxi. 26), lightning (Job xxxvii. 3), and there is every reason to believe that light, heat, and electricity are only modifications of the same force, we may be warranted in embracing all the three in its significance.

Ver. 4.—**And God saw the light, that it was good.** The anthropomorphism of this verse is suggestive, as teaching that from the first, the absolute and all-sufficient Elohim was an intelligent Spectator of the operation of his own laws and forces, and was profoundly interested in the results which they achieved—an amount and degree of inter-ʿerence with the vast machine of nature which would satisfy any rational theist of to-day. God *saw*, i. e. examined and judged the newly-finished product, investigated its nature and its properties, contemplated its uses, admired its excellences, noted its correspondence with his own Divine idea ; and in all these respects he pronounced it *good*. Afterwards it is the particular arrangement effected, or condition induced, by the creative word that evokes the Divine commendation ; here it is the creature itself—" perhaps as the one object in nature which forms the fittest representation of the Creator himself, who is Light, and in whom is no darkness at all (1 John i. 5), and of the true Light, which lighteth every man (John i. 9)" (Macdonald). **And God divided between the light and the darkness.** The celestial bodies not having been constituted " light-holders " for the earth until the fourth day forbids the supposition that the luminous matter, on being eliminated from the chaotic mass, was forthwith transported towards and concentrated in the sun. The sun itself, it is now well known, is "a solid mass of highly igneous matter engirt by a bed of dense clouds, on the top of which there lies, encircling all, a floating phosphorescent or luminous atmosphere, the lower part of it splendid, but the upper of lustre altogether dazzling, from which streams the flood of light that enlivens all surrounding spheres " (Nichol's ' Cyclopedia,' art. Sun). "If, therefore, with Laplace, we may assume that the physical history of the sun was the archetype of that of the various planetary bodies that compose our system, we must think of them also, in the process of condensation, developing luminous atmospheres, which would continue encircling them, and in fact making them suns, until, through their further condensation, those phosphorescent bands were broken up, and, becoming disengaged from their parent globes, were attracted towards, and subsequently centralised in, the photosphere of the sun. So far as our earth is concerned, that happened on the fourth day. On the first day the light would either ensphere it in a radiant cloud, or exist apart from it, like a sun, though always in the plane of its orbit " (Delitzsch). If the former, then mani-festly, though revolving on its axis, the earth would not experience the vicissitude of day and night, which some conjecture was not at this time established ; if the latter, then the same succession of light and darkness would be begun as was afterwards rendered permanent by the fourth day's work. The chief reasons for the latter alternative are the supposed necessity of understanding the term day as a period of twenty-four hours, and the apparent impossibility of explaining how the light could be divided from the darkness otherwise than by the diurnal revolution of the earth. The Hiphil of בָּדַל, however, means to disjoin what was previously mixed, and may simply refer to the separation of the luminous particles from the opaque mass. By that very act the light was divided from the darkness. It was henceforth to be no more commingled. "The light denotes all that is simply illuminating in its efficacy, all the luminous element ; the darkness denotes all that is untransparent, dark, shadow-casting ; both together denote the polarity of the created world as it exists between the light-formations and the night-formations—the constitution of the day and night" (Lange).

Ver. 5.—**And God called** (literally, called to) **the light Day, and** (literally, to) **the darkness he called Night.** "None but superficial thinkers," says Delitzsch, "can take offence at the idea of created things receiving names from God. The name of a thing is the expression of its nature. If the name be given by man, it fixes in a word the impression which it makes upon the human mind ; but, when given by God, it expresses the reality, what the thing is in God's creation, and the place assigned it there by the side of other things." The things named were the light and the darkness ; not the durations, but the phenomena. The names called were day, *yom*, and night, *layela*, which, again, were not time-measures, but character-descriptions. Ainsworth suggests that *yom* was intended to express "the tumult, stir, and business of the day," in all probability connecting it with *yam*, which depicts the foaming or the boiling of the sea ; and that *layela*, in which he seems to detect the Latin *ululare*, is indicative of "the yelling or the howling of wild beasts at night." Gesenius derives the former from the unused root *yom*, which signifies to glow with heat, while the latter he associates with *lul*, also unused, to roll up, the idea being that the night wraps all things in obscurity. Macdonald sees in the naming of the creatures an expression of sovereignty and lordship, as when Adam named the beasts of the field. **And the evening and the morning were the first day.** Literally, *And evening was, and* *morning was, day one.* Considerable diversity of sentiment prevails with regard to the exact interpretation of these words. On the one hand, it is assumed that the first creative period is here described as an ordinary astronomical or sidereal day of twenty-four hours' duration, its constituent parts being characterised in the usual way, as an evening and a morning. In the judgment of Kalisch and others the peculiar phrase, "Evening was, and morning was," is simply equivalent to the later Hebrew compound "evening-morning" (Dan. viii. 14), and the Greek νυχθήμερον (2 Cor. xi. 25), both of which denote a natural or civil day, though this is challenged, in the case of the Hebrew compound, by Macdonald. The language of the fourth commandment (Exod. xx. 11) is also appealed to as removing it beyond the sphere of doubt that the evening and the morning referred to are the component sections of an earthly day. As to the proper *terminus a quo* of this initial day, however, the advocates of this interpretation are at variance among themselves; Delitzsch taking the terms *ereb* (literally, " the setting," from *arab*, (1) to mix ; (2) to set, to depart, like the sun) and *boker* (literally, " the breaking forth," from *bakar*, to cleave, to open) in an active sense, and applying the former to the first fading of the light, and the latter to the breaking of the dawn after the first interval of darkness has passed, thus reckoning the creative days from daybreak to daybreak ; while Murphy and Kalisch, who agree with him in regarding the days as ordinary solar days, declare they must be reckoned, *Hebraico more*, from sunset to sunset. But if the first day commenced with an *evening* or obscure period (Has *ereb* no connection with *arab*, to mix ? May it not describe the condition of things when light and darkness were commingled ?), that can be discovered only in the chaotic *darkness* out of which the light sprang. Hence, on the other hand, as it seems improbable that this was of no more than twelve hours' duration, and as the presumption is that the light-period would be commensurate in length, it has been argued that day one was not a sun-measured day, but a period of indefinite extent. Of course the length of day one practically determines the length of all the six. If it was a solar day, then they must be considered such. But as the present sidereal arrangements for the measurement of time were not then established, it is clearly gratuitous to proceed on the assumption that it was. Hence, neither is it to be accepted without demonstration that they were not likewise periods of prolonged duration. It is obvious they were if it was ; and that it was appears to be suggested by the terms in which it is described. This conclusion, that

the creation days were long periods, and not simply solar days, is confirmed by a variety of considerations. 1. In the creation record itself (chs. i., ii. 4) the term is employed with an obvious latitude of meaning ; standing for *light* as opposed to darkness (ver. 5) ; *day* as distinguished from night ; and for a period of *twenty-four hours*, as in the phrase " for days and years " (ver. 14) ; and again for the whole creation period of six days, or, as is more probable, for the second and third days (ch. ii. 4). 2. General Scripture usage sanctions this interpretation of the word *day* as a period of indefinite duration ; *e. g.* Zech. xiv. 6, 7, which speaks of the time of our Lord's coming, and indeed of the entire gospel dispensation, as אֶחָד יוֹם *unus dies*, i. e. a day together unique, the only day of its kind (Delitzsch) ; and characterises it as one of God's days, " known to the Lord," as if to distinguish it from one of man's ordinary civil days (cf. Deut. ix. 1 ; Ps. xc. 4 ; xcv. 8 ; Isa. xlix. 8 ; John ix. 4 ; Heb. xiii. 8 ; 2 Pet. iii. 8). 3. The works ascribed to the different days can with difficulty be compressed within the limits of a solar day. Taking the third day, *e. g.*, if the events assigned to it belong *exclusively* to the region of the supernatural, nothing need prevent the belief that twenty-four hours were sufficient for their accomplishment ; but if the Divine *modus operandi* during the first half of the creative week was through " existing causes " (even vastly accelerated), as geology affirms that it was during the second half, and as we know that it has been ever since its termination, then a considerably larger space of time than twice twelve hours must have been consumed in their execution. And the same conclusion forces itself upon the judgment from a consideration of the works allotted to the sixth day, in which not only were the animals produced and Adam made, but the former, being collected in Eden, were passed in review before the latter to be named, after which he was cast into a sleep by Jehovah Elohim, a rib extracted from his side and fashioned into a woman, and the woman presented to him as a partner. 4. The duration of the seventh day of necessity determines the length of the other six. Without anticipating the exposition of ch. ii. 1—4 (*q. v.*), it may be said that God's sabbatic rest is understood by the best interpreters of Scripture to have continued from creation's close until the present hour ; so that consistency demands the previous six days to be considered as not of short, but of indefinite, duration. 5. The language of the fourth commandment, when interpreted in accordance with the present theory, confirms the probability of its truth. If the six days in Exod. xx. 11 are simply natural days, then the seventh day, in which God is represented as having rested from his creative labours, must likewise be a natural or solar day ; and if so, it is proper to observe what follows. It follows (1) that the events recorded in the first five verses of Genesis must be compressed into a single day of twenty-four hours, so that no gap will remain into which the short-day advocates may thrust the geologic ages, which is for them an imperative necessity ; (2) that the world is only 144 hours older than man, which is contrary to both science and revelation ; (3) that the statement is incorrect that God finished all his work at the close of the sixth day ; and (4) that the fossiliferous remains which have been discovered in the earth's crust have either been deposited there since man's creation, or were created there at the first, both of which suppositions are untenable. But now, if, on the contrary, the language signifies that God laboured in the fashioning of his cosmos through six successive periods of indefinite duration (olamim, æons), and entered on the seventh day into a correspondingly long period of sabbatic rest, we can hold the opposite of every one of these conclusions, and find a convincing argument besides for the observance of the sabbath in the beautiful analogy which subsists between God's great week of olamim and man's little week of sun-measured days. 6. Geology declares that the earth must have been brought to its present condition through a series of labours extending over indefinitely long epochs ; and, notwithstanding the confident assertion of Kalisch and others that it is hopeless to harmonise science and revelation, the correspondence between the contents of these geologic ages and those of the Mosaic days is so surprising as to induce the belief that the latter were, like the former, extended periods. First, according to geology, travelling backward, comes the Cainozoic era, with the remains of animals, but not of man ; next is the Mesozoic era, with the remains of fish and fowl, but not of animals ; and underneath that is the Palæozoic era, with its carboniferous formations, but still with traces of aquatic life at its beginning and its end.

Now, whether the vegetation of the third day is to be sought for in the carboniferous formations of the Palæozoic age (Hugh Miller), or, as is more probable, in the age which saw the formation of the metamorphic rocks (Dawson), the order disclosed is precisely that which the Mosaic narrative affirms was observed—first plants, then fish and fowl, and finally animals and man ; so that if the testimony of the rocks be admissible at all upon the subject, it is unmistakably in favour of the long-period day. 7. The opinion of neither Jewish nor Christian antiquity was entirely on the side of the natural-day theory. Josephus and Philo lent their sanction to the other view. Origen perceived the difficulty of having a first, second, and third day, each with an evening and a morning, without the sun, moon, and stars, and resolved it by saying that these celestial luminaries were appointed "οὐκετι εἰς ἀρχας τῆς ἡμέρας καὶ τῆς νυκτὸς, ἀλλ' εἰς τὴν ἀρχην τῆς ἡμέρας καὶ τῆς νυκτός" (' Com. in Genesin,' i. 16). Augustine similarly writes, "Qui dies cujusmodi sint, aut perdifficile nobis, aut etiam impossibile est cogitare, quanto magis dicere . . . . Illorum autem priores tres sine sole peracti sunt, qui quarto die factus refertur" (' De Civitate Dei,' lib. xi. 6, 7). Bede likewise remarks, "Fortassis hic diei nomen totius temporis nomen est, et omnia volumina seculorum hoc vocabulo includit." 8. Heathen cosmogonies may also be appealed to as an indirect confirmation of the preceding evidence. Egyptian, Persian, Indian, and Etruscan legends represent the elaboration of the world as having been accomplished in a series of ages of prolonged duration. "God created in the first thousand years heaven and earth ; in the second the vault of heaven ; in the third the sea and the other waters of the earth ; in the fourth the sun, moon, and stars ; in the fifth the inhabitants of the air, of the water, and of the land ; and in the sixth man," is the creation story of Etruria ; and although in itself it has no validity, yet, as a traditional reflection of the Mosaic narrative it is not entirely destitute of weight.

HOMILETICS.

Ver. 4.—*The value of light.* I. A DIVINE CREATURE. 1. *Mysteriously fashioned.* Philosophers can analyse light, unfold the seven prismatic hues that lie concealed in its pure bosom, theorise with much exactitude concerning its transmission, calculate its incredible velocity, elucidate the laws of its dispersion, utilise the wondrous potencies that are treasured up in its mystic beams; but they can neither make light nor explain its production. Notwithstanding all the restless activity of modern scientific discovery, Jehovah's two interrogations (Job xxxviii. 19, 24) remain unanswered "Where is the way where light dwelleth ?" and, "By what way is the light parted, which scattereth the east wind upon the earth ?" 2. *Exquisitely beautiful.* The first made of God's creatures, it is likewise one of the most radiantly fair. Streaming forth direct from the golden sun, or reflected in silver beams from the pale moon, painting the orient dawn with roseate hues, or bathing the western hills in a sea of glory, shimmering in whiteness through the summer air, or lying across the rain-cloud in its many-coloured bow, it fascinates the eye of every intelligent beholder with its incomparable splendour. 3. *Essentially immaculate.* "Hail, holy light, offspring of Heaven, first born!" sings the immortal bard. "Bright effluence of bright essence," it could scarce be other than stainless in its purity. It is the one of all God's mundane creatures that has carried with it none of the chaotic darkness. Effectually divided from the darkness at the first, it now descends upon this lower earth from celestial realms. And being pure in itself, wherever it appears it communicates its own bright nature; it refines, beautifies, and purifies. 4. *Absolutely incorruptible.* As it brings no contamination in its beams, so it can receive none. The atmosphere may be polluted, the land may be defiled, the waters of the ocean may be rendered impure, it can in no degree be tainted. Excluded from our presence, admitted to the darkest and the foulest abodes, captivated and compelled to be our servant, absorbed by the dull sod, stored away in coal-fields—all these it may be, but not touched by earth's impurity.

II. A DIVINE GIFT. 1. A *universal* gift. It belongs to no one nation, country, class, or condition, being equally the heritage of all—the wise and the unwise, the unthankful and the grateful, the evil and the good (Matt. v. 45). It was God's first gift to the race. 2. A *free* gift. It costs nothing. The poorest beggar as well as the grandest monarch enjoys it on the same terms—"without money and without price." So free was it to the first man that it anticipated his arrival on the earth; and to this day the seeing eye is ever preceded by the light wherewith to see. And, like the light, all God's gifts are free. "He simply gives unto all men;" and, anticipative of man's wants, "he prevents us with his goodness." 3. A *useful* gift. Many of man's gifts are worthless; not so this of God's. Directly or indirectly, all the earth's glory is dependent on the light. Without light, neither would the loveliness of form be discerned, nor the beauty of colour exist. Light is indispensable for the production, preservation, and enjoyment of life. In almost every department of human industry its aid is sought. It is serviceable to the man of science, to the agriculturist, to the mechanic, to the sailor, to the traveller. "Upon whom does not his light arise?" inquires Bildad. We may ask, "Unto whom is not his light useful?" 4. A *silent* gift. It is ever gentle and noiseless in its coming; with incredible velocity rushing through the depths of space, yet with no appearance of hurry or confusion. Almost instantaneous in its swiftness, as if, having been the first to come in contact with the living word of the Creator, it had caught the Divine property of annihilating space. 5. A *welcome* gift. "Truly the light is sweet," &c. (Eccles. xi. 7). Welcome by all, it is specially so by them that "wait for the morning" (Ps. cxxx.).

III. A DIVINE EMBLEM. 1. Of God (1 John i. 5), in respect of its glorious appearance, pure essence, diffusive character, quickening influence. 2. Of Christ (John ix. 3), as enlightening, healing, purifying, directing. 3. Of the Holy Spirit (Acts ii. 3), in respect of its celestial origin, mysterious nature, sudden and unexpected movements.

Light an emblem of the gospel. I. THE APPROPRIATENESS OF THE METAPHOR. Light and the gospel resemble one another in respect of—1. Their *source*—God. 2. Their *purity*. 3. Their *influence*. 4. Their *gentleness*.

II. GOD'S WILL RESPECTING LIGHT. 1. That the world should be filled with gospel light. 2. That every man should have the light. 3. That Christians should be the light.

Application:—1. Have you this light in your hearts, in your families, in your neighbourhoods? 2. Are you doing what you can to diffuse the light?

EXPOSITION.

Ver. 6.—*Day two.* The work of this day consisted in the formation of that immense gaseous ocean, called the atmosphere, by which the earth is encircled. **And God said, Let there be a firmament** (*rakiya*, an expanse, from *rakah*, to beat out; LXX., στερέωμα; Vulgate, *firmamentum*) **in the midst of the waters.** To affirm with Knobel, Gesenius, and others that the Hebrews supposed the atmospheric heavens to be a metallic substance (Exod. xxiv. 10), a vault fixed on the water-flood which surrounds the earth (Prov. viii. 27), firm as a molten looking-glass (Job xxxvii. 18), borne by the highest mountains, which are therefore called the pillars and foundations of heaven (2 Sam. xxii. 8), and having doors and windows (ch. vii. 11; xxviii. 17; Ps. lxxviii. 23), is to confound poetical metaphor with literal prose, optical and phenomenal language with strict scientific statement. The Vulgate and English translations of *rakiya* may convey the idea of solidity, though it is doubtful if στερέωμα (LXX.) does not signify that which *makes* firm as well as that which is *made* firm (McCaul, Wordsworth, W. Lewis), thus referring to the well-known scientific fact that the atmosphere by its weight upon the waters of the sea keeps them down, and by its pressure against our bodies keeps them up; but it is certain that not *solidity*, but *expansiveness*, is the idea represented by *rakiya* (cf. Scottish, *rax*, to stretch; Job xxxvii. 18; Ps. civ. 2; Isa. xl. 22).

"The firmament, expanse of liquid, pure,
 Transparent, elemental air, diffused
 In circuit to the uttermost convex
 Of this great round."
            (Milton, 'Par. Lost,' Bk. vii.)

And let it divide the waters from the waters. What these waters were, which were designed to be parted by the atmospheric firmament, is explained in the verse which follows.

Ver. 7.—**And God made the firmament.** How the present atmosphere was evolved from the chaotic mass of waters the Mosaic narrative does not reveal. The primary intention of that record being not to teach science, but to discover religious truth, the thing of paramount importance to be communicated was that the firmament was of God's construction. This, of course, does not prevent us from believing that the elimination of those gases (twenty-one parts of oxygen and seventy-nine of nitrogen, with a small proportion of carbonic acid gas and aqueous vapour) which compose our atmosphere was not effected by natural means;

and how far it may have been assisted by the action of the light upon the condensing mass of the globe is a problem in the solution of which science may legitimately take an interest. **And divided the waters which were under the firmament from the waters which were above the firmament.** The *upper* waters are not the material of the stars (Delitzsch, Wordsworth), although Jupiter is of the same density as water, and Saturn only half its density; but the waters floating about in the higher spaces of the air. The *under* waters are not the lower atmospheric vapours, but the oceanic and terrestrial waters. How the waters are collected in the upper reaches of the atmosphere, Scripture, no less than science, explains to be by means of evaporation (Gen. ii. 6; Job xxxvi. 27; xxxvii. 16). These latter passages suggest that the clouds are balanced, suspended, upheld by the buoyancy of the air in exact accordance with scientific principles. **And it was so.** Six times these words occur in the creation record. Sublimely suggestive of the resistless energy of the Divine word, which speaks, and it is done, commands, and it standeth fast, they likewise remind us of the sweet submissiveness of the creature to the all-wise Creator's will, and, perhaps, are designed as well to intimate the fixed and permanent character of those arrangements to which they are attached.

Ver. 8.—**And God called the firmament heaven.** Literally, the heights, *shamayim*, as in ver. 1. "This," says Principal Dawson, "may be regarded as an intimation that no definite barrier separates our film of atmosphere from the boundless abyss of heaven without;" and how appropriate the designation "heights" is, as applied to the atmosphere, we are reminded by science, which informs us that, after rising to the height of forty-five miles above the earth, it becomes imperceptible, and loses itself in the universal ether with which it is surrounded. **And the evening and the morning were the second day.** For the literal rendering of this clause see on ver. 5. It is observable that in connection with the second day's work the usual formula, "And God saw that it was good," is omitted. The "καὶ εἶδεν ὁ θεος ὅτι καλόν" of the Septuagint is unsupported by any ancient version. The conceit of the Rabbis, that an expression of the Divine approbation was omitted because on this day the angels fell, requires no refutation. Aben Ezra accounts for its omission by making the second day's work terminate with ver. 10. Lange asks, "Had the prophetic author some anticipation that the blue vault was merely an appearance, whilst the savans of the Septuagint had no such anticipation, and therefore proceeded to doctor the passage?" The explanation of Calvin, Delitzsch, Macdonald, and Alford, though declared by Kalisch to be of no weight, is probably the correct one, that the work begun on the second day was not properly terminated till the middle of the third, at which place, accordingly, the expression of Divine approbation is introduced (see ver. 10).

HOMILETICS.

Ver. 7.—*The atmospheric firmament.* I. THE CREATURE OF GOD. 1. From God it received its being (ver. 7). Not here alone, but in other parts, Scripture declares the firmament to be the Divine handiwork (Ps. xix. 1; civ. 2). Whence we may note—(1) That not *it, the creature,* should receive our worship, but *he, its Maker,* who is God over all, blessed for ever. (2) That since the firmament was made by God, *it must belong to him.* If at the present moment it is the special abode of the prince of the power of the air (Ephes. ii. 2), it must be a usurped dominion. The air with all its beams and showers, quite as much as the earth with all its trees and flowers, is God's property (Gen. xiv. 22; Ps. xxiv. 1, &c.). (3) That in all its movements *it only carries out the will of its Creator.* The air does nothing of itself. Under the reign of law as all created things are, the law that reigns is itself beneath the rule of God. The Hebrew mind never mistook things for persons, or creatures for the Creator (Ps. cxlviii. 8); it is only modern science that degrades the Creator from his throne, and puts the creature in his seat. 2. From God it received its function (ver. 6),—to divide between the upper and the lower waters,— which was—(1) *Simple,* i. e. in the sense of not being complex. Though its uses are manifold, they are all contained in this, that it floats up and sustains the vapours rising from the earth at a sufficient distance from the terrestrial waters. (2) *Necessary.* Without a clear body of atmospheric air between the waters, human life could not have existed. And equally without the watery clouds swimming in the atmosphere, both vegetable and animal life would perish. " Were the air absolutely dry, it would cause the water in plants to evaporate from their leaves more rapidly than it could be supplied to them by the soil and the roots. Thus they would speedily become flaccid, and the whole plant would droop, wither, and die." Similarly, " were the air which man draws into his lungs entirely free from watery fluid, he would soon breathe out the fluids which fill up his tissues, and would dry up into a withered and ghastly mummy " ('Chemistry of Common Life,' vol. i. p. 13). (3) *Beneficent.* Collecting the vapours of the earth in the form of clouds, it is thus enabled to throw them down again in the shape of rain, snow, or dew, according as it is required. 3. From God it received its name. (1) *Suitable.* "Heights," significant of the reality. (2) *Suggestive.* "The love, the power, the majesty of God, his thoughts, his ways, his purposes when compared with man's, are set forth to us by the height of the heaven above the earth."

II. THE SERVANT OF MAN. 1. *Indispensable.* Without the air man could not live. His physical being would perish without its oxygen. Without its pressure his bodily structure would fall to pieces. 2. *Valuable.* The uses of the atmosphere to man as a resident on earth are manifold. It supports animal and vegetable life around him. It conveys, refracts, and decomposes light. It transmits sound. It draws up noxious vapours from the soil, and disperses them by its winds. It assists him in a variety of his mechanical, chemical, commercial, and scientific enterprises. 3. *Willing.* Great as are its powers of service and its capacities of rebellion when excited with tempest, for the most part it is meek and docile, ever ready to acknowledge man as its master, and to execute his slightest wish. 4. *Unwearied.* Ever since it received its appointment from God to minister to the happiness of man it has unrestingly performed that task, and betrays no more signs of weariness to-day than it did at the first. 5. *Gratuitous.* It gives its services, as its great Creator gives his blessings, without money and without price.

Let us learn—1. To be thankful for the air we breathe. 2. To admire God's wisdom in the wonderful adjustments of the air. 3. To make the best use we can of that life which the air supports and subserves.

EXPOSITION.

Ver. 9.—*Day three.* The distribution of land and water and the production of vegetation on this day engaged the formative energy of the word of Elohim. **And God said, Let the waters under heaven be gathered together into one place, and let the dry land appear.** To explain the second part of this phenomenon as a consequence of the first, the disclosure of the solid ground by the retirement of the waters from its surface, and not rather *vice versâ*, is to reverse the ordinary processes of nature. Modern analogy suggests that the breaking up of the hitherto universal ocean into seas, lakes, and rivers was effected by the upheaval of the land through the action of subterranean fires, or the subsidence of the earth's crust in consequence of the cooling and shrinking of the interior mass. Ps. civ. 7 hints at electric agency in connection with the elevation of the mountains and the sinking of the ocean beds. "At thy rebuke they (the waters) fled : at the voice of thy thunder they hasted away (were scattered). The mountains rose, the valleys sank (ἀναβαίνουσιν ὄρη καὶ καταβαίνουσι πεδία—LXX. ; ascendunt montes, et descendunt campi—Jerome) to the place which thou hadst established for them" (Perowne). The gathering of the waters into one place implies no more than that they were, from this day forward, to be collected into one vast body, and restrained within bounds in a place by themselves, so as to admit of the exposure of the earth's soil. The "place founded for them" was, of course, the depths and hollows in the earth's crust, into which they were immediately withdrawn, not through direct supernatural agency, but by their own natural gravitation. The configuration of the dry land is not described ; but there is reason to believe that the original distribution of land and water was the same, or nearly the same, as it is at present. Physical geographers have observed that the coast lines of the great continents and the mountain ranges generally run from north-east to south-west, and that these lines are in reality parts of great circles, tangent to the polar circle, and at right angles to a line drawn from the sun's centre to the moon's, when these bodies are either in conjunction or in opposition. These circles, it has further been remarked, are "the lines on which the thin crust of a cooling globe would be most likely to be ruptured by its internal tidal wave." Hence, though considerably modified by the mighty revolutions through which at successive periods the earth has passed, "these, with certain subordinate lines of fracture, have determined the forms of continents from the

beginning" (Dawson, 'O. W.,' p. 184 ; cf. 'Green's Geology,' p. 512). **And it was so.** Though the separation of the dry land from the waters and the distribution of both were effected by Divine agency, nothing in the Mosaic narrative obliges us to think that these works were instantaneously completed. "There is truly no difficulty in supposing that the formation of the hills kept on through the succeeding creative days" (Lange). "Generally the works of the single creative days consist only in laying foundations ; the birth process that is introduced in each extends its efficacy beyond it" (Delitzsch). "Not *how long,* but *how many times,* God created is the thing intended to be set forth" by the creative days (Hoffman). Scripture habitually represents the world in an aspect at once natural and supernatural, speaking of it as *natura* and *creatura,* φύσις and κτίσις (cf. Martensen's 'Dogmatics,' § 63) ; and although the latter is the view exhibited with greatest prominence, indeed exclusively, in the Mosaic cosmogony, yet the former is not thereby denied. Not immediateness, but certainty of execution, is implied in the "it was so" appended to the creative fiat.

Ver. 10.—**And God called the dry land Earth.** In opposition to the firmament, which was named "the heights" (*shamayim*), the dry land was styled "the flats," "Aretz" (cf. Sansc., *dhara ;* Pehlev., *arta ;* Latin, *terra ;* Gothic, *airtha ;* Scottish, *yird ;* English, *earth ;* vid. Gesenius). Originally applied to the dry ground as distinguished from the seas, as soon as it was understood that the solid earth was continuous beneath the water masses, by an easy extension of meaning it came to signify the whole surface of the globe. **And the gathering together of the waters called he Seas.** *Yamim,* from *yōm,* to boil or foam, is applied in Scripture to any large collection of water (cf. Gen. xiv. 3 ; Num. xxxiv. 11 ; Deut. iv. 49 ; Joel ii. 20). "The plural form *seas* shows that the *one place* consists of several basins" (Murphy). **And God saw that it was good.** The waters having been permanently withdrawn to the place founded for them by the upheaval of the great mountain ranges, and the elevation of the continental areas, the work thus accomplished is sealed by the Divine approval. The separation of the land and water was *good,* as a decided advance towards the completion of the *cosmos,* as the proper termination of the work commenced upon the previous day, as the production of two elements in themselves beautiful, and in separation useful as abodes of life, with which they were in due course to be replenished. "To our view," says Dawson, "that primeval dry land would scarcely have seemed good. It was a world of bare, rocky peaks and verdureless valleys— here active volcanoes, with their heaps of scoriæ, and scarcely cooled lava currents— there vast mud-flats, recently upheaved from the bottom of the waters—nowhere even a blade of grass or a clinging lichen. Yet it was good in the view of its Maker, who could see it in relation to the uses for which he had made it, and as a fit preparatory step to the new wonders he was soon to introduce. . . . . ." Besides, "the first dry land may have presented crags, and peaks, and ravines, and volcanic cones in a more marvellous and perfect manner than any succeeding continents, even as the dry and barren moon now, in this respect, far surpasses the earth" ('O. W.,' p. 181).

Ver. 11.—**And God said, Let the earth bring forth grass, the herb yielding seed, and the fruit tree yielding fruit after his kind, whose seed is in itself, upon the earth: and it was so.** Three terms are employed to describe the vegetation here summoned into existence. Kalisch regards the first as a generic term, including the second and the third ; but they are better understood as distinct classes :—(1) grass, *deshe*, first sprouts of the earth, tender herb, in which the seed is not noticed, as not being obvious to the eye ; "tenera herba sine semine saltem conspicuo" (Rosenmüller) ; probably the various kinds of grasses that supply food for the lower animals (cf. Ps. xxiii. 2) ; (2) "the herb (*eseb*) yielding seed," the more mature herbage, in which the seed is the most striking characteristic ; the larger description of plants and vegetables (cf. ch. ix. 3) ; and (3) "the fruit tree yielding fruit after his kind, whose seed is in itself, upon (or above) the earth." The first clause describes its *specific nature*—"fruit-bearing ;" the second, its *peculiar characteristic*—enclosing the seed in its fruit ; the third, its *external appearance*—rising above the ground. "This division is simple and natural. It proceeds upon two concurrent marks, the structure and the seed. In the first the green blade is prominent ; in the second, the stalk ; in the third, the woody texture. In the first the seed is not conspicuous ; in the second it is conspicuous ; in the third it is enclosed in a fruit which is conspicuous" (Murphy). The phrase "after his kind," appended to the second and third, seems to indicate that the different species of plants were already fixed. The modern dogma of the origin of species by development would thus be declared to be *unbiblical*, as it has not yet been *proved* to be scientific. The utmost that can be claimed as established is that "species," *qua* species,

have the power of variation along the line of certain characteristics belonging to themselves, but not that any absolutely new species has ever been developed with power indefinitely to multiply its kind.

Ver. 12.—**And the earth brought forth grass, and herb yielding seed after his kind, and the tree yielding fruit, whose seed was in itself, after his kind.** It is noticeable that the vegetation of the third day sprang from the soil in the same natural manner in which all subsequent vegetation has done, viz., by growth, which seems to resolve the well-known problem of whether the tree was before the seed, or the seed before the tree, in favour of the latter alternative, although in the order of nature the parent is always before the offspring. In all probability the seed forms were in the soil from the first, only waiting to be vitalised by the *Ruach Elohim*—The Spirit of God ; or they may have been then created. Certainly they were not evolved from the dead matter of the dry land. Scripture, no more than science, is acquainted with Abiogenesis. Believing that "if it were given to her to look beyond the abyss of geologically recorded time," she might "witness the evolution of living protoplasm from not living matter," science yet honestly affirms "that she sees no reason for believing that the feat (of vitalising dead matter) has been performed yet" (Huxley's 'Brit. Association Address,' 1871) ; and Scripture is emphatic that, if it is protoplasm which makes organised beings, the power which manufactures protoplasm is the *Ruach Elohim*, acting in obedience to the *Divine Logos*. The time when the earth put forth its verdure, viz., towards the close of the third day, after light, air, earth, and water had been prepared and so adjusted as to minister to the life of plants, was a signal proof of the wisdom of the Creator and of the naturalness of his working.

Ver. 13.—**And the evening and the morning were the third day.** For exposition *vid.* ver. 5. Has modern geological research any trace of this third day's vegetation ? The late Hugh Miller identified the long-continued epoch of profuse vegetation, since then unparalleled in rapidity and luxuriance, which deposited the coal-measures of the carboniferous system, with the latter half of this Mosaic day. Dana, Dawson, and others, rejecting this conclusion of the eminent geologist on the ground that the underlying Devonian, Silurian, and Cambrian systems yield abundant fossiliferous remains of aquatic life, infer that the third day's vegetation is to be sought for among the "unresolved schists" of the Azoic period. The metamorphic rocks, it is true, have not as yet yielded any absolutely certain traces of vegetable life ; and. indeed, it is an open question.

among geologists whether any of the earliest formed metamorphic rocks now remain (cf. Green's 'Geology,' p. 308) ; but still it is susceptible of almost perfect demonstration that plants preceded animals upon the earth. 1. Among the hypozoic strata of this early period limestone rocks and graphite have been discovered, both of these being of organic origin. 2. In the process of cooling the earth must have been fitted for vegetable life a long time before animals could have existed. 3. As the luxuriant vegetation of the coal period prepared the way for the subsequent introduction of animal life by ridding the atmosphere of carbonic acid, so by the presence of plants must the ocean have been fitted to be the abode of aquatic life. 4. Vegetation, being directly, or mediately, the food of animals, must have had a previous existence. On these grounds Professor Dana concludes that the latter part of the Azoic age of geology corresponds with

the latter half of the third creative day. In the Creation Series of Chaldean tablets are two fragments, which George Smith conjectures have a reference to the first part of the third day's work. The one is—

1. When the foundation of the ground of rock (thou didst make)

2. The foundation of the ground thou didst call . . .

3. Thou didst beautify the heaven . . .

4. To the face of the heaven . . .

5. Thou didst give . . .

The other, which is much more mutilated and obscure, describes the god Sar (or Assur) as saying—

7. Above the sea which is the sea of . . .

8. In front of the *esara* (firmament) which I have made.

9. Below the place I strengthen it

10. Let there be made also *e-lu* (earth ?) for the dwelling of [man ?]

('Chaldean Genesis,' p. 68.)

HOMILETICS.

Vers. 9—12.—*Sea, land, and vegetation, contrasted and compared.* I. Contrasted, in respect of — 1. Their *constitutions;*—sea being matter liquid and mobile, land matter solid and dry, vegetation matter organised and living. All God's creatures have their own peculiar natures and characteristic structures. Each one's nature is that which makes it what it is. A change of constitutional characteristics would be equivalent to an alteration of being. The nature and structure of each are assigned it by God. Whence may be gathered—(1) that if all creatures are not the same, it is because God has so willed it ; (2) that God has so willed it, for this among other reasons, that he delights in variety ; (3) that no separate creature can be other than its individual nature will allow ; (4) that to wish to be different from what God has made us is to be guilty of a foolish as well as sinful discontent ; and (5) that a creature's highest function is to act in accordance with its God-assigned nature. 2. Their *situations;* which were all different, yet all adapted to their respective natures and uses, and all wisely appointed. The waters were gathered into the earth's hollows, the lands raised above the ocean's surface, the plants spread upon the ground. It is the nature of water to seek the lowest levels ; and, collected into ocean, lake, and river beds, it is of infinitely greater value than it would have been had it continued to overspread the globe. Similarly, submerged beneath the waters, neither could the *land* have been arrayed in verdure, or made a habitation for the beasts, much less a home for man ; nor could the *plants* have grown without a dry soil to root in, while their beauty would have been concealed and their utility destroyed. And then each one has the place assigned it by God, out of which it cannot move, and against which it need not fret. The place founded for the waters has received them, and God has set a bound to them that they cannot pass. The dry land still maintains its elevation above the sea ; and, as if in obedience to the Divine Creator's will, the waves are continually building up terraces and raised beaches in compensation for those they are taking down. Nor does it seem possible to shake off the vegetation from the soil. Scarcely has a square inch of ground been recovered from the waters, than it begins to deck itself in green. Let us learn here (1) that every creature of God, man included, has its own place ; which is (2) best suited to its nature, functions, and uses on the earth ; and (3) assigned it by God. Also, (4) that to vacate that place would be to run counter to God's ordinance and to God's wisdom, as well as to its own nature and usefulness ; and (5) that it becomes every one to abide in that sphere of life in which he has been placed by God contentedly, cheerfully and diligently seeking to glorify his Creator. 3. Their *operations;* which are as diversified as are their natures and places. The sea moves, the land rests, the plant grows. The sea fertilises and beautifies the soil, the soil sustains and nourishes the plant, the plant decorates the land and gives food to man and beast. The sea fills the clouds, the clouds fill the rivers and the streams, the rivers and the streams slake the thirst of the valleys, the valleys yield their substance to the corn and the wine and the oil, and these again deliver up their treasures to their master—man. The sea divides the land into continents, which, in turn, are broken up into countries by rivers; and thus nationalities are formed, and peace promoted by division. As the great highway of the nations, too, the sea helps to diffuse abroad the blessings of civilisation, and to teach men their interdependence. So, likewise, the land has its specific functions in the economy of nature, being assigned to support, sustain, enrich, instruct, and comfort man. And different from both are the uses of the plants. All which is fitted to suggest wisdom. (1) That each separate creature has its own separate work to do, for which it has been fitted with appropriate powers—a lesson of diligence. (2) That there are many different ways of serving God in this world—a lesson of charity. (3) That God does not wish all his creatures either to be or to serve alike— a lesson of contentment. (4) That the best way to serve God is to be ourselves and use the powers we possess, without condescending to imitate our neighbours— a lesson of individuality. (5) That though each separate creature has its own nature, place, and power, yet each is subservient to the other, and all to the whole— a lesson of co-operation.

II. Compared, in respect of — 1. Their *natures*, as being God's creatures. Land, sea, and vegetation all owe their existence to his Almighty fiat, and all equally proclaim themselves to be his handiwork. Hence they are all God's property—the earth with its fulness, the sea with its treasures, the plants with their virtues. Consequently man should (1) reverently worship him who made the sea and formed the dry land, and caused the grass to grow; (2) thankfully receive those highly serviceable creatures at God's hand; and, (3) remembering whose they are, and that himself is but a steward, faithfully employ them for their Creator's glory. 2. Their *characters*, as being obedient to the Divine word. "Gathered be the seas," said the word, and the seas were gathered. "Let the dry land appear," and it appeared. "Let the grass grow," and the grass grew. Let the land, sea, and plants be our teachers. Obedience the first duty of a creature. Nothing can compensate for its want (1 Sam. xv. 22). And this obedience must be prompt, complete, and continual, like that of sea, land, and vegetation. 3. *Their varieties.* The seas were divided into oceans, lakes, rivers; the land into mountains, hills, and valleys . the plants into grasses, herbs, and trees. God loves diversity in unity. As in a great house there are vessels of small quantity and vessels of large quantity (Isa. xxii. 24), so in the world are the creatures divided into more important and less. In society men are distributed into ranks and classes according to their greatness and ability; in the Church there are "babes" and there are "perfect men" in Christ; there are those possessed of many talents and much grace, and those whose endowments and acquirements are of smaller dimensions. 4. Their *qualities*, as being all good in their Creator's estimation. The highest excellence of a creature is to be approved by its Maker, not simply commended by its fellow-creature; to be good in the judgment of God, and not merely in the sight of men.

EXPOSITION.

Vers. 14, 15.—*Day four.* With this day begins the second half of the creative week, whose works have a striking correspondence with the labours of the first. Having perfected the main structural arrangements of the globe by the elimination from primeval chaos of the four fundamental elements of light, air, water, and land, the formative energy of the Divine word reverts to its initial point of departure, and, in a second series of operations, carries each of these forward to completion—the light by permanently settling it in the sun, the air and water by filling them with fowl and fish, and the land by making animals and man. The first of these engaged the Divine Artificer's attention on the fourth creative day. **And God said, Let there be lights** (literally, places where light is, light-holders, Ps. lxiv. 16 ; φωστῆρες, LXX. ; *luminaria,* Vulgate ; spoken of lamps and candlesticks, Exod. xxv. 6 ; Num. iv. 9, 16) **in the firmament** (literally, the expanse) **of the heaven.** יְהִי in the singular with מְאֹרֹת in the plural is explained by Gesenius on the ground that the predicate precedes the subject (vid. 'Gram.,' § 147). The scientific accuracy of the language here used to describe the celestial luminaries relieves the Mosaic cosmogony of at least one supposed irreconcilable contradiction, that of representing light as having an existence independent of the sun. Equally does it dispense exegesis from the necessity of accounting for what appears a threefold creation of the heavenly bodies—in the beginning (ver. 1), on the first day (ver. 3), and again on the fourth (ver. 14). The reference in the last of these verses is not to the original creation of the matter of the supramundane spheres (Gerlach), which was performed in the beginning, nor to the first production of light, which was the specific work of day one ; but to the permanent appointment of the former to be the place, or centre of radiation, for the latter. The purpose for which this arrangement was designed, so far, at least, as the earth was concerned, was threefold :—1. **To divide the day from the night.** Literally, between the day and the night ; or, as in ver. 18, to divide the light from the darkness, to continue and render permanent the separation and distinction which was effected on the first day. 2. **And let them be for signs, and for seasons, and for days, and years.** The celestial lights were to serve—(1) For *signs. Othôth,* from *oth,* anything engraved, hence a mark (Gen. iv. 15 ; 2 Kings xx. 8), is employed to designate a *portent,* or sign of warning or instruction (Ps. lxv. 8 ; Isa. viii. 18 ; xx. 3 ; LXX., σημεῖον ; cf. Luke xxi. 25 ; Acts ii. 19), and here probably refers to the subsequent employment of the heavenly bodies " as marks or signs of important changes and occurrences in the kingdom of Providence" (Macdonald). " That they may have been designed also to subserve important purposes in the various economy of human life, as in affording signs to the mariner and husbandman, is not improbable, though this is not so strictly the import of the original " (Bush). Still less, of course, does the word refer to mediæval astrology or to modern meteorology. (2) For *seasons. Moradhim,* set times, from *ya'ad,* to indicate, define, fix, is used of yearly returning periods (Gen. xvii. 21 ; xviii. 14)—the time of the migration of birds (Jer. viii. 7), the time of festivals (Ps. civ. 19 ; Zech. viii. 19). (3) For *days* and *years,* i. e. for the calculation of time. Luther, Calvin, Mercer, Piscator, Delitzsch, Murphy, Macdonald, *et alii* re-

gard the three phrases as co-ordinate ; Rosenmüller, Gesenius, De Wette, Baumgarten take the first two as a *hendiadys* for "signs of the seasons ;" Kalisch considers the second to be in opposition to the first ; Tuch translates, " for signs, as well for the times as also for the days and years." The first, which accords with the English version, is the simplest, and, most probably, the correct interpretation. 3. **And let them be for lights in the firmament of the heaven to give light upon the earth.** Not to introduce light for the first time to this lower world, but to serve as a new and permanent arrangement for the distribution of the light already called into existence. **And it was so.** Like every other fiat which Elohim issued, this was in due time followed by complete realisation.

Ver. 16.—**And God made two great lights.** Perhaps no part of the material universe more irresistibly demands a supreme Intelligence as its only proper origin and cause. "Elegantissima hæcce solis, planetarum et cometarum compages non nisi consilio et dominio entis intelligentis et potentis oriri potuit " (Newton, 'Principia,' lib. iii. sub fin. Ed. of Le Seur and Jacquier, vol. ii. p. 199). **The greater light to rule** (literally, to make like ; hence to judge ; then to rule. *Mashal ;* cf. βασιλεύω—Gesenius) **the day, and the lesser light to rule the night.** The greater light is obviously the sun, which is sometimes denominated *chammah,* "the warm " (Ps. xix. 7 ; Isa. xxx. 26); sometimes *cheres,* "the glistering " (Job ix. 7); but usually *shemesh,* "the minister" (Deut. iv. 19 ; xxxiii. 14). Here it is described by its bulk or magnitude, which is larger than that of the moon, the second of the two luminaries, which is also spoken of as great relatively to the stars, which, though in reality immensely exceeding it in size, yet appear like little balls of light (*kokhavim*) bestudding the blue canopy of night, and are so depicted—the Biblical narrative being geocentric and phenomenal, not heliocentric or scientific. How the work of this day was effected does not fall within the writer's scope to declare, the precise object of revelation being to teach not astronomy, or any other merely human *gnosis,* but religion. Accepting, however, the guidance of physical astronomy, we may imagine that the cosmical light of day one, which had up to this point continued either encompassing our globe like a luminous atmosphere, or existing at a distance from it, but in the plane of the earth's orbit, was now, if in the first of these positions, gradually broken up, doubtless through the shrinking of the earth's mass and the consequent lessening of its power of attraction, and slowly drawn off towards, and finally concentrated, as a photosphere round the sun, which was thereby constituted chief luminary or "light-holder" for the system, the moon and planets becoming, as a necessary consequence, "light-holders" in the secondary sense of "light-reflectors." It is interesting to note that some such explanation as this appears to have suggested itself to Willet, who wrote before the birth of Newton, and at a time when solar physics and spectrum analysis were things of the remote future. "It is not unlike," says he, "but that this light (of the first day), after the creation of the celestial bodies, might be drawn upward and have his reflection upon the beame of the sunne and of other starres." And again, "Whereas the light created the first day is called ōr, but the starres (meaning the heavenly bodies) are called meōrōth, as of the light, hence it may appear that these lightsome (i. e. luminous) bodies were made the receptacles of that light then created, which was now increased and united to these lights" ('Hexapla,' vers. 3, 14, London, 1632); an explanation which, though certainly hypothetical, must be regarded as much more in accordance with the requirements of the sacred text than that which discovers in the making of the lights only a further dissipation of terrestrial mists so as to admit not the light-bringing beams of the celestial bodies alone, but the forms of those shining orbs themselves (Speaker's 'Commentary'). He made **the stars also.** Though the stars are introduced solely because of their relation to the earth as dispensers of light, and no account is taken of their constitution as suns and planets, it is admissible to entertain the opinion that, in their case, as in that of the chief luminary of our tellurian heavens, the process of "sun" making reached its culmination on the fourth day. Perhaps the chief reason for their parenthetical introduction in this place was to guard against the notion that there were any luminaries which were not the work of Elohim, and in particular to prevent the Hebrews, for whom the work was written, from yielding to the heathen practices of star-gazing and star-worship. " The superstition of reading the destiny of man in the stars never took root among the Israelites; astrology is excluded by the first principle of Mosaism—the belief in one all-ruling God, who is subject to no necessity, no fate, no other will. Jeremiah warns the Hebrews not to be afraid of the 'signs of heaven,' before which the heathen tremble in vain terror (Jer. x. 2); and Isaiah speaks with taunting irony against the 'astrologers, star-gazers, and monthly prognosticators,' in whose counsel it is folly and wickedness to rely (Isa. xlvii. 13). But the Israelites had not moral strength enough to resist the example of star-worship in general;

they could not keep aloof from an aberration which formed the very focus of the principal Eastern religions; they yielded to that tempting influence, and ignominious incense rose profusely in honour of the sun and the hosts of heaven—Jer. xix. 13; Ezek. viii. 16; Zeph. i. 5; Wisd. xiii. 2" (Kalisch).

Vers. 17, 18. — **And God set** (literally, gave) **them** (i. e. sun, moon, and stars) **in the firmament of the heaven to give light upon the earth, and to rule over the day and over the night, and to divide the light from the darkness.** An intimation that on this day the astronomical arrangements for the illumination of the globe and the measurement of time were permanently settled. **And God saw that it was good.** Laplace was inclined to question the Divine verdict with regard at least to the moon, which he thought might have been so placed as to be always full, whereas, at its present distance from the earth, we are sometimes deprived of both its light and the sun's together. But not to dwell upon the fact that to remove the moon four times its present distance from the earth, which it would require to be in order to be always full, would necessitate important changes in the other members of the solar system which might not be for the earth's advantage, the immediate effect of such a disposition of the lunar orb would be to give us a moon of only one sixteenth the size of that which now dispenses its silver beams upon our darkened globe (Job xi. 12).

Ver. 19.—**And the evening and the morning were the fourth day.** The Scripture references to this day's work are both numerous and instructive (cf. Job ix. 9; xxxvii. 31; Ps. viii.; xix.; civ.; cxlvii.). The Hebrew writers supply no information as to the astronomical theories which were prevalent in their time; yet "from other sources we have facts leading to the belief that even in the time of Moses there was not a little practical astronomy in the East, and some good theory. The Chaldeans at a very early period had ascertained the principal circles of the sphere, the position of the poles, and the nature of the apparent motions of the heavens as the results of revolution on an inclined axis. The Egyptian astronomers, whom we know through Thales, 640 B.C., taught the true nature of the moon's light, the sphericity of the earth, and the position of its five zones. Pythagoras, 580 B.C., knew, in addition, the obliquity of the ecliptic, the identity of the evening and morning star, and the earth's revolution round the sun" (Dawson, 'O. W.,' p. 207). Modern astronomy, though possessed of highly probable theories as to the formation of the universe, is still unable to speak with absolute precision with regard to this fourth day's work. Yet there are not wanting indirect corroborations of the truth of the Mosaic narrative from both it and geology. According to the sacred writer, the presently existing atmosphere, the distribution of land and water, the succession of day and night, and the regular alternation of the seasons, were established prior to the introduction of animal life upon the earth; and Sir Charles Lyell has demonstrated nothing more successfully than the dominion of "existing causes" from the Eozoic era downwards, and the sufficiency of these causes to account for all the changes which have taken place in the earth's crust. Again, geology attests the prevalence on our globe in prehistoric times of a much more uniform and high temperature than it now possesses, so late as the Miocene era a genial tropical climate having extended up beyond the Arctic circle, and in the earliest eras of the history of the globe, in all probability, the entire sphere being so favoured with excessive heat. Different causes have been suggested for this phenomenon ; as, *e. g.*, the greater heat of the cooling globe (the earliest geologists), a different distribution of land and water (Lyell), variations in the eccentricity of the earth's orbit (Herschell and Croll), changes in the earth's axis (Evans, Drayson, Bell), and the greater intensity of the sun's heat (Sir W. Thomson, 'Trans. Geolog. Soc.,' Glasgow, 1877). The Biblical narrative, by distinctly teaching that the sun was perfected on the fourth day, renders it intelligible that his influence on the surface of the earth was then at its greatest, causing tropical climates to prevail and tropical vegetation to abound, both of which have gradually disappeared from the polar regions in consequence of the sun's diminished heat. It remains only to note that the Chaldean Genesis preserves a striking reminiscence of this day's work ; the obverse of the fifth creation tablet reading

1. It was delightful, all that was fixed by the great gods.
2. Stars, their appearance (in figures) of animals he arranged.
3. To fix the year through the observation of their constellations.
4. Twelve months (or signs) of stars in three rows he arranged.
5. From the day when the year commences unto the close.
6. He marked the positions of the wandering stars (planets) to shine in their courses.

.   .   .   .

12. The god Uru (the moon) he caused to rise out, the night he overshadowed,
13. To fix it also for the light of the night, until the shining of the day.

.   .   .   .

19. When the god Shamas (the sun) in the horizon of heaven in the east.
20. .   .   . formed beautifully and   .   .
21. .   . to the orbit Shamas was perfected.

"It appears that the Chaldean record contains the review and expression of satisfaction at the head of each tablet, while the Hebrew has it at the close of each act" ('Chaldean Genesis,' pp. 69—73).

HOMILETICS.

Ver. 16. — *The celestial luminaries.* I. Display the DIVINE WISDOM. "The heavens declare the glory of God " (Ps. xix. 1). M. Comte believed they declared no other glory than that of Hipparchus, Kepler, Newton, and their successors. Newton agreed with the Hebrew poet (*vid.* Expos. on ver. 16). The astronomical argument in behalf of theism has always been impressive, if not absolutely conclusive. Certainly, granting the Divine existence, nowhere does God's glory shine out more conspicuously ; and perhaps the attribute which most imperiously arrests attention is that of *wisdom.* This would seem to be the aspect of the Divine glory which a contemplation of the midnight heavens discovered to the writer of Ps. civ. (*vid.* ver. 24, which is introduced after a poetic version of the fourth day's work) and of Ps. cxxxvi. (*vid.* ver. 7 in the same connection ; cf. Prov. iii. 19 ; viii. 27 ; Jer. li. 15). Many things about the orbs of heaven evince their Creator's wisdom : these specially—1. Their *formation,* as explained by the highly credible teachings of physical astronomy. 2. Their *varieties*—consisting of sun, moon, planets, comets, nebulæ. 3. Their *motions :* in elliptical and parabolic orbits. 4. Their *dispositions :* the suns, moons, and planets in systems ; the stars in constellations, clusters, galaxies.
II. Attest the DIVINE GOODNESS. Displayed chiefly by the threefold purpose the celestial orbs were designed to serve :—1. *To give light upon the earth.* Even the stars could scarcely be dispensed with without a sense of loss. Feeble as their light is, owing to their immense distance from the earth, they are yet invaluable to voyagers and travellers (Acts xxvii. 20). Still less could the *moon's* light, so pale and silvery in its whiteness, be spared. The night without its chaste beams would

be shrouded in thick gloom, while with them an air of cheerfulness is imparted to the darkened earth. And, of course, least of all could the *sun* be wanted (for 'The Value of Light' *vid.* p. 13). 2. *To distinguish day and night.* The beneficence of this arrangement appears by reflecting on the inconvenience of either of the other two alternatives, perpetual day and perpetual night. The disadvantages of the latter have been indicated; those of the former are scarcely less numerous. The alternation of darkness—(1) Introduces variety in nature, which is always pleasing. Continuous day would be in danger of becoming monotonous, at least in this mundane world, if not in the celestial (Isa. lx. 20; Rev. xxii. 5). (2) Meets the necessities of creature life, by supplying constantly-recurring periods of repose, which are eminently beneficial for the growth of plants, animals, and man. "Vegetable sleep is that relaxation of the vital processes which is indicated by the folding together and drooping of the leaves as night approaches" (Leo Grindon, 'Life : its Nature,' &c., p. 306). The animal tribes generally, with the exception of the wild beasts (Ps. civ. 20), seek repose with the shades of evening. And man, without the recuperative slumber which darkness brings, would speedily exhaust his energies. (3) Solemnises the mind of man, by suggesting thoughts of his frailty, of his end in the sleep of death, but also of his resurrection to the light of a better morning. 3. *To mark times and seasons.* That the different seasons of the year are somehow connected with the celestial bodies is perhaps all that the Mosaic narrative can be made to teach. But we know them to be dependent on the earth's revolution round the sun. And the fact that God has so arranged the earth's relation to the sun as to produce these seasons is a signal proof of the Divine goodness. Another is that God has so fixed and determined their movements as to enable man to measure time by their means. Without the help of sun, moon, and stars chronology would be impossible.

III. Proclaim the DIVINE POWER. More than any other science, astronomy enables us to realise the physical omnipotence of the Deity. Imagination becomes bewildered by the effort to represent the quantity of force required to propel a globe like our earth through the depths of space at the immense velocity of 65,000 miles an hour. What, then, must be the strength of that arm which, in addition, hurls Jupiter, equal in weight to 1400 earths, along his orbit with a velocity of 29,000 miles an hour? And not Jupiter alone, but suns immensely greater, at rates of motion that transcend conception. Well said Job (ch. xxvi. 14). Yet, perhaps, the Divine power is as much evinced by the *perpetuation* of these celestial masses and movements as by their first production. Not only has God made the sidereal firmament, with its stupendous globes and amazing velocities, but he has so established them that since the beginning they have kept on their mystic paths without rebellion and without confusion (Ps. cxlvii. 5).

IV. Reflect the DIVINE BEAUTY. Perhaps glory is the better word. The counterpart of glory in the Creator is beauty in the creature. The celestial luminaries were approved as good, doubtless, for their uses, but likewise for themselves, as being of incomparable splendour. "God hath made everything beautiful in his time" (Eccles. iii. 11). Nothing that God does make can be otherwise than beautiful; and by their splendour, their order, their unity, they seem to mirror forth the majesty, and purity, and oneness of him to whom they owe their being.

HOMILIES BY VARIOUS AUTHORS.

Vers. 14—19.—*The fourth day.* Notice—

I. GOD PREPARES HEAVEN AND EARTH FOR MAN. Light needed for the vegetable world. But when the higher life is introduced, then there is an order which implies intelligence and active rational existence. The signs are for those that can observe the signs. The seasons, days, and years for the being who consciously divides his life.

II. THE LUMINARIES ARE SAID TO RULE THE DAY AND NIGHT. The concentration of light is the appointed method of its diffusion, and adaptation to the purposes of man's existence. So in the moral world and in the spiritual world. There must be rule, system, diversities of gifts, diversities of operations. Distinctions of glory—of the sun, moon, stars. As the *light,* so is the *rule.* Those possessed of much power to enlighten others ought to be rulers by their Divinely-appointed place and work. But all the light which flows from heavenly bodies has first been communicated to them. We give out to others what we receive.

III. This setting out of time reminds us that THE EARTHLY EXISTENCE IS NOT SUPREME, but ruled over until it is itself lifted up into the higher state where day and night and diurnal changes are no more. The life of man is governed here largely by the order of the material universe. But as he grows into the true child of God he rises to a dominion over sun, moon, and stars. 1. *Intellectual.* By becoming master of many of the secrets of nature. 2. *Moral.* The consciousness of fellowship with God is a sense of moral superiority to material things. The sanctified will and affections have a sphere of rule wider than the physical universe, outlasting the perishable earth and sky. 3. *Spiritual.* Man is earthly first, and then heavenly. Human nature is developed under the rule of sun, moon, and stars. In the world where there shall be no more night the consciousness of man will be that of a spirit, not unwitting of the material, but ruling it with angelic freedom and power.—R.

EXPOSITION.

Ver. 20.—*Day five.* The waters and the air, separated on the second day, are on this filled with their respective inhabitants. **And God said.** Nature never makes an onward movement, in the sense of an absolutely new departure, unless under the impulse of the word of Elohim. These words distinctly claim that the creatures of the sea and of the air, even if evolved from material elements, were produced in obedience to Divine command, and not spontaneously generated by the *potentia vitæ* of either land, sea, or sky. **Let the waters bring forth abundantly the moving creature.** Literally, swarm with swarmers, or crawl with crawlers. The fundamental signification of *sharatz* is to creep or swarm, and hence to multiply (Gesenius); or, *vice versâ*, to multiply in masses, and hence to swarm or abound (Fürst; cf. ch. viii. 17; Exod. i. 7; viii. 3). The *sheretzim*, though including small aquatic creatures that have short or no legs, are obviously "all kinds of living creatures inhabiting either land or water which are oviparous and remarkable for fecundity" (Bush). We may, therefore, understand the creative fiat of the fifth day as summoning first into existence the insect creation (in Lev. xi. 20—23 defined as *flying sheretzim*), the fishes of the sea (*sheretzim* of the waters, Lev. xi. 9, 10), and the reptiles and saurians of sea and land (*sheretzim* of the land, Lev. xi. 41, 42). Dawson concludes that "the prolific animals of the fifth day's creation belonged to the three Cuvierian sub-kingdoms of the radiata articulata, mollusca, and to the classes of fish and reptiles among the vertebrata. **That hath life.** *Nephesh chayyah;* literally, a living breath. Here the creatures of the sea are distinguished from all previous creations, and in particular from vegetation, as being possessed of a vital principle. This does not, of course, contradict the well-known

truth that plants are living organisms. Only the life principle of the animal creation is different from that of the vegetable kingdom. It may be impossible by the most acute microscopic analysis to differentiate the protoplasmic cell of vegetable matter from that of animal organisms, and plants may appear to be possessed of functions that resemble those of animals, yet the two are generically different—vegetable protoplasm never weaving animal texture, and plant fibre never issuing from the loom of animal protoplasm. That which constitutes an animal is the possession of respiratory organs, to which, doubtless, there is a reference in the term *nephesh*, from *naphash*, to breathe. **And fowl that may fly.** Literally, let "winged creatures" fly. The fowls include all tribes covered with feathers that can raise themselves into the air. The English version produces the impression that they were made from the waters, which is contrary to ch. ii. 19. The correct rendering disposes of the difficulty. **Above the earth in the open firmament of heaven.** Not above the firmament like the clouds (Von Bohlen, Baumgarten), but in the concave vault (Tuch, Delitzsch), or before the surface of the expanse (Kalisch).

Ver. 21.—**And God created** (*bara*, as in ver. 1, to indicate the introduction of an absolutely new thing, viz., the principle of animal life) **great whales.** *Tanninim*, from *tanan;* Greek, τείνω; Latin, *tendo;* Sansc., *tan*, to stretch. These were the first of the two classes into which the *sheretzim* of the previous verse were divided. The word is used of serpents (Exod. vii. 9; Deut. xxxii. 33; Ps. xci. 13; Jer. li. 34), of the crocodile (Ezek. xxix. 3; xxxii. 2), and may therefore here describe "great sea monsters" in general: τὰ κήτη τὰ μεγάλα (LXX.); "monstrous crawlers that wriggle through the water or scud along the banks" (Murphy); whales, crocodiles, and other sea monsters (Delitzsch); gigantic aquatic and amphibious reptiles (Kalisch, Macdonald). **And every living creature** (*nephesh chayyah*) **which moveth.** Literally, the moving, from *ramas*, to move or creep. This is the second class of *sheretzim.* The term *remes* is specially descriptive of creeping animals (ch. ix. 2), either on land (ch. vii. 14) or in water (Ps. lxix. 35), though here it clearly signifies aquatic tribes. **Which the waters brought forth abundantly after their kind.** The generic terms are thus seen to include many distinct orders and species, created each after its kind. **And every winged fowl after his kind.** Why fowls and fish were created on the same day is not to be explained by any supposed similarity between the air and the water (Luther, Lyra, Calvin, &c.), or any fancied resemblance between the bodily organisms of birds and fishes, but by the circumstance that the firmament and the waters were separated on the second day, to which it was designed that this day should have a correspondence. **And God saw that it was good.** As in every other instance, the productions of this day approve themselves to the Divine Creator's judgment; but on this day he marks his complacency by a step which he takes for the first time, viz., that of pronouncing a benediction on the newly-created tribes. Nothing could more evince the importance which, in the Creator's judgment, attached to this day's work.

Ver. 22.—**And God blessed them.** To bless is to wish well to (ch. xxvii. 4; Num. vi. 23). In the case of God blessing inanimate things, it signifies to make them to prosper and be abundant (Exod. xxiii. 25; Job i. 10; Ps. lxv. 11). The nature of the blessing pronounced upon the animal creation had reference to their propagation and increase. **Be fruitful, and multiply, and fill the waters in the seas, and let fowl multiply in the earth.** The paronomastic combination, *be fruitful and multiply*, became a regular formula of blessing (cf. ch. xxiv. 60; xxxv. 11; xlviii. 4; Ps. cxxviii. 3, 4). The Divine benediction was not simply a wish; but, adds Calvin, "by the bare intimation of his purpose he effects what men seek by entreaty." Nor was it meaningless that the words of benediction were addressed to the creatures; it was designed to teach that the "force of the Divine word was not meant to be transient, but, being infused into their natures, to take root and constantly bear fruit" (Calvin).

Ver. 23.—**And the evening and the morning were the fifth day.** If of the previous creative days geological science has only doubtful traces, of this it bears irrefragable witness. When the first animal life was introduced upon our globe may be said to be as yet *sub judice.* Principal Dawson inclines to claim for the gigantic foraminifer, *eozoon canadense*, of the Laurentian rocks, the honour of being one of the first aquatic creatures that swarmed in terrestrial waters, though Professor Huxley believes that the earliest life is not represented by the oldest known fossils ('Critiques and Addresses,' ix. 1873); but, whether then or at some point of time anterior introduced, geology can trace it upwards through the Palæozoic and Mezozoic eras with the result that is here so exactly defined. Throughout the long ages that fill the interval between the Azoic period of our earth's history and that which witnessed the appearance of the higher animals she is able to detect an unbroken succession of aquatic life, rising gradually from lower to higher forms—from the trilobites and molluscs of the Cambrian and Silurian systems, up through the ganoid fishes of the Devonian and the amphibians of the Carboniferous to the saurian reptiles of the Permian periods. At this point certain ornithic tracks in the superincumbent Triassic strata reveal the introduction upon the scene of winged creatures, and with this accession to its strength and volume the stream of life flows on till the higher animals appear. Thus geology confirms the Scripture record by attesting (1) the priority of marine animals and birds to land animals; (2) the existence of a period when the great sea monsters, with the smaller aquatic tribes and winged fowls of the air, were the sole living creatures on the globe; and (3) that, precisely as Elohim designed life has continued in unbroken succession since the time of its first introduction. It may also be noted that the Palæontological history of the earth's crust suggests a number of considerations that enable us to form a conception of the fifth day's work, which, though not contravened by the Mosaic narrative, is yet by it not explicitly disclosed. For example, whereas it might seem to be the teaching of the inspired writer that the *tanninim*, the *remes*, and the *birds* were created simultaneously, and so were synchronous in their appearance, the testimony of the rocks rather points to a series of creative acts in which successive species of living creatures were summoned into being, as the necessary conditions of existence were prepared for their reception, and indeed with emphasis asserts that the order of creation was not, as in ver. 21, first the great sea monsters, and then the creepers, and then the birds; but first the smaller aquatic tribes, and then the monsters of the deep, and finally the winged creatures of the air. This, however, is not to contradict, but to elucidate, the word of God.

HOMILETICS.

Vers. 20—22.—*The mystery of life.* I. Its ORIGIN. 1. *Not dead matter.* Scripture, equally with science, represents life as having a physical basis ; but, unlike modern evolutionists, never confounds vital force with the material mechanism in which it resided, and through which it operates. Advanced biologists account for life by molecular arrangement, chemical combination, spontaneous generation, or some such equally insufficient hypothesis. The rigorous necessities of truth and logic, however, compel them to admit that neither the action of material forces nor the ingenuity of man has been able to produce a bioplasmic cell. "The chasm between the not living and the living the present state of knowledge cannot bridge" (Huxley). "Most naturalists of our time have given up the attempt to account for the origin of life by natural causes" (Häeckel). But—2. *The living God.* All existing life has proceeded from some antecedent life, is the latest verdict of biological science. Every bioplast has been produced by a previous bioplast: *omnis cellula e cellula.* Essentially that is the teaching of revelation. The Maker of the first bioplast was God. If the present narrative appears to recognise the doctrine of mediate creation by saying, "Let the waters bring forth," "Let the earth bring forth," it is careful to affirm that, in so far as material forces contributed to the production of life, they were directly impelled thereto, and energized therefor, by the creative word. The hypothesis that matter was originally possessed of, or endowed with, "the potency of life" (Tyndall) is expressly negatived by ver. 21, which represents life as the immediate creation of Elohim.

II. Its NATURE. Scripture vouchsafes no information as to what constitutes the *vis viva* of organised beings. Beyond characterising the beings themselves as "living creatures," it leaves the subject wrapped in profoundest mystery. And the veil of that mystery science has not been able to penetrate. The microscope has indeed conclusively shown that living matter, or bioplasm, is that which weaves the endlessly varied structures of animal forms ; but as to what that is which imparts to the transparent, structureless, albuminous fluid, called bioplasm, the power of self-multiplication and organisation it is silent. "We fail to detect any organisation in the bioplasmic mass, but there are movements in it and life" (Huxley). The utmost that science can give as its definition of life is, "that which originates and directs the movements of bioplasm" (cf. 'Beale on Protoplasm ;' Cook's 'Lectures on Biology'). Scripture advances a step beyond science, and affirms that life in its last analysis is the power of God (Ps. civ. 30 ; Isa. xxxviii. 16).

III. Its MANIFESTATION. 1. *Abundant.* The creatures of the sea were produced in swarms, and probably the birds appeared in flocks. This was—(1) Predictive of their natures as gregarious animals. Though afterwards prolific, they might have been created in small numbers ; but, as if to maintain a correspondence between the characteristic properties of the creatures and their first production, they were made, the fish in shoals, the fowl in broods. (2) Expressive of the Creator's joy. God finds a part of His happiness in surrounding himself with living creatures. Had there been no other end to serve by the fish and fowl of the fifth day, this would have been cause sufficient for their creation. (3) Anticipative of man's arrival on the scene. Not only was it a step in advance on the work of the previous day, and as such preliminary to the advent of man, but the aquatic and aerial creatures were designed to be subservient to man's needs and uses. 2. *Varied.* (1) In its form. The living creatures of the fifth day were diverse in their physical structures. Though in the initial stages of their embryonic condition fish and fowl may not be widely dissimilar, yet their completed organisms are not the same. Each class, too, consists of an endlessly diversified array of species, and the variations among individual members of the same species are practically limitless. (2) In its functions. Although all living creatures have certain essential characteristics in common, resembling one another in their chemical constituents, in their living by respiration, in their growth by intersusception of nutriment, in their capability of reproduction, yet the ordinary functions they are meant to perform through their respective organs are different in different kinds of animals. The fowls, *e. g.*, were designed to fly through the atmosphere ; the fish to swim in water. (3) In its sphere. The different living creatures are differently located,—the fish in the sea, the birds in the air,—each one's sphere being adapted to its nature. 3. *Progressive.* Science, no less than Scripture, attests that in the introduction of life to our globe there has been a regular and continuous gradation from lower to higher forms of organisation, and has ventured to propose, as its solution of the problem of vital progression, external conditions, embryonic phases, use and disuse of organs, natural selection, &c. These theories, however, are declared by competent authorities to be insufficient (*vid.* Page's ' Philosophy of Geology,' p. 108). The solution of Scripture —*special creation*—has at least the merit of being sufficient, and has not yet been disproved or displaced by modern research.

IV. ITS EXCELLENCE. God saw that it was good—1. As *the handiwork of God.* Nothing that God makes can be otherwise than beautiful and good (Eccles. iii. 11 ; 1 Tim. iv. 4). 2. As *an ornament to nature.* Without the vegetation of the third day the world would present an extremely uninteresting and uninviting appearance. Much more would it be devoid of attraction and cheerfulness if the myriads of sentient beings with which it is peopled were absent. 3. As *the servant of man.* From the first it was prepared with the express intention of being subjected to man's dominion, and doubtless the Creator's approbation had regard to this beneficent design.

V. ITS PERPETUATION. " Of the causes which have led to the origination of living matter," says Huxley, " we know absolutely nothing ; but, postulating the existence of living matter endowed with that power of hereditary transmission and with that tendency to vary which is found in all matter, Mr. Darwin has shown good reason for believing that the interaction between living matter and surrounding conditions, which results in the survival of the fittest, is sufficient to account for the gradual evolution of plants and animals from their simplest to their most complex forms " (' Ency. Brit.,' art. Biology). Moses accounts for the origination of living creatures by a Divine creation, and for their continuance by the Divine benediction which made it the law of their being to propagate their kind and to multiply in masses. The remarkable fecundity which by the blessing of Elohim was conferred upon both fish and fowl is graphically portrayed by Milton (' Par. Lost,' vii. 387). That from neither the aquatic nor aerial creatures has this power of kind-multiplication departed naturalists attest. " All organised beings have enormous powers of multiplication. Even man, who increases slower than all other animals, could, under the most favourable circumstances, double his numbers every fifteen years, or a hundred-fold in a century. Many animals and plants could increase their numbers from ten to a thousand-fold every year " (Wallace ' on Natural Selection,' p. 265).

Lessons :—1. Adore him who is the Author and Preserver of all life in the creatures. 2. Respect the mystery of life ; and what we cannot give let us be careful not to destroy. 3. Appreciate the value of the living creatures.

HOMILIES BY VARIOUS AUTHORS.

Vers. 20—23.—*The fifth day.* I. LIFE UNDER THE BLESSING OF GOD. 1. *Abundance.* Swarming waters, swarming air, preparing for the swarming earth. " Be fruitful, and multiply." The absence of all restraint because as yet the absence of sin. God's law is liberty. The law of life is the primary law. If there be in man's world a contradiction between the multiplication of life and the happiness of life, it is a sign of departure from the original order. 2. *Growth,* improvement, advancement towards perfection. The fish, fowl, beast, man exist in a scheme of things ; the type of animal life is carried up higher. The multiplication is not for its own sake, but for the future. Generations pass away, yet there is an abiding blessing. Death is not real, though seeming, destruction. There is a higher nature which is being matured. 3. *Service of the lower for the higher.* God blesses the animal races for the sake of man, the interpreter of creation, the voice of its praise. He blesses the lower part of human life for the sake of the soul.

II. LIFE UNDER THE GOVERNMENT OF GOD. The immense productiveness of nature would become a curse, not a blessing, unless restrained by its own laws. The swarming seas and air represent at once unbounded activity and universal control by mutual dependence and interaction. So in the moral world. It is not life, existence, alone that betokens the blessing of God, but the disposition of life to fulfil its highest end. We should not desire abundance without the grace which orders its use and controls its enjoyment.—R.

EXPOSITION.

Ver. 24. — *Day six.* Like day three, this is distinguished by a double creative act, the production of the higher or land animals and the creation of man, of the latter of which it is perhaps permissible to see a mute prediction in the vegetation which closed the first half of the creative week. **And God said, Let the earth bring forth the living creature after his kind.** In these words the land animals are generically characterised as *nephesh chayyah*, or animated beings ; in the terms which follow they are subdivided into three well-defined species or classes. **Cattle.** *Behemah ;* literally, the dumb animal, *i. e.* the larger grass-eating quadrupeds. **And creeping thing.** *Remes ;* the moving animal, *i. e.* the smaller animals that move either without feet or with feet that are scarcely perceptible, such as worms, insects, reptiles. Here it is land-creepers that are meant, the *remes* of the sea having been created on the previous day. **And beast of the earth** (*chayyah* of the earth) **after his kind.** *I. e.* wild, roving, carnivorous beasts of the forest. In these three comprehensive orders was the earth commanded to produce its occupants ; which, however, no more implied that the animals were to be developed from the soil than were the finny tribes generated by the sea. Simply in obedience to the Divine call, and as the product of creative energy, they were to spring from the plastic dust as being essentially earth-born creatures. **And it was so.** Modern evolutionists believe they can conceive—they have never yet been able to demonstrate—the *modus operandi* of the supreme Artificer in the execution of this part of the sixth day's work. Revelation has not deemed it needful to do more than simply state that they were—not, by an evolutionary process carried on through inconceivably long periods of time, developed from the creatures of the fifth day, but—produced directly from the soil by the fiat of Elohim.

Ver. 25. — **And God made** (*asah*, not *bara*, the principle of life being not now introduced for the first time, as in ver. 21) **the beast of the earth** (the *chayyah*) **after his kind, and cattle** (*behemah*) **after their kind, and every thing that creepeth on the earth** (literally, every *remes* of the ground) **after his kind.** The order of creation (ver. 25) differs from that in which they were summoned into existence (ver. 24). The latter may be the order of time, the former the order of rank ; or there may have been two divisions of the work, in the former of which the *herbivora* took the lead, and in the latter the *carnivora.* According to the witness of geology, "the quadrupeds did not all come forth together. Large and powerful *herbivora* first take the field, with only a few *carnivora.* These pass away. Other *herbivora,* with a larger proportion of *carnivora,* next appear. These also are exterminated, and so with others. Then the *carnivora* appear in vast numbers and power, and the *herbivora* also abound. Moreover, these races attain a magnitude and number far surpassing all that now exist. As the mammalian age draws to a close, the ancient *carnivora* and *herbivora* of that era all pass away, excepting, it is believed, a few that are useful to man. New creations of smaller size people the groves" (Dana. Quoted by Dawson, 'O. W.' p. 224). **And God saw that it was good.** As in the third day's work each branch is sealed by the Divine approbation, so in this. The creation of the higher animals completed the earth's preparation for the advent of man ; to which, doubtless, the Creator's commendation of his finished work had a special reference. Everything was in readiness for the *magnum opus* which was to close his creative labour and crown his completed cosmos.

Ver. 26.—The importance assigned in the Biblical record to the creation of man is indicated by the manner in which it is introduced. **And God said, Let us make man.** Having already explained the significance of the term *Elohim,* as suggesting the fulness of the Divine personality, and foreshadowing the doctrine of the Trinity (ver. 1), other interpretations, such as that God takes counsel with the angels (Philo, Aben Ezra, Delitzsch), or with the earth (Maimonides, M. Gerundius), or with himself (Kalisch), must be set aside in favour of that which detects in the peculiar phraseology an allusion to a sublime *concilium* among the persons of the Godhead (Calvin, Macdonald, Murphy). The object which this *concilium* contemplated was the construction of a new creature to be named *Adam;* descriptive of either his *colour,* from *adam,* to be red, (Josephus, Gesenius, Tuch, Hupfeld) ; or his *appearance,* from a root in Arabic which signifies "to shine," thus making Adam "the brilliant one ;" or his *compactness,* both as an individual and as a race, from another Arabic root which means "to bring or hold together" (Meier, Fürst) ; or his *nature* as God's image, from *dam,* likeness (Eichorn, Richers) ; or, and most probably, his *origin,* from *adamah,* the ground (Kimchi, Rosenmüller, Kalisch). **In our image, after our likeness.** The precise relationship in which the nature of the *Adam* about to be produced should stand to *Elohim* was to be that of a *tselem* (shadow—*vid.* Ps. xxxix. 7 ; Greek, σκιά, σκίασμα) and a *damuth* (likeness, from *damah,* to bring together, to compare—Isa. xl. 8). As nearly as possible the terms are synonymous. If any distinction does exist between them, perhaps *tselem* (image) denotes the shadow outline of a figure, and *damuth* (likeness) the correspondence or resemblance of that shadow to the figure. The early Fathers were of opinion that the words were expressive of separate ideas : *image,* of the body, which by reason of its beauty, intelligent aspect, and erect stature was an adumbration of God ; *likeness,* of the soul, or the intellectual and moral nature. According to Augustine *image* had reference to the *cognitio veritatis ; likeness* to *amor virtutis.* Irenæus, Clement, and Origen saw in the first man nature as originally created, and in the second what that nature might become through personal ethical conflict, or through the influence of grace. Bellarmine thought "imaginem in natura, similitudinem in probitate et justitia sitam esse," and conceived that " Adamum peccando non imaginem Dei, sed similitudinem perdidisse." Hävernick suggests that *image* is the concrete, and *likeness* the abstract designation of the idea. Modern expositors generally discover no distinction whatever between the words ; in this respect following Luther, who renders *an image that is like,* and Calvin, who denies that any difference exists between the two. As to what in man constituted the *imago Dei,* the reformed theologians commonly held it to have consisted (1) in the spirituality of his being, as an intelligent and free agent ; (2) in the moral integrity and holiness of his nature ; and (3) in his dominion over the creatures (cf. West. Conf., ch. iv. 2). In this connection the profound thought of Maimonides, elaborated by Tayler Lewis (*vid.* Lange, *in loco*), should not be overlooked, that *tselem* is the specific, as opposed to the architectural, form of a thing; that which inwardly makes a thing what it is, as opposed to that external configuration which it actually possesses. It corresponds to the *min,* or kind, which determines species among animals. It is that which constitutes the genus *homo.* **And let them have dominion.** The relationship of man to the rest of creation is now defined to be one of rule and supremacy. The employment of the plural is the first indication that not simply an individual was about to be called into existence, but a race, comprising many individuals. The range of man's authority is further specified, and the sphere of his lordship traced by an enumeration in ascending order, from the lowest to the highest, of the subjects placed beneath his sway. His dominion should extend **over the fish of the sea, and over the fowl of the air** (literally, the heavens), **and over the cattle** (the *behemah*), **and over all the earth, and over every creeping thing** (*remes*) **that creepeth upon the earth.**

Ver. 27.—**So** (or *and*) **God created** (*bara,* as in vers. 1, 21, *q. v.*) **man** (literally, the *Adam* referred to in ver. 26) **in his** own **image, in the image of God created he him ; male and female created he them.** The threefold repetition of the term "created" should be observed as a significant negation of modern evolution theories as to the descent of man, and an emphatic proclamation of his Divine original. The threefold parallelism of the members of this verse is likewise suggestive, as Umbreit, Ewald, and Delitzsch remark, of the jubilation with which the writer contemplates the crowning work of Elohim's creative word. Murphy notices two stages in man's creation, the general fact being stated in the first clause of this triumphal song, and the two particulars—first his relation to his Maker, and second his sexual distinction—in its other members. In the third clause Luther sees an intimation "that the woman also was created by God, and made a partaker of the Divine image, and of dominion over all."

Ver. 28.—**And God blessed them.** Not *him,* as LXX. As on the introduction of animal life the Divine Creator conferred on the creatures his blessing, so when the first pair of human beings are formed they are likewise enriched by their Creator's benediction. **And God said unto them, Be fruitful, and multiply.** As in the case of the lower creatures the Divine blessing had respect in the first instance to the propagation and perpetuation of the species, "which blessing," says Calvin, "may be regarded as the source from which the human race has flowed," a thought in full accord with Scripture teaching generally (cf. Ps. cxxvii. 3) ; yet by making one man and one woman an important distinction was drawn between men and beasts as regards the development of their races and the multiplication of their kind (Mal. ii. 7).

" Certe frænum viris et mulieribus non laxavit, ut in vagas libidines ruerent, absque delectu et pudore ; sed a sancto castoque conjugio incipiens, descendit ad generationem" (Calvin). **And replenish the earth.** The new-created race was intended to occupy the earth. How far during the first age of the world this Divine purpose was realised continues matter of debate (ch. x.). After the Flood the confusion of tongues effected a dispersion of the nations over the three great continents of the old world. At the present day man has wandered to the ends of the earth. Yet vast realms lie unexplored, waiting his arrival. This clause may be described as *the colonist's charter*. **And subdue it.** The commission thus received was to utilise for his necessities the vast resources of the earth, by agricultural and mining operations, by geographical research, scientific discovery, and mechanical invention. **And have dominion over the fish of the sea,** &c. *I. e.* over the inhabitants of all the elements. The Divine intention with regard to his creation was thus minutely fulfilled by his investiture with supremacy over all the other works of the Divine hand. Ps. viii. is the "lyric echo" of this original sovereignty bestowed on man.

Ver. 29.—Provision for the sustenance of the newly-appointed monarch and his subjects is next made. **And God said, Behold, I have given you every herb bearing seed,** which is upon the face of all the earth, and every tree, in the which is the fruit of a tree yielding seed ; to you it shall be for meat. Of the three classes into which the vegetable creation was divided, grass, herbs, and trees (ver. 12), the two last were assigned to man for food. Macdonald thinks that without this express conveyance man would have been warranted to partake of them for nourishment, warranted by the necessities of his nature. The same reasoning, however, would have entitled him to kill the lower animals if he judged them useful for his support. Murphy with more truth remarks, "Of two things proceeding from the same creative hand, neither has any original or inherent right to interfere in any way with the other. The absolute right to each lies in the Creator alone. The one, it is true, may need the other to support its life, as fruit is needful to man ; and, therefore, the just Creator cannot make one creature dependent for subsistence on another without granting to it the use of that other. But this is a matter between Creator and creature, and not by any means between creature and creature." The primitive charter of man's common property in the earth, and all that it contains, is the present section of this ancient document. Among other reasons for the formal conveyance to man of the herbs and trees may be noted a desire to keep him mindful of his dependent condition. Though lord of the creation, he was yet to draw the means of his subsistence from the creature which he ruled. Whether man was a vegetarian prior to the fall is debated. On the one hand it is contended that the original grant does not formally exclude the animals, and, in fact, says nothing about man's relation to the animals (Macdonald) ; that we cannot positively affirm that man's dominion over the animals did not involve the use of them for food (Murphy) ; and that as men offered sacrifices from their flocks, it is probable they ate the flesh of the victims (Calvin). On the other hand it is argued that the Divine language cannot be held as importing more than it really says, and that ch. ix. 3 distinctly teaches that man's right to the animal creation dates from the time of Noah (Kalisch, Knobel, Alford, &c.). Almost all nations have traditions of a golden age of innocence, when men abstained from killing animals (cf. Ovid, 'Met.,' i. 103—106). Scripture alone anticipates a. time when such shall again be a characteristic of earth's inhabitants (Isa. xi. 7 ; lxv. 25).

Ver. 30.—**And to every beast of the earth, and to every fowl of the air, and to every thing that creepeth upon the earth, wherein** there is life, I have given **every green herb for meat.** The first of the three classes of plants, grass, was assigned to the animals for food. From this Delitzsch infers that prior to the introduction of sin the animals were not predaceous. The geological evidence of the existence of death in prehistoric times is, however, too powerful to be resisted ; and the Biblical record itself enumerates among the pre-adamic animals the chayyah of the field, which clearly belonged to the carnivora. Perhaps the most that can be safely concluded from the language is "that it indicates merely the general fact that the support of the whole animal kingdom is based on vegetation" (Dawson).

Ver. 31.—**And God saw every thing that he had made, and, behold, it was very good.** Literally, lo ! good very ! Not simply good, but good exceedingly. It is not man alone that God surveys, but the completed cosmos, with man as its crown and glory, *decus et tutamen*. "It is not merely a benediction which he utters, but an expression of admiration, as we may say without any fear of the anthropomorphism — *Euge, bene preclare!*" (T. Lewis). **And the evening and the morning were the sixth day.** It seems unnecessary to add that this day corresponds to the Cainozoic or tertiary era of geology, the Palæontological remains of which sufficiently attest the truth of the Divine record in asserting that animals were anterior to man in their appearance on the earth, and that man is of comparatively recent origin.

The alleged evidence of prehistoric man is too fragmentary and hypothetical to be accepted as conclusive ; and yet, so far as the cosmogony of the present chapter is concerned, there is nothing to prevent the belief that man is of a much more remote antiquity than 6000 years. As of the other days, so of this the Chaldean tablets preserve an interesting monument. The seventh in the creation series, of which a fragment was discovered in one of the trenches at Kouyunjik, runs:—

1. When the gods in their assembly had created . . . .

2. Were delightful the strong monsters. .
3. They caused to be living creatures . .
4. Cattle of the field, beasts of the field, and creeping things of the field . . . .
5. They fixed for the living creatures . .
6. . . . . . Cattle and creeping things of the city they fixed . . . .

 . . . .
9. . . . . . And the god Nin-si-ku (the lord of noble face) caused to be two . . . in which it is not difficult to trace an account of the creation of the animal kingdom, and of the first pair of human beings.

HOMILETICS.

Ver. 27.—*The greatness of man.* I. THE TIME OF HIS APPEARANCE. The latest of God's works, he was produced towards the close of the era that witnessed the introduction upon our globe of the higher animals. Taking either view of the length of the creative day, it may be supposed that in the *evening* the animals went forth "to roar after their prey, and seek their meat from God," and that in the *morning* man arose upon the variegated scene, "going forth to his work and to his labour until the evening" (Ps. civ. 20—23). In this there was a *special fitness,* each being created at the time most appropriate to its nature. Man's works are often mistimed ; God's never. Likewise in man's being ushered last upon the scene there was *peculiar significance;* it was a virtual proclamation of his greatness.

II. THE SOLEMNITY OF HIS MAKING, which was preceded by a Divine consultation: "Let us make man," &c. The language of—1. *Resolution.* As if, in the production of the other creatures, the all-wise Artificer had been scarcely conscious of an effort, but must now bestir himself to the performance of his last and greatest work. 2. *Forethought.* As if his previous makings had been, in comparison with this, of so subordinate importance that they might be executed instantaneously and, as it were, without premeditation, whereas this required intelligent arrangement and wise consideration beforehand. 3. *Solicitude.* As if the insignificance of these other labours made no special call upon his personal care and attention, whereas the vastness of the present undertaking demanded the utmost possible watchfulness and caution. 4. *Delight.* As if the fashioning and beautifying of the globe and its replenishing with sentient beings, unspeakably glorious as these achievements were afforded him no satisfaction in comparison with this which he contemplated, the creating of man in his own image (cf. Prov. viii. 31).

III. THE DIGNITY OF HIS NATURE. "Created after God's image and likeness," suggesting ideas of—1. *Affinity,* or kinship. The resplendent universe, with its suns and systems, its aerial canopy and green-mantled ground, its Alps and Himalayas, its oceans, rivers, streams, was only as plastic clay in the hands of a skilful potter. Even the innumerable tribes of living creatures that had been let loose to swarm the deep, to cleave the sky, to roam the earth, were animated by a principle of being that had no closer connection with the Deity than that which effect has with cause ; but the life which inspired man was a veritable outcome from the personality of God (Gen. ii. 7). Hence man was something higher than a creature. As *imago Dei* he was God's son (Mal. ii. 10 ; Acts xvii. 28). 2. *Resemblance.* A distinct advance upon the previous thought, although implied in it. This likeness or similitude consisted in—(1) Personality. Light, air, land, sea, sun, moon, stars were "things." Plants, fishes, fowls, animals were "lives," although the first are never so characterised in Scripture. Man was a "person." (2) Purity. The image of absolute holiness must itself be immaculate. In this sense Christ was "the *express* image of God's person" (Heb. i. 3) ; and though man is not now a complete likeness of his Maker in the moral purity of his nature, when he came from the Creator's hand he was. It is the object of Christ's work to renew in man the image of his Maker (Ephes. iv. 24). (3) Power. That man's Creator was a God of power was implied in his name, ELOHIM, and demonstrated by his works. Even fallen man we can perceive to be possessed of many elements of power that are the shadows of that which resided in Elohim—the power of self-government, and of lordship over the creatures, of language and of thought, of volition and of action, of originating, at least in a secondary sense, and of combining and arranging. In the first man they resided in perfection. 3. *Representation.* Man was created in God's image that he might be a visible embodiment of the Supreme to surrounding creatures. "The material world, with its objects sublimely great or meanly little, as we judge them; its atoms of dust, its orbs of fire; the rock that stands by the seashore, the water that wears it away; the worm, a birth of yesterday, which we trample underfoot; the sheets of the constellations that gleam perennial overhead; the aspiring palm tree fixed to one spot, and the lions that are sent out free—these incarnate and make visible all of God their natures will admit." Man in his nature was intended as the highest representation of God that was possible short of the incarnation of the Word himself.

IV. THE GRANDEUR OF HIS DOMINION. Man was designed to be God's image in respect of royalty and lordship; and as no one can play the monarch without a kingdom and without subjects, God gave him both an empire and a people. 1. *An empire.* (1) Of wide extent. In the regal charter reaching to the utmost bounds of this terrestrial sphere (ver. 26). (2) Of available character. Not a region that was practically unconquerable, but every square inch of it capable of subjugation and occupation. (3) Of vast resources. Everything in heaven, earth, and sea was placed at his command. (4) Of incalculable value. Nothing was absolutely useless, and many things were precious beyond compare. (5) Of perfect security. God had given it to him. The grant was absolute, the gift was sure. 2. *A people.* (1) Numerous. "Every living thing" was subjected to his sway. (2) Varied. The fishes, fowls, and beasts were his servants (3) Submissive. As yet they had not broken loose against their master. (4) Given. They were not acquired by the sword, but donated by their Maker.

HOMILIES BY VARIOUS AUTHORS.

Vers. 24—31.—*The sixth day.* We pass from the sea and air to the earth. We are being led to man. Notice—

I. THE PREPARATION IS COMPLETE. Before the earth receives the human being, it brings forth all the other creatures, and God sees that they are good—good in his sight, good for man.

II. THE PURPOSE OF THE WORK IS BENEVOLENT. Cattle, creeping thing, beast of the earth. So man would see them distinguished—the wild from the domestic, the creeping from the roaming, the clean from the unclean. The division itself suggests the immense variety of the Divine provision for man's wants.

III. The incompleteness of the earth when filled with the lower creatures is A TESTIMONY TO THE GREATNESS OF MAN'S SPIRITUAL NATURE; for in comparison with the animal races he is in many respects inferior—in strength, swiftness, and generally in the powers which we call instinct. Yet his appearance is the climax of the earth's creation. "Man is one world, and hath another to attend him." Vegetable, marine, animal life generally, the whole earth filled with what God "saw to be good," waits for the rational and spiritual creature who shall be able to recognise their order and wield dominion over them. Steps and stages in creation lead up to the climax, the "paragon of animals," the god-like creature, made to be king on the earth.—R.

Vers. 26, 27.—*The creation of man.* Take it—I. As a revelation of God in his relation to man. II. As a revelation of man to himself.

I. GOD IN RELATION TO MAN. 1. As the *Father* as well as *Creator.* As to the rest of creation, it is said, "Let be," and "it was." As to man, "Let us make in our image." Closely kin by original nature, man is invited to intercourse with the Divine. 2. The *spirituality* of God's highest creature is the bond of union and fellowship. The language, "Let us make," suggests the conception of a heavenly council or conference preparatory to the creation of man; and the new description of the being to be created points to the introduction of a new order of life—the spiritual life, as above the vegetable and animal. 3. God intrusts *dominion* and authority to man in the earth. Man holds from the first the position of a vicegerent for God. There is trust, obedience, responsibility, recognition of Divine supremacy, therefore all the essential elements of religion, in the original constitution and appointment of our nature and position among the creatures. 4. The ultimate *destiny* of man is included in the account of his beginning. He who made him in his image, " one of us," will call him upward to be among the super-earthly beings surrounding the throne of the Highest. The possession of a Divine image is the pledge of eternal approximation to the Divine presence. The Father calls the children about himself.

II. MAN REVEALED TO HIMSELF. "The image and likeness of God." What does that contain? There is the ideal humanity. 1. There is an *affinity* in the intellectual nature between the human and the Divine. In every rational being, though feeble in amount of mental capacity, there is a sense of eternal necessary truth. On some lines the creature and the Creator think under the same laws of thought, though the distance be immeasurable. 2. Man *is by original creation absolutely free from moral taint*. He is therefore a fallen being in so far as he is a morally imperfect being. He was made like God in purity, innocence, goodness. . 3. The resemblance must be in *spirit* as well as in intellect and moral nature. Man was made to be the companion of God and angels, therefore there is in his earthly existence a super-earthly, spiritual nature which must be ultimately revealed. 4. *Place and vocation* are assigned to man on earth, and that in immediate connection with his likeness to God. He is ruler here that he may be prepared for higher rule elsewhere. He is put in his rank among God's creatures that he may see himself on the ascent to God. Man belongs to two worlds. He is like God, and yet he is male and female, like the lower animals. He is blessed as other creatures with productive power to fill the earth, but he is blessed for the sake of his special vocation, to subdue the earth, not for himself, but for God. 5. Here is the *end of all our endeavour* and desire—to be perfect men by being like God. Let us be thankful that there is a God-man in whom we are able to find our ideal realised. We grow up into him who is our Head. We see Jesus crowned with glory and honour. When all things are put under him, man will see the original perfection of his creation restored. 6. Man is taught *that he need not leave the earthly sphere to be like God*. There has been a grand preparation of his habitation. From a mere chaotic mass the earth has by progressive stages reached a state when it can become the scene of a great moral experiment for man's instruction. The god-like is to rule over all other creatures, that he may learn the superiority of the spiritual. Heavenly life, communion, society, and all that is included in the fellowship of man with God, may be developed in the condition of earth. Grievous error in early Church and Eastern philosophy—confusion of the material and evil. Purity does not require an immaterial mode of existence. Perfection of man is perfection of his dominion over earthly conditions, matter in subjection to spirit. Abnormal methods, asceticism, self-crucifixion, mere violence to original constitution of man. The "second Adam" overcame the world not by forsaking it, but by being in it, and yet not of it. 7. God's commandments to man are *commandments of Fatherly love*. "*Behold, I have given you*," &c. He not only appoints the service, but he provides the sustenance. "*Seek ye first the kingdom of God*," &c. Here is the union of creative power and providential goodness. We are blessed in an earthly life just as we take it from the hand of God as a trust to be fulfilled for him. And in that obedience and dependence we shall best be able to reach the ideal humanity. The fallen world has been degrading man, physically, morally, spiritually; he has been less and less what God made him to be. But he who has come to restore the kingdom of God has come to uplift man and fill the earth with blessedness.—R.

Ver. 31.—*Perfection*. The first chapter closes with a review of the whole work of the six days. God saw it. Behold, it was very good!

I. The SATISFACTION was in the completion of the earthly order in man, the highest earthly being. For God's "*good*" is not, like man's "*good*," a compromise, too

often, between the really good and the really evil, but the attainment of the *highest*
—the fulfilment of his Divine idea, the top-stone placed upon the temple with shout-
ings : " Grace, grace unto it."

II. " The evening and the morning were the sixth day." OUT OF THE NIGHT OF
THE INFINITE PAST CAME FORTH THE DAWN OF THE INTELLECTUAL AND SPIRITUAL
WORLD. And when God saw that, then he said, It is very good. So let us set our
faces towards that light of heaven on earth, the *day of Divine revelation*, Divine
intercourse with man, the pure and perfect bliss of an everlasting paradise, in which
God and man shall find unbroken rest and joy in one another.—R.

EXPOSITION.

CHAPTER II.

Ver. 1.—**Thus the heavens and the earth
were finished.** Literally, And finished were
the heavens and the earth, the emphatic
position being occupied by the verb. With
the creation of man upon the sixth day the
Divine Artificer's labours were brought to a
termination, and his work to a completion.
The two ideas of cessation and perfection
are embraced in the import of *calah*. Not
simply had Elohim paused in his activity,
but the Divine idea of his universe had been
realised. The finished world was a cosmos,
arranged, ornamented, and filled with organised, sentient, and rational beings, with
plants, animals, and man ; and now the resplendent fabric shone before him a magnificent success — "lo ! very good." This
appears to be by no means obscurely hinted
at in the appended clause, **and all the host
of them,** which suggests the picture of a
military armament arranged in marching
order. *Tsebaam*, derived from *tsaba*, to go
forth as a soldier (Gesenius), to join together
for service (Fürst), and applied to the angels
(στρατία οὐράνιος, Luke ii. 13. 1 Kings xxii.
19 ; 2 Chron. xviii. 18 ; Ps. cxlviii. 2) and
to the celestial bodies (δύναμεις τῶν οὐρανῶν,
Matt. xxiv. 29. Isa. xxxiv. 4 ; xl. 26 ;
Dan. viii. 10), here includes, by Zeugma,
the material heavens and earth with the
angelic and human races (cf. Neh. ix. 6). If
the primary signification of the root be splendour, glory, like *tsavah*, to come forth or
shine out as a star (T. Lewis), then will the
LXX. and the Vulgate be correct in translating πᾶς ὁ κόσμος αὐτῶν and *omnis ornatus
eorum*, the conception being that when the
heavens and the earth were completed they
were a brilliant array.

Ver. 2.—**And on the seventh day God**
(Elohim) **ended his work which he had
made.** To avert the possibility of imagining
that any portion of the seventh day was
consumed in working, which the English
version seems to favour, the LXX., the
Samaritan, and Syriac versions insert the
sixth day in the text instead of the seventh.
Calvin, Drusius, Le Clerc, Rosenmüller, and
Kalisch translate *had finished*. Others understand the sense to be *declared* the work to
be finished, while Baumgarten and Delitzsch
regard the resting as included in the completion of the work, and Von Bohlen thinks
"the language is not quite precise." But
calah followed by *min* signifies to cease
from prosecuting any work (Exod. xxxiv. 33 ;
1 Sam. x. 13 ; Ezek. xliii. 23), and this was,
negatively, the aspect of that sabbatic rest
into which the Creator entered. **And he
rested on the seventh day from all his work**
which he had made. *Shavath*, the primary
idea of which is to sit still, depicts Elohim
as desisting from his creative labours, and
assuming a posture of quiescent repose. The
expression is a pure anthropomorphism. " He
who fainteth not, neither is weary " (Isa. xl.
28), can be conceived of neither as resting
nor as needing rest through either exhaustion
or fatigue. Cessation from previous occupation is all that is implied in the figure, and
is quite compatible with continuous activity
in other directions. John v. 17 represents the
Father as working from that period onward
in the preservation and redemption of that
world which by his preceding labours he had
created and made.

Ver. 3.—**And God blessed the seventh day.**
The blessing (cf. ch. i. 22, 28) of the seventh
day implied—1. That it was thereby declared
to be the special object of the Divine favour.
2. That it was thenceforth to be a day or
epoch of blessing for his creation. And—3.
That it was to be invested with a permanence
which did not belong to the other six days—
every one of which passed away and gave
place to a successor. **And sanctified it.** Literally, declared it holy, or set it apart for holy
purposes. As afterwards Mount Sinai was
sanctified (Exod. xix. 23), or, for the time
being, invested with a sacred character as the
residence of God ; and Aaron and his sons
were sanctified, or consecrated to the priestly
office (Exod. xxix. 44) ; and the year of Jubilee
was sanctified, or devoted to the purposes of
religion (Levit. xxv. 10), so here was the
seventh day sanctified, or instituted in the
interests of holiness, and as such proclaimed
to be a holy day. **Because that in it he had**

rested from all his work which God had **created and made.** Literally, *created to make,* the exact import of which has been variously explained. The " *ὧν ἤρξατο ὁ Θεός ποιῆσαι*" of the LXX. is obviously incorrect. Calvin, Ainsworth, Bush, *et alii* take the second verb *emphatice,* as intensifying the action of the first, and conveying the idea of a perfect creation. Kalisch, Alford, and others explain the second as *epexegetic* of the first, as in the similar phrases, "spoke, saying, literally, spoke to speak" (Exod. vi. 10), and "laboured to do" (Eccles. ii. 11). Onkelos, the Vulgate (*quod Deus creavit ut faceret*), Calvin, Tayler Lewis, &c. understand the infinitive in a *telic* sense, as expressive of the purpose for which the heavens and the earth were at first created, viz., that by the six days' work they might be fashioned into a cosmos. It has been observed that the usual concluding formula is not appended to the record of the seventh day, and the reason has perhaps been declared by Augustine : "Dies autem septimus sine vespera est, nec habet occasum, quia sanctificasti eum ad permansionem sempiternam" ('Confess.,' xiii. 36). But now what was this seventh day which received Elohim's benediction? On the principle of interpretation applied to the creative days, this must be regarded as a period of indefinite duration, corresponding to the human era of both Scripture and geology. But other Scriptures (Exod. xx. 8 ; xxiii. 12 ; Deut. v. 12, &c.) show that the Hebrews were enjoined by God to observe a seventh day rest in imitation of himself. There are also indications that sabbatic observance was not unknown to the patriarchs (ch. xxix. 27, 28), to the antediluvians (ch. viii. 6—12), and to Cain and Abel (ch. iv. 3). Profane history likewise vouches for the veracity of the statement of Josephus, that "there is not any city of the Grecians, nor any of the barbarians, nor any nation whatsoever, whither our custom of resting on the seventh day hath not come" ('Contra Apionem,' ii. 40). The ancient Persians, Indians, and Germans esteemed the number seven as sacred. By the Greeks and Phenicians a sacred character was ascribed to the seventh day. The Assyrians, Babylonians, Egyptians, and other nations of antiquity were acquainted with the hebdomadal division of time. Travellers have detected traces of it among the African and American aborigines. To account for its existence among nations so widely apart, both chronologically and geographically, recourse has been had to some violent hypotheses ; as, *e. g.,* to the number of the primary planets known to the ancients (Humboldt), the division of a lunar month into four nearly equal periods of seven days (Ideler, Baden Powell, &c.), Jewish example (Josephus). Its true genesis, however, must

be sought for in the primitive observance of a seventh day rest in accordance with Divine appointment. Precisely as we reason that the early and widespread prevalence of sacrifice can only be explained by an authoritative revelation to the first parents of the human family of such a mode of worship, so do we conclude that a seventh day sabbath must have been prescribed to man in Eden. The question then arises, Is this sabbath also referred to in the Mosaic record of the seventh day? The popular belief is that the institution of the weekly sabbath alone is the subject spoken of in the opening verses of the present chapter ; and the language of Exod. xx. 11 may at first sight appear to warrant this conclusion. A more careful consideration of the phraseology employed by Moses, however, shows that in the mind of the Hebrew lawgiver there existed a distinction between God's seventh day and man's sabbath, and that, instead of identifying the two, he meant to teach that the first was the reason of the second ; as thus—"In six days God made . . . . and rested on the seventh day ; wherefore God blessed the (weekly) sabbath day, and hallowed it." Here it is commonly assumed that the words are exactly parallel to those in ch. ii. 3, and that the sabbath in Exodus corresponds to the seventh day of Genesis. But this is open to debate. The seventh day which God blessed in Eden was the first day of human life, and not the seventh day ; and it is certain that God did not rest from his labours on man's seventh day, but on man's first. We feel inclined then to hold with Luther that in Gen. ii. 3 Moses says nothing about man's day, and that the seventh day which received the Divine benediction was God's own great æonian period of sabbatic rest. At the same time, for the reasons above specified, believing that a weekly sabbath was prescribed to man from the beginning, we have no difficulty in assenting to the words of Tayler Lewis: "'And God blessed the seventh day.' Which seventh day, the greater or the less, the Divine or the human, the æonian or the astronomical? Both, is the easy answer ; both, as commencing at the same time, so far as the one connects with astronomical time ; both, as the greater including the less ; both, as being (the one as represented, the other as typically representing) the same in essence and idea." It does not appear necessary to refute the idea that the weekly sabbath had no existence till the giving of the law, and that it is only here proleptically referred to by Moses.

In addition to the above-mentioned historical testimonies to the antiquity of the Sabbath, the Fifth Tablet in the Chaldean Creation Series, after referring to the fourth day's work, proceeds :—

" On the seventh day he appointed a holy day,
　　And to cease from all business he com-
　　manded.
　Then arose the sun in the horizon of heaven
　　in (glory)."

thus apparently affirming that, in the opinion of the early Babylonians, the institution of the sabbath was coeval with the creation. (*Vid.* 'Records of the Past,' vol. ix. p. 117.)

HOMILETICS.

Ver. 3. *The two sabbaths: the Divine and the human.* 1. THE SABBATH OF GOD. A period of—1. *Cessation from toil,* or discontinuance of those world-making operations which had occupied the six preceding days (Heb. iv. 4). Never since the close of the creative week has God interfered to fundamentally rearrange the material structure of the globe. The Deluge produced no alteration on the constitution of nature. Nor is there evidence that any new species have been added to its living creatures. 2. *Holy delight.* On the seventh day Elohim rested and was " refreshed" (Exod. xxxi. 17) ; which refreshment consisted partly in the satisfaction he experienced in beholding the cosmos—a satisfaction prefigured and anticipated by the solemn pauses intervening at the end of each creative day, accompanied by the "good," "lo! very good," of Divine approbation ; and partly in the pleasure with which he contemplated the peculiar work of blessing his creation which lay before him, a work which also had its foreshadowings in the benedictions pronounced on the living creatures of the fifth day, and on man on the sixth. 3. *Beneficent activity.* Even man, unless where his intellectual and moral faculties are dormant, finds it difficult to rest in indolence and inactivity. Absence of motion, with complete negation of effort, may constitute the refreshment of the physical system. The mind seeks its rest in change of occupation. Still less can the supreme Intelligence, who is pure Spirit, rest in absolute inaction ; only the Divine energy is now directed towards the happiness of his creatures (Ps. cxlv. 9). Having finished his creative labours, what else could Elohim do but outpour his own blessedness upon his creatures, in proportion to their capacities to receive it? His nature as God necessitated such communication of good to his creatures (Ps. xxxiv. 8 ; James i. 5, 17). The capacities of his creatures for such blessing required it. Hence God's rest may be said to have been man's birthright. He was created in that rest, as the sphere of his existence. 4. *Continuous duration.* That which secures its perpetuity is the Divine resolution to bless it, *i. e.* constitute it an era of blessing for man, and in particular to sanctify it, or devote it to the interests of holiness. And in this Divine determination lies *the pledge of man's salvation.* Without it God's rest might have been broken into by man's sin, and the era of blessing ended. But, because of it, man's sin could not change the character of God's seventh day, so as to prevent it from dropping down gifts and exercising holy influences on the creature for whose sake it was appointed. *The security of the world as a cosmos* may also be said to be involved in the permanence of God's sabbath. So long as it continues nothing shall occur to resolve the present goodly framework of this globe into another lightless, formless, lifeless chaos, at least until the Divine purpose with the human race has been fulfilled.

II. THE SABBATH OF MAN. 1. Of *Divine institution* (Exod. xx. 8 ; Levit. xix. 30 ; Ps. cxviii. 24). That God had a right to enact a weekly sabbath for man is implied in his relation to man as Creator and Lawgiver. For man, therefore, to withhold the seventh portion of his time is to be guilty of disobedience against God as a moral Governor, ingratitude towards God as Creator and Preserver, robbery of God as the original Proprietor of both man's powers and time's days. As an institution of God's appointing, the sabbath deserves our honour and esteem. To neglect to render this God counts a sin (Isa. lviii. 13). 2. Of *sacred character.* Among the Israelites its sanctity was to be recognised by abstinence from bodily labour (Exod. xx. 10 ; xxxiv. 21, &c.) and holy convocations (Levit. xxiii. 3). That this was the manner of its observance prior to the giving of the law may be judged from the regulations concerning the manna (Exod. xvi. 22). That from the beginning it was a day of rest and religious worship may be reasonably inferred. That it was so used by Christ and his apostles the Gospels attest (Luke iv. 16). That the same character was held to attach to the first day of the week after Christ's resurrection may be deduced from the practice of the apostolic Church (Acts xx. 7).   The sanctity of the sabbath may be profaned, *positively*, by prosecuting one's ordinary labours in its hours (Isa. lviii. 13; Jer. xvii. 24); *negatively*, by neglecting to devote them to Divine worship and spiritual improvement (Ezek. xliv. 24).   Christianity has not obliterated the distinction between the sabbath and the other days of the week; not even by elevating them to the position of *holy* days.   An attempt to equalise the seven days always results in the degradation of the seventh, never in the elevation of the other six.   3. Of *beneficent design* (Mark ii. 27).   The sabbath is adapted to the wants of man physically, intellectually, socially, politically. Innumerable facts and testimonies establish the beneficial influence of a seventh day's rest from toil upon the manual labourer, the professional thinker, the social fabric, the body politic, in respect of health, wealth, strength, happiness.   It is, however, chiefly man's elevation as a religious being at which it aims.   In the paradisaiacal state it was designed to hedge him round and, if possible, prevent his fall; since the tragedy in Eden it has been seeking his reinstatement in that purity from which he fell.   4. Of *permanent obligation.* · Implied in the terms of its institution, its permanence would not be affected by the abolition of the Decalogue. The Decalogue presupposed its previous appointment.   Christianity takes it up, just as Judaism took it up, as one of God's existing ordinances for the good of man, and seeks through it to bring its higher influences to bear on man, just as Judaism sought, through it, to operate with its inferior agency.   Till it merges in the rest of which it is a shadow by the accomplishment of its grand design, it must abide.

III. THE CONNECTION OF THE TWO.   God's rest is—1. The *reason* of man's sabbath. The Almighty could have no higher reason for enjoining a seventh day's rest upon his creature than that by so resting that creature would be like himself.   2. The *pattern* of man's sabbath.   As God worked through six of his days and rested on the seventh, so should man toil through six of his days and rest on the seventh. As God did *all* his work in the six creative days, so should *all* man's labour be performed in the six days of the week.   As God employs his rest in contemplation of his finished work and in blessing his creature man, so should man devote his sabbath to pious meditation on his past life and to a *believing* reception of God's gifts of grace and salvation.   3. The *life* of man's sabbath.   Whatever blessing comes to man on his weekly day of rest has its primal fountain in the rest of God. As man himself is God's image, so is man's sabbath the image of God's rest; and as man lives and moves and has his being in God, so does man's sabbath live and move and have its being in God's rest.   4. The *end* of man's sabbath.   The reinstatement of man in God's rest is the purpose at which man's sabbath aims, the goal towards which it is tending.   God's rest remains on high (Heb. iv. 9), drawing men towards it.   Man's weekly sabbath will ultimately lose itself in God's eternal rest.

HOMILIES BY VARIOUS AUTHORS.

Vers. 1—3.—*Rest and Light.*   The finished heavens and earth and their host prepare the day of rest.   God ended his work as an interchange of darkness and light.

I. THE REST OF THE SABBATH IS NOT INACTION, BUT THE CESSATION FROM THE LOWER ORDER OF WORK FOR THE HIGHER.   The idea of the first proclamation seems to be that creation was perfectly adjusted through the six days into a settled harmony which puts heaven and earth in their abiding relation to one another.

II. Then THERE IS NO MORE SAID OF EVENING AND MORNING.   The seventh day is only *light.*   God's rest is complacency in his works.   The blessing on the seventh day which hallowed it is the blessing on that which the day represents—perfect peace between heaven and earth, God satisfied in his creation, and inviting his intelligent creatures to "*enter into his rest*" by communion with him.   It seems quite unnecessary to vindicate such a sanctification of the seventh day from the insinuations of critics that it was a late addition made by the Jewish legislator to support the fourth commandment.   In that case the whole cosmogony must be renounced.   Such an observance of a day of rest seems a natural antecedent to the patriarchal as well as the Mosaic economy.   We have already intimated that the whole account of creation is placed at the commencement of revelation because it has a bearing upon the positive ordinances of religion. It is not either a scientific or poetic sketch of the universe; it is the broad, fundamental outline of a system of religious truth connected with a body of Divine commandments. The sabbath is thus described in its original breadth. The sanctification of it is—1. *Negative.* It is separation *from* the lower conditions of work, which in the case of man are the characteristics of days which are sinful days—days of toil and conflict, of darkness and light mingled. 2. *Positive.* It is the restful enjoyment of a higher life, a life which is not labouring after emancipation from bondage, but perfect with a glorious liberty; the true *day,* "*sacred, high, eternal noon,*" God and man rejoicing in one another, the creature reflecting the glory of the Creator.—R.

§ 2. THE GENERATIONS OF THE HEAVENS AND OF THE EARTH (CH. II. 4—IV. 26).

EXPOSITION.

THE subject handled in the present section is the primeval history of man in his paradisaical state of innocence, his temptation and fall, and his subsequent development, in two diverging lines, of faith and unbelief, holiness and sin. On the ground of certain obvious, well-defined, and readily-explained characteristics which distinguish this from the preceding portion of the narrative, it is usual with the higher criticism to allege diversity of authorship; and, indeed, these same characteristics, magnified by misapplied ingenuity into insoluble contradictions, are the chief buttress of the documentary hypothesis of Astruc, Hupfeld, Tuch, Ewald, and others. Now the hypothesis that Moses, in the composition of the Pentateuch, and of this Book of Origins in particular, made use of existing documents that may have descended from a remote antiquity is, *à priori*, neither incredible nor impossible; but, on the contrary, is extremely probable, and may be held as admitted; only the alleged peculiarities of the different portions of the narrative do not justify the reckless confidence with which it has been resolved by Stähelin, Bleek, De Wette, Knobel, Ewald, and Davidson into its so-called original fragments; and, in the case of Ewald, primordial atoms (*vid.* Introd., p. ii.). The occurrence of the name *Jehovah Elohim,* instead of simply *Elohim,* as in the preceding section, is the chief peculiarity of the present portion of the narrative, so far as style and language are concerned; its alleged irreconcilable differences in subject-matter are skilfully and succinctly put by Kalisch. "In the first cosmogony vegetation is immediately

produced by the will of God; in the second its existence is made dependent on rain and mists and the agricultural labours: in the first the earth emerges from the waters, and is, therefore, saturated with moisture; in the second it appears dry, sterile, and sandy: in the first man and his wife are created together; in the second the wife is formed later, and from a part of man: in the former man bears the image of God, and is made ruler of the whole earth; in the latter his earth-formed body is only animated by the breath of life, and he is placed in Eden to cultivate and to guard it: in the former the birds and beasts are created before man; in the latter man before birds and beasts." For a reply to these "insoluble contradictions," which, though "too obvious to be overlooked or denied," are mostly, if not solely, due to a false exegesis and a misapprehension of the guiding purpose of the writer, see the Exposition following, which attempts no "artificial solution" such as Kalisch deprecates, and proposes no ingenious reconciliation of essentially opposing statements, but simply shows that, when naturally and literally interpreted, the narrative is free from those internal antagonisms which a microscopic criticism imagines it has detected in it. The *internal unity* of the present writing, or second document, as it is called, is apparent. The internecine struggle between the seed of the woman and the seed of the serpent, which the fratricidal act of Cain inaugurated (ch. iv.), is the legitimate and necessary outcome of the sin and the grace revealed in Eden (ch. iii.), while the melancholy story of the temptation and the fall presupposes the paradisaical innocence of the first pair (ch. ii.). Thus homogeneous in itself, it likewise *connects with the preceding section* through ch. ii., which, as a monograph on man, supplies a more detailed account of his creation than is given in the narrative of the six days' work, and, by depicting man's settlement in Eden as a place of trial, prepares the way for the subsequent recital of his seduction and sin, and of his consequent expulsion from the garden.

Ver. 4.—**These are the generations** is the usual heading for the different sections into which the Book of Genesis is divided (*vid.* ch. v. 1; vi. 9; x. 1; xi. 10, 27; xxv. 12, 19; xxxvi. 1; xxxvii. 2). Misled by the LXX., who render *tōldōth* by ἡ βίβλος γενέσεως, Ranke, Tiele, Hävernick, Tuch, Ewald, and Stähelin disconnect the entire verse from the second section, which says nothing about the origination of the heavens and the earth, and append it to the preceding, in which their creation is described. Ilgen improves on their suggestion by transferring it to the commencement of ch. i., as an appropriate superscription. Dreschler, Vaihinger, Bohlen, Oehler, Macdonald, *et alii* divide the verse into two clauses, and annex the former to what precedes, commencing the ensuing narrative with the latter. All of these proposals are, however, rendered unnecessary by simply observing that *tōldōth* (from *yaladh*, to bear, to beget; hence begettings, procreations, evolutions, developments) does not describe the antecedents, but the consequents, of either thing or person (Rosen., Keil, Kalisch). The *tōldōth* of Noah are not the genealogical list of the patriarch's ancestry, but the tabulated register of his posterity; and so the generations **of the heavens and the earth** refer not to their original production (Gesenius), but to their onward movements from creation downwards (Keil). Hence with no incongruity, but with singular propriety, the first half of the present verse, ending with the words **when they were created**, literally, *in their creation*, stands at the commencement of the section in which the forward progression of the universe is traced. The point of departure in this subsequent evolution of the material heavens and earth is further specified as being **in the day that the Lord God** (Jehovah Elohim) **made the earth and the heavens;** not the heavens and the earth, which would have signified the universe (*vid.* on ch. i. 1), and carried back the writer's thought to the initial act of creation; but the earth and the atmospheric firmament, which indicates the period embracing the second and (possibly) the third creative days as the *terminus a quo*

of the generations to be forthwith recorded. Then it was that the heavens and the earth in their development took a clear and decided step forward in the direction of man and the human family (was it in the appearance of vegetation?); and in this thought perhaps will be found the key to the significance of the new name for the Divine Being which is used exclusively throughout the present section—**Jehovah Elohim.** From the frequency of its use, and the circumstance that it never has the article, **Jehovah** may be regarded as the proper personal name of God. Either falsely interpreting Exod. xx. 7 and Levit. xxiv. 11, or following some ancient superstition (mysterious names of deities were used generally in the East; the Egyptian Hermes had a name which (Cic. 'de Natura Deorum,' 8, 16) durst not be uttered: Fürst), the later Hebrews invested this *nomen tetragrammaton* with such sanctity that it might not be pronounced (Philo, 'Vit. Mosis,' iii. 519, 529). Accordingly, it was their custom to write it in the sacred text with the vowel points of *Adonai*, or, if that preceded, Elohim. Hence considerable doubt now exists as to its correct pronunciation. Etymologically viewed it is a future form of *havah*, an old form of *hayah*; uncertainty as to what future has occasioned many different suggestions as to what constituted its primitive vocalisation. According to the evidence which scholars have collected, the choice lies between (1) Jahveh (Gesenius, Ewald, Reland, Oehler, Macdonald, the Samaritan), (2) Yehveh or Yeheveh (Fürst, W. L. Alexander, in Kitto's 'Cyclopedia'), and (3) Jehovah (Michaelis, Meyer, Stier, Hoelmann, Tregelles, Murphy). Perhaps the preponderance of authority inclines to the first; but the common punctuation is not so indefensible as some writers allege. Gesenius admits that it more satisfactorily accounts for the abbreviated syllables יְהוֹ and יָהּ than the pronunciation which he himself favours. Murphy thinks that the substitution of Adonai for Jehovah was facilitated by the agreement of their vowel points. The *locus classicus* for its signification is Exod. iii. 14, in which God defines himself as "I am that I am," and commands Moses to tell the children of Israel that *Ehyeh* had sent him. Hengstenberg and Keil conclude that absolute self-existence is the essential idea represented by the name (cf. Exod. iii. 14; ὁ ὤν, LXX.; Rev. i. 4, 8; ὁ ὢν καὶ ὁ ἦν καὶ ὁ ἐρχόμενος, *vid.* Fürst, 'Lex. sub nom.'). Baumgarten and Delitzsch, laying stress on its future form, regard it as = the Becoming One, with reference to the revelation, rather than the essence, of the Divine nature. Macdonald, from the circumstance that it was not used till after the fall, discovers a pointing forward to Jehovah as ὁ ἐρχόμενος in connection with redemption.

Others, deriving from a hiphil future, take it as denoting "he who causes to be, the Fulfiller," and find in this an explanation of Exod. vi. 3 (Exell). May not all these ideas be more or less involved in the fulness of the Divine name? As distinguished from Elohim, *Deus omnipotens*, the mighty One, Jehovah is the absolute, self-existent One, who manifests himself to man, and, in particular, enters into distinct covenant engagements for his redemption, which he in due time fulfils. In the present section the names are conjoined partly to identify Jehovah with Elohim, and partly because the subject of which it treats is the history of man.

Ver. 5.—**And every plant of the field before it was** (literally, not yet) **in the earth, and every herb of the field before it grew** (literally, had not yet sprouted). Following the LXX., the English Version suggests an intention on the writer's part to emphasise the fact that the vegetation of the globe—here comprehended under the general terms, *shiah*, shrub, and *eseb*, herb—was not a natural production, but, equally with the great earth and heavens, was the creation of Jehovah Elohim—a rendering which has the sanction of Tayler Lewis; whereas the writer's object clearly is to depict the appearance of the earth at the time when the man-ward development of the heavens and the earth began. Then not a single plant was in the ground, not a green blade was visible. The land, newly sprung from the waters, was one desolate region of bleak, bare lava-hills and extensive mud-flats. Up to that point the absence of vegetation is accounted for by the circumstance that the presently existing atmospheric conditions of the globe had not then been established, **for the Lord God had not caused it to rain upon the earth**, and the ordinary agricultural operations on which its production was afterwards to depend had not then been begun, **and there was not a man to till the ground.**

Ver. 6.—**But there went up a mist from the earth, and watered the whole face of the ground.** The dry land having been separated from the waters, and the atmospheric ocean uplifted above them both, vaporous exhalations began to ascend to the aerial regions, and to return again in the shape of rain upon the ground. Jehovah thus *caused it to rain* upon the ground, and so prepared it for the vegetation which, in obedience to the Almighty fiat, sprung up at the close of the third day, although the writer does not mention its appearance, but leaves it to be inferred from the preceding section. That soon after its emergence from the waters the land should be "dry, sterile, and sandy" will not be thought remarkable if we remember the highly igneous condition of our planet at the time when the dry land was upheaved and the waters gathered into the subsiding valleys. Nothing would more naturally follow that event than the steaming up of vapours to float in the aerial sea. In fact, the rapidity with which evaporation would be carried on would very speedily leave the newly-formed land hard and dry, baked and caked into a crust, till the atmosphere, becoming overcharged with aqueous vapour, returned it in the shape of rain. To talk of insuperable difficulty and manifest dissonance where everything is clear, natural, and harmonious is to speak at random, and betrays an anxiety to create contradictions rather than to solve them.

Ver. 7.—**And the Lord God** (Jehovah Elohim) **formed man of the dust of the ground.** Literally, dust from the ground. Here, again, Bleek, Kalisch, and the theologians of their school discover contrariety between this account of man's creation and that which has been given in the preceding chapter. *In that* man is represented as having been created by the Divine word, in the Divine image, and male and female simultaneously; whereas *in this* his creation is exhibited as a painful process of elaboration from the clay by the hand of God, who works it like a potter (*asah;* LXX., πλάσσω), and, after having first constructed man, by a subsequent operation forms woman. But the first account does not assert that Adam and Eve were created together, and gives no details of the formation of either. These are supplied by the present narrative, which, beginning with the construction of his body from the fine dust of the ground, designedly represents it as an evolution or development of the material universe, and ends by setting it before us as animated by the breath of God, reserving for later treatment the mode of Eve's production, when the circumstances that led to it have been described. **And** (the Lord God) **breathed into his nostrils the breath of life.** Literally, the breath of lives. "The formation of man from the dust and the breathing of the breath of life must not be understood in a mechanical sense, as if God first of all constructed a human figure from the dust" (still less does it admit of the idea that man's physical nature was evolved from the lower animals), "and then, by breathing his breath of life into the clod of earth which he had shaped into the form of a man, made it into a living being. The words are to be understood θεοπρεπῶς. By an act of Divine omnipotence man arose from the dust; and in the same moment in which the dust, by virtue of creative omnipotence, shaped itself into a human form, it was pervaded by the Divine breath of life, and created a living being, so that we cannot say the body was earlier than the soul" (Delitzsch). **And man became a**

living soul. *Nephesh chayyah,* in ch. i. 21, 30, is employed to designate the lower animals. Describing a being animated by a ψυχή or life principle, it does not necessarily imply that the basis of the life principle in man and the inferior animals is the same. The distinction between the two appears from the difference in the mode of their creations. The beasts arose at the almighty fiat completed beings, every one a *nephesh chayyah.* "The origin of their soul was coincident with that of their corporeality, and their life was merely the individualisation of the universal life with which all matter was filled at the beginning by the Spirit of God" (Delitzsch).

Man received his life from a distinct act of Divine inbreathing; certainly not an inbreathing of atmospheric air, but an inflatus from the Ruach Elohim, or Spirit of God, a communication from the whole personality of the Godhead. In effect man was thereby constituted a *nephesh chayyah,* like the lower animals; but in him the life principle conferred a personality which was wanting in them. Thus there is no real contradiction, scarcely even an "apparent dissonance," between the two accounts of man's creation. The second exhibits the foundation of that likeness to God and world-dominion ascribed to him in the first.

HOMILETICS.

Ver. 7.—*The first man.* I. MADE FROM THE DUST. This does not imply that in the composition of humanity there is nothing but particles of dust, or "molecules of matter." Simply it designs to state that the point of departure in man's creation was the soil out of which all other living creatures were produced; that, so to speak, man was constructed from beneath upwards, the Divine Artificer proceeding with his creation in the same ascending scale of activity that had been observed in the production of the rest of the universe—first the material body, and then the immaterial soul; and that, so far as the former is concerned, man is wholly and solely of the earth, earthy,—an assertion which the researches of chemistry and physiology abundantly confirm,—the elements of organised bodies being the same as those which constitute the inorganic world, viz., carbon, hydrogen, oxygen, nitrogen, lime, iron, sulphur, and phosphorus. The statement is fitted to impress man with thoughts—1. Of his *lowly origin.* While the Scripture in general labours to imbue his mind with correct ideas of his obscure nativity, comparing him to a wind, to a vapour, to a flower, to the beasts, to a worm, the sentiment of Moses takes him lower yet for his birthplace—to the dust of the ground, above which the wind blows, from which the vapours rise, on which the flowers bloom, across which the beasts roam, out of which the worm creeps. 2. Of his *essential frailty.* Being composed of little particles of dust, held together by what science calls "organisation," but Holy Writ designates the power of God, it requires but the loosening of God's hand, as it were, for the framework of his body, so wondrously fashioned, so delicately carved, so finely articulated, so firmly knit, to resolve itself into a heap of dust. 3. Of his *final destiny.* Every mundane thing returns to the place whence it proceeded (Eccles. i. 5, 7). The vapours climb into the sky, but descend again upon the hills, and seek the plains. The flowers bloom, but, after dispensing their fragrance, shed their leaves upon the earth. The young lions, that, as it were, are sprung from the soil, find a grave at last within their forest dens. As it is with the flowers and the beasts, so is it also with man. "All are of the dust, and all turn to dust again" (Eccles. iii. 18, 20; Job x. 9; Ps. ciii. 14).

Lessons:—1. Humility of spirit (Job iv. 19; Ps. cxliv. 3, 4; Isa. li. 1). "Holy living" (Taylor, § iv. 9). 2. Care for the body—protecting its frailty from injury (Levit. xix. 28) and its materiality from mastery (Rom. xii. 1; 1 Cor. vi. 13; 1 Thess. iv. 4). 3. Preparation for death (Ps. xxxix. 4; xc. 12).

II. FASHIONED BY THE HAND OF GOD. Made from the dust, the first man neither sprung from the slime of matter, according to naturalism (οἱ αὐτόχθονες), nor was evolved from the τὸ πᾶν of pantheism, but was specifically formed by Divine creative power. This marked the first degree of man's superiority over other living creatures. Deriving existence, equally with man, from the creative power of God, it is not said of them that they were "formed" by God. Let this remind man—1. Of *the Divine origin of the body.* If the physical structures of the lower organisms display such admirable proportions and striking adaptations as to evince the action of Divine intelligence, much more may a Creator's hand be recognised in the form and symmetry, proportion and adjustment of the human body. An examination of the hand, eye, or brain, of the muscular or nervous systems, instinctively awakens the devout feelings of the Psalmist: "I will praise Thee, O Lord; for I am fearfully and wonderfully made" (Ps. cxxxix. 14). 2. Of *the Divine estimate of the body.* Shown by the personal care and attention which God devoted to its construction, since he designed it to be the noblest of his works, the shrine of an immortal spirit, a prophecy and type of the body of his Son, in the fulness of the times to be prepared by another special act of creation (1 Cor. xi. 6, Heb. x. 6). This estimate he has in many ways confirmed: by abundantly and generously sustaining it, although a partner in the spirit's sin (Gen. i. 29; ix. 3); guarding its life with the strictest and severest penalties (Gen. ix. 5, 6); taking it into union with himself, in the person of his Son (Heb. ii. 6); redeeming it, as well as the soul it enshrines, through his Son's blood (Rom. viii. 21, 23); and constituting it, as well as the immaterial spirit, a partaker of resurrection glory (1 Cor. xv. 42).

Learn—1. The true nobility of man's descent, and the duty of walking worthy of it. 2. The high value of the body, and the consequent obligation of neither dishonouring nor abusing it.

III. ANIMATED BY THE BREATH OF LIFE. The second degree of man's superiority to the lower animals. Like them, a living soul, his life is different from theirs— 1. *In its nature.* Theirs was a portion of that common life principle which God has been pleased to communicate to matter; his a direct afflatus from the personality of God. 2. *In its impartation.* Theirs was bestowed directly and immediately by the fiat of omnipotence; his conveyed into his material framework by a special Divine operation. 3. *In its effect.* Theirs constituted them "living souls;" his conferred on him personality. Theirs made them creatures having life; his caused him to become a spirit having life. Theirs left them wholly mortal; his transformed him into an immortal (Eccles. iii. 21).

Let man consider—1. That his body is a temple of the Holy Ghost (1 Cor. vi. 19). 2. That his spirit is the creation and the gift of God (Eccles. xii. 7; Isa. lvii. 16; Zech. xii. 1). 3. That with both it becomes him to glorify his Divine Creator (1 Cor. vi. 20).

HOMILIES BY VARIOUS AUTHORS.

Vers. 4—7.—*Man the living soul.* 1. Life is a Divine bestowment. 2. Dust which is Divinely inspired is no longer mere dust; the true life is neither grovelling on the earth, nor so much away from the earth as to be no longer the life of a living soul. 3. The creature who is last formed, and for whom all other things wait and are prepared, is made to be the interpreter of all, and the glory of God in them.—R.

EXPOSITION.

Ver. 8.—In accordance with a well-known characteristic of Hebrew composition, the writer, having carried his subject forward to a convenient place of rest, now reverts to a point of time in the six days antecedent to man's appearance on the earth. In anticipation of his arrival, it was needful that a suitable abode should be prepared for his reception. Accordingly, having already mentioned the creation of plants, trees, and flowers, the narrative proceeds to describe the construction of Adam's early home. **And the Lord God** (Jehovah Elohim) **planted** — *i. e.* specially prepared—**a garden** (*gan*, a place protected by a fence, from *ganan*, to cover; hence a garden: cf. Deut. ii. 10; 1 Kings xxi. 2; Isa. li. 3; LXX., παράδεισος; Vulgate, *paradisus;* whence English, paradise,

Luke xxiii. 43) **eastward** (*mekedem*, literally, from the front quarter, not from the beginning,—ἀπο ἀρχῆς, Aquila; ἐν πρῶτοις, Theodotion; *a principio*, Vulgate,—but in the region lying towards the east of Palestine — LXX., κατ᾽ ἀνατολὰς) **in** (not *of*, as Murphy, who renders "in the east of Eden") **Eden** (delight; Greek, ἡδονή: cf. Hedenesh, or Heden, the birthplace of Zoroaster—Kalisch). The word is not merely descriptive of the beauty and fertility of the garden (*paradisus voluptatis*, Vulg., cf. παράδεισος της τρυφης, LXX. (Joel ii. 3). On the ground of possessing similar qualities, other districts and places were subsequently termed Edens: cf. 2 Kings xix. 12; Isa. xxxvii. 12; li. 3; Ezek. xxvii. 23; Amos i. 5), but likewise indicates its locality, which is afterwards more exactly defined (vers. 10, 14). In the mean time it is simply noted that, this enchanting paradise having been specially prepared by Jehovah, **there he put the man** (Adam) **whom he had formed.**

Ver. 9.—**And out of the ground made the Lord God** (Jehovah Elohim) **to grow every tree that is pleasant to the sight**—literally, lovely to see ; *i. e.* beautiful in form and colour—**and good for food.** In the preparation of man's pristine abode respect was had to ornamentation as well as utility. Every species of vegetation that could minister to his corporeal necessities was provided. Flowers, trees, and shrubs regaled his senses with their fragrance, pleased his eye with their exquisite forms and enchanting colours, and gratified his palate with their luscious fruits. Hence the garden of the Lord became the highest ideal of earthly excellence (Isa. li. 3). In particular it was distinguished by the presence of two trees, which occupied a central position among its multifarious productions. **The tree of life also in the midst of the garden, and the tree of knowledge of good and evil.** That these were not two separate trees, but only one tree distinguished by different names, has been maintained, though with no weightier reason than the statement of Eve in ch. iii. 3. The opinion of Witsius, Luther, Kennicott, and Hengstenberg, that classes of trees, and not individual trees, are meant by the phrases " tree of life " and " tree of knowledge," is precluded by the language of Jehovah Elohim in ch. ii. 17 and ch. iii. 24. As regards their significance, consistency requires that they should both be explained on the same principle. This, accordingly, disposes of the idea that the tree of life (literally, the tree of the lives : cf. ξύλον τῆς ζωῆς, Rev. ii. 7; xx. 19) is simply a Hebraism for *a living tree*, as by no sort of ingenuity can the tree of knowledge be transformed into *a knowing tree.* It likewise militates against the notion that the two trees were styled from the peculiar effects of their fruits, the one conferring physical immortality on Adam's body (Scotus, Aquinas, Fairbairn, Kalisch, Luther), and the other imparting moral and intellectual intuitions to his soul (Josephus, Kalisch). But even if the life-giving properties of the one tree could be demonstrated from ch. iii. 24, proof would still be required with regard to the other, that the mere physical processes of manducation and digestion could be followed by results so immaterial as those of " rousing the slumbering intellect, teaching reason to reflect, and enabling the judgment to distinguish between moral good and moral evil " (Kalisch). Besides, if this was the immediate effect of eating the forbidden fruit, it is difficult to perceive either why it should have been prohibited to our first parents at all, it being " for their good to have their wits sharpened " (Willet) ; or in what respect they suffered loss through listening to the tempter, and did not rather gain (Rabbi Moses) ; or wherein, being destitute of both intellectual and moral discernment, they could be regarded as either guilty of transgression or responsible for obedience. Incapacity to know good and evil may be a characteristic of unconscious childhood and unreflecting youth (Deut. i. 39 ; Isa. vii. 15 ; Jonah iv. 11), or of debilitated age (2 Sam. xix. 36), but is not conceivable in the case of one who was created in God's image, invested with world-dominion, and himself constituted the subject of moral government. Unless, therefore, with ancient Gnostics and modern Hegelians, we view the entire story of the probation as an allegorical representation of the necessary intellectual and ethical development of human nature, we must believe that Adam was acquainted with the idea of moral distinctions from the first. Hence the conclusion seems to force itself upon our minds that the first man was possessed of both immortality and knowledge irrespective altogether of the trees, and that the true character which belonged to these trees was symbolical or sacramental, suggestive of the conditions under which he was placed in Eden. " Arbori autem vitæ nomen indidit, non quod vitam homini conferret, qua jam ante præditus erat ; sed ut symbolum ac memoriale esset vitæ divinitus acceptæ " (Calvin). For a further exposition of the exact significance of these trees see below on vers. 16, 17.

Ver. 10.—The precise locality of Eden is indicated by its relation to the great watercourses of the region. **And a river** (literally, a flowing water, applicable to large oceanic floods—Job xxii. 16 ; Ps. xxiv. 2 ; xlvi. 5 ; Jonah ii. 4—as well as to narrow streams) **went out** (literally, going out) **of Eden to water the garden.** To conclude from this that the river had its source within the limits of the garden is to infer more than the premises will warrant. Nothing more is implied in the language than that a great watercourse proceeded through the district of Eden, and served to irrigate the soil. Probably it intersected the garden, thus occasioning its remarkable fecundity and beauty. **And from thence** (*i. e.* either on emerging from which, or, taking מ in its secondary sense, outside of, or at a distance from which) **it was parted** (literally, divided itself), **and became into four heads.** *Roshim*, from *rosh*, that which is highest; either principal waters, arms or branches (Tayler Lewis, Alford), or beginnings of rivers, indicating the sources of the streams (Gesenius, Keil, Macdonald, Murphy). If the second of these interpretations be adopted, Eden must be looked for in a spot where some great flowing water is subdivided into four separate streams ; if the former be regarded as the proper exegesis, then any great river which is first formed by the junction of two streams, and afterwards disperses its waters in two different directions, will meet the requirements of the case.

Vers. 11, 12.—**The name of the first** (river **is**) **Pishon, or "the full flowing."** This is the first of those marks by which the river, when discovered, must be identified. It was palpably a broad-bosomed stream. A second is derived from the region through which it flows. **That is it which compasseth** (not necessarily surrounding, but skirting in a circular or circuitous fashion—Num. xxi. 4 ; Judges xi. 8) **the whole land of Havilah.** Havilah itself is described by three of its productions. **Where there is gold.** *I. e.* it is a gold-producing country. **And the gold of that land is good.** Of the purest quality and largest quantity. **There also is bdellium.** Literally *bedolach*, which the manna was declared to resemble (Exod. xvii. 14 ; Num. xi. 7). The LXX., supposing it to be a precious stone, translate it by ἄνθραξ in the present passage, and by κρυστάλλος in Num. xi. 7—a view supported by the Jewish Rabbis and Gesenius. The majority of modern interpreters espouse the opinion of Josephus, that it was an odorous and costly gum indigenous to India, Arabia, Babylonia, and Bactriana. The third production is **the onyx** (*shoham*, from a root signifying to be pale or delicate in colour, like the finger-nails), variously conjectured to be the beryl, onyx, sardonyx, sardius, or emerald. From this description it appears that Havilah must be sought for among the gold-producing countries of Asia. Now among the sons of Joktan or primitive Arabs (Gen. x. 29)—"whose dwelling was from Mesha, as thou goest, unto Sephar, a mount of the east"—are Ophir and Havilah, whence Gesenius concludes that India, including Arabia, is meant. Other countries have their advocates, such as Arabia Felix, Susiana, Colchis, &c.; and other rivers, such as the Ganges (Josephus, Eusebius), the Phasis (Reland, Jahn, Rosenmüller, Winer), the Indus (Schulthess, Kalisch).

Ver. 13.—**And the name of the second** is **the Gihon,** or "the bursting," from גּיח, to break forth. "Deep-flowing," T. Lewis renders it, connecting it with ὠκεανός, and identifying it with Homer's βαθυρρόος Ὠκεανός. **The same is it that compasseth the whole land of Ethiopia** (Cush). Under the impression that the African Cush was meant, the Alexandrine Jews discovered the Gihon in the Nile — an opinion in which they have been followed by Schulthess, Gesenius, Fürst, Bertheau, Kalisch, and others. But Cush, it is now known, describes the entire region between Arabia and the Nile, and in

particular the southern district of the former lying between the Persian Gulf and the Red Sea. Hence Tayler Lewis finds the Gihon in the ocean water sweeping round the south coast of Arabia. Murphy detects the name Kush in the words Caucasus and Caspian, and, looking for the site of Eden about the sources of the Euphrates and the Tigris in Armenia, thinks the Gihon may have been the leading stream flowing into the Caspian. Delitzsch advocates the claim of the Araxis to be this river.

Ver. 14.—**And the name of the third river** is the **Hiddekel,** or "the darting," from חד and דקל, a sharp and swift arrow, referring to its rapidity. It is unanimously agreed that this must be identified with the Tigris ; in the present language of the Persians designated *tir,* which signifies an arrow. It is styled in Aramaic *diglath* or *diglah.* **That is it which goeth towards the east of Assyria.** Its identity is thus placed beyond a question. **And the fourth** river is **Euphrates,** or "the sweet," from an unused root, *parath,* signifying to be sweet, referring to the sweet and pleasant taste of its waters (Jer. ii. 18). Further description of this great water was unnecessary, being universally known to the Hebrews as "the great river" (Deut. i. 7 ; Dan. x. 4), and "the river" *par excellence* (Exod. xxiii. 31 ; Isa. vii. 20). The river still bears its early name. In the cuneiform inscriptions deciphered by Rawlinson it is called "Ufrata." Recurring now to the site of Eden, it must be admitted that, notwithstanding this description, the whole question is involved in uncertainty. The two solutions of the problem that have the greatest claim on our attention are, (1) that which places Eden near the head of the Persian Gulf, and (2) that which looks for it in Armenia. The latter is favoured by the close proximity to that region of the sources of both the Euphrates and the Tigris ; but, on the other hand, it is hampered by the difficulty of discovering other two rivers that will correspond with the Gihon and the Pison, and the almost certainty that Cush and Havilah are to be sought for in the vicinity of the Persian Gulf. The former (Calvin, Kalisch, T. Lewis) is supported by this last consideration, that Cush and Havilah are not remote from the locality, though it too has its incumbrances. It seems to reverse the idea of יצא, which according to Le Clerc indicates the direction of the stream. Then its advocates, no more than the supporters of the alternate theory, are agreed upon the Gihon and the Pison : Calvin finding them in the two principal mouths of the Euphrates and the Tigris, which Sir Charles Lyell declares to be of comparatively recent formation ; Kalisch identifying them with the Indus and the Nile ; and Tayler Lewis regarding them as the two sides of the Persian Gulf. Sir H. Rawlinson, from a study of the Assyrian texts, has pointed out the coincidence of the Babylonian region of Karduniyas or Gàrduniyas with the Eden of the Bible ; and the late George Smith finds in its four rivers, Euphrates, Tigris, Surappi, and Ukui, its known fertility, and its name, Gandunu, so similar to Gan-eden (the garden of Eden), "considerations all tending towards the view that it is the paradise of Genesis" (' Chald. Gen.,' pp. 3—305).

Ver. 15.—Having prepared the garden for man's reception, **the Lord God took the man.** "Not physically lifting him up and putting him down in the garden, but simply exerting an influence upon him which induced him, in the exercise of his free agency, to go. He went in consequence of a secret impulse or an open command of his Maker" (Bush). **And put him into the garden;** literally, caused him to rest in it as an abode of happiness and peace. **To dress it.** *I. e.* to till, cultivate, and work it. This would almost seem to hint that the *aurea œtas* of classical poetry was but a dream—a reminiscence of Eden, perhaps, but idealised. Even the plants, flowers, and trees of Eden stood in need of cultivation from the hand of man, and would speedily have degenerated without his attention. **And to keep it.** Neither were the animals all so peaceful and domesticated that Adam did not need to fence his garden against their depredations. Doubtless there is here too an ominous hint of the existence of that greater adversary against whom he was appointed to watch.

Vers. 16, 17.—**And Jehovah Elohim commanded the man** (Adam), **saying.** Whether or not these were the first words listened to by man (Murphy), they clearly presuppose the person to whom they were addressed to have had the power of understanding language, *i. e.* of interpreting vocal sounds, and representing to his own mind the conceptions or ideas of which they were the signs, a degree of intellectual development altogether incompatible with modern evolution theories. They likewise assume the pre-existence of a moral nature which could recognise the distinction between "thou shalt" and "thou shalt not." **Of every tree of the garden thou mayest freely eat;** literally, eating, thou shalt eat. Adam, it thus appears, was permitted to partake of the tree of life ; not, however, as a means of either conferring or preserving immortality, which was already his by Divine gift, and the only method of conserving which recognised by the narrative was abstaining from the tree of knowledge ; but as a symbol and guarantee of that immortality with which he had been endowed, and which would continue to be his so long as he maintained his personal integrity. This, of course, by

the very terms of his existence, he was under obligation to do, apart altogether from any specific enactment which God might enjoin. As a moral being, he had the law written on his conscience. But, as if to give a visible embodiment to that law, and at the same time to test his allegiance to his Maker's will, which is the kernel of all true obedience, an injunction was laid upon him of a positive description—**But of the tree of the knowledge of good and evil, thou shalt not eat of it.** Speculations as to what kind of tree it was, whether a vine, a fig, or an apple tree, are more curious than profitable. There is no reason to suppose that any noxious or lethiferous properties resided in its fruit. The death that was to follow on transgression was to spring from the *eating*, and not from the *fruit ;* from the sinful act, and not from the creature, which in itself was good. The prohibition laid on Adam was for the time being a summary of the Divine law. Hence the tree was a sign and symbol of what that law required. And in this, doubtless, lies the explanation of its name. It was a concrete representation of that fundamental distinction between right and wrong, duty and sin, which lies at the basis of all responsibility. It interpreted for the first pair those great moral intuitions which had been implanted in their natures, and by which it was intended they should regulate their lives. Thus it was for them a tree of the knowledge of good and evil. It brought out that knowledge which they already possessed into the clear light of definite conviction and precept, connecting it at the same time with the Divine will as its source and with themselves as its end. Further, it was an intelligible declaration of the duty which that knowledge of good and evil imposed upon them. Through its penalty it likewise indicated both the good which would be reaped by obedience and the evil which would follow on transgression. **For in the day that thou eatest thereof thou shalt surely die;** literally, dying, thou shalt die. That this involved death physical, or the dissolution of the body, is indicated by the sentence pronounced on Adam after he had fallen (ch. iii. 19). That the sentence was not immediately executed does not disprove its reality. It only suggests that its suspension may have been due to some Divine interposition. Yet universal experience attests that permanent escape from its execution is impossible. In the case of Adam it was thus far put in force on the instant, that henceforth he ceased to be immortal. As prior to his fall his immortality was sure, being authenticated for him by the tree of life, so now, subsequent to that catastrophe, his mortality was certain. This, more than immediateness, is what the language implies. For the complete theological significance of this penalty see ch. iii. 19.

HOMILETICS.

Ver. 8.—*The garden of Eden.* I. A SCENE OF BEAUTY. Whether situated in Armenia or Babylonia (see Exposition), it was a fair spot in a sunny region of delights (Eden). This beauty was—1. *Luxuriant.* Milton has lavished all the wealth of his creative genius in an attempt to depict "the happy rural seat of the first pair" ('Par. Lost,' bk. iv.). Yet it is questionable if even he has succeeded in reproducing the gorgeous spectacle, the endlessly diversified assortment of lovely forms and radiant colours that seemed to compress "in narrow room nature's whole wealth," entitling Eden to be characterised as "a heaven on earth." 2. *Divinely prepared.* Jehovah Elohim caused it to spring up and bloom before the wondering eye of man. All the world's beauty is of God. The flowers and the herbs and the trees have all their symmetry and loveliness from him. God clothes the lilies of the field ; the raiment, outshining the glory of royal Solomon, in which they are decked is of his making. If nature be the loom in which it is woven, he is the all-wise ὑφάντης or Weaver by whom its wondrous mechanism is guided and energised. Let us rejoice in the earth's beauty, and thank God for it. 3. *Exceptional.* We are scarcely warranted, even by ch. iii. 17, to suppose that, prior to the fall, the whole world was a paradise. Rather, geologic revelations give us reason to believe that from the first the earth was prepared for the reception of a sinful race, death and deformity having been in the world anterior to man's arrival upon the scene (cf. Bushnell, 'Nat. and Super.,' ch. vii.), and that the Edenic home was what the Bible says it was—a fair spot, specially planted and fenced about, for the temporary residence of the innocent pair, who were ultimately, as transgressors, to be driven forth to dwell upon a soil which was cursed because of sin. Let it humble us to think that the earth is not a paradise solely because of human sin. 4. *Prophetic.* Besides being a picture of what the world would have been, had it been prepared for a sinless race, it was also a foreshadowing of the renovated earth when sin shall be no more, when "this land that was desolate shall have become like the garden of Eden." Let it stimulate our hope and assist our faith to anticipate the *palingenesia* of the future, when this sterile and disordered world shall be refitted with bloom and beauty.

II. A SPHERE OF WORK. Adam's work was—1. *God-assigned.* So in a very real sense is every man's life occupation appointed by God. "To every man his work" is the law of God's world as well as of Christ's kingdom. This thought should dignify "the trivial round, the common task," and enable us, "whether we eat or drink, or whatsoever we do, to do all to the glory of God." 2. *Pleasant.* And so should all work be, whether arduous or easy, especially to a Christian. To be sure, Adam's work was light and easy in comparison with that which afterwards became his lot, and that which now constitutes ours. But even these would be joyous and exhilarating if performed by the free spirit of love, instead of, as they often are, by the unwilling hands of bondmen. 3. *Necessary.* Even in a state of innocence it was impossible that man could be suffered to live in indolence ; his endowments and capacities were fitted for activity. His happiness and safety (against temptation) required him to be employed. And if God who made him was ever working, why should he be idle ? The same arguments forbid idleness to-day. Christianity with emphasis condemns it. "If a man will not work, neither shall he eat."

III. AN ABODE OF INNOCENCE. This abode was—1. *Suitable.* It was not suitable for sinners, just as the world outside would not have been adapted for a pair who were sinless ; but it was peculiarly appropriate for their innocence. He who appointeth to all men the bounds of their habitation always locates men in spheres that are exactly suited to their natures and needs. 2. *Provisional.* Their possession of it was contingent on their remaining sinless. If their souls continued pure, their homes would continue fair. It is man's own sin that defaces the beauty and mars the happiness of man's home. When men find themselves in positions that are not compatible with their happiness and usefulness, it is sin that has placed them there. 3. *Quickly lost.* How long they continued innocent is useless to conjecture, though probably it was not long. More important is it to observe that not much was required to deprive them of their lovely home—one act of disobedience! See the danger of even one sin. 4. *Ultimately recoverable.* This truth was taught by the stationing of the cherubim at its gate (*q. v.*). Rev. xxii. 1 tells us it has been regained for us by Christ, and will in the end be bestowed on us.

IV. A HOME OF HAPPINESS. 1. Everything was absent that might mar man's felicity. No sin, no error, no sorrow. 2. Everything was present that could minister to his enjoyment. There was ample gratification for all the different parts of his complex nature. (1) For his bodily senses, the fair scenes, melodious sounds, crystal streams, and luscious fruits of the garden. (2) For his mental powers, the study of the works of God. (3) For his social affections, a loving and lovely partner. (4) For his spiritual nature, God. To reproduce the happiness of Eden, so far as that is possible in a sinful world, there is needed (*a*) communion with a gracious God; (*b*) the felicity of a loving and a pious home; (*c*) the joy of life— physical, intellectual, moral.

V. A PLACE OF PROBATION. This probation was—1. *Necessary.* Virtue that stands only because it has never been assaulted is, to say the least of it, not of the highest kind. Unless man had been subjected to trial it might have remained dubious whether he obeyed of free choice or from mechanical necessity. 2. *Easy.* The specific commandment which Adam was required to observe was not severe in its terms. The limitations it prescribed were of the smallest possible description— abstinence from only one tree. 3. *Gracious.* Instead of perilling the immortality of Adam and his posterity upon every single act of their lives, he suspended it upon the observance, doubtless for only a short space of time, of one easily-obeyed precept, which he had the strongest possible inducement to obey. If he maintained his integrity, not only would his own holiness and happiness be confirmed, but those of his descendants would be secured; while if he failed, he would involve not himself alone, but all succeeding generations in the sweep of a terrific penalty. The clearness with which that penalty was made known, the certainty of its execution, and the severity of its inflictions, were proofs of the grace of God towards his creature man.

HOMILIES BY VARIOUS AUTHORS.

Vers. 8—17.—*Man's first dwelling-place.* The description of Eden commences an entirely new stage in the record. We are now entering upon the history of humanity as such.

I. The first fact in that history is a state of "PLEASANTNESS." The garden is planted by God. The trees are adapted to human life, to support it, to gratify it; and in the midst of the garden the two trees which represent the two most important facts with which revelation is about to deal, viz., immortality and sin.

II. OUTSPREAD BLESSING. The RIVER breaks into four fountains, whose description carries us over enormous regions of the world. It is the river which went out of Eden to water the garden; so that the conception before us is that of an abode of man specially prepared of God, not identical with Eden in extent, but in character; and the picture is carried out, as it were, by the channels of the outflowing streams, which bear the Eden life with them over the surface of the earth, so that the general effect of the whole is a *prophecy of blessing*, Eden-like beauty, and pleasantness, *over the whole extent of the world.*

III. THE PREPARED GARDEN WAITED FOR ITS INHABITANT. "And the Lord God took the man, and put him into the garden of Eden" (literally, made him to rest in the garden) "to dress it and to keep it." Perhaps the simplest view of these words is the most significant. Man is led into a life of pleasantness, with only such demands upon him as it will be no burden to meet; and in that life of pure happiness and free activity he is made conscious, not of mere dependence upon his Creator for existence, not of laws hanging over him like threatening swords, but of a Divine commandment which at once gave liberty and restrained it, which surrounded the one tree of knowledge of good and evil with its circle of prohibition, not as an arbitrary test of obedience, but as a Divine proclamation of eternal righteousness. "Evil is death.'

"Thou shalt not eat of it," for this reason, that "in the day that thou eatest thereof thou shalt surely die." It is not a subjection of a new-made creature to a test. It would be a harsh demand to make of Adam, unless he understood that it was founded on the nature of things.

IV. THE TREE OF LIFE AND THE TREE OF DEATH STAND TOGETHER in the midst of the garden. They hold the same position still in every sphere of human existence. But the book of Divine grace, as it teaches us how the sin-stricken, dying world is restored to a paradise of Divine blessedness, reveals at the last, in the vision of the Christian seer, only the *tree of life* beside *the water of life ;* the evil cast out, and the death which it brought with it, and the new-made inhabitants "*taking freely*" of "the pleasures which are for evermore."—R.

Vers. 9, 10.—*The tree of life and the water of life.* These two features of Eden claim special attention.

I. THEIR RECURRENCE IN SCRIPTURE. They link the paradise of unfallen man to that of redeemed man. Actual channels of life and blessing, they were also figures of that salvation which the history of the world was gradually to unfold. But sin came, and death ; present possession was lost. What remained was the promise of a Saviour. We pass over much of preparation for his coming : the selection of a people ; the care of God for his vineyard ; the ordinances and services foreshadowing the gospel. Then a time of trouble : Jerusalem a desolation ; the people in captivity ; the temple destroyed ; the ark gone ; sacrifices at an end. "Where is now thy God?" Where thy hope? Such the state of the world when a vision given to Ezekiel (Ezek. xlvii. 1—12), reproducing the imagery of Eden, but adapted to the need of fallen man. Again we have the stream ; now specially to heal. Its source the mercy-seat (comp. Ezek. xliii. 1—7; xlvii. 1; Rev. xxii. 1). And the trees ; not different from the tree of life (Ezek. xlvii. 12: "*It* shall bring forth new fruit"); varied manifestations of grace ; for food and for medicine. But observe, the vision is of a coming dispensation. Again a space. Our Saviour's earthly ministry over. The Church is struggling on. The work committed to weak hands ; the treasure in earthen vessels. But before the volume of revelation closed, the same symbols are shown in vision to St. John (Rev. xxii. 1, 2). The "river of water of life" (cf. "living water," John iv. 10), and the tree whose fruit and leaves are for food and healing. Meanwhile our Lord had said, "Blessed are they which do hunger and thirst after righteousness." A link to connect this with Gen. ii. is Rev. ii. 7 (cf. also Rev. xii. 11). And again, the word used for "tree" in all these passages is that used for the cross in Gal. iii. 13 and 1 Pet. ii. 24.

II. THEIR SPIRITUAL SIGNIFICANCE. The tree with its fruit and leaves are the manifestation of Christ to the soul—to sinners pardon, to the weak support and guidance, to saints communion. And the stream is the gospel (the four-parted river in Eden has been likened to the four Gospels), spreading throughout the world, bringing healing, light, and life ; enabling men to rejoice in hope. But mark, the drops of which that stream is composed are living men. The gospel spreads from heart to heart, and from lip to lip (cf. John vii. 38). Forming part of that healing flood are preachers of the gospel in every place and way ; and thinkers contending for the faith ; and men mighty in prayer ; and those whose loving, useful lives set forth Christ ; and the sick silently preaching patience ; and the child in his little ministry. There is helping work for all. The Lord hath need of all. To each one the question comes, Art thou part of that stream? Hast thou realised the stream of mercy, the gift of salvation for thine own need? And canst thou look at the many still unhealed and be content to do nothing? Thou couldst not cause the stream to flow ; but it is thine to press the "living water" upon others, to help to save others Art thou doing this? Is there not within the circle of thy daily life some one in grief whom Christian sympathy may help, some anxious one whom a word of faith may strengthen, some undecided one who may be influenced? There is thy work. Let the reality of Christ's gift and his charge to thee so fill thy heart that real longing may lead to earnest prayer ; then a way will be opened.—M.

EXPOSITION.

Ver. 18.—In anticipation of the ensuing narrative of the temptation and the fall, the historian, having depicted man's settlement in Eden, advances to complete his *dramatis personæ* by the introduction upon the scene of the animals and woman. In the preliminary creation record (I. 27) it is simply stated that God created man, male and female ; there is a complete absence of details as to the Divine *modus operandi* in the execution of these, his last and greatest works. It is one object, among others, of the second portion of the history to supply those details. With regard to man (Adam), an account of his formation, at once minute and exhaustive, has been given in the preceding verses (7—17) ; now, with like attention to antecedent and concomitant circumstances and events, the sacred penman adds a description of the time, reason, manner, and result of the formation of woman. **And the Lord God said, It is not good for man to be alone.** While the animals were produced either in swarms (as the fishes) or in pairs (as the birds and beasts), man was created as an individual ; his partner, by a subsequent operation of creative power, being produced from himself. With the wild phantasies and gross speculations of some theosophists, as to whether, prior to the creation of Eve, Adam was androgynic (Bohme), or simply *vir in potentia*, out of which state he passed the moment the woman stood by his side (Ziegler), a devout exegesis is not required to intermeddle. Neither is it needful to wonder how God should pronounce that to be not good which he had previously (i. 31) affirmed was good. The Divine judgment of which the preceding chapter speaks was expressed at the completion of man's creation ; this, while that creation was in progress. For the new-made man to have been left without a partner would, in the estimation of Jehovah Elohim, have been for him a condition of being which, if not necessarily bad in itself, yet, considering his intellectual and social nature, "would eventually have passed over from the negative not good, or a manifest want, into the positive not good, or a hurtful impropriety" (Lange). "It was not good for man to be alone ; not, as certain foolish Rabbis conceited, lest he should imagine himself to be the lord of the world, or as though no man could live without a woman, which is contrary to Scripture ; but in respect of (1) mutual society and comfort, (2) the propagation of the race, (3) the increase and generation of the Church of God, and (4) the promised seed of the woman (Willet). Accordingly, Jehovah Elohim,

for whom (seeing that his nature is to dispense happiness to his creatures) no more than for Adam would it have been good that man, being what he was, should remain alone, said, **I will provide a help meet for him ;** literally, an helper, as over against him, *i. e.* corresponding to him, βοηθὸν κατ' αὐτόν ; ver. 20, ὅμοιος αὐτῷ, LXX. The expression indicates that the forthcoming helper was to be of similar nature to the man himself, corresponding by way of supplement to the incompleteness of his lonely being, and in every way adapted to be his co-partner and companion. All that Adam's nature demanded for its completion, physically, intellectually, socially, was to be included in this *altera ego* who was soon to stand by his side. Thus in man's need, and woman's power to satisfy that need, is laid the foundation for the Divine institution of marriage, which was afterwards prescribed not for the first pair alone, but for all their posterity.

Ver. 19.—**And out of the ground the Lord God formed every beast of the field, and every fowl of the air.** To allege that the Creator's purpose to provide a helpmeet for Adam seeks realisation through the production of the animals (Kalisch, Alford) proceeds upon a misapprehension of the proper *nexus* which binds the thoughts of the historian, and a want of attention to the peculiar structure of Hebrew composition, besides exhibiting Jehovah Elohim in the character of an empiric who only tentatively discovers the sort of partner that is suitable for man. It is not the time, but simply the fact, of the creation of the animals that the historian records. The *Vav.* consec. does not necessarily involve time-succession, but is frequently employed to indicate thought-sequence (cf. ii. 8 ; 1 Kings ii. 13, &c.). The verb (pret.) may also quite legitimately be rendered "had formed" (Bush). "Our modern style of expressing the Semitic writer's thought would be this—'And God brought to Adam the beasts which he had formed'" (Delitzsch). It is thus unnecessary to defend the record from a charge of inconsistency with the previous section, by supposing this to be the account of a second creation of animals in the district of Eden. Another so-called contradiction, that the present narrative takes no account of the creation of aquatic animals, is disposed of by observing that the writer only notices that those animals which were brought to Adam had been previously formed by God from the ground, and were thus in the line of the onward evolutions of the heavens and the earth which led up to man. As to why the fishes were not brought into the garden, if other reason is required besides that of physical impossibility, the ingenuity of Keil suggests that these were not so nearly related to Adam as the fowls and the beasts, which, besides, were the animals specially ordained for his service. **And brought** them (literally, brought; not necessarily all the animals in Eden, but specimens of them) **unto Adam.** We agree with Willet in believing that "neither did Adam gather together the cattle as a shepherd doth his sheep, nor did the angels muster them, nor the animals come themselves, and, passing by, while he sat on some elevation, bow their heads at his resplendent appearance; nor were Adam's eyes so illuminate that he beheld them all in their places—all which," says he, "are but men's conceits;" but that through the secret influence of God upon their natures they were assembled round the inmate of paradise, as afterwards they were collected in the ark. The reasons for this particular action on the part of God were manifold; one of them being stated in the words which follow—**to see what he would call them**; literally, to them. Already man had received from God his first lesson in the exercise of speech, in the naming of the trees and the imposition of the prohibition. This was his second—the opportunity afforded him of using for himself that gift of language and reason with which he had been endowed. In this it is implied that man was created with the faculty of speech, the distinct gift of articulate and rational utterance, and the capacity of attaching words to ideas, though it also seems to infer that the evolution of a language was for him, as it is for the individual yet, a matter of gradual development. Another reason was to manifest his sovereignty or lordship over the inferior creation. **And whatsoever Adam** (literally, the man) **called every living creature** (i. e. that was brought to him), **that was the name thereof.** That is to say, it not only met the Divine approbation as exactly suitable to the nature of the creature, and thus was a striking attestation of the intelligence and wisdom of the first man, but it likewise adhered to the creature as a name which had been assigned by its master.

Ver. 20.—**And Adam gave names to all cattle, and to the fowl of the air, and to every beast of the field.** The portrait here delineated of the first man is something widely different from that of an infantile savage slowly groping his way towards the possession of articulate speech and intelligible language by imitation of the sounds of animals. Speech and language both spring full-formed, though not completely matured, from the *primus homo* of the Bible. As to the names that Adam gave the animals, with Calvin we need not doubt that they were founded on the best of reasons, though what they were it is impossible to discover, as it is not absolutely certain that Adam spoke in Hebrew. **But for Adam there was not found an help meet for him.** This was the chief reason for assembling the creatures. It was meant to reveal his loneliness. The longing for a partner was already deeply seated in his nature, and the survey of the animals, coming to him probably in pairs, could not fail to intensify that secret hunger of his soul, and perhaps evoke it into conscious operation.

Ver. 21.—**And the Lord God caused a deep sleep to fall upon Adam, and he slept.** This was clearly not a sleep of weariness or fatigue, in consequence of arduous labours undergone, but a supernatural slumber, which, however, may have been superinduced upon the natural condition of repose. Lightfoot, following the LXX., who translate *tardemah* (deep sleep) by *ecstasy*, ἔκστασις, imagines that the whole scene of Eve's creation was presented to Adam's imagination in a Divinely-inspired dream, which has at least the countenance of Job iv. 13 Such a supposition, however, is not required to account for Adam's recognition of his bride. There is more of aptness in the observation of Lange, that in the deep sleep of Adam we have an echo of the creative evenings that preceded the Divine activity. "Everything out of which some new thing is to come sinks down before the event into such a deep sleep," is the far-seeing and comprehensive remark of Ziegler. **And he took one of his ribs** (*tsela* = something bent, from *tsala*, to incline; hence a rib), **and closed up the flesh** (literally, flesh) **instead thereof.** Whether Adam was created with a superfluous rib, or his body was mutilated by the abstraction of a rib, is a question for the curious. In the first, Calvin finds nothing "which is not in accordance with Divine providence," while he favours the latter conjecture, and thinks that Adam got a rich compensation—"quum se integrum vidit in uxore, qui prius tantum dimidius erat." Luther inclines to think that Adam's language in ver. 23 implies that not the bare rib, but the rib with the accompanying flesh, was extracted.

Ver. 22.—**And the rib, which the Lord God had taken from man, made he** (literally, builded into; *ædificavit*, Vulgate; ᾠκοδόμησεν, LXX.) **a woman.** The peculiar phraseology employed to describe the formation of Adam's partner has been understood as referring to the physical configuration of woman's body, which is broadest towards the middle (Lyra); to the incompleteness of Adam's being, which was like an unfinished building until Eve was formed (Calvin); to the part of the female in building up the family (Delitzsch, Macdonald), to the building up of the Church, of which she was designed to be a type (Bonar);—yet it may be doubted if there is not as much truth in the remark that "by the many words used in the generation of mankind, as *creating* (ch. i. 27), *making* (ch. i. 26), *forming* and *inspiring* (ch. ii. 7), and now *building*, Moses would set forth this wondrous workmanship for which the Psalmist so laudeth God," Ps. cxxxix. 14 (Ainsworth). **And brought her unto the man.** *I. e.* led, conducted, and presented her to Adam. "The word implies the solemn bestowment of her in the bonds of the marriage covenant, which is hence called the covenant of God (Prov. ii. 17); implying that he is the Author of this sacred institution" (Bush). On awaking from his slumber Adam at once recognised the Divine intention, and joyfully welcomed his bride.

Ver. 23.—**And Adam said.** Either as being possessed, while in a sinless state, of a power of intuitive perception which has been lost through the fall, or as speaking under Divine inspiration (*vide* Matt. xix. 4—6). **This now.** Literally, this tread, step, or stroke, meaning either this time, looking back to the previous review of the animal creation, as if he wished to say, At last one has come who is suitable to be my partner (Calvin); or, less probably, looking forward to the ordinary mode of woman's production, this time she is supernaturally formed (Bush). "The thrice repeated *this* is characteristic. It vividly points to the woman on whom, in joyful astonishment, the man's eye now rests with the full power of first love" (Delitzsch). Instinctively he recognises her relation to himself. **Bone of my bone, and flesh of my flesh.** The language is expressive at once of woman's derivation from man (γυνὴ ἐξ ἀνδρός, 1 Cor. xi. 8, 12) and likeness to man. The first of these implies her subordination or subjection to man, or man's headship over woman (1 Cor. xi. 3), which Adam immediately proceeds to assert by assigning to her a name; the second is embodied in the name which she receives. **She** (literally, to this) **shall be called Woman** (*isha*, i. e. maness, from *ish*, man. Cf. Greek, ἀνδρίς (Symmachus), from ἀνήρ; Latin, *vir-ago*, *viræ* (old Latin), from *vir;* English, woman (wombman, Anglo-Saxon), from man; German, *männinn*, from *mann;* Sanscrit, *nari*, from *nara;* Ethiopic, *beesith*, from *beesi*), **because she** (this) **was taken from Man.** *Ish*, the name given by Adam to himself in contradistinction to his spouse, is interpreted as significant of man's authority (Gesenius), or of his social nature (Meier); but its exact etymology is involved in obscurity. Its relation to *Adham* is the same as that of *vir* to *homo* and ἀνήρ to ἄνθρωπος.

Ver. 24.—**Therefore shall a man leave his father and mother, and shall cleave unto his wife.** There is nothing in the use of such

terms as father and mother, or in the fact that the sentiment is prophetic, to prevent the words from being regarded as a continuation of Adam's speech, although, on the other hand, the statement of Christ (Matt. xix. 5) does not preclude the possibility of Moses being their author; but whether uttered by the first husband (Delitzsch, Macdonald) or by the historian (Calvin, Murphy), they must be viewed as an inspired declaration of the law of marriage. Its *basis* (fundamental reason and predisposing cause) they affirm to be (1) the original relationship of man and woman, on the platform of creation; and (2) the marriage union effected between the first pair. Its *nature* they explain to be (1) a forsaking (on the part of the woman as well as the man) of father and mother—not filially, in respect of duty, but locally, in respect of habitation, and comparatively, in respect of affection; and (2) a cleaving unto his wife, in a *conjugium corporis atque animæ*. Its *result* is stated in the words which follow: **and they shall be one flesh** (literally, into one flesh; εἰς σάρκα μίαν, Matt. xix. 5, LXX.). The language points to a unity of persons, and not simply to a conjunction of bodies, or a community of interests, or even a reciprocity of affections. Malachi (ch. ii. 15) and Christ (Matt. xix. 5) explain this verse as teaching the indissoluble character of marriage and condemning the practice of polygamy.

Ver. 25.—**And they were both naked.** Not partially (Pye Smith), but completely destitute of clothing. Diodorus Siculus and Plato both mention nakedness as a feature of the golden age and a characteristic of the first men (*vide* Rosenmüller, *Scholia in loco*). **The man and his wife.** The first pair of human beings are henceforth recognised in their relationship to one another as husband and wife. **And they were not ashamed.** Not because they were wholly uncultivated and their moral insight undeveloped (Knobel, Kalisch); but because their souls were arrayed in purity, and "their bodies were made holy through the spirit which animated them" (Keil). "They were naked, but yet they were not so. Their bodies were the clothing of their internal glory; and their internal glory was the clothing of their nakedness" (Delitzsch).

It is not surprising that the primeval history of mankind should have left its impress upon the current of tradition. The Assyrian tablets that relate to man are so fragmentary and mutilated that they can scarcely be rendered intelligible. So far as they have been deciphered, the first appears on its obverse side "to give the speech of the Deity to the newly-created pair (man and woman), instructing them in their duties," in which can be detected a reference to something which is eaten by the stomach, to the duty of daily invocation of the Deity, to the danger of leaving God's fear, in which alone they can be holy, and to the propriety of trusting only a friend ; and on its reverse what resembles a discourse to the first woman on her duties, in which occur the words, With the lord of thy beauty thou shalt be faithful : to do evil thou shalt not approach him" ('Chaldean Genesis,' pp. 78 — 80). The Persian legend describes Meschia and Meschiane, the first parents of our race, as living in purity and innocence, and in the enjoyment of happiness which Ormuzd promised to render perpetual if they persevered in virtue. But Ahriman, an evil demon (Dev), suddenly appeared in the form of a serpent, and gave them of the fruit of a wonderful tree. The literature of the Hindoos distinguishes four ages of the world, in the first of which Justice, in the form of a bull, kept herself firm on her four feet ; when Virtue reigned, no good which the mortals possessed was mixed with baseness, and man, free from disease, saw all his wishes accomplished, and attained an age of 400 years. The Chinese also have their age of happy men, living in abundance of food, and surrounded by the peaceful beasts ('Kalisch on Genesis,' p. 87). In the Zendavesta, Yima, the first Iranic king, lives in a secluded spot, where he and his people enjoy uninterrupted happiness, in a region free from sin, folly, violence, poverty, deformity. The Teutonic Eddas have a glimpse of the same truth in their magnificent drinking halls, glittering with burnished gold, where the primeval race enjoyed a life of perpetual festivity. Traces of a similar belief are found among the Thibetans, Mongolians, Cingalese, and others (Rawlinson's 'Hist. Illustrations of Scripture,' p. 10). The Western traditions are familiar to scholars in the pages of Hesiod, who speaks of the golden age when men were like the gods, free from labours, troubles, cares, and all evils in general ; when the earth yielded her fruits spontaneously, and when men were beloved by the gods, with whom they held uninterrupted communion (Hesiod, 'Opera et Dies,' 90). And of Ovid, who adds to this picture the element of moral goodness as a characteristic of the *aurea ætas* ('Metam.,' i. 89). Macrobius ('Somn. Scipionis,' ii. 10) also depicts this period as one in which reigned *simplicitas mali nescia et adhuc astutiæ inexperta* (Macdonald, 'Creation and the Fall,' p. 147). "These coincidences affect the originality of the Hebrew writings as little as the frequent resemblance of Mosaic and heathen laws. They teach us that all such narratives have a common source ; that they are reminiscences of primeval traditions modified by the different nations in accordance with their individual culture" (Kalisch)

HOMILETICS.

Ver. 22.—*The first marriage.* I. THE LONELY MAN. 1. *Nobly born.* Sprung from the soil, yet descended from above. Fashioned of the dust, yet inspired by a celestial breath. Allied to the beasts, yet the offspring of God. 2. *Comfortably placed.* His native country a sunny region of delights (Eden, ch. ii. 8) ; his home a beautiful and fertile garden (ch. iii. 5) ; his supplies of the amplest possible description (ch. i. 30 ; ii. 16) ; his occupation light and pleasant (ch. ii. 15) ; his restrictions slight and trivial (ch. ii. 17) ; his privileges large (ch. ii. 16). 3. *Richly endowed.* With immortality (ch. ii. 17), intelligence (ch. ii. 19), social capacities and instincts (ch. ii. 18), the faculty of speech (ch. ii. 20). 4. *Highly exalted.* As God's offspring, he was invested with world-dominion (ch. i. 28 ; Ps. viii. 6), symbolised in his naming of the creatures (ch. ii. 20). Yet—5. *Essentially alone.* Not as entirely bereft of companionship, having on the one hand the society of Jehovah Elohim, and on the other the presence of the animals ; but in neither the Creator nor the creatures could he find his other self—his counterpart and complement, his consort and companion. On the one hand Jehovah Elohim was too high, while on the other the creatures were too low, for such partnership as Adam's nature craved. And so Adam dwelt in solitude apart from both. "But for Adam there was not found an help meet for him."

II. THE PROVIDED PARTNER. 1. *Divinely fashioned* (ver. 22). (1) Woman was the last of God's creative works ; presumably, therefore, she was the best. "Eve's being made after Adam puts an honour upon that sex as the glory of the man (1 Cor. xi. 7). If man is the head, she is the crown—a crown to her husband, the crown of the visible creation" (M. Henry). (2) Woman was not made till everything was in the highest state of readiness for her reception. Before her creation, not only must there be a home for her reception, provision for her maintenance, and servants to attend upon her bidding; there must likewise be a husband that feels the need of her sweet society, that longs for her coming, and that can appreciate her worth. Hence he who seeks a partner should first find a house in which to lodge her, the means to support her, but specially the love wherewith to cherish her.   (3) Woman was formed out of finer and more precious material than man, being constructed of a rib taken from his side.   "The man was dust refined, but the woman was dust double refined, one remove further from the earth" (M. Henry).   This was not because of any supposed excellence residing in the matter of a human body.   It was designed to indicate woman's unity with man as part of himself, and woman's claim upon man for affection and protection.   She was made of a rib taken from his side—"not made out of his head, to rule over him; nor out of his feet, to be trampled on by him; but out of his side, to be equal with him; under his arm, to be protected; and near his heart, to be beloved" (Henry).   (4) Woman was constructed with the greatest possible care.   The entire operation was carried through, not only under God's immediate superintendence, but exclusively by God's own hand.   Adam neither saw, knew, nor took part in the work.   God cast him into a deep sleep, "that no room might be left to imagine that he had herein directed the Spirit of the Lord, or been his counsellor" (Henry).   Then by God's own hand Adam's side was opened, a rib extracted, the flesh closed in its stead, and finally, the rib thus removed from Adam's side—

> "Under his forming hands a creature grew,
> Man like, but different sex; so lovely fair,
> That what seemed fair in all the world, seemed now
> Mean, or in her summed up, in her contained,
> And in her looks; . . . . .
> Grace was in all her steps, heaven in her eye,
> In every gesture dignity and love" (Milton, 'Par. Lost,' Bk. viii. 469).

2. *Divinely presented* (ver. 22).   "The Lord brought her unto the man." "Wherein we have exemplified the three great causes of marriage.   (1) The father's consent, in God's giving.   (2) The woman's consent, in Eve's coming.   This was no forced marriage; the woman comes freely.   (3) The man's consent, in Adam's receiving.   'And Adam said, This is at last bone of my bone'" (Hughes).   And without these human marriages are sinfully contracted.   Love for the bride is one of the signs which God vouchsafes of his approval of a marriage; the bride's affection for the bridegroom is another; while a third is the approbation and the blessing of the parents of both.

III. THE WEDDED PAIR.   1. *Married by God.*   "God is the best maker of marriages" (Shakespeare).   Nay, unless God unites there is no real marriage, but only an unhallowed connection, legitimised by man's laws, it may be, but not sanctioned by God's.   As this wedding was of God's arranging, so likewise was it of his celebrating.   What celestial benedictions were outbreathed upon the young and innocent pair, as they stood there before their Maker, radiant in beauty, tremulous with joy, full of adoration, we are left to imagine.   Happy they whose nuptials are first sanctioned and then celebrated by the living God!   2. *United in love.*   This first marriage was certainly something more than a social or a civil contract; something other than a union of convenience or a diplomatic alliance; something vastly different from a legalised connubium.   It was the realisation of what our Laureate pictures as the ideal marriage:—

> "Each fulfils
> Defect in each, and always thought in thought,
> Purpose in purpose, will in will, they grow,
> The single, pure, and perfect animal;
> The two-cell'd heart beating, with one full stroke,
> Life" ('Princess,' vii.).

3. *Clothed in innocence.*   Never had bridal pair so beautiful and radiant apparel. The unclothed bodies of our first parents we can imagine were enswathed in ethereal and transfiguring light; in their case the outshining of their holy souls, which, as yet,

were the undimmed and unmarred image of their Maker, capable of receiving and reflecting his glory. Alas, never bridal pair has stood in robes so fair! The beauty of holiness, the lustre of innocence, the radiance of purity have departed from the souls of men. Never till we stand in the celestial Eden, where they neither marry nor are given in marriage, will garments of such incomparable splendour be ours. Meantime, let us thank God there is a spotless raiment in which our guilty souls may be arrayed, and in which it were well that every bridal pair were decked. Happy they who, when they enter into married life, can say, "I will greatly rejoice in the Lord, my soul shall be joyful in my God; for he hath clothed me with the garments of salvation, he hath covered me with the robe of righteousness, as a bridegroom decketh himself with ornaments, and as a bride adorneth herself with jewels." 4. *Housed in paradise.* United by the hand of God, they began their married life in Eden.

> "And there these twain upon the skirts of time
> Sat side by side, full summ'd in all their powers,
> Dispensing harvest, sowing the to-be.
> Self-reverent each, and reverencing each;
> Distinct in individualities,
> But like each other, ev'n as those who love" (Tennyson's 'Princess,' vii.).

And so may any wedded pair be housed in Eden who, putting on the Lord Jesus Christ, fill their home, however humble, with the light of love.

HOMILIES BY VARIOUS AUTHORS.

Vers. 18—25.—*The true life of man.* The commencement of human society. First we see man surrounded by cattle, fowl, and beast of the field, which were brought to him by God as to their lord and ruler, that he might name them as from himself. "What *he* called every living creature was the name thereof." Nothing could better represent the organisation of the earthly life upon the basis of man's supremacy. But there is no helpmeet for man ("*as before him,*" the reflection of himself) in all the lower creation.

I. HUMAN SOCIETY MUST SPRING OUT OF SOMETHING HIGHER THAN ANIMAL LIFE AND MAN'S MERE EARTHLY POSITION. The deep sleep, the Divine manipulation of man's fleshly frame, the formation of the new creature, not out of the ground, but out of man, the exclamation of Adam, This is another self, my bone and my flesh, therefore she shall be called *woman*, because so closely akin to man—all this, whatever physical interpretation we give to it, represents the fact that companionship, family life, man's intercourse with his fellow, all the relations which spring from the fleshly unity of the race, are of the most sacred character. As they are *from God*, and specially of God's *appointment*, so they should be *for God*.

II. There, in home life, torn off, as it were, from the larger sphere, that it may be THE NEW BEGINNING OF THE NEW WORLD TO US, should be the special recognition of God, the family altar, the house of man a house of God.

III. The Divine beginning of human life is the foundation on which we build up society. THE RELATIONS OF THE SEXES WILL BE PUREST AND NOBLEST the more the heart of man unfolds itself in the element of the heavenly love.—R.

EXPOSITION.

CHAPTER III.

Vers. 1—7.—How long the paradisiacal state of innocence and felicity continued the historian does not declare, probably as not falling within the scope of his immediate design. Ps. xlix. 12 has been thought, though without sufficient reason, to hint that man's Eden life was of comparatively short duration. The present chapter relates the tragic incident which brought it to a termination. Into the question of the origin of moral evil in the universe it does not enter. The metaphysical problem of how the first thought of sin could arise in innocent beings it does not attempt to resolve. It seeks to explain the genesis of evil with reference to man. Nor even with regard to this does it aim at an exhaustive dissertation, but only at such a statement of its beginnings as shall demonstrate that God is not the author of sin, but that man, by his own free volition, brought his pristine state of purity and happiness to an end. A due regard to this, the specific object of the Mosaic narrative, will go far to answer not a few of the objections which have been taken to its historic credibility. Like the Mosaic record of creation, the Biblical story of the fall has been impugned on a variety of grounds. 1. The *doctrine* of a fall, which this chapter clearly teaches, has been assailed as inconsistent with the dictates of a speculative philosophy, if not also with the tenets of a Scriptural theology. While in the present narrative the origin of sin is distinctly traced back to the free volition of man acting without constraint, though not without temptation, in opposition to the Divine will, a more exact psychological analysis, it is alleged, declares it to have been from the first a necessity, either (1) *metaphysically*, as being involved in the very conception of a finite will (Spinoza, Leibnitz, Baur) ; or (2) *historically*, "as the expression of the necessary transition of the human race from the state of nature to that of culture" (Fichte, Kant, Schiller), or as developing itself in obedience to the law of antagonism and conflict (John Scotus Erigena, Hegel, Schleiermacher, Schelling) ; or (3) *theologically*, as predetermined by a Divine decree (supralapsarianism). Without offering any separate refutation of these anti-Scriptural theories, it may suffice to say that in all questions affecting man's responsibility, the testimony of the individual consciousness, the ultimate ground of appeal, apart from revelation, affirms moral evil to be no all-controlling necessity, but the free product of the will of the creature. 2. The *narrative* of the fall has been impugned—(1) On the ground of its *miraculous character*. But unless we are prepared to equate the supernatural with the impossible and incredible, we must decline to admit the force of such objections. (2) On the ground of its *mythical form*, resembling as it does, in some slight degree, Oriental traditions, and in particular the Persian legend of Ormuzd and Ahriman (*vide infra*, 'Traditions of the Fall'). But here the same remark will apply as was made in connection with the similarity alleged to exist between the Mosaic and heathen cosmogonies : it is immeasurably easier and more natural to account for the resemblance of Oriental legend to Biblical history, by supposing the former to be a traditional reflection of the latter, than it is to explain the unchallengeable superiority of the latter to the former, even in a literary point of view, not to mention ethical aspects at all, by tracing both to a common source—the philosophic or theologic consciousness of man. (3) There are also those who, while neither repudiating it on the ground of miracle, nor discrediting it as a heathen myth, yet decline to accept it as other than a *parabolic* or allegorical narration of what transpired in the spiritual experience of the first pair. History is often a parable of truth.

Ver. 1.—**Now** (literally, and) **the serpent.** *Nachash*, from *nachash* — (1) in Kal, to hiss (unused), with allusion to the hissing sound emitted by the reptile (Gesenius, Fürst), though it has been objected that prior to the fall the serpent could hardly have been called by a name derived from its present constitution (Delitzsch) ; (2) in Piel, to whisper, use sorcery, find out by divination (ch. xxx. 27), suggestive of the creature's wisdom (Bush), which, however, is regarded as doubtful (Fürst); (3) to shine (unused, though supplying the noun *nechsheth*, brass, ch. iv. 22), referring to its glossy shining appearance, and in particular its bright glistening eye : cf. δράκων from δέρκομαι, and ὄφις from ὄπτομαι (T. Lewis) ; (4) from an Arabic root signifying to pierce, to move, to creep, so that *nachash* would be Latin *serpens* (Fürst). The presence of the article before *nachash* has been thought to mean *a certain serpent*, but " by eminent authorities this is pronounced to be unwarranted" (Macdonald). **Was more subtil.** *'Arum*—(1) Crafty (cf. Job v. 12; xv. 5); (2) prudent, in a good sense (cf. Prov. xii. 16), from *'aram*—(*a*) To make naked ; whence *arom*, plural *arumim*, naked (ch. ii. 25). (*b*) To be crafty (1 Sam. xxiii. 22). If applied to the serpent in the sense of πανοῦργος (Aquila, Keil, Lange, Macdonald), it can only be either (1) metaphorically for the devil, whose instrument it was ; or (2) proleptically, with reference to the results of the temptation; for in itself, as one of God's creatures, it must have been originally good. It seems more correct to regard the epithet as equivalent to φρόνιμος (LXX.), and to hold that Moses, in referring to the subtlety of this creature, "does not so much point out a fault as attribute praise to nature" (Calvin), and describes qualities which in themselves were good, such as quickness of sight, swiftness of motion, activity of the self-preserving instinct, seemingly intelligent adaptation of means to end, with perhaps a glance, in the use of 'arum, at the sleekness of its glossy skin ; but which were capable of being perverted to an unnatural use by the power and craft of a superior intelligence (cf. Matt. x. 16: γίνεσθε οὖν φρόνιμοι ὡς οἱ ὄφεις). **Than any** (literally, *was subtil more than any*) **beast of the field which the Lord God had made.** The comparison here instituted is commonly regarded as a proof that the tempter was a literal serpent, though Macdonald finds in the contrast between it and all other creatures, as well as in the ascription to it of pre-eminent subtlety, which is not now a characteristic of serpents, " an intimation that the reptile was no creature of earth, or one that received its form from God," an opinion scarcely different from that of Cyril (c. Julian., lib. 3), that it was only the *simulacrum* of a serpent.   But (1) the curse pronounced upon the serpent (ch. iii. 14) would seem to be deprived of all force if the subject of it had been only an apparition or an unreal creature ; and (2) the language of the New Testament in referring to man's temptation implies its literality (cf. 2 Cor. xi. 3).   "We are perfectly justified in concluding, from this mention of the fall, that Paul spoke of it as an actual occurrence" (Olshausen).   Adam Clarke contends with much enthusiasm that the tempter was not a serpent, but an ape or ourang outang.   **And he said.**   Not as originally endowed with speech (Josephus, Clarke), or gifted at this particular time with the power of articulation (' Ephrem., lib. de paradiso,' c. 27, quoted by Willet), but simply as used by the devil (Augustine, Calvin, Rosenmüller, *et alii*), who from this circumstance is commonly styled in Scripture "the serpent," "the old serpent," "that old serpent" (cf. Rev. xii. 9 ; xx. 2).   Nor is it more difficult to understand the speaking of the serpent when possessed by Satan, than the talking of Balaam's ass when the Lord opened its mouth (Num. xxii. 28—30).   Equally with the idea that the devil was the only agent in man's temptation, and that the serpent is purely the allegorical dress in which the historian clothes him (Eusebius, Cajetan, Quarry, Alford), must the notion be rejected that there was nothing but a serpent (Aben Ezra, Kalisch, Knobel). Why, if there was an evil spirit manipulating the reptile, the historian did not say so has been explained (1) on the ground that the belief in the devil was then foreign to the Hebrews (Knobel) ; (2) that up to this point in the narrative there is no mention of the

devil (White of Dorchester) ; (3) that Moses simply wished to be *rei gestæ scriptor non interpres* (Pererius) ; (4) that it was unnecessary, those for whom he wrote being sufficiently capable of discerning that the serpent was not the prime mover in the transaction (Candlish) ; (5) that " by a homely and uncultivated style he accommodates what he delivers to the capacity of the people" (Calvin) ; (6) that his object being merely to show that God had no hand in man's temptation, but that Adam sinned of himself, it was not needful to do more than recite the incident as it appeared to the senses (White) ; (7) that he wished " to avoid encouraging the disposition to transfer the blame to the evil spirit which tempted man, and thus reduce sin to a mere act of weakness" (Keil). **Unto the woman.**   As the weaker of the two, and more likely to be easily persuaded (1 Tim. ii. 14 ; 1 Pet. iii. 7).   Cf. Satan's assault on Job through his wife (Job ii. 9). Milton's idea that Eve desired to be independent, and had withdrawn herself out of Adam's sight, it has been well remarked, " sets up a beginning of the fall before the fall itself" (Lange).   **Yea.** אַף כִּי.   Is it even so that? (Gesenius). Is it really so that ? (Ewald, Fürst, Keil).   *Etiamne, vel Itane* (Calvin). A question either (1) spoken in irony, as if the meaning were, " Very like it is that God careth what you eat !" or (2) inquiring the reason of the prohibition (LXX., τί ὅτι εἶπεν ὁ θεὸς ; Vulgate, *cur præcepit vobis Deus*) ; or (3) simply soliciting information (Chaldee Paraphrase) ; but (4) most likely expressing surprise and astonishment, with the view of suggesting distrust of the Divine goodness and disbelief in the Divine veracity (Ewald, Rosenmüller, Kalisch, Keil, Macdonald, Lange).   The conversation may have been commenced by the tempter, and the question " thrown out as a feeler for some weak point where the fidelity of the woman might be shaken" (Murphy) ; but it is more likely that the devil spoke in continuation of a colloquy which is not reported (Kalisch, Macdonald), which has led some, on the supposition that already many arguments had been adduced to substantiate the Divine severity, to render " yea" by " *quanto magis*," as if the meaning were, " How much more is this a proof of God's unkindness !" (Aben Ezra, Kimchi).   **Hath God said.**   " The tempter felt it necessary to change the living personal God into a merely general *numen divinum* " (Keil) ; but the Elohim of ch. i. 1 was not a mere *numen divinum*.   As much astray is the observation that Satan wished to avoid profaning the name of Jehovah (Knobel).   Better is the remark that the serpent could not utter the name Jehovah, as his assault was directed against the paradisiacal covenant of God with man (Lange). By using the name Elohim instead of Jehovah the covenant relationship of God towards man was obscured, and man's position in the garden represented as that of a subject rather than a son. As it were, Eve was first placed at the furthest distance possible from the supreme, and then assailed. **Ye shall not eat of every tree of the garden.** *I. e.* either accepting the present rendering as correct, which the Hebrew will bear,—"Are there any trees in the garden of which you may not eat?" "Is it really so that God hath prohibited you from some?" (Calvin),—or, translating *lo-kol* as *not any*—Latin, *nullus* (Gesenius, § 152, 1)—"Hath God said ye shall not eat of any?" (Macdonald, Keil). According to the first the devil simply seeks to impeach the Divine goodness; according to the second he also aims at intensifying the Divine prohibition. The second rendering appears to be supported by the fitness of Eve's reply.

Vers. 2, 3.—And the woman said unto the serpent. Neither afraid of the reptile, there being not yet any enmity among the creatures; nor astonished at his speaking, perhaps as being not yet fully acquainted with the capabilities of the lower animals; nor suspicious of his designs, her innocence and inexperience not predisposing her to apprehend danger. Yet the tenor of the reptile's interrogation was fitted to excite alarm; and if, as some conjecture, she understood that Satan was the speaker, she should at once have taken flight; while, if she knew nothing of him or his disposition, she should not have opened herself so freely to a person unknown. "The woman certainly discovers some unadvisedness in entertaining conference with the serpent, in matters of so great importance, in so familiar a manner" (White). **We may eat of the fruit of the trees of the garden.** (1) Omitting the Divine name when recording his liberality, though she remembers it when reciting his restraint; (2) failing to do justice to the largeness and freeness of the Divine grant (cf. with ch. ii. 16);—which, however, charity would do well not to press against the woman as symptoms of incipient rebellion. **But of the fruit of the tree which is in the midst of the garden, God hath said, Ye shall not eat of it, neither shall ye touch it.** An addition to the prohibitory enactment, which may have been simply an inaccuracy in her understanding of Adam's report of its exact terms (Kalisch); or the result of a rising feeling of dissatisfaction with the too great strictness of the prohibition (Delitzsch), and so an indication "that her love and confidence towards God were already beginning to waver" (Keil); or a proof of her anxiety to observe the Divine precept (Calvin); or a statement of her un-

derstanding "that they were not to meddle with it as a forbidden thing" (Murphy). **Lest ye die.** Even Calvin here admits that Eve begins to give way, reading פֶּן as *forte*, with which Macdonald appears to agree, discovering "doubt and hesitancy" in her language; but—(1) the conjunction may point to a consequence which is certain—indeed this is its usual meaning (cf. ch. xi. 4; xix. 5; Ps. ii. 12); (2) "Where there are so many *real* grounds for condemning Eve's conduct, it is our duty to be cautious in giving those which are problematical" (Bush); and, (3) "she would have represented the penalty in a worse rather than a softened form had she begun to think it unjust" (Inglis).

Ver. 4.—And the serpent said unto the woman. "As God had preached to Adam, so Satan now also preaches to Eve. . . . . The object of Satan was to draw away Eve by *his word* or saying from that which God had said" (Luther). **Ye shall not surely die.** *Lō-mōth temūthun* (the negative *lō* preceding the infinitive absolute, as in Ps. xlix. 8 and Amos ix. 8; its position here being determined by the form of the penalty, ch. ii. 17, to which the devil's language gives the direct negative. *Vide* Ewald, 'Heb. Synt.,' § 312). Thus the second step in his assault is to challenge the Divine veracity, in allusion to which it has been thought our Saviour calls Satan a liar (cf. John viii. 44: ὅταν λαλῇ τὸ ψεῦδος, ἐκ τῶν ἰδίων λαλεῖ· ὅτι ψεύστης ἐστὶν καὶ ὁ πατὴρ αὐτοῦ). "Here, as far as we know, is his first begottten lie" (Bush).

Ver. 5.—For (כִּי—*nam*, γαρ, for, because; assigning the reason (1) for the devil's statement, and so, (2) by implication, for the Divine prohibition) **God doth know.** Thus the serpent practically charges the Deity with with (1) envy of his creatures' happiness, as if he meant to say, Depend upon it, it is not through any fear of your dying from its fruit that the tree has been interdicted, but through fear of your becoming rivals to your Master himself; and (2) with falsehood—(*a*) in affirming that to be true which he knew to be false; (*b*) in doing this while delivering his law; (*c*) in pretending to be careful of man's safety while in reality he was only jealous of his own honour. **That in the day ye eat thereof.** Cf. the Divine prohibition (ch. ii. 17), the exact terms of which are again used —a mark of growing aggressiveness towards the woman, and of special audacity towards God. The prohibition employs the singular number, being addressed to Adam only; the devil employs the plural, as his words were meant not for Eve alone, but for her husband with her. **Your eyes shall be opened.** "To open the eyes," the usual Biblical phrase for restoring sight to the blind (2 Kings vi. 17, 20 ; Ps. cxlvi. 8 ; Isa. xlii. 7), is also used to denote the impartation of power to perceive (physically, mentally, spiritually) objects not otherwise discernible (cf. ch. xxi. 19 ; Isa. xxxv. 5). Here it was designed to be ambiguous ; like all Satan's oracles, suggesting to the hearer the attainment of higher wisdom, but meaning in the intention of the speaker only a discovery of their nakedness. The same ambiguity attaches to the devil's exposition of his own text. **And ye shall be as gods.** Literally, as *Elohim ;* not ὡς θεοὶ (LXX.), *sicut dii* (Vulgate), as gods (A. V.), as the angels (R. Jonathan), as the devils (Ainsworth), *dæmonibusque, diisve similes* (Rosenmüller), as princes (White) ; but as the supreme Deity (Calvin, Keil, Kalisch, *et alii*)—ostensibly a promise of divinity. **Knowing good and evil.** As they knew this already from the prohibition, the language must imply a fulness and accuracy of understanding such as was competent only to Elohim (*vide* on ver. 22).

Ver. 6.—**And** (when) **the woman saw.** "An impure look, infected with the poison of concupiscence" (Calvin) ; cf. Joshua vii. 21. **That the tree was good for food.** "The fruit of this tree may have been neither poisonous nor beautiful, or it may have been both ; but sin has the strange power of investing the object of desire for the time being, whatever its true character, with a wonderful attraction" (Inglis). **And that it** (was) **pleasant.** Literally, a desire (Ps. x. 17), a lust (Num. xi. 4). **To the eyes.** Ἀριστὸν τοῖς ὀφθαλμοῖς (LXX.) ; *pulchrum oculis* (Vulgate) ; lustye unto the eyes (Coverdale) ; *i. e.* stimulating desire through the eyes (cf. 1 John ii. 16). **And a tree to be desired to make** (one) **wise.** לְהַשְׂכִּיל (from שָׂכַל—(1) to look at, to behold ; hence (2) to be prudent, 1 Sam. xviii. 30. Hiph., (1) to look at ; (2) to turn the mind to ; (3) to be or become understanding, Ps. ii. 10) being susceptible of two renderings, the clause has been taken to mean "a tree desirable to look at" (Syriac, Onkelos, Vulgate, Gesenius, Kalisch, Wordsworth), or, more correctly, as it stands in the English Version, the external loveliness of the tree having been already stated in the preceding clause (LXX., Aben Ezra, Calvin, Hengstenberg, Macdonald). This is the third time the charms of the tree are discerned and expressed by the woman—a significant intimation of how far the Divine interdict had receded from her consciousness. **She took of the fruit thereof, and did eat.** Thus consummating the sin (James i. 15). **And gave also to her husband.** Being desirous, doubtless, of making him a sharer in her supposed felicity. The first time Adam is styled Eve's husband, or man ; perhaps designed to indicate the complete perversion by Eve of the Divine purpose of her marriage with Adam, which was to be a help-meet for him, and not his destroyer. **With her.** An indication that Adam was present throughout the whole preceding scene (Delitzsch, Wordsworth), which is not likely, else why did he not restrain Eve ? or that he arrived just as the temptation closed (Calvin), which is only a conjecture ; better regarded as a reference to their conjugal oneness (Macdonald). **And he did eat.** And so involved himself in the criminality of his already guilty partner ; not simply as being "captivated with her allurements" ("fondly overcome with female charms"—Milton, 'Par. Lost,' Book x.), which 1 Tim. ii. 14 is supposed to justify ; but likewise as being "persuaded by Satan's impostures," which doubtless Eve had related to him. This much is distinctly implied in those Scriptures which speak of Adam as the chief transgressor (*vide* Rom. v. 12 ; 1 Cor. xv. 21, 22).

Ver. 7.—**And the eyes of them both were opened.** The fatal deed committed, the promised results ensued, but not the anticipated blessings. (1) The eyes of their minds were opened to perceive that they were no longer innocent, and (2) the eyes of their bodies to behold that they were not precisely as they had been. **And they knew that they were naked.** (1) Spiritually (cf. Exod. xxxii. 25 ; Ezek. xvi. 22 ; Rev. iii. 17), and (2) corporeally, having lost that enswathing light of purity which previously engirt their bodies (*vide* ch. ii. 25). **And they sewed.** Literally, fastened or tied by twisting. **Fig leaves.** Not the pisang tree (*Musa Paradisiaca*), whose leaves attain the length of twelve feet and the breadth of two (Knobel Bohlen) ; but the common fig tree (*Ficus Carica*), which is aboriginal in Western Asia, especially in Persia, Syria, and Asia Minor (Kalisch, Keil, Macdonald). **Together, and made themselves aprons.** Literally, girdles, περιζώματα (LXX.), *i. e.* to wrap about their loins. This sense of shame which caused them to seek a covering for their nudity was not due to any physical corruption of the body (Baumgarten), but to the consciousness of guilt with which their souls were laden, and which impelled them to flee from the presence of their offended Sovereign.

TRADITIONS OF THE FALL.

I. ORIENTAL. 1. *Babylonian.* "There is nothing in the Chaldean fragments indicating a belief in the garden of Eden or the tree of knowledge ; there is only an obscure allusion to a thirst for knowledge having been a cause of man's fall." . . . The details of the temptation are lost in the cuneiform text, which "opens where the gods are cursing the dragon and the Adam or man for his transgression.". . . "The dragon, which, in the Chaldean account, leads man to sin, is the creature of Tiamat, the living principle of the sea and of chaos, and he is an embodiment of the spirit of chaos or disorder which was opposed to the deities at the creation of the world." The dragon is included in the curse for the fall; and the gods invoke on the human race all the evils which afflict humanity—family quarrels, tyranny, the anger of the gods, disappointment, famine, useless prayers, trouble of mind and body, a tendency to sin ('Chaldean Genesis,' pp. 87—91). 2. *Persian.* For a time the first pair, Meschia and Meschiane, were holy and happy, pure in word and deed, dwelling in a garden wherein was a tree whose fruit conferred life and immortality; but eventually Ahriman deceived them, and drew them away from Ormuzd. Emboldened by his success, the enemy again appeared, and gave them a fruit, of which they ate, with the result that, of the hundred blessings which they enjoyed, all disappeared save one. Falling beneath the power of the evil one, they practised the mechanical arts, and subsequently built themselves houses and clothed themselves with skins. Another form of the legend represents Ahriman as a serpent. So close is the resemblance of this legend to the Scriptural account, that Rawlinson regards it not as a primitive tradition, but rather as "an infiltration into the Persian system of religious ideas belonging properly to the Hebrews" ('Hist. Illus. of the Old Testament,' p. 13). 3. *Indian.* In the Hindoo mythology the king of the evil demons, "the king of the serpents," is named Naga, the prince of the Nagis or Nacigs, "in which Sanscrit appellation we plainly trace the Hebrew Nachash." In the Vishnu Purana the first beings created by Brama are represented as endowed with righteousness and perfect faith, as free from guilt and filled with perfect wisdom, wherewith they contemplated the glory of Vishnu, till after a time they are seduced. In the legends of India the triumph of Krishna over the great serpent Kali Naga, who had poisoned the waters of the river, but who himself was ultimately destroyed by Krishna trampling on his head, bears a striking analogy to the Mosaic story (Kitto's 'Daily Bible Illustrations').

II. OCCIDENTAL. 1. *The story of Pandora.* According to Hesiod the first men lived wifeless and ignorant, but innocent and happy. Prometheus ("Forethought") having stolen fire from heaven, taught its use to mankind. To punish the aspiring mortals, Zeus sent among them Pandora, a beautiful woman, whom he had instructed Hephæstus to make, and Aphrodite, Athena, and Hermes had endowed with all seductive charms. Epimetheus ("Afterthought"), the brother of Prometheus, to whom she was presented, accepted her, and made her his wife. Brought into his house, curiosity prevailed on her to lift the lid of a closed jar in which the elder brother had with prudent foresight shut up all kinds of ills and diseases. Forthwith they escaped to torment mankind, which they have done ever since (Seemann's 'Mythology,' p. 163). 2. *The apples of the Hesperides.* These golden apples, which were under the guardianship of the nymphs of the West, were closely watched by a terrible dragon named Ladon, on account of an ancient oracle that a son of the deity would at a certain time arrive, open a way of access thither, and carry them off. Hercules, having inquired his way to the garden in which they grew, destroyed the monster and fulfilled the oracle (*ibid.*, p. 204). 3. *Apollo and the Python.* "This Python, ancient legends affirm, was a serpent bred out of the slime that remained after Deucalion's deluge, and was worshipped as a god at Delphi. Eminent authorities derive the name of the monster from a Hebrew root signifying to deceive." As the bright god of heaven, to whom everything impure and unholy is hateful, Apollo, four days after his birth, slew this monster with his arrows.

"What shall we say then to these things? This—that the nations embodied in these traditions their remembrances of paradise, of the fall, and of the promised salvation" (Kitto, 'Daily Bible Illustrations' p. 67).

HOMILETICS.

Ver. 6.—*The first sin.*—I. The TEMPTATION. 1. The *fact.* That sin is possible even in pure beings without the intervention of solicitation, at least *ab extra*, must be held to be the doctrine of Scripture (*vide* James i. 14 and Jude 6). Hence man might have fallen, even had he not been tempted. The fact, however, that he was tempted is explicitly revealed; a circumstance which notes an important distinction between his sin and that of the angels. Does this explain Heb. ii. 16 and 2 Pet. ii. 4 ? 2. *The author.* Though ostensibly a serpent, in reality the devil. Besides being expressly stated in the inspired word, it is involved in the very terms of the Mosaic narrative. If the *reptile* possessed the malice to conceive and the skill to manage such an assault upon the first pair as this book describes, then clearly it was not a *serpent*, but a *devil.* It is doubtful if all man's temptations come from the devil, but many, per-haps most, do. He is pre-eminently styled "the tempter" (Matt. iv. 3 ; 1 Thess. iii. 5). From the days of Adam downward he has been engaged in attempting to seduce the saints ; *e. g.* David (1 Chron. xxi. 1); Job (ch. ii. 7) ; Christ (Luke iv. 13) ; Ananias and Sapphira (Acts v. 3). At the present moment he is labouring to deceive the whole world (Rev. xii. 9). 3. The *instrument.* The serpent, which was a proof of Satan's skill, that particular reptile being specially adapted for his pur-pose (N.B.—The devil can always find a tool adapted to the work he has in hand); and is an indication of our danger, it being only a reptile, and therefore little likely to be suspected as a source of peril ; whence we may gather that there is no quarter so unexpected, and no instrument so feeble, that out of the one and through the other temptation may not leap upon us. 4. The *nature.* This was threefold. A tempta-tion (1) to suspect the Divine goodness (ver. 1); (2) to disbelieve the Divine word (ver. 4) ; (3) to emulate the Divine greatness (ver. 5). (Cf. the three assaults upon the Second Adam (Matt. iv. 1 ; Luke iv. 1), which were essentially the same.) The first aimed a death-blow at their filial confidence in God ; the second removed the fear of punishment from their path ; the third fired their souls with the lust of ambition. Separation from God, disobedience of God, opposition to or rivalry with God—the devil's *scala cœli.* 5. The *subtlety.* That great art should have been dis-played in the conduct of this campaign against the citadel of human holiness is what might have been expected from such a general. In these respects it was evinced. (1) The assault was commenced before use and practice had confirmed the first pair in obedience. (2) He began with the woman, who was the weaker of the two. (3) He attacked her when alone—the best time for temptation. Beware of solitude. (4) He selected the best ground for delivering his first blow—when the woman was in full sight of the tree. (5) He was extremely cautious so to moderate his onset as not to excite alarm—beginning with a casual inquiry. (6) He advanced by degrees as he obtained a footing in the woman's heart. (7) He never revealed the proper scope and drift of his observations, but always couched them in obscure and ambiguous language. (8) He never seemed to lead, but always to be following the woman's thought. (9) In all he said and did he pretended to be seeking his victim's good. (10) He chose the best of all possible baits to captivate the woman's fancy and ex-cite her cupidity—the hope of gaining knowledge.

II. The TRANSGRESSION. 1. Its guilty *perpetrators.* Not the serpent or the devil, but the first pair. The devil may tempt man to sin, but he cannot sin for man. A creature may be the unconscious instrument of leading man aside from the path of virtue, but it cannot possibly compel man to go astray. Men are prone to blame other things and persons for their sins, when the true criminals are themselves. 2. Its impelling *motive.* No temptation, however skilfully planned or powerfully applied, can succeed until it finds a footing in the nature that is tempted. Unless the devil's logic and chicanery had produced the effect described in ver. 6, it is more than probable that Eve would have stood. But first it wrought a change upon herself, and then it transformed the tree. First it created the need for sinful motives, and then it supplied them. So works temptation still. As with Eve, so with us. Sinful motives are (1) demanded by the heart ; (2) supplied by the evil which the heart contemplates ; and (3) are generally as weak and insufficient as Eve's. 3.

Its essential *wickedness*, as consisting of (1) unbelief, revealing itself in disobedience; (2) selfishness, making self the centre of all things; (3) desire, love of the world, gratification of the senses, the fundamental elements in all sin, corresponding to the three fundamental elements of man's being and consciousness—spirit, soul, body (cf. Auberlen's 'Divine Revelation,' Part I., § 3, ch. ix.). 4. Its sad *results*. (1) A discovery of *sin*. "Their eyes were opened," as the devil said, and as he meant. They felt that they had fallen, and that they had lost their purity. It is impossible to sin and not to have this knowledge and feel this loss. (2) A consciousness of *guilt*. "They knew that they were naked." Sin reports itself quickly to the conscience, and conscience quickly discovers to the guilty soul its true position as an unprotected culprit before the bar of God. (3) A sense of *shame*, which impelled them to seek a covering for their persons. "They sewed fig leaves together, and made themselves girdles." A picture of men's fruitless efforts to find a covering for their guilty souls.

Lessons :—1. The responsibility of man. 2. The duty of guarding against temptation. 3. The contagious character of moral evil. 4. The havoc wrought by a single sin.

HOMILIES BY VARIOUS AUTHORS.

Ver. 1.—*The tempter.* I. WHO TEMPTS? 1. Not the mere serpent. 2. A higher power of evil. 3. This higher power a person. 4. The leader of the fallen angels.

II. WHY PERMITTED? Easy to see why *moved ;* why permitted, a *mystery*. But we may note—1. That the intercourse of mind with mind is a general law of nature. To exclude the devil, therefore, from gaining access to man might have involved as great a miracle as preventing one mind from influencing another. 2. That the good as well as the evil angels have access to us. Can we estimate their influence, or be sure that Adam's position or the world's would have been better if both had been excluded? 3. That possibly by this sin *under* temptation we were saved from a worse sin *apart* from temptation. 4. That God magnifies his grace and vindicates his power against the devil's in raising fallen man above his first place of creatureship into that of sonship.

III. WHY EMPLOY THE SERPENT? 1. Because not permitted to assume a higher form—his masterpiece of craft, "an angel of light" (2 Cor. xi. 14), or his masterpiece of power, a mighty prince (Matt. iv. 1). 2. Because of all animals the serpent seemed the fittest for his purpose.—W.

Vers. 1—7.—*The moral chaos before the moral restoration.* Hitherto the moral nature of man may be said to be absorbed in his religious nature. He has held intercourse with his Creator. He has ruled earth as "the paragon of animals." The introduction of a helpmeet was the commencement of society, therefore of distinctly moral relations. It is in the moral sphere that sin takes its origin, through the helpmeet, and as a violation at the same time of a direct Divine commandment, and of that social compact of obedience to God and dependence upon one another which is the root of all true moral life. The woman was away from the man when she sinned. Her sin was more than a sin against God ; it was an offence against the law of her being as one with her husband. There are many suggestive points in the verses (1—7) which we may call the return of man's moral state into chaos, that out of it may come forth, by Divine grace, the new creation of a redeemed humanity.

I. As it is only IN THE MORAL SPHERE THAT SIN IS POSSIBLE, SO IT IS BY THE CONTACT OF A FORMER CORRUPTION WITH MAN that the evil principle is introduced into the world. The serpent's subtlety represents that evil principle already in operation.

II. While the whole transaction is on the line of moral and religious responsibility IT IS IMPOSSIBLE TO DISCONNECT THE ANIMAL NATURE FROM THE FIRST TEMPTATION. The serpent, the woman, the tree, the eating of fruit, the pleasantness to taste and sight, the effect upon the fleshly feelings, all point to the close relation of the animal and the moral. There is nothing implied as to the nature of matter, but it is plainly taught that the effect of a loss of moral and spiritual dignity is a sinking back into the lower grade of life ; as man is less a child of God he is more akin to the beasts that perish.

III. THE TEMPTATION IS BASED ON A LIE; first soliciting the mind through a question, a perplexity, then passing to a direct contradiction of God's word, and blasphemous suggestion of his ill-will towards man, together with an excitement of pride and overweening desire in man's heart. The serpent did not directly open the door of disobedience. He led the woman up to it, and stirred in her the evil thought of passing through it. The first temptation is the type of all temptation. Notice the three points:—(1) *falsification of fact and confusion of mind*; (2) *alienation from God* as the Source of all good and the only wise Ruler of our life; (3) *desire* selfishly exalting itself above the recognised and appointed limits. Another suggestion is—

IV. THE IMPOSSIBILITY THAT SIN SHOULD NOT FRUCTIFY IMMEDIATELY THAT IT BECOMES A FACT OF THE LIFE. Temptation is not sin. Temptation resisted is moral strength. Temptation yielded to is an evil principle admitted into the sphere of its operation, and beginning its work at once. The woman violated her true position by her sin; it was the consequence of that position that she became a tempter herself to Adam, so that the helpmeet became to Adam what the serpent was to her. His eating *with* her was, as Milton so powerfully describes it, at once—(1) a testimony to their oneness, and therefore to the power of that love which might have been only a blessing; and (2) a condemnation of both alike. The woman was first in the condemnation, but the man was first in the knowledge of the commandment and in the privilege of his position; therefore the man was first in *degree* of condemnation, while the woman was first in the *order of time*.

V. THE WORK OF SIN UPON THE WHOLE NATURE IS IMMEDIATE. The knowledge of good and evil is the commencement of a conflict between the laws of nature and the laws of the human spirit in its connection with nature, which nothing but the grace of God can bring to an end in the "peace which passeth understanding." That springing up of shame in the knowledge of natural facts is a testimony to a violation of God's order which he alone can set right. "Who told thee," God said, "that thou wast naked?" God might have raised his creature to a position in which shame would have been impossible. He will do so by his grace. Meanwhile the fall was what the word represents — a forfeiture of that superiority to the mere animal nature which was man's birthright. And the results of the fall are seen in the perpetual warfare between the natural world and the spiritual world in that being who was made at once a being of earth and a child of God. "They sewed fig-leaves together, and made themselves aprons." In the sense of humiliation and defeat man turns to the mere *material* protection of surrounding objects, forgetting that a *spiritual* evil can only be remedied by a *spiritual* good; but the shameful helplessness of the creature is the opportunity for the gracious interposition of God.—R.

Ver. 4.—*The tempter's chief weapon.* Narrative of the fall is of interest not only as the record of how mankind became sinful, but as showing the working of that "lie" (2 Thess. ii. 11) by which the tempter continually seeks to draw men away (2 Cor. xi. 3). Eve's temptation is in substance our temptation; Eve's fall illustrates our danger, and gives us matter whereby to try ourselves and mark how far we "walk by faith."

The SUBSTANCE OF THE TEMPTATION was suggesting doubts—(1) As to God's love. (2) As to God's truth. The former led to self-willed desire; the latter gave force to the temptation by removing the restraining power. We are tempted by the same suggestions. The will and unbelief act and react upon each other. Where the will turns away from God's will doubt more easily finds an entrance, and having entered, it strengthens self-will (Rom. i. 28). Unbelief is often a refuge to escape from the voice of conscience. But mark—the suggestion was not, "God has not said," but, It will not be so; You have misunderstood him; There will be some way of avoiding the danger. Excuses are easy to find: human infirmity, peculiar circumstances, strength of temptation, promises not to do so again. And a man may live, knowing God's word, habitually breaking it, yet persuading himself that all is well. Note two chief lines in which this temptation assails:—1. *As to the necessity for Christian earnestness.* We are warned (1 John ii. 15; v. 12; Rom. viii. 6—13). What is the life thus spoken of? Nothing strange. A life of seeking the world's prizes, gains, pleasures. A life whose guide is what others do; in which the example of Christ and guidance of the Holy Spirit are not regarded; in which religion is kept apart, and confined to certain times and services. Of this God says it is living death (cf. 1 Tim. v. 6); life's work neglected; Christ's banner deserted. Yet the tempter persuades—times have changed, the Bible must not be taken literally, ye shall not die. 2. *As to acceptance of the gift of salvation.* God's word is (Mark xvi. 15; Luke xiv. 21; John iv. 10) the record to be believed (Isa. liii. 5, 6; 1 John v. 11). Yet speak to men of the free gift, tell them of present salvation; the tempter persuades—true; but you must do something, or feel something, before it can be safe to believe;—God has said; but it will not be so. In conclusion, mark how the way of salvation just reverses the process of the fall. Man fell away from God, from peace, from holiness through doubting God's love and truth. We are restored to peace through believing these (John iii. 16; 1 John i. 9), and it is this belief which binds us to God in loving service (2 Cor. v. 14).—M.

EXPOSITION.

Ver. 8.—**And they heard the voice of the Lord God.** Either (1) the noise of his footsteps (cf. Levit. xxvi. 33; Num. xvi. 34; 2 Sam. v. 24; Knobel, Delitzsch, Keil, Kalisch, Macdonald); or (2) the thunder that accompanied his approach (cf. Exod. ix. 23; Job xxxvii. 4, 5; Ps. xxix. 3, 9; Murphy, Bush); or (3) the sound of his voice (Calvin, Lange, Wordsworth); or (4) probably all four. **Walking in the garden.** If the voice, then increasing in intensity (cf. Exod. xix. 19; Bush); if Jehovah, which is better, then "wandering or walking about in a circle" within the garden bounds (Macdonald). **In the cool** (literally, the wind) **of the day.** The morning breeze (Calvin); the evening breeze (Kalisch, Macdonald); τὸ δειλινόν (LXX.); *auram post meridiem* (Vulgate); cf. *hōm ha' yōm*, "the heat of the day" (Gen. xviii. 1). **And Adam and his wife hid themselves.** Not in humility, as unworthy to come into God's presence (Irenæus); or in amazement, as not knowing which way to turn (Augustine); or through modesty, (Knobel Bohlen); but from a sense of guilt. **From the presence of the Lord.** From which it is apparent they expected a visible manifestation.

Vers. 9, 10.—**And the Lord God called unto Adam.** Adam's absence was a clear proof that something was wrong. Hitherto he had always welcomed the Divine approach. **And said unto him, Where art thou?** Not as if ignorant of Adam's hiding-place, but to bring him to confession (cf. ch. iv. 9). **And I was afraid, because I was naked.** Attributing his fear to the wrong cause—the voice of God or his insufficient clothing; a sign of special obduracy (Calvin), which, however, admits of a psychological explanation, viz., that "his consciousness of the effects of sin was keener than his sense of the sin itself" (Keil), "although all that he says is purely involuntary self-accusation" (Delitzsch), and "the first instance of that mingling and confusion of sin and punishment which is the peculiar

characteristic of our redemption-needing humanity" (Lange). **And I hid myself.**

Vers. 11, 12.—**And he said.** "To reprove the sottishness of Adam" (Calvin); "to awaken in him a sense of sin" (Keil). **Who told thee that thou** wast **naked?** Delitzsch finds in מִי an indication that a personal power was the prime cause of man's disobedience; but, as Lange rightly observes, it is the occasion not of sin, but of the consciousness of nakedness that is here inquired after. **Hast thou eaten of the tree** (at once pointing Adam to the true cause of his nakedness, and intimating the Divine cognisance of his transgression) **whereof I commanded thee that thou shouldest not eat?** "Added to remove the pretext of ignorance" (Calvin), and also to aggravate the guilt of his offence, as having been done in direct violation of the Divine prohibition. The question was fitted to carry conviction to Adam's conscience, and had the instantaneous effect of eliciting a confession, though neither a frank one nor a generous. **And the man said** (beginning with apology and ending with confession,—thus reversing the natural order, and practically rolling back the blame on God), **The woman whom thou gavest to be with me** (accusing the gift and the Giver in one), **she gave me of the tree.** Cf. with the cold and unfeeling terms in which Adam speaks of Eve the similar language in Gen. xxxvii. 32; Luke xv. 30; John ix. 12. "Without natural affection" is one of the bitter fruits of sin (cf. Rom. i. 31). Equally with the blasphemy, ingratitude, unkindness, and meanness of this excuse, its frivolity is apparent; as if, though Eve gave, that was any reason why Adam should have eaten. **And I did eat.** Reluctantly elicited, the confession of his sin is very mildly stated. "A cold expression, manifesting neither any grief nor shame at so foul an act, but rather a desire to cover his sin" (White).

Ver. 13.—**And the Lord said unto the woman**—without noticing the excuses, but simply accepting the admission, and passing on, "following up the transgression even to the root—not the psychological merely, but the historical" (Lange): **What is this** that **thou hast done?** Or, "Why hast thou done this?" (LXX., Vulgate, Luther, De Wette). "But the Hebrew phrase has more vehemence; it is the language of one who wonders as at something prodigious, and ought rather to be rendered, 'How hast thou done this?'" (Calvin). **And the woman said** (following the example of her guilty husband, omitting any notice of her sin in tempting Adam, and transferring the blame of her own disobedience to the reptile), **The serpent beguiled me.** Literally, caused me to forget, hence beguiled, from נָשָׁה, to forget a thing (Lam. iii. 17), or person (Jer. xxiii. 39; Stanley Leathes, 'Gram.,' App. 197); or, caused me to go astray, from נָשָׁא (unused in Kal), kindred to כָשָׁה, perhaps to err, to go astray (Gesenius, Fürst); ἠπάτησέ (LXX.), ἐξαπάτησεν (2 Cor. xi. 3). **And I did eat.** "A forced confession, but no appearance of contrition. 'It's true I did eat, but it was not my fault'" (Hughes).

Ver. 14.—Confession having thus been made by both delinquents, and the arch-contriver of the whole mischief discovered, the Divine Judge proceeds to deliver sentence. **And the Lord God said unto the serpent.** Which he does not interrogate as he did the man and woman, "because (1) in the animal itself there was no sense of sin, and (2) to the devil he would hold out no hope of pardon" (Calvin); "because the trial has now reached the fountain-head of sin, the purely evil purpose (the demoniacal) having no deeper ground, and requiring no further investigation" (Lange). **Because thou hast done this.** *I. e.* beguiled the woman. The incidence of this curse has been explained as —1. The serpent only (Kalisch). 2. The devil only (Macdonald). 3. Partly on the serpent and partly on Satan (Calvin). 4. Wholly upon both (Murphy, Bush, Candlish). The difficulties attending these different interpretations have thus been concisely expressed: — "1. Quidam statuunt maledictionem latam in serpentem solum, quia hic confertur cum aliis bestiis, non in diabolum, quia is antea maledictus erat. 2. Alii in diabolum solum, quia brutus serpens non poterat justé puniri. 3. Alii applicant ver. 14 ad serpentem, ver. 15 in diabolum. At vero tu et te idem sunt in utroque versu. 4. Alii existimant eam in utrumque latam" (Medus in 'Poli Commentar.,' quoted by Lange). The fourth opinion seems most accordant with the language of the malediction. **Thou art cursed.** The cursing of the irrational creature should occasion no more

difficulty than the cursing of the earth (ver. 17), or of the fig tree (Matt. xi. 21). Creatures can be cursed or blessed only in accordance with their natures. The reptile, therefore, being neither a moral nor responsible creature, could not be cursed in the sense of being made susceptible of misery. But it might be cursed in the sense of being deteriorated in its nature, and, as it were, consigned to a lower position in the scale of being. And as the Creator has a perfect right to assign to his creature the specific place it shall occupy, and function it shall subserve, in creation, the remanding of the reptile to an inferior position could not justly be construed into a violation of the principles of right, while it might serve to God's intelligent creatures as a visible symbol of his displeasure against sin (cf. ch. ix. 5; Exod. xxi. 28—36). **Above.** Literally, *from*, i. e. separate and apart from all cattle (Le Clerc, Von Bohlen, Tuch, Knobel, Keil); and neither *by* (Gesenius, De Wette, Baumgarten) nor *above* (Luther, A. V., Rosenmüller, Delitzsch), as if the other creatures were either participators in or the instruments of the serpent's malediction. **All cattle, and above** (apart from) **every beast of the field.** The words imply the materiality of the reptile and the reality of the curse, so far as it was concerned. **Upon thy belly.** Ἐπὶ τῷ στήθει σου καὶ τῇ κοιλίᾳ (LXX.); "meaning with great pain and difficulty." "As Adam's labour and Eve's conception had pain and sorrow added to them (vers. 16, 17), so the serpent's gait" (Ainsworth). **Shalt thou go.** "As the worm steals over the earth with its length of body," "as a mean and despised crawler in the dust," having previously gone erect (Luther), and been possessed of bone (Josephus), and capable of standing upright and twining itself round the trees (Lange), or at least having undergone some transformation as to external form (Delitzsch, Keil); though the language may import nothing more than that whereas the reptile had exalted itself against man, it was henceforth "to be thrust back into its proper rank," "recalled from its insolent motions to its accustomed mode of going," and "at the same time condemned to perpetual infamy" (Calvin). As applied to Satan this part of the curse proclaimed his further degradation in the scale of being in consequence of having tempted man. "Than the serpent trailing along the ground, no emblem can more aptly illustrate the character and condition of the apostate spirit who once occupied a place among the angels of God, but has been cast down to the earth, preparatory to his deeper plunge into the fiery lake (Rev. xx. 10; Macdonald). **And dust shalt thou eat.** *I. e.* mingling dust with all it should eat. "The great scantiness of food on which serpents can subsist gave rise to the belief entertained by many Eastern nations, and referred to in several Biblical allusions (Isa. lxv. 25 ; Micah vii. 17)—that they eat dust" (Kalisch). More probably it originated in a too literal interpretation of the Mosaic narrative. Applied to the devil, this part of the curse was an additional intimation of his degradation. To "lick the dust" or "eat the dust" "is equivalent to being reduced to a condition of meanness, shame, and contempt" (Bush) ; "is indicative of disappointment in all the aims of being" (Murphy) ; "denotes the highest intensity of a moral condition, of which the feelings of the prodigal (Luke xv. 16) may be considered a type" (Macdonald ; cf. Ps. lxxii. 9). **All the days of thy life.** The degradation should be perpetual as well as complete.

Ver. 15.—**And I will put enmity between thee and the woman.** Referring—1. To the fixed and inveterate antipathy between the serpent and the human race (Bush, Lange) ; to that alone (Knobel). 2. To the antagonism henceforth to be established between the tempter and mankind (Murphy) ; to that alone (Calvin, Bonar, Wordsworth, Macdonald). **And between thy seed and her seed.** Here the curse manifestly outgrows the literal serpent, and refers almost exclusively to the invisible tempter. The hostility commenced between the woman and her destroyer was to be continued by their descendants—the seed of the serpent being those of Eve's posterity who should imbibe the devil's spirit and obey the devil's rule (cf. Matt. xxiii. 33 ; 1 John iii. 10) ; and the seed of the woman signifying those whose character and life should be of an opposite description, and in particular the Lord Jesus Christ, who is styled by pre-eminence "the Seed" (Gal. iii. 16, 19), and who came "to destroy the works of the devil" (Heb. ii. 4 ; 1 John iii. 8). This we learn from the words which follow, and which, not obscurely, point to a seed which should be individual and personal. **It**—or he; αὐτος (LXX.); not *ipsa* (Vulgate, Augustine, Ambrose, Gregory the Great ; later Romish interpreters understanding the Virgin)—**shall bruise.** 1. Shall crush, trample down—rendering שׁוּף by *terere* or *conterere* (Vulgate, Syriac, Samaritan, Tuch, Baumgarten, Keil, Kalisch). 2. Shall pierce, wound, bite—taking the verb as = שָׁפַף, to bite (Fürst, Calvin). 3. Shall watch, lie in wait = שָׁאַף (LXX., τηρήσει—Wordsworth suggests as the correct reading τερήσει, from τερέω, *perforo*, *vulnero* — Gesenius, Knobel). The word occurs only in two other places in Scripture—Job ix. 17 ; Ps. cxxxix. 11—and in the latter of these the reading is doubtful (cf. Perowne on Ps. *in loco*). Hence the

difficulty of deciding with absolute certainty between these rival interpretations. Ps. xci. 13 and Rom. xvi. 20 appear to sanction the first; the second is favoured by the application of the same word to the hostile action of the serpent, which is not treading, but biting; the feebleness of the third is its chief objection. **Thy head.** *I. e.* the superior part of thee (Calvin), meaning that the serpent would be completely destroyed, the head of the reptile being that part of its body in which a wound was most dangerous, and which the creature itself instinctively protects ; or the import of the expression may be, He shall attack thee in a bold and manly way (T. Lewis). **And thou shalt bruise his heel.** *I. e.* the inferior part (Calvin), implying that in the conflict he would be wounded, but not destroyed ; or "the biting of the heel may denote the mean, insidious character of the devil's warfare" (T. Lewis).

Ver. 16.—**Unto the woman he said.** Passing judgment on her first who had sinned first, but cursing neither her nor her husband, as "being candidates for restoration" (Tertullian). The sentence pronounced on Eve was twofold. **I will greatly multiply thy sorrow and thy conception.** A hendiadys for "the sorrow of thy conception" (Gesenius, Bush), though this is not necessary. The womanly and wifely sorrow of Eve was to be intensified, and in particular the pains of parturition were to be multiplied (cf. Jer. xxxi. 8). The second idea is more fully explained in the next clause. **In sorrow shalt thou bring forth children.** Literally, *sons*, daughters being included. The pains of childbirth are in Scripture emblematic of the severest anguish both of body and mind (cf. Ps. xlviii. 7 ; Micah iv. 9, 10 ; 1 Thess. v. 3 ; John xvi. 21; Rev. xii. 2). The gospel gives a special promise to mothers (1 Tim. ii. 15). "By bringing forth is also meant bringing up after the birth, as in ch. l. 23" (Ainsworth). **And thy desire shall be to thy husband.** תְּשׁוּקָה, from שׁוּק to run, to have a vehement longing for a thing, may have the same meaning here as in Cant. vii. 10 (Dathe, Rosenmüller, Delitzsch, Keil, Bohlen, Kalisch, Alford); but is better taken as expressive of deferential submissiveness, as in ch. iv. 7 (Luther, Calvin, Le Clerc, Lange, Macdonald, Speaker's 'Commentary'.) Following the LXX. (ἀποστροφή), Murphy explains it as meaning, "The determination of thy will shall be yielded to thy husband." According to the analogy of the two previous clauses, the precise import of this is expressed in the next, though by many it is regarded as a distinct item in the curse (Kalisch, Alford, Clarke, Wordsworth). **And he shall rule over thee.** Not merely a prophecy of woman's subjection, but an investiture of man with supremacy over the woman; or rather a confirmation and perpetuation of that authority which had been assigned to the man at the creation. Woman had been given him as an helpmeet (ch. ii. 18), and her relation to the man from the first was constituted one of dependence. It was the reversal of this Divinely-established order that had led to the fall (ch. iii. 17). Henceforth, therefore, woman was to be relegated to, and fixed in, her proper sphere of subordination. On account of her subjection to man's authority a wife is described as the possessed or subjected one of a lord (ch. xx. 3; Deut. xx. 22), and a husband as the lord of a woman (Exod. xxi. 3). Among the Hebrews the condition of the female sex was one of distinct subordination, though not of oppression, and certainly not of slavery, as it it too often has been in heathen and Mohammedan countries. Christianity, while placing woman on the same platform with man as regards the blessings of the gospel (Gal. iii. 28), explicitly inculcates her subordination to the man in the relationship of marriage (Ephes. v. 22; Col. iii. 18; 1 Pet. iii. 1).

Ver. 17.—**And unto Adam he said.** The noun here used for the first time without the article is explained as a proper name (Keil, Lange, Speaker's 'Commentary'), though perhaps it is rather designed to express the man's representative character (Macdonald). **Because thou hast hearkened unto the voice of thy wife.** Preceding his sentence with a declaration of his guilt, which culminated in this, that instead of acting as his wife's protector prior to her disobedience, or as her mentor subsequent to that act, in the hope of bringing her to repentance, he became her guilty coadjutor through yielding himself to her persuasions. **And hast eaten of the tree of which I commanded thee, saying, Thou shalt not eat of it.** For which a twofold judgment is likewise pronounced upon Adam. **Cursed is the ground.** *Ha' adamah,* out of which man was taken (ch. ii. 7); *i. e.* the soil outside of the garden. The language does not necessarily imply that now, for the first time, in consequence of the fall, the physical globe underwent a change, "becoming from that point onward a realm of deformity and discord, as before it was not, and displaying in all its sceneries and combinations the tokens of a broken constitution" (*vide* Bushnell, 'Nature and the Supernatural,' ch. vii.); simply it announces the fact that, because of the transgression of which he had been guilty, he would find the land beyond the confines of Eden lying under a doom of sterility (cf. Rom. viii. 20). **For thy sake.** בַּעֲבוּרֶךָ. 1. Because of thy sin it required to be such a world. 2. For thy good it was better that such a curse should lie upon the ground. Reading ד instead of ר, the LXX. translate ἐν τοῖς ἔργοις; and the Vulgate, *In opere tuo.* **In sorrow.** Literally, *painful labour* (cf. ver. 16; Prov. v. 10). **Shalt thou eat of it.** *I. e.* of its fruits (cf. Isa. i. 7; xxxvi. 16; xxxvii. 30). "Bread of sorrow" (Ps. cxxvii. 2) is bread procured and eaten amidst hard labour. **All the days of thy life.**

Ver. 18.—**Thorns also and thistles.** Terms occurring only here and in Hosea x. 8 = the similar expressions in Isa. v. 6; vii. 23 (Kalisch, Keil, Macdonald). **Shall it bring forth to thee.** *I. e.* these shall be its spontaneous productions; if thou desirest anything else thou must labour for it. **And thou shalt eat the herb of the field.** "Not the fruit of paradise" (Wordsworth), but "the lesser growths sown by his own toil" (Alford)—an intimation that henceforth man was "to be deprived of his former delicacies to such an extent as to be compelled to use, in addition, the herbs which had been designed only for brute animals;" and perhaps also "a consolation," as if promising that, notwithstanding the thorns and thistles, "it should still yield him sustenance" (Calvin).

Ver. 19.—**In the sweat of thy face** (so called, as having there its source and being there visible) **shalt thou eat bread.** *I. e.* all food (*vide* Job xxviii. 5; Ps. civ. 14; Matt. xiv. 15; Mark vi. 36). "To eat bread" is to possess the means of sustaining life (Eccles. v. 16; Amos vii. 12). **Till thou return unto the ground** (the mortality of man is thus assumed as certain); **for out of it thou wast taken.** Not declaring the reason of man's dissolution, as if it were involved in his original material constitution, but reminding him that in consequence of his transgression he had forfeited the privilege of immunity from death, and must now return to the soil whence he sprung. Ἐξ ἧς ἐλήφθης (LXX.); de qua sumptus es (Vulgate); "out of which thou wast taken" (Macdonald, Gesenius). On the use of כִּי as a relative pronoun = אֲשֶׁר cf. Gesenius, 'Lex. sub nom.,' who quotes this and ch. iv. 25 as examples. *Vide* also Stanley Leathes, 'Heb. Gram.,' p. 202; and 'Glassii Philologiæ,' lib. iii. tr. 2, c.xv. p. 335. This use of כִּי, however, appears to be doubtful, and is not necessary in any of the examples quoted.

HOMILETICS.

Vers. 8—19.—*The first judgment scene.* I. THE FLIGHT OF THE CRIMINALS. 1. *It is the instinct of sinful men to flee from God.* "Adam and his wife hid themselves from the presence of the Lord God" (ver. 8). So "Jonah rose up to flee unto Tarshish from the presence of the Lord" (Jonah i. 3). (1) Through a consciousness of *guilt.* A perception of their nakedness caused our first parents to seek the shelter of the garden trees (ver. 10). Doubtless it was the burden lying on Jonah's conscience that sent him down into the ship's hold (Jonah i. 5). So awakened sinners ever feel themselves constrained to get away from God. (2) From a dread of *punishment.* Not perhaps so long as they imagine God to be either unacquainted with or indifferent to their offence, but immediately they apprehend that their wickedness is discovered (cf. Exod. ii. 15). The sound of Jehovah's voice as he came towards our first parents filled them with alarm. How much more will the full revelation of his glorious presence in flaming fire affright the ungodly! 2. *It is God's habit to pursue transgressors.* As he pursued Adam and Eve in the garden by his voice (ver. 9), and Jonah on the deep by a wind (Jonah i. 4), and David by his prophet (2 Sam. xii. 1), so does he still in his providence, and through the ministry of his word, and by his Spirit, follow after fleeing sinners—(1) to apprehend them (cf. Phil. iii. 12) ; (2) to forgive and *save* them (Luke xix. 10) ; (3) if they will not be forgiven, to *punish* them (2 Thess. i. 8). 3. *It is the certain fate of all fugitives to be eventually arrested.* Witness Adam and Eve (ver. 9), Cain (ch. iv. 9), David (2 Sam. xii. 1), Ahab (1 Kings xxi. 20), Jonah (ch. i. 6). Distance will not prevent (Ps. cxxxix. 7). Darkness will not hinder (Ps. cxxxix. 11). Secrecy will not avail (Heb. iv. 13). Material defences will not ward off the coming doom (Amos ix. 2, 3). The lapse of time will not make it less certain (Num. xxxii. 23).

II. THE EXAMINATION OF THE CRIMINALS. 1. *God's questions are always painfully direct and searching.* "Adam, where art thou?" (ver. 9). "Who told thee thou wast naked? Hast thou eaten of the tree?" (ver. 11). "What hast thou done?" (ver. 13). (1) Because he knows the fact of the sinner's guilt. The nature and aggravation, the time, circumstances, manner, and reason of the sinner's transgression are perfectly understood. (2) Because he aims at the sinner's conviction ; *i. e.* he desires to bring sinners to a realisation of the sinfulness of their behaviour corresponding to that which he himself possesses. (3) Because he wishes to elicit a confession from the sinner's mouth. Without this there can be no forgiveness or salvation (Prov. xxviii. 13 ; 1 John i. 9). 2. *Man's apologies are always extremely weak and trifling.* (1) As attempting to excuse that which must for ever be inexcusable, viz., disobedience to God's commandment. Nothing can justify sin. God's authority over man being supreme, no one can relieve man from his responsibility to yield implicit submission to the Divine precepts. Jehovah's question rests special emphasis on the fact that Adam's sin was a transgression of his commandment (ver. 11). (2) As seeking to transfer the burden of guilt from himself to another. Adam blames his wife ; Eve blames the serpent ; and ever since, sinners have been trying to blame anything and everything except themselves—the companions God has given them ; the circumstances in which God has placed them ; the peculiar temperaments and dispositions with which God has endowed them. (3) As failing to obliterate the fact of transgression. Even Adam and Eve both discern as much as this. Beginning with apologies, they were obliged to end with avowal of their guilt. And if man can detect the worthlessness of his own hastily-invented pleas, much more, we may be sure, can God pierce through all the flimsy and trifling arguments that sinners offer to extenuate their faults. (4) As not requiring to be answered. It is remarkable that Jehovah does not condescend to answer either Adam or his wife ; the reason being, doubtless, that any reply to their foolish speeches was unnecessary. 3. *The Divine verdict is always clear and convincing.* (1) Though in this case *unspoken*, it was yet *implied.* Adam and Eve did not require to be informed of their culpability. And neither will sinners need to be informed of their guilt and condemnation when they stand before the great white throne. It is a special mark of mercy that God informs sinners in the gospel of the nature of the verdict which has been pronounced against them (John iii. 18, 19). (2) It was so *convincing* that it was *not denied.* Adam and Eve we can suppose were speechless. So was the disobedient wedding guest (Matt. xxii. 12). So will all the condemned be in the day of judgment (Rev. vi. 17).

III. THE SENTENCE OF THE CRIMINALS. 1. On the serpent—*judgment without mercy.* (1) Degradation on both the reptile and the tempter. (2) Hostility between the serpent's brood and the woman's seed. (3) Ultimate destruction of the tempter by the incarnation and death of the woman's seed. 2. On the sinning pair—*mercy, and then judgment.* (1) Mercy for both. *Great* mercy—the restitution of themselves and of their seed (or at least a portion of it) by the complete annihilation of their adversary through the sufferings of a distinguished woman's seed. *Certain* mercy— the entire scheme for their recovery was to depend on God, who here says, "I will put . . ." *Free* mercy—neither solicited nor deserved by Adam or his wife. (2) Judgment for each. For the *woman,* sorrow in accomplishing her womanly and wifely destiny, combined with a position of dependence on and submission to her husband. For the *man,* a life of sorrowful labour, a doom of certain death.

Learn—1. The folly of attempting to hide from God. It is better to flee to God than to run from God, even when we sin (Ps. cxliii. 9). 2. The expediency of confessing to God. It is always the shortest path to mercy and forgiveness (Ps. xxxii. 5). 3. The gentle treatment which men receive from God. Like David, we have all reason to sing of mercy as well as, and even rather than, judgment (Ps. ci. 1).

HOMILIES BY VARIOUS AUTHORS.

Ver. 8.—*The working of the sin-stricken conscience.* I. GOD THE JUDGE REVEAL- ING HIMSELF. The *voice of the Lord God* represents to men the *knowledge* of them- selves, which, like *light,* would be intolerable to the shamefaced.

II. MAN HIDING FROM THE JUDGE BECAUSE UNABLE TO MEET HIM. While the darkness of the thick foliage was regarded as a covering, hiding nakedness, it is yet from *the presence of the Lord God* that the guilty seek refuge.

III. MAN'S SELF AGAINST HIMSELF. The *instinctive* action of *shame* is a testimony to the moral nature and position of man. So it may be said—

IV. GUILT is itself God's witness, comprehending the *sense of righteousness* and the *sense of transgression* in the same being. (Perhaps there is a reference to the working of the conscience in the description of the voice of God as mingling in the facts of the natural world; " *the cool of the day* " being literally the " evening breeze," whose whispering sound became articulate to the ears of those who feared the per- sonal presence of their Judge.)—R.

Ver. 9.—*The searching question.* We can picture the dread of this question. Have you considered its love—that it is really the first word of the gospel? Already the Shepherd goes forth to seek the lost sheep. The Bible shows us — 1. The original state of man; what God intended his lot to be. 2. The entry of sin, and fall from happiness. 3. The announcement and carrying out God's plan of restoration.

THE GOSPEL BEGINS not with the promise of a Saviour, but WITH SHOWING MAN HIS NEED. Thus (John iv. 15—18) our Saviour's answer to " Give me this water " was to convince of sin: " Go, call thy husband." That first loving call has never ceased. Men are still straying, still must come to themselves (Luke xv. 17). We hear it in the Baptist's teaching; in the preaching of St. Peter at Pentecost; and daily in his life-giving work the Holy Spirit's first step is to convince of sin. And not merely in conversion, but at every stage he repeats, "Where art thou?" To welcome God's gift we must feel our own need; and the inexhaustible treasures in Christ are discerned as we mark daily the defects of our service, and how far we are from the goal of our striving (Phil. iii. 13, 14). Hence, even in a Christian con- gregation, it is needful to press " Where art thou? " to lead men nearer to Christ. We want to stir up easy-going disciples, to make Christians consider their calling, to rouse to higher life and work. Our Saviour's call is, "Follow me." How are you doing this? You are pledged to be his soldiers; what reality is there in your fighting? How many are content merely to do as others do! What do ye for Christ? You have your Bible; is it studied, prayed over? What do ye to spread its truth? Ye think not how much harm is done by apathy, how much silent teaching of unbelief there is in the want of open confession of Christ. Many are zealous for their own views. Where is the self-denying mind of Christ, the spirit of love? Many count themselves spiritual, consider that they have turned to the Lord, and are certainly in his fold. Where is St. Paul's spirit of watchfulness? (1 Cor. ix. 26, 27). "Where art thou?" May the answer of each be, Not shut up in myself, not following the multitude, but "looking unto Jesus."—M.

Vers. 14, 15.—*The doom of Satan and the hope of man.* I. THE DOOM OF DEGRADATION (ver. 14).

II. THE DOOM OF HOSTILITY (ver. 15). Three stages:—1. The enmity. 2. The conflict. 3. The victory.

Lessons:—1. See the wondrous mercy of God in proclaiming from the first day of sin, and putting into the forefront, a purpose of salvation. 2. Have we recognised it to the overcoming of the devil?—W.

Vers. 9—24.—*The word of God in the moral chaos.* These verses bring before us very distinctly the elements of man's sinful state, and of the redemptive dispensation of God which came out of it by the action of his brooding Spirit of life upon the chaos.

I. THE WORD OF GOD ADDRESSED TO THE PERSONAL CONSCIOUSNESS IS THE BEGINNING OF THE NEW WORLD. "The Lord God called unto Adam, and said unto him, *Where art thou?*" Before that direct intercourse between the Spirit of God and the spirit of man there is no distinct recognition of the evil of sin, and no separation of its moral and physical consequences. The "*Where art thou?*" begins the spiritual work.

II. THE PROCESS OF THE WORK OF GOD IN THE CONSCIENCE IS ONE THAT LEADS US FROM THE OUTSIDE CIRCLE OF RESPONSIBILITY TO THE INNERMOST CENTRE OF CONVICTION AND CONFESSION. "I was naked," "I was afraid," "I hid myself," "The woman gave me of the tree," "I did eat;" so at last we get to the *central fact*—I broke the commandment, I am guilty towards God. Each lays the blame on another—the man on the woman, the woman on the serpent. But the main fact is this, that when once the voice of God deals with us, when once the Spirit of light and life broods over the chaos, there will be truth brought out, and the beginning of all new creation is confession of sin. After all, both the transgressors admitted the fact: "*I did eat.*" Nor do they dare to state what is untrue, although they attempt to excuse themselves; for there may be a true confession of sin before there is a sense of its greatness and inexcusableness.

III. The transgression being clearly revealed, next comes THE DIVINE CONDEMNATION. It is upon the background of judgment that redemption must be placed, that it may be clearly seen to be of God's free grace. The *judgment upon the serpent* must be viewed as a fact in the sphere of *man's* world, not in the larger sphere of the *superhuman* suggested by the later use of the term "serpent." God's condemnation of Satan is only *shadowed forth* here, not actually described. The cursed *animal* simply represents the cursed *agent* or *instrument*, and therefore was intended to embody the curse of sin *to the eyes of man.* At the same time, the fifteenth verse must not be shorn of its spiritual application by a merely *naturalistic* interpretation. Man's inborn detestation of the serpent brood, and the serpent's lurking enmity against man, as it waits at his heel, is rightly taken as symbolically representing (1) the antagonism between good and evil introduced into the world by man's fall; (2) the necessity that that antagonism should be maintained; and (3) the purpose of God that it should be brought to an end by the destruction of the serpent, the removing out of the way both of the evil principle and of the besetments of man's life which have arisen out of it. This "*first promise,*" as it is called, was not given in the form of a promise, but of a *sentence.* Are we not reminded of the cross, which itself was the carrying out of a *sentence,* but in which was included the redeeming mercy of God? *Life in death* is the mystery of Christ's sacrifice. "*It pleased the Lord to bruise him"* (Isa. liii. 10). *" Through death he destroyed him that had the power of death,"* &c. (Heb. ii. 14). It must have been itself like a revelation of redeeming love that God pronounced sentence *first* upon the *serpent,* not upon *man,* thereby teaching him that he was in the sight of God a *victim* of the evil power, to be delivered by the victorious seed of the woman, rather than an *enemy* to be crushed and destroyed. The sentence seemed to say, Thou, *the serpent,* art the evil thing to be *annihilated ; man* shall be *saved,* though wounded and bruised in the heel ; the " woman's seed" shall be the conqueror,—which was the prediction of a renovation of humanity in a second Adam, a dim forecasting of the future, indeed, but a certain and unmistakable proclamation of the continuance of the race, notwithstanding sin and death ; and in that continuance it was declared there should be a realisation of entire deliverance. The *sentence upon the woman,* which follows that upon the serpent, as she was the first in the transgression, is a sentence which, while it clearly demonstrates the evil of sin, at the same time reveals the mercy of God. The woman's sorrow is that which she can and does forget, for "joy that a man is born into the world." Her desire to her husband and her submission to his rule do come out of that fall of her nature in which she is made subject to the conditions of a fleshly life ; but from the same earthly soil spring up the hallowed blossoms and fruits of the affections, filling the world with beauty and blessing. So have the law of righteousness and the law of love from the beginning blended together in the government of God. In like manner, the *sentence upon the man* is the same revelation of Divine goodness in the midst of condemnation. The ground is cursed for man's sake. *To thee* it shall bring forth thorns and thistles, *i. e.* thy labour shall not be the productive labour it would have been—thou shalt put it forth among difficulties and obstacles. Thou shalt see thine own moral perversity reflected in the stubborn barrenness, the wilderness growth of nature. Yet thou shalt eat the herb of the field, and depend upon it. With sweat of thy face all through thy life thou shalt win thy bread from an unwilling earth. And at last the dust beneath thy feet shall claim thee as its own ; thy toil-worn frame shall crumble down into the grave. It was (1) a sentence of death, of death in life ; but at the same time it was (2) a merciful appointment of man's most peaceful and healthy occupation—to till the ground, to grow the corn, to eat the bread ; and it was (3) a proclamation of welcome release from the burden "when the dust shall return to the earth as it was, and the spirit shall return-to God who gave it." There is no allusion in any of these sentences to spiritual results of transgression, but that is only because the whole is a representation of the fall, *objectively regarded.* Just as the serpent is spoken of *as though* it were only an animal on the earth, so man's sin is spoken of *as though* it were only his life's error, to be paid for in his life's suffering ; but as in the former case the deeper spiritual meaning lies behind the form of the serpent, so in the latter the condemnation which brings toil and suffering and death upon man's bodily frame brings upon his whole nature that which the external infliction symbolises and sets forth. The life goes down into the dust, but it is the life which by sin had become a smitten, cursed thing ; that hiding of it in the dust is the end, so far as the mere sentence is concerned. We must, however, wait for the revelation which is to be made in the new man,—the life coming forth again,—which, though but dimly promised, is yet suggested in the story of paradise. Adam gave a new name to his wife when she became to him something more than *" a help-meet for him."* He called her, first, *woman,* because she was taken out of man. He called her, afterwards, *" Eve,"* as the life-producing, *" because she was the mother of all living."* The coats of skin—which were not, like the fig-leaves sewn together, man's own device for hiding shame, but God's preparation for preserving that reverence between the sexes so vital to the very continuance of the race itself—betokened again the mingling of mercy with judgment ; for, apart altogether from any theory as to the slain animals whose skins were employed, the Divine origin of clothing is a most significant fact. When we are told that "the Lord God made them coats of skins, and clothed them," we must interpret the language from the standpoint of the whole narrative, which is that of an objective representation of the mysteries of man's primeval life. It would not be in harmony with the tone of the whole book to say in what method such Divine interposition was brought about. To the Biblical writers a spiritual guidance, a work of God in the mind of man, is just as truly God's own act as though it were altogether apart from any human agency. The origin of clothing was an inspiration. Perhaps it is not putting too much into the language to see in such a fact an allusion to other facts. Man is directed to use skins; might he not have been directed to slay animals? If so, might not such slaughter of animals have been first connected with religious observances, for as yet there is no allusion to the use of animal food, save in the indirect form of dominion over the lower creation? In the fourth chapter, in the extra paradisaic life, the keeping of herds and flocks is mentioned as a natural sequel. Doubtless from the time of the fall the mode of life was entirely changed, as was its sphere. Before sin man was an animal indeed, but with his animal nature in entire subordination; after his fall he was under the laws of animal life, both as to its support and propagation. Death became the ruling fact of life, as it is in the mere animal races. Man is delivered from it only as he is lifted out of the animal sphere and becomes a child of God. The expulsion from Eden was part of the Divine sentence, but it was part of the redemptive work which commenced immediately upon the fall. The creature knowing good and evil by disobedience must not live for ever in that disobedience. He must die that he may be released from the burden of his corruption. An immortality of sin is not God's purpose for his creature. *Therefore* the Lord God shut up Eden.—R.

EXPOSITION.

Ver. 20.—Arraigned, convicted, judged, the guilty but pardoned pair prepare to leave their garden home—the woman to begin her experience of sorrow, dependence, and subjection; the man to enter upon his life career of hardship and toil, and both to meet their doom of certain, though it might be of long-delayed, death. The impression made upon their hearts by the Divine clemency, though not directly stated by the historian, may be inferred from what is next recorded as having happened within the precincts of Eden ere they entered on their exile. **And Adam called** (not prior to the fall, reading the verb as a pluperfect (Calvin), nor after the birth of Cain, transferring the present verse to ch. iv. 2 (Knobel), but subsequent to the promise of the woman's seed, and preceding their ejection from the garden) **his wife's name Eve**. *Chavvah*, from *chavvah = chayyah*, to live (cf. with the organic root *chvi* the Sanscrit, *gîv;* Gothic, *quiv;* Latin, *vivo, gigno, vigeo;* Greek, ζάω, &c., the fundamental idea being to breathe, to respire —Fürst), is correctly rendered life—ζωή by the LXX., Josephus, Philo, Gesenius, Delitzsch, Macdonald, &c. Lange, regarding it as an abbreviated form of the participle *mechavvah*, understands it to signify "the sustenance, *i. e.* the propagation of life;" while Knobel, viewing it as an adjective, hints at woman's peculiar function—חַיָּה וָרָע —to quicken seed (ch. xix. 32) as supplying the explanation. Whether appended by the narrator (Delitzsch, Lange) or uttered by Adam (Kalisch, Macdonald), the words which follow give its true import and exegesis. **Because she was the mother** (*am*—Greek, μαμμα; Welsh, *mani;* Copt., *man;* Ger-

man and English, *mama;*—Gesenius) **of all living**. (1) Of Adam's children, though in this respect she might have been so styled from the beginning; and (2) of all who should truly live in the sense of being the woman's seed, as distinguished from the seed of the serpent. In Adam's giving a second name to his wife has been discerned the first assertion of his sovereignty or lordship over woman to which he was promoted subsequent to the fall (Luther), though this seems to be negatived by the fact that Adam exercised the same prerogative immediately on her creation; an act of thoughtlessness on the part of Adam, in that, "being himself immersed in death, he should have called his wife by so proud a name" (Calvin); a proof of his incredulity (Rupertus). With a juster appreciation of the spirit of the narrative, modern expositors generally regard it as a striking testimony to his faith.

Ver. 21.—**Unto Adam also and to his wife did the Lord God make coats** (*cathnōth*, from *cathan*, to cover; cf. χιτών; Sanscrit, *katam;* English, *cotton*) **of skin** ('*or*, the skin of a man, from *ūr*, to be naked, hence a hide). Neither their bodies (Origen), nor garments of the bark of trees (Gregory Nazianzen), nor miraculously-fashioned apparel (Grotius), nor clothing made from the serpent's skin (R. Jonathan), but tunics prepared from the skins of animals, slaughtered possibly for food, as it is not certain that the Edenic man was a vegetarian (ch. i. 29), though more probably slain in sacrifice. Though said to have been made by God, "it is not proper so to understand the words, as if God had been a furrier, or a servant to sew clothes" (Calvin); God being said to make or do what he gives orders or instructions to be made or done. Willet and Macdonald, however, prefer to think that the garments were actually fashioned by God. Bush finds in the mention of Adam and his wife an intimation that they were furnished with different kinds of apparel, and suggests that on this fact is based the prohibition in Deut. xxii. 5 against the interchange of raiment between the sexes. **And clothed them.** "1. To show them how their mortal bodies might be defended from cold and other injuries. 2. To cover their nakedness for comeliness' sake; *vestimenta honoris* (Chaldee Paraphrase). 3. To teach them the lawfulness of using the beasts of the field, as for food, so for clothing. 4. To give a rule that modest and decent, not costly or sumptuous, apparel should be used. 5. That they might know the difference between God's works and man's invention—between coats of leather and aprons of leaves; and, 6. To put them in mind of their mortality by their raiment of dead beasts' skins—talibus indici oportebat peccatorem ut essent mortalitatis indicium: Origen" (Willet). 7. "That they might feel their degradation—quia vestes ex ea materia confectæ, belluinum quiddam magis saperent, quam lineæ vel laneæ—and be reminded of their sin" (Calvin). "As the prisoner, looking on his irons, thinketh on his theft, so we, looking on our garments, should think on our sins" (Trapp). 8. A foreshadowing of the robe of Christ's righteousness (Delitzsch, Macdonald, Murphy, Wordsworth, Candlish; cf. Ps. cxxxii. 9, 16; Isa. lxi. 10; Rom. xiii. 14; Ephes. iv. 24; Col. iii. 10). Bonar recognises in Jehovah Elohim at the gate of Eden, clothing the first transgressors, the Lord Jesus Christ, who, as the High Priest of our salvation, had a right to the skins of the burnt offerings (Levit. vii. 8), and who, to prefigure his own work, appropriated them for covering the pardoned pair.

Ver. 22.—**And the Lord God said.** *Verba insultantis* (Augustine); *ironica reprobatio* (Calvin). But "irony at the expense of a wretched, tempted soul might well befit Satan, but not the Lord" (Delitzsch), and is altogether inconsistent with the footing of grace on which man was placed immediately upon his fall. **Behold, the man is become as one of us.** Not the angels (Kalisch), but the Divine Persons (cf. ch. i. 26). It is scarcely likely that Jehovah alludes to the words of the tempter (ch. iii. 5). **To know good and evil.** Implying an acquaintance with good and evil which did not belong to him in the state of innocence. The language seems to hint that a one-sided acquaintance with good and evil, such as that possessed by the first pair in the garden and the unfallen angels in heaven, is not so complete a knowledge of

the inherent beauty of the one and essential turpitude of the other as is acquired by beings who pass through the experience of a fall, and that the only way in which a finite being can approximate to such a comprehensive knowledge of evil as the Deity possesses without personal contact—can see it as it lies everlastingly spread out before his infinite mind—is by going down into it and learning what it is through personal experience (cf. Candlish, *in loco*). **And now, lest he put forth his hand, and take also of the tree of life, and eat, and live for ever.** On the meaning of the tree of life *vide* ch. ii. 9. Neither (1) lest by eating of the fruit he should recover that immortal life which he no longer possessed (Kalisch), as "it is certain that man would not have been able, had he even devoured the whole tree, to enjoy life against the will of God" (Calvin); nor (2) lest the first pair, through participation of the tree, should confer upon themselves the attribute of *undyingness*, which would not be the ζωὴ αἰώνιος of salvation, but its opposite, the ὄλεθρον αἰώνιον of the accursed (Keil, Lange, T. Lewis, Wordsworth); but either (3) lest man should conceive the idea that immortality might still be secured by eating of the tree, instead of trusting in the promised seed, and under this false impression attempt to take its fruit, which, in his case, would have been equivalent to an attempt to justify himself by works instead of faith (Calvin, Macdonald); or (4) lest he should endeavour to partake of the symbol of immortality, which he could not again do until his sin was expiated and himself purified (cf. Rev. xxii. 14; Candlish). The remaining portion of the sentence is omitted, *anakoloutha* or *aposiopesis* being not infrequent in impassioned speech (cf. Exod. xxxii. 32; Job xxxii. 13; Isa. xxxviii. 18). The force of the ellipsis or expressive silence may be gathered from the succeeding words of the historian.

Vers. 23, 24.—**Therefore** (literally, and) **the Lord God sent** (or *cast*, *shalach* in the Piel conveying the ideas of force and displeasure; cf. Deut. xxi. 14; 1 Kings ix. 7) **him forth from the garden of Eden to till the ground** (*i. e.* the soil outside of paradise, which had been cursed for his sake) **whence he was taken.** *Vide* ver. 19. **So** (and) **he drove out the man** (along with his guilty partner); **and he placed** (literally, caused to dwell) **at the east of the garden of Eden Cherubim.** 1. *Griffins*, like those of Persian and Egyptian mythology, which protected gold-producing countries like Eden; from *carav*, to tear in pieces; Sanscrit, *grivh;* Persian, *giriften;* Greek, γρυπ, γρυφ; German, *grip, krip, greif* (Eichhorn, Fürst). 2. *Divine steeds;* by metathesis for *rechubim*, from *rachab*, to ride (Ps. xviii. 11; Gesenius, Lange). 3. "Beings who approach to God and minister to him," taking *cerub* = *karov*, to come near, to serve (Hyde). 4. The engravings or carved figures; from *carav* (Syriac), to engrave (Tayler Lewis) ; from an Egyptian root (Cook, *vide* Speaker's Commentary). Biblical notices describe them as living creatures (Ezek. i. 5 ; Rev. iv. 6) in the form of a man (Ezek. i. 5), with four (Ezek. i. 8 ; ii. 23 ; x. 7, 8—21) or with six wings (Rev. iv. 8), and full of eyes (Ezek. i. 18 ; x. 12 ; Rev. iv. 8) ; having each four faces, viz., of a man, of a lion, of an ox, of an eagle (Ezek. i. 10 ; x. 16) ; or with one face each—of a man, of a lion, of a calf, and of an eagle respectively (Rev. iv. 7). Representations of these *chay'ath*—LXX., ζωά— were by Divine directions placed upon the Capporeth (Exod. xxv. 17) and curtains of the tabernacle (Exod. xxvi. 1, 31; xxxvi. 8, 35), and afterwards engraved upon the walls and doors of the temple (1 Kings vi. 29, 32, 35). In the Apocalypse they are depicted as standing in the immediate neighbourhood of the throne (Rev. iv. 6; v. 6; vii. 11), and as taking part in the acts of adoration and praise in which the heavenly hosts engage (*ibid.* v. 11), and that on the express ground of their redemption (*ibid.* v. 8, 9). Whence the opinion that most exactly answers all the facts of the case is, that these mysterious creatures were

symbolic not of the fulness of the Deity (Bahr), nor of the sum of earthly life (Hengstenberg), nor of the angelic nature (Calvin), nor of the Divine manhood of Jesus Christ (Wordsworth), but *of redeemed and glorified humanity* (Jamieson, Fairbairn, Macdonald, Candlish). Combining with the intelligence of human nature the highest qualities of the animal world, as exhibited in the lion, the ox, and the eagle, they were emblematic of creature life in its most absolutely perfect form. As such they were caused to dwell at the gate of Eden to intimate that only when perfected and purified could fallen human nature return to paradise. Meantime man was utterly unfit to dwell within its fair abode. **And a flaming sword, which turned every way.** Literally, *the flame of a sword turning itself;* not brandished by the cherubim, but existing separately, and flashing out from among them (cf. Ezek. i. 4). An emblem of the Divine glory in its attitude towards sin (Macdonald). **To keep** (to watch over or guard ; cf. ch. ii. 15) **the way of the tree of life.** "To keep the tree of life might imply that all access to it was to be precluded ; but to keep *the way* signifies to keep the way *open* as well as to keep it *shut*" (Macdonald).

HOMILETICS.

Vers. 20—24.—*First fruits of the promise.* I. Faith (ver. 20). The special significance of Adam's renaming his wife at this particular juncture in his history is best discerned when the action is regarded as the response of his faith to the antecedent promise of the woman's seed. 1. It is the *place* of faith to succeed, and not to precede, the promise. Faith being, in its simplest conception, belief in a testimony, the testimony must ever take precedence of the faith. "In whom ye also trusted after that ye heard the word of truth, the gospel of your salvation" (Ephes. i. 13). 2. As to the *genesis* of faith, it is always evoked by the promise, not the promise by the faith. Adam's faith was the creation of God's promise ; so is that of every true believer. "Faith cometh by hearing, and hearing by the word of God" (Rom. x. 17). 3. With regard to the *function* of faith, it is not that of certifying or making sure the promise, but simply of attesting its certainty, which it does by reposing trust in its veracity. "He that receiveth his testimony hath set to his seal that God is true" (John iii. 33). And this was practically what was done by Adam when he called his wife's name Eve. 4. The *power* of faith is seen in this, that while it cannot implement, it is able to anticipate the promise, and, as it were, to enjoy it beforehand, in earnest at least, as Adam did when he realised that his spouse should be the mother of all living. Even so "faith is the substance of things hoped for" (Heb. xi. 1).

II. Acceptance (ver. 21). 1. In the Divine scheme of salvation *acceptance ever follows on the exercise of faith.* See the language of the New Testament generally on the subject of a sinner's justification. The covering of our first parents with coats of skin, apart altogether from any symbolical significance in the act, could scarcely be regarded as other than a token of Jehovah's favour. 2. According to the same scheme *the clothing of a sinner ever accompanies the act of his acceptance.* In New Testament theology the Divine act of justification is always represented as proceeding on the ground that in the eye of God the sinner stands invested with a complete covering (the righteousness of Christ) which renders him both legally and morally acceptable.

That all this was comprehended with perfect fulness and clearness by the pardoned pair it would be foolish to assert ; but, in a fashion accommodated to their simple intelligences, the germ of this doctrine was exhibited by the coats of skin with which they were arrayed, and it is at least possible that they had a deeper insight into the significance of the Divine action than we are always prepared to allow. 3. In the teaching of the gospel scheme *the providing of a sinner with such a covering as he requires must ever be the work of God.* Though not improbable that the coats of skin were furnished by the hides of animals, now for the first time offered in sacrifice by Divine appointment, the simple circumstance that they were God-provided, apart from any other consideration, was sufficient to suggest the thought that only God could supply the covering which was needed for their sin.

III. DISCIPLINE (vers. 22—24). Rightly interpreted, neither the language of Jehovah nor that of Moses warrants the idea that the expulsion was designed as a penal infliction ; but rather as a measure mercifully intended and wisely adapted for the spiritual edification of the pardoned pair. Three elements were present in it that are seldom absent from the discipline of saints. 1. *Removal of comforts.* The initial act in the discipline of Adam and his wife was to eject them from the precincts of Eden. And so oftentimes does God begin the work of sanctification in his people's hearts by the infliction of loss. In the case of Adam and his spouse there were special reasons demanding their removal from the garden, as, *e. g.*, (1) its non-suitability as a home for them now that their pure natures were defiled by sin ; and (2) the danger of their continuing longer in the vicinity of the tree of life. And the same two reasons will frequently be found to explain God's dealings with his people when he inflicts upon them loss of creature comforts ; the non-suitability of those comforts to their wants as spiritual beings ; and the presence of some special danger in the things removed. 2. *Increase of sorrow.* Besides being ejected from the garden, the first pair were henceforth to be subjected to toil and trouble. Adam in tilling the ground, and Eve in bearing children. And this, too, was a part of God's educational process with our first parents ; as, indeed, the sufferings of this present life inflicted on his people generally are all commissioned on a like errand, viz., to bring forth within them the peaceable fruits of righteousness, and to make them partakers of his holiness. 3. *Sentence of death.* The words " whence he was taken " have an echo in them of " dust thou art," &c., and must have extinguished within the breasts of Adam and his wife all hope of returning to Eden on this side the grave ; perhaps, too, would assist them in seeking for a better country, even an heavenly. To prevent saints from seeking Edens on the earth seems to be one of the main designs of death.

IV. HOPE (ver. 24). Though excluded from the garden, man was not without cheering ingredients of hope in his condition. 1. *The Divine presence was still with him.* The cherubim and flaming sword were symbols of the ineffable majesty of Jehovah, and tokens of his presence. And never since has the world been abandoned by the God of mercy and salvation. 2. *Paradise was still reserved for him.* The cherubim and flaming sword were appointed " to keep the way of the tree of life ; " not simply to guard the entrance, but to protect the place. So is heaven a reserved inheritance (1 Pet. i. 4). 3. *The prospect of readmission to the tree of life was yet before him.* As much as this was implied in the jealous guarding of the gate so long as Adam was defiled by sin. It could not fail to suggest the idea that when purified by life's discipline he would no longer be excluded (cf. Rev. xxii. 14). 4. *The gate of heaven was still near him.* He was still permitted to reside in the vicinity of Eden, and to commune with him who dwelt between the cherubim, though denied the privilege as yet of dwelling with him in the interior of his abode. If debarred from the full inheritance, he had at least its earnest. And exactly this is the situation of saints on earth, who, unlike those within the veil, who see the Lord of the heavenly paradise face to face, can only commune with him, as it were, at the gate of his celestial palace.

Learn—1. To believe God's promise of salvation. 2. To be grateful for God's gift of righteousness. 3. To submit with cheerfulness to God's paternal discipline. 4. To live in hope of entering God's heaven.

HOMILIES BY VARIOUS AUTHORS.

Ver. 21.—*Covering.* God's chief promises generally accompanied by visible signs or symbolical acts ; *e. g.*, bow in the cloud, furnace and lamp (Gen. xv. 17), passover, &c. The time here spoken of specially called for such a sign. Man had fallen ; a Deliverer was promised ; it was the beginning of a state of grace for sinners. Notice four facts :—1. Man unfallen required no covering. 2. Man fallen became conscious of need, especially towards God. 3. He attempted himself to provide clothing. 4. God provided it. Spiritual meaning of clothing (Rev. iii. 18 ; vii. 14 ; 2 Cor. v. 3). And note that the root of "atonement" in Hebrew is "to cover." Thus the covering is a type of justification ; God's gift to convicted sinners (cf. Zech. iii. 4, 5 ; Luke xv. 22 ; and the want of this covering, Matt. xxii. 11). With Adam's attempt and God's gift compare the sacrifices of Cain and Abel. Abel's sacrifice of life accepted through faith (Heb. xi. 4), *i. e.* because he believed and acted upon God's direction. Thus atonement, covering, through the sacrifice of life (cf. Levit. xvii. 11), typical of Christ's sacrifice, must have been ordained of God. And thus, though not expressly stated, we may conclude that Adam was instructed to sacrifice, and that the skins from the animals thus slain were a type of the covering of sin through the one great sacrifice (Rom. iv. 7). We mark then—

I. THE HELPLESSNESS OF MAN TO SAVE HIMSELF FROM SIN. The natural thought of a heart convicted is, "Have patience with me, and I will pay thee all." Vain endeavour. The "law of sin" (Rom. vii. 21, 24) is too strong ; earnest striving only makes this more clear (cf. Job ix. 30 ; Isa. lxiv. 6). History is full of man's efforts to cover sins. Hence have come sacrifices, austerities, pilgrimages, &c. But on all merely human effort is stamped failure (Rom. iii. 20).

II. THE LOVE OF GOD FOR SINNERS (Rom. v. 8). A common mistake that if we love God he will love us. Whereas the truth is, 1 John iv. 10—19. We must believe his free gift before we can serve him truly. The want of this belief leads to service in the spirit of bondage.

III. THE PROVISION MADE BY GOD (John iii. 14—17). That we might be not merely forgiven, but renewed (2 Cor. v. 21). The consciousness that "Christ hath redeemed us" is the power that constrains to willing service (1 John iii. 3).—M.

Ver. 24.—*The dispensation of redemption.* Notice—

I. THE MERCY WITH JUDGMENT. He did not destroy the garden ; he did not root up its trees and flowers.

II. He "DROVE OUT THE MAN" into his curse that he might pray for and seek for and, at last, by Divine grace, obtain once more his forfeited blessing.

III. AT THE EAST OF THE GARDEN HE PLACED THE CHERUBIMS AND THE FLAMING SWORD TURNING EVERY WAY, emblems of his natural and moral governments, which, as they execute his righteous will amongst men, do both debar them from perfect happiness and yet at the same time testify to the fact that there is such happiness for those who are prepared for it. Man outside Eden is man under law, but man under law is man *preserved* by Divine mercy.

IV. The PRESERVING MERCY IS THE REDEEMING MERCY. The redemption is more than deliverance from condemnation and death ; it is *restoration to eternal life.* "*Paradise lost*" is not *paradise destroyed*, but shall be hereafter "*paradise regained.*"

V. There is a special significance in the description of "THE WAY OF THE TREE OF LIFE" as *closed* and *guarded*, and therefore a way which can be afterwards *opened* and made *free.*

VI. Without pressing too closely figurative language, it is impossible, surely, to ignore in such a representation the reference to a POSITIVE REVELATION as the MEDIUM OF HUMAN DELIVERANCE AND RESTORATION. The whole of the Scripture teaching rests upon that foundation, that there is "*a way, a truth, and a life*" which is Divinely distinguished from all others. Gradually that eastward gate of Eden has been opened, that road leading into the centre of bliss has been made clear in "*the man Christ Jesus.*"—R.

EXPOSITION.

CHAPTER IV.

Ver. 1.—Exiled from Eden, o'er-canopied by grace, animated by hope, assured of the Divine forgiveness, and filled with a sweet peace, the first pair enter on their life experience of labour and sorrow, and the human race begins its onward course of development in sight of the mystic cherubim and flaming sword. **And Adam knew Eve, his wife.** I. e. "recognised her nature and uses" (Alford; cf. Num. xxxi. 17). The act here mentioned is recorded not to indicate that paradise was "non nuptiis, sed virginitate destinatum" (Jerome), but to show that while Adam was formed from the soil, and Eve from a rib taken from his side, the other members of the race were to be produced "neque ex terra neque quovis alio modo, sed ex conjunctione maris et fœminæ" (Rungius). **And she conceived.** The Divine blessing (ch. i. 28), which in its operation had been suspended during the period of innocence, while yet it was undetermined whether the race should develope as a holy or a fallen seed, now begins to take effect (cf. ch. xviii. 14; Ruth iv. 13; Heb. xi. 11). **And bare Cain.** *Acquisition* or *Possession*, from *kanah*, to acquire (Gesenius). Cf. Eve's exclamation. Kalisch, connecting it with *kūn* or *kīn*, to strike, sees an allusion to his character and subsequent history as a murderer, and supposes it was not given to him at birth, but at a later period. Tayler Lewis falls back upon the primitive idea of the root, to create, to procreate, generate, of which he cites as examples ch. xiv. 19, 22; Deut. xxxii. 6, and takes the derivative to signify the *seed*, explaining Eve's exclamation *kanīthī kain* as equivalent to τετοκα τοκον, *genui genitum* or *generationem*. **And said, I have gotten a man from the Lord.** The popular interpretation, regarding *kani-thī* as the emphatic word in the sentence, understands Eve to say that her child was a thing achieved, an acquisition gained, either from the Lord (Onkelos, Calvin) or by means of, with the help of, the Lord (LXX., Vulgate, Jerome, Dathe, Keil), or for the Lord (Syriac). If, however, the emphatic term is Jehovah, then *eth* with Makkeph following will be the sign of the accusative, and the sense will be, "I have gotten a man—Jehovah" (Jonathon, Luther, Baumgarten, Lewis); to which, perhaps, the chief objections are— (1) that it appears to anticipate the development of the Messianic idea, and credits Eve with too mature Christological conceptions (Lange), though if Enoch in the seventh generation recognised Jehovah as the coming

One, why might not Eve have done so in the first? (Bonar); (2) that if the thoughts of Eve had been running so closely on the identity of the coming Deliverer with Jehovah, the child would have been called Jehovah, or at least some compound of Jehovah, such as Ishiah—אִישׁ and יהוה—or Coniah—קִין and יהוה (Murphy); (3) si scivit Messiam esse debet Jovam, quomodo existimare potuit Cainam esse Messiam, quem sciebat esse ab Adamo genitum? (Dathe); and (4) that, while it might not be difficult to account for the mistake of a joyful mother in supposing that the fruit of her womb was the promised seed, though, "if she did believe so, it is a caution to interpreters of prophecy" (Inglis), it is not so easy to explain her belief that the promised seed was to be Jehovah, since no such announcement was made in the Prot-evangel. But whichever view be adopted of the construction of the language, it is obvious that Eve's utterance was the dictate of faith. In Cain's birth she recognised the earnest and guarantee of the promised seed, and in token of her faith gave her child a name (cf. ch. iii. 20), which may also explain her use of the Divine name *Jehovah* instead of *Elohim*, which she employed when conversing with the serpent. That Eve denominates her infant a man has been thought to indicate that she had previously borne daughters who had grown to womanhood, and that she expected her young and tender babe to reach maturity. Murphy thinks this opinion probable; but the impression conveyed by the narrative is that Cain was the first-born of the human family.

Ver. 2.—**And she again bare** (literally, *added to bear*, a Hebraism adopted in the New Testament; *vide* Luke xx. 11) **his brother Abel.** *Habel* (vanity), supposed to hint either that a mother's eager hopes had already begun to be disappointed in her elder son, or that, having in her first child's name given expression to her faith, in this she desired to preserve a monument of the miseries of human life, of which, perhaps, she had been forcibly reminded by her own maternal sorrows. Perhaps also, though unconsciously, a melancholy prophecy of his premature removal by the hand of fratricidal rage, to which it has been thought there is an outlook by the historian in the frequent (seven times repeated) and almost pathetic mention of the fact that Abel was Cain's brother. The absence of the usual expression וַתַּהַר, as well as the peculiar phraseology *et addidit parere* has suggested that Abel was Cain's twin brother (Calvin, Kimchi, Candlish), though this is not necessarily implied in the text. **And Abel was a keeper of sheep** (ποιμὴν προβάτων, LXX.; the latter term includes goats—Levit. i. 10), **but Cain was a tiller of the ground.** These occupations, indirectly suggested by God in the command to till the ground and the gift of the clothes of skin (Keil), were doubtless both practised by the first man, who would teach them to his sons. It is neither justifiable nor necessary to trace a difference of moral character in the different callings which the young men selected, though probably their choices were determined by their talents and their tastes. Ainsworth sees in Abel a figure of Christ "in shepherdy as in sacrificing and martyrdom."

Ver. 3.—**And in process of time.** Literally, *at the end of the days*, i. e.—1. Of the year (Aben Ezra, Dathe, De Wette, Rosenmüller, Bohlen), at which season the feast of the ingathering was afterwards kept—Exod. xxiii. 16 (Bush). Aristotle, 'Ethics,' viii. 2, notes that anciently sacrifices were offered after the gathering of the fruits of the earth (Ainsworth). 2. Of the week (Candlish). 3. Of an indefinite time, years or days (Luther, Kalisch). 4. Of some set time, as the beginning of their occupations (Knobel). **It came to. pass** (literally, it was) **that Cain brought of the fruit of the ground an offering.** Θυσία, LXX.; *oblatio*, Vulgate; *speis-opfer*, Luther. The *mincha* of Hebrew worship was a bloodless sacrifice, consisting of flour and oil, or flour prepared with frankincense (Levit. ii. 1). All tree fruits and garden produce were excluded; it was limited to the productions of agriculture and vine growing (cf. Kurtz, 'Sacrificial Worship,' § 140). Here it includes both meat offerings and animal sacrifices (cf. ver. 4). **Unto the Lord.** Probably to the gate of the garden, where the cherubim and flaming sword were established as the visible monuments of the Divine presence.

Ver. 4.—**And Abel, he also brought of the firstlings of his flock.** Either the firstborn, which God afterwards demanded (Exod. xiii. 12), or the choicest and best (Job xviii. 13; Jer. xxxi. 19; Heb. xii. 23). **And the fat thereof.** Literally, *the fatness of them*, i. e. the fattest of the firstlings, "the best he had, and the best of those best" (Inglis; cf. Gen. xlv. 18; Num. xviii. 2; Ps. clxvii. 14); a proof that flesh was eaten before the Flood, since "it had been no praise to Abel to offer the fatlings if he used not to eat of them" (Willet), and "si antepposuit Abel utilitate suæ Deum, non dubium quia solitus sit ex labore suo utilitatem percipere" (Justin). **And the Lord had respect.** Literally, *looked upon;* ἐπεῖδεν, LXX. (cf. Num. xvi. 15); probably consuming it by fire from heaven, or from the flaming sword (cf. Levit. ix. 24; 1 Chron. xxi. 26; 2 Chron. vii. 1;

1 Kings xviii. 38; Jerome, Chrysostom, Cyril). Theodotion renders ἐνεπύρισεν, *inflammant;* and Heb. xi. 4, μαρτυροῦντος ἐπὶ τοῖς δώροις, is supposed to lend considerable weight to the opinion. **Unto Abel and his offering.** Accepting first his person and then his gift (cf. Prov. xii. 2; xv. 8; 2 Cor. viii. 12). "The sacrifice was accepted for the man, and not the man for the sacrifice" (Ainsworth); but still "without a doubt the words of Moses imply that the matter of Abel's offering was more excellent and suitable than that of Cain's," and one can hardly entertain a doubt that this was the idea of the author of the Epistle to the Hebrews" (Prof. Lindsay, 'Lectures on Hebrews,' Edin. 1867). Abel's sacrifice was πλείονα, fuller than Cain's; it had more in it; it had faith, which was wanting in the other. It was also offered in obedience to Divine prescription. The universal prevalence of sacrifice rather points to Divine prescription than to man's invention as its proper source. Had Divine worship been of purely human origin, it is almost certain that greater diversity would have prevailed in its forms. Besides, the fact that the mode of worship was not left to human ingenuity under the law, and that will-worship is specifically condemned under the Christian dispensation (Col. ii. 23), favours the presumption that it was Divinely appointed from the first.

Ver. 5.—**But unto Cain and to his offering he had not respect.** Because of the absence of those qualities which distinguished Abel and his offering; not because the heart of Cain was "no more pure," but "imbued with a criminal propensity" (Kalisch), which it was not until his offering was rejected. The visible sign, whatever it was, being awanting in the case of Cain's oblation, its absence left the offerer in no dubiety as to the Divine displeasure with both himself and his offering. In the rejection of Cain's offering Bohlen sees the animus of a Levitical narrator, who looks down slightingly on offerings of the fruits and flowers of earth; but, as Havernick well remarks, the theocracy was essentially based on agriculture, while the Mosaic institute distinctly recognised the legality and value of bloodless offerings. **And Cain was very wroth** (literally, *it burned with Cain exceedingly*), **and his countenance fell.** In fierce resentment against his brother, possibly in disappointed rage against himself, almost certainly in anger against God (cf. Neh. vi. 16; Job xxix. 24; Jer. iii. 12, and contrast Job xi. 15). There was apparently no sorrow for sin, "no spirit of inquiry, self-examination, prayer to God for light or pardon, clearly showing that Cain was far from a right state of mind" (Murphy). Yet the Lord does not forthwith abandon the contumacious and insensate transgressor, but patiently expostulates with and instructs him as to how he too might obtain the same blessing of acceptance which his younger brother enjoyed.

Vers. 6, 7—**And the Lord** (Jehovah) **said unto Cain.** Speaking either mediately by Adam (Luther), or more probably directly by his own voice from between the cherubim where the flaming sword, the visible symbol of the Divine presence, had been established (cf. Exod. xx. 24). **Why art thou wroth? and why is thy countenance fallen?** The ensuing verse is a veritable *crux interpretum*, concerning which the greatest diversity of sentiment exists. Passing by the manifest mistranslation of the LXX., "If thou hast offered rightly, but hast not divided rightly, hast thou not sinned? Rest quiet; toward thee is his (or its) resort, and thou shalt rule over him (or it)," which Augustine, Ambrose, and Chrysostom followed, at the same time "wearying themselves with many interpretations, and being divided among themselves as to how Cain divided not rightly" (Willet), the different opinions that have been entertained as to the meaning of its several clauses, their connection, and precise import when united, may be thus exhibited. **If thou doest well.** Either (1) if thou wert innocent and sinless (Candlish, Jamieson), or (2) if thou, like Abel, presentest a right offering in a right spirit (Vulgate, Luther, Calvin), or (3) if thou retrace thy steps and amend thine offering and intention (Willet, Murphy). **Shalt thou not be accepted?** Literally, *Is there not lifting up?* (*seâth,* from *nasa,* to raise up). Either—1. Of the *countenance* (Gesenius, Fürst, Dathe, Rosenmüller, Knobel, Lange, Delitzsch). 2. Of the *sacrifice,* viz., by acceptance of it (Calvin); akin to which are the interpretations—Is there not a lifting up of the burden of guilt? Is there not forgiveness? (Luther); Is there not acceptance with God? (Speaker's Commentary); Is there not a bearing away of blessing? (Ainsworth). Vulgate, Shalt thou not receive? (sc. the Divine favour). "Verum quamvis נָשָׂא עָוֹן peccatum condonare significet, nusquam tamen שְׂאֵת veniam sonat" (Rosen.). 3. Of the *person,* i. e. by establishing Cain's pre-eminency as the elder brother, to which reference is clearly made in the concluding clause of the verse (Bush). **And if thou doest not well, sin**—*chattath,* from *chata,* to miss the mark like an archer, properly signifies a sin (Exod. xxviii. 9; Isa. vi. 27; cf. Greek, ἄτη); also a sin offering (Levit. vi. 18, 23); also penalty (Zech. xiv. 19), though this is doubtful. Hence it has been taken to mean in this place 1. Sin (Dathe, Rosenmüller, Keil, Kalisch, Wordsworth, Speaker's Commentary, Murphy). 2. The punishment

of sin (Onkelos, Grotius, Cornelius à Lapide, Ainsworth), the guilt of sin, the sense of unpardoned transgression; "interius conscientiæ judicium, quod hominem convictum sui peccati undique obsessum premit" (Calvin). 3. A sin offering (Lightfoot, Poole, Magee, Candlish, Exell)—**lieth** (literally, *רֹבֵץ: robets, from rabats, to couch as a* beast of prey; cf. ch. xxix. 2; xlix. 9) **at the door.** Literally, at the opening = at the door *of the conscience,* expressive of the nearness and severity of the Divine retribution (Calvin); *of the soul,* indicating the close contiguity of the devouring monster sin to the evil-doer (Kalisch); *of paradise* (Bonar); *of Abel's fold* (Exell), suggesting the locality where a sacrificial victim might be obtained; *of the house,* conveying the ideas of publicity and certainty of detection for the transgressor whose sin, though lying asleep, was only sleeping at the door, *i. e.* "in a place where it will surely be disturbed; and, therefore, it is impossible but that it must be awoke and roused up, when as a furious beast it will lay hold on thee" (Luther); *h. e.* "statim se prodet, peccatum tuum non magis celari potest, quam id quod pro foribus jacet" (Rosenmüller). **And unto thee** shall be **his**—*i. e.* (1) Abel's (LXX. (?), Chrysostom, Ambrose, Grotius, Calvin, Ainsworth, Bush, Speaker's, Bonar, Exell); or (2) sin's (Vulgate (?), Luther, Rosenmüller, Von Bohlen, Kalisch, Keil, Delitzsch, Murphy); or (3) the sin offering's (Faber, Candlish)—**desire** (*vide* ch. iii. 16), **and thou shalt rule over him.** *I. e.,* according to the interpretation adopted of the preceding words—(1) thou shalt maintain thy rights of primogeniture over Abel, who, as younger son, shall be obsequious and deferential towards thee; or, (2) "the entire submission and service of sin will be yielded to thee, and thou shalt make thyself master of it," *sc.* by yielding to it and being hurried on to greater wickedness— a warning against the downward course of sin (Murphy); or, while sin lurks for thee like a beast of prey, and "the demon of allurement" thirsts for thee to gratify thy passion, thou shalt (or mayst) rule over it, *sc.* by giving up thy wrath and restraining thine evil propensities—a word of hopeful encouragement to draw the sinner back to holy paths (Keil); or, "peccatum tanquam mulier impudica sistitur, quæ hominem ad libidinem suam explendam tentet, cui igitur resistere debeat" (Rosenmüller); or, (3) the sacrificial victim is not far to seek, it is already courting thine acceptance, and thou mayst at once avail thyself of it (Candlish). Of the various solutions of this "difficillimus locus," all of which are plausible, and none of which are entirely destitute of support, that appears the most entitled to acceptance which, excluding any reference either to Abel or to a sin offering, regards the language as warning Cain against the dangers of yielding to sin.

Ver. 8.—**And Cain talked with** (literally, *said to*) **his brother.** Διέλθωμεν εἰς τὸ πεδίον (LXX.) ; *egrediamur foras* (Vulgate). The Samaritan and Syriac versions interpolate to the same effect. The Jerusalem Targum explains—"Cainum cum Abele contendisse de vita æterna, de extremo judicio, et providentia divina," inserting a long conversation commencing, "Veni, egrediamur ad superficiem agri ; " but the obvious supplement is to be found in the subject matter of the previous verse (Hieronymus, Aben Ezra, Gesenius). It is not against this that it argues too much moral goodness in Cain to suppose that he would tell his younger brother of Jehovah's admonition (Knobel) ; and it certainly relieves us from the necessity of adding to the moral turpitude of the unhappy fratricide by depicting him as deliberately planning his favoured brother's murder, carrying the fell purpose within his guilty bosom, watching his opportunity (Böttcher and Knobel, who substitute שָׁמַר, *he watched*, for אָמַר, *he said*), and at last accomplishing his unhallowed purpose by means of treachery. Beyond all question the historian designs to describe not an act of culpable homicide, but a deed of red-handed murder ; yet the impression which his language conveys is that of a crime rather suddenly conceived and hurriedly performed than deliberately planned and treacherously executed. **And it came to pass, when they were in the field, that Cain rose up against Abel his brother, and slew him.**

Ver. 9.—**And the Lord said unto Cain.** "Probably soon after the event, at the next time of sacrifice, and at the usual place of offering" (Bonar). **Where is Abel thy brother?** "A question fitted to go straight to the murderer's conscience, and no less fitted to rouse his wrathful jealousy, as showing how truly Abel was the beloved one" (*ibid*). Whether spoken by Adam (Luther), or whispered within his breast by the still small voice of conscience, or, as is most probable, uttered from between the cherubim, Cain felt that he was being examined by a Divine voice (Calvin). **And** (in reply) **he said** (adding falsehood, effrontery, and even profanity to murder), **I know not : am I my brother's keeper?** The inquiry neither of ignorance nor of innocence, but the desperate resort of one who felt himself closely tracked by avenging justice and about to be convicted of his crime. "He showeth himself *a lyer* in saying, ' I know not ;' *wicked and profane* in thinking he could hide his sin from God ; *unjust* in denying himself to be his brother's keeper ; *obstinate and desperate* in not confessing his sin" (Willet ; cf. Ps. x.).

Ver. 10.—Satisfied that the guilty fratricide is resolved to make no acknowledgment of his deed, the omniscient Judge proceeds to charge him with his sin. **And he**—*i. e.* Jehovah—**said, What hast thou done?** Thus intimating his perfect cognisance of the fact which his prisoner was attempting to deny. What a revelation it must have been to the inwardly trembling culprit of the impossibility of eluding the besetting God ! (Ps. cxxxix. 5). **The voice of thy brother's blood** (literally, *bloods*, *i. e.* of this and all subsequent martyrs—Chald. Par.) **crieth unto me.** A common Scriptural expression concerning murder and other crimes (ch. xviii. 20, 21 ; xix. 13 ; Exod. iii. 9 ; Heb. xii. 24 ; James v. 4). The blood crying is a symbol of the soul crying for its right to live (Lange). In this instance the cry was a demand for the punishment of the murderer ; and that cry has reverberated through all lands and down through all ages, proclaiming vengeance against the shedder of innocent blood (cf. ch. ix. 5). "Hence the prayer that the earth may not drink in the blood shed upon it, in order that it may not thereby become invisible and inaudible" (Knobel). Cf. Job xvi. 18 ; Isa. xxvi. 21 ; Ezek. xxiv. 7 ; also Eschylus, 'Chœphoræ,' 310, 398 (quoted by T. Lewis in Lange). **From the ground.** Into which it had disappeared, but not, as the murderer hoped, to become forgotten.

Vers. 11, 12.—Convicted, if not humbled, the culprit is speechless, and can only listen in consternation to the threefold judgment which pronounced him "cursed in his soul, vagabond in his body, and unprosperous in his labours" (Willet). **And now**—either *at this time*, already (cf. Josh. xiv. 11 ; Hosea ii. 10), or *for this cause*, because thou hast done this (ch. iii. 14 ; cf. ch. xix. 9 ; Exod. xviii. 19)—**art thou cursed.** *The first curse pronounced against a human being.* Adam and Eve were not cursed, though the serpent and the devil were. If we may not conclude that Cain was thereby for ever excluded from the hope of salvation if he should repent, still less must we explain the Divine judgment down to a simple sentence of banishment from Eden. The fratricide was henceforth to bear the displeasure and indignation of his Maker, whose image in Abel he had slain ; of which indignation and displeasure his expatriation was to be a symbol. Different explanations have been offered of the clause, **from the earth**, or *ground*, *Adhamah*, which, however, cannot mean *more than the ground*, which already had been cursed (ch. iii. 17 ; Lange), since "the curse of the soil and the misery of man cannot well be compared with each other" (Kalisch) ; or simply *away from the district*, the scene of his crime (Kalisch, Speaker's, Rosenmüller,

Tuch, Gerlach, Delitzsch), as if all that the sentence implied was banishment from Eden; but must involve in addition the idea that the curse was to leap upon him *from the earth*, or ground, in general (Aben Ezra, Kimchi, Knobel, Alford, Murphy). **Which hath opened her mouth to receive thy brother's blood from thy hand.** The terrible significance of this curse is further opened in the words which follow. The earth was to be against him — 1. *In refusing him its substance.* **When thou tillest** (literally, *shalt till*) **the ground, it shall not henceforth yield** (literally, *add to give*) **unto thee her strength.** Neither a double curse upon the entire earth for man's sake (Alford), nor a doom of sterility inflicted only on the district of Eden (Kalisch); but a judgment on Cain and his descendants with respect to their labours. Their tillage of the ground was not to prosper, which ultimately, Bonar thinks, drove the Cainites to city-building and mechanical invention. 2. *In denying him a home.* **A fugitive and a vagabond—** literally, *moving and wandering;* "groaning and trembling" (LXX., erroneously), "banished and homeless" (Keil)—**shalt thou be in the earth.** "As robbers are wont to be who have no quiet and secure resting-place" (Calvin); driven on by the agonising tortures of a remorseful and alarmed conscience, and not simply by "the earth denying to him the expected fruits of his labour" (Delitzsch). The ban of wandering, which David pronounced upon his enemies (Ps. lix. 12; cix. 10), in later years fell upon the Jews, who "for shedding the blood of Christ, the most innocent Lamb of God, are vagabonds to this day over the face of the earth" (Willet). Thus the earth was made the minister of God's curse, not a partaker of it, as some have strangely imagined, as if by drinking up the blood of Abel it had become a participant of Cain's crime (Delitzsch).

Vers. 13, 14.—**And Cain said unto the Lord, My punishment** (or my sin) **is greater than I can bear.** Or, than can be borne away. Interpreted in either way, this is scarcely the language of confession, "sufficiens confessio, sed intempestiva" (Chrysostom); but, as the majority of interpreters are agreed, of desperation (Calvin). According to the first rendering Cain is understood as deploring not the enormity of his sin, but the severity of his punishment, under which he reels and staggers as one amazed (Aben Ezra, Kimchi, Calvin, Keil, Delitzsch, Murphy, Alford, Speaker's, Kalisch). According to the second, from the terrific nature of the blow which had descended on him Cain awakens to the conviction that his sin was too heinous to be forgiven (margin, Septuagint, Vulgate, Theodotion, Arabic, Syriac, Onkelos, Samaritan, Gesenius, Wordsworth).

The first of these is favoured by the remaining portion of his address, which shows that that which had paralysed his guilty spirit was not the wickedness of his deed, but the overwhelming retribution which had leapt so unexpectedly from its bosom. The real cause of his despair was the sentence which had gone forth against him, and the articles of which he now recapitulates. **Behold, thou hast driven me this day**—"Out of the sentence of his own conscience Cain makes a clear, positive, Divine decree of banishment" (Lange)—**from the face of the earth.** Literally, *the ground*, i. e. the land of Eden. "Adam's sin brought expulsion from the inner circle, Cain's from the outer" (Bonar). **And from thy face shall I be hid.** Either (1) from the place where the Divine presence was specially manifested, *i. e.* at the gate of Eden, which does not contradict (Kalisch) the great Biblical truth of the Divine omni-presence (cf. Exod. xx. 24); or, (2) more generally, from the enjoyment of the Divine favour (cf. Deut. xxxi. 18). "To be hidden from the face of God is to be not regarded by God, or not protected by his guardian care" (Calvin). **And I shall be a fugitive and a vagabond.** "A vagabond and a runagate" (Tyndale, Coverdale, 'Bishops' Bible'). *Vagus et profugus* (Vulgate); *vagus et infestus agitationibus* (Tremellius and Junius). **In the earth.** The contemplation of his miserable doom, acting on his guilty conscience, inspired him with a fearful apprehension, to which in closing he gives expression in the hearing of his Judge. **And it shall come to pass, that every one**—not beast (Josephus, Kimchi, Michaelis), but person—**that findeth me shall slay me.** "Amongst the ancient Romans a man cursed for any wickedness might be freely killed (Dionysius Halicarnass., 1. 2). Amongst the Gauls the excommunicated were deprived of any benefit of law (Cæsar. 'de Bello Gallico,' 1. 6; cf. also Sophocles, 'Œdip. Tyrannus')" (Ainsworth). The apprehension which Cain cherished has been explained as an oversight on the part of the narrator (Schumann and Tuch); as a mistake on the part of Cain, who had no reason to know that the world was not populated (T. Lewis); as referring to the blood avengers of the future who might arise from his father's family (Rosenmüller, Delitzsch); and also, and perhaps with as much probability, as indicating that already, in the 130 years that had gone, Adam's descendants were not limited to the two brothers and their wives (Havernick).

Ver. 15.—The condemned fratricide's apprehensions were allayed by a special act of grace. **And the Lord said unto him, Therefore** (the LXX., Symm., Theodotion,

Vulgate, Syriac, Dathius, translate Not so—οὐχ οὕτως, *nequaquam*, reading לֹא בֵן instead of לָכֵן) **whosoever slayeth Cain, vengeance shall be taken on him sevenfold.** *I. e. fully*, sevenfold vengeance—complete vengeance (cf. Levit. xxvi. 28). In the case of Cain's murderer there was to be no such mitigation of the penalty as in the case of Cain himself; on the contrary, he would be visited more severely than Cain, as being guilty not alone of homicide, but of transgressing the Divine commandment which said that Cain was to live (Willet). As to why this special privilege was granted to Cain, it was not because "the early death of the pious Abel was in reality no punishment, but the highest boon" (Kalisch), nor because banishment from God's presence was the greatest possible punishment, "having in itself the significance of a social human death" (Lange), nor because it was needful to spare life for the increase of posterity (Rosenmüller); but perhaps — 1. To show that "Vengeance is mine; I will repay, saith the Lord." 2. To prove the riches of the Divine clemency to sinful men. 3. To serve as a warning against the crime of murder. To this probably there is a reference in the concluding clause. **And the Lord set a mark upon**—gave a sign to (LXX.)—**Cain, lest any finding him should kill him**. Commentators are divided as to whether this was a visible sign to repress avengers (the Rabbis, Luther, Calvin, Piscator, &c.), or an inward assurance to Cain himself that he should not be destroyed (Aben Ezra, Dathe, Rosenmüller, Gesenius, Tuch, Kalisch, Delitzsch). In support of the former it is urged that an external badge would be more likely to repel assailants; while in favour of the latter it is pleaded that of seventy-six times in which *ōth* occurs in the Old Testament, in seventy-five it is translated *sign*. If there was a visible mark upon the fugitive, it is impossible to say what it was; that it was a shaking (LXX.), or a continual fleeing from place to place (Lyra), or a horn in the head (Rabbis), a peculiar kind of dress (Clericus), are mere conceits. But, whatever it was, it was not a sign of Cain's forgiveness (Josephus), only a pledge of God's protection. Cf. the Divine prophetic sentence against the Jewish Cain (Ps. lix. 11).

Ver. 16.—**And Cain went out from the presence of the Lord.** Not simply ended his interview and prepared to emigrate from the abode of his youth (Kalisch); but, more especially, withdrew from the neighbourhood of the cherubim (*vide* on ver. 14). **And dwelt in the land of Nod.** The geographical situation of Nod (Knobel, China?) cannot be determined further than that it was **on the east of Eden**, and its name, *Nod*, or wandering (cf. vers. 12, 14; Ps. lvi. 8), was clearly derived from Cain's fugitive and vagabond life (*vide* Michaelis, 'Suppl.,' p. 1612; and cf. Fürst, 'Lex.,' *sub voce*), "which showeth, as Josephus well conjectureth, that Cain was not amended by his punishment, but waxed worse and worse, giving himself to rapine, robbery, oppression, deceit" (Willet).

HOMILETICS.

Vers. 1—15.—*The first brothers.* I. THE BROTHERS AT HOME. 1. The *first* home. Of Divine appointment, and among the choicest blessings that have survived the fall, homes are designed for—(1) The increase of the human family. Of all animals, the offspring of man is least fitted to provide for itself in infancy. Without the shelter of a home man would be born only to die. (2) The happiness of the race. Considering man's weakness and wants, miseries and dangers, as a fallen being existing in a sin-cursed world, the family constitution, which secures the interdependence of individuals, largely enhances his comfort. Whether the same amount of happiness would have been attainable had the race been created, like the angelic, as a multitude of separate individuals may be difficult to determine. (3) The training of children. Being God's gift, they should be highly prized, tenderly cherished, carefully nurtured, intelligently counselled by the father, anxiously cared for by the mother, lovingly, perseveringly, prayerfully reared by both; educated not for themselves, or the world, or even for their parents, but for God; trained to *work*, as indolence is a sin, and to *worship*, as piety is a duty. 2. A *pious* home. Its *locality*, though outside the garden, was still in Eden, which was a mercy, and probably not far from the cherubim, Adam's gate of heaven, which was hopeful. When man founds a home it should never be far removed from God, heaven, or the Church. Its *structure*, mayhap, was humble,—another garden likely, but this time man-made, and not so fair as that which God had planted,—but its precincts were hallowed by the rites of religion. It is one mark of a pious home when God has an altar in it (Ps. cxviii. 15). Its *inmates* were fallen creatures, but still pardoned sinners, who, having believed the Divine promise, had become partakers of the Divine mercy.   There is no true piety where there is no humble faith in the gospel.   3. A *happy* home.   At least it had all the elements that were needful to surround them with earthly felicity: the only true foundation on which a happy home can rest—religion (Ps. cxii. 1; Prov. xv. 25; xxiv. 3); the best blessing a home can receive—the Divine favour (Prov. iii. 33); the best ornaments a home can possess—children (Ps. cxxviii. 3),

II. THE BROTHERS AT WORK.   These works were—1. *Necessary*.   God's commands, man's powers and needs, the earth's condition, render toil indispensable.   No one is born to sloth.   Every one should have a calling.   Those whom God's bounty relieves from the necessity of toiling for daily bread should still labour in some specific occupation for God's glory and man's good.   2. *Various*.   The first instance of division of labour.   Diversity of employments, rendered necessary by individual capacities and tastes, promotes excellence of workmanship, facility of production, and rapidity of distribution; contributes to the unity and stability of the social fabric by teaching the interdependence of its several parts; multiplies the comforts, stimulates the energies, and generally advances the civilisation of mankind.   3. *Useful*.   Most trades and professions are useful; but some more so than others.   Parents should select for their children, and young persons for themselves, occupations that contribute to the good of man rather than those which enhance their own profit.   A calling that flourishes on the world's luxuries is less remunerative, besides being less honourable, than one which supplies men's necessities.   4. *Healthful*.   These brothers both worked in the open air.   Out-of-door employment more conducive to physical vigour and mental activity than toiling in mines, factories, warehouses, and shops.   Men should study health in their secular pursuits.

III. THE BROTHERS AT WORSHIP.   Born in the same home, educated by the same parents, trained to the same duty of devotion, the first brothers became worshippers of the same God, at the same time, and in the same place, at the same altar, and in the same way, viz., by the presentation of oblations, yet their service was essentially diverse.   1. Their *offerings*.   These were not the same — (1) In *matter*.   Cain brought of the fruit of the ground; Abel of the firstlings of his flock, and of the fat thereof.   The one was bloodless, the other bloody.   Each one's offering was connected with, perhaps suggested by, his daily calling.   So the trades, temperaments, abilities of men determine the kinds of their religious service and devotion.   This diversity in men's oblations is natural, appropriate, beautiful, right.   God requires the consecration to himself of the first-fruits of men's powers and callings (Prov. iii. 9). (2) In *measure*.   Abel offered unto God a more excellent (literally, a greater) sacrifice than Cain (Heb. xi. 4).   Cain brought *of the fruit*, not *fruits*, of the earth—offering with a penurious hand, as many of God's worshippers do still.   Abel brought of the fattest and the best of his flocks; so should all God's worshippers reserve for him the first-fruits of their years, powers, labours, increase.   (3) In *meaning*.   The elder brother's offering was an acknowledgment of dependence upon God, an expression, probably (?), of gratitude to God, possibly also a recognition of God's claim to be worshipped; the younger son's declared consciousness of sin, faith in atoning blood, hope in Divine mercy.   2. Their *worship*.   The state of the heart is the essential thing in worship.   If the offering of the hand be the husk, the devotion of the soul is the kernel of true religion.   Not only was Abel's offering better than Cain's; it was offered in a better way.   (1) In faith, trusting in the promise, having an outlook towards the woman's seed (Heb. xi. 4).   Without faith in the Lamb of God who died for sin no worship can be accepted.   (2) In obedience.   Abel's worship was offered in the way prescribed.   God does not leave men to invent forms of religion.   Christianity condemns will-worship (Col. ii. 18).   The most costly offerings will not suffice for obedience to Divine prescription (1 Sam. xv. 22).   (3) In sincerity.   Cain was a formalist; Abel a worshipper of God in spirit and in truth.   Only such can worship God (John iv. 24).   Hypocrisy and formalism, though accompanied with splendid ritual, God rejects (Prov. xxi. 27; Isa. i. 13—15; Matt. vi. 5).   3. Their *receptions*.   These were—(1) *Diametrically opposite*.   Abel was accepted by God, received into Divine favour, regarded as righteous, considered as a justified person. Cain was not accepted; not because the fruits of the earth were in themselves unworthy of God's acceptance, but because, in presenting them, he virtually proclaimed his disbelief in God's promise and repudiation of God's way of salvation. (2) *Visibly proclaimed.* By some outward sign God expressed in the one case his approbation, and in the other his displeasure. By the gospel he now solemnly declares his reception of the true and rejection of the false worshipper (John iii. 36). More reliable are the announcements which God now makes through his word than those which he then delivered through the medium of signs. (3) *Distinctly understood.* Neither Cain nor Abel was in any dubiety as to his position. The mind of God had been explicitly revealed. The one was assured that he was righteous ; the other knew that he was reprobate. So may every one ascertain his standing in God's sight who listens to the inspired declarations of the Divine word (John iii. 18 ; Rom. iii. 20 ; iv. 5).

IV. THE BROTHERS AT VARIANCE. Divided in daily toils, religious worship, Divine acceptance, they were now also divided in fraternal regards. This estrangement was—(1) *Unseemly* in its character, existing, as it did, between brothers. Where, if not within the hallowed circle of home, should mutual love prevail? Who, if not brothers, should preserve the unity of the Spirit in the bonds of peace? (Ps. cxxxiii. 1). Brothers were meant for friendship and helpfulness, not for envy and destruction. Let us thank God there is a Friend that sticketh closer than a brother (Prov. xviii. 24). (2) *Unjustifiable* in its cause. It sprang from *religion.* Alas, that which was heralded as the bringer of peace on earth and good-will among men has often been the cause of strife and contention, separation and estrangement, as Christ foretold (Matt. x. 34—36). What a signal proof of the corruption of the human heart! It was occasioned through *envy.* Cain was wroth because his brother was accepted. Unbelievers often take offence at believers because of blessings they affect to despise. (3) *Wrathful* in its manifestation. Because his brother's person and service were approved Cain grew enraged ; because himself and his offerings were refused he was angry with God. Hypocrites and sinners are always displeased with those who are better than themselves. (4) *Murderous* in its termination. Envy, wrath, murder—the beginning, middle, end of a wicked man's life. The last act lies enfolded in the second, and the second in the first, as the fruit in the tree, and the tree in the seed. Hence wrath is murder in the thought (1 John iii. 15) ; and "who is able to stand before envy ?" (Prov. xxvii. 4). Therefore *obsta principiis.* Cultivate fraternal affection. Let brotherly love continue. Follow younger brothers in their piety rather than hate them for their prayers.

V. THE BROTHERS AT THE JUDGMENT BAR. 1. Both *went* there. The spirit of the first martyr ascended to God, and God came to arraign the red-handed murderer. So must we all appear before the judgment-seat of Christ. 2. Both were *judged* there. The righteous Abel's character and conduct were approved ; for God espoused his cause, and heard the cry of his innocent blood. The guilty Cain was condemned. So will all before the great white throne be judged according to their works ; of every one of which God is now a witness, as he was of the fratricidal act of Cain. 3. Both were *sentenced* there. Abel was received into glory, and his blood avenged ; Cain banished from God's presence, transformed into a wandering fugitive, in mercy spared from immediate destruction, but in reality, with his scarred brow, doomed to a lifetime of woe—fit emblem of the doom of the ungodly ; as the award of righteous Abel was of the honour of the righteous (Matt. xxv. 46).

Lessons :—1. Value the Divine gift of home. 2. Provide things honest in the sight of all men. 3. Serve the Lord with gladness. Present your bodies a living sacrifice. Come into his courts, and bring an offering with you. 4. Follow peace with all men, and holiness, without which no man shall see the Lord. 5. Live in anticipation of, and preparation for, the judgment-day. 6. Learn that nothing will keep a man right in life and safe in death except faith in atoning blood. Cain had pious parents, a good home, an honourable calling, a religious profession, and yet was lost. Abel had a short life and a sad death, but he was safe. Faith in Christ (the woman's seed) made the difference.

Ver. 9.—*Am I my brother's keeper?* I. The *world* says, No! 1. Every man's brother ought to keep himself. 2. If a man's brother cannot keep himself, he deserves to perish. 3. No man's brother will be at the trouble to keep him. 4. Every man has enough to do to keep himself. Such is *the gospel of selfishness* proclaimed and practised by the world.

II. *God* says, YES ! 1. Because he is your brother. *Affection* should prompt you. 2. Because he may get lost without your keeping. *Humanity* should incline you. 3. Because I expect you. *Religion* commands you. Such is *the gospel of love* which God preaches and charges us to practise.

HOMILIES BY VARIOUS AUTHORS.

Vers. 1—8.—*The kingdom of God.* Another "genesis" is now described, that of *sinful society*, which prepares the way for the description of the rising *kingdom of God.*

I. THE DEVELOPMENT OF MORAL EVIL IS CONTEMPORANEOUS WITH HUMAN SOCIETY. We must still bear in mind that the aim of the narrative is not scientific, but religious and didactic. The sketch of the first family in vers. 1 and 2 is plainly an outline to be filled in. The keeper of sheep and the tiller of the ground are out in the broad world. We are not told that there were no other human beings when they were grown up. Probably from their employment it is meant to be inferred that the human family had already grown into something like a community, when there could be a division of labour. The production of animal and vegetable food in quantities can only be explained on the presupposition that man had increased on the earth. Then, in ver. 3, we are led on still further by "*the process of time.*"

II. THE COMMUNITY OF MEN, THUS EARLY, HAS SOME PROVISION FOR RELIGIOUS WORSHIP. The two men, Cain and Abel, "*brought*" their offerings apparently to one place. The difference was not the mere difference of their occupations. Abel brought not only "the firstlings of the flock," but "*the fat thereof*," an evident allusion to the appointment of some sacrificial rites. The Lord's respect to Abel's offering was not merely a recognition of Abel's state of mind, though that is implied in the reference to the person, as distinct from the offering, but it was approval of Abel's *obedience* to the religious prescription which is in the background. The Lord remonstrates with Cain when his countenance fell and he was wroth. "If thou doest well, shalt thou not be accepted? and if thou doest not well, sin lieth at the door" (croucheth like a beast of prey ready to be upon thee). This may be taken either (1) retrospectively or (2) prospectively—sin as guilt, or sin as temptation; in either case it is *at the door*—not necessarily a welcome guest, but ready to take possession. Sin forgiven, temptation resisted, are placed in apposition to acceptance. "Unto thee shall be his desire,"—*i. e.* Abel's, as the younger,—"and thou shalt rule over him," *i. e.* the natural order shall be preserved. Notice—1. Divine love providing acceptance in the Divine order, in which religion is preserved, and natural life, with its appointments. 2. Divine mercy rescuing a fallen creature from the results of his own blind disobedience. 3. The righteousness of God maintained in the disorder and passion which spring out of human error and corruption. Sin is at the door; judgment close upon it. Yet God is justified though man is condemned. There is no great sin committed but it has been seen at the door first. 4. *Doing not well* precedes the direct *presumptuous sin.* "Cleanse thou me from secret faults." Cain was warned by God himself before his fallen countenance darkened his heart with crime and stained his hand with a brother's blood. What a picture of the *gradual degradation* of the conscience. Notice—(1) The disobedience of a Divine commandment in some minor point. (2) Sense of estrangement from God—loss of his "respect unto us." (3) Sullen, brooding enmity against God and man. (4) All these culminating in the violent outbreak of self-assertion, his own works evil, his brother's righteous, therefore he hated him. Ver. 8 is again an epitome. The talk of the two men with one another may represent a long period of angry debate. "*It came to pass*," on some occasion, in the field, the angry thoughts found their vent in angry words. "Cain rose up against Abel his brother, and slew him." The first blood shed had a religious occasion for its origin. The protomartyr was slain as a testimony to the truth. Mark the significant omen for the subsequent human history. Marvel not if the world hate those to whom God shows special respect. The type is here of all religious wars. The Cain spirit is not mere bloody-mindedness, but *all* defiance of God, and self-assertion, as against his will and word. *Infidelity* has been as bloody as *superstition.* Both meet in the same *perverted worship of self.*—R.

Ver. 9.—*Care for our brethren.* How terrible this question to the murderer! He thought, perhaps, his act was hidden, and strove to put it out of mind. Perhaps did not anticipate effect of his stroke; but now brought face to face with his sin. "Where is Abel?" He knew not. He knew where the body lay; but that was not Abel. Had sent him whence he could not call him back. "Where is thy brother?" is God's word to each of us. It expresses the great law that we are responsible for each other's welfare. "Am I my brother's keeper?" some would ask. Assuredly yes. God has knit men together so that all our life through we require each other's help; and we cannot avoid influencing each other. And has created a bond of brotherhood (cf. Acts xvii. 26), which follows from our calling him "Father." What doing for good of mankind? Not to do good is to do harm; not to save is to kill. Love of Christ works (Rom. x. 1; 2 Cor. v. 14).

I. WE ARE CALLED TO CARE FOR THOSE AFAR OFF. "Who is my neighbour?" We might answer, Who is not thy neighbour? Everywhere our brethren. Thousands passing away daily. Abel, a vapour, the character of human life (Ps. ciii. 15). Whither are they going? And we know the way of salvation. Light is given to no one for himself only (Matt. v. 13, 14). We are to hold it forth; to be as lights in the world (Phil. ii. 15). It is God's will thus to spread his kingdom. Are we answering the call? Test yourselves (cf. 1 John iii. 17). Deliver us from blood-guiltiness, O God. Thank God, the question speaks to us of living men. There are fields still to be reaped. The heathen, our brethren, claim a brother's help. How many varieties of Cain's answer:—You cannot reclaim savages; you just make them hypocrites; we must look at home first. And the lost masses at home are our brethren. Oh, it is in vain to help them; they will drink; they hate religion; they only think what they can get from those who visit them. Test these objections. Single out in thought one soul; compare his case with yours. You have instruction, ordinances, influences; and he the darkness of heathenism, or surroundings of vice. Yet Christ died for that soul. Can you let it depart without some effort, or even earnest prayer?

II. WE ARE CALLED TO CARE FOR THOSE AROUND US. For their sake, watchfulness and self-restraint (cf. Rom. xiv. 15). We teach more by what we do than by what we say. The loving life teaches love; the selfish, ungodliness. Inconsistencies of Christians hinder Christ's cause. What art thou at home? Is thy life pointing heavenward? "None of us liveth to himself." "Where is thy brother?"—M.

Vers. 9—15.—*The condemnation and judgment of the first murderer.* Notice—
I. The Divine APPEAL TO CONSCIENCE, affording opportunity to repentance and confession, and therefore to the exercise of mercy.
II. THE BLINDING EFFECT OF A GREAT SIN. The man who knew that God knew all persisting in a lie, and insulting the Divine majesty at the very throne of judgment, *i. e.* defying God by the monstrous extravagance of self-assertion, which is the effect of indulged sin, not only hardening the heart, but filling it with a mad desperation. So we find great criminals still, to the very last, adding sin to sin, as though they had come to think that the deeper they sunk into it the more chance they had of escaping its punishment, or by daring the whole extremity might the sooner know the worst.
III. There is great significance in the INTIMATE CONNECTION SET FORTH BETWEEN THE CRIME AND PUNISHMENT OF CAIN AND THE EARTH AND THE GROUND. The blood speaks from the ground, crying to God. Cain is cursed from the ground. The ground opened her mouth to receive the brother's blood. The ground refuses to serve the murderer. On the earth he shall be a fugitive and vagabond. From the face of the earth he is driven. His punishment is greater than he can bear. Surely all that is intended to place in vivid contrast the righteousness of God and the unrighteousness of man; the one witnessed by the *steadfast earth,* with its unbroken

laws, its pure, unfallen, peaceful state, with its communities of creatures innocent of all sin; the other witnessed by the cursed, wandering, suffering, hunger-pinched, miserable man, flying from his neighbour, flying from himself.

IV. As in the expulsion of man from Eden, so in the expulsion of Cain from society, there is MERCY MINGLED WITH JUDGMENT. The mark set upon Cain by the Lord was at once the mark of rejection and the mark of protection; it threatened sevenfold vengeance on the murderer of the murderer; it was an excommunication for the sake of the sinner as well as for the sake of the community. We must not expect to find in these primeval records more than a dim intimation of the Divine mind. But here, at the outset of the human race, there is the germ of that distinction and separation among mankind on the moral and spiritual ground which really is the essential fact of the kingdom of God. "The blood of sprinkling speaketh better things than that of Abel." Yet it is a good thing that God should say to us, in however fearful a manner, that that which is destructive of human society, which rises up against a brother's life, which hates and works out its hatred in cruel act, shall be, can be, separated from the world into which it has come, and cast out. We must look at the whole narrative from the side of the Abel element, not from the side of the Cain element; and the blessed truth contained in it is that God purges society of its evil men and evil principles, and makes its very martyrs' blood to be a consecration of the earth to proclaim his righteousness. We have not to answer the question, How about Cain? He is protected from violence. He is permitted to repent and return, though for a time an outcast. Out of the conflict of the two worlds will come forth the purpose of God—evil separated, good eternally triumphant.—R.

EXPOSITION.

Ver. 17.—Domiciled in Nod, whither, impelled by woman's love, his wife had accompanied him, the unhappy fugitive began to seek, if not to find, relief from the gnawing agonies of remorse in the endearments of conjugal felicity and the occupations of secular industry. **And Cain knew his wife.** Who must have been his sister, and married before the death of Abel, as "after that event it can scarcely be supposed that any woman would be willing to connect herself with such a miserable fratricide" (Bush). Though afterwards forbidden, the tendency of Divine legislation on the subject of marriage being always in the direction of enlarging rather than restricting the circle of prohibited relationships, the union of brothers and sisters at the first was clearly indispensable, if the race was to multiply outwards from a common stock. "Even in much later times, and among very civilised nations, such alliances were not considered incestuous. The Athenian law made it compulsory to marry the sister if she had not found a husband at a certain age. Abraham married his half-sister, Sarah; and the legislator Moses himself was the offspring of a matrimony which he later interdicted as unholy" (Kalisch). **And she conceived.** For even from the unbelieving and unthankful, the disobedient and the reprobate, God's providential mercies are not entirely withheld (Ps. cxlv. 9; Matt. v. 45). **And bare Enoch.** *Chanoch*, "dedicated," "initiated," from *chanach*, to instruct (Prov.

xxii. 6) and to consecrate (Deut. xx. 5; 1 Kings viii. 63). Candlish detects in the name the impious pride of the first murderer; with more charity, Keil and Kalisch see a promise of the renovation of his life. The latter thinks that Cain called his son "Initiated" or "Instructed" to intimate that he intended to instruct him from his early years in the duties of virtue, and his city "Dedicated" to signify that he now recognised that "the firstling of his social prosperity belongs to God." If Luther's conjecture be correct, that the child received its name from its mother, it will touchingly express that young mother's hope that the child whom God had sent might be an augury of blessing for their saddened home, and her resolution both to consecrate him from his youth to God and to instruct him in God's fear and worship. **And he builded.** Literally, *was building*, i. e. began to build, "but never finished, leading still a runagate life, and so often constrained to leave the work, as the giants did who built the tower of Babel" (Willet). **A city.** Vater, Hartmann, and Bohlen discover in the city-building of Cain "a main proof of the mythical contents of the narrative," an advanced state of civilisation "utterly unsuitable to so early a period;" but ancient tradition (Phœnician, Egyptian, and Hellenic) is unanimous in ascribing to the first men the invention of agriculture and the arts, with the discovery of metals, the origin of music, &c. (*vide* Havernick's 'Intro.,' § 16).

Of course the עִיר which Cain erected was
not a city according to modern ideas, but a
keep or fort, enclosed with a wall for the
defence of those who dwelt within (Murphy).
It was the first step in the direction of civilisation, and Kalisch notes it as a deep trait
in the Biblical account that the origin of
cities is ascribed not to the nomad, but to
the agriculturist. Impelled by the necessities
of his occupation to have a fixed residence,
he would likewise in course of time be constrained by the multiplication of his household to insure their protection and comfort.
It is possible also that his attempt to found
a city may have been dictated by a desire to
bid defiance to the curse which doomed him
to a wandering life ; to create for his family
and himself a new point of interest outside
the holy circle of Eden, and to find an outlet
for those energies and powers of which, as an
early progenitor of the race, he must have
been conscious, and in the restless activity
of which oblivion for his misery could alone
be found. If so, it explains the action which
is next recorded of him, that **he called the
name of the city after the name of his son,
Enoch.** *I. e.* he consecrated it to the realisation of these his sinful hopes and schemes.

Ver. 18.—Years passed away, the family
of Cain grew to manhood, and, in imitation
of their parents, founded homes for themselves. **And unto Enoch** (whose wife probably would also be his sister, few caring at
this early stage to intermarry with the accursed race) **was born Irad.** *Townsman,*
citizen, *urbanus civilis* (Keil, Lange); fleet
as a wild ass (Murphy); ornament of a city,
from Ir, a city (Wordsworth). **And Irad
begat Mehujael.** Smitten of God (Keil,
Gesenius, Murphy), the purified or formed
of God (Lange). **And Mehujael begat
Methusael.** Man of God (Gesenius, Lange),
man asked or man of El (Murphy), man of
prayer (Keil). **And Methusael begat Lamech.**
Strong youth (Gesenius, Lange) ; man of
prayer, youth (Murphy); king, by metathesis
for *melech* (Wordsworth). The resemblance
between these names and those in the line of
Seth has been accounted for by supposing a
commingling of the two genealogies, or one
common primitive legend in two forms
(Ewald, Knobel). But—1. The similarity
of the names does not necessarily imply the
identity of the persons. Cf. *Korah* in the
families of Levi (Exod. vi. 21) and Esau
(ch. xxxvi. 5); *Hanoch* in those of Reuben
(ch. xlvi. 9) and Midian (ch. xxv. 4); *Kenaz*
in those of Esau (ch. xxxvi. 11) and Judah
(Num. xxxii. 12). 2. The similarity of the
names only proves that the two collateral
branches of the same family did not keep
entirely apart. 3. The paucity of names at
that early period may have led to their repetition. 4. The names in the two lines are

only similar, not identical (cf. with Irad,
Jared, descent ; with Mehujael, Mahalaleel,
praise of God ; with Methusael, Methuselah,
man of the sword). 5. The particulars related
of Enoch and Lamech in the line of Seth
forbid their identification with those of the
same name in the line of Cain.

Ver. 19. — **And Lamech took unto him
two wives.** Being the first polygamist of
whom mention is made, the first by whom
"the ethical aspect of marriage, as ordained
by God, was turned into the lust of the eye
and lust of the flesh " (Keil). Though afterwards permitted because of the hardness of
men's hearts, it was not so from the beginning. This was "a new evil, without even
the pretext that the first wife had no children, which held its ground until Christianity
restored the original law—Matt. xix. 4—6"
(Inglis). The names of Lamech's wives were
suggestive of sensual attractions. **The name
of the one Adah,** the Adorned (Gesenius),
and the name of the other Zillah, the shady
or the tinkling (Keil), the musical player
(Lange), the shadow (Wordsworth). "Did
Lamech choose a wife to gratify the eye with
loveliness ? and was he soon sated with that
which is so short-lived as beauty, and then
chose another wife in addition to Adah ?
But a second wife is hardly a wife; she is
only the shadow of a wife" (*ibid.*).

Ver. 20.—**And Adah bare Jabal.** Either
the Traveller or the Producer, from *yabhal,* to
flow; poetically, to go to walk ; hiphil, to
produce ; descriptive, in the one case, of his
nomadic life, in the other of his occupation
or his wealth. **He was the father**—*av,*
father ; used of the founder of a family or
nation (ch. x. 21), of the author or maker of
anything, especially of the Creator (Job
xxxviii. 28), of the master or teacher of any
art or science (ch. iv. 21)—**of such as dwell
in tents, and** of such as have **cattle.** *Mikneh,*
literally, possession, from *kanah,* to acquire,
as in ver. 1; hence cattle, as that was the
primitive form of wealth (cf. *pecus, pecunia*);
by which may be meant that Jabal was the
first nomad who introduced the custom of
living in tents, and pasturing and breeding
not sheep merely, but larger quadrupeds as
well, for the sake of wealth.

Ver. 21.—**And his brother's name was
Jubal.** Player on an instrument, the musician. Cf. *jobel,* an onomatopoetic word signifying *jubilum,* a joyful sound. Cf. Greek,
ὀλολύζειν, ἀλαλάζειν ; Latin, *ululare ;* Swed-
ish, *iolen ;* Dutch, *ioelen ;* German, *juchen*
(Gesenius). **He was the father of all such
as handle the harp.** The *kinnor,* a stringed
instrument, played on by the plectrum according to Josephus ('Ant.,' 7, 12, 3), but in
David's time by the hand (1 Sam. xvi. 23;
xviii. 10; xix. 9), corresponding to the modern
lyre. Cf. κινύρα, κιννύρα, cithara ; German,

knarren; so named either from its tremulous, stridulous sound (Gesenius), or from its bent, arched form (Fürst). **And the organ.** '*Ugabh,* from a root signifying to breathe or blow (Gesenius), or to make a lovely sound (Fürst); hence generally a wind instrument—*tibia, fistula, syrinx;* the shepherd's reed or bag-pipe (Keil); the pipe or flute (Onkelos); the *organon,* 1. e. an instrument composed of many pipes (Jerome). Kalisch discovers a fitness in the invention of musical instruments by the brother of a nomadic herdsman, as it is "in the happy leisure of this occupation that music is generally first exercised and appreciated." Murphy sees an indication of the easy circumstances of the line of Cain ; Candlish, "an instance of the high cultivation which a people may often possess who are altogether irreligious and ungodly ;" Bonar, a token of their deepening depravity—" it is to shut God out that these Cainites devise the harp and the organ."

Ver. 22.—**And Zillah, she also bare Tubal-cain.** Worker in brass or iron ; related to Persian, *túpal,* iron dross (Gesenius, Rödiger, Delitzsch). Keil and Fürst think this Persian root cannot be regarded as the proper explanation of the name. Fürst suggests that the tribe may have been originally named Tubal, and known as inventors of smith-work and agricultural implements, and that Cain may have been afterwards added to them to identify them as Cainites (*vide* ' Lex. sub nom.'). The name Tubal, like the previous names Jabal and Jubal, is connected with the root *yabal,* to flow, and probably was indicative of the general prosperity of the race. Their ancestor was specially distinguished as **an instructor** (literally, *a whetter*) **of every artificer** (instrument, LXX., Vulgate, Kalisch) **in brass** (more correctly copper) **and iron.** בַּרְזֶל, according to Gesenius a quadrilateral from the ch. בָּרַן, to transfix, with ל appended; according to Fürst out of בְּזַל, from בָּזַל, to be hard, by resolving the dagesh into *r.* **And the sister of Tubal-cain was Naamah**—the lovely. Considering the general significance of names, we shall scarcely go astray if with Kalisch we find in the name of the sister of Tubal-cain, "the beautiful," as compared with that of Adam's wife, "the living," a growing symptom of the degeneracy of the times. Beauty, rather than helpfulness, was now become the chief attraction in woman. Men selected wives for their lovely forms and faces rather than for their loving and pious hearts. The reason for the introduction of Naamah's name into the narrative commentators generally are at a loss to discover. Inglis with much ingenuity connects it with the tragedy which some see in the lines that follow.

Vers. 23, 24.—**And Lamech said unto his wives.** The words have an archaic simplicity which bespeak a high antiquity (*vide* Hävernick's ' Introd.,' p. 105), naturally fall into that peculiar form of parallelism which is a well-known characteristic of Hebrew poetry, and on this account, as well as from the subject, have been aptly denominated *The Song of the Sword* (Ewald, p. 267).

Adah and Zillah, Hear my voice ;
Ye wives of Lamech, hearken unto my
    speech :
For I have slain a man to my wounding (for
    my wound),
And a young man to my hurt (because of
    my strife).
If (for) Cain shall be avenged sevenfold,
Truly (and) Lamech seventy and sevenfold.

Origen wrote two whole books of his commentary on Genesis on this song, and at last pronounced it inexplicable. The chief difficulty in its exegesis concerns the sense in which the words כִּי הָרַגְתִּי are to be taken. 1. If the verb be rendered as a preterite (LXX., Vulgate, Syriac, Kalisch, Murphy, Alford, Jamieson, Luther), then Lamech is represented as informing his wives that in self-defence he has slain a young man who wounded him (not two men, as some read), but that there is no reason to apprehend danger on that account ; for if God had promised to avenge Cain sevenfold, should any one kill him, he, being not a wilful murderer, but at worst a culpable homicide, would be avenged seventy and sevenfold. 2. If the verb be regarded as a future (Aben Ezra, Calvin, Kiel, Speaker's. "The preterite stands for the future . . . (4) In protestations and assurances in which the mind of the speaker views the action as already accomplished, being as good as done"—Gesenius, ' Heb. Gram.,' § 126), then the father of Tubal-cain is depicted as exulting in the weapons which his son's genius had invented, and with boastful arrogance threatening death to the first man that should injure him, impiously asserting that by means of these same weapons he would exact upon his adversary a vengeance ten times greater than that which had been threatened against the murderer of Cain. Considering the character of the speaker and the spirit of the times, it is probable that this is the correct interpretation. 3. A third interpretation proposes to understand the words of Lamech hypothetically, as thus :— "If I should slay a man, then," &c. (Lange, Bush) ; but this does not materially differ from the first, only putting the case conditionally, which the first asserts categorically. 4. A fourth gives to כִּ the force of a question (*vide* Stanley Leathes, ' Heb. Gram.,' p. 202), and imagines Lamech to be assuring his wives, who are supposed to have been apprehensive of some evil befalling their husband through the use of Tubal-cain's dangerous weapons, that there was no cause for their anxieties and alarms, as he had not slain a man, that he should be wounded, or a young man, that he should be hurt ; but this interpretation, it may be fairly urged, is too strained to be even probably correct. Vers. 25, 26.—The narrative now reverts to the fortunes of the doubly saddened pair. **And Adam knew his wife again.** Having mournfully abstained for a season *à thoro conjugali* (Calvin) ; not necessarily implying that Adam and Eve had not other children who had grown to man's estate prior to the death of Abel (cf. ch. v. 4). **And she bare a son, and called his name Seth.** *Sheth*, from *shîth*, to put or place ; hence appointed, put, compensation. **For God,** said she, **hath appointed me another seed**—*semen singulare* (Calvin); *filium*, Eve having borne daughters previously (Onkelos, Jonathon, Dathe, Rosenmüller)—**instead of Abel.** Her other children probably had gone in the way of Cain, leaving none to carry on the holy line, till this son was born, whom in faith she expects to be another Abel in respect of piety, but, unlike him, the head of a godly family (Calvin). **Whom Cain slew.** Literally, *for Cain killed him* (Kalisch). The A. V. follows the LXX., ὃν ἀπέκτεινε καϊν, and has the support of Gesenius, who renders כִּי = אֲשֶׁר (see 'Lex. sub nom.') ; of Rosenmüller, who says, " Conjunctio enim causalis כִּי sæpius pro relativo pronomine usurpatur," quoting, though without much aptness, Ps. lxxi. 15 (*com. in loco*) ; and of Sal. Glass, who supplies several so-called examples of the relative force of כִּי, every one of which is perfectly intelligible by translating the particle as *quia* ('Sac. Phil.,' iii. 2, xv.) ; and of Stanley Leathes ('Heb. Gram.,' ch. xii. 16). There seems, however, no sufficient reason for departing from the ordinary casual signification of the particle. Fürst does not recognise the meaning which Gesenius

attaches to כִּי (cf. Ewald's 'Heb. Syntax,' § 353). **And to Seth, to him also there was born a son.** Thus the expectations of Eve concerning her God-given son were not disappointed, but realised in the commencement and continuance of a godly line. The pious father of this succeeding child, however, had either begun to realise the feebleness and weakness of human life, or perhaps to be conscious of the sickly and infirm state in which religion then was. **And he called his** (son's) **name Enos.** *Enosh*, "man" (Gesenius) ; "mortal, decaying man" (Fürst) ; "man, sickly" (Murphy). **Then began men.** Literally, *it was begun*. *Huchal* third preterite *hophal* of *chalal* (Greek, χαλάω, λύω), to open a way. Hence " the literal sense of the word is, a way was now opened up, and an access afforded, to the worship of God, in the particular manner here described" (Wordsworth). **To call upon the name of the Lord.** Either (1) to invoke by prayer the name of Jehovah, *i. e.* Jehovah himself as he had been pleased to discover his attributes and character to men, referring to the formal institution of public worship. " The expression is elsewhere used to denote all the appropriate acts and exercises of the stated worship of God— ch. xii. 8 ; xiii. 4 ; xxi. 33 ; 1 Chron. xvi. 8 ; Ps. cv. 1" (Bush). Or (2) to call themselves by the name of Jehovah—cf. Num. xxxii. 42 ; Judges xviii. 29 ; Ps. xlix. 12 ; Isa. xliv. 5 (margin). Other renderings need only be mentioned to be set aside. (*a*) Then began men profanely to call upon the name of God (Onkelos, Jonathan, Josephus), referring to the institution of idolatry. (*b*) Then men became so profane as to cease to call (Chaldee Targum). (*c*) Then he hoped to call upon the name of the Lord ; οὗτος ἤλπισεν ἐπικαλεῖσθαι τὸ ὄνομα Κυρίον τοῦ θεοῦ (LXX). (*d*) Then the name Jehovah was for the first time invoked (Cajetan), which is disproved by ch. iv. 3.

HOMILETICS.

Vers. 17—26.—*The progress of the race.* I. ITS INCREASE IN POPULATION. Starting from a single pair in Eden, in the course of seven generations the human family must have attained to very considerable dimensions. At the birth of Seth, Adam was 130 years old, and in all probability had other sons and daughters besides Cain and his wife. If Lamech, the seventh from Adam in the line of Cain, was contemporaneous with Enoch, the seventh from Adam in the line of Seth, at least 600 years had passed away since the race began to multiply ; and " if Abraham's stock in lesse than 400 yeares amounted to 600,000, Cain's posterity in the like time might arise to the like multitude " (Willet). If to these the descendants of Seth be added, it will at once appear that the earth's population in the time of Lamech was considerably over 1,000,000 of inhabitants. Let it remind us of the reality and power of God's blessing (ch. i. 28).

II. ITS ADVANCEMENT IN INTELLIGENCE. " It is a curious fact that while all modern writers admit the great antiquity of man, most of them maintain the very recent development of his intellect, and will hardly contemplate the possibility of men equal in mental capacity to ourselves having existed in prehistoric (?) times " (Wallace, Brit. Assoc. Address, 1876). For prehistoric write antediluvian, and the sentiment is exactly true. The circumstance that we have no remains of antediluvian civilisation is no sufficient evidence that such did not exist. Speaking of certain earthworks of great antiquity that have been discovered in the Mississippi valley,— camps, or works of defence, sacred enclosures, with their connected groups of circles, octagons, squares, ellipses, polished and ornamented pottery, &c.,—the same distinguished writer says, " The important thing for us is, that when North America was first settled by Europeans, the Indian tribes inhabiting it had no knowledge or tradition of any races preceding themselves of higher civilisation. Yet we find that such races existed ; that they must have been populous, and have lived under some established government ; while there are signs that they practised agriculture greatly, as indeed they must have done to have supported a population capable of executing such gigantic works in such vast profusion." The exhumation by Dr. Schliemann on the plains of Troy of three successive civilisations, of which two were not known to have previously existed, and the third (the Ilium of Homer) had been almost regarded by archæologists as fabulous, is conclusive demonstration that the absence of all traces of primeval civilisation is no more a proof that such civilisation did not exist, than is the absence of all traces of the third day's vegetation a proof that it did not exist. The passage under consideration unmistakably reveals that the human intellect in those early times was not asleep. Within the compass of ten verses we read of the building of cities, of the laying out of farms and the acquisition of property, of the beginning of the mechanical arts and the manufacture of metallic weapons, of the rise of music and the cultivation of poetry. It may strike one as peculiar that this great intellectual development is represented as taking place exclusively in the line of Cain. From this some have inferred that the Bible means to throw disparagement upon human industry, commercial and agricultural enterprise, and all kinds of mechanical and inventive genius, and even sanctions the idea that religion is incompatible with business talent, poetical genius, and intellectual greatness. There is, however, no reason to suppose that this advancement in intelligence was confined to the Cainitic branch of the Adamic race. The prophecy of Enoch (*vide* Expos.) and the incidental allusion to metallic weapons in the name of Methuselah (man of the dart) suggest that the Sethitic line kept pace with their ungodly contemporaries in the onward march of civilisation, though that was not their chief distinction. Let us learn—1. That there is no essential antagonism between intelligence and piety. 2. That in God's estimation righteousness is of much higher value than material prosperity. 3. That where, as in the Cainitic line, there is no true godliness there is apt to be too intense devotion to culture or business.

III. ITS DECLENSION IN WICKEDNESS. 1. We can trace it in their *names*. Enoch, Irad, Mehujael, Lamech being suggestive of qualities, principles, characteristics such as are approved by the spirit of worldliness ; and Adah and Zillah (*vide* Expos.) being indicative of sensual attractions. 2. Their *works* proclaim it. It would be wrong to say that cities are necessarily evil things. On the contrary, they are magnificent monuments of man's constructive genius, and immensely productive of man's comfort. A city too is a type of heaven's gathering of redeemed humanity. Still it cannot be doubted that the need for cities was a proof of sin, as the building of the first city was an act of sin. The acquisition of property, and the uprise of such ideas as the rights of property, are likewise indications of a state of life that is not purely innocent (cf. Acts iv. 32). And though certainly it cannot be sinful either to make or to handle a harp, or to cultivate poetry, yet when we put all these things together—beautiful wives, iron weapons, musical instruments, and warlike ballads, if not bacchanalian songs—it is not difficult to perceive a deepening of that devotion to the things of this life which invariably proclaims a departure from the life of God. 3. Their immoral *lives* attest it. A growing disregard for the marriage law is evinced by the polygamy of Lamech ; in the manufacture and use of offensive weapons we see the rising of a turbulent and lawless spirit ; and these two things, licentiousness and lawlessness, always mark the downward progress of an age or people.

IV. ITS PROGRESS IN RELIGION ; at least in a section of its population, the godly line of Seth, in whom the piety of Abel was revived. Yet the narrative would seem to indicate that even they were not entirely free from the prevailing wickedness of the times. In the third generation the pressure of the worldly spirit upon the company of the faithful was so great that they felt obliged, as it were, in self-defence, to buttress their piety by a double wall of protection ; viz., *separation from their ungodly associates in the world* by the formation of a distinct religious community, and by *the institution of stated social worship* (ch. iv. 26). And without these declension in true religion is as certain as with them advancement is secure. They are the New Testament rules for the cultivation of piety (2 Cor. vi. 14—18 ; Ephes. iv. 11—13 ; Heb. x. 25).

Lessons :—1. The downward progress of sin. 2. The danger of intellect and civilisation when divorced from piety. 3. The only right use of earth and earthly things is to make all subservient to the life of grace. 4. The danger of conformity to the world. 5. The only safety for the people of God, and especially in these times of great intellectual activity and mechanical and scientific skill, is to make deep and wide the line of distinction between them and the world, and steadfastly to maintain the public as well as private ordinances of religion.

HOMILIES BY VARIOUS AUTHORS.

Vers. 16—24.—*The kingdom of God contrasted with the kingdom of this world.* Society without the Lord. The banished Cain and his descendants.

I. MULTIPLICATION apart from Divine order is no blessing.

II. CIVILISATION without religion is a chaos of conflicting forces, producing violence, bloodshed, working out its own ruin. Compare France in the seventeenth and eighteenth centuries. Arts of life may grow from a mere natural root. Music, mechanical skill, scientific discovery, and invention, in themselves contain no moral life. Luxury turns to corruption, and so to misery.

III. RELIGION IS THE BASIS OF SOCIAL PROSPERITY. It is the true defence against the "inhumanity of man." Lamech, with his artificial protection against violent revenge, suggests the true safety in the presence of the Lord and observance of his commandments.—R.

Ver. 25, 26.—*Revelation in history.* The reappearance of the redeeming purpose. The consecrated family of Adam. The Divinely blessed line of descent preserved leading onward to the fulfilment of the first promise. "*Then began men to call upon the name of Jehovah.*"

I. THE COMMENCEMENT OF REGULAR WORSHIP, possibly of distinct Church life. 1. The name of the Lord is the true centre of fellowship—including *revelation, redemption, promise.* 2. The pressure of outward calamity and danger, the multiplication of the unbelievers, the necessary separation from an evil world, motives to call upon God.

II. RENOVATION AND RE-ESTABLISHMENT OF RELIGIOUS LIFE WORKS OUT GOD'S BLESSING ON THE RACE. The separated seed bears the promise of the future. See the repetition of the message of grace in the names of the descendants of Seth, "*the appointed.*"

III. The worship which was maintained by men was ENCOURAGED AND DEVELOPED BY REVELATIONS and special communications from Jehovah. Probably there were prophets sent. Methuselah, taking up the ministry of Enoch, and himself delivering the message to Noah, the preacher of righteousness. It is the method of God throughout all the dispensations to meet men's call upon his name with gracious manifestations to them.

IV. THE PERIOD OF AWAKENED RELIGIOUS LIFE and of special messengers, culminating in the long testimony and warning of Noah, preceded the period of outpoured judgment. So it is universally. There is no manifestation of wrath which does not vindicate righteousness. He is long-suffering, and waits. He sends the spirit of life first. Then the angel of death.—R.

§ 3. The Generations of Adam (ch. v. 1—vi. 8)

EXPOSITION.

CHAPTER V.

The present section carries forward the inspired narrative another stage, in which the onward progress or development of the human race is traced, in the holy line of Seth, from the day of Adam's creation, through ten successive generations, till the point is reached when the first great experiment of attempting to save man by clemency rather than by punishment is brought to a termination, and Jehovah, whose mercy has been spurned and abused, determines to destroy the impenitent transgressors. First, in brief and somewhat monotonous outline, the lives of the ten patriarchs are sketched, scarcely more being recorded of them than simply that they were born, grew to manhood, married wives, begat children, and then died. In only two instances does the history diverge from this severely simple style of biographical narration, namely, in the cases of Enoch, who, as he eclipsed his predecessors, contemporaries, and successors in the elevation of his piety during life, was honoured above them in the mode of his departure from the earth ; and of Noah, whose birth was welcomed by his parents as a happy omen in a time of social degeneracy and religious declension, but who lived to see the hopes of reform which his pious parents cherished disappointed, and the world for its wickedness overwhelmed by a flood. Then, after sketching the uneventful lives of the patriarchs in a few bold strokes, the sacred penman sets before us a vividly arresting and profoundly impressive picture of the wickedness of the human race on the eve of that appalling catastrophe, at once indicating the cause of the earth's degeneracy in morals, and representing that degeneracy as a sufficient justification for the threatened judgment. Throughout the genealogical register the name Elohim is employed to designate the Deity, the subject being the evolutions of the Adam who was created in the image of Elohim. In the paragraph depicting the growth of immoral-ity among men, and recording the Divine resolution to destroy man, the name Jehovah is used, the reason being that in his sin and in his punishment man is viewed in his relations to the God of redemption and grace.

Vers. 1, 2.—**This is the book.** *Sepher*, a register, a complete writing of any kind, a book, whether consisting of a pair of leaves or of only a single leaf (Deut. xxiv. 1, 3 ; "a bill of divorcement ;" LXX., βίβλος ; cf. Matt. i. 1 ; Luke iii. 36, 38). The expression presupposes the invention of the art of writing. If, therefore, we may conjecture that the original compiler of this ancient document was Noah, than whom no one would be more likely or better qualified than he to preserve some memorial of the lost race of which he and his family were the sole survivors, it affords an additional corroboration of the intelligence and culture of the antediluvian men. It is too frequently taken for granted that the people who could build cities, invent musical instruments, and make songs were unacquainted with the art of writing ; and though certainly we cannot affirm that the transmission of such a family register as is here recorded was beyond the capabilities of oral tradition, it is obvious that its preservation would be much more readily secured by some kind of documentary notation. **Of the generations** —*i. e.* evolutions (*tol'doth ;* cf. ch. ii. 4)—**of Adam.** In the preceding section the *tol'doth* of the heavens and the earth were exhibited, and accordingly the narrative commenced with the creative labours of the third day. Here the historian designs to trace the fortunes of the holy seed, and finds the point of his departure **in the day that God** (Elohim) **created man** (Adam), *i. e.* the sixth of the creative days. More particularly he calls attention to the great truths which had been previously included in his teaching concerning man ; viz., *the dignity of his nature,* implied in the fact that **in the likeness of Elohim made he him** ; *his sexual distinction*—**male and female created he them;** *their Divine benediction*—**and blessed them** (cf. ch. i. 27, 28) ; at the same time adding a fourth circumstance, which in the first document was not narrated, that their Maker gave to them *a suitable and specific appellation*—**and called their name Adam** (*vide* ch. i. 26), **in the day when they were created.**

Vers. 3—5.—At the head of the Adamic. race stands the first man, whose career is summarised in three short verses, which serve as a model for the subsequent biographies. **And Adam lived an hundred and thirty years.** *Shanah,* a repetition, a return of the sun's circuit, or of similar natural phenomena ; from *shanah,* to fold together, to repeat ; hence a year (Gesenius, Fürst). Cf. Latin, *annus;* Greek, ἐνιαυτός; Gothic, *iar, jar, jer;* German, *jahr;* English, *year*—all of which " seem to carry the same thought, viz., that which comes again" (T. Lewis). "*Shanah* never means month" (Kalisch). **And begat** *a son* **in his own likeness,—***damuth* (cf. ch. i. 26)—**after his image** — *tselem* (cf. ch. i. 26) ; not the Divine image in which he was himself created (Kalisch, Knobel, Alford), but the image or likeness of his own fallen nature, *i. e.* the image of God modified and corrupted by sin (Keil, Murphy, Wordsworth). "A supernatural remedy does not prevent generation from participating in the corruption of sin. Therefore, according to the flesh Seth was born a sinner, though he was afterwards renewed by the Spirit of grace" (Calvin). The doctrine of inherited depravity or transmitted sin has been commonly held to favour the theory which accounts for the origin of the human soul *per traducem* (Tertullian, Luther, Delitzsch), in opposition to that which holds it to be due to the creative power of God (Jerome, Augustine, Calvin, Beza, Turretin). Kalisch thinks the statement "Adam begat Seth in his own image" decisive in favour of Traducianism, while Hodge affirms "it only asserts that Seth was like his father, and sheds no light on the mysterious process of generation" ('Syst. Theol.,' Part I. ch. iii. § 2). The truth is that Scripture seems to recognise both sides of this question. *Vide* Ps. li. 5 in favour of Traducianism, and Ps. cxxxix. 14—16 ; Jer. i. 5 in support of Creationism (cf. Martensen's 'Dogmatics,' § 74), though there is much force in the words of Augustine—"De re obscurissima disputatur, non adjuvantibus divinarum scripturarum certis clarisque documentis." **And called his name**—probably concurring in the name selected by Eve (ch. iv. 25)—**Seth.**—Appointed, placed, substituted ; hence compensation (ch. iv. 25). **And the days of Adam after he had begotten** — literally, *his begetting*—Seth **were eight hundred years: and he begat sons and daughters.** " In that primitive time the births did not rapidly follow each other—a fact which had not a physical, but only an ethical ground " (Delitzsch). The comparatively mature age at which the parent begat the son (in most instances probably the firstborn) through whom the promise was transmitted seems

to indicate that his having a posterity at all was conditioned by the ripeness of his faith. At the same time the lateness of paternity among these primeval men may have been partly due to a physical cause as well, " since in exact accordance with the increasing degeneracy and rankness of human life is there, in a literal sense, the increase of a numerous and wretched offspring " (Lange). **And all the days that Adam**—not the whole tribe (Gatterer, *vide* Bohlen ; cf. Balgarnie, 'Expositor,' vol. viii.), "as in this case Enoch must have been taken to heaven with his whole family " (Kalisch) ; but the individual bearing that name — **lived were nine hundred and thirty years.** The remarkable longevity of the Macrobii has been explained — 1. *On the supposition of its non-authenticity.* (1) As a purely mythical conception (Knobel, Bauer, Hartmann, Bohlen) ; which, however, may be safely rejected as an altogether inadequate hypothesis. (2) As due to an error in the traditional transmission of the genealogical registers, several names having fallen out, leaving their years to be reckoned to those that remained (Rosenmüller) ; but against this conjecture stands the orderly succession of father and son through ten generations. (3) As representing not the lifetimes of individuals, but dynastic epochs (*vide supra*) ; and (4) as signifying lesser spaces of time— *e. g.* three months (Hensler), or one month (Raske)—than solar years ; but even Knobel admits that " no shorter year have the Hebrews ever had than the period of a year's time." 2. *On the basis of its historic credibility;* as attributable to—(1) The original immortality with which man was endowed, and which was now being frayed away by the inroads of sin (Kalisch). (2) The superior piety and intelligence of these early fathers of the race (Josephus, 'Antiq.,' I. iii. 9). (3) The influence of the fruit of the tree of life which, while in the garden, Adam ate (Whately, 'Ency. Brit.,' eighth ed., Art. Christianity). (4) The original vigour of their physical constitutions, and the greater excellence of the food on which they lived (Willet). But if the first and second opinions are correct, then the Cainites should have died earlier than the Sethites, which there is no reason to believe they did ; while the third is a pure conjecture (*vide* ch. ii. 9), and the fourth may contain some degree of truth. We prefer to ascribe the longevity of these antediluvian men to a distinct exercise of grace on the part of God, who designed it to be (1) a proof of the Divine clemency in suspending the penalty of sin ; (2) a symbol of that immortality which had been recovered for men by the promise of the woman's seed ; and (3) a medium of transmission for the faith, for the benefit of both the Church and the world. **And he died.** "The solemn toll of the patriarchal funeral bell" (Bonar). Its constant recurrence at the close of each biography proves the dominion of death from Adam onward, as an immutable law (Rom. v. 11; Baumgarten, Keil, Lange); "warns us that death was not denounced in vain against men" (Calvin); "is a standing demonstration of the effect of disobedience" (Murphy); "was intended to show what the condition of all mankind was after Adam's fall" (Willet). The expression is not appended to the genealogical list of the Fathers after the Flood, doubtless as being then sufficiently understood; and it is not said of the descendants of Cain that they died, "as if the inheritance of the sons of God were not here on earth, but in death, as the days of the deaths of martyrs are held in honour by the Church as their birthdays" (Wordsworth).

Vers. 6—20.—The lives of the succeeding patriarchs are framed upon the model of this Adamic biography, and do not call for separate notice. The names of the next six were **Seth** (ver. 6; *vide* ch. iv. 25); **Enos** (ver. 9; *vide* ch. iv. 26); **Cainan**, possession (Gesenius); a child, one begotten (Fürst); a created thing, a creature, a young man (Ewald); possessor, or spearsman (Murphy; ver. 12); **Mahalaleel**, praise of God (Gesenius, Fürst, Murphy; ver. 15); **Jared**, descent (Gesenius); low ground, water, or marching down (Fürst); going down (Murphy; ver. 18); **Enoch**, dedicated, initiated (ver. 19; cf. ch. iv. 17).

Ver. 21. — The dedicated and initiated child grew up, like an Old Testament Timothy let us hope, to possess, illustrate, and proclaim the piety which was the distinguishing characteristic of the holy line. At the comparatively early age of sixty-five he **begat** ("forbidding to marry" being unknown then) **Methuselah.** Man of a dart (Gesenius), man of military arms (Fürst), man of the missile (Murphy), man of the sending forth—sc. of water (Wordsworth), man of growth (Delitzsch). **And Enoch walked with God** (Elohim). The phrase, used also of Noah, (ch. vi. 9), and by Micah (ch. vi. 8. Cf. the similar expressions, "to walk before God," ch. xvii. 1; Ps. cxvi. 9, and "to walk after God," Deut. xiii. 4; Ephes. v. 1), portrays a life of singularly elevated piety; not merely a constant realisation of the Divine presence, or even a perpetual effort at holy obedience, but also "a maintenance of the most confidential intercourse with the personal God" (Keil). It implies a situation of nearness to God, if not in place at least in spirit; a character of likeness to God (Amos iii. 3), and a life of converse with God. Following the LXX. (εὐηρέστησε δὲ Ἐνὼχ τῷ θεῷ), the writer to the Hebrews describes it as a life that was "pleasing to God," as springing

from the root of faith (Heb. xi. 5). Yet though pre-eminently spiritual and contemplative, Jude tells us (vers. 14, 15) the patriarch's life had its active and aggressive outlook towards the evil times in which he lived. **After he begat Methuselah.** "Which inti mates that he did not begin to be eminent for piety till about that time; at first he walked as other men" (Henry). Procopius Gazeus goes beyond this, and thinks that before his son's birth Enoch was "a wicked liver," but then repented. The historian's language, however, does not necessarily imply that his piety was so late in commencing, and it is more pleasing to think that from his youth upwards he was "as a shining star for virtue and holiness" (Willet). **Three hundred years.** As his piety began early, so likewise did it continue long; it was not intermittent and fluctuating, but steadfast and persevering (cf. Job xvii. 9; Prov. iv. 18; 1 Cor. xv. 58). **And begat sons and daughters.** "Hence it is undeniably evident that the state and use of matrimony doth very well agree with the severest course of holiness, and with the office of a prophet or preacher" (Poole). **And all the days of Enoch were three hundred and sixty-five years.** "A year of years" (Henry); "the same period as that of the revolution of the earth round the sun. After he had finished his course, revolving round him who is the true light, which is God, in the orbit of duty, he was approved by God, and taken to him" (Wordsworth). Modern critics have discovered in the age of Enoch traces of a mythical origin. They conclude the entire list of names to be not older than the time of the Babylonian Nabonassar, and believe it to be not improbable that "the Babylonians regulated the calendar with the assistance of an Indian astrologer or *ganaka* (arithmetician) of the town of *Chanoge*" (Von Bohlen). But "it would be strange indeed if just in the life of Enoch, which represents the purest and sublimest unity with God, a heathen and astrological element were intentionally introduced;" and, besides, "it is almost generally admitted that our list contains no astronomical numbers; that the years which it specifies refer to the lives of individuals, not to periods of the world; and that none of all these figures is in any way reducible to a chronological system" (Kalisch). **And Enoch walked with God.** "*Non otiosa ταυτολογία,*" but an emphatic repetition, indicative of the ground of what follows. **And he was not.** Literally, *and not he* (cf. ch. xii. 36; Jer. xxxi. 15; καὶ οὐχ εὑρίσκετο, LXX.). "Not absolutely he was not, but relatively he was not extant in the sphere of sense." "Non amplius inter mortales apparuit" (Rosenmüller). "If this phrase does not denote annihilation, much less does the phrase 'and he died.' The one denotes absence from the world of sense, and the other indicates the ordinary way in which the soul departs from this world" (Murphy). **For God** (Elohim) **took him.** Cf. 2 Kings ii. 3, 5, 9, 10, where the same word לָקַח is used of Elijah's translation ; ὅτι μετέθηκεν αὐτὸν ὁ θεός, LXX.). Though the writer to the Hebrews (ch. xi. 5) adopts the paraphrase of the LXX., yet his language must be accepted as conveying the exact sense of the words of Moses. Analysed, it teaches (1) that the patriarch Enoch did not see death, as did all the other worthies in the catalogue; and (2) that in some mysterious way " he was taken up from this temporal life and transfigured into life eternal, as those of the faithful will be who shall be alive at the coming of Christ to judgment" (Keil). The case of Elijah, who was also taken up, and who afterwards appeared in glory on the mount of transfiguration (Matt. xvii. ; Mark ix. ; Luke ix.), appears to determine the locality into which Enoch was translated (which Kalisch willingly leaves to antiquaries to decide) to be neither the terrestrial Eden (certain Popish writers) nor the heavenly paradise where the pious dead are now assembled—*sheol* (Delitzsch and Lange), but the realm of celestial glory (Keil). That the departure of the good man was witnessed by his contemporaries we may infer from what occurred in the case of Elijah ; and, indeed, unless it had been so it is difficult to see how it could have served the end for which apparently it was designed, which was not solely to reward Enoch's piety, but to demonstrate the certainty and to stimulate the hope of immortality. That the memory of an event so remarkable should have survived not merely in Jewish (Ecclus. xliv. 16) and Christian tradition (Jude 15), but also in heathen fable, is nothing marvellous. The Book of Enoch, compiled probably by a Jew in the days of Herod the Great, describes the patriarch as exhorting his son Methuselah and all his contemporaries to reform their evil ways ; as penetrating with his prophetic eye into the remote future, and exploring all mysteries in earth and heaven; as passing a retired life after the birth of his eldest son in intercourse with the angels and in meditation on Divine matters; and as at length being translated to heaven in order to reappear in the time of the Messiah, leaving behind him a number of writings on religion and morality. " The Book of Jubilees relates that he was carried into paradise, where he writes down the judgment of all men, their wickedness and eternal punishment " (Kalisch). Arabic legend declares him to have been the inventor of writing and arithmetic. The Phrygian sage Annacus (Ἄνακος: "nomen detortum ab Chanoch ") is said by Stephanus

Byzantinus, and Suidas, who corrupts the name into Nannacus, to have lived before the flood of Deucalion, to have attained an age of more than 300 years, to have foreseen the flood, gathered all the people into a temple and made supplication to God, and finally to have been translated into heaven. " Classical writers also mention such translations into heaven ; they assign this distinction among others to Hercules, to Ganymede, and to Romulus (liv. i. 16 : "nec deinde in terris fuit "). But it was awarded to them either for their valour or their physical beauty, and not, as the translation of Enoch, for "a pious and religious life." Nor is " the idea of a translation to heaven limited to the old world ; it was familiar to the tribes of Central America ; the chronicles of Guatemala record four progenitors of mankind who were suddenly raised to heaven ; and the documents add that those first men came to Guatemala from the other side of the sea, from the East" (cf. Rosenmüller and Kalisch, *in loco*).

Vers. 25—32.—The shortest life was followed by the longest, Methuselah begetting, at the advanced age of 187, **Lamech,**—strong or young man (Gesenius) ; overthrower, wild man (Fürst); man of prayer (Murphy),—continuing after his son's birth 782 years, and at last succumbing to the stroke of death in the 969th year of his age, the year of the Flood. Lamech, by whom the line was carried forward, was similarly far advanced when he begat a son, at the age of 182, and called his name **Noah,**—" rest," from *nuach*, to rest (cf. ch. viii. 4),—not " The Sailor," from the Latin *no*, and the Greek ναῦς (Bohlen), but at the same time explaining it by saying, **This** same **shall comfort**—*nacham*, to pant, groan, Piel to comfort. " *Nuach* and *nacham* are stems not immediately connected, but they both point back to a common root, *nch*, signifying to sigh, breathe, rest, lie down " (Murphy)—**us concerning our work and toil of our hands.** To say that Lamech anticipated nothing more than that the youthful Noah would assist him in the cultivation of the soil (Murphy) is to put too little into, and to allege that " this prophecy his father uttered of him, as he that should be a figure of Christ in his building of the ark, and offering of sacrifice, whereby God smelled a sweet savour of rest, and said he would not curse the ground any more for man's sake, ch. viii. 21 " (Ainsworth), is to extract too much from his language. Possibly he had nothing but a dim, vague expectation of some good thing— the destruction of sinners in the Flood (Chrysostom), the use of the plough (R. Solomon), the grant of animal food (Kalisch), the invention of the arts and implements of husbandry (Sherlock, Bush)—that God was about to bestow upon his weary heritage ; or at most a hope that the promise would be fulfilled in his son's day (Bonar), if not in his son himself (Calovius). The fulfilment of that promise he connects with a recall of the penal curse which Jehovah had pronounced upon the soil. **Because of the ground which the Lord**—*Jehovah*, by whom the curse had been pronounced (ch. iii. 17)—**hath cursed**. The clause is not a Jehovistic interpolation (Bleek, Davidson, Colenso), but a proof "that the Elohistic theory is unfounded" ('Speaker's Commentary').

Ver. 32.—**And Noah was five hundred years old**. Literally, a son of 500 years, *i. e.* going in his 500th year (cf. ch. vii. 6 ; xvii. 1). The "son of a year" (Exod. xii. 5) means "strictly within the first year of the life" (Ainsworth). **And Noah begat**—*i. e.* began to beget (cf. ch. xi. 26)—**Shem**,—name (Gesenius), fame (Fürst)—**Ham**, —*cham ;* hot (Gesenius, Murphy), dark-coloured (Fürst)—**and Japheth**—spreading (Gesenius, Murphy) ; beautiful, denoting the white-coloured race (Fürst). That the sons are mentioned in the order of their ages (Knobel, Kalisch, Keil, Colenso) may seem to be deducible (1) from the fact that they usually stand in this order (cf. ch. vi. 10 ; vii. 13 ; ix. 18 ; x. 1 ; 1 Chron. i. 4) ; (2) from the circumstance that it is commonly the eldest son's birth which is stated in the preceding list, though this is open to doubt ; (3) from ch. x. 21, which, according to Calvin, Knobel, Keil, and others, describes Shem as Japheth's elder brother ; and ch. ix. 24, which, according to Keil, affirms Ham to be

the younger son of Noah ; (4) from ch. x. 2—31, in which the order is reversed, but not otherwise altered. But there is reason to believe that Japheth was the eldest and Ham the youngest of the patriarch's children (Michaelis, Clarke, Murphy, Wordsworth, Quarry). According to ch. xi. 10 Shem was born 97 years before the Flood, while (ch. vi. 11) Noah was 600 years old at the time of the Flood. Hence, if Noah began to beget children in his 500th year, and Shem was born in Noah's 503rd year, the probability is that the firstborn son was Japheth. In accordance with this ch. x. 21 is understood by LXX., Vulgate, Michaelis, Lange, Quarry, and others to assert the priority in respect of age of Japheth. In the narrative Shem is placed first as being spiritually, though not physically, the firstborn. Ranke perceives in the mention of the three sons an indication that each was subsequently "to lay the foundation of a new beginning."

THE ANTIQUITY OF MAN.—The chronology of the present chapter represents man as having been in existence at the time of the Deluge exactly 1656 years. According to the Septuagint, which Josephus follows except in one particular (the age of Lamech), and which proceeds, again with two exceptions (the age of Jared, which it leaves untouched, and that of Lamech, which it increases by six), upon the principle of adding 100 to the Hebrew numbers, the age of man at the date of that catastrophe was 2262 (*vide*

	HEBREW.		SAMARITAN.		SEPTUAGINT.		JOSEPHUS.	
	Age at son's birth.	Age at death.	Age at son's birth.	Age at death.	Age at son's birth.	Age at death.	Age at son's birth.	Age at death.
ADAM	130	930	130	930	230	930	230	930
SETH	105	912	105	912	205	912	205	912
ENOS	90	905	90	905	190	905	190	905
CAINAN	70	910	70	910	170	910	170	910
MAHALALEEL	65	895	65	895	165	895	165	895
JARED	162	962	62	847	162	962	162	962
ENOCH	65	365	65	365	165	365	165	365
METHUSELAH	187	969	67	720	187	969	187	969
LAMECH	182	777	53	653	188	753	182	777
NOAH	500	950	500	950	500	950	500	950
SHEM	100		100		100		100	
DELUGE	1656		1307		2262		2256	

Chronological Table). The dates of the Samaritan Pentateuch, being manifestly incorrect, need not be considered. Adding to the above dates the subsequent chronological periods from the Deluge to the call of Abram (Hebrew, 367 ; LXX., 1017), from the call

of Abram to the exodus from Egypt (430 years according to one calculation, LXX. ; 730 according to another, Kalisch), from the exodus to the birth of Christ (1648, Hales ; 1593, Jackson ; 1491, Ussher ; 1531, Petavius ; 1320, Bunsen), the antiquity of man, according to the Biblical account, is not less than 5652 and not more than 7536 years. The conclusion thus reached, however, is somewhat scornfully repudiated by modern science, as affording, on either alternative, an altogether inadequate term of existence for the human race. 1. The evidence of geology is supposed irrefragably to attest that man must have been upon the earth at least 1000 centuries, and probably ten times as long (Wallace on 'Natural Selection,' p. 303). The data for this deduction, as stated by Sir Charles Lyell, are chiefly the discovery, in recent and post-pliocene formations of alleged great antiquity, of fossil human remains and flint implements along with bones of the mammoth and other animals long since extinct ('Antiquity of Man,' chs. i.—xix.). But (1) "So far as research has been prosecuted in the different quarters of the globe, no remains of man or of his works have been discovered till we come to the lake-silts, the peat-mosses, the river-gravels, and the cave-earths of the post-tertiary period," which seems at least an indirect confirmation of the Biblical record. (2) "The tree canoes, stone hatchets, flint implements, and occasional fragments of the human skeleton," upon which so much is based, "have been chiefly discovered within the limited area of Southern and Western Europe," while "we have scarcely any information from the corresponding deposits of other regions;" consequently, "till these other regions shall have been examined—and especially Asia, where man flourished long prior to his civilisation in Europe—it were premature to hazard any opinion as to man's first appearance on the globe." (3) "It is true that the antiquity of some of the containing deposits, especially the river drifts, is open to question, and it is also quite possible that the remains of the extinct quadrupeds may in some instances have been reassorted from older accumulations." (4) "Historically we have no means of arriving at the age of these deposits; geologically we can only approximate the time by comparison with existing operations; while palæontologically—the differences between these extinct pachyderms and those still existing are not greater than that which appears between the several living species, and would therefore indicate no great palæontological antiquity—nothing that may not have taken place within a few thousand years of the ordinarily received chronology" (Page on 'The Philosophy of Geology,' ch. xii. pp. 114—117). With these undesigned replies from a late eminent authority in geological science, the Bible student will do well to pause before displacing the currently-received age of man by the fabulous duration claimed for him by the first-named writers.

HOMILETICS.

Vers. 1—32.—*The antediluvian saints.* I. DESCENDANTS OF ADAM. As such they were—1. A *sinful* race. Adam's son Seth was begotten in his father's image. Though still retaining the Divine image (1 Cor. xi. 7) as to nature, in respect of purity man has lost it. Inexplicable as the mystery is of inherited corruption, it is still a fact that the moral deterioration of the head of the human family has transmitted itself to all the members. The doctrine of human depravity, however unpleasant and humbling to carnal pride, is asserted in Scripture (Gen. vi. 5, 12; viii. 21; Job xv. 14; xxv. 4; Ps. xiv. 2, 3; li. 5; Isa. liii. 6; Rom. iii. 23), implied in the universal prevalence of sin and death (Rom. v. 12—21), assumed in the doctrines of regeneration, which is declared to be necessary absolutely and universally (John iii. 3), and redemption, of which one part of the design was to deliver men from the power as well as guilt of sin (Ephes. v. 25—27; Titus ii. 14; Heb. ix. 12—14; xiii. 12), and abundantly confirmed by experience, which testifies that "the wicked are estranged from the womb, and go astray as soon as they be born, speaking lies" (Ps. lviii. 3). 2. A *long-lived* race. Whether their remarkable longevity was due to the original vigour of the *primus homo*, or to the influence of the tree of life, or to the eminency of the Sethites' piety, it was—(1) A great privilege, affording to themselves ample opportunity for self-cultivation and family training; to the world enlarged facilities for advancement in intelligence and civilisation; and to the Church the means of transmitting truth from age to age, and of drawing more closely together the bonds of religious communion. (2) An unexpected privilege. Upon the mind and heart of

Adam in particular it must have come with much surprise to find that life, which had been forfeited by sin, prolonged to well-nigh a millennium of years ; and this impression, though perhaps it might become less as patriarch succeeded patriarch, would not, we think, entirely disappear.   And so let us hope they came to recognise it as (3) a gracious privilege, due not to any secondary cause whatsoever, but primarily and solely to the infinite mercy of God, who had given them the promise of a woman's seed to sustain their faith and hope.   And as such also (4) a suggestive privilege, emblematic of the immortality they had lost by sin, but received again through grace.   3. A *dying* race.   Though a sinful, they were yet a pardoned race ; but though a pardoned, they were yet a mortal race.   A portion of the original penalty remains to remind man of his past history and present condition ; and so although the Sethites "lived many hundred yeares, yet none of them filled up a thousand, lest they should have too much flattered themselves in long life ; and seeing a thousand is a number of perfection, God would have none of them to attain to a thousand, that we might know that nothing is perfect here" (Willet).

II. MEMBERS OF THE CHURCH OF GOD.   Great as was the former distinction, it is completely eclipsed by this.   It is a great thing to be born, but a greater to be born again.   To be in God's world is much, to be in God's Church is more.   To be of the line of Adam by nature is questionable honour, to be of Adam's line by grace is unquestionable glory.   These ten names from Adam to Noah represent the leaders of the Church of God in the primeval age of the world.   Whether distinguished by rare talent, great wealth, or high position, whether they invented arts, built cities and composed hymns like the Cainites, is not said.   Their chief distinction lay in— 1. *Their possession of faith in God.*   Not perhaps all with the same tenacity, but all with the same reality, they clung to the promise of the woman's seed.   This it was which made them members of the antediluvian Church.   Without faith it is impossible to please God (Heb. xi. 6).   2. *Their observance of religious worship.*   From the beginning of the world the practice of sacrificial worship was maintained by believers.   For two generations it appears to have been private rather than public in its character.   In the days of Enos, according to one of the interpretations of ch. iv. 26, the Sethites began to worship God in social assemblies, as a means at once of fostering their own piety and of defending themselves against the rising tide of ungodliness ; and we cannot doubt the godly practice would continue till the number of believers became so small that Noah could discover no one of like heart and spirit with himself to participate in his devotions.   3. *Their nonconformity to the world.*   According to another reading of ch. iv. 26, in the third generation the holy seed began to make clearer and more distinct the lines of demarcation between themselves and the Cainites by calling themselves by the name of Jehovah, *i. e.* by adopting to themselves the appellation of the worshippers of the Lord.   The fact that "the sons of God" are mentioned in ch. vi. 1 lends a sanction to this view.   If it was so, doubtless the assumption of this particular title was only a sign or symptom of a great religious movement that began to effect the age,—a movement of separation in heart and life from the unbelievers of the time,—and that with a greater or lesser intensity perpetuated itself through each successive generation, not even dying away when there was only one man to be affected by it.   4. *Their witness-bearing against the wickedness of the ungodly world.*   This comes out not indeed here, but in other Scriptures, in connection with two patriarchs, Enoch and Noah ; the first of whom prophesied of the coming of the Lord (Jude 14), and the second of whom was a preacher of righteousness to the men of his generation (2 Pet. ii. 5) ; and what was true of them was doubtless characteristic in a measure of them all.   They were unquestionably prophets, priests, and kings in their families and in relation to their contemporaries.   5. *Their eminently godly lives.*   As much as this is implied in what has been already said.   But of two of them it is distinctly stated that they walked with God : of Enoch, that before his translation he had this testimony, that he pleased God ; and of Noah, that he was a perfect man and an upright ; and though not perhaps entitled to say that all of them lived at the same spiritual elevation as did those two fathers, yet we are fairly warranted to conclude that all of them maintained a holy walk and conversation in a rapidly degenerating age.

III. PROGENITORS OF THE PROMISED SEED. This was the chief distinction of these saintly men, and the real reason why their names and ages have been so carefully preserved to the Church of God. They were all links in the chain leading on to the woman's seed. So to speak, they were the ten first heralds sent out to proclaim the approach of the king ; the ten first shadows or adumbrations of the great Prophet, Priest, and King to whom the faith of the Church was looking forward. True, it is not much that we know about them beyond their names, and certainly there is considerable vagueness and uncertainty about their import ; but still, accepting those meanings which have the greatest probability in their favour, it is interesting to note how they all indicate points of character or features of history which met in Christ. Adam we know was a prophecy of Christ, the second Adam, in more than his name (1 Cor. xv. 45). Abel, the first martyr, prefigured him in dying by a brother's hand. Seth, the Substituted One, was a shadow of him who took our room and stead (Rom. v. 8) ; Enos, the Frail One, of him who, as to his human nature, was as "a tender plant, and a root out of a dry ground" (Isa. liii. 2) ; Cainan, Possession, of him who was the gift of God (2 Cor. ix. 15). Mahalaleel, Praise of God, of him who "was not ashamed to call us brethren, saying, I will declare thy name unto my brethren, in the midst of the church will I sing praise unto thee" (Heb. ii. 11, 12) ;   Jared, Descent, of him who came down from heaven (John vi. 38) ; Enoch, the dedicated and instructed child who walked with God, and was translated that he should not see death, of him who for his people "sanctified himself" (John xvii. 19), "in whom were hid all the treasures of wisdom and knowledge" (Col. ii. 3), who with regard to his Father could say, "I do always those things that please him" (John viii. 29), and who, after accomplishing his Divine mission on the earth, was received up into glory (Acts i. 11) ; Methuselah, Man of the Dart, of him of whom the royal psalmist sang, "Thine arrows are sharp in the heart of the king's enemies" (Ps. xlv. 5); Lamech, Strong Youth, of the strong One whom David saw in vision raised up for Israel's help (Ps. lxxxix. 19) ; Noah, Rest, of him in whose sacrifice God smelled a sweet savour of rest (Ephes. v. 2).

Lessons :—1. As descendants of Adam, let us remember we are sinners, and, repenting, believe the gospel; let us measure our days, and, observing their shortness, apply our hearts unto wisdom ; let us think of our mortality, and prepare for the narrow house appointed for all the living. 2. As members of the Church of Christ, have we the marks that distinguished these antediluvian saints ? 3. As the spiritual posterity of Jesus Christ, do we reflect him as his progenitors foreshadowed him?

Vers. 22—24.—*Enoch.* I. The CHARACTER of his piety. 1. Walking with God. 2. Witnessing for God.

II. The EXCELLENCE of his piety. 1. It began in early boyhood. 2. It flourished in evil times. 3. It grew in spite of scanty privileges. 4. It continued to the close of life.

III. The REWARD of Enoch's piety. He was translated that he should not see death. 1. A visible proof of immortality. 2. A solemn confirmation of the gospel. 3. A striking prophecy of Christ's ascension.

HOMILIES BY VARIOUS AUTHORS.

Ver. 24.—*Walking with God.* Whole chapter a reproof of the restless ambitions of men. Of these long lives the only record is a name, and the fact, "he died." Moral of the whole, "Dust thou art" (cf. 1 Cor. xv. 50). Yet a link between life here and life above. Enoch translated (Heb. xi. 5). The living man passed into the presence of God. How, we need not care to know. But we know why. He "walked with God." Who would not covet this ? Yet it may be ours. What then was that life ? Of its outward form we know nothing. But same expression (ch. vi. 9) tells us that Noah's was such. Also Abraham's, "the friend of God" (ch. xvii. 1) ; and St. Paul's (Phil. i. 21) ; and St. John (1 John i. 3) claims "fellowship with the Father" not for himself only (cf. John xiv. 23).

I. ESSENTIAL FEATURES OF A WALK WITH GOD. Not a life of austerity or of contemplation, removed from interests or cares of world. Noah's was not ; nor Abraham's. Nor a life without fault. Elijah was " of like passions as we are ; " and David ; and St. John declares, 1 John i. 8—10. 1. It is a life of faith, *i. e.* a life in which the word of God is a real power. Mark in Heb. xi. how faith worked in different circumstances. To walk with God is to trust him as a child trusts ; from belief of his fatherhood, and that he is true. With texts before us such as John iii. 16 ; 1 John i. 9 ; ii. 2, why are any not rejoicing ? Or with such as John iv. 10 ; Luke xi. 13, why are any not asking and receiving to the full ? God puts no hindrance (Rev. iii. 20). But (1) too often men do not care. To walk with God is of less importance than to be admired of men. (2) If they do care, they often will not take God's way. The simple message (2 Cor. v. 20 ; 1 John v. 11) seems too simple. They look for feelings, instead of setting God's message before them and grasping it. 2. To walk with God implies desire and effort for the good of men. In an ungodly world Enoch proclaimed the coming judgment (Jude 14 ; cf. Acts xxiv. 25). Spiritual selfishness often a snare to those who have escaped the snare of the world. It is not the mind of Christ. It springs from weakness of faith. Knowing the gift so dearly purchased, so freely offered to all, our calling is to persuade men. Not necessarily as teachers (James i. 19), but by intercession and by loving influence.

III. ENOCH WAS TRANSLATED. But apostles and saints died. Yet think not that their walk with God was less blessed. Hear our Lord's words (John xi. 26), and St. Paul (2 Tim. i. 10). Hear the apostle's desire (Phil. i. 23). Enoch walked with God on earth, and the communion was carried on above. Is not this our Saviour's promise ? (John xiv. 21—23 ; xvii. 24). Death is not the putting off that which is corruptible ; it is separation from the Lord. Assured that we are his for ever, we may say, " O death, where is thy sting ? "—M.

Ver. 24.—*A great example and a great reward.* Notice the three distinctions in this patriarchal prophet.

I. HIS distinguished PIETY—walking with God ; faith giving him knowledge, confidence in God, enjoyment of God.

II. HIS comparatively SHORT LIFE, and therefore speedy deliverance from the imperfection and suffering of this world, though his son lived the longest antediluvian life, and perhaps was a disciple of his father, teaching his doctrine. Those who " *initiate* " (Enoch) great moral movements are seldom long-lived men.

III. HIS distinguished END—*translation.* God took him because he loved him. The anticipation of the resurrection was itself a prophecy. The seventh from Adam is taken to heaven without death, though all the rest died, however long they lived, as though to vivify the promise of the redeeming seed. It seems better to supply the word " *died* " rather than " *was.*" " *And he died* not ; *for God took him* " —referring to the common formula of the patriarchal history, " *and he died.*" [Walking with God is walking to God.] Those who are like Enoch in their life will not be very different from him in their end ; for the peace and triumph of a good man's end is little short of translation. The first of the prophets is thus gloriously signalised. Was it not like a special blessing from the beginning of the world on the life of consecrated ministration to God ? Walking with God may be the description of any kind of service, but especially of the prophets'.—R.

EXPOSITION.

CHAPTER VI.

Vers. 1, 2.—**And it came to pass.** Literally, *it was ;* not in immediate sequence to the preceding chapter, but at some earlier point in the antediluvian period ; perhaps about the time of Enoch (corresponding to that of Lamech the Cainite), if not in the days of Enos. Hävernick joins the passage with ch. iv. 26. **When men**—*ha'adham,* i. e. the human race in general, and not the posterity of Cain in particular (Ainsworth, Rosenmüller, Bush)—**began to multiply**—in virtue of the Divine blessing (ch. i. 28)—**on** (or over) **the face of the earth.** "Alluding to the population spreading itself out as well as increasing " (Bonar). **And daughters were born unto them.** Not referring to any special increase of the female sex (Lange), but simply indicating the quarter whence the danger to the pious Sethites rose: "who became snares to the race of Seth" (Wordsworth). **That the sons of God.** *Bene-ha Elohim.* 1. Not young men of the upper ranks, as distinguished from maidens of humble birth (Onk., Jon., Sym., Aben Ezra); an opinion which "may now be regarded as exploded" (Lange). 2. Still less the angels (LXX.,—some MSS. having ἄγγελοι τοῦ θεοῦ,—Philo, Josephus, Justin Martyr, Clement, Tertullian, Luther, Gesenius, Rosenmüller, Von Bohlen, Ewald, Baumgarten, Delitzsch, Kurtz, Hengstenberg, Alford); for (1) they are either *good* angels, in which case they might be rightly styled sons of God (Ps. xxix. 1 ; lxxxix. 7 ; Job i. 6 ; ii. 1 ; xxxviii. 7 ; Dan. iii. 25), though it is doubtful if this expression does not denote their official rather than natural relationship to God, but it is certain they would not be guilty of the sin here referred to ; or they are *bad* angels, in which case they might readily enough commit the sin, if it were possible, but certainly they would not be called "the sons of God." (2) The statement of Jude (vers. 6, 7), though seemingly in favour of this interpretation, does not necessarily require it ; since (*a*) it is uncertain whether the phrase "τὸν ὅμοιον τούτοις τρόπον ἐκπορνεύσασαι καὶ ἀπελθοῦσαι ὀπίσω σαρκὸς ἑτέρας" refers to the angels or to "αἱ περὶ αὐτὰς πόλεις," in which case the antecedent of τούτοις will not be the ἀγγέλοι of ver. 6, but Σόδομα καὶ Γόμορρα of ver. 7 ; (β) if even it refers to the angels it does not follow that the parallel between the cities and the angels consisted in the "going after strange flesh," and not rather in the fact that both departed from God, "the sin of the apostate angels being in God's view a sin of like kind spiritually with Sodom's going away from God's order of nature after strange flesh" (Fausset); (γ) again, granting that Jude's language describes the sin of the angels as one of carnal fornication with the daughters of men, the sin of which the sons of Elohim are represented as guilty is not πορνεία, but the forming of unhallowed matrimonial alliances. Hence (3) the assertion of our Lord in Luke xx. 35 is inconsistent with the hypothesis that by the sons of God are meant the angels ; and (4) consistent exegesis requires that only extreme urgency, in fact absolute necessity (neither of which can be alleged here), should cause the sons of God to be looked for elsewhere than among the members of the human race. 3. The third interpretation, therefore, which regards the sons of God as the pious Sethites (Cyril of Alexandria, Theodoret, Augustine, Jerome, Calvin, Keil, Hävernick, Lange, Murphy, Wordsworth, Quarry, 'Speaker's Commentary '), though not without its difficulties, has the most to recommend it. (1) It is natural, and not monstrous. (2) It is Scriptural, and not mythical (cf. Numbers xxv. ; Judges iii. ; 1 Kings xi., xvi. ; Rev. ii., for sins of a similar description). (3) It accords with the designation subsequently given to the pious followers of God (cf. Deut. xiv. 1 ; xxxii. 5 ; Ps. lxxiii. 15 ; Prov. xiv. 26 ; Luke iii. 38 ; Rom. viii. 14 ; Gal. iii. 26). (4) It has a historical basis in the fact that *Seth* was regarded by his mother as a son from God (ch. iv. 25), and in the circumstance that already the Sethites had begun to call themselves by the name of Jehovah (ch. iv. 26). Dathius translates, "qui de nomine Dei vocabantur." (5) It is sufficient as an hypothesis, and therefore is entitled to the preference. **Saw the daughters of men** (not of the Cainitic race exclusively, but of men generally) **that they** were **fair**, and had regard to this alone in contracting marriages. "Instead of looking at the spiritual kinsmanship, they had an eye only to the pleasure of sense" (Lange). "What the historian condemns is not that regard was had to beauty, but that *mera libido regnaverit* in the choice of wives" (Calvin). **And they took them wives.** *Lakach isha,* "a standing expression throughout the Old Testament for the marriage relationship established by God at the creation, is never applied to πορνεία, or the simple act of physical connection, which is sufficient of itself to exclude any reference to angels" (Keil ; cf. ch. iv. 19 ; xii. 19 ; xix. 14 ; Exod. vi. 25 ; 1 Sam. xxv. 43). **Of all whom they chose.** The emphasis on מִכֹּל (of all) signifies that, guided by a love of merely sensual attractions, they did not confine themselves to the beautiful daughters of the Sethite race, but selected their brides from the fair women of the Cainites, and perhaps with a preference for these. The opinion that they selected "both virgins and wives, they cared not whom," and "took them by violence" (Willet), is not warranted by the language of the historian. The sons of God were neither the Nephilim nor the Gibborim afterwards described, but the parents of the latter. The evil indicated is simply that of promiscuous marriages without regard to spiritual character.

Ver. 3.—**And the Lord**—Jehovah ; not because due to the Jehovist (Tuch, Bleek, Colenso), but because the sin above specified was a direct violation of the footing of grace on which the Sethites stood — **said,** — to himself, *i. e.* purposed,—**My spirit**—neither "ira, seu rigida Dei justitia" (Venema), nor "the Divine spirit of life bestowed upon man, the principle of physical and ethical, natural and spiritual life" (Keil) ; but the Holy Ghost, the Ruach Elohim of ch. i. 2 —**shall not always strive.** *Lo-yadon :*—1. Shall not dwell (LXX., οὐ μὴ καταμείνῃ ; Vulgate, *non permanebit;* Syriac, Onkelos).

2. Shall not be humbled, *i. e.* by dwelling in men (Gesenius, Tuch). 3. More probably, shall not rule (De Wette, Delitzsch, Kalisch, Fürst), or shall not judge (οὐ κρίνει), as the consequence of ruling (Symmachus, Rosenmüller, Keil), or shall not contend in judgment (*arguere, reprehendere;* cf. Eccles. vi 10), *i. e.* strive with a man by moral force (Calvin, Michaelis, Dathe, 'Speaker's Commentary,' Murphy, Bush). **With man, for that he also**—*beshaggam.* Either *be*, *shaggam*, inf. of *shagag*, to wander, with pron. suff. = "in their wandering" (Gesenius, Tuch, Keil)—the meaning being that men by their straying had proved themselves to be flesh, though a plural suffix with a singular pronoun is inadmissible in Hebrew (Kalisch); or *be, sh* (contracted from *asher*), and *gam* (also) = *quoniam.* Cf. Judges v. 7; vi. 17; Song of Sol. i. 7 (A. V.). Though an Aramaic particle, "it must never be forgotten that Aramaisms are to be expected either in the most modern or *in the most ancient portions of Scripture*" ('Speaker's Commentary')—is **flesh.** Not "transitory beings" (Gesenius, Rosenmüller, Tuch), or corporeal beings (Kalisch), but sinful beings; *bashar* being already employed in its ethical signification, like σάρξ in the New Testament, to denote "man's materiality as rendered ungodly by sin" (Keil). "The doctrine of the carnal mind (Rom. viii.) is merely the outgrowth of the thought expressed in this passage" (Murphy). **Yet his days**—not the individual's (Kalisch), which were not immediately curtailed to the limit mentioned, and, even after the Flood, extended far beyond it (*vide* ch. xi.); but the races, which were only to be prolonged in gracious respite (Calvin)—**shall be an hundred and twenty years.** Tuch, Colenso, and others, supposing this to have been said by God in Noah's 500th year, find a respite only of 100 years, instead of 120; but the historian does not assert that it was then God either formed or announced this determination.

Ver. 4. — **There were.** Not *became*, or arose, as if the giants were the fruit of the previously-mentioned mesalliances; but *already existed* contemporaneously with the sons of God (cf. Keil, Havernick, and Lange). **Giants.** *Nephilim,* from *naphal,* to fall; hence supposed to describe the offspring of the daughters of men and the fallen angels (Hoffman, Delitzsch). The LXX. translate by γίγαντες; whence the "giants" of the A. V. and Vulgate, which Luther rejects as fabulous; but Kalisch, on the strength of Num. xiii. 33, accepts as the certain import of the term. More probable is the interpretation which understands them as men of violence, roving, lawless gallants, "who fall on others;" robbers, or tyrants (Aquila, Rosenmüller, Gesenius, Luther, Calvin, Kurtz, Keil, Murphy, 'Speaker's Commentary'). That they were "monsters, prodigies" (Tuch, Knobel), may be rejected, though it is not unlikely they were men of large physical stature, like the Anakim, Rephaim, and others (cf. Num. xiii. 33). In the earth. Not merely on it, but largely occupying the populated region. **In those days.** Previously referred to, *i. e.* of the mixed marriages. **And also**—*i. e.* in addition to these *nephilim*—**after that,**—*i. e.* after their uprising—**when the sons of God came in unto the daughters of men, and they bare children to them, the same** became **mighty men.** *Ha'gibborim,* literally, the strong, impetuous, heroes (cf. ch. x. 8). "They were probably more refined in manners and exalted in thought than their predecessors of pure Cainite descent" (Murphy). **Which** were **of old.** Not "of the world," as a note of character, taking *olam* as equivalent to αἰών, but a note of time, the narrator reporting from his own standpoint. **Men of renown.** Literally, *men of the name;* "the first nobility of the world, honourable robbers, who boasted of their wickedness" (Calvin) · or gallants, whose names were often in men's mouths (Murphy). For contrary phrase, "men of no name," see Job xxx. 8.

Ver. 5.—**And God** (Jehovah, which should have been rendered 'the Lord') **saw**—indicative of the long-continued patience (Calvin) of the Deity, under whose immediate cognizance the great experiment of the primeval age of the world was wrought out—**that the wickedness** (*ra'ath;* from the root *raa*, to make a loud noise, to rage, hence to be wicked) **of man** (literally, *of the Adam:* this was the *first* aggravation of the wickedness which God beheld; it was the tumultuous rebellion of the being whom he had created in his own image) was **great** (it was no slight iniquity, but a wide-spread, firmly-rooted, and deeply-staining corruption, the *second* aggravation) **in the earth.** This was the *third* aggravation; it was in the world which he had made, and not only in it, but pervading it so "that integrity possessed no longer a single corner" (Calvin). **And that every imagination**—*yetzer,* a device, like pottery ware, from *yatza,* to fashion as a potter (ch. ii. 7; viii. 19). Cf. *yotzer,* a potter, used of God (Ps. xciv. 9, 20). Hence the fashioned purpose (ἐνθύμησις) as distinguished from the thought out of which it springs—"a distinction not generally or constantly recognised by the mental philosopher, though of essential importance in the theory of the mind" (Murphy)—**of the thoughts** — *mahshevoth;* from *hashal,* to think, to meditate = ἔννοια; cf. Heb. ix. 12 (T. Lewis)—**of his heart**—*lev*, the heart, the seat of the affections and emotions of the mind. Cf. Judges xvi. 15 (love); Prov. xxxi. 11 (confidence); Prov. v. 12 (contempt); Ps. civ. 15 (joy). Here "the feeling, or deep mother heart, the state of soul, lying below all, and giving moral character to all (Lewis). Cf. the psychological division of Heb. iv. 12— was **only evil continually.** Literally, *every day.* "If this is not total depravity, how can language express it?" Though the phrase does not mean "from infancy," yet "the general doctrine" (of man's total and universal depravity) "is properly and consistently elicited hence" (Calvin).

Ver. 6.—**And it repented the Lord.** *Yinnahem;* from *naham,* to pant, to groan; Niph., to lament, to grieve because of the misery of others, also because of one's own actions; whence to repent (cf. German, *reuen;* English, *rue:* Gesenius); = "it grieved him at his heart." "Verbum nostræ pravitatæ accommodatum" (Chrysostom); "non est perturbatio, sed judicium, quo irrogatur pœna;" and again, "pœnitudo Dei est mutandorum immutabilis ratio" (Augustine). "Deus est immutabilis; sed cum ii, quos curat, mutantur, mutat ipse res, prout iis expedit quos curat" (Justin Martyr: Latin Version). "The repentance here ascribed to God does not properly belong to him, but has reference to our understanding of him" (Calvin). "The repentance of God does not presuppose any variableness in his nature or purposes" Keil). "A peculiarly strong anthropopathic expression, which, however, presents the truth that God, in consistency with his immutability, assumes a changed position in respect to changed man" (Lange). **That he had made man on the earth.** *I. e.* that he had created man at all, and in particular that he had settled him on the earth. **And it grieved him at his heart.** A touching indication that

God did not hate man, and a clear proof that, though the Divine purpose is immutable, the Divine nature is not impassible.

Ver. 7.—**And the Lord said,**—"Before weird (doom) there's word: Northern Proverb" (Bonar)—**I will destroy**—literally, *blot or wipe out by washing* (cf. Num. v. 23; 2 Kings xxi. 13; Prov. xxx. 20; Isa. xxv. 8). "The idea of destroying by washing away is peculiarly appropriate to the Deluge, and the word is chosen on account of its significance" (Quarry)—**man whom I have created from the face of the earth.** An indirect refutation of the angel hypothesis (Keil, Lange). If the angels were the real authors of the moral corruption of the race, why are they not sentenced as the serpent was in ch. iii. 14 ? **Both man, and beast, and the creeping thing.** Literally, *from man unto beast,* &c. The lower creatures were involved in the punishment of man neither because of any moral corruption which had entered into them, nor as sharing in the atonement for human sins (Knobel); but rather on the ground of man's sovereignty over the animal world, and its dependence on him (Keil, Lange), and in exemplification of that great principle of Divine government by which the penal consequences of moral evil are allowed to extend beyond the immediate actor (cf. Rom. viii. 20). **For it repenteth me that I have made them.** *Vide supra* on ver. 6.

Ver. 8.—**But Noah found grace.** *Hēn;* the same letters as in Noah, but reversed (cf. ch. xviii. 3; xxxix. 4; 1 Kings xi. 19). The present is the first occurrence of the word in Scripture. "Now for the first time *grace* finds a tongue to express its name" (Murphy); and it clearly signifies the same thing as in Rom. iv., v., Ephes. ii., Gal. ii., the gratuitous favour of God to sinful men.

HOMILETICS.

Vers. 1—8.—"*The days that were before the flood*" (Matt. xxiv. 38). I. SIN INCREASING. 1. *Licentiousness* raging. The special form it assumed was that of sensuous gratification, leading to a violation of the law of marriage. In the seventh age Lamech the Cainite became a polygamist. By and by the sons of God, captivated by the charms of beauty, cast aside the bonds of self-restraint, and took them wives of all whom they chose. (1) They married with ungodly women,—beautiful, perhaps talented and accomplished, like the Adahs, Naamahs, and Zillahs of the race of Cain, but unbelieving and ungodly,—which, as the professing followers of Jehovah, they should not have done. Holy Scripture forbids the union of believers with unbelievers (2 Cor. vi. 14). (2) They married to please their fancies, leaving altogether out of reckoning, as necessary qualifications in their partners, spiritual affinity, intellectual compatibility, and even general suitability, and fixing their eyes only on what charmed the senses, physical loveliness. (3) They married as many wives as they desired. Lamech, the first polygamist, was satisfied with two; the degenerate sons of Seth, having yielded to self-indulgence, only limited their wives by the demands of their passion. 2. *Violence* prevailing. Those who begin by breaking the laws of

God are not likely to end by keeping those of man.⌉ From the beginning a characteristic of the wicked line (witness Cain and Lamech), lawlessness at length passed over to the holy seed.   What with the Nephilim on the one hand (probably belonging to the line of Cain) and the Gibborim on the other (the offspring of the degenerate Sethites), the world was overrun with tyrants. *Sheer brute force was the ruler*, and the only code of morals was "Be strong." ⌈Moral purity alone has a God-given right to occupy the supreme seat of influence and power upon the earth.⌉ ⌈After that, intellectual ability.⌉ Mere physical strength, colossal stature, immense bulk, were designed for subjection and subordination.   The subversion of this Divinely-appointed order results in tyranny ; and, of all tyrannies, that of strong, coarse, passion-driven animalism is the worst.   And this was the condition of mankind in these antediluvian ages.   And what was even a worse symptom of the times, *the people loved to have it so.*   Those lawless robbers and tyrants and these reckless, roving gallants were men of name and fame, in everybody's mouth, as the popular heroes of the day. ⌈As mere physical beauty was woman's pathway to marriage, so was sheer brute force, displaying itself in feats of daring and of blood, man's road to renown.⌉ 3. *Corruption* deepening.   Most appalling is the picture sketched by the historian of the condition of the Adam whom God at first created in his own image, implying—(1) Complete extinction of the higher nature.   Through persistence in the downward path of sin it had at length become lost, swallowed up, in the low, carnal portion of his being called the "flesh."   (2) Complete supremacy of evil—evil in the imaginations, evil in the thoughts, evil in the heart, nothing but evil ; and that not temporarily, but always ; nor in the case of one or two individuals merely, but in the case of all, with one solitary exception.   (3) Complete insensibility to Divine influences.   Hence the withdrawal of God's Spirit.   There was no use for further striving to restrain or improve them ; they were "past feeling" (Ephes. iv. 19).

II. God repenting. 1. A *mysterious* fact.   "We do not gain much by attempting to explain philosophically such states or movements of the Divine mind.   They are strictly ἄρρητα—ineffable.   So the Scripture itself represents them—Isa. lv. 9" (Tayler Lewis).   What is here asserted of the Divine thoughts is likewise true of the Divine emotions ; like the Deity himself, they are past finding out.   2. A *real* fact.   The language describes something real on the part of God.   If it is figurative, then there must be something of which it is the figure ; and that something is the Divine grief and repentance.   These, however, are realities that belong to a realm which the human intellect cannot traverse.   As of the Divine personality man's personality is but an image or reflection, so of the Divine affections and emotions are man's affections and emotions only shadows.   Man repents when he changes his mind, or his attitude, or his actions.   God repents when his thoughts are changed, when his feelings are turned, when his acts are reversed.   But God is "of one mind, and who can turn him ? "   He is "without variableness and shadow of turning ; " "the same yesterday, to-day, and for ever."   Hence we rather try to picture to ourselves the Divine penitence as expressive of the changed attitude which the immutable Deity maintains towards things that are opposite, such as holiness and sin.   3. An *instructive* fact, telling us (1) that the Divine nature is not impassible ; (2) that sin is not the end of man's creation ; and (3) that a sinful man is a disappointment to God.   4. An *ominous* fact.   As thus explained, the grief and penitence of God describe the effect which human sin ever have upon the Divine nature.   It fills him with heart-felt grief and pity.   It excites all the fathomless ocean of sympathy for sinning men with which his infinite bosom is filled.   But at the same time, and notwithstanding this, it moves him to inflict judicial retribution.   "And the Lord said, I will destroy man."

III. Grace operating. 1. *In restraining sinners.*   It was impossible that God could leave men to rush headlong to their own destruction without interposing obstacles in their path.   In the way of these apostates of the human race he erected quite a series of barriers to keep them back from perdition.   He gave them (1) a gospel of mercy in the promise of the woman's seed ; (2) a ministry of mercy, raising up and maintaining a succession of pious men to preach the gospel, and warn them against the ways of sin ; (3) a Spirit of mercy to strive within them ; (4) a providence of mercy, (*a*) measuring out to them a long term of years, yet (*b*) solemnly reminding them of their mortality, and finally (c) giving them a reprieve, even after they were sentenced to destruction. 2. *In saving believers.* (1) Accepting them as he accepted Noah; (2) preserving them amid the general defection of the times, as he did Noah, who without Divine assistance must have been inevitably swept away in the general current of ungodliness; (3) providing for their safety against the coming judgment. They were all removed by death before the flood came, and Noah was delivered by the ark.

Lessons :—1. The terrible degeneracy of human nature. 2. The danger of mixed marriages. 3. God may pity, but he must likewise punish, the evil-doer. 4. The day of grace has its limits. 5. If a soul will go to perdition, it must do so over many mercies. 6. God never leaves himself without a witness, even in the worst of times.

HOMILIES BY VARIOUS AUTHORS.

Vers. 1—8.—*The work of sin.* The moral chaos out of which the new order is about to be evolved. We find these features in the corrupt state depicted.

I. ILL-ASSORTED MARRIAGES. The sons of God—*i. e.* the seed of the righteous, such men as the patriarchs described in ch. v., men who walked with God, and were his prophets—fell away from their allegiance to the Divine order, and went after the daughters of the Cainites. The self-will and mere carnal affections are denoted by the expression " all whom they chose."

II. VIOLENCE AND MILITARY AMBITION. The giants were the "nephilim," those who assaulted and fell upon their neighbours. The increase of such men is distinctly traced to the corrupt alliances.

III. THE WITHDRAWAL by judgment of THE DIVINE SPIRIT from man, by which may be meant not only the individual degeneracy which we see exemplified in such a case as Cain, driven out from the presence of the Lord, given up to a reprobate mind, and afterwards in Pharaoh; but the withdrawal of prophecy and such special spiritual communications as had been given by such men as Enoch.

IV. THE SHORTENING OF HUMAN LIFE. Since the higher moral influence of Christianity has been felt in society during the last three centuries, it is calculated that the average length of human life has been increased twofold. The anthropomorphism of these verses is in perfect accordance with the tone of the whole Book of Genesis, and is not in the least a perversion of truth. It is rather a revelation of truth, as anticipating the great central fact of revelation, God manifest in the flesh. But why is God said to have determined to destroy the face of the earth, the animal creation with the sinful man? Because the life of man involved that of the creatures round him. "The earth is filled with violence." To a large extent the beasts, creeping things, and fowls of the air participate in the disorder of the human race, being rendered unnaturally savage and degenerate in their condition by man's disorderly ways. Moreover, any destruction which should sweep away a whole race of men must involve the lower creation. The defeat of a king is the defeat of his subjects. In all this corruption and misery there is yet, by the grace of God, one oasis of spiritual life, the family of Noah. He found grace not because he earned it, but because he kept what had been given him, both through his ancestors and by the work of the Spirit in his own heart.—R.

Vers. 1—5.—*The demoralisation of the race.* This was due to—

I. THE LONG LIVES OF THE ANTEDILUVIANS. Long life, if helpful to the good, is much more injurious to the wicked. Giants in health and life are often giants in wickedness.

II. THE UNHOLY ALLIANCES OF THE SETHITES AND CAINITES. Nothing so demoralising as marriage with an evil woman. Its bad effects are commonly transmitted to, and intensified in, posterity.

III. THE DEPRAVITY INDUCED BY THE FALL, which was universal in its extent, and gradually deepening in its intensity.

Lessons :—1. The inherent evil of our natures. 2. The curse clinging to ungodliness. 3. The true function of worldly sorrows and of frequent and early death.—W. R.

Ver. 3.—*Probation, approbation, and reprobation.* "And the Lord said, My spirit shall not always strive with man," &c. The life of man, whether longer or shorter, is a time during which the Spirit of God strives with him. It is at once in judgment and in mercy that the strife is not prolonged; for where there is continued opposition to the will of God there is continual laying up of judgment against the day of wrath. The allotted time of man upon the earth is sufficient for the required probation, clearly manifesting the direction of the will, the decided choice of the heart. Here is—

I. THE GREAT MORAL FACT OF MAN'S CONDITION IN HIS FLESHLY STATE. The striving of God's Spirit with him. 1. In the order of the world and of human life. 2. In the revelation of truth and positive appeals of the Divine word. 3. In the constant nearness and influence of spiritual society. 4. In the working of conscience and the moral instincts generally.

II. THE DIVINE APPOINTMENT OF SPIRITUAL PRIVILEGE at once a righteous limitation and a gracious concentration. [That which is unlimited is apt to be undervalued.] *Not always* shall the Spirit strive. 1. *Individually* this is testified. A heart which knows not the day of its visitation becomes hardened. 2. In the history of spiritual work *in communities*. Times of refreshing generally followed by withdrawments of power. The limit of life itself is before us all. *Not always* can we hear the voice and see the open door.

III. THE NATURAL AND THE SPIRITUAL ARE INTIMATELY RELATED TO ONE ANOTHER IN THE LIFE OF MAN. He who decreed the length of days to his creature did also strive with the evil of his fallen nature that he might cast it out. The hundred and twenty years are seldom reached; but is it not because the evil is so obstinately retained? Those whose spirit is most in fellowship with the Spirit of God are least weighed down with the burden of the flesh, are strongest to resist the wearing, wasting influence of the world.

IV. THE STRIVING OF GOD'S SPIRIT WITH US MAY CEASE. What follows? To fall on the stone is to be broken, to be under it is to be crushed. The alternative is before every human life—to be dealt with as with God or against him. "Woe unto him that striveth with his Maker!" The progressive revelations of the Bible point to the winding up of all earthly history. *Not always* strife. Be ye reconciled to God.—R.

Ver. 3.—*The striving of the Spirit* implies—
I. THE DOCTRINE OF HUMAN DEPRAVITY.
II. THE GRANTING OF GOD'S SPIRIT TO OUR FALLEN WORLD.
III. That God's Spirit is OPPOSED BY MAN.
IV. That the effort of God's Spirit for man's salvation, even though not successful, COMES TO AN END.
V. That the striving of God's Spirit comes to an end not because God's willingness to help comes to an end, but because HUMAN NATURE SINKS BEYOND THE POSSIBILITY OF HELP.
VI. That it belongs to God as Sovereign to FIX THE DAY OF GRACE.

Learn—1. The richness of Divine mercy. 2. The possibility of falling away beyond the hope of repentance. 3. The fact that our day of grace is limited. 4. The certainty that, however short, the day of grace which we enjoy is available for salvation.—W. R.

§ 4. THE GENERATIONS OF NOAH (CH. VI. 9—IX. 29).

EXPOSITION.

Ver. 9.—**These are the generations of Noah.** "Novi capitis initium" = "hæc est historia Noachi" (Rosenmüller; cf. ch. v. 1). **Noah** (*vide* ch. v. 29) **was a just man.** צַדִּיק: not of spotless innocence (Knobel); but upright, honest, virtuous, pious (*vir probus*);

from צָדַק, to be straight, hence to be just; Piel to render just or righteous (Eccl. Lat., *justificare*), to declare any one just or innocent (Gesenius); better "justified" or declared righteous, being derived from the Piel form of the verb (Fürst). "Evidently the righteousness here meant is that which represents him as justified in view of the judgment of the Flood, by reason of his faith, Heb. xi. 7" (Lange). "To be just is to be right in point of law, and thereby entitled to all the blessings of the acquitted and justified. When applied to the guilty this epithet implies pardon of sin among other benefits of grace" (Murphy). **And perfect.** תָּמִים: complete, whole (τέλειος, *integer*) ; *i. e.* perfect in the sense not of sinlessness, but of moral integrity (Gesenius, Calvin). It describes "completeness of parts rather than of degrees in the renewed character" (Bush). "The just is the right in law, the perfect is the tested in holiness" (Murphy). If, however, the term is equivalent to the τελείωσις of the Christian system (1 Cor. ii. 6 ; Heb. vii. 11), it denotes that complete readjustment of the being of a sinful man to the law of God, both legally and morally, which is effected by the whole work of Christ for man and in man ; it is " the establishment of complete, unclouded, and enduring communion with God, and the full realisation of a state of peace with him which, founded on a true and ever valid remission of sins, has for its consummation eternal glory"(Delitzsch on Heb. vii. 11). **In his generations.** בְּדֹרֹתָיו, from דּוּר, to go in a circle ; hence a circuit of years ; an age or generation (*generatio, seculum*) of men. The clause marks not simply the sphere of Noah's virtue, among his contemporaries, or only the duration of his piety, throughout his lifetime, but likewise the constancy of his religion, which, when surrounded by the filth of iniquity on every side, contracted no contagion (Calvin). "It is probable, moreover, that he was of pure descent, and in that respect also distinguished from his contemporaries, who were the offspring of promiscuous marriages between the godly and the ungodly" (Murphy). **And Noah walked with God.** The special form in which his just and perfect character revealed itself amongst his sinful contemporaries. For the import of the phrase see on ch. v. 22. Noah was also a preacher of righteousness (2 Pet. ii. 5), and probably announced to the wicked age in which he lived the coming of the Flood (Heb. xi. 7).

Ver. 10.—**And Noah begat three sons, Shem, Ham, and Japheth** (cf. ch. v. 32). Here (in the story of the Flood) if anywhere, observes Rosenmüller, can traces be detected of two distinct documents (*duorum monumentorum*), in the alternate use of the names of the Deity, the frequent repetitions of the same things, and the use of peculiar forms of expression; and in vers. 9—13, compared with ch. vi. 5—8, Bleek, Tuch, Colenso, and others find the first instance of needless repetition, on the supposition of the unity of the narrative, but a sure index

of the Elohistic pen, on the hypothesis of different authors ; but the so-called " repetition " is explained by remembering that ch. vi. 5—8 forms the close of a section " bringing down the history to the point at which the degeneracy of mankind causes God to resolve on the destruction of the world," while the new section, which otherwise would begin too abruptly, introduces the account of the Deluge by a brief description of its cause (cf. Quarry, p. 367). The structure of the narrative here is not different from what it appears elsewhere (cf. ch. ii. 4 ; v. 1).

Ver. 11.—**The earth**—(1) its inhabitants, as in ver. 11 (cf. Gen. xi. 1)—mankind being denominated earth because wholly earthly (Chrysostom) ; (2) the land, which had become defiled through their wickedness (vers. 12, 13 ; cf. Ps. cvii. 34)—**also** (literally, *and the earth*) **was corrupt**—in a moral sense, the causes and forms of which corruption have already been detailed in the preceding paragraph. The term is elsewhere applied to idolatry, or the sin of perverting and depraving the worship of God (Exod. xxxii. 7 ; Deut. xxxii. 5 ; Judges ii. 19 ; 2 Chron. xxvii. 2) ; but the special sins of the antediluvians were rather licentiousness and lawlessness—**before God**—*i. e.* openly, publicly, flagrantly, and presumptously (cf. ch. x. 9) ; noting the intensity of their wickedness, or intimating the fact that God had *seen* their corruption, and so commending the Divine long-suffering (Calvin), —**and the earth was filled with violence.** " The outward exhibition of inward carnality " (Murphy) ; "injurious and cruel dealing, the violating of duties towards men, 'rapines or robberies (Chaldee)'" (Ainsworth). Cf. ch. xlix. 5; Joel iii. 19 ; Obad. x.

Ver. 12.—**And God looked upon the earth.** "God knows at all times what is doing in our world, but his looking upon the earth denotes a special observance of it, as though he had instituted an inquiry into its real condition" (Bush ; cf. Ps. xiv. 2 ; xxxiii. 13, 14 ; liii. 2, 3). **And, behold, it was corrupt.** " Everything stood in sharpest contradiction with that good state which God the Creator had established " (Delitzsch, quoted by Lange). The nature of this corruption is further indicated. **For all flesh** — *i. e.* the human race, who are so characterised here not so much for their frailty (Isa. xl. 5, 6) as for their moral and spiritual degeneracy (Gen. vi. 3, q. v.) — **had corrupted** — *shachath* (καταφθείρω, LXX.) ; literally, had destroyed, wrecked, and ruined, wholly subverted and overthrown — **his way** — *derech* (from *darach*, to tread with the feet), a going; hence a journey, a way ; *e. g.* (1) of living or acting (Prov. xii. 15 ; 1 Sam. xviii. 44) ; (2) of worshipping God—ὁδὸς, Acts xix. 9, 23 (Ps. cxxxix. 24 ; Amos viii. 14). Here it signifies the entire plan and course of life in all its ethical and religious aspects as designed for man by God (cf. Ps. cxix. 9 ; and contrast "the way of Cain," Jude 11 ; "the way of Balaam," 2 Pet. ii. 15)—upon the earth.

Ver. 13.—And God said unto Noah, The end. קֵץ (from Hophal of קָצַץ, to cut off), that which is cut off, the end of a time (Gen. iv. 3) or of a space (Isa. xxxvii. 24) ; specially the end or destruction of a people (Ezek. vii. 2 ; Amos viii. 2), in which sense it is to be here understood (Gesenius, Rosenmüller). The rendering which regards kêtz as, like τέλος = the completion, consummation, fulness of a thing (here of human fleshliness or wickedness), and the following clause as epexegetic of the present (Bush), though admissible in respect of Scriptural usage (cf. Jer. li. 13 ; Eccles. xii. 13 ; Rom. x. 4) and contextual harmony, is scarcely so obvious ; while a third, that the end spoken of is the issue to which the moral corruption of the world was inevitably tending (Keil, Lange), does not materially differ from the first. Of all flesh. I. e. of the human race, of course with the exception of Noah and his family, which "teaches us to beware of applying an inflexible literality to such terms as all, when used in the sense of ordinary conversation" (Murphy). Is come before me. Literally, before my face. Not "a me constitutus est" (Gesenius), "is decreed before my throne" (Kalisch) ; but, "is in the contemplation of my mind as an event soon to be realised" (Murphy), with perhaps a glance at the circumstance that man's ruin had not been sought by God, but, as it were, had thrust itself upon his notice as a thing that could no longer be delayed. If בָּא לְפָנַי = the similar expression בָּא אֶל, which, when applied to rumours, signifies to reach the ear (cf. ch. xviii. 21 ; Exod. iii. 9 ; 1 Kings ii. 28 ; Esther ix. 11), it may likewise indicate the closeness or near approach of the impending calamity. For the earth is filled with violence through them. More correctly, "from their faces;" "a facie eorum" (Vulgate). That is, "the flood of wickedness which comes up before God's face goes out from their face" in the sense of being perpetrated openly (Lange), and "by their conscious agency" (Alford). And, behold, I will destroy them. Literally, and behold me destroying them. The verb is the same as is translated "corrupt" in ver. 12, q. v., as if to convey the idea of fitting retribution (cf. 1 Cor. iii. 17 : εἴ τις τὸν ναὸν τοῦ θεοῦ φθείρει, φθερεῖ τοῦτον ὁ θεός ; Rev. xi. 18 : καὶ διαφθεῖραι τοὺς διαφθείροντας τὴν γῆν). Whether this destruction which was threatened against the antediluvian sinners extended to the loss of their souls throughout

eternity may be reasoned (pro and con) from other Scriptures, but cannot be determined from this place, which refers solely to the extinction of their bodily lives. With the earth. Not from the earth (Samaritan), or on the earth (Syriac, Rosenmüller), or even the earth, "thus identifying the earth with its inhabitants" (Bush), but, together with the earth (Kalisch, Keil, Alford; cf. ch. ix. 11 ; καὶ τὴν γῆν, LXX.). The universality of representation which characterises this section (vers. 9—13) is regarded by Davidson, Colenso, and others as contradictory of ch. vi. 5, which depicts the corruption as only human, and limits the destruction to the race of man. But as the two accounts belong to different subdivisions of the book, they cannot properly be viewed as contradictory (cf. ' Quarry on Genesis,' pp. 370, 371).

Ver. 14.—Make thee an ark. תֵּבַת, constr. of תֵּבָה, etymology unknown (Gesenius); of Shemitic origin, from תָּבָה, to be hollow (Fürst) ; of Egyptian derivation, a boat being called tept (Keil, Kalisch, Knobel) ; from the Sanscrit pota, a pot or boat (Bohlen) ; "a peculiar archaic term for a very unusual thing, like מַבּוּל, the term for the Flood itself" (T. Lewis) ; translated κιβωτός, θίβη (LXX.), arca (Vulgate), λάρναξ (Nicolas Damascenus), πλοῖον (Berosus) ; not a ship in the ordinary acceptation of the word, but a box or chest (cf. Exod. ii. 3) capable of floating on the waters. "Similar vessels, generally, however, drawn by horses or men, were and are still used in some parts of Europe and Asia" (Kalisch). Of gopher wood. Literally, woods of gopher (גֹּפֶר : ἅπαξ λεγ., the root of which, like כָּפַר, seems to signify to cover (Kalisch) ; ligna bituminata (Vulgate); pitch trees, resinous trees, such as are used in ship-building (Gesenius) ; most likely cypress, κυπάρισσος (Bochart, Celsius, Keil), which was used "in some parts of Asia exclusively as the material for ships, in Athens for coffins, and in Egypt for mummy cases" (Kalisch). "It is said too that the gates of St. Peter's Church at Rome (made of this wood), which lasted from the time of Constantine to that of Eugene IV., i. e. 1100 years, had in that period suffered no decay" (Bush). Rooms— kinnim, nests, applied metaphorically to the chambers of the ark—shalt thou make in the ark, and shalt pitch it within and without with pitch. וְכָפַרְתָּ בַכֹּפֶר : literally, shalt cover it with a covering. The substance to be employed will probably bitumen or asphalt (ἄσφαλτος, LXX. ; bitumen, Vulgate). The root (cf. English, cover) signifies also to pardon sin, i. e. to cover them from God's sight (Ps. lxv. 3 ; lxxviii. 38 ; 2 Chron. xxx. 18), and to make expiation for sin, i. e.

to obtain covering for them (ch. xxxii. 20 ; Dan. ix. 24) ; whence *copher* is used for a ransom (Exod. xxi. 30 ; xxx. 12), and *capporeth*, the covering of the ark (Exod. xxv. 17), for the mercy-seat (ἱλαστήριον, LXX. ; *propitiatorium*, Vulgate).

Ver. 15.—**And this** is the fashion **which thou shalt make it of.** The shape of it is not described, but only its dimensions given. **The length of the ark** shall be **three hundred cubits,**—a cubit = the length from the elbow to the middle finger (Deut. iii. 11) ; nearly twenty-two inches, if the sacred cubit ; if the common, eighteen inches,—**the breadth of it fifty cubits, and the height of it thirty cubits.** With a cubit of twenty-one inches, the length would be 525 feet, the breadth 87 feet 6 inches, dimensions not dissimilar to those of the *Great Eastern* which is 680 feet long, 83 feet broad, and 58 feet deep. The cubic contents of the ark with these dimensions would be 2,411,718·75 feet, which, allowing forty cubic feet per ton, would give a carrying capacity equal to 32,800 tons. P. Jansen of Holland, in 1609, proved by actual experiment that a ship constructed after the pattern of the ark, though not adapted for sailing, would in reality carry a cargo greater by one-third than any other form of like cubical content. The difficulty of building a vessel of such enormous magnitude, T. Lewis thinks, may be got over by remembering the extreme simplicity of its structure, the length of time allowed for its erection, the physical constitution of the builders, and the facilities for obtaining materials which may have existed in abundance in their vicinity. Bishop Wilkins ('Essay towards a Philosophical Character and Language'), Dr. A. Clarke, and Bush are satisfied that the ark was large enough to contain all the animals directed to be taken into it, along with provision for a twelvemonth ; but computations founded on the number of the species presently existing must of necessity be precarious ; and besides, it is at least doubtful whether the Deluge was universal, or only partial and local, in which case the difficulty (so called) completely vanishes.

Ver. 16.—**A window**—עֹהַר, from צָהַר, to shine, hence light (עָהֳרַיִם, double light, or light of midday—ch. xliii. 16 ; Jer. vi. 4). Not the window which Noah afterwards opened to let out the dove, which is called הַלּוֹן (ch. viii. 6), but obviously a lighting apparatus, which may have been a series of windows (Gesenius), scarcely one (Theodotion, θύραν ; Symmachus, διαφανές ; Vulgate, *fenestram* ; Kimchi, Luther, Calvin) ; or an opening running along the top of the sides of the ark, occupied by some translucent substance, and sheltered by the eaves of the

roof (Knobel) ; or, what appears more probable, a light opening in the upper deck, stretching along the entire length, and continued down through the different stories (Baumgarten, Lange) ; or, if the roof sloped, as is most likely, an aperture along the ridge, which would admit the clear light of heaven (*tsōhar*), and serve as a meridional line enabling Noah and the inmates of the ark to ascertain the hour of noon (Tayler Lewis). Keil and Murphy think we can form no proper conception of the light arrangement of the ark. The conjecture of Schultens, which is followed by Dathius, Michaelis, Rosenmüller, and others, that the *tsōhar* meant the covering (*tectum, dorsum*), "quo sane hoc ædificium carere non potuit, propter pluviam tot dierum continuam," is obviously incorrect—**shalt thou make to the ark, and in a cubit**—to a cubit, *i. e.* all but a cubit (T. Lewis) ; into a cubit, *i. e.* to the extent of a cubit (Ainsworth) ; by the cubit, *i. e.* by a just measure (Kalisch)—**shalt thou finish it**—not the window (Gesenius, Ewald, Tuch), the feminine suffix agreeing with *tebah*, which is feminine, and not with *tsōhar*, which is masculine ; but the ark—**above.** Literally, *from above to above;* i. e., according to the above interpretations of the preposition, either the roof, after the construction of the windows, should be regularly finished "by the just measure" (Kalisch) ; or the roof should be arched but a cubit, that it might be almost flat (Ainsworth) ; or from the eaves up toward the ridge it should be completed, leaving a cubit open or unfinished (T. Lewis). **And the door of the ark**—the opening which should admit its inmates—**shalt thou set in the side thereof;** with **lower, second, and third** stories. The word stories is not in the original, but some such word must be supplied. Lange thinks that each flat or story had an entrance or door in the side.

Ver. 17.—**And, behold, I, even I.** More correctly, "And I, behold, I," an emphatic assertion that what was coming was a Divine visitation, and not simply a natural occurrence. **Do bring.** Literally, *bringing,* the participle standing in place of the finite verb to indicate the certainty of the future action (*vide* Gesenius, 'Gram.,' § 134). **A flood of waters upon the earth.** מַבּוּל, pronounced by Bohlen "far-fetched," "is an archaic word coined expressly for the waters of Noah (Isa. xliv. 9), and is used nowhere else except Psalm xxix. 10 — waters upon the earth" (Keil). The first intimation of the means to be employed in inflicting judgment on the morally corrupted world. **To destroy all flesh, wherein is the breath of life, from under heaven ; and every thing that is in the earth shall die.** The fishes only being excepted, "either (1) because they did not live in the same element wherein man lived and sinned; or (2) because they were not so instrumental in man's sins as the beasts might be; or (3) because man had a greater command over the beasts than over the fishes, and greater service and benefit from them " (Poole).

Ver. 18.—**But with thee will I establish my covenant.** בְּרִית (διαθήκη, LXX.; *fœdus*, Vulgate; *testamentum*, N. T.), from בָּרָא, to cut or carve; hence a covenant, from the custom of passing between the divided pieces of the victims slain on the occasion of making such solemn compacts (cf. ch. xv. 9; Gesenius); from בָּרָה, to eat, hence an eating together, a banquet (cf. ch. xxxi. 54; Lee). On the Bible idea of covenant see ch. xv. 9. My covenant = the already well-known covenant which I have made with man. **And thou shalt come into the ark, thou, and thy sons, and thy wife, and thy sons' wives with thee.** This was the substance of the covenant agreement so far as Noah was concerned. The next three verses describe the arrangements about the animals.

Vers. 19—21.—**And of every living thing** of all flesh, two of every sort (literally, *by twos*, i. e. in pairs) **shalt thou bring into** —or cause to enter, *i. e.* receive them when they come (ver. 20)—**the ark, to keep them alive**—literally, *to cause to live; ἵνα τρέφῃς* (LXX.); in order to preserve alive (sc. the animals)—**with thee; they shall be male and female. Of fowls after their kind** (literally, *of the fowl after its kind*), **and** of cattle after their kind (literally, *of the cattle after its kind*), **of every creeping thing of the earth after its kind, two of every** sort **shall come unto thee.** "Non hominis actu, sed Dei nutu" (Augustine). Perhaps through an instinctive presentiment of the impending calamity (Lange, 'Speaker's Commentary'). **And take thou unto thee of all food that is eaten, and thou shalt gather it to thee** (collecting sufficient for a twelvemonth's sustenance); **and it shall be for food for thee, and for them.**

Ver. 22.—**Thus did Noah; according to all that God** (Elohim; in ch. vii. 5 it is Jehovah) **commanded** (with respect to the building of the ark, the receiving of the animals, the collecting of provisions) **him, so did he.**

HOMILETICS.

Vers. 9—22.—*The building of the ark.* I. THE MAN AND HIS CONTEMPORARIES. A common saying, and one possessed of a show of wisdom, that a person seldom rises far above the average goodness, or sinks far below the average wickedness, of the age in which he lives. Yet it is precisely in proportion as individuals either excel or fall beneath their generation that they are able to affect it for good or evil. All epoch-making men are of this stamp. Noah, it is obvious, was not a man whose character was shaped by his contemporaries. In respect of three things, the contrast between him and them was as great and decided as could well be imagined. 1. *Legal standing.* Noah was a just man, *i. e.* a sinner justified by his believing acceptance of the gospel promise of the woman's seed; while they were corrupt, or had declined into infidelity. 2. *Spiritual character.* Noah was perfect in the sense that his heart was right with God, and his nature was renewed by Divine grace; they were wanting in all the essential characteristics of true being, "alienated from the life of God through the ignorance that was in them, because of the hardness of their hearts." 3. *Outer walk.* As a consequence the daily life of Noah was one of eminent piety—a walking with God, like that of Enoch; while theirs was one of impious defiance of the laws of God, and ruthless oppression of the rights of men. Learn (1) that it is quite possible to be pious in the midst of evil times; and (2) that only a life of close communion with God will prevent one from being overborne by the wickedness of his age.

II. THE EVENT AND ITS OCCASION. The event was—1. *Appalling in its form.* The destruction of a world by a flood of waters. "In the beginning," at God's command, the goodly fabric had risen from the waters (ch. i. 2; 2 Pet. iii. 5), radiant in beauty, swimming in a sea of light, rejoicing its Creator's heart (ch. i. 31); now it was about to return to the dark and formless matrix whence it sprang. If the world's birth woke music among the morning stars (Job xxxviii. 7), surely its destruction was enough to make the angels weep! 2. *Universal in its sweep.* Without engaging at present in any controversy as to the actual extent of the Deluge, we may notice that Elohim represents it as destructive of the entire human race (Noah and his family excepted). Considering the impression made upon our hearts by the report of some sudden accident (the explosion of a mine, the sinking of a ship, the collision of a train), in which a number of lives are lost, it is not wonderful that the echo of this stupendous catastrophe should have vibrated through the world (see 'Traditions of the Deluge'). 3. *Supernatural in its origin.* It was not an ordinary occurrence, but a distinctly miraculous phenomenon. "Behold, I, even I, do bring a flood of waters upon the earth." 4. *Punitive in its purpose.* Its retributive character was distinctly implied in the form of its announcement— "I will destroy." All temporal calamities are not of this description. That all suffering is penal was the mistake of Job's friends (Job iv. 7, *et passim*), though not of Job himself, and certainly it is not the teaching of the Bible (cf. Job xxxiii. 29; Ps. xciv. 12; Rom. viii. 28; 2 Cor. iv. 17). But this was — 5. *Melancholy in its occasion*—the total, absolute, and radical corruption of the earth's inhabitants. Through unbelief and disobedience they had ruined the moral nature which God had given them; and now there was no help for it but that they should be swept away. 6. *Inevitable in its coming.* Implied in one interpretation of the words "the end of all flesh" (*vide* Expos.). Sin ever carries its own retribution in its bosom; not merely, however, in recoiling upon itself with inward misery, sense of loss, weakness, depravation; but likewise in necessitating the infliction on the part of Elohim of positive retribution. 7. *Near in its approach.* "Behold, I am bringing!" as if it were already at hand. See here (1) the danger of sin; (2) the certainty of retribution; (3) the righteousness of the wrath of God; (4) the mercy of God in making this known to sinners, as he foretold the Flood to the antediluvians.

III. THE COMMISSION AND ITS EXECUTION. 1. *It related to the safety of the Church* (ver. 18). At that time the antediluvian Church was small, consisting only of Noah and his family (ch. vii. 1), and in all probability uninfluential and despised, by the Gibborim and Nephilim of the day ridiculed and oppressed. Endangered by the immorality and violence of the times, it was likewise imperilled by the impending Deluge. Yet God never leaves his people unprotected or unprovided for (Deut. xxxiii. 12; Ps. xxxiv. 15; xlvi. 5; Zech. ii. 5; 2 Pet. ii. 9). The Church of God and Christ is imperishable (Isa. liv. 17; Matt. xvi. 18; xviii. 14). That was symbolised to Israel by the burning bush (Exod. iii. 2), and to all postdiluvian time by the ark. It was impossible that God could be unconcerned about the safety of the believing remnant in antediluvian times. The commission which came to Noah concerned the rescue of himself and children. 2. *It was Divinely given* (vers. 13, 14). Salvation is of the Lord (Ps. iii. 8; Jonah ii. 9). Manifestly only God could have provided for the safety of Noah and his family. Directions from any other quarter, or even expedients devised by himself, must have proved both futile and presumptuous. So, whatever instructions may be given to man with a view to salvation must come from God, if they are to be successful. Schemes of redemption may be beautiful, ingenious, attractive, hopeful; if they are not God's schemes they are worthless (Isa. xliii. 11; Hosea xiii. 4). 3. *It was minutely detailed* (vers. 14—16). The plan which God proposed to Noah for the salvation of himself and house was building of an ark according to Divinely-prepared specifications. In its construction there was no room left for the exercise of inventive genius. Like the tabernacle in the wilderness, it was fashioned according to a God-given pattern. And so, in all that concerns the salvation of sinful men, from first to last the plan is God's, admitting neither of addition nor subtraction, correction nor improvement, at the hands of the men themselves. 4. *It was believingly received* (Heb. xi. 7). Perhaps the last device that would ever have suggested itself to the mind of Noah, very likely ridiculed by his contemporaries as an act of folly, probably at times regarded with considerable misgivings by the patriarch himself, and certainly an undertaking that would involve immense labour, patient endurance, heroic self-sacrifice, it was yet accepted in a spirit of meek and unquestioning faith. And so should it be with us. When God speaks we should hear. When he directs we should obey. 5. *It was obediently carried through* (ver. 22). This was the best test of his faith. Where obedience is absent, faith is not present. Faith always discovers its existence by obedience (Heb. xi. 8). Learn—(1) God's care of his people. (2) The sufficiency of God's plan of salvation. (3) The wisdom of implicitly following God's directions.

Ver. 22.—*The obedience of Noah.* I. Pious in its PRINCIPLE. II Prompt in its OPERATION. III. Laborious in its EXERCISE. IV. Universal in its EXTENT. V. Persevering in its COURSE. VI. Successful in its END.

HOMILIES BY VARIOUS AUTHORS.

Vers. 9—22.—*Righteousness and peace.* The description of Noah is very similar to that of Enoch, just and perfect in his generation, that is, blameless in his walk before men, which is saying much of one who lived in a time of universal corruption. And he walked with God, *i. e.* devout and religious, and, from the analogy of the preceding use of the words, we may say, a prophet. He preached righteousness both with lip and life. To this good and great prophet the announcement is made of the coming judgment. "The secret of the Lord is with them that fear him, and he will show them his covenant." The earth is filled with violence through men, and therefore with man must be destroyed. With the message of judgment there is also the message of mercy, as at the first.

The ark, an emblem of salvation by grace, as afterwards (cf. 1 Pet. iii. 19—22). The offer of salvation was a trial of faith. God did not himself provide the ark; it was made by the hands of men, of earthly materials, with ordinary earthly measurements and appointments, and prepared as for an ordinary occasion. There was nothing in the visible ark to stumble faith; but, as it was connected with a positive commandment and prophecy, it was a demand on the simple faith of the true child of God, which is of the nature of obedience. We cannot doubt that this Divine message to Noah was the Bible of that time. It appealed to faith as the word of God. And, as in all times, with the written or spoken word there was the unwritten law, the *lex non scripta ;* for we are told that "Noah did according to all that God commanded him, so did he." In this primitive dispensation notice these things:—1. The righteousness of God is the foundation. 2. The accordance of the world with God's heart, as at once commanding righteousness and hating violence, is the condition of its preservation. 3. The mercy of God is connected with his special revelations in and by the men who have found grace in his sight. 4. The provisions of redemption are embodied in an ark, which is the symbol of Divine ordinances and the associated life of believers. 5. The salvation of man is the real end and aim of all judgments. 6. With the redeemed human race there is a redeemed earth—creatures kept alive in the ark to commence, with the family of God, a new life. 7. While we must not push the symbology of the Flood too far, still it is impossible to overlook the figure which the Apostle Peter saw in the ark floating on the waters—the Church of Christ as washed by the Holy Ghost in those waters, which represent not the putting away of the filth of the flesh, but the answer of a good conscience toward God.—R.

Ver. 14.—*The way of safety.* Prediction of deluge and way of escape were alike trials of faith ; beyond reach of foresight; rejected or neglected by the world. Key to the typical meaning, 1 Pet. iii. 20, 21. Baptism the initial seal of the Christian covenant. Text therefore sets forth salvation through Christ.

I. "Make thee an ark." Why? Because sentence of death rests upon all men (Rom. v. 12). As in the destruction of first-born (Exod. xi. 5). No exceptions. Covenant people saved only by the blood ; so here (cf. Job ix. 30). Men, even now, are slow to believe this. Maxims of society contradict it. From childhood trained to live as if no danger, as if many things more important than salvation. And when preacher proclaims (Acts ii. 40), men listen and approve and go on as before. Yet this is the first step towards salvation, the first work of the Holy Spirit—to convince careless (Matt. xvi. 26) and well-living people that they cannot save themselves. Until this is done Christ has no attractiveness (Isa. liii. 2). Who would shut himself up in the ark if no deluge coming? Who would trust it if another way would afford safety?

II. "Make thee an ark." It is God's appointed way of safety. "The Lord hath made known his salvation." As surely as the deluge is according to his word, so surely is the way of deliverance (Rom. v. 20). But mark the way. Can you trust that which seems so frail? At the root of sin lies unbelief of God's truth. This caused the fall. God says, Will you trust me? One will say, I live a good life; is not that the main thing? (cf. 1 Cor. iii. 11). Another, I pray that God would love me, and be reconciled to me. Does he not love thee? (Titus iii. 4). Is he not longing for thee? (Isa. i. 18). And is not this unbelief of what God says? Thou needest indeed to pray that the Holy Spirit should open thine eyes to what God has done. But that thy prayer may be answered there must be the will to be taught (Ps. lxxxv. 8).

III. "Make thee an ark." THE TEST OF FAITH. There is a faith which does nothing, which merely accepts a doctrine. Such was not that of Noah. His life's work was to act on what he believed. The object of our faith is Jesus Christ, the personal, living, loving Saviour; not merely the doctrine that he died and rose again. "Make thee an ark" is more than knowledge that he is the Deliverer. It is taking refuge in him, and walking in his steps.—M.

EXPOSITION.

CHAPTER VII.

Ver. 1.—**And the Lord.** *Jehovah*, since Elohim now appears as the covenant God, though this change in the Divine name is commonly regarded by modern critics as betraying the hand of a Jehovist supplementer of the fundamental document of the Elohist (Bleek, Vaihinger, Davidson, Kalisch, Colenso, Alford); but "that the variations in the name of God furnish no criterion by which to detect different documents is evident enough from the fact that in ver. 5 Noah does as Jehovah commands him, while in ver. 16 Elohim alternates with Jehovah" (Keil). **Said unto Noah.** At the end of the 120 years, when the building of the ark had been completed, and only seven days before the Flood—doubtless by an audible voice still speaking to him from between the cherubim, which we can suppose had not yet vanished from the earth. **Come thou and all thy house into the ark.** *I. e.* prepare for entering; the actual entry taking place seven days later. So God ever hides his people before the storm bursts (cf. Isa. xxvi. 20). **For thee have I seen righteous** (*vide* ch. vi. 9) **before me.** Literally, *before my face;* not merely notifying the Divine observance of Noah's piety, but announcing the fact of his justification in God's sight. "To be righteous before God," the usual Scriptural phrase for justification (cf. Ps. cxliii. 2). **In this generation.** *Vide* ch. vi. 9. Indicating not alone the sphere of Noah's godly life, but its exceptional character; "involving an opposing sentence of condemnation against his contemporaries" (Lange).

Ver. 2.—**Of every clean beast.** That the distinction between clean and unclean animals was at this time understood is easier to believe than that the writer would perpetuate the glaring anachronism of introducing in prediluvian times what only took its rise

several centuries later (Kalisch). That this distinction was founded on nature, "every tribe of mankind being able to distinguish between the sheep and the hyena, the dove and the vulture" ('Speaker's Commentary'), or "on an immediate conscious feeling of the human spirit, not yet clouded by any ungodly and unnatural culture, which leads it to see in many beasts pictures of sin and corruption" (Keil), has been supposed; but with greater probability it was of Divine institution, with reference to the necessities of sacrifice (Ainsworth, Bush, Wordsworth; cf. ch. viii. 20). To this was appended in the Levitical system a distinction between clean and unclean in respect of man's food (Levit. xi. 3). **Shalt thou take**—inconsistent with ch. vi. 20, which says the animals were to come to Noah (Colenso); but ch. vi. 19, which says that Noah was to bring them, *i. e.* make them go (at least nearly equivalent to take), clearly recognises Noah's agency (Quarry)—**to thee by sevens.** Literally, *seven, seven;* either seven *pairs* (Vulgate, LXX., Aben Ezra, Clericus, Michaelis, De Wette, Knobel, Kalisch, Murphy, Alford, Wordsworth, 'Speaker's Commentary'), or seven individuals (Chrysostom, Augustine, Theodoret, Calvin, Pererius, Willet, Delitzsch, Rosenmüller, Keil, Lange, Bush); both parties quoting the next clause in support of their particular interpretation. Davidson, Colenso, and Kalisch challenge both interpretations as "irreconcilable with the preceding narrative" (ch. vi. 19); but the obvious answer is, that while in the first communication, which was given 120 years before, when minute instructions were not required, it is simply stated that the animals should be preserved by pairs; in the second, when the ark was finished and the animals were about to be collected, it is added that, in the case of the few clean beasts used for sacrifice, an exception should be made to the general rule, and not one pair, but either three pairs with one over, or seven pairs, should be preserved. **The male and his female.** This seems to be most in favour of the first interpretation, that pairs, and not individuals, are meant. **And of beasts that are not clean by two, the male and his female.** *Ish veishto.* Cf. ch. ii. 25, where the phrase denotes the ethical personality of human beings, to which there is here an approximation, as the preserved animals were designed to be the parents of subsequent races. The usual phrase for male and female, which is employed in ch. i. 28 (a so-called Elohistic) and ch. vii. 3 (a so-called Jehovistic section), refers to the physical distinction of sex in human beings.

Ver. 3.—**Of fowls also of the air by sevens, the male and the female.** *I. e.* of clean fowls, "which he leaves to be understood out of the foregoing verse" (Poole). The Samaritan, Syriac, and LXX. (not so Vulgate, Onkelos, Arabic) insert the word "clean" unnecessarily, and also add, "καὶ ἀπὸ πάντων τῶν πετεινῶν τῶν μὴ καθαρῶν δύο δύο ἄρσεν καὶ θῆλυ," manifestly to make the verse resemble the preceding. **To keep seed alive upon the face of all the earth.**

Vers. 4, 5.—**For yet seven days.** Literally, *for to days yet seven*—after seven days; thus giving Noah time to complete his preparations, and the world one more opportunity to repent, which Poole thinks many may have done, though their bodies were drowned for their former impenitency. **And I will cause it to rain**—literally, *I causing it*, the participle indicating the certainty of the future action (cf. ch. vi. 17 ; Prov. xxv. 22 ; cf. Ewald's 'Heb. Synt.,' § 306)— **upon the earth forty days and forty nights.** The importance assigned in subsequent Scripture to the number forty, probably from the circumstance here recorded, is too obvious to be overlooked. Israel wandered forty years in the wilderness (Num. xiv. 33). The scouts remained forty days in Canaan (Num. xiii. 26). Moses was forty days in the mount (Exod. xxiv. 18). Elijah fasted forty days and forty nights in the wilderness of Beersheba (1 Kings xix. 8). A respite of forty days was given to the Ninevites (Jonah iii. 4). Christ fasted forty days before the temptation (Matt. iv. 2), and sojourned forty days on earth after his resurrection (Acts i. 3). It thus appears to have been regarded as symbolical of a period of trial, ending in victory to the good and in ruin to the evil. **And every living substance—**

yekûm; literally, standing thing, *omne quod subsistit,* i. e. "whatever is capable by a principle of life of maintaining an erect posture" (Bush) ; ἀνάστημα (LXX. ; cf. Deut. xi. 6 ; Job xxii. 20)—**that I have made will I destroy**—literally, *blot out* (cf. ch. vi. 7)— **from off the face of the earth. And Noah did according to all that the Lord** (Jehovah, the God of salvation, who now interposed for the patriarch's safety ; in ch. vi. 22, where God is exhibited in his relations to all flesh, it is Elohim) **had commanded him.**

Ver. 6.—**And Noah was six hundred years old.** Literally, *a son of six hundred years,* i. e. in his 600th year (cf. ver. 11). The number six " is generally a Scriptural symbol of suffering. Christ suffered on the sixth day. In the Apocalypse the sixth seal, the sixth trumpet, the sixth vial introduce critical periods of affliction" (Wordsworth). **When the flood of waters was upon the earth.**

Ver. 7.—**And Noah went in.** *I. e.* began to go in a full week before the waters came (*vide* ver. 10). "A proof of faith and a warning to the world." **And his sons, and his wife, and his sons' wives with him.** In all eight persons (1 Pet. iii. 20) ; whence it is obvious that " each had but one wife, and that polygamy, as it began among the Cainites, was most probably confined to them" (Poole). **Into the ark, because of the waters of the flood.** Literally, *from the face* of the waters, being moved with fear and impelled by faith (Heb. xi. 7).

Vers. 8, 9.—**Of clean beasts, and of beasts that are not clean, and of fowls, and of every thing that creepeth upon the earth, there went in two and two into the ark, the male and the female.** In obedience to a Divine impulse. Nothing short of Divine power could have effected such a timely and orderly entrance of the creatures into the huge vessel (cf. their mode of exit, ch. viii. 18). The seeming inconsistency of this verse with ver. 2, which says that the clean animals entered the ark by sevens, will be at once removed by connecting vers. 7 and 8 instead of 8 and 9, and commencing a new sentence with ver. 9. It favours this, that "of" is awanting before "everything that creepeth," and that the LXX. begin ver. 8 with "and" (cf. Quarry, p. 373). **As God had commanded Noah.**

Ver. 10.—**And it came to pass after seven days** (literally, *at the seventh of the days*), **that the waters of the flood were upon the earth.**

HOMILETICS.

Vers. 1—9.—*The ark entered.* I. THE INVITATION OF JEHOVAH. "Come thou and all thy house into the ark." This invitation was—1. *Timely.* It was given on the finishing of the ark, and therefore not too soon ; also seven days before the Flood, and therefore not too late. God's interventions in his people's behalf are always opportune : witness the exodus from Egypt, the deliverance at the Red Sea, the destruction of Sennacherib's army ; Christ's walking on the sea, sleeping in the boat, rising from the dead. 2. *Special.* It was addressed in particular to Noah. "Come thou." "The Lord knoweth them that are his." "The Good Shepherd calleth his own sheep by name, and leadeth them out." So is the invitation of the gospel of the same personal and individual description (Matt. xiii. 9; Rev. iii. 6). Men are not summoned to believe in masses, but as individuals. 3. *Comprehensive.* "And all thy house." Whether Shem, Ham, and Japheth were at this time believers is not known. The noticeable circumstance is that the invitation was not addressed immediately to them, but mediately through their father. If Noah stood alone in his piety, their summons to enter the ark reminds us of the advantage of belonging to a pious family, and being even only externally connected with the Church (cf. Luke xix. 9; Acts xvi. 32). 4. *Gracious.* Given to Noah certainly, in one sense, because of his piety, (ch. vii. 1). But since his godliness was the fruit of faith, and his faith nothing more than a resting on the Divine covenant or promise, it was thus purely of grace. So is God's invitation in the gospel all of grace (Gal. i. 6; Ephes. iii. 8). 5. *Urgent.* Only seven days, and the Flood would begin. There was clearly not much time to lose. Only a seventh of the time given to the men of Nineveh (Jonah iii. 4). But not even seven days are promised in the gospel call (Matt. xxiv. 36; Rom. xiii. 12; Phil. iv. 5; James v. 9).

II. THE OBEDIENCE OF NOAH. "And Noah did according unto all that the Lord commanded him." This obedience was—1. *Immediate.* It does not appear that Noah trifled with the Divine summons, or in any way interposed delay ; and neither should sinful men with the invitation of the gospel (2 Cor. vi. 2; Heb. iii. 7). 2. *Believing.* It had its inspiration in a simple credence of the Divine word that safety could be secured only within the ark ; and not until the soul is prepared to accord a hearty trust to the statement that Christ is the heaven-provided ark of salvation for a lost world does it yield to the gospel call, and enter into the safe shelter of his Church by believing on his name (Ephes. i. 13). 3. *Personal.* Noah himself entered in. Had he not done so, not only would his own salvation have been missed, but his efforts to induce others to seek the shelter of the ark would have been fruitless. So the first duty of a herald of the gospel or minister of salvation is to make his own calling and election sure, after which his labours in behalf of others are more likely to be efficacious (1 Cor. ix. 27; 1 Tim. iv. 16). 4. *Influential.* The entire household of the patriarch followed his example. It is doubtful if at this time any of them were possessors of his faith. Yet all of them complied with the heavenly invitation, probably impelled thereto by the example and exhortation of their parent. When the head of a household becomes a Christian he in effect brings salvation to the house. He brings all its inmates into at least a nominal connection with the Church, encircles them with an atmosphere of religion emanating from his own character and conduct, and frequently through Divine grace is honoured to be the instrument of their salvation (Luke xix. 9; Acts xi. 14; xvi. 31). 5. *Minute.* Noah's entry into the ark in all particulars corresponded with the Divine invitation. The animals went in two and two, as God commanded. Men are not expected or allowed to deviate from the plain prescriptions of the word of God concerning the way of faith and salvation (Acts x. 33).

Learn—1. The unwearied diligence of God in saving men. 2. The personal nature of God's dealings with men. 3. The extreme solicitude with which he watches over them, who are his. 4. The indispensable necessity of obedience in order to salvation.

HOMILIES BY VARIOUS AUTHORS.

Vers. 1—6.—*God the Saviour inviting faith.* "Come thou and all thy house into the ark," &c. Covenant mercy. A type of the Christian Church, with its special privilege and defence, surrounded with the saving strength of God.

I. DIVINE PREPARATION. *Providence.* The ark. 1. Human agency under inspired direction. The word of God. The institutions of religion. The fellowship of saints.   2. A preparation made in the face of and in spite of an opposing world. The history of the Church from the beginning.   3. The preparation is safety and peace to those who trust in it, notwithstanding the outpoured judgment.

II. DIVINE FAITHFULNESS.   "Come *thou;* for *thee* have I seen righteous."   *Not* the merit of man is the ground of confidence, but the Lord's grace.   I have seen thee righteous because I have looked upon thee as an obedient servant, and have counted thy faith for righteousness.   Faithfulness in God is an object of man's trust as con nected with his spoken word and the preparation of his mercy.

III. DIVINE SUFFICIENCY.   The weak creatures in the ark surrounded by the destroying waters.   A refuge opened in God.   His blessing on the household.   His redemption succouring the individual soul, the life and its treasures, family peace and prosperity, &c.   The ark a type of the prepared salvation, carrying the believer through the flood of earthly cares and troubles, through the deep waters of death, to the new world of the purified heaven and earth, wherein dwelleth righteousness.—R.

Vers. 7—16.—*Realised salvation.*   "And Noah went in," &c.   "And the Lord shut him in" (vers. 7, 10, 16).

I. The CONTRAST between the position of the BELIEVER and that of the UNBELIEVER.   The difference between a true freedom and a false.   "*Shut in*" by the Lord to obedience, but also to peace and safety.   The world's judgment *shut out.* The restraints and privations of a religious life only temporary.   The ark will be opened hereafter.

II. THE METHOD OF GRACE ILLUSTRATED.   He that opens the ark for salvation shuts in his people for the completion of his work.   We cannot shut ourselves in. Our temptation to break forth into the world and be involved in its ruin.   The misery of fear.   Are we safe ?   Perseverance not dependent upon our self-made resolutions or provisions.   By various means we are shut in to the spiritual life.   Providentially ; by ordinances ; by bonds of fellowship.   We should look for the Divine seal.—R.

EXPOSITION.

Vers. 11, 12.—**In the six hundredth year of Noah's life, in the second month.**   Not (1) of Noah's 600th year (Knobel) ; but either (2) of the theocratic year, which began with Nisan or Abib (Exod. xii. 2 ; xiii. 4 ; xxiii. 15 ; xxxiv. 18 ; Deut. xvi. 1 ; Neh. ii. 1), either in March or April (Rabbi Joshua, Ambrose, Luther, Calvin, Mercerus, Hävernick, Kalisch, Alford, Wordsworth) ; or (3) of the civil year, which commenced with the autumnal equinox in the month Tisri, "called of old the first month, but now the seventh" (Chaldee Paraphrase ; Exod. xxiii. 16 ; xxxiv. 22), corresponding to September or October (Josephus, Rabbi Jonathan, Kimchi, Rosenmüller, Keil, Murphy, Bush, Ainsworth, 'Speaker's Commentary').   In support of the former may be alleged the usual Biblical mode of reckoning the sacred year by numbers, and in defence of the latter that the ecclesiastical year did not begin till the time of the Exodus.   **In the seventeenth day of the month.**   "The careful statement of the chronology, which marks with such exactness day and month in the course of this occurrence, puts all suspicion of the history to shame" (Hävernick).   **The same day were all the fountains of the great deep**—*i. e.* the

waters of the ocean (Job xxxviii. 16, 30 ; xli. 31 ; Ps. cvi. 9) and of subterranean reservoirs (Job xxviii. 4, 10 ; Ps. xxxiii. 7 ; Deut. viii. 7)—**broken up.**   "By a metynomy, because the earth and other obstructions were broken up, and so a passage opened for the fountains" (Poole).   "The niphal or passive form of בָּקַע denotes violent changes in the depths of the sea, or in the action of the earth—at all events in the atmosphere" (Lange).   **And the windows of heaven were opened.**   *Arubboth,* from *arabh,* to twine— network or lattices ; hence a window, as being closed with lattice-work instead of glass (Eccles. xii. 3) ; here the flood-gates of heaven, which are opened when it rains (cf. ch. viii. 2 ; 2 Kings vii. 19 ; Isa. xxiv. 18 ; Mal. iii. 10).   **And the rain was**—literally, *and there was* (happened, came) *violent rain;* גֶּשֶׁם, different from מָטָר, which denotes any rain, and is applied to other things which God pours down from heaven (Exod. ix. 18 ; xvi. 4)—**upon the earth forty days and forty nights** (cf. ch. vii. 4).   Though the language is metaphorical and optical, it clearly points to a change in the land level by which the ocean waters overflowed the depressed continent, accompanied with heavy and continuous rain, as the cause of the Deluge (contrast with this the works of the third and fourth creative days); yet "the exact statement of the natural causes that concurred in the Deluge is a circumstance which certainly in no wise removes the miraculous nature of the whole fact—who has unveiled the mysteries of nature?—but which certainly shows how exact was the attention paid to the external phenomena of the Deluge" (Hävernick).

Vers. 13, 14.—In the selfsame day—literally, *in the bone*, or *strength*, or *essence* (ch. ii. 23) *of that day*—in that very day (cf. ch. xvii. 23, 26); "about noonday, *i. e.* in the public view of the world" (Poole); "a phrase intended to convey the idea of the utmost precision of time" (Bush)—entered Noah, and Shem, and Ham, and Japheth, the sons of Noah, and Noah's wife, and the wives of his three sons with them, into the ark. Not inconsistent with vers. 4, 5, which do not necessarily imply that the actual entry was made seven days before the Flood; but merely that Noah then began to carry out the Divine instructions. The threefold recital of the entry—first in connection with the invitation or command (ver. 5), and again in the actual process during the seven days (ver. 7), and finally on the day when the Flood began (ver. 15),—besides lending emphasis to the narrative, heightens its dramatic effect. They, and every beast after his kind, and all the cattle after their kind, and every creeping thing that creepeth upon the earth after his kind, and every fowl after his kind, every bird of every sort (literally, *wing*). The creatures here specified correspond with the enumeration—viz., chay-yah, behemah, remes—in ch. i. 25, *q. v.* The last clause, *kol-canaph*, Kalisch, following Clericus, translates, though, according to Rosenmüller, without satisfactory reasons, "every winged creature," and so makes "three classes of winged beings—the eatable species (עוֹף), the birds which people the air and enliven it by the sounds of their melodies (עִפוֹר), and the endless swarms of insects (בָּנָף), the greatest part of which possess neither the utility of the former nor the beauty of the latter." Gesenius, however, translates it "birds of all kinds," and Knobel regards it as synonymous with "every bird." The LXX. give the sense of the two clauses: καὶ πᾶν ὄρνεον πετεινὸν κατὰ γένος αὐτοῦ.

Ver. 15.—And they went in unto Noah into the ark (cf. ch. vi. 20, which affirmed they should come), two and two of all flesh, wherein is the breath of life. Cf. the three expressions for an animated creature—חַיָּה נֶפֶשׁ (ch. i. 30), יְקוּם (ch. vii. 4), רוּחַ חַיִּים אֲשֶׁר־בּוֹ.

Ver. 16.—And they that went in, went in male and female of all flesh, as God (Elohim) had commanded him. This evidently closed an Elohistic passage, according to Colenso, as the ensuing clause as manifestly belongs to the Jehovistic interpolator; but the close connection subsisting between the two clauses forbids any such dislocation of the narrative as that suggested. "On the supposition of an independent Jehovistic narrative, Bishop Colenso feels it necessary to interpolate before the next statement the words, 'And Noah and all his house went into the ark'" (Quarry, p. 379). And the Lord (Jehovah) shut him in. Literally, *shut behind him*, i. e. closed up the door of the ark after him (ἔκλεισε τὴν κιβωτὸν ἔξωθεν αὐτοῦ, LXX.); doubtless miraculously, to preserve him both from the violence of the waters and the rage of men. The contrast between the two names of the Deity is here most vividly presented. It is Elohim who commands him about the beasts; it is Jehovah, the covenant God, who insures his safety by closing the ark behind him.

Vers. 17—19.—And the flood was forty days upon the earth. Referring to the forty days' and nights' rain of ver. 4 (τεσσαράκοντα ἡμέρας καὶ τεσσαράκοντα νύκτας, LXX.), during which the augmentation of the waters is described in a threefold degree. And the waters increased. Literally, *grew great*. The *first degree* of increase, marked by the *floating* of the ark. And bare up the ark, and it was lift up above the earth. Literally, *it was high from upon the earth*, i. e. it rose above it. And the waters prevailed. Literally, *were strong;* from גָּבַר, to be strong; whence the Gibborim of ch. vi. 4. And were increased greatly on the earth. Literally, *became great, greatly*. The *second degree* of increase, marked by the *going* of the ark. And the ark went—*i. e.* floated along; καὶ ἐπεφέρετο, LXX. (Ps. civ. 26)—upon the face of the waters. And the waters prevailed exceedingly. Literally, *and the waters became strong, exceedingly*. The *third degree* of increase, marked by the *submergence* of the mountains. And all the high hills, that were under the whole heaven, were covered. A clear assertion of the universality of the Flood (Keil, Kalisch, Alford, Bush, Wordsworth); but the language does not necessarily imply more than that all the high hills beneath the spectator's heaven were submerged (cf. ch. xli. 57; Exod. ix. 25; x. 15; Deut. ii. 25; 1 Kings x. 24; Acts ii. 5; Col. i. 25, for instances in which the universal terms *all* and *every* must be taken with a limited signification); while it is almost certain that, had the narrator even designed to record only the fact that all the heights within the visible horizon had disappeared beneath the rising waters, he would have done so by saying that "all the high hills under the whole heaven were covered." While, then, it is admitted that the words may depict a complete submergence of the globe, it is maintained by many competent scholars that the necessities of exegesis only demand a partial inundation (Poole, Murphy, Tayler Lewis, 'Speaker's Commentary,' Inglis).

Ver. 20.—**Fifteen cubits upward**—half the height of the ark—**did the waters prevail.** Literally, *become strong;* above the highest mountains obviously, and not above the ground simply ; as, on the latter alternative, it could scarcely have been added, **and the mountains were covered.**

Vers. 21, 22 describe the effect of the Deluge in its destruction of all animal and human life. **And all flesh died that moved upon the earth.** A general expression for the animal creation, of which the particulars are then specified. **Both of fowl, and of cattle, and of beast, and of every creeping thing that creepeth on the earth.** Literally, *in* fowl, and in cattle, &c. (cf. ver. 14). **And every man.** *I. e.* all the human race (with the exception of the inmates of the ark), which is further characterised as **all in whose nostrils** was **the breath of life.** Literally, *the breath of the spirit of lives,* i. e. all mankind. A clear pointing backwards to ch. ii. 7, which leads Davidson to ascribe vers. 22, 23 to the Jehovist, although Eichhorn, Tuch, Bleek, Vaihinger, and others leave them in the fundamental document, but which is rather to be regarded as a proof of the internal unity of the book. **Of all that** was **in the dry** land,—a further specification of the creatures that perished in the Flood,—**died.** It is obvious the construction of vers. 21, 22 may be differently understood. Each verse may be taken as a separate sentence, as in the A. V., or the second sentence may commence with the words, "And every man," as in the present exposition. Thus far the calamity is simply viewed in its objective result. In the words which follow, which wear the aspect of an unnecessary repetition, it is regarded in its relation to the Divine threatening.

Ver. 23. — **And every living substance was destroyed**—literally, *wiped out (of ch.* vi. 7; vii. 4)—**which was upon the face of the ground, both man, and**—literally, *from man unto*—**cattle, and the creeping things, and the fowl of the heaven; and they were destroyed**—wiped out by washing (cf. ch. vi. 7)—**from the earth : and Noah only remained alive, and they that were with him in the ark.** The straits to which the advocates of the documentary hypothesis are sometimes reduced are remarkably exemplified by the fortunes of these verses (21—23) in the attempt to assign them to their respective authors. Astruc conjectures that ver. 21 was taken from what he calls monumentum B, ver. 22 from "monument" A, and ver. 23 from monument C. Eichhorn ascribes vers. 21, 22 to an Elohistic author, and ver. 23 to a Jehovistic. Ilgen assigns vers. 21, 22 to the first, and ver. 23 to the second Elohist. Bleek, all three to the Elohist ; and Davidson ver. 21 to the Elohist, vers. 22, 23 to the Jehovist. Amid such uncertainty it will be reasonable to cling to the belief that Moses wrote all the three verses, at least till the higher criticism knows its own mind.

Ver. 24.—**And the waters prevailed upon the earth an hundred and fifty days**. Additional to the forty days of rain (Murphy), making 190 since the commencement of the Flood ; or more probably inclusive of the forty days (Knobel, Lange, Bush, Wordsworth, 'Speaker's Comment.,' Inglis), which, reckoning thirty days to the month, would bring the landing of the ark to the seventeenth day of the seventh month, as stated in ch. viii. 4.

HOMILETICS.

Ver. 19.—*Was the Flood universal ?* I. The Biblical account. Unquestionably the language of the historian appears to describe a complete submergence of the globe beneath a flood of waters, and is capable of being so understood, so far as exegesis can determine. Unquestionably also that this was the writer's meaning would never have been challenged had it not been for certain difficulties of a scientific nature, as well as of other kinds, which were gradually seen to attach to such hypothesis. But these difficulties having arisen in men's minds led to a closer and more careful investigation of the Scripture narrative, when it was found—1. That the language of the historian did not necessarily imply that the catastrophe described was of universal extent (*vide* Exposition). 2. That, if it had been only partial and local in its operation, in all probability the same, or at least closely similar, terms would have been selected to depict its appearance, as observed by a spectator. 3. That the purpose for which, according to the inspired record, the Deluge was sent could have been completely effected without the submergence of the entire globe— that purpose being the destruction of the human race, which, it is believed, had not at that time overspread the earth, but was confined to a limited region contiguous to the valley of the Euphrates. That this last conjecture is not of recent origin, but was early entertained by theologians, is proved by the facts that Aben Ezra "confuteth the opinion of some who in his days held the Deluge not to have been universal" (Willet); that Bishop Patrick notes (ch. vii. 19) that "there were those anciently, and they have their successors now, who imagined the Flood was not universal,—ἀλλ' ἐν ᾧ οἱ τότε ἄνθρωποι ᾤκουν,—but only there where men then dwelt;" that Matt. Poole writes, "Peradventure this Flood might not be universal over the whole earth, but only over all the habitable world, where either men or beasts lived, which was as much as either the meritorious cause of the Flood, men's sins, or the end of it, the destruction of all men and beasts, required" (Synopsis, ch. vii. 19); and that Bishop Stillingfleet in his 'Origines Sacræ' remarks, "I cannot see any necessity, from the Scriptures, to assert that the Flood did spread itself over all the surface of the earth. That all mankind (those in the ark excepted) were destroyed by it is most certain, according to the Scriptures; but from thence follows no necessity at all of asserting the universality of it as to the globe of the earth, unless it be sufficiently proved that the earth was peopled before the Flood, which I despair of ever seeing proved" (vide 'Quarry on Genesis,' p. 184). This opinion, it is almost needless to observe, has been adopted by the majority of modern scholars. 4. That subsequent Scriptural references to this primeval catastrophe are at least not decidedly at variance with the notion of a limited Deluge. Gen. ix. 15 places emphasis on the fact that the waters will no more become a flood to destroy all flesh, i. e. all mankind. Isa. liv. 9, pointing back to Gen. ix. 15, says that as God swore in the days of Noah that the earth would be no more inundated as to carry off the entire population, so did he swear then that he would not rebuke Israel. The language does not, as Wordsworth thinks, imply the universality of the Deluge. 2 Pet. ii. 5; iii. 6 refers to the destruction of the ἀρχαῖος κόσμος, i. e. the world of men, the κόσμος ἀσεβῶν specially mentioned in the former of these passages. So far then as Scripture is concerned we are not shut up to the necessity of regarding the Deluge as universal.

II. SCIENTIFIC DIFFICULTIES. 1. *Astronomical.* It is urged that, as there is no sufficient evidence of any general subsidence of the earth's crust, the theory proposed by some harmonists, that the land and water virtually exchanged places (this was supposed to be borne out by the existence of shells and corals at the top of high mountains), having now been completely abandoned (that the outlines of the great continental seas have been substantially the same from the beginning—vide ch. i. ver. 9, Expos.), the entire surface of the globe could be covered only by a large increase of water being added to the earth's mass. Kalisch supposes eight times the aggregate of water contained in all the seas and oceans of the earth; that this must have produced such a shock to the solar system as to have caused a very considerable aberration in the earth's orbit, of which, however, no trace can be detected; and that, consequently, it is unphilosophical to imagine that such a disturbance of the entire stellar world as would necessarily follow on that event would be resorted to in order to destroy a race of sinful beings in one of the smallest planets of the system. But—(1) Biblical science, which recognises an incarnation of the Word of God in order to save man, will always hesitate to pronounce anything too great for the Almighty to permit or do in connection with man. (2) It is gratuitous to infer that because a general subsidence of the earth's crust cannot now be traced, there was none. Absence of evidence that a thing was is not equivalent to presence of proof that a thing was not. Witness the third day's vegetation and antediluvian civilisation. (3) If even the earth's surface were covered with water, it is doubtful if it would be much more in effect than the breaking out of a profuse sweat upon the human body, or the filling up with water of the indentures on the rough skin of an orange, in which case it is more than probable that the apprehended disturbance of the solar system would prove in great part imaginary. 2. *Geological.* At one time believed to afford incontestable evidence of a universal deluge in the drift formations, the diluvium of the earlier geologists (of late, with better reason, ascribed to the influence of a glacial period which prevailed over the greater part of Central and Northern Europe in prehistoric times), geological science is now held to teach exactly the opposite. The extinct volcanoes of Languedoc and Auvergne are believed to have been in operation long anterior to the time of man's appearance on the earth, the remains of extinct animals being found among their scoriæ; and yet the lava cones are in many instances as perfect as when first thrown up, while the dross lies loose upon their sides, which it is scarcely supposable would be the case had they been subjected to any cataclysmal immersion such as is presupposed in the Deluge. But here the mistake is that of imagining the Noachic Flood to have been of any such violent torrential character. On the contrary, the Scripture narrative represents the waters as having risen and subsided slowly, and the whole phenomenon to have been of such a kind as, while destroying human life, to effect comparatively little change upon the face of nature; and, besides, careful scientific observers have declared that the volcanic scoriæ in question is not so loose as is sometimes alleged (Smith's 'Bib. Dict.,' art. Noah). 3. *Zoological.* This refers to the difficulty of accommodating all the animals that were then alive. So long of course as Raleigh's computation of eighty-nine distinct species of animals was accepted as correct, the task imposed upon apologists was not of a very formidable character. But of mammalia alone there are now known to exist 1658 different species, thus making about 4000 and upwards of individuals (the clean beasts being taken in sevens or seven pairs) that required to be stalled in the ark; and when to these are added the pairs of the 6000 birds, 650 reptiles, and 550,000 insects that are now recognised by zoologists, the difficulty is seen to be immensely increased. An obvious remark, however, in connection with this is that there is a tendency among modern zoologists unnecessarily to multiply the number of species. But in truth a prior difficulty relates to the collection of these multitudinous creatures from their respective habitats. If the entire surface of the globe was submerged, then must the fauna belonging to the different continents have been conveyed across the seas and lands towards the ark, and reconducted thence again to their appropriate settlements in some way not described and impossible to imagine; whereas if the inundated region extended (through the subsidence of the earth's crust) to the Mediterranean on the west, and the Indian Ocean on the south and east, it is apparent that neither would this difficulty have proved insuperable, nor would the collection of the animals have been rendered unnecessary, the devastated country being so wide that only by preservation of the species could it have been speedily replenished.

III. The CONCLUSION, therefore, seems to be that, while Scripture does not imperatively forbid the idea of a partial Deluge, science appears to require it, and, without ascribing to all the scientific objections that are urged against the universality of the Flood that importance which their authors assign to them, it may be safely affirmed that there is considerable reason for believing that the *mabbul* which swept away the antediluvian men was confined to the region which they inhabited.

Ver. 23.—*The Deluge.* I. A STRIKING TESTIMONY TO THE DIVINE FAITHFULNESS. 1. *In respect of threatenings against the wicked.* Whether the faith of Noah ever betrayed symptoms of wavering during the long interval of waiting for the coming of the Flood it is impossible to say; it can scarcely be doubted that the men who for six score years had seen the sun rise and set with unwearied regularity, that had watched the steady and continuous movement of nature's laws and forces throughout the passing century, oftentimes exclaimed, "Where is the promise of his coming, for all things continue as they were from the beginning?" And yet God kept his word, and fulfilled his threatening. "The flood came, and took them all away" (Matt. xxiv. 39). Cf. the Divine threatenings against Babylon (Jer. li. 33), against Tyre (Isa. xxiii. 12), against Jerusalem (2 Kings xxi. 13; Jer. xxvi. 18), against the Jews (Deut. xxviii. 49). Let impenitent sinners thereby be reminded that there is one more word of doom which he will yet cause to come to pass (Ps. ix. 17; 2 Thess. i. 8; 2 Pet. iii. 10). 2. *In respect of promises to the saints.* At the same time that he foretold to Noah the destruction of his licentious and violent contemporaries, he distinctly promised that he would establish his covenant with Noah, and preserve both him and his amid the general overthrow. And that too he implemented in due time and to the letter. Let the saints then learn to trust the precious promises of God

(2 Pet. i. 4) which have been given to enable them to escape the corruption that is in the world through lust (τῆς ἐν κόσμῳ ἐν ἐπιθυμίᾳ φθορᾶς, i. e. the destruction that is already operating in the world and coming out of, as it is carried in, the world's lust).

II. A SIGNAL DISPLAY OF THE DIVINE POWER. 1. *In controlling his creatures.* (1) *In collecting the animals,* which he did, doubtless, by making use of their instincts which led them to apprehend the coming danger. *Vide* Job xxxix.—xli. for God's power over the animal creation. (2) *In using the powers of nature*—breaking up the flood-gates of the deep, and opening the windows of heaven. The phenomenon was distinctly miraculous; but if God made the world, causing it to stand together out of the water and through the water, the supernatural character of the Deluge should not occasion difficulty. Nor should the power of God be overlooked in the ordinary phenomena of nature. "Nature is but another name for an effect whose cause is God." In the miracle God reveals what he is always silently and imperceptibly doing in the natural event. Nothing happens in the realm of providence without the concurrence of Almighty power (Amos iii. 6; Matt. x. 29). Let God's power exhibited over nature's forces remind us of his ability to bring the present terrestrial economy to an end as he has promised (2 Pet. iii. 10, 11). (3) *In destroying the lives of men.* In every case life is a gift of God, and can only be recalled by him (Deut. xxxii. 39; 2 Sam. ii. 6). Yet, unless when God interposes to destroy on a large scale,—*e. g.* by famine, pestilence, war, accident,—his absolute and unchallengeable control over men's lives (Ps. xxxi. 15) is apt to be forgotten. And with what infinite ease he can depopulate the fairest and most crowded regions he has often shown; witness, in addition to the Flood, the destruction of the cities of the plain (ch. xix. 24, 25), of the first-born in Egypt (Exod. xii. 29), of the army of Pharaoh (Exod. xiv. 27), of the host of Sennacherib (2 Kings xix. 35). 2. *In punishing his enemies.* That appalling visitation is fitted to remind us that God is able to execute vengeance—(1) *On the greatest sinners.* Having cast down the sinning angels, and drowned the world of the ungodly, and burnt up the filthy Sodomites, it is scarcely likely that any criminal will be beyond his power to apprehend and chastise (2 Pet. ii. 9; Jude 15). (2) *In the severest forms.* Having all the resources of nature at his command,—the gleaming thunderbolt, the sweeping flood, the sleeping volcano, the tempestuous hurricane, all the several and combined potencies of fire, air, earth, and water,—he can never want a weapon wherewith to inflict upon his adversaries "the tribulation and wrath, indignation and anguish," he has decreed for their portion (Rom. ii. 8, 9; 2 Thess. i. 8, 9; Rev. xx. 15; xxi. 8). (3) *At the most unexpected times.* Few things connected with the Noachic Deluge are more impressive and paralysing to the mind than the suddenness of the surprisal with which it sprang upon the wicked generation that for 120 years had been disbelieving its reality and ridiculing the warnings of the patriarch. "SO ALSO SHALL THE COMING OF THE SON OF MAN BE." (4) *With the most inevitable certainty.* Tempted by their long lives to imagine that the penalty of death was cancelled or had become inoperative, or at least would not really be put in force against them, these men of the first age were recalled from their delusive reasonings. The Deluge was God's proclamation that the penalty was still in force against sinners, God's explanation of what that penalty meant, God's certification that that penalty was sure. 3. *In protecting his people.* The ark floating on the waters was a visible sermon to all time coming of God's ability to save them who believe and obey him. And, like the shelter enjoyed by Noah, the salvation which God bestows upon his people is (1) *gracious*—flowing from the Divine mercy; (2) *free*—with no condition attached except that men shall, like Noah, believe and obey; (3) *adequate*—containing all that is required for their spiritual necessities, as the ark held abundant provision for the voyage; (4) *secure*—"the Lord shut him in." So says Christ, "I give unto them eternal life, and they shall never perish" (John x. 28).

III. A SOLEMN ATTESTATION OF THE DIVINE HOLINESS. Proclaiming—1. *That the Divine character was holy.* A deity who is himself subject to imperfection is inconceivable. But sinful men are prone to forget that God is of purer eyes than to look upon iniquity. In this last age of the world God has discovered that to men by sending forth an image or likeness of himself in the person of his Son, who was holy, harmless, undefiled, and separate from sinners (cf. John xiv. 9).   In the first age he announced the same great truth by the water-flood.   2. *That the Divine law was holy.*   That, besides being himself personally pure, he requires sinless obedience at the hands of his creatures, the Almighty has in every separate era or epoch of human history taken pains to inform men ; in Edenic times by the forbidden tree ; in ante-diluvian by the Deluge ; in Mosaic by Mount Sinai ; in Christian by the cross of Calvary.   3. *That the Divine government was holy.*   That from the first the world has been governed in the interests of holiness is unmistakably the doctrine of Scripture. If any in Noah's time believed either that God was indifferent to righteousness, or that it was possible for "the throne of iniquity to have fellowship" with him, they must have been terribly undeceived when the crack of doom was heard above their heads.   So will it be when the righteous Judge reveals himself a second time in flaming fire to render unto every man according to his deeds.

Lessons :—1. "It is impossible for God to lie" (Heb. vi. 18).   2. "There is nothing too hard for the Lord" (Gen. xviii. 14).   3. "It is a fearful thing to fall into the hands of the living God" (Heb. x. 31).

HOMILIES BY VARIOUS AUTHORS.

Ver. 16.—*The believer's safety.*   Parable of the ten virgins speaks of a final separation.   "The door was shut."   There our thoughts are turned to those without ; here, to those within.   The time was come when the choice must be made.   "Come thou and all thy house into the ark."   The broad and narrow way.   The confinement of the ark or the freedom of home ; and, in view of the flood, the frail vessel or the mountains.   Trust in Christ or trust in self (cf. Rom. x. 3).   He chose the way of faith.   God shut him in (cf. Isa. xxvi. 3).   He knew he was safe.   The world saw no good in it.   The pause of seven days (ver. 10) illustrates the present state. Believers rejoicing in their safety ; the world unconvinced of danger.

I. CHRIST OFFERS SAFETY TO ALL.   The ark was prepared that all might be saved. The condemnation was because they did not care (John iii. 19).   There was room and welcome for all who would come (cf. Luke xiv. 22).   Noah did not preach impossible things.   When Jericho was destroyed Rahab was saved.   When Sodom, Lot.   God bids all seek and find refuge in Christ (Rom. iii. 22).

II. CHRIST IS A REFUGE FROM THE CONVICTION OF SIN.   How many are living without serious concern.   Not rejecting the gospel ; they hear it, and approve, and think that all is well.   Like St. Paul, "alive without the law."   God's commandments not understood ; his holiness not known.   Let such a one be led to see how God's law reaches to the springs of life and feeling, and to feel the working of the "law of sin" in his members ; then what a flood.   "Who will show us any good ?" Good deeds cannot give peace.   Worldly good as wormwood.   Conscience repeats, He has been knocking, and I have not opened (Prov. i. 26).   Yet, hark ! his voice again : "Come unto me."   It is not too late.   Even now, if thou wilt, the Lord will shut thee in.

III. THE SAFETY OF THOSE WHO BELIEVE, whom God shuts in.   Who shall lay anything to their charge ?   Who shall condemn ?   Who shall separate ? (Rom. viii. 33—35).   The flood is without.   Noah is weak and helpless as the world.   His safety is God's refuge.   The Christian is surrounded by evil influences, messengers of Satan.   Temptations to worldliness or to spiritual pride ; cares and anxieties hindering prayer ; suggestions of unbelief, and hard thoughts of God ; the fainting of nature because so little progress made.   But in Christ is safety.   Coming to him daily as we are ; with weak faith, with many perplexities, with the marks of many falls.   His word is, "I will never leave thee nor forsake thee."   In the trials of life "we are more than conquerors through him that loved us."—M.

EXPOSITION.

CHAPTER VIII.

Ver. 1.—**And God**. *Elohim*, i. e. God in his most universal relation to his creatures. The supposition of two different accounts or histories being intermingled in the narrative of the Flood (Bleek, Eichhorn, Hupfeld, Kalisch, Alford, Colenso) is not required for a sufficient explanation of the varying use of the Divine names. **Remembered**. From a root signifying to prick, pierce, or print, *e. g.*, upon the memory; hence to remember. "Not that there is oblivion or forgetfulness with God, but then God is said to remember when he showeth by the effects that he hath taken care of man" (Willet). He remembers man's sins when he punishes them (Ps. xxv. 7; cf. 1 Kings xvii. 20), and his people's needs when he supplies them (cf. Neh. v. 19). The expression is an anthropopathism designed to indicate the Divine compassion as well as grace. Calvin thinks the remembrance of which Moses speaks "ought to be referred not only to the external aspect of things (*i. e.* the coming deliverance), but also to the inward feeling of the holy man," who, through grace, was privileged to enjoy "some sensible experience of the Divine presence" while immured in the ark. **Noah,** —cf. the Divine remembrance of Abraham and Lot (ch. xix. 29), the request of the Hebrew psalmist (Ps. cxxxii. 1)—**and every living thing,**—chayyah, or wild beast (*vide* ch. i. 25; vii. 14)—**and all the cattle that was** with **him in the ark**. A touching indication of the tenderness of God towards his creatures (cf. Deut. xxv. 4; Ps. xxxvi. 6; cxlv. 9, 15, 16; Jonah iv. 11). As a proof that God remembered the lonely inmates of the ark, he at once takes steps to accomplish their deliverance, which steps are next enumerated. **And God made a wind** — *ruach*. Not the Holy Ghost, as in ch. i. 2 (Theodoret, Ambrose, LXX.— πνεῦμα), nor the heat of the sun (Rupertus); but a current of air (ἄνεμος), which "would promote evaporation and aid the retreat of the waters" (Murphy):—the ordinary method of driving away rain and drying the ground (*vide* Prov. xxv. 23); the special instrumentality employed to divide the waters of the Red Sea (Exod. xiv. 21)—**to pass over the earth, and the waters assuaged,** or *began to grow calm*, after a period of commotion (cf. Esther ii. 1; vii. 10)—the first stage in the returning of the waters. Καὶ ἐκόπασε τὸ ὕδωρ, and the water grew tried (LXX.). Cf. ἐκόπασεν ὁ ἄνεμος, Matt. xiv. 32; Mark iv. 39; vi. 51.

Ver. 2.—**The fountains also of the deep, and the windows of heaven were stopped.**

וַיִּסָּכְרוּ, from סָכַר = סָגַר, to surround, to enclose; literally, *were shut up; ἐπεκαλύφθησαν* (LXX.). Their opening was described in ch. vii. 11. **And the rain from heaven was restrained.** וַיִּכָּלֵא, literally, *was shut up,* from כָּלָא, to close. Cf. κλείω, κωλύω, κολούω, *celo, occulo* (Gesenius, Fürst), συνεσχέθη (LXX.). At the end of the forty days (ch. vii. 12; Augustine, Willet); at the end of the 150 days (Aben Ezra, Murphy).

Ver. 3.—**And the waters returned from off the earth continually**. Literally, *going and returning.* "More and more" (Gesenius). The first verb expresses the continuance and self-increasing state of the action involved in the second; cf. ch. xxvi. 13; 1 Sam. vi. 12; 2 Kings ii. 11 (Fürst). Gradually (Murphy, Ewald). The expression "denotes the turning-point after the waters had become calm" (T. Lewis). May it not be an attempt to represent the undulatory motion of the waves in an ebbing tide, in which the water seems first to advance, but only to retire with greater vehemence, reversing the movement of a flowing tide, in which it first retires and then advances—in the one case returning to go, in the other going to return? The LXX., as usual, indicates the visible effect rather than the actual phenomenon: καὶ ἐνεδίδου τὸ ὕδωρ πορευόμενον ἀπὸ τῆς γῆς. **And after the end of the hundred and fifty days the waters were abated.** Literally, *were cut off,* hence diminished; *imminutæ sunt* (Vulgate); ἠλαττονοῦτο τὸ ὕδωρ (LXX.). The first stage was the quieting of the waters; the second was the commencement of an ebbing or backward motion; the third was a perceptible diminution of the waters.

Ver. 4.—**And the ark rested**. Not stopped sailing or floating, got becalmed, and remained suspended over (Kitto's 'Cyclop.,' art. Ararat), but actually grounded and settled on (Tayler Lewis) the place indicated by עַל (cf. ver. 9; also Exod. x. 14; Numb. x. 36; xi. 25, 26; Isa. xi. 2). **In the seventh month, on the seventeenth day of the month**. *I. e.* exactly 150 days from the commencement of the forty days' rain, reckoning thirty days to a month, which seems to confirm the opinion expressed (ch. vii. 24) that the forty days were included in the 150. Supposing the Flood to have begun in Marchesvan, the second month of the civil year (about the beginning of November), "we have then the remarkable coincidences that on the 17th day of Abib (about the beginning of April) the ark rested on Mount Ararat, the Israelites passed over the Red Sea, and our Lord rose again from the dead" ('Speaker's Commentary'). **Upon the mountains.** *I. e.* one of the mountains. "Pluralis numerus pro singulari ponitur" (cf. ch. xxi. 7 ; xlvi. 7 ; Judges xii. 7 ; vide Gloss, Ebilel Soon Tract,' 1 aap xiv. p. 866). **Of Ararat.** 1. It is agreed by all that the term *Ararat* describes a region. 2. This region has been supposed to be the island of Ceylon (Samaritan), Aryâvarta, the sacred land to the north of India (Von Bohlen, arguing from Gen. xi. 2) ; but "it is evident that these and such like theories have been framed in forgetfulness of what the Bible has recorded respecting the locality" (Kitto's 'Cyclopedia,' art. Ararat). 3. The locality which appears to have the countenance of Scripture is the region of Armenia (cf. 2 Kings xix. 37 ; Isa. xxxvii. 38 ; Jeremiah li. 27 ; Aquila, Symmachus, Theodotion, Vulgate). 4. In Armenia three different mountains have been selected as the site on which the ark grounded. (1) The modern Ararat, which rises in Northern Armenia, about twelve miles south of Erivan, in the form of two majestic cones, the one 16,254, and the other 12,284 feet (Parisian) in height above the level of the sea (Hieronymus, Fürst, Kalisch, Keil, Delitzsch, and Lange). All but universal tradition has decided that the loftiest of these two peaks (called Macis in Armenian ; Aghri-Dagh, *i. e.* the difficult or steep mountain, by the Turks ; Kuchi Nuch, *i. e.* the mountain of Noah, by the Persians) was the spot where the sacred vessel first felt the solid land. Travellers describe the appearance of this amazing elevation as of incomparable and overpowering splendour. "It appeared as if the highest mountains in the world had been piled upon each other to form this one sublime immensity of earth and rocks and snow. The icy peaks of its double head rose majestically into the clear and cloudless heavens ; the sun blazed bright upon them, and the reflection sent forth a radiance equal to other suns" (Ker Porter's 'Travels,' i. 132 ; ii. 636). "Nothing can be more beautiful than its shape, more awful than its height. All the surrounding mountains sink into insignificance when compared to it. It is perfect in all its parts ; no hard, rugged feature, no unnatural prominences ; everything is in harmony, and all combines to render it one of the sublimest objects in nature" (Morier's 'Journey,' i. 16 ; ii. 312, 345). The ascent of the Kara Dagh, or Greater Ararat, which the Armenians believe to be guarded by angels from the profane foot of man, after two unsuccessful attempts, was accomplished in 1829 by Professor Parrot, a German, and five years later, in 1834, by

the Russian traveller Automonoff. In 1856 five English travellers, Majors Stewart and Frazer, Rev. Walter Thursby, Messrs. Theobald and Evans, performed the herculean task. The latest successful attempt was that of Prof. Bryce of Oxford in 1876 (*vide* 'Transcaucasia and Ararat:' London: Macmillan and Co, 1877) (?) An unknown mountain in Central Armenia between the Araxes and lakes Van and Urumiah (Vulgate, *super montes Armeniæ;* Gesenius, Murphy, Wordsworth, Bush, 'Speaker's Commentary'). (3) A peak in the Gordyæan mountains, or Carduchian range, separating Armenia on the south from Kurdistan (Chaldee Paraphrase, Onkelos, Syriac, Calvin), near which is a town called Naxuana, the city of Noah (Ptolemy), Idshenan (Moses Chorenensis), and Nachidshenan, the first place of descent (the Armenians), which Josephus translates by ἀποβατήριον, or the place of descent. Against the first is the inaccessible height of the mountain; in favour of the third is the proximity of the region to the starting-place of the ark.

Ver. 5.—**And the waters decreased continually**—literally, *were going and decreasing*—**until the tenth month : in the tenth** month, **on the first** day **of the month,**—*chodesh,* a lunar month, beginning at the new moon, from *châdâsh,* to be new ; νεομηνία, LXX. (cf. Exod. xiii. 5). *Chodesh yâmim,* the period of a month (cf. ch. xxix. 14 ; Num. xi. 20, 21)—**were the tops of the mountains seen.** "Became distinctly visible" (Tayler Lewis, who thinks they may have previously projected above the waters). *Apparuerunt cacumina montium* (Vulgate). The waters had now been subsiding ten weeks, and as the height of the water above the highest hills was probably determined by the draught of the ark, we may naturally reason that the subsidence which had taken place since the seventeenth day of the seventh month was not less than three hundred and fifteen inches, at twenty-one inches to the cubit, or about four and one-third inches a day.

Vers. 6, 7.—**And it came to pass**—literally, *it was*—**at the end of forty days.** Delaying through combined fear and sorrow on account of the Divine judgment (Calvin) ; to allow sufficient space to undo the effect of the forty days' rain (Murphy) ; probably just to be assured that the Deluge would not return. **That Noah opened the window** — *chalôn,* a window, "so called from being perforated, from *chalal,* to bore or pierce" (Gesenius) ; used of the window of Rahab's house (Josh. ii. 18) ; not the window (*tsôhar*) of ch. vi. 16, *q. v.*—**of the ark which he had made : and he sent forth a raven.** Literally, *the orev,* "so called from its black colour' (Gesenius ; cf. Cant. v. 11), Latin, *corvus,* a raven or crow ; the article being used either (1) because the species of bird is intended to be indicated (Kalisch), or (2) because there was only one male raven in the ark, the raven being among the unclean birds (Levit. xi. 15; Deut. xiv. 14; Lange); but against this is "the dove" (ver. 8); or (3) because it had come to be well known from this particular circumstance (Keil). Its peculiar fitness for the mission imposed on it lay in its being a bird of prey, and therefore able to sustain itself by feeding on carrion (Prov. xxx. 17). To the incident here recorded is doubtless to be traced the prophetic character which in the ancient heathen world, and among the Arabians in particular, was supposed to attach to this ominous bird. **Which went to and fro.** Literally, *and it went forth going and returning*, i. e. flying backwards and forwards, from the ark and to the ark, perhaps resting on it, but not entering into it (Calvin, Willet, Ainsworth, Keil, Kalisch, Lange, Bush, 'Speaker's Commentary'); though some have conceived that it no more returned to the ark, but kept flying to and fro throughout the earth (LXX., "καὶ ἐξελθὼν οὐκ ἀνέστρεψεν;" Vulgate, "qui egrediebatur et non revertebatur;" Alford, "it is hardly probable that it returned;" Murphy, "it did not need to return"). **Until the waters were dried up from off the earth.** When of course its return was unnecessary. Cf. for a similar form of expression 2 Sam. vi. 23. Whether it entirely disappeared at the first, or continued hovering round the ark, Noah was unable from its movements to arrive at any certain conclusion as to the condition of the earth, and accordingly required to adopt another expedient, which he did in the mission of the dove.

Vers. 8, 9.—**Also he sent forth**—ver. 10 seems to warrant the inference that this was after an interval of seven days (Baumgarten, Knobel, Keil, Lange)—**a dove.** Literally, *the* dove. The Scriptural references to the dove are very numerous: cf. Ps. lxviii. 14 (its beautiful plumage); Levit. v. 7; xii. 6 (its sacrificial use); Isa. xxxviii. 14; lix. 11 (its plaintive notes); Ps. lv. 6 (its power of flight); Matt. x. 16 (its gentleness); *vide* also the metaphorical usage of the term in Cant. i. 15; v. 12 (beautiful eyes); Cant. v. 2; vi. 9 (a term of endearment). **From him.** *I. e.* from himself, from the ark; not ὀπίχω αὐτοῦ (LXX.), *post eum* (Vulgate); *i. e.* after the raven. Lange thinks the expression indicates that the gentle creature had to be driven from its shelter out upon the wide waste of water. **To see if the waters were abated**—literally, *lightened*, i. e. decreased (ver. 11)—**from off the face of the ground; but the dove found no rest for the sole of her foot.** The earth being not yet dry, but wet and muddy, and doves delighting to settle only on such places as are dry and

clean; or the mountain tops, though visible, being either too distant or too high, and doves delighting in valleys and level plains, whence they are called *doves of the valleys* (Ezek. vii. 16). **And she returned unto him into the ark, for the waters** were **upon** (literally, *waters upon;* a much more graphic statement than appears in the A. V.) **the face of the whole earth : then** (literally, *and*) **he put forth his hand, and took her, and pulled her in** (literally, *caused her to come in*) **unto him into the ark.**

Ver. 10. — **And he stayed.** וַיָּחֶל, fut. apoc., Hif. of חוּל, to turn, to twist, to be afraid, to tremble, to wait (Fürst); fut. apoc. Kal (Gesenius). **Yet other seven days.** עוֹד, prop. the inf. absol. of the verb עוּד, to go over again, to repeat; hence, as an adverb, conveying the idea of doing over again the action expressed in the verb (cf. ch. xlvi. 29; Ps. lxxxiv. 5). **And again he sent forth**—literally, *he added to send* (cf. vers. 12, 21)—**the dove out of the ark.**

Ver. 11.—**And the dove came in unto him.** Literally, *to him.* As the manner of doves is, partly for better accommodation both for food and lodging than yet he could meet with abroad, and partly from love to his mate (Poole). **In the evening** (of the seventh day). **And, lo, in her mouth was an olive leaf plucked off.** Not as if "Deo jubente, uno die germinavit terra" (Ambrose), but because the olive leaves kept green under water (Chrysostom). Rosenmüller, Lange, and Kalisch quote Pliny (xiii. 50) and Theophrastus ('Hist. Plant.,' iv. 8) to this effect. That the olive tree grows in Armenia is proved by the testimony of Strabo (xi. 575), Horace (Od. I. vii. 7), Virgil (Georg. ii. 3), Diodorus Siculus (i. 17), &c. On this point *vide* Kalisch. The leaf which the dove carried towards the ark was "taraf," freshly plucked; hence rightly translated by "viride" (Michaelis, Rosenmüller) rather than by "decerptum" (Chaldee, Arabic) or "raptum" (Calvin). Κάρφος (LXX.) is just the opposite of "fresh," viz., withered. **So Noah knew that the waters were abated from off the earth.**

Ver. 12.—**And he stayed.** וַיִּיָּחֶל; Niph. fut. of יָחַל (Gesenius); cf. וַיָּחֶל (ver. 10), Hiph. fut. of חוּל (Fürst, Delitzsch). Tayler Lewis, following Jewish authorities, would derive both from יָחַל; with Aben Ezra making the first a regular Niphal, and with Rashi the second a contracted Piel (*vide* Lange, p. 308; Clark's 'For. Theol. Lib.'). **Yet other seven days.** The frequent repetition of the number seven clearly points to the hebdomadal division of the week, and the institution of Sabbatic rest (*vide* ch. ii.

1—3, Expos.). **And sent forth the dove.** "The more we examine these acts of Noah, the more it will strike us that they must have been of a religious nature. He did not take such observations, and so send out the birds, as mere arbitrary acts, prompted simply by his curiosity or his impatience ; but as a man of faith and prayer he inquired of the Lord. What more likely then that such inquiry should have its basis in solemn religious exercises, not arbitrarily entered into, but on days held sacred for prayer and religious rest?" (T. Lewis). **Which returned not again** (literally, *and it added not to return*) **unto him any more.**
Ver. 13.—**And it came to pass** (literally, *it was*) **in the six hundredth and first year** (of Noah's life ; so LXX.), **in the first** month, — τοῦ πρώτου μηνὸς, (LXX.) ; the word for month (expressed in vers. 4, 14) being omitted in the Hebrew text for brevity,—**the first** day **of the month, the waters were dried up**—the root signifies to burn up or become dry in consequence of heat (Fürst) ; "it merely denotes the absence of water" (Gesenius)—**from off the earth : and Noah removed the covering of the ark**—*mikseh,* from *kasah,* to cover ; used of the covering of the ark (Exod. xxvi. 14) and of the holy vessels (Num. iv. 8, 12), and hence supposed to be made of skins (Knobel, Bush) ; but "the deck of an ark on which the rain-storms spent their force must surely have been of as great stability as the ark itself (Lange)— **and looked, and, behold, the face of the ground was dry.**
Ver. 14.—**And in the second month, on the seven and twentieth day of the month, was the earth dried.** יָבְשָׁה. The three Hebrew verbs employed to depict the gradual cessation of the floods express a regular gradation ; קָלַל (ver. 11), to be lightened, signifying their abatement or diminution (κεκόπακε τὸ ὕδωρ, LXX.) ; חָרַב (ver. 13), to be dried up, indicating the disappearance of the

water (ἐξέλιπε τό ὕδωρ, LXX.) ; יָבֵשׁ (ver. 14), to be dry, denoting the desiccation of the ground (ἐξηράνθη ἡ γῆ, LXX.). Cf. Isa. xix. 5, where there is a similar gradation : וְנָהָר יֶחֱרַב וְיָבֵשׁ, and the river shall be wasted and dried up.

CHRONOLOGY OF THE FLOOD.

(Reckoning from the first day of the year.)

		mos.	days	days
I.	Beginning of the Flood	1	17 =	47
	Continuance of Rain		=	40
	Prevalence of Waters		=	110
II.	The Ark touches Ararat	6	17 =	197
III.	The Mountains seen	9	=	270
	Raven sent after 40 days		=	310
	Dove sent ,, 7 ,,		=	317
	Dove sent ,, 7 ,,		=	324
	Dove sent ,, 7 ,,		=	331
IV.	The Waters dried up	12	=	360
V.	The Earth dry	13	27 =	417

The data are insufficient to enable us to determine whether the Noachic year was solar or lunar. It has been conjectured that the year consisted of twelve months of thirty days, with five intercalated days at the end to make up the solar year of three hundred and sixty-five days (Ewald) ; of seven months of thirty days and five of thirty-one (Bohlen) ; of five of thirty and seven of twenty-nine (Knobel) ; but the circumstance that the period from the commencement of the Deluge to the touching of Ararat extended over five months exactly, and that the waters are said to have previously prevailed for one hundred and fifty days, naturally leads to the conclusion that the months of Noah's year were equal periods of thirty days.

HOMILETICS.

Vers. 4, 18.—*Mount Ararat, or the landing of the ark.* That disembarkment on the mountain heights of Ararat was an emblem of another landing which shall yet take place, when the great gospel ship of the Christian Church shall plant its living freight of redeemed souls upon the hills of heaven. Everything that Mount Ararat witnessed on that eventful day will yet be more conspicuously displayed in the sight of God's believing people who shall be counted worthy of eternal life.

I. SIN PUNISHED. *Mount Ararat was a solemn witness to the severity of God's judgments upon a guilty world.* Never had the world looked on such a vindication of the insulted holiness and offended justice of Almighty God, and never will it look upon another till the hour strikes when "the heavens, being on fire, shall dissolve" (2 Pet. iii. 10), and "the Lord himself shall be revealed in flaming fire" (2 Thess. i. 7).

II. GRACE REVEALED. *Mount Ararat saw Divine grace displayed to sinful men.* Pre-eminently Noah and his family were debtors to Divine grace that day when they stepped forth from the ark; and who can doubt that a sense of the richness of Divine grace in saving them will be one of the first feelings to take possession of the souls of the ransomed on reaching heaven?

III. SALVATION ENJOYED. *Mount Ararat beheld salvation enjoyed by believing sinners.* The deliverance of Noah and his family was a type of the salvation of the saints, which, however, is immeasurably grander than that of Noah. 1. In *kind*, as being a spiritual, and not merely a temporal, deliverance. 2. In *degree*, as being complete; whereas Noah's was at the best an imperfect deliverance—a deliverance from the Flood, but not from that which caused the Flood—sin. 3. In *duration*. Noah's deliverance was only for a time—in the end he descended to the grave; the deliverance of the saints is for ever (Luke xx. 36).

IV. GRATITUDE EXPRESSED. *Mount Ararat heard the adorations and thanksgivings of a redeemed family.* In Noah's sacrifice was a wonderful commingling of ideas and emotions,—(1) faith, (2) penitence, (3) thanksgiving, (4) consecration,— all of which will have a place within the bosoms of the ransomed host who yet shall sit upon the sea of glass. If not the offering up of sacrificial victims, as the expression of the soul's faith, there will be (1) in the midst of the throne a Lamb as it had been slain; (2) the continual offering up of broken and of contrite hearts; (3) the chanting of perpetual hosannas and hallelujahs; and (4) the eternal consecration of our redeemed hearts to God.

V. SAFETY CONFIRMED. *Mount Ararat listened to the voice of God confirming the salvation of his people.* In two ways was it confirmed. (1) By a voice, and (2) by a sign—the rainbow. And so is the eternal happiness of God's believing people secured (1) by the sure word of promise (Rev. xxi. 3) and (2) by the covenant of grace (Rev. iv. 3).

Vers. 10—12.—*Hoping and waiting.* I. The PATIENCE of Noah's hope. 1. Patience a characteristic of all true hope (Rom. viii. 25). 2. Faith in the Divine covenant is the secret of hope's patience (Heb. xi. 1). 3. The patience of hope is always proportioned to the brightness of faith's vision.

II. The EAGERNESS of Noah's hope. 1. While waiting God's time he kept a steady outlook for the coming of the promise. 2. He employed different methods to discover its approach—the raven and the dove. 3. He sanctified the means he used by devotion.

III. The REWARD of Noah's hope. In due time the dove returned with an olive leaf, which was—1. A timely answer. 2. An intelligible answer. 3. A joyous answer; and—4. A sufficient answer.

Ver. 14.—*The returning of the waters, or the recall of Divine judgments.* I. GOD'S JUDGMENTS HAVE THEIR SPECIFIC PURPOSES. 1. *Separation*—the elimination of the righteous from the wicked. Under the present condition of the world there is a strange intermingling of the good and the evil. The tares and the wheat, the drawnet with good and bad fish (Matt. xiii.) are suggestive emblems of this mixed state of society. The grand object contemplated by Christianity is the elimination of the saintly element from that which is corrupt. For this end it lays a special injunction on the former to withdraw themselves from the company and contagion of the latter (2 Cor. vi. 17; 2 Thess. iii. 6; 1 Tim. vi. 5). Only it forbids men, under cover of real or pretended zeal for righteousness, to attempt any forcible separation of the commingled elements (Matt. xiii. 30). Yet what the hand of man cannot do the hand of God can—winnow the chaff from the wheat. He did so by the Flood. He did so by the incarnation (Matt. iii. 12). He will do so at the second advent (Matt. xiii. 30; xxv. 32). 2. *Condemnation*—the infliction of retribution on the finally impenitent. Undisguisedly was this the design of the fell catastrophe which overtook "the world of the ungodly" in the time of Noah. It was sent for the specific purpose of punishing their evil deeds. And so have all Divine judgments of a like kind, what we misname accidents,—catastrophes, floods, famines, pestilences, &c.,—a terrible ou look of wrath and judicial retribution to them who forget to humble themselves beneath the mighty hand of God. So certainly will the last great judgment, of which Noah's flood was a prophetic symbol and warning, have as its specific purpose the complete destruction of the finally impenitent (Rom. ii. 5; 2 Thess. i. 7; Heb.

x. 27 ; 2 Pet. iii. 7). 3. *Preservation*—the salvation of the faithful. This may be said to be the aim of all those minor troubles and afflictions that befall God's people on the earth (Rom. viii. 28 ; 2 Cor. iv. 17). It is specially so when on a larger scale he interposes to inflict his judgments on the world (Isa. xxvi. 9). When he over-throws the wicked (whether nation or individual) suddenly as in a moment, it is with an eye to the deliverance of his people. Examples—Pharaoh, Goliath, Haman, Herod, Belshazzar. It was so with Noah. The destruction of the antediluvian sinners was necessary, if the remnant of the primitive Church was to be saved. Or may it be said that the future overthrow of the wicked is indispensable, if the eternal happiness of the redeemed is to be secured.

II. GOD'S JUDGMENTS HAVE THEIR APPOINTED TIMES. 1. Their *times of coming.* The hour of the commencement of the Flood was both fixed and announced 120 years before the event. Though not revealed, as in the case of the Noachic Deluge, the date of every event is as truly predetermined (cf. Gen. xviii. 14 ; Exod. ix. 5 ; Job vii. 1 ; Eccles. iii. 1 ; Jer. viii. 7 ; Acts xvii. 26). And God's judgments always keep their set times of coming, as the Flood came in the predicted hour for its arrival. 2. Their *times of continuance.* The flood of waters lingered on the earth for a season, but not for ever. From the moment when the first rain-drop fell from the leaden sky, after the Lord had shut the patriarch with his family and living creatures into the ark, till it could be said the earth was dry, one year and ten days passed away. So have all God's judgments, at least here, their limits. Upon sinful men his wrath is not poured out without measure. 3. Their *times of recall.* In the future world we do not read that there will be any recall of the Divine judgments ; everlasting punishment (Matt. xxv. 46), fire that never shall be quenched (Mark ix. 43), everlasting destruction (2 Thess. i. 9) are some of the expressions employed to depict the fire-deluge of eternity. But here on earth God's judgments, being only for a set time, are subject to recall ; and as they cannot anticipate the hour appointed for their coming, so neither can they linger beyond the moment assigned for their departure. Their recall too is, as in the case of Noah's flood—(1) An act of *grace* (Gen. viii. 1). "God remembered Noah." "It is of the Lord's mercies we are not consumed" (Lam. iii. 22 ; cf. 2 Kings xiii. 23 ; Mark i. 41). (2) An act of *power* (vers. 2, 3). As in order to roll back the tide of waters he sent forth a wind and stopped up the flood-gates of the deep and the windows of heaven, so is he able to lay his hand upon all the powers and forces of the material universe, and make them cease their working as easily as he set them in operation.

III. GOD'S JUDGMENTS HAVE THEIR APPROPRIATE SIGNS. 1. *Signs of their approach,* which are commonly—(1) *The growing wickedness of man,* as in the days of Noah (ch. vi. 11, 12). When an individual or a nation is becoming mature in sin, then that individual or that nation is becoming ripe for judgment. So it was with Pharaoh, and afterwards with Israel, with Babylon, Nineveh, Greece, Rome. So will it be in the end of the world (cf. Rev. xiv. 15). (2) *Prelusive chastisements from God,* again as in the days of Noah (ch. vii. 10). The Deluge began with a rain-shower, which gradually became more violent as the days passed, and with the bursting forth of subterranean floods, which swelled the rivers, lakes, and oceans ; all which must have been ominous indications that the long-threatened judgment was at last approaching. So the full outpouring of God's wrath is commonly heralded by anticipatory inflic-tions. 2. *Signs of their departure,* which are usually—(1) *The accomplishment of their mission.* Immediately it could be said, "All in whose nostrils was the breath of life died" (ch. vii. 22), it was added, "And God made a wind to pass over the earth, and the waters asswaged" (ver. 1). (2) *The mitigation of their violence.* The quieting of the waters (ver. 1) was the first symptom of the passing of the storm to Noah ; and so, when God's retributive judgments are about to be withdrawn, their severity begins to relax. (3) *The removal of their causes.* The second sign to Noah was the cessation of the rain and the retirement of the floods (ver. 2). So, when God's judgments are about to disappear, the agencies that brought them are visibly recalled. (4) *The arrival of little foretastes of deliverance.* Such was the grounding of the ark to Noah and his imprisoned family (ver. 4). (5) *The per-ceptible return of the previous condition of affairs.* This was symbolised by the reappearance of the mountain-tops (ver. 5).

IV. God's judgments have their interested observers. Possibly the wicked are indifferent to the Divine judgments when they happen to be abroad upon the earth; but not so the righteous, to whom everything connected with them is of the utmost importance. Observers of God's judgments should be like Noah—1. *Hopeful*— expecting them to pass. Had Noah not anticipated the complete removal of the waters, he had not made a single experiment to discover how that removal was pro- gressing. Let the saints learn from Noah to cherish hope in God. 2. *Prayerful.* There is good reason for believing that Noah sent forth the raven and the dove on the day of weekly rest, and after solemn religious exercises (*vide* Expos.). The saint's inquiries into God's judgments should always be conducted in a spirit of devotion. 3. *Intelligent*—i. e. capable of reading the signs of the times. When the dove came home to Noah with the fresh-gathered olive leaf, "he knew that the waters were abated from off the earth" (ver. 11). So God ever vouchsafes to devout souls, who seek them by faith, appropriate and adequate signs of his move- ments, which it becomes them to study and interpret. 4. *Patient*—seeking neither to outrun God's leading nor to anticipate God's directing, but, like Noah, calmly waiting the Divine order to advance to the new sphere and the new duty which the passing of his judgments may reveal. Noah waited fifty-seven days after the drying up of the waters before he left the ark, and then he only did so at God's command; wherefore, "be ye not unwise" by being over-hasty, "but understanding what the will of the Lord is" (Ephes. v. 17).

HOMILIES BY VARIOUS AUTHORS.

Ver. 1.—*God's infinite care.* In the experience of Christians the joy of first believing is often followed by a time of discouragement. Freshness of feeling seems to fade. The "law of sin" makes itself felt. Yet it is just the training by which firmer faith and fuller joy are to be reached. Deep must have been the thankfulness of those in the ark; safe in the midst of the flood. But their faith was tried. Five months, and still no abatement. Noah may well have had misgivings (cf. Matt. xi. 3). But God had not forgotten him (cf. Mark vi. 48; John x. 14). He remembered not Noah only, but every creature in the ark (cf. Luke xii. 6). He saves to the uttermost (Heb. vii. 25). The time of trial was a prelude to complete deliverance (cf. Acts xiv. 22). I. There are times when believers are tempted to feel forgotten. When troubles gather, and prayers seem unanswered, it is hard to keep faith firm. The warning Heb. xii. 6, 7 often needful. Christians would fain be led in smooth ways. And when their course is irksome and discouraging they sometimes see the wind boisterous, and begin to sink. Still more surely does the feeling follow sin. The disciple has forgotten to watch; has trusted to his own strength; has ventured into temptation, and fallen. Then God is felt to be afar off (cf. Exod. xxxiii. 7). And there are times of discipline, when spiritual freedom seems denied, and the soul cannot cry Abba, and prayer seems choked (cf. Isa. xlix. 14). Perhaps it is to teach humility; perhaps to show some root of evil; perhaps to excite more hunger for communion with God. II. But God does not forget. A creature's love may fail (Isa. xlix. 15), a crea- ture's watchfulness may faint, but not God's. He made us; can he forget our wants? His purpose is our salvation; will he neglect any step? He gave his own Son for us; is anything else too great for his goodness? Not even thy coldness and unbelief can make him cease to care. III. God's care extends to the least. Our Lord welcomed (1) those of small account (Matt. xxi. 16; Mark x. 49; Luke xviii. 16), and (2) the undeserving (Luke vii. 39; xv. 10; xix. 7). He cares also for small matters (cf. Luke xii. 28—30). What treasures of wisdom and love surround us on every side! These are not beneath his care. Will he not fulfil? (Rom. viii. 28). IV. Freedom through the work of the Holy Spirit. God's time not always what we should choose (cf. John vii. 6). Noah a prisoner of hope. God showed that the hope was well founded. The agent of deliverance "a wind"—the same word, both in Hebrew and in the LXX., as is used in Gen. i. 2 for the Spirit of God.

Doubtless the agent in drying up the water was a wind.   But in the spiritual lesson we are reminded of the Holy Spirit.   His work at first brought life on the earth ; and his work prepared for repeopling it, and completed the work of Noah's deliverance. And his work gives us freedom, showing us the work of Christ, and our position as children of God.—M.

Vers. 1—5.—*Grace and providence*   The powers of material nature are obedient servants of God, and those who are the objects of his regard, remembered by him, are safely kept in the midst of the world's changes.   "All things work together for their good."   There is an inner circle of special providence in which the family of God, with those whose existence is bound up in it, is under the eye of the heavenly Father, and in the hollow of his hand.   "And the ark rested" (ver. 4).   We speak of the cradle of the human race being set on Mount Ararat ; is it not well to remember—1. The new world came out of an ark of Divine grace.   Religion is the real foundation of society.   2. The waves of the flood bore the ark to its resting-place.   So the waters of affliction, though they heave our vessel and trouble our hearts with fear, carry us onward to a new and often higher standpoint of know-ledge and faith.   3. While the flood bore the ark, God himself chose out the spot where it should end its awful journey.   The Ararat of the new world was like the paradise of the first man—the nursery of a rising humanity ; but whereas in the state of innocence it is a garden, in the case of the redeemed man it is a mountain, with its steep, rough places, its heights and depths, its trials and dangers.   The humanity which started from Ararat carried with it at once the good and the evil of the old world which had passed away, and the mountain symbolised the complex treasury of possibilities, mingled with liabilities, which were laid up in the rescued race.—R.

Vers. 6—12.—*The dispensations of righteousness and love.* The raven and the dove. While this passage has its natural, historical fitness, we cannot overlook its symbolical significance.   It seems to set forth the two administrations of God, both of them going forth from the same centre of his righteousness in which his people are kept safe. The one represented by the carrion bird, the raven, is THE ADMINISTRATION OF JUDG-MENT, which goes forth to and fro until the waters are dried up from off the earth— finding a resting-place in the waters of destruction, though not a permanent rest; returning to the ark, as the beginning and the end of judgment is the righteousness of God.   The dove is the emblem of DIVINE GRACE, spiritual life and peace.   It can-not find rest in the waters of judgment until another seven days, another period of gracious manifestation, has prepared the world for it ; then it brings with it the plucked-off olive leaf, emblem of retiring judgment and revealed mercy ; and when yet another period of gracious manifestation has passed by, the dove shall return no more to the ark, for the ark itself is no more needed—the waters are abated from off the face of the earth.   So we may say the raven dispensation was that which pre-ceded Noah.   Then followed the first sending forth of the dove unto the time of Moses, leading to a seven days' period of the ark life, waiting for another mission of grace.   The dove brought back the olive leaf when the prophetic period of the old dispensation gave fuller promise of Divine mercy.   But yet another period of seven days must transpire before the dove is sent forth and returns no more to the ark, but abides in the earth.   After the two sacred intervals, the period of the law and the period of the prophets, which were both immediately connected with a special limited covenant such as is represented in the ark, there followed the world-wide mission of the Comforter.   The waters were abated.   The "*Grace and Truth*" took posses-sion of man's world, cursed by sin, redeemed by grace.—R.

EXPOSITION.

Vers. 15—17.—**And God spake unto Noah, saying, Go forth of the ark.** For which command doubtless the patriarch waited, as he had done for instructions to enter in (ch. vii. 11), "being restrained by a hallowed modesty from allowing himself to enjoy the bounty of nature till he should hear the voice of God directing him to do so" (Calvin). **Thou, and thy wife, and thy sons, and thy sons' wives with thee.** The order is different in ch. vii. 7, whence Ambrose noteth, "non commiscetur sexus in introitu, sed commiscetur in ingressu." **Bring forth with thee**—God having preserved alive the creatures that a twelvemonth before had been taken into the ark, and were now to be restored to their appropriate habitations on the earth—**every living thing that is with thee, of all flesh,** both **of fowl, and of cattle, and of every creeping thing that creepeth upon the earth** (cf. ch. vii. 21 ; ix. 10) ; **that they may breed abundantly**—*sharatz,* to creep or crawl, used of reptiles and small water animals (ch. i. 20 ; vii. 21) ; hence to swarm, or multiply (ch. ix. 7)—**in the earth, and be fruitful** (ch. i. 22), **and multiply**—literally, *become numerous*—**upon the earth.** Vers. 18, 19.—**And Noah went forth,**—in obedience to the Divine command,—**and his sons, and his wife, and his sons' wives with him,**—in obedience to Noah, to whom alone the Divine instructions were communicated ; —an early instance of filial subjection to parents. **Every beast, every creeping thing, and every fowl,** and **whatsoever creepeth upon the earth.** *I. e.* the chayyah, the remes, the 'oph, all creepers upon the ground (cf. ch. i. 26 ; vii. 8, 14), all of which had previously entered in. **After their kinds.** Hebrew, *families, tribes* (ch. x. 18) ; *i. e.* not confusedly, but in an orderly fashion, as they had come in, each one sorting to its kind. **Went forth out of the ark.** Ver. 20.—**And Noah builded an altar.** *Mizbëach,* a place for slaying sacrifices, from *zabach,* to slaughter animals (ch. xxxi. 54), to slay in sacrifice (Levit. ix. 4 ; 1 Sam. i. 4), as θυσιαστήριον, from θύειν, is the first altar mentioned in history. The English term (from *altus,* high) signifies a high place, because the altar was commonly a raised structure or mound of earth or stones (Exod. xx. 24). Keil thinks that altars were not required prior to the Flood, the Divine presence being still visibly among men at the gate of Eden, " so that they could turn their offerings and their hearts towards that abode." Poole, Clarke, Bush, and Inglis hold that the antediluvian sacrifices presupposed an altar. **Unto the Lord.** *Jehovah,* the God of salvation. **And took of every clean beast, and of every clean fowl.** *Vide* ch. vii. 2. " Seldom has there been a more liberal offering in proportion to the means of the giver. His whole stock of clean animals, wherewith to fill the world, was seven pairs of each " (Inglis). **And offered.** By Divine appointment, since his service was accepted ; and "all religious services which are not perfumed with the odour of faith are of an ill savour before God" (Calvin) ; but "God is peculiarly well pleased with free-will offerings, and surely if ever an occasion existed for the exercise of grateful

and adoring sentiments, the present was one" (Bush). **Burnt offerings.** '*ōlōth,* literally, *things that ascend,* from '*ālāh,* to go up, alluding not to the elevation of the victims on the altar, but to the ascension of the smoke of the burnt offerings to heaven (cf. Judges xx. 40 ; Jer. xlviii. 15 ; Amos iv. 10). **On the altar.** Ver. 21—**And the Lord** (Jehovah) **smelled** —as is done by drawing the air in and out through the nostrils ; from the root *ruach,* to breathe ; hiph., to smell—**a sweet savour.** *Rëach hannichoach,* literally, an odour of satisfaction, acquiescence, or rest ; from *nuach,* to rest, with an allusion to Noah's name (*vide* ch. v. 29) ; ὀσμὴν εὐωδίας (LXX.) ; (cf. Levit. ii. 12 ; xxvi. 31 ; Num. xv. 3 ; Ezek. vi. 13). The meaning is that the sacrifice of the patriarch was as acceptable to God as refreshing odours are to the senses of a man ; and that which rendered it acceptable was (1) the feeling from which it sprang, whether gratitude or obedience ; (2) the truths which it expressed—it was tantamount to an acknowledgment of personal guilt, a devout recognition of the Divine mercy, an explicit declaration that he had been saved or could only be saved through the offering up of the life of another, and a cheerful consecration of his redeemed life to God ; (3) the great sacrifice of which it was a type. Paul, by using the language of the LXX. (Ephes. v. 2), shows that he regarded the two as connected. **And the Lord said in his heart.** *I. e.* resolved within himself. It is not certain that this determination on the part of Jehovah was at this time communicated to the patriarch (cf. ch. vi. 3, 7 for Divine inward resolves which were not at the moment made known), unless the correct reading be *to his* (*Noah's*) *heart,* meaning the Lord *comforted* him (cf. Judges xix. 3 ; Ruth ii. 13 ; Isa. xl. 2 ; Hosea ii. 14), which is barely probable. **I will not again curse the ground any more for man's sake.** Literally, *I will not add to curse.* Not a revocation of the curse of Gen. iii. 17, nor a pledge that such curse would not be duplicated. The language refers solely to the visitation of the Deluge, and promises not that God may not sometimes visit particular localities with a flood, but that another such world-wide catastrophe should never overtake the human race. **For the imagination of man's heart is evil from his youth.** Ch. vi. 5 assigns this as the reason for man's destruction ; a proof of inconsistency between the Elohistic author and his Jehovistic editor (Bleek). " Hic inconstantiæ videtur Deus accusari posse" (Luther). " God seems to contradict himself by having previously declared that the world must be destroyed because its iniquity was desperate" (Calvin). Some endeavour to remove the incongruity by translating כִּי as *although* (Bush, Inglis), but "there are few (if any) places were כִּי can be rendered *although*" (T. Lewis). Others connect it with "for man's sake," as explanatory not of the promise, but of the past judgment (Murphy), or as stating that any future cursing of the ground would not be for man's sake (Jacobus). The true solution of the difficulty appears to lie in the clause "from his youth," as if God meant to say that whereas formerly he had visited man with judicial extermination on account of his absolute moral corruption, he would now have regard to the circumstance that man inherited his depravity through his birth, and, instead of smiting man with punitive destruction, would visit him with compassionate forbearance (Keil, 'Speaker's Commentary'). Tayler Lewis regards the expression as strongly anthropopathic, like ch. vi. 6, and indicative of the Divine regret at so calamitous an act as the Deluge, although that act was absolutely just and necessary. **Neither will I again smite any more every living thing, as I have done.** There should be no more deluge, but—

Ver. 22.—**While the earth remaineth.** Literally, *as yet, all the days of the earth*, i. e. henceforth, so long as the earth continues, עֹד expressing the ideas of repetition and continuance (*vide* ver. 12). **Seed-time and harvest,**—from roots signifying to scatter, *e. g.* seed, and to cut off, specially grain ; σπέρμα καὶ θερισμὸς (LXX.)—**and cold and heat,**—ψύχος καὶ καῦμα (LXX.)—**and summer and winter.** Properly the cutting off of fruits, from a root meaning to cut off, hence summer ; and the time when fruits are plucked, hence autumn (including winter) ; the import of the root being to gather, to pluck off ; θέρος καὶ ἔαρ (LXX.). The first term of each pair denotes the first half of the year, and the second term of each pair the second half. **And day and night** (cf. ch. i. 5) **shall not cease.** Hebrew, *lo yishbothu*, shall not sabbatise, or keep a day of rest ; *i. e.* they shall continue ever in operation and succession. This Divine promise to conserve the orderly constitution and course of nature is elsewhere styled "God's covenant of the day and of the night" (cf. Jer. xxxiii. 20, 25).

TRADITIONS OF THE DELUGE.

1. The *Babylonian*. (1) From the Chaldean monuments. As deciphered from the eleventh tablet of the Izdubar series, the story of the Flood is briefly this :—Izdubar, whom George Smith identifies with Nimrod, the founder of Babylonia, is informed by Hasisadra, whom the same authority believes to represent Noah, of a Divine commandment which he had received to construct a ship after a specified pattern, in which to save himself and "the seed of all life," because the city Surippak wherein he dwelt was to be destroyed. After first attempting to excuse himself, as he explains to Izdubar, on the ground that "young and old will deride him," Hasisadra builds the ship, and causes to go up into it "all my male servants and my female servants, the beast of the field, the animal of the field, the sons of the people, all of them," while the god Shamas makes a flood, causing it to rain heavily. The flood destroys all life from the face of the earth. Six days and nights the storm rages ; on the seventh it grows calm. Twelve measures above the sea rises the land. The ship is stopped by a mountain in the country of Nizir. After seven days Hasisadra sends forth a dove, "which went and turned, and a resting-place it did not find, and it returned ;" then a swallow, and finally a raven. On the decrease of the waters he sends forth the animals, and builds an altar on the peak of the mountain, and pours out a libation ('Chaldean Genesis,' ch. xvi. ; 'Records of the Past,' vol. vii. 133—141). (2) From Berosus. The god Kronos appeared to Xisuthrus, the tenth king of Babylon, in a vision, and warned him of an approaching deluge upon the fifteenth day of the month Desius, by which mankind would be destroyed. Among other things the god instructed him to build a vessel for the preservation of himself and friends, and specimens of the different animals. Obeying the Divine admonition, he built a vessel five stadia in length and two in breadth, and conveyed into it his wife, children, and friends. After the flood had been upon the earth he three times sent out birds from the vessel, which returned to him the second time with mud upon their feet, and the third time returned to him no more. Finding that the vessel had grounded on a mountain, Xisuthrus disembarked with his wife and children, and, having constructed an altar, offered sacrifices to the gods, in reward for which he was raised immediately to heaven ('Chaldean Genesis,' ch. iii. ; Kalisch, p. 202 ; 'Encyclopedia Britannica,' art. Deluge, ninth edition).

2. The *Egyptian*. Though commonly

alleged to be entirely unknown in the Nile valley, it is certain that the germs of the Deluge story are to be discovered even there. According to the Egyptian historian Manetho, quoted by Eusebius, Thoth, the first Hermes, erected certain pillars with inscriptions, which, *after the Deluge*, were transcribed into books. Plato also states in the Timæus (chap. v.) that a certain Egyptian priest informed Solon that the gods, when wishing to purify the earth, were accustomed to overwhelm it by a deluge, from which the herdsmen and shepherds saved themselves on the tops of the mountains. Josephus ('Ant.,' I. iii. 9) certifies that Hieronymus the Egyptian refers to the Flood. A conception altogether analogous to that of Genesis is likewise to be found in a myth belonging to the archaic period of Seti I., which represents Ra, the Creator, as being disgusted with the insolence of mankind, and resolving to exterminate them (*vide* Inscription of the Destruction of Mankind, 'Records of the Past,' vol. vi. p. 103). In short, the Egyptians believed not that there was no deluge, but that there had been several. The absence of any indications of this belief in the recovered literature of ancient Egypt is not sufficient to set aside the above concurrent testimonies to its existence (Kitto, 'Bible Illustrations,' vol. i. p. 150; Rawlinson's 'Historical Illustrations of O. T.;' 'Encycl. Britan.,' art. Deluge, ninth edition).

3. The *Indian.* Through the theft of the sacred Vedas by the giant Hayagrivah, the human race became fearfully degenerate, with the exception of seven saints and the good King Satyavrata, to whom the Divine spirit Vishnu appeared in the form of a fish, informing him of his purpose to destroy the earth by a flood, and at the same time to send a ship miraculously constructed for the preservation of himself and the seven holy ones, along with their wives, and one pair of each of all the irrational animals. After seven days the rain descended, when Satyavrata, confiding in the promises of the god, saw a huge ship drawing near, into which he entered as directed. Then the god appeared in the form of a fish a million miles long, with an immense horn, to which the king made the ship fast, and, drawing it for many years (a night of Brahma), at length landed it upon the highest peak of Mount Himavâu. When the flood abated the god arose, struck the demon Hayagrivah, recovered the sacred books, instructed Satyavrata in all heavenly sciences, and appointed him the seventh Manu, from whom the second population of the earth descended in a supernatural manner, whence man is styled Manudsha (born of Manu). *Vide* Kalisch, p. 203; Auberlen's 'Divine Revelation,' p. 169 (Clark's 'For. Theol. Lib.').

4. The *Grecian.* It is sufficient here to refer to the well-known story of Deucalion and Pyrrha, first given in Pindar, and afterwards related by Apollodorus, Plutarch, Lucian, and Ovid, whose account bears so close a resemblance to the Biblical narrative as to suggest the probability of access to Hebrew or Syrian sources of information. The previous corruption of manners and morals, the eminent piety of Deucalion, the determination "genus mortale sub undis perdere," the construction of a boat by Divine direction, the bursting of the storm, the rising of the waters, the universal ocean in which "jamque mare et tellus nullum discrimen habebant," the subsidence of the flood, the landing of the boat on Parnassus with its double peak, the consultation of the Deity "per sacras sortes," and the answer of the god as to how the earth was to be re-peopled "ossaque post tergum magnæ jactate parentis," are detailed with such graphic power as makes them read "like amplified reports of the record in Genesis." Indeed, by Philo, Deucalion was distinctly regarded as Noah. Cf. Ovid, 'Metamorph.,' lib. i. f. vii.; 'Kalisch on Genesis,' p. 203; Kitto's 'Bible Illustrations,' p. 150 (Porter's edition); 'Lange on Genesis,' p. 294, note by Tayler Lewis; Smith's 'Dictionary of the Bible,' art. Noah.

5. The *American.* Traditions of the Flood appear to be even more numerous in the New World than the Old. The Esquimaux in the North, the Red Indians, the Mexicans and the Brazilians in the central parts of America, and the Peruvians in the South have all their peculiar versions of the Deluge story. Chasewee, the ancestor of the Dogrib Indians, on the Mackensie river, according to Franklin, escaped in a canoe from a flood which overflowed the earth, taking with him all manner of four-footed beasts and birds. The Astecs, the Mixtees, the

Zapotees, and other nations inhabiting Mexico all have, according to Humboldt, their Noahs, Xisuthrus, or Manus (called Coxcox, Teocipactli, or Tezpi), who saves himself by a raft, or in a ship, which lands upon the summit of Colhuacan, the Ararat of the Mexicans. The legends of the Tamanacks relate that a man and woman saved themselves from the Deluge, and repeopled the earth by casting behind them the fruits of the Mauritia palm tree (Kalisch, p. 205 ; Auberlen's ' Divine Revelation,' p. 171 ; Smith's ' Dictionary,' art. Noah).

What, then, is the conclusion to be drawn from this universal diffusion of the Deluge story ? The theory of Schirren and Gerland, as stated by the writer of the article Deluge in the ' Encyclopedia Britannica,' is that the Deluge stories were originally ether-myths, descriptive of the phenomena of the sky, which have been transferred from the celestial regions to the earth ; but, as Kalisch justly observes, " the harmony between all these accounts is an undeniable guarantee that the tradition is no idle invention ; " or, as is forcibly stated by Rawlinson, of a tradition existing among all the great races into which ethnologists have divided mankind,—the Shemites, the Hamites, the Aryans, the Turanians,— " but one rational account can be given, viz., that it embodies the recollection of a fact in which all mankind was concerned."

HOMILETICS.

Vers. 15—22.—*The saint and the Saviour.* I. THE SAVIOUR'S INJUNCTION TO THE SAINT (ver. 15). The command which God addressed to Noah and the other inmates of the ark to go forth and take possession of the renovated earth may be regarded as emblematic of that Divine instruction which shall yet be given to the saints to go forth and take possession of the new heavens and the new earth, when the great gospel ship of the Christian Church, now floating on the troubled sea of life, shall have landed with its living freight upon the coasts of bliss. The Divine command to Noah was an order to pass—1. *From a situation of comparative peril to a position of perfect safety.* Though, certainly, before the bursting of the storm the only available shelter was that afforded by the ark, " all flesh and all in whose nostrils was the breath of life " that remained without having perished, yet even inside the ark must have seemed to the inexperienced voyagers to be at the best of only doubtful security. But now whatever danger had been connected with their twelve months' drifting across a trackless sea was at an end. And so, though only within the shelter of the Christian Church can safety be enjoyed, yet at the best it is not entirely free from peril. What with temptations and afflictions, " fears within and foes without," there always is a risk of making shipwreck of the soul (1 Tim. i. 19) ; but when life's voyage has been finished, and the new heavens and the new earth have been revealed, the salvation of the saints will be complete. 2. *From a period of patient hoping to a season of delightful enjoying.* It is doubtful if we always sufficiently realise the greatness of the strain to which the faith of the patriarch was subjected when he was shut up within the ark and left there for over a twelvemonth without any direct communication from God, with nothing for his faith to rest upon but the simple promise that he and his should be saved. At the best it was only little foretastes or earnests of God's complete salvation which he enjoyed : first in being sheltered from the storm ; next in being floated above the waters ; then in touching land upon Ararat ; and again in getting signs of the approaching deliverance. Throughout the entire period he could only live in hope and patiently endure. But here at length was the time of full fruition come. Go forth from the ark. And so it is with Christ's saints universally. Here are only earnests of the inheritance (Ephes. i. 14) ; there alone is the inheritance itself (Col. i. 12). Now is the time for hoping and waiting (Rom. viii. 25) ; then is the season for seeing and enjoying (1 John iii. 2). Here the saints rest upon the promise as their guarantee (2 Tim. i. 1 ; Heb. iv. 1) ; there the saints behold and experience its realisation (Heb. vi. 12). 3. *From a condition of restrained activity to a sphere of higher and freer service.* Not that Noah's life within the ark could in any sense have been one of idleness, and neither are the lives of Christians on the earth and in the Church below ; but Noah entered on another and a nobler kind of work when he left the ark than that which had engaged his powers within its precincts, and so do they who are counted worthy of attaining to Christ's kingdom and glory. Here, like Noah's, the saint's powers of service are limited and confined; there they shall attain to greater freedom and fuller scope (1 Cor. xiii. 9 —12; Rev. iv. 8).

II. THE SAINT'S RESPONSE TO THE SAVIOUR (ver. 18). The command to leave the ark which God addressed to Noah was obeyed—1. *Immediately.* We can imagine that everything was in a state of readiness for departure when the marching orders came, so that there was no need to interpose delay. So was it with the Hebrews when the Lord led them forth from Egypt (Exod. xii. 11); so should Christians be always ready for their Master's summons, whether to pass from affliction (Isa. lii. 11) or into it (ch. xxii. 1; Acts xxi. 13), to enter upon a new sphere of work (Isa. vi. 8) or retire from an old one into silence (1 Kings xvii. 3); to go down into the grave (2 Tim. iv. 6) and wait for the apocalypse of the saints (Job xiv. 14), or to go up into glory and partake of the inheritance of the saints in light (Matt. xxiv. 44). 2. *Universally.* Not the patriarch alone, but all his family and all the creatures came forth; so did all God's people come forth from the house of bondage (Exod. x. 26); and so will all Christ's redeemed ones who have entered into the salvation ark of his Church emerge at last into the light and felicity of heaven (Isa. li. 11; Luke xii. 32; 1 Cor. xv. 22; 1 Thess. iv. 14). 3. *Joyfully.* This we may infer. After the twelve months' isolation, and confinement, and comparative peril we need not doubt that Noah and his family exulted with delight, and that even the lower creatures were not strangers to agreeable sensations. It was a picture of the happiness which even here the saints enjoy in the Divine interpositions on their behalf; but especially of the universal thrill of gladness which God's redeemed family, and even "the creature itself," shall experience in the palingenesia of the heavens and the earth (Isa. xxxv. 10; Rom. viii. 19—23). 4. *Finally.* They were never more to return to the ark, because never again should there be a flood. It was a delightful symbol of the completeness and finality of God's salvation when the saints shall have been landed on the heights of bliss (Rev. xxi. 4; xxii. 3—5).

III. THE SAINT'S WORSHIP OF THE SAVIOUR (ver. 20). As Noah's first act on stepping forth from the ark was to build an altar unto the Lord, so the saint's first work on reaching heaven will be to worship; and this worship will be—1. *Believing.* This was implied in the very thought of offering up a sacrifice to Jehovah, but specially so in the circumstances in which the patriarch was then placed. The visible symbol of the Divine presence had retired to its original dwelling-place in the heavens, and yet Noah had as little doubt as ever he had that there was a God to worship. The building of an altar, therefore, just then and there was an explicit declaration of his faith. Without faith there can be no worship of God either here or there, on earth or in heaven (Heb. xi. 6). 2. *Thankful.* The offering of Noah was designed as an expression of his gratitude for the Lord's mercy, and so should the worship of the saints on earth be characterised by the same spirit (Phil. iv. 6), as we know the adorations of the saints before the throne are (Rev. vii. 12). 3. *Generous.* Noah took of every clean beast and every clean fowl, *i. e.* one of seven or one of fourteen (*vide* Expos.), in either case a munificent tribute to the God of his salvation. How seldom is the like liberality exhibited by Christ's worshippers on earth! What a blessed thought it is that among the saints above there will be no temptation to such meanness as is often practised by the saints below! 4. *Sincere.* It was no merely formal service that the patriarch presented. The burnt offering was a symbolic declaration of his self-consecration—body, soul, and spirit—to the God who had redeemed him. Of this sort is the service which Christ expects and believers should render on the earth (Matt. xvi. 24; Luke xiv. 26; Rom. xii. 1; 1 Cor. vi. 20). Of such kind will be the worship of the saints in heaven (Rev. xxii. 3).

IV. THE SAVIOUR'S RESPONSE TO THE SAINT (vers. 21, 22). As the sacrifice of Noah was well-pleasing unto God, so will the worship of the saints find acceptance in his sight. And this acceptance of the sacrifices of the glorified, like the reception of Noah's offering—1. *Will consist in* the cherishing by God of a feeling of sweet complacency towards the worshippers. As from the burning victims upon Noah's altar there came up into the Divine nostrils a savour of rest, so from the spiritual sacrifices of Christians even here there ascends an odour of a sweet smell unto God (Phil. iv. 18), while in the upper sanctuary the services of the redeemed go up con-

tinually before God like the smoke of incense (Rev. viii. 4).   2. *Will be based upon*
the odour of the sacrifice of Christ, of which Noah's was the type.   It was not the
actual service of Noah, considered as an *opus operatum*, that produced the feeling of
complacency in God (Micah vi. 7), but the sacrificial work of Christ, to which the
faith of the patriarch had an outlook (Ephes. v. 2).   For the sake of that offering up
of himself once for all in the end of the world that was to be accomplished by the
woman's seed, and which Noah's faith truly, however dimly, embraced, God accepted
him and his.   That same offering is the ground or basis on which all the saints'
sacrifices are accepted either on earth (1 Pet. ii. 5) or in heaven (Rev. v. 6).   3.
Will express itself through the perpetuation of the worshipper's safety.   (1) By
averting all evil.   " There shall be no more curse " (Rev. xxii. 3), as God determined
in his heart (ver. 21), and afterwards expressed to Noah (ch. ix. 15), never more to
curse the ground or flood the earth.   (2) By securing all good, which was symbolised by the confirmation of the covenant of day and night.

   Lessons :—1. Live in a state of readiness for the glorious appearing of the Son of
man (Titus i. 13).   2. Expectantly wait for the manifestation of the sons of God
(Rom. viii. 19).   3. Learn the nature of the saint's service in the heavenly world
(Rev. v. 8).   4. Note the security for the perpetuity of heaven's blessedness—
Christ's sacrifice and God's covenant.

HOMILIES BY VARIOUS AUTHORS.

   Vers. 13—19.—*Rest and restoration.*   Noah (Rest) comes forth from the ark in
the sabbath century of his life, the six hundred and first year.   He lived after
the Flood 350 years, the half week of centuries ; his life represented *a* rest, but not
the rest, a half sabbath, promise of the *rest* which remains to the people of God.

   I. An example of faith.   1. Not until God spake did Noah dare to do more than
lift off the covering and look.   2. At the heavenly word the family, redeemed by
grace, takes possession of the redeemed habitation.

   II. The redeemed life in its new appointment.   Go forth of the ark into the
new world.   There is the keynote of the Bible.   Man redeemed is man living by
every word of God.   1. By Divine commandment going into the prepared refuge.
2. By Divine commandment taking down old bounds and occupying new places.
3. *Going forth* into a promised land rejoicing in a *pledged future.*   4. Carrying with
him all lower creatures into a new, progressive, God-blessed inheritance.   The whole
creation groaning and travailing, the whole creation participating in the Divine
deliverance.—R.

   Vers. 20—22.—*The sanctification of the earth.*   The sweet savour of man's burnt
offerings—(1) not the offerings of caprice, but the fulfilment of *Divine commands*,
(2) the reciprocation of Heaven's *communications*—(3) ascends from the earth-built
altar and fills the Lord with *satisfaction.*   In return for that obedience and devotion
the curse is removed, the earth is sealed with the saving strength of God in a
covenant of peace.

   I. Religious life is acceptable to God when it is (1) grateful acknowledgment of his mercy ; (2) humble obedience to his own revealed will ; (3) consecration
of place, time, life, possessions to him.

   II. Union and communion between God and man is the foundation on which all
earthly happiness and security rest.

   III. The forbearance and mercy of God in his relation to those whose hearts are
yet full of evil is at once probation and grace.   The ground is not cursed any more for
man's sake, but, the more evidently, that which falls upon the ground may fall upon
man himself.   The higher revelations of God in the post-Noachic period were certainly
larger bestowments of grace, but at the same time they involved a larger responsibility.   So the writer of the Epistle to the Hebrews reasons as to the punishment
of those who trample underfoot the covenant of the gospel.   The progressive
covenants which make up the history of God's grace recorded in the Scriptures are
progressive separations of the evil and the good, therefore they point to that
complete and final separation in which God's righteousness shall be eternally
glorified.—R.

EXPOSITION.

CHAPTER IX.

Ver. 1.—**And God**—*Elohim*, not because belonging to the Elohistic document (Bleek, Tuch, Colenso); but rather because throughout this section the Deity is exhibited in his relations to his creatures—**blessed**—a repetition of the primal blessing rendered necessary by the devastation of the Flood (cf. ch. i. 28)—**Noah and his sons,**—as the new heads of the race,—**and said unto them,**—audibly, in contrast to ch. viii. 21, 22, which was not addressed to the patriarch, but spoken by God to himself in his heart, as if internally resolving on his subsequent course of action,—**Be fruitful, and multiply.** A favourite expression of the Elohist (cf. ch. i. 28 ; viii. 17 ; ix. 1, 7 ; xvii. 20 ; xxviii. 3 ; xxxv. 11 ; xlvii. 27 ; xlviii. 14), (Tuch); but (1) the apparently great number of passages melts away when we observe the verbally exact reference of ch. viii. 17 ; ix. 1, 7 to i. 28 ; and of ch. xlviii. 4 to xxxv. 11 ; (2) the Elohist does not always employ his "favourite expression" where he might have done so, as, *e. g.*, not in ch. i. 22 ; xvii. 6 ; xxviii. 14 ; (3) the Jehovist does not avoid it where the course of thought necessarily calls for it (*vide* Levit. xxvi. 9), (Keil). **And replenish the earth.** The words, " and subdue it," which had a place in the Adamic blessing, and which the LXX. insert here in the Noachic (καὶ κατακυριεύσατε αὐτῆς), are omitted for the obvious reason that the world dominion originally assigned to man in Adam had been forfeited by sin, and could only be restored through the ideal Man, the woman's seed, to whom it had been transferred at the fall. Hence says Paul, speaking of Christ : " καὶ πάντα ὑπέταξεν ὑπὸ τοὺς πόδας αὐτοῦ (Ephes. i. 22) ; and the writer to the Hebrews : νῦν δὲ οὔπω ὁρῶμεν αὐτῷ (*i. e.* man) τὰ πάντα ὑποτεταγμένα, τὸν δὲ βραχύ τι παρ' ἀγγέλους ἠλαττομένον βλέπομεν Ἰησοῦν, διὰ τὸ πάθημα τοῦ θανάτου, δόξῃ καὶ τιμῇ ἐστεφανωμένον (*i. e.* the world dominion which David, Ps. viii. 6, recognised as belonging to God's ideal man) ὅπως χάριτι θεοῦ ὑπὲρ παντὸς γεύσηται θανάτου (ch. ii. 8, 9). The original relationship which God had established between man and the lower creatures having been disturbed by sin, the inferior animals, as it were, gradually broke loose from their condition of subjection. As corruption deepened in the human race it was only natural to anticipate that man's lordship over the animal creation would become feebler and feebler. Nor, perhaps, is it an altogether violent hypothesis that, had the Deluge not intervened, in the course of time the beast would have become the master and man the slave. To prevent any such apprehensions in the future, as there was to be no second deluge, the relations of man and the lower creatures were to be placed on a new footing. Ultimately, in the palingenesia, they would be completely restored (cf. Isa. xi. 6) ; in the mean time, till that glorious consummation should arrive, the otherwise inevitable encroachments of the creatures upon the human family in its sin-created weakness should be restrained by a principle of fear. That was the first important modification made upon the original Adamic blessing.

Ver. 2.—**And the fear of you and the dread of you.** Not simply of Noah and his sons, but of man in general. **Shall be.** Not for the first time, as it could not fail to be evoked by the sin of man during the previous generations, but, having already been developed, it was henceforth to be turned back upon the creature rather than directed against man. **Upon.** The verb *to be* is first construed with עַל, and afterwards with בְּ. The LXX. render both by ἐπί, though perhaps the latter should be taken as equivalent to ἐν, in which case the three clauses of the verse will express a gradation. The dread of man shall first overhang the beasts, then it shall enter into and take possession of them, and finally under its influence they shall fall into man's hand. **Every beast of the earth, and upon every fowl of the air, upon** (literally, *in ;* vide *supra*. Murphy translates *with*) **all that moveth** upon **the earth, and upon** (literally, *in*) **all the fishes of the sea.** This does not imply that the animals may not sometimes rise against man and destroy him (cf. Exod. viii. 6, 17, 24 ; Levit. xxvi. 22 ; 1 Kings xiii. 24, 25 ; xx. 36 ; 2 Kings ii. 24 ; Ezek. xiv. 15 ; Acts xii. 23, for instances in which the creatures were made ministers of Divine justice), but simply that the normal condition of the lower creatures will be one of instinctive dread of man, causing them rather to avoid than to seek his presence—a statement sufficiently confirmed by the facts that wherever human civilisation penetrates, there the dominion of the beasts retires ; that even ferocious animals, such as lions, tigers, and other beasts of prey, unless provoked, usually flee from man rather than assail him. **Into your hand are they delivered.** Attested by (1) man's actual dominion over such of the creatures as are either immediately needful for or helpful to him, such as the horse, the ox, the sheep, &c. ;

and (2) by man's capability of taming and so reducing to subjection every kind of wild beast—lions, tigers, &c.

Ver. 3.—**Every**—obviously admitting of "exceptions to be gathered both from the nature of the case and from the distinction of clean and unclean beasts mentioned before and afterwards" (Poole)—**moving thing that liveth**—clearly excluding such as had died of themselves or been slain by other beasts (cf. Exod. xxii. 31 ; Levit. xxii. 8) —**shall be meat for you.** Literally, *to you it shall be for meat.* Though the distinction between unclean and clean animals as to food, afterwards laid down in the Mosaic code (Levit. xi. 1—31), is not mentioned here, it does not follow that it was either unknown to the writer or unpractised by the men before the Flood. **Even as the green herb have I given you all things.** An allusion to ch. i. 29 (Rosenmüller, Bush) ; but *vide infra*. The relation of this verse to the former has been understood as signifying— 1. That animal food was expressly prohibited before the Flood, and now for the first time permitted (Mercerus, Rosenmüller, Candlish, Clarke, Murphy, Jamieson, Wordsworth, Kalisch)—the ground being that such appears the obvious import of the sacred writer's language. 2. That, though permitted from the first, it was not used till postdiluvian times, when men were explicitly directed to partake of it by God (Theodoret, Chrysostom, Aquinas, Luther, Pererius)—the reason being that prior to the Flood the fruits of the earth were more nutritious and better adapted for the sustenance of man's physical frame, propter excellentem terræ bonitatem præstantemque vim alimenti quod fructus terræ suppeditabant homini, while after it such a change passed upon the vegetable productions of the ground as to render them less capable of supporting the growing feebleness of the body, invalidam ad bene alendum hominem (Pererius). 3. That whether permitted or not prior to the Flood, it was used, and is here for the first time formally allowed (Keil, Alford, 'Speaker's Commentary'); in support of which opinion it may be urged that the general tendency of subsequent Divine legislation, until the fulness of the times, was ever in the direction of concession to the infirmities or necessities of human nature (cf. Matt. xix. 8). The opinion, however, which appears to be the best supported is—4. That animal food was permitted before the fall, and that the grant is here expressly renewed (Justin Martyr, Calvin, Willet, Bush, Macdonald, Lange, Quarry). The grounds for this opinion are —(1) That the language of ch. i. 29 does not explicitly forbid the use of animal food. (2) That science demonstrates the existence of carnivorous animals prior to the appearance of man, and yet vegetable products alone

were assigned for their food. (3) **That shortly after the fall animals were slain by Divine direction for sacrifice, and probably also for food**—at least this latter supposition is by no means an unwarrantable inference from ch. iv. 4 (*q. v.*). (4) That the words, "as the green herb," even if they implied the existence of a previous restriction, do not refer to ch. i. 29, but to ch. i. 30, the green herb in the latter verse being contrasted with the food of man in ch. i. 29. Solomon Glass thus correctly indicates the connection and the sense : "ut viridem herbam (illis), sic illa omnia dedi vobis " (' Sacr. Phil.,' lib. iii. tr. 2, c. xxii. 2). (5) That a sufficient reason for mentioning the grant of animal food in this connection may be found in the subjoined restriction, without assuming the existence of any previous limitation.

Ver. 4.—**But**—אַךְ, an adverb of limitation or exception, as in Levit. xi. 4, introducing a restriction on the foregoing precept—**flesh with the life thereof,** which is **the blood thereof.** Literally, *with its soul, its blood ;* the blood being regarded as the seat of the soul, or life principle (Levit. xvii. 11), and even as the soul itself (Levit. xvii. 14). The idea of the unity of the soul and the blood, on which the prohibition of blood is based, comes to light everywhere in Scripture. In the blood of one mortally wounded his soul flows forth (Lam. ii. 12), and he who voluntarily sacrifices himself pours out his soul unto death (Isa. liii. 12). The murderer of the innocent slays the soul of the blood of the innocent (ψυχὴν αἵματος ἀθώου, Deut. xxvii. 25), which also cleaves to his (the murderer's) skirts (Jer. ii. 34 ; cf. Prov. xxviii. 17, blood of a soul ; cf. Gen. iv. 10 with Heb. xii. 24 ; Job xxiv. 12 with Rev. vi. 9 ; *vide* also Ps. xciv. 21 ; Matt. xxiii. 35). Nor can it be said to be exclusively peculiar to Holy Scripture. In ancient Egyptian hieroglyphics the hawk, which feeds on bloods, represents the soul. Virgil says of a dying person, "purpuream vomit ille animam" ('Æneid,' ix. 349). The Greek philosophers taught that the blood was either the soul (Critias), or the soul's food (Pythagoras), or the soul's seat (Empedocles), or the soul's producing cause (the Stoics) ; but only Scripture reveals the true relation between them both when it declares the blood to be not the soul absolutely, but the means of its self-attestation (*vide* Delitzsch's ' Bib. Psychology,' div. iv. sec. xi.). **Shall ye not eat.** Not referring to, although certainly forbidding, the eating of flesh taken from a living animal (Raschi, Cajetan, Delitzsch, Luther, Poole, Jamieson)—a fiendish custom which may have been practised among the antediluvians, as, according to travellers, it is, or was, among modern Abyssinians ; rather interdicting the flesh of slaughtered animals from which the blood has not been properly ·drained (Calvin, Keil, Kalisch, Murphy, Wordsworth). The same prohibition (commonly regarded by the Hebrew doctors as the seventh of the Noachic precepts which were enjoined upon all nations; *vide infra*, ver. 6) was afterwards incorporated in the Mosaic legislation (cf. Levit. iii. 17; vii. 26, 27; xvii. 10—14; xix. 26; Deut. xii. 16, 23, 24; xv. 23), and subsequently imposed upon the Gentile converts in the Christian Church by the authority of the Holy Ghost and the apostles (Acts xv. 28, 29). Among other reasons, doubtless, for the original promulgation of this law were these : — 1. A desire to guard against the practice of cruelty to animals (Chrysostom, Calvin, 'Speaker's Commentary'). 2. A design to hedge about human life by showing the inviolability which in God's eye attached to even the lives of the lower creatures (Calvin, Willet, Poole, Kalisch, Murphy). 3. The intimate connection which even in the animal creation subsisted between the blood and the life (Kurtz, 'Sacr. Worship,' I. A. 5). 4. Its symbolic use as an atonement for sin (Poole, Delitzsch, 'Bib. Psy.' iv. 11; Keil, Wordsworth, Murphy). That the restriction continues to the present day may perhaps be argued from its having been given to Noah, but cannot legitimately be inferred from having been imposed on the Gentile converts to Christianity as one τῶν ἐπάναγκες τούτων, from the burden of which they could not be excused (Clarke), as then, by parity of reasoning, meat offered to idols would be equally forbidden, which it is not, except when the consciences of the weak and ignorant are endangered (Calvin).

Ver. 5. — **And surely.** Again the conjunction אַךְ introduces a restriction. The blood of beasts might without fear be shed for necessary uses, but the blood of man was holy and inviolable. Following the LXX. (καὶ γάρ), Jerome, Pererius, Mercerus, Calvin, Poole, Willet give a causal sense to the conjunction, as if it supplied the reason of the foregoing restriction—a sense which, according to Fürst ('Heb. Lex.,' *sub nom.*) it sometimes, though rarely, has; as in 2 Kings xxiv. 3; Ps. xxxix. 12; lxviii. 22; but in each case אַךְ is better rendered "surely." **Your blood of your lives.** (1) *For* your souls, *i. e.* in requital for them—*lex talionis*, blood for blood, life for life (Kalisch, Wordsworth, Bush); (2) *for* your souls, *i. e.* for their protection (Gesenius, Michaelis, Schumann, Tuch); (3) *from* your souls—a prohibition against suicide (Samaritan); (4) *with reference to* your souls,—לְ =*quoad* (Ewald, 'Heb. Syn.,' 310 *a*),—as if specifying the particular blood for which exaction would be made (Keil); (5) *of* your souls, belonging to them, or residing in

them (LXX., Syriac, Vulgate, A. V., Calvin, Rosenmüller (qui ad animas vestras pertinet), Murphy, 'Speaker's Commentary')— although, according to Kalisch, לְ cannot have the force of a genitive after הַדְּמְכֶם, a substantive with a suffix; but *vide* Levit. xviii. 20, 23; cf. Ewald, 'Heb. Syn.,' p. 113. Perhaps the force of לְ may be brought out by rendering "your blood *to the extent of* your lives ;" *i. e.* not all blood-letting, but that which proceeds to the extent of taking life (cf. ver. 15 : "There shall no more be waters *to the extent of* a flood "). **Will I require.** Literally, *search after*, with a view to punishment ; hence avenge (cf. ch. xlii. 22 ; Ezek. xxxiii. 6 ; Ps. ix. 13). **At** (literally, *from*) **the hand of every beast will I require it.** Not "an awful warning against cruelty to the brute creation !" (Clarke), but a solemn proclamation of the sanctity of human life, since it enacted that that beast should be destroyed which slew a man—a statute afterwards incorporated in the Mosaic legislation (Exod. xxi. 28—32), and practised even in Christian times ; "not for any punishment to the beast, which, being under no law, is capable of neither sin nor punishment, but for caution to men" (Poole). If this practice appears absurd to some moderns (Dr. H. Oort, 'The Bible for Young People,' p. 103), it was not so to Solon and Draco, in whose enactments there was a similar provision (Delitzsch, Lange). **And at** (*from*) **the hand of man ; at** (or *from*) **the hand of every man's brother.** Either (1) *two* persons are here described—(*a*) the individual man himself, and (*b*) his brother, *i. e.* the suicide and the murderer (Maimonides, Wordsworth, Murphy), or the murderer and his brother man, *i. e.* kinsman, or *goël* (Michaelis, Bohlen, Baumgarten, Kalisch, Bush), or the ordinary civil authorities (Kalisch, Candlish, Jamieson)—or (2) *one*, viz., the murderer, who is first generically distinguished from the beast, and then characterised as his victim's brother ; as thus—"at" or from "the hand of man," as well as beast ; "from the hand of the individual man, or every man (cf. ch. xlii. 25 ; Num. xvii. 17 for this distributive use of אִישׁ) his brother," supplying a new argument against homicide (Calvin, Knobel, Delitzsch, Keil, Lange). The principal objection to discovering Goëlism in the phraseology is that it requires מִיַּד to be understood in two different senses, and the circumstance, that the institution of the magistracy appears to be hinted at in the next verse, renders it unnecessary to detect it in this. **Will I require the life** (or *soul*) **of man.** The specific manner in which this inquisition after blood should be carried out is indicated in the words that follow.

Ver. 6.—**Whoso sheddeth.** Literally, *he shedding*, i. e. wilfully and unwarrantably; and not simply *accidentally*, for which kind of manslaughter the law afterwards provided (*vide* Num. xxxv. 11); or *judicially*, for that is commanded by the present statute. **Man's blood.** Literally, *blood of the man*, human blood. **By man.** Not openly and directly by God, but by man himself, acting of course as God's instrument and agent—an instruction which involved the setting up of the magisterial office, by whom the sword might be borne ("Hic igitur fons est, ex quo manat totum jus civile et jus gentium." —Luther. Cf. Num. xxxv. 29—31; Rom. xiii. 4), and equally laid a basis for the law of the *goël* subsequently established in Israel (Deut. xix. 6; Josh. xx. 3). The Chaldee paraphrases, "with witnesses by sentence of the judges." The LXX. substitutes for "by man" ἀντὶ τοῦ αἵματος αὐτοῦ—an interpretation followed by Pro-

fessor Lewis, who quotes Jona ben Gannach in its support. **Shall.** Not merely a permission legalising, but an imperative command enjoining, capital punishment, the reason for which follows. **For in the image of God made he man.** To apply this to the magistracy (Bush, Murphy, Keil), who are sometimes in Scripture styled Elohim (Ps. lxxxii. 6), and the ministers of God (Rom. xiii. 4), and who may be said to have been made in the Divine image in the sense of being endowed with the capacity of ruling and judging, seems forced and unnatural; the clause obviously assigns the original dignity of man (cf. ch. i. 28) as the reason why the murderer cannot be suffered to escape (Calvin, Poole, Alford, 'Speaker's Commentary,' Candlish, Lange)

Ver. 7.—**And you, be ye fruitful, and multiply; bring forth abundantly in the earth, and multiply therein.** *Vide* on ver. 1.

HOMILETICS.

Vers. 1—7.—*New arrangements for a new era.* I. PROVISION FOR THE INCREASE OF THE HUMAN FAMILY. 1. *The proximate instrumentality* — the ordinance of marriage (vers. 1, 7), which was — (1) A *Divine* institution appointed by God in Eden (cf. ch. ii. 22, and Matt. xix. 5). (2) A *sacred* institution. Every ordinance of God's appointment, it may be said, is in a manner holy; but a special sanctity attaches to that of marriage. God attested the estimation in which he held it by visiting the world's corruption, which had principally come through its desecration, with the waters of a flood. (3) A *permanent* institution, being the same in its nature, uses, and ends that it had been from the beginning, only modified to suit the changing circumstances of man's condition. Prior to the fall it was exempt from any of those imperfections which in human experience have clung to it ever since. Subsequent to the melancholy entrance of sin, there was superadded to the lot of woman an element of pain and sorrow from which she had been previously free; and though anterior to the Flood it had been grossly abused by man's licentiousness, after it, we cannot doubt, it was restored in all its original purity, though still with the curse of sorrow unremoved. 2. *The originating cause*—the Divine blessing (vers. 1, 7), without which—(1) *The marriage bed would not be fruitful* (Ps. cxxvii. 3). Cf. the case of Rachel (ch. xxx. 2), of Hannah (1 Sam. i. 11), of Ruth (Ruth iv. 13). (2) *The married life would not be holy.* What marriage is and leads to when dissociated from the fear of God had already been significantly displayed upon the theatre of the antediluvian world, and is abundantly declared in Scripture, both by precept (ch. xxiv. 3; xxviii. 1; Exod. xxxiv. 16; Deut. vii. 3, 4; Josh. xxiii. 12, 13; 2 Cor. vi. 14) and example; *e. g.*, the Israelites (Judges iii. 6, 7), Samson (Judges xiv. 1—16), Solomon (1 Kings iii. 1), Jews (Ezra ix. 1—12). (3) *The marriage tie would not be sure.* As ungodliness tends to violate the marriage law by sins of polygamy, so, without the fear of God, there is no absolute security that the bond may not be broken by adultery and divorce (cf. ch. xix. 5, 8; xxxv. 22; 2 Sam. xi. 1—5; Mark vi. 17, 18).

II. PROVISION FOR THE PROTECTION OF THE HUMAN FAMILY. 1. Against *the world of animals.* (1) In Eden such protection was *not required*, man having been constituted lord of the inferior creation, and the beasts of the field never rising to dispute his authority, his rule being characterised by gentleness and love (ch. ii. 20). (2) After the fall such protection was *incomplete.* A change having passed upon the master, there is reason to suppose that a corresponding change transpired upon the servant. The moral order of the world having been dislocated, a like instability would doubtless invade those economical arrangements that depended on man for their successful administration.   As man sank deeper into the mire of corruption, his supremacy over the beasts of the field would appear to have been more frequently and fiercely disputed (ch. vi. 11).   But now, the Flood having washed away the sinning race, (3) such protection was henceforth to be rendered *secure* by imbuing the brute nature with an instinctive dread of man which would lead the animals to acknowledge his supremacy, and rather flee from his presence than assail his dominion.   The operation of this law is proved to-day by the facts that man retains unquestioned his lordship over all those domesticated animals that are useful to him ; that there is no creature, however wild and ferocious, that he cannot tame ; and that wherever man appears with his civilising agencies the wild beast instinctively retires.   2. Against *the world of men*.   Ever since the fall man has required to be protected against himself.   Prior to the Flood it does not appear that even crimes of murder and bloodshed were publicly avenged.   Now, however, the previous laxness, if it was such, and not rather Divine clemency, was to cease, and an entirely new arrangement to come into operation.   (1) The *law* was henceforth to inflict CAPITAL PUNISHMENT on its murderers ; not the law of man simply, but the law of God.   Given to Noah, this statute was designed for the universal family of man until repealed by the Authority that imposed it.   Not having been exclusively a Jewish statute, the abrogation of the Mosaic economy does not affect its stability. Christ, having come not to destroy the fundamental laws of Heaven, may be fairly presumed to have left this standing.   Inferences from the spirit of Christianity have no validity as against an express Divine commandment.   (2) The *reasons* for the law were to be the essential dignity of man's nature (ver. 6 ; cf. homily on the greatness of man, ch. i. 26) and the fundamental brotherhood of the race (ver. 5), a point which appears not to have received sufficient prominence in prediluvian times (cf. Acts xvii. 26).   (3) The *execution* of the law was neither to be retained in the Divine hand for miraculous administration, nor to be left in that of the private individual (the kinsman) to gratify revenge, but to be intrusted to society for enforcement by means of a properly-constituted tribunal.   This was the commencement of social government among men, and the institution of the magisterial office, or the power of the sword (*vide* Rom. xiii. 1—5).

III. PROVISION FOR THE SUSTENANCE OF THE HUMAN FAMILY.   1. The *rule*.   It is not certain that animal food was interdicted in Eden ; it is almost certain that it was in use between the fall and the Flood.   At the commencement of the new era it was expressly sanctioned.   2. The *restriction*.   While the flesh of animals might be used as food, they were not to be mutilated while alive, nor was the blood to be eaten with the flesh.   Note the bearing of the first of these on the question of vivisection, which the Divine law appears explicitly to forbid, except it can be proved to be indispensable for the advancement of medical knowledge with a view to the healing of disease, and, in the case of extending a permission, imperatively requires to be carried on with the least possible infliction of pain upon the unresisting creature whose life is thus sacrificed for the good of man ; and of the second of these, on the lawfulness of eating blood under the Christian dispensation, see Expos. on ver. 4.   3. The *reason*.   (1) For the rule, which, though not stated, may be judged to have been (*a*) a concession to the moral weakness of man's soul, and (*b*) a provision for the physical infirmity of man's body.   (2) For the restriction— (*a*) to prevent cruelty to animals ; (*b*) to fence about man's life by showing the criminality of destroying that of the beast ; (*c*) to assert God's lordship over all life ; (*d*) because of its symbolic value as the sign of atoning blood.

Lessons :—1. God's clemency towards man.   2. God's care for man.   3. God's goodness to man.   4. God's estimate of man.

HOMILIES BY VARIOUS AUTHORS.

Vers. 1—7.—*The new life of man on the earth* under a new revelation of the Divine favour.   The chief points are—

I. UNLIMITED POSSESSION OF THE EARTH, and use of its inhabitants and products, whether for food or otherwise ; thus supplying—1. The scope of life.   2. The enjoyment of life.   3. The development of life.

II. Absolute RESPECT FOR HUMAN LIFE, and preservation of the gentler feelings (the blood being forbidden as injurious to man in this case), promoting—1. The supremacy of the higher nature over the lower. 2. The revelation of the ethical law. 3. The preparation of the heart for Divine communications.

III. Man living in BROTHERHOOD, (1) revealing the image of God, (2) observing God's law, (3) rejoicing in his blessing, he shall multiply and fill the earth. The earth waits for such inhabitants ; already by Divine judgments prepared for them.—R.

EXPOSITION.

Ver. 8.—**And God spake**—in continuation of the preceding discourse—**unto Noah, and to his sons with him, saying.**

Ver. 9.—**And I, behold, I establish**—literally, *am causing to rise up or stand; ἀνίστημι* (LXX.)—**my covenant** (cf. ch. vi. 18) **with you, and with your seed after you.** *I. e.* the covenant contemplated all subsequent posterity in its provisions, and, along with the human family, the entire animal creation.

Ver. 10.—**And with every living creature** —literally, *every soul* (or breathing thing) *that liveth,* a generic designation of which the particulars are now specified—**that is with you, of the fowl, of the cattle, and of every beast of the earth**—literally, *in fowl,* &c. ; *i. e.* belonging to these classes of animals (cf. ch. i. 25, 30 ; vi. 20 ; viii. 17)— **with you ; from all that go out of the ark,** —not necessarily implying ('Speaker's Commentary,' Murphy), though in all probability it was the case, that there were animals which had never been in the ark ; but simply an idiomatic phrase expressive of the totality of the animal creation (Alford)—**to every beast of the earth.** *I. e.* wild beast (ch. i. 25), the chayyah of the land, which was not included among the animals that entered the ark (Murphy) ; or living creature (ch. ii. 19), referring here to the fishes of the sea, which were not included in the ark (Kalisch). That the entire brute creation was designed to be embraced in the Noachic covenant seems apparent from the use of the prepositions—בְּ describing the classes to which the animals belong, as in ch. vii. 21 ; מִן in- dicating one portion of the whole, the *ter- minus a quo,* and לְ the *terminus ad quem*— in their enumeration (*vide* Fürst, 'Hebrew Lex.,' sub לְ, p. 715 ; cf. Keil *in loco*). Kalisch thinks the language applies only to the animals of Noah's time, and not to those of a later age, on the ground that "the destiny of the animals is everywhere connected with that of the human race ;" but this is equivalent to their being included in the covenant.

Ver. 11.—**And I will establish my cove- nant with you.** Not form it for the first time, as if no such covenant had existed in antediluvian times (Knobel) ; but cause it to stand or permanently establish it, so that it shall no more be in danger of being over- thrown, as it recently has been. The word " my " points to a covenant already in existence, though not formally mentioned until the time of Noah (ch. vi. 18). The promise of the woman's seed, which formed the substance of the covenant during the interval from Adam to Noah, was from Noah's time downwards to be enlarged by a specific pledge of the stability of the earth and the safety of man (cf. ch. viii. 22). **Neither shall all flesh**—including the human race and the animal creation. Cf. כָּל־בָּשָׂר, mankind (ch. vi 12), the lower creatures (ch. vii. 21)—**be cut off any more by the waters of a flood.** Literally, *the* flood just passed, which would no more return. **Neither shall there any more be a flood** (of any kind) **to destroy the earth.** Regions might be devastated and tribes of animals and men swept away, but never again would there be a universal destruction of the earth or of man.

Ver. 12.—**And God said, This is the token** —אוֹת (*vide* ch. i. 14 ; iv. 15)—**of the cove- nant which I make**—literally, *am giving* (cf. ch. xvii. 2)—**between me and you and every living creature that is with you, for perpetual generations.** *Le'dôrôth* (*vide* ch. vi. 9) ; '*ôlam* (from '*alam,* to hide, to conceal), pr. *that which is hidden;* hence, specially, time of which either the beginning or the end is uncertain or undefined, the duration being usually determined by the nature of the case (*vide* Gesenius, 'Heb. Lex.,' *sub voce*). Here the meaning is, that so long as there were circuits or generations of men upon the earth, so long would this covenant endure.

Ver. 13.—**I do set.** Literally, *I have given, or placed,* an indication that the atmospheric phenomenon referred to had already frequently appeared (Syriac, Arabic, Aben Ezra, Chrysostom, Calvin, Willet, Murphy, Wordsworth, Kalisch, Lange). The contrary opinion has been maintained that it now for the first time appeared (Bush, Keil, Delitzsch), or at least that the historian thought so (Knobel) ; but unless there had been no rain, or the laws of light and the atmospheric conditions of the earth had been different from what they are at present, it must have been a frequent spectacle in the primeval heavens. **My bow.** *I. e.* the rainbow, τόξον (LXX.), (cf. Ezek. i. 28). The ordinary rainbow consists of a series of successive zones or bands of polarised light, forming little concentric circles in the sky, and having a common centre almost always below the horizon, and diametrically opposite to the sun. It is produced by the refraction and reflection of the sun's light through the spherical raindrops on which the rays fall, and, accordingly, must always appear, with a greater or a lesser degree of visibility, when the two material agencies come in contact. The part of the sky on which the rainbow is thrown is much more bright within than without the bow. The outer space is dark, almost black; and the inner space, on the contrary, melts into the violet almost insensibly (Nichol's 'Cyclopedia of the Sciences,' art. Rainbow). It is here styled God's bow, as being his workmanship (cf. Ecclus. xliii. 12), and his seal appended to his covenant (ch. ix. 17). **In the cloud.** עָנָן, *that which veils the heavens*, from a root signifying to cover (Gesenius). **And it shall be for a token.** לְאוֹת = εἰς σημεῖον (LXX.). In Greek mythology the rainbow is designated by a name (Iris) which is at least connected with εἴρω, to speak, and εἰρήνη, peace; is represented as the daughter of Thaumas (wonder), and Electra (brightness) the daughter of Oceanus; is assigned the office of messenger to the king and queen of Olympus; and is depicted as set in heaven for a sign (Homer, 'Il.,' xi. 27; xvii. 547, 548; xxiv. 144, 159; Virgil, 'Æn.,' iv. 694; v. 606; Ovid, 'Met.,' i. 270; xi. 585). The Persians seem to have associated the rainbow with similar ideas. An old picture, mentioned by Stolberg, represents a winged boy on a rainbow with an old man kneeling in a posture of worship. The Hindoos describe the rainbow as a warlike weapon in the hands of Indras their god, "with which he hurls flashing darts upon the impious giants;" but also as a symbol of peace exhibited to man "when the combat of the heavens is silenced." By the Chinese it is regarded as the harbinger of troubles and misfortunes on earth, and by the old Scandinavians as a bridge uniting earth and heaven ('Kalisch on Genesis,' pp. 223, 224). Traditional reflections of the Biblical narrative, they do not "account for the application in the Pentateuch of the rainbow to a very remarkable purpose," or "explain why the New Testament represents the rainbow as an attribute of the Divine throne," or "why angels are sent as messengers on earth" (Kalisch); but are themselves accounted for

and explained by it. The institution of the rainbow as a sign clearly negatives the idea (Aquinas, Cajetan) that it was originally and naturally a sign; which, if it was, "it was a lying sign," since the Flood came notwithstanding its prognostications (Willet). **Of a covenant.** "The bow in the hands of man was an instrument of battle (ch. xlviii. 22; Ps. vii. 12; Prov. vi. 2; Zech. ix. 10); but the bow bent by the hand of God has become a symbol of peace" (Wordsworth). **Between me and the earth.**

Ver. 14.—**And it shall come to pass, when I bring a cloud over the earth.** Literally, *in my clouding a cloud*, i. e. gathering clouds, which naturally signify store of rain (1 Kings xviii. 44, 45). Clouds are often used to denote afflictions and dangers (cf. Ezek. xxx. 3, 18; xxxii. 7; xxxiv. 12; Joel ii. 2). **That the bow shall be seen in the cloud.** Literally, *and the bow is seen*, which it always is when the sun's rays fall upon it, if the spectator's back is towards the light, and his face towards the cloud. Thus at the moment when danger seems to threaten most, the many-coloured arch arrests the gaze.

Ver. 15.—**And I will remember** (cf. ch. viii. 1). An anthropomorphism introduced to remind man that God is ever faithful to his covenant engagements (Calvin). "God is said to remember, because he maketh us to know and to remember" (Chrysostom). **My covenant** (*vide* on ver. 11), **which is between me and you and every living creature of all flesh; and the waters shall no more become a flood**—*hayah* with *le* = to become (cf. ch. ii. 7); literally, *shall no more be* (i. e. grow) to a flood; or, "and there shall no more be the waters to the extent of a flood"—**to destroy all flesh.**

Ver. 16.—**And the bow shall be in the cloud; and I will look upon it, that I may remember the everlasting covenant.** Literally, *the covenant of eternity*. One of those pregnant Scripture sayings that have in them an almost inexhaustible fulness of meaning, which does not at first sight disclose itself to the eye of the unreflecting reader. In so far as the Noachic covenant was simply a promise that there should be no recurrence of a flood, the covenant of eternity had a corresponding limit in its duration to the period of this present terrestrial economy. But, rightly viewed, the Noachic covenant was the original Adamic covenant set up again in a different form; and hence, when applied to it, the phrase **covenant of eternity** is entitled to retain its highest and fullest significance, as a covenant reaching from eternity to eternity. **Between God and every living creature of all flesh that is upon the earth.**

Ver. 17.—**And God said unto Noah, This**

is **the token of the covenant.** Murphy thinks that God here directed the patriarch's attention to an actual rainbow; it seems more natural to conclude that from the beginning of the interview (ch. viii. 20) the ark, altar, and worshippers were encircled by its variegated arch. Kalisch compares with the rainbow the other signs which God subsequently appended to his covenants; as, *e. g.*, circumcision (ch. xvii. 11), the passover (Exod. xii. 13), the sabbath (*ibid.* xxxi. 13). The Noachic covenant being universal, the sign was also universal—"τέρας μερόπων ἀνθρώπων" (Il., xi. 27), a sign to men of many tongues. The later covenants being limited to Israel, their signs were local and provisional, and have now been supplanted by the higher symbolism of the Christian Church, viz., baptism, the Lord's Supper, and the Christian sabbath. **Which I have established.** The different verbs used in this passage in connection with בְּרִית may be here brought together. 1. נָתַן (ver. 12) representing the covenant as a gift of Divine grace. 2. קוּם (Hiph. ; vers. 9, 11, 17) exhibiting the covenant as something which God has both caused to stand and raised up when fallen. 3. זָכַר (ver. 15) depicting the covenant as always present to the Divine mind. Tuch, Stähelin, and Delitzsch detect an idiosyncrasy of the Elohist in using the first and second of these verbs instead of כָּרַת, the favourite expression of the Jehovist. But כָּרַת is used by the Elohist in ch. xxi. 27, 32, while in Deut. iv. 18 the Jehovist uses הֵקִים. **Between me and all flesh that is upon the earth.**

HOMILETICS.

Ver. 16.—*The covenant renewed.* I. THE AUTHOR OF THE COVENANT. God. This is evident from the nature of the case. In ordinary language a covenant signifies "a mutual contract between two (or more) parties" (Hodge, 'Syst. Theol.,' vol. ii. p. 355); cf. ch. xxi. 27 (Abraham and Abimelech); Josh. xxiv. 25 (Joshua and Israel); 1 Sam. xviii. 3 (Jonathan and David) ; 1 Kings xx. 34 (Ahab and Benhadad); "comprehending a promise made by the one to the other, accompanied with a condition, upon the performance of which the accepter becomes entitled to the fulfilment of the promise" (Dick's 'Theol. Lect.,' xlv.). Applied, however, to those transactions between God and man which took their rise subsequent to the fall, a covenant is an arrangement or disposition originated by God under which certain free and gracious promises are made over to man, which promises are ratified by sacrifice and impose certain obligations on their recipients, while they are usually connected with institutions illustrative of their nature (cf. 'Kelly on the Covenants,' lect. i. p. 12). But, taking either definition of the term, it is obvious that the initial movement in any such transaction must belong to God ; and with special emphasis does God claim to be the sole Author of the covenant established with Noah and his descendants (vers. 9, 11, 12, 17).

II. THE PARTIES TO THE COVENANT, *i. e.* the persons interested in the covenant; viz., Noah and his posterity. But Noah and his sons at that time were—1. *The heads of the race.* Hence the covenant may be said to have possessed a worldwide aspect. Because of their connection with Noah the entire family of man had an interest in its provisions. 2. *The fathers of the Church.* As believers Noah and his family had been saved ; and with them, in the character of believers, the covenant was made. Hence it had also a special outlook to the Church, for whom it had a blessing quite distinct from that which it conferred upon the world as such.

III. THE SUBSTANCE OF THE COVENANT. Calling it so frequently as he does "my covenant" (ch. vi. 18; vii. 9, 11), the Author of it seems desirous to connect it in our thoughts with that old covenant which, more than sixteen centuries earlier, he had established with mankind immediately after the fall. Now that covenant was in substance an arrangement, disposition, proposal, or promise of mercy and salvation ; and that has been the essential element in every covenant that God has made with man. So to speak, God's covenant is just another name for his formal conveyance to mankind sinners of the free gift of Christ and his salvation.

IV. THE FORM OF THE COVENANT. While in every age essentially the same, the form of the covenant has been changing with the changing eras of human history. When we speak of a change of dispensation, the thing meant is a change upon the outward form or mode of representing the covenant—a dispensation being a Divine arrangement for communicating blessing. In prediluvian times the form which the covenant assumed was the promise of the woman's seed. From the Deluge onwards it was a promise of forbearance—"Neither shall all flesh be cut off any more by the waters of a flood; neither shall there be any more a flood to destroy the earth." In the patriarchal era it became the promise of a son "in whom all the families of the earth should be blessed" (ch. xii. 3; xviii. 18; xxii. 18). Under the Mosaic dispensation the promise of a prophet like unto Moses (Deut. xviii. 15); during the monarchy the promise of a king to sit upon David's throne (2 Sam. vii. 12); in the time of Isaiah the promise of a suffering servant of the Lord (Isa. xlii., liii.); in the fulness of the times it assumed its permanent form, viz., that of the incarnation of the Lord Jesus Christ as the woman's seed, as Abraham's child, as David's son, as Jehovah's servant.

V. THE SEAL OF THE COVENANT. Covenant transactions under the old or Levitical dispensation were invariably accompanied with the offering up of sacrificial victims, as a public attestation of the binding character of the arrangement. The covenant which God made with Noah had also its sacrificial seal. 1. *The meritorious sacrifice.* The propitiatory offering of the Lord Jesus Christ, on the sole ground of which he is well pleased with and mercifully disposed towards the race of sinful man. 2. *The typical sacrifice.* The offering of Noah upon Ararat after emerging from the ark.

VI. THE SIGN OF THE COVENANT. The rainbow, which was—1. A *universal* sign. The covenant having been made with the entire family of man, it was in a manner requisite that the sign should be one which was patent to the race; not limited and local and national, like circumcision, afterwards given to the Hebrews or Abrahamidæ, but universal, ubiquitous, cosmopolitan; and such was the rainbow. This was a first mark of kindness on the part of God towards the family which he had taken into covenant with himself. 2. An *attractive* sign. Such as could not fail to arrest the gaze of those whose special interest it was to behold it. Nothing is more remarkable than the quickness with which it attracts the eye, and the pleasurable feelings which its sight enkindles. In its selection, then, to be a sign and symbol of his covenant, instead of something in itself repulsive or even indifferent, we can detect another proof of kindness on the part of God. 3. A *seasonable* sign. At the very moment, as it were, when nature's elements are threatening another deluge, the signal of heaven's clemency is hung out upon the watery sky to rebuke the fears of men. Another token of special kindness on the part of God. 4. A *suggestive* sign—suggestive of the covenant of grace. Possibly this was the chief reason why the rainbow was selected as the sign of the covenant; a further display of kindness on the part of God.

VII. THE PERPETUITY OF THE COVENANT. 1. *To eternity* (ver. 16). In so far as it was a spiritual covenant with the believing Church, it was designed to be unto, as it had actually been from, everlasting. 2. *For perpetual generations* (ver. 12). In so far as it was a providential covenant with the race, it was designed to continue to the end of time.

Lessons:—1. The exceeding riches of Divine grace in dealing with men by way of a covenant. 2. The exceeding faithfulness of God in adhering to his covenant, notwithstanding man's sinfulness and provocation. 3. The exceeding hopefulness of man's position in being placed beneath a covenant of mercy.

HOMILIES BY VARIOUS AUTHORS.

Vers. 8—17. — *The new Noachic covenant established.* I. It is a COVENANT OF LIFE. It embraces all the posterity of Noah, *i. e.* it is—1. *The new foundation* on which humanity rests. 2. It passes through man *to all flesh,* to all living creatures. 3. The sign of it, *the rainbow in the cloud,* is also the emblem of the *salvation* which may be said to be typified in the deliverance of Noah and his family. 4. The background is the same element wherewith the world was destroyed, representing *the righteousness of God* as against the sin of man. *On that righteousness God sets the sign of love,* which is produced by the rays of light—the sun being the emblem of Divine goodness — radiating from the infinite centre in the glorious Father of all.

"*And it shall come to pass, when I bring a cloud over the earth, that the bow shall be seen in the cloud.*"

II. GOD'S REVELATION SET BEFORE OUR FAITH. 1. It is *waiting to be recognised.* When we place ourselves in *right relation* to the revelations and promises of Jehovah we can always see the bow on the cloud of sense, on events—*bright* compassion on the *darkest* providence. 2. There is an *interdependence* between the *objective* and *subjective.* The rainbow is the natural result of an adjustment between the sun, the earth, the cloud falling in rain, and man, the beholder. Take *the earth* to represent the abiding laws of man's nature and God's righteousness, *the falling cloud* to represent the condemnation and punishment of human sin, *the sun* the revealed love and mercy of God sending forth its beams in the midst of the dispensation of judgment; then let there be *faith in man* to *look up* and rejoice in that which is set before him, and he will *behold the rainbow of the covenant* even on the very background of the condemnation.

III. TRANSFIGURED RIGHTEOUSNESS IN REDEMPTION. The cross at once condemnation and life. The same righteousness which once destroyed the earth is manifested in Christ Jesus—"*righteousness unto all and upon all them that believe.*"

IV. UNION OF GOD AND MAN. God himself is said to look upon the sign of the covenant that he may *remember.* So *man looking* and *God looking* to the *same pledge* of salvation. "God was in Christ reconciled," &c. Their reconciliation is complete and established.—R.

Ver. 13.— *The bow in the cloud.* With deep joy and yet with awe must Noah have looked around him on leaving the ark. On every side signs of the mighty destruction; the earth scarcely dried, and the busy throng of men (Luke xvii. 27) all gone. Yet signs of new life; the earth putting forth verdure, as though preparing for a new and happier chapter of history. His first recorded act was sacrifice—an acknowledgment that his preserved life was God's gift, a new profession of faith in him. Then God gave the promise that no such destruction should again befall the earth, and so ordered the sign that the rain-cloud which might excite the fear should bring with it the rainbow, the pledge of the covenant. But as ch. vi. 18 foreshadowed the Christian covenant (1 Pet. iii. 21) in its aspect of deliverance from destruction, the text points to the same in its bearing on daily life and service. The Godward life and renewal of the will which the law could not produce (Rom. viii. 3) is made sure to believers through the constraining power of the love of Christ (cf. 1 John iii. 3; Rev. xii. 11). And if clouds should cause fear, and God's face be hidden, and the energy of dedication grow languid, we are reminded (Rom. vi. 14; Gal. v. 24). And in the vision of the glorified Church (Rev. iv. 3) the rainbow again appears, pointing back to the early sign, connecting them as parts of one scheme, and visibly setting forth the glory of God in his mercy and grace (cf. Exod. xxxiii. 19; xxxiv. 6; John i. 14).

I. THE COVENANT WAS MADE WITH NOAH AND HIS SEED AS CHILDREN OF FAITH. They had believed in God's revealed way of salvation and entered the ark (cf. Num. xxi. 8). The root of a Christian life is belief in a finished redemption (2 Cor. v. 14; 1 John v. 11); not belief that the doctrine is true, but trust in the fact as the one ground of hope. Hast thou acted on God's call; entered the ark; trusted Christ; none else, nothing else? Waitest thou for something in thyself? Noah did not think of fitness when told to enter. God calleth thee as unfit (cf. 1 Tim. i. 15). Try to believe; make a real effort (cf. Matt. xv. 28; Mark ix. 23).

II. THE POWER OF A CHRISTIAN LIFE; FAITH AS A HABIT OF THE MIND. Look to the bow. "Looking unto Jesus." The world is the field on which God's grace is shown; we are the actors by whom his work is done. How shall we do this? Beset by hindrances—love of the world, love of self, love of ease. We cannot of ourselves (cf. Luke xxii. 33, 34; Rom. xi. 20). We are strong only in trusting to the power of the Lord (cf. 2 Cor. xii. 10; Phil. iv. 13).

III. IN THIS THE HOLY SPIRIT IS OUR HELPER. His office is to reveal Christ to the soul. His help is promised if sought for.—M.

EXPOSITION.

Ver. 18.—**And the sons of Noah, that went forth of the ark, were Shem, and Ham, and Japheth,** who are here again mentioned as the heads of the nations into which the family of man developed, the writer having described the important modifications made upon the law of nature and the covenant of grace, and being now about to proceed with the onward course of human history. The present section, extending to ver. 27, is usually assigned to the Jehovistic author (Tuch, Bleek, Kalisch, Colenso, Kuenen), though by Davidson it is ascribed to a so-called redactor, with the exception of the present clause, which is recognised as the Jehovist's contribution to the story. The ground of this apportionment is the introduction of the name Jehovah in ver. 26 (*q. v.*), and certain traces throughout the paragraph of the style of writing supposed to be peculiar to the supplementer. **And Ham is the father of Canaan.** *Kena'an,* the depressed or low one ; either the Lowlander or inhabitant of a low coast country, as opposed to the loftier regions (Aram) ; from *kana'*, to be low, depressed, in situation, as of land (Gesenius) ; or more probably the servile one in spirit (Fürst, Murphy, Keil, Lange). The reason for the insertion of this notice here, and of the similar one in ver. 22, was obviously to draw attention to the circumstance, not " that the origin of Israel's ascendancy and of Canaan's degradation dates so far back as the family of the second founder of the human race," as if the writer's standpoint were long subsequent to the conquest (Kalisch), but that, " as Israel was now going to possess the land of Canaan, they might know that now was the time when the curse of Canaan and his posterity should take place " (Willet).

Ver. 19.—**These are the three sons of Noah ; and of them was the whole earth** —*i. e.* the earth's population (cf. ch. xi. 1 ; xix. 31)—**overspread.** More correctly, *dispersed themselves abroad.* Διεσπάρησαν ἐπὶ πᾶσαν τὴν γῆν (LXX.) : *disseminatum est omne genus hominum* (Vulgate).

Ver. 20.—**And Noah began to be an husbandman.** Literally, *a man of the ground.* *Vir terræ* (Vulgate) ; ἄνθρωπος γεωργὸς γῆς (LXX.) ; Chald., נְבַר פָּלַח בְּאַרְעָא = *vir colens terram ; agriculturæ dediturus.* Cf. Josh. v. 4, "a man of war ;" 2 Sam. xvi. 7, "a man of blood ;" Gen. xlvi. 32, "a man of cattle ;" Exod. iv. 10, "a man of words." **And he planted a vineyard.** So Murphy, Wordsworth, Kalisch. Keil, Delitzsch, and Lange regard *ish ha' Adamah,* with the art., as in apposition to Noah, and read, "And Noah, the husbandman,

began and planted a vineyard," i. e. *cœpit plantare* (cf. Gesenius, 'Gram.,' § 142, 3 ; Glass, ' Sacræ Philologiæ,' lib. iii. tr. iii. can. 34). Neither interpretation presupposes that husbandry and vine cultivation were now practised for the first time. That Armenia is a wine-growing country is testified by Xenophon ('Anab.,' iv. 4, 9). That the vine was abundantly cultivated in Egypt is evident from representations on the monuments, as well as from Scriptural allusions. The Egyptians say that Osiris, the Greeks that Dionysus, the Romans that Saturn, first taught men the cultivation of the tree and the use of its fruit.

Ver. 21. — **And he drank of the wine.** יַיִן; "perhaps so called from bubbling up and fermenting ;" connected with יָוָן (Gesenius). Though the first mention of wine in Scripture, it is scarcely probable that the natural process of fermentation for so many centuries escaped the notice of the enterprising Cainites, or even of the Sethites ; that, "though grapes had been in use before this, wine had not been extracted from them " (Murphy) ; or that Noah was unacquainted with the nature and effects of this intoxicating liquor (Chrysostom, Theodoret, Keil, Lange). The article before יַיִן indicates that the patriarch was "familiar with the use and treatment " of the grape (Kalisch) ; and Moses does not say this was the first occasion on which the patriarch tasted the fermented liquor (Calvin, Wordsworth). **And was drunken.** The verb שָׁכַר (whence *shechar,* strong drink, Num. xxviii. 7), to drink to the full, very often signifies to make oneself drunken, or simply to be intoxicated as the result of drinking ; and that which the Holy Spirit here reprobates is not the partaking of the fruit of the vine, but the drinking so as to be intoxicated thereby. Since the sin of Noah cannot be ascribed to ignorance, it is perhaps right, as well as charitable, to attribute it to age and inadvertence. Six hundred years old at the time of the Flood, he must have been considerably beyond this when Ham saw him overtaken in his fault, since Canaan was Ham's fourth son (ch. x. 6), and the first was not born till after the exit from the ark (ch. viii. 18). But from whatever cause induced, the drunkenness of Noah was not entirely guiltless ; it was sinful in itself, and led to further shame. **And he was uncovered.** Literally, *he uncovered himself.* Hithpael of גָּלָה, to make naked, which more correctly indicates the personal guilt of the patriarch than the A. V., or the LXX., ἐγυμνώθη. That intoxication tends to sensuality cf. the cases of Lot (ch. xix. 33), Ahasuerus (Esther i. 10, 11), Belshazzar (Dan. v. 1—6). **Within his tent.** 'Εν τῷ οἴκῳ αὐτοῦ (LXX.).

Ver. 22.—**And Ham, the father of Canaan, saw the nakedness.** *Pudenda,* from a root (עָרָה) signifying to make naked, from a kindred root to which (שׁוּם) comes the term expressive of the nakedness of Adam and Eve after eating the forbidden fruit (ch. iii. 7). The sin of Ham—not a "trifling and unintentional transgression" (Von Bohlen)—obviously lay not in seeing what perhaps he may have come upon unexpectedly, but (1) in wickedly rejoicing in what he saw, which, considering who he was that was overcome with wine,—"the minister of salvation to men, and the chief restorer of the world,"—the relation in which he stood to Ham,—that of father,—the advanced age to which he had now come, and the comparatively mature years of Ham himself, who was "already more than a hundred years old," should have filled him with sincere sorrow; "sed nunquam vino victum patrem filius risisset, nisi prius ejecisset animo illam reverentiam et opinionem, quæ in liberis de parentibus ex mandato Dei existere debet" (Luther); and (2) in reporting it, doubtless with a malicious purpose, to his brethren. **And told his two brethren without.** Possibly inviting them to come and look upon their father's shame.

Ver. 23.—**And Shem and Japheth took a garment.** Literally, *the robe,* i. e. which was at hand (Keil, Lange); the *simlah,* which was an outer cloak (Deut. x. 18; 1 Sam. xxi. 10; Isa. iii. 6, 7), in which, at night, persons wrapped themselves (Deut. xxii. 17). Sometimes the letters are transposed, and the word becomes *salmah* (cf. Exod. xxii. 8; Micah ii. 8). **And laid it upon both their shoulders, and went backwards, and covered the nakedness of their father; and their faces** were **backward, and they saw not the nakedness of their father;** thereby evincing "the regard they paid to their father's honour and their own modesty" (Calvin).

Ver. 24. — **And Noah awoke from his wine.** *I.e.* the effects of his wine (cf. 1 Sam. i. 14; xxv. 37); ἐξένηψε (LXX.); "became fully conscious of his condition" (T. Lewis). **And knew.** By inspiration (Alford); more probably by making inquiries as to the reason of the simlah covering him. **What his younger son.** Literally, *his son, the little one,* i. e. the youngest son (Willet, Murphy, Wordsworth, T. Lewis, Alford, Candlish), or the younger son (Keil, Bush, Kalisch); cf. ch. v. 32. Generally believed to have been Ham, though by many Canaan is understood (Aben Ezra, Theodoret, Procopius, Scaliger, Poole, Jamieson, Inglis,

Lewis). Origen mentions a tradition that Canaan first saw the shame of Noah, and told it to his father. Wordsworth, following Chrysostom, believes Canaan may have been an accomplice. 'The Speaker's Commentary' thinks it would solve the difficulty which attaches to the cursing of Canaan.

Ver. 25.—**And he said.** Not in personal resentment, since "the fall of Noah is not at all connected with his prophecy, except as serving to bring out the real character of his children, and to reconcile him to the different destinies which he was to announce as awaiting their respective races" (Candlish); but under the impulse of a prophetic spirit (Poole, Keil, Lange, Candlish, Murphy, and expositors generally), which, however, had its historical occasion in the foregoing incident. The structure of the prophecy is perfectly symmetrical, introducing, in three poetical verses, (1) the curse of Canaan, (2) the blessing of Shem, and (3) the enlargement of Japheth, and in all three giving prominence to the doom of servitude pronounced upon the son of Ham. **Cursed.** The second curse pronounced upon a human being, the first having been on Cain (ch. iv. 11). Colenso notices that all the curses belong to the Jehovistic writer; but *vide* ch. xlix. 6, 7, which Tuch and Bleek ascribed to the Elohist, though, doubtless in consequence of the "curse," by Davidson and others it is now assigned to the Jehovist. That this curse was not an imprecation, but a prediction of the future subjection of the Canaanites, has been maintained (Theodoret, Venema, Willet), chiefly in consequence of its falling upon Canaan; but (1) as the contrary "blessing" implies the inheritance of good in virtue of a Divine disposition to that effect, so does "cursing" import subjection to evil by the same Divine power; and (2) if we eliminate the moral element from the doom of Canaan, which clearly referred to a condition of temporal servitude, there seems no reason why the language of Noah should not be regarded as a solemnly pronounced and Divinely guaranteed infliction; while (3) as the curse is obviously aimed at the nations and peoples descending from the execrated person, it is not inconsistent to suppose that many individuals amongst those nations and peoples might attain to a high degree of temporal and spiritual prosperity. **Be Canaan.** (1) Not Ham, the father of Canaan (Arabic Version); nor (2) all the sons of Ham, though concentrated in Canaan (Hävernick, Keil, Murphy); but (3) Canaan alone, though indirectly, through him, Ham also (Calvin, Bush, Kalisch, Lange, *et alii*). For the formal omission of Ham many different reasons have been assigned. (1) Because God had preserved him in the ark (Jewish commentators). (2) Because if Ham had been mentioned all his other sons would have been implicated (Pererius, Lange). (3) Because the sin of Ham was comparatively trifling (Bohlen). For the cursing of Canaan instead of Ham, it has been urged — (1) That he was Ham's youngest son, as Ham was Noah's (Hoffman and Delitzsch); surely a very insufficient reason for God cursing any one! (2) That he was the real perpetrator of the crime (Aben Ezra, Procopius, Poole, Jamieson, Lewis, &c.). (3) That thereby the greatness of Ham's sin was evinced (Calvin). (4) That Canaan was already walking in the steps of his father's impiety (Ambrose, Mercerus, Keil). (5) That Noah foresaw that the Canaanites would abundantly deserve this visitation (Calvin, Wordsworth, Murphy, Kalisch, Lange). We incline to think the truth lies in the last three reasons. **A servant of servants.** A Hebraism for the superlative degree; cf. " King of kings," "holy of holies," "the song of songs" (vide Gesenius, § 119). I. e. "the last even among servants" (Calvin); " a servant reduced to the lowest degree of bondage and degradation " (Bush); " vilissima servitute pressus " (Sol. Glass); " a most base and vile servant " (Ainsworth); "a working servant" (Chaldee); "the lowest of slaves" (Keil); παῖς οἰκέτης (LXX.), which " conveys the notion of permanent hereditary servitude " (Kalisch). Keil, Hengstenberg, and Wordsworth see an allusion to this condition in the name Canaan (q.v., supra), which, however, Lange doubts. **Shall he be to his brethren.** A prophecy which was afterwards abundantly fulfilled, the Canaanites in the time of Joshua having been partly exterminated and partly reduced to the lowest form of slavery by the Israelites who belonged to the family of Shem (Josh. ix. 23), those that remained being subsequently reduced by Solomon (1 Kings ix. 20, 21); while the Phenicians, along with the Carthaginians and Egyptians, who all belonged to the family of Canaan, were subjected by the Japhetic Persians, Macedonians, and Romans (Keil).

Ver. 26.—**And he said**—not " Blessed of Jehovah, my God, be Shem " (Jamieson), as might have been anticipated (this, equally with the omission of Ham's name, lifts the entire patriarchal utterance out of the region of mere personal feeling), but—**Blessed**— בָּרוּךְ when applied to God signifies an ascription of praise (cf. Ps. cxliv. 15; Ephes. i. 3); when applied to man, an invocation of good (cf. ch. xiv. 19, 20; Ps. cxxviii. 1; Heb. vii. 6)—be **the Lord God**—literally, Jehovah, Elohim of Shem (cf. ch. xxiv. 27); Jehovah being the proper personal name of God, of whom it is predicated that he is the Elohim of Shem; equivalent to a statement not simply that Shem should

enjoy " a rare and transcendent," " Divine or heavenly," blessing (Calvin), or " a most abundant blessing, reaching its highest point in the promised Seed" (Luther); but that Jehovah, the one living and true God, should be his God, and that the knowledge and practice of the true religion should continue among his descendants, with, perhaps, a hint that the promised Seed should spring from his loins (Œcolampadius, Willet, Murphy, Keil, &c.)—**of Shem.** In the name Shem (name, renown) there may lie an allusion to the spiritual exaltation and advancement of the Semitic nations (vide ch. v. 32).

And Canaan shall be his servant. לָמוֹ == לָהֶם (Chaldee, Syriac, Arabic), i. e. the two brothers (Delitzsch), their descendants (Knobel, Keil), Shem and Jehovah (Bush); or more probably = לוֹ, as a collective singular (cf. Gesenius, § 103, 2), i. e. Shem, including his descendants (LXX., αὐτοῦ; Kalisch, Lange, Murphy).

Ver. 27.—**God.** Elohim. If vers. 18—27 are Jehovistic (Tuch, Bleek, Colenso, et alii), why Elohim? Is this a proof that the Jehovistic document was revised by the Elohistic author, as the presence of Jehovah in any so-called Elohistic section is regarded as an interpolation by the supplementer? To obviate this inference Davidson assigns vers. 20 — 27 to his redactor. But the change of name is sufficiently explained when we remember that " Jehovah, as such, never was the God of Japheth's descendants, and that the expression would have been as manifestly improper if applied to him as it is in its proper place applied to Shem " (Quarry, p. 393). **Shall enlarge Japheth.** יַפְתְּ לְיֶפֶת; literally, shall enlarge or make room for the one that spreads abroad; or, " may God concede an ample space to Japheth " (Gesenius). " Wide let God make it for Japheth " (Keil). " God give enlargement to Japheth" (Lange). So LXX., Vulgate, Chaldee, Syriac, Arabic. The words form a paronomasia, — both the verb and the noun being connected with the root פָּתָה, to spread abroad; Hiph., to cause to lie open, hence to make room for,—and refer to the widespread diffusion and remarkable prosperity of the Japhetic nations. The familiar interpretation which renders " God will persuade Japheth, the persuadible," i. e. incline his heart by the gospel so that he may dwell in the tents of Shem (Junius, Vatablus, Calvin, Willet, Ainsworth), is discredited by the facts (1) that the verb never means to persuade, except in a bad sense (cf. 1 Kings xxii. 20), and (2) that in this sense it is never followed by לְ, but always by the accusative (vide Gesenius, sub. nom.; cf.

Bush, p. 109). The fulfilment of the prophecy is apparent from the circumstance that "præter Europam" ($\epsilon\dot{\nu}\rho\dot{\omega}\pi\eta =$ wide, extensive) "maximam Asiæ partem, totum demique novum orbem, veluti immensæ magnitudinis auctarium, Japheto posterique ejus in perpetuam possessionem obtigisse" (Fuller, 'Sac. Miscel.,' lib. ii. c. 1, quoted by Glass); cf. ch. x. 2—5, in which Japheth is given as the progenitor of fourteen peoples, to which are added the inhabitants of the lands washed by the sea. The expansive power of Japheth "refers not only to the territory and the multitude of the Japhethites, but also to their intellectual and active faculties. The metaphysics of the Hindoos, the philosophy of the Greeks, the military prowess of the Romans, and the modern science and civilisation of the world are due to the race of Japheth" (Murphy). **And he**—not *Elohim* (Philo., Theodoret, Onkelos, Dathe, Baumgarten, *et alii*), which (1) substantially repeats the blessing already given to Shem, and (2) would introduce an allusion to the superiority of Shem's blessing in what the context requires should be an unrestricted benediction of Japheth ; but *Japheth* (Calvin, Rosenmüller, Delitzsch, Keil, Lange, Kalisch, Murphy, Wordsworth, 'Speaker's Commentary') — **shall dwell.** יִשְׁכֹּן, from שָׁכַן, to dwell ; used of God inhabiting the heavens (Isa. lvii. 15), dwelling in the bush

(Deut. xxx. 16), residing, or causing his name to dwell, in the tabernacle (Deut. xii. 11) ; hence supposed to favour the idea that Elohim is the subject ; but it was as Jehovah (not Elohim) that God abode between the cherubim (Exod. xl. 34). **In the tents of Shem.** Not the tents of celebrity (Gesenius, Vater, Michaelis, De Wette, Knobel), but the tents of the Shemitic races, with allusion not to their subjugation by the Japhethites (Clericus, Von Bohlen, Bochart), which would not be in keeping with the former blessing pronounced upon them (Murphy), but to their subsequent contiguity to, and even commingling with, but especially to their participation in the religious privileges of, the Shemites (the Fathers, Targum Jonathan, Hieronymus, Calvin, Keil, Lange, 'Speaker's Commentary,' Murphy, Candlish). The fulfilment of the prophecy is too obvious to call for illustration. **And Canaan shall be his servant.**

Vers. 28, 29.—**And Noah lived after the flood three hundred and fifty years.** *I. e.* to the fifty-eighth year of the life of Abram, and was thus in all probability a witness of the building of the tower of Babel, and of the consequent dispersion of mankind. **And all the days of Noah were nine hundred and fifty years : and he died.** Tuch, Bleek, and Colenso connect these verses with ver. 17, as the proper continuation of the Elohist's work.

HOMILETICS.

Vers. 20—29.—*The future unveiled.* I. A PAGE FROM HUMAN HISTORY. The prominent figure an old man (of 620 years or upwards)—always an object of interest, as one who has passed through life's vicissitudes, and worthy of peculiar honour, especially if found walking in the paths of righteousness and peace ; an old saint who had long been distinguished for the elevation of his piety, who had long maintained his fidelity to God in the midst of evil times, who had just enjoyed a special deliverance at the hand of God, and who up to the period referred to in our text had brought neither stain upon his piety nor cloud upon his name ; the second head of the human family, and in a manner also the second head of the Church of God ; an old disciple, who probably had seen Seth, the son of Adam, and walked with Enoch, and spoken with Methuselah, and who lived, as the Scripture tells us, to the days of Abram ; clearly one of the most distinguished figures that, looking back, one is able to detect upon the canvas of time. Well, in connection with this venerable patriarch we learn—1. That *he engaged in a highly honourable occupation.* (1) *It was to his credit that he had an occupation.* Being an old man, he might have reasoned that his working days were done, and that the evening of life might as well be spent in leisure and meditation. Having three stalwart sons, he might have deemed it proper to look to them for aid in his declining years. And knowing himself to be an object of Heaven's peculiar care, he might have trusted God would feed him without his working, since he had saved him without his asking. But from all these temptations—to idleness, to dependence, to presumption—Noah was delivered, and preferred, as all good Christians should do, to labour to the last, working while it is called to-day, to depend upon themselves rather than their friends and neighbours, and to expect God's assistance rather when they try to help themselves than when they leave it all to him. Then, (2) *The calling he engaged in was an honest one.*

He was a man of the soil, and he planted a vineyard (*vide* Exposition on vine cultivation). God's people should be careful in selecting honest trades and professions
for themselves and their children (Rom. xii. 17). No social status, or public estimation, or profitable returns can render that employment honourable which, either in its
nature or in the manner of its carrying or, violates the law of God; while that calling
has a special glory in itself and a special value in the sight of Heaven which, however
humble and unremunerative, respects the rights of men and the rules of God. 2. That
he indulged in a perfectly legitimate gratification. "He drank of the wine." There
was nothing wrong in Noah eating of the ripe grapes which grew upon his vines,
or drinking of their juice when transformed into wine (cf. Deut. xxv. 4; 1 Cor. ix.
7). The sinfulness of making fermented liquors cannot be established so long as
fermentation is a natural process for the preservation of the produce of the grape,
and Scripture, in one set of passages, speaks of its beneficial influence upon man's
physical system (Judges ix. 13; Ps. civ. 15; Prov. xxxi. 6; 1 Tim. v. 23), and
God himself employs it as a symbol of the highest and choicest blessings, both
temporal and spiritual (Gen. xxvii. 28, 37; Prov. ix. 2; Isa. xxv. 6; Matt. xxvi.
28, 29), and Christ made it at the marriage feast of Cana (John ii. 9, 10). Nor is
the drinking of wines and other fermented liquors condemned in Scripture as a
violation of the law of God. That there are special seasons when abstinence from
this as well as other gratifications of a physical kind is a duty (cf. Levit. x. 9;
Judges xiii. 4, 14; Ezek. xliv. 21; Dan. i. 5, 8, 16; Rom. xiv. 21; 1 Cor. x. 28),
and that it is competent to any Christian, for the sake of his weaker brethren, or as
a means of advancing his own spiritual life, or for the glory of God, to renounce his
liberty in respect of drinks, no intelligent person will doubt. But that total abstinence is imperatively required of every one is neither asserted in Scripture nor was
it taught by the example of Christ (Matt. xi. 19), and to enforce it upon Christian
men as a term of communion is to impose on them a yoke of bondage which Christ
has not sanctioned, and to supplant Christian liberty by bodily asceticism. 3. That
he fell beneath a pitifully sad humiliation. (1) *He drank to the extent of intoxication.* Whatever extentuations may be offered for the action of the patriarch, it
cannot be regarded in any other light than a sin. Considering the age he had come
to, the experience he had passed through, the position which he occupied as the
head of the race and the father of the Church, he ought to have been specially upon
his guard. While permitting man a moderate indulgence in the fruit of the vine,
the word of God especially condemns the sin of drunkenness (cf. Prov. xxiii. 20;
Isa. v. 11, 22; Luke xxi. 34; Rom. xiii. 13; 1 Cor. v. 11; vi. 10; Gal. v. 21;
Ephes. v. 18; 1 Thess. v. 8). (2) *His immodesty.* The veil of modesty in which
God designs that every sinful human being should be wrapt should be jealously
guarded from infringement by any action either of ourselves or others.

Lessons:—1. "Let him that thinketh he standeth take heed lest he fall" (1 Cor.
x. 12). Remember Adam, Noah, Abraham, David, Peter. 2. "Be not drunk with
wine, wherein is excess; but be filled with the Spirit" (Ephes. v. 18). There is
scarcely a sin to which intoxication may not lead; there is no infallible cure for
drunkenness but being filled with the Spirit. 3. "Be sure thy sin will find thee out"
(Num. xxxii. 23). "There is nothing covered that shall not be revealed; neither
hid that shall not be known."

II. A REVELATION OF HUMAN CHARACTER. On the threshold of the new world,
like the Lord Jesus Christ in the opening of the gospel dispensation (Luke ii. 35),
the patriarch Noah appears to have been set for the fall and rising again of many,
and for a sign to be spoken against that the thoughts of many hearts might be
revealed. All unconsciously to him his vine-planting and wine-drinking become the
occasion of unveiling the different characters of his sons in respect of—1. *Filial
piety,* which Shem and Japheth remarkably displayed, but of which Ham, the
youngest son, appears to have been destitute. There was nothing sinful in Ham's
having witnessed what should never have been exposed to view, and there is no
reason to credit any of the idle rabbinical legends which allege that Ham perpetrated a particular outrage upon his father; but Ham was manifestly wanting in
that filial reverence and honour which were due to his aged parent, in that he gazed
with delight upon the melancholy spectacle of his father's shame — in singular
contrast to the respectful and modest behaviour of Shem and Japheth, who "went

with their faces backward," so that "they saw not their father's nakedness." 2. *Tender charity.* In addition to the mocking eye which gloated over the patriarch's infirmity, there was present in the heart of Ham an evil and malicious spirit, which led him to inflict another and a severer indignity upon his father's fame. The faults of even bad men are required by religion to be covered up rather than paraded in public view. Much more the indiscretions, failings, and sins of good men. Most of all the faults of a father. But, alas, instead of sorrowing for his father's overthrow, Ham obviously took pleasure in it; instead of charitably trying to excuse the old man, nay, without even waiting to ascertain whether an explanation of his conduct might be possible, he appears to have put the worst construction on it; instead of doing what he could to hide his father's sin and shame, he rushes forth and makes it known to his brothers. But these brothers, with another spirit, without offering any apology for their father's error, perhaps instinctively perceiving it to be altogether unjustifiable, take the first loose garment they can find, and, with a beautiful modesty as well as a becoming piety, casting it around their shoulders, enter their father's presence with their faces backward, and cover up his prostrate form. Let the incident remind us—(1) That if nothing can extenuate a father's falling into sin, much more can nothing justify a son for failing in respect towards his father. (2) That it is a sure sign of depravity in a child when he mocks at a parent's infirmities and publishes a parent's faults. (3) That filial piety ever seeks to extenuate and to hide rather than to aggravate and blaze abroad a parent's weaknesses and sins. (4) That children in the same family may be distinguished by widely different dispositions. (5) That a son may have pious parents and experience many providential mercies for their sakes, and yet be at heart a child of the devil. (6) That that which makes one son differ from another in the same family is Divine grace ; and (7) that the characters of children, and of men in general, are oftentimes revealed at the most unexpected times, and by the most improbable events.

III. A DISCLOSURE OF HUMAN DESTINY. Awaking from his wine, the patriarch became aware of what had taken place. Discerning in the conduct of his sons an indication of divergence in their characters, recognising in their different characters a repetition of what had taken place at the commencement of the first era of the world's history, viz., the division of mankind into a holy and a wicked line, foreseeing also, through the help of inspiration, the development of the world's population into three different tribes or races, he foretells, acting in all under the Spirit's guidance, the future destinies that should await them. His utterance takes the form of a prediction, in which he declares—1. *The degradation of Canaan.* "Cursed be Canaan; a servant of servants shall he be to his brethren." (1) So far as Ham was concerned this judgment was *severe*, as being imposed upon his youngest and probably his best beloved son ; *appropriate*—he for whose sake it had been inflicted having been his father's youngest son ; *merciful*, as falling not on all his race, but only upon one son and his descendants. N.B.—God's judgments upon sinful men are always proportioned in severity to the guilt which brings them, adjusted to the natures of the sins for which they come, and mixed with mercy in the experience of the persons on whom they fall. (2) So far as Canaan was concerned the doom of servitude was *sovereignly imposed.* There is no evidence that Canaan was at all connected with the incident that happened in his grandfather's tent. That the penalty of his father's offence was made to fall on him of all his father's sons was in virtue of that high prerogative which belongs to God alone of assigning to men and nations their lots on earth (cf. Ps. lxxv. 7 ; Isa. xli. 2 ; Dan. v. 19 ; iv. 35 ; Acts xvii. 26). *Richly merited.* Whether Canaan had begun by this time to display any of the dispositions of his father cannot certainly be known ; but in after years, when the prophecy was nearing its accomplishment, it is well known that the peculiar sins for which the Canaanites were destroyed or subjected to bondage were allied to those which are referred to in the text (*vide* Levit. xviii. 27). *Exactly fulfilled* by the subjugation of the land of Canaan under Joshua and David, though here it should be noted that the enslavement of the African negro, who, though a Hamite, is not a Canaanite, was a daring defiance of those limits within which the supreme Judge had confined the sentence pronounced upon the Hamite race. *Mercifully cancelled* by the later promise which was given to Abraham, and is now fulfilled in the incarnation of the Lord Jesus Christ—of a seed in whom all the families of the earth should be blessed (Gen. xxii. 18). 2. *The exaltation of Shem.* " Blessed be Jehovah, the Elohim of Shem," &c., in which description was the promise of a threefold exaltation. (1) To *supremacy in the Church*, as being possessed of the knowledge of the true religion, as being enriched with the fulness of blessing that is in Jehovah Elohim, as being the Divinely-appointed medium through which the first promise of the woman's seed was to be fulfilled, and he was to come whose name should be above every name. (2) To *dominion in the world*. In virtue of the religious ascendancy conferred upon him, Shem was to be possessed of power to influence other nations for good, and in particular to receive into his service, for education as well as for assistance, the descendants of Canaan. (3) To *renown throughout all time*. As much as this perhaps is hinted at in the name Shem ; and to this day the glory which encircled the Shemitic nations of antiquity has not faded, but continues to shine down the centuries with undiminished lustre. 3. *The enlargement of Japheth.* "God shall enlarge Japheth, and he shall dwell in the tents of Shem, and Canaan shall be his servant." A promise of—1. *Territorial expansion.* While the Shemite tribes should remain in a manner concentrated in the valley of the Tigris and Euphrates, the Japhethites should spread themselves abroad westward as the pioneers of civilisation. 2. *Spiritual enrichment*, by being brought ultimately to share in the religious privileges and blessings of the Shemites—a prediction which has been abundantly fulfilled by the admission of the Gentiles to the Christian Church. 3. *Civilising influence*. As Canaan was subjected to Shem in order, while he served, to be instructed in the faith of his master, so does he seem to have been placed beneath the sway of Japheth, that Japheth might lead him forth to a participation of the peculiar blessings which he has been commissioned to bestow upon the other nations of the earth.

HOMILIES BY VARIOUS AUTHORS.

Vers. 18—29.—*The threefold distribution of the human race*—into the Shemitic, Hamitic, and Japhetic families. The fall of Noah was through wine ; not, indeed, a forbidden product of the earth, but, like the fruit of the tree of knowledge of good and evil, representing a *tremendous responsibility*.

I. THE FERTILITY OF SIN. It was out of *drunkenness* that the widespread curse of the Hamitic nations came forth. And the drunkenness is closely connected with other sins — (1) shameful *degradation both of father and son*, (2) *alienation of brethren*, and (3) *human slavery*. What a picture of the forthcoming results of intemperance and self-indulgence !

II. THE CONTRAST BETWEEN THE BLESSING AND THE CURSE IN THEIR WORKING OUT. Noah's prediction of the blessing on Shem and Japheth and the curse upon Ham may be taken as an outline of the religious history of the world. 1. The *Shemitic races* are the source of religious light to the rest. " *Blessed be the Lord God of Shem.*" "*Jehovah*," the Shemitic revelation, is the foundation of all other. 2. The *Japhetic races* are the great *colonisers* and *populators* of the world, overflowing their own boundaries, dwelling in the tents of Shem, both as inquirers after Shemitic light and in friendly co-operation with Shemitic civilisation. 3. The *Hamitic races* are *servants of servants* unto their brethren, partly by their *degradation*, but partly also by their *achievements*. The Phœnician, Assyrian, Egyptian, Ethiopian, and Canaanitish races, although by no means always in a lower *political* state than the rest of the world, have yet been subdued by Japhetic and Shemitic conquerors, and handed down their wealth and acquirements to the Northern, Western, and Eastern world.

III. THE RENOVATION OF THE EARTH UNDER THE NEW-COVENANT. After the Flood Noah lived the half week of centuries, and thus laid firmly the *foundations of a new earth*. Yet, prolonged as was that life of him who had "*found grace in the eyes of the Lord*," it came to an end at last. *He died.* The *one* became the *three*. 1. The *blessing handed on.* The type of *rest* and *comfort* was spread through the redeemed earth. And from henceforth we have to deal not with the *small beginnings* of the rescued race, but with the *vast multitude* of human beings. 2. *New sphere of trial.* Under the light of the new covenant again the new race were placed upon their trial, that again the redeeming mercy of him who willeth not the death of his creatures may be made manifest in the midst of the teeming earth, with its *threefold humanity*, spreading eastward, westward, northward, and southward.—R.

PART II.

THE POST-DILUVIAN AGE OF THE WORLD. CH. X. 1—XI. 26.

FROM THE DELUGE TO THE CALL OF ABRAM.

§ 5. THE GENERATIONS OF THE SONS OF NOAH (CH. X. 1—XI. 9).

I. THE *historical credibility* of the present section has been challenged. 1. On account of a fancied resemblance to the ethnographic mythologies of Greece, the genealogical table of the nations has been relegated to the category of fictitious invention. It has been assigned by many critics to a post-Mosaic period, to the days of Joshua (Delitzsch), to the age of Hebrew intercourse with the Phenician Canaanites (Knobel), to the era of the exile (Bohlen); and the specific purpose of its composition has been declared to be a desire to gratify the national pride of the Hebrews by tracing their descent to the first-born son of Noah, that their rights might appear to have a superior foundation to those of other nations (Hartmann). But the primogeniture of Shem is at least doubtful, if not entirely incorrect, Japheth being the oldest of Noah's sons (*vide* ch. v. 32 ; x. 21); while it is a gratuitous assumption that not until the days of the monarchy, or the exile, did the Israelites become acquainted with foreign nations. The authenticity and genuineness of the present register, it is justly remarked by Hävernick, are guaranteed by the chronicler (ch. i. 1). "In the time of the chronicler nothing more was known from antiquity concerning the origin of nations than what Genesis supplied. Supposing, then, that some inquiring mind composed this table of nations from merely reflecting on the nations that happened to exist at the same period, and attempting to give them a systematic arrangement, how could it possibly happen that his turn of mind should be in such complete harmony with that of the other? This could only arise from the one recognising the decided superiority of the other's account, which here lies in nothing else than the historical truth itself belonging to it" (Intro., § 17). And the historical truthfulness of the Mosaic document is further strikingly authenticated by the accredited results of modern ethnological science, which, having undertaken by a careful analysis of facts to establish a classification of races, has divided mankind into three primitive groups (Shemitic, Aryan, Turanian or Allophylian), corresponding not obscurely to the threefold arrangement of the present table, and presenting in each group the leading races that Genesis assigns to the several sons of Noah ; as, *e. g.*, allocating to the Indo-European family, as Moses has done to the sons of Japheth, the principal races of Europe, with the great Asiatic race known as Aryan ; to the Shemitic, the Assyrians, Syrians, Hebrews, and Joktanite Arabs, which appear among the sons of Shem in the present table ; and to the Allophylian, the Egyptians, Ethiopians, Southern Arabs, and early Babylonians, which the primitive ethnologist of Genesis also writes among the sons of Ham (cf. Rawlinson's 'Hist. Illus. of O. T.,' p. 23). 2. The narrative of the building of the tower of Babel has also been impugned, and that chiefly on two grounds : viz., (1) an incorrect derivation of the term Babel, which is now said to have no connection whatever with the confusion of tongues, but to be the word "Bab-il," the house or gate of God, or "Bāb-Bel," the gate or court of Belus ; and (2) an incorrect explanation of the present diversity of tongues among mankind, which modern philology has now shown to be due to local separation, and not at all to a miraculous interference with the organs or the faculty of speech. To each of these objections a specific reply will be returned in the exposition of the text (*q. v.*); in the mean time it may be stated that there are not wanting sufficiently numerous testimonies from ancient history, archæological research, and philological inquiry to authenticate this most interesting portion of the Divine record.

II. The *literary unity* of the present section has been assailed. Tuch ascribes ch. x. to the Elohist and ch. xi. 1—9 to the Jehovist; and with this Bleek and Vaihinger agree, except that they apportion ch. x. 8—12 to the Jehovist. Davidson assigns to him the whole of ch. x., with the exception of the expression "every one after his tongue" (ver. 5), the similar expressions (vers. 20, 31), the story of Nimrod commencing at "he began" (ver. 8), ver. 21, and the statement beginning "for" (ver. 25), all of which, with ch. xi. 1—9, he places to the credit of his redactor. But the literary unity of the entire section is so apparent that Colenso believes both passages, "the table of nations" and "the confusion of tongues," to be the work of the Jehovist; and certainly the latter narrative is represented in so intimate a connection with the former that it is much more likely to have been composed by the original historian than inserted later as a happy afterthought by a post-exilian editor.

EXPOSITION.

CHAPTER X.

It is impossible to exaggerate the importance of this ethnological table. Whether regarded from a geographical, a political, or a theocratical standpoint, "this unparalleled list, the combined result of reflection and deep research," is "no less valuable as a historical document than as a lasting proof of the brilliant capacity of the Hebrew mind." Undoubtedly the earliest effort of the human intellect to exhibit in a tabulated form the geographical distribution of the human race, it bears unmistakable witness in its own structure to its high antiquity, occupying itself least with the Japhetic tribes which were furthest from the theocratic centre, and were latest in attaining to historic eminence, and enlarging with much greater minuteness of detail on those Hamitic nations, the Egyptian, Canaanite, and Arabian, which were soonest developed, and with which the Hebrews came most into contact in the initial stages of their career. It describes the rise of states, and, consistently with all subsequent historical and archæological testimony, gives the prominence to the Egyptian or Arabian Hamites, as the first founders of empires. It exhibits the separation of the Shemites from the other sons of Noah, and the budding forth of the line of promise in the family of Arphaxad. While thus useful to the geographer, the historian, the politician, it is specially serviceable to the theologian, as enabling him to trace the descent of the woman's seed, and to mark the fulfilments of Scripture prophecies concerning the nations of the earth. In the interpretation of the names which are here recorded, it is obviously impossible in every instance to arrive at certainty, in some cases the names of individuals being mentioned, while in others it is as conspicuously those of peoples.

Ver. 1.—**Now these** are **the generations of the sons of Noah** (cf. ch. v. 1; vi. 9), **Shem, Ham, and Japheth.** Not the order of age, but of theocratic importance (*vide* ch. v. 32). **And unto them were sons born** (cf. ch. ix. 1, 7, 19, 22) **after the flood.** An indication of the *punctum temporis* whence the period embraced in the present section takes its departure.

Ver. 2.—**The sons of Japheth** are first mentioned not because Japheth was the eldest of the three brothers, although that was true, but because of the greater distance of the Japhetic tribes from the theocratic centre, the Hamites having always been much more nearly situated to and closely connected with the Shemites than they. The immediate descendants of Japheth, whose name, Ἰάπετος, occurs again in the mythology of a Japhetic race, were fourteen in number, seven sons and seven grandsons, each of which became the progenitor of one of the primitive nations. **Gomer.** A people inhabiting "the sides of the north" (Ezek. xxxviii. 6); the Galatæ of the Greeks (Josephus, 'Ant.,' i. 6); the Chomarii, a nation in Bactriana on the Oxus (Shulthess, Kalisch); but more generally the Cimmerians of Homer ('Odyss.,' xi. 13—19), whose abodes were the shores of the Caspian and Euxine, whence they seem to have spread themselves over Europe as far west as the Atlantic, leaving traces of their presence in the Cimbri of North Germany and the Cymri in Wales (Keil, Lange, Murphy, Wordsworth, 'Speaker's Commentary'). **And Magog.** A fierce and warlike people presided over by Gog (an appellative name, like the titles Pharaoh and Cæsar, and corresponding with the Turkish Chak, the Tartarian Kak, and the Mongolian Gog: Kalisch), whose complete destruction was predicted by Ezekiel (chs. xxxviii. xxxix.); generally understood to be the Scythians, whose territory lay upon the borders of the sea of Asoph, and in the Caucasus. In the Apocalypse (ch. xx. 8—10) Gog and Magog appear as two distinct nations combined against the Church of God. **And Madai.** The inhabitants of Media (Mada in the cuneiform inscriptions), so called because believed to be situated περὶ μεσην τὴν 'Ασίαν (Polyb. v. 44) on the south-west shore of the Caspian. **And Javan.** Identical with 'Ιάων (Greek), Javana (Sanscrit), Juna (Old Persian), Jounan (Rosetta Stone); allowed to be the father of the Greeks, who in Scripture are styled Javan (vide Isa. lxvi. 19; Ezek. xxvii. 13; Dan. viii. 21; x. 20; Joel iii. 6). **And Tubal, and Meshech.** Generally associated in Scripture as tributaries of Magog (Ezek. xxxviii. 2, 3; xxxix. 1); recognised as the Iberians and Moschi in the north of Armenia, between the sources of the Tigris and Euphrates, and the Black Sea (Josephus, Knobel, Lange, Kalisch). **And Tiras.** The ancestor of the Thracians (Josephus), of the Tyrrheni, a branch of the Pelasgians (Tuch), of the Asiatic tribes round the Taurus (Kalisch), in support of which last is a circumstance mentioned by Rawlinson, that on the old Egyptian monuments *Mashuash* and *Tuirash*, and upon the Assyrian *Tubal* and *Misek*, stand together as here. Tiras occurs nowhere else in Scripture.

Ver. 3.—**And the sons of Gomer; Ashkenaz.** Axenus, the ancient name of the Euxine, is supposed to favour Phrygia and Bithynia as the locality possessed by Askenaz (Bochart); Iskus, equivalent to Ask, Ascanios, the oldest son of the Germanic Mannus, to point out Germany as his abode (Jewish commentators); but Jer. li. 27 seems to indicate the region between the Euxine and the Caspian. Kalisch, following Josephus, identifies the name with the ancient town Rhagæ, one day's journey to the south of the Caspian. Murphy and Poole, on the authority of Diodorus Siculus, believe the Germans may have been a colony of the Ashkenians. **And Riphath.** Diphath (1 Chron. i. 6)—the Paphlagonians (Josephus); more generally the tribes about the Riphæan mountains, on the north of the Caspian (Knobel, Kalisch, Clericus, Rosenmüller,

Murphy, 'Speaker's Commentary'); but both are uncertain (Keil). **And Togarmah.** Mentioned again in Ezek. xxvii. 14; xxxviii. 6; the Phrygians (Josephus), the Cappadocians (Bochart), the Armenians (Michaelis, Gesenius, Rosenmüller), the Taurians, inhabiting the Crimea (Kalisch). The tradition preserved by Moses Chorensis, that the ancestor of the Armenians was the son of Thorgom, the son of Gomer, is commonly regarded as deciding the question.

Ver. 4.—**And the sons of Javan; Elishah.** The isles of Elishah are praised by Ezekiel (xxvii. 7) for their blue and purple; supposed to have been Elis in the Peloponnesus, famous for its purple dyes (Bochart); Æolis (Josephus, Knobel); Hellas (Michaelis, Rosenmüller, Kalisch); without doubt a maritime people of Grecian stock ('Speaker's Commentary'). **And Tarshish.** Tarsus in Cilicia (Josephus); but rather Tartessus in Spain (Eusebius, Michaelis, Bochart, Kalisch). Biblical notices represent Tarshish as a wealthy and flourishing seaport town towards the west (vide 1 Kings x. 22; Ps. xlviii. 7; lxxii. 10; Isa. lx. 9; lxvi. 19; Jer. x. 9; Ezek. xxvii. 12). **Kittim.** Chittim (Num. xxiv. 24); Citium in Cyprus (Josephus), though latterly the name appears to have been extended to Citium in Macedonia (Alexander the Great is called the king of Chittim, 1 Macc. i. 1; viii. 5), and the colonies which settled on the shores of Italy and Greece (Bochart, Keil, Kalisch). Isa. xxiii. 1, 12; Dan. xi. 30 describe it as a maritime people. **And Dodanim.** Dordona in Epirus (Michaelis, Rosenmüller); the Dardanians, or Trojans (Gesenius); the Daunians of South Italy (Kalisch); the Rhodani in Gaul, reading as in 1 Chron. i 7 (Bochart). Josephus omits the name, and Scripture does not again mention it.

Ver. 5.—**By these were the isles of the Gentiles.** Sea-washed coasts as well as islands proper (cf. Isa. xlii. 4 with Matt. xii. 21). Isaiah (ch. xx. 6) styles Canaan an isle (cf. Peloponnesus). The expression signifies maritime countries. **Divided in their lands; every one after his tongue.** Indicating a time posterior to the building of Babel (ch. xi. 1). **After their families.** 'Εν ταῖς φυλαῖς αὐτῶν (LXX.); in their tribes or clans, a lesser subdivision than the next. **In their nations.** The division here exhibited is fourfold: (1) geographical, (2) dialectical, (3) tribal, and (4) national. The first defines the territory occupied, and the second the language spoken by the Japhethites; the third their immediate descent, and the fourth the national group to which they severally belonged.

Ver. 6.—**And the sons of Ham.** These, who occupy the second place, that the list might conclude with the Shemites as the line of promise, number thirty, of whom only four were immediate descendants. Their territory generally embraced the southern portions of the globe. Hence the name Ham has been connected with חֹם, to be warm, though Kalisch declares it to be not of Hebrew, but Egyptian origin, appearing in the Chmé of the Rosetta Stone. The most usual ancient name of the country was *Kem*, the *black* land. Scripture speaks of Egypt as the land of Ham (Ps. lxxviii. 51 ; cv. 23 ; cvi. 22). **Cush.** Ethiopia, including Arabia " quæ mater est," and Abyssinia "quæ colonia" (Michaelis, Rosenmüller). The original settlement of Cush, however, is believed to have been on the Upper Nile, whence he afterwards spread to Arabia, Babylonia, India (Knobel, Kalisch, Lange, Rawlinson). Murphy thinks he may have started from the Caucasus, the Caspian, and the Cossaei of Khusistan, and migrated south (to Egypt) and east (to India). Josephus mentions that in his day Ethiopia was called Cush ; the Syriac translates ἀνὴρ 'Aἰθίοψ (Acts viii. 27) by Cuschaeos ; the ancient Egyptian name of Ethiopia was *Keesh*, Kish, or Kush (' Records of the Past,' iv. 7). The Cushites are described as of a black colour (Jer. xiii. 23) and of great stature (Isa. xlv. 14). **And Mizraim.** A dual form probably designed to represent the two Egypts, upper and lower (Gesenius, Keil, Kalisch), though it has been discovered in ancient Egyptian as the name of a Hittite chief (*circa* B.C. 1300, contemporary with Rameses II.), written in hieroglyphics *M'azrima*, Ma being the sign for the dual. The old Egyptian name is *Kemi, Chemi*, with obvious reference to Ham ; the name Egypt being probably derived from *Kaphtah*, the land of Ptah. The singular form Mazor is found in later books (2 Kings xix. 24 ; Isa. xix. 6 ; xxxv. 25), and usually denotes Lower Egypt. **And Phut.** *Phet* (Old Egyptian), *Phaiat* (Coptic) ; the Libyans in the north of Africa (Josephus, LXX., Gesenius, Bochart). Kalisch suggests *Buto'* or *Butos*, the capital of the delta of the Nile. **And Canaan.** Hebrew, *Kenaan* (*vide* on ch. ix. 25). The extent of the territory occupied by the fourth son of Ham is defined in vers. 15—19.

Ver. 7.—**And the sons of Cush ; Seba.** Merce, in Nubia, north of Ethiopia (Josephus, 'Ant.,' ii. 10). **And Havilah.** Eὐϊλὰ (LXX.); may refer to an African tribe, the Avalitae, south of Babelmandeb (Keil, Lange, Murphy), or the district of Chaulan in Arabia Felix (Rosenmüller, Kalisch, Wordsworth). Verse 29 mentions Havilah as a Shemite territory. Kalisch regards them as " the same country, extending from the Arabian to the Persian Gulf, and, on account of its vast extent, easily divided into two distinct parts" (cf. ch. ii. 11). **And Sabtah.** The Astaborans of Ethiopia

(Josephus, Gesenius, Kalisch) ; the Ethiopians of Arabia, whose chief city was Sabota (Knobel, Rosenmüller, Lange, Keil). **And Raamah.** 'Ῥέγμα (LXX.) ; Ragma on the Persian Gulf, in Oman (Bochart, Rosenmüller, Kalisch, Lange). **And Sabtechah.** Nigritia (Targum, Jonathan), which the name *Subatok*, discovered on Egyptian monuments, seems to favour (Kalisch) ; on the east of the Persian Gulf at Samydace of Carmania (Bochart, Knobel, Rosenmüller, Lange). **And the sons of Raamah ; Sheba.** The principal city of Arabia Felix (1 Kings x. 1 ; Job i. 15 ; vi. 19 ; Ps. lxxii. 10, 15 ; Isa. lx. 6 ; Jer. vi. 20 ; Ezek. xxvii. 22 ; Joel iii. 8) ; occurs again (ch. v. 28) as a son of Joktan ; probably was peopled both by Hamites and Shemites. **And Dedan.** Daden on the Persian Gulf (*vide* Isa. xxi. 13 ; Jer. xlix. 8 ; Ezek. xxv. 13 ; xxvii. 12—15).

Ver. 8.—**And Cush begat**—not necessarily as immediate progenitor, any ancestor being in Hebrew styled a father—**Nimrod** ; the rebel, from *maradh*, to rebel ; the name of a person, not of a people ;—*Namuret* in ancient Egyptian. Though not one of the great ethnic heads, he is introduced into the register of nations as the founder of imperialism. Under him society passed from the patriarchal condition, in which each separate clan or tribe owns the sway of its natural head, into that (more abject or more civilised according as it is viewed) in which many different clans or tribes recognise the sway of one who is not their natural head, but has acquired his ascendancy and dominion by conquest. This is the principle of monarchism. Eastern tradition has painted Nimrod as a gigantic oppressor of the people's liberties and an impious rebel against the Divine authority. Josephus credits him with having instigated the building of the tower of Babel. He has been identified with the Orion of the Greeks. Scripture may seem to convey a bad impression of Nimrod, but it does not sanction the absurdities of Oriental legend. **He began to be a mighty one**—*Gibbor* (*vide* ch. vi. 4) ; what he had been previously being expressed in ver. 5—**in the earth.** Not ἐπι τῆς γῆς (LXX.), as if pointing to his gigantic stature, but either among men generally, with reference to his widespread fame, or perhaps better "in the land" where he dwelt, which was not Babel, but Arabia (*vide* ver. 6).

Ver. 9. — **He was a mighty hunter.** Originally doubtless of wild beasts, which, according to Bochart, was the first step to usurping dominion over men and using them for battle. "Nempe venationum prætextu collegit juvenum robustam manum, quam talibus exercitus ad belli labores induravit" (' Phaleg.,' liv. 12). **Before the Lord.** 1. 'Ἐναντίον κυρίου (LXX.), in a spirit of defiance (Augustine, Keil, Murphy, Bush). 2. *Coram Deo*, in God's sight, as an aggravation of his sin—cf. ch. xiii. 3 (Cajetan). 3. As a superlative, declaring his excellence—cf. ch. xiii. 10 ; xxx. 8 ; xxxv. 5 ; 1 Sam. xi. 7 ; John iii. 3 ; Acts vii. 20 (Aben Ezra, Kimchi, Kalisch, 'Speaker's Commentary'). 4. With the Divine approbation, as one who broke the way through rude, uncultivated nature for the institutions of Jehovah (Lange). Cf. ch. xvii. 18 ; xxiv. 40 ; 1 Sam. xi. 15 ; Ps. xli. 12. Probably the first or the third conveys the sense of the expression. **Wherefore it is said, Even as Nimrod the (a) mighty hunter before the Lord.** The precise import of this is usually determined by the view taken of the previous phrase.

Ver. 10. — **And the beginning of his kingdom.** Either his first kingdom, as contrasted with his second (Knobel), or the commencement of his sovereignty (Keil, Kalisch), or the principal city of his empire (Rosenmüller) ; or all three may be legitimately embraced in the term *reshith*, only it does not necessarily imply that Nimrod *built* any of the cities mentioned. **Was Babel.** Babylon, "the land of Nimrod" (Micah v. 6), the origin of which is described in ch. xi. 1, grew to be a great city covering an area of 225 square miles, reached its highest glory under Nebuchadnezzar (Dan. iv. 30), and succumbed to the Medo-Persian power under Belshazzar (Dan. v. 31). The remains of this great city have been discovered on the east bank of the Euphrates near Hillah, where there is a square mound called "Babil" by the Arabs (Rawlinson's 'Ancient Monarchies,' vol. i. ch. 1). **And Erech.** The Orchoe of Ptolemy, identified by Rawlinson as Wurka, about eighty miles south of Babylon. **And Accad.** 'Αρχάδ (LXX.) ; the city Sittace on the river Argade (Bochart) ; Sakada, a town planted by Ptolemy below Ninus (Clericus) ; Accete, north of Babylon (Knobel, Lange) ; identified with the ruins of Niffer, to the south of Hillah (Keil) ; with those of Akkerkoof, north of Hillah (Kalisch). Rawlinson does not identify the site ; George Smith regards it as "the capital of Sargon, the great city Agadi, near the city of Sippara on the Euphrates, and north of Babylon" ('Assyrian Discoveries,' ch. xii.). **And Calneh.** Calno (Isa. x. 9) ; Canneh (Ezek. xxvii. 23) ; Ctesiphon, east of the Tigris, north-east of Babylon (Jerome, Eusebius, Bochart, Michaelis, Kalisch) ; identified with the ruins of Niffer on the east of the Euphrates (Rawlinson). **In the land of Shinar.** Babylonia, as distinguished from Assyria (Isa. xi. 11), the lower part of Mesopotamia, or Chaldæa.

Ver. 11.—**Out of that land went forth Asshur**, the son of Shem (ver. 22 ; LXX., Vulgate, Syriac, Luther, Calvin, Michaelis, Dathe, Rosenmüller, Bohlen) ; *i. e.* the early Assyrians retired from Babylon before their Cushite invaders, and, proceeding northward, founded the cities after mentioned ; but the marginal rendering seems preferable : "Out of that land went (Nimrod) into Asshur," or Assyria, the country north-east of Babylon, through which flows the Tigris, and which had already received its name from the son of Shem (the Targums, Drusius, Bochart, Le Clerc, De Wette, Delitzsch, Keil, Kalisch, Lange, *et alii*). **And builded Nineveh.** The capital of Assyria, opposite Mosul on the Tigris, afterwards became the largest and most flourishing city of the ancient world (Jonah iii. 3 ; iv. 11), being fifty-five miles in circumference (Diod., ii. 3), and is now identified with the ruins of Nebbi-yunus and Kouyunjik (Layard's 'Nineveh,' vol ii. pp. 136 ff.). **And the city Rehoboth.** *Rehoboth-ir*, literally, the streets of the city (cf. Platæa, a city in Bœotia), a town of which the site is unknown. **And Calah.** The mounds of Nimroud (Layard and Smith), though Kalisch and Murphy prefer Kalah Shergat (about fifty miles south of Nineveh), which the former authorities identify with Asshur, the original capital of the country.

Ver. 12.—**And Resen**, *i. e.* Nimroud, between Kalah Shergat and Kouyunjik (Kalisch) ; but if Calah be Nimroud, then Resen may be Selamiyeh, a village about half way, **between Nineveh and Calah**, *i. e.* Kouyunjik and Nimroud, *ut supra* (Layard). **The same.** Resen (Kalisch), which will suit if it was Nimroud, whose remains cover a parallelogram about 1800 feet in length and 900 feet in breadth ; but others apply it to Nineveh with the other towns as forming one large composite city (Knobel, Keil, Lange, Wordsworth). **Is a great city.** With this the record of Nimrod's achievements closes. It is generally supposed that Nimrod flourished either before or about the time of the building of the tower of Babel ; but Prof. Chwolsen of St. Petersburg, in his 'Ueber die Ueberreste der Altbabylonischen Literatur,' brings the dynasty of Nimrod down as late as 1500 B.C., relying principally on the evidence of an original work composed by Qût'âmi, a native Babylonian, and translated by Ibn-wa'hschijjah, a descendant of the Chaldæans, and assigned by Chwolsen to one of the earlier periods of Babylonian history, in which is mentioned the name of Nemrod, or Nemroda, as the founder of a Canaanite dynasty which ruled at Babylon (*vide* an excellent paper on this subject in Turner's 'Biblical and Oriental Studies,' Edin., A. and C. Black, 1876). Perhaps the hardest difficulty to explain in connection with the ordinary date assigned to Nimrod is the fact that in ch. xiv., which speaks of the reigning monarchs in the

Euphrates valley, there is no account taken of Nineveh and its king—a circumstance which has been supposed to import that the founding of the capital of Assyria could not have been anterior to the days of Abraham. But early Babylonian texts confirm what ch. xiv. seems to imply—the fact of an Elamite conquest of Babylonia, B.C. 2280, by Kudur-nanhundi (Kudurlagamar, the Chederlaomer of Genesis), who carried off an image of the goddess Nana from the city Erech (*vide* 'Assyrian Discoveries,' ch. xii. ; 'Records of the Past,' vol. iii.), so that this difficulty may be held to have disappeared before the light of archæological discovery. But at whatever period Nimrod flourished, the Biblical narrative would lead us to anticipate a commingling of Hamitic and Shemitic tongues in the Euphrates valley, which existing monuments confirm (cf. 'Records of the Past,' vol. iii. p. 3).

Ver. 13.—**And Mizraim begat Ludim.** An African tribe, a colony of the Egyptians, like the next seven, which are "nomina non singulorum hominum sed populorum" (Aben Ezra, Michaelis, Rosenmüller, Kalisch, Murphy); probably referred to in connection with Tarshish and Put (Isa. lxvi. 19), with Kush and Put (Jer. xlvi. 9), and in connection with Put (Ezek. xxvii. 10 ; xxx. 5). Lud (ver. 22) was Shemitic. **And Anamim.** Not elsewhere mentioned ; the inhabitants of the Delta (Knobel). **And Lehabim.** Lubim (2 Chron. xii. 3 ; Dan. ii. 43 ; Nahum iii. 9) ; Libyans (Dan. xi. 43) ; probably the Libyans west of Egypt (Michaelis, Kalisch, Murphy). **And Naphtuhim.** Nephthys, near Pelusium, on the Lake Sirbonis (Bochart) ; the Libyan town Napata (Kalisch) ; the people of Middle Egypt (Knobel).

Ver. 14.—**And Pathrusim.** Pathros in Upper Egypt. **And Casluhim.** The Colchians, of Egyptian origin (Bochart, Gesenius) ; the inhabitants of the primitive Egyptian town Chemnis, later Panoplis (Kalisch). **Out of whom came Philistim.** The Philistines on the Mediterranean from Egypt to Joppa, who had five principal cities — Gaza, Ashdod, Ashkelon, Gath, and Ekron. They are here described as an offshoot from Casluhim. The name has been derived from an Ethiopic root *fălăsă*, to emigrate ; hence "immigrants" or "emigrants." Jer. xlvii. 4 and Amos ix. 7 trace the Philistines to the Caphtorim. Michaelis solves the difficulty by transposing the clause to the end of the verse ; Bochart by holding the Casluhim and Caphtorim to have intermingled ; Keil and Lange by the conjecture that the original tribe the Casluhim was subsequently strengthened by an immigration from Caphtor. Against the Egyptian origin of the Philistines the possession of a Shemitic tongue and the non-observance of circumcision have been urged ; but the first may have been

acquired from the conquered Avim whose land they occupied (Deut. ii. 23), and the exodus from Egypt may have taken place prior to the institution of the rite in question. **And Caphtorim.** Cappadocia (Bochart), Syrtis Major (Clericus), Crete (Calmet, Ewald), Cyprus (Michaelis, Rosenmüller), Coptos, Kouft or Keft, a few miles north of Thebes (Kalisch).

Ver. 15.—**And Canaan begat Sidon his firstborn.** A famous commercial and maritime town on the coast of Syria (1 Kings v. 6 ; 1 Chron. xxii. 4 ; Isa. xxiii. 2, 4, 12 ; Ezek. xxvii. 8) ; here including Tyre. From the mention of the circumstance that Sidon was Canaan's firstborn, we may infer that in the rest of the table the order of seniority is not followed. **And Heth.** The father of the Hittites (ch. xxiii. 3, 5), identified by Egyptologers with the Kheta, a powerful Syrian tribe.

Ver. 16.—**And the Jebusite.** Settled at and around Jerusalem (Josh. xv. 8 ; Judges xix. 10, 11 ; 1 Chron. xi. 4, 5). **And the Amorite.** On both sides of the Jordan, though dwelling chiefly in the Judæan mountains (ch. xiv. 7 ; Josh. x. 5), to which the name "mountaineer," from "Amor," elevation (Gesenius), is supposed to refer. **And the Girgasite.** The n me nly is preserved (Josh. xxiv. 11).

Ver. 17.—**And the Hivite.** "Villagers" (Gesenius) ; "settlers in cities" (Ewald) ; their localities are mentioned in ch. xxxiv. 2 ; Josh. ix. 1, 7 ; xi. 3 ; Judges vi. 3. **And the Arkite.** Inhabitants of Arka, a city of Phœnicia (Josephus) : afterwards called Cæsarea Libani ; its ruins still exist at Tel Arka, at the foot of Lebanon. **And the Sinite.** The inhabitants of Sin. Near Arka are a fortress named Senna, ruins called Sin, and a village designated Syn.

Ver. 18.—**And the Arvadite,**—dwelt in Arvad, Aradus, now Ruad (Josephus)—**and the Zemarite,**—Simyra, a city of Phœnicia (Bochart, Michaelis, Gesenius, Kalisch) whose ruins are still called Sumrah—**and the Hamathite.** The inhabitants of Hamath, called Hammath Rabbah (Amos vi. 2) ; Epiphaneia by the Greeks ; now Hamah. **And afterwards**—*i. e.* subsequent to the formation of these distinct tribes by the confusion of tongues—**were the families of the Canaanites spread abroad.**

Ver. 19.—**And the border of the Canaanites was from Sidon** (its northern boundary), **as thou comest**—*i. e.* as thou goest, in the direction of—**to Gerar,**—between Kadesh and Shur (ch. xx. 1)—**unto Gaza** (now called Guzzeh, at the south-west corner of Palestine) ; **as thou goest, unto Sodom, and Gomorrah, and Admah, and Zeboim** (*vide* ch. xix. 24), **even unto Lasha**—Callirrhoe (Hieronymus, Jerusalem Targum, Josephus, Rosenmüller, Keil, Kalisch) ; possibly a variation of Laish and Leshem, a Sidonian city near the sources of the Jordan (Murphy).

Ver. 20.—**These are the sons of Ham, after their families, after their tongues, in their countries**, and in their nations (*vide* ver. 5).

Ver. 21.—**Unto Shem also, the father of all the children of Eber,**—as Ham of Canaan (ch. ix. 22; *vide* ver. 24)—**the brother of Japheth the elder.** Either the eldest brother of Japheth (Syriac, Arabic, Vulgate, Gesenius, Rosenmüller, Kalisch); or the brother of Japheth who was older (LXX., Symmachus, Onkelos, Raschi, Aben Ezra, Luther, Clericus, Michaelis, Dathe); or the elder of Japheth's brothers, as distinguished from Ham the younger, *i. e.* the son who was older than Ham, but younger than Japheth (Murphy, Quarry; *vide* ch. v. 32). **Even to him were children born.**

Ver. 22.—**The children of Shem** were twenty-six in number, of whom five were sons. **Elam.** Elymais, a region adjoining Susiana and Media, stretching from the Persian Gulf to the Red Sea; the people first met with as Persians. **And Asshur.** The ancestor of the Assyrians (*vide* ver. 11). **And Arphaxad.** A region in the north of Assyria; the Arrhapacitis of Ptolemy (Rosenmüller, Keil, Kalisch). The explanation of the name is "fortress of the Chaldæans" (Ewald); "highland of the Chaldæans" (Knobel). **And Lud.** The Lydians of Asia Minor, to which they appear to have migrated from the land of Shem (Josephus, Bochart, Keil, Kalisch). **And Aram.** "The high land;" Mesopotamia being the Aram of the two rivers, and Syria the Aram of Damascus.

Ver. 23.—**And the children of Aram; Uz,** from whom was named the land of Uz (Job i. 1), south-east of Palestine, a tract of the Arabia Deserta. **And Hul.** In Armenia (Josephus); that part called Cholobetene, or house of Hul (Bochart); the Hylatæ of Syria, near the Emesenes (Delitzsch); Cœlesyria (Michaelis); Huleh, near the sources of the Jordan (Murphy). **And Gether**—of uncertain situation—**and Mash**—traced in Mons Masius of Armenia (Bochart).

Ver. 24.—**And Arphaxad begat Salah.** The nation descended from him has not been identified, though their name, "Extension," may imply that they were early colonists. **And Salah begat Eber.** The father of the Hebrews or "Emigrants" (*vide* ver. 21).

Ver. 25.—**And unto Eber were born two sons: the name of one was Peleg.** "Division," from *palag*, to divide; cf. πέλαγος and *pelagus*, a division of the sea. **For in his days**

was the earth divided. At the confusion of tongues (Bochart, Rosenmüller, Keil, Lange, Murphy); at an earlier separation of the earth's population (Delitzsch), of which there is no record or trace. **And his brother's** name was Joktan. Father of the Arabians, by whom he is called Kachtan.

Vers. 26-30. **And Joktan begat Almodad.** Usually said to be Yemen. **And Sheleph.** The Salapenoi of Ptolemy, belonging to the interior of Arabia. **And Hazarmaveth.** Hadramaut, south-east of Arabia (Bochart, Michaelis). **And Jerah.** Contiguous to Hadramaut. **And Hadoram.** Adramitæ of Ptolemy, or the Atramitæ of Pliny (Bochart). **And Uzal.** Awzal, the capital of Yemen (Bochart). **And Diklah.** The palm-bearing region of Arabia Felix (Bochart); a tribe between the mouth of the Tiber and the Persian Gulf (Michaelis). **And Obal, and Abimael,** whose settlements are not known. **And Sheba.** *Vide supra,* ver. 7. **And Ophir.** In Arabia; probably in Oman, on the Persian Gulf (Michaelis, Rosenmüller, Kalisch, Keil), though it has also been located in India (Josephus, Vitringa, Gesenius, Delitzsch). The gold of Ophir celebrated (1 Kings ix. 27, 28; 2 Chron. ix. 10, 13, 21). **And Havilah.** The Chaulan in Arabia Felix, but *vide supra,* ver. 7. **And Jobab.** The Jobabitæ of Ptolemy, near the Indian Sea (Michaelis, Rosenmüller); but more probably a tribe in Arabia Deserta if Jobab = Arabic *jebab,* a desert (Bochart, Gesenius, Kalisch). **All these were the sons of Joktan. And their dwelling was from Mesha.** The seaport of Muza (Bochart); Messene, at the mouth of the Tigris (Michaelis, Rosenmüller, Kalisch). **As thou goest into Zephar.** Zafar or Dhafari, on the coast of the Hadramut. The difficulty of identifying a seaport town with a mountain is got over (Kalisch) by reading "to the" instead of a mount of the east—the thuriferous range of hills in the vicinity.

Vers. 31, 32.—**These are the sons of Shem, after their families, after their tongues, in their lands, after their nations.** The pedigree of the Shemite tribes is closed with the customary formula (*vide* ver. 5); that which follows being the concluding formula for the entire table of nations. **These are the families of the sons of Noah, after their generations** (literally, *according to their Thôldôth, or historical developments*), **in their nations: and by these** (literally, *from these*) **were the nations divided** (or, did the nations scatter themselves) **in the earth after the flood.**

HOMILETICS.

Ver. 32.—*The ethnological register.* I. PROCLAIMS THE UNITY OF THE RACE. 1. It *declares* all the successive families of mankind to have sprung from a common stock. Diverse as they now are in their geographical situations, ethnic relations, physical capabilities, national peculiarities, according to the doctrine of this genealogical table they all trace their origin to Noah and his sons.   2. It *condemns* all those theories which derive man from several pairs.   Equally the heathen superstition which assigned to each particular region its own *Autochthones,* and the modern scientific dogma of varieties of species and distinct centres of propagation is here condemned.   Even now ethnologists, archæologists, and philologists of the highest repute lend their sanction to the sublime sentiment of the great Mars' hill preacher, that " God hath made of one blood all nations of men for to dwell upon all the face of the earth."   The anatomical structure of the human frame, especially of the brain and skull, the physiological properties and functions possessed by the body, the psychological nature of man, and the power of indefinite propagation, which are the same in all nations, with the ascertained results of comparative grammar, which have already traced back all existing languages to three primitive branches, tend in a powerful degree to confirm the doctrine which this table teaches.   3. It *implies* certain other truths on which Scripture with equal emphasis insists, such as the brotherhood of man, the universal corruption of the race, and the necessity and universality of Christ's redemption.

II. ATTESTS THE DIVISION of the RACE.   1. It *asserts the fact* of the division.   It states that in the days of Peleg the earth's population was divided.   The means employed are described in the succeeding chapter.   2. It *confirms the truth* of this division.   Had the confusion at Babel not occurred, and the subsequent dispersion not followed, this table could not have been written.   Its existence as a literary document in the time of Moses authenticates the fact which it reports.   3. It *defines the extent* of this division.   It shows that the scattered race were to be split up into nations, families, tongues.

III. ILLUSTRATES THE DISTRIBUTION OF THE RACE.   The geographical distribution of the earth's population was—1. *Effected in an orderly manner.*   They were neither scattered promiscuously nor suffered to wander and settle at hazard.   Divided into tribes and nations according to their tongues and dialects of speech, they were allocated to distinct portions of the earth's surface.   2. *Specially adapted to the characters and destinies of the several nations.*   The operation of purely natural principles makes it impossible that tribes can permanently settle in countries that are either incapable of yielding to them a maintenance or affording an outlet to their powers.   More extensive information would doubtless enable the suitability of each locality in this table to the occupying people to be exhibited ; but in broad outline it is perceptible even here—Japheth, whose destiny it was to spread abroad, being established on the coasts of the Euxine, the Caspian, and the Mediterranean ; Ham finding rest in the warmer climates, whose enervating influences tended largely to develop his peculiar character, and ultimately to lay him open to subjection by the more vigorous races of the North ; and Shem, whose function in the Divine economy it was to conserve religion and religious truth, being concentrated mainly in the Tigris and Euphrates valley.   3. *The result of Divine appointment.*   Moses (Deut. xxxii. 8) and Paul (Acts xvii. 26) conspire to represent the allocation of territory to the different races of mankind as the handiwork of God (the special means employed for the breaking up of the originally united family of Noah's sons is detailed in the ensuing chapter) ; the import of which is, that nations have a God-assigned title to the countries which they occupy.   4. The Divinely-ordered distribution of the earth's population is *capable of being disturbed by the sinful interference of man.*   Instances of this appear in the present table, *e. g.* the intrusion of the Cushite into Shinar, and of the Canaanite into what originally belonged to Shem.

IV. PREDICTS THE FUTURE OF THE RACE.   As it were, the separation of the earth's population into races and the moving of them outward to their respective habitations was the starting of them on the lines along which it was designed they should accomplish their respective destinies and common work.   They were meant to overspread the globe ; and this was the initiation of a great movement which would only terminate in the complete occupation of their God-given heritage.

*Lessons :—*1. The equal rights of men.   2. The sinfulness of wars of aggression. 3. The hopefulness of emigration.

HOMILIES BY VARIOUS AUTHORS.

Ver. 8.—*Nimrod.* 1. His ancestral pedigree—a Cushite. 2. His early occupation —a hunter of wild beasts, a pioneer of civilisation. 3. His rising ambition—he began to be a "Gibbor," or mighty one. 4. His regal authority—the beginning of his kingdom was Babel. 5. His extending empire—out of that land went he forth into Asshur. 6. His posthumous renown: "Wherefore it is said, Even as Nimrod."—W

Vers. 15—19.—*The Canaanites.* I. DESCENDANTS OF A WICKED FATHER. II. IN- HERITORS OF AN AWFUL CURSE. III. POSSESSORS OF A FAIR DOMAIN. IV. USURPERS OF ANOTHER'S LAND.
Lessons:—1. Wicked men and nations may greatly prosper. 2. Prosperity some- times leads to greater wickedness. 3. The greatest prosperity cannot turn aside the punishment of sin.—W.

Ver. 25.—*Peleg, or the division of the people.* I. WHEN IT TOOK PLACE. In the fourth generation after the Flood.
II. HOW IT WAS EFFECTED. 1. By the Divine interposition. 2. By the confusion of tongues.
III. FOR WHAT IT WAS DESIGNED. 1. To punish sin. 2. To separate the Church. 3. To occupy the earth.
IV. BY WHAT IT WAS REMEMBERED. The naming of Eber's son.
Learn—1. To read well the signs of the times. 2. To understand well the cause of God's judgments. 3. To remember well the gift of God's mercies.—W.

Ver. 32.—*Nations.* I. THEIR ROOTS. Individuals.
II. THEIR RISE. 1. As to time, after the Flood. 2. As to cause, Divine impulse. 3. As to instrumentality, variation of speech.
III. THEIR CHARACTERISTICS. 1. A common head. 2. A common tongue. 3. A common land.
IV. THEIR DESTINIES. To overspread the earth.—W.

EXPOSITION.

CHAPTER XI.

Ver. 1.—**And the whole earth.** *I. e.* the entire population of the globe, and not simply the inhabitants of the land of Shinar (Inglis ; cf. ch. ix. 29). **Was.** Prior to the dis- persion spoken of in the preceding chapter, though obviously it may have been subse- quent to that event, if, as the above-named author believes, the present paragraph refers to the Shemites alone. **Of one language.** Literally, *of one lip,* i. e. one articulation, or one way of pronouncing their vocables. **And of one speech.** Literally, *one* (kind of) *words,* i. e. the matter as well as the form of human speech was the same. The primi- tive language was believed by the Rabbins, the Fathers, and the older theologians to be Hebrew ; but Keil declares this view to be utterly untenable. Bleek shows that the family of Abraham spoke in Aramaic (cf. Jegar-sahadutha, ch. xxxi. 47), and that the patriarch himself acquired Hebrew from the Canaanites, who may themselves have adopted it from the early Semites whom they displaced. While regarding neither the Aramaic, Hebrew, nor Arabic as the original tongue of mankind, he thinks the Hebrew approaches nearest the primitive Semite language out of which all three were developed.

Ver. 2.—**And it came to pass, as they journeyed.** Literally, *in their journeyings.* The root (עָקַע, to pull up, as, *e. g.,* the stakes of a tent when a camp moves, Isa. xxxiii. 20) suggests the idea of the migration of nomadic hordes (cf. ch. xii. 9 ; xxxiii. 17). **From the east.** *Ab oriente* (Ancient Versions, Calvin, *et alii*), meaning either that they started from Armenia, which was in the east *respectu terræ Canaan* (Luther), or from that portion of the Assyrian empire which was east of the Tigris, and called Orientalis, as distinguished from the Occidentalis on the west (Bochart) ; or that they first tra- velled westwards, following the direction of the Euphrates in one of its upper branches (Bush) ; or that, having roamed to the east of Shinar, they ultimately returned *occi- dentem versus* (Junius). The phrase, how- ever, is admitted to be more correctly rendered *ad orientem* (Drusius, Lange, Keil, Murphy), as in ch. xiii. 11. Kalisch interprets gener- ally *in oriente,* agreeing with Luther that the migrations are viewed by the writer as taking place in the east; while T. Lewis prefers to read from one front part (the original meaning of *kedem*) to another— onwards. **That they found a plain.** בִּקְעָה; not a valley between mountain ranges, as in Deut. viii. 7; xi. 11; Ps. civ. 8, but a widely-extended plain (πεδίον, LXX.), like that in which Babylon was situated (Herod., lib. i. 178, κέεται ἐν πεδίῳ μεγάλῳ; cf. Strabo, lib. ii. 109). **In the land of Shinar.** Babylonia (cf. ch. x. 10). The derivation of the term is unknown (Gesenius), though it probably meant the land of the two rivers (Alford). Its absence from ancient monuments (Rawlinson) suggests that it was the Jewish name for Chaldæa. **And they dwelt there.**

Ver. 3.—**And they said one to another.** Literally, *a man to his neighbour;* ἄνθρωπος τῷ πλησίον αὐτοῦ (LXX.). **Go to.** A hortatory expletive = come on (Anglicè). **Let us make brick.** *Nilbenah lebenim;* literally, let us brick bricks; πλινθεύσωμεν πλίνθους (LXX.); *laterifecimus lateres* (Calvin); *lebenah* (from *laban*, to be white), being so called from the white and chalky clay of which bricks were made. **And burn them thoroughly.** Literally, *burn them to a burning; venisrephah lisrephah*, a second alliteration, which, however, the LXX. fails to reproduce. Bricks were usually sun-dried; these, being designed to be more durable, were to be calcined through the agency of fire, a proof that the tower-builders were acquainted with the art of brick-making. **And they had**—literally, *and there was to them*—**brick for stone.** Chiefly because of the necessities of the place, the alluvial plain of Babylon being void of stones and full of clay; a proof of the greatness of their crime, seeing they were induced to undertake the work *non facilitate operis, nec aliis commodis, quæ se ad manum offerrent* (Calvin); scarcely because bricks would better endure fire than would stones, the second destruction of the world by fire rather than water being by this time a common expectation (Corn. à Lapide). Josephus, 'Ant.,' lib. i. cp. 4; Herod., lib. i. cp. 179; Justin, lib. i. cp. 2; Ovid, 'Metam.,' iv. 4; and Aristoph. in Avibus (περιτευχίζειν μεγάλαις πλίνθοις ὁπταῖς, ὥσπερ Βαβυλῶνα), all attest that the walls of Babylon were built of brick. The mention of the circumstance that brick was used instead of stone "indicates a writer belonging to a country and an age in which stone buildings were familiar, and therefore not to Babylonia" (Murphy). **And slime.** *Chemer*, from *chamar*, to boil up; ἄσφαλτος (LXX.); the bitumen which boils up from subterranean fountains like oil or hot pitch in the vicinity of Babylon, and also near the Dead Sea (*lacus asphaltites*). Tacitus, 'Hist.,' v. 6; Strabo, xvi. p. 743; Herod., lib. i. c. 179; Josephus, 'Antiq.,' lib. i. c. 4;

Pliny, lib. xxxv. c. 15; Vitruvius, lib. viii. c. 3, are unanimous in declaring that the brick walls of Babylon were cemented with bitumen. Layard testifies that so firmly have the bricks been united that it is almost impossible to detach one from the mass ('Nineveh and Babylon,' p. 499). **Had they.** Literally, *was to them.* **For mortar.** *Chomer.* The third instance of alliteration in the present verse; possibly designed by the writer to represent the enthusiasm of the builders.

Ver. 4.—**And they said.** Being impelled by their success in making bricks for their dwellings (Lange), though the resolution to be mentioned may have been the cause of their brick-making (Bush). **Go to, let us build us a city.** Cf. ch. iv. 17, which represents Cain as the first city builder. **And a tower.** Not as a distinct erection, but as forming a part, as it were the Acropolis, of the city (Bochart). **Whose top** may reach **unto heaven.** Literally, *and his head in the heavens*, a hyperbolical expression for a tower of great height, as in Deut. i. 28; ix. 1 (cf. Homer, 'Odys.,' v. 239, ἐλάτη τ' ἦν οὐρανομήκης). This tower is commonly identified with the temple of Belus, which Herodotus describes (i. 181) as being quadrangular (two stadia each way), and having gates of brass, with a solid tower in the middle, consisting of eight sections, each a stadium in height, placed one above another, ascended by a spiral staircase, and having in the top section a spacious temple with a golden table and a well-furnished bed. Partially destroyed by Xerxes (B.C. 490), it was attempted unsuccessfully to be rebuilt by Alexander the Great; but the remaining portion of the edifice was known to be in existence five centuries later, and was sufficiently imposing to be recognised as the temple of Belus (Pliny, vi. 30). The site of this ancient tower is supposed by George Smith to be covered by the ruin "Babil," a square mound about 200 yards each way, in the north of the city; and that of the tower of Babel to be occupied by the ruin Birs-Nimrud (situated six miles south-west of Hillah, which is about forty miles west of Bagdad), a tower consisting of seven stages, said by inscriptions on cylinders extracted from the ruin to have been "the Temple of the Seven Planets, which had been partially built by a former king of Babylon, and, having fallen into decay, was restored and completed by Nebuchadnezzar" ('Assyrian Discoveries,' xii. p. 59; 'Chaldæan Genesis,' p. 163; cf. Layard's 'Nineveh and Babylon,' chap. xxii. p. 496). It is, however, *primâ facie*, unlikely that either Babil or Birs-Nimrod is the exact site of Babel. The original building was never finished, and may not have attained any great dimensions. Perhaps the most that can be said is that these existing mounds enable us to picture what sort of erection the tower of Babel was to be. **And let us make us a name.** שֵׁם; neither an idol temple, שֵׁם being = God, which it never is without the article, הַשֵּׁם —cf. Levit. xxiv. 11 (Jewish writers); nor a monument, as in 2 Sam. viii. 13 (Clericus); nor a metropolis, reading עִיר instead of שֵׁם, as in 2 Sam. xx. 19 (Clericus); nor a tower that might serve as a sign to guide the wandering nomads and guard them against getting lost when spread abroad with their flocks, as in 2 Sam. viii. 13; Isa. lv. 13 (Perizonius, Dathe, Ilgen); but a name, a reputation, as in 2 Sam. viii. 13; Isa. lxiii. 12, 14; Jer. xxxii. 20; Dan. ix. 15 (Luther, Calvin, Rosenmüller, Keil, Lange, Murphy, Wordsworth, Kalisch). This was the first impelling motive to the erection of the city and tower. The offspring of ambition, it was designed to spread abroad their fame *usque ad ultimos terrarum fines* (Calvin). According to Philo, each man wrote his name upon a brick before he built it in. The second was to establish a rallying point that might serve to maintain their unity. **Lest we be scattered abroad.** Lest = *antequam*, πρό, before that, as if anticipating that the continuous increase of population would necessitate their dispersion (LXX., Vulgate), or as if determined to distinguish themselves before surrendering to the Divine command to spread themselves abroad (Luther); but the more exact rendering of פֶּן is μή, *ne*, lest, introducing an apodosis expressive of something to be avoided by a preceding action (cf. Gesenius, 'Heb. Gram.,' § 152, and Fürst, 'Lex.,' *sub voce*. What the builders dreaded was not the recurrence of a flood (Josephus, Lyra), but the execution of the Divine purpose intimated in ch. ix. 1, and perhaps recalled to their remembrance by Noah (Usher), or by Shem (Wordsworth), or by Eber (Candlish); and what the builders aimed at was resistance to the Divine will. **Upon the face of the whole earth.** Over the entire surface of the globe, and not simply over the land of Shinar (Inglis), or over the immediate region in which they dwelt (Clericus, Dathe, *et alii, ut supra*).

Ver. 5.—**And the Lord came down.** Not in visible form, as in Exod. xix. 20; xxxiv. 5 (Onkelos), but "*effectu ostendens se propinquiorem quem absentem esse judicabant*" (Poole), an anthropomorphism (cf. ch. xviii. 21; Ps. cxliv. 5). "It is measure for measure (*par pari*). Let us build up, say they, and scale the heavens. Let us go down, says God, and defeat their impious thought" (Rabbi Schelomo, quoted by T. Lewis). **To see** (with a view to judicial action) **the city and the tower which the children of men— sons of Adam;** neither the posterity of Cain,

i. e. the Hamites exclusively, as the Sethites were called sons of God, ch. vi. 2 (Augustine), nor wicked men in general (Junius, Piscator), imitators of Adam, i. e. *rebellantes Deo* (Mede, Lyra), since then the Shemites would not have been participators in the undertaking (Drusius), which some think to have been their work exclusively (Inglis); but the members of the human race, or at least their leaders—**builded.**

Ver. 6.—**And the Lord said**—within himself, and to himself (*vide* ver. 8); expressive of the formation of a Divine resolution (cf. ch. vi. 7)—**Behold, the people**—עַם, from root signifying to bind together, expresses the idea of association; גּוֹי, from a root signifying to swell (Lange), to flow together (Gesenius), to gather together (Fürst), conveys the notion of a *confluxus hominum*. T. Lewis connects it with the sense of interiority, or exclusion, which is common in the Chaldee and Syriac—**is one, and they have all one language; and this they begin to do.** One race, one tongue, one purpose. The words indicate unity of effort, as well as concentration of design, on the part of the builders, and a certain measure of success in the achievement of their work. **And now nothing will be restrained from them.** Literally, *there will not be cut off from them anything;* οὐκ ἐκλείψει ἀπ' αὐτῶν πάντα (LXX.); *non desistent a cogitationibus suis* (Vulgate, Luther); *i. e.* nothing will prove too hard for their daring. It can hardly imply that their impious design was on the eve of completion. **Which they have imagined to do.**

Ver. 7.—**Go to.** An ironical contrast to the "Go to" of the builders (Lange). **Let us** (cf. ch. i. 26) **go down, and there confound their language** (*vide infra*, ver. 9), **that they may not understand** (literally, *hear;* so ch. xlii. 23; Isa. xxxvi. 11; 1 Cor. xiv. 2) **one another's speech.** Not referring to individuals (*singuli homines*), since then society were impossible, but to families or nations (*singulæ cognationes*), which each had its own tongue (Poole).

Ver. 8.—**So** (literally, *and*) **the Lord scattered them abroad** (as the result of the confusion of their speech) **upon the face of all the earth : and they left off to build the city.** *I. e.* as a united community, which does not preclude the idea of the Babylonians subsequently finishing the structure.

Ver. 9.—**Therefore is the name of it called Babel.** For *Balbel*, confusion (σύγχυσις, LXX., Josephus), from *Balal*, to confound; the derivation given by the sacred writer in the following clause (cf. for the elision of the letter *l*, *totaphah* for *tophtaphah*, Exod. xiii. 16, and *cochav* for *covcav*, Gen. xxxvii. 9). Other derivations suggested are *Bab-Bel*, the gate or court of Belus (Eichhorn, Lange), an explanation of the term which Fürst thinks not impossible, and Kalisch declares

" can scarcely be overlooked ;" and *Bab-il*, the gate of God (Rosenmüller, Gesenius, Colenso) ; but the first is based upon a purely mythical personage, *Bel*, the imaginary founder of the city ; and the second, if even it were supported by evidence, which it is not, is not so likely as that given by Moses. **Because the Lord did there confound** —how is not explained, but has been conjectured to be by an entirely inward process, viz., changing the ideas associated with words (Koppen) ; by a process wholly outward, viz., an alteration of the mode of pronouncing words (Hoffman), though more probably by both (Keil), or possibly by the first insensibly leading to the second—**the language of all the earth : and from thence did the Lord scatter them.** As the result not simply of their growing discord, *dissensio animórum, per quam factum sit, ut qui turrem struebant distracti sint in contraria studia et consilia* (Vitringa) ; but chiefly of their diverging tongues—a statement which is supposed to conflict with the findings of modern philology, that the existing differences of language among mankind are the result of slow and gradual changes brought about by the operation of natural causes, such as the influence of locality in changing and of time in corrupting human speech. But (1) modern philology has as yet only succeeded in explaining the growth of what might be called the sub-modifications of human speech, and is confessedly unable to account for what appears to be its main division into a Shemitic, an Aryan, and a Turanian tongue, which may have been produced in the sudden and miraculous way described ; and (2) nothing prevents us from regarding the two events, the confusion of tongues and the dispersion of the nations, as occurring simultaneously, and even acting and reacting on each other. As the tribes parted, their speech would diverge, and, on the other hand, as the tongues differed, those who spoke the same or cognate dialects would draw together and draw apart from the rest. We may even suppose that, prior to the building of Babel, if any of the human family had begun to spread themselves abroad upon the surface of the globe, a slight diversity in human speech had begun to show itself ; and the truthfulness of the narrative will in no wise be endangered by admitting that the Divine interposition at Babel may have consisted in quickening a natural process which had already commenced to operate ; nay, we are rather warranted to conclude that the whole work of subdividing human speech was not

compressed into a moment of time, but, after receiving this special impulse, was left to develop and complete itself as the nations wandered farther and ever farther from the plains of Shinar (cf. Kurtz, ' Hist. of the Old Covenant,' vol. i. pp. 108—117 (Clark's For. Theol. Lib.), and 'Quarry on Genesis,' pp. 195—206).

CHALDÆAN LEGEND OF THE TOWER OF BABEL.—Berosus, indeed, does not refer to it. and early writers are obliged to have recourse to somewhat doubtful authorities to confirm it. Eusebius, *e. g.*, quotes Abydenus as saying that "not long after the Flood, the ancient race of men were so puffed up with their strength and tallness of stature that they began to despise and contemn the gods, and laboured to erect that very lofty tower which is now called Babylon, intending thereby to scale the heavens. But when the building approached the sky, behold, the gods called in the aid of the winds, and by their help overturned the tower, and cast it to the ground ! The name of the ruin is still called Babel, because until this time all men had used the same speech ; but now there was sent upon them a confusion of many and diverse tongues " (' Praep. Ev.,' ix. 14). But the diligence of the late George Smith has been rewarded by discovering the fragment of an Assyrian tablet (marked K. 3657 in British Museum) containing an account of the building of the tower, in which the gods are represented as being angry at the work and confounding the speech of the builders. In col. i., lines 5 and 6 (according to W. St. C. Boscawen's translation) run—

" Babylon corruptly to sin went, and Small and great mingled on the mound ;"

while in col. ii., lines 12, 13, 14, 15, are—

" In his anger also the secret counsel he poured out
   To scatter abroad his face he set
     He gave a command to make strange their speech
     . . . their progress he impeded."

(' Records of the Past,' vol. vii. p. 131 ; cf. ' Chaldæan Genesis,' p. 160.)

HOMILETICS.

Ver. 4.—*The tower-builders of Babel.* I. THE IMPIETY OF THEIR DESIGN. **1.** *Ambition.* They were desirous of achieving fame, or "a name" for themselves. Whether in this there was a covert sneer at the exaltation promised to the Shemites, or simply a display of that lust of glory which natively resides within the fallen heart, it was essentially a guilty purpose by which they were impelled. In only one direction is ambition perfectly legitimate, viz., in the direction of moral and spiritual goodness, as distinguished from temporal and material greatness (cf. 1 Cor. xii. 31). Only then may the passion for glory be exuberantly gratified, when its object is the living God instead of puny and unworthy self (cf. Jer. ix. 23, 24 ; 1 Cor. i. 29, 31). 2. *Rebellious*, setting its head among the clouds, "exalting its throne above the stars," it was designed to be an act of insolent defiance to the will of Heaven. The city and the tower of Babel had their origin in deliberate, determined, enthusiastic, exulting hostility to the Divine purpose that they should spread themselves abroad over the face of the whole earth. And herein lies the essence of all impiety : whatever thought, counsel, word, or work derives its inspiration, be it only in an infinitesimal degree, from antagonism to the mind of God is sin. Holiness is but another name for obedience.

II. The magnitude of their enterprise. The undertaking of the tower-builders was—1. *Sublimely conceived.* The city was to ward off invasion from without, and to counteract disruption from within. Gathering men of a common tongue into a common residence, engaging them in common pursuits, and providing them with common interests was the sure way to make them strong. If this was the creative idea out of which cities sprung, the Cainites, if not pious, must at least have been possessed of genius. Then the tower was to touch the skies. Unscientific perhaps, but scarcely irrational ; "an undertaking not of savages, but of men possessed with the idea of somehow getting above nature." And though certainly to aspire after such supremacy over nature in the spirit of a godless science which recognises no power or authority superior to itself was the very sin of these Babelites, yet nothing more convincingly attests the essential greatness of man than the ever-widening control which science is enabling him to assert over the forces of matter. 2. *Hopefully begun.* The builders were united in their language and purpose. The place was convenient for the proposed erection. The most complete preparations were made for the structure. The work was commenced with determination and amid universal enthusiasm. It had all the conditions of success, humanly speaking—one mind, one heart, one hand. 3. *Suddenly abandoned.* "They left off to build the city." So the most prosperous undertakings often terminate in miserable failure. The mighty enterprise was mysteriously frustrated. So have all such wicked combinations in times past been overthrown. Witness the great world empires of Babylon, Persia, Greece, Rome. So in the end will the great mystery of iniquity, of which that early Babel was the first type.

III. The inspection of their work. 1. *No work of man can hope to escape the eye of God.* Even now he is minutely acquainted with the thoughts, and words, and works, and ways of every individual on the earth (Prov. xv. 3 ; Heb. iv. 13), while there is a day coming when "there is nothing covered that shall not be revealed" (Matt. x. 26). 2. *Every work of man shall be judged at the bar of God* (Eccles. xii. 14 ; 1 Cor. iii. 13). The Divine verdict upon human undertakings will often strangely conflict with the judgments of men.

IV. The confusion of their tongues. 1. As a fact in the experience of the builders, it was—(1) *Unchallengeable.* They could not understand one another, so that they could not doubt that a change of some kind had passed upon their speech ; and observation convinces us that as men have now a variety of tongues, something must have broken up the original unity of speech. (2) *Mysterious.* It is not likely that these primitive builders understood how their language had been transmuted. Modern philology has no certain word to utter upon the subject yet. (3) *Supernatural.* It was effected by the immediate agency of God. If even natural causes had begun to operate, they were quickened by the Divine action. Believers in a God who made the tongue of man should have no difficulty in believing in a God who changed the tongue of man. 2. As a judgment on the persons of the builders, it was—(1) *Unexpected in its coming*, as are all God's judgments, like the Flood and like the coming of the Son of man. (2) *Deserved by its subjects.* Caught, as it were, in the very act of insubordination, guilty of nothing short of treason against the King of heaven, they were visited with summary and condign chastisement. So are all God's punishments richly merited by those on whom they fall. (3) *Appropriate in its character.*

It was fitting that they who had abused their oneness of speech, which was designed for their good, to keep them in the Church, should be punished with variety of tongues. (4) *Effectual in its design.* Sent to scatter them abroad, it succeeded in its aim. Man's designs often fail; God's never.

V. THE DISPERSION OF THEIR RANKS. 1. *Judicial in its character.* In its incidence on the builders it wore a punitive aspect. Providences that are full of blessings for the good are always laden with curses to the wicked. 2. *Beneficial in its purpose.* The scattering of the earth's population over the surface of the globe was originally intended for what it has eventually turned out to be, a blessing for the race. 3. *Unlimited in its extent.* Though the original dispersion could not have carried the tribes to any remote distances from Shinar, the process then begun was intended not to rest until the earth was fully occupied by the children of men.

VI. THE MEMORIAL OF THEIR FOLLY. This was—1. *Exceedingly expressive.* The unfinished tower was designated Babel, or Confusion. It is well that things should be called by their right names. The name of Babel was an epitome of the foolish aim and end of the builders. The world is full of such monuments of folly. 2. *Self-affixed.* So God often compels "men of corrupt minds" and "reprobate concerning the faith" not only to manifest, but also to publish, their own folly. 3. *Long-enduring.* It continued to be known as Babel in the days of Moses and long after—an emblem of that shame which shall eventually be the portion of all the wicked.

Learn—1. The sinfulness of ambition. 2. The folly of attempting to resist God. 3. The power of God in carrying out his purposes. 4. The mercy of God in dividing the nations. 5. The ability of God to regather the divided nations of the earth.

HOMILIES BY VARIOUS AUTHORS.

Vers. 1—9.—*Order brought forth.* We are now to trace the rise of the kingdom of God among the nations. Already in the case of Nimrod, the mighty hunter before the Lord, that is, by permission of Divine providence, the antagonism between the kingdom of God and the kingdoms of this world has been symbolised. Now we find the concentration of the world's rebellion and ungodliness in the false city, type of the worldly power throughout the Scriptures. It is on the plain of Shinar to which the early migration from the East directed the course of mankind. We are not told at what time the settlement in Shinar took place. As the account of the confusion of tongues is introduced between the larger genealogy and the lesser, we may infer that its object is to account for the spread of nations. Whether we take this Babel to be Nimrod's Babel or an earlier one is of very little consequence. The whole narrative is full of Divine significance. Notice—

I. MAN'S BABEL IS A LYING PRETENSION. It rests on an attempt to substitute his own foundation of society for God's; it is—1. False safety—the high tower to keep above the flood. 2. False ambition—reaching unto heaven, making a name with bricks and mortar. 3. False unity—"lest we be scattered abroad." These are the characteristics of all Babel despotisms. Material foundations to rest upon; lying structures built upon them.

II. GOD'S KINGDOM IS NOT REALLY HINDERED BY MAN'S REBELLION. He suffers the Babel structure to be reared, but by his judgments scatters both the men and their projects, making the rebellious conspiracy against himself prepare the way for his ultimate universal triumph. So it has been all through the history of the world, and especially immediately before the coming of the Lord Jesus Christ. The confusion of tongues was a judgment and at the same time a mercy. Those that are filled with such ambitions and build upon such foundations are not fit to dwell together in one place. It is better they should be divided. The investigations into comparative grammar and the genesis of human language point to some primitive seat of the earliest form of speech in the neighbourhood indicated. It was certainly the result of the false form of society with which men began, the Nimrod empire, that they could not remain gathered in one community; and as they spread they lost their knowledge of their original language, and were confounded because they understood not one another's speech. It is remarkable that in the beginning of the kingdom of Christ, the true city of God which shall overspread the world, the Spirit bestowed the gift of tongues, as if to signify that the Babel of man's lying ambitions was to cease, and in the truth of the gospel men would be united as one family, "understanding one another's speech."—R.

Ver. 1.—*Unity of language.* 1. The original birthright of the human race. 2. The lost inheritance of sinful men. 3. The ultimate goal of the Christian dispensation. 4. The recovered heritage of redeemed humanity.—W.

Ver. 2.—Note—1. The benefit of a wandering condition. It sometimes prevents the rise of sinful thoughts and wicked deeds. So long as the primitive nomads were travelling from station to station they did not think of either rebellion or ambition. So Israel followed God fully in the wilderness. 2. The danger of a settled state. Established in the fat plain of Shinar, they wanted a city and a tower. So Israel in Canaan waxed fat and kicked. So Moab, having been at ease from his youth, retained his scent unchanged. So comfortable surroundings often lead men from God.—W.

Ver. 3.—*Ancient brickmakers.* I. IN SHINAR. Examples of (1) ingenuity, (2) earnestness, (3) perseverance, (4) unity in sin.
II. IN EGYPT (Exod. v. 7). Illustrations of (1) the bondage, (2) the degradation, (3) the misery, (4) hopelessness, of sin.—W.

Ver. 4.—*The tower of Babel.* I. A MONUMENT OF MAN'S—1. Sinful ambition. 2. Laborious ingenuity. 3. Demonstrated feebleness. 4. Stupendous folly.
II. A MEMORIAL OF GOD'S—1. Overruling providence. 2. Resistless power. 3. Retributive justice. 4. Beneficent purpose.—W.

Ver. 4.—*God's city or man's city.* "And they said, Go to, let us build us a city and a tower, whose top may reach unto heaven; and let us make us a name, lest we be scattered abroad upon the face of the whole earth." In the world after the Flood we trace the outlines of the gospel dispensation. To Noah was revealed " good will toward men;" the acceptance of sacrifice; faith as the condition and channel of blessing; and work, to spread the knowledge of and trust in his name, *i. e.* what he is pleased to reveal concerning himself. But "the carnal mind" was there resisting the Spirit. Noah and his seed were to replenish the earth (ch. ix. 1; cf. Mark xvi. 15). They were promised safety from beasts, of whom, if separated, they might be afraid (ch. ix. 2; cf. Matt. x. 29, 31; Luke x. 19). Here was a trial of faith and obedience (cf. Exod. xxxiv. 24). But men had not faith, would not trust, would not go forth at his word. Their calling was to seek God's city (Heb. xi. 10—16), to live as citizens of it (Phil. iii. 20). They chose a city for themselves; earthly security, comforts, luxuries. Called to glorify God's name, their thought was to make a name for themselves. Self was the moving power. The name of God is the trust of his people (Ps. xx. 7; Prov. xviii. 10); a centre of unity to all his children in every place. They trusted in themselves; would be like God to themselves. The tower, the work of their own hands, was to be their centre of unity; and the name of it came to be Babel, *i. e.* confusion (cf. Matt. xv. 13). Love draws mankind together. Self-seeking tends to separation. God bade them spread that they might be united in faith and in work. They chose their own way of union, and it led to dispersion with no bond of unity.
I. WE ARE CALLED TO BUILD THE CITY OF GOD (Heb. xii. 22). To prepare the way for Rev. xxi. 3. The gifts of Christ are made effectual by the work of men. That city, built of living stones (1 Pet. ii. 5), cemented not with slime, but by unity of faith (Ephes. iv. 3). And a tower, a centre of unity, the "good confession" (Rom. xiv. 11; Phil. ii. 11). And to obtain a name, to be confessed by the Lord before the angels, to be acknowledged as his "brethren," and stamped with the "new name." And a promise given, as if pointing to Babel: "Your labour is not in vain in the Lord."
II. MANY HAVE NO MIND TO BUILD. They love ease and have no earnestness, triflers with time, or direct their earnestness to earthly prizes—a name among men.
III. EVEN BELIEVERS ARE OFTEN THUS HINDERED. There may be spiritual selfishness along with really spiritual aims. The multitude of cares may distract the soul. Temptations may wear the garb of zeal, or of charity, or of prudence. Watch and pray. God's faithfulness will not fail (1 Cor. x. 13).—M.

Ver. 5.—*The cities of men and the city of God* (Gen. xi. 5; Heb. xi. 16). I. THEIR BUILDERS. Of the first, men—mostly wicked men; of the second, the Architect of the universe.

II. THEIR ORIGIN. Of the first (Enoch, ch. iv. 17; and Babel, ch. xi. 5), hostility to God; of the second, love to man.

III. THEIR DESIGN. Of the first, to be a bond of union among sinners; of the second, to be a residence for God's children.

IV. THEIR APPEARANCE. Of the first, that of slime, mud, bricks, or at best stones; of the second, that of gold and pearls.

V. THEIR DURATION. Of the first, it is written that with all the other works of man, they shall be burnt up; of the second, that it shall be everlasting.—W.

Ver. 6.—*Vain imaginings*—1. Commonly spring from misused blessings. A united people, with a common language, and enjoying a measure of success in their buildings, the Babelites became vain in their imaginings. So do wicked men generally misinterpret the Divine beneficence and leniency which suffers them to proceed a certain length with their wickedness (cf. Rom. i. 21; 2 Tim. iii. 9). 2. Are never unobserved by him against whom they are directed (Deut. xxxi. 21; 1 Chron. xxviii. 9). 3. Are doomed to certain and complete frustration (Ps. ii. 1; Luke i. 51; 2 Cor. x. 5).—W.

Ver. 7.—*Babel and Zion.* 1. Confusion, division, dispersion. 2. Gathering the dispersed, uniting the divided, restoring order to the confused.—W.

§ 6. THE GENERATIONS OF SHEM (CH. XI. 10—26).

EXPOSITION.

Ver. 10.—**These are the generations of Shem.** The new section, opening with the usual formula (cf. ch. ii. 4; v. 1; vi. 9; x. 1), reverts to the main purpose of the inspired narrative, which is to trace the onward development of the line of promise; and this it does by carrying forward the genealogical history of the holy seed through ten generations till it reaches Abram. Taken along with ch. v., with which it corresponds, the present table completes the chronological outline from Adam to the Hebrew patriarch. **Shem was an hundred years old** (literally, *the son of an hundred years*, i. e. in his hundredth year), **and begat Arphaxad.** The English term is borrowed from the LXX., the Hebrew being Arpachshadh, a compound of which the principal part is כשׁד, giving rise to the Chashdim or Chaldæans; whence Professor Lewis regards it as originally the name of a people transferred to their ancestor (cf. ch. x. 22). **Two years after the flood.** So that in Noah's 603rd year Shem was 100, and must accordingly have been born in Noah's 503rd year, i. e. two years after Japheth (cf. ch. v. 32; x. 21). The mention of the Flood indicates the point of time from which the present section is designed to be reckoned.

Ver. 11.—**And Shem lived after he begat Arphaxad five hundred years** (making his life in all 600 years), **and begat sons and daughters** (concerning whom Scripture is silent, as not being included in the holy line).

Vers. 12, 13.—**And Arphaxad lived five** and thirty years (the first indication of a change having transpired upon human life after the Flood, the average age of paternity prior to that event being 117, the earliest 65, and the latest 187), **and begat Salah.** *Shalach*, literally, *emission*, or the sending forth, of water, a memorial of the Flood (Bochart); or of an arrow or dart (*vide* ch. x. 24). **And Arphaxad lived after he begat Salah four hundred and three years** (making a total of 438, i. e. 339 years less than the youngest complete life in the prediluvian table,—Enoch's, of course, being excepted,—and 162 less than Shem's: a second indication of the shortening of the period of existence), **and begat sons and daughters.**

Vers. 14, 15.—**And Salah lived thirty years, and begat Eber.** Literally, *the region on the other side* (πέραν); from עֵבֶר, to pass over (cf. ὑπέρ, Greek; *über*, German; *over*, Saxon). The ancestor of the Hebrews (ch. x. 21), so called from his descendants having crossed the Euphrates and commenced a southward emigration, or from the circumstance that he or another portion of his posterity remained on the other side. Prof. Lewis thinks that this branch of the Shemites, having lingered so long in the upper country, had not much to do with the tower building on the plain of Shinar. **And Salah lived after he begat Eber four hundred and three years** (in all 433 years, or five years less than Arphaxad), **and begat sons and daughters.**

Vers. 16, 17.—**And Eber lived four and thirty years, and begat Peleg.** *Division;* from *palag*, to divide. For the reason of this cognomen *vide* ch. x. 25. **And Eber lived after he begat Peleg four hundred and thirty years** (thus reaching the age of 464, the longest-lived of the postdiluvian fathers), **and begat sons and daughters.**

Vers. 18, 19.—**And Peleg lived thirty years, and begat Reu.** *Friend* (sc. of God, or of men), or *friendship;* from a root signifying to pasture, to tend, to care for. Bochart traces his descendants in the great Nisæan plain Ragau (Judith i. 6), situated on the confines of Armenia and Media, and having, according to Strabo, a city named Ragæ or Ragiæ. **And Peleg lived after he begat Reu two hundred and nine years** (thus making his entire age 239 years), **and begat sons and daughters.**

Vers. 20, 21.—**And Reu lived two and thirty years, and begat Serug.** *Vine-shoot,* from *sarag,* to wind (Gesenius, Lange, Lewis, Murphy); *strength, firmness,* from the sense of twisting which the root bears (Fürst). **And Reu lived after he begat Serug two hundred and seven years** (in all 239), **and begat sons and daughters.**

Vers. 22, 23.—**And Serug lived thirty years, and begat Nahor.** *Panting* (Gesenius); from *nachar,* to breathe hard, to snort. *Piercer, slayer* (Fürst); from an unused root signifying to bore through. **And Serug lived after he begat Nahor two hundred years** (or 230 in all), **and begat sons and daughters.**

Vers. 24, 25.—**And Nahor lived nine and twenty years, and begat Terah.** *Terach,* or turning, tarrying; from *tarach,* an unused Chaldæan root meaning to delay (Gesenius);

singularly appropriate to his future character and history, from which probably the name reverted to him. Ewald renders *Terach* by "migration," considering *Tarach = arach,* to stretch out. **And Nahor lived after he begat Terah an hundred and nineteen years** (148 in all, the shortest liver among the postdiluvian patriarchs), **and begat sons and daughters.**

Ver. 26.—**And Terah lived seventy years, and begat Abram.** First named on account of his spiritual pre-eminence. If Abram was Terah's eldest son, then, as Abram was seventy-five years of age when Terah died (ch. xii. 4), Terah's whole life could only have been 145 years. But Terah lived to the age of 205 years (ch. xi. 32); therefore Abram was born in Terah's 130th year. This, however, makes it surprising that Abraham should have reckoned it impossible for him to have a son at 100 years (ch. xvii. 17); only, after having lived so long in childless wedlock, it was not strange that he should feel somewhat doubtful of any issue by Sarai. Kalisch believes that Stephen (Acts vii. 4) made a mistake in saying Terah died before his son's migration from Charran, and that he really survived that event by sixty years; while the Samaritan text escapes the difficulty by shortening the life of Terah to 145 years. **And Nahor,** who must have been younger than Haran, since he married Haran's daughter. **And Haran,** who, as the eldest, must have been born in Terah's seventieth year. Thus the second family register, like the first, concludes after ten generations with the birth of three sons, who, like Noah's, are mentioned not in the order of their ages, but of their spiritual pre-eminence.

CHRONOLOGICAL TABLE.

NAMES OF PATRIARCHS.	HEBREW TEXT.			SAMARITAN.			SEPTUAGINT.		
	Age at son's birth.	Rest of life.	Total no. of years.	Age at son's birth.	Rest of life.	Total no. of years.	Age at son's birth.	Rest of life.	Total no. of years.
SHEM	100	500	600	100	500	600	100	500	600
ARPHAXAD	35	403	438	135	303	438	135	400	535
(Καϊνᾶν)							130	330	460
SALAH	30	403	433	130	303	433	130	330	460
EBER	34	430	464	134	270	404	134	270	404
PELEG	30	209	239	130	109	239	130	209	339
REU	32	207	239	132	107	239	132	207	339
SERUG	30	200	230	130	100	230	130	200	330
NAHOR	29	119	148	79	69	148	179	125	304
TERAH	70	135	205	70	75	145	70	135	205
	390			1040			1270		

From this table it appears that 292 years, according to the Hebrew text, passed away between the Flood and the birth, or 292 + 75 = 367 between the Flood and the call of Abraham. Reckoning, however, the age of Terah at Abram's birth as 130 (*vide* Exposition), the full period between the Deluge and the patriarch's departure from Haran will be 367 + 60 = 427 years, which, allowing five pairs to each family, Murphy computes, would in the course of ten generations yield a population of 15,625,000 souls ; or, supposing a rate of increase equal to that of Abraham's posterity in Egypt during the 400 years that elapsed from the call to the exodus, the inhabitants of the world in the time of Abraham would be between seven and eight millions. It must, however, be remembered that an element of uncertainty enters into all computations based upon even the Hebrew text. The age of Terah at the birth (apparently) of Abram is put down at seventy. But it admits of demonstration that Abram was born in the 130th year of Terah. What guarantee then do we possess that in every instance the registered son was the firstborn? In the case of Arphaxad this is almost implied in the statement that he was born two years after the Flood. But if the case of Eber were parallel with that of Terah, and Joktan were the son that he begat in his thirty-fourth year, then obviously the birth of Peleg, like that of Abram, may have happened sixty years later ; in which case it is apparent that any reckoning which proceeded on the minute verbal accuracy of the registered numbers would be entirely at fault. This consideration might have gone far to explain the wide divergence between the numbers of the Samaritan and Septuagint as compared with the Hebrew text, had it not been that they both agree with it in setting down seventy as the age of Terah at the date of Abram's birth. The palpable artificiality also of these later tables renders them even less worthy of credit than the Hebrew. The introduction by the LXX. of Cainan as the son of Arphaxad, though seemingly confirmed by Luke (Luke iii. 35, 36), is clearly an interpolation. It does not occur in the LXX. version of 1 Chron. i. 24, and is not found in either the Samaritan Pentateuch, the Targums or the ancient versions, in Josephus or Philo, or in the Codex Beza of the Gospel of Luke. Its appearance in Luke (and probably also in the LXX.) can only be explained as an interpolation. Wordsworth is inclined to regard it as authentic in Luke, and to suppose that Cainaan was excluded from the Mosaic table either to render it symmetrical, as Luke's table is rendered symmetrical by its insertion, or because of some moral offence, which, though necessitating his expulsion from a Hebrew register, would not prevent his reappearance in his proper place under the gospel.

HOMILETICS.

Vers. 10—26.—*From Shem to Abram.* I. THE SEPARATION OF THE GODLY SEED. The souls that constitute the Church of God upon the earth are always, as these Hebrew patriarchs—1. *Known to God ;* and that not merely in the mass, but as individuals, or units ; nor simply superficially and slightly, but minutely and thoroughly. He knows the fathers they descend from, the families they belong to, the names by which they are designated, the number of years they live, and the children they leave behind them on the earth (cf. Ps. i. 6 ; 2 Tim. ii. 19). 2. *Separated by God.* This was one of the great ends contemplated by the division of the people which happened in the days of Peleg, which was designed to eliminate the Shemites from the rest of mankind. Then the migration of the sons of Eber contributed further to the isolation of the children of the promise. And, lastly, the selection of the son, not always the firstborn, through whom the hope of the gospel was to be carried on tended in the same direction. So God afterwards separated Israel from the nations. So he still by his providence and his word calls out and separates his people from the world (cf. 1 Kings viii. 53 ; 2 Cor. vi. 17). 3. *Honoured before God ;* by being selected as the vessels of his grace, the channels of his promise. the ministers of his gospel, and the messengers of his covenant, while others are passed by ; and by being written in God's book of remembrance, while others are forgotten (cf. 1 Sam. ii. 30 ; Ps. xci. 15 ; Mal. iii. 16 ; Matt. x. 32 ; 2 Tim. ii. 20 ; Rev. iii. 5).

II. THE SHORTENING OF HUMAN LIFE. A second characteristic of the postdiluvian era. 1. *A patent fact.* Even Shem, the longest liver of the men of this period, did not continue on the earth so long as Lamech, the shortest liver of the previous age, by 177 years; while the life of Arphaxad was shorter than that of his father by 162 years, and the days of Terah at the close dwindled down to 205 years. 2. *A potent sermon.* Whether the comparative brevity of life immediately after the Flood was due to any change in the physical constitution of man, or to the altered conditions of existence under the Noachic covenant, or to the gradual deterioration of the race through the lapse of time, or to the direct appointment of Heaven, it was admirably fitted to remind them of—(1) *The reality of sin.* With its penalty descending so palpably and frequently it would seem impossible to challenge the fact of their being a guilty and condemned race. (2) *The necessity of repentance.* Every death that happened would sound like a trumpet-call to sinful men to turn to God. (3) *The vanity of life.* The long terms of existence that were meted out to men before the Flood might tempt them to forget the better country, even an heavenly, and to seek a permanent inheritance on earth; it would almost seem apparent to these short livers that no such inheritance could be obtained below. Alas that the shortness of man's career beneath the sun is now so familiar that it has well nigh ceased to impress the mind with anything! (4) *The certainty of death.* When men's lives were counted by centuries it might be easy to evade the thought of death. When decades came to be enough to reckon up the longest term of existence, it could scarcely fail to remind them that " it was appointed unto all men once to die "

III. The nearing of the gospel promise. Ten generations further down the stream of time do we see the promise carried in this second genealogical table. It was—1. *A vindication of the Divine faithfulness* in adhering to his promise. Already twenty generations had come and gone, and neither was the promise forgotten nor had the holy line been allowed to become extinct. Ever since Adam's day in Eden the covenant-keeping Jehovah had found a seed to serve him, even in the darkest times, and had been careful to raise up saints who would transmit the hope of the gospel to future times. It was a proof to the passing generations that God was still remembering his promise, and was intending to make it good in the fulness of the times. 2. *A demonstration of God's ability* to keep his promise. Not once through all the bygone centuries had a link been found wanting in the chain of saintly men through whom the promise was to be transmitted. It was a clear pledge that God would still be able to supply the necessary links that might be required to carry it forward to its ultimate fulfilment.

HOMILIES BY VARIOUS AUTHORS.

Vers. 10—26.—*The order of grace* is—1. Determined by God, and not by man. 2. Arranged after the Spirit, and not according to the flesh. 3. Appointed for the world's good as well as for the Church's safety.—W.

Vers. 10—32.—*Divine traditions.* A genealogy of Shem and of Terah, in order to set forth clearly the position of Abraham and that of his nephew Lot, and their connection with Ur of the Chaldees and Canaan. The chosen family is about to be separated from their country, but we are not told that there was no light of God shining in Ur of the Chaldees. Probably there was the tradition of Shem's knowledge handed down through the generations. Arphaxad was born two years after the Flood; Salah, thirty-seven years; Eber, sixty-seven years; Peleg, one hundred and one years; Reu, one hundred and thirty-one years; Serug, one hundred and sixty-three years; Nahor, one hundred and ninety-three years; Terah, the father of Abraham, two hundred and twenty-two years—no great length of time for traditions to be preserved. The call of Abram was not merely his separation from idolatry, but his consecration to the special vocation of founding the religious institutions which were to be connected with his family.—R.

PART III

THE PATRIARCHAL AGE OF THE WORLD. Ch. XI. 27—L. 26.

§ 7.   The Generations of Terah (Ch. XI. 27—XXV. 11).

Ver. 27.—**Now** (literally, *and*, intimating the close connection of the present with the preceding section) **these** are **the generations** —the commencement of a new subdivision of the history (Keil), and neither the winding-up of the foregoing genealogy ('Speaker's Commentary') nor the heading only of the brief paragraph in vers. 27—32 (Lange; *vide* ch. ii. 4)—**of Terah.** Not of Abram; partly because mainly occupied with the career not of Abram's son, in which case "the generations of Abram" would have been appropriate, but of Abram himself, Terah's son; and partly owing to the subsidiary design to indicate Nahor's connection, through Rebekah, with the promised seed (cf. Quarry, p. 415). **Terah begat Abram**, "Father of Elevation," who is mentioned first not because he happened to be Terah's eldest son (Keil), which he was not (*vide* ch. xi. 26), or because Moses was indifferent to the order in which the sons of Terah were introduced (Calvin), but because of his spiritual preeminence as the head of the theocratic line (Wordsworth). **Nahor**, "Panting," not to be confounded with his grandfather of the same name (ver. 25). **Haran**, "Tarrying," the eldest son of Terah (ver. 26), and, along with Abram and Nahor, reintroduced into the narrative on account of his relationship to Lot and Milcah. That Terah had other sons (Calvin) does not appear probable. **And Haran begat Lot.** לוֹט; of uncertain etymology, but may be = לוּט, a concealed, *i. e.* obscure, low one, or perhaps a dark-coloured one (Fürst).

Ver. 28.—**And Haran died before his father.** Literally, *upon the face of his father*; ἐνώπιον τοῦ πατρὸς αὐτοῦ (LXX); while his father was alive (Munster, Luther, Calvin, Rosenmüller); perhaps also in his father's presence (Keil, Lange), though the Jewish fable may be discarded that Terah, at this time an idolater, accused his sons to Nimrod, who cast them into a furnace for refusing to worship the fire-god, and that Haran perished in the flames in his father's sight. The decease of Haran is the first recorded instance of the natural death

of a son before his father. **In the land of his nativity.** Ἐν τῇ γῇ ᾗ ἐγεννήθη (LXX.). **In Ur of the Chaldees.** *Ur Kasdim* (ch. xi. 31; xv. 7; Neh. ix. 7). The *Kasdim* —formerly believed to have been Shemites on account of (1) Abram's settlement among them, (2) the preservation of the name *Kesed* among his kindred (ch. xxii. 22), (3) the close affinity to a Shemite tongue of the language known to modern philologists as Chaldee, an Aramæan dialect differing but slightly from the Syriac (Heeren), and (4) the supposed identity or intimate connection of the Babylonians with the Assyrians (Niebuhr)—are now, with greater probability, and certainly with closer adherence to Biblical history (ch. x. 8—12), regarded as having been a Hamite race (Rawlinson, Smith); an opinion which receives confirmation from (1) the statement of Homer ('Odyss.,' i. 23, 24), that the Ethiopians were divided and dwelt at the ends of the earth, towards the setting and the rising sun, *i. e.*, according to Strabo, on both sides of the Arabian Gulf; (2) the primitive traditions (*a*) of the Greeks, who regarded Memnon, King of Ethiopia, as the founder of Susa (Herod., v. 54), and the son of a Cissian woman (Strabo, xv. 3, § 2; (*b*) of the Nilotic Ethiopians, who claimed him as one of their monarchs; and (*c*) of the Egyptians, who identified him with their King Amunoph III., whose statue became known as the vocal Memnon (*vide* Rawlinson's 'Ancient Monarchies,' vol. i. p. 48); (3) the testimony of Moses of Chorene ('History of Armenia,' i. 6), who connects in the closest way Babylonia, Egypt, and Ethiopia Proper, identifying Belus, King of Babylon, with Nimrod, and making him the son of Mizraim, or the grandson of Cush; and (4) the monumental history of Babylonia, which shows the language of the earliest inscriptions, according to Rawlinson "differing greatly from the later Babylonian," to have been that of a Turanian people (cf. 'Records of the Past,' vol. iii. p. 3). The term *Ur* has been explained to be identical with 'Ir, a city (Rawlinson); the Zend Vare, a fortress (Gesenius); *Ur*, the light country, *i. e.* the land of the sun-rising (Fürst); and even *Ur*, fire, with special reference to the legendary furnace already referred to (Talmudists). Whether a district (LXX., Lange, Kalisch) or a city (Josephus, Eusebius, Onkelos, Drusius, Keil, Murphy, 'Speaker's Commentary'), its exact site is uncertain. Rival claimants for the honour of representing it have appeared in (1) a Persian fortress (Persicum Castellum) of the name of Ur, mentioned by Ammianus Marcellinus (lxxv. c. 8) as lying between Nisibis and the Tigris (Bochart, Michaelis, Rosenmüller, Delitzsch); (2) the modern Orfah, the Edessa of the Greeks, situated "on one of the bare, rugged spurs which descend from the mountains of Armenia into the Assyrian plains" (Stanley's 'Jewish Church,' i. 7); and (3) Hur, the most important of the early capitals of Chaldæa, now the ruins of Mugheir, at no great distance from the mouth, and six miles to the west, of the Euphrates (Rawlinson's 'Ancient Monarchies,' i. 15, 16; Smith's 'Assyrian Discoveries,' xii. 233; 'Records of the Past,' vol. iii. p. 9). Yet none of them is quite exempt from difficulty. A military fort, to take the first-named location, does not appear a suitable or likely place for a nomade horde to settle in; while the second has been reckoned too near Charran, the first place of encampment of the emigrants; and the third, besides being exceedingly remote from Charran, scarcely harmonises with Stephen's speech before the Sanhedrim (Acts vii. 2). Unless, therefore, Stephen meant Chaldæa when he said Mesopotamia (Dykes), and Abraham could speak of Northern Mesopotamia as his country (ch. xxiv. 4), when in reality he belonged to Southern Babylonia, the identification of Ur of the Chaldees with the Mugheir ruin though regarded with most favour by archæologists, will continue to be doubtful; while, if the clan march commenced at Edessa, it will always require an effort to account for their coming to a halt so soon after starting and so near home; and the Nisibis station, though apparently more suitable than either in respect of distance, will remain encumbered with its own peculiar difficulties. It would seem, therefore, as if the exact situation of the patriarchal town or country must be left undetermined until further light can be obtained.

Ver. 29.—**And Abram and Nahor took them wives** (cf. ch. vi. 2): **the name of Abram's wife** was **Sarai**. "My princess," from *sarah*, to rule (Gesenius, Lange); "Strife" (Kalisch, Murphy): "Jah is ruler" (Fürst). The LXX. write Σάρα, changing afterwards to Σάρρα to correspond with Sarah. That Sarai was Iscah (Josephus, Augustine, Jerome, Jonathan) has been inferred from ch. xx. 12; but,

though receiving apparent sanction from ver. 31, this opinion "is not supported by any solid argument" (Rosenmüller). **And the name of Nahor's wife, Milcah** (Queen, or Counsel), **the daughter of Haran**, *i. e.* Nahor's niece. Marriage with a half-sister or a niece was afterwards forbidden by the Mosaic code (Levit. xviii. 9, 14). **The father of Milcah, and the father of Iscah,** whose name "Seer" may have been introduced into the narrative like that of Naamah (ch. iv. 22), as that of an eminent lady connected with the family (Murphy). Ewald's hypothesis, that Iscah was Lot's wife, is pure conjecture.

Ver. 30. — **But Sarai was barren; she had no child.** Perhaps in contrast to Milcah, who by this time had begun to have a family (Murphy).

Ver. 31.—**And Terah took**—an act of pure human volition on the part of Terah (Kalisch); under the guidance of God's ordinary providence (Keil); but more probably, as Abram was called in Ur (*vide infra*), prompted by a knowledge of his son's call, and a desire to participate in his son's inheritance (Lange)—**Abram his son, and Lot the son of Haran his son's son, and Sarai his daughter-in-law, his son Abram's wife.** The Samaritan reads, "and Milcah his daughter-in-law, the wives of Abram and Nahor his sons," with an obvious intention to account for the appearance of Nahor as a settler in Charran (ch. xxiv. 10); but it is better to understand the migration of Nahor and his family as having taken place subsequent to Terah's departure. **And they went forth with them.** *I. e.* Lot and Sarai with Terah and Abram (Keil); or, better, Terah and Abram with Lot and Sarai (Jarchi, Rosenmüller, Murphy, 'Speaker's Commentary'); though best is the interpretation, "and they went forth with each other" (Lange, Kalisch). For the reflexive use of the personal pronoun *vide* ch. iii. 7; xxii. 3, and cf. Gesenius, 'Gram.,' § 124. Other readings are, "and he led them forth" (Samaritan, LXX., Vulgate, Dathius), and "and they (the unnamed members of the family) went forth with those named" (Delitzsch). **From Ur of the Chaldees, to go into the land of Canaan.** Expressive of the Divine destination, rather than of the conscious intention of the travellers (Heb. xi. 8), though Canaan was not at this time unknown to the inhabitants of the Tigris and Euphrates valley (*vide* ch. xiv. 1—12). **And they came into Haran.** *Charran*, Κάῤῥαι, Carrae, in north-west Mesopotamia, about twenty-five miles from Edessa, one of the supposed sites of Ur, and celebrated as the scene of the overthrow of Crassus by the Parthians (B.C. 53). **And dwelt there.** Probably in consequence of the growing infirmity of Terah, the period of their sojourn being differently computed according as Abram is regarded as having been born in Terah's 70th or 130th year.

Ver. 32.—**And the days of Terah were two hundred and five years.** So that if Abram was born in Terah's 70th year, Terah must have been 145 when Abram left Haran, and must have survived that departure sixty years (Kalisch, Dykes); whereas if Abram was born in his father's 130th year, then Terah must have died before his son's departure from Haran, which agrees with Acts vii. 4. **And Terah died in Haran.**

HOMILETICS.

Ver. 31.—*The migration of the Terachites.* I. THE DEPARTURE OF THE EMIGRANTS. The attendant circumstances of this migration—the gathering of the clan, the mustering of the flocks, the farewells and benedictions exchanged with relatives and friends, the hopes and fears of the adventurous pilgrims—imagination may depict; the reasons which prompted it may be conjectured to have been—1. *The spirit of emigration*, which since the dispersion at Babel had been abroad among the primitive populations of mankind. The arms of a Trans-Euphratean state had already penetrated as far west as the circle of the Jordan, and it has been surmised that this Terachite removal from Chaldæa may have been connected with some larger movement in the same direction. 2. *The oppression of the Hamites*, who, besides being the most powerful and enterprising of the early tribes, and having seized upon the fattest settlements, such as Egypt, Canaan, and Chaldæa, had wandered farthest from the pure Noachic faith, and abandoned themselves to a degraded polytheism, based for the most part upon a study of the heavenly bodies. That the Cushite conquerors of Southern Babylonia were not only idolaters, but, like Nimrod, their leader, destroyers of the liberties of the subject populations, has at least the sanction of tradition. 3. *The awakening of religious life* in the breasts of the pilgrims. That Abram had by this time been called we are warranted on the authority of Stephen to hold, and though Terah is expressly said to have been an idolater in Ur, it is by no means improbable that he became a sharer in the pure faith of his distinguished son. At least it lends a special interest to this primitive migration to connect it with the call of Abram.

II. THE JOURNEY OF THE EMIGRANTS. Though upon the incidents and experiences of the way, as upon the circumstances and reasons of the departure, the inspired record is completely silent, yet the pilgrimage of the Chaldæan wanderers was—1. *From an idolatrous land*, which could not fail to secure, even had it not already received, the Divine approbation. Not that flight from heathen countries is always the clear path of duty, else how shall the world be converted? But where, as was probably the case with the Terachites, the likelihood of doing good to is less than that of receiving hurt from the inhabitants, it is plainly incumbent to withdraw from polluted and polluting lands. 2. *By an unknown way.* Almost certainly the road to Canaan was but little understood by the exiles, if even Canaan itself was not entirely a *terra incognita.* Yet in setting forth upon a path so uncertain they were only doing what mankind in general, and God's people in particular, have always to do in life's journey, viz., travel by a way that they know not; while for comfort they had the sweet assurance that their path was steadily conducting them from idols and oppression, and the certain knowledge that they were journeying beneath the watchful and loving superintendence of the invisible Supreme. Happy they whose path in life, though compassed by clouds and darkness, ever tends away from sin and slavery, and never lacks the guidance of Abram's God! 3. *To a better country.* In comparison with the rich alluvial soil of Southern Babylonia, the land of Canaan might be only a bleak succession of barren hills; but, in respect of liberty to worship God, anywhere, in the eyes of men whose hearts were throbbing with new-found faith, would seem superior to idolatrous Chaldæa. Without endorsing Luther's fancy, that Shem and his followers had already withdrawn to Palestine, and that Terah and his family were setting forth to place themselves beneath the patriarch's rule, we may reasonably suppose that, like the Pilgrim Fathers of a later age, they were seeking a new land where they might worship God in peace.

III. THE HALTING OF THE EMIGRANTS. In the absence of definite information as to the motives which induced it, this sudden stoppage of their journey at Haran is usually ascribed to either—1. *The irresolution of Terah*, who, having become wearied by the fatigues and perils of the way, and having found a comfortable location for himself and flocks, preferred to bring his wanderings to a close, as many a noble enterprise is wrecked through weak-kneed vacillation, and many a Christian pilgrimage broken short by faint-hearted indecision; or—2. *The unbelief of Terah*, who, in the first flush of excitement produced by Abram's call, had started on the outward journey with strong faith and great zeal, but, as enthusiasm subsided and faith declined, was easily persuaded to halt at Haran—an emblem of other pilgrims who begin their heavenward journey well, but pause in mid career through the cooling of their ardour and declining of their piety; or—3. *The infirmity of Terah*, who was now an old man, and unable further to prosecute his journey to the promised land, thus making the delay at Haran a beautiful act of filial piety on the part of Abram, and on that of Terah an imperious necessity.

See in this migration of the Terachites—1. An emblem of the changefulness of life. 2. An illustration of God's method of distributing mankind. 3. An example of the way in which an overruling Providence disseminates the truth. 4. A picture of many broken journeys on the face of earth.

HOMILIES BY VARIOUS AUTHORS.

Vers. 29, 30.—*Two weddings.* I. THE TWO BRIDEGROOMS—Abram and Nahor. 1. Younger sons in Terah's family. 2. Eminent men in Ur of the Chaldees. 3. Favoured saints in the Church of God. Marriage is honourable in all.

II. THE TWO BRIDES—Sarai and Milcah. 1. Near relations of their husbands. Though permissible at that early stage of the world's history, the intermarriage of relatives so close as half-sister and niece is not now sanctioned by the law of God. 2. Attractive ladies in themselves. As much as this may be inferred from their names. It is both allowable and desirable to seek as wives women distinguished for beauty and intelligence, provided also they are noted for goodness and piety. 3. Descendants of the holy line. Doubtless this was one cause which led to the choice of Abram and Nahor. So Christians should not be unequally yoked with unbelievers.

III. THE TWO HOMES. Formed it might be at the same time, and under similar benignant auspices, they were yet divided. 1. And from the first in their constitutions. This was of necessity. 2. And afterwards in their fortunes. Sarai had no child; Milcah was the mother of a family. "Lo, children are the heritage of the Lord." 3. And eventually in their locations. Nahor and Milcah remained in Ur, and ultimately moved to Haran; Abram and Sarai pitched their tent and established their home in Canaan. So God parts the families of earth.—W.

EXPOSITION.

CHAPTER XII.

Vers. 1—5.—Designed to trace the outward development of God's kingdom on the earth, the narrative now concentrates its attention on one of the foregoing Terachites, whose remarkable career it sketches with considerable minuteness of detail, from the period of his emigration from Chaldæa to his death at Hebron in the land of Canaan. Distinguished as a man of undoubted superiority both of character and mind, the head of at least two powerful and important races, and standing, as one might say, on the threshold of the historical era, it is yet chiefly as his life and fortunes connect with the Divine purpose of salvation that they find a place in the inspired record. The progress of infidelity during the four centuries that had elapsed since the Flood, the almost universal corruption of even the Shemite portion of the human family, had conclusively demonstrated the necessity of a second Divine interposition, if the knowledge of salvation were not to be completely banished from the earth. Accordingly, the son of Terah was selected to be the founder of a new nation, in which the light of gospel truth might be deposited for preservation until the fulness of the times, and through which the promise of the gospel might be conducted forward to its ultimate realisation in the manifestation of the woman's seed. Partly to prepare him for the high destiny of being the progenitor of the chosen nation, and partly to illustrate the character of that gospel with which he was to be intrusted, he was summoned to renounce his native country and kinsmen in Chaldæa, and venture forth upon an untried journey in obedience to the call of Heaven, to a land which he should afterward receive for an inheritance. In a series of successive theophanies or Divine manifestations, around which the various incidents of his life are grouped—in Ur of the Chaldees (Acts vii. 2), at Moreh in Canaan (Gen. xii. 7), near Bethel (*ibid.* xiii.), at Mamre (*ibid.* xv., xvii.), and on Moriah (*ibid.* xxii.)—he is distinctly promised three things—a land, a seed, and a blessing—as the reward of his compliance with the heavenly invitation; and the confident persuasion both of the reality of these gracious promises and of the Divine ability and willingness to fulfil them forms the animating spirit and guiding principle of his being in every situation of life, whether of trial or of difficulty, in which he is subsequently placed. The miraculous character of these theophanies indeed has been made a ground on which to assail the entire patriarchal history as unhistorical. By certain writers they have been represented as nothing more than natural occurrences embellished by the genius of the author of Genesis (Eichhorn, Bauer, Winer), as belonging to the domain of poetical fiction (De Wette), and therefore as undeserving of anything like serious consideration. But unless the supernatural is to be *in toto* eliminated from the record, a concession which cannot possibly be granted by an enlightened theism, the Divine appearances to Abraham cannot be regarded as in any degree militating against the historical veracity of the story of his life, which, it may be said, is amply vouched for by the harmony of its details with the characteristics of the period to which it belongs (cf. Havernick's 'Introduction,' § 18). Nor does the employment of the name Jehovah in connection with these theophanies warrant the conclusion that the passages containing them are interpolations of a post Mosaic or Jehovistic editor (Tuch, Bleek,

Colenso, Davidson). "Such a hypothesis," says Keil, "can only be maintained by those who misunderstand the distinctive meaning of the two names, Elohim and Jehovah (*q. v.* on ch. ii. 4), and arbitrarily set aside the Jehovah in ch. xvii. 1, on account of an erroneous determination of the relation in which El Shaddai stands to Jehovah." Indications of the literary unity of the patriarchal history will be noted, and replies to objections given, in the progress of the Exposition.

Ver. 1.—**Now the Lord.** Jehovah = the God of salvation, an indication that the narrative is now to specially concern itself with the chosen seed, and the Deity to discover himself as the God of redemption. The hypothesis that vers. 1—4 were inserted in the fundamental document by the Jehovist editor is not required for a satisfactory explanation of the change of the Divine name at this particular stage of the narrative. **Had said.** Literally, *said.* In Ur of the Chaldees, according to Stephen (Acts vii. 2), reverting, after the usual manner of the writer, to the original point of departure in the Abrahamic history (Aben Ezra, Mede, Piscator, Pererius, Calvin, Willet, Rosenmüller, Dathius, Alford, Murphy, 'Speaker's Commentary'); or in Haran, after Terah's death, as the first call given to the patriarch (LXX., Chaldee, Syriac, Raschi, Lyra, Keil, Kalisch, Dykes), or as a repetition of the call addressed to him in Ur (Clarke, Wordsworth, Inglis). Luther conjectures that the call in Ur was given "*fortasse per patriarcham Shem;*" but if the authority of Stephen be recognised, this was the occasion of the first theophany vouchsafed to Abram. **Get thee out.** Literally, *go for thyself,* a frequent Hebraism, expressive of the way in which the action of the verb returns upon itself, is terminated and completed (cf. ch. xxi. 16; xxii. 2; Isa. xxxi. 8; Cant. ii. 11; *vide* Ewald's 'Hebrew Syntax,' § 314); hence, though not necessarily emphatic, it may be equivalent to "Go *thou,*" whoever else remains behind (Jarchi, Ainsworth, Bush). **Of thy country.** A proof that the date of the call was while Abram was in Ur (Calvin), though if Ur was at Edessa (*vide supra*) the patriarch could scarcely have been said to be from home. **And from thy kindred.** At Ur in all probability Nahor and Milcah were left behind; at Haran, Nahor and his family, if they had already arrived thither, and according to some (Kalisch, Dykes) Terah also. **And from thy father's house.** *I. e.* if they will not accompany thee. No Divine interdict forbade the other members of the family of Terah joining in the Abrahamic emigration,

Unto a (literally, *the*) **land that I will show thee.** Through a revelation (Lange), or simply by the guidance of providence. The land itself is left unnamed for the trial of the patriarch's faith, which, if it sustained the proof, was to be rewarded by the exceeding great and precious promises which follow: —according to one arrangement, seven in number, one for each clause of the next two verses (Cajetan, Willet) ; according to another, four, corresponding to the clauses of the second verse, the last of which is expanded in the third (Keil) ; according to a third, six, forming three pairs of parallels (Alford) ; according to a fourth, and perhaps the best, two, a lower or personal blessing, comprising the first three particulars, and a higher or public blessing, embracing the last three (Murphy).

Vers. 2, 3.—**And I will make of thee a great nation.** A compensation for leaving his small kindred. The nation should be great (1) numerically (Keil, Rosenmüller), (2) influentially (Kalisch, Inglis), (3) spiritually (Luther, Wordsworth). **And I will bless thee.** Temporally (Pererius, Murphy), with every kind of good (Rosenmüller), in particular with offspring (Vatablus) ; but also spiritually (Rupertus, Bush), in the sense, *e. g.*, of being justified by faith, as in Gal. iii. 8 (Candlish). The blessing was a recompense for the deprivations entailed upon him by forsaking the place of his birth and kindred (Murphy). **And make thy name great.** Render thee illustrious and renowned (Rosenmüller) ; not so much in the annals of the world as in the history of the Church (Bush); in return for leaving thy father's house (Murphy). So God made David a great name (2 Sam. vii. 9 ; cf. Prov. xxii. 1 ; Eccles. vii. 3). **And thou shalt be a blessing.** *I. e.* "blessed," as in Zech. viii. 12 (Chaldee, Syriac, LXX., Dathe, Rosenmüller, Gesenius) ; or "a type or example of blessing," so that men shall introduce thy name into their formularies of blessing (Kimchi, Clericus, Knobel, Calvin) ; but, best, "a source of blessing' (spiritual) to others" (Tuch, Delitzsch, Keil, Kalisch, Murphy). The sense in which Abram was to be a source of blessing to others is explained in the next verse. First, men were to be either blessed or cursed of God according as their attitude to Abram was propitious or hostile. **And I will bless them** —grace expecting there will be many to bless (Delitzsch)—**that bless thee, and curse** (with a judicial curse, the word being the same as in ch. iii. 14 ; iv. 11) **him**—only an individual here and there, in the judgment of the Deity, being likely to inherit this malediction (Delitzsch)—**that curseth** (literally, *treateth lightly*, or *despiseth*. The verb is applied in ch. viii. 11 to the diminution of

the waters of the flood) **thee.** The Divine Being thus identifies himself with Abram, and solemnly engages to regard Abram's friends and enemies as his, as Christ does with his Church (cf. Acts i. 4). **And in thee shall all the families of the earth be blessed.** Not bless themselves by thee or in thy name (Jarchi, Clericus) ; but in thee, as the progenitor of the promised seed, shall all the families of the ground (which was cursed on account of sin, ch. iii. 17) be spiritually blessed—cf. Gal. iii. 8 (Calvin, Luther, Rosenmüller, Keil, Wordsworth, Murphy, 'Speaker's Commentary'). Thus the second sense in which Abram was constituted a blessing lay in this, that the whole fulness of the Divine promise of salvation for the world was narrowed up to his line, by which it was in future to be carried forward, and at the appointed season, when the woman's seed was born, distributed among mankind.

Ver. 4.—**So** (literally, *and*) **Abram departed**—from Ur of the Chaldees, or from Haran (*vide supra*) — **as the Lord had spoken unto him; and Lot went with him.** Lot's name being repeated here because of his connection with the ensuing narrative. **And Abram was seventy and five years old**—literally, *a son of five years and seventy years* (cf. ch. vii. 6)—**when he departed**—literally, *in his going forth* upon the second stage of his journey—**from Haran.**

Ver. 5.—**And Abram took** (an important addition to the foregoing statement, intimating that Abram did not go forth as a lonely wanderer, but accompanied by) **Sarai his wife, and Lot his brother's son, and all the substance** — *recush*, acquired wealth, from *racash*, to gain (cf. ch. xiv. 11, 16, 21 ; xv. 14), which consisted chiefly in cattle, Lot and Abram being nomads—**that they had gathered** (not necessarily implying a protracted stay, as some allege), **and the souls** —here slaves and their children (cf. Ezek. xxvii. 13)—**that they had gotten** "not only as secular property for themselves, but as brethren to themselves, and as children of the one heavenly Father" (Wordsworth) ; that they had converted to the law (Onkelos) ; that they had proselyted (Raschi, Targum Jonathan, and Jerusalem Targum)—**in Haran; and they went forth to go into the land of Canaan;** —a prolepsis (cf. ch. xi. 31, *q. v.*)—**and into the land of Canaan they came**—a distance of 300 miles from Haran, from which their course must have been across the Euphrates in one of its higher affluents, over the Syrian desert, southwards to Lebanon and Damascus (cf. ch. xv. 2), where, according to Josephus, the patriarch reigned for some considerable time, "being come with an army from the land of the Chaldæans" ('Ant.,' i. 7), and a village survived to his day called "Abraham's habitation." According to the partitionists (Tuch, Bleek, Colenso, Davidson) this verse belongs to the Elohist or fundamental document ; but if so, then the Jehovist represents Abram (ver. 6) as journeying through the land without having previously mentioned what land (cf. Quarry, p. 420).

HOMILETICS.

Ver. 4.—*The Chaldæan emigrant.* I. THE CALL OF GOD. Whether spoken in a dream or distinctly articulated by a human form, the voice which summoned Abram to emigrate from Ur was recognised by the patriarch to be Divine ; and so is the gospel invitation, which through the medium of a written word has been conveyed to men, essentially a message from the lips of God. The call which Abram received was—1. *Distinguishing and selecting*—coming to him alone of all the members of Terah's family, of all the descendants of the line of Shem, of all the citizens of Ur, of all the inhabitants of earth ; and the gospel invitation which men now receive, in its widest no less than in its narrowest acceptation, is differentiating and elective, passing by one nation and falling on another, addressing itself to one individual and allowing another to remain uncheered by its joyful sound (Rom. ix. 16). 2. *Separating and dividing*—summoning the patriarch to disentangle himself from the idolatries of his native land, and even sever his connection with the nearest and the dearest, rather than imperil his salvation by remaining in Chaldæa ; and in a like spirit does the voice of Jesus in the gospel direct men to forsake the world (spiritually regarded the land of their nativity), to relinquish its infidelities, iniquities, frivolities ; to renounce its possessions, occupations, amusements ; yea, to dissolve its friendships and endearing relationships, if they would now be numbered among his disciples, and eventually enter into life (Luke xiv. 26). 3. *Commanding and directing*—enjoining on the patriarch a long and arduous pilgrimage, that must necessarily be attended with many difficulties and dangers, and perhaps with not a few sorrows and privations that would require the most heroic fortitude and the most enduring patience, and that could only be accomplished by minutely following the Divine instructions, and taking each successive step in faith ; and of a like character is the journey to which the follower of Christ is invited in the gospel—a journey as painful and laborious in its nature, as much demanding self-sacrifice and heroic resolution, as repugnant to the carnal heart, and as unprofitable to the eye of sense, as uncertain in its various steps, and as much dependent on the principle of faith (2 Cor. v. 7). 4. *Cheering and encouraging*—assigning to the patriarch a number of exceeding great and precious promises which should abundantly compensate for the sacrifices and deprivations that should be entailed upon him by compliance with the heavenly invitation—a great inheritance, a great posterity, a great salvation, a great renown, a great influence ; and in the gospel, too, are held forth to stimulate and comfort heaven's pilgrims, a variety of rich rewards that shall more than recompense them for all that they may do or suffer in yielding to the call of Christ.

II. THE FAITH OF ABRAM. As the heavenly invitation which the patriarch received was designed to be symbolic of the gospel call which is addressed to us, so the faith of the patriarch, which responded to the voice of God, was intended for a pattern of that hearty trust with which by us the gospel message should be embraced. The faith of Abram was — 1. *Submissive and obedient.* Summoning his household, gathering his flocks, and taking with him his aged father Terah, he departed. Without this indeed he could not have been possessed of faith. Whenever the Divine testimony contains a precept and a promise, the faith that is sincere must yield obedience to the precept as well as cling to the promise. In the gospel message both are present : a promise of salvation, a full, free, and generous offer of eternal life ; and along with this a precept of separation from the world, of consecration to a life of faith, holiness, and love ; and the second must be obeyed, while the first is embraced to render faith complete. 2. *Prompt and unhesitating.* Without question or complaint, without the slightest shadow of reluctance, so far at least as the narrative reveals, the Chaldæan flock-master puts Jehovah's order into execution ; and in this respect again he is worthy of imitation. The same promptitude which he displayed should be exhibited by us in responding to the gospel call, and all the more that in our case there is less room than there was in his to doubt that the voice which calls is Divine. 3. *Intelligent and reasonable.* Even if Abram had departed from Chaldæa purely *suâ sponte*, in order to escape contamination from its idolatries, instead of being open to a charge of folly because he had gone forth, " not knowing whither he went," he would have been entitled to be regarded as having performed an act of highest prudence. Much more then was his conduct wise and commendable when he was acting in obedience to Heaven's express command—going forth beneath the guidance and protection of Almighty strength and Omniscient love. And just as little can Christian faith be challenged as fanatical and rash, possessing as it does the same sanction and supervision as that of the father of the faithful. 4. *Patient and persevering.* Delayed at Haran, the traveller was not diverted from his path. Undaunted by prospective perils, he had left Chaldæa to go to a land which God was to show him ; unconquered by actual hardships and trials, he halted not till he set his foot within the promised land. And so we learn that faith to begin the Christian life is not enough ; not he who commences the heavenward pilgrimage, but he who endureth to the end, shall be saved.

HOMILIES BY VARIOUS AUTHORS.

Vers. 1—5.—*The preparations of grace.* We may call this the genesis of the kingdom of God.

I. It is FOUNDED in the word of the Divine covenant, the faith given by Divine grace to individuals, the separation unto newness of life.

II. The one man Abram gathers round him a small SOCIETY, kindred with him by the flesh, but bound to him doubtless by spiritual bonds as well. Thus God has sanctified the family life by making it as the nidus of the spiritual genesis. When the new kingdom began its course in the Messiah, he drew to himself those who were previously associated by neighbourhood, relationship, and familiar intercourse in Galilee. The Divine does not work apart from the human, but with it and by it.

III. The PROMISE was that of Abram should be made a great nation, that he should be blessed and a blessing, and his blessing should be spread through all families of the earth. The structure which Divine grace rears on the foundation which itself lays is a structure of blessed family and national life.

IV. The land of CANAAN may not have been indicated with positive certainty to the migrating children of God, but it was enough that he promised them a land which he would hereafter show them. " A land that I will show thee." There was the certainty that it was a *better* land : Get thee out of thy country, because I have another for thee. The day-by-day journey under Divine direction was itself a help to faith to make the promise definite. The stay at Haran, from whence the pilgrimage might be said to make a true start, was itself a gathering of " souls " and " substance " which predicted a large blessing in the future. When once we have followed the word of God's grace and set our face towards Canaan we soon begin to get pledges of the future blessings, laid-up riches of soul and substance, which assure us of the full glory of the life to come.

V. Even in that first beginning of the kingdom, that small Church out of Ur of the Chaldees, there is the evidence of that individual VARIETY OF CHARACTER AND ATTAINMENT and history which marks the whole way of the people of God. Lot was a very different man from Abram. As the story of this little company of travellers develops itself we soon begin to see that the grace of God does not obliterate the specialities of human character. Out of the varieties of men's lives, which to us may seem incapable of reconciliation, there may yet be brought the onward progress of a Divine order and a redeeming purpose.—R.

Ver. 1.—*The voices of God at the opening of the world's eras.* I. AT THE OPENING OF CREATION. " And God said, Let there be light."

II. AT THE OPENING OF REDEMPTION. " And God said, I will put enmity between thee and the woman," &c.

III. AT THE OPENING OF THE OLD DISPENSATION. " And God said to Abram, Get thee out of thy country."

IV. At the opening of the Christian era. "And God said, This is my beloved Son."

V. At the opening of the eternal state God will say, "Come, ye blessed of my Father."—W.

Ver. 1.—*Abraham called.* "Now the Lord God had said unto Abraham, Get thee out of thy country," &c. The record of Abraham's life is second only in beautiful simplicity to that of Christ. There are certain correspondences between the two.

I. A summons was given to Abraham. It was from the Lord. We know not the form. It was explicit. He was to leave all. It was an *unmistakable* summons, and it was repeated. Such calls are generally opposed to carnal inclinations. Dangers beset the one who should respond to the call, for "the Canaanite was then in the land."

II. The summons was sustained by a promise of guidance to *the* land. The first call was to a land, the second to a definite place. God did not at first tell Abraham that he would give him the land, but only "show" it. God does not reveal all the riches of his grace at once. The promise was sufficient. Abraham went forth from the plain of Chaldea to the land which God would make through him and his descendants the most renowned in the world. Ever listening to a voice unheard by others Abraham was led. Sublime faith of the patriarch; he looked for "a city that had foundations."—H.

Ver. 2.—*Abraham useful.* "And thou shalt be a blessing." This is part of the sixfold promise given to Abraham. He was to be a blessing to all nations. It is a very great joy to a devout soul to become a blessing temporally or spiritually to others.

I. Every man of faith is a centre of blessing. Men who yield to their carnal natures cannot bless others. The Christian should not incidentally, but intentionally, bless others. Where a man is corrupt his working will be injurious; purity is a benediction to mankind.

II. A devout and faithful man is a blessing chiefly to those who can receive his influence. The light of the sun causes one substance to decay, another to fructify. The life of a servant of God may only provoke a sneer and opposition in some souls; but in others joy, thankfulness, love, and effort at imitation. To some an apostle was "a savour of death unto death."

III. The measure of our faith is the measure of the blessing we shall transmit to others. We sometimes hinder the operation of God's promise by our self-righteous humility, which ignores the fact that God often uses the "weak things of the world to confound the things that are mighty." There must be faith in God's continued working. He can make the future fruitful in proportion to our faith. Look at what he made of Paul, Luther, Wesley, and Whitfield because they were all men of strong faith.

IV. To be a blessing through the power and favour of God is the highest honour in the world. It was God who "made" Abraham a blessing; he gave him the power, fostered his faith, and perpetuated his influence. What honour could Abraham have comparable with this? It is probable that Abraham thought little of the honour which would come to him; but God adapted his promise to that which he knew to be the desire of the secret soul of Abraham. Seeing a longing in the heart to lift men to a higher level, he gratifies it by making Abraham a blessing. All should cherish such desires. The help we can give to others morally is far greater than that we can bestow materially. To live an aimless life is a disgrace and sin, but to live to bless others is Divine.—H.

Vers. 2, 3.—*Sevenfold promises.* I. Of the pre-incarnate Jehovah to Abram. 1. A great inheritance. 2. A great posterity. 3. A great name. 4. A great blessing. 5. A great alliance. 6. A great defence. 7. A great influence.

II. Of the incarnate Word to his disciples. 1. The kingdom of heaven. 2. Divine consolation. 3. Inheritance of the earth. 4. Divine satisfaction. 5. Divine mercy. 6. The vision of God. 7. A place in God's family (see Matt. v. 1—9).

III. OF THE GLORIFIED CHRIST TO HIS CHURCH. 1. The tree of life. 2. A crown of life. 3. Hidden manna, the white stone, and a new name. 4. Power over the nations, and the morning star. 5. White raiment. 6. The distinction of being made a pillar in God's temple. 7. A seat on Christ's throne (see Rev. ii., iii.).—W.

EXPOSITION.

Ver. 6. And Abram passed through— literally, passed over, or travelled about as a pilgrim (cf. Heb. xi. 9) in—the land unto (or as far as) the place of Sichem. A prolepsis for the place where the city Shechem (either built by or named after the Hivite prince, ch. xxxiv. 2) was afterwards situated, viz., between Ebal and Gerizim, in the middle of the land ; "the most beautiful, perhaps the only very beautiful, spot in Central Palestine" (Stanley's 'Sinai and Palestine,' v. 234). The modern name of Sichem is Nâblus, a corruption of Neapolis. Unto the plain. אֵלוֹן, from אוּל or אֵיל, to be strong, a strong, hardy tree: the terebinth, as opposed to the oak, אַלוֹן, from אָלַל (Celsius, Michaelis, Rosenmüller, Keil) ; the oak, as distinguished from אֵלָה, the turpentine tree, or terebinth (Gesenius, Kalisch, Murphy). But it seems demonstrable that these and the other cognate terms, אֵיל, אֵלָה, are frequently used as synonymous for any large, strong tree (cf. ch. xxxv. 5 ; Judges ix. 9 ; xxiv. 26 ; Josh. xix. 33 with Judges iv. 11), though commonly אֵלוֹן, oak, is opposed to אֵלָה, terebinth, as in Isa. vi. 13 ; Hosea iv. 13. The translation of אֵלוֹן by plain (Targums, A. V.) is inaccurate, though "the truth is it was both a plain and set with oaks" (Willet). Of Moreh. Like Mamre (ch. xiii. 18), the name of the owner of the oak-grove (Murphy, Kalisch, Alford); probably a priestly character (Moreh signifying a teacher, Judges vii. 1 ; 2 Kings xvii. 28 ; Isa. ix. 15) who instituted the Divine cultus in the locality (Luther); though it has also been regarded as the name of the place (Calvin), which may be here given to it by anticipation (Wordsworth), being derived from *raah*, to see, and equivalent to the place of vision (Samaritan), because God there appeared to the patriarch (Fagius), and showed him the land of Canaan (Masius, Lyra). Knobel renders "the oak of the teacher," comparing it with "the oak of the witches" (Judges ix. 37). The LXX. translate by ὑψηλήν, lofty, and the Vulgate by *illustrem*. And the Canaanite was then in the land. A sign of post-Mosaic authorship (Tuch, Bleek, Colenso) ; an interpolation (Aben Ezra ; rather (1) a proclamation of the miserable exile in which the patriarch lived (Luther) ; or (2) a reminder to Abram of his heavenly country, seeing he was a stranger

in his earthly one (Calvin); or, better, (3) an intimation of the fact that *already* the Canaanites were in possession of the land which bore their name (Kalisch), or perhaps simply (4) a declaration that the land was not a stretch of unoccupied territory, but a populated region (Hengstenberg), thus making the fulfilment of the ensuing promise all the more difficult, and all the greater a trial to the faith of the patriarch (Keil, Murphy, Wordsworth, Alford) ; or (5), but not so good, an explanation of the previous selection of the oak of Moreh as his habitation (Lange, Hävernick, *vide* Introduction, § 18).

Ver. 7.—And the Lord appeared. The first mention of a theophany, though Acts vii. 2 alleges that such a Divine manifestation had previously occurred in Ur of the Chaldees. Though not a direct vision of Jehovah (John i. 18), that there was some kind of outward appearance may be inferred from the subsequent Divine manifestations to the patriarch (ch. xviii. 2, 17, 33 ; xxii. 11—18), to Hagar (ch. xvi. 7—14 ; xxi. 17, 18), and to Jacob (ch. xxxi. 11—13 ; xxxii. 24—30). On the relation of the angel of Jehovah to Jehovah *vide* ch. xvi. 17. Unto Abram. "Jam pæne fatigato Abraha isto duro exsilio et perpetuis migrationibus" (Luther). And said, Unto thy seed—to himself God gave "none inheritance in it, no, not so much as to set his foot on" (Acts vii. 5) ; the land was promised to his seed "when as yet he had no child"—will I give this land Now occupied by the Canaanites. Undoubtedly a great promise, that the Canaanites should be dispossessed, and their country given to the offspring of a childless old man already over seventy-five years. The apparent improbability of its ever being accomplished rendered it a strong trial to the patriarch's faith. And there builded he an altar. "Constituit certum locum, in quo conveniat ecclesia, auditura verbum Dei, factura preces, laudatura Deum, sacrificatura Deo' (Luther). "Altare forma est Divini cultus ; invocatio autem substantia et veritas" (Calvin). "The rearing of an altar in the land was, in fact, a form of taking possession of it on the ground of a right secured to the exercise of his faith" (Bush). "It is often said of Abraham and the patriarchs that they built altars to the Lord ; it is never said they built houses for themselves" (Wordsworth). Unto the Lord who had appeared to him.

Ver. 8. — **And he removed** — literally, *caused* (i. e. his tent) *to be broken up* (cf. ch. xxvi. 22—**from thence**—no cause for which being assigned, the hostility of his neighbours (Luther, Calvin) and the commencement of the famine (Alford, Keil) have been conjectured as the probable reasons—**unto a** (literally, *the*) **mountain east of Bethel.** Here proleptically named "house of God," being called in the time of Abram Luz (ch. xxviii. 19). Its present name is Beitin. **And pitched his tent** (cf. ch. ix. 21), having **Bethel on the west**—literally, *sea-ward*, the Mediterranean being the western boundary of Palestine (cf. ch. xxviii. 14 ; Exod. x. 19 ; xxvi. 22 ; Ezek. xlviii. 1, 2)—**and Hai**—Ai (עַי ; עָי, Neh. xi. 31 ; עָיָה, Isa. x. 28) ; with the article, because signifying "the heap of ruins," near which it was no doubt built ;

the scene of the first Israelitish defeat under Joshua (ch. vii. 2) : its ruins still exist under the name of *Medinet Gai*—**on the east** (about five miles from Bethel) : **and there he builded an altar unto the Lord** (*vide supra*), **and called upon the name of the Lord** (*vide* ch. iv. 26).

Ver. 9.—**And Abram journeyed** (literally, *broke up*, e. g., his encampment), **going on still**—literally, *going on and breaking up* (cf. ch. viii. 3) ; "going and returning"—**towards the south.** *Negeb*, the dry region, from *naqabh*, to be dried, the southern district of Palestine (ch. xiii. 3 ; xx. 1 ; xxiv. 62). The LXX. render, ἐστρατοπέδευσεν ἐν τῇ ἐρήμῳ.

Of this section vers. 5, 6, 8*a* are commonly assigned to the Elohist ; and 7, 8*b*, and 9 to the Jehovist.

HOMILETICS.

Vers. 6—10.—*The promised land.* I. WANDERINGS. Entering Canaan from the north, the Chaldæan emigrant directs his progress steadily towards the south, removing from station to station till he reaches the furthest limit of the land. This wandering life to the patriarch must have been (1) *unexpected*. Leaving Ur at the Divine command, and journeying many hundreds of miles, he must have eagerly anticipated rest in Canaan ; but instead he finds that he must journey still. So is life to God's people always full of disappointments. Yet was it also (2) *inevitable.* The land was in possession of the Canaanites, and, even though it had been free and untenanted, it was famine-stricken, both of which circumstances necessitated frequent removal. And for causes not dissimilar must the saints ever wander, the world for the most part belonging to their enemies, and the produce of earth being insufficient to meet their souls' needs. Then to the patriarch himself it was meant to be (3) *prophetic*. The promised land being designed not so much for a possession in itself as for an emblem of the better country towards which his spirit with its new-found faith was travelling, it was not intended that life in Canaan for the father of the faithful should be one of absolute repose, but rather one of wandering and unrest ; and of that he had a foretaste, or earnest, immediately he stepped across the borders of the land. And still further was it purposed to be (4) *emblematic.* In the fortunes of Abram it was contemplated that God's believing people in every age should behold, in main characteristic at least, an outline or shadow of their own. As to him the land of Canaan was not the better country, but only its anticipation, so to them is it not so much a type of heaven as of the visible Church, and the patriarchal wanderings an emblem not of the beatific life of the redeemed in glory, but of the experiences of the saints on earth.

II. TRIALS. Along with ceaseless peregrinations, more or less exacting in their nature, trials of another and severer sort entered into the texture of the patriarch's experience in the promised land. The peculiar circumstances in which he found himself were such as to make a vehement assault upon his faith. 1. *His childless condition* seemed to render all but impossible belief in the mighty nation of which Jehovah talked. And so are saints sometimes tempted to indulge a suspicion of the Divine goodness and veracity, because of the absence of certain creature comforts which they see God bestowing upon others. 2. *The occupation of the land* appeared to negative the idea of its ever becoming his ; and not unfrequently because a saint cannot discern how a promise is to be fulfilled, he begins to challenge the Divine resources, and ends by impeaching the Divine faithfulness. 3. *The prevalence of famine* was calculated to excite doubts in his mind as to whether after all the land was worth either having or desiring ; and in this life the saints are not unacquainted with temptations, arising from the pressure of outward circumstances, such as extreme poverty or long-continued affliction, to admit the apprehension that after all the blessings of religion and the glories of the future life may not be worth the sacrifices made to secure them.

III. CONSOLATIONS. If a field of wanderings and a scene of trials, the promised land was likewise a place of consolation. Abram enjoyed—1. The comfort of *the Divine presence.* Though unseen, the companionship of Jehovah was understood by the patriarch to be a grand reality on which he might depend; and so says Christ to his believing people, "Lo, I am with you always, even unto the end of the world." 2. The joy of *Divine manifestations.* As Jehovah appeared to Abram, probably in the form of a man, so already has God appeared to his Church in the person of the man Christ Jesus; and so does Christ promise still to appear spiritually to his people, and to disclose to them the treasures of his grace and love (John xiv. 21). 3. The consolation of *Divine worship.* Wherever Abram wandered he built an altar and called upon the name of the Lord who had appeared unto him; and without any altar may the saint at any moment enter into closest communion with the Lord Jesus Christ, who in the fulness of the times was manifested to take away our sins, and who is ever ready, through the medium of his Holy Spirit, to interpose for his people's aid.

Learn—1. That a saint's wanderings are of God's appointing. 2. That a saint's trials are of God's permitting. 3. That a saint's consolations are of God's sending.

HOMILIES BY VARIOUS AUTHORS.

Vers. 6—9.—*Revelations.* We here enter upon the more special history of Divine appearances. Hitherto the word is described simply as a word—"The Lord said;" now we connect with the word distinct appearances. The plain of Moreh will be ever memorable as the first scene of such revelations. The altar which Abram erected was to the Lord who appeared unto him, *i. e.* in commemoration of the vision. Thus the long line of theophanies commences. The great lesson of this record is the worship of man proceeding from the gracious revelation of God. True religion is not a spontaneous product of man's nature, but rather a response to God's grace. He appears; the believer to whom the vision is vouchsafed raises an altar not "to the unknown God," but to the God who has appeared to him. Another point in the record is the connection of the promise with the revelation. The Lord appeared, and when he appeared he gave his word of promise : "Unto thy seed will I give this land." Are we not reminded thus early in the history of religion that for its maintenance there is required not only a revelation to the mind and heart by the Spirit, but also a seat of its institutions and community? Religion without a people of God dwelling in the land of privilege, and bound together by the sacred bonds of a Divine fellowship, is no true religion at all. Abram builds altars at the various stages of his pilgrimage, still going south. Although we are not told of a distinct vouchsafement of God in connection with every altar, we may well suppose, especially as the "mountain" is specified, that the altars marked out not mere resting-places, but the scenes of special communion with Jehovah.—R.

Ver. 6.—*The first wanderer and the second, or Cain and Abram compared and contrasted.* I. COMPARED. Each wandered—1. From the place of his nativity—Cain from Eden, Abram from Ur. 2. Accompanied by his wife, who in each instance was his sister. 3. In obedience to the word of Jehovah. He who called Abram had previously banished Cain. 4. Beneath the protection of Heaven—Cain defended by his scarred brow, Abram shielded by the arm of God. 5. To the close of life; neither finding a permanent habitation on the earth.

II. CONTRASTED. While both wandered—1. The one, Cain, travelled from God; the other, Abram, journeyed with God.. 2. The one roamed across the face of earth; the other walked within the borders of the promised land. 3. The one fled beneath the curse of Heaven; the other was o'ercanopied by Heaven's favour. 4. The one was an emblem of the sinner seeking rest and finding none; the other was a picture of the saint, who must travel through the world to his home.

Lessons :—1. There are wanderings and wanderings among men upon the earth. 2. He who would not become a fugitive like Cain must, like Abram, become a pilgrim. 3. They who choose the lot of Abram need never fear the doom of Cain.—W.

Vers. 6—20.—*The strength and weakness of Abram.* I. A THREEFOLD SOURCE OF STRENGTH. 1. His enjoyment of gracious visits from God. 2. His exercise of faith in God. 3. His cultivation of communion with God. II. A THREEFOLD SOURCE OF WEAKNESS. 1. An unwarrantable fear of man. 2. A heedless reliance on worldly policy and craft. 3. A sinful preference of self-interest to the happiness and welfare of others.—W.

Ver. 7.—*Abraham worshipping.* "And there he builded an altar unto the Lord, who appeared unto him." Abraham is at length Divinely informed that he is *in* the land hereafter to be his. He was at the spot where the great temple, to be set up by his descendants, would stand. Here he builds an altar. It was doubtless a very plain altar of rough stones, but large enough for the sacrifices to be offered. It would have little attraction in the eyes of many, but it would be approved of by God.

I. IT WAS REARED ENTIRELY IN THE HONOUR OF GOD. There was no self-glorifying in it. It was erected as a spontaneous act of gratitude. The men of Babel by the tower-building sought to get themselves a name; Abraham by his altar-building seeks to honour God's name. His act was a protest against the prevalent and surrounding idolatry. This was the first altar reared in Canaan to the great I AM.

II. IT WAS AN EXPRESSION OF ABRAHAM'S DESIRE TO ACKNOWLEDGE THE DIVINE GUIDANCE IN HIS PAST LIFE. He found it a joy to be under the leadership of God. "Wherever Abraham had his tent God had his altar." In how many families is the altar in need of repair! In many it has not even been set up.

III. IT EXPRESSED ABRAHAM'S DEPENDENCE ON THE MERCY REVEALED THROUGH A PROPITIATORY SACRIFICE. He evidently believed in an atonement. He offered an heifer, goat, ram, turtle-dove, and pigeon. After the rude manner of that day he offered sacrifices for his own sins and for those of his household. He found that God was brought nearer through the sacrifice, even as we discover that fact through the Christ of Calvary.

IV. IT EXPRESSED ALSO ABRAHAM'S READINESS TO CONSECRATE HIMSELF ENTIRELY TO GOD. An altar that failed to express this would have been a mockery. God is not flattered by an outward show of reverence. He must have inner and absolute consecration if we are to know the heights of spiritual power.

V. IT EXPRESSED THE PATRIARCH'S FAITH IN THE FULFILMENT OF THE DIVINE PROMISES. Abraham was already in the land of promise, and could leave the future to his God. He was, by rearing that altar, taking possession of the land for himself, and of the world for God, even as Columbus, with befitting pomp, planted in the newly-discovered continent a cross, and named the land San Salvador, thus consecrating it to the holy Saviour.—H.

Ver. 8.—*Abraham's altar.* "And there he builded an altar unto the Lord, and called upon the name of the Lord." There is a solemn word (Matt. x. 32, 33). The distinction is not between Christians and heathen; it is within the visible Church. To confess Christ is more than professing Christianity. It must be in the life, not merely in religious services. No doubt these have their use; without them spiritual life would wither and die, like a light under a vessel. They are as food; but "the life is more than meat." The world acquiesces in such services as respectable and proper. But it is a poor Christianity that raises no opposition. A Christian life may constrain respect, but it must differ from worldly (1) as to its object—*first* the kingdom of God; (2) as to its means—God's promises and help trusted to as real. Mark Abraham's example: dwelt among Canaanites on sufferance; they idolaters. Prudence would suggest keeping his religion secret. Many try to keep their faith secret; afraid to confess it, but unwilling to give it up. In vain; faith ashamed of brings no comfort or strength. Abram did not hide his faith. Wherever he sojourned he built an altar; confessed whom he trusted. We are told

—1. He built an altar, *i. e.* made open confession of his faith. 2. "Called on the name," &c., *i. e.* spoke to God as a living person, a real helper.

I. WHAT IS IT TO CONFESS GOD? 1. In the heart; firmly to believe what he has revealed. His promises were given to be trusted. The fool puts away belief (Ps. xiv. 1). It may be from dislike of truth (cf. Rom. i. 28); it may be despondingly (cf. Gen. xlii. 36), afraid to take God at his word. The voice of true wisdom, Ps. lxii. 1, 2. 2. In the life; acting upon "ye are not your own." We cannot go far without being tried: in business, in companionship, in bearing what we do not like, in resisting self-will and self-seeking, in standing firm against the world's scorn or well-meant persuasions. Passing events constantly put the question whom we serve (cf. Dan. iii. 15; Acts v. 28, 29). And not merely in matters that seem great. Little things show whom we have first in our hearts.

II. CLOSELY CONNECTED WITH THIS IS CALLING ON THE NAME OF THE LORD. We must look below the surface. Among professing Christians some prayer is a matter of course; but is it used as a real means to obtain? It is one thing to believe the doctrine of God's providence, and of the use of prayer, and another to pray as a practical power and to feel our Father's care. Yet St. Paul connects prayer and peace (Phil. iv. 6, 7). When Hannah had prayed she was no more sad (1 Sam. i. 18). The Bible has many encouragements to pray, but not one warning against asking too much.

III. EFFECT OF THIS ON THE CHARACTER. Abraham's character as eminently faithful was built up by exercising faith. He walked with God not by any constraining power, nor by reason of special manifestations; then he would be no example for us. Each acknowledgment of God increased his communion. Each altar marked a step in his own life, and a work in the world. He who is faithful in little gains more power (cf. Matt. xiii. 12).—M.

EXPOSITION.

Ver. 10.—**And there was a famine.** רָעָב, from a root signifying to hunger, the primary idea appearing to lie in that of an ample, *i. e.* empty, stomach (Gesenius, Fürst). The term is used of individuals, men or animals (Ps. xxxiv. 11; l. 12); or of regions (Ps. xli. 55). **In the land.** Of Canaan, which, though naturally fertile, was, on account of its imperfect cultivation, subject to visitations of dearth (cf. ch. xxvi. 1; xli. 56), especially in dry seasons, when the November and December rains, on which Palestine depended, either failed or were scanty. The occurrence of this famine just at the time of Abram's entering the land was an additional trial to his faith. **And Abram went down to Egypt.** Mizraim (*vide* ch. x. 6) was lower than Palestine, and celebrated then, as later, as a rich and fruitful country, though sometimes even Egypt suffered from a scarcity of corn, owing to a failure in the annual inundation of the Nile. Eichhorn notes it as an authentication of this portion of the Abrahamic history that the patriarch proposed to take himself and his household to Egypt, since at that time no corn trade existed between the two countries such as prevailed in the days of Jacob (*vide* Hävernick's Introduction, § 18). The writer to the Hebrews remarks it as an instance of the patriarch's faith that he did not return to either Haran or Ur (Heb. xi.

15, 16). **To sojourn there.** To tarry as a stranger, but not to dwell. Whether this journey was undertaken with the Divine sanction and ought to be regarded as an act of faith, or in obedience to his own fears and should be reckoned as a sign of unbelief, does not appear. Whichever way the patriarch elected to act in his perplexity, to leave Canaan or reside in it, there was clearly a strain intended to be put upon his faith. **For the famine was grievous** (literally, *heavy*) **in the land.**

Vers. 11—13.—**And it came to pass** (literally, *it was*), **when he was come near to enter into Egypt** (that he had his misgivings, arising probably from his own eminence, which could scarcely fail to attract attention among strangers, but chiefly from the beauty of his wife, which was calculated to inflame the cupidity and, it might be, the violence of the warm-blooded Southrons, and) **that he said unto Sarai his wife.** The arrangement here referred to appears (ch. xx. 13) to have been preconcerted on first setting out from Ur or Haran, so that Abram's address to his wife on approaching Egypt may be viewed as simply a reminder of their previous compact. **Behold now, I know that thou art a fair woman to look upon.** Literally, *fair of aspect* (cf. 1 Sam. xvii. 42). Though now upwards of sixty-five years of age, she was still in middle life (ch. xxiii. 1), and her

constitution had not been impaired by bearing children. Besides, the clear complexion
of Sarah would render her specially attractive
in the eyes of the Egyptians, whose women,
though not so dark as the Nubians and Ethiopians, were yet of a browner tinge than the
Syrians and Arabians. Monumental evidence
confirms the assertion of Scripture that a fair
complexion was deemed a high recommenda-
tion in the age of the Pharaohs (*vide* Hengstenberg's 'Egypt and the Books of Moses,'
p. 200). **Therefore** (literally, *and*) **it shall
come to pass, when** (literally, *that*) **the
Egyptians**—notorious for their licentiousness
(*vide* P. Smith's 'History of the World,' vol.
i. ch. vi. p. 71)—**shall see thee, that** (literally, *and*) **they shall say, This is his wife:
and they will kill me**—in order to possess
thee, counting murder a less crime than
adultery (Lyra). An unreasonable anxiety,
considering that he had hitherto enjoyed the
Divine protection, however natural it might
seem in view of the voluptuous character of
the people. **But** (literally, *and*) **they will
save thee alive**—for either compulsory marriage or dishonourable use. **Say, I pray thee,**
—translated in ver. 11 as "now;" " verbum
obsecrantis vel adhortantis " (Masius)—**thou
art my sister.** A half truth (ch. xx. 12),
but a whole falsehood. The usual apologies,
that he did not fabricate, but " cautiously
conceal the truth " (Lyra), that perhaps he
acted in obedience to a Divine impulse
(Mede), that he dissembled in order to protect his wife's chastity (Rosenmüller), are not
satisfactory. On the other hand, Abram must
not be judged by the light of New Testament
revelation. It is not necessary for a Christian
in every situation of life to tell all the truth,
especially when its part suppression involves
no deception, and is indispensable for self-
preservation ; and Abram may have deemed
it legitimate as a means of securing both his
own life and Sarah's honour, though how
he was to shield his wife in the peculiar circumstances it is difficult to see. Rosenmüller
suggests that he knew the preliminary ceremonies to marriage required a considerable
time, and counted upon being able to leave
Egypt before any injury was done to Sarah.
The only objection to this is that the historian represents him as being less solicitous
about the preservation of his wife's chastity
than about the conservation of his own life.
That it may be well (not with thee, though
doubtless this is implied, but) **with me for thy
sake** (the import of which is declared in the
words which follow) ; **and my soul shall live
because of thee.** " No defence can be offered
for a man who, merely through dread of
danger to himself, tells a lie, risks his wife's
chastity, puts temptation in the way of his
neighbours, and betrays the charge to which the
Divine favour had summoned him " (Dykes).

Vers. 14, 15.—**And it came to pass, that,
when Abram was come into Egypt, the
Egyptians beheld the woman that she was
very fair. The princes also**—literally, *and
the princes* (שָׂרֵי, mas. of Sarah), chief men
or courtiers, who, in accordance with the
ancient custom of Egypt that no slave should
approach the priestly person of Pharaoh,
were sons of the principal priests (*vide* Hävernick, § 18)—**of Pharaoh.** The official title of
the kings of Egypt (cf. Cæsar, the designation
of the Roman emperors, and Czar, that of
the Emperor of Russia), who are never introduced in the Pentateuch, as in later books,
by their individual names (1 Kings iii. 1 ;
ix. 40) ; an indirect evidence that the author
of Genesis must at least have been acquainted
with the manners of the Egyptian Court.
The term Pharaoh, which continued in use
till after the Persian invasion—under the
Greek empire the Egyptian rulers were styled
Ptolemies—is declared by Josephus to signify
"king" ('Ant.,' viii. 6, 2), which agrees with
the Koptic Pouro (*Pi-ouro ;* from *ouro,* to
rule, whence *touro,* queen), which also means
king. Modern Egyptologers, however, incline to regard it as corresponding to the
Phra of the inscriptions (Rosellini, Lepsius,
Wilkinson), or to the hieroglyphic *Peraa,* or
Perao, "the great house" (M. de Rougé,
Brugsch, Ebers), an appellation which belonged to the Egyptian monarchs, and with
which may be compared "the Sublime
Porte," as applied to the Turkish sultans
(cf. Canon Cook in 'Speaker's Commentary,'
vol. i. p. 477). The particular monarch
who occupied the Egyptian throne at the
time of Abram's arrival has been conjectured
to be Necao (Josephus, 'Bell. Jud.;' v. ix. 4),
Ramessemenes (Syncellus, p. 101), Phare-
thones (Euseb., ' Praep. Ev.,' ix. 8), Apappus
(Wilkinson, ' Anc. Egypt.,' vol. i. p. 13, note
5, Dr. Birch's edition), Achthoes, the sixth
king of the eleventh dynasty (Osburn, 'Mon.
Hist. of Egypt,' vol. i. ch. vii. p. 375),
Salatis or Saïtas, the first king of the fifteenth
dynasty, whose reign commenced B.C. 2080
(Stuart Poole in 'Smith's Dict.,' art. Pharaoh),
a monarch belonging to the sixteenth dynasty
of shepherd kings (Kalisch), and a Pharaoh
who flourished between the middle of the
eleventh and thirteenth dynasties, most probably one of the earliest Pharaohs of the
twelfth (Canon Cook in 'Speaker's Commentary,' vol. i. p. 447). Amid such conflicting
testimony from erudite archæologists it is
apparent that nothing can be ascertained with
exactitude as to the date of Abram's sojourn
in Egypt ; though the last-named writer, who
exhibits the latest results of scholarship on the
question, mentions in support of his conclusion a variety of considerations that may be
profitably studied. **Saw her.** So that she
must have been unveiled, which agrees with

monumental evidence that in the reign of the Pharaohs the Egyptian ladies exposed their faces, though the custom was discontinued after the Persian conquest (*vide* Hengstenberg's 'Egypt and the Books of Moses,' p. 199). **And commended her before Pharaoh: and the woman was taken.** *Capta* (Targum of Jonathan), *rapta* (Arab.), *abducta* (Pagnini), *capta et deducta* (Rosenmüller) ; all implying more or less the idea of violence, which, however, besides being not warranted by the text, was scarcely likely in the circumstances, the king being perfectly honourable in his proposals, and Abram and Sarai by their deception having rendered it impossible to object without divulging their secret. **Into Pharaoh's house.** Or harem, with a view to marriage as a secondary wife. Cf. the Papyrus D'Orbiney, now in the British Museum, but belonging to the age of Rameses II., in which the Pharaoh of the time, acting on the advice of his counsellors, sends two armies to fetch a beautiful woman by force, and then to murder her husband. A translation by M. Renouf will be found in The Tale of the Two Brothers, in 'Records of the Past,' vol. ii. p. 138.

Ver. 16.—**And he entreated Abram well**— literally, *did good to Abram ; εὖ ἐχρήσαντο* (LXX., Hieronymus, Poole) supposes that the court of Pharaoh or the Egyptian people generally conferred favours on the patriarch, which is not at all so probable as that Pharaoh did—**for her sake.** Marriage negotiations in Oriental countries are usually accompanied by presents to the relatives of the bride as a sort of payment. "The marriage price is distinctly mentioned in Scripture (Exod. xxii. 15, 16 ; Ruth iv. 10 ; 1 Sam. xviii. 23, 25 ; Hosea iii. 2) ; was commonly demanded by the nations of antiquity, as by the Babylonians (Herod., i. 196), Assyrians (Ælian V. H., iv. 1 ; Strabo, xvi. 745), the ancient Greeks ('Odyss.,' viii. 318 ff.), and the Germans (Tacit., 'German.,' xviii.) ; and still obtains in the East to the present day" (*vide* Kitto's 'Cyclopedia,' art. Marriage, by Dr. Ginsburg). **And he had**—literally, *there was* (given) *to him*—**sheep, and oxen.** Flocks of small cattle and herds of larger quadrupeds, together constituted the chief wealth of nomads (cf. ch. xiii. 5 ; Job i. 3). **And he asses.** *Chamōr*, so named from the reddish colour which in southern countries belongs not only to the wild, but also to the common or domestic, ass (Gesenius). The mention of asses among Pharaoh's presents has been regarded as an "inaccuracy" and a "blunder," at once a sign of the late origin of Genesis and a proof its author's ignorance of Egypt (Bohlen, Introd., ch. vi.) ; but (1) asses were among the most common of Egyptian animals, a single individual, according to Wilkinson (vol. iii. p. 34), possessing

sometimes as many as 700 or 800 ; and (2) it is certain that asses appear on the early monuments (cf. 'Records of the Past,' vol. ii. p. 26). **And men-servants, and maid-servants, and she asses.** *Athōn ;* from *athan,* to walk with short steps ; so named from its slowness (ch. xxxii. 16), though "the ass in Egypt is of a very superior kind, tall, handsome, docile, swift" (Kitto's 'Cyclopedia,' art. Egypt). **And camels.** *Gāmāl* (from *gāmāl,* to repay, because the camel is an animal that remembers past injuries (Bochart) , or from a cognate Arabic root *hamala,* meaning he or it carried, with reference to its being a beast of burden (Gesenius) ; both of which derivations Stuart Poole declares farfetched, and proposes to connect the term with the Sanskrit *kramêla,* from *kram,* to walk or step, which would then signify the walking animal (*vide* Kitto, art. Camel). Cf. with the Hebrew the Sanskrit as above, the Arab *jemel* or *gemel,* the Egyptian *sjamoul,* Greek *κάμηλος,* Latin *camelus*) is the well-known strong animal belonging to Palestine (Ezra ii. 67), Arabia (Judges vii. 12), Egypt (Exod. ix. 3), Syria (2 Kings viii. 9), which serves the inhabitants of the desert for travelling (ch. xxiv. 10 ; xxxi. 17) as well as for carrying burdens (Isa. xxx. 6), and for war-like operations (ch. xxi. 7), and in which their riches consisted (Job i. 3 ; xlii. 21). Though the camel does not thrive well in Egypt, and seldom appears on the monuments, the historian has not necessarily been guilty of an "inaccuracy and a blunder" in assigning it to Abram as one of Pharaoh's presents (Bohlen) ; for (1) the camel thrives better in Egypt than it does anywhere else out of its own proper habitat ; (2) if camels were not generally kept in Egypt, this Pharaoh may have been "one of the shepherd kings who partly lived at Avaris, the Zoan of Scripture," a region much inhabited by strangers (Poole in Kitto, art. Camel) ; and (3) if camels have not been discovered among the delineations on the monuments, this may have been because of its connection with the foreign conqueror of Egypt, which caused it to be regarded as a beast of ill omen ; though (4) according to Heeren they do appear on the monuments (Hävernick, § 18, p. 142). That horses, though the glory of Egypt, were not included among the monarch's gifts was doubtless owing to the fact that they could not have been of much service to the patriarch.

Ver. 17.—**And the Lord plagued** (literally, *struck*) **Pharaoh and his house with great plagues** (or *strokes,* either of disease or death, or some other calamity—an indication that Pharaoh was not entirely innocent) **because of Sarai Abram's wife.** The effect of this was to lead to the discovery, not through the aid of the Egyptian priests (Josephus), but either through a special revelation granted to him, as afterwards (ch. xx. 6) to Abimelech in a dream (Chrysostom), or through the confession of Sarai herself (À Lapide), or through the servants of Abraham (Kurtz).

Vers. 18, 19.—**And Pharaoh called Abram and said, What is this that thou hast done unto me? why didst thou not tell me she was thy wife?** In which case we are bound to believe the monarch that he would not have taken her. **Why saidst thou, She is my sister? so I might have taken her to me to wife** (which as yet he had not done; an indirect proof both of the monarch's honourable purpose towards Sarai and of Sarai's unsullied purity): **now therefore behold thy wife, take her, and go thy way.** According to Josephus ('Bell. Jud.' v. ix. 4) Sarah was only one night in Pharaoh's house; but this is obviously incorrect.

Ver. 20.—**And Pharaoh commanded** his men (i. e. certain officers designated for the purpose) **concerning him** (to see to his departure): **and they sent him away, and his wife, and all that he had.**

The partitionists assign this entire section to the Jehovist.

HOMILETICS.

Ver. 10.—*The descent into Egypt.* I. THE STORY OF A GOOD MAN'S FALL. 1. *Experiencing disappointment.* Arrived in Canaan, the patriarch must have felt his heart sink as he surveyed its famine-stricken fields and heathen population; in respect of which it was so utterly unlike the fair realm of his imaginings. So God educates his children, destroying their hopes, blighting their expectations, breaking their ideals, "having provided some better thing for them," some loftier and more beautiful ideal than they have ever ventured to conceive. 2. *Declining in faith.* In presence of the famine the patriarch must have found himself transfixed upon the horns of a terrible dilemma. The promised land, to all appearance, was only fit to be his grave, like the wilderness, in later years, to his descendants. To return to Ur or Haran was impossible without abandoning his faith and renouncing Jehovah's promise. The only harbour of refuge that loomed before his anxious vision was the rich corn-land of Egypt, and yet going into Egypt was, if not exhibiting a want of trust in God, voluntarily running into danger. So situated, unless the spiritual vision of the patriarch had suffered a temporary obscuration he would not have quitted Canaan. A calm, steady, unwavering faith would have perceived that the God who had brought him from Chaldæa could support him in Palestine, even should his flocks be unable to obtain pasture in its fields; and, besides, would have remembered that God had promised Canaan only to himself, and not at all to his herds. 3. *Going into danger.* The descent into Egypt was attended by special hazard, being calculated not only to endanger the life of Abram himself, but also to jeopardise the chastity of Sarai, and, as a consequence, to imperil the fulfilment of God's promise. Yet this very course of action was adopted, notwithstanding its peculiar risks; another sign that Abram was going down the gradient of sin. Besides being in itself wrong to court injury to our own persons, to expose to hurt those we should protect, or occupy positions that render the fulfilment of God's promises dubious, no one who acts in either of these ways need anticipate the Divine favour or protection. Saints who rush with open eyes into peril need hardly look for God to lift them out. 4. *Resorting to worldly policy.* Had Abram and Sarai felt persuaded in their own minds that the proposed journey southwards entirely met the Divine approval, they would simply have committed their way to God without so much as thinking of "crooked ways." But instead they have recourse to a miserable little subterfuge of their own, in the shape of a specious equivocation, forgetting that he who trusts in his own heart is a fool, and that only they whom God keeps are perfectly secure. 5. *Practising deception.* Cunningly concocted, the little scheme was set in operation. Crossing into Egypt, the Mesopotamian sheik and his beautiful partner represented themselves as brother and sister. It is a melancholy indication of spiritual declension when a saint condescends to equivocate, and a deplorable proof of obliquity of moral vision when he trusts to a lie for protection. 6. *Looking after self.* Anxious about his wife's chastity, the patriarch, it would appear, was much more solicitous about his own safety. The tendency of sin is to render selfish; the spirit of religion ever leads men to prefer the interests of others to their own, and in particular to esteem a wife's happiness and comfort dearer than life. 7. *Caught in his own toils.*

The thing which Abram feared actually came upon him. Sarai's beauty was admired and coveted, and Sarai's person was conducted to the royal harem. So God frequently " disappoints the devices of the crafty," allows transgressors to be taken in their own net, and causes worldly policy to outwit itself.

II. THE STORY OF A GOOD MAN'S PROTECTION. 1. *God went down with Abram into Egypt.* Considering the patriarch's behaviour, it would not have been surprising had he been suffered to go alone. But God is always better to his people than their deserts, and, in particular, does not abandon them even when they grieve him by their sins and involve themselves in trouble by their folly. On the contrary, it is at such times they most require his presence, and so he never leaves them nor forsakes them. 2. *God protected Sarai in Pharaoh's house.* Not perhaps for Sarai's or Abram's sake, who scarcely deserved consideration for the plight into which they had fallen, but for his own name's sake. The fulfilment of his own promise and the credit, as it were, of his own character necessitated measures for securing Sarai's honour. Accordingly, the house of Pharaoh was subjected to heavy strokes of affliction. So God can protect his people in every time and place of danger, and always finds a reason in himself, when he is able to discover none in them, for interposing on their behalf. 3. *God delivered both in his own time and way.* To all God's afflicted ones deliverance sooner or later comes. " The Lord knoweth how to deliver the godly out of temptations," and how to make a way of escape when his time arrives.

III. THE STORY OF A GOOD MAN'S REPROOF. 1. *By his own conscience.* Profoundly ashamed must the patriarch have been when he reflected on Sarai's peril in the house of Pharaoh, and on his own craven spirit which had bartered her good name for the sake of saving his own skin. It is difficult to harmonise with conscientious qualms his acceptance of the monarch's gifts. But if Abram had any manhood left after parting with Sarai, besides being humiliated before God for his wickedness, he must have been dishonoured in his own eyes for what looked like selling a wife's purity for flocks and herds. No doubt conscience exacted vengeance from the guilty soul of the patriarch, as it does from that of every sinner. 2. *By his unbelieving neighbour.* Though not entirely guiltless, Pharaoh was unquestionably less blameworthy than Abram. And yet Abram was a saint who had been favoured with Divine manifestations and enriched with Divine promises ; whereas Pharaoh was a heathen, a consideration which must have added keenness to the pang of shame with which the patriarch listened to the monarch's righteous rebuke. So Christians by their worldly craft, mean duplicity, and gross selfishness, if not by their open wickedness, occasionally expose themselves to the merited censures of irreligious neighbours.

Learn—1. That the best of men may fall into the greatest of sins. 2. That the worst of sins committed by a saint will not repel the grace of God. 3. That the severest of the world's censures are sometimes deserved by the Church.

HOMILIES BY VARIOUS AUTHORS.

Vers. 10—20.—*The Church and the world.* The genesis of intercourse and controversy between the kingdom of God and the world power, as represented in the great southern kingdom of Egypt.

I. THE PRESSURE OF EARTHLY NECESSITIES FORMS THE OCCASION OF THE SOJOURN IN EGYPT. We are not told that Abram was sent by Divine direction amongst the temptations of the South ; still there is providential protection even where there is not entire Divine approval. The Lord suffers his people to mingle with the world for their trial, and out of the evil brings ultimate good. Abram went for corn, but obtained much more—the wealth and civilisation of Egypt.

II. SOJOURN IN THE MIDST OF WORLDLY POWER GENERALLY INVOLVES SOME COMPROMISE OF SPIRITUAL LIBERTY, some lowering of spiritual principle. Jehovah's servant condescends to prevarication and dissembling not for protection only, but "that it may be well with him." The danger to Sarai and to Abram was great. All compromise is danger.

III. IN THE SUBORDINATE SPHERE OF SOCIAL MORALITY THERE HAVE BEEN MANY INSTANCES OF CONSCIENCE ACTING MORE POWERFULLY WHERE THE LIGHT OF TRUTH HAS SHONE LESS CLEARLY. Pharaoh was a heathen, but he compares to advantage with Abram. Notice that these early plagues of Egypt mentioned in ver. 17 were very different from the later, although they illustrate the same truth, that by means of judgments God preserves his people and carries forward his kingdom, which is the truth exhibited in every apocalypse.

IV. The dismission of the little company of believers from Egypt was AT THE SAME TIME JUDGMENT AND MERCY. The beginning of that sojourn was wrong, the end of it was disgraceful. A short stay among the world's temptations will leave its results among the people of God, as the subsequent history testifies. Abram became very rich, but his riches had been wrongly obtained. There was trouble in store for him. God's method is to perfect his people not apart from their own character and ways, but by the gracious ordering of their history, so that while good and evil are mingled together, good shall yet ultimately be triumphant.—R.

Ver. 10.—*Famines.* 1. Not even the Holy Land is exempt from famine. Neither is the saint's condition free from suffering, nor the believer's portion on earth from defects. 2. Lands naturally fertile can be rendered barren by a word from God. So circumstances that might conduce to the Church's comfort can be made to disappear when God wills. 3. The drought was sent on Canaan just as Abram arrived. So God often sends his judgments on the world for the sake of his people, and can always time them to meet their spiritual necessities. 4. Famines never come in all lands together, for that were a violation of the covenant; and so neither do God's judgments fall on all men or all saints at once, for that too were to gainsay his promise.—W.

Ver. 13.—*Abraham and carnal policy.* "Say, I pray thee, that thou art my sister: that it may be well with me." These words were partially true (ch. xi. 20). Abraham had real ground for saying that Sarah was his sister, but he hid the fact that she was his wife. He asked her to consent to an equivocal statement and to repeat it.

I. CONTEMPLATE THE NATURE OF CARNAL POLICY. A truth which is part a lie is ever a dangerous lie. The temptation to this carnal policy came (1) from his mingling with the worldly Egyptians on equal terms, (2) from his very prosperous state, and (3) from his having lately come from a religious observance in which he had had high spiritual revelations. Possibly he presumed upon his visions and the Divine promises. David fell also shortly after he had attained the kingdom and been delivered from great dangers.

II. SEE HOW ALL CARNAL POLICY IS SURE IN THE LONG RUN TO FAIL. Abraham did not foresee all the consequences of his equivocations. He even made the path clear for Pharaoh to ask for Sarah. He had afterwards to know that his name was a by-word among the Egyptians. (1) He lost self-respect; (2) he had to be rebuked by a Pharaoh, and (3) to feel that God was dishonoured by his act. Abraham repeated his sin. That God delivered Abraham should teach us that we are not to reject others, who have committed a special sin, as past hope. God does not cast us off for one sinful action. Still Divine forbearance and love should never lead to presumption and to a tampering with carnal policy.—H.

Ver. 20.—*Abram and Israel; a parallel.* 1. Both were driven into Egypt by a famine. 2. To both the land of Egypt proved a house of bondage. 3. In each case the Pharaoh of the time was subjected to plagues. 4. Both were sent away by the alarmed monarchs who were made to suffer for their sakes. 5. Both went up from Egypt laden with the spoils of those among whom they had sojourned. 6. On leaving Egypt both directed their steps to Canaan.—W.

EXPOSITION.

CHAPTER XIII.

Ver. 1.—**And Abram went up out of Egypt, he and his wife.** A special mercy that either of them returned, considering the sin they had committed and the peril in which they had been placed. **And all that he had.** Referring principally to the souls, "domestici" (Poole), acquired in Haran (ch. xii. 5, 16), his material wealth being mentioned afterwards. **And Lot** (who does not appear in the preceding paragraph, no part of which relates to him, but is now reintroduced into the narrative, the present portion of the story being connected with his fortunes) **with him into the south** (sc. of Canaan, vide ch. xii. 9).

Ver. 2. — **And Abram was very rich.** Literally, weighty; used in the sense of abundance (Exod. xii. 38 ; 1 Kings x. 2 ; 2 Kings vi. 14). **In cattle.** Mikneh, from kana, to acquire by purchase, may apply to slaves as well as cattle (cf. ch. xvii. 12, 13, 23). **In silver and gold.** Mentioned for the first time in Scripture ; implying an acquaintance among the Egyptians with the operations of mining and the processes of refining the precious metals. Cf. the instructions of Amenemhat I., which speak of that monarch, belonging to the twelfth dynasty, as having built for himself a palace adorned with gold (vide 'Records of the Past,' vol. ii. p. 14).

Vers. 3, 4.— **And he went on his journeys.** Literally, in his journeyings or stations (cf. ch. xi. 2 ; Exod. xvii. 1 ; Num. x. 6, 12). The renderings καὶ ἐπορεύθη ὅθεν ἦλθεν (LXX.) and reversus est per iter quo venerat (Vulgate) imply without warrant that he used the same camping grounds in his ascent which he had previously occupied in his descent. **From the south even to Bethel** (vide ch. xii. 8), **unto the place where his tent had been at the beginning.** Before his demigration into Egypt, i. e. not to Shechem, the site of his first altar, where probably he had not encamped for any length of time, if at all, but to a spot **between Bethel and Ai** (the exact situation being more minutely described as) **unto the place of the altar, which he had made there at the first.** After entering the promised land. In reality it was the second altar he had erected (vide ch. xii. 7, 8). **And there Abram called on the name of the Lord.** Professed the true and pure worship of God (Calvin) ; preached and taught his family and Canaanitish neighbours the true religion (Luther). Vide ch. xii. 8 ; iv. 26.

Vers. 5, 6.—**And Lot also** (literally, and also to Lot), **who went with Abram** (literally, going with Abram), **had** (were) **flocks and herds and tents.** The uncle's prosperity overflowed upon the nephew. Rosenmüller includes in the tents the domestics and servants, qui in tentoriis degebant (cf. 1 Chron. iv. 11). **And the land was not able to bear them.** Literally, did not bear, i. e. support their households and flocks. **That they should dwell together.** In consequence partly of the scarce pasturage, the land probably having not yet sufficiently recovered from the drought, but chiefly because of their increasing wealth. **For their substance** (vide ch. xii. 5) **was great, so that they could not** (literally, and they were not able to) **dwell together.**

Ver. 7.—**And there was a strife** (originating doubtless in the scarcity of pasture, and having for its object the possession of the best wells and most fertile grounds) **between the herdmen of Abram's cattle and the herdmen of Lot's cattle: and the Canaanite** —the lowlander (vide ch. ix. 22 ; xii. 6)— **and the Perizzite**—the highlander, or dweller in the hills and woods of Palestine (Josephus, Bochart) ; in the open country and in villages, as opposed to the Canaanites, who occupied walled towns (Kalisch, Wordsworth ; a tribe of wandering nomads (Murphy), the origin of whose name is lost in obscurity (Keil), who, though not mentioned in ch. x., are commonly introduced with the Canaanites (Gen. xv. 20 ; xxxiv. 30 ; Exod. iii. 8, 17), as dividing the land between them, and are probably to be regarded as the remnant of an early Shemite race displaced by the Hamite invaders of Palestine. Their introduction here is neither a sign of post-Mosaic authorship nor an interpolation, but an explanation of the difficulty of finding pasture — the land was occupied (vide ch. xii. 6)—**dwelt then in the land.**

Ver. 8.—**And Abram said unto Lot.** Perceiving probably that Lot's face was not towards him as usual, and being desirous to avert the danger of collision between his nephew and himself. **Let there be no strife, I pray thee, between me and thee, and** (i. e. either identifying himself and his nephew with their subordinates, or fearing that the strife of their subordinates might spread to themselves, hence, as) **between my herdmen and thy herdmen; for we be brethren.** Literally, men brethren (cf. ch. xi. 27, 31 ; Exod. ii. 13 ; Ps. cxxxiii. 1). Abram and Lot were kinsmen by nature, by relationship, and by faith (vide ch. xi. 31 ; 2 Pet. ii. 7).

Ver. 9.—**Is not the whole land before thee ?** The Bethel plateau commands an extensive view of Palestine (vide on ver. 10).

Separate thyself, I pray thee, from me. Thus giving Lot the choice of the country. **If** thou wilt take **the left hand** (literally, *if to the left hand* (sc. thou wilt go), the Hebrew term being in the accusative after a verb of motion (Kalisch, p. 344)—**then I will go to the right; or if** thou depart **to the right hand, then I will go to the left.**

HOMILETICS.

Ver. 9.—*The magnanimity of Abram.* I. WHEN IT WAS EVOKED. 1. *On returning to the land of Canaan.* Departing into Egypt, the better nature of the patriarch became obscured and enfeebled, and he himself became the subject of timorous emotions, the deviser of guileful machinations, and the perpetrator of unworthy actions; retracing his erring footsteps to the holy soil, he seems as it were immediately to have recovered the nobility and grandeur of soul which he had lost in the land of Ham. When saints wander into sinful ways they inflict a hurt upon their spirits from which they cannot recover till they seek the good old paths. Sublime deeds of spiritual heroism are not to be expected at the hands of believers who conform to the world. The true champions of the faith, who by their personal behaviour can illustrate its godlike character, are only to be found among those who walk as strangers and pilgrims on the earth, and do not stray from God's commandments. 2. *After having committed a great sin.* The recoil which Abram's spirit must have experienced when, in the light of God's merciful interposition, he came to perceive the heinous nature of the transgression into which his fears had betrayed him in Egypt, had doubtless something to do with that lofty elevation of soul to which he soon afterwards climbed upon the heights of Bethel. So oftentimes a saint, through grace, is profited by his backslidings. The memory of the matter of Uriah had its influence in ripening the piety of David, and the recollection of the judgment-hall of Pilate assisted Peter to a height of spiritual fortitude he might not otherwise have attained. 3. *After an experience of rich mercy.* After all, God's kindnesses to Abram and Sarai were the principal instrumentalities that quickened the better nature of the patriarch; and so it is generally in proportion as we meditate upon and partake of Divine mercy that our hearts are ennobled and enabled. It is the love of God in Christ that constrains a saint to holy and unselfish deeds.

II. HOW IT WAS OCCASIONED. 1. *By the danger of collision between himself and Lot.* The strife which had arisen between his nephew's herdsmen and his own was liable, unless promptly extinguished, to communicate its bad contagion to himself and Lot. But the patriarch, with that insight which belongs to simple minds, discerned a method of avoiding so unseemly a calamity, and, with that self-forgetful heroism which ever characterises noble souls, had the fortitude and magnanimity to put it into execution. It indicates an advanced stage of Christian maturity when what might prove temptations to sin are, by spiritual discernment and unshrinking self-sacrifice, transformed into occasions for holy acting and suffering. 2. *By the necessity of separation which had come on him and Lot,* which necessity was owing— (1) To their increasing wealth. If the present history shows that good men may become rich, and sometimes in dubious ways, it also reveals that wealth has its dangers. The character of Lot was demonstrably injured by prosperity; while if Abram escaped corruption through wealth, that wealth was indirectly the power which deprived him of his kinsman. It is a poor bargain when one grows rich at the expense of his better nature, as did Lot; or even, like Abram, at the expense of affection. Better remain poor and keep friends than become rich and lose friends! (2) To the quarrels of their servants. Though possibly occasioned by devotion to their masters' interests, the contention of the herdsmen was wrong. Not even for the sake of employers should workmen and dependents become involved in strife. And still less should masters and mistresses become entangled in the wranglings of employés and domestics. Better part than fight!

III. BY WHAT IT WAS PRECEDED. 1. *By a solemn act of devotion.* Suitable at all seasons, prayer is specially needful and becoming in times of danger and trial like those in which the patriarch was situated. Nothing is better calculated to soothe the troubled heart, to allay irritation, to prevent strife, to enable the assaulted spirit to resist temptation, to brace the soul for arduous duty and magnanimous self-renunciation, than communion with God. Had Abram's discernment of the growing danger to which he and Lot were exposed, and Abram's contemplation of the necessity of yielding Lot the choice of the land their influence in taking him back to Bethel with its altar? 2. *By an earnest deprecation of the rising strife.* If the Spirit's fruits will not flourish in the stagnant marsh of a dead soul, neither will they in the breast of an angry Christian. A peaceful mind and a quiet heart are indispensable pre-requisites to grace's motions. Heavenly virtue cannot prosper in an atmosphere of wrath and contention. But where saints cultivate a gentle and forgiving spirit it is not uncommon to find them strengthened to perform deeds of holy valour. The conciliatory disposition of the elder of the two travellers was an admirable preparation for, almost a foreshadowing of, the magnanimous act that followed; as the perpetuation of the strife or the indulgence of anger on the part of Abram would have rendered it impossible.

IV. IN WHAT IT WAS DISPLAYED. 1. *A sublime act of self-renunciation.* (1) In preferring Lot's interests to his own, though Lot was the younger, and a dependent on himself, and in a manner only in the land by sufferance; in this exemplifying the very spirit which Christ and his apostles afterwards enjoined upon New Testament believers (Matt. xx. 26; Rom. xii. 10; Phil. ii. 3); and (2) in renouncing Canaan for the sake of peace, which was practically what he did when he gave Lot the choice of the land, the greatness of which act of self-abnegation appears when it is remembered that already God had given him the land, so that he, and not Lot, was entitled to elect to what quarter he should turn, and that this concession of his rights was intended to disarm Lot's hostility, and preserve the unity of the Spirit in the bonds of peace. 2. *A signal illustration of self-resignation,* in which, when he beheld the meanness of Lot, and saw the best portion of the soil abstracted from him, there was neither a display of feeling towards his nephew nor the uprising of a pang of discontentment and regret at the result, but the most humble and self-satisfied acquiescence in what he knew to be the allotment of Heaven.

Learn—1. That soul-wealth is greater than material prosperity. 2. That a man becomes spiritually rich in proportion as he practises self-renunciation. 3. That the higher one rises in true spiritual greatness, the less is he affected by the loss of earth's goods.

HOMILIES BY VARIOUS AUTHORS.

Vers. 1—13.—*The separation between Abram and Lot.* [Return to Bethel—to the altar. The circumstances of the patriarch were very different. He was very rich. Lot is with him, and the sojourn in Egypt had far more depraving effect upon his weaker character than upon that of his uncle. We should remember when we take the young into temptation that what may be comparatively harmless to us may be ruinous to them. The subsequent misery of Lot's career may be all traced to the sojourn in Egypt.]

I. The root of it lay in WORLDLY WEALTH LEADING TO CONTENTION. "They could not dwell together."

II. THE DIVERGENCE OF CHARACTER IS BROUGHT OUT IN THE COMPLICATION OF EXTERNAL CIRCUMSTANCES. Lot is simply selfish, wilful, regardless of consequences, utterly worldly. Abram is a lover of peace, a hater of strife, still cherishes the family feeling and reverences the bond of brotherhood, is ready to subordinate his own interests to the preservation of the Divine order, has faith to see that Canaan with the blessing of God is much to be preferred to the plain of Jordan with Divine judgments hanging over those who were wicked and sinners before the Lord exceedingly.

III. LESSONS OF PROVIDENCE ARE NOT LOST ON THOSE WHO WAIT UPON GOD, and can be learnt in spite of infirmities and errors. Abram could not forget what Egypt had taught him; rich as he was, he did not put riches first. He had seen that that which seems like a garden of the Lord in external beauty may be a cursed land after all. There are people of God who pitch their tents towards Sodom still, and they will reap evil fruits, as Lot did. It is a most terrible danger to separate ourselves from old religious associations. In doing so we cannot be too careful where we pitch our tent.—R.

Ver. 8.—*Abraham, the peaceable man.* "Let there be no strife, I pray thee, between me and thee." Abraham had a nephew who attached himself to his fortunes and shared his fate. Food, fodder, and water became scarce. The flocks of Lot and of Abraham are more than the land can sustain; the herdsmen of each strive together. Servants will often be more bitter towards the servants of a rival of their master, than those immediately concerned. Pathetic is the appeal of the patriarch for the maintenance of peace.

I. It is a most desirable thing to live in peace with others. We are commanded to do so: "As much as lieth in you live peaceably with all men." We may not sacrifice any good principle for the sake of ease, but we are to strive to maintain peace. In matters of faith a man may have to take up at times such a position that others will speak ill of him, but in regard to the neighbourly life he must by all means cultivate amity and concord. Little is ever gained by standing on "our rights." Scandal is always the fruit of quarrelling. The worldly-minded are sure to plume themselves on their superior goodness when the spiritually-minded contend. In many homes there is jangling, sneering, and strife; scathing remarks like hot cinders from Vesuvius fall carelessly around. Tyrannous tempers become like tornados, and moodiness kills like the choke-damp of an ill-ventilated mine. Among nations there should be maintenance of peace. The common sense of most should "hold the fretful realm in awe." In the Church strife should cease. It will when each sect seeks to make men Christlike and not uniform bigots.

II. There are always means of maintaining peace when it is desired. Abraham acted most unselfishly with this view; he yielded his claim to a choice. Lot owed much to Abraham, yet he seized an advantage. Lot looks towards Sodom; the strip of green beside the lake and reaching to Jordan reminds him of the land of Nile. The spirit of Egypt, whence he had lately come, is in him; he chooses Sodom, but with its green pastures he has to take its awful corruption. Abraham turns away in the direction alone left to him. He has his tent, his altar, the promises, and his God; he will live in peace. His Father will not forsake him; indeed God very speedily renews his promises to Abraham, and thus the unselfishness of a peaceful man met with an appropriate reward.—H.

EXPOSITION.

Ver. 10.—**And Lot lifted up his eyes.** *Circumspexit;* with a look of eager, lustful greed (cf. ch. iii. 6). The same expression is afterwards used of Abram (ver. 14), where perhaps also the element of satisfaction, though in a good sense, is designed to be included. **And beheld all the plain.** Literally, *all the circle*, or surrounding region כִּכָּר, from כָּרַר, to move in a circle; cf. *arrondissement*, Fr.; *kreis* or *bezirk*, Ger.); περίχωρος (LXX., Matt. iii. 5); now called El Ghôr, the low country (Gesenius). **Of Jordan.** Compounded of Jor-Dan, the names of the two river sources (Josephus, Jerome); but, accordng to modern etymologists, derived from יָרַד, to go down, and signifying the Descender, like the German Rhine, from *rinnen*, to run. The largest river of Palestine, rising at the foot of Antilibanus, and passing, in its course of 200 miles, over twenty-seven rapids, it pours its waters first into the lake of Merom, and then into the sea of Galilee, 653 feet, and finally into the Lacus Asphaltites,

1316 feet below the level of the Mediterranean (cf. Stanley's 'Sinai and Palestine,' ch. vii. p. 282). It is now called Esh-Sheri'ah, *i. e.* the ford, as having been of old crossed by the Israelites (Gesenius). **That it** was **well-watered everywhere.** Not by canals and trenches, as old interpreters imagined, but by copious streams along its course, descending chiefly from the mountains of Moab. **Before the Lord destroyed**—the same word is used for the destruction of all flesh in what is styled the Elohistic account of the Deluge (ch. vi. 13, 17; ix. 11, 15; cf. 'Quarry on Genesis,' p. 423)—**Sodom and Gomorrha** (*vide* ch. xiv. 2). Even **as the garden of the Lord.** Paradise in Eden, with its four streams (ch. ii. 10; Calvin, Lange, Keil); though by some this is deemed unsatisfactory (Quarry), and the phrase taken as = *hortus amœnissimus* (Rosenmüller), and in particular Mesopotamia, which was a land of rare fecundity (Grotius, Junius). **Like the land of Egypt**—which was irrigated by the Nile and by canals from it as well as by machines (Deut. xi. 10, 11)—**as thou comest unto Zoar**—at the south-east corner of the Dead Sea (*vide* ch. xiv. 3).

Ver. 11.—**Then Lot chose him all the plain of Jordan.** Allured by its beauty and fertility, and heedless of other or higher considerations. **And Lot journeyed east,** מִקֶּדֶם = *versus orientem* (cf. ch. xi. 2). **And they separated themselves the one from the other.** Literally, *a man from his brother.*

Ver. 12.—**Abram dwelled in the land of Canaan.** Strictly so called; in its larger sense Canaan included the circle of the Jordan. **And Lot dwelled in the cities of the plain.** Being desirous of a permanent settlement within the gates, or at least in the immediate neighbourhood, of the wealthy cities of the land; in contrast to his uncle, who remained a wanderer throughout its borders, sojourning as in a strange country (Heb. xi. 9). **And** (with this purpose in contemplation, he) **pitched** his **tent toward** (*i. e.* in the direction of, and as far as to) **Sodom.**

Ver. 13.—**But** (literally, *and*) **the men of Sodom** were **wicked and sinners** — their wickedness is more specifically detailed in ch. xix., *q. v.*)—**before the Lord**—literally, *to Jehovah* = before the face of Jehovah; ἐναντίον τοῦ θεοῦ (LXX.), *vide* ch. x. 9; an aggravation of the wickedness of the Sodomites—**exceedingly.** Their vileness was restrained neither in quantity nor quality. As it passed all height in arrogance, so it burst all bounds in prevalence.

HOMILETICS.

Ver. 10.—*The choice of Lot.* I. THE EXCELLENCE OF LOT'S CHOICE. 1. *Beautiful.* Viewed from the Bethel plateau, at the moment perhaps gilded with the shimmering radiance of the morning sun, the Jordan circle was a scene of enchanting loveliness; and in yielding to the fascinations of the gorgeous panorama that spread itself out on the distant horizon it cannot be affirmed that Lot committed sin. The Almighty Maker of the universe loves beauty, as his works attest (Eccles. iii. 11), and hath implanted the like instinct in the soul of man. Hence, so far from being a signal of depravity, the capacity of admiring and appreciating mere physical and external grace and symmetry betokens a nature not yet completely disempowered by sin; and so far from its being wrong to surround oneself with objects that are pleasing to the eye, it is rather incumbent so to do, provided always it can be accomplished without sin. 2. *Productive.* As there is no sin in having elegant mansions, fair gardens, and fine pictures to look upon, so neither is there evil in desiring fertile fields instead of barren rocks to cultivate. Sentenced to eat bread in the sweat of his brow, the Christian is not thereby required to prefer a tract of moorland to a farm of rich alluvial soil. Monkish asceticism may enjoin such self-mortification on its devotees; Christianity invites men to enjoy the good things which have been freely given to them by God. The well-watered fields of the Jordan circle were as open to the choice of Lot as were the bleak Judæan hills. 3. *Suggestive.* Already it had recalled to his memory the luxuriant plains of Egypt which he had lately visited, and to his imagination the resplendent Eden of man's primeval days; and doubtless it was such a region as could scarcely fail to inspire a devout mind with lofty thoughts, pure emotions, and holy aspirations, so leading the entranced worshipper from nature up to nature's God. Since the human soul cannot choose but be insensibly affected for good or evil by its material as well as moral environment, it is well, when Divine providence gives us the election, that we select for our abodes scenes and places that shall elevate and refine rather than deteriorate and depress.

II. THE DRAWBACKS OF LOT'S CHOICE. 1. *Bad neighbours.* The inhabitants of the Jordanic Pentapolis were sinners of an aggravated type. And while it may not be possible to avoid all contact with wicked men (1 Cor. v. 10), it becomes God's people to keep as far aloof as possible from the ungodly, and especially from transgressors like the Sodomites. Mingling with and marrying into the families of the ungodly ruined the antediluvian world. The chief injury done to the Church of Christ arises from a throwing down of the wall of separation between it and the world. Separation from and nonconformity to the world, and much more the wicked portion of it, is the duty of believers (Rom. xii. 2; 1 Cor. vi. 17). 2. *Moral contamination.* Though Lot was a good man, his piety would not prevent the gradual deterioration of his nature through the evil influence of his neighbours. There is a contagion, for good or evil, in example which is well nigh irresistible. "He that

walketh with wise men shall be wise ; but the companion of fools shall be destroyed."
3. *Bitter sorrow.* Precisely in proportion to the eminence of his religious character
would this be inevitable. The immoralities and infidelities of the Sodomites would
plunge him into grief, if they did not cause " rivers of water " to run down his eyes.
And so it eventually came to pass (2 Pet. ii. 8).

III. THE SINFULNESS OF LOT'S CHOICE. 1. *Avaricious in its origin.* Thus it was
a sin against God. Had no drawbacks attended it, had it in all other respects been
commendable and prudent, the lust of cupidity out of which it sprang would have
condemned it. Few things are more frequently and emphatically reprehended in the
word of God than the inordinate desire of possession (Luke xii. 15; Ephes. v. 3; Col.
iii. 5; Heb. xiii. 5). 2. *Selfish in its character.* Thus, besides being a sin against
God, it was an offence against his uncle. Had Abram and Lot stood upon a platform
of equality, religious principle should have dictated to Lot the propriety of either
returning the right of choice to Abram, or himself selecting what he believed to be
the inferior quarter (Rom. xii. 10; Phil. ii. 3) ; but Abram was Lot's superior in age,
and therefore entitled to take precedence of one who was younger ; Lot's uncle, and,
in virtue of that relationship, deserving of his nephew's honour ; Lot's guardian and
benefactor, and, as a consequence, worthy of acknowledgment and gratitude at the
hands of one whom he had enriched ; and, what was more important for the settlement of the question, the actual heir and owner of the land, to whom accordingly
belonged the prerogative of claiming not its fattest portion only, but its entire
domain. All these considerations rendered Lot's choice offensive in the extreme. 3.
Dangerous in its issues. As such it was a sin against himself as well as against
God. Even though evil should not come of it, it was not open to Lot, as a good man,
to establish himself where injury to his spiritual interests was possible. That he did
not reckon the moral bearings of his choice was an aggravation rather than an extenuation of his sin. He had time to calculate the chances of material prosperity ;
he should also have counted up the moral hazards before he elected to drive his flocks
and herds to Sodom.

Lessons :—1. All is not gold that glitters ; hence the supreme unwisdom of judging
either things or persons according to appearance. 2. In every man's lot there is a
crook ; hence the propriety of moderating our desires concerning everything. 3. It
is possible to pay too dear a price for material prosperity. "What shall it profit a
man if he shall gain the whole world and lose his own soul ? " 4. It is a poor outcome of piety which prefers self-interest to the claims either of affection or religion ;
the man who loves himself better than his neighbour is still devoid of the spirit of
Christ. 5. In the long run the spirit of selfishness is certain to overreach itself and
accomplish its own ruin.

HOMILIES BY VARIOUS AUTHORS.

Vers. 10—13.—*The choice of Lot.* I. WHAT LOT TOOK INTO ACCOUNT. 1. His own
worldly circumstances ; and, 2. The suitability of the Jordan circle to advance them.
II. WHAT LOT DID NOT TAKE INTO ACCOUNT. 1. The reverence due to his uncle.
2. The greater right which Abram had to the soil of Canaan. 3. The danger, in parting with Abram, of separating himself from Abram's God. 4. The risk of damage
to his spiritual interests in settling in the Jordan circle.

Learn—1. That while it may be right, in life's actions, to take our worldly interests
into account, it is wrong and dangerous to take nothing else. 2. That no amount of
purely worldly advantage can either justify or recompense the disregard of the
higher interests of the soul. 3. That though good men may oftentimes find reasons
for neglecting the soul's interests, they cannot do so with impunity.—W.

Vers. 10, 13.—*Sodom and the Sodomites, or the place and the people.* 1. The
physical beauty of the Jordan valley. 2. The moral corruption of its inhabitants.
Lessons :—1. The weakness of nature as a moral educator. 2. The true design of
nature as a moral educator.—W.

Ver. 11.—*The parting of the friends.* I. The SADNESS of this parting. It was a parting—1. Of kinsmen (men, brethren).   2. Of kinsmen in a foreign land.   3. Of kinsmen by their own hand.

II. The CAUSE of this parting.   1. The difficulty of finding sustenance together. 2. The danger of collision if they kept together.

III. The MANNER of this parting.   1. After prayer.   2. In peace.   3. With magnanimity on the part of Abram.   4. With meanness on that of Lot.

Lessons:—1. It is sad when brethren cannot dwell together in unity.   2. It is better that brethren should separate than quarrel.—W.

Ver. 11.—*Lot's unwise choice.*   "Then Lot chose him all the plain of Jordan." To Lot no doubt this seemed but a matter of prudence, a choice of pastures, yet it stamped his after life.   He was a godly man.   We miss the point if we think of him as careless.   The lesson is for God's people.   At first guided by his uncle, but time came when he must act alone.   Pastures of Bethel not sufficient. Strife between the herdsmen.   God uses little things to work his will.   In every life times when choice must be made.   Perhaps definite and distinct, *e. g.* leaving home, or choice of a profession ; perhaps less marked, as in the choice of friends and associates, or the habits imperceptibly formed.   We must be thus tried ; needful for our training (James i. 12).   A sevenfold blessing "to him that overcometh" (Rev. ii., iii.).

I. EVIL OF LOT'S CHOICE.   He chose the best pasture.   Why should he not?   The fault lay in the motive, the want of spiritual thought in a secular matter.   He broke no positive law, but looked only to worldly good.   The evil of Sodom was disregarded.   No prayer for guidance ; no thought how he could best serve God (cf. James i. 14).

II. EFFECT OF LOT'S CHOICE.   1. No real happiness.   His soul vexed (2 Pet. ii. 8). His life ; fretting at evil which he had not resolution to escape from.   2. Real injury.   His character enervated.   From dwelling in plain came into the city ; formed connections there.   Irresolute and lingering when warned to flee.   His prayer for himself only.   Was saved " as by fire " (1 Cor. iii. 15).   We are tried daily, in the valley or on the mountain.   We cannot avoid trials ; not good for us if we could. The one way of safety : " Seek first the kingdom of God."   There is an evil terribly widespread—of seeking first the world ; thinking not to neglect God, but putting Christianity into corners of the life.   What saith the world?   Haste to be rich, or great ; take thine ease ; assert thyself ; be high-spirited.   And the customs of society and much of education repeat the lesson.   But what saith Christ?   Look unto me. Not at stated times, but always.   The cause of much dispeace, of many spiritual sorrows (1 Tim. vi. 10), is want of thoroughness in taking Christ as our guide.   Lot was preserved.   Will any say, "I ask no more"?   "Remember Lot's wife."   How narrow the line between his hesitation and her looking back !   The grain *may* sprout through thorns (Matt. xiii. 22), but the thorns are ever growing.—M.

Ver. 12.—*Going to Sodom.*   I. HOW IT MAY HAVE LOOKED TO LOT.   1. As a matter of business it was good.   2. In its moral aspects the step was dangerous.   But—3. Doubtless at first Lot did not intend entering the city.   And perhaps—4. Lot may have justified his doubtful conduct by hoping that he would have opportunities of doing good to the Sodomites.

II. HOW IT MUST HAVE LOOKED TO THE SODOMITES.   It must have—1. Surprised them to see a good man like Lot coming to a neighbourhood so bad.   2. Led them to think adversely of a religion that preferred worldly advantage to spiritual interest. 3. Rendered them impervious to any influence for good from Lot's example.

Lessons:—1. It is perilous to go towards Sodom if one wants to keep out of Sodom.   2. It is useless preaching to Sodomites while gathering wealth in Sodom. —W.

Going towards Sodom.   1. An inviting journey.   2. A gradual journey.   3. A sinful journey.   4. A dangerous journey.—W.

EXPOSITION.

Vers. 14, 15.—**And the Lord said**—speaking probably with an articulate voice ; the third occasion on which the patriarch was directly addressed by God. The narrative, however, does not affirm that there was any actual theophany—**unto Abram**—who could readily recognise the voice which had twice already spoken to him. **After that Lot was separated from him.** Thus God approved that separation (Poole), and administered consolation to the troubled heart of the patriarch (Calvin), though Divine revelations are rather wont to be made to minds already quiet and sedate (Lyra). **Lift up now thine eyes.** Perhaps a studied reference to the act of Lot, which Moses describes in similar language (ver. 10), and possibly designed to suggest the greater satisfaction which would be imparted to the soul of Abram by the survey about to be made. **And look from the place where thou art.** Between Bethel and Ai, on one of the mountain peaks (cf. ch. xii. 8 ; xiii. 3), from which a commanding view of almost the entire country could be obtained. **Northward**—towards "the hills which divide Judæa from the rich plains of Samaria"—**and southward**—as far as to the Hebron range—**and eastward**—in the direction of the dark mountain wall of Moab, down through the rich ravine which leads from the central hills of Palestine to the valley of the Jordan, and across that very "circle" into which Lot has already departed with his flocks—**and westward**—literally, *towards the sea.* Cf. on the view from the stony but fertile plateau between Bethel and Ai, Stanley's 'Sinai and Palestine,' ch. iv. p. 218. **For all the land which thou seest—** *i. e.* the entire country, a part being put for the whole—**to thee will I give it.** To avoid an apparent conflict between this Divine declaration and the words of Stephen (Acts vii. 5), it is proposed by some to read the next clause as epexegetic of the present (Ainsworth, Bush) ; but the land was really given to Abram as a nomade chief, in the sense that he peacefully lived for many years, grew old, and died within its borders (Clericus, Rosenmüller, 'Speaker's Commentary'), while it was assigned to his descendants only because it had been first donated to him. **And to thy seed.** Not his bodily posterity alone, to whom the terrestrial Canaan was given, but also and chiefly his spiritual family, to whom was made over that better country, even an heavenly, of which the land of promise was a type. **For ever.** *'Adh 'ōlam* (*vide* on ch. ix. 16) = in perpetuity ; *i.e.* (1) to the close of that 'olam or period which was already measured out in the secret counsels of Jehovah for the duration of the seed of Abraham as a people, "quum terra in

seculum promittitur, non simpliciter notatur perpetuitas, sed quæ finem accepit in Christo" (Calvin) ; and (2) unto eternity, in so far as it was a promise of a spiritual inheritance to Abraham's believing children. Thus as the promise did not preclude the expulsion of unbelieving Israel from the land, so neither does it guarantee to existing Jews a return to the earthly Paradise (Keil).

Ver. 16.—**And I will make thy seed as the dust of the earth.** "As the land shall be great for thy people, thy posterity, so thy people shall be great or innumerable for the land" (Lange). Afterwards the seed of Abram is likened to the stars of heaven for multitude (ch. xv. 5). **So that if a man can number the dust of the earth,** then **shall thy seed also be numbered.**

Ver. 17.—**Arise.** According to a common mode of Oriental speech, pleonastically affixed to verbs of going, going forward, and of setting about anything with impulse (Gesenius, p. 727 ; cf. ch. xxii. 3 ; Job i. 20). **Walk through the land in the length of it and in the breadth of it.** To be understood not as a literal direction, but as an intimation that he might leisurely survey his inheritance with the calm assurance that it was his. **For I will give it unto thee.**

Ver. 18.—**Then** — literally, *and*, acting immediately as the heavenly voice directed —**Abram removed**—or rather pitched (cf. ver. 12)—his **tent, and dwelt**—settled down, made the central point of his subsequent abode in Canaan (Wordsworth)—**in the plain** —בְּאֵלֹנֵי = oaks (Gesenius) or terebinths (Celsius); *vide* ch. xii. 6—**of Mamre**—an Amorite chieftain who afterwards became the friend and ally of Abram (ch. xiv. 13, 24), and to whom probably the grove belonged—**which is in Hebron**—twenty-two miles south of Jerusalem on the way to Beersheba, a town of great antiquity, having been built seven years before Zoan, in Egypt (Numb. xiii. 22). As it is elsewhere styled *Kirjath-arba*, or the city of Arba (ch. xxiii. 2 ; xxxv. 27), and appears to have been so called until the conquest (Josh. xiv. 15), the occurrence of the name *Hebron* is regarded as a trace of post-Mosaic authorship (Clericus, *et alii*); but it is more probable that *Hebron* was the original name of the city, and that it received the appellation *Kirjath-arba* on the arrival in the country of Arba the Anakite, perhaps during the sojourn of Jacob's descendants in Egypt (Rosenmüller, Baumgarten, Hengstenberg, Keil, Kurtz). The place is called by modern Arabs El Khalil, the friend of God. **And built there an altar unto the Lord.**

HOMILETICS.

Vers. 14—18.—*Magnanimity rewarded, or Divine compensations.* I. A REVELA-
TION GIVEN. Immediately on Lot's departure Jehovah approaches, the appearance
of the heavenly Friend compensating for the loss of the earthly kinsman, as often
happens in the Divine dealings with men and saints. The revelation now afforded
to the patriarch was—1. *Personal.* Essentially a self-revealing God, only through
the medium of a person can Jehovah give a full and clear unveilment of himself.
Of this description was the theophany accorded to the solitary flock-master on the
Bethel plateau; and in the man Christ Jesus have the saints a like disclosure of the
person and character of the unapproachable Supreme. 2. *Gracious.* The dignity
of him who thus appeared to the patriarch, the all-sufficient and self-existent Deity,
and the character of him to whom such revelation was vouchsafed, the father of the
faithful, but still a mere creature, and, apart from Divine grace, exposed to just
condemnation, attest its stupendous condescension. Yet "such honour have all the
saints" to whom, notwithstanding their personal insignificance and deep unworthiness, the supreme Deity has approached and unveiled himself in Christ. 3. *Opportune.* At the time when it was made the patriarch's heart, we can imagine, was the
seat of mingled emotions. Saddened by the loss of a kinsman who had been long
his companion, and perhaps pained by the recollection of that kinsman's avarice,
dejected as he realised his solitude among hostile neighbours and in a foreign land,
though, doubtless, also sustained by a consciousness of having acted well in parting
with his nephew, the patriarch was much in need of Divine consolation and succour.
And so are Christ's visits to his people ever seasonable (Luke xxiv. 15; John vi. 20)
and suitable to their wants. 4. *Comforting.* This was proved by his subsequent
behaviour. Plucking up the stakes of his tent, he resumed his travels, and at his
next encampment built an altar for the worship of the Lord. It is a good sign that
gracious visits to needy souls are having their desired effect when those souls are able
to attend to the ordinary but necessary duties of life, and to preserve their relish for
the public and private rites of religion.

II. A LAND GRANTED. For the loss of the Jordan circle the patriarch receives an
express donation of the entire territory of Canaan. So Christ promises to reward his
self-sacrificing followers in kind as well as quantity, and in the life that now is as
well as in that which is to come (Matt. xix. 29). The grant made to Abram was—
1. *Magnificent.* The grant of a land; of the land of Palestine in the first instance,
and in the second of the better country, even an heavenly, of which the earthly
Canaan was a type (Heb. xi. 8—10). The like grant is made to believers in the
gospel (Matt. v. 5; 1 Cor. iii. 22; 2 Tim. ii. 12). 2. *Certain.* The complete isolation of the patriarch, the occupation of the land, and especially the barrenness of
Sarai, were all calculated to make the Divine donation of the country before him but
a doubtful gift after all. And so sometimes to Christians may the heavenly inheritance appear highly problematical. But the ground of certainty for them is precisely
what it was to Abram, the word of the living God; and as Abram staggered not at
the promise of God through unbelief, so neither should they. 3. *Perpetual.* To
thee, and to thy seed for ever, were the terms in which the earthly Canaan was conveyed to the patriarch. That is, so long as the seed of Abram according to the flesh
existed as a separate nation they should occupy the land of Canaan; while for his
spiritual posterity the heavenly Canaan should continue an inalienable possession. So
earth to the believer is a perpetual inheritance in the sense that "the world is his,"
while heaven is an eternal country from which he shall go no more out.

III. A SEED PROMISED. The magnanimity of the patriarch had deprived him of a
brother's son; the grace of God rewarded him by promising a child of his own. No
man ever comes off a loser who makes sacrifices for God. The seed promised was to
be—1. *Numerous.* A multitude instead of one; exemplified in the untold millions
of Abram's natural descendants. So God delights to reward his people, returning to
them a hundredfold for what they give to him (Matt. xix. 20; Ephes. iii. 20). 2.
Spiritual. An offspring united to him by bonds of grace in lieu of a kinsman connected with him by ties of blood; a prediction realised in the myriads of his believing

children. Another principle which regulates the Divine compensations bestowed on saints is to take the less and give the greater, to remove the material and impart the spiritual (John xvi. 7 ; xix. 26). 3. *Eminent.* If Lot was renowned for wealth and worldly prudence, the unborn seed of Abram should be distinguished in the annals of both Church and world for riches of a more enduring character and wisdom of a nobler kind ; a prophecy fulfilled in Israel after the flesh, which as a nation has always been more distinguished for intelligence and capacity than for numbers ; in Israel after the spirit, or the Church of God, whose characteristics have ever been rare spiritual illumination and high moral potency; and in Israel's Saviour, "in whom are hid all the treasures of wisdom and knowledge,"[1] and "in whom dwelleth all the fulness of the Godhead bodily."

Learn—1. That God is the ever-present though unseen Spectator of noble deeds. 2. That every act of self-sacrifice performed for his sake elicits his approbation. 3. That while he who keeps his life shall lose it, he who, for Christ's sake and the gospel's, loses it shall ultimately find it.

EXPOSITION.

CHAPTER XIV.

Ver. 1.—And it came to pass. After the separation of Abram and Lot, the latter of whom now appears as a citizen of Sodom, and not merely a settler in the Jordan circle ; perhaps about the eighty-fourth year of Abram's life (Hughes). The present chapter, "the oldest extant record respecting Abraham" (Ewald), but introduced into the Mosaic narrative by the Jehovistic editor (Knobel, Tuch, Bleek, Davidson), possesses traces of authenticity, of which not the least is the chronological definition with which it commences (Hävernick). **In the days of Amraphel.** Sanscrit, *Amrapâla,* keeper of the gods (Gesenius) ; *Arphaxad* (Fürst) ; powerful people (Young, 'Analytical Concordance') ; root unknown (Murphy, Kalisch). **King of Shinar.** *Babel* (Onkelos) ; *Bagdad* (Arabic version of Erpenius) ; *Pontus* (Jonathan) ; the successor of Nimrod (*vide* ch. x. 10). **Arioch.** Sanscrit, *Arjaka,* venerated (Bohlen, Gesenius, Fürst) ; probably from the root אֲרִי, a lion, hence leonine (Gesenius, Murphy). The name, which reappears in Dan. ii. 14, has been compared, though doubtfully, with the *Urukh* of the inscriptions (*vide* 'Records of the Past,' vol. iii. p. 9). **King of Ellasar.** *Pontus* (Symmachus, Vulgate) ; the region between Babylon and Elymais (Gesenius); identified with Larsa or Laranka, the Λάρισσα or Λαράχων of the Greeks, now *Senkereh,* a town of Lower Babylonia, between *Mugheir* (Ur) and *Warka* (Erech), on the left bank of the Euphrates (Rawlinson). **Chedorlaomer.** A "handful of sheaves," if the word be Phœnicio-Shemitic, though probably its true etymology should be sought in ancient Persian (Gesenius, Fürst). The name has been detected by archæologists in *Kudur-mapula,* the Ravager of the West, whom monu-

mental evidence declares to have reigned over Babylon in the twentieth century B.C. ; and "*Kudurnanhundi* the Elamite, the worship of the great gods who did not fear," and the conqueror of Chaldæa, B.C. 2280 ; but in both instances the identifications are problematical. The name Chedorlaomer in Babylonian would be *Kudur-lagamer;* but as yet this name has not been found on the inscriptions (*vide* 'Records of the Past,' vol. iii. pp. 7, 19). **King of Elam.** East of Babylonia, on the north of the Persian Gulf (cf. ch. x. 22). **And Tidal.** "Fear, veneration" (Gesenius) ; terror (Murphy) ; "splendour, renown" (Fürst) ; though the name may not be Shemitic. **King of nations.** The Scythians (Symmachus) ; the Galilean heathen (Clericus, Rosenmüller, Delitzsch), which are inappropriate in this connection ; nomadic races (Rawlinson) ; probably some smaller tribes so gradually subjugated by Tidal as to render it "impossible to describe him briefly with any degree of accuracy " (Kalisch).

Ver. 2.—That these **made war.** The LXX. connect the present with the preceding verse by reading "that Arioch," &c. Ewald interpolates "of Abram" before "that Amraphel." **With Bera.** "Gift"= בֶּן־רַע (Gesenius). **King of Sodom.** "Burning, conflagration," as being built on bituminous soil, and therefore subject to volcanic eruptions ; from סְדֹם, conjectured to mean to burn (Gesenius). "Lime place," or "enclosed place ;" from סְדָה, to surround (Fürst). A mountain with fossil salt at the present day is called Hágv Usdûm ; and Galen also knew of a Sodom mountain. **And with Birsha** = בֶּן־רֶשַׁע "son of wickedness" (Gesenius) ; "long and thick" (Murphy) ; "strong, thick" (Fürst). **King of Gomorrah.** Γομόῤῥα (LXX.) ; perhaps "culture, habitation" (Gesenius) ;

"rent, fissure" (Fürst). **Shinab.** "Father's tooth" (Gesenius); "splendour of Ab" (Fürst); "coolness" (Murphy). **King of Admah.** Fruit region, farm city (Fürst). **And Shemeber.** "Soaring aloft" (Gesenius). **King of Zeboiim.** Place of hyenas (Gesenius); gazelles (Murphy); a wild place (Fürst). **And the king of Bela.** "Devoured," or "devouring" (Gesenius). **Which is Zoar.** "The small," a name afterwards given to the city (ch. xix. 22), and here introduced as being better known than the more ancient one.

Ver. 3.—**All these**—the last-named princes — **were joined together**—i. e. as confederates (sc. and came with their forces)—**in** (literally, *to*) **the vale of Siddim.** The salt valley (LXX.); a wooded vale (Vulgate); a plain filled with rocky hollows (Gesenius), with which ver. 10 agrees; the valley of plains or fields (Onkelos, Raschi, Keil, Murphy). **Which is the salt sea.** *I. e.* where the salt sea afterwards arose, on the destruction of the cities of the plain—ch. xix. 24, 25 (Keil, Hävernick; cf. Josephus, 'Bell. Jud.,' iv. 8, 4); but the text scarcely implies that the cities were submerged—only the valley (cf. Quarry, p. 207). The extreme depression of the Dead Sea, being 1300 feet below the level of the Mediterranean ("the most depressed sheet of water in the world:" Stanley's 'Sinai and Palestine,' ch. vii.), conjoined with its excessive saltness (containing 26¼ per cent of saline particles), renders it one of the most remarkable of inland lakes. Its shores are clothed with gloom and desolation. Within a mile from its northern embouchure the verdure of the rich Jordan valley dies away. Strewn along its desolate margin lie broken canes and willow branches, with trunks of palms, poplars, and other trees, half embedded in slimy mud, and all covered with incrustations of salt. At its south-western corner stands the mountain of rock salt, with its columnar fragments, which Josephus says in his day was regarded as the pillar of Lot's wife.

Ver. 4.—**Twelve years**—dating from the commencement of his reign (Murphy)—**they served**—and paid tribute (cf. 2 Kings xviii. 7)—**Chedorlaomer.** If the king of Elam was a Shemite prince, this was in accordance with the Noachic prophecy (ch. ix. 26); but according to the monuments the Elamite dynasty was Turanian. **And in the thirteenth year**—during the whole of the thirteenth year (*vide* Ewald's 'Heb. Synt.,' § 300, *a.*; cf. ver. 5)—**they rebelled,** or had rebelled.

Ver. 5.—**And in** (or during) **the fourteenth year came Chedorlaomer, and the kings that** were **with him, and smote** (because of actual or probable rebellion) **the Rephaims.** Γίγαντας (LXX.), a tribe of

gigantic stature (from an Arabic root, to be high), the iron bed of whose last king, Og, measured nine yards in length and four in breadth (Deut. iii. 11); forming a portion of the aboriginal inhabitants of Palestine prior to the invasion of the Canaanites, though existing as a remnant as late as the conquest (ch. ii. 20; iii. 11, 13). **In Ashteroth Karnaim.** Literally, *Ashteroth of the Two Horns;* so called either from its situation between two horn-shaped hills (Jewish interpreters), or because of the horned cattle with which it abounded (Hillery), or in honour of the goddess Ashtaroth, Astarte, or Venus, whose image was such as to suggest the idea of a horned figure (Λ Lapido, Gesenius, Kalisch); identified by some with the capital of Og (Keil), but by others distinguished from it (Wetstein); of uncertain site, though claimed to survive in the ruins of *Tell Ashtereh*, near the ancient Edrei (Ritter); in those of *'Afineh*, eight miles from Buzrah (Porter); in the modern village *Mesarib* (Burckhardt); or in *El Kurnem* or *Ophein* in Ledsha (Robinson). **And the Zuzims.** Probably the Zamzummims between the Arnon and the Jabbok (Deut. ii. 20). **In Ham.** "Possibly the ancient name of Rabba of the Ammonites (Deut. iii. 11), the remains being still preserved in the ruins of Ammân" (Keil). **And the Emims.** *Fearful and terrible men*, the primitive inhabitants of Moab (Deut. ii. 10, 11); called also Rephaims, as being of colossal stature. **In Shaveh Kiriathaim.** Literally, *the plain of Kiriathaim*, or *the plain of the two cities*, situated in the district afterwards assigned to Reuben (Numb. xxxii. 37); identified with *Coraiatha*, the modern *Koerriath* or *Kereyat*, ten miles west of Medebah (Eusebius, Jerome, Kalisch), which, however, rather corresponds with *Kerioth*, in Jer. xlviii. 24 (Keil).

Ver. 6.—**And the Horites.** Literally, *dwellers in caves;* from *chor*, a cave. **In their mount Seir.** Literally, wooded (Gesenius); hairy (Fürst); rugged (Lange); probably with reference to the thick brushwood and forests that grew upon its sides. The cave men of Seir were the earlier inhabitants of the region lying between the Dead Sea and the Gulf of Elam, afterwards taken possession of by the Edomites (Deut. ii. 12; Jer. xlix. 16; Obad. 3, 4). **Unto El-paran.** *I. e.* the oak or terebinth of Paran, **Which is by the wilderness.** Between the land of Edom and the fertile country of Egypt, and to the southward of Palestine, identified as the plateau of the *Tih*, across which the Israelitish march lay from Sinai (Stanley, 'Sinai and Palestine,' p. 92).

Ver. 7.—**And they returned**—from the oak of Paran, the southernmost point reached by the invaders—**and came to En-**

mishpat—the Well of Judgment, regarded as a prolepsis by those who derive the name from the judgment pronounced on Moses and Aaron (A Lapide) ; but more probably the ancient designation of the town, which was so styled because the townsmen and villagers settled their disputes at the well in its neighbourhood (Kalisch)—**which is Kadesh,** of which (Numb. xx. 14) the exact site cannot now be ascertained, though the spring *Ain Kades*, on the heights of *Jebel Halal,* twelve miles east-south-east of *Moyle*, the halting-place of caravans (Rowland, Keil, Kalisch), and *Petra* (Josephus, Stanley), have been suggested as marking the locality. **And smote all the country of the Amalekites.** *I. e.* afterwards possessed by them, to the west of Edom. Amalek was a grandson of Esau (*vide* ch. xxxvi. 12). **And also the Amorites.** The mountaineers, as distinguished from the Canaanites or lowlanders (cf. ch. x. 16). **That dwelt in Hazezon-tamar.** "The pruning of the palm ;" afterwards Engedi, "the fountain of the wild goat," situated midway up the western shore of the Dead Sea, and now called *Ainjidy* (cf. Josh. xv. 62; 1 Sam. xxiv. 1, 2 ; 2 Chron. xx. 2 ; Ezek. xlvii. 10).

Vers. 8, 9.—**And there went out** (to resist the onslaught of the victorious Asiatics) **the king of Sodom, and the king of Gomorrah, and the king of Admah, and the king of Zeboiim, and the king of Bela (the same is Zoar);** (*i. e.* the five revolted monarchs of the Pentapolis) **and they joined battle with them in the vale of Siddim**

(*vide* ver. 3) ; **with Chedorlaomer the king of Elam, and with Tidal king of nations, and Amraphel king of Shinar, and Arioch king of Ellasar; four kings with five.**

Ver. 10.—**And the vale of Siddim was full of slime-pits.** Literally, *was pits, pits* (cf. 2 Kings iii. 16 ; Ezek. xlii. 12 for examples of repeated nouns) *of slime,* bitumen or asphalte, and therefore unfavourable for flight. "Some of the wells near the Dead Sea are 116 feet deep, with a stratum of bitumen fifteen feet in depth, and as black as jet" (Inglis). **And the kings of Sodom and Gomorrah fled and fell there.** Stumbled into the pits and perished (Keil, Lange, Murphy), though if the king of Sodom escaped (ver. 17), the language may only mean that they were overthrown there (Knobel, Rosenmüller, Bush, 'Speaker's Commentary'). **And they that remained fled to the mountain,** of Moab, with its numerous defiles.

Ver. 11. — **And they** (the conquering kings) **took all the goods of Sodom and Gomorrah, and all their victuals, and went their way,** ascending up the valley of the Jordan *en route* for Damascus.

Ver. 12.—**And they took Lot, Abram's brother's son, who dwelt in Sodom.** The last view of Lot saw him driving off his flocks and herds from Bethel. It betokens a considerable declension in spiritual life to behold him a citizen of Sodom. **And his goods** (all the property he had acquired through his selfish choice of the Jordan circle), **and departed.**

HOMILETICS.

Ver. 12.—*The capture of Lot, or Nemesis pursuing sin.* I. AN EXAMPLE OF THE BITTER FRUITS OF WAR. 1. *War is sometimes justifiable in its origin and objects.* When undertaken to achieve or preserve national independence, to vindicate the liberties and secure the rights of men, or to repel the aggressions of ambitious despots, even war with all its bloody horrors may become an imperious and fierce necessity. It is difficult to determine whether on either side the campaign in the vale of Siddim was entitled to be so characterised. The kings of the Pentapolis were fighting for emancipation from a foreign yoke, and so far perhaps were entitled to be regarded as having right upon their side; yet they had themselves been invaders of a land which had originally been assigned to the tribes of Shem. But however the question of right may be settled as between these ancient warriors, it is certain their successors on the battle-fields of earth have much more frequently had the wrong upon their sides than the right. 2. *Victory does not always favour those who seem to have the best cause.* The maxim of the great Napoleon, that God is always on the side of the strongest battalions, is as wide astray from the exact truth on this important subject as is the prevailing sentiment that God always defends the right. The doctrine of Scripture is that the Lord of Hosts is independent of both regiments and rifles, can save by many or by few, and giveth the victory to whomsoever he will ; and that not always does he choose to render those arms triumphant which are striking for the holiest cause, but sometimes, for reasons of his own (it may be to chastise a nation for its sins, or to move them to faith and prayer, or to teach them some important lesson), permits the wrong to trample down the right. The history of Israel and the records of modern warfare supply numerous examples. 3. *Disastrous and terrible are the usual concomitants of war.* Not that God does not frequently overrule the hostilities of contending nations, and evolve from the murderous designs of monarchs results the most beneficial, making war the pioneer of civilisation, and even of religion; but the immediate effects of international strife are ever ruinous and appalling—fruitful fields devastated, fair cities sacked, valuable property destroyed, lives of men wasted, a nation's blood and treasure poured out like water, lamentation, mourning, and woe commissioned to many homes, and a burden of care and sorrow laid on all. All this was exemplified in the present instance. 4. *When war arises the innocent largely suffer with the guilty.* Had the campaign against the kings of the Pentapolis not been prepared, it is probable that the Rephaims, Zuzims, Emims, Horites, Amalekites, and Amorites would not have suffered at the hands of Chedorlaomer, and it is certain that Lot would not have been made a prisoner by the victorious monarch. Now, so far as the primal reason of this invasion was concerned, all these were innocent of any offence against the Asiatic king, and yet they were amongst the victims of his wrath against the rebels of the Jordan circle.

II. AN INSTANCE OF DIVINE RETRIBUTION. 1. *Deserved.* Although Lot was a righteous man, he had egregiously sinned, (1) in choosing the Jordan circle as his portion, (2) in making his abode in Sodom, (3) in continuing amongst the inhabitants when he ascertained their ungodly character. Consequently God avenged himself upon his erring servant by allowing him to lose his property, and to come near the losing of his life as well in the sacking of the city. So "the face of the Lord is set against them that do evil." 2. *Unexpected* probably as to its cause, Lot thinking he had committed nothing worthy of chastisement, for sin has a strange power of obscuring the moral vision and deadening the voice of conscience; almost certainly as to its time, God's judgments for the most part taking men unawares (cf. Ps. lxxiii. 18, 19), and evil-doers being commonly snared in an evil time, like the fishes of the sea (Eccles. ix. 12), walking like blind men because they have sinned against the Lord (Zeph. i. 17); and more than likely as to its form, those who anticipate the outpouring of Divine indignation being seldom able to discern beforehand the special character it will assume. 3. *Appropriate.* Lot had chosen the Jordan circle as the most advantageous locality for thriving in his flocks and herds, and Chedorlaomer's armies swept his folds and stalls entirely clean. He had elected to live among the filthy Sodomites, and so he is compelled to fare as they. God's recompenses to evil-doers (whether saints or sinners) are never unsuitable, though man's often are. 4. *Merciful.* He might have lost his life in the general massacre of the city's inhabitants, but he only lost his property, or rather it was not yet lost, although, doubtless, Lot imagined that it was; only pillaged and carried off along with himself, his wife, and daughters. So God ever mingles mercy with judgment when dealing with his people. 5. *Premonitory.* Though all retribution is not designed to admonish and reprove, this was. The vengeance taken on the wicked at the day of judgment will be purely punitive; that which falls upon transgressors while on earth is aimed at their amendment. Unhappily, however, as in the case of Lot, it is sometimes inefficacious. Instead of taking warning at what might have proved his ruin, Lot was no sooner rescued than he returned to Sodom. So great providential judgments and great providential mercies are often equally despised.

HOMILIES BY VARIOUS AUTHORS.

Ch. xiv.—*The kingdom of God in its relation to the contending powers of this world.* I. GOD'S JUDGMENTS ARE ALREADY BEGINNING TO FALL. War is made by confederate kings or princes against the people of the wicked cities of the plain, who by their propinquity would naturally be leagued together, but by their common rebellion against Chedorlaomer were involved in a common danger. Notice the indication of the future judgment given in the course of the narrative—"the vale of Siddim was full of slime-pits." God's vengeance underlies the wicked, ready to burst forth on them in due time.

II. THE UNFAITHFUL LOT IS INVOLVED IN THE JUDGMENT. He and his goods are taken. For while before it is said he pitched his tent near to Sodom, now we find that he is *in* Sodom.

III. The MEDIATION OF ABRAM, representative of that of God's people in the world, procures the deliverance of the backsliding. He has already succeeded in drawing strength to himself; and doubtless Abram the Hebrew represented a nucleus of higher life even in that land of the idolatrous and degenerate which was recognised as in some sense a refuge to which men could appeal.

IV. The VICTORY OF THE CHILD OF GOD, with his small company, over the great army of heathen is typical. It represents, like the victory of David over Goliath, &c., the superior might of the spiritual world (cf. 1 Cor. i. 27—31).

V. The HOMAGE PAID TO ABRAM as the conqueror both by the heathen king of Sodom and the priest-king of Salem is typical of the superior position of the covenant people. Abram gave tithes to Melchizedek (cf. Heb. vii. 1—7) as an acknowledgment of the superiority of the position of Melchizedek, but Melchizedek blessed Abram as the possessor of the promise. The idea is that Melchizedek was the priest of a departing dispensation, Abram the recipient of the old and the beginning of the new.

VI. ABRAM'S STRICT SEPARATION from the worldly power, which he rested on an oath of faithfulness to God, shows that he is decidedly advancing in spiritual character. The contrast is very striking between his conduct and that of Lot. He at the same time does not attempt to enforce his own high principle upon others. The Church of God has suffered much from its attempts to apply its own high rules to the world instead of leaving the world to find out for itself their superiority and adopt them.—R.

EXPOSITION.

Ver. 13.—**And there came one that had escaped.** Literally, *the fugitive party,* the article denoting the genus, as in "the Canaanite," ch. xii. 6 (*vide* Ewald's 'Hebrew Syntax,' § 277, *a.*). **And told Abram the Hebrew.** "The immigrant" *transfluvialis,* ὁ περάτης, from beyond the Euphrates, if applied to the patriarch by the inhabitants of Palestine (LXX., Aquila, Origen, Vulgate, Keil, Lange, Kalisch); but more probably, if simply inserted by the historian to distinguish Abram from Mamre the Amorite, "the descendant of Eber" (Lyra, Drusius, Calvin, Bush, Candlish, Murphy, 'Speaker's Commentary;' *vide* on ch. x. 21). **For he dwelt**—literally, *and* (sc. at that time) *he was dwelling*—**in the plain** — rather "oak groves" (*vide* ch. xiii. 18)—**of Mamre the Amorite, the brother of Eshcol, and brother of Aner,** concerning whom nothing is certainly known beyond the fact that they were Canaanitish chieftains (probably possessing some remnant of the true faith, like Melchisedeck) with whom the patriarch entered into an offensive and defensive alliance. **And these** were **confederate**—literally, *lords of covenant,* i. e. masters or possessors of a treaty (cf. "lord or possessor of dreams," ch. xxxvii. 19; "lords or masters of arrows," 2 Kings i. 8); rendered συνωμόται (LXX.) = lords of the oath, as in Neh. vi. 18, ἔνορκοι (LXX.)—**wit Abram.**

Ver. 14.—**And when Abram heard that his brother**—so called as his brother's son, or

simply as his relative (ch. xiii. 8)—**was taken captive, he**—literally, *and he*—**armed**—literally, *caused to pour forth,* i. e. drew out in a body, from a root signifying "to pour out" (Gesenius, Fürst); from a root meaning to unsheath or draw out anything as from a scabbard, and hence equivalent to *expedivit,* he got ready (Onkelos, Saadias, Rosenmüller, Bush, 'Speaker's Commentary'). Kalisch connects both senses with the root. The LXX., Vulgate, and others translate "numbered," reading יָדֶק for יָרֶק, **his trained**—literally, *initiated,* instructed, but not necessarily practised in arms (Keil); perhaps only familiar with domestic duties (Kalisch), since it is the intention of the writer to show that Abram conquered not by arms, but by faith—servants, **born in his own house**—i. e. the children of his own patriarchal family, and neither purchased nor taken in war—**three hundred and eighteen**—which implied a household of probably more than a thousand souls—**and**— along with these and his allies (*vide* ver. 24)—**pursued** them—the victorious Asiatics—**unto Dan**—which is here substituted for its older name Laish, for which *vide* Josh. xix. 47 (Ewald), though regarded by some as not the Laish Dan conquered by the Danites, but probably Dan-jaan, mentioned in 2 Sam. xxiv. 6 (Hävernick, Keil, Kalisch); against which, however, is the statement of Josephus ('Ant.,' i. 10), that this Dan was one of the sources of the Jordan. Murphy regards

Dan as the original designation of the town, which was changed under the Sidonians to Laish (lion), and restored at the conquest. Clericus suggests that the Jordan fountain may have been styled Dan, "Judge," and the neighbouring town Laish, and that the Danites, observing the coincidence of the former with the name of their own tribe, gave it to the city they had conquered. Alford is doubtful whether Dan-jaan was really different from Laish.

Ver. 15.—**And he divided himself** (i. e. his forces) **against them, he and his servants** (along with the troops of his allies), **by night, and** (falling on them unexpectedly from different quarters) **smote them, and pursued them unto Hobah.** A place Choba is mentioned in Judith xv. 5 as that to which the Assyrians were pursued by the victorious Israelites. A village of the same name existed near Damascus in the time of Eusebius, and is "probably pre-served in the village *Hoba*, mentioned by Troilo, a quarter of a mile to the north of Damascus" (Keil); or in that of *Hobah*, two miles outside the walls (Stanley, 'Syria and Palestine,' 414, k.), or in *Burzeh*, where there is a Moslem wely, or saint's tomb, called the sanctuary of Abraham (Porter's 'Handbook,' p. 492). **Which is to the left of** (i. e. to the north of, the spectator being supposed to look eastward) **Damascus.** The metropolis of Syria, on the river Chrysorrhoas, in a large and fertile plain at the foot of Antilibanus, the oldest existing city in the world, being possessed at the present day of 150,000 inhabitants.

Ver. 16.—**And he brought back all the goods.** *Col-harecush.* The LXX. translate τὴν ἵππον, as if they read רְכֻשׁ for רְכֻשׁ. **And also brought again his brother Lot, and his goods.** Καὶ πάντα τὰ ὑπάρχοντα αὐτοῦ (LXX.). **And the women also, and the people.**

HOMILETICS.

Vers. 13—16.—*The kinsman deliverer, or Abram's military expedition.* I. ABRAM'S ELEVATED PIETY. 1. *Self-forgetful magnanimity.* Had the patriarch possessed a less noble soul, the tidings of his nephew's capture would almost certainly have kindled in his breast a secret feeling of complacency. But not only in his behaviour on the occasion was there the complete absence of any such revengeful disposition as gloats with satisfaction over the punishment of a wrong-doer, there was something like a manifest unconsciousness of having ever suffered injury at Lot's hands at all. 2. *Brotherly compassion.* If he did sometimes admit to himself that his nephew had scarcely acted handsomely towards him, any feeling of resentment with which that reflection may have been associated was completely swallowed up by the sorrow which he felt for that nephew's fate. After all Lot was his dead brother's son, and was a child of God as well, and he could not choose but be affected by the melancholy news. Besides being self-forgetful, the piety of Abram was sympathetic. 3. *Active benevolence.* Meekly patient of injuries when inflicted on himself, the patriarch was ever ready to redress the wrongs of others, even of the undeserving. Nor was his philanthropy of that weakly benevolent sort which is always going to do some act of kindness to others, but never does it, or is so unaccountably slow in doing it that it comes to be practically of little use, or that would willingly extend a helping hand to the unfortunate if it could only be done without much trouble; on the contrary, it was prompt, decisive, energetic, and carried through with much labour, and at considerable risk to his own personal safety.

II. ABRAM'S MILITARY GENIUS. 1. *Unexpectedly evoked.* The last thing which ordinary minds would anticipate as an element in the character of one so good, pious, benevolent, and magnanimous as Abram the Hebrew, there is yet no essential incongruity between the talents of a soldier and the graces of a Christian; while as for the patriarch suddenly discovering all the qualities of a great commander, it is perhaps sufficient to reply that hitherto the crisis had not arrived to call them forth. The annals of warfare, both ancient and modern, attest that true military genius has not always been confined to professors of the soldier's art, but has oftentimes been discovered, of the rarest kind, in persons who, till summoned forth by Providence, have been engaged in peaceful callings. 2. *Brilliantly displayed.* In the gallant exploit of the patriarch are exhibited the tactics that from time immemorial have been adopted by all great generals—by Miltiades and Themistocles of Greece, by Julius Cæsar, by Belisarius, the general of Justinian, by Oliver Cromwell, by Napoleon, by Stonewall Jackson and Sherman of America, and again by Von Moltke of Prussia—celerity of movement, suddenness of attack, skilful division of forces, outflanking and outmarching of the enemy (cf. Lange, p. 405). 3. *Completely successful.* The foe was defeated, the prisoners and spoil were recaptured, and it does not appear that Abram or his allies lost a man. That generalship is the best which accomplishes its object at the least expense of soldiers' blood and subjects' treasure.

III. ABRAM'S WONDER-WORKING FAITH. It afforded—1. *A sufficient ground* on which to go to war. The question as to Abram's right to mingle in this contest in the Sodom valley is fairly answered by replying that Abram had the right (1) of natural affection to attempt the rescue of his relative, (2) of a sacred humanity to liberate the captive and punish the oppressor, and (3) of faith. Already God had given him the land, and we are fully warranted in regarding him as acting in this heroic expedition in the capacity of (under God) lord-paramount of the soil. 2. *The necessary power* with which to prosecute the war. Possessed of military genius though the patriarch was, it is not supposable that he entered upon this campaign against the trained armies of the conquering kings, pursuing them along a difficult and dangerous track, without first casting himself on the Almighty arm as his strength. And if that Almighty arm, in order to succour him, took the way of developing the capabilities for warfare which had hitherto been lying dormant in his soul, it was none the less true that the help which he received was Divine. 3. *The splendid victory* which resulted from the war. Whether the writer to the Hebrews (ch. xi. 34) thought of Abram when he spoke of faith's heroes subduing kingdoms and waxing valiant in the fight, it is apparent that Isaiah (ch. xli. 2, 3) ascribed the triumph of the son of Terah to the grace of God, which thus rewarded the faith which, in obedience to a Divine impulse, sprang to the relief of Lot.

IV. ABRAM'S TYPICAL CHARACTER. The symbolic foreshadowing of the great kinsman Deliverer is too obvious to be overlooked. 1. In his person the Lord Jesus Christ, like Abram, was the kinsman of those whom he delivered. 2. The work he undertook, like that of Abram, was the emancipation of his brethren. 3. As in the case of Abram, that work consisted in despoiling the principalities and powers of evil. 4. The motive by which he was impelled on this arduous warfare was, like that which inspired the patriarch, love for his kinsmen. 5. The promptitude of Christ in coming to the aid of men was typified by Abram's celerity in hastening to the rescue of Lot. 6. As the campaign of Abram, so the warfare of Christ was carried through at great expense of toil and suffering to himself. 7. In the faith of Abram was shadowed forth the calm reliance of the Saviour that all he did was in obedience to his Father's will. 8. The success with which the patriarch was rewarded was emblematic of the higher victory of Christ.

Learn—1. To imitate the piety of Abram. 2. To admire in him, if we cannot in ourselves, the possession of superior abilities. 3. To covet earnestly the wonder-working faith which he displayed. 4. To trust in the great kinsman Deliverer of which he was the type.

HOMILIES BY VARIOUS AUTHORS.

Vers. 13—16.—*Abram's expedition a sermon for the New Testament Church.* I. THE LITTLE ARMY; emblematic of the handful of Christ's disciples at the first, and of the comparative feebleness of the Church still; yet "God's strength is ever made perfect in weakness," and so "the weakness of God becomes stronger than men."

II. THE TRUSTY CONFEDERATES; regarding the Amorite chieftains as possessors of the true faith, suggestive of the united purpose and action by which the Church of Christ in all its parts should be governed, and of the weakness that springs from divided counsels.

III. THE RAPID MARCH; a picture of the holy celerity and earnest zeal with which the Church should set about her enterprise of conquering the world for Christ; a reminder of how much may be lost by delay.

IV. THE SKILFUL TACTICS; proclaiming the same doctrine as Christ—that his people should be wise as serpents; revealing the necessity for the Church making use of the most brilliant abilities she can command on all her different fields of action.

V. THE SPLENDID VICTORY; a foreshadowing of the final triumph which awaits the Church, and of the blessing which, through its instrumentality, will eventually descend upon the world.—W.

EXPOSITION.

Ver. 17.—**And the king of Sodom**—Bera, or his successor (*vide* ver. 10)—**went out to meet him** (*i. e.* Abram) **after his return from the slaughter** (perhaps too forcible an expression for mere defeat) **of Chedorlaomer, and the kings that were with him** (the entire clause from "after" is parenthetical), **at the valley of Shaveh.** A valley about two stadia north of Jerusalem (Josephus, 'Ant.,' viii. 10), supposed to be the valley of the Upper Kedron, where Absalom's pillar was afterwards erected (2 Sam. xviii. 10); which may be correct if the Salem afterwards mentioned was Jerusalem (*vide infra*); but if it was not, then the exact site of Shaveh must be left undetermined. **Which is the king's dale.** Or valley (*emek*); so styled because suitable for kingly sports or military exercises (Onkelos); because of its beauty (Poole); because Melchisedeck had his camp and palace there (Malvenda); or most likely because of the interview between him and Abram which there occurred (Keil, Lange), with which agrees the rendering τὸ πεδίον τῶν βασιλέων (LXX.).

Ver. 18.—**And Melchisedeck.** "King of righteousness" (Heb. vii. 2); an indication that the Canaanitish language was Shemitic, having been probably adopted from the original Shemite inhabitants of the country. Not a titular designation, like Augustus, Pharaoh, or Malek-ol-adel (*rex justus*) of the Mohammedan kings (Cajetan), but the name of a person; neither an angel (Origen), nor the Holy Ghost (Hieracas), nor some great Divine power (the Melchisedecians), all of which interpretations are baseless conjectures; nor Christ (Ambrose), which is contrary to Heb. vi. 20; nor Shem (Targums, Lyra, Willet, Luther, Ainsworth), which Heb. vii. 3 sufficiently negatives; but most probably a Canaanitish prince by whom the true faith was retained amid the gloom of surrounding heathenism (Josephus, Irenæus, Eusebius, Calvin, À Lapide, Delitzsch, Keil, Rosenmüller, Candlish, Bush), though it has been suggested that "the enlightenment of the king of Salem was but a ray of the sun of Abram's faith" (Kalisch), an opinion difficult to harmonise with Heb. vii. 4. **King of Salem** = "king of peace" (Heb. vii. 1). The capital of Melchisedeck was either Jerusalem, of which the ancient name was Salem, as in Ps. lxxvi. 2 (Josephus, Onkelos, Aben Ezra, Kimchi, Knobel, Delitzsch, Keil, Kalisch, Murphy, Bush); or a city on the other side Jordan *en route* from Damascus to Sodom (Ewald); or, though less likely, as being too remote from Sodom and the king's dale, Salem in the tribe of Ephraim, a city near Scythopolis, where the ruins of Melchisedeck's palace were said to exist (Jerome), and near to which John baptized (Bochart). **Brought forth bread and wine.** As a refreshment to the patriarch and his soldiers (Josephus, Calvin, Clarke, Rosenmüller), which, however, was the less necessary since the spoils of the conquered foe were in possession of Abram and his men (Kalisch); hence mainly as a symbol, not of his transference of the soil of Canaan to the patriarch, bread and wine being the chief productions of the ground (Lightfoot), or of his gratitude to Abram, who had recovered for the land peace, freedom, and prosperity (Delitzsch), or of the institution of the Supper by the Lord Jesus Christ (Bush); but of the priestly benediction which followed and of the spiritual refreshment which it conferred upon the soul of Abram (Kalisch, Murphy). The Romish idea, that the act of Melchisedeck was sacrificial, is precluded by the statement that he brought forth the bread and wine before the people, and not before God. **And he was the priest.** *Cohen;* one who undertakes another's cause, hence one who acts as mediator between God and man, though the primary signification of the root is doubtful and disputed. The necessity for this office has its ground in the sinfulness of man, which disqualifies him for direct intercourse with a holy Being (cf. Kurtz, 'Sacrificial Worship,' ch. i. *b.*). The occurrence of this term, here mentioned for the first time, implies the existence of a regularly-constituted form of worship by means of priests and sacrifices. Hence the Mosaic cultus afterwards instituted may only have been a resuscitation and further development of what had existed from the beginning. **Of the most high God.** Literally, *El-Elion*, a proper name for the Supreme Deity (occurring only here, in the narrative of Abram's interview with the kings); of which the first term, *El*, from the same root as Elohim (ch. i. 1, *q. v.*), signifies the Strong One, and is seldom applied to God without some qualifying attribute or cognomen, as El-Shaddai, or El, the God of Israel; and the second, *'Elion* (occurring frequently afterwards, as in Num. xxiv. 16; Deut. xxxii. 18; Ps. vii. 18; ix. 2), describes God as the High, the Highest, the Exalted, the Supreme, and is sometimes used in conjunction with Jehovah (Ps. vii. 18), and with Elohim (Ps. lvii. 3), while sometimes it stands alone (Ps. xxi. 8). Most probably the designation here describes the name under which the Supreme Deity was worshipped by Melchisedeck and the king of Sodom, whom Abram recognises as followers of the true God by identifying, as in ver. 22, El-Elion with Jehovah (cf. Quarry, p. 426).

Ver. 19.—**And he blessed him** (in which act appears his distinctively sacerdotal character), **and said** (the form of the benediction is poetical, consisting of two parallel stanzas), **Blessed be Abram**—so Isaac blessed Jacob (ch. xxvii. 27), and Jacob Joseph (ch. xlviii. 15), conveying in each case a Divine benediction—**of the most high God**—ל after a passive verb indicating the efficient cause (*vide* Gesenius, § 143, 2, and cf. Gen. xxxi. 15; Prov. xiv. 20)—**possessor**—so Onkelos and Calvin; but *koneh*, from *kanah*, to erect, set up, hence found or create, means founder and creator (Gesenius), combines the meanings of κτίζειν and κτᾶσθαι (Keil), contains no indistinct allusion to the doctrine of ch. i. 1 (Murphy), and is rendered ὃς ἔκτισε (LXX.) and *qui creavit* (Vulgate)—**of heaven and earth.**

Ver. 20.—**And blessed be the most high God** (cf. ch. ix. 26), **who hath delivered**—*miggen*, a word peculiar to poetry = *nathan* (cf. Prov. iv. 9; Hosea xi. 8)—**thine enemies**—*tsarecha*, also a poetical expression = *'ōyeb* (cf. Deut. xxxii. 27; Job xvi. 9; Ps. lxxxi. 15)—**into thy hand. And he**—not Melchisedeck (Jewish interpreters), but Abram (Josephus, LXX., Jonathan, Heb. vii. 6)—**gave him** (not Abram, but Melchisedeck) **tithes**—"tenths." These, being the customary offering to the Deity, were an acknowledgment of the Divine priesthood of Melchisedeck. The practice of paying tithes, primarily a voluntary tax for the servants of the sanctuary, appears to have obtained among different nations from the remotest antiquity (*vide* Dr. Ginsburg in 'Kitto's Cyclopedia,' art. Tithes). The tithal law was afterwards incorporated among the Mosaic statutes (Levit. xxvii. 30—33; Numb. xviii. 21—32)—**of all**—the spoils which he had taken (Heb. vii. 4.)

Ver. 21.—**And the king of Sodom** (who, though first coming, appears to have retired in favour of the greater personage, Melchisedeck, and to have witnessed the interview between him and Abram, but who now, on its termination, advances—**said unto Abram,** —perhaps anticipating that like donations from the spoils might be made to him as to Melchisedeck, in which case he evinced a

remarkable degree of generosity—**Give me the persons**—literally, *the souls*, i. e. those of my people whom you have recovered (cf. ch. xii. 5, in which the term is employed to describe domestic slaves)—**and take the goods to thyself** (which, Michaelis observes, he was justly entitled to do by right of conquest).

Ver. 22.—**And Abram said unto the king of Sodom, I have lift up mine hand**—a common form of swearing (Deut. xxxii. 40; Ezek. xx. 5, 6; Dan. xii. 7; Rev. x. 5, 6; cf. Virg., 'Æn.,' xii. 195)—**unto the Lord** (*Jehovah;* which, occurring in the present document, proves the antiquity of its use as a designation of the Deity), **the most high God,** —*El-Elion;* thus identifying Jehovah with the God of Melchisedeck, and perhaps of the king of Sodom (*vide supra*)—**the possessor of heaven and earth.**

Ver. 23.—**That I will not** take—literally, *if* (sc. I shall take); an abbreviation for "May God do so to me, if . . . !" (cf. 1 Sam. iii. 17; 2 Sam. iii. 35). The particle אם has the force of a negative in adjuration—**from a thread even to a shoe-latchet, and that I will not take any thing** (literally, *and if I shall take anything*) **that is thine,**—literally, *of all that* (sc. belongs) *to thee*—**lest thou shouldest say** (literally, *and thou shalt not say*), **I have made Abram rich.** Though not averse to accept presents from heathen monarchs (ch. xii. 16), the patriarch could not consent to share in the wealth of the impious Sodomites; in this a striking contrast to Lot.

Ver. 24.—**Save** — בִּלְעָדַי, compounded of בַּל, not, and עַד, unto = not unto; a particle of deprecation, meaning, "nothing shall come unto me" (cf. ch. xli. 16)—**only that which the young men**—עֲ, a primitive word (cf. Sanscrit, *nara*, man; *narî, nârî*, woman; Zend., *nære;* Greek, ἀνήρ), applied to a new-born child (Exod. ii. 26; 1 Sam. iv. 21), a youth of about twenty (ch. xxxiv. 19; xli. 12), a servant, like παῖς (ch. xxxvii. 2; 2 Kings v. 20), a common soldier (1 Kings xx. 15, 17, 19; 2 Kings xix. 6)—**have eaten, and the portion of the men who went with me, Aner, Eshcol, and Mamre; let them take their portion.**

HOMILETICS.

Vers. 17—24.—*Visited by kings.* I. THE KING OF SALEM. 1. *His exalted person.* Neither a supramundane being, an angel, the Holy Ghost, or Christ; nor one of the early patriarchs, such as Enoch or Shem; but a Canaanitish (Shemite?) prince, whose capital was Salem (Jerusalem), and who united in his person the double function of priest and monarch of his people; probably the last official representative of the primitive religion, who here advances to meet and welcome the new faith in the person of Abram, as at a later period John Baptist recognised and saluted

Christ. 2. *His twofold designation.* Melchisedeck, king of Salem, *i. e.* king of righteousness and king of peace (Heb. vii. 2) ; descriptive of—(1) *Personal excellence.* Pious in spirit and peace-loving in disposition, he was not only fitted to be a type of the Meek and Holy One, but admirably qualified to be a governor of men and a minister of religion. Happy the land whose throne is filled by purity and love, and the Church whose teachers illustrate by their lives the religion they profess! (2) *Regal sway.* Righteous in principle, as a consequence his kingly rule was peaceful in administration; thus again constituting him an eminent foreshadowing of the righteous King and Prince of peace, as well as an instructive pattern and guide to earth's rulers. When righteousness and peace occupy the throne they seldom fail to reign throughout the land. (3) *Priestly work.* The specific function of his sacerdotal office being to make peace between God and sinful men, probably by means of sacrifice, and thus to cover with righteousness as with a garment those who were exposed to condemnation, he a third time symbolised the great King-Priest of the New Testament Church ; while at the same time he seemed to proclaim this important truth, that they who labour in the priest's office should diligently strive for the salvation of souls. 3. *His mysterious appearance.* Of unknown parentage, of unrecorded genealogy, of unchronicled existence, the unique personality of this grand old king-priest flashes meteor-like across the path of the conquering patriarch, emerging from the gloom of historical obscurity, and almost instantaneously vanishing into inscrutable seclusion. Spirit-taught writers of later times discerned in this ancient figure, so enigmatical and mysterious, a Divinely-appointed type of the ever-living High Priest, " the Son who is consecrated for evermore." 4. *His regal hospitality.* Whatever additional significance attached to the banquet on the plain of Shaveh, it was clearly designed as a refreshment for the victorious patriarch and his wearied soldiers. So should earthly monarchs gratefully and sumptuously reward those who at the risk of their lives maintain the cause and vindicate the rights of the oppressed within their borders. So does heaven's King provide for his toiling followers. 5. *His priestly benediction.* (1) The blessing conferred on Abram was not simply the expression of a wish, but the actual conveyance by Divine authority of the good which it proclaimed ; and so is Christ invested with supreme power to bless and save. (2) The ascription of praise to God was a sincere declaration of the patriarch's gratitude for the heavenly succour vouchsafed in connection with his military expedition ; and so should God's redeemed ones, whom he has delivered out of the hands of the enemy, cherish a lively recollection of Divine mercies, and offer heartfelt thanksgivings through the one Mediator. 6. *His public recognition.* In presence of the king of Sodom and his people, his confederates and their forces, as well as of his own domestics, the patriarch delivered into the hands of Melchisedeck a tenth part of the spoils. Designed as a solemn act of worship to Jehovah, it was both an acknowledgment of the claim which God's minister had upon his countenance and support, and a symbol of the service,—the voluntary devotement of a liberal portion of their substance,—which should by all saints be yielded to him who has been constituted a Priest for ever after the order of Melchisedeck.

II. THE KING OF SODOM. 1. *His courteous behaviour.* Displayed in retiring before Melchisedeck's advance, and deferring the prosecution of his suit till the termination of the king-priest's interview with the patriarch, it may be regarded as suggesting (1) the politeness which in all ranks of society, but especially in intelligent and educated circles, should regulate the intercourse of man with man; (2) the deference which should be paid, by even kings and those in authority, to the ministers of religion; (3) the homage which, though unwillingly, the world sometimes is obliged to render to the Church ; and (4) the preference which should ever be assigned to heaven's business over that of earth. 2. *His generous proposal.* Made to Abram, this evinced—(1) *Lively gratitude* towards the patriarch for his distinguished services. Persons of known profligacy of character and life at times discover sparks of true nobility which proclaim them not entirely lost; and not unfrequently individuals not professing to be pious outshine the followers of Christ in acts of self-renunciation, and in thankful acknowledgment of benefits (Luke xvii. 17). (2) *Peaceful disposition* in himself, which, while it might have claimed the entire spoil, and perhaps vindicated the justness of such claim by an appeal to arms, was forward to avoid strife by asking only the persons. Even the world may occasionally instruct the Church how to follow peace with all men. (3) *Remarkable discernment* as to the respective values of men and things, being prepared to forego the goods and chattels if only the persons were restored to his dominion. 3. *His rejected liberality.* Generous as from the king of Sodom's standpoint the proposal was, it was repudiated by the patriarch—(1) *In absolute entirety,* without the reservation of so much as a thread or shoe-latchet; another proof of the wholly unworldly character of the patriarch, another instance of self-sacrificing magnanimity, of a piece with his surrender of the land to Lot. (2) *With shuddering apprehension,* lest his fair name should be contaminated by participation in the wealth of Sodom. So should God's people not let their good be evil spoken of, and in particular look well to the channels through which the treasures that enrich them come. There is ever an important difference between the wealth which proceeds from the devil and that which is bestowed by the hand of Christ. (3) *With unmistakable sincerity,* as revealed by his solemn adjuration. God's name, while to be taken in vain by none, may on appropriate occasions be appealed to by his servants to vindicate their truth-fulness. (4) *After equitable reservation* of the just claims of others, of the rations of his soldiers, which were not to be repaid, and the portions of his allies, which were not to be appropriated unless with their consent. The sacrifices made by God's people should be composed of their own, and not of their neighbour's property.

Learn—1. That God's faithful servants are sure to win the approbation of good men and the benediction of Heaven. 2. That the friendship of wicked men and the congratulations of the world should never be desired by the saints.

HOMILIES BY VARIOUS AUTHORS.

Vers. 18—20.—*A king-priest.* "And Melchizedek king of Salem brought forth bread and wine: and he was the priest of the most high God. And he blessed Abraham," &c. When the king of Sodom was beaten in a war with Chedorlaomer, Lot was involved in the overthrow. Chedorlaomer was a warrior of great power, and his very name was terrible. Five confederate kings had in vain resisted him with his three auxiliaries. He whom kings could not oppose the simple patriarch Abraham, with armed herdsmen, will attack and conquer. His kinsman Lot is in captivity; Abraham will deliver him or die in the attempt. How nobly shines the character of Abraham in this determination. Lot had separated from him through a misunderstanding, and had chosen the most fertile district, and left Abraham the least promising, yet Abraham forgets all, when his relative is in danger. At great risk he undertakes his deliverance. He armed his "trained servants," pursues the enemy, comes upon them "by night," divides his small band into three companies, and makes an assault at once on the right, the centre, and flank of the enemy. He routs and pursues them, smiting many and taking much spoil. He accomplishes above all his one desire, the restoration of Lot to liberty. As Abraham returns, flushed with conquest, he is met at the gates of Salem by Melchizedek, bringing to him bread, wine, and the Divine benediction.

I. THE DESIGNATION AND CHARACTER OF MELCHIZEDEK. He is king and priest. His name means, king of righteousness. He dwells in Salem, the place of peace. He did not go out to war; and he had no part in the quarrel between Chedorlaomer and the king of Sodom. He had lost no relatives, and had no reason for fighting. Had cunning foes attacked his city of peace, he would doubtless have driven them off if possible. A king of righteousness, he would not think it his duty to submit to unrighteousness. He was, however, left unattacked by the fierce Chedorlaomer, and took care to provoke no quarrel. Perhaps he was not assailed because universally respected as a man of peace and a priest of God. This reason may have availed in that early age, and in respect to the first war of which we have any account, but it is not certain that it would be accounted a sufficient reason now. Various have been the speculations as to who Melchizedek was. Some believed that he was Enoch come back to earth, or Job, the tried one; others, that he was Shem, the best son of Noah. This is possible, as, according to calculations made, Shem survived Abraham forty years; but it is improbable, because Moses would have spoken of

Shem by his proper name, and because that would not apply which is said of Melchizedek, in Heb. vii. 3—that he was "without father, without mother, without descent, having neither beginning of days, nor end of life." We know the ancestry of Shem, but not that of Melchizedek. The difficult passage, the third of the seventh chapter of Hebrews, means, probably, merely this—that his descent was not known, and that his priesthood was not inherited or derived from others, but one resting in his individual character. Thus Noah, Job, Hobab or Jethro, and Balaam acted as independent priests, and their offerings were recognised by God. Melchizedek, in his maintenance of the worship of God, came to be accepted as a priest, and his life was like a star shining amid the general heathenism of Canaan. He also came like a streak of light, neither the coming nor the going of which could easily be discerned. We are told of him that he was "without beginning of days or end of life." Some have therefore thought that Melchizedek was an angel or a pre-incarnation of Christ; if so, Christ would have been the type and the antitype. But that which is thought to be spoken of the man refers to his office; it was without definite beginning or ending. The Levitical priesthood had a definite beginning and ending; that of Melchizedek is never ended. The one stood in carnal ceremonies, the other in the power of a holy character. The Levitical was introduced because of the unfitness of all to become "kings and priests unto God;" but that of Melchizedek, being according to character, has no "end of days." It foreshadowed the priesthood of Christ, whose work never passeth away, but who abideth a priest continually. Melchizedek was a type of Christ, the one great High Priest, the holiest of all on earth, and who enters for us into the holiest place. The omissions concerning parentage or the beginning of his priesthood were probably designed by God, that in Melchizedek—the most prominent of patriarchal priests—there might be a more significant type of him who is a Priest for ever after the order of Melchizedek. This would explain the force of the prophecy in Ps. cx., and the words in Heb. vii. Indeed the Levitical priesthood could not supply a perfect type, for it had no one who was at once a priest and king. Moses claimed not to be priest or king. David ventured not to intrude into the priestly office. Solomon, at the dedication of the temple, when he blessed the people, gave sacrifices for the priests to offer, but he slew them not. Uzziah attempted to intrude into the priestly office, but was stricken with leprosy. Under the Jewish dispensation there was no one who in his person could represent the twofold character of Christ as the only High Priest and universal King. Under the patriarchal dispensation, and in Melchizedek, there is this very plain type of Christ in his priestly and regal character. Melchizedek may never have imagined how great was the dignity put upon him as a type of Christ. Living a quiet, pure, and devoted life, he becomes accepted by his fellows as a priest of the Most High, and becomes the type of him who was the Saviour of the world.

II. THE SIGNIFICANCE IN THE RECORDED ACTS OF MELCHIZEDEK. 1. Refreshing the weary. "Brought forth bread and wine," that Abraham might eat and be strengthened. Possibly part of the wine was poured out as an oblation. When those who met wished to seal a friendship, they brake bread or partook of a meal together. Thus the Lord's Supper is the indication of our union with Christ—of a friendship on his part for us sinners, cemented by his suffering. He gave himself to be the Bread of Life for us. We are in a spiritual sense to eat of his flesh and drink of his blood, or we have no life in us. Christ oft thus comes forth to meet the weary pilgrims and soldiers of the cross. We must remember that it is the previous weary march, the confusion and the conflict, that fits us for the enjoyment of the sacred ordinance of the Lord's Supper. We have had to battle with temptations of various kinds, and come stained with the dust and blood of battle to the table of our Lord, and here he meets us and refreshes us. We begin here to see the meaning of all the conflict and burden of life. His word acquires more meaning, and his Spirit rests upon us with greater power, as, just outside the gates of the heavenly Jerusalem, we sit and rest awhile ere pursuing our way and battling again with sin. What thoughtfulness there was in this act of Melchizedek! Single acts like these tell what is the character of a man. How it hints at the thoughtfulness of Christ for us in all our spiritual struggles! 2. Melchizedek also "blessed" Abraham. He pronounced upon him the blessing which belongs to an unselfish performance of duty. God's blessing is Abraham's great reward, and a man was its mouthpiece. Because God's approval was his reward he would not retain the spoil, although urged by the king of Sodom to keep the goods, and simply hand over the persons of his captive subjects. The approval of God expressed through conscience or the words of the good should be the Christian's one desired reward. The blessing will always come in the way of duty. 3. Melchizedek claimed the honour of the victory for God. "Blessed be the most high God, who hath delivered thine enemies into thine hand." Before the king of Sodom Abraham is reminded of his dependence on God; thus before the world the Christian shows forth his dependence on the Spirit's help and "on the Lord's death till he come." We may never be ashamed to confess Christ. Abraham readily recognised the claim of God. He gave as a thank offering a tenth part of all he had taken. That which he gave, was his by custom and right. He gives it to God. God would not accept that which is wrung, by force, from another. He would say, "Who hath required this at your hand?" "I hate robbery for burnt offering." God only accepts that which is righteously and willingly offered. If taxes are imposed men pay them, but often when it is left to their conscience they neglect their duty. Better, however, that no tenth or tithings, no ratings and taxings, should be paid than that God's cause should be sustained unwillingly. As God gives us all we possess in love, as he sustains and pardons us in love, the least we can do is to love him and readily serve in return. We should devote all we are and have to Christ. Talents and possessions are his, and should be held in stewardship as from him. Let us not, however, make the mistake of thinking that it is by our gifts or good works we are saved. Many err here. It is only through Christ that our doings or persons can be accepted, even as Abraham's gifts were through Melchizedek. Christ is our Priest and Sacrifice. Do not attempt to slight him. Trust in his merits, work, and intercession. Let him have the pre-eminence. Christ must rule in our hearts and lives. The will must be given into his hands. Life must be held as a gift from him, and eternal life will be his certain bestowal hereafter. 4. Melchizedek gave to Abraham cheering words and stimulus. This was more almost than the refreshment. Here, as we meet in communion with one another and with Christ, we have great joy. Christ cheers us. We feel we can go forth boldly, and that when sin meets us we can, in Christ's strength, say, "Stand aside;" when hopes are cut off, as Lot was from his home, we can recover them through the cross. Thus our arms are nerved and hearts made strong for the future conflict. All the joy, however, is only a foretaste of that which will be ours when Christ shall meet us at the gate of the New Jerusalem, and shall lead us in to sit down with Abraham, Isaac, Jacob, Melchizedek, and all those who have been faithful to him. What will be our joy when we shall enter to abide in the "city of peace" with the "King of righteousness" for ever! May none of us know what will be the bitter pain of those who shall vainly call from without, because the door is shut, and the Master has entered in with those who were ready.—H.

Ver. 19.—*Melchizedek blessing Abraham.* "And he blessed him, and said, "Blessed be Abram of the most high God, possessor of heaven and earth." Wherever in Scripture Melchizedek is spoken of, it is as a type of Christ (Ps. cx. 4; Heb. v., vi., vii.). We may so regard him here, and consider his act in its typical light. Outwardly the transaction was of little mark. A band of men under Chedorlaomer carried off Lot, along with other spoil, from Sodom. Abram, on learning this, armed his household, pursued the invaders, routed them, and set the captives free. On his return Melchizedek, the head of a tribe near the line of march, came out to offer refreshment to his men; and as priest of his tribe he blessed Abram. Whether the type was understood by Abram or Melchizedek matters not. These things are written for our learning. We see in them Christ bestowing his blessing.
I. THE OCCASION OF THE BLESSING. After conflict. Our Lord the antitype of Melchizedek, as King of peace (Isa. ix. 6; cf. Luke ii. 14; John xiv. 27). Yet the Christian life is emphatically one of warfare (Ephes. vi. 11—13; 2 Tim. ii. 3; cf. Gen. xxxii. 24; 1 Pet. v. 8; also Rev. ii., iii.—"to him that overcometh," &c.). The nature of that fight is against temptations to unbelief. The fight of faith (1 Tim.

vi. 12). The renewal under Christ of the battle lost in Eden (2 Tim. iv. 7 ; 1 John v. 4). Circumstances may vary. The trial may be apparent or not. There may be no outward suffering, no visible hindrance. But what a struggle is implied in 2 Cor. x. 5. It is the struggle against unbelief ; to resist the power of things seen ; to overcome "How can these things be?" to realise habitually the "city which hath foundations" (cf. Phil. iii. 20) ; to rest on God's promises in simplicity (Phil. iii. 7). As often as this struggle is honestly waged a blessing is bestowed (James i. 2 ; cf. Matt. vii. 13 , xvi. 21 , Acts xiv. 22). We naturally love spiritual ease, but trial is better (Ps. cxix. 71).

II. THE SOURCE OF THE BLESSING. "The most high God, possessor," &c. 1. All blessing is from God. We acknowledge this ; but Isa. x. 13 is a natural feeling. We instinctively look to second causes ; yet without this "looking upward" we cannot truly pray, "Thy will be done ;" we cannot really live a Godward life. Compare Melchizedek's words with our Lord's (John xiv. 13—16 ; xvi. 23), and their fulfilment in his receiving for men (Ps. lxviii. 18) all needful gifts—forgiveness, sonship, right to pray, means of grace, opportunities of work. 2. All creation used by him as means of bestowing his blessing (cf. Rom. viii. 28). Sorrows (Rom. v. 3 ; Heb. xii. 11) and joys (Rom. ii. 4) are alike instruments of good (cf. Ps. cxvi. 12 ; cxix. 67).

III. THE FRUIT OF THE BLESSING. Closer walk with God. The events of this chapter were followed by more vivid spiritual manifestations to Abram. And thus our spiritual life advances. The blessing is God's free gift ; but through conflict with evil the soul is prepared to receive it (cf. Ps. xcvii. 10). As in natural life powers are increased by exercise, or rather by God's gift on this condition, so in the spiritual the conflict of self-denial, our Saviour's blessing, and the "spirit of adoption" are inseparably linked together. "Grace for grace" should be the Christian's motto ; ever pressing onwards. And as we can assign no limits to God's blessing, so neither is there any limit to our nearness to him.—M.

Ver. 20.—*The Church militant.* I. THE ENEMIES OF THE CHURCH. Like Abram's —1. Numerous. 2. Formidable. 3. Exulting.

II. THE TRIUMPH OF THE CHURCH. Like Abram's—1. Certain. 2. Complete. 3. Final.

III. THE THANKSGIVING OF THE CHURCH. Like Abram's—1. Due to God most high. 2. Offered through the priest of the most high God. 3. Expressed in self-consecration to the service of God.—W.

Vers. 22, 23.—*Abraham's independent spirit.* "And Abraham said to the king of Sodom, I have lift up my hand unto the Lord, the most high God, the possessor of heaven and earth, that I will not take from a thread even to a shoelatchet," &c. When Lot chose the plains of Sodom he knew not what trials awaited him there. The king of Sodom was attacked and defeated. He escaped, but many of his subjects were either slaughtered or made captive. Lot was carried away by the invading host. Abraham delivers him. On his return, flushed with victory, he is met by two persons—Melchizedek and the king of Sodom. To the first he gives tithes, as a thank offering ; from the second he will not receive anything for all the risk he had run in the conflict. If Abraham had taken all the spoil, it would only have been in accordance with the general practice of that age ; but a principle, and not a custom, is his guide.

I. ABRAHAM WISHED TO AVOID PLACING HIMSELF UNDER OBLIGATION TO A WORLDLY MAN.

II. ABRAHAM WISHED TO AVOID THE APPEARANCE OF TOO GREAT INTIMACY WITH AN UNRIGHTEOUS MAN.

III. ABRAHAM WISHED TO SHOW THAT THE SERVANT OF THE MOST HIGH GOD CAN DO GOOD WITHOUT HOPE OF REWARD.

IV. ABRAHAM WISHED TO SHOW HOW UNDESIRABLE A PRACTICE IT WAS, TO GAIN BY THE MISFORTUNES OF OTHERS.

V. ABRAHAM WISHED TO SHOW THAT GOD, AND A SPIRIT OF CONTENTEDNESS, WERE A GOOD MAN'S TRUE RICHES.

How much better to act thus than to permit the ungodly to point the finger of scorn and say, with respect to professedly religious men, that they are just as greedy and worldly as the most irreligious.—H.

EXPOSITION.

CHAPTER XV.

Ver. 1.—**After these things**—the events just recorded—**the word of the Lord**—*Debar Jehovah;* the first occurrence of this remarkable phrase, afterwards so common in the Hebrew Scriptures (Exod. ix. 20 ; Numb. iii. 16 ; Deut. xxxiv. 5 ; 1 Sam. iii. 1 ; Ps. xxxiii. 6, *et passim*). That this was a personal designation of the pre-incarnate Logos, if not susceptible of complete demonstration, yet receives not a little sanction from the language employed throughout this narrative (cf. vers. 5, 7, 9, 13, 14, &c.). At least the expression denotes "the Lord manifesting himself by speech to his servant" (Murphy ; *vide* ch. i. 3)—**came** (literally, *was*) **unto Abram in a vision**—a night vision, but no dream (*vide* ver. 5). Biblically viewed, the vision, as distinguished from the ordinary dream, defines the presentation to the bodily senses or to the mental consciousness of objects usually beyond the sphere of their natural activities ; hence visions might be imparted in dreams (Numb. xii. 6), or in trances (Numb. xxiv. 4, 16, 17). **Saying, Fear not, Abram.** With allusion, doubtless, to the patriarch's mental dejection, which was probably occasioned by the natural reaction consequent upon his late high-pitched excitement (cf. 1 Kings xix. 4), which might lead him to anticipate either a war of revenge from the Asiatic monarchs (Jonathan), or an assault from the heathen Canaanites, already jealous of his growing power, or perhaps both. Wordsworth observes that the words here addressed to Abram are commonly employed in Scripture to introduce announcements of Christ (Luke i. 13, 30 ; ii. 10 ; John xii. 15 ; cf. St. John's vision, Rev. iv. 1). **I am thy shield,** and **thy exceeding great reward.** Literally, *thy reward, exceeding abundantly,* the hiphil inf. abs. הַרְבֵּה being always used adverbially (cf. Neh. ii. 2 ; iii. 33). The other rendering, "thy reward is exceeding great" (LXX., Rosenmüller, Delitzsch, Ewald), fails to give prominence to the thought that the patriarch's reward was to be the all-sufficient Jehovah himself. It is not needful to suppose with Lange an actual vision of a shield and treasure.

Ver. 2.—**And Abram said, Lord God.** *Adonai Jehovah;* the first use of these terms in combination, the second, which usually has the vowel-points of the first, being here written with the vocalisation of

Elohim. *Adonai,* an older plural form of *Adonim, pluralis excellentiæ* (Gesenius), though by some the termination is regarded as a suffix (Ewald, Fürst), is a term descriptive of the Divine sovereignty, from *adan* = *dun,* or *din,* to rule or judge ; connected with which is the Phœnician *adon,* an honorary epithet of deity, and recognised as such in Deut. x. 17 (*vide* Fürst, 'Hebrew Lexicon,' *sub voce*). **What wilt thou give me, seeing I go** — literally, *and I going* = ἐγὼ δὲ ἀπολύομαι (LXX., Jonathan) ; *ex hac vita discedam* (Rosenmüller) ; but this, though the word "go" is sometimes used in the sense of "die" (Ps. xxxix. 14), does not seem necessary—**childless**—solitary, desolate, hence devoid of offspring, as in Levit. ch. xx. 20, 21 ; Jer. xxii. 30 — **and the steward**—*Ben-Meshek;* either (1) the son of running (from *shakak,* to run) = *filius discursitatis,* i. e. the steward who attends to my domestic affairs (Onkelos, Drusius) ; or, and with greater probability, (2) the son of possession (from *mashak,* to hold), *i. e.* the possessor of my house, or heir of my property (Gesenius, Fürst, Delitzsch, Keil, Kalisch)—**of my house is this Eliezer of Damascus.** Literally, *Dammesek Eliezer.* The paronomasia of this utterance is apparent, and was obviously designed to impart a touch of pathos to the patriarch's grief by pointing out the coincidence that the *Ben-Meshek* of his house was either *Dammesek* (Damascus) in the person of Eliezer (Delitzsch, Keil), or the Damascene Eliezer (Onkelos, Syriac, Aben Ezra, Calvin, Lange, Murphy), or *Dammesek-Eliezer* as one word (Kalisch).

Ver. 3.—**And Abram said, Behold, to me thou hast given no seed : and, lo, one born in my house** (literally, *the son of my house,* i. e. Eliezer) **is mine heir.** The language of the patriarch discovers three things : (1) a natural desire to have a child of his own ; (2) a struggle to hold on by the promise in face of almost insuperable difficulties ; and (3) an obvious unwillingness to part with the hope that the promise, however seemingly impossible, would eventually be realised. This unwillingness it was which caused him, as it were, so pathetically to call the Divine attention to his childless condition ; in response to which he received an assurance that must have thrilled his anxious heart with joy.

Ver. 4.—**And, behold, the word of the Lord** came **unto him, saying, This shall not** be thine heir; but he that shall come forth out of thine own bowels shall be thine heir. Ver. 5.—**And he** (Jehovah, or "the Word of the Lord") **brought him forth abroad, and said, Look now toward heaven, and tell the stars, if thou be able to number them** (a proof that Abram's vision was not a dream): **and he said unto him, So shall thy seed be.** Hence it has been inferred that Abram's vision was miraculously quickened to penetrate the depths of space and gaze upon the vastness of the stellar world, since the stars visible to the naked eye would not represent an innumerable multitude (Candlish). Ver. 6.—**And he believed in the Lord.** The hiphil of the verb *aman*, to prop or stay, signifies to build upon, hence to rest one's faith upon; and this describes exactly the mental act of the patriarch, who reposed his confidence in the Divine character, and based his hope of a future seed on the Divine word. **And he counted it to him.** Ἐλογίσθη αὐτῷ (LXX.), which is followed by nearly all the ancient versions, and by Paul in Rom. iv. 3; but the suffix ה (a feminine for a neuter, as in Job v. 9; Ps. xii. 4; xxvii. 4;

vide Glass, ' Phil.,' lib. iii. cp. i. 19), clearly indicates the object of the action expressed by the verb הָשַׁב, to think, to meditate, and then to impute (λογίζομαι), followed by לְ of pers. and acc. of the thing (cf. 2 Sam. xix. 20; Ps. xxxii. 2). The thing in this case was his faith in the Divine promise. For righteousness צְדָקָה — εἰς δικαιοσύνην (LXX.); neither for merit and justice (Rabbi Solomon, Jarchi, Kalisch), nor as a proof of his probity (Gesenius, Rosenmüller); but unto and with a view to justification (Rom. iv. 3), so that God treated him as a righteous person (À Lapide), not, however, in the sense that he was now "correspondent to the will of God both in character and conduct" (Keil), but in the sense that he was now before God accepted and forgiven (Luther, Calvin, Murphy, Candlish), which "passive righteousness," however, ultimately wrought in him an "active righteousness of complete conformity to the Divine will" ('Speaker's Commentary').

HOMILETICS.

Vers. 1—6.—*Under the stars with God.* I. DEJECTED BEFORE GOD. 1 *Apprehensive of danger.* Victorious over the Asiatic monarchs, Abram nevertheless dreaded their return. Signal deliverances are not seldom followed by depressing fears; e. g. David (1 Sam. xxvii. 1) and Elijah (1 Kings xix. 10). Having emancipated the people of the land by breaking "the yoke of their burden, and the staff of their shoulder, the rod of their oppressor," he yet feared an outbreak of their hostility. The enmity of those they serve is not an infrequent reward of patriots: witness Moses (Exod. xvii. 4) and Christ (John x. 31). 2. *Disappointed in hope.* Notwithstanding repeated assurances that he would one day become a mighty nation, the long-continued barrenness of Sarai appears to have lain upon his heart like a heavy burden. Partaking to all more or less of the nature of a deprivation, the lack of offspring was to Abram an acute grief and serious affliction. The pent-up yearnings of his nature, rendered the more intense by reason of the promise, could not longer be restrained. In language full of pathos he complains to God about his childless condition. So "hope deferred maketh the heart sick" (Prov. xiii. 12). 3. *Anxious about the promise.* He could not discern the possibility of its fulfilment, with years rapidly advancing on himself and Sarai. It is doubtful if any saints, more than Abram, can predict beforehand how the Divine promises shall be accomplished. Yet a recollection of whose promises they are should enable them, as it might have assisted him, to perceive that not a single word of God's can fall to the ground. But, owing partly to limitations in the human mind and imperfections in the human heart, doubts insensibly insinuate themselves against even the clearest and the strongest evidence. And when danger, disappointment, and doubt conjoin to invade the soul, dejection must inevitably follow.

II. COMFORTED BY GOD. 1. *A shield for his peril.* Divinely given, all sufficient, ever present. "I," Jehovah, "am," now and always, "thy shield"—*i. e.* thine impregnable defence. And the like protection is vouchsafed to Abram's children when imperilled: as to character, Divine (Prov. xxx. 5); as to extent, complete, universal, defending from all forms of evil, warding off assaults from all quarters (Ps. v. 12); as to duration, perpetual (Ps. cxxi. 8). 2. *A solace for his sorrow.* Happy as the birth of an heir in Sarai's tent would make him, Jehovah gives him to understand that not that was to be his recompense for the trials he had passed through, the sacrifices he had made, and the feats he had performed since leaving Ur, but himself. God's saints are prone to seek their happiness in God's gifts, rather than in the Giver. Here they are recalled along with Abram to the sublime thought that God himself is his people's best reward, and that the possession and enjoyment of his friendship should abundantly compensate for the absence of creature comforts, however dearly prized and ardently desired. 3. *A son for his heir.* Instead of Eliezer, whom in his perplexity he thought of adopting as his son, a veritable child of his own is promised. Let saints learn how blind is human reason, and how feeble faith becomes when it tries to walk by sight; let them also notice and consider how sure are God's promises, and how inexhaustible are God's resources.

III. BELIEVING IN GOD. 1. The *object* of Abram's faith. That at this stage of the patriarch's history attention is so markedly directed to his faith can only be explained on the supposition that he now for the first time clearly and implicitly received, embraced, and rested in the promise of a seed, and consequently of a Saviour. And the faith which justifies and saves under the gospel dispensation has an outlook nothing different from that of Abram. The object which it contemplates and appropriates is not simply the Divine promise of salvation, but the specific offer of a Saviour. God is the Justifier of him who believes in Jesus (Rom. iii. 26). 2. The *ground* of Abram's faith. Neither reason nor sense, but the solemnly given, clearly stated, perfectly sufficient, wholly unsupported word of God. And of a like description is the basis of a Christian's faith—God's promise in its naked simplicity, which promise (of a Saviour, or of salvation through Jesus Christ) has, like that delivered to Abram, been solemnly announced, clearly exhibited, declared to be perfectly sufficient, but left wholly unsupported in the gospel (John iii. 36). 3. The *acting* of Abram's faith. It was instantaneous, accepting and resting on the Divine promise the moment it was explicitly made known; full-hearted, without reservation of doubt or uncertainty, implicitly reposing on the naked word of God; and conclusive, not admitting of further opening of the question, "being fully persuaded that God was able also to perform that which he had promised" (Rom. iv. 21).

IV. ACCEPTED WITH GOD. Whatever exegesis be adopted of the clause, "it was counted unto him for righteousness," the transaction which took place beneath the starry firmament is regarded in the New Testament as the pattern or model of a sinner's justification, and employed to teach—1. The *nature* of justification, which is the reckoning of righteousness to one in himself destitute of such excellence, and, on the ground of such imputed righteousness, the acquittal in the eye of the Divine law of one otherwise obnoxious to just condemnation. Possessing no inherent righteousness of his own, Abram had the righteousness of another (not at that time revealed to him) set to his account, and was accordingly justified or declared righteous before God. 2. The *condition* of justification, which is not works, but faith, Abram having been accepted solely on the ground of belief in the Divine promise (Rom. iv. 2—5); not, however, faith as an *opus operatum* or meritorious act, but as a subjective condition, without which the act of imputation cannot proceed upon the person. 3. The *time* of justification, which is the instant a soul believes, whether that soul be cognisant of the act or not, Abram again being justified, according to the Scripture, from the moment he accepted the Divine promise, though it is not said that Abram at the time was aware of the indemnatory act passed in his favour in the court of heaven.

Lessons:—1. God's saints may sometimes be cast down in God's presence (Ps. xliii. 5). 2. It is God's special character and care to comfort those who are cast down (2 Cor. vii. 6). 3. God's promises are the wells of comfort which he has opened for the solace of dejected saints.

HOMILIES BY VARIOUS AUTHORS.

Ch. xv.—*Faith.* The substance of this chapter is the special intercourse between Jehovah and Abram. On that foundation faith rests. It is not feeling after God, if haply he be found; it is a living confidence and obedience, based upon revelation, promise, covenant, solemn ratification by signs, detailed prediction of the future. God said, " I am thy shield and thy exceeding great reward "—*i. e.* I am with thee day by day as the God of providence ; I will abundantly bless thee hereafter.   The promise of a numerous offspring, of descendants like the stars for multitude, was not a merely temporal promise, it was a spiritual blessing set in the framework of national prosperity.   " Abram believed in the Lord ; and he counted it to him for righteousness" (ver. 6 ; cf. Rom. iv. ; Gal. iii. ; Heb. xi.).

I. It was a FAITH IN THE PERSONAL, revealed, covenant Jehovah ; not merely in a word, or in a sign, or in a prospect, but " in the Lord."

II. The GRACIOUS BOND OF RELATIONSHIP AND OF COVENANT.   Faith on the one side, God dealing with a sinful creature as righteous on the other.   The elements of that bond are (1) gracious acceptance, (2) gracious revelation, (3) gracious reward of obedience—in each case vouchsafed to faith.   Thus the faith which justifies is the faith which sanctifies, for the sanctification, as the Apostle Paul shows in Rom. viii., is as truly the outcome of the grace which accepts as the acceptance itself.—R.

Ver. 1.—*What the Lord is to his people.*   I. A SHIELD against—1. The charges of the law (Isa. xlv. 24).   2. The accusations of conscience (Rom. xv. 13).   3. The force of temptation (Rev. iii. 10).   4. The opposition of the world (Rom. viii. 31). 5. The fear of death (Heb. ii. 15).

II. A REWARD—1. For sufferings patiently endured (2 Tim. ii. 12).   2. For sacrifices cheerfully made (Matt. xix. 28).   3. For service faithfully accomplished (Rev. ii. 28).

Lessons :—1. Admire the exceeding richness of Divine grace.   2. Appreciate the fulness of Divine salvation.   3. Realise the height of Divine privilege accorded to the saint.—W.

Ver. 6.—*Faith and Righteousness.*   "And he believed in the Lord ; and he counted it to him for righteousness."   Even by itself this passage claims attention. How does the idea of righteousness come into it at all?   What is meant by "counting" or "imputation"?   And what is the connection between belief and imputed righteousness?   But it does not stand alone.   (1) In Ps. cvi. 30 (cf. Num. xxv. 7) the same " counting " takes place on an act of an entirely different character ; and (2) it is thrice quoted in the New Testament as an example of the action of faith in the spiritual life.   Imputation must not be explained away.   Its meaning is seen in Levit. vii. 18 ; xvii. 4 ; 2 Sam. xix. 19.   There is here the germ of "the Lord our righteousness."   In Rom. iv. 3—5, 23—25, St. Paul refers to it as an instance of justification by faith, connecting it with "the reward ;" and this again with forgiveness and acceptance (Ps. xxxii. 2), the psalm almost repeating the words of the text (see also Gal. iii. 6).   We need not suppose that now for the first time Abram was accepted of God, or that he alone was counted righteous.   Mark, Abram believed not merely the particular promise, but "in the Lord."   This instance is specially noticed by St. Paul as an instance of faith, because from the nature of the case there was no opportunity of action.

I. THE WORKING OF FAITH — simple belief of what God has said, because he is true ; casting all care upon him.   No merit in this.   Faith is the channel, not the source of justification.   By the look of faith the dying Israelites lived (Num. xxi. 9), but the healing was from God.   God offers salvation freely (John vii. 37 ; Rev. xxii. 17), because he loves us even while in our sins (Ephes. ii. 4).   What hinders that love from being effectual is unbelief.   Many "believe a lie"—*e. g.* that they must become better ere they can believe (cf. Acts xv. 1).   Primary lesson of practical Christianity is that we must begin by receiving, not by giving ; must learn to believe his word because it is his word.   This delivers from the spirit of bondage (Rom. viii. 15), and enables to ask with confidence (Rom. viii. 32).   And this faith is counted for righteousness.

II. FAITH GROWS BY USE.   It is the gift of God (Ephes. ii. 8), but it is given according to laws.   Sometimes it springs up suddenly—*e. g.* Nathanael, St. Paul, the Philippian jailer ; but usually it is like the growth of the seed, hardly to be traced— a gradual growth from efforts to live by faith.   Let none think, I can believe when I will.   The endeavour delayed will meet with many difficulties, suggestions of doubt, or habits of indecision. And let none despise the training which prepares the soul to believe. It may seem to be labour in vain, yet the Holy Spirit may be working unseen to prepare the soul for life and peace.

III. FAITH LEADS TO HOLINESS. It renders possible a service which cannot otherwise be given. The faith which was counted to Abram for righteousness formed the character which enabled him afterwards to offer up Isaac (cf. James ii. 21—23). Thus growth in holiness is the test of real faith. There is a faith which has no power (cf. James ii. 19; 1 Cor. xiii. 2; 2 Tim. iv. 10). It is with the heart that man believes unto righteousness (cf. Ps. lxxxiv. 6,7; Prov. iv. 23).—M.

EXPOSITION.

Ver. 7.—**And he** (Jehovah, or the Word of the Lord) **said unto him** (after the act of faith on the part of the patriarch, and the act of imputation or justification on the part of God, and in explication of the exact nature of that relationship which had been constituted between them by the spiritual transaction so described), **I am the Lord that brought thee out of Ur of the Chaldees** (vide ch. xi. 28), **to give thee this land to inherit** (or, to possess) **it.**

Ver. 8.—**And he said, Lord God** (Adonai Jehovah; vide ver. 2), **whereby shall I know that I shall inherit it?** Not the language of doubt, though slight misgivings are not incompatible with faith (cf. Judges vi. 17; 2 Kings xx. 8; Luke i. 34), and questioning with God "is rather a proof of faith than a sign of incredulity" (Calvin); but of desire for a sign in confirmation of the grant (Luther), either for the strengthening of his own faith (Chrysostom, Augustine, Keil, 'Speaker's Commentary'), or for the sake of his posterity (Jarchi, Michaelis), or for some intimation as to the time and mode of taking possession (Murphy). Rosenmüller conceives the question put in Abram's mouth to be only a device of the narrator's to lead up to the subject following.

Ver. 9.—**And he said unto him, Take me** (literally, for me, i. e. for my use in sacrifice) **an heifer of three years old.** So rightly (LXX., Syriac, Samaritan, Arabic, Josephus, Bochart, Rosenmüller, Keil); not three heifers (Onkelos, Jarchi, Kimchi, et alii). **And a she goat of three years old, and a ram of three years old.** These offerings, afterwards prescribed by the law (Exod. xxix. 15; Num. xv. 27; xix. 2; Deut. xxi. 3), were three in number, and of three years each, to symbolise him who was, and is, and is to come (Wordsworth); perhaps rather to indicate the perfection of the victim in respect of maturity (Murphy). Cf. Ganymede's offering (in 'Lucian's Dialogues') of a three years old ram for a ransom. **And a turtle-dove, and a young pigeon**—also prescribed by the law (Levit. i. 14; Luke ii. 24).

Ver. 10.—**And he took unto him all these, and divided** (a word occurring only here in Genesis, and supposed by Michaelis to have been taken by Moses from the ancient document from which he transcribed this portion of his work. The word is afterwards found in Cant. ii. 17, and Jer. xxxiv. 18) **them in the midst,**—μέσα (LXX.); in equal parts (Onkelos)—**and laid each piece one against another: but the birds divided he not.** So afterwards in the Mosaic legislation (Levit. i. 7). Wordsworth detects in the non-dividing of the birds an emblem of "the Holy Spirit, the Spirit of peace and love, which is a Spirit of unity," and of "Christ's human spirit, which was not divisible." Kalisch, with more probability, recognises as the reason of their not being divided the fact that such division was not required, both fowls being regarded as one part of the sacrifice only, and each, as the half, being placed opposite the other. Wordsworth numbers seven parts in the sacrifice, and sees a symbol of completeness and finality, the number seven being the root of shaba, to swear (Gesenius, p. 802); Kalisch reckons four, which he regards as "denoting perfection, but rather the external perfection of form than the internal one of the mind," and pointing "to the perfect possession of the Holy Land." The ritual here described is the same which was afterwards observed among the Hebrews in the formation of covenants (cf. ch. xxxiv. 18), and appears to have extensively prevailed among heathen nations (cf. 'Iliad,' b. 124, "ὅρκια πιστὰ ταμόντες;" and the Latin phrase, "fœdus icere").

Ver. 11.—**And when the fowls**—literally, and the bird of prey, a collective singular with the article, as in ch. xiv. 13, symbolising the Egyptians and other adversaries of Israel, as in Ezek. xvii. 3, 7, 12; xxxix. 4, 17; Rev. xix. 17, 18 (Knobel, Rosenmüller, Lange, Keil, Kalisch), which may be regarded as probable if the divided victims represented Israel in affliction, which is doubtful (vide supra). It does not appear necessary to attach any special significance to the descent of the vultures, which are always attracted towards carrion, and the introduction of which here completes the naturalness of the scene—**came down upon the carcases** (the

LXX. interpolates, ἐπὶ τὰ διχοτομήματα), **Abram drove them away.** Literally, *caused them to be blown away,* i. e. by blowing. "Though Abram is here represented as the instrument, yet the effect is to be ascribed primarily to the tutelar agency of omnipotence" (Bush ; cf. Exod. xv. 10 ; Ezek. xxi. 31). The act of scaring the voracious birds has been taken to represent the ease with which Abram or Israel would ward off his enemies (Jonathan, Targums, Rosenmüller, Bush) ; the averting of destruction from the Israelites through Abram's merit (Kalisch, Keil) ; Abram's religious regard for and observance of God's treaty (Wordsworth) ; the patriarch's expectation that God was about to employ the sacrificial victims for some holy purpose (Alford) ; simply his anxiety to preserve the victims pure and unmutilated for whatever end they might have to serve (Murphy).

Ver. 12.—**And when the sun was going down.** Literally, *was about to go down* (cf. Gesenius, § 132). The vision having commenced the previous evening, an entire day has already passed, the interval being designed to typify the time between the promise and its fulfilment (Kalisch). **A deep sleep**—*tardemah* (cf. Adam's sleep, ch. ii. 21) ; ἔκστασις (LXX.) ; a supernatural slumber, as the darkness following was not solely due to natural causes—**fell upon Abram**; **and, lo, an horror of great darkness**—literally, *an horror, a great darkness,* i. e. an overwhelming dread occasioned by the dense gloom with which he was encircled, and which, besides being designed to conceal the working of the Deity from mortal vision (Knobel), was meant to symbolise the Egyptian bondage (Grotius, Calvin, Rosenmüller, Keil, Kalisch), and perhaps also, since Abram's faith embraced a larger sphere than Canaan (Heb. xi. 10, 14, 16), and a nobler seed than Sarah's son (John viii. 56), the sufferings of Christ (Wordsworth, Inglis) —**fell upon him.**

Ver. 13.—**And he said unto Abram, Know of a surety**—literally, *knowing know* (cf. ch. ii. 17 ; *vide* Ewald's 'Hebrew Syntax,' § 312)—**that thy seed shall be a stranger in a land which is not theirs** (literally, *not to them,* viz., Egypt, or Egypt and Canaan, according to the view which is taken of the point of departure for the reckoning of the 400 years), **and shall serve them** (*i. e.* the inhabitants of that alien country) ; **and they** (*i. e.* these foreigners) **shall afflict them**— three different stages of adverse fortune are described : — (1) exile ; (2) bondage ; (3) affliction (Murphy) ; or the two last clauses depict the contents of the first (Kalisch)— **four hundred years.** The duration not of their affliction merely, but either of their bondage and affliction, or more probably of their exile, bondage, and affliction ; either a round number for 430 (Calvin, Rosenmüller, Keil, Alford), to be reckoned from the date of the descent into Egypt (Kalisch, Lange), as Moses (Exod. xii. 39) and Stephen (Acts vii. 6) seem to say, and to be reconciled with the statement of Paul (Gal. iii. 17) by regarding the death of Jacob as the closing of the time of promise (Lange, Inglis) ; or an exact number dating from the birth of Isaac (Willet, Murphy, Wordsworth), which was thirty years after the call in Ur, thus making the entire interval correspond with the 430 years of Paul, or from the persecution of Ishmael (Ainsworth, Clarke, Bush), which occurred thirty years after the promise in ch. xii. 3.

Ver. 14.—**And also that nation** (the name of which he does not reveal, in case of seeming to interfere with the free volition of his creatures, who, while accomplishing his high designs and secret purposes, are ever conscious of their moral freedom), **whom they shall serve, will I judge :**—*i. e.* punish after judging, which prediction was in due course fulfilled (Exod. vi. 11)—**and afterward shall they come out with great substance**—*recush* (cf. ch. xiii. 6 ; *vide* Exod. xii. 36).

Ver. 15.—**And thou shalt go to thy fathers in peace** (cf. ch. xxv. 8 ; xxxv. 29 ; xlix. 33). Not a periphrasis for going to the grave (Rosenmüller), since Abram's ancestors were not entombed in Canaan ; but a proof of the survival of departed spirits in a state of conscious existence after death (Knobel, Murphy, Wordsworth, 'Speaker's Commentary,' Inglis), to the company of which the patriarch was in due time to be gathered. The disposal of his remains is provided for in what follows. **Thou shalt be buried in a good old age.**

Ver. 16.—**But in the fourth generation**— τετάρτῃ δὲ γενεᾷ (LXX.) ; but, more correctly, *the fourth generation,* calculating 100 years to a generation. "Caleb was the fourth from Judah, and Moses from Levi, and so doubtless many others" (Bush). Drs. Oort and Kuenen, reckoning four generations as a far shorter space of time than four centuries, detect a contradiction between this verse and ver. 13, and an evidence of the free use which the ancient and uncritical Israelitish author made of his materials ('Bible for Young People,' vol. i. p. 158). On the import of דור *vide* ch. vi. 9—**they shall come hither again** (literally, *shall return hither*): **for the iniquity of the Amorites is not yet full.** Literally, *for not completed the iniquity of the Amorites* (vide ch. xiv. 7 ; here put for the entire population) *until then* (the same word as "hither," which is its usual signification).

Ver. 17.—**And it came to pass, that, when the sun went down,**—literally, *and it was* (*i. e.* this took place), *the sun went down* ; less accurately, ἐπεὶ δὲ ὁ ἥλιος ἐγένετο πρὸς δυσμὰς (LXX.), which was the state of matters in ver. 12. Here the sun, which was then setting, is described as having set—**and it was dark,**—literally, *and darkness was, i. e.* a darkness that might be felt, as in ver. 12 ; certainly not φλὸξ ἐγίνετο (LXX.), as if there were another flame besides the one specified in the description—**behold a smoking furnace,**—the תַּנּוּר, or Oriental furnace, had the form of a cylindrical fire-pot (cf. Gesenius, p. 869 ; Keil *in loco*)—**and a burning lamp**—a lamp of fire, or fiery torch, emerging from the smoking stove ; an emblem of the Divine presence (cf. Exod. xix. 18)—**that passed between those pieces**—in ratification of the covenant.

Vers. 18—21.—**In that day the Lord made a covenant**—literally, *cut a covenant* (cf. ὅρκια τέμνειν, *fœdus icere*). On the import of בְּרִית *vide* ch. ix. 9)—**with Abram, saying, Unto thy seed have I given this land, from the river of Egypt**—the Nile (Keil, Kurtz, Hengstenberg, Kalisch) rather than the *Wady el Arish*, or Brook of Egypt (Knobel, Lange, Clarke), at the southern limits of the country (Numb. xxxiv. 5 ; Josh. xv. 4 ; Isa. xxvii. 12)—**unto the great river, the river Euphrates.** The ideal limits of the Holy Land, which were practically reached under David and Solomon (*vide* 1 Kings iv. 21 ; 2 Chron. ix. 26), and which embraced the following subject populations, ten in number, " to convey the impression of universality without exception, of unqualified completeness" (Delitzsch). **The Kenites,**—inhabiting the mountainous tracts in the south-west of Palestine, near the Amalekites (Numb. xxiv. 21 ; 1 Sam. xv. 6 ; xxvii. 10) ; a people of uncertain origin, though (Judges i. 16 ; iv. 11) Hobab, the brother-in-law of Moses, was a Kenite—**and the Kenizzites,**—mentioned only in this passage ; a people dwelling apparently in the same region with the Kenites (Murphy), who probably became extinct between the times of Abraham and Moses (Bochart), and cannot now be identified (Keil, Kalisch), though they have been connected with Kenaz the Edomite, ch. xxxvi. 15, 42 (Knobel)—**and the Kadmonites,**—never again referred to, but, as their name implies, an Eastern people, whose settlements

extended towards the Euphrates (Kalisch)—**and the Hittites,**—the descendants of Heth (*vide* ch. x. 15) ; identified with the Kheta and Katti of the Egyptian and Assyrian monuments, and supposed by Mr. Gladstone to be the Kheteians of the 'Odyssey;' a powerful Asiatic tribe who must have early established themselves on the Euphrates, and spread from thence southward to Canaan and Egypt, and westward to Lydia and Greece, carrying with them, towards the shores of the Ægean Sea, the art and culture of Assyria and Babylon, already modified by the forms and conceptions of Egypt. The northern capital of their empire was Carchemish, about sixteen miles south of the modern Birejik ; and the southern Kadesh, on an island of the Orontes (Prof. Sayce in ' Frazer's Magazine,' August, 1880, art. ' A forgotten Empire in Asia Minor ')—**and the Perizzites, and the Rephaims** (*vide* ch. xiii. 7 ; xiv. 5), **and the Amorites, and the Canaanites, and the Girgashites, and the Jebusites** (*vide* ch. x. 15—19). The boundaries of the Holy Land as here defined are regarded by some (Bohlen) as contradictory of those designated in Numb. xxxiv. 1—12. But (1) the former may be viewed as the ideal (or poetical), and the latter as the actual (and prosaic), limits of the country assigned to Israel (Hengstenbreg, Keil) ; or (2) the former may represent the maxima, and the latter the minima, of the promise, which admitted of a larger or a smaller fulfilment, according as Israel should in the sequel prove fit for its occupation (Augustine, Pererius, Willet, Poole, Gerlach, Kalisch, and others) ; or, (3) according to a certain school of interpreters, the former may point to the wide extent of country to be occupied by the Jews on occasion of their restoration to their own land, as distinguished from their first occupation on coming up out of Egypt, or their second on returning from Babylon ; or (4) the rivers may be put for the countries with which the promised land was coterminous (Kurtz, Murphy) ; or (5) strict geographical accuracy may not have been intended in defining the limits of the land of promise ('Speaker's Commentary,' Inglis).

HOMILETICS.

Ver. 18.—*Taken into covenant.* I. THE BLESSING OF THE COVENANT. 1. The *ultimate* blessing, to which, in both the commencement and close of the present section, the prominence is assigned, was *a splendid inheritance*—the land of Canaan for his descendants, and for himself the better country, of which that earthly possession was a type. 2. The *mediate* blessing, through which alone the last could be reached, was *a distinguished seed*—a numerous posterity to occupy the land, and a living Saviour to secure for himself the better country. 3. The *proximate* blessing, to be enjoyed while as yet the second and the third were unfulfilled, was *a celestial alliance* by which Jehovah himself engaged to be his shield and exceeding great reward.   It is obvious that these are the blessings which the gospel confers on believers—a heavenly Friend, an all-sufficient Saviour, a future inheritance; whence the Abrahamic covenant was nothing different from the covenant of grace.

II. THE REASON OF THE COVENANT.   The essential idea in a covenant being a visible pledge for the fulfilment of a promise, the necessity for such a guarantee on the present occasion, it is apparent, could not lie with God.   On the contrary, the proposal on the part of God to bind himself by a superadded engagement to implement his own gracious and spontaneous promise was an explicit condescension, if not to the feebleness of the patriarch's faith, at least to the weakness of his human nature. Perhaps the recollection of who Jehovah was, and what he had already accomplished in bringing Abram from Ur, should have proved sufficient to authenticate the promise; but it would almost seem as if human nature, in its innocent no less than in its fallen state, instinctively craved the assistance of external symbols to enable it to clearly apprehend and firmly grasp the unseen and spiritual blessings that are wrapt up in God's promises.   In the garden of Eden the tree of life was Adam's sacramental pledge of immortality; after the Flood the many-coloured rainbow was a sign to Noah; in the Hebrew Church material symbols of unseen verities were not awanting; while in the Christian Church the passover and circumcision have been replaced by the Lord's Supper and baptism.   The reasons that required the institution of these external signs may be held as having necessitated the solemn ritual which was exhibited to Abram.

III. THE SYMBOLS OF THE COVENANT.   1. *The sacrificial victims.*   Seeing that these were afterwards prescribed in the Mosaic legislation, which itself was a shadow of the good things to come, to be employed as propitiatory offerings, it is impossible not to regard them, though not necessarily understood as such by Abram, as types (not of Israel, Abram's seed after the flesh simply, nor of the Church of God generally, *i. e.* Abram's seed according to the spirit, though perhaps neither of these should be excluded, but) of Abram's greater Seed, whose perfect, Divinely-appointed, and substitutionary sacrifice alone constitutes the basis of the everlasting covenant.   2. *The smoking furnace and the burning lamp.*   Compared with the smoke and fire that afterwards appeared on Sinai when Jehovah descended to covenant with Israel, and the pillar of cloud and fire that led the march of Israel from Egypt, these at once suggest their own interpretation.   They were emblems of God's presence, and may be viewed as suggesting (1) the combination of justice and mercy in the Divine character, and (2) the twofold attitude in which the Deity exhibits himself to men according as they are his enemies or friends.

IV. THE IMPORT OF THE COVENANT.   Partly through visible sign, partly in spiritual vision, partly by audible words, the patriarch was instructed as to—1. *The objective basis of his own justification,* which was neither personal merit nor faith considered as an *opus operatum,* but the Divinely-appointed sacrifice which God was graciously pleased to accept in propitiation for human sin.   2. *The true security for God's fulfilment of the promise,* which was not any outward sign or token, but the everlasting covenant which in mysterious symbol had been unfolded to him.   3. *The interval of discipline allotted to the heirs of the land;* for his descendants three generations of exile, servitude, and affliction, to prepare them for receiving Canaan in the fourth; and for himself a continual sojourning, without a final settling within its borders; in both cases emblematic of the saint's experience after justification and before glorification.   4. *The ultimate assumption of the inheritance by his seed*—a Divine voice solemnly foretelling their return from captivity, as it afterwards declared that his spiritual descendants should be emancipated and brought back to their celestial abode, and a Divine vision unfolding to his gaze the wide extent of territory they should eventually possess—perhaps the limits of the earthly land melting away, as his spirit stood entranced before the gorgeous panorama, into the confines of the better country.   5. *His own certain passage to the heavenly Canaan,* for which he was even at that time looking—a promise which belongs individually to all who are the children of Abram by faith in Jesus Christ.

See from this subject—1. The fulness of Divine blessing which the covenant contains.   2. The depth of Divine condescension which the covenant reveals.   3. The glorious securities which the covenant affords.

HOMILIES BY VARIOUS AUTHORS.

Vers. 7, 8.—*The strength and weakness of faith.* I. FAITH'S SOURCE OF STRENGTH. 1. Looking up to the Divine character—"I am the Lord." 2. Looking back to the Divine grace—"that brought thee out of Ur of the Chaldees." 3. Looking out to the Divine promise—"to give thee this land to inherit it."

II. FAITH'S OCCASION OF WEAKNESS. 1. Looking forward—the fulfilment of the promise seeming far away. 2. Looking in—discovering nothing either in or about itself to guarantee its ultimate realisation.—W.

Ver. 11.—*The silent worshipper.* I. THE NATURE OF ABRAM'S WORSHIP. 1. Divine in its appointment. 2. Simple in its ritual. 3. Sacrificial in its character. 4. Believing in its spirit. 5. Patient in its continuance. 6. Expectant in its attitude.

II. THE INTERRUPTIONS OF ABRAM'S WORSHIP. 1. *What they were.* The descent of the fowls may be regarded as emblematic of those obstructions to communion with God which arise from—(1) The principalities and powers of the air. (2) The persecutions and oppressions (or, where these are absent, the pleasures and engagements) of the world. (3) The disturbances and distractions of vain thoughts and sinful motions in the heart. 2. *How they were removed.* (1) By watchfulness. (2) By opposition. (3) By perseverance. (4) By Divine help—the breath of Abram's mouth being probably accompanied by a wind from God.

III. THE ACCEPTANCE OF ABRAM'S WORSHIP. This was proved—1. By the approach of God at night-fall towards the scene. 2. By the supernatural revelation accorded to the patriarch. 3. By the passage of the symbol of Jehovah's presence between the divided victims. 4. By the announcement that God had taken him into covenant with himself. 5. By the vision of the land which was granted to him.

Learn—1. The sinfulness and worthlessness of all forms of worship except that which God has appointed. 2. The need for self-examination and Divine assistance when engaged in serving God. 3. The certain acceptance and spiritual enrichment of those who worship God in spirit and in truth.—W.

Vers. 12—17.—*Abraham's watch and vision.* "And when the sun was going down, a deep sleep," &c. The great blessings promised are still afar off. As yet Abraham has no son to hand down his name to posterity. By means of a vision God strengthened his faith. Weird is the picture in this fifteenth chapter. See the solitary sheik in the desert offering his varied sacrifice, then watching until the sun goes down to drive off the vultures from the slain offerings. His arms become weary with waving and his eyes with their vigils. As the sun sinks below the wide-spread horizon, and night quickly steals over the desert, a horror of great darkness creeps over his spirit. Then a deep sleep falls upon him, and in that sleep come visions and a voice. The vision was of a furnace and a shining lamp moving steadily between the divided emblems. Look at the meaning of that vision.

I. It indicated the ACCEPTANCE OF THE OFFERINGS. Fire in the East is generally understood to be a solemn witness to any engagement. To confirm an oath some Orientals will point to the lamp and say, "It is witness." Nuptial ceremonies are sometimes solemnised by walking round a fire three times, and the parties uttering certain words meanwhile.

II. The furnace may have referred to THE NEED FOR PURIFICATION, AND THE LAMP TO THE CERTAINTY OF DIVINE GUIDANCE. 1. Both the Israel after the flesh and that after the spirit had to pass through the fire of persecution; but the lamp of truth had always been kept alight by the prophets, apostles, martyrs, and confessors of the Church. 2. The life and work of Christ may also have been shadowed forth in that furnace and lamp. Christ knew the bitterness of betrayal, denial, and death; but he knew also the joy of conscious sinlessness, complete self-sacrifice, and unending power of salvation. 3. They illustrated the character of the life of many believers. Trial and joy must be intermingled. As Abraham saw the vision in connection with sacrifice, so on Calvary shall we best learn the meaning of the smoking furnace and burning lamp.—H.

EXPOSITION.

CHAPTER XVI.

Ver. 1.—**Now Sarai Abram's wife bare him no children** (literally, *bare not to him*, notwithstanding the promise; the barrenness of Sarai being introduced as the point of departure for the ensuing narrative, and emphasised as the cause or occasion of the subsequent transaction): **and she had**—literally, *to her* (there was)—**an handmaid, an Egyptian** (obtained probably while in the house of Pharaoh (ch. xii. 16)—**whose name was Hagar**—"flight," from *hagar*, to flee. Cf. Hegirah, the flight of Mahomet. Not her original designation, but given to her afterwards, either because of her flight from Egypt (Ambrose, Wordsworth), or because of her escape from her mistress (Michaelis, Bush, 'Speaker's Commentary'). Though not the imaginary or mythical (Bohlen), it is doubtful if she was the real (Ainsworth, Bush), ancestor of the Hagarenes (1 Chron. v. 10, 19, 20; xxvii. 31; Ps. lxxxiii. 6, 8).

Ver. 2.—**And Sarai said unto Abram, Behold now, the Lord hath restrained me from bearing.** Literally, *hath shut me up* (*i. e.* my womb, ch. xx. 18; συνέκλεισέ με, LXX.) *from bearing.* Her advancing age was rendering this every day more and more apparent. **I pray thee go in unto my maid** (cf. ch. xxx. 3, 9). It is so far satisfactory that the proposal to make a secondary wife of Hagar did not originate with Abram; though, as Sarai's guilt in making it cannot altogether be excused, so neither can Abram be entirely freed from fault in yielding to her solicitations. **It may be that I may obtain children by her.** Literally, *be built up by her;* from *banah*, to build, whence *ben*, a son (Deut. xxv. 9; Ruth iv. 11). Calvin notes that Sarai's desire of offspring was not prompted by natural impulse, but by the zeal of faith which made her wish to secure the promised benediction. As yet it had not been clearly intimated that Sarai was to be the mother of Abram's child; and hence her recourse to what was a prevalent practice of the times, while unjustifiable in itself, was a signal proof of her humility, of her devotion to her husband, and perhaps also of her faith in God. **And Abram hearkened to the voice of Sarai.** "The faith of both was defective; not indeed with regard to the substance of the promise, but with regard to the method in which they proceeded" (Calvin).

Ver. 3.—**And Sarai Abram's wife took Hagar her maid the Egyptian, after Abram had dwelt ten years in the land of Canaan** (*i. e.* in his eighty-fifth, and her seventy-fifth year; a note of time introduced, probably, to account for their impatience in waiting for the promised seed), **and gave her to her husband Abram to be his wife.** Afterwards styled a *pilgash* or concubine (ch. xxv. 6), she is here improperly called a wife *quæ præter Dei logom in aliimum thorum inducitur* (Calvin), from whom the *pilgash* or concubine differed (1) in power over the family, which belonged solely to the true wife, not to the secondary; (2) in the manner of espousal, which in the case of the former was accompanied with solemn rites of espousal and liberal gifts of dowry; and (3) in privilege of issue, the offspring of the secondary wife having no title to inherit. The act of Sarai (cf. the similar behaviour of Stratonice, the wife of King Deiotarus, who, according to Plutarch, gave her maid Electra to her husband, and so obtained an heir to the crown) is as little to be imitated as the conduct of Abram. The apparent repetitions in vers. 1—3 do not require the hypothesis of different authorship (Tuch, Colenso, Bleek, Davidson) for their explanation, but are characteristic of the genius of Hebrew composition (cf. ch. vii. 1—10), and may even be considerably removed by connecting vers. 1, 2 with ch. xv., and commencing the new sub-section with ch. xvi. 3 (Quarry, p. 331).

Ver. 4.—**And he went in unto Hagar.** בּוֹא אֶל, a linguistic peculiarity of the Jehovist, occurring ch. xxix. 21, 30; xxx. 3, 4; xxxviii. 2, 9, 16 (Vaihinger, Davidson); but by some partitionists chs. xxix. and xxx. are assigned to the Elohist (Tuch, Bleek, De Wette). **And she conceived: and when she saw that she had conceived, her mistress was despised in her eyes.** As Hannah by Peninnah (1 Sam. i. 6); barrenness among the Hebrews having been regarded as a dishonour and reproach (ch. xix. 31; xxx. 1, 23; Levit. xx. 20), and fecundity as a special mark of the Divine favour (ch. xxi. 6; xxiv. 60; Exod. xxiii. 26; Deut. vii. 14). Whether Hagar imagined Sarai to be through her barrenness "*tanquam a Divino promisso repudiatam*" (Lyra), or anticipated Sarai's displacement from her position as Abram's wife (Inglis), she, immediately on perceiving her condition, became insolent (cf. Prov. xxx. 23).

Ver. 5.—**And Sarai said unto Abram, My wrong** be upon thee. Ἀδικοῦμαι ἐκ σοῦ (LXX.); *inique agis contra me* (Vulgate); My injury is upon thee, *i. e.* thou art the cause of it (Jonathan, Rosenmüller, Ainsworth, Clarke, 'Speaker's Commentary'); or, it belongs to thee as well as to me (Clericus, Bush, Alford); or, perhaps better, May the injury done to me return upon thee! cf.

xxvii. 13 (Keil, Kalisch, Lange, Wordsworth) —the language of passionate irritation, indicating repentance of her previous action and a desire to both impute its guilt to, and lay its bitter consequences on, her husband, who in the entire transaction was more innocent than she. **I have given my maid into thy bosom** (very imprudent, even had it not been sinful ; the result was only what might have been expected) ;—**and when she saw that she had conceived, I was despised in her eyes : the Lord judge between me and thee** (cf. 1 Sam. xxiv. 15 ; Judges xi. 27). An irreverent use of the Divine name on the part of Sarai (Calvin), and a speech arguing great passion (Ainsworth).

Ver. 6. — **But Abram said unto Sarai, Behold, thy maid is in thy hand** (regarding her still as one of Sarai's servants, though elevated to the rank of secondary wife to himself) ; **do to her as it pleaseth thee.** Literally, *the good in thine eyes ;* in which conduct of the patriarch may be seen perhaps (1) an evidence of his peaceful disposition in doing violence to his feelings as a husband in order to restore harmony to his disquieted household (Calvin), and (2) a proof that he had already found out his mistake in expecting the promised seed through Hagar (Calvin) ; but also (3) an indication of weakness in yielding to Sarai's passionate invective (Willet, Bush), and (4) an unjustifiable wrong inflicted on the future mother of his child (Candlish). **And when Sarai dealt hardly with her** — (literally, *afflicted her*, by thrusting her back into the condition of a slave (Lange, Candlish) ; though probably by stripes or maltreatment of some sort in addition (Ainsworth, Bush) —**she fled from her face.**

HOMILETICS.

Ver. 3.—*Crooked ways, or marrying with Hagar.* I. The specious proposal. 1. The *author* of it ; Sarai, the wife of Abram, a daughter of the faith, the mistress of a household. To the first, the suggestion referred to in the narrative should have been impossible ; in the second, it was inconsistent ; while, proceeding from the third, it was calculated to be harmful. 2. The *wickedness* of it. It was (1) a clear violation of the law of God (cf. ch. ii. 24 ; Matt. xix. 5 ; 1 Cor. vi. 16 ; Ephes. v. 28, 31) ; (2) a direct offence against the soul of Abram, being in reality the placing of a dangerous temptation in his way (Deut. xiii. 6 ; Rom. xiv. 13) ; and (3) an unjustifiable invasion of the liberties of Hagar. Though permitted in the providence of God to be a bondmaid in the house of Sarai, she was not in the power of her mistress to be disposed of in the way proposed, without consent either asked or obtained. 3. The *extenuations* of it. (1) The practice was common. Secondary wives being then in vogue, the scheme recommended by Sarai may not have been regarded by her as sinful. (2) The motive was good. It had its origin undoubtedly in a firm belief in the promise, and a strong desire that her husband should no longer be debarred from its realisation through her apparently permanent sterility. (3) The self-denial was great. The entire conduct of Sarai, in giving Hagar to her husband, evinced certain truly engaging features in her personal and wifely character, which must not be overlooked in forming an estimate of her peculiar action ; such as genuine humility in yielding to another the honour of being the mother of Abram's seed, and intense devotion to her husband in submitting for his sake to a displacement which must have carried anguish to her breast.

II. The sinful compliance. "Abram hearkened unto the voice of Sarai." 1. *Deliberately.* He was not surprised into this secondary marriage with the Egyptian maiden. The scheme of Sarai appears to have been talked over between them ; and if at first he had scruples in complying with her proposition, they were eventually overcome. 2. *Inconsiderately.* That is, the ulterior consequences were not taken into account in assenting to this device for the anticipation of the promised seed ; only its immediate feasibility and superficial recommendations. So men are morally shortsighted, and cannot see afar off when confronted by some sweet temptation. Had Abram only dimly discerned the outcome of Sarai's counsel, he would have seen that the thing was not of God. A perception of the coming whirlwind would often hinder the sowing of the wind. 3. *Inexcusably.* Though not dictated by carnal desire, Abram's acquiescence in Sarai's scheme was far from being faultless. It evinced a want of faith, and, indeed, a want of true spiritual discernment in supposing that what God had promised as a gift of grace could be surreptitiously snatched from his Divine hand in the way proposed, or even by any purely human stratagem ;

and a want of patience in not calmly waiting for the accomplishment of God's word in God's own time and way.

III. The SORROWFUL RESULT. 1. *Humiliation to Sarai.* Elated by the prospect of maternity, the young Egyptian slave-girl despised her mistress ; by haughtiness of carriage, perhaps silently discovering contempt for Sarai's sterility, and possibly assuming airs of superiority, as if, in consequence of approaching motherhood, anticipating her displacement from the throne of Abram's love (Prov. xxx. 23). 2. *Misery to Abram.* The womanly nature of Sarai, stung to jealousy by the success of her own plan, and incapable of longer enduring the scornful triumph of a maiden whom her own hands had transformed into a favoured rival, with something like vindictive heat turned upon her meek, submissive, and in this matter wholly innocent lord, reproaching him as, if not the cause of her barrenness, at least the patient and half-satisfied witness of her humiliation ; she almost called down upon him the judgment of Heaven. To a noble spirit like that of Abram the anguish of Sarai must have been distressing to behold ; and the pain which it occasioned must have been intensified when he came to realise the painful dilemma in which he stood between her and Hagar. 3. *Oppression to Hagar.* Reminding Sarai that Hagar, though a wife to him, was still a maid to her, the patriarch unwisely extended sanction to whatever remedy the heated breast of Sarai might devise. The result was that the favoured maiden was at once thrust back into her original condition of servitude, deprived of whatever tokens of honour and affection she had received as Abram's wife, and subjected to injurious treatment at the hands of her incensed mistress and rival, from which she ultimately sought refuge in flight.

Learn—1. That eminent saints may lapse into grievous sins. 2. That a child of God is specially liable to temptation after seasons of high religious privilege. 3. That the strongest temptations sometimes proceed from the least expected quarters. 4. That trying to anticipate the Divine promise is not an uncommon form of temptation. 5. That when God's people take to crooked ways, nothing but evil can come of it.

HOMILIES BY VARIOUS AUTHORS.

Ch. xvi.—*Hagar.* The history of Hagar has its two sides—that which is turned towards God and illustrates Divine grace, that which is turned towards man and illustrates human infirmity and sinfulness. Jehovah brought forth compassionate bestowments of revelation and promise out of his people's errors. Abram and Sarah both sinned. Hagar sinned. The angel of the Lord, representative of the continuous gracious revelation of Jehovah as a covenant God, appeared in the cloud of family sorrow, drawing once more upon it the rainbow of promise. Until the heir came there was a call for patience. Unbelief appeared at work—in the patriarch's weakness, in Sarah's harshness, in Hagar's pride and rebellion, for she was, as a member of the household, partaker of the covenant. In the wilderness appeared the messenger of grace.

I. The NAME OF THE LORD WAS THE TESTIMONY. Thou God seest me ; or, Thou God of vision. The idea is that the sight of God was deliverance. Hagar's seeing God was God seeing her. The vision was both objective and subjective. So the world has wearied itself in the wilderness of its own ignorance and moral helplessness (cf. Gal. iv. 22—31). The unspiritual, carnal mind is the bond slave, which must give way to the true heir. All true religious life is a response to revelation. In his light we see light.

II. The REVELATION TO HAGAR MAY BE CONNECTED WITH HER PERSONAL HISTORY. She turned back with a new light in her heart. Submission and obedience are commanded, but abundant reward is promised. Our life is under the eye of Jehovah and in his hand. "Thou God seest me" is the cry of a grateful memory, the note of a bright future. The nearness of God, his knowledge, may be not terror, but blessing, angels round about us, gracious sunshine of love in which we are invited to walk as children of light.—R.

Vers. 1—6.—*The maid, the mistress, and the master.* I. HAGAR'S SINS. 1. Pride. 2. Contempt. 3. Insubordination. 4. Flight.

II. SARAI'S FAULTS. 1. Tempting her husband. 2. Excusing herself. 3. Appealing to God. 4. Afflicting her servant.
III. ABRAM'S INFIRMITY. 1. Yielding to temptation. 2. Perpetrating injustice.
3. Acquiescing in oppression.—W.

EXPOSITION.

Ver. 7.—**And the angel of the Lord.** *Maleach Jehovah*, elsewhere styled *Maleach Elohim* (ch. xxi. 17 ; xxxi. 11) ; supposed but wrongly to be a creature angel (Augustine, Origen, Jerome, Hofmann, Baumgarten, Tholuck, Delitzsch, Kurtz), for the reasons chiefly (1) that the term angel commonly designates a class of spiritual beings (ch. xix. 1 ; xxxii. 1 ; Job iv. 18 ; Ps. xci. 11 ; Matt. xiii. 41 ; John xx. 12, *et passim*) ; (2) that the ἄγγελος κυρίου of the New Testament (Matt. i. 20 ; Luke ii. 9 ; Acts xii. 7) is always a created angel ; (3) that the meaning of the term מַלְאָךְ, one sent, from לָאַךְ, to depute (Gesenius), one through whom work is executed, from לָאַךְ, to work (Keil), implies a certain degree of subordination, which is afterwards more distinctly recognised (1 Chron. xxi. 27 ; Zech. i. 12) ; (4) that the distinction between the unrevealed and the revealed God was not then developed as in later times, and particularly since the advent of Christ—to every one of which arguments, however, it is comparatively easy to reply (cf. Keil and Lange *in loco*). With more force of reason believed to have been the Divine Being himself, who already as Jehovah had appeared to Abram (the Fathers, the Reformers, Hengstenberg, Keil, Lange, Hävernick, Nitzsch, Ebrard, Steir, Kalisch, Ainsworth, Bush, Wordsworth, Candlish), since—1. The *Maleach Jehovah* explicitly identifies himself with Jehovah (ver. 10) and Elohim (ch. xxii. 12). 2. Those to whom he makes his presence known recognise him as Divine (ch. xvi. 13 ; xviii. 23—33 ; xxviii. 16—22 ; Exod. iii. 6 ; Judges vi. 15, 20—23 ; xiii. 22). 3. The Biblical writers constantly speak of him as Divine, calling him Jehovah without the least reserve (ch. xvi. 13 ; xviii. 1 ; xxii. 16 ; Exod. iii. 2 ; Judges vi. 12). 4. The doctrine here implied of a plurality of persons in the Godhead is in complete accordance with earlier foreshadowings (ch. i. 26 ; xi. 7) and later revelations of the same truth. 5. The organic unity of Scripture would be broken if it could be proved that the central point in the Old Testament revelation was a creature angel, while that of the New is the incarnation of the God-Man. **Found her by a fountain of water in the wilderness.** Properly an uninhabited district suitable for pasturing flocks, from a root signifying to lead to pasture ; hence a sterile, sandy country, like that here referred to, Arabia Deserta, bordering on Egypt (ch. xiv. 6 ; Exod. iii. 1). **By the fountain.** The article indicating a particular and well-known spring. **In the way to Shur.** "Before Egypt, as thou goest toward Assyria" (ch. xxv. 18) ; hence not Pelusium on the Nile (Jos., 'Ant.,' vi. 7, 3), but probably the modern Dschifar in the north-west of Arabia Deserta (Michaelis, Rosenmüller, Keil, Lange). Hagar was clearly directing her flight to Egypt.

Ver. 8. — **And he said, Hagar, Sarai's maid.** Declining to recognise her marriage with the patriarch, the angel reminds her of her original position as a bondwoman, from which liberty was not to be obtained by flight, but by manumission. **Whence camest thou ? and whither wilt thou go ? And she said, I flee from the face of my mistress Sarai.** "Her answer testifies to the oppression she had experienced, but also to the voice of her own conscience" (Lange).

Ver. 9.—**And the angel of the Lord said unto her**—as Paul afterwards practically said to Onesimus, the runaway slave of Philemon (*vide* Phil. 12)—**return to thy mistress, and submit thyself**—the verb here employed is the same as that which the historian uses to describe Sarah's conduct towards her (ver. 6) ; its meaning obviously is that she should meekly resign herself to the ungracious and oppressive treatment of her mistress—**under her hands.**

Ver. 10.—**And the angel of the Lord said unto her** (after duty, promise), **I will multiply thy seed exceedingly** (literally, *multiplying I will multiply thy seed ;* language altogether inappropriate in the lips of a creature), **that** (literally, *and*) **it shall not be numbered for multitude.**

Ver. 11.—**And the angel of the Lord said unto her, Behold, thou art with child, and thou shalt bear a son, and shalt call his name Ishmael.** "God shall hear," or, "Whom God hears," the first instance of the naming of a child before its birth (cf. afterwards ch. xvii. 19 ; 1 Kings xiii. 2 ; 1 Chron. xxii. 9 ; Matt. i. 21 ; Luke i. 13). **Because the Lord hath heard thy affliction.** Τῇ ταπεινώσει σου (LXX.), "thy prayer" (Chaldee), of which there is no mention, though men's miseries are said to cry when men themselves are mute (Calvin ; cf. Exod. i. 24 ; iii. 7).

Ver. 12.—**And he will be a wild man.** Literally, *a wild ass (of a) man ;* the פֶּרֶא,

onager, being so called from its swiftness of foot (cf. Job xxxix. 5—8), and aptly depicting "the Bedouin's boundless love of freedom as he rides about in the desert, spear in hand, upon his camel or his horse, hardy, frugal, revelling in the varied beauty of nature, and despising town life in every form" (Keil). As Ishmael and his offspring are here called "wild ass men," so Israel is designated by the prophet "sheep men" (Ezek. xxxvi. 37, 38). **His hand** will be **against every man, and every man's hand against him.** Exemplified in the turbulent and lawless character of the Bedouin Arabs and Saracens for upwards of thirty centuries. "The Bedouins are the outlaws among the nations. Plunder is legitimate gain, and daring robbery is praised as valour" (Kalisch). **And he shall dwell in the presence of**—literally, *before the face of*, i. e. to the east of (Rosenmüller, Gesenius, Tuch, Knobel, Delitzsch) ; or, "everywhere before the eyes of" (Kalisch, Wordsworth) ; or, independently of (Calvin, Keil, Lange, Murphy) **—all his brethren.** The Arabs of to-day are "just as they were described by the spirit of prophecy nearly 4000 years ago" (Porter's 'Giant Cities of Bashan,' pp. 28, 31, 324).

Ver. 13.—**And she called the name**—not invoked the name (Chaldee, Lapide), though occasionally קָרָא שֵׁם has the same import as קָרָא בְשֵׁם (*vide* Deut. xxxii. 3)—**of the Lord**—*Jehovah*, thus identifying the *Maleach Jehovah* with Jehovah himself—that **spake unto her, Thou God seest me.** Literally, *Thou* (art) El-Roi, *a God of seeing*, meaning either the God of my vision, i. e. the God who revealest thyself in vision (Gesenius, Fürst, Le Clerc, Dathe, Rosenmüller,

Keil, Kalisch, Murphy), or, though less correctly, the God who sees all things, and therefore me (LXX., Vulgate, Calvin, Ainsworth, Candlish, Hofmann, Baumgarten, Delitzsch, Wordsworth). **For she said, Have I also here looked after him that seeth me ?** Literally, *Have I also hitherto seen ?* i. e. Do I also still live after the vision ? (Onkelos, Gesenius, Fürst, Keil, Kalisch, Rosenmüller, Murphy).

Ver. 14.—**Wherefore the well was called** —in all likelihood first by Hagar—**Beerlahai-roi,** or the well of him that liveth and seeth me (A. V.) ; but either (1) the well of the living one of vision, i. e. of God, who appeared there (Onkelos, Rosenmüller, Lange) or (2) the well of the life of vision, i. e. where after seeing God life was preserved (Gesenius, Keil, Kalisch, Murphy), or where in consequence of seeing God a new life was imparted (Inglis). **Behold, it is between Kadesh** (*vide* ch. xiv. 7) **and Bered.** Of uncertain situation ; but the well has probably been discovered in *Ain Kades* (called by the Arabs *Moilahi Hagar*), to the south of Beersheba, and about twelve miles from Kadesh (cf. Keil *in loco*).

Ver. 15.—**And Hagar bare Abram a son : and Abram called his son's name**—a peculiarity of the Elohist to assign the naming of a child to the father (Knobel) ; but the present chapter is usually ascribed to the Jehovist, while the instances in which the name is given by the mother do not always occur in Jehovistic sections (cf. ch. xxx. 6, which Tuch imputes to the Elohist)—**which Hagar bare, Ishmael** — thus acknowledging the truth of Hagar's vision.

Ver. 16.—**And Abram was fourscore and six years old, when Hagar bare Ishmael to Abram.**

HOMILETICS.

Ver. 7.—*The capture of the runaway, or Hagar and the angel of the Lord.* I. THE FUGITIVE ARRESTED. 1. *The agent of her capture.* The angel of Jehovah (*vide* Exposition), whose appearance to Hagar at this particular juncture was doubtless—(1) *Unexpected.* Those who flee from duty seldom anticipate the encountering of God in their career (Jonah i. 3). (2) *Instantaneous.* The Invisible Supreme, who ever compasses our paths, only requires to either open his creatures' eyes, or veil his uncreated glory in a finite form, to make his presence known (Ps. cxxxix. 7 ; Luke xxiv. 15). (3) *Familiar.* Though here mentioned, angelic visitation need not now have occurred for the first time. Hagar probably had learnt something in the patriarch's household of the character, existence, and form of this celestial visitant. (4) *Opportune.* Whether regarded in this light or not, the present Divine manifestation to Hagar was highly seasonable, as God's visits to men ever are, in both the world and the Church. 2. *The place of her capture.* (1) *In the wilderness*, a very different locality from Abram's tent. But all regions are equally accessible to God's providence and grace ; and God's angel of mercy and salvation can find his way to disconsolate wanderers across the wilderness of a barren world as easily as to eminent saints within the sacred precincts of the Church. (2) *On the way to Shur*, i. e. going back to Egyptian worldliness and idolatry. Her chances of reaching the land of Ham were indeed small, considering her bodily condition; but thither was her destination, and hence her arrestment by the angel of the Lord was a special mercy. So Divine grace interposes to prevent those who have been once enlightened from relapsing to their old natural condition of worldliness and sin. (3) *By a fountain of water*, beside which it may be imagined she had cast herself in sheer exhaustion; an emblem of those springs of refreshment, or wells of Baca, which God has provided for the spiritually disconsolate, and one of which was being opened by Jehovah's visit for the comfort of the unhappy bondmaid.

II. THE FOUNDLING INTERROGATED. 1. *The question of the angel.* (1) The designations used, Hagar, Sarai's maid, reveal the minuteness of the Divine knowledge. God is acquainted with the names and the homes, the conditions in life, and the constituent elements in the history of all men (Ps. cxxxix. 1 5). (2) The reference to Hagar's original condition of servitude implies disapprobation of her union with Abram. No transaction can be safely passed as blameless until it has been reviewed and judged by God. (3) The inquiries addressed to Hagar were designed to convict her of sin. Whence had she come? From Abram's house, where the name of God was worshipped; from the presence of Sarai, who had a lawful claim upon her service; from the land of Canaan, the inheritance of Abram's seed, of which, as she fondly hoped, she was about to become the mother—in all which she was clearly committing wrong. Then whither was she going? Back again to Egypt, as the ultimate goal of her flight, while in the mean time she was exposing herself and her unborn child to serious peril. Doubtless these and other considerations of a similar sort arose within the breast of Hagar as she listened to Jehovah's questionings. When God examines souls they are truly, minutely, and completely searched. 2. *The answer of Hagar.* (1) Promptly given. There was no sign of hesitancy or reluctance. The utmost frankness and cordiality should characterise a sinner's dealings with God. (2) Briefly expressed. "She was fleeing from the face of Sarai her mistress." Comprehensive brevity should signalise our responses to God's interrogations. (3) Honestly declared. She had run away. If it was wrong, she made no attempt at concealment. Guileless acknowledgment of sin is a true mark of contrition.

III. THE WANDERER DIRECTED. 1. *To return to Abram's house.* The tent of Sarai, though to Hagar's quick Southron blood a place of humiliation, was nevertheless for her the true place of safety, both physically and spiritually. The first counsel that God's word and spirit give to those who flee from duty, forsake the company of saints, and venture out upon perilous and sinful courses is "to stand in the ways, and ask for the old paths" (Jer. vi. 16). 2. *To submit to Sarai's yoke.* Her alliance with the patriarch could not in God's sight alter her original position as a slave. Though soon to be the mother of Abram's seed, she was still a bondwoman, whose duty was submission, however galling to her hot blood, and however unreasonable it might seem in the case of one whose child might yet inherit Canaan. God's people are required to abide in those stations in life in which they have been called, until they can be honourably released from them (1 Cor. vii. 20—22), and to endure those afflictions which God in his providence may impose, rather than impetuously and sinfully endeavour to escape from them (Matt. xvi. 24).

IV. THE DISCONSOLATE COMFORTED. 1. The richness of the offered consolation. (1) *A gracious assurance*—that she was an object of the Divine regard, as this very visit proved; of the Divine observation, since the Lord knew her condition; and of the Divine compassion, for already he had heard her affliction—than which no sweeter consolation can be offered to either penitent backslider or dejected sufferer. (2) *A comfortable promise*—that she should live to be the mother of Abram's seed, that her unborn babe should be a son, and that her son should develop into a bold, courageous, and prosperous man, and that through him she herself, an Egyptian slave-girl, should become the ancestress of a numerous and mighty people. God is able, even in respect of material and temporal benefits, to compensate for life's sorrows and tribulations, and to make up in one direction for what he takes away in another. (3) *An important instruction*—to name her child "Ishmael" when it should be born; partly as a memorial to herself of the Divine mercy, and partly as a reminder to her child of the sure Source of prosperity, both personal and national, temporal and spiritual. God's people should remember the right hand of the Most High (Ps. lxxvii. 10), and seek advancement from him alone (Ps. lxxv. 6, 7). 2. The efficacy of the offered consolation. (1) *Adoring gratitude.* Hagar was amazed at the Divine condescension in permitting her to see God and yet live—a mercy denied to Moses on the mount (Exod. xxxiii. 20); and the Divine grace which had imparted life and hope to her soul through this celestial visitation. (2) *Mercy remembered.* Hagar called the well Beer-lahai-roi, *i. e.* the well of seeing and living. The Divine loving-kindness is worthy of memorials, which also should be written on the tablets of the heart when they cannot be expressed in words or enshrined in deeds. (3) *Cheerful submission.* Hagar returned to Abram's house, submitted to Sarai's hand, and in due time gave birth to Ishmael. The best evidence that grace has comforted the human heart is prompt compliance with the will of God.

See in the angel's appearance to Hagar—1. An adumbration of the incarnation of our Lord Jesus Christ. 2. An illustration of God's care of those who are within his Church. 3. An indication of the kind of people that most attract the Divine notice and compassion. 4. A revelation of the tenderness with which he deals with sinners. 5. A proclamation of God's gracious readiness to forgive the erring.

HOMILIES BY VARIOUS AUTHORS.

Ver. 7.—*Wells in the wilderness.* 1. God provides them for the rest and refreshment of pilgrims. 2. God visits them to meet with weary and afflicted pilgrims. 3. God dispenses from them life and hope to all repenting and believing pilgrims. Compare with the angel of Jehovah and Hagar at the fountain of Shur, Christ and the woman of Samaria at Jacob's well (John iv. 6).—W.

Vers. 7—13.—*Glimpses of the Godhead.* 1. Divine condescension. God visits men as the angel visited Hagar. 2. Divine omniscience. God knows men as the angel knew Hagar. 3. Divine compassion. God pities and comforts men as the angel did Hagar. 4. Divine wisdom. God instructs men as the angel directed Hagar. 5. Divine grace. God pardons and accepts men as the angel did Hagar.—W.

Ver. 8.—*God pleading with wanderers.* "Hagar, Sarai's maid, whence camest thou? and whither wilt thou go?" She knew not, cared not. Undisciplined, smarting under effects of her own wilfulness (ver. 4), she thought only of escaping pain—a type of those weary, yet unconverted (cf. Jer. ii. 13; v. 3). But God saw her. The Shepherd sought her (cf. Gen. iii. 9; Luke xv. 9). Though not of the chosen race, and having no claim upon his care, of his own mercy he calls her (cf. Ps. cxlv. 9; Ephes. ii. 4; Titus iii. 5). The angel of the Lord; in ver. 13 called the Lord; the messenger of the covenant (Mal. iii. 1)—sent to carry out the Father's purpose (cf. John iii. 17; Luke iv. 18). The same who speaks in the voice of awakened conscience, that he may give peace (cf. Matt. xi. 28). "Hagar, Sarai's maid," expresses God's full knowledge of her (cf. Exod. xxxiii. 12; John x. 3). The name distinguishes the individual. She a stranger, a slave, a fugitive; yet God's eye upon her; all her life before him (cf. Ps. cxxxix. 1—4). A word for those following their own ways, feeling as if hidden in the multitude. Nothing glaring in their lives; men see nothing to find fault with; will God? (cf. Ps. xciv. 7). He knows thee altogether; thy whole life, the selfishness underlying a fair profession, the unconfessed motives, the little duplicities, the love of worldly things; or it may be thy spiritual pride and self-trusting. He sees thee through. But wilt thou seek to escape the thought of him? For what does he search thee out? Is it not to bring thee to peace? A word of comfort to him who is cast down because of weakness in faith, little progress, want of spirituality. He sees all (cf. Luke xix. 5). Not as man—men see the failures; God sees the battle, the longing desire for better things, the prayers (Ps. xxviii. 1; cxxx. 1), the searching of heart, the sorrow because of failure. Even in the wilderness he is present to help (Gal. vi. 9).

I. "WHENCE CAMEST THOU?" Is the wilderness better than the home thou hast left? (cf. Isa. v. 4). Thou hast left safety and plenty (cf. Num. xxi. 5), impatient of God's discipline. A goodly possession was thine—the place of a child (1 John

iii. 1), the right always to pray (Luke xviii. 1; John xv. 7; Heb. iv. 16; James iv. 2), the promise of guidance (Ps. xxxii. 8; Isa. xxx. 21). For what hast thou given up all this? Is thy present lot better? In deepest love these questions are asked. God pleads by providence (Ps. cxix. 67), by the entering of the word (Ps. cxix. 130; Heb. iv. 12), by the "still small voice" of the Holy Spirit.

II. "WHITHER WILT THOU GO?" How many have never really considered. Hast thou renounced thy heavenly portion? God forbid. Then is thy life heavenward? Are thy sins blotted out? Hast thou accepted the free gift of salvation? I am not sure of that. And why not? Is it not that thou hast not cared enough to entertain the question as a practical one? (cf. Ezek. xx. 49; xxxiii. 32). Meanwhile thou art not standing still. The day of grace is passing away (cf. Jer. viii. 20). Still Christ pleads (Rev. iii. 20). But day by day the ear becomes more dull, and the aims and habits of life more hard to change. "Return," was the Lord's word to Hagar. Take again thy place in God's family (cf. Luke xv. 20). Fear not to bear thy cross. There is a welcome and joy in heaven over every returning wanderer.—M.

EXPOSITION.

CHAPTER XVII.

Ver. 1.—**And when Abram was ninety years old and nine**—consequently an interval of thirteen years had elapsed since the birth of Ishmael; the long delay on the part of God being probably designed as chastisement for Abram's second nuptials (Calvin), and at least corresponding with Abram's undue haste (Lange)—**the Lord appeared to Abram**—lest he should regard Ishmael's birth as a complete fulfilment of the promise (Menochius), and be satisfied with Hagar's child as the expected seed (Calvin)—**and said to him, I** am **the Almighty God**—*El Shaddai*, found six times in Genesis and thirty-one times in Job, composed of *El*, God, and *Shaddai;* not a *nomen compositum* (from שַׁ = אֲשֶׁר and דִּי) signifying *qui sufficiens est* (Aquinas, Symmachus, Theodoret, Saadias, Maimonides, Calvin), but either a *pluralis excellentiæ*, from the singular שַׁד, powerful—root שָׁדַד, to be strong (Gesenius, Rosenmüller, Wordsworth), or a singular from the same root with the substantive termination ‘ַ, as in הַגַּי, the festal, שִׁישִׁי, the old man, סִינַי, the thorn-grown (Keil, Oehler, Lange); descriptive of God as revealing himself violently in his might, hence correctly rendered παντοκράτωρ by the LXX. in Job (Oehler); distinguishing Jehovah, the God of salvation, from Elohim, the God who creates nature so that it is and supports it that it may stand, as "the God who compels nature to do what is contrary to itself, and subdues it to bow and minister to grace" (Delitzsch); characterising Jehovah the covenant God, "as possessing the power to realise his promises, even when the order of nature presented no prospect of their fulfilment, and the powers of nature were insufficient to secure it" (Keil); perhaps, like Elohim and Adonai, one of the world-wide titles of the Most High since it was known to Balaam (Numb. xxiv. 4, 16), and is constantly used in Job ('Speaker's Commentary'). Said in Exod. vi. 2, 3 to have been the name by which God was known to the patriarchs, it is regarded by the partitionists as characteristic of the Elohist (Tuch, Bleek, Colenso, Davidson, Ewald), and accordingly to that writer the present chapter is assigned, and the Jehovah of this verse explained as an alteration of the original Elohist's narrative; but the πρῶτον ψεῦδος of this criticism lurks in the identification of El-Shaddai with Elohim, whereas it is not Elohim, but Jehovah, who reveals himself as El Shaddai not alone in the Pentateuch, but in the historical and prophetical books as well (cf. Ruth i. 20, 21; *vide* Keil's Introduction, pt. i. § 2; div. i. § 25). **Walk before me.** Literally, *set thyself to walk*, as in ch. xiii. 17, *in my presence*, as if conscious of my inspection and solicitous of my approval; not behind me, as if sensible of shortcomings, and desirous to elude observation. The phrase intimates a less exalted piety than the corresponding phrase used of Enoch (v. 24) and Noah (ch. vi. 9). **And be thou perfect.** *Tamim*, ἄμεμπτος (LXX.), used of Noah in ch. vi. 9, and rendered τέλειος (LXX.), while perhaps retrospectively glancing at Abram's sin in marrying Hagar, indicates that absolute standard of moral attainment, viz., completeness of being in respect of purity, which the supreme Lawgiver sets before his intelligent creatures (cf. Matt. v. 8).

Ver. 2.—**And I will make my covenant between me and thee.** Literally, *I will give* (cf. ch. ix. 9, 11, 12). Neither an additional covenant to that described in ch. xv. (Rosenmüller), nor a different traditional account of the transaction contained in ch. xv. (Tuch, Bleek), nor the original Elohistic narrative of which that in ch. xv. was a later imitation (Knobel); but an intimation that the covenant already concluded was about to be carried into execution, and the promise of a son to be more specifically determined as the offspring of Sarai (Keil). **And will multiply thee exceedingly** (*vide* ch. xii. 2 ; xiii. 16 ; xv. 5).

Ver. 3.—**And Abram fell on his face**—in reverential awe and worship (*vide* ver. 17 ; cf. ch. xxiv. 52 ; Numb. xvi. 22 ; Mark xiv. 35). Other attitudes of devotion are mentioned (1 Kings viii. 54 ; Mark xi. 25 ; 1 Tim. ii. 8). **And God**—*Elohim*, the third name for the Deity within the compass of as many verses, thus indicating identity of being—**talked with him, saying**—

Ver. 4.—**As for me.** Literally, *I*, standing alone at the beginning of the sentence by way of emphasis (cf. 2 Kings x. 29 ; Ps. xi. 4 ; xlvi. 5 ; *vide* Ewald's ' Hebrew Syntax,' § 309). Equivalent to " So far as I am concerned," or, " I for my part," or, " So far as relates to me." **Behold, my covenant** is **with thee, and thou shalt be** — literally, *shalt become* (cf. ch. ii. 7), or grow to (cf. ch. ix. 15)—**a father of many** (or of a multitude of) **nations.**

Ver. 5.—**Neither shall thy name any more be called Abram,**—Ab-ram, *i. e.* high father (*vide* ch. xi. 26) ; **but Abraham**—Ab-raham (in Arabic signifying a multitude) ; hence " the father of a multitude," as the next clause explains—**for a father of many** (or a multitude of) **nations have I made thee.**

Ver. 6.—**And I will make thee exceeding fruitful, and I will make nations of thee,**—a promise fulfilled in the Ishmaelites, the descendants of Keturah, the Edomites, and the Israelites—**and kings** (*e. g.* David and Solomon) **shall come out of thee.**

Ver. 7.—**And I will establish my covenant between me and thee and thy seed after thee in their generations for an everlasting covenant,**—literally, *for a covenant of eternity* (*vide* ch. ix. 16)—**to be a God unto thee, and to thy seed after thee.** Literally, *to be for Elohim ;* a formula comprehending all saving benefits ; a clear indication of the spiritual character of the Abrahamic covenant (cf. ch. xxvi. 24 ; xxviii. 13 ; Heb. xi. 16).

Ver. 8.—**And I will give unto thee, and to thy seed after thee, the land wherein thou art a stranger,**—literally, *of thy sojournings* (ch. xii. 9 ; Acts vii. 5 ; Heb. xi. 9)—**all the land of Canaan** (*vide* ch. x. 19),—**for an everlasting possession.** Literally, *for a possession of eternity ;* i. e. the earthly Canaan should be retained by them so long as the arrangement then instituted should continue, provided always they complied with the conditions of the covenant ; and the heavenly Canaan should be the inheritance of Abraham's spiritual children for

ever (*vide* ch. ix. 16 ; xiii. 15). **And I will be their God.** Literally, *to them for Elohim* (*vide supra*).

Ver. 9.—**And God said unto Abraham, Thou** —literally, *and thou*, the other party to the covenant, the antithesis to *I* (ver. 4)—**shalt keep my covenant**—literally, *my covenant thou shalt keep*—therefore, **thou, and thy seed after thee in their generations.**

Ver. 10.—**This** is **my covenant** (*i. e.* the sign of it, as in ch. ix. 12), **which ye shall keep** (*i. e.* observe to do), **between me and you and thy seed after thee ; Every man child among you shall be circumcised.** Literally, *circumcise among* (or *of*) *you every male*, the inf. abs. הִמּוֹל, when it stands abruptly at the commencement of a sentence, having the force of a command (cf. Ewald's ' Hebrew Syntax,' § 328 ; Gesenius, ' Grammar,' § 130).

Ver. 11.—**And ye shall circumcise the flesh of your foreskin.** עָרְלָה, ἀκροβυστία, *membrum praeputiatum*, from עָרֵל, to be naked, bare, hence to be odious, unclean, impure, was regarded afterwards as unclean (Deut. x. 16 ; Isa. lii. 3 ; Jer. iv. 4), and is here directed to be deprived of the skin covering its extremity, not because through it sin first discovered its effects (Poole), and original corruption is still transmitted (Lapide, Augustine), or to promote cleanliness (Philo), or to express detestation of certain idolatrous rites which were paid to it by the Egyptians and other heathen nations (Lyra, Kalisch), but (1) as a sign of the faith that Christ should be descended from him (Lapide) ; (2) as a symbolic representation of the putting away of the filth of the flesh and of sin in general (Calvin). Hence it served a variety of uses : (1) to distinguish the seed of Abraham from the Gentiles, (2) to perpetuate the memory of Jehovah's covenant, (3) to foster in the nation the hope of the Messiah, (4) to remind them of the duty of cultivating moral purity (Deut. x. 16), (5) to preach to them the gospel of a righteousness by faith (Rom. iv. 11), (6) to suggest the idea of a holy or a spiritual seed of Abram (Rom. ii. 29), and (7) to foreshadow the Christian rite of baptism (Col. ii. 11, 12). **And it shall be a token of the covenant**—literally, *for a token of covenant* (cf. ch. ix. 12 ; Acts vii. 8 ; Rom. iv. 11)—**betwixt me and you.**

Ver. 12.—**And he that is eight days old**— —literally, *and the son of eight days* (cf. ch. xvii. 1)—**shall be circumcised among you** (Levit. xii. 3 ; Luke ii. 21 ; Phil. iii. 5), **every man child** —" The fact that several times the circumcision of the males only is enjoined may point to the legislator's intention to exclude that rite in the other sex, though it was customary among many ancient nations, but not universal among the Egyptians" (Kalisch). Though not administered to both, the symbol was ordained for the sake of both sexes (Calvin)—**in your generations, he that is born in the house, or bought with money of any stranger, which is not of thy seed.** Not only a proof of the Divine benignity to Abraham in embracing all the members of his household within the pale of the visible Church now constituted, but likewise a hint of the world-wide aspect of the Abrahamic covenant, a first-fruits as it were of the "all the families of the earth" that should be blessed in Abram.

Ver. 13.—**He that is born in thy house, and he that is bought with thy money, must needs be circumcised.** Literally, *circumcised, must be circumcised*, he that is born, &c., the niph. inf. abs. with the finite verb occupying the place of emphasis at the beginning of the sentence (*vide* Gesenius, 'Grammar,' § 131). **And my covenant shall be in your flesh for an everlasting covenant.**

Ver. 14. — **And the uncircumcised man child whose flesh of his foreskin is not circumcised, that soul shall be cut off from his people.** Ἐξολοθρευθήσεται ἐκ τοῦ γένους αὐτῆς (LXX.), *i. e.* shall be destroyed from amongst his nation, from among his people (Levit. xvii. 4, 10 ; Numb. xv. 30), from Israel (Exod. xii. 15 ; Numb. xix. 13), from the congregation of Israel (Exod. xii. 19), by the infliction of death at the hands of the congregation, the civil magistrate, or of God (Abarbanel, Gesenius, Clericus, Michaelis, Rosenmüller, Keil, Wordsworth, Alford) ; or shall be excommunicated from the Church, and no longer reckoned among the people of God (Augustine, Vatablus, Piscator, Willet, Calvin, Knobel, Murphy, Kalisch, Inglis). That excision from one's people was in certain cases followed by the death penalty (Exod. xxxi. 14 ; Levit. xviii. 29 ; Numb. xv. 30) does not prove that the capital infliction was an invariable accompaniment of such sentence (*vide* Exod. xii. 19 ; Levit. vii. 20, 21 ; Numb. xix. 13). Besides, to suppose that such was its meaning here necessitates the restriction of the punishment to adults, whereas with the alternative signification no such restriction requires to be imposed on the statute. The uncircumcised Hebrew, whether child or adult, forfeited his standing in the congregation, *i. e.* ceased to be a member of the Hebrew Church. **He hath broken my covenant.**

HOMILETICS.

Vers. 1—14.—*The covenant renewed.* I. THE COVENANT CONFIRMED. 1. *The time.* "When Abram was ninety years old and nine," *i. e.* thirteen years after Ishmael's birth. Mark the penalty of striving to anticipate Divine promises. Human ingenuity, even when not directly sinful, can only retard, not accelerate, Jehovah's purpose. 2. *The Author.* "El Shaddai," *i. e.* the Being who, though ordinarily operating silently and invisibly in nature, is able to break through nature in order to accomplish his designs. Nature is not superior to God, but *vice versâ*—the Almighty transcends his own handiwork ; and much as Nature discloses of God's eternal power and Godhead in her ordinary workings, she does not by means of these reveal the infinite fulness of his Divine resources. 3. *The condition.* "Walk before me, and be thou perfect," *i. e.* follow holiness as well as trust my word. Though grace is the prime mover in all Heaven's bargains or contracts with sinful men, they are invariably conditioned by man's obedience to and trust in the Divine Covenanter. The meaning briefly is, that if God's grace does not conquer man's unbelief and sin, man's unbelief and sin will ultimately cancel God's grace.

II. THE COVENANT EXPLAINED. 1. *The promise of a seed.* An old promise recapitulated, since God gives "line upon line," "precept upon precept" (Isa. xxviii. 10) ; with little additional clearness of definition, beyond the hint, conveyed by the words "nations" and "kings," that something more than Ishmael and his descendants was to be expected, since the Revealer of the Father (the Word of Jehovah, Christ, the Word of God) only discovers truth to the human mind as it can bear (Mark iv. 33). 2. *The promise of a land.* This too was an old promise redelivered, with the old particularity of description and the old solemnity of donation ; partly to inform the hearer's mind, partly to allay whatever anxious thoughts might remain, but chiefly to prepare for the imposition of the obligations that were about to be declared. Covenant mercies, at least in God's contracts, always go before covenant duties. 3. *The promise of a blessing.* This too had been included in the gracious provisions of the covenant from the first ; but now a slight advance is made in the elucidation of its nature. The blessing is to be distinctly spiritual. Jehovah is to be a God to

Abram and his seed. Hence the inference which Paul draws (Gal. iii. 14—18) was designed to be deduced by the patriarch—that the true and proper recipients of the covenanted mercies were not to be his natural, but spiritual descendants. See the prominence in respect of clearness of revelation which God assigns to things spiritual.

III. THE COVENANT ATTESTED. 1. The imposition of a new name. (1) Its *significance*. Instead of high-father, a personal appellation descriptive of the elevation of his rank as a chieftain, or of his character as a man, he was henceforth to be styled father of a multitude, a federal or representative designation, defining his relation to both his natural and spiritual descendants. It were well if names always were thus suggestive and symbolic; but only names assigned by God, directly or indirectly, can be relied on as expressive of reality. (2) Its *intention*. This was to indicate that God's covenant was made not with Abram the Chaldæan chieftain, but with Abraham the believer. It was thus a symbol of the new position before God which Abraham occupied, and the new nature which as a believer in God Abraham possessed; *i. e.* of Abraham's justification and regeneration. It was also a reminder that God's covenant was made not with the offspring of Abram as a man, *i. e.* with his natural descendants, except, indeed, provisionally and typically; but with the children of Abraham the believer, *i. e.* with his spiritual posterity, all of whom, like himself, must have new names, *i. e.* occupy new positions and possess new natures, in other words, be justified and regenerated children of God by faith in Jesus Christ. 2. The attachment of a new sign. (1) Its *nature*. Circumcision. On the origin of the rite of circumcision see Exposition. (2) Its *import*. As regarding the grand blessing of the covenant, the promise of a seed, it was designed for a sign that that seed was to be not a child of the flesh, but a child of the promise; not the offspring of nature, but the gift of grace. Hence it served as an adumbration of the sinless humanity of the Lord Jesus Christ, and an intimation of the holy character of his seed. Then, as administered to the patriarch, it was intended as a practical declaration of his faith in the coming seed, and a symbolic representation of his personal devotement to holiness. In every one of these respects its place has been supplied by the Christian rite of baptism, with only this difference, that baptism is a visible token of faith not in a coming, but a crucified and risen, Saviour. (3) Its *incidence*. The ceremony was appointed to be administered first to Abraham, and then to all his household, including Ishmael and his male domestics, and subsequently to all his posterity through the promised son. So the obligations of the covenant rest on all within the Church, and descend from age to age upon believers.

HOMILIES BY VARIOUS AUTHORS.

Ver. 1.—*God's call to believers.* "And when Abram was ninety years old and nine, the Lord appeared to Abram, and said unto him, I am the Almighty God; walk before me, and be thou perfect." In what sense are we to take this? None can keep God's law perfectly (Rom. vii. 23). And why at this point in Abram's history the emphatic "I am?" &c. The character of his life was faith (cf. Heb. xi. 6) resting on the promises made him (Gen. xii. 7; xiii. 16; xv. 5). The last of these was a special instance of faith. But the triumph was followed by a fall—impatience, would not wait God's time (cf. Ps. xxvii. 14; xxxi. 15). An instance of a common fault —partial faith (cf. Matt. iv. 4; xiv. 28—31). The result was disappointment. Thirteen years passed. Must we not connect this with his fault? Want of faith delayed the blessing (cf. Num. xiv. 33). Then came the word of the Lord—a gentle rebuke (cf. Matt. viii. 26), and a precept: "Walk before me," &c. Return to thy first faith; let it be perfect, not partial (cf. Prov. iii. 5; Matt. xvii. 20).

I. A LESSON FOR BELIEVERS. Watch lest faith grow cold. Some like not to retain God in their thoughts. They hide themselves from him amid the vanities of the world. But his people, who have known his love (1 John iii. 1), why should they ever shrink from opening their whole heart to him? Yet, imperceptibly perhaps, there is a change. The faith is held, but the sunshine is gone. The desire to tell all to God is not there. Why? The man has set his heart upon something, and cannot trust God's love; or he is drawn to something he cannot approve, and listens to what can be said for it (cf. Rom. xiv. 4); or he has fallen into self-sufficiency. Then reserve towards God. The hidden life becomes disordered. No longer the desire that he should know all and guide all. And thus uneasiness, reserve, distance. Then follow plans to quiet the uneasiness—business, ceremony, theology, or work in some other direction. But no real communion with God in all this.

II. The remedy. "Walk before me." Recognise the evil. Believe the cause. Be not faithless. Bear in mind God's presence (cf. Ps. lxii. 1—7). Seek not to hide from him, or to justify self. And "be perfect," i. e. matured; not in any high or strange attainment, but in that which a child may learn—in trusting God's truth and love; in bringing thoughts, wants, and wishes before him. Towards this active obedience and following Christ are means; and, above all, sincerity, and a real definite dedication of the life to God.

III. Encouragement. "I am the Almighty God"—all-powerful (Isa. lix. 1; Luke i. 37) and all-loving (Ps. xxxvii. 5; Rom. viii. 32). This, really believed, would remove anxious care. What is it that leads thee to seek another way? The consciousness of having wandered. Has he not made provision for this? (1 Tim. i. 15; 1 John ii. 1). Or is it that the blessing long desired is not given? Some power, some opportunity for God's work, and still the door is closed; or it may be some spiritual gift, some token of growth in grace, and still the evil of thy nature is unsubdued. Be patient (James i. 4). Thy Father in heaven will not fail thee (Rom. vi. 14). Walk before him. Tell him all that is in thy mind. In his time thou shalt find peace (Phil. iv. 6; 1 John v. 4; Rev. xxi. 7).—M

Vers. 1, 2.—*The true life of faith set forth.* I. Commencing with gracious appearance of God to his creature. 1. The revelation one in a continued series of *progressive manifestations.* 2. Accompanied with direct *promise,* which in the form of covenant appeals to reciprocal fellowship and confidence. 3. Embracing both present and future blessedness. The blessing upon the earthly lot, as preparatory to the higher blessedness, a foundation on which the higher life is built up.

II. The method of the life of faith. Walk before me; be perfect, &c. 1. Constant *reference to God*—his will, his truth, his covenant. 2. *Distinction* from the world. Abram the pilgrim. Walk among the heathen, and yet before me. The consciousness of a chosen aim a great preservative. The sustaining favour of God. Development of the Divine in the human. 3. A life which is worked out as a *trust for others.* The representative man holds a special position towards God not for his own sake alone, but as the depositary of the blessing. Great help to walk before God and be perfect, that we are called to be the channel through which blessings flow. Confirmation of the covenant will be sent to us in the way, when there is lack of promise in appearances, notwithstanding the evidence of our own infirmity. We walk in the light towards a future which shall abundantly reward patient continuance in well doing.—R.

EXPOSITION.

Ver. 15.—**And God said unto Abraham, As for Sarai thy wife,**—who, not having hitherto been mentioned in any of the promises, is now expressly taken into covenant, and accordingly receives a new name (cf. ver. 5; ch. xxxii. 28; Rev. iii. 12)—**thou shalt not call her name Sarai,**—"my princess" (Gesenius); "princely, noble" (Ikenius, Rosenmüller, Keil, Delitzsch); "the heroine" (Knobel); "strife, contention" (Ewald, Murphy), with special reference to her struggle against sterility (Kalisch)—**but Sarah**—"princess" (Gesenius), the meaning being that, whereas formerly she was Abram's princess only, she was henceforth to be recognised as a princess generally, i. e. as the mother of the Church (Jerome, Augustine), or as princess to the Lord, the letter h being taken from the name Jehovah, as in the change of Abram into Abraham (the Rabbis); though Ikenius and Rosenmüller derive from an Arabic root, *sara,* to have a numerous progeny—shall **her name** be.

Ver. 16.—**And I will bless her, and give thee a son also of her** (the first intimation that the promised seed was to be Sarai's child), **and she shall be a mother of nations;** —literally, *she shall become nations* (cf. ver. 4)—**kings of people shall be of her.**

Ver. 17.—**Then Abraham fell upon his face** (*vide* ver. 3), **and laughed.** וַיִּצְחָק, from

צָחַק, to laugh. Cf. καχάζω καγχάζω, *cachinnor*, German, *kichern; καὶ ἐγέλασε* (LXX.); rejoiced (Onkelos); marvelled (Jerome, Targums); laughed for joy (Arabic version, Augustine, Calvin, Delitzsch, Keil, Murphy, *et alii*); not a smile of incredulity (Jerome, Chrysostom) or of diffidence (Kalisch), as partitionists assert in order to produce a contradiction between the Elohist and Jehovist of ch. xv. **And said in his heart, Shall a child be born unto him that is** (literally, *to the son of*) **an hundred years old?** A suggestion of natural reason which was overruled by faith (Calvin, Wordsworth), though better regarded as the exclamation of holy wonder, or as an illustration of believing not for joy (Inglis; cf. Luke xxiv. 41). **And shall Sarah, that is ninety years old, bear?** Yes. What reason declared impossible was possible to faith. "He considered not the deadness of Sarah's womb" (Rom. iv. 19).

Ver. 18.—**And Abraham said unto God, O that Ishmael might live before thee!** Not implying that Abram was content with Hagar's child as the promised seed without waiting for Sarai's son (Jerome, Calvin, Kalisch); scarcely that he feared lest God might remove Ishmael by death now that Isaac had been promised (Wordsworth); but probably that he desired that Ishmael might not only live and prosper (Bush), but share with Sarah's son in the blessings of the covenant (Keil, Lange, Rosenmüller, Murphy, 'Speaker's Commentary,' Inglis).

Ver. 19.—**And God said, Sarah thy wife shall bear thee a son indeed; and thou shalt call his name Isaac.** "Laughter," or "he laughs"(the third person future (*yitsak*) being frequently employed in personal designations; cf. Jacob, Jair, Jabin, &c.), with obvious reference to Abraham's laughter (*vide* ver. 17). Cf. on naming before birth ch. xvi. 11. **And I will establish my covenant with him for an everlasting covenant, and with his seed after him.**

Ver. 20—**And as for Ishmael, I have heard thee** (meaning, also, "and will grant thy prayer;" an allusion to the significance of the name Ishmael, "God hears"): **Behold, I have blessed him, and will make him fruitful, and will multiply him exceedingly; twelve princes shall he beget** (*vide* ch. xxv. 12—16), **and I will make him a great nation.**

Ver. 21.—**But my covenant will I establish with Isaac, whom Sarah shall bear unto thee at this set time in the next year** (cf. ch. xxi. 2).

Ver. 22.—**And he** (*i. e.* God) **left off talking with him** (Abraham), **and God went up** —into heaven (*vide* ch. xxxv. 13)—**from Abraham.**

Ver. 23.—**And Abraham took Ishmael his son, and all that were born in his house, and all that were bought with his money, every** **male among the men of Abraham's house; and circumcised the flesh of their foreskin in the self-same day.** Literally, *in the bone of that day*, an expression occurring in ch. vii. 13, which is commonly regarded as Jehovistic, while this is Elohistic; though Quarry suggests that the ensuing section should commence with this verse, in which case the present paragraph would also be Jehovistic, and the appearance of unnecessary repetition in its statements avoided by viewing them as the customary recapitulations that mark the opening of a new division of the history (*vide* 'Genesis,' p. 440); against which, however, is the name of God which continues to be here employed. **As God** (Elohim) **had said unto him.**

Ver. 24.—**And Abraham was ninety years old and nine,**—literally, *a son of ninety years and nine* (cf. ch. vii. 6; xvi. 16)—**when he was circumcised in the flesh of his foreskin.**

Ver. 25.—**And Ishmael his son** was **thirteen years old** (the same form of expression as above), **when he was circumcised.** Hence among the Arabs the ceremony is usually delayed till the thirteenth year (cf. Josephus, 'Ant.,' i. 13).

Vers. 26, 27.—**In the selfsame day was Abraham circumcised, and Ishmael his son. And all the men of his house, born in the house, and bought with money of the stranger, were circumcised with him.** The usual charges of needless repetition which are preferred against the closing verses of this chapter may be disposed of by observing that ver. 23 intimates that the sacrament of circumcision was administered to the patriarch and his household on the very day that God had enjoined it, *i. e.* without delay; that vers. 24, 25 declare the respective ages of Abraham and Ishmael when they received the Divinely-appointed rite; and that vers. 26, 27 state the fact that the entire household of the patriarch was circumcised simultaneously with himself.

THE ORIGIN OF CIRCUMCISION. The determination of this question does not appear of paramount importance, yet the ascertained results may be briefly indicated. (1) According to Herodotus (ii. 104) circumcision was observed as a custom of primitive antiquity among the Colchians, Ethiopians, and Egyptians, by the last of whom it was communicated to the Syrians of Palestine and the Phœnicians. It is, however, uncertain whether among the Egyptians the practice was universal, as Philo and Herodotus assert, or limited to the priesthood, as Origen believed; and equally doubtful whether the Egyptians themselves may not have adopted it from the Hebrews in the time of Joseph, instead of from the Ethiopians, as appears to be the judgment of Kalisch. Against the idea that circumcision was a national and universal observance among the Egyptians in the time of Abraham, it has been urged that the male servants of the patriarch, some of whom were Egyptians (ch. xii. 16), were not circumcised till Abraham was commanded to perform the rite; that Ishmael, the son of an Egyptian mother, remained uncircumcised till the same time; and that the daughter of Pharaoh recognised Moses as a Hebrew child, which, it is supposed, she could not have done had circumcision been generally practised among her own people. On the other hand, it is contended that the absence of details as to how the rite should be performed seems to imply that already circumcision was familiar to Abraham; and by some modern Egyptologists it is asserted that an examination of ancient mummies and sculptures, in which circumcision is a distinctive mark between the Egyptians and their enemies, shows that the ceremony must have been in use not among the priests only, but throughout the nation generally so early as the time of the fourth dynasty, i. e. 2400 B.C., or considerably earlier than the time of Abraham. Still (2) though it should be held as indubitably established that circumcision was a prevalent custom among the Egyptians in the time of Abraham, it would not follow that the Hebrews adopted it from them. On the contrary, the Biblical narrative expressly mentions that its observance by the patriarch and his household was due to a Divine command, and was connected with a religious significance which was altogether foreign to the Egyptians and others by whom that rite was practised. Among the reasons for its adoption by the heathen nations of antiquity have been assigned, among the Ethiopians, a prophylactic design to ward off certain painful, and often incurable, disorders; among the Egyptians, a regard to cleanliness; and perhaps among the priesthood of the latter country a semi-religious idea (the deification of the generative powers) was associated with a practice which was commonly regarded as enhancing productivity; but the import of the ceremony as enjoined upon the father of the faithful was as widely as possible removed from every one of these ideas, being connected with spiritual conceptions of which the heathen world was entirely ignorant. That a heathen custom should have been adopted by Jehovah and elevated to the rank and connected with the spiritual significance of a religious sign will not occur as a difficulty to those who remember that the rainbow, a well-known natural phenomenon, was selected as the sign for Noah's covenant, and that Christian baptism is a similar transformation of a previously existing ceremony by which Gentile proselytes were admitted to the Hebrew Church.

HOMILETICS.

Vers. 15—27.—*The covenant completed.* I. THE ADMISSION OF SARAI. 1. *The changed name.* As on entering within the covenant the name of Abram was changed to Abraham, so, to signalise the reception of his spouse, Sarai was transformed into Sarah (vide Exposition), the transformation having in her case the same significance as it had in Abraham's. In particular it proclaimed that, like Abraham, Sarah was now a justified and regenerated believer in the Divine promise. *N. B.* There is only one gate of entrance to Christ's Church, viz., faith or conversion. 2. *The guaranteed blessing.* What is here affirmed of Sarai is that she should not only be received into the Church, but made a sharer of Abraham's blessing, i. e. become entitled to all the gracious provisions of the covenant. The blessing of Abraham belongs to all who are possessed of Abraham's faith. Christ's salvation is the common property of believers. And to all it is certain, as it was to Sarai. The "yea" concerning Sarai has now become for Christ's people "yea and amen." 3. *The promised son.* This was the first intimation that Sarai was to be the mother of the seed. The Eternal never hastens. God's disclosures of his own plans are ever slow, gradual, progressive, and mostly regulated by the faith of the recipients. When the fulness of the time arrives he is able to be minute, explicit, emphatic, as he was in intimating Isaac's birth : (1) by the time—a year hence, and (2) by the name—Isaac. 4. *The rejoicing husband.* The laugh of gladness which escaped the patriarch, though partly owing to the reiterated promise of a son, was chiefly due to the announcement that Sarah was to be its mother. It was the joy of a husband in the happiness of a beloved wife, long tried, but at length about to be rewarded ; it was also the joy of a believing husband in the well-founded assurance of his wife's interest in the covenant of grace.

II. THE EXCLUSION OF ISHMAEL. 1. The prayer of Abraham—(1) *Reveals a note of sorrow.* The displacement of Hagar's child by the son of Sarah, though for Sarah's sake thrilling him with joy, appears to have raised a tender sympathy in his breast for the disappointment which was to fall upon the lad and his mother. For years he had himself no other thought than that Ishmael might be the seed, and now he cannot put aside the cherished hope without regret. Let fathers learn that though it is beautiful to feel for children's griefs, it is dangerous to construct plans for children's greatness. (2) *Breathes an earnest spirit.* Deeply concerned for the welfare of his son, Abraham was also filled with longing that God would listen to his prayer. If there is anything about which a parent's heart should be sincerely passionate, it is the happiness and prosperity of his offspring ; and if there is one season more than another in which a parent's heart should be possessed by strong emotion, it is when pleading for his children at a throne of grace (Ps. lxxviii. 2). (3) *Craves a heavenly blessing.* Though Ishmael was to be denied the honour of serving as a medium for the transmission of the blessings of the covenant to future ages, his father supplicated for him a personal participation in those blessings. The chief ambition of a parent should be the conversion and spiritual advancement of his children (3 John 4). 2. The answer of God—(1) *Assures the praying father of acceptance.* Ishmael, though not admitted to the succession of the holy seed, should not be excluded from the gifts of grace. If Hagar's child, though born of the flesh, should become possessed of faith, he too would share in the spiritual benediction of the covenant. Let parents be encouraged to pray for their children. (2) *Promises great temporal prosperity to the son.* Abraham had sought spiritual life for Ishmael ; God bestowed in addition temporal renown. So God did with Solomon (1 Kings iii. 11), and still does with saints (Ephes. iii. 20).

III. THE ACQUIESCENCE OF ABRAHAM. This was signified by the patriarch's observance of the rite of circumcision, in regard to which his obedience was—1. *Immediate.* There was no delay, no reluctance, no considering the question, but instantaneous compliance with the Divine directions. On the self-same day as God explained to him the provisions and conditions of the covenant, he declared his consent before God by the acceptance of the suggested sign. His behaviour in this respect should be taken as a model by believers. 2. *Cheerful.* The rite of circumcision was of course attended with pain and something approaching to personal humiliation, and yet self-abasement and suffering were joyously assented to in view of the coming gift of the covenant. So should Christians delightedly accept tribulation and any sort of bodily indignity that God may impose, considering them as nothing in comparison with the eternal weight of glory. 3. *Thorough-going.* Prompt as to its time, willing in its spirit, the obedience of Abraham was also minute in its performance. The appointed ordinance was administered to himself, his son Ishmael, and every male domestic in his house, as God had said unto him. So God's people are required to observe all things written in the book of the covenant.

HOMILIES BY VARIOUS AUTHORS.

Ver. 15.—"Thou shalt not call her name Sarai, but Sarah shall her name be," &c. "Mother of nations ;" "kings of peoples shall be of her."

I. EXALTATION OF THE LOWLY. A pilgrim and stranger, made a princess. A mother of nations, though once desolate, mourning, ready to murmur. The lamentation turned into laughter.

II. THE FREEDOM OF DIVINE GRACE. The blessing unexpected, apart from creature strength, notwithstanding blind and foolish attempts to obtain blessing in our own way—the Ishmael, not the Isaac. Though many things "*said in our heart*," the one thing Divinely purposed the only true fulfilment of that heart's desire.

III. FOREGLEAMS OF THE COMING GLORY. The seed of the woman, specially representing the promise of God, supernaturally given, coming as the royal seed, son of a princess and forerunner of kings of peoples. God-given heir, God-given inheritance. The birth of the child of promise, so manifestly Divine, points to the yet greater glory: "Unto us a Son is born."—R.

EXPOSITION.

CHAPTER XVIII.

Ver. 1.—**And the Lord**—*Jehovah*, the Divine name employed throughout the present and succeeding chapters, which are accordingly assigned to the Jehovist (Tuch, Bleek, Davidson, Colenso), with the exception of ch. xix. 29, which is commonly regarded as a fragment of the original Elohist's narration (*vide infra*)—**appeared unto him.** The absence of Abraham's name has been thought to favour the idea that the present chapter should have begun at ch. xvii. 23 (Quarry). That the time of this renewed Divine manifestation was shortly after the incidents recorded in the preceding chapter is apparent, as also that its object was the reassurance of the patriarch concerning the birth of Isaac. **In the plains of Mamre.** Literally, *in the oaks of Mamre* (*vide* ch. xiii. 18). **And he sat in the tent door.** Literally, *in the opening of the tent*, a fold of which was fastened to a post near by to admit any air that might be stirring. **In the heat of the day.** *I. e.* noontide (cf. 1 Sam. xi. 11), as the cool of the day, or the wind of the day (ch. iii. 8), means eventide. "The usual term for noon is *Tsoharim* (ch. xliii. 16), that is, the time of 'double or greatest light,' while a more poetical expression is 'the height of the day' (Prov. iv. 18), either because then the sun has reached its most exalted position, or because it appears to stand still in the zenith" (Kalisch). Among the Orientals the hour of noon is the time of rest (cf. Cant. i. 7) and the time of dinner (ch. xliii. 16, 25). In this case the patriarch had probably dined and was resting after dinner, since, on the arrival of his visitors, preparations had to be commenced for their entertainment.

Ver. 2.—**And he lift up his eyes and looked, and, lo, three men stood by him.** Not in addition to (Kalisch), but including (Keil), Jehovah, whose appearance to the patriarch, having in the previous verse been first generally stated, is now minutely described. That these three men were not manifestations of the three persons of the Godhead (Justin Martyr, Ambrose, Cyril), but Jehovah accompanied by two created angels (Keil, *et alii*), may be inferred from ch. xix. 1. When first perceived by the patriarch they were believed to be men, strangers, who were approaching his tent, and indeed were already close to it, or

standing by him. **And when he saw them** (*i. e.* understood that one of them was Jehovah, Jarchi rightly explaining that the word translated above "looked," *i. e.* with the bodily vision, now implies an act of mental perception), **he ran to meet them from the tent door, and bowed himself toward the ground.** The expression denotes the complete prostration of the body by first falling on the knees, and then inclining the head forwards till it touches the ground. As this was a mode of salutation practised by Orientals towards superiors generally, such as kings and princes (2 Sam. ix. 8), but also towards equals (ch. xxiii. 7 ; xxxiii. 6, 7 ; xlii. 6 ; xliii. 26), as well as towards the Deity (ch. xxii. 5 ; 1 Sam. i. 3), it is impossible to affirm with certainty (Keil, Lange) that an act of worship was intended by the patriarch, and not simply the presentation of human and civil honour (Calvin). If Heb. xiii. 2 inclines to countenance the latter interpretation, the language in which Abraham immediately addresses one of the three men almost leads to the conclusion that already the patriarch had recognised Jehovah.

Ver. 3.—**And said, My Lord**—Adonāi, literally, Lord, as in ch. xv. 2, *q. v.* (LXX., κύριε ; Vulgate, *Domine ;* Syriac, Onkelos, Kalisch, Alford, Lange), though the term may have indicated nothing more than Abraham's recognition of the superior authority of the Being addressed (Murphy). The readings Adoni, my Lord (A. V., Dathius, Rosenmüller), and Adonăi, my lords (Gesenius), are incorrect—**if now I have found favour in thy sight** — not implying dubiety on Abraham's part as to his acceptance before God (Knobel), but rather postulating his already conscious enjoyment of the Divine favour as the ground of the request about to be preferred (Delitzsch, Lange). Those who regard Abraham as unconscious of the Divinity of him to whom he spake see in his language nothing but the customary formula of Oriental address (Rosenmüller ; cf. ch. xxx. 27 ; 1 Sam. xx. 29 ; Esther vii. 3)— **pass not away, I pray thee, from thy servant.** The hospitality of the Eastern, and even of the Arab, has been frequently remarked by travellers. Volney describes the Arab as dining at his tent door in order to invite passers-by ('Trav.,' i. p. 314). "The virtue of hospitality is one of the great redeeming virtues in the character of the Bedouins"

(Kalisch). "Whenever our path led us near an encampment, as was frequently the case, we always found some active sheikh or venerable patriarch sitting 'in his tent door,' and as soon as we were within hail we heard the earnest words of welcome and invitation which the Old Testament Scriptures had rendered long ago familiar to us, 'Stay, my lord, stay. Pass not on till thou hast eaten bread, and rested under thy servant's tent. Alight and remain until thy servant kills a kid and prepares a feast'" (Porter's 'Giant Cities of Bashan,' p. 326 ; cf. *ibid.* p. 87).

Ver. 4.—**Let a little water, I pray you, be fetched, and wash your feet.** Feet washing was a necessary part of Oriental hospitality (cf. ch. xix. 2 ; xxiv. 32 ; xliii. 24). "Among the ancient Egyptians the basins kept in the houses of the rich for this purpose were sometimes of gold" (Freeman, Bible Manners, 'Homiletic Quarterly,' vol. i. p. 78). "In India it is considered a necessary part of hospitality to wash the feet and ankles of the weary traveller, and even in Palestine this interesting custom is not extinct. Dr. Robinson and party on arriving at Ramleh repaired to the abode of a wealthy Arab, where the ceremony was performed in the genuine style of ancient Oriental hospitality" (*vide* Kitto's 'Bible Illustrations,' vol. i. p. 230). **And rest yourselves** (literally, *recline* by resting on the elbow) **under the tree.**

Ver. 5.—**And I will fetch a morsel of bread,**—a modest description of what proved a sumptuous repast (*vide* vers. 6, 8)—**and comfort ye your hearts;**—literally, *strengthen* or support them, *i. e.* by eating and drinking (Judges xix. 5 ; 1 Kings xxi. 7)—**after that ye shall pass on: for therefore**—כִּי־עַל־כֵּן, introduces the ground of what has already been stated, something like *quando quidem*, forasmuch as (Ewald, 'Heb. Synt.,' § 353), since, or because (Kalisch), and not=עַל־בֵּן־כִּי, for this cause that (Gesenius, 'Gram.,' § 155), or "because for this purpose" (Keil)—**are ye come to** (literally, *have ye passed before*) **thy servant.** The patriarch's meaning is not that they had come with the design of receiving his gifts (LXX., A. V.), but either that, unconsciously to them, God had ordered their journey so as to give him this opportunity (Calvin, Bush, Wordsworth, 'Speaker's Commentary,' Keil), or perhaps simply that since they had passed by his tent they should suffer him to accord them entertainment (Kalisch, Rosenmüller). **And they said, So do, as thou hast said.** Therefore we must believe that Abraham washed the men's feet, and they did eat (ver. 8). Here is a mystery (Wordsworth).

Ver. 6.—**And Abraham hastened into the tent unto Sarah, and said, Make ready quickly three measures** — Hebrew, three seahs, a seah being a third of an ephah, and containing 374 cubic inches each (Keil) ; a third of a bushel (Kalisch)—**of fine meal,** —literally, *of flour, fine flour;* σεμίδαλις (LXX.) ; the first term when alone denoting flour of ordinary quality (cf. Levit. ii. 1 , v. 11 ; Num. vii. 13)—**knead it, and make cakes upon the hearth**—*i. e.* "round unleavened cakes baked upon hot stones" (Keil).

Ver. 7.—**And Abraham ran unto the herd, and fetcht a calf tender and good,**—the greatness of the honour done to the strangers was evinced by the personal activity of the patriarch, and the offering of animal food, which was not a common article of consumption among Orientals — **and gave it unto a young man;**—*i. e.* the servant in attendance (cf. ch. xiv. 24)—**and he hasted to dress it.**

Ver. 8.—**And he took butter,**—חֶמְאָה, from the root חמא, to curdle or become thick, signifies curdled milk, not butter (βούτυρον, LXX.; *butyrum*, Vulgate), which was not used among Orientals except medicinally. The word occurs seven times in Scripture with four letters (Deut. xxxii. 14 ; Judges v. 25 ; 2 Sam. xvii. 29 ; Isa. vii. 15, 22 ; Prov. xxx. 33 ; Job xx. 17), and once without א (Job xxix. 6 ; *vide* Michaelis, 'Supplement,' p. 807)—**and milk,**—חָלָב, milk whilst still fresh, or containing its fatness, from a root signifying to be fat (cf. ch. xlix. 12 ; Prov. xxvii. 27)—**and the calf which he**—*i. e.* the young man—**had dressed, and set it before them; and he stood by them under the tree,**—a custom still observed among the Arabs, who honour their guests not by sitting to eat with, but by standing to wait upon, them—**and they did eat.** Not seemed to eat (Josephus, Philo, Jonathan), nor simply ate after an allegorical fashion, as fire consumes the materials put into it (Justin Martyr), but did so in reality (Tertullian, Delitzsch, Keil, Kurtz, Lange). Though the angel who appeared to Manoah (Judges xiii. 16) refused to partake of food, the risen Saviour ate with his disciples (Luke xxiv. 43). Physiologically inexplicable, this latter action on the part of Christ was not a mere φαινόμενον or simulation, but a veritable manduction of material food, to which Christ appealed in confirmation of the reality of his resurrection ; and the acceptance of Abraham's hospitality on the part of Jehovah and his angels may in like manner have been designed to prove that their visit to his tent at Mamre was not a dream or a vision, but a genuine external manifestation.

Ver. 9.—**And they said unto him** (*i. e.* the Principal One of the three, speaking for the others, interrogated Abraham during the progress, or perhaps at the close of, the meal saying), **Where** is **Sarah thy wife?** (thus indicating that their visit had a special reference to her). **And he said, Behold, in the tent.** It is obvious that if at first Abraham regarded his visitors only as men, by this time a suspicion of their true character must have begun to dawn upon his mind. How should ordinary travellers be aware of his wife's name? and why should they do so unusual a thing, according to Oriental manners, as to inquire after her? If thus far their behaviour could not fail to surprise the patriarch, what must have been his astonishment at the subsequent communication?

Ver. 10. — **And he said** (the Principal Guest, as above, who, by the very nature and terms of his announcement, identifies himself with Jehovah), **I will certainly return unto thee according to the time of life.** Literally, *at the time reviving;* i. e. when the year shall have been renewed, in the next year, or rather spring (*vide* Ewald, 'Heb. Synt.,' § 337; Rosenmüller, Drusius, Keil, Kalisch, Lange, Ainsworth, 'Speaker's Commentary'); though other interpretations of the phrase have been suggested, as, *e. g.*, "according to the time of that which is born," *i. e.* at the end of nine months (Willet, Calvin, Bush, Murphy). **And, lo, Sarah thy wife shall have a son.** *I. e.* at the time specified. **And Sarah heard it in the tent door, which** was **behind him.**

Ver. 11.—**Now Abraham and Sarah** were **old** and **well stricken in age.** Literally, *gone into days,* i. e. into years. This was the first natural impediment to the accomplishment of Jehovah's promise; the second was peculiar to Sarah. **And it ceased to be with Sarah after the manner of women** (*vide* Levit. xv. 19, 25).

Ver. 12.—**Therefore** (literally, *and*) **Sarah laughed within herself** — Abraham had laughed in joyful amazement (ch. xvii. 17) at the first mention of Sarah's son; Sarah laughs, if not in unbelief (Calvin, Keil, 'Speaker's Commentary,' Wordsworth), at least with a mingled feeling of doubt and delight (Lange, Murphy) at the announcement of her approaching maternity—**saying, fter I am waxed old shall I have pleasure, my lord being old also?**—literally, *and my lord,* i. e. my husband, is *old.* The reverential submission to Abraham which Sarah here displays is in the New Testament commended as a pattern to Christian wives (1 Pet. iii. 6).

Ver. 13.—**And the Lord said unto Abraham, Wherefore did Sarah laugh,**—a question which must have convinced Abraham of the Speaker's omniscience. Not only had he heard the silent, inaudible, inward cachinnation of Sarah's spirit, but he knew the tenor of her thoughts, and the purport of her dubitations—**saying, Shall I of a surety bear a child, which** (literally, *and I*) **am old?** Sarah's mental cogitations clearly showed that the temporary obscuration of her faith proceeded from a strong realisation of the weakness of nature, which made conception and pregnancy impossible to one like her, who was advanced in years; and accordingly her attention, as well as that of her husband, was directed to the Divine omnipotence as the all-sufficient guarantee for the accomplishment of the promise.

Ver. 14.—**Is any thing too hard for the Lord?** Literally, *Is any word too wonderful,* *i. e.* impossible, for Jehovah? μὴ ἀδυνατήσει παρὰ τῷ θεῷ ῥῆμα (LXX.), with which may be compared Luke i. 37. **At the time appointed I will return unto thee, according to the time of life** (*vide supra,* ver. 10), **and Sarah shall have a son.**

Ver. 15.—**Then Sarah** (who had overheard the conversation, and the charge preferred against her, and who probably now appeared before the stranger) **denied, saying, I laughed not.** Sarah's conduct will admit of no other explanation than that which the sacred narrative itself gives. **For she was afraid.** The knowledge that her secret thoughts had been deciphered must have kindled in her breast the suspicion that her visitor was none other than Jehovah. With this a sense of guilt would immediately assail her conscience for having cherished even a moment any doubt of the Divine word. In the consequent confusion of soul she tries what ever seems to be the first impulse of detected transgressions, viz., deception (cf. ch. iii. 12, 13). **And he said, Nay; but thou didst laugh.** With a directness similar to that which he employed in dealing with the first culprits in the garden, not contending in a multiplicity of words, but solemnly announcing that what she said was false. The silence of Sarah was an evidence of her conviction; her subsequent conception was a proof of her repentance and forgiveness.

HOMILETICS.

Vers. 1—15.—*Noontide at Mamre, or angels' visits.* I. THE ARRIVAL OF THE STRANGERS. 1. *The appearance they presented.* Seemingly three men, they were in reali'y three angels, or, more correctly, Jehovah accompanied by two celestial attendants, who, at an unexpected moment, were making for Abraham's tent. So are the homes of saints ofttimes visited by angels unawares (Heb. i. 14), and, greater honour still, by him who claims the angels as his ministers (Ps. viii. 4; Isa. lvii. 17). 2. *The reception they obtained.* Immediately that Abraham discerned their approach, he hastened to accord them most respectful and courteous salutation, in true Oriental fashion, falling on his knees and bowing till his head touched the ground; an illustration of that beautiful politeness towards one's fellow-men (if as yet he only regarded his visitors as men), or of that reverential self-abasement before God (if already he had recognised the superior dignity of the principal figure of the three) which ought especially to characterise God's believing and covenanted people (see Ps. xcv. 6; 1 Pet. iii. 8). 3. *The invitation they received.* Probably oppressed by the sultry beams of the noonday sun, if not otherwise travel-stained and weary, they were, with genuine Arab-like hospitality, entreated by the patriarch to avail themselves of such refreshment and repose as his cool-shaded, well-furnished tent might be able to afford. And this invitation of the patriarch was—(1) *Humbly proffered,* as if their acceptance of it would be more an act of grace conferred on him than a benefit enjoyed by themselves. (2) *Modestly described,* as if it were only a trifle after all that he was asking them to accept, while all the time his liberal heart was devising liberal things. (3) *Piously enforced,* by the consideration that he recognised in their arrival at his tent a special call to the discharge of the duty of hospitality. (4) *Promptly accepted,* without apologies or deprecations of any sort, but with the same generous simplicity as it was offered. "So do as thou hast said."

II. The ENTERTAINMENT OF THE STRANGERS. In the banquet which Abraham extemporised for his celestial guests beneath the umbrageous oak at Mamre were three things which should be studied by all who would use hospitality. 1. *Joyous alacrity.* That the patriarch's invitation was no mere conventional remark which was meant to pass unheeded by those to whom it was addressed was proved by the expeditious cordiality with which he set about the preparations needed for the proffered repast, enlisting Sarah's practised hands in baking cakes, and commissioning a trusty servant of the house to kill and dress a young and tender calf selected by himself from the flocks. Here was no reluctance or half-heartedness with Abraham in the work of kindness to which Providence had called him. So ought Christians to manifest a spirit of cheerfulness and a habit of promptitude in doing good (Rom. xii. 8, 13; 2 Cor. ix. 7). 2. *Unstinted liberality.* Modestly characterised as a little repast, it was in reality a sumptuous banquet which was set before the strangers. Abraham entertained his guests with princely munificence. The modern virtue of stinginess, or niggardliness, supposed by many to be a Christian grace, had not been acquired by the patriarch, and should with as much speed as possible be unlearned by Christ's disciples. Hospitality towards the saints and beneficence towards all men, but especially towards the poor, should be practised with diligence, and even with a holy prodigality, by all who are of Abraham's seed (Luke xiv. 12—14; Rom. xii. 13; 1 Tim. iii. 2; Heb. xiii. 2). 3. *Personal activity.* Though the master of a large household, with 300 trained domestics, and the noble Eliezer at their head, the patriarch does not think of relegating the important work of preparing the entertainment to his subordinates, but himself attends to its immediate execution. Indeed, in all the bustling activity which forthwith pervades the tent his figure is always and everywhere conspicuous. And when the meal is ready he reverently serves it with his own hand; again a true pattern of humility, as if he had caught up by anticipation the spirit of our Saviour's words (Matt. xx. 26); and a true preacher of Christian duty, saying that in God's work personal service is ever better than labouring by proxy.

III. The COMMUNICATION OF THE STRANGERS. The noonday meal over, or perhaps while it was advancing, the principal of the three guests, who certainly by this time was recognised as Jehovah, made an important announcement to the patriarch, which, however, was specially intended for Sarah, who was listening behind the dark fold of the camel's-hair tent, viz., that next year the promised seed should be born. That announcement was—1. *Authoritatively made.* It was made by him who is the faithful and true Witness, with whom it is impossible to lie, and who is able also to perform that which he has promised. 2. *Unbelievingly received.* The laugh of Sarah was altogether different from that of Abraham (ch. xvii. 17). While Abraham's was the outcome of faith, hers was the fruit of latent doubt and incredulity. There are always two ways of receiving God's promises; the one of which secures, but the other of which imperils, their fulfilment (Mark ix. 23; xi. 23). 3. *Solemnly confirmed.* (1) By an appeal to the Divine omnipotence. The thing promised was not beyond the resources of Jehovah to accomplish. (2) By a further certification of the event. As it were a second time the Divine faithfulness was pledged for its fulfilment. (3) By an impressive display of miraculous power, first in searching Sarah's heart, and second in arresting Sarah's conscience. The result was that Sarah's unbelief was transformed into faith.

Learn—1. The duty and profit of entertaining strangers (Heb. xiii. 2). 2. The beauty and nobility of Christian hospitality (Rom. xii. 13). 3. The excellence and acceptability of personal service in God's work. 4. The condescension and kindness of God in visiting the sons of men. 5. The admirable grace of Jehovah in repeating and confirming his promises to man. 6. The right way and the wrong way of listening to God's words of grace and truth.

HOMILIES BY VARIOUS AUTHORS.

Vers. 1—15.—*The theophany at Mamre.* I. THE DIVINE VISIT TO THE PATRIARCH. 1. A remarkable proof of the Divine condescension. 2. A striking adumbration of the incarnation of Christ. 3. An instructive emblem of God's gracious visits to his saints. II. THE DIVINE FEAST WITH THE PATRIARCH. 1. The courteous invitation. 2. The sumptuous provision. 3. The ready attention. III. THE DIVINE MESSAGE FOR THE PATRIARCH. 1. Its delivery to Abraham. 2. Its reception by Sarah. 3. Its authentication by Jehovah.—W.

Vers. 1—15.—*The theophany at Mamre.* "The Lord appeared unto him" (ver. 1). I. THE PREPARATION FOR DIVINE MANIFESTATION. 1. Abraham stands on a higher plane of spiritual life. He is endeavouring to fulfil the commandment given (ch. xvii. 1): "Walk before me," &c. The appearances and communications are more frequent and more full. 2. The concentration of the believer's thought at a particular crisis. His place at the tent door, looking forth over the plains of Mamre, representing his mental attitude, as he dwelt on the promises and gazed into the future. 3. There was a coincidence between the conjuncture in the history of the neighbouring cities and the crisis in the history of the individual believer. So in the purposes of God there is preparation for his manifestation both in external providence and in the events of the world on the one hand, and on the other in the more personal and private history of his people. II. THE MANIFESTATION ITSELF. 1. It was very *gracious* and *condescending.* The angels did not appear in angelic glory, but in human likeness. They came as guests, and, in the fragrant atmosphere of a genial hospitality, at once quickened confidence and led forward the mind to expect a higher communication. The household activity of Abraham and Sarah on behalf of the three visitors, while it calmed and strengthened, did also give time for thought and observation of the signs of approaching opportunity. 2. There was from the first an *appeal to faith.* Three persons, yet one having the pre-eminence. The reverential feeling of the patriarch called out at the manner of their approach to his tent. The coincidence possibly between the work of the Spirit in the mind of the believer and the bestowment of outward opportunity. 3. The communication of the Divine promise in immediate connection with the facts of human life. The great trial of faith is not the appeal to accept the word of God in its larger aspect as his truth, but the application of it to our own case. We may believe that the promise will be fulfilled, and yet we may not take it to heart. "I will return unto *thee.*" "Sarah shall have a son." The strength made perfect *in* weakness, not merely *for* weakness. The Divine in the Scripture revelation does not overwhelm and absorb the human; the human is taken up into the Divine and glorified. Taking the narrative as a whole, it may be treated—(1) *Historically*—as it holds a place in the history of the man Abraham and in the progressive development of revelation. (2) *Morally*—suggesting lessons of patience, reverence, humility, truthfulness, faith. (3) *Spiritually*—as pointing to the Messiah, intimating the incarnation, the atonement, the prophetic, priestly, and kingly offices of the promised Redeemer ; the freedom and simplicity of the fellowship of God with man ; the great Christian entertainment—man spreading the meal before God, God accepting it, uniting with man in its participation, elevating it into that which is heavenly by his manifested presence.—R.

Ver. 12.—"Sarah laughed within herself." 1. The incongruity between a Divine promise and the sphere of its fulfilment is temptation to unbelief. 2. A disposition to measure the reality and certainty of the Divine by a human or earthly standard is sure to lead us to irreverence and sinful doubt. 3. There may be an inward and concealed working, known to God though not outwardly expressed, which is still both an insult to him and an injury to us. 4. The root of unbelief is in the ground of the soul. Sarah laughed because she was not prepared for the gracious promise. She was afraid of her own thoughts because they were not such as became her, and did dishonour to God's sufficiency and love. "She denied, saying, I laughed not." A more receptive and spiritual mind would have both risen above the incongruity and been incapable of the dissimulation.—R.

Ver. 14.—"Is anything too hard for the Lord?" I. TAKE IT AS THE QUESTION WHICH GOD ASKS OF MAN. 1. *Remonstrance.* The history of Divine manifestations proves that nothing is demanded of faith which is not justified by the bestowments of the past. 2. *Invitation.* We connect the question with the promise. He opens the gate of life ; is it too hard for him to give us the victory? "At the time appointed" his word will be fulfilled. He would have us rest on *himself.* "Believe that he *is,* and that he is the *rewarder,*" &c. What he is, what he says, are blended into one in the true faith of his waiting children.

II. TAKE THE QUESTION AS ONE WHICH MEN ASK OF ONE ANOTHER. 1. When they set forth the goodness of Divine truth. The possibility of miracles. The hardness of the world's problems no justification of unbelief. 2. When they proclaim a gospel of supernatural gifts, a salvation not of man, but of God. Why should we doubt conversion? Why should a regenerated, renewed nature be so often mocked at? 3. When they would encourage one another to persevere in Christian enterprise. The methods may be old, but the grace is ever new. The world may laugh, but the true believer should see all things possible. The times are our measures. Eternity is God's.—R.

EXPOSITION.

Ver. 16.—**And the men rose up from thence,**—Mamre (*vide supra,* ver. 1)—**and looked towards Sodom.** Literally, *toward the face* (Rosenmüller), or towards the plain (Keil), of Sodom, as if intending to proceed thither. **And Abraham went with them**—across the mountains on the east of Hebron, as far as *Caphár-barucha,* according to tradition, whence a view can be obtained of the Dead Sea—*solitudinem ac terras Sodomæ* (vide Keil, *in loco*)—**to bring them on the way.** Literally, *to send them away,* or accord them a friendly convoy over a portion of their journey.

Ver. 17.—**And the Lord said** (to himself), **Shall I hide from Abraham**—the LXX. interpolate, τοῦ παιδός μου ; but, as Philo observes, τοῦ φιλοῦ μου would have been a more appropriate designation for the patriarch (cf. 2 Chron. xx. 7 ; Isa. xli. 8 ; James ii. 23)—**that thing which I do.** *I. e.* propose to do, the present being used for the future, where, as in the utterances of God, whose will is

equivalent to his deed, the action is regarded by the Speaker as being already as good as finished (*vide* Ewald, 'Heb. Synt.,' § 135 ; Gesenius, § 126).

Ver. 18. — **Seeing that Abraham shall surely become** (literally, *becoming shall become*) **a great and mighty nation** (cf. ch. xii. 2 ; xvii. 4—6), **and all the nations of the earth shall be blessed in him?** The import of Jehovah's self-interrogation was, that since Abraham had already been promoted to so distinguished a position, not only was there no sufficient reason why the Divine purpose concerning Sodom should be concealed from him, but, on the contrary, the gracious footing of intimacy which subsisted between himself and his humble friend almost necessitated some sort of friendly communication on the subject, and all the more for the reason next appended.

Ver. 19.—**For I know him, that**—literally, *for I have known* (or chosen, יְדַעְתִּיו being = *dilexi,* as in Amos iii. 2) *him to the end that*

(לְמַעַן conveying the idea of purpose; vide Ewald, § 357), the language expressing the idea that Abraham had been the object of Divine foreknowledge and election (Gesenius, Rosenmüller, Delitzsch, Keil, Oehler, Kalisch, Lange), although the reading of the text is substantially adopted by many (LXX., Vulgate, Targums, Luther, Calvin, Dathe, et alii). The latter interpretation assigns as the reason of the Divine communication the knowledge which Jehovah then possessed of Abraham's piety; the former grounds the Divine resolution on the prior fact that Divine grace had elected him to the high destiny described in the language following. It is generally agreed that this clause connects with ver. 17; Bush regards it as exhibiting the means by which the future promised to Abraham in ver. 18 should be realised—he will (rather, may) command his children and his household after him (by parental authority as well as by personal example), and they shall keep (rather, that they may keep) the way of the Lord, — i. e. the religion of Jehovah (cf. Judges ii. 22; 2 Kings xxi. 22; Ps. cxix. 1; Acts xviii. 25), of which the practical outcome is—to do justice and judgment;—or righteousness and judgment, that which accords with right or the sense of oughtness in intelligent and moral beings, and that which harmonises with the Divine law (cf. Ezek. xviii. 5)—that (literally, to the end that, in order that, לְמַעַן, ut supra) the Lord may bring upon Abraham that which he hath spoken of him.

Ver. 20.—And the Lord said, Because the cry of Sodom and Gomorrah is great. Literally, the cry of Sodom and Gomorrah (cf. ch. iv. 10), because it is (not, it is indeed, Baumgarten, Keil) multiplied; the place of emphasis being conceded to the subject of discourse, viz., the cry of Sodom's wickedness. And because their sin is very great.

Literally, and their sin, because it is heavy, i. e. abundant and heinous.

Ver. 21.—I will go down now (cf. ch. xi. 5), and see (judicial investigation ever precedes judicial infliction at the Divine tribunal) whether they have done altogether—literally, whether they have made completeness, i. e. carried their iniquity to perfection, to the highest pitch of wickedness (Calvin, Delitzsch, Keil); or consummated their wickedness, by carrying it to that pitch of fulness which works death (Ainsworth, Kalisch, Rosenmüller). The received rendering, which regards כלה as an adverb, has the authority of Luther and Gesenius—according to the cry of it, which has come unto me; and if not, I will know. The LXX. render ἵνα γνῶ, meaning, "should it not be so, I will still go down, that I may ascertain the exact truth;" the Chaldee paraphrases, "and if they repent, I will not exact punishment." The entire verse is anthropomorphic, and designed to express the Divine solicitude that the strictest justice should characterise all his dealings both with men and nations.

Ver. 22.—And the men turned their faces from thence, and went toward Sodom (i. e. two of the three proceeded on their way towards the Jordan valley, while the third was detained by the patriarch, probably on the heights overlooking the plain, for a sublime act of intercession which is thus briefly but suggestively described): but Abraham stood yet before the Lord. According to the Masorites the text originally read, "And the Lord stood before Abraham," and was changed because it did not seem becoming to speak of God standing in the presence of a creature. This, however, is a mere Rabbinical conceit. As Abraham is not said to have stood before the three men, the expression points to spiritual rather than to local contiguity.

HOMILETICS.

Ver. 17. — Sodom's doom revealed. I. THE REASON OF THE REVELATION. 1. Abraham's new position. Having been lately taken into covenant with God, allied by the holy tie of a celestial friendship to Jehovah, the patriarch seemed in the Lord's eyes to occupy a footing of intimacy before him that demanded the disclosure of Sodom's impending doom. That footing the patriarch no doubt owed to Divine grace—sovereign, unmerited, free; but still, having been accorded to him, it is, by a further act of grace, represented as laying God himself under certain obligations towards his servant. So "the secret of the Lord is with them that fear him, and he will show them his covenant" (Ps. xxv. 14). 2. Abraham's new prospects. About to become the head of a great nation, it was natural to suppose that Abraham would be profoundly interested in all that concerned mankind. As the head of the Old Testament Church too, which had just been constituted (ch. xvii.), there existed a special reason for his being properly instructed as to the impending judgment of Sodom. Upon him would devolve the interpretation to the men of his day of the significance of that event. Rightly viewed, this is one of the proper functions of the Church on earth—to explain God's judgments to the unbelieving world. Hence "the Lord God doeth nothing but he revealeth his secret unto his servants the prophets" (Amos iii. 7). 3. Abraham's *new responsibilities.* These were the cultivation of personal and family religion, which devolved upon him with a new force and a heavier degree of obligation than they did before in consequence of his new standing as a Church member. God having graciously assigned this position within the Church in order that he might command his children and his household after him, by means of religious instruction as well as through the influence of personal example, to fear God, it was needful that he should be informed as to the ground, at least, of the coming judgment on the cities of the plain.

II. The reason of the retribution. This was the wickedness of Sodom, which was—1. *Exceedingly heinous as to its character.* Minutely detailed in the ensuing chapter, it is here only indirectly mentioned as something grievous in the sight of God. All sin is inherently offensive in the eyes of the Almighty; but some forms of wickedness are more presumptuously daring or more intrinsically loathsome than others, and of such sort were the sins of Sodom (ch. xix. 1). 2. *Exceedingly abundant as to its measure.* It was "multiplied" iniquity of which the Sodomites were guilty; and this not simply in the sense in which the sins of all may be charac-terised as beyond computation (Ps. xix. 12; xl. 12), but in the sense that their hearts were set in them to do evil (Eccles. viii. 11), so that they worked all manner of uncleanness with greediness (Ephes. iv. 19). 3. *Exceedingly clear as to its com-mission.* Though God speaks of making investigation into the sins of Sodom, this was really unnecessary. The moral degeneracy of the inhabitants of the Jordan valley was one of the "all things" that are ever "naked and manifest" unto his eye. So nothing can hide sin from God (2 Chron. xvi. 9; Prov. xv. 3; Amos ix. 8). 4. *Exceedingly patent as to its ill desert.* This was the reason why God employed the language of ver. 21. He meant that though the guilt of Sodom was great, he would not let loose his vengeance until it should be seen to be perfectly just. Nothing would be done in haste, but all with judicial calmness.

Lessons:—1. The impotence of anything but true religion to purify the heart or refine a people. 2. God is specially observant of the wickedness of great cities. 3. When great cities sink to a certain depth in their wickedness they are doomed to perish. 4. When God's judgments overtake a nation they are ever characterised by justice.

HOMILIES BY VARIOUS AUTHORS.

Vers. 16—33.—*Abraham's intercession for Sodom.* The whole wonderful scene springs out of the theophany. Abraham's faith has given him a special position with the Lord. "Shall I hide from Abraham that thing which I do?" &c. The true priesthood and mediatorship is friendship with God. The grace of God first gives the likeness and then exalts it. The Lord knew Abraham because Abraham knew the Lord. The superior angel, the Lord, remains behind his companions that Abraham might have the opportunity of intercession; so the Lord lingers in his providence that he may reveal his righteousness and mercy. As to the pleading of the patriarch and the answers of the Lord to it, we may take it—

I. As it bears on the character of God. 1. He is open to entreaty. 2. He is unwilling to destroy. 3. He spares for the sake of righteousness. 4. He "does right" as "Judge of the earth," even though to the eyes of the best men there is awful mystery in his doings.

II. As it reveals the characteristics of patriarchal piety. 1. It was bold with the boldness of simplicity and faith. 2. It was full of true humanity while deeply reverential towards God. Abraham was no fanatic. 3. It waited for and humbly accepted Divine judgments and appointments not without reason, not without the exercise of thought and feeling, but all the more so as it prayed and talked with ·God. 4. The one living principle of the patriarchal religion was that entire con-fidence in God's righteousness and love, in separating the wicked and· the good, in both his judgments and his mercy, which is the essence of Christianity as well. "*The right*" which the Judge of all the earth will do is not the right of mere blind

law, or rough human administration of law, but the right of him who discerneth
between the evil and the good, "too wise to err, too good to be unkind."—R.

Ver. 19.—*God's rule in the family.* "For I know him, that he will command
his children and his household after him, and they shall keep the way of the Lord."
The promise to Abraham included—(1) understanding of God's acts ; (2) that he
should become a mighty nation ; (3) that he should be ancestor of the promised
Seed ; (4) that he himself should be a blessing to others. Of these points two at
least are not confined to him personally, but belong to all who will. To know what
God doeth a man must be taught of the Spirit (1 Cor. ii. 14 ; cf. Isa. vii. 12). There
is a wide difference between seeing an event, or even foreseeing it, and understanding
God's lessons therein. To be able in everything to mark the love, and care, and
wisdom of God ; to walk with him as a child, accepting what he sends not merely
as inevitable, but as loving ; to learn lessons from all that happens, and through the
works of his hands to see our Father's face—this is peace, and this is what the
wisdom of this world cannot teach (Matt. xi. 25 ; 1 Cor. i. 20, 21). Again, Abraham
was to be not merely the ancestor of a nation, but the father of a spiritual family
by influence and example (Matt. iii. 9 ; Gal. iii. 7). In this his calling is that of
every Christian (Dan. xii. 3 ; Matt. v. 13, 14). Text connects the godly rule of a
family with both these blessings. Christianity is not to be a selfish, but a diffusive
thing (Matt. v. 15 ; xiii. 33) ; and the influence must needs begin at home (cf.
Num. x. 29 ; Acts i. 8), among those whom God has placed with us.
I. THINGS NEEDFUL FOR THIS WORK. 1. *Care for his own soul.* If that is not
cared for a man cannot desire the spiritual good of others. He may desire and try
to train his children and household in honesty and prudence ; to make them good
members of society, successful, respected ; and may cultivate all kindly feelings ;
but not till he realises eternity will he really aim at training others for eternity.
Might say that only one who has found peace can fully perform this work. A man
aroused with desire that his family should be saved. But he cannot press the full
truth as it is in Jesus. 2. *Love for the souls of others.* Christians are sometimes
so wrapped up in care for their own souls as to have few thoughts for the state of
others. Perhaps from a lengthened conflict the mind has been too much turned
upon its own state. But this is not the mind of Christ (1 Cor. x. 24). It is not a
close following of him. It tells of a halting in the "work of faith" (2 Cor. v. 13, 14 ;
cf. Rom. x. 1). 3. *Desire to advance the kingdom of Christ.* When a man has this
he sees in every one a soul for which Christ died (cf. John iv. 35), and those with
whom he is closely connected must chiefly call forth this feeling.
II. THE MANNER OF THE WORK. Family worship ; acknowledgment of God as
ruling in the household ; his will a regulating principle and bond of union. Let this
be a reality, not a form. Let the sacrificial work of Christ be ever put forward in
instruction and in prayer. Personal example—constantly aiming at a holy life. To
pray in the family and yet to be evidently making no effort to live in the spirit of
the prayer is to do positive evil ; encouraging the belief that God may be worshipped
with words, without deeds ; and tending to separate religion from daily life. Prayer
in private for each member—children, servants, &c. ; and watchfulness to deal with
each as God shall give opportunity (Prov. xv. 23). Let prayer always accompany
such efforts.—M.

Ver. 19.—*Abraham and family training.* "For I know him, that he will command his children and his household after him," &c. Under the shady terebinth
celestial visitants partake, or appear to do so, of a meal hastily provided by the
patriarch. The whole narrative is given in such a way that,—after the manner of
the time,—to God are ascribed human passions, desires, hesitancy, and resolve.
Hence God is described as resolving, on two grounds, to reveal to Abraham that
which he is about to do in the destruction of Sodom and Gomorrah: (1) that he
would become a great and mighty nation ; (2) that he would direct his household to
follow in the ways of righteousness and truth. Notice—
I. THE VALUE GOD PLACES ON EARLY SPIRITUAL TRAINING. Children and servants
are both to be brought under spiritual influence. The heart will not become pure

naturally, any more than the boat left to itself would make headway against a strong current. The set of the world-tide is in an evil direction. Abraham had no written book to aid him in his work. His unwritten Bible was the tradition of God's dealings with the race and with himself. He could tell of the promises of God and of the way of approach to him by sacrifice. Evidently there had been careful training in this respect; for when Isaac was going with his father to the mount of sacrifice he noticed that, although the fire and wood were carried, they had no lamb for a burnt offering.

II. God notices how spiritual training is carried on. "I know him." He could trust Abraham, for he would "command," &c., not in the dictatorial tones of a tyrant, but by the power of a consistent life. Many children of religious parents go back to the world because of the imperious style of training they have received. In training, every word, look, and act tells. In many homes there is, alas, no training given and no holy example set. Parents are held accountable for failure, and should therefore be firm and loving in training. They should not readily delegate to others the work of training, either in secular or religious knowledge. Sunday-school teaching should supplement, not supplant, home training.

III. God made the bestowment of intended blessings contingent on the faithful discharge of duty. "That the Lord may bring upon Abraham that which he hath spoken of him." If Abraham had not been faithful his name would have died out, and there would have been no handing on of the narrative of his devoted life and tenacious hold of the Divine promises. Isaac followed in his father's steps and was a meditative man. Jacob cherished the promises and handed them on to his sons. The Jews preserved a knowledge of God when all other races were sunk in polytheism. From them came the One who was the Saviour of the world. All, however, depended on the right training of Isaac. The rill flowed to the streamlet, the streamlet to the creek, the creek to the river, the river to the ocean. Influence ever widened, and God's aim with respect to Abraham was carried out. Let all strive so to act that the character of the life may not undo the teachings of the lip.—H.

EXPOSITION.

Ver. 23.—**And Abraham drew near.** *I. e.* to Jehovah; not simply locally, but also spiritually. The religious use of בָּגַשׁ as a performing religious services to God, or a pious turning of the mind to God, is found in Exod. xxx. 20; Isa. xxix. 13; Jer. xxx. 21; and in a similar sense ἐγγίζω is employed in the New Testament (cf. Heb. iv. 16; x. 22; James iv. 8). The Jonathan Targum explains, "and Abraham prayed." **And said.** Commencing the sublimest act of human intercession of which Scripture preserves a record, being moved thereto, if not by an immediate regard for Lot (Lange), at least by a sense of compassion towards the inhabitants of Sodom, "*communis erga quinque populos misericordia*" (Calvin), which was heightened and intensified by his own previous experience of forgiving grace (Keil). **Wilt thou also destroy the righteous with the wicked?** The question presupposes that God had, according to the resolution of ver. 17, explained to the patriarch his intention to destroy the cities of the plain. The object the patriarch contemplated in his intercession was not simply the preservation of any godly remnant that might be found within the doomed towns, but the rescue of their entire populations from the impending judgment,—only he does not at first discover

his complete design, perhaps regarding such an absolute reversal of the Divine purpose as exceeding the legitimate bounds of creature supplication; but with what might be characterised as holy adroitness he veils his ulterior aim, and commences his petition at a point somewhat removed from that to which he hopes to come. Assuming it as settled that the fair Pentapolis is to be destroyed, he practically asks, with a strange mixture of humility and boldness, if Jehovah has considered that this will involve a sad commingling in one gigantic overthrow of both the righteous and the wicked.

Ver. 24. — **Peradventure there be fifty righteous within the city.** A charitable supposition, as the event showed, though at first sight it might not appear so to Abraham; and the bare possibility of Sodom's — not Sodom alone (Kalisch), but the Pentapolis— containing so many good men was enough to afford a basis for the argument which followed. **Wilt thou also destroy and not spare**—literally, *take away* (sc. the iniquity) *i. e.* remove the punishment from — the **place** (not the godly portion of the city merely, but the entire population; a complete discovery of Abraham's design) **for the fifty righteous that** are **therein?**

Ver. 25.—**That be far from thee**—literally

to profane things (be it) *to thee* = nefas sit tibi = *absit a te!* an exclamation of abhorrence, too feebly rendered by μηδαμῶς (LXX.)—**to do after this manner** (literally, *according to this word*), **to slay the righteous with the wicked : and that the righteous should be as the wicked** (literally, *and that it should be—as the righteous, so the wicked*), **that be far from thee : Shall not the Judge of all the earth do right?** The patriarch appeals not to Jehovah's covenant grace (Kurtz), but to his absolute judicial equity (Keil). It does not, however, follow that the Divine righteousness would have been compromised by consigning pious and wicked to the same temporal destruction. This must have been a spectacle not unfrequently observed in Abraham's day as well as ours. Yet the mind of Abraham appears to have been perplexed, as men's minds often are still, by the magnitude of the proposed illustration of a common principle in Providence. Though prepared to admit the principle when its application is confined to solitary cases, or cases of no great amplitude, yet instinctively the human mind feels that there must be a limit to the commingling of the righteous and the wicked in calamity, though it should be only of a temporal description. That limit Abraham conceived, or perhaps feared that others might conceive, would be passed if good and bad in Sodom should be overwhelmed in a common ruin ; and in this spirit the closing utterance of his first supplication may be regarded as giving expression to the hope that Jehovah would do nothing that would even seem to tarnish his Divine righteousness. Abraham of course regarded this as impossible, consequently he believed that Sodom might be spared.

Ver. 26.—**And the Lord said, If I find in Sodom fifty righteous within the city** (thus accepting the test proposed by Abraham, but not necessarily thereby acquiescing in the absolute soundness of his logic), **then I will spare** (not as an act of justice, but as an exercise of mercy, and not because of any suspicions that might otherwise attach to my rectitude, but solely in vindication of my clemency) **all the place** (not the righteous merely, which was all that justice could have legitimately demanded) **for their sakes,** *i. e.* because of the claims upon my mercy which grace admits the righteous to prefer.

Ver. 27.—**And Abraham answered and said** (being emboldened by the success of his first petition), **Behold now, I have taken upon me**—literally, *I have begun*, though here perhaps used in a more emphatic sense : I have undertaken or ventured (*vide* Gesenius, p. 326)—**to speak unto the Lord**—Adonai (ch. xv. 2)—**which am but dust and ashes.** "Dust in his origin and ashes in his end" (Delitzsch ; *vide* ch. iii. 19).

Ver. 28.—**Peradventure there shall lack five of the fifty righteous : wilt thou destroy all the city for lack of five?** Literally, *on account of five,* i. e. because they are wanting. A rare example of holy ingenuity in prayer. Abraham, instead of pleading for the city's safety on account of forty - five, deprecates its destruction on account of five. **And he said, If I find there forty and five, I will not destroy** it.

Ver. 29. — **And he spake unto him yet again**—literally, *and he added yet to speak to him* (cf. ch. iv. 2 ; viii. 10, 12 ; xxv. 1)—and said (increasing in his boldness as God abounded in his grace), **Peradventure there shall be forty found there.** Does Abraham hesitate to add the query, "Wilt thou also?" &c., as if fearing he had at last touched the limit of the Divine condescension. If so, he must have been surprised by the continued gracious response which his supplication received. **And he said, I will not do** it **for forty's sake.**

Ver. 30.—**And he said unto him, Oh let not the Lord be angry,**—literally, *let not be burning with anger to the Lord* (Adonai)—**and I will speak : Peradventure there shall thirty be found there. And he said, I will not do it, if I find thirty there.**

Ver. 31.—**And he said, Behold now, I have taken upon me** (*vide* ver. 27) **to speak unto the Lord** (Adonai): **Peradventure there shall be twenty found there. And he said, I will not destroy it for twenty's sake.**

Ver. 32.—**And he said, Oh let not the Lord be angry** (*vide supra*), **and I will speak but this once** (literally, *only this time more*, as in Exod. x. 17): **Peradventure ten shall be found there. And he said, I will not destroy** it **for ten's sake.**

Ver. 33.—**And the Lord** (Jehovah) **went his way,**—*i. e.* vanished (Keil) ; not to avoid further entreaties on the part of Abraham (Delitzsch), but for the reason specified in the next words—**as soon as he had left' communing with Abraham** (because Abraham's supplications were ended): **and Abraham returned unto his place** (viz., Mamre near Hebron).

HOMILETICS.

Vers. 23—33.—*Abraham's intercession.* I. THE OBJECT OF HIS INTERCESSION. Not simply the rescue of Lot from the doomed cities, but the salvation of the cities themselves, with their miserable inhabitants. A request evincing—1. *Tender sympathy.*

Though doubtless the righteous character of the impending retribution had been explained to him, its appalling severity was such as to thrill his feeling heart with anguish, which would certainly not be lessened, but intensified, if he allowed his thoughts to dwell upon the future into which that overwhelming calamity would forthwith launch its unhappy victims. 2. *Unselfish charity.* Not blindly shutting his eyes to the miseries of the Sodomites, as many would have done, on the plea that they were richly merited, or that they were no concern of his, or that it was little he could do to avert them, he actively bestirs himself, if possible, to prevent them. Nor does he say that, having delivered them once from the devouring sword of war, without their having profited by either the judgment or the mercy that had then been measured out to them, he will now leave them to be engulfed by the approaching storm of Almighty wrath; but, on the contrary, he rather seeks a second time to effect their rescue. 3. *Amazing catholicity.* Not content with asking Lot's deliverance, or the rescue of the righteous, he aims at nothing short of the complete preservation of the cities. He solicits not a few of their inhabitants only, but their entire population. One wonders whether to admire most the greatness of the love or the grandeur of the faith herein displayed.

II. THE SPIRIT OF HIS INTERCESSION. 1. *Holy boldness.* Abraham "drew near." The expression intimates confidential familiarity, earnestness of entreaty, unrestrained freedom of discourse, almost venturesome audacity in prayer; all of which characteristics should be found in a believer's prayers, especially when interceding in behalf of others (Heb. x. 22). 2. *Reverent humility.* Three times he deprecates Jehovah's anger, and acknowledges personal unworthiness; and that this self-abasement was not affected, but real, is apparent from the circumstance that the more his supplication prospers, the deeper does he sink in self-prostration. Gracious souls are ever humble under a sense of God's mercies: Jacob (ch. xxxii. 10), David (2 Sam. vii. 18; cf. Luke vii. 6). 3. *Fervent importunity.* With a sanctified dexterity he, as it were, endeavours to shut up the heart of God to grant the deliverance he solicits. Nor does he rest contented with the first response to his entreaty, but with greater vehemence returns to the charge, increasing his demands as God enlarges his concessions (cf. Matt. xv. 22).

III. THE LOGIC OF HIS INTERCESSION. 1. The *argument.* The principle on which the patriarch stands is not the grace of the covenant, but the righteousness of the Judge. His meaning is that in moral goodness there is a certain dynamic force which operates towards the preservation of the wicked, and which the Divine righteousness itself is bound to take into its calculations. Where this force reaches a certain limit in intensity, a regard to judicial equity seems to require that it shall be allowed to exercise its legitimate sway—a principle which God admitted to the patriarch when he said that the Amorites were spared because their iniquity was not full (ch. xv. 16), and which he here endorses by consenting to spare Sodom if even ten righteous men can be found within its gates. 2. The *application.* The patriarch conducts his case with singular directness, going straight to the logical issues of the principle with which he starts; with marvellous ingenuity pitching the hypothetical number of pious Sodomites so high as to insure a favourable response, and gradually diminishing as grace enlarges, and with unwearied assiduity refusing to discontinue his holy argument so long as a chance remains of saving Sodom.

IV. THE SUCCESS OF HIS INTERCESSION. 1. *He got all he asked.* He did not crave the unconditional sparing of the city, but only its preservation on certain suggested conditions. Those conditions too were of his own framing; and yet against them not so much as one single caveat was entered by God. 2. *He ceased asking before God stopped giving.* It may be rash to speculate as to what would have happened had Abraham continued to reduce the number on which he perilled the salvation of Sodom; but for God's glory it is only just to observe that it was not he who discontinued answering the patriarch's petitions, so much as the patriarch himself, who felt that he had reached the limit of that liberty which God accords to believing suppliants at his throne.

Lessons:—1. The liberty which saints have to approach God in prayer. 2. The Divinely-taught art of wrestling with God in prayer. 3. The great encouragement which saints have to pray without ceasing. 4. The profound interest which saints should ever take in the welfare of their fellow-men.

EXPOSITION.

CHAPTER XIX.

Ver. 1.—**And there came two angels**—literally, *the two angels*, i. e. the two men of the preceding chapter who accompanied Jehovah to Mamre ; οἱ δύο ἄγγελλοι (LXX.)—**to Sodom at even** (having left the tent of Abraham shortly after noon) ; **and Lot**—last heard of in the narrative as captured by the Asiatic kings, and delivered by his uncle (ch. xiv. 12, 16) **sat in the gate of Sodom.** שַׁעַר, from the idea of opening, signified the gateway or entrance of a camp (Exod. xxxii. 26, 27), of a palace (Esther ii. 19), of a temple (Ezek. viii. 5), of a land (Jer. xv. 7), or of a city (Josh. ii. 7). Corresponding to the ancient forum of the Romans, or agora of the Greeks, the city gate among the Hebrews was the customary place of resort for the settlement of disputes, the transaction of business, or the enjoyment of ordinary social intercourse (cf. ch. xxxiv. 20 ; Deut. xxi. 19 ; xxii. 15 ; Ruth iv. 1 ; Prov. xxxi. 23). It was probably an arch with deep recesses, in which were placed chairs for the judges or city magistrates, and seats or benches for the citizens who had business to transact. So Homer describes the Trojan elders as sitting at the Scæan gate (iii. 148). In what capacity Lot was sitting in the gate is not narrated. That he was on the outlook for travellers on whom to practise the hospitality he had learned from his uncle (Poole, Calvin, Willet, Lange) is perhaps to form too high an ideal of his piety (Kalisch) ; while the explanation that he had been promoted to the dignity of one of the city judges, though not perhaps justified as an inference from ver. 9, is not at all unlikely, considering his relationship to Abraham. **And Lot seeing** them (and recognising them to be strangers by their dress and looks) **rose up to meet them ;**—having not yet abandoned the practice of hospitality, or forgotten, through mingling with the Sodomites, the respectful courtesy which was due to strangers, since the writer adds—**and he bowed himself with his face toward the ground** (cf. ch. xviii. 2).

Ver. 2.—**And he said, Behold now, my lords,**—*Adonâi* (vide ch. xviii. 3). As yet Lot only recognised them as men—**turn in, I pray you, into your servant's house, and tarry all night, and wash your feet** (cf. ch. xviii. 4), **and ye shall rise up early, and go on your ways.** Though an act of kindness on the part of Lot, his invitation was not accepted by the angels obviously with a view to try his character (cf. Luke xxiv. 28). **And they said, Nay ; but we will abide in the street all night.** Literally, *for in the*

broad open spaces (i. e. the streets of the town) *we will pass the night ;* no great hardship in that climate.

Ver. 3. — **And he pressed upon them greatly.** Being himself sincerely desirous to extend to them hospitality, and knowing well the danger to which they would be exposed from the violence and licentiousness of the townsmen. **And they turned in unto him, and entered into his house ; and he made them a feast,**—*mishteh*, from *shathah*, to drink, is rightly rendered πότον (LXX.), a drink, or refreshing beverage (cf. Esther v. 6 ; vii. 7)—**and did bake unleavened bread**—literally, *bread of sweetness*, that is, bread not soured by leaven. The banquet was thus of the simplest kind, chiefly, it may be hoped, for the sake of dispatch. **And they did eat.**

Ver. 4.—**But before they lay down, the men of the city, even the men of Sodom, compassed the house round, both old and young, all the people from every quarter.** *I. e.* of the town, as in Jer. li. 31 (Lange) ; from the extremity, or extremities, of the town (Kalisch) ; from the extremities, *i. e.* all the population contained within the extremities (Rosenmüller) ; all the citizens to the last man (Keil). The text probably conveys the writer's idea.

Ver. 5.—**And they called unto Lot, and said unto him, Where are the men which came in to thee this night ?** Josephus supposes them to have been of beautiful countenances ('Ant.,' i. 11, 3), which excited the lust of the Sodomites, and caused them to assault Lot's house with shameful cries. **Bring them out unto us, that we may know them.** The sin here euphemistically referred to (cf. Judges xix. 22) was exceedingly prevalent among the Canaanites (Levit. xviii. 22) and other heathen nations (Rom. i. 27). Under the law of Moses it was punishable by death.

Vers. 6—8.—**And Lot went out at the door unto them,**—literally, *at the doorway, or opening* (*pethach*, from *pathach*, to open ; cf. *pateo*, Latin ; πρόθυρον, LXX.) ; in which the gate or hanging door (*dĕlĕth*, from *dalal*, to be pendulous) swings, and which it closes (*vide* Gesenius, p. 201)—**and shut the door** (*deleth*, ut supra ; θύρα, LXX.) **after him,**—to protect his visitors, which he also sought to accomplish by personal exhortation—**and said, I pray you, brethren, do not so wickedly**—and also by an infamous proposal which nothing can extenuate and the utmost charity finds difficult to reconcile with any pretence of piety on the part of Lot. **Behold now, I have two daughters which have not known man ;**—*i. e.* unmarried (cf. ch. iv. 1), though, according to some, already betrothed to two Sodomites (ver. 14) —**let me, I pray you, bring them out unto you, and do ye to them as is good in your eyes.** The usual apologies—that in sacrificing his daughters to the Sodomites instead of giving up his guests to their unnatural lust Lot (1) selected the lesser of two sins (Ambrose); (2) thereby protected his guests and discharged the duties of hospitality incumbent on him (Chrysostom); (3) believed his daughters would not be desired by the Sodomites, either because of their well-known betrothal (Rosenmüller), or because of the unnatural lust of the Sodomites (Lange); (4) acted through mental perturbation (Augustine)—are insufficient to excuse the wickedness of one who in attempting to prevent one sin was himself guilty of another (Delitzsch), who in seeking to be a faithful friend forgot to be an affectionate father (Kalisch), and who, though bound to defend his guests at the risk of his own life, was not at liberty to purchase their safety by the sacrifice of his daughters ('Speaker's Commentary').

Only unto these men—הָאֵל, an archaic form of הָאֵלֶּה, a proof of the antiquity of the Pentateuch (cf. ver. 25; xxvi. 3, 4; Levit. xviii. 27; Deut. iv. 42; vii. 22; xix. 11)—**do nothing** (i. e. offer to them neither violence nor dishonour); **for therefore** (vide ch. xviii. 5) **came they under the shadow of my roof**—in order to find protection. Ver. 9.—**And they said, Stand back.** Ἀπόστα ἐκεῖ (LXX.); recede illuc (Vulgate); "Make way," i. e. for us to enter (Keil,

Knobel, Gesenius); Approach hither (Baumgarten, Kalisch); Come near, farther off ('Speaker's Commentary'). **And they said** again, **This one** fellow (literally, the one, an expression of the Sodomites' contempt) **came in to sojourn, and he will needs be a judge:** —literally, and shall he judge, judging; shall he continually play the judge, referring doubtless to Lot's daily remonstrances against their wickedness (cf. 2 Pet. ii. 7, 8)—**now will we deal worse with thee, than with them. And they pressed sore upon the man**, even **Lot** (literally, upon Lot, who appears to have offered a sturdy resistance to their violence no less than to their clamours), **and came near to break** (שָׁבַר, to break to pieces, to shiver) **the door.**

Ver. 10.—**But the men** (i. e. the angels) **put forth their hand, and pulled Lot into the house to them, and shut to the door**—deleth (vide ver. 6).

Ver. 11.—**And they smote the men that were at the door**—the pethach, or opening (vide ver. 6)—**of the house with blindness,** —סַנְוֵרִים (sanverim), from an unused quadrilateral signifying to dazzle, is perhaps here intended not for natural blindness, but for confused or bewildered vision, involving for the time being loss of sight, and accompanied by mental aberration; what Aben Ezra calls "blindness of eye and mind" (cf. 2 Kings vi. 18)—**both small and great: so that they wearied themselves to find the door** —which they would hardly have done had it been natural blindness only (Augustine).

HOMILETICS.

Vers. 1—11.—*Warning lights in Sodom.* I. THE FLICKERING LIGHT OF LOT'S PIETY. 1. That the light of Lot's piety was *still burning*, though he had long been subjected to the moral contamination of the licentious Pentapolis, is apparent from— (1) *The practice of hospitality which he appears to have maintained,* having probably learnt it while in his uncle's tent. So men often cling to the outward forms of religion when its living power is ceasing to exert an influence upon the heart; and though adherence to the former is not to be mistaken for the latter, yet it renders the decline of the latter less rapid and disastrous than it would otherwise be. (2) *The kindly reception which he extended to his celestial visitors.* If scarcely so elaborate as the sumptuous entertainment of Abraham at Mamre, the banquet of Lot was at least as outwardly reverential and as unaffectedly sincere and earnest. It clearly testified that Lot had not yet become insensible to the practical duties of religion, as at that time understood. Early religious training is exceedingly difficult to eradicate. (3) *The courageous defence which he made of his threatened guests.* At the risk of his personal safety he endeavoured to repel the violence with which the citizens assailed them; and by the proffer of a sacrifice, the greatest surely that a parent could make, he sought to beguile the infamous designs which the townsmen cherished. Whatever may be said of Lot's conduct in this latter action, his behaviour throughout towards the angels proved that the life of grace within his soul was not quite extinct. 2. That the light of Lot's piety, though still burning, was *fast fading,* may be gathered from the circumstances—(1) *That he had remained so long among the*

Sodomites. Unless a process of moral deterioration had been going on within the soul of Lot, residence among a people so depraved would eventually have become impossible. Instead of being merely vexed in his righteous soul while in Sodom, he would have taken the earliest opportunity to escape from Sodom. (2) *That he had betrothed his daughters to two of Sodom's citizens*. That his prospective sons-in-law were infected by the bad taint of the city may be inferred from their subsequent behaviour, as well as from the preceding judgment of God on the universal corruption of the city's inhabitants. Hence Lot should rather have kept his daughters virgins than have suffered them to enter into matrimonial engagements with ungodly suitors. (3) *That he actually offered to sacrifice his daughters' purity to the lust of the Sodomites*. Whatever apology may be offered for so extraordinary a proposal on the part of Lot, nothing can be plainer than that it implied a strange obliquity of moral vision, and a serious deadening of fine moral feeling. It was a clear proof that the immoral contagion had begun to affect Lot, and that it was high time for him to leave Sodom.

II. THE LURID LIGHT OF SODOM'S IMPIETY. Already well enough known as to its character, the wickedness of Sodom is at length unveiled in all its revolting features and frightful dimensions. The history of that last night in the doomed city proclaimed the sin of Sodom to be—1. *Unnatural*. In the unbridled licence of their appetites they had far outstripped common sinners; even the natural brute beasts they had left behind; they had sunk to a monstrosity of wickedness of which shame forbids to speak. Paul enumerates their sin amongst the forms of impurity by which the heathen world has at times defiled itself (Rom. i. 26, 27). 2. *Shameless*. Disgusting and repulsive as their wickedness was, instead of shrinking into darkness and doing it in secret, they openly proclaimed their filthiness, and would have gratified their lusts in public. It is a lower deep in moral degradation when one not only does "those things which are not convenient," but glories in his shame (Phil. iii. 19). 3. *Violent*. This marked a third degree in the wickedness of Sodom, that, rather than be baulked of their lewd design, the citizens were prepared to set at nought the laws of hospitality, which insured the safety of strangers within their city, and, if need were, the rights of property, by breaking into Lot's house, and, still further, the liberties of the person, by laying hands on the objects of their unhallowed lusts. Ordinary sinners are satisfied if they can gratify an unholy impulse without an undue expenditure of crime; these were ready to trample on all laws of God and man to accomplish their desire, "adding sin to sin" (Isa. xxx. 1). 4. *Obdurate*. Even when struck with blindness they did not discontinue their impious attempt. They wearied themselves groping about in the darkness, but it was still in an endeavour "to find the door." Common sinners pause when confronted with the just judgments of Heaven; these were only maddened into greater fury (Ps. lxxiii. 7). And, to complete the picture, this appalling wickedness was—5. *Universal*. From all quarters and of all ages they clustered and clamoured round the door of Lot's house. There does not seem to have been any dissension in the multitude. They were all of one mind. Could anything more signally attest Sodom's ripeness for destruction?

Learn—1. How rapidly a good man can deteriorate in evil company. 2. How completely a nation can resist the ameliorating influences of its good men. 3. How disgustingly repulsive sin is when fully developed.

EXPOSITION.

Vers. 12, 13.—**And the men said unto Lot,**—after the incident recorded in the preceding verses. Lot by this time had doubtless recognised their celestial character; accordingly, the Codex Samaritanus reads "angels"—**Hast thou here any besides?** (*i. e.* any other relatives or friends in the city in addition to the daughters then present in the house) **son in law, and thy sons, and thy daughters, and whatsoever** (not of things, but of persons) **thou hast in the city, bring** them **out of this place: for we will destroy this place** (literally, *for destroying this place are we*, i. e. we are here for that purpose), **because** the **cry of them** — not "the outcry on account of them," *i. e.* which the men of Sodom extort from others (Gesenius), but the cry against them which ascends to heaven, the cry for vengeance on their iniquities (cf. ch. iv. 10; xviii. 20—**is waxen** great before the face of the Lord (cf. ch. vi. 11 ; x. 9) ; and the Lord (Jehovah) hath sent us (language never employed by the *Maleach Jehovah*) to destroy it.

Ver. 14.—And Lot went out (obviously that same evening), and spake unto his sons in law, which married his daughters,—literally, *those taking his daughters*, meaning either those who had taken them (LXX., Targums, Knobel, Delitzsch), or more probably those intending to take them, their affianced husbands (Josephus, Vulgate, Clericus, Rosenmüller, Ewald, Keil, Kalisch)—and said, Up, get you out of this place; for the Lord (Jehovah) will destroy this (literally, *the*) city. But (literally, *and*) he seemed as one that mocked—as one that made laughter ; from the same root as the word Isaac (ch. xvii. 19 ; cf. Judges xvi. 25) —unto his sons in law.

Vers. 15, 16.—And when the morning arose,—literally, *as soon as the dawn* (from שָׁחַר, to break forth as the light) *went up*, *i. e.* on the first appearance of the morning twilight—then the angels hastened Lot, saying, Arise, take thy wife, and thy two daughters, which are here;—literally, *which are found;* not implying the existence of other daughters (Knobel), but contrasting with the sons in law (Keil, Kalisch)—lest thou be consumed in the iniquity (or punishment, as in Isa. v. 18) of the city. And while he lingered,—Lot's irresolution would have been his ruin but for his attendants. His heart manifestly clung to the earthly possessions he was leaving. The angels made no mention of his attempting to save a portion of his greath wealth—the men laid hold upon his hand, and upon the hand of his wife, and upon the hand of his two daughters; the Lord being merciful to him: —literally, *in the mercy*, or gentleness, *of Jehovah to him;* the primary idea of the verb from which the noun is derived being that of softness (cf. Isa. lxiii. 9)—and they brought him forth, and set him without the city.

Ver. 17.—And it came to pass, when they had brought them (*i. e.* Lot and his family) forth abroad (literally, *without;* sc. the city), that he—one of the angels (Rabbi Solomon, Jarchi, Rosenmüller, Lange, 'Speaker's Commentary'); the one that had taken Lot's hand (Inglis); Jehovah speaking through the angel (Delitzsch) ; the angel speaking in the name of God (Keil, Kalisch) ; Jehovah himself, who, though not mentioned, had now appeared upon the scene (Ainsworth, Candlish)—said, Escape for thy life (literally, *for thy soul ;* and clearly in this case the loss of the soul in the higher sense must have been involved in the destruction of the life) ; look not behind thee. From the event it may be inferred that this injunction was

also given to Lot's wife and daughters ; perhaps to hide God's working in the fiery judgment from mortal vision (Knobel), but more likely to express detestation of the abhorred city (Bush), to guard against the incipience of any desire to return (Lange), and to stimulate their zeal to escape destruction. Neither stay thou in all the plain— or "circle" (*vide* ch. xiii. 10). Once so attractive for its beauty, it must now be abandoned for its danger. Escape to the mountain (the mountain of Moab, on the east of the Dead Sea), lest thou be consumed.

Ver. 18.—And Lot said unto them, Oh, not so, my Lord. *Adonai*, which should rather be translated Lord ; whence it would almost seem as if Lot knew that his interlocutor was Jehovah. Keil admits that Lot recognised a manifestation of God in the angels, and Lange speaks of a miraculous report of the voice of God coming to him along with the miraculous vision of the angels. That the historian uses "them" instead of "him" only proves that at the time Jehovah was accompanied by the angels, as he had previously been at Mamre (*vide* ch. xviii. 1).

Ver. 19.—Behold now, thy servant hath found grace in thy sight (cf. ch. xviii. 3), and thou hast magnified thy mercy (language inappropriate to be addressed to the angels, though exactly suitable if applied by Lot to Jehovah), which thou hast showed unto me in saving my life ; and I cannot escape to the mountain, lest some evil (more correctly, *the evil*, i. e. the destruction threatened upon Sodom) take me, and I die.

Ver. 20.—Behold now, this city is near to flee unto (literally, *thither*), and it is a little one : Oh, let me escape thither, (is it not a little one ?) and my soul shall live. Lot's meaning was that since Zoar was the smallest of the cities of the Pentapolis, it would not be a great demand on God's mercy to spare it, and it would save him from further exertions for his safety. A singular display of moral obtuseness and indolent selfishness on the part of Lot.

Ver. 21.—And he said unto him, See, I have accepted thee (literally, *I have lifted up thy face*, the petitioner usually supplicating with his face toward the ground, so that the elevation of his countenance expressed the granting of his request) concerning this thing also, that I will not overthrow this city, for the which thou hast spoken.

Ver. 22. — Haste thee, escape thither; for I cannot do anything till thou be come thither. Therefore the name of the city was called Zoar. *I. e.* "The Little ;" obviously from Lot's remark concerning it (ver. 20) ; Σηγώρ (LXX.). The original name of the city was Bela (ch. xiv. 2, *q. v.*). It has been sought for in the Wady Zuweirah, a pass leading down from Hebron to the Dead Sea, on the west side of the lake (De Sancey) ; in the *Ghor-el-Mezraa*, i. e. upon the southern peninsula, which projects a long way into the Dead Sea (Robinson) ; and in the *Ghor-el-Szaphia*, at the south-eastern end of the sea, at the opening of the *Wady-el-Raumer* (Keil) ; but has now been identified with Zi'ara, at the northern extremity of the lake (Tristram, 'Land of Moab,' p. 330 ; *vide infra*, ver. 28, on the site of cities of the plain.

Ver. 23.—**The sun was risen upon the earth**—literally, *the sun went forth*, i. e. it was now above the horizon. Lot had left Sodom with the first streak of dawn ; but, having lingered, it was clear morning—**when Lot entered into Zoar**, or "went towards Zoar," *i. e.* when the angel left him (Keil).

Ver. 24.—**Then the Lord rained**—literally, *and Jehovah caused it to rain*; καὶ κύριος ἔβρεξε (LXX.), which latter term is adopted by Luke in describing this event (ch. xvii. 29) —**upon Sodom and upon Gomorrah**—and also upon Admah and Zeboim (Deut. xxix. 23 ; Hosea xi. 8), Bela, or Zoar, of the five cities of the Jordan circle (ch. xiv. 2, 8) being exempted—**brimstone and fire**—גָּפְרִית ; properly pitch, though the name was afterwards transferred to other inflammable materials (Gesenius) ; וָאֵשׁ, and fire, which, though sometimes used of lightning, as in 1 Kings xviii. 38 ; 2 Kings i. 10, 12, 14 ; Job i. 16, may here describe a different sort of igneous agency. Whether this Divinely-sent rain was "burning pitch" (Keil), or lightning which ignited the bituminous soil (Clericus), or a volcanic eruption which overwhelmed all the region (Lynch, Kitto), it was clearly miraculous in its nature, and designed as a solemn punitive infliction on the cities of the plain—**from the Lord**—*i. e. Jehovah* (the Son) rained down from *Jehovah* (the Father), as if suggesting a distinction of persons in the Godhead (Justin Martyr, Tertullian, Athanasius, *et alii*, Delitzsch, Lange, Wordsworth) ; otherwise the phrase is regarded as "an elegancy of speech" (Aben Ezra), "an emphatic repetition" (Calvin), a more exact characterisation of the storm (Clericus, Rosenmüller) as being **out of heaven.**

Ver. 25.—**And he overthrew** — literally, *turned over*, as a cake ; whence utterly destroyed (cf. Deut. xxix. 23 ; κατέστρεψε, LXX. ; *subvertit*, Vulgate). In Arabic "the overthrown" is a title applied, κατ' ἐξοχὴν, to Sodom and Gomorrah (Gesenius). From the use of the expression καταστροφή (2 Pet. ii. 6), Wordsworth thinks an earthquake may have accompanied the burning—**those cities**,—that they were submerged as well as overthrown (Josephus) is a doubtful inference from ch. xiv. 3 (*vide infra*, ver. 28, on the site of cities of the plain). The archaic

הָאֵל is again employed (cf. ch. xix. 8)—**and all the plain**,—*kikkar*, circle or district (ch. xiii. 10)—**and all the inhabitants of the cities**,—a proof of their entire corruption (ch. xviii. 32)—**and that which grew upon the ground**—literally, *that which sprouts forth from the ground*, the produce of the soil ; thus converting "a fruitful land into barrenness for the wickedness of them that dwell therein" (Ps. cvii. 34).

Ver. 26.—**But his wife looked back from behind him**, — *i. e.* went behind him and looked back ; ἐπίβλεψεν (LXX.), implying wistful regard ; *respiciens* (Vulgate) ; an act expressly forbidden by the angel (ver 17)— **and she became** (literally, *she was*, conveying an idea of complete and instantaneous judgment) **a pillar of salt.** נְצִיב מֶלַח ; στήλη ἁλός (LXX.); a statue or column of fossil salt, such as exists in the neighbourhood of the Dead Sea. That she was literally transformed into a pillar of salt (Josephus, Calvin, Rosenmüller, Kalisch, Wordsworth), though not impossible, is scarcely likely. A more probable interpretation is that she was killed by the fiery and sulphurous vapour with which the atmosphere was impregnated, and afterwards became encrusted with salt (Aben Ezra, Keil, Lange, Murphy, Quarry), though against this it has been urged (1) that the air was not filled with "salt sulphurous rain," but with fire and brimstone ; and (2) that the heaven-sent tempest did not operate in the way described on the other inhabitants of Sodom (Inglis). A third explanation regards the expression as allegorical, and intimating that the fate of Lot's wife was an *everlasting* monument of the danger of disregarding the word of the Lord, either as a covenant of salt signifies a perpetual covenant (Clark), or with reference to the salt pillars which, in a similar manner, attest the destruction of the cities (Inglis). The notion that Lot's wife, returning to the city, stuck fast *in terra salsuginosa*, like a salt pillar (Dathius), and that she perished in the flames, having afterwards erected to her memory a monument of the salt stone of the region (Michaelis), may be disregarded.

Ver. 27.—**And Abraham gat up early in the morning** (of the catastrophe) **to the place** (*i. e.* and went to the place) **where he stood before the Lord** (*vide* on ch. xviii. 22).

Ver. 28.—**And he looked toward**—literally, *towards the face*, or visible side (cf. ch. xviii. 16 where the same phrase is employed to describe the act of the angels on leaving Mamre)—**Sodom and Gomorrah, and toward all the land of the plain**, or Jordan circle. The cities of the plain are commonly believed to have been situated at the southern extremity of the Dead Sea. The principal reasons assigned for this conclusion may be stated. 1. Josephus and Jerome, the one representing Jewish, and the other Christian, tradition, both speak of a Zoar as existing in that locality. 2. The difference of level between the northern and southern ends of the lake, the one according to Lynch being 1800 feet, and the other not more than 10 feet, seems to favour the idea that the latter is of recent formation, having been, in fact, submerged at the time of the overthrow of the cities. 3. A ridge of rock-salt on the west of the Vale of Salt is called by the name *Jebel Usdum*, in which a trace of the word Sodom is by some detected ; and the pillars of salt that in that region have from time to time been detached from the salt cliffs have been designated by the name of Lot's wife (*Bint Sheikh Lot*). 4. The statement of ch. xiv. 3 appears to imply that the Salt Sea now covers what was originally the vale of Siddim. 5. The expression "like the land of Egypt as thou comest to Zoar" (ch. xiii. 10) is suggestive rather of the southern than of the northern extremity of the lake as the site of the Pentapolis. It may be added that this opinion has received the sanction of Robinson, Stanley, Porter, Thomson ('The Land and the Book'), and other eminent geographers. On the other hand, there are reasons for believing that the true site of the cities was at the north, and not the south, of the Dead Sea. 1. The circle of the Jordan was visible from the Bethel plateau (ch. xiii. 10); the southern extremity of the Dead Sea is not. 2. From the heights above Hebron or Mamre, though the actual circle is not visible, "yet the depression between the nearer hills and those of Gilead can be perceived, and Abraham could at once identify the locality whence the smoke arose," after Sodom's burning. 3. Chedorlaomer's route (ch. xiv. 7—14) was from Kadesh to Hazezon-tamar, midway up the western shore of the Dead Sea, from Haze-

zon-tamar to the vale of Siddim, and from Siddim to Dan, the natural conclusion being that on reaching Hazezon-tamar he did not turn southward, but continued marching northwards. 4. Moses from Mount Nebo (Deut. xxxiv. 3) beheld "the south, and the plain of the valley of Jericho, the city of palm trees, unto Zoar," which was certainly possible if Zoar was in the line of vision with the plain and the city of Jericho, but as certainly impossible if it was at the southern extremity of the lake. This view has been advocated by Grove (Smith's 'Biblical Dictionary,' art. Zoar) and by Tristram ('Land of Israel,' pp. 354—358, and 'Land of Moab,' pp. 330—334), and has been adopted by Drew ('Imp. Bible Dict.,' art. Sodom), Dykes ('Abraham, the Friend of God,' p. 185), and Inglis ('Genesis,' p. 168). **And beheld, and, lo, the smoke of the country went up as the smoke of a** (literally, *of the*) **furnace.** Thus the appalling catastrophe proclaimed its reality to Abraham ; to subsequent ages it stamped a witness of its severity (1) *upon the region itself*, in the bleak and desolate aspect it has ever since possessed ; (2) *upon the page of inspiration*, being by subsequent Scripture writers constantly referred to as a standing warning against incurring the Almighty's wrath (Deut. xxix. 22 ; Isa. xiii. 19 ; Jer. xlix. 18 ; l. 40 ; Lam. iv. 6 ; Amos iv. 11 ; 2 Pet. ii. 6 ; Jude 7) ; and (3) *upon the course of ancient tradition*, which it powerfully affected. Cf. Tacitus, 'Hist.,' v. 7 : "Haud procul inde campi, quos ferunt olim uberes, magnisque urbibus habitatos, fulminum jactu arsisse ; et manere vestigia ; terramque ipsam specie torridam vim frugiferam perdidisse ; nam cuncta atra et inania velut in cinerem vanescunt. Ego, sicut inclitas quondam urbes igne celesti flagrasse concesserim." For traditional notices of this event by Diodorus Siculus, Strabo, Pliny, Ovid, &c. *vide* Rosenmüller (Scholia I. ch. xix. 25).

HOMILETICS.

Ver. 24.—*The judgment of fire.* I. THE DELIVERANCE OF LOT. 1. *Mercifully warned.* The intimation conveyed by the angels was—(1) Explicit ; the city was to be destroyed. The cry for vengeance could no longer be resisted. The cup of its iniquity was full. (2) Emphatic ; there was no dubiety about the announcement. Already the doom had been decreed, and they had come to be the ministers of its execution. (3) Merciful ; it was designed to secure the escape of himself and friends from the impending overthrow. "Whatsoever thou hast, bring them out of this place." (4) Timely ; there was still ample opportunity for not only getting clear out of the perilous region himself, but for alarming his daughters' intended husbands. So are sinners warned clearly, expressly, graciously, and opportunely in the gospel to flee from the wrath to come, to escape from the city of destruction. 2. *Urgently hastened.* Notwithstanding the angel's warning, it is obvious that Lot trifled, probably from a latent apprehension that there was plenty of time, if not from any secret dubiety as to the need for the celestial exhortation ; and so do sinners dally yet with the solemn announcement of the gospel, which necessitates that they be vehemently pressed, like Lot, with—(1) Earnest admonition. "Arise!" "Up!" "Get thee out of this place!" (2) Serious caution. "Lest thou be consumed in the iniquity of the city." 3. *Graciously assisted.* Even the urgency displayed by the angels would not have sufficed to rescue Lot, had they not extended to him and his worldly-minded partner a helping hand. Hankering after Sodom, perhaps thinking of the wealth they had to leave, the good man and his wife still lingered, and were at last only dragged forth by main force beyond the precincts of the doomed city. It reminds us that few, probably none, would ever escape from the city of destruction if Divine grace were not practically to lay hold of them and drag them forth; and even this Divine grace would not do unless the Lord were specially merciful to them, as he was to Lot. 4. *Minutely directed.* To the further prosecution of their journey they were not left without most careful instructions as to how they might secure their safety; and neither are awakened sinners, who have been aroused to see their peril and to start upon the way of life, permitted to struggle on without celestial guidance as to how to make their calling and election sure. Like the fleeing Lot and his wife, they are counselled (1) to be in earnest, seeing it is their life for which they flee; (2) to beware of backsliding, since he who looketh back is not fit for the kingdom of God; (3) to indulge in no delay, since so long as one continues in the plain of his natural condition he stands in imminent peril; and (4) to persevere until he reaches the mount of salvation in Jesus Christ.

II. THE OVERTHROW OF SODOM. 1. *Supernatural.* Whatever the natural forces employed in the destruction of the fair cities of the Jordan circle, their employment with such severity and at such a time, viz., precisely at the moment when the moral degradation of the people showed them to be ripe for judgment, was a signal demonstration of the miraculous character of the catastrophe; as indeed the narrative alleges it to have been a phenomenon altogether out of the common course of events: "Jehovah rained down fire from Jehovah." 2. *Unexpected.* It does not appear that the inhabitants of Sodom generally were warned of the approaching fire-storm, though, if Lot's sons-in-law may be accepted as an indication of the temper in which the people at that time were, any such announcement would only have been listened to with mocking incredulity. So was it in the days of Noah (Matt. xxiv. 38); so will it be in the end of the world (2 Pet. iii. 3, 4). 3. *Complete.* The cities with their inhabitants, the fields with their vegetation, were engulfed in the sulphureous baptism and "turned into ashes." As overwhelming in its kind, though not as sweeping in its extent, as had been the previous submergence of the world by a flood of water, the devastation sent upon the fair Pentapolis of the Jordan circle was a ghastly shadow and premonition of that vengeance of eternal fire which shall yet devour the ungodly (2 Thess. i. 8). 4. *Righteous.* It was a just judgment which had been richly merited, as the visit of the angels had convincingly demonstrated. Indeed that previous unveiling of the filthiness of Sodom which had taken place may be viewed as having been designed to supply a visible justification of the righteousness of the great Judge in consigning them to so disastrous an overthrow. And so before the infliction of the great day of wrath upon the impenitent and the ungodly there will be a revelation of the secret characters of all hearts and lives, that "thou mightest be justified when thou speakest, and be clear when thou judgest" (Ps. li. 3). 5. *Public.* In particular, besides being experienced by the unhappy sufferers and observed by the trembling fugitives who had sought refuge in Zoar, it was witnessed by Abraham, who gat him up early, and, looking towards Sodom, saw the smoke of the country ascending like the smoke of a furnace to heaven—a fit emblem of the terrible publicity which will invest the final judgment of a sinful world (Matt. xxv. 31—46; 2 Thess. i. 7—10; Rev. xviii. 9).

III. THE FATE OF LOT'S WIFE. 1. *Intensely melancholy.* Overtaken by the sulphureous storm, she was transfixed where she stood, and in a moment after wrapt in a sheet of saline incrustation. Affecting in itself, her doom was rendered all the more impressive from the circumstance that she had so nearly escaped. Alas, nearly saved means wholly lost! 2. *Truly deserved.* Contrary to the angel's instructions, she had looked behind. Thus she had brought her tragic fate upon herself. Obedience would have saved her; disobedience proved her ruin. Whether she was lost eternally it is not safe to say, but her temporal destruction had been righteously incurred. 3. *Solemnly suggestive.* It was doubtless designed to teach many lessons, such as the danger of disobedience, the folly of delay, the severity of the Divine judgments, and the intensity of the Divine displeasure against sin.

Lessons :—1. The difficulty of saving a good man (1 Pet. iv. 18). 2. The ability of God to punish sin (Heb. x. 31). 3. The danger of looking back (Heb. x. 26, 27, 28). 4. The possibility of being nearly saved, yet wholly lost (Mark xii. 34).

HOMILIES BY VARIOUS AUTHORS.

Vers. 23—25.—*The righteousness of God revealed.* The judgment of God upon Sodom and the cities of the plain. The deliverance of Lot. The reception of the two angels by Lot was a great contrast to that of the three by Abraham. The scene of the Divine judgment is suggestive. The plain of the Jordan was well watered, attracted Lot by its beauty and promise. Early civilisation gathered about such spots, but civilisation without religion is a blasting influence. There are hidden fountains of judgment ready to burst forth and pour the fire of Divine wrath upon the sinners. The man who "pitched his tent towards Sodom" became at last a townsman, "vexed with the filthy conversation," yet, but for Divine mercy, involved in its punishment. The whole narrative teaches important lessons, especially on the following points :—

I. A TRULY RELIGIOUS LIFE is not a mere secret of the soul, but HAS ITS APPROPRIATE PLACE AND SURROUNDINGS.

II. THE HOUSEHOLD of the true believer IS A LARGE ENOUGH CIRCLE IN WHICH .TO MANIFEST SINCERITY AND FAITHFULNESS, yet must we take heed that our house is well defended against the invasions of the corrupt world.

III. HOW GREAT A RESULT COMES OUT OFTEN FROM A SMALL BEGINNING OF ERROR! The selfishness of Lot's first choice of his residence was the seed of evil which multiplied into all the subsequent suffering and wrong.

IV. " Behold the GOODNESS and SEVERITY OF GOD "—mingled judgment and mercy, but not mingled in a confused manner, with perfect order. The man who had joined with Abraham in the covenant with Jehovah, who with all his faults was yet a believer, is warned, rescued by angels ; able by his intercession to obtain mercy for others.

V. The DIVINE JUSTICE which is manifested on the large scale as BETWEEN THE CHURCH AND THE WORLD is also revealed in the smaller sphere of HOUSEHOLDS and families. Lot's wife is an apostate, and becomes involved in the destruction of the wicked. His sons-in-law mock at the Divine warning. His daughters become the incestuous originators of nations which afterwards greatly trouble the history of the people of God.

VI. THE SAME STEADFASTNESS OF GOD HAS TWO SIDES OR ASPECTS OF IT. "The sun was risen upon the earth when Lot entered Zoar." The same day, while the sun was serenely smiling on the city of refuge, the storm of fire and destruction from heaven was gathering over the doomed people and ready to burst upon them. "When God destroyed the cities of the plain, God remembered Abraham, and sent Lot out of the midst of the overthrow."—R.

Ver. 26.—*The danger of falling back.* " But his wife looked back from behind him, and she became a pillar of salt." Every part of this narrative suggestive of lessons. Reminded how "the righteous scarcely saved," and of the danger of an amiable weakness. In Lot's sons-in-law we see how the world receives the gospel (cf. Ezek. xx. 49 ; James i. 24). In his wife, one convinced, but not converted ; seeking safety, but with a divided aim (James i. 8). In the angel's help, God's watchful care, even where the need is unknown. Text teaches the responsibility of those who hear the gospel. Dangers surrounding us, but a way of safety (Ps. ci. 1 ; 2 Cor. ii. 16). But not enough to be roused (Matt. x. 22 ; Heb. xii. 1). Many are awakened to flee, yet look back (Luke ix. 62). Lot's wife not deaf to the call ; did not think it fancy ; really believed ; felt the danger, and fled (2 Cor. vi. 17 ; Rev.

xviii. 4). But the sun rose.; the valley beautiful; home attractive; no signs of danger. *Must* she leave all; and at once? She paused. That pause was death.

I. May be roused by ALARM OF CONSCIENCE and yet look back (cf. Matt. xii. 43—45). Some, intent on the world, think not of the future. Preaching seems only a venerable form; prayer a proper homage to God. But as to anything more, no hurry. But a time of anxiety comes. Perhaps a wave of revival, or some special occurrence—illness, bereavement, care. Eternity is brought near, false confidence dispelled (Isa. xxviii. 17). Then in earnest to seek the true refuge (Heb. vi. 18). The Bible read; prayer a real pleading. But the sun arises. The immediate cause passes away. Fears fade away. Then a looking back. Surely some of you can remember times of earnestness. Perhaps in hours of anxious watching, or in preparation for communion, or God has spoken directly to the soul and made you feel his presence (Gen. xxviii. 16, 17). Then the blessedness of accepted salvation was felt. The message was not a parable then. The Bible and prayer were precious then. But time went on. The immediate influence gone. All as before. Old ways asserted their power; hard to give them up. In mercy the call once more. Awake; the storm is at hand, though thou, seest it not. Pray that the Holy Spirit may transform thy heart.

II. May be moved by EXAMPLE OF OTHERS, yet turn back. She felt her husband's earnestness, and went with him, but so far only. We know the power of example. When we see those we love affected, we are moved to be as they. So at the preaching of John the Baptist. So at times of missions. Have any felt this influence; been stirred to read and pray? It is well. But has it lasted? For a real saving change there must be a personal transaction with the Lord as a living Saviour; a laying hold of him, a real desire and effort that the will and whole nature be submitted to him.

III. A MIGHTIER POWER STILL MAY ACT UPON THE SOUL. While Lot lingered angels laid hold of hands. There are times when God pleads urgently. One refuge after another swept away. Call upon call, sign upon sign, till the will seems conquered. But all is not done (Phil. iii. 13). Such pleadings neglected, cease. Observe, God led Lot out of Sodom, not to Zoar. There is work still to be done (2 Pet. i. 10). The question is not as to the past, but as to the present. It will not save a man that he was once anxious. Look not back. Look to Jesus (Heb. xii. 2). Let earnestness in every part of Christian life testify that you are not looking back (Heb. x. 39).—M.

EXPOSITION.

Ver. 29.—**And it came to pass**—not a pluperfect (Rosenmüller), as if a direct continuation of the preceding narrative, but a preterite, being the commencement of a new subdivision of the history in which the writer treats of Lot's residence in Zoar—**when God** —Elohim. Hence, as a fragment of the original Elohist's composition, the present verse is by the pseudo-criticism connected with ch. xvii. 27 (Ilgen, Tuch, Bleek); but "a greater abruptness of style and a more fragmentary mode of composition" than this would indicate "could not easily be imagined" (Kalisch). The change in the Divine name is sufficiently explained by the supposition that the destruction of the cities of the plain was not at the moment viewed by the writer in its connection with the Abrahamic covenant and intercession, but as a sublime vindication of Divine justice (cf. Quarry, p. 444) — **destroyed** (literally, *in he destroying by Elohim*, or in Elohim's destroying) **the cities of the plain, that God**

remembered Abraham. If the narrative containing the intercession of Abraham and the overthrow of Sodom was due to the Jehovist, how came the earlier author to know anything about those events? The obvious allusions to them in the present verse could only have been made by one acquainted with them. Either, therefore, the present verse proceeded from the hand of the so-called Jehovist, or it requires explanation how in the original document this should be the first and only occasion on which they are referred to (cf. Quarry, p. 445). **And**—in answer to Abraham's prayer (ch. xviii. 23)—**sent Lot out of the midst of the overthrow** (there is no reason to suppose that Abraham was aware of his nephew's escape), **when he overthrew**—literally, *in the overthrowing of the cities*, the inf. being construed with the case of its verb (*vide* Gesenius, § 133)—**the cities in the which**—one of which (cf. Judges xv. 7)—**Lot dwelt.**

Ver. 30.—**And Lot went up out of Zoar** (probably soon after), **and dwelt in the moun-**

tain (*i. e.* of Moab, on the east of the Dead Sea), **and his two daughters**—step-daughters, it has been suggested, if Lot married a widow who was the mother of the two girls (Starke) **—with him; for he feared to dwell in Zoar** —from which the panic-stricken inhabitants may have fled towards the mountains (Murphy), either because at that time it was shaken by an earthquake (Jerome, Rosenmüller); or because he dreaded the conflagration which devoured the other cities might spread thither (Poole, Kalisch, Wordsworth), or the rising waters of the Dead Sea which engulfed them might reach to it (Bush) —apprehensions which were groundless and unbelieving, since God had granted Zoar for an asylum (Lange); or because he saw the wickedness of the inhabitants, who had not been improved by Sodom's doom (Vatablus, Inglis); or simply because he was driven by "a blind anxiety of mind" (Calvin). **And he dwelt in a cave,**—*i. e.* in one of those cavernous recesses with which the Moabitish mountains abound, and which already had been converted into dwelling-places by the primitive inhabitants of the region (cf. ch. xiv. 6)—**he and his two daughters.**

Ver. 31.—**And the firstborn said unto the younger,**—showing that she had not escaped the pollution, if she had the destruction, of Sodom. "It was time that Lot had left the cities of the plain. No wealth could compensate for the moral degradation into which his family had sunk" (Inglis)—**Our father is old,**—an indirect confirmation of the inference (*vide* ch. xi. 26) that Abram was younger than Haran, since Lot, Haran's son, is now an old man—**and there is not a man in the earth** — not in the entire world (Origen, Irenæus, Chrysostom, Kalisch), which is scarcely probable, since they knew that Zoar had been spared ; but either in the district whither they had fled (Calvin, Willet), being under the impression that, living in so desolate a region, they could have no more intercourse with mankind ; or in the land of Canaan (Ainsworth, Bush), meaning that there were no more godly men with whom they might marry ; or perhaps they meant that no man would now care to unite himself with them, the remnant of a curse-stricken region (Knobel, Keil)—**to come in unto us after the manner of all the earth.**

Ver. 32.—**Come, let us make our father drink wine,**—either, therefore, Lot had not left Sodom totally unprovided (Inglis), or some little time had elapsed after his escaping to the mountain cave, since his daughters are provided with this intoxicating beverage— **and we will lie with him.** Considering the town in which the daughters of Lot had been reared, the mother of whom they were the offspring, and the example they had received from their father (ver. 8), "we can under-

stand, though we cannot cease to abhor, their incestuous conduct" (Kalisch). Their proposal was revolting and unnatural in the extreme. By subsequent Mosaic legislation a transgression of such enormity was rendered punishable by death. Even in the present instance the perpetrators were not wholly unconscious of the wickedness of their conduct. The fact that they required a stratagem for the attainment of their purpose shows that at least they could not calculate on their father's approbation. The entire story has been regarded as the invention of later Jewish hatred to the Moabites and Ammonites (De Wette), a conjecture believed by some to be "not improbable" (Rosenmüller); but if so, how should the same writer exhibit Abraham (ch. xviii. 23) as filled with compassionate tenderness towards the cities of the plain ? (Hävernick). **That we may preserve seed of our father.** Literally, *quicken or vivify seed* (cf. ver. 34). Lot's daughters may be credited with whatever virtue may be supposed to reside in this motive for their conduct.

Ver. 33.—**And they made their father drink wine that night**—which was sinful both in them and him (*vide* Isa. v. 11 ; Prov. xx. 1 ; Hab. ii. 15)—**and the firstborn went in, and lay with her father; and he perceived not when she lay down, nor when she arose.** That it was his own daughter *quacum concumberet* (Rosenmüller), being so intoxicated that he could not discern who it was to whom he had approached, or even what he was doing (Keil). The reading "when *he* lay down and when he arose" (LXX.) is incorrect, and the explanations that Lot was a mere unconscious instrument in this disgraceful transaction (Kalisch), that he was entirely ignorant of all that had taken place (Chrysostom, Cajetan), that he was struck on account of his intemperance with a spirit of stupor (Calvin), are not warranted by the text.

Ver. 34.—**And it came to pass on the morrow, that the firstborn said unto the younger, Behold, I lay yesternight with my father: let us make him drink wine this night also; and go thou in, and lie with him, that we may preserve seed of our father.**

Ver. 35.—**And they made their father drink wine that night also.** The facility with which Lot allowed himself to be inebriated by his daughters Clericus regards as a sign that before this the old man had been accustomed to over-indulgence in wine. The inference, however, of Kalisch, that because "Lot's excess in the enjoyment of wine is no more blamed than it was in Noah," "the narrative exempts him from all serious reproach," can scarcely be admitted. **And the younger arose, and lay with him** (following the bad example of her sister) ; **and he perceived not when she lay down, nor when she arose** (*vide supra,* ver. 33).

Ver. 36.—**Thus were both the daughters of Lot** (who after this disappears from sacred history, not even his death being recorded) **with child by their father.**

Ver. 37.—**And the firstborn bare a son, and called his name Moab** = *Meab*, from the father, alluding to his incestuous origin (LXX., which adds λέγουσα ἐκ τοῦ πατρός μοῦ ; Augustine, Jerome, Delitzsch, Keil) ; though *Mo* (= water, an Arabic euphemism for the *semen virile*) and *ab* has been advanced as a more correct derivation (Rosenmüller). **The same is the father of the Moabites**—who originally inhabited the country north-east of the Dead Sea, between the Jabbok and the Arnon (Deut. ii. 20), but were afterwards driven by the Amorites south of the Arnon— **unto this day.** This phrase, indicating a variable period from a few years to a few centuries (cf. ch. xlviii. 13 ; Exod. x. 6 ; Numb. xxii. 39 ; Josh. xxii. 3), cannot be regarded as a trace of post-Mosaic authorship (De Wette, *et alii*), since in Genesis it is

always used of events which had taken place several centuries before the time of Moses, as in ch. xxvi. 33 ; xxxv. 20 ; xlvii. 26 (cf. Keil, ' Introduction,' part i. § 2, div. 1, § 38).

Ver. 38.—**And the younger, she also bare a son, and called his name Ben-ammi.** *I. e.* son of my people (LXX., Jerome, Augustine), meaning that her child was the offspring of her own kind and blood (Rosenmüller), or the son of her relative (Kalisch), or of an unmixed race (' Speaker's Commentary '). **The same is the father of the children of Ammon**—an unsettled people who occupied the territory between the Jabbok and the Arnon, from which they had ejected the Rephaims or Zamzummims (Deut. ii. 22), and in which they possessed a strong city, Rabbah (2 Sam. xi. 1) ; in their habits more migratory and marauding than the Moabites (Isa. xv., xvi. ; Jer. xlviii.), and in their religion worshippers of Molech, "the abomination of the Ammonites" (1 Kings xi. 7)— **unto this day.**

HOMILETICS.

Ver. 29.—*The last days of Lot.* I. HAUNTED BY TERROR. 1. *The terror of Divine judgment.* The appalling spectacle of Sodom's overthrow had no doubt filled him with alarm. And so are God's judgments in the earth designed to put the souls of men in fear (Ps. ix. 20 ; xlvi. 8—10 ; cxix. 120). 2. *The terror of men.* Dwelling in Zoar, he apprehended an outburst of wrath from the citizens, who probably regarded him as the cause of the ruin which had invaded Sodom. So are better men than Lot sometimes overtaken by the fear of man (2 Sam. xxii. 5 ; Ps. xviii. 4), though they should not (Isa. li. 12). 3. *The terror of conscience.* That Lot enjoyed while in Zoar a calm and undisturbed repose of heart and mind is scarcely supposable. Rather it may be safely conjectured that after the storm and the fire and the earthquake through which he had lately passed, the still small voice of conscience spoke to him in awe-inspiring accents, unveiling his past life, reproving him of sin, and piercing him through with many sorrows ; and that under the agitations produced by its accusations and reproaches he became afraid, and withdrew to the mountains. "Thus conscience doth make cowards of us all."

II. SOUNDING THE LOWER DEEPS. 1. *Descending into unbelief.* God had promised to spare Zoar for him, and him in Zoar, and one would have thought Lot had been sufficiently warned of the sin of distrusting God. Yet he is scarcely established in the city which God had granted in response to his own prayer than he begins to think it hardly safe to remain within its precincts. How inveterate is unbelief ! 2. *Plunging into sin.* The details of the present story clearly show that Lot, when he went to the mountain cave, endeavoured to escape from his terrors not by carrying them to God's throne, but by drowning them in dissipation. The wretched man, who had once been a saint in God's Church, must have been in the habit of drinking to excess, else his daughters would never have thought of their abominable stratagem. Only one little gleam of virtue can be detected as entitled to be laid to Lot's account, viz., that his daughters apparently believed that unless their father was drunk he would never be brought to assent to their lewd proposal. 3. *Sinking into shame.* Twice overcome by wine, he is twice in succession dishonoured by his daughters ; and twice over, while in his drink stupor, he allows himself to commit an act which almost outSodoms Sodom. To what depths a saint may fall when once he turns his back on God !

III. DISAPPEARING INTO OBLIVION. Nothing could more distinctly mark the Divine disapprobation with Lot's conduct than the fact that after this he was suffered—1. *To live an unrecorded life*, being never heard of again in the pages of Holy Scripture.

2. *To die an unnoticed death.* Where and how he met his end the historian does not condescend to state. 3. *To sink into an unknown grave.* Whether buried in his mountain cave or entombed in the Jordan valley no man knoweth unto this day. See—1. The danger of turning aside from God and good men (Heb. iii. 12; x. 25). 2. The melancholy end of a worldly life (1 Cor. x. 6; Phil. iii. 19; 2 Tim. iv. 10). 3. The bitter fruits of parental neglect (1 Sam. ii. 27—36; Prov. xxix. 15—17).

HOMILIES BY VARIOUS AUTHORS.

Ver. 29.—*The destruction of Sodom and Gomorrah.* I. THE VISIBLE JUDGMENT. "God overthrew the cities in the which Lot dwelt." 1. The reason. 2. The instrumentality. 3. The reality. 4. The lessons of the overthrow.

II. THE UNKNOWN MERCY. "He sent Lot out of the midst of the overthrow." To Abraham this was—1. A great mercy. 2. A mercy granted in answer to prayer. But—3. An unknown mercy, there being no reason to believe that Abraham ever saw Lot again, or knew of his deliverance.

Learn—1. That God always mixes mercy with his judgments. 2. That his mercies are not always so perceptible to the eye of sense and reason as his judgments. 3. That God's people get more mercies poured into their cups than they are at all times cognisant of.—W.

EXPOSITION.

CHAPTER XX.

Ver. 1.—**And Abraham journeyed** (*vide* ch. xii. 9) **from thence.** Mamre (ch. xviii. 1). In search of pasture, as on a previous occasion (Keil); or in consequence of the hostility of his neighbours (Calvin); or because he longed to escape from the scene of so terrible a calamity as he had witnessed (Calvin, Willet, Murphy); or in order to benefit as many places and peoples as possible by his residence among them (À Lapide); or perhaps being impelled by God, who designed thereby to remind him that Canaan was not intended for a permanent habitation, but for a constant pilgrimage (Poole, Kalisch). **Toward the south country.** *Negeb*, the southern district of Palestine (ch. xii. 9; xiii. 1); the central region of Judæa being called *Hahor*, or the Highlands; the eastern, towards the Dead Sea, *Midhbar;* and the western *Shephelah* (Lange). **And dwelled between Kadesh and Shur** (*vide* ch. xvi. 14 and xvi. 7), **and sojourned in Gerar** (*vide* ch. x. 19).

Ver. 2.—**And Abraham said of Sarah his wife, She is my sister.** As formerly he had done on descending into Egypt (ch. xii. 13). That Abraham should a second time have resorted to this ignoble expedient after the hazardous experience of Egypt and the richly-merited rebuke of Pharaoh, but more especially after the assurance he had lately received of his own acceptance before God (ch. xv. 6), and of Sarah's destiny to be the mother of the promised seed (ch. xvii. 16), is well nigh unaccountable, and almost irreconcilable with any degree of faith and piety. Yet the lapse of upwards of twenty years since that former mistake may have deadened the impression of sinfulness which Pharaoh's rebuke must have left upon his conscience; while altogether the result of that experiment may, through a common misinterpretation of Divine providence, have encouraged him to think that God would watch over the purity of his house as he had done before. Thus, though in reality a tempting of God, the patriarch's repetition of his early venture may have had a secret connection with his deeply-grounded faith in the Divine promise (cf. Kalisch *in loco*). **And Abimelech**—*i. e. Father-king,* a title of the Philistine kings (ch. xxi. 22; xxvi. 1; Psalm xxxiv. 1), as Pharaoh was of the Egyptian (ch. xii. 15), and Hamor of the Shechemite (ch. xxxiv. 4) monarchs; cf. *Padishah* (father-king), a title of the Persian kings, and *Atalik* (father, properly paternity), of the Khans of Bokhara (Gesenius, p. 6)—**king of Gerar sent, and took Sarah.** *I. e.* into his harem, as Pharaoh previously had done (ch. xii. 15), either having been fascinated by her beauty, which, although she was twenty years older than when she entered Egypt, need not have been much faded (*vide* ch. xii. 11; Calvin), or may have been miraculously rejuvenated when she received strength to conceive seed (Kurtz); or, what is as probable, having sought through her an alliance with the rich and powerful nomade prince who had entered his dominions (Delitzsch).

Ver. 3.—**But God**—*Elohim;* whence the present chapter, with the exception of ver. 18, is assigned to the Elohist (Tuch, De Wette, Bleek, Davidson), and the incident at Gerar explained as the original legend, of which the story of Sarah's abduction by Pharaoh is the Jehovistic imitation. But (1) the use of Elohim throughout the present chapter is sufficiently accounted for by observing that it describes the intercourse of Deity with a heathen monarch, to whom the name of Jehovah was unknown, while the employment of the latter term in ver. 18 may be ascribed to the fact that it is the covenant God of Sarah who there interposes for her protection; and (2) the apparent resemblance between the two incidents is more than counterbalanced by the points of diversity which subsist between them—**came to Abimelech in a dream**—the usual mode of self-revelation employed by Elohim towards heathen. Cf. Pharaoh's dreams (ch. xli. 1) and Nebuchadnezzar's (Dan. iv. 5), as distinguished from the visions in which Jehovah manifests his presence to his people. Cf. the theophanies vouchsafed to Abraham (ch. xii. 7; xv. 1; xviii. 1) and to Jacob (ch. xxviii. 13; xxxii. 24), and the visions granted to Daniel (Dan. vii. 1—28; x. 5—9) and the prophets generally, which, though sometimes occurring in dreams, were yet a higher form of Divine manifestation than the dreams—**by night, and said to him, Behold, thou** art but **a dead man,**—literally, *behold thyself dying*, or *about to die* = σὺ ἀποθνήσκεις (LXX.). Abimelech, it is probable, was by this time suffering from the malady which had fallen on his house (*vide* ver. 17)—**for** (*i. e.* on account of) **the woman which thou hast taken; for she** is **a man's wife**—literally, *married to a husband*, or under lordship to a lord (cf. Deut. xxii. 22).

Ver. 4. — **But Abimelech had not come near her.** Apparently withheld by the peculiar disease which had overtaken him. The statement of the present verse (a similar one to which is not made with reference to Pharaoh) was clearly rendered necessary by the approaching birth of Isaac, who might otherwise have been said to be the child not of Abraham, but of the Philistine king. **And he said, Lord,**—*Adonai* (*vide* ch. xv. 2)—**wilt thou slay also a righteous nation?** Anticipating that the stroke of Divine judgment was about to fall upon his people as well as on himself, with allusion to the fate of Sodom (Knobel), which he deprecates for his people at least on the ground that they are innocent of the offence charged against him (cf. 2 Sam. xxiv. 17). That Abimelech and his people, like Melchisedeck and his subjects, had some knowledge of the true God, and that the Canaanites generally at this period had not reached the depth of moral degradation into which the cities of the Jordan circle had sunk before their overthrow, is apparent from the narrative. The comparative virtue, therefore, of these

tribes was a proof that the hour had not arrived for the infliction on them of the doom of extermination.

Ver. 5.—**Said he not unto me, She is my sister? and she, even she herself said, He is my brother.** From which it is clear that the Philistine monarch, equally with the Egyptian Pharaoh, shrank from the sin of adultery. **In the integrity of my heart and innocency of my hands have I done this.** *I. e.* he assumes the right of kings to take unmarried persons into their harems.

Ver. 6.—**And God said unto him in a dream,**—"It is in full agreement with the nature of dreams that the communication should be made in several, and not in one single act; cf. chs. xxxvii. and xli.; Matt. ii." (Lange)—**Yea, I know that thou didst this in the integrity of thy heart**—*i. e.* judged from thy moral standpoint. The words do not imply a Divine acquittal as to the essential guiltiness of the act, which is clearly involved in the instruction to seek the mediation of God's prophet (ver. 7). **For I also withheld thee from sinning against me: therefore suffered I thee not to touch her** (*vide* on ver. 4).

Ver. 7.—**Now therefore restore the man his wife.** Literally, *the wife of the man,* God now speaking of Abraham *non tanquam de homine quolibet, sed peculiariter sibi charum* (Calvin). **For he** is **a prophet.** *Nabi*, from *naba*, to cause to bubble up; hence to pour forth, applied to one who speaks by a Divine afflatus (Deut. xiii. 2; Judges vi. 8; 1 Sam. ix. 9; 1 Kings xxii. 7). The office of the Nabi was twofold—to announce the will of God to men (Exod. iv. 15; vii. 1), and also to intercede with God for men (ver. 7; Jer. vii. 16; xi. 14; xiv. 11). The use of the term Nabi in this place neither proves that the spirit of prophecy had not existed from the beginning (cf. ch. ix. 25—27), nor shows that the Pentateuch, which always uses this term, cannot be of greater antiquity than the time of Samuel, before which, according to 1 Sam. ix. 9, the prophet was called a seer (Bohlen, Hartmann). As used in the Pentateuch the term describes the recipient of Divine revelations, and as such it was incorporated in the Mosaic legislation. During the period of the Judges the term *Roeh* appears to have come into use, and to have held its ground until the reformation of Samuel, when the older theocratic term was again reverted to (*vide* Hävernick, § 19). **And he shall pray for thee** (*vide supra*), **and thou shalt live.** Literally, *live thou*, the imperative being used for the future in strong prophetic assurances (cf. Ps. cxxviii. 5; *vide* Gesenius, § 130). **And if thou restore her not, know thou that thou shalt surely die,**—literally, *dying thou shalt die* (cf. ch. ii. 17)—**thou, and all that are thine.**

Ver. 8.—**Therefore Abimelech rose early in the morning,**—an evidence of the terror into which he had been cast by the Divine communication, and of his earnest desire to carry out the Divine instructions—**and called all his servants, and told all these things in their ears:**—confessed his fault, explained his danger, and affirmed his intention to repair his error ; a proof of the humility of this God-fearing king (Lange)—**and the men were sore afraid.** It spoke well for the king's household that they received the communication with seriousness.

Ver. 9.—**Then Abimelech called Abraham, and said unto him** (in the presence of his people), **What hast thou done unto us?**—identifying himself once more with his people, as he had already done in responding to God (ver. 4)—**and what have I offended thee** (thus modestly allowing that he may himself have unwittingly occasioned the sin of Abraham), **that thou hast brought on me and on my kingdom a great sin?** The gravamen of Abimelech's accusation was that Abraham had led him and his to offend against God, and so to lay themselves open to the penalties of wrong-doing. **Thou hast done deeds unto me that ought not to be done.** Literally, *deeds which ought not to be done thou hast done with me* (cf. ch. xxxiv. 7 ;. Levit. iv. 2, 13 ; *vide* Glass, 'Philol. Tract., l. iii. t. iii. c. vi.). The king's words were unquestionably designed to convey a severe reproach.

Ver. 10.—**And Abimelech said unto Abraham, What sawest thou,**—either, What hadst thou in view? (Knobel, Delitzsch, Keil, Murphy, *et alii*), or, What didst thou see? Didst thou see any of my people taking the wives of strangers and murdering their husbands? (Rosenmüller, 'Speaker's Commentary')—**that thou hast done this thing?**

Ver. 11.—**And Abraham said** (offering as his first apology for his sinful behaviour the fear which he entertained of the depravity of the people), **Because I thought,**—literally, *said* (sc. in my heart)—**Surely the fear of God is not in this place**;—otherwise, *there is not any fear of God*, רק having usually a confirming sense with reference to what follows (cf. Deut. iv. 6 ; 1 Kings xiv. 8 ; *vide* Gesenius, p. 779)—**and they will slay me for my wife's sake.**

Ver. 12.—**And yet indeed she is my sister.** This was the second of the patriarch's extenuating pleas, that he had not exactly lied, having uttered at least a half-truth. **She is the daughter of my father** (Terah), **but not the daughter of my mother.** That Sarah was the grand-daughter of Terah, *i. e.* the daughter of Haran, and sister of Lot, in other words, Iscah, has been maintained

(Josephus, Augustine, Jerome, Jonathan). That she was Terah's niece, being a brother's daughter adopted by him, has received some support (Calvin) ; but there seems no reason for departing from the statement of the text, that she was her husband's half-sister, *i. e.* Terah's daughter by another wife than Abraham's mother (Rosenmüller, Kalisch, Keil, Knobel). **And she became my wife.**

Ver. 13.—**And it came to pass, when God caused me to wander** (or to go on pilgrimages) **from my father's house,**—*Elohim*, usually construed with a singular verb, is here joined with a verb in the plural, as an accommodation to the polytheistic standpoint of Abimelech (Keil), as a proof that Elohim is to be viewed as a *Pluralis Majestaticus* (Kalisch), as referring to the plurality of Divine manifestations which Abraham had received (Lange), as showing that Elohim here signifies angels (Calvin), or, most likely, as an instance of the literal meaning of the term as the supernatural powers (Murphy). Cf. ch. xxxv. 7 ; Exod. xxii. 8 ; 2 Sam. vii. 23 ; Ps. lviii. 12—**that I said unto her, This is thy kindness which thou shalt show unto me.** The third plea which the patriarch presented for his conduct; it had no special reference to Abimelech, but was the result of an old compact formed between himself and Sarah. **At every place whither we shall come, say of me, He is my brother** (cf. ch. xii. 13).

Ver. 14.—**And Abimelech**—as Pharaoh did (ch. xii. 16), but with a different motive—**took sheep, and oxen, and men-servants, and women-servants.** The LXX. and Samaritan insert "a thousand didrachmas" after "took," in order to include Sarah's present mentioned in ver. 16 ; but the two donations are separated in order to distinguish them as Abraham's gift and Sarah's respectively (Rosenmüller, Delitzsch), or the sum of money may indicate the value of the sheep and oxen, &c. which Abraham received (Keil, Knobel, Lange, 'Speaker's Commentary'). **And gave them unto Abraham.** To propitiate his favour for the wrong he had suffered. Pharaoh's gifts were "for the sake of Sarah" (ch. xii. 16). **And restored him Sarah his wife.**

Ver. 15.—**And Abimelech said, Behold, my land is before thee : dwell where it pleaseth thee.** Literally, *in the good in thine eyes ;* the generous Philistine offering him a settlement within his borders, whereas the Egyptian monarch hastened his departure from the country (ch. xii. 20).

Ver. 16.—**And unto Sarah he said, Behold, I have given thy brother a thousand** pieces **of silver.** Literally, *a thousand of silver*, the exact weight of each piece being uncertain. If sacred shekels (Gesenius, Keil, Kalisch) their value would be over £130, if shekels ordinary somewhat less. **Behold, he**—*i. e.* thy brother; or it, *i. e.* the present (LXX., Vulgate, Targums, Syriac)—is **to thee a covering of the eyes.** כְּסוּת עֵינַיִם (from a root signifying to cover over) has been understood as (1) a propitiatory gift = τιμή (LXX.), or (2) a veil for the protection of the face; and, according as the subject of the sentence has been regarded as Abraham or the sum of money, the sense of the clause has been given as either (1) he, *i. e.* thy brother, will be to thee a protection, hiding thee like a veil, from the voluptuous desires of others (Aben Ezra, Cajetan, Calvin, Kalisch); or (2) it, *i. e.* this present of mine, will be to thee a propitiatory offering to make thee overlook my offence (Chrysostom, Gesenius, Fürst, Knobel, Delitzsch, Keil, Murphy); or (3) a declaration of thy purity, and so a defence to thee against any calumnious aspersions (Castalio); or (4) the purchase-money of a veil to hide thy beauty, lest others be ensnared (Vulgate, Arabic, Kitto, Clark); or (5) the means of procuring that bridal veil which married females should never lay aside (cf. ch. xxiv. 65; Dathe, Vitringa, Michaelis, Baumgarten, Rosenmüller). The exact sense of this difficult passage can scarcely be said to have been determined, though of the above interpretations the choice seems to lie between the first and second. **Unto all that** are **with thee, and with all** other. *I. e.* in presence of thy domestics and of all with whom thou mayest yet mingle, either Abraham will be thy best defence, or let my gift be an atonement, or a veil, &c. **Thus she was reproved.** וְנֹכָחַת. If a third person singular niph. of נכח (Onkelos, Arabic, Kimchi, Gesenius, Rosenmüller, Fürst), then it is the historian's statement signifying that Sarah had been convicted, admonished, and left defenceless (Gesenius); or, connecting the preceding words וְאֶת־כֹּל), that, with regard to all, right had been obtained (Fürst), or that all had been done that she might be righted (Murphy); but if a second person singular niph. (LXX., Vulgate, Delitzsch, Keil, Lange, Murphy, Kalisch), then it is a continuation of Abimelech's address, meaning neither καὶ πάντα ἀλήθευσον (LXX.), nor *memento te deprehensam* (Vulgate), but either, "and thou art reproved" (Wordsworth), or, "and thou wilt be recognised" (Kalisch), or, again connecting with the preceding words, "and with all, so thou art justified or set right" (Delitzsch, Keil, Lange), or, "and all this that thou mayest be righted" (Murphy) or "reproved" (Ainsworth).

Ver. 17.—**So Abraham prayed unto God.** Literally, *the Elohim*, the personal and true God, and not Elohim, or Deity in general, to whom belonged the cure of Abimelech and his household (Keil), as the next clause shows. **And God** (*Elohim*, without the art.) **healed Abimelech, and his wife, and his maid-servants;**—*i. e.* his concubines, as distinguished from the women servants (ver. 14) — **and they bare** children. The verb may apply to both sexes, and the malady under which they suffered may be here described as one which prevented procreation, as the next verse explains.

Ver. 18.—**For the Lord** (*Jehovah;* vide *supra* on ver. 3) **had fast closed up all the wombs**—*i. e.* prevented conception, or produced barrenness (cf. ch. xvi. 2; Isa. lxvi. 9; 1 Sam. i. 5, 6; for the opposite, ch. xxix. 31; xxx. 22); "pœna convenientissima; quid enim convenientius esse poterat, quam ut amittat, qui ad se rapit aliena" (Musculus). *Vide* Hävernick, § 19—**of the house of Abimelech, because of Sarah Abraham's wife**—the motive obviously being to protect the purity of the promised seed.

HOMILETICS.

Vers. 1—18.—*Abraham in Gerar, or two royal sinners.* I. THE SIN OF THE HEBREW PATRIARCH. 1. *An old sin repeated.* "Abraham said of Sarah his wife, She is my sister." Twenty years before the same miserable equivocation had been circulated in Egypt. A sin once committed is not difficult to repeat, especially if its legitimate consequences, as in the case of Abraham and Sarah, have been mercifully averted. One is apt to fancy that a like immunity will attend its repetition. 2. *A worthless lie propagated.* "Abimelech, king of Gerar, sent and took Sarah." Designed for protection in both Egypt and Gerar, the ignoble expedient of the patriarch was in both places equally ineffectual. So does all sin tend to outwit itself, and in the end generally proves abortive in its designs. 3. *A deliberate fraud practised.* As Abraham explained to Abimelech, it was no sudden impulse on which he acted, but a preconcerted scheme which he had put in operation. Intended for the extenuation of his fault, this was in reality an aggravation. Sin leisurely and knowingly gone about is ever more heinous than that into which the heart and will are surprised. 4. *An unjustifiable suspicion entertained.* All the preceding sins had their origin in what the event proved to be an altogether unwarranted estimate of Abimelech and his people. The patriarch said to himself, " Surely the fear of God is not in this place, and they will slay me for my wife's sake," without reflecting that he was not only deciding without evidence, but doing an injustice to the monarch and the people into whose land he was crossing. Learn—1. How hard it is to lay aside one's besetting sin. The character of the patriarch, otherwise so noble, appears to have had a natural bias towards deception. 2. How difficult it is to lead a life of faith. One would have thought that by this time every vestige of carnal policy would have been eliminated from the walk of Abraham. 3. How possible it is for an eminent saint to relapse into great sin. If Abraham illustrated the virtues, he likewise remarkably exemplified the weaknesses of God's believing people. 4. How wrong it is to cherish and act upon uncharitable views of others. True religion always leans to the side of charity in judging of the characters of men.

II. THE SIN OF THE HEATHEN PRINCE. 1. A *common* sin. The popularity of an action, though not sufficient to make it good, may serve, in some degree, to extenuate its guilt where it is wrong. 2. An *unconscious* sin. The narrative distinctly represents Abimelech as a prince who feared God and shrank from incurring his displeasure—a character which all kings should study to possess. Abimelech himself claimed to have perpetrated no offence against the law of God in acting as he did, which shows that the voice of conscience always speaks according to its light. The avowal which he makes of his integrity is admitted by Jehovah as correct—a proof that God judges men according to their privileges. Yet it was—3. A *great* sin. Implied in the Divine direction to seek the friendly intercession of the patriarch, it was admitted by Abimelech when once his mind was enlightened as to the true character of the deed he had committed.

See here—1. A lesson of charity concerning peoples and individuals outside the visible Church. 2. A proof that men are not necessarily free from guilt because their consciences fail to accuse them. 3. A good sign of true contrition, viz., the acknowledgment of sin when it is pointed out.

III. GOD'S DEALINGS WITH THE PRINCE AND WITH THE PATRIARCH. 1. With the prince. (1) *Restraining* grace. God withheld him from proceeding to further sin by doing injury to Sarah, the means employed being disease which was sent upon both the monarch and his house. So God frequently interposes by afflictive dispensations to prevent those who fear him from running into sins of which perhaps they are not aware. (2) *Illuminating* grace. Appearing in a dream, Elohim disclosed the true character of his offence, and quickened his conscience to apprehend the guilt and danger which had been incurred. Sincere souls who fear God and are faithful to the light they have are never left to wander in darkness, but in God's time and way are mysteriously guided to the path of safety and duty (Ps. xxv. 12—14). (3) *Directing* grace. Finding the heathen monarch's heart susceptible of good impressions, God further counselled him how to act in order to obtain forgiveness, viz., to solicit the mediating services of Abraham, who in this matter was a type of heaven's great High Priest and Intercessor (Heb. vii. 25). Cf. God's way of dealing with erring men (Job xxxii. 14—33). 2. With the patriarch. (1) *Protection*. A second time he shielded his erring servant from the consequences of his own folly. A mark of God's tender pity towards sinful men. (2) *Reproof*. Besides being much needed, it was exceedingly severe, and must have been deeply humiliating. God often permits his people to be rebuked by the world for their good. (3) *Honour*. God is ever better to his people than their deserts. Not only did he direct Abimelech to ask the help of Abraham, but he constituted Abraham the medium of bestowing blessings on Abimelech. So does God honour Abraham's seed, Christ, by exalting him in the world's sight as the one Mediator between God and man; and Abraham's children, the Church, by making them the instruments of drawing down blessings on the world. Learn—1. That God's dealings with sinning men are always adapted to the peculiar characters of their respective sins. 2. That God never chastises men, either by affliction or rebuke, for his pleasure, but for their profit. 3. That God never pardons sin without bestowing blessing on the sinner.

HOMILIES BY VARIOUS AUTHORS.

Ver. 2.—*Falsehood the fruit of unbelief.* "Abraham said of Sarah his wife, She is my sister." Notice how imperfectly the obligation of truth recognised in Old Testament times. Not only among heathen, or those who knew little of God (Josh. ii. 5 ; 2 Kings x. 18), but godly men among God's own people (ch. xxvi. 7 ; 1 Sam. xxvii. 10). Yet the excellence of truth was known, and its connection with the fear of God (Exod. xviii. 21 ; Ps. xv. 2). Not until manifested in Christ does truth seem to be fully understood (cf. John viii. 44 ; 1 John iii. 8). This gives force to " I am the truth." Some see in text an act of faith ; trust that God would make the plan (ver. 13) successful. But faith must rest on God's word. Trust in what God gives no warrant for believing is not faith, but fancy, e. g. to attempt what we have no reason to believe we can accomplish, or to incur liabilities without reasonable prospect of meeting them. More natural and better to look on it as a breach of truth under temptation ; the failure of a godly man under trial. His words were true in letter (ver. 12), but were spoken to deceive, and did deceive.

I. ROOT OF HIS FAULT—UNBELIEF ; want of all-embracing trust. His faith was real and vigorous (cf. 1 Cor. x. 12), but partial (cf. ch. xxvii. 19 ; Matt. xiv. 28). Shrank from trusting God fully. Turned to human devices, and thus turned out of the way (Prov. iii. 5). Partial distrust may be found even where real faith. A very common instance is trusting in God for spiritual blessings only. A large part of our actions, especially in little things, springs not from conscious decision, but from habitual modes of thought and feeling. We act instinctively, according to what is the natural drift of thought. Abraham had so dwelt on the danger that he forgot the help at hand (Ps. xxxiv. 7 ; Rom. viii. 28). Bold in action, his faith failed when danger threatened. To endure is a greater trial of faith than to do. To stand firm amid secularising influences, ridicule, misconstruction is harder than to do some great thing. St. Peter was ready to fight for his Master, but failed to endure (Mark xiv. 50—71 ; Gal. ii. 12). So to St. Paul's "What wilt thou have me to do?" the Lord's word was, " I will show him how great things he must suffer."

II. FORM OF HIS FAULT—UNTRUTH. Contrary to the mind of Christ. May be without direct statement of untruth. May be by true words so used as to convey a wrong idea ; by pretences, e. g. taking credit unduly for any possession or power ; by being ashamed to admit our motives ; or by untruth in the spiritual life, making unreal professions in prayer, or self-deceiving. Every day brings numberless trials. These can be resisted only by the habit of truthfulness, gained by cultivating " truth in the inward parts," aiming at entire truthfulness. Nothing unpractical in this. May be said, Must I tell all my thoughts to every one? Not so. Many things we have no right to speak ; e. g. things told in confidence, or what would give unnecessary pain. Concealment when it is right is not untruth. No doubt questions of difficulty may arise. Hence rules of casuistry. But a Christian should be guided by principles rather than by rules (Gal. v. 1) ; and wisdom to apply these rightly is to be gained by studying the character of Christ, and prayer for the Holy Spirit's guidance (Luke xi. 13 ; John xvi. 14).—M.

Vers. 15, 16.—*Abraham and Abimelech at Gerar.* I. THE UNIVERSALITY OF DIVINE GRACE. The varieties in moral state of nations a testimony to God's forbearing mercy. There was evidently a great contrast between such people as dwelt under Abimelech's rule and the cities of the plain, which helps us to see the extreme wickedness of the latter. It was probably no vain boast which the king-uttered when he spoke of "*the integrity of his heart and innocency of his hands.*" Moreover, God *appeared* to him by dreams, and it is implied that he would have the greatest reverence for Jehovah's prophet. Abraham testified the same ; although he declared that the fear of God was not in the place, still he sojourned in Gerar, and after Lot's experience he would not have done so unless he had believed it to be very different from Sodom.

II. THE CHARACTER OF GOD'S CHILDREN IS NOT THE GROUND OF THEIR ACCEPTANCE WITH HIM. It is strange that the Egyptian experience should not have taught the patriarch simply to trust in God. But the *imperfect* faith *justifies;* the *grace of God* alone *sanctifies.* The conduct of Abimelech is throughout honourable and straightforward. Abraham's equivocation is not excusable. It sprang from fear, and it was no sudden error, but a deliberate policy which betokened weakness, to say the least.

III. THE LORD BRINGS GOOD OUT OF EVIL. Abimelech's character is a bright spot in the terrible picture of evil and its consequences. By the discipline of Providence the errors and follies of men are made the opportunities for learning God's purposes and character. The contact of the less enlightened with the more enlightened, though it may humble both, gives room for Divine teaching and gracious bestowments. Again we are reminded "the prayer of a righteous man availeth much" not because he is himself righteous, but because he is the channel of blessing to others, chosen of God's free grace.—R.

EXPOSITION.

CHAPTER XXI.

Ver. 1.—**And the Lord**—*Jehovah;* not because the verse is Jehovistic (Knobel, Bleek, *et alii*), but because the promise naturally falls to be implemented by him who gave it (*vide* ch. xviii. 10)—**visited**—remembered with love (Onkelos), ἐπισκέψατο (LXX.; cf. ch. l. 24; Exod. iv. 31; 1 Sam. ii. 21; Isa. xxiii. 17); though it sometimes means to approach in judgment (*vide* Exod. xx. 5; xxxii. 34). Alleged to be peculiar to the Jehovist (the term used by the Elohist being זָכַר: ch. viii. 1; xix. 29; xxx. 20), the word occurs in ch. l. 24, which Tuch and Bleek ascribe to the Elohist—**Sarah as he had said** (ch. xvii. 21; xviii. 10, 14),—God's word of promise being ever the rule of his performance (cf. Exod. xii. 25; Luke i. 72)—**and the Lord did unto Sarah as he had spoken**—*i. e.* implemented his promise; the proof of which is next given (cf. Numb. xxiii. 19; Heb. vi. 18).

Ver. 2.—**For Sarah conceived,**—through faith receiving strength from God for that purpose (Heb. xi. 11); the fruit of the womb, in every instance God's handiwork (Isa. xliv. 2), being in her case a special gift of grace and product of Divine power—**and bare**—the usual construction (ch. xxix. 32; xxx. 5) is here somewhat modified by the Jehovist (Kalisch); but the clause may be compared with ch. xxx. 22, 23, commonly assigned to the Elohist—**Abraham** (literally, *to Abraham*) **a son in his old age,**—literally, *to his old age;* εἰς τὸ γῆρας (LXX.)—**at the set time** (*vide* ch. xvii. 21; xviii. 10, 14) **of which God had spoken to him.** God's word gave Abraham strength to beget, Sarah to conceive, and Isaac to come forth. Three times repeated in two verses, the clause points to the supernatural character of Isaac's birth.

Ver. 3.—**And Abraham called the name of his son**—the naming of a child by its father is, according to partitionists, a peculiarity of the Elohist as distinguished from the Jehovist,

who assigns that function to the mother; but *vide* ch. xvi. 15—**that was born unto him, whom Sarah bare to him** (the latter clause being added to distinguish him from Hagar's child), **Isaac** — *laughter;* the name appointed for him by God before his birth (ch. xvii. 19).

Ver. 4.—**And Abraham circumcised** (*vide* on ch. xvii. 11, and note at the end of that chapter) **his son Isaac being eight days old** (literally, *a son of eight days*), **as** (not only because, but in the manner in which) **God had commanded him.**

Ver. 5.—**And Abraham was an hundred years old** (cf. ch. xvii. 1, 17), **when his son Isaac was born unto him.** Literally, *at the time of bearing to him* (ἐν τῷ τεκεῖν) *Isaac* (*vide* Gesenius, 'Gram.,' § 143). Thus Abraham had waited twenty-five years for the fulfilment of the promise—a remarkable instance of faith and patience (Rom. iv. 20), as Isaac's birth was a signal display of Divine power (Rom. iv. 17; Heb. xi. 12). Whether Isaac was born at Gerar or at Beersheba cannot with certitude be inferred.

Ver. 6.—**And Sarah said,**—the spiritual elevation of her soul being indicated by the poetical form of her speech. Differing from Mary's magnificat in having been uttered after, and not before, the birth of the promised seed, the anthem of Sarah was obviously designed as a prelude to that loftier song of the Virgin (cf. Luke i. 46). It consists of two sentences, the first containing two, and the second three lines—**God hath made me to laugh.** Or, retaining the order of the Hebrew, *To laugh hath made me Elohim;* the emphatic position of צְחֹק, containing an allusion to the name Isaac, probably indicating that Sarah's laughter was of a different character now from what it had previously been (ch. xviii. 12); and her ascription of it to Elohim intimating that him whom she formerly mistook for a traveller she now recognised to be Divine ('Speaker's Commentary'). So that all that hear me will laugh with me. Not, will laugh at me, *deridebit me* (Poole), a sense the words will bear (Rosenmüller, 'Speaker's Commentary'), though in the instances adduced (Job v. 22 ; xxxix. 7, 18, 22) צָחַק לְ rather conveys the idea of despising difficulties (Kalisch) ; but, will laugh with me, συγχαρεῖταί μοι, *congaudebit mihi* (LXX., Vulgate, Targums, Calvin, Dathe, Keil).

Ver. 7.—**And she said, Who would have said unto Abraham,**—מִלֵּל, the poetic word for דָּבַר, is introduced by מִי in order to express astonishment ; the meaning being that what had happened was altogether out of the ordinary course of nature, was, in fact, God's work alone (Vatablus, Calvin, Rosenmüller, Keil, Kalisch, 'Speaker's Commentary'). Less happy are τίς ἀναγγελεῖ τῷ Ἀβραὰμ (LXX.); *quis auditurum crederet Abraham quod* (Vulgate) ; *quam fidelis est ille qui dixit Abrahamo* (Onkelos)—**that Sarah should have given children suck?** Literally, *Sarah suckleth sons.* " Many of the greatest saints in Holy Scripture, and even our Lord himself, were nursed by their own mothers " (Wordsworth). **For I have born** him **a son in his old age.** Literally, *I have born a son to his old age.* The LXX. incorrectly render ἐν τῷ γήρᾳ μου.

Ver. 8.—**And the child grew,**—καὶ ηὐξήθη τὸ παιδίον (LXX.) : imitated by Luke concerning Christ : τὸ παιδίον ηὔξανε (Luke ii. 40)—**and was weaned.** The verb *gamal* originally signifies to do good to any one, to do completely ; hence to finish, or make completely ready, as an infant ; hence to wean, since either at that time the period of infancy is regarded as complete, or the child's independent existence is then fully reached. The time of weaning is commonly believed to have been at the end of the second or third year (cf. 1 Sam. i. 22—24 ; 2 Chron. xxxi. 16 ; 2 Macc. vii. 27 ; Josephus, 'Ant.,' ii. 9, 6). **And Abraham made a great feast the same day that Isaac was weaned.** Literally, *in the day of the weaning of Isaac ;* probably, therefore, when Isaac was three years old and Ishmael seventeen. "It is still customary in the East to have a festive gathering at the time a child is weaned. Among the Hindoos, when the time for weaning has come, the event is accompanied with feasting and religious ceremonies, during which rice is formally presented to the child " ('Bible Manners and Customs,' by Rev. J. A. Freeman, M.A., 'Homiletical Quarterly,' vol. i. p. 78 ; cf. Roberts' 'Oriental Illustrations,' p. 24).

HOMILETICS.

Vers. 1—8.—*The son of promise, or a young child's biography.* I. THE BIRTH OF ISAAC. 1. *A surprising phenomenon.* "Who would have said that Sarah should have suckled sons ? " Motherhood at ninety was certainly unusual, especially when conjoined with paternity at a hundred. In a world presided over by a personal Deity there must always be room for surprises. 2. *A miraculous production.* That the conception and birth of Isaac were due to Divine interposition—that, in fact, the child of promise was a special supernatural creation—is asserted by Paul as well as Moses (Rom. iv. 17). 3. *An accomplished prediction.* Not only the fact of Isaac's birth, but the exact time was specified beforehand. And now the long-looked-for child had arrived. A signal proof of the Divine veracity, it was another pledge to God's people in every age of the Divine fidelity in implementing his gracious word of promise. 4. *A joyous inspiration.* Isaac's birth not simply woke laughing echoes in Sarah's tent, but opened founts of song in Sarah's breast ; which was not wonderful, considering that the tender infant over which she exulted was the child of her own and Abraham's old age, the child of promise, the fruit of faith and the gift of grace, and the Heaven-appointed heir of the covenant blessing. 5. *A prophetic intimation.* Sarah's anthem contained a higher note of melody than that occasioned by a mother's joy ; there was in it too the gladness of a faith that saw in Isaac the harbinger and pledge of another and greater Seed. Like the birth of Isaac, that of Christ was fore-announced by God, waited for in faith, accomplished through Divine power, and welcomed with bursts of joy.

II. THE CIRCUMCISION OF ISAAC. 1. The *import* of the rite (see on ch. xvii. 10). It implied the formal reception of the party upon whom it was imposed within the pale of the Old Testament Church ; it signified the putting away of the filth of the flesh ; it took the subject of it bound to a holy life. Of a like import is the Christian sacrament of baptism, which, however, differs from the Hebrew rite in looking back upon a Christ already manifested, instead of forward to a Christ that was still to come. 2. The *authority* for the rite. This was exclusively the Divine command-ment — the sole reason that can be assigned for the observance of the Christian sacraments, which in themselves are only symbols of spiritual transactions, and have no validity apart from the appointment of Christ. 3. The *index* to the rite. This was contained in the name generally given on the occasion of its observance : cf. Abraham (ch. xvii. 5), John the Baptist (Luke i. 60), Jesus (Luke ii. 21). With this ancient custom must be connected the Christian practice of naming children at baptism.

III. The weaning of Isaac. 1. *A mother's duty fulfilled.* The first duty of a mother is to her babe, and to withhold the sustenance God has provided for her babe's necessities is both to violate Divine law and to perpetrate a fraud upon her helpless offspring. Sarah, though a princess, was not above discharging the duties of a nurse—an example which Sarah's daughters should diligently follow. 2. *A child's independence begun.* From the moment of weaning a child may be said to enter on a separate and as it were independent existence, attaining then for the first time to a distinct individuality of being. 3. *A father's joy expressed.* The interest-ing event was celebrated by a festal entertainment, at which, if not Shem, Mel-chisedek, and Selah, according to the Rabbis, the inmates of Abraham's household were doubtless present. "God's blessing upon the nursing of children, and his pre-servation of them during the perils of infant age, are signal instances of the care and tenderness of Divine providence, which ought to be acknowledged to its praise" (Henry).

*Lessons :—*1. The right of parents to rejoice in their children. 2. The duty of parents to introduce their children to the Church of God. 3. The propriety of parents recognising the separate individualities of children.

HOMILIES BY VARIOUS AUTHORS.

Vers. 1—8.—*Birth, circumcision, and weaning of Isaac.* Here is—
I. The faithfulness of Jehovah. "As he had spoken." "At the set time." "God hath made me to laugh."
II. The faith of his servant, which was evidenced in waiting, hoping, naming the son born unto him, obeying the commandment.
III. The gift of God was the revelation of God : his love, his power, his purpose, his patience.
IV. Taken typically, the foreshadowing of the miraculous conception, the kingdom of God, as originating in the sphere of human infirmity and helplessness ; as being the introduction of bright hope and cheerful promise into the gloomy barrenness of human life ; as the lifting up of man's state into the covenant of God, sealed with his appointed ordinance, surrounded with the promised blessings. Isaac was the type of Christ, Sarah of Mary, Abraham of the people and Church of God.
V. Sarah's song, the first cradle hymn of a mother's thankful joy, representing the Divine delight in the pure and simple happiness of those who are children of God. Abraham rejoiced to see the brightness of the future (John viii. 56).
VI. The weaning feast. All called in to share in the joy. Household joy should be widespread. We may suppose that such a banquet was religious in its character. If so, not only is it a sanction of religious festivals, but it reminds us that we should connect the events of the family life immediately with the word and ordinances of God.—R.

Vers. 8—21.—*The separation of the bondwoman's son from the promised seed.* It was necessary that this should take place for the accomplishment of the Divine plan. Human conduct is employed, as in so many other cases, as the instrument or occasion. There was mockery or unbelief in Ishmael. It was not personal merely, but a mockery of Jehovah and of his Church. Sarah saw it. The mother's keen affections were sharpened to detect the scorn of her joy. Abraham and Sarah were both severely tried. Their lack of faith must yield fruit of sorrow. The separation was pain to the father, but it was part of the gracious work of God for Isaac. Abraham was being prepared by such discipline for his great climax of trial. There is beautiful tenderness and simplicity in Abraham's conduct (ver. 14). It is—1. Entire obedience. 2. Kind and gentle consideration for Sarah and Hagar. 3. Strong faith : he committed her to God according to his word. 4. The master and the servant at the door of the house in the early morning; the master himself placing the bottle of water on the bondwoman's shoulder as a sign of continued affinity. God commands separations. In obedience to him they may involve severe struggle with self. Should still be carried out with as little wounding of human affections as possible.—R.

EXPOSITION.

Ver. 9.—**And Sarah saw**—at the feast already mentioned (Knobel, Keil); probably also on different occasions since the birth of Isaac—**the son of Hagar the Egyptian, which she had born unto Abraham, mocking.** Παίζοντα μετὰ Ἰσαὰκ τοῦ υἱοῦ αὐτῆς (LXX.), *ludentem cum Isaaco filio suo* (Vulgate), playing like a child (Aben Ezra, Knobel, Tuch, Ilgen), playing and dancing gracefully (Gesenius); but the stronger sense of the word, implying mockery, scoffing, irritating and deriding laughter (Kimchi, Vatablus, Grotius, Calvin, Rosenmüller, Keil, Kalisch, 'Speaker's Commentary,' Murphy), besides being admissible (cf. ch. xix. 14; xxvi. 8; xxxix. 14, 17; Exod. xxxii. 6), seems involved in the Piel form of the participle מְצַחֵק (Kurtz), and is demanded by Gal. iv. 29. That Ishmael ridiculed the banquet on the occasion of Isaac's weaning (Malvenda), quarrelled with him about the heirship (Fagius, Piscator), and perhaps made sport of him as a father of nations (Hengstenberg), though plausible conjectures, are not stated in the text. Ainsworth dates from this event the 400 years of Israel's oppression (*vide* ch. xv. 13).

Ver. 10.—**Wherefore she said**—though with an admixture of sinful feelings, *non dubito arcano Spiritus instinctu gubernatam fuisse ejus linguam et mentem* (Calvin); *vide* Gal. iv. 30—**unto Abraham, Cast out**—by some kind of legal act (as divorce: cf. Levit. xxi. 7, 14; xxii. 13; Isa. lvii. 20), which should insure the disinheriting of Ishmael (Bush); though probably this is to import later Mosaic legislation into the records of primitive times —**this bondwoman**—a term ill befitting Sarah, who had given Hagar to her husband as a wife (ch. xvi. 3)—**and her son** (who was Abraham's offspring, though not the promised seed; a consideration which should have mitigated Sarah's anger): **for the son of this bondwoman** (a repetition evincing the bitterness of her contempt and the intensity of her choler) **shall not be heir with my son,** even **with Isaac.** Notwithstanding the assurance (ch. xvii. 21) that the covenant was made with Isaac, Sarah was apprehensive lest Ishmael should contrive to disinherit him; an act of unbelief into which she was mani-

festly betrayed by her maternal fears and womanly jealousy.

Ver. 11.—**And the thing** (literally, *the word*, i. e. Sarah's proposal) **was very grievous** (literally, *evil exceedingly;* for the contrary phrase *vide* ch. xx. 15) **in Abraham's sight** (literally, *in the eyes of* Abraham) **because of his son**—who, besides being bound to him by the ties of natural affection, had for years been regarded as the Heaven-appointed heir of the promise (*vide* ch. xvii. 18).

Ver. 12.—**And God said unto Abraham,**—probably in a dream, or night vision (*vide* ver. 14)—**Let it not be grievous in thy sight because of the lad, and because of thy bondwoman;**—who was never recognised by God as Abraham's wife (cf. ch. xvi. 8)—**in all that Sarah hath said unto thee, hearken unto her voice.** Though Sarah's counsel was approved by God, it does not follow that her conduct was. On a former occasion Abraham's hearkening unto Sarah's voice had led to sin (ch. xvi. 2); this time it would lie exactly in the line of duty. **For in Isaac shall thy seed be called.** Literally, *in Isaac shall seed* (i. e. posterity) *be called to thee;* meaning neither, "by Isaac shall thy seed be called, or named" (Hofmann, Kalisch, Ainsworth), nor, "in Isaac shall thy seed be called into existence" (Dreschler); but, "in Isaac shall there be posterity to thee which shall pass as such," *i. e.* be called or recognised as such (Keil); or, more simply, "in Isaac," *i. e.* in the line of Isaac, "shall be called to thee a seed," *i. e.* a seed *par excellence*, the seed already promised (Bleek, Delitzsch, Rosenmüller, Alford, Murphy).

Ver. 13.—**And also of the son of the bondwoman will I make a nation.** Literally, *to a nation I will set or put him;* a promise already given (ch. xvii. 20), but here repeated to render Ishmael's dismissal easier. **Because he is thy seed.** "Thy son according to the flesh, though not after the promise, as Isaac was" (Ainsworth); a proof that men may sometimes receive mercies for their fathers' sakes.

Ver. 14.—**And Abraham rose up early in the morning,**—hastening to put in force the Divine instructions (cf. ch. xix. 27; xxii. 3,

Abraham; ch. xx. 8, Abimelech; ch. xxviii. 18, Jacob)—**and took bread, and a bottle of water,**—the bottle, from a root signifying to enclose (Fürst); ἀσκόν (LXX.), was composed of skin, the material of which the earliest carrying vessels were constructed (cf. Josh. ix. 4, 13; Judges iv. 19; 1 Sam. xvi. 20; Matt. ix. 17). "The monuments of Egypt, the sculptures of Mesopotamia, and the relics of Herculaneum and Pompeii afford ample opportunities to learn the shape and use of every variety of bottles, often surprising us both by their elegance and costliness" (Kalisch)—**and gave** it **unto Hagar, putting** it **on her shoulder,**—the usual place for carrying such vessels among Oriental women. According to Herodotus (ii. 35), Egyptian women carried burdens on their shoulders, Egyptian men upon their heads—**and the child,**—not placing the child, now a youth

of over seventeen years, upon her shoulder (LXX., Schumann, Bohlen); but giving him, along with the bottle (Hävernick, Kalisch, À Lapide, Ainsworth), or, as well as the bread (Keil, Murphy), to Hagar, not to be carried as a burden, but led as a companion—**and sent her away**:—divorced her by the command of God (À Lapide); but as Hagar was never recognised by God as Abraham's wife, her sending away was not a case of divorce (Wordsworth)—**and she departed** (from Beersheba, whither Abraham had by this time removed, and where, in all probability, Isaac had been born), **and wandered—**i. e. lost her way (cf. ch. xxxvii. 15)—**in the wilderness** (the uncultivated waste between Palestine and Egypt) **of Beer-sheba**—introduced here by anticipation, unless the incident in vers. 22—33 had previously taken place (*vide* on ver. 31).

HOMILETICS.

Vers. 9—14.—*The expulsion of Ishmael.* I. THE CAUSE. 1. *The persecution of Isaac.* "Sarah saw the son of Hagar the Egyptian mocking." That this was no mere sportive pleasantry may be inferred from the deep feeling it aroused in Sarah, the summary chastisement it brought on Ishmael, and the severe language in which it is characterised by Paul. The emphasis laid by Sarah on the heirship suggests the probability that Ishmael's offence partook of the nature of wicked, irritating laughter at the position and prospects of Sarah's son, springing partly from envy and partly from unbelief. 2. *The apprehensions of Sarah.* That Sarah was actuated by personal dislike of Hagar's boy, or inspired solely by maternal jealousy, is a gratuitous assumption. It is more satisfactory to ascribe her seemingly harsh counsel to the clearness with which she recognised that Isaac alone was the Heaven-appointed heir, and that nothing must be allowed to either damage his position or endanger his prospects. 3. *The commandment of God.* Considering the patriarch's former experience of "hearkening to Sarah," his acquiescence in her counsel on this occasion would in all probability have been problematical, had not God interposed to recommend its adoption. It would both secure the happiness of Isaac and remove temptation from the path of Ishmael; while it would serve to educate the patriarch himself for the coming sacrifice on Mount Moriah. To facilitate the patriarch's compliance with the Divine injunction, the promise of future greatness to Ishmael is renewed, and in the end Hagar and her boy are dismissed.

II. THE MANNER. 1. With *pain to himself.* "The thing was very grievous in Abraham's sight because of his son." Parental affection must have urged him to retain his first-born son. Conjugal love must have interceded for her who had been to him as a wife. Self-interest may have represented the advisability of still clinging to Ishmael for the fulfilment of the promise, in case the line of Isaac should fail. Yet grace and faith triumphed. "All things are possible to him that believeth." 2. With *tenderness towards the outcasts.* Making provision for their immediate necessities, and either then or afterwards adding gifts (ch. xxv. 6), he sends them away, doubtless with many prayers and tears. Nature and grace both enjoin tenderness in dealing with those whom God in his providence calls to suffer. 3. With *submission to the will of God.* The moment the mind of God was ascertained, internal controversy ceased and determined. The patriarch was never irresolute in following when God led. Obedience is the first duty of faith.

III. THE TYPICAL SIGNIFICANCE. 1. *Ishmael and Isaac* representatives of Abraham's natural descendants and Abraham's spiritual posterity; Israel after the flesh and Israel after the spirit; souls in legal bondage and souls enjoying spiritual freedom. 2. *Ishmael's mockery of Isaac* foreshadowed the persecuting spirit of the unbelieving Jews, who adhered to the system of Moses, towards the disciples of the New Testament faith, who sought salvation through Christ; hence ·also the antagonism of the sinful principle in man to the renewed life of grace. 3. *Ishmael's separation from Isaac* prefigured the ultimate removal of unbelievers from believers, of the world from the Church, of those in a state of nature or of legal bondage from those who are children of the promise and of the heavenly Jerusalem.

Learn—1. The wickedness and danger of mocking at sacred persons and things. 2. The superior spiritual insight not unfrequently exhibited by woman. 3. The necessity of trying all human opinions by God's revealed will. 4. The care God takes to guide sincere souls as to the path of duty. 5. The proper function of faith, which is to hear and obey. 6. The impossibility of any compromise existing between the world and the Church. 7. The final casting out of the wicked from the congregation of the righteous.

EXPOSITION.

Ver. 15.—**And the water was spent in** (literally, *from*) **the bottle,** — so that the wanderers became exhausted, and were in danger of fainting through thirst—**and she cast the child**—a translation which certainly conveys an erroneous impression, first of Ishmael, who was not an infant, but a grown lad (*vide supra*, ver. 14), and secondly of Ishmael's mother, whom it represents as acting with violence, if not with inhumanity; whereas the sense probably is that, having, as long as her rapidly diminishing strength permitted, supported her fainting son, she at length suddenly, through feebleness, released his nerveless hand as he fell, and in despair, finding herself unable to give him further assistance, left him, as she believed, to die where he had flung himself in his intolerable anguish—**under one of the shrubs.**

Ver. 16.—**And she went, and sat her down**—וַתֵּשֶׁב לָהּ, the pronoun being added to the verb, as an ethical dative, to indicate that the action was of special importance to her, meaning, "she, for herself, or for her part, sat down" (*vide* Ewald's 'Heb. Synt.,' § 315, *a.*; and Glass, 'Phil. Tract.,' l. iii. tr. ii. c. 6; and cf. Gen. xii. 1; xxii. 5)—**over against** him **a good way off.** The hiph. inf. of רָחַק, to go far away, to recede from any one, is here used adverbially, as in Josh. iii. 16 (Gesenius, Fürst, Kalisch), though by others it is understood as explaining the action of the previous verbs, and as equivalent to a gerund in *do*, or a participle, *elongando se* (Rosenmüller), or simply "removing to a distance" (Ewald; *vide* 'Heb. Synt.,' § 280 *a.*). **As it were a bowshot.** Literally, *as those who draw the bow*, i. e. as far off as archers are accustomed to place the target (Keil). The sense is correctly given by the LXX.: μακρόθεν, ὡσεὶ τόξου βολήν. **For she said, Let me not see**—i. e. look upon with anguish (cf. Num. xi. 15)—**the death of the child**—τοῦ παιδίου μου (LXX.). **And she sat over against** him, **and lift up her voice,**

and wept. The verbs, being feminine, indicate that it is Hagar's grief which is here described, and that the rendering, "and the child lifted up his voice and wept" (LXX.), is incorrect; although the next verse may suggest that Ishmael, like his mother, was also dissolved in tears.

Ver. 17.—**And God**—*Elohim;* Hagar and Ishmael having now been removed from the care and superintendence of the covenant God to the guidance and providence of God the ruler of all nations (Keil)—**heard the voice of the lad;**—praying (Inglis), or weeping, *ut supra*—**and the angel of God**—*Maleach Elohim;* not *Maleach Jehovah*, as in ch. xvi. 7—13, for the reason above specified (Hengstenberg, Quarry)—**called to Hagar out of heaven,**—it may be inferred there was no external appearance or *theophaneia*, such as was vouchsafed to her when wandering in the wilderness of Shur (ch. xvi. 7)—**and said unto her, What aileth thee** (literally, *What to thee?*) **Hagar? fear not;**—so the word of Jehovah addressed Abram (ch. xv. 1), Isaac (ch. xxvi. 4), Daniel (Dan. x. 12), and John (Rev. i. 17)—**for God hath heard the voice of the lad**—i. e. the voice (perhaps the mute cry) of the lad's misery, and in that also the audible sob of Hagar's weeping. It is not said that either Ishmael or his mother prayed to God in their distress. Hence the Divine interposition on their behalf *non quid a se peterent, sed quid servo suo Abrahae de Ismäele pollicitus foret, respexit* (Calvin)—**where he is**—an ellipsis for from, or in the place where he is; ἐκ τοῦ τόπου οὗ ἐστιν (LXX.); *ex loco ubi est* (Calvin); meaning either "in his helpless condition" (Keil), or out in the desolate wilderness, as contrasted with the house of Abraham (Calvin).

Ver. 18.—**Arise, lift up the lad, and hold him in thine hand.** Literally, *bind fast thy hand to him*, i. e. give him thy support now, and take care of him till he reaches manhood. Cf. God's promise to Israel (Isa. xlii.

6). **For I will make him** (literally, *to*) **a great nation** (*vide* ver. 13 ; and cf. ch. xvi. 10 ; xvii. 20).

Ver. 19.—**And God opened her eyes.** Not necessarily by miraculous operation ; perhaps simply by providentially guiding her search for water, after the administered consolation had revived her spirit and roused her energies. **And she saw a well of water.** בְּאֵר, as distinguished from בּוֹר, a pit or cistern, meant a fountain or spring of living water (cf. ch. xxiv. 11, 20 ; xxvi. 19, 20, 21). It had not been previously observed by Hagar, either because of her mental agitation (*dolore quasi cæca*, Rosenmüller), or because, as was customary, the mouth of the well was covered—**and she went, and filled the bottle with water, and gave the lad drink**—which was certainly the first of the youth's necessities, being needful to the preservation of his life and the reviving of his spirits.

Vers. 20, 21.—**And God was with the lad.** Not simply in the ordinary sense in which he is with all men (Ps. cxxxix. 3—9 ; Acts xvii. 27, 28) ; not, certainly, in the spiritual sense in which he had promised to be with Isaac (ch. xvii. 21), and in which he is with believers (ch. xxvi. 24 ; Isa. xli. 10 ; Matt. xxviii. 20) ; but in the particular sense of exercising towards him a special providence, with a view to implementing the promise made concerning him to Abraham and Hagar. **And he grew** (literally, *became great*, i. e. progressed towards manhood), **and dwelt in the wilderness** (*i. e.* led a roving and unsettled life), **and became an archer.** Literally, *and he was* רֹבֶה קַשָּׁת ; *i. e.* deriving רֹבֶה from רָבָה, to grow great or multiply, either (1) when he grew up, an archer, or man using the bow (Gesenius, Keil) ; (2) growing an archer, or acquiring skill as a bowman (Kalisch, Wordsworth) ; or (3) growing, or multiplying into, a tribe of archers (Murphy). With the first of these substantially agree the renderings καὶ ἐγένετο τοξότης (LXX.), and *factus est juvenis sagittarius* (Vulgate). Others, connecting רֹבֶה with רָבַב, in the sense of to cast arrows (cf. ch. xlix. 23), read, (1) "and he was a shooter of arrows from the bow" (Jarchi, Kimchi, Rosenmüller), though in this case קֶשֶׁת would have to be read for קַשָּׁת (Fürst) ; (2) a marksman, archer, i. e. a marksman skilled in using the bow (Ewald, *vide* ' Heb. Synt.,' § 287). Baumgarten translates, a hero (or great one), an archer. **And he dwelt in the wilderness of Paran :**—the desert of *El-Tih*, on the south of Canaan (cf. ch. xiv. 6)—**and his mother took him a wife out of the land of Egypt** (cf. ch. xxiv. 4, 55 ; Exod. xxi. 10).

HOMILETICS.

Vers. 15—21.—*Hagar and Ishmael, or the fortunes of the outcasts.* I. THE LONELY WANDERERS. 1. *Banished from home.* Hitherto the household of Abraham had been to Hagar and her boy such a pleasant and doubtless much-prized abode ; henceforth their connection with the patriarch's encampment was to be completely severed. So God in his mysterious providence and in many different ways frequently bereaves men of the shelter and society of home. 2. *Separated from the Church.* Practically the expulsion of this Egyptian slave-mother and her son from the household of Abraham, if it did not involve a casting off from God's mercy, amounted to extrusion from the patriarchal Church. 3. *Lost in the wilderness.* Whether because the region through which they travelled was unfamiliar, or because, impelle by indignation and excitement, they simply drifted on with aimless feet, the narrative depicts the unhappy pair as having "wandered," turned aside into unfrequented paths, and become lost ; in that touchingly portraying the sad condition of thousands of homeless and churchless wanderers to-day, roaming purposeless and perplexed across the trackless waste of life.

II. THE FAINTING YOUTH. 1. *Perishing through thirst.* Extreme thirst one of the most excruciating torments to which the physical frame can be subjected, and a fellow-creature dying for lack of water, one of the commonest of God's mercies, as sad a spectacle as any on which the eye of man can gaze. 2. *Sobbing in anguish.* Too exhausted to weep aloud, the poor disheartened lad moans out his misery. Happy they who, if they cannot relieve, can at least understand and be affected by their necessities. To recognise and make complaint of one's spiritual destitution is better than to be callous and indifferent to one's dying condition. 3. *Praying to God.* Though not certain that the "voice" of the lad meant more than the rude cry of his distress, charity may hope that in the day of his calamity he directed his prayer to God. Prayer generally precedes deliverance.

III. THE WEEPING MOTHER. 1. *The voice of heathen superstition.* "Let me not see the death of the lad." To a Christian mother Hagar's behaviour is simply inexplicable. It is doubtful if Sarah would have been a bow-shot removed from Isaac had he been expiring. But then Hagar, though she had been Abraham's wife, was still a poor untutored slave-girl. It may assist us to understand our indebtedness to the humanising influences of Christ's religion. 2. *The cry of maternal affection.* "She sat over against her boy, and lifted up her voice and wept." Even in the breast of this Egyptian bondmaid nature asserted her supremacy. Everywhere beautiful and sacred is a mother's love, worthy of being cherished and reciprocated by those who know its sweetness and strength, never failing to bring down retribution on those by whom it is rejected and despised.

IV. THE COMFORTING GOD. 1. *Sympathising with the sorrowful.* "What aileth thee, Hagar?" What a glimpse into the infinite pitifulness of the Divine nature! Only when Christ came was it surpassed in clearness and fulness. 2. *Listening to the suppliant.* As the prayer of Ishmael came up into the wakeful ear of God, so the cries of dying men and perishing souls never fail to do. 3. *Consoling the dejected.* As to Hagar the angel spoke words of encouragement, and renewed the formerly-given assurance concerning the future greatness of her son, so God revives the drooping spirits of his people by directing them to his exceeding great and precious promises. 4. *Providing for the destitute.* "God opened her eyes, and she saw a well of water." And so by the leadings of his providence, the teachings of his word, and the illumination of his Spirit does God guide the meek to the wells of salvation. 5. *Abiding with the homeless.* "God was with the lad." Ejected from Abraham's house, he was not deserted by Abraham's God. Happy they who amid life's wanderings can count on God's companionship. For desertions of friends and deprivations of goods it will prove ample compensation.

Learn—1. To prize the blessing of a home and the privilege of a Church. 2. To commiserate and succour those who have neither. 3. To use God in all the revealed aspects of his gracious character.

HOMILIES BY VARIOUS AUTHORS.

Ver. 17.—*Hagar, a weary outcast.* "What aileth thee, Hagar?" Hagar is sent away from Abraham's tents. In the wilderness wandering she is lost. In despair she sinks down and weeps. An angel's voice is heard inquiring, "What aileth thee, Hagar?"

I. HAGAR MAY BE TAKEN AS REPRESENTING THE SOULS STILL CHRISTLESS. They are— 1. Weary. 2. Thirsty. 3. Apparently man-forsaken and God-forsaken. 4. Their dearest comforts slipping from them, as Hagar's child, by death. 5. Death expecting.

II. HAGAR'S ACT INDICATES HOW SUCH SOULS SHOULD ACT IN TROUBLE. 1. Realise it. 2. Seek deliverance from above. God nearer to us than we imagine. He feels for us, hears us, helps us. He gives sustenance, cheer, guidance.—H.

Vers. 17—19.—*God's appearance to Hagar.* The greatest truths in the Bible put before us in a setting of human interest and feeling. Our hearts strangely touched by the picture of the desolate woman and the helpless child. The fatherly character of God exhibited. He heard the voice of the lad. All such facts point to the greatest fact, the union of God and man in the man Christ Jesus. We see here—

I. GOD'S NOTICE OF AND COMPASSION FOR HUMAN SUFFERING: our example. The object of pity apart from antecedents.

II. THE WORKING OUT OF DIVINE PURPOSES notwithstanding, and to some extent by means of, human infirmities, errors, and sins. Ishmael must be preserved, and has his part to play in the future.

III. Taken TYPICALLY, Hagar and Ishmael represent the life of man apart from the covenant of God, outside the circle of special privilege. There is God in the wilderness. The eyes which are darkened with ignorance and self-will may yet be mercifully opened to see the well of water. The angel of deliverance follows even the bondwoman and her son. But the way to God through the wilderness is a hard way, a way of suffering, a way of danger. God was with Ishmael. He was with him through Abraham, for Abraham's sake. The course of Ishmael's life illustrates the contrast between a truly religious career and one given up to natural impulse. Cf. Esau and Joseph's brethren.—R.

Ver. 19.—*Hagar in the wilderness.* "And God opened her eyes, and she saw a well of water." Hagar in the wilderness. Why? She had no pleasure in her home; would not accept her position there. Hence Ishmael's mocking. Compare working of pride in Eden—" Ye shall be as gods;" and its result—Adam and Eve driven out. Observe—a soul despising the position of a child of God is driven into the wilderness by its own act. Pride rebels against terms of salvation (Rom. x. 3)— a free gift to sinners seeking it as such (Mark ii. 17). Hagar felt her misery, like many who find no peace. " All is vanity." She sat down and wept. Did she cry to God? He had met her there before. Past mercies should move to trust (Ps. xlii. 6). But pride and unbelief hinder prayer (Exod. xvii. 3—6). But God had not forgotten her (cf. Matt. xviii. 11). " What aileth thee?" Compare our Lord's dealing with those he helped. 1. Himself taking the first step. 2. Requiring a confession of their want. 3. Rousing expectation (John iv. 14; vii. 37).

I. THE WELL WAS NEAR HER, BUT SHE SAW IT NOT. So is it with the water of life. Why are so many without peace? The well is beside them; the sound of the gospel is familiar to them. The Bible is read in their hearing, but it speaks nothing to them (2 Cor. iii. 15). Christ died for all (2 Cor. v. 14). His blood the ransom for all (1 John i. 7). We have not to go to seek a Saviour (Rom. x. 6—8). No sin too deep for cleansing, no sorrow too great for comfort; nothing required to give a right to trust him (Isa. lv. 1; Luke xv. 2). Why without peace? The eyes are closed to the truth (1 Cor. ii. 14). Human teaching cannot give life (Ezek. xxxvii. 8). What is wanted is not a new fountain, but opened eyes. And it is disbelief of this that keeps so many in anxiety. To them the well is not there; they want God to give it. They look for something they are to do to find a Saviour. Important to know what is wanted—spiritual discernment. To many this seems a mere fancy; but they whose eyes are opened know it to be a passing from darkness to light (cf. 2 Tim. i. 10). Words often read become full of new meaning.

II. GOD OPENED HER EYES. It is blindness that causes trouble; but as blind cannot see by his own will, so neither can the unspiritual. The way of salvation is before him, but while it commends itself to his reason it brings him no joy. Are we then without effort to sit still? No; all is ready on God's part. " Wilt thou be made whole?" Want of will alone hinders. Often men would like to drink, but not at God's fountain. Make an effort to believe, and power will be given.

III. WHAT SHE SAW. The well of life; the revelation of Jesus Christ to the soul —this is peace. Not our own powers or wisdom, not our own holiness or advance in grace; but trust in him. No more fears. True, the wilderness is there; the work has to be done, temptations overcome, sorrows borne, graces cultivated; but we can do all through Christ. Now troubles become helps (Ps. lxxxiv. 6), for they make us flee to Christ (2 Cor. xii. 9). And who can count the blessings revealed to him whose eyes are opened? A Father in everything—protection, teaching, guidance. Everything surrounding him, every event that happens to him, are inlets of ever-increasing knowledge of God, whom to know is life eternal.—M.

Ver. 20.—*God's care for Ishmael.* " And God was with the lad." The encampment of Abraham was the scene of joy and festivity on the occasion of the recognition of Isaac publicly as his heir. It is said in Jewish lore that Abraham called a number of the patriarchs to the feast, and that Melchizedek, Nahor, and even Noah were present. Ishmael had been heir-presumptive up to that time. He was then put in the position of a subject to the son of Sarah. He and his mo'her despised the weakling and nursling. They " mocked." This roused the indignation of Sarah, and she insisted on the banishment of both. Abraham was very unwilling to consent to the proposal, for he had great affection for Ishmael. No wonder that he loved him, for he was, if not the child of promise, at least the son who first roused in his breast the pride and joy of paternity. He seems to have hoped that Ishmael would be the one through whom the great blessings promised to him would be bestowed.

Hence he had prayed, "O that Ishmael might live before thee" (ch. xvii. 18).
Perhaps unbelief had much to do with the expression of the hope. He indicated
his own contentment with that mode of fulfilment of the promises; God, however,
has another. Abraham evidently loved the lad, and now that he is grown to be a
stalwart youth of about sixteen, it is strongly against his inclination to send him
away. Sarah insists. She in her indignation will not even speak of him by his
name, but calls him contemptuously "the son of this bondwoman" (ch. xxi. 10).
Abraham was very grieved (ver. 11), but he can see that there is no prospect of any
peace in his encampment unless he should do as Sarah wishes. Two jealous women
are enough to embitter his life, and bring discord eventually among his retainers.
For typical reasons the banishment was permitted by God (ver. 12), and Abraham
sends both away, laden probably not only with trinkets, which shall suffice for barter,
but with a flask of water and strings of small loaves. Abraham had thus to sacrifice
his own inclinations in Ishmael, his son after the flesh, as afterwards his will in
offering up Isaac, his child of promise. Away towards Egypt Hagar and Ishmael
travel. They enter the wilderness of Beersheba. Happiness and home is behind;
desolateness, dreariness, lonely journeyings, imminent dangers from the wild beasts
and fierce hordes of men, with Egypt, before them. Hagar, with bread dry and
water spent, losing her way, waits for some one to guide. Unable to proceed, she
and her son sink down to die, to perish in the scorching heat from that most fearful
of all deprivations, water. Hagar, with bitter memories of lost happiness and
unjust treatment crowding, cannot bear the sight of her son's woe and sound of his
moaning, therefore removes to a slight distance, that she might not see his death nor
disturb it as she sought to ease her poor heart with tears. Oh, what moral beauty
blossoms in the desert in the maternal love of this outcast bondwoman. No human
eye detects it, but God notices and hears her voice, and that of the child. Then
comes the direction from heaven, and the promise, "I will make of him a great
nation." We are told immediately afterwards in the brief record concerning Ishmael
that "God was with the lad," and so the promise was fulfilled. We notice *God's
care even for an Ishmael*, for one who would appear to be outside all covenant blessings. He was one whose "hand was to be against every man, and every man's
against him" (ch. xvi. 12). God manifested care, however, to this Ishmael—

I. BY PRESERVING HIS LIFE. He heard his cry in distress. He knew his needs.
God always knows our needs; whence to supply them, and where to find us even in
the wilderness. A well of water is unexpectedly pointed out to the mother. Her
eyes were opened to see its whereabouts. So God teaches many a mother, that she
may lead her children to the well of living water. Every life preserved is only
through the mercy of God. "In his hand our breath is" (Dan. v. 23). There is a
well for bondsmen as well as free. God's living well is to be reached in any position
of life. It is near to us when we think it far off. "The word is nigh thee, in thine
heart," &c. (Rom. x. 8). If we are to see the treasure, our spiritual understanding
must be quickened, our "eyes opened" by the Holy Spirit. If we desire to know
the way and well of life, we can pray for that opening. Only as we have this
spiritual sight and life can we rejoice in the present existence, in our preservation.
God preserved Ishmael that he might know him.

II. GOD ADVANCED HIM IN LIFE. He was with him as he grew up, and gave him
favour in the sight of others. God is ever seeking by his Holy Spirit to mould the
character of the worst for good. If we have any prosperity and grow up to influence,
we should remember that it is from God. The darkest hour for Ishmael had ushered
in the dawning of the brightest day. God knew what he would do with Ishmael.
Ishmael is to found a nation. It is remarkable that he was the ancestor of the same
number of tribes as was Israel (ch. xxv. 16). He found various scattered people in
the Arabian desert, but the tribes descended from him seem to have absorbed all
others. What an honour to be the founder of a house, a dynasty; how much more
of a nation! This God granted to an Ishmael.

III. GOD GAVE HIM SKILL. "He became an archer." He had to learn to defend
himself, and secure for himself, by God's help, a position. The fighting power is not
the highest, but man has always had to protect himself before he could make progress in civilisation. Alas, when he supposes himself to be civilised he often clings

to the old habit, and still loves the fighting. The archers, like Ishmael, have their sphere as well as the shepherds, like Isaacs. The fiery defenders of faith and the controversial champions of the truth have their sphere as well as the pious, plodding pastors of Christ's flock. If men have skill for the one thing, let them not despise the powers of others. We have all to learn to appreciate diversity of talents, and to remember that skill in any work is the outcome of independence, resolution, and energy Ishmael had been endowed with these by God.

IV. GOD FURNISHED ISHMAEL WITH A PLACE OF HABITATION. He gave to him the desert for his domain. Here he might roam and pitch his tent at his own suggestion. God knew that the hot blood of his Egyptian mother, which coursed in his veins, would find its most fitting sphere in the desert. Instead of mingling with gentle herdsmen, he had to dwell among the fierce and untrained spirits of the desert. He became an ancestor of those who despised town life, and who were hardy and frugal enough to exist where others would have perished. Thus to Ishmael, the desert, with its widespread, sun-scorched sands, its scant herbage, its infrequent wells and scattered oases, became a fitting home. God chose for him his dwelling-place, and defined for him the bounds of his habitation. And is it not best for us to leave ourselves in God's hands? He knows best where to place any of us, and what work to give us to do, what sphere to fill. We might prefer the green pasture and hills flowing with milk and honey of the Canaan of prosperity, but the desert of trial and loneliness may be the best for training our spirits. We may have losses to endure outwardly, but if we can acquire a spirit of content and faith, that is great gain. That spirit will lead us to say, "He shall choose our inheritance for us."

V. GOD ALSO INSURED ISHMAEL'S HONOUR AMONG HIS BRETHREN. He was to "dwell in the presence of his brethren" (ch. xvi. 12). Though cast out by Abraham, he was not cast off by God or cut off from all interchange with others. We find (ch. xxv. 6) that Abraham gave portions to the sons of his second wife, Keturah, and sent them away. Doubtless he gave a portion to Ishmael, for we find him uniting with Isaac in the funeral obsequies of his father (ch. xxv. 9). The two sons were not at enmity now. Further, he seems to have kept up his union with his brother, for his daughter Bashemath (ch. xxxvi. 3) married Esau, Isaac's son. Thus two families in the line of promise, but who had cast themselves out—Esau by his indifference, and Ishmael by his mocking—were united. Thus, although of fierce and fiery nature, Ishmael "dwelt in the presence of his brethren." God was with him. He had a shorter life than Isaac. Ishmael died at 130 years old, Isaac at 180. Evidently the active, restless, wandering, hazardous life was more wearing and consuming than the calm and meditative life of the pastoral Isaac. But when he died God cared for him as well as for Isaac, only his purposes with respect to Isaac were different. Isaac was an ancestor after the flesh of the Messiah, but Ishmael had not that honour. Still we must not think that God had cast off Ishmael, and left him utterly and everlastingly to perish. Our God cares for those outside the pale of the Church, even as for those within. The former have not taken up their privileges, nor seen how Christ loves them. They are suffering great loss, and are in danger of further loss, but God cares for and pities them. He wills not the death of a sinner. He pitied the people of Nineveh, sent them a warning, and gave them space for repentance. He healed a Naaman; sent his prophet to dwell with a woman of Sarepta, and so conferred honour upon her; and he brought a Nebuchadnezzar to his right mind by a judicious infliction. All this was mercy shown outside the pale of Israel to those who would be accounted as Ishmaelites. Oh, how much more widely flows the channel of Divine mercy and love than we imagine! How little we conceive the depth of the Father's love to all his creatures! In every heart he is seeking to find a reflection of his image. By the side of every soul, however much of an Ishmaelite, he is seeking by his Holy Spirit to walk, that he may win back to the fold of love and mercy. Oh, ye who think yourselves too sinful to have a share in the Divine compassion, see God's treatment of an Ishmael. Remember that Christ came "not to call the righteous, but sinners to repentance." God is merciful even to thoughtless sinners, and gives streams in the desert. If this be the spirit of our God and Saviour, should it not teach us to take an interest in all? As the sun when setting in the west throws his golden and purple rays not only over the broad ocean, but on the dank ditches of the meadows and the puddles of the street, so should we remember that there is no heart so depraved but the love of God in Christ may light it up. If only we looked at our fellows thus, with deeper sympathy, we should see them won to Christ.—H.

EXPOSITION.

Ver. 22.—**And it came to pass at that time,** —possibly in immediate sequence to the incident of the preceding chapter, but, "according to the common law of Hebrew narrative, probably not long after the birth of Isaac" (Murphy)—**that Abimelech**—the king of Gerar (ch. xx. 2; xxvi. 1, 16)—**and Phichol**—if the name be Shemitic, "mouth of all," *i. e.* spokesman of all (Murphy), ruler of all (Gesenius); or "the distinguished" (Fürst); believed to have been a titular designation of the Philistine monarch's grand vizier or prime minister (Lange, 'Speaker's Commentary'), who was also—**the chief captain of his host** (*i. e.* the commander-in-chief of his forces) **spake unto Abraham** (having come from Gerar for the purpose), **saying, God is with thee in all that thou doest**—a conviction derived from his former acquaintance with the patriarch (ch. xx.), his knowledge of Isaac's birth, and his general observation of the patriarch's prosperity.

Ver. 23.—**Now therefore swear unto me here by God**—the verb to swear is derived from the Hebrew numeral seven, inasmuch as the septennary number was sacred, and oaths were confirmed either by seven sacrifices (ch. xxi. 28) or by seven witnesses and pledges,—**that thou wilt not deal falsely with me,**—literally, *if thou shalt lie unto me;* a common form of oath in Hebrew, in which the other member of the sentence is for emphasis left unexpressed (cf. Ruth i. 17, and *vide* ch. xiv. 23). As a prince, Abimelech was afraid of Abraham's growing power; as a good man, he insures the safety of himself and his dominions not by resorting to war, but by forming an amicable treaty with his neighbour—**nor with my son, nor with my son's son**:—σπέρμα καὶ ὄνομα (LXX.); *posteri et stirps* (Vulgate); offspring and progeny (Kalisch); kith and kin (Murphy)—but **according to the kindness that I have done unto thee** (*vide* ch. xx. 15), **thou shalt do unto me, and to the land wherein thou hast sojourned**—the land being put for the people (cf. Numb. xiv. 13).

Ver. 24.—**And Abraham said, I will swear.** Only before concluding the agreement there was a matter of a more personal character that required settlement.

Ver. 25.—**And Abraham reproved** (literally, *reasoned with,* and proved to the satisfaction of) **Abimelech** (who was, until informed, entirely unacquainted with the action of his servants) **because of a well of water, which Abimelech's servants had violently taken away.** The greatest possible injury of a material kind that could be done to a nomade chief was the abstraction of his water supplies. Hence "the ownership of wells in Palestine was as jealously guarded as the possession of a mine in our own" (Inglis). Contests for wells "are now very common all over the country, but more especially in the southern deserts" (Thomson, 'Land and Book,' p. 559).

Ver. 26.—**And Abimelech said, I wot not who hath done this thing.** There is no reason to question the sincerity of the Philistine monarch in disclaiming all knowledge of the act of robbery committed by his servants. **Neither didst thou tell me, neither yet heard I of it, but to day.** The prince rather complains that Abraham had done him an injustice.

Ver. 27.—**And Abraham took sheep and oxen, and gave them unto Abimelech.** As the usual covenant presents (cf. 1 Kings xv. 19; Isa. xxx. 6; xxxix. 1). **And both of them made a covenant.** As already Mamre, Aner, and Eshcol had formed a league with the patriarch (*vide* ch. xiv. 13).

Vers. 28—30.—**And Abraham set seven ewe lambs of the flock by themselves** (designing by another covenant to secure himself against future invasion of his rights). **And Abimelech said unto Abraham, What mean these seven ewe lambs which thou hast set by themselves? And he said, For these seven ewe lambs shalt thou take of my hand, that they may be a witness unto me,**—that this peculiar kind of oath never occurs again in Old Testament history is no proof of the mythical character of the narrative (Bohlen); on the contrary, "that the custom existed in primitive Hebrew times is shown by the word נִשְׁבַּע, which had early passed into the language, and which would be inexplicable without the existence of such a custom" (Hävernick)—**that I have digged this well.**

Ver. 31.—**Wherefore he called that place Beer-sheba.** *I. e.* "the well of the oath," φρέαρ ὁρκισμοῦ (LXX., Gesenius, Fürst, Rosenmüller), or the well of the seven (Keil), rather than the seven wells (Lange); discovered by Robinson in *Bir-es-seba,* in the Wady-es-seba, twelve miles to the south of Hebron, with two deep wells of excellent water. "The great well has an internal diameter at the mouth of twelve feet six inches, or a circumference of nearly forty feet. The shaft is formed of excellent masonry to a great depth until it reaches the rock, and at this juncture a spring trickles perpetually. Around the mouth of the well is a circular course of masonry, topped by a annular parapet of about a foot high ; and at a distance of ten or twelve feet are stone troughs placed in a concentric circle with the well, the sides of which have deep indentions made by the wear of ropes on the upper edges. The second well, about 200 yards farther south, is not more than five feet in diameter, but is formed of equally good masonry, and furnishes equally good water" (vide 'Byeways in Palestine,' by James Finn, M.R.A.S., p. 190). **Because there they sware both of them.**

Ver. 33.—**And** Abraham **planted**—as a sign of his peaceful occupation of the soil (Calvin) ; as a memorial of the transaction about the well ('Speaker's Commentary') ; or simply as a shade for his tent (Rosenmüller) ; scarcely as an oratory (Bush, Kalisch)—**a grove**—the אֵשֶׁל—wood, plantation (Targums, Vulgate, Samaritan, Kimchi) ; a field, ἄρουραν

(LXX.)—was probably the *Tamarix Africanæ* (Gesenius, Fürst, Delitzsch, Rosenmüller, Kalisch), which, besides being common in Egypt and Petræa, is said to have been found growing near the ancient Beer-sheba—**in Beer-sheba, and called there** (not beneath the tree or in the grove, but in the place) **on the name of the Lord,**—Jehovah (vide ch. xii. 8 ; viii. 4). **the everlasting God.** Literally, *the God of eternity* (LXX., Vulgate, Onkelos) ; not in contrast to heathen deities, who are born and die (Clericus), but "as the everlasting Vindicator of the faith of treaties, and as the infallible Source of the believer's rest and peace" (Murphy).

Ver. 34.—**And Abraham sojourned in the Philistines' land many days.** The apparent contradiction between the statement of this verse and that of ver. 32 may be removed by supposing either, (1) that as the land of the Philistines had no fixed boundary toward the desert, Beer-sheba may at this time have been claimed for the kingdom of Gerar (Keil); or, (2) that as Beer-sheba was situated on the confines of the Philistines' territory, Abraham must frequently have sojourned in their country while pasturing his flocks (Rosenmüller).

HOMILETICS.

Vers. 22—34. — *Abimelech and Abraham, or ancient covenanters.* I. THE POLITICAL ALLIANCE. 1. *The contemplated object.* Peace. What modern monarchs mostly desire at the close of exhausting campaigns is here sought before campaigns begin. 2. *The covenanting parties.* Two powerful princes, in their conduct exemplifying the spirit of unity and peace which should bind together private persons in their daily intercourse, as well as kings and nations in their political alliance. 3. *The impelling motives.* Worldly policy may have urged Abimelech to cement a league with the powerful chieftain in his neighbourhood, but religious affinity would also seem to have exercised an influence in drawing him to seek the friendship of one who appeared to enjoy celestial protection. Good men mostly desire to have the saints as friends, and even the wicked can perceive an advantage in being allied to the righteous. Abraham's acquiescence in the king's proposal was no doubt dictated by a peaceable disposition, a sense of equity, a spirit of contentment, and an unwavering confidence in God. 4. *The public ceremonial.* The alliance was contracted (1) by means of amicable conference, and (2) with the sanctions of religion.
II. THE FRIENDLY REMONSTRANCE. 1. *The palpable injury.* The herdsmen of the king had appropriated Abraham's well. God's people, though expected meekly to suffer wrong, cannot always help seeing that it is wrong they suffer. Nor are they called upon to bear what by lawful means they are able to redress. A good man is entitled to be careful of his property, to preserve it from damage, protect it from theft, and recover it when stolen or lost. 2. *The mistaken charge.* Abraham, thinking the herdsmen had acted on their master's orders, reproved Abimelech. This, however, was an error, which shows (1) that a person cannot always be held responsible for what his servants do, (2) that it is wrong to judge on insufficient evidence with reference to the characters and conduct of others, and (3) that in making charges or preferring complaints it is well to avoid both heat of temper and severity of language. 3. *The satisfactory explanation.* Abimelech declared himself perfectly unacquainted with the wrong which had been done to Abraham, and immediately returned the well, which discovers how easily misunderstandings might be

removed if, instead of harbouring enmity, men would resort to friendly conference. It is as much the duty of him who has a grievance to reveal it, as it is the duty of him who has caused the grievance to remove it. 4. *The prudent measure.* Abraham gave Abimelech seven ewe lambs as a witness that he had digged the well, and consequently had a right to its possession. Seemingly betraying a secret suspicion of the prince's veracity, the act aimed at preventing any recurrence of the grievance, and in this light it appears to have been regarded by Abimelech. Good men should not only rectify the wrongs they do to one another, but adopt all wise precautions against their repetition.

III. THE PLEASING RESULT. 1. *Peace established*, Abimelech and Phichol, having accomplished their mission, returned to Philistia. " Blessed are the peace-makers," and " beautiful upon the mountains are the feet of him that publisheth peace." 2. *Peace commemorated.* Abraham instituted two memorials of the important transactions, naming the well Beersheba, and planting a tamarisk beside his tent. It is good to remember God's mercies, of which national and civil quietude is one of the greatest, and it is becoming to erect memorials of both privileges and obligations. 3. *Peace enjoyed.* Abraham called on the name of the everlasting God. As a planter of tamarisks, the patriarch has been styled the father of civilisation; it is more important to remark that he never neglected to worship God himself and publish his salvation to others. Happy they who can do both in peace !

HOMILIES BY VARIOUS AUTHORS.

Vers. 22—34.—*A covenant between the patriarch and the Philistine king.* Abraham a sojourner in that land, afterwards the troubler of Israel; for his sake as discipline, for their sakes as opportunity. 1. God's care for those beyond the covenant. A Beersheba in a heathen land. 2. The things of this world made a channel of higher blessings. The covenant arising out of bodily wants a civil agreement. The oath a testimony to God where reverently made. 3. He is not far from every one of us. The neighbourhood of Beersheba, the revelation of Jehovah, the little company of believers. 4. The blessing made manifest. The days spent in Philistia left behind them some enlightenment. 5. Adaptation of Divine truth to those to whom it is sent. Abraham's name of God, Jehovah El Olam; the two revelations, the God of nature and the God of grace. The name of the Lord itself an invitation to believe and live. Paul at Athens adapted himself in preaching to the people's knowledge while leading them to faith.—R.

EXPOSITION.

CHAPTER XXII.

Ver. 1.—**And it came to pass**—the alleged mythical character of the present narrative (De Wette, Bohlen) is discredited not more by express Scripture statement (Heb. xi. 17 —19) than by its own inherent difficulties— **after**—how long after may be conjectured from the circumstance that Isaac was now a grown lad, capable of undertaking a three days' journey of upwards of sixty miles—**these things** (literally, *words*, of benediction, promise, trial that had gone before—**that God**— literally, *the Elohim*, i. e. neither Satan, as in 1 Chron. xxi. 1, compared with 2 Sam. xxiv. 1 (Schelling, Stanley), nor Abraham himself, in the sense that a subjective impulse on the part of the patriarch supplied the formal basis of the subsequent transaction (Kurtz, Oehler); but the El-Olam of ch. xxi. 32, the term Elohim being employed

by the historian not because vers. 1—13 are Elohistic (Tuch, Bleek, Davidson,)—a hypothesis inconsistent with the internal unity of the chapter, "which is joined together like cast-iron " (Oehler), and in particular with the use of Moriah in ver. 2 (Hengstenberg),—but to indicate the true origin of the after-mentioned trial, which proceeded neither from Satanic instigation nor from subjective impulse, but from God (Keil)— **did tempt**—not solicit to sin (James i. 13), but test or prove (Exod. xvi. 4 ; Deut. viii. 2 ; xiii. 3 ; 2 Chron. xxxii. 31 ; Ps. xxvi. 2) —**Abraham, and said unto him,**—in a dream-vision of the night (Eich-horn, Lange), but certainly in an audible voice which previous experience enabled him to recognise—**Abraham : and he said, Behold**, here I am. " These brief introductions of the conversation express the great tension and application of the human mind in those moments in a striking way, and serve at the same time to prepare us for the importance of the conversation" (Lange).

Ver. 2.—**And he said, Take now**—"the נָא modifies the command, and seems to express that Elohim wished to receive the sacrifice as a free-will offering" (Lange)—**thy son** (not a lamb, but thy child), **thine only son**—not ἀγαπητὸν (LXX.), but *unigenitum* (Vulgate), meaning the only son of Sarah, the only legitimate offspring he possessed, the only heir of the promise, the only child that remained to him after Ishmael's departure (cf. ὁ μονογενὴς, John i. 18)—**Isaac, whom thou lovest,**—or, *whom thou lovest, Isaac;* the order and accumulation of the terms being calculated to excite the parental affection of the patriarch to the highest pitch, and to render compliance with the Divine demand a trial of the utmost severity—**and get thee**—literally, *go for thyself* (cf. ch. xii. 1; xxi. 16)—**into the land of Moriah.** Moriah = vision (Vulgate, Symmachus, Samaritan), worship (Onkelos, Jonathan), high (LXX.), rebellious (Murphy); but rather a compound of יְ and מֹרִי, meaning God is my instructor, alluding to the temple from which the law should afterwards proceed (Kalisch), or, better, of יה and רָאָה, and signifying "the shown of Jehovah," *i. e.* the revelation or manifestation of Jehovah (Hengstenberg, Kurtz, Keil, &c.); or "the chosen," *i. e.* "pointed out of God," with reference to its selection as the site of the Divine sanctuary (Gesenius), or rather because there God provided and pointed out the sacrifice which he elected to accept (Lange). **And offer him there for a burnt offering**—not make a spiritual surrender of him in and through a burnt offering (Hengstenberg, Lange), but actually present him as a holocaust. That Abraham did not stagger on receiving this astounding injunction may be accounted for by remembering that the practice of offering human sacrifices prevailed among the early Chaldæans and Canaanites, and that as yet no formal prohibition, like that of the Mosaic code, had been issued against them—**upon one of the mountains**—not Moreh in Sichem (Tuch, Michaelis, Stanley, Grove, *et alii*), which was too distant, but Moriah at Jerusalem (Hengstenberg, Kurtz, Keil, Kalisch), where subsequently God appeared to David (2 Sam. xxiv. 16), and the temple of Solomon was built (2 Chron. iii. 1)—**which I will tell thee of**—*i. e.* point out (probably by secret inspiration) as thou proceedest.

Ver. 3.—**And Abraham rose up early in the morning,**—a habit of the patriarch's after receiving a Divine communication (cf. ch. xix. 27; xx. 8; xxi. 14)—**and saddled his ass, and took two of his young men**

with him (the ass for the wood, and the young men for the ass), **and Isaac his son** (explaining to him as yet only his intention to offer sacrifice upon a distant mountain), **and clave the wood for the burnt offering** (obviously with his own hands), **and rose up** (expressive of resolute determination), **and went unto** (or towards) **the place of which God had told him**—literally, *the Elohim had spoken to him.* The accumulation of brief, sententious clauses in this verse admirably represents the calm deliberation and unflinching heroism with which the patriarch proceeded to execute the Divine command.

Ver. 4.—**Then on the third day**—Jerusalem, being distant from Beersheba about twenty and a half hours' journey according to Robinson, could easily be within sight on the third day—**Abraham lifted up his eyes,**—not implying that the object of vision was above him (cf. ch. xiii. 10)—**and saw the place** (which Calvin conjectures he had previously beheld in vision) **afar off.** Though Mount Moriah cannot be seen by the traveller from Beersheba till within a distance of three miles (Stanley, 'Sinai and Palestine,' p. 251), the place or region where it is can be detected (Kalisch).

Ver. 5.—**And Abraham said unto his young men, Abide ye** (for similar forms of expression cf. ch. xii. 1; xxi. 6; xxii. 2) **here with the ass;**—partly because the beast required watching, though chiefly because the contemplated sacrifice was too solemn for any eyes but God's to witness—**and I and the lad will go yonder and worship, and come again to you.** An act of dissimulation on the part of Abraham (Knobel, Kalisch, Murphy); an unconscious prophecy (Lyra, Junius, Rashi); the expression of a hopeful wish (Lange); a somewhat confused utterance (Calvin, Keil); the voice of his all-conquering faith (Augustine, Calvin, Wordsworth, Bush, 'Speaker's Commentary,' Inglis), which last seems the teaching of Heb. xi. 19.

Ver. 6.—**And Abraham took the wood of the burnt offering, and laid it upon Isaac his son;**—instinctively the mind reverts to the cross-bearing of Abraham's greater Son (John xix. 17)—**and he took the fire in his hand, and a knife** (to him terribly suggestive weapons); **and they went both of them together.** Doubtless in silence on Abraham's part and wonder on Isaac's, since as yet no declaration had been made of the true purpose of their journey.

Ver. 7.—**And Isaac spoke to Abraham his father,**—during the progress of the journey, after leaving the young men, solitude inviting him to give expression to thoughts which had been rising in his bosom, but which the presence of companions had constrained him to suppress—**and said, My father :**—a term

THE BOOK OF GENESIS.

of filial reverence and endearment that must have lacerated Abraham's heart. As used by Isaac it signified a desire to interrogate his parent—**and he said, Here am I, my son** (literally, *Behold me, my son* = Well, my son, what is it? in colloquial English). **And he said, Behold the fire and the wood : but where is the lamb for a burnt offering.** Another hint that the sacrificial system did not originate with Moses.

Ver. 8.—**And Abraham said, My son, God will provide himself a lamb for a burnt offering :**—the utterance of heroic faith rather than the language of pious dissimulation (*vide* on ver. 5)—**so they went both of them together.** To see in this twice-repeated expression a type of the concurrence of the Father and the Son in the work of redemption (Wordsworth) is not exegesis.

Ver. 9.—**And they came to the place which God had told him of; and Abraham built an altar there,**—*i. e.* upon the mountain summit or slope (ver. 2)—**and laid the wood in order** (it is scarcely likely that Isaac was permitted to assist in these affecting preparations), **and bound Isaac his son,**—who must have acquiesced in his father's purpose, and thereby evinced his faith in the Divine commandment. The term "bound," though seeming to convey the idea of violence, derives its significance from the binding of the sacrificial victim—**and laid him on the altar on the wood.** The feelings of the patriarch throughout this transaction are simply inconceivable.

Ver. 10.—**And Abraham stretched forth his hand, and took the knife to slay his son** —who even in the last moment offers no resistance, but behaves like a type of him who was led like a lamb to the slaughter (Isa. liii. 7).

Ver. 11.—**And the angel of the Lord**— Maleach Jehovah (*vide* ch. xvi. 7); introduced into the narrative at this point not as a Jehovistic alteration (Bleek, Kalisch, *et alii*), but because the God of redemption now interposes for the deliverance of both Isaac and Abraham (Hengstenberg)—**called unto him out of heaven, and said, Abraham, Abraham** (the repetition denotes urgency, as contrasted with ver. 1): **and he said, Here am I.**

Ver. 12.—**And he said, Lay not thine hand upon the lad, neither do thou any thing unto him.** Abraham's surrender of the son of his affections having been complete, there was no need to push the trial further. The voice from heaven has been accepted as evidence of God's rejection of human sacrifices (Lange, Murphy), only that is not assigned as the reason for Isaac's deliverance. **For now I know**—literally, *have known;* not caused thee to know (Augustine), but caused others to know

(Lange); or the words are used anthropomorphically (Calvin)—**that thou fearest God,**— *Elohim;* the Divine intention being to characterise the patriarch as a God-fearing man, and not simply as a worshipper of Jehovah (cf. Quarry 'on Genesis,' p. 460)— seeing—literally, *and* (sc. in proof thereof)— **thou hast not withheld thy son, thine only son from me.** Καὶ οὐκ ἐφείσω τοῦ υἱοῦ σοῦ ἀγαπητοῦ δι᾽ ἐμέ (LXX.). Cf. ὅς γε τοῦ ἰδίου υἱοῦ οὐκ ἐφείσατο (Rom. viii. 32), as applied to the sacrifice of Christ. In this verse the angel of Jehovah identifies himself with Elohim.

Ver. 13.—**And Abraham lifted up his eyes** (in the direction of the voice), **and looked, and behold behind** him—either at his back (Fürst, Keil, Lange, Murphy), or in the background of the altar, *i. e.* in front of him (Gesenius, Kalisch). The LXX., Samaritan, Syriac, mistaking אַחַר for אֶחָד, read "one," which adds nothing to the sense or picturesqueness of the composition—**a ram**—אַיִל ; in the component letters of which cabalistic writers find the initial letters of יְרָאֶה־לּוֹ אֱלֹהִים, God will provide for himself (ver. 8 ; *vide* Glass, 'Phil. Tract.,' p. 196). In the animal itself the Fathers (Augustine, Tertullian, Origen, Chrysostom, Theodoret, Ambrose) rightly discerned a type of Christ, though it is fanciful to detect a shadow of the crown of thorns in the words that follow —**caught in a thicket by his horns** (the *sebach* being the intertwined branches of trees or brushwood): **and Abraham went and took the ram, and** (though not directed what to do, yet with a fine spiritual instinct discerning the Divine purpose) **offered him up for a burnt offering in the stead of his son**—whom he thus received from the dead as in a figure (Heb. xi. 19).

Ver. 14.—**And Abraham called the name of that place Jehovah-jireh :**—*i. e.* the Lord will provide (Jonathan, Calvin, Rosenmüller, Keil, &c.), rather than the Lord selects, or looks out, *i. e.* the sacrifices to be afterwards offered in the temple worship on Moriah (Kalisch) ; or, the Lord shall appear (Oort, Kuenen), which overlooks the manifest allusion to ver. 8—**as it is said** to **this day,**—or, so that it is said ; cf. ch. xiii. 16 (Keil)—**In the mount of the Lord it shall be seen**—or "it shall be provided" (Gesenius, Rosenmüller, Dathe, 'Speaker's Commentary '), though by competent authorities it has been otherwise rendered. "In the mount the Lord shall appear, or be seen" (LXX.) ; "in the mount the Lord will see, or provide" (Vulgate, Syriac, Samaritan) ; "in the mount of the Lord he will be seen" (Murphy) ; "in the mount of the Lord one shall be seen," or "people appear," *i. e.* the people of God shall gather on this mountain for worship

(Kalisch); "on the mountain where Jehovah appears" (Keil). Amidst such a conflict of interpretations absolute certainty is perhaps unattainable; but the sense of the proverb will probably be expressed by understanding it to mean that on the mount of Abraham's sacrifice Jehovah would afterwards reveal himself for the salvation of his people, as he then interposed for the help of Abraham—a prophecy which was afterwards fulfilled in the manifestations of the Divine glory given in the Solomonic temple and in the incarnation of Jesus Christ.

Vers. 15—18.—**And the angel of the Lord called unto Abraham out of heaven the second time,**—the object of the first call having been to arrest the consummation of the fatal deed which threatened Isaac's life, and to declare the Divine satisfaction with the patriarch's complete spiritual surrender of his son, the purpose of the second was to renew the promise in reward for his fidelity and obedience—**and said, By myself have I sworn,** — by my word (Onkelos); by my name (Arabic); equivalent to by himself, by his soul (Jer. li. 14), or by his holiness (Amos iv. 2)—an anthropomorphism by which God in the most solemn manner pledges the perfection of his Divine personality for the fulfilment of his promise; an act which he never again repeats in his intercourse with the patriarchs. The oath here given to Abraham (frequently referred to in later Scripture: ch. xxiv. 7; xxvi. 3; l. 24; Exod. xiii. 5, 11; xxxii. 13; xxxiii. 1; Isa. xlv. 23; Heb. vi. 13) is confirmed by the addition of—**saith the Lord,**—literally, *the utterance of Jehovah;* like the Latin *ait, inquit Dominus,* the usual prophetic phrase accompanying Divine oracles (cf. Isa. iii. 15; Ezek. v. 11; Amos vi. 8), though occurring in the Pentateuch only here and in Num. xiv. 28—**for because thou hast done this thing, and hast not withheld thy son, thine only** son (*vide supra,* ver. 12; from which the LXX., Syriac, and Samaritan insert here the words "from me"): **that in blessing I will bless thee, and, multiplying, I will multiply thy seed as the stars of heaven, and as the sand which is upon the sea shore;** —literally, *upon the lip of the sea;* a repetition and accumulation of the promises previously made to the patriarch concerning his seed (cf. ch. xii. 2, 3; xiii. 14—16; xv. 5; xvii. 1—8), with the special amplification following—**and thy seed shall possess** (*i. e.* occupy by force) **the gate of his enemies;**—shall conquer their armies and capture their cities (Keil, Murphy); though that the spiritual sense of entering in through the doorway of their susceptibilities in conversion (Lange) is not to be overlooked may be inferred from the appended prediction—**and in thy seed shall all the nations of the earth be blessed** (*vide* ch. xii. 3, where "families of the ground" occur as the equivalent of "nations of the earth"); **because thou hast obeyed my voice.** Originally unconditional in its grant, the promise is here distinctly declared to be renewed to him as one who, besides being justified and taken into covenant with Jehovah, had through trial and obedience attained to the spiritual patriarchate of a numerous posterity.

Ver. 19.—**So Abraham returned unto his young men, and they rose up and went together to Beer-sheba; and Abraham dwelt at Beer-sheba.**

HOMILETICS.

Vers. 1—19.—*Mount Moriah, or the mount of sacrifice.* I. ABRAHAM'S TRIAL. 1. *Divine in its origin.* However explained, the appalling ordeal through which the patriarch at this time passed was expressly created for him by Elohim. Only he who made the human heart can adequately search it; and he alone who has a perfect understanding of the standard of moral excellence can pronounce upon the intrinsic worth of his creatures. 2. *Unexpected in its coming.* After all that had preceded, it might have been anticipated that not only were the patriarch's trials over, but that the need for such discipline in his case no longer existed. It shows that neither length of years nor ripeness of grace, neither conscious enjoyment of Divine favour nor previous experience of suffering, can exempt from trial or place beyond the need of testing; and that mostly "temptations" come at unexpected times, and in unlooked-for ways. 3. *Severe in its form.* Trials to be efficient must be graduated to the strength of those they design to test. Only a temptation of great force could be of service in the case of moral heroism like Abraham's. The intensity of the strain put upon his soul by the astounding order to make a holocaust of Isaac simply baffles description. Even on the supposition that Abraham was not unfamiliar with the practice of offering human victims, as it prevailed among the Canaanites and early Chaldæans, painful doubt must have insinuated itself into his mind (1) as to the character of Jehovah, who in making such a barbarous and inhuman demand might seem little superior to the heathen deities around; (2) as to his own enjoyment of the Divine favour, which could scarcely fail to be staggered by such an excruciating stab to his natural affection; but, (3) and chiefly, as to the stability of the promise, which reason could not but pronounce impossible of fulfilment if Isaac must be put to death. Yet, overwhelming as the trial was, it was—4. *Needful in its design.* The great covenant blessing was still conditioned on the exercise by the patriarch of full-hearted trust in the naked word of God. Not until that standpoint had been reached by Abraham in his spiritual development was he able to become the parent of Isaac; and now that Isaac was born there was still the danger lest Isaac, and not the naked word of God, should be the ground of the patriarch's confidence. Hence the necessity arose for testing whether Abraham could resign Isaac and yet cling to the promise.

II. ABRAHAM'S VICTORY. 1. The *splendour* of it. The tremendous act of self-immolation was performed not without pain, else Abraham must have been either more or less than human, but (1) with unhesitating promptitude—"Abraham rose up early in the morning," and "went unto the place of which God had told him;" (2) with literal exactness—"Abraham laid the wood in order, and bound Isaac his son, and laid him upon the altar on the wood;" (3) in perfect sincerity—"Abraham stretched forth his hand to slay his son;" yet (4) without ostentation—Abraham went alone with his son to the mount of sacrifice. 2. The *secret* of it. This was faith. He accounted that, though Isaac should be slain, God was able to raise him up again from the dead. Hence, though prepared to plunge the knife into his son's breast, and to reduce his beloved form to ashes, he "staggered not at the promise."

III. ABRAHAM'S REWARD. 1. *The deliverance of Isaac.* (1) The time of it. At the moment when the sacrifice was about to be consummated, neither too soon for evincing the completeness of Abraham's obedience, nor too late for effecting Isaac's preservation. (2) The reason of it. Because the piety and faith of the patriarch were sufficiently demonstrated. God often accepts the will for the deed. (3) The manner of it. By the substitution of a ram, a type of the Lord Jesus Christ, through whose atoning death the Isaac of the Church is delivered from condemnation. (4) The teaching of it. If Abraham's surrender of Isaac was a shadow of the sacrificing love of the eternal Father in sparing not his only Son, and the bound Isaac typical of the Church's condemned condition before the sacrifice of Christ on Calvary, and the substituted ram was emblematic of him who, though he knew no sin, was made a sin offering for us, the deliverance of Isaac was symbolic both of the resurrection life of Christ and of the new life of his redeemed people. 2. *The confirmation of the blessing.* (1) A renewal of the promises—of a numerically great, territorially prosperous, and spiritually influential posterity, and more particularly of that distinguished seed in whom all the families of the earth should be blessed; (2) a specification of the ground on which they were held, viz., the patriarch's believing obedience to the Divine commandment; and (3) a solemn oath in guarantee of their fulfilment.

Lessons:—1. The certainty of trial. 2. The omnipotence of faith. 3. The blessedness of obedience.

HOMILIES BY VARIOUS AUTHORS.

Ver. 12.—*Abraham's perfect faith.* "Now I know that thou fearest God, seeing thou hast not withheld thy son, thine only son from me." "The word of God," says Coleridge, "speaks to man, and therefore it speaks the language of the children of men. This has to be kept in mind in studying the remarkable incident recorded in this chapter. When God is represented as "tempting" Abraham, it only means that he tried or tested him.

I. THE TESTING OF FAITH. Abraham was to be the head of the faithful and type of the justified, therefore it was essential he should be tested. Entire obedience is the test of perfect faith. Abraham had shown his faith when he left his own land, and when he waited patiently for a son; now he has to show it in a different way. In the two former testings he had a promise to rest on; now he must go far without any promise to buoy him up in the perplexing sea of trial. "Take now thy son," &c. Surely there is some mistake! Must Abraham offer a human sacrifice? This event has perplexed many, and they have only escaped from the difficulties presented by regarding the event—(1) As exceptional for the purpose of securing a unique type of the future sacrifice of Christ.   (2) As never intended to be actually carried out, God having foreseen the faith of his servant, and having determined at the right moment to interfere and prevent any disaster.   There is also a miraculous element in the narrative, both in the special voice and the ram caught in the thicket.   Some have thought that the impulse was from Abraham's own mind—that, seeing human sacrifices around, he wished to rise above all others in devotion to the one God.   Had this been the case, the Scriptures would not have represented the testing as from God.   In that age a father's right to do as he would with his son was as unquestioned as his right to do what he would with his slave.   The command of God was not out of harmony with this idea, but it helped to correct the mistake.   A single act of such self-sacrifice becomes of the highest value ; it is even a means of education to the world. God elicited the highest exercise of faith, but not the blood of Isaac.   What it must have cost the patriarch to submit to the Divine command !   With one blow he must slay his boy and his own ardent hopes.   The only gleam of light was in the thought that God who first gave Isaac could also restore him from death.   This is indicated in the words he uttered to the young man, " *We* will come again to you."   Tradition says that the mount was the same on which Adam, Abel, and Noah had offered sacrifice.   Here possibly Abraham found an altar to repair or rebuild.   Isaac helps in rebuilding the altar and in arranging the wood.   Silent prayers ascend from father and son.   Isaac wonders where the lamb is to come from.   He finds out when his father has bound him and laid him on the altar.   The knife gleams aloft, and, but for the arresting voice, would have been plunged in Isaac.   The test was satisfactory.

II. God's manifest approval of the patriarch's faith and perfect obedience. 1. It was by a voice from heaven.   2. It was manifested also by the way in which God took away any pain consequent on obedience to his command.   It is remarkable how those who appear to have little faith can become, when trial falls, perfectly submissive to the Divine will.   3. The approval was seen also in the way in which God provided a sacrifice.   4. And God repeated his promise of blessing, confirming it by a solemn covenant.   " By myself have I sworn," &c.   No such voice comes to us, and no such promise is audibly given ; still we can have, in the inner calm of the soul, an evidence of the Divine approval.   When our faith is strongest, after passing through some trial, we get a clearer view of the glory of God's working, both in our lives and in the world.   What approval have we won ?   Does not Abraham put us to shame ?   Too many will laud the obedience of Abraham who will never try to emulate it.   Abraham was glad to have his Isaac spared ; so would the Father have been, but he gave up his " only-begotten, well-beloved Son " for us.   Our readiness to accept and follow the Saviour given is only another way of showing how we bear the testing of faith.   " Thy will be done" should be the utterance of each believer.   Perfect faith in the heart should be exhibited by perfect obedience in life.—H.

Ver. 14.—*The Lamb of God.*   " And Abraham called the name of that place Jehovah-jireh."   The key to this narrative is John i. 29.   It sets forth in type the way of salvation.   Whether Abraham understood this we need not inquire. The lesson is for us.   Isaac, *i. e.* laughter (cf. Luke ii. 10), the child of promise (Rom. ix. 7), type of " the children of the kingdom," is yet condemned to die (cf. Rom. v. 12).   So in Egypt the Israelites were not exempted ; God's gift to them was a way of escape.   What is that way ? (cf. Micah vi. 6).   Every age of the world has asked this question.   A sense of separation from God has led to many efforts for its removal.   Hence sacrifices, offerings, austerities, &c., but all in vain (Heb. x. 4). Still the soul asked, " Where is the Lamb ?" the effectual sacrifice for sin.   The answer of prophecy, *i. e.* God's answer, " God will provide himself a lamb " (cf. John i. 29 ; viii. 56).   Man has no claim upon God, yet his need is a plea (cf. Exod. xxxiv. 6, 7).   We know not what was in Abraham's mind ; perhaps he was escaping from the direct answer, unable to utter it ; perhaps there was a hope that God would in some way preserve or restore his son (cf. Heb. xi. 19).   There are many instances of prophecy unconsciously uttered (cf. John xi. 50).   Isaac was bound—

type of man's helplessness to escape from the curse (cf. Luke iv. 18), or from the law of sin in the members. The law of God of itself can only condemn. It can only be fulfilled by one who loves God; but he who is not at peace with God cannot love him. The sacrifice was now complete as far as Abraham could offer it. He had cast down self-will (cf. Matt. xxvi. 39); he had sacrificed himself (Rom. xii. 1). This is the state of mind of all others most prepared to receive blessings (cf. 2 Kings iv. 3—6). "Lay not thine hand upon the lad." God's purpose our deliverance (Rom. viii. 1). The work of the law, bringing home the conviction of sin, is the prelude to the knowledge of life (cf. Rom. vii. 10—13)—life through death. God's way of deliverance (Isa. liii. 6). The type, the ram caught in the thicket; the antitype, Christ fulfilling the Father's will (Matt. xxvi. 54; Mark xv. 31). The practical application of this shown in brazen serpent (John iii. 14). Marvellous love of God (Rom. v. 8). We had no claim on him, yet he would not that we should perish (Ezek. xxxiii. 11). He wanted, for the fulness of his blessedness, that we should partake of it, and therefore Christ came that he might die in our stead; and now in him we are dead (2 Cor. v. 4). Do not dilute the truth by saying he died for believers only. This is to miss the constraining power of his love. If there is any doubt of his death being for each and all, the gospel is no longer felt to be "whosoever will" (Rev. xxii. 17). Behold the Lamb. We need not now to say, "God will provide;" he has provided (1 John ii. 2). The universe could not purchase that propitiation. No efforts could make thee worthy of it, yet it is freely offered to thee to-day. And mark what that gift includes (Rom. viii. 32)—the help of the Holy Spirit (Luke xi. 13), wisdom (James i. 5), help in trials (1 Cor. x. 13), peace (Rom. viii. 33), needs of this life (Luke xii. 30). Bring all thy sins, thy wants, thy hindrances to the mercy-seat (Heb. iv. 16). The Lord will see, will look upon thy need; and ere thy prayer is offered he has provided what that need requires.—M.

Vers. 15—19.—*The great trial and the great revelation.* In such a history the representative character of Abraham must be remembered. He was tried not only for his own sake, but that in him all the families of the earth might be blessed.

I. The PREPARATION for this great grace God and Abraham recognising each other; the servant called by name, responding with the profession of readiness for obedience.

II. The COMMANDMENT is itself a secret communication, a covenant. Do this, and I will bless thee; follow me in this journey "as I tell thee," and thou shalt see my salvation.

III. The simple, childlike OBEDIENCE of the patriarch is reflected in the quiet demeanour of Isaac bearing the wood of the burnt offering, type of Jesus bearing his cross, inquiring for the lamb with lamb-like innocence and patience. "They went both of them together" (vers. 6 and 8)—"together" in the beginning of the journey, "together" in the end, in the trial and in the blessing.

IV. FAITH which accepts the will of God and takes up the Divine mission WILL COMMIT THE FUTURE TO THE GRACIOUS PROVISION ON WHICH IT DEPENDS. "My son, God will provide himself a lamb for a burnt offering" (ver. 8). Already Abraham was saying, "The Lord will provide." We say it sometimes with a fearful burden upon our heart; but when we go steadfastly and hopefully forward we say it at last with the remembrance of a great deliverance sending its glory along the way of our future.

V. THE TRIAL OF THE TRUE HEART IS OFTEN STRETCHED OUT TO ITS LAST EXTREMITY, that the revelation which rewards faithfulness may be the more abundant and wonderful (vers. 9, 10). We must take God at his word, otherwise we shall not experience the promised deliverance. "Take thy son, and offer him there" (ver. 2). "And Abraham stretched forth his hand and took the knife to slay his son." What else could he do? The commandment must be obeyed. The obedience must be "good and perfect and acceptable" as the will of God.

VI. AT THE POINT OF ENTIRE SURRENDER APPEARS THE ANGEL, is heard the voice of relief, the assurance of acceptance, the change in the method of obedience, the opened eyes, the provided sacrifice, THE RETURNING JOY OF SALVATION (vers. 11—13). There is a blindness of self-sacrifice which leads to a sight of immeasurable joy.

Abraham saw nothing before him but the plain path of obedience ; he went on, and at last "lifted up his eyes, and looked, and behold" the self-sacrifice changed into peaceful offering of an appointed substitute (ver. 13) " *in the stead of his son.*"

VII. THE CLIMAX OF OUR EXPERIENCE AND OF DIVINE MERCY BECOMES TO US A NEW NAME OF JEHOVAH. We know him henceforth by that knowledge of fact. " Jehovah-jireh (the Lord will provide) : as it is said to this day, In the mount of the Lord it shall be provided " (or seen) (ver. 14). 1. *Not before the mount*, but *in the mount ;* therefore go to the summit and wait. 2. What the Lord will provide will be *better every way than what we could provide.* 3. The offering on the mount is *the great provision*, the whole burnt offering for the sins of the world, by which the true humanity is redeemed and the true "joy" (" Isaac," laughter) is retained. 4. The last name of Jehovah which Abraham gave him was *Jehovah the Everlasting ;* now he adds to that name that which brings the Everlasting into the sphere of daily life—"*Jehovah-jireh, the Lord will provide.*" We name that name when we *reach the mount* where the great sacrifice was provided—*Mount Moriah, Mount Calvary.* 5. *The end* of the great trial and obedience was a renewal, a *solemn republication, of the covenant.* "God could swear by no greater ; he sware by himself" (Heb. vi. 13). On the foundation of *practical faith* is built up *the kingdom of heaven*, which the Lord swears shall include all nations, and be supreme in all the earth. The *notes of that kingdom* are here in the history of the patriarch—(1) *acceptance of the word of God*, (2) *self-sacrifice*, (3) *faith instead of sight*, (4) *withholding nothing*, (5) *perseverance to the end.* Beersheba became now a new place to Abraham, for he carried to the well and grove which he had named after the oaths of himself and Abimelech the remembrance of the Divine oath, on which henceforth he rested all his expectations. After this the man in whom all nations shall be blessed looks round and finds the promise being already fulfilled, and his kindred spreading widely in the earth.—R.

EXPOSITION.

Ver. 20.—**And it came to pass after these things** (probably not long after his return to Beersheba), **that it was told** (by some unknown messenger or accidental traveller from Mesopotamia) **Abraham, saying, Behold, Milcah** (*vide* ch. xi. 29), **she hath also born children unto thy brother Nahor**—as Sarah has born a son to thee. From this it would almost seem as if Milcah had not begun to have her family at the time Abram left Ur of the Chaldees ; but *vide* ch. xi. 30. The present brief table of Nahor's descendants is introduced for the sake of showing the descent of Rebekah, who is soon to become Isaac's wife.

Ver. 21.—**Huz his firstborn,**—(*vide* ch. x. 23, where Uz appears as a son of Aram ; and ch. xxxvi. 28, where he recurs as a descendant of Esau. That he was a progenitor of Job (Jerome) has no better foundation than Job i. 1—**and Buz his brother,**—mentioned along with Dedan and Tema as an Arabian tribe (Jer. xxv. 23), and may have been an ancestor of Elihu (Job xxxii. 2)—**and Kemuel the father of Aram.** "Not the founder of the Arameans, but the forefather of the family of Ram, to which the Buzite Elihu belonged ; Aram being written for Ram, like Arammim, in 2 Kings viii. 29, for Rammim, in 2 Chron. xxii. 5 " (Keil).

Ver. 22.—**And Chesed,**—according to Jerome the father of the Chasdim or Chaldees (ch. xi. 28) ; but more generally regarded as the head of a younger branch or offshoot of that race (Keil, Murphy, Lange ; cf. Job i. 17)—**and Hazo, and Pildash, and Jidlaph** (concerning whom nothing is known), **and Bethuel**—"man of God " (Gesenius) ; dwelling of God (Fürst) ; an indication probably of his piety.

Ver. 23.—**And Bethuel begat Rebekah**—*Ribkah ;* captivating, ensnaring (Fürst) ; "a rope with a noose," not unfit as the name of a girl who ensnares men by her beauty (Gesenius). Rebekah was the child of Isaac's cousin, and being the daughter of Nahor's youngest son, was probably about the same age as her future husband. **These eight Milcah did bear to Nahor, Abraham's brother.**

Ver. 24.—**And his concubine** (*vide* on ch. xvi. 3), **whose name** was **Reumah,**—raised, elevated (Gesenius) ; pearl or coral (Fürst)—**she bare also Tebah, and Gaham, and Thahash, and Maachah**—whence probably the Maachathites (Deut. iii. 14 ; Josh. xlii. 5). That three of Terah's descendants (Nahor, Ishmael, and Jacob) should each have twelve sons has been pronounced "a contrived symmetry, the intentional character of which cannot be mistaken" (Bohlen) ; but "*what* intention the narrator should have connected with it remains inconceivable, unless it was to state the fact as it was, or (on the supposition that some of them had more than twelve sons) to supply a round number easily retainable by the memory " (Hävernick).

HOMILETICS.

Vers. 20—24.—*Good news from a far country.* I. THE JOYFUL BUDGET. 1. *Tidings from home.* For nearly half a century Abraham had been a wanderer in Palestine, and with something like an emigrant's emotion on receiving letters from the old country would the patriarch listen to the message come from Haran beyond the river. 2. *News concerning Nahor.* It demands no violent exercise of fancy to believe that Abraham regarded his distant brother with intense fraternal affection, and that the unexpected report of that distant brother's prosperity struck a chord of joy within his aged bosom. 3. *A message about Milcah.* When the two brothers parted it would seem that neither of their spouses had begun to have a family. Now information reaches the patriarchal tent that the union of Nahor and Milcah, like that of himself and Sarai, has been blessed with offspring ; and, in particular, that the second generation had begun to appear in Nahor's house, the queenly grace of Milcah being reproduced in her captivating grandchild Rebekah.

II. THE WELCOME MESSENGER. 1. *His unknown name.* One is curious to know who it was that brought the tidings from the old home. Some spirited adventurer who at the distance of half a century sought to emulate the Chaldæan chieftain who left the valley of the Euphrates for the bleak hills of Palestine ; some Mesopotamian Stanley whom Nahor, now a wealthy Emir, had despatched upon a mission of inquiry after his long-lost brother ; or some chance traveller who had come across the patriarch's tent. 2. *His timely arrival.* Whoever he was, his appearance at this particular juncture was exceedingly opportune, when, the great trial having passed, Isaac's marriage must have loomed in the prospect as a near possibility. To Abraham it must have seemed not a fortuitous occurrence, but a providential arrangement.

Learn—1. That no passage of Scripture can be said to be entirely useless. 2. That joy and sorrow mostly lie in close contiguity in human life. 3. That it becomes good men and women to be interested in each other's welfare. 4. That in God's government of the world there are no such things as accidents. 5. That it becomes good men to keep an outlook upon the leadings of Divine providence.

EXPOSITION.

CHAPTER XXIII.

Ver. 1.—**And Sarah was an hundred and seven and twenty years old** (literally, *and the lives of Sarah were an hundred and twenty and seven years*) ; so that Isaac must have been thirty-seven, having been born in his mother's ninetieth year. Sarah, as the wife of Abraham and the mother of believers (Isa. li. 2 ; 1 Pet. iii. 6), is the only woman whose age is mentioned in Scripture. These were **the years of the life of Sarah** — an emphatic repetition designed to impress the Israelitish mind with the importance of remembering the age of their ancestress. Ver. 2.—**And Sarah died in Kirjath-arba** —or city of Arba, Abraham having again removed thither after an absence of nearly forty years, during which interval Murphy thinks the reign of Arba the Anakite may have commenced, though Keil postpones it

to a later period (cf. Josh. xiv. 15). **The same is Hebron**—the original name of the city, which was supplanted by that of Kirjath-arba, but restored at the conquest (Keil, Hengstenberg, Murphy ; *vide* ch. xiii. 18)— **in the land of Canaan**—indicating that the writer was not then in Palestine ('Speaker's Commentary') ; perhaps rather designed to emphasise the circumstance that Sarah's death occurred not in the Philistines' country, but in the promised land (Rosenmüller, Keil, Murphy). **And Abraham came**—or went ; ἦλθε (LXX.), *venit* (Vulgate); not as if he had been absent at her death (Calvin), either in Beersheba, where he retained a location (Clarke), or in Gerar, whither he had gone to sell the lands and other properties he held there (Luther), or in the pasture grounds adjoining Hebron (Keil, Murphy) ; but as addressing himself to the work of mourning for his deceased wife (Vatablus, Rosenmüller), or perhaps as going into Sarah's tent (Maimonides, Ainsworth, Wordsworth, 'Speaker's Commentary')—**to mourn for Sarah, and to weep for her.** "To arrange for the customary mourning ceremony" (Keil); the first verb, סָפַד (cf. σφαδάζω), referring to the beating of the breast as a sign of grief (cf. 1 Kings xiv. 13), and the second, בָּכָה, to flow by drops, intimating a quieter and more moderate sorrow. Beyond sitting on the ground and weeping in presence of (or upon the face of) the dead, no other rites are mentioned as having been observed by Abraham; though afterwards, as practised among the Hebrews, Egyptians, and other nations of antiquity, mourning for the dead developed into an elaborate ritual, including such ceremonies as rending the garments, shaving the head, wearing sackcloth, covering the head with dust and ashes (vide 2 Sam. iii. 31, 35; xxi. 10; Job i. 20; ii. 12; xvi. 15, 16). Cf. the mourning for Patroclus ('Il.,' xix. 211—213).

Ver. 3.—**And Abraham stood up**—during the days of mourning he had been sitting on the ground; and now, his grief having moderated (Calvin), he goes out to the city gate—**from before** (literally, from over the face of) **his dead,**—"Sarah, though dead, was still his" (Wordsworth)—**and spake unto the sons of Heth,**—the Hittites were descendants of Heth, the son of Canaan (vide ch. x. 15). Cf. "daughters of Heth" (ch. xxvii. 46) and "daughters of Canaan" (ch. xxviii. 1)—**saying.**

Ver. 4.—**I am a stranger and a sojourner with you.** Gêr, one living out of his own country, and Thoshabh, one dwelling in a land in which he is not naturalised; advena et peregrinus (Vulgate); πάροικος καὶ παρ' ἐπίδημος (LXX.). This confession of the heir of Canaan was a proof that he sought, as his real inheritance, a better country, even an heavenly (Heb. xi. 13). **Give me a possession of a burying-place with you.** The first mention of a grave in Scripture, the word in Hebrew signifying a hole in the earth, or a mound, according as the root is taken to mean to dig (Fürst) or to heap up (Gesenius). Abraham's desire for a grave in which to deposit Sarah's lifeless remains was dictated by that Divinely planted and, among civilised nations, universally prevailing reverence for the body which prompts men to decently dispose of their dead by rites of honourable sepulture. The burning of corpses was a practice common to the nations of antiquity; but Tacitus notes it as characteristic of the Jews that they preferred interment to cremation ('Hist.,' v. 5). The wish to make Sarah's burying-place his own possession has been traced to the instinctive desire that most nations have

evinced to lie in ground belonging to themselves (Rosenmüller), to an intention on the part of the patriarch to give a sign of his right and title to the land of Canaan by purchasing a grave in its soil—cf. Isa. xxii. 16 (Bush), or simply to anxiety that his dead might not lie unburied (Calvin); but it was more probably due to his strong faith that the land would yet belong to his descendants, which naturally led him to crave a resting-place in the soil with which the hopes of both himself and people were identified (Ainsworth, Bush, Kalisch). **That I may bury my dead out of my sight**—decay not suffering the lifeless corpse to remain a fit spectacle for grief or love to gaze on.

Vers. 5, 6.—**And the children of Heth answered Abraham, saying unto him, Hear us, my lord.** My lord (Adoni) = sir, monsieur, or mein herr. One acts as the spokesman of all; the number changing from plural to singular. The LXX., reading לֹא instead of לוֹ, after the Samaritan Codex, render μὴ κύριε, Not so, my lord; but hear us. **Thou** art **a mighty prince among us.** Literally, a prince of Elohim; not of Jehovah, since the speakers were heathen whose ideas of Deity did not transcend those expressed in the term Elohim. According to a familiar Hebrew idiom, the phrase might be legitimately translated as in the A. V.—cf. "mountains of God," i. e. great mountains, Ps. xxxvi. 6; "cedars of God," i. e. goodly cedars, Ps. lxxx. 10 (Calvin, Kimchi, Rosenmüller, 'Speaker's Commentary'); but, as employed by the Hittite chieftains, it probably expressed that they regarded him as a prince or phylarch, not to whom God had given an elevated aspect (Lange), but either whom God had appointed (Gesenius), or whom God manifestly favoured (Kalisch, Murphy). This estimate of Abraham strikingly contrasts with that which the patriarch had formed (ver. 4) of himself. **In the choice of our sepulchres bury thy dead; none of us will withhold from thee his sepulchre, but that thou mayest bury thy dead.** This remarkable offer on the part of the Hittites Thomson ('Land and Book,' p. 578) regards as having been merely compliment, which Abraham was too experienced an Oriental not to understand. But, even if dictated by true kindness and generosity, the proposal was one to which for many reasons—faith in God, love for the dead, and respect for himself being among the strongest—the patriarch could not accede. With perfect courtesy, therefore, though likewise with respectful firmness, he declines their offer.

Ver. 7. — **And Abraham stood up** (the customary posture among Orientals in buying and selling being that of sitting), **and bowed himself to the people of the land,** even **to the children of Heth**—an act of respect quite accordant with modern Oriental manners (*vide* Thomson, 'Land and Book,' p. 579).

Vers. 8, 9.—**And he communed with them, saying, If it be your mind**—literally, *if it be with your souls*, the word *nephesh* being used in this sense in Ps. xxvii. 12; xli. 3; cv. 22—**that I should bury my dead out of my sight; hear me, and intreat for me to Ephron the son of Zohar.** The ruler of the city (Keil); but this is doubtful (Lange). "There is scarcely anything in the habits of Orientals more annoying to us Occidentals than this universal custom of employing mediators to pass between you and those with whom you wish to do business. Nothing can be done without them. A merchant cannot sell a piece of print, nor a farmer a yoke of oxen, nor any one rent a house, buy a horse, or *get a wife*, without a succession of go-betweens. Of course Abraham knew that this matter of the field could not be brought about without the intervention of the neighbours of Ephron, and therefore he applies to them first" ('Land and Book,' p. 579). **That he may give me the cave of Machpelah,**—Machpelah is regarded as a proper noun (Gesenius, Keil, Kalisch, Rosenmüller), as in ch. xlix. 30, though by others it is considered as an appellative, signifying that the cave was double (LXX., Vulgate), either as consisting of a cave within a cave (Hamerus), or of one cave exterior and another interior (Aben Ezra), or as having room for two bodies (Calvin), or as possessing two entrances (Jewish interpreters). It is probable the cave received its name from its peculiar form,—**which he hath** (Ephron's ownership of the cave is expressly recognised, and its situation is next described), **which is in the end of his field**—"so that the cession of it will not injure his property" (Wordsworth). At the same time Abraham makes it clear that an honest purchase is what he contemplates. **For as much money as it is worth**—literally, *for full silver* (1 Chron. xxi. 22). Cf. *siller* (Scotch) for money. This is the first mention of the use of the precious metals as a medium of exchange, though they must have been so employed at a very early period (*vide* ch. xiii. 2)—**he shall give it me for a possession of a burying-place amongst you.** The early Chaldæans were accustomed to bury their dead in strongly-constructed brick vaults. Those found at Mughheir are seven feet long, three feet seven inches broad, and five feet high, are composed of sun-dried bricks embedded in mud, and exhibit a remarkable form and construction of arch, resembling that occurring in Egyptian buildings and Scythian tombs, in which the successive layers of brick are made to overlap until they come

so close that the aperture may be covered by a single brick (Rawlinson's 'Ancient Monarchies,' vol. i. p. 86). In the absence of such artificial receptacles for the dead, the nearest substitute the patriarch could obtain was one of those natural grottoes which the limestone hills of Canaan so readily afforded.

Ver. 10.—**And Ephron dwelt among the children of Heth.** Not *habitabat* (Vulgate), in the sense of resided amongst, but *sedebat*, ἐκάθητο (LXX.); was then present sitting amongst the townspeople (Rosenmüller), but whether in the capacity of a magistrate or councillor is not stated. **And Ephron the Hittite answered Abraham in the audience of the children of Heth, even of all that went in at the gate of his city,**—this does not imply that he was the chief magistrate (Keil), but only that he was a prominent citizen (Murphy). On the gate of the city as a place for transacting business *vide* ch. xix. 1—**saying**—

Ver. 11.—**Nay, my lord, hear me: the field give I thee, and the cave that is therein, I give it thee**—an Oriental mode of expressing willingness to sell. Ephron would make a present of cave and field to the patriarch,—"and just so have I had a hundred houses, and fields, and horses given to me" ('Land and Book,' p. 578),—the design being either to obtain a valuable compensation in return, or to preclude any abatement in the price (Keil), though possibly the offer to sell the entire field when he might have secured a good price for the cave alone was an indication of Ephron's good intention (Lange). At least it seems questionable to conclude that Ephron's generous phrases, which have now become formal and hollow courtesies indeed, meant no more in that simpler age when the ceremonies of intercourse were newer, and more truly reflected its spirit (Dykes, 'Abraham, the Friend of God,' p. 287). **In the presence of the sons of my people give I it thee** (literally, *have I given*, the transaction being viewed as finished): **bury thy dead.**

Vers. 12, 13.—**And Abraham bowed down himself before the people of the land.** To express his sense of their kindness, and appreciation of Ephron's offer in particular; after which he courteously but firmly urged forward the contemplated purchase. **And he spake unto Ephron in the audience of the people of the land, saying, But if thou wilt give it, I pray thee, hear me.** Literally, *if thou, I would that thou wouldst hear me,* the two particles אִם and לוּ being conjoined to express the intensity of the speaker's desire. **I will give thee money for the field.** Literally, *money of the field,* i. e. the value of the field in money. This seems to indicate that Abraham at least imagined

Ephron's offer of the field and cave as a gift to be not wholly formal. Had he regarded Ephron as all the while desirous of a sale, he would not have employed the language of entreaty. **Take it of me, and I will bury my dead there.** Vers. 14, 15. — **And Ephron answered Abraham, saying unto him, My lord, hearken unto me : the land is worth four hundred shekels of silver.** The word "shekel," from *shakal*, to weigh, here used for the first time, was not a stamped coin, but a piece of metal of definite weight, according to Exod. xxx. 13, equal to twenty gerahs, or beans, from *garar*, to roll. Coined money was unknown to the Hebrews until after the captivity. In the time of the Maccabees (1 Macc. xv. 6) silver coins were struck bearing the inscription שֶׁקֶל יִשְׂרָאֵל. According to Josephus ('Ant.,' iii. 8, 2) the shekel in use in his day was equal to four Athenian drachmæ ; and if, as is believed, these were one-fifth larger than the old shekels coined by Simon Maccabeus, the weight of the latter would be equal to three and one-third drachms, or two hundred grains, reckoning sixty grains to a drachm. It is impossible to ascertain the weight of the shekel current with the merchant in the time of Abraham ; but reckoning it at a little less than 2*s*. 6*d*. sterling, the price of Ephron's field must have been somewhat under £50 ; a very considerable sum of money, which the Hittite merchant begins to depreciate by representing as a trifle, saying, **What is that betwixt me and thee ?**—words which are still heard in the East on similar occasions (*vide* 'Land and Book,' p. 578)—**bury therefore thy dead.** Ver. 16.—**And Abraham hearkened unto Ephron** (either as knowing that the price he asked was reasonable, or as being in no humour to bargain with him on the subject); **and Abraham weighed to Ephron the silver,** —"Even this is still common ; for although coins have now a definite name, size, and value, yet every merchant carries a small apparatus by which he weighs each coin to see that it has not been tampered with by Jewish Clippers" ('Land and Book,' p. 578) —**which he had named in the audience of the sons of Heth** (the stipulation and the payment of the money were both made in the presence of witnesses), **four hundred shekels of silver, current money with the merchant**—literally, *silver passing with the merchant*, or goer about, *i. e.* with merchandise ; from *sachar*, to go about (cf. ἔμπορος, ἐμπορεύομαι). The Canaanites, of whom the Hittites were a branch, were among the earliest traders of antiquity (cf. Job xl. 30 ; Prov. xxxi. 24) ; and the silver bars employed as the medium of exchange in their mercantile transactions were probably stamped in some rude fashion to indicate their weight.

Vers. 17, 18.—**And the field of Ephron, which** was **in Machpelah,**—here the word is used as a proper name (*vide supra*)—**which** was **before Mamre,—**לִפְנֵי = over against (Lange), to the east of (Keil), the oak grove—**the field, and the cave which** was **therein, and all the trees that were in the field, that were in all the borders round about,—**"In like manner the *specifications* in the contract are just such as are found in modern deeds. It is not enough that you purchase a well-known lot; the contract must mention everything that belongs to it, and certify that fountains or wells in it, trees upon it, &c., are sold with the field" ('Land and Book,' p. 578)—**were made sure**—literally, *stood up or arose, i. e.* were confirmed (cf. Levit. xxvii. 14, 19)—**unto Abraham for a possession in the presence of the children of Heth, before all that went in at the gate of his city.** "This also is true to life. When any sale is now to be effected in a town or village, the whole population gather about the parties at the usual place of concourse, around or near the gate where there is one. There all take part and enter into the pros and cons with as much earnestness as if it were their own individual affair. By these means the operation, in all its circumstances and details, is known to many witnesses, and the thing is made *sure* without any written contract" ('Land and Book,' p. 579).

Ver. 19.—**And after this, Abraham buried Sarah his wife**—with what funeral rites can only be conjectured. Monumental evidence attests that the practice of embalming the dead existed in Egypt in the reign of Amunophth I. (B.C. 1500), though probably originating earlier (Sharpe's 'Egypt,' vol. i. p. 31) ; and an examination of the Mugheir vaults for burying the dead shows that among the early Chaldæans it was customary to place the corpse upon a matting of reed spread upon a brick floor, the head being pillowed on a single sun-dried brick, and the body turned on its left side, the right arm falling towards the left, and the fingers resting on the edge of a copper bowl, usually placed on the palm of the left hand (*vide* Rawlinson's 'Ancient Monarchies,' vol. i. p. 87)—**in the cave of the field of Machpelah before Mamre.** In which also in succession his own remains and those of Isaac, Rebekah, Jacob, and Leah were deposited, Rachel alone of the great patriarchal family being absent. This last resting-place of Abraham and his sons, as of Sarah and her daughters, has been identified with *Ramet-el-Kalil*, an hour's journey to the north of Hebron (which is too distant), where the foundations of an ancient heathen temple are still pointed out as Abraham's house ; but is more probably to be sought for in the Mohammedan mosque

Haram, built of colossal blocks, and situated on the mountain slope of Hebron towards the east (Robinson, Thomson, Stanley, Tristram), which, after having been for 600 years hermetically sealed against Europeans, —only three during that period having gained access to it in disguise,—was visited in 1862 by the Prince of Wales and party (*vide* Stanley, 'Lectures on Jewish Church,' App. ii.).   **The same is Hebron in the land of Canaan** (*vide* ver. 2).

Ver. 20. — **And the field, and the cave that is therein, were made sure unto Abraham for a possession of a burying-place by the sons of Heth.**   The palpable discrepancy between the statements of the Hebrew historian in this chapter concerning the patriarchal sepulchre and those of the Christian orator when addressing the Jewish Sanhedrim (Acts vii. 16) has been well characterised as *prægravis quædam et perardua, et quorundam judicio inextricabilis quæstio* (Pererius).   Of course the Gordian knot of difficulty may be very readily cut by boldly asserting that a mistake has been committed somewhere ; either by Stephen, the original speaker, under the impulse of emotion confounding the two entirely different stories of Abraham's purchase of Machpelah and Jacob's buying of the field near Shechem (Bede, Clarke, Lange, Kalisch, Alford, and others) ; or by Luke, the first recorder of the Martyr's Apology, who wrote not the *ipsissima verba* of the speech, but simply his own recollection of them (Jerome); or by some subsequent transcriber who had tampered with the original text, as, *e. g.*, inserting Αβραὰμ, which Luke and Stephen both had omitted, as the nominative to ὠνήσατο (Beza, Calvin, Bishop Pearce). The last of these hypotheses would not indeed be fatal to the inspiration of the record ; but the claims of either Luke or Stephen to be authoritative teachers on the subject of religion would be somewhat hard to maintain if it once were admitted that they had blundered on a plain point in their own national history.   And yet it is doubtful if any of the proposed solutions of the problem is perfectly satisfactory ; such as (1) that the two purchases of Abraham and Jacob are here intentionally, for the sake of brevity, compressed into one account (Bengel, Pererius, Willet, Hughes) ; or (2) that Abraham bought two graves, one at Hebron of Ephron the Hittite, as recorded by Moses, and another at Shechem of the sons of Hamor the father of Shechem (Wordsworth) ; or (3) that the words "which Abraham bought for a sum of money" should be regarded as a parenthesis, and the sentence read as intimating that Jacob and the fathers were carried over into Shechem, and (afterwards) by the sons of Hamor the father of Shechem interred in Abraham's sepulchre at Hebron (Cajetan).   Obvious difficulties attach to each of them ; but the facts shine out clear enough in spite of the encompassing obscurity, viz., that Abraham bought a tomb at Hebron, in which first the dust of Sarah was deposited, and to which afterwards the bodies of himself, Isaac and Rebekah, Jacob and Leah were consigned, while Joseph and the twelve patriarchs, who all died in Egypt, were brought over to the promised land and buried in Jacob's field at Shechem.

HOMILETICS.

Vers. 1—20.—*The death and burial of Sarah.*   I. THE DEATH OF SARAH.   1. *The mournful event.*   The death of—(1) An aged woman.   "Sarah was an hundred and twenty-seven years old."   (2) A distinguished princess.   As the wife of Abraham and the mother of the promised seed, Sarah was doubly ennobled.   (3) An eminent saint.   Sarah, like her husband, was renowned for faith and piety ; indeed in these respects only second to the mother of our Lord, whom she conspicuously typified, and proposed by the Holy Spirit as a pattern for Christian women.   (4) A beloved wife.   Sarah's married life extended over the greater part of a century, and the tender and constant love which gilded it with happiness through all the passing years shines on every page of the inspired narrative.   (5) A revered parent.   In the death of Sarah Isaac lost a loving and a much-loved mother.   2. *The attendant circumstances.*   Sarah died—(1) In the land of Canaan. If not the place of her birth, Canaan had become the country of her adoption, and the scene of her spiritual nativity.   A special sadness attaches to death upon a foreign shore, and among heathen peoples.   Sarah may be said to have expired upon her own inheritance, and in Jehovah's land.   (2) In the bosom of her family.   If Sarah was not spared the anguish of dying in the absence of her noble husband, her latest moments, we may be sure, were soothed by the tender ministries of her gentle son.   (3) In the exercise of faith.   Sarah was one of those "all" who "died in faith," looking for a better country, even an heavenly.   Hence the last enemy, we cannot doubt, was encountered with quiet fortitude and cheerful resignation.

II. The BURIAL OF SARAH. 1. *The days of mourning.* "Abraham came to mourn and to weep for Sarah." The sorrow of the patriarch was—(1) Appropriate and becoming. Lamentation for the dead agreeable to the instincts of nature and the dictates of religion. Witness Joseph (ch. l. 1), David (2 Sam. xii. 16), Job (ch. i. 20), the devout men of Jerusalem (Acts viii. 2), Christ (John xi. 35). (2) Intense and sincere. Though partaking of the nature of a public ceremonial, the patriarch's grief was none the less real and profound. Simulated sorrow is no less offensive than sinful. (3) Limited and restrained. If there is a time to mourn and a time to weep, there is also a time to cast aside the symbols of sorrow, and a time to refrain from tears. Nature and religion both require a moderate indulgence in the grief occasioned by bereavement. 2. *The purchase of a grave.* Here may be noted—(1) The polite request. Its object—a grave for a possession; its purpose—to bury his dead; its plea—his wandering and unsettled condition in the land. (2) The generous proposal; prefaced with respect, proffered with magnanimity; teaching us the respect owing neighbours, the honour due superiors, and the kindness which should be shown strangers. (3) The courteous refusal. Unwilling to acquiesce in the proposed arrangement, Abraham declines with much respectfulness (ver. 12), expresses his desire with greater clearness (ver. 13), and urgently requests the friendly intercession of the people of the land (ver. 8). Abraham's politeness a pattern for all. (4) The liberal donation. Ephron indicates his wish to bestow the cave upon the patriarch as a gift. Liberality a Christian virtue which may sometimes be learnt from the men of the world. (5) The completed purchase. Abraham weighs out the stipulated sum, neither depreciating Ephron's property nor asking an abatement in the price; an example for merchants and traders. (6) The acquired possession. The field and cave were made sure to Abraham for ever. The only thing on earth a man can really call his own is his grave. 3. *The last rites of sepulture.* "After this Abraham buried Sarah his wife in the cave of the field of Machpelah;" with unknown funeral rites, but certainly with reverence, with sadness, with hope.

Learn—1. The duty of preparing for death. 2. The propriety of moderate indulgence in grief. 3. The obligation resting on surviving relatives to carefully dispose of the lifeless bodies of the dead. 4. The wisdom of good men acquiring as soon as possible for themselves and their families a burial-place for a possession.

HOMILIES BY VARIOUS AUTHORS.

Vers. 19, 20.—*The death and burial of Sarah.* I. TRUE RELIGION SANCTIFIES NATURAL RELATIONSHIPS. Those who know themselves blessed of God do not only feel that their human affections are precious and true, but do, in obedience to his will, preserve the greatest respect for their bodily frame, and for their dead who died in the Lord, and whose dust is committed tenderly to his keeping.

II. THE PEOPLE OF GOD WERE UPHELD BY FAITH IN THEIR CARE FOR THE DEAD. They looked beyond the grave. Some say there is no evidence of the doctrine of immortality in the Old Testament until after the captivity. Surely Abraham's feelings were not those of one who *sorrowed without hope.* The purchase of the field, the securing possession for all time of the burying-place, pointed to faith, not the lack of it. Where there is no sense of immortality there is no reverence for the dead.

III. The PURCHASE OF THE FIELD was not only its security, but a testimony to the heathen that the people of God held in reverence both the memory of the dead and the rights of the living. All social prosperity has its root in religious life.—R.

Ver. 20.—*Lessons from the sepulchre.* "And the field, and the cave that is therein, were made sure unto Abraham for a possession of a burying-place." Abraham's first and only possession in Canaan, a sepulchre. The importance of the purchase appears in the careful narrative of the transaction. For himself he was content to live as a stranger and pilgrim (cf. 1 Pet. v. 7); but Sarah's death led him to acquire a burying-place. Declining the offer to use any of the sepulchres of the people of the land (cf. the separation at death between God's people and aliens), he bought the field and the cave, and carefully prepared the evidence of the purchase.

The purchase showed his faith in God's truth; one of the branches of Adam's tempt-ation (Gen. iii. 4). It had been promised that his seed, after dwelling in a land not theirs, should return and possess that whereon he stood (cf. Jer. xxxii. 14, 15). Type of entrance into rest after pilgrimage (cf. 2 Cor. v. 1). It showed also his faith in a resurrection (cf. Ps. xvi. 10). The desire that he and his family should lie in the same sepulchre speaks of a life beyond the present. Parted by death, they were one family still. Sarah was to him "my dead." There was a link between them still. The living and dead still one family. Doctrine of communion of saints (cf. Matt. xxii. 32). Death was the gate of life (cf. 1 Thess. iv. 16). Canaan a type of the rest which remaineth; Abraham of the "children of the kingdom," pilgrims with a promise. No rest here. Life full of uncertainties. One thing sure, we must die. But—

I. WE ENTER THE HEAVENLY REST THROUGH DEATH; THE CITY OF GOD THROUGH THE VALLEY OF BACA. Here we walk by faith. Great and glorious promises for our encouragement, that we may not make our home here; yet we know not what we shall be. Sight cannot penetrate the curtain that separates time from eternity. Thus there is the trial, do we walk by faith or by sight? We instinctively shrink from death. It is connected in our mind with sorrow, with interruption of plans, with breaking up of loving companionship; but faith bids us sorrow not as those without hope. It reminds that it is the passing from what is defective and transitory to what is immortal. Here we are trained for the better things beyond, and our thoughts are turned to that sepulchre in which the victory over death was won; thence we see the Lord arising, the pledge of eternal life to all who will have it.

II. THE SEPULCHRE WAS MADE SURE TO ABRAHAM. In time he should enter it as one of the company gathered there to await the resurrection day; but meanwhile it was his. And if we look upon this as typical of our interest in the death of Christ, it speaks of comfort and trust. He took our nature that he might "taste death for every man." His grave is ours (2 Cor. v. 14). We are "buried with him," "planted together in the likeness of his death." The fact of his death is a possession that cannot be taken from us (Col. iii. 3, 4). He died that we might live. If frail man clings to the tomb of some dear one; if the heart is conscious of the link still endur-ing, shall we not rejoice in our union with him whose triumph makes us also more than conquerors?

III. THE FIELD AND CAVE. How small a part did Abraham possess in his life-time, but it was an earnest of the whole; he felt it so, and in faith buried his dead (cf. Gen. l. 25; Heb. xi. 22). An earnest is all we possess here, but still we have an earnest. In the presence of the Lord (John xiv. 23), in the peace which he gives, in the spirit of adoption, we have the "substance of things hoped for," a real fragment and sample of the blessedness of heaven.—M.

EXPOSITION.

CHAPTER XXIV.

Ver. 1.—**And Abraham was old**, and **well stricken in age** :—literally, *gone into days* (cf. ch. xviii. 11), being now about 140 (*vide* ch. xxv. 20)—**and the Lord**—*Jehovah ;* not because the chapter is the exclusive composition of the Jehovist (Tuch, Bleek, Kalisch), but because the writer aims at showing how the God of redemption pro-vided a bride for the heir of the promise (Hengstenberg)—**had blessed Abraham in all things.**

Vers. 2—4.—**And Abraham said unto his eldest servant of his house, that ruled over all that he had,**—literally, *to his servant, the old man*, ancient or elder, *of his house, the ruler over all which* (sc. belonged) *to him.* The term וְקֵן (an old man) is in most

languages employed as a title of honour,—cf. *sheikh, senatus,* γέρων, *presbyter,* signor, seigneur, señor, sir (Gesenius, p. 252),—and is probably to be so understood here. Eliezer of Damascus, upwards of half a century previous regarded as heir presumptive to Abraham's house (ch. xv. 2), is commonly considered the official meant, though the point is of no importance — **Put, I pray thee, thy hand under my thigh : and I will make thee swear.** This ancient form of adjuration, which is mentioned again only in chap. xlvii. 29, and to which nothing analogous can elsewhere be discovered,—the practice alleged to exist among the modern Egyptian Bedouins of placing the hand upon the *membrum virile* in solemn forms of asseveration not forming an exact parallel,—was probably originated by the patriarch.

The thigh, as the source of posterity (cf. ch. xxxv. 11 ; xlvi. 26 ; Exod. i. 5), has been regarded as pointing to Abraham's future descendants (Keil, Kalisch, Lange), and in particular to Christ, the promised seed (Theodoret, Jerome, Augustine, Luther, Ainsworth, Bush, Wordsworth), and the oath to be equivalent to a swearing by him that was to come. By others the thigh has been viewed as euphemistically put for the generative organ, upon which the sign of circumcision was placed, and the oath as an adjuration by the sign of the covenant (Jonathan, Jarchi, Tuch). A third interpretation considers the thigh as symbolising lordship or authority, and the placing of the hand under it as tantamount to an oath of fealty and allegiance to a superior (Aben Ezra, Rosenmüller, Calvin, Murphy). Other explanations are modifications of the above. **By the Lord** (*Jehovah ;* since the marriage to which this solemn adjuration was preliminary was not an ordinary alliance, such as might have taken place under the providence of Elohim, but the wedding of the heir of the promise), **the God of heaven, and the God of the earth** (a clause defining Jehovah as the supreme Lord of the universe, and therefore as the sole Arbiter of human destiny), **that thou shalt not take a wife unto my son**—not investing him with authority to provide a wife for Isaac in the event of death carrying him (Abraham) off before his son's marriage, but simply explaining the negative side of the commission with which he was about to be intrusted. If it evinced Isaac's gentle disposition and submissive piety, that though forty years of age he neither thought of marriage, but mourned in devout contemplation for his mother (Lange), nor offered resistance to his father's proposal, but suffered himself to be governed by a servant (Calvin), it was also quite in accordance with ancient practice that parents should dispose of their children in marriage (cf. ch. xxviii. 2)—**of the daughters of the Canaanites, among whom I dwell.** Being prompted to this partly by that jealousy with which all pastoral tribes of Shemitic origin have been accustomed to guard the purity of their race by intermarriage (Dykes; cf. Thomson, 'Land and Book,' p. 591), and partly no doubt by his perception of the growing licentiousness of the Canaanites, as well as his knowledge of their predicted doom, though chiefly, it is probable, by a desire to preserve the purity of the promised seed. Intermarriage with the Canaanites was afterwards forbidden by the Mosaic legislation (Exod. xxxiv. 16 ; Deut. vii. 3). **But** (literally, *for,* i. e. the former thing must not be done because this must be done) **thou shalt go unto my country** (not **Ur of the Chaldees,** but the region beyond

the Euphrates generally), **and to my kindred, and take a wife unto my son Isaac.** Though enforced by religious considerations, this injunction to bring none but a relative for Isaac's bride "was in no sense a departure from established usages and social laws in regard to marriage" ('Land and Book,' p. 591).

Ver. 5.—**And the servant said unto him** (not having the same faith as his master), **Peradventure** (with perhaps a secret conviction that he ought to say, "Of a surety") **the woman will not be willing to follow me unto this land.** *Primâ facie* it was a natural and reasonable hypothesis that the bride elect should demur to undertake a long and arduous journey to marry a husband she had never seen ; accordingly, the ancient messenger desires to understand whether he might not be at liberty to act upon the other alternative. **Must I needs bring thy son again unto the land from whence thou camest?** In reply to which the patriarch solemnly interdicts him from attempting to seduce his son, under any pretext whatever, to leave the land of promise.

Vers. 6—8.—**And Abraham said, Beware thou**—literally, *beware for thyself,* the pleonastic pronoun being added by way of emphasis (cf. ch. xii. 1 ; xxi. 16 ; xxii. 5)— **that thou bring not my son thither again.** Literally, *lest thou cause my son to return thither;* Abraham speaking of Isaac's going to Mesopotamia as a return, either because he regarded Isaac, though then unborn, as having come out with him from Mesopotamia, cf. Heb. vii. 10 (Wordsworth), or because he viewed himself and his descendants as a whole, as in ch. xv. 16 (Rosenmüller). **The Lord God of heaven, who took me from my father's house, and from the house of my kindred,**—*vide* ch. xii. 1. This was the first consideration that prevented the return of either himself or his son. Having emigrated from Mesopotamia in obedience to a call of Heaven, not without a like instruction were they at liberty to return—**and who spake unto me,**—*i. e.* honoured me with Divine communications (*vide supra*)—**and** (in particular) **that sware unto me,**—*vide* ch. xv. 17, 18 ; the covenant transaction therein recorded having all the force of an oath (cf. ch. xxii. 16)—**saying, Unto thy seed will I give this land.** Here was a second consideration that negatived the idea of Isaac's return,—he was the God-appointed heir of the soil,—and from this, in conjunction with the former, he argued that the Divine promise was certain of fulfilment, and that accordingly the mission for a bride would be successful. **He shall send his angel before thee,**—*i. e.* to lead and protect, as was afterwards promised to Israel (Exod. xxiii. 20), and to the Christian Church (Heb.

i. 14)—**and thou shalt take a wife unto my son from thence** (meaning, thy mission shall be successful). **And if the woman will not be willing to follow thee, then shalt thou be clear of this my oath** (*i. e.* at liberty to hold thyself as no longer under obligation in the matter ; thy responsibility will at that point cease and determine) : **only bring not my son thither again** — or, observing the order of the Hebrew words, *only my son bring not again to that place;* with almost feverish entreaty harping on the solemn re-frain that on no account must Isaac leave the promised land, since in that would be the culmination of unbelief and disobedience.

Ver. 9.—**And the servant** (understanding the nature of his mission, and feeling satisfied on the points that impinged upon his conscience) **put his hand under the thigh of Abraham his master, and sware to him concerning that matter**—to be true to his master and his mission, and to the hope and promise of the covenant.

HOMILETICS.

Vers. 1—9.—*A bride for the heir.*—1. *Abraham and Eliezer, or the mission for the bride.* I. THE TRUSTY MESSENGER. 1. *His designation.* (1) From official position, a servant. (2) From venerable age, the old man or ancient of the house. (3) From superior dignity, the steward or ruler over Abraham's property. 2. *His qualification.* (1) Obedient, as became a slave or servant. (2) Faithful, as was required of a steward. (3) Prudent, as might have been expected of age.

II. THE IMPORTANT COMMISSION. 1. The *purport* of it. "To take a wife for Isaac." A step of greatest moment for the happiness of Isaac, the fulfilment of the promise, and the onward development of the Church. 2. The *reason* of it. (1) Abraham's advancing years. The patriarch was "gone into days," and had no time to waste if he desired to see Isaac well married before he followed Sarah to Machpelah. (2) Abraham's prosperous estate. "The Lord had blessed him in all things," left nothing that his soul could desire to complete the cup of his terrestrial happiness, except the wedding of his son to a godly partner. (3) Isaac's obvious disinclination to seek a wife for himself, his placid and pensive temperament disposing him rather to cling with mournful tenderness to the memory of a beloved mother than to anticipate the felicities of conjugal affection. (4) Eliezer's admirable fitness for the contemplated mission.

III. THE SOLEMN ADJURATION. 1. The *form* of the oath. "Put, I pray thee, thy hand under my thigh." For the significance of this ancient ceremony consult Exposition. 2. The *power* of the oath. This was derived from the character of the Divine Being—the Lord God of heaven and of earth—in whose presence it was taken, to whose witness it appealed, and whose wrath it invoked in case of failure to perform what was vowed. 3. The *tenor* of the oath. (1) Negative—not to marry Isaac to a daughter of the Canaanites, an already doomed race ; and (2) positive—to seek a wife for Sarah's son among his kinsmen in Padan-aram, amongst whom as yet the knowledge of the true God was retained.

IV. THE REASONABLE APPREHENSION. 1. *Natural.* A priori there was little probability that a modest girl would consent on the invitation of a stranger to leave her home and kindred, accompany him into a distant land, and wed a man (even though a relative) whom she had never seen ; and in a similar way reason can make out a case against almost every step in the distinctly Christian life as being unlikely, improbable, imprudent. 2. *Unbelieving.* The aged ambassador's anxiety was not shared in by the patriarch, whose faith had already reasoned out the successful termination of the contemplated expedition. And so again in the Christian life, difficulties which to sagacious reason appear insurmountable, to simple-minded faith cease to exist. 3. *Unnecessary.* When discovered and interrogated, the maiden was quite willing to become Isaac's bride. Many of the saint's fears are of his own making, like this of Abraham's servant, and in the end are found to have been superfluous.

V. THE RESOLUTE PROHIBITION. "Beware that thou bring not my son thither again." To do so would be—1. *To reverse the Divine call* which had brought the patriarch from Mesopotamia. 2. *To endanger the inheritance* by exposing Isaac to the temptation of remaining in Mesopotamia, should his wife prove unwilling to return.

Learn—1. The interest which should be taken by pious parents in the marriage of their children. 2. The care which should be exercised by those who marry to secure pious partners. 3. The lawfulness of imposing and taking oaths on important occasions, and for sufficient reasons. 4. The clearer sight which belongs to faith than to sense and reason. 5. The folly of anticipating difficulties that may never arise. 6. The danger of taking any step in life without Divine guidance or instruction. 7. The sin of renouncing one's religion for the sake of a wife.

HOMILIES BY VARIOUS AUTHORS.

Ch. xxiv.—*The unfolding of the Divine purpose.* I. THE EXPANDED BLESSING. The first line of the web of sacred history stretches itself out to Mesopotamia. The aged patriarch, blessed of Jehovah in all things, is fading from our sight. We must look on a new generation and see the blessing expanded.

II. THE DIVINE GUIDANCE. The angel shall be sent before Isaac, and he will overrule the events and wills which seem to stand in the way. The marriage of Isaac was a matter of most solemn moment. The earthly bonds are blessed only when they are held up by the Divine covenant.

III. MAN'S FAITH REWARDED BY SPECIAL DIRECTION. The servant *prayed* for good speed, because it was in the spirit of *dependence upon Jehovah* that the whole errand was undertaken. We have no ground for expecting supernatural indications of the future, but when we commit our way unto the Lord we may ask him to show it. If it be well for us to see it beforehand, which it sometimes is not, he will send us "*kindness*" both in the occurrences and persons we meet.

IV. EARTHLY RELATIONSHIPS ARE UNDER HEAVEN'S SUPERINTENDENCE. The fair Mesopotamian is a suitable companion for the heir of the patriarch. She is full of graciousness and activity, free from pride, gentle, unsuspicious, generous, patient, self-sacrificing, benevolent. Such characteristics are what the children of God desire to transmit to their descendants. In the sight of so much that was lovely both in person and character, the servant held his peace with wondering thoughtfulness, waiting for and already anticipating the blessing of the Lord.

V. THE TRUE PIETY WATCHES FOR GOD AND WORSHIPS. On receiving the simple answer to his inquiry, and perceiving how the hand of the Lord had been guiding him, he *bowed his head and worshipped* (vers. 26, 27). Those who wait for "the mercy and the truth" will not be left destitute of it. Oh to be able at every step and stage of life to say, "*Blessed be the Lord!*" to hear the salutation rendered us, "*Come in, thou blessed of the Lord!*"

VI. GOD IN HISTORY. The kingdom of God had its points of connection from this moment with the thread of human affection, sanctified by the grace of God, uniting them together. The house of Abraham, the house of Bethel, are widely separated from one another in the measurement of space, but closely bound together henceforth by the spiritual ties of a common faith and obedience in the name of Jehovah. The same Divine purpose which directed the servant's way moved the heart of the damsel. "*She said, I will go.*" She went out of the midst of pure family affections; she was welcomed by one who saw her coming when he was "meditating in the field at eventide," doubtless in the spirit of prayerful expectation; and who took her to his mother Sarah's tent, where she might be sure one who so tenderly mourned the loss of a mother would know how to cherish a wife sent of God to comfort him. "He loved her." Religion is the only true guardian of domestic happiness, the only deep soil in which the affections flourish.—R.

Ver. 6.—*No turning back.* "And Abraham said unto him, Beware thou that thou bring not my son thither again." Abraham's care to prevent the leaven of idolatry entering his family (cf. Exod. xxxiv. 16; 1 Cor. xv. 33; James i. 27). Worldly wisdom would have led him to seek a wife for his son among the families of Canaan, so as to give him a firmer footing in the land; but he solemnly charged his steward, in sending him on a marriage embassy, not to do this (cf. 1 Kings xi. 3; 2 Cor. vi. 14). A wife was to be sought from his brother's family. Out of the earnestness of this godly desire came the trial of his faith. An obvious difficulty ; what if the damsel should not be willing to follow a stranger ? There had been little intercourse between the families. The news in ch. xxii. 20 was plainly the first for many years. Must Isaac go in person to take a wife from her father's house ? Much might be urged in favour of this. If the presence of Isaac were of importance, might he not return for a little, though Canaan was his appointed home ? Was it not hindering the very thing Abraham desired, to refuse to do so ? Was it not unreasonable to look for a blessing and yet to neglect obvious means for obtaining it ? Not for a moment would Abraham listen to the suggestion. At God's call he had left Mesopotamia for ever. To send his son back would be contrary to the principle of his whole life. It would be to put expediency above faith, to distrust God's promise, to think his will changeable (cf. 1 Kings xiii. 19). Contrast the faithlessness of the Israelites in their wilderness journeys. Abraham would not allow even a temporary return. They " in their hearts turned back again into Egypt " (cf. Luke ix. 62).

I. IN A GODLY LIFE THERE IS OFTEN A TEMPTATION TO TURN BACK FOR A LITTLE. With a laudable aim, some step which seems likely to lead to it is not quite what in itself we know to be right. To gain the means of doing good, some little departure from truth may seem almost necessary. In the eagerness of some plan of usefulness the time for prayer can hardly be found, or the ordinary daily duties of life seem to interrupt the greater and higher work ; or, to gain an influence over the gay and worldly, it may seem the course of wisdom to go, a little way at least, with them. And is not a Christian, under the law of liberty, freed from strict observance of the letter ? Does not that savour of the spirit of bondage ? Nay, " to obey is better than sacrifice." Always danger when men seek to be wiser than God (Prov. xiv. 12). We cannot foresee the difficulties of returning.

II. TRUE FAITH POINTS TO IMPLICIT OBEDIENCE. Can we not trust God to order all—not only the ends towards which he would have us strive, but the means to be used ? We are to live by every word of God, not by some special saying only. Promise and precept, instruction and direction, are alike his words, by which every step should be guided. It is want of faith which leads to departure from obedience ; want of full trust in God which leads to ways of fancied wisdom. We have to do with efforts, not with results ; these are in God's hand. Where obedience is not in question we rightly use our judgment ; reason was given us to be our guide, but not to take the guidance out of God's hands.—M.

EXPOSITION.

Ver. 10.—**And the servant took ten camels of the camels of his master,**—to bear the presents for the bride, to enhance the dignity of his mission, and to serve as a means of transport for the bride and her companions on the return journey. On the word *Gamal vide* ch. xii. 16 — **and departed.** Either from Hebron (ch. xxiii. 19), or from the south country, near Beer-lahai-roi (ch. xxiv. 62). **For all the goods of his master** were **in his hand.** Literally, *and every good thing of his master in his hand;* meaning that he selected (*sc.* as presents for the bride) every best thing that belonged to his master —cf. 2 Kings viii. 9 (LXX., Vulgate, Murphy, Kalisch), though some regard it as explaining how he, the servant, was able to start upon his journey with such an equipage, viz., because, or for, he had supreme command over his master's household (Calvin, Rosenmüller, ' Speaker's Commentary '). **And he** arose, and went—if along the direct route, then " through Palestine along the west side of the Jordan and the lakes, into the Buk'ah, and out through the land of Hamath to the Euphrates, and thence " (' Land and Book,' p. 591) — **to Mesopotamia,** — *Aram-Naharaim,* i. e. the Aram of the two rivers ; Aram meaning the high region, from *aram,* to be high—an ancient and domestic name for Syria, not altogether unknown to the Greeks ; *vide* Hom., ' Il.,' ii. 783 ; Hes., ' Theog.,' 304 ; Strabo, xiii. 4 (Gesenius). Standing alone it signifies Western Syria (Judges iii. 10 ; 1 Kings x. 29 ; xi. 25 ; xv. 18), and especially Syria of Damascus (2 Sam. viii. 6 ; Isa. vii. 1, 8 ; Amos i. 5) ; when Mesopotamia is intended it is conjoined with *Naharaim* (upon Egyptian monuments Naharina ; *vide* ' Records of the Past,' vol. ii. pp. 32, 61, 67), the two rivers being the Tigris and the Euphrates, or *Padan,* the field or plain, as in ch. xxv. 20. The latter is not an Elohistic expression as distinguished from the former, which some ascribe to the Jehovist (Knobel, *et alii*), but a more exact description of a portion of Mesopotamia, viz., of that where Laban dwelt. **Unto the city of Nahor**—*i. e.* Haran, or Charran (ch. xxviii. 10, *vide* ch. xi. 31). Nahor must have migrated thither either along with or shortly after Terah.

Ver. 11.—**And he made his camels to kneel down**—"a mode of expression taken from actual life. The action is literally kneeling; not stooping, sitting, or lying down on the side like a horse, but kneeling on his knees; and this the camel is taught to do from his youth" (Thomson, 'Land and Book,' p. 592)—**without the city by a well of water.** "In the East, where wells are scarce and water indispensable, the existence of a well or fountain determines the site of the village. The people build near it, but prefer to have it outside the city, to avoid the noise, dust, and confusion always occurring at it, especially if the place is on the highway" (*Ibid.*). **At the time of the evening,** *even* **the time that women go out to draw** *water*. Literally, *that women that draw go forth*. "It is the work of *females* in the East to draw water both morning and evening; and they may be seen going in groups to the wells, with their vessels on the hip or on the shoulder" (Roberts' 'Oriental Illustrations,' p. 27). "About great cities men often carry water, both on donkeys and on their own backs; but in the country, among the unsophisticated natives, *women only* go to the well or the fountain; and often, when travelling, have I seen long files of them going and returning with their pitchers "at the time when women go out to draw water" (Thomson, 'Land and Book,' p. 592).

Vers. 12—14.—**And he said,**—commencing his search for the maiden by prayer, as he closes it with thanksgiving (ver. 26)—a beautiful example of piety and of the fruits of Abraham's care for the souls of his household, ch. xviii. 19 (Wordsworth)—**O Lord God of my master Abraham, I pray thee, send me good speed this day.** Literally, *cause to meet* (or come before) *me*, i. e. what I wish, the maiden of whom I am in quest; hence εὐόδωσον ἐναντίον ἐμοῦ, make the way prosperous before me (LXX.); less accurately, *occurre obsecro mihi* (Vulgate). **And show kindness unto my master Abraham.** The personal humility and fidelity displayed by this aged servant are only less remarkable than the fervent piety and childlike faith which discover themselves in the method he adopts for finding the bride. Having cast the matter upon God by prayer, as a concern which specially belonged to him, he fixes

upon a sign by which God should enable him to detect the bride designed for Isaac. **Behold, I stand here by the well of water;**—literally, *Behold me standing* (cf. ver. 43) —**and the daughters of the men of the city come out to draw water** (*vide* on ver. 11, and cf. ch. xxix. 9; Exod. ii. 16): **and let it come to pass that the damsel** הַנַּעַר‎, with the vowels of the Keri; the word used for Abraham's young men (cf. ch. xiv. 24; xviii. 7; *q. v.*). In the Pentateuch it occurs twenty-two times, without the feminine termination, meaning a girl (*vide* ch. xxiv. 16, 28, 55; xxxiv. 3, 12; Deut. xx. 15, &c.); a proof of the antiquity of the Pentateuch, and of this so-called Jehovistic section in particular, since in the latter books the distinction of sex is indicated by the affix ה‎ being appended when a girl is intended ('Speaker's Commentary'); but this happens at least once in the Pentateuch (Deut. xxii. 19)—**to whom I shall say, Let down thy pitcher, I pray thee, that I may drink; and she shall say, Drink, and I will give thy camels drink also:**—the sign fixed upon was the kindly disposition of the maiden, which was to be evinced in a particular way, viz., by her not only acceding with promptitude to, but generously exceeding, his request It is probable that the servant was led to choose this sign not by his own natural tact and prudence, but by that Divine inspiration and guidance of which he had been assured (ver. 7) before setting out on his important mission—**let the same be she that thou hast appointed for thy servant Isaac.** "The three qualifications in the mind of this venerable domestic for a bride for his master's son are a pleasing exterior, a kindly disposition, and the approval of God" (Murphy). **And thereby**—ἐν τούτῳ (LXX.), *per hoc* (Vulgate); but rather, by her, *i. e.* the damsel—**shall I know that thou hast showed kindness unto my master.**

Ver. 15.—**And it came to pass** (not certainly by accident, but by Divine arrangement), **before he had done speaking, that,** —his prayer was answered (cf. Isa. lxv. 24; Dan. ix. 20, 21). From ver. 45 it appears that the servant's prayer was not articulately spoken, but offered "in his heart;" whence the LXX. add ἐν τῇ διανοίᾳ αὐτοῦ—**behold, Rebekah came out, who was born to Bethuel, son of Milcah, the wife of Nahor, Abraham's brother** (*vide* ch. xxii. 23), **with her pitcher** —the *cad* (cf. κάδος, *cadus*) was a pail for drawing water, which women were accustomed to carry on their shoulders; it was this sort of vessel Gideon's men employed (Judges vii. 20) — **upon her shoulder** — in exact correspondence with Oriental custom— the Egyptian and the negro carrying on the head, the Syrian on the shoulder or the hip (*vide* Thomson, 'Land and Book,' p. 592).

Ver. 16.—**And the damsel was very fair to look upon.** Literally, *good of countenance*, like Sarah (ch. xii. 11) and Rachel (ch. xxix. 17 ; cf. ch. xxvi. 7 of Rebekah). **A virgin.** *Bethulah*, i. e. one separated and secluded from intercourse with men ; from *bathal*, to seclude (cf. Deut. xxii. 23, 28 ; 2 Sam. xiii. 2, 18). **Neither had any man known her.** A repetition for the sake of emphasis, rather than because *bethulah* sometimes applies to a married woman (Joel i. 8). **And she went down to the well,**—"nearly all wells in the East are in wadys, and have steps down to the water" (Thomson, 'Land and Book,' p. 592)—**and filled her pitcher, and came up**—probably wholly unconscious of the old man's admiration, though by no means unprepared for his request, which immediately followed.

Vers. 17—19.—**And the servant ran to meet her, and said, Let me, I pray thee, drink a little water of thy pitcher** (a request which was at once complied with). **And she said, Drink** (and with the utmost politeness), **my lord** (and with cheerful animation): **and she hasted, and let down her pitcher upon her hand, and gave him drink.** "Rebekah's address to the servant will be given you in the exact idiom by the first gentle Rebekah you ask water from ; but I have never found any young lady so generous as this fair daughter of Bethuel" ('Thomson,' 'Land and Book,' p. 592). **And when she had done giving him drink, she said, I will draw** water **for thy camels also, until they have done drinking**—thus proving that the kindly disposition within her bosom was "not simply the reflex of national customs, but the invisible sun beaming through her mind, and freely bringing forward the blossoms of sterling goodness" (Kalisch).

Ver. 20.—**And she hasted, and emptied her pitcher into the trough** (or gutter made of stone, with which wells were usually provided, and which were filled with water when animals required to drink), **and ran again unto the well to draw** water, **and drew for all his camels.** "At one point we came upon a large village of nomade Bedouins dwelling in their black tents. For the first time we encountered a shepherd playing on his reeden pipe, and followed by his flock. He was leading them to a fountain, from which a maiden was meanwhile drawing water with a rope, and pouring it into a large stone trough. She was not so beautiful as Rebekah" ('In the Holy Land,' by Rev. A. Thomson, D.D. p. 198).

Ver. 21.—**And the man wondering at her** —gazing with attention on her (LXX., Vulgate, Gesenius, Fürst) ; amazed and astonished at her (Rosenmüller, Delitzsch, Keil,

Lange, Calvin)—**held his peace, to wit**—i. e. that he might know—silence being the customary attitude for the soul in either expecting or receiving a Divine communication (cf. Levit. x. 3 ; Ps. xxxix. 2 ; Acts xi. 18) —**whether the Lord had made his journey prosperous or not.** This inward rumination obviously took place while the whole scene was being enacted before his eyes—the beautiful young girl filling the water-troughs, and the thirsty camels sucking up the cooling drink. The loveliness of mind and body, both which he desired in Isaac's bride, was manifestly present in Rebekah ; but still the questions remained to be determined, Was she one of Abraham's kindred? was she single? and would she follow him to Canaan?—points of moment to the solution of which he now proceeds.

Vers. 22—27.—**And it came to pass, as the camels had done drinking,**—"If it is remembered that camels, though endowed in an almost marvellous degree with the power of enduring thirst, drink, when an opportunity offers, an enormous quantity of water, it will be acknowledged that the trouble to which the maiden cheerfully submitted required more than ordinary patience" (Kalisch) —**that the man took a golden earring of half a shekel weight,**—the נֶזֶם was neither a pendant for the ear (LXX., Vulgate) nor a jewel for the forehead (A.V., margin), but a ring for the nose (ver. 47), the side cartilage, and sometimes the central wall, of which was pierced for the purpose of admitting it (cf. Ezek. xvi. 11, 12). Such rings are still worn by Oriental women, and in particular "the nose-ring is now the usual engagement present among the Bedouins" (Delitzsch). The weight of that presented to Rebekah was one בֶּקַע, or half (sc. shekel), from בָּקַע, to divide—**and two bracelets for her hands of ten** skekels **weight of gold ;**—the עָמִיד, from צָמַד, to bind or fasten, meant a circle of gold for the wrist or arm. So favourite an ornament is this of Oriental ladies, that sometimes the whole arm from wrist to elbow is covered with them ; sometimes two or more are worn one above the other ; and not unfrequently are they so numerous and heavy as almost to appear burdensome to the fair owners (Kalisch)— **and said, Whose daughter** art **thou? tell me, I pray thee: is there room in thy father's house for us to lodge in?** The production of the bridal presents, and the tenor of the old man's inquiries, indicate that already he entertained the belief that he looked upon the object of his search. All dubiety was dispelled by Rebekah's answer. **And she said unto him, I am the daughter of Bethuel the son of Milcah,** — to show that she was not descended from Nahor's concubine (cf. ver. 15)—**which she bare unto Nahor.** This appears to have been the stage at which the jewels were presented (ver. 47). **She said moreover unto him, We have both straw and provender enough, and room to lodge in.** It was now conclusively determined, by her answering all the pre-arranged criteria, that the Lord had heard his prayer and prospered his way, and that the heaven-appointed bride stood before him. **And the man bowed down his head, and worshipped the Lord.** The first verb expressing reverent inclination of the head, and the second complete prostration of the body, and both combining "to indicate the aged servant's deep thankfulness for the guidance of the Lord." **And he said, Blessed be the Lord God of my master Abraham** (on the import of בָּרוּךְ *vide* ch. ix. 26), **who hath not left destitute my master of his mercy and his truth :**—literally, *who hath not taken away*

his grace (i. e. the free favour which bestows) *and his truth* (i. e. the faithfulness which implements promises) *from* (= from the house of, as in Exod. viii. 8, 25, 26 ; Gesenius) *my master* (cf. Ps. lvii. 3 ; cxv. 1 ; Prov. xx. 28)—**I** being **in the way, the Lord led** (or, hath led) **me to the house of my master's brethren.**

Ver. 28.—**And the damsel**—הַנַּעֲרָ (*vide* on ver. 16)—**ran** (leaving the venerable stranger in the act of devotion), **and told** them of **her mother's house**—a true touch of nature. With womanly instinct, discerning the possibility of a love-suit, she imparts the joyful intelligence neither to her brother nor to her father, but to her mother and the other females of the household, who lived separately from the men of the establishment—**these things** — in particular of the arrival of a messenger from Abraham. Perhaps also the nose-jewel would tell its own tale.

HOMILETICS.

Vers. 10—28.—*A bride for the heir.*—2. *Eliezer and Rebekah, or the finding of the bride.* I. THE MATRIMONIAL EMBASSY. 1. *The departure from Hebron.* With promptitude and alacrity, as became a servant executing the instructions of a master —attended by a cavalcade of ten camels and their drivers, as ambassadors of princes are wont to signalise their dignity by ample retinues ; and laden with the choicest of his master's goods as presents for the bride, since they who go to woo must not neglect to carry gifts—the venerable steward issued forth upon his mission. 2. *The journey northwards.* Up the Jordan valley towards "the Eye of the East" would probably be the route followed by Eliezer of Damascus ; thence closely skirting the spot where in after years Tadmor in the wilderness arose with its palaces and temples, now magnificent in their ruins, till at length, crossing the Euphrates, he would reach Aram of the Two Rivers. 3. *The arrival at Haran.* If the time at which the patriarchal envoy reached the city of Nahor, viz., at sunset, when the maidens sally forth to draw, was an indication of the guiding hand of Providence, perhaps the spot at which he halted and partially unloaded his weary camels, viz., at the well, was a testimonial to his own shrewd sagacity, which discerned that for meeting with the virgins of the district, and in particular the females of Nahor's family, no better place could be selected than the city well, which was besides the customary resting-place for travellers.

II. THE PRAYER AT THE WELL. 1. *Its reverent humility.* Not only does he adore the Divine greatness, but, leaving himself altogether out of account, he bespeaks an interest in the Divine favour entirely as an act of kindness to his master. 2. *Its childlike simplicity.* He proposes a test by which he may be able to recognise the bride whom God has selected for his master's son. In doing so he practically casts the matter over upon God, asking him in the fashion indicated to point out the object of his search, thus exemplifying the very spirit of the Christian rule, "In everything by prayer and supplication let your requests be made known unto God." 3. *Its immediate answer.* "Before he had done speaking, Rebekah came out" to the well, and acted precisely as he had desired that the bride should do. It was a striking illustration of the promise, "Whiles they are yet speaking I will hear."

III. THE MEETING WITH REBEKAH. 1. *A description of her person.* As to parentage, the daughter of Bethuel ; in respect of condition, of virgin purity ; with regard to appearance, very fair to look upon ; concerning education, trained to domestic duties. 2. *An account of her kindness.* Coming up from the well, she graciously complies with the servant's request to be allowed to take a draught from her pitcher. Then with winning sweetness she promptly offers to fill the stone troughs for his wearied animals. And finally, when asked her name, she with ingenuous frankness tells it, adding, in reply to a request for lodging, that in Bethuel's house there was not only room for himself and camels, but sumptuous hospitality for both. Such spontaneous acts of kindness to an unknown and aged stranger bespoke a tender and susceptible heart within the breast of the fair Rebekah. 3. *The impression which she made on Eliezer.* (1) Her appearance arrested him and made him run to meet her (ver. 17) with his pre-arranged request. Clearly this old man had a singular discernment of character as well as a quick eye for beauty. (2) Her kindness touched him, and made him silent in wonder (ver. 21), struck dumb with amazement at her minute fulfilment of every one of his stipulated conditions. (3) Her invitation overpowered him, causing him to bow his head and worship (ver. 26), acknowledging God's goodness in so quickly leading him to the house of his master's brethren, and so unmistakably pointing out the bride.

Learn—1. The fidelity and devotion to the interests of masters and mistresses which should be evinced by servants. 2. The spirit of prayer and supplication which Christians should display in all the perplexing and difficult paths of life. 3. The kind of brides which young men should select, viz., maidens distinguished by Rebekah's amiable and obliging disposition, even should they not be gifted with Rebekah's grace of form.

HOMILIES BY VARIOUS AUTHORS.

Ver. 21.—*Eliezer, or a wife-seeker.* "And the man wondering at her held his peace, to wit whether the Lord had made his way prosperous or not." "The man" spoken of was probably the Eliezer of Damascus mentioned in ch. xv. 2. He had been selected by Abraham to be his heir, but of course when Isaac was born he could not hold that position. He became honoured and trusted as "the eldest servant of (Abraham's) house, who ruled over all that he had" (ch. xxiv. 2). To him was committed the delicate business recorded in this chapter; and the way in which it was executed was just that which would be expected from one who had so won the confidence of Abraham as to be selected as heir. We cannot but admire the thoughtfulness of Abraham for his son. He sought to prevent Isaac from being brought under the polluting influence of the Canaanitish people in the midst of whom he dwelt. He also desired to prevent Isaac from going back to the country from which he had himself been Divinely led. Hence he sends his steward to select from among his kindred one who shall be a suitable life-companion for his son. He takes an oath of his steward that he will in no wise permit a wife to be taken from among the Canaanites, or lead Isaac to Mesopotamia again. The mission of Eliezer was indeed difficult and delicate. We must not think of it according to the customs of our land. In Oriental nations to this day it is the practice to employ a third person to negotiate a marriage between those who seem by report to be suitable for such relationship. Eliezer undertook the affair with every desire to gratify his master, and to serve well even the one who had supplanted him in heirship. We cannot too highly praise "the man" for his unselfishness, or too warmly admire the devoutness which characterised his whole conduct.

I. HE SEEKS BY PRAYER SUCCESS FROM GOD. The prayer recorded here was probably not the first offered with respect to the subject. His mission was not only delicate, but rather indefinite. He is sent to the relations of his master to choose from among them a wife for Isaac. He knows that much of the satisfaction of Abraham and welfare of Isaac will depend on his right performance of the duty. He feels the responsibility resting upon him, and makes every needful preparation for discharging it. He starts on the camels prepared, and carries with him presents suitable. After a long journey he arrives at a city in Mesopotamia where dwelt Nahor, his master's brother. It is eventide when he reaches the well outside the city. The graceful daughters of the city, with pitchers poised on their shoulders, are just coming forth to draw water for their households. The camels turn their long necks and weary eyes in the direction of the approaching maidens. They know that on their arrival the dry troughs, which only tantalised thirst, will be filled. The shade from the palms avails not now to break the fierce rays of the sun setting so rapidly in the west. Long shadows are over the landscape. Eliezer stands with the golden light about him. He feels that this may be the moment of great import. Clasping firmly his hands, and lifting fervently his face heavenward, he breathes the beautiful prayer, "O Lord God of my master Abraham, I pray thee, send me good speed this day, and show kindness unto my master Abraham." It was—1. Brief prayer, because there was not time to say much more, but it was most appropriate. He asked for what he felt he needed. He did not use prayer as a mere mystical method of pleasing God, but as the expression of a felt need. This is true prayer. God does not want fine words, long sentences, and wearying repetitions. None are heard for their much speaking. That is a heathenish notion. God is not glorified by the length of time we remain on our knees, or the number of things we can crowd into a certain time. The longest prayers are often the most unmeaning. This is true of prayers in the home and in the Church. Brief, earnest, sincere prayer is that which wings its way to heaven. When Peter was sinking in the waters his cry was brief and pointed enough: "Lord, save; I perish." 2. Eliezer did not hesitate to ask God's guidance in respect to a subject which many would have accounted as quite within the scope of their own judgment to decide. Many also would have thought it beneath the notice of God. Many would have made their way direct into the city to Nahor's house to choose for themselves. And many would have left the matter to be decided by chance; but Eliezer seeks guidance from God. Only those who are ignorant of the value of trifles, of their relative power, or who are ignorant of the fact that there are no trifles but which may become all-important circumstances, would think of such an affair as that Eliezer had in hand, as beneath God's notice. If not beneath God's notice, it may be the subject of prayer. Many who contemplate forming relationships might with the greatest advantage imitate the example of Eliezer in this case, and seek direction from God. Were this the practice there would be fewer unhappy marriages. Eliezer, in carrying out his master's wish, seeks success from God.

II. NOTICE HOW GOD OVERTAKES OUR PRAYERS. At the most opportune time the steward prays. He committed his way unto the Lord at the juncture when he felt he needed the guidance. God honours the man's trust. "It came to pass that before he had done speaking Rebekah came out." She was the very one whom God had appointed. She knew not that she was moving to fulfil the intention of God. In her acts and in her words she was doing that which was in harmony with the sign the man had asked. Courteously, on being asked for a draught from her vessel, she had offered even to draw for the camels also. In the first one addressed Eliezer had the answer to his prayer. Cf. Isa. lx. 54: "Before ye call I will answer," &c.; and Dan. ix. 23: "At the beginning of thy supplication the commandment came forth." We lose much of the comfort of prayer because, after having put up a petition, we either forget to look for the answer, or because we have but a semi-belief in the power of prayer. If prayer be a reality to us, it is no less so in God's sight. Some put up prayers in the spirit which seems to say, "Now I will see whether God will answer that." God is not to be subject to mere testings. Christ showed that, when on earth he refused to gratify the curiosity or submit to the testings the Pharisees prepared for him. Where God is perfectly trusted the answer will, in some way or other, overtake, or even anticipate, the prayer.

III. SEE HOW THE RAPIDITY OF THE ANSWER STAGGERS BELIEF. "He, wondering at her, held his peace," waiting to know whether the "Lord had made his journey prosperous or not." God had not only answered speedily, but in the manner desired. Sometimes he sends the answer, but in a way so different from that we expected, that we discern not the fact that we have an answer. But what heavenly telegraphy is here! No sooner the petition sent than the answer is given. The very correspondence between the sign desired and its rapid fulfilment only sets Eliezer speculating as to whether it may not have been simply a very remarkable coincidence rather than a Divine response. Meanwhile he acts as though he believed. He offers to Rebekah the gifts which indicated already his business. He offers such as shall become the character of his master, who was princely in his possessions as well as position. He offers and waits. The man "held his peace." He knows that if God has answered in part ne will also answer fully. God's dealings should always induce awe and patient waiting. He will often surprise us with the blessings of goodness. In our lives we have probably known like surprisingly rapid answers to prayer. We have even disbelieved in the answer. What if God had withdrawn the help or blessing given because received in such unbelief! There are times when we, like Eliezer, and like the Israelites on the shores of the Red Sea, have to be still and know that the Lord is God. Then God's action staggers belief.

IV. SEE HOW GRACIOUSLY GOD CONFIRMS HIS SERVANT'S WONDERING HOPE. Eliezer inquires of the maiden whether there is room in her father's house for him to lodge. After the manner of the Orientals, she readily replies, "We have both straw and provender enough, and room to lodge in." He follows Rebekah. Laban acts as host in place of his father Bethuel. He welcomes Eliezer heartily. "Come in, thou blessed of the Lord," &c. Eliezer enters and attends to the wants of his men and camels, but will not attend to his own until he has unburdened his mind. He tells of his errand, of the meeting with Rebekah at the well, of his praying, of the speedy answer, and of the sign fulfilled. Laban and Bethuel are surprised, and see in it God's hand. They say, "The thing proceedeth from the Lord; we cannot speak unto thee good or ill." Then the man "bowed his head and worshipped." Rebekah consented to accompany him and become the wife of Isaac, his master's son. Everything fell out better than the steward could have expected; he could only see in it God's hand, God's mercy in guiding him and in confirming his hope.

1. God is as willing to answer us as to answer Eliezer of Damascus. 2. Prayer can overcome difficulties that seem insurmountable. When the cup of sorrow is not removed the strength is given to bear it, and so prayer is answered. If the way we expected does not open up in answer to our supplication, another and better is sure to be made plain. Prayer also "makes the darkened cloud withdraw." 3. When in the other world we look at our past life, we shall all see that God had answered all prayers that it would have been for our good to have answered, and that in others the withholdment has been kindliest response. There we shall "bow our heads and worship" him who made our earthly journey prosperous, and who had brought us to the "city which hath foundations." Whatever, then, our anxiety, trial, perplexity, let us lay all before God. If we are earnestly trying for the salvation of members of our own family, or for the advancement of God's kingdom, let us by prayer and supplication make our requests known to God, and he will send us an answer of peace, even as he did to Eliezer.—H.

EXPOSITION.

Ver. 29.—**And Rebekah had a brother, and his name** was **Laban.** "White," whose character has been considerably traduced, the Biblical narrative not representing him as "a monster of moral depravity," but rather as actuated by generous impulses and hospitable dispositions (Kalisch). **And Laban ran out unto the man, unto the well.** That Laban, and not Bethuel, should have the prominence in all the subsequent transactions concerning Rebekah has been explained by the supposition that Bethuel was now dead (Josephus), but vide ver. 50; that he was altogether an insignificant character (Lange, Wordsworth); that firstborn sons enjoyed during their father's lifetime a portion of his authority, and even on important occasions represented him (Kalisch); that in those times it was usual for brothers to take a special interest in sisters' marriages —cf. ch. xxxiv. 13; Judges xxi. 22; 2 Sam. xiii. 22 (Rosenmüller, Michaelis).

Ver. 30.—**And it came to pass, when he saw the earring and bracelets upon his sister's hands** (vide ver. 22), **and when he heard the words of Rebekah his sister, saying, Thus spake the man unto me; that he came unto the man** (this explains the cause of the action mentioned in the previous verse); **and, behold, he stood by the camels at the well.**

Ver. 31.—**And he said, Come in, thou blessed of the Lord.** בָּרוּךְ יְהוָֹה (cf. ch. xxvi. 29; Numb. xxiv. 9); the usual form being לַיהוָֹה (vide ch. xiv. 19; Ruth ii. 20; 1 Sam. xv. 13). Though Laban was an idolater (ch. xxxi. 30), it seems more satisfactory to regard him as belonging to a family in which the worship of Jehovah had originated, and by which it was still retained (Murphy, Wordsworth), than to suppose that he first learnt the name Jehovah from the servant's address (Keil, Lange, Hengstenberg).

Wherefore standest thou without? (as if his not accepting Rebekah's invitation were almost a reflection on the hospitality of the house of Abraham's kinsmen) **for** (literally, *and*, in expectation of thine arrival) **I have prepared the house,**—or, put the house in order, by clearing it from things in confusion (cf. Levit. xiv. 36)—**and room** (*i. e.* place) **for the camels.**

Ver. 32.—**And the man came into the house: and he** (*i. e.* Laban) **ungirded his** (literally, *the*) **camels, and gave straw**—cut up by threshing for fodder (cf. Job xxi. 18; Isa. xi. 7; lxv. 25)—**and provender for the camels, and water to wash his feet** (cf. ch. xviii. 4; xix. 2), **and the men's feet that were with him**—the first intimation that any one accompanied the messenger, though that assistants were necessary is obvious from the narrative.

Ver. 33.—**And there was set**—*appositus est* (Vulgate); *i. e.* if the first word be taken, as in the Keri, as the hophal of שׂוּם; but if the Kethib be preferred, then וַיִּישֶׂם is the fut. Kal of יָשַׂם, signifying, "and he set;" παρέθηκεν (LXX.)—meat **before him to eat** (the crowning act of an Oriental reception): **but he said, I will not eat, until I have told mine errand.** Oriental politeness deferred the interrogation of a guest till after he had supped ('Odyss.' iii. 69); but Abraham's servant hastened to communicate the nature of his message before partaking of the offered hospitality—an instance of self-forgetful zeal of which Christ was the highest example (*vide* Mark vi. 31; John iv. 34). **And he** (*i. e.* Laban) **said, Speak on.**

Vers. 34—49.—Availing himself of the privilege thus accorded, the faithful ambassador recounted the story of his master's prosperity, and of the birth of Isaac when Sarah his mother was old (literally, *after her old age*); of the oath which he had taken to seek a wife for his master's son among his master's kindred, and of the singularly providential manner in which he had been led to the discovery of the chosen bride. Then with solemn earnestness he asked for a decision. **And now if ye will deal kindly and truly**—literally, *if ye are doing*, i. e. are ready or willing to extend kindness and truth (cf. ver. 27)—**with** (or, to) **my master, tell me: and if not, tell me; that I may turn** (literally, *and I will turn*) **to the right hand, or to the left**—in further prosecution of my mission, to seek in some other family a bride for my master's son.

Vers. 50—52.—**Then Laban and Bethuel** (*vide* on ver. 29) **answered and said, The thing proceedeth from the Lord:**—*Jehovah* (*vide* on ver. 31)—**we cannot speak unto thee bad or good**—*i. e.* they could not demur to a proposal so clearly indicated by

Divine providence; a proof of the underlying piety of those descendants of Nahor. **Behold, Rebekah is before thee, take** her, **and go,**—that the consent of the maiden is not asked was not owing to the fact that, according to ancient custom, Oriental women were at the absolute disposal, in respect of marriage, of their parents and elder brothers (Bush), but to the circumstance that already it had been tacitly given by her acceptance of the bridal presents (Kalisch), or, from her amiable and pious disposition, might be taken for granted, since she, no more than they, would resist the clearly-revealed will of Jehovah (Lange, Wordsworth)—**and let her be thy master's son's wife, as the Lord hath spoken.** Words which again kindled the flame of reverential piety in the old man's heart, so that **he worshipped the Lord, bowing himself to the earth**—literally, *he prostrated himself to the earth to Jehovah* (cf. ver. 26).

Vers. 53, 54.—**And the servant brought forth jewels**—literally, *vessels* (σκεύη, LXX.), the idea being that of things finished or completed; from כָּלָה, to finish (cf. ch. xxxi. 37; xlv. 20)—**of silver, and jewels** (or vessels) **of gold, and raiment,**—covering garments, *e. g.* the outer robes of Orientals (ch. xxxix. 12, 13, 15; xli. 42); especially precious ones (1 Kings xxii. 10)—**and gave** them **to Rebekah**—as betrothal presents, which are absolutely essential, and usually given with much ceremony before witnesses (*vide* 'Land and Book,' p. 593). **He gave also to her brother and to her mother** (here mentioned for the first time) **precious things.** מִגְדָּנֹת—from מֶגֶד, precious, occurring only elsewhere in 2 Chron. xxi. 3 and Ezek. i. 6; both times, as here, in connection with gold and silver—probably describes valuable articles in general. **And** (having thus formally concluded the engagement) **they did eat and drink,**—*i. e.* partook of the victuals which had been set before them at an earlier stage (ver. 33)—**he and the men that** were **with him, and tarried all night;**—literally, *and passed the night* (cf. ch. xix. 2; xxiv. 25)—**and they rose up in the morning** (indicative of alacrity and zeal), **and he said, Send me away unto my master**—being impatient to report to Abraham the success of his expedition.

Ver. 55.—**And her brother and her mother** —Laban as usual (ver. 50) having the first place; probably because of the prominence which from this time he assumes in the theocratic history—**said, Let the damsel abide with us** a few **days, at least ten.** Literally, *days, at least* (Vulgate, *saltem*); as it were (LXX., ὡσεί); perhaps (Murphy); or (Fürst, Ewald, Kalisch), if she wish, with the idea of choice (Gesenius); *a ten*, or decade of days; the עָשׂוֹר being used as a measure of time analogous to the שָׁבוּעַ or hebdomad. That ten months are meant (Chaldee, Arabic, Ainsworth) is probably incorrect. **After that she shall go.**

Vers. 56—60.—Still urging his suit for permission to depart, Laban and the mother of Rebekah proposed that the maiden should be left to decide a matter so important for her by her own inclinations. When consulted she expressed her readiness at once to accompany the venerable messenger to his distant home ; and accordingly, without more delay, she was dismissed from her mother's tent, attended by a faithful nurse (ch. xxxv. 8) and enriched by the blessing of her pious relatives, who said unto her, **Thou art our sister, be thou** the mother **of thousands of millions** (literally, *our sister thou, become to thousands of myriads,* i. e. let thy descendants be very numerous), **and let thy seed possess the gate** (*vide* ch. xxii. 17) **of those which hate them.**

HOMILETICS.

Vers. 29—60.—*A bride for the heir.*—3. *Eliezer and Laban, or proposals for the bride.* I. THE HOSPITABLE BROTHER. 1. *The eager invitation.* "Come in, thou blessed of the Lord!" (1) The speaker was Laban, Rebekah's brother, who on hearing his sister's call had hurried to the well. (2) The motive which impelled him was not unlikely a little greed of filthy lucre, the appetite for which a sight of Rebekah's jewels may have whetted ; a little feeling of friendship, since he would learn from Rebekah that the stranger had come from Abraham ; and a little sense of religion, as the family of Nahor appear still to have retained the knowledge of Jehovah. Most people's motives are mixed, and so probably were Laban's. 2. *The kindly reception.* (1) Eliezer's camels were unpacked, stalled, and fed—a proof of Laban's humanity (Prov. xii. 10). (2) His men's feet and his own were refreshed by washing—a necessary part of Oriental hospitality, evincing Laban's thoughtfulness (cf. Luke vii. 44). (3) Meat and drink were set before himself and his companions—the crowning act of an Eastern reception, showing that Laban and the other members of the household were accustomed to "use hospitality without grudging."

II. THE AGED WOOER. 1. *Impatient.* The nature of his mission urged him to despatch, as knowing well that his master was old, that Isaac was needful of a bride, that coy maidens are soonest caught by fervent suitors, and that successful wooing brooks no delay. 2. *Skilful.* The first recorded speech in the Bible, Eliezer's bride-wooing cannot fail to be admired for its wisdom. (1) He secures the sympathy of his auditors by declaring himself to be the servant of Abraham ; (2) he details to them the wealth of his master, reasoning probably that no mother would ever think of sending away her daughter into a foreign country to be a poor man's bride ; (3) he advances to the great religious consideration that Isaac's wife must be a worshipper of God ; and (4) he narrates the singular providence that had pointed out Rebekah as the destined bride. 3. *Pious.* The religious character of this wooing is apparent from the reverent use of the Divine name throughout the old man's speech, the importance assigned to piety as one of the bride's qualifications, the devout recognition of God's hand in prospering his journey, and the impression he conveys that Jehovah has himself selected Rebekah.

III. THE CONSENTING RELATIVES. The acquiescence of Laban, Bethuel, and the mother of Rebekah was—1. *Unhesitatingly given.* "Behold, Rebekah is before thee, take her, and go, and let her be thy master's son's wife." A little reluctance on their part would not have been surprising. 2. *Piously dictated.* "The thing proceedeth from the Lord!" Not the eligibility of the match, but the approbation of Heaven, secured their consent. 3. *Thankfully acknowledged.* "Abraham's servant worshipped the Lord, bowing himself to the earth." How eminent the piety which traces every blessing to its primal source ; how beautiful the religion which, the more it gets, the more it stoops! 4. *Richly rewarded.* "The servant brought forth jewels of silver," &c. (ver. 53). While adoring the original Giver, he did not neglect the second cause. Young men who receive fair Rebekahs in marriage should not forget to recompense with love and gifts the fathers and mothers who have given them up.

IV. THE WILLING MAIDEN. 1. *The proposed delay.* "Let the damsel abide with us a few days, at least ten." This was natural, and would be convenient both for the preparation of the bride's trousseau and for the gratification of friends who might wish to bid her farewell. 2. *The urgent request.* "Hinder me not; send me away." The old man accepted his prosperity in wooing as an indication that God intended his immediate return. 3. *The important question.* "Wilt thou go with this man?" No maiden, however urged by relatives and friends, should contract a forced and unwilling marriage. 4. *The decisive answer.* "I will go." After this there could be no mistaking how Rebekah's heart inclined. It augured well for the coming marriage that it would prove a union of love, and not simply of convenience. 5. *The fraternal benediction.* "Thou art our sister, be thou the mother of thousands of millions."

HOMILIES BY VARIOUS AUTHORS.

Ver. 30.—*Laban's eye of greed.* "And when he saw the bracelets," &c. One thing moved Laban to offer hospitality to a stranger—the vision of gold on his sister's form.

I. COVETOUSNESS MAKES A MAN CALCULATING WHEN APPEARING TO BE GENEROUS. Laban had not been so pressingly urgent in his invitation if he had not cherished a hope of further advantages. He was a churlish man. He said, "Come in, thou blessed of the Lord," &c., because he saw that which was to him the greatest sign of blessing—wealth. Laban helped the more readily to ungird Eliezer's camels because he hoped thereby to loosen the girdle-purse of his visitor. He had the eye of greed. He could not see anything valuable belonging to another without wishing to possess it.

II. COVETOUSNESS MAKES A MAN, GENERALLY, SHORT-SIGHTED WITH RESPECT TO HIS OWN BEST INTERESTS. Laban gave Eliezer a bad impression of himself. The latter would soon see through such a man as Laban. He showed this when he gave presents not only to the sister and mother, but to the brother (ver. 53). He knew that it would not be advisable to overlook Laban. Eliezer knew he could be bought. Laban, when treating with Jacob, was just as short-sighted. He gave Leah and Rachel to Jacob as wives only after years of service for which he stipulated. He changed Jacob's wages ten times. Through his greed he at last lost Jacob. He confessed how great a helper Jacob had been. "The Lord hath blessed me for thy sake" (ch. xxx. 27). Jacob would not tarry with him, and even the daughters were glad enough to get away from such a father. Covetousness is opposed to our temporal and eternal interests. We lose by it the respect of others here and of God hereafter.

III. COVETOUSNESS IS EVER INDIFFERENT TO THE RIGHTFUL CLAIMS OF OTHERS. It will ignore those claims altogether, if possible. 1. We find Laban thus ignored the influence of his father throughout the whole transaction. Perhaps Bethuel was infirm or aged, but he is, consistently with the character of Laban, thrust into the background. Laban also takes all presents, and there is no mention of any being given to his father. 2. We find also he was in great measure indifferent to the happiness of his sister. He was subtle in tongue, and spoke of the Lord arranging things, but he believed in the arrangement because his family was the gainer. A good chance is offered by the Damascene stranger, and Rebekah soon saw that it was a foregone conclusion that she should go with him. Covetousness will make parents careless as to the physical, mental, and moral well-being of their children, and employers careless of the state of their servants. It is covetousness also that leads many to spread temptations, too strong to be resisted, before others, and one nation to get rich out of that which is sapping the life-blood of another.

IV. COVETOUSNESS NEVER SATISFIES, AND OFT MAKES MEN MOST MISERABLE. "He that is greedy of gain troubleth his house." "Envy is rottenness to the bones." Misers perish in the midst of plenty. Riches possessed, the desire for more is generally intensified. The desire is no more checked than a lamp is extinguished by added oil.

V. COVETOUSNESS IS SURE, SOONER OR LATER, TO BE REBUKED. The greed in Laban's eye which glistened at the sight of the golden ornaments on his sister's form deepened with the passage of years. At last, in his pursuit of Jacob, he was rebuked by God in a vision, and afterwards by the man he had wronged. Learn, therefore, that medium prosperity is better than great riches gained by greed. Despise not the comforts of life, but live for something higher. What is gained in the world is speedily gone. If we gain much and ruin our souls, we shall not only be rejected by God, but shall bitterly condemn ourselves.—H.

Ver. 31.—*Laban, the solicitous host.* "Wherefore standest thou without?" The character of Laban has been well explained by Blunt in his 'Coincidences.' It is one of consistent greed. He was sincere in inviting Eliezer because he saw the bracelets on his sister's arm, and expected still further favours from a guest who can so lavishly bestow gifts. Christ asks us to enter his kingdom, but he expects nothing from us in return but love. We may adapt this inquiry of Laban to souls as yet outside the Church.

I. THE POSITION OCCUPIED. "Without." Probably they have no realised pardon, no enjoyment in religion, no future prospects of joy. Life is a dread mystery to them. They are saying, "Who will show us any good?" They may be just awakened spiritually, like the Philippian jailor. They may be under the condemnings of law and conscience, and in dread of the consequences of sin. Those within the true Church know in whom they have believed, and rejoice in forgiveness and the prospect of heaven. They are no longer outside the gates of mercy. We may be in a visible Church without being of Christ's fold. It is penitence, faith, and character that determine our position, and not birth, rank, or ceremonial observances.

II. THE REASONS WHEREFORE MANY RETAIN A POSITION OUTSIDE THE CHURCH. 1. Accustomed to the state, and unwilling to change. They are like the prisoner who, after many years' imprisonment in the Bastile, was liberated, and went forth only to find all his friends gone and himself a mere burden to society. He went back and entreated to be allowed to retain his cell until he should pass out of the world. 2. Many, because they are ignorant of the fulness of Divine mercy. 3. Others, because they think there is so much to be done ere they can be fitted to be received within, and are looking to their own efforts to prepare themselves. 4. Many, because they fear their opportunity of admittance is past. 5. Others, because undecided as to whether they shall give up the pleasures of the world for the privileges of Christian fellowship. 6. Others, because they lack faith in their faith and its power to justify. 7. Many stand outside because they think themselves as secure outside as within. They forget that Christ demands open confession, and that to be united openly to his Church is one way of confessing his name before men. Let there be a personal and searching inquiry, "Wherefore standest *thou* without?" The invited guest passed within, and found his highest expectations more than realised, because God "had prospered his journey."—H.

EXPOSITION.

Ver. 61.—**And Rebekah arose** (expressive of the promptitude, celerity, and decision of her departure), **and her damsels,**—probably a company, at least two, though Laban afterwards only gave each of his daughters one (ch. xxix. 24, 29)—**and they rode upon camels** (most likely those which Abraham's servant had brought), **and followed the man** (not in fear, but in hope): **and the servant took** (in the sense of undertook the charge of) **Rebekah** (who, in his eyes, would now be invested with additional charms, as his young master's intended bride), **and went his way**—returning by the road he came.

Ver. 62.—**And** (when the bridal train was nearing home) **Isaac came from the way of the well Lahai-roi;**—Hagar's well (ch. xvi. 7, 14)—**for he dwelt in the south country—**

on the Negeb (*vide* ch. xii. 9). Abraham may by this time have removed from Hebron; or, if Hebron be included in the south country, Isaac may have been only on a visit to Hagar's well (Lange).

Ver. 63.—**And Isaac went out to meditate** —לָשׂוּחַ; to think (LXX., Vulgate, Murphy, Kalisch); to pray (Onkelos, Samaritan, Kimchi, Luther, Keil); to lament (Knobel, Lange); doubtless to do all three, to commune with his heart and before God; not, however, about agricultural affairs, or the improvement of his property (Knobel), but concerning his deceased mother, whom he still mourned (ver. 67), though chiefly, it is probable, anent the marriage he contemplated (Keil)—**in the field at the eventide.** Literally, *at the turning of the evening* (cf. Deut. xxiii. 12; and for corresponding phrase, "when the morning draws on," Exod. xiv. 27; Judges xix. 26; Ps. xlvi. 6). **And he lifted up his eyes, and saw, and, behold, the camels** were **coming.** The bride's first glimpse of her intended spouse being, with artless simplicity though with dramatic picturesqueness, described in similar terms.

Ver. 64.—**And Rebekah lifted up her eyes, and when she saw** (literally, *and she saw,* though as yet she did not know that it was) **Isaac, she lighted**—literally, *fell;* the word signifying a hasty descent (cf. 1 Sam. xxv. 23; 2 Kings v. 21); κατεπήδησεν (LXX.); *descendit* (Vulgate)—**off the camel.** "The behaviour of Rebekah was such as modern etiquette requires" (*vide* Thomson, 'Land and Book,' p. 593).

Ver. 65.—**For she had said** (literally, *and she said;* not before, but after alighting) **unto the servant** (of Abraham), **What man is this that walketh in the field to meet us?**—Isaac having obviously hastened forward to give a welcome to his bride. On learning who it was **she took a veil**—"the cloak-like veil of Arabia" (Keil), which covers not merely the face, but, "like a kind of large wrapper, nearly the whole form, rendering it impossible to recognise the person" (Kalisch)—**and covered herself.** That married ladies did

not always use the veil when travelling appears from the case of Sarah (ch. xx. 16); but that brides did not discover their faces to their intended husbands until after marriage may be inferred from the case of Leah (ch. xxix. 23, 25). Thus modestly attired, she meekly yields herself to one whom she had never before seen, in the confident persuasion that so Jehovah willed.

Ver. 67.—**And Isaac**—receiving an account (ver. 66) from his father's faithful ambassador of all things that he had done—**brought her into his mother Sarah's tent** (which must have been removed from Hebron as a precious relic of the family, if by this time they had changed their abode), **and took Rebekah, and she became his wife** — the primitive marriage ceremony consisting solely of a taking before witnesses (*vide* Ruth iv. 13). **And he loved her.** And he had every reason; for, besides being beautiful and kindly and pious, she had for his sake performed a heroic act of self-sacrifice, and, better still, had been both selected for and bestowed upon him by his own and his father's God. **And Isaac was comforted after his mother's** death. Literally, *after his mother;* the word *death* not being in the original, "as if the Holy Spirit would not conclude this beautiful and joyful narrative with a note of sorrow" (Wordsworth).

HOMILETICS.

Vers. 61—67.—*A bride for the heir.*—4. *Rebekah and Isaac, or the wedding of the bride.* I. THE PENSIVE BRIDEGROOM. 1. *Mourning for his mother.* Isaac's meditation clearly includes this. Good mothers, when they die, should be deeply and affectionately sorrowed for by grateful and loving sons. A son who loves his mother living forgets not to lament her dead. The best testimonial of filial piety is to know that a son tenderly regards his mother while she lives, and cherishes her memory when she is gone. 2. *Musing on his bride.* This too the language will admit. Scarcely could the thought of Eliezer's mission be excluded from Isaac's mind. Doubtless he would often, during the interval of his absence, have his silent wonderings about its return with the God-provided spouse. Almost certainly too his prayers would ascend to heaven on her behalf. He who asks a wife from God is most likely to receive one, and he who frequently prays for the wife of his youth is most likely to love her when she comes. Note that Isaac's mournings and musings were in the field at eventide. While any place and time will suffice for heart exercises, some places and times are more suitable than others, and none more so than the solitude of nature and the darkening of eve.

II. THE VEILED BRIDE. Springing from her camel at the sight of her intended husband, "she took a veil and covered herself." The actions indicated—1. *Rebekah's politeness.* Etiquette required both. It was satisfactory at least that Isaac was about to receive as his wife a lady, one acquainted with the gentle manners of the day. Refinement, while desirable in all, is specially beautiful in woman. Elegance of manners are only second to beauty of form in a bride. 2. *Rebekah's modesty.* Nothing can palliate immodesty in any, least of all in the gentler sex. Hence, not only should maidens be educated with the greatest possible attention to the cultivation of pure and delicate emotions, but nothing should ever tempt them to cast aside that shield of maidenly reserve which is one of their surest protections in the midst of life's dangers and seductions.

III. THE PRIMITIVE WEDDING. 1. *The giving of the bride.* This we can suppose was performed by Eliezer, who, by his recital of "all things that he had done," practically certified that Rebekah was the maiden whom Jehovah had provided, and now in formal act handed over to him to be his wife. 2. *The taking of the bride.* "Isaac took Rebekah," *i. e.* publicly and solemnly accepted her in the presence of witnesses as his bride. Thus, without elaborate or expensive ceremonial, Rebekah "became his wife." 3. *The home-coming of the bride.* "Isaac brought her into his mother Sarah's tent," and thus installed her in the honours as well as invested her with the privileges of matron of his house.

IV. The happy home. 1. Isaac *loved* Rebekah. "So ought husbands to love their wives as their own bodies" (Ephes. v. 28). It is their duty; it ought to be their happiness; it certainly will prove their interest. 2. Rebekah *comforted* Isaac. So ought wives not merely "to reverence their husbands" (Ephes. v. 33), but to soothe their sorrows, cure their cares, and dispel their despondencies.

Learn—1. That the son who sorrows for a mother will likely prove a husband that can love a wife. 2. That maidens' charms are most attractive when seen through a veil of modesty. 3. That those marriages are most auspicious which are made by God. 4. That those homes are happiest where husband and wife love and comfort one another.

HOMILIES BY VARIOUS AUTHORS.

Ver. 63.—*Isaac in the field.* "And Isaac went out to meditate in the field at eventide." Isaac was one of the less prominent among the patriarchs. He seems to have lacked energy of character, but there was great devoutness. His life was like a toned picture, lacking garish colouring, but having a depth of interest. Possibly the fact that an uplifted knife had once gleamed death upon him, and that he had so narrowly escaped, may have had great influence in giving a sober tinge to his life. Not only so, but training by such a father as Abraham must have inculcated a ready obedience to God's will, and a constant desire to know that will. In the passage above we have—

I. A godly habit indicated. "Went out to meditate"—to pray. There is a great difference between reverie and meditation. The one is aimless dreaming, the other, thought tending to an object. Prayer is the thought expressed. Meditation is the "nurse of prayer." Meditation stirs up the spiritual fire within. It brings us nearer to the Divine. It should be cultivated as a habit rather than be left to spasmodic impulses.

II. A place well adapted to prayer selected. The field or open country, where we can get away from men, is the place for fellowship with God. A free prospect lets God's power be more plainly seen. It is an advantage to get out to sea, and, leaning over the bulwark of a vessel, to realise the width of the world, the vastness of the universe and greatness of God. We should seek some place where we can specially realise the presence and power of God. "Enter into thy closet" is a command which many find it difficult to obey. At school, in business houses, there is little or no provision for solitary meditation; but with a book in hand the believer may in spirit get alone with God.

III. The time chosen for prayer was most fitting. Isaac went into the field at eventide. When the fret and toil of the day were over; when the sun was setting, glorified by crimson clouds, or shaded by the purplish haze; when the blossoms were closing, and flocks were being folded; when the moon was just showing, and the stars beginning to shine out; when a hush was over nature and entering into the soul—then Isaac sought to pray; then he sought to realise the certainty of the Divine promises and the faithfulness of the Divine performance. The time accorded well with his own feelings. He still mourned for his mother (ver. 67). Sorrow makes solitude congenial. Moreover, he was anticipating a change of state. He knew his father had sent Eliezer to seek for him a wife from among his own kindred, and he may have been praying that God would send him a suitable partner for life. While he was praying the answer was approaching. By prayer Isaac was prepared also to bear with the selfishness and wrong-doing of others. In ch. xxvi. we see how he avoided quarrelling with the Philistines. Gentleness made him great, and that gentleness was intensified by prayer.—H.

EXPOSITION.

CHAPTER XXV.

Ver. 1.—**Then again Abraham took a wife,** —literally, *and Abraham added and took a* אִשָּׁה (*i. e. a secondary wife, as concubine,* *pilgash;* vide ver. 6 and 1 Chron. i. 28, 32); but whether after (Kalisch, Lange, Murphy) or before (Calvin, Keil, Alford, Bush) Sarah's death it is impossible to decide—**and her name was Keturah**—"Incense" (Gesenius); probably a servant in the family, as Hagar had been, though not Hagar herself (Targums), whom Abraham had recalled after Sarah's death (Lyra), since ver. 6 speaks of concubines.

Ver. 2.—**And she bare him** (since the patriarch's body at 100 years was practically dead, it is almost certain that his marriage with Keturah took place after the renewal of his powers; and it is easier to suppose that his physical vigour remained for some years after Sarah's death than that, with his former experience of concubinage, and his parental joy in the birth of Isaac, he should add a second wife while Sarah lived) **Zimran,** —identified with *Zabram,* west of Mecca, on the Red Sea (Knobel, Keil); or the *Zimareni,* in the interior of Arabia (Delitzsch, Kalisch) —**and Jokshan,**—the *Kassamitæ,* on the Red Sea (Knobel); or the Himarytish tribe Jakish, in Southern Arabia (Keil)—**and Medan, and Midian,**—*Modiana,* on the east of the Elamitic Gulf, and *Madiana,* north of this (Rosenmüller, Keil, Knobel)—**and Ishbak,**— perhaps preserved in Schobeck, in the land of the Edomites (Knobel, Keil)—**and Shuah**— for which the epithet Shuhite (Job ii. 11) may point to Northern Idumæa (Keil, Knobel, Kalisch).

Ver. 3.—**And Jokshan begat Sheba,**—probably the Sabeans: Job i. 15; vi. 19 (Keil) —and **Dedan**—probably the trading people mentioned in Jer. xxv. 23 (Keil). **And the sons of Dedan were Asshurim,**—who have been associated with the warlike tribe of the *Asir,* to the south of Hejas (Keil)—**and Letu- shim,**—the *Bann Leits* in Hejas (Keil)—**and Leummim**—the tribe *Bann Lâm,* which extended even to Babylon and Mesopotamia (Keil).

Ver. 4.—**And the sons of Midian; Ephah** (*vide* Isa. lx. 6), **and Epher** (Beni Ghifar in Hejas), **and Hanoch** (Hanakye, three days north of Medinah), **and Abidah, and Eldaah** —the tribes of Abide and Vadaa in the neighbourhood of Asir. Keil adds that all these identifications are uncertain. **All these were the children of Keturah**—six sons, seven grandsons, three great-grandsons; in all sixteen descendants.

Vers. 5, 6.—**And Abraham gave all that he had unto Isaac.** *I. e.* constituted him his chief heir, according to previous Divine appointment (ch. xv. 4), and made over to him the bulk of his possessions (ch. xxiv. 36). **But unto the sons of the concubines** (Hagar and Keturah), **which Abraham had, Abraham gave gifts,**—"doubtless established them as youthful nomads" (Lange) — **and sent them away from Isaac his son,**—Ishmael's dismissal took place long before (ch. xxi. 14); probably he then received his portion-· **while he yet lived** (*i. e.* during Abraham's lifetime), **eastward, unto the east country** (or Arabia in the widest sense; to the east and south-east of Palestine).

Ver. 7.—**And these are the days of the years of Abraham's life which he lived,**— an impressive and appropriate expression for the computation of life (cf. ch. xlvii. 9)— **an hundred and threescore and fifteen years** —*i. e.* 175 years; so that he must have lived seventy-five years after Isaac's birth and thirty-eight years after Sarah's death. "His grandfather lived 148 years, his father 205, his son 180, and his grandson 147; so that his years were the full average of that period" (Murphy).

Vers. 8—10.—**Then Abraham gave up the ghost** (literally, *breathed out,* sc. the breath of life), **and died in a good old age,**—literally, *in a good hoary age,* i. e. "with a crown of righteousness upon his hoary head" (Hughes)—**an old man, and full** of years. Literally, *and satiated,* i. e. satisfied not merely with life and all its blessings, but with living. The three clauses give an elevated conception of the patriarch's life as that of one who had tasted all the sweets and realised all the ends of a mundane existence, and who accordingly was ripe and ready for transition to a higher sphere. **And was gathered to his people.** An expression similar to "going to his fathers" (ch. xv. 15, *q. v.*), and to "being gathered to one's fathers" (Judges ii. 10). "The phrase is constantly distinguished from departing this life and being buried, denotes the reunion in Sheol with friends who have gone before, and therefore presupposes faith in the personal continuance of a man after death" (Keil). Abraham died in the hope of a better country, even an heavenly (Heb. xi. 13—16). **And his sons Isaac and Ishmael**—Isaac as the heir takes precedence; but Ishmael, rather than the sons of Keturah, is associated with him at his father's funeral; probably because he was not so distant as they from Hebron (Lange), or because he was the subject of a special blessing, which they were not (Keil,

Murphy); or perhaps simply Ishmael and Isaac united as the eldest sons to perform the last rites to a parent they revered (Kalisch). " Funerals of parents are reconciliations of children (ch. xxxv. 29), and differences of contending religionists are often softened at the side of a grave " (Wordsworth)—**buried him** (*vide* on ch. xxiii. 19) **in the cave of Machpelah, in the field of Ephron the son of Zohar the Hittite, which is before Mamre** (*vide* on ch. xxiii. 3—20); **the field which Abraham purchased of the sons of Heth** (a repetition which augments the importance of the statement that Abraham did not sleep in a borrowed tomb): **there was Abraham buried, and Sarah his wife.**

Ver. 11.—**And it came to pass after the death of Abraham, that God**—*Elohim;* whence the preceding section is ascribed to the Elohist; but the general name of God is here employed because the statement partakes merely of the nature of an intimation that the Divine blessing descended upon Isaac by inheritance (Hengstenberg), and the particular blessing of which the historian speaks is not so much the spiritual and eternal blessings of the covenant, as the material and temporal prosperity with which Isaac, in comparison with other men, was enriched (Murphy)—**blessed his son Isaac; and Isaac dwelt by the well Lahai-roi** (*vide* ch. xvi. 14; xxiv. 62).

HOMILETICS.

Vers. 1—11.—*The last days of Abraham.* I. ABRAHAM'S OLD AGE. 1. *The taking of a second wife.* (1) Her name: Keturah, recorded because of her relationship to Abraham. Connection with God's people confers honours as well as privileges. (2) Her marriage: of the second degree. Succeeding to Sarah's marriage bed, Keturah did not succeed to her social status. Neither did her issue possess legal claim to Abraham's inheritance. Concubinage, though permitted, was not necessarily approved by God. (3) Her children: numerous and (in some instances) distinguished. The common seed of the flesh may often be more enlarged than the special seed of grace; but the descendants of good men, other things being equal, are likelier to come to honour than the families of the wicked. 2. *The making of his will.* (1) Isaac, the son of Sarah, he constitutes his heir, in accordance with the Divine counsel, not attempting to interpose on behalf of Ishmael, his first-born. Primogeniture may involve certain rights in the world; it has no superiority in grace, or in the Church. (2) The sons of Hagar and Keturah he endows with portions from his ample pastoral wealth before he dies, and sends away to settle as independent nomads in the unoccupied territory lying on the east of Palestine, thus providing for the prosperity of his children and the peace of his family after he is gone—two things which pious parents should as far as possible secure before they die.

II. ABRAHAM'S DEATH. 1. *Before death.* The age to which the patriarch had attained was—(1) Numerically great, viz., 175 years. Mark the tendency of piety to prolong life (Ps. xxxiv. 12). (2) Morally good. Neither beautiful nor desirable in itself, when associated with corresponding ripeness in grace old age is both delightful to look upon and pleasant to enjoy (Prov. xvi. 31). (3) Completely satisfying. He had experienced the Divine goodness and mercy for 175 years, had God's covenant established with himself and family, beheld Isaac born, married, and, the father of two promising sons, and seen Sarah away before him to the better land; now he had no desire left unfulfilled but one, viz., to depart. 2. *At death.* His end was peaceful; he " breathed out his spirit " into the hands of Jehovah. So did Isaac (ch. xxxv. 29), Jacob (ch. xlix. 33), David (Ps. xxxi. 5), Christ (Luke xxiii. 46). " Mark the perfect, and behold the upright " (Ps. xxxvii. 37). 3. *After death.* He was gathered to his people—a significant intimation of (1) the immateriality of the soul; (2) the conscious existence of the soul after death; (3) the gathering of pious souls into one society beyond the grave; (4) the mutual recognition of the glorified; (5) the complete separation of the righteous from the wicked.

III. ABRAHAM'S FUNERAL. 1. *The chief mourners.* Whether Keturah's boys were present at the affecting ceremonial is not stated, but the prominent positions were occupied by Ishmael and Isaac. It is a duty which surviving children owe deceased parents to see their remains deposited with reverence in the grave, and it is beautiful when fraternal estrangements are removed round a father's tomb. 2. *The place of sepulture.* The cave of Machpelah had three attractions for the patriarch : it was in the promised land, it was his own tomb, and it contained the dust of Sarah.　3. *The bereaved son.* Isaac, from his sensitive disposition and the unexciting character of his occupation, would feel his father's loss more keenly than Ishmael. Perhaps this explains the statement of ver. 11. It is God's special care to comfort orphans (Ps. xxvii. 10).

Learn—1. That though secondary wives are not agreeable to the word of God, second marriages are not against the will of God.　2. That good men ought to make a just disposition of their temporal affairs before they die.　3. That whether God's saints die soon or late, they are always satisfied with living.　4. That in whatever sort of tomb a saint's dust may lie, his immortal spirit goes to join the company of just men made perfect.　5. That the loss of earthly parents is more than compensated by the blessing of a father's God.

HOMILIES BY VARIOUS AUTHORS.

Vers. 1—18.—*The line of blessing.* Although Abraham has many descendants, he carefully distinguishes the line of the Divine blessing. His peaceful end at 175 years set the seal upon a long life of faith and fellowship with God. His two sons, Isaac and Ishmael, met at their father's grave, although living apart. The influence of such a character as Abraham's is very elevating and healing, even in the sphere of the world. Ishmael is not entirely forgotten, but Isaac, as the true heir of Abraham, hands on the blessing of the covenant.—R.

§ 8. The Generations of Ishmael (CH. XXV. 12—18).

EXPOSITION.

Ver. 12.—**Now these are the generations of Ishmael,**—the opening of a new section (cf. ch. ii. 4), in which the fortunes of Abraham's eldest son are briefly traced before proceeding with the main current of the history in the line of Isaac (cf. 1 Chron. i. 29 —31)—**Abraham's son,**—because of his relation to Abraham it was that Ishmael attained subsequent historical development and importance (*vide* ch. xxi. 13)—**whom Hagar the Egyptian, Sarah's handmaid, bare unto Abraham** (*vide* ch. xvi. 1, 15).

Ver. 13.—**And these are the names of the sons of Ishmael, by their names, according to their generations : the firstborn of Ishmael, Nebajoth ;**—"Heights ;" the *Nabathæans*, a people of Northern Arabia, possessed of abundant flocks (Isa. lx. 7), and, according to Diodorus, living by merchandise and rapine (Gesenius). From Petræa they subsequently extended as far as Babylon (Keil)—**and Kedar,**—"Black Skin ;" the Cedrei of Pliny (Gesenius, Keil, Rosenmüller) ; characterised as good bowmen (Isa. xxi. 17), and dwelling between Arabia Petræa and Babylon—**and Adbeel,**—"Miracle of God" (Gesenius) ; of whom nothing is known—**and Mibsam,**—"Sweet Odour" (Gesenius) ; equally uncertain.

Ver. 14.—**And Mishma,**—"Hearing" (Gesenius) ; Masma (LXX., Vulgate) ; connected with the *Maisaimeneis*, north-east of Medina (Knobel)—**and Dumah,**—"Silence ;" same as Stony Dumah, or Syrian Dumah, in Arabia, on the edge of the Syrian desert (Gesenius) ; mentioned in Isa. xxi. 11—**and Massa,**—"Burden ;" north-east of Dumah are the *Massanoi*.

Ver. 15. — **Hadar,** — "Chamber" (Gesenius) ; Hadad (1 Chron. i. 30, LXX., Samaritan, and most MSS.) ; though Gesenius regards Hadar as probably the true reading in both places ; identified with a tribe in Yemen (Gesenius) ; between Oman and Bahrein, a district renowned for its lancers (Keil)—**and Tema,**—"Desert" (Gesenius) ; Θαιμὰν (LXX.) ; the Θεμοί, on the Persian Gulf, or the tribe Bann Teim, in Hamasa (Knobel) ; a trading people (Job vi. 19 ; Isa. xxi. 14 ; Jer. xxv. 23)—**Jetur,** —"Enclosure" (Gesenius) ; the Itureans (Gesenius, Kalisch, Keil) — **Naphish,** — "Breathing" (Murphy) ; "Refreshment" (Gesenius) ; not yet identified—**and Kedemah** —"Eastward" (Gesenius) ; unknown.

Ver. 16.—**These are the sons of Ishmael, and these are their names, by their towns,** —unwalled encampments, from *hatzar*, to surround ; used of the movable villages of nomadic tribes (cf. Isa. xlii. 11)—**and by their castles ;**—fortified keeps (Murphy) ; tent villages (Keil) ; nomadic camps (Kalisch). Cf. Num. xxxi. 10 ; 1 Chron. vi. 39 ; Ps. lxix. 26 ; Ezek. xxv. 4)—**twelve princes**— this does not imply that Ishmael had only twelve sons, like Israel—a very suspicious circumstance (De Wette) ; but only that these twelve became phylarchs (Hävernick).

The Egyptian dodecarchy rested on a like earlier division of names. Homer mentions a similar case among the Phœnicians ('Odyss.,' viii. 390) ; Thucydides another in ancient Attica (ii. 15) ; vide Hävernick's ' Introd.,' § 18—**according to their nations** (or tribe divisions).

Vers. 17, 18.—**And these** are **the years of the life of Ishmael, an hundred and thirty and seven years :**—a life shorter by nearly half a century than that of Isaac (ch. xxxv. 21) ; does this prove the life-prolonging influence of piety ?—**and he gave up the ghost and died ; and was gathered unto his people** (vide on ver. 8). **And they dwelt from Havilah unto Shur, that is before Egypt, as thou goest toward Assyria** (vide ch. x. 29 ; xvi. 7) : and **he died**—literally, fell down ; not expired (Vulgate, à Lapide, Aben Ezra, et alii), but settled down, had his lot cast (Calvin, Keil, Kalisch); κατῴκησε (LXX.) —**in the presence of all his brethren** (a fulfilment of ch. xvi. 12).

HOMILETICS.

Vers. 12—18.—*The generations of Ishmael, or the biography of a prince.*
I. THE PRINCE'S NAME. Ishmael. 1. The *significance* of his name. "God hears." It was thus a perpetual reminder to its bearer of a grand religious truth, that God is essentially a hearer of prayer, and that he is never far from any of his intelligent and needy creatures. 2. The *occasion* of his getting it. (1) Before his birth, because the Lord had heard the affliction of his mother. (2) At his birth, because his father believed the report of Hagar concerning the instruction of the angel. 3. The *verification* of his name. When he lay beneath the shrub God heard the voice of his distressful cry (ch. xxi. 17).

II. THE PRINCE'S LINEAGE. Abraham's son. That—(1) *Proclaimed his dignity.* Though not a prince in the Church, he was a prince in the world, being Abraham's immediate descendant. Grace runs not in the blood, earthly rank does. (2) *Bespoke his privilege.* Jehovah reckoned it a great thing for Ishmael that he was Abraham's seed. To be the offspring of those who are exalted in earthly station is a special honour, though not so great an honour as to be descended from those who are eminent in grace. (3) *Implied his responsibility.* Degrees of rank in society are of God's ordaining, and involve the recipients thereof in corresponding obligations (Luke xii. 48).

III. THE PRINCE'S FAMILY. 1. *Princely in rank.* This quality they received by birth, being Ishmael's sons. 2. *Many in number.* They were twelve princes, and as such they developed into large and flourishing tribes and nations. This characteristic was due to grace, God having promised that kings and nations should spring from Hagar's son. 3. *Influential in power.* The twelve princes mentioned were powerful chieftains of as many clans.

IV. THE PRINCE'S DEATH. 1. *The time.* At 137 years. The days of all, even of princes, in this life are numbered. 2. *The manner.* "He expired." "There is no man that hath power over the spirit to retain the spirit" in the day of his death. 3. *The result.* "He was gathered unto his people," passing to the company of those who were like-minded with himself in the unseen world, as Abraham went to enjoy the society of those who were of kindred spirit with him.

V. THE PRINCE'S DOMINIONS. "His lot was cast in the presence of all his brethren," i. e. his empire was—1. *Outside of Canaan.* He had no part or lot in the inheritance of Issac. Neither have the world's princes as such any share in the heritage of heaven's peers. 2. *Among the tribes of earth.* And so the worldly man's portion is of the earth, earthy.

See—1. How comparatively unimportant the world's biographies are in the judgment of the Spirit. 2. How the children of the wicked often outnumber the offspring of the pious. 3. How it is appointed unto all men once to die, though not to all to die alike. 4. How certain it is that the wicked and the good shall be separated after death, since at death both are gathered unto their respective peoples. 5. How clearly and minutely God fulfils the promises he makes to wicked men no less than to good.

§ 9. The Generations of Isaac (ch. xxv 19—xxxv. 29).

EXPOSITION.

Ver. 19.—**And these** are **the generations of Isaac, Abraham's son.** The usual formula for the opening of a new section (cf. ch. ii. 4). **Abraham begat Isaac.** A reiteration in perfect harmony not only with the style of the present narrative, but of ancient historiography in general; in this instance specially designed to connect the subsequent streams of Isaac's posterity with their original fountain-head in Abraham.

Ver. 20.—**And Isaac was forty years old when he took Rebekah to wife,**—the valuable chronological fact here stated for the first time proves that Isaac was married three years after his mother's death (cf. ch. xxiii. 1)—**the daughter of Bethuel the Syrian of Padan-aram, the sister to Laban the Syrian** (vide on ch. xxii. 23 ; xxiv. 29). Though a descendant of Arphaxad (ch. x. 24), Bethuel is styled a Syrian, or Aramæan, from the country of his adoption. On Padan-aram vide ch. xxiv. 10.

Ver. 21.—**And Isaac entreated**—from a root signifying to burn incense, hence to pray, implying, as some think (Wordsworth, 'Speaker's Commentary'), the use of incense in patriarchal worship ; but perhaps only pointing to the fact that the prayers of the godly ascend like incense (Gesenius): cf. Tobit xii. 12 ; Acts x. 4. The word is commonly regarded as noting *precum multiplicationem, et vehementiam et perseverantiam* (Poole): cf. Ezek. xxxv. 13—**the Lord**—*Jehovah ;* not because vers. 21— 23 are the composition of the Jehovist (Tuch, Bleek, Davidson, *et alii*), but because the desired son was to be the heir of promise (Hengstenberg). The less frequent occurrence of the Divine name in the Thol'-doth of Isaac than in those of Terah has been explained by the fact that the historical matter of the later portion furnishes less occasion for its introduction than that of the earlier ; and the predominance of the name *Elohim* over that of *Jehovah* in the second stage of the patriarchal history has been partly ascribed to the employment after Abraham's time of such like equivalent expressions as "God of Abraham" and "God of my father" (Keil)—**for his wife,**—literally, *opposite to* his wife, *i. e.* beside his wife, placing himself opposite her, and conjoining his supplications with hers (Ainsworth, Bush) ; or, better, in behalf of his wife (LXX., Vulgate, Calvin, Keil, Kalisch), *i. e.* setting her over against him as the sole object to which he had regard in his intercessions (Luther)—**because she** was **barren :** —as Sarah had been before her (*vide* ch. xi. 30) ; the long-continued sterility of both

having been designed to show partly that "children are the heritage of the Lord" (Ps. cxxvii. 3), but chiefly that the children of the promise were to be not simply the fruit of nature, but the gift of grace — **and the Lord was entreated of him, and Rebekah his wife conceived** (cf. Rom. ix. 10).

Ver. 22. — **And the children struggled together within her.** The verb is expressive of a violent internal commotion, as if the unborn children had been dashing against one another in her womb. Cf. the story of Acrisius and Prœtus, who quarrelled before birth about their subsequent dominion (Apollod., II. ii. 1). *Vide* Rosenmüller, Scholia, *in loco*. **And she said, If it be so, why am I thus ?** Literally, *If so, why thus* (am) *I ?* Of obscure import, but probably meaning, "If so," *i. e.* if it is the case that I have conceived, "for what am I thus ?" what is the reason of these unwonted sensations that accompany my pregnancy ? (Aben Ezra, Calvin, Lange, Murphy) ; rather than, "If such be the sufferings of pregnancy, why did I seek to conceive ? " (Rashi, Rosenmüller), or, why have I conceived ? (Vulgate, Onkelos, Bush, Ainsworth), or, why do I yet live ? (Syriac, Keil, Kalisch, Delitzsch). **And she went to inquire of the Lord.** Not by *Urim* (Bohlen), since this method of inquiring at the Deity did not then exist (Numb. xxvii. 21) ; but either through a prophet, — Shem (Luther), Melchisedeck (Jewish interpreters), Heber (Lyra) ; more likely Abraham (Grotius, Ainsworth, Wordsworth, Kalisch, 'Speaker's Commentary'), or Isaac, the prophet nearest her (Lange),— or through herself by prayer, as in Ps. xxxiv. 5 (Calvin, Rosenmüller, Lange, Murphy, Inglis). The language seems to imply that by this time there was a regularly-appointed place for the worship of God by prayer and sacrifice—Theodoret suggests the family altar ; Delitzsch, Hagar's well.

Ver. 23.—**And the Lord said unto her,**— in a dream (Hävernick), a form of revelation peculiar to primitive times (ch. xv. 1 ; xx. 6 ; xxviii. 12 ; xxxvii. 5 ; xl. 5 ; xli. 1 ; xlvi. 2 ; cf. Job iv. 13 ; xxxiii. 15) ; but whether communicated directly to herself, or spoken through the medium of a prophet, the Divine response to her interrogation assumed an antistrophic and poetical form, in which she was informed that her unborn sons were to be the founders of two mighty nations, who, "unequal in power, should be divided in rivalry and antagonism from their youth" —**Two nations are in thy womb** (*i. e.* the ancestors and founders of two nations, viz., the Israelites and Idumeans), **and two manner of** people shall be separated from thy bowels; —literally, *and two peoples from thy bowels* (or womb) *are separated*, i. e. proceeding from thy womb, they shall be divided from and against each other—and the one **people shall be stronger than** the other **people** (literally, *and people shall be stronger than people*, i. e. the one shall prevail over the other); **and the elder shall serve the younger**—*i. e.* the descendants of the elder shall be subject to those of the younger. *Vide* inspired comments on this oracle in Mal. i. 2, 3 and Rom. ix. 12—33.

Ver. 24.—**And when her days to be delivered were fulfilled,**—literally, *and were fulfilled her days to bring forth;* ἐπλήρώ- θησαν αἱ ἡμέραι τοῦ τεκεῖν αὐτήν (LXX.; cf. Luke i. 57; ii. 6). Jarchi accounts for the different phrase used of Thamar (ch. xxxviii. 27), who also bore twins, by supposing that she had not completed her days, but gave birth to Pharez and Zarah in the seventh month (*vide* Rosenmüller, *in loco*) —**behold, there were twins in her womb** (cf. ch. xxxviii. 27, where the full form of the word for twins is given).

Ver. 25.—**And the first came out red,**— *Adhmoni*, πυῤῥάκης (LXX.), *rufus* (Vulgate), red-haired (Gesenius), of a reddish colour (Lange), containing an allusion to *Adham*, the red earth — **all over like an hairy garment.** Literally, *all of him as a cloak of hair* (not, as the LXX., Vulgate, *et alii*, all of him hairy, like a cloak); the fur cloak, or hair mantle, forming one notion (Gesenius). The appearance of the child's body, covered with an unusual quantity of red hair, was "a sign of excessive sensual vigour and wildness" (Keil), "a foreboding of the animal violence of his character" (Kalisch), "the indication of a passionate and precocious nature" (Murphy). **And they called his name Esau** — "the hairy one," from an unused root signifying to be covered with hair (Gesenius).

Ver. 26.—**And after that came his brother out, and his hand took hold on Esau's heel.** The inf. constr. standing for the finite verb (Ewald's 'Heb. Synt.,' § 304). Not simply followed close upon the heels of Esau (Kalisch), but seized Esau's heel, as if he would trip him up (Keil, Murphy). It has been contended (De Wette, Schumann, Knobel) that such an act was impossible, a work on obstetrics by Busch maintaining that an hour commonly intervenes between the birth of twins; but practitioners of eminence who have been consulted declare the act to be distinctly possible, and indeed it is well known that "a multitude of surprising phenomena are connected with births" (Hävernick), some of which are not greatly dissimilar to that which is here recorded. Delitzsch interprets the language as meaning only that the hand of Jacob reached out in the direction of his brother's heel, as if to grasp it; but Hosea xii. 3 explicitly asserts that he had his brother's heel by the hand while yet in his mother's womb. **And his name was called**—literally, *and he* (i. e. one) *called his name;* καὶ ἐκάλεσε τὸ ὄνομα αὐτοῦ (LXX.); *id circo appellavit eum* (Vulgate; cf. ch. xvi. 14; xxvii. 36)—**Jacob.** Not "Successor," like the Latin *secundus*, from *sequor* (Knobel, Kalisch); but "Heel-catcher" (Rosenmüller, Gesenius, Keil, Lange, Murphy), hence Supplanter (cf. ch. xxxvii. 36). **And Isaac was threescore years old when she bare them.** Literally, *in the bearing of them*, the inf. constr. taking the case of its verb (*vide* Gesenius, § 133) = when she (the mother) bare them; ὅτε ἔτεκεν αὐτοὺς Ῥε- βέκκα (LXX.); *quum nati sunt parvuli* (Vulgate); though, as Rebekah's name does not occur in the immediate context, and ילד is applied to the father (ch. iv. 18; x. 8, 13) as well as to the mother, the clause may be rendered *when he* (Isaac) *begat them* (Kalisch, Alford).

HOMILETICS.

Vers. 19—26.—*The childless pair.* I. THE DISAPPOINTED HUSBAND. 1. *The grievous affliction.* Rebekah, the wife of Isaac, was barren. Though neither uncommon nor unjust, this was to Isaac (1) a specially severe affliction, from its long continuance, from his love for Rebekah, from his own natural desire of offspring, but chiefly from his faith in the promise; (2) a highly beneficial affliction, serving to instruct and discipline his faith as to the true character of the children of the promise, to refine and intensify his affection for Rebekah, to purify and elevate his own spiritual life, and to enable him to realise his complete dependence on the grace of God. 2. *The earnest intercession.* "Isaac entreated the Lord for his wife." Isaac's supplication was (1) directed to the right quarter, since "children are the heritage of the Lord;" (2) conceived in the right spirit, the word "entreated" implying earnest and repeated application to the heavenly throne; (3) stated in the right way, with plainness and simplicity of speech; and (4) seconded by the right helper, Rebekah, according to one reading of the text, joining her entreaties with her husband's. Husbands and wives should be helpers, not hinderers, of each other's prayers. 3. *The gracious response.* "The Lord was entreated of Isaac, and Rebekah conceived." Note the character of God as the Hearer of prayer, the habitual practice of God, which is to listen to his people's supplications, the power which belongs to prayer of being able to prevail with God, and the special virtue which resides in united prayer (Matt. xviii. 19).

II. THE ANXIOUS WIFE. 1 *The unwonted experience.* In two respects the pregnancy of Rebekah was unusual. First, she had never conceived before; and secondly, the attendant sensations were uncommon. Great mercies are often accompanied by great discomforts to prevent gracious souls from resting in the gifts and neglecting the Giver. 2. *The remarkable interrogation.* "Rebekah went to inquire of the Lord." Her conduct was remarkable for the impatience it displayed, the piety it evinced, the faith it implied. If in her querulous exclamation there was sin, in her seeking to God with her anxiety there were grace and faith. 3. *The mysterious oracle.* This contained three distinct announcements: the first hopeful, that Rebekah should be the mother of twins; the second painful, that, besides being mutually antagonistic from their birth, her two sons should develop into hostile nations; the third unusual, that the elder should serve the younger.

III. THE HAPPY MOTHER. 1. *Her days were fulfilled.* A special mercy which pregnant mothers can appreciate. 2. *Her sons were born.* Another cause of rejoicing to a mother (John xvi. 21). (1) Their names. "Esau and Jacob." Names of men are sometimes prophetic of both character and condition. (2) Their birth: remarkable for the singular phenomenon by which it was accompanied. Jacob's holding of Esau's heel was intended to foreshadow the early character of Jacob, his future over-reaching of Esau, and his ultimate precedence in grace. *N.B* The first in nature is often last in grace. Between nature and grace there is perpetual antagonism. The great achievements of gracious souls have sometimes foreshadowings in nature. (3) Their appearance. Esau red like a hairy cloak; Jacob catching Esau's heel. The boy is oft the father of the man. 3. *Her husband was spared.* "Isaac was threescore years old when she bare them." A third mercy not always granted to mothers, to retain their husbands to participate in their maternal joys (1 Sam. iv. 19).

Learn—1. That children in a home are a special mark of Divine favour. 2. That anxious wives and mothers should carry their troubles to God's throne. 3. That the future histories and destinies of children are known to God, if not to their parents. 4. That mothers of families have peculiar joys as well as special sorrows.

HOMILIES BY VARIOUS AUTHORS.

Vers. 19—34.—*Divine purposes unfolded.* We are now entering a new stage of the sacred history, where we are looking less upon the development of one man's character than upon the unfolding purposes of Jehovah in the family with which he has made his covenant. Again we are in the region of—1. *Gracious interposition.* 2. *Supernatural assistance of human infirmity.* 3. *Prophetic announcements.* The atmosphere is that of the covenant. The children in the womb are two nations. The history of great peoples is anticipated.—R.

EXPOSITION.

Ver. 27.—**And the boys grew: and Esau was a cunning hunter,**—literally, *skilled in hunting; εἰδὼς κυνηγεῖν* (LXX.); *gnarus venandi* (Vulgate); a sportsman—**a man of the field;**—not a husbandman, *homo agricola* (Vulgate), who is differently denominated—*ish haadhamah* (ch. ix. 20); but one addicted to roaming through the fields in search of sport—*ἀγροικὸς* (LXX.); an indication of the rough, fiery nature and wild, adventurous life

of the elder of the two brothers—**and Jacob was a plain man,**—םֵת = *ἄπλαστος* (LXX.); *simplex* (Vulgate); *integer*, i. e. *mitis*, of mild and gentle manners (Rosenmüller); blameless, as a shepherd (Knobel); pious (Luther); righteous (Kalisch); obviously intended to describe Jacob as, both in character and life, the antithesis of Esau—**dwelling in tents**—i. e. loving to stay at home, as opposed to Esau, who loved to wander afield;

preferring a quiet, peaceable, domestic, and pious manner of existence to a life of "excitement, adventure, and danger," such as captivated Esau.

Ver. 28.—**And Isaac loved Esau, because he did eat of** his **venison**:—literally, *because his hunting* (i. e. its produce) *was in his mouth;* ὅτι ἡ θήρα αὐτοῦ βρῶσις αὐτῷ (LXX.); not perhaps the sole reason for Isaac's preference of Esau, though mentioned here because of its connection with the ensuing narrative. Persons of quiet and retiring disposition, like Isaac, are often fascinated by those of more sparkling and energetic temperament, such as Esau; mothers, on the other hand, are mostly drawn towards children that are gentle in disposition and home-keeping in habit. Accordingly it is added—**but Rebekah loved Jacob.**

Ver. 29.—**And Jacob sod pottage**:—literally, *cooked something cooked;* ἕψησε δὲ Ἰακὼβ ἕψημα (LXX.); prepared boiled food, of lentiles (*vide* on ver. 34)—**and Esau came from the field, and he** was **faint**—exhausted, the term being used of one who is both wearied and languishing (cf. Job xxii. 7 ; Ps. lxiii. 2 ; Prov. xxv. 25).

Ver. 30.—**And Esau said unto Jacob, Feed me** (literally, *let me swallow*, an expression for eating greedily), **I pray thee, with that same red** pottage ;—literally, *of that red, red* (*sc.* pottage), or thing, in his excitement forgetting the name of the dish (Knobel), or indicative of the haste produced by his voracious appetite (Wordsworth, Luther), though the duplication of the term *red* has been explained as a witty play upon the resemblance of the lentil broth to his own red skin, as thus : " Feed with that red me the red one" (Lange)—**for I** am **faint** (*vide supra*, ver. 29): **therefore was his name called Edom**—*i. e.* red. "There is no discrepancy in ascribing his name both to his complexion and the colour of the lentil broth. The propriety of a name may surely be marked by different circumstances" (A. G. in Lange). The Arabians are fond of giving surnames of that kind to famous persons. Cf. *Akil-al Murar*, which was given to Hodjr, king of the Kendites, owing to his wife saying in a passion, " He is like a camel that devours bushes" (*vide* Hävernick, ' Introduction,' § 18).

Ver. 31.—**And Jacob said, Sell me this day**—literally, *as the day;* as clearly as the day (Jarchi, Kimchi, Drusius); immediately, *statim* (Rosenmüller) ; perhaps simply to-day, σήμερον (LXX., Glassius, Gesenius, Kalisch ; cf. 1 Sam. ix. 13, 27 ; 1 Kings i. 49)—**thy birthright.** The right of primogeniture in the family of Abraham implied (1) succession to the earthly inheritance of Canaan ; (2) possession of the covenant bless-

ing transmitted through the paternal benediction ; and (3) progenitorship of the promised seed. Under the Mosaic institute the privileges of the firstborn were clearly defined. They involved succession to (1) the official authority of the father; (2) a double portion of the father's property ; and (3) the functions of the domestic priesthood (*vide* ch. xxvii. 4, 19, 27—29 ; xlix. 3 ; Exod. xxii. 29 ; Numb. viii. 14—17 ; Deut. xxi. 17).

Ver. 32.—**And Esau said, Behold, I** am **at the point to die**:—literally, *going to die;* meaning, " on the eve of expiring," through hunger ; " *ex animo testetur se mortis sensu urgeri*" (Calvin) ; or, " liable to death," through the dangerous pursuits of his daily calling (Ainsworth, Bush, Rosenmüller); or, what is most probable, " on the way to meet death "—uttered in a spirit of Epicurean levity, " Let us eat and drink, for to-morrow we die " (Keil, Kalisch)—**and what profit shall this birthright do to me?**—literally, *of what* (use) *this* (thing) *to me,* (called) *a birthright?* signifying, according to the sense attached to the foregoing expression, either, Of what use can a birthright be to a man dying of starvation ? or, The birthright is not likely ever to be of service to me, who am almost certain to be cut off soon by a violent and sudden death ; or, What signifies a birthright whose enjoyment is all in the future to a man who has only a short time to live ? I prefer present gratifications to deferred felicities.

Ver. 33.—**And Jacob said, Swear to me this day.** On the expression " this day " *vide supra*, ver. 31. The conduct of Jacob in this transaction is difficult to defend Though aware of the heavenly oracle that assigned to him the precedence in his father's house, he was far from being justified in endeavouring, by " cautious, prudent, and conciliatory proposals " (Murphy), but rather by unbelieving impatience, despicable meanness, and miserable craft, to anticipate Divine providence, which in due time without his assistance would have implemented its own designs. **And he sware unto him.** If Jacob's demand of an oath evinced ungenerous suspicion, Esau's giving of an oath showed a low sense of honour (Lange). **And he sold his birthright unto Jacob**—thus meriting the appellation of βέβηλος (Heb. xii. 16).

Ver. 34.—**Then Jacob gave Esau bread and pottage of lentiles**. "Lentiles (עֲדָשִׁים ; *Ervum lens*) were and are extensively and carefully grown in Egypt, Syria, and Palestine (2 Sam. xvii. 28 ; xxiii. 11) ; those of Egypt were, at a later period particularly famous ; and the manner of cooking them is even immortalised on monuments " (Kalisch). " The lentil does not grow more than six or eight inches high, and is pulled like flax, not cut with the sickle. When green it resembles an incipient pea-vine, only the leaves are differently arranged, smaller and more delicate—somewhat like those of the mimosa, or sensitive plant" (Thomson, ' Land and Book,' p. 596). **And he did eat and drink, and rose up, and went his way.** A graphic portrait of an utterly carnal mind, which lives solely in and for the immediate gratification of appetite. **Thus Esau despised his birthright—** and thus Scripture both proclaims his guilt and describes his offence.

HOMILETICS

Vers. 27—34.—*The twin brothers.* I. THE GROWING LADS. 1. *Diverse in daily calling.* Esau elected to follow the adventurous and roving life of a hunter ; Jacob, the simpler and less exciting occupation of keeping sheep. The principles that guided their respective choices are not explained ; but, like the selection of trades by other inexperienced youths, these were doubtless due to physical constitution, mental temperament, the influence of example, the effect of parental counsel, and above all the over-ruling providence of God. Cf. Cain and Abel (ch. iv. 2). 2. *Unlike in personal character.* Esau was a wild man in disposition no less than in action, a youth of strong animal propensities and essentially mundane proclivities. Jacob, without being religious, was quiet, sedate, fond of home life, and studious of peace, though not without a vein of duplicity in his soul's texture. This diversity in character, not due to parentage, birth, or education, which in both were alike, modern science would explain by molecular arrangement. Biblical theology goes a step behind, and traces it to God (Rom. ix. 11). 3. *Divided in parental favour.* Esau was loved by Isaac, Jacob by Rebekah. Besides being sinful in itself—scarcely anything can justify partiality in parental affection—the conduct of Isaac and Rebekah was more than likely hurtful to the lads, leaving on their consciences a sense of injustice, estranging them from each other in fraternal regard, and helping them unconsciously to fulfil the untoward destiny of mutual rivalry and jealousy already predicted for them.

II. THE TIRED HUNTER. 1. *His famishing condition.* If Esau was really faint, it indicated too great eagerness in following his sports. Even in honourable callings and profitable pursuits moderation is a duty. Rom. xii. 11 will assist traders and merchants to preserve the golden mean between slothfulness and slavishness in business. If Esau was not really faint, but only fatigued and hungry, it was an instance of exaggerated talking which with some is common, but by all should be avoided. 2. *His ravenous request.* This indicated an impatient spirit, which the words attempt to reproduce—a spirit characteristic of ill-balanced natures, resulting in most instances from unsubdued selfishness, betraying frequently into sins and faults that might otherwise be avoided, and at all times ill-befitting noble souls and renewed hearts. It also discovered a gluttonous appetite. The glutton's god is his belly, the glutton's temple his kitchen, the glutton's high priest his cook, the glutton's ritual, Let us eat and drink. Let saints beware of gluttony (Prov. xxiii. 2).

III. THE DESPISED BIRTHRIGHT. 1. *The base proposal.* "Sell me this day thy birthright." Jacob's desire to deprive Esau of his right of primogeniture was envious, unbrotherly, and, in the light of the pre-natal oracle, impatient and unbelieving. The conditions of sale were mean, exacting, and selfish. That Jacob's conduct was the fruit of grace or faith is difficult to credit, though God, who often works with despicable instruments, over-ruled it for the accomplishment of his own designs. 2. *The foolish answer.* "Behold, I am at the point to die : and what profit shall this birthright do to me ? " An ejaculation discovering both contempt for spiritual and doubt of future things ; the very essence of epicureanism, whether ancient or modern. 3. *The unholy oath.* "Swear to me this day ; and he sware unto him." On the part of both giver and receiver this was wrong. Neither had Esau right to part with his birthright until God in his providence took it from him ; nor had Jacob the right to accept that birthright until God transferred it to his hands. 4. *The unequal exchange.* Jacob got the birthright ; Esau got the pottage. Esau the type of many who accept the devil's bargain of the world (mostly an infinitesimal fragment of it) for a soul.

HOMILIES BY VARIOUS AUTHORS.

Ver. 27.—The "*cunning hunter*" is set over against the "*plain man dwelling in tents.*" I. THE TWO KINGDOMS, that of *material force* and that of *moral power*, are thus represented in contrast and rivalry.

II. GOD'S WAYS AND MAN'S WAYS CONTRASTED. The partialities of the parents foster the special faults of the children. *Esau* is *more* the *man of fleshly impulse* because Isaac loved him for his venison. *Jacob* is *more* the *crafty supplanter* because Rebekah by her favouritism encouraged him to take advantage of his brother.

III. THE IMPORTANCE OF HOME LIFE IN THE DEVELOPMENT OF CHARACTER. The sins of parents are generally in some form transmitted to children. *Esau's* new name was *Edom*, memento of his selfish succumbing to appetite. *Jacob's* new name was *Israel*, memento of the victory which by the grace of God he obtained. "*Esau despised his birthright.*" It was the natural working of a sensual nature. We begin by yielding to the lower impulses without thinking how they bind their cords round us. At last we lose the power of distinguishing a mere passing evil from an overwhelming danger, and when we ought to fight, cry, *I am at the point to die ;* then in wretched collapse all goes. What is this birthright, *what profit?* 1. *The loss of the sense of responsibility.* 2. *The absorbing hunger after present gratification.* 3. *The blindness to all proportion in life.* 4. The *dulness and stupidity* of the animalism which does not even care for the very birthright itself, though it is an earthly advantage. These are the *fearful payments* which they have to render who, like Esau, give themselves up to a mere *life of the flesh.*—R.

Ver. 32.—*Esau, the spiritually indifferent.* "What profit shall the birthright do to me ?" There was very much in Esau which would be greatly admired. He was of good humour, off-handed, manly, open, daring, and fond of field sports. He, and not Jacob, would in society have carried off the palm. He was a fair sample of a worldling. He knew nothing of the consecration of heart to God, or of spiritual aspirations. In the narrative we see how he showed indifference to the birthright, which carried with it certain spiritual advantages. He came in faint from the field, and the wafted odour of Jacob's savoury lentils filled him with longing. For a share in a mess of pottage he parted with his birthright.

I. THE UNRENEWED HEART ALWAYS UNDERVALUES MATERIAL, NATURAL, AND SPIRITUAL BLESSINGS. We may enjoy all the blessings God may shower upon us and not think of them as coming from God. We undervalue the gift of *life*, and the various means by which God has arranged that life shall be sustained. Then we forget that God preserves to us reason and the power of acquiring knowledge. But there are spiritual advantages analogous to those which Esau despised which we may treat indifferently. 1. Authority and honour as the firstborn. 2. A double portion of his father's possessions. 3. The privilege of the priesthood. Evidently the eldest son acted as the priest of the family in offering the sacrifices, and the priestly garb was kept for him. It was this that Rebekah had by her, and which she put on Jacob to deceive Isaac. 4. The peculiar blessing of his father, which was bestowed with solemnity. A covenant was ratified by eating, and hence Isaac sent out Esau to prepare venison; but Rebekah forestalled him. 5. Included in that blessing of Isaac was the promise made by God to Abraham, and which was to be handed on from one generation to another. It was for this Jacob longed. He rightly appraised the spiritual advantages connected with it. Though there was much that was mean in his character at first, he had these spiritual desires and faith in God not possessed by his brother. These brothers were twins, yet how diverse their character. It may have been that Jacob, knowing he was of equal age, felt he had an equal right to be accounted the firstborn. This may be said by way of excuse for that which otherwise would appear outrageous and mean. Probably when Esau said he was "at the point of death" he only meant it in the same way that we say "we are dying of hunger." Jacob asked the transfer because he knew his brother cared little about it, and because he may have heard him express his indifference to it. Jacob could not have taken it by violence, and Esau should have refused the suggestion with an emphatic "no;" say, "I will rather die than part with that." Esau may have even smiled at Jacob for caring so much about that which was of such little worth to him A depraved heart made him profane, indifferent, ungrateful, and rash.

II. A TIME IS SURE TO COME WHEN THE GOOD WE UNDERVALUED BECOMES OF GREATEST WORTH, AND WHEN IT MAY BE BEYOND OUR REACH. It was probably about twenty years after Esau had parted with his birthright that Isaac felt one day that his end was approaching, and desired to bless his son before he died. He was ignorant of the transfer which had been made. Esau deceived his father. He ignored a solemn compact. He would now rob his brother. He comes back perspiring and exhausted from the field, thinking that anyhow he has earned his father's blessing. He finds that Jacob has acted in his right and obtained the blessing. His own mother frustrates him, believing that she was acting rightly for her son Jacob. We can see how questionable were her doings, but we must not measure her nor Jacob by present moral standards. Esau weeps, "What, no blessing for thy firstborn?" He gets a blessing, but not the best. Deep his regret. He sees now his folly in its true light. "No place for repentance," &c. means no chance of repairing the mischief. Thus things done thoughtlessly in youth may have fearful after-consequences. Neglect of educational advantages, incurring of debt, acquirement of habits, rejection of appeals, and withstanding religious impressions. As the icicle freezes one drop at a time, so character is gradually formed. It depends on the water as to what the icicle will be. If muddy and tinged, the frozen mass will not be transparent; clear or thick, it is frozen and fixed, and will never be altered until dissolved altogether. Where are the warm rays that are to change our character? Esau sought to change his father's mind, but it was useless. Our heavenly Father is always willing to forgive if there be true repentance, but his forgiveness may not conquer the fixed evil habit. So long as there is life none should despair. See how David sinned, but he repented too. Esau lacked contrition. His sorrow was only remorse. What if we are risking the loss of some great spiritual advantage like to Esau's! We shall discover it on the death-bed or at the judgment bar. There is then a serious warning—1. To those who are trifling with religion. Can you push the cross aside, and laugh on Calvary's mount? 2. To those hardening their hearts in neglect. An old man once said to me, "It is no use talking of religion to me now; I am past it. There was a time once when I felt, but now I cannot." 3. To those who think it will be easier to repent and do the right later in life. God promises pardon when we repent, but he does not promise to prolong life. Probably there is not one present who has not heard this warning before, therefore it is to be feared it will be as unavailing as the preceding. Oh, Holy Spirit, forbid that it should.—H.

Ver. 34.—*Neglect of heavenly things.* "Thus Esau despised his birthright." Strange and sad that truths so important as those bearing on eternal life, even where believed, often exercise so slight influence. Yet so it is. How many like to hear the gospel in its fulness, and to be warned against neglecting it, yet in their lives show little of its power (Ezek. xxxiii. 32). How many live, content to know truth, forgetting that all our daily life tells for good or ill on our eternal life, and that opportunities are passing away. How many, believing that in every being there is a soul to be saved or lost, can yet see multitudes living in ungodliness without effort or even prayer for their recovery (cf. Luke xix. 41). Is not the spirit of Esau in these? He is called (Heb. xii. 16) a "profane person." Yet no crime or great fault is laid to his charge. There is an attractiveness in his character. We see in him an impulsive, thoughtless man; not what would be called a bad son; his father's favourite; having some regard to his parent's wishes (ch. xxviii. 8, 9); but swayed by passing things, and without self-denial. Hungry and weary with the chase, he craved the food he saw (cf. Matt. iv. 3). But the price? His birthright, the claim to a special benediction, the domestic priesthood (cf. Exod. xxii. 29), were as nothing. He did not realise their value (cf. Heb. xi. 1). The present was everything (cf. 1 Cor. xv. 32). The pleasant, genial, headlong man is pronounced "profane." Observe—

I. THE GRADUAL EFFECT OF SELF-INDULGENCE (cf. Matt. xix. 24). The birthright despised not through sudden temptation or any marked step of sin, but by worldly interests taking up the thoughts. Customs and maxims of the world tend to neglecting the birthright (cf. Matt. vi. 33). This is no ideal danger. No sharp line to tell when danger begins. Things perfectly allowable, even laudable, may choke spiritual life. Even in good work the mind may be so engrossed in the work itself that communion with God fades. There is need of habitual self-denial (John vi. 38) ; of keeping guard over the tendencies of daily life ; of definite aims, not passing wishes ; of making personal communion with God an essential part of each day's work.

II. THE DEADENING EFFECT IN RELATION TO REPENTANCE. "Time enough" is a fatal mistake (Acts xxiv. 25 ; 2 Cor. vi. 2). So far as we know Esau never repented. Even when Jacob received the blessing he was sorry, but there was no real change, no confession of error. Self was still the ruling power.

III. THE CALL TO CONSIDER OUR BIRTHRIGHT (Rom. viii. 17 ; 1 John iii. 2). Not merely a future blessing. Thinking of it thus leads to its being left out of view. Now there is reconciliation, peace, spirit of adoption, the Spirit's witness in our hearts, freedom of access in prayer, and promises to be realised in growing likeness to Christ and communion with him. Few would deliberately postpone to the end of life the claiming their birthright and making sure of it, the work of repentance and faith, and the casting away what has hindered. But many without set purpose do delay. Each time the call is put away is a victory for the tempter.—M.

EXPOSITION.

CHAPTER XXVI.

Ver. 1.—**And there was a famine in the land** (of Canaan), **beside the first** (*i. e.* first recorded) **famine that was in the days of Abraham**—at least a century previous (*vide* ch. xii. 10). **And Isaac**—who, since his father's death, had been residing at Hagar's well in the wilderness of Beersheba (ch. xxv. 11)—**went unto Abimelech king of the Philistines unto Gerar** (cf. ch. xx. 1, 2 ; xxi. 22). Seventy or eighty years having elapsed since Abraham's sojourn in Gerar, it is scarcely probable that this was the monarch who then reigned.

Ver. 2.—**And the Lord** (Jehovah, *i. e.* the God of the covenant and of the promise) **appeared unto him,**—only two Divine manifestations are mentioned as having been granted to the patriarch. Either the peaceful tenor of Isaac's life rendered more theophanies in his case unnecessary ; or, if others were enjoyed by him, the brief space allotted by the historian to the record of his life may account for their omission from the narrative. Though commonly understood as having occurred in Gerar (Keil, Lange, Murphy), this appearance is perhaps better regarded as having taken place at Lahai-roi, and as having been the cause of Isaac's turning aside into the land of the Philistines (Calvin) —**and said, Go not down into Egypt**—whither manifestly he had been purposing to migrate, as his father had done on the occasion of the earlier dearth (ch. xii. 10). Jacob in the later famine was instructed to go down to Egypt (ch. xlvi. 3, 4) ; Abraham in the first scarcity was left at liberty to think and act

for himself. **Dwell in the land which I will tell thee of** (*i. e.* Philistia, as appears from the preceding verse).

Ver. 3.—**Sojourn in this land,**—viz., Philistia (Murphy, Alford), though otherwise regarded as Canaan (Lange, Keil, Calvin)— **and I will be with thee, and will bless thee.** Of this comprehensive promise, the first part was enjoyed by, while the second was distinctly stated to, Abraham (cf. ch. xii. 2). God's presence with Isaac of higher significance than his presence with Ishmael (ch. xxi. 20). **For unto thee, and unto thy seed, will I give all these**—הָאֵל, an archaism for הָאֵלֶּה (cf. ch. xix. 8, 25)—**countries** (*i. e.* Canaan and the surrounding lands), **and I will perform the oath** (*vide* ch. xxii. 16) **which I sware unto Abraham thy father.**

Ver. 4.—**And I will make thy seed to multiply as the stars of heaven** (*vide* ch. xv. 1—6), **and will give unto thy seed all these countries** (*i. e.* the territories occupied by the Canaanitish tribes) ; **and in thy seed shall all the nations of the earth be blessed** (cf. ch. xii. 3 ; xxii. 18).

Ver. 5.—**Because that Abraham obeyed** (literally, *hearkened to*) **my voice** (a general description of the patriarch's obedience, which the next clause further particularises), **and kept my charge,** — *custodierit custodiam* (Calvin) ; observed my observances (Kalisch) ; the charge being that which is intended to be kept — **my commandments,** — *i. e.* particular injunctions, specific enactments, express or occasional orders (cf. 2 Chron. xxxv. 16)—**my statutes,**—or permanent ordinances, such as the passover ; literally, *that which is* *graven on tables or monuments* (compare Exod. xii. 14)—**and my laws**—which refer to the great doctrines of moral obligation. The three terms express the contents of the Divine observances which Abraham observed.

Ver. 6.—**And Isaac dwelt in Gerar**—as God had shown and enjoined him.

HOMILETICS.

Vers. 1—6.—*A good man's perplexity.* I. THE CONTEMPLATED JOURNEY. 1. *Its projected destination.* Egypt. Renowned for fertility, the land of the Pharaohs was yet no proper resort for the son of Abraham, the heir of Canaan, and the friend of God. It was outside the land of promise; it had been to Abraham a scene of peril, and it was not a place to which he was directed to turn. Considerations such as these should have operated to deter Isaac from even entertaining the idea of a pilgrimage to Egypt. But the behaviour of this Hebrew patriarch is sometimes outdone by that of modern saints, who not simply project, but actually perform, journeys, of pleasure or of business, across the boundary line which separates the Church from the world, into places where their spiritual interests are endangered, and that too not only without the Divine sanction, but sometimes in express violation of that authority. 2. *Its ostensible occasion.* The famine. A severe trial, especially to a flock-master. It was yet by no means an exceptional trial, but one which had occurred before in the experience of the inhabitants of Canaan, and in particular of his father, and might possibly recur to himself, just as life's afflictions generally bear a singular resemblance to one another (1 Cor. x. 13; 1 Pet. iv. 12). It was not an accidental trial, but had been appointed and permitted by that Divine wisdom without whose sanction no calamity can fall on either nation or individual, saint or sinner (Deut. xxxii. 39; Ps. lxvi. 11; Amos iii. 6). And just as little was it purposeless, being designed to initiate Isaac in that life discipline from which no child of God can escape (Acts xiv. 22; Heb. xii. 11; James i. 2, 3). 3. *Its secret inspiration.* Unbelief. Jehovah, who had given the land to Isaac, could easily have maintained him in it notwithstanding the dearth, had it been his pleasure not to provide a way of escape. Had Isaac not at this time been walking somewhat by sight, it is probable his thoughts would not have turned to Egypt. Most of the saint's doubtful transactions and dangerous projects have a secret connection with the spirit of unbelief which causes to err.

II. THE DIVINE INTERPOSITION. 1. *Prohibiting.* "Go not down into Egypt." That Jacob subsequently went down to Egypt in obedience to Divine instructions is no proof that Isaac would have been blameless had he gone down without them. Abraham did so, but it is not certain that God approved of his conduct in that matter. Besides, though it could be shown that Abraham incurred no guilt and contracted no hurt by residence in Egypt, it would not follow that his son might venture thither with impunity and without sin. Hence the proposed journey was interdicted. So God in his word debars saints from going down to the unspiritual and unbelieving world to endamage or imperil their souls' higher interests. 2. *Prescribing.* "Dwell in the land which I shall tell thee of: sojourn in this land." It is always safest for the saint in seasons of perplexity to wait for and to follow the light from heaven. Sufficient guidance God has promised, through his Spirit, by his word, and in his providence, to enable gracious ones who wait upon his teaching to detect the path of duty and the place of safety. 3. *Promising.* For Isaac's encouragement the various promises of the Abrahamic covenant are repeated, renewed, and confirmed to himself for his father's sake; embracing promises of the Divine presence—" I will be with thee "—and the Divine blessing—" and will bless thee ; " in which latter are comprehended the inheritance,—" all these countries,"—the seed,—" I will make thy seed to multiply,"—and the universal salvation—" in thy seed shall all the nations of the earth be blessed," which had been promised and guaranteed to Abraham by oath. So has God given to believers " exceeding great and precious promises " for Christ's sake, because of the covenant made with him, on the ground of the obedience rendered, and for the merit of the sacrifice presented, by him.

III. THE FILIAL OBEDIENCE. "Isaac dwelt in Gerar," having removed thither in compliance with the Divine instructions. Like Abraham's, Isaac's obedience was—

1. *Minute*, exactly following the Divine prescription.   2. *Prompt*, putting into immediate execution the Divine commandment.   3. *Patient*, remaining in the land of the Philistines till God in his providence indicated it was time to remove.   So should Christ's followers obey.

HOMILIES BY VARIOUS AUTHORS.

Ch. xxvi.—*Line upon line, in God's teaching.*   Isaac, like his father, has his time of sojourn among the Philistines.   The events of his intercourse with the Abimelech of his day resemble those of the former patriarch, though there are differences which show that the recurrence is *historical*.

I. GOD REPEATS HIS LESSONS that they may make the deeper impression.   The intention of the record is to preserve a certain *line of Divine guidance.*   Isaac trod in the footsteps of Abraham.   We have Isaac's *wells, oaths, feast, Shebah*—all following close upon those of the preceding generation.

II. The SAME PRESERVATION OF THE COVENANT RACE in the midst of heathens confirms that covenant.   The same lesson of *special providential protection and blessing* is thus repeated and enforced.   Again the same *contrast of man's infirmity with God's unchangeableness.*   The perversity of the fleshly-minded man forming a marriage connection with heathen people, and bringing grief of mind to his parents, reveals the distinctness of *the world* from *the kingdom of God.—R.*

EXPOSITION.

Ver. 7.—**And the men of the place** (*i. e.* the inhabitants of Gerar) **asked** him (literally, *asked*, or made inquiries ; probably first at each other, though ultimately the interrogations might reach Isaac himself) **of his wife** (being in all likelihood fascinated by her beauty) ; **and he said,**—falling into the same infirmity as Abraham (ch. xii. 13 ; xx. 2)—**She** is **my sister** :—which was certainly an equivocation, since, although sometimes used to designate a female relative generally (*vide* ch. xxiv. 60), the term "sister" was here designed to suggest that Rebekah was his own sister, born of the same parents.   In propagating this deception Isaac appears to have been actuated by a similar motive to that which impelled his father—**for he feared to say,** She is **my wife ; lest,** said he (*sc.* to himself, the words describing the good man's secret apprehensions), **the men of the place should kill me for Rebekah ;**—the historian adding, as the explanation of his fears—**because she** was **fair to look upon** (*vide* ch. xxiv. 16).

Ver. 8.—**And it came to pass, when he had been there a long** time (literally, *when were prolonged to him there the days*), **that Abimelech king of the Philistines looked out at a window, and saw, and, behold, Isaac** was **sporting with Rebekah his wife**—*i. e.* caressing and using playful liberties with her, which showed she was not a sister, but a wife—παιζοντα (LXX.), *jocantem* (Vulgate).

Ver. 9.—**And Abimelech called Isaac, and said, Behold, of a surety she** is **thy wife: and how saidst thou, She** is **my sister?** **And Isaac said unto him, Because I said** (*sc.* in my heart, or to myself), **Lest I die for her.**

Ver. 10.—**And Abimelech said, What is this thou hast done unto us? one of the people might lightly have lien with thy wife,**—literally, *within a little* (cf. Ps. lxxiii. 2 ; cxix. 87) *one of the people might have lain with thy wife*—**and thou shouldest**—*i. e.* (within a little) *thou mightest*—**have brought** (or caused to come) **guiltiness upon us** (cf. ch. xx. 9, where הָטָאָת is used instead of אָשָׁם).

Ver. 11.—**And Abimelech charged all** his (literally, *the*) **people, saying, He that toucheth**—in the sense of injureth (cf. Josh. ix. 19 ; Ps. cv. 15)—**this man or his wife shall surely be put to death.**   The similarity of this incident to that related in ch. xx. concerning Abraham in Gerar may be explained without resorting to the hypothesis of different authors.   The stereotyped character of the manners of antiquity, especially in the East, is sufficient to account for the danger to which Sarah was exposed recurring in the case of Rebekah three quarters of a century later.   That Isaac should have resorted to the miserable expedient of his father may have been due simply to a lack of originality on the part of Isaac ; or perhaps the recollection of the success which had attended his father's adoption of this wretched subterfuge may have blinded him to its true character.   But from whatever cause resulting, the resemblance between the two narratives cannot be held as destroying the credibility of either, and all the more that a careful scrutiny will detect sufficient dissimilarity between them to establish the authenticity of the incidents which they relate.

HOMILETICS.

Vers. 7—11.—*A good man's transgression.* I. A LIE TOLD. 1. An *unmitigated* lie. It was scarcely entitled to claim the apology of being what Abraham's falsehood was, an equivocation, Rebekah not being Isaac's half-sister, but cousin. 2. A *deliberate* lie. Asked about his relations to Rebekah, he coolly replies that they are sister and brother. He had no right to suppose his interrogators had ulterior designs against Rebekah's honour. 3. A *cowardly* lie. All falsehoods spring from craven fear—fear of the consequences that may flow from telling the honest truth. 4. A *dangerous* lie. By his wicked suppression of the truth he was guilty of imperilling the chastity of her whom he sought to protect. Almost all falsehoods are perilous, and most of them are mistakes. 5. An *unnecessary* lie. No lie ever can be necessary ; but least of all could this have been, when God had already promised to be with him in the land of the Philistines. 6. An *unbelieving* lie. Had Isaac's faith been active, he would hardly have deemed it needful to disown his wife. 7. A wholly *worthless* lie. Isaac might have remembered that twice over his father had resorted to this miserable stratagem, and that in neither instance had it sufficed to avert the danger which he dreaded. But lies generally are wretched hiding-places for endangered bodies or anxious souls.

II. A LIE DETECTED. 1. God by his providence assists in the detection of liars. By the merest accident, as it might seem, Abimelech discovered the true relationship of Isaac and Rebekah ; but both the time, place, and manner of that discovery were arranged by God. So the face of God is set against them that do evil, even though they should be his own people. 2. Liars commonly assist in their own detection. Truth alone is sure-footed, and never slips ; error is liable to stumble at every step. It is difficult to maintain a disguise for any lengthened period. The best fitting mask is sure in time to fall off. Actions good in themselves often lead to the detection of crimes.

III. A LIE REPROVED. The conduct of Isaac Abimelech rebukes—1. With *promptitude.* Sending for Isaac, he charges him with his sin. It is the part of a true friend to expose deception whenever it is practised, and, provided it be done in a proper spirit, the sooner it is done the better. Sin that long eludes detection is apt to harden the sinning heart and sear the guilty conscience. 2. With *fidelity.* Characterising it as (1) a surprising inconsistency on the part of a good man like Isaac ; (2) a reckless exposure of his wife's person, which was far from becoming in a kindly husband ; and (3) an unjustifiable offence against the people of the land, who, by his carelessness and cowardice, might have been led into grievous wickedness. 3. With *forgiveness.* That Abimelech did not intend to exact punishment from Isaac, or even cherish resentment against him in consequence of his behaviour, he proved by charging his people to beware of injuring in any way either Isaac or Rebekah. It is good and beautiful when mercy seasons judgment, and the reproofs of friendship are accompanied by messages of love.

EXPOSITION.

Ver. 12.—**Then Isaac sowed in that land,** —viz., Philistia. Though a distinct advance on the purely nomadic life pursued by Abraham, this did not imply fixed property in, or even permanent settlement on, the soil, "but only annual tenancy" thereof. Robinson (i. 77) mentions a colony of the Tawarah Arabs, about fifty families, living near Abu Zabel, in Egypt, who cultivated the soil and yet dwelt in tents. "The Biblical patriarchs were not mere Bedawîn wanderers, like those who now occupy the Eastern deserts. They had large herds of cattle, which genuine Bedawîns have not ; they

tilled the ground, which these robbers never do ; and they accommodated themselves, without difficulty or reluctance, to town and city when necessary, which wild Arabs cannot endure" ('Land and Book,' p. 296)— **and received in the same year an hundredfold**—literally, *an hundred measures,* i. e. for each measure of that which he sowed ; an exceptional return even for Philistia, though "the country is no less fertile than the very best of the Mississippi Valley" ('Land and Book,' p. 557) ; and Arab grain stores at *Nŭttâr-abu-Sŭmâr,* in the vicinity of Gaza, still proclaim the remunerative yield of its harvests (Robinson, vol. i. p. 292). Herodotus (i. 193) speaks of two and three hundred-fold as having been reaped on the plain of Babylonia ; but in Palestine the usual rate of increase was from thirty to a hundred-fold (*vide* Matt. xiii. 23). The reading "an hundred of barley" (LXX., Syriac, Michaelis) is not to be preferred to that in the Textus Receptus. **And the Lord blessed him**—as he had promised (ver. 3).

Ver. 13.—**And the man waxed great,**— like his father before him (cf. ch. xxiv. 1, 35)—**and went forward,**—literally, *went going*, the verb followed by the infinitive expressing constant growth or progressive increase (cf. ch. viii. 3 ; xii. 9 ; Judges iv. 24)—**and grew until he became very great** —"as any other farmer would who reaped such harvests" ('Land and Book').

Ver. 14.—**For he had** (literally, *there was to him*) **possession of flocks, and possession of herds, and great store of servants :**— γεώργια πολλά (LXX.), *i.e.* much husbandry, the abstract being put for the concrete, "implying all manner of work and service belonging to a family, and so servants and tillage of all sorts" (Ainsworth) ; but the reference rather seems to be to the number of his household, or domestic slaves, *plurimum familiæ* (Vulgate)—**and the Philistines envied him.** The patriarch's possessions (*mikneh*, from *kanah*, to acquire) excited jealous feeling (from root *kana*, to burn) in the breasts of his neighbours (cf. Eccles. iv. 4).

Ver. 15.—**For all the wells which his father's servants had digged in the days of Abraham his father** (*vide* ch. xxi. 30), **the Philistines had stopped them, and filled them with earth.** This act, commonly regarded as legitimate in ancient warfare, was practically to Isaac an act of expulsion, it being impossible for flocks and herds to exist without access to water supplies. It was probably, as the text indicates, the outcome of envy, rather than inspired by fear that Isaac in digging and possessing wells was tacitly claiming the ownership of the land.

Ver. 16.—**And Abimelech said unto Isaac** (almost leading to the suspicion that the Philistine monarch had instigated the outbreak of hostilities amongst his people), **Go from us** (a royal command rather than a friendly advice) ; **for thou art much mightier than we.** The same apprehension of the growing numbers and strength of Isaac's descendants in Egypt took possession of the heart of Pharaoh, and led to their enslavement (*vide* Exod. i. 9).

Ver. 17.—**And Isaac**—perhaps not without remonstrance, but without offering resistance, as became a saint (Matt. v. 5 ; Rom. xii. 17, 18 ; Heb. xii. 14 ; 1 Pet. iii. 9)

—**departed thence** (*i. e.* from Gerar), **and pitched his tent in the valley of Gerar,** —a valley or *nahal* meant a low, flat region watered by a mountain stream. The Wady Gerar has been identified with the *Joorf-el-Gerar*, the rush or rapid of Gerar, three hours south-east of Gaza—**and dwelt there.**

Ver. 18. — **And Isaac digged again** — literally, *returned and digged*, i. e. re-dug (cf. 2 Kings xx. 5)—**the wells of water, which they** (the servants of Abraham) **had digged in the days of Abraham his father;** —from which it appears that Abraham had digged other wells besides that of Beersheba (ch. xxi. 31)—**for the Philistines had stopped them after the death of Abraham :**—which was a violation of the league into which Abimelech had entered with the patriarch (*vide* ch. xxi. 23)—**and he called their names after the names by which his father had called them**—and with which Isaac was sufficiently acquainted.

Ver. 19.—**And Isaac's servants digged in the valley, and found there a well of springing water.** Literally, *living water* (cf. Levit. xiv. 5, 6 ; Zech. xiv. 8 ; Rev. xxi. 6).

Ver. 20.—**And the herdmen of Gerar**— i. e. Abimelech's servants (ch. xxi. 25)—**did strive with Isaac's herdmen,**—as Lot's with those of Abraham (ch. xiii. 7)—**saying, The water is ours :**—literally, *to us* (belong) *the waters*—**and he called the name of the well Esek** ("Strife") ; **because they strove with him**—the verb being עָשַׂק, to strive about anything.

Ver. 21.—**And they digged another well** (Isaac having yielded up the first), **and strove for that also :**—"The beginning of strife is as when one letteth out water" (Prov. xvii. 14)—**and he called the name of it Sitnah**—"Contention" (from שָׂטַן, to lie in wait as an adversary ; whence Satan) ; probably in *Wady-es-Shutein*, near Rehoboth (*vide infra*).

Ver. 22.—**And he removed from thence** (yielding that too), **and digged another well ; and for that they strove not** (perhaps as being beyond the boundaries of Gerar) : **and he called the name of it Rehoboth ;**— i. e. "Wide spaces" (hence "streets," ch. xix. 2) ; from רָחַב, to be or become broad ; conjectured to have been situated in the *Wady Ruhaibeh*, about eight and a half hours to the south of Beersheba, where are still found a well named *Bir-Rohebeh* and ruins of a city of the same name (Robinson, vol. i. p. 289 ; Thomson, 'Land and Book,' p. 558)—**and he said, For now the Lord hath made room** (literally, *hath made a broad space*) **for us, and we shall be fruitful in the land.**

HOMILETICS.

Vers. 12—22.—*A good man's prosperity.* I. WHENCE IT PROCEEDED. 1. *The industry of Isaac.* "Isaac sowed in that land, and received in the same year an hundredfold." An intimate connection subsists between diligence and prosperity. (1) As there is no harvest without a seed-time, so there is no increase of wealth without the putting forth of personal labour in its acquisition (cf. Prov. x. d; xiii. 4; xxviii. 19). (2) As by God's appointment harvest follows seed-time, so commonly "the hand of the diligent maketh rich" (cf. Prov. xiii. 4; xxi. 5; xxviii. 19). 2. *The blessing of God.* "And the Lord blessed him." As without Divine assistance the best contrived and most laboriously applied means may fail in the accumulation of material goods, so with heavenly succour the least likely instruments can achieve success. The harvests of the farmer depend more upon the goodness of God than upon the excellence of the plough (cf. Ps. cxxvii. 1, 2).

II. IN WHAT IT RESULTED. 1. *The envy of the Philistines.* Envy, one of the works of the flesh (Gal. v. 19; James iv. 5), a frequent characteristic of evil men (1 Cor. iii. 3; Titus iii. 3), an occasional infirmity of pious souls (1 Cor. iii. 3; Phil. i. 15; 1 Pet. ii. 1), and straitly forbidden by the law of God (Exod. xx. 17; Ps. xxxvii. 1; James v. 9), is commonly excited by observing the prosperity of others (Ps. xxxvii. 7; lxxiii. 7; Eccles. iv. 4; cf. Rachel and Leah, ch. xxx. 1, 15; Joseph's brethren, ch. xxxvii. 4—11, 19, 20; Acts vii. 9; Miriam and Aaron, Num. xii. 1—10; the princes of Darius, Dan. vi. 4), is usually accompanied with some degree of hatred (Cain, ch. iv. 4—8; Sarah, ch. xvi. 5, 6; Laban, ch. xxxi. 5), and inevitably tends, as in the case of the Philistines, to hostility, secret or open. 2. *The suspicion of Abimelech.* The growing power of the patriarch had filled the monarch's mind with alarm. Interpreting the character of Isaac by his own, he conceived it impossible to possess large resources without using them to acquire dominion over others. Modern kings and statesmen are scarcely further advanced, the prosperity of neighbouring empires being commonly regarded as a menace to the liberties of their own. It is the mission of Christianity, as regards both nations and individuals, to show how power of every kind can be possessed without injury, and wielded with advantage, to the highest interests of others.

III. HOW IT WAS MAINTAINED. By—1. *Patience,* or the exhibition of a meek and unresisting spirit in submitting to injury. When Abimelech requested him to leave the town of Gerar, he left. When the Philistines filled up his father's wells, he quietly dug them out again. When the herdmen of Gerar wrangled with his shepherds about a spring, he simply gave it up, and sought another; and when this too was disputed, he retired and sank a third. And all the while his flocks and herds kept on multiplying. A beautiful example of the spirit which Christ has enjoined (Matt. v. 39—42), and of the promise which Christ has made (Matt. v. 5) to his followers. 2. *Perseverance,* or the diligent exercise of means in selecting pasture grounds and digging wells; not permitting himself to be discouraged by the opposition of his neighbours, but, while peacefully allowing himself to be despoiled, steadily attending to his business. An illustration of that quiet, determined, and unwearied application which often contributes more to success in life than brilliant abilities. 3. *Piety,* or the grateful recognition of God's hand in putting an end to the irritation and annoyance of his neighbours, and giving him at last a comfortable settlement at Rehoboth. It is grace in God which affords quiet neighbourhoods to reside in, easy circumstances to live in, and hopeful futures to trust in; and it is piety in us to acknowledge that grace.

Learn—1. That there is only one royal road to material prosperity, viz., diligence and devotion. 2. That if material prosperity can procure comforts, it is also attended by drawbacks. 3. That material prosperity is often thrown away in litigation when it might be preserved by submission. 4. That material prosperity should stir the heart's gratitude to God.

HOMILIES BY VARIOUS AUTHORS.

Ver. 22.—*Digging wells of salvation.* "And he removed from thence, and digged another well." Historically, an instance of a meek and quiet spirit in contact with the world. Wells precious. Often formed with much labour. Herdsmen of Gerar took what Isaac had digged. Twice he yielded for the sake of peace. Then he digged another, and for it they strove not. His example (cf. Matt. v. 39; 1 Cor. vi. 7). But we may also observe a typical significance. Wells, fountains, sources of "living water" (Isa. xii. 3; Zech. xiii. 1) connected with spiritual blessings (cf. 1 Cor. x. 4 with John iv. 14, and vii. 39).

I. Isaac digged, to find "the gift of God" (common Eastern name for water). The gift is from God alone (Isa. xliv. 3; Zech. xii. 10). His will to bless appears through the whole Bible—in the first formation of man, and in care for the salvation of sinners (Luke xix. 10). But many, though thirsty, do not seek living water. They have not peace. Separation from God brings unrest (Isa. lvii. 20). But the cause is not believed, and the way of comfort not loved. Many try all ways to find peace except the right one. They will follow preachers, or take up systems, or join associations. But Christ's word is "Come unto me." Again, many will not dig; content merely to wish. God who bestows the gift has appointed means (Matt. xi. 12). These do not really desire a work of grace in their souls. Want to be made safe, not to be renewed; to be delivered from fear, but not disturbed just now. Hence do not search their Bibles (Ps. cxix. 130), or pray for the Holy Spirit (Ezek. xxxvii. 9), or care for the salvation of others (1 John iii. 17). It is God's will we should dig. He may send a blessing unsought. But usually he works through means. The Bible, prayer, the Lord's table, Christian converse, Christian work (Prov. xi. 25), all are as wells, means for getting the water of life; nothing in themselves, yet made effectual where the blessing is desired.

II. Hindrances. Let none expect to possess wells of salvation without. They form the trial of faith (1 Pet. i. 7). From those who love not God. A Christian member of a worldly family, or cast among careless associates, meets many hindrances. They may be open or veiled; in opposition or in mistaken kindness. And time for prayer is intruded on, and work for God is hindered, and a constant opposing influence is felt to chill the love of God. Or the hindrance may be from within. In prayer the mind overpowered by intrusive thoughts; besetting sins constantly gaining the victory; our spirits not in harmony with the "still small voice." Remember it is God's will through trial to give victory (1 Cor. x. 13). Amalek fought against Israel (Exod. xvii.) as the herdsmen strove against Isaac, but the way of victory was the same in both instances—trust and perseverance.

III. Digged another well (Gal. vi. 9). Will the Lord fail his people though surrounded by hindrances? Is some means of grace debarred? Is some line of Christian work, some way of Christian progress, closed against thee? Dig another well. Seek and pray for other channels in which to consecrate thy life. Perhaps the real foe hindering thee was self-will, and God has helped thee to put down self. Jesus cried, "Come unto me and drink." Whatever be the well, he is the source of its spring. Make it clear to your own heart that you are pressing to him. Tell God that it is indeed so. Then in some form or other the prayer, "Spring up, O well," shall have an abundant answer.—M.

EXPOSITION.

Ver. 23. — **And he** (viz., Isaac) **went up from thence** (Rehoboth, where latterly he had been encamped) **to Beer-sheba**—a former residence of Abraham (ch. xxi. 33), situated "near the water-shed between the Mediterranean and the Salt Sea" (Murphy), hence approached from the low-lying wady by an ascent.

Ver. 24.—**And the Lord appeared unto him the same night** (*i. e.* the night of his arrival at Beersheba), **and said** (in a dream or vision), **I** (the pronoun is emphatic) am **the God** (the Elohim) **of Abraham thy father** (the language is expressive not alone of the covenant relationship which subsisted between Jehovah and the patriarch while the latter lived, but also of the present continuance of that relationship, since Abraham, though dead, had not ceased to be) : **fear not** (cf. ch. xv. 1, in which the same encouraging admonition is addressed to Abraham after his battle with the kings), **for I am with thee, and will bless thee, and multiply thy seed**—a repetition of promises already given to himself (*vide* vers. 3, 4)—**for my servant Abraham's sake**—a reason declaring God's gracious covenant, and not personal merit, to be the true source of blessing for Isaac.

Ver. 25.—**And he** (*i. e.* Isaac, in grateful response to the Divine Promiser who had appeared to him) **builded an altar there,**—the first instance of altar building ascribed to Isaac ; "those erected by his father no doubt still remaining in the other places where he sojourned" (Inglis) — **and called upon the name of the Lord,**—*i. e.* publicly celebrated his worship in the midst of his household (*vide* on ch. xii. 7, 8)—**and pitched his tent there** (the place being now to him doubly hallowed by the appearance of the Lord to himself as well as to his father) : **and there Isaac's servants digged a well**—a necessary appendage to a flockmaster's settlement.

Ver. 26.—**Then** (literally, *and*) **Abimelech went to him from Gerar,** — the object of this visit was to resuscitate the alliance which had formerly existed between the predecessor of Abimelech and Abraham (ch. xxi. 22—32) ; yet the dissimilarity between the two accounts is so great as to discredit the hypothesis that the present is only another version of the earlier transaction—**and Ahuzzath one of his friends,**—מֵרֵעֵהוּ ; neither ὁ νυμφαγωγὸς αὐτοῦ (LXX.), nor a suite or number of his friends (Onkelos), nor one of his friends (A. V.) ; but his friend, and probably his privy councillor (Keil, Kalisch, Murphy), whose presence along with the monarch and his general marks the first point of difference between the present and the former incident—**and Phichol** (*vide* ch. xxi. 22) **the chief captain of his army.**

Ver. 27. — **And Isaac said unto them, Wherefore**—מַדּוּעַ, contr. from מָה יָדוּעַ, **what** is taught ? = for what reason (cf. τί μαθών) —**come ye to me, seeing** (literally, *and*) **ye hate me, and have sent me away from you?** While animadverting to the personal hostility to which he had been subjected, Isaac says nothing about the wells of which he had been deprived : a second point of difference between this and the preceding narrative of Abraham's covenant with the Philistine king.

Ver. 28.—**And they said, We saw certainly**—literally, *seeing we saw*, i. e. we assuredly perceived, or, we have indeed discovered (*vide* Ewald's ' Heb. Synt.,' § 312).

Abimelech and his ministers first explain the motive which has impelled them to solicit a renewal of the old alliance—**that the Lord was with thee** :—the use of Jehovah instead of Elohim, as in ch. xxi. 22, does not prove that this is a Jehovistic elaboration of the earlier legend. Neither is it necessary to suppose that the term Jehovah is a Mosaic translation of the epithet employed by Abimelech (Rosenmüller). The long-continued residence of Abraham in Gerar and Beersheba afforded ample opportunity for Abimelech becoming acquainted with the patriarch's God. The introduction of Jehovah into the narrative may be noted as a third point of dissimilarity between this and the previous account—**and we said, Let there be now an oath**—*i. e.* a treaty secured by an oath or self-imprecation on the transgressor (cf. ch. xxiv. 41 ; Deut. xxix. 11, 13)—**betwixt us,** even **betwixt us and thee,** —a farther particularisation of the parties to the covenant for the sake of emphasis— **and let us make a covenant with thee.** The phrase " to cut a covenant," here used in a so-called Jehovistic portion of the history, occurs in ch. xxi. 27, 32, which confessedly belongs to the fundamental document.

Ver. 29.—**That thou wilt do us no hurt,** —literally, *if thou wilt do us evil* (sc. thy curse come upon thee !) ; the force being to negative in the strongest way possible any intention of injury (cf. ch. xxi. 23)—**as we have not touched thee,**—*i. e.* injured thee ; which was not true, as they, through their servants, had robbed Isaac of at least two wells — **and as we have done unto thee nothing but good,**—Abimelech's estimate of his own behaviour, if exceedingly favourable to himself, is at least natural (*vide* Prov. xvi. 2)—**and have sent thee away in peace** (without open violence certainly, because of Isaac's yielding, but scarcely without hostility) : **thou** art **now the blessed of the Lord.** Regarded by some as an instance of adroit and pious flattery, these words are perhaps better understood as explaining either why Isaac should overlook the injuries which they had done to him (Calvin, Bush), or why he should grant them the oath which they desired (Ainsworth),—he requiring no guarantee of safety from them, since Jehovah was on his side (Murphy),— or why they had been stirred up to seek his favour and alliance (Rosenmüller).

Ver. 30.—**And he made them a feast,**—so Lot did to the angels (ch. xix. 3). There is no mention of any banquet in the case of Abraham's covenant, which may be noted as another point of difference between the two transactions. A similar entertainment accompanied Jacob's covenant with Laban (ch. xxxi. 54) ; while in the Mosaic system the sacrificial meal formed an integral part of the regularly-appointed sacrificial worship (Levit. vii. 15, 31 ; Deut. xii. 7, 17 ; *vide* Kurtz, 'Sacrificial Worship,' § 79)—**and they did eat and drink.**

Ver. 31.—**And they rose up betimes in the morning, and sware one to another :**—literally, *a man to his brother.* On the derivation of the verb to swear from the word for seven, see ch. xxi. 23—**and Isaac sent them away, and they departed from him in peace.**

Ver. 32.—**And it came to pass the same day** (*i. e.* the day of the treaty), **that Isaac's servants came, and told him concerning the well which they had digged,** — the operation of sinking this well had probably commenced on the day of Abimelech's arrival at Beersheba (*vide* ver. 25). Almost immediately on the king's departure the well-diggers returned to the patriarch's encampment to report the success of their operations—**and said unto him, We have found water.** The LXX., mistaking לוֹ, to him, for לֹא, not, read, "We have not found water ;" the incorrectness of which is sufficiently declared by what follows.

Ver. 33. — **And he called it Shebah** ("Oath ;" which he would certainly not have done had it not been a well): **therefore the name of the city** (which ultimately gathered round the well) **is Beersheba —** *i. e.* the well of the oath (*vide* ch. xxi. 31). Isaac must have perfectly understood that the place had been so named by his father three quarters of a century previous ; but either the name had been forgotten by others, or had not come into general use amongst the inhabitants, or, observing the coincidence between his finding a well just at the time of covenanting with Abimelech and the fact that his father's treaty was also connected with a well, he wished to confirm and perpetuate the early name which had been assigned to the town. It is not certain that this was Abraham's well which had been rediscovered ; the probability is that it was another, since at Bir-es-Sheba two wells are still in existence (*vide* ch. xxi. 31)—**unto this day**—an expression used throughout Genesis to describe events separated from the age of Moses by several centuries (*vide* ch. xix. 37, 38 ; xxii. 14 ; xxxii. 32).

Ver. 34.—**And Esau was forty years old**—literally, *a son of forty years ;* the age of Isaac when he married Rebekah (ch. xxv. 20)—**when he took to wife Judith** (*Jehudith*, "Celebrated," "Praised," if Shemitic; but the name is probably Phœnician) **the daughter of Beeri**—("of a well" ? "The Well-finder," *vide* ch. xxxvi. 24)—**the Hittite, and Bashemath** ("Sweet-smelling," "Fragrant"?) **the daughter of Elon the Hittite**)—adding to them afterwards Mahalath the daughter of Ishmael, and sister of Nebajoth (ch. xxviii. 9). On Esau's wives *vide* ch. xxxvi. 2, 3.

Ver. 35.—**Which were a grief of mind** (literally, *bitterness of spirit*) **unto Isaac and to Rebekah**—possibly because of their personal characters, but chiefly because of their Canaanitish descent, and because in marrying them Esau had not only violated the Divine law which forbade polygamy, but also evinced an utterly irreligious and unspiritual disposition.

HOMILETICS.

Vers. 23—35.—*A good man's environment.* I. ISAAC AND JEHOVAH. 1. *Jehovah's grace to Isaac.* (1) Revealing his presence. "The Lord appeared unto him." Similar discoveries are now made to saints in "night" seasons, and at localities like Beersheba, previously consecrated by gracious revelations of himself. (2) Proclaiming his character. "I am the God of thy father ;" an appellation that must have sounded dear to Abraham's son, but not more than the God of our Lord Jesus Christ is to Christians. (3) Comforting his servant. "Fear not, for I am with thee." So a Christian has the best right to preserve equanimity amid life's vicissitudes and tribulations, Christ's command (Matt. x. 31 ; Luke xii. 32) ; and the best reason, Christ's presence (Matt. xviii. 20 ; xxviii. 20). (4) Renewing his promises. "I will bless thee and multiply thy seed." God renews his promises when he revives their impressions on the heart, which he does for his own glory as the faithful Promiser, and for his people's comfort as necessity requires. 2. *Isaac's gratitude to Jehovah.* (1) Building an altar; an act expressive of Isaac's personal devotion (1 Thess. v. 18). (2) Invoking God's name ; referring to the public recital of God's goodness (*vide* ch. xii. 8). It becomes saints to remember God's mercies (Ps. xlviii. 9 ; ciii. 1, 2), and to speak of them to others (Ps. lxvi. 16 ; lxxviii. 4). (3) Pitching a tent and digging a well ; indicative of Isaac's confidence in God. Grateful acknowledgment of past mercies, public celebration of present mercies, hopeful expectation of future mercies, are duties incumbent upon all, but especially on saints.

II. ISAAC AND ABIMELECH. 1. *Abimelech's request of Isaac.* (1) The nature of it: a demand for a formal alliance confirmed by the sanctions of religion. "Let there be now an oath betwixt us, and let us make a covenant with thee." (2) The object of it: his own rather than Isaac's protection. "That thou wilt do us no hurt." Most men suspect their neighbours sooner than themselves. Christianity requires saints to be as careful of their neighbour's interests as of their own (Phil. ii. 4). (3) The motive of it: partly selfish fear, and partly a recognition of Isaac's goodness. "Thou art now the blessed of the Lord." 2. *Isaac's reception of Abimelech.* (1) Cautious inquiry. "Wherefore come ye to me?" It is prudent to try injurious men before we trust them. (2) Generous entertainment. "He made them a feast." Overlooking, as became a good man, their too favourable account of themselves, he gave them welcome to his hospitable board. God's people should not be censorious even in judging enemies; when obliged to suffer, they should forget as well as forgive injuries, and never should they disdain overtures for peace, though made by those who have done them wrong. 3. *Solemn adjuration.* "And they sware one to another." Though religion does not lie within the sphere of politics, politics lie within the sphere of religion. Nothing should be done by a good man that he cannot sanctify by the word of God and prayer (Col. iii. 17, 23). 4. *Peaceful dismissal.* "Isaac sent them away, and they departed from him in peace." Those who come for peace should never go without peace. It is the saint's interest as well as duty to follow after peace (Matt. v. 9). No sooner had Isaac dismissed Abimelech and his ministers, than his servants came with tidings of their successful operations in sinking a well. Peace-makers seldom fail to find a recompense (James iii. 18).

III. ISAAC AND ESAU. 1. *Esau's sinful marriage.* (1) He took more wives than one, which was against the fundamental law of marriage (ch. ii. 24; Matt. xix. 5); (2) he married Canaanitish women, which was against the will of God, as expressed by Abraham in regard to Isaac's marriage, and doubtless also by Isaac with reference to Esau's; and (3) he acted contrary to his parents' counsel in the matter, which was a violation of that filial duty which he owed his aged parents. 2. *Isaac's bitter grief.* (1) Deeply seated as to its intensity, being bitterness of spirit (Prov. xviii. 14); (2) truly religious as to its character, being occasioned chiefly by the circumstance that Esau's ill-assorted marriages were not such as Heaven could approve; and (3) sympathisingly shared by Rebekah, whose motherly bosom was also stricken with sorrow at her son's impiety.

Learn—1. That God's gracious visits to his people are always admirably suited to their needs in respect of time, place, and manner. 2. That when a man's ways please God he maketh even his enemies be at peace with him. 3. That while a wise son maketh a glad father, a foolish son is the heaviness of his mother.

EXPOSITION.

CHAPTER XXVII.

Ver. 1.—**And it came to pass, that when Isaac was old,**—according to the generally-accepted calculation, in his one hundred and thirty-seventh year. Joseph, having been introduced to Pharaoh in his thirtieth year (ch. xli. 46), and having been thirty-nine years of age (ch. xlv. 6) when his father, aged one hundred and thirty (ch. xlvii. 9), came down to Egypt, must have been born before Jacob was ninety-one; consequently, as his birth occurred in the fourteenth year of Jacob's sojourn in Mesopotamia (cf. ch. xxx. 25 with xxix. 18, 21, 27), Jacob's flight must have taken place when he was seventy-seven. But Jacob was born in Isaac's sixtieth year (ch. xxv. 26); hence Isaac was now one hundred and thirty-seven. There are,

however, difficulties connected with this reckoning which lay it open to suspicion. For one thing, it postpones Jacob's marriage to an extremely late period. Then it takes for granted that the term of Jacob's service in Padan-aram was only twenty years (ch. xxxi. 41), whereas it is not certain whether it was not forty, made up, according to the computation of Kennicott, of fourteen years' service, twenty years' assistance as a neighbour, and six years of work for wages. And, lastly, it necessitates the birth of Jacob's eleven children in the short space of six years, a thing which appears to some, if not impossible, at least highly improbable. Adopting the larger number as the term of Jacob's sojourn in Mesopotamia, Isaac would at this time be only one hundred and seventeen (*vide* 'Chronology of Jacob's Life,'

xxxi. 41)—**and his eyes were dim,**—literally, *were failing in strength*, hence becoming dim (1 Sam. iii. 2). In describing Jacob's decaying vision a different verb is employed (ch. xlviii. 10)—**so that he could not see,** —literally, *from seeing;* מֵ with the inf. constr. conveying the idea of receding from the state of perfect vision (cf. ch. xvi. 2 ; xxxi. 29 ; *vide* Gesenius, 'Hebrew Grammar,' § 132)—**he called Esau his eldest son,** —Esau was born before his twin brother Jacob (ch. xxv. 25)—**and said unto him, My son :**—*i. e.* my special son, my beloved son, the language indicating fondness and partiality (ch. xxv. 28)—**and he (Esau) said unto him, Behold,** here am I.

Ver. 2.—**And he** (*i. e.* Isaac) **said, Behold now, I am old, and know not the day of my death.** Isaac had manifestly become apprehensive of the near approach of dissolution. His failing sight, and probably the recollection that Ishmael, his half-brother, had died at 137 (if that was Isaac's age at this time ; *vide supra*), occasioned the suspicion that his own end could not be remote, though he lived forty-three or sixty-three years longer, according to the calculation adopted, expiring at the ripe age of 180 (*vide* ch. xxx. 28).

Ver. 3.—**Now therefore take, I pray thee, thy weapons,**—the word "weapon" signifying a utensil, vessel, or finished instrument of any sort (cf. ch. xxiv. 53 ; xxxi. 37 ; xlv. 20). Here it manifestly denotes weapons employed in hunting, and in particular those next specified—**thy quiver**—the ἅπαξ λεγόμενον, תְּלִי from תָּלָה to hang, properly is "that which is suspended ;" hence a quiver, φαρέτραν (LXX.), *pharetram* (Vulgate), which commonly depends from the shoulders or girdle (Aben Ezra, Rosenmüller, Keil, Kalisch, *et alii*), though by some it is rendered "sword" (Onkelos; Syriac)—**and thy bow** (*vide* ch. xxi. 16), **and go out to the field,**—*i. e.* the open country inhabited by wild beasts, as opposed to cities, villages, or camps (cf. ch. xxv. 27)—**and take me some venison**—literally, *hunt for me hunting,* i. e. the produce of hunting, as in ch. xxv. 28.

Ver. 4.—**And make me savoury meat,**— "delicious food," from a root whose primary idea is to taste, or try the flavour, of a thing. Schultens observes that the corresponding Arabic term is specially applied to dishes made of flesh taken in hunting, and highly esteemed by nomade tribes (*vide* Gesenius, p. 467)—**such as I love** (cf. ch. xxv. 28, the ground of his partiality for Esau), **and bring it to me, that I may eat;**—"Though Isaac was blind and weak in his eyes, yet it seemeth his body was of a strong constitution, seeing he was able to eat of wild flesh, which is of harder digestion" (Willet)—**that**—the

conjunction בַּעֲבוּר followed by a future commonly expresses a purpose (cf. Exod. ix. 14) —**my soul may bless thee**—notwithstanding the oracle (ch. xxv. 23) uttered so many (fifty-seven or seventy-seven) years ago, Isaac appears to have clung to the belief that Esau was the destined heir of the covenant blessing ; *quædam fuit cæcitatis species, quæ illi magis obstitit quam externa oculorum caligo* (Calvin)—**before I die.**

Ver. 5. — **And Rebekah** (who, though younger than Isaac, must also have been old) **heard when Isaac spake**—literally, *in the speaking of Isaac;* בְּ with the inf. forming a periphrasis for the gerund, and being commonly rendered by *when* (ch. xxiv. 30 ; xxxiii. 18), the subordinated noun being changed in translation into the subject of the sentence (*vide* Ewald, 'Heb. Synt.,' § 304)—**to Esau his son** (to which the "her son" of ver. 6 stands in contrast). **And Esau went to the field to hunt for venison,** —literally, *to hunt hunting* (*vide* on ver. 3) and **to bring it**—*i. e.* "the savoury meat" or "delicious food," as directed (ver. 4).

Vers. 6, 7.—**And Rebekah** (having already formed a plan for diverting the patriarchal blessing from Esau, whose habit of life and utterly unspiritual character may perhaps have recalled to her mind and confirmed the declaration of the oracle concerning Jacob's precedence) **spake unto Jacob her son,**—*i. e.* her favourite, in contrast to Esau, Isaac's son (ver. 5)—**saying, Behold, I heard thy father speak unto Esau thy brother, saying, Bring me venison** (*vide* on ver. 3), **and make me savoury meat, that I may eat** (literally, *and I shall eat*), **and bless thee** — the lengthened form of the future in this and the preceding verb (cf. וְאֹכֵלָה in ver. 4) is expressive of Isaac's self-excitement and emphatic determination—**before the Lord.** The word Jehovah, by modern criticism regarded as a sign of divided authorship, is satisfactorily explained by remembering that Rebekah is speaking not of the blessing of God's general providence, but of the higher benediction of the covenant (Hengstenberg). The phrase, though not included in Isaac's address to Esau, need not be regarded as due to Rebekah's invention. She may have understood it to be implied in her husband's language, though it was not expressed (cf. ch. xxiv. 20). That it was designedly omitted by Isaac in consequence of the worldly character of Esau appears as little likely as that it was deliberately inserted by Rebekah to whet her favourite's ambition (Kalisch). As to meaning, the sense may be that this patriarchal benediction was to be bestowed sincerely (Menochius), in presence and by the authority of God (Ainsworth, Bush, Clericus) ; but the use of the term

Jehovah rather points to the idea that Rebekah regarded Isaac simply "as the instrument of the living and personal God, who directed the concerns of the chosen race" (Hengstenberg). **Before my death.** Since Rebekah makes no remark as to the groundlessness of Isaac's fear, it is not improbable that she too shared in her bed-ridden husband's expectations that already he was "in the presence of" his end.

Ver. 8.—**Now therefore, my son,**—Jacob at this time was not a lad, but a grown man of mature years (if Isaac was 137, he must have been 77), which shows that in the following transaction he was rather an accomplice than a tool—**obey my voice according to that which I command thee.** We can scarcely here think of a mother laying her imperative instructions on a docile and unquestioning child ; but of a wily woman detailing her well-concocted scheme to a son whom she discerns to be possessed of a like crafty disposition with herself, and whom she seeks to gain over to her stratagem by reminding him of the close and endearing relationship in which they stand to one another.

Vers. 9, 10.—**Go now to the flock, and fetch me**—literally, *take for me,* i. e. for my purposes (cf. ch. xv. 9)—**from thence two good kids of the goats.** According to Jarchi kids were selected as being the nearest approach to the flesh of wild animals. Two were specified, it has been thought, either to extract from both the choicest morsels (Menochius), or to have the appearance of animals taken in hunting (Rosenmüller), or to make an ample provision as of venison (Lange), or to make a second experiment, if the first failed (Willet). **And I will make them**—probably concealing any difference in taste by means of condiments, though Isaac's palate would not be sensitive in consequence of age and debility—**savoury meat for thy father, such as he loveth** (*vide* ver. 4): **and thou shalt bring it to thy father, that he may eat** (literally, *and he shall eat*), **and that he may bless thee**—בַּעֲבֻר אֲשֶׁר, in order that, from the idea of passing over to that which one desires to attain ; less fully in ver. 4—**before his death.** Clearly Rebekah was anticipating Isaac's early dissolution, else why this indecent haste to forestall Esau? There is no reason to surmise that she believed any connection to subsist between the eating and the benediction, though she probably imagined that the supposed prompt obedience of Isaac's son would stimulate his feeble heart to speak (Rosenmüller).

Ver. 11.—**And Jacob** (who was not yet such an adept at trickery as he afterwards became, and who, if he had no scruples of conscience in either imposing on a senile parent or despoiling an open-hearted brother, was yet averse to being detected in his frauds, as deceivers usually are) **said to Rebekah his mother, Behold, Esau my brother is a hairy man** (*vide* ch. xxv. 25) **and I am a smooth man**—חָלָק, smooth (opposed to שָׂעִיר, hairy); the primary idea of which is to cut off the hair. Cf. χαλκός, χάλιξ, κόλαξ, γλυκύς, γλοῖος, γλίσχρος ; *glacies, glaber, gladius, glisco ;* gluten, glatt, gleiten, glas—all of which convey the notion of smoothness (*vide* Gesenius, p. 283).

Ver. 12. — **My father peradventure will feel me, and I shall seem to him as a deceiver ;**—literally, *shall be in his eyes as a scoffer* (Keil, Lange), with the idea of mocking at his aged sire's infirmities—ὡς καταφρονῶν (LXX.) ; or *as a deceiver,* an impostor, one who causes to go astray (Vulgate, Rosenmüller, Ainsworth, Murphy) ; though perhaps both senses should be included, the verb תָּעַע, to scoff, meaning primarily to stammer, and hence to mislead by imperfect speech, and thus to cause to wander or lead astray, תָּעָה (*vide* Gesenius, p. 870, and Kalisch, p. 506)—**and I shall bring a curse**—קְלָלָה (from קָלַל, to be light, hence to be despised) signifies first an expression of contempt, and then a more solemn imprecation—**upon me, and not a blessing.**

Ver. 13.—**And his mother said unto him, Upon me** be **thy curse, my son** (cf. ch. xliii. 9 ; 1 Sam. xxv. 24 ; 2 Sam. xiv. 9 ; Matt. xxvii. 25). Tempted to regard Rebekah's words as the utterance of a bold and unscrupulous woman (Aben Ezra), we ought perhaps to view them as inspired by faith in the Divine promise, which had already indicated that of her two sons Jacob should have the precedence (Willet, Calvin, Lange), and that accordingly there was every reason to anticipate not a malediction, but a benediction. **Only obey my voice** (*i. e.* do as I direct you, follow my instructions), **and go fetch me** them—or, go and take for me (*sc.* the two kids I spoke of).

Ver. 14.—**And he went** (*sc.* to the flock), **and fetched,**—or, rather, took (*sc.* the two kids as directed) **and brought** them (after slaughter, of course) **to his mother : and his mother made savoury meat, such as his father loved.** All this implies that Rebekah reckoned on Esau's absence for a considerable time, perhaps throughout the entire day.

HOMILETICS.

Vers. 1—14.—*The stolen blessing: a domestic drama.*—1. *Isaac and Rebekah, or plotting and counterplotting.* I. THE SCHEME OF ISAAC. 1. *Its sinful object.* The heavenly oracle having with no uncertain sound proclaimed Jacob the theocratic heir, the bestowment of the patriarchal benediction on Esau was clearly an unholy design. That Isaac, who on Mount Moriah had evinced such meek and ready acquiescence in Jehovah's will, should in old age, from partiality towards his firstborn, or forgetfulness of Jehovah's declaration, endeavour to thwart the Divine purpose according to election affords a melancholy illustration of the deceitfulness of sin even in renewed hearts, and of the deep-seated antagonism between the instincts of nature and the designs of grace. 2. *Its secret character.* The commission assigned to Esau does not appear to have been dictated by any supposed connection between the gratification of the palate, the reinvigoration of the body, or the refreshment of the spirit and the exercise of the prophetic gift, but rather by a desire to divert the attention of Rebekah from supposing that anything unusual was going on, and so to secure the necessary privacy for carrying out the scheme which he had formed. Had Isaac not been doubtful of the righteousness of what he had in contemplation, he would never have resorted to manœuvring and secrecy, but would have courted unveiled publicity. Crooked ways love the dark (John iii. 20, 21). 3. *Its urgent motive.* Isaac felt impelled to relieve his soul of the theocratic blessing by a sense of approaching dissolution. If it be the weakness of old men to imagine death nearer, it is the folly of young men to suppose it farther distant than it is. To young and old alike the failure of the senses should be a premonition of the end, and good men should set their houses in order ere they leave the world (ch. xxv. 6; 2 Kings xx. 1; Isa. xxxviii. 1). 4. *Its inherent weakness.* That Isaac reckoned on Rebekah's opposition to his scheme seems apparent; it is not so obvious that he calculated on God's being against him. Those who meditate unholy deeds should first arrange that God will not be able to discover their intentions.

II. THE STRATAGEM OF REBEKAH. 1. *The design was legitimate.* Instead of her behaviour being represented as an attempt to outwit her aged, blind, and bed-ridden husband (for which surely no great cleverness was required), and to stealthily secure the blessing for her favourite, regard for truth demands that it should rather be characterised as an endeavour to prevent its surreptitious appropriation for Esau. 2. *The inspiration was religious.* Displaying a considerable amount of woman's wit in its conception and execution, and perhaps largely tainted by maternal jealousy, Rebekah's stratagem ought in fairness to be traced to her belief in the pre-natal oracle, which had pointed to Jacob as the theocratic heir. That her faith, however mixed with unspiritual alloy, was strong seems a just conclusion from her almost reckless boldness (ver. 13). 3. *The wickedness was inexcusable.* Good as were its end and motive, the stratagem of Rebekah was deplorably wicked. It was an act of cruel imposition on a husband who had loved her for well-nigh a century; it was a base deed of temptation and seduction, viewed in its relations to Jacob—the prompting of a son to sin against a father; it was a signal offence against God in many ways, but chiefly in the sinful impatience it displayed, and in the foolish supposition that his sovereign designs needed the assistance of, or could be helped by, human craft in the shape of female cunning.

III. THE RIVAL ACC MPLICES. 1. *The confederate of Isaac.* The guilt of Esau consisted in seeking to obtain the birthright when he knew (1) that it belonged to Jacob by Heaven's gift, (2) that he had parted with any imaginary title he ever had to expect it, (3) that he was utterly unqualified to possess it, and (4) that he was endeavouring to obtain it by improper means. 2. *The tool of Rebekah.* That Jacob in acting on his mother's counsel was not sinless is evinced by the fact that he (1) perceived its hazardous nature (vers. 11, 12), (2) discerned its criminality, and yet (3) allowed himself to carry it through.

Lessons:—1. The wickedness of trying to subvert the will of Heaven—exemplified in Isaac. 2. The sinfulness of doing evil that good may come—illustrated by the conduct of Rebekah. 3. The criminality of following evil counsel, in opposition to the light of conscience and the restraints of Providence—shown by the conduct of both Esau and Jacob.

EXPOSITION.

Ver. 15.—**And Rebekah took goodly raiment of her eldest son Esau,**—literally, *the robes of Esau her son the elder—the desirable,* i. e. the handsome ones. The בֶּגֶד was an outer garment worn by the Oriental (ch. xxxix. 12, 13, 15 ; xli. 42),—στολή, LXX.,—and was often made of beautiful and costly materials (cf. 1 Kings xxii. 10). That the clothes mentioned as belonging to Esau were sacerdotal robes possessed by him as heir of the patriarchal priesthood (Jewish Rabbis), though regarded by many as a probable conjecture (Ainsworth, Bush, Candlish, Clarke, Wordsworth, 'Speaker's Commentary,' Inglis), is devoid of proof, and ,may be pronounced unlikely, since the firstborn did not serve in the priesthood while his father lived (Willet, Alford). They were probably festive garments of the princely hunter (Kalisch)—**which** were **with her in the house,**—not because Esau saw that his wives were displeasing to his parents (Mercerus, Willet), or because they were sacred garments (Ainsworth, Poole), but probably because Esau, though married, had not yet quitted the patriarchal household (Kalisch)—**and put them upon Jacob her younger son.** The verb, being in the hiphil, conveys the sense of causing Jacob to clothe himself, which entirely removes the impression that Jacob was a purely involuntary agent in this deceitful and deeply dishonourable affair.

Ver. 16.—**And she put the skins of the kids of the goats**—not European, but Oriental camel-goats, whose wool is black, silky, of a much finer texture than that of the former, and sometimes used as a substitute for human hair (cf. Cant. iv. 1); *vide* on this subject Rosenmüller's 'Scholia,' and commentaries generally—**upon his hands, and upon the smooth of his neck**—thus cautiously providing against detection, in case, anything occurring to arouse the old man's suspicions, he should seek, as in reality he did, to test the accuracy of his now dim sight and dull hearing by the sense of touch.

Ver. 17.—**And she gave the savoury meat and the bread, which she had prepared, into the hand of her son Jacob**—who forthwith proceeded on his unholy errand.

Ver. 18.—**And he came unto his father,**—by this time a bed-ridden invalid (*vide* ver. 19)—**and said, My father.** If he attempted to imitate the voice of Esau, he was manifestly unsuccessful ; the dull ear of the aged patient was yet acute enough to detect a strangeness in the speaker's tone. **And he said, Here am I : who art thou, my son ?** "He thought he recognised the voice of Jacob ; his suspicions were aroused ; he knew the crafty disposition of his younger son too well ; and he felt the duty of extreme carefulness" (Kalisch).

Ver. 19.—**And Jacob** (either not observing or not regarding the trepidation which his voice caused, but being well schooled by his crafty mother, and determined to go through with what perhaps he esteemed a perfectly justifiable transaction) **said unto his father, I am Esau thy firstborn.** A reply for which laborious excuses have been invented ; as that Jacob spoke mystically, meaning not that he individually, but that his descendants, the Church, were Isaac's firstborn (Augustine) ; or figuratively, as importing that since he had already bought Esau's birthright, he might justly regard himself as standing in Esau's place (Theodoret, Aquinas). It is better not to attempt vindication of conduct which to ordinary minds must ever appear questionable, but rather to hold that "Jacob told an officious lie to his father" (Willet). **I have done according as thou badest me.** If the former assertion might be cleared of mendacity, it is difficult to see how this can. By no conceivable sophistry could he convince his conscience that he was acting in obedience to his father, while he was knowingly implementing the instructions of his mother. This was Jacob's second lie. **Arise, I pray thee, sit and eat of my venison.** Lie three. One lie commonly requires another to support or conceal it. Few who enter on a course of deception stop at one falsehood. **That thy soul may bless me.** It was the blessing of the Abrahamic covenant he craved.

Vers. 20, 21.—**And Isaac** (still dissatisfied, but still resolving to proceed with caution) **said unto his son, How is it that thou hast found it so quickly, my son ?** Giving expression to a natural surprise at the speedy success which had attended Esau's hunting expedition ; an interrogation to which Jacob replied with daring boldness (Murphy), with consummate effrontery (Bush), not without perjury (Calvin), and even with reckless blasphemy (Kalisch, Alford). **And he said, Because the Lord thy God brought it to me.** Literally, *caused it to come before me ;* by the concurrence, of course, of his providence ; which, though in one sense true, yet as used by Jacob was an impious falsehood. Solemn as this declaration was, it failed to lull the suspicions or allay the disquiet of the aged invalid. **And Isaac said unto Jacob, Come near, I pray thee, that I may feel thee, my son,**—the very thing which Jacob had suggested as likely to happen (ver. 12)—**whether thou be my very son Esau** (literally, *this, my son Esau*) **or not.**

Vers. 22, 23.—**And Jacob** (with a boldness worthy of a better cause) **went near unto Isaac his father; and he** (*i. e.* Isaac) **felt him** (*i. e.* Jacob), **and said, The voice is Jacob's voice, but** (literally, *and*) **the hands are the hands of Esau. And he discerned him not, because his hands were hairy, as his brother Esau's hands: so he blessed him.** Isaac must either have forgotten the heavenly oracle which announced the destinies of his sons at their birth, and distinctly accorded the precedence to Jacob, or he must not have attached the same importance to it as Rebekah, or he may have thought that it did not affect the transmission of the covenant blessing, or that it did not concern his sons so much as their descendants. It is hard to credit that Isaac either did not believe in the Divine announcement which had indicated Jacob as the heir of the promise, or that, believing it, he deliberately allowed paternal partiality to interfere with, and even endeavour to reverse, the will of Heaven.

Vers. 24—26.—**And he said** (showing that a feeling of uneasy suspicion yet lingered in his mind), **Art thou my very son Esau?** Luther wonders how Jacob was able to brazen it out; adding, "I should probably have run away in terror, and let the dish fall;" but, instead of that, he added one more lie to those which had preceded, saying with undisturbed composure, **I am**—equivalent to an English *yes;* upon which the blind old patriarch requested that the proffered dainties might be set before him. Having partaken of the carefully-disguised kid's flesh, and drunk an exhilarating cup of wine, he further desired that his favourite son should approach his bed, saying, **Come near now, and kiss me, my son**—a request dictated more by paternal affection (Keil, Kalisch) than by lingering doubt which required reassurance (Lange).

Ver. 27.—**And he came near, and kissed him.** Originally the act of kissing had a symbolical character. Here it is a sign of affection between a parent and a child; in ch. xxix. 13 between relatives. It was also a token of friendship (Tobit vii. 6; x. 12; 2 Sam. xx. 9; Matt. xxvi. 48; Luke vii. 45; xv. 20; Acts xx. 37). The kissing of princes was a symbol of homage (1 Sam. x. 1; Ps. ii. 12; Xenoph., 'Cyrop.,' vii. 5, 32). With the Persians it was a mark of honour (Xenoph., 'Agesil.,' v. 4). The Rabbins permitted only three kinds of kisses—the kiss of reverence, of reception, and of dismissal.

The kiss of charity was practised among disciples in the early Christian Church (Rom. xvi. 16; 1 Cor. xvi. 20; 2 Cor. xiii. 12; 1 Thess. v. 26; 1 Pet. v. 14; *vide* Kitto's 'Cyclopedia,' art. Kissing). **And he smelled the smell of his raiment,**—not deliberately, in order to detect whether they belonged to a shepherd or a huntsman (Tuch), but accidentally while in the act of kissing. The odour of Esau's garments, impregnated with the fragrance of the aromatic herbs of Palestine, excited the dull sensibilities of the aged prophet, suggesting to his mind pictures of freshness and fertility, and inspiring him to pour forth his promised benediction —**and blessed him** (not a second time, the statement in ver. 23 being only inserted by anticipation), **and said,**—the blessing, as is usual in elevated prophetic utterances, assumes a poetic and antistrophical form (cf. Esau's blessing, vers. 39, 40)—**See, the smell of my son is as the smell of a field**—the first clause of the poetic stanza clearly connects with the odour of Esau's raiment as that which had opened the fount of prophetic song in Isaac's breast, so far at least as its peculiar form was concerned; its secret inspiration we know was the Holy Ghost operating through Isaac's faith in the promise (*vide* Heb. xi. 20)—**which the Lord hath blessed.** The introduction of the name Jehovah instead of Elohim in this second clause proves that Isaac did not mean to liken his son to an ordinary well-cultivated field, but to "a field like that of Paradise, resplendent with traces of the Deity—an ideal field, bearing the same relation to an ordinary one as Israel did to the heathen—a kind of enchanted garden, such as would be realised at a later period in Canaan, as far as the fidelity of the people permitted it" (Hengstenberg).

Ver. 28.—**Therefore God give thee of the dew of heaven,**—literally, *and the Elohim will give thee,* with an optative sense; *i. e.* and may the Elohim give thee! The occurrence of הָאֱלֹהִים in what is usually assigned to the Jehovist (Tuch, Bleek, Davidson) is not to be explained as a special Jehovistic formula (Colenso), or as a remnant of the fundamental Elohistic writing (Kalisch), or as indicating that the personal God, and not Jehovah, the God of the covenant, was the source of the blessing (Keil, Gosman in Lange), or as intimating a remaining doubt as to whether Esau was the chosen one of Jehovah (Lange); but as identifying Jehovah with Elohim, the art. being the art. of reference, as in ch. xxii. 1 (Hengstenberg; cf. Quarry 'on Genesis,' p. 483). The blessing craved was substantially that of a fertile soil, in Oriental countries the copious dew deposited by the atmosphere supplying the place of rain. Hence dew is employed in

Scripture as a symbol of material prosperity (Deut. xxxiii. 13, 28 ; Zech. viii. 12), and the absence of dew and rain represented as a signal of Divine displeasure (2 Sam. i. 21 ; 1 Kings xvii. 1 ; Haggai i. 10, 11)—**and the fatness of the earth,**—literally, *of the fatnesses,* or choicest parts, *of the earth* (ch. xlv. 18)—**and plenty of corn and wine** ？ ？ abundance of the produce of the soil (cf. Deut. xxxiii. 28).

Ver. 29.—**Let people serve thee** (literally, *and will serve thee, peoples ;* at once a prayer and a prophecy; fulfilled in the political subjection of the Moabites, Ammonites, Syrians, Philistines, and Edomites by David ; the thought being repeated in the next clause), **and nations bow down to thee** (in expression of their homage): **be lord over thy brethren,** —literally, *be a lord* (from the idea of power; found only here and in ver. 37) *to thy brethren.* Pre-eminence among his kindred as well as

dominion in the world is thus promised— **and let thy mother's sons bow down to thee** (a repetition of the preceding thought, with perhaps a hint of his desire to humble Jacob, the favourite of Rebekah): **cursed** be **every one that curseth thee, and blessed** be **he that blesseth thee** —framed on the model of the Abrahamic benediction (ch. xii. 8), but not so full as that, either because Isaac felt that after all Esau was not to be the progenitor of the holy seed (Murphy), or because, not being actuated by proper feelings towards Jehovah and his promises, the patriarch could not rise to that height of spiritual benediction to which he afterwards attained—ch. xxviii. 3, 4 (Keil), or because the prerogative of pronouncing the Abrahamic blessing in all its fulness Jehovah may have reserved to himself, as in ch. xxviii. 14 (' Speaker's Commentary ').

HOMILETICS.

Vers. 15—29.—*The stolen blessing : a domestic drama.*—2. *Isaac and Jacob, or the successful stratagem.* I. JACOB'S DECEPTION OF ISAAC. Jacob's personation of Esau was—1. *Deftly prepared.* The ingenious Rebekah, having dressed him in the fragrant festal robes of the princely hunter, covered his smooth skin with the soft, silky hide of the camel-goat, and put into his hand the simulated dainty dish which she had cooked. It is a melancholy thing when either woman's wit or man's sagacity is prostituted to unholy ends. 2. *Boldly avowed.* Entering his father's tent, and approaching within easy reach of the invalid's couch, at the same time imitating Esau's intonations, the heartless impostor calls upon his aged parent to arise and eat of his son's venison, in response to his father's inquiry also openly declaring himself to be Esau ; in which was a fourfold offence—against his venerable father, against his absent brother, against himself, and against God. Never is a lie, and seldom is a sin of any kind, single or simple in its criminality. That scheme cannot be a good one of which the first act is a lie. 3. *Persistently maintained.* In the face of his father's searching interrogation, careful examination, and manifest trepidation, Jacob brazens out the imposture he had begun, covering his first falsehood by a second, and his second by a third, in which he verges on the limits of blasphemy, allowing himself to be handled by his aged parent without betraying by a word or sign the base deception he was practising, and at length capping his extraordinary wickedness by a solemn asseveration of his identity with Esau that carried with it in the hearing of Isaac much of the impressiveness and weight of an oath,—" I am thy very son Esau ! " It is amazing to what depths of criminality those may fall who once step aside from the straight paths of virtue. 4. *Completely successful.* Critical as the ordeal was through which he passed, he was not detected. So God sometimes allows wicked schemes to prosper, accomplishing his own designs thereby, though neither approving of the schemes nor holding the schemers guiltless.

II. ISAAC'S BENEDICTION OF JACOB. The patriarchal blessing which Isaac uttered was—1. *Divinely inspired as to its origin.* It was not within the power of Isaac to either conceive or express it in any arbitrarily selected moment, or in any particular way or place that he might determine. Least of all was it the production of Isaac's ordinary faculties under the physical or mental impulse of delicious viands or paternal affection. It was the outcome of an unseen afflatus of the Divine Spirit upon the venerable patriarch's soul (Heb. xi. 20). 2. *Providentially directed as to its destination.* Intended for the firstborn, it was pronounced upon the younger of his sons. Had Rebekah and Jacob not interposed with their miserable trick, there is reason to suppose that God would have discovered means of defeating the misguided patriarch's design; perhaps by laying an embargo upon his lips, as he did on Balaam (Numb. xxii. 38); perhaps by miraculously guiding his speech, as afterwards he guided Jacob's hands (ch. xlviii. 14). But none the less is the Divine finger discernible in carrying the heavenly blessing to its predestined recipient, that he does not interfere with Rebekah's craft, but allows it, beneath the guidance of his ordinary providence, to work out its appropriate result. 3. *Richly laden as to its contents.* It embraced — (1) Material enrichment, represented by the dew, corn, and wine, which may also be regarded as symbolic of spiritual treasures; (2) personal advancement in the world and the Church, foreshadowing both the political supremacy and ecclesiastical importance to which Israel should afterwards attain; (3) spiritual influence, emblematic of the religious priesthood enjoyed first by the Hebrew people as a nation, and latterly by Christ, the true Seed of Abraham, and Isaac, and Jacob. 4. *Absolutely permanent as to its duration.* Though Isaac subsequently learnt of the deception which had been practised towards him, he felt that the words he had spoken were beyond recall. This was proof decisive that Isaac spake not of himself, but as he was moved by the Holy Ghost. His own benediction, uttered purely by and from himself, might, and, in the circumstances, probably would, have been revoked; the blessing of Jehovah transmitted through his undesigned act he had no power to cancel.

Learn—1. That those who attempt to deceive others are not unfrequently themselves deceived. 2. That those who enter on a sinful course may speedily sink deeper into sin than they intended. 3. That deception practised by a son against a father, at a mother's instigation, is a monstrous and unnatural display of wickedness. 4. That God can accomplish his own designs by means of man's crimes, without either relieving them of guilt or himself being the author of sin. 5. That the blessing of God maketh rich and addeth no sorrow therewith. 6. That the gifts and calling of God are without repentance.

EXPOSITION.

Ver. 30.—**And it came to pass** (literally, *and it was*), **as soon as Isaac had made an end of blessing Jacob, and Jacob was yet scarce gone out**—literally, *and it was* (sc. as soon as, or when) *Jacob only going forth had gone;* i. e. had just gone out (Ewald, Keil), rather than was in the act of coming out (Murphy), since the narrative implies that the brothers did not meet on this occasion—**from the presence of Isaac his father, that** (literally, *and*) **Esau his brother came in from his hunting.**

Ver. 31.—**And he also had made savoury meat** (*vide* ver. 4), **and brought it unto his father, and said unto him, Let my father arise, and eat of his son's venison**—compared with Jacob's exhortation to his aged parent (ver. 19), the language of Esau has, if anything, more affection in its tones—**that thy soul may bless me.** Esau was at this time a man of mature age, being either fifty-seven or seventy-seven years old, and must have been acquainted with the heavenly oracle (ch. xxv. 23) that assigned the precedence in the theocratic line to Jacob. Either, therefore, he must have supposed that his claim to the blessing was not thereby affected, or he was guilty of conniving at Isaac's scheme for resisting the Divine will. Indignation at Jacob's duplicity and baseness, combined with sympathy for Esau in

his supposed wrongs, sometimes prevents a just appreciation of the exact position occupied by the latter in this extrordinary transaction. Instead of branding Jacob as a shameless deceiver, and hurling against his fair fame the most opprobrious epithets, may it not be that, remembering the previously-expressed will of Heaven, the real supplanter was Esau, who as an accomplice of his father was seeking secretly, unlawfully, and feloniously to appropriate to himself a blessing which had already been, not obscurely, designated as Jacob's? On this hypothesis the miserable craft of Jacob and Rebekah was a lighter crime than that of Isaac and Esau.

Ver. 32.—**And Isaac his father said unto him, Who** art thou? The language indicates the patriarch's surprise. **And he said, I am thy son, thy firstborn Esau.** The emphatic tone of Esau's answer may have been dictated by a suspicion, already awakened by Isaac's question, that all was not right (Inglis). Esau's claim to be regarded as Isaac's firstborn, after having bartered away his birthright, is considered by some to be unwarranted (Wordsworth); but it is doubtful if Esau attached the importance to the term "firstborn" which this objection presupposes.

Ver. 33.—**And Isaac trembled very ex-**

ceedingly,—literally, *feared a great fear, to a great degree;* shuddered in great terror above measure (Lange). The renderings ἐξέστη δὲ Ἰσαὰκ ἔκστασιν μεγάλην σφόδρα (LXX.), *Expavit stupore, et ultra quam credi potest admirans* (Vulgate), "wondered with an exceedingly great admiration" (Onkelos), emphasise the patriarch's astonishment, the first even suggesting the idea of a trance or supernatural elevation of the prophetic consciousness (Augustine); whereas that which is depicted is rather the alarm produced within the patriarch's breast, not so much by the discovery that his plan had been defeated by a woman's wit and a son's craft — these would have kindled indignation rather than fear—as by the awakening conviction not that he had blessed, but that he had been seeking to bless, the wrong person (Calvin, Willet)—and said, Who? where is he—*quis est et ubi est?* (Jarchi); but rather, who then is he? (Rosenmüller, Kalisch, Lange)—that hath taken venison, — literally, *the one hunting prey* = that hunted, or has hunted, the part. having the force of a perfect (*vide* Ewald's 'Heb. Synt.,' § 335)—and brought it me, and I have eaten of all before thou camest, and have blessed him? yea, and he shall be blessed—thus before Jacob is named he pronounces the Divine sentence that the blessing is irrevocable (Lange).

Ver. 34. — And when Esau heard the words of his father, he cried with a great and exceeding bitter cry—literally, *he cried a cry, great and bitter exceedingly;* expressive of the poignant anguish of his soul (Kalisch, Bush), if not also of his rage against his brother (Philo, Eusebius), of his envy of the blessing (Menochius, Lapide), and of the desperation of his spirit (Calvin). Cf. Heb. xii. 17—and said unto his father, Bless me, even me also, O my father. A proof of Esau's blind incredulity in imagining it to be within his father's power to impart benedictions promiscuously without and beyond the Divine sanction (Calvin); a sign that he supposed the theocratic blessing capable of division, and as dependent upon his lamentations and prayers as upon the caprice of his father (Lange); an evidence that "now at last he had learned in some measure adequately to value" the birthright (Candlish); but if so it was *post horam.*

Ver. 35.—And he (*i. e.* Isaac) said, Thy brother came with subtilty,—with wisdom (Onkelos); rather with fraud, μετὰ δόλου (LXX.)—and hath taken away thy blessing —*i. e.* the blessing which I thought was thine, since Isaac now understood that from the first it had been designed for Jacob.

Ver. 36.—And he (Esau) said, Is he not rightly named Jacob?—literally, *is it that*

one has called his name Jacob? הֲכִי being employed when the reason is unknown (*vide* Ewald, 'Heb. Synt.,' § 324). On the meaning of Jacob cf. ch. xxv. 26—for (literally, *and*) he hath supplanted me (a paronomasia on the word Jacob) these two times — or, already twice; זֶה being used adverbially in the sense of *now* (Gesenius, 'Grammar,' § 122). The precise import of Esau's exclamation has been rendered, "Has he not been justly (δικαίως, LXX.; *juste,* Vulgate; rightly, A. V.) named Supplanter from supplanting?" (Rosenmüller). "Is it because he was named Jacob that he hath now twice supplanted me?" (Ainsworth, Bush). "Has he received the name Jacob from the fact that he has twice outwitted me?" (Keil). "Shall he get the advantage of me because he was thus inadvertently named Jacob?" (Lange). "Has in truth his name been called Jacob?" (Kalisch). All agree in bringing out that Esau designed to indicate a correspondence between Jacob's name and Jacob's practice. He took away my birthright;— this was scarcely correct, since Esau voluntarily sold it (ch. xxv. 33)—and, behold, now he hath taken away my blessing. Neither was this exactly accurate, since the blessing did not originally belong to Esau, however he may have imagined that it did. And he said, Hast thou not reserved a blessing for me? The question indicates that Esau had no proper conception of the spiritual character of the blessing which his brother had obtained.

Ver. 37.—And Isaac answered and said unto Esau (repeating the substance of the blessing already conferred on Jacob), Behold, I have made him thy lord,—literally, *behold, a lord* (vide on ver. 29) *have I constituted him to thee;* Isaac hereby intimating that in pronouncing the words of blessing he had been speaking under a celestial impulse, and therefore with absolute authority—and all his brethren have I given to him for servants (for the fulfilment *vide* 2 Sam. viii. 14), and with corn and wine have I sustained him :—*i. e.* declared that by these he shall be sustained or supported (cf. ver. 28) —and what shall I do now unto thee, my son?

Ver. 38.—And Esau said unto his father, Hast thou but one blessing, my father? Not as desiring either the reversal of the patriarchal sentence upon Jacob, which he appears to have understood to be irrevocable, or an extension of its gracious provisions, so as to include him as well as Jacob; but as soliciting such a benediction as would place him, at least in respect of temporalities, on a level with the favourite of Rebekah, either because he did not recognise the spiritual character of the covenant blessing, or because, though recognising it, he was willing to let it go. **Bless me, even me also, O my father. And Esau lifted up his voice, and wept** (cf. Heb. xii. 17). "Those tears expressed, indeed, sorrow for his forfeiture, but not for the sinful levity by which it had been incurred. They were ineffectual (*i. e.* they did not lead to genuine repentance) because Esau was incapable of true repentance" (*vide* Delitzsch on Heb. xii. 17).

Ver. 39.—**And Isaac his father** (moved by the tearful earnestness of Esau) **answered and said unto him,** — still speaking under inspiration, though it is doubtful whether what he spoke was a real, or only an apparent, blessing — (*vide infra*) — **Behold, thy dwelling shall be the fatness of the earth, and of the dew of heaven from above.** Literally, *from* (מִן) *the fatnesses* (or fat places) *of the earth, and from the dew of heaven;* a substantial repetition of the temporal blessing bestowed on Jacob (ver. 28), with certain important variations, such as the omission of plenty of corn and wine at the close, and of the name of Elohim at the commencement, of the benediction (Vulgate, Luther, Calvin, Ainsworth, Rosenmüller, 'Speaker's Commentary'); though, by assigning to the preposition a privative rather than a partitive sense, it is readily transformed into "a modified curse"—*behold, away from the fatnesses of the earth,* &c., *shall thy dwelling be,* meaning that, in contrast to the land of Canaan, the descendants of Esau should be located in a sterile region (Tuch, Knobel, Kurtz, Delitzsch, Keil, Kalisch, Murphy). In support of this latter rendering it is urged (1) that it is grammatically admissible; (2) that it corresponds with the present aspect of Idumæa, which is "on the whole a dreary and unproductive land;" (3) that it agrees with the preceding statement that every blessing had already been bestowed upon Jacob; and (4) that it explains the play upon the words "fatness" and "dew," which are here chosen to describe a state of matters exactly the opposite to that which was declared to be the lot of Jacob. On the other hand, it is felt to be somewhat arbitrary to assign to the preposition a partitive sense in ver. 28 and a privative in ver. 39. Though called in later times (Mal. i. 3) a waste and desolate region, it may not have been originally so, or only in comparison with Canaan; while according to modern travellers the glens and mountain terraces of Edom, covered with rich soil, only want an industrious population to convert the entire region into "one of the wealthiest, as it is one of the most picturesque, countries in the world."

Ver. 40.—**And by thy sword shalt thou live,**—literally, *upon thy sword shalt thou be,* i. e. thy maintenance shall depend on thy sword; a prediction that Esau's descendants should be a warlike and tumultuous people of predatory habits (cf. Josephus, B. I., iv. 4)—**and shalt serve thy brother;**—a prediction afterwards fulfilled (cf. 1 Sam. xiv. 47; 2 Sam. viii. 14; 1 Kings xi. 16; 2 Kings xiv. 7—10; 2 Chron. xx. 22—25)—**and it shall come to pass when thou shalt have the dominion, that thou shalt break his yoke from off thy neck.** The verb רוּד, used of beasts which have broken the yoke and wander freely about (Gesenius, Fürst), appears to hint at an incessant restlessness on the part of Edom while under Israel's yoke which should eventually terminate in regaining their independence. The exact rendering of the clause is obscure, but perhaps means that when Edom should roam about as a freebooter (Lange), or should revolt (Alford), or should toss, shake, or struggle against the yoke (Vulgate, Keil, Hengstenberg, 'Speaker's Commentary), he should succeed. Other renderings are, when thou shalt bear rule (Kimchi), when thou shalt repent (Jarchi), when thou shalt be strong (Samaritan), when thou prevailest (Murphy), when thou shalt truly desire it (Kalisch), when thou shalt pull down (LXX.); because thou art restless (Hävernick).

HOMILETICS.

Vers. 30—40.—*The stolen blessing: a domestic drama.*—3. *Isaac and Esau, or the hunter's lamentation.* I. ISAAC'S STARTLING DISCOVERY. 1. *Unexpectedly made.* The return of Esau from the hunting-field with a dish of venison was a sudden and most unpleasant revelation to the aged patriarch, showing that in some inexplicable manner he had been out-manœuvred, and, as it were, constrained against his will to bestow the blessing upon Jacob. So in common life it is not unfrequently seen that the unexpected is that which happens, that wicked schemes prove abortive, that the deceiver is himself deceived—"the engineer hoist on his own petard,"—and that men are often made the involuntary and unconscious instruments of furthering the will of Heaven. 2. *Tremblingly received.* Apprehending what had taken place, the blind old invalid "feared a great fear exceedingly," saddened with an inward horror, not through disappointment at the failure of his scheme, or indignation at the wicked craft and heartless duplicity of Rebekah's favourite, but alarm at his own sinful intention which God had thus manifestly seen and thwarted. It is well when the soul trembles at a discovery of its own wickedness. Gracious souls dread nothing more than standing on the verge of sin. 3. *Pathetically acknowledged.* "Thy brother came with subtilty, and hath taken away thy blessing;" and, "I have blessed him: yea, and he shall be blessed." It becomes parents to commiserate their children's misfortunes, and especially to sorrow if they miss the blessings of salvation. They who lack these, even when they do not wish to obtain them, are objects of profoundest pity. 4. *Meekly acquiesced in.* Recognising the hand of God in the remarkable transaction in which he had been an actor, with true humility and faith the venerable patriarch bowed before the will of the Supreme. Neither Esau's prayers and tears, nor his own paternal affections, could stimulate so much as a wish to undo what had been done. To a truly pious heart the will of God is final. "Thy will be done" is the language of faith.

II. ESAU'S SINGULAR BEHAVIOUR. 1. *His bitter lamentation for himself.* Esau's "great and exceeding bitter cry" was expressive not of heartfelt grief for his sinful levity in parting with the birthright, or guileful behaviour in attempting to secure the blessing; but (1) of deep mortification at being over-reached by his crafty brother; (2) of remorseful chagrin at not recovering the blessing he had practically surrendered in the sale of the birthright; (3) of earnest desire to induce Isaac to revoke the words he had spoken. The repentance which he sought carefully with tears (Heb. xii. 17) was not his own change of heart, but his father's change of mind. 2. *His wrathful indignation against his brother.* "Is he not rightly named Jacob? for he hath supplanted me these two times." A statement not quite accurate; but angry men are seldom remarkable for accuracy of statement; a statement also expressive of hatred against Jacob, and incensed brothers often call each other bad names. Good men should be angry and sin not. Indignation, even when righteous, should be restrained. 3. *His tearful request to his father.* "Bless me, me also, O my father!" Having lost the blessing of the covenant, he was still desirous of possessing some sort of blessing. Wicked men often covet the material advantages of religion who have no desire to share in its spiritual enrichments.

III. ISAAC'S SOLEMN DECLARATION. 1. *Of Esau's subjection to Jacob.* "Behold, I have made him thy lord." A prediction of (1) political subordination, afterwards fulfilled in the conquests of Israel; and (2) of possible salvation to Esau and his descendants through believing recognition of the spiritual ascendancy of Jacob and his seed. 2. *Of Esau's portion from God.* (1) A fat soil. God appoints to all men, individuals and nations, the bounds of their habitation. Inhabitants of fertile regions have a special call to thankfulness. (2) A roving life. Though the warlike character of Esau's descendants was of God's appointment and permission, it is no just inference that savage tribes are as useful as those of settled and improved habits, or that God does not desire the diffusion of civilisation and the elevation of the race. (3) Ultimate independence. Though some nations have been placed in subjection, it is God's will that all should aspire to freedom. Revolt, rebellion, insurrection are sometimes a people's highest duty.

Lessons:—1. The blessing of the covenant is not of him that willeth or of him that runneth, but of God that showeth mercy. 2. Those who despise God's salvation in youth cannot always obtain it in manhood or age. 3. Those who finally come short of eternal life will have no one to blame but themselves. 4. No one need sue in vain for Heaven's favour, since the blessing is not now for one, but for all. 5. There is a difference between penitence and remorse. 6. Though no man can hope to change the mind of God, it is within the power of all men to desire and to effect a change upon their own hearts. 7. The prediction of a nation's or a person's future does not interfere with the free operation of the human will.

HOMILIES BY VARIOUS AUTHORS.

Ver. 33.—*Jacob's deceit. Esau supplanted.* In this familiar narrative the following points may be distinguished:—

I. ISAAC'S ERROR—connecting a solemn blessing with mere gratification of the senses, neglect of the Divine word, favouritism towards the son less worthy.

II. JACOB'S SUBTILTY and selfishness. The birthright had been sold to him; he might have obtained the blessing by fair agreement. His fear of Esau lay at the root of his deceit. One sin leads on to another. Those who entangle themselves with the world are involved more and more in moral evil.

III. REBEKAH'S AFFECTION was perverted into unmotherly partiality and unwifely treachery to Isaac. The son's guilt rested much on the mother's shoulders, for she laid the plot and prepared the execution of it. All were sad examples of self-assertion destroying the simplicity of faith. And yet—

IV. THE COVENANT GOD over-rules the weakness and error of his people. The blessing was appointed for Jacob. Although pronounced by an instrument blind, foolish, sinful, deceived, it yet is the blessing, which, having been lodged in Isaac, must pass on to the true heir of Isaac, who, according to the promise and prediction, is Jacob.

V. The lower character and standing of Esau and his inferior blessing represents the distinction between THE CHOSEN PEOPLE AND THOSE WHO, WHILE NOT INCLUDED IN THE COMMONWEALTH OF ISRAEL, may yet by connection and intercourse with it derive some portion of the Divine benediction from it. Both in pre-Christian and Christian times there have been nations thus situated.

VI. The LATE REPENTANCE of the supplanted Esau. He found no possibility of averting the consequences of his own error (Heb. xii. 17), no place where repentance would avail to recover that which was lost. The " great and exceeding bitter cry " only reveals the shame, the blessing taken away. Those who, like Esau, despise their place in the family of God are driven out into the fierce opposition of the world ; " by their sword " they must live and " serve their brethren."

VII. THE END OF DECEIT IS HATRED, passion, fear, flight, individual and family disorder and suffering. Yet again the merciful hand interposes to over-rule the errors of man. Jacob's flight from Esau's hatred is his preservation from ungodly alliance with heathen neighbours, and the commencement of a wholesome course of discipline by which his character was purged of much of its evil, and his faith deepened and developed.—R.

Ver. 36.—*Unfaithfulness in believers.* " Is not he rightly named Jacob ? " Jacob, Israel—how widely different the thoughts suggested by the two names. Both tell of success. But one is the man of craft, who takes by the heel to trip up. The other, as a prince of God (cf. Luke i. 15), prevails through believing prayer. Yet Jacob became Israel, and Israel had once been Jacob. The plant of faith has often to struggle through a hard soil. To understand the lessons of his life, remember—1. In contrast to Esau, he was a man of faith. His desire was for a future and spiritual blessing. He believed that it was to be his, and that belief influenced his life. But—2. His faith was imperfect and partial in its operation, and this led to inconsistencies (cf. Matt. xiv. 29, 30 ; Gal. ii. 12). Naturally quiet, his life was passed chiefly at home. Godly influences undisturbed by outward life taught him to worship God, and to prize his promise. But he had not proved his armour (cf. 1 Cor. x. 12) ; and, as often happens, the object of his faith was the means of his trial. His father's purpose in favour of Esau shook his faith (cf. 1 Pet. iv. 18). He yielded to the suggestion to obtain by deceit what God had promised to give (Isa. lix. 1), and earned his brother's taunt, " Is not he rightly named Jacob ? " Yet it does not appear that he was conscious of having failed in faith. Consider—

I. THE DANGER OF SELF-DECEIVING (cf. Ezek. xiii. 10). One brought up among godly influences may seem to possess faith. Ways of faith, hopes of faith, may be familiar to him. He may really embrace them, really desire a spiritual prize. But not without cause are we warned (1 Cor. x. 12). Some plan of worldly wisdom, some point of self-seeking or self-indulgence, attracts him ; only a little way ; not into anything distinctly wrong. Or he falls into indolent self-sufficiency. Then there is a shrinking from close walk with God. Formality takes the place of confidence. All may seem outwardly well ; but other powers than God's will are at work within. And if now some more searching trial is sent, some more distinct choice between God and the world, a self-satisfying plea is easily found. And the self-deceit which led to the fall makes it unfelt. And the path is lighted, but not from God (Isa. l. 11).

II. The harm done to others by unfaithfulness of Christians (cf. Rom. ii. 24; xiv. 16). The world is quick to mark inconsistencies of believers. They form an excuse for the careless, a plea for disbelieving the reality of holiness. And for weak Christians they throw the influence of example on the wrong side (cf. 1 Cor. viii. 9). Deeds have more power than words; and the course of a life may be turned by some thoughtless yielding. Nor can the harm be undone even by repentance. The failure is visible, the contrition and seeking pardon are secret. The sins of good men are eagerly retailed. The earnest supplication for pardon and restoration are known to few, and little cared for. The man himself may be forgiven, and rise stronger from his fall; but the poison in the soul of another is still doing its deadly work.

III. The way of safety. Realise the living Christ (Ephes. iii. 17). Rules of themselves can do little; but to know the love of Christ, to bear it in mind, is power.—M.

EXPOSITION.

Ver. 41.—**And Esau hated Jacob**—a proof that he was not penitent, however disappointed and remorseful (cf. Obad. 10, 11; 1 John iii. 12, 15)—**because of the blessing wherewith his father blessed him** :—notwithstanding the fact that he too had received an appropriate benediction; a display of envy as well as wrath, another proof of his ungracious character (Gal. v. 21; James iv. 5)—**and Esau said in his heart,—**i. e. secretly resolved, though afterwards he must have communicated his intention (*vide* ver. 42)—**The days of mourning for my father are at hand.** The LXX. interpret as a wish on the part of Esau that Isaac might speedily die, in order that the fratricidal act he contemplated might not pain the old man's heart; another rendering (Kalisch) understands him to say that days of grief were in store for his father, as he meant to slay his brother; but the ordinary translation seems preferable (Rosenmüller, Keil, Murphy, *et alii*), that Esau only deferred the execution of his unholy purpose because of the near approach, as he imagined, of his father's death. Isaac, however, lived upwards of forty years after this. **Then will I slay my brother Jacob.** That which reconciled Isaac and Ishmael (ch. xxv. 9), the death of a father, is here mentioned as the event which would decisively and finally part Esau and Jacob. Esau's murderous intention Calvin regards as a clear proof of the non-reality of his repentance for his sin, the insincerity of his sorrow for his father, and the intense malignity of his hate against his brother.

Ver. 42.—**And these** (literally, *the*) **words of Esau her elder son were told to Rebekah:**—not likely by revelation (Augustine), but by some one to whom he had made known his secret purpose (Prov. xxix. 11)—**and she sent and called Jacob her younger son** (to advise him of his danger, being apprehensive

lest the passionate soul of the enraged hunter should find it difficult to delay till Isaac's death), **and said unto him, Behold, thy brother Esau, as touching thee, doth comfort himself,** purposing **to kill thee.** Literally, *behold thy brother Esau taking vengeance upon thee* (the hithpael of נָחַם meaning properly to comfort oneself, hence to satisfy one's feeling of revenge) *by killing thee.* The translations ἀπειλεῖ (LXX.) and *minatur* (Vulgate), besides being inaccurate, are too feeble to express the fratricidal purpose of Esau.

Vers. 43—45.—**Now therefore, my son, obey my voice;**—i. e. be guided by my counsel; a request Rebekah might perhaps feel herself justified in making, not only by her maternal solicitude for Jacob's welfare, but also from the successful issue of her previous stratagem (*vide* on ver. 8)—**and arise, flee thou**—literally, *flee for thyself* (cf. ch. xii. 1; Numb. xxiv. 11; Amos vii. 12)—**to Laban my brother to Haran** (*vide* ch. xi. 31; xxiv. 29); **and tarry with him a few days,**—literally, *days some.* The few days eventually proved to be at least twenty years (*vide* ch. xxxi. 38). It is not probable that Rebekah ever again beheld her favourite son, which was a signal chastisement for her sinful ambition for, and partiality towards, Jacob—**until thy brother's fury turn away; until thy brother's anger turn away from thee,**—the rage of Esau is here described by two different words, the first of which, חֵמָה, from a root signifying to be warm, suggests the heated and inflamed condition of Esau's soul, while the second, אַף, from אָנַף, to breathe through the nostrils, depicts the visible manifestations of that internal fire in hard and quick breathing—**and he forget that which thou hast done to him.** Rebekah apparently had conveniently become oblivious of her own share in the transaction by which Esau had been wronged. **Then will I send, and fetch thee from thence** —which she never did. Man proposes, but God disposes. **Why should I be deprived also of you both in one day?** *I. e.* of Jacob by the hand of Esau, and of Esau by the hand of the avenger of blood (ch. ix. 6; cf. 2 Sam. xiv. 6, 7; Calvin, Keil, Rosenmüller, Kalisch), rather than by his own fratricidal act, which would for ever part him from Rebekah (Lange). Ver. 46. — **And Rebekah said to Isaac** (perhaps already discerning in the contemplated flight to Haran the prospect of a suitable matrimonial alliance for the heir of the promise, and secretly desiring to suggest such a thought to her aged husband),

I am weary of my life because of the daughters of Heth :—referring doubtless to Esau's wives (cf. ch. xxvi. 35)—**if Jacob take a wife of the daughters of Heth, such as these** which are **of the daughters of the land, what good shall my life do me?** Literally, *for what to me life,* i. e. what happiness can I have in living? It is impossible to exonerate Rebekah altogether from a charge of duplicity even in this. Unquestionably Esau's wives may have vexed her, and her faith may have perceived that Jacob's wife must be sought for amongst their own kindred; but her secret reason for sending Jacob to Haran was not to seek a wife, as she seems to have desired Isaac to believe, but to elude the fury of his incensed brother.

HOMILETICS.

Vers. 41—46.—*The stolen blessing: a domestic drama.*—4. *Rebekah and Esau, or fratricide frustrated.* I. THE MURDEROUS DESIGN OF ESAU. 1. *The ostensible reason.* "Because of the blessing wherewith his father had blessed Jacob." No argument can justify wilful and deliberate homicide; least of all an excuse so lame and feeble as that of Esau. The blessing Jacob had obtained was one which he himself had formerly despised and practically sold. If Jacob had been guilty of stealing it from him, as he imagined, it was only what he had been attempting to do with reference to Jacob. Besides, in so far as the blessing was an object of desire to Esau, viz., for its material advantages, he had himself received a blessing not greatly dissimilar. There was therefore no sufficient cause for Esau's hostility towards his brother. 2. *The impelling motive.* "Hate"—the essential spirit of murder (Matt. v. 22; 1 John iii. 15). Esau's causeless hatred of Jacob was typical of the world's enmity against the Church: in its ground, the Church's enjoyment of the blessing; in its spirit, bitter and implacable; in its manifestation, persecution and oppression (1 John iii. 13). 3. *The decorous restraint.* "The days of mourning for my father are at hand; then will I slay my brother." Wicked men who resist all the influences of piety are not always able to surmount the barriers of public opinion. Though Esau had no scruples on the score of conscience as to killing Jacob, he had some scruples on the ground of decency as to doing it while his father lived. Persons who have no religion not unfrequently do homage to the appearance of religion. 4. *The providential discovery.* Though Esau originally resolved on Jacob's murder in secret, he appears to have inadvertently disclosed his purpose to another, who forthwith communicated his intention to Rebekah. Those who have secrets to keep should tell them to no one; but Divine providence has wisely and mercifully arranged that guilty secrets should be ill to keep. "Murder will out." 5. *The inglorious defeat.* The information brought to Rebekah enabled her to counterwork Esau's design, and thus a second time was Esau outwitted by a woman. It is obvious that some sons are not so clever as their mothers. II. THE PRUDENT COUNSEL OF REBEKAH. 1. *Hastily formed.* The shrewd sagacity of Isaac's wife at once perceived an outlet from the snare. The woman's wit that had cheated Isaac was not likely to be baffled with blustering Esau. Calling Jacob from the herds, she told him of his brother's murderous design, and detailed her own scheme for his protection. 2. *Clearly explained.* He should immediately betake himself to Haran, and seek shelter for a season beside his uncle Laban and his cousins. Though Rebekah does not mention the propriety of looking for a wife, it is apparent that the possibility of Jacob's finding one was present to her thoughts. 3. *Skilfully urged.* Arguments were not long in coming to Rebekah's aid. (1) His brother's anger would soon burn out. (2) His absence accordingly would not require to be long. (3) If he did not go he was certain to be killed, in which case

Esau would fall a victim to judicial retribution, and she, a heart-broken mother, would be deprived of both her sons in one day. (4) She was his mother, and her advice should be received with filial reverence and submission. 4. *Adroitly carried through.* Securing her son's compliance, there was still the difficulty how to obtain the assent of Isaac. This she does by leading Isaac himself to suggest the propriety of Jacob's going north to Padan-aram in search of a wife ; and to this she turns the thoughts of Isaac by expressing the hope that Jacob will not imitate his brother by marrying daughters of the land, a calamity, she informs her husband, which would render her already miserable life scarcely worth retaining. It was prudent in Rebekah to direct the mind of Isaac to the propriety of getting Jacob married, but there is not wanting a trace of that craftiness which was Rebekah's peculiar infirmity.

Learn—1. That the world's hostility to the Church is wholly unreasonable and unjustifiable. 2. That wicked devices against God's people are sure eventually to be overturned. 3. That bad men sometimes wear a semblance of religion. 4. That good mothers grieve for the wickedness of bad, and work for the safety of good, sons. 5. That while wicked matches in their children are a burden to gracious parents, it should be a parent's aim to secure pious wives for their sons, and Christian husbands for their daughters.

HOMILIES BY VARIOUS AUTHORS.

Ver. 46.—*Rebekah, the disappointed.* " What good shall my life do me ? " Rebekah as a mother doubtless promised herself much joy in her children. They grew up. Esau becomes wayward, Jacob becomes a wanderer. Rebekah yielded to favouritism (ver. 13), and schemed to carry her point. She cherished a treacherous spirit, and led Jacob to sin. She was ambitious not for herself, but for Jacob. This is like woman ; she lives in others. She was reckless as to results, but when they came she found them bitter. " She loved Jacob more than truth, more than God." This was idolatry. No wonder she utters the exclamation, " What good shall my life do me ? " She was a disappointed woman. Her favourite son was in hiding from the wrath of a wronged brother, and Esau was indifferent towards her and angry. If life is not to be a disappointment we must beware of—

I. Unscrupulous scheming.

II. Affections that care more for happiness than honour.

III. Of idolatry, covetousness, and neglect of God's claims.

IV. Of ignoring the rights of others.

V. Of ignorance as to the true elements of success.

Rebekah began well. Her advent unto the encampment was a " comfort " to Isaac. She seems to have been " weary of life," and asks " what good it shall do her." Some who ask at this day " whether life is worth living " may find a suggestion in Rebekah's conduct as to the reason wherefore they ask the question.—H.

EXPOSITION.

CHAPTER XXVIII.

Ver. 1.—**And Isaac** (recognising the wisdom and propriety of Rebekah's suggestion that a bride should now be sought for him whom God had so unmistakably declared to be the heir of the theocratic promise) **called Jacob** (to his bed-side), **and blessed him,**—in enlarged form, renewing the benediction previously given (ch. xxvii. 27)—**and said unto him, Thou shalt not take a wife of the daughters of Canaan** (cf. ch. xxiv. 3). Intermarriage with the women of the land was expressly forbidden to the theocratic heir,

while his attention was directed to his mother's kindred.

Ver. 2.—**Arise, go to Padan-aram** (*vide* ch. xxiv. 10 ; xxv. 20 ; xxvii. 43), **to the house of Bethuel thy mother's father ;**— (*vide* ch. xxiv. 24). If yet alive, Bethuel must have been very old, since he was Isaac's cousin, and probably born many years before the son of Abraham—**and take thee a wife from thence**—though Isaac's wife was found for him, he does not think of imitating Abraham and despatching another Eliezer in search of a spouse for Rebekah's son. Probably he saw that Jacob could attend to that business sufficiently without assistance from others—**of the daughters of Laban thy mother's brother** (*vide* ch. xxiv. 29). "Isaac appears to entertain no doubt of Jacob's success, which might be the more probable since the same reason which kept Jacob from marrying in Canaan might prevent Laban's daughters from being married in Haran, the worshippers of the Lord being few" (Inglis). Ver. 3.—**And God Almighty**—El Shaddai (*vide* ch. xvii. 1)—**bless thee,**—the Abrahamic benediction in its fullest form was given by El Shaddai (*vide* ch. xvii. 1—8)—**and make thee fruitful, and multiply thee, that thou mayest be**—literally, *and thou shalt become* (or grow to)—**a multitude**—an assembly, or congregation, or crowd called together, from a root signifying to call together (Gesenius), or to sweep up together (Fürst) ; corresponding to ἐκκλησία in Greek—**of people.** Ver. 4.—**And give thee the blessing of Abraham,**—*i. e.* promised to Abraham (*vide* ch. xii. 2 ; xxii. 17, 18). The additions of τοῦ πατρός μου (LXX.), אָבִיךָ = τοῦ πατρὸς σου (Samaritan), are unwarranted—**to thee, and to thy seed with thee; that thou mayest inherit the land wherein thou art a stranger,**—literally, *the land of thy sojournings* (ch. xvii. 8)—**which God gave unto Abraham**—by promise (cf. ch. xii. 7 ; xiii. 15 ; xv. 7, 18 ; xvii. 8). Ver. 5. — **And Isaac sent away Jacob**

(Rebekah only counselled, Isaac commanded): **and he went to Padan-aram unto Laban, son of Bethuel the Syrian** (*vide* Hosea xii. 12), **the brother of Rebekah, Jacob's and Esau's mother.** The historian here perhaps intentionally gives the first place to Jacob. Vers. 6—9.—**When** (literally, *and*) **Esau saw that Isaac had blessed Jacob, and sent him away to Padan-aram, to take him a wife from thence ; and that as he blessed him he gave him a charge,**—literally, *in his blessing him* (forming a parenthesis), *and he commanded him*—**saying, Thou shalt not take a wife of the daughters of Canaan ; and that** (literally, *and*) **Jacob obeyed his father and his mother, and was gone** (or went) **to Padan-aram ; and Esau seeing that** (more correctly, *saw that*) **the daughters of Canaan pleased not** (literally, *were evil in the eyes of*) **Isaac his father;** then (literally, *and*) **went Esau unto Ishmael** (*i. e.* the family or tribe of Ishmael, aiming in this likely to please his father), **and took unto the wives which he had** (so that they were neither dead nor divorced) **Mahalath** (called Bashemath in ch. xxxvi. 3) **the daughter of Ishmael** (and therefore Esau's half-cousin by the father's side, Ishmael, who was now dead thirteen years, having been Isaac's half-brother) **Abraham's son, the sister of Nebajoth,**—Ishmael's firstborn (*vide* ch. xxv. 13)—**to be his wife.**

HOMILETICS.

Vers. 1—9.—*Jacob and Esau, or diverging paths.* I. JACOB'S JOURNEY TO PADAN-ARAM. 1. *The path of duty.* Entered on in obedience to his mother's wish and his father's commandment, it was an evidence of filial piety. It is the token of a good son that he "hears the instruction of his father, and forsakes not the law of his mother" (Prov. i. 8). Sons come to mature age should respect and, where not inconsistent with allegiance to God, yield submission to parental authority (Prov. vi. 20 ; Mal. i. 6 ; Ephes. vi. 1—3). 2. *The path of blessing.* The benediction already bestowed upon Jacob was repeated with greater amplitude and tenderness before he left the patriarchal tent. Happy the youth who enters upon life's journey carrying on his head and in his heart a father's blessing ! much more who goes forth beneath the canopy of Heaven's benediction ! and this is ever the experience of him who travels by the way of filial obedience. Pious children seldom fail to come to honour, and never want the favour of the Lord (Ps. xxxvii. 26 ; Prov. iv. 20—22 ; viii. 32). 3. *The path of promise.* In addition to his father's blessing and the Almighty's benediction, Jacob carried with him as he left Beersheba the promise of a seed and an inheritance to be in due time acquired ; and in like manner now has the saint exceeding great and precious promises to cheer him in his heavenward pilgrimage, promises the full realisation of which is attainable only in the future (John xiv. 2 ; 1 Pet. i. 4). 4. *The path of hope.* Sad and sorrowful as Jacob's heart must have been as he kissed his mother and bade farewell to Isaac, it was at least sustained by pleasant expectation. Gilding the horizon of his future was the prospect of a wife to love as Isaac had loved Rebekah, and to be the mother of the seed of promise. So the pathway of the children of promise, though often painful, arduous, and protracted, is always lighted by the star of hope, and always points to a bright and beautiful beyond. II. ESAU'S MARRIAGE WITH MAHALATH. 1. *The way of sin.* His former wives being neither dead nor divorced, the conduct of Esau in adding to them a third was wrong. 2. *The way of shame.* In the selection of Ishmael's daughter he hoped to please his father, but was apparently indifferent about the judgment of either Rebekah or Jehovah. Daring transgressors, like Esau, rather glory in their shame than feel abashed at their wickedness. 3. *The way of sorrow.* If not to himself, at least to his pious parents, this fresh matrimonial alliance could not fail to be a grief. The daughter of Ishmael was certainly better than a daughter of the Hittites, being almost as near a relative on Isaac's side as Rachel and Leah were on Rebekah's ; but, unlike Rachel and Leah, who belonged to the old family stock (the Terachites) in Mesopotamia, Mahalath descended from a branch which had been removed from the Abrahamic tree.

Learn—1. The care which pious parents should take to see their sons well married. 2. The piety which children should delight to show to their parents. 3. The connection which subsists between true religion and prosperity. 4. The inevitable tendency of sin to produce shame and sorrow. 5. The wickedness of violating God's law of marriage.

HOMILIES BY VARIOUS AUTHORS.

Vers. 1—9.—*Life with, and life without, God.* The divergence of the two representative men is seen in this short statement of their marriage relations. 1. Domestic life under the blessing of God and apart from that blessing. 2. The true blessing is the blessing of Abraham, the blessing which God has already provided, promised, and secured. 3. The heir of the blessing must be sent away and learn by experience how to use it. 4. The disinherited man, who has scorned his opportunity, cannot recover it by his own devices. Esau is still Esau. Polygamy was suffered, but never had the blessing of God upon it.—R.

EXPOSITION.

Ver. 10.—**And Jacob went out from Beersheba,** — in obedience to his father's commandment to seek a wife (ver. 2), but also in compliance with his mother's counsel to evade the wrath of Esau (ch. xxvii. 43 ; cf. Hosea xii. 12. On Beersheba *vide* ch. xxi. 31 ; xxvi. 33—**and went towards Haran**—probably along the route traversed by Abraham's servant (cf. ch. xxiv. 10).

Ver. 11.—**And he lighted upon a certain place,**—literally, *he struck upon the place;* *i. e.* either the place best suited for him to rest in (Inglis), or the place appointed for him by God (Ainsworth, Bush), or more probably the well-known place afterwards mentioned (Keil, Wordsworth, 'Speaker's Commentary'). Situated in the mountains of Ephraim, about three hours north of Jerusalem, it was not reached after one, but after several days' journey (cf. ch. xxii. 4)—**and tarried there all night, because the sun was set ;**—being either remote from the city Luz when overtaken by darkness, or unwilling to enter the town ; not because he hated the inhabitants (Josephus), but because he was a stranger—**and he took of the stones of that place,**—*i. e.* one of the stones (*vide* ver. 18). "The track (of pilgrims) winds through an uneven valley, covered, as with gravestones, by large sheets of bare rock ;

some few here and there standing up like the cromlechs of Druidical monuments" (Stanley's 'Sinai and Palestine,' p. 219 ; cf. 'Lectures on Jewish Church,' p. 59)—**and put them for his pillows,**—literally, *and put for his head-bolster,* the word signifying that which is at the head of any one (cf. 1 Sam. xix. 13 ; xxvi. 7, 11, 16 ; 1 Kings xix. 6)—**and lay down in that place to sleep** (cf. ch. xix. 4 ; 1 Sam. iii. 5, 6, 9).

Ver. 12.—**And he dreamed.** This dream, which has been pronounced "beautifully ingenious," "clever," and "philosophical," the work of a later Hebrew poet, and not of Jacob (De Wette), was not wonderful considering the state of mind and body in which he must have been—fatigued by travel, saddened by thoughts of home, doubtless meditating on his mother, and more than likely pondering the great benediction of his aged and, to all appearance, dying father. Yet while these circumstances may account for the mental framework of the dream, the dream itself was Divinely sent. **And behold a ladder**—the rough stones of the mountain appearing to form themselves into a vast staircase (Stanley, Bush) — **set up on the earth, and the top of it reached to heaven:** —symbolically intimating the fact of a real, uninterrupted, and close communication between heaven and earth, and in particular between God in his glory and man in his solitude and sin—**and behold the angels of God**—literally, *the messengers of Elohim*, i. e. the angels (Ps. ciii. 20, 21; civ. 4; Heb. i. 14)—**ascending and descending on it** —*vide* John i. 51, which shows that Christ regarded either the ladder in Jacob's vision as an emblem of himself, the one Mediator between God and man (Calvin, Luther, Ainsworth, 'Speaker's Commentary,' Murphy), or, what is more probable, Jacob himself as a type of him, the Son of man, in whom the living intercourse between earth and heaven depicted in the vision of the angel-trodden staircase was completely fulfilled (Hengstenberg, Baumgarten, Lange, Bush).

Ver. 13.—**And, behold,**—"the dream-vision is so glorious that the narrator represents it by a threefold הִנֵּה"(Lange)—**the Lord stood above it,**—the change in the Divine name is not to be explained by assigning vers. 13—16 to the Jehovistic editor (Tuch, Bleek) or to a subsequent redactor (Davidson), since without it the Elohistic document would be abrupt, if not incomplete (Kalisch), but by recalling the fact that it is not the general providence of the Deity over his creature man, but the special superintendence of the God of Abraham and of Isaac over his chosen people, that the symbolic ladder was intended to depict (Hengstenberg)—**and said, I am the Lord God of Abraham thy father, and the God of Isaac:**—thus not simply proclaiming his personal name Jehovah, but announcing himself as the Elohim who had solemnly entered into covenant with his ancestors, and who had now come, in virtue of that covenant, to renew to him the promises he had previously given them—**the land whereon thou liest, to thee will I give it, and to thy seed**—given to Abraham, ch. xiii. 15; to Isaac, ch. xxvi. 3.

Ver. 14.—**And thy seed shall be as the dust of the earth,**—promised to Abraham, ch. xiii. 16; to Isaac, under a different emblem, ch. xxvi. 4—**and thou shalt spread abroad** (literally, *break forth*) **to the west, and to the east, to the north, and to the south :**—(cf. ch. xiii. 14; Deut. xii. 20). In its ultimate significance this points to the world-wide universality of the kingdom of Christ (Murphy)—**and in thee and in thy seed shall all the families of the earth be blessed** (*vide* ch. xii. 3; xviii. 18; xxii. 18 (Abraham); xxvi. 4 (Isaac).

Ver. 15.—**And, behold, I am with thee,**—spoken to Isaac (ch. xxvi. 24); again to Jacob (ch. xxxi. 3); afterwards to Christ's disciples (Matt. xxviii. 20)—**and will keep thee in all** places **whither thou goest,**—literally, *in all thou goest* = in all thy goings (cf. ch. xlviii. 16; Ps. cxxi. 5, 7, 8)—**and will bring thee again into this land ;**—equi-

valent to an intimation that his present journey to Padan-aram was not without the Divine sanction, though apparently it had been against the will of God that Isaac should leave the promised land (*vide* ch. xxiv. 6, 8)—**for I will not leave thee,**—a promise afterwards repeated to Israel (Deut. xxxi. 6, 8), to Joshua (ch. i. 5), to Solomon (1 Chron. xxviii. 20), to the poor and needy (Isa. xli. 17), to Christians (Heb. xiii. 7)—**until I have done** that **which I have spoken to thee of**—cf. Balaam's testimony to the Divine faithfulness (Numb. xxiii. 19), and Joshua's (ch. xxi. 45), and Solomon's (1 Kings viii. 56). It is impossible, in connection with this sublime theophany granted to Jacob at Bethel, not to recall the similar Divine manifestation vouchsafed to Abraham beneath the starry firmament at Hebron (*vide* ch. xv. 1).

Ver. 16.—**And Jacob awaked out of his sleep** (during which he had seen and talked with Jehovah), **and he said, Surely the Lord is in this place; and I knew it not.** Jacob does not here learn the doctrine of the Divine omnipresence for the first time (Knobel), but now discovers that the covenant God of Abraham revealed himself at other than consecrated places (Rosenmüller, Keil, Lange, Murphy); or perhaps simply gives expression to his astonishment at finding that whereas he fancied himself alone, he was in reality in the company of God—*se plus adeptum esse quam sperare ausus fuisset* (Calvin).

Ver. 17.—**And he was afraid,**—so were Moses (Exod. xx. 18, 19), Job (ch. xlii. 5, 6), Isaiah (ch. vi. 5), Peter (Luke v. 8), John (Rev. i. 17, 18), at similar discoveries of the Divine presence—**and said, How dreadful is this place !**—*i. e.* how to be feared! how awe-inspiring ! φοβερὸς (LXX.), *terribilis* (Vulgate)—**this is none other but the house of God, and this is the gate of heaven.** Not literally, but figuratively, the place where God dwells, and the entrance to his glorious abode (Keil); the idea that Jacob was "made aware by the dream that he had slept on one of those favoured spots singled out for a future sanctuary, and was fearful that he had sinned by employing it for a profane purpose" (Kalisch), being fanciful.

Ver. 18.—**And Jacob rose up early in the morning** (cf. ch. xix. 27; xxii. 3), **and took the stone that he had put for his pillows** (*vide supra*), **and set it up for a pillar** —literally, *set it up, a pillar* (or something set upright, hence a statue or monument); not as an object of worship, a sort of fetish, but as a memorial of the vision (Calvin, Keil, Murphy; cf. ch. xxxi. 45; xxxv. 14; Josh. iv. 9, 20; xxiv. 26; 1 Sam. vii. 12)—**and poured oil upon the top of it.** *Quasi signum consecrationis* (Calvin), and not because he regarded it as in itself invested with any degree of sanctity. The worship of sacred stones (Bætylia), afterwards prevalent among the Greeks, Romans, Hindoos, Arabs, and Germans, though by some (Kuenen, Oort ; *vide* 'The Bible for Young People,' vol. i. p. 231) regarded as one of the primeval forms of worship among the Hebrews, was expressly interdicted by the law of Moses (cf. Exod. xxiii. 24 ; xxxiv. 13 ; Levit. xxvi. 1 ; Deut. xii. 3 ; xvi. 22). It was probably a heathen imitation of the rite here recorded, though by some authorities (Keil, Knobel, Lange) the Bætylian worship is said to have been connected chiefly with meteoric stones which were supposed to have descended from some divinity ; as, *e. g.*, the stone in Delphi sacred to Apollo ; that in Emesa, on the Orontes, consecrated to the sun ; the angular rock at Pessinus in Phrygia worshipped as hallowed by Cybele ; the black stone in the Kaaba at Mecca believed to have been brought from heaven by the angel Gabriel (*vide* Kalisch *in loco*). That the present narrative was a late invention, "called into existence by a desire" on the part of the priests and prophets of Yahweh (Jehovah) "to proclaim the high antiquity of the sanctuary at Bethel, and to make a sacred stone harmless" ('The Bible for Young People,' vol. i. p. 231), is pure assumption. The circumstance that the usage here mentioned is nowhere else in Scripture countenanced (except in ch. xxxv. 14, with reference to this same pillar) forms a sufficient pledge of the high antiquity of the narrative (*vide* Hävernick's ' Introd.,' § 20).

Ver. 19. — **And he called the name of that place Bethel** — *i. e.* house of God. Rosenmüller and Kalisch find a connection between Bethel and Bætylia, the former regarding Bætylia as a corruption of Bethel, and the latter viewing Bethel as the Hebraised form of Bætylion. Keil objects to both that the interchange of τ in βαιτύλιον and θ in βαιθήλ would be perfectly inexplicable. On the site of Bethel (Beitin) *vide* ch. xii. 8. **But the name of that city** was called **Luz at the first.** Originally the Canaanitish town, built according to Calvin after this event, was called Luz, or "almond tree," a name it continued to bear until the conquest (Judges i. 23). From the circumstances recorded in the narrative, Jacob called the spot where he slept (in the vicinity of Luz) Bethel—the designation afterwards extending to the town (ch. xxxv. 6). Until the conquest both titles appear to have been used—Luz by the Canaanites, Bethel by the Israelites. When the conquest was completed the Hebrew name was substituted for the Hittite, the sole survivor of the captured city building another Luz in another part of the country (*vide* Judges i. 26).

Vers. 20, 21.—**And Jacob vowed a vow,**—

not in any mercenary or doubtful spirit, but as an expression of gratitude for the Divine mercy (Calvin), as the soul's full and free acceptance of the Lord to be its own God (Murphy), as the instinctive impulse of the new creature (Candlish)—**saying, If** (not the language of uncertainty, but equivalent to "since," or "forasmuch as ;" Jacob by faith both appropriating and anticipating the fulfilment of the preceding promise) **God** (Elohim ; for the reason of which *vide infra*) **will be with me,**—as he has promised (ver. 15), and as I believe he will—**and will keep me in this way that I go,**—a particular appropriation of the general promise (ver. 15) —**and will give me bread to eat, and raiment to put on** (*i. e.* all the necessaries of life, included, though not specially mentioned, in the preceding promise), **so that I come again to my father's house**—also guaranteed by God (ver. 15), and here accepted by the patriarch—**in peace** (*i. e.* especially free from Esau's avenging threats); **then shall the Lord be my God**—literally, *and Jehovah will be to me for Elohim* (Rosenmüller, Hengstenberg, Keil, Kalisch, 'Speaker's Commentary'), though the received translation is not without support (LXX., Vulgate, Syriac, Calvin, Michaelis, Lange, Murphy, Wordsworth) ; but to have bargained and bartered with God in the way which this suggests before assenting to accept him as an object of trust and worship would have been little less than criminal. Accordingly, the clause is best placed in the protasis of the sentence, which then practically reads, "if Elohim will be Jehovah to me, and if Jehovah will be to me Elohim" (*vide* Hengstenberg, 'Introduction,' vol. i. p. 358).

Ver. 22.—**And** (or then, the apodosis now commencing) **this stone which I have set for a pillar** (*vide* on ver. 18) **shall be God's house** — Bethel, meaning that he would afterwards erect there an altar for the celebration of Divine worship — a resolution which was subsequently carried out (*vide* ch. xxxv. 1, 15). "The pillar or cairn or cromlech of Bethel must have been looked upon by the Israelites, and may be still looked upon in thought by us, as the precursor of every "house of God" that has since arisen in the Jewish and Christian world—the temple, the cathedral, the church, the chapel ; nay, more, of those secret places of worship that are marked by no natural beauty and seen by no human eye—the closet, the catacomb, the thoroughfare of the true worshipper" (Stanley's ' Jewish Church,' lect. iii. p. 60). **And of all that thou shalt give me I will surely give the tenth unto thee.** Literally, *giving I will give the tenth* (cf. ch. xiv. 20). The case of Jacob affords another proof that the practice of voluntary tithing was known and observed antecedent to the time of Moses

HOMILETICS.

Vers. 10—22.—*Jacob at Bethel, or heaven opened.* I. THE LONELY SLEEPER. 1. *His desolate condition.* Exiled from home, fleeing from the murderous resentment of a brother, o'er-canopied by the star-lit firmament, remote from human habitation, and encompassed by a heathen population, on the bleak summit of the Bethel plateau, upwards of sixty miles from Beersheba, the wandering son of Isaac makes his evening couch with a stone slab for his pillow, an emblem of many another footsore and dejected traveller upon life's journey. 2. *His inward cogitations.* The current of his thoughts needs not be difficult to imagine. Mingling with the sadness of leaving home, and the apprehension with which he regarded the uncertain future, there could not fail to be a sense of security, if not a gleam of hope, arising from the consciousness that he carried with him his father's blessing ; in this again affording a reflex of most men's lives, in which joy and sorrow, hope and fear, continually meet and strangely blend. 3. *His heavenly visitation.* If the dream by which Jacob's slumber was disturbed was occasioned by unusual cerebral excitement, if its psychological framework was supplied by the peculiar colour of his meditations, it is still true that it was made the medium of a Divine theophany and revelation. So God, who is "never far from any one of us," is specially near to his children in solitude and sorrow, "in dreams, in visions of the night, when deep sleep falleth upon men, in slumberings upon the bed, opening the ears of men, and sealing their instruction" (Job xxxiii. 15, 16).

II. THE MIDNIGHT DREAM. 1. *The celestial vision.* (1) A ladder reaching from earth to heaven ; suggesting the thought of an open pathway of communication between God and man, and in particular between the heirs of the promise and their covenant God. (2) The angels of God ascending and descending upon it ; symbolising God's providential government of the world by means of the celestial hosts (Ps. ciii. 20, 21 ; civ. 4), but especially the ministry of angels towards the heirs of salvation (Ps. xci. 11 ; Heb. i. 14). A truth henceforward to be exemplified in the experience of Jacob, and afterwards more fully, indeed completely and ideally, realised in Christ. (3) Jehovah standing above it. The situation occupied by the symbolic presence of Jehovah was designed to indicate two things : first, that Jehovah was the true and only source whence blessing could descend to man ; and, second, that the pathway which had been opened up for sinful man conducted straight into God's immediate presence. Thus it was a visible unveiling of the grace and glory comprehended in the covenant, and now fully revealed by the gospel. 2. *The accompanying voice.* (1) Proclaiming the Divine name; as the covenant God of Abraham and of Isaac, of which the New Testament interpretation is the God and Father of our Lord and Saviour Jesus Christ, the true seed of Abraham. (2) Renewing the covenant promises—of a land, of a seed, of a blessing. (3) Personally engaging to extend to Jacob continual attendance,—" Behold, I am with thee,"—constant protection,—" and will keep thee in all thy goings,"—complete fidelity,—" I will not leave thee," &c. ; in all which again the voice was but an anticipatory echo of the heavenly voice that sounds in the gospel.

III. THE AWE-STRUCK AWAKENING. 1. *Devout impression.* The night having passed in contemplation of the unseen world, the morning found the startled sleeper with a strong sense of the supernatural upon his soul, which filled him with alarm. Even to God's reconciled children awe-inspiring (cf. Job xlii. 6 ; Isa. vi. 5 ; Luke v. 8 ; Rev. i. 17), a vivid realisation of the Divine presence is to the sinful heart overwhelmingly terrible. 2. *Reverent adoration.* "This is none other but the house of God "—implying ideas of Divine residence,—"Surely the Lord is in this place ! "— Divine provision,—the thoughts of "bread to eat and raiment to put on " appear to have been suggested to Jacob's mind,—and Divine communion—Jacob realises as never before the conception of personal intercourse between Jehovah and his people ; —" and the gate of heaven "—in which lie embedded the fundamental notions of nearness, vision, entrance. 3. *Grateful commemoration.* (1) He sets up the stone slab on which his head had rested as a visible memorial of the sublime transaction which had there occurred, and in token of his gratitude pours the only gift he carried with him on it, viz., oil. Sincere piety demands that God's merciful visitations should be remembered and thankfully acknowledged by offerings of the choicest and best of our possessions. (2) He calls the name of the place Bethel: in the mean time with a view to his own comfort and satisfaction, but also, there is little doubt, with an eye to the instruction and encouragement of his descendants. It is dutiful in saints not only to rejoice their own hearts by the recollection of Divine mercies, but also to take measures for transmitting the knowledge of them to future generations.

IV. THE SOLEMN VOW. 1. *Faith's expectation.* In a spirit not of mercenary stipulation, but of believing anticipation, Jacob expresses confidence in henceforth enjoying (1) Divine companionship—"If," or since, "God will be with me;" (2) Divine protection—"and will keep me in this way that I go;" (3) Divine sustenance—"and will give me bread to eat, and raiment to put on;" (4) Divine favour—"so that I come again to my father's house in peace;" and (5) Divine salvation—"then," or rather, and since, "Jehovah shall be my God;"—five things promised to the poorest and most desolate of heaven's pilgrims. 2. *Faith's resolution.* Confidently anticipating the fulfilment of God's promises, Jacob resolves—(1) To erect an altar at Bethel on returning to the Holy Land, a vow which he afterwards fulfilled. Whatever vows God's people make should be paid, and no vows are more agreeable to God's will than those which have for their objects the cultivation of personal piety and the perpetuation and spread of his religion among men. (2) To consecrate the tenth part of his increase to God, *i. e.* to the maintenance of God's worship—an example of pious liberality which has seldom been approached by Christ's followers, though, considering their higher privileges and obligations, it ought to have been frequently surpassed.

HOMILIES BY VARIOUS AUTHORS.

Vers. 10—22.—*Jacob's dream.* Where revelations had been vouchsafed it was supposed that they would be repeated. The stony pillow on which the weary head rested may be changed by the visitation of Divine grace into the meeting-place of heaven and earth. The morning beams breaking in upon the shadowy refuge of the night are transfigured into a dream of covenant blessing. The ladder set up on the earth, the top of it reached to heaven. Angels of God on the way of mediation, ascending, descending, carrying up the wants and services of the man of God, bringing down the messages of consolation, the vouchsafements of help and deliverance. "Behold, the Lord stood above it," as the source of all the blessing, standing ready to work for his chosen. This is the first direct communication of Jehovah to Jacob, the first in a long line of revelations of which he was the recipient. It is a renewal of the covenant made to his fathers, it is a republication of the promises. But we require to hear the Lord say to us, " I am with *thee*, I will not leave thee," especially when we are already on the journey of faith, when we are obeying the commandment of God, and of the father and mother speaking in his name. Such a place as Jacob found may be made known to us—

I. IN PROVIDENTIAL INTERPOSITIONS. We journey on through the wilderness and light upon a certain place where we think we are only among stony facts, where we can find but a harsh welcome; but the Lord is in the place, though we know it not till he reveals himself. Then we cry with trembling gratitude, This is the house of God, &c.

II. IN SEASONS OF RELIGIOUS OPPORTUNITY. The ordinary and customary is lifted up by special gift of the Spirit into the opened heaven, the visiting angels, the vision of the throne of God. "The house of God, the gate of heaven." Such may be the awaking of our soul in the sanctuary of our own private devotions or of our public worship.

III. Jacob is A TYPE OF THE LORD'S PEOPLE REGARDED AS A WHOLE. The Church has often laid itself down upon the stones and slept with weariness in its passage through the desert, and the Lord has revealed the ladder of his covenant, connecting together that very place and time of hardship with the throne of grace and glory, and the ascending and descending angels.

IV. Jesus himself employed this dream of the patriarch as A TYPICAL PROPHECY OF THE KINGDOM OF GOD. "Heaven open, and the angels of God ascending and descending upon the Son of man," the true Jacob, the Prince prevailing with God and with men (John i. 51). The cross is the ladder of mediation. It was set up on the earth. It was not of earthly origin as a means of atonement, but its foot was on the earth as it came forth out of the method and course of earthly history in connection with Divine counsels. Its top reached to heaven, for it was a Divine Mediator whose sacrifice was offered upon it. Angels of God ascended and descended upon the ladder, for only through the atoning merit of Christ is angelic ministration maintained. It is for them "who shall be heirs of salvation." At the summit of the cross, representing the whole mediatorial work of Christ, is the Lord standing, speaking his word of covenant, and stretching forth his right hand on behalf of his people. Resting at the foot of the cross we hear the voice of a faithful Guide, saying, "I will not leave thee," &c. In every place one who is conscious of surrounding covenant mercy can say, "This is none other but the house of God," &c.—R.

Ver. 12.—*A stairway to heaven.* "And he dreamed, and behold a ladder set up on the earth, and the top of it reached to heaven." Jacob in fear of his life leaves home. The last kiss of his mother is taken. During the day Jacob goes forward cheerfully. Night comes on at length. The path is no longer distinct. The wind moans sadly. A sense of loneliness creeps over him. Fear of Esau haunts him. He sees the figure of his brother behind this shrub and that rock. Had Esau outrun to murder him in that lonely spot? He trembles at every shadow, and shudders at every sound. He thinks of the God of his father and mother, and prays. He lies down in the desert; a furze-bush is his only shelter, and a stone his hard pillow. He looks up into the dark vault all glittering with the silent stars. More intense becomes his loneliness, for the stars have no voice for him. Plotting and far-seeing Jacob had deep home-longings, mystic inquirings, and a wealth of affection in his nature. Of such God can make something; to such God can reveal something. To idolatrous, carnal Esaus how little can God make known. Selfishness hinders. Here in the desert Jacob draws his camel-hair robe more tightly over his feet, and dreams of parents and home, and heaven and God. It might surprise us that he could have such sweet dreams when he was fleeing from the one whom he had undoubtedly wronged. God would over-rule the wrong, and therefore sent him this vision.

I. ALL HAVE DREAMS OF A HEAVEN. A heaven is that for which all men are seeking, whether sought in the way of business, or pleasure, or politics, or literature. Even sceptics have their heaven in their doubt and intellectual pride. That which is our highest object is our heaven. As water cannot rise above its level, so the heaven of some cannot be above their thoughts. There will be a future state answering to the highest longings of the believer, a place of existence in glory far beyond anything here.

II. ACTUAL COMMUNICATION WITH HEAVEN IS POSSIBLE. One author (Hazlitt) says, "In the days of Jacob there was a ladder between heaven and earth, but now the heavens are gone further and become astronomical." True science opens up an infinite number of worlds and densely-peopled spaces. Material discoveries lessen the sense of spiritual realities. It need not be so. If the universe is great, how great also is the soul, which can embrace in its thoughts the universe! And it is in the soul that God can and does reveal heaven. Peace, hope, love is the spirit of heaven, and that is revealed by Christ. Purify the spirit and heaven comes near.

III. EARNEST EFFORT IS NEEDED TO MAINTAIN COMMUNICATION WITH HEAVEN. In the dream of Jacob he saw a picture of his own struggling ascent in life. Angels might flit up and down, but man had to *struggle* and put forth earnest effort to maintain the union. Early in life the ascent seems easy. A mountain never appears so far to its summit as it is in reality. As we go on we become more conscious of the difficulties in the way of maintaining the open communications. Often we find ourselves with heads between our hands, pondering whether we shall ever overcome the evil and attain to the good.

IV. THERE IS ALWAYS HELP FROM THE HEAVENS IN THE EFFORT TO MAINTAIN THE COMMUNICATION. A voice comes to Jacob. A promise of guidance and support was given. Christ in his conversation with Nathaniel shows us how all good comes through him. In Christ all goodness centres. All heaven rays out from him in the pardon and reconciliation he has brought. He is the Word made flesh. He is the Divine voice from above. Through him the Holy Spirit is given, and that Holy Spirit shows us things to come, makes heaven plain, and the way direct. One day we shall be called to follow the way the angels go, and after death shall ascend that stairway which "slopes through darkness up to God."—H.

Ver. 15.—*God's providential care.* "Behold, I am with thee, and will keep thee in all places whither thou goest." Among things believed, but not sufficiently realised, is the truth of God's constant overruling care. We can trace cause and effect a little way, then lose the chain, and feel as if it went no further, as if events had no special cause. This a common evil in the life of Christians. Its root, walking by sight more than by faith. Jacob—what made him try craft? Did not trust God fully. Had no habit of faith. But God had not forgotten him. And as he slept on the stone at Bethel the reality of God's presence was made known to him (Isa. xliii. 2; Matt. xxviii. 20) and recorded for our learning.

I. GOD DOES ALWAYS WATCH OVER AND GUIDE. The ladder was not a new thing; it had existed always. The vision showed what exists everywhere (2 Kings vi. 17). The ladder shows the truth which should stamp our lives. God is love, and love means care. This is for all. Not our love that causes it. Our love, trust, life spring from that truth. The living God is close to us. His hand touches our life at every point. How is it that we are unconscious of this?

II. GOD'S WORKING IS HIDDEN AND SILENT. Jacob was startled to find him near. Because year by year the world goes on as before, unbelievers deny God's active presence, worldly men think not of it, and even godly men sometimes forget; for we cannot see the top of the ladder. But God, there, directs all.

III. HIS PURPOSES ARE ACCOMPLISHED BY MANY AGENTS. Many angels, messengers (Ps. civ. 4; Heb. i. 14); natural agents, the elements, &c.; human agents, men good and bad alike carrying out his will; spiritual beings (Ps. xci. 11). How often those who pray for spiritual blessings forget that common things also are ruled by God. Thus a great door of communion is closed.

IV. BUT THERE IS SO MUCH CONFUSION IN THE WORLD. We often cannot trace God's hand. How often is trust confounded, wise schemes frustrated, earnest self-denial in vain; prayers, real and intense, without apparent answer. Nay, these are but seeming confusions, to teach the lesson of faith. Through all these, by all these, God's purposes are surely carried out. One great truth is the key of all—the love of God revealed in Christ. This is the ladder from which he proclaims, "Lo, I am with thee" (cf. Rom. viii. 32). He who wrought out redemption, can he fail?

V. GOD'S GOVERNANCE IS FOR OUR SALVATION, in the fullest sense of the word, giving us the victory over evil. God was with Jacob. He had been from the first, though not recognised. He was so to the end. Not giving uninterrupted prosperity. Many a fault and many a painful page in his history; but through all these he was led on. The word to each who will receive it—"Behold, I am with thee." Not because of thy faith, still less of thy goodness. Oh that every Christian would practise trust (Ps. v. 3); hearing our Father's voice, "Commit thy way unto the Lord," and gladly believing "the Lord is my Shepherd."—M.

Vers. 18—22.—*The grateful retrospect and the consecrated prospect.* I. THE TRUE LIFE is that which starts from the place of fellowship with God and commits the future to him. We can always find a pillar of blessed memorial and consecration. *The Bethel.* 1. Providential care. 2. Religious privilege. 3. Special communications of the Spirit. God with us as a fact. Our pilgrimage a Bethel all through.

II. THE TRUE TESTIMONY that which erects a stone of witness, *a Bethel,* where others can find God. 1. *Personal.* The pillow of rest the pillar of praise. 2. *Practical.* The testimony which speaks of the journey and the traveller.

III. THE TRUE COVENANT. 1. Coming out of fellowship. 2. Pledging the future at the house of God, and in sight of Divine revelation. 3. Blessed exchange of gifts, confirmation of love. Jehovah keeping and guiding and feeding ; his servant serving him and giving him a tenth of all he received. The patriarch's vow was the result of a distinct advance in his religious life. The hope of blessing became the covenant of engagement, service, worship, sacrifice. The highest form of religious life is that which rests on a solemn vow of grateful dedication at Bethel. The end before us is *"our Father's house in peace."*—R.

EXPOSITION.

CHAPTER XXIX.

Ver. 1.—**Then Jacob went on his journey** (literally, *lifted up his feet*—a graphic description of travelling. Inspired by new hopes, and conscious of loftier aims than when he fled from Beersheba, the lonely fugitive departed from Bethel), **and came into the land of the people of the east**—literally, *the land of the sons of the east,* i. e. Mesopotamia, about 450 miles distant from Beersheba.

Ver. 2.—**And he looked** (either to discover where he was, or in search of water), **and behold a well in the field,**—not the well at which Eliezer's caravan halted, which was a well for the village maidens, situated in front of the town, and approached by steps (*vide* ch. xxiv.), but a well in the open field for the use of flocks, and covered at the time of Jacob's arrival with a huge stone—**and, lo, there were three flocks of sheep lying by it.** A frequent Oriental scene (cf. ch. xxiv. 11 ; Exod. ii. 16). "Who that has travelled much in this country has not often arrived at a well in the heat of the day which was surrounded with numerous flocks of sheep waiting to be watered ? I once saw such a scene in the burning plains of Northern Syria. Half-naked, fierce-looking men were drawing up water in leather buckets ; flock after flock was brought up, watered, and sent away ; and after all the men had ended their work, then several women and girls brought up their flocks, and drew water for them. Thus it was with Jethro's daughters ; and thus, no doubt, it would have been with Rachel if Jacob had not rolled away the stone and watered her sheep" ('Land and Book,' p. 589). **For out of that well they watered the flocks : and a great stone** was upon the **well's mouth.** "Most of the cisterns are covered with a large thick, flat stone, in the centre of which a hole is cut, which forms the mouth of the cistern. This hole, in many instances, we found covered with a heavy stone, to the removal of which two or three men were requisite" (Robinson, ii. p. 180).

Ver. 3.—**And thither were all the flocks gathered.** "Fifteen minutes later we came to a large well in a valley among the swells, fitted up with troughs and reservoirs, with

flocks waiting around" (Robinson, iii. p. 21). **And they rolled the stone from the well's mouth, and watered the sheep, and put the stone again upon the well's mouth in his place.** From the middle of ver. 2 the words are parenthetical, the watering of the flocks not having taken place till Rachel had arrived (ver. 9) and Jacob had uncovered the well (ver. 10).

Ver. 4.—**And Jacob said unto them** (the shepherds of the three flocks), **My brethren** (a friendly salutation from one who was himself a shepherd), **whence be ye ?** Anticipating that their reply would reveal his whereabouts. **And they said, Of Haran** are we. This could scarcely fail to remind Jacob of God's promise to guide him in his journey.

Ver. 5.—**And he said unto them** (with the view of discovering his kinsmen), **Know ye Laban the son of Nahor ?**—i. e. the grandson, Laban's father having been Bethuel, who, however, here, as in ch. xxiv., retires into the background. **And they said, We know** him. The language of the shepherds being Chaldæan (*vide* ch. xxxi. 47), Jacob, who spoke Hebrew, was able to converse with them either because he had learnt Chaldee from his mother (Clericus), or, as is more probable, because the dialects were not then greatly dissimilar (Gosman in Lange).

Ver. 6.—**And he said unto them,** Is **he well ?** Literally, *is there peace to him?* meaning not simply bodily health, but all manner of felicity ; *ὑγιαίνει* (LXX.) ; *sanusne est ?* (Vulgate). Cf. the Christian salutation, *Pax vobiscum.* **And they said,** He is **well** (literally, *peace*): **and, behold, Rachel**— "Ewe" (Gesenius)—**his daughter cometh with the sheep.**

Ver. 7.—**And he said, Lo,** it is **yet high day** (literally, *the day is yet great,* i. e. much of it still remains), **neither** is it **time that the cattle should be gathered together** (*i. e.* to shut them up for the night): **water ye the sheep, and go** and **feed** them—being desirous to get the shepherds away from the well that he might meet Rachel alone (Keil, Lange, Murphy), though perhaps his words with as much correctness may be traced to that prudent and industrious habit of mind which afterwards shone forth so conspicuously in himself, and which instinctively caused him to frown upon laziness and inactivity (Starke, Kalisch, Bush).

Ver. 8.—**And they said, We cannot,**—not because of any physical difficulty (Kalisch), since three men could easily have accomplished what Jacob by himself did, but because they had agreed not to do so (Rosenmüller, Murphy), but to wait—**until all the flocks be gathered together** (when the watering was done at once, instead of at so many different times), **and till they roll the stone from the well's mouth ;**—more correctly rendered, *and* (*sc.* then, *i. e.* when the flocks are assembled) *they* (i. e. the shepherds) *roll away the stone* —**then** (or, and) **we water the sheep.** The object of watering the flocks collectively may have been, as above stated, for convenience, or to prevent the well from being opened too frequently, in which case dust might rapidly accumulate within it (Kalisch), or perhaps to secure an equal distribution of the water (Murphy).

Ver. 9—**And while he yet spake with them** (literally, *he yet speaking with them*), **Rachel came with her father's sheep: for she kept them**—or, *she* was *a* shepherdess, the part. רֹעָה being used as a substantive (Gesenius, ' Lex.,' sub. nom.).

Ver. 10.—**And it came to pass, when Jacob saw Rachel the daughter of Laban his mother's brother,**—" the term mother's brother is not unintentionally repeated three times in this verse to describe with the greatest possible stress that Jacob had met with his own relations, with " his bone and his flesh" (Kalisch) — **and the sheep of Laban his mother's brother** (Jacob from the first takes particular notice of Laban's flock, perhaps regarding them as a sign of Laban's wealth. If Laban's daughter had her attractions for the son of Isaac, so also had Laban's sheep), **that Jacob went near, and rolled the stone from the well's mouth** (probably disregarding the shepherds' rule to wait for the gathering of all the flocks, unless, indeed, Rachel's was the last), **and watered the flock of Laban his mother's brother.** The threefold repetition of this phrase does not prove that Jacob acted in all this purely as a cousin (Lange). The phrase is the historian's, and Jacob had not yet informed Rachel of his name.

Ver. 11.—**And Jacob kissed Rachel,**—in demonstration of his cousinly affection. If Jacob had not yet discovered who he was to the fair shepherdess, his behaviour must have filled her with surprise, even allowing

for the unaffected simplicity of the times ; but the fact that she does not resent his conduct as an undue liberty perhaps suggests that he had first informed her of his relationship to the inmates of Laban's house (Calvin). On kissing *vide* ch. xxvii. 26— **and lifted up his voice, and wept**—partly for joy at finding his relatives (cf. ch. xliii. 30 ; xlv. 2, 14, 15) ; partly in grateful acknowledgment of God's kindness in conducting him to his mother's brother's house.

Ver. 12.—**And Jacob told** (or, had told, *ut supra*) **Rachel that he** was **her father's brother,**—as Lot is called Abraham's brother, though in reality his nephew (ch. xiii. 8 ; xiv. 14, 16)—**and that he** was **Rebekah's son** (this clause would explain the meaning of the term " brother" in the former): **and she ran and told her father.** Like Rebekah, believing the stranger's words and running to report them, though, unlike Rebekah, first relating them to her father (cf. ch. xxiv. 28).

Ver. 13.—**And it came to pass, when Laban heard the tidings** (literally, *heard the hearing*, or *thing heard*, i. e. the report of the arrival) **of Jacob his sister's son,**—he acted very much as he did ninety-seven years before, when Abraham's servant came to woo his sister (ch. xxiv. 20, 30)—**that** (literally, *and*) **he ran to meet him, and embraced him,** —so afterwards Esau did Jacob (ch. xxxiii. 4), and Jacob the two sons of Joseph (ch. xlviii. 10)—**and kissed him, and brought him to his house**—thus evincing the same kindness and hospitality that had characterised him on the previous occasion. **And he** (Jacob) **told Laban all these things**—what his mother had instructed him to say to attest his kinship (Calvin) ; the things related in the immediate context (Keil) ; more likely the entire story of his life, and in particular of his exile from home, with its cause and object (Rosenmüller, Kalisch, Lange).

Ver. 14.—**And Laban said unto him** (giving utterance to the impression Jacob's recital had produced upon his mind), **Surely thou art my bone and my flesh**—*i. e.* my blood relation (cf. Judges ix. 2 ; 2 Sam. v. 1). Laban meant that Jacob had satisfactorily proved himself Rebekah's son. **And he abode with him the space of a month**—literally, *a month of days* (cf. ch. xli. 1 ; Numb. xi. 20), or a month as regards time, " the second substantive describing the general notion of which the first is a specification" (Kalisch).

HOMILETICS.

Vers. 1—14.—*Jacob at the well of Haran: a romantic adventure.* I. JACOB'S MEETING WITH THE SHEPHERDS. 1. *The providential discovery.* The well in the field with the three flocks of sheep lying by it enabled Jacob to ascertain his whereabouts, and ultimately led to his finding Rachel. God guides the steps of his people without interfering with the ordinary course of nature, simply directing them in the exercise of sense and intelligence; and doubtless Jacob recognised in his lighting on the Haran well a first instalment of that celestial guidance he had been lately promised. Saints should practise the art of discerning the movement of God's finger in the minutest and commonest events of life. 2. *The friendly conversation.* Saluting the shepherds as his brethren, *i. e.* as masters of a common craft, Jacob gathers from their frank communications that he was on the outskirts of Haran, in which his uncle Laban was a prosperous and wealthy citizen, and that his cousin Rachel was on the road to that very well beside which he stood with a flock of her father's sheep. Great is the virtue of asking questions, especially when they are prefaced with politeness. Seldom anything is lost, but frequently much is gained, by courteous inquiries. 3. *The prudent counsel.* Observing his friends disposed to indolence, and perhaps desirous of meeting Rachel alone, Jacob recommends them to uncover the well, water their flocks, and drive them off again to pasture, since much of the day yet remained. If it was their advantage he sought, his advice was good; if it was his own interest he served, the stratagem was ingenious. God's people should be wise as serpents, but harmless as doves.

II. JACOB'S FIRST SIGHT OF RACHEL. 1. *The gallant action.* The lovely shepherdess arriving made a deep impression on her cousin's heart. Springing to his feet, he rolls the stone from the well's mouth, fills the troughs, and waters Laban's sheep—impelled thereto, shall we say, as much by consideration for the fair girl who attended them as for the rich flock-master who possessed them. Kindly acts proceeding from loving hearts are sometimes largely assisted by the attractions of their recipients. 2. *The loving salutation.* "And Jacob kissed Rachel." If before explaining who he was, it must have taken her by surprise even in those unconventional times; but it is probable he may have first announced his name, in which case his behaviour was only in accordance with the manners of the age. Suitable expressions of affection to friends beseem both grace and nature. 3. *The irrepressible emotion.* "And Jacob lifted up his voice and wept"—expressive both of joy at finding his relatives, and of gratitude for God's goodness in guiding him to the house of his mother's brother. Unexpected good and eminent providences kindle transports of delight in gracious souls. 4. *The important communication.* "Jacob told Rachel that he was her father's brother, and that he was Rebekah's son: and she ran and told her father." Friends, and much more Christians, meeting on life's journey, should with frankness discover themselves to each other, and give each other hearty welcome.

III. JACOB'S INTRODUCTION TO LABAN. 1. *The uncle's reception of his nephew,* "Laban ran to meet his sister's son, and embraced him, and kissed him, and brought him to his house." Kinship and kindness should ever be allied. Laban's hospitality to Jacob was grounded on the fact of their relationship. So is Christ's entertainment of his people based upon the circumstance that they are "members of his body, of his flesh, and of his bones." 2. *The nephew's return to his uncle.* Ingenuous confidence—"Jacob told Laban all these things"—and faithful service. It is implied in ver. 15 that during the month Jacob abode with Laban he served in keeping Laban's sheep. God's people should endeavour as far as in them lies to requite the kindnesses of relatives and friends.

HOMILIES BY VARIOUS AUTHORS.

Ch. xxix. — *Jacob among his mother's kindred.* Taught by experience to be patient. His own craft reflected in Laban. Lessons to be learned.

I. THE CONNECTION BETWEEN THE TEACHING OF GOD IN THE INNER MAN AND HIS LEADINGS IN PROVIDENCE. Jacob learned what he needed to learn—dependence, self-humiliation. Saw the evil of selfishness; understood that the Divine purposes must not be identified in our thought with our personal feelings and desires. We must wait on God to know what his will is.

II. THE INDEPENDENCE OF GOD'S GRACE. The chosen instruments not chosen for their own sake. Often that which displeases us is our special help. Leah, not chosen by Jacob, bore him sons. Rachel, whom he loved, was barren. Even in such mixed soil as these characters the seed of Divine life will grow. Leah gave names to her children which betokened an increasing faith. Jacob's willingness to serve was a gracious victory over self, preparing him for higher things. Thwarted man is taught to wait upon God.

III. PRACTICAL LESSONS ON THE RELATIONS OF THE SEXES AND MARRIED LIFE, &c. The misery of all that interferes with the sanctity of affection and its supremacy. The certainty that lack of candour and truthfulness will be fruitful in evil results. The importance of right feeling in sustaining religious character; how difficult, where the relationship is not founded on affection, to maintain truth, purity, and a lofty standard of life. We must try to see disappointments from a higher point of view. God may withhold what we desire, but only to give afterwards a fuller blessing.—R.

EXPOSITION.

Ver. 15.—**And Laban said unto Jacob** (probably at the month's end), **Because thou art**—literally, *is it not that thou art* (cf. ch. xxvii. 36; 2 Sam. xxiii. 19)—**my brother,** —my kinsman (*vide* on ver. 12)—**shouldest thou therefore serve me for nought?** (literally, *and thou servest me gratuitously*) **tell me, what** shall **thy wages** be? A proof of Laban's generosity and justice (Kalisch); of his selfishness and greed (Keil); of his prudence and sagacity in opening up the way for a love-suit (Lange).

Ver. 16.—**And Laban had two daughters** (the wife of Laban is not mentioned in the story): **the name of the elder** was **Leah,**— "Wearied" (Gesenius); "Dull," "Stupid" (Fürst); "Pining," "Yearning" (Lange)— **and the name of the younger** was **Rachel** —"Ewe" (Gesenius).

Ver. 17.—**Leah was tender eyed.** Literally, *the eyes of Leah were tender*, i. e. weak, dull; ἀσθενεῖς (LXX.), *lippi* (Vulgate); cf. 1 Sam. xvi. 12. Leah's face was not ugly (Bohlen), only her eyes were not clear and lustrous, dark and sparkling, as in all probability Rachel's were (Knobel). **But Rachel was beautiful and well favoured.** Literally, *beautiful in form* (i. e. in outline and make of body; cf. ch. xxxix. 6; also 1 Sam. xvi. 18—"a man of form," *i. e. formosus*, well made) *and beautiful in appearance* (i. e. of a lovely countenance). "If authentic history was not in the way, Leah, as the mother of Judah, and of the Davidic Messianic line, ought to have carried off the prize of beauty after Sarah and Rebekah" (Lange).

Ver. 18.—**And Jacob loved Rachel** (it is more than probable that this was an illustration of what is known as "love at first sight" on the part of Rachel as well as Jacob); **and said, I will serve thee seven years for Rachel thy younger daughter.** Having no property with which to buy his wife, according to Oriental custom (Kalisch), or to give the usual dowry for her to her father (Keil),—cf. ch. xxiv. 53; xxxiv. 12;

1 Sam. xviii. 25,—Jacob's offer was at once accepted by his grasping uncle, though he was that uncle's "brother" (ver. 15).

Ver. 19.—**And Laban said, It is better that I give her to thee, than that I should give her to another man.** Orientals commonly prefer alliances within the circle of their own relatives. Burckhardt, Volney, Layard, and Lane testify that this is still the case among the Bedouins, the Druses, and other Eastern tribes. **Abide with me**— a formal ratification of the compact on the part of Laban.

Ver. 20.—**And Jacob served**—hard service (ch. xxxi. 40, 41), in keeping sheep (Hosea xii. 12)—**seven years for Rachel.** The purity and intensity of Jacob's affection was declared not alone by the proposal of a seven years' term of servitude,—a long period of waiting for a man of fifty-seven, if not seventy-seven, years of age,—but also by the spirit in which he served his avaricious relative. Many as the days were that required to intervene before he obtained possession of his bride, they were rendered happy by the sweet society of Rachel. **And they seemed unto him** but **a few days, for the love he had to her.** "Words breathing the purest tenderness, and expressing more emphatically than the flowery hyperboles of romantic phraseology the deep attachment of an affectionate heart" (Kalisch); words too which show the lofty appreciation Jacob had of the personal worth of his future bride.

Ver. 21.—**And Jacob said unto Laban** (who, though the term of servitude had expired, appeared to be in no haste to implement his part of the bargain), **Give** me **my wife** (*i. e.* my affianced wife, as in Deut. xxii. 23, 24; Matt. i. 20), **for my days are fulfilled** (*i. e.* my term of service is completed), **that I may go in unto her**—*quo significat intactam adhuc esse virginem* (Calvin); a proof that Jacob's love was pure and true.

Ver. 22.—**And Laban** (unable to evade or delay the fulfilment of his agreement with Jacob) **gathered together all the men of the**

place (not the entire population, but the principal inhabitants), **and made a feast**—a "mishteh," or drinking (cf. ch. xix. 3), *i. e.* a wedding banquet (cf. bride-ale = bridal), which commonly lasted seven days (Judges xiv. 10 ; Tobit xi. 18), though it appears to have varied according to the circumstances of the bridegroom.

Ver. 23.—**And it came to pass in the evening, that he took Leah his daughter, and brought her to him.** The deception practised on Jacob was rendered possible by the fact that the bride was usually conducted into the marriage chamber veiled ; the veil being so long and close as to conceal not only the face, but much of the person (*vide* ch. xxiv. 65). **And he went in unto her.** The conduct of Laban is perfectly intelligible as the outcome of his sordid avarice ; but it is difficult to understand how Leah could acquiesce in a proposal so base as to wrong her sister by marrying one who neither sought nor loved her. She must herself have been attached to Jacob ; and it is probable that Laban had explained to her his plan for bringing about a double wedding.

Ver. 24.—**And Laban gave unto his daughter Leah Zilpah**—"the Dropping"? (Gesenius), "Myrrh-juice" (Fürst)—**his maid** (according to Gesenius the word is closely connected with an unused root signifying to spread out, hence a maid-servant) for **an handmaid.** This was in accordance with Oriental custom (*vide* ch. xxiv. 61). That Leah obtained only one damsel need not be ascribed to Laban's parsimonious character, but to his already-formed intention to bestow a second on Rachel.

Ver. 25.—**And it came to pass, that in the morning, behold, it was Leah.** If Jacob's deception, even with the veiled bride, may still be difficult to understand, it is easy to perceive in Leah's substitution for Rachel a clear instance of Divine retribution for the imposition he had practised on his father. So the Lord oftentimes rewards evil-doers *according* to their wickedness (cf. 2 Sam. xii. 10—12). **And he said to Laban** (who, Calvin conjectures, had given Jacob a splendid entertainment the night before to make him say nothing about the fraud), **What is this thou hast done unto me? did not I serve with thee for Rachel? wherefore then hast thou beguiled me?** It says much for Jacob that he did not seek to repudiate the marriage. Perhaps he saw the hand of God in what had happened, and probably considered that, though he had chosen Rachel, God had se-

lected Leah as his wife. If so, it must be set to Jacob's credit that at the call of God, thus providentially addressed to him, he was prepared to sacrifice his best affections to the claims of religion and duty. It is not Jacob, but Laban, who proposes that he should also marry Rachel.

Ver. 26.—**And Laban said, It must not be so done**—the future expresses the thought that the custom has grown into a strong moral obligation (Kalisch)—**in our country** (Hebrew, *place*), **to give the younger before the firstborn.** The same custom exists among the Indians (Rosenmüller ; cf. Roberts, 'Oriental Illustrations,' p. 34), Egyptians (Lane), and other Oriental countries (Delitzsch).

Ver. 27. — **Fulfil her week,** — literally, *make full the week of this one,* i. e. of Leah, if Leah was given to Jacob on the first night of the festivities (Calmet, Rosenmüller, Keil, Kalisch, Lange, Ainsworth) ; but if Leah was married at the close of the seven days, then it must refer to Rachel's week (Bush, Murphy) —**and we** (including Laban's wife and eldest son, as in ch. xxiv. 50, 55) **will give thee this also** (*i. e.* Rachel) **for the service which thou shalt serve with me yet seven other years.** Almost every motive that is mean, base, and despicable appears in this behaviour of Laban's ; if he attached little value to his daughters' affections, he had a keen appreciation of Jacob's qualities as a shepherd.

Ver. 28.—**And Jacob did so, and fulfilled her week.** Literally, *the week of this one,* either of Leah or of Rachel, as above. Rosenmüller, assigning the first week (ver. 27) to Leah, refers this to Rachel ; but the expression can scarcely have two different meanings within the compass of two verses. **And he gave him Rachel his daughter to wife also.** The polygamy of Jacob, though contrary to the law of nature (ch. ii. 21—25), admits of some palliation, since Rachel was the choice of his affections. The marriage of sisters was afterwards declared incestuous (Levit. xviii. 18).

Ver. 29.—**And Laban gave to Rachel his daughter Bilhah** — "Bashful," "Modest" (Gesenius)—**his handmaid to be her maid.**

Ver. 30.—**And he went in also unto Rachel, and he loved also Rachel more than Leah** (implying, however, that Leah had a place in his affections), **and served with him yet seven other years.** The seven years cunningly exacted for Leah was thus the second fraud practised upon Jacob (ch. xxx. 26 ; xxxi. 41 ; Hosea xii. 12).

HOMILETICS.

Vers. 15—30.—*Jacob and Laban, or the deceiver deceived.* I. JACOB'S CONTRACT WITH LABAN. 1. *The promised service*—seven years of pastoral assistance. (1) Freely offered. "I will serve thee seven years." Contracts are legally and morally invalid where freedom in the promisor does not exist. (2) Faithfully rendered. Jacob "served seven years," as he had stipulated. Voluntary engagements should be deemed sacred. (3) Readily accepted. Laban both appreciated Jacob's merits as a shepherd and regarded Jacob's terms as easy. If Laban's words in closing with Jacob's offer did not indicate his guile, they were at least evidence of his greed. (4) Harshly exacted. Jacob testifies as much on leaving Laban. Covetous souls do not shrink from making hard bargains even with relatives and friends. 2. *The stipulated wages*—Rachel in marriage as a wife. This part of the contract was— (1) Eagerly desired by Jacob. "Jacob loved Rachel," who was beautiful both in face and form. It is not sinful either to appreciate or desire personal symmetry and grace in those to whom we yield our affections. Female loveliness, though it may enkindle love, need not render the heart that loves less pure. (2) Patiently waited for by Jacob. This was a testimony to the purity, tenderness, and strength of Jacob's affection. Besides transforming seven years into a few days, and making pleasant and lightsome labour of what would otherwise have been galling bondage, it enabled him to wait God's time for receiving his bride. (3) Cheerfully assented to by Laban. "It is better that I give her to thee than that I should give her to another man." Yet—(4) Guilefully withheld by Laban. Avaricious men seldom scruple at deceiving others for the sake of profit. Greed of gain is commonly accompanied by guile of men.

II. LABAN'S DECEPTION OF JACOB. 1. *The just request.* "Give me my wife." "The labourer is worthy of his hire," and the servant is entitled to his wages. 2. *The marriage festival.* "Laban made a feast." Seemingly assenting to his nephew's request, the crafty uncle prepares a wedding banquet. Feasting and rejoicing are both becoming and allowable in connection with marriage celebrations. 3. *The substituted bride.* Either at the end of the first day or at the close of the festivities, "Laban took Leah and brought her," veiled and in silence, to the bridal chamber. For the wickedness of Laban in breaking his promise, defrauding his nephew, wronging his younger daughter, and practically prostituting his elder, excuse is impossible; for Leah's acquiescence in her father's plot explanation, though not apology, may be found in her manifest love for Jacob, and perhaps in her belief that Laban had secured Jacob's consent to the arrangement. The man who could sell one daughter's affections and sacrifice another's would not stick at deceiving both, if he could. 4. *The discovered fraud.* "In the morning, behold, it was Leah." The day manifests what the night hides—the sins of men; and the light of the great day will disclose what the darkness of time conceals. 5. *The lame excuse.* Interrogated by Jacob, Laban offers in extenuation of his heartless deception that popular custom demanded the marriage of an elder sister before a younger. So public opinion, prevailing habit, universal practice, are often pled in apology for offences against the law of God. But the conventional maxims of society are of no weight when set against Divine commandments. 6. *The righteous retribution.* Though indefensible on the part of Laban, the substitution of Leah for Rachel was a deserved punishment of Jacob. Having wronged Esau his brother, he is in turn wronged by "a brother"—Laban. Having substituted the younger (himself) for the older (Esau), he is recompensed by having the older put into the place of the younger. As Isaac knew not when he blessed Jacob, so Jacob knows not when he marries Leah. As Jacob acted at the instigation of his mother, Leah yields to the suggestion of her father. 7. *The amicable settlement.* Jacob celebrates the week of festival for Leah, and then receives Rachel as a wife, engaging to serve another term of seven years for her who had lightened the labour of the previous seven. If Jacob's conduct evinced sincere attachment to Rachel and peaceful disposition towards Laban, it displayed doubtful regard for the law of God.

HOMILIES BY VARIOUS AUTHORS.

Ver. 20.—*The power of true affection.* "And Jacob served seven years for Rachel," &c. I. THE INWARD SPRING OF THE OUTWARD LIFE. Power of the heart over the will, over the circumstances, over flesh. Time measured by the motions of our thought. The world needs to be taught that the material rests on the immaterial.

II. THE SERVICE OF LOVE THE CONSECRATION AND CONSUMMATION OF HUMAN ENERGY. Christ the highest object of affection. The life of his servant compared with the life of selfish caprice.

III. THE GREAT EXAMPLE OF LOVE SUGGESTED. Jacob a type of Christ; Rachel, of his Church. He served for her. His love made obedience, even unto death, his delight.

IV. SPECIAL TRIAL HAS ITS SPECIAL REWARD. Jacob served doubly for Rachel; but his service was amply paid afterwards, although for a time the veil of disappointment hid the purpose of God. While Leah, as the mother of Judah, was the true ancestress of Messiah, still it was in Joseph, the son of Rachel, that Jacob's heart was satisfied, and that the history of the kingdom of God was most manifestly carried on and its glory set forth. As in the case of Sarah and Rebekah, so in that of Rachel, the birth of the representative seed is connected with special bestowments of grace.—R.

Ver. 20.—*Christ's love for the Church.* "And Jacob served seven years for Rachel." On the surface this is a step in Jacob's training, in the fulfilment of God's promise at Bethel. It shows a new feature in his character. We see not the man of cunning devices, but one full of pure, self-sacrificing love. Fourteen years of service willingly given to purchase, according to Eastern custom, his bride. But Jacob's love suggests the deeper and purer love of Christ for the Church. Rachel a type of the Bride; a shepherdess and "fairest among women" (Cant. i. 7, 8); sharer of the sufferings of the Church (Jer. xxxi. 15; Matt. ii. 18; Rev. xii. 17). For the Church's sake (Ephes. v. 25) Christ "served" (Phil. ii. 7); became a Shepherd (John x. 11); with his service and life-blood, "obedient unto death," he purchased her (Acts xx. 28), to unite her to himself for ever.

I. THE LORD "SERVED" BECAUSE HE LOVED HIS CHURCH. In condescending to unite himself with human nature; in bearing the infirmities of childhood and state of subjection; in bearing the contradiction of sinners and the wrath of God. And still in standing and knocking (Rev. iii. 20); in bearing with half-hearted believers (2 Pet. iii. 9); in pleading with and for the wayward (1 John ii. 1; 2 Cor. v. 20); in seeking and following individual sheep. The love which led to this was free, not deserved or purchased. Rachel brought no dowry to Jacob. The Church has of its own no spiritual wealth (Isa. lxiv. 6; Rom. iii. 23). The Bridegroom had to sanctify and cleanse it. By nature unholy, at variance with God's will; yet, knowing this, he loved it (cf. Rom. viii. 35). For love to Rachel Jacob gave the labour of fourteen years. For the Church Christ grudged nothing—gave himself. Sacrifice a mark of true love. How many will not sacrifice anything—will not leave a gain, a companion, an amusement—to "win Christ." In the garden his human nature shrank from the bitterness of the cup, but he persevered. Why?

II. THE LORD "SERVED" THAT HE MIGHT UNITE US TO HIMSELF. Marriage, the closest earthly tie, used as a type. No mere removal of condemnation satisfied that love, nor even our being made happy; he became such as we are, that we might become such as he is. The Church is his Bride (Ephes. v. 27; Rev. xxi. 9), sharer of his kingdom (Rev. iii. 21; xx. 4), of his blessedness and glory (John xvii. 22—24). And this belongs to its humblest and weakest member. A union in this life (Cant. ii. 16; John xv. 4); peace in committing all cares to him, even our own steadfastness (John x. 28; Rom. viii. 35; Heb. xiii. 6). A union after our departure more close (Phil. i. 23). Here we see dimly (1 Cor. xiii. 12). The conditions of mortal life hinder clear visions (Exod. xxxiii. 20). The law of sin in our members hinders perfect union. Then no impediment (Luke xxiii. 43). Union perfected after the resurrection (1 Thess. iv. 7). The body, which now limits conscious union, shall then minister to its completeness. Not till then shall we be perfectly like him in his human nature.

III. HE "SERVED" THAT WE MIGHT HAVE CONFIDENCE IN HIS LOVE. Jacob's love not shaken by time, or by the deceit practised upon him, a type of Christ's. Often forgetful, often faithless, we might well think, How dare I trust to a love so often neglected? But his love is not wearied out (Isa. xlix. 15). He has graven us with the nail-prints on his hands. His word is still, "Look unto me;" trust my love (Ps. xxxvii. 5).—M

EXPOSITION.

Ver. 31—**And when the Lord saw**—literally, *and Jehovah saw*. As Eve's son was obtained from Jehovah (ch. iv. 1), and Jehovah visited Sarah (ch. xxi. 1), and was entreated for Rebekah (ch. xxv. 21), so here he again interposes in connection with the onward development of the holy seed by giving children to Jacob's wives. The present section (vers. 31—35) is by Davidson, Kalisch, and others assigned to the Jehovist, by Tuch left undetermined, and by Colenso in several parts ascribed to the Elohist. Kalisch thinks the contents of this section must have found a place in the earlier of the two documents—**that Leah** was **hated,**—*i. e.* less loved (cf. Mal. i. 3)—**he opened her womb** (cf. 1 Sam. i. 5, 6; Ps. cxxvii. 3): **but Rachel was barren**—as Sarai (ch. xi. 30) and Rebekah (ch. xxv. 21) had been. The fruitfulness of Leah and the sterility of Rachel were designed not so much to equalise the conditions of the sisters, the one having beauty and the other children (Lange), or to punish Jacob for his partiality (Keil), or to discourage the admiration of mere beauty (Kalisch), but to prove that "the origin of Israel was to be a work not of nature, but of grace" (Keil).

Ver. 32.—**And Leah conceived, and bare a son, and she called his name Reuben** (literally, *Reu-ben*, Behold a Son! an expression of joyful surprise at the Divine compassion): **for she said, Surely the Lord hath looked upon my affliction.** Though not directly contained in the term Reuben, the sense of these words is implied (Kalisch). As Leah's child was an intimation that she had been an object of Jehovah's compassion, so did she expect it to be a means of drawing towards herself Jacob's affection. **Now therefore** (literally, *for now*) **my husband will love me.** She was confident in the first flush of maternal joy that Jacob's heart would turn towards her; she believed that God had sent her child to effect this conversion of her husband's affections; and she regarded the birth of Reuben as a signal proof of the Divine pity.

Ver. 33.—**And she conceived again, and bare a son** (probably the following year); **and said, Because the Lord hath heard that I was hated** (the birth of Reuben had obviously not answered Leah's expectations in increasing Jacob's love), **he hath therefore given me this** son also (the faith and piety of Leah are as conspicuous as her affection for Jacob): **and she called his name Simeon** —*i. e. Hearing*, because God had heard that she was hated (*ut supra*).

Ver. 34.—**And she conceived again** (say, in the third year of her marriage), **and bare a son; and said, Now this time will my husband be joined unto me,—**לָוָה, to join, is the root from which comes לֵוִי (Levi), her son's name—**because I have born him three sons: therefore was his name called Levi—** Associated, or Joined.

Ver. 35.—**And she conceived again, and bare a son** (possibly in the fourth year of marriage, and in Jacob's eighty-eighth year of age, he having been seventy-seven when he arrived in Haran, and eighty-four when he was united to Laban's daughters): **and she said, Now will I praise the Lord.** Well she might; for this was the ancestor of the promised seed (Murphy). There cannot be a doubt that her excellence of character as well as eminence of piety eventually wrought a change upon her husband (*vide* ch. xxxi. 4, 14; xlix. 31). **Therefore she called his name Judah** (*i. e.* Praise); **and left bearing.** Literally, *stood still*, i. e. ceased, *from bearing*. Not altogether (ch. xxx. 16); only for a time, "that she might not be unduly lifted up by her good fortune, or attribute to the fruitfulness of her own womb what the faithfulness of Jehovah, the covenant God, had bestowed upon her" (Keil.)

HOMILETICS.

Vers. 31 — 35. — *Leah and Rachel, or the two wives.* I. RACHEL THE BELOVED. "Jacob loved Rachel more than Leah." That Leah was not hated in the sense of being regarded with aversion, the numerous family she bore to Jacob proves; that she occupied a lower place than Rachel in her husband's affections is explicitly declared. This preference of Rachel to Leah was—1. *Natural in Jacob.* Rachel had been his heart's choice from the first, while Leah had been thrust upon him against his inclination. But even had this been otherwise, as no man can serve two masters, so can no husband love two wives equally—an argument against polygamy. 2. *Painful to Leah.* Had Leah loved Jacob less than she manifestly did, it is doubtful if the undue regard shown to Rachel would not have inflicted a grievous wound upon her wifely heart; but, entertaining towards him an affection strong and tender, she yearned for a larger share of his esteem, and at each successive child's birth gave utterance to a hope that he would yet be joined to her. No heavier blow can be dealt by a husband to the tender heart of a loving wife than to withdraw from her his love, or even to be cold and indifferent in its expression. 3. *Sinful in the sight of God.* Though not so beautiful as Rachel, Leah was yet entitled to an equal share with her in Jacob's affection. Equally with Rachel she was Jacob's wife. It was Jacob's sin that he had married her at all when he did not either love or desire her. On detecting the fraud he should have instantly repudiated the engagement. But having publicly ratified the contract with Leah by fulfilling her week, he owed to Leah a full share of his affection as a husband. Nay, though not the wife his inclination had selected, there is reason for believing that Leah, rather than Rachel, was the bride God had chosen (Leah was the ancestress of the Saviour); hence doubly was Jacob bound to love Leah equally with Rachel.

II. LEAH THE FRUITFUL. While Rachel enjoyed the highest place in Jacob's affection, she was "barren"—a grievous affliction to one who might possibly be the mother of the promised Seed. The fruitfulness of Leah was—1. *Expressly caused by God.* The Lord, who had decreed temporary barrenness for Rachel the fair, opened the womb of Leah the despised; neither to compensate Leah for the loss of Jacob's love, nor to punish Jacob for his sinful partiality; but to manifest his power, to show that children are the heritage of the Lord, to vindicate his sovereignty, to attest that God giveth families to whomsoever he will, and to suggest that the line of promise was designed to be not the fruit of nature, but the gift of grace. 2. *Thankfully acknowledged by Leah.* While cherishing the hope that her children would eventually unite Jacob's heart to her own, she delightedly recognised her exceptional fruitfulness as a special mark of Jehovah's favour, and gave expression to her gratitude in the naming of her sons: Reuben, see, a son! Simeon, hearing; Levi, joined; Judah, praise. 3. *Enviously beheld by Rachel.* This appears from the opening statement in the ensuing chapter; and this, though perhaps as natural as Leah's sense of pain at Rachel's preference by Jacob, was yet as sinful as Jacob's excessive partiality towards herself.

Learn—1. The sinfulness and sorrow of having more wives at once than one. 2. The wickedness of wedding where one does not love. 3. The sovereignty of God in giving and withholding children. 4. The cruelty and criminality of showing partiality towards those who possess an equal claim on our affections. 5. The duty and profit of remembering and acknowledging family mercies.

EXPOSITION.

CHAPTER XXX.

Ver. 1.—**And when Rachel saw** (apparently after, though probably before, the birth of Leah's fourth son) **that she bare Jacob no children** (literally, *that she bare not to Jacob*), **Rachel envied her sister** (was jealous of her, the root referring to the redness with which the face of an angry woman is suffused); **and said unto Jacob, Give me children** (sons), **or else I die**—literally, *and if not, I am a dead woman;* i.e. for shame at her sterility. Rachel had three strong reasons for desiring children—that she might emulate her sister,

become more dear to her husband, and above all share the hope of being a progenitrix of the promised Seed. If not warranted to infer that Rachel's barrenness was due to lack of prayer on her part and Jacob's (Keil), we are at least justified in asserting that her conduct in breaking forth into angry reproaches against her husband was unlike that of Jacob's mother, Rebekah, who, in similar circumstances, sought relief in prayer and oracles (Kalisch). The brief period that had elapsed since Rachel's marriage, in comparison with the twenty years of Rebekah's barrenness, signally discovered Rachel's sinful impatience.

Ver. 2.—**And Jacob's anger was kindled against Rachel** (not without just cause, since she not only evinced a want of faith and resignation, but wrongfully imputed blame to him): **and he said, Am I in God's stead,** —*i. e.* am I omnipotent like him? This you yourself will surely not presume to believe. The interrogative particle conveys the force of a spirited denial (*vide* Ewald, 'Hebrew Syntax,' § 324)—**who hath withheld from thee the fruit of the womb?** Rachel herself understood that God alone could remove sterility (ver. 6); but to this fact jealousy of Leah appears for the moment to have blinded her.

Ver. 3.—**And she said,**—resorting to the sinful expedient of Sarah (ch. xvi. 2), though without Sarah's excuse, since there was no question whatever about an heir for Jacob; which, even if there had been, would not have justified a practice which, in the case of her distinguished relative, had been so palpably condemned—**Behold my maid Bilhah** (*vide* ch. xxix. 29), **go in unto her; and she shall bear upon my knees,**—*i. e.* children that I may place upon my knees, as mothers do (Piscator, A Lapide, Calvin, Rosenmüller, Lange, Ainsworth); the literal sense of the words being too absurd to require refutation —**that I may also have children**—literally, *be builded up* (cf. ch. xvi. 2)—**by her.**

Ver. 4.—**And she gave him Bilhah her handmaid to wife: and Jacob went in unto her.** "Whence we gather that there is no end of sin where once the Divine institution of marriage is neglected" (Calvin). Jacob began with polygamy, and is now drawn into concubinage. Though God overruled this for the development of the seed of Israel, he did not thereby condone the offence of either Jacob or Rachel.

Ver. 5.—**And Bilhah conceived, and bare Jacob a son.** "Conception and birth may be granted to irregular marriages" (Hughes). "So God often strives to overcome men's wickedness through kindness, and pursues the unworthy with his grace" (Calvin).

Ver. 6.—**And Rachel said, God hath judged me,**—"hath chastened me," as in ch. xv. 14 (Ainsworth, Wordsworth); better, "hath procured for me justice," as if reckoning her sterility an injustice by the side of Leah's fecundity (Keil, Lange); or, hath carried through my cause like a patron, *i. e.* hath vindicated me from the reproach of barrenness (Munster, Rosenmüller); or, hath dealt with me according to his sovereign justice, withholding from me the fruit of the womb while I was forgetful of my dependence on him, and granting me posterity when I approached him in humble supplication (Murphy), which it is obvious from the next clause that Rachel did—**and hath also heard my voice, and hath given me a son.** With undue

severity older interpreters regard Rachel as using the Divine name *more hypocritarum,* who, when their schemes prosper, think that God favours them (Vatablus, Calvin). The employment of Elohim by Jacob and Rachel, supposed to mark the first thirteen verses as belonging to the primitive document (Tuch, Bleek, Kalisch), though by others (Davidson, Colenso) they are ascribed to the Jehovist, is sufficiently explained by Rachel's consciousness that in a large measure her handmaid's son was rather the fruit of her own impious device than the gift of Jehovah (Hengstenberg). **Therefore called she his name Dan**— *i. e.* "Judge," one decreeing justice, *vindex,* from דִּין, to judge (Gesenius, Keil, Lange, *et alii*), though, as in other proper names, *e. g.* Joseph, Zebulun, in which two verbs are alluded to, Michaelis thinks *non a judicando solum, sed et ab audiendo nomen accepisse Danem,* and connects it with another verb, a denominative from an Arabic root, signifying to hear (*vide* 'Suppl.,' p. 425).

Vers. 7, 8.—**And Bilhah Rachel's maid conceived again, and bare Jacob a second son. And Rachel said, With great wrestlings have I wrestled with my sister,**— literally, *wrestlings of God have I wrestled with my sister,* meaning, by "wrestlings of Elohim;" not great wrestlings in rivalry with Leah (A. V., Vatablus, Ainsworth, Rosenmüller, Calvin), nor wrestlings in the cause of God, as being unwilling to leave the founding of the nation to her sister alone (Knobel), but wrestlings with God in prayer (Delitzsch, Lange, Murphy, Kalisch), wrestlings regarding Elohim and his grace (Hengstenberg, Keil), in which she at the same time contended with her sister, to whom apparently that grace had been hitherto restricted— **and I have prevailed** (scarcely in the sense of achieving a victory over Leah, who had already borne four sons, but in the sense of drawing the Divine favour, though only indirectly, towards herself): **and she called his name Naphtali**—*i. e.* "My Wrestling."

Ver. 9.—**When Leah saw that she had left bearing** (literally, *stood from bearing,* as in ch. xxix. 35), **she took Zilpah her maid, and gave her to Jacob to wife**—being in this led astray by Rachel's sinful example, both as to the spirit of unholy rivalry she cherished, and the questionable means she employed for its gratification.

Vers. 10, 11.—**And Zilpah Leah's maid bare Jacob a son. And Leah said, A troop cometh.** בָּגָד, for בְּגָד, in or with good fortune; ἐν τύχῃ (LXX.); *feliciter,* so this happens to me (Vulgate), a translation which has the sanction of Gesenius, Fürst, Rosenmüller, Keil, Kalisch, and other competent authorities—the Keri, which is followed by Onkelos and Syriac, reading בָּא גָד,

fortune cometh. The Authorised rendering, supported by the Samaritan, and supposed to accord better with ch. xlix. 19, is approved by Calvin, Ainsworth, Bush, and others. **And she called his name Gad**—*i. e.* Good Fortune.

Vers. 12, 13.—**And Zilpah Leah's maid bare Jacob a second son. And Leah said, Happy am I,**—literally, *in* my happiness, *sc.* am I ('Speaker's Commentary'); or, *for* or *to* my happiness (Keil, Kalisch)—**for the daughters will call me blessed** (or, happy): **and she called his name Asher**—*i. e.* Happy.

HOMILETICS.

Vers. 1--13.—*Rachel and Leah, or unholy rivalry.* I. RACHEL'S ENVY OF LEAH. 1. *The insufficient cause.* "She saw that she bare Jacob no children," while Leah had begun to have a family. Though commonly regarded by Hebrew wives as a peculiarly severe affliction, childlessness was not without its compensations, which Rachel should have reckoned. Then the motherhood of Leah was the good fortune of a sister, in which Rachel should have lovingly rejoiced; and both the barrenness and the fruitfulness were of God's appointment, in which Rachel should have piously acquiesced. 2. *The querulous complaint.* "Give me children, or else I die." To inordinately long for children was, on Rachel's part, a great sin; to depreciate the gift of life with its manifold blessings because of their absence was a greater sin; to express her bitter and despondent feeling in reproachful language against her husband was a sin still greater; but the greatest sin of all was to overlook the hand of God in her affliction. 3. *The merited rebuke.* "Am I in God's stead?" If Jacob sinned in being angry with Rachel, evincing want of sympathy and patience with her womanly distress, if even he erred in infusing a too great degree of heat into his words, he yet acted with propriety in censuring her fault. It is the province of a husband to reprove grievous misdemeanours in a wife, only not with severity, as Jacob, yet with Jacob's fidelity. 4. *The sinful expedient.* "Behold my maid Bilhah." Sanctioned by popular custom, the plan adopted by Rachel for obtaining children might almost seem to have been sanctified by the conduct of Sarah. But the circumstances in which the two wives were placed were widely different. Yet, even though they had been the same, Rachel was not at liberty, any more than Sarah, to tempt her husband to a violation of the marriage law. The bad example of a saint no more than the evil practice of the world can justify a sin. 5. *The apparent success.* "Rachel's maid conceived." God often allows wicked schemes to prosper, without approving of either the schemes or the schemers. Sometimes their success is needful, as in this case, to manifest their wickedness and folly. 6. *The mistaken inference.* "God hath judged me." Rachel is not the only person who has reckoned God upon his side because of outward prosperity. The world's standard of morality is success. But moral triumphs are frequently achieved through material defeats.

II. LEAH'S IMITATION OF RACHEL. 1. *Of Rachel's bad feeling.* She might have borne with her sister's exultation over the happiness of reaching motherhood by proxy, might have allowed Rachel to have her little triumph, but she could not. Immediately foreseeing the possibility of being out-distanced by her favoured rival, she became a victim of green-eyed jealousy. The envy stirring in the heart of Rachel had at length spread its contagion to her. 2. *Of Rachel's sinful conduct.* "Leah took Zilpah her maid, and gave her Jacob to wife." One never knows where the influence of a bad example is to end. When one saint steps aside from the straight path others are sure to follow. The more eminent the first transgressor is, the easier sinning is to his successors. 3. *Of Rachel's wrong reasoning.* "The daughters will call me blessed." Faulty logic (at least in morals) seems as easy to copy as improper feelings or wicked deeds. The connection between much happiness and many children is not absolute and inevitable. The hopes of rejoicing mothers are sometimes sadly blighted, and their expectations of felicity strangely disappointed. She is truly happy whom not the daughters, but Jehovah, pronounces blessed.

Lessons:—1. The bitterness of envy. 2. The wickedness of polygamy. 3. The contagiousness of sin.

HOMILIES BY VARIOUS AUTHORS.

Ver. 1.—*Envy working in God's people.* "Rachel envied her sister." Jacob's love for Rachel a type of Christ's love for his Church. We cannot doubt that his love was returned. There was thus the chief element of conjugal happiness. But her sister, less favoured in this, had a blessing which was denied her, and "Rachel envied her sister." It was not that she feared to lose her husband's love. Of that she had abundant proof. It was a selfish sorrow. Her husband's children were growing up, but they were not hers. Rachel's envy has its counterpart among Christians. Love for Christ may take the form of selfish zeal; unwillingness to acknowledge or rejoice in work for God in which we take no part. In the spiritual history of the world a blessing often seems to rest upon means irregular or unlikely. Where efforts that promised well have failed, God makes his own power felt; and many think this cannot be right (cf. John ix. 16), and would rather have the work not done than done thus (cf. Numb. xi. 28; Mark ix. 38). Contrast the spirit of St. Paul (Phil. i. 18). Examples of this: unwillingness to rejoice in good done by some other communion, or some other party than our own; inclination to look at points of difference rather than at those held in common; the work of others doubted, criticised, or ignored; eagerness to warn against this or that. Self lies at the root of this. Perhaps the harvest of another seems to diminish ours. Perhaps our own thoughts are to us the measure of God's plans (cf. Mark xiv. 4). Men see the outside of others' work, and judge as if they knew both the motives and the full results. Yet with this there may be much real zeal and love for the Lord. The failure lies in the want of complete acceptance of his will. To rejoice in work for Christ, by whomsoever done, is not inconsistent with decided views as to the objects to be aimed at, and the means to be used (1 Thess. v. 21). 1. We are called to enlarge the household of God; to be the means of making enemies into children (cf. Ps. lxxxvii. 4, 5) through producing faith (cf. John i. 12). Each responsible for the faithful use of the powers given to us, and bidden to examine ourselves as to sincerity. But the visible results are as God pleases. Here a test of singleness of mind. Can we rejoice in success of a work in which we have no share, or when another's success appears greater than ours? (Gal. v. 26). 2. As an exercise of unselfishness, be careful not to provoke envy by parading distinctive peculiarities (Rom. xii. 18) or exalting our own work. 3. Be not discouraged that work of others seems more blessed (John iv. 36, 37). Faithfulness is within the power of all. It is that which God regards (Matt. xxv. 21). The result we cannot judge of here. The fruit delayed may prove a greater blessing.—M.

EXPOSITION.

Ver. 14.—**And Reuben** (at this time four or five years old) **went** (probably accompanying the reapers) **in the days of wheat harvest** (in the beginning of May), **and found mandrakes**—דּוּדָאִים, μῆλα μανδραγορῶν (LXX., Josephus), apples of the mandragora, an herb resembling belladonna, with a root like a carrot, having white and reddish blossoms of a sweet smell, and with yellow odoriferous apples, ripening in May and June, and supposed, according to Oriental superstition, to possess the virtue of conciliating love and promoting fruitfulness (*vide* Gesenius, p. 191, and cf. Rosenmüller's 'Scholia,' and Kalisch *in loco*)—**in the field** (when at his childish play), **and brought them unto his mother Leah** (which a son of more mature years would not have done). **Then Rachel** (not exempt from the prevailing superstition) **said to Leah, Give me, I pray thee, of thy son's mandrakes** (in the hopes that they would remove her sterility).

Ver. 15—**And she** (Leah) **said unto her,** —*stomachose* (Calvin)—**Is it a small matter that thou hast taken my husband?**—literally, *Is it little thy taking away my husband?* meaning that Rachel had been the cause of Jacob's forsaking her (Leah's) society—**and wouldest thou take away** (literally, *and to take also* = wouldst thou take? expressive of strong surprise) **my son's mandrakes also?** Calvin thinks it unlikely that Jacob's wives were naturally quarrelsome; *sed Deus confligere eas inter se passus est ut polygamiæ pœna ad posteras extaret.* **And Rachel said** (in order to induce Leah's compliance with her request), **Therefore he shall lie with thee to-night for thy son's mandrakes.**

Ver. 16.—**And Jacob came out of the field in the evening,**—*i. e.* the harvest-field (ver. 14)—**and Leah went out to meet him, and said, Thou must come in unto me** (the Samaritan codex adds "this night," and the LXX. "to-day"); **for surely I have hired thee** (literally, *hiring I have hired thee*) **with my son's mandrakes. And** (assenting to the arrangement of his wives) **he lay with her that night.**

Ver. 17.—**And God hearkened unto Leah,** —*i. e.* unto Leah's prayers (Onkelos, Jerome, Rosenmüller, Murphy), which Calvin thinks doubtful—*quis enim putaret, dum odiose sorori suæ negat Lea fructus a puero collectos, et hoc pretio noctem mariti mercatur, ullum esse precibus locum.* The historian employs the term Elohim to show that Leah's pregnancy was not owing to her son's mandrakes, but to Divine power (Keil, Lange)— **and she conceived, and bare Jacob the fifth son** — or, counting Zilpah's, the seventh ; while, reckoning Bilhah's, this was Jacob's ninth child.

Ver. 18.—**And Leah said, God**—Elohim ; a proof of the lower religious consciousness into which Leah had fallen (Hengstenberg), though perhaps on the above hypothesis an evidence of her piety and faith (Keil, Lange) —**hath given me my hire, because I have given my maiden to my husband :**—*i. e.* as a reward for my self-denial (Keil, Murphy) ; an exclamation in which appears Leah's love for Jacob (Lange), if not also a tacit acknowledgment that she had her fears lest she may have sinned in asking him to wed Zilpah (Rosenmüller) — **and she called his name Issachar**—" There is Reward," or " There is Hire ; " containing a double allusion to her hire of Jacob and her reward for Zilpah

Vers. 19, 20.—**And Leah conceived again, and bare Jacob the sixth son. And Leah said, God** (Elohim ; *vide supra*) **hath endued me with a good dowry.** Δεδώρηται μοι δῶρον καλον (LXX.), *dotavit me dote bona* (Vulgate), hath presented me with a goodly present. The word זֶבֶד is a ἅπαξ λεγόμενον. **Now will my husband dwell with me.** זָבַל, also a ἅπαξ λεγ., signifies to be or make round (Gesenius), to limit round or encompass (Fürst) ; hence, according to both,

to cohabit or dwell together as husband and wife. The LXX. render αἱρετιεῖ, the meaning being that Leah's six sons would, in her judgment, be an inducement sufficiently powerful to cause Jacob to select her society instead of that of her barren sister. **And she called his name Zebulun**—*i. e.* Dwelling ; from *zabal*, to dwell with, with a play upon the word זָבַל, to hire, which, commencing with the same letter, was regarded as similar in sound to זָבַד, the ד and the ל being sometimes interchangeable (Keil, Kalisch).

Ver. 21. — **And afterwards she bare a daughter, and called her name Dinah**—*i. e.* Judgment. Dinah (the female Dan) may not have been Jacob's only daughter (*vide* ch. xxxvii. 35 ; xlvi. 7). Her name is here recorded probably because of the incident in her history afterwards related (ch. xxxiv. 1).

Vers. 22 — 24. — **And God remembered Rachel** (cf. ch. viii. 1 ; 1 Sam. i. 19), **and God hearkened to her,**—as to Leah (ver. 17)— **and opened her womb**—as he had previously done to Leah (ch. xxix. 31). Rachel's barrenness had not continued so long as either Sarah's or Rebekah's. **And she conceived, and bare a son ; and said, God hath taken away my reproach**—*i. e.* of sterility. The mandrakes of Leah having proved inefficacious, Rachel at length realises that children are God's gift, and this thought sufficiently explains the use of the term Elohim. **And she called his name Joseph ;**—יוֹסֵף, either, "he takes away," with allusion to the removal of her reproach, or, "he shall add," with reference to her hope of another son. Perhaps the first thought is not obscurely hinted at, though the second appears from the ensuing clause to have occupied the greater prominence in Rachel's mind—**and said, The Lord** — Jehovah ; a trace of the Jehovistic pen (Tuch, Bleek, *et alii*) ; rather an outcome of the higher spiritual life of Rachel, who had now got emancipated from all such merely human devices as resorting to mandrakes, and was able to recognise her complete dependence for offspring on the sovereign grace of the covenant God of Abraham and Isaac and Jacob (Hengstenberg, Keil)—**shall add to me another son.**

HOMILETICS.

Vers. 14—24.—*The story of the mandrakes.* I. A YOUNG CHILD'S INNOCENCE. " Reuben found mandrakes in the field, and brought them to his mother." Nature, with its beautiful sights and harmonious sounds, possesses a wonderful fascination for the infant mind. In proportion as man sinks beneath the power of sin does he fall out of sympathy with God's fair world. Strong and tender is the bond of love which unites a child to its mother. The true depositary for a child's treasures is the mother's lap, for a child's joys and sorrows the mother's heart. Yet a child's inexperience and simplicity may sometimes cause a parent to err, though the true source of temptation lies in the parent, and not in the child. "To the pure all things are pure ; but to them that are defiled is nothing pure."

II. A GROWN WOMAN'S SUPERSTITION. "Give me of thy son's mandrakes." Rachel obviously shared the popular belief that Reuben's fragrant herbs would have an influence in removing her sterility. It is useless inquiring how such a notion originated. Superstitions commonly arise from mistaking as cause and effect what are only coincident occurrences. Of more importance it is to note that Rachel was of mature years, had been born and nurtured in what may be regarded as a religious home, was now the wife of an intelligent and pious (if also encompassed with infirmities) man, and yet she was the victim of delusive beliefs. In this Rachel was perhaps scarcely to be charged with blame. Superstition is essentially a fault of the intellect resulting from defective information. But Rachel erred in calling superstition to her aid in her unholy rivalry with Leah ; all the more when she knew that God alone could remove her reproach.

III. A JEALOUS WIFE'S BARGAIN. On the part both of Rachel and Leah it was a miserable compact ; and a pitiable spectacle it surely was, that of two rival wives contracting with one another about their husband's society. Rachel disposes of Jacob for a night in consideration of a handful of mandrakes, and Leah counts herself entitled to Jacob's favours as a boon which she had purchased with Reuben's yellow apples. Not to speak of the humiliation in all this to Jacob, and the continual misery to which he must have been subjected between his ardent sister-wives, think of the wretchedness it must have entailed upon the women themselves, and the dispeace it must have brought into the rival homes. A more powerful condemnation of polygamy it will be difficult to find, or a more signal illustration of the retribution which sooner or later follows on the heels of transgression.

IV. A SOVEREIGN GOD'S DECISION. The two wives were seemingly uncertain whether to ascribe virtue to the mandrakes or not. God determined the problem in a way that must have fully convinced them. 1. That the mandrakes could not remove sterility he demonstrated by allowing Rachel's barrenness to continue at least two years longer, though she had made use of Reuben's apples, and by opening Leah's womb without them. 2. That he alone could bestow offspring on married people he showed by remembering Rachel in his own time, and causing her reproach to depart.

Learn—1. That things and persons innocent and pleasant in themselves may lead astray. 2. That out of small occasions great events may spring. 3. That much infirmity may cling to good men and women. 4. That things desirable in themselves may be sought in wrong ways. 5. That God's hand should be recognised in the giving or withholding children.

HOMILIES BY VARIOUS AUTHORS.

Vers. 22—24.—*The life of faith and its reward.* The Scripture teaches us to put the facts of common life in the light of God's countenance. The true foundation on which family welfare rests is God's faithfulness and favour. The intense desire of the Hebrew women for children, especially sons, a testimony to the Divine covenant ; the original promise pervading all the national life.

I. The birth of Joseph a REWARD OF FAITH AND ANSWER TO PRAYER. God remembers, though we think he forgets. Reproach may lie awhile on the true believer, but is taken away at last. Syrophenician woman ; seeming neglect calls out stronger expression of faith. Pray without ceasing.

II. BLESSINGS WAITED FOR are the more appreciated and the richer WHEN THEY COME. "*Joseph*" a type of him who, though he was sent after many prophets and long tarrying, was greater than all his brethren. The Rachel, the true beloved, the chosen bride, the Church in whom the true Jacob finds special delight, waits and prays. When God shall show that he has remembered and hearkened, the elect one shall be abundantly satisfied. "God hath taken away my reproach."

III. All experience of Divine faithfulness is a great help, in looking forward, to cherish expectation. "The Lord shall add to me another son." We ask for more when we know that our prayer is heard.—R.

EXPOSITION.

Ver. 25.—**And it came to pass, when Rachel had born Joseph,**—either at or about the expiry of the second term of seven years. Jacob's family now consisted in all of eleven sons and one daughter, unless Dinah's birth occurred later in the next term of service (Keil). Since these were all born within seven years, the chronological cannot be the order observed by the historian in recording the events of the preceding paragraphs. Rather the births of the children are arranged in connection with the mothers from whom they sprang. Hence the possibility of acquiring so large a family in so short a time. The six sons of Leah might be born in the seven years, allowing one year's complete cessation from pregnancy, viz., the fifth ; Bilhah's in the third and fourth years ; Zilpah's in the beginning of the sixth and seventh ; and Rachel's toward the end of the seventh, leaving Dinah to be born later (cf. Keil *in loco*)—**that Jacob said unto Laban** (if not immediately, certainly soon, after Joseph's birth), **Send me away** (meaning that Laban should permit him to depart), **that I may go** (literally, *and I will go*) **unto mine own place, and to my country**—to Canaan in general, and to that part of it in particular where he had formerly resided (cf. ch. xviii. 33 ; xxxi. 55).

Ver. 26.—**Give** me (suffer me to take) **my wives and my children, for whom I have served thee, and let me go** (literally, *and I will go*): **for thou knowest my service which I have done thee**—implying that he had faithfully implemented his engagement, and that Laban was aware of the justness of his demand to be released from further servitude.

Ver. 27. —**And Laban said unto him** (having learnt by fourteen years' acquaintance with Jacob to know the value of a good shepherd), **I pray thee, if I have found favour in thine eyes** (the clause is elliptical, the A. V. rightly supplying), tarry : for (this word also is not in the original), **I have learned by experience** — literally, *I have divined* (נִחַשְׁתִּי, from נָחַשׁ, to hiss as a serpent, hence to augur) ; not necessarily by means of serpents (Gesenius, Wordsworth, 'Speaker's Commentary'), or even by consulting his gods (Delitzsch, Kalisch), but perhaps by close observation and minute inspection (Murphy, Bush). The LXX. render οἰωνισάμην ; the Vulgate by *experimento didici* — **that the Lord** — Jehovah. Nominally a worshipper of the true God, Laban was in practice addicted to heathen superstitions (cf. ch. xxxi. 19, 32)—**hath blessed me** (with material prosperity) **for thy sake.**

Ver. 28.—**And ne said, Appoint me thy wages.** Literally, *distinctly specify* (from a root signifying to bore, hence to declare accurately) *thy hire upon me,* i. e. which I will take upon me as binding. Laban's caution to be clear and specific in defining the terms of any engagement he might enter into was much needed, and would doubtless not be neglected by Jacob, whose past experience must have taught him he was dealing with one who, in respect of covenants and contracts, was eminently treacherous. **And I will give** it.

Ver. 29.—**And he** (Jacob) **said unto him** (Laban), **Thou knowest how** (literally, *what*) **I have served thee, and how thy cattle was with me**—literally, *and what thy cattle has been* (or become) *with me,* i. e. to what a number they have grown.

.Ver. 30.—**For it was little which thou hadst before I** came,—literally, *for little* (it was) *which was to thee before me ;* i. e. not in place, ἐναντίον ἐμοῦ (LXX.), but in time, *i. e.* before my arrival—**and it is now increased**—literally, *broken forth* (cf. ver. 43)—**unto a multitude; and the Lord** (Jehovah) **hath blessed thee since my coming** (literally, *at my foot,* i. e. wherever I have gone among your flocks): **and now when shall I provide** (literally, *do*) **for mine own house also ?**

Ver. 31.—**And he** (Laban, unwilling to part with so profitable an assistant) **said, What shall I give thee?** He was apparently prepared to detain Jacob at his own terms. **And Jacob said, Thou shalt not give me anything.** Jacob did not design to serve Laban gratuitously, but chose rather to trust God than Laban for recompense (Wordsworth, Gosman in Lange); or he may have meant that he would have no wages of Laban's setting, but only of his own proposing (Hughes). **If thou wilt do this thing for me** (accede to this stipulation), **I will again feed** and **keep thy flock**—literally, *I will turn, I will tend thy flock, I will keep* (sc. it).

Ver. 32. — **I will pass through all thy flock to-day,**—wrongly rendered παρελθέτω πάντα τὰ πρόβατα σου (LXX), *gyra per omnes greges tuos* (Vulgate), as if Jacob proposed that the separation of the flocks should be effected by Laban, and not by himself—**removing from thence**—not "remove thou," as if the verb were imperative (Rosenmüller, Murphy, Kalisch), but "to remove," the verb being in the inf. (Keil; cf. Ewald, 'Heb. Synt.,' § 279)—**all the speckled and spotted cattle, and all the brown cattle among the sheep, and the spotted and speckled among**

the goats. Since in Oriental countries sheep are commonly white and goats black, the number of speckled and spotted animals (*i. e.* sheep with little spots and large patches of black, and goats with little or large points of white, in their hair) would be unusually small. **And of such shall be my hire** *i. e.* the dark spotted or entirely black sheep and white or white-speckled goats were to be Jacob's reward (Knobel, Delitzsch, Keil, Lange), which was to be subsequently increased by whatever speckled animals might appear among the one-coloured flocks ; but it seems more probable that Jacob only claimed the latter, and, both to make the bargain more attractive to Laban and to show that he wanted nothing from Laban but only what God might be pleased in accordance with this arrangement to bestow, he suggested that the flocks and herds should be purged of all such speckled and spotted animals to begin with (Tuch, Baumgarten, Kurtz, Rosenmüller, Kalisch, Candlish, Murphy, 'Speaker's Commentary,' Clarke, Bush).

Ver. 33.—**So shall my righteousness** (literally, *and my righteousness*) **answer for me** (or bear testimony in my behalf) **in time to come,** — literally, *in the day, to-morrow ;* meaning in the future (Gesenius) rather than the day following (Delitzsch)—**when it shall come for my hire before thy face.** Either, (1) for it (my righteousness) shall come, concerning my wages, before thy face, *sc.* for consideration (Calvin) ; or, (2) when thou shalt come to my reward, connecting "before thy face" with the previous clause (Chaldee, Rosenmüller, Ainsworth, Lange) ; or, (3) when thou shalt come to my wages before thee (Murphy), or to inspect it (Kalisch). **Every one that is not speckled and spotted among the goats, and brown among the sheep, that shall be counted stolen with me**—and therefore to be delivered up to thee.

Ver. 34.—**And Laban said, Behold, I would it might be according to thy word.** Jacob's chances of obtaining speckled animals by this arrangement were so small that Laban, with his customary selfishness, had no difficulty in closing with the offered bargain. As originally proposed by Jacob it seems to have been an honest desire on his part to commit the question of wages to the decision rather of God's providence than of his kinsman's greed. That at this time Jacob's mind "had already formed the whole fraudulent procedure by which he acquired his wealth" (Kalisch) does not accord with the statement subsequently made.

Ver. 35.—**And he**—Laban (Rosenmüller, Keil, Delitzsch, Kalisch, Murphy, *et alii*) ; Jacob (Lange)—**removed that day** (that the smallest possible chance of success might remain to his nephew) **the he-goats that**

were ringstraked (striped or banded) **and spotted, and all the she-goats that were speckled and spotted, and every one that had** some **white in it, and all the brown among the sheep,**—four sorts of animals were to be removed : (1) the dotted, (2) the patched, (3) the ring-marked or striped, and (4) the black or brown, **and gave them into the hand of his** (Laban's or Jacob's, *ut supra*) **sons.**

Ver. 36.—**And** (as if to insure the impossibility of the two flocks mingling and breeding) **he set three days' journey betwixt himself** (with his sons and the parti-coloured animals) **and Jacob : and Jacob fed the rest of Laban's flocks**—out of which he was to pay himself as best he could in accordance with the contract.

Ver. 37.—**And Jacob took him rods of green poplar**—literally, *a rod* (the singular being used collectively for rods) *of* לִבְנֶה, (from לָבַן, to be white, meaning either the) *poplar* (LXX., in Hosea iv. 13 ; Vulgate, Kalisch) *or the storax* (LXX. *in loco*, Keil ; cf. Michaelis, 'Suppl.,' p. 1404) *fresh or green*—**and of the hazel**—לוּז, the hazel tree (Raschi, Kimchi, Arabic, Luther, Fürst, Kalisch) or the almond tree (Vulgate, Saadias, Calvin, Gesenius, 'Speaker's Commentary') —**and chesnut tree ;**—עַרְמוֹן, the plane tree (LXX., Vulgate, *et alii*), so called from its height — **and pilled white strakes in them** (literally, *peeled off in them peeled places white*), **and made the white appear** (literally, *making naked the white*) **which** was **in the rods.**

Ver. 38.—**And he set the rods which he had pilled before the flocks in the gutters** (רְהָטִים ; literally, *the canals or channels through which the water ran*, from a root signifying to run) **in the watering troughs** (שְׁקָתוֹת, *i. e.* the troughs which contained the water, to which the animals approached) **when the flocks came to drink, that they should conceive** (literally, *and they became warm*, in the sense expressed in the A. V.) **when they came to drink**—this was Jacob's first artifice to overreach Laban.

Ver. 39.—**And the flocks conceived** (*ut supra*) **before the rods, and brought forth cattle ringstraked, speckled, and spotted.** The fact is said to have been frequently observed that, particularly in the case of sheep, whatever fixes their attention in copulation is marked upon the young. That Jacob believed in the efficacy of the artifice he adopted is apparent ; but the multiplication of parti-coloured animals it will be safer to ascribe to Divine blessing than to human craft.

Ver. 40.—**And Jacob did separate the**

lambs (*i. e.* the speckled lambs procured by the foregoing artifice he removed from the main body of the flock), **and set the faces of the flocks toward the ringstraked, and all the brown in the flock of Laban** (this was Jacob's second artifice, to make the speckled lambs serve the same purpose as the pilled rods) ; **and he put his own flocks by themselves, and put them not unto Laban's cattle**—so that they were not exposed to the risk of producing offspring of uniform colour.

Ver. 41.—**And it came to pass, whensoever the stronger cattle did conceive,** — literally, *in every heating of the cattle, the bound ones,* i. e. the firm, compact sheep, "the spring flock" (Luther), which, being conceived in spring and dropped in autumn, are supposed to be stronger than those conceived in autumn and dropped in spring ; but this is doubtful—**that Jacob laid the rods before the eyes of the cattle in the gutters, that they might conceive among the rods.** Jacob's third artifice aimed at securing for himself a vigorous breed of sheep.

Ver. 42.—**But when the cattle were feeble,** —literally, *in the covering* (sc. with wool ; hence weakening) *of the flock,* which took place in autumn—**he put** them **not in** (partly to prevent the introduction of feeble animals amongst his parti-coloured flocks, but partly also, it is thought, to avoid prematurely exciting Laban's suspicion): **so the feebler were Laban's, and the stronger Jacob's.**

Ver. 43.—**And**—as the apparent result of the triple stratagem, though *vide supra,* ver. 38, and cf. ch. xxxi. 12—**the man increased exceedingly,**—literally, *broke forth greatly* (vide ver. 30)—**and had much cattle, and maid-servants, and men-servants, and camels, and asses**—like Abraham (ch. xiii. 2) and Isaac (ch. xxvi. 13, 14). Thus far the historian simply narrates the fact of the patriarch's prosperity, and the steps which led to it, "without expressing approbation of his conduct or describing his increasing wealth as a blessing from God. The verdict is contained in what follows" (Keil).

HOMILETICS.

Vers. 25—43.—*Jacob and Laban, or craft* versus *greed.* 1. JACOB'S RESPECTFUL REQUEST OF LABAN. At the close of fourteen years' harsh and exacting service, Jacob desires permission to take his wives and children and return to Canaan. The motives which induced him were probably—1. The termination of his contract, which released him from a servitude both galling and oppressive. 2. The remembrance of God's covenant, which had assigned him the land of promise as his true inheritance. 3. The joy occasioned by the birth of Rachel's child, whom he seems to have regarded as the theocratic heir. 4. A desire to provide for his now rapidly-increasing household.

II. JACOB'S SELFISH HINDRANCE BY LABAN. That Jacob's uncle and father-in-law was unwilling to acquiesce in his departure and solicitous to retain him was due to— 1. His appreciation of Jacob's qualities as a flock-master. Jacob felt he could appeal to "the service he had done" for the past fourteen years. 2. His discovery of a latent connection between Jacob's presence and his own augmenting prosperity. Laban, poor enough before his nephew's arrival, had shrewdly noted that the day of Jacob's coming had been the day of fortune's turning in his favour, and that, wherever his clever "brother" went, flocks and herds broke out beside him. 3. His secret hope of effecting easy terms with Jacob. Though ostensibly willing to take him at his own price, he was clearly calculating that he would not have much difficulty in over-reaching the man whom already he had cheated in the matter of his daughters.

III. JACOB'S REMARKABLE CONTRACT WITH LABAN. He agrees to serve a third time with Laban on condition of receiving all the speckled and spotted, ringstraked and brown, animals that Laban's flocks might produce, after all of those sorts had been previously removed. 1. The proposal of such a singular condition on the part of Jacob was an act not of folly, but of faith, being tantamount to a committal of his cause to God instead of Laban. 2. The acceptance of it on the part of Laban was a pitiful display of greed, and a proof that the bygone years of prosperity had both awakened in his soul the insatiable demon of avarice and extinguished any spark of kindly feeling towards Jacob that may have once existed in his breast.

IV. JACOB'S CUNNING STRATAGEM AGAINST LABAN. 1. The *nature* of it. This was the employment of a triple artifice : (1) by means of pilled rods to produce parti-coloured animals in Laban's flock ; (2) on securing these, so to use them as to increase their number ; and (3) to direct the animals in such a fashion that the stronger and healthier portion of the flock should be his, and the feebler Laban's. 2. The *success* of it. That Jacob's stratagem did not fail is apparent; but how far it was due to the particular expedient employed cannot be so easily determined. That impressions made upon the minds of sheep at rutting time affect the fœtus seems a well-established fact; but the extraordinary rapidity with which brown and speckled animals were produced appears to point to the intervention of a special providence in Jacob's behalf. 3. The *rightness* of it. That in what Jacob did there was nothing fraudulent may be inferred from the fact that he acted under the Divine approval (ch xxxi. 12), and made use of nothing but the superior knowledge of the habits of animals which he had acquired through his long experience in keeping sheep.

V. JACOB'S ULTIMATE ADVANCEMENT OVER LABAN. This comes out with greater prominence in the ensuing chapter; the present notices his amazing prosperity. "The man increased exceedingly;" and, in spite of Laban's craft and avarice combined, eventually eclipsed him in the possession of flocks and herds.

Learn—1. The attractive influence of home, both temporal and spiritual. 2. The danger of material prosperity—exemplified in Laban. 3. The wisdom of trusting God in all things, even in secular callings. 4. The value of all kinds of knowledge, but especially of the best. 5. The advantage of having God upon our side in all our bargains—notably when dealing with the selfish and mean. 6. The right to use all lawful means to preserve our interests—particularly against such as would invade them. 7. The possibility of the last outstripping the first—in the Church as well as in the world.

HOMILIES BY VARIOUS AUTHORS.

Ver. 43.—*Jacob's history an illustration of the blending together of the natural and the supernatural in God's dealings.* "And the man increased exceedingly," &c.

I. The PROMISE TO GUIDE, protect, and bless fulfilled in connection with the employment of ordinary faculties and instrumentalities. Jacob's craft partly natural, but in this instance specially assisted that he might be helped in an emergency. The "supplanter" in this case represented the better cause.

II. HUMAN DEVICES only apparently, and not really, thwart the purposes of God. Jacob represents the people of God. The victory is appointed them. Their interests must be served by the kingdoms of this world, though for a season the advantage appears on the side of the mere calculating, selfish policy. The true wisdom is that which cometh from above.

III. INCREASE in the best sense is God's promise. It will be sent as he wills and when he wills, but will be found the true answer to prayer and the true manifestation of love. On all that belongs to us the blessing rests. Spiritual prosperity carries with it all other. Though the individual may be called to suffer for the sake of the community, the promise to the Church must be fulfilled. "It is our Father's good pleasure to give us the kingdom." "The meek shall inherit the earth."—R.

EXPOSITION.

CHAPTER XXXI.

Ver. 1.—**And he**—Jacob had now served twenty years with Laban, and must accordingly have been in his ninety-seventh or seventy-seventh year (*vide* ch. xxvii. 1)—**heard the words of Laban's sons,**—who were not at this time only small youths about fourteen years of age (Delitzsch), since they were capable of being entrusted with their father's flocks (ch. xxx. 35)—**saying** (probably in a conversation which had been overheard by Jacob), **Jacob hath taken away** (by fraud is what they meant, an opinion in which Kalisch agrees; but it is not quite certain that Jacob was guilty of dishonesty in acting as he did) **all that was our father's;** —this was a manifest exaggeration; *sed hoc morbo laborant sordidi et nimium tenaces, ut sibi ereptum esse putent quicquid non ingurgitant* (Calvin)—**and of** that which was **our father's hath he gotten** (literally, *made,* in the sense of acquiring, as in ch. xii. 5; 1 Sam. xiv. 48) **all this glory.** כָּבוֹד (from כָּבֵד, to be heavy, hence to be great in the sense of honoured, and also to be abundant) signifies either glory, splendour, renown, δόξα (LXX.), as in Job xiv. 21; or, what seems the preferable meaning here, wealth, riches, *facultates* (Vulgate), as in Ps. xlix. 13 ; Nahum ii. 10. The two ideas appear to be combined in 2 Cor. iv. 17 ; βάρος δόξης (cf. Wordsworth, *in loco*).

Ver. 2.—**And Jacob beheld the counten-ance of Laban, and, behold, it** (*i. e.* either Laban or his countenance) **was not toward him** (literally, *with him*) **as before**—literally, *as yesterday and the day before.* The evident change in Laban's disposition, which had previously been friendly, was obviously em-ployed by God to direct Jacob's mind to the propriety of returning to the land of his inheritance ; and the inclination thus started in his soul was further strengthened and confirmed by a revelation which probably soon after, if not the night following, was sent for his direction.

Ver. 3.—**And the Lord**—Jehovah ; since the entire journey to Padan-aram had been conducted under his special care, *vide* ch. xxviii. 15 (Hengstenberg), and not because the first three verses of this chapter have been inserted or modified by the Jehovist (Tuch, Bleek, *et alii*)—**said unto Jacob,**—probably in a dream (cf. vers. 5, 10, 11)—**Return unto the land of thy fathers** (*i. e.* Canaan), **and to thy kindred ; and I will be with thee.** So Jehovah had promised at Bethel twenty years before (ch. xxviii. 15).

Ver. 4.—**And Jacob sent**—being unwilling to approach the house lest Laban should dis-cover his design (Rosenmüller)—**and called Rachel and Leah**—Rachel may be placed first as the beloved wife of Jacob (Words-worth, Lange), scarcely as the principal wife in comparison with Leah, who was *adventitia* (Rosenmüller ; cf. ver. 14)—**to the field unto his flock.** The expression " his flock " indi-cates that Jacob had abandoned Laban's sheep and taken possession of those which belonged to himself—probably in preparation for his departure.

Ver. 5.—**And said unto them, I see your father's countenance, that it** is **not toward me as before** (*vide supra*) ; **but the God of my father**—literally, *and the Elohim of my father,* the term Elohim employed by Jacob not being due to " the vagueness of the re-ligious knowledge " possessed by his wives (Hengstenberg), but to a desire on his own part either to distinguish the God of his father from the gods of the nations, or the idols which Laban worshipped ('Speaker's Commentary'), or perhaps, while using an expression exactly equivalent to Jehovah, to bring out a contrast between the Divine favour and that of Laban (Quarry)—**hath been with me**—literally, *was with me ;* not the night before simply, but during the past six years, as he explains in ver. 7.

Ver. 6.—**And ye know that with all my power I have served your father.** The term Jacob here uses for power is derived from an

unused onomatopoetic root, signifying to pant, and hence to exert one's strength. If, there-fore, the assertion now made to his wives was not an unblushing falsehood, Jacob could not have been the monster of craft and de-ception depicted by some (Kalisch) ; while. if it was, it must have required considerable effrontery to appeal to his wives' knowledge for a confirmation of what they knew to be a deliberate untruth. The hypothesis that Jacob first acquired his great wealth by " consummate cunning," and then piously " abused the authority of God in covering or justifying them" (Kalisch), presupposes on the part of Jacob a degree of wickedness in-conceivable in one who had enjoyed the sub-lime theophany of Bethel.

Ver. 7.—**And your father hath deceived me,**—הֵתֶל, the hiph. of תָּלַל, means to rob or plunder (Fürst), or to cause to fall, as in the cognate languages, whence to deceive (Gesenius)—**and changed my wages ten times ;**—*i. e.* many times, as in Numb. xiv. 22 ; Job xix. 3 (Rosenmüller, Bush, Kalisch, Lange) ; as often as possible, the number ten expressing the idea of completeness (Keil, Murphy)—**but God** (Elohim, Jacob purposing to say that he had been protected, not by human stratagem, but by Divine interposi-tion) **suffered him not to hurt me**—literally, *to do evil to me.* The verb here construed with עָמַד = עָם is sometimes followed by עַל (1 Kings xvii. 20), and sometimes by בְּ (1 Chron. xvi. 22).

Ver. 8.—**If he** (*i. e.* Laban) **said thus, The speckled shall be thy wages ;**—by the original contract Jacob had been promised all the parti-coloured animals (ch. xxx. 32) ; here it seems as if Laban, struck with the re-markable increase of these, took the earliest opportunity of so modifying the original stipulation as to limit Jacob's portion to one sort only, viz. the speckled. Yet this dis-honourable breach of faith on the part of Laban was of no avail ; for, when the next lambing season came—**then** (it was discovered that) **all the cattle bare speckled : and if he said thus** (changing the sort of animals assigned to his son-in-law), **The ringstraked shall be thy hire** (the result was as before) ; **then bare all the cattle ringstraked.**

Ver. 9.—**Thus**—literally, *and* (as the result of this)—**God hath taken away the cattle of your father, and given** them **to me.** In ascribing to God what he had himself effected by (so-called) fraud, this language of Jacob appears to some inexcusable (Kalisch) ; in passing over his own stratagem in silence Jacob has been charged with not telling the whole truth to his wives (Keil). A more charitable consideration of Jacob's statement, however, discerns in it an evidence of his piety, which recognised and gratefully acknowledged that not his own "consummate cunning," but Jehovah's watchful care had enabled him to outwit the dishonest craft of Laban (Rosenmüller, Ainsworth, Bush, Candlish, Murphy).

Ver. 10.—**And it came to pass at the time that the cattle conceived** (this obviously goes back to the commencement of the six years' service), **that I lifted up mine eyes, and saw in a dream, and, behold, the rams**—עֲתֻּדִים, he-goats, from an unused root, to be ready, perhaps because ready and prompt for fighting (Gesenius, *sub voce*)—**which leaped** (literally, *going up*) **upon the cattle** were **ringstraked, speckled, and grisled.** The grisled (*beruddim*, from *barad*, to scatter hail) were spotted animals, as if they had been sprinkled with hail, not a fifth sort in addition to the four already mentioned (Rosenmüller), but the same as the *teluim* of ch. xxx. 35 (Kalisch). Wordsworth observes that the English term grisled, from the French word *grêle*, hail, is a literal translation of the Hebrew. Gesenius connects with the Hebrew root the words πάρδος, *pardus*, leopard (so called from its spots), and the French *broder*, to embroider. The LXX. understand the עֲתֻּדִים to include both sheep and goats, and translate οἱ τράγοι καὶ οἱ κριοὶ ἀναβαίνοντες ἐπὶ τὰ πρόβατα καὶ τὰς αἶγας.

Ver. 11.—**And the angel of God**—literally, *the angel* (or *Maleach*) *of Elohim*, i. e. of the God who was with me and protecting me, though himself continuing unseen—**spake unto me in a dream,** saying, **Jacob: And I said, Here am I** (*vide* ch. xx. 1, 11).

Ver. 12.—**And he said, Lift up now thine eyes, and see, all the rams which leap upon the cattle are ringstraked, speckled, and grisled.** Since all the parti-coloured animals had already been removed (ch. xxx. 35), this vision must have been intended to assure him that the flocks would produce speckled and spotted progeny all the same as if the ringstraked and grisled rams and he-goats had not been removed from their midst (cf. Kurtz, § 78). To insist upon a contradiction between this account of the increase of Jacob's flocks and that mentioned in ch. xxx. 37 is to forget that both may be true. Equally arbitrary does it seem to be to accuse Jacob of fraud in adopting the artifice of the pilled rods (Kalisch). Without resorting to the supposition that he acted under God's guidance (Wordsworth), we may believe that the dream suggested the expedient referred to, in which some see Jacob's unbelief and impatience (Kurtz, Gosman in Lange), and others a praiseworthy instance of self-help (Keil). **For I have seen all that Laban doeth unto thee.** If the preceding clause appears to imply that the vision was sent to Jacob at

the beginning of the six years' service, the present clause seems to point to the end of that period as the date of its occurrence ; in which case it would require to be understood as a Divine intimation to Jacob that his immense wealth was not to be ascribed to the success of his own stratagem, but to the blessing of God (Delitzsch). The difficulty of harmonising the two views has led to the suggestion that Jacob here mixes the accounts of two different visions accorded to him, at the commencement and at the close of the period of servitude (Nachmanides, Rosenmüller, Kurtz, 'Speaker's Commentary,' Murphy, Candlish).

Ver. 13.—**I am the God of Beth-el,**—the angel here identifies himself with Jehovah (*vide* ch. xxviii. 13). Contrary to usual custom, הָאֵל, though in the construct. state, has the art. (*vide* Ewald, ' Heb. Synt.,' § 290) —**where thou anointedst the pillar,** and **where thou vowedst a vow unto me: now arise, get thee out from this land, and return unto the land of thy kindred**—i. e. to the land of Canaan, which was Jacob's true inheritance.

Vers. 14—16. — **And Rachel and Leah** (*vide* on ver. 4) **answered and said unto him** (Kalisch overdoes his attempt to blacken Jacob's character and whitewash Laban's when he says that Rachel and Leah were so entirely under their husband's influence that they spoke about their father "with severity and boldness bordering on disrespect." It rather seems to speak badly for Laban that his daughters eventually rose in protest against his heartless cruelty and insatiable greed), *Is there* **yet any portion or inheritance for us in our father's house?** The interrogative particle indicates a spirited inquiry, to which a negative response is anticipated (cf. ch. xxx. 2 ; *vide* Ewald, ' Heb. Synt.,' § 324). Kalisch obviously regards it as preposterous that Rachel and Leah should have expected anything, since "married daughters in the East never had any such claim where there were sons." But Laban had not treated Jacob's wives even as daughters. **Are we not counted of him strangers? for he hath sold us** (however much they loved Jacob they could not but resent the mercenary meanness of Laban, by which they, the free-born daughters of a chieftain, had been sold as common serfs), **and hath quite devoured also our money**—literally, *and hath eaten up, yes, even eating up, our money,* tho inf. abs., אָכוֹל, after the finite verb, expressing the continuance (Keil) and intensity (Kalisch) of the action (*vide* Ewald, ' Heb. Synt.,' § 280). For—כִּי is by some interpreters rendered but (Jarchi), so that (Keil), indeed (Kalisch), though there is no sufficient reason for departing from the usual meaning "for" (Rosenmüller)—**all the riches which God hath taken from our father,—**thus Rachel and Leah also recognise the hand of God (Elohim) in Jacob's unusual prosperity — **that is ours, and our children's** (Rachel and Leah mean to say that what Jacob had acquired by his six years of service with their father was no more than would have naturally belonged to him had they obtained their portions at the first): **now then, whatsoever God hath said unto thee, do.** It is clear that, equally with himself, they were prepared for breaking off connection with their father Laban.

Vers. 17, 18.—**Then** (literally, *and*) **Jacob rose up** (expressive of the vigour and alacrity with which, having obtained the concurrence of his wives, Jacob set about fulfilling the Divine instructions), **and set his sons**—his children, as in ch. xxxi. 1; xxxii. 12, including Dinah, if by this time she had been born (*vide* ch. xxx. 21)—**and his wives upon camels.** Since neither were able to undertake a journey to Canaan on foot, his oldest son being not more than thirteen years of age, and his youngest not more than six. On the camel, *vide* ch. xii. 16. **And he carried away**—the verb נָהַג, to pant, which is specially used of those who are exhausted by running (Gesenius, *sub voce*), may perhaps indicate the haste with which Jacob acted—**all his cattle,—***Mikneh,* literally, *possession,* from *kanah,* to procure, always used of cattle, the chief wealth of a nomad (cf. ch. xiii. 2; xxvi. 14) — **and all his goods which he had gotten,—***Recush,* literally, *acquisition,* hence substance, wealth in general, from *racash,* to acquire (*vide* ch. xiv. 11, 16, 21; xv. 14), which, however, is more specifically described as—**the cattle of his getting, which he had gotten** (both of the above verbs, *kanah* and *racash,* being now employed) **in** (*i. e.* during his stay in) **Padan-aram, for to go to Isaac his father in the land of Canaan.**

Ver. 19. — **And Laban went** — or, Now Laban had gone, probably to the other station, which was three days' journey from Jacob's flocks (*vide* ch. xxx. 36; and cf. ch. xxxi. 22)—**to shear his sheep.** In this work he would probably be detained several days, the time of shearing being commonly regarded as a festal season (cf. ch. xxxviii. 12; 1 Sam. xxv. 4; 2 Sam. xiii. 23), at which friendly entertainments were given. Whether Jacob's absence from the festivities is to be explained by the dissension existing between him and Laban, which either caused him to be uninvited or led him to decline the invitation (Kurtz), or by the supposition that he had first gone and subsequently left the banquet (Lange), the fact that Laban was so engaged afforded Jacob the opportunity he desired for making his escape. **And Rachel had stolen** (or, "and Rachel stole," availing herself likewise of the opportunity presented by her father's absence) **the images that** were **her father's.** The teraphim, from an unused root, *taraph,* signifying to live comfortably, like the Sanscrit *trip,* Greek τρέφειν, Arabic tarafa (Gesenius, Fürst, *sub voce*), appear to have been small human figures (cf. ch. xxxi. 34), though the image in 1 Sam. xix. 13 must have been nearly life-size, or at least a full-sized bust, sometimes made of silver (Judges xvii. 4), though commonly constructed of wood (1 Sam. xix. 13 —16); they were worshipped as gods (εἴδωλα, LXX.; *idola,* Vulgate, cf. ch. xxxi. 30), consulted for oracles (Ezek. xxi. 26; Zech. x. 2), and believed to be the custodians and promoters of human happiness (Judges xviii. 24). Probably derived from the Aramæans (Fürst, Kurtz), or the Chaldeans (Ezek. xxi. 21, Kalisch, Wordsworth), the worship of teraphim was subsequently denounced as idolatrous (1 Sam. xv. 23; 2 Kings xiii. 24). Cf. with Rachel's act that ascribed to Æneas :—

"Effigies sacræ divûm, Phrygiique Penates,
     Quos mecum a Troja, mediisque ex ignibus urbis,
Extuleram" (Virg., 'Æn.,' iii. 148—150).

Rachel's motive for abstracting her father's teraphim has been variously ascribed to a desire to prevent her father from discovering, by inquiring at his gods, the direction of their flight (Aben Ezra, Rosenmüller), to protect herself, in case of being overtaken, by an appeal to her father's gods (Josephus), to draw her father from the practice of idolatry (Bazil, Gregory, Nazianzen, Theodoret), to obtain children for herself through their assistance (Lengerke, Gerlach), to preserve a memorial of her ancestors, whose pictures these teraphim were (Lightfoot); but was probably due to avarice, if the images were made of precious metals (Pererius), or to a taint of superstition which still adhered to her otherwise religious nature (Chrysostom, Calvin, 'Speaker's Commentary'), causing her to look to these idols for protection (Kalisch, Murphy) or consultation (Wordsworth) on her journey.

Ver. 20.—**And Jacob stole away unawares to Laban the Syrian,** —literally, *stole the heart of Laban the Syrian,* i. e. deceived his mind and intelligence, like κλέπτειν νόον, Hom., 'Il.,' xiv. 227 (cf. vers. 26, 27); hence = ἔκρυψε (LXX.); so Calvin, Rosenmüller, Keil, Gesenius, and others. Lange fancifully understands by the heart of Laban which Jacob stole either Laban's daughters or his favourite Rachel. Gerlach contrasts Jacob's stealing with that of Rachel, in which Jacob had no part. The exact import of Jacob's stealing is declared by the words that follow—**in that he told him not** (Lange and Bush interpret הִגִּיד impersonally, as signifying in that or because it was not told; but in this among expositors they stand alone) **that he fled.**

Ver. 21.—**So** (literally, *and*) **he fled with** (literally, *and*) **all that he had; and he rose up, and passed over the river,—**i. e. the Euphrates, which was called by pre-eminence the river (cf. 1 Kings iv. 21; Ezra iv. 10, 16) — **and set his face toward the mount Gilead.** גִּלְעָד, according to Gesenius, "the hard, stony region," from an unused quadrilateral root, signifying to be hard, though, according to the historian (by a slight change in the punctuation), "The hill, or heap of witness," from the transaction recorded in verses 45—47, which name it here proleptically receives, was not the mountain-range to the south of the Jabbok, now styled Jebel Jilâd (Gesenius), Jebel or Ssalt (Robinson), Jebel osha (Tristram), since Jacob had not yet crossed the river, but that upon its northern bank, called Jebel Ajlun, and situated near Mahanaim (Delitzsch, Keil, Kalisch, Porter).

HOMILETICS.

Vers. 1—21.—*Jacob's flight from Laban.* I. THE HOMEWARD DESIRE. The longing to revisit Canaan, which six years previously Laban's exactions and Joseph's birth (ch. xxx. 25) had combined to inspire within the heart of Jacob, returned upon him with an intensity that could no longer be resisted. Accelerated in its vehemence partly by the interposed delay to which it had been subjected, partly by his further acquaintance with the meanness and craft of his uncle, and partly by his own rapidly-accumulating wealth, it was now brought to a head by—1. *The calumnious remarks of Laban's sons.* Inheriting the sordid and avaricious nature of their parent, they were filled with envy at the remarkable prosperity which had attended Jacob during the past six years. If good men are sometimes "envious at the foolish," it is not surprising that wicked men should occasionally begrudge the success of saints. Then from sinful desires they passed to wicked thoughts, accusing Jacob of having by superior craft out-manœuvred their designing father, and appropriated the flocks and herds that ought to have been his; which, however, was a manifest exaggeration, since Jacob had not taken away *all* their father's "glory," and an unjustifiable calumny, since it was not Jacob's stratagem, but God's blessing, that had multiplied the parti-coloured flocks. And lastly, from wicked thoughts they advanced to evil words, not only accusing Jacob in their minds, but openly vilifying him with their tongues, adding to the sin of private slander that of public defamation—conduct which the word of God severely reprehends (Prov. xxx. 10; 1 Cor. vi. 10; Titus iii. 2; James iv. 11). 2. *The manifest displeasure of Laban.* During the fourteen years that Jacob kept the flocks for Rachel and Leah, Laban regarded him with evident satisfaction; not perhaps for his own sake, but for the unprecedented increase in his (Laban's) pastoral wealth which had taken place under Jacob's fostering care. He was even disposed to be somewhat pious so long as the flocks and herds continued multiplying (ch. xxx. 27). But now, when at the end of six years the relative positions of himself and Jacob are reversed,—when Jacob is the rich man and he, comparatively speaking at least, the poor one,—not only does his piety towards God disappear, but his civility towards man does not remain. There are many Labans in the Church, whose religion is but the shadow that waits upon the sun of their prosperity, and many Labans in the world, whose amiability towards others is only the reflection of their complacent feeling towards themselves. 3. *The explicit command of God.* Twenty years before, at Bethel, God had promised to bring Jacob back again to Canaan, and now he issues formal instructions to his servant to return. As really, though not as visibly and directly, God orders the footsteps of all his children (Ps. xxxii. 8; xxxvii. 23). If it is well not to run before God's providence, as Jacob would have done had he returned to Canaan at the end of the fourteenth year, it is also well not to lag behind when that providence has been clearly made known. The assurance given to Jacob of guidance on his homeward journey is extended to all who, in their daily goings forth, obey the Divine instructions and follow the Divine leadings.

II. THE CONFERENCE IN THE FIELD. 1. *The explanation of Jacob.* Three contrasts complete the sum of Jacob's announcements to his wives. First, between the growing displeasure of Laban their father and the manifest favour of the Elohim of his father (ver. 5); second, between the unwearied duplicity of their father, notwithstanding Jacob's arduous service, and the ever-watchful protection of God against his injurious designs (vers. 6, 7); and third, between the diminishing herds of Laban and the multiplying flocks of himself, Jacob, both of which were traceable to Divine interposition (vers. 8, 10, 12). After enlarging on these contrasts, he informs them of the Divinely-given order to return (ver. 13). 2. *The answer of Rachel and Leah.* Acknowledging the mean and avaricious spirit of their father, who had not only sold them as slaves, but unjustly deprived them of the portions to which, as the daughters of a chieftain, they were entitled (vers. 14, 15), they first confess that Jacob's wealth was nothing more than it would have been had they been honourably dowered at the first; second, recognise the hand of God in thus punishing their father and restoring to their husband what was practically his; and, third, encourage him to yield complete and prompt obedience to the Divine commandment (ver. 16). III. THE HASTY DEPARTURE. In this there were four things discernible. 1. *Faith.* In setting his face towards Canaan he was acting in obedience to Divine instructions; and respect unto God's commandments is an essential characteristic of living faith. 2. *Love.* In determining "to go to Isaac his father" he was actuated by a true spirit of filial piety. 3. *Wisdom.* In stealing away unawares to Laban, while Laban was providentially detained at the sheep-shearing, there was commendable prudence, which, if possible, a good man should never lack. 4. *Sin.* Not indeed on Jacob's part, but on that of Rachel, who, taking advantage of her father's absence, carried off his Penates or household images.

Learn—1. That the love of country and friends is deeply implanted in the human breast. 2. That it is a great trial for worldly men to see good fortune go past their doors. 3. That the love of money, or the greed of gain, is the root of every kind of evil. 4. That the promises of God, however long delayed, are certain of fulfilment. 5. That loving husbands should consult their wives in all important steps in life. 6. That daughters should avoid speaking ill of parents, even should those parents deserve it. 7. That wives should always study to encourage their husbands in doing God's will. 8. That those who flee from oppression should seek for safety in paths of God's appointing. 9. That thriving and prosperous sons should not forget their parents in old age. 10. That daughters should not steal from their fathers, even to the extent of pilfering worthless images.

HOMILIES BY VARIOUS AUTHORS.

Ver. 19.—*Teraphim.* "Rachel had stolen the images that were her father's." This the first direct mention of images in connection with worship, though tradition speaks of Nimrod as an idolater (cf. Josh. xxiv. 2). Laban calls them his gods (ver. 30); yet he and his family knew the Lord. His use of them was a corruption of worship.

I. THE IMAGES. Teraphim. Had some resemblance to the human form (1 Sam. xix. 13). Of different sizes and materials. The manner of their use not very clear, but used in some way for worship. Apparently not as intentional rebellion against God. Rather as a help to worship him, but a help chosen in self-will. It was the error forbidden in the second commandment; a departure from the way of Abel, Noah, Abraham; the device of a soul out of harmony with spiritual things, and unable to realise God's presence in worship (cf. Exod. xxxii. 4; Judges viii. 27; xvii. 3; 1 Kings xii. 28). We live in midst of things claiming attention. Necessities of life compel it. And the good effect of diligence is quickly felt. This not evil, but becomes a snare unless spiritual life vigorous (Matt. xiii. 22; 1 Cor. vii 29—31). The habit of looking earthward grows. The walk with God becomes less close. Then unreality in worship. Then the attempt by material aids to reconcile worship with an unchanged life. Hence, in the old time, teraphim; in our days, will worship.

II. THE EFFECT OF THIS ON THE MORAL CHARACTER AND ON THE SPIRITUAL LIFE; exemplified in Laban. Compare him as presented in ch. xxiv. with what he now appears. There he is hospitable, frank, and liberal; here he is sordid, ungenerous, deceitful even to his own nephew. There he acknowledges the Lord as the Guide of actions (ch. xxiv. 50, 51); here he speaks of "the God of your father," and of "my gods." The love of wealth had made God no longer first in his thoughts (cf. Ps. x. 4; Phil. iii. 19). Thus worship became a thing of times and seasons, a thing separate from daily life, and therefore possessing no influence on daily life. So in the Christian Church great attention to external aids and extravagant symbolism were the resources of a pervading spirit less spiritual than in times before; and these too often were as clouds hiding the face of God.

III. RACHEL'S ACT. Stole teraphim. Why? Some have thought to wean her father from them. More probably wished to make use of them. Had not escaped her father's influence. Hence the want of a submissive spirit (cf. ch. xxx. 1 with 1 Sam. i. 11). The evil spread in Jacob's household (ch. xxxv. 2). The necessity for making a stand against it (Josh. xxiv. 23).

IV. THE LESSON FOR OUR TIMES. The second commandment meets a real danger in every age—of leaning upon secondary means in religious service. Teraphim no longer tempt us. But amid whirl of active life, danger of leaning too much on outward impressions for spiritual life; of cultivating the emotions in place of spiritual earnestness (Ps. cxxx. 6; Matt. xi. 12); of putting religious services (1 Sam. xv. 22) or work (Matt. vii. 22) in place of walk with God. Amid much apparent religious activity the striving against self (Luke ix. 23) and growth in grace may become languid (1 John v. 21).—M.

Vers. 20, 21.—*The separation from Laban.* "And Jacob stole away unawares to Laban the Syrian," &c. A great lesson on—

I. THE EVIL OF DISSIMULATION. Hatred and wrong the fruits of crafty ways. Family dissensions where the things of this world uppermost. Separations which are made in the spirit of dependence on God rend no true bond, but rather strengthen affection.

II. THE FORBEARANCE OF GOD. No justification of Laban, much imperfection in Jacob; yet the shield of Divine patience and mercy thrown over the man who vowed the vow of service, in whom his grace would yet be abundantly revealed. Laban's action controlled by God. He forbad the evil design. He stilleth the enemy and the avenger. "Take thou heed that thou speak not to Jacob either good or bad" (ver. 29). "Touch not mine anointed," &c. When we are doing God's work and walking towards his chosen end we may leave it with him to speak with those who would hinder or harm us.—R.

EXPOSITION.

Vers. 22, 23.—**And it was told Laban on the third day**—*i. e.* the third after Jacob's departure, the distance between the two sheep-stations being a three days' journey (*vide* ch. xxx. 36)—**that Jacob was fled. And he took his brethren**—*i. e.* his kinsmen, or nearest relations (cf. ch. xiii. 8; xxix. 15)—**with him, and pursued after him** (Jacob) **seven days' journey** (literally, *a way of seven days*); **and they overtook him in the mount Gilead.** The distance between Padan-aram and mount Gilead was a little over 300 miles, to perform which Jacob must at least have taken ten days, though Laban, who was less encumbered than his son-in-law, accomplished it in seven, which might easily be done by travelling from forty to forty-five miles a day, by no means a great feat for a camel.

Vers. 24, 25.—**And God**—Elohim is here employed, neither because the section belongs to the fundamental document (Tuch, Bleek, Colenso, *et alii*), nor because, though Laban had an outward acquaintance with Jehovah (*vide* ver. 49), his real religious knowledge did not extend beyond Elohim (Hengstenberg), but simply because the historian wished to characterise the interposition which arrested Laban in his wrath as supernatural (Quarry)—**came to Laban the Syrian in a dream by night,**—(cf. ch. xx. 3; Job xxxiii. 15; Matt. i. 20). This celestial visitation occurred the night before the fugitives were overtaken (*vide* ver. 29). Its intention was to guard Jacob, according to the promise of ch. xxviii. 15, against Laban's resentment—**and** (accordingly God) **said unto him, Take heed**—literally, *take heed for thyself*, the verb being followed by an ethical dative, as in ch. xii. 1; xxi. 16, *q. v.*—**that thou** speak not to Jacob—literally, *lest thou speak with Jacob*; μή ποτε λαλήσῃς μετὰ 'Ιακὼβ (LXX.)—either good or bad. Literally, *from good to bad*, meaning that on meeting with Jacob he should not pass from peaceful greetings to bitter reproaches (Bush, Lange), or say anything emphatic and decisive for the purpose of reversing what had occurred (Keil) ; or, perhaps more simply, say anything acrimonious or violent against Jacob (Rosenmüller, Murphy), the expression being a proverbial phrase for opposition or interference (Kalisch). (Cf. ch. xxiv. 50 ; 2 Sam. xiii. 23). Then (literally, *and*) Laban overtook Jacob. Now (literally, *and*) Jacob had pitched his tent—this was done by means of pins driven into the ground, the verb תָּקַע signifying to fasten, or fix anything by driving (cf. Judges iv. 21 ; Isa. xxii. 23, 25) —in the mount (*vide supra*, ver. 21): and Laban with his brethren (kinsmen, *ut supra*) pitched—his tent ; not ἔστησε τοὺς ἀδελφοὺς (LXX.)—in the mount of Gilead (*vide supra*, ver. 21).

Vers. 26—30.—And Laban (assuming a tone of injured innocence) said to Jacob, What hast thou done, that thou hast stolen away unawares to me, — literally, *and* (meaning, in that) *thou hast stolen my heart* (*vide supra*, ver. 20 ; and cf. ver. 27)—and carried away (*vide* ver. 18) my daughters, as captives taken with the sword ? Literally, *as captives of the sword*, i. e. *invitis parentibus* (Rosenmüller) ; language which, if not hypocritical on Laban's part, was certainly hyperbolical, since he had already evinced the strength of his parental affection by selling his daughters to Jacob ; and besides, so far as it concerned either Jacob or his wives, it was quite untrue, Rachel and Leah having voluntarily accompanied their husband in his flight. Wherefore didst thou flee away secretly,—literally, *wherefore didst thou hide thyself to flee away;* חָבָא (niph.), with an inf. following, corresponding to the similar construction in Greek of λανθάνειν with a part., and being correctly rendered in English by an adverb (*vide* Gesenius, 'Gram.,' § 142)—and steal away from me (literally, *and steal me*, ut supra); and didst not tell me, that I might (literally, *and I would*) have sent thee away with mirth, and with songs, — in Oriental countries those about to make a long journey are still sent away *cantionibus et musicorum instrumentorum concentu* (Rosenmüller) — with tabret,—the toph was a drum or timbrel, consisting of a wooden circle covered with membrane, and furnished with brass bells (like the modern tambourine), which Oriental women beat when dancing (cf. Exod. xv. 20 ; Judges xi. 34 ; Jer. xxxi. 4)—and with harp ? For a description of the *kinnor* see

ch. iv. 21. And hast not suffered me to kiss my sons (*i. e.* the children of Leah and Rachel) and my daughters ? It is perhaps judging Laban too severely to pronounce this complete hypocrisy and cant (Alford, Bush, Candlish, Gerlach), but equally wide of the truth is it to see in Laban's conduct nothing but generosity of feeling (Kalisch) ; probably there was a mixture of both paternal affection and crafty dissimulation (Delitzsch). Thou hast now done foolishly in so doing. The charge of folly in Old Testament Scriptures commonly carries with it an imputation of wrong-doing (cf. 1 Sam. xiii. 13 ; 2 Sam. xxiv. 10). It is in the power of my hand—so the phrase יֶשׁ־לְאֵל יָדִי (cf. Deut. xxviii. 32; Neh. v. 5 ; Micah ii. 1) is rendered by competent authorities (Gesenius, Fürst, Rosenmüller, Kalisch, Murphy, *et alii*), with which agree ἰσχύει ἡ χείρ μου (LXX.), and *valet manus mea* (Vulgate), though the translation "My hand is for God," *i. e.* my hand serves me as God (cf. Job xii. 6 ; Hab. i. 11), is by some preferred (Keil, Knobel, Jacobus)—to do you hurt : but the God of your father—the use of this expression can be rightly regarded neither as a proof of Elohistic authorship (Tuch, Bleek, Colenso, Davidson) nor as a sign of Laban's spiritual degeneracy (Hengstenberg, Wordsworth), since it is practically equivalent to Jehovah (*vide* ch. xxviii. 13), but is probably to be viewed as a play upon the sound and sense of the preceding clause, as thus :—" It is in the El of my hand to do you evil, but the Elohim of your father spake to me." Another instance of this play upon the sound and sense is to be found in vers. 19, 20—" Rachel stole the teraphim that were her father's ; and Jacob stole the heart of Laban the Syrian " (cf. Quarry on Genesis, p. 498)—spake unto me yesternight, saying, Take thou heed that thou speak not to Jacob —literally, *guard or keep thee for thyself* (the pleon. pron. being added *ut supra*, ver. 24) *from speaking with Jacob*—either good or bad (*vide* on ver. 24). And now, though thou wouldest needs be gone (literally, *going thou didst go* = thou hast indeed gone), because thou sore longedst after thy father's house (literally, *because desiring thou didst desire*. The verb כָּסַף, to be pale (whence כֶּסֶף, silver, so called from its pale colour), expresses the idea of pining away and languishing through strong inward longing), yet wherefore hast thou stolen my gods ? Laban had probably gone to consult his teraphim and so discovered their loss. Augustine calls attention to this as the first Scripture reference to heathen gods, and Calvin probably supplies the right explanation of the sense in which they were so styled by Laban, *non quia deitatem illic putaret esse inclusam, sed quia in honorem deorum imagines illas colebat; vel potius quod Deo sacra facturus, vertebat se ad illas imagines* (cf. Exod. xxxii. 4; 1 Kings xii. 28). "This complaint of Laban, that his 'gods were stolen,' showeth the vanity of such idolatry" (Ainsworth). Cf. Judges vi. 31; xvi. 24; Jer. x. 5, 11, 15.

Vers. 31, 32. **And Jacob answered**—"in an able and powerful speech" (Kalisch)—**and said to Laban** (replying to his first interrogation as to why Jacob had stolen away unawares), **Because I was afraid: for I said** (*sc.* to myself), **Peradventure** (literally, *lest*, i. e. I must depart without informing thee *lest*) **thou wouldest** (or shouldest) **take by force**—the verb signifies to strip off as skin from flesh (*vide* Mic. iii. 2), and hence to forcibly remove—**thy daughters from me** (after which, in response to Laban's question about his stolen gods, he proceeds). **With whomsoever thou findest thy gods, let him not live.** If Jacob meant he shall not live, but I will slay him with mine own hand (Aben Ezra), let God destroy him (Abarbanel), I give him up to thee to put to death (Rosenmüller), let him instantly die (Drusius), he was guilty of great unadvisedness in speech. Accordingly, the import of his words has been mollified by regarding them simply as a prediction, "he will not live," *i. e.* he will die before his time (Jonathan), a prediction which, the Rabbins note, was fulfilled in Rachel (*vide* ch. xxxv. 16, 18); or by connecting them with clause following, "he will not live before our brethren," *i. e.* let him be henceforth cut off from the society of his kinsmen (LXX., Bush). Yet, even as thus explained, the language of Jacob was precipitate, since he ought first to have inquired at his wives and children before pronouncing so emphatically on a matter of which he was entirely ignorant (Calvin). **Before our brethren**—not Jacob's sons, but Laban's kinsmen (ver. 23)—**discern thou**—literally, *examine closely for thyself*, the hiph. of נָכַר (to be strange) meaning to press strongly into a thing, *i. e.* to perceive it by finding out its distinguishing characteristics (*vide* Fürst, *sub voce*)—**what is thine with me, and take it to thee. For** (literally, *and*) **Jacob knew not that Rachel had stolen them**—otherwise he would have spoken with less heat and more caution.

Ver. 33.—**And Laban went into Jacob's tent, and into Leah's tent, and into the two maid-servants' tents;**—the clause affords an interesting glimpse into the manners of the times, showing that not only husbands and wives, but also wives among themselves, possessed separate establishments)—**but he found them not. Then went he out of Leah's tent** (he probably commenced with Jacob's and those of the hand-maids, and

afterwards passed into Leah's), **and entered into Rachel's tent**—last, because she was the favourite. Cf. ch. xxxiii. 2, in which a similar partiality towards Rachel is exhibited by Jacob (*vide* Thomson's 'Land and Book,' i. 370).

Ver. 34.—**Now Rachel had taken the images** (teraphim), **and put them in the camel's furniture,**—the camel's furniture was not *stramentà cameli* (Vulgate), "the camel's straw" (Luther), but the camel's saddle (LXX., Onkelos, Syriac, Calvin, Rosenmüller, Keil, and others), here called כַּר, from כָּרַר, an unused root signifying either to go round in a circle, hence to run (Gesenius), or to be firmly wound together, hence to be puffed up as a bolster (Fürst). The woman's riding-saddle was commonly made of wicker-work and had the appearance of a basket or cradle. It was usually covered with carpet, and protected against wind, rain, and sun by means of a canopy and curtains, while light was admitted by openings in the side (cf. Gesenius, *sub voce;* Kalisch *in loco*). "That which is now customary among the Arabs consists of a large closed basket-work, with a place for sitting and reclining, and a window at the side; one of this kind hangs on each side of the camel" (Gerlach)—**and sat upon them.** "To us the picture of Rachel seated upon the camel furniture is true to life, for we have often seen its counterpart. The saddle-bags and cushions which were to be set upon the camel lay piled on the floor, while she sat upon them" (Van Lennep, quoted by Inglis, p. 254). **And Laban searched**—the word means to feel out or explore with the hands (cf. ch. xxvii. 12; Job xii. 25)—**all the tent, but found them not.**

Ver. 35.—**And she said to her father,**—"covering theft by subtlety and untruth" (Kalisch), and thus proving herself a true daughter of Laban, as well as showing with how much imperfection her religious character was tainted—**Let it not displease my lord** literally, *let it not burn with anger* (יִחַר, from חָרָה, to glow, to burn) *in the eyes of my lord* (Adoni)—**that I cannot rise up before thee;**—Oriental politeness required children to rise up in the presence of their parents (*vide* Levit. xix. 32; and cf. 1 Kings ii. 19). Hence Rachel's apology was not unnecessary—**for the custom of women**—(literally, *the way of women;* a periphrasis for menstruation (cf. ch. xviii. 11) which, under the law, required females, as ceremonially unclean, to be put apart (Levit. xv. 19). That, prior to the law, this particular statute concerning women was in force among the Aramæans appears from the present instance; and that it was not exclusively Jewish, but shared in by other nations of antiquity, is the opinion of the best authorities (*vide* Kurtz, 'History of the Old Covenant,' § 79; 'Sacrificial Worship of the Old Testament,' § 213; Keil *in loco;* both of whom quote Bähr's 'Symbolik of the Mosaic Cultus,' ii. 466). Roberts mentions that under similar circumstances with Rachel no one in India goes to the temple or any religious ceremony ('Oriental Illustrations,' p. 37)—is **upon me.** It is just possible Rachel may have been speaking the exact truth, though the probability is she was guilty of fabrication. **And he searched** (everywhere except among the camel's furniture, partly from fear of defilement, but chiefly as regarding it impossible that Rachel in her then state would sit upon his gods), **but found not the images** (teraphim). The three times repeated phrase "he found not," emphasises the completeness of Laban's deception.

Vers. 36—42.—**And Jacob was wroth,**— literally, *and it burned, sc.* with indignation (same word as used by Rachel, ver. 35), *to Jacob,* i. e. he was infuriated at what he believed to be Laban's unjustifiable insinuation about his lost teraphim—**and chode**—or contended; the fundamental signification of the root, רוב or רִיב, being to seize or tear, *e. g.* the hair, hence to strive with the hands (Deut. xxxiii. 7), or with words (Ps. ciii. 9). The two verbs, וַיִּחַר and וַיָּרֶב, give a vivid representation of the exasperation which Jacob felt—**with Laban: and Jacob answered and said to Laban,**—in words characterised by "verbosity and self-glorification" (Kalisch), or "acute sensibility and elevated self-consciousness" (Delitzsch, Keil), according as one inclines to an unfavourable or favourable view of Jacob's character—**What is my trespass? what is my sin, that thou hast so hotly pursued after me?** The intensity of Jacob's feeling imparts to his language a rythmical movement, and leads to the selection of poetical forms of expression, such as דָּלַק אַחֲרֵי, to burn after, in the sense of fiercely persecuting, which occurs again only in 1 Sam. xvii. 53 (*vide* Gesenius and Fürst, *sub voce;* and cf. Keil, *in loco*), causing the reader at times to catch "the dance and music of actual verse" (Ewald). **Whereas thou hast searched all my stuff,**—literally (*sc.* What is my sin) *that thou hast felt all my articles* (LXX., Kalisch)? the clause being co-ordinate with the preceding; though by others כִּי is taken as equivalent to כַּאֲשֶׁר, *quando quidem,* since (A. V., Ainsworth), or *quando,* when (Calvin, Murphy)—**what hast thou found of all thy household stuff? set it here before my brethren and thy brethren** (*i. e.* Laban's kinsmen who accompanied him, who were also of necessity kinsmen to Jacob), **that they may judge betwixt us both**—which

of us has injured the other. **This twenty years** have I been **with thee** (*vide infra*, ver. 41); **thy ewes** (רָחֵל, a ewe, whence Rachel) **and thy she goats**—עֵז, a she-goat; cf. Sanscrit, *adsha,* a he-goat; *adshâ,* a she-goat; Goth., *gáitsa;* Anglo-Saxon, *gât;* German, *geis;* Greek, αἴξ; Turkish, *gieik* (Gesenius, *sub voce*)—**have not cast their young, and the rams of thy flock have I not eaten.** Roberts says that the people of the East do not eat female sheep except when sterile, and that it would be considered folly and prodigality in the extreme to eat that which has the power of producing more (*vide* 'Oriental Illustrations,' p. 37). **That which was torn** of beasts (טְרֵפָה, a coll. fem., from טָרַף, to tear in pieces, meaning that which is torn in pieces, hence cattle destroyed by wild beasts) **I brought not unto thee; I bare the loss of it;**—אֲחַטֶּנָּה, literally, *I made expiation for it,* the piel of חָטָא, signifying to make atonement for a thing by sacrifice (Levit. ix. 15), or by compensation, as here; hence equivalent to "I bare the loss of it" (Rashi, Fürst), or ἐγὼ ἀπετίννυον (LXX.), or, perhaps, "I will bear the loss of it, or pay it back" (Kalisch)—**of my hand didst thou require it,**—otherwise, " of my hand require it" (Kalisch)—whether **stolen by day, or stolen by night.** Without adhering literally to the text, the LXX. give the sense of this and the preceding clause as being, "From my own I paid back the stolen by day and the stolen by night." Thus **I was;** (*i. e.* I was in this condition that) **in the day the drought consumed me, and the frost by night.** קֶרַח, ice, so called from its smoothness, hence cold. The alternation of heat and cold in many eastern countries is very great and severely felt by shepherds, travellers, and watchmen, who require to pass the night in the open air, and who in consequence are often obliged to wear clothes lined with skins (cf. Ps. cxxi. 6; Jer. xxxvi. 30). "The thermometer at 24° Fahr. at night, a lump of solid ice in our basins in the morning, and then the scorching heat of the day drawing up the moisture, made the neighbourhood, convenient as it was, rather a fever-trap, and premonitory symptoms warned us to move" (Tristram, 'The Land of Moab,' p. 217). "The night air at Joaiza was keen and cold; indeed there was a sharp frost, and ice appeared on all the little pools about the camp" (Thomson, 'The Land and the Book,' p. 364). "Does a master reprove his servant for being idle, he will ask, 'What can I do? the heat eats me up by day, and the cold eats me up by night'" (Roberts' 'Oriental Illustrations,' p. 37; cf. Paxton's 'Illustrations,' vol. i. p. 30). **And my sleep departed from mine eyes.** "Syrian shepherds were compelled to watch their flocks often both night and day, and for a whole month together, and repair into long plains and deserts without any shelter ; and when reduced to this incessant labour, they were besides chilled by the piercing cold of the morning, and scorched by the succeeding heats of a flaming sun, the opposite action of which often swells and chafes their lips and face " (Paxton's 'Illustrations of Scripture,' vol. i. p. 30). **Thus have I been**—literally, *this to me* (or for myself, *vide infra*)—**twenty years in thy house; I served thee fourteen years for thy two daughters, and six years for thy cattle.** The majority of expositors understand the twenty years referred to in ver. 38 to be the same as the twenty spoken of here as consisting of fourteen and six. Dr. Kennicott, regarding the twenty years of ver. 38 as having intervened between the fourteen and the six of ver. 41, makes the entire period of Jacob's sojourn in Padan-aram to have been forty years. In support of this he contends —(1) that the particle הֶז, twice repeated (in ver. 38 and in ver. 41), may be legitimately rendered, "This (one) twenty years I was with thee" (ver. 38), *i. e.* taking care of thy flocks ; and "this for myself (another) twenty years in thy house," *i. e.* serving for thy daughters and thy cattle (cf. Exod. xiv. 20 ; Job xxi. 23, 25 ; Eccles. vi. 5) ; (2) that on this hypothesis more time is afforded for the birth of Jacob's family, viz. twenty-seven years instead of seven ; and (3) that it relieves the narrative of certain grave chronological difficulties in connection with Judah and his family, which, on the supposition of the shorter period, subsequently emerge, such as that Judah and his sons must have been quite children when they married (*vide* ch. xxxviii. 1—11). But, on the other hand, in favour of the accepted chronology it may be urged—(1) that the interposition of a second twenty years in the middle of the first is unnatural ; (2) that, though legitimate, the proposed rendering of הֶז does not at first sight suggest itself as that which Jacob intended ; (3) that it is not impossible for Jacob's family to have been born in the short space of seven years (*vide* ch. xxvii. 1 ; xxx. 35) ; (4) that in reality the difficulties connected with Judah and his sons are not removed by the hypothesis of a forty years' sojourn in Padan-aram any more than by a sojourn of only twenty years, since Judah must have married either after the sale of Joseph, in which case only twenty-two years remain for the birth and marriage of Er and Onan, for Pharez and Zarah, Judah's children by Tamar, to grow to manhood, and for Pharez to have two sons, Hezron and Hamul, before descending to Egypt, unless indeed, as Kürtz supposes, Judah's grandchildren were born in Egypt ; or before the sale of Joseph—indeed, if Hezron and Hamul were born in Canaan, before the birth of Joseph, *i. e.* while Judah was yet in Padan-aram, which is contrary to the narrative (*vide* ch. xxxviii. 1, 2). For these reasons, though adopted by some excellent authorities (Bishop Horsley, Adam Clarke, 'Speaker's Commentary,' Inglis), the computation of Dr. Kennicott does not appear of sufficient weight to set aside the ordinary reckoning, which is followed by interpreters of equal credit (Keil, Kalisch, Kürtz, Lange, Murphy, Wordsworth). **And thou hast changed my wages ten times** (*vide* ver. 7). **Except** (לוּלֵי, if not, *i. e.* unless, introducing the protasis of the sentence) **the God of my father, the God of Abraham, and the fear of Isaac,**—*i. e.* the object of Isaac's fear, not "terror" (Oort and Kuenen, *vide* 'The Bible for Young People,' vol. i. p. 243), viz. God ; פַּחַד being used metonymically of that which inspires reverence or fear, like σέβας and σέβασμα. The entire clause is a periphrasis for Jehovah of ver. 3, which is usually ascribed to the Jehovist, while the present verse belongs, it is alleged, to the fundamental document—**had been with**—or, for (cf. Ps. cxxiv. 1, 2)—**me** (during the whole period of my sojurn in Padan-aram, but especially during the last six years), **surely** (כִּי, then, commencing the apodosis) **thou hadst sent me away now empty** (as by thy stratagem in changing my wages thou didst design ; but) **God hath seen mine affliction** (cf. ch. xxix. 32 ; Exod. iii. 7) **and the labour**—especially that which is wearisome, from a root signifying to toil with effort so as to become fatiguing (cf. Job xxxix. 11)—**of my hands, and rebuked**—*i. e.* reproved, *sc.* thee, as in ch. xxi. 25 (LXX., Vulgate, A. V., Calvin, Ainsworth, Lange, Kalisch, and others) ; or judged, *sc.* it, *i. e.* mine affliction, in the sense of pronouncing an opinion or verdict on it, as in 1 Chron. xii. 17 (Keil, Murphy) ; or proved, *sc.* it, viz. that he had seen my affliction (Dathius, Poole) ; or decided, *sc.* betwixt us, as in ver. 37 (Fürst, Gesenius) **thee yesternight.**

Vers. 43, 44.—**And Laban answered and said unto Jacob,**—neither receiving Jacob's torrent of invective with affected meekness (Candlish), nor proving himself to be completely reformed by the angry recriminations of his "callous and hardened" son-in-law (Kalisch) ; but perhaps simply owning the truth of Jacob's words, and recognising that he had no just ground of complaint (Calvin), as well as touched in his paternal affections by the sight of his daughters, from whom he felt that he was about to part for ever—These **daughters**—literally, *the daughters* (there)—are **my daughters, and** these (literally, *the*) **children** are **my children, and** these (literally, *the*) **cattle** are **my cattle; and all that thou seest is mine.** Not as reminding Jacob that he had still a legal claim to his (Jacob's) wives and possessions (Candlish), or at least possessions (Kalisch), though prepared to waive it, but rather as acknowledging that in doing injury to Jacob he would only be proceeding against his own flesh and blood (Calvin, Rosenmüller, Gerlach, Alford). **And what can I do this day unto these my daughters,**—literally, *and as for* (or to) *my daughters, what can I do to these this day?* The LXX., connecting "and to my daughters" with what precedes, reads, καὶ πάντα ὅσα σὺ ὁρᾷς, ἐμά ἐστι, καὶ τῶν θυγατέρων μου—or **unto their children which they have born?**

—*i. e.* why should I do anything unto them? *An ego in viscera mea sævirem?* (Calvin)— **Now therefore**—literally, *and now,* νῦν οὖν (LXX.)—**come thou,**—לְכָה, imper. of יֵלֵךְ = age, go to, come now (cf. ch. xix. 32)—**let us make a covenant,**—literally, *let us cut a covenant,* an expression which, according to partitionists (Tuch, Stähelin, Delitzsch, *et alii*), is not used by the Elohist until after Exod. xxiv. 8; and yet by all such authorities the present verse is assigned to the Elohist (cf. Keil's 'Introduction,' part I. § ii., div. i. § 27)—**I and thou; and let it be for a witness between me and thee.**

HOMILETICS.

Vers. 22—44.—*Laban's pursuit of Jacob.* I. THE HOSTILE PREPARATION. Learning of his son-in-law's departure, Laban at once determines on pursuit; not alone for the purpose of recovering his household gods, but chiefly with the view of wreaking his pent-up vengeance on Jacob, whom he now regarded as the spoiler of his fortunes, and if possible to capture and detain the much-coveted flocks and herds which he considered had been practically stolen by his nephew. Mustering his kinsmen by either force or fraud,—by command enjoining those belonging to his household, and by misrepresentation probably beguiling such as were independent of his authority,—he loses not a moment, but starts upon the trail of the fugitives. Worldly men are seldom slow in seeking to repair their lost fortunes, and angry men are seldom laggard in exacting revenge. It is only God's vengeance that is slow-footed.

II. THE DIVINE INTERPOSITION. Six days the wrathful Laban follows in pursuit of Jacob, and now the distance of one day is all that parts him from the fugitives. In a dream by night he is warned by Elohim to speak neither good nor bad to Jacob. The incident reminds us of the Divine superintendence of mundane affairs in general, and of God's care for his people in particular; of the access which God ever has to the minds of his dependent creatures, and of the many different ways in which he can communicate his will; of his ability at all times to restrain the wrath of wicked men, and check the hands of evil-doers, who meditate the spoiling of his Church or the persecution of his saints.

III. THE STORMY INTERVIEW. 1. *The pompous harangue of Laban.* Laban gives way to—(1) Passionate reproach; charging Jacob with having clandestinely departed from his service and violently carried off his daughters, in the first of which Jacob did nothing wrong, while the second was a pure exaggeration (*vide* ver. 16). (2) Hypocritical affection; declaring that Jacob, had he, Laban, only known, might have been sent away with public demonstrations of rejoicing, while Rachel and Leah might have carried with them a parent's kiss, if not a father's blessing. But if Jacob's leave-taking would in any way have excited Laban's jubilation, it is doubtful if this would not have been traceable less to Laban's regard for his son-in-law than to Laban's anxiety about his flocks, which, in the absence of the spoiler, he might hope would become prolific as before; while as for Laban's love for his daughters, one might fairly claim indemnity for suspecting an affection so recent in its origin, and so palpably contradicted by his previous behaviour. (3) Boastful assertion; passing on, like all weak natures who love to be considered formidable, to brag about his power to inflict injury on Jacob (ver. 29), and to hint that he only forbears to do so out of respect for God, who had appeared to him on the previous night. (4) Direct accusation; ere he closes his oration, deliberately impeaching Jacob with having abstracted his teraphim. 2. *The ingenuous response of Jacob.* In this are discernible virtues worthy of imitation, if also infirmities deserving reprobation. If Jacob's candour in declaring the reasons of his flight (ver. 31) and willingness to restore to Laban whatever property belonged to him (ver. 32) are examples to be copied, on the other hand, the over-confident assertion that no one had Laban's gods, and the over-hasty imprecation on any who should be found possessing them, are not to be commended.

IV. THE FRUITLESS SEARCH. 1. *The missing gods.* On the nature, probable origin, and uses of the teraphim see Exposition, ver. 19. The existence of these silver or wooden images in Laban's tent was a proof of the religious declension, if not complete apostasy, of this branch of the family of Terah. Scripture never represents Idolatry as an upward effort of the human heart, as a further development in the onward evolution of the soul (Sir J. Lubbock on the 'Origin of Civilisation,' p. 256); but always as a deterioration, or a retrogression, or a falling away of the human spirit from its rightful allegiance. The loss of Laban's manufactured deities was a ridiculous commentary on the folly of worshipping or trusting in a god that could be stolen—a complete *reductio ad absurdum* of the whole superstructure of idolatry (cf. 1 Kings xviii. 27; Ps. cxv. 4, 8; Isa. xliv. 19; xlvi. 6, 7; Jer. x. 5). 2. *The anxious devotee.* Invited by Jacob to make a search for his lost teraphim, Laban begins with Jacob's tent, then with the tents of Bilhah and Zilpah, after which he passes into Leah's, and finally comes to Rachel's; but everywhere his efforts to recover his gods are defeated. What a spectacle of infinite humour, if it were not rather of ineffable sadness—a man seeking for his lost gods! The gospel presents us with the opposite picture—the ever-present God seeking for his lost children. 3. *The lying daughter.* If the conduct of Rachel in carrying off the images of her father was open to serious question (*vide* Exposition, ver. 19), her behaviour towards her father in the tent was utterly inexcusable. Even if she spoke the truth in describing her condition, she was guilty of bare-faced deception. This particular passage in Rachel's history is painfully suggestive of the disastrous results of worldliness and irreligion in the training of children. Laban's craft and Laban's superstition had both been factors in Rachel's education. 4. *The deceived parent.* Worse than being disappointed in his gods, Laban was dishonoured by his daughter. But what else could he expect? Laban was only reaping as he had sowed. Marvellous and appropriate are God's providential retributions.

V. THE PASSIONATE INVECTIVE. It was now Jacob's turn to pour out the vials of his wrath upon Laban, and certainly it burned all the hotter because of its previous suppression. 1. He *upbraids* Laban with the unreasonableness of his persecution (ver. 36). 2. He *taunts* Laban with the fruitlessness of his search (ver. 37). 3. He *reminds* Laban of the faithful service he had given for twenty years (vers. 38—41). 4. He *recalls* the crafty attempts to defraud him of which Laban had been guilty (ver. 41). 5. He *assures* Laban that it was God's gracious care, and neither his honesty nor affection, that had prevented him from being that day a poor man instead of a rich emir (ver. 42). 6. He somewhat fiercely *bids* Laban accept the rebuke which God had addressed to him the previous night.

VI. THE AMICABLE SETTLEMENT. Doubtless much to Jacob's surprise, the wrath of Laban all at once subsided, and a proposal came from him to bury past animosities, to strike a covenant of friendship with one another, and to part in peace. The seven days' journey, affording time for reflection; the Divine interposition, inspiring him with fear; the mortification resulting from his fruitless search, convincing him that he had really overstepped the bounds of moderation in accusing Jacob; the voice of conscience within his breast re-echoing the words of Jacob, and declaring them to be true; and perhaps the sight of his daughters at last touching a chord in the old man's heart;—all these may have contributed to this unexpected collapse in Laban; but whether or not, Jacob, as became him, cordially assented to the proposition.

Lessons:—1. The reality of God's care for his people—illustrated by the appearances of Elohim to Jacob and to Laban. 2. The miserable outcome of a worldly life—exemplified in Laban. 3. The efficacy of a soft answer in turning away wrath—proved by Jacob's first response. 4. The difficulty of restraining angry speech within just bounds—exemplified by both. 5. The folly of idolatry, as seen in Laban's lost teraphim. 6. The evil fruits of bad parental training, as they appear in Rachel. 7. The proper way of ending quarrels—exhibited by Laban and Jacob in their covenant agreement.

EXPOSITION.

Ver. 45.—**And Jacob took a stone, and set it up** *for* **a pillar**—or *Matzebah,* as a memorial or witness of the covenant about to be formed (ver. 52); a different transaction from the piling of the stone-heap next referred to (cf. ch. xxviii. 18; Josh. xxiv. 27).

Ver. 46. — **And Jacob said unto his brethren,** — Laban's kinsmen and his own (*vide* ver. 37)—**Gather stones; and they took stones, and made an heap :**—*Gal,* from *Galal,* to roll, to move in a circle, probably signified a circular cairn, to be used not as a seat (Gerlach), but as an altar (ver. 54), a witness (ver. 48), and a table (ver. 54), since it is added—**and they did eat there**—not immediately (Lange), but afterwards, on the conclusion of the covenant (ver. 54)—**upon the heap.**

Ver. 47. — **And Laban called it Jegarsahadutha :** — A Chaldaic term signifying "Heap of testimony," βουνὸς τῆς μαρτυρίας (LXX.) : *tumulum testis* (Vulgate) — **but Jacob called it Galeed**—compounded of *Gal* and *'ed* and meaning, like the corresponding Aramaic term used by Laban, "Heap of witness," βουνὸς μάρτυς (LXX.); *acervum testimonii* (Vulgate). "It is scarcely possible to doubt," says Kalisch, "that an important historical fact," relating to the primitive language of the patriarchs, "is concealed in this part of the narrative ;" but whether that fact was that Aramaic, Syriac, or Chaldee was the mother-tongue of the family of Nahor, while Hebrew was acquired by Abraham in Canaan (Bleek, Delitzsch, Keil), or that Laban had deviated from the original speech of his ancestors (Jerome, Augustine), or that Laban and Jacob both used the same language with some growing dialectic differences (Gosman in Lange, Inglis), Laban simply on this occasion giving the heap a name which would be known to the inhabitants of the district (Wordsworth), seems impossible to determine with certainty. The most that can be reasonably inferred from the term *Jegar-sahadutha* is that Aramaic was the language of Mesopotamia (Rosenmüller); besides this expression there is no other evidence that Laban and Jacob conversed in different dialects ; while it is certain that the word Mizpah, which was probably also spoken by Laban, is not Chaldee or Aramaic but Hebrew.

Vers. 48—50.—**And Laban said, This heap is a witness between me and thee this day.** The historian adding — **Therefore was the name of it called** (originally by Jacob, and afterwards by the Israelites from this transaction) **Galeed** (*vide* on ver. 21). The stony character of the region may have suggested the designation. **And Mizpah;**—watchtower, from Tsaphah, to watch. Mizpah afterwards became the site of a town in the district of Gilead (Judges x. 17 ; xi. 11, 19, 34); which received its name, as the historian intimates, from the pile of witness erected by Laban and his kinsmen, and was later celebrated as the residence of Jephthah (Judges xi. 34) and the seat of the sanctuary (Judges xi. 11). Ewald supposes that the mound (Galeed) and the watch tower (Mizpah) were different objects, and that the meaning of the (so-called) legend is that, while the former (the mountain) was piled up by Jacob and his people, the latter (now the city and fortress of Mizpah on one of the heights of Gilead) was constructed by Laban and his followers (*vide* 'History of Israel,' vol. i. p. 347) ; but the "grotesqueness" of this interpretation of the Hebrew story is its best refutation—**for he** (*i. e.* Laban) **said, The Lord**—Jehovah ; a proof that vers. 49, 50 are a Jehovistic interpolation (Tuch, Bleek, Colenso, Kalisch) ; an indication of their being a subsequent insertion, though not warranting the inference that the entire history is a complication (Keil) ; a sign that henceforth Laban regarded Jehovah as the representative of his rights (Lange) ; but probably only a token that Laban, recognising Jehovah as the only name that would bind the conscience of Jacob (Hengstenberg, Quarry), had for the moment adopted Jacob's theology ('Speaker's Commentary'), but only in self-defence (Wordsworth) — **watch between me and thee, when we are absent one from another** — literally, *a man from his companion.* **If thou shalt afflict my daughters, or if thou shalt take** other **wives beside my daughters** (Laban's concern for his daughters, though hitherto not conspicuous, may, in the hour of parting from them, have been real : his language shows that he was not quite at ease as to Jacob's integrity. Perhaps the remembrance that he had been the cause of Jacob's taking two wives made him anxious to secure that Jacob should not improve upon his evil instructions), **no man is with us;**—either then they stood apart from Laban's clan followers (Inglis) ; or his meaning was that when widely separated there would be no one to judge betwixt them, or perhaps even to observe them (Rosenmüller), but—**see, God** (Elohim in contrast to man) is **witness betwixt me and thee.**

Ver. 51—53.—**And Laban said to Jacob,** —according to Ewald the last narrator has transposed the names of Laban and Jacob (*vide* 'History of Israel,' vol. i. p. 346)— **Behold this heap, and behold** this **pillar, which I have cast** (same word as in ver. 45.

The Arabic version and Samaritan text read *yaritha*, thou hast erected, instead of *yarithi*, I have erected or cast up) **betwixt me and thee; this heap be witness, and this pillar be witness,** that (literally, *if*, here = *that*) **I will not pass over this heap to thee, and that thou shalt not pass over this heap and this pillar** (Laban bound himself never to pass over the heap which he had erected as his witness; whereas Jacob was required to swear that he would never cross the pillar and the pile, both of which were witnesses for him) **unto me, for harm.** The emphatic word closes the sentence. **The God of Abraham, and the God of Nahor, the God of their father, judge**—the verb is plural, either because Laban regarded the Elohim of Nahor as different from the Elohim of Abraham (Rosenmüller, Keil, Kalisch, Wordsworth, 'Speaker's Commentary'), or because, though acknowledging only one Elohim, he viewed him as maintaining several and distinct relations to the persons named (cf. Quarry, p. 499)—**betwixt us.** Laban here invokes his own hereditary Elohim, the Elohim of Abraham's father, to guard his rights and inter-

ests under the newly-formed covenant; while Jacob in his adjuration appeals to the Elohim of Abraham's son. **And Jacob sware by the fear of his father Isaac** (*vide supra*, ver. 42).

Ver. 54.—**Then Jacob offered sacrifice**—literally, *slew a slaying*, in ratification of the covenant **upon the mount, and called his brethren** (Laban's followers, who may have withdrawn to a distance during the interview) **to eat bread.** The sacrificial meal afterwards became an integral part of the Hebrew ritual (Exod. xxiv. 3—8; xxix. 27, 28; Levit. x. 14, 15). **And they did eat bread, and tarried all night in the mount.**

Vers. 55. — **And early in the morning Laban rose up, and kissed his sons and his daughters,**—*i. e.* Rachel and Leah and their children. It does not appear that Laban kissed Jacob on taking final leave of him as he did on first meeting him (ch. xxix. 39)—**and blessed them** (cf. ch. xxiv. 60; xxviii. 1): **and Laban departed, and returned unto his place** — Padan-aram (cf. ch. xviii. 33; xxx. 25).

HOMILETICS.

Vers. 45—55.—*Galeed and Mizpah, or the covenant of peace.* I. THE COVENANT MEMORIALS. 1. *The pillar of remembrance.* The erection of the stone slab appears to have been the act of Jacob alone, and to have been designed to commemorate the important transaction about to be entered into with Laban. It is well to keep note of those engagements we make with our fellow-men in order to their punctual fulfilment; much more of those we make with God. It does not appear that any name was given to the column, and this may have been because it was intended chiefly for himself. 2. *The pile of witness.* This was the work both of Laban and Jacob, which they conjointly performed through the instrumentality of their brethren; and being of the nature of a public monument, it was further characterised by a name— Laban calling it Jegar-sahadutha, and Jacob styling it Galeed, both expressions signifying heap of witness, and perhaps both of them naming it Mizpah, or watch-tower, from the nature of the oath which they both took on the occasion. Men who are truly sincere in their covenant engagements are never afraid to bind themselves by public attestations of their good faith, though it is certain that of all men these least require to be so bound.

II. THE COVENANT WORDS. 1. *The solemn engagements.* On the one hand Laban undertakes never to pass the stone heap on Gilead to do injury to Jacob—not mentioning the pillar, which was purely of Jacob's construction, and therefore supposed to have a religious significance solely for Jacob; and on the other hand Jacob records his vow never to cross the pillar and the pile to inflict wrong on Laban, and in addition, as Laban might be injured in his daughters without crossing the forbidden line, never to afflict Rachel and Leah by taking other wives besides them. The engagement on both sides is to abstain from doing injury of any sort to each other; and to this all men are bound by both natural and revealed religion without the formality of an oath; and much more than other men, are Christians taken bound by God's grace and Christ's blood to live peaceably with all men and be at peace amongst themselves. 2. *The impressive oaths.* If it is dubious whether Laban appealed to God or only to the stone-heap to witness his sincerity in promising not to harm Jacob, it is certain that he appealed to God to keep a strict eye on Jacob (ver. 49), and in a semi-superstitious way united the God of Abraham and the God of Nahor, the God of their fathers, to judge between them. Jacob does not mention either pile or pillar, but swears by the fear of his father Isaac.

III. THE COVENANT ACTIONS. 1. *The sacrifice.* The offering of sacrifice was essential to the formation of a covenant. As between God and man, it virtually proclaimed that God could enter into amicable relations with sinful man only on the basis of an atonement. As between man and man, it was equivalent to an acknowledgment by the covenanting parties that both required to be covered with the blood of propitiation. That Jacob, and not Laban, offered sacrifice intimates that these truths were already in some degree appreciated by Jacob, though possibly they were not understood by Laban. 2. *The feast.* In making this feast Jacob may only have been following the example of his father Isaac, who similarly entertained Abimelech and his statesmen at Beersheba on the occasion of the treaty which was there formed between them; but the sacrificial feast afterwards became an important element in the Mosaic cultus, and was designed to express the idea of house and table fellowship between the covenanting parties.

IV. THE COVENANT RESULTS. 1. *The kiss of reconciliation.* It is not certain that Laban kissed Jacob when he prepared for his departure in the morning; perhaps that was too much to expect; but he kissed Rachel and Leah and their children. It was a sign of forgiveness not alone to them, but through them also to Jacob. 2. *The paternal benediction.* Laban, whose better nature appears to have returned as the result of the covenant, or of the feast, or of the contemplated parting with his daughters, poured out his feelings in a farewell blessing on their heads. It is the last we hear or see of Laban in the Scripture narrative. Let us hope it was the revival of early kindness and piety in the old man's heart.

HOMILIES BY VARIOUS AUTHORS.

Vers. 51—55.—*Final covenant between Jacob and Laban.* I. ENTIRE SEPARATION FROM TEMPTATION IS THE ONLY SAFETY. Very imperfect knowledge in the Mesopotamian family. Rachel's theft of the household gods a sign of both moral and spiritual deficiency. The religion of Jacob and his descendants must be preserved from contamination. Intercourse with the unenlightened and unsanctified, though necessary for a time and in some degree, must not be suffered to obscure the higher light, or surround us with practical entanglements which hinder our faithfulness to God.

II. WHEREVER THE SPIRITUAL LIFE IS FEEBLE IT IS WELL THAT THERE SHOULD BE SOLEMN PUBLIC ACTS OF COVENANT AND TESTIMONY. We want the Galeed and the Mizpah, the heap of witness and the watch-tower of faith. Many united together in the covenant, and thus became witnesses in whose presence the oath was taken. We are helped to faithfulness by the publicity of our vows. But the higher the spiritual life, the less we shall call in material things to support it. Jacob with Laban is not the true Jacob. All dependence upon the symbol and rite is more or less compromise.

III. THE CONTACT OF THE HIGHER FORM OF RELIGION WITH THE LOWER ONE, OF THE MEANS OF PREPARING THE WORLD FOR THE TRUTH. Laban and his family types of the lower order of religious knowledge and life. The covenant between the father-in-law and son-in-law in the name of the God of Abraham and the God of Nahor points to a rising light in the Mesopotamian family. We may be sure that the influence of Christianity will be supreme wherever it is brought face to face with men's religions. That influence may be embodied in matters of common life, in covenants between man and man, in laws and commercial regulations and social arrangements.

IV. THE SEED OF THE DIVINE LIFE IS PLANTED IN THE SOIL OF NATURE, BUT REVEALS ITS SUPERIORITY TO NATURE BY BRINGING ALL THINGS AND MEN INTO SUBJECTION TO ITSELF. Jacob, Rachel, and afterwards Joseph, present to the Spirit of God elements of character which require both elevation and renovation. The grace is given. On a natural foundation inherited from others God rears by his grace a lofty structure. The crafty and the thoughtful are often nearly allied. It is one of the spiritual dangers to which specially energetic and subtle minds are exposed, that they may so easily fall into an abuse of their superior mental quickness to the injury of their moral purity and simplicity. Jacob and Laban making their covenant together, and erecting their witnessing monuments, are another illustration of the homage which even very imperfect characters pay to the God of truth. They appeal to him, and they do so in the presence of a world which they know will justify God, and not the sinner. The God of Abraham, the God of Nahor, the God of Isaac, judged between them. Jacob offered sacrifice upon the mount, and invited his brethren to a sacrificial banquet; and it was in that atmosphere of mingled reverence for God and human affection that the heir of the covenant bade farewell to all that held him in restraint, and set his face once more towards the land of promise.—R.

EXPOSITION.

CHAPTER XXXII.

Ver. 1.—**And Jacob** (after Laban's departure) **went on his way** (from Galeed and Mizpah, in a southerly direction towards the Jabbok), **and the angels of God**—literally, *the messengers of Elohim,* not chance travellers who informed him of Esau's being in the vicinity (Abarbanel), but angels (cf. Ps. civ. 4)—**met him.** Not necessarily came in an opposite direction, *fuerunt ei obviam* (Vulgate), but simply fell in with him, lighted on him as in ch. xxviii. 11, σὖνήν-τησαν αὐτῷ (LXX.), forgathered with him (Scottish); but whether this was in a waking vision (Kurtz, Keil, Inglis) or a midnight dream (Hengstenberg) is uncertain, though the two former visions enjoyed by Jacob were at night (cf. ch. xxviii. 12; xxxi. 10). Cajetan, approved by Pererius, translating בּ as "in him," makes it appear that the vision was purely subjective, *non fuisse visionem corporalem, sed internam:* the clause interpolated by the LXX., καὶ ἀναβλέ-ψας, εἶδε παρεμβολὴν θεοῦ παρμεβεβληκυῖαν, seems rather to point to an objective manifestation. The appearance of this invisible host may have been designed to celebrate Jacob's triumph over Laban, as after Christ's victory over Satan in the wilderness angels came and ministered unto him (Rupertus, Wordsworth), or to remind him that he owed his deliverance to Divine interposition (Calvin, Bush, Lange), but was more probably intended to assure him of protection in his approaching interview with Esau (Josephus, Chrysostom, Rosenmüller, Keil, Murphy, 'Speaker's Commentary'), and perhaps also to give him welcome in returning home again to Canaan (Kurtz), if not in addition to suggest that his descendants would require to fight for their inheritance (Kalisch).

Ver. 2.—**And when Jacob saw them, he said, This is God's host:**—Mahaneh Elohim; *i. e.* the army (cf. ch. l. 9; Exod. xiv. 24) or camp (1 Sam. xiv. 15; Ps. xxvii. 3) of God, as opposed to the Mahanoth, or bands of Jacob himself (*vide* ver. 7, 10)— **and he called the name of that place Mahanaim.**—*i. e.* Two armies or camps, from the root חָנָה, to decline or bend, and hence to fix oneself down or encamp; meaning either a multitudinous host, reading the dual for a plural (Malvenda), or two bands of angels, one before, welcoming him to Canaan, and another behind, conducting him from Mesopotamia (Jarchi and others), or one on either side to typify the completeness of his protection, as in Ps. xxxiv. 8 (Calvin, Bush, Gerlach, 'Speaker's Commentary'), or, as the best expositors interpret, his own company and the heavenly host (Aben Ezra, Clericus, Dathe, Keil, Lange, Rosenmüller, Kalisch, Murphy). Mahanaim, afterwards a distinguished city in the territory of Gad (Josh. xiii. 26), and frequently referred to in subsequent Scripture (2 Sam. ii. 8; xvii. 24, 27; xix. 32; 1 Kings iv. 14), as well as mentioned by Josephus ('Ant.' vii. 9, 8), as a strong and beautiful city, has been identified with Mahneh, a deserted ruin six or seven miles north-west by north of Ajlûn (Mount Gilead), and about twenty miles from the Jabbok (*vide* 'Robinson,' vol. iii. App. 166; and cf. Tristram, 'The Land of Israel,' p. 483); but the narrative appears to say that Mahanaim lay not north of Galeed, but between that place and Jabbok. Hence Porter suggests Gerasa, the most splendid ruin east of the Jordan, and bordering on the Jabbok, as occupying the site of Mahanaim (*vide* Kitto's 'Cyclopedia,' art. Mahanaim, and cf. 'Handbook for S. and P.' ii. 311, *seq.*).

Ver. 3.—**And Jacob sent messengers** (with the messengers of Jacob, the messengers of Elohim form a contrast which can scarcely have been accidental) **before him to Esau his brother unto the land of Seir,**— *vide* on ch. xiv. 6. Seir, nearly equivalent in force to Esau (Ewald), and meaning the rough or bristling mountain (Gesenius), was originally occupied by the Horites, but afterwards became the seat of Esau and his descendants (Deut. ii. 4; 2 Chron. xx. 10), though as yet Esau had not withdrawn from Canaan (ch. xxxvi. 5—8)—**the country** (literally, *plain or level tract* = Padan (*vide* Hosea xii. 13) **of Edom,** as it was afterwards called.

Vers. 4, 5.—**And he commanded them,**

saying, Thus shall ye speak unto my lord Esau; Thy servant Jacob saith thus;—the expression "my lord" may have been designed to intimate to Esau that he (Jacob) did not intend to assert that superiority or precedency which had been assigned him by Isaac's blessing (ch. xxvii. 29), at least so far as to claim a share in Isaac's wealth (Calvin, Bush, Gerlach), but was probably due chiefly to the extreme courtesy of the East (Gerlach), or to a desire to conciliate his brother (Keil), or to a feeling of personal contrition for his misbehaviour towards Esau (Kalisch), and perhaps also to a secret apprehension of danger from Esau's approach (Alford, Inglis) — I have sojourned with Laban, and stayed—אֵחַר, the fut. Kal. of אָחַר, occurring only here, is a contraction for אֶאֱחַר, like תּֽהִמָּ֫ךָ for תּֽאהֵמָ֫ךָ (Ps. civ. 29; vide Gesenius, § 68, 2)—there until now: and I have (literally, there are to me, so that I stand in need of no further wealth from either thee or Isaac) oxen, and asses, flocks, and menservants, and womenservants:—cf. xii. 16 (Abraham); xxvi. 13, 14 (Isaac) — and I have sent to tell my lord, that I may find grace in thy sight (cf. xxxiii. 8, 15; xxxix. 4; and vide vi. 8; xviii. 3).

Ver. 6. And the messengers returned to Jacob, saying, We came to thy brother Esau, and also he cometh to meet thee (vide ch. xxxiii. 1), and four hundred men with him. That Esau was attended by 400 armed followers was a proof that he had grown to be a powerful chieftain. If the hypothesis be admissible that he had already begun to live by the sword (ch. xxvii. 40), and was now invading the territory of the Horites, which he afterwards occupied (Delitzsch, Keil, Kurtz), it will serve to explain his appearance in the land of Seir, while as yet he had not finally retired from Canaan. That he came with such a formidable force to meet his brother has been set down to personal vanity, or a desire to show how powerful a prince he had become (Lyra, Menochius); to fraternal kindness, which prompted him to do honour to his brother (Poole, Calvin, Clarke), to a distinctly hostile intention (Willet, Ainsworth, Candlish), at least if circumstances should seem to call for vengeance (Keil), though it is probable that Esau's mind, on first hearing of his brother's nearness, was simply excited, and "in that wavering state which the slightest incident might soothe into good will, or rouse into vengeance" (Murphy).

Vers. 7, 8.—Then Jacob was greatly afraid and distressed:—literally, it was narrow to him; i. e. he was perplexed. Clearly the impression left on Jacob's mind by the report of his ambassadors was that he had nothing to expect but hostility—and he divided the people that was with him, and the flocks, and herds, and the camels, into two bands; —according to Gerlach, caravans are frequently divided thus in the present day, and for the same reason as Jacob assigns— And said, If Esau come to the one company, and smite it, then the other company which is left shall escape. It is easy to blame Jacob for want of faith in not trusting to God instead of resorting to his own devices (Candlish), but his behaviour in the circumstances evinced great self-possession, non ita expavefactum fuisse Jacob quin res suas componeret (Calvin), considerable prudence (Lange), if not exalted chivalry (Candlish), a peaceful disposition which did not wish vim vi armata repellere (Rosenmüller), and a truly-religious spirit ('Speaker's Commentary'), since in his terror he betakes himself to prayer.

Vers. 9—12.—And Jacob said,—the combined beauty and power, humility and boldness, simplicity and sublimity, brevity and comprehensiveness of this prayer, of which Kalisch somewhat hypercritically complains that it ought to have been offered before resorting to the preceding precautions, has been universally recognised—O God of my father Abraham, and God of my father Isaac, the Lord—Jacob's invocation is addressed not to Deity in general, but to the living personal Elohim who had taken his fathers Abraham and Isaac into covenant, i. e. to Jehovah who had enriched them with promises of which he was the heir, and who had specially appeared unto himself (cf. ch. xxviii. 13; xxxi. 3, 13)—which saidst unto me, Return unto thy country, and to thy kindred, and I will deal well with thee: —here was a clear indication that Jacob had in faith both obeyed the command and embraced the promise made known to him in Haran—I am not worthy of the least of (literally, I am less than) all the mercies, and (of) all the truth, which thou hast shewed unto thy servant;—the profound humility which these words breathe is a sure indication that the character of Jacob had either undergone a great inward transformation, if that was not experienced twenty years before at Bethel, or had shaken off the moral and spiritual lethargy under which he too manifestly laboured while in the service of Laban—for with my staff (i. e. possessing nothing but my staff) I passed over this Jordan (the Jabbok was situated near, indeed is a tributary of the Jordan); and now I am become two bands (or Machanoth). Deliver me, I pray thee, from the hand of my brother, from the hand of Esau (thus passing from thanksgiving to direct petition, brief, explicit, and fervent): for I fear him, lest he will come and smite me (i. e. my whole clan, as Ishmael, Israel,

Edom signify not individuals, but races), and **the mother with the children**. Literally, *mother upon the children*, a proverbial expression for unsparing cruelty (Rosenmüller, Keil), or complete extirpation (Kalisch), taken from the idea of destroying a bird while sitting upon its young (cf. Hosea x. 14). **And thou saidst, I will surely do thee good**,—literally, *doing good, I will do good to thee* (vide ch. xxviii. 13). Jacob here pleads the Divine promises at Bethel (ch. xxviii. 13—15) and at Haran (ch. xxxi. 3), as an argument why Jehovah should extend to him protection against Esau—conduct at which Tuch is scandalised as "somewhat inaptly reminding God of his commands and promises, and calling upon him to keep his word;" but just this is what God expects his people to do (Isa. xliii. 26), and according to Scripture the Divine promise is always the petitioner's best warrant—**and make thy seed as the sand of the sea**,—this was the sense, without the *ipsissima verba* of the Bethel promise, which likened Jacob's descendants to the dust upon the ground, as Abraham's seed had previously been compared to the dust of the earth (ch. xiii. 16), the stars of heaven (ch. xv. 5), and the sand upon the sea-shore (ch. xxii. 17)—**which cannot be numbered for multitude.**

Ver. 13.—**And he lodged there that same night; and took**—not by random, but after careful selection; separavit (Vulgate)—**of that which came to his hand**—not of those things which were in his hand, ὧν ἔφερεν (LXX.), such as he had (Ainsworth), *quæ in manu erant* (Rosenmüller), but of such things as had come into his hand, *i. e.* as he had acquired (Keil, Alford, 'Speaker's Commentary,' Inglis)—**a present** (Minchah ; used in ch. iv. 3, 4, 5, as a sacrifice to Jehovah, *q. v.*) **for Esau his brother.**

Ver. 14, 15—**Two hundred she goats, and twenty he goats, two hundred ewes, and twenty rams, thirty milch camels** (specially valuable in the East on account of their milk, which was peculiarly sweet and wholesome) **with their colts, forty kine, and ten bulls, twenty she asses, and ten foals.** The selection was in harmony with the general possessions of nomads (cf. Job i. 3 ; xlii. 12), and the proportion of male to female animals was arranged according to what the experience of the best ancient authorities has shown to be necessary for the purposes of breeding (Rosenmüller, Keil, Kalisch).

Ver. 16.—**And he delivered** them into the hand of his servants, every drove by them-selves (literally, *drove and drove separately*) ; and said unto his servants, **Pass over** (the river Jabbok) **before me, and put a space** (literally, *a breathing-place*) **betwixt drove and drove**—as is still the manner with Oriental shepherds (cf. 'Land and Book,' p. 331).

Vers. 17—20.—**And he commanded the foremost, saying** (with admirable tact and prudence), **When Esau my brother meeteth thee, and asketh thee, saying, Whose art thou? and whither goest thou? and whose** are **these before thee?** then thou shalt say, They be **thy servant Jacob's ; it is a present sent unto my lord Esau : and, behold, also** he (Jacob) **is behind us. And so commanded he the second, and the third, and all that followed the droves, saying, On this manner shall ye speak unto Esau, when ye find him** —literally, *in your finding of him*. **And say ye** (literally, *and ye shall say*) **moreover, Behold, thy servant Jacob is behind us—** "for he thought that this would convince Esau that he went to meet him with complete confidence, and without apprehension" (Kalisch)—**for he said** (the historian adds the motive which explained Jacob's singular behaviour), **I will appease him** (literally, *I will cover his face*, meaning I will prevent him from seeing my past offences, *i. e.* I will turn away his anger or pacify him, as in Prov. xvi. 14) **with the present that goeth before me**,—literally, *going before my face*. So Abigail appeased David with a present (1 Sam. xxv. 18—32)—**and afterward I will see his face ; peradventure he will accept of me**—literally, *lift up my face ;* a proverbial expression for granting a favourable reception (cf. ch. xix. 21 ; Job xlii. 8). "Jacob did not miscalculate the influence of his princely offerings, and I verily believe there is not an emeer or sheikh in all Gilead at this day who would not be appeased by such presents ; and from my personal knowledge of Orientals, I should say that Jacob need not have been in such great terror, following in their rear. Far less will now 'make room,' as Solomon says, for any offender, however atrocious, and bring him before great men with acceptance" ('Land and Book,' p. 371).

Ver. 21—23.—**So** (literally, *and*) **went the present over before him : and himself lodged that night in the company. And he rose up that night**,—*i. e.* some time before daybreak (*vide* ver. 24) — **and took his two wives, and his two womenservants** (Bilhah and Zilpah), **and his eleven sons** (Dinah being not mentioned in accordance with the common usage of the Bible), **and passed over the ford** — the word signifies a place of passing over. Tristram ('Land of Israel,' p. 558) speaks of the strong current reaching the horses' girths at the ford crossed by himself and twenty horsemen—**Jabbok.** Jabbok, from *bakak*, to empty, to pour forth (Kalisch), or from *abak*, to struggle (Keil), may have been so named either from the natural appearance of the river, or, as is more probable, by prolepsis from the wrestling which took place upon its banks. It is now called the *Wady Zerka*, or Blue River, which flows into the Jordan, nearly opposite Shechem, and midway between the Lake Tiberias and the Dead Sea. The stream is rapid, and often completely hidden by the dense mass of oleander which fringes its banks ('Land of Israel,' p. 558). **And he took them, and sent them** (literally, *caused them to pass*) **over the brook, and sent over** **that he had** — himself remaining on the north side (Delitzsch, Keil, Kurtz, Murphy, Gerlach, Wordsworth, Alford), although, having once crossed the stream (ver. 22), it is not perfectly apparent that he recrossed, which has led some to argue that the wrestling occurred on the south of the river (Knobel, Rosenmüller, Lange, Kalisch).

HOMILETICS.

Vers. 1—23.—*Mahanaim, or preparing for Esau.* 1. THE ANGELIC APPARITION. 1. *The time when it occurred.* (1) After Jacob had concluded a covenant of peace with Laban. Celestial visitations of a peaceful and encouraging character are never vouchsafed to those who are living in a state of enmity with their fellow-men. The troubled sea reflects not the shining face of heaven, and neither does the wrathful soul invite approaches of God. (2) When Jacob was proceeding on his way to Canaan. The road which Jacob now pursued was the path of duty, inasmuch as it had been prescribed by God, and led to the covenant inheritance; and only then need the saints expect to meet with either God or his angels, when they are walking in the way of his commandments, and making for the better country, even an heavenly. 2. *The impression which it made.* Whether completely surrounding him, or divided into two companies, one on either side of him, Jacob's angelic visitors, from their number, their orderly array, their military dispositions, assumed the appearance of a heavenly army lying encamped over against his own; and the sight of the two companies immediately suggested the ejaculation, "This is God's host," and caused him to name the place Mahanaim. 3. *The purpose which it served.* For an enumeration of the different ends which this sublime vision is supposed to have been intended to subserve the Exposition may be consulted. The greatest probability attaches to that which regards it as having been designed to prepare Jacob for his rapidly-approaching interview with Esau. It was fitted to remind him of the heavenly reinforcements that are always at hand to succour saints in their extremities (cf. 2 Kings vi. 17; Ps. xxxiv. 6; Zech. ix. 8; Heb. i. 14).

II. THE FRIENDLY EMBASSY. 1. The *despatch* of the messengers. (1) Their destination—to Mount Seir, to Esau; (2) their instructions—to inform Esau of Jacob's prosperous estate and immediate return; (3) their design—to deprecate the wrath of Esau, and find grace for Jacob in his sight. 2. The *return* of the messengers. (1) Their alarming report—that Esau was on the way with 400 men; (2) the terror it produced—Jacob was greatly afraid and distressed; (3) the acts to which it led—stratagem, supplication, conciliation.

III. THE SUDDEN STRATAGEM. Jacob divided the people that were with him, and the flocks and herds and camels, into two bands. 1. An evidence of Jacob's *self-possession.* The fear inspired by Esau's approach had not been so great as to make him lose command of his faculties. Men that have God upon their side should not allow themselves to be thrown by evil tidings into excessive trepidation (Ps. xxvii. 1—3; Rom. viii. 31). 2. A proof of Jacob's *prudence.* The division of his company into two bands afforded to one at least of the portions a chance of escaping the sword of Esau. Though contrary to the Divine word to resist evil, it is not wrong to use all lawful endeavours to avoid it. 3. A testimony to Jacob's *chivalry.* In a time of danger he thinks of the safety of others, of the women and children, rather than of himself. 4. A sign of Jacob's *meekness.* He contemplates not armed resistance to the onset of his infuriated brother, but prepares by peaceful means to elude at least the full force of his attack.

IV. THE EARNEST PRAYER. Characterised by—1. *Lofty faith.* Jacob addresses himself to God as to a living personality, and not as to an impersonal force; to the God of the covenant,—"O God of my father Abraham," &c.,—and not simply to God in the abstract, as the inscrutable power that presides over men and things, and bases his appeal upon the promises which God in virtue of that covenant had extended to himself. 2. *Profound humility.* He not only acknowledges the

Divine hand in his remarkable prosperity, which is always difficult for the proud spirit of the worldling to do, but he distinctly describes "all the mercies" he has received to the pure, unmerited grace of God, declaring himself to be utterly less than the least of them. Language such as this is either impious hypocrisy or lowly humility. 3. *Beautiful simplicity.* Plain, direct, artless, and confiding, it is such a prayer as a loving child might breathe into a mother's ear when driven by impending danger to seek shelter in her bosom :—" Deliver me, I pray thee, from the hand of Esau my brother: for I fear him."

V. THE CONCILIATORY PRESENT. "A man's gift maketh room for him," says Solomon (Prov. xviii. 16) ; and again, "A gift in secret pacifieth anger, and a reward in the bosom strong wrath" (Prov. xxi. 14). The gift of Jacob to his brother was—1. *Handsomely prepared.* It was munificently and generously selected from the best of the flocks and herds in his possession. 2. *Skilfully arranged.* The sheep, goats, camels, asses, kine that composed it were drawn up in a series of droves, which were despatched in succession under the care of as many drivers. 3. *Promptly despatched.* The measures just recited were adopted on the very day that Jacob's messengers returned, and the several droves despatched upon their journey ere the night fell. 4. *Peacefully designed.* They were meant to appease the wrath of Esau.

Lessons:—1. The ministry of angels. 2. The courage inspired by true religion. 3. The value of prayer. 4. The use of a present.

HOMILIES BY VARIOUS AUTHORS.

Vers. 1, 2.—*Divine protection.* The pilgrim on his way is met by the angels of God. They are two hosts—"Mahanaim," that is, twofold defence, before and behind. There was fear in the man, but there was trust and prayer. He saw the objective vision, but the inward preparation of heart enabled him to see it. On our way we may reckon on supernatural protection—protection for ourselves, protection for those who are Divinely appointed to be with us. The double host is an emblem of that angelic guardianship which we are told (Ps. xxxiv. and xci.) "encampeth round about them that fear the Lord, and delivereth them," "keepeth them in all their ways."—R.

Vers. 3—8.—*Faith and fellowship.* Jacob's preparation against danger betokened his sense of duty to do his utmost under the circumstances, and his sense of past errors and ill desert towards his brother. There is an exercise of our own judgment in times of distress and extremity which is quite consistent with dependence upon God.—R.

Vers. 9—12.—*Jacob's prayer.* 1. It was the prayer of *humility.* 2. Of *faith*— faith in a covenant God, faith in him who had already revealed himself, faith in promises made to the individual as well as to God's people generally, faith founded on experience of the past, faith which has been mingled with obedience, and therefore lays hold of Divine righteousness. He has commanded me to return ; I am in the way of his commandments. Faith in the great purpose of God and his kingdom : " I will make thy seed as the sand of the sea," &c. So Luther, in his sense of personal weakness in a troubled world, cried, "The Lord must save his own Church." 3. It was the prayer of *gratitude.* "*I was alone ; I am now two bands ;*" "not worthy of the least of thy mercies," &c., "yet abundantly blessed."—R.

Vers. 13—23.—*The crisis at hand.* Jacob understood the human heart.

I. KINDNESS WILL WORK WONDERS. "I will appease him with the present that goeth before me, and afterward I will see his face." It gave Esau time to think of an altered state of things, a changed brother, and his own brotherly affection, not entirely destroyed.

II. IMPORTUNITY IN DOING GOOD. The repeated strokes upon the iron changes its nature. We may learn a lesson from Jacob to prepare human hearts for the reception of the gospel by the same importunity. Kind deeds and kind words will often open the way for a more direct face-to-face pleading for God.

III. EXPERIENCE SANCTIFIES. The trials of Jacob's life were working a deeper and more loving *wisdom*—working *out* the more selfish craft, and transmuting the natural features of a character, far from pure and simple at first, into such as blended more really with the work of grace. So in the course of providence family cares and anxieties deliver us from lower thoughts, or may do so, if we serve God, and help us to walk steadfastly in the way of faith.

IV. THE TRUE LOVE PROVIDES FOR ITS OBJECTS. The shepherd with his flocks, and family, with his little bands of precious ones, fearing for them, and yet working for them, and putting them before him in the hands of God, is a type of the great Shepherd of the sheep, who was " not ashamed to call them brethren ; " and saying, as he stood in their midst,—partaker of their infirmities, representative of their wants and sorrows, guardian of their safety, " I will put my trust in him. Behold I and the children which God hath given me " (Heb ii. 13).

V. THE TWO WORLDS. If Esau be taken as a type of the kingdoms of this world threatening the kingdom of God, Jacob represents the little flock to whom the promise of victory and peace has been given. The true *mediator* must be left alone by the ford Jabbok. The place of his intercession and prevailing is where none of the people is with him, can be with him.—R.

EXPOSITION.

Ver. 24.—**And Jacob was left alone** (probably on the north bank of the Jabbok ; but *vide* on ver. 23) ; **and there wrestled**—thus assaulting in his strong point one who had been a wrestler or heel-catcher from his youth (Murphy). The old word נֶאֱבַק, niph. of אָבַק, unused, a denom. from הָבָק, dust, because in wrestling the dust is raised (Aben Ezra, Gesenius), or a weakened form of חָבַק, to wind round, to embrace (Fürst), obviously contains an allusion to the Jabbok (*vide* on ver. 22)—**a man**—called an angel by Hosea (ch. xii. 4), and God by Jacob (ver. 30) ; but *vide infra*—**with him until the breaking of the day** — literally, *the ascending of the morning.*

Ver. 25.—**And when he** (the unknown wrestler) **saw that he prevailed not against him, he touched**—not struck (Knobel)—**the hollow of his thigh** (literally, *the socket of the hip*) ; **and the hollow of Jacob's thigh was out of joint, as he wrestled with him** —literally, *in his wrestling with him.*

Ver. 26.—**And he** (the man) **said, Let me go** (literally, *send me away;* meaning that he yielded the victory to Jacob, adding as a reason for his desire to depart), **for the day breaketh**—literally, *for the morning or the dawn ascendeth ;* and therefore it is time for thee to proceed to other duties (Willet, Clarke, Murphy), *e. g.* to meet Esau and appease his anger ('Speaker's Commentary'). Perhaps also the angel was unwilling that the vision which was meant for Jacob only should be seen by others (Pererius), or even that his own glory should be beheld by Jacob (Ainsworth). Calvin thinks the language was so shaped as to lead Jacob to infer *nocturna visione se divinitus fuisse edoctum.* **And he said, I will not let thee go, except**

thou bless me. The words show that Jacob now clearly recognised his mysterious Antagonist to be Divine, and sought to obtain from him the blessing which he had previously stolen from his aged father by craft.

Ver. 27.—**And he said unto him, What is thy name ?** (not as if requiring to be informed, but as directing attention to it in view of the change about to be made upon it) **And he said, Jacob**—*i. e.* Heel-catcher, or Supplanter (*vide* ch. xxv. 26).

Ver. 28.—**And he said, Thy name shall be called no more** (*i. e.* exclusively, since both he and his descendants are in Scripture sometimes after this styled) **Jacob, but Israel: —**יִשְׂרָאֵל, from שָׂרָה, to be chief, to fight, though, after the example of Ishmael, God hears, it might be rendered " God governs " (Kalisch), yet seems in this place to signify either Prince of El (Calvin, Ainsworth, Dathe, Murphy, Wordsworth, and others), or wrestler with God (Fürst, Keil, Kurtz, Lange, *et alii*), rather than warrior of God (Gesenius), if indeed both ideas may not be combined in the name as the princely wrestler with God ('Speaker's Commentary,' Bush), an interpretation adopted by the A. V.—**for as a prince hast thou power with God**—literally, *for thou hast contended with Elohim* (Keil, Alford, &c.), ὅτι ἐνίσχυσας μετὰ θεοῦ (LXX.), *contra deum fortis fuisti* (Vulgate), thou hast obtained the mastery with God (Kalisch), rather than, thou hast striven to be a prince with God (Murphy)—**and with men, and hast prevailed.** So are the words rendered by the best authorities (Keil, Kalisch, Murphy, Wordsworth), though the translation καὶ μετὰ ἀνθρώπων δυνατὸς ἔσῃ (LXX.), *quanto magis contra homines prevalebis* (Vulgate) is by some preferred (Calvin, Rosenmüller, &c.).

Ver. 29.—**And Jacob asked** him, **and said, Tell** me, **I pray thee, thy name.** A request indicating great boldness on the part of Jacob—the boldness of faith (Heb. iv. 16; x. 19); and importing a desire on Jacob's part to be acquainted, not merely with the designation, but with the mysterious character of the Divine personage with whom he had been contending. **And he** (the mysterious stranger) **said, Wherefore** is it **that thou dost ask after my name?** Cf. Judges xiii. 18, where the angel gives the same reply to Manoah, adding, "seeing it is secret;" literally, *wonderful*, i. e. incomprehensible to mortal man; though here the words of Jacob's antagonist may mean that his name, so far as it could be learnt by man, was already plain from the occurrence which had taken place (Murphy, 'Speaker's Commentary,' Bush). **And he blessed him there.** After this, every vestige of doubt disappeared from the soul of Jacob.

Ver. 30.—**And Jacob called the name of the place Peniel** (i. e. "the face of God." Its situation must have been close to the Jabbok. The reason given for its designation follows): **for I have seen God** (Elohim) **face to face, and my life is preserved** (cf. ch. xvi. 13; Exod. xxiv. 11; xxxiii. 20; Judges vi. 22; xiii. 22; Isa. vi. 5).

Ver. 31.—**And as he passed over Penuel**— this some suppose to have been the original name of the place, which Jacob changed by the alteration of a vowel, but it is probably nothing more than an old form of the same word—**the sun rose upon him,**—"there was sunshine within and sunshine without. When Judas went forth on his dark design, we read, 'It was night,' John xiii. 30" (Inglis) —**and he halted upon his thigh**—thus carrying with him a memorial of his conflict, as Paul afterwards bore about with him a stake in his flesh (2 Cor. xii. 7).

Ver. 32.—**Therefore the children of Israel eat not of the sinew which shrank,**—the *gid hannasheh,* rendered by the LXX. τὸ νεῦρον ὅ ἐνάρκησεν, the nerve which became numb, and by the Vulgate *nervus qui emarcuit,* the nerve which withered, is the long tendon or sinew *nervus ischiaticus* (the tendo Achillis of the Greeks) reaching from the spinal marrow to the ankle. The derivation of *hannasheh* is unknown (Gesenius), though the LXX. appear to have connected it with *nashah,* to dislocate, become feeble; Ainsworth with *nashah,* to forget (i. e. the sinew that forgat its place), and Fürst with *nashah,* to be prolonged (vide 'Michaelis Suppl.', p. 303)—**which is upon the hollow of the thigh, unto this day:**—i. e. the day of Moses; though the custom continues to the present time among the Hebrews of cutting out this sinew from the beasts they kill and eat (vide Ainsworth *in loco*); but, according to Michaelis (Suppl., p. 303), *eo nemo omnino mortalium, si vel nullo cognationis gradu Jacobum attingat, nemo Græcus, nemo barbarus vesci velit*—**because he** (i. e. the angel) **touched the hollow of Jacob's thigh in the sinew that shrank.**

HOMILETICS.

Vers. 24—32.—*Peniel, or the mysterious contest.* I. THE DESCRIPTION OF THE STRUGGLE. 1. *The scene.* The north bank of Jabbok (vide Exposition). 2. *The time.* Night; the most suitable season for soul exercises, such as self-examination (Ps. iv. 4), meditation (Ps. lxiii. 6), devotion (Luke vi. 12). 3. *The circumstances.* Jacob was alone. In solitude the human soul discovers most of itself, and enjoys most frequent interviews with God (Ps. lxxvii. 6; Dan. x. 8; John xvi. 32). 4. *The combatants.* (1) Jacob: by nature the supplanter, by grace the heir of the covenant; who in early life by craft had overreached his brother Esau in the matters of the family birthright and theocratic blessing, and who had now, by the despatch of his munificent present to "my lord Esau," renounced both, so far at least as renunciation was possible, i. e. in respect of material and temporal advantages. (2) A man, i. e. one who in outward appearance wore the form of a man, though in reality "the visible revealer of the invisible God" (Delitzsch); the angel of Jehovah, who had previously appeared in like guise to Abraham at Mamre (ch. xviii. 1), and who subsequently, in the fulness of the times, incarnated himself as the Word made flesh (John i. 14). 5. *The combat.* (1) Its commencement. When precisely this mysterious conflict began, and how Jacob was engaged at the moment of the unknown wrestler's approach, are points upon which the narrative is silent, though it is probable that Jacob was employed in fervent supplication, and that, without knowing how, he suddenly became conscious of being involved in a close physical struggle with a powerful antagonist. Perhaps this was designed to suggest that God's approaches to the praying soul are mostly sudden and inexplicable (cf. John iii. 8). (2) Its character. Though unquestionably depicted in the narrative as a veritable contest between two human beings, it is apparent that underlying the physical struggle, and related to it as the substance to the shadow, as the soul to the body, was another spiritual contending carried on by means of prayers and tears (Hosea xii. 4). (3) Its continuance. Beginning probably at midnight, it was protracted until dawn, a circumstance suggestive of Jacob's earnestness and determination, and yet attesting the severe character of all true spiritual conflicts, and the extraordinary difficulty of achieving victories with God (Matt. xii. 12). (4) Its course. Four stages are discernible in this mysterious struggle. (*a*) The wrestlers appear to be equally balanced in their strength and skill, so that the stranger finds himself unable to prevail against Jacob, and laying his finger on his adversary's hip, puts it out of joint—a hint to Jacob that though seemingly the victory inclined towards him, it was due not so much, or even at all, to his wisdom and prowess, but rather to the stranger's grace and good-will. (*b*) Jacob having thus been disabled, his mysterious antagonist, as if owning that the mastery remained with him, requests permission to depart, alleging as a reason that the ascending dawn proclaimed the day's return, and called to other duties—a valuable reminder that religion has other necessary works for God's saints besides devotion and contemplation; but Jacob, who by this time recognised his antagonist as Divine, objected to his departure without confirming the blessing he had formerly received at Bethel—and this, the personal reception and enjoyment of the blessing of the covenant, should be the end and aim of all the saint's contendings with God and communings with Heaven. (*c*) Inquiring Jacob's name, the Divine adversary now discovers his true personality by authoritatively changing that name to Israel, prince of El, in token of his victory— an outward symbol of the completed spiritual renovation which had taken place in Jacob since God first met with him at Bethel. (*d*) Probably excited, or spiritually elevated, by what had just transpired, Jacob ventures, either with holy boldness or with unthinking curiosity, to inquire after his heavenly antagonist's name, but is answered that in the mean time he must rest satisfied with the blessing which was then and there pronounced. It was either a rebuke to Jacob's presumption, or, and with greater probability, a reminder that even holy boldness has its limits, beyond which it may not intrude. (5) Its close. Suddenly and mysteriously as the stranger came did he also disappear, leaving Jacob in possession of the blessing indeed, but also of a dislocated limb. So God frequently accompanies spiritual enrichment with material and temporal deprivation, in order both to evince his own sovereignty and to keep his saints humble (cf. 2 Cor. xii. 7). (6) Its commemoration. By Jacob, who called the place Peniel; by Jacob's descendants, who to this day eat not of the sciatic nerve in animals they kill for food.

II. The REALITY OF THE STRUGGLE. The question arises whether the contest just described had an objective reality (Hävernick, Kurtz, Murphy, Alford, &c.), or partook of a purely subjective character, being in fact an allegorical description of a spiritual conflict in the soul of Jacob (Kalisch), or a wrestling which took place only in a dream (Hengstenberg), or in an ecstasy (Delitzsch, Keil, Lange), for the idea of its being a myth (Bohlen, De Wette, Oort, Kuenen) may be discarded. 1. Against the notion of a dream-vision it is sufficient to remark that if Jacob's wrestling was a dream, so also were his victory and his blessing dreams. Besides, limbs do not usually become dislocated in dreams. 2. To read the passage as an allegory is both forced and unnatural, and "little better than trifling with the sacred narrative" (Alford). 3. There is no insuperable objection to the idea of an ecstasy, provided it is not intended to exclude the objective manifestation; yet, 4. There does not seem sufficient reason for departing from the obvious and literal sense of the passage, according to which there was a *bonâ fide* corporeal contest between Jacob and the angel of Jehovah in human form; for (1) the narrative gives no indication that it was designed in this part to be interpreted otherwise than literally and historically, as in the surrounding context; (2) unless on the hypothesis that the supernatural is the unreal, there is no imperative necessity why exception should be taken to the objective character of this remarkable struggle; (3) the dislocation of Jacob's thigh points to an actual physical contest; and (4) the other events in the narrative appear to require that the historic credibility of Jacob's wrestling be maintained.

III. The SIGNIFICANCE OF THE STRUGGLE. That a momentous crisis had arisen in

Jacob's history is universally admitted. He was now returning to the land of Canaan a man of mature age, being in his ninety-seventh year, and of a singularly diversified experience, both natural and spiritual. In his early life he had twice supplanted Esau by means of craft, depriving him of his birthright and blessing, and now he was on the eve of meeting that formidable brother whom he had wronged. That the prospective interview filled him with alarm is explicitly declared (ch. xxxii. 7) ; but it likewise drove him to take refuge in prayer, in which exercise it is scarcely doubtful he was engaged when his mysterious assailant approached. What then did this extraordinary combat signify in the spiritual consciousness of Jacob? Putting together those views which do not necessarily exclude one another, and which appear to contain an element of truth, it may be said that this remarkable experience through which the patriarch passed at Jabbok was designed to have a threefold bearing. 1. *On his fear of Esau.* Apprehensive of his brother, he now learns that not Esau, but Jehovah, was his real adversary (Keil, Kurtz, Gerlach, Candlish), and that before he can ever hope to triumph over Esau he must first conquer God. 2. *On his retention of the blessing.* Having previously, as he thought, obtained the birthright and its accompanying blessing by means of carnal policy and worldly stratagem, he now discovers that it cannot be received, or, if he renounced it in the act of homage done to Esau (Lange), cannot be recovered except directly from the lips of God, and by means of earnest cries and entreaties (Keil)—a truth taught him, according to Kurtz, by the dislocation of his thigh, which caused him to discontinue his corporeal wrestling, and resort to prayers and tears. 3. *On his personal character.* Jacob during all his past career, from his birth, when he caught his brother by the heel, to his last years in Haran, when he overreached the crafty and avaricious Laban, having been a person who sought to overcome by means of self-reliance and personal effort, it was now designed to teach him that, as the heir of the covenant, the weapons of his warfare were not to be carnal, but spiritual, and that his advancement to the place predestined for him of pre-eminence over his brethren was to be brought about by earnest reliance upon God (Murphy).

HOMILIES BY VARIOUS AUTHORS.

Vers. 24—32.—"*Peniel.*" "*The face of God.*" The patriarchal revelation at its best. The main point, the personal wrestling of the believer with the angel of deliverance. Through that scene Jacob passed as by a baptism (ford Jabbok) into the full enjoyment of confidence in Jehovah, into the theanthropic faith. A man wrestled with him. The faith of Jacob was now to be a faith resting not upon tradition alone, nor upon promises and commandments alone, nor upon past experience alone, but upon a living, personal union with God. The wrestling was a type of that intimate fellowship which spiritually identifies the individual child of God with the Father through the man Christ Jesus. The pilgrim on his way is henceforth the prince, having power with God and with men. It is a great lesson on prevailing prayer. 1. *The prayer of faith.* 2. *The prayer of importunity.* 3. *The prayer of intense desire.* "I will not let thee go, except thou bless me." Bless me for myself, bless me for my family, bless me for the world. But Jacob was a type of the true Prince of God prevailing for his people. He wrestled, he wrestled alone, he wrestled to his own suffering and humiliation, although into victory. He obtained the blessing as the Mediator. Although the patriarch was not allowed to know the name of the angel, he was himself named by the angel. Although we cannot with all our searching find out God, and even the revelation of Christ leaves much unknown, still we are "known of him." He gives us one name, and by that name we know him to be ours, which is the true saving knowledge. Peniel, the face of God, is the name not of God himself, but of the blessed revelation of God. We know where we may find him. We may each one start afresh from our Peniel, where we have been blessed of God, and have through Christ prevailed against the darkness of the future and the helplessness of our own impotence. Nor must we forget that this wrestling was reconciliation—the reconciliation between man and God, preceding the reconciliation between man and man. The lameness of the patriarch symbolised the life of dependence upon which he henceforth entered with much more entire surrender than before. " As the sun rose upon him, he halted upon his thigh." It was the morning of a new life—the life of man's confessed nothingness and God's manifested sufficiency. In such a light we can see light. The day may have dangers in it, but it will be a day of mighty deliverance, Divine blessedness, rejoicing in personal salvation and peaceful life.—R.

Ver. 28.—*A new name.* " Thy name shall be called no more Jacob, but Israel." Twenty years before Jacob learned at Bethel to know God as a living and present Protector. This a great step in spiritual life ; belief of God in heaven, becoming consciousness of God " in this place," guiding all events. It is the first step towards walking with God. But his training not yet complete. Truth is usually grasped by degrees. Unbelief, cast out, returns in new forms and under new pretences. A common mistake at beginning of Christian life is to think that the battle is at an end when decision made. The soul may have passed from death to life ; but much still to be done, much to be learned. Many a young Christian little knows the weakness of his faith. During these years Jacob shows real faith, but not perfect reliance (ch. xxx. 37 ; xxxi. 20). Returning home greatly enriched, he heard of Esau at hand. He feared his anger. No help in man ; God's promise his only refuge. Could he trust to it ? His wrestling. We cannot picture its outward form ; but its essence a spiritual struggle. His endurance tried by bodily infirmity (cf. Job ii. 5) and by the apparent unwillingness of the Being with whom he strove (cf. Matt. xv. 26). His answer showed determination (cf. 2 Kings iv. 30). This prevailed ; weak as he was, he received the blessing (cf. Heb. xi. 34). And the new name was the sign of his victory (cf. Matt. xxi. 22 ; 1 John v. 4).

I. THE STRUGGLE. Why thus protracted ? It was not merely a prolonged prayer, like Luke vi. 12. There was some hindrance to be overcome (cf. Matt. xi. 12) ; not by muscular force, but by earnest supplication. Where Scripture is silent we must speak cautiously. But probable explanation is the state of Jacob's own mind. Hitherto faith had been mixed with faithlessness ; belief in the promise with hesitation to commit the means to God. Against this divided mind (James i. 8) the Lord contended. No peace while this remained (cf. Isa. xxvi. 3). And the lesson of that night was to trust God's promise entirely (cf. Ps. xxxvii. 3). When this was learned the wrestling of the Spirit against the double mind was at an end. Such a struggle may be going on in the hearts of some here. A craving for peace, yet a restless disquiet. The gospel believed, yet failing to bring comfort. Prayer for peace apparently unanswered, so that there seemed to be some power contending against us. Why is this ? Most probably from failing to commit all to God. Perhaps requiring some sign (John xx. 25), some particular state of feeling, or change of disposition ; perhaps looking for faith within as the ground of trust ; perhaps choosing the particular blessing—self-will as to the morsel of the bread of life to satisfy us, instead of taking every word of God. There is the evil. It is against self thou must strive. Behold thy loving Saviour ; will he fail thee in the hour of need ? Tell all to him ; commit thyself into his hands ; not once or twice, but habitually.

II. THE NEW NAME (cf. Rev. iii. 12). No more Jacob, the crafty, but Israel, God's prince (cf. Rev. i. 6). The token of victory over distrust, self-will, self-confidence. In knowledge of poverty is wealth (Matt. v. 3) ; in knowledge of weakness, strength (2 Cor. xii. 10). That name is offered to all. The means, persevering prayer ; but prayer not to force our will upon God, but that trust may be so entire that our wills may in all things embrace his.—M.

EXPOSITION.

CHAPTER XXXIII.

Vers. 1, 2.—**And Jacob**, having the day before despatched his conciliatory gift to Esau, turned his back upon the Jabbok, having crossed to the south bank, if the previous night had been spent upon its north side, passed over the rising ground of Peniel (*vide* Tristram's ' Land of Israel,' p. 558), and advanced to meet his brother, richly laden with the heavenly blessing he had won in his mysterious conflict with Elohim, and to all appearance free from those paralysing fears which, previous to the midnight struggle, the prospect of meeting Esau had inspired. Having already prevailed with God, he had an inward assurance, begotten by the words of his celestial antagonist, that he would likewise prevail with man, and so he **lifted up his eyes** (*vide* on ch. xiii. 10), **and looked, and, behold, Esau came, and with him four hundred men** (*vide* ch. xxxii. 6). **And he** (*i. e.* Jacob) **divided the children unto Leah, and unto Rachel, and unto the two handmaids**, Bilhah and Zilpah, thus omitting no wise precaution to insure safety for at least a portion of his household, in case Esau should be still incensed and resolved on a hostile attack. **And he put the handmaids and their children foremost, and Leah and her children after, and Rachel and Joseph hindermost**, as being most beloved (Kalisch, Murphy, Lange, and others) or most beautiful (Bush).

Vers. 3, 4.—**And he** (the introduction of the pronoun giving emphasis to the statement) **passed over before them** (*i. e.* passed on in front of them, thus chivalrously putting himself in the place of danger), **and bowed himself to the ground**—not completely prostrating the body, as Abraham did in ch. xix. 1, but bending forward till the upper part of it became parallel with the ground, a mode of expressing deep reverence and respect, which may be seen to life in Oriental countries at the present day (Roberts, 'Oriental Illustrations,' p. 41)—**seven times** (not in immediate succession, but bowing and advancing), **until he came near to his brother.** The conduct of Jacob was dictated neither by artful hypocrisy nor by unmanly timidity; but by true politeness and a sincere desire to conciliate. **And** as such it was accepted by Esau, who **ran to meet him, and**, his better feelings kindling at the sight of his long-absent brother, **embraced him, and fell on his neck, and kissed him**—as Joseph afterwards did to Benjamin (ch. xlv. 14, 15), though the *puncta extraordinaria* of the Masorites over the word "kissed" seem to indicate either that in their judgment Esau was incapable of such fraternal affection (Delitzsch, Kalisch), or that the word was suspicious, Origen appearing not to have found it in his codices (Rosenmüller, Keil), unless indeed the conjecture be correct that the word was marked to draw attention to the power of God's grace in changing Esau's heart (Ainsworth). **And they wept** — the LXX. adding *both*. "All this is beautiful, natural, Oriental" ('Land and Book,' p. 372).

Ver. 5.—**And he** (*i. e.* Esau) **lifted up his eyes**,—corresponding to the act of Jacob (ver. 1), and expressive of surprise—**and saw the women and the children; and said, Who are those with thee?** (literally, *to thee*, i. e. whom thou hast). **And he** (Jacob) **said, The children which God** (Elohim ; *vide infra* on ver. 10) **hath graciously given**—the verb חָנַן being construed with a double accusative, as in Judges xxi. 22 ; Ps. cxix. 29 **thy servant.**

Vers. 6, 7.—**Then** (literally, *and*) **the handmaidens came near, they and their children** (since they occupied the front rank in the procession which followed Jacob), **and they bowed themselves** (after his example). **And Leah also with her children came near, and bowed themselves: and after came Joseph near and Rachel, and they bowed themselves.** The remark of Lange, that the six-year old lad who comes before his mother seems to break through all the cumbrous ceremonial, and to rush confidently into the arms of his uncle, is as fanciful and far-fetched as that of Jarchi, that Joseph took precedence of his mother because he feared lest Esau, who was a *homo profanus*, should be fascinated by his mother's beauty, and seek to do her wrong ; in which case he would try to hinder him.

Ver. 8.—**And he said, What** meanest **thou by all this drove**—literally, *What to thee all this camp* (Mahaneh)—**which I met?**—*i. e.* yesterday, referring to the droves which had been sent on by Jacob as a present to my lord Esau (ch. xxxii. 16). **And he said,** These are **to find grace in the sight of my lord** (*vide* ch. xxxii. 5).

Ver. 9.—**And Esau said, I have enough** (literally, *Here is to me abundance*), **my brother** (it is impossible not to admire the generous and affectionate disposition of Esau) ; **keep that thou hast unto thyself** (literally, *let be to thee what is to thee*, i. e. what belongs to thee).

Vers. 10, 11.—**And Jacob said, Nay, I pray thee, if now I have found grace in thy sight, then receive my present at my hand: for therefore**—פִּי־עַל־כֵּן, because (Gesenius, Rosenmüller, Quarry), or, for this purpose (Keil, Kalisch, Hengstenberg, Lange, Ewald. *Vide* ch. xviii. 5 ; xix. 8 ; xxxviii. 26)—**I have seen thy face, as though I had seen the face of God,**—literally, *as a vision of the face of Elohim*, in which language Jacob neither uses adulation towards his brother (Tostatius), nor calls him a god in the sense in which heathen potentates are styled deities (Vatablus, Arabic, Chaldee), nor simply uses a superlative expression to indicate the majesty (Menochius) or benevolence (Ainsworth) of Esau's countenance, nor signifies that he had recognised the person of Esau in the angel who contended with him at the Jabbok (Bush) ; but either that he had received from

Esau the same friendly welcome that one coming into God's presence would receive from him (Rosenmüller, Keil, Murphy, 'Speaker's Commentary'), or that he had come into Esau's presence with the same feelings of penitence as if he had been coming before God (Kalisch), or that, as he had already seen the face of God and his life was preserved, so now he had seen the face of Esau, and the anticipated destruction had not been inflicted on him (Quarry), either of which accords with the words that follow—**and thou wast pleased with me**—literally, *thou hast graciously received me*, the unexpressed thought being, as already I have been favourably accepted by Elohim. Hence Jacob with greater urgency renews his entreaty that Esau would not decline his proffered gift, saying, **Take, I pray thee, my blessing** (*i. e.* my present, the word signifying, as in 1 Sam. xxv. 27; xxx. 26; 2 Kings v. 15, a gift by which one seeks to express good - will) **that is brought to thee;**—or, which has been caused to come to thee, adding, as a special reason to induce him to accept—**because God hath dealt graciously with me,**—Elohim, it has been thought, is used here and in ver. 5 by Jacob instead of Jehovah, either " to avoid reminding Esau of the blessing of Jehovah which had occasioned his absence" (Delitzsch, Keil), or " because Jehovah was exalted far above the level of Esau's superficial religion" Hengstenberg) ; but it is just possible that by its employment Jacob only wished to acknowledge the Divine hand in the remarkable prosperity which had attended him in Haran—**and because I have enough**—literally, *there is to me all*, i. e. everything I can wish (Murphy), all things as the heir of the promise (Keil). The expression is stronger than that used by Esau (ver. 9), and is regarded by some (Ainsworth) as indicating a more contented spirit than that evinced by Esau. **And he urged him.** In Eastern countries the acceptance of a gift is equivalent to the striking of a covenant of friendship. If your present be received by your superior you may rely on his friendship ; if it be declined you have everything to fear. It was on this ground that Jacob was so urgent in pressing Esau to accept his present (cf. A. Clarke *in loco*). **And he took it**, and so gave Jacob an assurance of his complete reconciliation.

Ver. 12.—**And he** (*i. e.* Esau) said (in further token of his amity), **Let us take our journey, and let us go,** — but whether he intended to accompany Jacob on his way (Keil, Kalisch, *et alii*) or invited Jacob to go with him to Mount Seir (Ainsworth, Clericus) is uncertain. On the first hypothesis it is difficult to explain how Esau came to be travelling in the same direction as his

brother, while the adoption of the second will serve in some measure to elucidate Jacob's language in ver. 14. But whichever way the words of Esau are understood, they amounted to an offer to be an escort to Jacob through the desert regions with which his excursions had made him familiar, since he added, **and I will go before thee**—*i. e.* to lead the way.

Ver. 13.—**And he** (Jacob, politely declining Esau's society and protection, though apparently accepting his invitation to go to Mount Seir) **said unto him, My lord knoweth that the children** are tender (Joseph at this time being little over six years of age), **and the flocks and herds with young** (literally, *giving milk;* עָלוֹת, from עוּל, to give suck) are **with me,**—literally, *upon me*, i. e. are an object of my special care, because of their condition (Rosenmüller, Keil)—**and if men should over-drive them** — literally, *and they* (sc. the shepherds) *will over-drive them*, i. e. in order to keep pace with Esau's armed followers they must do so, and in that case, if they were to do so for only—**one day, all the flock** (literally, *and all the flock*) **will die.** Thomson says that Oriental shepherds gently lead along the mothers when in the condition spoken of by Jacob, knowing well that even one day's over-driving would be fatal to them, and, from the fact that Jacob's ewes were giving milk, infers that it was winter time, since then alone the flocks are in that condition—an inference which he further confirms by observing that at Succoth Jacob constructed booths for their protection ('Land and Book,' p. 205).

Ver. 14.—**Let my lord, I pray thee,**—it is perhaps too much to explain Jacob's obsequious and deferential address to his brother (my lord) as the sign of a guilty conscience (Kalisch, Alford), when possibly politeness and humility will suffice—**pass over**—not cross the Jordan (Alford), since Esau was not journeying to Canaan ; but simply pass on, as in ver. 3—**before his servant: and I will lead on softly** (literally, *I will go on at my slow pace*), **according as the cattle that goeth before me and the children be able to endure,**—literally, *according to the foot*, i. e. the pace, *of the property* (here, cattle), *and according to the foot of the children;* i. e. as fast as flocks and children can be made with safety to travel—**until I come unto my lord unto Seir.** It is apparent that Jacob at first intended to accept Esau's invitation to visit him at Seir, either immediately (Clericus, Kalisch), or, as is more probable, afterwards (Keil, Murphy, 'Speaker's Commentary '), though, if afterwards, the historian has preserved no record of any such journey, while, if presently such was his intention, he must have been providentially led, from some cause not mentioned, to alter his determination (Bush, Inglis, Clarke), unless we either think that he really went to Seir, though it is not here stated (Patrick), or entertain the, in the circumstances, almost incredible hypothesis that Jacob practised a deception on his generous brother in order to get rid of him, by promising what he never meant to fulfil, viz., to visit him at Mount Seir (Calvin), or leave it doubtful whether it is the old Jacob or the new Israel who speaks (Lange).

Ver. 15.—**And Esau said, Let me now leave** (literally, *set*, or *place*) **with thee** (as an escort or guard) some **of the folk**—*i. e.* armed followers (*vide* ver. 1)—**that are with me.** But of even this proposal Jacob appears to have been apprehensive. **And he said, What needeth it?** (literally, *For what*, or *wherefore, this?*) let me find grace in the sight of my lord—meaning either, I am satisfied, since thou art gracious to me (Vatablus), —ἱκανὸν, ὅτι εὖρον χάριν ἐναντίον σου, κύριε (LXX.); *hoc uno tantum indigeo, ut inveniam gratiam in conspectu tuo* (Vulgate),—or, be gracious to me in this also, and leave none of thy followers (Ainsworth, Patrick), though the two clauses might perhaps be connected thus : "Wherefore do I thus find grace in the eyes of my lord?" (Kalisch).

Vers. 16, 17.—**So** (literally, *and*, complying with his brother's request) **Esau returned that day on his way unto Seir**—from which he had come to meet Jacob (*vide* ch. xxxii. 3). **And Jacob journeyed to Succoth.** Succoth, so called here by anticipation, and afterwards belonging to the tribe of Gad, was situated in the valley of the Jordan, on the east side of the river, and to the south of the Jabbok (Josh. xiii. 27 ; Judges viii. 4, 5), and consequently is not to be identified with Sakût, on the western side of the Jordan, ten miles north of the Jabbok, and opposite the Wady Yâbis (Robinson, vol. iii. p. 175 ; Thomson, 'Land and Book,' p. 456) ; but is to be sought for at the ford opposite the Wady-el-Fariah, "down which the little stream from Shechem drains into the Jordan" (Tristram, 'Land of Israel,' p. 144 ; Porter in Kitto's 'Cyclop.,' art. Succoth ; cf. Keil and Kalisch *in loco*). **And built him an house.** This was an indication that Jacob purposed some considerable stay at Succoth ; and, indeed, if a period of repose was not now demanded by the state of Jacob's health after his long servitude with Laban, his exhausting conflict with the angel, and his exciting interview with Esau (Lange), an interval of some years appears to be imperatively required by the exigencies of the ensuing narrative concerning Dinah, who could not at this time have been much over six years

of age (Murphy, Alford, Gosman, *et alii*). **And made booths for his cattle.** Porter states that he has frequently seen such booths (Succoth, from *saccac*, to entwine) occupied by the Bedâwin of the Jordan valley, and describes them as rude huts of reeds, sometimes covered with long grass, and sometimes with a piece of tent (*vide* Kitto's 'Cyclop.,' *ut supra*). **Therefore the name of the place is called** (literally, *he called the name of the place*) **Succoth**—*i. e.* booths.

Ver. 18.—**And Jacob** (leaving Succoth) **came to Shalem**—the word שָׁלֵם, rendered by some expositors as here (LXX., Vulgate, Syriac, Luther, Calvin, Poole, Wordsworth), is better taken as an adverb signifying in peace or in safety (Onkelos, Saadias, Rashi, Dathius, Rosenmüller, Gesenius, Keil, Kalisch, *et alii*), meaning that Jacob was now sound in his limb (Jarchi) and safe in his person, being no more endangered by Esau (Gerundensis in Drusius), or that he had hitherto met with no misfortune, though soon to encounter one in the instance of Dinah (Patrick), or that the expectations of Jacob expressed in ch. xxviii. 21 (to which there is an obvious allusion) were now fulfilled (Keil)—**a city of Shechem**,—if Shalem be the name of the town, then probably Shechem is the name of the person referred to in ch. xxxiv. 2, viz., the son of Hamor the Hivite (Drusius, Poole) ; but if Shalem mean *incolumis*, then the present clause must be rendered "to the city of Shechem," the city being already built and named—**which is in the land of Canaan**,—Bush thinks that Jacob had originally contemplated entering Canaan from the south after rounding the Dead Sea, probably with a view to reach Beersheba, but that, after his interview with Esau, he suddenly altered his route, and entered Canaan directly by crossing the Jordan and driving up his flocks and herds to Shechem, the first halting-place of Abraham (*vide* ch. xii. 6), which may perhaps lend additional interest to, if they do not explain, the words that follow—**when he came from Padan-aram** (as Abraham previously had done) ; **and** (he) **pitched his tent before the city**—because he did not wish to come in contact with the inhabitants (Lyra), or because his flocks and herds could not find accommodation within the city walls (Murphy), or perhaps simply for convenience of pasturage (Patrick).

Ver. 19.—**And he bought a parcel of a field**,—literally, *the portion* (from a root signifying to divide) *of the field*—**where he had spread his tent**,—and in which he afterwards sank a well (cf. John iv. 6)—**at the hand of the children of Hamor, Shechem's father** (after whom the town was named, *ut supra*), **for an hundred pieces of money**—or kesitahs, the etymology of which is uncertain (Kalisch), though connected by some philologists (Gesenius, Fürst) with *kasat*, to weigh ; translated lambs (Onkelos, LXX., Vulgate), but believed to have been a certain weight now unknown (Michaelis, 'Suppl.,' p. 2207), or a piece of money of a definite value, perhaps the price of a lamb (Murphy), which, like the shekel, was used for purposes of commercial exchange by the patriarchs (Gesenius)—probably a coin stamped with the figure of a lamb (Bochart, Münter) ; but coined money does not appear to have been

of so great antiquity (Rosenmüller, Wordsworth, Alford).

Ver. 20.—**And he erected there an altar,** —as Abram his ancestor had done (ch. xii. 7)—**and called it**—not invoked upon it, *invocavit super illud* (Vulgate), ἐπεκαλήσατο (LXX.), but named it (Dathe, Rosenmüller, Keil, &c.)—**El-elohe-Israel**—*i. e.* God, the God of Israel ; meaning, he called it the altar of God, the God of Israel (Rosenmüller), or, reading *el* as a preposition, "To the God of Israel" (Quarry, p. 508).

HOMILETICS.

Vers. 1—20.—*Jacob and Esau, or the brothers reconciled.*   I. THE MEETING OF THE BROTHERS.   1. *The approach of Esau.* (1) Conscious of his greatness, being attended by 400 armed followers ; (2) thirsting for revenge, remembering the wrongs he had endured at Jacob's hands ; (3) longing to see his brother, from whom he had been parted now for upwards of twenty years.   It is probable that all three emotions—pride, anger, affection—swelled within the breast of my lord Esau, struggling to obtain the mastery.   Which of them should conquer another moment would decide.   2. *The advance of Jacob.* (1) With commendable caution, dividing his company into three several groups—first the handmaids and their boys, next Leah and her children, and last Rachel and Joseph ; (2) with rare chivalry, placing himself in front of the foremost, which may be placed to his account as a set-off against his supposed partiality to Rachel and Joseph ; (3) with profound respect, bowing and advancing seven times, with true Oriental politeness, until he came to Esau.   3. *The reconciliation of both.*   The conflict of emotions in the breast of Esau was brought to a decision by the sight of Jacob, which at once cast the balance on the side of fraternal affection.   Old memories of boyhood and home revived in the bosom of the stalwart hunter as he looked on his twin-brother, and, under the impulse of generous and noble feeling, he ran and embraced him, and fell on his neck and kissed him.   Nor was the heart of Jacob less susceptible of such tender emotion.   Reciprocating his manly brother's embrace, he too yielded to a rush of kindly sentiment, and they both wept.   What a study for a painter !   Cf. Jonathan and David (1 Sam. xx. 41), and the prodigal and his father (Luke xv. 20).

II. THE CONVERSE OF THE BROTHERS.   1. *Esau's inquiries and Jacob's answers.* (1) Esau asks about the women and the children in Jacob's train ; and Jacob, piously acknowledging the Divine hand that had surrounded him with so many precious objects of affection, instructs them to do obeisance to their kinsman, which with beautiful politeness, following his own courteous example, they do.   It bespeaks a devout heart when domestic as well as other blessings are traced to the all-bountiful Giver, a well-ordered home when its inmates imitate the good conduct of its head, and a fine sensibility when the claims of relatives to courtesy and kindness are recognised and honoured.   (2) Esau requests to be informed about the droves which he had met, and Jacob explains that he had sent them as a present to conciliate his favour.   At first declining with a praiseworthy magnanimity to deprive his brother of any of his hard-earned wealth, Esau is afterwards constrained to accept the proffered gift, on learning that Jacob would not otherwise be sure of his forgiveness and friendship.   .It is beautiful when brothers emulate each other in noble acts.   2. *Esau's invitations and Jacob's promise.*   It appears most satisfactory to understand Esau as soliciting his brother to accompany him to Seir, where for the time he was residing, and Jacob as engaging to drive on slowly after the roving chieftain, according as the tender age of his children and the condition of his flocks and herds would admit, with the view of ultimately paying him a visit in his mountain home ; but whether he fulfilled that promise now or afterwards, or at all, cannot be ascertained.   If he did not, we may rest satisfied that he had good reasons for breaking his word, which, alas, promise-breakers seldom have.   3. *Esau's offer and*

Jacob's declinature. Esau anxiously desires to leave a convoy of his troopers to assist his brother in the further prosecution of his journey; but Jacob with respectful firmness refused to accept of his kindness—perhaps because, being a man of peace, he did not care for the society of soldiers, but chiefly, we apprehend, because, having Jehovah as a guide, he did not need the help of roving buccaneers (cf. Ezra viii. 22).

III. THE PARTING OF THE BROTHERS.   1. *Esau returned unto Mount Seir.* (1) Immediately, that day; but (2) not as yet finally, since his ultimate withdrawal from the land of Canaan appears to have taken place at a subsequent period.   2. *Jacob journeyed to Succoth,* where he built himself a house, constructed booths for his cattle, and remained a considerable time, *afterwards moving up to Shechem,* where he (1) pitched his tent outside the city, for convenience or for safety; (2) purchased a field from the chief man of the place, honestly paying for his purchase, as became a just man; and (3) erected an altar, which he named El-elohe-Israel.

See here—1. The strength of fraternal affection.   2. The beauty of forgiveness and reconciliation.   3. The possibility of combining politeness and piety.   4. The power of kindness in disarming enmity and opposition.   5. The advantage of conference for promoting good understanding and exciting kindly feeling.   6. The tender care which the strong should exercise towards the weak.   7. The sad partings which Providence effects between friends.   8. The propriety of taking God with us on all our journeys.   9. The duty of affectionately remembering God's mercies.

HOMILIES BY VARIOUS AUTHORS.

Ch. xxxiii.—*The fruits of prayer.* The *"prince"* who has been lifted by the grace of God out of the humiliation of his fear and shame to the height of his favour at the throne of the Most High now reveals his princely power.   He takes captive Esau's heart; he blesses him in the name of God, he bestows his gifts upon him. Notice the *fruits of Divine discipline in the patriarch.*

I. THE THEOCRATIC FEELING IS ALIVE IN JACOB'S HEART.   He puts the handmaids first, Leah next, Rachel and Joseph hindermost.   He placed them in the order of his own affection; but it represented also the Divine order, for it was in Joseph that the kingdom of God was about to be especially manifested.   "I have seen thy face," he said to Esau, "as though I had seen the face of God."   He saw the favour of God going on before him, and like the sunshine it rested on the face of the enemy, and cast out the darkness and turned it into light.

II. Jacob's entire STEADFASTNESS AS A SERVANT OF GOD and believer in the covenant. Seen in his refusal to mingle his family and people with those of Esau.

III. SPECIAL GRACE MEETS THE TRUE SERVANT.   "*Succoth*" is better than "*Seir;*" and it is *on the way to "Shalem,"* peace.   There it is that the patriarch finds *rest,* and *builds an altar,* calling it "*El-elohe-Israel.*"   Not merely an *altar to God,* but to him who had *revealed himself* as the *faithful God,* the *God of Israel,* the *God of his people.*—R.

Ver. 12.—*Worldly companionship.*   "And he said, Let us take our journey, and let us go, and I will go before thee."   The offer probably made with kindly intention.   No sign of bitterness in Esau's feelings; but ignorance of the necessities of Jacob's march.   Jacob knew it was not possible with safety (cf. Ps. cxxxvii. 4; 1 Pet. iv. 4).   Reminds us of the attitude of many worldly persons towards Christians. "The carnal mind is enmity against God."   Yet worldly men may have sincere regard for Christian men; bear unconscious testimony to excellence of Christianity. And here a danger to Christians.   Let us journey together.   I like you; you are unselfish, trustworthy.   And why not?   Because in journeying with Esau he must be leader, or he would cease to be Esau.   The world's good-will does not mean a changed heart.   Without any pronounced dislike to higher aims, it shares them not, and knows not anything more real than earth.   There is a journey we all take in company: in the thousand ways in which men are dependent on each other; in the courtesies and good offices of life; in what belongs to our position as citizens or family men.   But in what constitutes the road of life—its stamp and direction, its motives and aims—no union. We have another Leader (Heb. xii. 2). The pillar of fire led Israelites not according to human judgment.

I. THIS DOES NOT IMPLY KEEPING ALOOF FROM MEN, OR FROM HUMAN INTERESTS. We are called to be the salt of the earth. It is an error to shrink from contact with the world as dangerous to us. This of old led to monasticism. But there may be a spiritual solitude even when living in the throng of a city. In secular matters refusing to take an interest in what occupies others (cf. Luke vi. 31), as if God had nothing to do with these ; or in spiritual things avoiding Christian intercourse with those who do not in all points agree with us ; or being engrossed with our own spiritual welfare, and turning away from all concern for the welfare of others (cf. 1 Cor. ix. 20—22).

II. IT DOES IMPLY A REAL CONSCIOUSNESS OF BEING REDEEMED, set free, bought with a price ; OF HAVING A DEFINITE WORK TO DO FOR GOD, WITH WHICH NOTHING MUST INTERFERE ; a real way to walk in, from which nothing must make us turn aside. And in order to this, watchfulness over self, that in seeking to help others we ourselves are not ensnared.

III. SOME WAYS IN WHICH THE WORLD IN ITS FRIENDSHIP TEMPTS CHRISTIANS. 1. By the plea, there is no harm in this or that. We must not think that all actions can be brought to an absolute standard of right and wrong. This is the spirit of legality, the spirit of bondage, and leads to partial service instead of entire dedication (cf. Luke xv. 29). Loyalty to Christ must direct the Christian's life ; desire not merely to avoid direct disobedience, but to use our time and powers for him who loved us and gave himself for us. 2. By the display of good feelings as the equivalent of Christian graces. Esau's kindliness and frankness are very attractive. Yet he was a "profane person ; " not because of his anger or any sinful act, but because he thought little of God's blessing. 3. By making Christians familiar with worldly aims and maxims, and thus insensibly blunting their spiritual aspirations. The way of safety is through prayer for the Holy Spirit's help, to maintain the consciousness of Christ's presence.—M.

EXPOSITION.

CHAPTER XXXIV.

Ver. 1.—**And Dinah the daughter of Leah, which she bare unto Jacob,**—if Dinah was born before Joseph (ch. xxx. 21) she was probably in her seventh year when Jacob reached Succoth (ch. xxxiii. 17) ; but it does not follow that she was only six or seven years of age when the incident about to be described occurred (Tuch, Bohlen). If Jacob stayed two years at Succoth and eight in Shechem (Petavius), and if, as is probable, his residence in Shechem terminated with his daughter's dishonour (Lange), and if, moreover, Joseph's sale into Egypt happened soon after (Hengstenberg), Dinah may at this time have been in her sixteenth or seventeenth year (Kurtz). Yet there is no reason why she should not have been younger, say between thirteen and fifteen (Keil, Lange, Kalisch, Murphy, et alii), since in the East females attain to puberty at the age of twelve, and sometimes earlier (Delitzsch)—**went out** —it is not implied that this was the first occasion on which Dinah left her mother's tent to mingle with the city maidens in Shechem : the expression is equivalent to "once upon a time she went out" (Hengstenberg)—**to see the daughters of the land** —who were gathered at a festive entertainment (Josephus, 'Ant.,' i. 21, 1), a not improbable supposition (Kurtz), though the language rather indicates the paying of a friendly visit (Lange), or the habitual practice of associating with the Shechemite women (Bush), in their social entertainments, if not in their religious festivals.

Ver. 2.—**And when Shechem the son of Hamor the Hivite, the prince of the country, saw her** (literally, *and Shechem . . . saw her, and*) **he took her.** "Dinah paid the full penalty of her carelessness. She suffered the fate which Sarah and Rebekah encountered in the land of Pharaoh and Abimelech ; she was seen and taken by the son of the prince" (Kalisch) ; forcibly, *i. e.* against her will in the first instance, though not, it is apparent, without the blandishments of a lover. **And lay with her, and defiled her**—literally, *oppressed her*, offered violence to her, whence humbled her—ἐταπεί-νωσεν (LXX.), *vi opprimens* (Vulgate).

Vers. 3, 4.—**And his soul clave** (*vide infra* on ver. 8) **unto Dinah the daughter of Jacob,** —it was in some degree an extenuation of the wickedness of Shechem that he did not cast off the victim of his violence and lust, but continued to regard her with affection—

and he loved the damsel,—on the use of *na'ar* for a youth of either sex *vide* ch. xxiv. 14—**and spake kindly unto the damsel**—literally, *spoke to the heart of the damsel*, ἐλάλησε κατὰ τὴν διάνοιαν τῆς παρθένου αὐτῇ (LXX.), *i. e.* addressed to her such words as were agreeable to her inclinations (cf. on the import of the phrase ch. 1. 21; Judges xix. 3; Isa. xl. 2; Hosea ii. 14), probably expressing his affection, and offering the reparation of honourable marriage, as may be legitimately inferred from what is next recorded of his behaviour. **And Shechem spake unto his father Hamor, saying, Get me this damsel to wife**—cf. the case of Samson (Judges xiv. 2).

Ver. 5.—**And Jacob heard**—most likely from some of Dinah's companions (Patrick), since she herself was still detained in Shechem's house (ver. 26)—**that he** (Hamor's son) **had defiled**—the verb here employed conveys the idea of rendering unclean (cf. vers. 13, 27; Numb. xix. 13; 2 Kings xxiii. 10; Ps. lxxix. 1; that in ver. 2 expresses the notion of violence)—**Dinah his daughter.** It was an aggravation of Shechem's wickedness that it was perpetrated not against any of Jacob's handmaids, but against his daughter. **Now** (literally, *and*) **his sons were with his cattle in the field**—perhaps that which he had lately purchased (ch. xxxiii. 19), or in some pasture ground more remote from the city. **And Jacob held his peace**—literally, *acted as one dumb*, i. e. maintained silence upon the painful subject, and took no measures to avenge Shechem's crime (cf. ch. xxiv. 21; 1 Sam. x. 27; 2 Sam. xiii. 22); either through sorrow (Ainsworth, Calvin), or through caution (Murphy, Lange), or through perplexity, as not knowing how to act (Kalisch), or as recognising the right of his sons by the same mother to have a voice in the settlement of so important a question (Kurtz, Gerlach), to which undoubtedly the next clause points—**until they were come**—literally, *until their coming.*

Ver. 6.—**And** (meantime) **Hamor the father of Shechem went out**—accompanied by Shechem (ver. 11)—**unto Jacob**—who was encamped in the outskirts of the city (ch. xxxiii. 18)—**to commune with him** concerning Dinah's marriage with his son.

Ver. 7.—**And the sons of Jacob** (*i. e.* Leah's children, Dinah's full brothers, for certain, though perhaps also her half brothers) **came out of the field when they heard it** (Jacob having probably sent them word): **and the men were grieved,**—literally, *grieved themselves*, or became pained with anger, the verb being the hithpael of עָצַב, to toil or labour with pain. The LXX. connect this with the preceding clause, ὡς δὲ ἤκουσαν, κατενύγησαν οἱ ἄνδρες, implying that they did not learn of their sister's seduction till

they came home—**and they were very wroth,**—literally, *it burned to them greatly* (cf. ch. xxxi. 36; 1 Sam. xv. 11; 2 Sam. xix. 43). Michaelis mentions an opinion still entertained in the East which explains the excessive indignation kindled in the breasts of Dinah's brothers, viz., that "in those countries it is thought that a brother is more dishonoured by the seduction of his sister than a man by the infidelity of his wife; for, say the Arabs, a man may divorce his wife, and then she is no longer his; while a sister and daughter remain always sister and daughter" (*vide* Kurtz, 'Hist. of Old Covenant,' § 82)—**because he** (*i. e.* Shechem)—**had wrought folly**—the term *folly* easily passes into the idea of wickedness of a shameful character (1 Sam. xxv. 25; 2 Sam. xiii. 12), since from the standpoint of Scripture sin is the height of unreason (Ps. lxxiv. 22; Jer. xvii. 11), and holiness the sublimest act of wisdom (Ps. cxi. 10; Prov. i. 4)—**in** (or against) **Israel**—the word, here applied for the first time to Jacob's household, afterwards became the usual national designation of Jacob's descendants; and the phrase here employed for the first time afterwards passed into a standing expression for acts done against the sacred character which belonged to Israel as a separated and covenanted community, especially for sins of the flesh (Deut. xxii. 21; Judges xx. 10; Jer. xxix. 23), but also for other crimes (Josh. vii. 15)—**in lying with Jacob's daughter.** The special wickedness of Shechem consisted in dishonouring a daughter of one who was the head of the theocratic line, and therefore under peculiar obligations to lead a holy life. **Which thing ought not to be done**—literally, *and so is it not done* (cf. ch. xxix. 26). Assigned to the historian ('Speaker's Commentary'), or to the hand of a late redactor (Davidson, Colenso, Alford), there is no reason why these words should not have been spoken by Jacob's sons (Keil, Murphy, and others) to indicate their sense of the new and higher morality that had come in with the name of Israel (Lange).

Vers. 8—10.—**And Hamor communed** (literally, *spake*) **with them** (*i. e.* the whole family, or Jacob and his sons), **saying, The soul of my son Shechem longeth for**—the root (חָשַׁק) signifies to join together, intrans., to be joined together, hence to cleave to another in love (cf. Deut. vii. 7, 10, 15; xxi. 11); of similar import to the word (דָּבַק) employed in ver. 3, which means to be devotedly attached to any one, as, *e. g.*, to God (Deut. x. 20), to a king (2 Sam. xx. 2), to a wife (1 Kings xi. 2)—**your daughter.** The words are addressed to Jacob's sons as well as Jacob himself, the brothers equally with the father being regarded as the natural guardians of a sister. **I pray you give her**

him to wife. The absence of any apology for Shechem's atrocious outrage against Dinah need not be regarded as indicating some measure of consent on the part of Dinah, but may be explained on the supposition that Hamor's proposal was considered by himself as a practical admission of his son's guilt. **And make ye marriages with us,**—literally, *contract affinity with us by marriage*, the verb *chathan* being spoken of the father-in-law (*chothen*), who makes the alliance (*vide* Fürst, 'Lex.,' *sub voce*)— **and give your daughters unto us,**—from this it has been inferred that Jacob had other daughters besides Dinah, which is not improbable (ch. xlvi. 7), but the words may not imply more than that Hamor thought he had—**and take our daughters unto you. And** (as an inducement to form this alliance) **ye shall dwell with us: and the land shall be before you; dwell and trade ye therein, and get you possessions therein**—*i. e.* he offers them the privilege of unrestricted movement throughout his dominions, with the right of establishing settlements, carrying on trade, and acquiring property.

Vers. 11, 12.—**And Shechem said unto her father and unto her brethren** (speaking with becoming deference and earnestness, and manifestly prompted by fervent and sincere love), **Let me find grace in your eyes,** —*i. e.* let my suit be accepted (*vide* ch. xxxiii. 15)—**and what ye shall say unto me I will give. Ask me never so much dowry and gift,**—literally, *multiply upon me exceedingly dowry and gift;* the dowry (*mohar*) being the price paid for a wife to her parents (cf. Exod. xxii. 16; 1 Sam. xviii. 25), and the gift (*mathan*) the presents given to the bride (Gesenius, Fürst, Rosenmüller, Gerlach, Alford); or the dowry being the bride's present, and the gift the wife's price (Michaelis, Keil, Murphy); or the dowry being given to the parents, and the gift to the kindred (Patrick); or the two being the same thing, viz., the compensation offered to the relatives of the bride (Lange)—**and I will give according as ye shall say unto me: but give** (or, and ye will give) **me the damsel to wife.**

Vers. 13—17.—**And the sons of Jacob** (manifestly without the knowledge of their father) **answered Shechem and Hamor his father deceitfully, and said,**—the object of the verb *said* is to be found in the next verse, "we cannot do this thing," the clause commencing "because" being parenthetical (Rosenmüller, Fürst), so that it is unnecessary either to take רַבֵּד in the unusual sense of *dolos struere* (Schultens, Gesenius, Keil), or to supply after *said* "with deceit" from the preceding clause (Onkelos, Ainsworth, Murphy, *et alii*)—**because he had defiled Dinah their sister** (to be taken parenthetically, as already explained): **and they said**

unto them (these words revert to the preceding verse), **We cannot do this thing, to give our sister to one that is uncircumcised** (*vide* ch. xvii. 11); **for that** were a **reproach unto us.** The ground on which they declined a matrimonial alliance with Shechem was good; their sin lay in advancing this simply as a pretext to enable them to wreak their unholy vengeance on Shechem and his innocent people. The treacherous character of their next proposal is difficult to be reconciled with any claim to humanity, far less to religion, on the part of Jacob's sons; so much so, that Jacob on his death-bed can offer no palliation for the atrocious cruelty to which it led (ch. xlix. 6, 7). **But in this** (*i. e.* under this condition) **will we consent unto you: If ye will be as we be, that every male of you be circumcised** (literally, *to have circumcision administered to you every male*); **then will we give our daughters unto you, and we will take your daughters to us** (*i. e.* to be our wives), **and we will dwell with you, and we will become one people.** This proposal was sinful, since (1) they had no right to offer the sign of God's covenant to a heathen people; (2) they had less right to employ it in ratification of a merely human agreement; and (3) they had least right of all to employ it in duplicity as a mask for their treachery. **But if ye will not hearken unto us, to be circumcised; then** (rather, *sc.* then we will not consent to your proposal, and) **we will take our daughter,**—who was still in Shechem's house (ver. 26)—**and we will be gone.**

Vers. 18, 19.—**And their words pleased** (literally, *were good in the eyes of*) **Hamor, and** (literally, *in the eyes of*) **Shechem, Hamor's son. And the young man deferred not** (*i. e.* delayed not) **to do the thing** (literally, *the word*, i. e. to submit to circumcision. This is stated here by anticipation), **because he had delight in Jacob's daughter: and he** was **more honourable**—literally, *more honoured*, doubtless because more worthy of regard (cf. 1 Chron. iv. 9)—**than all the house of his father.**

Vers. 20—23.—**And Hamor and Shechem his son came** (or went) **unto the gate of their city** (*vide* on ch. xix. 2; xxiii. 10), **and communed with** (or spake to) **the men of their city, saying, These men** (*i. e.* Jacob and his sons) **are peaceable with us** (literally, *peaceable are they with us*. This is the first argument employed by Hamor and Shechem to secure the consent of the citizens to the formation of an alliance with Jacob and his sons); **therefore let them dwell in the land, and trade therein;**—literally, *and they will dwell in the land, and trade in it* (*sc.* if you permit)—**for** (literally, *and*) **the land, behold, it is large enough**—literally, *broad of hands*, i. e. on both sides (cf. Isa.

xxxiii. 21 ; Ps. civ. 25)—**for them** (literally, *before them*, i. e. for them to wander about with their flocks and herds. This was the second argument employed by Hamor and his son) ; **let us take their daughters to us for wives, and let us give them our daughters. Only herein** (or under this condition) **will the men consent unto us for to dwell with us, to be one people, if every male among us be circumcised** (literally, *in the circumcising to or by us of every male*), **as they are circumcised.** After which statement of the indispensable condition of the alliance proposed, they advance as a third argument for its acceptance the material advantages which such an alliance would inevitably secure for them. **Shall not their cattle and their substance and every beast of theirs** (the *mikneh* refer to flocks and herds; the *behemah* to asses and camels) **be ours ?** —literally, *Shall not these* (be) *to us ?*—**only let us consent unto them, and they will dwell with us.**

Ver. 24. — **And unto Hamor and unto Shechem his son hearkened all that went out of the gate of his city.** The ready acquiescence of the Shechemites to the proposal of Jacob's sons has not unreasonably been regarded as a proof that they were already acquainted with circumcision as a social, if not religious, rite (Kurtz, Keil, &c.). **And every male was circumcised, all that went out of the gate of his city.** Knobel notes it as remarkable that the Hivites were not circumcised, since, according to Herodotus, the rite was observed among the Phenicians, and probably also the Canaanites, who were of the same extraction, and thinks that either the rite was not universally observed in any of these ancient nations where it was known, or that the Hivites were originally a different race from the Canaanites, and had not conformed to the customs of the land (*vide* Lange *in loco*). Murphy thinks the present instance may point out one way in which the custom spread from tribe to tribe.

Ver. 25.—**And it came to pass on the third day, when they were sore,**—literally, *in their being in pain;* ὃτε ἦσαν ἐν τῷ πόνῳ (LXX.). Inflammation and fever commonly set in on the third day, which was for that reason regarded as the critical day—**that two of the sons of Jacob, Simeon and Levi, Dinah's brethren** (*i. e.* sons of the same mother, Leah), **took each man his sword, and came upon the city**—accompanied by their servants (Keil), or their father's men (Murphy), but this is doubtful (Lange). That the other sons of Jacob and brethren of Dinah did not pursue their thirst for vengeance to the same extremity as Simeon and Levi seems apparent from ver. 27; yet it is quite possible that they joined with Simeon and Levi in the assault upon the city (Rosenmüller, 'Speaker's

Commentary') which they made—**boldly,**—i. e. either they themselves feeling confident of success because of the sickness which lay upon the inhabitants (Ainsworth, Dathe, Rosenmüller, Murphy, &c.), or, while the city was lulled into security in consequence of the treaty (Onkelos, Josephus, Keil, Lange), or perhaps referring only to the fact that they encountered no opposition, and came in safety (ἀσφαλῶς) to the city (LXX., Kalisch)—**and slew all the males.** Probably the town was small.

Ver. 26.—**And they slew Hamor and Shechem his son with the edge** (literally, *the mouth*) **of the sword,**—without excusing the inhuman barbarity of this remorseless massacre, Kurtz offers an elaborate and interesting analysis of the complex motive of which it was the outcome, in particular showing how in Jacob's sons that strange admixture of religious zeal and carnal passion, of lofty faith and low craft, existed which formed so large a portion of the character of the patriarch himself (*vide* ' Hist. of the Old Covenant,' vol. i. § 82)—**and took Dinah out of Shechem's house,**—in which up to this time she had been detained against her will (Alford), though this may be open to question (Kalisch)—**and went out.**

Vers. 27—29.—**The sons of Jacob**—not all except Simeon and Levi (Delitzsch), nor Simeon and Levi alone (Kalisch, Inglis), but Simeon and Levi along with the others (Rosenmüller, Keil, Lange)—**came upon the slain,**—the absence of the ‎ו conjunctive at the commencement of this verse, which partitionists account for by the hypothesis that vers. 27—29 are an interpolation, is explained by Keil as designed to express the subjective excitement and indignation of the historian at the revolting character of the crime he was narrating—**and spoiled the city, because they** (*i. e.* the inhabitants being regarded, on the well-known principle of the solidarity of nations, as involved in the crime of their ruler) **had defiled their sister,** and so exposed themselves to reprisals, in which **they** (*i. e.* the sons of Jacob) **took their sheep, and their oxen, and their asses, and that which** was **in the city, and that which** was **in the field, and all their wealth, and all their little ones,**—*taph,* a collective noun for boys and girls, who are so called from their brisk and tripping motion (Gesenius)—**and their wives took they captive, and spoiled even all that** was **in the house.** The words describe a complete sacking of the city, in which every house was swept of its inmates and its valuables.

Ver. 30.—**And Jacob said to Simeon and Levi, Ye have troubled me** (*i. e.* brought trouble upon me) **to make me to stink**—or, to cause me to become hateful ; μισητόν με πεποιήκατε (LXX.)—**among the inhabitants of the land, among the Canaanites and the**

Perizzites (*vide* ch. xiii. 7): **and I** (*sc.* with my attendants) being **few in number,**—literally, *men of number,* i. e. that can be easily numbered, a small band (cf. Deut. iv. 27; Ps. cv. 12; Jer. xliv. 28)—**they** (literally, *and they*) **shall gather themselves together against me, and slay me; and I shall be destroyed, I and my house.** That Jacob should have spoken to his sons only of his own danger, and not of their guilt, has been ascribed to his belief that this was the only motive which their carnal minds could understand (Keil, Gerlach); to a remembrance of his own deceitfulness, which disqualified him in a measure from being the censor of his sons (Kalisch, Wordsworth); to the lowered moral and spiritual tone of his own mind (Candlish, 'Speaker's Commentary'); to the circumstance that, having indulged his children in their youth, he was now afraid to reprove them (Inglis). That Jacob afterwards attained to a proper estimate of their bloody deed his last prophetic utterance reveals (ch. xlix. 5—7). By some it is supposed that he even now felt the crime in all its heinousness (Kalisch), though his reproach was somewhat leniently expressed in the word "trouble" (Lange); while others, believing Jacob's abhorrence of his sons' fanatical cruelty to have been deep and real, account for its omission by the historian on the ground that he aimed merely at showing "the protection of God (ch. xxxv. 5), through which Jacob escaped the evil consequences of their conduct" (Hengstenberg, Kurtz).

Ver. 31.—**And they said, Should he deal with our sister as with an harlot?** But Shechem offered Dinah honourable marriage.

HOMILETICS.

Vers. 1—31.—*The tragedy at Shechem.* I. DINAH AND SHECHEM. 1. *A young girl's indiscretion.* "Dinah went out to see the daughters of the land." If Dinah's object was to witness the manners of the people, she was guilty of objectionable curiosity; if to exhibit herself, of distressing vanity; if to mingle in their entertainments, of improper levity; and for all these reasons, considering the character of the family to which she belonged, and the wickedness of the people with whom she mingled, of exceedingly heinous sin. 2. *A young prince's wickedness.* Shechem saw her, and took her, and lay with her, and defiled her. The sin of Shechem had many aggravations. It was done by a prince, whose very rank should have preserved him from such degradation. Those whom God makes elevated in station should make themselves eminent in virtue. Goodness should always accompany greatness. Then it was done without the least excuse, since Shechem was at liberty by God's law and man's to have a wife whenever he desired. Again, it was done against a young and comparatively helpless girl whom circumstances had placed within his power. Further, it was done in violation of the laws of hospitality, which required him to protect, rather than to injure, a stranger's good name. And, lastly, it was done to one belonging to a family whose members were invested with a high degree of sanctity. Still the crime of Shechem was not without its extenuations. First, he loved the maiden whom he had dishonoured. Second, he offered the reparation of an honourable marriage. Third, he treated her with kindness while he detained her in his palace.

II. JACOB AND HIS SONS. 1. *The impression made on Jacob by Dinah's misfortune.* (1) He held his peace; in stupefaction, in sorrow, in meditation, in indecision. (2) He sent for his sons, who, as recognised guardians of their sister, were entitled to be consulted in all that concerned her welfare. 2. *The effect produced on Jacob's sons by their sister's shame.* (1) They were grieved for what had happened—for Dinah's, for their father's, for their own sake. (2) They were angry at its perpetrator; not so much, however, for the sin he had committed, as for the fact that he had committed it against Jacob's daughter.

III. JACOB'S SONS AND HAMOR'S SON. 1. *The honourable proposal of Shechem.* First through the medium of his father, and afterwards in his own person, he solicits Jacob and his sons to give him Dinah in marriage, and to enter in turn into matrimonial alliances with them, offering as an inducement unrestricted liberty to settle, trade, and acquire property in the land, and promising to pay whatever dowry or gift might be demanded for the damsel. 2. *The deceitful reply of Jacob's sons.* First they declared it impossible that Dinah should become the wife of one who was uncircumcised. Then they consented to the proposition on condition that Hamor, Shechem, and the Shechemites would submit to circumcision. And yet all the while it was only part of a deep-laid plot for exacting revenge.

IV. Hamor and the Shechemites. 1. *The condition prescribed by Jacob's sons explained.* This was done by the ruling sovereign and the crown prince in a public assembly convened at the city gate. 2. *The condition accepted by the Shechemites.* Trusting to the good faith of the Hebrew strangers, they assented to the proposition that all the male inhabitants should be circumcised, and in good faith it was carried out by both prince and people.

V. The sons of Jacob and the Shechemites. 1. *The massacre of the inhabitants by Dinah's brethren.* Three days after, when, in consequence of the painful operation to which they had submitted, the male part of the population was unable to stir in their defence, Simeon and Levi, confident of success in their nefarious deed, fell upon the unsuspecting city, and slew all the males. It was a heartless, ruthless, treacherous, diabolic massacre, fit to rank with the St. Bartholomews and Glencoes of modern times. 2. *The spoliation of the city by Jacob's sons.* If Simeon and Levi were alone responsible for the massacre, the sacking of the city was the work of all the brethren (Joseph and Benjamin doubtless excepted). Not only did they make captives of the wives and children, but they carried off every live thing they could find of any value; and not only did they ransack the houses, from the palace to the cottage, but they appear to have stripped even the very dead. The annals of uncivilised warfare scarcely record a more atrocious crime.

VI. Jacob and Dinah's brethren. 1. *The feeble reproof of Jacob.* He only complains that their cruel deed would cause his name to be abhorred in the land, and perhaps lead to their extermination as a people. For the different views that have been entertained of Jacob's words the Exposition may be consulted. 2. *The insufficient reply of Dinah's brethren.* Shechem certainly had wronged Dinah, but he never meant to treat her as a harlot.

Learn—1. The danger of unrestrained social intercourse between the Church and the world in general, and in particular between the daughters of the pious and the sons of the ungodly—exemplified in Dinah, who, going to see the daughters of the land, lost her fair fame, and brought trouble on her father's house. 2. The misery of yielding to unholy passion—illustrated in Shechem, whose unbridled lust bore bitter fruit to all concerned: to Dinah dishonour, to Jacob shame and sorrow, to Jacob's sons the thirst for revenge, to Hamor and the Shechemites as well as to himself overwhelming retribution. 3. The wickedness of which good men when left to themselves may be guilty—exhibited in the conduct of Jacob's sons, who in this lamentable affair were chargeable with treachery, sacrilege, murder, spoliation, oppression. 4. The possibility of the innocent suffering with and for the guilty—shown in the massacre of the Shechemites for the sin of Shechem. 5. The certainty that a man's worst foes are often those of his own household—of which the case of Jacob was a melancholy instance, whose name was more dishonoured by his sons' atrocities than by his daughter's misfortune.

HOMILIES BY VARIOUS AUTHORS.

Ch. xxxiv.—*Good out of evil.* The whole of this miserable story has its place in the development of the kingdom of God. No alliance can be true and safe which is not upon the foundation of the Divine covenants. Circumcision without faith is a mere carnal ordinance, working evil. The sin of Shechem was avenged, but it was avenged by the commission of a greater sin by Simeon and Levi. It was not thus that the kingdom of God was to be spread. "Ye have troubled me," Jacob said. And so have all worldly agencies and methods troubled the true Church. It is better to suffer at the hands of the wicked than to make compromising alliance with them. The worldly Church has filled the world with misery. Abuse of Divine things has been the source of innumerable evils, not only among the people of God, but even in the sphere of men's secular life. But notwithstanding the sin of Simeon and Levi, their prompt execution of the Divine judgment upon the sin of Shechem must have produced a wholesome fear in the country, and connected that fear with moral purity. The sins of unchastity and violation of family rights were monstrously prevalent among the heathen people of Canaan, and it was doubtless ordered that this outbreak of human passion should bear witness for God as the God of purity and the God of households, who blesses the life which is free from the defilement of sensual indulgence, and in which the bonds of relationship and virtuous marriages and the sanctities of home are deeply reverenced. We read afterwards (ch. xxxv. 5), "the terror of God was upon the cities that were round about them."—R.

Ver. 30.—*Anger unrestrained.* "And Jacob said to Simeon and Levi, Ye have troubled me." It was not merely the fear of retaliation by neighbouring tribes. He felt the act was wrong (ch. xlix. 5—7); God's blessing could not rest upon it (cf. Ps. xxxiv. 7); and he and his family were involved in that wrong (cf. Josh. vii. 13; 1 Cor. xii. 26). But was not the anger of Simeon and Levi just? No doubt there was cause, and no doubt a measure of righteous indignation. But (1) they thought more of the wrong against themselves than of the sin against God (ver. 31). (2) Their anger was unrestrained by mercy, or even by justice (ver. 25). (3) It led them into acts of sin—deceit, murder, robbery. (4) It was soiled by selfish gain (ver. 27). Anger may be right; but need of special watchfulness (Ephes. iv. 26). For under its influence the heart is not in a state fitted to judge; and much danger of self-deception, of mistaking a selfish for a godly anger.

I. A JUST CAUSE FOR ANGER DOES NOT EXCUSE ITS EXCESS. Anger may be called for (1) as a protest against wrong; (2) to deter others from wrong. But vengeance, retribution, belongs to God (Rom. xii. 19). He alone has the knowledge to apportion it, looking both to the past and to the future. But anger tempts to retaliation (Matt. v. 38). The wrong fills the mind. Our own errors and acts of wrong (cf. John viii. 7), and the plea, Thine anger brings harm to the innocent, are unheeded. The fact that there was cause for anger blinds to its real nature; for unrestrained anger is in truth an offering to self-love. The plea of zeal for right and of godly indignation may seem sincere; but "ye know not what manner of spirit ye are of."

II. A JUST CAUSE FOR ANGER DOES NOT EXCUSE WRONG-DOING. God's laws cannot be set aside. And he who takes on himself the office of judge should be especially watchful not to transgress (Ps. xxxvii. 3). To do wrong on the plea of doing God's work is to distrust his providential care (Rom. xii. 19—21). It is to do evil that good may come; a form of being drawn aside by our own lusts (cf. 1 Sam. xxiv. 7; xxvi. 9). Such acts of wrong are especially evil in Christians. They are "a city set on an hill." Men are ever ready to point to their errors as excusing their own. Men see and judge the act, but cannot estimate the provocation, or, it may be, the sorrow, for a hasty action.

III. WORKS DONE IN ANGER HINDER THE WORK OF THE CHURCH. That work is to draw men together in one (John xvii. 21). The power by which this is done is love. The love of Christ reflected in us (1 John iv. 7). Love wins men's hearts, reason only their minds. And the presence of anger hinders love; not merely in him against whom it is directed; like a stone thrown into still water, it disturbs its surface far and wide.

IV. THE POWER BY WHICH ANGER MUST BE CONTROLLED. Dwelling on the work and example of Christ. He bore all for us. Is not wrath rebuked in the presence of his patience? And if as a "strange work" we are constrained to indignation, must we not watch and pray that no selfish feeling may mingle with it; and, knowing in how many things we offend, that we be "slow to wrath," ready to forgive, and ever "looking unto Jesus"?—M.

EXPOSITION.

CHAPTER XXXV.

Ver. 1.—**And God**—Elohim. The employment of this name for the Deity throughout the present chapter has been deemed conclusive evidence that, with some Jehovistic alterations, it belongs to the fundamental document (Tuch, Bleek, Delitzsch, Kalisch, *et alii*); but the frequent allusions to ch. xxviii. 13—16, which by partitionists is almost universally assigned to the Jehovist, prove that both sections have proceeded from the same author, and that, "though the mention of the name is avoided, this chapter, there is no doubt, substantially relates to Jehovah" (Hengstenberg), while the name Elohim may simply indicate that Jacob's journey from Shechem was undertaken in obedience to a Divine intimation (Quarry)—said unto Jacob (shortly after the incidents recorded in the preceding chapter), Arise, go up to Bethel,—about thirty miles distant (ch. xii. 8 ; xiii. 3 ; xxviii. 19), to which, some thirty years previous, he had solemnly vowed to return (ch. xxviii. 22)—a vow which he appeared somewhat dilatory in performing, although its conditions had been exactly fulfilled (Keil, Kurtz, Kalisch, &c.) — and dwell there (the massacre of the Shechemites had obviously rendered longer residence in that neighbourhood unsafe): and make there an altar—this Jacob had substantially promised to do in his vow (vide ch. xxviii. 22) —unto God, that appeared unto thee—i. e. unto Jehovah (vide ch. xxviii. 13)—when thou fleddest from the face of Esau thy brother. The words contained an assurance that the same Divine arm which had shielded him against the enmity of Esau and the oppression of Laban would extend to him protection on his future way.

Vers. 2, 3.—Then Jacob said unto his household (i. e. those more immediately belonging to his family), and to all that were with him (referring probably to the captured Shechemites), Put away the strange gods—literally, the gods of the stranger, including most likely the teraphim of Laban, which Rachel still retained, and other objects of idolatrous worship, either brought by Jacob's servants from Mesopotamia, or adopted in Canaan, or perhaps possessed by the captives —that are among you, and be clean,—literally, cleanse yourselves. The word is that which afterwards describes the purifications of the law (Numb. xix. 11, 12 ; Levit. xiv. 4 ; xv. 13). Aben Ezra interprets it as meaning that they washed their bodies ; and Michaelis views the rite as a kind of baptism, signifying their adoption of the true religion of Jehovah—a quasi baptism of repentance, like that afterwards preached by John (vide 'Suppl.,' p. 1000) — and change your garments. The directions here given are very similar to those which were subsequently issued at Sinai (Exod. xix. 10), and were meant to symbolise a moral and spiritual purification of the mind and heart. And let us arise, and go to Bethel. "This is obviously not the first time Jacob acquainted his family with the vision at Bethel" (Inglis). And I will make there an altar unto God,—El is probably employed because of its proximity to and connection with Bethel, or house of El, and the intended contrast between the El of Bethel and the strange Elohim which Jacob's household were commanded to put away (cf. Quarry, p. 512)—who answered me in the day of my distress,—this seems to imply that Jacob prayed at Bethel before he slept, if it does not refer to his supplication before meeting,

Esau (ch. xxxii. 9)—and was with me in the way which I went. This language clearly looks back to Bethel (vide ch. xxviii. 20).

Ver. 4.—And they gave unto Jacob all the strange gods—Rosenmüller thinks these must have been many, since the historian would not otherwise have used the term כל —which were in their hand (i. e. which they possessed), and all their earrings which were in their ears;—i. e. those employed for purposes of idolatrous worship, which were often covered with allegorical figures and mysterious sentences, and supposed to be endowed with a talismanic virtue (Judges viii. 24 ; Isa. iii. 20 ; Hosea ii. 13)—and Jacob hid them—having probably first destroyed them, since they do not appear to have been ever after sought for or resumed by the parties who gave them up (Hughes) —under the oak which was by Shechem. Whether the oak, or terebinth, under which Abraham once pitched his tent (ch. xii. 6), that beneath whose shade Joshua afterwards erected his memorial pillar (Josh. xxiv. 26), the oak of the sorcerers (Judges ix. 37), and the oak of the pillar at Shechem (Judges ix. 6) were all the tree under which Jacob buried the images and earrings cannot with certainty be determined, though the probability is that they were.

Ver. 5.—And they journeyed (from Shechem, after the work of reformation just described) : and the terror of God—meaning not simply a great terror, as in ch. xxiii. 6 ; xxx. 8 (Dathe, Bush), but either a supernatural dread inspired by Elohim (Ainsworth, Clericus, Rosenmüller, Keil, Kalisch, and others), or a fear of Elohim, under whose care Jacob manifestly had been taken (Murphy, Quarry)—was upon the cities that were round about them,—literally, in their circuits, i. e. wherever they went—and they did not pursue after the sons of Jacob—as might have been expected.

Ver. 6.—So (literally, and) Jacob came to Luz (vide ch. xxviii. 19), which is in the land of Canaan (this clause is added to draw attention to the fact that Jacob had now accomplished his return to Canaan), that is, Bethel, he and all the people that were with him—i. e. his household and the captured Shechemites.

Ver. 7.—And he built there an altar,—thus redeeming his vow (cf. Eccles. v. 4)—and called the place El-beth-el :—i. e. God of Bethel. Not he called the place of God, or the place sacred to God, Bethel (Michaelis, 'Suppl.,' p. 2174), nor he called the altar (Keil, Kalisch, Gerlach, &c.), but he called the place where the altar was El-beth-el ; i. e. either he devoted the place as sacred to the El of Bethel (Rosenmüller), or he gave to the place the name of (sc. the place of) the El of Bethel, reading the first El as a genitive (Lange) ; or he called it El-Beth-el metaphorically, as Jerusalem afterwards was styled Jehovah Tsidkenu (Jer. xxxiii. 16) and Jehovah Shammah (Ezek. xlviii. 35 ; Inglis). It has been proposed, after the LXX., to avoid the seeming incongruity of assigning such a name to a place, to read, he invoked upon the place the El of Bethel (Quarry, p. 513)—**because there God appeared unto him,**—the El of Bethel was Jehovah (*vide* ch. xxviii. 13 ; xxxi. 13)— **when he fled from the face of his brother.**

Ver. 8.—**But Deborah**—Bee (Gesenius, Fürst) **Rebekah's nurse** (*vide* ch. xxiv. 59) **died**—at a very advanced age, having left Padan-aram for Canaan along with Rebekah, upwards of 150 years ago. That she is now found in Jacob's household may be accounted for by supposing that Rebekah had sent her, in accordance with the promise of ch. xxvii. 45 (Delitzsch) ; or that Jacob had paid a visit to his father at Hebron, and brought her back with him to Shechem, probably because of Rebekah's death (Lange) ; or that on Rebekah's death she had been transferred to Jacob's household (Keil, Murphy, Alford) ; or that Isaac, "who had during the twenty years of his son's absence wandered in different parts of the land" (?), had "at this period of his migrations come into the neighbourhood of Bethel" (Kalisch). **And she was buried beneath Bethel**—which was situated in the hill country, whence Jacob is instructed to "go up" to Bethel (ver. 1)— **under an oak.** More correctly, the oak or terebinth, *i. e.* the well-known tree, which long after served to mark her last resting-place, which some have without reason identified with the palm tree of Deborah the prophetess (Judges iv. 5), and the oak of Tabor mentioned in 1 Sam. x. 3 (Delitzsch, Kurtz, &c.). **And the name of it was called** —not "he," *i. e.* Jacob, "called it" (Ainsworth), but "one called its name," *i. e.* its name was called (Kalisch)—**Allon-bachuth** (*i. e.* the oak of weeping).

Vers. 9, 10.—And God appeared unto Jacob again,—this was a visible manifestation, in contrast to the audible one in Shechem (ver. 1), and in a state of wakefulness (ver. 13), as distinguished from the dream vision formerly beheld at Bethel (ch. xxviii. 12)— **when he came** (or had come) **out of Padan-aram** (as previously he had appeared to the patriarch on going into Padan-aram), **and blessed him**—*i. e.* renewed the promises of the covenant, of which he was the heir. **And God said unto him, Thy name is Jacob :** —or Supplanter (*vide* ch. xxv. 26). Lange reads, Is thy name Jacob ?—**thy name shall not be called any more Jacob, but Israel** (*vide* ch. xxxii. 28) **shall be thy name : and he called his name Israel.** The renewal of

the name given at Peniel may possibly indicate a revival in the spiritual life of Jacob, which had been declining in the interval between the former interview with God and the present (Murphy), but was probably designed as a confirmation of the former interview with God, and of the experience through which he then passed. Cf. the twice - given name of Peter (John i. 42 ; Matt. xvi. 16—19).

Vers. 11, 12.—**And God said unto him** (repeating substantially the promises made to Abraham), **I am God Almighty :**—El Shaddai (cf. ch. xvii. 1)—**be fruitful and multiply ;**—" Abraham and Isaac had each only one son of promise ; but now the time of increase was come" (Murphy ; cf. ch. i. 28) —**a nation and a company of nations shall be of thee** (cf. ch. xvii. 5 ; xxviii. 3), **and kings shall come out of thy loins** (cf. ch. xvii. 6, 16) ; **and the land which I gave Abraham and Isaac** (*vide* ch. xii. 7 ; xiii. 15 ; xxvi. 3, 4), **to thee I will give it** (cf. ch. xxviii. 13), **and to thy seed after thee will I give the land.** The time of their entering on possession was specified to Abraham (ch. xv. 16).

Ver. 13.—**And God went up from him**— showing this to have been a visible manifestation (cf. ch. xvii. 22)—**in the place where he talked with him.**

Ver. 14.—**And Jacob set up a pillar**—the former pillar (ch. xxviii. 18) having probably fallen down and disappeared—**in the place where he** (God) **talked with him** (to commemorate the interview), even **a pillar of stone.** The setting up of pillars, according to Tuch a peculiarity of the Elohist, appears to have been a favourite practice of Jacob's : witness the first pillar at Bethel (ch. xxviii. 18), the pillar on Galeed (ch. xxxi. 45), the second pillar at Bethel (ch. xxxv. 14), the pillar over Rachel's grave (ch. xxxv. 20). **And he poured a drink offering thereon.** This is the first mention of those sacrificial libations which afterwards became so prominent in connection with the Mosaic ritual (Exod. xxix. 40, 41 ; Levit. xxiii. 13, 18, 37 ; Numb. vi. 15 ; and elsewhere). Under the law the נֶסֶךְ —σπονδεῖον, σπονδή (LXX.) *libamentum, libamen* (Vulgate) ; frankopfer (Luther)—consisted of a fourth part of a hin of wine, which was equal to about a third of a gallon. **And he poured oil thereon**—as he did on the previous occasion (ch. xxviii. 18, *q. v.*).

Ver. 15.—**And Jacob called the name of the place where God spake with him, Bethel.** This name was first given after the dream vision of the ladder (ch. xxviii. 19) ; already on this occasion it had been changed into El-beth-el (ver. 7) ; now its old name is reimposed.

HOMILETICS.

Vers. 1—15.—*Bethel revisited.* I. JACOB'S JOURNEY TO BETHEL. 1.. The *occasion* of the journey. The crime of his sons had made it necessary that Jacob should leave Shechem and its neighbourhood; but it is doubtful if in the circumstances Jacob would have thought of going to Bethel without an express invitation from Heaven, which, however, he got. ? The *object* of the journey. This was stated by the Divine communication which Jacob received to be the fulfilment of the vow which twenty years before he had made to erect an altar on the spot where he enjoyed the vision of the ladder and the angels. Vows do not lose their obligatory character by lapse of years. Men may, but God never does, forget the promises which are made to him. Hence the counsel of the Preacher (Eccles. v. 4, 5). 3. The *preparation* for the journey. The removal of the strange gods—(1) Was needful if God was to be sincerely worshipped by Jacob and his household. The necessity of having no other gods but Jehovah was afterwards enjoined upon Israel as a nation. In the gospel the law is equally imperative. God and Christ demand the undivided homage of the human heart. (2) Was counselled by Jacob to his household. It is well when heads of families have the ability as well as inclination to direct their children and dependents in the duties of religion. (3) Was cheerfully assented to by Jacob's household. The silver and wooden images (the teraphim) that Rachel had abstracted from her father's tent, the idolatrous objects that the Shechemites may have brought with them, and the earrings that were in their ears, were at once and completely given up, and by Jacob's own hand buried beneath the oak of Shechem. (4) Was symbolised in Jacob's household by the acts of washing and putting on of clean apparel. Under the law corporeal ablutions and beautified habiliments were typical of spiritual renovation and the putting on of the righteousness of the saints (cf. Ezek. xxxvi. 25; Heb. x. 22; Jude 23; Rev. xix. 2). 4. The *experience* of the journey. Wherever the travellers went they found themselves unmolested, and the cities round about them alarmed, and afraid to pursue. The terror of Elohim was upon the people of the land, and thus the care of Jehovah was around his saints. 5. The *completion* of the journey. Jacob and all the people that were with him came to Luz in the land of Canaan, which is Bethel. Many journeys are begun that never end. Some that promise well at the outset are overwhelmed in disaster before they terminate. It is only he who keeps Israel that can preserve a good man's going out and coming in.

II. JACOB'S RESIDENCE AT BETHEL. 1. *The building of an altar.* This was on the part of Jacob (1) an act of obedience, since it was done in accordance with Divine instructions (ver. 1); (2) an act of justice, inasmuch as it was executed in fulfilment of a vow (ch. xxviii. 22); (3) an act of gratitude, being designed to give expression to Jacob's thankfulness for God's mercies (vers. 3, 7). 2. *The death of Deborah.* (1) Her life-work: Rebekah's nurse. (2) Her death: this must have taken place at an advanced age. (3) Her burial: the place of sepulture was on the slope of Bethel hill, beneath the shadow of a wide-spreading oak. (4) Her memorial: the tree was named Allon-bachuth, oak of weeping. 3. *The appearance of Elohim.* (1) The blessing renewed (ver. 9;) (2) the new name confirmed (ver. 10); (3) the promises repeated (ver. 11). 4. *The erection of a pillar.* The old column having probably been thrown down, this was (1) set up as a memorial of the interview with God which had just been enjoyed; (2) employed as an altar for the worship of Elohim—"he poured a drink offering thereon;" and (3) consecrated as an object of reverential regard by pouring oil thereon. 5. *The renaming of the place.* The name given twenty years previously is renewed, Bethel (ver. 15), with a slight modification, El-Bethel (ver. 7), to connect it with the altar just erected.

Learn—1. That good men sometimes require to be reminded by God of their duty. 2. That acts of Divine worship should be preceded by heart purification and life reformation. 3. That God is perfectly able to protect his people when they are walking in his appointed paths. 4. That good men when serving God are not exempt from the afflictions of life. 5. That faithful servants should be tenderly cherished by their masters when old, decently buried when dead, and lovingly remembered when entombed. 6. That God never forgets either his promises or his people. 7. That God should not be forgotten by those whom he remembers.

HOMILIES BY VARIOUS AUTHORS.

Vers. 1—15.—*God with us.* Jacob's settlement with his family at Bethel. This was a solemn renewal of the covenant to the patriarch at the end of his pilgrimage. It was the occasion for a new dedication of himself and his household by vows and offerings, and by separation of themselves from all heathen things and thoughts around the newly-erected altar *El-Bethel.*

I. REVELATION the basis of faith. God went up from him after he had spoken with him, and there he set up a pillar of stone, and poured a drink offering thereon, and he poured oil thereon.

II. PERSONAL EXPERIENCE the background of a consecrated life. We should make the *memory of God's goodness* the foundation on which we build up the monuments of our life. Mark the places by offerings. Let the Bethel of our worship be the Bethel of his praise.—R.

Vers. 1, 2.—*Spiritual renovation.* Spiritual life is a thing of growth; never finished here (Phil. iii. 13; Heb. vi. 1). No doubt the all-important question is, Art thou in Christ? And in every Christian life there is a point, known to God, when the soul passes from death to life (1 John v. 12). For by nature children of wrath. Still there is a life's work. The spirit may have chosen Christ; but the flesh is weak, and the law of sin still works. Most commonly in such a life certain times will stand out, connected with special lessons and special dealings, when some window of the soul has been opened to heavenly light, some line of action pressed upon the mind.

I. THE LESSON LEARNED BY JACOB HIMSELF. We know not when his spiritual life began. Probably before he left home; for with all his faults he desired a spiritual blessing. But at Bethel and Penuel great steps were made. He learned the presence of God, and the protecting care of God, as he had never known them before. Yet the lessons were chiefly subjective; they regarded his own attitude towards God. And this generally comes first, but it is not all. "Arise, go up to Bethel." Take up again the lesson book. Is there not more to be learned from it? Those angels ascending and descending, were they charged with thy good only? The Lord who stood above, did he care only for thee? With all thy possessions thou art in "a solitary way" (Ps. cvii. 4). Here Jacob seems first to realise his responsibility for the spiritual state of others (cf. Ps. cxix. 136). The Christian character is not thoroughly formed till it is felt that the possession of truth binds us to use it for the good of others. Being "bought with a price," we are debtors to all (Rom. i. 14); and chiefly to those with whom we are connected (1 Tim. v. 8).

II. THE WORK HE TOOK IN HAND. To press upon his household—1. Single-hearted service of God. "Put away the strange gods." Sincerity lies at the root of all real renovation. Hitherto the semi-idolatry of teraphim seems to have been tacitly allowed. Jacob's fondness for Rachel may have kept him from forbidding it. Hence a divided service (2 Kings xvii. 33; Mark vii. 7). Putting away does not refer only to formal worship. It is putting away service of the god of this world: covetousness (Col. iii. 5), worldly aims (John v. 44), gratification of self (Luke xii. 19; xiv. 11), traditional maxims of conduct and judgment (Mark iii. 21; 1 Pet. iv. 4). It is seeking first the kingdom of God, and resting in him (Ps. xxxvii. 5). 2. "Be clean." No toleration of evil (Matt. v. 48). Christians are to be a holy people (1 Pet. ii. 9). This is much more than a mere upright and honourable life. The Levitical rules, strict and minute as they were, faintly shadowed the extent of the law of righteousness. See the Sermon on the Mount. Vast difference between an upright life and a holy life. The one is a following of rules, the other a walk with God. 3. "Change your garments." Under the law this a necessary part of purification. Contrast the garments, Ps. cix. 18 and Isa. lxi. 10. The explanation, Zech. iii. 4. In New Testament language, "put on Christ." The root is atonement, the covering of sins (Ps. xxxii. 1), the forgiveness of the sinful (Rom. iii. 26). No real renovation without this change—casting away self-righteousness, and clinging to the work of Christ (Jer. xxiii. 6 ; Rom. x. 4). Many have said trust in free grace points to sin. God's word from end to end declares it is the only way of holiness.—M.

Ver. 2.—*Jacob's preparation for acceptable worship.* "Put away the strange gods that are among you, and be ye clean, and change your garments: and let us arise, and go up to Bethel." "When thou vowest a vow, defer not to pay it," says Ecclesiastes (ch. v. 4); but Jacob had deferred. He made a vow at Bethel, and he seems afterwards to have ignored it. If he thought of it, a number of things had been ever ready to present themselves as excuses for delay. His faithful services given constantly to Laban, his efforts to make good his position in the land, and then to avert the anger of Esau, had apparently absorbed so much of his attention that he had forgotten his vows. These solemn promises had been made at a very critical period of his life, and God had not forgotten them. He reminds Jacob of them in a very emphatic manner. Jacob had failed to see in the circumstances in which he was placed with respect to the people among whom he dwelt that there was a hint of neglected duty. God permitted Jacob to be made uncomfortable that he might be made considerate. The way in which his sons had treated the Shechemites had brought him into great danger. He and all his were likely to be cut off by these enraged inhabitants of the land. He is reminded of the danger in which he was once placed from the vengeance of Esau. The similarity of the circumstances forcibly and very naturally turn his thoughts to the One who alone can be his defence. Thus circumstances and Divine communications impel to the performance of duty. How merciful is God in his treatment of souls ! how he leads the wanderer back to duty ! Jacob, when about to strike his tents and remove to Bethel, wishes that his sons and servants should go up with him, and that they should go up in the right spirit. He therefore says to them, " Put away the strange gods," &c.

I. NEGLECTED DUTY IS A HINDRANCE TO APPROPRIATE AND ACCEPTABLE WORSHIP. That Jacob should have been obliged to give such an injunction to his household shows that he had not sufficiently kept before his sons and servants the duty they owed to God. He had allowed himself to strive for worldly success until they might have even imagined that he was no better than the rest of them or their neighbours ; but deep down in the heart of this man was a reverence for God and a desire to do his will. His neglect to carefully instruct his sons had borne bitter fruit. Had he instilled into his sons more in accordance with the character of the God he served, they would not have taken such mean methods as are mentioned of revenging themselves on those they had come to dislike. His neglect necessitates the sudden and difficult effort now put forth to induce his sons to seek with him to serve God. He feels that he cannot rightly worship God unless his children and household are with him in spirit. He wishes to foster in them a belief in his own sincerity. To have one in a family looking on indifferently or sneeringly is death to successful worship. Jacob's neglect had led to carelessness by his sons of the Divine service. He could not himself enter heartily on the service until he had discharged, in a measure, his duty as guide and instructor to his family.

II. ANOTHER HINDRANCE IS THE ATTACHMENT TO OBJECTS WRONGLY HELD IN REVERENCE. The sons of Jacob had admitted false gods into their affections. Idolatry was rife among them. Even his wife Rachel had so much faith in her father's idols that she stole them when she left home. The sons caught the spirit of the mother, and indulged in the worship of strange gods. Perhaps they worshipped secretly the gods which Rachel cherished, or they may have given adoration to the idols they found among the spoils of the Shechemites. They may have had little images which they carried about with them, as many superstitious Christians carry the crucifix. Amulets and charms they seem to have worn on their hands and in their ears, all indicating superstition, false worship, and wrong ideas. God is spoken of in the Bible as " jealous." This is with respect to worship given to representations of gods having no existence. The jealousy is right, because it would be an evil thing for man himself to think there were many gods, or to select his own god. When, in after ages, the descendants of these sons of Jacob yielded to the sin of worshipping other gods, ten of the tribes were swept away, and have never been rediscovered. Indeed the stream was tainted in source, and " grew no purer as it rolled along." When Achan brought the Babylonish garment into the camp of Israel, the chosen of God could not stand before their enemies, but when it was removed they were again victorious. So strange gods must be removed from our homes and from our hearts, or we can never be successful in the conflict against sin, or in the acceptability of the worship we offer. It is for each Christian to search his soul, and to see whether there is any desire, habit, or practice which in the least militates against the worship of God. Many who were incorporated with Jacob's household were Syrians, who brought their evil practices with them. When any enter God's Church they must leave behind them the practices of the world; nor possessions nor position must be the gods then worshipped. " If any man love the world, the love of the Father is not in him."

III. The harbouring of any special sin will be a sure hindrance. The sons of Jacob had not only outward false objects of reverence, but inward evil propensities. They were treacherous, cruel, lustful, envious, murderous. See how they treated the Shechemites, and in after years their own brother Joseph. What scandalising, jealousy, and even opposition, are found in some homes! How hard it is to alienate sinful habits from the heart and the home! how hard to get the right tone for devout service in the home! Certain habits of temper, ridicule, sarcasm will chill and check all worship. Jacob urged his sons to be " clean,"—pure,—" to change their garments." They had need to do the latter, for they had been spotted with the blood of the men they had murdered. Jacob meant that they were to put on the garments kept for the worship of God. Rebekah had garments by her in which Esau as eldest son worshipped God, and which she put on Jacob. It is probable that it was the practice under the patriarchal dispensation to perform certain ceremonial ablutions prior to entering on the solemn worship. " Cleanliness is next to godliness." It leads to it. The need of purity in the worship of God is thus indicated by ablutions and change of garments. But how easily we may have the outward without the inward. We need cleansing in the holy fountain opened by Christ, and to be clothed by his righteousness.

IV. A great hindrance to successful worship is having low ideas of the dignity of the act, and the majesty and holiness of him whom we worship. God must be made to appear great to us. He is " high and lifted up." He made not only these frames of ours, but this vast universe. He is worshipped by worlds of intelligent spirits, and has been worshipped from the depths of eternity. He is holy and full of majesty. Shall we be indifferent as to the duty or the mode of worship? What a marvel that we should be permitted to have fellowship with our Creator! If we have it, it must be in the way and place he appoints. For Jacob it was at Bethel, for the Jews at Jerusalem, for Christians at the cross. To Jacob and the Jews it was by annual sacrifices, to us it is by the offering of Christ " once for all."—H.

EXPOSITION.

Ver. 16.—**And they journeyed**—not in opposition to the Divine commandment (ver. 1), which did not enjoin a permanent settlement at Bethel, but in accordance probably with his own desire, if not also Heaven's counsel, to proceed to Mamre to visit Isaac—**from Bethel** (southwards in the direction of Hebron); **and there was but a little way** (literally, *there was yet a space of land;* probably a few furlongs (Murphy), about four English miles (Gerlach). The Vulgate translates, "in the spring-time," and the LXX. render, ἐγένετο δὲ ἡνίκα ἤγγισεν εἰς χαβραθὰ, both of which are misunderstandings of the original —**to come to Ephrath**:—Fruitful; the ancient name of Bethlehem (*vide infra,* ver. 19)—

and **Rachel travailed, and she had hard labour**—literally, *she had hard labour in her parturition,* which was perhaps all the more severe that sixteen or seventeen years had elapsed since her first son, Joseph, was born.

Ver. 17.—**And it came to pass, when she was in hard labour** (literally, *in her labouring hard in her parturition*), **that the midwife said unto her, Fear not; thou shalt have this son also**—literally, *for also this to thee a son;* meaning either that she would certainly have strength to bring forth another son, or, what is more probable, that the child was already born, and that it was a son.

Ver. 18.—**And it came to pass, as her soul was in departing,**—literally, *in the depart-*

ing of her soul; not into annihilation, but into another (a disembodied) state of existence (*vide* ch. xxv. 8)—**for she died** (a pathetic commentary on ch. xxx. 1), **that she called his name Ben-oni** (" son of my sorrow," as a memorial of her anguish in bearing him, and of her death because of him): **but his father called him Benjamin**—" son of my right hand; " either " the son of my strength " (Clericus, Rosenmüller, Murphy), or " the son of my happiness or good fortune " (Gesenius, Keil, Kalisch), with allusion to Jacob's now possessing twelve sons; or as expressive of Jacob's unwillingness to see a bad omen in the birth of Rachel's child (Candlish); or " the son of my days," *i. e.* of my old age (Samaritan), an interpretation which Lange passes with a mere allusion, but which Kalisch justly pronounces not so absurd as is often asserted (cf. ch. xliv. 20); or " the son of my affection " (Ainsworth; cf. ch. lxxx. 18).

Ver. 19. — **And Rachel died, and was buried in the way to Ephrath, which** is Bethlehem—or House of Bread, about seven miles south of Jerusalem. It afterwards became the birthplace of David (1 Sam. xvi. 18) and of Christ (Matt. ii. 1). The assertion that this clause is a later interpolation (Lange) is unfounded (Kalisch, Kurtz).

Ver. 20.—**And Jacob set a pillar upon her grave** (*vide* on ver. 14): **that is the pillar of Rachel's grave unto this day**—*i. e.* unto the times of Moses ; but the site of Rachel's sepulchre was known so late as the age of Samuel (1 Sam. x. 2); and there seems no reason to question the tradition which from the fourth century has placed it within the Turkish chapel Kubbet Rachil, about half-an-hour's journey north of Bethlehem (Robinson, vol. i. p. 322 ; Tristram, ' Land of Israel,' p. 404; Thomson, ' Land and Book,' p. 644; Stanley, ' Sinai and Palestine,' p. 149).

Ver. 21.—**And Israel** (or Jacob) **journeyed** (from Ephrath, after the funeral of Rachel), **and spread**—*i. e.* unfolded (ch. xii. 8; xxvi. 25)—**his tent beyond the tower of Edar**—literally, *to,* i. e. not *trans* (Vulgate), ultra (Dathe), but *ad,* usque (Rosenmüller), as far as Migdol Edar, the Tower of the Flock —probably a turret, or watch-tower, erected for the convenience of shepherds in guarding their flocks (2 Kings xviii. 8 ; 2 Chron. xxvi. 10 ; xxvii. 4),—the site of which is uncertain, but which is commonly supposed to have been a mile (Jerome) or more south of Bethlehem. The LXX. omit this verse.

Ver. 22.—**And it came to pass, when Israel dwelt in that land, that Reuben went and lay with Bilhah his father's concubine :**—an act of incest (Levit. xviii. 8) for which he

was afterwards disinherited (ch. xlix. 4 ; 1 Chron. v. 1) — **and Israel heard it.** The hiatus in the text and the break in the MS. at this point may both have been designed to express Jacob's grief at the tidings. The LXX. add feebly καὶ πονηρὸν ἐφάνη ἐναντίον αὐτοῦ, which surely fails to represent the mingled shame and sorrow, indignation and horror, with which his eldest son's wickedness must have filled him. **Now the sons of Jacob were twelve**—a separate verse in the LXX., which is certainly more in accordance with the sense than the division in the text.

Vers. 23—26.—**The sons of Leah; Reuben, Jacob's firstborn, and Simeon, and Levi, and Judah, and Issachar, and Zebulun** (cf. ch. xxix. 32—35 ; xxx. 18—20 ; xlvi. 8—15 ; Exod. i. 2, 3). **The sons of Rachel; Joseph, and Benjamin** (cf. ch. xxx. 22—24 ; xxxv. 18 ; xlvi. 19). **And the sons of Bilhah, Rachel's handmaid; Dan, and Naphtali** (cf. ch. xxx. 4—8). **And the sons of Zilpah, Leah's handmaid; Gad, and Asher** (cf. ch. xxx. 9—13) : **these are the sons of Jacob, which were born to him in Padan-aram.** All except Benjamin were born there. Either this is an instance of the summary style of Scripture in which minute verbal accuracy is not always preserved (Inglis), or the whole period of Jacob's pilgrimage to Mesopotamia and back is intended by his residence in Padan-aram (Kalisch).

Ver. 27.—**And Jacob came unto Isaac his father unto Mamre** (on the probability of Jacob's having previously visited his father, *vide* ver. 8), **unto the city of Arbah** (ch. xiii. 18 ; xxiii. 2, 19; Josh. xiv. 15 ; xv. 13), **which is Hebron, where Abraham and Isaac sojourned.**

Ver. 28.—**And the days of Isaac were an hundred and fourscore years.** At this time Jacob was 120 ; but at 130 he stood before Pharaoh in Egypt, at which date Joseph had been 10 years governor. He was therefore 120 when Joseph was promoted at the age of 30, and 107 when Joseph was sold ; consequently Isaac was 167 years of age when Joseph was sold, so that he must have survived that event and sympathised with Jacob his son for a period of 13 years.

Ver. 29.—**And Isaac gave up the ghost, and died, and was gathered unto his people,** —cf. the account of Abraham's death (ch. xxv. 8)—**being old and full of days** (literally, *satisfied with days.* In ch. xxv. 8 the shorter expression *satisfied* is used) : **and his sons Esau and Jacob buried him** — Esau arriving from Mount Seir to pay the last service due to his deceased parent, and Jacob according to him that precedence which had once belonged to him as Isaac's firstborn.

HOMILETICS.

Vers. 16—29. — *From Bethel to Mamre.* I. THE DEATH OF RACHEL. 1. *The travailing woman.* Rachel, overtaken by the pains of childbirth, had hard labour. In every instance an inheritance derived from mother Eve (ch. iii. 16), the sorrow of maternity was in her case providentially intensified; perhaps by her advanced age, or by the discomforts of travel, or by feebleness of health, or possibly by special appointment of God as a rebuke for her inordinate desire for children (ch. xxx. 1), or as a means of shortening her life. 2. *The comforting midwife.* Though her name is not recorded, wherever this pathetic story is recited, there shall her kindly offices to the dying Rachel be remembered. Chosen to assist Rachel in her bodily struggle, she was likewise helpful to Rachel in her soul's conflict. Sympathising with the sufferer in her pain, she sought to minister comfort to the drooping heart in its despondency. They who tend the sick and dying should be tender in their feelings and hopeful in their words, as well as skilful and gentle in their acts. 3. *The departing mother.* Though Rachel's child was born, Rachel herself died; in which were some circumstances of sadness, as (1) that it happened on a journey,—"in the way to Ephrath,"—and near its end—"there was but a little way to come to Ephrath," where it is likely Jacob had intended to rest a while for Rachel's convenience; (2) that it occurred on the occasion of her confinement, death in child-bed being a comparatively rare experience in the history of mothers, though, considering the severity of the ordeal, it is a special mercy that any mothers survive; and (3) that it removed her from her newly-born son, than which no greater grief can agitate a dying mother's heart, and the thought of which perhaps gave added poignancy to the bitter anguish with which she named her child Ben-oni—the son of my sorrow. Yet in Rachel's death were certain elements of gladness, as (1) that she died in the presence of her husband, Jacob being by her couch to catch her latest breath; (2) that she died not before she gave him another son, to be to him whom she loved a Benjamin, though to herself Ben-oni; and (3) that she died in the hope of a glorious immortality, her soul departing to the better country, even an heavenly. 4. *The bereaved husband.* (1) Cheering the drooping heart of his dying wife. This is probably the correct view to be taken of what otherwise interpreted cannot fail to seem strangely inconsistent—Jacob's naming Rachel's child Benjamin, the son of my right hand, the son of my affection, of my prosperity, a token of good hope and happy fortune, while Rachel called him Ben-oni. " In vain the broken-hearted father—refusing to take in the terrible fact passing under his eye—determined to be sanguine to the last, and let no evil omen touch either mother or child—whispers hope in the dull ear of death, and welcomes the last pledge of an undying love as no " son of sorrow," but "the son of the right hand" (Candlish). (2) Burying the lifeless body of his beloved spouse, which doubtless he would do with reverent affection and with heart-felt mourning. (3) Erecting a pillar above her lonely grave—to demonstrate his affection for her who slept beneath, to show that though she lay not in the family tomb, she was not forgotten, and to mark the last resting-place of an ancestress of Israel.

II. THE SIN OF REUBEN. 1. *The enormity of Reuben's wickedness.* The act which he committed was that of incest, since Bilhah had been the wife of Jacob. It was a sin punishable by death under Moses' law (Levit. xviii. 8), and such a sin as should not be named among Christians (1 Cor. v. 1). It is not likely that Bilhah was innocent in this matter, but it is certain that Reuben was guilty of heinous transgression. 2. *The impression it produced on Jacob.* " Israel heard." We may supply the hiatus by saying, (1) with inexpressible grief — grief that a son and wife of his should have committed such a horrible iniquity; (2) with bitter shame—was this to be the end of all God's mercies to his house, and of all his efforts to piously direct his household? (3) with silent submission, as recognising God's hand in the dispensation. More bitter and crushing was this last stroke than the death of Rachel or even the ravishment of Dinah; and Jacob's silence under it may be interpreted as the silence of devout resignation:—" I was dumb, because thou didst it."

III. THE DEATH OF ISAAC. 1. *He was spared to see his son's return.* " Jacob came unto Isaac his father unto Mamre" at least a considerable period before his death. According to calculations (*vide* Exposition), Isaac survived the sale of Joseph thirteen years. Hence Jacob's coming home must have taken place while Isaac had yet many years to live. It is a mercy which God does not grant to all, to see their children and their children's children around them before they die. 2. *He was privileged to reach a good old age.* "The days of Isaac were an hundred and fourscore years." Piety has a special tendency to prolong life (Ps. xxxiv. 12), while the wicked live not half their days (Ps. lv. 23). 3. *He was favoured with a peaceful and a blessed end.* "Isaac gave up the ghost, and died, and was gathered unto his people." See Homily on the death of Abraham (ch. xxv. 8). 4. *He was honoured with a decent and respectful funeral.* "Esau and Jacob buried him." They laid him beside his ancestral dust in the family burying-place of Machpelah, where already slept the lifeless bodies of Abraham and Sarah, awaiting the resurrection, while his spirit went to company with theirs in the better country, even an heavenly.

Learn — 1. That bereavements, like the rest of life's afflictions, are of God's ordering, both as to time, place, and manner. 2. That in human families they who are most beloved are frequently removed first. 3. That the sick and dying should be ministered to with sympathy and tender attention. 4. That good men should love their wives when living, and remember them when dead. 5. That faith should always try to see the bright light of blessing in the cloud of earth's afflictions. 6. That worse calamities may overtake a saint than bereavements. 7. That pious children do not cast off their parents in old age.

HOMILIES BY VARIOUS AUTHORS.

Vers. 16—29. These *family records* mingle well with the story of God's grace. The mother's "*Benoni*" is the father's "*Benjamin*." Out of the pain and the bereavement sometimes comes the consolation. A strange blending of joy and sorrow is the tale of human love. But there is a higher love which may draw out the pure stream of peace and calm delight from that impure fountain. Jacob and Esau were separated in their lives, but they met at their father's grave. Death is a terrible divider, but a uniter too. Under the shadow of the great mystery, on the borders of an eternal world, in the presence of those tears which human eyes weep for the dead, even when they can weep no other tears, the evil things of envy, hatred, revenge, alienation do often hide themselves, and the better things of love, peace, brotherhood, amity come forth. Jacob was with Isaac when he died, and Esau came to the grave.—R.

§ 10. The Generations of Esau (CH. XXXVI. 1—XXXVII. 1).

EXPOSITION.

CHAPTER XXXVI.

Ver. 1.—**Now these** are **the generations** (cf. ch. ii. 4 ; v. 1, &c.) **of Esau**,—Hairy (*vide* ch. xxv. 25)—**which is Edom**—Red (*vide* ch. xxv. 30).

Vers. 2, 3.—**Esau took his wives** (the expression refers in this place not to the marriage, but to the removal, of his wives) **of the daughters of Canaan ;**—*i. e.* who were of the daughters of Canaan (*vide* ch. xxvi. 34)— **Adah**—"Ornament," "Beauty" (Gesenius); the name also of one of Lamech's wives (cf. ch. iv. 19)—**the daughter of Elon**—"Oak" (Gesenius)—**the Hittite, and Aholibamah**— "Tent of the High Place" (Gesenius)—**the daughter of Anah**—"Answering" (Gesenius)

—**the daughter**—*i. e.* the grand-daughter, though, after the LXX. and the Samaritan, some read the son, as in ver. 24 (Gesenius, Kalisch, Fürst, *et alii*)—**of Zibeon**—"Coloured" (Gesenius) ; "Wild," "Robber" (Fürst) — **the Hivite ; and Bashemath** — "Sweet-smelling" (Gesenius) — **Ishmael's daughter, sister of Nebajoth**—"High Place" (Gesenius). The difference between this account and that previously given (ch. xxvi. 34 ; xxviii. 9) will appear at a glance by setting the two lists of wives in parallel columns :—

1. Judith, daughter of Beeri the Hittite.	1. Aholibamah, daughter of Anah, daughter of Zibeon the Hivite.

2. Bashemath, daughter of Elon the Hittite.
3. Mahalath, daughter of Ishmael, sister of Nebajoth.

2. Adah, daughter of Elon the Hittite.
3. Bashemath, Ishmael's daughter, sister of Nebajoth.

The two lists agree in saying (1) that Esau had three wives, (2) that one of them was the daughter of Elon the Hittite, (3) that another of them was Ishmael's daughter, the sister of Nebajoth, and (4) that the name of one of them was Bashemath. The discrepancy between the two is greatest in respect of the first wife, who appears with a different name and a different parentage in the two lists ; while with reference to the second and the third wives, it is only the difference of name that requires to be accounted for. Now since the two lists belong to the so-called Elohistic document (Tuch, Bleek, Stähelin, Davidson, *et alii*), the hypothesis must be discarded "that the Hebrew text, though containing several important coincidences, evidently embodies two accounts irreconcilably different" (Kalisch)— a conclusion which can only be maintained by ascribing to the author the most absolute literary incompetence. Equally the conjecture must be set aside that the two lists refer to different persons, the second three being names of wives which Esau took on the decease of the first. The solutions that appear most entitled to acceptance, though all are more or less conjectural, proceed upon the supposition that Esau had only three wives, or at most four. 1. On the hypothesis that Esau had not more than three wives, it is only needful to presume that each of them had two names, a not unusual circumstance in Oriental countries (Rosenmüller, Hävernick)—one of them, probably that contained in the present list, bestowed on the occasion of marriage ; and that Anah, the father of Aholibamah, was the same person with Beeri, or the Well-Man, who received that cognomen from the incident related in ver. 24, viz., that he discovered certain hot springs while feeding his father's asses (Hengstenberg, Keil, Kurtz) — the peculiarity that in one place (ch. xxvi. 34) he is styled a Hittite, in another (ch. xxxvi. 2) a Hivite, and in a third (ch. xxxvi. 20) a Horite, being explained by the conjecture that the first was the generic term for the race, the second the specific designation of the tribe, and the third the particular name for the inhabitants of the district to which he belonged (Keil, Lange, 'Speaker's Commentary'). 2. Another solution gives to Esau four wives, by supposing Judith to have died without issue (Murphy, Jacobus), or, in consequence of being childless, though still living, to have been passed over in silence in the former genealogical register (Quarry), and Aholibamah to have been the fourth partner whom Esau espoused. The Samaritan version reads Mahalath for Bashemath in the second list, which it regards as an error of transcription (W. L. Alexander in Kitto's 'Cyclopedia ') ; while others think that Adah has been written by inadvertence for Bashemath (Inglis)'; but such conjectures are as unnecessary as they are manifestly arbitrary.

Vers. 4, 5. — **And Adah bare to Esau Eliphaz ;**—" The Strength of God " (Gesenius) ; afterwards the name of one of Job's friends (Job ii. 11 ; iv. 1 ; xv. 1)— **and Bashemath bare Reuel ;**—" The Friend of God " (Gesenius) ; the name of Moses' father-in-law (Exod. ii. 18)—**and Aholibamah bare Jeush,**—"Collector" (Fürst, Lange) ; "whom God hastens" (Gesenius) ; afterwards the name of a son of Rehoboam (2 Chron. xi. 19)—**and Jaalam,**—"whom God hides" (Gesenius) ; " Ascender of the Mountains " (Fürst)—**and Korah :**—" Baldness " (Fürst, Gesenius) ; the name of a family of Levites and singers in the time of David to whom ten of the psalms are ascribed—**these are the sons of Esau, which were born unto him in the land of Canaan**—not necessarily implying that other sons were born to him in Edom, but rather intimating that all his family were born before he left the Holy Land.

Ver. 6.—**And Esau took his wives, and his sons, and his daughters, and all the persons** (literally, *souls*) **of his house, and his cattle** (*mikneh*), **and all his beasts** (*behemah*), **and all his substance** (literally, *all his acquisitions*), **which he had got in the land of Canaan ; and went into the country**— literally, *into a land ;* not ἐκ τῆς γῆς (LXX.), or *in alteram regionem* (Vulgate), but either into the land, *sc.* of Seir (Keil), or, taking the next as a qualifying clause, into a land apart (Murphy, Lange)—**from the face of**— or, on account of (Rosenmüller, Kalisch)—**his brother Jacob.**

Ver. 7.—**For their riches were more than that they might dwell together ; and the land wherein they were strangers**—literally, *of their wanderings* (cf. ch. xxviii. 4 ; xxxvii. 1)—**could not bear them because of their cattle.** This does not necessarily imply that Jacob was established in Canaan before Esau removed. Esau may have recognised the impossibility of two so rich and powerful chieftains as himself and his brother occupying Canaan, and may have retired before Jacob actually took possession (Keil, Inglis).

Ver. 8.—**Thus dwelt Esau in mount Seir** (ch. xxxii. 3 ; Deut. ii. 5 ; Josh. xxiv. 4): **Esau is Edom** (*vide* ch. xxv. 30). The obvious continuation of this verse is to be found in ch. xxxvii. 1, so that vers. 9—40 are parenthetical in their character ; but whether originally written by Moses, or inserted by a late redactor, as some maintain, may legitimately be regarded as an open question.

Ver. 9.—**And these** are **the generations of Esau**—"the repetition of this clause shows that it does not necessarily indicate diversity of authorship, or a very distinct piece of composition" (Murphy) **the father of the Edomites** (*i. e.* the founder of the Edomitish nation) **in mount Seir.**

Vers. 10—12.—**These** are **the names of Esau's sons ; Eliphaz the son of Adah the wife of Esau, Reuel the son of Bashemath the wife of Esau** (*vide* ver. 4). **And the sons of Eliphaz were Teman,**—the name was afterwards given to a district of Idumea (Jer. xlix. 20), and borne by one of Job's friends (Job ii. 11)—**Omar,**—"Eloquent" (Gesenius), "Mountain-dweller" (Fürst)—**Zepho,**—"Watch-tower" (Gesenius) ; called Zephi in 1 Chron. i. 36—**and Gatam,**—"their touch" (Gesenius), "dried up" (Fürst)—**and Kenaz**—"Hunting" (Gesenius). **And Timna** — "Restraint" (Gesenius, Fürst, Murphy)—**was concubine**—*pilgash* (vide ch. xvi. 3 ; xxv. 6)—**to Eliphaz Esau's son ;**—perhaps given to him by Adah, so that her children were reckoned Adah's (Hughes)—**and she bare to Eliphaz Amalek**—"Inhabitant of the Valley," or "Warrior" (Fürst) ; "a nation of head-breakers" (Lange) ; "Labouring" (Gesenius, Murphy). It is probable that this was the founder of the Amalekite nation who attacked Israel at Horeb (Keil, Kalisch, Murphy), though by others (Gesenius, Michaelis, Fürst) these have been regarded as a primitive people, chiefly on the grounds that Amalek is mentioned in ch. xiv. 7 as having existed in the days of Abraham, and that Balaam calls Amalek the first of nations (Numb. xxiv. 20) ; but the first may simply be a prolepsis (Hengstenberg), while the second alludes not to the antiquity of the nation, but either to its power (Kalisch), or to the circumstance that it was the first heathen tribe to attack Israel (Keil). **These** (including Eliphaz for the reason specified above) were **the sons of Adah Esau's wife.**

Ver. 13.—**And these** are **the sons of Reuel ; Nahath,**—Nachath, "Going down"—**and Zerah,**—or Zerach, "Rising" — **Shammah,**—"Wasting" (Gesenius, Murphy) ; "Fame," "Renown" (Fürst)—**and Mizzah :**—"Trepidation" (Gesenius) ; "Fear," "Sprinkling" (Murphy) ; if from *mazaz*, "Fear," if from *nazah*, "Joy" (Fürst)—**these were the sons of Bashemath Esau's wife.**

Ver. 14.—**And these were the sons of Aholibamah, the daughter of Anah the daughter of Zibeon, Esau's wife** (*vide* ver. 2) : **and she bare to Esau Jeush, and Jaalam, and Korah** (*vide* ver. 5).

Vers. 15, 16.—**These** were **dukes of the sons of Esau.** The אַלּוּפִים, derived probably from אָלַף, to be familiar, whence to join together, or associate, were Edomite and Horite phylarchs or tribe-leaders, ἡγεμόνες, (LXX.), chieftains of a thousand men (Gerlach). At a later period the term came to be applied to the Jewish chiefs or governors of the Restoration (Zech. ix. 7 ; xii. 5). **The sons of Eliphaz the firstborn** son **of Esau ; duke Teman, duke Omar, duke Zepho, duke Kenaz** (*vide* on ver. 11), **duke Korah,**—inserted here probably by clerical error from ver. 18 (Kennicott, Tuch, Knobel, Delitzsch, Keil, Murphy, Quarry), and accordingly omitted in the Samaritan Pentateuch and Version, though still retained by Onkelos and the LXX., and on the hypothesis of its genuineness explained by some as the name of a nephew of Eliphaz (Junius) ; of a son by another mother (Ainsworth) ; of a son of Korah (ver. 18) by the widow of Timna (1 Chron. i. 36), who, having died without issue, left his wife to his brother (Michaelis) ; of some descendant of Eliphaz by intermarriage who subsequently rose to be the head of a clan (Kalisch),—**duke Gatam** (*vide* ver. 11), and **duke Amalek** (*vide* ver. 12) : **these** are **the dukes** that came **of Eliphaz in the land of Edom ; these** were **the sons of Adah.**

Ver. 17.—**And these** are **the sons of Reuel Esau's son ; duke Nahath, duke Zerah, duke Shammah, duke Mizzah : these** are **the dukes** that came **of Reuel in the land of Edom ; these** are **the sons of Bashemath Esau's wife** (*vide* on ver. 13).

Ver. 18.—**And these** are **the sons of Aholibamah Esau's wife ; duke Jeush, duke Jaalam, duke Korah : these** were **the dukes** that came **of Aholibamah the daughter of Anah, Esau's wife.** In the two previous instances it is the grandsons of Esau that become the alluphim or heads of tribes, while in this it is the sons, which Hävernick regards as a mark of authenticity (*vide* 'Introd.,' § 20).

Ver. 19.—**These** are **the sons of Esau, who** is **Edom, and these** are **their dukes**

Vers. 20, 21.—**These** are **the sons of Seir the Horite, who inhabited the land.** The primitive inhabitants of Idumea were Horites (*vide* ch. xiv. 6), of whom the ancestor, Seir ("Rugged"), either gave his name to, or took his name from, the district in which he lived. Though ultimately driven out by the Edomites (Deut. ii. 12), they were probably only gradually dispossessed, and not until a portion of them had coalesced with their conquerors, as Esau himself had a Horite wife, Aholibamah, and his son Eliphaz a Horite concubine of the name of Timna. They were, as the name Horite, from *chor*, a hole or cavern, imports a race of troglodytes or cave men, who dwelt in the sandstone and limestone caves with which the land of Edom abounds. The cave palaces, temples, and tombs that have been excavated in Mount Seir are still astonishing in their grandeur. **Lotan,**—" Wrapping up" (Gesenius)—**and Shobal,** — "Flowing" (Gesenius) — and **Zibeon, and Anah** (this Anah was the uncle of the Anah mentioned in ver. 25), **and Dishon,**—"Gazelle" (Gesenius, Fürst)—**and Ezer,**—"Treasure" (Gesenius)—**and Dishan** : — same as Dishon (Gesenius, Fürst) ; "Threshing" (Murphy)—**these are the dukes of. the Horites, the children of Seir in the land of Edom.**

Ver. 22.—**And the children of Lotan were Hori**—the name of the tribe (ver. 20)—**and Hemam :**—or Homam (1 Chron. i. 39) ; "Destruction" (Gesenius), "Commotion" (Fürst, Murphy)—**and Lotan's sister was Timna**—probably the concubine of Eliphaz (ver. 12).

Ver. 23.—**And the children of Shobal were these ; Alvan,**—or Alian (1 Chron. i. 40) ; "Unjust" (Gesenius), "Lofty" (Fürst, Murphy)—**and Manahath,**—" Rest " (Gesenius)—**and Ebal,**—"Stripped of leaves" (Gesenius, Murphy) ; " Bare Mountain " (Fürst)—**Shepho,**—or Shephi (1 Chron. i. 40) ; " Nakedness" (Gesenius)—**and Onam**— " Strong " (Gesenius).

Ver. 24.—**And these are the children of Zibeon ; both Ajah,**—"Screamer" (Gesenius) —**and Anah :**—the father-in-law of Esau (ver. 2)—**this was that Anah that found the mules in the wilderness,**—neither invented the procreation of mules (Aben Ezra, Kimchi, Luther, Calvin, Willet, Clarke, Ainsworth, &c.), since מָצָא does not signify to invent, but to light upon or discover (Keil), and there were no horses at that time in those regions (Michaelis), and it is not said that Anah was feeding his father's horses and asses, but only asses (Rosenmüller) ; nor overcame the giants (Onkelos, Samaritan, Bochart),which would have required אֵימִים (ch. xiv. 5 ; Deut. ii. 11) ; nor found out salt water (Oleaster, Pererius), a useful herb (Mais), or 'Ιαμείν as a proper name (LXX.) ; but discovered the warm springs, the ἅπαξ λεγόμενον, יֵמִם, being now generally taken to mean aquæ callidæ (Vulgate, Dathius, Gesenius, Rosenmüller, Hengstenberg, Keil, Kalisch, Murphy), of which there were various in the vicinity, as, e. g., the springs of Callirrhoe in the Wady Zerka Maein, and those in the Wady-el-Ahsa to the south-east of the Dead Sea, and those in the Wady Hamad between Kerek and the Dead Sea—**as** he fed (literally, in his feeding) **the asses of Zibeon his father.** "The whirlpool of Karlsbad is said to have been discovered through a hound of Charles IV. which pursued a stag

into a hot spring, and attracted the huntsmen to the spot by its howling" (Keil in loco ; cf. Tacitus, 'Hist.,' v. 3).

Ver. 25.—**And the children of Anah**—the brother of Zibeon (ver. 20)—were **these ; Dishon,**—named after his uncle (ver. 21)—**and Aholibamah the daughter of Anah.** This Aholibamah was not Esau's wife, but the cousin of Esau's wife's father.

Ver. 26.—**And these are the children of Dishon ;**—the son of Seir (ver 21)—**Hemdan,** —or Amram (1 Chron. i. 41) ; "Pleasant" (Gesenius)—**and Eshban,** — or Heshbon ; "Reason," " Understanding" (Gesenius) ; "Intelligent," "Hero" (Fürst)—**and Ithran,** —the same as Jethro and Jithron ; "the Superior or Excellent One" (Gesenius, Fürst, Murphy, Lange)—**and Cheran** —"Harp" (Gesenius), "Companion" (Fürst).

Ver. 27.—**The children of Ezer are these ; Bilhan,**—"Modest" (Gesenius), "Tender" (Fürst)—**and Zaavan,**—" Disturbed " (Gesenius)—**and Akan**—Jakan (1 Chron. i. 42) ; "Twisting" (Gesenius, Murphy).

Ver. 28.—**The children of Dishan are these ; Uz,**—"Sandy" (Gesenius, Fürst)— **and Aran** — " Wild Goat" (Gesenius) ; "Power," "Strength" (Fürst).

Vers. 29, 30.—**These** are **the dukes that came of the Horites ; duke Lotan, duke Shobal, duke Zibeon, duke Anah, duke Dishon, duke Ezer, duke Dishan : these are the dukes that came of Hori, among** (rather, according to) **their dukes in the land of Seir.**

Ver. 31.—**And these** (which follow) are **the kings that reigned in the land of Edom, before there reigned any** (literally, before the reigning of a) **king over** (or, to) **the children of Israel.** 1. The reference to Israelitish kings in this place has been explained as an evidence of post - Mosaic authorship (Le Clerc, Bleek, Ewald, Bohlen, et alii), or at least as a later interpolation from 1 Chron. i. 43 (Kennicott, A. Clarke, Lange), but is sufficiently accounted for by remembering that in ch. xxxv. 11 kings had been promised to Jacob, while the blessing pronounced on Esau (ch. xxvii. 40) implied that in his line also should arise governors, the historian being understood to say that though the promised kings had not yet arisen in the line of Jacob, the house of Esau had attained at a somewhat early period to political importance (Calvin, Michaelis, Rosenmüller, Keil, Kalisch, Gerlach, Hävernick, and others). 2. The difficulty of finding room for the dukes (seven, four and three, all grandsons of Esau, vers. 15—19), the kings (eight in number, vers. 32—39), and again the dukes (in all eleven, vers. 40 —43), that intervened between Esau and Moses disappears if the kings and dukes existed contemporaneously, of which Exod. xv.

15, as compared with Numb. xx. 14, affords probable evidence. 3. As to the character of the Edomitish kings, it is apparent that it was not a hereditary monarchy, since in no case does the son succeed the father, but an elective sovereignty, the kings being chosen by the dukes, alluphim, or phylarchs (Keil, Hengstenberg, Kalisch, Gerlach), though the idea of successive usurpations (Lange) is not without a measure of probability.

Ver. 32.—**And Bela the son of Beor** (cf. ch. xiv. 2, where Bela is the name for Zoar ; and Numb. xxii. 5, where Balaam's father is called Beor, whence the LXX. has here Βαλάκ) **reigned in Edom** (as the first sovereign): **and the name of his city was Dinhabah**—"Concealment," or "Little Place" (Fürst) ; a place of plunder (Gesenius), the situation of which has not been identified.

Ver. 33.—**And Bela died, and Jobab**—probably meaning "Desert," or "Shout" (Gesenius) ; identified with Job (LXX., Augustine, Ambrose)—an opinion which Michaelis declares to be *insignis error, nec historicus solum, sed et grammaticus,* Jobab being derived from the root בבי (*vide* 'Suppl.,' p. 40) ; the name of a region of the Joktanite Arabs (ch. x. 29)—**the son of Zerah** (who may have been the duke Zerah mentioned in ver. 17, and is here described by the territory over which he ruled as) **of Bozrah**—"Fort" (Gesenius) ; afterwards an important city of the Edomites (Isa. xxxiv. 6 ; lxiii. 1 ; Jer. xlix. 13) ; still to be traced in El-Busaireh, a village and castle in Arabia Petræa, about twenty-five miles south by east of the Dead Sea (Robinson, vol. ii. pp. 570, 571 ; Gesenius, 'Lex.,' p. 135 ; Porter in Kitto's 'Cyclopedia')—**reigned in his stead**—literally, *under him,* i. e. in succession to him.

Ver. 34.—**And Jobab died, and Husham**—Hushai ; "Haste" (Gesenius)—**of the land of Temani** (a province in Northern Idumea, with a city Teman which has not yet been discovered) **reigned in his stead.**

Ver. 35.—**And Husham died, and Hadad**—"Shouting," *e. g.* for joy (Gesenius) ; whence "Conqueror" (Fürst)—**the son of Bedad,**—"Separation" (Gesenius)—**who smote Midian** (*vide* ch. xxv. 2) **in the field of Moab** (*vide* ch. xix. 37), **reigned in his stead: and the name of his city was Avith**—"Ruins" (Gesenius), "Twisting" (Murphy), "Hut-Village" (Fürst). An attempt has been made (Bohlen) to identify this monarch with the Edomite of the same name who rose against Solomon (1 Kings xi. 14) ; but (1) this Hadad was not of royal blood, while Solomon's contemporary was ; (2) this Hadad was a king, while Solomon's adversary was only a pretender ; (3) this Hadad was a conqueror of the Midianites, while in Solomon's time the Midianites had vanished

from history ; and (4) this Hadad lived and reigned before Israel had any kings (*vide* Hengstenberg, 'On the Genuineness of the Pentateuch,' vol. ii. dissert. 6 ; and cf. Hävernick's 'Introd.,' § 20, and Keil *in loco*).

Ver. 36.—**And Hadad died, and Samlah**—"Covering," "Garment," (Gesenius, Fürst, Murphy)—**of Masrekah**—"Vineyard" (Gesenius)—**reigned in his stead.**

Ver. 37.—**And Samlah died, and Saul**—"Asked" (Gesenius)—**of Rehoboth by the river**—Rehoboth (literally, *wide spaces*) of the River is so called to distinguish it from the Asshurite settlement of the same name in ch. x. 11 (Rosenmüller), though by some it is identified with Rehoboth Ir (Ainsworth). If the river spoken of be the Euphrates (Onkelos, Keil, Kalisch), then it is probably to be sought for in the Errachabi or Rachabeh near the mouth of the Chaboras (Keil), though the river may be some small *nahar* in Idumea (Lange), in which case the site will be uncertain—**reigned in his stead.**

Ver. 38.—**And Saul died, and Baal-hanan**—"Lord of Benignity" (Gesenius)—**the son of Achbor**—"Mouse" (Gesenius)—**reigned in his stead.**

Ver. 39.—**And Baal-hanan the son of Achbor died, and Hadar**—Hadad (1 Chron. i. 50)—**reigned in his stead : and the name of his city was Pau;**—Pai (1 Chron. i. 50) ; "Bleating" (Gesenius), "Yawning" (Fürst), with which accords Φογώρ (LXX.)—**and his wife's name was Mehetabel,**—"Whom God benefits" (Gesenius)—**the daughter of Matred,**—"Pushing" (Gesenius)—**the daughter of Mezahab**—"Water of Gold" (Gesenius). That the death of this king, which a later chronicler records (1 Chron. i. 51), is not here mentioned by the historian is commonly regarded (Rosenmüller, Hävernick, Hengstenberg, Keil, Kalisch, *et alii*) as a proof that he was then alive, and that in fact he was the king of Edom to whom Moses sent ambassadors requesting permission to pass through the land (Numb. xx. 14).

Vers. 40—43.—**And these are the names of the dukes that came of Esau, according to their families, after their places, by their names.** It is now generally agreed that this and the ensuing verses contain not a second list of dukes who rose to power on the overthrow of the preceding monarchical institutions (Bertheau, Ainsworth, Patrick), or a continuation of the preceding list of dukes, which had simply been interrupted by a parenthesis about the kings (Bush) ; but either an enumeration of the hereditary phylarchs who were contemporaneous with Hadar, and in all probability formed his council (Murphy), or a territorial catalogue of the districts in which the original alluphim who sprang from Esau (vers. 15—19) exercised their sovereignty

(Keil, Kalisch, Lange, 'Speaker's Commentary '). **Duke Timnah,** — according to the explanation just given this should perhaps be read duke of Timnah = Amalek, whose mother was Timna (Lange), but this is conjectural — **duke Alvah,** — or of Alvah, or Aliah, closely allied to Alvan (ver. 23)— **duke (of) Jetheth,** — " Nail " (Gesenius), " Subjugation " (Fürst)—**duke (of) Aholibamah,**—*vide* ver. 2 ; perhaps Esau's wife as well as Eliphaz's concubine gave her name to the district over which her son ruled— **duke Elah,**—"Strength " (Fürst), " Terebinth " (Murphy)—**duke Pinon,**—probably equal to Pımon, dark (Gesenius)—**duke Kenaz** (*vide* ver. 11), **duke Teman** (ver. 15), **duke Mibzar,**—"Fortress," " Strong City" (Gesenius)—**duke Magdiel,** —" Prince of God " (Gesenius)—**duke Iram :**—" Citizen " (Gesenius)—**these** be **the dukes of Edom, according to their habitations** (*i. e.* their capitals, or districts) **in the land of their possessions.** The word seems to indicate an independent sovereignty within their respective provinces or principalities. **He is Esau the father of**

the Edomites. The clause is equivalent to saying, This Esau (already referred to) was the ancestor of these Edomites.

CHAPTER XXXVII.

Ver. 1.—**And Jacob dwelt in the land wherein his father was a stranger** (literally, *in the land of the sojournings of his father*), **in the land of Canaan.** This verse is not the commencement of the ensuing (Keil, Kalisch, Lange, &c.), but the concluding sentence of the present, section, the adversative particle וֹ, corresponding to the δε of the LXX., introducing a contrast between Esau, who dwelt in Mount Seir, and Jacob, who dwelt in the land of Canaan, and the following verse beginning the next division of the book with the customary formula, " These are the generations " (LXX., some MS., Quarry, p. 523). Rosenmüller less happily connects the present verse with ch. xxxv. 29 ; the Vulgate begins the next section with ver. 3. A similar division of verses to that proposed will be found in ch. xxv. 11.

HOMILETICS.

Ch. xxxvi. 1—xxxvii. 1.—*The last of the house of Esau.* I. THE REMOVAL OF ESAU'S HOUSE FROM CANAAN. 1. A *complete* removal. " Esau took his wives, and his sons, and his daughters, and all the persons of his house, and his cattle, and all his beasts, and all his substance, which he had got in the land of Canaan ; and went into a land apart from the face of his brother." 2. A *necessary* removal. Two things rendered the withdrawal of Esau from Canaan imperative—(1) that which was patent to Esau's sense, viz., that the land of Canaan was too strait to afford accommodation to two so powerful chieftains as his brother and himself ; and (2) that which appears to have been accepted by Esau's faith, viz., that the decision of Divine providence was against him, and that the land belonged to Jacob. Hence for this twofold reason his retirement from Canaan is said to have taken place on account of his brother. 3. A *peaceful* removal. Though in one sense compulsory, in another aspect of it Esau's departure was voluntary. Instead of disputing possession of the land with his brother, which, humanly speaking, he might have done with some considerable hope of success, he quietly ceded what perhaps he saw he could not ultimately retain. Still it was to his credit that, instead of wrangling with Jacob about its present occupation, he peacefully withdrew to the wild mountain region of Seir. A *permanent* removal. Esau established his settlements altogether outside the limits of the Holy Land, and never again appeared as a claimant for its possession, leaving it finally in the free and undisputed ownership of Jacob. Hence, while it is said that " Esau dwelt in Mount Seir," it is appropriately added by the historian, in concluding the present section, "And Jacob dwelt in the land wherein his father was a stranger, in the land of Canaan."

II. THE DEVELOPMENT OF ESAU'S HOUSE IN EDOM. 1. A *numerous* race. Though Esau's sons were not so many as those of Jacob, yet his descendants developed into a people much more rapidly than did those of Jacob. This may have been partly due to the circumstance that they were—2. A *mixed* race, having obviously incorporated amongst themselves a portion at least of the original Horites, whose land they appropriated, and whose political life they appear to have adopted. Then it is apparent that they were—3. An *aristocratic* race. At the time of their invasion by the Esahites, the cave-dwellers of Mount Seir had attained to something like a settled government by means of alluphim, phylarchs, or tribe princes, each of whom enjoyed a sort of independent sovereignty ; and, as has often happened since, though obliged to retire before the more powerful Canaanitish tribe, they succeeded in imposing on their conquerors their own political institutions.　No fewer than fourteen of Esau's grandsons became reigning dukes in the country.　Still further, it may be inferred that they were—4. A *progressive* race.　The impulse towards a national life thus communicated by the Seirites does not appear to have exhausted itself by simply the formation of small independent principalities, which, as civilisation advances, are always felt to be a source of weakness rather than strength to the country whose social and political unity is thus broken up, and which eventually call for the reverse process of a unification of the different fragments, whether by free confederation or by imperial subordination.　In the case of the Edomites the phylarchs were succeeded by kings, whether elective monarchs or foreign usurpers cannot be determined, though the preponderance of sentiment among interpreters is in favour of the former hypothesis.　And then, finally, they were—5. An *exiled* race ; that is to say, though sprung from the soil of Canaan, they developed outside its limits—Jacob's family alone, as the Heaven-appointed heirs, remaining within the borders of the Holy Land.

Learn—1. That God is able to bring about his purposes in peaceful ways when he so desireth.　2. That natural men often exemplify great virtues in their conduct. 3. That abundance of wealth is frequently a cause of separation among friends.　4. That political greatness is much more easily attained, by nations as well as individuals, than spiritual pre-eminence.　5. That a nation's advancement in civilisation is no certain guarantee of its continuance.　6. That in nature, as well as grace, the first is often last, and the last first.　7. That the heirs of the covenant are certain in the long run to obtain the inheritance.

HOMILIES BY VARIOUS AUTHORS.

Ver. 8.—*Esau separates from Jacob.*　I. GOD REQUIRES ENTIRE DEVOTEDNESS AND FAITH.　*Edom* is *allied* to the true kingdom, but is not *one with it.*　We may keep in mind the relationship between the descendants of the two brothers, that we may learn the more clearly to distinguish the *true heirs* of the blessing.

II. THE TRUE BELIEVERS SET APART BY SPECIAL GRACE.　The rest of the Book of Genesis follows the course of *the one family* in whose midst the *ark of the covenant*, as it were, was already resting, where was (1) *the revelation of God* and (2) the *special manifestation* of his favour, and out of which should come forth (3) the *people among the peoples,* the kingdom among the kingdoms; the Goshen in the Egypt, the seed of life in the world of death.—R.

Ver. 31.—*Delay in fulfilment of God's promises.*　Between two stages of the history of the covenant family stands the genealogy of Esau's descendants.　The text suggests a contrast between their course and that of the family of Jacob.　On the death of Isaac Esau departed from Canaan with family and possessions (cf. ch. xxvii. 40).　The desert and the valleys of Seir were more attractive than quietness of Canaan.　Prosperity, such as he cared for, attended him.　Among his family we read of dukes, or heads of tribes, and of kings.　And what of the line of promise ?—kings foretold to them (ch. xvii. 6 ; xxxv. 11).　Yet while kings were reigning in Edom, Israelites were slaves in Egypt or wanderers in the desert.　Is God slack to fulfil his word ? (1 Pet. iii. 4).　This is often a trial to believers (Ps. lxxiii. 3).　But God's promises are sure, though the time may seem long.　The fulfilment of promises of great blessings has almost always been slow, as we count it.　Abraham waited long (ch. xii. 2).　It was long ere the kingdom of Israel arose ; far longer ere the promise of a Saviour fulfilled (ch. iii. 15 ; Gal. iv. 4) ; and still we wait for the Lord's return.　The same truth appears in nature.　Great and precious things are of slow growth (cf. Mark iv. 5).

Doctrinal lessons :—1. Delay serves for the trial and strengthening of faith.　Faith grows by enduring trial.　Mark how often the faith of eminent saints has been tried. Without faith we cannot please God ; for faith believes God's truth and love, and embraces his will.　Unbelief charges God with untruth (ch. iii. 4 ; 1 John v. 10).

Even in believers a leaven of unbelief may be at work. Trials are sent to cause faith to develop into other graces (James i. 3). 2. What springs up quickly is apt to fade quickly (cf. Exod. iii. 11 with Haggai i. 2). Danger lest what seems to be faith be merely feeling. 3. The time that seems so long is not mere delay, but preparation. While the seed lies in the earth a process is going on, though unseen, without which the perfect plant could not be formed. Compare the expression, " the fulness of time" (Gal. iv. 4), and the way in which all previous history prepared the way for the coming of Christ. These lessons apply equally to God's dealings with the world and with individuals.

Practical lessons:—1. Encouragement if disheartened by slow progress of Christ's kingdom: much labour among the heathen with little apparent result; or many efforts at home, yet ungodliness not checked. We have promises (Isa. lv. 11; 1 Cor. xv. 58). In his own time God will make them good. 2. In like manner if our own striving for personal holiness, or for good of others, seems to have little success. We require the training of disappointment to check pride (2 Cor. xii. 7), and God will see to the result (Gal. vi. 9). 3. To bear in mind that we are but instruments in the Lord's hand (1 Cor. iii. 6). Every work to be performed " looking unto Jesus " (2 Cor. xii. 10).—M.

§ 11. THE GENERATIONS OF JACOB (CH. XXXVII. 2—L. 26).

EXPOSITION.

1. HAVING disposed, in the preceding section, of the line of Esau by a brief sketch of its historical development during the two and a half centuries intervening between the founding of the Edomite empire by Esau's withdrawing to Mount Seir, and the days of Moses, the narrative reverts to the fortunes of the house of Jacob, the story of which, after having suffered a temporary interruption, it likewise carries forward to the same point of rest, viz., to the period of the sojourn in Egypt. Commencing with a glance at the inner family life of the patriarch at Mamre in the vale of Hebron, where, on returning from Padan-aram, he had finally established himself beside his aged and bed-ridden father Isaac, it recites the tragic incidents connected with the sale of Joseph by his brethren, after which, first rehearsing the further wickedness of Jacob's sons in the matter of Tamar, it pursues his eventful career from the moment of his entering Egypt as a slave in the household of Potiphar to the time when, arrayed in fine linen and decorated with a golden necklace, he rode in the second state chariot as Pharaoh's prime minister and ruler over all the land. Then, detailing the various circumstances arising from the famine which led to his discovery of his brethren, it ends by describing the descent of Jacob and his sons into Egypt and their settlement in Goshen, the death of Jacob after delivering his last prophetic blessing to his sons, and finally the decease of Joseph himself at the age of 110 years, when, as we learn from the subsequent narrative in Exodus, having lost their protector at the Court, and a dynastic change having taken place upon the throne, of Pharaoh, the sons of Israel gradually sank into oppressive and exhausting bondage.

2. By those who repudiate the Mosaic authorship of Genesis the present section is variously distributed among the alleged candidates for the honour of its composition. Beyond the ascription of ch. xxxviii. to the Jehovist, there is the most complete absence of unanimity among partitionists as to whom the different portions are to be assigned. Ch. xxxvii. 2—36, which Tuch declares to be the work of the Elohist, Bleek affirms to have been tampered with by the Jehovist, while Davidson divides it between a younger Elohist, the Jehovist, and a subsequent redactor. Ch. xxxix. is, according to Davidson, almost exclusively the composition of the Jehovist; while, according to Bleek, it has proceeded nearly entire from the pen of the Elohist, and Tuch divides it pretty evenly between the two. Tuch again thinks that chs. xl.—l. have been supplied by the fundamental document, and Bleek recognises alterations by the hand of the supplementer; but Davidson apportions most of them to the

Jehovist, giving the fragments that remain to the younger Elohist and the late redactor. The insufficient character of the grounds on which such assignments are made will be noted in the opposition ; in the mean time the ,remark is pertinent that their very diversity is one of the strongest indirect proofs of the Mosaic authorship of the entire composition.

Ver. 2. — **These** are **the generations of Jacob.** The opening of a new section (cf. ch. ii. 4 ; v. 1, &c.). **Joseph,**—the son of Rachel, and born in Padan-aram (ch. xxx. 24)—being **seventeen years old,**—literally, *a son of seventeen years,* thus making Jacob 108—**was feeding the flock with his brethren ;**—literally, *was shepherding ;* not his brethren (Bush), but with his brethren, in, or among, the flock—**and the lad** was—literally, *and he a lad, ætate, moribus et innocentia* (Lyra), *non tantum ætate sed et ministerio* (Poole), but most probably designed simply as a note of his age. Pererius, following the Vulgate, connects the clause with what precedes ; Calvin, Dathius, Lange, Murphy, Kalisch, and others conjoin it with the words that follow ; the LXX., Willet, Rosenmüller, Keil, Ainsworth, Bush, &c. regard it as a parenthetical statement—**with**—not in the capacity of a servant (Vatablus) or of a ward (Kalisch), but of a companion—**the sons of Bilhah, and with the sons of Zilpah, his father's wives.** With these rather than the sons of Leah, as being less supercilious and haughty than the children of the first wife (Lawson), or as being less opposed to him than they (Lange), or more probably as being nearer to his own age than they (Keil), or perhaps as having been brought more into contact with the handmaids' children, and in particular with those of Bilhah, Rachel's maid, who may have been to him as a mother after Rachel's death (Rosenmüller). **And Joseph brought unto his** (rather, their) **father their evil report.** Not *accusavit fratres suos apud patrem crimine pessimo* (Vulgate), or κατήνεγκαν ψόγον πονηρὸν πρὸς Ἰσραὴλ τὸν πατέρα αὐτῶν (LXX.), as if Joseph drew down upon himself their calumnious reports, but carried to his father an evil report concerning them (Kalisch) ; not informed him of what he himself saw of their ·evil deeds (Lawson), though this need not be excluded, but repeated the דִּבָּה, or *fama,* always of a bad character (Rosenmüller), which was circulating in the district respecting them — *malos rumores qui subinde de iis spargebantur* (Dathius) ; — the noun being derived from an onomatopœtic root, דָּבַב, signifying to go slowly, or to creep about.

Ver. 3.—**Now** (literally, *and*) **Israel loved Joseph more than all his children** (literally, *sons*), **because he** was **the son of his old age** —literally, *a son of old age* (was) *he to him ;* not a son possessing the wisdom of advanced years (Onkelos), but a son born in his old age (Rosenmüller, Keil, Kalisch, *et alii*), which was literally true of Joseph, since he was born in his father's ninety-first year. Yet as Joseph was only a year or two younger than the children of Bilhah and Zilpah, and as Benjamin was still later born than he, the application of this epithet to Joseph has been explained on the ground that Benjamin was at this time little more than a child (Keil), and had not much come into notice (Murphy), or perhaps was not born when this portion of the narrative was originally written ('Speaker's Commentary') ; or that Joseph had obtained the name before Benjamin's birth, and that it had clung to him after that event (Inglis). Josephus ('Ant.,' ii. 2, 1) gives another reason for Jacob's partiality which is not inconsistent with the statement in the text, viz., the beauty of his person and the virtue of his mind, διὰ τε τὴν τοῦ σώματος εὐγένειαν, καὶ διὰ ψυχῆς ἀρετῆς. **And he made him a coat of** many **colours** —literally, *a coat* (*kithoneth,* from *kathan,* to cover ; *vide* ch. iii. 21) *of ends* (Keil, Lange), *i. e.* a tunic reaching to the ancles, and with sleeves reaching to the wrists, and commonly worn by boys and girls of the upper ranks (Josephus, 'Ant.,' vii. 8, 1 ; 2 Sam. xiii. 18), or a coat of pieces (Kalisch, T. Lewis, Wordsworth) ; hence a variegated garment, χιτὼν ποικίλος (LXX.), *tunica polymita* (Vulgate), a coat of many colours (Murphy, 'Speaker's Commentary'). "Such garments are represented on some of the monuments of Egypt. At Beni-Hassan, for example, there is a magnificent excavation forming the tomb of Pihrai, a military officer of Osirtasen I., in which a train of foreign captives appears, who are supposed to be Jebusites, an inscription over one person in the group reading, "The Chief of the Land of the Jebusites." The whole of the captives are clad in parti-coloured garments, and the tunic of this individual in particular may be called "a coat of many colours" (Thornley Smith, 'Joseph and his Times,' p. 12). It has been supposed that Jacob's object in conferring this distinction on Joseph was to mark him out as the heir to whom the forfeited birthright of Reuben (1 Chron. v. 1) was to be transferred (Kurtz, Lange, Gerlach, Bush, Wordsworth, 'Speaker's Commentary,' &c.) ; but the historian only mentions it as a token of affection, such as was customary in those times for princes to bestow upon their subjects, and parents on their children (*vide* Thornley Smith, 'Joseph and his Times,' p. 11). Roberts says the same thing is still done among the Hindoos, crimson, purple, and other colours being often tastefully sewed together for beautiful or favoured children (*vide* 'Oriental Illustrations,' p. 43).

Ver. 4.—**And when** (literally, *and*) **his brethren saw that their father loved him more than all his brethren, they** (literally, *and they*) **hated him,**—as Esau hated Jacob (ch. xxvii. 41 ; cf. ch. xlix. 23)—**and could not speak peacably unto him**—literally, *they were not able to speak of him for peace,* i. e. they could not address him in such a way as to wish him well ; they could not offer him the customary salutation of *Shalom,* or Peace.

Ver. 5.—**And Joseph dreamed a dream** (in which, though, as the sequel shows, intended as a Divine communication, there was nothing to distinguish it from an ordinary product of the mind), **and he told it to his brethren:**—not in pride, since there is no reason to suppose that Joseph as yet understood the celestial origin of his dream, but in the simplicity of his heart (Kalisch, Murphy), though in doing so he was also guided, unconsciously it may be, but still really, by an overruling providence, who made use of this very telling of the dream as a step towards its fulfilment (Lawson)—**and they hated him yet the more**—literally, *and they added again to hate him.*

Ver. 6.—**And he said unto them, Hear, I pray you, this dream which I have dreamed.** Though Joseph did not certainly know that his dream was supernatural, he may have thought that it was, the more so as dreams were in those times commonly regarded as mediums of Divine communication ; and in this case it was clearly his duty to impart it to the household, and all the more that the subject of it seemed to be for them a matter of peculiar importance. In the absence of information to the contrary, we are warranted in believing that there was nothing either sinful or offensive in Joseph's spirit or manner in making known his dreams. That which appears to have excited the hostility of his brethren was not the mode of their communication, but the character of their contents.

Ver. 7.—**For** (literally, *and*), **behold, we** were **binding sheaves**—literally, *binding things bound,* i. e. sheaves, *alumim,* from *alam,* to bind ; the order of the words and the participial form of the verb indicating that the speaker describes the vision as it appeared to his mind (*vide* Ewald, 'Heb. Synt.,' § 342)—**in the field,**—literally, *in the middle of the field ;* from which it would appear that Jacob was not a mere nomad, but carried on agricultural operations like his father Isaac (ch. xxvi. 12)—**and, lo,**—" the הִנֵּה, as repeated in his narration, shows that he had a presentiment of something great "

(Lange)—**my sheaf arose, and also stood upright** (literally, *stood,* i. e. placed itself upright, and remained so) ; **and, behold, your sheaves stood round about, and made obeisance**—*i. e.* bowed themselves down (cf. ch. xxiii. 7, Abraham bowing to the Hethites)—**to my sheaf.** The fulfilment of this dream occurred in Egypt (*vide* ch. xlii. 6 ; xliii. 26 ; xliv. 14).

Ver. 8.—**And his brethren** (who had no difficulty in interpreting the symbol's significance) **said to him** (with mingled indignation and contempt), **Shalt thou indeed reign over us?**—literally, *reigning, wilt thou reign?* i. e. wilt thou actually *reign* over us ? the emphasis resting on the action of the verb (*vide* Ewald, ' Heb. Synt.,' § 312*a*)—**or shalt thou indeed have dominion over us ?** The form of expression is the same as that of the preceding clause. **And they hated him yet the more** (literally *and they added again to hate him*) **for** (*i. e.* on account of) **his dreams, and for** (or, on account of) **his words.**

Ver. 9.—**And he dreamed yet another dream,** — the doubling of the dream was designed to indicate its certainty (cf. ch. xli. 32) — **and told it his brethren, and said, Behold, I have dreamed a dream more ; and, behold, the sun** (הַשֶּׁמֶשׁ, the minister, from Chaldee root שְׁמַשׁ, the pael of which occurs in Dan. vii. 10) **and the moon** — קָיְרַח, probably, if the word be not a primitive, the circuit-maker, from the unused root יָרַח = אָרַח, to go about (Fürst) ; or the yellow one, from יָרַח = יָרַק, to be yellow, ה and ק being interchanged (Gesenius) — **and the eleven stars**—rather, eleven stars, כּוֹכָבִים, globes, or balls, from כָּבַב, to roll up in a ball (*vide* ch. i. 16)—**made obeisance to me**—literally, *bowing themselves to me,* the participles being employed *ut supra,* ver. 7. It is apparent that Joseph understood this second dream, even more plainly than the first, to foreshadow, in some way unexplained, his future supremacy over his brethren, who were unmistakably pointed out by the eleven stars of the vision ; and this remarkable coincidence between the number of the stars and the number of his brethren would facilitate the inference that his parents were referred to under the other symbols of the sun and moon. In the most ancient symbology, Oriental and Grecian as well as Biblical (Numb. xxiv. 17), it was customary to speak of noble personages, princes, &c., under such figures ; and the employment of such terminology by a nomadic people like the Hebrew patriarchs, who constantly lived beneath the open sky, may almost be regarded as a water-mark attesting the historic credibility of this page at least of the sacred record (*vide* Hävernick, 'Introd.,' § 21), in opposition to Bohlen, who finds in the symbolical character of Joseph's dreams an evidence of their unreality, and De Wette, who explains them as the offspring of his aspiring mind.

Ver. 10.—**And he told it to his father, and to his brethren**—whom it manifestly concerned, as, for the like reason, he had reported the first dream only to his brethren. That he does not tell it to his mother may be an indication that Rachel was by this time dead. **And his father rebuked him,**—either to avoid irritating his brethren (Calvin), or to repress an appearance of pride in Joseph (Lange, Murphy, Inglis), or to express his own surprise (Candlish) or irritation (Keil), or sense of the absurdity of the dream (Lawson), which he further demonstrated when he added—**and said unto him, What** is **this dream that thou hast dreamed? Shall I and thy mother**—(1) "Rachel, who was neither forgotten nor lost" (Keil), who may possibly have been living at the date of the dream ('Speaker's Commentary'), though then Joseph could not have had eleven brothers; who, being dead, was referred to in order to show the impossibility of its ever

being fulfilled (Kalisch, Pererius); or (2) Leah, as the chief mistress of Jacob's household (Willet, Hughes, Inglis); or (3) Bilhah, Rachel's maid, who had probably acted as Joseph's mother after Rachel's death (Jewish interpreters, Grotius, and others); or, what seems more probable, (4) the term "mother" is here introduced simply for the sake of giving completeness to the symbol (Kurtz, Murphy)—**and thy brethren indeed come to bow down ourselves to thee**—Joseph's brethren ultimately did so in Egypt (ch. xli. 6); Joseph's father practically did so when he recognised Joseph's greatness and depended on him for support (ch. xlvii. 12). It is certain that Leah died before the immigration to Egypt (ch. xlix. 31), and it cannot be determined whether Bilhah or Zilpah went to Egypt—**to the earth.** Jacob seems here, by intensifying Joseph's language, to resent the claim which it conveyed.

Ver. 11.—**And his brethren envied him.** The verb קָנָא (unused in Kal), to become red in the face, seems to indicate that the hatred of Joseph's brethren revealed itself in scowling looks. **But his father observed the saying**—literally, *kept the word*, διετήρησε τὸ ῥῆμα (LXX.). Cf. Dan. vii. 28; Luke ii. 51.

HOMILETICS

Vers. 2—11.—*Joseph in his father's house.* I. JOSEPH EMPLOYED WITH HIS BRETHREN. 1. *With them in the sense of as well as them.* That is to say, Joseph no more than the other sons of his father was trained to indolence. It is the duty of parents to educate their children in some useful and honourable calling. Even when not required for procuring daily bread, it is of advantage as a means of withdrawing one from temptations which would otherwise beset him, while it largely enhances the enjoyment of existence, and enables one to contribute more or less directly to the sum of human happiness. Adam, Noah, Abraham, Isaac, and even Laban, all brought up their sons to honest toil. 2. *With them in the sense of like them.* That is, he was, as they had been before him, instructed in the business of a husbandman and shepherd. There is evidence that Jacob combined the callings of an agriculturist as well as sheep-farmer, and trained his boys to sow and reap and bind sheaves as well as tend the flocks and herds on his estate. From this, however, it were wrong to argue that all the children in a family should be trained alike, or put to learn the same craft or profession. In Jacob's day and Joseph's there was little choice of openings for young men who had aspirations above the crook or the plough. But in these times the avocations of men are as diverse as their gifts; and in all respects it is better—more beneficial to society at large, and more advantageous for the individual—that a wise discrimination be exercised by parents and guardians in selecting spheres of labour for those dependent on or intrusted to them that shall be suited to their gifts and tastes. 3. *With them in the sense of beside them.* Joseph accompanied his brethren when they tended the flocks or reaped the ripened grain, and in particular associated himself, for reasons suggested in the Exposition, with the sons of Bilhah and Zilpah. It was a privilege which Joseph enjoyed that he did not need to go from home to learn his trade; and doubtless Joseph's amiable disposition would make the society of his father's sons more agreeable to him than the company of strangers.

II. JOSEPH PREFERRED ABOVE HIS BRETHREN. 1. *By his father.* (1) The ground of Jacob's partiality for Joseph.   He was the son of Jacob's old age.   However this expression may be explained (*vide* Exposition), the amount of it seems to be that Joseph had come to gladden Jacob's heart after a considerable period of waiting, and at a time when Jacob was beginning to feel himself an old man.   Hence more than to any of his other children Jacob's affections went out to the firstborn of Rachel, and this affection could not fail to strengthen after Rachel's death.   It is just possible also that it was kept alive and fostered by a reminiscence of Rachel's beauty, which he saw reproduced in the well-proportioned frame and finely-cut features of the growing lad.   Anyhow, Jacob's fondness for Joseph was palpable; and without affirming that it was right, it may at least be contended that it was natural, the more especially when Joseph's piety is contrasted with the notorious wickedness of Jacob's other sons.   (2) The exhibition of Jacob's partiality for Joseph.   Many parents who find themselves in Jacob's situation, drawn to one child more than another in their families, make an effort at least to conceal a preference which in their inmost hearts they cannot but feel to be justifiable.   But Jacob, with a sad lack of prudence, displayed his superior estimation of Rachel's son by presenting him with a rich and valuable coat of ends or pieces (*vide* Exposition).   As might have been expected, such a mark of preference was distasteful to his other children, and, had it not been for Joseph's superior character, might have been morally hurtful to Joseph himself.   As it was, it was no kindness to Joseph, but only a foolish gratification to Joseph's father.   2. *By God*.   Joseph was honoured to receive dreams prophetic of his future greatness.   The first, the dream of the bowing sheaves, was a Divine foreshadowing of his advancement above his brethren; and the second, the dream of the nodding orbs, of his elevation above all the members of his family.   Even had they not concerned himself at all, to have been made the recipient of Divine communications was an honour; much more when these communications related to his own exaltation.   This preference of Joseph was unquestionably gracious, but it was also natural (1 Sam. ii. 30)

III. JOSEPH HATED BY HIS BRETHREN.   1. *The cause of their hatred*.   This was—(1) The superior place which he enjoyed in their father's affection (ver. 4).   Parents may here observe the danger of cherishing, and especially of manifesting, a preference of one member of the family above another.   Unless in very exceptional circumstances, all are equally entitled to a father's care and a mother's love.   (2) The superior piety he displayed above themselves.   It is difficult to credit the actors in the Shechemite and Dothan tragedies with anything in the shape of religion.   Certainly they were not looked upon as exemplary characters by those who had the misfortune to live beside them.   Out of their father's sight they shook off any little restraint which his presence may have inspired.   Their scandalous behaviour became the talk of every neighbourhood they chanced to visit; and Joseph hearing it, as in duty bound, reported it to Jacob.   Not that the mere reporting of it at home would much concern these reckless youths.   Possibly it would exasperate their minds against their brother.   But the thing which would incense them most would be the disinclination which he showed to run with them into the same excess of riot.   (3) The superior honour he received from God.   The brethren clearly enough understood the dreams to contain a prognostication of Joseph's future, else why did they allow themselves to become inflamed with anger on account of a foolish boy's fancies?   At least they believed Joseph regarded them in this light, and they hated him on that account.   2. *The progress of their hatred*.   (1) They omitted to give him the customary salutation of Shalem.   It is a bad sign when a man declines to exchange friendly greetings with his neighbour, and much more with his brother.   (2) They passed on to deep and bitter hatred.   They hated him yet the more for his dreams and his words.   Evil passions have a tendency to grow, and should be nipped in the bud.   *Obsta principiis*.   (3) They envied him; the fierce malignity of their enraged spirits burning in their bosoms, suffusing their countenances with ominous looks and angry scowls, and generally expressing itself in dislike, irritation, and annoyance.   3. *The end of their hatred*.   It was impossible that the gathering storm should continue long without bursting.   All things mundane, evil as well as good, strive after completeness.   "Lust, when it hath conceived, bringeth forth sin: sin, when it is finished, bringeth forth death" (James i. 15).   Hence, "whosoever hateth his brother is a murderer"

(1 John iii. 15); initially in thought, and ultimately, granting time and opportunity, in deed. The murderous feeling of Joseph's brethren very speedily found occasion to become the fratricidal act.

HOMILIES BY VARIOUS AUTHORS.

Ch. xxxvii.—*The representative man.* Jacob may be said to fall into the background from this time until his parting benediction. The kingdom of God is represented in Joseph and his history. The main points in this chapter are—

I. GOD'S DISTINGUISHING GRACE TO JOSEPH, separating him from his brethren in character, in his father's affection, in the method of his life, in the communications of the Spirit. Joseph is the type of the believer, faithful to the covenant, amongst both the Canaanitish heathen and the unfaithful children of the covenant, the patriarchs.

II. THE WORKING OF EVIL PASSIONS AND MORAL IMPURITY BROUGHT TO A CLIMAX THROUGH THE DEVELOPMENT OF GOD'S GRACE IN THE INDIVIDUAL. Joseph brought the evil report to Jacob. Joseph dreamed. Joseph was evidently both in himself superior to his brethren and more favoured by God. That is the old story—the Cain spirit developed by contact with the Abel spirit. A time of special grace is always a time of special wickedness and judgment. Witness the advent of the Lord, the Reformation period, the revival of religion in the last century, leading on to the outburst of both wickedness and judgment at the end.

III. THE DREAMS OF THE PIOUS LAD WERE THEMSELVES STEPS IN THE COURSE OF REVELATION. The dominion which was foreshadowed was that of the spiritual kingdom over the unspiritual.

IV. THE PROVIDENTIAL FULFILMENT OF THE PROMISE. Partly through the personal character of Joseph, partly through the evil passions of his brethren, partly through the apparently casual incidents of the neighbourhood, partly through the Spirit of righteousness working in the heart of Reuben, partly through the weakness and fondness of Jacob. How strangely "all things work together" in God's hands! He weaves the web composed of many single threads into one united, orderly pattern as a whole in which we are able to trace his own thought and purpose.

V. Joseph in the pit while his brethren sit down to eat bread represents THE BELIEVER SUFFERING IN THE MIDST OF AN UNBELIEVING WORLD. A type of Jesus cast into the pit of his humiliation, while the Jewish people despised and rejected his claims, his prophetic words, his evident favour with God, and by their transactions with Gentiles, the Romans, gave him up to what *seemed* to them ruin, but what *was* the crowning of his head with glory. We begin to see at this point that, as the Psalmist sang, "the word of the Lord tried him."

VI. THE DELIVERANCE of Joseph and his transference to the sphere of his future triumph are EFFECTED THROUGH JUDAH IMMEDIATELY, THROUGH THE OTHER BRETHREN AND THE ISHMAELITES OR MIDIANITES SECONDARILY. These names of Judah, Ishmael, Midian remind us that the fleshly links which bind the descendants of Abraham together are not lost sight of by God, are called in to serve the purposes of grace, but not to take the place of the true spiritual work, which goes on in its own appointed channel. So in the history of the Church, while there are many secondary influences at work, still there is a remnant according to the election of grace in which there is the real continuity of Divine dealings.

VII. The genuine grief of Reuben, the barbarous inhumanity towards their father of the fallen sons, THE OVERWHELMING SORROW OF THE AGED, HEART-BROKEN JACOB, the rising up of all his sons and daughters to comfort him, are all beautiful and significant touches of nature in this history, which remind us that we are not "following cunningly-devised fables," and that God's gracious kingdom of truth and love does not annihilate the human in order to reveal the Divine, but puts its rainbow on the cloud.

VIII. THE INTRODUCTION OF EGYPT again into the history. Egypt is the type of the world, as built upon the foundation of fallen humanity alone, without the special grace of God. Into that bulk of the unrenewed race the leaven of the kingdom must be put. The connection between the covenant family and Egypt, which we trace in the history of Abraham, Isaac, and Jacob, as afterwards in their descendants, represents at once (1) the thoroughly human character of the kingdom that God would set up in the earth, for the people of God found much in Egypt which they carried away with them afterwards, and assimilated to their own specially-communicated faith; (2) the breadth of the promises of God—the separation of the one people was for the sake of all the families of the earth.—R.

Vers. 2—4.—*Joseph at home.* "Joseph, being seventeen years old," &c. Picturesque scene is the encampment of Jacob. How well the dark camel-hair tents harmonise with the general character of the spots in which they are pitched. Peace and purity should dwell there. Ten men of the tribe of Jacob are most depraved, but their characters only threw into brighter prominence that of Joseph. It is probable that Jacob gave greater attention to the training of Joseph than to that of his brethren. He showed favouritism also. His act of giving him a garb of varied colour may not altogether have been so foolish and weak as sometimes it has been supposed to be. It was simply an ordinary Eastern way of indicating that Joseph was to be the future leader and sheik of the encampment. Think of Joseph's home life, and learn—

I. THAT AT HOME WE SHOULD, LIKE JOSEPH, LEARN TO PREPARE FOR FUTURE LIFE. Doubtless Jacob would tell Joseph of the promises of God to Abraham, of the tradition of the Deluge and the Fall; probably also of his own fleeing from home, and his dream in the desert, when he saw "the great altar-stair sloping through darkness up to God," and the angels ascending and descending. Joseph always afterwards has great faith in dreams. No book had he. The Bible was not written. Traditions and oral teaching formed his mental training.

II. AT HOME WE SHOULD ALWAYS HAVE SOME EMPLOYMENT. His father loved him too dearly to allow him to grow up in habits of idleness. He learned to handle the crook and to become a faithful messenger. No work is to be despised, for all may be a preparation for future usefulness.

III. AT HOME WE SHOULD NOT WILLINGLY BE WITNESSES OF WRONG-DOING. The lives of Joseph's brethren were sinful, and their doings deceitful. Some things he is obliged to know about of which it is dangerous to keep silence. The welfare of the whole tribe was being risked by the elder brothers, and Joseph, fearing that, tells his father, or seeks counsel that he may be strengthened to resist evil influence.

IV. AT HOME WE MAY HAVE GLOWING VISIONS OF THE FUTURE. The two dreams concerning the sheaves, and the sun and moon and stars, brought hate from his brethren, but they had an influence on Joseph's after life. They were remarkably fulfilled. We all have some such visions. We build "castles in the air." The stern realities of life tone down our dreams. It is well to have some such dreams. Without them few make any advance in life. We are not to be like mere senseless stones, but growing plants. Better is it to bear fruit than to wait to become only the sport of circumstances.—H.

EXPOSITION.

Ver. 12.—**And his brethren went to feed their father's flock in Shechem**—*i. e.* the modern Nâblous, in the plain of Muknah, which belonged to Jacob partly by purchase and partly by conquest (*vide* ch. xxxiii. 19; xxxiv. 27). Shechem was at a considerable distance from the vale of Hebron, where the patriarchal family at this time resided.

Ver. 13.—**And Israel** (*vide* ch. xxxii. 28; xxxv. 10) **said unto Joseph, Do not thy brethren feed** the flock (literally, *Are not thy brethren shepherding?*) **in Shechem? come, and I will send thee unto them.** Either he was solicitous of the safety of his sons while in the vicinity of Shechem (Lawson), or he

hoped to effect a reconciliation between them and Joseph (Candlish). **And he** (*i. e.* Joseph, in response to this invitation, expressed a willingness to undertake a mission to his brethren, and) **said to him, Here am I.**

Ver. 14.—**And he** (Jacob) **said to him, Go, I pray thee, see whether it be well with thy brethren** (literally, *see the place of thy brethren*), **and well with the flocks** (literally, *and the peace of the flock*); **and bring me word again. So** (literally, *and*) **he sent him out of the vale of Hebron** (*vide* ch. xxxv. 27), **and he came to Shechem**—a distance of sixty miles.

Vers. 15, 16.—**And a certain man** (or simply

a man) found him, and, behold, he was wandering in the field (obviously seeking some thing or person) : and the man asked him, saying, What seekest thou ? And he said, I seek my brethren :—or, more emphatically, My brethren I (sc. am) seeking—tell me, I pray thee, where they feed their flocks —or, Where (are) they shepherding ?

Ver. 17.—And the man said, They are departed hence; for I heard them say, Let us go to Dothan — Dothaim, "the Two Wells," a place twelve miles north of Samaria in the direction of the plain of Esdraelon, situated on the great caravan road from Mount Gilead to Egypt, the scene of one of the greatest miracles of Elisha the prophet (2 Kings vi. 13—18), and, though now a deserted ruin, still called by its ancient name. And Joseph went after his brethren, and found them in Dothan. " Just beneath Tell Dothan, which still preserves its name, is the little oblong plain, containing the best pasturage in the country, and well chosen by Jacob's sons when they had exhausted for a time the wider plain of Shechem " (Tristram, 'Land of Israel,' p. 132 ; cf. Thomson, 'Land and Book,' p. 466).

Ver. 18.—And when (literally, and) they saw him afar off, even (or, and) before he came near unto them, they (literally, and they) conspired against him (or, dealt with him fraudulently) to slay him.

Ver. 19.—And they said one to another (literally, a man to his brother), Behold, this dreamer—literally, this lord of dreams (cf. ch. xiv. 13 ; Exod. xxiv. 14)—cometh —expressive of rancour, contempt, and hatred.

Ver. 20.—Come now therefore, and let us slay him, and cast him into some pit (literally, into one of the pits or cisterns in the neighbourhood), and we will say (sc. to his father and ours), Some (literally, an) evil beast hath devoured him (which will account for his disappearance); and we shall see what will become of his dreams—or, what his dreams will be.

Vers. 21, 22.—And Reuben (the eldest son, and therefore probably regarding himself as in some degree responsible for Joseph's safety) heard it, and he delivered him out of their hands; and said, Let us not kill him—literally, Let us not destroy his life (nephesh). And Reuben said (further) unto them, Shed no blood, but cast him into this pit that is in the wilderness (i. e. into a dry pit that was near), and lay no hand upon him; that (the adverb indicates the purpose Reuben had in view) he might rid him (translated above deliver him) out of their hands, to deliver him (or, more correctly, to return him) to his father again.

Ver. 23.—And it came to pass, when Joseph was come unto his brethren, that they stript Joseph out of his coat, his coat of many colours—i. e. his coat of ends, or coat of pieces (vide on ver. 3)—that was on him.

Vers. 24, 25.—And they took him, and cast him into a pit : and the pit was empty, there was no water in it. Cisterns when empty, or only covered with mud at the bottom, were sometimes used as temporary prisons (Jer. xxxviii. 6 ; xl. 15). And—leaving him, as they must have calculated, to perish by a painful death through starvation, with exquisite cold-bloodedness, paying no heed to his piteous outcries and appeals (ch. xli. 21)—they sat down (the callous composure of the act indicates deplorable brutality on the part of Joseph's brethren) to eat bread (perhaps with a secret feeling of satisfaction, if not also exultation, that they had effectually disposed of the young man and his dreams): and they lifted up their eyes and looked, and, behold, a company — orchath, from arach, to walk ; a band of travellers, especially of merchantmen ; a caravan ; συνοδία, ὁδοιπόροι (LXX. ; cf. Job vi. 19)—of Ishmaelites—Arabs descended from Ishmael, who occupied the district lying between Egypt and Assyria (ch. xxv. 18), and, as appears from the record, carried on a trade with the former country. That Ishmael's descendants should already have developed into a trading nation will not be surprising (Bohlen) if one reflects that Ishmael may have married in his eighteenth or twentieth year, i. e. about 162 years before the date of the present occurrence, that four generations may have been born in the interval, and that, if Ishmael's sons had only five sons each, his posterity in the fifth generation (not reckoning females) may have amounted to 15,000 persons (Murphy). But in point of fact the Ishmaelites spoken of are not described as nations—simply as a company of merchants, without saying how numerous it was (Hävernick, 'Introd.,' § 21)—came (literally, coming) from Gilead (vide ch. xxxi. 21) with (literally, and) their camels bearing spicery —נְכֹאת, either an infinitive from נָכָא, to break, to grind (?), and signifying a pounding, breaking in pieces, hence aromatic powder (Gesenius) ; or a contraction from נְכָאוֹת (Ewald), meaning that which is powdered or pulverised. Rendered θυμιάματα (LXX.), aromata (Vulgate), στύραξ (Aquila), it was probably the gum tragacanth, many kinds of which appear in Syria (Fürst, Gesenius, Rosenmüller, Keil, Kalisch, Lange, Murphy), or storax, the resinous exudation of the styrax officinale, which abounds in Palestine and the East (Aquila, Bochart, Bush, 'Speaker's Commentary,' Inglis)—and balm —צְרִי (in pause צֳרִי, after vau of union צְרִי), mentioned as one of the most precious fruits of Palestine (ch. xliii. 11), rendered ῥητίνη (LXX.) and *refina* (Vulgate), and derived from צוּף, to flow, to run (hence, literally, *an outflowing*, or out-dropping), was unquestionably a balsam, but of what tree cannot now be ascertained, distilling from a tree or fruit growing in Gilead, and highly prized for its healing properties (Jer. viii. 22 ; xlvi. 11). *Vide* Lexicons (Gesenius and Fürst) *sub voce;* Michaelis, 'Suppl.,' p. 2142 ; Kalisch *in loco*—**and myrrh,**—לֹט, στακτή (LXX.), *stacte* (Vulgate), *pistacia* (Chaldee, Syriac, Michaelis, 'Suppl.,' p. 1424), was more probably ladanum (Gesenius, Fürst, Rosenmüller, Keil, Kalisch, *et alii*),

an odoriferous gum formed upon the leaves of the cistus-rose, a shrub growing in Arabia, Syria, and Palestine (*vide* Herod., iii. 112 ; Pliny, 'N. H.,' xii. 37 ; Celsius, 'Hierob.,' i. 280—288)—**going**—the caravan route from Gilead crossed the Jordan in the neighbourhood of Bersan, and, sweeping through Jenin and the plain of Dothan, joined another track leading southwards from Damascus by way of Ramleh and Gaza (*vide* Robinson, iii. 27, and cf. Tristram, 'Land of Israel,' p. 132)—**to carry** it **down to Egypt.** At that time the land of the Pharaohs was the chief emporium for the world's merchandise.

HOMILETICS.

Vers. 12—25.—*Joseph among his brethren at Dothan.* I. THE FRIENDLY MISSION. 1. *Its local destination.* This was Shechem, at a distance of sixty miles from Hebron, where Jacob had previously resided for a number of years and acquired a small estate (ch. xxxiii. 18, 19), where Jacob's sons had committed, a few years before, the terrible atrocity which made the name of Israel stink throughout the land (ch. xxxiv. 26—30); and where now Joseph's brethren were shepherding their flocks, having gone thither either on account of the excellent pasture, or in order to be beyond the reach of Joseph and his tale-bearing, or perhaps with a mind to keep an eye on their father's estate. 2. *Its kindly intention.* Joseph was despatched to this important sheep-station in the north to inquire after the welfare of his brethren. That Jacob should have sent a son so tender and beloved on a journey so arduous and an errand so fraught with danger to himself, considering the well-known hostility of his brethren towards him, if a proof of Jacob's want of consideration, was also a mark of his parental solicitude for his sons' behaviour, as well as a sign of his apprehensions for their safety, venturing, as they had, to revisit the scene of their former crimes, and perhaps it may be added, an indication of his desire to effect a reconciliation between Joseph and his brethren. 3. *Its cheerful susception.* Though realising better than his father did the perilous character of the enterprise, in consequence of knowing more exactly than his father the depth of malignant feeling entertained towards him by his brethren, Joseph did not hesitate to comply with his father's instructions, but, making nothing of the long journey, and keeping silent as to the risks of increased hatred, if nothing more, which he must have known that mission would entail upon him, cheerfully replied, Here am I. What a bright example of true filial piety and obedience ! 4. *Its successful completion.* Arriving at Shechem, he first failed to find his brethren, and then lost his way, but ultimately, on being directed by a stranger, discovered them at Dothan. The perseverance of Joseph in carrying through his father's commission may be profitably studied, as a pattern to all to whom any sort of work, but more especially Christian work, is intrusted.

II. THE DIABOLICAL CONSPIRACY. 1. *Its innocent occasion*—the approach of Joseph in his long-sleeved and long-skirted tunic. Like a gunpowder train that has been carefully prepared, and only wants the application of a spark to produce an explosion, the brethren of Joseph were only needing some trifling incident to elicit all the fratricidal hate which was already growing in their bosoms, and that incident was supplied by the sight of the coat of ends. It was a striking illustration of how great results frequently proceed from apparently insignificant causes (James iii. 4, 5). 2. *Its murderous character.* It aimed at the destruction of Joseph's life. With unexampled unanimity, not a voice was raised against the proposal (perhaps made by Simeon) to kill him and cast his lifeless body into a pit. The proposal of Reuben must have been understood by the others as only a more excruciatingly cruel way of inflicting death, viz., by starvation. See here in Jacob's family a development of the same spirit of murder as existed in Adam's. Like Cain, the sons of Jacob were of that wicked one, and slew (in intention at least) their brother, and for the same reason (1 John iii. 12). 3. *Its impious design*—to spoil his dreams. From this it is evident that they regarded his dreams as a Heaven-sent prognostication of his future greatness ; else, if they regarded them as purely boyish fancies, why should they have felt annoyed at what was so evidently groundless ? Hence, in seeking to prevent the realisation of his dreams they were actually fighting against God. But it is just precisely in proportion as wicked men see God's hand in any prophecy or programme that they take measures to insure its defeat (cf. 1 Sam. xix. 1 ; 2 Kings vi. 14). 4. *Its ruthless execution.* They took him and cast him into a pit. The crime was perpetrated (1) with insolent humiliation—they stripped the poor lad of his pretty coat ; (2) with violent brutality—they cast him into the pit ; Jeremiah was let down by cords (Jer. xxxviii. 6) ; (3) with relentless cruelty—they heeded not his outcries and entreaties (ch. xlii. 21, 22) ; and (4) with exquisite cold-bloodedness—having despatched their infernal business, with infinite nonchalance the ruffians sat down to eat bread, to regale their appetites after a good day's work.

III. THE ATTEMPTED RESCUE. The stratagem of Reuben was—1. *Mercifully designed.* Reuben, in some respects not a person to be greatly admired, weak and vacillating in his character, and easily drawn aside by stronger natures into sinful courses, appears in this matter to have been the only one of Joseph's brethren in whom the natural affections of a brother were not completely overborne. Though he wanted the courage to resist his stronger-minded brothers, he seems to have conceived the purpose of saving, if he could, the life of Joseph. So far the stratagem was good, only it was—2. *Timidly planned.* The narrative would almost seem to convey that Reuben in the first onset of his opposition to his brother's nefarious intentions had succeeded in wresting Joseph from their hands. Had he at that moment asserted himself with vigour and boldness, as became the firstborn of the house, he might have saved Joseph altogether. But, alas, true to his feeble and pusillanimous character, he allowed himself to be overcome by the clamours of his fiercer-natured brethren, and only proposed that instead of imbruing their hands in Joseph's blood they should inflict on him the horrors of starvation. In making such a proposal of course Reuben hoped to be able to effect his deliverance, in which he might have succeeded, had he acted with promptitude and decision. But instead his stratagem was—3. *Weakly carried through.* Where Reuben was when his brethren were comforting their hearts with a dinner after Joseph's consignment to the cistern, and concocting the matter of his sale, the narrative does not say ; but most likely he was by himself, deliberating, and resolving, and hesitating, and delaying, instead of acting. Hence his stratagem was—4. *Completely defeated.* By the time he had got his mind made up to act it was too late. When he returned to the pit Joseph was gone, and, like many another procrastinator, he could only bemoan his own folly.

HOMILIES BY VARIOUS AUTHORS.

Vers. 14, 15.—*Joseph leaving home.* " Go, I pray thee, see whether," &c. Joseph left home unexpectedly. He knew not when he left it to seek his brethren that he would never come back again. After a longer journey than he anticipated Joseph finds his brethren.

I. Like many leaving home, Joseph MET WITH FAITHFUL GUIDES. There are generally companions, teachers, ministers to help.

II. Like many leaving home, Joseph FELL INTO SNARES. He ·could not help himself. The snares were not such as were willingly entered. The wicked entrapped him. On this youth, far from home, defenceless, and kindly-intentioned, nine cowardly men fell.

III. Like many away from home, Joseph FOUND THAT GOD CARED FOR HIM WHEN HIS EARTHLY FATHER COULD NOT. Reuben was the means of saving him from death. Sold into slavery, he was still on the highway to eminence. We have to beware of hateful and murderous thoughts, remembering " that he that hateth his brother is " (so far as intent goes) " a murderer." In all journeyings we have to commit our way unto the Lord, and he will guide and defend.—H.

Vers. 20, 21.—*God's providence and man's responsibility.* I. GOD'S PURPOSES CARRIED OUT BY MEN IRRESPECTIVE OF THEIR OWN PLANS. The word to Abraham (ch. xv. 13) does not seem to have been thought of by Jacob. After long wandering he seemed to be settled in Canaan. But God was bringing to pass his word. Jacob's injudicious fondness for Joseph, the anger and murderous design of his brethren (cf. John xi. 50; Acts iii. 17), Reuben's timid effort for his deliverance (cf. Acts v. 38), Judah's worldly wise counsel (cf. Luke xiii. 31), Joseph's imprisonment by Potiphar, the conspiracy in Pharaoh's household, were so many steps by which the sojourn in Egypt was brought about. So in the founding of the Christian Church. The writing on the cross (John xix. 20) pointed to three separate lines of history, two of them pagan, which combined to bring about the sacrifice of Christ and the spread of the gospel. So in the case of individuals. God's promises are sure (2 Cor. i. 20). There may seem to be many hindrances, from ourselves (Ps. lxv. 3) or from circumstances; but no cause for doubt (Luke xii. 32; xxii. 35). Unlikely or remote causes are often God's instruments. The envy of the Jews opened for St. Paul, through his imprisonment, a door to the Gentiles which otherwise he would not have had (Acts xxi. 28; Phil. i. 13). II. IT IS NO EXCUSE FOR WRONG-DOING THAT IT HAS WORKED GOOD (cf. Rom. ix. 19). The cruel act of his brethren brought about the realising of Joseph's dreams, his greatness in Egypt, the support of the whole family during the famine, and the fulfilment of God's word; but not the less was it wrong (ch. xlii. 21; cf. Matt. xxvi. 24). Moral guilt depends not upon the result, but on the motive. God has given the knowledge of redemption to move our will, and the example of Christ and the moral law to guide our lives. The fulfilment of his purposes belongs to himself. He needs not our help to bring it to pass. It is not his will that we should forsake his immutable rules of right and wrong, even for the sake of bringing on the fulfilment of prophecy. Much evil has sprung from neglect of this—*e. g.* the maxim, Faith need not be kept with heretics. God's will and promise, Ps. xxxvii. 3—5. III. TO EACH ONE THERE IS A HISTORY WITHIN A HISTORY. Our actions lead to their appropriate results (Gal. vi. 8) at the same time that they tend to carry out God's purposes, whether we will or not. Each one is a factor in the great plan which in the course of ages God is working out (John v. 17). Men such as they are, wise or ignorant, guided by the Spirit or resisting him, loving or selfish, pressing upwards or following worldly impulses, all are so directed by a power they cannot comprehend that they bring about what he wills (Ps. ii. 2—4). But along with this there is a history which concerns ourselves, which we write for ourselves, the issues of which depend immediately upon ourselves. To each a measure of time, knowledge, opportunity has been given, on the use of which the line of our course depends. Nothing can turn aside the course of God's providence; but upon our faithfulness or unfaithfulness depends our place and joy in it. Hence encouragement to work for Christ, however small our powers (1 Sam. xiv. 6). The little is accepted as well as the great; and as " workers together with him " (2 Cor. vi. 1) our work cannot be in vain.—M.

EXPOSITION.

Vers. 26, 27. — **And Judah** (apparently shrinking from the idea of murder) **said unto his brethren, What profit** is it if (literally, *what of advantage that*) **we slay our brother, and conceal his blood ?** (*i. e.* and hide the fact of his murder). **Come, and let us sell him to the Ishmaelites, and let not our hand be upon him** (literally, *and our hand, let it not be upon him,* i. e. to slay him); **for he is our brother** and **our flesh**— or, more ex-

pressly, our brother and our flesh he (cf. ch. xxix. 14). **And his brethren were content** —literally, *hearkened,* viz., to the proposal. Ver. 28.—**Then there passed by Midianites merchantmen;**—literally, *and passed by the men, Midianites* (by country), *merchants* (by profession). On the different appellations given to the traders *vide infra,* ver. 36— **and they**—not the Midianites (Davidson), but Joseph's brethren—**drew and lifted up**

Joseph out of the pit, and sold Joseph to the Ishmaelites for twenty pieces of silver — literally, *for twenty* (sc. shekels) *of silver =* £2 10s. ; the price afterwards fixed for a boy between five and twenty (Levit. xxvii. 5), the average price of a slave being thirty shekels (Ezek. xxi. 32), and Joseph only bringing twenty because he was a lad (Kurtz), because the Midianites desired to make money by the transaction (Keil), perhaps because his brethren wished to avoid the reproach of having acted from love of gain (Gerlach), but most probably because Joseph's brethren cared little what they had for him, if so be they were rid of him (Lawson). On the term *keseph* vide ch. xx. 16. And they brought Joseph into Egypt—where they in turn disposed of their purchase, doubtless at a profit (ver. 36).

Vers. 29, 30.—And Reuben (in whose absence apparently the scheme of sale had been concocted and carried through) returned to the pit (obviously with a view to deliver Joseph) ; and, behold, Joseph was not in the pit ; and he rent his clothes—in token of his mingled grief and horror at the discovery (cf. ver. 34 ; xliv. 13 ; 2 Sam. xiii. 31 ; 2 Kings xviii. 37 ; Job i. 20). And he returned unto his brethren, and said, The child (or young man, as in ch. iv. 23, where יֶלֶד in the one hemistich is equivalent to אִישׁ in the other) is not ; and I, whither shall I go—*i. e.* however shall I account for his disappearance ?

Vers. 31, 32. — And they—*i. e.* Joseph's brethren, including Reuben, to whom manifestly the matter had been explained (Candlish thinks Reuben may have been deceived by his brethren), and who wanted the courage either to expose their wickedness or to dissent from their device for deceiving Jacob— took Joseph's coat, and killed a kid of the goats, — more correctly, a he-goat of the goats, since the name of goat seems to have belonged in a wider sense to other animals also (Gesenius) ; usually understood to mean the somewhat older he-goat which was used as a sin offering—Levit. xvi. 9 ; xxiii. 19 ; Numb. vii. 16 ; xv. 24 (Fürst)—and dipped the coat in the blood ; and they sent the coat of many colours (*vide* on ver. 3), and they brought it (or caused it to be brought by the hands of a servant) to their father, and said (of course by the lips of the messenger), This have we found: know now whether it be thy son's coat or no. Either Jacob's sons had not the fortitude to witness the first outburst of his grief, or they had not the effrontery requisite to carry through their scheme in their own persons, and were accordingly obliged to employ another, probably a slave, to carry home the bloody coat to Jacob in Hebron.

Ver. 33.—And he knew it, and said, It is my son's coat; an evil beast (*vide* ver. 20) hath devoured him (this was precisely what his sons meant him to infer) ; Joseph is without doubt rent in pieces — טָרֹף טֹרַף, the inf. abs. Kal with the Pual expressing undoubted certainty.

Ver. 34. And Jacob rent his clothes, and put sackcloth upon his loins,—שַׂק (cf. σάκος, σάκκος, *saccus*), the usual dress of mourners (2 Sam. iii. 31 ; Neh. ix. 1 ; Esther iv. 1), was a coarse, thick haircloth, of which corn sacks were also made (ch. xlii. 25), and which in cases of extreme mental distress was worn next the skin (1 Kings xxi. 27)— and mourned for his son many days. Though twenty-two years elapsed before Jacob again beheld his son, and though doubtless the old man's grief for the premature and violent death, as he imagined, of Rachel's child was little abated by the lapse of time, yet the expression "many days" may only be employed to mark the intensity of Jacob's sorrow, which continued longer than the customary mournings of the period.

Ver. 35.—And all his sons—the criminals become comforters (Lange) — and all his daughters—either Jacob had other daughters besides Dinah (Kalisch, Gerlach, 'Speaker's Commentary'), or these included his daughters-in-law, the word being employed as in Ruth i. 11, 12 (Willet, Bush, Murphy), or the term is used freely without being designed to indicate whether he had one or more girls in his family (Augustine)—rose up to comfort him (this implies the return of Jacob's brethren to Hebron) ; but he refused to be comforted ; and he said (here the thought must be supplied : It is vain to ask me to be comforted), For I will go down into the grave unto my son mourning—or, retaining the order of the Hebrew words, which is almost always more expressive than those adopted by our translators, I will go down to my son mourning to, or towards, in the direction of, Sheol. The term שְׁאֹל—more fully שְׁאוֹל, an inf. absol. for a noun, either (1) from שָׁאַל = שָׁעַל, to go down, to sink (Gesenius, Fürst), signifying the hollow place ; or, (2) according to the older lexicographers and etymologists, from שָׁאַל, to ask, and meaning either the region which inexorably summons all men into its shade, the realm that is always craving because never satisfied (Keil, Murphy, Lange), or the land that excites questioning and wonder in the human heart, "the undiscovered country from whose bourne no traveller returns" (T. Lewis)—is not the grave, since Jacob's son had no grave, but the place of departed spirits, the unseen world (᾽Αδης, LXX.) into which the dead disappear, and where they consciously exist (2 Sam. xii. 23). **Thus** (literally, *and*) **his father** (not Isaac) **wept for him.**

Ver. 36.—**And the Midianites**—or Medanites, descendants of Medan, a brother of Midian, both of whom were sons of Abraham by Keturah (ch. xxv. 2). That the Arabian merchants are called Ishmaelites (ver. 27), Midianites (ver. 28), and Medanites (ver. 36), is explained as an evidence of varying legends (Tuch, Bleek, Davidson, Colenso), but is better accounted for as indicating that the traders were composed of men of various nations (Clericus); that the Midianites, Ishmaelites, and Medanites were often confounded from their common parentage and closely similar habits (Keil); that the narrator did not intend to lay stress upon the nationality, but upon the occupation, of the travellers (Hävernick); that the proprietors of the caravan were Ishmaelites, and the company attending it Midianites or Medanites (Lange); that the Ishmaelites were the genus, and the Midianites and Medanites the species, of the same nation (Rosenmüller, Quarry); that the Midianites or Medanites were the actual purchasers of Joseph, while the caravan took its name from the Ishmaelites, who formed the larger portion of it (Murphy)—**sold him into Egypt** (*i. e.* having brought him into Egypt, perhaps, as Luther conjectures, passing through Hebron on the way, sold him) **unto Potiphar,**—the name is abbreviated from Poti-Phera (ch. xli. 50), *i. e.* he who belongs to the sun (Gesenius, *sub voce*). The LXX. render Πετεφρής or Πετεφρῆ—**an officer—סָרִיס**, from **סָרַם**, an unused root signifying to pull up by the roots, originally means a eunuch (Isa. lvi. 3, 4), such as Oriental monarchs were accustomed to set over their harems (Esther ii. 3, 14, 15; iv. 5), but is here employed to denote an officer or courtier generally, without any reference to the primary signification, since Potiphar was married—**of Pharaoh's** (*vide* ch. xii. 15), and **captain of the guard**—literally, *captain of the slaughterers*, i. e. chief officer of the executioners, the nature of whose duties may be understood from the fact that he was keeper of the State prison, "where the king's prisoners were bound" (ch. xxxix. 20).

HOMILETICS.

Vers. 26—36.—*Joseph carried by Midianites to Egypt.* I. THE INFAMOUS SALE. 1. *The wicked proposal.* "Come, and let us sell him." By whatever motives Judah was actuated, the notion that either he or his brethren had a right thus to dispose of Joseph's life was not simply an open violation of the Divine law which constituted all men with equal rights, and in particular made every man his brother's keeper, not his brother's destroyer or proprietor, but a hideous discovery of the utter perversion of moral nature which had taken place in the case of Joseph's brethren. So low had they now sunk, that they were become not alone without humanity, but without natural affection as well. 2. *The double reason.* (1) The advantageous character of the proposed transaction is exhibited by Judah, who doubtless understood the sort of arguments that would weigh most powerfully with his brethren. Simply to assassinate the hated stripling and conceal his blood might indeed gratify their feelings of revenge, but would not do much to enrich them. Might it not be possible to dispose of him more profitably than by the coarse way of killing him? Then (2) the humane aspect of the proposed transaction is pathetically dwelt upon by Judah,—"he is our brother and our flesh,"—in which perhaps may also be detected Judah's subtle knowledge of human nature, in reasoning that men who cared nothing for the claims of humanity and brotherhood in themselves might be induced to do a little cheap philanthropy by sparing Joseph, after they had first been made to see that it would likewise be profitable. Judah's last remark was a master-stroke which overbore every vestige of opposition: "his brethren were content." 3. *The favourable opportunity.* Many wicked schemes are happily never carried through because the opportunity is wanting—thanks to Divine providence! But, on the other hand, thousands of nefarious crimes are born of the opportunity—thanks to the sinful ingenuity of the fallen heart! The scheme of Judah was clearly suggested by the providential circumstance that at the moment an Ishmaelitish caravan was passing by on its way with gums and spicery to Egypt. That caravan was God's chariot sent to convey Joseph to the throne of Egypt. Judah asked his brethren to see in it a prison van to take their brother into slavery in Egypt. Wicked men and God may often seem to play at cross purposes with one another, but God always triumphs. Man proposes; God disposes. 4. *The accomplished transaction.* "They drew and lifted Joseph up out of the pit, and sold him to the Midianites for thirty pieces of silver." The first recorded specimen of a transaction which has frequently been repeated in the history of mankind. Slave markets have often imitated, but seldom surpassed, the wickedness of which Joseph's brethren were guilty. It was not simply a fellow-creature that they sold, but a brother; and they had not even the poor apology of getting a good bargain, as they sold him for twenty shekels—little over forty shillings! 5. *The unforeseen result.* Joseph's purchasers conveyed him into Egypt, and sold him, as probably his brethren expected; it is scarcely likely they anticipated he would find his way into so honourable service as that of a high officer of state. But God was taking Joseph thereby a step nearer to his predicted elevation.

II. THE DOLEFUL TIDINGS. 1. *The ominous symbol.* The coat of ends, the token of a father's love for his darling son, the insensate ruffians, after dipping it in blood, caused to be conveyed into their father's presence by the hands of a swift-footed messenger. This was rather a proof of their cowardice than of their consideration for Jacob's feelings. 2. *The pretended discovery.* The bearer of the blood-stained tunic was directed to say that the brethren had found the robe, and to ask, with expressions of their deep concern, whether or not it was the coat of his beloved son. Their intention we cannot think was to stab their father's heart, but to mislead his judgment. 3. *The expected inference.* As they designed, the old man concluded that his son was devoured: "Joseph is without doubt rent in pieces." Seldom do villains' plots succeed so well.

III. THE SORROWING PARENT. 1. *The bitter grief.* The depth and tenderness of Jacob's mourning for his lost son was—(1) visibly expressed: "he rent his clothes, and put sackcloth on his loins;" (2) long continued: "he mourned for his son many days;" and, if we accept a proposed reading of the last clause of ver. 35, (3) lovingly shared: "his father," the blind Isaac, who still survived, "wept for him" —for Rachel's dead child and Jacob's lost son. 2. *The ineffectual consolation.* "All his sons and all his daughters rose up to comfort him; but he refused to be comforted." For this Jacob was (1) to be excused, since his comforters were mostly hypocrites, whose proffered consolations must have sounded strangely hollow in his ears; but also (2) to be blamed, since although God in his providence had taken away Joseph, that was no reason why he should give way to despairing grief. Not so did Abraham when he thought of losing Isaac.

HOMILIES BY VARIOUS AUTHORS.

Ver. 28.—*Drawn from the pit.* "And they drew and lifted up Joseph out of the pit." As a compromise Joseph had been thrown into a pit. His brothers at first intended to murder him. Their intention was almost as bad as a murder. The Scriptures tell us that "he that hateth his brother is a murderer." And one writer says, "Many a man who has not taken a brother's life, by indulgence of malevolence, is in the sight of God a more sinful man than many who have expiated their guilt on a scaffold." Joseph only was the gainer in that life was spared. To the brothers deep guilt appertained. They threw him into a pit to perish, thinking possibly to lessen guilt by avoiding the actual shedding of blood.

I. WE MUST EXPECT TO FIND PITFALLS IN LIFE. To Joseph the snare came suddenly. He was forced in. He had acted as he believed rightly in revealing the wicked deeds of his brethren, and he suffers for it. His brothers seize the first opportunity of bringing reprisals upon him for what they considered his officiousness. When alone they seized him. They were ten men to one stripling. Coward brothers! "In with him," they say. In the pit's depth is security, in its dryness speedy death. The pitfalls into which many stumble or into which they are drawn are such as these: circumstances being altogether unfavourable in life; or severe and overpowering temptations to some special sin, as intemperance, passion, or lust; or greed, or ambition, or spiritual pride. Debt, loss of character, and despondency are also deep pitfalls. If we come to love evil for itself, that is a very deep pit, and it adjoins that state which is hopeless. Many are drawn into these pits by carelessness, indifference, and neglect, while others are so entangled by circumstances and conditions of birth that the wonder is that they ever escape.

II. THERE IS OFTEN DELIVERANCE FROM THE DEEPEST PITFALLS. To Joseph it came at the right moment. It came in response to earnest desire. The brothers thought to make a profit by his deliverance, but God was saving him through their avarice and timidity. Joseph was helpless. His brothers had to lift him out. We must feel our helplessness, and then Christ is sure to deliver us from the pit of sin and despair. The brothers of Joseph had low and mercenary aims in lifting up their brother; Jesus is all love and self-sacrifice in the effort to save us. Nothing but the long line of his finished work and fervent love could reach souls. When brought up from the pit we shall not be inclined to praise ourselves. We shall ascribe all the glory to him who "brought us up out of the deep pit and miry clay, and placed our feet upon a rock, and established our goings."—H.

EXPOSITION.

CHAPTER XXXVIII.

Ver. 1.—**And it came to pass.** The present chapter appears to interrupt the continuity of the narrative of Joseph's history. Partly on this account, and partly because the name Jehovah occurs in it (vers. 7, 10), it has been pronounced a later Jehovistic interpolation (Tuch, Bleek, Davidson, Colenso). Its design has been explained as an attempt to glorify the line of David by representing it as sprung from Judah (Bohlen), or to disclose the origin of the Levirate law of marriage among the Jews (Knobel); but the incidents here recorded of Judah and his family are fitted to reflect dishonour instead of glory on the ancestry of David (Hävernick); and the custom here mentioned of raising up seed to a dead brother by marrying his widow, though the idea may have originated with Judah (Lange), is more likely to have descended from earlier times (Delitzsch, Keil). Rightly understood, the object of the present portion of the record appears to have been not simply to prepare the way for the subsequent (ch. xlvi. 8—27) genealogical register (Gerlach), or to contrast the wickedness of Judah and his sons with the piety and chastity of Joseph in Egypt (Wordsworth), or to recite the private history of one of Christ's ancestors (Bush, Murphy, 'Speaker's Commentary'), or to show that the pre-eminence of Judah in the patriarchal family was due exclusively to grace (Candlish), but also and chiefly to justify the Divine procedure in the subsequent deportation of Jacob and his sons to Egypt (Keil). The special danger to which the theocratic family was exposed was that of intermarrying with the Canaanites (ch. xxiv. 3; xxviii. 6). Accordingly, having carried forward his narrative to the point where, in consequence of Joseph's sale, a way begins to open up for the transference of the patriarchal house to the land of the Pharaohs, the historian makes a pause to introduce a passage from the life of Judah, with the view of proving the necessity of such removal, by showing, as in the case of Judah, the almost certainty that, if left in Canaan, the descendants of Jacob would fall before the temptation of marrying with the daughters of the land, with the result, in the first instance, of a great and rapid moral deterioration in the holy seed, and with the ultimate effect of completely obliterating the line of demarcation between them and the surrounding heathen world. How the purity of the patriarchal family was guarded till it developed into a powerful nation, first by its providential withdrawment in infancy from the sphere of temptation (ch. xlvi. 5), then by its separate establishment in Goshen beside a people who regarded them with aversion (ch. xlvi. 34), and latterly by its cruel enslavement under Pharaoh (Exod. i. 10), is a subject which in due course engages the attention of the writer. **At that time.** (1) If the date of Judah's marriage, as is most probable, was shortly after the sale of Joseph (Keil, Kurtz, Lange, Alford, Wordsworth, Quarry), since at the time of that atrocity Judah was still living with his brethren, the only difficulty calling for solution is to account for the birth of Judah's grandchildren, Hezron and Hamul (the sons of Pharez, the twin child of Judah by Tamar), in the short interval of twenty-two years which preceded Jacob's descent into Egypt without making Er and Onan marry in comparative boyhood. The case becomes a little less perplexing if Hezron and Hamul, though said to have come into Egypt (ch. xlvi. 27; Exod. i. 1; Deut. x. 22), may be regarded as having been born there (Hengstenberg), since twenty-two years afford sufficient space for the birth of Judah's three sons, Er, Onan, and Shelah, which may have taken place during the first three years after their father's marriage, and for the birth of Pharez and Zarah, even if Er married as late as eighteen. Of course if the narrative requires the birth of Hezron and Hamul to have taken place in Canaan (Kalisch), it is simply impossible to hold that all this occurred within little more than a score of years.   Hence (2) the date of Judah's marriage has been placed before the sale of Joseph (Augustine, Aben Ezra, Rosenmüller, Drechsler, Baumgarten, Gerlach, Ainsworth, Candlish, Murphy, Inglis); but even on this assumption the task is arduous to make the birth of Hezron and Hamul occur before the emigration of their great-grandfather to Egypt.   For as Judah was not more than four years older than Joseph (cf. ch. xxix. 35 with xxx. 25), his age at the time of Joseph's sale could not have been more than twenty-one.   But placing Judah's marriage at the earliest possible date, viz., in his fifteenth year, only substitutes an interval of twenty - eight years instead of one of twenty-two, in which Judah's son Er must be born, grow up to manhood, (say at fifteen) marry, die, and leave his widow Tamar, who, after marrying with Onan and waiting for Shelah (which would consume at least another year), must become the mother of twin sons by her father-in-law (for which another year would be required), and must see the elder of the two married at ten years of age, if his sons are to be born upon the soil of Canaan.   On either hypothesis, therefore, it seems indispensable to hold that Judah's grandsons were born in Egypt ; and in this case there is little gained by putting Judah's marriage earlier than Joseph's sale, i. e. in Judah's twenty-first year.   **That Judah went down**—from Hebron (ch. xxxvii. 14), or the mountains (Keil), towards the south (Aben Ezra, Rosenmüller) — **from his brethren,**—setting up a separate and independent establishment apart from them ; "not only immediately after Joseph was sold, but also on account of it," "in a fit of impenitent anger" (Kurtz), in a spirit of remorse (Lange)—**and turned in to a certain Adullamite,**—literally, *and pitched* (sc. his tent, ch. xxvi. 15) *up to,* as far as, or close by, a man, *an Adullamite,* i. e. belonging to Adullam, a town in the Hebron valley (Josh. xv. 35) ; in the time of the conquest the seat of a Canaanitish king (Josh. xii. 15), afterwards celebrated for its connection with the history of David (1 Sam. xxii. 1, 2 ; 2 Sam. xxiii. 13), subsequently mentioned in Scripture (2 Chron. xi. 7 ; Neh. xi. 30 ; Micah i. 15), but never successfully identified (*vide* 'Land and the Book,' pp. 606, 607 ; Robinson, ii. 175)—**whose name** was **Hirah** —"Nobility" (Gesenius).

Ver. 2.—**And Judah saw there the daughter of a certain** (literally, *of a man, a*) **Canaanite,**—not of a merchant (Onkelos), but of an inhabitant of the land of Canaan—**whose name was Shuah ;** — "Wealth,"

"Riches," "Cry for Help" (Gesenius). This was not the name of Judah's wife (LXX.), but of her father—(*vide* ver. 12)—**and he took her,**—i. e. married her (*vide* ch. vi. 2 ; xxiv. 67)—**and went in unto her.**

Ver. 3.—**And she conceived, and bare a son ; and he called his name Er**—" Watcher " (Gesenius).   What is commonly regarded as an Idiosyncrasy of the Elohist, *viz.,* the naming of a child by its father, here occurs in a so-called Jehovistic section.

Ver. 4.—**And she conceived again, and bare a son ; and she called his name Onan** —"Strength" (Gesenius).   The naming of a child by its mother a peculiarity of the so-called Jehovist ; but *vide* ch. xvi. 15.

Ver. 5.—**And she yet again conceived** (lit., *and she added again*), **and bare a son ; and called his name Shelah :** — "Prayer" (Gesenius), "Peace" (Fürst)—**and he** (*i. e.* Judah) **was**—sc. absent (Gerlach) ; or, translating impersonally, *it was,* i. e. the event happened (Murphy)—**at Chezib,**—probably the same as Achzib (Josh. xv. 44 ; Micah i. 14, 15) and Chezeba (1 Chron. iv. 22), which in the partitioning of the land fell to the sons of Shelah, and was here mentioned that Shelah's descendants might know the birthplace of their ancestor (Keil) ; or the fact of Judah's absence at the birth of his third son may be recorded as the reason of the name, "Peace," "Rest," "Prosperity," which the child received (Gerlach) — **when she bare him**—literally, *in her bearing of him.*

Ver. 6.—**And Judah took a wife** (cf. ch. xxi. 21 ; xxiv. 4) **for Er his firstborn,**—" by the early marriage of his sons Judah seems to have intended to prevent in them a germinating corruption " (Lange)—**whose name** was **Tamar**—"Palm tree" (Gesenius).   Though the name was Shemitic, it does not follow that the person was.   Cf. Melchisedeck and Abimelech.   Yet she is not expressly called a Canaanite, though it is more than probable she was.   Lange conjectures that she may have been of Philistine descent, and thinks the narrative intends to convey the impression that she was a woman of extraordinary character.

Ver. 7.—**And Er, Judah's firstborn, was wicked in the sight of the Lord.**   The connection between Er's name (עֵר) and Er's character· (רַע) is noticeable.   The special form which his wickedness assumed is not stated ; but the accompanying phrase suggests that, as in the case of the Sodomites (ch. xiii. 13 ; xix. 5), it was some unnatural abomination.   **And the Lord slew him**— literally, *caused him to die ;* not necessarily by direct visitation ; perhaps simply by allowing him to reap the fruits of his youthful indulgence in premature and childless death, which yet was so rapid and so evidently entailed by his evil courses as immediately to suggest the punitive hand of God.

Ver. 8.—**And Judah said unto Onan** (obviously after a sufficient interval), **Go in unto thy brother's wife, and marry her,**—literally, *and perform the part of levir, or husband's brother, to her.* The language seems to imply that what was afterwards in the code Mosaic known as the *Lex Leviratus* (Deut. xxv. 5, 6) was at this time a recognised custom. The existence of the practice has been traced in different forms among Indians, Persians, and other nations of Asia and Africa—**and raise up seed to thy brother.** As afterwards explained in the Hebrew legislation, the first-born son of such a Levirate marriage became in the eye of the law the child of the deceased husband, and was regarded as his heir.

Vers. 9, 10.—**And Onan knew that the seed should not be his; and it came to pass, when**—literally, *and it was if,* i. e. whenever (cf. Ewald, 'Heb. Synt.,' § 3456)—**he went in unto his brother's wife, that he spilled it on the ground** (literally, *destroyed to the ground*), **lest that he should** (or, so as not to) **give seed to his brother. And the thing which he did displeased** (literally, *was evil in the eyes of*) **the Lord :**—the word Jehovah is employed not because the writer was a late interpolater, but because the sin of Onan was an offence against the sanctity and prosperity of the theocratic family (Hengstenberg) — **wherefore he** (i. e. Jehovah) **slew him also** (*vide supra*).

Ver. 11.—**Then said Judah to Tamar his daughter-in-law, Remain a widow**—*almanah*, from *alam*, to be solitary, forsaken, signifies one bereft of a husband, hence a widow (cf. Exod. xxii. 21)—**at thy father's house** (cf. Levit. xxii. 13), **till Shelah my son be grown.** It is implied that this was merely a pretext on the part of Judah, and that he did not really intend to give his third son to Tamar, considering her an unlucky woman (Delitzsch, Keil, Kalisch), or, at least, not at present, under the impression that the deaths of Er and Onan had been occasioned by their too early marriages (Lange). The reason of his failure to release Tamar from her widowhood is added in the ensuing clause. **For he said** (*sc.* in his heart), **Lest peradventure he die also, as his brethren** did. **And Tamar went and dwelt in her father's house.**

Ver. 12.—**And in process of time**—literally, *and the days were multiplied* (cf. ch. iv. 3), which is rendered by the same words in the A. V.—**the daughter of Shuah Judah's wife died; and Judah was comforted** (or, comforted himself, ceased to mourn), **and went up unto his sheep-shearers** (*vide* ch. xxxi. 19) **to Timnath,**—a border town between Ekron and Bethshemesh (Josh. xv. 10) in the plain of Judah (Kalisch, Wordsworth,

W. L. Alexander in Kitto's 'Cyclopedia'); but more probably here a town (Josh. xv. 57) in the mountains of Judah (Robinson, ii. 343, Keil, Alford, 'Speaker's Commentary')—**he and his friend**—ὁ ποιμὴν αὐτοῦ (LXX.)—**Hirah the Adullamite.**

Ver. 13.—**And it was told Tamar, saying, Behold thy father-in-law**—חָם, a father-in-law, from חָמָה, unused, to join together. Cf. γαμβρός for γαμερός, a son-in-law, or generally one connected by marriage, from γαμέω —**goeth up to Timnath to shear his sheep.**

Ver. 14.—**And she put her widow's garments off from her** (to prevent detection by Judah), **and covered her with a vail,**—to conceal her features, after the fashion of a courtesan (ver. 15; cf. Job xxiv. 15) — and **wrapped herself,**—possibly with some large mantle (Alford)—**and sat in an open place,**—literally, *in the opening* (i. e. gate) *of Enaim* (LXX., Gesenius, Keil, Kalisch, Lange, *et alii*) ; less happily, in the opening of the eyes, *i. e.* in a public and open place (Calvin), in the parting of the ways, *in bivio itineris* (Vulgate), in the opening (or breaking forth) of the two fountains (Aben Ezra, Rosenmüller)—**which is by** (or upon) **the way to Timnath ;** — "close to the site of Thamna, now Tibneh, three miles to the east, on an ancient road coming from Adullam, the very road by which the patriarch Judah would have come from Adullam to Timnah, is a ruin called Allin, or Anim, or Ainim" ('Palestine Exploration,' quoted by Inglis) —**for she saw that Shelah was grown** (he was probably not much younger than either of his brothers who had died), **and she was not given unto him to wife**—literally, *for a wife.*

Ver. 15.—**When** (literally, *and*) **Judah saw her, he** (literally, *and he*) **thought her to be an harlot ;**—literally, *thought her* (i. e. took her for) *an harlot,* like λογίζεσθαί τινα εἰς τι (cf. 1 Sam. i. 13 ; Job xiii. 24), or זוֹנָה (fem. part. of זָנָה, to commit fornication) ; *vide* ch. xxxiv. 31—**because she had covered her face**—*more meretricis.*

Ver. 16.—**And he turned unto her by the way, and said, Go to, I pray thee, let me come in unto thee ; (for he knew not that she** was **his daughter-in-law).** Though willing to commit adultery or fornication, Judah would have shrank from the sin of incest. **And she said, What wilt thou give me, that thou mayest come in unto me?** The conduct of Tamar, though in every way reprehensible, is not to be attributed to mere lust, or inordinate desire for offspring, if not from the son Shelah, then from the father Judah, but was probably traceable to a secret wish on the one hand to be avenged on Judah, and on the other hand to assert her right to a place amongst the ancestresses of the patriarchal family. Yet Tamar was really guilty of both adultery and incest, though Lange thinks the wickedness of Er and Onan renders this open to question.

Ver. 17.—**And he said, I will send** thee **a kid from the flock**—literally, *a kid of the goats* (ver. 20; cf. Judges xv. 1). **And she said, Wilt thou give me a pledge, till thou send it ?**—literally, *if thou wilt give me a pledge* (עֵרָבוֹן, from עָרַב, to give in pledge, a word peculiar to traders which the Greeks and Romans appear to have borrowed from the Phenicians, the originators of traffic: cf. ἀῤῥαβών, *arrhabo:* vide Gesenius, p. 652) *until thy sending* (sc. then I consent to thy proposal).

Ver. 18.—**And he said, What pledge shall I give thee ? And she said, Thy signet,**— the *chotham*, or signet, was either worn on the finger, δακτυλίον (LXX.) or suspended round the neck by a *pithil*, or silk string. Its impression was a sign of property and a means of security (cf. Matt. xxvii. 66 ; John iii. 33 ; Ephes. i. 13, &c.). Among the ancient Babylonians it was customary for every one to wear such a ring (Herod., i. 195) ; and modern Arabians in towns wear a seal-ring on the finger, or fastened by a cord round the neck, the impression of which serves as a signature (Robinson, i. 52). The seals and signets that have been brought to light by the excavations in Assyria and Babylon (Layard, 'Nin. and Bab.,' 152—159, 602— 608) are of various forms and materials. They show the art of engraving to have been of great antiquity ; but whether Judah's signet was marked with alphabetical characters cannot be determined, though it may have been, since alphabetical writing was as old at least as the time of Abraham (*vide* Keil, 'Introd.,' Part I. sect. i. ch. i. § 4)—**and thy bracelets** (rather, thy chain, *pithil*, ut supra), **and thy staff** (the *mateh*, or rod, was so called from the idea of stretching out, the root being *natah*, to stretch out or extend) **that is in thine hand.** This too every Babylonian carried (Herod., i. 195). "It was necessarily adorned with some device carved upon it, and consisting in a flower or a fruit, a bird, or some other animal" (Kalisch). **And he gave** it her, **and came in unto her, and she conceived by him.**

Ver. 19.—**And she arose, and went away, and laid by her vail from her, and put on the garments of her widowhood.**

Ver. 20.—**And Judah sent the kid**— literally, *the kid of the goats,* which he had promised (ver. 17)—**by the hand of his friend the Adullamite, to receive** his pledge **from the woman's hand : but** (literally, *and*) he (*i. e.* Hirah) **found her not.**

Ver. 21.—**Then he asked the men of that place, saying, Where is the harlot,**—liter-

ally, *the consecrated,* the prostitute being regarded as "one devoted to the worship of Astarte, a goddess of the Canaanites, the deification of the generative and productive principle of nature," corresponding to the Babylonian Ashtarte, whose worship was of a grossly libidinous character (Herod., i. 199). Cf. Deut. xxiii. 19 ; Numb. xxv. 1 ; Hosea iv. 14 ; and *vide* Keil on Deut. xxiii. 10 that was openly by the way side ?—or, that was in Enajim on the way, *ut supra*, ver. 14). **And they said, There was no harlot** (or *kedeshah*) **in this** place.

Ver. 22.—**And he returned to Judah, and said, I cannot find her ; and also the men of the place said, that there was no harlot** (or *kedeshah*) **in this** place.

Ver. 23.—**And Judah said, Let her take** it **to her,**—literally, *let her take to herself* (sc. the pledge)—**lest we be shamed** (literally, *become a contempt,* i. e. by inquiring after her. Though not afraid to sin against God, Judah was pained at the idea of losing his reputation before men) : **behold, I sent this kid** (*i. e.* I take you to witness that I have fulfilled my promise), **and thou hast not found her.**

Ver. 24.—**And it came to pass about three months after** (the usual time at which pregnancy is certainly determined), **that it was told Judah, saying, Tamar thy daughter-in-law hath played the harlot** (or, acted as a *zonah*) ; **and also, behold, she is with child by whoredom. And Judah said** (altogether unmindful of his own iniquity three months previous), **Bring her forth, and let her be burnt.** Under the law stoning was the punishment allotted to the crime of Tamar (Deut. xxii. 20—24), burning being added only in cases of excessive criminality (Levit. xx. 14 ; xxi. 9). It is obvious that the power of life and death lay in the hand of Judah, as the head of his family.

Ver. 25.—**When she was brought forth** (literally, *she was brought forth, and*), **she sent to her father-in-law** (who apparently had not the heart to witness the execution of his own sentence), **saying, By the man, whose these are, am I with child : and she said, Discern, I pray thee, whose are these, the signet, and bracelets** (or chain), **and staff.**

Ver. 26.—**And Judah acknowledged** (or discerned, *ut supra*, i. e. recognised) **them, and said, She hath been more righteous than I ;**—though Tamar was far from innocent (*vide* ver. 16), she was by no means as culpable as Judah—**because that** (כִּי־עַל־כֵּן, for, for this cause, *i. e.* that so it might happen to me : vide ch. xviii. 5) **I gave her not to Shelah my son. And** (in token of his penitence) **he knew her again no more.**

Ver. 27.—**And it came to pass in the time**

of her travail, that, behold, twins were in her womb. Cf. the case of Rebekah (ch. xxv. 24).

Ver. 28.—**And it came to pass, when she travailed,**—literally, *in her bringing forth* (cf. ch. xxxv. 17)—**that the one put out his hand :**—literally, *and it* (sc. the child) *gave a hand,* i. e. it was an abnormal and dangerous presentation — **and the midwife** (*vide* ch. xxxv. 17) **took and bound upon his hand a scarlet thread, saying, This came out first.**

Ver. 29.—**And it came to pass, as he drew back his hand, that, behold, his brother came out : and she** (*i. e.* the midwife) **said,**

How hast thou broken forth ? this **breach** be **upon thee :**—literally, *What a breach hast thou made !* upon thee, a breach ! or, Why hast thou broken forth for thyself a breach (Delitzsch)? or, How hast thou made for thee a breach ? (Murphy)—**therefore his name was called Pharez**—or Breach (cf. ch. xlvi. 12; Numb. xxvi. 20 ; 1 Chron. ii. 4 ; Matt. i. 3).

Ver. 30.—**And afterward came out his brother, that had the scarlet thread upon his hand : and his name was called Zarah** —Splendour.

HOMILETICS.

Vers. 1—30.—*The house of Judah : a family record of sin and shame.* I. THE WICKEDNESS OF ER AND ONAN. 1. *Early.* On any hypothesis Er and Onan can have been little more than boys when they were married, and yet they appear to have arrived at a remarkable precocity in sin. Nor was it simply that they had shed the innocence and purity of youth, but they had also acquired a shameful proficiency in vice. Young scholars are mostly apt learners, especially in the devil's school. 2. *Unnatural.* Though not described, the wickedness of Judah's first son had relation to some perversion of the ordinance of marriage ; that of his second is plainly stated to have been uncleanness and self-pollution. Neither against nature nor contrary to grace are the endearments of the married state, but every act outside of the Divine permissions concerning woman is both. 3. *Heinous.* The act of Er is characterised as " wicked in the sight of the Lord," while that of Onan is said to have displeased the Lord. Hence it may be reasonably inferred that the essential criminality in both cases was the same. They were both perversions of a natural ordinance. They both militated against the purity and development of the theocratic family. Both indicated a contemptuous unbelief in the promise of the covenant, and a sacrilegious disregard for the calling of Israel as the progenitor of the promised seed. Hence both were deserving of Divine reprobation. 4. *Disastrous.* The tendency of all sin is ruinous, both for body, soul, and spirit. Whether as a natural result of indulgence in vice, or as a direct punitive visitation from God, Er and Onan were consigned to premature graves ; and this, it should be noted by young persons of both sexes, is the almost inevitable consequence of indulgence in secret vice, and in particular of the practice of which Onan was guilty. Yielded to, it debilitates the physical constitution by a wasting of the vital powers, it impairs the mental faculties, it corrupts the moral nature, it sears and petrifies the conscience, and finally, what might have been a fair specimen of noble and virtuous manhood or womanhood it covers up, a poor, wasted, shivering skeleton, beneath the clods of the valley, causing it to lie down among the sins of its youth.

II. THE SIN OF TAMAR. The conduct of Judah's daughter-in-law, the young widow of Er and Onan, though not without its extenuations, in having been partly provoked by Judah's reluctance to marry her to Shelah, and partly inspired by a desire to take her place among the ancestresses of the promised seed, was yet in many respects reprehensible. 1. She discovered *impatience.* Although Judah did manifest a temporary unwillingness to give her Shelah for a husband, she might have reasoned that, after losing two sons, it was not unnatural that he should hesitate about exposing a third to the same risk of destruction. 2. She manifested *unbelief.* If Tamar did regard herself as wronged, as most undoubtedly she was, instead of taking measures to right herself, she should have left her cause to God, who had already vindicated her against the wickedness of her youthful husbands, and who in his own time and way would doubtless have interposed to assert her prerogative as a widow belonging to the family of Israel. 3. She practised *deception.* Laying aside her widow's garments, and assuming the attire of a harlot, she took her station at the gate of Enajim, on the way to Timnath, and pretended to be a prostitute. Tamar manifestly was not a woman of refined and delicate sensibilities; but then she was a Canaanite, and had been the wife of Er and Onan, who were not calculated to improve her modesty. 4. She was guilty of *temptation*. It is true the narrative does not represent her as having been guilty of solicitation, like the "foolish woman" described by Solomon (Prov. vii. 6—23; ix. 14—18). Perhaps she knew that Judah would not require solicitation; but if so, she was all the more guilty in placing temptation in Judah's way. 5. She committed *incest*. The guilt of an incestuous connection which rested on Judah unconsciously she had knowingly and willingly taken on herself.

III. THE TRANSGRESSIONS OF JUDAH. More numerous, if not more heinous, than those of either his sons or his daughter-in-law were the offences of Judah. Jacob's fourth son sinned—1. *In marrying a Canaanitish wife*. Though Judah's marriage with Shuah's daughter was blessed by God, who made it fruitful, it does not follow that it was approved by God. 2. *In withholding Shelah from Tamar*. Although it does not appear as yet to have been commanded that in default of issue a widow should be married by her deceased husband's brother, it is obvious that Judah recognised that it should be so, both by his own act in giving Onan to Tamar after Er's death, and by his own subsequent confession with regard to Shelah (ver. 26). 3. *In deceiving Tamar*. Instead of frankly telling her that he did not intend his third son to become her husband, he bound her to remain a widow, and sent her home to her father's house (instead of keeping her in his own) under the impression that Shelah was only withheld from her on the score of youth. 4. *In committing sin with Tamar*. Though in reality Judah committed incest, yet so far as his intention went it was only adultery, or fornication. Yet all forms of unchastity are forbidden in the law of God. And it gives a very low conception of the morality of Judah that he, a member of the consecrated family of Israel, who had himself been married, should have so openly, and deliberately, and coolly turned aside to seek the company of a common strumpet, as he imagined Tamar to be. Judah should have acted on the principle afterwards stated by Paul (1 Cor. vii. 9). 5. *In condemning Tamar*. "Bring her forth, and let her be burnt," said the indignant patriarch. It is obvious the sentence was excessive in its severity. It was not imperative, else it could not have been remitted; and a recollection of his visit to Timnath three months previously should have inclined him to lean to mercy's side. But the virtuous Angelos of society always procure indulgence for themselves by damning their fellow-sinners (*Measure for Measure*, Act II.). Scripture counsels differently (Matt. vii. 3; Rom. ii. 22; Gal. vi. 1).

Vers. 12—26.—*Judah's sin with Tamar*. I. COMMITTED. 1. *Suddenly*. It was occasioned by the sight of a supposed courtesan. Much evil enters by the eye (cf. 2 Sam. xi. 2). Great need for the prayer of David (Ps. cxix. 37). 2. *Openly*. Judah was in the company of Hirah, his friend, when he beheld Tamar sitting in the gate of Enajim, and, without attempting to hide it from his friend, went to seek her society. Shamelessness in sin betokens great depravity. 3. *Wilfully*. Though in a manner surprised by the temptation, Judah was not inadvertently betrayed into commission of his sin with Tamar, but, on the contrary, went about it in a remarkably deliberate manner. 4. *Inexcusably*. There was no reason why Judah should not have sought a second wife to succeed Shuah's daughter, rather than consort with prostitutes.
II. DETECTED. 1. *Quickly*. No doubt Judah thought he had heard the last of his indiscretion on the way to Timnath; but lo! in three short months his guilt is discovered. Not every offender is so speedily arrested; but sooner or later detection is inevitable for all. "Be sure thy sin will find thee out." 2. *Unexpectedly*. Judah never imagined that his own signet, and chain, and staff would be produced as witnesses against him; and criminals never can be sure from what quarter testimony shall arise to condemn them. 3. *Completely*. There was no possibility of Judah's evading the charge of Tamar. By no sort of ingenuity could he repudiate the articles of dress with which probably his household were familiar. 4. *Publicly*. At the very moment when Tamar was produced for execution Judah was obliged to confess his guilt in presence of his assembled household; and in like manner will the wicked yet be openly convicted in the sight of an assembled world.

III. CONFESSED. 1. *Candidly.* Found out, Judah did not attempt either to deny
or to palliate his guilt, but frankly acknowledged that Tamar's condition was due to
him. 2. *Promptly.* Nor did he hesitate to own his guilt, but immediately confessed what he had done. 3. *Penitently.* This we may infer from the statement
of the historian that the offence was not again repeated.

IV. FORGIVEN. It does not fall within the scope of the historian's design to indicate whether Judah obtained mercy; but this may be reasonably concluded from—
1. *The promptness of his confession.* 2. *The sincerity of his penitence.* 3. *The
reality of his faith*—as evinced by the fact that he was reckoned among the ancestors of our Lord.

Vers. 27—30.—*Tamar's twins.* I. POINTS OF RESEMBLANCE. (1) The offspring
of the same parents; (2) the fruit of the same sin; (3) the gift of the same God.

II. POINTS OF DISTINCTION. (1) The order of their birth; (2) the import of their
names; (3) the purpose of their lives—the first being an ancestor of the promised
seed.

HOMILIES BY VARIOUS AUTHORS.

Ch. xxxviii.—*The goodness and severity of God.* These occurrences in the family
of Judah would seem (1) to betoken the *retributive judgment of God*, and (2) *illustrate his grace. Joseph* is lost, and still Divinely protected. *Judah* is a wanderer
from his brethren, a sensual, self-willed, degenerate man; yet it is in the line of
this same wanderer that the promised seed shall appear. The whole is a lesson
on the evil of *separation from the people of God.* Luther asks why such things
were placed in Scripture, and answers, (1) That no one should be *self-righteous*,
and (2) that no one should *despair*, and (3) to remind us that *Gentiles by natural
right* are brothers, mother, sisters to our Lord; the word of salvation is a word for
the whole world.—R.

EXPOSITION.

CHAPTER XXXIX.

Ver. 1.—**And Joseph was brought down
to Egypt.** The narrative now preparing to
recite the fortunes of Joseph in Egypt, which
eventually led, through his elevation to be
Pharaoh's prime minister, first to the salvation of the patriarchal family, and finally to
their settlement in Goshen, the historian
reverts, in accordance with his usual practice, to a point of time antecedent to the
incidents contained in the preceding chapter,
and makes a new departure in his story from
the moment of Joseph's crossing into Egypt.
**And Potiphar, an officer of Pharaoh, cap-
tain of the guard** (*vide* ch. xxxvii. 36), **an
Egyptian,**—literally, *a man of Mitzraim.*
This implies that foreigners were sometimes
employed to fill responsible offices about the
Court of Pharaoh. The phrase "is not a
superfluous addition, as the population of
Heliopolis, from remote times, included a considerable admixture of Arabians" (Kalisch)—
bought him of the hands of the Ishmaelites
(*vide* ch. xxxvii. 36), **which had brought him
down thither.**
Ver. 2. — **And the Lord** — Jehovah, as
usual, because the entire chapter is the work
of the Jehovist (Tuch, Colenso), with the

exception of a few alterations by the redactor
(Davidson), or because, though the work of
the Elohist, it has been modified by the
Jehovistic editor (Bleek, Vaihinger); but
more likely because the advancement of
Joseph in Egypt was a special fruit of the
theocratic promise which belonged to the
patriarchal family (Hengstenberg, Quarry)—
was with Joseph (cf. ver. 21; xxi. 20; xxvi.
24; xxviii. 15), **and he was a prosperous
man** (literally, *a man prospering*); **and he
was in the house of his master the Egyptian**—*i. e.* as a domestic servant.
Ver. 3.—**And his master saw that the
Lord** (Jehovah) **was with him**—this does not
imply that Potiphar was acquainted with
Jehovah, but simply that he concluded
Joseph to be under the Divine protection—
and that the Lord (Jehovah) **made all that
he did to prosper in his hand.** That which
led to the conviction of Potiphar concerning
Joseph was the remarkable success which
he saw attending all his efforts and undertakings.
Ver. 4.—**And Joseph found grace in his
sight,**—*vide* ch. vi. 8; xviii. 3; xix. 19;
xxxix. 21. Most men are pleased with a
good servant. Even Laban had no objections to Jacob so long as he divined that

Jehovah was multiplying his flocks for Jacob's sake (ch. xxx. 27)—**and he served him** (*i. e.* he waited on Potiphar, or acted as his personal attendant and comptroller of his household) : **and he** (*i. e.* Potiphar) **made him overseer over his house,**—a position corresponding to that occupied by Eliezer in the household of Abraham (ch. xxiv. 2). Egyptian monuments attest the existence of such an officer in wealthy houses at an early period ; a tomb at Kum-el-Ahmar exhibiting the account books, writing materials, and clerks that pertain to the office of a steward, and another at Beni-hassan, besides displaying his accustomed implements, styling him the Overseer (Wilkinson's ' Ancient Egyptians,' vol. i. p. 372, ed. 1878 ; Hengstenberg's 'Egypt and the Books of Moses,' p. 24). A sepulchral inscription belonging to the period of the eleventh dynasty also mentions among the officers comprising the household of Ameni the chancellor Athorsi, the barber Khentikhrati, the slave Gefahapi, the lady's maid Khui, the steward Ameni, the steward Santit (*vide* ' Records of the Past,' vol. vi. p. 3). Joseph had also, after his exaltation, a ruler or steward of his house (cf. ch. xliii. 16, 19 ; xliv. 1)—**and all that he had he put into his hand**=literally, *and all which was to him he gave into his hand*, i. e. he intrusted to Joseph's care).

Ver. 5.—**And it came to pass from the** time that **he had made** (literally, *from that time he made*) **him overseer in his house, and over all that he had, that** (literally, *and*) **the Lord** (Jehovah) **blessed the Egyptian's house for Joseph's sake** (cf. ch. xxx. 12); **and the blessing of the Lord** (Jehovah) **was upon all that he had in the house, and in the field.** It is observable that throughout this chapter, when the historian is speaking in his own name the term Jehovah is used to designate the Supreme Being (cf. vers. 21, 23), whereas when Joseph replies to his mistress it is the word Elohim which he employs, the reason of which is sufficiently obvious.

Ver. 6—**And** (accordingly, encouraged by the admirable success attending Joseph's management) **he left all that he had in Joseph's hand** (*i. e.* gave him unrestricted control over all his temporal affairs); **and he knew not ought he had** (literally, *he knew not anything with him,* i. e. he shared not the care of anything along with him), **save the bread which he did eat.** This was necessitated by the laws of caste which then prevailed among the Egyptians, and in particular by the fact that "the Egyptians might not eat with the Hebrews" (ch. xliii. 32). **And Joseph was a goodly** person, **and well favoured**—literally, *beautiful in form and beautiful in appearance,* like his mother Rachel (ch. xxix. 17).

HOMILETICS.

Vers. 1—23.—*Joseph in the house of Potiphar.* I. PURCHASED AS A SLAVE. 1. A *sad* lot. Worse even than being kidnapped by strangers, Joseph had been first sold by his brethren ; carried into Egypt, he had there been exposed for sale in a slave-market ; and now, as if he had been a beast of burden or a captive taken in war, he had been a second time purchased for money. Few fortunes are more touchingly sorrowful or more deeply humiliating than this which was now measured out to Jacob's youthful son. 2. A *common* lot. Happily in our land, and indeed wherever the gospel prevails, it is not a spectacle that can now be beheld—that of men trafficking in each other's flesh. But in those days the horrors of the auction block were not unfrequent sights, and Joseph, in being sold and bought like goods and chattels, was only experiencing a fate which had been undergone by many previous to his times, and has by myriads been suffered since. 3. An *appointed* lot. As everything on earth is, so was Joseph's sad and sorrowful estate assigned him by Heaven ; and the recognition of this doubtless it was by Joseph that prevented him from murmuring, and apparently inspired him with a cheerful confidence, even in the darkest times.

II. EMPLOYED AS A SERVANT. 1. *Eminently prosperous.* (1) The extent of this prosperity. All that he did prospered. Everything he put his hand to appeared to thrive. Success seemed to wait upon him like his shadow. It is seldom such a measure of good fortune is meted out to any of God's people on the earth, or even of the devil's children. For the first they would probably be spoiled by such indulgence, while for the second they mostly fail in the conditions that are needful for such distinction. (2) The means of this prosperity. That Joseph was attentive, diligent, and conscientious in the performance of his household duties, as well as faithful and devoted to the interests of his master, may be reasonably inferred, since success seldom waits upon the negligent, the idle, or the unprincipled. (3) The source of this prosperity. The historian is careful to note that the true mainspring of Joseph's, as of every other person's, prosperity was the Divine blessing on his labours. " The Lord made all that he did to prosper in his hand." 2. *Greatly rewarded*. Joseph was—(1) Noticed by his master. It is a pleasure to true and faithful servants when those they serve regard their work with favourable observation. (2) Accepted by his master. It says a great deal for Potiphar that he treated Joseph kindly, even though it was largely on account of his excellent qualities as a servant. (3) Promoted by his master. From being humble valet to the great man's person, he was exalted to the high position of steward or comptroller of the great man's house. (4) Trusted by his master. Everything connected with the management of Potiphar's establishment, in his mansion and on his farm, was unreservedly committed to the care of Joseph. Potiphar troubled himself about nothing " save the bread which he did eat."

III. BLESSED AS A MAN. 1. He enjoyed *Divine companionship* in his sad captivity. " The Lord was with him ; " a compensation rich enough to be set against the miseries of bondage and exile, as God's people, when similarly situated, have not unfrequently experienced (cf. Acts xvi. 25 ; 2 Tim. iv. 17). 2. He obtained *Divine assistance* in his arduous duties. When the circumstances of Joseph's lot might have induced despondency, indifference, inaction, carelessness, and inattention, Divine grace so upheld and cheered him that he was able to go about his duties with alacrity and cheerfulness, so that everything he turned his hand to succeeded. 3. He received *Divine favour* in the eyes of his master. For Joseph himself to have secretly known that God approved of his person and behaviour would have been an ample consolation to his sad heart ; but to obtain the good-will of Heaven so conspicuously that even his heathen master could not avoid observing it was surely a signal honour. 4. He attracted *Divine blessing* towards his fellow-men. " The Lord blessed the Egyptian's house for Joseph's sake." Here was a clear experience by Joseph of the truth of the Abrahamic blessing (ch. xii. 2, 3). In this also Joseph was an eminent type of Christ.

Lessons :—1. Patience under suffering. 2. Contentment with one's lot. 3. Fidelity in service. 4. The secret of prosperity. 5. The obligations of masters towards servants. 6. The value of religion to a workman. 7. The profit of a pious servant.

Vers. 1—23.—*Sunshine and shadow.* I. THE BRIGHTENING SKY. The advancement of Joseph in the house of Potiphar. 1. To Joseph's sense it was a lightening in his bondage. 2. To Joseph's faith it was the smiling of Jehovah's face. 3. To Joseph's hope it was the dawning of a better day.

II. THE THREATENING CLOUD. The temptation of Joseph by his mistress. Here was—1. An assault upon his virtue, which, unless it were overcome, would deprive him of Jehovah's favour, and consequently put an end to any prospect he might have of deliverance ; and, 2. An attack upon his safety, which, however it resulted, whether in his defeat or his victory, would likely terminate his enjoyment of his master's favour, if not altogether cost him his life.

III. THE FALLING DARKNESS. The accusation of Joseph by his mistress. 1. Though untrue, it was almost certain to be believed. 2. If believed, it would certainly involve him in punishment. 3. If deemed deserving of punishment, he would almost certainly be put to death.

IV. THE STARLIGHT NIGHT. The history of Joseph in the prison. 1. He had not been executed, but only imprisoned. 2. God was with him in the dungeon, as he had been in the palace. 3. If the favour of his master had been lost, the confidence of his keeper had been gained. 4. Misfortune might seem to be always lying in wait for him, but, on the other hand, prosperity appeared to be ever following close upon his heels.

HOMILIES BY VARIOUS AUTHORS.

Ch. xxxix.—*The righteous man.* Again the word of the Lord tries Joseph, but not so much now as the word of prophecy, but as the word of command, the doctrine of righteousness. " The Egyptian's house is blessed for Joseph's sake."

"The Lord was with Joseph, and he was a prosperous man." A lesson on the true method of prosperity. A prosperous man is one who has the Lord with him— 1. To give him favour with fellow-men. 2. To teach him wisdom, and put things into his hand. 3. To give him the faculty of rule, and dispose others to trust him entirely. 4. To keep him pure from the vicious besetments of the world, both by his own personal chastity and by his courage and self-command in hours of temptation. 5. By delivering him when he is entangled in the meshes of the evil-minded. The bad woman's determination is thwarted. Mercy is shown him in the prison. 6. By making him a messenger of peace and truth, even in the very prison-house of shame and misery.

Notice again the *elevation of Joseph's character*. 1. His *love of God*. "How can I do this great wickedness, and sin against God?" 2. His *love of man*. "My master hath committed all to me"—how can I wrong him so? 3. His *confidence in the blessing of God* on the upright and holy life. He knew that God would vindicate him. 4. His *self-control*. His circumstances were fearful temptation. Had he not been a virtuous man in his heart of hearts, he would have succumbed, and then pleaded, as so many do, the power of the flesh and of the tempting circumstances.

Notice also how these *characteristics do help one another* when they are in the character, and how, when a man casts himself upon God, *God makes the way of escape*. Joseph was safer in prison than he was in his master's house.—R.

EXPOSITION.

Ver. 7.—**And it came to pass after these things.** — Joseph had by this time been nearly ten years in Potiphar's house (*vide* ch. xli. 46)—**that his master's wife cast her eyes** (lasciviously) **upon Joseph ; and she said, Lie with me.** According to monumental evidence (Wilkinson's 'Ancient Egyptians,' vol. i. p. 392, ed. 1878; Hengstenberg's 'Egypt and the Books of Moses,' i. 25; Kalisch, p. 631) and historical testimony (Herod., ii. 111), Egyptian females, even though married, were distinguished for licentiousness and immorality, and were not condemned to live in seclusion (Bohlen), but were allowed freely to mix in promiscuous society, which facts perfectly account for Joseph's temptation by his mistress.

Vers. 8, 9.—**But he refused,**—"it may be that the absence of personal charms facilitated Joseph's resistance (Kalisch); but Joseph assigns a different reason for his non-compliance with her utterly immoral proposition—**and said unto his master's wife,**— "for her unclean solicitation he returneth pure and wholesome words" (Hughes)— **Behold, my master wotteth not what is with me in the house** (literally, *knoweth not, along with me, what is in the house*), **and he hath committed all that he hath to my hand,** (literally, *and all that is to him he hath given to or placed in my hand*) ; **there is none greater in this house than I ; neither hath he kept back anything from me but thee, because thou art his wife: how then can I do this great wickedness, and sin** (cf. ch. xx. 6 ; 2 Sam. xii. 13 ; Ps. li. 4 for the estimate of this act taken by God and good men) **against God?**—Elohim, since

Jehovah would have been unintelligible to a heathen woman.

Ver. 10.—**And it came to pass, as she spake**—or, though she spake (Kalisch)—**to Joseph day by day, that he hearkened not unto her, to lie by her** (a euphemistic expression), **or** (which is not in the original, and may be omitted) **to be with her.**

Vers. 11, 12.—**And it came to pass about this time** (literally, *at this day*, i. e. it one day happened), **that Joseph went into the house to do his business** (*i. e.* to attend to his accustomed duties) **; and there was none of the men of the house there within** (or, in the house). **And she caught him by his garment** (this was probably the long loose robe or mantle, with short sleeves, used in Oriental full dress), **saying, Lie with me: and he left his garment in her hand, and fled, and got him out**—literally, *and went forth into the place without*, i. e. out of the house and into the street.

Vers. 13—15.—**And it came to pass, when she saw that he had left his garment in her hand** (a very indiscreet act on the part of Joseph, considering the possible use that might be made of it), **and was fled forth, that she called unto the men of her house, and spake unto them, saying, See, he hath brought in** (literally, *one has brought in*, the subject of the verb being indefinite) **an Hebrew** (literally, *a man, an Heberw*) **unto us to mock us** (the verb צָחַק, from which comes Isaac, is here used in a bad sense ; not the same as in ch. xxvi. 8) **; he came in unto me to lie with me, and I cried with a loud voice: and it came to pass, when he heard that I lifted up my** voice and cried, that he left his garment with me (literally, *by my side*), and fled, and got him out (or, went forth into the street, *ut supra*).

Vers. 16—18.—**And she laid up his garment by her** (literally, *by her side*), **until his lord came home** (literally, *until the coming of his lord to his house*). **And she spake unto him according to these words, saying, The Hebrew servant, which thou hast brought unto us** (here she charges her husband with being indirectly at least the cause of the alleged affront which had been put upon her), **came in unto me to mock me:** —"she seemed too modest to speak in plain terms of Joseph's crime (Lawson) — **and it came to pass, as I lifted up my voice and cried, that he left his garment with me and fled out** (*i. e.* went forth into the street, *ut supra*).

Ver. 19.—**And it came to pass, when his master heard the words of his wife, which she spake unto him, saying, After this manner** (literally, *according to these words*) **did thy servant to me; that his wrath was kindled.** A papyrus consisting of nineteen pages of ten lines of hieratic writing (purchased from Madame D'Orbiney, and presently in the British Museum), belonging probably to the nineteenth dynasty, contains a tale of two brothers, in which incidents occur very similar to those here narrated. While the two are ploughing in the field, the elder sends the younger brother, who appears to have acted in the capacity of general superintendent, to fetch seed from the house. "And the younger brother found the wife of the elder sitting at her toilet." . . . . "And she spoke to him, saying, What strength there is in thee ! indeed I observe thy vigour every day. Her heart knew him. . . . She seized upon him, and said to him, Come, let us lie down for an instant. Better for thee . . . beautiful clothes." "The youth became like a panther with fury on account of the shameful discourse which she had addressed to him. And she was alarmed exceedingly." . . . "Her husband returned home at evening, according to his daily wont. He came to the house, and he found his wife lying as if murdered by a ruffian." Inquiring the reason of her distress, he is answered as Potiphar was answered by his deceitful spouse. "And

the elder brother became like a panther ; . . . he made his dagger sharp, and took it in his hand " (*vide* 'Records of the Past,' vol. ii. p. 139).

Ver. 20.—**And Joseph's master took him, and put him into the prison,** — literally *house of enclosure ; sohar*, from *sahar*, to encircle, meaning probably a turreted, arched, or rounded building for the confinement of prisoners—**a place where the king's prisoners** (*i. e.* State offenders) were **bound: and he was there in the prison.** This, which some regard as having been a mild punishment (Delitzsch, Keil), since, according to Diodorus Siculus, the laws of the Egyptians were specially severe in their penalties for offences against women, is represented by a Hebrew psalmist (Ps. cv. 18) as having been accompanied with bodily tortures, at least for a time ; for his speedy elevation to a place of trust within the prison almost gives countenance to the idea (Kurtz, Lange, &c.) that Potiphar did not believe his wife's story, and only incarcerated Joseph for the sake of appearances. That Joseph was not immediately punished with death is not improbable (Bohlen), but exceedingly natural, since Joseph was Potiphar's favourite (Hävernick).

Ver. 21.—**But** (even if Joseph was harshly treated in the tower of Heliopolis) **the Lord** —Jehovah (*vide* on ver. 5)—**was with Joseph** (*vide* ver. 2), **and shewed him mercy** (literally, *extended kindness unto him*), **and gave him favour in the eyes of the keeper (or** captain) **of the prison** (or round house).

Vers. 22, 23.—**And the keeper of the prison** (captain of the round house, or chief officer of the tower) **committed to Joseph's hand all the prisoners that were in the prison; and whatsoever they did there, he was the doer** of it — literally, *and all that they* (the prisoners) *were doing there, he was the person doing it, or attending to it ;* i. e. the keeper gave him charge to see that the prisoners obeyed whatever orders were issued for their regulation ; and, having implicit confidence in Joseph's probity, **the keeper of the prison looked not to anything** that was **under** (or in) **his hand** (*i. e.* he did not trouble himself about anything intrusted to Joseph); **because the Lord** (Jehovah) **was with him, and that which he did, the Lord** (Jehovah) **made it to prosper.**

HOMILETICS.

Vers. 7—23.—*Joseph and the wife of Potiphar.* I. THE GREAT TEMPTATION. 1. The *time* of it. Never perhaps had Joseph's prospects been brighter since he left his father's house than towards the close of that decade of years which he spent in the Egyptian officer's employ ; and yet then it was that, like a thunderbolt shot from a clear sky, a fierce temptation burst upon him. 2. The *occasion* of it. This was the beauty of Joseph's person. Things innocent and lovely in themselves may sometimes be a source of danger, and, if not guarded against, a cause of sin, to their possessors. In particular the good looks of men and women are often snares to others as well as fraught with peril to themselves, as the cases of Sarah (ch. xii. 14), Rebekah (ch. xxvi. 10), and Dinah (ch. xxxiv. 2) testify. Hence beauty of the person should neither be too eagerly coveted nor too proudly worn by either sex, as by each its charms in the other should be moderately admired, and its allurements earnestly resisted. 3. The *form* of it. The special trial to which the young man Joseph was now subjected partook of the character of an assault upon his chastity. It is, however, a mistake to suppose that a good man is always assaulted at the point where he is weakest. On the contrary, it is one of the devil's blunders that, in directing his attacks against saints, he for the most part mistakenly selects the point where they are strongest. Joseph was permitted to be assailed by his lascivious mistress not because his own personal virtue was doubtful, but because in that direction he was best prepared to repel the fiercest onset of temptation. 4. The *strength* of it. There were elements in this assault upon Joseph's virtue which were calculated to impart to it a vehemence that in ordinary circumstances, *i. e.* with persons of less robustness of moral principle than Joseph, must have proved overwhelming. These were—(1) The person by whom it was directed, viz., Joseph's mistress, the wife of a high officer of state, whose smile might have turned the head and intoxicated the heart of a young man who was only her slave. (2) The vehement importunity with which it was urged, his mistress speaking to him day by day, and even by act as well as word endeavouring to prevail. (3) The convenient opportunity which was almost always presented, seeing that Joseph's master was mostly absent, and the domestics often out of the way. (4) The danger he might incur by offending one so high in rank as his master's wife. (5) The advantages he might expect to reap from complying with her pleasure.

II. THE SPLENDID VICTORY. 1. The *manner* of Joseph's refusal. (1) Promptly, without the slightest hesitation or appearance of dallying with the tempting bait. Had Joseph hesitated, he might have been lost; had he trifled with the forbidden fruit, he might have plucked and ate. (2) Firmly. There was no sound of wavering or indecision about the reply of Joseph. It was not the answer of a man who was only half-hearted in putting away from him a thing which he secretly desired. In Joseph's "no" there was the clear, full-toned ring of a man who had made up his mind intelligently and finally. (3) Kindly. Joseph behaved towards his mistress with as much tenderness as his moral indignation and disgust at her behaviour would allow ; his considerateness shining out conspicuously in this, that he studiously endeavoured to be as much as possible out of the unhappy woman's sight, in the hope, doubtless, that her unholy passion might abate. (4) Bravely. Joseph was prepared to run any risk rather than accede to the base proposal of his mistress, as was proved by his fleeing from the house without his doublet, when the impudent woman sought by catching hold of him to secure compliance with her request. 2. The *reason* of Joseph's refusal. (1) The greatness of the trust reposed in him by his master. Potiphar had committed everything to his (Joseph's) care ; and how then could he repay with treachery so abominable a confidence so great ? (2) The extent of the power delegated to him. Potiphar had kept back nothing from him except his wife ; how then, having privileges so extensive, should he covet the one thing forbidden ? (3) The sacredness of the relationship existing between his mistress and Potiphar. "Thou art his wife ;" and by the covenant of marriage thou belongest to him only, and not to me. (4) The heinousness of the sin of which he would be guilty. "How can I do this great wickedness, and sin against God ?"

III. THE REMARKABLE REWARD. 1. *The slander of his mistress.* The disappointed strumpet, thirsting for revenge, resolves upon accomplishing the ruin of the fair youth of whom the moment before she affected to be enamoured. But indeed all illicit passion, whether gratified or baulked, has a tendency sooner or later to become transformed into hate. Laying up the garment which Joseph had indiscreetly dropped in his haste, she makes use of it to trump up a charge against Joseph of having attempted a violation of her chastity. There is no length to which the fierce resentment of a wicked woman will not proceed against those who have incurred her hate. It will commonly go hard with her if out of a straw her infernal ingenuity cannot manufacture a rope wherewith to strangle her victim. 2. *The wrath of his master* Potiphar, as was natural, at first felt inclined to believe his wife and to suppose that Joseph had foully betrayed the trust reposed in his honour. In this, of course, he acted hastily, and therefore sinfully. Even from the nearest and the dearest reports affecting injuriously the characters of others should not be accepted without investigation. But that second thoughts prevailed with Potiphar, who, remembering the bad reputation of Egyptian ladies generally, and knowing something possibly of the slenderness of his own wife's virtue, as well as recalling the previous high character of Joseph, began to doubt the truth of what was alleged against his favourite, and to think it more likely that his wife lied than that Joseph sinned, has been inferred from the circumstance that Joseph was not forthwith remitted to the executioner's block, but only committed to the tower. 3. *The mercy of his God.* As before, Jehovah went with Joseph to the prison, and comforted him with gracious thoughts concerning his affliction, with speedy favour in the sight of his keeper, so that the severity of his confinement was considerably mitigated, and with ultimate promotion to a position of trust within the prison, the charge of all the criminals being committed to his care. And finally, the Lord made him prosperous and successful as before in all his undertakings.

HOMILIES BY VARIOUS AUTHORS.

Ver. 21.—*Joseph in slavery.* "But the Lord was with Joseph," &c. Men would have thought, as they looked on the Hebrew slave, that he was God-forsaken. Not so. God blessed him. This was evidenced in the character he developed. The Lord was with him.

I. DISCRETION, THE RESULT OF A SENSE OF THE DIVINE PRESENCE. He did not betray trust, or presume on the confidence placed in him, or the kind treatment he received; nor did he unwisely run into danger.

II. DILIGENCE, THE OUTCOME OF A SENSE OF THE DIVINE PRESENCE. Toil kept off much temptation. If a slave by circumstances, he will yet do what he can to benefit his master. He worked under apparently hopeless conditions.

III. DEVOUTNESS, THE CERTAIN CONSEQUENCE OF A SENSE OF THE DIVINE PRESENCE. Joseph lived as under the eye of God. Hence when special temptations came he repelled them in the Divine strength. "How can I do this great wickedness?" &c. Joseph was neither to be persecuted out of his religion nor enticed from it. This is the brightest chapter in Joseph's life. He would not sin against himself, nor against God, who was with him.—H.

Ver. 21.—*God's presence with his servants.* Joseph in slavery, yet the Lord was with him (cf. Rev. i. 9). Twice stated in this chapter. Outward prosperity is no test of God's presence (cf. Rom. v. 3; 2 Cor. xii. 9). Often in times of trial God's presence is most clearly felt. When all dark below, the eye is drawn upwards. The world's good seen to be unprofitable (James iv. 4). There is a sense in which God is always with all. He guides men's actions and course of life, whether they will or not. But while unbelief derives no comfort from this (Zeph. i. 12), the knowledge of his presence gives peace to his people (Isa. xxvi. 3—12).

I. CHARACTER OF HIM WITH WHOM GOD WAS THUS PRESENT. A Godward mind— habitually living as in the sight of God, though left alone (cf. Gal. iv. 28). Fulfilled what his hand found to do. God's will was his rule of life. He resisted temptation (James i. 12); was faithful in the charge committed to him, though not of his own choice. Did not look upon the wrong he had suffered as excusing him from fidelity. This faithful spirit can spring only from thorough belief in God's love and care (1 John iv. 19).

II. THE BLESSING OF GOD'S PRESENCE EXTENDED TO EVERY PART OF HIS LIFE. Not merely in the fact of his being carried to Egypt (cf. Acts xxiii. 11), but in every incident God's hand is seen. His management of Potiphar's affairs was a training for rule over Egypt. His unjust accusation was a step towards his standing before Pharaoh. His experience in prison prepared him to be the deliverer of a nation (cf. Heb. ii. 18; iv. 15). Thus God's presence is something better and higher than merely a prosperous course. It is the certainty that everything that happens is ordered by infinite wisdom and love—is a step towards the fulness of joy (Deut. viii. 2). This holds good in spiritual experience not less than in temporal. A Christian is often led through times of darkness. Communion with God seems to be interrupted (Ps. lxv. 3; Rom. vii. 24). Temptation, opposition, difficulty in prayer make the soul sad. Yet the Lord is not absent; and these are all parts of the training by which he is preparing his servant for the fulness of blessing.

III. HE WITH WHOM THE LORD ABIDES (John xiv. 23; Rev. iii. 20) IS A BLESSING TO OTHERS. So it was with Joseph. Potiphar, the jailer, Pharaoh, the Egyptian nation, were blessed through him. There is no such thing as keeping a blessing to ourselves; the very attempt destroys it as a blessing. Temporal possessions and powers, used selfishly, become vanity. They pass away, and leave no good, no joy behind. And so with spiritual good. He who has experienced the grace of God must care for others, or his own state will suffer (Prov. xi. 24). The more we partake of the mind of Christ, the more we learn that wherever he leads us, it is that we may be channels of blessing to others.—M.

Ver. 22.—*Joseph as prison warder.* "And the keeper of the prison committed to Joseph's hands all the prisoners that were in the prison," &c. Joseph is unjustly treated and thrown into prison. Here he makes the best of circumstances. He gains the confidence of the keeper. The keeper of the State prison is glad to find one like Joseph, to whom he can delegate much toil and responsibility.

I. DUTY DISCHARGED IN A SYMPATHETIC SPIRIT. He admits many to prison, and feels for all. He sees that it is but a step from the presence-chamber of Pharaoh to a vile prison. To those who found higher places slippery, and those who found the temptations of poverty too strong, he shows his pity. His own bitter separation from friends makes him sympathetic.

II. DUTY DISCHARGED IN A CHEERFUL SPIRIT. Generally he had a smile for the prisoners. They looked for it, and responded to it. The heart can give to the sad that which is better than gold—a cheerful helpfulness. Our gloom can lay extra burdens on others.

III. DUTY DISCHARGED IN A COURTEOUS SPIRIT. He would not trample on those already fallen. He inquires even into the cause of the sadness of the prisoners, and interprets for them dreams which had perplexed them. His own dreams had made him at one time elate, but they seem as yet far from being fulfilled. Still this only leads him to be more courteous to those who may also be doomed to disappointment. The sympathy, cheerfulness, and courtesy of Joseph made him eventually prime minister of Egypt.—H.

EXPOSITION.

CHAPTER XL.

Ver. 1.—**And it came to pass** (literally, *and it was*) **after these things** (literally, *words*, i. e. after the transactions just recorded), that **the butler**—מַשְׁקֵה, the hiph. part. of שָׁקָה, to drink, signifies one who causes to drink, hence cupbearer (cf. ver. 11)—**of the king of Egypt and his baker**—the אֹפֶה (part. of אָפָה, to cook or bake) was the officer who prepared the king's food. The monuments show that the Egyptians had carried the arts of the confectioner and cook to a high degree of perfection (*vide* Hengstenberg, 'Egypt and the Books of Moses,' p. 27; Wilkinson, 'Ancient Egyptians,' ii. 33—39, ed. 1878)—**had offended** (or sinned against) **their lord** (literally,

against, the preposition being repeated) **the king of Egypt**—whom they had attempted to poison (the Targum of Jonathan), though this of course is only a conjecture in the absence of specific information.

Ver. 2.—**And Pharaoh was wroth**—literally, *broke forth* (sc. into anger)—**against two of his officers** (*vide* ch. xxxvii. 36), **against the chief**—*sar :* the word occurs in one of the oldest historical documents of ancient Egypt ('Inscription of Una,' line 4, sixth dynasty), meaning chief or eunuch (*vide* 'Records of the Past,' ii. 3)—**of the butlers,** —an office once filled by Nehemiah in the Court of Persia (Neh. i. 11), and Rabshakeh (Aramaic for "chief of the cupbearers") in the Court of Assyria (2 Kings xviii. 17)— **and against the chief of the bakers.** Oriental monarchs generally had a multitude of butlers and bakers, or cupbearers and Court purveyors, the chiefs in both departments being invested with high honour, and regarded with much trust (Herod., iii. 34 ; Xenoph., 'Cyrop.,' i. 3, 8).

Ver. 3.—**And he put them in ward** (or in custody) **in the house of the captain of the guard,**—*i. e.* Potiphar (*vide* ch. xxxvii. 36)—**into the prison,**—literally, *house of enclosure* (*vide* ch. xxxix. 20)—**the place where Joseph was bound.** The word אֵסוּר, from אָסַר, to make fast by binding, seems to corroborate the Psalmist's assertion (Ps. cv. 18) that Joseph had been laid in iron and his feet hurt with fetters ; but this could only have been temporarily (*vide* vers. 4, 6).

Ver. 4.—**And the captain of the guard charged Joseph with them** (literally, *set Joseph with them,* i. e. as a companion or servant ; to wait upon them, since they were high officers of State, not to keep watch over them as criminals), **and he served them** (*i. e.* acted as their attendant): **and they continued a season in ward** (literally, *and they were days,* i. e. an indefinite period, *in prison*).

Ver. 5.—**And they dreamed a dream both of them** (on dreams cf. ch. xx. 3), **each man his dream in one night** (this was the first remarkable circumstance connected with these dreams—they both happened the same night), **each man according to the interpretation of his dream** (*i. e.* each dream corresponded exactly, as the event proved, to the interpretation put on it by Joseph, which was a second remarkable circumstance, inasmuch as it showed the dreams to be no vague hallucinations of the mind, but Divinely-sent foreshadowings of the future fortunes of the dreamers), **the butler and the baker of the king of Egypt, which** were **bound in the prison.**

Vers. 6, 7.—**And Joseph came in unto them in the morning** (a proof that Joseph at this time enjoyed comparative freedom from corporeal restraint in the prison), **and looked upon them, and, behold, they** were **sad.** The word זֹעֲפִים from זָעַף, to be angry, originally signifying irate, wrathful, τεταραγμένοι (LXX.), is obviously intended rather to convey the idea of dejection, *tristes* (Vulgate). **And he asked Pharaoh's officers that** were **with him in the ward of his lord's house, saying, Wherefore look ye** so **sadly to-day ?**—literally, *knowing what* (מַדּוּעַ = מָה יָדַע = τί μαθών) *are your faces evil, or bad* (πρόσωπα σκυθρωπά, LXX. ; *tristior solito,* Vulgate), *to-day ?*

Ver. 8.—**And they said unto him, We have dreamed a dream, and** there is **no interpreter of it**—literally, *a dream have we dreamt, and interpreting it there is none.* This must be noted as a third peculiarity

connected with these dreams, that both **of** their recipients were similarly affected by them, though there was much in the butler's dream to inspire hope rather than dejection. **And Joseph said unto them, Do** not **interpretations** belong **to God ?**—literally, *Are not interpretations to Elohim?* i. e. the Supreme Being (cf. ch. xli. 16 ; Dan. ii. 11, 28, 47). The Egyptians believed ὅτι ἀνθρώπων μὲν οὐδενὶ προσκέεται ἡ τέχνη μαντική, τῶν δὲ θεῶν μετεξετέροισε (Herod., ii. 83). **Tell me** them, **I pray you.** Joseph's request implies that the consciousness of his Divine calling to be a prophet had begun to dawn upon him, and that he was now speaking from an inward conviction, doubtless produced within his mind by Elohim, that he could unfold the true significance of the dreams.

Vers. 9—11.—**And the chief butler told his dream to Joseph, and said to him, In my dream, behold, a vine** was **before me**—literally, *in my dream* (sc. I was), *and behold a vine* (*gephen*, from the unused root *gaphan*, to be bent, a twig, hence a plant which has twigs, especially a vine ; cf. Judges ix. 13 ; Isa. vii. 43 ; xxiv. 7) *before me.* The introduction of the vine into the narrative, which has been pronounced (Bohlen) an important factor in proof of its recent composition, since, according to Herodotus (ii. 77), the vine was not cultivated in Egypt, and, according to Plutarch ('De Is. et Osir.,' 6), it was not till after Psammetichus, *i. e.* about the time of Josiah, that the Egyptians began to drink wine, has now by more accurate study been ascertained to be in exact accordance, not only with Biblical statements (Numb. xx. 5 ; Ps. lxxviii. 47 ; cv. 33), but likewise with the testimony of Herodotus, who affirms (ii. 37) that wine (οἶνος ἀμπέλινος) was a privilege of the priestly order, and with the representations on the monuments of vines and grapes, and of the entire process of wine-making (*vide* Hävernick's 'Introduction,' § 21 ; Wilkinson's 'Ancient Egyptians,' i. 379, *et seqq.* 430, 431, ed. 1878 ; Hengstenberg, 'Egypt,' p. 13 ; Rawlinson, 'Hist. Illus.,' p. 49 ; Thornley Smith, 'Joseph and his Times,' p. 58). **And in the vine** were **three branches :**—*sarigim,* tendrils of a vine, from *sarag,* to intertwine (ver. 12 ; Joel i. 7)—**and it** was **as though it budded, and her blossoms shot forth ;**—literally, *as it budded* (Murphy) ; or, as though blossoming (Rosenmüller, Keil, Kalisch) ; it shot forth its blossom (Keil) ; or, its blossoms shot forth (Rosenmüller, Kalisch, Murphy)—**and the clusters thereof brought forth ripe grapes :**—more correctly, its stems caused to ripen, or matured, clusters, the אֶשְׁכֹּל being the stalk of a cluster, as distinguished from the עֲנָבִים, or clusters themselves (Gesenius, 'Lex.,' p. 85), though interpreters generally (Kalisch, Keil, Murphy) regard the first as the unripe, and the second as the ripe, cluster—**and Pharaoh's cup**— כּוֹס, a receptacle or vessel, either contracted from כָּנַס, like אִישׁ for אֱנִישׁ (Gesenius), or derived from כּוֹס, to conceal, to receive, to keep, connected with the idea of bringing together, collecting into a thing (Fürst)— was **in my hand : and I took the grapes, and pressed them**—ἐξέθλιψα (LXX.), *expressi* (Vulgate), a translation adopted by the most competent authorities (Gesenius, Fürst, Rosenmüller, Keil, Kalisch, *et alii*), though the sense of diluting with water is advocated by Dathe, Hävernick ('Introd.,' § 21), and others as the most appropriate signification of שָׂחַט, which occurs only here. That Pharaoh is represented as drinking the expressed juice of grapes is no proof that the Egyptians were not acquainted with fermentation, and did not drink fermented liquors. In numerous frescoes the process of fermentation is distinctly represented, and Herodotus testifies that though the use of grape wine was comparatively limited, the common people drank a wine made from barley : οἴνῳ δ᾽ ἐκ κριθέων πεποιημένῳ (ii. 77)—**into Pharaoh's cup, and I gave the cup into Pharaoh's hand** — literally, *I placed the cup upon Pharaoh's palm*, כַּף, used of Jacob's thigh-socket (ch. xxxii. 26), meaning something hollowed out.

Vers. 12—15.—**And Joseph** (acting no doubt under a Divine impulse) **said unto him, This is the interpretation of it** (cf. ver. 18 ; xli. 12, 25 ; Judges vii. 14 ; Dan. ii. 36 ; iv. 19): **The three branches** (*vide supra*, ver. 10) **are three days** :—literally, *three days these* (cf. ch. xli. 26)—**yet within three days** (literally, *in yet three days*, i. e. within three more days, before the third day is over) **shall Pharaoh lift up thine head,** — not μνησθήσεται τῆς ἀρχῆς σου (LXX.), *recordabitur ministerii tui* (Vulgate), a rendering which has the sanction of Onkelos, Samaritan, Jarchi, Rosenmüller, and others ; but shall promote thee from the depths of thy humiliation (Gesenius, Fürst, Keil, Kalisch, &c.), to which there is an assonance, and upon which there is an intentional play, in the opposite phrase employed to depict the fortunes of the baker (*vide infra*, ver. 19)— **and restore thee unto thy place** :—epexegetic of the preceding clause, the כֵּן (or pedestal, from כּוּן, unused, to stand upright, or stand fast as a base) upon which the butler was to be set being his former dignity and office, as is next explained—**and thou shalt deliver Pharaoh's cup into his hand, after the former manner when thou wast his butler.** After which Joseph adds a request for himself. **But think on me when it shall be well with**

thee (literally, *but, or only, thou shalt remember me with thee, according as, or when, it goes well with thee*), **and shew kindness, I pray thee, unto me** (cf. Josh. ii. 12 ; 1 Sam. xx. 14, 15 ; 2 Sam. ix. 1 ; 1 Kings ii. 7), **and make mention of me unto Pharaoh,**—literally, *bring me to remembrance before Pharaoh* (cf. 1 Kings xvii. 18 ; Jer. iv. 16 ; Ezek. xxi. 28)—**and bring me out of this house :** **for indeed I was stolen** (literally, *for stolen I was stolen*, i. e. I was furtively abducted, without my knowledge or consent, and did not voluntarily abscond in consequence of having perpetrated any crime) **away out** (literally, *from*) **of the land of the Hebrews :**— i. e. the land where the Ibrim live (Keil) ; an expression which Joseph never could have used, since the Hebrews were strangers and sojourners in the land, and had no settled possession in it, and therefore a certain index of the lateness of the composition of this portion of the narrative (Bleek, 'Introd.,' § 80) ; but if Abram, nearly two centuries earlier, was recognised as a Hebrew (ch. xiv. 13), and if Potiphar's wife could, in speaking to her Egyptian husband and domestics, describe Joseph as an Hebrew (ch. xxxix. 14, 17), there does not appear sufficient reason why Joseph should not be able to characterise his country as the land of the Hebrews. The Hebrews had through Abraham become known at least to Pharaoh and his Court as belonging to the land of Canaan (ch. xii. 15 —20) ; and it is not a violent supposition that in Joseph's time " the land of the Hebrews " was a phrase quite intelligible to an Egyptian, as signifying not perhaps the entire extent of Palestine, but the region round about Hebron and Mamre (Nachmanides, Clericus, Rosenmüller)—scarcely as suggesting that the Hebrews had possession of the land prior to the Canaanites (Murphy). **And here also have I done nothing** (*i. e.* committed no crime) **that they should** (literally, *that they have*) **put me into the dungeon.** The term בּוֹר is here used to describe Joseph's place of confinement, because pits or cisterns or cess-pools, when empty, were frequently employed in primitive times for the incarceration of offenders (cf. Jer. xxxviii. 6 ; Zech. ix. 11).

Vers. 16, 17.—**When** (literally, *and*) **the chief baker saw that the interpretation was good, he** (literally, *and he*, encouraged by the good fortune predicted to his fellow-prisoner) **said unto Joseph, I also was in my dream, and, behold, I had three** (literally, *and behold three*) **white baskets**—literally, *baskets of white bread ;* LXX., κανᾶ χονδριτῶν ; Vulgate, *canistra farinæ ;* Aquila, κόφινοι γύρεως (Onkelos, Pererius, Gesenius, Fürst, Keil, Kalisch, Murphy, *et alii*) ; though the rendering "baskets of holes," *i. e.* wicker baskets, is preferred by some (Symmachus

Dathius, Rosenmüller, and others), and accords with the evidence of the monuments, which frequently exhibit baskets of wickerwork (vide Wilkinson's 'Ancient Egyptians,' ii. 34, ed. 1878)—**on my head.** According to Herodotus (ii. 35), Egyptian men commonly carried on their heads, and Egyptian women, like Hagar (ch. xxi. 14), on their shoulders. **And in the uppermost basket** (whose contents alone are described, since it alone was exposed to the depredations of the birds) there was **of all manner of bakemeats for Pharaoh**—literally, *all kinds of food for Pharaoh, the work of a baker.* The monuments show that the variety of confectionery used in Egypt was exceedingly extensive (Hengstenberg, p. 27). **And the birds** —literally, *the bird;* a collective sing., as in ch. i. 21, 30 (cf. ver. 19)—**did eat them out of the basket upon my head.**

Vers. 18, 19.—**And Joseph answered and said** (with what reluctance and pathos may be imagined), **This is the interpretation thereof** (the exposition was supplied by God, and, however willing or anxious Joseph might be to soften its meaning to his auditor, he could not deviate a hair's-breadth from what he knew to be the mind of God): **The three baskets are three days: yet within three days**—literally, *in three days more* (ut supra, ver. 13)—**shall Pharaoh lift up thy head from off thee** (*i. e.* deprive thee of life, the phrase containing a resemblance to that employed in ver. 13, and finding its explanation in the words that follow), **and shall hang thee on a tree**—*i. e.* after decapitation (cf. Deut. xxi. 22, 23 ; Josh. x. 26 ; 2 Sam. iv. 12), which was probably the mode of execution at that time practised in Egypt (Michaelis, Clarke, Keil, Murphy, Alford, Inglis, Bush), though some regard the clause as a description of the way in which the baker's life was to be taken from him, viz., either by crucifixion (Onkelos, Rosenmüller, Ainsworth) or by hanging (Willet, Patrick, T. Lewis), and others view it as simply pointing to capital punishment, without indicating

the instrument or method (Piscator, Lapide, Mercerus, 'Speaker's Commentary'). **And the birds shall eat thy flesh from off thee.** "The terror of approaching death would be aggravated to the poor man by the prospect of the indignity with which his body was to be treated" (Lawson).

Ver. 20.—**And it came to pass** (literally, *and it was,* as Joseph had predicted) **the third day** (literally, *in, or on, the third day*). which was **Pharaoh's birthday,**—literally, *the day of Pharaoh's being born,* the inf. hophal being construed with an accusative (*vide* Gesenius, 'Grammar,' § 143)—**that he made a feast**—a *mishteh,* i. e. a drinking or banquet (*vide* ch. xix. 3)—**unto all his servants.** "The birthdays of the kings of Egypt were considered holy, and were celebrated with great joy and rejoicing. All business was suspended, and the people generally took part in the festivities' (Thornley Smith, 'Joseph and his Times,' p. 62 ; *vide* Herod., i. 133 : Ἡμέρην δὲ ἀπασέων μάλιστα ἐκείνην τιμᾶν νομίζουσι, τῇ ἕκαστος ἐγένετο ; and cf. Matt. xiv. 6 ; Mark vi. 21). **And he lifted up the head**—here the one phrase applies equally, though in different senses, to both. A similar expression occurs in the annals of Assur-nasir-pal (Sardanapalus), column ii. line 43: "Their heads on the high places of the mountain I lifted up" ('Records of the Past,' vol. iii. p. 54)—**of the chief butler and of the chief baker among his servants** — literally, *in their midst,* as a public example.

Vers. 21, 22.—**And he restored the chief butler unto his butlership again; and he gave the cup into Pharaoh's hand** (literally, *set the cup upon Pharaoh's palm*): **but he** (*i. e.* Pharaoh) **hanged the chief baker** (*vide supra,* ver. 19): **as Joseph had interpreted to them.**

Ver. 23.—**Yet did not the chief butler remember Joseph** (as Joseph had desired, and as he doubtless had promised), **but forgat him**—as Joseph might almost have expected (cf. Eccles. ix. 15, 16).

HOMILETICS.

Vers. 1—23.—*Joseph in the round house at Heliopolis.* I. THE PRISONERS AND THEIR ATTENDANT. 1. *The prisoners.* (1) Their rank. They were high officers of state—the chief of the butlers and the chief of the bakers, *i. e.* the principal cupbearer and Court purveyor. (2) Their offence. They had sinned against their lord the king of Egypt ; in what way it is of no importance to inquire, since " we would have heard nothing about them had their story not been connected with that of Joseph" (Lawson), though the Rabbis allege that they had been detected in an attempt at poisoning their master. (3) Their punishment. "The king's wrath is as the roaring of a lion," and " as messengers of death" (Prov. xix. 12 ; xvi. 14) ; and the two offenders were immediately arrested and thrown into prison, committed to the keeping of the captain of the round house, where Joseph was bound. (4) Their privilege. Their punishment was tempered with clemency. In consideration of their official rank, the governor of the tower appointed Joseph to wait upon them and act as their servant. 2. *Their attendant.* In this new capacity Joseph behaved himself wisely and with discretion. With regard to his illustrious companions in misfortune, he—(1) Served them faithfully. "Joseph had been unjustly enslaved, unjustly imprisoned, unjustly detained in his prison, and yet he declined not the work enjoined by his master" (Lawson). Joseph appears to have always acted on the principle commended by the royal preacher (Eccles. ix. 10), and on that recommended by Christ (Luke xlv. 11). "Joseph was a better man than the men whom he served. He was sprung from noble ancestors, and knew that he would one day be exalted above them; but at this time he cheerfully performed to them every service in his power" (Lawson). (2) Sympathised with them sincerely. Though bearing his own misfortunes with unmurmuring resignation and manly fortitude, because sustained by God's grace and the possession of truly religious principles, the amiability of Joseph's nature led him to commiserate his fellow-prisoners who had no such inward supports and consolations as were enjoyed by him. In particular on one occasion mentioned in the text he was so struck with their dejected countenances that he feelingly inquired the cause of their sadness. (3) Directed them wisely. Learning that they were troubled on account of dreams which they had dreamt over-night, and of which they could not find the explanation, he piously exhorted them to look to God for the desired interpretations.

II. THE DREAMS AND THEIR INTERPRETATIONS. 1. *The dreams*—(1) Agreed in the time when they occurred, happening on the same night; in the impressions they produced, filling the hearts of both dreamers with forebodings; in the person by whom they were explained, Joseph giving equally the key to both; and in the interval required for their fulfilment, only three days being allowed for the accomplishment of each. (2) Differed in the imagery of which they were composed—that of the butler consisting of a tableaux in which himself and his royal master appeared beneath the shadow of a blooming vine, Pharaoh sitting on his throne, and himself pressing the ripe clusters into Pharaoh's cup and setting it on Pharaoh's hand; and that of the baker representing himself also engaged in the performance of his official duties, bearing into Pharaoh's presence three wicker baskets of pastries and confections, out of the uppermost of which the birds came to eat;—in the character of the events which they foreshadowed—the butler's dream prognosticating speedy restoration to his butlership, and the baker's dream most ominously pointing to early execution. 2. *Their interpretations.* These were—(1) Revealed by God. Joseph did not claim to be able of himself to interpret the significance of either of the dreams, but explicitly affirmed that to do so was exclusively the prerogative of Elohim. (2) Declared by Joseph. Thus Joseph was authenticated as a prophet of the Lord in that heathen land. (3) Fulfilled by Pharaoh. Pharaoh was no doubt unconscious that he was accomplishing a Divine prediction. So God is able to accord to men the completest liberty of action, and yet realise his own sovereign purpose. Exactly as Joseph had interpreted, both as to time and as to results, the dreams came true.

III. THE INTERPRETER AND HIS REWARD. 1. *The interpreter's request.* Joseph desired in return for his services to the butler that a word should be spoken for him to the king by that officer when restored to his occupation, in the hope that it might lead to his release from confinement. For this conduct Joseph has been blamed by some censorious critics; but (1) his request was natural. Though required to endure the crosses laid on him by Divine providence with meekness and resignation, he was under no obligation to stay a moment longer in prison than he could justly help, but was rather bound to use all legitimate means to insure his deliverance. Then, (2) his request was moderate. He did not ask much at the butler's hand in return for his own great service, only that his name should be mentioned to Pharaoh. Joseph was not exacting in his demands. Again, (3) his request was touching. As he tells the butler, in the hope of moving him to pity, he was a stranger in a strange land, who had been forcibly abducted, though he does not say by whom. What a token of the kindly charity and truly forgiving spirit cherished by Joseph towards his brethren! And finally, (4) his request was just. He had done nothing to deserve imprisonment in that or any other dungeon. 2. *The interpreter's reward.* "Yet did not the chief butler remember Joseph, but forgat him." This must have been (1) a painful experience to Joseph, probably as cruel and unkind a blow as any he had yet received; as certainly it was (2) a monstrous iniquity on the part of the butler, indicating a callous, ungrateful, and truly base disposition, though unfortunately it is (3) a frequent occurrence in human life.

Learn—1. That God's saints are sometimes thrown !by Divine providence into companionship with the worst of men. 2. That the excellent of the earth are often found filling the very humblest situations. 3. That God has many different methods of discovering his mind to men. 4. That God is able to fulfil his own predictions. 5. That wicked men sometimes meet their deserts in this life. 6. That God's people should sympathise with and succour their fellow-men. 7. That they who do good to others should hope for nothing again.

HOMILIES BY VARIOUS AUTHORS.

Ch. xl.—*The inspired man.* Joseph is already supreme in the narrow sphere of the prison : "all was committed to his hand." The narrow sphere prepares him for the wider. The spiritual supremacy has now to be revealed. "Do not interpretations belong to God ?" The dreams are partly of man and partly of. God. Each man dreamed of things connected with his life. The butler of the wine coming from the grape-clusters, pressed into Pharaoh's cup, given into his hand. The baker of the white baskets and bakemeats, plucked from him while upon his head by the birds of prey. To a certain extent the interpretation was natural, but as at once communicated to Joseph it was inspired. The sphere of inspiration is concentric with the sphere of the natural intelligence and wisdom, but goes beyond it. The request of Joseph, that his spiritual superiority should be recognised and rewarded, was not fulfilled by the ungrateful man ; but, as an act of obedience to the Spirit of God, it was committed to him who seeth in secret and rewardeth openly. Joseph is still being tried by the word of God. It is committed to him as a messenger and witness for the covenant people. It tries his faith and patience. The whole is a parable, setting forth—1. The order of the world, as resting on the Divine foreknowledge and appointment in connection with the elect instrumentalities, bringing the things of Egypt under the dominion of the kingdom of God. 2. The providential hiding of gracious purposes. Joseph the seer in the prison, waiting for the hour of redemption, sending forth messages of truth to do their errands. 3. Invisible links between the rulers of this world and the representatives of the kingdom of God to be revealed in due time. 4. Discipline in the lives of God's people fruitful in blessed results, both for them and for all.—R.

Ver. 8.—*The interpreter of God's message.* We cannot but notice the importance often assigned in the Bible to dreams, as channels of revelation from God. The dreams of Jacob and of Pharaoh, and passages such as Deut. xiii. 1 and Joel ii. 28, show this. It may be that in the absence of the written word, which in its completeness is our heritage, God's message was thus given to them in portions. Applying this thought to the circumstances of the text, we see men who had received a message from God which they believed was of importance ; but they could not understand it, and they are sad because there is no interpreter.

I. THE DEEP IMPORTANCE OF GOD'S MESSAGE. How many questions does life present ! What and where are we ? Whither going ? What lies beyond the present ? I see that all things decay ; yet on all sides life from death. Is there such revival for me ? Can the active, thinking spirit be as though it had never been—passed from existence ere the frail body began to decay ? And if there be a life beyond the present, what is its nature ? and what the preparation for it ? Vainly does human wisdom try to answer these questions. He who made all things alone can explain his works (Ps. xciv. 9—12), and the Bible is his answer to our questions, wherein he tells us what we are, for what created, and how to fulfil the object of our being (Ps. cxix. 105).

II. But WE NEED AN INTERPRETER. It may be asked, Why ? The Bible is open. Its words are such as any one can understand. This is true, as far as regards facts, and precepts, and doctrines. There is a knowledge of the word which the natural man can attain to; but the Holy Spirit alone can so open it as to make it "the power of God." It is one thing to know the doctrines of sin and of salvation, and quite another to know ourselves as sinners, and Christ as the Saviour. The one puffs up with pride of knowledge, the other leads to the one Foundation. There is no more dangerous snare than of ignoring this work of the Holy Spirit. Too often men do not believe their need of it, and do not believe in his help. And thus the Bible is found dull, and its teaching departed from in daily life.

III. How to get the interpreter's help. "Tell me." Think of our Lord watching his disciples in the boat. So he watches over thee, ready to help. Hast thou found it so? Has the light of God's love entered thy heart? It is the special work of the Holy Spirit to guide into all truth (John xvi. 13); not in solving mysteries and hard questions, but in revealing Christ to the heart. Have you sought this; sought with expectation the full gift; sought to know Christ (Phil. iii. 10), and the transforming power of belief in his love? Will you seek? There lies the difficulty—the want of earnestness. Men seem afraid of being earnest. But it is the earnest (Matt. xi. 12, βιασταί) who enter the kingdom of heaven.—M.

Ch. xl. 23; xli. 9.—*Pharaoh's forgetful butler.* "Yet did not the chief butler remember Joseph, but forgat him." "I do remember my faults this day." Good men have sometimes had to bear painful imprisonments. Think of Bunyan and Baxter shivering behind the bars of a narrow cell, where light and air were almost excluded, and where disease and death held sway. How much brightness, however, has broken at times from behind prison bars! We might not have had the 'Pilgrim's Progress,' unless Bunyan had been incarcerated on the banks of the Ouse. Nor might the patience and kindness of Joseph's disposition have shone out so brilliantly but for his prison life. In a work entitled 'Five Years' Penal Servitude' a most vivid description is given of how the criminals of the clever and cultured class have to mingle and work with those of ignorant and most sensual type. Defaulting cashiers have to undergo the same treatment as cowardly garotters and desperate burglars. Breaking the law brings any under its rigorous clutches, and levels all distinctions of class or education. Thus Joseph, a Hebrew slave, although not a criminal, would be despised by the chief butler of Pharaoh, but the butler had to associate with him. Indeed the former became his superior in prison, and was in a position to render to a State official certain kindness.

I. The forgetful ingrate. This man was a courtier, a permitted adviser of the Pharaoh of Egypt, but he is sent to the common prison. Joseph gives him much cheer, attention, and kindness. He seeks in every way to relieve the monotony of prison life, and becomes a prophet and religious helper. He sees the butler one day sad of countenance, and learns the reason. Readily he, by Divine help, interpreted the perplexing dream. His words are verified. The chief butler was doubtless profuse in his thanks and promises, but we see how he kept them. Perhaps the forgetfulness was convenient. He did not wish, after his restoration, to remind his monarch—even by making a request—of his having been formerly in disfavour. He possibly never intended to make any effort, unless it should be a gain to himself. He is a very different man in prison and out. This is the way of men in life. Favours slip from the memory like floods from a smoothly-worn rock. We might here possibly find out certain things in our own conduct which would indicate a similar forgetfulness of favours. For example, Christ came as the good Joseph to share our captive state. Think of what love he showed in bearing so much suffering for us. Do not put aside the thought of it as not being definitely for you. It was for each one, as if there were none other for whom to suffer. Some have not believed, have not come out from prison, but have preferred the darkness to light, have thought that the atonement was all unnecessary. They cannot understand how evil is their state until brought out of it. A beggar would not be troubled about his patches and rags in the common lodging-house; but let him be taken into a room of decently-arrayed people, and he then feels the difference, and shudders at his degraded appearance. When once brought into Christ's light we see from what we have been saved, and should be grateful to him. Some have been brought into union with him, and afterwards have declined from his way. Dangerous state,

We should blame others who were ungrateful; what if we have been! The longer action is postponed, the deeper the ingratitude, and the less likelihood is there that the favour will be felt. The longer postponed, the harder to acknowledge. Thus the butler may have hesitated to speak of Joseph because he would have to reveal his own ingratitude. Possibly he hoped Joseph was dead. Not so; Joseph lives. Forgotten by man, he is not forgotten by God.. God will yet bring the forgetful one and his benefactor face to face.

II. AROUSED MEMORIES. Wonderful is that faculty of the mind whereby we can imagine ourselves to exist in the past. Some have weak memories, others strong. Some have memories for places and thoughts, others for dates, figures, and words. Whether memory be strong or weak, the power of association is such that at times facts long past will be brought back most vividly. Revisiting places of interest, traversing certain countries, will bring to memory past friendships, and perhaps even subjects of conversation formerly held there. A house in which one has been born or trained becomes a complete history in time. Certain seasons arouse memories of the past, as birthdays, wedding days, Christmas time, or Easter. Certain circumstances also arouse memory. Pharaoh's perplexity concerning his dream forcibly reminded the butler of his morning of sadness in the prison. "I do remember," &c. The butler implied that he repented of his sins and of his forgetfulness. He may not have been very sincere, but as a courtier he introduces a subject in that way. Let us remember our faults, our inconsistencies as Christians, our hesitation to confess Christ, our excusing ourselves on the ground of the doings of others. Let us be plain with ourselves. Let us not see the motes in the eyes of others, and forget the beams in our own. Let us remember them that we may be humbled, may gain experience of how to avoid them in the future, may gain strength to resist, may gain pardon for past faults, and learn thereby more of the infinite forbearance and love of God, who is so willing to blot out our transgressions, and even the memory of our sins.—H.

EXPOSITION.

CHAPTER XLI.

Ver. 1.—**And it came to pass at the end of two full years** (literally, *two years of days*, i. e. two complete years from the commencement of Joseph's incarceration, or more probably after the butler's liberation), **that Pharaoh**—on the import of the term *vide* ch. xii. 15. Under what particular monarch Joseph came to Egypt is a question of much perplexity, and has been variously resolved by modern Egyptologers in favour of—1. Osirtasen I., the founder of the twelfth dynasty, a prosperous and successful sovereign, whose name appears on a granite obelisk at Heliopolis (Wilkinson, 'Ancient Egyptians,' i. 30, ed. 1878). 2. Assa, or Assis, the fifth king of the fifteenth dynasty of Shepherd kings (Stuart Poole in Smith's 'Bible Dict.,' art. Egypt). 3. Apophis, a Shepherd king of the fifteenth dynasty, whom all the Greek authorities agree in mentioning as the patron of Joseph (Osburn, 'Monumental History,' vol. ii. ch. 2; Thornley Smith, 'Joseph and his Times,' p. 42). 4. Thothmes III., a monarch of the eighteenth dynasty (Stanley Leathes in Kitto's 'Cyclopedia,' p. 744). 5. Rameses III., the king of Memphis, a ruler belonging to the twentieth dynasty (Bonomi in 'The Imperial Bible Dict.,' p. 488; Sharpe's 'History of Egypt,' vol. i. p. 35). It may assist the student to arrive at a decision with respect to these contending aspirants for the throne of Pharaoh in the time of Joseph to know that Canon Cook ('Speaker's Commentary,' vol. i. p. 451), after an elaborate and careful as well as scholarly review of the entire question, regards it as at least "a very probable conjecture" that the Pharaoh of Joseph was Amenemha III., "who is represented on the lately-discovered table of Abydos as the last great king of all Egypt in the ancient empire (the last of the twelfth dynasty), and as such receiving divine honours from his descendant Rameses"—**dreamed.** "For the third time are dreams employed as the agencies of Joseph's history: they first foreshadow his illustrious future; they then manifest that the Spirit of God had not abandoned him even in the abject condition of a slave and a prisoner; and lastly they are made the immediate forerunners of his greatness" (Kalisch). **And, behold, he stood by the river**—i. e. upon the banks of the Nile, the term יְאֹר (an Egyptian word signifying great river or canal, in the Memphitic dialect *yaro*, in the Sahidic *yero*) being used almost exclusively in Scripture for the Nile (Exod. i. 22; ii. 3; vii. 15; Gesenius, 'Lex.,' p. 326). **This** was the common name for the Nile among the Egyptians, the sacred being *Hapi* (Canon Cook in 'Speaker's Commentary,' p. 485).

Ver. 2.—**And, behold, there came up out of the river seven well-favoured kine and fat-fleshed.** According to Plutarch and Clement of Alexandria, the heifer was regarded by the ancient Egyptians as a symbol of the earth, agriculture, and the nourishment derived therefrom. It was therefore natural that the succession of seven prosperous years should be represented by seven thriving cows. That they appeared ascending from the river is explained by the circumstance that the Nile by its annual inundations is the cause of Egypt's fertility (cf. Hävernick, 'Introd.,' § 21). A hymn to the Nile, composed by Euna (according to the generality of Egyptologers a contemporary of Moses), and translated from a papyrus in the British Museum by Canon Cook (who ascribes to it an earlier date than the nineteenth dynasty), describes the Nile as "overflowing the gardens created by Ra, . . . giving life to all animals, . . . watering the land without ceasing . . . Lover of food, bestower of corn . . . Bringer of food ! Great Lord of provisions ! Creator of all good things !" (*vide* 'Records of the Past,' vol. iv. pp. 107, 108). **And they fed in a meadow**—בָּאָ֑חוּ, ἐν τῷ Ἄχει (LXX.), literally, *in the Nile or reed grass.* The word אָחוּ appears to be an Egyptian term descriptive of any herbage growing in a stream. It occurs only here and in ver. 18, and Job viii. 11.

Ver. 3.—**And, behold, seven other kine came up after them out of the river, ill-favoured and lean-fleshed.** The second seven cows, "evil to look upon," *i. e.* bad in appearance, and "thin (beaten small, *dakoth*, from *dakak*, to crush or beat small) of flesh," also proceeded from the river, since a failure in the periodical overflow of the Nile was the usual cause of scarcity and famine in Egypt. **And stood by the** other **kine upon the brink of the river.** The use of the term lip, שָׂפָה, for brink, common enough in Hebrew (ch. xxii. 17 ; Exod. xiv. 30 ; 1 Kings v. 9), occurs also in a papyrus of the nineteenth dynasty, "I sat down by the lip of the river," which appears to suggest the impression that the verse in the text was written by one who was equally familiar with both languages (Canon Cook in 'Speaker's Commentary,' p. 485).

Ver. 4.—**And the ill-favoured and lean-fleshed kine did eat up the seven well-favoured and fat kine**—without there being any effect to show that they had eaten them (ver. 21). So (literally, *and*) **Pharaoh awoke.**

Ver. 5.—**And he slept and dreamed the second time** (that same night) : **and, behold, seven ears of corn came up upon one stalk, rank** (*i. e.* fat) **and good.** This clearly pointed to the corn of the Nile valley, the *triticum compositum*, which bears seven ears upon one stalk. The assertion of Herodotus, that the Egyptians counted it a disgrace to live on wheat and barley (ii. 36), Wilkinson regards as incorrect, since "both wheat and barley are noticed in Lower Egypt long before Herodotus' time (Exod. ix. 31, 32), and the paintings of the Thebaid prove that they were grown extensively in that part of the country ; they were among the offerings in the temples ; and the king, at his coronation, cutting some ears of wheat, afterwards offered to the gods as the staple production of Egypt, shows how great a value was set on a grain which Herodotus would lead us to suppose was held in abhorrence" (Rawlinson's 'Herodotus,' vol. ii. p. 49).

Ver. 6.—**And, behold, seven thin ears and blasted with the east wind sprung up after them**—literally, *burnt up of the east,* קָדִים being put poetically for the fuller רוּחַ קָדִים. It has been urged that this displays a gross ignorance of the nature of the climate in Egypt (Bohlen), since a wind directly east is rare in Egypt, and when it does occur is not injurious to vegetation ; but, on the other hand, it is open to reply (1) that direct east winds may be rare in Egypt, but so are dearth and famine such as that described in the narrative equally exceptional (Kalisch) ; (2) that the Hebrews having only names to describe the four principal winds, the *kadim* might comprise any wind blowing from an easterly direction (Hengstenberg) ; and (3) that the south-east wind, "blowing in the months of March and April, is one of the most injurious winds, and of longest continuance" (Hävernick). Hengstenberg quotes Ukert as saying, "As long as the south-east wind continues, doors and windows are closed ; but the fine dust penetrates everywhere ; everything dries up ; wooden vessels warp and crack. The thermometer rises suddenly from 16° 20', up to 30° 36°, and even 38°, Reaumur. This wind works destruction upon everything. The grass withers so that it entirely perishes if this wind blows long" ('Egypt and the Books of Moses,' p. 10).

Ver. 7.—**And the seven thin ears devoured the seven rank** (*i. e.* fat) **and full ears. And Pharaoh awoke, and, behold,** it was **a dream** —manifestly of the same import as that which had preceded. The dream was doubled because of its certainty and nearness (ver. 32).

Ver. 8.—**And it came to pass in the morning that his spirit was troubled ;**— or, rather, his mind was agitated, ἐταράχθη ἡ χυχή αὐτοῦ (LXX.), *pavore perterritus* (Vulgate), the *ruach* being the seat of the senses, affections, and emotions of various kinds (cf. Dan. ii. 1 ; iv. 5, 19)—and he sent and called for all the magicians of Egypt,—the חַרְטֻמִּים, from חָרַט (unused), to engrave, whence חֶרֶט, a stylus (Gesenius), or from חוּר, to see or explain, and טוּם, to conceal, i. e. he who explains hidden or mysterious things (Kalisch), were sacred scribes, ἱερογραμματεῖς, belonging to the priestly caste, who were skilled in making and deciphering the hieroglyphics. Besides figuring in the Court of Pharaoh (Exod. vii. 11, 22 ; viii. 3 ; xiv. 15) in the time of Moses, they recur again at a later period in that of the Babylonian monarch Nebuchadnezzar (Dan. i. 20 ; ii. 2)—**and all the wise men thereof.** The חֲכָמִים, from חָכַם, the primary idea of which is that of judging (Gesenius), were persons capable of judging, hence persons endowed with pre-eminent abilities for the prosecution of the ordinary business of life, the cultivation of the arts and sciences, the practice of divination, the interpreting of dreams, and other kindred occupations. They were the sages of the nation. **And Pharaoh told them his dream ; but** there was **none that could interpret them unto Pharaoh.** The magicians of Egypt were not so conceited as their brethren in Babylon afterwards showed themselves to be, Dan. ii.. 4 (Lawson). That they could not explain the dream, though couched in the symbolical language of the time, was no doubt surprising ; but "the things of God knoweth no man, but the Spirit of God" (1 Cor. ii. 11), and they to whom the Spirit doth reveal them (1 Cor. ii. 10).

Vers. 9—13.—**Then spake the chief butler unto Pharaoh, saying, I do remember my faults this day :**—literally, *my faults I* (sc. am) *remembering to-day ;* but whether he understood by his faults his ingratitude to Joseph or his offence against Pharaoh commentators are not agreed, though the latter seems the more probable—**Pharaoh was wroth with his servants,**—literally, *broke out against them* (vide ch. xl. 2)—**and put me in ward in the captain of the guard's house,**—literally, *put me in custody of the house of the captain of the slaughterers* (cf. ch. xl. 3)—both **me and the chief baker: and we dreamed a dream in one night, I and he; we dreamed each man according to the interpretation of his dream** (vide ch. xl. 5). **And** there was **there with us a young man, an Hebrew, servant to the captain of the guard** (vide ch. xxxvii. 36) ; **and we told him** (sc. our dreams), **and he interpreted to us our dreams** (vide ch. xl. 12, 13, 18, 19) ; **to each man according to his dream he did interpret. And it came to pass, as he interpreted to us, so it was; me he** (not Pharaoh, but Joseph) **restored unto mine office, and him he hanged** (vide ch. xl. 21, 22).

Ver. 14.—**Then Pharaoh sent and called Joseph, and they brought him hastily** (literally, *caused him to run*) **out of the dungeon** (*vide* ch. xl. 15) : **and he shaved** himself,—this was exactly in accordance with Egyptian custom (Herod. ii. 36). Wilkinson states that "the custom of shaving the head as well as beard was not confined to the priests in Egypt, but was general among all classes" (Rawlinson's 'Herodotus,' vol. ii. p. 49 ; cf. 'Ancient Egyptians,' vol. ii. pp. 330—332, ed. 1878). That the verb is not more exactly defined by a term following, such as the head (Numb. vi. 9), the beard (2 Sam. x. 4), but stands alone (the only instance of its intransitive use), appears to suggest that the writer was familiar with the practice of shaving (*vide* Hävernick, 'Introd.,' § 21)—**and changed his raiment,**—as required by the customs of Egypt (*vide* Hengstenberg's 'Egypt,' p. 30 ; cf. ch. xxxv. 2)—**and came** (or went) **in unto Pharaoh.**

Ver. 15.—**And Pharaoh said unto Joseph, I have dreamed a dream, and** there is **none that can interpret it** (literally, *and interpreting it there is no one*) : **and I have heard say of thee,** that **thou canst understand a dream to interpret it**—literally, *I have heard of thee, saying, thou hearest a dream to interpret it.*

Ver. 16.—**And Joseph answered Pharaoh, saying,** It is **not in me** (literally, *not I*) : **God**—Elohim (cf. ch. xl. 8)—**shall give Pharaoh an answer of peace** — literally, *shall answer the peace of Pharaoh,* i. e. what shall be for the welfare of Pharaoh. The rendering Ἄνευ τοῦ θεοῦ οὐκ ἀποκριθήσεται τὸ σωτήριον Φαραώ (LXX.), though giving the sense, fails in accuracy of translation.

Vers. 17—24.—Pharaoh then relates his dreams in substantially the same terms as those in which they have already been recited, only adding concerning the lean kine that they were (ver. 19) **such as I never saw** (literally, *I never saw such as these*) **in all the land of Egypt for badness:** and that (ver. 21) **when they had eaten them** (*i. e.* the good kine) **up, it could not be known they had eaten them ;**—literally, *and they* (i. e. the good kine) *went into the interior parts,* i. e. the stomach (of the bad kine), *and it was not known that they had gone into the interior parts*—but **they** (the bad kine) **were still ill-favoured, as at the beginning**—literally, *and their appearance was bad as in the beginning,* i. e. previously ; and concerning the thin and blasted ears, that they were also (ver. 23) **withered**—צְנֻמוֹת, from צָנַם, to be hard, meaning either barren (Gesenius), dry (Fürst), or sapless (Kalisch)—a word which the LXX. and the Vulgate both omit. Onkelos explains by נָצָן, flowering, but not fruiting; and Dathius renders by *jejunæ.* After which he (*i. e.* Pharaoh) informs Joseph that the professional interpreters attached to the Court (the *chartummim,* or masters of the occult sciences) could give him no idea of its meaning.

Ver. 25.—**And Joseph said unto Pharaoh** (the inability of the magicians to read the dream of Pharaoh was the best proof that Joseph spoke from inspiration), **The dream of Pharaoh is one** (*i. e.* the two dreams have the same significance) : **God hath shewed Pharaoh what he is about to do** (literally, *what the Elohim is doing,* i. e. is about to do, *he causeth to be seen by Pharaoh*).

Vers. 26—32.—Proceeding with the interpretation of the dream, Joseph explains to Pharaoh that the seven good kine and the seven full ears point to a succession of **seven years of great plenty throughout all the land of Egypt** which were already coming (ver. 29), after which there should arise **seven years of famine,** in which all the plenty should be forgotten in the land, **and the famine should consume,** or make an end of, **the land** (ver. 30), **and the plenty should not be known in the land by reason of** (literally, *from the face of,* used of the efficient cause of anything, hence on account of) **that famine following**—literally, *the famine, that one, after* (things have happened) *so;* adding (ver. 32), **And for that the dream was doubled unto Pharaoh twice** (literally, *and as for the doubling of the dream to Pharaoh twice*); it is **because the thing is established by God,**—literally, *the word* (or thing spoken of) *is firmly fixed,* i. e. certainly decreed, *by the Elohim*—**and God will shortly bring it to pass**—literally, *and hastening* (is) *the Elohim to do it.*

Vers. 33—36.—**Now therefore** (adds Joseph, passing on to suggest measures suitable to meet the extraordinary emergency predicted) **let Pharaoh look out a man discreet** (נָבוֹן, niph. part. of בִּין, intelligent, discerning), **and wise, and set him over the land of Egypt.** Let Pharaoh do this, and let him **appoint officers** (literally, *let him set overseers,* פְּקִדִים, from פָּקַד, to look after, in hiph. to cause to look after) **over the land, and take up the fifth part of the land of Egypt**—literally, *let him fifth the land,* i. e. levy a tax upon its produce to that extent (LXX., Vulgate), which was double the annual impost exacted from Egyptian farmers, but which the unprecedented fertility of the soil enabled them to bear without complaint, if, indeed, adequate compensation was not given for the second tenth (Rosenmüller)—**in the seven plenteous years.** Diodorus mentions the payment of a fifth in productive years as a primitive custom (*vide* Hävernick, p. 219). **And let them** (the officers) **gather all the**

food of those good years that come, and lay up corn under the hand of Pharaoh, and let them keep food in the cities (or, food in the cities, and let them keep it). **And that food shall be for store** (literally, *something deposited*) **to the land against the seven years of famine, which shall be in the land of Egypt; that the land perish not through the famine**—literally, *and the land* (i. e. the people of the land) *shall not be cut off in,* or *by, the famine.*

Vers. 37, 38.—**And the thing was good in the eyes of Pharaoh, and in the eyes of all his servants.** The advice tendered recommended itself to the king and his ministers. **And Pharaoh said unto his servants, Can we find such a one as this is, a man in whom the Spirit of God is?** The Ruach Elohim, as understood by Pharaoh, meant the sagacity and intelligence of a deity (cf. Numb. xxvii. 18; Job xxxii. 8; Prov. ii. 6; Dan. iv. 8, 18; v. 11, 14; vi. 3).

Vers. 39, 40.—**And Pharaoh said unto Joseph, Forasmuch as** (literally, *after*) **God** (Elohim) **hath shewed thee** (literally, *hath caused thee to know*) **all this,** there is **none so discreet and wise as thou art: thou shalt be over my house, and according unto thy word shall all my people be ruled**—literally, *according to thy mouth shall all my people dispose themselves,* i. e. they shall render obedience to thy commands (LXX., Vulgate, Onkelos, Saadias, Pererius, Dathius, Rosenmüller, Keil, Kalisch, Lange, Murphy, and others); though by many competent authorities (Calvin, Schultens, Knobel, Ainsworth, Gesenius, Fürst, Wordsworth, *et alii*) the rendering is preferred, "upon thy mouth shall all my people kiss," against which, however, is the fact that not even then were governors accustomed to be kissed on the lips by their subjects in token of allegiance. The suggestion that the verb should be taken in the sense of "arm themselves," as in 2 Chron. xvii. 17 (Aben Ezra), does not meet with general acceptance. **Only in the throne** (or, more accurately, only as to the throne) **will I be greater than thou.**

Vers. 41—43.—**And Pharaoh said unto Joseph, See, I have set thee over all the land of Egypt.** This was the royal edict constituting Joseph grand vizier or prime minister of the empire: the formal installation in office followed. **And Pharaoh took off his ring from his hand,**—the use of a signet-ring by the monarch, which Bohlen admits to be in accordance with the accounts of classic authors ('Introd.,' p. 60), has recently received a remarkable illustration by the discovery at Koujunjik, the site of the ancient Nineveh, of a seal impressed from the bezel of a metallic finger-ring, two inches long by one wide, and bearing the image, name, and titles of the Egyptian king Sabaco (*vide*

Layard, 'Nineveh and Babylon,' p.156)—**and put it upon Joseph's hand** (thus investing him with regal authority), **and arrayed him in vestures of fine linen,**—שֵׁשׁ, βυσσίνη (LXX.), byssus, so called from its whiteness (probably a Hebrew imitation of an Egyptian word), was the fine linen of Egypt, the material of which the peculiar dress of the priestly caste was constructed: "*vestes ex gossypio sacerdotibus Ægypti gratissimæ*" (Pliny, 'Nat. Hist.,' xix. 1). Herodotus (ii. 81) agrees with Pliny in affirming the priestly costume to have been of linen, and not of wool—**and put a**—literally, *the*, the article showing that it was so done in accordance with a common custom (Hengstenberg, 'Egypt and the Books of Moses,' p. 30)—**gold chain about his neck** (cf. Dan. v. 7, 29). This was usually worn by persons of distinction, and appears in the monuments as a royal ornament; in the Beni-hassan sepulchral representations, a slave being exhibited as bearing one of them, with the inscription written over it, "Necklace of Gold" (*vide* Wilkinson, 'Ancient Egyptians,' ii. 343, ed. 1878; Hengstenberg, 'Egypt,' p. 30). **And he made him to ride in the second chariot which he had;**—"which is another genuine Egyptian custom, for on the monuments the king constantly appears in his war-chariot" (Hävernick) ;—**and they cried before him, Bow the knee:**—אַבְרֵךְ, regarded by most ancient translators as a Hebrew word, an inf. abs. hiph. from בְּרַךְ, meaning bow the knee (Vulgate, Aquila, Origen, Kimchi), is most probably an Egyptian word either altered by the writer (Gesenius) or pointed by the Masorites (Keil) to resemble Hebrew, and signifying "bow the head" (Gesenius), "bend the knee" (Fürst), "Governor or Viceroy" (Kalisch), "rejoice thou" (Canon Cook in 'Speaker's Commentary'), "Pure Prince" (Osburn), "Robed by the king" (Forster)—**and he made him** ruler —literally, *and he set him* (by the foregoing acts)—**over all the land of Egypt.**

Ver. 44.—**And Pharaoh said unto Joseph, I am Pharaoh, and without thee shall no man lift up his hand or foot in all the land of Egypt.** Joseph's authority was to be absolute and universal.

Ver. 45.—**And Pharaoh called Joseph's name Zaphnath-paaneah;**—an Egyptian word, of which the most accredited interpretations are χονθομφανήχ (LXX.) ; *Salvator Mundi* (Vulgate); "the Salvation of the World," answering to the Coptic P-sotem-ph-eneh—*P* the article, *sote* salvation, *m* the sign of the genitive, *ph* the article, and *eneh* the world (Fürst, Jablonsky, Rosellini, and others) ; "the Rescuer of the World" (Gesenius); "the Prince of the Life of the World" (Brugsch); "the Food of

Life," or "the Food of the Living" (Canon Cook in 'Speaker's Commentary')—**and he gave him to wife**—cf. the act of Rhampsinitus, who gave his daughter in marriage to the son of an architect on account of his cleverness (Herod., ii. 121)—**Asenath**— another Egyptian term, rendered 'Ασενέθ (LXX.), and explained by Egyptologers to mean, "She who is of Neith, *i. e.* the Minerva of the Egyptians" (Gesenius, Fürst), "the Worshipper of Neith" (Jablonsky), "the Favourite of Neith" (Canon Cook in 'Speaker's Commentary'), though by some authorities regarded as Hebrew (Poole in Smith's 'Dictionary,' art. Joseph) — **the daughter of Poti-pherah**—Poti-pherah ("devoted to the sun")= Potiphar (*vide* ch. xxxix. 1). The name is very common on Egyptian monuments (Hengstenberg's 'Egypt and the Books of Moses,' p. 32)—**priest**—or prince (Onkelos), as in 2 Sam. viii. 18, where the word כֹּהֵן, as explained by 1 Chron. xviii. 17, means a principal minister of State, though the probability is that Poti-pherah belonged to the priestly caste in Egypt— **of On**—or Heliopolis, 'Ηλιούπολις (LXX.), the name on the monuments being ta-Râ or pa-Râ, house of the sun. "The site of Heliopolis is still marked by the massive walls that surround it, and by a granite obelisk bearing the name of Osirtasen I., of the twelfth dynasty, dating about 3900 years ago" (Wilkinson in Rawlinson's 'Herod.,' ii. p. 8). The priests attached to the temple of the sun at Heliopolis enjoyed the reputation of being the most intelligent and cultured historians in Egypt (Herod., ii. 3). That a priest's daughter should have married with a foreign shepherd may have been distasteful to the prejudices of an intolerant priesthood (Bohlen), but in the case of Asenath and Joseph it was recommended by sundry powerful considerations. 1. Though a foreign shepherd, Joseph was a descendant of Abraham, whom a former Pharaoh had recognised and honoured as a prince, and 'The Story of Saneha,' a hieratic papyrus belonging to the twelfth dynasty, shows that Eastern foreigners might even become sons-in-law to the most powerful potentates under the ancient empire (*vide* 'Records of the Past,' vol. vi. pp. 135—150). 2. Though a foreign shepherd, Joseph was at this time grand vizier of the realm, with absolute control of the lives and fortunes of its people (*vide* ver. 44). 3. Though a foreign shepherd, he was obviously a favourite of Pharaoh, who, besides being monarch of the realm, was the recognised head of the priestly caste, over whom, therefore, he exercised more than a merely external authority. 4. Though a foreign shepherd Joseph had become a naturalised Egyptian, as may be gathered from ch. xliii. 32. And, 5. Though a foreign shepherd, he was circumcised, which, if this rite was already observed in Egypt, and did not originate with Joseph, would certainly not prove a bar to the contemplated alliance (*vide* Canon Cook in 'Speaker's Commentary,' vol. i. p. 480 ; Kurst, 'Hist. of Old Covenant,' § 88 ; Hengstenberg, 'Egypt and the Books of Moses,' pp. 32—35). As to the probability of Joseph consenting to become son-in-law to a heathen priest, it may suffice to remember that though marriage with idolaters was expressly forbidden by patriarchal commandment (ch. xxiv. 3 ; xxviii. 1), and afterwards by Mosaic statute (ch. xxxiv. 16 ; Deut. vii. 3), it was sometimes contracted for what seemed a perfectly adequate reason, viz., the furtherance of the Divine purposes concerning Israel, and apparently too with the Divine sanction (cf.

the cases of Moses, Exod. ii. 21, and Esther, ch. ii. 16) ; that Joseph may have deemed the religion of Egypt, especially in its early symbolical forms, as perfectly compatible with a pure monotheistic worship, or, if he judged it idolatrous, he may both have secured for himself complete toleration and have felt himself strong enough to resist its seductions ; that Asenath may have adopted her husband's faith, though on this, of course, nothing can be affirmed ; and lastly, that the narrator of this history pronounces no judgment on the moral quality of Joseph's conduct in consenting to this alliance, which, though overruled for good, may have been, considered in itself, a sin. **And Joseph went out over all the land of Egypt** in the discharge of his vice-regal duties.

HOMILETICS.

Vers. 1—45.—*Joseph before Pharaoh, or from the prison to the throne.* I. THE DREAMS OF THE MONARCH. 1. *His midnight visions.* Two full years have expired since the memorable birthday of Pharaoh which sent the baker to ignominious execution, but restored the butler to the favour of his royal master. Slumbering upon his bed, the king of Egypt seems to stand among the tall grass upon the banks of the Nile. First seven well-formed and full-fleshed heifers appear to climb up one after the other among the reeds from the river's edge, where they have probably been drinking, followed by seven lean and haggard animals, walking up in the same mysterious procession, till they stand side by side with their thriving predecessors, when they suddenly fall upon these predecessors and eat them up. Startled by the strangeness of the scene, the royal sleeper wakes only to discover it a dream. Then composing himself a second time to slumber, he finds himself still standing in the Nile valley, but now looking out towards its luxuriant corn-fields. Again a strange phenomenon occurs. Growing from the soil he sees a tall, massive stalk of corn, with seven fat ears depending from its top ; but scarcely has this arrested his attention, when he notices another by its side, spare and feeble, with its seven ears parched and empty, as if they had been burnt up by the hot south-east winds blowing up from the sandy wastes of Arabia. To his astonishment, as before, the fat ears are devoured by the thin. Awaking, he a second time discovers that he has been dreaming. 2. *His morning agitations.* The spirit of the king of Egypt was troubled first because of the dreams, which he obviously regarded as conveying to his royal mind some supernatural communication, which, however, he failed to understand ; and secondly because the interpretation of them appeared equally to baffle the penetration of all the wise men and magicians of his empire, whom he had summoned to assist him in deciphering their import.

II. THE INTERJECTION OF THE BUTLER. 1. *The recollection of his faults.* If this referred to his ingratitude to Joseph (which is scarcely likely), that was a shortcoming which should have been remembered at least two years before, though it was better he should recall it then than never. But it is more than probable the offence spoken of was the crime for which he had been previously imprisoned by Pharaoh, and of which he now confessed himself to be guilty, as without acknowledging the justness of his royal master's anger he could scarcely hope to experience the mildness of his royal master's favour. That he only remembers Joseph when he deems it possible by doing so to gratify his master and serve himself indicates a disposition as hypocritical and time-serving as ungrateful and unfeeling. 2. *The recital of his mercies.* Narrating the story of his imprisonment, he informs the anxious monarch that he and his late companion, the chief baker, while suffering the righteous penalty of their misdeeds in the round house or State prison, had each a dream on one and the self-same night; that a young man, then an inmate of the cells, a Hebrew, and a servant of the provost marshal, to whom they severally related their extraordinary dreams, volunteered to deliver their interpretation; and that the event, in the case of both himself and his companion, had turned out exactly as had been predicted—the chief baker had been hanged, while himself, the chief butler, through the royal clemency of Pharaoh, had been restored to his office.

III. THE APPEARANCE OF THE PRISONER. 1. *The opening of the interview.* In obedience to a royal summons, Joseph, after shaving and exchanging his prison garb for a costume suited to the high occasion, is hastily presented to the king. Regarding him with mingled feelings of respect and awe, the mighty potentate declares his dilemma,—he has dreamed a dream which has baffled the ingenuity of all the Court magicians,—and explains how he has heard of Joseph's rare skill as an interpreter of dreams, upon which Joseph, disclaiming all ability in himself, and pointing Pharaoh to the true Interpreter of dreams, assures him, speaking in the exercise of prophetic faith, that God would vouchsafe to him an answer that should tend at once to the happiness of his own person and the prosperity of his realm. 2. *The interpretation of the dreams.* Listening to the monarch's recitation of the singular phenomena of his nocturnal visions, Joseph (1) declares their import·to be the coming of seven years of plenty to the land, to be followed by seven years of famine, which should consume the land by reason of its severity; (2) affirms the certainty of this prediction as involved in the repetition of the dream; and (3) concludes by recommending as a precautionary measure that a fifth part of the produce of the seven years of plenty should be taken up and stored in granaries in the chief cities of the empire, to be distributed among the people during the seven years of famine—a measure which would necessitate the appointment of one competent officer with a requisite staff of assistants, and with supreme authority to enforce the tax or compel the sale, according as the king might determine to uplift the grain. 3. *The reward of the interpreter.* As became one who had proved of such incomparable service to the monarch and the State, Joseph was immediately and generously recompensed. (1) His counsel was accepted. "The thing," or advice tendered, "was good in the eyes of Pharaoh, and in the eyes of all his servants." It is ever a grief to God's prophets and Christ's ministers when their Divinely-sent communications are rejected, as the acceptance of their heavenly messages never fails to afford them occasion of rejoicing. (2) His person was exalted. (*a*) He was constituted grand vizier of the empire, in the historian's account of. which may be noticed the monarch's resolution and the reason of it—"Forasmuch as God hath showed thee all this, thou shalt be over my house, and according unto thy word shall all my people be ruled," or dispose themselves; the royal edict and the public attestation of it—"See, I have set thee over all the land of Egypt. And Pharaoh took off his ring," &c.; the extent of his authority and the limitation of it—his power was to be absolute over all the realm—"without thee shall no man lift up hand or foot"—only as to the throne was he to be subordinate to Pharaoh. (*b*) He was naturalised as an Egyptian prince by the assignment of a new name, Zaphnath-paaneah, for the import of which the Exposition may be consulted. (*c*) He was married to a daughter of the priestly caste, who formed the highest dignitaries in the State.

Learn—1. The marvellous facility with which God can accomplish his designs. God can make Pharaoh dream and the butler recollect his faults when it is time to bring Joseph out of prison. 2. The amazing incompetence of human wisdom to understand God's riddles. The world by wisdom knows not God, any more than Pharaoh's magicians could interpret his dreams. 3. The extraordinary insight which those have who receive their teaching from God. Joseph can interpret the dreams of the monarch and the dreams of his officers with a like promptitude and accuracy, and God's people have an unction from the Holy One that enables them to know all things. 4. The incomparable greatness to which Christ's followers will eventually be raised. Joseph stepped from the prison to the palace, from the tower to the throne, from the wearing of iron fetters to the wielding of regal power; and such honour will have all the saints in the day of the manifestation of the sons of God. Even now God "raiseth up the poor out of the dust, and lifteth the needy out of the dunghill, that he may set him with princes, even with the princes of his people;"

but then "to him that overcometh will I grant," saith the King, "to sit with me on my throne, even as I overcame, and am set down with my Father on his throne."

HOMILIES BY VARIOUS AUTHORS.

Ch. xli.—The tried man is now made ready by long experience for his position of responsibility and honour. He is thirty years old. He can commence his public ministry for the people of God and the world. Pharaoh's dreams, the kine and the ears of corn, like those of the butler and baker, have their natural element in them; but apart from the Spirit of God Joseph would not have dared to give them such an interpretation. Even had his intelligence penetrated the secret, he would not have ventured on a prophecy without God. Pharaoh himself acknowledged that the Spirit of God was manifestly in Joseph. We may be sure there was evidence of Divine authority in his words and manner. As a testimony to the existence of a spirit of reverence for Divine teaching, and a reference of all great and good things to God as their source, even in the minds of the Egyptians, such facts show that God had not left the world without light. The farther we go back in human history, the more simple and unsophisticated we find the minds of men, pointing to a primitive revelation, to the religious beginning of the human race, and to their corruption being the result of a fall, and not a mere negative state, the state of undeveloped reason. Joseph is lifted up out of the dungeon and made to sit among princes. He submits to the providential appointment, doubtless, under the guidance of the same Spirit which had given him his superiority. Moses refused to be called the son of Pharaoh's daughter because at that time to be so was to be separated from his people. Joseph the slave, already far from his home, is willing to be Pharaoh's prime minister that he may be the forerunner of his people's exaltation. The opportunity was not to be lost. "God," he said, "hath made me forget all my toil and all my father's house." "God hath caused me to be fruitful in the land of my affliction." The very names given to Manasseh and Ephraim were a testimony to his faith. His forgetting was only to a better remembering. We must sometimes hide power for the sake of its manifestation. "All countries came into Egypt to Joseph for to buy corn." "I, if I be lifted up, will draw all men unto me." As a type of the Lord Jesus Christ, the Hebrew slave exalted to the rule of the world and the saving of the world, from the cross to the throne. The whole story is full of analogies. He that distributes the bread of life to a perishing race was himself taken from prison, was treated as a malefactor, was declared the Ruler and Saviour because the Spirit of God was upon him, was King of kings and Lord of lords. His benefits and blessings distributed to the world are immediately identified with his kingdom. He gathers in that he may give out. He is first the all-wise and all-powerful ruler of the seven years of plenty, and then the all-merciful helper and redeemer in the seven years of famine. "Joseph is a fruitful bough."—R.

Ver. 14.—*The blessing of suffering wrongfully.* Joseph had probably been three years in prison (cf. ver. 1 with xl. 4). Sorely must his faith have been tried. His brothers, who had plotted his death, prosperous; himself a slave, spending the best years of his life in prison; and that because he had been faithful to God and to his master. We know the end, and therefore hardly realise his desolate condition when no sign of anything but that he should live and die uncared for and forgotten. But the trial comes more home to us when some one for whom we care, or perhaps ourselves, "endure grief, suffering wrongfully;" when unsuspecting frankness has been overreached, or trust betrayed, or feebleness oppressed. We feel not only that wrong has been done, but as if there had been a failure in God's care. It is one thing to acknowledge the doctrine of God's providence, and quite another to feel it under pressure of trouble. A frequent mistake to think of suffering as calling for immediate restitution. Since God beholds the wrong, should there not be some speedy token that he does so? The truth which faith has to grasp is that God is carrying out a plan, for which all these things are a preparation. We may not be able to trace it; but it is so. Thus it was with Joseph. All through these sad years God was guiding him. It was not merely that in time the cloud was removed; every

step of the way had its purpose (John xvi. 20). In the prison he was learning lessons
of the soul,—unlearning the spirit of censoriousness and of self-complacency (ch.
xxxvii. 2),—and, by obeying, learning how to rule. And the course of events bore
him on to what was prepared for him. Had he remained at home, or returned
thither, or had Potiphar not cast him into prison, he would not have been the head of
a great work in Egypt, the helper of his family, the instrument of fulfilling God's
promise. Not one step of his course was in vain; his sufferings were blessings.

I. IN SUFFERING WRONG WE ARE FOLLOWING CHRIST. He suffered for us, "leaving
us an example" (1 Pet. ii. 21) of willingness to suffer for the good of others. This is
the principle of self-sacrifice; not a self-willed sacrifice (Col. ii. 23), but the submission of the will to God (Luke xxii. 42; Heb. x. 7). "This is acceptable with
God"—to accept as from him what he sends, though we may not see its use (Heb. xii.
5—7).

II. FOR EVERY CHRISTIAN THE DISCIPLINE OF SUFFERING IS NEEDFUL. If it was so in
our Lord's sinless human nature (Heb. ii. 10), how much more in us, who must be
taught to subdue the flesh to the spirit! Without trial Christian courage and fruit-
bearing graces would fail (John xv. 2), as without the winter's cold the forest tree
would not form sound wood. And trial calls them into exercise (Rom. v. 3), and
through a sense of our weakness draws us nearer to God (2 Cor. xii. 7—9).

III. NOT ONLY TRIAL IN GENERAL, BUT EVERY PART OF IT WORKS GOOD. To every
part the promise applies (John xvi. 20). So it was with Joseph. God lays no stroke
without cause (Heb. xii. 10). The conviction of this works practical patience. This
particular suffering has its own loving message.

IV. WE OFTEN CANNOT FORESEE THE PURPOSE OF TRIALS. How different was the
end to which God was leading Joseph from anything he could have expected or
hoped for! Yet far better. We can see but a very little way along the path by which
God is leading us. We walk by faith that his guidance is unerring, and that which
he has provided is best (Ephes. iii. 20).—M.

Ver. 40.—*Joseph as prime minister.* "Thou shalt be over my house, and according unto thy word shall all my people be ruled: only in the throne will I be greater
than thou." Sudden elevations are often the precursors of sudden falls. It was not
so with Joseph. He filled satisfactorily his position, retaining it to the end of life.
He made himself indispensable to Pharaoh and to the country. He was a man of
decision. Seeing what had to be done, he hesitated not in commencing it. Going
from the presence of Pharaoh, he passed throughout the land, arranging for granaries
and appointing officers to grapple with the seven years of famine which were imminent. Doubtless he felt the weight of responsibility resting upon him, and would have
many restless nights in calculating how by means of the money then in the treasury
and by forced loans to meet the expenditure for granaries, grain, and official salaries.
He superintended everything. By method he mastered detail.

I. CONSIDER THE POLICY OF THIS EGYPTIAN PRIME MINISTER. Many things we admire
in Joseph, but we must not be blind to the fact that he thought more of binding the
people to the throne than of benefiting the people themselves. He was the first
statesman of that day. His policy determined in great measure what should be the
standard of internal prosperity, and what position the country should hold in the eyes
of other nations. He sought to make Pharaoh's rule absolute. He gave no benefit
without payment, no supplies without sacrifice. He took all the money first (ch.
xlvii. 14), then the cattle (*ibid.* ver. 16), then the lands and their persons (*ibid.* ver. 23).
He thus reduced the people of Egypt to the position of slaves. He made all the land
crown lands. Thus the monarch was pleased, and the priests, being exempt, were
flattered. It is possible that in this Joseph laid the foundation of that system
of mismanagement which has made the most flourishing spot in the world the
basest of kingdoms. He seems also to have striven to give some sort of pre-
eminence to his brethren, and to advance them. Exempt from the burdens pressing
on others, they gained power, and would have become eventually the dominant
race in Egypt, but that another Pharaoh arose who knew not Joseph, *i. e.* who,
although he knew of his having lived and served the nation, yet recognised not his
policy. The state to which Joseph reduced the Egyptians was that to which after-

wards his own descendants were reduced. Thus our plans are overthrown. Time tries success, and by removing dimness from our vision enables us to test it better.

II. CONSIDER THE PRIVATE LIFE OF THIS EGYPTIAN PRIME MINISTER. He was soon led to conform to the spirit and practice of an ungodly nation. He used a divining cup (ch. xliv. 15, 16), took his meals apart (ch. xliii. 32), recognising and sustaining class distinctions. He learned the mode of speech common among the Egyptians, swore by the life of Pharaoh (ch. xlii. 15), and was affianced to an idolatress, probably a priestess (ch. xli. 45). He made no effort to return to his own land, or to the pastoral life of his fathers. It was in his power also for nine years to have sent to make search for his father, who was sorrowing for him as dead, but he sent not. Not until trouble, by an apparent chance, drove his brethren to him did he appear to think of them, or of home and Jacob. When they came he was very slow to make known himself, as though he feared it might compromise him in the eyes of the Egyptians to be known to have relatives who were shepherds, an occupation which was abominable to the Egyptians (ch. xlvi. 34). When he revealed himself to them, it was without the knowledge or presence of the Egyptians. He removed his brethren also to a distant part of Egypt, that they might not constantly, by their presence, remind him and others of his origin. We fancy that Joseph had weaknesses and imperfections such as other men had. He had dwelt in Egypt and caught its spirit. In the names he gave to his children there seems some indication of regret at his forgetfulness and wonder at his fruitfulness. Amid views that might depress there is some brightness. His forgiveness of his brethren was noble. His affection for his father returned. His faith in God was pure at last. Dying, he "gave commandment concerning his bones." He showed that though outwardly an Egyptian, he was inwardly an Israelite.—H.

EXPOSITION.

Ver. 46.—**And Joseph** was **thirty years old when he stood before Pharaoh king of Egypt**—literally, *a son of thirty years in his standing before Pharaoh.* If, therefore, he had been three years in prison (ch. xl. 4 ; xli. 1), he must have served for ten years in the house of Potiphar. **And Joseph went out from the presence of Pharaoh** (in the performance of his official duties), **and went throughout all the land of Egypt**—superintending the district overseers.

Vers. 47, 48.—**And in the seven plenteous years the earth brought forth by handfuls** (*i. e.* abundantly). **And he** (Joseph, through his subordinates) **gathered up all the food** (*i. e.* all the portions levied) **of the seven years, which were in the land of Egypt, and laid up the food in the cities :**—men bringing corn into granaries appear upon the monuments at Beni-hassan (Wilkinson, 'Ancient Egyptians,' vol. i. p. 371, ed. 1878) — **the food of the field, which** was **round about every city** (literally, *the food of the field of the city, which was in its environs*), **laid he up in the same** (literally, *in the midst of it*).

Ver. 49.—**And Joseph gathered** (or heaped up) **corn as the sand of the sea,** an image of great abundance (cf. ch. xxxii. 12)—**very much, until he left numbering** (*i. e.* writing, or keeping a record of the number of bushels); **for it was without number.** "In a tomb at Eilethya a man is represented whose business it evidently was to take

account of the number of bushels which another man, acting under him, measures. The inscription is as follows ; 'The writer or registrar of bushels—Thutnofre," (Hengstenberg, 'Egypt and the Books of Moses,' p. 36).

Vers. 50, 51.—**And unto Joseph were born two sons before the years of famine came,** (literally, *before the coming of the years of famine*), **which Asenath the daughter of Poti-pherah priest of On bare unto him. And Joseph called the name of the firstborn Manasseh** ("Forgetting," from *nashah,* to forget) : **For God** (Elohim ; Joseph not at the moment thinking of his son's birth in its relations to the theocratic kingdom, but simply in its connection with the overruling providence of God which had been so signally illustrated in his elevation, from a position of obscurity in Canaan to such conspicuous honour in the land of the Pharaohs), said he, **hath made me forget all my toil, and all my father's house.** Not absolutely (Calvin, who censures Joseph on this account, *vix tamen in totum potest excusari oblivio paternæ domus*), as events subsequently proved, but relatively, the pressure of his former affliction being relieved by his present happiness, and the loss of his father's house in some degree compensated by the building of a house for himself.

Ver. 52.—**And the name of the second called he Ephraim :**—"Double Fruitfulness" (Keil), "Double Land" (Gesenius), " Fruit"

(Fürst)—For God (Elohim) hath caused me to be fruitful in the land of my affliction. This language shows that Joseph had not quite forgotten "all his toil."

Vers. 53, 54.—And the seven years of plenteousness, that was in the land of Egypt, were ended. And the seven years of dearth began to come,—the most complete parallel to Joseph's famine was that which occurred in A.D. 1064—1071, in the reign of Fátimee Khaleefeh, El-Mustansir-b-illáh, when the people ate corpses and animals that died of themselves; when a dog was sold for five, a cat for three, and a bushel of wheat for twenty deenars (vide Smith's 'Bib. Dict.,' art. Famine)—according as Joseph had said (thus confirming Joseph's character as a prophet): and the dearth was in all lands;—i. e. in all the adjoining countries, and notably in Palestine (vide ch. xlii. 1, 2)—but in all the land of Egypt there was bread.

Ver. 55.—And when (literally, and) all the land of Egypt was famished (literally, and), the people cried to Pharaoh for bread: —cf. the famine in Samaria (2 Kings vi. 26) —and Pharaoh said unto all the Egyptians, Go unto Joseph; what he saith to you, do.

Vers. 56, 57.—And the famine was over all the face of the earth (vide supra, ver. 54): And Joseph opened all the storehouses, —literally, all wherein was, i. e. all the magazines that had grain in them. The granaries of Egypt are represented on the monuments. "In the tomb of Amenemha at Beni-hassan there is the painting of a great storehouse, before whose door lies a great heap of grain already winnowed. Near by stands the bushel with which it is measured, and the registrar who takes the account" (Hengstenberg's 'Egypt and the Books of Moses,' p. 36)—and sold unto the Egyptians

(cf. Prov. ii. 26);—and the famine waxed sore (literally, became strong) in the land of Egypt. A remarkable inscription from the tomb at Eileythia of Bava, which Brugsch ('Histoire d'Egypte,' second ed., p. 174, seqq.) assigns to the latter part of the seventeenth dynasty, mentions a dearth of several years in Egypt ("A famine having broken out during many years, I gave corn to the town during each famine"), which that distinguished Egyptologer identifies with the famine of Joseph under Apophis, the shepherd king (vide 'Encyclopedia Britannica,' ninth edition, art. Egypt); but this, according to Bunsen ('Egypt's Place,' iii. 334), is rather to be detected in a dearth of several years which occurred in the time of Osirtasen I., and which is mentioned in an inscription at Beni-hassan, recording the fact that during its prevalence food was supplied by Amenee, the governor of a district of Upper Egypt (Smith's 'Dict.,' art. Joseph). The character of Chnumhotep (a near relative and favourite of Osirtasen I., and his immediate successor), and the recorded events of his government, as described in the Beni-hassan monuments, also remind one of Joseph:—"he (i. e. Chnumhotep) injured no little child; he oppressed no widow; he detained for his own purpose no fisherman; took from his work no shepherd; no overseer's men were taken. There was no beggar in his days; no one starved in his time. When years of famine occurred he ploughed all the lands of the district, producing abundant food; no one starved in it; he treated the widow as a woman with a husband to protect her" (vide 'Speaker's Commentary,' vol. i. p. 450). And all countries (i. e. people from all the adjoining lands) came into Egypt to Joseph for to buy corn; because the famine was so sore in all lands.

HOMILETICS.

Vers. 46—57.—Joseph on the second throne in Egypt. I. DURING THE SEVEN YEARS OF PLENTY. 1. His mature manhood (ver. 46). Thirteen years had elapsed since his brethren had sold him at Dothan, and during the interval what a chequered life had he experienced! Carried into Egypt by the spice caravan of the Midianitish traders, he had been sold a second time as a slave. Ten years had he served as a bondman, first as a valet to the provost marshal of the slaughterers, and then as overseer of the great man's household. Three years more he had spent in prison, having been incarcerated on a charge of which he was entirely innocent. And now, at the age of thirty, he is the wisest and the greatest man in Egypt. God has strange ways of developing the talents, maturing the experience, and advancing the honour of his sons. The case of Joseph is a signal illustration of the beneficial uses of adversity, and shows that the true road to success in life, to the acquisition of wisdom, or of power, or of wealth, or of fame, or of all combined, often lies through early hardships and trials, disasters and defeats. 2. His political activity (vers. 46—49). As grand vizier of the empire, Joseph's labours during this period must have been many and laborious: surveying the corn-producing land of the country, and dividing it for purposes of taxation into districts, appointing overseers in every district, erecting granaries or government stores in every city of any size or importance, and generally superintending in every corner of the empire the work of uplifting the fifth part of the superabundant harvests of these precious years when the earth brought forth by handfuls. The result was, that by the close of this period the Egyptian government had collected corn as the sand of the sea, very much, and without number. 3. *His domestic prosperity* (ver. 50). On the name of Joseph's wife, and the questions connected with the subject of her marriage with Joseph, the Exposition under ver. 45 may be consulted. That the marriage itself was approved by God there is no sufficient reason to doubt, and that it was a marriage of affection may be inferred from the sentiments expressed by Joseph on the occasion of his sons' births. The birth of his children also was interpreted by him to be a mark of Divine favour. What a signal reward for the fidelity and purity of Joseph's behaviour in the house of Potiphar three years before! Had Joseph at that time left the straight path of virtue, where had been his advancement and felicity now? Even in this life God puts a premium in the long run on a life of purity. 4. *His personal piety* (vers. 51, 52). To some indeed Joseph's language on the birth of Manasseh appears somewhat hard to reconcile at least with true *filial* piety. Why did not Joseph, on reaching his exalted station in Egypt, at once communicate with his father? Was this a just or generous reward for what he had experienced of the old man's parental affection, and, what he must have still felt assured of, the old man's sorrow for his imagined death? Yet Joseph talks as if he had forgotten his father's house, as well as all his toil, in the splendour of his fame and the exuberance of his happiness in Egypt. But that these words are not to be interpreted literally becomes apparent, not alone from the pathetic meeting with his brethren and his father, soon to be described, but also from the statement which he makes upon the birth of Ephraim, in which he still characterises Egypt as the land of his affliction. That Joseph did not at once declare his parentage and send a message home to Hebron may be explained by many reasons without resorting to the hypothesis that " Joseph was still unable to attain perfect calm and cherish sentiments of love and forgiveness" towards his brethren (Kurtz): as, *e. g.*, the comparative insecurity that must have attended his position in Egypt until the years of famine came, an unwillingness prematurely to reveal to his father the full depth of wickedness of which his brethren had been guilty, a secret impression made upon his mind by God that the time of disclosure was not yet. At all events Joseph's conduct in this matter discovers nothing essentially inconsistent with a piety which shines out conspicuously in the grateful recognition of the hand of God in turning for him the shadow of death into the morning.

II. DURING THE SEVEN YEARS OF DEARTH. 1. *His reputation as a prophet fully confirmed* (vers. 53, 54). God is always careful to maintain the honour of his own prophets. Whatever message he transmits to the world or the Church through a messenger of his sending, he will in due time see to its fulfilment. No true ambassador of heaven need entertain the slightest apprehensions as to the failure of the words which God provides for him to speak. If he is not always, like Samuel, established as a prophet of the Lord at the beginning of his ministry (1 Sam. iii. 20), his claim to that distinction will in due course be made good by the exact accomplishment of what God has through his lips foretold. 2. *His sagacity as an administrator clearly established* (ver. 55). If Pharaoh had any doubts as to the wisdom of Joseph's proposal during the seven years of plenty, assuredly he had none now. With a famishing population all around him, what could Pharaoh have done, how averted the destruction of his people, and possibly the overthrow of his own dynasty, if it had not been for the prudent forethought of Joseph? Happy are the kings who have wise men in their kingdoms, and who, when they have them, can trust them. 3. *His work as a saviour hopefully begun* (ver. 56). If it be asked why Joseph did not gratuitously distribute Pharaoh's corn among the perishing multitudes, the reply is obvious. (1) In all probability the grain had been previously purchased from the people. (2) The people had been warned of the impending calamity, and might have exercised a little of the forethought of Joseph, and by care and economy provided for the day of want. (3) To have given the corn gratuitously would have resulted in a too lavish distribution, and for the most part to the greedy and the prodigal rather than to the really necessitous. (4) By affixing to it a price the people were encouraged as long as possible to practise frugality and preserve independence. Wise governors will be slow in making paupers of their subjects. This is one of the dangers connected with the Poor Law Administration in our own land. (5) It enabled Joseph by a judicious husbanding of resources to extend the circle of relief to the starving populations of other countries who came to him to purchase corn.

Learn—1. The sin of national wastefulness. 2. The value of a wise statesman. 3. The compatibility of piety with both personal greatness and political activity. 4. The propriety of setting mercies over against misfortunes. 5. The proper end of all government and legislation—the happiness and safety of the people. 6. The true duty of a monarch—to sympathise with and direct his subjects. 7. The legitimate ambition for a nation—to be an object of attraction for good to surrounding countries.

HOMILIES BY VARIOUS AUTHORS.

Ver. 54.—*Destitution and abundance.* " And the dearth was in all lands ; but in all the land of Egypt there was bread." The time of harvest is, of all periods of the year, the most important. It is the point to which all previous operations of the cultivator have tended. He knows how much depends on the weather and God's mercy. Having done all he can, he has to wait, and the harvest-time determines results. Those who are not engaged in agriculture are concerned in a harvest. Suppose there were none ; non-producers must starve. Dwelling in great towns and cities, many who are engaged in traffic or manufacture may easily overlook harvest-time, and forget their dependence on God for daily bread. They see not the sown fields, they watch not the springing blade, they seize not the sharp sickle, they join not in piling up the pointed stacks, and are therefore likely to forget dependence on God. It is well that God forgets us not. He has ever kept his promise— " So long as the earth remaineth," &c. No year has passed without harvest-time being stinted in some land. Think over the contrast given in the text.

I. GENERAL DISTRESS. "The dearth was in all lands," *i, e.* all the lands then known to be peopled by the descendants of Noah. Their harvests had failed. Rain excessive, or drought prolonged, had ruined their crops. For several years there seems to have been disappointment. Not only did the husbandmen suffer, but those who could not toil. Dearth engenders disease, despair, death. See 2 Kings vi. 24—30, to what straits famine will reduce people. Even mothers consent together to eat their own offspring. In the lamentations of Jeremiah there is a description of the fearful consequences of famine, leading men to say, " Then was our skin black like an oven, because of the terrible famine." How painful must it be to have scanty platters and empty barns ; for parents to have children clinging to the skirts of their garments, crying, " Give, oh, give bread," and to have none wherewith to satisfy them ! We see the effect of famine on one family in the East. Jacob's sons " looked on one another, and were sad." Their looks were despairing. They had money, flocks, and herds, but no bread. They could not eat their money, and to have lived on their starving flocks alone would engender disease of frightful character. Many had not even flocks to fall back upon, and the dearth was in all lands. How men at such a time must have looked longingly at the heavens, and prayed that God would send them bread ! Sometimes such seasons of trial are sent that men may be reminded of the dependence on God. To have a moral and spiritual dearth is worse than to have outward destitution. The spiritual is more important than the physical. A more terrible death than all is that where there is a lack of a knowledge of God and his love, and of hearing the word of the Lord.

II. EXCEPTIONAL ABUNDANCE. But for this plentifulness in Egypt the whole race might have perished. There were several reasons for the abundance in Egypt. 1. God arranged it by that wondrous overflowing of the Nile. A difference in the rising a few feet makes all the difference as to the crops. Even at this date, so do the crops of Egypt affect the markets of the world, that the rising of the Nile is watched, and the height attained telegraphed to all parts. God, at the period referred to, had given seven years of plenty, followed by seven years of dearth ; but such had been the previous abundance, owing to the overflow of the river, that in the terrible time of dearth there was abundance of bread in Egypt. 2. The foresight and energy of one man had led to the husbanding of resources and storing of excessive crops. 3. Divine revelation caused Joseph to act. He could not have known of the impending danger unless it had been revealed. He had faith in God when in prison, and maintained it when he became the governor of Egypt. Indeed that faith shone as brightly when he was the approved of Pharaoh as when he was the slave of Potiphar and the object of passion's hate. His faith was rewarded when he was able to save multi tudes from starving. What a contrast is presented in the text! Dearth of many lands, abundance in one. Such contrasts are often seen. On one side of the ocean there may have been an abundant harvest, on the other side but scanty crops. The world is full of contrasts. Here is a wedding ; there is a funeral. In one family is love, thoughtfulness, harmony, and in that—perhaps separated only by the thin partition of hasty builders—bickering, jealousy, and hastiness of temper. Here sobriety, providence, and religion reign ; there nothing but indigence, drunkenness, and utter neglect of the claims of God. In one country is peace, activity in all its branches of industry, commercial confidence, progress in education and art, thoughtfulness for the untaught and criminal classes, and higher appreciation of the sacredness of life ; in another depression, mistrust, plotting of adventurers, rule of the conscienceless, national faithlessness, and the spreading pall of desolation. Forceful is the contrast presented by nations under the influence of a simple Christianity and those enslaved by superstition, as Spain or Austria ; or paralysed by fatalism, as Turkey and Asia Minor ; or darkened by idolatry, as India, China, Africa, and some of the islands of the seas. And such contrasts are seen in individuals. There walks one whose soul has no light, no hope, no peace ; here one who knows he is pardoned, and is sure of acceptance by Christ. At death what a contrast ! See one dying shrinking, doubting, fearing, grasping at any straw of comfort ; another rejoicing that he is soon to enter and tread the streets of the New Jerusalem. Let all be prepared for such a change. Seek Christ, who is the " Bread of life," the Saviour of our souls. Lack of appetite and numbness may come from excessive exhaustion. Hunger and thirst after righteousness, and be not like a lady who once said, " Sir, I have been so long without religion that I have, I fear, now no desire for it." If we come to Christ he will receive us readily. Joseph was glad to receive and help his brethren. So will Christ supply all our need out of the treasures of his rich grace. Remember, that if the need of other nations tested the charity of Egypt, so the need of souls is to test our earnestness. If we have found the riches in Christ, we are to seek to bless others. If little time remains to some of us in which to do much for Christ, let us act as those who, having much to write and little space, crowd the letters and words the closer. Let us be earnest as the husbandman, who, seeing winter coming apace, hastens in the few fine days remaining to garner his crops. Alas, many of our doings will have to stand useless, like earless, rotten sheaves, blackening dreary fields.—H.

EXPOSITION.

CHAPTER XLII.

Ver. 1.—**Now when Jacob saw**—literally, *and Jacob saw*, i. e. perceived by the preparations of others for buying corn in Egypt (Lange), but more probably learnt by the report which others brought from Egypt (ver. 2)—**that there was corn**—שֶׁבֶר, either that which is broken, *e. g.* ground as in a mill, from שָׁבַר, to break in pieces, to shiver (Gesenius), or that which breaks forth, hence sprouts or germinates, from an unused root, שָׁבַר, to press out, to break forth (Fürst), is here employed to denote not simply grain,

but a supply of it, *frumenti cumulus*, for sale and purchase. The LXX. render by πρᾶσις, and the Vulgate by *quod alimenta venderentur*—**in Egypt** (*vide* ch. xli. 54), Jacob (literally, *and Jacob*) **said unto his sons**,—using *verba non, ut multi volunt, increpantis, sed excitantis* (Rosenmüller)—**Why do ye look one upon another ?**—*i. e.* in such a helpless and undecided manner (Keil), which, however, there is no need to regard as springing from a consciousness of guilt (Lange), the language fittingly depicting the aspect and attitude of those who are simply *consilii inopes* (Rosenmüller).

Ver. 2.—**And he said, Behold, I have heard**

(this does not imply that the rumour had not also reached Jacob's sons, but only that the proposal to visit Egypt did not originate with them) **that there is corn**—שֶׁבֶר, *ut supra*, σῖτος (LXX.), *triticum* (Vulgate)—**in Egypt: get you down thither.** That Jacob did not, like Abraham (ch. xii. 10) and Isaac (ch. xxvi. 2), propose to remove his family to Egypt, may be explained either by the length of the journey, which was too great for so large a household, or by the circumstance that the famine prevailed in Egypt as well as Canaan (Gerlach). That he intrusted his sons, and not his servants, with the mission, though perhaps dictated by a sense of its importance (Lawson), was clearly of Divine arrangement for the further accomplishment of the Divine plan concerning Joseph and his brethren. **And buy** (*i. e.* buy corn, the verb being a denominative from שֶׁבֶר, corn) **for us from thence.** From this it is apparent that the hitherto abundant flocks and herds of the patriarchal family had been greatly reduced by the long-continued and severe drought, thus requiring them to obtain food from Egypt, if either any portion of their flocks were to be saved, or themselves to escape starvation, as the patriarch explained to his sons. **That we may** (literally, *and we shall*) **live, and not die.**

Ver. 3.—**And Joseph's ten brethren went down**—either it was for safety that all the ten went, or because, the corn being sold to individuals, the quantity received would depend on their numbers (Lange)—**to buy corn** —the word for corn, בָּר, if not a primitive, like the Latin *far* (Fürst), may be derived from בָּרַר, to separate, sever, choose out, hence purify (Aben Ezra, Kimchi, Gesenius), and may describe grain as that which has been cleaned from chaff, as in Jer. iv. 11—**in** (literally, *from*, i. e. corn to be brought from) **Egypt.**

Ver. 4.—**But** (literally, *and*) **Benjamin, Joseph's brother** (*vide* ch. xxxv. 18), **Jacob sent not with his brethren.** Not because of his youth (Patrick, Lange), since he was now upwards of twenty years of age, but because he was Joseph's brother, and had taken Joseph's place in his father's affections (Lawson, Lange, Murphy, &c.), causing the old man to cherish him with tender solicitude. **For he said** (to, or within, himself, perhaps recalling the fate of Joseph), **Lest peradventure mischief befall him.** אָסוֹן, from אָסָה, to hurt (Gesenius, Fürst), and occurring only elsewhere in ver. 38, ch. xliv. 29, and Exod. xxi. 22, 23, denotes any sort of personal injury in general, and in particular here such mischance as might happen to a traveller.

Ver. 5.—**And the sons of Israel came to buy** corn **among those that came**—literally, *in the midst of the comers;* not as being desirous to lose themselves in the multitudes, as if troubled by an alarming presentiment (Lange), which is forced and unnatural; but either as forming a part of a caravan of Canaanites (Lawson), or simply as arriving among others who came from the same necessity (Keil). **For the famine was in the land of Canaan.** The statements in this verse concerning the descent of Joseph's brethren to Egypt, and the prevalence of the famine in the land of Canaan, both of which have already been sufficiently announced (*vide* ver. 3; ch. xli. 57; xlii. 2), are neither useless repetitions nor proofs of different authorship, but simply the customary recapitulations which mark the commencement of a new paragraph or section of the history, viz., that in which Joseph's first interview with his brethren is described (cf. "Quarry on Genesis,' pp. 556, 557).

Ver. 6.—**And Joseph** was **the governor over the land.** The word שַׁלִּיט, from שָׁלַט, to rule, describes one invested with despotic authority, or a sultan (Gesenius), in which character the early Shemites appear to have regarded Joseph (Keil). It is probably the same idea which recurs in the name Salatis, which, according to Manetho, belonged to the first of the shepherd kings (Josephus, 'Contra Apionem,' i. 14). Occurring nowhere else in the Pentateuch, it reappears in the later writings of Eccles. (vii. 10; x. 5), Ezra (iv. 20; vii. 24), Dan. (ii. 15; v. 29), which, however, need not suggest an exilian or post-exilian authorship, but may be explained by the fact that the root is found equally in the Arabic and Aramæan dialects (Keil). **And he** it was **that sold to all the people of the land.** Not conducted the retail corn trade (Tuch, Oort, Kuenen), which was assigned to subordinates (ver. 25; ch. xliv. 1), but presided over the general market of the kingdom (Murphy), probably fixing the price at which the grain should be sold, determining the quantities to be allowed to purchasers, and examining the companies of foreigners who came to buy (Rosenmüller, Hävernick, Lange, Gerlach). **And Joseph's brethren came, and bowed down themselves before him** with **their faces to the earth.** And so fulfilled his early dream in Shechem (ch. xxxvii. 7, 8).

Ver. 7.—**And Joseph saw his brethren, and he knew them, but** (literally, *and*) **made himself strange unto them.** The root נָכַר, to be marked, signed, by indentation, hence to be foreign (Fürst), or simply to be strange (Gesenius), in the Hiphil signifies to press strongly into a thing (Fürst), to look at a thing as strange (Gesenius), or to recognise, and in the Hithpael has the sense of representing one's self as strange, *i. e.* of feigning one's self to be a foreigner. **And spake roughly unto them**—literally, *spake hard things unto them;* not from a feeling of revenge which still struggled in his breast with his brotherly affection (Kurtz), or in a spirit of duplicity (Kalisch), but in order to get at their hearts, and discover the exact state of mind in which they then were with regard to himself and Benjamin, whose absence it is apparent had arrested his attention, and perhaps roused his suspicions (Keil, Murphy, Wordsworth, 'Speaker's Commentary'). **And he said unto them,**—speaking through an interpreter (ver. 23)—**Whence come ye? And they said, From the land of Canaan** (adding, as if they feared Joseph's suspicions, and wished to deprecate his anger) **to buy food** (*i. e.* corn for food).

Ver. 8.—**And Joseph knew his brethren, but they knew not him.** The lapse of time since the tragedy of Dothan, twenty years before, the high position occupied by Joseph, the Egyptian manners he had by this time assumed, and the strange tongue in which he conversed with them, all conspired to prevent Jacob's sons from recognising their younger brother; while the facts that Joseph's brethren were all grown men when he had last looked upon them, that he was quite familiar with their appearances, and that he perfectly understood their speech, would account for his almost instantaneous detection of them.

Ver. 9.—**And Joseph remembered** (*i. e.* the sight of his brethren prostrating themselves before him recalled to his mind) **the dreams which he dreamed** (or had dreamed) **of them** (*vide* ch. xxxvii. 5) **and said unto them, Ye are spies** (literally, *ye are spying,* or going about, so as to find out, the verb רָגַל signifying to move the *feet*); **to see the nakedness of the land**—not its present impoverishment from the famine (Murphy), but its unprotected and unfortified state (Keil). Cf. *urbs nuda præsidio* (Cic., 'Att.,' vii. 13); *murus nudatus defensoribus* (Cæs., 'Bell. Gall.,' ii. 6); τεῖχος ἐγυμνώθη (Homer, 'Iliad,' xii. 399)—**ye are come.** The Egyptians were characteristically distrustful of strangers,—*Ægyptii præ aliis gentibus diffidere solebant peregrinis* (Rosenmüller),—whom they prevented, when possible, from penetrating into the interior of their country (Wilkinson's 'Ancient Egyptians,' vol. i. p. 328, ed. 1878). In particular Joseph's suspicion of his Canaanitish brethren was perfectly natural, since Egypt was peculiarly open to attacks from Palestine (Herodotus, iii. 5).

Vers. 10—12.—**And they said unto him, Nay, my lord, but to buy food are thy servants come.** "They were not filled with resentment at the imputation" cast upon them by Joseph; "or, if they were angry, their pride was swallowed up by fear" (Lawson). **We are all one man's sons; we are true men,** —*i. e.* upright, honest, *viri bonæ fidei* (Rosenmüller), rather than εἰρηνικοί (LXX.), *pacifici* (Vulgate)—**thy servants are no spies.** It was altogether improbable that one man should send ten sons at the same time and to the same place on the perilous business of a spy, hence the simple mention of the fact that they were ten brethren was sufficient to establish their sincerity. Yet Joseph affected still to doubt them. **And he said unto them, Nay, but to see the nakedness of the land ye are come**—assuming a harsh and almost violent demeanour not out of heartless cruelty (Kalisch), but in order to hide the growing weakness of his heart (Candlish).

Ver. 13.—**And they said, Thy servants are twelve brethren, the sons of one man in the land of Canaan; and, behold, the youngest**—literally, *the little one* (cf. ch. ix. 24) —**is this day with our father, and one**— literally, *the one,* i. e. the other one, ὁ δὲ ἕτερος (LXX.)—**is not**—*i. e.* is dead (cf. ch. v. 24; xxxvii. 30)—in which statement have been seen a sufficient proof that Joseph's brethren had not yet truly repented of their cruelty towards him (Keil); an evidence that time had assuaged all their bitter feelings, both of exasperation against Joseph and of remorse for their unbrotherly conduct (Murphy); a suppression of the truth (Wordsworth), if not a direct falsehood (Lawson), since they wished it to be understood that their younger brother was dead, while of that they had no evidence beyond their own cunningly-invented lie (ch. xxxvii. 20) and their own probable surmisings. But in point of fact the inference was natural and reasonable that Joseph was no more, since twenty years had elapsed without any tidings of his welfare, and there was no absolute necessity requiring them to explain to the Egyptian governor all the particulars of their early life. Yet the circumstance that their assertion regarding himself was incorrect may have tended to awaken his suspicions concerning Benjamin.

Vers. 14—16.—**And Joseph said unto them** (betraying his excitement in his language), **That is it that I spake unto you, saying, Ye are spies.** But Joseph knew by this time that they were not spies. Hence his persistent accusation of them, which to the brothers must have seemed despotic and tyrannical, and which cannot be referred to malevolence or revenge, must be explained by a desire on the part of Joseph to bring his brothers to a right state of mind. **Hereby** (or in this) **ye shall be proved: By the life of Pharaoh** — literally, *life of Pharaoh!* An Egyptian oath (LXX., Gesenius, Rosenmüller, Kalisch, Lange), in using which Joseph was not without blame, *aliquid esse fateor quod merito culpetur* (Calvin) though by some (Ainsworth, Wordsworth, Murphy, 'Speaker's Commentary') the expression is regarded simply as a strong asseveration (cf. 1 Sam. i. 26 ; xvii. 55)—**ye shall not go forth hence** (literally, *life of Pharaoh! if ye go from this*. The language is elliptical, meaning either, May Pharaoh perish if ye escape from punishment as spies, unless, &c. ; or, As surely as Pharaoh lives, may retribution fall on me if ye go from this place) **except your youngest brother come hither.** The condition, which must have appeared extremely frivolous to Joseph's brethren, was clearly designed to ascertain the truth about Benjamin. **Send one of you, and let him fetch your brother, and ye** (*i. e.* the rest of you) **shall be kept in prison** (literally, *shall be put in bonds*), **that your words may be proved** (literally, *and your words shall be proved*), **whether** there be any **truth in you ; or else** (literally, *and if not*) **by the life of Pharaoh surely ye** are **spies**—literally (*sc.* I swear), *that ye are spies.*

Ver. 17.—**And he put them all together into ward** (literally, *and he assembled them into prison*) **three days.** Ostensibly in consequence of their unwillingness to agree to his proposal, but in reality to give them an experience of the suffering which they had inflicted on him, their brother, and so to awaken in their hearts a feeling of repentance. Yet the clemency of Joseph appears in this, that whereas he had lain three long years in prison as the result of their inhumanity towards him, he only inflicts on them a confinement of three days.

Vers. 18—20.—**And Joseph** (whose bowels of mercy were already yearning towards them) **said unto them the third day, This do, and live ;**—*i. e.* this do that ye may live (*vide* Gesenius, 'Grammar,' § 130, 2 ; Ewald's 'Hebrew Syntax,' § 348b)—**for I fear God** —literally, *the Elohim I fear ;* the term Elohim being employed, since to have said Jehovah would have been to divulge, if not his Hebrew origin, at least his acquaintance with the Hebrew faith (Hengstenberg). ᵗ At the same time its use would arrest them more than the preceding adjuration, By the life of Pharaoh ! and, whether or not it implied that the true God was not yet unknown in Egypt (Murphy), was clearly designed to show that he was a religious and conscientious person, who would on no account condemn them on mere suspicion (Lange). **If ye be true men, let one of your brethren be bound in the house of your prison.** Joseph's first proposal, that one should go for Benjamin while nine remained as hostages for their good faith, is now reversed, and only one is required to be detained while the other nine return. If the severity of the first proposal filled them with consternation, the singular clemency of the second could not fail to impress them. Not only were the nine to be released, but their original demand for grain to carry home to Palestine was to be complied with, the grand vizier adding, to their undoubted amazement, *As for the rest of you*, **go ye, carry corn for the famine of your houses.** "How differently had they acted towards their brother, whom they had intended to leave in the pit to starve" (Keil). The Egyptian governor feels compassion for their famishing households, only he will not abandon his proposition that they must return with Benjamin. **But bring your youngest brother unto me**—or, more emphatically, and your brother, the little one, ye shall cause to come to me. That Joseph should have insisted on this stipulation, which he must have known would cause his aged father much anxiety and deep distress, is not to be explained as "almost designed" by Joseph as a chastisement on Jacob for his undue predilection in favour of Benjamin (Kalisch), but must be ascribed either to the intensity of his longing to see his brother (Murphy), or to a desire on his part to ascertain how his brethren were affected towards Benjamin (Lawson), or to a secret belief that the best mode of persuading his father to go down to him in Egypt was to bring Benjamin thither ('Speaker's Commentary'), or to an inward conviction that the temporary concern which Benjamin's absence might inflict on Jacob would be more than compensated for by the ultimate good which would thereby be secured to the whole family (Kurtz), or to the fact that God, under whose guidance throughout he acted, was unconsciously leading him in such a way as to secure the fulfilment of his dreams, which required the presence of both Benjamin and Jacob in Egypt (Wordsworth, 'Speaker's Commentary'). The reason which Joseph himself gave to his brethren was that Benjamin's presence was indispensable as a corroboration of their veracity. **So** (literally, *and*) **shall your words be verified, and ye shall not die** (the death due to spies). **And they did so**—*i. e.* they consented to Joseph's proposal.

Ver. 21.—**And they said one to another** (Joseph's treatment of them beginning by this time to produce its appropriate and designed result by recalling them to a sense of their former guilt), **We are verily guilty** —"this is the only acknowledgment of sin in the Book of Genesis" (Inglis)—**concerning our brother.** They had been guilty of many sins, but the special iniquity of which their reception by the Egyptian governor had reminded them was that which some twenty years before they had perpetrated against their own brother. Indeed the accusation preferred against them that they were spies, the apparent unwillingness of the viceroy to listen to their request for food, and their subsequent incarceration, though innocent of any offence, were all calculated to recall to their recollection successive steps in their inhuman treatment of Joseph. **In that** (or because) **we saw the anguish of his soul, when he besought us** (literally, *in his beseeching of us*, an incident which the narrator omits to mention, but which the guilty consciences of the brethren remember), **and we would not hear; therefore is this distress come upon us.** The retributive character of their sufferings, which they cannot fail to perceive, they endeavour to express by employing the same word, עָרָה, to describe Joseph's anguish and their distress.

Ver. 22.—**And Reuben**—who had not consented to, but had been altogether unable to prevent, the wickedness of his brethren (ch. xxxvii. 22, 29)—**answered them, saying, Spake I not unto you, saying, Do not sin against the child** (or lad); **and ye would not hear? therefore, behold, also his blood is required**—literally, *and also his blood, behold it is required*. This was in accordance with the Noachic law against bloodshed (ch. ix. 5), with which it is apparent that Jacob's sons were acquainted.

Ver. 23.—**And they knew not** (while they talked in what they imagined to be a foreign dialect to the Egyptian viceroy) **that Joseph understood** them;—literally, *heard* (so as to understand what was said)—**for he spake unto them by an interpreter**—literally, *for the interpreter* (הַמֵּלִיץ, the hiph. part., with the art., of לוּץ, to speak barbarously, in the hiph. to act as an interpreter), *i. e.* the official Court interpreter, ἑρμηνευτής (LXX.), *was between them*.

Ver. 24.—**And he turned himself about from them** (in order to hide his emotion), **and wept** (as he reflected on the wonderful leadings of Divine providence, and beheld the pitiful distress of his brethren); **and returned to them again** (having previously withdrawn from them a space), **and communed with them** (probably about the one of them that should remain behind), **and took from them**—by a rough act of authority, since they either could not or would not settle among themselves who should be the prisoner (Candlish)—**Simeon,**—passing by Reuben not because he was the firstborn (Tuch, Lengerke), but because he was comparatively guiltless (Keil, Kalisch, Lange, Candlish, and expositors generally), and selecting Simeon either as the eldest of the guilty ones (Aben Ezra, Keil, Lange, Murphy, Wordsworth, Alford, and others), or as the chief instigator of the sale of Joseph (Philo, Rosenmüller, Fürst, Kalisch, Gerlach, Lawson, *et alii*)—**and bound him before their eyes**—thus forcibly recalling to their minds what they had done to him (Wordsworth), and perhaps hoping to incite them, through pity for Simeon, to return the more speedily with Benjamin (Lawson).

Ver. 25.—**Then** (literally, *and*) **Joseph commanded to fill**—literally, *commanded, and they* (i. e. Joseph's men) *filled*—**their sacks** (rather, vessels or receptacles, כְּלִי) **with corn, and to restore every man's money** (literally, *their pieces of silver, each*) **into his sack,**—שַׂק, *saccus*, σάκος, σάκκος, sack (*vide* ch. xxxvii. 34). Joseph "feels it impossible to bargain with his father and his brethren for bread" (Baumgarten)—**and to give them provision for the way: and thus did he** (literally, *it was done*) **unto them.**

Ver. 26.—**And they laded their asses with the corn** (literally, *put their grain upon their asses*), **and departed** (or went) **thence.**

Ver. 27.—**And as one of them opened his sack**—literally, *and the one opened his sack*, i. e. they did not all open their sacks on the homeward journey, although afterwards, in reporting the circumstance to Joseph, they represent themselves as having done so (ch. xliii. 21); but only one at the wayside inn, and the rest on reaching home (ver. 35; *vide infra*, ch. xliii. 21)—**to give his ass provender in the inn** (the מָלוֹן, from לוּן, to pass the night, was not an inn in the modern sense of the term, but simply a halting-place or camping station where travellers were wont to lodge, without finding for themselves or animals any other food than they carried with them), **he espied his money; for, behold, it was in his sack's mouth**—literally, *in the opening of his amtachath*, אַמְתַּחַת, from מָתַח, to spread out, an old word for a sack (ch. xliii. 18, 21, 22), here used synonymously with שַׂק, from which it would seem that the travellers carried two sorts of bags, one for the corn called כְּלִי (ver. 25), and another for the asses' provender called אַמְתַּחַת. It was in the latter that the money had been placed.

Ver. 28.—**And he** (i. e. the one who had opened his sack) **said unto his brethren, My money is restored; and, lo, it is even in my sack** (*amtachath*): **and their heart failed** them (literally, *went forth;* as it were, leapt into their mouths through sudden apprehension), **and they were afraid, saying one to another** (literally, *they trembled each one to his brother*, a *constructio pregnans* for they turned trembling towards one another, saying), **What is this that God hath done unto us?** Elohim is used, and not Jehovah, because the speakers simply desire to characterise the circumstance as supernatural.

Vers. 29—34.—**And they came unto Jacob their father unto the land of Canaan,** and told him all that befell unto them (literally, *all the things happening to them*, the participle being construed with the accusative) ; **saying, The man,** who is **the lord of the land, spake roughly to us** (literally, *spake the man, lord of the country, with us harsh things*, the order and arrangement of the words indicating the strong feeling which their treatment in Egypt had excited), **and took us for spies of the country. And we said unto him, We** are true men ; **we are no spies : we be twelve brethren, sons of our father; one is not, and the youngest is this day with our father in the land of Canaan** (*vide* vers. 11, 13). **And the man, the lord of the country, said unto us, Hereby shall I know that ye** are **true** men ; **leave one of your brethren here with me, and take** food **for the famine of your households, and be gone.** It is observable that they do not mention Joseph's first proposal, probably because of Joseph's subsequent kindness; neither do they intimate the fact that Simeon was bound, perhaps through a desire to soften the blow as much as possible for their venerable parent. **And bring your youngest brother unto me : then shall I know that ye** are **no spies, but** that **ye are true** men : **so will I deliver you your brother, and ye shall traffic in the land** (cf. ch. xxxiv. 10).

Ver. 35.—**And it came to pass as they emptied** (literally, *they emptying*) **their sacks, that** (literally, *and*), **behold, every man's bundle of money** (or silver) **was in his sack : and when** (literally, *and*) **both they and their father saw the bundles of money, they** (literally, *and they*) **were afraid.**

Ver. 36.—**And Jacob their father said unto them, Me have ye bereaved** (or are ye bereaving) of my children : **Joseph is not, and Simeon is not** (Jacob appears to suspect that in some way or another his sons had been responsible for Joseph's disappearance as well as Simeon's), **and ye will take Benjamin** away : **all these things are against me**—literally, *upon me, as an heavy burden, which I must bear alone.*

Ver. 37.—**And Reuben spake unto his father, saying** (Reuben was probably actuated by an ardent brotherly affection, which

prompted him to endeavour to recover Simeon, as formerly he had sought to deliver Joseph), **Slay my two sons,**—as Reuben had four sons (ch. xlvi. 9), he must be understood as meaning two of my sons (Ainsworth, Murphy), either the two then present (Junius) or the two oldest (Mercerus)—**if I bring him** (*i. e.* Benjamin) **not to thee.** Reuben's proposal, though in one sense "the greatest and dearest offer that a son could make to a father" (Keil), was either only a sample of strong rhetoric (like Joseph's "By the life of Pharaoh !) " designed to assure his father of the impossibility of failure (Lawson, Candlish, Inglis), and of the fact that neither he nor his brethren entertained any injurious designs against Benjamin (Calvin); or, if seriously made, was not only inconsiderate and rash, spoken in the heat of the moment (Kurtz), but sinful and unnatural (Ainsworth), *plusquam barbarum* (Calvin), and absolutely worthless besides, as what consolation would it be to Jacob to add to the loss of a son the murder of his grandchildren ? (Calvin, Willet). **Deliver him into my hand, and I will bring him to thee again.** Reuben might have learned to avoid strong asseverations on this point. "It was his wish to bring Joseph home to his father, and yet he could not persuade his brethren to comply with his intentions. It was his desire to bring Simeon safe to his father, and yet he was compelled to leave him in Egypt" (Lawson).

Ver. 38.—**And he** (*i. e.* Jacob) **said, My son shall not go down with you ;**—not because he could not trust Reuben after the sin described in ch. xxxv. 22 (Wordsworth), or because he could not assent to Reuben's proposal (Ainsworth), but because of what is next stated—**for his brother** (*i. e.* by the same mother, viz., Joseph) **is dead** (cf. ver. 13 ; xxxvii. 33 ; xliv. 28), **and he is left alone :**—*i. e.* he alone (of Rachel's children) is left as a survivor—**if mischief befall him** (literally, *and mischief shall befall him*) **by the way in the which ye go, then shall ye** (literally, *and ye shall*) **bring down my gray hairs with sorrow to the grave**—*Sheol* (cf. ch. xxxvii. 35).

HOMILETICS.

Vers. 1—38.—*The first visit of Joseph's brethren to Egypt.* I. THE JOURNEY TO EGYPT (vers. 1—5). 1. *The famishing household.* Although Canaan was the land of promise, and the family of Jacob the Church of God, yet neither was the one nor the other exempted from the pressure of that heavy famine which had fallen on all surrounding lands and peoples. It is not God's intention that his people should escape participating in the ills of life. Besides enabling them, collectively and individually, to sympathise with their fellow-men, it is a means under God of advancing their own sanctification, and oftentimes as well of furthering the purposes of God concerning both the world and the Church. 2. *The perplexed brethren.* Reuben, Simeon, Levi, Judah, and the rest of them were manifestly at their wits' end what to do to keep themselves from starving. If the thought of Egypt had anything to do with their listlessness and inactivity, it may remind us how dangerous it is to sin, the memory of past transgressions having an uncomfortable habit of springing up at unexpected moments, like grim and shaggy lions in the path; if their spiritless dejection was in no way connected with the Dothan tragedy, it shows that saints are not necessarily a whit more talented or fertile in expedient than their ungodly neighbours, and are frequently as helpless as the rest of them in the face of sudden and overwhelming calamities. Grace, though it gives goodness, does not guarantee greatness. 3. *The parental exhortation.* Jacob heard that there was corn in Egypt, and forthwith proposed that his sons should undertake a journey thither to fetch a supply for their necessities, at the same time prefacing his sound advice with a word of brisk reproof at their want of push in the face of news so full of comfort and hope as that grain might be had for the purchase. Jacob clearly discerned that, while it was right in them to look to God for help in their distress, it was also expected of them by God that they should help themselves. Although God promises to give his people bread, he does not undertake to relieve them of all trouble in the matter. If he provides corn in Egypt, he expects men to go for it; and it is a mark of sound sense, if it is not a sign of grace, when men are able to detect in Egypt providential supplies for their necessities. 4. *The important mission.* Concerning which may be noticed—(1) The number of the travellers: Joseph's ten brethren. Whether it was for safety to themselves, or for the advantage of the household to enable them to return with larger supplies, it was clearly a wise providential arrangement that the ten brethren who had sinned against the son of Rachel should go down to Egypt. (2) The destination of the travellers: Egypt. In all probability Egypt was the last place that they would ever have thought of going to. It is scarcely likely that they had quite forgotten Joseph. Whether or not they suspected that Joseph might yet be alive, they knew that he had gone to Egypt as a slave. And now they were themselves upon the way to the scene of Joseph's captivity. If Joseph's brethren were thoughtful men at all, they must have had their reflections by the way. (3) The object of the travellers: to buy corn. This at least was a lawful and an honourable purpose, which is more than could be said of some of their previous adventures. But God's people, whether they abide in Canaan or go to Egypt, should follow peace with, and provide things honest in the sight of, all men. 5. *The paternal reservation.* "But Benjamin, Joseph's brother, Jacob sent not with his brethren." If Jacob's reason for detaining Benjamin was anxiety for himself, who was now an old man, and afraid to lose the lad who served him as the son of his old age, it may remind us of the feebleness and helplessness of age, and of the duty of the young to comfort and assist the old. If it was anxiety for Benjamin, whom he feared to expose to the fate of Joseph, it is a beautiful example of the tenderness and strength of a father's love, and may well suggest the duty of rewarding that love with true filial affection. If it was anxiety for his ten sons, lest in the case of Benjamin they should repeat the crime which they had perpetrated against Joseph, it shows how difficult it is to remove from the minds of others, even of those who have the most disposition to judge us with charity, unfavourable impressions concerning ourselves when once they have been formed. There is good reason for believing that a change had passed upon the characters of Joseph's brethren since the dark deed at Dothan. Yet the old man was afraid to trust them. If once by our wickedness we forfeit the confidence of our fellow-men, these are not to be blamed if in future they fail to trust our integrity and honour.

II. THE INTERVIEW WITH THE GOVERNOR (vers. 6—25). 1. *Humble homage to the governor.* Arriving in Egypt, the sons of Jacob were conducted to the presence of the viceroy, and they "bowed down before him with their faces." Such respectful behaviour was due to the majesty of him in whose presence they stood (Rom. xiii. 7), and was admirably fitted to the character in which they came. They who have a suit to press, at an earthly or a heavenly throne, should be "clothed with humility." 2. *Non-recognition of the governor.* The moment Joseph looked upon the Hebrew strangers he knew them to be his brethren. But they entirely failed to discern him; because (1) he spoke like a foreigner—"an interpreter was between them;" (2) he dressed like an Egyptian — he wore a garment of byssus, like an

Egyptian priest (ch. xli. 42) ; (3) he swore like a courtier—"By the life of Pharaoh," which certainly his brethren knew was not the language of Canaan. Yet, if they had been as anxious to see their lost brother as he had been to see them (it is just possible Joseph may have been on the outlook for his brethren, expecting them to arrive with every caravan that came from Canaan), not even these disguises would have concealed his identity. 3. *Harsh treatment by the governor.* (1) The nature of it. He spoke to them roughly, he questioned them straitly, he accused them directly, he proved them severely, he imprisoned them closely. (2) The reason of it. Scarcely revenge; ostensibly to test their sincerity; but really to conceal his own identity, in order to secure time for thought how to act, and, if possible, to penetrate into their characters. (3) The mitigation of it. At the end of three days he somewhat relaxed his proposition, asking them to leave only one of their brethren instead of nine, viz., Simeon, whom he took and bound before their eyes. 4. *Bitter grief before the governor.* (1) The remembrance of their sin. As a result of their rough handling by the Egyptian vizier, they began to think of Joseph and their early sin against him, which almost every step in their present experience vividly recalled. It is good when affliction brings sin to mind. (2) The confession of their guilt. "We are verily guilty concerning our brother." It is better when tribulation leads to an acknowledgment of ill desert. (3) The recognition of their punishment. They saw the hand of God pursuing them for their wickedness, and requiting them, as they imagined, for Joseph's blood. It is best when God's retributive dispensations make the soul sensitive and humble. 5. *Unexpected kindness from the governor.* Though he did not depart from his original demand that they should bring down Benjamin, and though he insisted on retaining Simeon as a hostage for their obedience, he yet granted their request for corn, and, unknown to them as yet, caused their money to be restored to their sacks. So Christ often deals with penitents ; first blows and buffetings, then benefits and blessings.

III. THE RETURN TO CANAAN (vers. 26—38). 1. *The startling discovery.* Resting for the night at a wayside khan, or lodging-place, one of the brethren, having had occasion to give his beast a little provender, opened out his sack, and lo! the silver money he had paid for his corn was in its mouth. The same discovery was made by the rest on reaching Hebron. The instruction which Joseph gave his steward had not been heard by them, and they had penetration to see how the circumstance might be turned to their disadvantage. They were innocent of any crime in this matter ; but how were they to explain it to the austere and impenetrable man who sat upon the throne of Egypt? "Thus conscience doth make cowards of us all." The best that can be said of them in this connection is that they had piety enough to see the hand of God in the untoward affair. 2. *The faithful report.* On arriving at Hebron, they related to their father Jacob all that had befallen them in Egypt, beginning with the rough reception they had gotten from the governor, and ending with the startling discovery they had just made ; in all which there was at least a symptom of improvement in the characters of those ten brethren. Here was none of the concealment and lying that marked them at an earlier stage in their history, as when they palmed off upon their aged parent the clever story of the wild beast and the bloody coat to account for Joseph's disappearance. They presented themselves as before without their brother, but this time they told the truth: Simeon was a hostage in Egypt for the bringing down of Benjamin. 3. *The parental sorrow.* In the anguish of the moment Jacob committed three mistakes. (1) About his sons who had returned from Egypt, whom he was manifestly blaming for the loss both of Simeon and Joseph,—"Me ye are bereaving,"—which should lead us to beware of passing hasty judgments upon the characters of others, of those even whom we may think we know best. (2) About the two who were detained in Egypt, Joseph and Simeon, the first of whom he thought he knew was already dead, and the second of whom he feared had shared the same fate ; whereas Joseph was in honour in Egypt, and Simeon was only languishing in temporary confinement. (3) About himself and Benjamin, that their separation would but be the beginning of sorrow for them both, whereas it was to be the means of leading both to happiness and honour. So God's providences are often misinterpreted by his saints. Contrast with Jacob's exclamation that of Paul in Rom. viii. 28. 4. *The filial security.* Reuben offers to undertake the charge of Benjamin, and to be responsible for his safe-conduct to Egypt and back again, and in so far the act of Reuben was generous and kindly towards both Jacob and Benjamin; but his proposal that Jacob should slay two of his sons if he failed to deliver Benjamin was rash, unnatural, and sinful, and accordingly was at once rejected by the patriarch.

See in this interesting narrative—1. The fact of an overruling providence, exemplified in God's bringing Joseph's brethren to Egypt. 2. The strength of human affection, illustrated by Joseph's emotion in presence of his brethren, and Jacob's pathetic fondness for Benjamin. 3. The power of a guilty conscience, exhibited in the mutual recriminations of the brethren with reference to the sale of Joseph. 4. The beneficial influence of the discipline of life, as portrayed in the good effects produced by Joseph's rough handling of his brethren. 5. The short-sightedness of sense and reason, as seen in Jacob's lamentation, "All these things are against me," while, on the contrary, all things were working together for his good.

HOMILIES BY VARIOUS AUTHORS.

Ch. xlii.—*God's trials of his people.* The trial of Joseph is over. Now comes the trial of his brethren and of Jacob. The Spirit of God is at work in all their hearts. True men they were and yet sinful men. Before they can be made partakers of the blessing of Joseph they must pass through the fire. He who is appointed minister of grace to them is the instrument of their trials. Notice—

I. The trial is one of CONSCIENCE. " We are verily guilty concerning our brother." "His blood is required." Face to face with one whom they supposed to be a heathen man, they are reproved. They have to tell facts which smite them with inward reproach.

II. The trial is one of HEART. To leave Simeon behind, to be afraid both for him and for themselves and for Benjamin. To be keenly perplexed and agonised for their old father. To be deeply wounded in the remembrance of their brother Joseph's anguish of soul and helpless cries for pity.

III. The trial is one of FAITH. "What is this that God hath done unto us?" In the midst of all the roughness, and the fear, and the trouble there is still the feeling that they are being dealt with in some mysterious way by God himself, and there is a mingling of faith with their fear. Reuben again represents the better element in their character, and as they follow him they are led into peace. Joseph's smile is the smile of the loving heart which sometimes dissembles that it may reveal itself the more fully when the opportunity comes. He wept behind their backs. He was hiding the intensest love and the most abundant forgiveness and pitifulness, while he appeared to be a rough enemy. Still there were signs mingled with the harsh treatment that it was not all harsh. The sacks were filled with corn, and the money was returned. A deeper faith would have penetrated the secret. But those that have to be led from the feeble faith to the strong, have to be tried with appearances that seem, as Jacob said, "*all against*" them. How often the believer says, "All these things are against me," when he is already close upon that very stream of events which will carry him out of his distress into the midst of plenty, peace, and the joy of a healed heart in its recovered blessedness. Jacob poured out his natural fears and complaints, yet how little they were founded on truth. The son for whom he mourned yet lived and closed his eyes, and his gray hairs went to the grave in peace.—R.

Vers. 1, 2.—*Man's want and God's provision.* The famine was part of God's plan to carry out his promise to Abraham (Gen. xv. 13, 14). But it is not merely a fact in the historical preparation for what he was bringing to pass; a link in the chain of events leading on to Christ. We must look upon it as part of a series of types foreshadowing gospel truths. The famine was a step towards the promised possession, and has its counterpart in the work of the Holy Spirit. It represents the spiritual want of man; conviction of sin (John xvi. 8; cf. Rom. vii. 9), leading to know the power of Christ's work (Matt. xviii. 11).

I. The first step is CONSCIOUSNESS OF FAMINE; that a man's life is more than meat;

more than a supply of bodily wants. It is realising that he has wants beyond the present life; that in living for time he has been following a shadow. This knowledge is not natural to us. Bodily hunger soon makes itself felt, but the soul's need does not; and until it is known, the man may be "poor and blind and naked," and yet suppose that he is "rich and increased with goods."

II. WE CANNOT OF OURSELVES SUPPLY THAT WANT. Gradually we learn how great it is. We want to still the accusing voice of conscience; to find a plea that shall avail in judgment; to see clearly the way of life that we may not err therein. In vain we look one on another, seeking comfort in the good opinion of men, in their testimony to our upright life. In vain we try to satisfy ourselves, by promises to do better, or by offerings of our substance or of our work. In vain is it to seek rest in unbelief, or in the persuasion that in some way all will be right. The soul cannot thus find peace. There is a voice which at times will make itself heard—" all have sinned "—thou hast sinned.

III. GOD HAS PROVIDED BREAD. "I have heard that there is corn in Egypt" (cf. Rom. x. 18), answers to the gospel telling of the bread of life. As to this we mark— 1. It was provided before the want arose (1 Pet. i. 20; Rev. xiii. 8). The gospel tells us of what has already been done, not of a gift to come into existence on certain conditions. The ransom of our souls has been paid. We have to believe and take (Rev. xxii. 17). 2. *How faith works.* They must go for that food which was ready for them. To take the bread of life must be a real earnest act, not a listless assent. The manna which was to be gathered, the brazen serpent to which the sick were to look, the command to the impotent "Rise, take up thy bed and walk," all show that it is not enough merely to wish, there must be the effort of faith (cf. 1 Thess. i. 3). This is a law of the spiritual kingdom. As natural laws regulate results within their domain, so spiritual results must be sought in accordance with spiritual laws. 3. *It is our Brother* who has made provision for us. This is our confidence. He waits to reveal himself when in humility and emptiness we come to him, and to give us plenty (1 Cor. iii. 21, 22).—M.

EXPOSITION.

CHAPTER XLIII.

Vers. 1, 2.—And the famine was **sore** (literally, *was heavy*) **in the land** (*sc.* of Canaan). **And it came to pass** (how long after the return of Joseph's brethren cannot be determined, as the quantity of grain they brought or the number that partook of it cannot possibly be estimated; but it may be reasonably inferred that several months had elapsed since their arrival at Hebron), **when they had eaten up**—literally, *had finished to eat up*, i. e. not nearly (Mercerus, Bush), but entirely consumed—**the corn which they had brought out of Egypt,**—it is probable that only Jacob's family partook of the Egyptian corn, the slaves supporting themselves on roots, vegetables, and milk (Calvin, Rosenmüller, Gerlach)—**their father said unto them, Go again, buy us a little food.** What they could buy would be little in proportion to their needs.

Ver. 3.—And Judah spake unto him, saying,—Judah now becomes the spokesman, either because Reuben's entreaty had been rejected, and Levi, who followed Reuben and Simeon in respect of age, had forfeited his father's confidence though his treachery to the Shechemites (Keil, Murphy); or because he could speak to his father with greater freedom, having a freer conscience than the rest (Lange); or because he was a man possessed of greater prudence and ability than the rest (Lawson), if indeed the suggestion is not correct that they all endeavoured to persuade their father, though Judah's eloquence alone is recorded (Calvin)—**the man** (*i. e.* the Egyptian viceroy) **did solemnly protest** (literally, *protesting did protest*, i. e. did earnestly protest) **unto us, saying,**—with an oath which is not here repeated (ch. xlii. 15) **—Ye shall not see my face, except your brother be with you.**

Vers. 4, 5.—If thou wilt send—literally, *if thou art sending*, i. e. if thou art agreeable to send (cf. ch. xxiv. 42, 49; Judges vi. 36) **—our brother with us, we will go down and buy thee food: but** (literally, *and*) **if thou wilt not send** him (a similar form of expression to the above, the two words בֵּישׁ, being, and אִין, not being, including the substantive verb, and being conjoined with a participle for the finite verb), **we will not go down: for the man said unto us, Ye shall not see my face, except your brother** be **with you.** Judah's peremptory language receives sufficient justification from the fact that he believed the Egyptian governor to be in thorough earnest when he declared that without Benjamin they should sue a second time in vain.

Ver. 6.—**And Israel said,**—this is the second time that Jacob is so designated in the history of Joseph, the first time being in ch. xxxvii., which recites the sad account of Joseph's disappearance from the family circle. The recurrence of what may eventually prove another breach in the theocratic family is probably the circumstance that revives the name Israel, which besides seems to prevail throughout the chapter (*vide* vers. 8, 11)—**Wherefore dealt ye** so **ill with me, as to tell the man whether ye had yet a brother?**—literally, *whether yet to you a brother* (sc. there was).

Ver. 7.—**And they said, The man asked us straitly of our state, and of our kindred, saying, Is your father yet alive? have ye** another **brother?** Though not appearing in the preceding narrative of the historian (ch. xlii. 13, 32), it must yet be held as accurate that the information given to Joseph about Jacob and Benjamin was supplied in answer to direct inquiries, since Judah afterwards gives the same account of it (ch. xliv. 19) when pleading before Joseph in behalf of Benjamin. **And we told him according to the tenor of these words**—literally, *according to these words,* i. e. either in conformity to his questions (Ainsworth, Rosenmüller, Keil), *κατὰ τὴν ἐπερώτησιν ταύτην* (LXX.), *juxta id quod fuerat sciscitatus* (Vulgate), or like those words we have told thee (Kalisch). **Could we certainly know** (literally, *knowing could we know*) **that he would say, Bring your brother down?**

Vers. 8—10.—**And Judah said unto Israel** his father, **Send the lad with me** (Benjamin, though styled a lad, must have been at this time upwards of twenty years of age), **and we will arise and go; that we may** (literally, *and we shall*) **live, and not die, both we, and thou,** and **also our little ones. I will be surety for him** (the verb conveys the idea of changing places with another); **of my hand shalt thou require him** (*vide* ch. ix. 5): **if I bring him not unto thee, and set him before thee,** —the words are even more emphatic than those of Reuben (ch. xlii. 37)—**then let me bear the blame for ever** — literally, *and I shall be a sinner* (i. e. liable to punishment as a sinner) *against thee all the days* (sc. of my life). The thought is elliptical. Judah means that if he does not return with Benjamin he shall both have failed in his promise and be guilty of a dire transgression against his father (cf. 1 Kings i. 21). **For except we had lingered, surely now we had returned this second time**—literally, *these two times.* The nobility of character which shines out so conspicuously in Judah's language is after-

wards signally illustrated in his pathetic pleading before Joseph, and goes far to countenance the suggestion that a change must have taken place in his inner life since the incidents recorded of him in chs. xxxvii. and xxxviii.

Ver. 11.—**And their father Israel said unto them, If it must be so now** (literally, *if so now*), **do this; take of the best fruits in the land** (literally, *of the song of the land,* i. e. of its choicest and most praised productions) **in your vessels, and carry down the man a present.** That Jacob could propose to send a handsome present of rich fruits to the Egyptian viceroy has been regarded as inconsistent with the prevalence of a famine in the land of Canaan for over two or three years (Bohlen); but (1) the failure of the cereal crops does not necessarily imply a like absence of fruit, and (2) it does not follow that, though Jacob selected the under-mentioned articles for his gift, they existed in abundance, while (3) if the fruit harvest was small, an offering such as is here described would only be all the more luxuriant and valuable on that account (Kurtz, Kalisch). **A little balm,**—balsam (*vide* ch. xxxvii. 25) —**and a little honey,**—דְּבַשׁ, grape honey, called by the Arabians *dibs,* and the Persians *dushab,* was prepared by boiling down must or new wine to a third or half; hence called by the Greeks ἕψημα, and by the Romans *sapa, defrutum.* It is still imported into Egypt from the district of Hebron. That it was not the honey of bees, μέλι (LXX.), *mel* (Vulgate), is rendered probable by the circumstance that Egypt abounds in this excellent production of nature (*vide* Michaelis, 'Suppl.,' p. 391)—**spices, and myrrh** (*vide* ch. xxxvii. 25), **nuts,**—בָּטְנִים, an oblong species of nut, so called from its being flat on one side and bellying out on the other (the *pistacia vera* of Linnæus), having an oily kernel which is most palatable to Orientals (*vide* Kalisch *in loco*)—**and almonds.** The שָׁקֵד or almond tree, so called because of all trees it is the first to arouse from the sleep of winter, the root being שָׁקַד, to be sleepless, (Gesenius), does not seem to have been indigenous in Egypt, while it flourishes in Syria and Palestine (Kalisch).

Ver. 12—**And take double money** (literally, *money of a second,* i. e. of the same, *amount;* not twice as much as the first time, but simply as much as the first time) **in your hand; and the money that was brought again** (or returned) **in the mouth of your sacks, carry** it **again in your hand; peradventure it** was **an oversight** (literally, *a something caused to wander,* a mistake, from a root signifying to go astray).

Vers. 13, 14.—**Take also your brother,**

and arise, go again unto the man: and God Almighty—El Shaddai, the covenant God of Abraham (ch. xvii. 1), and of Jacob himself (ch. xxxv. 11)—give you mercy (literally, *bowels*, hence very tender affection, the inward parts being regarded as the seat of the emotions) before the man, that he may send away—literally, *and he shall send with you* (Kalisch), or for you (Keil)—your other brother, and Benjamin. If I be bereaved of my children, I am bereaved—literally, *and I, if I am bereaved, I am bereaved*, an expression of the patriarch's acquiescence in the Divine will (cf. 2 Kings vii. 4; Esther iv. 16).

Ver. 15.—And the men took that present (which Jacob had specified), and they took double money (literally, *a doubling of the money*, i. e. the first money, and as much again for the new purchase; the phrase is different from that used in ver. 12, though the words are the same) in their hand, and Benjamin (*sc.* they took with them); and rose up, and went down to Egypt, and stood before Joseph (i. e. in the corn-market).

Ver. 16.—And when (literally, *and*) Joseph saw Benjamin with them, he (literally, *and he*) said to the ruler of his house,—literally, *to him who was over his house*, i. e. the steward (cf. ch. xxiv. 2; xxxix. 4; xliv. 1) —Bring these men home (i. e. conduct these men to my house, which was probably at some distance), and slay,—literally, *slay a slaughter*. The assertion that the narrator is here guilty of an inaccuracy in representing Joseph as having animal food prepared for himself and his guests (Bohlen) is refuted by Herodotus (ii. 37, 40) and by Wilkinson ('Ancient Egyptians,' vol. ii. ch. vii. pp. 22, 23, ed. 1878), who says that "beef and goose constituted the principal part of the animal food throughout Egypt," and that according to the sculptures "a considerable quantity of meat was served up at those repasts to which strangers were invited." "Though there was scarcely an animal which was not held sacred in some province, there was, perhaps with the only exception of the cow, none which was not killed and eaten in other parts of the land" (Kalisch) —and make ready; for these men shall dine with me at noon—literally, *at the double lights* (צָהֳרִים), i. e. at mid-day, the time of greatest splendour.

Vers. 17, 18.—And the man did as Joseph bade; and the man brought the men into Joseph's house. And the men were afraid, because they were brought into Joseph's house. "A more natural picture of the conduct of men from the country, when taken into the house of a superior, cannot be drawn. When they are told to go inside they at once suspect that they are about to be punished or confined" (Roberts' 'Oriental Illustrations,' p. 49). And they said (*sc.* to

themselves), Because of the money that was returned in our sacks at the first time are we brought in; that he may seek occasion against us,—literally, *that he may roll himself upon us* (cf. Job xxx. 14; Ps. xxii. 8; xxxvii. 5; Prov. xvi. 3). "To say a man rolls himself upon another is the Eastern way of saying he falls upon him" (Roberts' 'Oriental Illustrations,' p. 49)— and fall upon us, and take us for bondmen, and our asses. The brethren of Joseph were clearly apprehensive of some serious stratagem to deprive them of liberty.

Vers. 19—22.—And they came near to the steward of Joseph's house (literally, *the man who was over Joseph's house*), and they communed (or spake) with him at the door of the house (i. e. before they entered), and said, O sir,—literally, *Pray, my lord*; δεόμεθα κύριε (LXX.)—we came indeed down at the first time to buy food: and it came to pass, when we came to the inn,—or halting-place (*vide* ch. xlii. 27)—that we opened our sacks,—this was not strictly accurate, as only one sack had been opened at the wayside khan, while the others were not examined till they had reached home; though, as an explanation of the difficulty, it has been suggested (*vide* Keil's 'Introduction,' vol. i. p. 109, note by Prof. Douglas) that all the sacks may have been, and probably were, opened at the inn, but that only one man found his money in his sack's mouth, as the next clause explains — and, behold, every man's money was in the mouth of his sack, —literally, *a man's money in the mouth of his sack*, i. e. one of them found his money there, while the others discovered their money, which was not "in the sack's mouth," but "in the sack" (ch. xlii. 35), only on emptying their sacks at home—our money in full weight (literally, *according to its weight*): and we have brought it again in our hand. And other money (i. e. the second silver of ver. 12) have we brought down in our hands to buy food: we cannot tell who put our money in our sacks.

Ver. 23.—And he said, Peace be to you, fear not: your God (Elohim), and the God of your father,—an indication that Joseph's steward had been taught to fear and trust the God of the Hebrews (Wordsworth, Murphy)—hath given you treasure in your sacks: I had your money (literally, *your money came to me*). And he brought Simeon out unto them.

Ver. 24.—And the man (Joseph's steward) brought the men into Joseph's house, and gave them water, and they washed their feet (cf. ch. xviii. 4; xxiv. 32); and he gave their asses provender.

Ver. 25.—And they made ready the present against Joseph came at noon: for they heard that they should eat bread there. This must have been communicated to them after they had entered Joseph's palace, since they had obviously not learnt it upon the way thither (*vide supra*, ver. 18).

Ver. 26.—**And when Joseph came home** (after the despatch of public business), **they brought him the present which was in their hand** (*vide ver. 11*) **into the house, and bowed themselves to him to the earth.** Thus they fulfilled the dream of the sheaves (ch. xxxvii. 7 ; cf. ch. xviii. 2 ; xix. 1).

Ver. 27.—**And he asked them of** their **welfare** (literally, *peace*), **and·said, Is your father well** (literally, *Is there peace to your father?*), **the old man of whom ye spake ? Is he yet alive ?**

Ver. 28.—**And they answered, Thy servant our father is in good health, he is yet alive. And they bowed down their heads, and made obeisance.**

Ver. 29.—**And he** (*i. e.* Joseph) **lifted up his eyes, and saw his brother Benjamin, his mother's son, and said, Is this your younger brother, of whom ye spake unto me ? And he said** (without waiting for an answer), **God be gracious unto thee, my son.** The tenderness of this language was much fitted to encourage the brethren.

Ver. 30.—**And Joseph made haste ; for his bowels did yearn** (literally, *were becoming warm*, from intensity of love) **upon his brother: and he sought where to weep;—** the second occasion on which Joseph is represented as overcome by the strength of his inward emotion, the first having been when his brethren were speaking about their cruelty towards himself (ch. xlii. 24)—**and he entered into** his **chamber, and wept there.**

Ver. 31.—**And he washed his face** (an indication of the violence of his weeping), **and went out** (from his chamber), **and refrained himself** (keeping his tears in check), **and said, Set on bread**—an expression used at the present day in Egypt for bringing dinner (Wilkinson, 'Ancient Egyptians,' vol. ii. p. 41, ed. 1878).

Ver. 32.—**And they set on for him by himself, and for them by themselves, and for the Egyptians, which did eat with him, by themselves.** "Joseph eats apart from his brethren, keeping strictly to the Egyptian mode ; and the history does not omit to remark that in this point he adhered to the custom of the country" (Hävernick, § 21). **Because the Egyptians might not eat bread with the Hebrews.** Herodotus (ii. 41) affirms that the Egyptians would neither use

the knife, spit, or basin of a Grecian, nor taste the flesh of a clean cow if it happened to be cut with a Grecian knife. **For that is an abomination unto the Egyptians.** The reason for this separation from foreigners being that they dreaded being polluted by such as killed and ate cows, which animals were held in high veneration in Egypt.

Ver. 33.—**And they sat before him,**—that the Egyptians sat at meals is in exact accordance with the representations on the monuments, in which they are never exhibited as reposing on couches, but always as seated round a circular table resembling the *monopodium* of the Romans (*vide* Wilkinson, 'Ancient Egyptians,' vol. ii. pp. 40, 41, with Dr. Birch's note ; Hengstenberg's 'Egypt and the Books of Moses,' ch. i. p. 38)—**the firstborn according to his birthright, and the youngest according to his youth: and the men marvelled one at another**—probably thinking that Joseph must have been supernaturally enlightened to discover so exactly the ages of strangers.

Ver. 34.—**And he took** and sent (literally, *and he sent*) **messes**—*maseoth*, from *nasa*, to take or lift up, *i. e.* things taken or lifted up, hence portions or gifts (2 Sam. xi. 8)—**unto them from before him** (cf. 1 Sam. ix. 23). The practice of thus honouring guests was also observed among other nations (*vide* 'Iliad,' vii. 321). **But Benjamin's mess** (or portion) **was five times so much as any of theirs**—literally, *exceeded the portions of all of them five hands*, i. e. five times. Herodotus (vi. 57) mentions that among the Spartans the king received a double portion. The unusually large portion assigned to Benjamin was designed as an expression of his strong fraternal affection, and perhaps also as a test of his brethren to ascertain if they were now free from that spirit of envy which had prompted their former cruelty to him. **And they drank, and were merry with him**—literally, *and drank largely with him*. Though the verb שָׁכַר sometimes signifies to drink·to the full (Haggai i. 6 ; Cant. v. 1), and though intoxication was not unusual at Egyptian entertainments, there is no reason to suppose that either Joseph or his brethren were inebriated (Vulgate, Alford), or that more is meant than simply that their hearts became exhilarated "because their cares were dissipated by the kindness they were receiving, the presence of Simeon, and the attention paid to Benjamin" (Murphy).

HOMILETICS.

Vers. 1—34.—*The second visit of Joseph's brethren to Egypt.* I. THE SCENE IN JACOB'S HOUSE AT HEBRON (vers. 1—15). 1. *The second journey proposed.* "Go again, buy us a little food." It was necessitated by the long continuance of the famine, and the complete consumption of the corn they had brought from Egypt on the previous occasion. 2. *The second journey agreed on.* (1) The difficulty started. As explained by Judah, it was useless to go to Egypt unless accompanied by Benjamin, since the governor had solemnly protested and sworn that without him they should not only not obtain a grain of corn, but they should not even be admitted to his presence. But to speak of taking Benjamin to Egypt, as Jacob had already testified, and now again declared, was like driving a poniard into the old man's heart. As he thinks of it he can hardly forbear reproaching his stalwart sons for having heaped upon him one more unkindness in even mentioning the fact of Benjamin's existence. (2) The difficulty removed. Skilfully the eloquent Judah reasons with his aged sire, first pointing out that it was only in reply to the grand vizier's interrogations that they had referred to Benjamin at all, that, not suspecting any sinister motives on the part of their noble questioner, they had never dreamt of attempting concealment or evasion in their answers; urging the imperative necessity for Benjamin's going down with them if either they or their little ones were to be kept from starvation, solemnly engaging to be surety for the safe convoy of the beloved youth, and lastly delicately hinting that but for the delay occasioned by his (their father's) reluctance they might have been to Egypt and back since he first spoke of their going. 3. *The second journey prepared for* (vers. 11—13). Since it was inevitable that Benjamin must go, Jacob recommended them along with him to take (1) a present in their vessels for the great man whose favour they desired to secure; (2) second money, or money for the purchase of the grain they wished, to show that they came not as beggars, but as buyers; (3) the silver that had been returned in their sacks, to prove that they were honest, and regarded the matter simply as an oversight. It is well always to put the best construction on a dubious matter, and in particular to let not our good be evil spoken of. 4. *The second journey began* (vers. 14, 15). Listening to their father's prayer,—"God Almighty give you mercy before the man,"—witnessing their father's sorrowful resignation,—"If I be bereaved, I am bereaved,"—and observing faithfully their father's instructions, carrying a present of "the song of the land" and double money in their hands, the men rose up and went down to Egypt. 5. *The second journey completed* (ver. 15). In the providence of God they reached the land of Egypt and stood before Joseph. It is a special mercy to travellers when, escaping all the perils of the way, they arrive at their desired destinations in peace.

II. THE SCENE IN JOSEPH'S HOUSE IN EGYPT (vers. 16—34). 1. *The reception of the brethren* (vers. 16, 17). Scarcely had the brethren arrived at the public mart than they were observed by Joseph. Directing his eyes eagerly in search of Benjamin, he is gratified by noticing that he has not been left behind. Preserving as before his incognito, he gives instructions to his steward to convey them to his palace, and prepare a dinner for him and them at the hour of noon. 2. *The apprehensions of the brethren* (vers. 18—24). (1) The nature of them. They feared lest Joseph was only seeking occasion to fall upon them and take them for bondmen. (2) The ground of them. This was the money which had been discovered in their sacks, and for which as they imagined they were now being arrested. (3) The expression of them. Without directly saying what they dreaded, they begin to deprecate the wrath of the steward, and to offer explanations concerning the money (vers. 20—22). (4) The removal of them. Although the steward was not yet aware that the strangers were his master's brethren, he was perfectly cognisant of their innocence in the matter of the money, and of his master's desire to show them kindness. Accordingly he seeks to reassure them by encouraging them to dismiss their apprehensions—"Peace be to you, fear not;" by telling them to regard the treasure in their sacks as a Divine gift, since it was indubitable that he had received their money—"Your God hath given you treasure in your sacks: I had your money;" by producing Simeon before them, no doubt in the enjoyment of perfect health and happiness—"and he brought Simeon out unto them;" by exercising towards them the rights of hospitality—"the man gave them water, and they washed their feet;" and by providing for the wants of their beasts—"and he gave their asses provender." 3. *The homage of the brethren* (vers. 25—31). (1) Its presentation: with precious gifts—the delicacies of the land of Canaan; with dutiful obeisance

—"they bowed themselves to him to the earth." (2) Its acceptance; which was indicated by the friendly inquiries of the governor—"Is your father well, the old man of whom ye spake? Is he yet alive?" "Is this your younger brother, of whom ye spake unto me?" by the warm benediction he pronounced on Benjamin— "God be gracious unto thee, my son;" by the rising emotion which he could with difficulty repress—"his bowels did yearn upon his brother, and he sought where to weep;" and by the order which he issued to his servants—"Set on bread." 4. *The entertainment of the brethren.* (1) The separation of the guests, first from the host, and then from one another, the Egyptians from the Canaanites, and both from Joseph, the reason being that the Egyptians might not eat with foreigners in case of contracting pollution. (2) The order of the brethren, each being arranged before the governor in accordance with their ages, a circumstance which appears to have simultaneously evoked their wonder—"and the men marvelled one at another." (3) The portions from the host, one to each of the nine oldest, and five to the youngest, which were designed as marks of special favour. (4) The hilarity of the company. The fears of the brethren disappearing, and their enjoyment rising, as they talked and drank with the gracious governor who had brought them to his palace.

HOMILIES BY VARIOUS AUTHORS.

Ch. xliii.—*Lessons of life.* I. The chief lesson of this chapter is the MINGLING TOGETHER OF THE PROVIDENTIAL GOVERNMENT OF GOD WITH HIS PURPOSE OF GRACE. It was part of the Divine plan that Jacob and his family should be settled for a long period in Egypt. It could only be brought about by the transference in some way of the point of attraction to Jacob's heart from Canaan to the strange land. Hence "Jacob" is now "Israel," reminding us how the future is involved in all the events of this time. "Judah" is the chief agent in this matter. The very names are significant of Divine promises—"Judah," "Israel," "Joseph," "Benjamin." The conduct of Joseph cannot be explained except on the ground of his inspiration. He is not acting. He is not trifling with human feelings. He is not merely following the dictate of his own personal affections. He is, under Divine direction, planning for the removal of his father's house to Egypt that the people of God may pass through their season of trial in the house of bondage. Another point—

II. God's blessing on a TRUE HUMANITY. THE THOROUGHLY HUMAN CHARACTER OF THE NARRATIVE. The *tenderness*, the *pathos*, the *simplicity*, the *truthfulness*, especially in the case of Joseph himself. How little he had been spoiled by prosperity! That is the *criterion of real greatness*. The Bible histories help us to keep in mind that real religion does not suppress the human, but preserves and develops all that is best and noblest in the man.

III. THE GRACIOUS WISDOM OF THE GOOD MAN IN HIS CONDUCT TOWARDS OTHERS. Joseph's dealing with his brethren gradually preparing their minds for the great announcement which was soon to be made. Both his kindness to them and his particular inquiries after Jacob, and affectionate salute of Benjamin, must have *roused their curiosity* and *disarmed their terrors*. As they "drank and were merry" with the great Egyptian ruler, and their youngest brother rejoiced in the special mark of favour, which was favour to all, they must have felt the bondage of their previous apprehensions slipping away from them, and have anticipated some good thing in preparation for them. Moreover, there may have been the intention working in Joseph's mind of accustoming the Egyptians to the sight of those Hebrew people, and so opening the way to their subsequent elevation when as his brethren he should settle them in Goshen. There was great wisdom in all this lingering in divulging the great secret.

IV. THE MARK OF FAITH IS A SINGLE EYE TO GOD'S GLORY. We should endeavour to blend the *personal* with the *larger interests* of God's kingdom. *Family life* should be based upon *religious foundations.*—R.

Ver. 18.—*Distrust the fruit of sin.* Why should they be afraid? The invitation was an honour not unusual. Abraham was received at Pharaoh's court (Gen. xii. 15). And the brethren were evidently people of large possessions with a considerable retinue, as they were to carry food for so many ; and they had brought the proof required that they were true men. Had Joseph intended to do them harm he might have done it before. It was conscious guilt that made them fear. What they had done to their brother suggested similar treatment being meted to them. Perhaps they had almost forgotten it. But God left not himself without witness to bring their sin to remembrance. The stain of sin on the conscience is indelible. Time cannot remove it. Occupation may turn the thoughts from it, but it returns again and again. The act of wrong may be little thought of at the time. Only afterwards is it felt that it cannot be undone (cf. 1 Cor. xv. 9). This explains the attitude of so many toward God. Why is there such slowness to receive the gospel just as it is offered ? When men are bidden to their brother's table; when his will is declared they shall sup with me (cf. Rev. iii. 20), why is there such shrinking as if they were being led into danger ; as if God were laying some obligation on them which they cannot fulfil, to bring them into bondage for ever ? It is because of sin in the heart; perhaps unfelt, unthought of ; but it is there, the fact of a self-chosen life. And if these are invited to closer communion with God, straightway they are afraid ; suspicious of God. And hence, when the gospel invitation is pressed, and the Lamb of God held up, and the power of the blood of Christ and the welcome for all proclaimed, and they are bidden to trust, to accept salvation, men try to fortify their position : " O sir, we have done this or that " (cf. Matt. xviii. 26), clinging to distrust instead of striving against it.

I. THIS DISTRUST AND SUSPICION OF GOD ARISES FROM THE PRESENCE OF SIN NOT FULLY RECOGNISED AS SIN ; while the man is still trying to set good deeds against bad ones, or to find excuses for faults. It is the effect of sin before conviction by the Holy Spirit. Real conviction brings to God (Ps. li. 4 ; Luke xviii. 13). It is unacknowledged sin that separates.

II. DISTRUST IS REMOVED BY A REAL BELIEF IN THE ATONEMENT (Heb. ix. 25), God's plan for reconciling the sinful to himself (Rom. iii. 26). Hence this is the turning point of the spiritual life (John iii. 18) ; the great work (John vi. 29) out of which, as from a germ, the whole Christian life must grow.—M.

EXPOSITION.

CHAPTER XLIV.

Vers. 1, 2.—**And he** (*i. e.* Joseph) **commanded the steward of his house,**—literally, *him that was over his house* (ch. xliii. 15)—**saying, Fill the men's sacks with food, as much as they can carry, and put every man's money in his sack's mouth** (as before, but not this time as a test). **And put my cup,**—גְּבִיעַ, from an unused root, גָּבַע, conveying the sense of elevation or roundness ; hence a goblet or bowl, commonly of a large size (Jer. xxxv. 5), as distinguished from the כּוֹס, or smaller cup, into which, from the *gabia*, wine or other liquid was poured (cf. ch. xl. 11) —the silver cup,—τὸ κόνδυ τὸ ἀργυροῦν (LXX.). Bohlen mentions that the religious drinking utensil of the Indian priests is called *kundi*—**in the sack's mouth of the youngest, and his corn money**—literally, *the silver of his grain,* or of his purchase. **And he** (*i. e.* the steward) **did according to the word that Joseph had spoken.**

Vers. 3—5.—**As soon as the morning was light** (literally, *the morning became bright*), **the men** (literally, *and the men*) **were sent away, they and their asses.** That Joseph

did not make himself known to his brothers at the repast was not due to unnatural callousness which caused his heart to remain cold and steeled (Kalisch), or to a fear lest he should thereby destroy the character of his mission which made him the medium of retribution for his brothers (Kalisch), but to the fact that in his judgment either his brothers had not been sufficiently tested, or the time did not appear convenient for the disclosure of his secret. **And when they were gone out of the city** (literally, *they went forth out of the city*), **and not yet far off** (literally, *they had not gone far*), **Joseph** (literally, *and Joseph*) **said unto his steward** (or man over his house), **Up, follow after the men ; and when thou dost overtake them, say unto them** (literally, *and overtake them, and say to them*), **Wherefore have ye rewarded evil for good ?** The interpolation at this point of the words, " Why did you steal my silver goblet ? " (LXX., Vulgate, Syriac) is superfluous. **Is not this it in which my lord drinketh, and whereby indeed he divineth ?** —literally, *and divining he divineth,* or maketh trial, *in it,* the verb נָחַשׁ (from which is derived *nachash,* a serpent : *vide* ch. iii. 1) originally signifying to hiss or whisper, and hence to mutter incantations, to practise ophiomancy, and generally to divine. The special form of divination here referred to (κυλικομαντεία, or divining out of cups) was practised by the ancient Egyptians (Hengstenberg's 'Egypt and the Books of Moses,' p. 39). "Small pieces of gold or silver, together with precious stones, marked with strange figures and signs, were thrown into the vessel; after which certain incantations were pronounced, and the evil demon was invoked; the latter was then supposed to give the answer either by intelligible words, or by pointing to some of the characters on the precious stones, or in some other more mysterious manner. Sometimes the goblet was filled with pure water, upon which the sun was allowed to play; and the figures which were thus formed, or which a lively imagination fancied it saw, were interpreted as the desired omen" (Kalisch). Traces of this ancient practice of soothsaying have been detected by some writers in the magnificent vase of turquoise belonging to Jamsheed, the Solomon of Persia. Like Merlin's cup, described by Spenser ('Faery Queene,' iii. 2, 19)—

" It vertue had to show in perfect sight
  Whatever thing was in the world contained
  Betwixt the lowest earth and heven's hight,
  So that it to the looker appertaynd."

A similar account is given by Homer of the cup of Nestor; and Alexander the Great is reported to have possessed a mystic goblet of a like kind. It is said that in the storming of Seringapatam the unfortunate Tippoo Saib retired to gaze on his divining cup, and that after standing awhile absorbed in it he returned to the fight and fell (vide Kitto's 'Cyclopedia,' art. Divination). **Ye have done evil in so doing.**

Ver. 6.—**And he** (i. e. the steward) **overtook them, and he spake unto them these same words.**

Vers. 7—10.—**And they said unto him, Wherefore saith my lord these words?** God forbid that thy servants should do (literally, far be thy servants from doing) **according to this thing: behold, the money** (literally, the silver), **which we found in our sacks' mouths, we brought again unto thee out of the land of Canaan** (this was an irrefragable proof of their honesty): **how then should we steal out of my lord's house silver or gold?** They were even so confident of their innocence that they ventured on a rash proposition. **With whomsoever of thy servants it be found, both let him die, and we also will be my lord's bondmen**—literally, for servants to my lord. **And he** (the steward) **said, Now also**

let it be **according to your words.** So LXX., Vulgate, and commentators generally; but Kalisch reads it as an interrogation, " Is it right according to your words?" meaning that strict justice demanded only the punishment of the thief, as he explained. **He with whom it is found shall be my servant; and ye** (i. e. the others of you) **shall be blameless.**

Vers. 11—13.—**Then they speedily took down** (literally, and they hasted and took down) **every man his sack** (from off his ass) **to the ground, and opened every man his sack.** Thus as it were delivering them up for examination. **And he** (the steward) **searched, and began at the eldest, and left at the youngest** (in order thereby to mask the deception): **and the cup was found** (where the steward himself had put it) **in Benjamin's sack. Then** (literally, and) **they rent their clothes** (on the simlah vide ch. ix. 23), **and laded every man his ass** (by putting on the sack which had been taken down), **and returned to the city.**

Vers. 14—17.—**And Judah**—who is recognised as the leader in this second embassy to Egypt (ch. xliii. 8)—**and his brethren came to Joseph's house; for he** was yet there:— "awaiting, no doubt, the result which he anticipated" (Murphy)—**and they fell before him on the ground.** The expression indicates a complete prostration of the body. It was a token of their penitence, and a sign that they craved his forgiveness. **And Joseph said unto them,**—in a speech not of " cruel and haughty irony " (Kalisch), but simply of assumed resentment—**What deed is this that ye have done? wot ye not** (or, did you not know?) **that such a man as I can certainly divine?**—literally, divining can divine (vide on ver. 5). Though Joseph uses this language, and is represented by his steward as possessing a divining cup, there is no reason to suppose that he was in the habit of practising this heathen superstition. **And Judah said** (acting throughout this scene as the spokesman of his brethren), **What shall we say unto my lord? what shall we speak? or how shall we clear ourselves?** (i. e. justify ourselves, or purge ourselves from suspicion). **God** (literally, the Elohim) **hath found out the iniquity of thy servants: behold, we are my lord's servants** (literally, servants to my lord), **both we, and he also with whom the cup is found. And he** (i. e. Joseph) **said, God forbid that I should do so** (vide ver. 9): but **the man in whose hand the cup is found, he shall be my servant; and as for you, get you up in peace unto your father.** Thus they were once more tested as to whether they could, as before, callously deliver up their father's favourite, and so bring down the grey hairs of their father to the grave, or would heroically and self-sacrificingly offer their own lives and liberties for his protection (Rosenmüller, Keil, Lange, Murphy, and others). How nobly they stood the test Judah's pathetic supplication reveals.

Vers. 18—34.—**Then Judah came near to him, and said,**—the speech of Judah in behalf of his young brother Benjamin has been fittingly characterised as "one of the masterpieces of Hebrew composition" (Kalisch), "one of the grandest and fairest to be found in the Old Testament" (Lange), "a more moving oration than ever orator pronounced" (Lawson), "one of the finest specimens of natural eloquence in the world" (Inglis). Without being distinguished by either brilliant imagination or highly poetic diction, "its inimitable charm and excellence consist in the power of psychological truth, easy simplicity, and affecting pathos" (Kalisch)— **Oh my lord** (the interjection Oh! is the same as that used by Judah in ch. xliii. 20; q. v.), **let thy servant, I pray thee, speak a word in my lord's ears** (probably pressing towards him in his eagerness), **and let not thine anger burn against thy servant: for thou art even as Pharaoh** (i. e. one invested with the authority of Pharaoh, and therefore able, like Pharaoh, either to pardon or condemn). **My lord asked his servants, saying, Have ye a father, or a brother? And we said unto my lord, We have a father, an old man, and a child of his old age** (vide ch. xxxvii. 3), **a little one; and his brother is dead, and he alone is left of his mother, and his father loveth him.** Substantially this is the account which the brethren gave of themselves from the first (ch. xlii. 13); only Judah now with exquisite tact as well as resistless pathos dwells on the threefold circumstance that the little one whose life was at stake was inexpressibly dear to his father for his dead brother's sake as well as for his departed mother's and his own. **And thou saidst unto thy servants, Bring him down unto me, that I may set mine eyes upon him.** This last clause is also a rhetorical enlargement of Joseph's words, ἐπιμελοῦμαι αὐτοῦ (LXX.); the phrase, to set one's eyes on any one, being commonly used in a good sense, signifying to regard any one with kindness, to look to his good (cf. Ezra v. 5; Job xxiv. 23; Jer. xxxix. 12; xl. 4). **And we said unto my lord, The lad cannot leave his father: for if he should leave his father, his father would die.** Judah in this no doubt correctly reports the original conversation, although the remark is not recorded in the first account. **And thou saidst unto thy servants, Except your youngest brother come down with you, ye shall see my face no more** (cf. ch. xliii. 3—5). **And it came to pass** (literally, it was) **when we came up unto thy servant my father, we told him the words of my lord.** The effect upon

Jacob of their sad communication Judah does not recite (ch. xlii. 36), but passes on to the period of the commencement of the second journey. **And our father said** (i. e. after the consumption of the corn supply), **Go again, and buy us a little food** (vide ch. xliii. 2). **And we said, We cannot go down: if our youngest brother be with us, then will we go down: for we may not see the man's face, except our youngest brother be with us. And thy servant my father said unto us** (at this point Judah with increased tenderness alludes to the touching lamentation of the stricken patriarch as he first listens to the unwelcome proposition to take Benjamin from his side), **Ye know that my wife**—Rachel was all through her life the wife of his affections (cf. ch. xlvi. 19)—**bare me two sons**:—Joseph and Benjamin (ch. xxx. 22, 24; xxxv. 18)—**and the one** (Joseph) **went out from me** (and returned not, thus indirectly alluding to his death), **and I said, Surely he is torn in pieces; and I saw him not since.** Jacob means that had Joseph been alive, he would certainly have returned; but that as since that fatal day of his departure from Hebron he had never beheld him, he could only conclude that his inference was correct, and that Joseph was devoured by some beast of prey. **And if ye take this also from me** (in the sense which the next clause explains), **and mischief befall him, ye shall bring down my grey hairs with sorrow to the grave** — Sheol (vide ch. xxxvii. 35). **Now therefore** (literally, and now) **when I come** (or go) **to thy servant my father, and the lad be not with us; seeing that his life** (or soul) **is bound up in the lad's life** (or soul); **it shall come to pass, when he seeth that the lad is not** with us, **that he will die: and thy servants shall bring down the grey hairs of thy servant our father with sorrow to the grave. For thy servant became surety for the lad unto my father, saying, If I bring him not unto thee, then I shall bear the blame to my father for ever** (vide ch. xliii. 9). **Now therefore** (literally, and now), **I pray thee, let thy servant abide instead of the lad a bondman** (or servant) **to my lord; and let the lad go up with his brethren.** "There was no duty that imperiously prohibited Judah from taking the place of his unfortunate brother. His children, and even his wife, if he had been in the married state, might have been sent to Egypt. He was so far master of his own liberty that he could warrantably put himself in Benjamin's room, if the governor gave his consent" (Lawson). **For how shall I go up to my father, and the lad be not with me? lest peradventure I see the evil that shall come on** (literally, shall find) **my father.** The sublime heroism of this noble act of self-sacrifice on the part of Judah it is impossible to over-estimate. In behalf of one whom he knew was preferred to a higher place in his father's affection than himself, he was willing to renounce his liberty rather than see his aged parent die of a broken heart. The self-forgetful magnanimity of such an action has never been eclipsed, and seldom rivalled. After words so exquisitely beautiful and profoundly pathetic it was impossible for Joseph to doubt that a complete change had passed upon his brethren, and in particular upon Judah, since the day when he had eloquently urged, and they had wickedly consented, to sell their brother Joseph into Egypt. Everything was now ready for the denouement in this domestic drama. The story of Joseph's discovery of himself to his astonished brethren is related in the ensuing chapter.

HOMILETICS.

Vers. 1—34.—*Joseph's artifice to detain Benjamin, or the story of the silver goblet.* I. JOSEPH'S STRATAGEM (vers. 1—13). 1. *The formation of the plot* (vers. 1—5). (1) The singular nature of the plot. This was, after filling the men's sacks with corn, and putting each man's money in his sack's mouth as before, that the steward should secretly deposit in the amtachath of Benjamin the silver goblet from which Joseph was accustomed to fill his wine-cup when he drank. (2) The immediate object of the plot. It was designed that the company should be pursued under suspicion of theft, and that, on examination made, Benjamin should be arrested as a criminal. (3) The ultimate purpose of the plot. Not simply to detain Benjamin, whom Joseph longed to have beside him, but chiefly to try the others as to whether they could witness unmoved Benjamin's consignment to exile and probable imprisonment, as formerly with callous hearts they had beheld his (Joseph's) sale and departure as a bondman into Egypt. 2. *The execution of the plot* (vers. 6—12). (1) The cup was put into the sack of Benjamin, as arranged, and the men allowed to depart with the first streak of dawn in happy unconsciousness of what had been devised against them. (2) Overtaken by the steward, and abruptly charged with having stolen his master's divining cup, they indignantly repel the charge, and somewhat rashly suggest that their sacks should be searched on the spot, at the same time offering, so conscious were they of innocence, to deliver up the culprit to death, and themselves to a voluntary captivity. (3) Taking them at their word, and modifying their proposal to the extent that he would take the guilty one only as a servant, the sacks were opened out, and, as the steward of course expected, the missing vase was found where he himself had placed it, in the amtachath of Benjamin. 3. *The result of the plot* (vers. 13—16). (1) Utter consternation of mind: "they rent their clothes" to give expression to the anguish of their souls. (2) Instantaneous retracing of their steps: "they laded every man his ass, and returned to the city." (3) Abject acknowledgment of their offence: "What shall we say unto my lord? God hath found out the iniquity of thy servants." (4) Faithful fulfilment of their contract: "Behold, we are my lord's servants, both we, and he also with whom the cup is found."

II. BENJAMIN'S SENTENCE (ver. 17). 1. *Exceedingly severe.* He became a bond-man. Remark upon the sadness of slavery, even when most mitigated. 2. *Circumstantially justified.* Appearances were against him. But the evidence of circumstances is sometimes fallacious. 3. *Absolutely undeserved.* In every sense of the expression Benjamin was blameless. 4. *Wisely designed.* It was meant to assay the characters of both Benjamin and his brethren.

III. JUDAH'S SUPPLICATION (vers. 18—34). 1. *Deferential humility* (ver. 18). It is difficult to imagine language more respectful and deferential than that of Judah. Almost every word is so framed as to convey a sense of Joseph's lofty station, superior dignity, and just cause of indignation against the speaker. 2. *Artless simplicity* (vers. 19—26). Infinitely more powerful than either voluble rhetoric or closely-compacted argument is the plain and unsophisticated logic of truth. Without the most distant approach to sophistry, or even an attempt at persuasion, Judah confines himself to a bare recital of the facts of the case which were already well known to Joseph. 3. *Inimitable pathos* (vers. 28—32). Depicting his father's love for Benjamin for his dead mother's and his lost brother's sakes, he tells how he himself had become surety for the lad to his aged parent, and that if he should fail to take him back again in safety he would bring down his father's grey hairs with sorrow to the grave. 4. *Heroic self-sacrifice* (vers. 33, 34). Rather than that Benjamin should not go home again to Hebron, he would himself remain a bondman to my lord the governor for ever. Nay, he explicitly makes offer that he should take the young man's place, as he would rather die than see the sorrow which his absence would bring down upon his venerable sire. Noble Judah! thou art he whom thy brethren shall praise.

HOMILIES BY VARIOUS AUTHORS.

Ch. xliv.—*Character built on faith.* This chapter continues the same thread of Joseph's policy, and the same lessons are in it.

I. PRACTICAL WISDOM THE FRUIT OF PIETY. The true man is the strong man. With a deep knowledge of the human heart, Joseph felt quite sure that the only way to move Jacob from Canaan was to detain Benjamin.

II. THE SANCTITY OF THE AFFECTIONS. Real religion their only safeguard in the world's hardening and perverting influences. Joseph did *apparent* violence to his brethren's and his father's feelings that he might afterwards fill them with joy. There was a great deal of genuine family affection at the bottom of the scheme. He could not bear to part with Benjamin. He at first meant to maintain the dissembling till the old man was brought, but nature burst through the restraint. The whole a testimony to the real *purity* and *simplicity* of Joseph's heart, and therefore, in such circumstances of temptation as his, to his real religion.

III. CONTRAST BETWEEN GOD'S IDEAL OF GREATNESS AND THE WORLD'S. Great rulers and statesmen are not wont thus to cultivate the emotions. The tendency of high position is to harden the heart, and to change nature into policy, and the real into the artificial. Yet such instances as Joseph show the possibility of uniting the two spheres—the secular and the spiritual, and being great in both.—R.

Ver. 5.—*Probation.* Divination by cups was practised by the ancient Egyptians. But no reason to suppose that Joseph actually used this art. It would have been inconsistent with his habitual faithfulness to God, and with the ascription to him alone of the power to reveal secrets (ch. xl. 7—xli. 16). He was now acting a part. He spoke in the character of an Egyptian ruler, to whom the nation ascribed supernatural wisdom. We need not now inquire how far he was right in this. But his object was to try his brethren, whether, and how much, they loved their father and their young brother. He contrived that Benjamin should appear to have incurred the penalty of servitude. What would the rest do? Would they, as they had done to him, leave their brother in slavery? Would they go home and deceive their father by a false story of his death? Could they bear to renew his grief? Had they learned that God marked their actions, and ordained the things that happened to them? The cup hidden in Benjamin's sack was indeed that whereby he was divining their secret thoughts. They stood the test. They acknowledged God's hand, and refused to purchase their own safety at the price of their brother's freedom (contrast ch. xxxvii. 26, 27, with ch. xliv. 30, 34). Forthwith the clouds passed away. In him whom they feared they found a brother.

I. GOD BY HIS PROVIDENCE TRIES THE SPIRIT THAT IS IN US. The events of our lives are ordered so as to bring this about (Deut. viii. 2). They are to us as Joseph's cup. Daily work, family life, professional duties, the common intercourse of society, raise questions which are answered according as God or self rules the heart and guides the actions. Hence no part of our life is unimportant in a spiritual point of view. Things, in themselves of small account, test the character and motives of the life, as floating straws show the current; and this all the more because their spiritual bearing is not apparent. Kindness, truth, unselfishness, in little matters, reveal the man more truly than on greater and more conspicuous occasions (cf. 1 Cor. xiii. 3).

II. TRIALS ARE SENT IN LOVE AS INSTRUMENTS OF BLESSING (James i. 12). Through their operation the Christian life is matured (Rom. v. 3—5). Every grace must be exercised in order to grow, and trial is the opportunity of exercise. Without trial there could be no real victory over evil, no real submission of the will to God. We pray to be kept from temptation. To run into it is to court a fall. But where

God sends trial grace is provided (1 Cor. x. 13), answering every need; help for the falling or fallen as well as strength for the steadfast.

III. HOW TO STAND IN THE DAY OF TRIAL. In each of the messages to the Churches (Rev. ii., iii.) trial is implied—now of persecution, now of false doctrine, now of indolent spiritual ease. And the blessing is " to him that overcometh." How ? " By the blood of the Lamb " (Rev. xii. 11), *i. e.* by faith in it. Not merely belief in the doctrine, but realising what the work of Christ has won for us, and the love of the Father from which it proceeds, and the claim which the mercies of God make upon us (Rom. xii. 1). The first step is receiving with an undoubting spirit the love of God ; not letting in unbelief in the garb of humility. The next is keeping that truth present in the mind in the midst of daily work, that the love of Christ may constrain the direction of our life.—M.

Vers. 14—34.—*The conversion of Judah.* I. THE EVIDENCE OF IT. 1. The unexpected confession of guilt which he makes. " God hath found out the iniquity of thy servants." 2. The sensitive appreciation of the terrible blow which Benjamin's loss would be to Jacob. " When he seeth the lad is not with us he will die." 3. The noble sacrifice he proposes to make for Benjamin. " Let thy servant abide instead of the lad, a bondman to my lord."

II. THE CAUSE OF IT. 1. The memory of his old sin, which appears to have haunted his conscience. 2. The arrestment of Divine Providence, which in his Egyptian experience he suffered. 3. The inward operation of God's grace upon his heart.

Learn—1. That no living sinner is beyond the reach of conversion. 2. That for the most part the work of conversion is gradually consummated ; and—3. That when once it is completed it appears in a change of character and life.—W.

Ver. 32.—*A surety.* " For thy servant became surety for the lad unto his father." The brethren of Joseph had been surprised on their second visit to Egypt at the cordiality of their reception. They started homewards with well-laden sacks and trembling gladness. They had not gone far when they were overtaken, their sacks searched, and the cup found. With depressed spirits and dreary forebodings they were brought back to the city, and into the presence of Joseph. Joseph had several motives in his strange treatment of his brethren. He may have desired in some way to punish them for their sin against himself by letting them taste some of the bitterness he had experienced when, ruthlessly torn from his home, he was sent a shrinking slave into a distant land. Human nature was strong in Joseph as in others. His brethren had to learn the nature of their own sin by suffering. They have also to learn that their lives were forfeited by sin to justice. He wished also to bring them to a state of humility, so that they should afterwards behave rightly to each other. He may have had doubts as to the safety of his own brother Benjamin with them. He tests thus their interest in their half-brother, for they could have left with some sort of excuse Benjamin as a slave in Egypt. He tests also their regard for their father, and finds out also how they would look upon himself when he should reveal himself to them. Judah is the spokesman for the rest in the painful circumstances in which they are all placed. Joseph proposes to keep only Benjamin as a slave, but Judah draws near, and with deepest humility and heartfelt earnestness pleads with Joseph. Consider—

I. JUDAH'S PLEADING. 1. Judah pleads as surety for Benjamin, and as a brother. We find that it is Judah and not Reuben who pleads now for the life of a brother. Age has mellowed the fierce Judah. We cannot always tell from what a man is in his early years what he will be later on. (1) Judah admits the wrong, attempts no excuse or extenuation. All evidence was against Benjamin. Judah and the rest cannot tell what to think of the act. He admitted it. We must admit our sin. (2) Confessed that it was right that Benjamin and they should suffer. Some blame others for their circumstances and sins. To all appearance here Benjamin was alone to blame. (3) He throws himself on the righteousness and compassion of Joseph. This is all we can do before God. He pleads the pain which it will cause to his father. His appeal is most pathetic. Read it, and the fount of tears must be touched. In all the volumes of fiction ever written there is nothing to surpass the tenderness and pathos of this pleading of Judah.   2. We learn from this position and pleading of Judah as to how we should approach God.   We have sinned and can only throw ourselves on his mercy.   We see also how Christ pleads for us.   His pleading is real and earnest.   He prayed on earth for his disciples.   The present is a dispensation of mediation.   Hence Christ still pleads as our surety in heaven.

II. JUDAH'S OFFER.   He is ready to be bound for Benjamin.   It is one thing to talk, another to act.   He had promised his father to bring Benjamin again (ch. xliii. 9), and he wishes to keep his word.   He became surety, a guarantee, as one who is bound by signing a paper.   He was answerable to his father.   He is ready to give his service for Benjamin, his life for his brother.   His faithfulness was thus proved.   Christ is our surety.   He makes himself one with us (Heb. ii. 11).   He sprang from Judah (Heb. vii. 14).   He became one with us in nature and in temptation, and was accepted as our substitute, was bound, abused, and crucified.   He bore the curse for us (Gal. iii. 13).   He sacrificed himself for us.   Christ died for us who were below him. We may see in the success of Judah's pleading an indication of the success of Jesus' work.   Joseph needed no entreaty to be merciful to Benjamin.   He was nearer of kin to Benjamin than Judah was.   So God is *our Father*.   Joseph only wished to see the brethren in a fit state to be forgiven.   They were entirely forgiven (vers. 5—15).   He forgave freely, and wished them to forgive themselves. He knew very well that if they began to blame themselves too much, or to upbraid each other, they would never be happy.   Forgiveness should produce peace.   1. Let us see ourselves in those suppliant brothers of Joseph.   2. Let us see in Judah how Christ pleads for us, and with what power.   Certainly he excelled in his appeal, in wisdom, boldness, eloquence, tenderness, and self-sacrifice.   How much more should we not praise Jesus for his power, his life, his love, sufferings, death, and present intercession.   3. Let us then trust him.   What would have been thought of the others if they should have said to Judah, " You are not equal to being surety for him," or " You are not of sufficient standing, not above us, so as to speak in the name of the rest"? And is not Christ equal to the work of securing our salvation ?   If he can do it, shall we attempt to mar by our meddling ?   Full atonement is made, as well as powerful intercession offered.   What we have to do is to trust Christ's work.   Let us give up hope of preparing ourselves.   He is not like some who are sureties, and are unwilling to pay.   He *has* paid.   The law and justice have nothing to demand.   Should either present a claim, point to the cross, for that answers all demands.   Oh the mystery of redeeming love !   Oh the simplicity and yet the depth of meaning contained in that work of Christ !   It is a stumbling-block to the high-minded, but a salvation to the humble.—H.

EXPOSITION.

CHAPTER XLV.

Vers. 1, 2.—**Then** (literally, *and*) **Joseph could not refrain himself** (*i. e.* keep himself from giving way to the impulses of love) **before all them that stood by him** (*i.e.* the Egyptian officials of his household) **; and he cried** (or made proclamation, issued an instruction), **Cause every man to go out from me.   And there stood no man with him, while Joseph made himself known unto his brethren.**   It was true delicacy on the part of Joseph which prompted the discovery of himself to his brethren in private ; not simply because he did not wish to pain his brethren by a public reference to their past wickedness, *ne facinus illud detestabile multis testibus innotescat* (Calvin), but because the unrestrained outburst of emotion *erga fratres et parentem non posset ferre alienorum*

præsentiam et aspectum (Luther).   **And he wept aloud** (literally, *and he gave forth*, or uttered, *his voice in weeping*) : **and the Egyptians and the house of Pharaoh heard.** The meaning is that the Egyptian officials of Joseph's house, who were standing outside, heard, and reported it to the house of Pharaoh (Keil, Murphy).   It is not necessary to suppose that Joseph's residence was so close to the palace that his voice was heard by the inmates (Lange).

Ver. 3.—**And Joseph said unto his brethren, I am Joseph.**   The effect of this announcement can be better imagined than described.   Hitherto he had been known to his brethren as Zaphnath-paaneah.   Now the voice and the appearance of their long-lost brother would rush upon their minds at the first sound of the familiar name, and fill them with apprehension.   Probably Joseph's discernment of this in their countenances was the reason why he asked so abruptly after Jacob. **Doth my father yet live?** It is not now "the old man of whom ye spake" (ch. xliii. 27) for whom Joseph inquires, but his own beloved and revered parent—"my father." "Before it was a question of courtesy, but now of love" (Alford). **And his brethren could not answer him; for they were troubled** (or cast into a trepidation, hence terrified) **at his presence**—literally, *before his face.* Not only did his present greatness overawe them, but the recollection of their former crimes against him filled them with alarm.

Vers. 4—13.—**And Joseph said unto his brethren, Come near to me, I pray you.** It is probable they had instinctively shrunk from his presence on learning the astounding fact that he was Joseph, but felt reassured by the kindly tone of Joseph's words. **And they came near. And he said, I am Joseph your brother, whom ye sold into Egypt.** It was impossible to evade allusion to their early wickedness, and this Joseph does in a spirit not of angry upbraiding, but of elevated piety and tender charity. **Now therefore be not grieved, nor angry with yourselves** (literally, *let it not burn in your eyes,* as in ch. xxxi. 35), **that ye sold me hither** (their self-recriminations and heart upbraidings for their former wickedness Joseph in all probability saw depicted in their faces): **for God** (Elohim) **did send me before you to preserve life** (literally, *for the preservation of life*). **For these two years hath the famine** been **in the land** (literally, *in the midst of the land*): **and yet** there are **five years, in the which** there shall **neither** be **earing nor harvest**—literally, *neither ploughing nor reaping,* the term ploughing, or earing, *charish* (cf. ἄροσις, *aratio,* Anglo-Saxon, *erian*), being derived from a root signifying to cut. **And God** (Elohim, the use of which here and in ver. 5 instead of Jehovah is sufficiently explained by remembering that Joseph simply desires to point out the overruling providence of God in his early transportation to Egypt) **sent me before you to preserve you a posterity in the earth** (literally, *to keep for you a remnant on the earth,* i. e. to preserve the family from extinction through the famine), **and to save your lives by a great deliverance**—literally, *to preserve life to you to a great deliverance,* i. e. by a providential rescue (Rosenmüller, Kalisch, Murphy, 'Speaker's Commentary'), which is better than to a great nation or posterity, פְּלֵיטָה being understood, as in 2 Sam. xv. 14; 2 Kings xix. 30, 31, to mean a remnant escaped from slaughter (Bohlen), an interpretation which Rosenmüller thinks admissible, but Kalisch disputes. **So now** (liter-

ally, *and now*) it was **not you** that **sent me hither, but God**—literally, *for the Elohim* (sent me). Joseph's brethren sent him to be a slave; God sent him to be a saviour (Hughes). **And he hath made me a father to Pharaoh,**—i. e. a wise and confidential friend and counsellor (Keil, Kalisch, 'Speaker's Commentary;' cf. 1 Macc. xi. 32). Murphy explains the term as signifying "a second author of life," with obvious reference to the interpretation of his dreams and the measures adopted to provide against the famine—**and lord of all his house, and a ruler throughout all the land of Egypt** (*vide* ch. xli. 40, 41). **Haste ye, and go up to my father, and say unto him, Thus saith thy son Joseph, God** (Elohim) **hath made me lord of all Egypt: come down unto me, tarry not: and thou shalt dwell in the land of Goshen.** Goshen, Γεσὲμ 'Αραβίας (LXX.), was a region on the east of the Pelusiac branch of the Nile, extending as far as the wilderness of Arabia, a land of pastures (ch. xlvi. 34), exceedingly fertile (ch. xlvii. 6), styled also the land of Rameses (ch. xlvii. 11), and including the cities Pithon and Rameses (Exod. i. 11), and probably also *On,* or Heliopolis (Josephus, 'Ant.,' ii. 7, 6; Hengstenberg's 'Egypt and the Books of Moses,' p. 42; Gesenius, 'Lexicon,' p. 183). **And thou shalt be near unto me, thou, and thy children, and thy children's children, and thy flocks, and thy herds, and all that thou hast: and there will I nourish thee** (the verb is the Pilpel of כּוּל, to hold up, hence to sustain); **for yet** there are **five years of famine**; **lest thou, and thy household, and all that thou hast, come to poverty**—literally, *be robbed,* from יָרַשׁ, to take possession (Keil), or fall into slavery, i. e. through poverty (Knobel, Lange). **And, behold, your eyes see, and the eyes of my brother Benjamin, that** it is **my mouth that speaketh unto you. And ye shall tell my father of** (literally, *ye shall relate to my father*) all my **glory** (cf. ch. xxxi. 1) **in Egypt, and of all** (literally, *all*) **that ye have seen; and ye shall haste and bring down my father hither.** Calvin thinks that Joseph would not have made such liberal promises to his brethren without having previously obtained Pharaoh's consent, *nisi regis permissu;* but this does not appear from the narrative.

Vers. 14, 15.—**And he** (i. e. Joseph) **fell upon his brother Benjamin's neck, and wept; and Benjamin wept upon his neck.** "Benjamin is the central point whence leads out the way to reconciliation" (Lange). "Here brotherly affection is drawn out by affection, tear answering tear" (Hughes; cf. ch. xxxiii. 4). **Moreover he kissed all his brethren,**—"the seal of recognition, of reconciliation, and of salutation" (Lange)—**and wept upon them.** It has been thought that

Benjamin stood when Joseph embraced him, and that the two wept upon each other's neck, but that the brethren bowed themselves at Joseph's feet, causing the expression to be, "and he wept upon them" (Lange). **And after that his brethren talked with him**—feeling themselves reassured by such demonstrations of affection.

HOMILETICS.

Vers. 1—15.—*Joseph's discovery of himself to his brethren.* I. THE ANNOUNCEMENT. "I am Joseph, whom ye sold into Egypt." 1. *How it was made.* (1) *In privacy.* "There stood no man with Joseph, while he made himself known to his brethren." This was natural. The emotions of the moment were too strong and deep to be shared in or even witnessed by strangers. But it was also merciful. Joseph knew that he could not divulge his secret without a reference to the past, and he would not expose his brothers' guilt and shame in the presence of unsympathising lookers-on. (2) *With tears.* "Joseph could not refrain himself" even "before all them that stood before him," and scarcely had they withdrawn than "he wept aloud." From the first Joseph had a herculean task to perform in keeping his emotion within bounds. This was partly the explanation of the rough treatment he gave his brethren. Had he yielded to the tender feelings which the sight of Reuben and Judah and the others kindled in his breast, he would at once have been discovered. Yet it was all that he could do to avoid detection. Once and again he had to retire from their presence to relieve his bursting heart by "weeping" (cf. ch. xlii. 24 ; xliii. 30). But this time the rising flood of emotion was too strong to be repressed even long enough to admit of his escape. The pathetic eloquence of Judah, the earnest, tearful pleading combined with the sublime and affecting heroism of the man who offered himself to be a bond-man for ever, that his young brother might escape and that his father's heart might not be broken, was too much for the Egyptian viceroy, and he sobbed aloud. (3) *With forgiveness.* Few things are more touching in this wholly melting story than the considerate tenderness of Joseph in sparing his brethren's feelings, and the exquisite delicacy with which he leads them to understand that he cherishes against them not the least resentment. Scarcely has he made the startling disclosure that he was Joseph, than, as if to prevent them from thinking of their sin, he hurries on to ask about their father. Then, as he sees them shrinking in alarm from his presence, expecting doubtless that the hour of recompense for Dothan had arrived, he kindly asks them not to stand aloof from him, but to come near. Again, as he understands the impossibility of their ever shutting their eyes to their deplorable wickedness, he tries to lead them rather to contemplate the wonderful way in which the hand of God had overruled his captivity for the salvation of their entire household. "So now it was not you that sent me hither, but God." Beautiful sophistry of love ! I do not know that Joseph's brethren would believe it ; but it is obvious that in the enthusiasm of his forgiving love Joseph did. 2. *How it was received.* (1) With *surprise.* This was only to be expected. It must have fallen on Joseph's brethren like a thunderbolt. It manifestly struck them into silence. "They could not answer him." (2) With *alarm.* Apprehending vengeance, they were "troubled at his presence," and involuntarily shrank from before him. (3) With *pain.* They were grieved and angry with themselves, not that Joseph was alive, but that ever he had been sold. Many a time during the past years, and in particular since their first visit to Egypt, they had mourned over their sin against the child of Rachel. Now the anguish of their self-reproach was almost more than they could bear. And this was the best sign of its sincerity, that it was intensified rather than diminished by the sight of Joseph (cf. Zech. xii. 10). True penitence, as distinguished from remorse, is sorrow for sin, irrespective altogether of its consequences.

II. THE COMMISSION. 1. *To carry an invitation.* "Haste ye, and go up to my father, and say unto him, Thus saith thy son Joseph, God hath made me lord of all Egypt: come down unto me, and tarry not." 2. *To deliver a promise.* "And thou shalt dwell in the land of Goshen," and "there will I nourish thee." 3. *To explain a reason.* "For yet there are five years of famine ; lest thou, and thy household, and all that thou hast, come to poverty." 4. *To provide an authentication.* "And, behold, your eyes see, and the eyes of my brother Benjamin, that it is my mouth that speaketh unto you." 5. *To supply an encouragement.* "And ye shall tell my father of all my glory in Egypt." 6. *To return with an answer.* "And ye shall haste and bring down my father hither."

III. THE RECONCILIATION. 1. *With tears of joy.* "He fell upon his brother Benjamin's neck, and wept; and Benjamin wept upon his neck." Over the rest of his brothers also as they bowed before him "he wept." 2. *With kisses of love.* "Moreover he kissed all his brethren"—not even forgetting Simeon, who probably had bound him. 3. *With words of cheer.* "After that his brethren talked with him."

Lessons:—See in the character of Joseph, as portrayed in this touching scene, a brilliant constellation of heavenly virtues and holy graces. 1. Of fraternal affection in his tender dealing with his brethren. 2. Of filial piety in his considerate regard for his father. 3. Of eminent devotion in recognising the hand of God in all his past fortunes. 4. Of exquisite sensibility in being so quickly moved to tears.

HOMILIES BY VARIOUS AUTHORS.

Vers. 1—15.—*Darkness turned into light.* Joseph's revelation of himself to his brethren in the atmosphere of the purest brotherly affection and grateful acknowledgment of Divine goodness. Only small natures are ashamed of tears. At first the men who had a great sin upon their consciences were only troubled at the presence of their injured brother, but soon the free and full manifestation of his love turns all their fears into rejoicing. Joseph wept for joy at their return to him, and they were henceforth his brethren indeed. Although for a time we carry the burden of our sins and feel their weight, even though we believe that they are forgiven, still as God reveals himself to us and surrounds us more and more with the embrace of his love, we lose the constraint of our painful remembrance, and rejoice with all our hearts in present peace and future glory.—R.

Ver. 3.—*The great announcement.* Not a stranger, but a brother. Yet they were slow to receive comfort from it. The fact beyond all expectation; the suspicion of the unknown ruler attaching itself to the newly-found brother; the remembrance of their own former cruelty; the doubt whether indeed the past were forgiven, combined to make them "troubled at his presence." Akin to this is the slowness with which the great revelation of the gospel is received, our adoption as sons (Gal. iv. 5) through our brotherhood with Christ; members of Christ, and thus children of God. Not the doctrine, for we are familiar with its terms, but the practical reception of it. The gospel preached is "good-will to men;" the foundation on which it rests is the work whereby the eternal Son became our brother and representative (2 Cor. v. 14). The means of appropriation, belief that God has indeed done this thing for us (Matt. xi. 28). Yet even to those who are longing for peace and salvation the message often seems to bring no real comfort. The truth of the doctrine is admitted, but Jesus is not recognised as a personal, present Saviour. There is a feeling that something not declared lies behind; that there is some unexplained "if," some condition to be fulfilled, some part of the work to be done, ere it can be safe to trust. Conscious of sin, they do not fully receive the offer as made to them such as they are. The fact is, men often want to begin at the wrong end; to make some worthy offering to God ere they have it to give (cf. 1 Chron. xxix. 14; 1 Cor. iv. 7); want to gather fruit ere the tree is planted; to build a spiritual house ere the foundation is laid.

I. GOD'S OFFER PRECEDES FAITH. The gospel proclaims a fact—Christ crucified for us, the fulfilment of Isa. liii. 5. Its primary message is not of something to follow our faith, but of that on which our faith rests. The "foundation" of spiritual life is not our belief but Christ's work (1 Cor. iii. 11). But in practice many seem to regard the right to trust in Christ's work as depending on their being in a fitting state of mind. And thus their mind is turned away from Christ to their own state (cf. Matt. xiv. 30). No doubt there must be a conviction of need ere the Saviour can be welcomed (Matt. ix. 12). But the evidence of that conviction is not our feelings but laying our burden upon the Lord.

II. GOD'S OFFER MUST BE RECEIVED BY FAITH—that is, it must be accepted as it is made; not something else put in its place. God's message is, Trust in Christ.

To do this is to exercise faith. But the answer often is, I must first see whether I have faith. It is as if when our Lord bade the impotent arise, he had answered, I must first feel that I have the power. Faith depends not on accurate knowledge. The gospel is for the ignorant; and what it claims is that we receive it according to the measure of our knowledge, guided by those means of instruction which we possess.

III. GOD'S OFFER IS TO MAKE US WHAT WE OUGHT TO BE. Christ accepted, trusted, is made unto us wisdom, &c. (1 Cor. i. 30). Faith leads to more communion with Christ. The Bible becomes a living voice instead of a dead letter. Channels of knowledge are opened, and daily increasing powers are given where the will is to be really Christ's (John vi. 68).—M.

Ver. 5.—*Providence.* "Now therefore be not grieved," &c. I. THE END IS GOODNESS AND MERCY. 1. To preserve life. 2. To set the seed of the better society in the midst of the corruptions and imperfections of the old. 3. To prepare the way for the higher revelations of the future.

II. GOD'S METHOD OF INSTRUMENTALITIES HIS GLORY. 1. The history of his people, their persecutions, their apparent humiliations, their marvellous victories. 2. The transformation of men, whereby enemies are made friends, &c. 3. The biographies of distinguished servants of God illustrate his grace in bestowing fitness for appointed work.

III. MYSTERIES LOOKED AT FROM A HIGHER POINT OF VIEW BECOME REVELATIONS. 1. *Time* a great revealer. Wait for the Lord. 2. The narrow circle of a family history taken up into the higher sphere of Divine purposes concerning nations and humanity itself. 3. Ultimate vindication of the spiritual men and spiritual principles as against the merely earthly and selfish aims of individuals or communities.—R.

EXPOSITION.

Ver. 16.—**And the fame thereof**— literally, *the voice,* hence rumour (cf. Jer. iii. 9)—**was heard in Pharaoh's house** (having been brought thither doubtless by some of the Court officials), **saying, Joseph's brethren** —it is probable that they would style him Zaphnath-paaneah (cf. ch. xli. 45) — **are come** (*i. e.* are arrived in Egypt): **and it pleased Pharaoh well, and his servants** —literally, *it was good in the eyes of Pharaoh, and in the eyes of his servants* (cf. ch. xli. 37). The LXX. render ἐχάρη δὲ Φαραώ; the Vulgate, *gavisus est Pharao,* i. e. Pharaoh was glad.

Vers. 17, 18.—**And Pharaoh said unto Joseph, Say unto thy brethren, This do ye; lade your beasts, and go, get you unto the land of Canaan; and take your father and your households, and come unto me.** This may have been an independent invitation given by the Egyptian king to Joseph's relatives; but it is more than likely that Joseph had already told him of the proposal he had made to his brethren, and that he here receives a royal confirmation of the same). **And I will give you the good of the land of Egypt,**—*i. e.* the best part of the land, viz., Goshen (Rosenmüller, Lange, and others); though the phrase is probably synonymous with that which follows—**and ye shall eat the fat of the land.** The fat of the

land meant either the richest and most fertile portion of it (Lange, Kalisch), or the best and choicest of its productions (Gesenius, Keil). Cf. Deut. xxxii. 14; Ps. cxlvii. 14.

Vers. 19, 20.—**Now thou art commanded, this do ye;**—an apostrophe to Joseph, Pharaoh manifestly regarding the cause of Joseph and his brethren as one (Rosenmüller, Keil, Lange, and others)—**take you wagons out of the land of Egypt**—the carriages here referred to (עֲגָלוֹת, from עֶגֶל to roll) were small two-wheeled vehicles suitable for a flat country like Egypt, or for traversing roadless deserts. They were usually drawn by cattle, and employed for carrying agricultural produce. Herodotus mentions a four-wheeled car which was used for transporting the shrine and image of a deity (ii. 63; *vide* Rawlinson's edition, and note by Sir G. Wilkinson)— **for your little ones, and for your wives, and bring your father, and come.** Pharaoh meant them to understand that they had not only Joseph's invitation, but his (Pharaoh's) commandment, to encourage them to undertake so serious a project as the removal of their households to Egypt. **Also regard not your stuff**—literally, *and your eyes shall not* (i. e. let them not) *grieve for your utensils* (i. e. articles of domestic furniture), *although you should require to leave them behind* (LXX.,

Rosenmüller, Keil, Kalisch, Lange, *et alii*). The rendering of the Vulgate, *nec dimittatis quicquid de supellectili vestra*, conveys a meaning exactly the opposite of the true one, which is thus correctly expressed by Dathius: *Nec ægre ferrent jacturam supellectilis suæ.* **For the good of all the land of Egypt is yours**—literally, *to you it* (*sc.* shall belong). Ver. 21.—**And the children** (better, *sons*) **of Israel did so: and Joseph gave them wagons, according to the commandment** (literally, *the mouth*) **of Pharaoh, and gave them provision for the way.** Ver. 22.—**To all of them he gave each man changes of raiment;**—literally, *alterations of garments*, i. e. changes or suits of dress (Judges xiv. 12, 13 ; 2 Kings v. 5) ; probably dress clothes for special occasions (Keil, Lange, Murphy); δισσὰς στολὰς (LXX.) ; *binas stolas* (Vulgate)—**but** (literally, *and*) **to Benjamin he gave**—not to make amends for having given him a fright (Lange), but as a special token of fraternal affection (Murphy)—**three hundred pieces of silver,**—literally, *three hundred of silver* (cf. ch. xliii. 44)—**and five changes of raiment**—which renders it probable that the brothers only received two. Ver. 23.—**And to his father he sent after this manner ; ten asses** (*vide* ch. xii. 16) **laden with** (literally, *carrying*) **the good things of Egypt, and ten she asses laden with** (or carrying) **corn and bread and meat** —probably prepared meats, some sort of delicacy (Clarke)—**for his father by the way.** Ver. 24.—**So** (literally, *and*) **he sent his brethren away, and they departed: and he said unto them, See that ye fall not out by the way.** The verb רגז signifies to be moved or disturbed with any violent emotion, but in particular with anger (Prov. xxix. 9 ; Isa. xxviii. 21 ; cf. Sanscr. *rag*, to move oneself, Gr. ὀργή, anger, Lat. *frango*, Ger. *regen*), and is here generally understood as an admonition against quarrelling (LXX., μὴ ὀργίζεσθε ; Vulgate, *ne irascimini* (Calvin, Dathius, Rosenmüller, Keil, Murphy, Lange, Alford, *et alii*), although by others (Tuch, Baumgarten, Michaelis, Gese-

nius, Kalisch) it is regarded as a dissuasive against fear of any future plot on the part of Joseph.

Vers. 25—28.—**And they went up out of Egypt, and came into the land of Canaan unto Jacob their father, and told him, saying, Joseph is yet alive, and he** (literally, *and that he ;* an emphatic assurance which Keil, following Ewald, renders by "yea," and Kalisch by "indeed") **is governor over all the land of Egypt. And Jacob's** (literally, *his*, i. e. Jacob's) **heart fainted** (literally, *grew chill*, the primary idea of the root being that of rigidity through coldness ; cf. πηγνύω, to be rigid, and *pigeo*, *rigeo*, *frigeo*, to be chill. The sense is that Jacob's heart seemed to stop with amazement at the tidings which his sons brought), **for he believed them not.** This was scarcely a case of believing not for joy (Bush), but rather of incredulity arising from suspicion, both of the messengers and their message, which was only removed by further explanation, and in particular by the sight of Joseph's splendid presents and commodious carriages. **And they told him all the words of Joseph, which he had said unto them:**—*i. e.* about Joseph's invitation and promise (vers. 9—11) — **and when he saw the wagons**—probably royal vehicles (Wordsworth)—**which Joseph had sent to carry him, the spirit of Jacob their father revived** (literally, *lived ;* it having been previously numb and cold, as if dead) **: and Israel said,**—the change of name here is significant. The sublime theocratic designation, which had dropped into obscurity during the period of the old man's sorrow for his lost son, revives with the resuscitation of his dead hope (cf. ch. xliii. 6)—**It is enough** (one word, as if expressing his complacent satisfaction) **; Joseph my son is yet alive** (this is the one thought that fills his aged heart) **: I will go down**—"The old man is young again in spirit ; he is for going immediately ; he could leap ; yes, fly " (Lange) **—and see him** (a sight of Joseph would be ample compensation for all the years of sorrow he had passed through) **before I die.** He would then be ready to be gathered to his fathers.

HOMILETICS.

Vers. 16—28.—*Joseph's invitation to Jacob.* I. AUTHORISED BY PHARAOH. Though possessed of the liberty to issue such a commission as he had just intrusted to his brethren, Joseph felt that it would be right and proper to have his sovereign's sanction. Accordingly, on mentioning the matter to the king, the required consent was—1. *Immediately obtained.* "Say unto thy brethren, This do ye ; lade your beasts, and go, get you unto the land of Canaan ; and take your father and your households, and come unto me." It was also—2. *Sincerely given*, as was attested by the royal order to take Egyptian curricles in order to convey the immigrants. "Now thou art commanded, this do ye ; take you wagons out of the land of Egypt for your little ones, and for your wives, and bring your father, and come." And, still further, it was—

3. *Warmly urged*, by a handsome promise—" I will give you the good of the land of Egypt, and ye shall eat the fat of the land "—and an earnest exhortation—" Also regard not your stuff; for the good of all the land of Egypt is yours."

II. ATTESTED BY JOSEPH. Had the sincerity of Joseph stood in need of any demonstration, it would at once have been supplied by—1. The *splendid carriages* he sent from Egypt to convey his father. That they had such an influence upon the heart of Jacob is apparent from the narrative. At first the old man could not bring himself to credit the report which his sons brought; but when he saw the wagons which Joseph had sent to carry him, the spirit of Jacob their father revived. 2. The *valuable presents* he bestowed upon his brethren and sent to his father: to each of the ten " changes of raiment ; " to Benjamin 300 pieces of silver and five " changes of raiment ; " to his father ten asses laden with the good things of Egypt, and ten she-asses laden with corn and bread and meat for his father than Joseph's heart. 3. The *good counsel* he addressed to his brethren : " See that ye fall not out by the way." It was not likely if they disagreed among themselves that they would execute successfully the great commission Joseph had intrusted to them. It was a token of his anxiety for their accomplishing his mission that they should unitedly and lovingly address themselves to its performance.

III. REPORTED BY THE BRETHREN. On arriving at Hebron in the land of Canaan the sons of Jacob hastened to unburden themselves of their marvellous intelligence. The invitation of Joseph was detailed—1. *Faithfully*. On the last occasion on which they had returned to Hebron with tidings concerning Joseph they had lied, and their father believed them; this time, although the old man believed not, what they said was true : " Joseph is yet alive, and he is governor over all the land of Egypt," adding that he wished his venerable parent to go down to Egypt beside him. 2. *Fully*. " They told him all the words of Joseph which he had said unto them," not forgetting to deliver him the presents, and point him to the wagons or royal carriages which his son had sent for his conveyance thither.

IV. ACCEPTED BY JACOB. The strange tale to which the old man listened seemed on its first hearing to be incredible. Such a shock did it give to his feeble sensibilities that his heart almost stopped its beating. Apprehending that they were only mocking his already aged and bereaved spirit, he believed them not. But at length the splendid carriages carried conviction to his mind, and he believed—1. *With holy satisfaction*. " It is enough." Since this was true, he had no desires unsatisfied below. 2. *With paternal love*. " Joseph my son " (what tenderness in the words !) " is yet alive." 3. *With simple confidence*. " I will go down and see him before I die."

HOMILIES BY VARIOUS AUTHORS.

Vers. 16—28.—*The grace of God to his people*. We are now dealing no longer with Joseph's personal history, but brought out into the larger sphere of " *the children of Israel* " (ver. 21). Already it may be said the Egyptian period in the history of the children of Israel has commenced. Pharaoh comes upon the scene and his servants. All the wealth of Egypt is placed at the command of Israel. The men who had been the transgressors against Joseph are now the mediators of the great change in the condition and prospects of the Israelitish race. The effect upon the old man's heart.—R.

Vers. 25—28.—*The believer led to his reward*. Jacob's incredulity conquered. His spirit revived. His resolution taken.

I. OUR ENJOYMENT OF WHAT GOD HAS PREPARED FOR US IS DEPENDENT UPON OUR CONFIDENT BELIEF AND EXPECTATION. 1. Separation from the old for the new life involves a struggle with self, with circumstances, with fellow-men. 2. The future must be laid hold of. We must believe that the better place is prepared for us, that the will of God is good.

II. WE GAIN THE VICTORY OVER NATURAL FEARS, DOUBTS, AND DIFFICULTIES WHEN WE SIMPLY LOOK AT THE FACTS AS GOD HAS SET THEM BEFORE US, BOTH IN HIS WORD AND IN HIS PROVIDENCE. The men were deceivers. The facts, the wagons, the good things, the blessings plainly sent of God, earnest of the future, would not deceive.

III. THE TRUE FAITH IS THAT WHICH GRATEFULLY ACCEPTS THE INVITATION OF DIVINE GRACE, ACTING UPON IT, BOTH BY THE DECISION OF THE WILL AND BY THE DEVOTION OF THE LIFE. "*It is enough, I will go.*"

IV. THE REWARD WHICH IS PREPARED FOR THE TRUE OBEDIENCE IS MUCH GREATER THAN WE CAN ANTICIPATE. To *see Joseph* was the patriarch's anticipation. The purpose of God was much larger for him. Joseph and Jacob met in the abundance of Egypt. The earthly pilgrimage leads to the true Goshen. "*It is enough.*" We follow the voice of our God. It hath not entered into our heart to conceive what is before us.—R.

EXPOSITION.

CHAPTER XLVI.

Ver. 1.—**And Israel** (as the head of the theocratic family) **took his journey**—literally, *broke up*, sc. his encampment (cf. ch. xii. 9)—**with all that he had, and came**—from Hebron (ch. xxxvii. 14)—**to Beersheba,** —where Abraham (ch. xxi. 33) and Isaac (ch. xxvi. 25) had both sojourned for considerable periods, and erected altars to Jehovah—**and offered sacrifices unto the God** (the Elohim) **of his father Isaac.** Probably giving thanks to God for the tidings concerning Joseph (Ainsworth); consulting God about his journey to Egypt (Rosenmüller); it may be, pouring out before God his fear as well as gratitude and joy, more especially if he thought about the stern prophecy (ch. xv. 13) which had been given to Abraham (Kalisch); perhaps commending himself and family to the care of his covenant God (Keil), and certainly praying that God would confirm to him and his the covenant which had been made with his father's (Calvin).

Ver. 2.—**And God** (Elohim) **spake unto Israel in the visions of the night, and said, Jacob, Jacob**—the name Jacob being employed probably to remind Jacob of what he had been (Lawson, Bush, Wordsworth), and repeated *ut magis attentus reddatur* (Calvin). **And he said, Here** am **I**—literally, *behold me* (cf. ch. xxii. 1).

Ver. 3.—**And he said, I** am **God, the God of thy father**—literally, *I am the El* (the Mighty One), *the Elohim of thy father.* Though in consequence of this phrase the section (vers. 1—7), indeed the entire chapter, is usually assigned to the Elohist (Tuch, Bleek, Vaihinger), yet the contents of this theophany are felt to be so substantially Jehovistic in their import (Hengstenberg), that certain critics have been constrained to give verses 1—5 to the Jehovist (Colenso), or, omitting the last clause of ver. 5, to the redactor (Davidson). In ch. xxviii. 13 the designation used is "I am Jehovah, the God of Abraham thy father." As on that former occasion when setting out for Padan-aram, so now, when departing for Egypt, he receives a comforting assurance. **Fear not to go down**

into Egypt. There was reason for Jacob's apprehensions, since Abraham had been in peril in the land of the Pharaohs (ch. xii. 14—20), Isaac had been forbidden to go thither (ch. xxvi. 2), and Egypt had been foreshadowed as a place of servitude for his descendants (ch. xv. 13). מִרְדָה is an irregular infinitive רְדָה for רֶדֶת (cf. דֵעָה for דַעַת, Exod. ii. 4), with מִן prefixed after a verb of fearing (*vide* Ewald's 'Heb. Synt.,' § 336). **For I will there make of thee a great nation** —literally, *for to a great nation will I put thee there* (cf. ch. xxi. 13). Jacob had previously received the injunction, accompanied by the Divine benediction, to be fruitful and multiply (ch. xxviii. 3). Twice over had it previously been predicted that he should develop into a multitudinous people (ch. xxviii. 14; xxxv. 11). The present promise was an indication that the fulfilment of the prophecy was at hand.

Ver. 4.—**I will go down with thee into Egypt;**—not a proof that the Hebrews believed in a local deity following them when they changed their abodes, and confined to the district in which they happened for the time being to reside (Tuch, Bohlen), but simply a metaphorical expression for the efficiency and completeness of the Divine protection (Kalisch)—**and I will also surely bring thee up** again (literally, *and I will bring thee up also, bringing thee up;* a double emphasis lying in the use of the infinitive absolute, with גַּם preceding, as in ch. xxxi. 15, meaning that God would assuredly recover his body for interment in Canaan should he die in Egypt, and his descendants for settlement in the land of their inheritance): **and Joseph shall put his hand upon thine eyes**—*i. e.* will perform for thee the last offices of affection by closing thine eyes in death, a service upon which the human heart in all ages and countries has set the highest value (*vide* Homer, 'Il.,' xi. 453; 'Odys.,' xxiv. 294; Virg., 'Æn.,' ix. 487; Ovid, 'Epist.,' i. 162). "A father at the point of death is always very desirous that his wife, children, and grandchildren should be with him. Should there be one at a distance, he will be immediately sent for, and until he arrive the father will mourn and complain, 'My son, will you not come? I cannot die without you.' When he arrives, he will take the hands of his son, and kiss them, and place them on his eyes, his face, and mouth, and say, 'Now I die.'" (Roberts' 'Oriental Illustrations,' p. 52).

Vers. 5—7.—**And Jacob rose up**—having received new vigour from the vision (Calvin) —**from Beersheba** (it is not probable that his stay there was of more than a day or two's, perhaps only a night's, duration): **and the sons of Israel carried Jacob their father, and their little ones, and their wives,—** "Unlike the heathen tribes around them, and Oriental nations generally, the family of Jacob gave honour to the wife as to the weaker vessel" (Lawson)—**in the wagons which Pharaoh had sent to carry him** (vide ch. xlv. 19, 21). **And they took their cattle, and their goods** (including probably their servants), **which they had gotten in the land of Canaan,**—"Pharaoh had desired Jacob not to regard his stuff, because the good of all the land of Egypt was before him; but he wished not to take advantage of Pharaoh's goodness, or to owe greater obligations to him than he found necessary" (Lawson)— **and came into Egypt,**—a scene depicted on the tomb of Chnumhotep, the near relative and successor of Osirtasen I., at Beni-hassan, represents a company of immigrants, apparently Shemitic in their origin, entering Egypt with their goods, as well as women and children, borne upon asses. Without affirming that this was the Egyptian version of the descent of Israel into Egypt, it may serve as a striking illustration of that event (vide Wilkinson, 'Ancient Egyptians,' vol. i. p. 480, ed. 1878; Brugsch, 'Histoire d'Egypte,' p. 63; Hengstenberg's 'Egypt and the Books of Moses,' p. 37)—**Jacob, and all his seed** (i. e. his descendants) **with him: his sons, and his sons' sons with him, his daughters** (this need not imply that Jacob had more daughters than Dinah, but may include his sons' wives, who are not otherwise mentioned in this enumeration), **and his sons' daughters, and all his seed brought he with him into Egypt.** The date of this event was in the 130th year of Jacob's life (ch. xlvii. 9), and 215 years after the call of Abraham (ch. xii. 4), i. e. B. C. 1728 (Usher), 1885 (Hales); or A. M. 2276 (Usher), 3526 (Hales).

Ver. 8.—**And these** are **the names of the children of Israel, which came into Egypt.** The phrase "which came into Egypt" must obviously be construed with some considerable latitude, since in the appended list of seventy persons, "souls of the house of Jacob which came into Egypt," are reckoned Joseph, who undoubtedly came into Egypt, but not with Jacob, Hezron and Hamul, the sons of Pharez, as well as the descendants of

Benjamin, who probably, and Ephraim and Manasseh, the children of Joseph, who certainly, were born in Egypt. **Jacob and his sons: Reuben, Jacob's firstborn.**

Ver. 9.—**And the sons of Reuben; Hanoch,**—"Initiated or Dedicated;" the name also of Cain's firstborn (ch. iv. 17), and of the son of Jared (ch. v. 19)—**and Phallu,** —"Distinguished" (Gesenius)—**and Hezron,** —"Enclosed" (Gesenius), "Of the Court or Village" (Murphy), "Blooming One" (Fürst)—**and Carmi,** — "Vine-dresser" (Gesenius, Murphy), "Noble One" (Fürst).

Ver. 10.—**And the sons of Simeon; Jemuel,**—"Day of El" (Gesenius, Murphy); in 1 Chron. iv. 24, Nemuel—**and Jamin,**— "Right Hand" (Gesenius, Murphy)—**and Ohad,**—"Joined together" (Gesenius, Murphy)—**and Jachin,**—"Whom God strengthens" (Gesenius), "He shall establish" (Murphy), or Jarib (1 Chron. iv. 24)—**and Zohar,**—"Whiteness" (Gesenius, Murphy); named Zerah (1 Chron. iv. 24)—**and Shaul,**— "Asked for" (Gesenius)—**the son of a Canaanitish woman.** The wives of the other sons, except Judah, were probably from Mesopotamia.

Ver. 11.—**And the sons of Levi; Gershon,** —or Gershom,—"Expulsion" (Gesenius),— **Kohath,** or Kehath,—"Assembly" (Gesenius)--**and Merari,**—"Bitter," "Unhappy" (Gesenius), "Flowing" (Murphy), "Harsh One" (Lange).

Ver. 12.—**And the sons of Judah; Er, and Onan, and Shelah** (vide ch. xxxviii. 3), **and Pharez, and Zarah** (ch. xxxviii. 29; 1 Chron. ii. 4): **but Er and Onan died in the land of Canaan** (ch. xxxviii. 7, 10). **And the sons of Pharez were Hezron** (vide on ver. 9) **and Hamul,** — "One who has experienced mercy" (Gesenius).

Ver. 13.—**And the sons of Issachar; Tola,** — "Worm," "Scarlet" (Gesenius)—**and Phuvah,**—"Mouth"? (Gesenius)—**and Job,** —perhaps an incorrect reading for Jashub ("Turning Oneself"), as in Numb. xxvi. 24; 1 Chron. vii. 1 (Gesenius), which the LXX. adopts—**and Shimron,**—"Watch" (Gesenius).

Ver. 14. — **And the sons of Zebulun; Sered,** — "Fear" (Gesenius)—**and Elon,** — "Oak" — **and Jahleel,**—"Whom God has made sick" (Gesenius).

Ver. 15.—**These** be **the sons of Leah, which she bare unto Jacob in Padan-aram** (i. e. the descendants of Leah's sons which were born in Padan-aram), **with his daughter Dinah** (who probably had continued unmarried after her misfortune in Shechem, and is here mentioned as an independent member of Jacob's family): **all the souls of his sons and his daughters** (reckoning himself, and excluding Er and Onan) were **thirty and three.**

Ver. 16.—**And the sons of Gad; Ziphion,—**

"Expectation" (Gesenius) ; Zephon (Numb. xxvi. 15)—and **Haggi,**—"Festive" (Gesenius)—**Shuni,** — "Quiet" (Gesenius) — **and Esbon,**—"Toiling" (Murphy) ; named Ozni (Numb. xxvi. 16)—**Eri,**—"Guarding" (Gesenius)—**and Arodi,** — "Wild Ass" (Gesenius), "Rover" (Murphy), "Descendants" (Lange) ; styled Arod (Numb. xxvi. 17) **and Areli**—"Lion of El" (Murphy), "Son of a Hero" (Gesenius), "Heroic" (Lange).

Ver. 17.—**And the sons of Asher ; Jimnah,** —"Prosperity" (Gesenius)—**and Ishuah,**— "Even," "Level" (Gesenius)—**and Isui,**— "Even," "Level" (Gesenius) : they may have been twins—**and Beriah,**—"Gift" (Gesenius), "In Evil" (Murphy) — **and Serah**—"Abundance" (Gesenius), "Overflow" (Murphy)—**their sister: and the sons of Beriah ; Heber,** — "Fellowship" (Gesenius)—**and Malchiel**—"King of El" (Gesenius, Murphy), "My king is El" (Lange).

Ver. 18.—**These are the sons of Zilpah, whom Laban gave to Leah his daughter, and these she bare unto Jacob,** even six-teen souls.

Ver. 19.—**The sons of Rachel Jacob's wife** (cf. ch. xliv. 27); **Joseph and Benjamin.**

Ver. 20.—**And unto Joseph in the land of Egypt were born Manasseh and Ephraim, which Asenath the daughter of Poti-pherah priest of On bare unto him** (*vide* ch. xli. 50). The LXX., having probably transferred them from 1 Chron. vii. 14, append the words, Ἐγένοντο δὲ υἱοὶ Μανασσῆ, οὓς ἔτεκεν αὐτῷ ἡ παλλακὴ ἡ Συρα τὸν Μαχίρ. Μαχὶρ δὲ ἐγέννησε τὸν Γαλαάδ. Υἱοὶ δὲ Ἐφραῒμ ἀδελφοῦ Μανασσῆ· Σουταλαὰμ καὶ Ταάμ-Υἱοὶ δὲ Σουταλαὰμ Ἐδώμ. Since they are not to be found in the Samaritan text, Rosenmüller thinks they may have been originally written on the margin, and thence by some subsequent copyist transferred to the text.

Ver. 21.—**And the sons of Benjamin** were **Belah,** — "Devouring" (Gesenius) ; the an-cient name of Zoar, one of the cities in the Jordan circle (ch. xiv. 2)—**and Becher,**—"a Young Camel" (Gesenius)—**and Ashbel,**— "Opinion of God" (Gesenius), "Sprout" (Lange), "Short"? (Murphy)—**Gera,** — "a Grain" (Gesenius), "Fighter"? (Lange)— **and Naaman,** — "Pleasantness" (Gesenius) —**Ehi,**—"Brotherly" (Lange, Murphy) ; = Ehud, "Joining together" (Gesenius), 1 Chron. viii. 6 ; styled Ahiram (Numb. xxvi. 38)—**and Rosh,**—"Head" (Gesenius)—**Muppim,**—"Adorned One" (Lange) ; = Shupham (Numb. xxvi. 38) and Shephupham (1 Chron. viii. 5), "Serpent"? (Gesenius)—**and Huppim,**—"Coverings" (Gesenius), or Hupham (Numb. xxvi. 39) — **and Ard**—"Fugitive," "Rover" (Murphy), "Ruler"? (Lange). In Numb. xxvi. 40 Naaman and Ard are given as the sons of Bela, and the grandsons of Benjamin ; a plausible explanation of which is that Benjamin's sons died early, and were replaced in the list of heads of families by two of Bela's sons who had been named after them (Keil, Murphy, Inglis, *et alii*). In the same table of *mishpachoth* the names of Becher, Gera, and Rosh have been omitted, and that probably for a similar reason that they died either without issue, or without a number of descendants large enough to form inde-pendent families.

Ver. 22.—**These** are **the sons of Rachel, which were born to Jacob: all the souls** were **fourteen.**

Ver. 23.—**And the sons of Dan; Hushim** —"Those who make haste" (Gesenius) ; de-signated Shuham in Numb. xxvi. 42.

Ver. 24.—**And the sons of Naphtali; Jahzeel,**—"Allotted by God" (Gesenius)—**and Guni,** — "Painted" (Gesenius), "Dyed" (Murphy), "Protected" (Lange)—**and Jezer,** —"Image," "Form" (Gesenius, Lange, Murphy) — **and Shillem** — "Retribution" (Gesenius), "Avenger" (Lange).

Ver. 25.—**These** are **the sons of Bilhah,** which Laban gave unto Rachel his daughter, and she bare these unto Jacob: **all the souls** were **seven.**

Vers. 26, 27.—**All** the **souls that came with Jacob into Egypt, which came out of his loins, besides Jacob's sons' wives, all the souls** were **threescore and six; and the sons of Joseph, which were born him in Egypt,** were **two souls: all the souls of the house of Jacob, which came into Egypt,** were **threescore and ten.** Accord-ing to the LXX. the number of Joseph's sons was nine ; and the number of those who came with Jacob into Egypt seventy-five, a number adopted by Stephen (Acts vii. 14). The apparent confusion in these dif-ferent numbers, sixty-six, seventy, seventy-five, will disappear if it be observed that the first takes no account of Jacob, Joseph, Ma-nasseh, and Ephraim, while they are as pal-pably included in the second computation, and that Stephen simply adds to the seventy of ver. 27 the five grandsons of Joseph who are mentioned in the Septuagint version, from which he quoted, or to the sixty-six of ver. 26 the nine mentioned above, consisting of Jacob, Joseph, Manasseh, Ephraim, and Jo-seph's five grandsons, thus making seventy-five in all. There is thus no irreconcilable contradiction between the Hebrew historian and the Christian orator.

Ver. 28.—**And he sent Judah before him unto Joseph** (the noble qualities displayed by Judah had manifestly secured, as they had certainly merited, the affectionate admir-ation and hearty confidence of the aged patri-arch), **to direct his face unto Goshen;**—*i. e.* that Joseph might supply him with the necessary instructions for conducting the

pilgrims to their appointed settlement (Dathius, Rosenmüller, Keil, Lange, Ainsworth,
Murphy, 'Speaker's Commentary'), rather
than that Joseph might meet him in Goshen
(LXX., Vulgate, Samaritan, Kalisch) — and
(having received the necessary directions)
they came into the land of Goshen. The
LXX. read εἰς γῆν 'Ραμεσσῆ, as in ch. xlvii. 11.

Ver. 29. — **And Joseph made ready his
chariot, and went up to meet Israel his
father, to Goshen, and presented himself unto
him;**—literally, *he* (i. .e. Joseph) *appeared*
(the niph. form of the verb, which is commonly used of the appearance of God or his
angels, being here employed to indicate the
glory in which Joseph came to meet his
father: Keil) *unto him,* viz., Jacob—**and he
fell on his neck,**—*i. e.* Joseph fell upon Jacob's neck (LXX., Vulgate, Calvin, Dathe,
Keil, and commentators generally), though
Maimonides regards Jacob as the subject of
the verb *fell*—**and wept on his neck a good
while**—in undoubted transports of joy, feeling his soul by those delicious moments
abundantly recompensed for all the tears he
had shed since he parted from his father in
Hebron, upwards of twenty years before.

Ver. 30.—**And Israel** (realising something
of the same holy satisfaction as he trembled
in his son's embrace) **said unto Joseph, Now
let me die, since I have seen thy face, because thou** art **still alive**—literally, *I will
die this time, after I have seen thy face,
that* (Keil, Kalisch), *or since, thou art still
alive;* the meaning of the patriarch being
that, since with his own eyes he was now
assured of Joseph's happiness, he had nothing
more to live for, the last earthly longing of
his heart having been completely satisfied,
and was perfectly prepared for the last scene
of all—ready, whenever God willed, to be
gathered to his fathers.

Vers. 31, 32.—**And Joseph said unto his
brethren, and unto his father's house, I will
go up** (employed in ver. 29 to describe a
journey from the interior of the country to
the desert, or Canaan, the verb עָלָה is here
used in a courtly sense to signify a visit to a
sovereign or superior), **and shew Pharaoh**
(literally, *relate, or tell, to Pharaoh*), **and
say unto him, My brethren, and my father's
house, which** were **in the land of Canaan,
are come unto me; and the men are shepherds** (literally, *keepers of flocks*), **for their
trade hath been to feed cattle** (literally,
they are men of cattle); **and they have
brought their flocks, and their herds, and
all that they have.**

Vers. 33, 34.—**And it shall come to pass,
when Pharaoh shall call you, and shall say,
What is your occupation?** Pharaoh's inquiry was characteristically Egyptian, being
rendered necessary by the strict distinction of

castes that then prevailed. According to a
law promulgated by Amasis, a monarch of
the 26th dynasty, every Egyptian was obliged
to give a yearly account to the monarch or
State governor of how he lived, with the
certification that if he failed to show that he
possessed an honourable calling (δικαίην ζόην)
he should be put to death (Herod., ii. 177).
**That ye shall say, Thy servants' trade hath
been about cattle** (literally, *men of cattle
are thy servants*) **from our youth even until
now, both we,** and **also our fathers: that ye
may dwell in the land of Goshen.** Joseph
probably desired his brethren to settle in
Goshen for three reasons. (1) It was suitable
for their flocks and herds; (2) it would
secure their isolation from the Egyptians; and
(3) it was contiguous to Canaan, and would
be easier vacated when the time arrived for
their return. **For every shepherd is an
abomination unto the Egyptians.** These are
obviously the words not of Joseph, but of the
historian, and their accuracy is strikingly
corroborated by Herodotus (ii. 47, 164), who
affirms that the swine-herds, one of the seven
castes, classes, or guilds into which the Egyptians were divided, were regarded with such
abhorrence that they were not allowed to
enter a temple or contract marriage with any
others of their countrymen; and by existing
monuments, which show that though the
statement of Josephus ('Ant.,' ii. 7, 5) is incorrect that "the Egyptians were prohibited
from meddling with the keeping of sheep,"
yet those who tended cattle were greatly
despised, Egyptian artists evincing the contempt in which they were held by frequently
representing them as either lame or deformed,
dirty and unshaven, and sometimes of a most
ludicrous appearance (*vide* Wilkinson, 'Ancient Egyptians,' vol. ii. p. 444, ed. 1878).
It has been thought that the disrepute in
which the shepherd guild was held by the
Egyptians was attributable partly to the
nature of their occupation, and partly to the
feeling excited against them by the domination of the shepherd kings (Wilkinson,
Wordsworth, Murphy, and others); but (1)
while this might account for their dislike to
foreign shepherds, it would not explain their
antipathy to native shepherds; (2) if, as
some think, Joseph's Pharaoh was one of the
shepherd kings, it is not likely that this
rooted prejudice against shepherds would
then be publicly expressed, however violently
it might afterwards explode; (3) there is
good reason for believing that the descent
into Egypt occurred at a period much earlier
than the shepherd kings. Hence the explanation of this singular antipathy to shepherds or wandering nomads has been sought
in the fact that the Egyptians were essentially an agricultural people, who associated
ideas of rudeness and barbarism with the

very name of a shepherd (Hengstenberg, Keil, Kurtz), perhaps because from a very early period they had been exposed on their Eastern boundary to incursions from such nomadic shepherds (Rosenmüller), and per-

haps also because from their occupation shepherds were accustomed to kill the animals held sacred by the other classes of the community (Kalisch).

HOMILETICS.

Vers. 1—34.—*The descent of Jacob and his family into Egypt.* I. THE DEPARTURE FROM CANAAN (vers. 1—7). 1. *The journey to Beersheba.* Distant from Hebron somewhere over twenty miles, Beersheba lay directly in the way to Egypt. Yet doubtless the chief motive for halting at "the well of the oath" consisted in the fact that it had been, so to speak, consecrated by the previous encampments of Abraham and Isaac, by the altars they had there erected, and the revelations they had there enjoyed. It is both pleasurable and profitable to visit scenes and places that have been hallowed by the saints of former days; and though now under the Christian dispensation it is true that every place is holy ground, yet few there are who do not feel their religious emotions quickened when they stand upon some sacred spot where holy men have walked and prayed, or saintly martyrs bled and died. 2. *The stoppage at Beersheba.* (1) The solemn act of worship—"Jacob offered sacrifices unto the God of his father Isaac." This he did in obedience to Divine prescription, which had appointed the presentation of offerings as the only acceptable mode of worship, in imitation of the piety of his ancestors, in presence of his assembled household, in supplication of Divine direction with regard to his contemplated journey. (2) The midnight revelation. "I said not unto the seed of Jacob, Seek ye me in vain," was Jehovah's word to Israel in a later day (Isa. xlv. 19); and certainly he never said so either to Jacob's ancestors or to Jacob himself. As formerly he had appeared to Abraham and to Isaac on this very spot, so now he appeared to their descendant; *solemnly*, in the visions of the night; *audibly*, speaking to him in a voice articulate and clear; *earnestly*, saying, Jacob, Jacob, to which Jacob answered, Here am I; and *graciously*, discovering himself as the covenant God of his father Isaac. (3) The encouraging exhortation—"Fear not to go down to Egypt." Abraham had been formerly reproved for going into Egypt, and Isaac prevented from following his example; but here Jacob is both permitted and advised to go. No saint can safely guide himself by following the example of another. What is God's will concerning one man may be the opposite concerning another. It is best to imitate the patriarch, and after asking God's counsel follow where he, his Spirit, word, or providence, may lead. (4) The fourfold promise: "I will there make of thee a great nation"—"I will surely go down with thee"—"I will also surely bring thee up again"—"and Joseph shall put his hand upon thine eyes;" a promise of enlargement, protection, restoration, consolation; a promise, like all God's promises in the gospel, suited to the wants of his servant. 3. *The advance from Beersheba.* This took place with alacrity, for Jacob "rose up;" with unanimity, for they all went, carrying with them their wives and little ones; and with comfort, since they rode in Pharaoh's waggons; and with safety, for it is added that they "came into Egypt."

II. THE COMPANY OF THE TRAVELLERS (vers. 8—27). 1. *Their character.* (1) Descendants of Jacob. They came out of Jacob's loins. In the entire catalogue there is no name that cannot be traced down in a direct line from Jacob. (2) Immigrants into Egypt. The expression of course is used with a certain amount of latitude, since Joseph's sons were born in Egypt, and probably all the family of Benjamin. But the accuracy of the language may be defended on the principle that the historian represents the entire family as having done what was done by its head. (3) Ancestors of Israel. Jacob's sons were the heads of the tribes, and Jacob's grandsons of the families, that subsequently formed the nation. 2. *Their number.* (1) "All the souls were threescore and six;" (2) "all the souls of the house of Jacob were threescore and ten;" (3) according to Stephen the total of Jacob's kindred was "threescore and fifteen souls." For the reconciliation of these different accounts, see the Exposition.

III. THE ARRIVAL AT EGYPT (vers. 28—34). 1. *The mission of Judah.* "And he sent Judah before him unto Joseph," that he (Joseph) "might direct his face unto Goshen." 2. *The coming of Joseph.* (1) Joseph and his father. Learning of Jacob's arrival, Joseph "made ready his chariot and went up to meet Israel his father to Goshen." It was not ostentation, but the impatience of love that caused Joseph to drive to Goshen in the royal chariot. Presenting himself before his aged parent, he falls upon his neck and weeps, unable for a good while to control his tears ; while the old man is so overcome at having his long-lost Joseph once more in his embrace, that he is quite willing to depart: "Now let me die, since I have seen thy face, because thou art yet alive." (2) Joseph and his brethren. Informing them of his intention to report their arrival to Pharaoh, he explains to them that Pharaoh will inquire about their occupation, and directs them how to answer so as to secure their residence in Goshen ; a mark of duplicity in Joseph according to some, but rather a proof of the kindly and fraternal interest he took in his brothers' welfare.

HOMILIES BY VARIOUS AUTHORS.

Ch. xlvi. 1 — 4 ; xlvi. 28 — 30 ; xlvii. 7 — 10. — *The three meetings.* I. BETWEEN JACOB AND GOD. 1. A *gracious* meeting. In the visions of the night, at Beersheba, Jehovah, after a lapse of upwards of a quarter of a century, again makes known his presence to his servant. It was a signal act of gracious condescension on the part of God. 2. A *promised* meeting. As the God of Abraham and of Isaac, Jehovah had solemnly taken Jacob into covenant with himself, and engaged to be with him for guidance and succour wherever he might wander and whensoever he might need assistance ; and such an occasion had manifestly arisen then in the experience of the patriarch. 3. A *solicited* meeting. It is more than likely this was the explanation of Jacob's sacrifices at Beersheba. He was asking God to come to him with counsel and help at the important crisis which had come upon him. 4. An *encouraging* meeting. Jacob got all that he desired and more—words of cheer and promises of love, that sufficed at once to dispel his fears and animate his hopes.

II. BETWEEN JACOB AND JOSEPH. 1. A *longed-for* meeting. How earnestly father and son had yearned to behold one another we can imagine better than express. 2. An *expected* meeting. No doubt Joseph instructed Judah to inform Jacob that he (Joseph) would visit him at Goshen. 3. A *happy* meeting. Those who have passed through experiences in any degree similar to this of Joseph and Jacob meeting after many years, when each perhaps thought the other dead, will not be surprised at their emotion.

III. BETWEEN JACOB AND PHARAOH. 1. An *interesting* meeting. Of age with (probable) youth, of poverty with wealth, of lowly birth (at least, comparatively) with regal dignity, of piety with superstition. 2. An *instructive* meeting. No doubt the monarch would learn something of Jacob's by-past history, and let us hope too of Jacob's God ; and perhaps Jacob would discover something in what he heard from Pharaoh concerning Joseph that would lead him to recognise the Divine hand even more clearly than he did. 3. A *profitable* meeting. Pharaoh got a good man's blessing, and Jacob won a great man's smile.—W.

Vers. 1—7.—*God speaking in the visions of the night.* While there were providential intimations which were clear enough, still the direct revelation of God was necessary for Jacob's assurance. At Beersheba, the consecrated spot, Jacob offers sacrifices in the covenant spirit, and receives in return the message of the covenant God : "I will make of thee a great nation." "I will also surely bring thee up again," *i. e.* in thy descendants. The vision is not a mere personal matter for Jacob's consolation, it is another in the series of Divine revelations which are connected with the development of the covenant.—R.

Vers. 8—27.—*The beginning of the nation.* "The souls of the house of Jacob which came into Egypt were threescore and ten." The number seventy became afterwards a symbolic number among the Israelites — as in the seventy elders of Moses, the seventy of the Sanhedrim, the seventy of the Alexandrian version of the Scriptures, the seventy disciples of the Lord, the seventy heathen nations of the world according to the Jews. There may be something in the combination of numbers. Seventy is 7 × 10. Ten is the symbol of the complete development of humanity. Seven of perfection. Therefore seventy may symbolise the elect people of God as the hope of humanity—Israel in Egypt. In the twelve patriarchs and seventy souls we certainly see the foreshadowing of the Saviour's appointments in the beginning of the Christian Church. The small number of Israel in the midst of the great multitude of Egypt is a great encouragement to faith. "Who hath despised the day of small things?" R.

Vers. 28—34.—*The meeting of the aged Jacob and his lost son Joseph.* I. FUL-FILMENT OF DIVINE PROMISES. Both father and son examples of grace. Reminding us of *Simeon*, "Now lettest thou thy servant depart in peace," &c. (*Judah* is sent forward to Joseph—again a distinction placed upon the royal tribe). The meeting of father and son takes place in *Goshen*. For the people of God, although *in* Egypt must not be *of* it.
II. SEPARATION and DISTINCTION from the heathen world — enforced from the beginning. The policy of Joseph again is a mingling together of—
III. SIMPLICITY and WISDOM. He does not attempt to conceal from Pharaoh the low caste of the shepherds, but he *trusts in God* that what was an abomination unto the Egyptians will be made by his grace acceptable. It was a preservation at the same time from intermarriage with Egyptians, and a security to the Israelites of the pastoral country of Goshen. It was better to suffer reproach with the people of God than to be received among the highest in the heathen land, at the cost of losing the sacredness of the chosen people. A lesson this on the importance of preserving ourselves "*unspotted from the world.*"—R.

Vers. 3, 4.—*Guidance.* Convinced that Joseph really lived, Jacob's first impulse was to hasten to him. But at Beersheba, ere he left the land of Canaan, he sought guidance of God. The promise made him reminds of that at Bethel. Each on the occasion of leaving the land; each revealing God's protecting care. His presence is the only pledge of safety (cf. Exod. xxxiii. 14, 15). It was not a word for Jacob only. Had it been so it would have failed, for Jacob never returned to Canaan. It was like the promise to Abraham (Gen. xvii. 8; cf. Heb. xi. 9, 10). It was the assurance that God's word would not fail. Though he seemed to be leaving his inheritance, he was being led in the way appointed for its more complete possession. God was with him in all. This fully made known to us in Immanuel, without whom we can do nothing, but who by the Holy Spirit abides in his people (John xv. 4; xvi. 14).
I. JACOB'S EXAMPLE. Before taking a step of importance he solemnly drew near to God (cf. Neh. ii. 4; 2 Cor. xii. 8). Not even to see Joseph would he go without inquiring of the Lord. Christ by his Holy Spirit is to his people wisdom (1 Cor. i. 30). The habit of prayer for guidance, or for wisdom to discern the right way, rests on sure promises (Isa. xxx. 21; Luke xi. 13), and is a thoroughly practical resource. We look not for visions or direct manifestations. But guidance is given through channels infinitely varied, though our way may seem strange; and it may be long ere we find that our prayer has been all along answered in the course of events. Why so much neglect of this? so much uncertainty? Because often men do not really seek to be guided by God. Their real wish is to be led as they themselves wish.
II. They who would be sure of God's promises MUST LEAN ON HIS GUIDANCE. They may seem to be led far from what they hoped for. They would fain have great spiritual elevation, and are kept low. They would like to do great work, and are led through homely duties; to have great powers for God's service, and are made weak. The cross must be borne (Rev. iii. 19), and it is sure to take a form they do not like. Otherwise it would not be really a cross. Many would willingly endure pain or poverty if they might thereby gain fame.
III. GOD'S CARE FOR INDIVIDUALS. "I will go down with thee." The universe in its laws shows power, wisdom, and love. But what inspires trust is the confidence that each one is remembered and cared for by God, a confidence called forth by the human sympathy of Christ (Matt. ix. 36; Luke vii. 13; John xi. 35).—M.

EXPOSITION.

CHAPTER XLVII.

Ver. 1.—**Then Joseph came**—literally, *and Joseph went*, up to the royal presence, as he had proposed (ch. xlvi. 31)—**and told Pharaoh, and said, My father and my brethren, and their flocks, and their herds, and all that they have, are come out of the land of Canaan;**—as thou didst desire (ch. xlv. 17, 18)—**and, behold, they** are **in the land of Goshen** (*vide* ch. xlv. 10).

Ver. 2.—**And he took some of his brethren, even five men,**—literally, *from the end, or extremity, of his brethren;* not from the weakest, lest the king should select them for courtiers or soldiers (the Rabbis, Oleaster, Pererius, and others); or the strongest and most handsome, that the Egyptian monarch and his nobles might behold the dignity of Joseph's kindred (Lyra, Thostatus, and others); or the youngest and oldest, that the ages of the rest might be therefrom inferred (Calvin); but from the whole body of his brethren (Gesenius, Rosenmüller, Keil, Kalisch, *et alii*) he took five men—**and presented them unto Pharaoh** (cf. Acts vii. 13).

Ver. 3.—**And Pharaoh said unto his** (*i. e.* Joseph's) **brethren, What is your occupation?** (*vide* ch. xlvi. 33). **And they said unto Pharaoh,**—as directed (ch. xlvi. 34)—**Thy servants are shepherds, both we,** and **also our fathers.**

Ver. 4.—**They said moreover** (literally, *and they said*) **unto Pharaoh, For to sojourn in the land are we come;**—an unconscious fulfilment of an ancient prophecy (ch. xv. 13)—**for thy servants have no pasture for their flocks** (it was solely the extreme drought that had caused them for a season to vacate their own land); **for the famine is sore** (literally, *heavy*) **in the land of Canaan: now therefore, we pray thee, let thy servants dwell** (literally, *and now might thy servants dwell, we pray,* the future having here the force of an optative) **in the land of Goshen.**

Vers. 5, 6.—**And Pharaoh spake unto Joseph, saying, Thy father and thy brethren are come unto thee: the land of Egypt** is **before thee** (cf. ch. xx. 15); **in the best of the land make thy father and brethren to dwell.** Wilkinson thinks it possible that Jacob's sons "may have asked and obtained a grant of land from the Egyptian monarch on condition of certain services being performed by themselves and their descendants" ('Ancient Egyptians,' vol. i. ch. ii. p. 35). **In the land of Goshen let them dwell.** Robinson (ch. i. 78, 79) speaks of the province of es-Shar-Kiyeh, which corresponds as nearly as possible with ancient Goshen, as being even in modern times (1736) exceedingly productive and thickly populated. **And if thou knowest** any **men of activity among them,**—literally, *and if thou knowest, and there be among them, men of strength*—*chayil,* from *chul,* to twist (εἰλύω ἐλίσσω), the idea being that of strength as of twisted rope—**then make them rulers over my cattle**—literally, *and thou shalt make them masters of cattle over that which belongs to me.* "The shepherds on an Egyptian estate were chosen by the steward, who ascertained their character and skill previous to their being appointed to so important a trust" (Wilkinson, 'Ancient Egyptians,' vol. ii. p. 445, ed. 1878).

Ver. 7.—**And Joseph brought in Jacob his father, and set him before Pharaoh.** It has been thought that Jacob's presentation to the Egyptian king was deferred till after the monarch's interview with his sons because of the public and political character of that interview, relating as it did to the occupation of the land, while Jacob's introduction to the sovereign was of a purely personal and private description. **And Jacob**—in reply probably to a request from Pharaoh (Tayler Lewis), but more likely *suâ sponte*—**blessed Pharaoh.** Not simply extended to him the customary salutation accorded to kings (Rosenmüller, Kalisch, Alford, and others), like the "May the king live for ever!" of later times (2 Sam. xvi. 16; 1 Kings i. 25; Dan. ii. 4; iii. 9, &c.), but, conscious of his dignity as a prophet of Jehovah, pronounced on him a heavenly benediction (Murphy, 'Speaker's Commentary,' and others)—*hoc verbo non vulgaris et profana salutatio notatur, sed pia sanctaque servi Dei precatio* (Calvin).

Vers. 8, 9.—**And Pharaoh said unto Jacob, How old** art thou?—literally, *How many are the days of the years of thy life?* **And Jacob said unto Pharaoh, The days of the years of my pilgrimage** (literally, *of my sojournings,* wanderings to and fro without any settled condition) **are an hundred and thirty years.** Since Joseph was now thirty-seven years of age (ch. xlv. 6), it is apparent that he was born in his father's ninety-first year; and since this event took place in the fourteenth year of Jacob's residence in Padan-aram (ch. xxx. 25), it is equally apparent that Jacob was seventy-seven years of age when he left Beersheba after surreptitiously securing the patriarchal blessing (ch. xxviii. 1). **Few and evil have the days of the years of my life been, and have not attained unto the days of the years of the life of my fathers in the days of their pilgrimage.** As Jacob's life fell short of that of his ancestors in respect of duration (witness the 175 years of Abraham, and the 180 of Isaac), so it greatly surpassed theirs in respect of the miseries that were crowded into it.

Ver. 10.—**And Jacob blessed Pharaoh** (as he had done on entering the royal presence), **and went out from before Pharaoh.**

HOMILETICS.

Vers. 1—10.—*Jacob and his sons before Pharaoh.* I. JOSEPH'S BRETHREN BEFORE PHARAOH (vers. 1—6). 1. *Their arrival announced* (ver. 1). " My father and brethren are come out of the land of Canaan, and behold they are in the land of Goshen." 2. *Their persons presented* (ver. 2). "He took some of his brethren, even five men, and presented them to Pharaoh." The import of this selection of five is explained in the exposition. 3. *Their occupations declared* (ver. 3). In answer to the king's interrogation they replied that they were shepherds. They had no desire to deceive, although they had learnt that persons of their trades were not commonly regarded with favour. Joseph indeed had convinced them that in this instance honesty would be the best policy; but even had it been precisely the reverse there is no reason to suppose they would have attempted any sort of prevarication. 4. *Their purpose explained* (ver. 4). It was not their intention to settle permanently in Egypt, but only to find in it a temporary shelter during the years of famine. But while man proposes God disposes. 5. *Their wish stated* (ver. 4). "Now, therefore, let thy servants dwell in Goshen." Though Joseph might have had sufficient power to accord them this favour, it was only courteous to ask it from Pharaoh. "Honour to whom honour is due," is the dictate of right feeling as well as of true religion, and men seldom find themselves the losers by practising politeness. 6. *Their request granted* (ver. 6). Pharaoh at once responded—"The land of Egypt is before thee ; in the best of the land make thy father and brethren to dwell; in the land of Goshen let them dwell." Nay, Pharaoh even exceeded their desires or expectations. 7. *Their promotion indicated* (ver. 6). "If thou knowest any men of activity among them, make them rulers over my cattle." "Seest thou a man diligent in business? he shall stand before kings!"

II. JOSEPH'S FATHER BEFORE PHARAOH (vers. 7—11). 1. *The old man's blessing.* "And Jacob blessed Pharaoh." This was (1) a valuable gift. Once before he had sent a present to one whom he regarded as of vice-regal dignity; but now, when standing in the royal presence, he does not think of material offerings, but presents what must ever be beyond rubies, the intercession of a saintly heart with God on a fellow-creature's behalf. If the effectual fervent prayer of a righteous man availeth much, the simple benediction of an aged saint cannot profit little. (2) Earnestly given. This was shown by the promptitude with which it was bestowed. Immediately the venerable patriarch is ushered into the royal presence he breaks forth into the language of benediction, as if the inward emotion had just been trembling on the heart's lip and ready at the first agitation to overflow. And he for whom he prays was a benefactor indeed, but a monarch and a heathen; and so are Christ's people taught to pray for all men, for kings and such as are in authority, for unbelieving as well as believing, and not for friends and benefactors solely, but likewise for enemies and persecutors. (3) Solemnly confirmed. Spoken on the first entrance to the regal mansion, it was tremblingly re-uttered on departure. Never before had such a prayer been heard within an Egyptian palace. Yet the halls of princes no more than the hovels of peasants are unsuitable for intercessions and supplications. Everywhere and always should be the saint's motto in regard to prayer. 2. *The old man's history.* Gazing with tender interest on the venerable form of the patriarch as, leaning on the arm of his son, he softly steps across the threshold of the magnificent reception hall, the royal Pharaoh, probably struck with his aged and feeble appearance, kindly inquires, "How many are the days of the years of thy life?" to which Jacob with equal circumlocution, with perhaps a little of the garrulousness that is so natural and becoming in the old, but also with a true touch of pathos, replies, "The days of the years of my pilgrimage are an hundred and thirty years; few and evil have the days of the years of my life been, and have not attained unto the days of the years of the lives of my fathers in the days of their pilgrimage." His existence on the earth he characterises as having been—(1) A perpetual pilgrimage, a constant wandering, a continual sojourning, which in his case it had really been — from Beersheba to Padan-aram, from Padan-aram to Canaan, from one location in the land of promise to another, and finally from Canaan to Egypt—but which is no less true of all men's lives; "here we have no continuing city." (2) A short pilgrimage. Adding them up one by one, the days of the years of his pilgrimage might seem to be many; but in the retrospect they appeared what they really were, few and soon numbered; as life, which to the young in prospect looks long, to the old in retrospect is ever short. How amazing is the difference which a change of standpoint produces in the view which the mind takes of man's existence on the earth, as of other things! and how important that we should bear this in mind when numbering our days! (3) A sad pilgrimage. Not only had the days of Jacob's years been few, but they had also been evil, filled with trouble, sorrow, and vexation, more even than that of any of his predecessors. It was one more testimony to the fact that not only is man born unto trouble as the sparks fly upward, but that it is only through much tribulation that a child of God can enter the kingdom.

Learn—1. That prudence becomes a counsellor. This was strikingly exemplified in Joseph's conduct in presenting his brethren before Pharaoh. 2. That honesty advances a suppliant. In the long run Joseph's brethren were better served by their perfect integrity and straightforwardness in Pharaoh's presence than they would have been by resorting to duplicity and equivocation. 3. That piety adorns the old. How beautiful does the character of Jacob, the aged wanderer, appear as it stands before us in Pharaoh's palace, in the westering sunlight of his earthly pilgrimage! "The hoary head is a crown of glory, if it be found in the way of righteousness."

HOMILIES BY VARIOUS AUTHORS.

Vers. 1—10.—*The presentation to Pharaoh.* I. TESTIMONY TO POWER OF CHARACTER. Joseph's influence. The five brethren selected perhaps with a view to their *appearance*, and in the number *five*, which was regarded as a significant number among the Egyptians. The monarch's reception of the strangers due to Joseph's influence. Generally diffused. There is much *graciousness* in the heathen monarch, although partly to be ascribed to national characteristics, for the Egyptians were a very different race from the Canaanites; still we may believe that the conduct of Pharaoh was mostly due to the effect of Joseph's ministry and personal exemplification of the religious life. One true man is a great power in a country.

II. A CONSPICUOUS EXAMPLE of Divine grace. The old patriarch is presented. He plainly impressed the monarch as *extremely aged*, perhaps indicating that the centenarian was a great rarity then among heathen nations. His long life was a long course of gracious dealings. The *effect of a religious life* in prolonging the years is exemplified. It is said that since Christianity obtained its legitimate, or more of its legitimate influence in Europe, the average length of human life has been doubled. Yet, as Jacob confesses, he is *not as old as his fathers.* His life had been a *pilgrimage in a wilderness.* His days *few and evil*, compared with what they might have been. Seventeen years longer they were lengthened out—a testimony to the effect of peace and prosperity in preserving life when it is under the blessing of God. Jacob blessed Pharaoh. The less is blessed of the greater. The two princes stood face to face— the *prince of God*—the *prince of Egypt.*

III. A PROPHETIC FACT: the world shall be blessed through the heirs of the Divine promise. Jacob had much to be thankful for; and although he thanked God first, he teaches us by his example not to forget the claims of fellow-creatures in our gratitude, even though they be separated from us in faith and religion.—R.

Ver. 9.—*The discipline of life.* Few and evil, yet 130 years; and how many blessings temporal and spiritual had been received during their course. We need not suppose him unthankful. But blessings do not of themselves make a man happy. Some worm may be at the root. And in Jacob's case early faults cast a shadow over his whole life. The remembrance of early deceit, his natural shrinking from danger, his family cares, his mourning for Rachel (ch. xlviii. 7) and for Joseph, gave a tinge of melancholy not entirely to be taken away even by receiving his son as it were from the dead. The retrospect of his life seemed that of a suffering man.

I. ABIDING SORROW IS THE FRUIT OF EARLY FAULTS, THOUGH REPENTED OF (1 Cor. xv. 9). It does not necessarily imply separation from God, or doubt of personal salvation. If "a godly sorrow," it works repentance, i. e. a more complete turning to God. But just as early neglect of the laws affecting bodily health produces a lasting effect, however carefully these laws may be attended to in after years, so neglect of God's moral and spiritual laws produces sorrow, varying in kind, and in the channel by which it comes, but bearing witness to the truth of God's unceasing watchfulness.

II. THE DISCIPLINE OF LIFE IS NOT IN ANGER, BUT FOR OUR PURIFICATION. Thus suffering may be a blessing. But for sorrow Jacob might have sunk into taking his ease. His besetting danger was worldly carefulness (ch. xxx. 41). So sorrow, from outward circumstances or from inward reflection, often brings us nearer God. It teaches the vanity of earth that we may realise the blessedness of the inheritance above ; that frail and weary we may cling more closely to the promises of the rest which remaineth (Heb. iv. 9).

III. THIS LIFE IS INTENDED TO BE A PILGRIMAGE, NOT A REST. Its blessedness consists not in present enjoyment, but in preparation for the rest to come (Luke xii. 20, 21). We are reminded that there is a goal to be reached, a prize to be won (1 Cor. ix. 24 ; 1 Pet. i. 3—9), and that the time is short, that we may put forth all our efforts (Eccles. ix. 10) to overcome besetting faults and snares of worldliness. A pilgrim (Heb. xi. 14) is seeking a country not yet reached. The remembrance of this keeps the life Godward. True faith will work patience and activity ; true hope will work cheerfulness under hindrances, and, if need be, under sufferings. And the love of Christ (John xiv. 2, 3), and the consciousness that we are his, will constrain us " to walk even as he walked." For what are you striving ? to lade yourself with thick clay ? To gain honour, renown, admiration, bodily enjoyment ? or as a pilgrim (Num. x. 29) walking in Christ's way, and doing Christ's work ?—M.

EXPOSITION.

Ver. 11.—And Joseph placed his father and his brethren (i. e. gave them a settlement, the import of which the next clause explains), and gave them a possession (i. e. allowed them to acquire property) in the land of Egypt, in the best of the land, in the land of Rameses,—either that district of Goshen in which Jacob and his family first settled (Michaelis, Rosenmüller), or, what seems more probable, the land of Goshen itself (LXX., Keil, Hengstenberg, Kalisch, et alii), being so named proleptically from the town Rameses, which was subsequently built (Exod. i. 11), or, if the town existed in the time of Joseph, and was only afterwards fortified by the Israelites, deriving its designation from the name of its chief city—as Pharaoh had commanded.

Ver. 12.—And Joseph nourished—ἐσιτομέτρει (LXX.), i. e. gave them their measure of corn—his father, and his brethren, and all his father's household, with bread, according to their families—literally, to, or according to, the mouth of the little ones, meaning either in proportion to the size of their families (LXX., Keil, Kalisch, Murphy), or with all the tenderness with which a parent provides for his offspring (Murphy), or the whole body of them, from the greatest even

to the least (Calvin), or completely, down even to the food for their children (' Speaker's Commentary ').

Ver. 13.—And there was no bread in all the land ; for the famine was very sore (literally, heavy), so that the land of Egypt and all the land of Canaan fainted (literally, was exhausted, had become languid and spiritless) by reason of the famine. The introduction of the present section, which first depicts the miseries of a starving population, and then circumstantially describes a great political revolution forced upon them by the stern necessity of hunger, may have been due to a desire (1) to exhibit the extreme urgency which existed for Joseph's care of his father and brethren (Bush), (2) to show the greatness of the benefit conferred on Joseph's house (Baumgarten, Keil, Lange), and perhaps also (3) to foreshadow the political constitution afterwards bestowed upon the Israelites (Gerlach).

Ver. 14.—And Joseph gathered up—the verb, used only here of collecting money, usually signifies to gather things lying on the ground, as, e. g., ears of corn (Ruth iii. 3), stones (ch. xxxi. 46), manna (Exod. xvi. 14), flowers (Cant. vi. 2)—all the money (literally, silver) that was found in the land of Egypt, and in the land of Canaan, for the corn which they bought: and Joseph (who in this matter was simply Pharaoh's steward) **brought the money into Pharaoh's house** (*i. e.* deposited it in the royal treasury).

Ver. 15.—**And when money failed** (literally, *and the silver was consumed, or spent*) **in the land of Egypt, and in the land of Canaan, all** (literally, *and all*) **the Egyptians came unto Joseph, and said, Give us bread: for why should we die in thy presence? for the money faileth** (literally, *and why should we die in thy presence because silver faileth?* i. e. seeing that thou art able to support us).

Vers. 16, 17.—**And Joseph said, Give** (literally, *bring*) **your cattle; and I will give you** (*sc.* bread) **for your cattle, if money fail. And they brought their cattle unto Joseph: and Joseph gave them bread in exchange for horses, and for the flocks** (literally, *and for cattle of the flocks*), **and for the cattle of the herds, and for the asses** (the severity of these terms of sale and purchase was not so great as at first sight appears, since to a famishing people under-fed cattle and starving horses must have been comparatively worthless): **and he fed them**—literally, *led*, in the sense of cared for and maintained, *them* (cf. Ps. xxiii. 2; Isa. xl. 11)—**for all their cattle for that year**—this was the sixth year of the famine (*vide* ver. 23).

Vers. 18, 19.—**When that year was ended, they came unto him the second year** (not the second from the commencement of the dearth, but the second from the consumption of their money), **and said unto him, We will not hide it from my lord, how that**—literally, *for if* (sc. we should speak openly), hence equivalent to an intensified *but*—**our money** (literally, *the silver*) **is spent; my lord also hath our herds of cattle;**—literally, *our herds of cattle also* (sc. have come) *to my lord*—**there is not ought left in the sight of my lord, but our bodies, and our lands: wherefore shall we die before thine eyes, both we and our land? buy us and our land for bread, and we and our land will be servants unto Pharaoh: and give us seed, that we may** (literally, *and we shall*) **live, and not die, that the land be not desolate** (literally, *and the land shall not be desolate*).

Ver. 20.—**And Joseph bought all the land of Egypt for Pharaoh; for the Egyptians sold every man his field, because the famine prevailed over them: so** (literally, *and*) **the land became Pharaoh's.** From this it may be concluded that originally Pharaoh had no legal claim to the soil, but that the people had a valid title to its absolute possession, each man being regarded as the legitimate proprietor of the portion on which he had expended the labour of cultivation.

Ver. 21.—**And as for the people, he removed them**—not enslaved them, converted them into serfs and bondmen to Pharaoh (LXX., Vulgate), but simply transferred them, caused them to pass over—**to cities**—not from cities to cities, as if changing their populations (Onkelos, Rosenmüller, Kalisch), but either from the country districts to the towns (Targums Jonathan and Jerusalem, Lange, Schumann, Gerlach, Murphy), or according to the cities, *i. e.* in which the grain had been previously collected (Keil)—**from** one end of the borders of Egypt even to the other **end thereof.** Not that the people were transported from one side of the country to the other as a high stroke of policy to complete their subjugation (Jarchi, Grotius, Rosenmüller, Kalisch, and others), but that throughout the land they were moved into the nearest cities, as a considerate and even merciful arrangement for the more efficiently supplying them with food (Calvin, Keil, Lange, Wordsworth, Speaker's Commentary).

Ver. 22.—**Only the land of the priests** (so the LXX., Vulgate, and Chaldee render *cohen*, which, however, sometimes signifies a prince) **bought he not; for the priests had a portion**—not of land (Lange, Kalisch), but of food (Keil, Murphy)—assigned them **of Pharaoh** (not of Joseph, who must not, therefore, be charged with the sin of extending a State allowance to an idolatrous priesthood), **and did eat their portion which Pharaoh gave them: wherefore they sold not their lands,**—that is, in consequence of the State aliment which they enjoyed (during the period of the famine) they did not require to alienate their lands.

Vers. 23, 24.—**Then Joseph said unto the people, Behold, I have bought you this day and your land for Pharaoh: lo, here is seed for you, and ye shall sow the land.** This proves the time to have been the last year of the famine; and since the people obtained seed from the viceroy, it is reasonable to suppose that they would also have their cattle restored to them to enable them to till the ground. **And it shall come to pass in the increase, that ye shall give the fifth part unto Pharaoh, and four parts shall be your own, for seed of the field, and for your food, and for them of your households, and for food for your little ones.** This verse is a sufficient refutation of the oft-preferred charge that Joseph had despoiled the Egyptians of their liberties, and converted a free people into a horde of abject slaves. Slave-owners are not usually content with a tax of only twenty per cent. on the gross revenues of their estates. Nor does it seem reasonable to allege that this was an exorbitant demand on the part either of Joseph or of Pharaoh. If in the seven years of plenty the people could afford to part with a fifth part of their produce, might not an improved system of agriculture enable them, under the new regulations, to pay as much as that in the shape of rent, and with quite as much ease? At all events the people themselves did not consider that they were being subjected to any harsh or unjust exaction.

Ver. 25.—**And they said, Thou hast saved our lives** (literally, *thou hast kept us alive*): **let us find grace in the sight of my lord** (*i. e.* let us have the land on these favourable terms), **and we will be Pharaoh's servants.** "That a sort of feudal service is here intended—the service of free labourers, not bondmen—we may learn from the relationship of the Israelites to God, which was formed after the plan of this Egyptian model" (Gerlach).

Ver. 26.—**And Joseph made it a law over the land of Egypt unto this day** (*i. e.* the day of the narrator), **that Pharaoh should have the fifth** part; **except the land of the priests only,** which became not Pharaoh's. The account here given of the land tenure in Egypt, viz., (1) that after the time of Joseph the kings of Egypt became lords paramount of the soil, (2) that the only free landholders in the country were the members of the priestly caste, and (3) that the population generally occupied their farms at the uniform fixed rent of one fifth of their yearly produce, is abundantly corroborated by the statements of Herodotus (ii. 109), that Sesostris divided the soil of Egypt among the inhabitants, "assigning square plots of equal size to all, and obtaining his chief revenue from the rent which the holders were required to pay him year by year;" of Diodorus Siculus (i. 73), that the land in Egypt belonged either to the priests, to the king, or to the military order; and of Strabo (xvii. 787), that the peasants were not landowners, but occupiers of rateable land; as also by the monuments, which represent the king, priests, and warriors alone as having landed property (Wilkinson, Keil). Dr. Robinson quotes a modern parallel to this act of Joseph's, which both illustrates its nature and by way of contrast exhibits its clemency. Up to the middle of the present century the people of Egypt had been the owners as well as tillers of the soil. "By a single decree the Pasha (Mohammed Ali) declared himself to be the sole owner of all lands in Egypt; and the people of course became at once only his tenants at will, or rather his slaves." "The modern Pharaoh made no exceptions, and stripped the mosques and other religious and charitable institutions of their landed endowments as mercilessly as the rest. Joseph gave the people seed to sow, and required for the king only a fifth of the produce, leaving four-fifths to them as their own; but now, though seed is in like manner given out, yet every village is compelled to cultivate two-thirds of its lands with corn and other articles for the Pasha, and also to render back to him, in the form of taxes and exactions in kind, a large proportion of the produce remaining after" ('Biblical Researches,' i. 42).

Ver. 27.—**And Israel** (*i. e.* the people) **dwelt in the land of Egypt, in the country of Goshen; and they had possessions therein** (*i. e.* acquired holdings in it), **and grew** (or became fruitful), **and multiplied exceedingly** —or became very numerous. This was the commencement of the promise (ch. xlvi. 3).

HOMILETICS.

Vers. 11—27.—*Joseph's policy in Egypt.* I. Towards the Israelites. 1. *He gave them a settlement in Goshen.* Though in one sense the land of Goshen was Pharaoh's grant, it is apparent from the story that they owed it chiefly to the wise and prudent management of Joseph that they found themselves located in the fattest corner of the land. In thus providing for them Joseph had without doubt an eye to their enrichment, to their separation as a people from the Egyptian inhabitants of the land, and to their convenience when the day came for their return. Thus we see an evidence of Joseph's fervent piety. 2. *He supplied them with food while the famine lasted.* That he did so without charges to them the narrative explicitly asserts. Nor can Joseph's right so to provide for his own household be legitimately challenged, the more especially that it was owing purely to his wise administration that the king's granaries were filled with corn. That Joseph did so was a proof of his natural affection. 3. *He allowed them to acquire possessions.* That is to say, he secured them in their rights of property while they resided among strangers. He cast around them the protection of the law all the same as if they had been Egyptians. This was a testimony to Joseph's political equity.

II. Towards the Egyptians. 1. *Joseph's policy described.* (1) Before the coming of the famine. Joseph gathered up a fifth part of the produce of the land and stored it up in granaries against the succeeding years of famine, paying doubtless for what he took, and affording the inhabitants of the country an example of economy and foresight. (2) During the continuance of the famine he resold the grain which he had previously collected; in the first instance, for money; in the second instance, when the money failed, for horses and cattle; and in the third instance, when nothing remained between the people and starvation, for their lands and their persons. (3) At the close of the famine Joseph returned to the people their lands, along with seed, and of necessity also cattle for its cultivation, exacting from them in return as rent a fifth part of the produce, the same proportion that he had lifted from them during the seven prosperous years. 2. *Joseph's policy challenged.* It has been vigorously assailed, (1) for its severity; eloquent writers dilating with much indignation on its arbitrary, oppressive, tyrannical, and ferocious character, representing Joseph as little other than a semi-royal despot who little recked of the lives and liberties of his grovelling subjects so long as he could aggrandise himself and his royal patron; (2) for its injustice, being very different treatment from that which had been measured out to the Israelites, who were strangers and foreigners in the land, while they (the Egyptians) were the native population; and (3) for its impiety, Joseph having sinfully taken advantage of the necessities of the people to reduce them by one bold stroke to a condition of abject and helpless slavery. 3. *Joseph's policy defended.* (1) The alleged severity is greater in appearance than reality, since it is certain that Joseph did nothing harsh in selling corn for money so long as people had it, or horses and cattle when money failed, and it cannot be fairly proved that Joseph did not give them full value for their lands. (2) The imputation of partiality will disappear if it be remembered that Joseph's brethren were only expected to be temporary settlers in Egypt, and besides were few in number, so that a gratuitous distribution of corn amongst them was not at all an unwarrantable exercise of philanthropy, whereas to have pauperised a whole nation would have been to inflict upon them the greatest possible injury. (3) The charge of having enslaved a free people may be answered by stating first that the narrative when fairly construed implies nothing more than that Joseph changed the land tenure from that of freehold to a rent charge, and that for the convenience of supporting the people while the famine lasted he distributed them (*i. e.* the country folks) among the cities where the grain was stored; and secondly, that instead of complaining against Joseph as the destroyer of their liberties, the people applauded him as the saviour of their lives.

HOMILIES BY VARIOUS AUTHORS.

Vers. 11, 12.—*The settlement of the children of Israel in Goshen.* I. A CONSUMMATION. Distinctly the *act of Joseph*, under the command of Pharaoh. 1. The fruit of righteousness reaped. 2. The fulfilment of God's word.

Il. A NEW LIFE BASED UPON THE TESTIMONY OF DIVINE GRACE. The weak things have been *proved mighty*, the elect of God has been exalted. The "*best of the land*" is for the seed of the righteous: "The meek shall inherit the earth." Goshen the type of the Divine kingdom.

Vers. 13—26. The policy of Joseph is faithfully employed for his monarch. The advantage taken of the people's necessities to increase the power of the throne is quite Eastern in its character—not *commended* to general imitation, but *permitted* to be carried out through Joseph, because it gave him greater hold upon the government, and perhaps wrought beneficially on the whole in that early period of civilisation. The honour of the priesthood is a testimony to the sacredness which the Egyptians attached to religious persons and things. The earliest nations were the most religious, and there is no doubt that the universality of religion can be traced among the tribes of the earth. An atheistic nation never has existed, and never can exist, except as in France, at a revolutionary period, and for a short time.—R.

EXPOSITION.

Ver. 28.—**And Jacob lived in the land of Egypt seventeen years: so the whole age of Jacob was** (literally, *the days of Jacob, the years of his life, were*) **an hundred forty and seven years.** He had lived seventy-seven years in Canaan, twenty years in Padan-aram, thirty-three in Canaan again, and seventeen in Egypt, in all 147 years.

CH. XLVII. 28—31.]THE BOOK OF GENESIS.515

Ver. 29.—**And the time drew nigh that Israel** (*i. e.* Jacob) **must die** (literally, *and the days of Israel to die drew near*): **and he called his son Joseph, and said unto him, If now I have found grace in thy sight** (not as if Jacob doubted Joseph's affection, but simply as desiring a last token of his love, perhaps also as unconsciously recognizing his son's greatness), **put, I pray thee, thy hand under my thigh,**—an ancient form of adjuration (cf. ch. xxiv. 2)—**and deal kindly and truly with me; bury me not, I pray thee, in Egypt.** On the root קָבַר, to bury (cf. Eng. cover), *vide* ch. xxiii. 4.

Ver. 30.—**But I will lie with my fathers, and thou shalt carry me out of Egypt, and bury me in their burying-place.** The request of the venerable patriarch, while due in some respect to the deeply-seated instinct of human nature which makes men, almost universally, long to be buried in ancestral graves, was inspired by the clear faith that Canaan was the true inheritance of Israel, and that, though now obtaining a temporary refuge in Egypt, his descendants would eventually return to the land of promise as their permanent abode. **And he** (*i. e.* Joseph) **said, I will do as thou hast said**—literally, *according to thy word.*

Ver. 31.—**And he** (i. e. Jacob) **said, Swear unto me** (in the manner indicated in ver. 29). **And he** (*i. e.* Joseph) **sware unto him. And** (having concluded this touching and impressive ceremonial) **Israel bowed himself upon the bed's head.** Though supported by many eminent authorities (Chaldee Paraphrase, Symmachus, Vulgate, Calvin, Willet, Rosenmüller, Delitzsch, Keil, Kalisch, &c., &c.), the present rendering is not entirely free from difficulty, since not until the next chapter is there any mention of Jacob's sickness; while in favour of the reading, "And Israel bowed himself on the top of his staff" (LXX.), it may be urged (1) that it is adopted by the writer to the Hebrews (Heb. xi. 21), (2) that the Hebrew words for staff and bed differ only in the punctuation, and (3) that the action of leaning on his staff was quite as suitable to Jacob's circumstances as turning over and bowing on his bed's head.

HOMILETICS.

Vers. 28 — 31. — *Jacob's residence in Egypt.* I. Jacob's peaceful old age. "And Jacob lived in the land of Egypt seventeen years." After an eventful and chequered pilgrimage of 130 years, during which Jacob had made large experience of the ills of life, having encountered adversity in forms both more numerous and severe than are allotted to most, he had at length reached a happy harbour of rest in the calm contemplative evening of old age, exchanging the anxieties and toils of his previously wandering condition for a home of ease and comfort in the fat land of Goshen, and bidding farewell to all his past tears and sorrows in the enjoyment of the tender care and rich love of Joseph, Rachel's son. Verily, with this old weather-beaten traveller it had become light at eventide. It is noticeable that Jacob lived as long a time in Egypt as Joseph had spent in Jacob's home in Canaan—seventeen years—thus receiving an ample recompense for the affection he had lavished on his son. Let parents be encouraged thereby to love and care for their children in the tender years of infancy and youth; and let children see in Joseph an example of the rich return which they should give their parents, cherishing amid the infirmities of age those who have watched over them, and loved them, and prayed for them with so much solicitude and affection.

II. Jacob's approaching dissolution. "The time drew nigh that Israel must die." It was a time that Israel had now for some considerable period been anticipating. When he stood before Pharaoh he informed that august but benevolent monarch that he reckoned his earthly pilgrimage as good as closed. At least his words imply that he had no expectation of living to the age of his revered ancestors. Consequently he was not surprised, though he perceived that death was rapidly gaining ground upon his feeble steps. Perfectly aware that it was appointed unto all men once to die, he had been piously, while reposing beneath the shadow of Joseph's wing, reckoning up the number of his own days in particular, and had found that the allotted span was nearly passed. Nor does it appear that he was alarmed by the knowledge of that melancholy fact. The man who had fought with God and prevailed was not likely to be dismayed by the prospect of engaging with the king of terrors. He who had been so long in the enjoyment of Jehovah's friendship and salvation would scarcely regard it as a hardship to be translated to Jehovah's presence. Let the saints learn to number their days that so they may apply their hearts to heavenly wisdom ; to live in habitual contemplation of the end, that they may not be afraid when death comes, and to cultivate that holy alliance with the God of salvation which will enable them to say, "For we know that if our earthly house of this tabernacle were dissolved, we have a building of God, an house not made with hands, eternal in the heavens."

III. JACOB'S DYING REQUEST. "Bury me not in Egypt; but I will lie with my fathers, and thou shalt carry me out of Egypt and bury me in their burying-place." This request was addressed to his son Joseph, whom he had hastily summoned to his side. It is not quite certain that at this moment Jacob was confined to bed, or that he was actually so near his decease as he imagined. The probability is that he survived for some little while longer, but that with the knowledge that his departure from the earth could not be long delayed, he desired to leave his last instructions for his funeral with his honoured and beloved son. Accordingly, in a conversation, he explained that he was anxious that Joseph should convey his remains to the family vault at Hebron, and lay them beside the dust of Abraham and Isaac. It was a natural desire that the old man should seek to sleep among his kindred; but the wish had a higher origin than simply the instincts of nature. Canaan was the God-given inheritance of himself and his descendants; and though as yet a long interval must elapse before his children could enter on its possession, he would manifest his faith in the Divine promise by laying his bones in the sacred soil. It becomes God's people to imitate the patriarch in still holding on to God's sure word of promise, although the fulfilment should be long delayed, and in particular to remember that as with Jacob so with them, God's best promises will be realised not on earth, but in the better country, even an heavenly.

IV. JACOB'S DEEP ANXIETY. "And he said, Swear unto me." It might have been supposed that Joseph's word of promise, "I will do as thou hast said," would be sufficient to allay the aged patriarch's apprehensions, but it was not. Remembering the old form of oath which Abraham had employed in connection with Eliezer, he imposed it on his son, as if to bind him by the holiest obligations to fulfil his last request. Joseph, we may be sure, would have honoured his aged parent's wish without the additional ceremony of swearing; but inasmuch as it was not necessarily sinful, and it would tend to dispel his father's fears, he consented to the proposal, "and he sware unto him." Jacob perhaps might have dispensed with the oath, and certainly Christians should be satisfied with a simple "yea" or "nay," remembering that whatsoever is more than these cometh of evil; but sons may learn from Joseph to bear with an aged parent's infirmities and to humour his inclinations, when these are not sinful.

V. JACOB'S SOLEMN WORSHIP. "And Jacob bowed himself upon the bed's head," or "worshipped, leaning upon the top of his staff." But whatever was the exact position of the patriarch, his exercise was devotion. With reverent inclination of his aged head he poured out his soul in grateful adoration to his God, who had enabled him so successfully to arrange everything connected with his funeral that he had now nothing left to do but die. And in this too the patriarch might advantageously be followed by his spiritual children. Happy they who before being summoned to put off this tabernacle are able to say, "Father, I have finished the work thou gavest me to do!" It is a special mercy for which they may well give God thanks.

HOMILIES BY VARIOUS AUTHORS.

Vers. 27—31.—*The sunset of a long life.* There is a touching beauty in this scene between the veteran Israel and the prosperous Joseph.

I. An illustration of HUMAN INFIRMITY. The *supplanter,* the *prince of God,* must succumb at last to the King of Terrors. "*Israel must die.*" Yet he is not afraid of death.

II. STRENGTH IS MADE PERFECT IN WEAKNESS. Grace appears brightest at the end. His gray hairs have *not* been "brought with sorrow to the grave," although he feared they would. The lost son is the comforter of his last days; to him he commits his dust to be laid with his fathers.

III. PERSEVERANCE IS NOT THE FRUIT OF MAN'S PERFECTION, BUT OF GOD'S MERCY.

Jacob is faithful to the covenant spirit to the end, although in many respects his character was a mingled one. Yet he clung to the Divine word. Seventeen years could not wear out his love for the promised land. He knew the solemnity of an oath, for had he not himself sworn and changed not? He would leave behind him in his last wishes a *testimony* which would help to keep his children faithful. "*And Israel bowed himself upon the bed's head.*" The LXX., and the Syriac, and the Itala versions, with the reference in Heb. xi. 21, by a slight change in the Hebrew vowels, have rendered the words "*he worshipped upon the top of his staff*"—*i. e.* leaning on that which had borne him through his pilgrimage, and thus, as it were, declaring the long journey at an end. But whether he turned towards the bed's head, as it were away from the world towards God, or leaned on his staff, the idea is the same—he *bowed himself*, like Simeon, saying, "Now, Lord, lettest thou thy servant depart in peace." It was a lovely sunset after a day of many clouds and much weariness and fear.—R.

Vers. 28—31.—*Jacob's apprehension.* I. WHAT IT WAS. 1. It was *not anxiety about temporal support*, for that had been generously made sure to him by his son Joseph. 2. It was *not concern about the future fortunes of his family*, for these had been graciously taken under God's protection. 3. It was *not uncertainty as to his own personal acceptance with Jehovah*, for of that he had long ago been assured. 4. It was scarcely even *fear of his approaching death*, for besides being a thought with which Jacob had long been familiar, to a weary pilgrim like him the event itself would not be altogether unwelcome. 5. It was *dread lest his lifeless body should be interred in Egypt*, far from the graves of his ancestors in the holy land. II. WHENCE IT AROSE. 1. *From the deeply-seated instinct in human nature*, which makes men wish, if possible, to sleep beside their fathers and friends. Though religion teaches us to believe that every spot on earth is in a manner holy ground, yet it does not induce a spirit of indifference as to the last resting-place where we shall lie. 2. From *a firm faith in the Divine promise* that his descendants should yet return to Canaan. Even if Jacob did not anticipate that this would immediately occur, if, as is probable, he had already dark forebodings that the period of exile and servitude spoken of by Jehovah to Abraham was about to commence, he was yet able to detect a silver lining in the cloud, to see the happy time beyond, when his children, in accordance with the promise "I will surely bring thee up again," should return home to their presently abandoned inheritance. III. HOW IT WAS REMOVED. 1. By Joseph's *promise.* Requested by his aged parent to convey his body back to Canaan, when the life had departed, Joseph solemnly engages to carry out that parent's wishes to the letter. "I will do as thou hast said." 2. By Joseph's *oath.* As if to remove every possible ground of apprehension, the old man further binds his son by an appeal to heaven. "And he said, Swear unto me; and he (Joseph) sware unto him." The venerable patriarch's anxieties were at an end. "And Israel bowed himself upon the bed's head."—W.

EXPOSITION.

CHAPTER XLVIII.

Ver. 1.—**And it came to pass after these things** (*i. e.* the events recorded in the preceding chapter, and in particular after the arrangements which had been made for Jacob's funeral), **that one told Joseph,**—the verb וַיֹּאמֶר is here used impersonally, or passively, for "one told," or "it was told," to Joseph (LXX., ἀπηγγέλη; Vulgate, *nunciatum est;* Rosenmüller, Keil, Kalisch, Murphy, *et alii*); or probably emphatically, by way of calling attention to the circumstance—de-

noting perhaps a special messenger (Tayler Lewis) — **Behold, thy father is sick.** The word in the original conveys the idea of being worn down or becoming infirm through age or disease, and may suggest the notion that Jacob was now regarded as rapidly approaching dissolution. **And he took with him his two sons, Manasseh and Ephraim** —who at this time must have been about eighteen or twenty years of age (Keil), and who appear to have accompanied their father from respectful affection to their aged relative (Murphy), or to have been taken in the hope that "the words of their blessed grandfather would make an indelible impression on their hearts" (Lawson), rather than in order to obtain from Jacob "a pledge of their unqualified admission as members of his house," of their exclusion from which Joseph was not altogether groundlessly apprehensive, in consequence of their being the children of an Egyptian mother (Kalisch).

Ver. 2.—**And** one **told Jacob** (וַיַּגֵּד, also used impersonally, like וַיֹּאמֶר in ver. 1), **and said, Behold, thy son Joseph cometh unto thee: and Israel**—the significance of this change of name it is impossible to overlook (cf. ch. xlv. 27, 28)—**strengthened himself** (for the work which, as head of the theocratic family, he now felt himself inwardly moved to perform), **and sat upon the bed**—i. e. he raised himself up to a sitting posture.

Vers. 3, 4.—**And Jacob said unto Joseph,** —recalling the experiences of early days— **God Almighty**—El Shaddai (vide ch. xvii. 1) —**appeared unto me at Luz**—i. e. Bethel (vide ch. xxviii. 17, 19 ; xxxv. 6, 15)—**in the land of Canaan, and blessed me, and said unto me, Behold, I will make thee fruitful, and multiply thee, and I will make of thee a multitude of people ; and will give this land to thy seed after thee for an everlasting possession.** It is obvious that Jacob principally has in his mind the theophany at Bethel on his return from Padan-aram.

Vers. 5, 6.—**And now thy two sons, Ephraim and Manasseh, which were born unto thee in the land of Egypt** (vide ch. xli. 50—52) **before I came unto thee into Egypt,** — this would almost seem to imply that Jacob knew of Joseph's having had sons born to him since his (Jacob's) arrival at Goshen—**are mine** (i. e. I shall reckon them as my own sons, giving them an equal place with the other members of my family) ; **as Reuben and Simeon, they shall be mine**— literally, Ephraim and Manasseh, as Reuben and Simeon, shall be mine. The double portion thus conferred upon Joseph in the persons of his sons was a practical investiture of him with the birthright of which Reuben had been deprived (1 Chron. v. 1), in respect at least of the inheritance ; in respect of the honour of being the next connecting link in the chain of redemption, leading on and down to the coming of the Saviour, the birthright appears to have been transferred to Judah (ch. xlix. 8—10). **And thy issue, which thou begettest after them, shall be thine** (i. e. shall be reckoned in thine own family), and **shall be called after the name of their brethren in their inheritance.** They should not form heads of separate tribes, but be ranked under the banners of Ephraim and Manasseh. It is uncertain whether Joseph had more sons than two (vide supra) ; if he had, they were included in the

families of their brethren, as here directed (cf. Numb. xxvi. 28—37 ; 1 Chron. vii. 14—29).

Ver. 7.—**And as for me** (literally, and I, the pronoun being emphatic), **when I came from Padan,**—literally, in my coming, i. e. while on my journey, from Padan, or Padan-aram. This is the only place where the shorter designation is employed (cf. ch. xxv. 20)—**Rachel**—the mention to Joseph of his beloved mother could not fail to kindle emotion in his breast, as obviously it had revived a pang of sorrow in that of the old man—" the remembrance of the never-to be-forgotten one causing a sudden spasm of feeling" (Delitzsch)—**died by me**—not for me in the sense of sharing with me my toils and perils, and so bringing on herself the deadly travail which cut her off (Lange), which is too subtle and metaphysical in its refinement ; but either upon me, i. e. as an heavy affliction falling on me (Rosenmüller, Gesenius, Murphy, et alii) ; or at my side, i. e. near me (Keil, Wordsworth, 'Speaker's Commentary') ; or perhaps to me, meaning, This happened to me, or, I saw Rachel die (Kalisch) ; or possibly with a touch of tender emotion, Rachel to me, i. e. my Rachel died (Tayler Lewis)—**in the land of Canaan in the way, when yet** there was **but a little way**— literally, a length of ground ; the LXX. add ἱππόδρομος, meaning probably such a distance as a horse can go without being over-worked (vide ch. xxxv. 16)—**to come unto Ephrath : and I buried her there in the way of Ephrath ; the same is Bethlehem.**

Ver. 8.—**And Israel beheld Joseph's sons, and said, Who** are these ? The failing sight of the patriarch (ver. 10) probably was the reason why he did not sooner recognise his grandchildren, and the fact that he did not at first discern their presence shows that his adoption of them into the number of the theocratic family was prompted not by the accidental impulse of a natural affection excited through beholding the youths, but by the inward promptings of the Spirit of God.

Ver. 9.—**And Joseph said unto his father, They** are **my sons** (of whom you have just spoken), **whom God hath given me in this** place. It speaks highly in Joseph's favour that, after listening to Jacob's promise regarding Ephraim and Manasseh, he did not seek to draw his aged father's attention to the young men before him, but quietly waited for Jacob to take the initiative in any further communications of a personal nature that he might wish to address to them. **And he** (i. e. Jacob) **said Bring them, I pray thee, unto me, and I will bless them.**

Ver. 10.—**Now** (literally, and) **the eyes of Israel were dim** (literally, heavy) **for age,** so that he **could not see.** This explains why he did not earlier recognise his grandchildren, and why he asked them to be set close by his bed. **And he** (their father) **brought them near unto him ; and he** (their old grandfather) **kissed them, and embraced them** (cf. Isaac's blessing of Jacob, ch. xxvii. 26, 27).

Ver. 11.—**And Israel said unto Joseph, I had not thought to see thy face ; and, lo, God** (Elohim) **hath shewed me also thy seed.** The first half of Israel's utterance is rendered by the LXX. "'Ιδού τοῦ προσώπου σου οὐκ ἐστερήθην."

Ver. 12.—**And Joseph brought them out from between his knees** (literally, *from near his knees*, i. e. the knees of his father, who while in the act of embracing had drawn them into that position), **and he** (viz. Joseph) **bowed himself with his face to the earth.** The reading "and they bowed themselves," *i. e.* Ephraim and Manasseh (Samaritan, Michaelis),and the rendering καὶ προσκύνησαν αὐτῷ (LXX.), are incorrect.

Ver. 13.—**And Joseph took them both, Ephraim in his right hand toward Israel's left hand, and Manasseh in his left hand toward Israel's right hand, and brought them near unto him.** Joseph naturally expected that Jacob's right hand would fall upon the head of Manasseh, as the firstborn, although with regard to even this a doubt might have been suggested if he had remembered how Isaac had been preferred to Ishmael, and Jacob to Esau.

Ver. 14.—**And Israel stretched out his right hand, and laid it upon Ephraim's head,** —the first instance of the imposition of hands being used as a symbol of blessing. Though not necessarily connected with the form of benediction, it is not without a natural fitness to suggest the transmission of spiritual benefit. Accordingly it afterwards became the recognised mode of conveying to another some supernatural power or gift, and was employed in the Old Testament Church in the dedication of priests (Numb. xxviii. 18, 23 ; Deut. xxxiv. 9), and in the New in the ordination of Christian office-bearers (Acts vi. 6 ; viii. 17 ; 1 Tim. iv. 14 ; 2 Tim. i. 6), as well as by the Saviour and his apostles in the performance of many of their miracles (Matt. xix. 13 ; Mark viii. 23, 25 · Acts ix. 17 ; six. 6 ; xxviii. 8)—**who** was **the younger** (literally, *and he the little one*, i. e. the younger), **and his left hand upon Manasseh's head, guiding his hands wittingly ;**—literally, *he placed his hands prudently*, i. e. of set purpose, the piel of שָׂכַל, to look at, conveying the intensive signification of acting with prudence and deliberation (Gesenius, Fürst); *intelligere fecit manus suas hoc est, docte, scite, et perite imposuit eis manus* (Vatablus, *vide* Glass. ' Phil. Tract.,' p. 761) ; a rendering of

the words which has been adopted by the best scholars (Calvin, Dathe, Rosenmüller, Keil, Kalisch, Murphy, Tayler Lewis, and others), though the translation, "he crossed his hands," which regards שָׂכַל as the piel of an unused root signifying to intertwine, ἐναλλάξ τὰς χεῖρας (LXX.), *commutans manus* (Vulgate), is not entirely destitute of learned supporters (Targums of Jonathan and Jerusalem, Pererius, Knobel, Delitzsch, Gerlach, and others)—**for Manasseh was the firstborn.**

Vers. 15, 16.—**And he blessed Joseph** (*i. e.* in his sons), **and said, God,**—literally, *the Elohim.* The use of Elohim in a passage (vers. 15—19) which is undoubtedly Jehovistic in its import, and is by advanced critics (Davidson, Colenso) assigned to that writer, has been explained (Hengstenberg) as an indication that " the great spiritual Sun, Jehovah, was at that time," viz., at the entrance of the captivity, "concealed behind a cloud from the chosen race ;" but, without resorting to any such doubtful hypothesis, it is sufficient to observe that Jacob practically identifies the Elohim spoken of with Jehovah, while by using the former expression he conveys the thought that the blessing about to be pronounced proceeded forth, not from Deity in general, but from the particular Elohim who had graciously manifested himself in the manner after described—**before whom my fathers Abraham and Isaac did walk,**—(cf. ch. xvii. 1 ; xxiv. 40) the God here referred to was one who had "a face," or manifested presence ; in other words, was Jehovah—**the God which fed me**—literally, *the Elohim shepherding me* (cf. Ps. xxiii. 1 ; xxviii. 9)—**all my life long**—literally, *from as yet* (sc. I was), *i. e.* from the beginning of my existence, ἐξ νεότητος (LXX.)—**unto this day, the Angel**—the Maleach here spoken of cannot possibly be a creature, since he is explicitly identified with Elohim, but must have been the Jehovah Angel with whom Jacob wrestled at the ford of Jabbok (ch. xxxii. 23—29). The reading of the Samaritan codex, הַמֶּלֶךְ, the king, is open to suspicion—**which redeemed me from all evil,**—literally, *the* (sc. angel) *redeeming me;* the first use of the term *goël*, from גָּאַל, to buy back or redeem (Gesenius), to separate or untie (Fürst), or to stain as with blood, hence to be stained or polluted, as one who suffers a kinsman's blood to go unavenged, hence to remove the stain of blood by taking vengeance on the murderer (Tayler Lewis). Applied under the law to the next of kin (Levit. xxv. 25 ; xxvii. 13, 15, 19, &c., &c.), it is also used of God redeeming men, and especially Israel, from captivity (Exod. vi. 6 ; Isa. xliii. 1). In this sense it was employed by Jacob (cf. ch. xlviii.

16 with xlix. 18) and by Job (xix. 21) to describe the Divine Rescuer who had delivered them from ill both temporal and spiritual, and who was to complete his emancipating work by ultimately ransoming them from the power of the grave. The *Goël* to whom both Jacob and Job looked forward, and of whom both Moses and the prophets testified, was Christ (Gal. iii. 11 ; Titus ii. 14 ; 1 Pet. i. 18)—**bless the lads.** The singular verb suggests to Luther the reflection that the writer "*conjungit in uno opere benedicendi tres personas, Deum Patrem, Deum Pastorem, et Angelum,*" from which he draws the obvious conclusion, "*sunt igitur hi tres unus Deus et unus benedictor.*" **And let my name be named on them, and the name of my fathers Abraham and Isaac ;**—literally, *and my name and the name of my fathers shall be named in them,* i. e. they shall be counted my sons and the children of my ancestors, though born of thee (Calvin, Rosenmüller, Lawson, Murphy, Wordsworth, and others) ; or, May this name be preserved by them, and the race of Abraham propagated by them ! may the fathers and I live in them ! (Gerlach, Kalisch) ; or, what seems more appropriate than either, May the grace and salvation enjoyed by my fathers and myself be renewed in them ! (Keil, Lange) —**and let them grow into a multitude in the midst of the earth.** The original conveys the sense of swarming like the fishes of the sea, the ἅπαξ λεγόμενον, דָּגָה (from which comes the term דָּג, a fish, from being so wonderfully prolific), signifying to cover over with a multitude (*vide* Gesenius, 'Lexicon,' *sub voce*).

Ver. 17.—**And when** (literally, *and*) **Joseph saw that his father laid** (or was laying) **his right hand upon the head of Ephraim, it displeased him** :—literally, *and it was evil in his eyes* (cf. ch. xxviii. 8)—**and** (supposing his father had made a mistake) **he held up** (or took hold of) **his father's hand, to remove it from Ephraim's head unto Manasseh's head.**

Ver. 18.—**And Joseph said unto his father, Not so, my father : for this is the firstborn ; put thy right hand upon his head.** "From Joseph's behaviour we cannot certainly infer that, like Isaac, he loved the firstborn better than the youngest ; but he was sorry that an honour was not given to the eldest which he would naturally expect, and bestowed on the youngest, who did not expect it, and who would not have been hurt by the want of it" (Lawson).

Ver. 19.—**And his father refused, and said, I know** it, **my son, I know** it : **he also shall become a people, and he also shall be great : but truly** (literally, *and over against that* ; אוּלָם, the strongly adversative particle, signifying that which stands in front of, or opposite to, another thing) **his younger bro-**

ther **shall be greater than he** (cf. Numb. i. 33 with i. 35 ; ii. 19 with ii. 21), **and his seed shall become a multitude of nations**—literally, *shall be a fulness of nations.* In the time of Moses this prediction began to realise itself. In the first census which took place in the wilderness the tribe of Ephraim had 40,500 men, while that of Manasseh could only reckon 32,200 ; in the second the numbers received a temporary alteration, Ephraim counting only 32,500, and Manasseh 52,700 ; but after the conquest the ascendancy of Ephraim was restored, so that she easily assumed the lead among the ten northern tribes, and acquired a name and an influence only second to that of Judah (cf. Judges iv. 5 ; v. 14 ; viii. ; xii.).

Ver. 20.—**And he** (*i. e.* Jacob) **blessed them that day, saying, In thee** (*i. e.* in Joseph, who is still identified with his sons) **shall Israel** (the nation) **bless, saying, God** (Elohim, the supreme source of all blessing) **make thee as Ephraim and as Manasseh : and he set Ephraim before Manasseh** — "in the position of his hands, and the terms of the blessing" (Keil).

Ver. 21.—**And Israel** (Jacob) **said unto Joseph, Behold, I die : but God** (Elohim) **shall be with you, and bring you again unto the land of your fathers.** "For Joseph and his children a great promise and dispensation" (Lange).

Ver. 22.—**Moreover** (literally, *and*) **I have given**—or, I give (Keil), I will give (Kalisch), the preterite being used prophetically as a future, or even as a present, the event being regarded, from its certainty, as already accomplished. It is thus not absolutely clear that Jacob here alludes to any past transaction in his own personal history—**to thee one portion**—literally, *one shoulder,* or ridge, or elevated tract of land, שְׁכֶם ; *unam partem* (Vulgate), with which agree several of the ancient versions (Onkelos, Syriac)—**above thy brethren, which I took**—or take (Keil), or shall take (Kalisch)—**out of the hand of the Amorite**—a general name for the inhabitants of Canaan (*vide* ch. xv. 16)—**with my sword and with my bow.** As Scripture has preserved no account of any military exploit in the history of Jacob such as is here described, the patriarch's language has been understood as referring to the plot of ground at Shechem which Jacob purchased of Hamor the father of Shechem (ch. xxxiii. 19), and as signifying either that he had captured it by sword and bow, in the sense that his sons at the head of his armed retainers had put the inhabitants of the town to the sword, and so taken possession of the entire district (Calvin, Rosenmüller, Murphy) ; or that, though he had peacefully paid for it, he yet required at a subsequent period to recover it by force of arms from the Canaanites (Lawson, Bush, Wordsworth); or that after the terrible tragedy at Shechem, when God put a fear upon the surrounding cities, Jacob and his sons stood in the gate of Shechem in the armed expectation of a hostile attack, and so may be said to have taken it by sword and bow (Rabbi Solomon, Lyra, Willet). It seems, however, better to regard the words as a prophetic utterance pointing forward to the conquest of Canaan, which Jacob here represents himself, in the persons of his descendants, as taking from the Amorites by means of sword and bow, and as intimating that the tribes of Ephraim and Manasseh would receive a double portion of the inheritance, the word שְׁכֶם being probably designed to convey a hint that the tract to be in future assigned to Joseph's descendants would be the region round about the ancient city Shechem (Ainsworth, Keil, Kalisch, Lange, &c.).

HOMILETICS.

Vers. 1—22.—*Jacob's dying utterances.* I. AN OLD MAN'S SICK-BED. "It came to pass after these things, that one told Joseph, Behold, thy father is sick." In this the venerable patriarch—1. *Suffered an experience that is common to all.* For nearly three half-centuries had this weather-beaten pilgrim been able to maintain himself erect amid the numberless vicissitudes of life. Strong, healthy, vigorous, and active too, he appears to have been until now, notwithstanding the peculiarly trying and chequered career through which he had passed. But all the while, the rolling years, as they glided softly by, had been touching him with their invisible fingers, and leaving on him their ineffaceable impressions, imperceptibly but surely relaxing his corded muscles, whitening and diminishing his manly locks, loosening his joints, making his step less lithe and firm, and generally draining away his strength. And now, at length, he had arrived where all men must, sooner or later, come, if they have a death-bed at all, no matter how bright may be their eye, or how ruddy their countenance, or how stalwart their frame, or how herculean their strength, to that period of infirmity and sickness that precedes dissolution. 2. *Enjoyed a privilege accorded to few.* Immediately that he had fallen sick, a messenger, despatched from Goshen, carried tidings to the vice-regal palace in the great metropolis, and Joseph, his beloved son, accompanied by his two boys, Ephraim and Manasseh, at once descended to express his sympathy and lend his aid. Not to many is it granted, in this world of separations and bereavements, to have all their family around them when they breathe their last, or to have their Josephs even, to put their hands upon the sinking eyelids, and gently close them in the sleep of death. Venerable pilgrim! Much afflicted in thy riper years, thou wast greatly comforted in thy latter days.

II. AN OLD PILGRIM'S REMINISCENCES. Learning of Joseph's arrival, the aged father musters his rapidly failing strength, and, recognising within his withered bosom the stirrings of the old prophetic spirit, prepares himself, by sitting upright in his bed, for delivering whatever communication should be put into his trembling lips. Casting his thoughts back upon the past with that fond delight with which the aged recall the story of their younger years, he relates to Joseph—1. *How El Shaddai had appeared to him* at Luz, or Bethel, in the land of Canaan, as he returned from Mesopotamia. 2. *What God had promised him* on that memorable occasion, that he should grow into a multitude of people, who should eventually possess the land, adding by way of parenthesis, at this stage, that in view of that inheritance to come he intended to adopt the sons of Joseph as his own; and 3. *The great affliction that had happened to him* almost immediately after in the loss of Rachel, Joseph's mother, to whose premature death and affecting burial "in the way of Ephrath" the old man, even at that long distance of time, cannot refer without emotion. "As for me, Rachel died upon me in the land of Canaan in the way."

III. AN OLD SAINT'S BLESSING. It is probable that, though Jacob had already referred to Joseph's sons, he had not yet been conscious of their presence, for "the eyes of Israel were dim for age, so that he could not see." At length, however, discerning unfamiliar forms in the chamber, and ascertaining they were Ephraim and Manasseh, he proceeds to give them his patriarchal benediction. 1. *The actions of the patriarch.* (1) Requesting his grandchildren to be brought to his bedside, he tenderly embraces them, and kisses them with all an old man's affection, at the same time giving special thanks to Elohim for his superabundant mercy in permitting him to see Joseph's sons, and his beloved Rachel's offspring. (2) Guiding his hands wittingly, he sets them crosswise upon his grandsons' heads, the right hand upon that of Ephraim, the younger, and the left hand upon that of Manasseh, the elder. Supposing that the patriarch had erred, Joseph endeavours, by changing his father's hands, to rectify the mistake, saying, "Not so, my father: for this is the firstborn; put thy right hand upon his head." But the old man replies, thinking perhaps at the moment of himself and Esau, when they came before Isaac for his blessing, " I know it, my son, I know it," but refuses to comply with his son's suggestion. 2. *The contents of the blessing.* (1) The blessing upon Ephraim. This was the heirship of the theocratic blessing, the right of primogeniture, the place and power of the firstborn. "Truly his younger brother shall be greater than he, and his seed shall become a multitude of nations." (2) The blessing upon Manasseh. "He also shall become a people, and he also shall be great." (3) The blessing upon both. " The angel who redeemed me from all evil bless the lads "—a promise of spiritual blessing for themselves; and "In thee shall Israel bless, saying "—a promise of spiritual influence with others. (4) The blessing upon Joseph. Joseph was blessed in the blessing of his sons, by their adoption into Jacob's family,—" My name shall be named upon them, and the name of my fathers, Abraham and Isaac; " and by their reception of a double portion of the inheritance,—" Moreover, I have given to thee one portion above thy brethren, which I took out of the hand of the Amorite with my sword and with my bow."

IV. AN OLD PROPHET'S PREDICTION. "Behold, I die; but God shall be with you, and bring you again into the land of your fathers." 1. *The time when it was uttered.* When Jacob was on the eve of death. It is not at all improbable that the soul's vision of unseen (celestial and future) things becomes clearer as the obscuring veil of this mortal flesh wears thin; but the power of apprehending things to come, which Jacob in this instance displayed, was not due to such intensified spiritual penetration. Neither is it necessary to suppose that he received at this moment any special supernatural communication. Simply, he directed his dying gaze to the sure word of promise. 2. *The substance of what it said.* It announced nothing more than God already promised, viz., that he would continue with Jacob's descendants in Egypt, and eventually bring them up again to Canaan. 3. *The guarantee to which it pointed.* This was implicitly contained in the expression, " the land of your fathers." Canaan had been given in covenant to Abraham, and Isaac, and Jacob; and hence of necessity it would ultimately be restored to their seed according to the terms of the covenant.

HOMILIES BY VARIOUS AUTHORS.

Ch. xlviii.—We are admitted into the inner chamber of the patriarch's departing life, and we see there *the presence of Jehovah* with him. He is—1. *The subject of inspiration.* 2. The *mediator of the Divine promises.* He is under the control of purposes which have been swaying him all his life. 3. *A witness to Divine faithfulness.* The grandfather blessing the grandchildren. The blessing passes on to the third and fourth generation. Yet the human blessing is only the type of the Divine. " *The angel which redeemed me from all evil bless the lads.*" Jacob made a cross with his hands over the heads of the boys. It displeased Joseph, but it pleased God. The imposition of hands is also here. The *name of Jacob* is named upon them, the *symbol of the covenant.* Their prosperity is predicted, but it is connected immediately with their covenant standing. The elevated state of mind in the patriarch is a testimony to the sustaining power of religion in fleshly weakness. It points on too to the survival of the soul after the death of the body. The preference of Ephraim reminds us that all is ascribed to the grace of God.—R.

Vers. 15, 16.—*The threefold blessing.* Though the doctrine of the Trinity is not revealed in the Old Testament with the same clearness as in the New Testament, the light of the gospel reveals many indications of it. In Numb. vi. 24, 27, the "name " of God is put upon the children of Israel in a triple formula. A name suggests what we know of the person named. The "name" of God is what he has revealed concerning himself (cf. Exod. xxxiv. 5—7 ; Ps. xx. 1). The threefold benediction of Numb. vi. 24 (cf. Isa. vi. 3 ; Rev. iv. 8) answers to the apostolic benediction of 2 Cor. xiii. 14. And Jacob's solemn blessing of his grandsons in a threefold name of God, answers to the formula of Christian baptism (Matt. xxviii. 19) into (εἰς) the name of the Trinity ; while the word "bless," being in the singular, points to the unity of the Godhead. Whether the distinction of the Persons was known to Jacob matters little to us, if we believe that "these things were written for our learning." His prophetic blessing speaks to us of Fatherhood, Sanctification, Redemption, the blessings which we refer to the three Persons. The order of the two last is different from that which we usually observe ; but cf. 1 Cor. i. 30. "God before whom my fathers did walk." The well-spring of all grace and source of all blessing. Of his own inherent love, caring for us (1 Pet. v. 7). His purpose, that we should rejoice in hope (Rom. xii. 12) ; having communion with him here (Phil. iv. 6, 7), the foretaste of eternal joy. Creation the proof of this good will (Ps. xix. 1). The infinity of his power, and minuteness of his care. The application of this to us (Matt. x. 29—31). The Bible and nature agree in declaring God's fatherhood. On this rests the call to walk before him (Gen. xvii. 1; Mal. i. 6), which can be obeyed only through belief of his fatherhood and love (Rom. viii. 3). Therefore he gives the spirit of adoption (Rom. viii. 15), the personal application of the general truth of his love, whereby we realise our position as children by grace (Titus iii. 5). "The God which fed me." The Holy Ghost imparts to men the bread of life. 1. *Historically.* By his agency the eternal Son became incarnate to give his flesh as the living bread. 2. *Practically.* By his power we are fed. Christ's work is applied to our conscience (John xvi. 14) ; we receive the food of our souls. This is the way of sanctification. It cannot be enforced by rules or penalties. However these may constrain outward observance, they cannot bring about the surrender of the will, the desire "Thy will be done," which is the principle of holiness. "The angel which redeemed me from all evil." Reminded of Ps. xci. 11, and probably some such idea was in Jacob's mind. But there is a foresight of Christ, the Angel of the covenant (Mal. iii. 1), in whom God's name is (Exod. xxiii. 20) ; of a redemption going far beyond earthly danger ; "all evil." From sin and all its fruits of sorrow Christ redeemed us (Rom. vi. 14 ; Gal. iii. 13). Jacob, from his own experience, knew that "God is faithful." To us, a wider view of deliverance is given. And the pledge of God's faithfulness is Rom. viii. 32 ; and the assurance that it gives us 1 John vi. 2.—M.

EXPOSITION

CHAPTER XLIX.

Ver. 1.—And Jacob (having closed his interview with Joseph and his two sons) **called** (by means of messengers) **unto his sons** (*i. e.* the others who were then absent), **and said, Gather yourselves together,**—the prophet's last utterance must be a public one —**that I may tell you**—literally, *and I will tell you*—that **which shall befall you**—קְרָא, in the sense of happening or occurring to any one, is here equivalent to קָרָה (cf. ch. xlii. 4, 38)—**in the last days**—literally, *in the end of the days*, not simply in future time (Gesenius, Rosenmüller, Kalisch), or in the times intervening between the speaker and the end of the human race (Murphy), but in the last age, the closing period of time, the era of fulfilment (Kurtz, Hengstenberg), which era, however, must be judged from the standpoint of the speaker (Baumgarten). Hence the period must not be restricted to exclu-

sively Messianic times (Rabbi Nachmanides), ἐπ᾽ ἐσχάτων τῶν ἡμερῶν (LXX.), *in diebus novissimis* (Vulgate), but must commence with what to Jacob was the era of consummation, the days of the conquest (Baumgarten, Hengstenberg) ; while, on the other hand, it can as little be limited to these, but must be held as extending over *totum tempus ab exitu Ægypti ad Christi regnum* (Calvin), and even as reaching, though unconsciously to Jacob, to the very terminus of human history (Keil, Lange).

Ver. 2.—**Gather yourselves together,**—the repetition indicates at once the elevation of the speaker's soul, and the importance, in his mind, of the impending revelation—**and hear, ye sons of Jacob ; and hearken unto Israel your father.** The two clauses form a synthetic or synonymous parallel, numerous illustrations of which are to be found in the succeeding verses.

Vers. 3, 4.—**Reuben, thou art my first-**

born, my might, and the beginning of my strength, the excellency of dignity, and the excellency of power:—Jacob's patriarchal benediction takes the form of an elevated poem, or sublime religious hymn, exhibiting the well-known classes of parallelism, the synthetic, the antithetic, and the synonymous, not alone in its separate clauses, but sometimes also in its stanzas or verses. As was perhaps to be expected, it begins with Reuben, who is characterised by a threefold designation, viz., (1) by his position in the family, as Jacob's firstborn; (2) by his relation to Jacob, as the patriarch's "might," כֹּחַ, or *robur virile*, and "the beginning" of his "strength," not "of his sorrow" (Vulgate, Aquila, Symmachus), though אוֹן might be so translated (cf. ch. xxxv. 18), and the sense would sufficiently accord with the allusion of ver. 4, but, as required by the parallelism, "of his vigour," אוֹן being here equivalent to כֹּחַ (Rosenmüller, Kalisch, Keil, 'Speaker's Commentary,' *et alii*); and (3) by the natural prominence which as Jacob's eldest son belonged to him, "the excellency of dignity" or "elevation," *i. e.* the dignity of the chieftainship, and "the excellency of power," or authority, which the first-born claimed and received as his prerogative. Yet the natural advantages enjoyed by Reuben as Jacob's firstborn were to be taken from him, as the patriarch proceeded to announce—Unstable as water,—literally, *boiling over like water*, the import of which is not *effusus es sicut aqua* (Vulgate), but either ἐξύβρισας ὡς ὕδωρ (LXX.), or lasciviousness (*sc.* was to thee) as the boiling of water (Gesenius, Rosenmüller, Keil, Kalisch, &c.), the same root in Arabic conveying the notion of pride, and in Syriac that of wantonness—thou shalt not excel;—literally, *thou shalt not have the* יֶתֶר *or excellency* (ver. 3), *i. e.* the pre-eminence belonging to the firstborn, a sense which the versions have more or less successfully expressed: μὴ περισσεύσῃς (Aquila), οὐκ ἔσῃ περισσότερος (Symmachus), μὴ ἐκζέσῃς (LXX.), *non crescas* (Vulgate)—because thou wentest up to thy father's bed (*vide* ch. xxxv. 22; 1 Chron. v. 1); then defiledst thou it:—the verb is used absolutely, as meaning that Reuben had desecrated what ought to have been regarded by him as sacred (cf. Deut. xxvii. 20)—he went up to my couch—literally, *my couch he ascended;* the order of the words and the change from the second to the third person helping to give expression to the horror and indignation with which, even at that distance of time, the venerable patriarch contemplated the shameful deed.

Vers. 5—7.—Simeon and Levi are breth-ren (not in parentage alone, but also in their deeds; *e. g.* their massacre of the Shechemites (ch. xxxiv. 25), to which undoubtedly the next words allude); instruments of cruelty are in their habitations—literally, *instruments of violence their* מְכֵרֹת, a ἅπαξ λεγόμ. which has been variously rendered—(1) their dwellings, or habitations (Kimchi, A. V., Calvin, Ainsworth), in the land of their sojournings (Onkelos), for which, however, there does not seem to be much authority; (2) their machinations or wicked counsels, deriving from מָכַר, to string together, to take in a net, to ensnare (Nahum iii. 4), the cognate Arabic root signifying to deceive or practise stratagems (De Dieu, Schultens, Castelli, Tayler Lewis, and others); (3) their betrothals, or compacts of marriage, connecting with the same root as the preceding in the sense of "binding together" (Dathius, Clericus, Michaelis, Knobel, Fürst, *et alii*); (4) their rage, as suggested by the unused root כִּיד, to boil or seethe (Kalisch); (5) their swords, from כָּרָה = כּוּר, to dig or pierce through, cf. μάχαιρα (Vulgate, Luther, Gesenius, Rosenmüller, Keil, Murphy, and others). The preponderance of authority appears to be in favour of this last. O my soul, come not thou into their secret;—literally, *into their council or assembly* (סוֹד, from יָסַד, to set or sit) *come not, my soul*, or *my soul shall not come* (cf. Prov. i. 15, 16) —unto their assembly, mine honour, be not thou united:—literally, *with or in their assembly or congregation* (קָהָל from קָהַל, to call together: cf. ch. xxviii. 3; xxxv. 11; xlviii. 4), *mine honour or glory* (*i. e.* the soul as being the noblest part of man: Ps. xvi. 9; lvii. 9; cviii. 2—the term כְּבֹדִי is parallel with the preceding נַפְשִׁי), *do not join* (Keil), or *shall not join* (Kalisch)—for in their anger they slew a man,—literally, *man*, a collective singular for "men," the plural form of אִישׁ occurring rarely; only in Ps. cxli. 4; Prov. viii. 4; and Isa. liii. 3—and in their selfwill they digged down a wall —literally, *they houghed ox* (LXX., Gesenius, Fürst, Rosenmüller, Keil, Kalisch, Lange, Gerlach, T. Lewis, Murphy, &c., &c.), the singular שׁוֹר, the plural of which is only found once, in Hosea xii. 12, being retained here to correspond with אִישׁ. The received rendering, which is not without sanction (Onkelos, Targum of Jonathan, Syriac, Arabic, Aquila, Symmachus, Vulgate, Dathius, Calvin), reads שּׁוּר instead of שׁוֹר, and takes עָקַר in the primary sense of *destruere, evertere.* Cursed be their anger, for it was fierce; and their wrath, for it was

cruel:—the second synonym "wrath," literally, *outpourings*, indicates the fulness and
intensity of the tide of fury which by Simeon
and Levi was let loose upon the unsuspecting
Shechemites—**I will divide them in Jacob,
and scatter them in Israel.** While for the
sin (the deed, not the doers) Jacob has a curse,
for the sinners themselves he has a well-
merited chastisement. They had been confederate in their wickedness, they should in
future, when returning to occupy their God-
assigned inheritance, be disjoined. That
this prediction was exactly fulfilled Scripture
testifies. At the second census in the wilderness, shortly before the conquest, the tribe
of Simeon had become so reduced in its
numbers (reckoning only 22,000 as against
76,500 in Judah) as to be the smallest of the
twelve (Numb. xxvi. 14); to be passed over
entirely in the last blessing of Moses (Deut.
xxxiii.); to be accorded no independent allotment of territory in Canaan on the completion
of the conquest, having only a few cities
granted to it within the borders of Judah
(Josh. xix. 1—9); and to be ultimately absorbed in the more powerful and distinguished
tribe under whose protection and tutelage,
so to speak, it had been placed (1 Chron. iv.
27). The tribe of Levi also was deprived of
a separate inheritance, receiving only a
number of cities scattered here and there
among the possessions of their brethren
(Josh. xxi. 1, 40); and, though by its
election to the priesthood the curse may be
said to have been turned into a blessing, yet
of this signal honour which was waiting
Levi Jacob was completely silent, showing
both that no prophecy was of any private
interpretation (the seer seeing no further than
the Holy Spirit helped him), and that Jacob
spoke before the days of Moses. It is almost
incredible that a late writer would have
omitted to forecast the latter-day glory of
the tribe of Levi; and this opinion is confirmed by observing the very different strain
in which, after Levi's calling had been revealed, the benediction of Moses himself
proceeds (Deut. xxxiii. 8—11).

Vers. 8—12.—**Judah, thou** art he **whom
thy brethren shall praise**—literally, *Judah
thou, will praise thee thy brethren*, the word
יוֹדוּךָ being a palpable play on יְהוּדָה (cf.
ch. xxix. 35). Leah praised Jehovah for his
birth, and his brethren should extol him for
his nobility of character, which even in his
acts of sin could not be entirely obscured
(ch. xxxvii. 26; xxxviii. 26), and certainly
in his later days (ch. xliii. 8; xliv. 18—34)
shone out with undiminished lustre. **Thy
hand shall be in the neck of thine enemies**
(*i. e.* putting his foes to flight, Judah should
grasp them by the neck, a prediction remarkably accomplished in the victories of David
and Solomon); **thy father's children shall**

bow down before thee. Fulfilled in the elevation of the house of Judah to the throne,
which owned as its subjects not simply
Judah's mother's children, *i. e.* the tribes
descended from Leah, but also his father's,
i. e. all the tribes of Israel. **Judah is a
lion's whelp: from the prey, my son, thou
art gone up: he stooped down, he couched
down as a lion, and as an old lion; who
shall rouse him up?** By a bold and striking
figure Judah is compared to a young lion,
ripening into its full strength and ferocity,
roaming through the forests in search of prey,
repairing to his mountain den (ἐκ βλάστου
ἀνέβης, LXX.) when his booty has been
devoured, and there in quiet majesty, full of
dignified repose, lying down or crouching in
his lair, and calmly resisting all attempts to
disturb his leonine serenity. The effect of
the picture is also heightened by the alternative image of a lioness, which is particularly
fierce in defending its cubs, and which no
one would venture to assail when so employed. The use of such figures to describe
a strong and invincible hero is by no means
infrequent in Scripture (*vide* Ps. vii. 3; lvii.
5; Isa. v. 29; Ezek. xix. 2—9). **The sceptre
shall not depart from Judah,**—literally, *a
sceptre* (i. e. an emblem of regal command,
hence dominion or sovereignty; ἄρχων,
LXX., Theodotion; ἐξουσία, Symmachus)
shall not depart from Judah—**nor a lawgiver from between his feet**—literally, *and
a legislator* (sc. shall not depart) *from between his feet;* מְחֹקֵק, the poel part. of חָקַק,
to cut, to cut into, hence to decree, to ordain,
having the sense of one who decrees; hence
leader, as in Judges v. 44, *dux* (Vulgate),
ἡγούμενος (LXX.), or lawgiver, as in Deut.
xxxiii. 21 and Isa. xxxiii. 22 (Calvin,
Dathius, Ainsworth, Rosenmüller, Murphy,
Wordsworth, 'Speaker's Commentary'). In
view, however, of what appears the requirement of the parallelism, מְחֹקֵק is regarded
as not the person, but the thing, that determines or rules, and hence as equivalent to
the ruler's staff, or marshal's baton (Gesenius,
Fürst, Keil, Lange, Bleek, Tuch, Kalisch,
and others), in support of which is claimed
the phrase "from between his feet," which
is supposed to point to the Oriental custom,
as depicted on the monuments, of monarchs,
when sitting upon their thrones, resting their
staves between their feet (cf. Agamemnon,
'Iliad,' ii. 46, 101; Layard's 'Nineveh and
Babylon,' p. 195). But the words may likewise signify "from among his descendants,"
"from among his children's children"
(Onkelos), ἐκ τῶν μηρῶν αὐτοῦ (LXX.).
Until Shiloh come. This difficult clause has
been very variously rendered. 1. Taking
Shiloh as the name of a place, viz., Shiloh in
Ephraim (Josh. xviii. 1, 8, 9, 10; xix. 51;

Judges xviii. 31 ; 1 Sam. i. 3, 9, 24 ; ii. 14, &c.), the sense has been explained as meaning that the leadership of Judah over the other tribes of Israel should not cease until he came to Shiloh (Rabbi Lipmann, Teller, Eichhorn, Bleek, Fürst, Tuch, Delitzsch). But though וַיָּבֹא שִׁלֹה, and they came to Shiloh, a similar phrase, is found in 1 Sam. iv. 12, yet against this interpretation may be urged (1) the improbability of so obscure a locality, whose existence at the time is also problematical, being mentioned by Jacob, Zidon, the only other name occurring in the prophecy, having been, even before the days of Jacob, a city of renown (ch. x. 19) ; and (2) the inaccuracy of the historical statement which would thus be made, since the supremacy of Judah was in no way affected, and certainly not diminished, by the setting up of the tabernacle in Shiloh ; to obviate which objection Kalisch proposes to read עַד כִּי as "even if," or "even when," and to understand the prediction as intimating that even though a new empire should be established at Shiloh, as was eventually done, Judah should not forfeit her royal name and prerogative—only this sense of עַד כִּי is not clearly recognised by the best grammarians (Gesenius, Fürst), and is not successfully supported by the passages referred to (ch. xxviii. 15 ; Ps. cx. 1 ; cxii. 8), in every one of which the received rendering "until" is distinctly preferable.   2. Regarding Shiloh as an abstract noun, from שָׁלֵי to be safe, like גֹּלָה from גָּלָה, the import of the prophecy has been expressed as asserting that the sceptre should not depart from Judah, either until he (Judah) should attain to rest (Hofmann, Kurtz), or until tranquillity should come, i. e. until Judah's enemies should be subdued (Gesenius), an interpretation which Rosenmüller properly characterises as "languidum et pœne frigidum." Hence—3. Believing Shiloh to be the name of a person, the majority of commentators, both Jewish and Christian, and ancient as well as modern, agree that the Messiah is the person referred to, and understand Jacob as fore-announcing that the time of his appearance would not be till the staff of regal power had dropped from the hands of Judah ; only, the widest possible diversity exists among those who discover a Messianic reference in the prediction as to the exact significance of the term Shiloh.   Some render it his son, or progeny, or (great) descendant, from an imaginary root, שָׁל, which, after Chaldee and Arabic analogies, is supposed to mean "offspring" (Targum of Jonathan, Kimchi, Calvin, Ainsworth, and others) ; others, deriving it from שָׁלַה, to send, compare it with Siloam

(John ix. 7) and Shiloah (Isa. viii. 6), and interpret it as qui mittendus est (Vulgate, Pererius, À Lapide, Grotius) ; a third class of expositors, connecting it with שָׁלָה, to be safe or at rest, view it as a nomen appellatum, signifying the Pacificator, the Rest-giver, the Tranquilliser, the Peace (Luther, Venema, Rosenmüller, Hengstenberg, Keil, Gerlach, Murphy, &c.) ; while a fourth resolve it into אֲשֶׁר לוֹ, and conjecture it to signify, he to whom it (sc. the sceptre or the kingdom) belongs, or he whose right it is, as in Ezek. xxi. 27 (LXX., ἕως ἐὰν ἔλθῃ τα ἀποκείμενα αὐτῷ ; Aquila and Symmachus, ᾧ ἀπόκειται ; Onkelos, Syriac, Saadias, Targum of Jerusalem, et alii).   It seems indisputable that the preponderance of authority is in favour of the last two interpretations, and if שִׁילֹה be the correct reading, instead of שִׁלֹה (= שִׁלָה = אֲשֶׁר לוֹ), as the majority of MSS. attest, it will be difficult to withhold from the former, "the Tranquilliser," the palm of superiority. The translations of Dathius (quamdiu prolem habebit, ei gentes obedient), who professes to follow Gulcher, who understands the words as a prophecy of the perpetuity of Judah's kingdom, fulfilled in David (2 Sam. vii.), and of Lange ("until he himself comes home as the Shiloh or Rest-bringer"), who also discerns in Judah a typical foreshadowing of the Messiah, may be mentioned as examples of ingenious, but scarcely convincing, exposition.   And unto him shall the gathering of the people be.   Not "καὶ αὐτὸς προσδοκία ἐθνῶν" (LXX.), ipse erit expectatio gentium (Vulgate), with which also agrees the Syriac, or "to him nations will flock" (Samaritan), σύστημα λαῶν (Aquila), but to him, i. e. Shiloh, will be not aggregatio populorum (Calvin), but the submission or willing obedience (a word occurring elsewhere only in Prov. xxx. 17) of nations or peoples (Onkelos, Targum of Jonathan, Kimchi, Aben Ezra, Dathius, Rosenmüller, Keil, Kalisch, Gerlach, Murphy, Tayler Lewis, 'Speaker's Commentary').   Binding his foal unto the vine,— i. e. not Shiloh, but Judah.   The verb אֹסְרִי has the archaic י appended, as in ch. xxxi. 39 ; Deut. xxxiii. 16 ; Zech. xi. 17—and his ass's colt unto the choice vine.   The שֹׂרֵקָה (fem. of שֹׂרֵק) was a nobler kind of vine which grew in Syria, with small berries, roundish and of a dark colour, with soft and hardly perceptible stones (Gesenius, p. 796).   בְּנִי is an archaic form of the construct state which occurs only here.   He washed his garments in wine, and his clothes in the blood of grapes.   The word סוּת is a ἅπαξ λεγόμενον, and is either put by aphæresis for כְּסוּת, which occurs in the Samaritan

Version, or is derived from סָוָה, an uncertain root, signifying to cover (Gesenius, Kalisch). **His eyes** shall be **red with wine, and his teeth white with milk.** Otherwise rendered "redder than wine," and "whiter than milk" (LXX., Vulgate, Targum of Jerusalem, et alii), as a description of Judah's person, which scarcely seems so appropriate as the received translation (Calvin, Rosenmüller, Keil, Kalisch, Murphy, Lange, and others), which completes the preceding picture of Judah's prosperity. Not only would Judah's soil be so fertile that its vines should be employed for tying asses and colts to their branches, but the grapes of those vines should be so plentiful and luscious as to make wine run like the water in which he washed his clothes, while the wine and milk should be so exhilarating and invigorating as to impart a sparkling brilliance to the eyes and a charming whiteness to the teeth. The aged prophet, it has been appropriately remarked, has here no thought of debauchery, but only paints before the mind's eye a picture of the richest and most ornate enjoyment (Lange). *Minime consentaneum esse videtur profusam intemperiem et projectionem in benedictione conseri* (Calvin).

Ver. 13.—**Zebulun shall dwell at the haven of the sea ;**—not παρ' ὅρμον πλοίων (LXX.), in statione navium (Vulgate), but to, or at, or beside, the shore (from the idea of being washed by the waters of the ocean) of the waters, i. e. of the Galilean and Mediterranean seas—**and he shall be for an haven of ships ;**—literally, and he to, at, or on, a shore of ships, i. e. a shore where ships are unloaded (sc. shall dwell), the words being a repetition of the previous thought, with only the expansion, suggested by the term ships, that Zebulun's calling should be in the direction of commerce ;—**and his border** shall be **unto Zidon** — literally, and his side, or hinder part (sc. shall be, or extend), towards, rather than unto,—usque ad (Vulgate), ἕως (LXX.),—Zidon, since the territory subsequently allotted to Zebulun neither actually touched the Mediterranean, nor reached to Zidon—a circumstance that may be noted as an indirect hint that this prophecy was not spoken, or even first written, after the occupation of the land.

Vers. 14, 15.—**Issachar is a strong ass couching down between two burdens** — literally, an ass of bone—hence a strong, powerful animal, asinus fortis (Vulgate), asinus validi corporis (Gesenius), asinus robustus (Rosenmüller)—lying down between the folds, or cattle-pens, which received and protected the flocks by night, the dual being used probably because such pens were divided into two parts for different kinds of cattle (Gesenius, Keil, Kalisch, Murphy, 'Speaker's Comment-

ary,' &c.), though the word mishpetaim has been also rendered ἀνὰ μέσον τῶν κλήρων (LXX.), inter terminos (Vulgate, Rosenmüller), "within their own boundaries" (Onkelos, Targums of Jerusalem and Jonathan), "between two burdens" (A. V., Lange, Murphy, &c.). **And he saw that rest** was **good, and the land that** it was **pleasant.** Issachar was to manifest a keen appreciation of the land or portion of territory that should be assigned to him, and to renounce the warlike spirit and military enterprises of his brethren for the indolent and luxurious repose of his fat pastures, crouching between his sheep-folds, or rejoicing within his tents, like a lazy ass, capable indeed of mighty efforts, but too self-satisfied to put forth much exertion, devoting himself to agriculture and pastoral pursuits, and preferring rather to pay tribute to his brethren, in order to secure their protection, than to leave his ploughshare and cast aside his shepherd's crook to follow them into the tented field of war, as the patriarch next describes. **And bowed his shoulder to bear, and became a servant unto tribute**—or a tributary servant. The phrase מַס־עֹבֵד, though sometimes used of servitude under a foreign sovereignty (Deut. xx. 11 ; Josh. xvi. 10), commonly refers to tribute rendered by labour (1 Kings ix. 21 ; 2 Chron. viii. 8), and is correctly rendered ἄνθρωπος εἰς φόρον δουλεύων (Aquila), factusque est tributo serviens (Vulgate). The translation καὶ ἐγενήθη ἀνὴρ γεωργός (LXX.) discovers in the clause an allusion to Issachar's agricultural pursuits.

Vers. 16—18.—**Dan shall judge his people as one of the tribes of Israel.** With a play upon his name, the firstborn son of Rachel's handmaid, Bilhah, is described as one who should occupy an important place and exercise highly beneficial functions in the future commonwealth, enjoying independence and self-government as one of the tribes of Israel (Herder, and others), and performing the office of an administrator among the people not of his own tribe merely, but also of all Israel, a prediction pointing perhaps to the transient supremacy enjoyed by Dan over the other tribes in the days of Samson (Onkelos, et alii). **Dan shall be a serpent by the way, an adder in the path, that biteth the horse heels, so that his rider shall fall backward.** The שְׁפִיפֹן, from the Syriac שְׁפַף, to glide (Gesenius), from שׁוּף, to sting (Kalisch), שָׁפַף, to bite (Fürst), was the horned serpent, cerastes, of the colour of sand, and marked with white and black spots, which was exceedingly dangerous to passers-by, its bite being poisonous and fatal. The allusion has been almost unanimously explained as pointing to Samson (Judges xvi. 28), but the tribe in general appears not to have been entirely destitute of the treacherous and formidable characteristics here depicted (Judges xviii. 27). "It is certainly observable that the first introduction of idolatry in Israel is ascribed to the tribe of Dan (Judges xviii.), and that in the numbering of the tribes in Rev. vii. the name of Dan is omitted. From these or other causes many of the Fathers (Irenæus, Ambrose, Augustine, Theodoret) were led to believe that Antichrist should spring from the tribe of Dan " ('Speaker's Commentary'). **I have waited for thy salvation, O Lord.** To discover in this beautiful and tender ejaculation of the dying patriarch an apprehensive sigh lest his strength should be exhausted before his benediction was completed (Tuch), or a prayer that God might speedily effect his painless dissolution (Hengstenberg), or a device for dividing his benedictions, and separating the group of Judah from that of Joseph (Lange), is surely to fail in seizing its hidden spirit. It is doubtful if even the usual interpretation, that Jacob here expresses his hope and expectation that God would help and succour his descendants (Calvin, Rosenmüller, Keil, Kalisch, Murphy, and others), exhausts its rich significance. That, speaking in their name, he does anticipate the deliverance of Jehovah— " In thy help do I hope, O Jehovah ! "—is apparent ; but nothing surely can be more natural than to suppose that the dying patriarch, at the moment when he was formally transmitting to his children the theocratic blessing, had his thoughts lifted up towards that great salvation, of which all these material and temporal benedictions pronounced upon his sons were but the shadows and the types, and of which perhaps he had been incidentally reminded by the mention of the biting serpent, to which he had just likened Dan (' Speaker's Commentary '). It is noticeable that this is the first occurrence of the term salvation (יְשׁוּעָה, from the root יָשַׁע, unused in Kal, to be roomy or spacious, hence in the Hiphil to set free or deliver).

Ver. 19.—**Gad, a troop shall overcome him: but he shall overcome at the last.** The threefold alliteration of the original, which is lost in the received translation, may be thus expressed : " Gad—a press presses him, but he presses the heel" (Keil); or, " troops shall troop on him, but he shall troop on their retreat " (' Speaker's Commentary '). The language refers to attacks of nomadic tribes which would harass and annoy the Gadites, but which they would successfully repel.

Ver. 20.—**Out of Asher his bread** shall be **fat, and he shall yield royal dainties** — literally, *dainties of, or for, the king.* The first clause may be otherwise rendered: Of Asher the bread shall be fat (Kalisch); fat shall be his bread (Murphy); Out of Asher (cometh) fat his bread (Keil). The import of the blessing is that Asher should possess a specially productive soil.

Ver. 21.—**Naphtali is a hind let loose: he giveth goodly words.** The LXX., followed by Dathe, Michaelis, Ewald, Bohlen, and others, read, Naphtali is a tall terebinth, that putteth forth beautiful boughs ; but the word אַיָּלָה signifies a hind or gazelle, and is here employed, along with the qualifying epithet שְׁלֻחָה, let loose, running freely (Keil), or graceful (Kalisch), to depict Naphtali as a beautiful and agile warrior. In the appended clause he is represented as possessing in addition the capacity of " giving words of beauty," in which may be detected an allusion to the development in eloquence and song which afterwards took place in that northern tribe (Judges iv. 6—9 ; v. 1—31).

Vers. 22—26.—**Joseph** is **a fruitful bough, even a fruitful bough by a well;** whose **branches run over the wall**—literally, *son of a fruit tree, Joseph ; son of a fruit tree at the well ; daughters run* (each one of them : *vide* Gesenius, 'Grammar,' § 146, 4) *over the wall.* The structure of the clauses, the order of the words, the repetition of the thoughts, supply a glimpse into the fond emotion with which the aged prophet approached the blessing of his beloved son Joseph. Under the image of a fruit tree, probably a vine, as in Ps. lxxx., planted by a well, whence it draws forth necessary moisture, and, sending forth its young twigs or offshoots over the supporting walls, he pictures the fruitfulness and prosperity which should afterwards attend the tribes of Ephraim and Manasseh, as the twofold representative of Joseph, with perhaps a backward glance at the service which Joseph had performed in Egypt by gathering up and dispensing the produce of the land for the salvation of his family and people. **The archers have sorely grieved him, and shot** at him, **and hated him**—literally, *they provoked him, and shot at, and laid snares for him, masters of arrows,* though Kalisch translates וָרֹבּוּ, and they assembled in multitudes, which yields a sense sufficiently clear. It is sometimes alleged (Keil, Lange, ' Speaker's Commentary ') that the words contain no allusion to the personal history of Joseph, but solely to the later fortunes of the tribes of Ephraim and Manasseh ; but even if they do point to the subsequent hostilities which Joseph's descendants incur (Josh. xvii. 16—18 ; Judges xii. 4—6), it is almost morally certain that the image of the shooting archers which he selects to depict their adversaries was suggested to his mind by the early lot of his beloved son (Calvin,

Rosenmüller, Kalisch, Gerlach, Murphy, and others). **But his bow abode in strength, and the arms of his hands were made strong by the hands of the mighty** God **of Jacob.** Notwithstanding the multitudinous and fierce assaults which had been made on Joseph, he had risen superior to his adversaries; his bow had continued firm and unbroken (cf. 1 Sam. ii. 4, Job xii. 19, xxxiii. 19), and his arms had been rendered active and flexible—neither ἐξελύθη τὰ νεῦρα βραχιόνων χειρὸς αὐτῶν (LXX.), *dissoluta sunt vincula brachiorum et manuum* (Vulgate), as if Joseph's enemies were the subjects referred to; nor, "Therefore gold was placed upon his arms" (Onkelos, Rashi, and others), referring to the gift of Pharaoh's ring—by the hands of the Mighty One of Jacob, *i. e.* God, who had proved himself to be Jacob's Mighty One by the powerful protection vouchsafed to his servant. The title here ascribed to God occurs afterwards in Isa. i. 24. **From thence is the shepherd, the stone of Israel.** If the clause is parenthetical, it may signify either that from the time of Joseph's exaltation he became the shepherd (who sustained) and the stone of (*i. e.* the rock which supported) Israel (Oleaster); or that from God, the Mighty One of Jacob, Joseph received strength to become the shepherd and stone of Israel (Pererius, Ainsworth, Lawson, Patrick, and others), in which capacity he served as a prefiguration of the Good Shepherd who was also to become the Rock or Foundation of his Church (Calvin, Pererius, Candlish, &c.); but if the clause is rather co-ordinate with that which precedes and that which follows, as the introductory particle מִן appears to suggest, then the words "shepherd and stone of Israel" will apply to God, and the sentiment will be that the hands of Joseph were made strong from the hands of the Mighty One of Jacob, from there (*i. e.* from there where is, or from him who is) the Shepherd, the Stone of Israel (Keil, Kalisch, Murphy, Gerlach, Lange, *et alii*). Even **by the God of thy father, who shall help thee** (literally, *from the God of thy father, and he shall help thee*, i. e. who shall help thee); **and by the Almighty, who shall bless thee**—literally, *and with* (sc. the aid of) *the Almighty, and he shall bless thee.* It is unnecessary to change וְאֵת into וְאֵל (LXX., Vulgate, Samaritan, Syriac, Ewald), or to insert מִן before אֵת, as thus, מֵאֵת (Knobel, Rosenmüller, Kalisch), since אֵת may be understood here, as in ch. iv. 1; v. 24, in the sense of helpful communion (Keil)—**with blessings of heaven above, blessings of the deep that lieth under, blessings of the breasts, and of the womb.** "From the God of Jacob, and by the help of the Almighty, should the rain and dew of heaven (ch. xxvii. 28), and fountains and

brooks which spring from the great deep or the abyss of the earth, pour their fertilising waters over Joseph's land, so that everything that had womb and breast should become pregnant, bring forth and suckle" (Keil). **The blessings of thy father have prevailed above the blessings of my progenitors unto the utmost bound of the everlasting hills.** The meaning is, according to this rendering, which some adopt (the Targums, Vulgate, Syriac, Saadias, Rosenmüller, Lange, Murphy, *et alii*), that the blessings which Jacob pronounced upon Joseph surpassed those which he himself had received from Abraham and Isaac, either as far as the primary mountains towered above the earth (Keil, Murphy), or, while exceeding the benedictions of his ancestors, those now delivered by himself would last while the hills endured (Rosenmüller, 'Speaker's Commentary'). But the words may be otherwise rendered: "The blessings of thy father prevail over, are mightier than the blessings of the mountains of eternity, the delight, or glory, or loveliness of the hills of eternity" (LXX., Dathe, Michaelis, Gesenius, Bohlen, Kalisch, Gerlach, and others); and in favour of this may be adduced the beautiful parallelism between the last two clauses, which the received translation overlooks. **They shall be on the head of Joseph, and on the crown of the head of him that was separate from his brethren**—literally, *of him, the separated* (from *nazar*, to separate) *from his brethren* (Onkelos, Rashi, Rosenmüller, Keil, and others), though by some different renderings are preferred, as, *e. g.*, the crowned among his brethren (LXX. Syriac, Targum of Jerusalem, Kimchi, Kalisch, Gerlach), taking *nazir* to signify he who wears the *nezer*, or royal diadem.

Ver. 27.—**Benjamin shall ravin** as a **wolf** (literally, *a wolf, he shall tear in pieces*): **in the morning he shall devour the prey, and at night he shall divide the spoil.** The prediction alludes to the warlike character of the tribe of Benjamin, which was manifested in Ehud the judge (Judges iii. 15), and Saul the king of Israel (1 Sam. xi. 6—11; xiv. 13, 15, 47, 48), who both sprang from Rachel's younger son.

Ver. 28.—**All these** are **the twelve tribes of Israel** (the underlying thought is that in blessing his sons Jacob was really blessing the future tribes): **and this is it that their father spake unto them, and blessed them; every one according to his blessing he blessed them** (*i. e.* every one received his own appropriate benediction).

Vers. 29, 30.—**And he charged them, and said unto them, I am to be gathered unto my people** (*vide* on ch. xv. 15): **bury me with my fathers**—thus laying on them the injunction he had previously, with the superadded solemnity of an oath, laid on Joseph (ch. xlvii. 29—31)—**in the cave that is in the field of Ephron the Hittite, in the cave that is in the field of Machpelah, which is before Mamre, in the land of Canaan, which Abraham bought with the field of Ephron the Hittite for a possession of a burying-place** (*vide* ch. xxiii. 16—20). Jacob had learnt from his father and had carefully preserved all the details relating to the purchase of their family sepulchre. **There they buried Abraham and Sarah his wife ; there they buried Isaac and Rebekah his wife; and there I buried Leah.** From this it would appear that Leah had not descended into Egypt.

Ver. 32.—**The purchase of the field and of the cave that is therein** was from the **children of Heth.** Kalisch connects the present verse with the 30th, and reads ver. 31 as a parenthesis.

Ver. 33.—**And when Jacob had made an end of commanding his sons, he gathered up his feet into the bed** (having on the arrival of Joseph strengthened himself and sat up upon the bed, probably with his feet overhanging its edge), **and yielded up the ghost, and was gathered unto his people** (*vide* on ch. xxv. 8 ; xxxv. 29).

HOMILETICS.

Vers. 1—33.—*The patriarchal blessing, or the last words of Jacob.* I. THE SONS OF LEAH. 1. *The blessing on Reuben.* (1) A declaration of Reuben's natural precedence, as the first-born in Jacob's family, the beginning of Jacob's strength, and therefore the legitimate heir of Jacob's house. (2) A proclamation of Reuben's deposition from this honourable position : " Boiling as water, thou shalt not have the precedence," *i. e.* the birthright is taken from thee, and assigned to another. (3) A statement of Reuben's sin, as the reason of this forfeiture of the firstborn's place : " because thou wentest up to thy father's bed : then defiledst thou it ; he went up to my couch." 2. *The blessings on Simeon and Levi.* It is only by a species of irony that the words pronounced on the authors of the Shechem massacre can be styled a blessing. (1) The patriarch expresses his abhorrence of their atrocious wickedness, describing them with a refined sarcasm as brethren, confederates in sin as well as the offspring of common parents, characterising their swords, or their compacts, or their rage, or their machinations, according to the translation adopted, as instruments of violence, and shudderingly recoiling from the least association with two such reckless murderers, who in their wrathful fury spared neither man nor beast : " Man they slew, and ox they houghed." (2) He pronounces a solemn curse upon their sin. Not upon themselves, it is noticeable, but upon their deed, meaning that while God might mercifully pardon transgressors such as they had been, he could not do otherwise than reveal his wrath against appalling wickedness like theirs. (3) He allots to them a punishment appropriate to their offence : " I will divide them in Jacob, and scatter them in Israel." 3. *The blessing upon Judah.* Recalling probably the part which his fourth son had played with reference to Benjamin, Jacob fervently declares that Judah should be—(1) The admiration of his brethren : " Judah, thou art he whom thy brethren shall praise ; " and " thy father's children shall bow down unto thee." (2) The terror of his foes : " thy hand shall be in the neck of thine enemies ; " " Judah is a lion's whelp," &c. (3) The ancestor of the Messiah, whose character he defines by the term Shiloh, whose advent he marks by the time : " The sceptre shall not depart from Judah, nor a lawgiver (or ruler's staff) from between his feet, until Shiloh come ; " and the result of his appearance : " unto him shall the gathering of the people be." (4) The possessor of a prosperous domain, whose vine-trees should be abundant, and whose pasture grounds should be fertile. 4. *The blessing on Zebulun.* With allusion to the import of his name, Jacob prophesies that Leah's sixth son should be the ancestor of a flourishing community devoted to commercial pursuits, with a territory reaching towards the sea-coast, where ships should come to load and unload their cargoes of merchandise. 5. *The blessing on Issachar.* The last mentioned son of Leah, though the fifth in the order of birth, the patriarch predicts should develop into a powerful and sagacious tribe, capable of great exertion and warlike achievements, but addicted to pastoral pursuits, and so fond of luxuriant repose, that for the sake of resting among his sheepfolds and in his fat meadows he should be willing to fulfil the mute anticipation of his name, and render tribute to his more heroic brethren.

II. THE SONS OF THE CONCUBINES. 1. *The blessing on Dan.* Dan was the firstborn of Bilhah, the maid of Rachel; and concerning him the patriarch announces—(1) That though the child of a secondary wife, his descendants should attain to the position of an independent and self-governing tribe : " Dan shall judge his people, as one of the tribes of Israel "; (2) That if not as a tribe, yet as individuals, and if not permanently, yet occasionally, they should manifest the qualities of sudden, unexpected, and even treacherous attack that were so remarkably characteristic of the horned serpent; (3) That he should enjoy, in all the perils to which he might in future be exposed, the gracious succour of Jehovah—a thought which appears to elevate the speaker's soul to the contemplation of another and higher keeper, who was yet to come to heal the fatal bite of that great serpent the Devil, who had injected his mortal virus into the race.   2. *The blessing on Gad.*   The firstborn of Zilpah, Leah's handmaid, obtains the next place in the order of the sons, and concerning him it is declared with a threefold play upon his name, which signifies a troop, that—(1) He will be sore pressed on every side by troops of marauding foes ; but that—(2) He will in the end prove himself to be victorious over the fiercest and the boldest.   3. *The blessing on Asher.*   The happy one should be the occupier of a territory exceeding fertile, and capable of yielding rich and dainty fruits for royal tables.   4. *The blessing on Naphtali.*   Naphtali was Bilhah's child, which Rachel named in honour of her triumphant wrestling or contending with her sister ; and for him were reserved the gifts of a graceful exterior, agile movements, and attractive speech both in eloquence and song.

III. THE SONS OF RACHEL.   1. *The blessing on Joseph.*   With a fulness and tenderness of paternal emotion like that with which already he had spoken of Judah, the expiring patriarch declares the fortunes of Joseph, setting forth—(1) The general prosperity that awaited him, representing him as the son (or offshoot) of a fruit-tree planted by a well, and rushing up into such luxuriance of growth that its branches (or daughters) overhung the walls that gave it support ; (2) The severe adversity to which in early years he had been exposed, and of which in future his descendants should have experience, comparing him to one whom the archers shot at and hated, and fiercely persecuted ; (3) The heavenly succour which had enabled him to overcome his bitter trials, and which would yet advance his children to safety, viz., the assistance of the mighty God of Jacob, the Shepherd and Stone of Israel, the God of his fathers Abraham and Isaac ; (4) The wealth of Benediction that should descend upon the head of him who had been separated from his brethren, viz., blessings of heaven above, blessings of the deep that lieth under, blessings of the breasts and of the womb, blessings that should surpass those bestowed on any of his progenitors, or, according to the more correct rendering, that should outlast the everlasting hills.   2. *The blessing on Benjamin.*   Though latest born of Jacob's family, he should not be the least important, but should show himself possessed of a warlike and adventurous disposition, causing him with eagerness and animation to take the field against the foe, and to desist not from battle till he could lead back his legions as rejoicing conquerors, enriched with the spoils of glorious victory.

Learn—1. That God is the great arbiter of human destiny.   2. That each man's sphere in life, as well as each nation's place on earth, is adapted to his or its peculiar character.   3. That though fore-appointed and fore-known, the destinies of men and nations are freely wrought out by themselves.   And—4. That in Providence as well as Grace, it often happens that the first becomes last, and the last first.

HOMILIES BY VARIOUS AUTHORS.

Ch. xlix.—*Last words.*— Jacob's benediction on his sons was a prophetic treasure, to be kept in store by future generations, and a foundation on which much faith could afterwards be built.   It has been called " the last full bloom of patriarchal prophecy and theocratic promise."   The central point, the blessing on the royal tribe of Judah.   The corresponding eminence being given to Joseph.   The Israel blessing to the one, the Jacob blessing to the other.   In each case we distinguish—1. *The earthly basis of the blessing* in the tribe itself.   2. The *nearest fulfilments* of it in the temporal history.   3. The *symbolical import* pointing to a remoter fulfilment.   We may compare the many dying scenes of the Bible with this ; as the last words of *Isaac, Moses,*

Joshua, Samuel, David, Simeon, Stephen, Paul, Peter, and the *apocalyptic visions* of John.   Compare especially the *song of Moses,* and the *prophecy of Balaam.*   It seems possible that the beautiful exclamation, ver. 18, " *I have waited for thy salvation, O Lord,*" was intended to form a kind of middle point, separating the groups of blessings into one of seven, and another of five.   The first group has *a Messianic character,* the second a *wider, cosmopolitan.*   In the first, *Judah,* the royal tribe, represents the theocracy.   In the second, *Joseph,* the link of connection between Israel and Egypt, represents the kingdom of Christ becoming the universal kingdom, from thence is the shepherd, the stone of Israel.   The whole is a typical representation of " Israel " in the higher sense.   1. *It comes out of sinful human nature.*   2. *It is developed by the grace of God in human history.*   3. *It stands upon the Divine order* of the twelve tribes, the revealed truth, and the Divinely sanctioned religious life and institutions.   4. The *essential element* in the history, is the *Messiah coming out of Judah,* the shepherd of Israel, the stone of help out of Joseph, the Nazarite, the tried man, the blessed one.   5. *The kingdom of Christ is the universal blessedness* of the world.   When Jacob has handed on his blessing to his heirs, he gathers up his feet into the bed, yields up the ghost, and is gathered to his people.   When the carnal Israel is done with, the spiritual Israel remains.   When the promises of God shall be fulfilled, then there shall be no more concern with the earthly pilgrimage. " The blessings prevail unto the utmost bound of the everlasting hills."—R.

Vers. 8—12.—*Judah's portion.*   " Judah, thou art he whom thy brethren shall praise," &c.   This dying vision and the utterances of the dying patriarch seem in harmony with all the surroundings in this part of the sacred record.   The aged Jacob is dying.   He has passed through such changes, such trials and successes, has had such seasons of depression and of exultation, but now his soul is filled with rapture at what will be the future of his children.   He saw how he would live in his children. A man should not be indifferent to his name dying out.   Some are, but only such as are not of intense nature.   As a man nearing the close of life, great importance was attached, by his son, to his utterances.   On a farewell festive occasion, Isaac partook of venison before giving his blessing to Jacob and Esau.   Jacob called all his sons together, as he was dying, and seems to have had supernatural strength given to utter so many and distinct prophecies.   He knew the individual character of his sons, and so could better foretell, almost apart from Divine inspiration, what would be their future.   The words uttered on the borders of the other land seemed necessarily inspired.   Such a man as Jacob would no more pass away, if possible, without such utterances, than would a millionnaire think of dying without a will. No mere offspring of a disordered brain, or over-excited imagination, were these words.   They were actual prophecies.   Jacob was not only a patriarch, but a prophet.   He speaks under the influence of the God of his fathers (ch. xlviii. 15), and the future bore out what he had foretold.   We wish to consider chiefly the utterances concerning one tribe, Judah.

I. A PROPHECY OF POWER.   His enemies were " to flee before him," &c.   As victor he lays his hands on their necks, that they may be subject and yet live.   His brethren were to acknowledge his power.   He is to be as a young lion in agility, and as an old lion with the strength of years remaining, whom none will dare to anger.   All this seems to be the glorification of mere physical power.   Spiritual power is to be desired above the physical.   And this we have in Christ.

II. A PROPHECY OF PRECEDENCY.   Jacob seems to have come at last upon the one for whom he was seeking.   He speaks of Judah as one whom his brethren shall praise. This is said to be " a play upon the name, Judah, as meaning one who is celebrated." And the name of Judah was accepted afterwards by the whole nation.   We should have thought that if the firstborn, Reuben, had not been placed first, Joseph would have been.   Judah's character, however, was more noble in some things even than that of Joseph.   He did not delight in the wrong-doing of the brethren.   Jacob may in his mind have blamed Joseph, in that he had not sought to know whether his father was alive before circumstances of death drove him to know of his still being alive. Judah was always ever ready to sacrifice himself, to be bound for his brother.   There seems to have been much that was noble in him.   Hence, we can understand, in a

measure, the precedency accorded to him.   Precedency is not to be sought for its own
sake.   It is then only another form of vanity.   When precedency is forced on men, it
is because their worth and their usefulness to others is recognised by others, although
not by themselves.   How remarkable it is that God often selected the younger before
the elder, e. g. Abel, Jacob, Moses, David.   Judah is taken before Reuben.   A lesson
evidently taught in this, viz., that God is no respecter of persons, that he seeth not as
man seeth, that the course of spiritual feeling does not always follow the line of birth.

III. PROPHECY OF PERMANENCY. This permanency was comparative in one sense
and actual in another.   Judah lasted longer than any of the tribes as a distinct power,
and, since Christ came of that tribe, may be said to be permanent still.   Who thinks
of Naphtali, or Zebulun, or Issachar ? but Judah is a name most familiar.   The
" sceptre " is the sheik's staff, which, like a marshal's baton, indicates his right to
lead.   Judah was to lead, and to give the law until Shiloh came ; and he did.
Shiloh evidently points to the Messiah.   It is a mystic name (comp. ch. xlviii. 16 ;
Is. ix. 6 ; xi. 1).   Some render this passage, "Until he [Judah] comes as the rest-
giver;" others, " until he comes to whom it belongs."   Christ is the only rightful rest-
giver, and to him alone belongs all honour and praise.   We see that the aim of God
with respect to the descendants of Jacob was to provide a race which should keep
alive a knowledge of God in the world until the Messiah should come.   When that
race had fulfilled this mission, it dropped into line with the rest of the nations.   It is
no longer to lead.   We see that as ten tribes were broken off by Jeroboam from Judah,
they were carried captive by the Assyrians, and with that nation swallowed up in oblivion, never, probably, to be known of again.   And so with the Jews ; they no longer
lead.   Although still retaining much that is distinctive, they will gradually, we believe, assimilate with other nations, and, accepting Christ, be one with other Christians
in that one fold of mercy he has provided.   Christ unites us to God and to others,
breaks down middle walls of partition, gives to us also " life eternal," so that when
this life shall fail, we shall be received into " everlasting habitations," and know as
real a permanency as that of Judah.

IV. PROPHECY OF PROSPERITY.   In the eleventh verse, Jacob indicates the sort of
territory Judah will have,—one rich in vineyards and oliveyards.   He foretells his
prosperity during the period intervening between the prophecy and the advent of
Shiloh.   The twelfth verse means, that " his eyes should be redder than wine," i. e.
brilliant with joy.   The words "white as milk" refer to purity as well as prosperity.
Both are found in Christ.   True joy and purity shall draw souls to Christ.   " Unto
him shall the gathering of the people be."   His truth has " the promise of the life
that now is, and of that which is to come."   How much that is foretold of Judah is
only typical of Jesus.   He is the true conqueror, ruler, object of praise.   He is " the
Lion of the tribe of Judah " (Rev. v. 5), the " desire of all nations " (Hag. ii. 7), the
one who if lifted up would draw all unto him (John xii. 32), the one in whom all the
children of God are to be gathered in one (John xi. 52).

Learn—1. We find much to confirm faith in the way in which the prophecy of
Jacob was fulfilled.   2. We find much to lead us to seek to be in Christ, through whom
Judah obtained such blessings antecedently.   3. We find something to lead us to ask
as to whether we have grown in purity, power, and whether our souls prosper and are
in health.—H.

Ver. 10.—*The coming of Shiloh.* Remarkable agreement of ancient interpreters,
Jewish as well as Christian, to consider this a prophecy of Messiah.   The former of
special value, as being before the event.   The Targum of Onkelos renders the passage,
"until Messiah comes, whose is the kingdom."   Many others equally distinct.   Some
have observed that the words, "Shiloh shall come," make in Hebrew the same number
as the name " Messiah."   Ancient Christian writers all take the same view.   The
name Shiloh expresses rest or peace.   Observe how this answers the need of man.
Sin brought the curse of labour (ch. iii. 17—19), and unrest (Isa. lvii. 20, 21), and
want of peace.   Hence the frequent mention of rest, which, however, was only typical
and temporary (Heb. iv. 8).   Hence the common salutation, " Peace be unto you."
And rest and peace are ours through the coming of Christ (Matt. xi. 28 ; John x. 28 ·
Rom. viii. 38).

I. The history of Israel a preparation for the coming of Christ. The moral law convincing of sin (Gal. iii. 24). The ceremonial law foreshadowing restoration (Heb. x. 1); the prophets declaring God's purpose, and the person and work of Christ; the dispersion by the captivity, bringing the people into contact with other nations, and thus preparing for a universal Church; their sufferings and state of subjection after their return, keeping alive the expectation of "Messiah, the prince."

II. The history of the world a preparation for Christ. The colonising instinct of the Greeks making their language almost universal; the contact of Greek and Jewish learning at Alexandria and elsewhere, by which the heathen language was made capable of expressing Divine truth; the widespread power and organisation of the Romans, by which in so many ways the fulfilment of prophecy was brought about (Luke ii. 1; John xix. 36, 37).

III. For what Shiloh should come. To gather all nations unto himself (Isa. ii. 2, 3; John xi. 52; xii. 32). To redeem mankind, both Jews and Gentiles (Ps. xlix. 15; Isa. xxxv. 4—10; John x. 16; Gal. iv. 5). To bear the sins of mankind (Isa. liii. 11, 12; 2 Cor. v. 14; 1 Pet. ii. 24). To teach his people the way of life (Deut. xviii. 15; Matt. xi. 27; John iv. 25). To reign over his people (Dan. ii. 44; Rev. xi. 15). To give them victory (Ps. xliv. 5; 1 John v. 4; Rev. xii. 11).

IV. Lesson of encouragement. Why doubt God's acceptance of thee? or his readiness to help? Mark his desire that all should be saved (Ezek. xviii. 32; 1 Tim. ii. 4). Mark how this is the ruling principle running through the whole Bible. The work of Christ was no newly devised thing, but "that which was from the beginning" (1 Pet. i. 20). All our imperfections, all our weakness of faith is known to God, yet such as we are, he bids us trust in Christ's work. Judah himself was a very imperfect character. His descendants not less so. Yet of them the text was spoken. "Be not afraid, only believe."—M.

Ver. 18.—*God's salvation.* I. What it is. Deliverance from evil, succour against foes, victory over sin and death.

II. Whence it comes. The primal fountain is Jehovah, the covenant God of the believer. The salvation of the gospel is God's in its original conception and proclamation, in its subsequent procurement and donation, in its ultimate development and consummation.

III. How it is obtained. Not by merit, or by works, but by believing, and waiting, and hoping. "He that believeth shall be saved." "The Lord loveth them that hope in his mercy." "It is good for a man both to hope, and to quietly wait for the salvation of the Lord."—W.

Ver. 18.—*A dying saint's exercise.* I. Adoration. "O Lord!" Jehovah the God of redemption, the supreme object of worship.

II. Meditation. "Thy salvation!" What a theme for the thoughts to dwell on God's salvation in its origin, in its greatness, in its freeness, &c.

III. Expectation. "For thy salvation do I hope." Hope is the expectation of future good, and presupposes faith as its ground-work and support.—W.

Ver. 26.—*The separated one, or Joseph a type of Christ.* Joseph was separated from his brethren—

I. In his father's affections. Jacob loved him more than any of his other sons. So was Christ the only-begotten and well-beloved Son of the Father.

II. In his personal character. Joseph brought unto Jacob the evil report that he heard circulating about his brethren, thus proving that he had no sympathy with their wicked ways. So Christ was "holy, harmless, undefiled, and separate from sinners."

III. In his heavenly communications. Joseph was favoured above his brethren in being made the recipient of dreams, and the depositary, as it were, of Divine secrets. And Christ received not the Spirit by measure, so that of him it could be said, No man knoweth the Father but the Son.

IV. In his evil fortunes. Joseph was hated, sold, and practically given over to death by his brethren.   So was Christ not only despised and rejected by his brethren, but separated from all mankind in the character of his sufferings and death.

V. IN HIS FUTURE EXALTATION.   Joseph became the governor of Egypt, and the saviour of his family.   And Christ after his resurrection was exalted to be a Prince, and a Saviour for mankind.—W.

EXPOSITION.

CHAPTER L.

Ver. 1.—**And Joseph fell upon his father's face, and wept upon him, and kissed him.** Joseph had no doubt closed the eyes of his revered and beloved parent, as God had promised to the patriarch that he would (ch. xlvi. 4), and now, in demonstration both of the intensity of his love and of the bitterness of his sorrow, he sinks upon the couch upon which the lifeless form is lying, bending over the pallid countenance with warm tears, and imprinting kisses of affection on the cold and irresponsive lip.   It is neither unnatural nor irreligious to mourn for the dead; and he must be callous indeed who can see a parent die without an outburst of tender grief.

Ver. 2.—**And Joseph commanded his servants the physicians**—literally, *the healers*, הָרֹפְאִים from רָפָא, to sew together, to mend, hence to heal, a class of persons which abounded in Ancient Egypt, each physician being only qualified to treat a single disorder (Herod., ii. 84).   The medical men of Egypt were held in high repute abroad, and their assistance was at various times required by persons from other countries, as, *e. g.*, Cyrus and Darius (Herod., iii. 1, 132).   Their knowledge of medicines was extensive, and is referred to both in sacred (Jer. lxvi. 11) and profane (Homer, 'Odyssey,' iv. 229) writings.   The Egyptian doctors belonged to the sacerdotal order, and were expected to know all things relating to the body, and diseases and remedies contained in the six last of the sacred books of Hermes.   According to Pliny (vii. 56), the study of medicine originated in Egypt (*vide* Wilkinson in Rawlinson's 'Herodotus,' vol. ii. pp. 116, 117).   The physicians employed by Joseph were those attached to his own household, or the court practitioners—**to embalm his father:** —literally, *to spice or season* (the body of) *his father*, i. e. to prepare it for burial by means of aromatics; *ut aromatibus condirent* (Vulgate); ἐνταφιάσαι τὸν πατέρα αὐτοῦ (LXX.), which is putting part of a proceeding for the whole (Tayler Lewis).   According to Herodotus (ii. 86), the embalmers belonged to a distinct hereditary class or guild from the ordinary physicians; but either their formation into such a separate order of practitioners was of later origin (Hengstenberg, Kurtz,

Kalisch), or Jacob was embalmed by the physicians instead of the embalmers proper because, not being an Egyptian, he could not be subjected to the ordinary treatment of the embalming art ('Speaker's Commentary')—**and the physicians embalmed Israel.**   The method of preparing mummies in Ancient Egypt has been elaborately described, both by Herodotus (ii. 86) and Diodorus Siculus (i. 91), and, in the main, the accuracy of their descriptions has been confirmed by the evidence derived from the mummies themselves.   According to the most expensive process, which cost one talent of silver, or about £250 sterling, the brain was first extracted through the nostrils by means of a crooked piece of iron, the skull being thoroughly cleansed of any remaining portions by rinsing with drugs; then, through an opening in the left side made with a sharp Ethiopian knife of agate or of flint, the viscera were removed, the abdomen being afterwards purified with palm wine and an infusion of aromatics; next, the disembowelled corpse was filled with every sort of spicery except frankincense, and the opening sewed up; after that the stuffed form was steeped for seventy days in natrum or subcarbonate of soda obtained from the Libyan desert, and sometimes in wax and tanning, bitumen also being employed in later times; and finally, on the expiration of that period, which was scrupulously observed, the body was washed, wrapped about with linen bandages, smeared over with gum, decorated with amulets, sometimes with a network of porcelain bugles, covered with a linen shroud, and, in due course, transferred to a mummy case (*vide* Wilkinson's 'Manners and Customs of the Ancient Egyptians,' vol. iii. p. 471, ed. 1878; Rawlinson's 'Herodotus,' vol. ii. pp. 118—123).

Ver. 3.—**And forty days were fulfilled for him; for so are fulfilled the days of those who are embalmed: and the Egyptians mourned** (literally, *wept*) **for him threescore and ten days**—*i. e.* the whole period of mourning, including the forty days for embalming, extended to seventy days, a statement which strikingly coincides with the assertion of Diodorus Siculus (i. 72), that the embalming process occupied about thirty days, while the mourning continued seventy-two days; the first number, seventy, being seven decades, or ten weeks of seven days, and the second $12 \times 6 = 72$, the duodecimal calculation being also used in Egypt (*vide* Wilkinson in Rawlinson's 'Herodotus,' vol. ii. p. 121 ; and in ' Manners and Customs of the Ancient Egyptians ' vol. iii. p. 471, *et seqq.*, ed. 1878). The apparent discrepancy between the accounts of Genesis and Herodotus will disappear if the seventy days of the Greek historian, during which the body lay in *natrum*, be viewed as the entire period of mourning (Hengstenberg's ' Egypt and the Books of Moses,' p. 68 ; Sir G. Wilkinson in Rawlinson's 'Herodotus,' vol. ii. p. 121), a sense which the words ταῦτα δὲ ποιήσαντες ταριχεύουσι λίτρῳ, κρύψαντες ἡμέρας ἑβδομήκοντα (Herod. ii. 86) will bear, though Kalisch somewhat arbitrarily, but unconvincingly, pronounces it to be " excluded both by the context and Greek syntax."

Vers. 4, 5.—**And when the days of his mourning were past, Joseph spake unto the house of Pharaoh, saying, If now I have found grace in your eyes, speak, I pray you, in the ears of Pharaoh,**—that Joseph did not address himself directly to Pharaoh, but through the members of the royal household, was not owing to the circumstance that, being arrayed in mourning apparel, he could not come before the king (Rosenmüller), since it is not certain that this Persian custom (Esther iv. 2) prevailed in Egypt, but is supposed to have been due, either to a desire on Joseph's part to put himself on a good understanding with the priesthood who composed the courtly circle, since the interment of the dead was closely connected with the religious beliefs of Egypt (Hävernick), or, what was more likely, to the fact that Joseph, having, according to Egyptian custom (Herod. ii. 36), allowed his beard and hair to grow, could not enter the king's presence without being both shaven and shorn (Hengstenberg, Kurtz, Keil). It has been suggested (Kalisch) that Joseph's power may have been restricted after the expiration of the famine, or that another Pharaoh may have succeeded to the throne who was not so friendly as his predecessor with the grand vizier of the realm ; but such conjectures are not required to render Joseph's conduct in this matter perfectly intelligible—**saying, My father made me swear** (ch. xlvii. 29), **saying** (*i. e.* my father saying), **Lo, I die : in my grave which I have digged for me**—not bought (Onkelos, Drusius, Ainsworth, Bohlen, and others), but digged, ὤρυξα (LXX.), *fodi* (Vulgate). Jacob may have either enlarged the original cave at Machpelah, or prepared in it the special niche which he designed to occupy—**in the land of Canaan, there shalt thou bury me. Now therefore** (literally, *and now*) **let me go up, I pray thee** (the royal permission was

required to enable Joseph to pass beyond the boundaries of Egypt, especially when accompanied by a large funeral procession), **and bury my father, and I will come again.**

Ver. 6.—**And Pharaoh said, Go up, and bury thy father, according as he made thee swear.** Pharaoh's answer would, of course, be conveyed through the courtiers.

Vers. 7—9.—**And Joseph went up to bury his father: and with him went up all the servants of Pharaoh** (*i. e.* the chief officers of the royal palace, as the next clause explains), **the elders of his house** (*i. e.* of Pharaoh's house), **and all the elders of the land of Egypt** (*i. e.* the nobles and State officials), **and all the house of Joseph, and his brethren, and his father's house: only their little ones, and their flocks, and their herds, they left in the land of Goshen. And there went up with him** (as an escort) **both chariots and horsemen: and it was a very great company.** Delineations of funeral processions, of a most elaborate character, may be seen on the monuments. A detailed and highly interesting account of the funeral procession of an Egyptian grandee, enabling us to picture to the mind's eye the scene of Jacob's burial, will be found in Wilkinson's ' Manners and Customs of the Ancient Egyptians,' vol. iii. p. 444, ed. 1878. First servants led the way, carrying tables laden with fruit, cakes, flowers, vases of ointment, wine and other liquids, with three young geese and a calf for sacrifice, chairs and wooden tablets, napkins, and other things. Then others followed bearing daggers, bows, fans, and the mummy cases in which the deceased and his ancestors had been kept previous to burial. Next came a table of offerings, fauteuils, couches, boxes, and a chariot. After these men appeared with gold vases and more offerings. To these succeeded the bearers of a sacred boat and the mysterious eye of Osiris, as the god of stability. Placed in the consecrated boat, the hearse containing the mummy of the deceased was drawn by four oxen and by seven men, under the direction of a superintendent who regulated the march of the funeral. Behind the hearse followed the male relations and friends of the deceased, who either beat their breasts, or gave token of their sorrow by their silence and solemn step as they walked, leaning on their long sticks ; and with these the procession closed.

Ver. 10.—**And they came to the threshing-floor of Atad.** The threshing-floor, or *goren*, was a large open circular area which was used for trampling out the corn by means of oxen, and was exceedingly convenient for the accommodation of a large body of people such as accompanied Joseph. The goren at which the funeral party halted was named Atad (*i. e.* Buckthorn), either from the name of the owner, or from the quantity of buckthorn which grew in the neighbourhood. **Which is beyond Jordan**—literally, *on the other side of the Jordan*, i. e. west side, if the narrator wrote from his own standpoint (Jerome, Drusius, Ainsworth, Kalisch, 'Speaker's Commentary,' Wordsworth, *et alii*), in which case the funeral train would in all probability follow the direct route through the country of the Philistines, and Goren Atad would be situated somewhere south of Hebron, in the territory (afterwards) of Judah ; but east side of the river if the phrase must be interpreted from the standpoint of Palestine (Clericus, Rosenmüller, Hengstenberg, Kurtz, Keil, Lange, Gerlach, Hävernick, Murphy, and others), in which case the burial procession must have journeyed by the wilderness, as the Israelites on a latter occasion did, and probably for not dissimilar reasons. In favour of the former interpretation may be claimed ver. 11, which says the Canaanites beheld the mourning, implying seemingly that it occurred within the borders of Canaan, *i. e.* on the west of the Jordan ; while support for the latter is derived from ver. 13, which appears to state that after the lamentation at Goren Atad the sons of Jacob carried him into Canaan, almost necessarily involving the inference that Goren Atad was on the east of the Jordan ; but *vide infra*. If the former is correct, Goren Atad was probably the place which Jerome calls Betagla *tertio ab Hiericho lapide, duobus millibus ab Jordane;* if the latter is correct, it does not prove a post-Mosaic authorship (Tuch, Bohlen, &c.), since the phrase appears to have had an ideal usage with reference to Canaan in addition to the objective geographical one (Hengstenberg 'on the Genuineness of the Pentateuch,' vol. ii. p. 260 ; Keil's 'Introduction,' vol. i. p. 189 ; Kalisch 'on Genesis,' p. 776). **And there they mourned with a great and very sore lamentation.** The Egyptians were exceedingly demonstrative and vehement in their public lamentations for the dead, rending their garments, smiting on their breasts, throwing dust and mud on their heads, calling on the deceased by name, and chanting funeral dirges to the music of a tambourine with the tinkling plates removed (Wilkinson's 'Ancient Egyptians,' vol. iii. p. 440, ed. 1878). **And he made a mourning for his father seven days.** This was a special mourning before interment (cf. Ecclus. xxii. 11).

Ver. 11.—**And when** (literally, *and*) **the inhabitants of the land, the Canaanites, saw the mourning in the floor of Atad, they** (literally, *and they*) **said, This is a grievous mourning to the Egyptians: wherefore the name of it was called Abel-mizraim,**—*i. e.* the meadow (אָבֵל) of the Egyptians, with a play upon the word (אֵבֶל) *mourning* (Keil, Kurtz, Gerlach, Rosenmüller, &c.), if indeed the word has not been punctuated wrongly—אָבֵל instead of אֵבֶל (Kalisch), which latter reading appears to have been followed by the LXX. (πένθος Αἰγύπτου) and the Vulgate (*planctus Ægypti*)—**which is beyond Jordan** (*vide supra*).

Vers. 12, 13.—**And his sons**—the Egyptians halting at Goren Atad (Keil, Hävernick, Kalisch, Murphy, &c.); but this does not appear from the narrative—**did unto him according as he commanded them** (the explanation of what they did being given in the next clause): **for his sons carried him** —not simply from Goren Atad, but from Egypt, so that this verse does not imply anything about the site of the Buckthorn threshing-floor (*vide supra*, ver. 11)—**into the land of Canaan, and buried him in the cave of the field of Machpelah, which Abraham bought with the field for a possession of a burying-place of Ephron the Hittite, before Mamre** (*vide* ch. xxiii.).

Ver. 14.—**And Joseph returned into Egypt, he, and his brethren, and all that went up with him to bury his father, after he had buried his father.**

HOMILETICS.

Vers. 1—14.—*The funeral of Jacob.* I. THE PRIVATE SORROW. That a great and good man like Jacob, the father of a numerous family, the ancestor of an important people, the chieftain of an influential tribe, the head of the Church of God, should depart this life without eliciting from some heart a tribute of sorrow, is inconceivable. That any of his sons witnessed the last solemn act of this great spiritual wrestler, when he gathered up his feet into his bed and yielded up his spirit into the hands of God, without a tear and without a pang of grief, although it is only the emotion of Joseph that is recorded, is what we cannot for a moment believe. Less demonstrative than was that of Joseph, less deep too, probably, since the heart of Joseph appears to have been peculiarly susceptible of tender emotions, we may yet suppose that the grief of Joseph's brethren was not less real.

II. THE PUBLIC MOURNING. In accordance with the customs of the times, and of the country, it was needful that a public ceremonial should be observed, in honour of the dead. Accordingly, Joseph, as the first step required by the usages of the people amongst whom he lived, gave instructions to his court physicians to embalm his father. For details as to the process, which occupied a period of forty days, the Exposition may be consulted. Then, along with this, for seventy days, peculiar rites, supposed to be expressive of the heart's grief, such as rending the garments, smiting the breast, throwing dust upon the head, calling on the deceased, were maintained with the assistance of friends, neighbours, and professional mourners.

III. THE FUNERAL PROCESSION. 1. *The train of mourners.* This consisted of the state and court officials of Pharaoh's house, and of the land of Egypt, the members of the houses of Joseph and his brethren, and a troop of horsemen and charioteers for protection on the journey. 2. *The line of march.* This was either straight north, through the country of the Philistines, if Goren Atad was south of Hebron in Judea, or it was round about by the way of the wilderness, if the halting-place was east of Jordan. 3. *The lamentation at Goren Atad.* This was intended as a special demonstration before burial, and was conducted with such vehemence as to arrest the attention of the Canaanites, who called the place in consequence, Abel-Mizraim; *i. e.* the plain or the mourning of Mizraim. 4. *The advance to Hebron.* It is more than probable that the Egyptians, who had accompanied the funeral procession from Goshen, remained behind at Goren Atad, while Joseph and his brethren bore the patriarch's body on to Hebron.

IV. THE SOLEMN INTERMENT. His sons buried him in the ancestral vault of Machpelah. Reverently, affectionately, tearfully, yet hopefully, let us hope, they laid the weary pilgrim down to sleep till the resurrection morn beside the dust of his own Leah, and in the company of Abraham, and Sarah, and Isaac, and Rebekah. It must have been an affecting, as surely it was a sublime spectacle, this coming home of an aged exile to lay his bones in his native land, this returning of the heir of Canaan to claim his inheritance, this laying down of the last member of the great patriarchal family among the other inmates of Machpelah. With the burial of Jacob, the first patriarchal family was complete, and the tomb was closed. The members of the second household slept at Shechem.

HOMILIES BY VARIOUS AUTHORS.

Ch. l.—*Retrospect and prospect.* The fellowship of Egypt with the children of Israel in the burial of Jacob is full of significance. "A very great company went with them." "Abel-Mizraim" the Canaanites called it, "a grievous mourning to the Egyptians." It seemed to them altogether an Egyptian funeral. Yet we know that it was not. The work of God's grace will transform the world that it shall not be recognised. The funeral itself said, Egypt is not our home. It pointed with prophetic significance to the future of God's people. Canaan, the home of God's people, is the symbol of the everlasting home. Strange that the conscience should wake up in the brethren of Joseph after the father's death. How great the power of love in subduing fear! The true-hearted, tender piety of Joseph both towards God and towards his father and his kindred, is not influenced by such considerations as affected the lower characters of his brethren. They feared because they were not as true as he. "Joseph wept when they spake unto him," wept for them, wept to think they had not yet understood him. It is a great grief to a good man, a man of large, simple, loving nature, to be thought capable of unkindness and treachery. Joseph recognised that his life had been a Divine thing. He was only an instrument in the hands of God, in the place of God. He saw Providence working with grace. The influence of real religion is to sanctify and exalt natural affections. Joseph's end, like his father's, was a testimony to the faithfulness of God, and a fresh consecration of the covenant people to their Divine future. "I die, and God will surely visit you." He was a truly humble man to the last. His people's blessedness was not of his making. His death would be rather their gain than their loss. Yet "by faith he gave commandment concerning his bones" (Heb. xi. 22), not in any foolish feeling of relic worship, but because he would have the people while *in* Egypt not to be *of*

Egypt. Those who live on the promises of God will feel that "faith is the substance of things hoped for, the evidence of things not seen," and confess, not by word only but by deed, and to the last moment of life, "that they are pilgrims and strangers on the earth," "seeking a better city, even a heavenly."—R.

EXPOSITION.

Ver. 15. — **And when** (literally *and*) **Joseph's brethren saw that their father was dead, they** (literally, *and they*) **said, Joseph will peradventure hate us,**—literally, *If Joseph hated us*, or pursued us hostilely (*sc.* what would become of us ?), לוּ with the imperfect or future setting forth a possible but undesirable contingency (*vide* Ewald's 'Hebrew Syntax,' § 358*a* ; Gesenius, 'Lexicon,' *sub voce*)—**and will certainly requite us** (literally, *if returning he caused to return upon us*) **all the evil which we did unto him.** "What then ?" is the natural conclusion of the sentence. "We must be utterly undone."

Vers. 16, 17.—**And** (under these erroneous though not unnatural apprehensions) **they sent a messenger unto Joseph,**—literally, *they charged Joseph*, i. e. they deputed one of their number (possibly Benjamin) to carry their desires to Joseph—**saying, Thy father did command before he died, saying** (though not recorded, the circumstance here mentioned may have been historically true), **So shall ye say unto Joseph, Forgive, I pray thee now, the trespass of thy brethren, and their sin; for they did unto thee evil** (nothing is more inherently probable than that the good man on his death-bed did request his sons to beg their brother's pardon): **and now, we pray thee, forgive the trespass of the servants of the God of thy father.** Joseph's brethren in these words at once evince the depth of their humility, the sincerity of their repentance, and the genuineness of their religion. They were God's true servants, and they wished to be forgiven by their much-offended brother, who, however, had long since embraced them in the arms of his affection. **And Joseph wept when they spake unto him** — pained that they should for a single moment have entertained such suspicions against his love.

Ver. 18.—**And his brethren also went and fell down before his face; and they said, Behold, we be thy servants.** Both the attitudes assumed and the words spoken were designed to express the intensity of their contrition and the fervour of their supplication.

Ver. 19.—**And Joseph said unto them, Fear not: for am I in the place of God ?**—*i. e.* either reading the words as a question, Should I arrogate to myself what obviously belongs to Elohim, viz., the power and right of vengeance (Calvin, Kalisch, Murphy,

'Speaker's Commentary '), or the power to interfere with the purposes of God ? (Keil, Rosenmüller) ; or, regarding them as an assertion, I am in God's stead, *i. e.* a minister to you for good (Wordsworth).

Ver. 20.—**But as for you, ye thought evil against me; but God meant it unto good** (literally, *and ye were thinking or meditating evil against me; Elohim was thinking or meditating for good*, i. e. that what you did should be for good), **to bring to pass, as it is this day, to save much people alive** (*vide* ch. xlv. 5).

Ver. 21. — **Now therefore** (literally, *and now*) **fear ye not: I will nourish you, and your little ones.** Thus he repeats and confirms the promise which he had originally made to them when he invited them to come to Egypt (ch. xlv. 11, 18, 19). **And he comforted them, and spake kindly unto them**—literally, *to their hearts* (cf. ch. xxxiv. 3).

Ver. 22.—**And Joseph dwelt in Egypt, he, and his father's house: and Joseph lived an hundred and ten years.** Wordsworth notices that Joshua, who superintended the burial of Joseph in Shechem, also lived 110 years. Joseph's death occurred fifty-six years after that of Jacob.

Ver. 23. — **And Joseph saw Ephraim's children of the third** generation : — *i. e.* Ephraim's great-grandchildren (Kalisch, Lange), or Ephraim's great-great-grandsons (Keil, Murphy), which perhaps was not impossible, since Ephraim must have been born before Joseph's thirty-seventh year, thus allowing at least sixty-three years for four generations to intervene before the patriarch's death, which might be, if marriage happened early, say not later than eighteen— **the children also of Machir the son of Manasseh**—by a concubine (1 Chron. vii. 14)— **were brought up upon Joseph's knees**—literally, *were born upon Joseph's knees*, i. e. were adopted by him as soon as they were born (Kalisch, Wordsworth, 'Speaker's Commentary '), or were born so that he could take them also upon his knees, and show his love for them (Keil).

Vers. 24, 25.—**And Joseph said unto his brethren, I die: and God** (Elohim) **will surely visit you,**—literally, *visiting will visit you*, according to his promise (ch. xlvi. 4)— **and bring you out of this land unto the land which he sware to Abraham, to Isaac, and to Jacob. And Joseph took an oath of the children of Israel,**—as his father had done of him (ch. xlvii. 31),—**saying, God will surely visit you, and ye shall carry up my bones from hence.** The writer to the Hebrews (ch. xi. 22) refers to this as a signal instance of faith on the part of Joseph.

Ver. 26.—**So Joseph died, being an hundred and ten years old** (literally, *a son of a hundred and ten years*), **and they** (*i. e.* the children of Israel) **embalmed him** (*vide* on

ver. 2), **and he was put in a coffin** (or chest, *i. e.* a mummy case, which was commonly constructed of sycamore wood) **in Egypt,** where he remained for a period of 360 years, until the time of the Exodus, when, according to the engagement now given, his remains were carried up to Canaan, and solemnly deposited in the sepulchre of Shechem (Josh. xxiv. 32).

HOMILETICS.

Vers. 15—26.—*The last of the house of Jacob.* I. JOSEPH AND HIS BRETHREN (vers. 15—18). 1. *The unworthy suspicion.* After Jacob's death, Joseph's brethren began to fear lest he should seek to revenge himself on account of his early injuries. It was perhaps natural that such an apprehension should arise within their breasts, considering the enormity of the wickedness of which they had been guilty; but remembering all the tokens of Joseph's love which already they had received, it was surely unkind to Joseph to suffer such a thought for even a moment to find a lodgment in their breasts. 2. *The friendly embassage.* Deputing Benjamin, it is thought, to be the bearer of their wishes, they instructed him to remind Joseph of their dead father's desire that he should forgive the evil he had suffered at their hands, and to solicit an express assurance from his own lips that it was so. 3. *The voluntary humiliation.* Whether they allowed their messenger to return or followed close upon his heels cannot be certainly concluded. But they appear to have resorted in a body to Joseph's palace, and placed themselves unconditionally in his power : "Behold, we be thy servants," meaning, "Do with us what seemeth good in thy sight." 4. *The generous assurance.* As they desired, he explicitly declared, though with tears at their unkindness, that they had no cause whatever to anticipate his anger, that he was not in God's place that he should seek to punish them for a sin which had turned out so providentially for good, and that on the contrary he would continue to nourish them and their little ones so long as they remained in Egypt. II. JOSEPH AND HIS CHILDREN'S CHILDREN. 1. *The children of Ephraim.* He lived long enough to see the children of Ephraim's grandchildren born into this sinful world, and then he died at the good old age of 110 years. 2. *The children of Manasseh.* He saw the offspring of Manasseh's son born, and either adopted into his own family, or brought up in his own house. III. JOSEPH AND THE HOUSE OF ISRAEL. 1. *Joseph's premonition of approaching death.* "Joseph said unto his brethren,"—*i. e.* the descendants of his brethren, his actual brethren having in all probability predeceased him,—"I die." Along with this Joseph recalled to their minds the sacred promise that God would eventually visit them and cause them to return to their own land. It is well when death approaches to remember God's promises. The thoughts of God are very suitable for dying hours. 2. *Joseph's preparation for death.* He took an oath of the children of Israel that they would carry up his bones to Canaan, in this following the example and imitating the faith of his revered father Jacob. 3. *Joseph's falling asleep in death.* "Joseph died, the son of an hundred and ten years." He had lived a shorter life than any of the four great preceding patriarchs ; but his life had been eminently honoured and useful, and his death, we may be sure, would be beautifully calm and peaceful. 4. *Joseph's body after death.* It was embalmed, and the mummy put into a coffin for better preservation, until the time approached when it could be taken for consignment to the holy land.

Learn—1. How difficult it is to shake oneself free from the evil consequences of sin, even after it has been forgiven. 2. How painful to a loving heart it is to be suspected of cherishing a feeling of revenge. 3. How generously God sometimes rewards his servants on earth, by permitting them to see children's children, born and brought up, and sometimes also brought into the family of his Church. 4. How peacefully a child of God can die ; and 5. How hopefully he ought to look forward to the resurrection

HOMILIES BY VARIOUS AUTHORS.

Ver. 20.—*Intended bane an unintentional boon.* "Ye thought evil against me; but God meant it unto good." Joseph must have been deeply pained by the mistrust of his brethren. They implied that it was only out of consideration for his father that he had been kind to them. Yet Joseph had forgiven them. They could not so easily believe in the forgiveness; just as man now is forgiven by God, but he has the greatest difficulty in believing in the reconciliation. Joseph's brethren sent a messenger unto him, probably Benjamin. They who had once sold Joseph as a slave now offer to be his slaves. The offer is to him humiliating. Moreover, it is great pain to him. To a noble soul designing only good to others there is no greater offensiveness than to have his doings viewed with suspicion. Joseph repudiated the mistrust, and refused the offered self-enslavement. He assures his brethren of full forgiveness in words which must have been as softest balm to wounded spirits. In a spirit of the highest magnanimity he tries even to make them view with complacency the result of their wrong-doing. In the text we have the "grand golden key to the whole of his life's history." Notice how—

I. Intended bane often becomes unintentional boon. Evil works evil to others, but sometimes good. Intended evil is overruled by God when he has some good object in view. "Man proposes, God disposes." God always knows what the result of certain actions will be. If they are good actions they work in line with his will: if evil, he overrules them. If the horse keeps the road it feels not the rein, but if it will turn aside, the sharp bit must draw it back again. Whatever speculation there may be about our absolute freeness, we *feel* that we are free. It is the glory of God to be able to trust with freedom a being with such great powers for moral evil, like man. He would teach us to *use* our wills, by giving us full freedom. We frequently pain him by our misuse and our abuse of our powers. What evil we devise and strive to carry out! The brethren of Joseph even intended murder, and modified it by selling their brother into slavery. They acted more cruelly than some of the men-stealers of Africa. The latter steal strangers to sell them, but these ten men sold their own brother. They thought they were rid of him. Egypt was a long way off; Joseph was but a weakling, and might soon perish. They would be free from his presence, and could divide their guilty gains. They hardened themselves against his tears and entreaties; and even in malicious spite were ready to slay the weeping youth because he did not appreciate their considerateness in selling him into slavery instead of killing him outright. It was an evil deed. Those who looked on could see no good to come out of it. There were, however, several great results. 1. He was personally advanced in life, and was able to make the best of it. 2. He saved thousands of people from perishing. and among them his own family. 3. He was the means of bringing Israel into Egypt, where it developed as a people. Its deliverance gave occasion to the mightiest display of Divine power. 4. He became a type of the Messiah—rejected of men. Thus we know not the results of any of our acts. God can overrule, to the development of character and spiritual power, circumstances seemingly most opposed to our best interests. God knows what is best. He could break the plans of the evil in pieces. Instead of this he oft confounds the wicked by letting them see that the ends they did not desire have been attained in spite of their opposition, and even by the very existence, that the intended bane becomes an unintentional boon. Thus Joseph's brothers found it, and bowed their heads.

II. There are several lessons to be learned from the way in which, by God's overruling, intended bane becomes a boon. 1. It is a *dangerous* thing to scheme against others. Especially is it a dangerous thing when a good man is the object of the attack. It is likely to be checked and to recoil. "A greater power than we can contradict may thwart our plans." There are a thousand chances of check or change. Men have so noticed this that even a French moralist said, "I do not know what hidden force it is that seems to delight in breaking up human plans just at the moment when they promise to turn out well." Yes, there is a "hidden force," ever watchful, ever balancing human actions, ever ordaining, either in this world or the next, the just meed of praise or blame, of retribution or reward. See how the scribes and Pharisees held councils against Jesus, the gentle, pure, loving teacher of truth, and healer of diseases, They sought how they might kill him. They excommunicated him, they sent others to entrap him. They succeeded at length in nailing him to the cross. They carried out their evil intentions; but that cross became the throne of the Saviour's power, the salvation; and the death of Christ became the life of the world. They went by wagging their heads, but at last they had to wring their hands. They themselves were left in their sin, and their "house left unto them desolate," while unto the Christ they hated all men are being drawn. 2. That God overrules evil s no license to do evil. Many would say, "Let us do evil that good may come." This would suit carnal nature. They would say, " Sin is not so great an evil, since God can overrule it." To talk like this would be like throwing dust in our own eyes when we have reached an eminence from whence we might behold a beautiful landscape. It would be like a youth who, seeing a gardener pruning trees, should take a knife and cut and slash all the trunks. Or, it would be like the act of one who, seeing how an artist had wrought in a picture some blunder into a beauty, should take a brush and streak with black the brilliant sky. We are not at liberty to sin that God may bring good out of it. 3. That God overrules evil should make us *feel our dependence* on him. If we could succeed in good without him, if all we intended to do could surely be calculated upon, we should become proud. It is well that God sometimes even breaks up our good plans in order that we may learn this lesson. We might even intend good without him otherwise, and that would lead to evil in ourselves. But we are dependent on him to check the evil of our own lives and of others' intentions. 4. It should make us *hopeful* also with respect to our affairs. Surely out of this thought we may get "royal contentment," as knowing we are in the hands of a noble protector, "who never gives ill but to him who deserves ill." 5. It should make us hopeful with respect to the order and destiny of the world. In some way, far off, God's glory may be advanced, even by the way in which he will have subdued, by Christ, *all* things unto himself. 6. Intended good is not always a benefit to those for whom intended. God intends good to men, and provides a way to bless, but men refuse. See at what a cost the way has been provided. Those who refuse are under worse condemnation. " It were better for them not to have known the way of righteousness than, after they have known it, to turn from the holy commandment delivered unto them." 7. We must all face our wrong-doing some time or other. We shall find that the evil we have sown has produced a harvest of weeds, which we shall have sorrowfully to reap. We ought to pray earnestly, "Deliver us from evil."—H.

Ver. 26.—*The lessons of a life.* Joseph's life remarkable for the variety of his experience, and for the consistency of his character through all. A man full of human sympathy, who also walked with God. Here the charm of his history. We can thoroughly enter into his feelings. In his boyhood, deservedly loved by his father, and on that very account hated by his brethren (1 John iii. 13); in his unmerited sufferings; in his steadfast loyalty to God and to his master; in his exaltation, and the wisdom with which he ruled Egypt; and in his forgiveness of those who had sold him as a slave, we feel for him and with him. But Joseph died. His trials and his triumphs passed away. The scene where he had played so conspicuous a part is filled by other forms. And he who was the means of saving a nation must share the lot of the most commonplace life. One event happens to all (Eccles. ii. 15). I. THE UNCERTAIN TENURE OF EARTHLY GOOD. No care can keep away misfortune, not even care to walk uprightly before God. Sin brings sorrow sooner or later; but it is a great mistake to think that all sorrow springs from faults committed (Ps. lxxiii. 5). Joseph's slavery was because his Godward life condemned his brothers and made them angry. His being thrown into prison was because he would not yield to temptation. This often a stumbling-block. If God really marks all that is done, why are his most faithful servants often so sorely smitten? We can neither deny the fact nor trace the reason of the stroke. Enough to know that it is part of God's plan (Heb. xii. 6), to fit us for the end of our being. As Christ was perfected by suffering (Heb. ii. 10), so must we be. And just because to bear the cross is needful for a follower of Christ (Matt. xvi. 24)—and this is not the endurance of suffering at our own choice, but the willing receiving of what God is pleased to send—the uncertainty of life gives constant opportunity for that submission to his will which is the result of living faith.

II. THE ONE END OF ALL LIVING (Exod. i. 6). How varied soever the outward lot, wealth or penury, joy or mourning, one day all must be left behind. To what purpose then is it to labour for good, or to dread impending evil? Can we not remember many whose name was much in men's mouths, full of youthful vigour or mature wisdom? And they are gone, and the world goes on as before. Joseph, embalmed in Egypt with almost royal honours, was as completely separated from all his wealth and power as if he had never possessed them. Others filled his place and occupied his gains, in their turn to give them up, and awake from the dream of possessions to join the company of those who have left all these things behind. And is this all? Has life nothing worth striving for? Is there no possession that we can really regard as our own?

III. LIFE HAS ABIDING TREASURES. Was it nothing to Joseph that he possessed and showed a forgiving spirit (Matt. vi. 14, 15), and singleness of heart, and earnest benevolence, and watchful consciousness of God's presence? These are treasures the world thinks little of. But these are treasures indeed, ministering comfort without care. And when earthly things slip from the grasp these abide, reflections of the mind of Christ, and telling of his abiding in the soul (Rev. xiv. 13).—M.

HOMILETICAL INDEX

TO

THE BOOK OF GENESIS

EXODUS

EXPOSITION AND HOMILETICS BY

GEORGE RAWLINSON

HOMILIES BY VARIOUS AUTHORS

J. ORR   D. YOUNG
C. A. GOODHART   J. URQUHART
H. T. ROBJOHNS

THE
BOOK OF EXODUS

VOL. I.

INTRODUCTION

§ 1. TITLE AND CONTENTS.

THE Hebrew-speaking Jews have always designated the five books of the Pentateuch by their initial word or words; and, as they called the first book *Berêshith*, "In the Beginning," and the third *Vay-yikra*, "And he called," so they denominated the second *Ve-êleh shemôth*, "And these (are) the names." The title "Exodus" was first applied to the book by the Hellenistic, or Greek-speaking, Jews, who translated the Hebrew Bible into Greek at Alexandria in the third and second centuries B.C. Exodus (ἔξοδος) means "departure" or "outgoing," and was selected as an appropriate name for a work which treats mainly of the departure of the Children of Israel out of the land of Egypt. The earliest Latin translation of the Old Testament, which was made from the Greek, retained the Greek title untranslated; and hence it passed into the Vulgate of Jerome, and into the languages of modern Europe.

While the departure of the Israelites out of Egypt, and the mode in which it was brought about, constitute the main subject of the book, and occupy its middle portion (chs. ii.—xviii.), two other subjects are also treated of, which form the prologue and the epilogue of the principal drama. The former of these—the subject-matter of ch. i.—is the increase and growth of the Israelites—their development from a tribe into a nation. The latter, which in spiritual grandeur and importance holds a pre-eminent rank, is the adoption of Israel as God's peculiar people by the Law given and the Covenant entered into at Mount Sinai (chs. xix.—xl.). The contents are thus in part historical, in part legislative. Historically, the book contains the events of 360 years, which is the interval between the death of Joseph and the giving of the Law at Sinai. It embraces the formation of the people by a rapid increase, which may have been partly due to natural causes, but was also in some degree the result of God's blessing resting especially upon them; the alarm of the Egyptian monarch at their growing numbers; his plans for preventing their multiplication and the entire failure of those plans; the birth and education of Moses; his first unauthorised attempt to deliver his nation from oppression; his flight to the land of Midian, and Divine appointment to be the deliverer of his nation; his communications with the Egyptian king on the subject of the people's release; the ten successive plagues whereby the king's reluctance was ultimately overcome; the institution of the Passover, and the departure of the Israelites; Pharaoh's pursuit; the passage of the Red Sea and the destruction of the Egyptian host; the journey from the Red Sea to Sinai; the giving of the Decalogue and the acceptance of the "Book of the Covenant" by the people; the lapse into idolatry and its punishment (ch. xxxii.); the directions given for the construction of the Tabernacle, the freewill offerings made, and the execution of the work by Bezaleel and Aholiab (chs. xxxv.—xl. 33); followed by the Divine occupation of the new construction, and the establishment, in connection with it, of signs whereby the further journeyings of the people were directed (xl. 34—38). In its legislative aspect, the book occupies the unique position of being the very source and origin—*fons et origo*—alike of the moral and of the ceremonial law, containing in the Decalogue an inspired summary of the first principles of pure morality, and in the directions given with respect to the Passover (xii. 1—50) and other feasts (ch. xxiii. 14—17), the redemption of the firstborn (ch. xiii. 11—16), the materials and plan of the Tabernacle (ch. xxv. 10—ch. xxvii.), the vestments of the priests and high-priest (ch. xxviii.), the method of their consecration (ch. xxix.), and other similar matters, asserting and enforcing the necessity of a prescribed course of outward acts and forms for the sustentation of religious life in a community of beings so constituted as men are in this world.

It has been well observed, that "the contents of the Second Book of Moses include an extraordinary variety of matter, and offer to the inquiring mind an unusual extent" of subjects for investigation.[1] The historical sketch of Israel's position in Egypt invites inquiry into the dark and difficult problems of Egyptian history and chronology: the Ten Plagues open up to us the consideration of the natural phenomena of Egypt and the East generally; the journeyings of the Hebrews in Egypt and the Sinaitic peninsula lead the way to various geographical doubts and queries; the Decalogue and the Book of the Covenant give occasion for, if they do not necessitate, investigations connected with the sciences of ethics and jurisprudence; lastly, the account of the Tabernacle, the sacred utensils, and the sacerdotal dress and ornaments, involve the consideration of the previous history of art, and the existing state of proficiency in such handicrafts as weaving, embroidery, and metallurgy. Again, the language of Exodus, in common with that of the rest of the Pentateuch, has to some

[1] Kalisch, 'Historical and Critical Commentary on the Old Testament,' Introduction to Exdous, § 1, par. 3.

extent an Egyptian tinge, and involves philological inquiries of considerable difficulty and importance. Altogether the Book is one of extraordinary and diversified interest, and necessitates a number of disquisitions of a more or less abstruse character.

§ 2. Divisions.

It is usual to divide Exodus into two portions only, the first extending from ch. i. to the end of ch. xix., and treating of the circumstances under which the deliverance from Egypt was effected; the second, commencing with ch. xx. and reaching to the end of the book, containing an account of the giving of the Law, and the institutions by which the organisation of the people was completed. But, for the purposes of a comment such as the present, something more than this broad distinction and single line of demarcation is needed. It is not, however, necessary to have recourse to artificial or imaginary *termini*. The Book itself bears a markedly sectional character, which has been accounted for on the supposition that it was composed at different times, and written on separate parchments or papyri, each section being of such a length as suited it for congregational reading.[1] The first and second chapters together form such a section. Its main subject is the oppression of the Israelites by the Egyptians, with which is interwoven an account of the birth of Moses, and the first wholly abortive attempt which he made to right the wrongs of his people and improve their social position. This is followed by a section on the call of Moses, and the Divine commission given to him, whereby he was empowered to take the oversight of his people, to act for them, to plead for them with Pharaoh, and ultimately to lead them out of Egypt; the section terminating with the people's acknowledgment of his mission, and acceptance of him as their chief (ch. iv. 31). The third section is co-extensive with ch. v. It contains the record of Moses' first application to the king of Egypt on behalf of Israel, and of its unhappy result. Section 4 is the sequel to this. It consists of ch. vi. vers. 1 to 27, and tells of the depression of the people in consequence of their increased affliction, the encouragement vouchsafed by God to Moses, and the fresh "charge" given by God to him and Aaron to persist in their efforts and effect the people's release. The next section is a long one. It begins at verse 28 of ch. vi. and continues to the end of ch. xi. The subject is an account of the nine ineffectual plagues, against which Pharaoh "hardened his heart," prefaced by a description of the one miracle wrought as a mere sign to accredit the mission of the brothers, and followed by the announcement of the tenth and last plague, before which even Pharaoh's stubborn will was to bend. Section 6 contains the institution of the Passover, the tenth plague, and the actual hasty departure of the

---

[1] 'Speaker's Commentary,' vol. i. pp. 237—8.

Israelites from Rameses, when Pharaoh finally "thrust them out." It consists of the first forty-two verses of ch. xii. Section 7 contains directions with respect to the Passover and the sanctification of the firstborn. It extends from ch. xii. 43 to ch. xiii. 16, and constitutes a document apart, of a purely legal character, which was probably inserted at this point, as the fittest place for it, when the various sections were finally put together by their author. In the next section (ch. xiii. 17—ch. xv.), the historical narrative is resumed, and the march of the Israelites is traced from Succoth to the shores of the Red Sea ; their pursuit by the Egyptians is related, together with their miraculous passage across the bed of the sea, and the destruction of Pharaoh's host by the return of the waters. Section 9 contains the song of Moses and Miriam, and consists of the first twenty-one verses of ch. xv. In section 10 the further march of the Israelites is traced, and they are conducted from the Red Sea to Sinai, where God proposes to enter into a covenant with them (ch. xv. 22 to the end of ch. xix.). Section 11 contains the Decalogue, together with the "Book of the Covenant," and extends from ch. xx. 1 to ch. xxiii. 33. Section 12 comprises—the acceptance of the covenant ; the revelation of God's presence to Aaron, Nadab, Abihu, and the seventy elders ; together with the ascent of Moses into the cloud that covered the mountain, and his continuance there for forty days (ch. xxiv.). Section 13 contains the directions given by God for the construction of the Tabernacle, the Ark of the Covenant, the altar of burnt-offering, and the court of the Tabernacle ; for the sacerdotal garments, and the ceremonial of priestly consecration ; for the altar of incense ; and for the composition of the incense and of the oil of consecration (ch. xxv.—xxx.). Section 14 contains the appointment of Bezaleel and Aholiab as the artists to execute the required works ; the appointment of the Sabbath *as a sign;* and the delivery to Moses of the two Tables of stone, written with the finger of God. It is coincident with ch. xxxi. Section 15 is purely historical. It gives an account of the terrible sin of the people in setting up the golden calf, and the consequences of this dreadful sin—the breaking of the two Tables, the slaughter of three thousand guilty persons by the Levites, and the threat of the withdrawal of God's presence, which however was revoked at the prayer of Moses (chs. xxxii.—xxxiii.). Section 16 (ch. xxxiv.) is the sequel to section 15. It records the renewal of the two Tables of stone, and the descent of Moses from Sinai with them in his hand, and with a glory on his face that the people could not bear to look on, whence the necessity of his veiling himself. The remaining section (chs. xxxv.—xl.) contains the historical account of the construction of the Tabernacle, the Ark of the Covenant, the altars of incense and burnt-offering, the priests' dresses, etc., the setting of all things in their places, and the sanctification of the whole by the visible entrance of the Shechinah into the sacred dwelling-place.

§ 3. Unity of the work.

Much the same arguments have been employed to disprove the unity of Exodus, and to establish the theory that it is the work of at least two authors, as have been already examined in this COMMENTARY with respect to Genesis. "The Elohist" and "the Jehovist" are again paraded before us, as if they were admitted realities, instead of being, as they are, pure figments, the creations of a captious and over-refining pseudo-criticism. There is the same want of agreement among the various advocates of the theory, which has been already noticed in the comment on Genesis, as to which passages are the work of the Elohist, and which of the Jehovist, whole chapters being assigned to one of them by some critics, and by others to the other.[1] Moreover, curiously enough, in their application to Exodus, the very *raison d'être* of the names disappears, passages being ascribed to the Jehovist in which the only name of God is *Elohim*, and others to the Elohist in which the only name used is *Jehovah*.[2] Under these circumstances it would only be reasonable that the terms Elohist and Jehovist should be relinquished, and the confession made that the theory on which they are based has broken down; but "the higher criticism," as it delights to call itself, seems not greatly to affect the virtue of candour. The real question now raised with regard to Exodus is not whether it can be divided into two sets of passages, Elohistic and Jehovistic respectively, in the former of which may be recognised the original document, while the latter are the work of an editor, supplementer, or compiler; but whether any division at all can be made, whether there are any clear traces of a second hand, or whether the "book" has not, in its structure, style, and method such clear and unmistakable marks of unity as to point distinctly to a single author.[3]

Now the book has one clear and plain purpose, which is to give an account of the circumstances under which the Israelites quitted Egypt, and became God's peculiar people, bound to him by a covenant, and granted his continuous presence with them to guide and direct them. The narrative flows on without a break. If there are some chronological gaps in the earlier portion,[4] they are necessitated by the fact that nothing occurred

---

[1] As ch. xx., which is assigned to the Elohist by De Wette, Stähelin, and Von Lengerke, but to the Jehovist by Knobel ('Exegetisches Handbuch,' vol. ii. p. xvii.).

[2] *E.g.* Ex. i. 15—22 is assigned to the Jehovist by Knobel, De Wette, Von Lengerke, and others, though God appears as Elohim in vers. 17, 20 and 21, and the name Jehovah does not appear at all. Similarly chs. xxv.—xxviii. are ascribed to the Elohist, though Jehovah occurs in them five times, and Elohim not at all. Less extreme cases are those of ch. iii. and chs. xxx.—xxxi., both called Elohistic; though in the former Jehovah occurs twenty times, and Elohim seven only; in the latter, Jehovah occurs fifteen times, and Elohim only twice.

[3] Against the disintegrating views of so many German critics may well be set the conviction of Kalisch:—"We see the completest harmony in all parts of Exodus; we consider it as a perfect whole: pervaded throughout by one spirit and the same leading ideas." ('Hist. and Crit. Commentary,' p. x. E. T.)

[4] As between the death of Joseph (ch. i. 6) and the accession of the "new king, which knew not Joseph" (*ib.* 8); between the adoption of Moses by Pharaoh's daughter (ch. ii. 5—10) and

during the omitted periods which either advanced or hindered the action which it is the writer's business to relate. He is not a secular historian, bent on recording all the circumstances in the early life of his nation, but a sacred writer, a religious teacher, bound to confine his attention to their *theocratic* history, or in other words to God's providential dealings with them. These consist for some centuries in two things only—the rapid increase of the race, despite all attempts to hinder it; and the severe oppression to which after a time they were subjected. The former is important as giving them the strength to do what they did; the latter as supplying the motive. So these two things are put on record; but their life before the oppression began, and even the time that the oppression lasted, which an ordinary historian would of course have noted, are omitted as unimportant for the theocratic history. Similarly, with regard to Moses, the leader of the Exodus, while those circumstances which prepared him for his task—his education at the court, which gave him ready access to Pharaoh, and his sojourn in Midian, which made him familiar with life in the desert—are clearly marked; all the details of his early career, covering a space (according to St. Stephen, Acts vii. 23) of "full forty years," and all but the barest outline of his life in Midian, occupying another similar term, are suppressed, as not helping on the people's deliverance, or conducing to their reception into covenant. But, from the time that the deliverance begins, *i.e.* from the date of Moses' call, there are no gaps, no omissions— every step of the history is traced with the utmost minuteness, because each furthers the great ends which the writer has in view—first, the people's deliverance—then, their acceptance into covenant at Sinai—finally, the completion of the covenant on God's part by the visible location of the Shechinah in the Tabernacle.

And as there is this unity of historical aim in the whole of Exodus, so is there a great unity of style. Historical narrative indeed, and the details of legislation and construction, being subjects exceedingly diverse, cannot well be treated in the same way; and it would be fanciful to maintain, that either "the Book of the Covenant" or the description of the Tabernacle is manifestly from the same hand as the account of the oppression of Israel or of the plagues; but wherever in the later chapters a narrative passage occurs (*e.g.* chs. xxiv.; xxxii.—xxxiv. 8; xxxiv. 28—35; xl. 16—38), the resemblances to the style of the earlier portion of the book (chs. i.—xix.) are numerous and striking;[1] and similarly, wherever in the early portion

his "going out unto his brethren" (*ib.* 11); and between the birth of Gershom (*ib.* 22) and the miracle of the burning bush (ch. iii. 2).

[1] It would be tedious to exhibit this agreement, and it seems to be unnecessary. No arguments of any weight have been adduced by the opponents of the unity, based upon style. When Stähelin says, "Wherever I find mention of a 'pillar of fire,' or of a 'cloud,' or an 'angel of Jehovah,' or the phrase 'flowing with milk and honey,' . . . when mention is made of a 'coming down of God,' or when the Canaanite nations are numbered, or the Tabernacle supposed to be without the camp, I feel tolerably certain that I am reading the words of the

legislation is introduced (*e.g.* ch. xii. 1—20 ; 43—50 ; ch. xiii. 1—16 ; ch. xx.), the style and mode of expression recall the general tone of the Book's later sections. Style indeed is so much a matter of instinctive perception and feeling, and unity of style is a thing so little admitting of proof, that no writer can do much more than state his own impressions on the subject, it being quite impossible adequately to represent the grounds of them. For our own part, we feel bound to echo the conclusion of Kalisch, who says— " We see the completest harmony in all parts of Exodus ; we consider it as a perfect whole, pervaded throughout by one spirit and the same leading ideas." [1]

The only reasonable ground which exists for any doubt or hesitation on the question of the unity is the fact, already noted,[2] of the markedly sectional character of the work—its division into a number of distinctly separate portions, not very skilfully or artistically joined together. But this peculiarity is exactly what might have been looked for in a work which was written by snatches in the rare intervals of leisure allowed by a life of extreme and almost constant activity, and under circumstances that precluded attention to literary finish. If the writer of Exodus was a con- temporary, who from time to time placed on record the series of events whereof he was a witness, soon after their occurrence, and who ultimately arranged his various pieces into a volume, the result would naturally be that which the Book of Exodus presents to us.[3] Had a compiler, a mere man of letters, effected the arrangement, it is probable that the result would have been, in a literary point of view, better, *i.e.* more artistic—the breaks in the narrative would have been fewer and less abrupt ; repetitions would have been avoided ; the roughness inseparable from a work hastily accom- plished in odds and ends of time would have been smoothed down, and we should have had a more finished literary composition. Thus, the " frag- mentary character" of Exodus is an important and precious indication that we have the work in its original form—the statue as it was rough-hewn in the quarry—and that it has not undergone the process of polishing and smoothing at the hands of a redactor, compiler, or supplementarist.

§ 4. MOSAIC AUTHORSHIP.

It is an axiom of sound criticism that books are to be attributed to the authors to whom tradition assigns them, unless *very* strong reasons can be shown to the contrary.[4] Exodus, and indeed the Pentateuch generally, has

author of the Second Legislation," it is perfectly clear that the supposed notes of authorship are wholly arbitrary and fanciful.

[1] 'Historical and Critical Commentary,' Introduction, p. x.

[2] See above, § 2, p. iii.

[3] Compare Rosenmüller, " Prolegomena in Exodum," § 2, in his ' Scholia in Vetus Testa mentum,' vol. ii. pp. 2—4.

[4] See ' Aids to Faith,' Essay vi. § 3 ; pp. 238—9

been assigned to Moses by a unanimous tradition, current alike among Pharisees and Sadducees, among Jews and Samaritans, among those who ascribed a sacred character to the work and those who regarded it as a mere human production. No other author has ever been put forward as a rival candidate to Moses;[1] and we must either ascribe the work to a wholly unknown and nameless writer,[2] who, with a marvellous humility and self-abnegation, while composing the most important treatise which the world had seen, concealed himself so effectually as to secure his own complete oblivion, or we must admit that the tradition is in the right, and that Moses, the hero of Exodus, and of the three following books, was also their composer.

It has sometimes been argued that the historical Moses, considering the time when he lived, and the condition of the world at that period, could not possibly have been the author even of a single book of the Pentateuch. Some have supposed that alphabetic writing was not at the time invented, and that if the Egyptian hieroglyphic system was anterior to Moses, it could not have been employed to embody with any definiteness the articulate sounds of the Hebrew language.[3] Others, without going these lengths, have maintained that so grand a work as the Pentateuch could not possibly have been produced at so early a period of the world's history, when literature, like everything else, must have been in its infancy. Thus De Wette urges that the Pentateuch is altogether beyond the literary capabilities of the age, containing within it, as he says it does, " every element of Hebrew literature in the highest perfection to which it ever attained, and so necessarily belonging to the acme and not to the childhood of the nation." It is absurd, he thinks, to suppose that in so rude and primitive a time the Hebrew nation should have produced a writer possessing such powers of mind, and such a mastery over his native language as to " leave nothing for succeeding authors but to follow in his footsteps."[4]

In answer to these preliminary objections it is to be noted—first, that alphabetic writing is a much earlier discovery than has sometimes been supposed, and that there is every reason to believe that its use was widely spread over the world in ages long anterior to Moses. Berosus believed it to have been an antediluvian invention, and related that Xisuthrus, or

---

[1] When Jerome says that the Pentateuch may be considered either the work of Moses or of Ezra, he does not mean to ascribe to the latter anything more than that sort of verbal revision (modernising of language, explanation or possibly alteration of obsolete names, and the like) which tradition connects with his name. He distinctly calls Moses the " author " and Ezra the " restorer " of the work.

[2] It does not much mend the matter if we suppose, with Ewald, half-a-dozen such writers, all equally reticent; while this theory introduces the fresh difficulty that the patchwork of six or seven different hands is found to be pervaded by a marked unity of style and of design.

[3] See Norton, 'Genuineness of the Gospels,' vol. ii. Appendix, Note D, § 3; pp. 439—441

[4] De Wette, ' Einleitung in d. alt. Test.,' § 163, sub fin.

Hasis-adra, his "Noah," consigned to writing the learning of the old world before the Flood, impressing it on tablets of baked clay, which he buried at Sippara, and exhumed after the Flood had subsided.[1] Existing Babylonian inscriptions upon bricks and gems[2] are believed to date from before B.C. 2000. Ewald remarks,[3] that the words expressive of "writing" (כתב), "book" (ספר), and "ink" (דיו), are common to all the branches and dialects of Semitic speech, except that the Ethiopic and the Southern Arabian have צחק for "to write," and deduces from this fact the conclusion that writing in a book with ink must have been known to the earliest Semites before they separated off into their various tribes, nations, and families.[4] The Hittites were certainly acquainted with letters before the time of Moses; for not only had they written treaties with the Egyptians at a period anterior to the Exodus,[5] but a Hittite author is mentioned by Pentaour, a royal scribe of the reign of Rameses the Great.[6] Alphabetic writing was probably an art well known in the greater part of Western Asia from a date preceding not only Moses but Abraham.

The Egyptian system of hieroglyphic writing was also beyond all doubt complete several centuries before Abraham. This system is sometimes supposed to be little more than a representation of ideas by pictorial forms; but in reality it is almost wholly phonetic.[7] There would be no difficulty in transliterating the Pentateuch into hieroglyphic characters,[8] which one familiar with them would read off so as to be intelligible to a Jew. If Moses, therefore, did not possess an alphabetic system of his own, and was acquainted with the hieroglyphic system, which is not impossible, since he was bred up at the court, and "learned in all the wisdom of the Egyptians" (Acts vii. 22), he might have written the Pentateuch in that character. At any rate, it would have been easy for him to adopt the cursive hieratic character, which, while based upon the hieroglyphics, presents no pictures of objects, but only a set of straight or curvilinear lines. The hieratic writing was certainly in use as early as the time of the twelfth or thirteenth dynasty,[9] and therefore long anterior to the Exodus.

With regard to the objection of De Wette, that a work so perfect as the Pentateuch is altogether beyond the literary capabilities of the age of Moses,

---

[1] Frag. 7 (in C. Müller's 'Fragm. Hist. Græc.,' vol. ii. p. 501).

[2] Rawlinson, 'Ancient Monarchies,' vol i. pp. 80, 87, 199; 'History of Herodotus,' vol. i. pp. 360—2, 2nd edition.

[3] 'Geschichte des Volkes Israel,' vol. i. p. 77.

[4] The argument is analogous to those drawn by Professor Max Müller from the words common to all Aryan dialects, and seems to be quite unanswerable

[5] 'Records of the Past,' vol. iv. pp. 27—32.

[6] Brugsch, 'Histoire d'Égypte,' p. 139.

[7] Lenormant, 'Manuel d'Histoire Ancienne,' vol. i. p. 500; Birch, in Bunsen's 'Egypt,' vol. v. pp. 599—617.

[8] For the details of the process, see Canon Cook's essay 'On Egyptian Words in the Pentateuch,' published in the 'Speaker's Commentary,' vol. i. pp. 476—492.

[9] 'Records of the Past,' vol. vi. p. 134. Compare Birch, 'Ancient Egypt,' p. 49.

the present writer may perhaps be allowed to quote a passage which he wrote twenty years ago, and which he has never seen answered :—" De Wette's statement is a gross exaggeration of the reality. Considered as a literary work, the Pentateuch is not the production of an advanced or refined, but of a simple and rude age. Its characteristics are plainness, inartificiality, absence of rhetorical ornament, and occasional defective arrangement. The only style which it can be truly said to bring to perfection, is that simple one of clear and vivid narrative which is always best attained in the early dawn of a nation's literature, as a Herodotus, a Froissart, and a Stow sufficiently indicate. In other respects it is quite untrue to say that the work goes beyond all later Hebrew efforts. We look in vain through the Pentateuch for the gnomic wisdom of Solomon, the eloquent denunciations of Ezekiel and Jeremiah, or the lofty flights of Isaiah. It is absurd to compare the song of Moses, as a literary production, even with some of the psalms of David, much more to parallel it with Ezekiel's eloquence and Homeric variety, or Isaiah's awful depth and solemn majesty of repose. In a literary point of view it may be questioned whether Moses did so much for the Hebrews as Homer for the Greeks, or whether his writings had really as great an influence on the after productions of his countrymen. And if his literary greatness still surprises us, if Hebrew literature still seems in his person to reach too suddenly a high excellence, albeit not so high a one as has been argued—let us remember, in the first place, that Moses was not, any more than Homer, the first writer of his nation, but only happens to be the first whose writings have come down to us. 'Vixere fortes ante Agamemnona.' Moses seems so great because we do not possess the works of his predecessors, and so are unable to trace the progress of Hebrew literature up to him. Had we the 'Songs of Israel' (Num. xxi. 17), and the 'Book of the Wars of the Lord' (*ib.* 14), which he quotes, we might find him no literary phenomenon at all, but as a writer merely on a level with others of his age and nation." [1] Moreover, recent research has shown that in Egypt, long prior to the time at which Moses wrote, literature had become a profession, and was cultivated in a variety of branches with ardour and considerable success. Morality, history, epistolary correspondence, poetry, medical science, novel‑writing, were known as separate studies, and taken for their special subjects by numerous writers, from a date anterior to Abraham.[2] In the times of the eighteenth and nineteenth dynasties, under one or the other of which the Exodus almost certainly took place, Egyptian literature reached its acme : lengthy works were composed, such as that contained in the " Great Harris Papyrus," which is 133 feet long by nearly seventeen inches broad; [3] writers enjoyed

[1] 'Aids to Faith,' Essay vi. pp. 245—6 (published in 1861).
[2] See Goodwin, in 'Cambridge Essays' for 1858, pp. 230—260.
[3] 'Records of the Past,' vol. vi. p. 21.

a high status and reputation; their compositions were engraved upon temple walls;[1] and it passed into a proverb that literature was the first and best of all employments.[2] Moses, educated at the court under one or other of these dynasties, and intended doubtless for official life, would necessarily receive a literary training, and would be perfectly competent to produce an extensive literary work, the exact merit of which would of course depend on his ability and genius.

If then there is no obstacle arising out of the circumstances of the time when Moses lived, to hinder our regarding him as the author of Exodus, and if tradition is unanimous in assigning it to him, nothing remains but to ask what internal evidence the book itself offers upon the subject— does it support, or does it make against, the hypothesis of the Mosaic authorship?

And first, as to language and style. We have already noticed[3] the simplicity of style observable in Exodus and the Pentateuch generally, which places it on a par with the early writings of other nations, and proves it to belong to the dawn of Hebrew literature. The language is generally allowed to be archaic, or at any rate to contain archaisms; and though some writers deny this, and assert that the unusual forms and words which characterise the Pentateuch are "not so much archaisms as peculiarities," yet this conclusion is contrary to the general opinion of Hebrew scholars,[4] and has the appearance of being rather a position forced on its maintainers by the exigencies of controversy, than one assumed spontaneously from a dispassionate consideration of the linguistic facts. Such features as the employment of the pronoun הוא for the third person of both genders, of נַעַר for "girl" as well as "boy," and of the full form וּן instead of the abraded וּ for the termination of the third person plural of the preterite, are by the very nature of things and the universal laws of language, archaic. The archaic character of other peculiar forms is also indicated by the fact that several of them occur besides only in Joshua, while some are common to the Pentateuch with none but very late books, e.g. Chronicles and Ezekiel, books written in the decay of the language, when it is notorious that writers studiously imitate the old forms.[5] Exodus has its full share of these peculiarities, which we must venture, with the bulk of Hebrew critics, still to term "archaisms," and has therefore at least

---

[1] As the poem of Pentaour, which may to this day be·read on the walls of the great Temple of Karnak.

[2] In the 'Praise of Learning' we read—"Consider that there is not anything beyond letters" ('Records of the Past,' vol. viii. p. 147); and again—"Love letters as thy mother; it is a greater possession than all employments" (ib. p. 148); and—"Consider, there is not an employment destitute of superior ones, except the scribe's, which is the first" (ib. p. 153).

[3] Supra, p. x.

[4] The archaic character of the language of Exodus and the Pentateuch generally is maintained by Jahn, Fritzsche, De Wette, Hävernick, Keil and Delitzsch, Marsh, Stuart, Bishop Harold Browne, Canon Cook, Dean Perowne, and others; it is impugned by Vater, Gesenius, and a few more.

[5] Perowne, in Dr. Smith's 'Dictionary of the Bible,' vol. ii. p. 783.

as much claim as any other of the five books to be regarded as Mosaic on this ground.

The language of Exodus has also another peculiarity, which, if it does not prove the Mosaic authorship, fits in exactly with it, viz. the frequent occurrence of Egyptian words and phrases. This subject has been treated elaborately by Canon Cook[1] and M. Harkavy,[2] who have proved beyond all question that in that part of his narrative which deals with Egyptian matters, words are constantly used by the author of Exodus which are either pure Egyptian, or common to Egyptian with Hebrew. From thirty to forty such words occur in the first sixteen chapters.[3] Subsequently they are more rare; but a certain number of Egyptian words occur even in the later chapters,[4] showing how familiar the writer was with the language, and how naturally he had recourse to it where the vocabulary of his native tongue was defective. Egyptian phrases are also not unfrequently used, as "the lip of the river" (ch. ii. 5) for "the brink of the river;" "chiefs of tribute" (ch. i. 11) for "taskmasters;" an "ark of bulrushes" (ii. 3); "making persons' savour to stink" (v. 21); "consuming enemies *as stubble*" (ch. xv. 7), etc.

Next, with respect to the matter of the book, it is to be remarked that the writer—whoever he was—shows a notable acquaintance with the customs, climate, and productions of Egypt; an acquaintance such as to imply long residence in the country, and the sort of familiarity which it takes years to acquire, with the natural phenomena, the method of cultivation, the religious ideas, and other habits and usages of the people. Under this head it is important to observe that large additions are constantly being made to the stock of our Egyptian knowledge by learned research into the native documents, which are copious, even for the time anterior to Moses, with this result hitherto—that fresh illustrations of the truthfulness with which Egypt and the Egyptians are portrayed in Exodus continually reveal themselves, while contradictions of the narrative, discrepancies, even difficulties, are almost wholly absent. There was a time when the author of the Pentateuch was boldly taxed with ignorance of Egyptian customs,[5] and when it was argued on this ground that he could not possibly be Moses. Now, no one ventures on such an assertion. The works of Hengstenberg[6] and Canon Cook[7] are sufficient to preclude the

---

[1] 'Appendix to Exodus,' Essay ii. 'On Egyptian Words in the Pentateuch,' in the 'Speaker's Commentary,' vol. i. pp. 476—492.

[2] See an article entitled 'Les Mots Égyptiens de la Bible,' published in the 'Journal Asiatique' for March, 1870.

[3] Cook, in the 'Speaker's Commentary,' vol. i. p. 244, note ·

[4] E.g. *Shesh*, in ch. xxv. 4; *tacharah*, in ch. xxviii. 32; *thummim*, in ch. xxviii. 30; and *hin*, in ch. xxix. 40.

[5] Von Bohlen, 'Commentar,' p. 360

[6] 'Aegypten und Moses,' Berlin, 1840. Translated by Robbins, with additional notes by Dr Cooke Taylor, in Clark's Edinburgh Series, Edinburgh, 1845.

[7] 'Comment on Exodus' in the 'Speaker's Commentary,' vol. i. London, 1871

possibility of the revival of this line of attack; but the counter-evidence continually accumulates. Not a year passes without the discovery of fresh passages in Egyptian literature, which harmonise with and illustrate the narrative delivered to us in Exodus.

It is further observable that the writer, who has this wide and exact acquaintance with Egypt and the Egyptians, is also perfectly familiar with the character of the Sinaitic peninsula, with its vegetable and animal products, with its natural phenomena, as that of the manna, with its rare springs, sometimes sweet, sometimes "bitter" (ch. xv. 23), its wells, its occasional palm-groves (ib. 27), its acacia trees (ch. xxv. 10, 23; xxvi. 15, etc.), its long stretches of dry sand, its bare rocks and lofty mountains. It has been well said that " the chapters of Exodus which belong either to the early sojourn of Moses or to the wanderings of the Israelites, are pervaded by a peculiar tone, a local colouring, an atmosphere (so to speak) of the desert, which has made itself felt by all those who have explored the country, to whatever school of religious thought they may have belonged." [1]

This double knowledge of Egypt and of the Sinaitic peninsula, joined to the antique character of the work, seems to amount to a *proof* that the book of Exodus was written either by Moses or by one of those who accompanied him in his journey from the land of Goshen to the borders of Palestine. There was no period between the Exodus and the reign of Solomon when an Israelite—and the writer was certainly an Israelite—was likely to be familiar either with Egypt or with the Sinaitic peninsula, much less with both. There was little intercourse between the Hebrews and Egypt from the time of the passage of the Red Sea to that of Solomon's marriage with Pharaoh's daughter; and if occasionally during this period an Israelite went down into Egypt and sojourned there (1 Chr. iv. 18), it was a very unlikely thing that he should visit the region about Sinai, which lay above 150 miles out of his route. Add to this the dangers of the journey and the absence of any conceivable motive for it, and the conclusion seems almost certain that only one of those who, after being brought up among the Egyptians, traversed the " wilderness of the wanderings " on his way to Palestine, can have composed the existing record.

The conclusion thus reached is, for all critical purposes, sufficient. If the narrative is from the pen of an eye-witness, it must possess the highest degree of historical credibility,[2] and, so far as accuracy and trustworthiness are concerned, can gain nothing, or at any rate very little, by being ascribed to one of the emigrants rather than another. We trust the last book of the ' De Bello Gallico ' no less than the remainder, though written by Hirtius and not by Cæsar; and the authenticity of Exodus would be no whit

---

[1] Canon Cook, in the ' Speaker's Commentary,' vol. i. p. 244.
[2] See the writer's ' Bampton Lectures,' pp 21, 22, and compare Cornewall Lewis on the ' Credibility of Early Roman History,' vol i. p. 16.

diminished by Joshua or Caleb being its author instead of Moses. Could we suppose it written by a mere ordinary Israelite, the case would be somewhat different; but it is evidently impossible, considering the circumstances of the time, to ascribe a work of such high literary merit, and one evidencing such varied and extensive knowledge, to any one below the rank of a high officer, a leading man among the people.

The absolute *Mosaic* authorship of Exodus is thus a matter not so much of historical importance as of literary curiosity. Still it is of interest to know the real author of any great book, and essential to a right estimate of the character and work of Moses that we should understand whether or no he added to his other eminent qualities the literary ability and power which "Exodus" displays. What then does the Book itself reveal to us on this subject? In the first place it shows us the ability of Moses to write (ch. xxiv. 4); in the next it informs us that he was expressly commanded by God to write an account of some of those very matters which are contained in Exodus (ch. xvii. 14; xxxiv. 27); in the third place it distinctly tells us in one passage that he "wrote all the words of the Lord" (ch. xxxiv. 4), these "words" being (according to almost all commentators) the passage which extends from ch. xx. 22 to the end of ch. xxiii.; finally, it speaks of a "book" which it calls "*the* book"[1] (the expression used being בַּסֵּפֶר and not בְּסֵפֶר), wherein one of his writings was to be inserted, whereby it would seem that at the time of the war with Amalek (ch. xvii. 8—14) Moses already had a book in which he was putting on record the circumstances of the Israelites' deliverance—a book, as Keil says,[2] "appointed for the record of the glorious works of God." The question naturally occurs to a candid mind, Why should not this be the book which we possess? why go out of our way to suppose a second author unnamed and unnameable, when here is one distinctly proclaimed—an author more competent to the task than any other Israelite then living—and moreover the very man to whom an ancient and uniform tradition has always ascribed the work in question? There should be some very cogent arguments, derivable from the contents of the book, to set against this evident *prima facie* probability, in order even to raise a doubt on the subject, and make it worth while to pursue the inquiry any further.

What then is there said to be of this kind, constituting a difficulty in our acceptance of the Mosaic authorship? First, the fact that Moses is always spoken of in the third person. Now, as Xenophon and Cæsar, in writing histories of which they were the heroes, spoke of themselves always

---

[1] Knobel argues that the expression, "write this in the book," merely means "put this into writing" ('Exegetisches Handbuch,' vol. ii. p. 178), and quotes Num. v. 23; 1 Sam. x. 25; Jer. xxxii. 10; and Job xix. 23, as bearing out this explanation; but of these passages only the last is to the point, and there the LXX. have ἐν βιβλίῳ, not ἐν τῷ βιβλίῳ, as if their copies had had the reading בְּסֵפֶר.

[2] 'Commentary on the Old Testament,' vol. ii p. 81.

in the third person, it is at least not unnatural for a man who has to write this sort of history to do so. Nay, it may rather be said to be distinctly natural. Perpetual egotism is wearisome to the reader, and disagreeable to the writer who is not puffed-up by a sense of his own importance. The use of the third person throws a veil, at any rate, over the egotistic character of a work, softens it down, half obliterates it. We forget the writer in his work, when the first person does not constantly obtrude him on us, and pardon his being the hero of his own narrative when he is sufficiently modest to preserve an *incognito*. Moreover, speaking of oneself in the third person was common in Egypt in Moses' day. The inscriptions which kings set up to commemorate their conquests were sometimes written wholly in the third person,[1] sometimes partly in the third and partly in the first.[2] The inscriptions placed by private individuals on their tombs generally began in the third person.[3] With such examples before him, it cannot be regarded as surprising that Moses avoided altogether the use of the first person in his narrative and confined himself wholly to the third.

Secondly, it is said that Moses is spoken of—at any rate in one place (ch. xi. 3), perhaps also in ch. vi. 26, 27—in a way in which he would not be likely to have spoken of himself. The objection taken may, in both instances, be allowed, but without the conclusion following which is supposed to follow. For the passages are both of them parenthetic, and also abnormal. They do not speak of Moses as he is commonly spoken of; and they are so isolated from the context that their removal would leave no gap, produce no difficulty. They are thus exactly such passages as may have been introduced on that review of the book which is ascribed to Ezra by ancient authorities,[4] and generally allowed to have taken place by moderns. The question whether Moses or a nameless contemporary is to be regarded as the author of Exodus cannot properly be ruled by reference to one or two passages—especially parenthetic passages. We must look upon the matter more broadly. We must ask ourselves, Is the entire presentation of the personal character and qualifications of the great Israelite leader which the book offers more consonant with the view that Moses himself wrote it, or with the theory that it was composed by one of the younger and subordinate Israelite leaders, as Joshua or Caleb? Now, nothing is more striking in that presentation than the humble estimate made of the character, gifts, powers,

---

[1] As the statistical tablet of Karnak, or 'Annals of Thothmes III.,' published in the ' Records of the Past,' vol. ii. pp. 19—28, and the inscription of Pianchi Mer-amon in the same volume (pp. 81—104).

[2] This is the case in the long inscription of Thothmes III. (' Records of the Past,' vol. ii. pp. 35—58), where the person changes on page 53; and again in the ' Annals of Rameses III.' (' Records,' vol. vi. pp. 23—70), where changes of person occur on pp. 34, 50, 52, 59, and 69.

[3] For specimens, see the ' Records,' vol. vi. p. 7; vol. x. pp. 3, 7, etc. Sometimes a funereal inscription is entirely in the third person, as that of Ameni (' Records,' vol. vi. pp. 3, 4).

[4] Tertullian, ' De Cultu Femin.' § 3; Clem. Alex. ' Strom.' i. 22; Hieronym. ' Ad Helvid.' vol. ii. p. 212; etc.

and even of the personal conduct of the great leader. From first to last he is never praised; once only (in the passage objected to) he is said to have come to be " very great in the sight of Pharaoh's servants " and the Egyptian people. His faults are set forth without any disguise or extenuation : his hastiness and unjustifiable violence in " slaying the Egyptian " (ch. ii. 12); his foolish assumption of authority over his brethren (*ib.* 13); his timidity when he found that he was likely to be punished for his crime (*ib.* 14, 15); his unwillingness to undertake the mission which God assigned to him (ch. iv. 1—13); his neglect of the covenant of circumcision (*ib.* 24—26); his irreverent remonstrance when success did not attend his first application to Pharaoh (ch. v. 22—24); and his want of self-control when on account of the sin of his people in worshipping the golden calf he " cast the Tables " —written by the finger of God—" out of his hands and brake them " (ch. xxxii. 19). Nothing is said of his possessing any remarkable ability. On the contrary, he is represented as insisting, over and over again, on his incompetency, on his want of eloquence (ch. iv. 10), his insignificance ("Who am I?" ch. iii. 11), and his inability to persuade even his own people (ch. iv. 1; vi. 12). No credit is assigned to him for anything that he does; for his bold and courageous behaviour before Pharaoh; for that organisation of the people which must have preceded the Exodus; [1] for his conduct of the march; or for that faith which never wavered, even when he and his people were shut in between the irresistible host of Pharaoh and the waters of an apparently untraversable sea (ch. xiv. 13, 14). While it is in complete harmony with the general practice of the sacred writers, and with the spirit of true religion, that such reticence and such a disparaging tone should be employed by a writer respecting himself, it is quite inconceivable that either Joshua or any other companion of Moses should have written of him in this style. To his contemporaries, to those who had seen his miracles, and who owed their lives and liberties to his bold and successful guidance, Moses must have been a hero, a paladin, the first, the greatest, and the most admirable of men. We may see what they thought of him by the words with which Deuteronomy closes—" There arose not a prophet since in Israel like unto Moses, whom the Lord knew face to face, in all the signs and the wonders which the Lord sent him to do in the land of Egypt to Pharaoh, and to all his servants, and to all his land, and in all that mighty hand, and in all the great terror which Moses showed in the sight of all Israel " (Deut. xxxiv. 10—12).

If then the style and diction of Exodus, combined with the knowledge which it exhibits both of Egypt and of the Sinaitic peninsula, indicate unmistakably for its author either Moses or one of the other leading Israelites of Moses' time, there cannot be any reasonable doubt towards

---

[1] See the remarks of Canon Cook in the 'Speaker's Commentary,' vol. i. p. 305, " Note on v. 18."

which of the two theories the balance of the internal evidence inclines. It is simply inconceivable that one of those who looked up to Moses with the reverence and admiration that he must have inspired in his followers, could have produced the unflattering portraiture which Exodus presents to us of one of the very greatest of men. It is, on the other hand, readily conceivable, and completely in accordance with what experience teaches of the thoughts and words of great saints concerning themselves, that Moses should have given such a representation of himself. The internal evidence is thus in harmony with the external. Both alike point to Moses as the author of this Book and of those which follow.

§ 5. Chronology.

The internal chronology of the Book of Exodus is a matter of great simplicity, presenting only a single point of doubt or difficulty. This is the question whether the Hebrew text of ch. xii. 40 is to be regarded as sound and genuine, or whether it is to be corrected from the Samaritan version and the Septuagint. In the Hebrew text we read: "Now the sojourning of the children of Israel, who dwelt in Egypt, was four hundred and thirty years;" or more literally, "Now the sojourning of the children of Israel, which they sojourned in Egypt,[1] was 430 years." But in the Septuagint the passage runs thus: "The sojourning of the children of Israel, which they sojourned in Egypt *and in the land of Canaan*, was 430 years;"[2] and in the Samaritan thus: "The sojourning of the children of Israel *and of their fathers*, which they sojourned *in the land of Canaan and* in the land of Egypt, was 430 years." If the Hebrew text is sound we must count 430 years from the descent of Jacob into Egypt to the Exodus; if it is corrupt, and to be corrected from the two ancient versions, the time of the sojourn will be reduced one-half, for it was a space of exactly 215 years from the entrance of Abraham into Canaan to the descent of Jacob into Egypt.[3]

In favour of the short period it is urged, first, that the genealogies contained in the Pentateuch, and especially the genealogy of Moses and Aaron (Ex. vi. 16—20), will not admit of the longer term;[4] and, secondly,

---

[1] The verb and the substantive used are cognate; and the passage is correctly, as well as literally, rendered by the LXX.: ἡ δὲ κατοίκησις τῶν υἱῶν Ἰσραὴλ, ἣν κατῴκησαν ἐν γῇ Αἰγύπτῳ.

[2] In some copies of the Septuagint (*e.g.* the Codex Alexandrinus) the reading is—" The sojourning of the children of Israel, which *they and their fathers* sojourned in Egypt *and in the land of Canaan*, was 430 years," which approaches to the Samaritan, but still differs from it.

[3] From the entrance of Abraham into Canaan to the birth of Isaac was twenty-five years (Gen. xii. 4; xvii. 1, 21); from the birth of Isaac to that of Jacob was sixty years (*ib.* xxv. 26). Jacob was 130 years old when he went into Egypt (*ib.* xlvii. 9). But 25 + 60 + 130 = 215.

[4] So Kennicott, Pool, Houbigant, Geddes, Morinus, Cappellus, Deyling, Köppen, Usher, Marsham, Buddæus, Bengel, Knobel, Colenso, etc. The last-named writer, who has collated *all* the genealogies contained in the Pentateuch, has shown that they vary between four and six names, tending thus, in some degree, to confirm the estimate of four generations from Levi to Moses

that St. Paul reckoned no more than 430 years from the call of Abraham to the Exodus (Gal. iii. 17). Now, certainly, if the genealogies are complete, and especially that of Moses and Aaron, the longer term of years cannot have been reached, since even if Kohath was but a year old at the time of his being carried into Egypt (Gen. xlvi. 11), and if Amram was born in the last year of Kohath's life, and Moses in the last year of Amram's, the eightieth year of Moses, in which the Exodus took place (Ex. vii. 7), would be only the 350th from the descent into Egypt and not the 430th.[1] But the ordinary Jewish practice with regard to genealogies was to contract them; and it is quite possible that in *all* the recorded genealogies of this period, except that of Joshua (1 Chr. vii. 22-27), there are omissions. The number of generations in the genealogy of Joshua is ten, an amount very much more consonant with the period of 430 than with that of 215 years; and this number we are bound to accept as historical, since there could be no possible reason why the writer of Chronicles should have invented it; so that, on the whole, the argument to be drawn from the Scriptural genealogies is rather in favour of the long period than against it. It is the Oriental practice to call any male descendant a son, any female descendant a daughter;[2] it is the Jewish practice to contract genealogies by means of omissions;[3] it is unheard-of to expand a genealogy by thrusting in unhistorical names: there must consequently have been ten generations from Joseph to Joshua. Ten generations would certainly, at this period of Jewish history, represent 400 years, and might easily cover 430, giving an average of forty-three years to a generation, instead of the thirty-three years of later times.[4]

With respect to St. Paul's estimate (Gal. iii. 17), it would simply show that, in writing to Greek-speaking Jews, whose only Bible was the Septuagint version, he made use of that translation. It would not even prove his own opinion upon the point, since the chronological question is not pertinent to his argument, and, whatever he may have thought upon it, he would certainly not have obtruded upon his Galatian disciples a wholly irrelevant discussion.

In favour of the longer term the *great* argument is the general one, that

---

[1] Colenso's statement is correct—"Now supposing that Kohath was only an infant, when brought down by his father to Egypt with Jacob, and that he begat Amram at the very end of his life, when 133 years old, and that Amram, in like manner, begat Moses when he was 137 years old, still these two numbers added to eighty years, the age of Moses at the time of the Exodus, would only amount to 350 years, instead of 430 " ('The Pentateuch and the Book of Joshua,' Part I., p. 92).

[2] No one would suppose that " a daughter of Levi " in Ex. ii. 1 meant more than a female descendant of Levi; yet when exactly the same phrase is used of the same person in Num. xxvi 59, it has been argued that an actual daughter must be intended.

[3] In the genealogy of Ezra (Ezr. vii. 1—5) at least seven names are omitted; in that of our Lord (Matt. i. 2–16) at least three, probably more. A comparison of 1 Chr. ix. 4—19 with Nehem. xi. 4—22, gives additional evidence of the practice of omission.

[4] Herod. ii. 142—γενεαὶ τρεῖς ἀνδρῶν ἑκατὸν ἔτεά ἐστι. Compare Clem. Alex. ' Strom.' i. 21, p. 145

the Hebrew text is to be taken as the true original unless it contains internal signs of imperfection, and that here there are no such signs. On the other hand, there are signs that the Septuagint and Samaritan texts are interpolated—viz. first, their variations;[1] and secondly, the fact that the length of the sojourn in Egypt is alone naturally before the writer's mind at this point of his narrative. A further argument is furnished by Gen. xv. 13—16, where the term of the Egyptian sojourn is prophetically given (in *round* numbers) as 400 years; a passage quoted by St. Stephen (Acts vii. 6), who clearly regards the prophecy as fulfilled. It has been argued that "the 400 years is meant to refer to the time during which the ' seed of Abraham' should be sojourners in a strange land," rather than to the time during which they should suffer oppression, and so, that the sojourn in Canaan is included;[2] but this exposition, which is admitted to be contrary to the apparent sense,[3] cannot possibly be allowed, since Gen. xv. 13—16 speaks of one land and one nation—a nation which should "afflict" them, and which they should "serve," and which at the end of the 400 years should be "judged"—whereas the Canaanites did not "afflict" them, for quarrels about wells (Gen. xxvi. 15—21) are not an "affliction" in the language of Scripture,[4] and certainly they did not "serve" the Canaanites— neither could it possibly be of the Canaanites that it is said, "That nation, whom they shall serve, will I judge, and *afterward* shall they come out with great substance" (Gen. xv. 14). Finally, the long term is most consonant alike with the estimate formed of the entire number of the grown males at the time of the Exodus (600,000, Ex. xii. 37), and with the details given of particular families in the Book of Numbers, as especially those of the families of the Levites, in ch. iii. 21—39.

If, upon these grounds, the longer term of 430 years for the sojourn in Egypt be preferred to the shorter term of 215 years, the details of the chronology must be arranged as follows:[5]—

	Years.
From the descent of Jacob into Egypt to the death of Joseph . . .	71
„ death of Joseph to the birth of Moses	278
„ birth of Moses to his flight into Midian	40
„ flight of Moses into Midian to his return to Egypt . .	40
„ return of Moses to the Exodus	1
	430

It is a different, and a much more intricate, question, how the chronology of this period is to be attached to the general chronology of mundane

---

[1] See above, p. xvii.

[2] Colenso, 'The Pentateuch and the Book of Joshua,' Part I., p. 94.

[3] *Ibid.*

[4] Note the constant use of the terms "affliction" and "afflict" with reference to Egypt in the Pentateuch (Gen. xli. 52; Ex. i. 11, 12; iii. 7, 17; iv. 31; Deut. xxvi. 6, 7). They are never used in reference to any suffering the Israelites may have undergone in Canaan

[5] See Keil and Delitzsch, 'Commentary on the Old Testament,' vol. i. p. 414, E. T. ; and Kalisch, 'Comment on Exodus,' Introduction, pp. xi.—xiii.

affairs, or even how it is to be united with the later chronology of the Jewish nation. If complete reliance could be placed on the genuineness of a particular text (1 Kings vi. 1), the difficulties indeed of this latter problem would in a great measure disappear; for, having fixed the date of the commencement of Solomon's temple, which was certainly begun *about* B.C. 1000, we should only have to add to the exact date on which we decided, the number 480, in order to obtain an equally exact date for the Exodus. It was in this way that Archbishop Ussher produced his date of B.C. 1491, which is still maintained by Kalisch,[1] and with an unimportant variation by Keil.[2] But the genuineness of the words in 1 Kings vi. 1— "in the 480th year after the children of Israel were come out of the land of Egypt"—is open to serious question.[3] They stand alone, unsupported by anything analogous in the whole of the rest of Scripture.[4] They were apparently unknown to Josephus, to Theophilus of Antioch, and to Clemens of Alexandria, who would necessarily have quoted them, had they existed in their copies.[5] They are also at variance with the tradition glanced at by St. Paul (Acts xiii. 20), that from the partition of Canaan to Samuel was a space of 450 years. But if, on these grounds, we surrender the genuineness of 1 Kings vi. 1, we are launched at once upon an open sea of conjecture. St. Paul's statement is defective both in consequence of his using the expression "about," and in consequence of his not marking whether he means to include the judgeship of Samuel in the 450 years or to exclude it. His statement leaves moreover the space between the death of Moses and the partition of Canaan unestimated. The detailed statements in the books of Scripture from Joshua to Kings are defective, since in the first place they leave many periods unestimated,[6] and further, they are expressed to a large extent in *round* numbers,[7] which are fatal to exact computation. It has been calculated that, on the most probable estimate, the details of Joshua, Judges, and Samuel would produce for the period between the Exodus and the foundation of the Temple, 600, 612, or 628 years.[8] On the other hand, it has been argued with considerable force that these estimates are greatly in excess of the real time—that different judges bore office

---

[1] 'Historical and Critical Commentary,' Introduction, p. xiv.

[2] By lengthening the duration of the kingdom of Judah by one year, Keil makes the date B.C. 1492 ('Biblical Commentary,' vol. i. p. 414).

[3] Hales says—"The period of 480 years is a forgery, foisted into the text" ('Chronology,' vol. ii. p. 287). The date is also rejected by Jackson, Clinton, Stuart Poole, Bunsen, Lepsius, Lenormant, Brugsch, and others, but defended by Canon Cook and Mr. Greswell.

[4] The words involve the assumption of the Exodus *as an era* from which to date events. But the idea of an era nowhere else appears in Scripture, and was unknown to the nations of antiquity until the time of Thucydides.

[5] See the writer's note on the passage in the 'Speaker's Commentary,' vol. ii. pp. 51—59.

[6] As the periods during which Joshua, Shamgar and Samuel judged Israel; the time between the death of Joshua and the first servitude; and the reign of Saul (estimated at forty years by St Paul, Acts xiii. 21).

[7] Forty years (Judg. iii. 11; v. 31; viii. 28; xiii. 1; 1 Sam. iv. 18); twenty years (Judg. v. 3; xvi. 31; 1 Sam. vii. 2); eighty years (Judg. iii. 30); 300 years (ib. xi. 26).

[8] Clinton, 'Fasti Hellenici' vol i p. 312

simultaneously in different parts of Palestine,[1] and that the actual period which elapsed from the Exodus to Solomon's accession did not much exceed 300 years. The result is that the best and most learned of modern critics vary in their dates for the Exodus by as much as 332 years, some placing it as late as B.C. 1300, and others as early as B.C. 1632.

It might have been supposed that the difficulties of the Scriptural chronology would have received light from the parallel chronology of Egypt, or even have been set at rest by it; but Egyptian chronology has difficulties of its own which render it one of the most abstruse of studies, and preclude the possibility of any positive conclusions being formed respecting it, unless by the method of arbitrary selection from among co-equal authorities. Hence it is not yet a settled point among Egyptologists, under which dynasty, much less under which king, the Exodus took place, some placing it as early as Thothmes III., the fifth king of the eighteenth dynasty, and others as late as Seti-Menephthah, the fifth king of the nineteenth. An interval of above two centuries separates these reigns. On the whole, the preponderance of authority is in favour of the Exodus having fallen under the nineteenth, rather than the eighteenth dynasty, and under either Seti-Menephthah or his father Menephthah,[2] who were the fifth and fourth kings. The Egyptian tradition upon the subject, recorded by Manetho,[3] Chæremon,[4] and others, points evidently to one or other of these kings, and has generally been taken as decisive in favour of the father. But a hieratic inscription,[5] deciphered and translated by Dr. Eisenlohr of Heidelberg in 1872, has been thought by some to incline the scale towards the son, Seti-Menephthah, whose reign seems to have been followed by a period of revolution and disturbance, described in terms almost identical with those in which Manetho speaks of the time that followed the Exodus.

If we accept Manetho's account of the period in Egyptian history to which the Exodus belongs, we shall have as the probable date of the event, calculated from Egyptian sources,[6] about B.C. 1300, or from that to B.C. 1350. Four hundred and thirty years before this will bring us to the eighteenth century B.C., when Egypt was, according to all writers,[7] under the dominion of the Shepherd kings. This will agree well with the tradition, which George the Syncellus says was universal,[8] that Joseph governed Egypt in

---

[1] Bunsen, 'Egypt's Place in Universal History,' vol. iii. pp. 282—288; Canon Cook, in the 'Speaker's Commentary,' vol. i. p. 248.

[2] This is the view of Lepsius, Bunsen, Lenormant, Brugsch, and Birch—a combination of authority which it is difficult to resist. The last-named writer says of Menephthah—" It is *generally admitted* that the Exodus took place in his reign."

[3] 'Ap. Joseph. c. Apion.' i. 26, 27.   [4] *Ibid.* i. 32.

[5] See the 'Transactions of the Society of Biblical Archæology,' vol. i. pp. 355—384· and compare 'Records of the Past,' vol. viii. pp. 45—47.

[6] Brugsch makes the year of Menephthah's accession B.C. 1300 ('History of Egypt,' vol. ii. p. 314); Wilkinson, B.C. 1245; Lenormant, B.C. 1350 ('Manuel d'Histoire Ancienne,' vol. i. pp. 404, 428).

[7] So Brugsch, Lenormant, Bunsen, Wilkinson, Birch, etc.   [8] Chronographia, p. 62, B.

the time of King Apophis, who was the last king of the seventeenth or great Shepherd dynasty. Joseph probably outlived Apophis, and saw the commencement of the eighteenth dynasty, so that the founder of that dynasty, Aahmes, cannot be the "king that knew not Joseph" (Ex. i. 8). Nor could the Israelites have been by that time so numerous as to rouse the king's fears. The Pharaoh intended is probably the founder of the nineteenth dynasty, Rameses I., or his son Seti, the great conqueror. If Moses was born under this monarch, his flight to Midian would have taken place under Rameses II., Seti's son and successor; and his return, forty years later, on the death of the Pharaoh who sought his life, would fall in the reign of Menephthah, the son and successor of Rameses II. It may have been the exhaustion of Egypt through the double loss of the firstborn and of the great bulk of the armed force in the Red Sea, together with the discontent caused by the unwise conduct of the king, that led shortly afterwards to those troubles which supervened on the death of Menephthah —first disputes with regard to the succession, and then a period of complete anarchy.[1] The Israelites were in the Sinaitic peninsula at this time. When the Egyptian troubles came to an end, and Rameses III. began his conquests, they were engaged in their wars on the eastern side of Palestine, and profited by his attack, which weakened their enemies. After Rameses III. Egypt declined; and hence no more is heard of her in the Biblical history till the reign of Solomon. The subjoined table will show at a glance the view here taken of the synchronisms between the Egyptian and the Israelite history from the time of Joseph to the entrance into Canaan.

Circa B.C.	Egyptian History.	Hebrew History.
1900—1700	Egypt under the Shepherd Kings Dynasty XVII.	Joseph in Egypt. His brethren join him. Commencement of the 430 years, about B.C. 1740.
1700	Accession of Dynasty XVIII. .	Joseph dies about B.C. 1670.
1400	Accession of Dynasty XIX. (Rameses I. first king).	
1395	Seti I. (great conqueror) . . .	Rise of "king who knew not Joseph." Pithom and Rameses built.
1385	Rameses II. (associated) . . .	Birth of Moses (*circa* B.C. 1390). Flight of Moses to Midian (*circa* B.C. 1350).
1320	Menephthah I.	Moses returns from Midian (*circa* 1311).
1305	Seti II. (Seti-Menephthah) . .	The Exodus (*circa* B.C. 1310).
1300—1280	Revolution in Egypt. Short reigns of Amon-meses and Siphthah. Period of anarchy.	
1280	Accession of Dynasty XX. Set-Nekht.	
1276	Rameses III. (conqueror) . .	The Israelites enter Canaan (*circa* B.C. 1270).
1255	Rameses IV.	

[1] Birch, 'Egypt from the Earliest Times,' pp. 135—7; Brugsch, 'History of Egypt,' vol. ii pp. 130—6.

On Early Egyptian History and Chronology.

The admitted uncertainty of the proper mode of synchronising Egyptian with Biblical history makes it desirable to add in this place a few remarks on the main features of Egyptian chronology and history in the earlier times, that so the reader may be able to judge for himself between the various synchronistic theories which come under his notice, and form his own scheme, if that in the text (*supra*, p. xxii.) does not satisfy him.

It is allowed on all hands that civilisation, kingly government, architecture of a remarkable kind, and fairly advanced mimetic art, existed in Egypt from a time considerably anterior to Abraham. The lowest date that has been assigned, so far as we are aware, by any modern scholar [1] to the commencement of the civilised monarchical Egypt, is B.C. 2250, or from that to B.C. 2450. Some of the most learned writers raise the date by one thousand or two thousand years.[2] But, setting aside such extravagances, we may state it as universally agreed upon among historians of the present day that the history of Egypt goes back *at least* to the date mentioned above. It is maintained by many that, in this early period, the country was for the most part split up among several distinct kingdoms; but on the other hand it is allowed that at times a single monarchy held the whole, and kings possessed of great power and resources ruled Egypt from the Tower of Syene to the waters of the Mediterranean. Manetho assigned to the period no fewer than fourteen dynasties, and though some of these may be purely mythical,[3] and others [4] may represent lines of petty princes who bore sway in some obscure province, yet a certain number—as the fourth, fifth, sixth, eleventh and twelfth—were beyond a doubt dynasties of great power, dominant over the whole or the greater part of Egypt, and possessed of resources which enabled them to erect monuments of an extraordinary character. The two greatest of the Pyramids belong to the fourth dynasty, and must have been seen by Abraham when he visited Egypt, about B.C. 1950. The Third Pyramid in its present state is the work of a queen of the sixth dynasty. A king of the twelfth erected the obelisk which still stands at Heliopolis, as well as another which lies prostrate in the Fayoum. The artificial Lake Mœris, the Fayoum pyramids, and the celebrated Labyrinth belong to the same period. Egypt from B.C. 2450 (or at any rate from B.C. 2250) to about B.C. 1900 was in a flourishing condition: unattacked by foreign foes, she developed during this time the chief features of her

---

[1] See the author's 'Origin of Nations,' p 31, where he has suggested that "the establishment of a settled monarchy in Egypt fell between B.C. 2450 and B.C. 2250." The date suggested by Mr. R. S. Poole is B.C. 2717; that preferred by Sir G. Wilkinson, B.C. 2691.

[2] Bunsen gives B.C. 3059, Lepsius B.C. 3892, Dr. Brugsch B.C. 4400, Mariette and Lenormant B.C. 5004.

[3] As the first three, which have left no remains and no history.

[4] As the seventh, eighth, ninth and tenth.

architecture and of her sculpture, carried to perfection her complex system of hieroglyphics—and attained very considerable proficiency in most of the useful and ornamental arts. The period of this civilisation was designated by Manetho that of "the Old Empire;" and the phrase has been preserved by some modern historians of Egypt[1] as indicative of a very important reality.

The period of "the Old Empire" was followed by that of "the Middle Empire." At a date variously estimated, but believed by the present writer to have been about B.C. 1900, Egypt was conquered by a pastoral Asiatic people, which destroyed the old civilisation, defaced the monuments, burnt the cities, and completely demolished the temples. The whole country was plunged for a time into utter ruin and desolation. All the less massive buildings disappeared—literature, unless enshrined in pyramids or buried in sepulchral chambers, ceased to exist—architecture, mimetic art, even the ornamental arts, finding no demand, died out—for a century or more utter barbarism settled down generally over the land, and if it had not been that in a few places native Egyptian dynasties were suffered to drag on a dependent and precarious existence, all the old knowledge would have perished. It was as when the Goths and Vandals and Alans and Alemanni and Burgundians swept over the Roman Empire of the West, and brought in those "Dark Ages" of which so much has been said and so little is known. Egypt for a century or more was crushed under the iron heel of her conquerors. Then, by slow degrees, there was a revival. The barbarism of the invaders yielded to the softening influences of that civilisation which it had nearly, but not quite, annihilated. First the useful, then the ornamental arts, were recalled into life. Temples were built, sphinxes were carved, even statues were attempted by the rude race which had at first despised all arts but war, and all trades but that of the armourer. The court of the invaders, held at Tanis in the Delta, became assimilated to that of the old Egyptian Pharaohs. No great works, however, were attempted; and the memorials of the period which remain are few and insignificant. How long the foreign domination lasted is uncertain, but the five centuries of some writers[2] are reduced by others to two centuries or two centuries and a half.[3] The present writer inclines to the shorter estimate, and would assign to the "Middle Empire" or "Hyksos rule" the period between B.C. 1900 and 1700—or at most that between B.C. 1925 and B.C. 1675.

---

[1] See Bunsen, 'Egypt's Place in Universal History,' *passim*; Birch, 'Egypt from the Earliest Times,' pp. 23—56; etc.

[2] As Brugsch ('History of Egypt,' vol. ii. p. 314), Lenormant ('Manuel d'Histoire Ancienne,' vol. i. p. 321), and Wilkinson (in the author's 'Herodotus,' vol. ii. pp 297, 298).

[3] The arguments for the shorter period are well stated by Canon Cook in his Essay on the Bearings of Egyptian History upon the Pentateuch ('Speaker's Commentary,' vol. i. part i pp. 447—8).

The yoke of the invaders was thrown off about B.C. 1700—1675 by an uprising of the native Egyptians against them, under a leader named Aahmes, who had his capital at Thebes. The most brilliant period in Egyptian history—the time of the "New Empire"—now set in. Under the eighteenth dynasty, which consisted of twelve kings and a queen, Egyptian fleets explored the Mediterranean and the Red Seas, commerce flourished, Palestine and Syria were conquered, the Euphrates was crossed, Assyria invaded, and the Khabour made the eastern limit of the Empire. At the same time architecture and all the arts revived; great temples were built, lofty obelisks erected, huge colossi upreared. The duration of the dynasty is variously estimated at from two to three centuries. In assigning to it the period from B.C. 1700 to B.C. 1400 we follow the high authority of Dr. Brugsch. Other writers [1] have assigned it the space from B.C. 1703 to B.C. 1462—from B.C. 1633 to B.C. 1412—and from B.C. 1520 to B.C. 1324.

In the ensuing dynasty—the nineteenth—Egyptian art and literature culminated, while in arms there was a slight retrogression. Seti I. and Rameses II. erected the most magnificent of all Egyptian buildings. Seti was a conqueror, but Rameses was content to resist attack. Towards its close the dynasty showed signs of weakness. Internal troubles broke out. The succession to the crown was disputed; and three or four short reigns were followed by a time of complete anarchy. The dynasty probably held the throne from about B.C. 1400 to B.C. 1280.

Under the twentieth dynasty a rapid decline set in. The second king, Rameses III., was a remarkable monarch, successful in his wars, and great in the arts of peace. But with him the glorious period of the Egyptian monarchy came to an end—his successors rapidly degenerated, and for more than two centuries—until the time of Solomon—there was not the slightest sign of a revival. Architecture, art, literature—all pass under a cloud; and, but for the dynastic lists and the excavated tombs of the kings, we might have supposed that some sudden calamity had engulfed and destroyed the Egyptian people.

It is agreed on all hands that the period within which the Israelites and their ancestors came into contact with Egypt prior to their settlement in Canaan fell within the space occupied in Egyptian history by the dynasties between the twelfth and the twentieth inclusively. Abraham's visit to Egypt is generally assigned to the period called above that of "the Old Empire," Joseph's residence to the "Middle Empire," the oppression of the Israelites and the Exodus to the "New Empire." The chief controversy raised is with respect to the Exodus, which some assign to the nineteenth, some to the eighteenth, some to a period anterior to the eighteenth dynasty. The materials at present existing seem insufficient to determine this controversy; and perhaps the unlearned reader will do best to follow the

---

[1] Lenormant gives the first of these estimates, Bunsen the second, and Wilkinson the third.

balance of authority, which certainly at present points to the nineteenth as the dynasty, and to Menephthah, son of Rameses II., as the king, under whom the "going forth" of the Israelites took place.

TABULAR VIEW OF THE CHIEF EVENTS IN EGYPTIAN HISTORY FROM THE TWELFTH TO THE TWENTIETH DYNASTY, WITH APPROXIMATE DATES.

About B.C.	Dynasties.	Chief Kings.	Events.
2150	Accession of the 12th Dynasty (Theban).	Usurtasen I.	Obelisks erected at Heliopolis and in the Fayoum. Great Temple of Karnak commenced
		Usurtasen III	Ethiopia conquered. Frontier advanced to the Second Cataract.
		Amenemhat III.	Construction of the Labyrinth, and the artificial Lake Mœris.
1960	Accession of the 13th Dynasty (Theban).		Egypt invaded by nomadic races from Asia.
1900	Accession of the 17th Dynasty (Shepherds).	Set (or Saïtes).	Great Shepherd invasion under Set. Destruction of Egyptian monuments and records.
		Apepi (or Apophis).	
1700	Accession of the 18th Dynasty (Theban).	Aahmes.	Shepherds driven out. Avaris taken.
		Thothmes I.	Southern frontier advanced. Asia invaded. Campaign in Mesopotamia. Temple of Karnak enlarged. Obelisks erected.
		Queen Hatasu.	Egyptian ships navigate the Red Sea.
		Thothmes III.	Campaigns in Asia. Syria and Western Mesopotamia conquered. Assyria invaded and forced to pay a tribute. Great additions made to the Karnak temple. Erection of numerous obelisks[1] and colossi. A fleet employed in the Mediterranean.
		Amenophis III.	Conquests of Thothmes III maintained. Luxor temple erected. The two great sitting colossi set up.
		Amenophis IV. (or Khuenaten), Saanekht, Ai, and Tutankhamen (heretic kings).	Disk-worship introduced.
		Hor-em-het.	Restoration of the Old Religion.
1400	Accession of the 19th Dynasty (Theban).	Rameses I.	Campaign in Syria. Treaty with Hittites.
		Seti I.	Great victories over the Shasu (Arabs), Hittites, and natives of N. Africa. Egyptian power re-established in Mesopotamia. Splendid additions made to the Temple of Karnak. Rameseum and city of Pa-Ramesu commenced.

[1] Among these were included the tallest existing one, that before the Church of S. John Lateran at Rome, and the obelisk recently placed on the Thames Embankment.

TABULAR VIEW OF THE CHIEF EVENTS IN EGYPTIAN HISTORY FROM THE TWELFTH TO THE TWENTIETH DYNASTY, WITH APPROXIMATE DATES.—*Continued.*

ABOUT B.C.	DYNASTIES.	CHIEF KINGS.	EVENTS.
1400		Rameses II, (reigns 67 years).	Acme of Egyptian civilisation, architecture, and art. Military decline begins. Peace made with the Hittites on terms of perfect equality. Mesopotamia relinquished. Great magnificence in building. Rameseum completed and adorned with huge colossi. Rock-temple of Ipsambul constructed. Canal completed between the Nile and the Red Sea. City of Pa-Ramesu completed.
		Menephthah.	Great attack on Egypt from the north and north-west repulsed. Friendly relations maintained with the Hittites. Expulsion of the "lepers" from Egypt according to Manetho. Reign terminates in troubles and disturbances.
		Seti II. (or Seti-Menephthah).	Crown claimed by a pretender, called Amon-mes, and afterwards by another called Siphthah. Long struggle, terminating in anarchy.
1280	Accession of the 20th Dynasty (Theban).	Set-Nekht.	
		Rameses III. (reigns 31 years).	Combined attack on Egypt of Asiatics and Europeans by land and sea from the north-east repulsed. Nations of N. Africa defeated. Syria overrun, and power of Egypt re-established as far as Carchemish. Temple of Ammon at Medinet Abou built. Commerce encouraged.
1100	Close of the 20th Dynasty	Rameses IV. to XIII.	General decline of Egypt. No wars. No great works. Scarcely any literature. The kings gradually sink into *fainéants*, and power passes into the hands of the high-priests of Ammon.

ON THE GEOGRAPHY OF THE EXODUS AND OF THE WANDERINGS AS FAR AS SINAI.

The difficulties in the way of tracing the route whereby the Israelites passed from the Land of Goshen to Sinai, always considerable, have been recently much enhanced by the propounding of an entirely new line of march by a scholar of high reputation, Dr. Heinrich Brugsch.[1] It is true

---

[1] See a paper read before the International Congress of Orientalists in London, Sept. 17, 1874, and afterwards published under the title 'L'Exode et les Monuments Egyptiens,'

that the same theory was put forward many years ago by two other learned Germans, Messrs. Unruh and Schleiden, but their views attracted little attention, having no great local knowledge to recommend them, whereas Dr. Brugsch is probably the highest authority living on the subject of Egyptian geography, and a view which has his support cannot possibly be ignored or passed over. We must, then, commence the examination of the subject before us by discussing the theory of Dr. Brugsch, which is regarded in some quarters as "a brilliant one," and as having "at any rate *prima facie* much to recommend it." [1]

Dr. Brugsch supposes that the "Rameses" from which the Israelites started (Ex. xii. 37; Num. xxxiii. 3) was the same place as Tanis or Zoan, now *San,* a large town situated on the Tanitic branch of the Nile, about lat. 31° and long. 31° 50' E. from Greenwich. He brings abundant proof to show that this town, which was rebuilt by Rameses II., was known in his reign and in that of his son, Menephthah, as Pa-Ramesu, or "the city of Rameses," that it was a place of great importance, and a common residence, if not *the* common residence, of the court at that period. Placing the Exodus, as we do ourselves, in the reign of Menephthah, he naturally concludes that the miracles of Moses and his interviews with the Egyptian king took place at this city, the only "city of Rameses" known to have existed at the time, and that it was the starting-point from which he and his company commenced their journey. In proof that he is right, he very properly adduces the statement of the psalmist, probably Asaph, that the miracles of Moses were wrought "in the field of Zoan" (Ps. lxxviii. 12, 43). These arguments are of so much weight that we, at any rate, do not care to dispute them, and we shall assume as highly probable, if not absolutely certain, that the Rameses from which the Israelites started was Zoan-Rameses, the capital city of Rameses II. and Menephthah, now marked by the extensive ruins at San-el-Hagar, which have lately been visited and described by Mr. Greville Chester. [2]

The children of Israel journeyed "from Rameses to Succoth" (Ex. xii. 37). Dr. Brugsch assumes the identity of this word, Succoth, with an Egyptian name, *Thuku* or *Thukot,* which he finds applied to the marshy district east and south-east of Tanis, and suggests that the place where the Israelites encamped was a certain fort, called "the barrier of Thukot," which, he says, is mentioned in papyri, and which he believes to have lain to the south-east of Tanis, halfway between that place and the modern Tel-Defneh, the ancient Daphnæ. We quite agree as to the direction in

Leipzig, 1875. An English translation of the work is appended to the 'History of Egypt,' by the same writer, translated by the late Mr. H. Danby Seymour and Mr. Philip Smith, and published by Mr. Murray, London, 1879.

[1] See an article by Mr. Greville Chester in the 'Quarterly Statement of the Palestine Exploration Fund,' for July, 1880, p. 134

[2] *Ibid.* pp. 140—4.

which Succoth is to be sought, since the wilderness, for which Moses was bound, lay south-east of Tanis; we demur, however, to the identification of Succoth with Thuku,[1] and we regard seven and a-half miles, which is half the distance between San and Tel-Defneh, as too short a march for the people to have made in the first freshness of their powers and the first warmth of their zeal. We should incline to double the distance, and to place Succoth at Tel-Defneh, an elevated spot of ground in a marshy district, where the cultivators of the soil would be likely to fix their "booths" of sedge and brushwood.[2]

The third station named in the journey of the Israelites is Etham (Ex. xiii. 20) "in the edge of the wilderness." Having identified Succoth with "the barrier of Thukot," about seven or eight miles from San, Dr. Brugsch not unnaturally places Etham at Tel-Defneh, seven or eight miles further on in the same direction. Here there was, he says, in the time of Rameses II., a "Khetam," or fort, to guard the passage of the easternmost branch of the Nile, whence (according to him) the Hebrew name, Etham. Khetam, however, with a strong guttural *kh*, is not Etham, אתם, which commences with the light breathing, *aleph*. And Khetam, again, is not a local name, but a descriptive word, meaning "fort" or "stronghold."[3] Consequently there were many Khetams, especially towards the frontier; and even granting the identity of the words, there is nothing to mark the identity of the Biblical Etham with the Khetam, or fortress, at Tel-Dafneh. We should incline to place Etham at El-Kantara, on the line of the Suez Canal, about eleven or twelve miles from Tel-Defneh, almost due east. El-Kantara is truly "in the edge of the wilderness" proper, which commences as soon as the Suez Canal is crossed; and the ruins show it to have been a place of some importance in the time of Rameses II.[4]

At Etham the Israelites were commanded to change their route. "Speak unto the children of Israel," said God to Moses, "that they *turn* and encamp before Pi-hahiroth, between Migdol and the sea, over against Baal-zephon" (Ex. xiv. 2). Dr. Brugsch believes that the "turn" was made to the left—that from Tel-Defneh the south-east course was changed to a north-east one, and a march made which brought the Israelites close to the Mediterranean Sea at the western extremity of Lake Serbônis. The distance to this point from Tel-Defneh, his Etham, is by the shortest route considerably over forty miles—yet Dr. Brugsch appears to regard this distance as accomplished in one day.

---

[1] We believe that the Egyptian *t* (*th*) never replaces the sharp Hebrew sibilant *samech*, which is the initial letter of Succoth.

[2] Succoth is more properly "booths" than "tents," and is so translated in Gen. xxxiii. 17; Lev. xxiii. 42; Neh. viii. 14, 16. The natives of the marsh district to this day lodge in "huts made of reeds" ('Quarterly Statement of Pal. Exp. Fund,' p. 144).

[3] See Dr. Birch's 'Dictionary of Hieroglyphics,' in vol. v. of Bunsen's 'Egypt's Place, p. 558, *ad voc.* Khetmu.

[4] Greville Chester, in the 'Quarterly Statement' above quoted, p. 147.

Pi-hahiroth is described (Ex. xiv. 2) as "between Migdol and the sea," and as "over against Baal-zephon." Dr. Brugsch finds a Migdol some twenty miles from the western end of Lake Serbônis, to the south-west, and conjectures that Baal-zephon was a Phœnician settlement, situated at the modern Ras Kazeroun, the ancient Mons Casius. As this place is distant from his site for Pi-hahiroth some twenty-five miles in the opposite direction from Migdol, he regards the description of Ex. xiv. 2 as sufficiently answered, and even places the three sites accordingly. Almost all other expositors have felt that the three places must have been very near together —indeed, so near that the encampment beside Pi-hahiroth (Ex. iv. 9) was regarded as "pitching before Migdol" (Num. xxxiii. 7).

We approach now the main feature of Dr. Brugsch's theory, to which all the rest is subordinate. He believes that the Israelites, having reached the shores of the Mediterranean at the point opposite the western extremity of Lake Serbônis, found stretching before them a long tongue of land, which formed the regular road from Egypt to Palestine,[1] and that immediately, without having to wait for a miracle, they entered upon it. The Egyptians followed them. After the Hebrews, marching on foot, had successfully traversed the entire neck of land to the point where it (as he supposes) re-joined the continent, "a great wave from the Mediterranean took by surprise the Egyptian cavalry, and the captains of the war-chariots."[2] Thrown into disorder, their pathway obliterated, they became entangled in the soft mud of the Serbonian Lake, which was, he says, "a lagoon of weeds,"[3] and thence called *Yam-Suph*—they suffered the calamity which befel the soldiers of Artaxerxes Ochus,[4] and to which Milton alludes in 'Paradise Lost'[5]—they perished in the waters of Serbônis.

The objections to this entire view are numerous, and of various kinds. In the first place, it gives no reason for the Pharaoh's sudden resolve to pursue the Israelites, since, instead of being "entangled in the land," they were, according to Brugsch, on the shortest and readiest road leading out of Egypt to Palestine. In the second place, it contradicts the statement[6] that "God led them not the way of the Philistines, but led the people the way of the Yam-Suph," since it makes the way of the Philistines and the way of the Yam-Suph one and the same, and it makes God lead them out of Egypt by the way which conducted most directly to Palestine, or the country of the Philistines. Thirdly, it leaves no place for the miracle of dividing the sea (Ex. xiv. 21), since it regards the tongue of land as a regular road constantly used. Fourthly, it contradicts the natural features

---

[1] Brugsch, 'History of Egypt,' vol. ii. p. 360 :—" A long tongue of land, which in ancient times formed the only road from Egypt to Palestine." This point is essential to Dr. Brugsch's theory, since he could not otherwise suppose that the Israelites would have pent themselves up in such a corner as that between the Mediterranean and Lake Serbônis.

[2] *Ibid.* p. 364.　　　　[3] *Ibid.* p. 360.　　　　[4] Diod. Sic. xvi. 46.
[5] Book II. ll. 592—4.　　　　　　　　　　　　　　　[6] Ex. xiii. 17.

of the place, since (1) the Lake Serbônis contains no weeds, sedge, or rushes of any kind,[1] and (2) it is, and always must be, so long as it is a lake, fed by a deep channel connecting it with the Mediterranean, so that the tongue of land is not continuous, and cannot be used as a road, unless by an army carrying pontoons, or a small company of travellers, who might be conveyed across the channel in boats. Fifthly, it assumes that the expression *Yam-Suph* is used by the writer of the Pentateuch of two quite different pieces of water, since no one can possibly deny that *Yam-Suph* in Num. xxxiii. 10, 11, is used of the Red Sea. Finally, it is in the teeth of a twofold tradition, Egyptian[2] and Jewish,[3] which unhesitatingly made the upper end of the Red Sea the scene of the disaster.

On the destruction of the Egyptians, the Israelites, according to Dr. Brugsch, turned sharp to the south from Baal-zephon, or the Mons Casius, and entered the wilderness of Shur, now the Tih, in long. 32° 50′ nearly. A recent examination of the locality has shown such a movement to have been impossible, since the Lake Serbônis continues in an unbroken line from long. 32° 32′, where it commences, to long. 33° 20′, where it terminates, at a place called El Saramit.[4] Even at this point there is no escaping from the tongue of land on which the Israelites are supposed to have entered, without crossing the channel connecting Lake Serbônis with the Mediterranean,[5] so that, having reached the end of the spit, the Israelites would have had no course open to them but to have turned back and retraced their steps to the supposed site of Pihahiroth.

From the Mons Casius, his Baal-zephon, Dr. Brugsch, having conducted the Israelites across a tongue of land which does not exist, makes them enter the wilderness of Shur, and travel three days in a south-west direction to Marah, which he identifies with the "Bitter Lakes." It seems to have escaped him that the distance is one of at least seventy miles, which could not certainly have been accomplished under five days, and being through an arid desert would probably have taken six. He also fails wholly to account for the extraordinary change of mind on the part of the Israelites, who, having marched out of Egypt thirty miles on the direct road to Palestine, suddenly turn round and go back to the very confines of Egypt,

---

[1] Greville Chester, in the 'Quarterly Statement,' p. 155 :—"The clear bright water of Lake Serbônis is as devoid of lacustrine vegetation as the Dead Sea itself. Of it there is *no trace whatsoever*. But more, it is matter of fact that Lake Serbônis is *almost equally devoid of marine vegetation*."

[2] The Egyptian tradition appears in Polyhistor, who reports the people of Memphis as maintaining that the passage of the sea was made by Moses watching the *ebb of the tide*, ('Fragm. Hist. Gr.' vol iii. p. 223), which could only be done on the Red Sea side of Egypt, not on the side of the Mediterranean, which is tideless.

[3] The Jewish tradition has never been doubted. It appears by the regular translation of Yam-Suph by the LXX., in every place but one where it occurs, by ἡ ἐρυθρὰ θάλασσα, "the Red Sea."

[4] Greville Chester, in the 'Quarterly Statement,' p. 154.

[5] *Ibid.* p. 157

taking a line from Etham to Marah which must have measured at least 140 miles, when the two places (according to him) were not much above thirty miles apart.

It seems needless to pursue Dr. Brugsch's theory any further. It is alike in contradiction with tradition, geography, and common sense. Its apparent foundation is a string of geographical names, supposed to be identical in the nomenclature of ancient Egypt and in that of the writer of Exodus. But on careful examination the agreement is found to be strained and forced. Only one of the Scriptural names (Migdol) really occurs upon Dr. Brugsch's line of march, and that name is of a generic character (*migdol* meaning simply "a tower"), and so likely to have been borne by more than one place.[1] The other names are either pure inventions, not found in Egyptian geography, as Baal-zapouna and Pi-hakhirot,[2] or names not really the same as the Hebrew, *e.g.* Thukot and Khetam. Common sense forbids belief in a route which involves the making of a circuit of 140 miles to reach a place thirty miles off, the performance of a six or seven days' journey in the space of three, and the assignment by one and the same writer of one and the same name to two quite different sheets of water, without any note of distinction or indication that two "seas" are meant.

Returning then to Etham, which we have placed conjecturally at El-Kantara, and which must certainly have been either there or in the neighbourhood, perhaps toward Ismailia, we have now to trace the further march from Etham to Sinai. We imagine, then, that on the command being given, —"Speak unto the children of Israel that they *turn* and encamp before Pi-hahiroth, between Migdol and the sea, over against Baal-zephon" (Ex. xvi. 2), the direction of the route was altered from east or south-east to due south—the "Bitter Lakes" were placed on the left hand, and the march continued southwards along the western shore of the Red Sea until an extensive camping-ground was reached, lying between a place called Migdol, quite distinct from the northern Migdol, and another called Pi-hahiroth, which was on or near the Red Sea. An exact location of these places is impossible, since neither in ancient nor modern geography have we any clear trace of the names,[3] and the position of the northern extremity of

---

[1] There were two Migdols in Palestine, distinguished as Migdol-El, and Migdol-Gad. Lepsius and Stuart Poole maintain that there were at least two in Egypt. It is in favour of this contention that the northern Migdol had a descriptive epithet, being called in the Egyptian writings "the Migdol of King Seti-Menephthah" (Brugsch, 'Hist. of Egypt,' vol. ii. p. 359).

[2] Baal-zapouna is found in the Egyptian texts as an epithet of the god Ammon, but not as the name of a place. Pi-hakhirot is not found at all, but is supposed by Dr. Brugsch to be a name that might have been given to a place situated at "the entrance of the gulfs" (*ib.* p. 363). But Jablonsky's etymology—"the place where sedge grows"—seems to be quite as probable.

[3] The ancient geographers (Hecatæus, Fr. 282; 'Itin. Antonin.' p. 76, ed. Parthey) have a Magdôlus which corresponds to the *northern* Egyptian Migdol: Herodotus has a Magdôlus (ii. 159), which seems to represent Megiddo. But there is no trace of the southern Egyptian

the Gulf of Suez at the time of the Exodus is open to question. On the whole, it is perhaps most probable that the Bitter Lakes were then a portion of the Red Sea inlet,[1] being connected with it by a narrow and shallow channel, which is now dried up. We should ourselves place the passage somewhere near the present site of Suez, and we should suppose the point of landing to have been about five or six miles north of the Ayûn Musa, about which, for the sake of the water, the host would no doubt have encamped. To the objection that the site of Suez is too far south, since the distance from Etham, as we have now placed it, is above forty miles, which could not have been accomplished in a day, we answer that in the Scriptural narrative there is no mention of days, and that it is quite a gratuitous supposition that the number of camping-places mentioned marks the number of days spent on the journey. In point of fact only six camping-places are mentioned between Rameses and the wilderness of Sin; yet it is expressly stated that the journey took a full month (Ex. xvi. 1). We should suppose at least three days to have been occupied by the march from Etham to Pi-hahiroth.

The Red Sea crossed, and the Ayûn Musa reached, there was no doubt a halt of at least a day, while Moses composed his "Song," and thanksgiving was offered, and Miriam and the other women danced and sang for joy (Ex. xv. 1—21). The Israelites were then led out into "the wilderness of Shur" (ib. ver. 22), or, as it is elsewhere called, "the wilderness of Etham" (Num. xxxiii. 8). These names seem to have been applied, indifferently, to the whole western portion of the great desert-tract which separates Egypt from Palestine. It was called "the wilderness of Etham," because Etham lay "in its edge" (Ex. xiii. 20), at the point where it was most accessible from Egypt; and it was called "the wilderness of Shur," probably from a name, Zor, which the Egyptians applied to the tract within which Etham was situated.[2] Through this tract, or rather through the south-western portion of it, which lay along the eastern side of the Gulf of Suez, the Israelites proceeded for three entire days without finding any water (ib.). Travellers tell us that this is the exact character of the tract east of the Gulf from the Ayûn Musa to the source, called Howarah,[3] which lies at the distance of about thirty-eight or thirty-nine miles. Most critics agree that this was the line of route pursued, and identify Marah (ib. ver. 23) with Howarah or its neighbourhood, which has several springs that are

---

Migdol. In modern geography, some low hills near Suez are said to be called Muktala (Stanley, 'Sinai and Palestine,' p. 65), which may be a reminiscence of Migdol, but points to no exact site. Of the names Pi-hahiroth and Baal-zephon there is no trace at all.

[1] So Canon Cook ('Speaker's Commentary,' vol. i. pt. i. p. 435), and Mr. R. Stuart Poole ('Dictionary of the Bible,' vol. iii. p. 1016).

[2] Brugsch, 'History of Egypt,' vol. ii. p. 357.

[3] Robinson, 'Biblical Researches,' vol. i. pp. 91—96; Stanley, 'Sinai and Palestine,' p. 66; Wilson and Palmer 'Our Work in Palestine,' p. 275; etc.

remarkably "bitter."[1] We incline to agree with them, though it must be allowed that in the space of three thousand years many physical changes are likely to have occurred, and that an exact correspondence between the present condition of the country and the description of Moses is not to be expected.

The next camping-place after Marah was Elim, which means "trees" according to some critics.[2] Here were twelve springs of water and a grove of seventy palm-trees[3] (Ex. xv. 27)—pleasing objects to the traveller who has spent three or four consecutive days in the true wilderness. Elim has been identified with three distinct sites—Wady Ghurundel, Wady Useit, and Wady Shubeikah,[4] all of which have trees and water. They are distant from Howarah, respectively, six miles, ten miles, and sixteen miles. To us it seems that Wady Ghurundel, which would be reached first, and which is the most beautiful of the three, has the best claim of the three to represent the camping-place of Elim, the short distance from Howarah furnishing no objection now that there was no need of haste, and the abundance of shade, pasturage, and water rendering the place most attractive. We are inclined to believe that a considerable stay was made in this locality, more especially for the refreshment of the flocks and herds, which must have suffered severely during the three days' march without water.[5]

The next notice of movement which we have in Exodus is remarkably vague, and but for the light thrown upon the subject by the summary in Numbers might be misleading. "They took their journey," we are told, "from Elim, and all the congregation of the children of Israel came unto the wilderness of Sin, which is between Elim and Sinai" (Ex. xvi. 1). From this it might have been supposed that the next encampment after Elim was in the wilderness of Sin, which must then have been looked for within twelve or fifteen miles of Wady Ghurundel. But there is no suitable tract within the distance. We find, however, by Numbers (xxxiii. 10, 11), that there was at least one encampment between Elim and the Sin desert. "They removed from Elim," it is said, "and encamped by the Red Sea;

---

[1] The bitterness of Ain Howarah is recognised by all travellers, from Burckhardt ('Travels in Syria,' p. 473) downwards. Winer (Realwörterbuch, ad voc. Marah) says that a still bitterer well lies east of Marah. Mention is also made of an exceedingly bitter spring south of Marah ('Dictionary of the Bible,' vol ii. p. 233).

[2] Stanley, 'Sinai and Palestine,' pp. 22, 508; Highton, in Smith's 'Dictionary of the Bible, vol. ii. p. 532, note, etc.

[3] Palms are still found in these parts, both at Wady Ghurundel and Wady Useit. They are "either dwarf, i. e. trunkless, or else with savage hairy trunks and branches all dishevelled" (Stanley, p. 68).

[4] Shubeikah is preferred by Lepsius ('Travels,' vol. i. p. 27); Useit by Laborde ('Geographical Commentary on Exodus,' xv. 27); Ghurundel, or Ghurundel together with Useit, by Dean Stanley (p. 68); Ghurundel positively by Canon Cook, the Rev. S. Clark, Kalisch, Knobel, and most others.

[5] It is our conviction that the cattle of the Israelites rapidly decreased as they pursued their march. Many were probably killed for food; others died of thirst, or pined away from the insufficiency of the pasturage.

and they removed from the Red Sea and encamped in the wilderness of Sin." This makes it certain that Wady Ghurundel was reached at some distance inland,[1] and that after leaving it the route was deflected towards the right, and the coast of the Red Sea reached, probably either at the mouth of Wady Ethal or of Wady Shubeikah. As Wady Ethal is only ten miles from Ghurundel, and Shubeikah is less than fifteen, the latter would seem to be the more probable,[2] unless indeed there was more than one encampment on the sea-shore.

We have now to identify " the wilderness of Sin." Within eleven or twelve miles of the mouth of Wady Shubeikah are two tracts fairly suitable. One of these is the plain of El Markha,[3] an open sandy space, about thirteen miles long by three broad, intervening between the mountains and the sea, which may be reached from Wady Shubeikah by a march along the shore in about three or four hours. The other is the Debbet er Ramleh, an inland tract, " bare, wild, and desolate,"[4] extending about twenty-five miles from N.W.W. to S.E.E., between long. 33° 20′ and 33° 40′, and varying in width from two to seven miles. This tract may be reached from Wady Shubeikah by a succession of wadys, rough but practicable, in a march of about three hours. The conductors of the recent Sinai Survey Expedition, having examined both localities, are strongly of opinion that the way by the shore and El Markha is the one most likely to have been pursued by so large a body as the Israelites,[5] and that El Markha consequently is " the wilderness of Sin," where the quails were brought and the manna was first given (Ex. xvi. 4—36). The opinion of scientific observers has so much weight, that, though some coincidences of name have been noted on the rival route,[6] we incline to accept the line by El Markha as that which the Israelites most probably took.

From some part of the plain El Markha they must have turned inland. Three wadys lead out of it, the Wady Shellal towards the north, the Wady Feiran on the south, and the Wady Seih-Sidreh, halfway between the two. Wadys Shellal and Seih-Sidreh unite in the Wady Magharah, where the Egyptians had an important settlement for the working of the copper-mines, defended by a fortress and a garrison.[7] It is probable that the

---

[1] The whole of the coast-line is arid. The wadys are entered from the shore up a steep dry incline (Stanley, p. 10), and it is not till some distance inland that vegetation is found.

[2] Shubeikah has trees, water, and pasturage. It is, next to Ghurundel, the most fertile of the outer wadys.

[3] Cook, in the 'Speaker's Commentary,' vol. i. pt. i. p. 438; Stanley, 'Sinai and Palestine,' p. 70.　　[4] Cook, p. 436.

[5] Palmer, 'Desert of the Exodus,' vol. i. pp. 232—9.

[6] *Debbet* is said to have exactly the same meaning as *Sin* (Cook, in the ' Speaker's Commentary,' vol. i. pt. i. p. 436), *Dophkah* (Num. xxxiii. 12) to correspond to *Sih*, the name of a wady which communicates with the Debbet, and *Alush* to be the same as *El Esh*, another wady further on (*ibid.* pp. 437—8).

[7] Brugsch, 'History of Egypt,' vol. i. p. 65 ; Cook, in the 'Speaker's Commentary,' vol. i. pt. i. p. 438 ; Stanley, ' Sinai and Palestine,' p. 28.

Israelites would wish to avoid a collision with a disciplined force, and would therefore prefer the southern route, which, though circuitous, and said to be at the present time ill-watered, was spacious and free from enemies. Three encampments brought them to Rephidim, which, if we have correctly divined the movements of the host up to this point, must have been in the Wady Feiran, a valley declared to be " richer in water and vegetation than any other in the peninsula." [1] Here, consequently, abundant water was expected, but none was found; the watercourse was dry (Ex. xvii. 1). Hence the extreme anger of the people against Moses, followed by the miracle of bringing water out of the rock (*ib.* vers. 2—6), and soon afterwards by the battle with the Amalekites. Wady Feiran, of great value in itself on account of its fertility, was also of extreme importance as giving access to the entire group of valleys about Sinai, which formed an oasis in the stony wilderness. It has been well observed that " if the Israelites passed through Wady Feiran, it seems improbable that they should not have come into collision with the natives." [2] Here were " the tombs and storehouses of the Amalekites; " [3] here probably was the ancient sanctuary of the nation; [4] here certainly, and in the neighbourhood, was one of the best grazing districts, for which a nomadic horde will fight, if it fights for anything. Here, finally, is a spot fitting well the description of the battle and its attendant circumstances. " Every one who has seen the valley of Feiran will at once recognise the propriety of the 'hill' (Ex. xvii. 9, 10), if applied to the rocky eminence which commands the palm-grove, and on which, in early Christian times, stood the church and palace of the bishops of Paran. Thus, if we can attach any credence to the oldest known tradition of the peninsula, that Rephidim is the same as Paran, then Rephidim, 'the resting-place,' is the natural name for the paradise of the Bedouins in the adjacent palm-grove; then the hill of the church of Paran may fairly be imagined to be " the hill " on which Moses stood, deriving its earliest consecration from the altar which he built; the Amalekites may thus have naturally fought for the oasis of the Desert and the sanctuary of their gods; and Jethro may well have found his kinsmen encamping after their long journey amongst the palms 'before the mount of God' (Serbal), and acknowledged that the Lord was greater even than all the gods who had from ancient days been thought to dwell on the lofty peaks which overhung their encampment." [5]

The Wady Feiran bifurcates at its eastern extremity, sending off the Wady esh Sheikh to the left, and to the right the Wady Solaf, both of them

[1] Highton, in Smith's ' Dictionary of the Bible,' vol. iii. p. 1030.
[2] Cook, in the ' Speaker's Commentary,' l.s.c.
[3] Rev. F. W. Holland, quoted in the same work, vol. i. pt. i. p. 438, note [1]. (Compare Our Work in Palestine,' p. 282.)
[4] Ritter, ' Sinai,' pp. 728–44; Stanley, ' Sinai and Palestine,' p. 40.
[5] Stanley, pp. 41-2.

practicable routes, but the former the easier. It is a reasonable suggestion that both may have been utilised, and that the two portions of the congregation, reuniting where the above-mentioned wadys converge, thus entered the Wady er Rahah, "the enclosed plain in front of the magnificent cliffs of Ras Sufsâfeh,"[1] which is now generally admitted to be "the wilderness of Sinai" (Ex. xix. 1), the camping-ground in which the Israelites assembled to see the Lord "come down upon Mount Sinai" (ib. ver. 11). The southern extremity of the mountain, once preferred by many[2] as the probable scene of the descent, is found to have no plain at all at its base, and no place within moderate distance at all suited for a great assembly.[3] Er Rahah and Ras Sufsâfeh, on the other hand, answer all the conditions. "No one," says Dean Stanley,[4] "who has approached the Ras Sasâfeh (Sufsâfeh) through that noble plain, or who has looked down upon the plain from that majestic height, will willingly part with the belief that these are the two essential features of the view of the Israelite camp. That such a plain should exist at all in front of such a cliff is so remarkable a coincidence with the sacred narrative as to furnish a strong internal argument, not merely of its identity with the scene, but of the scene itself having been described by an eye-witness. The awful and lengthened approach, as to some natural sanctuary, would have been the fittest preparation for the coming scene. The low line of alluvial mounds at the foot of the cliff exactly answer [?] to the 'bounds' which were to keep the people off from 'touching the mount.' The plain itself is not broken and uneven and narrowly shut in, like almost all others in the range, but presents a long retiring sweep, against which the people could 'remove and stand afar off.' The cliff, rising like a huge altar in front of the whole congregation, and visible against the sky in lonely grandeur from end to end of the whole plain, is the very image of 'the mount that might be touched,' and from which the voice of God might be heard far and wide over the stillness of the plain below, widened at that point to its utmost extent by the confluence of all the contiguous valleys." The opinion here stated rests upon such solid grounds that further exploration can scarcely shake it. The latest and most scientific explorers have given to it their full adhesion. And the trigonometrical survey which these explorers made of the entire neighbourhood has converted one,[5] who was strongly inclined to the rival view, into a zealous advocate of the opinion here set forth. Finally, the judgment of Sir Henry James, one of our best engineers, coincides with that of the

---

[1] Stanley, p. 42.

[2] As Ritter, Kalisch, Wellsted, Laborde, Strauss, and others.

[3] So far as I know, this was first pointed out by Dean Stanley in 1856 ('Sinai and Palestine, pp. 75—6). His judgment on the point was completely confirmed by the engineers who made the Ordnance Survey in 1868.

[4] 'Sinai and Palestine,' pp. 42–3.

[5] Canon Cook. (See the 'Speaker's Commentary,' vol. i. pt. i. pp. 440—1.)

officers who made the survey. Sir Henry believes that "no spot in the world can be pointed out which combines in a more remarkable manner the conditions of a commanding height and of a plain in every part of which the sights and sounds described in Exodus would reach an assembled multitude of more than two million souls." [1]

There would seem, therefore, to be no reasonable doubt that Sinai and its wilderness have been identified, and that the Law was given from Ras Sufsâfeh to the people of Israel assembled in the Wady of Er Rahah.

LITERATURE OF EXODUS.

The Book of Exodus is so closely connected with the remainder of the Pentateuch that it has but seldom, comparatively speaking, been made the subject of distinct and separate comment. The great bulk of those who have written upon it, have been either composers of "Introductions" to the whole of the Old Testament, like Eichhorn, Bertholdt, Carpzov, Hävernick, Keil and Delitzsch, De Wette, Jahn, Herbst, Michaelis, Bleek, and Stähelin, or writers of commentaries on the entire Pentateuch, like Vater, Knobel, Baumgarten, Marsh, Jahn (Aechtheit des Pentateuch), Hartmann, Fritzsche, Kalisch, and Bush. One English writer of repute, Graves, occupied somewhat narrower ground in his 'Lectures on the Last Four Books of the Pentateuch,' which in England was long reckoned among standard theological works. The volume devoted to Exodus by Kalisch, though part of a general commentary, stands on a somewhat peculiar footing, since it was written and published separately by one who viewed "Exodus" as "forming the centre of the Divine Revelation," and as being consequently "the most important volume which the human race possesses." As the comment of a Jew, a special interest attaches to this treatise, the author having certain advantages of intimate familiarity with the text and close acquaintance with Hebrew customs and ideas, which render his remarks deserving of attentive consideration.

Of comments on Exodus alone, the earliest which deserves mention is that of Rivet, entitled 'Commentarii in Exodum,' which will be found in his Opera Theologica, vol. i. published at Rotterdam in 1651. After this, no contribution of much value was made towards the right understanding of the work until Rosenmüller published his 'Scholia in Exodum' in 1822. The strictures of Von Bohlen in his 'Alte Indien' (1835) called forth in 1840 the excellent work of Hengstenberg, entitled 'Aegypten und Moses,' which, although containing reference to Genesis, is in the main a comment on Exodus, of great value in all that regards Egypt and the Egyptians. Thirteen years later Keil and Delitzsch commenced the publication of their great work, 'Einleitung in die Kanonischen Schriften des alten Testamentes,' by commentaries on Genesis and Exodus, which were translated into English in Clark's Edinburgh Series in the year 1864. Kalisch's 'Historical and Critical Commentary,' which has been already mentioned, appeared within two years of that of Keil and Delitzsch, but was written apparently without any knowledge of it, and shows throughout marks of original and independent thought. It was published simultaneously in English and in German, in the year 1855. In 1857, two years later, the editors of the 'Kurzgefasstes exegetisches Handbuch zum alten Testament,' published by Hirzel of Leipsic, gave to the world a still more elaborate comment than either of these, entitled 'Die Bücher Exodus und Leviticus erklärt von Augustus Knobel,' in which great and varied learning was brought to bear on the subject, and a view taken which, though rationalistic to a certain extent, was moderate in comparison with the older generation of German commentators, as De Wette, Von Lengerke, and Stähelin. Finally, in 1871, the first volume of the 'Speaker's Commentary' contained an Introduction and Explanatory Comment on

---

[1] 'Speaker's Commentary,' vol. i. p. 442

Exodus, accompanied by additional Notes and Essays—the joint production of Canon Cook and the Rev. S. Clark, remarkable for the great knowledge of Egyptian history and of the ancient Egyptian language which it displayed—a knowledge that at once placed the principal author in the first rank of European Egyptologers.

Some good collections have been made in recent years of the Jewish commentators upon Exodus, or the Pentateuch generally. Among these the most important are 'Mechilta, der älteste halach. und hagad. Commentar z. 2. Buch Moses, von J. H. Weiss,' Wien, 1865; 'Wehishir, gesammelte, erläuterte, Midrasch und Halachastokon z Buche Exodus des Pentateuch, von R. Chefez Aluf,' Leipzig, 1873; and 'Der Pentateuch, mit folgenden zehn Commentatoren, Raschi, Ibn Esra, Ramban, Raschbam, Balhaturim, Sefurus, Asvi Eser, Mesoras Targum, Paschegen, und dem Commentar Nesina-la-ger von R. Nathan Adler, ferner mit Targum und Toldos Aron,' Wilna, 1876.

Important works have also been written on portions of Exodus, e. g. that of Bryant, entitled 'Observations upon the Plagues inflicted upon the Egyptians,' 2nd edition, London, 1810, and that of Millington on the same subject; also Michaelis, 'Mosaisches Recht,' Frankfurt, 1775–80; and the following upon the Tabernacle—Friedrich, 'Symbolik der Mosaischen Stiftshütte,' Leipzig, 1841; and Neumann, 'Die Stiftshütte, Bild und Wort,' Gotha, 1861. Important light has also been thrown on this last-mentioned subject by Mr. James Fergusson, in Dr. Smith's 'Dictionary of the Bible' art. Temple.

THE
BOOK OF EXODUS.

INTRODUCTORY SECTION. CHAPTERS I., II.

The Oppression of Israel in Egypt, with the Birth and Early Life of Moses.

EXPOSITION.

CHAPTER I.

Vers. 1—6.—The Book of Exodus, being written in continuation of the history recorded in Genesis, is carefully connected with it by a recapitulation. The recapitulation involves three points :—1. The names of Jacob's children; 2. The number of Jacob's descendants who went down into Egypt; and 3. The death of Joseph. Verses 1—4 are a recapitulation of Gen. xxxv. 22–26; verse 5, of Gen. xlvi. 27; and verse 6, of Gen. l. 26. In no case, however, is the recapitulation exact, or (so to speak) mechanical. The "households" of verse 1 had not been mentioned previously; Joseph had not in Genesis been separated off from his brethren, as he is in verse 5; nor had the deaths of "his brethren" been recorded, much less of "all that generation." Thus there is here no "vain repetition." New facts come out in the course of the recapitulation; and the narrative advances while aiming especially at maintaining its continuity.

Ver. 1.—Now these are the names. Literally, "And these are the names." Compare Gen. xlvi. 8, where the phrase used is the same. We have here the first example of that almost *universal* practice of the writers of the Historical Scriptures to connect book with book in the closest possible way by the simple copulative "and." (Compare Josh. i. 1, Judg. i. 1, Ruth, Samuel, Kings, Ezra, Nehemiah, and Esther.) This practice, so unlike that of secular writers, can only be explained by the instinctive feeling of all, that they were contributors to *a single book*, each later writer a continuator of the narrative placed on record by his predecessor. In the Pentateuch, if we admit a single author, the initial *vau* will be less remarkable, since it will merely serve to join together the different sections of a single treatise. **Which came into Egypt.** The next two words of the original, "with Jacob," belong properly to this clause. The whole verse is best translated, "Now these are the names of the children of Israel which came into Egypt with Jacob; they came every man with his household." So the LXX., Pagnini, Kalisch, Geddes, Boothroyd, etc. **Every man and his household.** This is important in connection with the vexed question of the possible increase of the original band of so-called "Israelites" within the space of 430 years to such a number as is said to have quitted Egypt with Moses (ch. xii. 37). The "household" of Abraham comprised 318 adult males (Gen. xiv. 14). The "households" of Jacob, his eleven sons, and his numerous grown-up grandsons, have been with reason estimated at "several thousands." (Kurtz, 'History of the Old Covenant,' vol. ii p. 149, E. T.)

Vers. 2—5.—The sons of the legitimate wives Leah and Rachel are placed first, in the order of their seniority (Gen. xxix. 32–35; xxx. 18–20; xxxv. 18); then those of the secondary wives, or concubines, also in the order of their birth (*ib.* xxx. 6—13). The order is different from that observed in Gen. xlvi., and seems intended to do honour to legitimate, as opposed to secondary, wedlock. The omission of Joseph follows necessarily from the exact form of the opening phrase, "These are the names of the children of Israel, which *came into Egypt with Jacob.*"

Ver. 5.—**All the souls that came out of the loins of Jacob were seventy souls.** This is manifestly intended as a repetition of Gen. xlvi. 27, and throws the reader back upon the details there adduced, which make up the exact number of "seventy souls," by the inclusion of Jacob himself, of Joseph, and of Joseph's two sons, Ephraim and Manasseh. The inaccuracy by which Jacob is counted among his own descendants, is thoroughly Oriental and Hebraistic, however opposed to Western habits of thought. To stumble at it shows a narrow and carping spirit. (Compare note on Gen. xlvi. 15.) **For Joseph was in Egypt already.** Joseph, *i.e.*, has not been mentioned with the other sons of Jacob, since he did not "come into Egypt with Jacob," but was there previously. The transfer of the clause to the commencement of the verse, which is made by the LXX., is unnecessary.

Ver. 6. — **And Joseph died.** Or, "So Joseph died"—a reference to Gen. l. 26 —**and all his brethren.** All the other actual sons of Jacob—some probably before him; some, as Levi (ch. vi. 16), after him. Joseph's "hundred and ten years" did not constitute an extreme longevity. **And all that generation.** All the wives of Jacob's sons, their sister Dinah, and the full-grown members of their households who accompanied them into Egypt.

HOMILETICS.

Vers. 1—5.—*The patriarchal names.* I. THE NAMES IN THEMSELVES. Nothing seems to the ordinary reader of Holy Scripture so dry and uninteresting as a bare catalogue of names. Objections are even made to reading them as parts of Sunday or week-day "lessons." But "ALL Scripture," rightly viewed, "is profitable" (2 Tim. iii. 16). Each Hebrew name has a meaning, and was given with a purpose. What a wealth of joys and sorrows, hopes and fears, surmises, triumphs, jealousies, is hid up in the list before us! Jacob, the *supplanter* (Gen. xxvii. 36); Reuben, the son of God's gracious *regard* (*ib.* xxix. 32); Simeon, the proof that God *hears* prayers and answers them (*ib.* ver. 33); Levi, the bond of *association* between wife and husband; Judah, he for whom God is *praised*; Issachar, the son given as a *reward*; Zebulon, he who will make the husband and wife *dwell* together; Benjamin "son of my strength," otherwise Benoni, "son of my sorrow" (*ib.* xxxv. 16); Dan, the sign that there is a God who *judges* us; Naphtali, "one *wrestled* for"; Gad, "good fortune cometh"; Asher, "the happy one"! How the private life of Jacob, how the rivalries and heats and contentions of that polygamist household, come before us, as we read the names! How again, amid all these heats and contentions, is revealed on all sides a faithful trust in God, a conviction of his overruling providence, and an acceptance of that aspect of his character which the Apostle holds up to view, when he calls him "a rewarder of them that diligently seek him" (Heb. xi. 6). Again, how strong the feeling, that, whatever cares and troubles they bring with them, children are a blessing! What a desire is shown to have children! What a pride in the possession of many children! Already "the Desire of all nations" was looked for, and each Hebrew mother hoped that in the line of descent from her might be born that Mighty One, who would "bruise the serpent's head" (Gen. iii. 15), and in whom "all the nations of the earth would be blessed" (*ib.* xii. 3; xviii. 18). Thus this list of names, if we will consider the meaning of them and the occasion of their being given, may teach us many a lesson, and prove "profitable for doctrine, for reproof, for correction, for instruction in righteousness."

II. THE ORDER OF THE NAMES. The order in which the names are given assigns a just advantage to legitimate and true marriage over even the most strictly legal union which falls short of true marriage. Let men beware lest they forfeit God's blessing upon their domestic life, by contracting marriage in any but the most solemn way that is open to them. There is a sanctity in the relation of husband and wife, that should lead us to surround the initial contract with every sacred association and every holy form that the piety of bygone ages has provided for us.

Again, the order followed assigns a just and rightful advantage to priority of birth. Primogeniture is in a certain sense, a law of nature. The elder brother, superior in strength, in knowledge, and experience, rightfully claims respect, submission, reverence from those younger than himself. In a properly regulated family this principle will be laid down and maintained. Age, unless by misconduct it forfeits its privilege, will be assigned the superior position ; younger children will be required to submit themselves to elder ones ; elder children will be upheld and encouraged to exercise a certain amount of authority over their juniors. There will be a training within the domestic circle in the habits both of direction and submission, which will prepare the way for the after discipline of life in the world.

III. THE NUMBER OF THE NAMES. Whatever minor lessons he may have intended to teach in this opening paragraph, the *main* purpose of the writer was undoubtedly to show from what small beginnings God produces the greatest, most remarkable, nay, the most astounding results. From the stock of one man and his twelve sons, with their house-holds, God raised up, within the space of 430 years, a *nation*. Similarly, when " in the fulness of time " the New Dispensation succeeded the Old, from " the Twelve " and from " the Seventy " (Luke x. 1), the original " little flock " (*ibid.* xii. 32) was derived that " general assembly and church of the firstborn " (Heb. xii. 23) which is a " great multitude that no man can number " (Rev. vii. 9). And the growth was even more rapid. " We are but of yesterday," says Tertullian, in the third century after our Lord's birth, " and yet we fill all places—your cities, islands, forts, towns, villages ; nay, your camps, tribes, decuries—your palace, your senate, your forum." How wonderful is such increase in either case ! How clearly the consequence of Divine favour and blessing !

Ver. 5.—*Joseph in Egypt.* Exodus here points back to Genesis. So the present is always pointing back to the past. In the life of an individual, in the life of a family, in the life of a nation, there is a continuity : no past act but affects the present—no present act but affects the future. Joseph's descent into Egypt is at the root of the whole of Exodus, underlies it, forms its substratum. Without an in-coming, no out-going ; and it was at Joseph's instance that his brethren had come into the country (Gen. xlv. 9—24). Or our thoughts may travel further back. " Joseph in Egypt." How had he come there ? Through the envy and jealousy of brethren, provoked by the favouritism of a too fond father. Here are evils to be guarded against ; here are sins to be cast out. And yet of the evil good had come : " Ye thought evil against me ; but God meant it unto good " (Gen. l. 20). " The fierceness of men he turns to his praise ; and the fierceness of them he doth refrain " (Ps. lxxvi. 10). The cruel wrong done to Joseph had saved from starvation his father and his father's house, had pre-served the entire people of the Egyptians from extreme suffering, and had brought Joseph himself to the highest honour. " God's ways are not as our ways, nor his thoughts as our thoughts." He is potent to bring good out of evil, and to turn the worst calamity into the choicest blessing.

Ver. 6.—*Joseph in death with all his generation.* There are some sayings so trite that we can scarcely bring ourselves to repeat them, so vital that we do not dare to omit them. One of these is that immemorial one : " We must all die." Joseph, great as he had been, useful as his life had been to others, unspeakably precious as it had proved to his near kinsmen, when his time came, went the way of all flesh—died like any common man, and " was put in a coffin " (Gen. l. 26) and buried. So it must always be with every earthly support and stay ; it fails us at last, and if it does not betray us, at any rate deserts us ; suddenly it is gone, and its place knows it no more. This is always to be borne in mind ; and no excessive reliance is to be placed on individuals. The Church is safe ; for its Lord is always " with it," and so will be " even to the end of the world." But the men in whom from time to time it trusts are all mortal—may at any time be lost to it—may in one hour be snatched away. It is important therefore for the Church to detach itself from individuals, and to hold to two anchors—Christ and the Faith of Christ—which can never cease to exist, and can never fail it. For, when our Joseph dies, there die with him, or soon after him, " all his brethren, and all that generation." The great lights of an age are apt to go out at once, or if a few linger on, they burn with a dim lustre. And the generation that hung upon their words despairs, and knows not which way to turn itself, until the thought comes—" Lord, to whom shall we go? Thou hast the words of eternal life." Then, in resting upon Christ, it is well with us. Well, too, for each generation to remember, it will not long stay behind—it will follow its teachers. Joseph dies—his brethren die; wait a few years, and God will have taken to himself " all that generation."

HOMILIES BY VARIOUS AUTHORS.

Ver. 1.—*Removal to Egypt.* This early instance of emigration shows—
I. How the CALL to leave the land of one's fathers may sometimes be—1. Unexpected Jacob little expected to end his days in Egypt. 2. Trying. Canaan, the land of promise, where were the graves of his ancestors, etc. 3. Mysterious. An apparent reversal of the lines on which Providence had hitherto been moving. Yet—4. Distinct. Jacob had no doubt that God's call had come to him. It came first in providence, and was ratified by direct Divine permission (Gen. xlvi. 2—5). Many have the indirect call, who can scarcely doubt that it is also a direct one. Causes of emigration—Want and distress at home, with reasonable prospect of comfort and plenty abroad; opening of a better field for talents and energies; state of health, necessitating change of climate; persecution, as in case of Huguenots, Pilgrim Fathers, etc.
II. What CONSOLATIONS the emigrant may carry with him. 1. God accompanies him (Gen. xlvi. 4). 2. He can serve God yonder as well as here. 3. He is further-ing wise and beneficent purposes. Little doubt of that, if he is leaving at God's bidding. Israel's residence in Egypt secured for the tribes—(1) A home. (2) Provi-sion. (3) Room to grow. (4) Education in arts and letters. (5) Valuable discipline —all preparatory to settlement in Canaan, and the fulfilment of their spiritual mission to the world. 4. The terminus is not Egypt, but Canaan. Jacob never saw again the Canaan he had left, but, dying in faith, he and his sons became heirs of the better Canaan. Whatever his earthly destination, let the emigrant keep in view a " better country, that is, an heavenly " (Heb. xi. 16).
III. The ADVANTAGES of emigration. 1. It is not always advantageous. (1) Not always advantageous to the country left. A country that by misgovernment, bad laws, excessive taxation, or persecution, drives its best subjects from its soil, may be compared to a man who humours an insane bent by occasionally opening a vein. (2) Not always advantageous to the country settled in. Emigrants may carry with them—too often do—low and immoral habits, and prove a curse, rather than a blessing, to the populations in whose midst they settle. (3) Not always to the emigrant himself. His step may prove to have been hasty. He may have taken it on impulse, or on insufficient information, or in a spirit of adventure. He finds when too late that a sanguine disposition has deceived him. This is to go forth without a clear call. But—2. Emigration, wisely and judiciously conducted, is of great benefit to society. (1) It thins an overstocked country, and so relieves pressure on the means of subsistence. (2) It occupies territory needing population to develop its resources. (3) It affords room and scope for the vigorous expansion of a young race. (4) It benefits native populations. The Egyptians would profit by the residence of the Hebrews in their midst. (5) It may be made subservient to the diffusion of the knowledge of the true religion. How seldom is this thought of, yet what a responsibility rests on those who leave Christian shores, carrying with them, to lands sunk in the night of heathenism, the blessed truths of Christianity! The conclusion of the matter is: Let emigration be an act of faith. Do not, in so important a step in life, lean to your own understanding. Ask guidance and clear direction from on High. But if the way is open and the call plain, then, like Jacob, go forth, and go boldly, and in faith. Trust God to be with you. He goes before you to seek you out a place to dwell in, and will surely bless you in all you put your hand to (Deut. i. 33; xv. 10).—J. O.

Vers. 1—6.—*The twelve foundations.* The heads of the covenant race had hitherto been single individuals. Abraham—Isaac—Jacob. The one now expands into the twelve. Glance briefly at this list of the patriarchs.
I. THE MEN. Here we are struck—1. *With the original unfitness of most of these men for the position of dignity they were afterwards called to occupy.* How shall we

describe them! Recall Reuben's incest; Simeon and Levi's cruelty; Judah's lewdness; the "evil report" which Joseph brought to his father of the sons of the handmaids. The picture in the later chapters of Genesis is crowded with shadows, and it is chiefly the sins of these men which are the causes of them. Joseph is the one bright exception. The rest appear to have been men of a violent, truculent disposition, capable of selling their younger brother into Egypt, and afterwards, to screen their fault, of imposing by wilful falsehood on their aged father. Even in Benjamin, traits of character were discernible which gave ground for the tribal prediction: "Benjamin shall ravin as a wolf" (Gen. xlix. 17). How unlikely that men of so ungodly a stamp, who began so ill, should end by being exalted to be patriarch-heads of a covenant nation! And neither in truth were they, till, by God's grace, a great change had passed upon them. Their crime in selling Joseph was, in a sense, their salvation. It was an act for which they never forgave themselves. Compunction wrought in them a better disposition, and laid the basis for "a train of humiliating and soul-stirring providences, tending to force on them the conviction that they were in the hands of an angry God, and to bring them to repentance of sin and amendment of life." See—(1) The natural unfitness of man for God's service; "that which is born of the flesh is flesh" (John iii. 6). (2) What the grace of God can make even of very bad men. "By grace ye are saved" (Eph. ii. 5). (3) How those whom God designs for honour in his kingdom, he first prepares for that honour. Whatever disciplines are needful for that purpose—and they may not be few—he will not withhold. 2. *With the variety of gifts and dispositions found amongst them.* This variety is taken note of in the blessings of Jacob and of Moses, and is reflected in the history. Judah is from the first a leader. He and Joseph were heads of what subsequently became the royal tribes. Reuben's impulsiveness reminds us of Peter, but he lacked Peter's underlying constancy. Levi's zeal wrought at first for evil, but afterwards for good. The other brethren were less distinguished, but, as shown by the blessings, all were gifted, and gifted diversely. Does this not teach us? (1) That God *can use*, and (2) that God *requires*, every variety of gift in his service. Hence, (3) that there is both *room* and *need* in his kingdom for all types and varieties of character—for every species of gift. A type of religion is self-condemned which cannot find room in it for the play and development of every legitimate capability of human nature. This is but to say that the goal of God's kingdom is the perfecting of humanity, not in part, but in the *totality* of its powers and functions. Grace does not suppress individuality; it develops and sanctifies it. It does not trample on gifts, but lays hold upon, transforms, and utilises them. 3. *With the existence of a law of heredity in spiritual as in natural descent.* The characteristics of the patriarchs were stamped with remarkable distinctness on the tribes which bore their names. Reuben's instability, Judah's capacity of rule, Levi's zeal, Dan's agility, Benjamin's fierceness, etc. This reappearance of ancestral characteristics in the descendants is a fact with which we are familiar, and is only explained in part by inherited organisation. Inheritance of ideas, customs, family traditions, etc., plays quite as important a part in producing the result. A law this, capable of being the vehicle of much good, but also of much evil—as potent to punish as to bless.

II. THEIR NUMBER. The number twelve not to be regarded as fortuitous. Twelve (3×4), the symbol of the indwelling of God in the human family, of the interpenetration of the world by the Divinity. Three, the number of the Divine; four, the number of the world. Hence, twelve tribes, twelve cakes of shewbread, twelve apostles, twelve foundations and twelve gates of the New Jerusalem. The number twelve is kept up in spite of actual departures from it in fact. The "twelve tribes" are spoken of in the days of the apostles (Acts xxvi. 17; Jas. i. 1), though, counting Levi, there were really thirteen tribes, and after the Captivity only two. It was doubtless with reference to the twelve tribes of Israel, and therefore to the number of these patriarchs, that Christ chose the twelve apostles. View the patriarchs, accordingly, as representing the covenant race, not only—1. In its natural heads, but symbolically—2. In its spiritual privilege as a people of God, and 3. In its world-wide destiny.—J. O.

Ver. 6.—*An ending.* The descent into Egypt was—1. An ending. 2. A beginning. It closed one chapter in God's providence, and opened a new one. It terminated the sojourn in Canaan; brought to a harmonious conclusion the complicated series of events which separated Joseph from his father, raised him to power in Egypt, wrought for the purification of his brethren's character, and prepared the way for the ultimate settlement of the whole family in Goshen. It laid the foundation for new historical developments. There is now to be a pause, a breathing space, while the people are gradually multiplying, and exchanging the habits of nomadic life for those of agriculturists and dwellers in cities. The death of Joseph, and of his brethren, and of all that generation, is the proper close of this earlier period. Their part is played out, and the stage is cleared for new beginnings. 1. They died—*so must we all*. The common fate, yet infinitely pathetic when reflected on. 2. They died—*the end of earthly greatness*. Joseph had all he could wish for of earthly power and splendour, and he enjoyed it through a long lifetime. Yet he must part with it. Well for him that he had something better in prospect. 3. They died—*the end of earthly disciplines*. The lives of the brethren had been singularly eventful. By painful disciplines God had moulded them for good. Life to every one is a divinely ordained discipline. The end is to bring us to repentance, and build us up in faith and holiness. With some, the discipline succeeds; with others it fails. In either case death ends it. "After this the judgment" (Heb. ix. 27). The fact of discipline an argument for immortality. God does not spend a lifetime in perfecting a character, that just when the finishing touches have been put upon it, he may dash it into non-existence. Death ends discipline, but we carry with us the result and the responsibility. 4. They died—Joseph and his brethren—*happily in faith*. There was a future they did not live to see; but their faith grasped God's promise, and "Joseph, when he died . . . gave commandment concerning his bones" (Heb. xi. 22). And behind the earthly Canaan loomed something better—an inheritance which they and we may share together.—J. O.

Vers. 1—22.—*The prosperity of Israel*. This prosperity was not a mere appearance, nor a passing spurt of fortune. It was a deep, abiding, and significant reality. Nor was it something exaggerated in order to make an excuse for the cruelties of a suspicious tyrant. There was indeed only too much to make Pharaoh uneasy; but altogether apart from his alarms there is a plain and emphatic statement of the prosperity of Israel in ver. 7. It is a very emphatic statement indeed, summoning us in the most imperative way to a special notice of this remarkable prosperity. Let us therefore take a general view of Israel's prosperity as it is set before us in all the extent of this first chapter. Note—

I. THE INDICATIONS OF THIS PROSPERITY. The prosperity is not only plainly stated, but the chapter abounds in indications of Jehovah's favour towards Israel, and his peculiar watchfulness over it. 1. *The wonderful way in which God had brought a whole family into Egypt, and provided for their comfortable settlement in the land.* Families usually get scattered; but here are the children of Israel and children's children all kept together. The very means which they had employed in order to get rid of one of their number who was an offence to them, had ended in their being brought together more closely than ever. Joseph went before, and all unconsciously made a solid foundation for the building of their prosperity. Through all domestic jealousies, in the perils of famine, and in their journeyings between Canaan and Egypt, the Lord had preserved these twelve men so that not one of them was lacking in his contribution to the future excellency of Israel. 2. *The name by which they were described—the children of Israel.* God had said to Jacob (Gen. xxxii. 28), "Thy name shall be called no more Jacob, but Israel," and yet down to the end of his life he is sometimes called Jacob and sometimes Israel, as if to keep before our minds both his natural character and also his new position and privileges gained in the memorable wrestling at Peniel. These twelve men, the fathers of the tribes, were *children of Israel as well as sons of Jacob*. Jacob himself had done many things to show the meanness and corruption of fallen human nature, and his sons had been not one whit better than himself (consider the revengeful action of Simeon and Levi in Gen. xxxiv. 25; the conduct of Reuben in xxxv. 22; and especially the conduct of the brethren towards Joseph and the father who so doted upon him). But these sons of Jacob, with all their personal demerits, were also the children of him who by his sublime, persistent, courageous, and successful struggle had gained the name of Israel. It was a name to be transmitted from them to their children, full of significance, **recalling a glorious experience in the past and promising a still more** glorious experience in the future. It was a name not to be forfeited even in the greatest apostasies, and perhaps its chief splendour lay in this, that it pointed forward to a still more glorious fatherhood enjoyed by those who through the gracious work of him who taught Nicodemus concerning regeneration, are permitted to say, "Now are we the children and heirs of God." 3. *The apprehensive attitude of Pharaoh.* He is a witness to the greatness of Israel's prosperity, and to the Divine and miraculous origin of it, all the more valuable because he gives his evidence unconsciously. The more we consider his unaffected alarm and his continuous and energetic efforts to crush Israel, the more we feel what a real and Divine thing Israel's prosperity was, how it was nourished by the secret and unassailable strength of God. It should be a matter of great rejoicing to God's people when the world, in its hatred, suspicion, and instinctive sense of danger, takes to the instruments of persecution, for then there is unmistakable indication of prosperity within.

II. Wherein the prosperity consisted. It did not consist in *the accumulation of external possessions.* The Israelites might have remained comparatively few or have increased in a way such as to excite no attention. Their increase might have been in external wealth, and this would have been reckoned, by many, true prosperity. But it would not have been prosperity after a godly sort. It was the purpose of God to show in Israel how our true resources come, not from things outside of us, but from the quality of the life which he puts within. Hence the prosperity of Israel was not the result of industry, personal ability, and fortunate circumstances. It was shown by *the manifestation of a miraculous fulness of life.* The husbandman does not reckon it anything wonderful that there should be among the trees of his vineyard a certain increase of fruitfulness, corresponding to the carefulness of his cultivation. But if all at once certain trees begin to put forth a fulness of fruit altogether beyond expectation, the husbandman would not claim that such a result came from him. There is the greatest possible difference between the prosperity lying in mere external possessions and that which comes from the energy of a Divine life working in us. It needs no special help from God to make a man a millionaire. There are but few who can be such; but place them in favourable circumstances, and the immense results of their industry and attention are quite intelligible. But to produce such a result as appears in the peculiar prosperity of Israel in Egypt required a special influx of Divine energy. We have not only unmistakable indications of the prosperity of Israel; it is an equally important thing to notice that this prosperity in its peculiar character is an indication of the presence of God. He was doing what none but himself could do. Learn then that our spiritual prosperity must be something produced by God manifesting his power in our hearts. There is no chance of attributing it to our unaided industry, attention, and prudence. It is a growth more than anything else, and must show itself in the abundant and beautiful fruits of a Divine life within us.

III. A painful accompaniment of the prosperity. Such prosperity as is indicated in ver. 7 could not but produce apprehension and opposition on the part of Pharaoh—inevitably assuming, as it did, the appearance of a menace to his kingdom. But it was better for Israel to go on increasing with the increase of God, even in the midst of persecutions, than to be without the persecutions on condition of being without the increase. Spiritual prosperity not only may be, but must be, accompanied with afflictions of the natural life. That is a very doubtful spirituality which manages to keep clear of all temporal troubles. They that will live godly must suffer persecution. Let us pray for spiritual prosperity, and hail its coming, and secure its stay, whatever pains be suffered and whatever lesser comforts be lost. The more the life of God is in us, the more we must expect the powers of evil to be stirred against us.—Y.

Vers. 1—7. *Tarry thou the Lord's leisure.* Introduction to the Book of Exodus. How much summed up in so few words. When men *live* history, every month seems important; when God *records* history a few sentences suffice for generations. *Man's* standpoint in the midst of the tumult is so different from God's: he "sitteth above the waterflood" and seeth "the end from the beginning" (Ps. xxix. 10; Isa. xlvi. 10). From God's standpoint we have here as of main consequence—

I. A list of names, vers. 1—5. Names of certain emigrants. More in them than seems at first sight. If I say, "William, Arthur etc., came to England at such and such a time," not much. If I say, "William, a great warrior; Arthur, a great inventor," we feel at once that with them elements are introduced which may prove important. In these early times names are connected with the characters of the men who bear them. All these names are *significant*. Illustrate from their meaning as given in Gen. xxix., etc., and expanded in Jacob's blessing, Gen. xlix. We are supposed, too, to know something of the men from the previous history. The whole, taken together, shows us, as it were, a nation in embryo—a nation of which the characteristics were wholly different from those of the Egyptians. "Seventy souls," but—1. *Seed* souls; bound to develop through their offspring the characteristics they exhibited. 2. *United*, not isolated; a nation in embryo, not a collocation of units.

II. WHAT HAPPENED TO THE BEARERS OF THE NAMES, ver. 6. All died—Joseph and all that generation. The common lot, but, from God's standpoint, the ordained method of development (John xii. 24). What wailing, as each patriarch, in his own time, passed away! Yet with each death the harvest of the future was being ever more securely sown. Death, as it were, rounds off the life; *pedestals* it; sets it where it can become exemplary. So set it becomes fruitful; the old husk drops away, and the true life-grain is enfranchised. Gad, Asher, and the rest, very ordinary men, or, if not ordinary, not very high-class men; and yet, once dead, they are rightly reverenced as the fathers of their tribes. Which is better, the day of death or the day of birth? The day which makes life possible for us, or the day which, by sanctifying our memory, makes that life an ennobling influence for others?

III. HOW THE DESCENDANTS PROSPERED, ver. 7. So—through the vicissitudes of life; the varieties of character; the monotony of death—God works on, slowly but certainly, to his destined end. New generations, each more numerous, succeed the old. Power and prosperity, for a time, go hand-in-hand with increased numbers—the people "waxed exceeding mighty." [The shepherd life, even in Egypt, ensured some knowledge of warfare. Goshen, the border land—cf. "the borders" in the wars with Scotland. Perhaps Joseph had purposely placed his brethren as a defence to Egypt against raids from the desert.] Families grew into tribes, and the tribes learnt their first lessons in discipline and war. Egypt, God's Aldershot—the training-ground for his armies. Canaan had to be conquered and cleared, but God could take his own time about it. When at length the hour should come, it would find his preparations perfected.

Application:—Would that man—God's child—would be content to copy his Father's methods—slow; thorough; a definite end in view; quiet, persistent preparation. No haste, no hurry, no delay (Isa. xxviii. 16).—G.

EXPOSITION.

Vers. 7—14.—Here the real narrative of Exodus begins. The history of the Israelites from and after the death of Joseph is entered on. The first point touched is **their rapid multiplication**. The next, their falling under the dominion of a **new king**. The third, **his mode of action under the circumstances**. It is remarkable that the narrative contains no notes of time. How long the increase continued before the new king arose, how long it went on before he noticed it, how long the attempt was made to check it by mere severity of labour, we are not told. Some considerable duration of time is implied, both for the multiplication (ver. 7) and for the oppression (ver. 11—14); but the narrator is so absorbed in the matters which he has to communicate that the question what time these matters occupied does

not seem even to occur to him. And so it is with the sacred narrative frequently—perhaps we should say, generally. The chronological element is regarded as of slight importance; "A thousand years in the Lord's sight are but as yesterday"—"one day is as a thousand years, and a thousand years as one day." Where a profane writer would have been to the last degree definite and particular, a sacred writer is constantly vague and indeterminate. We have in the Bible nothing like an exact continuous chronology. Certain general chronological ideas may be obtained from the Bible; but in order to construct anything like a complete chronological scheme, frequent reference has to be made to profane writers and monuments, and such a scheme must be mainly dependent on these references. Archbishop

Ussher's dates, inserted into the margin of so many of our Bibles, are the private speculations of an individual on the subject of mundane chronology, and must not be regarded as in any way authoritative. Their primary basis is profane history ; and, though taking into consideration all the Scriptural numbers, they do not consistently follow any single rule with respect to them. Sometimes the authority of the Septuagint, sometimes that of the Hebrew text, is preferred ; and the result arrived at is in a high degree uncertain and arbitrary.

Ver. 7.—The multiplication of the Israelites in Egypt from " seventy souls " to " six hundred thousand that were men " (ch. xii. 37)—a number which may fairly be said to imply a total of at least two millions—has been declared to be " impossible," and to stamp the whole narrative of Exodus with the character of unreality and romance. Manifestly, the soundness of this criticism depends entirely on two things—first, the length of time during which the stay in Egypt continued ; and secondly, the sense in which the original number of the children of Israel in Egypt is said to have been " seventy souls." Now, as to the first point, there are two theories—one, basing itself on the Septuagint version of Ex. xii. 40, would make the duration of the Egyptian sojourn 215 years only ; the other, following the clear *and repeated* statement of the Hebrew text (Ex. xii. 40, 41), literally rendered in our version, would extend the time to 430 years, or exactly double it. Much may be said on both sides of this question, and the best critics are divided with respect to it. The longer period is supported by Kalisch, Kurtz, Knobel, Winer, Ewald, Delitzsch, and Canon Cook among moderns ; by Koppe, Frank, Beer, Rosenmüller, Hofmann, Tiele, Reinke, Jahn, Vater, and J. D. Michaelis among earlier critics ; the short period is approved by Calvin, Grotius, Buddeus, Morinus, Voss, Houbigant, Baumgarten ; and among our own countrymen, by Ussher, Marsham, Geddes, and Kennicott. The point cannot be properly argued in an " exposition " like the present ; but it may be remarked that both reason and authority are in favour of the simple acceptance of the words of the Hebrew text, which assign 430 years as the interval between Jacob's descent into Egypt and the deliverance under Moses.

With respect to the number of those who accompanied Jacob into Egypt, and were assigned the land of Goshen for a habitation (Gen. xlvii. 6), it is important to bear in mind, first of all, that the " seventy souls " enumerated in Gen. xlvi. 8—27 comprised only two females, and that " Jacob's sons' wives " are expressly mentioned as not included among them (*ib.* ver. 26). If we add the wives of 67 males, we shall have, for the actual family of Jacob, 137 persons. Further, it is to be borne in mind that each Israelite family which went down into Egypt was accompanied by its " household " (Ex. i. 1), consisting of at least some scores of dependants. If each son of Jacob had even 60 such retainers, and if Jacob himself had a household like that of Abraham (Gen. xiv. 14), the entire number which " went down into Egypt " would have amounted to at least 2000 persons.

According to Malthus, population tends to double itself, if there be no artificial check restraining it, every twenty-five years. At this rate, 2000 persons would expand into 2,048,000 in 250 years, 1000 would reach the same amount in 275 years, and 500 in 300 years ; so that, even supposing the " seventy souls " with their " households " to have numbered no more than 500 persons when they went down into Egypt, the people would, unless artificially checked, have exceeded two millions at the expiration of three centuries— that is to say, 130 years before the Exodus ! No doubt, the artificial checks which keep down the natural tendency of population to increase began to tell upon them considerably before that time. The " land of Goshen." a broad tract of very fertile country, became tolerably thickly peopled, and the rate of increase gradually subsided. Still, as the Delta was a space of from 7000 to 8000 square miles, and the land of Goshen was probably about half of it, a population of two millions is very much what we should expect, being at the rate of from 500 to 600 persons to the square mile.

It is an interesting question whether the Egyptian remains do, or do not, contain any mention of the Hebrew sojourn ; and if they do, whether any light is thereby thrown on these numbers. Now it is admitted on all hands that, about the time of the Hebrew sojourn, there was in Egypt a subject race, often employed in forced labours, called Aperu or Aperiu, and it seems impossible to deny that this word is a very fair Egyptian equivalent for the Biblical עברים, " Hebrews." We are forced, therefore, either to suppose that there were in Egypt, at one and the same time, two subject races with names almost identical, or to admit the identification of the Aperu with the descendants of Jacob. The exact numbers of the Aperu are nowhere mentioned ; but it is a calculation of Dr. Brugsch that under Rameses II., a little before the Exodus, the foreign races in Egypt, of whom the Aperu were beyond all doubt the chief, " amounted certainly to a third, and probably still more," of the whole population (' History of Egypt,' vol. ii. p. 100, E. T.), which is usually reckoned at from 7,000,000 to 8,000,000.

One-third of this number would be from 2,300,000 to 2,600,000.

The writer of Exodus does not, however, as yet, make anything like a definite calculation. He is merely bent on having it understood that there had been a *great* multiplication, and that the "family" had grown into a "nation." To emphasise his statement, he uses four nearly synonymous verbs ("**were fruitful, and increased abundantly, and multiplied, and waxed-mighty**"), adding to the last a duplicated adverb, *bim'ôd m'ôd,* "much, much." Clearly, an astonishing increase is intended.

Ver. 8.—**There arose up a new king.** It is asked, Does this mean merely another king, or a *completely different* king, one of a new dynasty or a new family, not bound by precedent, but free to adopt and likely to adopt quite new principles of government? The latter seems the more probable supposition; but it is probable only, not certain. Assuming it to be what is really meant, we have to ask, What changes of dynasty fall within the probable period of the Israelite sojourn in Egypt, and to which of them is it most likely that allusion is here made? Some writers (as Kalisch) have supposed the Hyksôs dynasty to be meant, and the "new king" to be Set, or Salatis, the first of the Hyksôs rulers. But the date of Salatis appears to us too early. If Joseph was, as we suppose, the minister of Apôphis, the last Hyksôs king, two changes of dynasty only can come into consideration— that which took place about B.C. 1700 (or, according to some, B.C. 1600), when the Hyksôs were expelled; and that which followed about three centuries later, when the eighteenth dynasty was superseded by the nineteenth. To us it seems that the former of these occasions, though in many respects suitable, is (*a*) too near the going down into Egypt to allow time for the multiplication which evidently took place before this king arose (see ver. 7), and (*b*) unsuitable from the circumstance that the first king of this dynasty was not a builder of new cities (see ver. 11), but only a repairer of temples. We therefore conclude that the "new king" was either Rameses I., the founder of the nineteenth dynasty, or Seti I., his son, who within little more than a year succeeded him. It is evident that this view receives much confirmation from the name of one of the cities built for the king by the Hebrews, which was Raamses, or Rameses, a name now appearing for the first time in the Egyptian dynastic lists.

Who knew not Joseph. Who not only had no personal knowledge of Joseph, but was wholly ignorant of his history. At the distance of from two to three centuries the benefits conferred by Joseph upon Egypt, more especially as they were conferred under a foreign and hated dynasty, were forgotten.

Ver. 9—**And he said unto his people,**

Behold, the children of Israel are more and mightier than we. Literally, "great and strong in comparison with us." Actual numerical superiority is not, perhaps, meant; yet the expression is no doubt an exaggerated one, beyond the truth—the sort of exaggeration in which unprincipled persons indulge when they would justify themselves for taking an extreme and unusual course.

Ver. 10.—**Come on.** The "Come then" of Kalisch is better. **Let us deal wisely.** "The children of this world are in their generation *wiser* than the children of light." Severe grinding labour has often been used as a means of keeping down the aspirations of a people, if not of actually diminishing their numbers, and has been found to answer. Aristotle (Pol. v. 9) ascribes to this motive the building of the Pyramids and the great works of Polycrates of Samos, Pisistratus of Athens, and the Cypselidæ of Corinth. The constructions of the last Tarquin are thought to have had the same object (Liv. i. 56; Niebuhr, 'Roman History,' vol. i. p. 479). **Lest, when there falleth out any war, they join also to our enemies.** At the accession of the nineteenth dynasty, though there was peace, war threatened. While the Egyptians, under the later monarchs of the eighteenth dynasty, had been quarrelling among themselves, a great nation upon their borders "had been growing up to an importance and power which began to endanger the Egyptian supremacy in Western Asia" (Brugsch, 'History of Egypt,' vol. ii. p. 2). Both Rameses I. and his son Seti had almost immediately after their accession to engage in a war, which was rather defensive than offensive, with the Khita, or Hittites, who were the great power of Syria (*ib.* pp. 9, 15, 16). At the commencement of his reign, Seti may well have feared a renewed invasion like that of the Hyksôs, which would no doubt have been greatly helped by a rising of the Israelites. **And so get them up out of the land.** Literally, "And go up out of the land." The Pharaoh already fears that the Israelites will quit Egypt. As men of peaceful and industrious habits, and in some cases of considerable wealth (Joseph. 'Ant. Jud.' ii. 9, § 1), they at once increased the strength of Egypt and the revenue of the monarch. Egypt was always ready to receive refugees, and loth to lose them. We find in a treaty made by Rameses II., the son of Seti, with the Hittites, a proviso that any Egyptian subjects who quit the country, and transfer themselves to the dominion of the Hittite king, shall be sent back to Egypt ('Records of the Past,' vol. iv. p. 30).

Ver. 11.—**They did set over them taskmasters.** Literally, "lords of tribute," or "lords of service." The term used, *sarey massim*, is the Egyptian official title for overlookers of forced labour. It occurs in this sense on the monument representing brick-making, which has been supposed by some to be a picture of the Hebrews at work. (See Cook, in the 'Speaker's Commentary,' vol. i. pt. i. p. 253, and compare Brugsch, 'History of Egypt,' vol. i. p. 376.) **To afflict them with their burdens.** Among the tasks set the labourers in the representation above alluded to are the carrying of huge lumps of clay and of water-jars on one shoulder, and also the conveyance of bricks from place to place by means of a yoke. **They built for Pharaoh treasure-cities, Pithom and Raamses.** By " treasure-cities " we are to understand " store-cities," or " cities of store," as the same word is translated in 1 K. ix. 19 and 2 Chr. viii. 4, Such cities contained depots of provisions and magazines of arms. They were generally to be found on all assailable frontiers in ancient as in modern times. (Compare 2 Chr. xi. 5, 12; xxxiii. 28, etc.) Of the cities here mentioned, which the Israelites are said to have " built," or helped to build, **Pithom** is in all probability the Patumos of Herodotus (ii. 158), which was not far from Bubastis, now Tel-Basta. Its exact site is uncertain, but if identical with the Thou, or Thoum, of the 'Itinerary of Antonine,' it must have lain north of the Canal of Necho, not south, where most maps place it. The word means " abode of the sun," or rather " of the setting sun," called by the Egyptians Tum, or Atum. Names formed on the model were very common under the nineteenth dynasty, Rameses II. having built a Pa-Ra, a Pa-Ammon, and a Pa-Phthah in Nubia (Brugsch, 'History of Egypt,' vol. ii. p. 90). Pa-Tum itself has not been found among the cities of this period (*ib.* p. 99), but appears in the records of the twentieth dynasty as a place where the Setting-Sun god had a treasury ('Records of the Past,' vol. vi. p. 54). The name **Raamses** is probably put for Pa-Rameses (as Thoum for Pa-Tum), a city frequently mentioned in the inscriptions of the nineteenth dynasty, and particularly favoured by Rameses II., whose city it was especially called ('Records of the Past,' vol. ii. p. 77; vol. vi. p. 13), and by whom it was greatly enlarged, if not wholly built. We incline to believe that the building was commenced by Seti, who named the place, as he did his great temple, the Rameseum, after his father. The city was, according to Brugsch, a sort of suburb of Tanis ('History of Egypt,' vol. ii. p. 94). It was a magnificent place, and under Rameses II. and his son Menephthah was the ordinary residence of the court. Hence the miracles of Moses are said to have been wrought " in the field of Zoan," *i.e.* the country about Tanis (Ps. lxxviii. 12, 43).

Ver. 12.—**They were grieved because of the children of Israel.** The word **grieved** very insufficiently renders the Hebrew verb, which " expresses a mixture of loathing and alarm " ('Speaker's Commentary,' vol. i. pt. 1, p. 251). Kalisch translates forcibly, if inelegantly—" They had a horror of the children of Israel."

Ver. 13.—**The Egyptians made the children of Israel to serve with rigour.** The word translated **rigour** is a very rare one. It is derived from a root which means " to break in pieces, to crush." The " rigour " would be shown especially in the free use of the stick by the taskmaster, and in the prolongation of the hours of work.

Ver. 14.—**They made their lives bitter with hard bondage, in morter and in brick.** While stone was the material chiefly employed by the Egyptians for their grand edifices, temples, palaces, treasuries, and the like, brick was also made use of to a large extent for inferior buildings, for tombs, dwelling-houses, walls of towns, forts, enclosures of temples, etc. There are examples of its employment in pyramids (Herod. ii. 136; Vyse, 'Pyramids of Gizeh,' vol. iii. pp. 57—71); but only at a time long anterior to the nineteenth and even to the eighteenth dynasty. If the Pharaoh of the present passage was Seti I., the bricks made may have been destined in the main for that great wall which he commenced, but did not live to complete, between Pelusium and Heliopolis, which was to secure his eastern frontier (Birch, 'Egypt from the Earliest Times,' p. 125). **All manner of labour in the field.** The Israelitish colony was originally employed to a large extent in tending the royal flocks and herds (Gen. xlvii. 6). At a later date many of them were engaged in agricultural operations (Deut. xi. 10). These, in Egypt, are in some respects light, *e.g.* preparing the land and ploughing, whence the remark of Herodotus (ii. 14); but in other respects exceedingly heavy. There is no country where care and labour are so constantly needed during the whole of the year. The inundation necessitates extreme watchfulness, to save cattle, to prevent the houses and the farmyards from being inundated, and the embankments from being washed away. The cultivation is continuous throughout the whole of the year; and success depends upon a system of irrigation that requires constant labour and unremitting attention. If the " labour in the field " included, as Josephus supposed (1.s.c.), the cutting of canals, their lives would indeed have been " made bitter." There is no such exhausting toil as that of working under the hot Egyptian sun, with the feet in water, in an open cutting, where there can be no shade, and scarcely a breath of air, from sunrise to sunset, as forced labourers are generally required to do. Mehemet Ali lost 20,000 labourers out of 150,000 in the construction of the Alexandrian Canal towards the middle of the present century.

HOMILETICS.

Vers. 7 and 12.—*God the Protector of his people.* I. THE MULTIPLICATION OF ISRAEL. All increase is of God, and comes to man by his blessing. As he gave the original command, " Be fruitful, and multiply, and replenish the earth " (Gen. i. 28), so he in every case gives the new lives by which the earth is replenished. " Children, and the fruit of the womb, are an heritage and gift that cometh of the Lord " (Ps. cxxviii. 3). He gives or withholds offspring as he pleases; enlarges families, tribes, nations, or causes them to decline, decay, and die out. Increase is a sign of his favour—1. To the individual—" Happy is the man that hath his quiver full of them " (Ps. cxxviii. 5); 2. To the nation—" I will multiply them and they shall not be few; I will also glorify them and they shall not be small " (Jer. xxx. 19); and 3. To churches—" Walking in the fear of the Lord, and the comfort of the Holy Ghost, they were multiplied " (Acts ix. 31). A nation or church that increases has, so far at any rate, a sign of God's approval of it, of his favour, of his having in his eternal counsels work for it to do for him in the present and the future. One which dwindles has, on the contrary, a note of God's disapproval—at the very least, a warning that all is not with it as it should be. Nations, when they can no longer do God service, die out; churches, when they become effete and useless, have their candlesticks removed (Rev. ii. 5). II. EFFECT OF PERSECUTION ON IT. Note, that the effect of persecution was the very opposite of what was intended. *The more they afflicted them, the more they multiplied.* So is it ever with God's people. Persecutions always " fall out for the furtherance of the Gospel " (Phil. i. 12). " They which were scattered abroad upon the persecution that arose about Stephen, travelled as far as Phœnice, and Cyprus, and Antioch preaching the word " (Acts xi. 19). Persecution brought Paul to Rome, and enabled him to proclaim the Gospel and make many converts in the very citadel of Satan, the headquarters of the enemy. So marked was the prevalence of the law, that among the early Christians it became a proverb, that " the blood of the martyrs was the seed of the Church." After each of the ten great Imperial persecutions, the Church was found within a brief space to be more numerous than ever. And so it will be to the end. " The gates of Hell " cannot prevail against the Church. Out of the last and greatest of all the persecutions, when Antichrist shall be revealed, the Church will issue triumphant, a " great multitude, which no man can number " (Rev. vii. 9).

Ver. 8.—*Joseph forgotten.* " The evil that men do lives after them—the good is oft interred with their bones." Had Joseph been a tyrant, a conqueror, an egotist who crushed down the Egyptians by servile toil for the purpose of raising a huge monument to his own glory, he would no doubt have remained fresh in the memory of the nation, and his name and acts would have been familiar even to a " new king," who was yet an Egyptian and an educated man. But as he had only been a benefactor of the nation, and especially of the kings (Gen. xlvii. 20—26), he was utterly forgotten—as some think, within sixty-five years of his death, but according to our calculations, not till about 275 years after it. This is about the space that separates us from Queen Elizabeth, who is certainly not forgotten, as neither are her ministers. So Christian nations would seem to have better memories than heathen ones. In time, however, every man is forgotten; and Christians should therefore not make their object the praise of men, or posthumous fame, but the praise and approval of God, which will continue for ever. " God is not unrighteous to forget " (Heb. vi. 10)

Vers. 10—12.—*The wisdom of the wise brought to nought.* God is wont to " destroy the wisdom of the wise, and bring to nothing the understanding of the prudent " (1 Cor. i. 19). He " makes the devices of the people of none effect " (Ps. xxxiii. 10). Humanly speaking, the Pharaoh had done " wisely," had counselled well : many a people has been crushed utterly under the yoke of an oppressor, ground down by hard labour—even after a time well-nigh exterminated. It was a clever and crafty plan to avoid the risk and discredit of a massacre of unoffending subjects, and at the same time to gain advantage by their heavy labours while effectually thinning their ranks through the severity of the toils imposed on them. Unless God had interfered, and by his secret help supported and sustained his people; enabled them to retain their health and strength under the adverse circumstances; induced them, bitter and hopeless as their lot seemed, still to contract marriages, and blessed those marriages, not only with offspring, but with superabundant offspring (see verses 12 and 20)—the result anticipated would without doubt have followed: the multiplication of the people would have been checked—their numbers would soon have begun to diminish. But God had determined that so it should not be. He had promised Abraham an extraordinary increase in the number of his descendants, and was not going to permit a cruel and crafty king to interfere with the carrying out of his designs, the performance of his gracious promises. So the more that Pharaoh and his obsequious subjects afflicted them, "the more they multiplied and grew"—"the little one became a thousand, and the small one a strong nation"—the Lord "hastened it in his time" (Is. lx. 22). Christians therefore need never fear the devices of their enemies, however politic they may seem. God has the power, and if he sees fit will exert it, to turn the wisdom of the world into foolishness, to upset all human calculations, confound all prudent counsels, and make each act done in opposition to his will help to work it out. In Israel's case, the hard labour and unceasing toil which made their lives bitter (ver. 14), was at once needed to wean their minds from the recollection of the "fleshpots" and other delights of Egypt, and so make them content to quit it; and also it was required to brace them for the severe life of the wilderness—the hard fare, the scant water, the scorching heat by day, the chill dews at night; to harden their frames, relaxed by a time of sensual indulgence (ch. xvi. 3), and nerve their minds to endurance.

HOMILIES BY VARIOUS AUTHORS.

Vers. 7—11.—*A multiplying people and a king's fears.* The increase of Israel in Egypt excited Pharaoh's jealousy. They were a useful people, and he dreaded their departure (ver. 10). But their staying was almost equally an occasion of uneasiness. Their position in Lower Egypt, so near the frontier, made them dangerous in case of wars. Revolutions were not infrequent, and many things were less likely than a future Hebrew dynasty. Hence the policy of breaking their power, and checking their increase, by reducing them to servitude.

I. VIEW ISRAEL'S INCREASE AS A WORK OF DIVINE POWER. While—1. Natural—that is, not miraculous, but due to the superabundant blessing of God on ordinary means—it was yet, 2. Extraordinary, and 3. Invincible—defying the efforts of the tyrant to check it. It may be legitimately viewed as a type of the spiritual increase of the Church. This also—1. *Excites astonishment.* So great a fruitfulness had never before been known. It was a marvel to all who witnessed it. Like surprise is awakened by the facts of the history of the Church. Consider (1) The smallness of the Church's beginnings. (2) The rapidity of her growth. (3) What opposition she has encountered. (4) What efforts have been made to crush her. (5) How she survives, and has from time to time renewed her youth. (6) How she has even thriven in the fires of persecution. (7) How, notwithstanding formidable resistance, and great internal lukewarmness and corruption, her progress is being steadily maintained. 2. *Awakens jealousy and fear.* The world does not relish the progress of the Gospel. It resents it as full of danger to itself. The filling of the land with sincere believers would mean the downfall of its power. Its spirit shown in opposition to revivals of religion, in decrying missions, in anger at bold and fearless preaching of Christ, followed by saving results, &c. 3. *Can only be accounted for by ascribing it to God as its author.* Naturalistic explanations have been offered. Gibbon has enumerated "secondary causes." So "secondary causes," might be pointed to in explaining the increase of Israel, yet these alone would not account for it. There was implied a Divine power, imparting to ordinary means an extraordinary efficacy. As little can the success of Christianity be explained on grounds of mere naturalism. 1. The Bible attributes it to Divine efficiency. 2. Those who experience its power unhesitatingly trace it to this source. 3. The Church is successful only as she relies on Divine assistance. 4. Naturalistic theories, one and all, break down in their attempts at explanation. Each new one that appears founds itself on the failure of its predecessors. It, in turn, is exploded by a rival. The supernatural hypothesis is the only one which accounts for all the facts.

II. VIEW PHARAOH'S POLICY AS A TYPE OF WORLDLY POLICY GENERALLY. Leave it to describe itself, and it is—1. Far-seeing. 2. Politic. 3. Unsentimental. Napoleon was unsentimental: "What are a hundred thousand lives, more or less, to me!" 4. A necessity of the time. Describe it as it ought to be described, and it appears in a less favourable light. 1. Ever awake to selfish interests. 2. Acute to perceive (or imagine) danger. 3. Unrestrained by considerations of gratitude. The new king "knew not Joseph." Nations, like individuals, are often forgetful of their greatest benefactors. 4. Regardless of the rights of others. 5. Cruel—stops at nothing. It will, with Pharaoh, reduce a nation to slavery; or, with Napoleon, deluge continents with blood. Yet—5. Is essentially short-sighted. All worldly policy is so. The King of Egypt could not have taken a more effectual means of bringing about the evils that he dreaded. He made it certain, if it was uncertain before, that in the event of war, the Hebrews would take part with his enemies. He set in motion a train of causes, which, as it actually happened, led to the departure of the whole people from Egypt. His policy thus outwitted itself, proved suicidal, proclaimed itself to be folly. Learn—1. The folly of trusting in man. "Beware of men" (Matt. x. 17). 2. How futile man's wisdom and cunning are when matched against God's power. 3. The short-sightedness of selfish and cruel action.—J. O.

Vers. 11—14.—*The bondage.* I. How EFFECTED? Doubtless, partly by craft, and partly by force. To one in Pharaoh's position, where there was the will to enslave, there would soon be found the way. 1. *The Israelites were politically weak.* "The patriarchal family had grown into a horde; it must have lost its domestic character, yet it had no polity . . . . a people in this state was ripe for slavery" (Maurice). 2. *And Pharaoh had no scruples.* Those engaged in tillage and keeping of cattle could easily be ruined by heaping on them tributes and exactions. Liberty once forfeited, they were at Pharaoh's disposal, to do with as he listed. Of the rest, large numbers were probably already employed—as forced labourers—on Pharaoh's works of construction. Over these (ver. 11) it was proposed to set "taskmasters"—"chiefs of tribute"—to afflict them with their burdens. 3. *Complaint was useless.* The Hebrews soon found, as expressed afterwards (ch. v. 19), that they were "in evil case"—that a general conspiracy, from the king downwards, had been entered into to rob, injure, and oppress them. Their subjugation in these circumstances was easily accomplished. Learn—1. A nation may outgrow itself. It will do so if intelligence and morals, with suitable institutions, do not keep pace with numbers. 2. Great prosperity is not always an advantage. It (1) excites jealousy; (2) tempts cupidity; (3) usually weakens by enervating.

II. WHY PERMITTED? This question may be answered by viewing the bondage 1. *As a punishment for sins.* The Hebrews had doubtless greatly corrupted themselves in Egypt, and had become in their masses very like the people around them. This was in them a sin that could not pass unpunished. God cannot suspend his moral laws even for his own people. If they do wrong, they must, no less than others, suffer for it. Nay, they will be punished with even greater severity than others are for similar offences. It is this which explains the bitter servitude of Israel. The nation is allowed to sink into a condition which is at once a fit retribution for its own sin, and an apt image of the condition of the sinner generally. For sin is slavery. It is inward bondage. It is degradation. It is rigorous service, and bitterness, and misery. God's law, the soul's own lusts, an exacting world, become in different ways taskmasters. It is unprofitable service. It sends a man to the husks, to the swine-troughs. It is slavery from which nothing but the power of God Almighty can redeem us. We bless God for our greater Moses, and the grander Exodus. 2. *As a trial of faith.* It would be so in a very especial degree to the godly portion of Israel. For why this long hiding of God's face—this keeping silence while his people were broiling and perishing under their terrible tasks? Did it not seem as though the promise had failed and God had *forgotten* to be gracious? (Ps. lxxvii. 8, 9.) Truly we need not wonder at anything in God's dealings with his Church when we reflect on how long and how fearfully Israel was afflicted. The faith which endured *this* trial must have come out of the furnace seven times purified. 3. *As a moral preparation.* It is now manifest, though it could hardly have been seen then, how needful was this affliction, protracted through successive generations—(1) To wean the people's hearts from Egypt. (2) To make them willing to leave it. (3) To make the thought of Canaan sweet to them. (4) To break up trust in self and man. (5) To lead them to cry mightily to God. The same reasons, in whole or part, serve to explain why God lays trials on ourselves ; indicate at least the ends which affliction is used to subserve. Had everything been prosperous, the hearts of Israel would naturally have clung to the fleshpots, their hopes would have been forgotten ; even their God would in time have been abjured.—J. O.

Vers. 7—14.—*Israel in Egypt.* The life of a people, like that of an individual, to a great extent *shaped* by circumstances. In Canaan the Israelites might learn hardihood, but no room for much growth; few opportunities for national organisation ; the tendency would be for the families to separate, each seeking pasturage for its own flocks (cf. Abraham and Lot). To become a nation they had to be placed (1) where they might increase and multiply, and (2) where their slightly connected elements might coalesce and be welded into one. To attain this object God led his people into Egypt. [Cf. (1) Hothouse where plants may strike and grow before being planted out, and (2) Deut. iv. 20. Furnace where metal may be smelted into one homogeneous mass and the worst of the dross removed.] We may notice in this view—

I. PROSPERITY AND ITS USES. Cf. ver. 7. In Goshen life simple and the means of subsistence plentiful, ample room and ample provision. Happy years without a history, passed in a land which even now yields the largest revenue in Egypt, and where the population still increases more rapidly than in any other province. Probably no incident of more importance than some occasional skirmish with border tribes. No wonder that " they increased abundantly and multiplied, and waxed exceeding mighty." Prosperity has its uses as well as adversity. The long unnoticed years through which the fruit-tree attains maturity are necessary antecedents to the fiery summers which see the fruit ripening. Not much to notice in such years. Still their *existence* is noteworthy. They make no small portion of the sum of human life, whether viewed in its national or individual aspect. History grows out of them even whilst it is compelled to forget them in its records. The fruit of Life draws from them its *substance*, though other years may give it its *colour* and *flavour*.

II. ADVERSITY AND ITS USES. Vers. 10—14 show how trouble came to Israel, and the nature of the trouble which did come. Originating in Pharaoh's natural jealousy at the increasing influence of an alien race, it took the form of enforced labour, such as—perhaps owing to Joseph's land law (Gen. xlvii. 23, &c.)—he clearly had the acknowledged right to levy at will from all his subjects. Pharaoh however was but the instrument which God used for the education of his people ; he knew that adversity was needed to carry on the work which prosperity had begun. Notice—1. *Affliction did not hinder progress.* We gather from ver. 12 that it really advanced it. Prosperity long continued may be a greater hindrance than adversity. It tends to produce a stagnant condition [cf. the opening poems in Tennyson's 'Maud']. The after-history shows us that Israel had, to some extent, *morally* deteriorated ; and moral deterioration in the long run must lead to physical degradation. When the stock needs pruning the pruning process stimulates growth. 2. *Affliction proved morally helpful.* The people had been getting careless and slothful, forgetting God (cf. Josh. xxiv. 14, Ezek. xx. 5—8) or paying him a merely nominal service. Now, however, cf. ii. 23—25, God could hear their cry because their cry was genuine ; he could have respect unto them because they were learning to have respect unto him. 3. *Affliction ensured national union.* Hitherto the people was just a collection of families, united by a common name and common traditions. Mutual need begets mutual helpfulness, and it is by mutual help that tribes are dovetailed into one another and come to form one nation. [Isolated fragments of ore need smelting in the furnace to produce the consolidated metal.] It is in the heat of the furnace of affliction that rivalries, jealousies, and all kinds of tribal littlenesses can alone be finally dissolved. And affliction still has such uses. Prosperity is good, no doubt, but, in this world, it requires to be complemented by adversity. " Why is trouble permitted ? " Because men cannot otherwise be perfected. It is just as necessary for our moral ripening as heat is necessary for the ripening of the fruit. (1) It need not hinder any man's progress; (2) If rightly used it should purge out the dross from us and make us morally better; (3) It tends to dissolve the barriers which selfishness erects between man and man, and works towards the formation of that holy brotherhood which embraces in one family all the nations of the earth.—G.

Vers. 8—14.—*Egypt's sin.* I. NATIONAL WRONG-DOING THE SEED OF NATIONAL DISASTER. The story of Egypt's suffering begins with the story of Egypt's injustice. There was wisdom in Pharaoh's statesmanship, and a sincere desire to serve his country, and yet he was his country's worst foe. The service rendered by wickedness is in the end rebuke and ruin.

II. THE CARE SOUGHT TO BE REMOVED BY SIN BECOMES GREATER (10—12). 1. The bondage was imposed to prevent their multiplying: "but the more they afflicted them the more they multiplied and grew." 2. The trouble was at first simply a possibility detected by the statesman's keen eye, and now all Egypt was "grieved because of the children of Israel." The way of wickedness is through a deepening flood.

III. WRONG GROWS INTO GREATER WRONG (13, 14). Egypt had gone too far to retreat. Israel's enmity was now a certainty, and they must be crushed. From being compelled to labour in the erection of strong cities, their lives are made bitter by all manner of hard bondage. Evil grows with an inward necessity. When a nation makes an unjust demand it does not mean murder, yet that is its next step. Satan dare not whisper all his counsel at first but by-and-by he can tell it all and have it all accomplished.—U.

EXPOSITION.

Vers. 15—22.—Some time—say five or six years—having elapsed and the Pharaoh's first plan having manifestly failed, it was necessary for him either to give up his purpose, or to devise something else. Persevering and tenacious, he preferred the latter course. He bethought himself that a stop might be put to the multiplication of the Israelites by means of infanticide on a large scale. Infanticide was no doubt a crime in Egypt, as in most countries except Rome; but the royal command would legitimate almost any action, since the king was recognised as a god; and the wrongs of a foreign and subject race would not sensibly move the Egyptian people, or be likely to provoke remonstrance. On looking about for suitable instruments to carry out his design, it struck the monarch that something, at any rate, might be done by means of the midwives who attended the Hebrew women in their confinements. It has been supposed that the two mentioned, Shiphrah and Puah, might be the only midwives employed by the Israelites (Canon Cook and others), and no doubt in the East a small number suffice for a large population: but what impression could the monarch expect to make on a population of from one to two millions of souls by engaging the services of two persons only, who could not possibly attend more than about one in fifty of the

births? The midwives mentioned must therefore be regarded as "superintendents," chiefs of the guild or faculty, who were expected to give their orders to the rest. (So Kalisch, Knobel, Aben Ezra, etc.) It was no doubt well known that midwives were not always called in; but the king supposed that they were employed sufficiently often for the execution of his orders to produce an important result. And the narrative implies that he had not miscalculated. It was the disobedience of the midwives (ver. 17) that frustrated the king's intention, not any inherent weakness in his plan. The midwives, while professing the intention of carrying out the orders given them, in reality killed none of the infants; and, when taxed by the Pharaoh with disobedience, made an untrue excuse (ver. 19). Thus the king's second plan failed as completely as his first—"the people" still "multiplied and waxed very mighty" (ver. 20).

Foiled a second time, the wicked king threw off all reserve and all attempt at concealment. If the midwives will not stain their hands with murder at his secret command, he will make the order a general and public one. "All his people" shall be commanded to put their hand to the business, and to assist in the massacre of the innocents—it shall be the duty of every loyal subject to cast into the waters of the Nile any

Hebrew male child of whose birth he has cognisance. The object is a national one—to secure the public safety (see ver. 10): the whole nation may well be called upon to aid in carrying it out.

Ver. 15.—**The Hebrew midwives.** It is questioned whether the midwives were really Hebrew women, and not rather Egyptian women, whose special business it was to attend the Hebrew women in their labours. Kalisch translates, " the women who served as midwives to the Hebrews," and assumes that they were Egyptians. (So also Canon Cook.) But the names are apparently Semitic, Shiphrah being " elegant, beautiful," and Puah, " one who cries out." And the most natural rendering of the Hebrew text is that of A. V.

Ver. 16.—**The stools.** The explanation furnished by a remark of Mr. Lane ('Modern Egyptians,' vol. iii. p. 142) is more satisfactory than any other. In modern Egypt, he says, " two or three days before the expected time of delivery, the midwife conveys to the house the *kursee elwilâdeh*, a chair of a peculiar form, upon which the patient is to be seated during the birth." A chair of the form intended is represented on the Egyptian monuments.

Ver. 17.—**The midwives feared God.** The midwives had a sense of religion, feared God sufficiently to decline imbruing their hands in the innocent blood of a number of defenceless infants, and, rather than do so wicked a thing, risked being punished by the monarch. They were not, as appears by ver. 19, *highly* religious—not of the stuff whereof martyrs are made ; they did not scruple at a falsehood, believing it necessary to save their lives ; and it would seem that they succeeded in deceiving the king.

Ver. 19.—**They are vigorous.** Literally, " they are lively." In the East at the present day a large proportion of the women deliver themselves ; and the services of professional accoucheurs are very rarely called in. The excuse of the midwives had thus a basis of fact to rest upon, and was only untrue because it was not the whole truth.

Vers. 20, 21.—**Therefore God did well to the midwives.** Literally, " *And* God did well," etc. (see ver. 21). Because they feared him sufficiently to disobey the king, and take their chance of a punishment, which might have been very severe—even perhaps death— God overlooked their weak and unfaithful divergence from truth, and gave them a reward.

He made them houses. He blessed them by giving them children of their own, who grew up, and gave them the comfort, support, and happiness which children were intended to give. There was a manifest fitness in rewarding those who had refused to bring misery and desolation into families by granting them domestic happiness themselves.

Ver. 22.—**Every son that is born.** The words are universal, and might seem to apply to the Egyptian, no less than the Hebrew, male children. But they are really limited by the context, which shows that there had never been any question as to taking the life of any Egyptian. With respect to the objection sometimes raised, that no Egyptian monarch would possibly have commanded such wholesale cold-blooded destruction of poor innocent harmless children, it is to be observed, first, that Egyptian monarchs had very little regard indeed for the lives of any persons who were not of their own nation. They constantly massacred prisoners taken in war—they put to death or enslaved persons cast upon their coasts (Diod. Sic. i. 67)—they cemented with the blood of their captives, as Lenormant says ('Manuel d'Hist. Anc.,' vol. i. p. 423), each stone of their edifices. The sacredness of human life was not a principle with them. Secondly, that tender and compassionate regard for children which seems to us Englishmen of the present day a universal instinct is in truth the fruit of Christianity, and was almost unknown in the ancient world. Children who were " not wanted " were constantly exposed to be devoured by wild beasts, or otherwise made away with (Döllinger, ' Jew and Gentile,' vol. ii. p. 246) ; and such exposition was defended by philosophers (Plat. 'Rep.' v. p. 460 c). In Syria and Carthage they were constantly offered to idols. At Rome, unless the father interposed to save it, every child was killed. It would probably not have cost an Egyptian Pharaoh a single pang to condemn to death a number of children, any more than a number of puppies. And the rule " Salus publica suprema lex," which, if not formulated, still practically prevailed, would have been held to justify anything. **The river.** Though, in the Delta, where the scene is laid throughout the early part of Exodus, there were many branches of the Nile, yet we hear constantly of " *the* river" (ch. ii. 3, 5 ; vii. 20, 21 ; viii. 3, etc.), because one branch only, the Tanitic, was readily accessible. Tanis (Zoan) was situated on it.

HOMILETICS.

Vers. 15—22.—*Steps in sin.* Bad men, when their designs are frustrated, and things fall out otherwise than as they wish, are far from suspecting that it is God who opposes them and brings their counsels to nought. They find fault with themselves or their advisers, and suppose that, if their end is not to be compassed in one way, it may be obtained in another. Like Balak (Num. xxii. xxiii.), they would outwit God; or rather, not realising his existence, they would force fortune by a combination of inventiveness, perseverance, and audacity. When one means fails, they do not lay aside their design, but seek another means. And their second plan is almost always more wicked than their first. Pharaoh follows up the cruel thought of grinding oppression by the still more cruel resolve to effect his purpose through murder. And not liking to incùr the odium of open murder, he devises a secret system, a *crypteia*, which shall rid him of a certain number of his enemies, and yet keep him clear, even of suspicion. The mid-wives, had they come into his plan, would of course have said that the children they murdered were stillborn, or died from natural causes. But this crafty scheme like-wise fails; and then what follows? His subtle brain invents a third plan, and it is the cruelest and wickedest of all. Grown shameless, he openly avows himself a murderer, takes his whole people into his confidence, compels them, so far as he can, to be a nation of murderers, and extends his homicidal project to all the males. "Every son that is born ye shall cast into the river." The Nile, according to his own religion, was a god, and no Egyptian corpse ever defiled it; but everything must give way that the king may work his wicked will, and the restraints of the national creed are as little regarded as those of natural morality. *Facilis descensus Averni*; the steps by which men go down the road to hell are easy; each is in advance of the other, a little further on in guilt; there is no startling transition; and so, by little and little, advance is made, and the neophyte becomes a graduate in the school of crime.

Ver. 17.—*Duty of opposing authority when its commands are against God's Law.* Few lessons are taught in Holy Scripture more plainly than this, that the wrongful commands of legitimate authority are to be disobeyed. "Saul spake to Jonathan his son, and to all his servants that they should kill David" (1 Sam. xix. 1). But Jonathan positively refused, and rebuked his father: "Wherefore wilt thou sin against innocent blood?" (*ib.* ver. 5). Uzziah would have usurped the priest's office; but Azariah the priest "withstood him" (2 Chr. xxvi. 16—21), and God signified his approval by smiting the king with leprosy. Ahasuerus commanded that a "reverence" trenching upon God's honour should be done to Haman (Esth. iii. 2). Mordecai "transgressed the king's commandment," and it is recorded of him to his credit. The "Three Children" disobeyed Nebuchadnezzar when he would have had them "worship the golden image which he had set up" (Dan. iii. 18) on the plain of Dura. Daniel disobeyed Darius the Mede when required to discontinue his daily prayers. The Apostles disobeyed the Sanhedrin, when forbidden "to preach at all or teach in the name of Jesus" (Acts iv. 18). God's law is paramount; and no human authority may require anything to be done which it forbids, or anything to be left undone which it commands. The argument is unanswerable: "Whether it be right in the sight of God to hearken unto you more than unto God, judge ye" (*ib.* ver. 19). So the midwives, because they "feared God," disobeyed the king. No doubt the lesson is to be applied with caution. We are not to be always flying in the face of authority, and claiming it as a merit. More especially, in States calling themselves Christian and retaining even partially a Christian character, opposition to the law is a serious matter, and, if resorted to, should only be resorted to under a clear and distinct conviction that the Divine law and the human are in absolute opposition. "Whatsoever is not of faith, is sin." If we are not sure of the Divine obligation we must accept the human one. Still, as the good man struggling against adversity is admitted to be one of the noblest of sights, so there is nothing grander, nothing finer, nothing more heroic, than the conscientious resistance of religious persons to the wicked and tyrannical commands of men, whether they be kings, or judges, or mobs. Daniel refusing to obey Darius, Peter and John rejecting the orders of the Sanhedrim, Socrates declining to take part in the arrests of the Thirty, the Seven Bishops refusing to read the proclamation of King James II., are among the most admirable and inspiriting facts of history. The men who rightfully resist authority are "the salt of the earth." They save the world from a rapid and complete corruption. The remembrance of their acts continues, and is a warning to authorities, preventing hundreds of iniquitous laws and orders, which would otherwise have been enjoined and enacted. Their example is an undying one, and encourages others on fitting occasion to do the like. All honour then to the noble band, who, when the crisis came, have "obeyed God rather than man," and taken their chance of the consequences! Not that the *final* consequences to themselves can be doubtful. "But and if ye suffer for righteousness' sake, blessed are ye!" (1 Pet. iii. 14). In this life, the consequence may be success, severe punishment, or (occasionally) neglect and oblivion. But in the world to come there will be a reward for rightful resistance undoubtedly. "God made the midwives houses." For all whom a tyrannical authority makes to suffer because they fear and obey him, he will reserve in his own house "mansions" where they will enjoy bliss eternal.

Vers. 18—21.—*God's acceptance of an imperfect obedience.* The midwives had not the courage of their convictions. They did not speak out boldly, like Daniel, and the "Three Children," and the Apostles. They did not say, "Be it known unto thee, O king, that we fear God, and will not do this thing." They cast about for an excuse, which should absolve them of the crime of disobedience, and so perhaps save them from punishment, and they found one which was no doubt partially true, but which by a *suppressio veri* was a *suggestio falsi.* Some have exonerated them from all blame under the circumstances; but though the circumstances may extenuate, they do not justify their conduct. It was a fault, but (especially if they were heathens) a venial fault. And it was perhaps repented of. At any rate God condoned it. He was not "extreme to mark what was done amiss." He accepted their good deeds and their reverent fear of him, though it was not accompanied by high courage and a heroic love of truth; that is to say, he accepted an *imperfect obedience.* And this is what he does in all cases. No man but One has rendered an obedience that was perfect. "All we, the rest, offend in many things; and if we say that we have no sin, deceive ourselves and the truth is not in us." Well for us that God, for his Son's sake, and through his atonement on the cross, can condone our offences, and despite our many misdeeds reward our acts of faithfulness! (See Matt. vi. 4; x. 42; xvi. 27; Luke vi. 35; 1 Cor. iii. 14; &c.)

HOMILIES BY VARIOUS AUTHORS.

Vers. 15—22.—*A king's edicts.* I. THE COMMAND TO THE MIDWIVES TO DESTROY THE MALES (ver. 16). This was a further stage in the persecution of the Hebrews. Happily the command was not obeyed. There is a limit even to the power of kings. Stronger than kings is—1. The power of *religion.* "The midwives feared God" (ver. 17). 2. The force of *patriotism.* They were "Hebrew midwives" (ver. 15), and would not, even at the king's bidding, be murderers of their race. 3. The instincts of *humanity.* These came in to thwart both this and the next expedient for destroying the children. 4. The cunning of *evasion.* It is hopeless to attempt to force laws upon a people determined not to obey them. The midwives had only to stay away, and let the Hebrew women help themselves, to reduce the king's decree to a dead letter. And this was probably what they did (ver. 19). The result shows how much better it is, even at some risk, to obey God than to obey man. The midwives—1. Lost nothing. 2. Retained a good conscience. 3. Were signally honoured and rewarded: God made them houses (ver. 21). Kindness shown to God's people never fails of its reward.

II. THE COMMAND TO THE PEOPLE TO CAST THE MALES INTO THE RIVER (ver. 22). He must indeed have been a foolish king, if he thought to secure obedience to so inhuman a decree. Parents would not obey it. The work was of a kind which would soon grow hateful even to those who might at first be willing to do it for reward. The hearts of the most abandoned ere long sicken at murder. Public sympathy does not appear to have gone with the edict, and the number of males at the Exodus makes it certain that it was not long in operation. Its chief fruit was one little contemplated by the tyrant—the salvation and courtly upbringing of Moses. Learn—1. How one cruelty leads to another, and increasingly hardens the heart. It is told of Robespierre that when judge at Arras, half-a-dozen years before he took his place in the popular mind of France and Europe as one of the bloodiest monsters of myth or history, he resigned his post in a fit of remorse after condemning a criminal to be executed. "He is a criminal, no doubt," he kept groaning to his sister, "a criminal no doubt; but to put a man to death!" (Morley). 2. The impotence of human devices. 3. The certainty of the Church surviving under the worst that man can do against it. The more Pharaoh persecuted, the more the people multiplied and grew (vers. 12, 20).— J. O.

Vers. 8—22.—*The policy of Pharaoh.* I. THE PRINCIPLE OF THE POLICY. This is indicated in vers. 9, 10. It was a policy of *selfish fear,* proceeding upon an unconcealed regard for the supremacy of Egypt. Whatever interfered with that supremacy was to be, if possible, swept completely out of the way. Pharaoh was dealing, not with the necessities of the present, but with the possibilities of the future. He made no pretence that Israel deserved to be dealt with in this merciless fashion. There was no attempt to cloak the cruelties of the tyrant under the aspect of needful severity against evil-doers. The fear of Pharaoh is seen in the very language he employs. It was not true as yet that the Israelites were more and mightier than the Egyptians: but Pharaoh feels that such a state of things is not improbable, and may not be remote. Something has already happened very different from what might have been expected. Who was to suppose that a handful of people from Canaan, instead of blending with the bulk of Egypt, would keep persistently separate and increase with such alarming rapidity? Seeing that such unexpected things have already happened, what may not be feared in the future? Who knows what allies Israel may ultimately find, and what escape it may achieve? Thus from this attitude and utterance of Pharaoh we learn—1. *Not to make our safety and our strength to consist in an unscrupulous weakening of others.* The true strength, ever becoming more and more sufficient, is to be gained within ourselves. Pharaoh would have done more for his own safety and the safety of his people by putting away idolatry, injustice, and oppression, than by all his frantic attempts to destroy Israel. It is a sad business, if we must hold our chief possessions at the expense of others. If my gain is the loss or suffering of some one else, then by this very fact the gain is condemned, and however large and grateful it may be at present, it will end in the worst of all loss. Surely the luxuries of the few would become utterly nauseous and abhorrent, if it were only considered how often they depend on the privation and degradation of the many. Pharaoh's kingdom deserved to perish, and so deserve all kingdoms and all exalted stations of individuals, if their continuance can only be secured by turning all possible enemies into spiritless and emasculated slaves. 2. *Not to set our affections on such things as lie at the mercy of others.* Pharaoh had to be incessantly watching the foundations of his vast and imposing kingdom. Other nations only saw the superstructure from a distance, and might be excused for concluding that the magnificence rested upon a solid base. But we may well believe that Pharaoh himself lived a life of incessant anxiety. The apprehensions which he here expresses must have been a fair sample of those continually passing through his mind. The world can give great possessions and many opportunities for carnal pleasure; but security, undisturbed enjoyment of the possession, it cannot give.

II. THE WORKING OUT OF THE POLICY. The thing aimed at was to keep the numbers of Israel within what were deemed safe bounds; and to this end Pharaoh began by trying to crush the spirits of the people. He judged—and perhaps not unwisely, according to the wisdom of this world—that a race oppressed as he proposed to oppress Israel would assuredly not increase to any dangerous extent. If only the rate of increase in Israel did not gain on the rate of increase in Egypt, then all would be safe. Pharaoh firmly believed that if only Egypt could keep more numerous than Israel, Egypt would be perfectly secure. Therefore he put these people into a state of bondage and oppression ever becoming more rigorous. Notice that he had peculiar advantages, from his point of view, in making this course of treatment successful. The Israelites had hitherto lived a free, wandering, pastoral life (Gen. xlvii. 3—6), and now they were cooped-up under merciless taskmasters and set to hard manual toil. If any human policy had success in it, success seemed to be in this policy of Pharaoh. Nevertheless it utterly failed, from Pharaoh's point of view, for, whatever depressing effect it had on the spirits of the Israelites, there was no diminution in their numbers. The extraordinary and alarming increase still went on. The more the taskmasters did to hinder Israel, the more, in this particular matter of the numerical increase, it seemed to prosper. It was all very perplexing and unaccountable, but at last Pharaoh recognises the failure, even while he cannot explain it, and proceeds to a more direct method of action, which surely cannot fail in a perfectly efficacious result. He commands the men-children of Israel to be slain from the womb. But here he fails even in a more conspicuous and humiliating way than before. He was a despot, accustomed to have others go when he said "Go," and come when he said "Come." Accordingly, when he commanded *men* to become the agents of his harsh designs, he found obedient servants in plenty, and probably many who bettered his instructions. But now he turns to *women*—weak, despised women, who were reckoned to obey in the most obsequious manner and he finds that they will not obey at all. It was an easy thing to do, if it had only been in their hearts to do it; for what is easier than to take away the breath of a new-born infant? They do not openly refuse; they even pretend compliance; but for all that they secretly disobey and effectively thwart Pharaoh's purpose. When we find others readily join with us in our evil purposes, then God interferes to disappoint both us and them; but we cannot always reckon even on the support of others. Notice lastly, that in carrying out this policy of defence against Israel, Pharaoh never seems to have thought of the one course which might have given him perfect safety. *He might have expelled Israel altogether out of his coasts.* But, so far from deeming this desirable, it was one of the very things he wished to guard against. Israel was a continual source of alarm and annoyance, a people beyond management, an insoluble problem; but it never occurred to him that Egypt would be better with them away. It would have had a very bad look to send them out of the land; it would have been a confession of inability and perplexity which those proud lips, so used to the privileged utterances of despotism, could not bring themselves to frame.

III. THE TOTAL RESULT OF THE POLICY. Though it failed in attaining the particular end which it had in view, it did not fail altogether; nay, it rather succeeded, and that with a most complete success, seeing that in doing so it effectually served the purpose of God. Pharaoh *failed* as dealing with *the children of Israel.* He called them the children of Israel, but in profound ignorance of all that this description involved. He did not know that Israel was the son of him who was born to Abraham and Sarah in their old age, contrary to all expectation and entirely of promise. But Pharaoh *succeeded* in a way he did not anticipate, in so far as he was dealing with the posterity of *Jacob,* the heirs of human infirmity. They did become, in the course of time, slaves in spirit as well as in body, personally so undeserving of freedom that when they had received it, they wished almost immediately to go back to the creature comforts of Egypt like a dog to its vomit, or a sow to her wallowing in the mire. Hence we see that God served himself, alike by Pharaoh's failure and Pharaoh's success. Pharaoh's failure showed how really and powerfully God was present with his people. It was another instance of the treasure being in an earthen vessel that the excellency of the power might be of God and not of men. And Pharaoh by his very success in making the iron to enter into the soul of Israel, was unconsciously working a way to make the stay of Israel in Egypt as full a type as possible of the tyrannous bondage of sin. As Egypt presented its pleasant side at first, so does sin. For a considerable time Egypt looked better than Canaan. There had been corn in Egypt; there had been a land of Goshen; there had been a reflected honour and comfort from the relation of the children of Israel to the all-powerful Joseph. But Joseph dies, and then little by little it becomes plain that Egypt will be anything but a land of happiness. What the Israelites might have become if Pharaoh had not persecuted them, it is vain to speculate, as vain as to speculate what might happen to the sinner if he could go on sinning without suffering. We have to thank Pharaoh for helping to set before us in such a clear way the bitter bondage of sin, and the greatness of that deliverance by which God will liberate us from it. God moves in a mysterious way. He fills Israel with a strength whereby even in bondage and oppression their numbers are miraculously increased, but he denies to them the strength whereby they might have overthrown their oppressors. We can now see the why and wherefore of all this mysterious dealing. By the work of his Son God fills us with a life which, through all the discomforts of the present state, goes on undestroyed and still increasing into a state where these discomforts will be unknown. But at the same time God makes it clear that we cannot escape all the sufferings that belong to sin. So far as we have sown to the flesh, we must also out of the flesh reap corruption. Our joy is that, even in this world, amid all tribulation and all reaping of the temporal results of sin, there is also the opportunity for another and better sowing, and the consequent opportunity for another and better reaping.—Y.

Vers. 15—21.—*The conduct of the midwives.* I. NOTICE WHAT WAS PRAISEWORTHY IN THEIR CONDUCT. "They did not as the king of Egypt commanded them, but saved the men-children alive," and this *conduct* was made possible because behind it there was a praiseworthy *feeling.* "The midwives feared God." They saw how real was the power of Pharaoh in enslaving and oppressing the Israelites, but they were not thereby misled into supposing the power of Pharaoh to be greater than the power of God. They had ample opportunity, even more than the rest of Israel, to mark the Hand that was producing this extraordinary ,increase in the numbers of the people. Their very professional experience was of a kind to impress them deeply with the fact that Israel was increasing at a rate not to be accounted for by the ordinary processes of nature. They could not see God as they saw Pharaoh, but his superior power was made evident by the things he did. Then, on the other hand, with all the manifestations of Pharaoh's power, it was impossible for him to conceal that he was afraid himself. Moreover, as the oppression and affliction of Israel increased, it became still clearer that God was with the people, and the more confirmed would the midwives be in their fear of him. Hence it would have been a very poor sort of prudence to comply with Pharaoh's order, to avoid his displeasure, perhaps to gain his rewards, and then find themselves face to face with an angry God, from whom there was no escape. What a rebuke, out of these depths of bondage and suffering, and out of a very imperfect moral state, these two women give to us! They feared God, and that fear kept them safe, and made them prosperous. The fear of man ever bringeth a snare; but a real, practical and all-dominating sense of the presence and the power of God takes snares and stumbling-blocks out of our path.

II. NOTICE WHAT WAS CENSURABLE IN THEIR CONDUCT. It must not be supposed that because they feared God, and God dealt well with them, everything therefore which they did was quite as it should be. With all their deep sense of God's presence, these women were living but in the twilight of the revelation, as far as they personally were concerned. They knew enough to *fear* God, *i.e.* they knew the reality and greatness of his power, but they did not know enough to *love* him. With them, conscience was in such a half-enlightened, half-awakened state, that while they felt it wrong to obey Pharaoh's command, and would probably not have obeyed it if the sword had been hanging over their heads, yet they have no scruple as to deceiving Pharaoh. Undoubtedly, women who had been fully instructed in all the will of God, and who were fully alive to all the round of duty, would have faced the king boldly, and said, "We cannot do this thing, come what may." But they were living, as we have already noticed, in a very imperfect moral state. They honestly felt that deceiving Pharaoh was a quite permissible way of showing their obedience to God. Hence, while upon certain considerations we may excuse their deception, we must not slur it over as a matter of no moment; and though it is said that God was pleased with them as it was, this does not prevent us from feeling that he would have been even better pleased if they had said straight out to Pharaoh, "How can we do this great wickedness and sin against God?"

III. CONSIDER THE CONDUCT OF THESE TWO WOMEN AS ILLUSTRATIVE OF A CERTAIN STAGE IN THE PROGRESS OF SINNERS TOWARDS GOD. There are many who have got so far as to fear God, and this is no small attainment. It may be that there is something slavish, terrifying, paralysing even in the fear; but, even so, it is better to have the fear than be as those who are completely destitute of it. For, with a feeling of real fear to lay hold of, God can do great things. He can gradually bring us nearer and nearer, so that we shall love as well as fear him. He can show us his loving spirit, and his power to fill our lives with blessing and ,surround them with security. He can show us that there is really no more reason to live in restless dread of him than there is for a little bird to fly hastily away at the approach of some kind-hearted human being. But where there is no fear of God, what can be done? When the chief thing you dread is the laughter of fools; or the censure of unsympathising friends and neighbours or threatening superiors; or the fear of temporal loss and pain in general; what can then be done? Be thankful if you have got so far as to fear God. Fearing him, dreading him, trembling before him, feeling his power more than any other of his attributes—this is a long way short of loving him, but nevertheless it is a stage toward that glorious state of the heart; and it is incomparably better than to have no feeling for God at all, and to let an arrogant world fill his place. It is a great point gained, when once we clearly perceive, and act upon the perception, that to be safe and right with man is a mere trifle to the great necessity of being safe and right with God. One Pharaoh goes and another comes, but the God of Israel, the God who is bringing all these men children to the birth, abides for ever. Before we begin to pity Shiphrah and Puah for their defective notions with regard to truth, we had better make sure that they do not rise in the judgment against us, on account of our gross indifference to the majesty and authority of God.—Y.

Vers. 15—22.—*The way of sin.* I. THE GROWING SHAMELESSNESS OF CRIME. 1. Murder was intended from the first—the hope was that the people *should* be diminished—but the intention was veiled. 2. (15, 16.) The crime was now looked in the face, but it was so arranged that it might be done secretly. 3. When this failed, then public proclamation was made that the murder should be deliberately and openly done (22). No man steps at first into shameless commission of sin. Every sin is a deadening of the moral sense and a deepening of shame. II. THOSE WHO REFUSE TO AID IN PHARAOH'S CRIME FIND BLESSING. 1. The refusal of the midwives was service to God. (1) It prevented secret murder. (2) It rebuked Pharaoh's sin. 2. Their refusal was justified because it sprang from obedience to a higher authority: "they feared God." Disobedience to human law must have a higher sanction than a factious spirit. 3. God gave them inheritance among his people. In that dread of sin and heroism for the right they were fit allies for God's people. Those who separate themselves from evil God will lead into the light. III. THOSE WHO AID IN BRING JUDGMENT UPON THEMSELVES. The king appeals to his people and they make his crime their own. But Egypt's sin is set at last in the light of Egypt's desolation. Obedience to unjust laws will not protect us from God's just judgment. The wrong decreed by authority becomes by obedience a nation's crime.—U.

EXPOSITION.

CHAPTER II

Vers. 1—10.—THE BIRTH, ESCAPE, AND EDUCATION OF MOSES. Some years before the Pharaoh issued his edict for the general destruction of the Hebrew male children, Amram of the tribe of Levi, had married Jochebed, his kinswoman (ch. vi. 20). They had already had two children—Miriam, a daughter, born probably soon after the marriage, and Aaron, a son, born some twelve years later. Soon after the issue of the edict, Jochebed gave birth to her third child, a son, who therefore came under its terms. Knowing as she did what fate was in store for him, if his existence became known to the Egyptians, she "hid him three months." Then, despairing of being able to keep him concealed much longer, she devised the plan related in vers. 3—4, which proved successful.

Ver. 1.—**There went a man.** The Hebrew language is deficient in tenses, and cannot mark *pluperfect* time. The meaning is, that "a man of the house of Levi *had* gone, some

time before, and taken to wife a daughter of Levi." Miriam must have been fourteen or fifteen at the time of the exposure of Moses. By **a daughter of Levi,** we must not understand an actual daughter, which is irreconcilable with the chronology, but one of Levi's descendants—"a wife of the daughters of Levi," as the LXX. translates.

Ver. 2.—**And the woman conceived.** Not for the first time, as appears from ver. 4, nor even for the second, as we learn from ch. vii. 7; but for the third. Aaron was three years old when Moses was born. As no difficulty had occurred with respect to him, we must regard the edict as issued between his birth and that of Moses. **When she saw that he was a goodly child.** Perhaps Jochebed would have done the same had Moses been ill-favoured, for mothers have often loved best their weakest and sickliest; but still it naturally seemed to her the harder that she was called upon to lose a strong and beautiful baby; and this is what the writer means to express—the clauses are not "simply co-ordinate." **She hid him**—*i.e.* kept him within the house—perhaps even in the female apartments. Egyptians were mixed up with the Israelites in Goshen—not perhaps in any great numbers, but still so that no Hebrew felt himself safe from observation.

Ver. 3.—**She took for him an ark of bul-rushes.** The words translated "ark" and "bul-rushes" are both of Egyptian origin, the former corresponding to the ordinary word for "chest," which is *teb*, *teba*, or *tebat*, and the latter cor-responding to the Egyptian *kam*, which is the same in Coptic, and designates the papyrus plant. This is a strong-growing rush, with a triangular stem, which attains the height of from 10 to 15 feet. The Egyptian paper was made from its pith. The rush itself was used for various purposes—among others for boat-building (Plin. 'H. N.' vi. 22 ; vii. 16 ; Theo-phrast. iv. 9 ; Plut. 'De Isid. et Osir.' § 18, etc.), as appears from the monuments. It would be a very good material for the sort of purpose to which Jochebed applied it. **She daubed it with slime and with pitch.** The word trans-lated "slime" is the same as that used in Gen. xi. 3, which is generally thought to mean "mineral pitch" or "bitumen." According to Strabo and Diodorus, that material was largely used by the Egyptians for the embalm-ing of corpses, and was imported into Egypt from Palestine. Boats are sometimes covered with it externally at the present day (Ker Porter, Travels, vol. ii. p. 260 ; Layard, 'Nineveh and its Remains,' pt. ii. ch. v.); but Jochebed seems to have used vegetable pitch — the ordinary pitch of commerce—for the purpose. Here again the Hebrew word is taken from the Egyptian. **She laid it in the flags.** "Suph," the word translated "flags," is a modification of the Egyptian *tufi*, which has that meaning. Water-plants of all kinds abound in the backwaters of the Nile and the marshy tracts communicating with it. The object of placing the ark in a thicket of reeds probably was, that it might not float away out of sight. **The river's brink.** Lite-rally, *the lip of the river* — an Egyptian idiom.

Ver. 4.—**His sister.** There can be no reasonable doubt that this is the "Miriam" of the later narrative (ch. xv. 20, 21 ; Num. xx. 1), who seems to have been Moses' only sister (Num. xxvi. 59). She was probably set to watch by her mother.

Ver. 5.—**The daughter of Pharaoh.** Pro-bably a daughter of Seti I. and a sister of Rameses the Great. Josephus calls her Ther-muthis; Syncellus, Pharia; Artapanus, Merrhis, and some of the Jewish commentators, Bithia —the diversity showing that there was no genuine tradition on the subject. There is nothing improbable in an Egyptian princess bathing in the Nile, at a place reserved for women. (See Wilkinson, 'Manners and Cus-toms of Ancient Egyptians,' vol. iii. p. 389.) The Nile was regarded as sacred, and its water as health-giving and fructifying (Strab. xv.

p. 695). **Her maidens.** Egyptian ladies of high rank are represented on the monuments as attended to the bath by a number of hand-maidens. As many as four are seen in one representation (Wilkinson, l. s. c.). **Her maid** is her special personal attendant, the others being merely women attached to her house-hold.

Ver. 6.—The princess herself **opened** the "ark," which was a sort of covered basket. Perhaps she suspected what she would find inside; but would it be a living or a dead child? This she could not know. She opened, and looked. It was a living babe, and **it wept.** At once her woman's heart, heathen as she was, went out to the child—its tears reached the common humanity that lies below all dif-ferences of race and creed—and she pitied it. "One touch of nature makes the whole world kin." **This is one of the Hebrews' children.** Hebrew characteristics were perhaps stamped even upon the infant visage. Or she formed her conclusion merely from the circumstances. No Egyptian woman had any need to expose her child, or would be likely to do so; but it was just what a Hebrew mother, under the cruel circumstances of the time, might have felt herself forced to do. So she drew her conclusion, rapidly and decidedly, as is the way of woman.

Vers. 7—9.—**Then said his sister.** Miriam had watched to some purpose. She had seen everything—she had drawn near as she beheld the "maid" go down to the water's edge, and take the ark out. She had heard the words of the princess; and thereupon she promptly spoke—**"Shall I go and call thee a nurse of the Hebrew women?"** No doubt, all had been prepared beforehand by the mother, who had selected the place and time of the expo-sure from a knowledge of the habits and character of the princess, had set her daughter to watch, and—so far as was possible—in-structed her what she was to say. But Miriam at least carried out the instructions given her with excellent judgment and tact. She did not speak too soon, nor too late. She did not say a word too much, nor too little. "Surely," exclaimed the princess, "this is one of the Hebrews' children." "Shall I fetch thee then a Hebrew mother to nurse him? is the re-joinder. Egyptians, it is implied, cannot properly nurse Hebrews—cannot know how they ought to be treated ; an Egyptian nurse would mismanage the boy—shall I fetch one of his own nation? And the princess, feeling all the force of the reasoning, answers in one short pregnant word—"Go." "Yes," she means, "do so; that will be best." And then the result follows—**"The maid (Miriam) went and called the child's mother."** So the scheming of the loving mother, and the skilful performance of the part assigned her by the clever sister, were crowned with success—

Moses' life was saved, and yet he was not separated from his natural guardian, nor given over to the tender mercies of strangers : the child went back to his own home, to his own apartment, to his own cradle ; continued to be nourished by his own mother's milk ; and received those first impressions, which are so indelibly impressed upon the mind, in a Hebrew family. **Pharaoh's daughter said, "Take this child away, and nurse it for me."** "Take him with you—take him to your own home for a while—and there nurse him *for me*, as long as he needs nursing." And to mark that he is mine, and not yours—to silence inquiry—to stop the mouths of informers—**"I will give thee thy wages."** Jochebed was more than content, and "**took the child and nursed it.**"

Ver. 10.—**The child grew.** Compare Gen. xxi. 8, where the full phrase is used—"The child grew, *and was weaned*." Jochebed had saved her son's life by a transfer of her mother's right in him to Pharaoh's daughter. She had received him back, merely as a hired nurse, to suckle him. When the time came, probably at the end of the second year, for him to be weaned, she was bound, whatever the sufferings of her heart may have been, to give him up—to restore him to her from whom she had received him, as a child put out to nurse. And we see that she made no attempt to escape her obligations. No sooner was the boy weaned, than "**she brought him unto Pharaoh's daughter**"—as it would seem, of her own accord. **And he became her son.** There is no evidence that formal "adoption" was a custom of the Egyptians ; and probably no more is here meant than that the princess took the child into her family, and brought him up as if he had been her son, giving him all the privileges of a son, together with such an education as a princess's son usually received. We obtain the best general idea of what such an education was from the words of St. Stephen (Acts vii. 21)—"Now Moses was learned in all the wisdom of the Egyptians." This "wisdom," though not perhaps very deep, was multiform and manifold. It included orthography, grammar, history, theology, medicine, arithmetic, geometry, astronomy, and engineering. Education began, as in most countries, with orthography and grammar. The hieroglyphical system was probably not taught, and the knowledge of it remained a special privilege of the priest-class : but the cursive character, known as the

hieratic, was generally studied, and all tolerably educated persons could read it and write it. Style was cultivated, and though no great progress was made in the graces of finished composition, the power of expressing thought and relating facts in a simple and perspicuous prose was acquired by the greater number. Much attention was paid to letter-writing ; and models of business and other letters were set before the pupil as patterns which he was to follow. By the more advanced, poetry was read, and poetic composition occasionally practised. Arithmetic and geometry, up to a certain point, were studied by all ; and a plain morality was inculcated. But history, theology, astronomy, medicine, and engineering, were viewed as special studies, to be pursued by those intended for certain professions, rather than as included within the curriculum of an ordinary education ; and it may well be doubted whether Moses' attention was much directed to any of them. He *may* indeed have been initiated into the mysteries, and in that case would have come to understand the esoteric meaning of the Egyptian myths, and of all that most revolts moderns in the Egyptian religion. But, on the whole, it is most probable that he was rather trained for active than for speculative life, and received the education which fitted men for the service of the State, not that which made them dreamers and theorists. His great praise is, that "he was mighty in words and deeds" (Acts, l.s.c.) ; and he was certainly anything rather than a recluse student. We should do wrong to regard him as either a scientific man or a philosopher. His genius was practical ; and his education was of a practical kind—such as fitted him to become the leader of his people in a great emergency, to deal on equal terms with a powerful monarch, and to guide to a happy conclusion the hazardous enterprise of a great national migration. **And she called his name Moses.** The Egyptian form of the name was probably Mesu, which signifies "born, brought forth, child," and is derived from a root meaning "to produce," "draw forth." Egyptian has many roots common to it with Hebrew, whereof this is one. The princess's play upon words thus admitted of being literally rendered in the Hebrew—"she called his name Mosheh (drawn forth) ; because, she said, I drew him forth (*meshithi-hu*) from the water." Mesu is found in the monuments as an Egyptian name under the nineteenth dynasty

HOMILETICS.

Vers. 1.—2.—§ 1. *The birth of Moses.* In the providence of God, great men are raised up from time to time, for the express object of working out his purposes. A great task is before them, but there is often nothing peculiar, nothing striking, in their birth or parentage. They come into the world with as little commotion, as little *éclat*, as other children. True history admits this. Legendary history conceals it, denies it, makes up a series of extraordinary events anterior to the birth, which shadow forth the coming greatness of the mighty one, and warn the world what to expect of him. The legends attaching to Cyrus, to Romulus, to Pericles (Herod. vi. 131) are cases in point. Contrast with such legends the extreme simplicity of vers. 1, 2;— "There went a man of the house of Levi, and took to wife a daughter of Levi; and the woman conceived and bare a son." Here is the founder of the Jewish nation, the originator of its independence, its lawgiver, historian, prophet, for the first time introduced to our notice; and not one word is said to exalt him, to challenge to him special attention, to show that he is the foremost man of his age, greater than Pentaour the poet, or Seti, or Rameses. His father and mother not even named—"a man"—"a daughter of Levi"—no rank assigned them, no epithet used— nothing recorded but the bare facts: a marriage, a birth, the child a male child, a son! Here at length a note is struck, which wakes a responsive echo in the heart of the reader. The last verse of ch. i. had told him of the barbarous edict issued by the cruel despot who wielded the sceptre of Egypt, and his interest is awakened for the poor babe born under such circumstances. Will he perish at once, or will he escape? Can it be possible to elude or defy the express order of an absolute monarch? And if so, how? The sequel shows, relating as it does his escape from death through the faithful, bold, and loving action of his mother. (See below, p. 27.)

Ver. 2.—§ 2. *The beauty of Moses.* Moses was "a goodly child"—beautiful to look upon—"fair to God," or "exceeding fair," as St. Stephen expresses it (Acts vii. 20). Though beauty be but "skin-deep," and if unaccompanied by loveliness of character is apt to be a snare and a curse, yet, in its degree, and rightly employed, it must be regarded as a blessing. The beauty of Old-Testament saints is often mentioned. Moses was "goodly," David "ruddy and of a beautiful countenance" (1 Sam. xvi. 12), Daniel "fair and well-favoured" (Dan. i. 4, 15), Esther "fair and beautiful" (Esth. ii. 7); Solomon was comely and "the chiefest among ten thousand" (Cant. v. 10); One greater than Solomon was "fairer than the children of men" (Ps. xlv. 2). It is an affectation to ignore beauty, and the influence which it gives. Those who possess it should be taught that they are answerable for it, as for other gifts, and are bound to use it to God's glory. Esther's example may help them in the details of conduct.

Vers. 3—9.—§ 3. *The escape of Moses.* The escape of Moses teaches three things especially—1. God's over-ruling providence, and his power to make wicked men work out his will; 2. The blessing that rests upon a mother's faithful love and care; and 3. The fact that natural virtue is acceptable in God's sight.

I. GOD'S OVER-RULING PROVIDENCE turned the cruel king's edict to the advantage of the child whom he designed for great things. Had it not been for the edict, Moses would never have been exposed, and Pharaoh's daughter would probably never have seen him. Had she not come down to the river when she did—had any little circumstance occurred to prevent her, as might easily have happened, the child might have died of hunger or exposure before she saw it, or might have been found by an unfriendly Egyptian and thrown from the ark into the water. Moreover, had the child not happened to be in tears when she opened the ark, it might not have moved her compassion, or at any rate not have so stirred it as to make her take the boy for her son. In any of these contingencies, Moses, even if saved by some further device of his mother's, would not have had the education which alone fitted him to be the nation's leader and guide, nor the familiarity with court life which enabled him to stand up boldly before the Pharaoh of his time and contend with him as an equal. Thus Pharaoh's pet weapon, the edict, was turned against himself, and brought about that Exodus of the Israelites which he was so anxious to hinder (ch. i. 10). It was an aggravation of his punishment that the hand by which his designs were frustrated was that of his own daughter, who unwittingly preserved the child which, of all others, he was most concerned to destroy.

II. GOD'S BLESSING ON A MOTHER'S FAITHFUL LOVE AND CARE. "By *faith* Moses, when he was born, was hid three months of his parents" (Heb. xi. 23). Disobedience to the edict of the king would in Egypt, if detected, have been punished either by death or mutilation. Amram and Jochebed, but especially Jochebed, who must have been the main agent in the concealment, braved these penalties—did not allow their fear of them to influence their conduct—had *faith* in God that he would, somehow or other, give success to their endeavours to preserve their child, and either save them from punishment or reward them in another world. And it was done to them according as they believed. The concealment of the birth was undetected for the long space of three months—the ark was placed, no one perceiving, among the flags at the edge of the river—the daughter of Pharaoh made her appearance at the time expected "had compassion" on the babe—accepted without hesitation Miriam's suggestion that she should fetch a nurse—accepted without demur or suspicion the mother as the nurse—gave him back to her care for a space of nearly two years—and finally assigned the child the highest position possible, almost that of a prince of the blood royal—allowed him to be called and considered her son—and had him educated accordingly. Jochebed's utmost hope had probably been to save her child's life. God's blessing brought it to pass that she not only obtained that result, but procured him the highest social rank and the best possible cultivation of all his powers, whether of mind or body. Mothers should lay this lesson to heart, and—whatever danger threatens their children—hope for the best, plan for the best, work for the best; they may not always, like Jochebed, find all their plans crowned with success; but they may trust God to bless their endeavours in his own way and in his own good time, if only they be made in faith, and with due submission of their own wills to his.

III. NATURAL VIRTUE ACCEPTABLE IN GOD'S SIGHT. There runs through both the Old and the New Testament a continual protest against the view that God is "a respecter of persons" in the sense of confining his favour to those who have been brought by the appointed mode into actual covenant with him. The lesson is taught with frequent iteration, that "in every nation he that feareth God and worketh righteousness is accepted with him" (Acts x. 35). Here it is an Egyptian—Pharaoh's daughter—that is evidently regarded favourably. Elsewhere it is Rahab of Jericho, or Ruth the Moabitess, or Araunah the Jebusite, or Darius the Mede, or Cyrus the Persian, or Artaxerxes, or the Syro-Phœnician woman, or Cornelius the centurion—all of whom are examples of the same universal law, which is, that God looks graciously upon all his creatures, and accepts every sincere effort towards good that is made by any of them. In his house are "many mansions"—in his future kingdom are many gradations. No one is shut out of his kingdom by the circumstances of his birth or profession. Let a man but seek honestly to do his will according to his lights, and persevere to the end, he will obtain acceptance, whatever the belief in which he has been brought up, and whatever his professed religion. His profession will not save him; but his love of goodness, his efforts to do what is right, his earnest cleaving to truth, and right, and virtue, will be accepted, through the merits of Christ, and counted to him for righteousness. Man may be very far gone from his original perfectness; but he was made in God's image—he has an instinctive sense of right and wrong. When he refuses the evil and chooses the good—whether he be in covenant with God or out of covenant—his conduct is pleasing and acceptable for Christ's sake, who has enlightened him and sustained him, and enabled him to do his good works, and presents them to the Father and obtains for them acceptance through his merits. Pharaoh's daughter stands to us here as a type of the heathen world—a world lying in wickedness, but still salvable, still on the verge of salvation—she has the approval of the writer, and of the Holy Spirit, who inspired him—she had only to continue to act compassionately, kindly—according to her lights, rightly—and she was secure of final acceptance by him who "judges the folk righteously, and governs all the nations upon earth" (Ps. lxvii. 4). We hear much in these days of God's supposed exclusiveness and favouritism. Scripture does not sanction any such views. He is there presented to us as "no respecter of persons," but "a rewarder of them that diligently seek him" (Heb. xi. 6).

Ver. 10.—§ 4. *The education of Moses.* Education is to fit us for the battle of life. The first and most important point is that a child be "virtuously brought up to lead a godly life." In Egypt morality was highly regarded; and some have gone so far as to say that "the laws of the Egyptian religion"—in respect of morality at any rate—

" fell short in nothing of the teachings of Christianity " (see Brugsch, 'History of Egypt,' vol. i. p. 20). This is, no doubt, an over-statement; but it is the fact, that correct and elevated ideas on the subject of morality were entertained by the Egyptian sages, and inculcated on the young by Egyptian teachers. To " give bread to the hungry, drink to the thirsty, to clothe the naked, set the wanderer in his path, resist the oppressor, and put a stop to violence," were regarded as the first elements of duty, the very alphabet of morality, which the most ignorant was expected to know and practise. To the more advanced such counsels as the following were given :—" If thou art become great after thou hast been humble, and if thou hast amassed riches after poverty, and art come to be the first man of thy city; if thou art known for thy wealth, and hast become a great lord : let not thy heart grow proud because of thy riches; for it is God who has given them to thee." " Despise not another who is as thou wast; be towards him as towards thine equal." " Happiness makes one content with any abode ; but a small disgrace darkens the life of a great man." " Good words shine more than the emerald which the hand of the slave finds among a heap of pebbles." " The wise man is satisfied with what he knows; content dwells in his heart, and his lips speak words that are good." " The son who accepts the words of his father will grow old in consequence; for obedience is of God, disobedience is hateful to God." " Let thy heart wash away the impurity of thy mouth : fulfil the word of thy master." Moses in the household of a virtuous Egyptian princess, the wife probably of a respected official, would be guarded from corrupting sights and sounds, would hear none but " good words," would learn courtesy, good manners, politeness, affability, gentlemanly ease ; while at the same time he would have inculcated upon him the duties of activity, diligence, truthfulness, benevolence, consideration for others, temperance, purity, courage. The peculiar circumstances of his position, as a foreigner, a foundling, a mere adopted child, would lay him open to many a reproach and innuendo on the part of those who were jealous of his good-fortune. In this way his path would be beset with difficulties, which would furnish the necessary discipline that might otherwise have been lacking to one brought up by a tender and indulgent mistress who assumed towards him the attitude of a mother. He would learn the virtues of reticence and self-control. As he grew to manhood, active duties would no doubt be assigned to him—he would have to exercise a certain amount of authority in the household, to undertake the management of this or that department, and thus acquire experience in the direction and government of men. Altogether, it is easy to see that the position wherein by God's providence he was placed would furnish an excellent training for the part which he was to be called upon to play, would naturally tend to make him at once outwardly gentle and inwardly firm and self-reliant; at once bold to rebuke kings and patient to govern a stiff-necked and refractory people.

To the moral training thus furnished was added a mental training, on which we have already enlarged. Book-learning is of little use towards the management of men. But when it is superadded to a good practical education, which has already given active habits and facility in dealing with all the various circumstances of life, it adds a grace and dignity to its possessor which are far from contemptible. Moses, without his Egyptian " learning," might have led his people out of Egypt and conducted them safely to Palestine; but he would have lost his most glorious titles and offices; he would scarcely have been the great legislator that he was; he could certainly not have been the great historian, or the great poet. Moses, to obtain the knowledge and the powers that he shows in his writings, must have been during his youth a most diligent student. In this respect he is a pattern to all the young, and most especially to those high-placed youths who are too apt to think that their wealth and rank put them above the necessity of hard work and diligent application. The truth is, that such a position lays its holder under a special obligation to diligence. " Noblesse oblige." Those who are highly placed, and will have many eyes on them, should endeavour to make their acquirements such as will bear close scrutiny and observation. " A city that is set on an hill cannot be hid " (Matt. v. 14).

HOMILIES BY VARIOUS AUTHORS.

Vers. 1—11.—*A child of providence.* This section recounts the birth, deliverance, and upbringing at the court of Pharaoh, of the future Deliverer of Israel. In which we have to notice— .

I. AN ACT OF FAITH ON THE PART OF MOSES' PARENTS. The faith of Moses' parents is signalised in the Epistle to the Hebrews (Heb. xi. 23). Observe 1. *The occasion of its trial.* The king's edict threatened the child's life. The case of Moses was peculiar, yet not entirely so. No infancy or childhood but lays a certain strain upon the faith of parents. The bark of a child's existence is so frail, and it sets out amidst so many perils! And we are reminded that this strain is usually more felt by the mother than the father, her affection for her offspring being in comparison deeper and more tender (cf. Is. xlix. 15). It is the *mother* of Moses who does all and dares all for the salvation of her babe. 2. *Its nature.* Both in Old and New Testaments it is connected with something remarkable in the babe's appearance (Acts vii. 20; Heb. xi. 23). Essentially, however, it must have been the same faith as upholds believers in their trials still—simple, strong faith in God, that he would be their Help in trouble, and would protect and deliver the child whom with tears and prayers they cast upon his care. This was sufficient to nerve Jochebed for what she did. 3. *Its working.* Faith wrought with works, and by works was faith made perfect (Jas. ii. 22). (1) It nerved them to disobey the tyrant's edict, and hide the child for three months. Terrible as was this period of suspense, they took their measures with prudence, calmness, and success. Religious faith is the secret of self-collectedness. (2) It enabled them, when concealment was no longer practicable, to make the venture of the ark of bulrushes. The step was bold, and still bolder if, as seems probable, Jochebed put the ark where she did, knowing that the princess and her maidens used that spot as a bathing-place. Under God's secret guidance, she ventured all on the hope that the babe's beauty and helplessness would attract the lady's pity. She would put Pharaoh's daughter as a shield between her child and Pharaoh's mandate. Learn—1. Faith is not inconsistent with the use of means. 2. Faith exhausts all means before abandoning effort. 3. Faith, when all means are exhausted, waits patiently on God. 4. Pious parents are warranted in faith to cast their children on God's care. It was a sore trial to Jochebed to trust her child out of her own arms, especially with that terrible decree hanging over him. But faith enabled her to do it. She believed that God would keep him—would make him his charge—would provide for him,—and in that faith she put the ark among the rushes. Scarcely less faith are parents sometimes called upon to exercise in taking steps of importance for their children's future. Missionaries in India, *e.g.,* parting with their children, sons leaving home, etc. Sorest trial of all, when parents on their deathbeds have to part with little ones, leaving them to care of strangers. Hard, very hard, to flesh and blood; but God lives, God cares, God will provide,—will watch the ark of the little one thus pushed out on the waters of the wide, wide world.

II. AN ACT OF PROVIDENCE ON THE PART OF MOSES' GOD. The faith of Moses' parents met with its reward. Almost "whiles" they were yet "praying" (Dan. ix. 20), their prayers were answered, and deliverance was vouchsafed. In regard to which observe—1. *How various are the instrumentalities employed by Providence in working out its purposes.* A king's edict, a mother's love, a babe's tears, a girl's shrewdness, the pity of a princess, Egyptian customs, etc. 2. *How Providence co-operates with human freedom in bringing about desired results.* The will of God was infallibly accomplished, yet no violence was done to the will of the agents. In the most natural way possible, Moses was rescued by Pharaoh's daughter, restored to his mother to nurse, adopted by the princess as her son, and afterwards educated by her in a way suitable to his position. Thus was secured for Moses—(1) Protection. (2) A liberal education. (3) Experience of court-life in Egypt. 3. *How easily the plans of the wicked can be turned against themselves.* Pharaoh's plans were foiled by his own daughter. His edict was made the means of introducing to his own court the future deliverer of the race he meant to destroy. God takes the wicked in their own net (Ps. ix. 15, 16). 4. *How good, in God's providence, is frequently brought out of evil.* The people might well count the issuing of this edict as the darkest hour of their night—the point of lowest ebb in their fortunes.   Yet see what God brought out of it !   The deliverance of a Moses—the first turning of the tide in the direction of help.   What poor judges we are of what is really for or against us ! 5. *How greatly God often exceeds our expectations in the deliverances he sends.*   He does for us above what we ask or think.   The utmost Moses' parents dared to pray for was doubtless that his life might be preserved.   That he should be that very day restored to his mother, and nursed at her bosom; that he should become the son of Pharaoh's daughter; that he should grow to be great, wise, rich, and powerful—this was felicity they had not dared to dream of.   But this is God's way.   He exceeds our expectations.   He gives to faith more than it looks for.   So in Redemption, we are not only saved from perishing, but receive "everlasting life" (John iii. 16)—honour, glory, reward.—J. O.

Vers. 1—9.—*The infancy of Moses.*   I. WE HAVE, IN THIS EXPERIENCE OF THE INFANT AND HIS MOTHER, A MOST AFFECTING ILLUSTRATION OF THE MISERABLE STATE TO WHICH ISRAEL HAD BEEN REDUCED.   We come down from the general statement of the first chapter to the particular instance of the second.   Moses was born, in all likelihood, just at the very height of Pharaoh's exasperation, and when the command of ch. i. 22 was in process of being carried out.   His servants, ever becoming more savage and brutal in disposition, as the very consequence of the harshness and severity they had daily to exercise, would be going about, watching the midwives and hanging round the abodes of the Israelites to listen for the first faint cry of the newborn child.   In such circumstances, the work of the midwives most likely fell into abeyance; for the midwife became the unwilling herald of the murderer. Thus mothers in the crisis of their greatest need might be left without any ministry or sympathy whatever; their greatest safety in solitude, their greatest comfort to know that the newborn infant's existence was utterly unknown to any Egyptian. No hour could well be darker, no circumstances more provocative of despair.   We may depend upon it that God meant much to be suggested to Israel in after generations, by the birth of Moses just at this time.   "In which time Moses was born" (Acts vii. 20). May we not well imagine that when in later years Moses stole away from time to time, out of the splendours and luxuries of his royal home, to spend an hour or two with his own mother, she would tell him that, for all his relation to Pharaoh's daughter and all his privileges about the court, he had been once, with many another helpless babe, the object of Pharaoh's bitterest animosity.   Things were in a very bad state when Moses was born.   Bad for Israel in point of present suffering; bad for Egypt itself, seeing what a merciless and unscrupulous man sat upon the throne; bad for the prospects of Moses and all the coming generation.   And so we cannot but feel that the whole world was in a very bad state when Jesus was born.   He was exposed to the risk of a Herod; and Herod was but one of many like-minded oppressors.   And worse than any cruelty and oppression from without was the state of the people in their hearts.   Jew and Gentile were alike utterly departed from God.   Romans, ch. i., does as much as human language can do to give us the measure of the universal corruption and degradation. We shall do well to mark in the New Testament the many things that show what unregenerate, vile, and apostate hearts were those with whom Christ and his apostles came in contact.   Then, when we have the dark, repulsive picture of the times well before us, we may imitate Stephen, and say—"in which time Christ was born."

II. WE HAVE A MOST AFFECTING INSTANCE OF THE PECULIAR CARES AND SORROWS WHICH BELONG TO THE MATERNAL RELATION.   "When she saw him that he was a goodly child, she hid him three months."   This can hardly mean that if he had been a puny dwarfling, she would have cast him aside as not worth anxiety.   We know that it is precisely the weakest, the least attractive to a stranger's eye, who most draws forth the mother's love; thus furnishing a sweet suggestion of that Divine affection which yearns, with the greatest tenderness, over those who may seem to others hopelessly lost.   But as Moses was a goodly child, she was bound by this fact to give all available chances for the promise that was in him.   Who can tell what anxieties and alarms filled her thoughts during these terrible three months, and how often she skirted the extreme edge of disaster, always feeling that with each succeeding week her task became more difficult?   How keen must have been the struggle before she brought her mind to face the dread necessity of exposure! We can imagine her being driven to decisive action at last, by seeing the agonies of some neighbouring mother, as the servants of Pharaoh discover her child and ruthlessly extinguish its delicate life. Here, in the sufferings of the mother of Moses, and of all the rest whom she but represents, we have something like the full significance set before us of that curse which first rested upon Eve. There may have been a measure of truth in what the midwives said concerning the ease with which the mothers in Israel had been delivered; but not so were they going to escape the curse. Their trouble only began when the man-child was born into the world. Not to them at least was the birth to be an occasion of joy, but the beginning of unspeakable solicitude (Matt. ii. 16—18; xxiv. 19; John xvi. 21). This poor woman exposed her tender infant, not because she was callous of heart, unnatural, and lacking in love; but because of the very intensity of her love. So wretched had the state of Israel become that its infants found no place so dangerous as the place that should have been safest—the warm bosom of the mother.

III. We have a most impressive illustration of womanly sympathy. The Scriptures, true to their character as being the fullest revelation not less of human nature than of the Divine nature, abound in illustrations of the demonstrativeness of womanly sympathy. To go no further afield, we have such an illustration in the previous chapter (the conduct of the midwives). But here there is an instance which is peculiarly impressive. It was the daughter of Pharaoh who showed the much-needed sympathy. She knew well how the babe came to be forsaken, and how, though it was forsaken, this waterproof ark had been so carefully provided for it. Somewhere in Israel she could see a mother anxiously speculating on the fate of this child; and she knew that all the strange discovery she had made came out of the stern, unrelenting policy of her own father. Some women indeed in her circumstances would have said, "Sad it may be that an infant should thus perish, but my father knows best. Leave it there." But compassion rose to flood-tide in her heart, and choked all thoughts of selfish policy, if they even so much as entered into her mind. Jesus says to his disciples, concerning one of the difficulties and pains of discipleship, that a man's foes shall be they of his own household. And the principle seems to hold good in the carrying out of worldly plans. If a man wants to be downright selfish, he also may find foes in his own household, not to be conquered, bribed, or persuaded. Pharaoh thinks he is closing-up the energies of Israel in a most effective fashion; but his own daughter opens a little window only large enough for an infant three months old to get through it, and by this in the course of time all the cunning and cruelty of her father are made utterly void.

IV. We have, in all these events connected with the infancy of Moses, a critical illustration of the reality of special providence. Notice that there is not a word about God in the narrative; indeed, he is not mentioned as having anything directly to do with Moses, until the interview, long after, at Horeb. There is plenty of mention of human beings, in the play of their affections, their desires, and their ingenuity. The mother, the child, the sister, the nurse, the mother by adoption, all come before us, but there is no mention of God. Yet who does not feel that the Lord of Israel, unmentioned though he be, is yet the central, commanding, and controlling figure in all that takes place! It was he who caused Moses to be born at that particular time. It was he who sheltered the infant during these three months, when perhaps others were being snatched away in close proximity on the right hand and the left. It was he who put into the heart of the mother to dispose of her child in this particular way, and taught her to make such a cradle as surely never was made before. It was he who gave the sister wisdom to act as she did—a wisdom possibly beyond her years. It was he who turned the feet of Pharaoh's daughter (of her and no one else) in that particular direction, and not in some other. All his excellent working in this matter is hidden from those who do not wish to see it; but how manifest it is, how wonderful and beautiful, to those whose eyes he himself has opened! How different is his working here from the working of the *Deus ex machinâ* in the tanglements and complications of classical fable. There, when things get to all appearance hopelessly disordered, a deity comes in visible form and puts them right. But in this real deliverance of Moses, the God who is the only true God works in a far different way. He works through natural means, and so silently, so unobtrusively, that if men wise in their own conceits are determined to ignore his presence, there is nothing to force it upon them.

V. This narrative, along with that of the midwives, has A VERY SPECIAL BEARING ON THE CAPABILITIES AND DUTIES OF WOMEN. We have here in the compass of some five-and-twenty verses a most encouraging instance of what women are able to do. So far, in this book of the Exodus, God is seen exalting the woman and abasing the man. Man, so far as he appears, is set before us a weak, thwarted creature; cruel enough in disposition, but unable to give his cruelty effect. Even a king with all his resources is baffled. But weak women set themselves to work, to shelter a helpless infant, and they succeed. Here as on other occasions the hand of God is manifest, taking the weak things of the world to confound the strong. What a lesson, what an appeal and warning to women! We are all only too readily inclined to say, "What can I do?"— women perhaps more than others, because of their inability to share in the bustle and strain of public life. Think then of what God enabled these women to do, simply following out the dictates of natural affection and pity. They did far more than they were conscious of. Might not women ask very earnestly if they are doing anything like what they ought to do, and have the opportunity to do, in bringing up children in the nurture and admonition of the Lord? Christian women, those who are themselves new creatures in Christ Jesus, able to have all the love and wisdom and every spiritual grace that belongs to the new creature, might do a work for the world, compared with which the work of these women whom we have been considering would look a small matter indeed.—Y.

Vers. 1—10.—*By works was faith made perfect.* Bad times; harsh decrees against the Israelites; doubts and misgivings which must have occurred to one in Amram's position; a hard *experience* and a dark *prospect.* Still the man believed in God, remembered the promises, and knew that God also must remember them; did not see *how* they were to be fulfilled, but was content to do his own duty and leave all else to God. See—

I. How HIS FAITH WAS MANIFESTED BY HIS WORKS. We have—1. *His. marriage.* Under all the circumstances he might well have been excused if he had decided to remain unmarried. Such advice as that of St. Paul to the Corinthians (1 Cor. vii. 25—28) would seem to apply to such a time. The matter, however, was not to be so easily settled. *Faith* will not permit marriage without prudence and due forethought, but neither will *Faith* permit abstinence from marriage merely because marriage will bring "trouble in the flesh." Improvidence and a too-calculating abstinence both prompted by selfishness. Faith looks forward and looks around, but she looks *up* also, and is guided by the result of that upward look. Theories of political economists, etc., are not to be despised, none the less Faith will act—her actions *regulated* to some extent, but not *fettered,* by calculation. Paul's teaching is to be qualified by Amram's example; Amram knew the times, foresaw the rocks ahead, yet he "took to wife a daughter of Levi." 2. *His choice of a wife.* Clear from narrative that the woman was the man's true helpmeet. Of the same family, they must have been well acquainted, and her conduct shows that her faith equalled his. Faith not only prompted marriage, but also directed choice. Amram and his wife did not marry merely for the sake of marrying, but "for the mutual society, help, and comfort which the one ought to have of the other both in prosperity and adversity." 3. *Conduct in the face of trial.* The two, man and wife, now as one : though the woman comes to the fore, no doubt her faith represents that of both. Aaron and Miriam, reared before the trial reached its height; then "a goodly child," just at the season of greatest danger. Note the action prompted by faith; how different from that which might have been suggested by fatalism. Fatalism would have said, "Let things be; if he must be killed he must." Cf. Eastern proverb, "On two days it skills not to avoid death, the appointed and the unappointed day." Faith, on the other hand, is ready and courageous, holding that God helps those who help themselves, or rather that he helps them *through* self-help. But notice—

II. How THIS LIVING FAITH WAS APPROVED AND JUSTIFIED. 1. The conduct of the wife justified her husband's choice. She *was* the helpmeet he hoped she would be. God gave her wisdom to comfort and strengthen him; *His* blessing added the third strand to that threefold cord which is not quickly broken. 2. Their united efforts for the preservation of their children were crowned by God with complete success. [Illustrate from the history—all happening, all *ordained* to happen, just as they hoped.] They had prepared, by carrying out the plan which faith prompted, a channel through which God's gracious and ready help might reach them; and God used the channel which they had prepared. The whole narrative shows how faith, when it is living, proves its life by works, and how in response to a living faith God shows that he is a living God. If Amram had walked by sight and not by faith, Moses might never have been born, Jochebed never have been married; as it was he walked by faith and not by sight, doing his duty and trusting God, and through him came redemption unto Israel—the child "*taken out of*" the water became the leader who should "*take*" his people "*out of*" bondage.—G.

Vers. 1—10.—*A picture of true faith.* I. WHAT TRUE FAITH IS. 1. There was obedience to a Divine impulse: her heart was appealed to, she saw he was a goodly child, and she hid him three months. She read in the child's appearance an intimation of future greatness, and that God did not mean him to die in accordance with the king's commandment. The work of faith begins in obeying the Spirit's prompting in the heart. 2. She was not daunted by difficulties. She might have asked what could this temporary concealment do but only prolong her misery. Faith is content if it has light but for one step. 3. Faith is fertile in expedients. The safety which is no longer to be had in the home may be found on the waters. 4. When it has done all, it waits, as with girded loins, for the dawning light. Miriam stood afar off.
II. HOW GOD JUSTIFIES OUR TRUST. When we have done all, and, knowing it is nothing, look unto him, then God appears for us. 1. The child's life was saved. 2. He was given back into his mother's arms. 3. The very might which before was raised to slay was now used to guard him. 4. He was freed from the unhappy lot of his countrymen, and set among the princes of the land. Our trust prepares a place where God may manifest himself. He "is able to do exceeding abundantly above all that we ask or think."—U.

Vers. 1—10.—*The child of the water.* "And she called his name Moses ... water."— Exod. ii. 10. Save Jesus, Moses is the greatest name in history. Compare with it Mahomet, or even that of Paul. As the founder of the Jewish religion—under God— his influence is felt to-day, not only by 6,000,000 Jews, but throughout the Christian Church. Here is the beginning of his career. This mighty stream of influence we can trace to its source; not like the Nile, whose origin is still in debate, a mystery. The text gives the name and its reason. The derivation is either Hebrew, and then= "Drawing out," so designating the act of the princess; or Egyptian, and then= "Saved from the water." The name a memorial of salvation. Happy, when children bearing distinguished names, shame them not in the after-years. We treat the subject in the order of the story: so its suggestiveness for heart and life will appear.
I. THE FAMILY OF THE CHILD. Amram and Jochebed, the father and mother; Miriam, much older, and Aaron, three years older, than Moses. Note: *Moses owed*— 1. *Little to his family.* Look at ver. 1. But the pre-eminence of Levi was not yet. The tribe did not make Moses; rather Moses (with Miriam and Aaron) the tribe. "Blue blood?" Yes! and No! There is a sense in which we may be proud of ancestry, a sense in which not. What to me that I descend from a Norman baron? Everything to me that I come from able, gifted, saintly parentage. See Cowper on "My Mother's Picture," lines 108—112. 2. *Little to his home.* Only a slave hut; the scene of toil, poverty, suffering, fear. Out of it brought one thing—sympathy with suffering. 3. *Little to his parents.* Biographers usually give us the attributes and history of ancestors, and show how they account for the career of the child. Nothing of that here. Even the names of the parents do not appear. Note omission in ver. 1. "A man," etc. "A daughter," etc. No doubt here a mental and moral heritage; but little training, because little opportunity. Generally, there is, under this head, a lesson of encouragement for those who have, or fancy they have, hard beginnings in life. Some of earth's noblest have risen out of disadvantage.
II. THE APPEARANCE OF THE CHILD. For traditions of predictions of his birth see Jos. Antiq. ii. 9. 2—4. Moses was—1. *No common child.* Scepticism objects that

Miriam and Aaron are not mentioned in vers. 1, 2 by name. But the motive and impulse of inspiration are to be taken into account. The object was to give the event which led to the Exodus, and to the constitution of the Jewish Church. From this point of view interest concentrates on Moses. Hence we infer the extraordinary greatness of his character and career. 2. *Born at a critical moment.* See Acts vii. 20. So the Jewish proverb: "When the tale of bricks is doubled, then comes Moses." Note:—(1) At the moment of deepest darkness God sends deliverance. (2) When he wants instruments he creates them. 3. *Of no common beauty.* Not only in his mother's eyes, which would be natural enough, but absolutely. See Acts vii. 20, as well as Exod. ii. 2; and for interesting illustration, Jos. Antiq. ii. 9. 6. All this the promise of a higher beauty of character that opened out with the years.

III. THE DANGER OF THE CHILD. The child born to great issues, and therefore must run the gauntlet of peril. Compare Jesus under the edict of Herod with Moses under that of Pharaoh. No sooner born than a battle for life. The two only infants, but full of possibilities. Pharaoh! the babe you may crush; hereafter the man shall ruin you. A seeming law in the case, to which witness the legends of many nations, *e.g.* Romulus and Remus, Cyrus, King Arthur.

IV. LOVE FENCING FOR THE CHILD. 1. *Of the mother.* (1) Concealing. Heb. xi. 23. How by faith? Went right on in the discharge of *common duty* to the child, not turning aside to observe the king's commandment. Then the love went to the other extreme :—(2) Exposing. Here narrate the facts, for which see the text and commentary above; *e.g.* impossibility of longer concealing a growing child, form and material of the ark, laid in a place of comparative safety, "in the flags" at "the lip of the river," the elements of danger—starvation, discovery—*not* crocodiles on the Tanitic branch of the river. But observe the feeling behind the facts. A mother's despair becoming hope, and then faith; but a faith *provident and workful*, for, living in the neighbourhood, she could not fail to know where the childless (so says tradition) princess was wont to bathe. *Just there* she placed the child. 2. *Of the sister.* Imagine her anxiety! The mother-heart in every girl. She was (1) Watchful: over the ark, against an enemy, for the princess; (2) Active; (3) Clever, full of resource; (4) Successful; (5) Became eminent; a prophetess, Ex. xv. 20. One of *the* three deliverers, Micah vi. 4. The adored of the people, Num. xii. 10—15. In childhood are laid the foundations of character. 3. *Of God.* Before all, over all, and behind all! Love to the child, sister, parents, to Israel, and to the world to be blest through him.

V. THE DELIVERANCE OF THE CHILD. This of God, but note the part played by each of the following instruments :—1. *The princess.* Note the independent status of an Egyptian princess, the custom then of bathing in the open river, the probable locality, Zoan (Ps. lxxviii. 43), that compassion was inculcated by the Egyptian religion, and the probable application to her of Acts x. 35. 2. *The sister.* 3. *The mother.* 4. *The princess* again; and possible lifelong parting from the mother.

Finally, observe—1. *The deliverances of God are wonderful.* Only *one* person in all the land of Egypt that could save Moses, and *she* came to the river. 2. *The object of God's deliverances does not centre and rest on the delivered.* It passes beyond: Moses for Israel, Israel for the Messiah, Messiah for the world. So Abraham, Gen. xii. 2. So with elect spirits and elect nations in all ages. None for himself. 3. *So is it with the great salvation.* Wonderful! The benediction thereof unresting, passing on from the first recipients. 4. *But the retributions of God are just as marvellous.* Moses was to be the ruin of the house of Pharaoh, and deservedly so. But in the providence of God the tyrant is made to pass by and even protect the instrument of his future punishment.—R.

EXPOSITION.

Vers. 11—15.—FIRST ATTEMPT OF MOSES TO DELIVER HIS NATION, AND ITS FAILURE. After Moses was grown up—according to the tradition accepted by St. Stephen (Acts vii. 23), when he was "full forty years old"

—having become by some means or other acquainted with the circumstances of his birth, which had most probably never been concealed from him, he determined to "go out" to his brethren, see with his own eyes what their treatment was, and do his best to alleviate it. He had as yet no Divine mission, no command from God to act as he did, but only a natural sympathy with his people, and a feeling perhaps that in his position he was bound, more than any one else, to make some efforts to ameliorate what must have been generally known to be a hard lot. It is scarcely likely that he had formed any definite plans. How he should act would depend on what he should see. Thus far, his conduct deserves nothing but praise. It only perhaps a little surprises us (if St. Stephen's tradition accords with fact) that he did not earlier in his life take some steps in the direction here indicated. We are bound to recollect, however, that we know very little of the restraints under which he would have been laid—whether a severe law of etiquette, or the commands of his benefactress, may not have hampered him, and caused the long delay which strikes us as strange. Living with the court—in Tanis probably—he would have been required to make a strong effort—to break through an established routine, and strike out for himself a new and unheard-of course, if he quitted the princess's household to make a tour of inspection among the enslaved Hebrews. The author of the Epistle to the Hebrews seems to consider that his act in "going out" to "look upon the burdens" of his people involved a renunciation of his court life—a refusal to be called any more the son of Pharaoh's daughter (Heb. xi. 24); a casting-in of his lot with his brethren, so as thenceforth to be a sharer in their afflictions (ib. ver. 24). If this were so, we can well understand a long period of hesitation before the resolve was made to take the course from which there was no retreating.

Ver. 11.—**When Moses was grown.** "When he had become a man of vigour and intelligence" (Kalisch). **He went out.** The expression is emphatic, and accords with the view above exhibited—that a complete change in the life of Moses was now effected, that the court was quitted, with its attractions and its temptations, its riches and its pleasures; and the position of adopted child of a princess forfeited. **He spied an Egyptian smiting a Hebrew.** It is not certain that this was one of the "taskmasters" (ch. i. 11); but most probably he was either a taskmaster, or one of the officers employed by them. Such persons are on the Egyptian monuments represented as armed with long rods, said to be "made of

a tough pliant wood imported from Syria" (Chabas, 'Voyage d'un Égyptien,' p. 119). It was their right to employ their rods on the backs of the idle, a right which was sure to degenerate in many cases into tyrannous and cruel oppression. We may assume that it was an instance of such abuse of power that excited the anger of Moses; "seeing one of them suffer *wrong*, he defended him, and avenged him that was *oppressed*" (Acts vii. 24). For a light fault, or no fault at all, a heavy chastisement was being inflicted.

Ver. 12.—**He looked this way and that way.** Passion did not so move him as to make him reckless. He looked round to see that he was not observed, and then, **when he saw there was no man, slew the Egyptian.** A wrongful act, the outcome of an ardent but undisciplined spirit; not to be placed among the deeds "which history records as noble and magnanimous" (Kalisch), but among those which are hasty and regrettable. A warm sympathetic nature, an indignant hatred of wrong-doing, may have lain at the root of the crime, but do not justify it, though they may qualify our condemnation of it. (See the remarks of St. Augustine quoted by Keil and Delitzsch, 'Commentary on the Pentateuch,' vol. i. p. 451: "I affirm that the man, though criminal and really the offender, ought not to have been put to death by one who had no legal authority to do so. But minds that are capable of virtue often produce vices also, and show thereby for what virtue they would have been best adapted, if they had but been properly trained," etc.) **And hid him in the sand.** There is abundant "sand" in the "field of Zoan," and in all the more eastern portion of the land of Goshen. (See the 'Quarterly Statement of the Palestine Exploration Fund' for July, 1880, p. 140.)

Ver. 13.—**The second day.** *I.e.* "the following day." See Acts vii. 26. **Him that did the wrong.** Literally, "the wicked one." **Wherefore smitest thou thy fellow?** Literally "thy *neighbour*." In interposing here Moses certainly did nothing but what was right. The strife was one in which blows were being exchanged, and it is the duty of everyone in such a case, by persuasion at any rate. to seek to stop the combat.

Ver. 14.—**Who made thee a prince and a judge over us?** It was not his interference now, but his wrongful act of the day before, that exposed Moses to this rebuke. There was no assumption of lordship or of judicial authority in the bare inquiry, "Why smitest thou thy neighbour?" nor in the fuller phrase reported by St. Stephen, "Sirs, ye are brethren. Why do ye wrong one to another?" (Acts vii. 26), unless as coupled with the deed of the preceding day. Thus the violence of to-day renders of no avail the loving persuasion of to-morrow; the influence for good which the education and position of Moses might have enabled him to exercise upon his nation was lost by the very act to which he had been urged by his sympathy with them; it was an act which could be thrown in his teeth, an act which he could not justify, which he trembled to find was known. The retort of the aggressor stopped his mouth at once, and made his interposition valueless.

Ver. 15.—**Pharaoh heard.** If we have been right in supposing the Pharaoh of the original oppression to have been Seti I., the present Pharaoh, from whom Moses flies when he is "full forty years old" (Acts vii. 23), and who does not die till Moses is near eighty, must be his son, the Great Rameses, Rameses II. This prince was associated by his father at the age of ten or twelve (Brugsch, 'History of Egypt,' vol. ii. pp. 24—5), and reigned sixty-seven years, as appears from his monuments. He is the only king of the New Empire whose real reign exceeded forty years, and thus the only monarch who fulfils the conditions required by the narrative of Exodus supplemented by St. Stephen's speech in the Acts. **He sought to slay Moses.** We need not understand from this expression that the Pharaoh's will was thwarted or opposed by anything but the sudden disappearance of Moses. As St. Stephen says (Acts vii. 29), "Then fled Moses *at this saying*," i.e. at the mere words of the aggressor, "Wilt thou slay me as thou didst the

Egyptian?" Moses fled, knowing what he had to expect, quitted Egypt, went to Midian; and the Egyptian monarch "sought to slay him" too late. **The land of Midian** is a somewhat vague expression, for the Midianites were nomads, and at different times occupied distinct and even remote localities. Their principal settlements appear to have been on the eastern side of the Elanitic Gulf (Gulf of Akabah); but at times they extended northwards to the confines of Moab (Gen. xxxvi. 35; Num. xxii. 4, 7, etc.), and westward into the Sinaitic peninsula, which appears to have been "the land of Midian" whereto Moses fled (see below, ch. iii. 1). The Midianites are not expressly mentioned in the Egyptian inscriptions. They were probably included among the Mentu, with whom the Egyptians contended in the Sinaitic region, and from whom they took the copper district north-west of Sinai. **And he sat down by a well.** Rather "and he *dwelt* by *the* well." He took up his abode in the neighbourhood of the principal well belonging to the tract here called Midian. The tract was probably one of no great size, an offshoot of the greater Midian on the other side of the gulf. We cannot identify the well; but it was certainly not that near the town of Modiana, spoken of by Edrisi and Abulfeda, which was in Arabia Proper, on the east of the gulf.

HOMILETICS.

Vers. 11, 12.—§ 1. *Moses as a would-be deliverer.* Moses, as a would-be deliverer, shows us how zeal may outrun discretion. Actuated by deep love for his brethren, he had quitted the court, resigned his high prospects, thrown in his lot with his nation, and "gone out" to see with his own eyes their condition. No doubt he came upon many sights which vexed and angered him, but was able to restrain himself. At last, however, he became witness of a grievous—an extreme—case of oppression. Some Hebrew, we may suppose, weaker than the generality, delicate in constitution or suffering from illness, rested awhile from his weary labour under the scorching sun, and gave himself a few moments of delightful, because rare, repose. But the eye of the taskmaster was on him. Suddenly his rest was interrupted by a shower of severe blows, which were rained pitilessly upon his almost naked frame, raising great wheals, from which the blood streamed down in frequent heavy drops. Moses could no longer contain himself. Pity for the victim and hatred of the oppressor surged up in his heart. "Many a time and oft" had he wished to be a deliverer of his brethren, to revenge their wrongs, to save them from their sufferings. Here was an opportunity to make a beginning. He would save at any rate this one victim, he would punish this one wrongdoer. There was no danger, for no one was looking (ver. 12), and surely the man whom he saved would not betray him. So, having a weapon in his belt, or finding one ready to his hand—a stone, it may be, or a working man's implement— he raised it, and striking a swift strong blow, slew the Egyptian. In thus acting he was doubly wrong. He acted as an avenger, when he had no authority from God or man to be one; and, had he had authority, still he would have inflicted a punishment disproportionate to the offence. Such a beating as he had himself administered the taskmaster may have deserved, but not to be cut off in his sins; not to be sent to his last account without warning, without time even for a repentant thought. The deed done, conscience reasserted herself: it was a deed of darkness; a thing which must be concealed: so Moses dug a hole in the sand, and hid the dreadful evidence of his crime. It does not appear that the man whom he had delivered helped him; he was perhaps too much exhausted with what he had suffered, and glad to creep to his home. Moses, too, returned to his own abode, well satisfied, as it would seem, on the whole, with what he had done. Having struck the blow, and buried the body unseen, he did not fear detection; and he probably persuaded himself that the man deserved his fate. He may have even had self-complacent thoughts, have admired his own courage and strength, and thought how he had at last come to be a deliverer indeed. In reality, however, he had disqualified himself for the office; he had committed a crime which forced him to quit his brethren and fly to a distance, and be thus unable to do anything towards mitigating their sufferings for the space of forty years! Had he been patient, had he been content with remonstrances, had he used his superior strength to rescue the oppressed without injuring the oppressor, he would have shown himself fit to be a deliverer, and God might not improbably have assigned him his mission at once. But his self-willed and wrongful mode of proceeding showed that he needed a long course of discipline before he could properly be entrusted with the difficult task which God designed him to accomplish. Forty years of almost solitary life in the Sinaitic wilderness chastened the hot spirit which was now too wild and untamed for a leader and governor of men.

Vers. 13—14.—§ 2. *Moses as a peacemaker.* A great sin disqualifies a man for many a long year from setting himself up to be a guide and teacher of others. It may at any time be *thrown in his teeth.* Nothing could be better intended than the efforts of Moses, on the day after his crime, to compose the quarrels of his brethren, and set the disputants at one. Nor is he fairly taxable with any want of equity, or even of tact, in the manner in which he set to work. He rebuked "him that did the wrong." His rebuke was mild in character—a mere expostulation; "Wherefore smitest thou," etc. Nay, according to St. Stephen (Acts vii. 26), it was not even an expostulation addressed to an individual, but a general address which avoided the assignment of special blame to either disputant. "Sirs, ye are brethren; why do ye wrong one to another?" Yet it had no effect; it failed utterly. The tables were at once turned on the expostulator by the inquiry, "Who made thee a prince and a judge over us? Intendest thou to slay me as thou didst the Egyptian?" Conscience makes cowards of us all. Moses, hearing this, had no more to say; he had essayed to pluck out the mote from his brother's eye, and behold! the beam was in his own eye. His brethren were quarrelsome and injurious; but he—he was a murderer.

Ver. 15.—§ 3. *Moses as a fugitive.* Men's sins are sure to "find them out." Moses had thought that he would not be detected. He had carefully "looked this way and that way" ere he struck the blow, and had seen "that there was no man." He had at once hidden the body of his victim underground. He had concluded that the Hebrew whom he had delivered from the oppressor would keep silence; if from no other reason, yet at any rate to save himself from being suspected. But the man, it appears, had chattered. Perhaps from no ill motive, but simply from inability to keep a secret. He had told his wife, or his daughter, or his neighbour; and at once "the thing was known." While Moses imagined his deed shrouded in deepest secrecy, it was the general talk. All the Hebrews knew of it; and soon the Egyptians knew also. Presently it came to the ears of the king, whose business it was to punish crime, and who, naturally and rightfully, "sought to slay Moses." But he had fled away; he had put seas and deserts between himself and the royal vengeance; he was a refugee in Midian. So, though he escaped the public execution which Egyptian law awarded to his crime, he had to expiate it by forty years of exile and of hard service, a hireling shepherd tending the flock of another man.

HOMILIES BY VARIOUS AUTHORS.

Vers. 11, 12.—*The choice of Moses.* Underlying this episode of killing the Egyptian there is that crisis in the history of Moses to which reference is made so strikingly in the eleventh of the Hebrews—" By faith Moses, when he was come to years, refused to be called the son of Pharaoh's daughter; choosing rather," etc. (Heb. xi. 24—27). Two views may be taken of the episode. Either, as might be held, the elements of decision were floating in an unfixed state in the mind of Moses, when this event happened, and precipitated a choice; or, what seems more likely, the choice had already been made, and the resolution of Moses already taken, and this was but the first outward manifestation of it. In either case, the act in question was a deliberate committal of himself to his brethren's side—the crossing of the Rubicon, which necessitated thereafter a casting-in of his lot with theirs. View this choice of Moses—

I. As a RESULT OF MENTAL AND MORAL AWAKENING. " When Moses was grown." With years came thought; with thought " the philosophic mind;" with this, power of observation. Moses began to think for himself, to see things with his own eyes. What he saw made evident to him the impossibility of halting longer between two opinions. He had not before felt the same necessity of definitely making up his mind whether he would be Hebrew or Egyptian. He had not seen in the same way the impossibility of retaining a sort of connection with both—sympathising with the Hebrews, yet enjoying Egypt's pleasures. Now there came awakening. The two spheres of life fell apart to his vision in their manifest incongruity—in their painful, and even, in some respects, hideous contrast. He may now be Hebrew *or* Egyptian; he can no longer be *both*. Up to this time choice could be staved off. Now it is forced upon him. To determine now not to choose, would be to choose for Egypt. He knows his duty, and it is for him to decide whether or not he will do it. And such in substance is the effect of moral awakening generally. 1. In most lives there is a time of thoughtlessness, at least of want of serious and independent reflection. It is not at this stage seen why religion should require so *very* decided a choice. God and the world seem not absolute incompatibles. It is possible to serve both; to agree with both. Christ's teaching to the contrary sounds strangely on the ears. 2. But an awakening comes, and it is now seen very clearly that this double service is impossible. The friendship of the world is felt to be enmity with God (Jas. iv. 4). The contrariety, utter and absolute, between what is in the world and love of the Father (John ii. 15) is manifest beyond dispute. Then comes the need for choice. God or the creature; Christ, or the world which crucified him; God's people or the friendship of those who deride and despise them. There is no longer room for dallying. Not to choose is already to have chosen wrongly —to have decided for the world, and rejected Christ.

II. As a VICTORY OVER STRONG TEMPTATION. It was no slight victory over the temptations of his position for Moses to renounce all at the call of duty, and cast in his lot with an oppressed and despised race. His temptation was obviously a typical one, including in it everything which tempts men still to refrain from religious decision, and to dissemble relationship to Christ and connection with his people; and his victory was also typical, reminding us of his who became poor that we might be rich (2 Cor. viii. 7), and who put aside " all the kingdoms of the world and the glory of them," when offered him on sinful terms (Matt. iv. 8—10). View it—1. As *a victory over the world*. Moses knew his advantages at the court of Pharaoh, and doubtless felt the full value of them. Egypt was to him the world. It represented to his mind (1) Wealth and position. (2) Ease and luxury. (3) Brilliant worldly prospects. (4) A sphere congenial to him as a man of studious tastes. And all this he voluntarily surrendered at the call of duty—surrendered it both in spirit and in fact. And are not we, as Christians, called also to surrender of the world? Renouncing the world, indeed, is not monkery. It is not the thoughtless flinging away of worldly advantages. But neither is it the mere renouncing of what is *sinful* in the world. It is the renouncing of it *wholly*, so far as use of it for selfish ends or selfish enjoyment is concerned : the sinking of its ease, its pleasures, its possessions, in entire self-surrender to Christ and duty. And this carries with it the ability for any outward sacrifice that may be needed. 2. As *a victory over the dread of reproach*. In renouncing Egypt,

Moses chose that which the multitudes shun as almost worse than death itself, viz. (1) Poverty. (2) Reproach. Yet how many stumble at reproach in the service of the Saviour! A measure of reproach is implied in all earnest religious profession. And it requires courage to face it—to encounter the moral crucifixion involved in being flouted and scouted by the world. It is when "tribulation and persecution ariseth because of the word" that "by and by" many are "offended" (Matt. xiii. 21). Yet to be able to encounter reproach is the true moral greatness—the mark of the spiritual hero. 3. As *a victory over private feelings and inclinations.* Not only was there much about his life in Egypt which Moses dearly loved (leisure, opportunities for self-culture, etc.); but there must have been much about the Hebrews which, to a man of his courtly up-bringing, would necessarily be repulsive (coarseness of manners, servility of disposition, etc.). Yet he cheerfully cast in his lot with them, taking this as part of his cross. A lesson for people of culture. He who would serve God or humanity must lay his account for much he does not like. Every reformer, every earnest servant of mankind, has to make this sacrifice. He must not be ashamed to call those "brethren" who are yet in every way "compassed with infirmity," about whom there is much that is positively distasteful. Here also, "no cross, no crown."

III. As an act of religious faith. The determining motives in Moses' choice were—1. *Patriotism.* This people was his people, and his blood boiled with indignation at the wrongs they were enduring. Only a nature dead to the last spark of nobleness could have reconciled itself to look on their sufferings and yet eat bread and retain favour at the court of their oppressor. 2. *Humanity.* "There was in him that nobleness of nature, which besides tending to sympathy with the oppressed, revolts from all that is selfish and cruel; and this nobleness was stirred up in him by seeing the state of his kindred, and comparing it with his own. This was his faith. Faith saved him from being content to be idle and useless, and gave him zeal and courage to play the part of a man and a hero in the liberation of his people" (Dr. J. Service). 3. *Religion.* We fail of a right view of Moses' conduct if we stop short of religious faith proper. Moses knew something of the history of his people. He knew them to be the people of God. He knew of the covenants and promises. He knew of their religious hopes. And it was this which weighed most of all with him in casting-in his lot among them, and enabled him to count their reproach greater riches than all the treasures of Egypt. His faith was—(1) Faith in God. He believed in the God of his fathers, and in the truth and certainty of his promise. (2) Faith in the spiritual greatness of his nation. He saw in these Hebrews, sweat-covered, down-trodden, afflicted as they were, the "people of God." Faith is not misled by the shows of things. It pierces to the reality. (3) Faith in duty. "It is of the essence of faith that he who has it feels himself to be in a world of better things than pleasures, whether innocent or sinful, which are only pleasures of sense; and in which to be right is greater and better than to be mighty or to be rich—feels, in a word, that the best of this life, and of all life, is goodness" (Dr. J. Service). (4.) Faith in the recompense of reward. Moses believed in future recompense—in immortality. A cardinal doctrine, even in Egyptian theology, it can scarcely be supposed to have been absent from his. How great was the reward of Moses, even in this life! "He was happier as the persecuted and despised worshipper of Jehovah, the avowed kinsman of slaves, than as the son of Pharaoh's daughter, and the admired proficient in all Egyptian wisdom. He felt that he was richer, despoiled of the treasures of Egypt. He felt that he was happier, divorced from the pleasures of sin. He felt that he was freer, reduced to the bondage of his countrymen. He was richer, because enriched with the treasures of grace; happier, because blessed with the smiles of an approving conscience; freer, because enfranchised with the liberty of the sons of God. The blessings he chose were richer than all the advantages he cast away" (Lindsay). How great has been his reward in history! "For ages past his name has outshone all the monarchs combined of the one-and-thirty dynasties" (Hamilton). But the eternal reward has been greatest of all. A glimpse of it in the glorious reappearance of Moses on the mountain of transfiguration. Wise choice, for honours like these to surrender riches and pleasures which were perishable! Through faith in God, Christ, duty, and eternity, let the same noble choice be repeated in ourselves!

J. O.

Vers. 11—15.—*Unfruitful effort.* I. MOSES' SELF-SACRIFICE (Heb. xi. 24—26).
1. He owned his relationship to the enslaved and hated people. 2. He cast in his lot
among them. God calls for the same sacrifice to-day; confession of Jesus and brotherhood with his people. 3. The result of a mother's influence: from her he must have
learned the truth regarding his descent and the hope of Israel. The seed sown outlived
the luxury, temptations, ambitions of the court. God's blessing rests on these efforts
of holiest love.
II. THE LESSONS OF HIS FAILURE. 1. True desire to serve is not the only requisite
for success. We may be defeated by mistakes of judgment, an ungoverned temper, etc.
2. There can be no true service without the heart's waiting upon God. In order to
guide we ourselves must follow. 3. The power which does not wait upon God comes
to nothing. Contrast the prince with the unknown wanderer in Midian. Not only
were means and influence lost, his very opportunity was gone. "Fret not thyself in
any wise to do evil."—U.

Vers. 11—15.—*Unpurified zeal.* We must certainly attribute the killing of the
Egyptian, not to Divine inspiration, but to the natural impetuosity of Moses' character.
At this stage Moses had zeal, but it was without knowledge. His heart burned with
indignation at the wrongs of his brethren. He longed to be their deliverer. Something
told him that "God by his hand would deliver them" (Acts vii. 25). But how to
proceed he knew not. His plans had taken no definite shape. There was no revelation,
and perhaps one was not expected. So, acting under impulse, he struck the blow which
killed the Egyptian, but did no service to the cause he had at heart. That he did not
act with moral clearness is manifest from the perturbation with which he did the deed,
and from his subsequent attempt to hide the traces of it. It completed his discomfiture
when, next day, he learned that the deed was known, and that his brethren, instead of
welcoming his interposition, were disposed to resent it. He had involved himself in
murder. He had sown the seeds of later troubles. Yet he had gained no end by it.
How true it is that violence seldom leads to happy issues! "The wrath of man
worketh not the righteousness of God" (Jas. i. 20). An exhibition of violence on our
own part is a bad preparation for interfering in the quarrels of others. He that does
the wrong will rarely fail to remind us of it. Learn lessons from the narrative—
I. AS TO THE CHARACTER OF MOSES. Moses, like every man of true, powerful, and
loving nature, was capable of vehement and burning anger. He was a man of great
natural impetuosity. This casts light upon the sin of Meribah (Num. xx. 10). An
outbreak of the old, long-conquered failing (cf. ch. iv. 13). The holier side of the same
disposition is seen in the anger with which he broke in pieces the Tables of the Law
(Ex. xxxii. 19). It casts light also on his meekness, and teaches us to distinguish
meekness from mere natural placableness and amiability. Meekness—the meekness
for which Moses is famed (Num. xii. 3)—was not a gift of nature, but the result of
passions, naturally strong, conquered and controlled—of long and studied self-
repression.
II. AS TO UNPURIFIED ZEAL. 1. *Unpurified zeal leads to hasty action.* It is
ungoverned. It acts from impulse. It is not schooled to bearing and waiting. It
cannot bide God's time, nor keep to God's ways. 2. *Unpurified zeal unfits for God's
service.* It relies too much on self. It takes events into its own hand. Hence Moses
is sent to Midian to spend forty years in learning humility and patience—in acquiring
power of self-control. He has to learn that the work is not his, but God's, and that
only God can accomplish it. 3. *Unpurified zeal, by its hasty action, retards, rather
than furthers, the accomplishment of God's purposes.* By driving Moses into Midian,
it probably put back the hour of Israel's deliverance.—J. O.

Vers. 11—12.—*Moses, the ardent but mistaken patriot.* We are not told much
of Moses in the first forty years of his life, just as we are not told much of Jesus
before he began his public ministry; but as it is with Jesus, so it is with Moses—what
we are told is full of light concerning their character, disposition, and thoughts of the
future. Just one action may be enough to show the stuff a man is made of. Moses,
grown to manhood, by this single action of killing the Egyptian makes clearly

manifest his spirit and his sympathies; shows to us in a very impressive way much that was good, and much also that was evil.

I. CONSIDER THE CONDUCT OF MOSES HERE AS CASTING LIGHT UPON CERTAIN QUALIFICATIONS FOR THE WORK TO WHICH HE WAS AFTERWARDS CALLED. 1. *Though he had been brought up amid Egyptian surroundings, he remained an Israelite in heart.* Very early he must have been made acquainted, in some way or other, with the strange romance that belonged to his infancy. Whatever Pharaoh's daughter brought to bear on him in the way of Egyptian influence one day, would be neutralised by what he heard from his own mother the next. For it was not likely that, after he was able to understand it, his nurse would long conceal the fact that she was his true mother. Perhaps the very ark of bulrushes had become one of his treasured possessions. His name, once explained, was a continual memento of infantile peril and deliverance. And as he grew onward to manhood, he would be inclined to reproach himself again and again for living so easily and comfortably with Pharaoh's daughter, while her father was treating with such harshness and injustice his own people, his own kinsfolk—Aaron his own brother being probably among them. Thus there was everything to keep the state of Israel incessantly in his mind; everything in the way of good soil to make the seed of patriotism grow, if only the seed were in his nature to begin with. And there it unquestionably was, growing with his growth and strengthening with his strength. 2. It is very important to notice *how clearly the vicarious element comes out in the relation of Moses to Israel during the years he spent with Pharaoh's daughter.* In one sense, he did not suffer himself. His life was not made "bitter with hard bondage, in morter, and in brick, and in all manner of service in the field." No taskmaster ever smote him. And yet, in another sense, he suffered perhaps even more than any of the Israelites. There are burdens of the spirit which produce a groaning and prostration far worse than those of any bodily toil. There is a laceration of the heart more painful, and harder to heal, than that of any bodily wound. Moses felt the sorrows of Israel as if they were his own. In all their affliction he was afflicted. Not one of them smarted more under a sense of the injustice with which they were treated than he did. It is a most precious, ennobling and fruitful feeling to have in the heart—this feeling which links the unsuffering to the suffering in a bond not to be broken. It brings together those who have the opportunity to deliver, and those who, fastened hand and foot, can do nothing for themselves. We find this feeling, in its purest, most operative, and most valuable expression in Jesus, in him who knew no sin, no defiling thoughts, no torture of conscience for his own wrong-doing; and who yet came to feel so deeply the misery and helplessness of a fallen world, that he descended into it for its deliverance, having an unspeakably keener sense of its calamities than the most observant and meditative of its own children. It is a grand thing to have this element of vicarious suffering in our hearts; for the more we have it the more we are able to follow Jesus in serving our needy fellow-men. Moses had this element; the prophets had it; Paul had it; every true and successful apostle and evangelist must have it (Rom. ix. 1—5). Every Christian in process of salvation should have this element as he looks round on those still ignorant and out of the way. The civilised should have it as he looks on the savage; the freeman as he looks on the slave; the healthy as he looks on the sick; the man as he looks on the brute creation. This element of vicarious suffering has been at the root of some of the noblest and most useful lives in all ages, and not least in modern times. A thousand times let us run the risk of being called sentimental and maudlin, rather than lack the element or cripple it in its vigorous growth. Certain it is, that we shall do but little for Christ without it. 3. *We have a very suggestive intimation of the superiority of Moses to the people whom he was about to deliver;* this superiority being not a mere matter of greater social advantages, but arising out of personal character. The brother whom he succoured treated him but badly in return. He did not mean to treat him badly; but simple thoughtlessness makes untold mischief. He must have known that Moses wished the act kept a secret, yet in a few hours it is known far and wide through Israel. Not all might have been so inconsiderate, but assuredly most would; and so this man may be taken as representative of his people. He had not the courage and energy to return the Egyptian's blow himself; nor had he the activity and forethought of mind to shelter the generous champion who did return the blow. Israel was in servitude altogether; not only in body, but in all the nobler faculties of life as well. *Hence, if Israel was to be saved, it must be by the condescending act of a superior and stronger hand.* And thus Moses slaying the Egyptian shadows forth a prime requirement in the greater matter of the world's redemption. Unless the Son of God had stooped from his brighter, holier sphere, to break the bonds of sin and death, what could we poor slaves have done?

II. CONSIDER THE CONDUCT OF MOSES HERE AS INDICATING THE PRESENCE IN HIM OF GREAT DEFECTS WHICH REQUIRED MUCH DISCIPLINE AND ENLIGHTENMENT TO REMOVE THEM. Moses, in respect of his ardent and sustained sympathy with Israel, was a man after God's own heart; but he had everything yet to learn as to how that sympathy was to be made truly serviceable. His patriotism, strong and operative as it had proved, was produced by entirely wrong considerations. His profound and fervent interest in Israel was a right feeling, and an indispensable one for his work; but it needed to be produced by quite different agencies, and directed to quite different ends. How had the feeling been produced? Simply by observing the cruelties inflicted on his brethren. He slew the Egyptian simply because he smote his brother, not because that brother belonged to the chosen people of God. The thing wanted was that he should come to understand clearly the connection of Israel with God, their origin and their destiny. He was to sympathise with Israel, not only as his brethren, but first and chiefly as the people of God. *Patriotism is a blessing or a curse just according to the form it takes.* If it begins to say, "Our country, right or wrong," then it is one of the greatest curses a nation can be afflicted with. Arrogance, conceit, and exorbitant self-assertion are as hideous in a nation as in an individual, and in the end correspondingly disastrous. *Our greatest sympathy with men is wanted in that which affects them most deeply and abidingly.* Sympathy has no full right to the name till it is the sympathy of forgiven sinners who are being sanctified and perfected, with those who are not only sinners, but still in the bondage of sin, and perhaps hardly conscious of the degradation of the bondage, and the firmness with which its fetters are fixed. Moses did not know *how much* his brethren were losing, because he did not know how much he himself was still lacking, even though in such comfortable freedom at Pharaoh's court. In his eyes, the main thing to be done for Israel was to get them freedom, independence, self-control in this world's affairs. And therefore *it was necessary for God to effect a complete and abiding change in Moses' way of thinking.* He needed to be made better acquainted with God, and with God's past revelations, and expressed purposes for Israel. Slaying the Egyptian did not advance the real interests of Israel a whit, except as God wove the action in with his own far-reaching plans. Considered *purely as a human action*, it was an aimless one, fruitful of evil rather than good. It was natural enough and excusable enough; but the wrath of man worketh not the righteousness of God; they that take the sword shall perish with the sword; and thus Moses in his carnal impetuosity made clear how dependent he was to be upon God for a really wise, comprehensive, practical plan of action. In the providence of God he was to come back to Israel, not to deal with some obscure subordinate, but with a Pharaoh himself; not to take the sword into his own hands, but to stand still himself, and make the people stand still also, that he and they together might see the salvation of God.—Y.

Vers. 13—15.—*Moses the hater of all oppression.* I. WE HAVE HERE FURTHER IMPORTANT REVELATIONS WITH RESPECT TO THE CHARACTER OF MOSES AND HIS FITNESS TO BE DELIVERER OF ISRAEL. 1. *It is evident that his conscience did not accuse him, as touching the slaying of the Egyptian.* Wrong as the action was, he made it clear that he had done it from a right motive. Although he had taken the life of a fellow-man, he had taken it not as a murderer, with malice in his heart against the individual, but as a patriot. Hence the conscience that makes cowards of us all—the consciousness, that is, of having done a wrong thing—was absent from his breast. It is a very great matter indeed not to go against conscience. Let conscience have life and authority, and God will take his own time and means to cure the blinded understanding. 2. *Moses felt continued interest in the state of Israel.* He went out the second day. He did not say, upon reflection, that these visits to his brethren were too perilous to be continued. He did not say, "I cannot trust my own indignant feelings, and therefore I must keep away from these oppressed countrymen of mine." His heart was wholly and steadily with them. Interest may be easily produced while the exhibition of an injury is fresh, or the emotions are excited by some skilful speaker. But we do not want the heart to be like an instrument, only producing music so long as the performer touches it. We want it to have such a continued activity within, such a continued thoughtfulness, as will maintain a noble and alert sympathy with men in all their varied and incessant needs. 3. *The conduct of Moses here shows that he was a hater of all oppression.* His patriotic feeling had been excited by the Egyptian smiting the Hebrew, and now his natural sense of justice was outraged by seeing one Hebrew smiting another. He beheld these men the victims of a common oppression, and yet one of them who happens to be the stronger adds to the already existing sufferings of his weaker brother instead of doing what he can to diminish them. The patriotism of Moses, even with all its yet unremedied defects, was founded not only in community of blood, but in a deep and ardent love for all human rights. We may conclude that if Moses had been an Egyptian, he would not have joined Pharaoh in his remorseless treatment of Israel, nor seconded a policy of oppression and diminution on the plea that it was one of necessity. If the Egyptians had been under the thraldom of the Hebrews, then, Hebrew though he was, he would have sympathised with the Egyptians.

II. CONSIDER THE OCCASION OF HIS REMONSTRANCE. It is a sad lesson Moses has now to learn, that the oppressed will be the oppressors, if only they can get the chance. Here we are in the world, all sinners together, with certain outward consequences of sin prevalent amongst us in the shape of poverty and sickness, and all such trials onward to death. Right feeling should teach us, in these circumstances, to stand by one another, to bear one another's burdens and do what we can, by union and true brotherliness, to mitigate the oppressions of our great enemy. While he is going about seeking whom he may devour, we, his meditated prey, might well refrain from biting and devouring one another. But what is the real state of things? The rich sinner afflicts the poor, and too often uses him in his helplessness for his own aggrandisement. The strong sinner is always on the look-out to make as much as he can out of every sort of weakness among his fellow-sinners. And what is worse still, when the sinner professes to have passed from death unto life, he does not always show the full evidence of it in loving the brethren as he is bound to do (1 John iii. 14). Some professed Christians take a long time to perceive, and some never perceive at all, that even simple self-indulgence is not only hurtful to self, but an ever-flowing spring of untold misery to others.

III. CONSIDER THE REMONSTRANCE ITSELF. 1. *Notice the person whom Moses addresses.* "He said to him that did the wrong." He does not pretend to come forward as knowing nothing of the merits of the quarrel. He does not content himself with dwelling in general terms on the unseemliness of a dispute between brethren who are also the victims of a common oppressor. It is not enough for him simply to beseech the disputants to be reconciled. One is clearly in the wrong, and Moses does not hesitate by implication to condemn him. Thus there appears in Moses *a certain disposition towards the judicial mind,* revealing the germs of another qualification for the work of his after-life. For the judicial mind is not only that which strives to bring out all the evidence in matters of right or wrong, and so to arrive at a correct conclusion; it is also a mind which has the courage to act on its conclusions, and without fear or favour pass the necessary sentence. By addressing one of these men rather than the other, Moses does in a manner declare himself perfectly satisfied that he is in the wrong. 2. *Notice the question which Moses puts.* He smote the Egyptian; he expostulated with the Hebrew. The smiting of one Hebrew by another was evidently very unnatural conduct in the eyes of Moses. When we consider *what men are,* there is of course nothing astonishing in the conduct of this domineering Israelite; he is but seizing the chance which thousands of others in a like temptation would have seized. But when we consider *what men ought to be,* there was great reason for Moses to ask his question, "Why smitest thou thy fellow?" Why indeed! There was no true reason he could give but what it was a shame to confess. And so we might often say to a wrong-doer, "Why doest thou this or that?" according to the particular wrong he is committing. "*Why?*" There might be great virtue in this persistent interrogation if only put in a spirit purged as far as possible from the censorious and the meddlesome. What a man does carelessly enough and with much satisfaction, upon the low consideration of self-indulgence, he might come to forsake if only brought face to face with high considerations of duty and love, and of conformity to the will of God and example of Christ. Everything we do ought to have a sufficient reason for it. Not that we are to be in a perpetual fidget over minute scruples. But, being by nature so ignorant, and by training so bound-in with base traditions, we cannot too often or too promptly ask ourselves whether we have indeed a sufficient reason for the chief principles, occupations and habits of life. 3. *Notice that the question put to the Hebrew wrong-doer might just as well have been put to the Egyptian.* He also had been guilty of indefensible conduct, yet he as well as the other was a man with powers of reflection, and the timely question, "Why smitest thou this Hebrew?" might have made him consider that really he had no sufficient reason at all to smite him. We must not too readily assume that enemies will persist in enmity, if only we approach them in a friendly manner. He that would change an enemy into a friend must show himself friendly. The plan may not always be successful; but it is worth trying to conquer our foes by love, patience and meekness. We must ever strive to get the selfish people *to think*, their thinking powers and all the better part of their humanity only too often get crushed into a corner before the rush of pride, appetite and passion.

IV. CONSIDER THE RESULT OF THE REMONSTRANCE. The wrong-doer has no sufficient and justifying answer to give; and so he tells Moses to his face that he is a mere meddler. When men are in a right course, a course of high and generous aims, they hail any opportunity of presenting their conduct in a favourable aspect. But when they are doing wrong, then they make a pretence of asserting their independence and liberty in order that they may fight shy of awkward confessions. If we wait till we are never found fault with as meddlers we shall do very little to compose quarrels and redress injuries, to vindicate the innocent or deliver the oppressed. Men will listen to a general harangue against tyranny, injustice and selfishness. They will look at us with great admiration as long as we shoot our arrows in the air; but arrows are not meant to be shot in the air; they are meant, at the very least, to go right into the crowd of men, and sometimes to be directly and closely personal.—Y.

Vers. 11—15.—*Moses "was grown."* According to the tradition he had already distinguished himself as a warrior—was "a prince and a judge" amongst the Egyptians, if not over the Hebrews (ver. 14). Learned, too, in all the wisdom of the day (cf. Acts vii. 22). At his age, forty years, with his influence, surely if ever he was to do anything for his people, *now* must be the time. Notice:

I. THE HASTY MISCALCULATION OF THE MAN. 1. *What he did, and why he did it.* "It came into his heart to visit his brethren." In the seminaries of the priests, in the palace, with the army, he had not forgotten his people; but he had scarcely realised the bitterness of their trial. Now his heart burns within him as he looks upon their burdens. He feels that he is the appointed deliverer trained for this very purpose. What is so plain to him must, he thinks, be equally plain to others (Acts vii. 25). A chance encounter gives him the opportunity of declaring himself; defending a Hebrew, he kills an Egyptian. The supposition that his brethren will understand proves to be a great mistake: "they understood not." Moses did that which we are all too ready to do: took it for granted that other people would look at things from his standpoint. A man may be all that he thinks himself to be; but he will fail in accomplishing his designs if he makes their success depend upon other people taking him at his own estimate; there is an unsound premiss in his practical syllogism which will certainly vitiate the conclusion. What we *should* do is to take pains to place ourselves at the standpoint of other people, and before assuming that they see what we see, make sure that at any rate we see what they see. Moses, the courtier, could see the weakness of the oppressor, and how little power he had *if* only his slaves should rise; the slaves, however, bowing beneath the tyranny, felt and exaggerated the tyrant's power—they could not see much hope from the aid of this self-constituted champion. 2. *What followed from his deed.* Life endangered, compulsory flight, a refuge amongst shepherds in a strange land, forty years' comparative solitude, life's prospects blighted through impatience. "More haste worse speed" is one of the world's wise proverbial generalisations. Moses illustrates the proverb—forty years' exile for an hour's hurry!

II. THE OVERRULING PROVIDENCE OF GOD. "There's a divinity that shapes our ends, rough-hew them as we will." The apparently wasted years not really wasted—no *needless* delay, only preparation and Divine discipline. Moses had learnt much, but he needed to learn more. God takes him from *the school* of Egypt, and places him in *the university* of Nature, with Time and Solitude and the Desert as his tutors. What did they teach him? 1. *The value of the knowledge gained already.* Well "to be learned in all the wisdom of the Egyptians." But wisdom improves by keeping—it needs time and solitude to ripen it. Intellectually and spiritually we are ruminants; silence and solitude are needed to appropriate and digest knowledge. 2. *New knowledge.* Few books, if any, of man's making, but the books of Nature invited study. The knowledge of the desert would be needed by-and-bye, together with much other knowledge which could be gained nowhere else. 3. *Meekness.* He not merely became a wiser man, he grew to be also a better man. The old self-confidence yielded place to entire dependence upon the will of God. God had delivered him from the sword of Pharaoh (cf. ver. 15 with ch. xviii. 3), and would help him still, though in a strange land. Nothing makes a man so meek as faith; the more he realises God's presence and confides in him, the more utterly does the "consuming fire" burn out of him all pride and selfishness.

Application:—Turning the pages of the book of memory, what records of delay occasioned by impatience! Yet how do the same pages testify to the way in which all along God has shaped our ends! It is a mercy that we are in such good hands, and not left to our own devices. Trusting in God, we can hope to make the best even of our errors. He can restore—ay, more than restore—even years which the locust hath eaten (Joel ii. 25).—G.

Vers. 11—15.—*Mistake in life's morning.* "He supposed his brethren would have," etc. (Acts vii. 25). The heart-abandonment of the throne must have taken place before Moses went out from the palace of the princess to inquire, and therefore before the enforced flight. Place therefore "the crisis of being" between Exod. ii. 10 and 11. Let no one fear to face this error in the life of the Lord's servant. Admit frankly that Moses was wrong. We are embarrassed by a notion that clings to us, that the Bible is a repertory of good examples. It is not so. Only One perfect. All other men and women in the Bible are imperfect and sinful, the subjects of God's grace, pardoning, correcting, sanctifying, glorifying. Never lower the moral standard to defend a Bible character. It gives occasion to the adversary, and brings no satisfaction to the believer. In this chapter of the biography of Moses observe in his conduct—

I. THE RIGHT. 1. *Inquiry.* No inclination to shrink from responsibility under the plea of want of knowledge. See the striking passage, Prov. xxiv. 11, 12. Moses going out to investigate for himself, argues that either his mother or his people, or both, had opened and maintained communication with him, informing him of his origin, teaching the doctrine of the true God, and awakening concern. 2. *Sympathy.* "He looked on their burdens." 3. *Indignation.* We may be angry and sin; but it is also true that we may not be angry, and sin even yet more deeply. For illustration cite modern instances of cruel oppression.

II. THE WRONG. 1. *Excess of indignant feeling.* 2. *Murder.* The "supposition" of Stephen is no justification, even if true; but it may not be true, or may be only partially true; for the utterance of Stephen, based on tradition, is not to be confounded with the inspired dictum of God. That furtive look "this way and that way" does not indicate an assured conscience. Note the true meaning and spirit of Rom. xiv. 23.

III. THE IMMEDIATE RESULTS. Failure—Peril—Fear—Flight—*Delay of Israel's deliverance.*

IV. THE FINAL OVERRULING. God originates no wrong, but, being done, lays on it the hand of the mighty. That enforced life in the desert became as important a part of the training of Moses as life at Avaris; acquainted him with "the Wilderness of the Wandering," its resources, mode of life; those other children of Abraham—the Midianites; gave him to wife a descendant of Abraham; led to an important policy for all the future of Israel (Ex. xviii.); and furnished an all-but-indispensable human helper and guide (Num. x. 29—31). Thus does the Eternal Mercy overrule and countervail the errors, even the sins, of penitent believers.—R.

EXPOSITION.

Vers. 16—22.—LIFE OF MOSES IN MIDIAN. Fugitives from Egypt generally took the northern route from Pelusium or Migdol to Gaza, and so to Syria, or the regions beyond. But in this quarter they were liable to be arrested and sent back to the Egyptian monarch. Rameses II. put a special clause to this effect into his treaty with the contemporary Hittite king (Brugsch, 'History of Egypt,' vol. ii. p. 73). It was, perhaps, the fear of extradition which made Moses turn his steps southeastward, and proceed along the route, or at any rate in the direction, which he afterwards took with his nation. Though Egypt had possessions in the Sinaitic peninsula, it was not difficult to avoid them; and before Sinai was reached the fugitive would be in complete safety, for the Egyptians seem never to have penetrated to the southern or eastern parts of the great triangle. "The well," by which Moses took up his abode, is placed with some probability in the neighbourhood of Sherm, about ten miles north-east of Ras Mahommed, the southern cape of the peninsula.

Ver. 16.—The priest of Midian. *Cohen* is certainly "priest" here, and not "prince," since the father-in-law of Moses exercises priestly functions in ch. xviii. 12. His **seven daughters** drew water for his flock, in accordance with Eastern custom. So Rachel "kept the sheep" of her father Laban, and watered them (Gen. xxix. 9). Such a practice agrees well with the simplicity of primitive times and peoples; nor would it even at the present day be regarded as strange in Arabia.

Ver. 17.—The shepherds came and drove them away. There is not much "natural politeness" among primitive peoples. The right of the stronger prevails, and women go to the wall. Even the daughters of their priest were not respected by these rude sons of the desert, who would not wait their turn, but used the water which Reuel's daughters had drawn. The context shows that this was not an accidental or occasional circumstance, but the regular practice of the shepherds, who thus day after day saved themselves the trouble of drawing. (See the next verse.) **Moses stood up and helped them.** Ever ready to assist the weak against the strong (*supra*, vers. 12, 13), Moses "stood up"—sprang to his feet—and, though only one man against a dozen or a score, by his determined air intimidated the crowd of wrong-doers, and forced them to let the maidens' sheep drink at the troughs. His dress was probably that of an Egyptian of rank; and they might reasonably

conclude from his boldness that he had attendants within call.

Ver. 18.—Reuel their father. Reuel is called "Raguel" in Num. x. 29, but the Hebrew spelling is the same in both places. The word means "friend of God," and implies monotheism. Compare ch. xviii. 9—12.

Ver. 19.—An Egyptian. Reuel's daughters judged by the outward appearance. Moses wore the garb and probably spoke the language of Egypt. He had had no occasion to reveal to them his real nationality. **Drew water enough for us.** The shepherds had consumed some of the water drawn by the maidens, before Moses could drive them off. He supplied the deficiency by drawing more for them—an act of polite attention.

Ver. 20.—Where is he? Reuel reproaches his daughters with a want of politeness—even of gratitude. Why have they "left the man"? Why have they not invited him in? They must themselves remedy the omission—they must go and "call him"—that he "may eat bread," or take his evening meal with them.

Ver. 21.—Moses was content to dwell with the man. Moses had fled from Egypt without any definite plan, simply to save his life, and had now to determine how he would obtain a subsistence. Received into Reuel's house, or tent, pleased with the man and with his family, he consented to stay with him, probably entered into his service, as Jacob into Laban's (Gen. xxix. 15—20), kept his sheep, or otherwise made himself useful (see ch. iii. 1); and in course of time Reuel **gave Moses his daughter,** accepted him for his son-in-law, so that he became not merely a member of his household, but of his family, was adopted probably into the tribe, so that he could not quit it without permission (ch. iv. 18), and, so far as his own intention went, cast in his lot with the Midianites, with whom he meant henceforth to live and die. Such vague ideas as he may previously have entertained of his "mission" had passed away; he had been "disillusioned" by his ill-success, and now looked forward to nothing but a life of peaceful obscurity.

Ver. 22.—Gershom. An Egyptian etymology has been assigned to this name ('Speaker's Commentary,' vol. i., p. 488); but Moses in the text clearly indicates that his own intention was to give his child a name significant in Hebrew. "He called his name Gershom, for he said, a stranger (*ger*) have I been," etc. The only question is, what the second element of the name, *shom*, means. This appears to be correctly explained by Kalisch and others as equivalent to *sham* "there"—so that the entire word would mean "(I was) a stranger there" —*i.e.* in the country where this son was born to me.

HOMILETICS.

Vers. 16—19. — § 1. *Moses a second time the champion of the oppressed.* His championship of an oppressed Hebrew, indiscreetly and wrongfully asserted, had driven Moses from the country of his birth. No sooner does he set foot in the land where he seeks a refuge, than his championship is again called forth. On the first occasion it was a weaker race oppressed by one more powerful that made appeal to his feelings; now it is the weaker sex, oppressed by the stronger, that rouses him. His Egyptian civilisation may have helped to intensify his aversion to this form of oppression, since among the Egyptians of his time women held a high place, and were treated with consideration. He springs forward therefore to maintain the rights of Reuel's daughters; but he has learnt wisdom so far that he restrains himself—kills no one, strikes no one—merely "helps" the victims, and has their wrong redressed. The circumstances of life give continual occasion for such interference as this; and each man is bound, so far as he can, to check oppression, and "see that they who are in need and necessity have right." If Moses is a warning to us in respect of his mode of action on the former occasion, he is an example here. The protection of women, whensoever and wheresoever they are wronged and ill-used, is a high Christian duty.

Vers. 21, 22.—§ 2. *Moses as husband and father.* The Midianites were descendants of Abraham (Gen. xxv. 2—4); and marriage with them was permitted, even under the Law (Num. xxxi. 18). Moses, in wedding Zipporah, obeyed the primeval command, "Be fruitful and multiply" (Gen. i. 28), while at the same time he gave himself the solace so much needed by an exile, of tender and loving life-long companionship. That Reuel was willing to give him one of his daughters indicates that he had approved himself as a faithful servant in the good priest's household, and was felt to deserve a reward. That Zipporah accepted him was perhaps mere filial obedience, for which she was rewarded when the fugitive and exile became the first man in a considerable nation. God blessed the marriage with male issue, a blessing fondly desired by each true Israelite, and certainly not least by Moses, who knew so well that in some descendant of Abraham "all the families of the earth should be blessed." A shade of sadness shows itself, however, in the name which he gave his firstborn—Gershom, "a stranger there." He himself had been for years, and, for aught that he could tell, his son might always be, "a stranger in a strange land"— far from his true home, far from his own people, a refugee among foreigners, who could not be expected to love him as one of themselves, or treat him otherwise than with coldness. Depression like this often assails us at moments of great joy, the good obtained making us feel all the more sensibly that other goods have been lost. Such depression, however, after a time, passes away, and the desponding cry of "Gershom" is followed (ch. xviii. 3, 4) by that of "Eliezer," or "my God helps."

HOMILIES BY VARIOUS AUTHORS.

Vers. 15—23.—*The long exile.* Moses took with him into Midian all the best elements of his character; he left some of the faulty ones behind. He may be assumed to have left much of his self-confidence, and to have been cured in part of his natural rashness. His after growth in meekness would almost imply that he had come to see the need of curbing his hot passions, and had, like David, purposed in his heart that he would not transgress (Ps. xvii. 3; xxxii. 1). But he carried with him all his nobleness, all his magnanimity and courtesy. This comes beautifully out in his defence of the women at the well (vers. 16, 17).

I. AN INSTANCE OF CHIVALRY. We have in the incident—1. The weak pushed aside by the strong. Rude, ill-mannered fellows thrust aside the daughters of the priest of Midian from the sheep-troughs, and shamelessly appropriate the water with which they had diligently filled them. 2. Brave championship of the weak. Moses takes their part, stands up to help them, and compels the shepherds to give way. Not content with this, he gives the maidens what assistance he is able. The two dispositions stand in fine contrast: the one all that is unmanly and contemptible, the other all that is chivalrous and noble. The instance teaches—1. That *the chivalrous disposition is also helpful.* The one grace sets off the other. But the bully is a churl, helping nobody, and filching from the weak. 2. That *the bully is to boot a coward.* He will insult a woman, but cringes in the presence of her vindicator. No true man need be afraid to beard him. 3. That *acts of kindness to the defenceless are often repaid in unexpected ways.* They are indeed their own reward. It revives one's spirit to maintain the cause of the needy. Moses, like Jesus, sat by the well; but this little act of kindness, like the Saviour's conversation with the woman of Samaria, did more to refresh his spirit than the sweetest draught he could have taken from it. It was good for him, defeated in resisting tyranny in Egypt, and discouraged by the reception he had met with from his brethren, to have this opportunity of reasserting his crushed manhood, and of feeling that he was still useful. It taught him, and it teaches us—(1) Not to despair of doing good. Tyranny has many phases, and when it cannot be resisted in one form, it may in another. And it taught him (2) Not to despair of human nature. Gratitude had not vanished from the earth, because his brethren had proved ungrateful. Hearts were still to be found, sensitive to the magic touch of kindness; capable of responding to it; ready to repay it by love. For the little deed of chivalry led to unexpected and welcome results. It prepared the way for the hospitable reception of Moses by Reuel; found for him a home in Midian; gave him a wife; provided him with suitable occupation.

II. THE RESIDENCE IN MIDIAN. Notice on this—1. The *place* of it. In or near the Peninsula of Sinai. Solitude and grandeur. Fit place for education of thought and heart. Much alone with God—with Nature in her more awful aspects—with his own thoughts. 2. The *society* of it. He had probably few companions beyond his immediate circle: his wife; her father, sheikh and priest,—pious, hospitable, kindly-natured; the sisters. His life simple and unartificial, a wholesome corrective to the luxury of Egypt. 3. The *occupation* of it. He kept flocks (ch. iii. 1). The shepherd's life, besides giving him a valuable knowledge of the topography of the desert, was very suitable for developing qualities important in a leader—watchfulness, skill, caution, self-reliance, bravery, tenderness, etc. So David was taken "from the sheepcote, from following the sheep," to be ruler over God's people, over Israel (2 Sam. vii. 8). It lets in light on Moses' character that he was willing to stoop to, and did not spurn, this lowly toil. He that could so humble himself was fit to be exalted. By faithfulness in that which was least, he served an apprenticeship for being faithful also in much (Luke xvi. 10). 4. The *duration* of it. Forty years was a long time, but not too long for the training God was giving him. The richest characters are slowest in coming to maturity, and Moses was all this while developing in humility, and in knowledge of God, of man, and of his own heart. The whole subject teaches us valuable lessons. Learn—1. *God's dealings with his servants are often mysterious.* Moses in Midian seems an instance of the highest gifts thrown uselessly away. Is this, we ask in surprise, the only use God can find for a man so richly gifted, so remarkably preserved, and on whom have been lavished all the treasures of Egypt's wisdom? Any ordinary man might be a shepherd, but how few could do the work of a Moses? Moses himself, in the meditations of these forty years, must often have wondered at the strange irony of his life. Yet how clear it was all made to him at last! Trust God to know better what is good for you than you do yourself. 2. *How little a man has, after all, to do with the shaping of his own history!* In one sense he has much, yea everything, to do with it. Had Moses, *e.g.*, not so rashly slain the Egyptian, his whole future would doubtless have borne a different complexion. Man is responsible for his acts, but once he has done them, they are taken in spite of himself out of his hands, and shaped in their consequences by overruling Providence. He who sent the princess to the river, sent also the priest's daughters to the well. 3. *It is man's wisdom to study contentment with his lot.* It may be humble, and not the lot we like, or had counted on. It may be a lot to which we never expected to be reduced. We may feel as if our gifts and powers were being wasted in it. Yet if it *is* our lot—the one meanwhile providentially marked out for us—our wisdom is cheerfully to accept of it, and make the best of the tasks which belong to it.

J. O.

Ver. 22.—*Gershom*. 1. *The good man in this world is often lonely at heart.* (1) When violence reigns unchecked. (2) When God's cause is in a depressed condition. (3) When repulsed in efforts to do good. (4) When severed from scenes of former labour. (5) When his outward lot is uncongenial. (6) When deprived of suitable companionships, and when he can find few to sympathise with him. 2. *God sends to the good man alleviations of his loneliness.* We may hope that Zipporah, if not without faults, formed a kind and helpful wife to Moses. Then, sons were born to him—the first, the Gershom of this text. These were consolations. A wife's affection, the prattle and innocence of children—have sweetened the lot of many an exile. Bunyan and his blind daughter.—J. O.

Vers. 15—22.—*Moses in Midian*. Moses had to flee. The hard, unworthy reproach, humiliating as he must have felt it to be, nevertheless gave him a timely warning. His flight seems to have been instantaneous; perhaps not even the opportunity to bid farewell to his friends. An utter rupture, a complete separation was his only safety. Consider—

I. WHAT HE LEFT BEHIND HIM. 1. *Possibly Pharaoh's daughter was still alive.* If so, we can imagine her sorrow and utter perplexity over the son of her adoption, and the reproaches she might have to bear from her own kindred. How often she may have heard that common expression which adds insult to bitter disappointment, "I told you so." We may be tolerably sure as to one result of the long sojourn of Moses in Midian, viz., that when he returned, she would be vanished from the scene, spared from beholding the son of her adoption the agent of such dreadful visitations to her own people. Yet even with this mitigation, the agony may have been more than she could bear. She had sheltered Moses, watched over him, and "nourished him for her own son," giving him the opportunity to become "learned in all the wisdom of the Egyptians;" only to find at last that a sword had pierced through her own soul (Luke ii. 35; Acts vii. 21, 22). 2. *He left his brethren in servitude.* Any expectation they may have had, from his present eminence and possibly greater eminence in the future, was now completely crushed. It is well to effect a timely crushing of false hopes, even if great severity has to be used. 3. *He left behind all difficulties that came from his connexion with the court.* Had he gone on staying in Egypt he would have had to make his election, sooner or later, between the Egyptians and his own people. But now he is spared having to decide for himself. We have to thank God that he sometimes takes painful and difficult decisions out of our hands, so that we have no longer to blame ourselves either for haste or procrastination; for rashness and imprudence, or cowardice and sloth. God in his providence does things for us, which we might find it very hard to do for ourselves.

II. WHAT HE FOUND BEFORE HIM. He went out, hardly knowing whither he went. The safest place was the best for him, and that safest place might not immediately appear. Yet how plain it is that God was guiding him, as really as he guided Abraham, though Moses was not conscious of the guiding. He fled because he had slain a fellow-man, yet he was not going forth as a Cain. Under the wrath of Pharaoh, he was not under that wrath of God which rests upon murderers. He was going to a new school, that was all—having learned all that could be learned in the old one. He probably asked himself as he fled, " Where can I go? Who will receive me? What story can I tell?" He would feel, now the homicide was known, that it was impossible to say how far the news had reached. Onward he sped—perhaps, like most fugitives of the sort, hiding by day and travelling by night—until at last he reached the land of Midian. Here he concluded to dwell, although it may have been in his mind only a temporary stage to a distant and safer abode. And now observe that with this fresh mention of what happened to him after his flight, there is *an immediate and still further revelation of his character, all in the way of showing his natural fitness for the great work of his life.* He has made an awful mistake in his manner of showing sympathy with Israel, and in consequence has exposed himself to a humiliating rebuff; but all this does not make him one whit less willing to champion the weak when the occasion comes. *He was a man always ready for opportunities of service;* and wherever he went there seemed to be something for him to do. He had fled from a land where the strong oppressed the weak, and come into another land where he found the same thing prevailing, and in one of its most offensive forms; for the tyranny was that of man over woman. The people of Midian had a priest who seems to have been himself a hospitable man and a judicious and prudent one (ch. xviii.); but there was so little reality of religion among the people, so little respect for the priest's office, that these shepherds drove his daughters away from the well—whom rather they should have gladly helped. It was not an occasional misadventure to the daughters, but a regular experience (ver. 18). None of these shepherds perhaps had ever killed a man, but for all that they were a pack of savage boors. Moses, on the other hand, even though he has slain a man, is not a mere bravo, one who puts little value on human life. One might have said of him as Chaucer says of one of his pilgrims in the 'Canterbury Tales,'

> "He was a veray parfit gentil knight."

Then, when Moses had helped the women, his difficulties and doubts were soon brought to an end. He had helped them, though they were utter strangers, because he felt it his duty so to do. He was not looking to them for a release from his difficulties, for how could a few weak women help him, those who had just been the objects of his own pity? But as women had been the means of protecting him in infancy, so they were the means of providing for him now. He did not seek Reuel; Reuel sought him. He needed no certificate of character; these daughters themselves were an epistle of commendation to their father. He might safely tell all his story now, for even the darkest chapter of it would be viewed in the light of his recent generous action.—Y.

Ver. 15.—*Sitting by the well: a suggestive comparison.* The very expression, "He sat down by a well," inevitably suggests that conversation beside the well at Sychar, in which Jesus took so important a part. Note the following points of resemblance, and then say if they can be considered as purely accidental. Are they not rather involved in the profound designs of him who presided over the construction of the Scriptures? 1. As we see Moses fleeing from the face of Pharaoh, so we see Jesus making a prudent departure from Judaea into Galilee, on account of the Pharisees. 2. Both Moses and Jesus are found sitting by a well. 3. As Moses comes in contact with seven women of *a different nation,* so Jesus with the woman of *Samaria.* And just as the daughters of Reuel made the difference seem greater still by calling Moses an Egyptian, which though a name partly appropriate, was yet particularly inappropriate at a time when he was the object of Pharaoh's bitterest hatred—so the woman of Samaria laid emphasis on the fact that Jesus was a Jew, being altogether ignorant how small a part was that of the truth concerning him. 4. The very difference in number is significant. Moses could help a number in the service that he rendered, because it was a mere external service. But Jesus needed to have the woman of Samaria alone, that he might deal effectually with her peculiar, individual need. There is a great difference in respect of the things to be said and done, according as we are dealing with one person or more than one. 5. The meeting of Moses with the daughters of Reuel led on to his becoming acquainted with Reuel himself; gaining his confidence and becoming his helper. So Jesus serving the woman of Samaria was led on to serve, not one only, but many of those connected with her. 6. Moses soon entered into a nearer relation still with Reuel, and Jesus in the course of his conversation with the woman asserted principles which were to break down the barriers between Jew and Samaritan, and every wall of partition separating those who should be united. Lastly, he who helped these women became a shepherd; and his dying thought was of a shepherd's work, as he prayed God to give him a successor who should be a true shepherd to Israel. And as to Jesus, we all know how he delighted to set himself before his disciples as the Good Shepherd, deeply concerned for the nourishment and security of his flock, and concerned most of all to seek and to save that which was lost (Matt. xviii. 11—13; Luke xv. 4; xix. 10).—Y.

Ver. 22.—*Life and its moods.* "He called his name Gershom," etc. (Ex. ii. 22), compared with—"And the name of the other was Eliezer," etc. (Ex. xviii. 4).

Note the isolation and misery of the earlier time, and the mercy of the later—each begetting its own tone and mood of mind; and further, the desirability of living above the mood of the passing day. Rev. C. Kingsley says ('Life,' i. 82): "Let us watch against *tones*. They are unsafe things. The tone of a man or woman's mind ought to be that of thoughtful reverence and love; but neither joy or sorrow, or activity or passiveness, or any other animal tone, ought to be habitual," etc.—R.

EXPOSITION.

Vers. 23—25.—Death of the Pharaoh from whom Moses fled—Continuance of the oppression of Israel—Israel's prayers —God's acceptance of them.—After a space of forty years from the time of Moses' flight from Egypt, according to the estimate of St. Stephen (Acts vii. 30), which is not, however, to be strictly pressed, the king whose anger he had provoked—Rameses II., as we believe—died. He had reigned sixty-seven years — about forty-seven alone, and about twenty in conjunction with his father. At his death, the oppressed Israelites ventured to hope for some amelioration of their condition. On his accession, a king in the East often reverses the policy of his predecessor, or at any rate, to make himself popular, grants a remission of burthens for a certain period. But at this time the new monarch, Menephthah I., the son of Rameses II., disappointed the hopes of the Israelites, maintained his father's policy, continued the established system of oppression, granted them no relief of any kind. They " sighed," therefore, in consequence of their disappointment, and "cried" unto God in their trouble, and made supplication to him more earnestly, more heartily, than ever before. We need not suppose that they had previously fallen away from their faith, and " now at last returned to God after many years of idolatrous aberration " (Aben Ezra, Kalisch). But there was among them an access of religious fervour; they "turned to God" from a state of deadness, rather from one of alienation, and raised a " cry " of the kind to which he is never deaf. God therefore " heard their groaning," deigned to listen to their prayers, and commenced the course of miraculous action which issued in the Exodus.

(This section is more closely connected with what follows than with what went before, and would better begin ch. iii. than terminate ch. ii.)

Ver. 23.—In process of time. Literally, " in those *many* days." The reign of Rameses II. was exceptionally long, as previously explained. He had already reigned twenty-seven years when Moses fled from him (ch. ii. 15). He had now reigned sixty-seven, and Moses was eighty! It had seemed a weary while to wait. **The children of Israel sighed.** If the time had seemed a weary while to Moses, how much more to his nation! He had escaped and was in Midian—they toiled on in Egypt. He kept sheep—they had their lives made " bitter" for them " with hard bondage, in morter, and in brick, and in all manner of service in the field" (ch. i. 14). He could bring up his sons in safety ; their sons were still thrown into the river. No wonder that " an exceeding bitter cry "went up to God from the oppressed people, so soon as they found that they had nothing to hope from the new king.

Vers. 24, 25.—God heard their groaning. God is said to " hear" the prayers which he accepts and grants ; to " be deaf " to those which he does not grant, but rejects. He now " heard " (*i.e.* accepted) the supplications of oppressed Israel ; and on account of the covenant which he had made with Abraham, Isaac, and Jacob—a covenant always **remembered** by him—he **looked upon** his people, made them the objects of his special **regard,** and entered on a course, which was abnormal, irregular, miraculous, in order to carry out his purposes of mercy towards them It is observed that anthropomorphic expressions are here accumulated ; but this is always the case when the love and tenderness of God towards man are spoken of, since they form the only possible phraseology in which ideas of love and tenderness can be expressed so as to be intelligible to human beings. **And God regarded them.** Literally, "and God knew." God kept the whole in his thoughts—bore in mind the sufferings, the wrongs, the hopes, the fears, the groans, the despair, the appeal to him, the fervent supplications and prayers —knew all, remembered all—counted every word and sigh—gathered the tears into his bottle—noted all things in his book—and for the present endured, kept silence—but was preparing for his foes a terrible vengeance— for his people a marvellous deliverance

HOMILETICS.

Ver. 23.—*Death comes at last, even to the proudest monarch.* Rameses II. left behind him the reputation of being the greatest of the Egyptian kings. He was confounded with the mythical Sesostris, and regarded as the conqueror of all Western Asia, of Ethiopia, and of a large tract in Europe. His buildings and other great works did, in fact, probably excel those of any other Pharaoh. His reign was the longest, if we except one, of any upon record. He was victorious, by land or sea, over all who resisted his arms. Yet a time came when he too "went the way of all flesh." "It is appointed unto all men once to die, and after that the judgment." After eighty years of life and sixty-seven of regal power, the Great Rameses was gathered to his fathers. Of what avail then was all his glory, all his wealth, all his magnificence, all his architectural display, all his long series of victories? Could he plead them before the judgment-seat of an all-righteous God? He could not even, according to his own belief, have pleaded them before the tribunal of his own Osiris. A modern writer says that every stone in the edifices which he raised was cemented with the blood of a human victim (Lenormant, 'Manuel d'Histoire Ancienne,' vol. i. p. 423). Thousands of wretches toiled incessantly to add to his glory, and cover Egypt with buildings, obelisks, and colossi, which still show forth his greatness. But what is the result of all, what advantage has he gained by it? On earth, he is certainly not forgotten; but History gibbets him as a tyrant and oppressor—one of the scourges of the human race. In the intermediate region where he dwells, what can be his thoughts of the past? what his expectations of the future? Must he not mourn continually over his misspent life, and unavailingly regret his cruelties? The meanest of his victims is now happier than he, and would refuse to change lots with him.

Vers. 24, 25.—*God is never deaf to earnest prayer for deliverance.* It was eighty years since the cruel edict went forth, "Every son that is born ye shall cast into the river" (ch. i. 22)—ninety, or perhaps a hundred, since the severe oppression began (*ib.* 11—14). Israel had sighed and groaned during the whole of this long period, and no doubt addressed many a prayer to God, which *seemed* unheard. But no earnest faithful prayer during the whole of the long space *was* unheard. God treasured them all up in his memory. He was "not slack, as men count slackness." He had to wean his people from their attachment to Egypt—he had to discipline them, to form their character—to prepare them to endure the hardships of the desert, and to face the fierce tribes of Canaan. When this was done—when they were fit—he gave effect to their prayers—"heard their groaning"—and just as they were on the point of despairing, delivered them. The lesson to us here is, that we never despair, never grow weary and listless, never cease our prayers, strive to make them more and more fervent. We can never know how near we are to the time when God will show forth his power—grant and accomplish our prayers.

HOMILIES BY VARIOUS AUTHORS.

Vers. 23—25.—*The hour of help.* 1. It was *long delayed.* (1) Till tyranny had done its worst. (2) Till the last hope of help from man had disappeared. Improvement may have been looked for at death of king. 2. It *came at last.* (1) When the bondage had served its ends. (2) When the people, in despair of man, were crying to God. 3. When *it did come*—(1) The man was found ready who was to bring it. (2) God was found faithful to his promise.—J. O.

Vers. 1—25.—*Moses and Christ.* Compare in circumstances of early life. 1. Obscurity of birth. 2. Peril in infancy. 3. Protection in Egypt. 4. Rejected by brethren. 5. Humble toil. The carpenter's shop—keeping sheep. 6. Long period of silent preparation. See F. W. Robertson's striking sermon on "The Early Development of Jesus" ('Sermons,' vol. ii.). The period was not so long in Christ's case as in the case of Moses, but had a like significance—preparation for future work.—J. O.

Vers. 23—25.—*A groaning Israel and an observant God.* I. THERE WAS SIGHING AND CRYING, YET NO REAL PRAYER. There was no supplication for help, no expression of confidence in a helper; seeing there was no real sense of trust in One who could keep, and therefore no possibility of real expectation from him. These Israelites did not wait as they that watch for the morning, sure that it will come at last (Ps. cxxx. 6), but rather as those who say in the morning, "Would God it were even!" and at even, "Would God it were morning!" (Deut. xxviii. 67). Their right attitude, if only they had been able to occupy it, was that which Jesus is said to have occupied (Heb. v. 7). They should have offered up prayers and supplications along with their strong crying and tears to him that was able to save them. But the God who had been so near to Abraham, Isaac, and Jacob, seemed now removed to a distance. No one appeared with whom the Israelites in their despair could wrestle until they gained the blessing of deliverance. And thus it has been in every generation, and still continues. The misery of the world cannot be silent, and in it all the saddest feature is, that the miserable have no knowledge of God, or, if they have, it is a knowledge without practical use. They are without hope in the world, because they are without God in the world. They go on groaning like a sick infant that neither knows the cause of its trouble nor where to look for help. And in the midst of all this ignorance, Jesus would lead men to true prayer—to intelligent and calm dependence upon God for things according to his will.

II. NOTICE THE REASON GIVEN FOR THE SIGHING AND CRYING. They sighed by reason of the bondage. Bodily restraint, privation, and pain—in these lay the reasons for their groaning. Their pain was that of the senses, not that of the spirit. Little wonder then that they were not susceptible to the presence of God. Contrast their painful experiences with those recorded in the following Psalms, xxxii., xxxviii., xxxix., li., cxix. 136. Jesus made it evident by his dealings with many of those who came to him that the bulk of men, like the Israelites of old, are sighing because of some temporal bondage. They think that pain would vanish, if only they could get all sensible comforts. The poor man thinks what a comfort wealth and plenty must be, yet a rich man came to Jesus, still unsatisfied in spite of his wealth, and was obliged to go away again, sad, because of what Jesus had said, *deeply disturbed and disappointed; and all because he had great possessions.* There was no chance of doing much good to Israel, as long as they were sighing simply because of the bondage. The pain of life which comes through the senses would sink into a matter of superficial insignificance, if only we felt as we ought to do the corruption and danger which come through sin. We should soon come to the true remedy for all our pains, if only we learnt to cry for the clean heart and the right spirit.

III. THOUGH THE SIGHING AND CRYING DID NOT AMOUNT TO A REAL PRAYER, YET GOD ATTENDED TO IT. God made allowance for the ignorance of the people. He knew what was wanted, even though they knew not. The father on earth, being evil, has to make the best guess he can at the interests of his children; our Father in heaven knows exactly what we want. God does not expect from the ignorant what can only be presented by those who know him; and he was about to deal with Israel so that they might know him. And first of all they must be made to feel that Egypt was in reality a very different place from what it appeared to Jacob and his sons, coming out of famine-stricken Canaan. The time had long past when there was any temptation to say, "Surely Egypt is better than Canaan; we shall be able to take our ease, eat, drink, and be merry." There had not only been corn in Egypt, but tyrants and taskmasters. We have all to find out what Egypt really is; and until we make the full discovery, we cannot appreciate the nearness of God and profit by it. God can do much for us when we come to the groaning-point, when the dear illusions of life not only begin to vacate their places, but are succeeded by painful, stern, and abiding realities. When we begin to cry, even though our cry be only because of temporal losses and pains, there is then a chance that we may attend to the increasing revelations of the presence of God, and learn to wait upon him in obedience and prayer.—Y.

Vers. 23—25.—As in streams the water is attracted to and swirls round various centres, so here the interest of the narrative circles about three facts. We have—

I. THE KING'S DEATH. Who the king was may be uncertain. [Some say Aahmes I. —see Canon Cook, in 'Speaker's Commentary;' others, Rameses II.—see R. S. Poole, in 'Contemporary Review,' March, 1879.] What he had done is sufficiently evident. Confronted with an alien people, of whose history he knew little and with whom he had no sympathy, he had treated them with suspicion and cruelty. Walking by sight he had inaugurated a policy which was sufficiently clever but decidedly unwise; he had hatched the very enmity he dreaded, by making those whom he feared miserable. Nevertheless, he, personally, does not seem to have been the loser in this life. He left a legacy of trouble for his successor, but probably to the last he was feared and honoured. Such lives were to the Egyptians, and must still be, suggestive of immortality. If evil can thus prosper in the person of a king, life must indeed be a moral chaos if it end with death and there be no hereafter. "The king of Egypt died:" what about the King of Heaven and Earth?

II. THE PEOPLE'S CRY. The inheritance of an evil policy accepted and endorsed by the new king. Results upon an oppressed people:—1. *Misery finds a voice.* "They sighed"—a half-stifled cry, which however gathers strength; "they *cried.*" Forty years of *silent* endurance seeks at length relief in utterance. The king's death brings the dawn of hope; the first feeling after liberty is the cry of anguish which cannot be suppressed. Such a cry, an inarticulate prayer which needed no interpreter to translate it—an honest and heartfelt prayer of which God could take cognizance. 2. *The voice of misery finds a listener.* The cry was a cry with wings to it—it "came up unto God." Too many so-called prayers have *no* wings, or at most clipped wings. They grovel on the earth like barn-yard fowls, and if they chance to pick up solace, it is, like themselves, of the earth earthy. Winged prayers, even when winged by sorrow, go up, and for a time seem lost, but they reach heaven and find harbour there.

III. GOD'S RESPONSE. 1. *Attention secured and the covenant remembered.* God had not been deaf before, nor had he been forgetful of his promise. For *practical* memory, however, there must be a *practical* claim upon that which is remembered. So long as the people are indifferent, their indifference suspends the fulfilment of the covenant. All the while God, by permitting the tyranny, had been stirring up their memory that they might stir up his. When *they* are aroused, he shows at once that *he* is mindful. 2. *The children of the covenant beheld, and respect paid to their necessities.* So far, God had looked upon a people of slaves, trying hard to make themselves content with servitude. Now that misery has aroused them to remember who and what they are, he sees once more the children of *Israel*—offspring of the wrestling Prince. People have to come to themselves before God can effectually look upon them. Content with servitude, he sees them slaves. Mindful of the covenant, he sees them as children. God is ready to help them directly they are ready to claim and to receive help from God.

Application :—Evil in this world often seems to triumph, because men submit to it, and try to make the best of it, instead of resisting it. The general will not fight the foe single-handed; in the interest of those who should be his soldiers, he must have them ready to fight under him. When we realise our true position, then God is ready at once to recognise it. Indifference, forgetfulness, delay, all really due to man. God the deliverer only *seems to be* that which man the sufferer *is.*—G.

SECTION II.—CHAPTERS III. IV.

THE CALL AND MISSION OF MOSES.

EXPOSITION.

CHAPTER III.

Vers. 1—22.—THE MISSION OF MOSES. After forty years of monotonous pastoral life, affording abundant opportunity for meditation, and for spiritual communion with God, and when he had attained to the great age of eighty years, and the hot blood of youth had given place to the calm serenity of advanced life, God at last revealed Himself to Moses "called him" (ver. 4), and gave him a definite mission. The present chapter is intimately connected with the next. Together, they contain an account of that extraordinary and indeed miraculous interchange of thought and speech between Moses and God himself, by which the son of Amram was induced to undertake the difficult and dangerous task of freeing his people, delivering them from their bondage in Egypt, and conducting them through the wilderness to that "land flowing with milk and honey," which had been promised to the seed of Abraham more than six centuries previously (Gen. xv. 18). Whatever hopes he had entertained of being his people's deliverer in youth and middle life, they had long been slumbered; and, humanly speaking, nothing was more improbable than that the aged shepherd, grown "slow of speech and of a slow tongue" (ch. iv. 10)—his manners rusticised—his practical faculties rusted by disuse—his physical powers weakened—should come forth from a retirement of forty years' duration to be a leader and king of men. Nothing less than *direct* supernatural interposition could—one may well believe—have sufficed to overcome the natural *vis inertiæ*.of Moses' present character and position. Hence, after an absolute cessation of miracle for more than four hundred years, miracle is once more made use of by the Ruler of the Universe to work out his ends. A *dignus vindice nodus* has arisen; and the ordinary laws of that Nature which is but one of his instruments are suspended by the Lord of All, who sees what mode of action the occasion requires, and acts accordingly.

Ver. 1.—**Moses kept the flock.** The Hebrew expresses that this was his regular occupation. Understand by "flock" either sheep or goats, or the two intermixed. Both anciently and at the present day the Sinaitic pastures support these animals, and not horned cattle. **Of Jethro, his father-in-law.** The word translated "father-in-law" is of much wider application, being used of almost any relation by marriage. Zipporah uses it of Moses in ch. iv. 25, 26; in Gen. xix. 12, 14, it is applied to Lot's "sons-in-law;" in other places it is used of "brothers-in-law." Its application to Jethro does not prove him to be the same person as Reuel, which the difference of name renders improbable. He was no doubt the head of the tribe at this period, having succeeded to that dignity, and to the priesthood, when Reuel died. He may have been either Reuel's son or his nephew. **The backside of the desert,** *i.e.* "behind" or "beyond the desert," across the strip of sandy plain which separates the coast of the Elanitic Gulf from the mountains, to the grassy regions beyond. **He came to the mountain of God, even Horeb.** Rather, "the mountain of God, *Horeb-way*," or "*towards* Horeb." By "the mountain of God" Sinai seems to be meant. It may be so named either by anticipation (as "the land of Rameses" in Gen. xlvii. 11), or because there was already a sanctuary there to

the true God, whom Reuel and Jethro worshipped (ch. xviii. 12).

Ver. 2.—**The angel of the Lord.** Literally, "an angel of Jehovah." Taking the whole narrative altogether, we are justified in concluding that the appearance was that of "the Angel of the Covenant" or "the Second Person of the Trinity himself;" but this is not stated nor implied in the present verse. We learn it from what follows. The angel "**appeared in a flame of fire** out of the midst of *the* thorn-bush"—not out of "*a* thorn-bush"—which may be explained by there being only one on the spot, which however seems improbable, as it is a common tree; or by Moses having so often spoken of it, that, when he came to write to his countrymen, he naturally called it "the bush," meaning "the bush of which you have all heard." So St. John says of the Baptist (iii. 24) that "he was not yet cast into *the* prison," meaning, the prison into which you all know that he was cast. *Seneh*, the word translated "bush," is still the name of a thorny shrub, a species of acacia, common in the Sinaitic district.

Ver. 3.—**I will turn aside.** Suspecting nothing but a natural phenomenon, which he was anxious to investigate. The action bespeaks him a man of sense and intelligence, not easily scared or imposed upon.

Ver. 4.—**When the Lord saw . . . God called.** This collocation of words is fatal to the entire Elohistic and Jehovistic theory, for no one can suppose that two different writers wrote the two clauses of the sentence. Nor, if the same term was originally used in both clauses, would any reviser have altered one without altering both. **Out of the midst of the bush.** A voice, which was the true voice of God, appeared to Moses to proceed out of the midst of the fire which enveloped the thorn-bush. An objective reality is described, not a vision. **Moses, Moses.** The double call implies urgency. Compare the call of Samuel (1 Sam. iii. 10).

Ver. 5.—**Draw not nigh.** The awful greatness of the Creator is such that his creatures, until invited to draw near, are bound to stand aloof. Moses, not yet aware that God himself spoke to him, was approaching the bush too close, to examine and see what the "great thing" was. (See ver. 3.) On the general unfitness of man to approach near to holy things, see the comment on ch. xix. 12. **Put off thy shoes.** Rather, "thy *sandals*." Shoes were not worn commonly, even by the Egyptians, until a late period, and would certainly not be known in the land of Midian at this time. The practice of putting them off before entering a temple, a palace, or even the private apartments of a house, was, and is, universal in the East—the *rationale* of it being that the shoes or sandals have dust or dirt attaching to them. The command given to

Moses at this time was repeated to Joshua (Josh. v. 15). **Holy ground.** Literally, " ground of holiness "—ground rendered holy by the presence of God upon it—not " an old sanctuary," as some have thought, for then Moses would not have needed the information.

Ver. 6 — **The God of thy father.** " Father " here is used collectively, meaning forefathers generally, a usage well known to Hebraists. (Compare ch. xv. 2, and ch. xviii. 4.) **The God of Abraham**, etc., *i.e.* the God who revealed himself to Abraham, Isaac, and Jacob, and entered into covenant with them (Gen. xv. 1—21; xxvi. 2—5; xxxv. 1—12). The conclusion which our Blessed Lord drew from this verse (Matt. xxii. 32) is not directly involved in it, but depends on his minor premiss, " God is not the God of the dead, but of the living." **Moses hid his face.** A natural instinctive action. So Elijah, on the same site (1 K. xix. 13) and the holy angels before God's throne in heaven (Is. vi. 2). In the religious system of Rome, the augurs when discharging their office, and all persons when offering a sacrifice, veiled their heads. (See Liv. i. 18; Virg. Æn. iii. 405; Juv. vi. 390.)

Ver. 7.—**I have surely seen.**' Literally " Seeing I have seen "—an expression implying continuance. On the force of the anthropomorphic terms " seeing, hearing, knowing," as used of God, see the comment on ch. ii. 24 —25. **Taskmasters.** Not the general superintendents of ch. i. 11, but subordinate officials, who stood over the labourers and applied the rod to their backs. (See above, ch. ii. 11.)

Ver. 8.—**I am come down.** Another anthropomorphism, and one very common in Scripture (Gen. xi. 5, 7; xviii. 21; Ps. xviii. 9; cxliv. 5, etc.), connected of course with the idea that God has a special dwellingplace, which is *above* the earth. **To bring them up.** Literally correct. Palestine is at a much higher level than Egypt. (Compare Gen. xii. 10; xiii. 1; xxxvii. 25; xxxix. 1; xlii. 2; xlvi. 3, 4; l. 25.) **A good land and a large.** The fertility of Palestine, though not equal to that of Egypt, was still very great. Eastward of Jordan, the soil is rich and productive, the country in places wooded with fine trees, and the herbage luxuriant. Vast tracts in the spring produce enormous crops of grain, and throughout the year pasturage of every kind is abundant. " Still the countless flocks and herds may be seen, droves of cattle moving on like troops of soldiers, descending at sunset to drink of the springs—literally, in the language of the prophet, " rams, and lambs, and goats, and bullocks, all of them fatlings of Bashan " (Stanley, ' Jewish Church,' pp. 217, 218). The western region is less productive, but by careful cultivation in terraces may be made to bear excellent crops of corn, olives, and figs. Palestine proper to a modern European seems small, being about the size of Belgium, less than Holland or Hanover, and not much larger than Wales. It contains about 11,000 square miles. To an Israelite of the age of Moses such a land would appear sufficiently " large ;" for it was considerably larger than the entire Delta of Egypt, whereof his nation occupied the smaller half; and it fell but little short of the entire cultivable area of the whole land of Egypt, which was the greatest and most powerful country known to him. It may be added that the land included in the covenant which God made with Abraham (Gen. xv. 18—21), and actually possessed by David and Solomon (1 K. iv. 21), was a " good land and a large," according even to modern notions, including (as it did) besides Palestine the whole of Syria, and thus containing an area of from 50,000 to 60,000 square miles. The phrase **flowing with milk and honey**, first used here, and so common in the later books (Num. xiii. 27; Deut. xxvi. 9, 15; xxxi. 20; Jer. xi. 5; xxxii. 22; Ezek. xx. 6, etc.) was probably a proverbial expression for " a land of plenty," and not intended literally. See what the spies say, Num. xiii. 27

The enumeration of the nations of Palestine here made is incomplete, five only of the ten whose land was promised to Abraham (Gen. xv. 19—21) being expressly mentioned. One, however, that of the Hivites, is added. We may suppose that they had succeeded to the Kenizzites or the Kadmonites of Abraham's time. The only important omission is that of the Girgashites, who hold their place in most other enumerations (Gen. x. 16; xv. 21; Deut. vii. 1; Josh. iii. 10; xxiv. 11, etc.), but seem to have been the least important of the " seven nations,"and are omitted in Judg. iii. 5. (" Girgashites " is introduced in the Samaritan version and the Sept.)

Ver. 9.—This is a repetition, in substance, of ver. 7, on account of the long parenthesis in ver. 8, and serves to introduce verse 10. The *nexus* is : " I have seen the oppression — I am come down to deliver them—come now, therefore, I will send thee "

Ver. 11.—**And Moses said . . . Who am I, that I should go**, etc. A great change had come over Moses. Forty years earlier he had been forward to offer himself as a " deliverer." He " went out " to his brethren and slew one of their oppressors, and " supposed his brethren would have understood how that God by his hand would deliver them " (Acts vii. 25). " But they understood not " (*ibid.*) They declined to accept him for leader, they reproached him with setting himself up to be " a ruler and a judge " over them. And now, taught by this lesson, and sobered by forty years of inaction, he has become timid and distrustful of himself, and shrinks from putting himself forward. **Who am I, that I should go to Pharaoh ?** What weight can I, a foreigner, forty years an exile, with the manners of a rough shepherd, expect to have with the mighty monarch of all Egypt—the son of Rameses the Great, the inheritor of his power and his glories? And again, **Who am I, that I should bring forth the children of Israel?** What weight can I expect to have with my countrymen, who will have forgotten me— whom, moreover, I could not influence when I was in my full vigour—who then "refused" my guidance and forced me to quit them? True diffidence speaks in the words used— there is no ring of insincerity in them; Moses was now as distrustful of himself as in former days he had been confident, and when he had become fit to be a deliverer, ceased to think himself fit.

Ver. 12.—**Certainly I will be with thee.** Literally, "*Since* I will be with thee." Moses had excused himself on the ground of unfitness. God replies—"Thou wilt not be unfit, *since* I will be with thee—I will supply thy deficiencies—I will impart all the qualities thou needest—**and this shall be a sign unto thee** of my power and faithfulness—this shall assure thee that I am not sending thee upon a fruitless errand—it is determined in my counsels that not only shalt thou succeed, and lead the people out, but after that—when thou hast so done—thou and they together **shall serve me on this mountain.**" The "sign" was one which appealed to faith only, like that given to Hezekiah by Isaiah (1 K. xix. 29), but, if accepted, it gave a full assurance—the second step involved the first—the end implied the means—if Moses was of a certainty to bring the Israelites to Sinai, he must first lead them out of Egypt—he must in some way or other triumph over all the difficulties which would beset the undertaking.

Ver. 13.—**What is his name?** It is not at all clear why Moses should suppose that the Israelites would ask him this question, nor does it even appear that they did ask it. Perhaps, however, he thought that, as the Egyptians used the word "god," generically, and had a special name for each particular god—as Ammon, Phthah, Ra, Mentu, Hor, Osiris, and the like—when he told his people of "the God of their fathers," they would conclude that he, too, had a proper name, and would wish to know it. The Egyptians set much store by the names of their gods, which in every case had a meaning. Ammon was "the concealed (god)," Phthah, "the revealer," Ra, "the swift," etc. Hitherto Israel's God had had no name that could be called a proper name more than any other. He had been known as "El," "The High;" "Shaddai," "The Strong;" and "Jehovah," "The Existent;" but these terms had all been felt to be descriptive epithets, and none of them had passed as yet into a proper name. What was done at this time, by the authority of God himself, was to select from among the epithets one to be distinctly a proper name, and at the same time to explain its true meaning as something more than "The Existent"—as really "The Alone Existent"—the source of all existence. Henceforth this name, which had previously been but little used and perhaps less understood, predominated over every other, was cherished by the Jews themselves as a sacred treasure, and recognised by those around them as the proper appellation of the one and only God whom the Israelites worshipped. It is found in this sense on the Moabite stone ('Records of the Past,' vol. xi., p. 166), in the fragments of Philo-Byblius, and elsewhere.

Ver. 14.—**I AM THAT I AM.** No better translation can be given of the Hebrew words. "*I will be* that I *will be*" (Geddes) is more literal, but less idiomatic, since the Hebrew was the simplest possible form of the verb substantive. "I am *because* I am" (Boothroyd) is wrong, since the word *asher* is certainly the relative. The Septuagint, 'Εγώ εἰμι ὁ ὤν, explains rather than translates, but is otherwise unobjectionable. The Vulgate, *sum qui sum*, has absolute exactness. The idea expressed by the name is, as already explained, that of real, perfect, unconditioned, independent existence. **I AM hath sent me to you.** "I am" is an abbreviated form of "I am that I am," and is intended to express the same idea.

Ver. 15.—**The Lord God.** In the original *Jehovah elohey*—"Jehovah, God of your fathers," etc. The name is clearly an equivalent of the "I AM" in the preceding verse. The exact mode of its formation from the old root *hava*, "to be," is still disputed among the best Hebraists. **This is my name for ever.** Henceforth there will be no change—this will be my most appropriate name so long as the world endures—"The Existent"—"The Alone Existent"—"He that is, and was, and is to come" (Rev. i. 4, 8; iv. 8; xi. 17; xvi. 5). **My memorial.** The name whereby I am to be spoken of.

Ver. 16.—**Gather the elders.** It is generally thought that we are to understand by "the elders" not so much the more aged men, as those who bore a certain official rank and position among their brethren, the heads of the various houses (ch. vi. 14, 25; xi. 21), who exercised a certain authority even during the worst times of the oppression. Moses was first to prevail on them to acknowledge his mission, and was then to go with them to Pharaoh and make his representation (ver. 18). **I have surely visited you.** The words are a repetition of those used by Joseph on his deathbed (Gen. l. 24), and may be taken to mean, "I have done as Joseph prophesied—I have made his words good thus far. Expect, therefore, the completion of what he promised."

Ver. 18.—**They shall hearken to thy voice.** Moses thought they would despise him—turn a deaf ear to his words—look upon him as unworthy of credit. But it was not so. The hearts of men are in God's hands, and he disposed those of the elders to receive the message of his servant, Moses, favourably, and believe in it. (See ch. iv. 29—31.) **Thou shalt come, thou and the elders of Israel, unto the king of Egypt.** This future is perhaps one of command rather than of prophetic announcement. The elders do not seem to have actually made their appearance before Pharaoh. (See ch. v. 1—4.) They may, however, have authorised Moses and Aaron to speak in their name. **The Lord God of the Hebrews hath met with us.** Through our representative Moses. "Met with us" is undoubtedly the true meaning. **That we may sacrifice.** There was reticence here, no doubt, but no falseness. It was a part of God's design that sacrifice, interrupted during the sojourn in Egypt for various reasons, should be resumed beyond the bounds of Egypt by His people. So much of his purpose, and no more, he bade Moses lay before Pharaoh on the first occasion. The object of the reticence was not to deceive Pharaoh, but to test him.

Ver. 19.—**I am sure.** Literally, "I know," a better rendering, since, "I am sure" implies something less than knowledge. **No, not by a mighty hand.** Or "not even by a mighty hand." Pharaoh will not be willing to let you go even when my mighty hand is laid upon him. (See ch. viii. 15, 19, 32; ix. 12, 35; x. 20, 27.) "But by strong hand" (*marg.*) is a rendering which the rules of grammar do not permit.

Ver. 20.—**I will stretch out my hand.** To encourage Moses and the people, to support them in what was, humanly speaking, a most unequal contest, this important promise is made. It is a confirmation, and to some extent, an explanation of the pledge already given, "Certainly I will be with thee" (ver. 12). It shows *how* God would be with him—he would **smite Egypt with all his wonders**—what those would be was left obscure. He would come to his people's aid, and openly assert himself, and afflict and strike terror into their enemies—until at last even Pharaoh's stubborn spirit would be broken, and he would consent to **let them go.**

Vers. 21, 22.—The "spoiling of the Egyptians" has called forth much bitter comment. (See Kalisch, note on Ex. iii. 22.) It has been termed a combination of "fraud, deception and theft"—"base deceit and nefarious fraud"—"glaring villainy," and the like. The unfortunate translation of a verb meaning "ask" by "borrow" in ver. 22, has greatly helped the objectors. In reality, what God here commanded and declared was this :—The Israelite women were told on the eve of their departure from Egypt to ask presents (*bakhsheesh*) from their rich Egyptian neighbours, as a contribution to the necessary expenses of the long journey on which they were entering ; and God promised that he would so favourably incline the hearts of these neighbours towards them, that, in reply to their request, articles of silver and of gold, together with raiment, would be freely and bounteously bestowed on them—so freely and so bounteously, that they might clothe and adorn, not only themselves, but their sons and daughters, with the presents ; and the entire result would be that, instead of quitting Egypt like a nation of slaves, in rags and penniless, they would go forth in the guise of an army of conquerors, laden with the good things of the country, having (with their own good-will) "spoiled the Egyptians." No fraud, no deceit, was to be practised—the Egyptians perfectly well understood that, if the Israelites once went, they would never voluntarily return—they were asked to give and they gave—with the result that Egypt was "spoiled." Divine justice sees in this a rightful nemesis. Oppressed, wronged, down-trodden, miserably paid for their hard labour during centuries, the Israelites were to obtain at the last something like a compensation for their ill-usage ; the riches of Africa were to be showered on them. Egypt, "glad at their departing," was to build them a bridge of gold to expedite their flight, and to despoil herself in order to enrich her quondam slaves, of whom she was, under the circumstances, delighted to be rid.

Ver. 22.—**Borrow.** The Hebrew word means simply "ask" (αἰτήσει, LXX. ; *postulabit*, Vulg.). **Of her neighbours.** The intermixture to some extent of the Egyptians with the Hebrews in Goshen is here again implied, as in chs. i. and ii. **And of her that sojourneth in her house.** Some of the Israelites, it would seem, took in Egyptian lodgers superior to them in wealth and rank. This implies more friendly feeling between the two nations than we should have expected ; but it is quite natural that, after their long stay in Egypt, the Hebrews should have made a certain number of the Egyptians their friends.

HOMILETICS.

Vers. 1, 2.—*The Burning Bush.*—All nations have seen in fire something emblematic of the Divine nature. The Vedic Indians made Agni (fire) an actual god, and sang hymns to him with more fervour than to almost any other deity. The Persians maintained perpetual fires on their fire-altars, and supposed them to have a divine character. Hephaistos in the Greek and Vulcan in the Roman mythology were fire-gods; and Baal, Chemosh, Moloch, Tabiti, Orotal, etc., represented more or less the same idea. Fire is in itself pure and purifying; in its effects mighty and terrible, or life-giving and comforting. Viewed as light—its ordinary though not universal concomitant—it is bright, glorious, dazzling, illuminative, soul-cheering. God under the Old Covenant revealed himself in fire, not only upon this occasion, but at Sinai (ch. xix. 18; xxiv. 17), to Manoah (Judg. xiii. 20), to Solomon (2 Chr. vii. 1—3), to Ezekiel (Ezek. i. 4—28), to Daniel (Dan. vii. 9, 10); under the New Covenant, he is declared to be "a consuming fire" (Heb. xii. 29), "the Light of the world" (John viii. 12), "the True Light" (ib. i. 9), "the Sun of Righteousness." Of all material things nothing is so suitable to represent God as this wonderful creation of his, so bright, so pure, so terrible, so comforting! To Moses God reveals himself not merely in fire, but in a "burning bush." In this respect the revelation is abnormal—nay, unique, without a parallel. Surely this was done, not merely to rouse his curiosity, but to teach him some lesson or other. It is well to consider what lesson or lessons may have been intended by it. First, Moses would see that "the ways of God were not as man's ways;" that, instead of coming with as much, he came with as little, display as possible; instead of showing all his glory and lighting up all Sinai with unendurable radiance, he condescended to appear in a small circumscribed flame, and to rest upon so mean, so poor, so despised an object as a thorn-bush. God "chooseth the weak things of the world to confound the strong;" anything is sufficient for his purpose. He creates worlds with a word, destroys kingdoms with a breath, cures diseases with clay and spittle or the hem of a garment, revolutionises the earth by a group of fishermen. Secondly, he would see the spirituality of God. Even when showing himself in the form of fire, he was not fire. Material fire would have burnt up the bush, have withered its fair boughs and blasted its green leaves in a moment of time; this fire did not scathe a single twig, did not injure even the most delicate just-opening bud. Thirdly, he might be led on to recognise God's tenderness. God's mercy is "over all his works," he will not hurt one of them unnecessarily, or without an object. He "careth for cattle" (Jonah iv. 11), clothes the lilies with glory (Matt. vi. 28—30), will not let a sparrow fall to the ground needlessly (ib. x. 29). Lastly, he might learn that the presence of God is "consuming" only of what is evil. Of all else it is preservative. God was present with his people in Egypt, and his presence preserved them in that furnace of affliction. God was present in each devout and humble heart of his true followers, and his presence kept them from the fiery darts of the Wicked One. God would be present through all time with his Church and with his individual worshippers, not as a destroying, but as a sustaining, preserving, glorifying influence. His spiritual fire would rest upon them, envelop them, encircle them, yet would neither injure nor absorb their life, but support it, maintain it, strengthen it.

Ver. 3.—*The impulse to draw nigh.* Moses saw a strange sight; one that he had never seen before; one that struck him with astonishment. His natural impulse was to inquire into its cause. God has implanted in us all this instinct, and we should do ill if we were to combat it. Natural phenomena are within reason's sphere; and Moses, who had never yet seen a supernatural sight, could not but suppose, at first beholding it, that the burning bush was a natural phenomenon. That he approached to examine is an indication that he was a man of spirit and intelligence; not a coward who might have feared some snare, not careless and unobservant, as too many country folk are. He drew near to see more clearly, and to use his other senses in discovering what the "great thing" was—acting like a sensible man and one who had had a good education.

Vers. 4—6.—*The prohibition, and the ground of it.* Suddenly the steps of the inquirer are arrested. Wonder upon wonder! a voice calls to him out of the bush, and calls him by his own name, "Moses, Moses!" Now must have dawned on him the conviction that it was indeed a "great thing" which he was witnessing; that the ordinary course of nature was broken in upon; that he was about to be the recipient of one of those wonderful communications which God from time to time had vouchsafed to his forefathers, as to Adam, Enoch, Noah, Abraham, Isaac, and

Israel.   Hence his submissive, child-like answer, "Here I am."   (Compare 1 Sam. iii. 4, 6.)   Then came the solemn prohibition, "Draw not nigh hither."   Man, until sanctified, until brought into covenant, must not approach near to the dread presence of the Supreme Being.   At Sinai Moses was commanded to "set bounds" to keep the people off, that no one might "go up into the mount, nor touch the border of it" (ch. xix. 12). The men of Bethshemesh were smitten with death, to the number of 50,070, for looking into the ark of the covenant (1 Sam. vi. 19).   Uzzah was slain for putting forth his hand to touch it, when he thought that there was danger of its falling (2 Sam. vi. 7).   God, under the Old Covenant, impressed on man in a multitude of ways his unapproachableness.   Hence all the arrangements of the Temple ; the veil guarding the sanctuary, into which only the high-priest could enter once in the year; the main temple-building, only to be entered by the priests; the courts of the Levites, of the Israelites, and of the Gentiles, each more and more remote from the Divine Presence. Hence the purifications of the priests and of the Levites before they could acceptably offer sacrifice; hence the carrying of the Ark by means of staves forming no part of it ; hence the side-chambers of the Temple, emplaced on "rests" in the walls, "that the beams should not be fastened in the walls of the house" (1 Kings vi. 6).   It was so needful to impress on men, apt to conceive of God as "such an one as themselves," his awful majesty, purity, and holiness, that artificial barriers were everywhere created to check man's rash intrusion into a Presence for which he was unfit.   Thus reverence was taught, man was made to know and to feel his own unworthiness, and, little by little, came to have some faint conception of the absolute perfectness and incomprehensible greatness of the Supreme One.   Further, God being such as this, each place where he makes himself manifest, becomes at once *holy ground.*   Though "heaven is his throne, and earth his footstool," and no "place" seems worthy of him or can contain him, yet it pleases him, in condescension to our infirmities and our finiteness, to choose some spots rather than others where he will make himself known and make his presence felt.   And these at once are sacred.   So was the mount to which Moses went up; so was Shiloh; so was Araunah's threshingfloor; so was Jerusalem.   And so in our own days are churches and the precincts of churches. God's presence, manifested in them, albeit spiritually and not materially, hallows them. And the reverent heart feels this, and cannot but show its reverence by outward signs.   In the East shoes were put off.   With us the head should be uncovered, the voice hushed, the eye cast down.   We should feel that "God is in the midst of us." So felt Moses, when God had proclaimed himself (ver. 6), and not only bared his feet as commanded, but shrouded his face in his robe—"for he was afraid to look upon God."   All his own sinfulness and imperfection rushed to his thought, all his unworthiness to behold God and live.   Jacob had once seen God "face to face," and had marvelled that "his life was preserved" (Gen. xxxii. 30).   Moses shut out the awful Vision.   So Elijah, on the same site, when he heard the "still small voice" (1 Kings xix. 13); and so even the seraphim who wait continually before God's Throne in heaven (Is. vi. 2).   Consciousness of imperfection forces the creature to stand abashed in the presence of the Creator.

Vers. 7—10.—*The call of Moses.*   With face covered, but with ears attent to hear, Moses stands before God to learn his will.   And God takes him, as it were, into counsel, not only calling him to a certain work, but revealing to him why he is called, what exactly he is to do, and what will be the issue of his enterprise.   1. WHY HE IS CALLED.   He is called because the affliction of Israel—their sufferings—from the constant toil, from the brutal taskmasters, from the cruel Pharaoh, from the apparent hopelessness of their position—had reached to such a point that God could allow it to go on no longer. There is a point at which he will interfere to vindicate the oppressed and punish the wrong-doers, even if the oppressed are too much crushed, too downtrodden, too absolutely in despair, to cry to him.   Their *case* calls to him; their "blood cries from the ground."   But in this instance actual despair had not been reached.   His people had "cried to him."   And here was a second reason why he should interfere.   God is never deaf to any prayers addressed to him for succour; he may not always grant them, but he hears them.   And if they are sustained, and earnest, and justified by the occasion, he grants them.   Such was the case now, and Moses was called because of the *extreme* affliction of the Israelites, and because of their prolonged and earnest cry to God under it. 2. Moses is told WHAT HE IS TO DO. He is to " bring forth the children of Israel out of Egypt" (ver. 10); and, as a preliminary step, he is to "go to Pharaoh" (*ibid.*). Thus he is directed to return to Egypt forthwith, and to put himself into communication with the new king who had succeeded the one from whom he had fled. So much is made clear to him. He, an exile for forty years, and a mere hireling shepherd of the desert during that space, is to seek an interview with the great monarch of all Egypt, and to plead the cause of his people before him—to endeavour to induce him to "let them go." A difficult enterprise, to say the least; humanly speaking, a hopeless one. How should a king be induced to allow the departure of 600,000 able-bodied labourers, whose condition was that of state slaves, who could be set to any work which the king had in hand—to keep cattle, or make bricks, or build cities, or erect walls, or excavate canals? What inducement was to be offered to him to make the sacrifice? Such thoughts would naturally occur to Moses under the circumstances, and would naturally have risen to his lips but for the distinct announcement made with regard to the further point. 3. WHAT WOULD BE THE ISSUE OF THE ENTERPRISE. The Divine declaration, "I am come down to deliver them, and to bring them up out of that land into a good land and a large," was so definite and clear a statement, so positive a promise of success, as to override all objections on the score of the task being an impossible one. God "had come down to deliver" his people, and would undoubtedly do it, whatever opposition was raised. Thus, to counteract the despondency which the consideration of the existing facts and circumstances was calculated to produce, there was held forth before Moses the positive assurance of success; the certainty that God would make good his word; would, however difficult it seemed, lead his people forth, deliver them out of the hand of the Egyptian, and make them the masters of another land, large and good, flowing with milk and honey, into possession of which they would enter through his might and by his irresistible assistance.

Ver. 11.—*Fitness of Moses to be God's instrument in delivering Israel.* The fitness of Moses to be Israel's deliverer will appear if we consider, first, What were the qualities which the part of deliverer required; secondly, how far they were united in him; and thirdly, what reasons there are for believing that, at the time, they were not united to the same extent in any other person. 1. NECESSARY QUALITIES OF THE DELIVERER. As having to deal, in the first instance, with a great king and his court, it was necessary that the Deliverer should be familiar with the habits of the court, should be able to assume its manners, speak its language, and not unwittingly infringe its etiquette. Not being set merely to petition, but to require—to prefer demands—it was requisite that he should feel himself, socially, on a par with the monarch, so as not to be timid or abashed before him, but able without difficulty to assert himself, to use freedom of speech, to talk as prince with prince, and not as mere courtier with monarch. Again, as having to meet and baffle Egyptian priests, and further, to be not only the Deliverer, but the Teacher and Educator of his nation, it was to the last degree necessary that he should be "learned in all the wisdom" of the time; that he should have had as good an education as any other man of the day; be able to foil the priests with their own weapons; and, after delivering his people out of bondage, be capable of elevating them, instructing them, advancing them from a rabble of slaves into an orderly, self-sufficient, fairly-enlightened, if not highly-civilised, nation. Once more: a moral fitness was necessary. The Deliverer needed to have high aspirations, a bold spirit, fervent zeal, and yet to have all these under control; to be calm, quiet, self-contained, imperturbable in danger, persevering, prompt, considerate. Moreover, he needed to be a religious man. Anyone not upheld by high religious principle, anyone not possessed of deep and true faith, would have fallen away in some of the trials through which the nation had to pass; would have despaired, or murmured, or "lusted after evil things" (1 Cor. x. 6), or waxed proud and wanton, or grown weary of seemingly interminable wanderings, and settled down in Arabia or even returned to Egypt. 2. MOSES' POSSESSION OF THESE QUALITIES. Moses was familiar with the customs of the Egyptian court, having been brought up in the household of a princess, and been himself a courtier until he was nearly forty years of age. Though he had subsequently spent forty years in the desert, this would not unfit him; since, in the first place, Egyptian manners and customs were unchanging; and secondly, life in the desert is at no time a bad school of manners. Arabian ,shepherds are not like European ones. As much politeness is often seen in the tent of a Bedouin as in the drawingroom of an empress. Moses probably *thought* that his forty years of seclusion rendered him less suited for the atmosphere of a court, but he was probably mistaken. What he may have lost in polish he gained in simplicity, directness, and general force of character. Moses, again, could speak with the Pharaoh almost as an equal, since as the adopted son of a princess he had been accounted a prince, and may even, before his flight, have met Menephthah´ in the royal palace on terms of social equality. On the education and "wisdom" of Moses we have already descanted, and it will scarcely be questioned that in these respects he was eminently fitted for the part assigned to him by Providence. His character, too, as chastened and ripened in Midian, made him exceptionally fit. Audacity, high aspirations, strong sympathies, a burning zeal, had shown themselves in the conduct that led to his exile. These had been disciplined and brought under control by the influences of desert life, which had made him calm, self-contained, patient, persevering, considerate, without quenching his zeal or taming his high spirit. And of his religious principle there is no question. If he angered God once by "speaking unadvisedly" (Ps. cvi. 33; Num. xx. 10), this does but show that he was human, and therefore not perfect. Apart from this one occasion his conduct as leader of the people is, as nearly as possible, blameless. And his piety is everywhere conspicuous. 3. NO ONE BUT MOSES POSSESSED THE NECESSARY QUALITIES. With the limited knowledge that we possess, the negative is incapable of positive proof. But, so far as our historical knowledge goes, there is no one who can be named as possessing any one of the necessary qualities in a higher degree than Moses, much less as uniting them all. No Hebrew but Moses had had, so far as we know, the advantages of education and position enjoyed by Moses. No Egyptian would have been trusted by the Hebrew nation and accepted as their leader. No one who was neither Egyptian nor Hebrew would have had any weight with either people. Thus Moses was the one and only possible deliverer, exactly fitted by Providence for the position which it was intended he should take: raised up, saved, educated, trained by God to be his instrument in delivering his people, and so exactly fitted for the purpose.

Vers. 11—12.—*Moses' timidity notwithstanding his fitness.* It is not often that those are most confident of their powers who are fittest for God's work. Great capacity is constantly accompanied by a humble estimate of itself. Jeremiah's reply when God called him was: "Ah! Lord God, I cannot speak, for I am a child" (Jer. i. 6). Newton seemed to himself a child gathering shells upon the shores of the ocean of Truth. The exclamation of Moses, "Who am I that I should go," etc. has been echoed by thousands. If, however, God's call is clear, the voice of self-depreciation is not to be much listened to. He knows best whether we are fit to work out his purposes, or no. Whether the call is to be an ordinary minister, or a missionary, or a bishop, or a civil leader, the foremost in a political movement, or a general at the crisis of a war, or anything else, too much timidity ought not to be shown. There is cowardice in shrinking from responsibility. If the call be, clearly from without, not courted by ourselves, not sought, not angled for, not assignable to any unworthy motive, then it is to be viewed as God's call; and the proper answer is "Speak, Lord, for thy servant heareth." Unfit as we may think ourselves, we may be sure that he will not leave us to ourselves—his grace will be sufficient for us—he will give us all the strength we need.

Vers. 13—15.—*God's revelation of himself under the name Jehovah, and the meaning of it.* At first sight the name by which God shall be called may seem unimportant, as it is unimportant whether a man be called Tully or Cicero. But, originally, each name that is given to God is significant; and according as one name or another is commonly used, one idea or another of the Divine nature will be prevalent. Hitherto God had been known mainly to the Semites as *El, Eliun, Elohim,* "Exalted, Lofty," or *Shaddai,* "Strong, Powerful." Another name known to them, but rarely used, was JHVH, "Existent." (The vocalisation of the name has been lost, and is uncertain.) God was now asked by Moses under what name he should speak of him to the Israelites, and was bidden to speak of him as JHVH. What, then, was the full meaning of JHVH, and why was it preferred to the other names? Probably as a security against polytheism. When words expressive of such attributes as exaltation, strength, knowledge, goodness, beautifulness, even creative energy, are made into names of God, there is a temptation at once to extend them from the one to the many, from the possessor of the attribute in the highest degree to others who possess it, or are supposed to possess it, in a high degree. Thus all such words come to be used in the plural, and the way is paved for polytheism. But if God is called "the Existent," this danger disappears; for there are but two kinds or degrees of existence, viz., self-existence, and created, dependent existence. "The Existent" must mean "the Self-Existent," who must necessarily be One. Hence JHVH never had a plural. The only way by which an Israelite could become a polytheist was by deserting Jehovah altogether and turning to *Elohim*. In vindicating to himself the name Jehovah, "He who exists," or "He who *alone* exists," God declared himself to be—1, eternal; 2, uncaused; 3, unconditioned; 4, independent; 5, self-sufficient. He placed a gulf, profound—not to be bridged—between himself and every other being. He indicated that all other gods were unrealities—breath, vapour, shadows of shades; that he alone was real, stable, to be trusted; and that in him his worshippers might have "quietness and assurance for ever."

Ver. 16.—*The Divine injunction to gather the elders.* God here added another injunction to those which he had previously given (ver. 10), as to the *modus operandi* which Moses was to adopt. He was to go to the children of Israel, but not immediately or as the first step. Before making any appeal to them he was, in the first instance, to "gather the elders of Israel together." In this is involved a principle of very general application. When great designs are on hand, consultation should first be with the few. With the few matters can be calmly and quietly discussed, without passion or prejudice; questions can be asked, explanations given. And the few will have influence with the many. This was the whole idea of ancient government, which was by a king, a council, and an assembly of the people, which last was expected to ratify the council's decision. Direct appeal to the masses is, as much as possible, to be avoided. The masses are always, comparatively speaking, ignorant, stolid, unimpressible. Great ideas take root and grow by being first communicated in their fulness to a "little flock," who spread them among their companions and acquaintance, until at length they prevail generally. So our Lord called first the Twelve, and then the Seventy, and made known his doctrine to them, leaving it to them to form the Church after his ascension.

Vers. 17, 18.—*The promises to the elders, and to Moses.* The elders were promised two things: (1) that they should be brought forth out of the affliction of Egypt, and (2) that they should be established in a good land, "a land flowing with milk and honey." Ordinary men—men who are, spiritually speaking, backward and undeveloped—require to be stirred to action by comparatively low motives. Escape from present suffering and unpleasantness, enjoyment of happiness in the future— these are practically the two chief moving powers of human action. Neither of them is a wrong motive; and Moses was instructed to appeal to each by a special promise. So may the preacher rightly do with his congregation, the minister with his flock, the father with his children. As long as men are what they are, appeals to the lower motives cannot be dispensed with *at first*. Care must, however, be taken that before each one, as he becomes fit for it, higher motives are set—such as duty, the love of goodness for goodness' sake, and—last, not least—the highest motive of all, the love of God, our Creator, Sustainer, Sanctifier, "in whom we live, and move, and have our being." Moses was promised at this point, to stimulate him to action, immediate success. He had doubted whether his people would listen to him, or regard him as anything but a dreamer. He is told, "they shall hearken unto thy voice." A great comfort to every one who feels that he has a mission is the acceptance of it by others. Each man, more or less, misdoubts himself, questions his own ability, sincerity, singleness of heart. The seal of an apostleship is the success of the apostolic efforts (1 Cor. ix. 2).

Direct promise of success at the mouth of God was, to one so faithful as Moses, as powerful to cheer, encourage, and sustain, as success itself.

Vers. 19, 20.—*Pharaoh's obduracy, and God's mode of overcoming it.* There are stubborn hearts which no warnings can impress, no lessons teach, no pleading, even of God's Spirit, bend. With such he " will not always strive." After they have resisted him till his patience is exhausted, he will break them, crush them, overrule their opposition, and make it futile. God's will surely triumphs in the end. But it may be long first. God is so patient, so enduring, so long-suffering, that he will permit for months, or even years, the contradiction of sinners against himself. He will not interfere with the exercise of their free-will. He will warn, chide, chasten, afflict, contend with the sinner; try him to the uttermost; seek to lead him to repentance; give him chance after chance. But he will not compel him to submit himself; man may resist to the last; and even " curse God and die " at war with him. The final success in such a struggle cannot, however, rest with man. God " will not alway be chiding, neither keepeth he his anger for ever." At the fitting time he " stretches forth his hand and smites " the sinner, strikes him down, or sets him aside, as the storm-wind sets aside a feeble barrier of frail rushes, and works his own will in his own way. Mostly he works by natural causes; but now and again in the history of the world he has asserted himself more openly, and has broken the power and chastised the pride of a Pharaoh, a Benhadad, or a Sennacherib, in a miraculous way. Such manifestations of his might produce a marked effect, causing, as they do, " all the kingdoms of the earth to know that he is the Lord God, and he only " (2 Kings xix. 19).

Vers. 21, 22.—*God brings good out of evil.* Had Pharaoh yielded at the first, the Egyptians would have seen the departure of Israel with regret, and would have in no way facilitated it. The opposition of the king and court, the long struggle, the ill-usage of the Israelites by the monarch who so often promised to release them, and so often retracted his word, awoke a sympathy with the Israelites, and an interest in them, which would have been altogether lacking had there been no opposition, no struggle, no ill-usage. Again, the plagues, especially the last, thoroughly alarmed the Egyptians, and made them anxious to be quit of such dangerous neighbours. " Egypt was glad of their departing, for they were afraid of them " (Ps. cv. 38). But for Pharaoh's obduracy the plagues would not have been sent; and but for the plagues the departing Israelites would not have been looked upon by the Egyptians with the " favour " which led to their going out laden with gifts. Thus Pharaoh's stubbornness, though it led to their sufferings being prolonged, led also to their final triumphant exit, as spoilers, not as spoiled, laden with the good things of Egypt, " jewels of silver and jewels of gold," and rich apparel, the best that the Egyptians had to offer. History presents an infinitude of similar cases, where the greatest advantages have been the result of oppression and wrong. Extreme tyranny constantly leads to the assertion of freedom; anarchy to the firm establishment of law; defeat and ill-usage by a conqueror to the moral recovery of a declining race or nation. Each man's experience will tell him of the good that has arisen to him individually from sickness, from disappointment, from bereavement, from what seemed at the time wholly evil. God brings good out of evil in a thousand marvellous ways; at one time by turning the hearts of oppressors, at another by raising the tone and spirit of the oppressed; now by letting evil run riot until it produces general disgust, anon by making use of adverse circumstances to train a champion and deliverer. Countless are the evidences that God causes evil to work towards good; uses it as an instrument—evolves his own purposes, in part, by its means, vindicating thus his absolute lordship over all, and showing that evil itself, though it fight against him, cannot thwart him.

HOMILIES BY VARIOUS AUTHORS.

Vers. 1—5.—*Moses at the bush.* We do not now see burning bushes, or hear voices calling to us from their midst. The reason is, that we do not need them. The series of historical revelations is complete. Revelation in the sense of the communication of new truth—of truth beyond the range of our natural faculties, or not capable of being derived, under the guidance of God's Spirit, from revelations already given—is not to be expected. The Bible is the sum of God's authoritative revelations to the race. This bush, *e.g.*, still burns for us in Scripture, where at any time we can visit it, and hear God's voice speaking out of it. But in another sense, revelation is not obsolete. It is not a tradition of the past, but a living reality. It has its *objective* side in the continuous (non-miraculous) revelation going on in nature (Ps. xix. 1; Rom. i. 19, 20) and history (Acts xvii. 26, 27); and in the tokens of a supernatural presence and working in the Church (Matt. xxviii. 20, 1 Thess. i. 3 10; Rev. ii. 1). And it has its *subjective* side in the revelation (mediate) of Divine things to the soul by the Holy Spirit (Eph. i. 17), and in the manifestation of God to the heart in private spiritual experience (John xiv. 21, 23; Rom. v. 5; viii. 16). The veil between the soul and the spiritual world is at all times a thin one. The avenues by which God can reach devout minds are innumerable. The Word, sacraments, and prayer are special *media*, the Divine Spirit taking of the things of Christ, and showing them to the soul (John xvi. 15), illuminating, interpreting, applying, confirming. But, in truth, God is "not far from every one of us" (Acts xvii. 27); and by events of providence, in workings of conscience, through our moral and spiritual intuitions, enlightened and purified as these are by the Word, by numberless facts of nature and life, he can still draw near to those who tarry for him; meets them in ways as unexpected and surprising as at the burning bush; awes them by his wonders; flashes to them the messages of his grace. Viewing this revelation at the bush as a chapter in spiritual history, consider—

I. THE CIRCUMSTANCES OF IT. The revelation came to Moses—(1) unexpectedly; (2) while in the way of duty—he "kept the flock;" (3) in a solemn place—"mountain of God," a natural oratory and place of sacred repute—and probably while revolving solemn thoughts; (4) from a most unlooked-for quarter—a common bush; and at first (5) impersonally. The bush burning had no apparent relation to Moses more than to another. It was there for him to look at, to inquire into, *if he chose*. It invited, but did not compel, or even ask for, his attention. All which circumstances are significant. 1. *The Divinity is ever nearer to us than we think.* So Jacob, as well as Moses, found it. "Surely God is in this place, and I knew it not" (Gen. xxviii. 16). 2. Revelations are not to be expected, *save in the way of duty.* 3. God may be met with anywhere (John iv. 24), but *some places are more favourable for communion with God than others*—the closet (Matt. vi. 6), the sanctuary (Ps. lxxiii. 16, 17), natural solitudes (Matt. xvi. 23). And revelations have usually a relation to the state of mind of those who receive them—answering questions, resolving perplexities, affording guidance, adapting themselves to psychological conditions (cf. Job ii. 12, 13; Dan. ii. 29; ix. 20, 21; x. 2—6; Acts x. 3, 10; 1 Cor. xii. 9; Rev. i. 10). It is in every way likely that Moses' thoughts were at that moment deeply occupied about Israel's future. 4. *God's discoveries of himself are marked by great condescension.* Lowliness of situation is no bar to the visits of the King of Heaven, while humility of heart is indispensable to our receiving them. He who dwelt in the bush will not refuse the dwelling place of the contrite heart (Is. lvii. 15). God's most wonderful discoveries of himself have been made through "base things of the world, and things which are despised" (1 Cor. ii. 28). The highest example of this is Christ himself, of whose incarnation the angel in the bush may be regarded as a prophecy. "He shall grow up before him as a tender plant, and as a root out of a dry ground; he hath no form nor comeliness," etc. (Is. liii. 2). 5. *God's revelations act as a moral test.* This applies to the objective revelation—to the tokens of the supernatural strewn everywhere around us in life and history, as well as to Nature and the Bible. We may pass them unheeded, or we may draw nearer to inquire. The Bible invites attention by the supernatural in its history, as well as by its teachings. It is only when we draw nearer to it that the Word becomes personal, and seizes on the conscience with spiritual power. Attention on man's part is rewarded by further self-discovery on God's.

II. ITS INTEREST FOR MOSES. We may connect his turning aside to see (ver. 4)— 1. *With an appeal to his faculty of wonder.* This is one function of miracle—to arrest attention, and awaken in the witness of it a powerful consciousness of the Divine presence. 2. *With a general habit of devout inquiry.* It may be true that "many a man has been led through the pale of curiosity into the sanctuary of reverence"

(Parker); but it is also true that to a merely curious disposition God usually reveals little, and to an irreverent one nothing. The habit of inquiry is as valuable, if one's ultimate aim is in all things to become acquainted with God and his will, as in science and philosophy, or any other form of the pursuit of knowledge; but let inquiry be devout. "Search the Scriptures" (John v. 39). Ponder thoughtfully events of providence and facts of history. Study Nature with an eye to spiritual suggestions—to underlying spiritual analogies. Give to whatever you read or hear, which seems to have truth or value in it, the attention it deserves. Inquiry throws the mind into the attitude most favourable for receiving Divine revelations. Moses was not called by name till he "turned aside to see." 3. *With the perception that in this circumstance God was specially calling him to inquire.* As Moses gazed, he would be prompted to ask about this bush—What means it? What invisible power is here manifesting itself? Why is it burning at this place, and at this time? What mystery is contained in it? Has it a message for *me?* And he would not be long in perceiving that it must be burning there with the special view of attracting his attention. And is it not thus that the Divine usually draws near to us? Attention is arrested by something a little aside from the course of ordinary experience, and the impression it makes upon us produces the conviction that it is not unintended; that it is, as we say, "sent;" that it has a meaning and message to us we do well to look into. Every man, at some point or another in his history, has felt himself thus appealed to by the supernatural. The impression may be made by a book we feel drawn to read, or by something we read in it; through a sermon, through some event of life, by a sickness, at a deathbed, by the sayings and doings of fellow-men, or in hours of solitude, when even Nature seems peopled with strange voices, and begins to speak to us in parables. But, originate as it may, there is plainly in it, as in all special dealings of God with us, a call to inquire, to question ourselves, to ask whether, from the midst of the mystery, God may not have some further message for our souls.

III. THE SIGHT ITSELF. The bush that burned (ver. 2) was—1. *A token of the Divine Presence.* Moses would soon feel that he was standing in presence of the Unseen Holy. 2. *A significant emblem.* It represented the Israelites in their state of affliction, yet miraculously surviving. Possibly, in the questionings of his spirit, Moses had not before sufficiently considered the "token for good" implied in this astonishing preservation of the nation, and needed to have his attention directed to it. It was a clear proof that the Lord had not cast off his people. If Israel was preserved, it could only be for one reason. The continued vitality, growth, and vigour of the nation was the infallible pledge of the fulfilment of the promise. 3. *An answer to prayer.* For what could be the meaning of this portent, but that the long, weary silence was at length broken; that the prayer, "O Lord, how long?" was at last to receive its answer? Faith can see great results wrapped up in small beginnings. For nothing in God's procedure is isolated. Beginnings with God mean endings too.

IV. THE PERSONAL CALL. As Moses wondered—1. *The revelation became personal.* He heard himself addressed by name, "Moses, Moses" (ver. 4). Solemnised, yet with that presence of mind which could only arise from long habituation to the idea of an invisible spiritual world, he answered, "Here am I." This was to place himself unreservedly at God's disposal. Mark the order—(1) God revealing (ver. 1); (2) man attending (ver. 2); (3) the revelation becoming personal (ver. 3). Then followed the direction (ver. 5), "Draw not nigh hither; put off thy shoes," etc. Thus Moses was instructed: 2. As to *the right attitude towards God's revelations.* (1) Self-surrender; (2) reverence; (3) obedience. Moses doubtless obeyed the injunction he received. These qualities meet in all true religion: humility in hearing what God has to say; submission of mind and heart to it when said; readiness to obey. Glance for a moment at the requirement of *reverence.* One can understand how in the tumult of his feelings at the moment—in the very eagerness of his spirit to hear what further God had to say to him—Moses should be in danger of neglecting the outward tokens of the reverence which no doubt he felt; but it is instructive to observe that God recalls his attention to them. We are thus taught that reverence becomes us, not only in relation to God himself, but in relation to whatever is even outwardly connected with his presence, worship, or revelation. *E.g.*, in our dealing with Scripture, in the use of Divine names and titles, in the ritual of Divine service. The attitude of the spirit is doubtless the main thing; but a reverent spirit will seek for itself suitable forms of expression; and respect for the forms is itself a duty, and an aid in the education of the sentiment. Those are greatly to be censured who, presuming on a supposed special intimacy with God not granted to others, venture to take liberties, and allow themselves in a demeanour and in a style of expression to the Almighty at the least irreverently familiar, and not unfrequently bordering on profanity. Raptures of piety, however sincere, do not justify us in forgetting that in communion with God we stand on "holy ground." J. O.

Vers. 1—5.—*The bush and its suggestions.* Glean here a few of the general suggestions of the passage :—

I. REVELATION. The appearance at the bush suggestive—1. Of the supernatural *in Nature.* Bushes are aglow all around us, if only we had eyes to see them. Christ's teaching an illustration of the spiritual suggestiveness of Nature. "Consider the lilies" (Matt. vi. 28). The parables. 2. Of the supernatural *in common life.* "Moses kept the flock of Jethro." The Higher Presence may be with us in the humblest occupations. 3. Of the supernatural *in the Church*—(1) As a whole; (2) Individual believers. The bush, burning but not consumed, an emblem of Israel—of the Church—enduring in tribulation. 4. Of *the higher supernatural of positive revelation.* Authoritative revelation is suspended, but the sum of its results is given in Scripture. The Bible is the Bush of revelation, to which the student of Divine things will do well to direct his attention.

II. PREPAREDNESS. Cultivate with Moses—1. A spirit of duty (ver. 1). 2. A spirit of devout inquiry (ver. 3). 3. A spirit of *humility* and *reverence* (vers. 5, 6). To such a spirit, God—1. Reveals himself. 2. Addresses calls to his service (ver. 4). 3. Gives work to do. 4. Honours in its work.—J. O.

Ver. 2.—*The bush in history.* The bush had primary reference to Israel, and the fire in the bush represented Jehovah's fiery presence in the midst of his people—1. For their *protection.* A fire flaming forth to consume the adversaries. 2. For their *purification.* God was in the fires that tried them, as well as in the power that upheld them. The fire was thus a figurative representation at once of destroying punishment and of refining affliction. But the bush, while burning, was not consumed. This involves the principle that nothing, however weak and perishable in itself, with which God connects his presence, or which he wills to continue in existence, can by any possibility be destroyed. From this point of view—a thoroughly legitimate one—the emblem admits of various applications, and directs our attention to a series of supernatural facts yet greater than itself, and well deserving our turning aside to see. 1. There is the obvious application to *the Church,* which to a thoughtful mind, pondering as it should the facts of history, is a veritable repetition of the wonder of the bush "burning but not consumed." The bush is an emblem of the Church in the other respect of outward plainness and unattractiveness. And it is noteworthy that the times when the Church has forgotten her calling to be meek and lowly in heart, and has aspired to great outward splendour, and been ambitious of worldly supremacy, have invariably been times of marked decline in purity and spirituality. She fares best when content with modest outward pretensions. 2. A second application is to *the nation of the Jews*—also a "sign and wonder" in history (see Keble's hymn, "The Burning Bush"). 3. A third is to *the Bible.* What enmity has this book encountered, and what fierce attempts have been made to disprove its claims, destroy its influence, sometimes even to banish it from existence! Yet the miraculous bush survives, and retains to this hour its greenness and freshness, as if no fire had ever passed upon it. 4. Yet another application is to *individual believers,* against whom, while tried by fiery trials (1 Pet. iv. 12), neither the enmity of man, the assaults of Satan, nor providential afflictions and calamities (Job i.) are permitted to prevail, but who, under all, enjoy a support, a peace, a comfort, plainly supernatural—"dying, and behold we live" (2 Cor. vi. 9). Flippant observers may see in these things nothing worthy of peculiar attention—nothing which cannot be explained by ordinary historical causes; but sober minds will not readily agree with them. They will regard the facts now referred to as truly "great sights," and will, like Moses, reverently turn aside to inquire into them further. Note—1. The true glory of the Church is God in her midst. 2. The outward weakness of the Church enhances the wonder of her preservation. 3. The Church has most reason to glory in those periods of her history when she has been most despised and persecuted (Matt. v. 11; 2 Cor. xii. 9; 1 Pet. iv. 14).—J. O.

Ver. 6.—*The God of the fathers.* "I am the God of thy father, the God of Abraham," etc. In these words—

I. GOD CONNECTS HIMSELF WITH THE DEAD PATRIARCHS. They imply—1. *Continued existence;* for God, who says here, not "I *was,*" but "I *am,* the God of thy father," is, as Christ reminds us, "not the God of the dead, but of the living" (Matt. xxii. 32). The personal relation was not dissolved. The patriarchs still lived to him. 2. The *resurrection of the body.* This will not appear a far-fetched inference, if we consider the nature of the Bible hope of immortality. The Bible has little or nothing to say of an abstract "immortality of the soul." It nowhere regards the disembodied state as in itself desirable. The immortality it speaks of is the immortality of the "man"—of man in his whole complex personality of body, soul, and spirit. This implies a resurrection. The life forfeited by sin was a life in the body, and so must be the life restored by Redemption. The covenant-promise could not fall below the hopes of the heathen; and even Egyptian theology held by the notion of a revival of the body, as essential to perfected existence. Hence the practice of embalming, with which compare the care of the body by the patriarchs.

II. CONNECTS THIS REVELATION WITH PAST REVELATIONS, AS ONE OF A SERIES. It introduces what is to be said as the fulfilment of what had been already promised.

III. CONNECTS HIMSELF WITH THE EXISTING GENERATION. The God of the fathers is, in virtue of the promise, the God of the children.—J. O.

Vers. 7—11.—*God's sympathy with the oppressed.* I. GOD IS EVER IN SYMPATHY WITH THE OPPRESSED, AND AGAINST THEIR OPPRESSORS (vers. 7, 9). This is now, thanks to the Bible, made as certain to us as any truth can be. God's sympathy may be viewed—1. As *implied in his moral perfection.* 2. As *certified to us by the pity of our own hearts.* He who put pity in these hearts must surely himself be pitiful. Yet, so much is there in the world which bears a different aspect, that—3. *It needs revelation to assure us of it*—to put the fact beyond all doubt. And the revelation has been given. No student of God's character in the Bible can doubt that he compassionates. (1) His words declare it. (2) His deeds attest it. (3) The Cross demonstrates it. And, whatever mystery surrounds God's ways at present, he will one day make it plain by exacting a terrible retribution for all wrongs done to the defenceless (Ps. xii. 5; Jas. v. 4). 1. Comfort for the oppressed. Not one of their sighs escapes the ear of God. 2. Warning to the oppressor.

II. GOD IS PECULIARLY IN SYMPATHY WITH THE OPPRESSED, WHEN THE OPPRESSED ARE HIS OWN PEOPLE (vers. 7, 10). Israel was God's people—1. *As Abraham's seed*—children of the covenant—far gone indeed from righteousness, yet beloved for the fathers' sake (Rom. xi. 28). 2. As *retaining, in however corrupt a form, the worship of the true God.* They were his people, in a sense in which the worshippers of Osiris, and Thoth, and the other gods of Egypt, were not. 3. *As containing many true believers.* There was a spiritual Israel within the natural—an "holy seed" (Is. vi. 13) —"a remnant according to the election of grace" (Rom. xi. 5). Therefore, because Israel was God's people, God was deeply interested in them. He knew their sorrows. He was zealous on their behalf, as One whose own honour was concerned in what they suffered. And as in all their affliction he was afflicted (Is. lxiii. 9), so when the time came, he would avenge them of their adversaries. Believers have the same consolation in enduring trial (2 Thess. 4—10).

III. GOD'S SYMPATHY WITH THE OPPRESSED IS SHOWN BY HIS MERCIFULLY INTERPOSING ON THEIR BEHALF. As he interposed for Israel—as he has often interposed for his Church since—as he interposed for the salvation of the world, when, moved by our pitiable state under sin—afflicted and "oppressed of the devil" (Acts x. 38; xxvi. 18; Eph. ii. 2; Col. i. 13)—he sent his Son that "we should not perish, but have everlasting life" (John iii. 16). His sympathy with his Church is shown, not only in the comforts he imparts, and the grace by which he upholds, but in the deliverances he sends; on which remark—1. God has his own times for them. 2. Till the time comes, his people must be content to wait. 3. When it comes, no power can hinder the execution of his purpose. 4. The deliverance will bring with it compensation for all that has been endured—" a good land," etc. The *ultimate* compensation, when God has brought his people up out of the Egypt of all their afflictions, and planted them in the land of perfected bliss, will be such as to clear his character from all imputations of injustice and unkindness.—J. O.

Vers. 10—12.—*Insufficiency.* A very different Moses this from the hero who was formerly so ready, even without a call, to undertake the work of Israel's deliverance. Probably failure in that first attempt led him to doubt whether he was the instrument ordained for so great a task. He may have concluded he was not, and learned his first lesson of acquiescence in the Divine will, by surrendering the hope. Or, he may have thought himself rejected for his fault. In any case, Moses had now much juster views of the magnitude of the work, and of his natural unfitness to undertake it. Who was he—a man of lonely, self-retired spirit—that he should brave the power of the Pharaohs, or think of bringing Israel out of Egypt?
Learn—1. *Conscious unfitness for our work is one of the best preparations for it.* The greatest of God's servants have had this feeling in a remarkable degree. They needed to be " thrust forth " to the harvest (Matt. x. 38, Gr.). 2. *Conscious unfitness for work grows with the clearness of our apprehensions of the Divine call to it.* The nearer we are brought to God, the less we feel fit to serve him (Is. vi. 5). 3. *God's call and promise are sufficient reasons for undertaking any work, however deep our consciousness of personal unfitness.* " Our sufficiency is of God " (2 Cor. iii. 6). The sign in ver. 12 was a pledge to Moses that God would " make all grace to abound toward " him (2 Cor. ix. 8).—J. O.

Vers. 15—16.—*The Name.* The request of Moses to know the name of the Being who had filled him with such unutterable awe (ver. 6), rested on ideas deeply rooted in ancient modes of thought. The " name " with us tends to become an arbitrary symbol—a mere vocable. But this is not the true idea of a name. A real name expresses the *nature* of that to which it is given. It is significant. This idea of the name is the ruling one in scientific nomenclature, where names are not imposed arbitrarily, but are designed to express exactly the essential characteristics of the object or fact of Nature for which a name is sought. The man of science interrogates Nature—allows it to reveal *itself*. He stands before his fact, asking—" Tell me, I pray thee, thy name ? " (Gen. xxxii. 29), and the name but expresses the properties which come to light as the result of the interrogation. Hence, as science progresses, old names are superseded by new ones—the former no longer proving adequate to the stage at which knowledge has arrived. This illustrates in some degree the ancient idea of a name, and the desire that was felt at each new stage of revelation for a new name of God. God's Name is the revelation of his attributes or essence—the disclosure of some part or aspect of the fulness of his Deity. The vocable is valueless in itself—its significance is derived from the fact of revelation of which it is the memorial. To know God's *absolute* Name—the Name, if one might so speak, wherewith he names himself, would be to wrest from him the secret of his absolute existence. And Jacob was rebuked when, in this sense, he sought to wrest from God his Name (Gen. xxxii. 29). God's *revealed* Name expresses that of his Nature which is communicable and comprehensible—his attributes in their relations to the intelligence and needs of the creature. Each of his names is but part of the whole—a ray. The whole Name is given in the completed revelation. (An illustration of the extent to which in ancient times name and reality were held to interpenetrate each other is furnished by the practice of conjuration—the name being viewed as so truly a living part of the Being, so bound up with his essence and qualities, that to know it was to obtain a certain power over him.)
I. THE NAME ASKED (ver. 13). Moses expected that this would be the first question the people would ask him—" What is his Name ? " 1. It was *natural* to expect that a Being announcing himself, would do so by *some* name, either a name by which he was already known, or a new one given in the revelation. 2. It was *probable*, in analogy with past history, that the name would be a new one, and would serve—(1) As

a memorial of the revelation; (2) As an exponent of its significance; (3) As a clue to God's purpose in it; and (4) As a name by which God might suitably be invoked in the new crisis of their nation's history.   And 3.   It was *certain* that the people would ask this question, familiarised as they were in Egypt with the practice of invoking the gods by the one or other of their many names which bore particularly on the wants and circumstances of the worshippers.   To Moses, however, this request for the Name had a much deeper significance.   It originated, we may believe, in the felt inadequacy of all existing names of God to syllable the deep and powerful impression made on him by this actual contact with the Divine.   Cf. Jacob at Peniel (Gen. xxxii. 24—30). God in that hour was nameless to the spirit of Moses—his experience of God went beyond any name he knew for him.   A multitude of ideas crowded on him, and he could not fix or express them.   Language thus fails us in moments of extraordinary experience, not always because none of the words we know would suit our purpose, but because language tends to become conventional, and the profounder meaning which lies in words gets rubbed off them.   The name which God gave was after all not a new one, but an old name with new life put into it.

II. THE NAME GIVEN (vers. 14, 15).   God grants his servant's request.   The name is given first *explicatively,*—" I am that I am " (ver. 14), then as a *denominative*— " Jehovah " (ver. 15); while he who gives it expressly claims for himself, as formerly (ver. 6), that he is the God of the old covenants—the " Jehovah God " of the fathers (vers. 15, 16).   1. The name, as above remarked, while new in this relation, *is itself an old one.*   This is already implied in the expression—" Jehovah God of your fathers " (ver. 16); and is proved by its occurrence in the earlier history, and by the name of Moses' own mother—Jochebed (ch. vi. 20), " she whose glory is Jehovah."   This old and half-obsolete name God revives, and makes it the key-word of a new era of revelation.   2. *He who assumes the name is the "Angel of Jehovah" of ver.* 1.   The Angel— " a self-presentation of Jehovah entering into the sphere of the creature, which is one in essence with Jehovah; and is yet again different from him " (Oehler).   The soundest view is that which regards the " Angel " as the Pre-incarnate Logos—the Divine Son. 3. The name was *eminently suitable and significant.*   The ideas awakened in Moses by the revelation he had received would be such as these—God's living Personality; his enduring Existence (the same God that spoke to the fathers of old, speaking to him at Horeb); his covenant-keeping Faithfulness; his Self-identity in will and purpose; his unfailing Power (the bush burning unconsumed); his Mercy and Compassion.   All these ideas are expressed in the name Jehovah, which represents the highest reach of Old Testament revelation.   That name denotes God as—1. Personal.   2. Self-existent. 3. Eternal.   4. Independent of his creatures.   5. Self-identical.   6. Self-revealing and gracious.   Hence—1. Changeless in his purpose.   2. Faithful to his promises. 3. Able to fulfil them.   4. Certain to do so.—J. O.

Vers. 16—22.—*The two messages.*   I. THE MESSAGE TO THE ELDERS OF ISRAEL (vers. 16—18).   Moses was to go *first* to the elders of the people.   First—before he went to Pharaoh; and first—before communicating with any of the people.   This arrangement was—1. *Necessary.*   The people's consent must be obtained to their own deliverance.   God would have them co-operate with him—(1) Freely. (2) Intelligently; would carry them with him as free agents in all he did.   This applies to the higher Redemption.   Men cannot be saved without their own consent.   We must, in the sense of Phil. ii. 12, work out our own salvation—must co-operate with God, by freely adopting and falling in with his method of grace.   There must be free choice of Christ as our Saviour, free compliance with the directions of the Gospel, free co-operation with the Spirit in the work of our sanctification.   2. *Wise.*   The elders were the representatives of the people.   They had a claim to be approached first.   They were men of experience, and were better able to judge deliberately of the proposals laid before them.   They had exceptional facilities for diffusing information, while communication with them would have the additional advantage of greater privacy.   If Moses could satisfy the elders of his Divine commission, and could gain *their* intelligent consent to his proposals, the consent of the people would readily be forthcoming.   So Paul, in going up to Jerusalem, communicated the Gospel he had received " privately to them which were of reputation,"—to " James, Cephas, and John, who seemed to be pillars" (Gal. ii. 2—9). And it was not till Jesus had been decisively rejected by the authorities in Jerusalem that he commenced a popular ministry in Galilee. Learn lessons—(1) Of the respect due to constituted authorities. (2) Of the value of representative institutions. (3) Of the need of prudence and caution in the initiation and conduct of public movements. 3. *Kindly.* No time was to be lost in carrying to the Israelites the tidings of approaching deliverance. The message brought to them was a true gospel. Mark its nature. It told how God had seen their affliction, and had visited them, and would redeem them from bondage. This gives no sanction to Ewald's theory, that the Exodus had its origin in a powerful movement in the nation itself—"the most extraordinary exertions, and most noble activities of the spirit wrestling for freedom." The narrative says nothing of this mighty spiritual movement, but represents the people as lying hopeless and helpless till God visited them ; their help did not come from themselves, but from God. The two views well illustrate the two ways of conceiving the possibility of man's deliverance from the woes that oppress him. The one—the humanitarian—trusts to recuperative powers inherent in the race, to its own "extraordinary exertions" and noble spiritual activities—and predicts for it a glorious future wrought out by its own efforts. The other—the Christian—has no such hope. It views the race as lying in a state of moral and spiritual helplessness, and recognises the necessity of a salvation coming to it from without. "We look," says Neander, "upon Christianity, not as a power that has sprung up out of the hidden depths of man's nature, but as one which descended from above, when heaven opened itself anew to man's long-alienated race ; a power which, as both in its origin and essence it is exalted above all that human nature can create out of its own resources, was designed to impart to that nature a new life, and to change it in its inmost principles."

II. THE MESSAGE TO PHARAOH (ver. 18). Moses, with the elders, was to go to Pharaoh, and demand of him that the Hebrews be allowed to take a three days' journey into the wilderness, there to sacrifice to Jehovah. Note on this request—1. Its *honesty.* The ultimate design was to lead Israel out of Egypt altogether. If this first request was studiously made moderate, it was not with the intention of deceiving Pharaoh, but that it might be the easier for him to grant it. The demand was made in perfectly good faith. What was asked sufficed to test° the king's disposition. Had Pharaoh yielded, no advantage would have been taken of his compliance to effect a dishonourable escape from Egypt. New announcements would doubtless have been made to him, rewarding him as amply for obedience to this first word of God as afterwards he was punished for disobedience to it, and informing him further of the Divine intentions. 2. Its *incompleteness.* For this demand bore on the face of it that it was not the whole. It told Pharaoh his immediate duty, but beyond that left matters in a position requiring further revelation. Whatever was to follow the three days' journey, it was certain that "the God of the Hebrews," who had met with them, would never consent to his worshippers being sent back again to bondage. *That* Pharaoh must plainly enough have perceived, and Moses made no attempt to dissemble it. Learn—(1) God's counsels are revealed to men bit by bit. (2) When present duty is revealed to us, we ought to act on that, though ignorant of all that is to follow. (3) God partially hides his counsels from men, that the spirit of obedience may be tested. (4) The gravest consequences may hang on *first* acts of obedience or disobedience.

III. PHARAOH'S REJECTION OF GOD'S MESSAGE (vers. 18—22). 1. It was foreseen by God (ver. 19). Yet—2. It did not hinder the execution of God's purpose (ver. 20). Whether Pharaoh willed or not, the Exodus would take place. If not with his consent, then against it, and "by a mighty hand." Pharaoh's disobedience would be overruled— (1) To God's glory. The clay cannot escape from the hand of the potter (Jer. xviii. 6 ; Rom. ix. 21). If Pharaoh will not be made a vessel unto honour, he will be moulded into a vessel unto dishonour, and made to subserve God's purpose in another way (ch. ix. 16). (2) To his own hurt (ver. 20). His disobedience would bring on him wrath and destruction. "Woe unto him that striveth with his Maker!" (Is. xlv. 9). (3) To the enrichment of the people (vers. 21—22). The Egyptians would be glad in the end to give the Hebrews whatever they wished. So would they "spoil the Egyptians." Believers' trials tend to their ultimate enrichment (2 Cor. iv. 18). And it is the saints of God who shall yet inherit the earth. Learn also that whatever is valuable in the world's learning, science, literature, or art, is not to be despised, but to be freely appropriated by the Church, and used in God's service.—J. O.

Vers. 1—5.—*The burning bush.* I. OBSERVE THE CIRCUMSTANCES IN WHICH GOD FINDS MOSES. He is still with Jethro, although forty years have passed since their first acquaintance. Though a fugitive, he had not become a mere wanderer. 1. *He continues, however, in a comparatively humble position.* His marriage to Jethro's daughter and his long stay in the country do not seem to have brought him much external prosperity. He has not reached even the modest point of success in the eyes of a Midianite shepherd, viz. to have a flock of his own. But this very humility of position doubtless had its advantages and its place in the providence of God with respect to him. With all the lowliness of his state, it was better to be a living man in Midian than to have been slain as the son of Pharaoh's daughter. God had brought him out of a king's house, so that he might be freed from all the temptations of soft raiment, and also to make manifest that, although among courtiers, he was not of them. But if during his stay in Midian he had increased in pastoral wealth, and become a second Job (Job i. 3), then, like Job, he might have had to go into humiliation because of his wealth. It was well for him that while he had the care of property, he had not the cares of it (Jam. i. 10, 11). 2. *God finds him engaged in faithful service,* leading his flock far into the desert that they might find suitable pasture. God comes to those who are diligently occupied in some useful work, even if it be as humble and obscure as that of Moses. He does not come with his revelations to day-dreamers; they are left to build their castles in the air. They who despise common and daily work, on the pretext that they are fitted for something much better, will at last be thrown into the corner among the refuse. "Let those that think themselves buried alive be content to shine like lamps in sepulchres, and wait till God's time comes for setting them in a candlestick" (Matt. iv. 18—22, ix. 9; Luke ii. 8).

II. GOD APPROACHES MOSES WITH A SUDDEN TEST. "The angel of the Lord appeared to him in a flame of fire, out of the midst of a bush" i.e. the flame of fire became a messenger of God to Moses. We are told in Psalm civ. that God is he who makes the clouds his chariot, walks upon the wings of the wind, makes the winds his messengers, and flaming fire into his ministers (Heb. i. 7). And so here God sends this flame of fire, encompassing and attacking the bush, *in order to discover what sort of man Moses is.* Certain features of his character, viz. his patriotism, his hatred of oppression, his prompt action to serve the weak, have hitherto been exhibited rather than tested. He had shown what sort of man he was in the ordinary experiences of life, such experiences as might come to any of us. But now he is face to face with an extraordinary experience, a sudden and unexpected test. The burning bush was to Moses what both miracles and parables were to those who came into contact with Jesus. To some the miracles were mere wonders; to others they revealed an open door of communication with God. To some the parables were only aimless narratives, mere story-telling. To others the Divine Teacher was able to say, "It is given unto you to know the mysteries of the kingdom of heaven" (Matt. xiii. 11). And, in a similar way, when Moses came suddenly upon the burning bush, there was also a sudden revelation of the state of his heart. He did not treat the phenomenon as a delusion; did not begin to suspect his own sanity; did not seek his kindred, that they might come and gape at this new wonder. It was impressed upon his mind exactly as it was meant to be impressed. He asked the very question that above all others needed to be asked—why this bush was not consumed. For observe that it was something which in ordinary circumstances would be easily and quickly consumed (ch. xxii. 6; Eccl. vii. 6; Matt. vi. 30). It was not some metal well used to the fire, but *a bush actually burning yet not burning away.* And as this burning bush was thus a test to Moses, so *the record of it is also a test to us.* Let us suppose the question put all round, "What would you have done if you had been there?" We know well the answer that would come from one class of minds: "There was no such thing; it was all Moses' own imagination." Thus the test comes in. As God tested Moses in exhibiting the burning bush as his messenger, so he tests us by the record of this and all other unusual occurrences with which the Scriptures are crowded. If we say at once concerning the burning bush and all that is supernatural that it is but delusion, then God's way to our hearts and our salvation is blocked at once. We must be loyal to fact wherever we find it. The very evidence of our own senses, and the accumulated testimony of honest and competent-witnesses, are not to be sacrificed to so-called first principles of rational inquiry. The right spirit is that shown by Peter and his companion in the house of Cornelius. They saw with their own eyes that the Holy Spirit fell on Cornelius and his household; and Peter made his inferences and his action to depend on this indisputable fact (Acts x. 44; xi. 18). When Moses-turned aside to see the great sight his eye was single; he did not quibble and double; and therefore his whole body was filled with light.

III. GOD MEETS A PROPER INQUIRY WITH PROPER TREATMENT. Moses is approaching the burning bush to investigate the difficulty by his natural faculties, when *God at once arrests him, making known his own presence, and enjoining such outward marks of reverence as became the place and the occasion.* And Moses, as we might expect, is immediately obedient. Those who have in them the spirit that seeks for truth, the spirit of faith and right inquiry, will also show a spirit ready at once to respond to the presence of God. Moses must have had those principles in his life which pointed on to perfect purity of heart. That purity he had in its beginnings, or he would not have gained such a sense of God's presence as was here bestowed on him. Note next, that *God does not proceed to answer the inquiry of Moses.* There was really no occasion to answer it. When Moses knew that the presence of God had to do with the miracle, he knew enough. To know exactly how God had done it was beyond him. Even God cannot explain the inexplicable. The secrets of creation cannot be penetrated by those who lack creative power. Man can make machines; therefore the man who makes a machine can explain the purpose and the parts of it to another man. Human beings are the parents of human beings; but as they have no power to make intelligently any living thing, so they cannot understand either how living things are brought into existence or sustained in it. God calls Moses now, not to explain why the bush is burning, but to subdue his mind into appropriate reverence and expectation. The search for truth must not degenerate into curiosity, nor be pursued into presumption.

IV. THOUGH GOD LEAVES THE INQUIRY FORMALLY UNANSWERED, YET THE BURNING BUSH DOES SERVE SOME FURTHER PURPOSE AS AN INSTRUMENT OF INSTRUCTION. *There was much teaching in this burning bush.* If the aim had been merely to arrest the attention of Moses, then any wonder would have served the purpose. But the wonders of God not only test; they also teach. They must be something unusual, or they would not test sufficiently; they must be something more than merely unusual, else they would not teach. *The bush was Israel in the flame of Egypt.* That bush had been burning now a century, more or less, yet it was not consumed. All that was essential to its nature, its growth, and its fruitfulness still remained. What was permanent in Israel was no more affected than the tree is by the fading and falling of its leaves in autumn. The leaves die, but the tree remains. Its roots are still in the soil and the sap still in the trunk. Thus, by this exhibition of the burning bush, God brought before Moses the great truth that, however natural forces may be gathered against his people, and however they may be intensified in their attack, there is nevertheless a power from on high which can resist them all—a secret, countervailing power in which we may ever put our trust. And this power is not only for preservation in the midst of affliction, but for ultimate deliverance from it. The power by which God can keep the bush from being consumed, is a power by which he can take it out of the fire altogether. Believe in this power, and trust it more and more, and God will lead you into sublime conclusions, and endow you with most precious privileges.—Y.

Ver. 6.—*The God of Abraham, Isaac, and Jacob.*—Having wakened the mind of Moses into full activity, given him a revelation of supernatural power, and brought him altogether into a state of the greatest reverence and awe, God proceeds to a revelation of himself in a particular aspect—an aspect which required and repaid the most earnest attention. Notice that, unlike the revelation of the name I AM (ver. 13), it was *unsolicited.*

I. CONSIDER THE SIGNIFICANCE OF THIS NAME TO MOSES AND THE CHILDREN OF ISRAEL. 1. *It was a confident reference to the past.* Moses might look back on his own career, or that of the people to whom he belonged, with a measure of shame, doubt, humiliation, and disappointment; but God could point back to all his dealings with men as consistent, glorious, and worthy of all remembrance. 2. *It provided a certain kind of mediatorship in the knowledge of God.* It gave the best way for Moses and Israel to think of God, at that particular time. It was as if God had said to Moses, "You are to gain your chief sense of my nearness to Israel and abiding interest in them by thinking of my actual, repeated, and recorded dealings with Abraham, Isaac, and Jacob." No devout Israelite could become acquainted with that section of Genesis, from the time when God first appeared to Abram down to the death of Jacob, without feeling that the God of these three men was even a more prominent figure in the history than they are themselves. We could as easily leave out the name of Abraham from the narrative, as leave out the name of God. What we are told of Abraham is nothing, save as the effect and expression of the will of God. Abram is as a mere name, till God comes in contact with him. It is not so much a life of Abraham we are reading, as a history of how God's purposes and power became manifest in his experience. 3. *It kept before Moses the connexion of God with the lives of individuals.* God made separate appearances to each of these three men, dealing with them according to their circumstances and their character. He showed his continual and unfailing observation of their lives, by revealing his presence at every critical point. 4. *There was a connexion of peculiar importance which God had with some individuals rather than with others.* He was the God of Adam, of Enoch, and of Noah; why not have associated himself with these illustrious names? The God of Abraham, Isaac, and Jacob stood towards Israel in the relation of one who had made large promises, allowed himself to become the source of large expectations, and imposed strict requirements. He was not only the God of Abraham, Isaac, and Jacob, taken separately, but of these three men, bound together in a very peculiar way. Not only did they stand in a lineal succession, Abraham being father to Isaac, and Isaac father to Jacob, but that succession was contrary to natural expectations and customary arrangements. Isaac was the son of Abraham, but also a son born when the resources of nature were exhausted. Jacob was the son of Isaac, but also the younger son, on whom, contrary to custom, the privileges of the firstborn alighted. Thus it became impossible to describe God as the God of Abraham and Ishmael, though in a certain sense he was the God of Ishmael (Gen. xvii. 20). Nor could he be called the God of Abraham, Isaac, and Esau, though assuredly he was the God of Esau also. The only name which would indicate to Moses all he had to bear in mind, was the name which God here employs. 5. *He was the God of these men in spite of great defects of character and great blots on conduct.* They were men in whom he found much that was evil, much that indicated a low moral state, but he found in them all, and particularly in the first of them, a spirit of faith which enabled him to begin, as from a certain definite point in history, that work which is to end in all nations of the earth being blessed. Already he had made a great nation out of Abram—a persecuted and oppressed nation indeed, but none the less a great one. And had he not spoken to Abram concerning this very bondage in Egypt? (Gen. xv. 13, 14). Some such revelation as this at Horeb, to some deliverer or other, might now be expected. It must surely have been often a perplexity to Moses, what had become of this God who had done so much for Abraham, Isaac, and Jacob.

II. CONSIDER THE SIGNIFICANCE OF THIS NAME TO US. We are not mere spectators of the way in which the God of Abraham, Isaac, and Jacob approved himself as also the God of Moses and the Israelites in Egypt and in the wilderness. To speak of the God of Abraham, Isaac, and Jacob is only another way of speaking of the God of those who really believe in him. Whenever a real believer ponders this name, then it becomes one of precious associations; it leads by the very mention of it, further and further onwards in subjection to the invisible. But after all, this name, so deeply impressed on Moses, is chiefly valuable to us as suggesting a name far richer in meaning and in power. We have a look into the past which Moses had not. He looked backward and saw God's dealings with Abraham, and found in them everything to inspire faith in God and expectation from him. We look backward and see, not only Abraham, but Christ; not only Isaac, but Christ; not only Jacob, but Christ. When we look back to these men of *Genesis*, we see faith standing out like an isolated mountain in the midst of a plain; but we see much also that we would rather not see. Whereas, when we look back to Christ we see not only a full believer, but a flawless life. In him there stands the chief of those that walk by faith, the *facile princeps* of them—he who, for the joy that was set before him, endured the cross, despising the shame. His faith was such a full, exalted element of his character, that it needs much effort on our part to grasp the fact that, while here below, Jesus, as much as all the rest of us, needed to walk by faith, and was constantly compelled to struggle with unbelief. The great Jehovah is the God and Father of our Lord Jesus Christ; also the God of Paul and every true apostle. Suppose Moses could have had the spirits of Abraham, Isaac, and Jacob appear to him in Horeb, and assure him that the God of the burning bush was the God who had dealt with them in the days of their flesh; would not this have been reckoned a most confirming and exhilarating testimony? And we, practically, have a testimony of this sort. We read of Jesus regarding God as his Father, habitually and in the most appropriating way. We have his actual experience for our comfort, our inspiration, and our guide. If an Israelite was asked what God he believed, tried to serve, and had his highest expectations from, his best answer was, "The God of Abraham, Isaac, and Jacob." So we, if asked a similar question, can give no better answer than "The God of Christ and the God of Paul: the God who has ever been the same through all vicissitudes of his Church; ever loving, faithful, and sustaining."—Y.

Vers. 7—9.—*A large promise for a great need.* I. THE GREAT NEED. *It is a need carefully observed by God and well known to him.* This has been recorded already, although hardly so emphatically, in ch. ii. 23—25. It is one thing to have intelligence of God's interest communicated by some third person; quite another to hear the words of pity warm and tender from God himself. Moses and many of the Israelites may have thought that they knew the need only too well, bitter as their experiences had been; but, with all their experiences, they knew not that need as God knew it, looking down from heaven, seeing all things with his searching eye, and having a correct and complete knowledge of them. It is with great force that God represents himself *seeing* as well as *hearing*. *Hearing* indicated that he noted the representation of their troubles and needs which the people themselves made; *seeing* indicated the investigation he made for himself. God was not dependent upon the complaints of the people for his knowledge of their troubles. The cries of men are not always worthy of pity, any more than the cry of a spoilt child. Such cries can only be left unheeded, with the hope that they may end in wisdom and submission. But the cry of Israel was the cry of the oppressed, the cry of God's people; and, as God saw their state, there was ample evidence of the oppression and the cruelty. When he came down to meet Moses at Horeb, he needed not to listen to a long account of Israel's troubles; he came not in order that he might inquire, but because of what he already fully knew.

II. THE LARGE PROMISE. God may be long unmanifested, but, when he appears, it is with indubitable proofs of his presence; he may be long silent, but when he speaks, it is with statements and promises worthy of himself. He does not merely utter an expression of sympathy with suffering Israel; that expression is only the starting word of a large undertaking for the future. He repeats, emphatically, the essence of all he had ever said to Abraham, Isaac, and Jacob concerning their posterity. He has distinctly in view, not only the removal of a burden, but a future of liberty, independence, and blessedness. Thus it became manifest that the deliverance had not come earlier in time because the matter of deliverance was not the only thing in question. It had to be considered how liberty should be used when acquired. Israel needed a leader, and the leaders whom God approves are not made in a day. Israel had to wait while Moses went through his eighty years of varied discipline. Then, moreover, the people were going into a good land and a large, a land flowing with milk and honey, a land of rich pastures and great fertility, a land inhabited by six strong and warlike nations; and therefore they must not go as a handful of people. Thus, while the people were going through these great afflictions, groaning as if in despair, God was doing two things of the greatest moment. He was training Moses and increasing Israel in numbers. What a lesson to us in the midst of our afflictions, with all their consequent murmuring and unbelief! If God seemed to have little to do with Israel during these years of oppression, it was that he might have all the more to do with them, manifestly, in the years to come. Little did either Moses or Israel dream how closely God would keep to them in the future. By the word of God to him here, the thoughts of Moses were brought as at one bound from the darkness of midnight to the blaze of noonday. God does not confine himself to telling Moses that he will deliver Israel. Deliverance for its own sake was as nothing; it was for the sake of what lay beyond it. He does not say that he will deliver, and wait till the time of deliverance comes, to speak of the glories and blessings of Canaan. All these things had been spoken of generations before. God was but taking, as it were, out of some muniment-room, his old plan, first shown to Abraham; unfolding it, and showing also to Moses that it still remained in all its integrity.—Y.

Vers. 10—12.—*The first difficulty:* "*Who am I?*" Divine promises are not long kept separated from human duty. Scarcely has God presented to Moses this welcome, almost dazzling prospect for Israel, when there breaks upon his ear an announcement of his own connection with it, and that in the most trying and responsible position. That he was to have some sort of connection with the liberation of Israel was just what he might expect. God assuredly had not chosen to visit him so far from Egypt, and in that solitary place, simply to give him the good news and leave him there. And now a duty indeed is laid upon him, the duty of duties; he who has not been near Israel for forty years is to be the chief agent in their deliverance.

I. CONSIDER THE RECEPTION WHICH MOSES GIVES TO GOD'S ANNOUNCEMENT. Observe —1. *The point on which Moses expresses no doubt.* He says no word of doubt as to the possibility of Israel being delivered from Egypt. The achievement is from the human point of view a great one, and how it is to be managed he has not yet the slightest clue, but he does not doubt that it will be managed. He might have asked, "How can a thing so great as this be done, and the thraldom of generations utterly cast off?" but he had profited already by the lesson of the burning bush, and no such question crossed his lips. For whether is easier, to preserve a bush amid the fierce flames, or to deliver a nation from bondage? The power that can do the one can do the other. 2. *The point on which he is full of doubt.* "Who am I?" etc. His mind is turned at once to his own qualifications. And what wonder? It was a great leap from being a shepherd in the wilderness to being an ambassador to a king, and a leader of men. The fact that Moses questioned his personal ability and personal worthiness is, though it may not at first appear so, a great indication of his very fitness for the post. He did not jump at the chance of distinction. He had a remembrance of his bad odour in Egypt. He had lived, too, at court, and knew how hard it is to get at kings. We can hardly call this doubt of Moses blameworthy, for he was spoken to as a sinful man, and God did not expect from him at this first opening of the interview a response such as could only come fittingly from an angel, ready at once to fly on any errand of the Almighty. A Gabriel would not have said, "who am I, that I should go to Pharaoh?" for angels cannot be spoken of as either humble or proud. But Moses was deeply conscious of his own faults. Indeed, if he had not been, God would not have chosen him. Men of a different sort, self-complacent and self-confident, were the last God would have looked to in such circumstances. The men he wants are such as feel keenly all natural defects—sensitive, may be, to criticism and harsh words of every kind; men, too, who for their own inclination, love the quiet and shady nooks of existence, and do not care to leave them, save under the pressure of some manifest public claim or some persistent voice of God to the tender conscience within. Such men are generally called, upon their first emergence into public, presumptuous, meddlesome, and fanatical; and they have to lay their account with these hard names. They are apt to meet with a great deal of gratuitous counsel, given on the grounds of what is called common sense. Moses well knew the difficulties that would come in his way. The one thing he had yet to learn was that God knew him far better than he did himself.

II. CONSIDER THE ENCOURAGEMENTS WHICH GOD GIVES TO MOSES. There is no word of rebuke in any way, but immediate and abundant encouragement. 1. *The emphatic assurance of God's presence and companionship.* The "I" of Moses is met by the "I" of God. Moses was to go to Pharaoh strong in the consciousness that the God who sent him was also with him. There would not be about him anything that ambassadors usually had—rich personal adornments, pomp of attendance, great profusion of presents, distinguished earthly rank. But the absence of these things only makes more manifest the presence and dignity of the invisible God. The less of earth was seen, the more of heaven; the less of man, the more of God. If God be for us, who can be against us? If God be with us, what need we care who forsake us? Because Moses felt his own deficiencies, compared with the greatness of the work before him, God gave him this promise, and the fulfilment of it gave both needed and sufficient strength during all his conflict with Pharaoh. What about our relation to Christ's promise, " Lo, I am with you alway, even unto the end of the world?" The mournful truth with respect to us may be that we do not feel, either the greatness of the work before us, or our utter lack of strength to do it. We must know the burdens and the bonds, the smitings and the contumely, the sighing and the crying, of spiritual Egypt, before we can appreciate the necessity and graciousness of Christ's parting promise to his people. 2. God adds something even more noticeable than the promise of his presence. We do not say it is more important, but it is certainly more noticeable. *He makes an intimation of a very helpful token to be exhibited in the future.* Moses needed no more tokens of God's power at present; he had a sufficient token in the burning bush. If this had failed to impress him, neither could he have been persuaded by any additional wonder. But God gave to Moses a word which would keep in his mind the prospect and hope of a great sign in the time to come. What a thought to take with him through all the dismal succession of the plagues, through all the steady progress towards deliverance—that somehow or other God would bring the large host of Israel to this very mountain; to this lonely place where few people lived, because few could live! *Moses would need a token by-and-bye even more than he had needed one now.* His greatest difficulties were to be, not with Pharaoh, but with Israel; not in getting them out of Egypt, but in leading them onward to Canaan. Some difficulties doubtless he would expect, but all the stubbornness, waywardness and carnality of Israel he did not yet foresee. So the Apostle found his greatest difficulties and sorrows, not from those who stoned him at Lystra, imprisoned him at Philippi, and conspired against him at Jerusalem; but from the fornicators, the litigious, the schismatical, the deniers of the resurrection at Corinth; from the pliable yielders to Jewish bigotry in Galatia; in short, from all who, having professed to receive the truth, acted in a way incompatible with their professions; and thus we see *God keeping Moses, as it were, ahead of the people.* He was forty years ahead of them already. The creature comforts of Egypt, for which Israel lusted so in the wilderness, were no temptation to him, seeing he had become used to the wilderness. And so, when he came again to Horeb, with all this vast host in his charge, it was to rejoice in the strength that came from a fulfilled promise of God.

III. Consider the expectation from Israel with which God looks forward to the giving of this token. Not only will God bring Israel to this mountain, but when they reach it, it will be to serve him. He says very little; only, " Ye shall serve God," but that little would be enough to set Moses thinking. And yet, with all his anticipations, they must have fallen far short of the reality. One small word from the lips of God has behind it a fulness of meaning far beyond present thoughts. We learn, by the time we come to the end of this book, that serving God meant gathering in solemn and timid awe around the smoking mount; meant for Moses himself forty days and nights of retirement with Jehovah; meant the construction of the Tabernacle with all its holy contents according to the pattern shown in the mount. What a difference in the knowledge, the obligations, and the outlook of the Israelites when they left Sinai! And if the word " service," looked at in the light of past experience, was a word of meaning so large with respect to them, is it not incumbent on us to do all we can for ourselves to fill the great terms of the Christian dispensation with the fulness of their meaning? Faith—atonement—the blood of Christ—regeneration— love—holiness—heaven: let these words represent to our minds an ever-growing, a devout and correct experience of the great body of the truth as it is in Jesus.—Y.

Vers. 13—17.—*The second difficulty: the God of Abraham, Isaac, and Jacob— what is his name?* Moses feels that when he goes among his brethren, one of their first questions will be as to the name of this God of Abraham, Isaac, and Jacob. Consider—

I. How it was that the possibility of such a question was suggested to his mind. All the deities of the other nations had names, and doubtless the gods of Egypt were well known by name to the Israelites. Part of the glory of each nation came from the fact that it was under the protection and favour of so renowned a being as its God. The feeling of Moses in asking this question may be illustrated from the clamour of the Ephesian mob against Paul. The Ephesians felt that it was a great deal to be able to say that Diana had a special interest in them. And so it seemed to Moses a reversal of the proper order of things to go to his brethren with no more indication of the Being who had sent him, than that he had been historically connected with Abraham, Isaac and Jacob. Moses could not believe that his own people would rest contented with such a representation as this; indeed, we may very reasonably go further, and assume that he himself was anxious to know the name of this unnamed God. He was not yet filled with the light and power of the pure monotheistic conception. Certainly he had just felt what real might there was with the God of his fathers, and probably there was no shadow of doubt in his mind that this God was powerful far beyond any of the rest; but he had yet to learn that he was God alone, and that all other deities, however imposing, were nothing more than the fictions of degraded and wayward imagination. When we bear in mind that Moses was only at the beginning of his personal acquaintance with God, then we shall see that there was nothing wonderful or unreasonable, from the point of his attainments at the time, in asking such a question. Observe also that *the very question is a revelation of how ignorant the Israelites were of God.* How clear the proof is that the thought of God, as Jehovah, came down from above, and did not rise out of the corrupted hearts of men. When we have much to do with persons, it is a matter of necessity to have names for them, and if they give us none, we must make them for ourselves. But the Israelites had no transactions with God, save as he came down and pressed his presence upon them; and even then all that they could see was such power as became manifest to the senses. It is very certain that if God had not revealed this name, there was no faculty among the Israelites to invent it.

II. The giving of the name. *We must bear in mind the purpose for which the name was given.* The question at once suggests itself—Would God have given this name, if he had not been asked? To this perhaps the best answer is that the difficulty out of which the question rose was sure to be felt, even if the question itself was not asked. Some name of the kind assuredly became needed for distinguishing purposes. It was a name as helpful to the people of idolatrous nations as to Israel itself. An Egyptian or a Philistine could say, "The Hebrews call their God Jehovah." What the Israelite understood by the name in itself, is, we may fairly say, a point impossible to settle. The wisdom of God is certainly evident in giving a name which, while it so well served a temporary purpose, remains still to suggest matters which no lapse of time can ever render indifferent. It is vain to discuss the form of the expression, with the aim of tying it down to mean some particular aspect of the Divine nature, to the exclusion of others. Far better is it for Christians to take it—and thus, surely, devout Israelites would take it—as suggesting all that it is fitted to suggest. There is the name; some will put into it more, and some less, but no one can pretend that he has filled it with the fulness of its import. It would be very helpful for the Israelites always to bear in mind *the occurrence of the first person* in this great distinguishing name. The God of Abraham, Isaac and Jacob, is one who can say "I." He is not represented by some dumb idol, voiceless save through the traditions of those who worship it. He who says "I am" thus registers in Holy Writ an expression which will have meaning and suggestiveness in every language under heaven. What an intimation is given to us of the permanent value of the expression when we come upon it so suddenly in the discussion between Jesus and the Jews! They had spoken haughtily concerning great names in the past—the dead Abraham and the dead prophets; when straightway, as by the breath of his mouth, Jesus shrivels up the glories of all mere mundane history by his declaration, "Before Abraham was, I am." (John viii. 58.) Abraham and all the rest of us have come into existence. But Jesus is one who, even here below, with the knowledge of what happened at Bethlehem, has that in him whereby he can say, "I am."

III. The giving of this name made it needful to reiterate and emphasise

THE NAME ALREADY GIVEN. There is nothing to indicate that the name for which Moses asked was to be mentioned to the Israelites unless they applied for it. The real necessity and value of it belonged to the future rather than the present. The name already given was the name of urgent importance for the present need. It could not for a moment sink into the background even before the name "I am." The one thing needful for Israel, at this time, was to get them into the past, and to bring before their minds with all possible freshness and impressiveness, the actions, the purposes and the claims of the God who had dealt with Abraham, Isaac and Jacob. Of what avail is it to know that there is an eternal immutable God, unless we, in our mutability, in our melancholy experiences of time, are brought into helpful connection with him? We may ponder over the name Jehovah without coming to any knowledge of the God of Abraham, Isaac and Jacob; but if we only begin by a devout consideration of the narrative concerning these men, then assuredly we shall come at last to a profitable and comforting knowledge of God. There are many good purposes to be served by studying the differences between created and uncreated existence, and by making ourselves acquainted with those subtle speculations concerning the Divine nature which have fascinated and too often tantalised the greatest intellects among men; and yet all these are as nothing unless from our acquaintance with them we advance, still searching and seeking, to a personal knowledge of the God and Father of our Lord Jesus Christ. It is well to have our minds lifted up to lofty conceptions; it is better still, coming to the Father through Christ, to have our hearts nourished, gladdened and consoled.—Y.

Vers. 18—22.— *The coming liberation: God indicates the method of it.* In this conversation between God and Moses, recorded in chaps. iii. and iv., we observe that God is occupied with something more than simply answering the questions of Moses. Answering these questions, he then goes on to give his own instructions besides. God's instructions to us, for right service, do not depend on our questions. These must be answered, that stumblingblocks may be taken out of the way; but when they are removed, then we must wait and listen, to find out the exact path according to the Divine will. Thus in the passage before us, God indicates to Moses the really critical part of the great enterprise. The questions of Moses show that it is in Israel, in himself and in his brethren, that Moses looks for the great difficulties. But now God would point out to him that the real struggle is to be in breaking down the proud, despotic resolution of Pharaoh. There was no occasion for Moses to doubt the concurrence of his own people. Nothing very taxing or trying is yet asked from them. "They shall hearken to thy voice." But, when they had hearkened, Moses had to go from them to a man who would not hearken, either to him or to God who had sent him. Observe—

I. THE INSTRUCTIONS FOR APPROACHING PHARAOH. Moses was not left to approach Pharaoh in any way that might seem best to himself. God ordered who the suppliants were to be, and what the exact petition they were to present. 1. *The suppliants.* They are Moses and the elders of Israel. There is a due, general and dignified representation of the whole people. Moses is to go, not only as the messenger of God, but undeniably as the spokesman of his enslaved brethren. God assures him that he will win the companionship and support of the older and experienced men among them. It is not to be some hot, rebellious crowd of youths that will seek to break in upon Pharaoh. A representative body, most if not all of them well up in years, and headed by a man of fourscore, are to approach him in a dignified way, respectful to him and respectful to themselves. Those who are the advocates of a righteous cause must not spoil or dishonour it by a rash, provocative and boisterous line of conduct. Pharaoh is to be made conscious that he is dealing with those who have every right and competency to speak. If he meets them in an angry, unyielding spirit, he will be left with no chance of finding excuse for himself in the spirit in which he has been approached. 2. *The petition.* The petitioners are to ask for only a small part of what is really required. The request has been called by some a deceptive one. It is wonderful how quick the worldly mind is, being so full of trickery and deceit itself, to find out deceit in God. If this had been purely the request of Israel, then it would have been deceitful, but it was emphatically God's request, and it served more purposes than one. In

the first place, the character of the boon desired indicated to Israel, and especially to
these responsible men the elders, what God was expecting from them. He who had
told Moses, in direct terms, concerning the service in " this mountain " (ver. 12), was
now intimating to them, indirectly, but not less forcibly, something of the same kind.
God has more ways than one of setting our duties before us. Secondly, the request
was a very searching test of Pharaoh himself. It was a test with regard to the spirit
and reality of his own religion. If to him religion was a real necessity, a real source of
strength, then there was an appeal to whatever might be noble and generous in his
heart not to shut out the Hebrews from such blessings as were to be procured in
worshipping Jehovah their God, and the request searched Pharaoh's heart in many
ways besides. God well knew beforehand what the result would be, and he chose such
an introductory message as would most completely serve his own purposes. These
threatened wonders were to start from plain reasons of necessity. We must constantly
bear in mind the comprehensiveness of the Divine plans, the certainty with which God
discerns beforehand the conduct of men. If we keep this truth before us we shall not
be deceived by the shallow talk of would-be ethical purists concerning the deceptions
found in Scripture. We must not argue from ourselves, wandering in a labyrinth of
contingencies, to a God who is above them all.

II. GOD NOW SEEKS TO MAKE CLEAR TO MOSES THAT WHAT PHARAOH EMPHATI-
CALLY REFUSES TO GRANT AT FIRST, HE WILL BE COMPELLED TO GRANT AT LAST.
Thus God makes luminous another important point in the future. That future now
stretches before Moses, like a road in the dark, with lamps fixed at certain intervals.
Between the lamps there may be much darkness, but they are sufficient to indicate the
direction of the path. God had lighted one lamp to assure Moses of a favourable
reception by his own people ; another to show the kind of treatment which would have
to be adopted towards Pharaoh ; a third to show the complete success of this treatment ;
and a fourth shining all the way from Sinai, to make plain that in due course Moses
and his liberated brethren would arrive there. God was quickly adding one thing after
another, to increase and assure the faith of his servant, and make him calm, courageous,
and self-possessed in the prosecution of a momentous enterprise. Only let Moses be
faithful in certain matters that are comparatively little, such as making a prompt
return to Egypt, and then delivering his messages, first of all to Israel and afterwards
to Pharaoh ; and God will take care of all the rest. At the beginning Pharaoh will
thunder forth a decided and apparently decisive " No !"—but in spite of all his present
resolution, the end will see Israel hurried out of the land by a nation smitten with
universal bereavement and terror. And, to make this point clearer still, God gives to
Israel the marvellous assurance that Egypt will rush from the one extreme of pitiless
extortion to the other of lavish generosity. God would secure to Israel much of its
own again, even in the secondary matter of external possessions. The Egyptian wealth
that had been gained by oppressing the people would be largely disgorged. They were
not to go out as impoverished fugitives, but as bearing the rich spoils of God's own
great battle. Thus does God invite his servant to bear in mind this mighty compelling
force. Pharaoh is great and rich and strong, but God is about to do things in the
midst of his land which will force him to confess that there is One far greater and far
stronger than himself.—Y.

Vers. 1—6.—Forty years since, Moses (ii. 11) had "turned aside " from court life in
Egypt to see how his brethren the children of Israel fared amid the furnace of trial. The
old life seems like a dream, so long ago ; the old language (iv. 10) grown unfamiliar.
The annual routine ; flocks to be driven to distant pasturage at the approach of summer.
God's hour at hand just when least expected.

I. THE PROPHETIC VISION. When God calls to the prophetic office, there is usually some
vision or appearance, through which the call is emphasised and its significance suggested. Cf. Is. vi. 1—7 ; Jer. i. 11—13 ; Ezek. i. 4 ; Matt. iii. 16 to iv. 11 ; Acts ix. 3—6.
So here : 1. *The vision.* A dry acacia bush on fire, not very singular. What is
singular is that the bush seems to flourish amidst the flame ! The mystery explained,
vers. 2—4. The bush is in the midst of the flame, but the angel of Jehovah is in the
midst of the bush. 2. *Its significance.* Israel " a root out of a dry ground." In the
furnace of affliction, yet flourishing amid the furnace (cf. i. 12). When Moses had

"turned aside to see" forty years before, he had supposed that his brethren would have recognised in him their deliverer; had not sufficiently recognised himself that it was God's angel in their midst who was really preserving them. Trouble, sorrow, persecution *may* consume and practically annihilate; whole peoples have been killed off and left hardly a trace in history. Though "the blood of the martyrs is the seed of the Church," yet there is no specially conservative power in suffering; it is only when God is with men that they can "walk through the fire and yet not be burned" (cf. Is. xliii. 2).

II. THE DIVINE REVELATION. 1. *Preliminary condition:* ver. 4. "Jehovah saw that he turned aside to see." (1) Revelations are not for the unobservant. God will give us eye-guidance if we will have it (Ps. xxxii. 8), but we must be alert to catch his glance. (2) Revelations are not for the cowardly; where *one* turned aside to see, *nine* might have turned aside in sheer terror to escape seeing. He that would hear God's voice must fight with and overcome his fears, otherwise he is likely to be classed with the unbelieving and the abominable (Rev. xxi. 7, 8). 2. *The call heard and answered.* To the man ready to receive it the call comes. God is going to reveal his own name to Moses, but calls Moses first by *his* name. The conviction that God knows us is the best preparation for learning more about him. Moses is on the alert; eager to listen, ready to obey. 3. *Reverence secured:* ver. 5. Interviews with God need preparation. Even when God calls, man cannot hear his voice aright save in the hush of utter reverence. To attain this for those who are in the body, material aids must not be despised; so long as men possess senses there must be a sensuous form for even the most spiritual worship. 4. *God declares himself:* ver. 6. Cf. Matt. xxii. 32. God in the midst of the nation, as in the midst of the bush, was preserving it *in its entirety.* Not like a bundle of green twigs, the relics of a perished stem. Stem and twigs, the ancestral stock no less than the offspring, all alike preserved—kept by him who can say, "I am their God." *Application:*—Has God ever declared himself to us? If not, whose the fault? Have we been on the outlook to catch his signs? Have we used due reverence in listening for his voice? Have we been ready to obey even the lightest indication of his will? Attention, reverence, obedience—all needed if we would hear God speak. We must be as Moses was—self stifled, the world silenced, a-hush to hear the Divine voice.—G.

Vers. 1—10.—*The Burning Bush.* "Behold the bush," etc. Ex. iii. 2. A very astonishing event; yet amply evidenced to us by those voluminous arguments which now more than ever establish the authenticity of Exodus; but in addition to this, we have here the special endorsement of the Truth Incarnate. See Mark xii. 26. [Examine this passage critically, and consider how full and valid the endorsement is! No mere acceptance of received legend.]

I. THE TIME. A solemn undertone in ver. 1. A great soul wandering under the starlight of a partial revelation. 1. *In the life of the Church.* A time of trial; Israel like leaves in autumn, like the foam of the sea, and that for long. Of deepening trial, see Ex. i. Deliverance apparently impossible. The government of the new Pharaoh now firm and strong. For evidence of depression see Ex. vi. 9. 2. *In the life of Moses.* Eighty years of age. Acts vii. 23, 30. Yet hardly any history of the man. In fact we have no continuous history. Died at 120. First forty years? Blank. So with second and third. *A history of four crises!* Birth; decision; entrance on service; death.

Learn: (1) *Crises in all lives.* Divergent roads! Crises fix what we are to be and do. Illustrate from life. Watch for them. Pass them on your knees. "Hold up my goings," etc. (2) *God determines them.* This came on Moses unexpectedly. Where? On the line of common duty. "He led the flock," etc. "So, rest in the Lord," etc. (3) *Leave life to God.*

II. THE SCENE. The following should be carefully observed, with the view of vivifying and realising this story of Divine manifestation. The scene was laid— 1. *In the desert.* See Stanley's 'Sinai and Palestine,' pp. 12—14, for the general characteristics of the desert. 2. *In the Midian section* of the desert. For exact definition of this, see "Midian," in Smith's ' Bibl. Dict.' 356a. 3. *In the Horeb range.* Horeb designates the range of mountains about Sinai; Sinai the solitary grandeur of

Jebel Músa. 'Desert of the Exodus,' p. 118. 4. *At Sinai.* Probably in Er Rahah, the wide wady north of Sinai, with the mighty pile of Rás Sufsâfeh towering on the south. 5. Generally—*amid mountains :* where oft, as on the sea at night, God seems so near. His face towards the sun, Sinai in grand altitude of shade before him, Moses saw the brightness and heard the word of the Logos, the manifested God.

III. THE VISION. Observe here two elements :—1. *The subjective.* Moses' state of mind. This would be determined by the known circumstances of Israel, and by his own : he was away from his people, seemingly out of the covenant, the Divine promise forgotten. 2. *The objective.* A lowly plant ; not a tree. Fire. No consuming ; no smoke, no ashes, no waste. In the Fire (ver. 4) the Angel-God of the Old Testament. Symbol of the Church of all time. Is. xliii. 2, 3.

IV. THE FIRST EFFECT. Intellectual curiosity. " I will now . . . *why* the bush," etc. This attention was better than indifference, but was probably nothing more than an intelligent curiosity. Still, this was not enough.

V. THE CHECK : vers. 4, 5.—The attitude of the mind should be that of reverent attention, face to face with Divine manifestations. " The word of the Lord always went along with the glory of the Lord, for every Divine vision was designed for Divine revelation." This the more necessary because over every revelation there is a veil. Hab. iii. 4. Distance becomes us. " Draw not nigh hither ! " So in Science, Psychology, History, the revelation of the Christ. The aim not to satisfy the curiosity, but to enlighten and empower the conscience, and direct the life.

VI. THE DRAWING into covenantal relations, notwithstanding the momentary check. This by making known—1. *The Divine Name :* ver. 6. The God of thy father; of the immortal dead too; therefore thy God. The effect of this tender revelation : " Moses hid his face," etc. 2. *The Divine sympathy.* " I know." Sense of the Divine Omniscience alone is an awful pressure from above on the soul ; but there is a restoration to equilibrium, by a pressure from beneath supporting, *i.e.* by a sense of Divine sympathy—" their sorrows." See Maurice, 'Patriarchs and Lawgivers,' p. 162. 3. *A Divine salvation.* " I am come down to deliver." 4. *Possibility of Divine service.* " Come now, therefore, and I will send *thee* unto Pharaoh : " ver. 10.—R.

Vers. 13—15.—*The proper Name of God.* " This is my name for ever," etc.— (Ex. iii. 15.) This incident of the burning bush teems with subjects susceptible of homiletic treatment. We name a few of the more important, which we ourselves do not linger to treat. 1. THE INDESTRUCTIBILITY OF THE CHURCH: ver. 2. 2. THE DOCTRINE OF THE ANGEL-GOD. Note in vers. 2—4 that " The Angel of Jehovah," " Jehovah," and " God," are one and the same. 3. THE RESTRICTION OF JUDAISM CONTRASTED WITH THE FREEDOM OF THE GOSPEL : ver. 5. For valuable hints on this, see 'Moses the Lawgiver,' by Dr. Taylor of New York, pp. 46, 47. 4. THE DOCTRINE OF IMMORTALITY IN THE OLD TESTAMENT : ver. 6, comp. with Matt. xxii. 31, 32. 5. SHRINKING AT THE DIVINE CALL. The reluctance of Moses ; his four reasons— incompetence, ver. 11; ignorance of the proper name of God, ver. 13 ; incredulity of the people, iv. 1 ; want of speaking power, iv. 10—and how they were severally overcome. 6. OUR LIFE WORK—*Preparation for it and possible late discovery of it :* ver. 10. It is in connection with the second disability of Moses that the Deity gives his proper name. Note, that whilst Elohim and other names are generic, this name " Jahveh," or more commonly " Jehovah," is the distinctive *proper* name of God. See Is. xlii. 8, in Heb. As a foundation it will be needful to exhibit, in a popular way, the connection between the Hebrew form for " I am " and " Jehovah." See exegesis of vers. 14, 15 above, and also the valuable Dissertation on the Divine Name, by Russell Martineau, M.A., in Ewald's 'History of Israel,' Eng. ed. vol. ii. 433. The writer of the hymn, " The God of Abraham praise ! " speaking of " Jehovah, great I Am," showed that he had perceived the etymological relation. The fundamental idea in the name is that of " Being," but around that idea plays many a prismatic light, something of which will now be exhibited. There are associated with " I am," " I am what I am," " Jahveh," the following ideas :—

I. EXISTENCE. How calm and solemn is this Divine affirmation in the silence of the desert, as in it God protests against being confounded with—1. *Idols.* Material or intellectual. Over against the teaching of the atheist positivist, pantheist agnostic, polytheist, God places his "*I am.*" 2. *Mere phenomena.* Who can separate always surely in nature between reality and appearance; or within the realm of mind, between certainty and illusion or delusion? But behind all phenomena is the Existence—God.

II. ETERNITY. The Existence is absolute, without any limit of time; so much so, that many are anxious to translate "Jahveh," or "Jehovah," everywhere by "The Eternal." See same idea of God in Rev. i. 4—8. In opening out the eternity and consequent immutability of God, we expound it, not metaphysically, but experimentally, that is, in relation to the actual experience of men, who need beyond everything the assurance of an unchanging Saviour and Father to trust, and love, and serve—"the same yesterday, to-day," etc.

III. CAUSATIVE ENERGY. "Jahveh," or "Jehovah," is from Hiphil, the causative form of the verb. Carries, then, in itself, not only the meaning "To be," but "To *cause* to be." The idea is not however merely, having *once for all* caused existence, but that of constantly creating. Note this mighty causative force operating—1. *In nature,* which is the momentary work of the ever-present God. 2. In creating *a people* for his praise, as now about to do in the desert of Sinai.

IV. PERSONALITY. The transcendently sublime egoism, "I am!" It is not necessary that we should be able to answer the question, What is a person? to know what personality is, or to be sure that there is personality in God. On this point see Wace's Boyle Lectures on "Christianity and Morality," p. 62, and, indeed, the whole of lecture iv. on "The Personality of God." "The question of immediate practical importance is, not what God's nature is, but how we may feel towards him, and how we may suppose him to feel towards us. The simple and perfectly intelligible answer given to these questions by the Jews was, that they could feel towards God in a manner similar to that in which they felt towards other beings whom they considered persons, and that he felt similarly towards them." Our true knowledge of personality is quite independent of our ability to define it in words. This meeting of the personality in Moses with the personality in God constituted for Moses a crisis in his history. So is it ever—the confronting of my spirit by the Spirit of God is the supreme moment of existence.

V. FIDELITY. The words in ver. 14 may be read: "I shall be what I shall be." From future to future the same; not like the gods of the heathen, fitful, capricious. What God was to the fathers, that he will be to children's children; not a promise broken or a purpose unfulfilled.

VI. COVENANTAL GRACE. Evidence that "Jahveh," or "Jehovah," is the covenantal name of God is accumulated in abundance in Smith's 'Bib. Dict.' under word "Jehovah," (sect. v.) p. 957. To the many striking illustrations there, add, that Jesus is equivalent to Joshua = Jehovah that saves.

VII. MYSTERY. God we may apprehend, never comprehend; touch, as with the finger, never grasp or embrace. "I am *what* I am." Job. xi. 7—9; Ps. lxxvii. 19; Hab. iii. 4.—R.

Observe generally on the name: 1. It was then *new*: Ex. vi. 3. Not absolutely new, but practically so. 2. It became *sacred.* The Jew never pronounced it. This savoured of superstition, and its ill effect is to be seen in the suppression of the name Jehovah, even in our English Bibles, and in the substitution for it of LORD in small capitals. We will enter into their reverence without showing their superstition. "Where the Spirit of the Lord is there is liberty." 3. The name is a *root*-designation in the revelation of God. Assumed universally in Judaism and Christianity, see Maurice's 'Patriarchs and Lawgivers,' pp. 165, 166. 4. The name sets forth *objective truth.* "This is my name for ever." It is the sign-manual of the Almighty across nature, in providence, on the cross. The name gives us a true idea of the Deity. 5. The name should be *subjectively cherished.* "This is my *memorial* to all generations." God's forget-me-not in the believer's heart. The name by which he would be remembered.—R.

Vers. 3—10.—I. HOW MOSES MET WITH GOD. 1. The marvel was marked and considered. He might simply have glanced at it and passed on; but he observed it till the wonder of it possessed his soul. There are marvels that proclaim God's presence in the earth to-day. Creation, the Bible, Christ's saving work. The first step towards conviction is to consider them. 2. "He turned aside to see." It was a matter to be inquired into and probed to the bottom. 3. God meets the earnest, sincere spirit: "When the Lord saw," etc., "God called unto him." The eunuch reading in his chariot, and Philip, etc. We cannot turn aside to consider these things with a sincere desire for light, and not meet at last with him who is Light. To all true seekers God will reveal himself.

II. WHAT FITS FOR GOD'S SERVICE. 1. We must rise from a mere seeking after God to the knowledge that we are known of God: his heart was thrilled by the cry, "Moses! Moses!" The cry proclaimed not only that God knew him, but that he was *his* God. The Lord claimed him in that cry as his servant, his son. Have we heard it? If not, we do not know God as the living God, as *our* God, and how can we serve him? 2. The sense of God's holiness and majesty, hallowing all things for us (ver. 5). The depth of our trust and our love may be measured by the depth of our adoration. 3. The vivid realisation of what God has done in the past (ver. 6). That is God's revelation of himself. The story of the past must yield strength to the present. 4. The assurance that God's purpose of redemption is behind our efforts: that we speak and labour because he *has surely* risen to redeem (vers. 7—10).—U.

Vers. 11—17.—*Hindrances to service and how God removes them.* 1. THE HINDRANCE FOUND IN THE SENSE OF OUR OWN WEAKNESS (vers. 11, 12). 1. Moses knew the pomp and pride of the Egyptian court. He remembered how Israel had rejected him when he was more than he was now. Once he had believed himself able for the task, but he was wiser now: "Who am I?" etc. He might serve God in the lowly place he held, but not there. Moses in this the type of multitudes. God's call for service is met on every hand by the cry, "Who am I that I should go?" 2. How God meets this sense of weakness. (1) By the assurance of his presence. It was not Moses only that should go, but God also. The conviction that he is with us, and that we speak for him, makes the meekest bold, the weakest strong. (2) By the assurance of success: "Ye shall serve God *upon this mountain.*" He is armed with *faith* and *hope.* From self let us look to God and his pledged word.

II. THE HINDRANCE FOUND IN THE SENSE OF OUR IGNORANCE (vers. 13—17). 1. His own thought of God was dim. How then could he carry conviction to the hearts of the people? The same lack of clear, living thought of God keeps tongues tied to-day. 2. How it may be removed. (1) God is THE UNCHANGING ONE. He had revealed himself to their fathers: he was all this still. It was his memorial for ever. Grasping this thought, all the past is God's revelation. (2) He takes with him a gospel for present need (vers. 16, 17), and these two things will be God's full revelation. We must make men apprehend the revelation which God has given of himself in the past, and proclaim him as the God of to-day. "I have surely visited you . . . and I will bring you up out of the affliction."—U.

Vers. 18—22.—I. THE REMOVAL OF MOSES' FEAR. His mission will be successful. 1. He will win the people's trust for God. They will not refuse to hear. 2. Their elders will accompany him into Pharaoh's presence: his request will become the people's. 3. The Lord will lead them out laden with the spoils of Egypt. Going on God's errand there is no possibility of failure. The fears which rise as we measure the greatness of the task and our own strength vanish when we look up into the face of God.

II. OPPOSITION WILL BE MET WITH, BUT IT WILL ONLY HEIGHTEN GOD'S TRIUMPH. "I am sure that the King of Egypt will not let you go . . . and I will stretch out my hand and smite Egypt with all my wonders." 1. We are not to expect that we shall sail over an unruffled sea, and that labour for Christ will be a continuously triumphal progress. "In the world ye shall have tribulation." 2. It is the occasion of the revealing of God's mighty power. Trial is God's school for deepening and purifying trust in himself. The triumph of Christianity in the first ages a consecration of the Church and a proof to the world of the Divine origin of our faith.

III. THE PLAN GOD FOLLOWS IN EFFECTING HIS PEOPLE'S DELIVERANCE. 1. A small demand is made: permission to go three days' journey into the wilderness. Great promises are given to the Church, but it does not now demand that the silver and the gold should be yielded for the service of God, and that the mighty should come down from their thrones and give them to his saints. It asks only for liberty to serve God and to declare his will. 2. The world's refusal brings down God's judgments; and then comes the glory and the enrichment of the sons of God.—U.

EXPOSITION.

CHAPTER IV.

Vers. 1—17.—The reluctance of Moses to undertake the part of leader, indicated by his first reply at his first calling, " Who am I that I should go ?" etc. (ch. iii. 11), was not yet overcome. God had promised that he would succeed ; but he did not see how he could succeed, either with the people or with Pharaoh. It was not enough for him that God had declared, " They (the people) shall hearken unto thy voice " (ib. 18); he does not, cannot believe this, and replies : " Behold, they will not believe, neither hearken unto my voice " (ch. iv. 1). This was plain want of faith ; but not unnatural, and not, in God's sight, inexcusable. God therefore condescended to the human weakness of his servant, and proceeded to show him how he intended that he should persuade the people of his mission. He should persuade them by producing the credentials of miracles (vers. 2—9). But the laggard heart finds yet a further objection. Moses feels that he labours under a personal defect, which (he thinks) is an absolute disqualification. He is " slow of speech and of a slow tongue " (ver. 10), has always been wanting in eloquence, and does not find himself any the more eloquent since God has been speaking with him. In vain does Jehovah promise to " be with his mouth " (ver. 12); Moses' last word indicates all the old feeling of self-distrust. " Send, I pray thee, by the hand of him whom thou wilt send " (ver. 13). Then at last the anger of the Lord is kindled against Moses, and God inflicts on him a sort of punishment—degrades him, as it were —deposes him from the position of sole leader, and associates Aaron with him in such sort that Aaron must have appeared, both to the Israelites and to the Pharaoh, as the chief leader rather than Moses. (See ch. iv. 30 ; vii. 2, 10, 19 ; viii. 6, 17, etc.)

At this point the interview between Moses and Jehovah ends, and the action of the Exodus commences. Moses obtains leave to quit Midian, and quits it — returns to Egypt, after escaping from a dangerous sickness on the way (vers. 24—26), is met by Aaron and takes him into his counsels, summons the elders and exhibits before them his miraculous powers, persuades them, and is finally accepted as having, with Aaron, a mission from God, both by the elders and the people.

Ver. 1.—**Behold, they will not believe.** Attempts have been made to soften down this contradiction of God's words in ch. iii. 18, and to represent Moses as merely saying, " What if the people will not hearken, etc. What shall I do then ? " (So the LXX., Geddes, Boothroyd, and others.) But the phrase is really emphatic and peremptory. As Rosenmüller says: " Vox est negantis et detractantis officium." **The Lord hath not appeared to thee.** It is quite probable that the Israelites would have so spoken, if Moses had had no sign to show. There had been no appearance of Jehovah to anyone for above four hundred years. And the Israelites, who had not seen Moses for forty years, would not know whether he was a veracious person or not.

Ver. 2.—**A rod.** Or " a staff." Some suppose the ordinary shepherd's staff, or crook, to be meant; but it is objected that this would have been an unfit object to have brought into the presence of Pharaoh (Kalisch), being unsuitable for a court, and emblematic of an occupation which the Egyptians loathed (Gen. xlvi. 34); and the suggestion is therefore made, that it was the bâton or long stick commonly carried by Egyptians of good position and especially by persons in authority. But Moses in Midian, forty years after he quitted Egypt, is not likely to have possessed such an article ; nor, if he had possessed it, would he have taken it with him when shepherding. Probably a simple staff, the natural support of a man of advanced years, is meant.

Ver. 3.—**It became a serpent.** The word here used for " serpent," nakhash, is a generic word applicable to any species of snake. We cannot assume that the cobra is the serpent meant, though no doubt Moses, when he fled from before it, believed it to be a venomous serpent. Various reasons for God's choice of this particular sign have been given. Perhaps the best is, that a trick of the kind was known to the Egyptian conjurors, who would be tempted to exhibit it in order to discredit Moses, and would then be discredited themselves by his stick swallowing theirs. (See ch. vii. 10—12.) It is fanciful to suppose a reference either to the serpent of Gen. iii. (Keil and Delitzsch) or to the uræus (*cobra*), which the Egyptian kings bore in their headdress as a mark of sovereignty (Canon Cook)

Ver 4.—**By the tail.** A snake-charmer will usually take up his serpents by the neck, so that they may not be able to bite him. Moses was bidden to show his trust in God by taking up his serpent by the tail. His courage, as well as his faith, is shown in his ready obedience. **It became a rod.** A veritable rod once more, not a mere stiffened snake like the "rods" of the magicians (ch. vii. 12)

Ver. 5.—**That they may believe.** The sign was to convince the Israelites, in the first instance, and cause them to accept the mission of Moses (see vers. 30, 31). It was afterwards to be exhibited before Pharaoh (ver. 21), to try him and prove him, but not to convince him.

Ver. 6.—**Furthermore.** The first sign is followed by a second, equally simple and easy of performance, and perhaps, in the eyes of the Israelites, even more marvellous. Leprosy in a developed form was regarded as absolutely incurable. (Celsus, 'De Re Medica,' v. 7—8.) Its instantaneous production and removal were contrary to all experience, and in themselves thoroughly astonishing. Further, while the first miracle was simply a sign of supernatural power—a credential, the second was a warning and a lesson. What might not he do to smite or to save on whom God had bestowed such power over the human organism? Each man would naturally fear to resist or disobey one so dangerously gifted. **Leprous as snow.** The Greek name for the worst form of leprosy, λεύκη, was based on this fact of whiteness. The loathsome disease is thus described by Kalisch:—"It begins with mealy crusts and scurfy scabs, originally not larger than a pin's point, a little depressed in the skin (Lev. xiii. 3, 30), and covered with white hairs (*ib*. 3, 20). These spots rapidly spread (*ib*. 8), and produce wild [proud?] flesh (*ib*. 10, 14). The leprous symptoms appear most frequently on the hairy parts of the body, and also on members which have been ulcerously affected. When the leprosy has gained ground, *the whole skin appears glossy white* at the forehead, nose, etc., tuberated, thickened, dry like leather, but smooth; sometimes it bursts, and ulcers become visible. The nails of the hands and feet fall; the eyelids bend backwards; the hair covers itself with a fetid rind, or goes off entirely (Lev. xiii. 42). All external senses are weakened: the eyes lose their brightness, become very sensitive, and are continually blearing; from the nostrils runs a fluid phlegm." ('Comment. on Exodus,' p. 50.)

Ver. 8.—**The voice of the first sign.** Some understand "the voice of Moses as he gave them the first sign;" but it is better to regard the sign itself as speaking to them. According to the sacred writers everything that can

teach us anything—day, night, the heavens, the firmament, the beasts, the fowls of the air, the fishes, nay, the very stones—have a voice. They teach us, speak to us, declare to us, cry out aloud, lift up their voice, shout, sing, proclaim God's will, whether man will hear or whether he will forbear. (See Ps. xix. 1—3; Job xii. 7, 8; Hab. ii. 11; Luke xix. 40, etc.) Equally, or rather much more, must a miracle be regarded as having a voice. God speaks to us by it.

Ver. 9.—**If they will not believe also.** "*Even*" would be a better translation than "also." **The river** is of course "the Nile." See the comment on ch. ii. 3. Of the three signs given, the first would probably convince all those who were religious, well-disposed, and fair-minded; the second, acting upon their fears, would move all but the desperately wicked, who despised Jehovah and put their trust in the gods of the Egyptians (Josh. xxiv. 14; Ezek. xx. 7, 8; xxiii. 3, 8, etc.). The third sign was for these last, who would regard the Nile as a great divinity, and would see in the conversion of Nile water into blood a significant indication that the God who had commissioned Moses was greater than any Egyptian one.

Ver. 10.—**And Moses said, O my Lord.** The phrase used by Moses is full of force. It is "vox dolentis et supplicantis" (Noldius). Joseph's brethren use it to the steward of Joseph's house, when they expect to be fallen upon and taken for bondsmen (Gen. xliii. 20); Judah used it (*ib*. xliv. 18) when pleading with Joseph for Benjamin; Aaron when pleading for Miriam (Num. xii. 11); Joshua when expostulating with God about Ai (Josh. vii. 8). There is a deprecatory idea in it, as well as a supplicatory one; an idea like that which Abraham expanded into the words, "Oh! let not the Lord be angry, and I will speak yet but this once" (Gen. xviii. 32). Moses feels that he is trying the patience of God to the uttermost; but yet he must make one more effort to escape his mission. **I am not eloquent.** Literally, as in the margin, "a man of words." "Words do not come readily to my tongue when I attempt to speak; I have never been a fluent speaker, neither yesterday (*i.e.* recently) nor the day before (*i.e.* formerly). Nor do I even find that I have become eloquent by divine inspiration since thou spakest with me. Still I remain **slow of speech** and slow of tongue." A question is raised whether the mere difficulty of finding words and giving them utterance—a difficulty felt at first by almost every speaker—is here meant, or something further, as "a natural impediment owing to defect in the organs of speech" (Kalisch), or a want of readiness, owing to disuse, in speaking the Hebrew language (Clarke). The latter suggestion is scarcely consistent with the ease and fluency with which Moses had carried on the conversation in Hebrew up to this point. The former is a possible meaning, though not a necessary one. According to a Jewish tradition, Moses had a difficulty in pronouncing the labials *b*, *v*, *m*, *ph*, *p*.

Vers. 11—13. — **Who hath made man's mouth?** God could and would have cured the defect in Moses' speech, whatever it was; could and would have added eloquence to his other gifts, if he had even at this point yielded himself up unreservedly to his guidance and heartily accepted his mission. Nothing is too hard for the Lord. He gives all powers—sight, and hearing, and speech included—to whom he will. He would have been " with Moses' mouth," removing all hesitation or indistinctness, and have " taught him what to say "—supplied the thought and the language by which to express it—if Moses would have let him. But the reply in ver. 13 shut up the Divine bounty, prevented its outpour, and left Moses the ineffective speaker which he was content to be. The words, **O my Lord, send, I pray thee, by the hand of him whom Thou wilt send**, are curt and ungracious; much curter in the original than in our version.[1] They contain a grudging acquiescence. But for the deprecatory particle with which they commence—the same as in ver. 10—they would be almost rude. And we see the result in the next verse.

Ver. 14.—**The anger of the Lord was kindled against Moses.** The expression used is a strong one, but does not perhaps here mean more than that God was displeased. At least, he did not punish the offender in any severer way than by the withholding of a gift that he was ready to bestow, and the partition between two of a position and a dignity which Moses might have had all to himself. Perhaps diffidence and self-distrust, even when out of place, are not altogether abhorrent to One whose creatures are continually offending him by presumption and arrogance. **Is not**

Aaron the Levite thy brother? I know, etc. This translation is wrong. The two clauses form one sentence, and should be rendered, " Do I not know that Aaron the Levite, thy brother, speaks well? " Aaron's designation as " the Levite " is remarkable, and seems to glance at the future consecration of his tribe to God's especial service. **Behold, he cometh forth to meet thee.** It has been conjectured that Aaron designed to visit Moses in Midian, in order to convey to him the intelligence that the king who had sought his life (ch. ii. 15) was dead. He did not, however, start on the journey till God gave him a special direction (ver. 27).

Ver. 15.—**Thou shalt speak unto him and put words in his mouth.** Moses was to tell Aaron what to say—furnish, *i.e.*, the matter of his speeches—and Aaron was to clothe this matter in fitting words. God promised to be with both of their mouths; with Moses', to make him give right directions to Aaron; with Aaron's, to make him utter them persuasively. Moses' position was still the more honourable one, though Aaron's might seem the higher to the people.

Ver. 16. — **He shall be thy spokesman.** Literally, " He shall speak for thee." **He shall be, even he.** It is the verb that is repeated, not the pronoun. Probably the meaning is, " he shall *surely* be." There is no comparison between Aaron and anyone else. **Thou shalt be to him instead of God.** Divine inspiration, that is, shall rest on thee; and it shall be his duty to accept thy words as Divine words, and to do all that thou biddest him.

Ver. 17.—**Thou shalt take this rod.** Not any rod, but the particular one which had already once become a serpent. **Wherewith thou shalt do signs.** Rather, " *the* signs," *i.e.* the signs which thou wilt have to do, as already declared in ch. iii. 20. It is quite gratuitous to suppose that God had already particularised them

HOMILETICS.

Vers. 1—5.—*The intent of the first sign.* Primarily, no doubt, the object was to empower Moses to show forth a sign easily, readily, without preparation, and so at any moment. He had come to the time of life at which he naturally carried a staff. That he should be able at his will to transform that dead piece of vegetable matter into an active, living organism, would show him endued with supernatural power over both the vegetable and animal worlds, and give him a means, always ready to his hand, of demonstrating the truth of his mission. This alone was a great matter. But the fact that his rod became a serpent, rather than any other living thing, was specially calculated to impress the Egyptians. In one form, the serpent with them meant " a king," or " a crown; " and the change of a staff into a snake would typify the conversion of a shepherd into a monarch. In another form it was a sign for a " multitude," and the transformation might remind them that the single stock or stem of Jacob was now

---

[1] They might perhaps be best translated—" Ah! my Lord, pray send by whom thou wilt."

become " millions." The great serpent, Apap, moreover, held a high position in their mythology, as powerful to destroy and punish, whence they might the more fear one who seemed able to create serpents at his pleasure. The Israelites would perhaps view the staff as a rod to smite with, and connect its change into a serpent with the notion that when rods or whips were not thought severe enough, rulers chastised with " scorpions " (1 Kings xii. 11). Altogether, the sign, if viewed as a type, was threatening and alarming; perhaps the more so on account of its vagueness. Forms ill-defined, seen through mist, affright men more than those which are clear and definite.

Vers. 6—8.—*The intent of the second sign.* If the first sign was powerful to convince, the second was still more powerful (ver. 8). It showed Moses able to produce, and cure, in a moment of time, the most virulent malady to which human nature was liable. The Egyptians greatly feared leprosy, and declared in their own accounts of the Exodus that they drove the Israelites out of their country because they were afflicted with that loathsome disease. The Israelites regarded it as the worst affliction that could befall a man. The hand of Moses made leprous within the folds of the garment that enwrapped his bosom typified perhaps the Israelitish nation, corrupted by the circumstances that enwrapped it around in Egypt. The cure indicated that Moses would, through the power committed to him, cleanse the people from their defilements, and restore them to a state of spiritual soundness. Thus it was at once a warning and a promise. The sign appears not to have been used in Moses' dealings with the Egyptians (ch. vii. 10—17), because it was inappropriate as respected them, since they were beyond cleansing—there was no healing of their wound. Thus by this sign were taught two things: 1. That there is a fountain opened for sin and for uncleanness which can wash away, under the condition of repentance, any defilement; and 2. That there is a state of sinfulness and corruption when repentance ceases to be possible, and the moral nature can no longer be restored, and nothing remains but that fearful looking-for of judgment to come whereof the Epistle to the Hebrews speaks (ch. x. 27). The signs of the serpent and the blood—signs of judgment—were for the Egyptians and the Israelites alike; the sign of the hand made leprous *and then restored*—a sign of mercy—was for the Israelites only.

Ver. 9.—*The intent of the third sign.*—Blood poured on the ground could symbolise nothing but war and destruction. That water should be turned into it implied that peace should be changed into war, prosperity into ruin, quiet and tranquillity into a horrible carnage. The special reference would be to the destruction of Pharaoh's host in the Red Sea; but the other ruinous plagues, as especially the fifth, the seventh, and the tenth, would be glanced at also. That the water became blood on touching the ground of Egypt would indicate that it was the land and people of Egypt who were to be the sufferers. A very dreadful vengeance was thus foreshadowed by the third sign, which should have warned the Pharaoh of the terrible results that would follow his resistance to God's will as proclaimed by Moses. To the Israelites, on the contrary, the sign was one assuring them of final triumph; that the blood of their enemies would be poured out like water in the coming struggle, and their resistance to God's will be signally punished.

Ver. 10.—*Slowness of speech a drawback on ministerial fitness, but not a disqualification.* It is remarkable that both Moses, the great prophet of the First Covenant, and St. Paul, the " chosen vessel" for the publication of the Second Covenant, were ineffective as speakers; not perhaps both " in presence base," but certainly both " in speech contemptible " (2 Cor. x. 1, 10). Speakers and preachers should lay the lesson to heart, and learn not to be overproud of the gift of eloquence. A good gift it is, no doubt—when sanctified, a great gift—which may redound to God's honour and glory, and for which they should be duly thankful, but not a necessary gift. The men of action, the men that have done the greatest things, and left their mark most enduringly upon the world, have seldom been " men of words." Luther indeed was mighty in speech, and John Knox, and Whitfield, and (though less so) John Wesley, but not our own Cranmer, nor Melancthon, nor Anselm, nor Bishop Cosin, nor John Keble. In the secular sphere of statesmanship and generalship the same principle holds even more decidedly. Demosthenes has to yield the palm to Alexander, Cicero to Cæsar, Pym to Cromwell, the Abbé Siéyès to Napoleon. On the whole it must be said that those who are great in deed are rarely great in speech. And without eloquence a man may do God good service in every walk of life, even as a minister. The written sermon may go as straight to the heart of the audience as the spoken one. Ministerial effort in house-to-house visiting may do as much to convert a parish as any number of extempore sermons. Example of life preaches better than palaver. Let no one who feels within him the ministerial call, who longs to serve God by bringing his fellow-men to Christ, be deterred by the thought that he is "slow of speech and of a slow tongue." God, without making him eloquent, can "be with his mouth," give his words force, make them powerful to the conversion of souls. It has been said that there are many "dumb poets." So are there many "dumb preachers," whose weak and hesitating words God blesses and renders effectual, so that in the end they have no cause to be ashamed, but may point to those whom they have brought to Christ, and exclaim with St. Paul, "Ye are our work, ye are our epistle, the seal of our apostleship are ye in the Lord" (1 Cor. ix. 1, 2; 2 Cor. iii. 2).

Vers. 13, 14.—*The sin of self-distrust, and its punishment.* Undoubtedly the general inclination of men is towards self-assertion and self-sufficiency, so that diffidence and distrust of self are commonly regarded as excellences. But there is a diffidence which is wrongful, a self-distrust which Scripture condemns. St. Paul calls it "a voluntary humility" (ἐθελοταπεινοφροσύνη)—a humblemindedness, that is, which has its root in the will; a man not choosing to think that he is fit for high things, and determining to keep down his aims, aspirations, hopes, endeavours. The same apostle exhorts his converts "not to think of themselves more highly than they ought to think" (Rom. xii. 3), but at the same time, by implication, not to think too humbly, for he tells them to think *soberly*, according as God has dealt to every one the measure of faith." We ought to take *true* views of ourselves, of our capacities, powers, faculties, even of the graces to which by God's mercy we have been able to attain; and not to deny them or depreciate them. If we do so we keep ourselves back from high things, and this is how God punishes us. Moses lost the gift of eloquence, which God would supernaturally have bestowed upon him (ver. 12), and lost one-half of his leadership (vers. 14—16), by his persistent diffidence and distrust. We prevent ourselves from attaining heights to which we might have attained, we keep ourselves down in this world and make our position low in the next, by similar folly. The youth who bore the banner with the word "excelsior" upon it, was wiser than most of us. If we would rise high we must aim high; if we would aim high we must not be too diffident of ourselves.

Ver. 14.—*The love of brothers.* Few things are more lovely than the affection of brothers. James and John, Simon and Andrew, Philip and Bartholomew, James and Jude, were sent out together by our Lord, that they might enjoy this sweet companionship. How touching is the love of Joseph for Benjamin! If there is "a friend that sticketh closer than a brother," the fact is noted for its rarity; and the force of the phrase depends on the known intensity of fraternal affection. Aaron, though so long parted from Moses, perhaps the more *because* so long parted, would at the sight of him be "glad in his heart." Though not brought up together, though educated so differently, and gifted so differently, though seemingly intended for such different walks in life, the two had a true affection, each for each, which had survived a long and—so far as we are told—complete separation. Here, and again in verse 27, it is the affection of Aaron which is especially noticed—perhaps because it was the more praiseworthy. Aaron, the elder brother, might naturally have felt some jealousy of Moses' advancement above himself, of his superior education, social position, privileges, etc. But he seems to have been entirely free from this feeling. Moses might, for aught that he knew, resume his old princely rank on his return to Egypt, and throw him once more into the shade. Aaron did not disquiet himself about this. God knew that he longed for the simple keen pleasure of *seeing* his brother ("when he seeth thee, he will be glad," etc.), of pressing him to his heart, and kissing him on the face (ver. 27). Well would it be, if among Christians all brothers were thus minded.

Vers. 14—16.—*Diversities of gifts a benefit both to individuals and to the Church.*—
After all, the self-distrust of Moses was turned by God to good. Without it Moses
would have been sole leader of the entire enterprise, must have appeared alone before
the elders and before the monarch, must have undertaken the entire charge, direction,
superintendence of everything, must have had upon his mind an unshared burden which
it would have been most trying to bear. God's strength might indeed have been
sufficient for his weakness. But his life could not but have been a weariness to him.
He would have lacked the unspeakable solace and comfort of a loved and loving
associate, to whom he might open—indeed, was bound to open (ver. 15)—all his mind,
and with whom he could constantly "take sweet counsel together." He would have
also lacked the support, so much needed by a shy man, of a companion and coadjutor in
crises and times of difficulty, as when he appeared first before the elders (vers. 29, 30),
and when he appeared first before Pharaoh (ch. v. 1). Thus the association of Aaron
with himself in the leadership must have been felt by Moses as a benefit. And to
Aaron it was an unmixed advantage. The gift with which God had endowed him, and
which he had no doubt sedulously cultivated, caused him to be placed almost on a par
with his brother—enabled him to be of use to him—gave him loving companionship—
and caused him to have a large part in the deliverance of his nation. After forty years
of separation, during which he had never ceased to long for the return of his brother,
Aaron found himself associated in the closest possible way with Moses, made his
"right-hand man," his other self, his constant aider and assister. After a wholly
undistinguished life, which had lasted eighty-three years (ch. vii. 7), he found himself
brought into a position of the highest dignity and responsibility. And the Church was
benefited greatly by the double leadership. Moses, the man of thought, was able to
devote himself exclusively to thinking out all the details of the great work entrusted to
him. Aaron, the man of words, was able to give all his attention to the framing of
addresses whereby he might advance the plans of his brother. So in the Christian
Church there have always been, and will always be, "diversities of gifts." At one time
they are "gifts of healing, tongues, prophecy, interpretation, discerning of spirits, faith,
wisdom, prudence" (1 Cor. xii. 8—10); at another, preaching power, administrative
energy, learning, scholarship, influence, and the like. Seldom are even two of these
gifts united in the same individual. The Church prospers by utilising the gifts of all,
assigning to each man the position suited to him, and taking care that he has a fair
field for the employment of his special gift. In this way, "the whole building fitly
joined together, and *compacted by that which every joint supplieth*, according to the
effectual working in the measure of every part, maketh increase of the body to the
edifying of itself in love" (Eph. iv. 16).

HOMILIES BY VARIOUS AUTHORS.

Ver. 1.—*Unbelief.* The objection started by Moses to the mission on which he was
sent was a very natural one. The people would not believe him, nor hearken to his
voice. For—

I. HE WAS AS YET UNFURNISHED WITH DISTINCT CREDENTIALS. In so grave a matter
Moses could not expect the people to believe his bare word. This was a real difficulty.
Before committing themselves to his proposals, the Hebrews would be entitled to ask
for very distinct proofs that the message brought to them had really come from God—
that there was no mistake, no deception. God acknowledges the justice of this plea, by
furnishing Moses with the credentials that he needed. From which we gather that it
is no part of the business of a preacher of the Gospel to run down "evidences."
Evidences are both required and forthcoming. God asks no man to confide in a message
as of Divine authority, without furnishing him with sufficient grounds for believing
that this character really belongs to it. The reality of revelation, the supernatural
mission of Christ, the inspiration of prophets and apostles, the authority of Scripture,
all admit of proof; and it is the duty of the preacher to keep this fact in view, and in
delivering his message, to exhibit along with the message the evidences of its Divine
original.

II. MORAL CAUSES, AS DISTINGUISHED FROM MERE DEFICIENCY OF EVIDENCE, WOULD

MAKE IT DIFFICULT FOR HIM TO SECURE CREDENCE. Moses anticipated being met, not simply with hesitation and suspense of judgment, which would be all that the mere absence of credentials would warrant, but by positive disbelief. "The Lord hath *not* appeared to thee." How account for this? 1. *The message he had to bring was a very wonderful one.* He had to ask the people to believe that, after centuries of silence, God, the God of the patriarchs, had again appeared to him, and had spoken with him. This in itself was not incredible, but it would assume an incredible aspect to those whose faith in a living God had become shadowy and uninfluential—who had learned to look on such appearances as connected, not with the present, but with a distant and already faded past. Credulous enough in some things, they would be incredulous as to this; just as a believer in witchcraft or fairies might be the hardest to convince of a case of the supernatural aside from the lines of his ordinary thinking and beliefs. It is a similar difficulty which the preacher of the Gospel has to encounter in the indisposition of the natural mind to believe in anything outside of, or beyond, the sphere in which it ordinarily works and judges,—the sphere of things sensible (John xiv. 17). The super-natural is strange to it. It pushes it aside as inherently incredible, or at least as of no interest to it. From this the advance is easy to that which is so peculiarly a charac-teristic of our age, the denial of the supernatural as such—the flat assertion that miracle is impossible. 2. *The announcement contained in his message was so good as almost to surpass belief.* Great good news has often this effect of producing incredulity. Cf. Gen. xlv. 26,—"Jacob's heart fainted, and he believed them not," and Ps. cxxvi. And would not the Hebrews require evidence for the great good news that God had visited them, and was about to bring them out of Egypt, and plant them in Caanan! In like manner, is it not vastly wonderful, almost passing belief, that God should have done for man all that the Gospel declares him to have done! Sending his Son, making atonement for sin, etc. 3. *The difficulties in the way of the execution of the purpose seemed insuperable.* Even with God on their side, it might seem to the Israelites as if the chances of their deliverance from Pharaoh were very small. True, God was omni-potent; but we know little if we have not learned how much easier it is to believe in God's power in the abstract, than to realise that this power is able to cope successfully with the actual difficulties of our position. The tendency of unbelief is to "limit the Holy One of Israel" (Ps. lxxviii. 41). And this tendency is nowhere more manifest than in the difficulty men feel in believing that the Gospel of the Cross is indeed the very "power of God unto salvation"—able to cope with and overcome the moral evil of the world, and of their own hearts. 4. *One difficulty Moses would not have to contend with,* viz.: *aversion to his message in itself.* For, after all, the message brought to the Israelites was in the line of their own fondest wishes—a fact which ought, if anything could, powerfully to have recommended it. How different with the Gospel, which, with its spiritual salvation, rouses in arms against itself every propensity of a heart at enmity against God! The Israelites must at least have *desired* that Moses' message would turn out to be true; but not so the mass of the hearers of the Gospel. They desire neither God nor his ways; have no taste for his salvation; are only eager to find excuses for getting rid of the unwelcome truths. To overcome an obstacle of this kind, more is needed than outward credentials—even an effectual working of the Holy Ghost.

III. INFERENCES FROM THESE CONSIDERATIONS. 1. *Preachers of the Gospel must prepare themselves for encountering unbelief.* It is the old complaint—"Who hath believed our report?" (Is. liii. 1). 2. *The success of Moses in overcoming the people's unbelief shows that he must have possessed decisive credentials of his mission.* The complaint of this verse does not tally with what is sometimes alleged as to the unlimited drafts that may be made on human credulity. Moses did not find the people all readiness to believe *him*. He was bringing them a message in the line of their dearest wishes, yet he anticipated nothing but incredulity. He had never much reason to complain of the over-credulity of the Israelites; his complaint was usually of their unbelief. Even after signs and wonders had been wrought, he had a constant battle to fight with their unbelieving tendencies. How then, unless his credentials had been of the clearest and most decisive kind, could he possibly have succeeded? For, mark— (1) It was not merely a few enthusiasts he had to carry with him, but the whole body of the people. (2) He was no demagogue, but a man of slow, diffident, self-distrustful nature, the last man who might be expected to play successfully on popular credulity or enthusiasm. (3) His plans were not to be laid before the multitude at all, but before the "elders"—the cool, cautious heads of the nation, who would be sure to ask him for very distinct credentials before committing themselves to a contest with Pharaoh. The inference is that there must have been a true supernatural in the founding of the Mosaic era; as afterwards there must have been a true supernatural in the founding of the Christian era. Imposture, credulity, the force of mere ideas, the commanding power of a great personality, are, together or apart, incapable of explaining all the facts. Wonders must have been wrought, alike in the accrediting of the mission of Moses and in the stupendous work of the deliverance itself.—J. O.

Vers. 1—10.—*A trilogy of signs.* In reply to his complaint that the people would not believe him, nor hearken to his voice, God gave Moses three signs. These are to be viewed—

I. As ATTESTATIONS OF HIS DIVINE COMMISSION (ver. 5, 8). Divine power is supernaturally exercised in proof of Moses' title to speak with Divine authority. This is a clear case of the use of miracles as credentials of a mission, and confutes those who reason that this view of miracles has no basis in Scripture. The *character* of the signs was not to be disregarded, but the immediate circumstance which gave them evidential value was the fact of supernatural origin. Practically, signs of the kind wrought by Moses would be felt to be incontestable proofs of his Divine commission; and it is difficult to see how otherwise his message could have been authenticated. Why should this be objected to? Why, if the message is worthy of God, and the work of power is also worthy of God, should the work of power not be employed to add authority to the word, as indicating with certainty the source from which it comes?

II. As SIGNIFICANT OR PARABOLIC ACTS. This is implied in their character as "signs." They had had of themselves a "voice." They told over again what Moses had explained in words, while they exhibited in symbol the superiority of Jehovah to the king and gods of Egypt. 1. *Sign 1st.*—*The impotence of Pharaoh against Jehovah's messenger.* This seems to be the import of the turning of the rod into the serpent (vers. 2—5). The serpent "was the symbol of the royal and divine power on the diadem of every Pharaoh." (1) The rod cast to the ground and changing into a serpent symbolised the effect of the challenge to Pharaoh. (2) Before this terrible apparition, with its gleaming eyes, inflated neck, hissing tongue, and vehemence of assault, Moses fled in natural terror. (3) But he is instructed not to fear it, but to seize it by the tail; when there is given a representation of Pharaoh's absolute power-lessness to hurt him in the reconversion of the serpent into the rod. The foe vanishes, and Moses remains master of the situation. The lesson is, that God's servants, charged with the execution of his mission, are more than a match for all the powers of ill that can be arrayed against them. God will bruise even Satan—"that old serpent"—under their feet shortly (Rom. xvi. 20). They wield an authority which gives them for the time a charmed existence, and ensures the defeat of those opposed to them. Cf. with this sign Mark xvi. 18; Acts xxviii. 5; Rev. xii. 6; and instance Luther before the Diet of Worms. 2. *Sign 2nd.*—*The power of Jehovah to smite and heal.* The symbol of this was at the same time an instance of it—viz. the sudden smiting of Moses' hand with leprosy, followed by as instantaneous a cure (vers. 6—8). Leprosy was peculiarly the theocratic punishment (Miriam, Uzziah, Gehazi). It was probably a common disease among the Israelites, who figure in Egyptian traditions as a nation of lepers, hateful to the gods on account of their pollutions. The obvious teaching of this sign would therefore be—(1) That Jehovah was able to smite with the most grievous plagues, yet (2) As able to heal when he had smitten. This conveyed both threat and promise. (1) If the people obeyed his voice, as he had healed the leprous hand, so would he heal them of their natural and spiritual disorders, and lift them out of their despised and unclean state in Egypt; while conversely, (2) If they resisted, great and sore strokes of the Divine anger would fall upon them; or, if Egypt resisted God's will, it in turn would be smitten by his plagues. The power in both cases was omnipotent and resistless. Thus we are instructed—1. To fear the stroke of the Divine anger. 2. That God who smites can also heal (Hos. vi. 1). 3. That God is more willing to remove judgments than to send them. 4. That God can heal the leprous heart. 5. To fear, above all, that most awful fulfilment of the leprosy symbol

—the adjudging of the soul, under Divine wrath, to the unchecked spread of its own corruptions—to the reign of sin within itself. *Sign 3rd.*—*The ruin that would descend on Egypt if God's will continued to be disobeyed.* The sign of the turning of a portion of the water of the Nile—the source of Egypt's beauty, fertility, and prosperity—into blood (ver. 9) could only have one meaning. It portended ruin to the state of Egypt. And such would be the inevitable consequence of a contest between Pharaoh and Jehovah, if protracted by the king's obstinacy. In this case there was no reversal of the sign. The end of strife with God is judgment without mercy—utter destruction. Lesson—the folly of striving with the Almighty.

III. AS A SERIES OF SIGNS ADAPTED TO REMOVE DOUBT AT DIFFERENT STAGES (vers. 8, 9). Though, strictly speaking, one sign was enough to attest the Divine commission of him who wrought it, yet God, who condescends to man's infirmity, added sign to sign, thus furnishing a superabundance and accumulation of evidences, and rendering unbelief wholly inexcusable. It has often been observed that the strength of the evidence for revelation lies, not in any single line of proof, but in the cumulative force of a great variety of evidences, some of which strike one class of minds as of peculiar cogency, while minds differently constituted are more impressed by others. In the case before us, a certain progression may be noted; each sign, by peculiar marks, carrying us a step further than its predecessor. 1. In the turning of the rod into the serpent, we have a work of Divine power, but not without a certain resemblance to the feats of the native serpent-charmers. The points of contrast were great, but it might be doubted whether the acts of the magicians were not competent to produce as great a wonder. 2. In the second sign—the stroke of leprosy—this doubt is eliminated, and the presence of Divine power conclusively demonstrated. But Egypt had her gods also, and the question, as it would present itself to those who believed in them, was not simply, Is Jehovah powerful? but, Is his power greater than theirs? 3. The last sign gives the final proof, by working a miracle on the water of the Nile—itself one of Egypt's greatest gods. The turning of that sacred water into blood was the death-blow to all hope of help from the Egyptian idols. Observe— 1. The anxiety of God to remove doubt. 2. The ample provision he has made for its removal. 3. The patience with which he bears with man's dulness and slowness of heart. 4. The inexcusableness of unbelief.—J. O.

Vers. 10—17.—*Slow of speech.* The longer Moses pondered the mission on which he was sent, the more he shrank from it. The difficulty which now oppressed him was his want of eloquence. It seemed to him that in this respect he was the least qualified person God could have chosen. There was needed for such a work a man of persuasive tongue, of fluent, forcible, and impressive speech; and his own utterance was hesitating and heavy. Overwhelmed with the sense of unfitness, he again appeals to God, and asks to be relieved from duty. We have here—

I. A FELT INFIRMITY. Moses was doubtless right in what he said of his natural difficulty of speech. But his error lay—1. *In exaggerating the value of a gift of mere eloquence.* He did not possess it—though Stephen calls him "mighty in words" (Acts vii. 22)—and he was apt to overrate its influence. He forgot that the man of deep silent nature has a power of his own, which expresses itself through the very ruggedness and concentration of his speech; and that oratory, while valuable for some purposes, is not the most essential gift in carrying through movements which are to leave a permanent impress on history. What is chiefly wanted is not power of speech, but power of action; and when it is felt that a man can act, a very limited amount of speech will serve his purpose (Cromwell, William the Silent, Bismarck, etc.). The smooth persuasive tongue, though pleasant to listen to, is not the weightiest in counsel. 2. *In forgetting that God knew of this infirmity when he called him to the work.* God knew all about his slowness of speech, and yet had sent him on this mission. Did not this carry with it the promise that whatever help he needed would be graciously vouchsafed? God has a purpose in sometimes calling to his service men who seem destitute of the gifts—the outward gifts—needful for his work. 1. The work is more conspicuously his own. 2. His power is glorified in man's weakness. 3. The infirmity is often of advantage to the servant himself—keeping him humble, driving him to prayer, teaching him to rely on Divine grace, rousing him to effort, etc.

(2 Cor. xii. 7—10). Paul was a man "rude in speech" (2 Cor. xi. 6), and came not with eloquence of words (1 Cor. ii. 1); but his defects of speech only made the Divine power which resided in his utterances the more conspicuous (2 Cor. ii. 4, 5).

II. A GRACIOUS PROMISE. God would be with his mouth, and teach him what to say (ver. 11). The Maker of speech, he might be trusted to aid its powers, when these were needed in his service. So Christ promises his disciples to give them in their hour of need what they shall speak (Matt. x. 19). Lips touched by Divine grace possess a simple, natural eloquence of their own, far excelling the attempts of studied oratory. Then there is the other fact, that gifts of speech are often latent till grace comes to evoke them. Moses' original awkwardness was no index to what, assisted by God's grace, he might ultimately have become, even as a speaker. His gift would probably have grown with the necessity. The greatest preachers of the Gospel, with Paul at their head, have not been men naturally eloquent. If they became so afterwards, it was grace that made them. Thus, we are told of Luther that at first he dared not enter the pulpit. "Luther, who subsequently preached with so much power,—who gave a new direction, and a force and elevation never before attained, to the whole system of German preaching,—who is still the unparalleled master of all who hope to effect more by the internal demonstrativeness of a discourse than by its external ornamentation,—this Luther was too humble, too modest, to take the place of a preacher. It was only at the solicitation of Slauptitz that he finally consented to preach—at first in the oratory of the convent, and afterwards in church" (Hagenbach). Knox was equally diffident about the exercise of his gifts, and when an unexpected appeal was made to him, at the age of forty-two—"the said John, abashed, burst forth in most abundant tears, and withdrew himself to his chamber" (Knox's 'History'). All may not be eloquent like these; but anyone possessed of earnest feeling and intense convictions, who is content to deliver a plain message with directness and simplicity, will be surprised at what God can sometimes make even of rude and unskilled lips.

III. A SINFUL SHRINKING FROM DUTY (ver. 13). The continued reluctance of Moses, after so gracious an assurance, was not to be excused. It was a direct act of disobedience, and argued, besides a want of faith, a certain measure of stubbornness. God was angry with him, yet forbore with his infirmity. And if God forbore with Moses, it is surely not for us to blame him, who are so often in "the same condemnation." Let him who has never shrunk from unwelcome duties, or who has never stumbled in believing that Divine grace will, under trying circumstances, be made sufficient for his needs, cast the first stone. Admire rather in this incident—1. The patience and forbearance of God in stooping to his servant's weakness, and 2. The "exceeding greatness" of the power which accomplished such mighty results by so unwilling an instrumentality. Nothing proves more clearly that the work of Israel's deliverance was not of man, but of God, than this almost stubborn reluctance of Moses to have anything to do with it.

IV. A SECOND-BEST ARRANGEMENT (vers. 14—17). The appointment of Aaron as spokesman to his brother, while in one view of it an act of condescension, and a removal of Moses' difficulty, was in another aspect of it a punishment of his disobedience. It took from Moses the privilege of speaking for God in his own person, and committed the delivery of the message to more eloquent, perhaps, but also to less sanctified, lips. 1. *The arrangement had its advantages.* (1) It supplied one's defect by another's gift. (2) It utilised a talent lying unemployed. (3) It gave Aaron a share in the honour of being God's messenger. (4) It formed a new link of sympathy between the brothers. But—2. *It was not the best.* (1) It prevented the development of the gift of speech in Moses himself. Had he relied on God's promise, he would doubtless have acquired a power of speech to which he was at first a stranger. (2) The message would lose in force by being delivered through an intermediary. This of necessity. How much of the power of speech lies in its being a direct emanation from the mind and heart of the speaker—something instinct with his own personality! As delivered by Aaron, the messages of God would lose much of their impressiveness. Fluency has its disadvantages. A mind burdened with its message, and struggling with words to give it utterance, conveys a greater impression of force than ready delivery charged with a message that is not its own. (3) Moses would be hampered in his work by the constancy of his dependence on Aaron. It limits a man, when he cannot act without continually calling in another to his assistance. (4) It divided Moses' authority, and gave Aaron an undue influence with the people (cf. Ex. xxxii.). (5) It was a temptation to Aaron himself to assume, or at least aspire to, greater authority than of right belonged to him (cf. Num. xii.). Learn—1. That it is not always good for us to have our wishes granted. 2. That God sometimes punishes by granting us our wishes (cf. Hos. xiii. 11). 3. That God's way is over the best. J. O.

Ver. 11.—*God the Giver of our faculties.* See—1. His power in the creation of them. "Who hath made," etc. Wisdom also. Eyes, ears, organs of speech—miracles of contrivance. 2. His goodness in the bestowal of them. A reason for thankfulness. 3. His providence in the deprivation of them. "Who maketh the dumb, or deaf," etc. A reason for not murmuring. 4. His perfection as mirrored in their functions. "He that planted the ear, shall he not hear? he that formed the eye, shall he not see?" (Ps. xciv. 9). An answer to the objection against positive revelation. He that formed the mouth, shall he not speak? And he that formed the ear, can he not address to it his own message? 5. Lesson—His ability to aid us in using them for his glory (ver. 12).—J. O.

Ver. 13.—*A servant's difficulties.* Observe—

I. WHAT THEY WERE. Moses' difficulties resolved themselves into three. 1. *The power of Pharaoh.* "Who am I that I should go to Pharaoh?" (ch. iii. 10). We may be staggered by the thought of the powers that are arrayed against us. 2. *The anticipated unbelief of the people* (ver. 1). The preacher has to encounter hard and unbelieving hearts, and this may enfeeble and dishearten him. 3. *His lack of gifts* (ver. 10). Humble natures are easily discouraged by the sense of their own short-comings—by the consciousness of ignorance, defective education, lack of gifts of speech, etc.

II. HOW THEY WERE MET. 1. God armed Moses with powers that made him more than a match for the mighty king of Egypt. 2. He gave him the means of overcoming the unbelief of the people. 3. He promised to endow him with power of speech; and, when that was rejected, supplied his defect by giving him a coadjutor. From which learn:—1. That while it is right to state our difficulties to God—to pour out all our hearts before him—it is wrong to make them an excuse for shrinking from duty. 2. That God, if relied on, will give us all sufficiency.—J. O.

Ver. 17.—*The rod.* The rod a fit emblem of " the word of the truth of the Gospel." 1. The rod was something definite. "This rod." Not any rod, but the one which God gives us. 2. The rod was perhaps the instrument of a despised calling. So is the preaching of the Cross "foolishness" (1 Cor. i. 21—25). 3. The rod was to be grasped and used: "in thine hand." Study, preach, expound, apply. 4. By the rod, Moses was to do signs: "wherewith thou shalt do signs." Spiritual miracles wrought by the preaching of the word. 5. The rod was efficient only as accompanied by Divine power (1 Cor. ii. 4).—J. O.

Vers. 1—9.—*The third difficulty: how is Moses to deal with an incredulous Israel?* With the mention of this third difficulty, we begin to see how much of doubt, self-distrust, and reluctance disturbed the mind of Moses. And no wonder. This revelation and commandment of God had come very suddenly upon him; and though strong assurances and sufficient information were readily given, yet he could not all at once receive the comforts which flowed from them. Had he attended to what God said by way of removing the difficulties already expressed he would never have given utterance to this third one. His perseverance in suggesting obstacles almost makes us feel that he hoped somehow to get out of the mission. But God meets him at every point. There is no weak place in the Divine plans. Even a matter which seems so uncertain as the reception of Moses by Israel is confidently taken altogether out of the region of uncertainties. God had already said (ch. iii. 18), "They shall hearken to thy voice," and if Moses had only waited, he would have been made to see how that hearkening would be brought about. The suggestion of this difficulty, therefore, showed how much he was still lacking in calm faith; nevertheless we must bear in mind that the difficulty was a real one. There was only too much reason to apprehend that Israel would receive him in the way he indicated. Consider—

I. THE POOR EXPECTATIONS MOSES HAD OF A FAVOURABLE RECEPTION FROM ISRAEL. Why should he have these gloomy anticipations? Was the cause of them to be looked for wholly in Israel or wholly in himself? Did he mean to blame his brethren for their unbelief, or did he thus take another way of indicating his own utter distrust of himself? As he expresses no blame of Israel it is not for us to assume that he intended it. He knew very well that to go to his brethren with such a story, would be the very way to make them reject him and laugh him to scorn. He could not but feel that if he had been in their position, he would probably have behaved in the same way. What could it appear but presumptuous to return after forty years' absence from the distant and half-barbarous Midian, and pretend that he had been chosen to deliver Israel—he, a mere weather-beaten shepherd? Truth is stranger than fiction, and for this very reason it is too often believed to be the most improbable of all fictions. Moses thus had every ground to expect that he would be treated either as insane or as the most impudent of impostors. He would have been more easily believed in telling some made-up story than when he told the simple truth. God had looked very kindly and favourably on Moses in all his deeply felt unworthiness; but the very things that commended him to God, hindered him with men. In what a humiliating aspect this word of Moses puts our fallen human nature! When the truth in which we are most of all concerned comes before us, we are tempted to neglect and repudiate it because the messenger does not look sufficiently dignified. Nor is unbelief our only danger. We must labour to have a state of mind in which we shall always not only receive the true but reject the false. We have to do with false apostles as well as true ones. The elders of Israel would have done very wrong if they had rushed into a welcome of Moses on his bare *ipse dixit*. We must not, in our anxiety to avoid unbelief, deliver ourselves over to credulity. If the world has in it only too many of the unbelieving spirit, so, alas! it has only too many of the deceiving spirit; all the more deceivers because thoroughly deceived themselves. We must try the spirits whether they be of God, and ever live in thankful use of the infallible tests which God has given us.

II. GOD GIVES TO MOSES AMPLE EVIDENCES TO PRODUCE FAITH IN ISRAEL. Observe that *God does not simply promise these signs.* He works them at once, at least the two that were possible, before the very eyes of Moses. Moses has faith enough to be sure that it is indeed God who is with him at the present hour; but what about the future? True, God had said, "Certainly I will be with thee" (ch. iii. 12), and he might have repeated these words rebukingly. But he remembered that Moses was as yet very ignorant of the fulness of the Divine nature; and he acted with all his own wisdom and tenderness, to cherish the real but as yet very feeble and struggling faith of his servant. When Moses comes into the presence of his brethren, it is to cast down a rod that has already been a serpent, and to stretch forth a hand that has already been snow-white with leprosy. "What is that in thine hand?"—as much as to say, "Take note of it, look at it well, make sure that it is the rough, easily replaced instrument of your daily work." Moses is to be taught that things are not what they seem. He who according to his good pleasure took some of the original matter of the universe, and from it made the rod-nature, and from other made the serpent-nature, now by the same power changes in a moment the dead rod into the living serpent, and the living serpent into the dead rod. The healthy hand is all at once infected with leprosy, and even while Moses is shuddering with the terrible experience, the leprosy is as suddenly taken away. It is a fearful thing to fall into the hands of the living God. As to *the significance of these miracles*, there is doubtless much that lies beyond our power to ascertain. Assuredly they had in them perfect propriety both as to their order and their nature. What the burning bush became to Moses, these three miracles might become to the Israelites; not only paving the way for Moses to act with full authority in their name, but giving many lessons to such as had eyes to see and hearts to understand. For instance how could they but perceive that when God began his dealings with Pharaoh, he began with two out of the three miracles which Moses had shown to them. Moses turned the rod into a serpent, and the water into blood before Israel, and Israel believed (vers. 28—31). He did the same things before Pharaoh, and he remained unmoved. Who can tell what terrible things Israel escaped by their timely acceptance of the mission of Moses? and yet that acceptance, as we discover by the rebellions in the wilderness, did not amount to very much. The belief that is produced by miracle, if there be not some more penetrating force behind the mere exhibition of the extraordinary, does not go very deep, nor does it last very long. The greatest benefit of these miracles was to such Israelites as could see in them, not only the power of God, but something of the purposes for which that power was used. Pharaoh caused great pain to Israel, but he did nothing else; he sought no blessed end for the people beyond the pain. God, on the other hand, though he turned a rod into a threatening serpent, and a clean and healthy hand into a leprous, loathsome mass, yet very speedily took these signs of destruction away. When God brings threatening and affliction very near to us, it is only to show how quickly and completely they may be removed. All untoward things are in his hands—all serpents, all diseases, all degrading transformations of what is good and beautiful.—Y.

Vers. 10—12.—*The fourth difficulty: Moses alleges defect of utterance.* The third time is often represented in Scripture as the final and decisive time (1 Sam. iii. 8; Matt. xxvi. 44, 45, 75; John xxi. 17; 2 Cor. xii. 8). But Moses is not yet either satisfied or even silenced. As fast as one difficulty is swept away, his fearful and fertile mind has another ready to take its place. He began with himself, in stating his objections and difficulties, pleading then his unworthiness in general terms; now in the end he comes back to himself with the mention of a special difficulty. Consider—

I. THE DIFFICULTY AS STATED BY MOSES. In the course of the conversation, God has laid before him such particulars of the work required as seem to show him, in his hasty view of them, that he will have much speaking to do. But for speaking he alleges himself to be peculiarly unfit. What he meant by this unfitness we have no means of exactly ascertaining. Perhaps he had some actual defect in the vocal organs; or it may have been nothing more than the well-nigh insurmountable difficulty which some men feel when called on to speak in public. In any case he was bringing the difficulty forward under mistaken views as to the importance of mere utterance. 1. *He was exaggerating the service of natural faculties.* To say that these are nothing at all would be of course the language of mock humility. God has shown often in the history of his work in the world that he welcomes great natural gifts, lovingly devoted to him and thoroughly sanctified. But the great temptation undoubtedly is, to make too much of natural gifts—too much of the intellect, the voice, the physical presence altogether, and too little of the purposes for which these instruments are to be used. How a thing is said is of much less moment than the thing itself. Better to stammer out a great truth than to deck lying, deception, and worldly vanities in the best-chosen words. When the Jews conspiring against Paul wanted some one to plead their cause before Felix, they sought, very wisely from their point of view, for the practised professional orator. It mattered nothing that he lacked the love of truth and justice. It was his business to do the best he could for even the worst of causes. God might easily have found elsewhere in Israel a thousand fluent and attractive speakers, more pleasant to the ear than Moses, and yet none of them sufficiently endowed, in other ways, for the great work required. 2. *He was underrating the power of God working through those whom he chooses for himself.* It is inevitable that if we exaggerate in one direction, we shall underrate in another. If we make too much of the work of man, we shall make too little of the work of God. Moses is not yet duly impressed with the fact that God has unmistakably and finally chosen him. He thinks he ought to be able to see clearly why he is chosen, and this is just what he cannot as yet get even a glimpse of. If only he had been able to feel conscious of some improvement in his natural faculties, it would have been a great encouragement, a great help to submission and prompt advance, at least so he thought. Depend upon it, we can never think of the power of God too highly. Nothing, so long as it is agreeable to his character, is beyond him. If he has chosen us for any work, he will always make his choice quite certain to our hearts; though, at the same time, to humble and try us, he may give much to perplex our intellects. In such moments our true and sufficient refuge is to remember the unfailing power of him who directs us. If Moses had only lived, say in the time of Paul, and been able to look back as Paul looked on all the Divine dealings recorded in the Scriptures, he would have seen at once, and gloried in the fact, that his very lack of fluent speech, so far from being against him, was rather in his favour (2 Cor. iv. 7).

II. GOD'S TREATMENT OF THIS PERSEVERING RELUCTANCE. Observe God's continued patience. So far there has not been a word of rebuke to Moses; no action such as corresponds with the smiting of a stupid or inattentive scholar. But it was really quite time for Moses to begin to reflect a little before he spoke. Moses seemed to hint in this latest appeal that it was desirable at once to confer on him what he judged to be the requisite powers of speech. But God saw that the real want was not speaking, but thinking; quiet, earnest, introspective thinking. There had been quite enough of speaking unadvisedly with the lips, only to be excused by the fact that Moses had become so recently acquainted with Jehovah. Now God gives his servant something to think about. Moses has said in effect, " Here am I, called to a great work, for which, through no fault of my own, I lack the necessary faculties." And God in return is not slow to meet Moses with a plain admission of the Divine responsibility for many things which *we count defects* in human nature. " Where," says the sceptic, " is the wisdom of that God who allows the world to abound in so many human beings deficient in one or another of their natural faculties?" God meets the charge himself, and meets it boldly. He not only allows man to be so, but he makes him so; in other words, what we call defects are not defects at all. The defect is in us, who are not able to look at them in a right and comprehensive way. There are defects and defects. Man, thinking of the blind, the deaf, the dumb, the lame, begins to wail what an imperfect thing creation is; yet he is only complaining of spots on the surface. Our outward senses, with all the knowledge and pleasure that they bring, are only subsidiary parts of humanity. Let Moses consider, and he will see that, inasmuch as these defects come from no fault of his own, God can easily make them up. The fact that Moses was so slow of heart to believe all that God had spoken was a far greater hindrance than all his slowness of speech. We find serious defects and hindrances where, so to speak, God rather finds helps; while the things that hinder God's work and stir his indignation it takes a great deal to make us conscious of. The worst obstacles to be encountered by Moses did not come from any of the things he had laid such emphasis on; they lay in his own heart—that heart into which the dawning of God's presence had only just begun to penetrate.—Y.

Vers. 13—16.—*Moses, taking a step too far, is suddenly arrested.* In ver. 13 we must evidently look at the spirit of the words, rather than the words themselves. There is nothing wrong in the words. Uttered in a different tone and in different circumstances they might have drawn forth the approval of God rather than his anger. They might be used as expressing the most devout submissiveness, the consciousness of one who, though he is treading forth into darkness and danger, is sure that he is filled with the fulness of God. But not so had Moses yet learned to speak. God has tried to call him away from the turmoil of his doubts, from his hasty conjectures and crude anticipations; but instead of obeying, instead of acquainting himself with God, and thereby being at peace, he flies in his face with this half-despairing half-defiant cry. It is the crisis of the struggle, and it is very instructive to notice how firmly and yet gently God deals with his servant. Observe, then, how we have here a *due mingling of righteous anger and compassionate aid.*

I. GOD'S MANIFESTED ANGER WITH MOSES. The expression is a strong and suggestive one. Not simply that God was angry, but that his anger was kindled. We may take it as meaning that there was some anger already, growing indeed hotter and hotter, but only now under this great provocation breaking into flame. The anger of God must inevitably rise at every contact with human ignorance and stubbornness, though it may be so veiled beneath love, pity, and patience as to be concealed from the man whose conduct excites it. And note in particular that there is no inconsistency in attributing to God anger with Moses. Moses himself was to be excused, as having only recently become acquainted with God; but he could not escape his share of the due effects arising out of the alienation of the entire human race from God. Besides, God's anger must be looked upon as one of his instruments in bringing us effectually to compliance with his will. God's anger is really part of the goodness which leads us to repentance; and if gentler methods fail, then the time will come at last when that anger must be decidedly manifested, even for our good. Moses could not but admit that so far he had been dealt with very gently indeed. God, quickly and tenderly responsive, had met every hint of difficulty with a strong encouragement. But all the encouragements had made no real difference in Moses' mood of mind. He turns upon God in the querulous unappreciative strain indicated in ver. 13. Thus he unconsciously signifies that the time has come for God to change the method of his action. Moses, like a persistently heedless scholar, must be made to feel that his master cannot be trifled with. God speaks, not that we may discuss and parley with him, but that we may obey. Let Moses now understand that the time has come for him at once to go forth.

II. The anger is mingled with a gracious promise of appropriate aid. God's anger with his own chosen ones is but a sudden darkness to make the following light more useful and esteemed. God, who has just shown his power to Moses in the burning bush and the following signs, now shows power in a way even more attractive. He is one who can at the same moment warn and comfort—not only smiting that he may heal, but able to blend smiting and healing together. Even though Moses has provoked his indignation, he does not leave him with a bare promise that somehow or other his defect of utterance will be supplied. God sweeps away this latest difficulty as completely as he had done the previous ones. And note moreover that he disposed of it in his own unexpected way. It was better to leave Moses as he was, and make Aaron his spokesman, than to enrich him in his own person with all gifts of utterance and leave him alone. By linking the two men together, God was constantly teaching them the need of mutual subordination. If they would only be companions in humility they should also be companions in prosperity and in gladness of heart. Sad and disastrous would be the day when Moses should be disposed to say to Aaron, "I have no need of thee," or Aaron to Moses, "I have no need of thee." Aaron had what Moses lacked. Moses had the matter of a Divine and gladsome message, but he felt utterly at a loss how he was to get it properly laid before all whom it concerned. Aaron, on the other hand, had voice and faculty of speech, but behind that voice there had hitherto been nothing of commandment, direction, and encouragement. Aaron, says the Lord, was a man who could speak well; that is, as we may take it, a man able to speak distinctly and impressively—one who could deliver any message entrusted to him in a way which would not obscure the message, nor draw ridicule on the utterer of it. Moses and Aaron went together like the musician and the instrument on which he plays. *Thus we see the way in which God binds us together by our very deficiencies.* He constitutes us so that we are always more or less dependent on our fellow-men, and sometimes the dependence is very marked indeed. It is well for us in the midway and strength of life to consider that there may be but a step between us and the need of the tenderest sympathy. When we are most independent there are possibilities lying before us—yes, there are even certainties—which should moderate our pride and self-sufficiency. Manly independence is one of the greatest blessings; egotistic isolation one of the greatest curses. They that are strong should bear the infirmities of the weak; there are none of us so strong but that in some emergency of life we may accept the relief; there are none of us so weak but that we may do something to provide the relief. In a world which is so full of temptations to discord and rivalry it is a great comfort to remember that God is constantly working to counteract them. He guides human affairs, even as he guides the planets themselves; the centripetal force is greater than the centrifugal. If every one of us were free to work out the desires of our selfish hearts, anarchy would come with fearful rapidity.—Y.

Ver. 17.—*The importance of the rod: God guards Moses against a very natural oversight.* "Thou shalt take this rod in thine hand." Was Moses, then, likely to forget it? That rod had just been pointed out to him as connected with his favourable reception by Israel. It was to be the instrument for helping to deliver him from one of his chief apprehensions. And yet it was as likely as not that in the hurry of gathering his household goods together, the rod would be thrown into a corner of the fold as a mere bit of wood that could easily be replaced if Moses had once again to become a shepherd. Notice—1. *That other things seemed, to the natural eye, of a great deal more consequence.* As Martha, when Jesus came to her house, was cumbered with much serving, and in the middle of it all was unwittingly neglecting the one thing needful, so Moses, amid the distracting questions that filled his mind, had no inducement to regard the rod with such attention as corresponded to its real importance. Here is one of the great difficulties in bringing the natural man to discern the things of the Spirit of God. Not only is man, by nature, indifferent to spiritual things, but he is absorbingly occupied in the desires, cares, and apprehensions of the natural life. When the disciples of Christ had their minds filled with carnal anticipations of the kingdom of heaven, they heard even such glorious news as that of the resurrection of their Master as if they heard it not. 2. *This rod seemed a thing of particularly little consequence.* Were not a thousand such within easy reach? Might not God be trusted to turn any rod Moses took up just as he had turned this? If it had only been some precious stone, something costly, elaborate, and rare, he would not have forgotten it. 3. *The real consequence of the rod appeared clearly in the light of after events.* Suppose Moses had left the rod behind him. The likelihood is that he would very quickly have been stopped on the way, even as he was stopped and threatened because of his uncircumcised son. And if he had been allowed to go on, assuredly he would have been put to shame on coming into the presence of Israel. God was beginning to teach Moses that strict, unflagging attention to details would be necessary when he again came to this mountain to take his part in serving God on it. 4. *The rod itself was a great sign that Israel was to be delivered not by human but by Divine operations.* It was probably not only the companion of Moses, but the constant companion. Ever in his hand, it was something by which he could readily turn his thoughts away from his own inability to the all-sufficing power of God. It is our folly, both as concerns our own salvation and the salvation of our fellow-men, that we go out without the rod. When the Israelites saw Moses coming among them with his rod, clinging to it, though there seemed no use for it, some of them perhaps said, "Throw that rod aside; why cumber yourself with it, and become a laughingstock and a puzzle to beholders." And in like manner how often have those put in trust with the Gospel been exhorted to lay aside those elements which to the natural man appear mere excrescences and deformities. We may well believe that to the first apostles, it was one of the hardest things in the world to keep firm to the essential parts of their message. What the rod was to Moses, going forth with it and working signs, that must the doctrine of the Cross be to all apostles. Christ crucified is to the Jews a stumblingblock and to the Greeks foolishness, but to them which are called, Christ the power of God and the wisdom of God.—Y.

Vers. 1—9.—*Weakness and strength for God's service.* I. FEAR OF THE REJECTION OF THE MESSAGE WE BEAR FOR GOD MAKES ITS DELIVERANCE IMPOSSIBLE. The tidings he was to bear were so wonderful that he believed his words would be listened to with utter incredulity. Our Gospel is more wonderful still. To speak it, our eye must rest less on the message, and more on God's power to chastise and to bless. We are not critics of, nor apologists for, the Gospel: we are messengers sent before God's face. Our Master is behind us.

II. MIRACLES BELONG TO THE INFANCY OF FAITH. The signs are given because of unbelief. Elijah and Elisha work miracles among the tribes which had almost wholly forsaken God; Isaiah, Jeremiah, John, work none. The Apostles alone were empowered to bestow miraculous gifts, and these died out with the men who received them from the Apostles' hands. To bring again the age of miracles would be retrogression, not advance.

III. THE MIRACLES AS SIGNS. 1. The rod cast upon the ground becomes a serpent; the serpent dealt with in obedience to God's command becomes a rod. They who reject God's guidance will be pursued by his terrors, and if we deal with our foes as God directs us they will help, not harm us. 2. The hand put in the bosom (the attitude of determined indifference) becomes leprous; placed again in obedience to God's command, it is made whole. God can make the strength of the disobedient a burden and horror; and if we rest in him our loathsomeness and weakness will be changed into health and strength. 3. The sweet Nile waters changed into blood. The delight of the land to which unbelief will cling will become a loathing and a curse.—U.

Vers. 10—17.—*God's wrath will fall where his service is declined.* I. MOSES' OBJECTION AND GOD'S ANSWER (10—12). 1. He deems himself unfit to occupy the place even of spokesman to the Lord. The objection was based upon a real infirmity, which so far God had not removed. The same objection urged as a reason to-day for not engaging in Sunday-school work, etc. The want of power may be real, but is it a sufficient reason for refusal? 2. God's answer. (1) He points to his power. Is that realised? (2) He gives the promise of help. Our weakness will merely afford a hold on which God's might and faithfulness will be manifested.

II. MOSES' REFUSAL AND GOD'S ANGER (13—17). 1. The disinclination to the service which lay behind his objections is at last manifested. That very name (Adonai) "my master," by which he addresses God, might have rebuked him. But Moses in this may be the type of ourselves. We acknowledge that all we have, that we ourselves, are his, and yet is there no service which no amount of reasoning or expostulation can prevail upon us to undertake for God? 2. God's anger. (1) A revelation of the judgment which awaits the slothful servant. Its shadows fall now in the withdrawal of his favour and the decay of spiritual life. (2) It left its mark upon the life of Moses although his refusal was followed by repentance. Aaron was joined with him, and where in the eye of Israel and the world there would have been one figure only, there is henceforth two. The mark of God's anger is left in a lessened glory.

III. THE POWER OF THE PAST FOR CHRISTIAN SERVICE. "Take this rod"—not another. It reminded him of the time when he contended with God, and ministered humility in the moments of mightiest triumph. The Cross of Jesus the memento of our stubbornness and guilt.—U.

Vers. 1—17.—*Divine supplements for human infirmity.* "Now therefore go, and I will be with thee," etc. (ver. 12.) It is not at all clear whether the four objections urged by Moses against receiving the Divine commission were presented at one interview with the manifested God, or whether the controversy recorded Ex. iii. 1—iv. 17, occupied weeks or months. The probabilities are in favour of some considerable time. See iv. 10, and specially in the Heb. In dealing with this particular plea, viz. the lack of eloquence, we must bear in mind that it is not for every man to be a Moses, or a preacher, or even a worker. True, there is a ministry for each and all; but some are called to, one of patience in suffering. Treat the subject therefore as one of Divine supplementing of human infirmity generally. Comp. 2 Cor. xii. 7—10.

I. SHRINKING FROM DIVINE SERVICE. Not a doubt of this in the case of Moses. Earlier he was not unwilling to put himself forward as the champion of Israel —Acts vii. 25; but diffidence came with years. So Jeremiah—Jer. i. 6. So all the prophets—their message a "burden"—something heavy to be carried, to which they braced themselves. So Paul, 1 Cor. ix. 16. Nor is the feeling unhealthy or undesirable. Self-confidence looks at first the best preparation for great enterprises. But is it so? Look at life. In all departments, to estimate aright the greatness of the work, the comparative feebleness of our resources, and yet the weight of our responsibility, is the condition of success; e g. Lord Clyde in India. The Christian minister. By the reluctance of Moses, measure the irresistible impulse upon his spirit. Nor is consciousness of incapacity always the reality of incapacity.

II. THE EXCUSE THAT IS OFFERED. Take ver. 10, translated thus: "And said Moses unto Jehovah, Let it please Thee, O Lord, not a man of words am I, either since yesterday, or since the day before, or since the time Thou hast spoken unto Thy servant; for heavy of mouth and heavy of tongue am I." 1. *The time-hint.* An intimation here of a long controversy between Moses and God. 2. *The meaning of Moses.* He was not a "man of words"—*not eloquent,* in the popular sense; he was heavy—doubly heavy—of lip and tongue. A great writer of poetry and prose, but not a speaker. This self-estimate just. Yet there were compensations. He was "*mighty* in word." Distinguish between fluency and power. He was, too, a man of *thought.* A man of *action.* 3. *A lesson* in passing: "Take heed *how* ye hear!"—"Take heed *what* ye hear." Compare the massive eloquence of the Puritan age, and the men it made, with what seems to be now the taste of many for the sensational—with present impatience of so-called "heavy" preaching. Where would Israel have been, had Israel turned its back on the " heavy " Moses, and followed the lead of the brilliant but perhaps shallow Aaron, who could make molten images under the very shadow of Sinai, the mount of God, ere reverberating thunders had died away in the desolation of the desert. 4. *The essence of his excuse.* The defect was to the mind of Moses fatal—eloquence was the one quality material to his mission. To many missions (*e.g.* military or administrative) eloquence is not essential. The mission of Moses was diplomatic—it needed tongue-power. " *Say* unto the elders of Israel !" " *Say* unto Pharaoh." He had to persuade a nation of slaves that *he* was the heaven-sent deliverer. He had to go into the audience-chamber of the greatest potentate of earth, and speak to him for a nation, and for Jehovah behind the nation. *Just the one thing he could not do ; and for which he had not the indispensable qualification.* So in thousands of other cases, of various forms of duty and responsibility, of sorrow and perplexity. " Tongue " and " lip " and " word " are what the service demands, and all are wanting.

III. THE DIVINE DECLINING OF EXCUSE. Notice—1. *The changing tone.* It is— (1) *Encouraging.* Vers. 11, 12. (2) *Indignant.* Moses said, ver. 13 : " Let it please Thee, O Lord, send I pray Thee by a hand Thou wilt send." (See the Heb.) This sounds submissive, as though Moses meant, " Send me." But from the translation of the LXX. the words seem to have carried a disloyal meaning, now lost in the Heb.: " I pray Thee, O Lord, prepare for Thyself another capable, whom Thou wilt send." And so Jehovah was indignant. Self-diffidence may be carried too far. Yet was not Moses wholly cast away—for Jehovah took up again a tone likely to woo him to his duty. (3) *Encouraging again :* vers. 14—17. 2. *The counter pleas.* God allows the truth of all we say, and then comes in with his own Divine counter pleas why he should not accept either our excuses or declining—of which the main articles are these : The glory of God will be manifested—(1) *In the use of man* at all. God might have glorified himself in breaking to pieces the empire of Egypt without the intervention of any human agency. Pietists have sometimes thought that they glorified God by making him everything, man nothing. But God glorifies himself more by using men, for men are such poor tools to work with. *E.g.* Quentin Matsys making the beautiful covering for the well that stands in front of Antwerp cathedral with only a file and hammer. How ! Such work with only file and hammer ? So great an overthrow here, and such a creation of nation and church by a man, and such a man ? The strength of God is evermore working by our weakness. (2) By *the imperfection* of our powers : vers. 11, 12. God the Creator of the imperfection as well as the power—the dumbness of the dumb, as well as the eloquence of the eloquent. He does this—*i.e.* supplements our imperfect power, by—i. *Other faculties in the man.* So here " the rod " of might in deed was to supplement the imperfect speech. [See also above, II. 2.] ii. *Other men.* Here by Aaron, vers. 14—16. iii. *Himself.* In the earlier part of this controversy it was, " Certainly I will be with thee "—a general declaration. Now it is, " I will be with *thy mouth,* and teach thee *what thou shalt say.*" The Almighty power goes along with the imperfect organ of the Divine will. Apply as suggested above to *all*— whether in the activity or in the patience of the Kingdom of Jesus Christ.—R.

EXPOSITION.

Vers. 18—23.—If Moses had, as we have supposed, been accepted into the Midianitish nation, he would need permission to withdraw himself from the tribal head. This head was now Jether, or Jethro, Moses' connexion by marriage, perhaps his brother-in-law, perhaps a less near connexion. Nations and tribes were at this time anxious to keep up their numbers, and jealous of the desertion even of a single member. Jethro, however, made no opposition to the return of Moses to Egypt, even though he designed to be accompanied

by his wife and sons (ver. 20). Scripture gives no indications of the motives which actuated him. Perhaps the Midianites were at this time straitened for want of room. Perhaps the peculiar circumstances of Moses were held to justify his application for leave.

Ver. 18.—**My brethren** probably means here " my relations " (compare Gen. xiii. 8 ; xxix. 12). Moses could scarcely doubt but that some of his countrymen were still living. It would not have been for the interest of the Egyptians to exterminate them. **Go in peace**

means, "you have my leave—I do not oppose your going."

Ver. 19.—**And the Lord said unto Moses in Midian, Go, return.** It would seem that Moses was still reluctant, and was delaying his departure, even after he had obtained Jethro's leave to go. Perhaps he was making it an excuse to himself for not getting out that if he returned he might still suffer death on account of the offence which had driven him into exile. To remove this last impediment, God assured him that " *all* the men were dead who had sought his life."

Ver. 20.—**His sons.** Gershom, already mentioned (ch. ii. 22), and Eliezer (ch. xviii. 4), who was probably an infant. **Set them upon an ass.** Literally, "the ass," *i.e.* the one ass that belonged to him. The word might best be translated " *his ass.*" When Moses is said to have *set them* upon " the animal, we need not understand " all of them." Probably Zipporah and her baby rode, while Gershom walked with his father. Though horses were known in Egypt before this, they could not be used in the Sinaitic peninsula, and the employment of an ass by Moses is thoroughly appropriate. **Returned.** *I.e.* " set out to return." **Took the rod of God in his hand.** This is of course the " rod " of ver. 2, which had become " the rod of God " by the miracle of vers. 3 and 4, and which God had commanded him to take to Egypt (ver. 17).

Vers. 21—23.—**And the Lord said, etc.** Now that Moses had at last given up his own will and entered on the path of obedience, God comforted him with a fresh revelation, and gave him fresh instructions as to what exactly he was to say to Pharaoh. The statements of ver. 21 are not new, being anticipated in ch. iii. 19—20; but the directions in vers. 22—23 are wholly new, and point to the greatest of all the miracles wrought in Egypt—the death of the firstborn.

Ver. 21.—**All those wonders.** The miracles wrought in Egypt are called *niphělôth*, " marvels," *môphěthim*, " portents," and *'ôthôth*, " signs." *Môphěthim*, the word here used signifies something out of the ordinary course of nature, and corresponds to the Greek τέρατα and the Latin *portenta*. It is a different word from that used in ch. iii. 20. In " all those wonders " are included, not only the three signs of ch. iv. 3—9, but the whole series of miracles afterwards wrought in Egypt, and glanced at in ch. iii. 20. **I will harden his heart.** This expression, here used for the first time, and repeated so frequently in chs. vii.— xiv., has given offence to many. Men, it is said, harden their own hearts against God; God does not actively interfere to harden the heart of anyone. And this is so far true, that a special interference of God on the occasion, involving a supernatural hardening of Pharaoh's heart, is not to be thought of. But among the natural punishments which God has attached to sin, would seem to be the hardening of the entire nature of the man who sins. If men " do not like to retain God in their knowledge, God gives them up to a reprobate mind " (Rom. i. 28); if they resist the Spirit, he " takes his holy Spirit from them " (Ps. li. 11); if they sin against light he withdraws the light; if they stifle their natural affections of kindness, compassion and the like, it is a law of his providence that those affections shall wither and decay. This seems to be the " hardening of the heart " here intended—not an abnormal and miraculous interference with the soul of Pharaoh, but the natural effect upon his soul under God's moral government of those acts which he wilfully and wrongfully committed.

Ver. 22.—**Thou shalt say unto Pharaoh, Israel is my son.** This would be addressing Pharaoh in language familiar to him. Each Egyptian monarch of this period was accustomed to style himself, " son of the Sun," and to claim and expect the constant favour and protection of his divine parent. It was also quite within the range of Egyptian ideas that God should declare himself by word of mouth to his special favourites, and give directions as to their actions. (See ' Records of the Past,' vol. iv. p. 43.) **My firstborn.** Not only " as dear to me as to a father his firstborn " (Kalisch), but the only nation that I have adopted, and taken into covenant, so as to be unto me " a peculiar people above all the nations that are upon the earth " (Deut. xiv. 2). Israel's sonship is here mentioned for the first time.

Ver. 23.—**I will slay thy son, even thy firstborn.** For the fulfilment of the threat, see ch. xii. 29. Moses did not utter it till all other arguments were exhausted, and he knew that he was having his last interview with the monarch (ch. x. 29; xi. 4, 5). In this reserve and in the whole series of his dealings with the Egyptian king, we must regard him as simply carrying out the special directions which, after his return to Egypt, he continually received from the Almighty. (See ch. vi. 11; vii. 9, 15 19; viii. 1, 5, 16, 20, etc.)

HOMILETICS.

Ver. 19.—*The fact of having a mission does not release a man from social obligations.* Direct communications with Jehovah, appointment to a great and glorious mission, with the power of working miracles, might have rendered many a man neglectful of ordinary obligations, might have seemed to place him above the necessity of asking anyone's permission to do as he pleased. But Moses read his duty differently. He had been received among the Midianites with great kindness, had been given a home and a wife, and probably enrolled formally as an adopted member of the tribe or nation. Though Reuel, the head of the tribe at the time of his coming, had ceased to hold that position, having probably died, the tribe had a new head, to whom he was bound, if not by all the obligations which had attached him to Reuel, yet by several very definite and tangible bonds. Jethro was his near relative and his tribal chief; he had perhaps sworn allegiance to him; he had certainly received from him protection, employment, sustenance (ch. iii. 1). To have quitted his service without permission, to have left his flock in the Sinaitic valleys, and proceeded straight to Egypt would have been easy, but would have been unkind, ungrateful, and contrary to the accepted standard of tribal morality at the time. Moses therefore went back to Midian from Sinai before proceeding to Egypt—made, that is, a considerable journey in the opposite direction to that which he was about to take—in order to obtain Jethro's consent to his going, thus acting the part of a faithful servant and a good subject. It would be well if all who believe themselves to have Divine missions, and to be highly gifted, would follow Moses' example, and not make their mission and high gifts an excuse for neglect of ordinary duties and obligations. Moses' example, and the words of One higher than Moses, should teach them that it becomes all men to "fulfil all righteousness" (Matt. iii. 15). If those with high missions neglect even small social duties, they "give an occasion to the adversary to blaspheme."

Reticence sometimes a duty. We are not bound in all cases to tell even those in authority over us the reasons, much less *all* the reasons, which actuate us. Moses wanted Jethro's permission to quit his adopted tribe, and return to his native country and his people. He gave a reason which was not untrue, but which was far from being his sole, or even his main, reason. If he had said more, if he had revealed his mission, he would probably have raised a storm of opposition to his departure. He would have been called a fanatic, a visionary, a madman; and everything would have been said that was possible to deter him from carrying out his projects. If Moses felt, as he may have felt, that he was too weak to encounter such a storm of opposition, he was wise to be silent and so not arouse it.

The reasonable wishes of a subordinate should be granted cheerfully. Jethro's answer, " Go in peace," may well be taken as a pattern by those in authority. It is kindly, gracious, and ungrudging. The chieftain of a tribe might naturally have demurred to the withdrawal of a family of subjects, the master to the loss of a valuable servant, the head of a household to parting with near kinsfolk. But Jethro, deeming Moses' plea a sufficient one, is careful not to mar the grace of his concession by a single word of objection, reproach, or querulousness. Nor is " Go in peace " even a bare consent, but a consent embodying a blessing. It is equivalent to " Go, and the Lord go with thee! " Note also the absence of inquisitiveness. Jethro does not pester Moses with questions— does not ask, " Is the reason thou hast assigned thy true reason," or "thy sole reason?" or, "When wilt thou return?" or, "Why take thy wife and children?" or, "How wilt thou live in Egypt?" or, "Art thou not afraid to return thither?" He will not pain his near connection by doubt or distrust, or even undue curiosity. He will not travel beyond the record. His consent has been asked. He gives it freely, fully cheerfully.

Vers. 19—23.—*Obedience brings a blessing.* There must have been something in the hesitation of Moses which caused it not to be wholly displeasing to God. Once he was " angered " (ch. iii. 14), but even then not greatly offended—content to show his anger by inflicting a slight penalty. Now, when Moses still delayed in Midian, how gentle the rebuke that is administered—" Go, return; " and to the rebuke moreover is appended an encouragement—" all the men are dead who sought thy life." Observe also that no sooner does Moses obey, than his reluctance seems wholly forgiven; the Lord appears afresh to him, and rewards his obedience by fresh revelations. " Israel is my son, even my firstborn." This tender relationship, never before acknowledged, is breathed into the prophet's ear as he enters on the path of obedience. What may he not expect, if he continues in it! Surely blessings upon blessings. Deliverance, triumph, continued, never-ending protection are assured to them whom God declares to be his children. Moses, as their leader, will have the glory of their success. Even the might of Pharaoh will be impotent if used against them. Should Pharaoh refuse to liberate God's " firstborn," he will lose his own.

HOMILIES BY VARIOUS AUTHORS.

Vers. 18—21.—*The return*. Weeks, perhaps months, intervened between the revelation at the bush and Moses' actual departure from Midian. Time was given for allowing the first agitation of his spirit to subside, for enabling him to take the just measure of the task entrusted to him, for the final overcoming of his involuntary reluctance. An interval is presupposed in ver. 10—" Neither heretofore, nor since thou hast spoken unto thy servant," and is implied again here. Events were not yet *quite* ready for his departure. The preparation of the man, and the preparation of events (ver. 19) were going on simultaneously. God would have his servant brought, not only to a clear apprehension of his message, but into a state of intelligent and entire sympathy with it, before actually starting him on his journey. The call would come at the proper time.

I. PERMISSION RECEIVED (ver. 18). The request to Jethro was couched in simple but courteous terms, and was as courteously responded to. Moses said nothing of the revelations he had received. 1. He had no *call* to say anything. His message was to the elders of Israel, not to Jethro. 2. It would have been a *breach of confidence* to have divulged what passed between him and God without permission. 3. It was not *advisable* to say anything. He would have required to have entered into explanations, and might have encountered unbelief and opposition. If Jethro perceived, as possibly he did, that there was something underlying Moses' request which he did not care to state, he had the good sense to refrain from prying too curiously into what did not concern him. The parting was courteous and friendly, creditable alike to both. Observe: 1. There are times when it is prudent to keep one's own counsel. 2. It is the mark of a wise man that he *can* keep his own counsel. 3. It is well to be reserved about private religious experience (Gal. i. 16, 17). 4. It is one's duty on all occasions to study friendliness and courtesy. 5. It is nearly as high a mark of character not to be too curious in prying into the secrets of others, as it is to be cautious in keeping silence about those entrusted to us.

II. THE WAY CLEARED (ver. 19). As suggested above, Moses had probably been instructed to wait a Divine intimation as to the time of his actual departure. In a work so important every step must be taken under direct Divine guidance. Cf. the movements of Mary and Joseph with the child Jesus (Matt. ii.). And the warning was not given till God was able to announce that all the men were dead who had formerly sought his life. This would be a comfort to Moses, and would remove at least one set of fears as to his personal safety. There may have been another reason for delaying to this point. Time had again brought matters to the condition of a *tabula rasa*. The conflict now to be begun was not to be demeaned by being mixed up with the spites and enmities of a buried past. Observe: 1. How God times events with a view to every class of conditions. 2. How God consults for the safety of his servants. 3. How God's purposes move with steady step to their accomplishment, while mortals, who thought to hinder them, drop into their graves, and are forgotten.

III. THE JOURNEY ENTERED UPON (ver. 20). 1. Moses took with him *his wife and two sons*. The desire to have them with him was natural, but he afterwards saw reason for sending them back. The work he was engaged in was of a kind not compatible with family entanglements. There are times when a man's hands need to be absolutely free; when it is his duty not to enter into relationships which would encumber him; or, if these already exist, to make the temporary sacrifice of comfort and affection which the exigencies of his work demand (Matt. viii. 21, 22; 2 Tim. ii. 4). 2. He took with him *the rod of God*. *This* was indispensable. By it he was to work signs (ver. 17). The rod of the Christian worker is his Bible. Armed with that, he can speak with Divine authority, work miracles in the souls of men and confound the mightiest of his enemies.—J. O.

Ver. 21.—*Hardening.* God communicates anew with Moses, fortifying his resolution to appear before Pharaoh, putting words into his mouth, and warning him of the effect his message would produce. He was not to fail to do all his wonders before Pharaoh, though the only effect would be to harden the monarch's heart—to confirm him in his resolution not to let the people go.

I. THE WORD OF GOD IS TO BE ADDRESSED TO MEN, WHATEVER RECEPTION IT MAY MEET WITH. It is to be set forth, and the evidence which attests it exhibited, "whether they will hear, or whether they will forbear" (Ezek. ii. 5); and this—1. That God's will may be made known. 2. That men's dispositions may be tested. 3. That if men disobey they may be left without excuse. 4. That ulterior purposes may be fulfilled. For men's unbelief cannot make the faith of God without effect (Rom. iii. 3). If men disbelieve and are hardened, God will use even their hardening as the point of attach ment for some new link in the chain of his providential developments.

II. GOD INFALLIBLY FOREKNOWS THE EFFECT OF EVERY APPEAL OR MESSAGE HE ADDRESSES TO HIS MORAL CREATURES. He knows those to whom his servants will be "the savour of death unto death," and those to whom they will be "the savour of life unto life" (2 Cor. ii. 16). But the knowledge that his Word will be rejected is not a reason for keeping it back. As respects these foreknown effects, we are not permitted to say either—1. That God wills (*i.e.* desires) that his Word should harden; or 2. That in any case it hardens by his *arbitrarily* withholding the grace which would have produced an opposite result. Yet Divine sovereignty is not to be denied in the effects produced by the preaching of the Word, or in God's dealings with men in mercy and judgment generally. He will be a bold student of Divine things who ventures to assert that by *no* means known to him could God have subdued the obstinacy even of a Pharaoh. Hearts as stubborn have yielded before now. We cannot solve these anomalies. Enough for us to know that God's sovereignty, however exercised, is ever righteous, holy, and, could we see all, loving.

III. GOD'S WORD, WHEN ITS MESSAGE IS RESISTED, HARDENS THE HEART THAT RESISTS IT. The hardening of the heart is here attributed to God, as in other places it is attributed to Pharaoh himself. The latter statement occasions no difficulty. It is the invariable law, and one which is constantly being exemplified, that he who resists grace and truth incurs the penalty of being hardened. That result follows from the constitution of the moral nature. But precisely in this fact lies the explanation of the other mode of statement, that the hardening of the heart is from God. For God is concerned in the results which flow from the operation of his own laws, and takes (providentially) the responsibility of them. We may go even further, and say that God *designs* that those who resist his truth *shall* be hardened by it; just as he designs that those who believe and obey it shall be saved. And the stronger way of putting the matter, harsh as it seems, has its own advantages. Resisters of the truth do well to remember that in their attitude of opposition they have to do, not merely with "laws," reacting to darken the mind and indurate the heart, but with a living God within and behind these laws, lending his solemn sanction to their operations, willing the results which flow from them, and righteously punishing sin by means of them. This explanation, indeed, is not complete. Other phases of the subject come into view later. Meanwhile the preacher of the Gospel is not to be astonished that his word, in many cases, produces hardening effects. This is foreseen by God, and is taken up into his plan. Learn also how a career of iniquity is often punished by the transgressor being brought into circumstances which, merciful in their own operation, yet lead to his greater hardening.—J. O.

Vers. 22, 23.—*Israel a type of sonship.* Consider—1. *The condescension of God in the establishing of this relationship.* A nation of slaves; in the eyes of the Egyptians little better than a nation of lepers; yet Jehovah says of them, "Israel is my son, my firstborn." "Behold what manner of love," etc. (1 John iii. 1). 2. *The privileges implied in it.* On this cf. Deut. i. 31—34; viii. 2—6; xxxii. 9—15. Reflect how Israel was led, fed, guided, trained, chastened, delivered from enemies, and conducted to a bountiful inheritance. These privileges have all their counterparts in the experience of the "children of God by faith in Christ Jesus" (Gal. iii. 26). 3. *The responsibilities it imposed on others.* Because Israel was God's son, his firstborn, Pharaoh was to refrain from oppressing his son, and if he did not he would be smitten in his own firstborn. (1) As men treat God's children so will God treat them. He notes, and he will reward, kindnesses done to his sons, and he will avenge their wrongs. (2) God's children may safely leave the avenging of their wrongs to God. It is not their work, but his, to avenge them; the rule for them is to avenge not themselves, but rather to give place to wrath; heaping coals of fire on the head of the enemy by returning him good for his evil (Rom. xii. 19—21).—J. O.

Vers. 18—23.—*True faith and its joy.* I. THE OBEDIENCE OF FAITH. 1. Note Moses' swift compliance with God's command. He tarried no longer: " He went and returned . . . and said . . . let me go." He does not seek advice. He does not even wait for a convenient opportunity of urging his request. We must wait neither upon time nor men. If God has spoken, we must obey. 2. His wise reticence. He said nothing of what he had seen and heard. These experiences are a holy place where the soul meets alone with God. Where this holy place is profaned the soul suffers loss. II. CONSOLATIONS ABOUND ALONG THE PATHWAY OF OBEDIENT FAITH. 1. Moses receives Jethro's permission and blessing. 2. Fears are removed (ver. 19). 3. He passes on with the consciousness of power: he " took the rod of God in his hand." 4. He has the assurance of victory. Pharaoh's heart will be hardened, yet there is one judgment in reserve which will bow that heart to compliance with the will of God (vers. 22, 23). The cause of God cannot be defeated. As we go on in obedience to God's commandment our advance is a continuous discovery of God's goodness. The lions which we saw in the distance are chained, and do not harm us.—U.

Vers. 24—31.—*The three meetings.* I. THE LORD'S MEETING WITH MOSES (vers. 24—26). 1. Moses' sin. (1) Circumcision was the solemnly expressed will of God (Gen. xvii. 9—14). (2) It was enforced by exclusion from the blessings of God's covenant. (3) Preparations had been made for the journey, but the circumcision of Eliezer was not among them. 2. The reason of the omission, weak yielding to the prejudices of his Midianitish wife. 3. His guilt. God looked beyond the sign to that which it signified and partially accomplished—the claiming of the life for himself and righteousness. Moses' disobedience was therefore murder by neglect, and life shall answer for life. The guilt of the unfaithful watchmen in Zion (Ezek. xxxiii. 7—9); of parents who never seek by instruction and example and prayer to have their children circumcised with the circumcision of Christ. 4. God will withstand the inconsistent worker. He will permit his work to be done only by the righteous and the faithful. This is seen both in churches and in individuals. II. THE MEETING OF MOSES AND AARON (vers. 27, 28). 1. Moses had to proceed alone (Ex. xviii. 2), the type of many who pass to service through loss. 2. God prepares consolation in the desert (Matt. xix. 27—29). 3. The marvels of God's providence. He makes their meeting with each other a meeting with himself. " They met at the mount of God." 4. Human love hallowed by the Divine love—" And Moses told Aaron," etc. III. THEIR MEETING WITH THE ELDERS OF ISRAEL (vers. 29—31). Where Moses dreaded failure he meets success. There is more faith waiting to receive God's word than we imagine: souls wait round us like the parched land for the showers.—U.

Ver. 19.—*The unsolicited removal of a source of great anxiety.* God assures Moses that he has no longer any cause to fear on account of the Egyptian slain forty years before. This last piece of information casts a flood of light on all the hesitation, reluctance, and perplexity which Moses has hitherto shown in his intercourse with Jehovah. It might have made a great deal of difference, if he had only known at the beginning that the men were dead who sought his life. Not but that Moses was honest enough in all the pleas he had started in order to escape from this mission and responsibility; but, deep under all other considerations, and very potent, even though he had been ashamed to confess it, lay his fear because of the slain Egyptian. He might even have got as far as the expressing of the fear, if God had not brought him sharply up by the kindling of his anger, and made him feel that of two perils it was wise to choose the lesser. Better run the risk from some Egyptian breathing vengeance than from the visitations of an angry God; and yet, though checked from speaking, he would be saying very earnestly in his heart, " Oh that I only knew myself to be safe in this matter." Remember the terror with which, after so long a time, Jacob approached his injured brother Esau. Certainly Jacob had the bitter consciousness of wrong-doing to heighten his fears, but Moses would have equally the consciousness of danger. Nor can it be too often impressed upon us, in considering this opening stage of Moses' acquaintance with God, that while he had a profound impression as to the real and awful Being with whom he had come in contact, the extent of his knowledge was not correspondent to the depth of his feeling. He had come into a real acquaintance with God; but it was at first, of necessity, a very imperfect and blundering one. The defective notions of Moses, with respect to God, find their New Testament parallel in the earth-born and earth-limited questions which the disciples so often addressed to Jesus. Hence, even though Moses has seen so much of God's power and promptitude in dealing with every difficulty he has raised, he still remains uncertain whether God has taken into account this peril from the slain Egyptian. It is no easy thing to get to a real and operative conviction that God knows even the smallest transaction in the past life of every one of us.—Y.

Vers. 18—31. — *Facing Egypt.* "And the people believed, and when," etc. (Ex. iv. 31). This section of the history may be homiletically treated under three geographical headings, which will keep the historical development prominent, without obscuring the moral and spiritual elements.

I. MIDIAN. From Sinai Moses returned to Midian. Reuel now dead, Jethro, probably his son, becomes priest and sheikh of the tribe. [We take Jethro to have been the brother-in-law of Moses. See 'Speaker's Commentary,' additional note on Exodus ii. 18.] In this part of the story it is of moment to observe the situation of Midian—east, and perhaps also west, of the Elanitic Gulf. Hence travellers from Egypt to Midian, or *vice versâ*, would come on the journey unto "the mount of God." Moses could not stay long in Midian. There was now pressing on him—1. The original impulse (ii. 11—14). 2. The commission of the Burning Bush. 3. The intelligence that it was now safe to go. [Ver. 19 furnishes a convenient opportunity for noticing the Old Testament formula, on the correct understanding of which so much depends, in which God is represented to have directly said and done what he *may* have done only mediately. Here, e.g., did God speak out of the air into the ear of Moses, or was the intelligence brought in the ordinary way, say by caravans across the desert? It is a large subject, but the following points are suggested: "God said," "God did" this or that, are to this day formulæ with the Arabs. This Oriental habit of the cousins of the Hebrews is the opposite of the Occidental. We suppress the name of God as much as possible; and if constrained to refer to the Divine Being, we allude to him as "Providence" or "Heaven." The Oriental habit is more direct and truer; for God is in the secondary cause, which fact some amongst ourselves ignore. The Arabian style of to-day was the Hebrew style, and the mode of the Old Testament. In the interpretation of this formula we must be careful not to assume always the direct or supernatural, though perhaps occasionally we shall have no other alternative. Indeed, no doubt that is so.] On the receipt of this news Moses paid fealty to the chief of the tribe which had given him a home for forty years; asked permission to return; obtained it, and set out with "rod," wife, two sons, and, no doubt, the usual service and attendants of a considerable caravan.

II. THE DESERT—ON THE ROAD. On the road, which passed through scenes of incomparable grandeur, several incidents of the first importance occurred. 1. *A word of Divine encouragement* (vers. 21—23). Jehovah inspired his servant with courage, warned him that success would not be immediate, and gave him the exact message for Pharaoh. [Whether all this came *direct* from God, or grew up in the mind of Moses, in the way of meditation, under the guidance of the Spirit, must be left to the decision of each.] But something may be here said on ver. 21: "I will harden," etc. The objection will occur to every one—How can God punish men for that which he himself causes or does? This "hardening" may be here considered once for all. The following considerations will have weight :—1. God is often in the Old Testament said to do what he only *permits* to be done. 2. In this passage of history (Ex. iv.—xiv.) God is said to harden Pharaoh's heart ten times, Pharaoh to harden his own three times; and the fact that Pharaoh's heart was hardened is stated five times. 3. Generally, until after the fifth plague, Pharaoh hardens his own heart; then, and only then, save in Ex. vii. 13, God is said to harden Pharaoh's heart. 4. The fact seems to be that at first Pharaoh sinfully hardened his own heart, and then God permissively allowed the process to go on and confirmed it. 5. It must also be borne in mind that the very same gracious influences will either harden or soften, according to the subject. The same sun melts wax and hardens clay. The final responsibility of the hardening lay with Pharaoh. The homiletic applications are obvious; but see a striking poem in Dr. Taylor's 'Moses' (p. 75), by Dr. J. A. Alexander, beginning: "There is a time, we know not when." Another lesson is obvious, as soon as mentioned: We are not justified in looking for results which God has not promised. The deliverance of Israel was promised and certain, but there was no promise that Pharaoh would voluntarily yield. 2. *A deed of Divine rebuke* (vers. 24—26). This passage is obscure, difficult, yet full of moral significance : must therefore be put in a true light. The incident shapes itself to our minds thus : Moses came on the journey to a caravanserai, burdened with a grievous memory of duty neglected, of the Divine covenant virtually repudiated (Gen. xvii. 9—14). The younger son had not been circumcised. This neglect was weak ; had been simply to please the Midianitish mother. Hence anxiety, contributing with other causes to fever and threatening death—"Jehovah met him," etc. Zipporah was persuaded to perform the rite. The "stone" would be a flint implement, considered more sacred than iron or bronze. To this day flint is used in New Guinea even for shaving the head. The task was performed unwillingly, hence her invective, twice repeated. Then Jehovah released Moses—"let him go." It was now clear that the wife in these matters was out of sympathy with Moses, and so, on the ground of moral incompatibility, was sent back with her children to the tents of Midian (Ex. xviii. 2), and the grand soul went on alone upon his mission. But the lesson :—The teachers of obedience must be themselves obedient. The law-giver must himself be marked by obedience to law. There is nothing small or great in questions of fidelity. How could Moses thereafter take a stand for righteousness if not himself above indictment ? Some moral defects may be absolutely fatal to moral strength. 3. *The meeting of the delivering allies*—of Moses and Aaron—not like that of Wellington and Blücher, after the battle, but before the campaign. The following points may be noted :—Aaron moved at a Divine intimation. The two met at Sinai. Moses communicated to his brother the revelation and conference connected with the burning bush. Had not told Jethro. With him no blatant speaking of the deepest mysteries of spiritual life.

III. EGYPT. Picture the familiarity of cities, monuments, and scenery, but the unfamiliar faces. No change, yet many changes. 1. *The assembling of the elders.* Moses, more wise than aforetime, knows that nothing can be done without the sympathy of the people. *Can* come into contact with them through the elders. This an argument for the organisation of the people. 2. *The prominence of Aaron.* At once takes his place. Note Moses' unfamiliarity now with Hebrew and Egyptian, after the lapse of so many years, as well as natural want of eloquence. 3. *The result.* Great success ! Belief ! Sensation at the coming down of the delivering God ! Every head bowed ! Worship ! God had said : They will believe—"they shall hearken to thy voice." Moses : "Behold, they will *not* believe me, nor hearken to my voice." BUT THEY DID. Success even beyond our hopes, and the fulfilments of God beyond all our fears.—R.

EXPOSITION.

Vers. 24—26.—The transition is abrupt from the promise of triumph over Pharaoh to the threat of instant death. But we must bear in mind that some days may have elapsed between the two, and that the sin which provoked the menace was probably not committed at the date of the promise. The narrative of verses 24—26 is obscure from its brevity ; but the most probable explanation of the circumstances is, that Zipporah had been delivered of her second son, Eliezer, some few days before she set out on the journey to Egypt. Childbirth, it must be remembered, in the East does not incapacitate a person from exertion for more than a day or two. On the journey, the eighth day from the birth of the child arrived, and his circumcision ought to have taken place; but Zipporah had a repugnance to the rite, and deferred it, Moses weakly consenting to the illegality. At the close of the eighth day, when Moses went to rest for the night, he was seized with a sudden and dangerous illness, which he regarded, and rightly regarded, as a God-inflicted punishment, sent to chastise his sin in breaking the Divine command (Gen. xvii. 10—12). Zipporah understood the matter in the same way; and, as her husband was too ill to perform the rite, she herself with her own hand cut off her boy's foreskin, and, still indignant at what she had been forced to do, cast it at her husband's feet, with the reproach —"Surely a bloody husband art thou to me." The rite once performed, however reluctantly, God remitted his anger, and allowed Moses to recover his health, and pursue his journey.

Ver. 24.—**It came to pass by the way in the inn.** "Inns," in our sense of the word, were unknown in the East for many ages after the time of Moses, and are still of very rare occurrence. Khans or caravanserais take their place. These are unfurnished buildings, open to all travellers, who thus obtain shelter *gratis*, but must provide themselves with food, bedding, and all other necessaries. It is questioned, however, if even such a place as this is here meant. Probably, the *mâlon* of Moses' time was a mere recognised halting-place, in the vicinity of a well, at which travellers were accustomed to pass the night. **The Lord met him and sought to kill him.** A sudden seizure, followed by a dangerous illness, is generally thought to be intended

(Knobel, Kalisch, Rosenmüller, Canon Cook); but the words seem more appropriate to a miraculous appearance, like that of the angel to Balaam (Num. xxii. 31). Still, it is quite possible that nothing more than an illness is meant.

Ver. 25.—**Zipporah took a sharp stone.** Literally "a stone." Stone knives were commonly used in Egypt for making the incisions necessary when bodies were embalmed, and were regarded as purer than iron or bronze ones. Joshua ordered the preparation of stone knives for the circumcision of those born in the wilderness (Josh. v. 2); and the Jews seem to have used stone for circumcision for many ages, though before the compilation of the Talmud they had changed their practice. **Cast it at his feet.** Not, certainly, the child's feet, but her husband's, to whom at the same moment she addresses herself. **A bloody husband.** Literally, "a bridegroom of blood." The words are clearly a reproach; and the gist of the reproach seems to be that Moses was a husband who cost her dear, causing the blood of her sons to be shed in order to keep up a national usage which she regarded as barbarous.

Ver. 26.—**So he let him go.** *I.e.* "God let Moses go"—allowed him to escape death, accepted Zipporah's tardy act as a removal of the cause of offence, and gave her husband back to her. **Then she said,** etc. This is not a second address of Zipporah to Moses, conceived in the same terms, but an explanation of her previous address. She called him "a bloody husband **because of the circumcision.**" Literally, "of the circumcisions." The two circumcisions, of Gershom in Midian, and of Eliezer on the way to Egypt, are especially in the writer's mind.

HOMILETICS.

Vers. 24—26. *One small duty neglected may frustrate the whole purpose of a life.* To an Israelite the circumcision of his male children on the eighth day was a plain practical duty, resting upon a positive precept, which was unambiguous and peremptory. (See Gen. xvii. 10—14.) Moses, probably in deference to the wishes of his wife, who disliked the custom, had allowed his son, Eliezer, to remain uncircumcised beyond the appointed time, perhaps making the excuse to himself that during a journey such a rite could not conveniently be performed, and intending that the thing should be done when they reached Egypt. But the precept was plain—"He that is eight days old shall be circumcised among you;" and nothing had been said by God of any circumstances under which the rite might be deferred. It was the appointed means by which the child was to be brought into covenant with God; and if he died before the performance of the rite, he would die out of covenant, and so suffer a wrong. Moses probably thought that his sin was a little matter—perhaps hardly recognised it as a sin at all. But it was the "little rift within the lute" which destroyed the whole value of the instrument. He who "shall keep the whole law, and yet offend in one point, is guilty of all" (Jam. ii. 10). God thought the neglect no small matter, and would have punished it, had it not been repaired, with death. It can never be a small matter to neglect any command of God, be it to perform a rite, or to undergo one, or to keep a particular day holy, or any other.

When a positive command is admitted to have come from God, the obligation to obey it, as Bishop Butler observes, is moral. And so this little duty neglected, had nearly cost Moses his life, Zipporah her husband, the child his natural protector. Moses' death at this period would have left the whole purpose of his life unaccomplished, have handed over the deliverance of Israel to another, and have caused his special powers and special training to have been wasted. Let men beware, then, of the neglect of little duties, the allowance in themselves of "little sins." Let them beware especially of being led into such "little sins," by over-complaisance to a wife, a friend, a companion. Many a man would have stood firm, but for such seductive influence. A man who is truly manly will resist it, and risk the loss of human affection, secure of the Divine approval.

HOMILIES BY VARIOUS AUTHORS.

Vers. 19—29.—"*My times are in Thy hand.*" Moses thought himself fit for his work at forty—eager to undertake it before the years increased; God waits until his self-confidence has abated, and then, at eighty, gives him his commission.

I. THE GREAT COMMISSION. His errand is to Pharaoh, as an ambassador from the King of heaven to the king of Egypt. Notice—1. *His credentials.* As coming in a king's name he must be accredited by the king who sends him. God gives him signs, very simple but very significant. (1) The shepherd's rod, emblem of his office, turned into a serpent, emblem of his new dignity. (2) A hand made leprous and cleansed, emblem of a people degraded but to be redeemed. (3) A libation of water turned to blood, emblem of life smitten by judgment. The signs are simple—a rod, a hand, a cup of water; so are most of God's signs; yet by the way in which he uses them they accredit the messenger, and attest the authenticity of his message. 2. *His message* corresponds with the last two signs :—(1) A command. Israel in slavery is to be released. God will have his son free, the leprous cleansed. (2) A threat. If Pharaoh refuse, *his* son shall be slain; the joy of his life turned to blood. Such the commission given to Moses, and to fulfil which he starts for Egypt.

II. THE GREAT TRIAL : vers. 24—26. [*Illustration :*—A man about to enter into battle carefully selects his best weapon. Is it, however, really trustworthy?—has it no weak points? He must prove it that he may know. Proving *looks* like seeking to break; it *is* seeking to discover if breakage is possible.] God having selected Moses, must *prove* him before he uses him; so if the proof brings out weak points they may at any rate be remedied. "The Lord met him and sought to kill him." Two weak points were immediately discovered :—1. *A broken covenant.* He who is selected to represent the covenant people, is himself shown to be a covenant-breaker! His son uncircumcised!! If judgment must fall on Egypt it must begin at the house of God. Moses must him- self be purified before he can be allowed to denounce Pharaoh. 2. *A refractory wife.* The secret of the broken covenant was clearly the wilful obstinacy of Zipporah. She is compelled to do through fear what she would not yield from love. A man's wife is meant for a help-meet; if not *that,* she may be his greatest hindrance. Let Zipporah return to Midian for the time (xviii. 2), and at least leave her husband unencumbered. So out of the trial God makes a way of escape; proves and reproves his servant that he may improve and approve him.

III. THE GREAT CONSOLATION : vers. 27, 28. God does not do, what kings and rulers too often do, treat his envoys as mere machines, forgetting their human needs and cravings. If Zipporah is no help-meet for Moses, he shall have a help-meet who will more than satisfy him. In Aaron he finds sympathy, ver. 27; to Aaron he can give his confidence, ver. 28. His own strength is doubled in the friendship of one who thus shares his burdens.

Application :—1. God gives us commissions, but they are always accompanied by credentials. You *say* God calls you to do this? Show then the signs of your calling. 2. God's envoys are not free from trials; rather, they are the more tried that they may be the more trustworthy. The Captain was perfected through suffering. 3. Whatever the commission, whatever the trial, God will empower us to fulfil the one and strengthen us to endure the other. One may well do without Zipporah when God sends him Aaron.—G.

Vers. 24—27.—*Interpretation of providence.* This mysterious passage in the life of Moses suggests various reflections. The facts are few. Moses, probably in deference to Zipporah's abhorrence of the rite, had neglected the circumcision of his child. This, in so eminent a servant of God, was a sin which could not be winked at. Least of all could it be overlooked at a time when the covenants were undergoing a species of resur-rection, and when Moses was on his way to Egypt for the very purpose of giving effect to them. Hence this incident at the inn. Moses, apparently, was seized by an illness which threatened to be mortal, and a fatal result was only averted by Zipporah, who, at once divining the cause of the affliction, used a sharp stone, and performed the neglected rite. Thus was Moses taught that he who represents God before men must himself be blameless—guiltless of gross neglect of Divine commandments ; taught also that service of God must be whole-hearted—that in the way of duty there is to be no conferring with flesh and blood—no pleasing of men at the cost of unfaithfulness to God. " He that loveth father or mother," etc. (Matt. x. 37). Besides these general lessons we draw from the incident such instruction as the following :—

I. GOD OFTEN TEACHES US THAT HE IS ANGRY WITH US BY VISITING US WITH AFFLICTIVE DESPENSATIONS, LEAVING US TO FIND OUT THE CAUSE. Even Moses, with whom God had so often spoken, received on this occasion no other warning of his displeasure than this severe illness which so unexpectedly overtook him. Huxley remarks on Nature's system of education—" Nature's discipline is not even a word and a blow, and the blow first ; but the blow without the word. It is left to you to find out why your ears are boxed." The words apply as fitly to the relation of outward providences to moral and spiritual conditions—a class of relations which this writer would reject, but which nevertheless exist.

II. CONSCIENCE, REMINDING US OF NEGLECTED DUTIES, OR OTHER SINS COMMITTED BY US, IS A READY INTERPRETER OF MANY OF GOD'S AFFLICTIVE PROVIDENCES. Zipporah guessed at once the cause of this trouble, and the result showed her guess to be correct. So Joseph's brethren (Gen. xlii. 21).

III. THE HOLIEST OF GOD'S SERVANTS ARE NOT EXEMPTED FROM SEVERE CHASTISE-MENTS. We may wonder that God should have chosen this particular time to put a valuable life in peril. It was, however, the summons to depart which brought matters to a crisis. Moses was not ignorant of this neglected duty, and to set out on so grave a mission, and leave it still neglected, was a sin calling for sharp rebuke. This is another illustration of the truth that God punishes sins in his own children with even greater severity than he does the like sins in others. Do we ask, What if Moses had died ? The question is needless. The Divine arrangements had all the facts in contemplation from the first. Had it been foreseen that the anticipated effect would not have followed from the stroke—that the trouble would have had a different ending—everything else would have been different to suit. Yet we may not doubt that Moses' life was for the time really in peril, and that, had repentance not supervened, God would not have receded, even at the cost of a Moses, from inflicting upon him the extreme penalty of his unfaith-fulness.

IV. TRUE REPENTANCE INCLUDES REPARATION FOR WRONG, AND WHERE THAT IS POSSIBLE, PERFORMANCE OF NEGLECTED DUTIES. Exemplified in Zipporah.

V. GOD IS ZEALOUS FOR THE OBSERVANCE OF HIS OWN ORDINANCES. It might be pleaded, this is only a ceremony, an outward rite ; what great importance is to be attached to it ? But God had commanded it, and had even made it the badge of his covenant ; therefore neglect of it was an act of disobedience, and implied a low esteem of covenant-privilege. The sacraments may be unduly and foolishly exalted ; but there is an opposite sin of disesteeming and neglecting them.—J. O.

Vers. 24—26.—*Neglect of the covenant on its human side.* In Gen. xvii. we find the covenant between God and Abram stated with great particularity and emphasis. On God's side there were large promises to Abram of an abundant posterity and an ever-lasting possession, and on man's side there was to be the faithful and regular practice of circumcision. Moses was going to Egypt now in virtue of this very covenant, and as the agent of God to advance it considerably towards its full effect ; and yet, strange to say, he had with him an uncircumcised son. No wonder that God visited him by the way, and—when we look into all the probabilities of the case—no wonder that God made as if he would kill him. The very obscurities of this strange incident help to make it more impressive and admonitory. Consider—

I. WHAT THERE MAY BE IN THE NARRATIVE TO THROW LIGHT ON THE CAUSE OF THE OMISSION. *It cannot have been that Moses was completely ignorant of God's requirement.* Had not God recalled the covenant to the particular attention of Moses ? He had done so in a sufficiently suggestive way, not by repeating the terms of the covenant in full, but simply by referring to himself as the God of Abraham, Isaac and Jacob. Having thus been reminded of the covenant, Moses was bound to make himself correctly acquainted with every provision and detail of it. This covenant had been delivered to Abram once for all, and was of such a kind that nothing but the most flagrant neglect could allow the sign of it on its human side to fall into disuse. It was a covenant written in the very body of every 'true Israelite. Doubtless Moses himself had been circumcised ; yet here he is, going as the messenger of God to make progress in fulfilling God's part of the covenant, and yet his own part, as a member of Israel, he is unmistakably neglecting. Hence we see that he could not have been ignorant ; and more than that, *neither could he have been forgetful.* We are led to infer that *easy-going compliance with his Midianite wife, Zipporah,* was at the bottom of this neglected duty. It would appear indeed as if Moses had circumcised one son and then left the other uncircumcised. If so, he had shown gross inconsistency. More might have been said for him if both had been uncircumcised. Probably Zipporah, having seen the pain of her firstborn, had struggled and pleaded only too successfully for exemption in the case of the second.

II. THE EXTREMELY MENACING MODE BY WHICH GOD BRINGS MOSES TO A SENSE OF THE OMISSION. "He sought to kill him." When God proceeds to such an extremity as this, it must be either because of some monstrous breach of duty, or to impress an important commandment by the most efficacious means that can be adopted. There is no need to suppose that Moses, knowing full well the importance of circumcision, yet deliberately omitted it. If so, his conduct would have been very bad indeed. There is a more reasonable and instructive aspect. He was brought nigh to death so that he might learn the truth—and learn it so as never to forget, never to neglect it—that no human being, whatever its claims and whatever its supplications, was to come between God and him. Let Moses now take his choice between pleasing his wife and obeying his God. He could only do God's work by the most hearty obedience and attention. Nor was he here only as the messenger of God to Israel and Egypt ; he was also the responsible head of a household. Leaders who are husbands and parents are watched in all their home relations. If Moses was going to let Zipporah rule and prevail by her womanly wiles in one instance, why not in others ? The only way to keep things right was for Zipporah to take her orders from him, and as Moses was to choose between his wife and his God, so Zipporah between her husband and her child. She has to put her child to a passing pain in order that she may spare her husband from impending death. Indeed, poor woman, she had been greatly tried of late : compelled to leave her father and her dear native land, and go on an expedition the reasons of which would be but indifferently comprehended by her. Whichever way she turns, and whatever she does, there is something to vex her soul. Dearly had she paid for that chivalrous service which Moses had rendered her and her sisters so many years before. The awkwardness of being unequally yoked is felt by the unbeliever as much as the believer.—Y.

EXPOSITION.

Vers. 27, 28.—The scene suddenly shifts. Moses is left in the wilderness to recover his strength and make such arrangements with respect to his wife and children as he thinks best under the circumstances. We are carried away to Egypt and introduced to Aaron, Moses' elder brother, of whom we have only heard previously that he could "speak well," and was to assist Moses as spokesman in his enterprise (ch. iv. 14—16). We now find God revealing himself to Aaron also, and directing his movements, as he had those of Moses. Aaron had perhaps already formed the design of visiting his brother (see ver. 14), and would have sought him in Midian but for the direction now given him. That direction was probably more definite than is expressed in the text, and enabled him to set forth confidently, without the fear of missing his brother. At any rate, under God's guidance he went and met him in the Sinaitic district. The joy of meeting is briefly described in the single phrase "he kissed him." The meeting was followed by a full explanation, on the part of Moses, both of the nature of his own mission and of the part which Aaron was to take in it.

Ver. 27.—**Go into the wilderness.** It is scarcely possible that this can have been the whole of the direction given, since the wilderness extended from the shores of the Mediterranean to the extreme point of the Sinaitic peninsula. The sacred writers study brevity, and leave much to be supplied by the common-sense of the reader. **He went and met him in the mount of God.** Compare above,

ch. iii. 1, which shows that Horeb is meant. Horeb seems to have been the name for the entire mountain region, of which Sinai was a part. **Kissed him.** So Esau kissed Jacob after their long separation (Gen. xxxiii. 4), and Joseph, Benjamin and his other brethren (*ib.* xlv. 14, 15). In the East men are more demonstrative than with us. Aaron's kiss showed the gladness that was in his heart (*supra*, ver. 14).

Ver. 28.—**Moses told Aaron all the words of the Lord.** Perfect confidence between the two brothers was absolutely necessary for the success of their enterprise; and Moses wisely, at their very first interview, made Aaron acquainted with the entire series of Divine revelations that had been made to him, keeping nothing back, but communicating to him "all the words of the Lord." **Who had sent him.** Rather, "which he had laid upon him." (So the LXX., the Vulgate, Knobel, Kalisch, and others.) **All the signs.** Compare verses 3—9 and verse 23.

HOMILETICS.

Ver. 27.—*God does not stint his help when he visits man.* It might have seemed that God had now done enough to set on foot the deliverance of his people. He had appeared to Moses, overcome his reluctance to be leader, given him the power of working some great miracles, and allowed him to devolve a portion of his duties upon his brother; Moses was on his way to Egypt to carry out his commission, and Aaron was minded to go forth to meet and greet him. Humanly speaking, nothing more was needed for the initiation of the work. But God, who "seeth not as man seeth," does not stint his arm when he has taken a business in hand. It would expedite matters if Aaron were to be directed where to meet Moses, and the two brothers were to have their conference at once, and arrange their course of proceedings. So Aaron is visited, probably by an angel, and sent to meet Moses, and told where he will find him; and by these means the meeting is brought about with all speed, Aaron enlightened as to his duties, and plans arranged to be put in act as soon as Egypt is reached. The two brothers gain the advantage of sweet companionship some days or weeks earlier than they would have done if left to themselves, and their first interview with Pharaoh is advanced correspondingly. And as with his miraculous, so with his ordinary help. God does not stint it. His grace is ever sufficient for men. He gives them all that they can possibly need, and more than they would ever think of asking. He loves to pour out his blessings abundantly on those that are true to him; makes "all things work together for their good;" goes out of his way to procure advantages for them; loads them with his favours.

Ver. 28.—*Full confidence necessary between fellow-workers.* Moses told Aaron "all the words of the Lord"—made "a clean breast" to him, kept back none of the counsel of God, so far as he had been made acquainted with it. A kind, a loving, and a prudent course. Half-confidences are valueless; they irritate rather than satisfy. If known to be half-confidences, they offend; if mistaken for full ones, they mislead and conduct to disaster. Those who are to be fellow-workers in any undertaking—more especially any great one—should have entire confidence each in each, and be wholly unreserved one towards the other. There is good sense and good advice in the motto, "Trust me not at all or all in all."

EXPOSITION.

Vers. 29—31.—Moses seems to have parted with Zipporah and his children in Horeb, and to have sent them back to Jethro (ch. xviii. 2), perhaps because they might have interfered with the work which he had to do, perhaps because he thought Egypt would be no pleasant residence for them during the coming struggle. He journeyed onward from Horeb with Aaron for his sole companion, and had abundant time for taking counsel with him, and exercising the influence over him which high intellect and education combined will always give to their possessor. The journey from Horeb to Goshen occupied probably some weeks. On arriving in Goshen, the two brothers, in obedience to the divine command (ch. iii. 16), proceeded at once to "gather together all the elders of Israel"—that is, all those who exercised local authority over their countrymen in the various districts which they inhabited. Through the mouth of Aaron, Moses declared all that had been revealed to him at the burning bush and subsequently, exhibiting at the same time the credentials which proved him an ambassador from God, i.e. the three miracles which he had been empowered to work at any moment (ch. iv. 2—8). The elders, being themselves convinced, summoned an assembly of the people, as is implied though not expressed in ver. 30 ; and the people, having heard the words of Aaron and seen the signs, were also convinced, and bowing their heads, worshipped the God whose ambassadors had appeared before them.

Ver. 29.—On the elders of Israel, see note upon ch. iii. 16. It is clear that the Israelitish nation, though in bondage to the Egyptians, had a certain internal organisation of its own, and possessed a set of native officers. These were probably the hereditary heads of families. Moses and Aaron could have no authority to gather these persons together ; but they issued an invitation, and it was accepted. The " elders " came to the meeting.

Ver. 30.—Aaron spake. Aaron at once entered on his office of " spokesman " (ver. 16), declaring to the elders all God's dealings with his brother. Aaron also, and not Moses, as we should have expected (ver. 17), did the signs, God, by allowing him to do them, sanctioning this delegation of power. On later occasions, we find Aaron more than once required by God to work the miracles. (See below, ch. vii. 19 ; viii. 5, 16.) In the sight of the people. It is not probable that the people were present at the first meeting of the elders ; but the sacred historian, anxious to compress his narrative, and bent simply on conveying to us the fact of Aaron's success with both elders and people, omits stages in the history which he supposes that any reader can supply, e.g. the doing of the signs in the sight of the elders, their belief in them, and their subsequent assembling of the people.

Ver. 31.—The people believed. This ready faith stands in strong contrast with the ordinary incredulous temper of the Israelitish people, who were "a faithless and stubborn generation"—a generation that " believed not in God, and trusted not in his salvation " (Ps. lxxviii. 22). It would seem that under the pressure of affliction—having, humanly speaking, no hope—the stubborn spirit of the people had given way, and they were content to look to Jehovah and accept his promises, and believe in his messengers, notwithstanding their natural scepticism. No doubt the novelty of miracles helped to produce this state of feeling ; and the fact that they were not called upon at present for any active exertion made acquiescence in what Moses put before them easier. When they heard that the Lord had visited—i.e. when the message contained in ch. iii. 16 was delivered to them. And that he had looked upon their affliction. Compare ch. iii. 7. They bowed their heads. Rather " they bowed down " (Kalisch), or " inclined themselves." And worshipped. Some understand an act of respect and homage done to Moses and Aaron, in token of their acceptance by the people as leaders ; but, though the words employed are sometimes used in this sense, the context is opposed to their having this sense in this place. " When the people heard that the Lord had visited the children of Israel, . . . they bowed down and worshipped." Whom? Surely, the Lord.

HOMILETICS.

Vers. 29—31.—*The blessing on obedience.* Moses and Aaron, on their return to Egypt in company, carried out exactly the Divine directions, doing neither less nor more. They summoned the elders as commanded (ch. iii. 16); they delivered God's message to them (*ib.*); they wrought the signs which they had been told to work (ch. iv. 17); they severally kept to their appointed offices ; and the result was complete success so far. The elders and people hearkened unto them, believed, gave in their unqualified assent and consent to all that was put before them. And this was according to the promise of God, "they shall hearken to thy voice" (ch. iii. 18). Moses had disbelieved the promise, and exclaimed, "Behold, they will not believe me, nor hearken unto my voice" (ch. iv. 1); but Moses was now proved mistaken. "The foolishness of God is wiser than men" (1 Cor. i. 25). God knew better than Moses; he was faithful; he kept his word. As Moses and Aaron had been true to him, and followed exactly his commands, so he proved himself true to them, and amply rewarded their obedience. Moses and Aaron were from this time the accepted leaders of the nation.

Ver. 31.—*Worship the proper outcome of thankfulness.* Israel, down-trodden, oppressed, crushed beneath an intolerable tyranny, no sooner hears the promise of deliverance, than it displays its gratitude by "bowing the head and worshipping." Many Christians talk of being thankful for God's blessings vouchsafed to them, but never think of showing forth their thankfulness by any extra act of worship, or even any increased intensity in that portion of their ordinary worship which consists in thanksgiving. A sad sign this of modern lukewarmness, an indication that the "last times" are drawing near, when "the love of many shall wax cold." Time was when each national success was at once celebrated by a "Te Deum," and when each blessing granted to an individual drew forth a special offering. The thankfulness that does not show itself in some such overt act must be a very poor thankfulness, a very weak and washed-out feeling.

HOMILIES BY VARIOUS AUTHORS.

Vers. 27, 28.—*A meeting of brothers.* 1. By Divine appointment (cf. ver. 14). 2. In a sacred place. 3. As co-operators in a good work. 4. With affection. 5. To exchange experiences.—J. O.

Vers. 29—31.—*Preaching and faith.* I. THE WORD SPOKEN. 1. Should be the Word of God. The preacher is not set to deliver his own speculations, but to convey a *message.* 2. Should be exhibited with its appropriate evidence. 3. Should be declared to all. II. THE WORD BELIEVED. The people—1. Appreciated the value of the word. 2. Believed the word. 3. Worshipped; a token of gratitude, submission, and obedience.—J. O.

SECTION III.—CHAPTER V.

FIRST APPEAL OF MOSES TO PHARAOH, AND INCREASE OF THE OPPRESSION.

EXPOSITION.

CHAPTER V

Vers. 1—5.—Having secured the adhesion of the Israelitish people, Moses and Aaron sought an interview with the Egyptian monarch who was now in possession of the throne. According to the bulk of modern authorities, and according to our own views of Egyptian history, this was Menephthah, the son and successor of Rameses II. Menephthah was a weak prince, whom events had favoured, and who had been thus led to have an exalted opinion of himself. A great invasion of Egypt had occurred at the

beginning of his reign, which had been met and completely repulsed, not by his own skill or valour, but by the skill and valour of his generals. Menephthah himself had pointedly avoided incurring any danger. He claimed to be in direct communication with the Egyptian gods, who revealed themselves to him in visions, and pleaded a distinct command of Phthah as preventing him from putting himself at the head of his army. Still, he counted as his own all the successes gained by his generals, and was as vainglorious and arrogant as if he had himself performed prodigies of valour. Such was the temper of the king before whom we believe that Moses and Aaron appeared. There would be no difficulty in any Egyptian subject, who had a prayer to make or a petition to present, obtaining an audience of the monarch, for it was an accepted principle of the administration that the kings were to hear all complaints, and admit to their presence all classes of the community.

Ver. 1.—**And afterward.** The interposition of some not inconsiderable space of time seems to be implied. Menophthah resided partly at Memphis, partly at Zoan (Tanis). Moses and Aaron may have had to wait until he returned from his southern to his northern capital. **Moses and Aaron went in, and told Pharaoh.** Aaron was, no doubt, the sole spokesman, but as he spoke for both, the plural is used. **Thus saith the Lord God of Israel.** Literally, "Thus saith Jehovah, God of Israel." Pharaoh would understand Jehovah to be a proper name, parallel to his own Phthah, Ra, Ammon, etc. **Let my people go.** The *rationale* of the demand is given in ch. viii. 26. The Israelites could not offer their proper sacrificial animals in the presence of the Egyptians without the risk of provoking a burst of religious animosity, since among the animals would necessarily be some which all, or many, of the Egyptians regarded as sacred, and under no circumstances to be killed. The fanaticism of the Egyptians on such occasions led to wars, tumults, and massacres. (See Plutarch, 'De Isid. et Osir.,' § 44.) To avoid this danger the "feast" must be held beyond the bounds of Egypt—in the adjacent "wilderness."

Ver. 2.—**And Pharaoh said, Who is the Lord?** Rather, "Who is Jehovah?" Either Pharaoh is actually ignorant, or he pretends to be. The former is possible, since Jehovah was a name but little employed, until the return of Moses to Egypt. The latter, however, is more probable. **That I should obey his voice.** Why am I to obey his voice? What is your Jehovah to me? What authority has he over me? He is, at best, your god, not mine. **I know not Jehovah.** I acknowledge him not. He is not within the range of my Pantheon.

Neither will I let Israel go, *i.e.* "nor even, if he were, would I consent to such a request as this from him." The Pharaohs assumed to be themselves gods, on a par with the national gods, and not bound to obey them.

Ver. 3.—**And they said.** Moses and Aaron are not abashed by a single refusal. They expostulate, and urge fresh reasons why Pharaoh should accede to their request. But first they explain that Jehovah is **the God of the Hebrews,** by which name the Israelites seem to have been generally known to the Egyptians (See ch. i. 15, 16, 19; ii. 6, 7.) Their God, they say, has **met with** them—made, that is, a special revelation of himself to them—an idea quite familiar to the king, and which he could not pretend to misunderstand and he has laid on them an express command. They are to go **a three days' journey into the desert** —to be quite clear of interruption from the Egyptians. Will not Pharaoh allow them to obey the order? If they do not obey it, their God will be angry, and will punish them, either by sending a **pestilence** among them, or causing an invader to fall upon them **with the sword.** The eastern frontier of Egypt was at this time very open to invasion, and was actually threatened by a vast army some ten or fifteen years later (Brugsch, 'History of Egypt,' vol. ii., pp. 147—9).

Ver. 4.—The king makes no direct reply to this appeal, but turns upon his petitioners, and charges them with an offence against the crown. Why do they, Moses and Aaron, by summoning the people to meet together, and exciting their minds with vague hopes, "**let the people from their works.**" This is damage to the crown, whose labourers the people are, and he, the Pharaoh, will not have it. "**Get you**—all of you, people and leaders together— to your appointed tasks—**your burdens.**"

Ver. 5.—**The people are many.** This is added as an aggravation of the offence charged in the last verse. The people are numerous. Therefore the greater damage is done to the crown by putting a stop to their labours. With these words the first interview between the Israelite leaders and the Egyptian monarch ends. Moses and Aaron, we must suppose, retired discomfited from the royal presence.

HOMILETICS.

Vers. 1—5.—*God's will often opposed by the great of the earth, and his servants rebuffed.* Encouraged by their success with the elders and with the people (ch. iv. 29—31), Moses and Aaron would step boldly into the presence of Pharaoh. It was, no doubt, known that they represented the feelings of an entire nation, a nation moreover of whom the Egyptians had begun to be afraid (ch. i. 9, 10). The courtiers would treat them, at any rate, with outward politeness and respect. They knew also that God was on their side, and would ultimately, if not at the first, give them success. Under these circumstances they made their request boldly and with much plainness (vers. 1 and 3). But they were met with the most complete antagonism. Pharaoh was in his own eyes not only the greatest king upon the face of the earth, but an actual god. If we are right in supposing him to be Menephthah, he was the son of a king who had set up his own image to be worshipped side by side with those of Ammon, Phthah, and Horus, three of the greatest Egyptian deities. He viewed the demand made of him as preposterous, and had probably not the slightest belief in the power of Jehovah to do him harm. Who was Jehovah? and what had he to fear from him? A god—if he was a god—who had not been able to prevent his people from becoming a nation of slaves. He therefore treated the petition of Moses with absolute contempt. And so it has ever been, and will ever be, with the great of the earth. They are so exalted above their fellows, that they think "no harm can happen unto them." They do not set themselves to inquire what is really God's will, but determinately carry out their own will in their own way. Even when they do not openly blaspheme, like this Pharaoh, and Sennacherib (2 Kings xviii. 29—35), and Herod Antipas (Luke xxiii. 11), they ignore God, reject the just demands of his ministers, refuse to be guided by their advice. Thus his servants are ever being rebuffed. They ask that slavery should everywhere cease, and are told that in some places it is a necessity. They plead against the licensing of vice, and are bidden not to interfere with sanitary arrangements. They ask for laws to restrain intoxication, and are denounced as seeking to lessen the national revenue. They cry for the abolition of vivisection, and are held up to ridicule as sickly sentimentalists. All this is to be expected, and should not discourage them. Let them, like Moses and Aaron, continually repeat their demands; urge them, in season and out of season. They may be sure that they will triumph at last. "The Lord is on their side;" they need not fear what flesh can do against them.

HOMILIES BY VARIOUS AUTHORS.

Vers. 1—21.—*Failure.* "I know not Jehovah," etc.: Exod. v. 2. We now come face to face with the king. As the king here becomes very prominent, we will keep him conspicuous in the outlining of this address.

I. AUDIENCE WITH THE KING. This is a convenient moment for introducing Pharaoh as the terrestrial representative of the Sun, as the vicegerent of Deity upon earth. Does it seem wonderful that men should receive a man in this capacity? But millions of professed Christians in this nineteenth century so receive the Pope. We will take the suggestions of the story in the time-order of the narrative. We have—1. *A lesson in courage.* The two went to their audience with the king at the peril of their lives. Some might have remembered Moses. Their demand touched the honour and revenues of the king. Courage in facing responsibility is the lesson; leave consequences to our poor selves to God. 2. A suggestion as to *the method of evangelic grace.* Jehovah here calls himself for the first time in relation to the nation, as distinguished from the man Jacob, "the God of Israel." A crowd was just becoming a State and a Church, when Jehovah calls himself their God. First he is their God: *then* all possibilities are before them. Their history begins well. So now: first adopted children, and then the obedience of children. 3. *A warning against want of catholicity.* The tone of Pharaoh is that of the vicegerent of Deity, as against a tutelary god he deigned not to acknowledge. But he was wrong even on the principles of enlightened pagandom, which was forward to acknowledge the gods of all nations. Compare the policy of imperial Rome. 4. Teaching as to *gradation in God's demands.* Here may be discussed the nature and propriety of the first demand for three days' absence. Looking at things after the events, it may appear to some that here was a demand which concealed the real intention, viz. to return no more. But this would be to impeach the veracity of God! The demand really was for "a whole day's prayer-meeting," with a day to go, a day to return. In the desert, as in consideration of Egyptian feeling; but probably within the frontier, for there were Egyptian garrisons in parts of the desert of Sinai. A moderate demand! One that Pharaoh might well have complied with. Compliance might have led to further negotiation; and this Pharaoh might have stood out in history as co-operating in the deliverance and formation of the Church of God. Instead of that he set himself against the small demand, and was unready for the greater (Exod. vi. 11) when it came. And so we see him through the mist of ages, "moving ghost-like to his doom." It is a picture of the method of God. He asks first for the simple, reasonable, easy etc. etc.

II. ORDERS FROM THE KING. "The very same day!" Such is the restlessness of the tyrant-spirit. The orders were addressed to the "drivers," Egyptians, and to the "clerks" of the works, Hebrews. Note the large employment of "clerks," as evidenced by the monuments. The appointment of these "clerks" would contribute much to the organisation of Israel, and so prepare for the Exodus. As to the orders—explain them. Bricks a government monopoly; witness the royal mark on many to this day. Same number of bricks as before, but people to gather in the corn-fields the straw (in harvest only the ear cut off) previously allowed by the government, chop it, and mix it with the clay. Terrible cruelty of these orders-in-council in such a climate.

III. OBEDIENCE TO THE KING. For the sake of vividly and pictorially bringing up the condition of the people, note the time of straw-collecting: time of harvest—end of April; then a hot pestilential sand-wind often blows over the land of Egypt for fifty days; the effects on health, tone, skin, eyes (in the land of ophthalmia), of so working in blazing sun, in clouds of dust, in hopeless slavery. They return to the horrid brickfields; fail; fierce punishments, as to this day in the same land.

IV. EXPOSTULATION WITH THE KING. The "clerks" of the works constitute a deputation to the king, perhaps by virtue of a "right of petition." The king accuses them of being "idle." To understand this, think of the gigantic public works, the terrific labour, the perishing of thousands, the likelihood that such a taunt would spring to tyrannical lips. The king refuses, perhaps threatens the lives of the "clerks." See ver. 21—" to put a *sword*," etc. Here again, that which seemed most against the people made for them. The treatment of the "clerks" brought them into sympathy with their enslaved brethren. Israel closed its ranks. The fellowship of suffering prepared for the companionship of pilgrimage. There was, too, a present blessing. Spiritual feelings were quickened, heaven came nearer, the pitying love of God became more precious. One can imagine such scenes as those in which the slaves of the Southern States, through horrid swamps and over mighty rivers, in the dead of night "stole away to Jesus."

> " In that hour, when night is calmest,
>   Sing they from some Sacred Psalmist,
>   In a voice so sweet and clear
>   That I cannot choose but hear.

> " And the voice of their devotion
>   Fills my soul with strange emotion;
>   For its tones by turns are glad,
>   Sweetly solemn, wildly sad."
>
> [*Adapted from* LONGFELLOW.]

V. CONSEQUENCES TO THE AMBASSADORS OF THE KING OF KINGS. Moses and Aaron, somewhere near the palace, were waiting to know the result of the audience of the "clerks" with the king. The "clerks," irritated and angry, turned on the God-given leaders: ver. 21. [Note in the Heb. the expression "to stink in *the eyes*," and the fact that pungent odours do affect the eyes.] A dreadful trouble to Moses and Aaron!

In conclusion, observe—1. *The cruelty that is ever incident to sin.* " Man's inhumanity to man" a universal fact. "The dark places of the earth are full," etc.; so places alight with modern civilisation. The incidents of any gin-palace! There is, too, a cruelty of word and manner. Soul-wounds deeper than sword-gashes. No cure save under the sanctifying power of the Cross of self-abnegating love. 2. *The pain that attends all emancipations.* The first efforts of Moses and Aaron led to nothing but disaster. See vi. 9. So with the agony of emancipation in America. So always and everywhere. So with reforms within the Church. So with crises of soul-history. 3. *The discouragement that may fall to leaders.* 4. *The encouragement we all have.* Note here—(1) The appointment of the "clerks;" (2) The personal danger into which they came; (3) The uniting all Israel into a fellowship of grief that they might dare the desert. All this came out of the oppression; but tended to salvation. Our darkest experiences may be our best friends. 5. *Through what sorrow all come to the final emancipation.*—R.

Chap. V.—The people of Jehovah detained and oppressed by the representative of the prince of this world; no doubt as to the strength of the latter—is it possible for his spoils to be wrested from him? The strong man armed has thus far kept his palace (Luke xi. 21), and his goods (cf. Rev. xviii. 13) have been in peace, so far as outward disturbance is concerned. Now comes one who claims to be the stronger. What may be expected to happen?

I. THE CHALLENGE DELIVERED. 1. *The tyrant.* Picture the king. Wholly self-satisfied, worshipped as a god, absolute ruler over the lives of thousands. Surrounded by obsequious servants—none to contradict him, none to disobey. Enthroned in palace. Enter—2. *The envoys.* Two men—one grown old in slavery, one for forty years a shepherd, looking now at all this pomp as a man who dimly recalls some dream. Does he think of what might have been, perhaps he himself seated upon the throne (cf. Heb. xi. 24)? Greater honour to be the unknown envoy of Jehovah than to be the Pharaoh who receives his message. 3. *The message.* Strange words for such a king to hear (1) a *command,* not a *request.* The sender of the message speaks as to a servant. (2) The slaves of Pharaoh claimed as the people of Jehovah; his right denied to the possession of his goods. 4. *The reply.* The demand met by a contemptuous refusal. Who is Jehovah? I know not Jehovah!" If the message is authoritative, yet the envoys are sufficiently humble—they even plead with him that, for the sake of the people, he will grant them permission and opportunity to sacrifice (ver. 3). All to no purpose; the strong man is secure in his possessions and means to keep them in his grasp.

II. HOSTILITIES COMMENCED. Pharaoh was not quite so indifferent as he seemed. If there is to be war, he will gain such advantage as may be gained by making the first hostile movement. His slaves at any rate shall be taught that rebellion is not likely to be successful. Effect of his policy:—1. *On people.* So long as he had been undisturbed his goods were in peace; now that he is disturbed the miserable peace of his chattels is disturbed too. [Man in prison, treated with greater rigour on the rumour of an attempted rescue.] Early spring, just after the corn has been cut; chopped straw needed to mix with the clay in brickmaking; let these discontented rebels gather their own. Israelites obliged to scatter themselves over the country; all complaints stifled with blows. Result, vers. 20, 21, great discouragement and distrust of Moses and Aaron. "This comes of interfering." Six months' worse tyranny than ever. 2. *On himself.* Six months to realise the success of his policy; feels more secure than ever; heart is harder; pride greater (cf. Rom. ii. 4, 5). 3. *On Moses.* Vers. 22, 23. Disheartened, but only for a little; repulsed by Pharaoh, suspected by the people, he is driven back on God; like the giant who gained strength each time he clasped the ground, so becoming more invincible with each new overthrow, finds God his *refuge* and his *strength* also. God is pledged to secure final victory. The slaves *must* be freed; not because *they* can win freedom, but because *God* has promised to free them. *Apply,* from our Lord's parable, Luke xi. 21, 22. Satan the strong man who has many slaves. His power seems at first to increase when moved by the rumour of redemption we attempt to follow the dictates of our Deliverer (cf. Rom. vii. 9—11). Content with slavery, there is quietude; trying after freedom we find trouble and affliction. [*Illustr.* A habit, not hard to *endure,* but hard to *break.* The chain of sin is easy to wear; they only know how fast it holds who try to struggle free of it.] Cf. again Rom. vii. with St. Paul as with Israel; the bondage seemed worse than ever when the hope of freedom was the most alluring. In either case the ground of hope, not *in* the sufferer, but away outside him. God prompts to the struggle against the oppressor, but he does not let victory depend on us; *that* rests with him. The promise to deliver is contained in the call to freedom. It is not, "I will help you when you are strong," nothing said about *our* strength at all; confidence rests on the fact that God is Jehovah, the *changeless* One (cf. Ex. vi. 2; Mal. iii. 6). Let Israel obey Moses, and God *must* redeem them from Pharaoh. Let us obey Christ, and God *must* redeem us from the power of Satan.—G.

Vers. 1—4.—*A first interview.* Accompanied by Aaron, Moses passes again through the halls of the Pharaohs from which he has been so long a stranger. Kings, courtiers, and people are different; but all else—gates and pillars, courts, corridors, and reception-rooms—how unchanged since first he knew them! The feelings of the *quondam* prince must have been strangely mingled, as, after forty years of exile, he trod the familiar pavements, and looked upon the old splendours. But the narrative, absorbed in its mightier theme, has no word to spare for the emotions of a Moses. The long contest between Pharaoh and Jehovah is on the eve of its commencement, and the interest centres in its opening scene. It is this which occupies the verses before us.

I. THE REQUEST (vers. 1, 3). Behold Pharaoh on his throne of state, while the brothers stand before him delivering Jehovah's message. The request preferred to him was—1. *Eminently righteous and reasonable.* No monarch has a right to deprive a people of the opportunity of worshipping God according to their consciences. If he does, the people have a right to protest against it. Pharaoh could not be expected to understand the modern views of rights of conscience, but even by the light of his own time people were entitled to be permitted to worship their own gods, and to honour them by appropriate festivals. But not only had Pharaoh deprived the Hebrews of their liberty, and ground them to the earth by cruel oppression—both offences against righteousness, but he had taken from them, we may be certain, the opportunity of observing in a proper manner the festivals of their God. Moses and Aaron would have been within their rights, even without Divine command, had they demanded that the whole nation be set at liberty. Much more when they only asked that they be allowed for a brief space to retire into the wilderness, there, unmolested by the Egyptians, to sacrifice to the Lord. 2. *Supported by Divine command.* "Thus saith the Lord God of Israel." Pharaoh, it is true, could plead that he did not know Jehovah; but when he saw these men's sincerity, and how they dreaded incurring their God's anger (ver. 3), it was his duty to have inquired further. The evil was that he did not care to know. He treated the whole matter with impious and disdainful contempt. 3. *Unaccompanied by signs.* Moses and Aaron had no occasion to exhibit signs. Pharaoh was not in a mood to pay the slightest attention to them. He did not even dispute that this was a *bonâ fide* message from Jehovah, but took the ground of simple refusal to obey it. Yet there may have been a reason for working no miracles at the opening of the conflict. God proceeds with men step by step. The first appeal is to be made, not to the king's fears, but to his sense of fairness, his humanity, and feeling of religion. He must be convicted on this lower ground before sterner measures are used to coerce him to submission. It might be true that purely moral considerations would have little effect upon him; but if so, this had to be made manifest. God deals with men first of all in the open court of conscience, and it is there—in the region of ordinary morals—that hardening usually begins.

II. PHARAOH'S REPLY (ver. 2). It was, as already stated, a haughty and angry refusal, showing total disregard of the rights and wishes of the Hebrews, and setting Jehovah at defiance. The king's disposition, as brought to light in it, is seen to be— 1. *Proud.* He probably regarded the request of the brothers as an instance of astounding audacity. Who were they, two slave-born men, that they should presume to ask from him, the lord of mighty Egypt, that the people be allowed to rest from their labours? His pride may have blinded him to the righteousness of their demand; but it could not lessen his responsibility. We are judged, not according to the impression which righteous and merciful appeals make upon us—that may be *nil*—but by the inherent righteousness of the appeals, and by the effects which they *ought* to have produced. 2. *Headstrong.* Before venturing so defiantly to scout Jehovah and his message, it would surely have been well for Pharaoh to have inquired a little further into the character and powers of this Being of whom the Hebrews stood so much in awe. He had not the excuse which many moderns would plead, that he did not believe in gods or in the supernatural in any shape. Pharaoh had no right, from his own point of view, to scout the possibility of "the God of the Hebrews" having met with them; and neither, so far as appears from the narrative, did he, though he chose to regard the story as a fiction. Many reject the Gospel, never having given its claims their serious attention; but this will not excuse them. They cannot plead that, had they believed it to be true, they would have acted otherwise. Their sin is that in their headstrongness they will not trouble themselves to inquire whether it *is* true. 3. *Profane.* After all, what Pharaoh's reply amounted to was this, that, let Jehovah be who or what he might, he (Pharaoh) set him at naught—would not obey him. The message might or might not come from a God, he did not care. Thus he "set his mouth against the heavens" (Ps. lxxiii. 9), and "exalted himself above all that is called God"

(2 Thess. ii. 4)—not an uncommon phase of pride. But the presumptuously wicked will do well to remember that, if Pharaoh thus exalted himself, it was to his own destruction. His very pride was a challenge to Jehovah to destroy him.—J. O.

Vers. 1—5.— *God's demand and Pharaoh's answer.*— I. THE DEMAND. 1. Its modesty. They merely ask liberty to depart on a three days' journey into the wilderness. 2. It was asked in good faith; it was not a cover for escape. God would give deliverance; but that was left in God's hand; and meanwhile they asked only for liberty to worship him. 3. Its reasonableness: they could not sacrifice the sacred animals of the Egyptians before their faces. 4. Its necessity. Pharaoh might not know Jehovah, but they knew him, and must serve him, "lest he fall upon us with the pestilence or the sword." The demand of the Church still is liberty to serve God in his own appointed way. It must be had. Luther's "God help me; I can do no other!" "We ought to obey God rather than men" (Acts v. 29).
II. THE REFUSAL. 1. Its presumption. *He* did not know Jehovah, and therefore the message was a lie! Unbelief makes the bounds of its knowledge the bounds of truth and possibility. The pretensions of modern agnosticism. 2. It was a refusal of justice; it was a resolve to continue oppression. Unbelief is the brother and helper of wrong-doing. 3. It was made with reproach and insult. They were encouraging idleness and sedition: "Get ye to your burdens." "These that have turned the world upside down are come hither also." 4. The rage of the wicked is often the best commendation of God's servants. It is a testimony to their faithfulness.—U.

Ver. 2.—*Pharaoh's first response: his answer in word.* Moses and Aaron, somehow or other, have found their way into Pharaoh's presence. All things, so far, have happened as God said they would happen. The very brevity and compactness of the record at the end of ch. iv. is an instructive comment on the way in which Moses had mistaken comparative shadows for substantial difficulties. The actual meeting of Moses with Israel is dismissed in a few satisfactory and significant words; as much as to say that enough space had already been occupied in detailing the difficulties started by Moses in his ignorance and alarm. It is when Moses and Pharaoh meet that the tug of war really begins. Moses addresses to Pharaoh the commanded request, and is met, as was to be expected, with a prompt and contemptuous defiance. Observe—
I. PHARAOH, IN HIS REJOINDER TO MOSES, PUTS A QUESTION WHICH GOD ALONE CAN PROPERLY ANSWER. "Who is the Lord that I should obey his voice to let Israel go?" *This was evidently in Pharaoh's opinion a question which needed no answer at all.* It had nothing interrogative about it, except the form. Taking the form of a question, it served to express more forcibly Pharaoh's defiant spirit. There was, in his opinion, really no need to consider or confer at all. "Am I not the great Pharaoh, successor to many great Pharaohs before me? Is not my power accepted and undisputed far and wide?" He could not so much as comprehend any danger unless it took the form of physical force; and not only so, but a form plainly visible—near, threatening, overwhelming. If only some great king had been approaching—strong with the strength of a large and victorious army—to demand the liberation of Israel, Pharaoh would not so have spoken. To him the invisible was as the unreal. Pharaoh listens to Moses, and what does he hear?—a claim that seems to dispute his supremacy, from this new deity, whose image he has never seen, whose name mayhap his priests have told him is not that of any deity worshipped in Canaan of which they have ever heard. Certainly it looks a large claim upon the first presentation of it, small as it is in comparison with what is to follow. This, then, is what he hears, and the audacity and presumption of it are not diminished by what he sees. There stand Moses and Aaron, completely devoid in person and surroundings of anything to impress the king with the peril of refusing their request. Surely if the men who say they are sent look so contemptible, the unseen being from whom they say they come may be safely neglected. Such is the reasoning, silently powerful, if not openly expressed, of those who despise and reject the claims of God. Christ is judged of, not as he is in himself, but by the superficial aspect of Christians. Because they are often low in station, or inconsistent in life, or lacking in disposition and ability to make much outward show, the world thinks that there is little or nothing behind them. It is the folly of only too many to take Pharaoh's stand. For the right reception of the things of God we need all possible humility and open-

mindedness; what then is to be done, if upon the very first approach of religion, we pooh-pooh it as mere superstition, folly, and delusion? 2. *This was a question to which Moses could have given a very effective and alarming answer if only he had been allowed opportunity.* Moses, fresh from the revelations and sanctities of Horeb, could have told Pharaoh such a story of the workings of Jehovah as would have been enough, and more than enough, to guide the steps of a right-minded listener. Not only his own personal experience; not only the sight of the burning bush, the rod transformed, the leprous hand, the blood where water ought to be; but also the fulness, the terrible fulness of Jehovah's power in the earlier days of the world, were within his reach to speak about. He could have told Pharaoh very admonitory things concerning Sodom and the Deluge if only he had been willing to listen. We may well believe that the effect of Pharaoh's defiant attitude would be to send Moses away striving to refresh and sustain his mind with the evidences, so available and so abundant, that in spite of this proud king's contempt, Jehovah, in his vast power and resources, was indeed no vain imagination. When the proud and self-sufficient ask this Pharaoh-question, it is for us to make such answer as may be reassuring to ourselves; not to doubt our own eyesight because others are blind, our own hearing because others are deaf.

> How few sometimes may know, when thousands err.

The truth which we may not be able to make even probable to others, we must strive so to grasp and penetrate, that more and more it may be felt as certain and satisfying to ourselves.

3. *Thus we see how the Lord himself needed to deal with this question.* Knowledge of God is of many kinds, according to the disposition of the person who is to be taught, and according to the use which God purposes to make of him. Pharaoh was evidently not going to be a docile scholar in God's school—one who comes to it willing and eager, thirsting for a refreshing knowledge of the living God. But still he had to be a scholar, willingly or not. He had to learn this much at least, that he was transgressing on the peculiar possessions of God when he sported with Israel in his despotic caprice. It is for no man to say that his present real ignorance gives assurance that he will never come to *some knowledge of God.* It may be as pitifully true of the atheist as it is encouragingly true of the godly, that what he knows not now, he will know hereafter. Now he knows not God, but in due time he will know him; not dubiously, not distantly, but in the most practical and it may be most painful and humiliating manner. Pharaoh says, with a sneer on his face, and derision in his voice, "Who is Jehovah?" That question is duly answered by Jehovah in signs and plagues, and the last answer we hear anything about on earth comes unmistakable and sublime, amid the roll of the Red Sea's returning waters.

II. But Pharaoh not only puts this defiant question; HE UTTERS A MOST DETERMINED RESOLUTION WHICH GOD ALONE CAN ALTER. "Neither will I let Israel go." What then are Israel's chances for the future? There was every certainty that, if left to himself, Pharaoh would go on, tyrannous and oppressive as ever. From a human point of view he had everything to help him in sticking to his resolution. His fears, if he had any— the wealth which he and his people had gained from the incessant toils of Israel—the great dislocations and changes which would have been produced by even a temporary withdrawal of Israel—all these things helped to a firm maintenance of the resolution. It was a resolution which had strong and active support in all the baser feelings of his own breast. It is just in the firmness and haughtiness of such a resolution, revealing as it does the spirit of the man, that we get the reason for such an *accumulation* of calamities as came upon his land. Here is another significant illustration of the manifold power of God, that he could break down so much proud determination. There was no change in Pharaoh's feeling; no conversion to an equitable and compassionate mind; he simply yielded, because he could not help himself, to continuous and increasing pressure, *and God alone was able to exert that pressure.* Pharaoh here is but the visible and unconscious exponent of that dark Power which is behind all evil men and cruel and selfish policies. That Power, holding men in all sorts of bitter disappointments and degrading miseries, virtually says, "I will not let them go." Our confidence ought ever to be, that though we can do nothing to break this bitter bondage, God, who forced the foe of Israel to relax his voracious grasp, will by his own means force freedom for us from every interference of our spiritual foe.   It was Pharaoh's sad prerogative to shut his own heart, to shut it persistently, to shut it for ever, against the authority and benedictions of Jehovah.   But no one, though he be as mighty and arrogant as a thousand Pharaohs, can fasten us up from God, if so be we are willing to go to him, from whom alone we can gain a pure and eternal life.—Y.

EXPOSITION.

Vers. 6—9.—Rulers are not always content simply to refuse inconvenient demands. Sometimes they set to work with much ingenuity and worldly wisdom to prevent their repetition. This is especially the case where they entertain a fear of their petitioners. The Spartans removed Helots, who had earned their freedom, by the Crypteia. The massacre of St. Bartholomew was caused by the Huguenot demand for freedom of worship and the difficulty of repressing it. The Pharaoh now is not content to let things take their course, but devises a plan by which he hopes to crush altogether the aspirations of the Hebrew people, and secure himself against the recurrence of any such appeal as that which had been made to him by Moses and Aaron. The Israelites had recently been employed chiefly in brickmaking. They had had to dig the clay and temper it, to mix it with straw, and mould it into the form of bricks; but the straw had been supplied to them. The king determined that this should be no longer done; the Israelites should find the straw for themselves. It has been estimated that by this change their labour was "more than doubled." (Canon Cook.) It was a not unreasonable expectation that under this system popular meetings would cease (ver. 9); and that Moses and Aaron, not being backed up by the voice of the people, would discontinue their agitation.

Ver. 6.—**The same day.** Pharaoh lost no time. Having conceived his idea, he issued his order at once—on the very day of the interview with the two leaders. It would be well if the children of light were as "wise" and as energetic on all occasions as the children of darkness. **Taskmasters and officers.** The word translated "taskmaster" here is not the same as the expression similarly rendered in ch. i. 11; and it is thought not to designate the same class. The *sarey massim* of the former passage are thought to be general superintendents of works, few in number and of high rank, the *nogĕshim* of the present place to be subordinates, numerous and inferior in position. Both of these classes were probably Egyptians. The "officers" (*shoterim*) were undoubtedly Hebrews. They were especially employed in keeping the tale of the bricks, and seeing that they reached the proper amount. Literally, the word *shoterim* means "scribes," and is so rendered in most passages.

Ver. 7.—**Straw to make brick.** Straw was used in Egypt to bind together the clay, or mud, which was, of course, the main material of the bricks. (See Wilkinson, in the author's 'Herodotus,' vol. ii. p. 213.) It is usually chopped into small pieces. **Let them go and gather straw.** This would involve the leaving of the brickfields, and the scattering of the people over the harvest-grounds, where alone they would be able to find straw in any quantity. There are so many harvests in Egypt, that straw would perhaps be obtainable somewhere during the greater part of the year.

Ver. 8.—**The tale of the bricks**—*i.e.* the number of the bricks. Exactly as many were to be required of each batch of workmen under the new regulation as previously. The demand was one with which, as the king well knew, it would be impossible to comply: **For they be idle.** There was so much ground for the charge as this—that hitherto their forced labours had not occupied the whole of their time. They had been able, apparently, to cultivate their own plots of ground (Deut. xi. 10), to raise crops of cucumbers, melons, leeks, onions, and garlic (Num. xi. 5), to catch fish (*ibid.*), and attend public meetings (Ex. iv. 30, 31). They had, in fact, had time which they could call their own. Now this was to be so no more. The Pharaoh, however, misrepresents and exaggerates, speaking as if their forced labours had been a mere nothing, and mere want of occupation had led them to raise the cry—"Let us go and sacrifice." It would have been far nearer the truth to say, that the severity and continuousness of their labours had made the notion of festival time, during which they would cease from their toils, generally popular.

Ver. 9.—**Let there more work be laid upon the men.** Rather, as in the margin, "Let the work be heavy upon the men." Let the tasks set them be such as to occupy all their time, and not leave them any spare moments in which they may be tempted to listen to mischievous talkers, like Moses and Aaron) who flatter them with vain (literally, *lying*, words. Pharaoh, no doubt, imagined that the hopes raised by the two brothers were vain and illusive. He was utterly blind as to the course which events were about to take.

HOMILETICS.

Vers. 6—9.—*The picture of a tyrant—crafty, energetic, and unsparing.* Scripture contains abundant portraitures, not only of good, but also of bad men, the Holy Spirit seeming to be as desirous of arousing our indignation against vice as our sympathy with virtue. Portraits are given us, as more effectual than precepts or general descriptions, appealing as they do to our feelings and imagination rather than to our intellect. The dramatic exhibition of a Pharaoh, an Ahab, a Sennacherib, a Judas Iscariot, is calculated at once to strike the soul and to remain indelibly impressed upon it. Here we have the portrait of a tyrant, characterised especially by three qualities—1. Craft or cleverness ; 2. Energy ; and 3. Mercilessness. (1.) Pharaoh's craft is shown, first in the skilful way in which he " turns the tables " upon Moses and Aaron, stopping their mouths with the charge that they are "letting the people from their labours," and "endamaging the king." (See Ezra iv. 13.) Secondly, it is shown in the rapidity and ingenuity of his thought—"More work must be laid upon the Israelites—let them be given no straw." Thirdly, it is shown further on in his attempts to secure the return of the Israelites by the detention of their children (ch. x. 10) or of their cattle (*ibid.* 24). (2.) Pharaoh's energy appears in the immediate steps that he took to carry his plan out by giving orders for the withholding of the straw without any diminution in the tale of bricks, "the same day" (verse 6). Finally, (3) his mercilessness is seen, first, in his refusing a very moderate request (verses 1, 2); secondly, in his meeting the demand for a relaxation of labour by an addition to it; thirdly and especially, in his making such an addition as was impossible of performance, and involved a continued series of punishments (verses 14—21). Pharaoh did not perhaps know the exact amount of misery which he was inflicting; but he was reckless in respect to it—he did not care what it might cost; the sighs and the groans of a whole nation were as nothing to him; and he adds insult to injury by the reproach (verses 8 and 17)—"Ye are idle, ye are idle."

Ver. 7.—*Bricks without straw.* The requirement of " bricks without straw " is not always made by a tyrannical *king.* All employers of labour who expect certain results without allowing sufficient time for them, and then complain that the work is scamped, are guilty of it. So is the father who expects his son to turn out a great scholar, without giving him the necessary books and the necessary instruction to make him one. So is the mistress who scolds her cook for not sending up a first-rate dinner, yet grudges every penny for the kitchen expenses. There are congregations which demand perpetual sermons of a high quality, yet do not either provide their pastors with sufficient money to buy books, or allow them sufficient leisure time for reading them. There are incumbents who act similarly by their curates, mercantile men who, *mutatis mutandis,* act so by their clerks, officials of all kinds who so treat their subordinates. The demand for bricks without straw is, unfortunately, far too common a demand. Let this note be set against it, that it is Pharaonic and tyrannical.

Ver. 9.—*Vain words.* There can be no doubt that "vain words" are unworthy of attention, deserve contempt, are foolish, unjustifiable. But what are "vain words"? What is the test whereby we are to know whether words are vain or not? Simply, the issue of them. Pharaoh thought that the promises of deliverance wherewith Moses and Aaron had excited the people were "vain words." Sennacherib described similarly the words of trust and confidence in God uttered by Hezekiah (2 Kings xviii. 20). The Athenians thought the same of St. Paul's words concerning the resurrection (Acts xvii. 32). But we know that, in none of these cases, were the words uttered " vain." The event justified or will justify them. When words then are uttered by any grave authority, especially if they are uttered in the name of God, we should hesitate to call them "vain." We should await the end. Full often, what the scoffer has called "vain words" turn out "words of truth and soberness"—words which tell with terrible force against those who have despised and rejected them—words which to have heard and despised is condemnation in the sight of the Almighty.

HOMILIES BY VARIOUS AUTHORS.

Vers. 4—10.—*Increased cruelty.* View Pharaoh's conduct as illustrative—

I. OF THE VIEW WHICH A WORLDLY MAN TAKES OF RELIGION. " Ye are idle " (ver. 8). This way of putting the matter was partly a pretext—a tyrant's excuse for adding to burdens already sufficiently heavy; but it had so far a ground in Pharaoh's real way of viewing things, that he doubtless regarded the desire to go and sacrifice as an idle, foolish notion, one which would not have come into the people's heads had they been worked hard enough, and which it was his interest to drive out again as soon as possible. Observe in this—1. *A total incapacity to understand the origin of religious aspirations.* Pharaoh had no better account to give of them than that they sprang from idleness. They were the fruit of a roving, unsettled disposition. The cure for them was harder work. This is precisely how the world looks on religion. It is the unpractical dream of people whose working faculties are not in sufficiently vigorous exercise. Of a true thirsting of the soul for God the world has not the slightest comprehension. 2. *A total want of sympathy with these aspirations.* Indulgence in them would be idling—a foolish and profitless waste of time. It is not idling to watch the markets, to speculate on stock, to read novels, to attend the Derby, to run to theatres, to spend evenings in the ball-room, to hunt, fish, shoot, or travel on the Continent, to waste hours in society gossip; but it would be idling to pray, or worship God, or engage in Christian work, or attend to the interests of the soul. To snatch an hour from business to attend a prayer-meeting would be reckoned egregious folly, and as little are the hours at one's disposal when business is over to be spent in such "foolishness." Even the Sabbath, so far as it cannot be utilised for pleasure, is deemed a day "wasted"—a weariness (Amos viii. 6; Mal. ii. 13). 3. *A total disregard of the rights of others in connection with these aspirations.* Thoroughgoing men of the world neither take pains to conceal their own contempt for religion (" vain words," ver. 9), nor trouble themselves with any scruples as to the rights of others. They will, without hesitation, take from the religiously-disposed their opportunities of serving God, if these stand in the way of their own interests. Gladly, had they the power, would they turn the Sabbath into a work-day for the many that it might become (as on the Continent) a play-day for the few. Their own domestics and workpeople are over-driven, and unscrupulously deprived of Sabbath and sanctuary privileges. Where even the plea of humanity is disregarded, the plea of religion is not likely to be allowed much weight.

II. OF THE ALARMS FELT BY A TYRANT AT THE UPRISING OF FREE ASPIRATIONS IN THE SUBJECTS OF HIS TYRANNY. Pharaoh shrewdly foresaw the consequences of a further spread of these new-fangled ideas among the people. The request to go and sacrifice would not be long in being followed by a demand for freedom. Despotism and the spirit of liberty cannot coalesce. The tyrant knows that his power is put in peril the moment people begin to think for themselves—to cherish dreams of freedom—to be moved by religious enthusiasms. His rule can only be maintained at the cost of the extinction in his subjects of the last vestige of mental and spiritual independence. If a spiritual movement like this which sprang up in Israel begins to show itself, it must be stamped out at once, and at whatever cost of suffering and bloodshed. Whatever tends to produce such movements is looked on with hostility. This applies to all kinds of despotisms—civil, ecclesiastical, industrial, social. Hence, under despotic governments, the gagging of the press, suppression of free institutions, restriction of liberty of speech, ostracism of men of public spirit, and opposition to progress and to liberal ideas generally. Hence the antagonism of the Roman Church to learning and science, with the baleful effects which have followed from that antagonism in countries where her influence is supreme (see Laveleye on ' Protestantism and Catholicism in their Bearings upon the Liberty and Prosperity of Nations '; and histories of the Reformation in Spain and Italy). " It has been wittily said, that in Madrid, provided you avoid saying anything concerning government, or religion, or politics, or morals, or statesmen, or bodies of reputation, or the opera, or any other public amusement, or any one who is engaged in any business, you may print what you please, under correction of two or three censors " (McCrie). Hence the antipathy of the slave-drivers of industry—those who grind the faces of the poor, making their profit out of their poverty and helplessness—to the diffusion of intelligence among the masses. Hence, in slave-holding countries, the laws against teaching slaves to read, etc. The slave-holder cannot afford to encourage the spread of intelligence, of anything which will enable his slave to realise his manhood. But tyranny of this kind is self-condemned. 1. As *unnatural*. It requires the extinction and suppression of everything noble and good in human nature. It sets itself in opposition to intelligence, freedom, progress, religion, and all holy and spiritual aspirations. 2. As *inhuman*. In consolidating its dominion, it stoops to perpetrate the grossest cruelties. Think of the work of the Inquisition! Think of the blood that has been shed on the shrine of civil liberty! Think of the George Harrises of slavery! "What business had his slave to be marching round the country, inventing machines, and holding up his head among gentlemen? He'd soon put a stop to it. He'd take him back, and put him to hoeing and digging, and see if he'd step about so smart?" ('Uncle Tom's Cabin.') See also, 3. Its *weakness*. Tyranny of this kind cannot endure. Under the influence of ideas from without, a mental and moral awakening is certain to come some day, and the tyrant's power is doomed.

III. OF THE PITILESS CRUELTY OF WHICH MEN GET TO BE CAPABLE IN THE PURSUIT OF INIQUITOUS ENDS: vers. 6—9. Pharaoh was determined to keep the Hebrews in slavery; and so, to suppress this new spirit of discontent which had broken out among them, he must heat their furnace sevenfold, and heap cruelty on cruelty. He may have urged the plea of state necessity, and justified himself by the reflection that less severe measures would not have served his purpose—that he was driven to cruelty by the logic of events. A vain plea in any case, and one which only a heart rendered callous by a long course of inhumanity could have brought itself to entertain. Yet Pharaoh was thus far right, that, once a career of inquity has been entered upon, events take the matter out of the sinner's hands, and leave him no alternative but either to abandon his evil courses, or be driven on from one cruelty to a worse. And, contemporaneously with the movement of events, there is going on a hardening of the heart, which makes the cruelty possible. It is wonderful what pitiless deeds men get to be capable of, who have others in their power, and who acknowledge no higher law than their own interests. We have only to recall the iniquities of the slave-trade, connived at by many of our most respectable merchants; the inhumanities attendant on the employment of women and young children in mines and factories, as brought to light by Parliamentary Commissions; the former semi-brutal condition of agricultural labourers; the underpaying of needle-women; the horrors of the "sweating system;" the instances of cruelty and rapacity exhibited in the emigration trade, which are described as "among the most atrocious that have ever disgraced human nature" (Chambers's 'Encyc.'); the reckless disregard of the lives of sailors in their being sent to sea in heavily-laden and untrustworthy ships (Plimsoll)—to see how far, even in a civilised country, the thirst of gain will carry men, under circumstances where they can count upon impunity, and evade the censure of public opinion. A Pharaoh could hardly do worse. "Small manufacturers, working with insufficient capital, and in times of depression not having the wherewith to meet their engagements, are often obliged to become dependants on the wholesale houses with which they deal; and are then cruelly taken advantage of . . . . He (the manufacturer) is obliged to work at the wholesaler's terms, and ruin almost certainly follows . . . . As was said to us by one of the larger silk-hosiers, who had watched the destruction of many of his smaller brethren—'They may be spared for a while as a cat spares a mouse; but they are sure to be eaten up in the end . . . .' We read that in Hindostan, the ryots, when crops fall short, borrow from the Jews to buy seed, and once in their clutches are doomed. It seems that our commercial world can furnish parallels" (H. Spencer).

Learn: 1. To avoid the *beginning* of a course of injustice. 2. To guard against the hardening of the heart by cruelty. 3. To have an open ear to the cry of the oppressed, and a readiness to support every righteous measure for their protection and relief. 4. See in Pharaoh's tyranny an image of the pitiless tyranny of Satan. He, too, is absolutely merciless in the power he obtains over us. His service is one which grows increasingly more rigorous. He, too, would have us make bricks without straw, driving us on by our lusts and passions in pursuit of ends impossible (in his service) of attainment. More acute than Pharaoh, he gets the sinner himself to believe that it is "idle" to sacrifice to God, and by this means lures him to his service, where he soon binds him in chains more terrible and galling than any which earthly tyrant ever put upon his slaves.—J. O.

Vers. 6—14.—*The increase of trouble for God's people no proof of the failure of his purpose.* I. THE DEMANDS OF GOD PROVOKE THE WRATH OF THE UNGODLY. The mad persistence of Pharaoh in his injustice is marked—1. In his haste: his commands were issued "the same day." 2. In the severity of the decree: they should find their own straw, and yet deliver the same number of bricks. 3. In his determination to have his commands obeyed. It is not meant to be an idle threat: the overseers are "straitly charged." When God's word is resisted the soul is inflamed to greater evil. The unregenerate spirit is the same everywhere. God's claim has only to be pressed home to be repelled in the same fashion.

II. THE WAY TO DELIVERANCE SOMETIMES LIES THROUGH DEEPER TROUBLE. Israel's case was now harder than it was before (vers. 11—14), and solely because God had arisen to fight for them: but it was the last struggle of a doomed foe. It is thus— 1. In the Church's struggle with the world of unbelief: God's message is met with scorn, repression, and opposition of science falsely so called. But these shall vanish away like smoke, and their utterances and deeds will at last be the monuments of their infamy. 2. In the contest with the dominion of sin in the soul. The might of sin is felt most when the Spirit's call is first heard; but God has said, "Let my people go," and the wrath of the enemy will soon be swallowed up in his destruction. 3. In the breaking of the yoke of death. When God's call is heard, "Come up higher," we wrestle in pain and mortal weakness with the dread adversary. He seems to triumph. But the last tie that bound us is broken, and we bid an eternal farewell to the bondage and the grief.—U.

EXPOSITION.

Vers. 10—14.—The command of Pharaoh had gone forth—no straw was to be provided for the Israelites, they were themselves to gather straw. The taskmasters could not soften the edict; they could only promulgate it (vers. 10, 11). And the Israelites could only choose between rebelling and endeavouring to obey. To rebel seemed hopeless; Moses and Aaron did not advise rebellion, and so the attempt was made to carry out Pharaoh's behest (ver. 12). But experience proved that obedience to it was impossible. Though the people did their best, and the native officers set over them did their best, and the Egyptian taskmasters hurried them on as much as possible (ver. 13), the result was that the tale of bricks fell short. Then, according to a barbarous practice said to be even now not unknown in Egypt (Kalisch), the native officers who had not delivered in the appointed "tale of bricks" were bastinadoed, suffering agonies for no fault of their own (ver. 16), but because the people had been set an impossible task.

Ver. 10.—**The taskmasters . . . went out,** *i.e.* quitted the royal palace to which they had been summoned (ver. 6), and proceeded to the places where the people worked. The vicinity of Zoan was probably one great brickfield.

Thus saith Pharaoh. The exact words of Pharaoh (ver. 7) are not repeated, but modified, according to men's ordinary practice in similar cases.

Ver. 11.—**Get you straw where ye can find it.** Straw was not valued in Egypt. Reaping was effected either by gathering the ears, or by cutting the stalks of the corn at a short distance below the heads; and the straw was then left almost entirely upon the ground. Grass was so plentiful that it was not required for fodder, and there was no employment of it as litter in farmyards. Thus abundance of straw could be gathered in the cornfields after harvest; and as there were many harvests, some sort of straw was probably obtainable in the Delta at almost all seasons of the year. To collect it, however, and chop it small, as required in brickmaking, consumed much time, and left too little for the actual making of the bricks.

Ver. 12.—**The people were scattered abroad throughout all the land of Egypt.** The expression used is hyperbolical, and not to be understood literally. A tolerably wide dispersion over the central and eastern portions of the Delta is probably intended. **Stubble instead of straw.** Rather, "stubble for the straw." *Teben,* the word translated straw, seems to be properly "chopped straw" (*stramenta minutim concisa,* Cook). The Israelites, who had been accustomed to have this provided for them, gathered now long stalks of stubble in the fields, which they had subsequently to make into *teben* by chopping it into short bits.

Vers. 13, 14.—**The taskmasters hasted them.** The Egyptian overseers, armed with rods, went about among the toiling Israelites continually, and "hasted them" by dealing out blows freely on all who made any pause in their work. The unceasing toil lasted from morning to night; yet still the required "tale" could not be produced; and consequently the native officers, whose business it was to pro-

duce the "tale," were punished by the bastinado at the close of the day not giving in the proper amount. Kalisch observes—"Even now the Arabic fellahs, whose position is very analogous to that of the Israelites described in our text, are treated by the Turks in the same manner. Arabic overseers have to give an account of the labours of their countrymen to the Turkish taskmasters, who often chastise them mercilessly for the real or imputed offences of the Arabic workmen."

HOMILETICS.

Vers. 10—14.—*A blind obedience to the commands of tyrants not laudable.* The Egyptian taskmasters seem to have carried out their monarch's orders to the full, if not with inward satisfaction, at any rate without visible repugnance. They published abroad the orders given without in any way softening them (vers. 10, 11), harassed the Israelite people all day long by "hasting them" (ver. 13), and bastinadoed the Israelite officers at night (ver. 14). How different their conduct from that of the midwives, when another Pharaoh sought to make them the instruments of his cruelty! Weak women defied the tyrant and disobeyed his commands. Strong sturdy men were content to be his slavish tools and accomplices. But so it is often. "Out of weakness God perfects strength." He "makes the weak things of the world to confound the strong." And the consequence is, that the weak, who show themselves strong, obtain his approval and the enduring praise of men, like the midwives; while the strong, who show themselves weak, are condemned by him, and covered with everlasting obloquy, like these taskmasters.

Ver. 14.—*Vicarious suffering.* Vicarious suffering is a blessed thing only when undergone voluntarily. In all other cases it is unjust, oppressive, cruel. At the English court under the early Stuarts there was a boy who had to receive all the punishments deserved by the heir-apparent. This was a piece of detestable tyranny. The execution of children for the offences of their parents, which prevailed under the judges (Josh. vii. 24, 25) and the kings of Israel (2 Kings ix. 26) was still worse; and had not even the show of justice about it, since it was not accepted in lieu of the parents' suffering, but was additional to it. The Oriental system of punishing "head men" for any offence or default of those under their jurisdiction, goes on the idea that they can and ought to prevent such sins of commission or omission. But this idea is not in accord with facts. Frequently they cannot; sometimes they neither can nor ought. In all such cases the punishment inflicted is an injustice; and the system itself must consequently be regarded as no better than an organised and licensed tyranny. Yet large tracts of Asia and Africa groan under it. "How long, O Lord, how long?"

HOMILIES BY VARIOUS AUTHORS.

Vers. 10—15.—*Bricks without straw.* Tyrants seldom lack subordinates, as cruel as themselves, to execute their hateful mandates. Not only are these subordinates generally ready to curry favour with their lord by executing his orders with punctilious rigour, but, when they get to know that particular persons are in disfavour, they find a positive delight in bullying and insulting the unhappy victims, and in subjecting them to every species of vexatious interference. The callous taskmasters entered heartily into Pharaoh's plans—withheld from the Israelites the straw, while requiring of them the full tale of bricks, and then mercilessly beating the officers for failing to get the people to accomplish the impossible. View in their behaviour—

I. A PICTURE OF THE NOT INFREQUENT TREATMENT OF MAN BY HIS FELLOW-MAN. Society abounds in tyrants, who, like Pharaoh's taskmasters—1. Demand the unreasonable. 2. Expect the impossible. And the unreasonable in extreme cases is one with the impossible. 3. Are insolent and violent in enforcing their unreasonable demands. The workman, *e.g.*, is scolded because he cannot, in a given time, produce work of given quantity and quality, though production to the extent required is shown to involve a physical impossibility. The public servant is abused because he has not wrought miracles in his particular department, though perhaps he has received neither the material nor the moral support to which he was entitled. The clergyman is blamed for deficiency in pulpit power, while endless calls are made upon him for work of other kinds, which dissipate his energies, and eat into his time for study. The wife is rated by her husband, because comforts and luxuries are not forthcoming, which his wasteful expenditure in other directions prevents her from obtaining. With like unreasonableness, buyers in commercial houses are rated because they cannot buy, and sellers because they cannot sell; and it is broadly hinted to the latter that if means are not discovered for effecting sales, and disposing of perhaps worthless goods, the penalty will be dismissal. And there are worse tyrannies behind. Most iniquitous of all is the system of exacting work from the necessitous, which imposes an unnatural and injurious strain upon their bodily and mental powers, while renumerating it by a pittance barely sufficient to keep soul and body together. The straw of which these bricks are made is the flesh and blood of living human beings—the fibre of despairing hearts. In short, bricks without straw are asked wherever work is required which overtaxes the strength and capability of those from whom it is sought, or where the time, means, or assistance necessary for accomplishing it is denied. To rage, scold, threaten, or punish, because feats which border on the impossible are not accomplished, is simply to play over again the part of Pharaoh's taskmasters.

II. A CONTRAST TO THE TREATMENT WHICH MAN RECEIVES FROM GOD. Unbelief and slothfulness, indeed, would fain persuade us of the opposite. Their voice is, " I knew thee that thou art a hard man, reaping where thou hast not sown," etc. (Matt. xxv. 24). And it may be pleaded in support of this that God's demands in respect of obedience go far beyond the sinner's powers. He inherits a depraved nature, yet he is held guilty for its actings, and the demand stands unchanged, " Thou shalt love the Lord thy God with all thy heart," etc. (Deut. vi. 5). The standard by which he is judged is that of absolute holiness, while yet it is admitted that he is naturally incapable of a single holy thought or resolve. But in this way of putting matters various things are forgotten. 1. The law of duty is a fixed quantity, and even God, by an act of will, cannot remove a sinner from under its obligations. 2. There is an obvious distinction between natural and moral inability. The hardened thief cannot plead his incorrigible thievishness as an excuse for non-fulfilment of the duties of honesty. It is his sin that he *is* thievish. 3. Depraved beings are condemned for being what they are (evil-disposed, cruel, lustful, selfish, etc.), and for the bad things which they do, not for the good things which they ought to do, but are now incapable of doing. The devil, *e.g.*, is condemned because he *is* a devil, and acts devilishly; not because it is still expected of him that he will love God with all his heart, etc., and because he fails to do this. But the true answer, as respects God's treatment of mankind, is a very different one. The sinner is not to be allowed to forget that if he has fallen and destroyed himself, God has brought him help. The very God against whom he has sinned desires his recovery, and has provided for it. He has made provision in Christ for the atonement (covering) of his sins. He asks nothing from him of a spiritual nature which his grace is not promised to enable him to accomplish. God presents himself in the Gospel, not as the sinner's exacting taskmaster, but as his friend and Saviour, ready, however multiplied and aggravated his offences—though they be as scarlet and red like crimson—to make them as the snow and wool (Is. i. 18). True, the sinner cannot renew his own heart, but surely he is answerable for the response he makes to the outward word, and to the teachings and drawings of the Spirit, who, given his submission, will willingly renew it for him. True also he cannot, even in the gracious state, render perfect obedience, but over and against this is to be put the truth that perfect obedience is not required of any in order to justification, and that, if only he is faithful, his imperfections will, for Christ's sake, be graciously forgiven him. And the same just and gracious principles rule in God's actings with his servants. Service is accepted "according to what a man hath, and not according to that he hath not" (2 Cor. viii. 12). No making bricks without straw here. The servant with the two talents is held only responsible for the two, not for five (Matt. xxv. 23). Justice, tempered by grace, is the rule for all.—J. O.

EXPOSITION.

Vers. 15—19.—Smarting under the sense of injustice, the Israelite officers "came and cried to Pharaoh" (ver. 15), supposing that he could not have intended such manifest unfairness and cruelty. They were conscious to themselves of having done their utmost, and of having failed simply because the thing required was impossible. Surely the king would understand this, if they pointed it out, and would either allow straw as before, or diminish the number of the bricks. But the king had no desire for justice, and did not even pretend to it. He asked for no particulars, ordered no inquiry into the ground of complaint; but turned upon the complainants with the cuckoo cry—"*Idle, idle* yourselves—else ye had no time to come here ; go, work—go, work." Then the officers felt that they were indeed "in evil case" (ver. 19)—the king was determined not to do justice—no hope remained—they must be beaten again and again, until they died of the punishment (ver. 21).

Ver. 15.—**Came and cried.** The shrill "cry" of Orientals when making complaint has often been noticed by travellers, and is probably here alluded to. **To Pharaoh.** See the "Introductory paragraph" at the beginning of the chapter, where it has been noticed that complainants had free access to the presence of Egyptian kings.

Ver. 16.—**They say to us.** Or, "they keep saying to us." The participle is used, which implies continuance or repetition. **The fault is in thine own people.** Literally, "Thine own people is in fault," or "sins."

Ver. 17.—**Ye are idle,** etc. Compare ver. 8. Pharaoh is evidently pleased with his "happy thought." It seems to him clever, witty, humorous, to tax overworked people with idleness ; and equally clever to say to religious people—"Your religion is a mere pretence. You do not want to worship. You want a holiday." We may remark further that idleness and hypocrisy were two sins of the deepest dye, according to Egyptian notions.

Ver. 18.—**Go therefore now and work**—*i.e.* "Off with you to the brickfields at once, and get to your own special work of superintendence, which you are neglecting so long as you remain here. It is useless to remain. I reject both of your requests. Straw shall not be given ; and the tale of bricks required shall be no less."

Ver. 19.—**The officers . . . did see that they were in evil case.** See the "Introductory paragraph" to this section, and comp. ver. 21.

HOMILETICS.

Vers. 15—18.—*A wicked man's persistence in wrong-doing.* Pharaoh when he first gave the order to withhold straw (ver. 7), may not have known the amount of misery he was causing. He may have meant no more than to give the people full occupation, and so prevent such gatherings as that from which Moses and Aaron had come (ch. iv. 29—31), when they appeared before him with their demands. He may not have realised to himself the idea that he was setting his bondsmen an impossible task. But now this fact was brought home to him, and he was asked, as a matter of simple justice, either to let straw be furnished as before, or to allow some diminution in the number of the bricks. It can scarcely be doubted that he knew and felt the demand made to be just. There were the officers before him with the wheals upon their backs. Would they have incurred the severe punishment, could they by any possibility have avoided it ? Pharaoh must have known that they would not. But he would not relent. As he had begun, he would continue. He had been more cruel than he meant ; but he did not care—it was only Hebrews and bondsmen who had suffered ; what mattered their agonies ? So he dismisses the complainants with jeers and scoffs : "Ye are idle, ye are hypocrites; go, work." So bad men almost always go on from bad to worse by a "facile descent;" severity deepens into cruelty, unkindness into injustice, religious indifference into impiety. Stop, then, the beginnings of wrong-doing. *Principiis obsta.* Crush the nascent germs of vice in thy heart, O man ! Master them, or they will master thee !

Ver. 16.—*Sufferings, even at the hand of lawful authorities, not always deserved.*
"Thy servants are beaten; but the fault is in thine own people." Punishment often
visits the wrong back. Kings commit injuries or follies, and their subjects suffer.
Employers are greedy of gain, and their "hands" must work overtime, go without sleep,
trench on the Sunday rest. Wholesale tradesmen adulterate goods, and retail traders
are blamed and lose custom. Justice itself is often at fault, and punishes the wrong
person—sometimes by a mere mistake, as when the wrong man is hanged for a murder;
but sometimes also through a defect in the law itself which judges have to administer;
as when Christians were delivered to the wild beasts for not sacrificing to the divinity
of the emperor, or Protestants were burnt at the stake for denying transubstantiation. It
is not to be assumed that the law is always right. The law of any country at any time
is only the expression of the will of those who are in authority at the time, and has no
more divinity or sacredness about it than they have. Those who transgress the law
will, of course, be punished for it; but that fact proves nothing as to their good- or ill-
desert. The greatest benefactors of mankind have had to set human law at defiance,
and to endure its penalties. Their answer to the authorities who persecute them might
constantly be, "Thy servants are beaten, but the fault is in thine own people."

HOMILIES BY VARIOUS AUTHORS.

Vers. 15—20.—*Unheeded expostulation.* Pharaoh's treatment of the officers of the
children of Israel, when they appeared before him to expostulate with him on his cruelty,
betrays his consciousness of the injustice of his cause.

I. AN UNJUST CAUSE BETRAYS ITSELF—1. *By refusal to listen to reason.* The
Hebrews had reason on their side, and Pharaoh had not. And because he had not, and
knew it, he would not hear them, would not enter into any argument with them. This
is the sure mark of a weak cause. People are usually willing enough to defend any of
their doings which they think defensible. But when causes are indefensible, and they
know this, they do not care to have the light let in upon them. "Every one that doeth
evil hateth the light, neither cometh to the light, lest his deeds should be reproved"
(John iii. 20). 2. *By clutching at flimsy and trumped-up pretexts.* "Ye are idle; ye
are idle; therefore ye say," etc. (ver. 17). Pharaoh knew as well as any that they were
not idle, but it served his purpose to put forward this pretence. 3. *By falling back in
the end on the right of the strong hand* (ver. 16). This is the tyrant's unfailing resort.
If he cannot argue, he can compel. If he cannot justify his courses, he can fall back
upon his power to enforce submission. His might is his right. Pharaoh had the power,
and he meant to use it, so the Israelites might save themselves the trouble of expostulating. This sort of authority, resting on force, without support in righteousness or
reason, is necessarily precarious. It can, in the nature of things, only last so long as the
power to compel remains with it. No throne is so insecure as that propped up on
bayonets.

II. AN UNJUST CAUSE ADHERED TO AND DEFENDED—1. *Reacts injuriously upon the
moral nature.* The refusal to listen to expostulation was a new stage in Pharaoh's
hardening. Besides fortifying his determination to brook no interference in his courses,
and strengthening the cruelty of his disposition—anew called into action by the increased
oppression of the Hebrews—it necessarily reacted to deprive him of a fresh portion of his
moral susceptibility. This is the Nemesis of sin; it leaves the sinner less susceptible
with each new appeal that is resisted; it darkens while it indurates; not only
strengthens him in evil courses, but increasingly disqualifies him for perceiving the truth
and reasonableness of the dissuasives that are addressed to him. Pharaoh's hardening still
moves in the region of ordinary morals (see on vers. 1—4). The first step in it was the
recoil of his pride and wilfulness against what he knew to be the righteous demand of
Moses and Aaron. Another step is the rejection of this righteous appeal. 2. *Exposes
the tyrant to the just judgment of God.* The Hebrews were helpless to resist Pharaoh,
but there was Another, whose question, "Wherefore dealest thou thus with thy servants?" he would not be able so easily to set aside. God was keeping the account, and
for all these things would yet call him to judgment (Eccl. xi. 9; xii. 14); while the
king's temporary success in his ways, building him up in a presumptuous self-

confidence, and confirming him in his boast of superiority to Jehovah, was a further step in his hardening—a ripening for destruction. 3. *Is a fresh call for God to interfere on behalf of the oppressed.* This new wrong, instead of leading the Israelites to despair, should only have lent fresh vehemence to their prayers, for it gave them a new plea with which to urge their cause. " For shall not God avenge his own elect, which cry to him day and night, though he bear long with them " (Luke xviii. 7).—J. O.

Vers. 4 18. *Pharaoh's first response: his answer in deed.* Pharaoh has given a proud verbal refusal to the request of Moses: but he is not contented to stop with words. The first result, discouraging and discrediting of Moses' application, is still further to increase burdens and hardships already scarcely tolerable.

I. CONSIDER HOW THIS ADDITIONAL SEVERITY TO ISRAEL ORIGINATED—that is, how it originated as far as Pharaoh's part in it was concerned. It came through *his utterly mistaken notions as to Moses and Israel.* Pharaoh, as an alert politician, was bound to inquire how it was that Moses had been led to prefer this request; and he came to the conclusion that the people had too much leisure time—did their work far too easily—and thus left an opportunity for the success of any designing demagogue, such as he judged Moses to be. And, indeed, Pharaoh's conjecture showed a very plausible appearance of shrewd insight into human nature. All such readers of this narrative as utterly disbelieve the reality of Divine intervention and supremacy in human affairs, will say that Pharaoh was not far wrong; whereas he was utterly wrong. Moses went into the presence of Pharaoh because the power of God constrained him. He would have gone anywhere to escape the task, if only he could have done it with safety and self-respect. Pharaoh little knew what a profound sense of unworthiness dwelt in the breast of Moses. Other feelings might come and go, mount to flow and sink to ebb; that remained, more penetrating and subduing the more he had to do with God, and the more he had to do with Israel. Pharaoh was also utterly mistaken *as to the people.* The request for liberty had not come from them. They of their own accord and carnal judgment would never have thought of such a request. As soon might the helpless victim of a raging beast of prey turn to it with a real expectation of mercy. The prisoner may devise many plans of escape: but he would reckon it a mere provocative of more painful and stringent captivity, if he addressed to his gaoler a formal request for liberty. Pharaoh then, in his ignorance of God, proved ignorant and mistaken in the whole of his policy. Every view is mistaken, egregiously mistaken, that leaves out the thought of God as a living, intimate, ever-watchful Power.

II. CONSIDER THAT ALL THIS CRUEL TREATMENT DID NOTHING AT ALL FOR PHARAOH. If it had done anything, however little, to delay the final disaster, it would have been something to say: but it did nothing at all. He treated Moses as a mere politician, and Israel as being only in a state of incipient insurrection. If such had been the reality of things, then his policy, however damnable for its cruelty, would have merited at least this admission, that there was a real adaptation of means to ends. But Pharaoh was as yet utterly unconscious of his real enemy. His mind was in a state of darkness, deep as that outward darkness which later overspread his land. All his efforts, summed up and stated in the largest way, simply came to this—that he was making very bitter the temporal life of a fleeting generation. But he himself had not arrested by a single step the advance of a righteous and omnipotent God. Struggling against the visible Moses and the visible Israel, he knew nothing of how to resist the invisible God. A man may rage about, putting out all candles and lamps, leaving us for awhile in darkness, but he has not retarded the sunrise by even the minutest fragment of time. This is our glory and our comfort, if we have the spirit of Christ dwelling in us, that we are contending against one who has only carnal weapons. *We* are not allowed to take carnal weapons; they are of no use to us; and never should we forget that they are of no use to those who are against us. Pharaoh did not delay God's liberating work; that work went on in all the majestic ease of its divinity, amid the smitings of the oppressor and the wailings of the oppressed. Making bricks without straw was mere child's-play compared with the enterprise on which Pharaoh was now embarked. He might as well have gone out with the sword and spear against the pestilence and the famine, as against Israel with a mere increase of oppression and cruelty.

III. THIS ADDITIONAL CRUELTY SHOWED THE IMPERATIVE NEED OF DIVINE INTERVENTION. If Pharaoh was powerless to delay the advance of God, he was very powerful to shut out interference from any other quarter. Help in God, sure and sufficient help, but help only in God, was one of the great lessons which all these painful years were meant to teach Israel. Pharaoh had unmistakable power of the human, despotic, might-makes-right sort over Israel. As the inquisitor by an easy nod signifies to give the thumbscrew another turn, so Pharaoh had only to send out his royal wish, and all the taskmasters had Israel at once in fresh agony. And just so we have to be taught by a bitter experience that as Christ is a Saviour from sin, with all its fatal fruits, so he is the only Saviour. The first attempt at a real protest and resistance against sin brings out all its power. Though the sinner's miseries do not begin when Christ the accredited deliverer makes his first approach to deliver, there is nevertheless a distinct accession to them. Christ cannot challenge the power of sin in any of us without rousing up into intense activity the evil already working in our breasts. Pharaoh was not really a more powerful ruler after the visit of Moses than he was before; but the disposition and power then became manifest. The hearts of the generation in the midst of which Christ lived and died were not of exceptional malignity or obduracy. The generation immediately before and the generation immediately after, would have treated him in exactly the same way. But it was necessary for him to draw out sin into a full revelation of its hideous potency, in order that it might be made perfectly clear that none but himself could deal with it. True, Pharaoh was glorying in what was only a fabric of delusions and a refuge of lies; but, frail though it was, no breath of man had strength enough to blow it down. None but God could make the effectual and dissipating storm to descend upon it.—Y.

Ver. 15—chap. vi. ver. 1.—*The troubled find consolation in God only. The three cries.* I. ISRAEL'S EXPOSTULATION WITH PHARAOH (15—19). They complain to him of the wrongs they suffer; but he who does not hear God will not listen to man. 1. It was reasonable to expect that their remonstrance might lead to redress. Pharaoh's decree might have been issued under momentary irritation. 2. They came with humility and modesty. They brought no railing accusation. They used no threats. They did not even make a silent show of their strength. And yet the only outcome of their appeal is deeper grief, more utter hopelessness (19). They who have no hope but in man will find little to sustain them. II. THEIR UPBRAIDING OF MOSES AND AARON (20, 21). 1. They spoke truth. The demand for liberty of worship had been seized by Pharaoh as a pretext for more oppressive measures. 2. They did not speak the whole truth. God and his purpose were kept out of sight. They were counted as nothing. How often is this done in our despondency and murmuring! 3. Their reproaches, though met by silence and grief equal to their own, brought no help to them. There is as little help in upbraiding friends for failure as in spreading their injustice before foes. III. MOSES' CRY TO GOD. 1. He "returned to the Lord." He did not seek to unburden his soul even to Aaron. The first step to help is to seek God's presence. 2. The holy boldness of his prayer. The grieved spirit is poured out. There is nothing kept back. God does not complain of our boldness, but of our restraining prayer before him. 3. God's answer (vi. 1). (1) This very failure shows God's truth (iv. 21). (2) God shall fight for them: "Now shalt thou see what *I* will do to Pharaoh." (3) Pharaoh's wrath and power will serve only to make their deliverance perfect. He will "drive them out of his land." Israel found no consolation; Moses does.—U.

EXPOSITION.

Vers. 20, 21.—On quitting the presence of Pharaoh, the officers of the Israelites, burning with the sense of the injustice done them, and deeply apprehensive with respect to their own future, found Moses and Aaron waiting in the precincts of the court to know the result of their application. It need cause no surprise that they poured out their pent-up indignation upon *them.* Were not Moses and Aaron the sole cause of the existing state of things? Did not the extreme affliction of the people, did not their own sufferings in the past, did not their apprehended sufferings in the future, originate wholly in the seductive words which the two brothers had addressed to them at the assembly of the people? (ch. iv. 29—31).

Accordingly, they denounced, almost cursed their officious would-be deliverers (ch. v. 21). "The Lord look upon you, and judge" between you and us, whether the blame of this whole matter does not lie upon you, its initiators—you have made us to be abhorred in the sight of Pharaoh, and of the Egyptians generally—you have brought us into danger of our lives—the Lord judge you!"

Ver. 20.—**Who stood in the way.** Rather, "who waited to meet them." It was not accident, but design, that had brought the two brothers to the spot. They were as anxious as the officers to know what course Pharaoh would take—whether he would relax the burthens of the people or no—whether he would have compassion or the contrary.

Ver. 21.—**They said unto them.** The officers were too full of their wrongs to wait until questioned. They took the word, and, without relating the result of their interview, implied it. **The Lord look upon you, and judge,** they said, meaning "the Lord (Jehovah)

consider your conduct, and judge it"—not exactly, "condemn it and punish it" (Keil and Delitzsch)—but "pass-sentence on it," "judge whether it has been right or not." We make this appeal **because** ye have at any rate done *us* a great injury—**ye have made our savour to be abhorred in the eyes of Pharaoh.** (Note the mixed metaphor, which shows perhaps rather that "in the eyes" had lost its original meaning, and come to signify no more than "with" or "in respect of," than that the literal meaning of "making a person's savour to stink" did not occur to the writer.) Nay, ye have done more—**ye have put a sword in the hand of his servants to slay us.** That is to say, "ye have armed them with a weapon wherewith we expect that they will take our lives." Either they will beat us to death—and death is a not infrequent result of a repeated employment of the bastinado—or when they find that punishment unavailing they will execute us as traitors. On the use of the bastinado as a punishment in Egypt, see Chabas, 'Mélanges Egyptologiques,' 3ᵐᵉ série, vol. i. pp. 100—6.

HOMILETICS.

Ver. 21.—*The servants of God liable to reproach from friends no less than enemies.* Moses and Aaron had borne the reproaches and scoffs of Pharaoh (vers. 4—8) without flinching. It was natural that an enemy should revile them. Pharaoh might tax them with idleness and insincerity in religion, if he pleased. The stab did not penetrate very deep, nor cause a very grievous smart. But when their brethren turned upon them and uttered reproaches, it was different. Then the wound went to the heart; the pain was bitter, scarce endurable. It made them misdoubt themselves. Had they really not acted for the best? Had they been self-seeking, or vainglorious, or reckless, or even injudicious? Such thoughts will always occur even to the best men, if on their plans seeming to have miscarried their friends reproach them. The best men best know their own frailty, and how easy it is for man to mar God's work by his own imperfections. It requires a very brave soul to bear up against the reproaches of friends, especially when there seems to be a ground for them. The more careful therefore should friends be not to reproach God's servants causelessly, or unless they can point out where they have been wrong. Actions are not to be always judged by their results, or, at any rate, not by their immediate results. Moses and Aaron had done quite right; they had obeyed God; they were bound to act as they had acted. It had not pleased God to give success to their efforts as yet. The officers should have had patience, should have prayed to God for relief, but should have forborne from reproaching the innocent.

HOMILIES BY VARIOUS AUTHORS.

Vers. 20—23.—*Murmuring and faith.* The Israelites were naturally sorely disappointed at the issue of the interview with Pharaoh; and with the unreasonableness so often seen in those whose expectations have received a check, they turned on Moses and Aaron, and accused these innocent men of being the authors of their misfortune. Moses and Aaron themselves were almost as dumbfounded as their accusers at the turn events had taken; but one of them, at least, behaved with wisdom. The Israelites accused men: Moses took his complaint to God, and opened up to *him* all the soreness of his heart. This portion of the narrative suggests the following reflections:—

I. GOD'S PROVIDENCE OFTEN ASSUMES AN ASPECT OF GREAT MYSTERY TO US. It did so to Moses and the Israelites (vers. 22, 23). They had concluded that now that

God had taken up their cause, their trials and sorrows were at an end; but in entertaining so comfortable a hope, they found they were deceived. The first step on the road to the promised deliverance had plunged them into a worse plight than ever. They had almost felt the breath of liberty on their cheeks, when suddenly their hopes are dashed from them, and the situation darkens till in its pitiless rigour it becomes well-nigh unendurable. So God's providence is often to the godliest a sore and perplexing mystery. It is not merely that things are not going as we wish, or as fast as we expect—this need not surprise us, though oftentimes it does—but that Jehovah seems acting contrary to his own perfections, to his character, to his revealed purpose, to the promise on which he has encouraged us to trust. The wicked prosper; the righteous are afflicted (Ps. xxxvii.; lxxiii.). Prayers seem unanswered, and the hopes we had begun to cherish, the expectations we had built upon his Word, are bitterly disappointed. The race seems to the swift, and the battle to the strong of this world, while "waters of a full cup are wrung out" to the saints whom God has pledged himself to bless and to protect. This is what distresses us, and the distress is not surprising.

II. THE MYSTERY WHICH MEETS US IN GOD'S PROVIDENCE ACTS AS A TEST OF CHARACTER. It drove Moses to prayer, but the multitude to murmurings and reproaches. As this storm burst over Israel, the thoughts of many hearts would be revealed (Luke ii. 35). Doubters would curse themselves for trusting to one whom, they would declare, they had always suspected of deceiving them; the timid would be heard reiterating, "We told you it would come to this; we saw it from the first!" while the profane would break out into open blasphemies, and the superficial crowd—those who had been most carried away by the enthusiasm—would groan and weep in utter disconsolateness, and pour out rash accusations against Heaven and against Moses and Aaron, who had brought them into all this trouble. Yet with foolish inconsistency they would call on the God they were mistrusting to judge between them and the men who had brought to them his message (ver. 21). Comp. Christian and Pliable at the Slough of Despond in 'Pilgrim's Progress.' Mystery in God's providence, in itself a moral necessity and inevitable, is thus used by him for important ends in the testing and disciplining of character. It brings to light our weaknesses; sifts the chaff from the wheat; educates us to trust; convinces us of ignorance; disenchants us of illusive hopes; leads us to prayer and wrestling with God. Thus it prepares us for further discoveries of the Divine wisdom when the time comes for the veil being removed, and educates us for higher service.

III. THE MYSTERY WHICH ENSHROUDS GOD'S PROVIDENCE ARISES FROM OUR PARTIAL AND IMPERFECT COMPREHENSION OF HIS PLAN. Had God's purpose been simply to get Israel out of Egypt in the easiest way possible, and with least cost of suffering to the people, the permission of this new cruelty would indeed have been inexplicable. But it is not in this way, or for such ends, or on these terms, that God conducts the government of his world. The error of Israel lay in looking on this one little bit of an unfinished work, and in judging of it without reference to the whole design of which it was a part. For God's purpose was not merely that the people should be delivered, but that they should be delivered in such a way, and with such accompaniments of power and judgment, as should illustriously glorify his own perfections, and print the memory of his goodness on their hearts for ever; while, as regards Pharaoh, his design was to glorify his power upon him (ch. ix. 16), and make him an example to all after ages of the folly of resisting the Almighty. This being the end, it was obviously indispensable that events should not be unduly hastened, but allowed, as far as possible, to take a natural course. Time and scope must be given to Pharaoh to develop his real disposition, and the development must not be prematurely interfered with. The people must be led by a way they knew not, and in paths they had not known; the way chosen could not be the absolutely shortest, but must include many turnings and windings, and even seem at times to be bending backwards; but the end would be "to make darkness light before them, and crooked things straight" (Is. xlii. 16). And this is truly the explanation of all our difficulties with regard to Divine providence. It is not God who is at fault, but our own haste and shortsightedness, that perceive not all the ends he has in view, nor how wonderfully he is working towards those ends by the very circumstances which perplex and baffle us. We know but "in part" (1 Cor. xiii. 12). The thoughts of Infinite Wisdom cannot all be made plain to us. The little that is before us we see, but how much lies beyond which is involved in the hiding of his power! (Hab. iii. 4.) Our walking must be " by faith," not " by sight " (2 Cor. v. 7).—J. O.

Vers. 19—21.—*Thoughtless smiters of a brother in adversity.* This whole chapter particularly abounds in illustrations of human ignorance and error. We have seen in what dense darkness was the mind of Pharaoh; and under what utter misapprehensions he multiplied the sorrows of Israel. Now we are introduced to the leaders of Israel, treating Moses with equal injustice, because they are not able to see the difference between the human instrument and the Divine hand that holds it. No more than Pharaoh can they pierce through Moses to the mighty God behind him. It says in ch. iv. 31, that when the people saw the signs they believed; here is conduct which shows for how little their faith counted. As soon as they were set to make bricks without straw, their faith utterly vanished. Yet surely the truth of God remained. Present *human cruelty*, let it press ever so hard, cannot alter past manifestations of *Divine power*. The God who gave his Son the parable of the Sower was prepared for such a lapse into unbelief on the part of his people. His signs were like the seeds which found no depth of earth; when persecution arose because of the message of Moses, the people were straightway offended. Consider—

I. In what a state of mind Moses would be when these officers attacked him. We know from his own language (vers. 22, 23) what his state of mind was *after the attack*; but even before it he must have been a prey to deep grief and gloomy apprehensions. We may be sure that when these officers came upon him, they did not find proofs of indifference and carelessness in his face. He must have been very popular just after he had wrought the signs; as popular as Jesus was after he had fed the five thousand. Aaron, doubtless, had been instructed by him to enlarge on the history of Abraham, Isaac and Jacob, and bring out into the boldest relief the terms of the Divine promises. Thus the confidence and expectation of the people—a reception altogether beyond his hopes—would lift him also into a confidence and expectation all the more precious because of his previous despondency. And now, as he sees the condition of his brethren, that despondency is more painful than ever. No imagination of ours can exaggerate the perplexity and sadness into which Moses would be thrown.

II. Thus we are called to notice the indifference of Moses' brethren to his painful position. He thought a great deal more upon their sorrows than they did upon his. The grief of selfish people, in the reckless abandonment with which it speaks and acts, furnishes as painful evidence as we can find of the extent to which human nature has fallen from its first estate. It is a greedy, insatiable feeling. It is an awful thing to consider that the very concentration of our thoughts on our own sufferings makes us to increase the sufferings of others. Why, even when others are to blame, we might safely leave them to the observant, unforgetting God, to their own consciences, and to the ultimate harvest which every doer of wrong must reap; and very often they are not to blame at all. If only these smarting Israelites had been able, in a right spirit, to look at the heart of Moses, they would have seen occasion for supporting him with the greatest tenderness, gratitude, and patient endurance. What right had they to complain of Moses? He had told them a coherent, straightforward story, given them the signs; and they, in return, had believed him for the very works' sake. If there is any time when we should be *slow to speak*, it is in our sorrow. We do well then to be silent, until such times as God has purged out of our minds all selfish desires and groundless expectations. When all these are gone, and the truth which he alone can plant is also ripened, then we shall be able to say, " It was *good* for us to be afflicted;" at present Israel said that it was *bad*—as bad as bad could be—and Moses was the convenient person on whom they could lay the blame.

III. These officers had not insight enough to look beyond first consequences. They could not look through the pain of the present to a future which was only attainable through that present. Thus the disciples spoke in deep perplexity and disappointment concerning their missing Master as if he had vanished like a dream of the night. " We trusted that it had been he which should have redeemed Israel." So they spoke, not having appreciated his recent word, " Except a corn of wheat fall into the ground and die, it abideth alone." We shall do well to consider in every enterprise, that *first consequences are very deceptive.* When they bring hardship we must not, therefore, turn back; when they bring pleasure, we must not therefore conclude that still greater pleasures lie beyond. Israel had no right to make any assumptions whatever as to the first consequences of Moses' visit to Pharaoh. The true and only safe position for Israel to take up was this : "Here are these signs; they are signs that Jehovah has sent Moses, and is with him; let us accept them in full and patient reliance." A man does not dispute the truth of the finger-post which points him into the right road, because soon after he has passed it he comes to a worse bit of travelling than any he has had before. There is a profound and admonitory generalisation in that way of indicating Christian experience which puts the Slough of Despond so early in the pilgrim's journey : and if first consequences that bring hardship are to be mistrusted, surely we must be even more cautious when the first consequences are full of pleasure. Though we be told to remember *our Creator* in the days of our youth—his claims, his expectations, and his judgment-day—the danger is that we shall only too easily forget all this, and remember only that we are strong, ambitious, able to enjoy, and with abundant opportunities for enjoyment. We must always mistrust the mere pleasure of our senses ; the pleasure of tastes and likings. Liking a thing is never a sufficient reason for doing it; disliking never a sufficient reason for refusing to do it. God appeals to our prudence, to our conscience, to our pity, to our fears, but never to our tastes. And be it ever remembered that there is one first consequence which never deceives nor disappoints those who put themselves in the way of it. Do that which is right in the sight of God, and there is an immediate and pure pleasure at the heart, which all the waves and billows of adversity cannot wash away. For instance, we cannot believe for a moment that Moses regretted his compliance with the commands of Jehovah. They had been clear and imperative, steady and unrelaxing in their pressure on his conscience. The pain from the reproaches of Israel was bad enough ; but it would have been a far worse pain, if he had sought to flee from the test of the burning bush, and, Jonah-like, bury himself with his sheep in the very depths of the wilderness.—Y.

EXPOSITION.

Vers. 22, 23.—The two brothers made no reply to the words of the officers. Perhaps their hearts were too full for speech ; perhaps they knew not what to say. Whatever faith they had, it did no doubt seem a hard thing that their interference, Divinely ordered as it was, should have produced as yet nothing but an aggravation of their misery to the Israelite people. They could not understand the course of the Divine action. God had warned them not to expect success at once (ch. iii. 19 ; iv. 21) ; but he had said nothing of evil consequences following upon their first efforts. Thus we can well understand that the two brothers (and especially Moses, the more impetuous of them) were bitterly grieved and disappointed. They felt their cup of sorrow to be full—the reproaches of the officers made it overflow. Hence the bitterness of the complaint with which this chapter terminates, and which introduces the long series of precious promise, contained in the opening section of ch. vi.

Ver. 22.—**Moses returned unto the Lord.** We are not to understand that Moses had forsaken God and now "returned" to him but simply that in his trouble he had recourse

to God, took his sorrow to the Throne of Grace, and poured it out before the Almighty. A good example truly, and one which Christians in all their trials would do well to follow. **Lord, wherefore,** etc. The words, no doubt, are bold. They have been said to "approach to irreverence." But there are parallels to them, which have never been regarded as irreverent, in the Psalms : *e.g.* "O God, why hast thou cast us off for ever ? Why does thine anger smoke against the sheep of thy pasture ? " (Ps. lxxiv. 1.) "How long wilt thou hide thyself ? Where are thy former lovingkindnesses ? Wherefore hast thou made all men for nought ?" (Ps. lxxxix. 46-9), and the like. Kalisch seems right in saying that " the desponding complaint of Moses was not the result of disbelief or doubt, but the effort of a pious soul struggling after a deeper penetration into the mysteries of the Almighty."

Ver. 23.—**He hath done evil to this people.** See above, vers. 7—9, and ver. 14. Pharaoh had increased the burdens of the whole nation, and in this way "done evil" to them. He had also brought the punishment of scourging on a number of the chiefs. **Neither hast thou delivered thy people at all.** The promised deliverance (ch. iii. 8, 20) had not come— there was no sign of it—the people was suffering under a more cruel bondage than ever.

HOMILETICS.

Vers. 22, 23.—*The religious soul takes its griefs straight to God.* When our hopes are disappointed, when matters fall out otherwise than as we wish, when our enemies resist us, and our friends load us with reproach, how sweet to have a safe refuge whither we may betake ourselves, even the bosom of our most loving God! "Truly God *is* loving unto Israel." His hand may be slack, "as men count slackness; but it is not crippled or paralysed—it is always "mighty to save." Worldlings take their difficulties and their troubles to counsellors whom they deem wise, or to friends whom they regard as powerful, or to subordinates whom they think to be crafty, but never to God. The religious soul's first instinct in deep trouble is to seek solitude, to fly from man, and to pour out all its grief before the Lord. It will even venture, like Moses, to expostulate— to ask to be shown the reason why God has disappointed it and troubled it—to demand "Why is thy wrath so hot?" and "When wilt thou comfort me?" It does not doubt but that in the end all will be right, that God will do as he has promised; but it wants to be sustained, upheld, comforted as to the intermediate time—to be assured that God "has not forgotten to be gracious," that he is still nigh at hand, that he "will not leave it nor forsake it."

SECTION IV.—CHAPTER VI. 1—27.

Depression of Moses, and confirmation of his mission.

EXPOSITION.

CHAPTER VI.

Vers. 1–8.—The expostulation of Moses did not offend God. God gave him, in reply to it, a most gracious series of promises and assurances, well calculated to calm his fears, assuage his griefs, and comfort his heart; and he confirmed the whole to him by his name JEHOVAH, "the Only Existent," and therefore "the Eternal and Immutable." This name he had previously revealed to Moses at Mount Sinai, as his peculiar name, and the one by which he would choose to be called (ch. iii. 13—15). He had also told him to proclaim this name to the people. This command is now repeated (ver. 6) very solemnly; and with it are coupled the promises above alluded to. 1. That God would certainly bring the Israelites out of Egypt, despite the unwillingness of Pharaoh (vers. 1 and 6), 2. That he would do this "with a stretched-out arm," and by means of "great judgments" (ver. 6); 3. That he would keep the covenant which he had made with the patriarchs to give their descendants the land of Canaan (ver. 4) and would assuredly "bring in" the Israelites to that land, and "give it them for an heritage" (ver. 8).

Ver. 1.—**Now shalt thou see.** There was encouragement in the very word "Now." Moses' complaint was, that God delayed his coming, would not show himself, was "slack concerning his promise." In reply he is told that there is to be no longer any delay—the work is just about to commence. "*Now* shalt thou see." **With a strong hand shall he let them go.** The "strong hand" is not Pharaoh's, but God's. "By means of my strong hand" (or "overpowering might") "laid upon him shall he be induced to let them go," and similarly with the other clause. **Drive them out.** This phrase well expresses the final anxiety of Pharaoh to be rid of the Israelites. (See ch. xii. 31, 22.)

Ver. 2.—**And God spake.** The promise of the first verse was, apparently, given first, and was quite distinct from all the others—perhaps separated from them by an interval of hours, or days. It was especially addressed to Moses. The rest was in the main (ver. 6—8) a message to the people. **I am the Lord.** Or, "I am JEHOVAH." Compare iii. 15, and note *ad loc.*

Ver. 3.—**I appeared unto Abraham, unto Isaac, and unto Jacob, by the name of God Almighty.** See Gen. xvii. 1 for the revelation of this name to Abraham, and Gen. xxxv. 11 for its repetition to Jacob. We do not find the full name used by God in any appearance to Isaac; but Isaac himself uses it in Gen. xxviii. 3. **By my name Jehovah was**

I not known unto them. The explanation of this passage is by no means easy. God himself, according to Gen. xv. 7, revealed himself to Abraham as Jehovah before declaring his name to be El-Shaddai (God Almighty) ; and again revealed himself to Jacob as Jehovah-Elohim (*ib*. xxxviii. 13). Abraham named the place where he had been about to sacrifice Isaac, "Jehovah-jireh" (*ib*. xxii. 14). That Moses regarded the name as known even earlier, appears from Gen. iv. 1. It was probably as old as language. The apparent meaning of the present passage cannot therefore be its true meaning. No writer would so contradict himself. Perhaps the true sense is, "I was known to them as a Being of might and power, not as mere absolute (and so eternal and immutable) existence." This meaning of the word, though its etymological and original meaning, may have been unknown to the patriarchs, who were not etymologists. It was first distinctly declared to Moses at Sinai (ch. iii. 14, 15).

Ver. 4.—I have established my covenant with them. Compare Gen. xv. 18—21 ; xvii. 7, 8 ; xxvi. 3 ; xxviii. 13. The land of Canaan, in a narrow acceptation, reached "from Sidon unto Gaza" (Gen. x. 19) ; in a wider sense it included the whole tract between "the river of Egypt (*Wady-el-Arish*) and the great river, the river Euphrates" (*ib*. xv. 18). It was this larger tract which was promised by God to Abraham. The land of their pilgrimage, wherein they were strangers. Literally, "the land of their sojourns wherein they sojourned." (So Kalisch.) It was by permission of the lords of the soil—the Canaanites, Perizzites, Hittites, and others, that Abraham and his descendants dwelt in Canaan to the time of Jacob's descent into Egypt. (See Gen. xii. 6 ; xiii. 7 ; xxiii. 7 ; xxvii. 46, etc.)

Ver. 5.—I have also heard the groaning. Compare ch. ii. 24 and iii. 9. The repetition is in consequence of Moses' expostulation (ch. v. 22, 23), and is to assure the Israelites that God has not forgotten them, but will sustain them under their afflictions, and will shortly deliver them.

Ver. 6.—Say unto the children of Israel. God felt for the disappointment which the people had suffered in finding no alleviation of their toils, but the reverse, after their hopes had been raised high by the words of Moses (ch. iv. 31). He therefore sent them an inspiriting and gracious message. "They *should* be rid of their bondage ; they *should* be brought out ; they *should* be redeemed and delivered by his mighty arm and miraculous intervention. He, Jehovah, had said it." Faith would lay hold on this assurance and cling to it, even though God still delayed his coming, and did not precipitate matters. A stretched-out arm. Arms are stretched out by men to help and save. An outstretched arm in the Egyptian writing meant "action." The phrase, elsewhere so common, is here used for the first time. (Compare, however, ch. iii. 20.) It was significant of active, energetic help. Great judgments. These had been previously hinted at (ch. iii. 20 and ch. iv. 22) but had not been previously called "judgments." Compare Gen. xv. 14 : "Also that nation whom they serve will I *judge*." The plagues of Egypt were not merely "wonders," but punishments inflicted on a proud and cruel nation by a Judge.

Vers. 7, 8.—The promises are continued, heaped one upon another. 1. God will take them for his own people. 2. He will be, in a special sense, their God. 3. They shall clearly know that it is he who brings them forth out of Egypt. 4. They shall be brought into the promised land. 5. The land shall be made over to them, and become their own inheritance. The Israelites were formally taken to be God's people at Sinai (ch. xix. 5, 6) ; where, at the same time, he became (specially but not exclusively) their God (ch. xx. 1 ; xxix. 45, 46). They had evidence that it was he who brought them forth in the pillar of fire and of a cloud (ch. xiii. 21 ; xiv. 19, 20, etc.). They were brought into the promised land by Joshua (Josh. iv. 1), and given the full possession of it by him and his successors —the various judges and kings, until at last, under David and Solomon, they held the entire tract that had been promised to Abraham (see 1 Kings iv. 21 ; 2 Chron. ix. 26).

Ver. 8.—The land which I did swear to give it to Abraham, etc. See Gen. xxii. 16—18 ; xxvi. 3, etc. The only formal oath is recorded in Gen. xxii. 16 ; but an oath is perhaps implied in every covenant between God and man. God's faithfulness is pledged to the performance of the terms of the covenant on his part. I will give it you for an heritage: I am the Lord. Rather, "I will give it you for an heritage, I the Lord" (or "I Jehovah," or "I the Eternal One"). "You have the pledge of my Eternity and Immutability that it shall be yours."

HOMILETICS.

Ver. 1.—*God's condescension to a weak faith.* As the Lord Jesus condescended to Thomas, and bade him "reach hither his finger and behold his hands, and reach hither his hand and thrust it into his side," so that he might be no longer "faithless, but believing" (John xx. 27), so Jehovah now declared to Moses that, if he could not walk by faith, sight should be vouchsafed to him. "Now shalt thou *see*," etc. Human infirmity is so great, man's faith is so weak, the best are so liable to accesses of distrust and despondency, that, if God were extreme to mark what is in this way done amiss, few indeed would be those who could "abide it." Therefore, in his mercy, he condescends. Well for man could he breathe continually the higher, rarer, atmosphere of faith. But, if he cannot, yet has Godward aspirations, so that he takes his distrust and his despondency to God, as Moses did, God will in no wise cast him out. He will not "break the bruised reed, nor quench the smoking flax." He will accept the imperfect service that is still service, and allow his servant to work in a lower sphere. Henceforth the faith of Moses was not much tried—he had soon sight to walk by. When once the series of plagues began, he could no longer ask, "Why is it that thou hast sent me?" He could *see* that the end was being advanced—the deliverance being extorted from the king—and that the day of final triumph was fast coming.

Vers. 2, 3.—*God's names and their importance.* With men a name is simply a "mark of difference"—a mode of distinguishing one individual from another; and the particular name that a man bears is, generally speaking, a matter of the very slightest importance. But with God the case is otherwise. The names of God have always been among all men significant names. If their signification is clear, or generally known, then men's views of the Supreme Being are vitally affected by the names under which they know him. Persons whose only name for God is *Dyaus* or *Tien*—"the heaven"—are not likely to be strongly apprehensive of the personality and spirituality of the Creator. If God is known as Ammon, the main idea of him will be, that he is a riddle and a mystery; if as Shaddai, that he is powerful; if as Mazda, that he is wise or bounteous. When monotheism is firmly established, it is well that God should be known by many names, as El, Elohim, Adonai, Eliun, Shaddai, Jehovah, because then his many and various attributes are better apprehended. If, however, God is to be known by one name only, or by one special name, while there is none more pure or lofty than Jehovah—"the Self-Existent"—there is none more tender and loving than our own English name, God —*i.e.* "the Good."

Vers. 4—8.—*God a keeper of covenants.* God is declared in Scripture to be one who "keepeth covenant and mercy, yea, to a thousand generations" (Deut. vii. 9). He is ever faithful. He cannot lie. He is not a man that he should repent. The bow which he set in the cloud, when he covenanted with Noah that the waters should no more become a flood to destroy all flesh, is still there, and the promise of which it was the sign has been kept—there has come no repetition of the Flood, no second destruction of mankind by water. God has kept the covenant which he made with Israel at Sinai— first, on the side of promise, in giving them all the good things which he said he would give them; and then, on the side of threatening, in bringing upon them all the calamities which he said he would bring. With Christians, too, God enters into covenant at their baptism, promising them protection, spiritual aid, and eternal life in heaven, on their maintaining faith and repentance. This covenant, like his others, he will assuredly keep. Let them be but true to him, and they need have no fear but that he will be true to them. The Promised Land will be theirs—he will give it to them for an heritage—he, Jehovah!

HOMILIES BY VARIOUS AUTHORS.

Vers. 1—9.—*A Divine commentary on a Divine name.* The antiquity of the name Jehovah, setting aside direct testimonies to its occurrence in earlier scriptures, is sufficiently proved by its etymology (from *havah*, an old—and, in the days of Moses, obsolete—form of the verb "to be"), and from its presence (in composition) in pre-Mosaic proper names (*e.g.* ver. 20). It is absurd to press this passage in proof of the ignorance of the patriarchs of this name of God, when one observes—1. That the context plainly relates to a commentary which God was about to give on this name *in deeds*. 2. That the name is not here *announced*, but is presupposed as known—"My name Jehovah." 3. That in ch. iii. 14—16, where it *is* announced, it is expressly referred to as a name of older date—God styling himself repeatedly, "Jehovah God of your fathers." The knowledge of God by this name in the present passage has obvious reference to a knowledge derived from manifestation of the attributes implied in the meaning of the name.

I. "JEHOVAH" IN CONTRAST WITH "EL-SHADDAI" (ver. 3). 1. El-Shaddai means, as translated, "God Almighty." It denotes in God the simple attribute of power—All-Mightiness—power exerted chiefly in the region of the natural life. 2. Jehovah, on the other hand, has a deeper and wider, an infinitely fuller and richer meaning. It denotes God as possessed of the perfections of the Absolute—self-identical and changeless because self-existent and eternal. God *is* eternally what he *is* (ch. iii. 14)—the Being who is and remains *one* with himself in all he thinks, purposes, and does. This implies, together with immutability, the attribute of self-determining freedom, and that unlimited rule (dominion, sovereignty) in the worlds of matter and mind, which is of the essence of the conception of the Absolute. Hence such passages as these :—" I am Jehovah, I change not " (Mal. iii. 6); " Whatsoever Jehovah pleased, that did he in heaven, and in earth, in the seas, and in all deep places " (Ps. cxxx. 6); " Jehovah, he is God in heaven above, and upon the earth beneath; there is none else " (Deut. iv. 39). Jehovah is, moreover, the God of *gracious* purpose. It is this which gave the name its depth of interest to the Hebrew bondsmen, who were not likely to be greatly influenced by purely ontological conceptions. *The chosen sphere for the manifestation of the attributes denoted by these names of God was that marked out by the promises of the Covenant.* El-Shaddai, *e.g.*, while declaring the possession by God of the attribute of power in general, had immediate reference to the manifestations of power which God would give in the birth of Isaac, and in the fulfilment of the promise to Abraham of a numerous posterity (Gen. xvi. 1—7). It was power working in the interests of grace, in subserviency to love. The same is true of the name Jehovah. A view of God in his bare absoluteness would awaken only a speculative interest ; but it is different when this self-existent, eternal Being is seen entering into history, and revealing himself as the God of compassionating love. Grace and mercy are felt to be no longer foreign to the meaning of the name, but to be as much a part of it as changelessness and freedom. This, accordingly, was what the name told to Israel; not simply that there was an Absolute, or even that he who had entered into covenant with the Fathers, and was now about to undertake their deliverance, was this absolute God ; but rather, that it was in the work of their salvation that his perfections *as* Absolute were to be surprisingly and surpassingly exhibited. Their redemption was to be a chosen field for the manifestation of his Jehovah attributes. There would be given in it a discovery and demonstration of these surpassing everything that had hitherto been known. And was not *this* glorious comfort to a nation lying in darkness and the shadow of death !

II. THE HISTORICAL EXHIBITION OF THIS CONTRAST. 1. *God revealed as El-Shaddai* (ver. 3). God was made known as El-Shaddai in the birth of Isaac (Rom. iv. 17—22), in the care exercised over the patriarchs in their wanderings (Gen. xxviii. 15), in the provision made for their temporal necessities (Gen. xlv. 5—9), in the increase and preservation of the chosen race in Egypt (Ex. i. 7, 12, 20 ; iii. 2). This name, however, was inadequate to express the richer aspects and relations of the Divine character brought to light in the Exodus, and in the subsequent experiences of the people. 2. *The transition from El-Shaddai to Jehovah.* Vers. 4—6 narrate the steps by which the way was prepared for the new and higher manifestation. The preparation involved—(1) The establishment of a covenant of promise (ver. 4). If God is revealed as Jehovah when seen acting with unbounded freedom in fulfilment of a purpose, then it was necessary, in order that the freedom and sovereignty of the worker might be rendered completely manifest, that the purpose should be previously declared. Only on the basis of a previously declared purpose could the Jehovah attributes be conspicuously and conclusively displayed. (See interesting remarks on this in Bruce's 'Chief End of Revelation,' ch. iv.). (2) The development of a crisis in the situation of Israel (ver. 5). This crisis was marked on the *human* side by the sufferings of Israel reaching a pitch of intensity which imperatively called for a Divine interposition ; and on the *Divine* side, by God arousing himself, and determining himself to interfere on their behalf (ch. ii. 23—25). We have already seen that the bondage was not without Divine permission. We have traced it in—(1) A punishment for sins, (2) A trial of faith, and (3) A moral preparation. We have now to view in it a situation providentially prepared with the design of affording the fullest possible scope for the display of the truth, grace, power, and all-embracing sovereignty of the great Being who was revealing himself in Israel's history. 3. *God revealed as Jehovah* (vers. 6—9). This revelation would embrace—(1) The deliverance of the people from the bondage and misery of Egypt, and this with great accompaniments of power and judgment (ver. 6). (2) Their adoption by God as a people to himself (ver. 7). (3) Their final settlement in Canaan, in fulfilment of promise (ver. 8). By such deeds would God make it manifest that he was indeed Jehovah, *their* God. He would display his might; would demonstrate his supremacy as Moral Ruler; would magnify his covenant-keeping faithfulness; would reveal himself as the Living Personal God, working freely in history in pursuance of gracious purposes, and, in spite of all human opposition, bringing them to pass.

Lessons :—1. How wonderful to contemplate God in the majesty of his perfections as the Great I Am—the absolute and unconditioned Being! But what language will express the condescension and grace displayed in the stooping down of this absolute Being to enter into covenant engagements with man, even to the extent of binding himself with *oaths* to fulfil the promises given by his own free goodness. 2. The manifestation of the Jehovah attributes in the deliverance of Israel from Egypt has its higher counterpart in the discovery of them since made in the redemption of men from sin and Satan through Christ. Christ redeems us from sin's burden and from Satan's tyranny. He does this in virtue of the " stretched-out arm" and "mighty judgments" with which, while on earth, he overcame the Prince of the power of this world; himself also enduring the judgment of God in being "made sin for us," " that we might be made the righteousness of God in him." By this atonement and victory, in the might of which he has now ascended on high, leading captivity captive, we, being reconciled to God, are formed into a people for his praise, and he becomes our God; the same power that redeemed us working in us to deliver us from sin in our members, and to prepare us for a heavenly inheritance; to which, as the goal of all God's leading of us, the promises immovably point forward (Rom. viii. 1, 2; 2 Cor. v. 21; Eph. iv. 8; Col. i. 12—15; ii. 15; 1 Pet. i. 3—10; ii. 9, 10).—J. O.

Ver. 7.—*A rich promise.* The promise is as rich as it is wonderful, and as wonderful as it is rich—" I will take you to me for a people, and I will be to you a God." It includes—1. *The highest honour.* Who speaks? The absolute God. To whom? A nation of bondsmen. Yet he says—" I will take you," etc. And he did it, even as he still takes sinners in Christ into union and fellowship with himself—adopting them as sons, admitting them to covenant, making them heirs, etc. 2. *The highest privilege.* All promise and all blessing, for time and for eternity, are wrapped up in this single but most comprehensive word—" I will be to you a God." 3. *The most indissoluble of relations.* It lasts through time, and extends into eternity, enduring as long as God and the soul and Christ endure, and that is for ever (cf. Matt. xxii. 31, 32).—J. O.

Ver. 8.—*God encourages Moses in his despondency.* We have here—

I. MOSES QUESTIONING THE PROCEDURE OF JEHOVAH. Observe—1. *Moses in all his perplexity still acts upon the firm assurance that there is a Jehovah to resort to.* " He returned unto the Lord." Neither the reproaches of the people nor his own disappointment made him at all to doubt that he was dealing with a glorious, awful, and Divine existence outside of himself. It seems just as much a matter of course for Moses to meet with Jehovah, as it had been for the Israelite officers to meet with Moses. This is one good result of all the discussion (for hardly any other term will sufficiently indicate it) which Moses has had with Jehovah concerning his own fitness. Every time God spoke he stood out before the mind of his servant more distinctly and impressively as a real existence. The troubled heart of Moses leads him here into a set of very ignorant questions; but these were a small evil compared with what might have happened, viz. a lapse into utter atheism. 2. *Moses, like the Israelite officers, makes the mistake of going by first consequences.* He does not rebuke the officers for wrong expectations and hasty conclusions. By his language in approaching God, he admits to the full that these officers have reason for their reproaches. They have appealed to Jehovah as against Moses; Moses in turn can only appeal to Jehovah, *not against them,* but—to justify himself. How easy it is for a man, even though fully persuaded of God's existence, to have utterly erroneous thoughts of his purposes and of his ways of working. Evidently it will need a gradual process—and not without temporary retrogressions—in order to lift Moses above such conceptions of deity as he had gained in Egypt and Midian, and by all his acquaintance with current idolatries. It is easier to remember the name I AM than to understand the thing signified by the name. 3. *In particular, Moses blundered in thinking of deliverance, not as a process, but as an act*—something to be achieved by a miracle as instantaneous and complete as those which he had wrought before Israel. One of the most pernicious misapprehensions of the Gospel is that which looks on salvation as an instantaneous thing—which speaks of the saved, instead of using the more exact description, " those who are being saved " (Rom. v. 10; 1 Cor. i. 18; Philipp. ii. 12; 1 Pet. i. 9). First of all, we put our shallow, unspiritual notions into the Word of God, and then turn round in amazement, because his actions do not correspond with our ideas of what they should be. 4. We see from this utterance of Moses, how *a man may make the first step towards freedom and Divine fulfilments of gracious purposes to him, and yet not know it.* Moses having gone to Pharaoh, had met with nothing but rebuff; and was further compelled to see his brethren treated more cruelly than ever. He thinks nothing has been done, because he can see nothing, but he is utterly mistaken. The Israelites, had they only known it, were nearer salvation—a great deal nearer—than when they first believed. " Wherefore hast thou so evil entreated this people ? " says Moses to Jehovah. Wherefore ? indeed !—only we should ever ask all-important questions in their proper order. First, " *Is it so ?* " and then, " Why is it so ? " It was not true that Jehovah was evilly entreating the people. The liberating work was really begun, even though Moses could see no sign of it. When, from the point of view given by the catastrophe of the Red Sea, we look back on this first interview, then we see that it was also the first step in a solemn gradation— for Moses and Israel, the first step upwards; and just as surely for Pharaoh, the first step downwards.

II. God gives an answer full of encouragement. 1. *Notice the absence of anything in the shape of rebuke.* These words of Moses had a very offensive and dishonouring sound, but we do not read that Jehovah's anger was kindled against Moses (ch. iv. 14), or that he sought to kill him (ch. iv. 24). When there is a want of due and prompt submission to the commandments of God, especially when they are plain and decisive ones, then God begins to threaten. But when the thing lacking is a want of understanding as to God's way, then he patiently extends sympathy, and endeavours to give light and truth. A commander severely punishes a subordinate when he neglects plain orders at a critical juncture ; but he would be very unreasonable if he expected him all at once to appreciate the plan of a campaign. Moses would have been very differently treated, if, after the reproaches of the officers, he had shown a spirit of disobedience towards Jehovah. 2. As to the substance of God's reply, what can be said that he has not said already ; save that *he puts the old truths and promises more emphatically, more comprehensively than ever ?* The first appeal to Moses is, *to rest as far as he can in an undisturbed sense of the power of God.* That power belongs to Jehovah is the one thing which Moses has seen most clearly, felt most deeply ; and God began by assuring him that he will yet be convinced how strong the Divine hand is. The strong man, violently and wastefully laying hold of Jehovah's possessions, will be utterly subdued by a far stronger than himself. The next point to be noticed is that though, as we have said, there was no expressed rebuke, yet there are elements in this reply of God, out of which Moses, reflecting on what was expressed, *could construct a rebuke for himself.* Moses is not showing a faith equal to that of Abraham, Isaac, and Jacob; and yet they were without the revelation of this name JEHOVAH. Moses, who had been told more of the Divine nature than Abraham was told, ought to have believed not less readily and steadily than Abraham. Rest if you can, Moses, in all the comforts that flow from a due consideration of this great and exhaustless Name ! Then God goes on to speak of his own faithfulness, *of the covenant which was constantly in the Divine mind.* Was it for Moses to speak as if God was unmindful of that covenant ; he to speak, who but lately had shown his own want of regard to the human side of it, and been in deadly peril because of his uncircumcised son ! The God of Abraham, Isaac, and Jacob, is Jehovah, the great I Am. If, then, he made a covenant with all its promises yesterday, be sure that to-day he is doing something to carry that covenant out.   If, yesterday, he expressed compassion for the oppressed, and wrath with the oppressor, be sure that he has not relapsed into cold indifference to-day.   These capricious sympathies are reserved for men and women who will weep over the mimic and exaggerated sorrows of the stage, and then go home to harden their hearts against the terrible sorrows of real life.   When we read over the words of Moses here, and compare them with the words of God, we see how contracted were the views of Moses, and how gloriously enlarged were the views of God.   Moses is thinking simply of deliverance—how to get the present generation from under the yoke of the oppressor; but God has in his mind a great plan, of which the deliverance from Pharaoh is but one stage in the development, and that a very brief stage.   To the completion of this plan the liberation of Israel was necessary, and therefore this liberation would assuredly be achieved.   Moses, so to speak, was low down in a hollow; he could get no proper view of the distances; he could not get a due impression of all this tract of time, from God's first appearing to Abraham down to the securing of the inheritance; and therefore he may well be excused if he speaks hastily.   But God looks down from his throne in eternity.   The whole stretch of the work lies before him, and thus beholding it, he can but reiterate his promises, exhibit the great features of his plan, and counsel Moses and Israel to do the one thing needful, *i.e.* continue obediently waiting upon him in the generation in which they live.   Let us do what God tells us, being perfectly sure that he sees what we cannot see, and that, because he is the God who cannot lie, he sets all things before us just as they are.   3. Another thing is to be considered here, which, though omitted from Jehovah's answer to Moses, ought not to be neglected by us.   For typical purposes, the welfare and future of Israel is the great thing spoken of; Pharaoh is looked at simply as the cruel adversary and oppressor of Israel.   Hence just those things are stated which most effectively show his complete downfall.   But we must remember that the things which are stated at any particular time are only a small part of what are in the mind of God.   He states not all the considerations which inspire his acts, but only such as it may be well for us to know.   Pharaoh had to be dealt with as a *man*, even though the record is emphatically constructed so as to set him forth merely as a *type*.   It would have been manifestly unjust to bring upon him sudden and terrible destruction of all his power, without an appearance of appeal to his voluntary action.—Y.

Vers. 2—8.—*The message to afflicted Israel.* I. THE WORD TO THE LEADER: vers. 2—5. The message must be from faith to faith.   The heart of God's servant must first be revived ere he can impart strength to the people.   1. He is reminded of God's faithfulness: "I am Jehovah."   We cannot grasp this truth without deliverance from fear. 2. The darkness will only make God's glory shine out the more resplendently.   Their present sufferings will mark a new era in God's revelation of himself.   Known before as the Almighty, he will now reveal himself as Jehovah, "the faithful One," who remembers and fulfils his promises.   3. Having grasped the truth regarding God's faithfulness he is led back to the promises by which the Lord has bound himself.   4. The assurance of present sympathy and speedy deliverance.   He has heard their groaning and called to remembrance his pledged word.   To dwell in these truths is to possess light and power. God's word will then be a joy to our hearts, and will be in our lips consolation and strength for the fainting ones around us.
II. THE WORD TO THE PEOPLE: vers. 6—8.   1. It is shut in between the reiterated assurance, "*I am Jehovah*," vers. 6—9.   For them, too, the truth to rest in is God's faithfulness.   2. The deliverance will be accompanied by the revelation of God's terribleness (ver. 6).   Israel never forgot those days, and never will.   3. God will wed them to himself.   He does not deliver us and then leave us: "I will take you to me for a people and I will be to you a God."   4. He will fulfil all the promises and give them the land for a heritage.   This is the Gospel message: Our bonds will be broken—God will bind us to himself and give us his people's heritage.   Have we received it?   Is it a living hope, an abiding joy to us?—U.

Vers. 2—3.—*The Lord thy God is one God.*   God appeared to the fathers of the race under one name; to their successors under another.   *Name* is more than *title*; it is the character, or aspect of character, denoted by the title. Jehovah would seem to have been a title of God before the time of Moses; but to him, and to the Israelites through him, was first revealed that aspect of the Divine character which explained and justified the title. Notice—

I. ONE MAY KNOW GOD WITHOUT KNOWING ALL ABOUT HIM. Abraham, Isaac, and Jacob certainly knew God. They believed in him as an Almighty Ruler—one who was ruling them, and who would fulfil his promise to them. His power and his trustworthiness were the characteristics they most relied on. Their faith centred in his name El-Shaddai, and as a living practical faith it tended to secure the righteousness for which —as seed for fruit—it was reckoned. [*Illustration:*—Certain medicines, in earlier years, were trusted and used successfully to produce certain effects; yet other uses remained unknown until long afterwards.] God was trusted by the patriarchs to the extent of their then knowledge, though they knew nothing of other characteristics which were to be afterwards revealed.

II. WE MAY KNOW GOD UNDER DIFFERENT ASPECTS, AND YET KNOW THE SAME GOD. No doubt the revelation of a new name, the fixing of the attention upon a new aspect of the Divine character, must have been, at first, somewhat startling to those who held by the old traditions. Those taught to believe in El-Shaddai may have held the new believers in Jehovah unorthodox. Yet both, in so far as their belief was genuine, knew and trusted the same God. Jehovah was El-Shaddai only viewed from a new standpoint. There was no contradiction between the two names—one God owned both.

III. WE MAY EXPECT AS THE OLD ORDER CHANGES TO VIEW GOD UNDER OTHER THAN THE OLD CONDITIONS. The new revelation resulted from new conditions. The old order having changed, a new standpoint was necessitated, whence God must be viewed under a new aspect. [*Illustration:*—The properties of a medicine are discovered little by little, as new diseases cause it to be applied in different ways.] New conditions must result in new discoveries as to the "properties" of God.

Application:—God is one; Truth is one; yet God and Truth are many-sided—we see them differently according to the position which we occupy. Some people are in a great hurry to denounce all novelty as heresy; but *novelty* may mean nothing more than a new point of view, whereas *heresy* results from distorted vision; it sees wrongly, through personal idiosyncrasy, that which, from the same standpoint, is seen clearly by the clear-eyed. We do well to suspect ourselves when our conclusions differ from those of others. We may test such conclusions in two ways:—1. What are the conditions under which they have been arrived at? If the conditions have changed, we may expect the conclusions to be different. 2. Do they *contradict* old beliefs? If so, they should be suspected —or, Do they merely embrace them within a wider faith? If so, they may sufficiently justify themselves. We may expect new revelations, but we must not hurriedly accept novelties. New names will be made known, but they are never really *inconsistent* with the old.—G.

EXPOSITION.

Ver. 9.—Hope deferred maketh the heart sick. The Israelites, who had expected a speedy deliverance, and found themselves only the more down-trodden for Moses' interference, were too much dispirited to be cheered even by the gracious promises and assurances which Moses was commissioned to give. They had no longer any trust in one who they thought had deceived them. He was a dreamer, a visionary, if no worse. They did not intend hearkening to him any more. "Anguish of spirit" possessed their souls, and "cruel bondage" claimed their bodies, day after day. They had not even the time, had they had the will, to hearken.

Ver. 9.—**Anguish of spirit.** Literally, "shortness." Compare Job xxi. 4. Their spirit was shortened—they had lost all heart, as we say, so cruel had been their disappointment. The contrast between their feelings now, and when Moses first addressed them (ch. iv. 31), is strong, but "fully accounted for by the change of circumstances". (Cook). **Cruel bondage.** Bondage, *i.e.*, far more oppressive and continuous than it had been (ch. v. 9—14). The Samaritan version adds: "And they said to him, Let us alone, and let us serve the Egyptians; for it is better for us to serve the Egyptians than die in a wilderness," an addition which receives some support from ch. xiv. 12.

HOMILETICS.

Ver. 9.—*Spiritual deadness produced by extreme physical need.* It is the worst result of long-continued oppression that it brings its victims into a state of apathy. Servile insurrections are rare—servile wars all but unknown. Slavery so crushes men, so brutalises, so deadens them, that they lose all heart, all spirit, all hope, almost all feeling. Defenders of slavery call the proper objects of the "institution" *live machines*, and "live machines" is exactly what it tends to make them. What is to stir a mass so sluggish and inert that it vegetates rather than lives? Not the name of God (ver. 3). It falls on closed ears—it has no meaning to them, conveys no idea, arouses no thought. Not the mention of a covenant (vers. 4, 5). They cannot realise so complex a notion—cannot understand what the word means. Not promises (vers. 6—8). A promise has no power unless embraced by faith; and the down-trodden have no faith, either in themselves or in others. So the most stirring appeals are made in vain—the brightest hopes and prospects presented to no purpose. And as with oppression, so with all extreme depression and destitution. Hopeless poverty, constant battle with the wolf at the door, continual striving to keep off starvation from themselves, their wives, and children, reduces a population to a condition in which it becomes dead to spiritual things, and not only appears to be, but is, unimpressible. It is so occupied with the cares of this life that it has no thought for another. It has bid farewell to hope, and with hope to fear. It is reckless. The preacher can do nothing with it until he has changed the physical conditions of its existence. He must first address himself to the people's physical wants. Let these be provided for, let the struggle for existence slacken, let hope dawn on the despairing souls, and all will at once be different. As the unbound earth opens to receive seed at the genial breath of spring, so these torpid souls may be brought to take in the seed of life, by having their bodies warmed and clothed and cared for.

HOMILIES BY VARIOUS AUTHORS.

Ver. 11, vi. 13.—*The new commission.* And Moses spoke so, etc. : Exod. vi. 9.

I. THE AUDACITY OF FAITH. Describe the *treatment* of Moses and Aaron. They acted under Divine direction, did their very best, but just because everything did not go well instantly, and that through the frowardness and waywardness of others, the people turned upon them, and upbraided them as accessories to their slavery. [See Matt. Henry for some valuable practical notes on this and other parts of this passage from ch. v. 22—vi. 13.] Moses felt this keenly, and in a moral sense *retreated* upon his base—that is, upon God. Compare Hezekiah and the letter. Alone with God, Moses *complained.* Moses is very bold—tells God to his face that he has not delivered Israel at all; that he has brought evil upon the nation, already oppressed to the border of despair; and challenges the Eternal as to his own commission. All this is high tragedy in the realms of spiritual life, and may well demand consideration. Consider—1. *The audacity* of Moses. See chap. v. 22, 23. Is this the language of enquiry or entreaty? Not at all. Of impetuosity, of remonstrance; it borders on the irreverent; the tone is angry, and nearly rebellious. [Note—Such a speech as this would never have been put into the mouth of Moses by any later writer—sure mark this, that we have the history under the hand of Moses.] Such expressions are not uncommon with Old Testament saints. See especially Jer. xx. 7, *et seq.* We learn that believers do not stand related to God as stones lying under a cast-iron canopy of destiny. They are quivering sensibilities in the presence of the Father of spirits. What they feel, they may say; better to say it. And if an earthly parent will make allowances for an angry, misapprehending child, shall not our Father in heaven? "Let us therefore come *boldly*," etc. 2. *The error* of Moses. God was all the time working in the direction of salvation for the people and of extraordinary eminence for Moses; but he thought everything looked the other way. A similar error may be ours. 3. *The accomplishment of the Divine purpose in Moses.* To draw him away from all secondary causes, to dependence on and communion with God.

II. THE CONDESCENDING FORBEARANCE OF GOD. In answer to the cry of Moses, God made five announcements of the very first importance. They were made with distinctness, formality, and solemnity. Note—There may have been an interval of months between the cry and these announcements. Note also, that this is not a second account of the revelation of the Burning Bush. The true explanation of the likeness between the two revelations is, that Moses having fallen into a desponding state of mind, God recalled to him first principles. So now, one cure at least for discouragement is to fall back on elemental Gospel truths. God announced—1. *His resolve:* ver. 1, see Hebrew ; and expound the true meaning. Pharaoh would be forced, not only to " *send* " Israel out, but to " *drive* " them out. 2. *His name.* First, God gave again his proper name, " Jehovah ;" and then we have a positive and a negative declaration—(1) Positive. To the fathers God had been known as El-Shaddai—God all-sufficient—that is, to and for them in their moving tents. (2) Negative. This may not mean that " Jehovah " had never fallen on their ear ; but this, that all in that name had not dawned on their intelligence. God's revelation of himself is always gradual. So it is in the gradual unfolding of the successive Bible economies. And so it is still. Modern science cannot give us a different idea of God ; but an enlarged idea, and one vastly illuminated. Dr. Chalmers when delivering his " Astronomical Discourses " had a grander idea of God than John Milton. Geology tells us of the æons through which he works. Microscopical revelations tell of the infinitude of his condescensions. As Diderot said : " Elargissez Dieu"—Enlarge your idea of God. 3. *His covenant:* ver. 4. 4. *His sympathy:* ver. 5. With new sorrows. 5. *His salvation:* vers. 6, 7, 8. It is impossible to read these verses without noting the parallel with a still greater salvation. God promised—(1) *Deliverance.* Note the " burden-bearing "(see the Heb.) of sin—its essential servitude—the redemption price—the power, the outstretched arm, with which salvation is wrought—the judgment on powers of darkness, Col. ii. 15. (2) *Adoption.* (3) *The land of rest.* These blessings for us, as for them, on the condition of implicit trust.

III. THE DEAFENING POWER OF SORROW : ver. 9. The contrast now and ch. iv. 31. " On a former occasion the people were comparatively at ease, accustomed to their lot, sufficiently afflicted to long for deliverance, and sufficiently free in spirit to hope for it." Now !—ver. 9. Observe the Heb., " shortness of breath," *i.e.* such as comes with anguish ; or may not the meaning be, " shortness of spirit," as we say " shortness of temper " ? This verse is against the theory that Israel, by sheer force of religious enthusiasm, emancipated itself. For them, as for us, no salvation save in Jehovah their God. Sorrow may shut out comfort. How many mistakenly stay away from the sanctuary because of their grief !

IV. THE PERSISTENCE OF THE DELIVERING GOD. In this extremity of woe, God appears. The demand once was for a three days' absence ; now God uncovers all his purpose. Ver. 11 is the ultimatum of God. This new commission overwhelms Moses with a deeper sense of incompetence. He pleads—1. *The aversion of his own people.* Effective homiletic use may here be made of the fact, that much of the strength of ministers, which might be used against the enemies of God, is used in dealing with the frowardness of his professed friends. 2. *His own infirmity.* There may be here a sense of moral unfitness—" uncircumcised lips "—and a latent reference to the disobedience, ch. iv. 24—26. God did not allow these pleas ; but put the two leaders forward once more into the position of responsibility, peril, and honour (ver. 13).—R.

Ver. 9.—*The pains of the lower life shutting out the blessings of the higher one.* " They hearkened not unto Moses for anguish of spirit, and for cruel bondage." Notice that this reason, and not some other, is stated for the indifference of Israel to the glorious words which Moses was commanded to repeat to them. We might fairly have expected some other reason to be stated ; as, for instance, " We have been deceived once, and are not again to be put off with fair words ;" or, " This array of promises is very grand and imposing, but there is nothing in them." But they are emphatically represented as not even attending to what Moses had to say. Their minds were effectually closed by preoccupation with something else. They were so much harassed in body and mind as to lack not only the inclination, but even the ability, to give Moses a proper hearing. And so Pharaoh's policy had this effect at least, that it prevented the people, *for a while,* from considering things belonging to their highest welfare. Only we must bear in mind that as the liberating advance of God was not in the least hindered by the cruelty of Pharaoh, so neither was it hindered by the negligence of Israel. A

Pharaoh could not hinder, so the people could neither help nor hinder. When they were yet without strength, utterly without strength, in due time God intervened to deliver them.

I. There is thus suggested to us how we should keep in mind ONE GREAT CAUSE OF HINDRANCE TO THE GOSPEL. A message like that of the Gospel of Christ finds great difficulty in its way from preoccupation of any kind, seeing that the mind of man cannot properly entertain two great topics of thought at the same time. Some one thing must hold a first place in thought; and when the heart is occupied with the presence of worldly cares, whatever form they take, then it must be peculiarly hard for the Gospel to find a foothold. God, when he seeks love and service from us, looks to find his rivals in ambition, in pleasure, in riches; and we are used to hear frequent warnings against these rivals. But what rival is more dangerous than (say) *poverty*, that cleaving, biting, pinching spirit, which, when once it gets hold of a man, never lets him forget that it is near. What chance is there then to bring out of the heart a deep conviction of sin and spiritual need? The difficulties of getting the natural man to attend to spiritual concerns are immensely increased by poverty as well as by riches. If, upon some considerations, it is seen to be hard for the rich to enter the kingdom of heaven, upon other considerations it is seen to be equally hard for the poor. The poor have the Gospel presented to them, but alas! it is often hard work to persuade them that it is a Gospel. Go to them, and how are you often met? It may be that your very exemption from a life-long struggle for daily bread blinds you to their peculiar difficulties. You are not able to see that grim wolf which is incessantly at the door, and never out of their thoughts. What wonder if at first—and indeed habitually—the poor should think that there is little or nothing in religion! Often they show their feeling very plainly by bitter and savage words. They want a gospel; but not your gospel. They do not care for a gospel which, while it makes large offers, makes also large demands. They do not care to be asked for self-denial, self-respect, contentment, and patient submission to hard conditions which cannot be easily or immediately altered. They want a gospel which will give, and give just what they choose to ask. The privations, the struggles, the agonies of the poor reduce them often nearer to the spirit of wild beasts than of human beings. Give them what indulges their appetites, and they will welcome you. Minister to the cravings of the flesh, and they will wait as long as you are disposed to supply. But proclaim unpalatable truths, and you might as well speak in a wilderness. We might pursue a similar line of thought in considering the anguish of spirit and cruel bondage of *heathendom*. The missionary often has to speak to those whose minds are oppressed with terrible visions of deities who can only be propitiated by laborious and agonising penances. Read what is said concerning the life-long austerities of some Hindoo devotees, and then consider whether you have not in them a bondage of spirit which may only too effectually shut out even the most attractive truths of the Gospel. We might speak also of the cruel bondage of *worldly conventions*; the incessant and weary struggle to keep up social position—a struggle which, however ridiculous it may be made to look, is, in the eyes of multitudes, a great necessity. And if a man feels a thing a necessity, then you must, at least in your first approaches to him, treat it as a necessity. And last, but not least, there is the anguish and bondage of *disease, physical pain, perhaps approaching death.* The sick send, or are supposed to send, for ministers of religion, but how plain it is in the great bulk of instances that such resorts are utterly ineffectual to bring the sick person to God! There may be an appearance of repentance, a pretence of understanding the way of salvation; but when we know that the actual motive is the fear of death, and not the bitter consciousness of sin, then we cannot but distrust all the action following upon the motive. When a human being, in youth, in health, and with the prospect of a long life, professes to be smitten with convictions of sin, and begins to seek for a Saviour, we know where we are in considering his position. His apparent motive has everything in the circumstances to approve itself as a real one. But when the appearance of interest in Divine things only comes consequent on the alarms of a dangerous, perhaps a fatal illness, then we suspect that the cry for salvation is a selfish and ignorant one; and how can we be sure that it will be anything but a vain one? A courteous pretence of listening to the message of God when there is no real apprehension of it is practically the same thing as not listening at all.

II. NOTE THE OBJECTION WHICH IS BROUGHT AGAINST THE GOSPEL FROM ITS INABILITY

TO DEAL IMMEDIATELY WITH ALL THIS ANGUISH AND BONDAGE OF MEN. There is a plausible argument—one very frequently urged, and alas! very easily deceiving—that the Gospel of Christ does nothing immediately for the social improvement of the world. What is more common than the cry, when some hideous blot and ulcer of society is suddenly revealed, "Here we stand, having only got so far, after more than eighteen centuries of Christianity!" And in hearing talk of this kind, which is sometimes sincere, but oftener is mere cant, we have not so much to reply to others as to enlighten and reassure ourselves. How easily it might have been said with respect to these Israelites, "God is no deliverer, else he would at once take these people—this living, suffering generation—out of all their pains." What God might have done we cannot tell; we only know what he actually did. The light of the whole transaction shows that Jehovah was unquestionably a deliverer; that however a single generation might suffer, the whole nation was in due time, and at the best time, fully redeemed. And in like manner, by the consideration of ultimate results as well as present experiences, we gain the assurance that God is truly the deliverer of men from all spiritual bondage, all spiritual pain. Our frequent folly as defenders of the faith is in saying more than there is any need to say. Let us keep within safe, practical, provable assertions, and these will give an answer enough for the present need. The Gospel of Christ, *we know*, does something, *immediately*, for every one who, in response to its great invitation, believes in the Lord Jesus Christ as his Saviour. Real belief in him will at once irradiate the meanest hovel, the most squalid circumstances, with a light which may most truly be described as

> The light that never was on sea or land.

No combination of favourable social surroundings will ever bring that light; nothing will bring it but the soul's own free and intelligent admission of Jesus as Saviour and Lord. His presence thus obtained gives joy in the midst of the bitterest anguish, liberty in the midst of the most grinding bondage. The more that people believe in Christ, the more we shall have of his effectual presence in the world; and the more we have of his effectual presence, the nearer we shall come to that perpetual summer when the ice that now wraps so many human hearts will be utterly and lastingly melted away. Social reformers who are not also humble Christians, with all their pretensions and all their zeal, are only touching secondary causes; relieving symptoms without cutting at the root of disease. No human being ever did or ever will get clear of anguish and bondage except by submitting to Christ. And no one ever submitted to Christ without having the certain assurance given, that in due time all sorrow and sighing would for ever flee away.—Y.

EXPOSITION

Vers. 10—12.—The Israelites having shown themselves, for the time, unimpressible, God commands Moses to make his next effort upon the Pharaoh. He is to enter into his presence once more, and demand, without circumlocution or obscurity, that the Israelites be allowed to quit the land (ver. 11). Moses, however, demurs. He had done God's will with respect to the people readily and at once, expecting that, as he had persuaded them before, so he would a second time. But he had been disappointed; the people had refused to listen to him. Immediately all his original self-distrust and diffidence recurred— even the old form of diffidence, distrust of his ability to persuade men (ch. iv. 10). How shall he expect to persuade Pharaoh, who had already rejected him (ch. v. 2—5), when he had just failed with his own countrymen, who

previously had "believed" his report (ch. iv. 31)?

Ver. 11.—**Out of his land.** Note the advance in the demand. No longer is there any limitation to a three days' journey, as at first (ch. iii. 18; v. 3). The children of Israel are to be let go altogether "out of the land." So generally, if God lays a light burthen upon us and we refuse it, we may expect him to exchange our light burthen for a heavier one. We had better accept the first cross he offers.

Ver. 12. — **Uncircumcised lips,** *i.e.* "lips inefficient for the purpose for which lips are given;" as "uncircumcised ears" are ears that cannot hearken (Jer. vi. 10), and an "uncircumcised heart" a heart that cannot understand (*ib.* ix. 26). The meaning is the same as in ch. iv. 10, where Moses says that he is "slow of speech and of a slow tongue." Nothing can be determined from the expression as to the exact cause of the imperfection of which complaint is made.

HOMILETICS.

Ver. 11.—*The servant of God must labour unceasingly.* Scarcely has Moses made one attempt at service and failed than God requires of him another service. "Go in, speak unto Pharaoh." In the career of God's servants there is "no rest, no pause." Failure here must be redeemed by effort there. And in this unceasing continuance of service one thing is especially remarkable. After failure, not a lighter but a heavier duty is commonly imposed on men. If they prove unable to convince their kindred, they are given a mission to strangers; if they fail with men of low degree, they are appointed to preach to princes. God will have them redeem failure by fresh effort. God knows the causes of their failure, and introduces them to new spheres, where those causes will not operate, or operate less. A man who has failed in a humble sphere not unfrequently succeeds in a higher one. The servant of God must not care greatly about the sphere to which he is called, but seek to do his best in each while he remains in it. He will thus—1. Be always labouring for God; 2. Be always exercising and so improving his own mental and spiritual gifts; and 3. Be of far more benefit to others than if he sat idle half his time waiting for such a call as seemed to him altogether fitting and suitable. "The time is short." We must "work while it is day—the night cometh when no man can work."

HOMILIES BY VARIOUS AUTHORS.

Vers. 9—14, 28—30.—*Shaken faith, and an unshaken purpose.* In these verses we have—

I. A PAINFUL RESULT OF AFFLICTIVE PROVIDENCE. The children of Israel, hard-driven by their taskmasters, and sunk in misery, were so stupefied with sorrow, as to have no longer any heart for their cheering tidings brought to them by Moses. Their despair had its ground in unbelief. They judged Moses a deceiver. They had trusted him before, and they reflected that the only outcome of it had been this unprecedented aggravation of their wretchedness. His fine promises must now go for what they were worth; they were past deriving comfort from them! Yet observe how in all this— 1. They *wronged God.* God had not deserted them as they thought. He was on the very eve of fulfilling every promise he had made them. We see the error in *their* case; it would be well if we could always see it as clearly in our own. 2. *Made their trials harder.* For if trials are hard enough to bear even *with* faith in the goodness and help of God, how much harder are they to bear *without* it! 3. *Shut themselves out from Divinely-sent consolation.* Their despondency led them, to refuse the very message which would have given them relief. How often is the same thing witnessed under severe affliction! There is a kind of perversity in grief, which leads it to "refuse to be comforted." God is mistrusted. The heart abandons itself to its despair. It sinks in gloom and wretchedness. It turns the very truth of God into a lie, and refuses Scripture and Gospel consolations. Unhappy condition! And as foolish as unhappy—for God is never nearer to the suffering spirit, never more ready to hear its cry, probably never nearer bringing it deliverance, than just when it is thus shutting out his consolations, and refusing him its confidence.

II. TYPICAL DISCOURAGEMENTS IN SPIRITUAL SERVICE (vers. 9, 13, 30). Moses was sorely discouraged—1. *At the unbelieving despair of the people.* He could make no impression on them. They seemed hardened in their misery. So swallowed up were they in their grief, so crushed with sorrow, that their minds seemed to have lost all elasticity, all power of responding to the gladdest of tidings. This is a difficulty one has often to contend with in spiritual work—the spiritless, despairing condition induced by long experience of misfortune. The city missionary, *e.g.,* has frequently to encounter it in going among the dwellings of the very poor. His heart sickens as he realises how little chance his Gospel has of finding acceptance in homes where all the surroundings are wretched, and where from year's end to year's end, there is being carried on the same heartless, monotonous "struggle for existence." But this insensibility to religion induced by suffering is not peculiar to the poor. Far from it. You will find it wherever men are sore beset with trouble, and have no firm, rooted faith in God to support them under it.

Absorbed in " the sorrow of the world," they have no ear for spiritual comfort, and almost spurn it as a mockery. 2. At *the prospect of having to go again before Pharaoh.* Having failed with the people, how should he hope to prevail with Pharaoh, emboldened as that monarch would be with the success of a previous refusal? The element of discouragement here is the depressing sense of *failure.* Moses had failed in the part of the work which seemed easiest, and in which on the former occasion he had succeeded; how, then, should he look for success in the more difficult part of it, where previously he had sustained defeat? Observe carefully that on this point Moses' plea was not admitted. (1) We are bad judges of what *is* failure. What Moses counted defeats were not defeats at all, but at most delays. The history of missions furnishes striking illustrations of the danger of too hastily concluding that a work has failed because no immediate fruits are visible. Nothing has been more common in missionary experience (South Seas, Madagascar, Tinnivelly, the Kohls, etc.) than times of extraordinary fruitfulness following upon long periods of seeming failure—ten, twenty, thirty years often passing without a single convert. These were seasons of trial of faith, and had the missions been abandoned, as timid counsellors advised, the whole blessing would have been lost. (2) It is the *doing* of our duty we are held responsible for, not the failure or success which may attend it. That remains with God. The lesson is that in spiritual work there must be no talk of abandonment; no putting of the hand to the plough and then looking back; no flinging away of our weapons because the outlook is discouraging. *Our* part is to labour on, believing that "in due season we shall reap if we faint not" (Gal. vi. 9). 3. By *the revived sense of personal deficiencies.* "How then shall Pharaoh hear me, who am of uncircumcised lips!" Moses had Aaron, it was true, to speak for him, but there was a certain clumsiness in this method of two men going in, the one to speak for the other, and Moses felt his deficiency only the more keenly on account of it. He seems to have despaired of having any influence with Pharaoh, who would look on him with contempt. Moses forgot that in work of this kind no man "goeth a warfare any time at his own charges" (1 Cor. ix. 7), and that, if God sent him, God would qualify and support him, would give him strength for every duty he had to perform (cf. ch. vii. 1—7).

III. GOD'S UNSHAKEN PURPOSE ASSERTING ITSELF IN THE MIDST OF HUMAN UNBELIEF AND INFIRMITY (vers. 11, 13, 29). This is a most remarkable feature in the narrative—how, high and clear above all notes of doubt and hesitancy on the side of man, and at the very time when things are wearing their most untoward aspect, God expresses himself with perfect decision as to the deliverance of the people. Hope in the hearts of the people seemed extinct; even the faith of a Moses was staggering at the obstacles to be encountered. These fears and tremblings, however, are all on the human side; he who names himself Jehovah is raised infinitely above them, and has clearly in his view not only the certainty of his purpose being fulfilled, but all the steps by which the fulfilment is to be brought about. How should this give us confidence when we are trembling for the cause of Truth! *We* cannot see the end from the beginning, but Jehovah can, and we can stay ourselves on *his* knowledge of what is dark to *us.* It is enough for us to know that no contingency can arise which he is not aware of and has not prepared himself to cope with; that no opposition can erect itself against his counsel, which it is not within his power to overthrow. The counsel of the Lord stands for ever—the one stable fact in the midst of earthly vicissitude and change, of all ebb and flow of human hopes and fears. That surely is enough to lean upon, in the dark and troubled hours of our own and of the world's existence.

IV. FRESH EVIDENCE OF THE SUPERNATURAL CHARACTER OF THE DELIVERANCE. Allusion has already been made to the theory that the Exodus had its origin, not in a supernatural interposition of God, but in some gigantic spiritual movement springing up among the people themselves. The facts in this chapter, if anything of the character of history belongs to them, conclusively dispose of that theory. So far from the people of Israel being in a state of hopeful enthusiasm, ready to make great efforts for their own deliverance, they appear as utterly crushed and broken-spirited—totally "without strength." There was doubtless a profound purpose in God's permitting them to be brought into this condition. 1. It made more manifest the fact that their deliverance did *not* originate with themselves. And 2. It furnishes a striking image of Gospel truth. We too were "without strength" when, "in due time, Christ died for the ungodly" (Rom. v. 6). There was the want of will as well as of power to do anything of ourselves. God has interposed, and done all for us.—J. O.

Ver. 10—chap. vii. 7.—*The uncircumcised lips.* I. " UNCIRCUMCISED LIPS." *Enquire what the significance of this strange expression may be, as coming from Moses.* It can hardly have been a current proverbial phrase adopted for the occasion by Moses, as a still more forcible statement of what he had said before on his felt inability as a speaker. There is no reason to suppose that up to this time there was any such feeling among the Israelites as would originate the expression "uncircumcised lips." They had, indeed, in one instance professed themselves very tenacious of the outward form (Gen. xxxiv. 15), but a general appreciation of the inward and spiritual meaning of this form was not to be expected. Hence we may take these words of Moses as giving a fresh, original and emphatic expression of how deeply Moses felt himself lacking in qualification for this serious enterprise. And evidently also, Moses was doing more than give a forcible variation of the old tale. The new expression goes deeper in its significance than " slow of speech and slow of tongue." It indicates that Moses had been pondering, as indeed he had reason to ponder, the meaning of circumcision. Circumcision was a separating sign, the sign of a peculiar destiny and inheritance, of peculiar duties and privileges. But so far it seemed only to have produced outward separation without inward differences, differences of feeling and disposition. Moses could not see that circumcision had done anything to give him ability for his peculiar task. His way of speaking may therefore be taken as a sign of advance in his appreciation of what was necessary to do Jehovah's work. Hitherto his great concern had been because of natural defects in mere organs of action. He had not thought so much of what was lacking in the life that lay behind the organs, and acted through them. But now we gain some hint that Moses sees what is really wanted. The thing wanted is not simply to be lifted up to the level of men who have all natural qualifications for effective speech, but to be lifted altogether above the ordinary level. Though Moses was " slow of speech, and of a slow tongue," others were not ; but they were all of " uncircumcised lips." Moses, we may take it, has now got beyond the personal reluctance which actuated him in his pleas at Horeb. The avengers of the slain Egyptian no longer frown upon him from the horizon of memory. But now comes in this new plea, urged in a worthier spirit, and with a mournful consciousness of its permanent force. It is a plea which is not a mere excuse, but possesses more of the dignity of a reason.

II. JEHOVAH IN HIS REPLY MAKES NO DIRECT REFERENCE TO THIS CIRCUMCISION OF THE LIPS. When Moses aforetime had spoken of his vocal defects, God at once reminded him that defects of this sort were beyond human responsibility, and he also indicated the clear provision through Aaron for the supply of them. Here, indeed, he again takes the opportunity of repeating to Moses that so far as vocal defects are concerned, Aaron will amply compensate for them. But as to the lips being uncircumcised, while this is indeed true, *it is a state of things which does not bear upon the present need.* Suppose the lips are circumcised—that is, suppose that Moses in his words is brought into full sympathy with the purposes of God—it will make no difference in the immediate results. Pharaoh's heart is being hardened ; his ears are being closed. It matters not with what purity, simplicity, devotion, and faithfulness we speak, if we speak to that which is insensible. Let us by all means blame ourselves for the faulty way in which we speak and live the message of God, but *our faults do not account for the indifference and the rejections of other men.* These faults bring us under censure for our unfaithfulness, but they do not excuse the unbeliever for his neglect. If but one clear word concerning Jesus be spoken—spoken only once—it is enough to fix responsibility on the auditor. " He that hath ears to hear, let him hear." If ever being on earth spoke with circumcised lips, it was Jesus himself, yet how idly fell all his solemn, weighty, truthful words upon the ear of Pharisee and Sadducee. Moses will have blame enough by-and-by, first, cruel and undeserved blame from Israel ; and next, the censure and penalty from Jehovah for the lapse at Meribah. At present, though he is speaking of an unquestionable defect, he is speaking of it in a premature and inapplicable way. He must indeed know the circumcision of the lip and of all other natural faculties ; for this is consequent on the circumcision of the heart. But the great object of all this circumcision is not to secure his acceptance with Pharaoh or with any other sinful or rebellious man. It is rather to secure his acceptance with God, and especially his full enjoyment of all that comes through this acceptance.

III. JEHOVAH POINTS OUT THE WAY IN WHICH PHARAOH SHALL BE EFFECTUALLY BROUGHT TO SUBMISSION. 1. *In the sight of Pharaoh, Moses is to become a God.* In effect Pharaoh has said that Jehovah is no God, and in his heart he thinks Moses a presumptuous impostor. Pharaoh is therefore in a state of mind in which it is impossible to reveal Jehovah to him, but Moses in his own person shall set forth—shall incarnate, so to speak—all that Pharaoh can understand or needs to understand of the Divine power. He shall be compelled to respect the ever-increasing power of Moses. He may hate it, he may make some attempts to resist it, but at the same time the very force of circumstances will bear it in on his mind as a tremendous reality. He shall see how all these successive devastations of his land are connected *in some inscrutable way* with the presence of Moses and the waving of his rod. Whatever the blindness of his heart so that seeing he does not perceive, he will be obliged to perceive that the strength of Moses does not lie in any visible, terrestrial forces. With all his obduracy, Pharaoh has a certain sense of awe before Moses, and doubtless this is the reason why no attempt is made to treat the person of Moses with violence. 2. *Notice the way in which God here applies the method of mediation.* Moses was not a mediator as from Pharaoh upwards to Jehovah, but he was a mediator from Jehovah downwards to Pharaoh. God thus seizes upon the disposition among the ignorant to venerate inscrutable power. Pharaoh will not listen to Moses speaking, but when the signs begin, and especially when they advance far beyond anything which his own magicians can simulate, he is ready to look on Moses as having something of a Divine nature. God looked for the impressible part in Pharaoh's mind and found it here. The way in which Pharaoh evidently came to regard Moses (God's word in ver. 1 being the voucher for the feeling) is illustrated by the attitude towards Paul and Barnabas of the Lystrans (Acts xiv. 8—13) and towards Paul of the Melitans (Acts xxviii. 6). 3. *Notice how God lays emphasis on Pharaoh's continued indifference to any verbal message.* "Pharaoh shall not hearken unto you." The thoughts of Moses are to be turned away more and more from his own lips or from any other faculty. He is to see that the great antagonists in this contest—even though he is made as a God to Pharaoh—are Jehovah and Pharaoh themselves. It is necessary that Pharaoh should have ample opportunity to show the extent of his passive strength, how long and how stiffly he can resist the constraints of Divine omnipotence. God stoops to a patient struggle with this obdurate monarch that he may thereby present, to all who read the Scriptures, an illustration of the complete way in which his power deals with the most stubborn assertions of human power. The Israelites, even with all their sufferings, had as yet seen only a part of what Pharaoh could do. They had seen him in cruel action; they had also to see him in stolid endurance. So Moses had seen signs of Divine power; but he had yet to see that power itself in extensive and awful operation. On the one hand Pharaoh is to be revealed, bringing out all his resources again and again, until at last they are swallowed in the catastrophe of the Red Sea. *Then*, he is done with, but the operations of Divine power are only as it were beginning. It is a great matter that we should thus see the powers arrayed against God, working at the utmost of their strength; that we may feel how immeasurably the power of God transcends them.—Y.

Vers. 9—12.—*The contagion of despair.* I. ISRAEL'S REJECTION OF THE PROFFERED CONSOLATION. They hearkened not "for anguish of spirit and for cruel bondage." 1. The sympathy of the Word of God. Their case stated not only fairly but with infinite compassion. 2. Israel's folly. Their anguish is permitted to stand between them and God their only helper—their sickness between them and the great Physician; multitudes will not hear because they have no sense of need, and multitudes again because their need is so very great. Israel in their folly typical: (1) The poor— "the lapsed masses." (2) Those passing through heavy trial. (3) The bereaved. (4) Those battling despairingly with besetting sin. How often have these no ear for the rich consolations of the promises of God!

II. THE WEAKNESS OF MOSES. 1. Failure among his own people crushes utterly hope of success among strangers and foes. If Israel will not hear, who have everything to gain, will Pharaoh, who has everything to lose? 2. The old sense of his insufficiency again overpowers him. Deaf ears, unmoved hearts, unconsecrated lives in the Church, paralyse the preacher in his appeals to those that are without.—U

EXPOSITION.

Vers. 13—27.—At this point the narrative is interrupted The author, or (it may be) the final compiler—perhaps Joshua—thought it desirable to insert here a genealogical section, taking up the *family* history of Israel from the point at which it was left in ch. i. 5, where the sons of Jacob were enumerated. The whole political system of Israel was based upon the tribal relation; and it was of the last importance, politically, to hand down the divisions and subdivisions of families. The lists here given, probably prepared by Moses in a separate document, had to be inserted somewhere. The present seemed a fitting place. The narrative had reached a turning-point. All the preliminaries were over—the action of the Exodus itself was about to begin. A dramatist would have made Act I. end and Act II. commence. A poet would have begun a new canto. In the imperfect bibliography of the time, it was thought best to make a division by a parenthetic insertion.

Ver. 13 seems to belong to what follows rather than to what precedes. There is no emphasis on the words **and to Aaron,** as if God, having found Moses singly to be irresponsive, had now given a charge to both the brothers conjointly (Rashi). Rather the verse is a concise summary of chs. iii.—v., prefixed to the genealogy when it was a separate document, and preserved when the compiler placed the document in the text

Ver. 14. - **These be the heads of their fathers' houses.** By "fathers' houses" are meant "families" (see 1 Chr. iv. 38; v. 13; vii. 40; ix. 9, etc.); and "the heads of fathers' houses" are simply the acknowledged chiefs and founders of families. The main families of the tribe of Reuben were those of **Hanoch, Pallu, Hezron, and Carmi,** actual sons of the patriarch (See Gen. xlvi. 9; and compare 1 Chr. v. 3.)

Ver. 15.—**The sons of Simeon.** The list corresponds exactly, both in the names and in the order, with that given in Gen. xlvi. 10, but differs considerably from 1 Chr. iv. 24, and Num. xxvi. 12. In both the latter places Jemuel appears as Nemuel, and Zohar as Zerah, while Obad is omitted. In 1 Chr. iv. 24, Jachin appears as Jarib. It would seem that the family of Obad died out and disappeared soon after the Israelites quitted Egypt. The family

of Shaul, on the other hand, increased and multiplied (1 Chr. iv. 25—27).

Ver. 16.—**The sons of Levi.** The same three sons are given in Gen. xlvi. 11; Num. iii. 17; and 1 Chr. vi. 2. **According to their generations.** This phrase is introduced because the writer does not here, stop at the sons, but proceeds on to the grandsons, great-grandsons, and other descendants. (See vers. 17—25.) He is concerned especially in this place with the descent of Moses, and therefore with the genealogy of the tribe of Levi, and has only inserted any account of the families descended from Reuben and Simeon, that he might not seem to disregard the claims of primogeniture. **The years of the life of Levi.** These began about forty or fifty years before the descent into Egypt, which took place after the birth of all his three sons, as appears from Gen. xlvi. 8—11. The length of Levi's life is recorded, not from any chronological considerations, but to show God's blessing upon the family of Moses, which gave such length of days to so many of his ancestors.

Ver. 17.—**The sons of Gershon.** The line of Gershon, as the eldest, is taken first. Moses and Aaron are descended from the second son. **Shimi** is called "Shimei" in 1 Chr. vi. 17; but there is no difference in the original.

Ver. 18.—**The sons of Kohath.** The same names are given in 1 Chr. vi. 2 and 18. **The years of the life of Kohath.** Kohath, who was probably about twenty at the time of the descent into Egypt, must have considerably outlived Joseph, who died about seventy years after the descent. His eldest son, Amram, is not likely to have been born much later than his father's thirtieth year. (See Gen. xi. 12—24.) Amram would thus have been contemporary with Joseph for above fifty years.

Ver. 19.—**The sons of Merari.** The same names occur in 1 Chr. vi. 19 and xxiii. 21, Mahali, by a difference of pointing, becoming Mahli. The Mahlites and Mushites were among the most important of the Levitical families (Num. iii. 33; xxvi. 58).

Ver. 20.—**Amram.** That this Amram is the "man of the house of Levi" mentioned in ch. ii. 1, cannot be doubted; but it is scarcely possible that he should be the Amram of ver. 18, the actual son of Kohath and contemporary of Joseph. He is probably a descendant of the sixth or seventh generation, who bore the same name, and was the head of the Amramite house. That house, at the time of the Exodus, numbered above two thousand males (Num. iii. 27, 28). See the excellent remarks of Keil and Delitzsch, 'Biblical Commentary,' vol. i. p. 470, E. T.; and compare Kurtz, 'History of Old Covenant,' vol. ii. p. 144, and Cook, in 'Speaker's Commentary,' vol. i. p. 274. **Jochebed his father's sister.** Marriages with aunts and nieces have been common in many countries, and are not forbidden by any natural instinct. They first became unlawful by the positive command recorded in Lev. xviii. 12. The name Jochebed is the earliest known compounded with Jah, or Jehovah. It means "the glory of Jehovah." **She bare him Aaron and Moses.** Aaron is placed first, as being older than Moses (ch. vii. 7). Miriam is omitted, since the object of the writer is confined to tracing descent in the male line.

Ver. 21.—**The sons of Izhar.** Korah is mentioned as a "son (descendant) of Izhar" in Num. xvi. 1 and 1 Chr. vi. 38. The other "sons" are not elsewhere mentioned. Zithri in this verse should be Zichri.

Ver. 22.—**The sons of Uzziel.** Mishael and Elzaphan are again mentioned as "sons of Uzziel" in Lev. x. 4. They were employed by Moses to carry the bodies of Nadab and Abihu out of the camp. Elzaphan, called Elizaphan, is mentioned as head of the Kohathites in Num. iii. 30.

Ver. 23. — **Elisheba, daughter of Amminadab.** Amminadab had not been previously mentioned. He was a descendant of Judah, through Pharez and Hezron, and held a place in the line of our Lord's ancestry. (See 1 Chr. ii. 3—10 · Matt. i. 5.) **Naashon** was at this

time "prince of the tribe of Judah" (Num ii. 3). **Nadab and Abihu.** On their fate, see Lev. x. 1, 2. **Eleazar** became high-priest upon the death of Aaron (Num. xx. 23—28). His death is related in Josh. xxiv. 33.

Ver. 24.—**The sons of Korah.** All Korah's sons were not cut off with him (Num. xxvi. 11). Three at least survived, and became the heads of "families of the Korhites."

Ver. 25.—**Eleazar...took him one of the daughters of Putiel to wife.** Putiel is not elsewhere mentioned. The name is thought to be half Egyptian (compare Poti-phar) and to mean "dedicated to God." **She bare him Phinehas.** This Phinehas became high priest on the death of Eleazar (Judg. xx. 28). **The heads of the fathers.** I.e. "the patriarchal chiefs."

Vers. 26, 27.—The genealogy being concluded as a separate document, its author appends a notice that the Aaron and Moses mentioned in it (ver. 20) are the very Aaron and Moses who received the Divine command to lead the children of Israel out of Egypt, and who appeared before Pharaoh, and "spoke to him" on their behalf. As the heading of the document was kept upon its insertion into the narrative of the Exodus (see the comment on ver. 13), so its concluding sentences were kept, though (according to modern ideas) superfluous.

Ver. 26.—**According to their armies.** The term "armies" had not been previously used of the Israelitish people; but it occurs in ch. vii. 4, which was probably in the mind of the writer who drew up the genealogy

HOMILETICS.

Vers. 13—27.—*The historical character of real revelation.* Among the religions of the world which are based on the contents of a written volume, none has such an historical character as the religion of Christians. Most nations have evolved their religion out of their internal consciousness, and have then, after a certain lapse of time, thrown into a narrative form the supposed revelations made to this or that individual secretly, and by him committed to writing. These revelations—to give them the name —are not connected with any series of events, are not, properly speaking, historical at all, but belong to the domain of thought, contemplation, philosophy. It is quite otherwise with the religion of the Bible. Both in the Old Testament and in the New our attention is directed primarily and mainly to a series of facts. Religion is not put before us in an abstract, but in a concrete form. The Bible represents to us "God in history." We learn the nature and the will of God from his dealings with nations and individuals at definite times and in definite places. It is a necessary consequence of such a mode of inculcating religious truth, that very dry and mundane details must from time to time be obtruded upon the reader, in order that the narrative may be clear, and that he may understand the circumstances of time and place with which each writer in his turn has to deal. In this way genealogies come in. History cannot be understood without them. We want to know who the individuals are who are introduced afresh at each new stage in the narrative, and in what relation they stand to those other individuals with whom the narrative is concerned before and after. Genealogies convey this knowledge. Many think them uninteresting; but they are not so to any thoughtful person. For (1) they raise the salutary thought of the rapid flight of time and the speedy passing away of one generation after another. Οἴη περ φυλλῶν γενέη, τοίηδε καὶ ἀνδρῶν. (2) They show us how good men and bad, great men and little, are intermixed in the world, arise under the same conditions, seem produced by the same circumstances; and thus they force us to see what a vast power the human will has in shaping human character, and even in determining the course of earthly events. Hence they remind us of our responsibilities. (3) They hold up to us warnings and examples —warnings in the names to which there is attached the savour of evil deeds never to be forgotten so long as the world endures—Nadabs, Abihus, Korahs; examples in those, familiar to us as household words, which we no sooner hear or see than there rush to our thought a crowd of glorious and heroic actions. Being dead, these men still speak to us—theirs is a death " full of immortality."

EXPOSITION.

Vers. 28 — 30 — The remainder of this chapter is scarcely more than a recapitulation. The author, or compiler, having interposed his genealogical section, has to take up the narrative from verse 12, where he broke off, and does so by almost repeating the words of verses 10—12. The only important addition is the insertion of the words —" I am the Lord " (ver. 29), and the only important variation, the substitution of " Speak thou unto Pharaoh *all that I say unto thee*" (ibid.), for " Speak unto Pharaoh . . . that he let the children of Israel go out of his land" (ver. 11).

Ver. 29.—**I am the Lord.** It is not improbable that every revelation made to Moses was authenticated by these initial words— which have the force of that initial phrase, so constant in the later prophets—" Thus saith the Lord."

Ver. 30.—**All that I say unto thee.** To the general command thus expressed, was probably appended the particular injunction of verse 11, not here repeated—" Speak thou unto Pharaoh, that he let the children of Israel go out of his land." The sacred historians continually abbreviate

HOMILIES BY VARIOUS AUTHORS.

Vers. 14—28.—*The genealogy of Moses and Aaron.* Beside its direct interest as setting in an exact light the descent and relationship of the two principal figures in the succeeding history—Moses, the Lawgiver of Israel, and Aaron, the head of the priesthood —this genealogical register presents us with several points deserving of attention. We are taught by it—

I. To RECOGNISE THE DIVINE SOVEREIGNTY IN THE SELECTION OF ITS INSTRUMENTS. 1. *The men selected*—Moses and Aaron (vers. 26, 27). Selection, as implying the previous or foreseen existence of variously qualified objects from which the selection is made is scarcely the fitting term to express the fact we have in view, viz. the preparing and raising up at this particular time and place, and from this particular stock, of a man of the special mould of Moses, with an eye to the accomplishment by him of a certain work. The appearance of great men at particular junctures of history is assuredly not to be attributed to chance. It is a shallow view of the Divine election which regards it as simply availing itself of happy varieties of character spontaneously presenting themselves in the course of natural development; as a workman might choose from a set of ready-made tools those best suited for his purpose. Election, if one may so speak, presides at the *making* of its object (Isaac, Jacob, David, etc.) as well as uses it when made (see Lange's ' Dogmatics'). The question is not simply how, a man of Moses' gifts and qualifications being given, God should use him in the way he did, but rather, how a man of this spiritual build came at that precise juncture to be there at all—broke out at that point in the genealogical tree and not at another. This is the true problem, and the solution can only be found in the Divine arrangements. 2. *The sovereignty of the selection.* We cannot but be struck by the almost studious departure in this list from the lines of descent which would imply natural pre-eminence. (1) Moses is not descended from Reuben and Simeon, the eldest sons of Jacob (vers. 14, 15). The only purpose, apparently, served by the introduction of these two names in the genealogy is to show that Moses did *not* spring from them. (2) Neither did he

spring from Judah or Joseph—the sons of Jacob who fell heirs to the birthright forfeited by the sin of Reuben (1 Chron. v. 1, 2). The genealogy stops, as having attained
its end, before it gets their length. (3) He sprang from Levi—a tribe originally
united with Simeon under a curse (Gen. xlix. 7)—yet not from the oldest branch of it,
but from Kohath, the second son (vers. 16—19). (4) Moses himself was not the
eldest son of Amram, but stood by descent in a secondary relation to Aaron, who was
afterwards to occupy so secondary a position in relation to *him*. What are we taught
by these facts, if not the lesson so strongly emphasised in Rom. ix., that mere natural
advantages constitute no ground of pre-eminence in the kingdom of God; that the
spiritual everywhere rules and controls the natural. Examples may be drawn from
every part of Scripture history. Isaac, not Ishmael; Jacob, not Esau; Ephraim, not
Manasseh; David, not his elder brothers; etc. The Jehovah attributes of freedom and
sovereignty, to which this chapter introduces us, find not their least conspicuous illustration in this section of it.

II. To TRACE, NOTWITHSTANDING, IN THE EXERCISE OF THE DIVINE SOVEREIGNTY,
VARIOUS SPIRITUAL LAWS. The sovereignty of God is degraded whenever it is viewed
as mere arbitrariness or caprice, as a liberty of indifference, or as anything else than the
perfectly free and self-determined action of an all-wise, all-holy, all-good Will, working
at every moment for the accomplishment of wise and good ends. Studied in this light,
it will be recognised that it has not only (1) its inherent laws of operation, but (2) its
self-imposed limitations. Partial glimpses of some of these laws are here afforded us.
1. *The natural, while subordinate to the spiritual, is taken as the basis of it.* There is
to be recognised a congruity between the instrument and the use to which it is to be
put; between the man, in respect of his physical, mental, and moral endowments, and
the work for which he is designed. Election works in the natural sphere prior to its
being revealed in the spiritual. Moses, for example, was, on his natural side, the product of a long line of causes operating through successive generations for the production
of just such a man as he was. He was a descendant of Levi, as truly as any other.
Inherited organisation was a fact of quite as capital importance in his case as in the
case of any of his contemporaries. It had as much to do with the kind and
quality of his manhood. Compare also Paul, separated from his mother's womb (Gal.
i. 15), and essentially the same man after his conversion as before it. The mould in
which he was cast by nature was that which specially fitted him for the work he had to
do as an apostle. 2. *The purpose of God is wrought out not fatalistically, but in
harmony with the laws of human freedom, and through man's moral self-determinations.*
This principle also receives striking illustration in the names of this list. The derivation of Moses from Levi, and not from Reuben or Simeon, has a connection with facts in
the moral history of the respective tribes. Reuben, Simeon, and Levi, the progenitors, were
all three originally of so wicked a disposition as virtually to undergo their father's curse.
Reuben lost the birthright, and Simeon and Levi were denied an inheritance with their
brethren (Gen. xlix. 3—8). The descendants of the two former followed closely in the
footsteps of their ancestors, and consequently never recovered themselves. It was
different with the tribe of Levi, which by earnest piety and zeal seems to have risen to
the rank of moral leadership even in Egypt, and was honoured to give birth to Moses
and Aaron. And greater honour still was in reserve for it; for while in its letter—
"I will divide them in Jacob, and scatter them in Israel"—the curse was not repealed, an
entirely new turn was given to it by the election of the tribe to the priesthood and
service of the sanctuary. The curse was changed into a blessing. Had Reuben and
Simeon followed in Levi's footsteps, who can doubt but that mercy would have been
shown to them also? 3. *Election flows by preference in the lines of pious descent.*
Moses and Aaron were the children of pious parents. The names of Moses' father—
Amram, "the kindred of the lofty one"—and of his mother—she "whose glory is
Jehovah" (ver. 20), testify to the piety of his ancestry. The instruction he received
from them in early life, and during the visits he paid to their home, would not be
without an important influence upon his character, and he had the benefit of their unceasing prayers. Aaron had even greater home advantages, in being with his parents
till character was fully formed. This also is an important fact in its bearing on God's
election of them to special service. The faith and prayers of parents have an important
influence on the salvation of their children. By far the larger number of pious men and

women in the world have come from pious homes. (See numerous illustrations of this in Dr. Norman MacLeod's 'Home School.') The Church historian, Neander, has noticed in how many cases "pious mothers" had to do with the planting of the seeds of Christianity in the souls of those who afterwards produced great effects as teachers of the Church. He instances Nonna, the mother of Gregory of Nazianzum; Arethusa of Antioch, the mother of Chrysostom; the mother of Theodoret; and Monica, the mother of Augustine. (See the whole passage in 'Church History,' vol. iii. sect. 2, I.)

III. THAT HONOUR IN GOD'S SIGHT IS DETERMINED BY SPIRITUAL CONSIDERATIONS. 1. As regards *position*. The true centre point of honour in this genealogy is ver. 20— that which includes the names of Moses and Aaron. It was the *spiritual* greatness of these men which secured for them this honour. 2. As regards *rise and fall*, Reuben was "the firstborn of Israel" (ver. 14), but he lost through sin the prerogatives of birth. He is eclipsed by Levi, who, through piety, rose from a degraded position to one of honour. Korah, whose name, from considerations of relationship, is honourably prominent in this select list (vers. 21—24), subsequently destroyed himself by his rebellion (Num. xvi.). His posterity, however (another illustration of the same law), rose to high spiritual honour in the minstrelsy of the temple. 3. As regards *relationship*. The families of the tribe of Levi, grouped around the names of Moses and Aaron, some in nearer, some in more distant relations, draw honour from the association. The chief prominence is given to the Kohathites, as most nearly related to the sons of Amram. This distinction was subsequently confirmed by the appointment of this family to the charge of the sacred Ark, and of the vessels of the sanctuary (Num. iv. 4—16). Relationship with the good thus confers honour, and secures privilege. The highest of all examples of this is the honour and privilege conferred through relationship to Christ.—J. O.

EXPOSITION.

CHAPTER VII.

Vers. 1—9.—Once more God made allowance for the weakness and self-distrust of Moses, severely tried as he had been by his former failure to persuade Pharaoh (ch. v. 1—5) and his recent rejection by the people of Israel (ch. vi. 9). He made allowance, and raised his courage and his spirits by fresh promises, and by a call upon him for immediate action. The process of deliverance, God assured him, was just about to begin. Miracles would be wrought until Pharaoh's stubbornness was overcome. He was himself to begin the series at once by casting his rod upon the ground, that it might become a serpent (ver. 9). From this point Moses' diffidence wholly disappears. Once launched upon his Heaven-directed course, assured of his miraculous powers, committed to a struggle with the powerful Egyptian king, he persevered without blenching or wavering until success crowned his efforts.

Ver. 1.—I have made thee a god to Pharaoh. Moses was diffident of appearing a second time before Pharaoh, who was so much his worldly superior. God reminds him that he is in truth very much Pharaoh's superior. If Pharaoh has earthly, he has unearthly power. He is to Pharaoh "as a god," with a

right to command his obedience, and with strength to enforce his commands. Aaron shall be thy prophet, *i.e.* "thy spokesman"— the interpreter of thy will to others. Compare ch. iv. 16.

Ver. 2.—Thou shalt speak. The Septuagint and the Vulgate have, "Thou shalt speak *to him*," which undoubtedly gives the true sense. Moses was to speak to Aaron, Aaron to Pharaoh. (See ch. iv. 15, 16.)

Ver. 3.—I will harden Pharaoh's heart. See the comment on ch. iv. 21. And multiply my signs and my wonders. The idea of a long series of miracles is here, for the first time, distinctly introduced. Three signs had been given (ch. iv. 3—9); one further miracle had been mentioned (*ib.* 23). Now a *multiplication* of signs and wonders is promised. Compare ch. iii. 20, and ch. vi. 6, which, however, are not so explicit as the present passage.

Ver. 4.—That I may lay my hand on Egypt. Pharaoh's obstinacy was foreseen and foreknown. He was allowed to set his will against God's, in order that there might be a great display of Almighty power, such as would attract the attention both of the Egyptians generally and of all the surrounding nations. God's glory would be thereby promoted, and there would be a general dread of interfering with his people. (See ch. xv. 14—16; Deut. ii. 25; xi. 25, etc.) Bring forth my armies. See the comment on ch. vi. 26. Great judgments. See above, ch. vi. 6.

Ver. 5.—**The Egyptians shall know that I am the Lord.** Rather, "that I am Jehovah" —*i.e.* that I answer to my Name—that I am the only God who is truly existent, other so-called gods being nonentities. They will know this and feel this **when I stretch forth mine hand upon Egypt,** as I am about to stretch it forth.

Ver. 6.—**Moses and Aaron did as the Lord commanded them.** This statement is general, and anticipative of the entire series of interviews beginning here (verse 10), and terminating (ch. x. 29) with the words, "I will see thy face no more." The obedience of Moses and Aaron was perfect and continuous from this time forward until Egypt was quitted.

Ver. 7.—**Fourscore years old.** This age is confirmed by the statement (in Deut. xxxi. 2; xxxiv. 7) that Moses was a hundred and twenty at his death. It is also accepted as exact by St. Stephen (Acts vii. 23, 30).

Moderns are surprised that at such an age a man could undertake and carry through a difficult and dangerous enterprise; but in Egypt one hundred and ten years was not considered a very exceptionally long life, and men frequently retained their full vigour till seventy or eighty.

Ver. 9.—**When Pharaoh shall speak to you, saying, Shew a miracle.** It is obvious that there would have been an impropriety in Moses and Aaron offering a sign to Pharaoh until he asked for one. They claimed to be ambassadors of Jehovah, and to speak in his name (ch. v. 1). Unless they were misdoubted, it was not for them to produce their credentials. Hence they worked no miracle at their former interview. Now, however, the time was come when their credentials would be demanded, and an express command was given them to exhibit the first "sign."

HOMILETICS.

Vers. 1, 2.—*God assigns to each man his intellectual grade.* Three different intellectual grades are here set before us—that of the thinker, that of the expounder, and that of the mere recipient. Pharaoh, notwithstanding his exalted earthly rank, occupies the lowest position. He is to hang on the words of Aaron, who is to be to him as a prophet of the Most High. Aaron himself is to hang on the words of Moses, and to be simply his mouthpiece. Moses is to stand to both (compare ch. iv. 16) as God. And here note, that the positions are not self-assumed—God assigns them. So there are leaders of thought in all ages, to whom God has given their intellectual gifts, whom he has marked out for intellectual pre-eminency, and whom he makes to stand to the rest of men as gods. Sometimes they are their own prophets—they combine, that is, the power of utterance with the power of thought. But very often they need an interpreter. Their lips are uncircumcised. They lack eloquence; or they even lack the power of putting their thoughts into words, and require a "prophet," to publish their views to the world. The "prophet-interpreter" occupies a position very much below theirs, but still one requiring important and peculiar gifts, such as God alone can give. He must have the intelligence to catch the true bearing, connection, and force of the ideas presented to him, often in rude and uncouth language, like statues rough-hewn. He must be able to work up the rough material into presentable form. He must have a gift of language, if not a gift of speech. The great mass of men occupy a lower rank than either of these; they can neither originate, nor skilfully interpret; it remains that they be content to receive. God has given to them their humble position, as he has given to the others their loftier ones. They should cultivate their receptivity. They should be satisfied to listen and learn. They should remember that if, on the one hand, οὗτος μὲν πανάριστος, ὃς αὐτὸς πάντα νοήσῃ—on the other, ἐσθλὸς δ' αὖ κἀκεῖνος ὃς εὖ εἰπόντι πίθηται.

Vers. 3—5.—*The fierceness of man turns to God's praise.* The most signal triumphs of Divine power are those in which the resistance to it is the most determined. The greatest of all victories was probably that which was gained when—after "war in heaven"—Satan was seen, like lightning, falling from heaven to earth. Since then, great triumphs, tending to God's praise, occur whenever the right and the truth succeed against seemingly insuperable opposition. When the boy shepherd with his sling and stone smites to the earth the gigantic Philistine—when the proud Sennacherib after all his boasts has to leave Jerusalem unhurt and fly to Nineveh—when Epiphanes is defied and baffled by a handful of Jewish mountaineers—when victory is finally gained by "Athanasius contra mundum," God's might is seen and recognised, as it would not have been, unless overwhelming strength had seemed to be arrayed against comparative weakness. When the "heathen rage," and the "kings of the earth and rulers" are on their side, and the cry of defiance goes forth : "Let us break God's bands asunder, and cast away his cords from us"—then God is most apt to show his might—to "refrain the spirit of princes," and make it manifest that he "is wonderful among the kings of the earth." The longer and fiercer the opposition, the more conspicuously is God's praise shown forth. Blow follows blow until the opposing power is shattered, smitten to the ground, laid prostrate. Then is the time for the song of triumph : "Be wise now therefore, O ye kings : be instructed, ye judges of the earth. Serve the Lord with fear, and rejoice with trembling. Kiss the Son, lest he be angry, and ye perish from the right way, when his wrath is kindled but a little. Blessed are all they that put their trust in him !" (Ps. ii. 10—12).

Ver. 9.—*Miracles the credentials of an ambassador from God.* It is not easy to see any way in which God could authenticate a message as coming from him, except by giving the messenger supernatural powers. Conceivably, he might proclaim his will from heaven directly, in terms of human speech. But even then doubts would be raised as to the words uttered ; men's recollections of them would differ ; some would question whether words were used at all, and would hold that it had "thundered" (John xii. 29). If, to avoid such results, he speaks to man through man, how is he to make it clear that his prophet has indeed been sent by him ? He cannot make his messenger impeccable, if he is still to be man. He cannot give him irresistible eloquence, for eloquence is at once suspected ; the reason rises up against it and resists it. What other course is there, but to impart to his messenger a portion of his own command over nature—in other words, to give him the power of working miracles ? The light of nature seems to have taught Pharaoh to ask for this proof. The same light taught Nicodemus to accept it—"No man can do these miracles that thou doest, except God be with him" (*ib.* iii. 2). So it will ever be with simple men in simple times. It is only when men have become sophisticated, when they have darkened the light that is in them by "foolish questionings" and "oppositions of science falsely so called," that they begin to see specious objections to miracles, and regard them as "difficulties in the way of receiving a revelation" rather than as convincing evidences of it. We may properly call upon an opponent to tell us what evidence of a Divine mission he would accept, if he rejects miracles as an evidence, and wait for his answer. We shall probably find that ὁ ἀναιρῶν ταύτην τὴν πίστιν οὐ πανὺ πιστότερα ἐρεῖ ("he who destroys this basis of belief will not discover a surer one").—Aristotle.

HOMILIES BY VARIOUS AUTHORS.

Vers. 1—8.—*A god to Pharaoh.* Moses was in the trying position of being sent out anew upon a mission in which hitherto he had not had the slightest particle of success. His discouragement was *natural.* Pharaoh, on a previous occasion, had repulsed him. He had lost the ear even of his own people. The situation, since his former interview with the monarch, had altered for the worse. To proceed further was like rowing against wind and tide, with little prospect of ever reaching shore. Discouragement *wrought in the usual way.* It led him to magnify difficulties. He brought up again his old objection of his deficiencies of speech. Even with Aaron as an intermediary, he felt how awkward it would be to appear in the presence of Pharaoh, and not be able to deliver his own message. His inability of speech would certainly, he thought, expose him to contempt. Yet observe, God *forebore* with him. His reluctance was not without sin, but God, who knows our frame, does not expect to find in us all at once the perfection of angels, and is compassionate of our weakness. We have here, therefore—

I. A DISHEARTENED SERVANT SUITABLY ENCOURAGED. God told Moses—1. *That he would clothe him with an authority which even Pharaoh would be compelled to respect.* "See, I have made thee a god to Pharaoh" (ver. 1). It was not with *words* only that Moses was sent to Pharaoh. Powers would be given him to enforce his words with *deeds.* The judgments he would bring upon the land would clothe him with a supernatural terror—make him a superhuman and almost a divine person—in the eyes of

Pharaoh and his servants. (Cf. ch. xii. 3.) So God gives attestation to his servants still, making it evident by the power of the Holy Ghost upon them, that they come in his name, and speak with his authority. He accompanies their word with Divine power, giving it efficacy to arrest, convict, and convert, and compelling the haughtiest of the earth to acknowledge the source of their message. So Felix trembled before Paul (Acts xxiv. 25). Paul's Gospel came to the Thessalonians, " not in word only, but also in power, and in the Holy Ghost, and in much assurance" (1 Thess. i. 5). 2. *That the work of deliverance would be no longer delayed.* This also was implied in what God said to Moses : the time had come for speech to be exchanged for action. Everything indicated that the "charge" with which Moses was now entrusted was to be the final one. It should encourage desponding servants to reflect that God has his "set time" for the fulfilment of every promise ; and that, when this period arrives, all their mourning will be turned into joy.

II. THE COURSE OF ISRAEL'S DELIVERANCE FORETOLD. 1. *Foretold because foreseen.* It is God's prerogative that he knows the end from the beginning (Is. xlii. 9). Nothing can take him by surprise. He knows all the way his purposes are to travel. The whole future lies mapped out, as in a clear-drawn chart, before him. 2. *Foreseen because pre-ordained.* God, like Christ in the miracle of the loaves, knew in himself what he would do (John vi. 6). Nothing was left to chance in his arrangements. The steps in his plan were fixed beforehand. What would be done would be according to God's "determinate counsel and foreknowledge" (Acts ii. 23)—would be "whatsoever (his) hand and (his) counsel determined before to be done" (Acts iv. 28). The deliverance was arranged in such a way as most to glorify the power and greatness of the Deliverer, and demonstrate his superiority to heathen idols. This in no wise implies that violence was in the very least done to human freedom, though it suggests that God can so interweave the volitions of men, in the situations in which he places them, into his purposes, as to leave not one of them outside his settled plan. The chief difficulty is in the hardening of Pharaoh's heart, here (ver. 3) represented as an ordained link in the chain of God's designs. But if this hardening simply means that God will place Pharaoh, already a bad man, in circumstances which he knows infallibly *will* harden his heart, and if this is done justly, and in punishment of former sins, the hardening taking effect through unalterable laws of the moral nature, which also are of God's ordainment, it is difficult to see what righteous objection can be taken to it. 3. *Foretold for wise ends.* Similar predictions of the course of the deliverance had been made at earlier stages (cf. ch. iii. 19—22; iv. 21—24; vi. 1—9). They are here repeated— (1) For the instruction of Moses, that he might be prepared for all that was to happen— that he might understand and co-operate with God in the execution of his designs. (2) For the re-invigoration of Moses' faith. (3) That it might be evidenced by the working-out of this fore-announced plan, that the God of Israel was indeed Jehovah, a free, personal Being, working in history for the accomplishment of gracious purposes. "The secret of the Lord is with them that fear him" (Ps. xxv. 14). God takes Moses into his counsel, and discovers to him something of his plan of operation. So he does in the Scriptures with his Church (Rev. i. 1).

II. A GLIMPSE OF GOD'S END IN PROVIDENTIAL GOVERNMENT (vers. 3, 4). The end is twofold—1. The manifestation of the utterly free and unconstrained character of his grace and mercy in the salvation of man ; and 2. What is the necessary counterpart of this, the manifestation of his power and justice in the infliction of judgments upon his enemies. Even evil is thus made to contribute indirectly to the ultimate and eternal establishment of the righteousness of God.—J. O.

Ver. 3.—*Heart-hardening.* On this subject, see above, and on ch. iv. 21. The present seems an appropriate place for a somewhat fuller treatment.

I. HARDENING AS PROCEEDING FROM GOD. "I will harden Pharaoh's heart." This, assuredly, is more than simple permission. God hardens the heart—1. *Through the operation of the laws of our moral constitution.* These laws, of which God is the author, and through which he operates in the soul, ordain hardening as the penalty of evil conduct, of resistance to truth, and of all misimprovement and abuse of privilege. 2. *Through his providence*—as when God, in the execution of his judgments, places a wicked man in situations which he knows can only have a hardening effect upon him.

He does this in righteousness. "God, having permitted evil to exist, must thereafter of necessity permit it also to run its whole course in the way of showing itself to be what it really is, as that which aims at the defeat of the Divine purpose, and the consequent dissolution of the universe." This involves hardening. 3. *Through a direct judgment in the soul of the individual,* God smiting him with a spirit of blindness and infatuation in punishment of obstinate resistance to the truth. This is the most difficult of all aspects of hardening, but it only cuts the knot, does not untie it, to put superficial meanings upon the scriptures which allege the reality of the judgment (*e.g.* Deut. xxviii. 28 ; 2 Thess. ii. 11). It is to be viewed as connected with what may be called the *internal* providence of God in the workings of the human mind ; his government of the mind in the wide and obscure regions of its involuntary activities. The direction taken by these activities, seeing that they do not spring from man's own will, must be as truly under the regulation of Providence, and be determined in quite as special a manner, as are the *outward* circumstances of our lot, or those so-called *fortuities* concerning which we are assured : " Are not two sparrows sold for a farthing ? and one of them shall not fall on the ground without your Father " (Matt. x. 29). It is a significant fact that, as sin advances, the sinner becomes less and less a free agent, falls increasingly under the dominion of necessity. The involuntary activities of the soul gain ground upon the voluntary. The hardening may be conceived of, partly as the result of a withdrawal of light and restraining grace ; partly as a giving of the soul up to the delusions of the adversary, " the spirit that now worketh in the children of disobedience " (Eph. ii. 2), whose will gradually occupies the region in the moral life vacated by the human will, and asserts there a correspondingly greater power of control ; and partly as the result of a direct Divine ordering of the course of thought, feeling, and imagination. Hengstenberg acutely remarks : " It appears to proceed from design, that the hardening at the beginning of the plagues is attributed, in a preponderating degree, to Pharaoh, and towards the end to God. The higher the plagues rise, so much the more does Pharaoh's hardening assume a supernatural character, so much the more obvious is it to refer it to its supernatural causality."

II. Hardening in itself considered. The heart is the centre of personality, the source of moral life, the seat of the will, the conscience, and the affections (Prov. iv. 23 ; Matt. xv. 18). The hardening of the heart may be viewed under two aspects : 1. More generally as the result of growth in sin, with consequent loss of moral and religious susceptibility ; and 2. As hardening against God, the author of its moral life. We have but to put these two things together—the heart, the *seat* of moral life, hardening itself against the *Author* of its moral life—to see that such hardening is of necessity fatal, an act of moral suicide. It may elucidate the subject to remark that in every process of hardening there is something which the heart *parts with,* something which it *resists,* and something which it *becomes.* There is, in other words— (1) That which the heart hardens itself *in,* viz. some evil quality, say injustice, cruelty, lust, hate, secret enmity to God, which quality gradually becomes a fixed element in character ; (2) that which the heart hardens itself *against,* viz. the influences of truth, love, and righteousness, in whatever ways these are brought to bear upon it, whether in the promptings of conscience, the movements of natural sensibility, the remonstrances of parents and friends, the Word of God, the internal strivings of the Spirit ; and (3) that which the heart *parts with* in hardening, viz. with its original susceptibility to truth, with its sensitiveness to moral influences, with its religious feeling, with its natural generosity, etc. The result is blindness, callousness, lostness to the feeling of right, to the sense of shame, to the authority of God, to the voice of truth, even to true self-interest. All hardening is thus *double-sided ;* hardening in hate, *e.g.,* being at the same time hardening against love, with a loss of the capacity of love ; hardening in injustice being a hardening against justice, with a loss of the capacity for moral discernment ; hardening in cruelty being a hardening against kindliness, with a corresponding destruction of the benevolent sensibilities ; hardening against God being at the same time hardening in self-hood, in egoism, with a loss of the capacity of faith. We hence conclude : 1. *All evil hardens,* and *all hardening in moral evil is in principle hardening against God.* The hardening may begin at the circumference of the moral nature, and involve the centre, or it may begin at the centre, and work out to the circumference. Men may be enemies to God in their mind *by wicked works* (Col. i. 21), they may have "the understanding darkened," and be "alienated from the life of God through the ignorance that is in them, because of the blindness (*marg.* hardness) of their hearts," and being "past feeling" may give "themselves over unto lasciviousness, to work all uncleanness with greediness" (Eph. iv. 17—19), and yet be strangers to God's revealed truth. All sin, all resistance to light, all disobedience to conscience, has this hardening effect (cf. Rom. i. 19—32). But it is a will which has broken from God which is thus in various ways hardening itself, and enmity to God is latent in the process. The moment the truth of God is brought to bear on such a nature, this latent enmity is made manifest, and, as in the case of Pharaoh, further hardening is the result. Conversely, 2. *Hardening against God is hardening in moral evil.* The hardening may begin at the centre, in resistance to God's known will, and to the scrivings of his Spirit, and thence spread through the whole moral nature. This is the deepest and fundamental hardening, and of itself gives a character to the being. A heart hardened in its interior against its Maker would be entitled to be called hard, no matter what superficial qualities of a pleasant kind remained to it, and no matter how correct the moral conduct. 3. *Hardening results in a very special degree from resistance to the Word of God, to Divine revelation.* This is the type of hardening which is chiefly spoken of in Scripture, and which gives rise to what it specially calls "the hard and impenitent heart" (Rom. ii. 5). All revelation of God, especially his revelation in Christ, has a *testing* power, and if resisted produces a hardness which speedily becomes obduracy. God may be resisted in his Word, his Spirit, his servants, his chastisements, and in the testimony to his existence and authority written on the soul itself. But the highest form of resistance—the worst and deadliest—is resistance to the Spirit drawing to Christ.

III. THE HARDENING OF PHARAOH COMPARED WITH HARDENING UNDER THE GOSPEL. Pharaoh stands out in Scripture as the typical instance of hardening of the heart. 1. He and Jehovah stood in direct opposition to each other. 2. God's will was made known to him in a way he could not mistake. He pretended at first to doubt, but doubt soon became impossible. 3. He resisted to the last. And the longer he resisted, his heart grew harder. 4. His resistance was his ruin. In considering the case of this monarch, however, and comparing it with our own, we have to remember—1. That Pharaoh was a *heathen king.* He was naturally prejudiced in favour of the gods of Egypt. He had at first no knowledge of Jehovah. But *we* have had from infancy the advantage of a knowledge of the true God, of his existence, his attributes, and his demands. 2. Pharaoh had a *heathen upbringing.* His moral training was vastly inferior to that which most have enjoyed who hear the Gospel. 3. The influences he resisted were *outward influences*—strokes of judgment. The hardening produced by resistance to the *inward* influences of Christianity, strivings of the Spirit, etc., is necessarily of a deeper kind. 4. What was demanded of Pharaoh was *the liberation of a nation of slaves*—in our case it is required that we part with *sins*, and yield up heart and will to the Creator and Redeemer. Outward compliance would have sufficed in his case; in ours, the compliance must be inward and spiritual. Here, again, inasmuch as the demand goes deeper, the hardening produced by resistance is of necessity deeper also. There is now possible to man the unpardonable sin of blasphemy against the Holy Ghost (Matt. xii. 32 ; Heb. vi. 4—6). 5. The *motives* in the two cases are not comparable. In the one case, God revealed in judgments; in the other, in transcendent love and mercy.

Conclusion :—"To-day, if ye will hear his voice, harden not your hearts" (Heb. iii. 7, 8, 13, 15, iv. 7). Beware, in connection with this hardening, of "the deceitfulness of sin." The heart has many ways of *disguising* from itself the fact that it is resisting God, and hardening itself in opposition to him. One form is *procrastination.* Not yet —a more convenient season. A second is *compromise.* We shall find attempts at this with Pharaoh. By conceding *part* of what is asked—giving up some sin to which the heart is less attached—we hide from ourselves the fact that we are resisting the chief demand. Herod observed John the Baptist, and "when he heard him, he did many things, and heard him gladly" (Mark vi. 20). The *forms* of *godliness*, as in the Pharisees, may conceal from the heart its denial of the power thereof. Conscience is quieted by church-membership, by a religious profession. There is disguised resistance in all *insincere repentance.* This is seen in Pharaoh's relentings. Even when the resistance becomes more avowed, there are ways of partially disguising the fact that it is indeed *God* we are resisting. Possibly the heart tries to wriggle out of the duty of submission by *cavilling at the evidence* of revelation. Or, objection is perhaps taken to something in the *manner* or *form* in which the truth has been presented; some alleged defect of taste, or infelicity of illustration, or rashness of statement, or blunder in science, or possibly a slip in grammar. Any straw will serve which admits of being clutched at. So conviction is pushed off, decision is delayed, resistance is kept up, and all the while the heart is getting harder less sensible of the truth, more ensnared in error. It is well also to remember that even *failure to profit by the word*, without active resistance to it (if such a thing is possible)—simple *want of care* in the cherishing of good impressions, and too rash an exposure to the influences which tend to dissipate and destroy them—will result in their disappearance, and in a consequent hardening of the heart. The impressions will not readily return with the same vividness. *To-day*, then, and *now*, hear and obey the voice of God.—J. O.

Chap. vi. ver. 28—chap. vii. ver. 7.—*God still glorified amid human weakness and sin.* I. MOSES' WEAKNESS (chap. vi. vers. 28—30). The command was—" Speak *thou* unto Pharaoh." Moses in his despondency is overpowered by the sense of his infirmity. He fears the ridicule of the Egyptian court. There are times when the sense of our unfitness for speaking God's words crushes us. Let us take heed lest lowly self-judgment pass into unbelief and disobedience. The loss of faith in ourselves is no reason why we should cease to trust God.

II. GOD'S REMEDY (chap. vii. vers. 1, 2). Moses' slowness of speech is veiled by unthought-of glory. He that feared the derision of Pharaoh is surrounded with dreadful majesty and made as God to him. To obedient faith, felt incompetency for the task God calls us to, will only be the occasion of his bestowing upon us more abundant honour. Our very defects can be transformed into power. A man's very awkwardness often disarms criticism and appeals to the heart as the most faultless elegance can never do.

III. JEHOVAH WILL BE GLORIFIED IN PHARAOH'S UNBELIEF (vers. 3—5). 1. They are forewarned of Pharaoh's stubborn refusal. We are not sent on God's errand with false expectations. 2. God's purpose will be accomplished, not defeated, by that opposition. His defiance will only call forth the revelation of God's terribleness. Where sin has sought to dwell and to reign, the terrors of God's judgment will alone be remembered. 3. Egypt will also know that God is Jehovah—the faithful One. God's name will be written in *their* punishment as well as in Israel's redemption.

IV. THE VERY AGE OF GOD'S SERVANTS WILL PRAISE HIM (ver. 7). The childhood of Samuel, the youth of Daniel, the old age of Moses and Aaron are arguments of unconquerable strength for the feeble and despised to trust and toil. 1. There is a place for all. 2. No man's day is over if he will only yield to God. The dying thief who believed in his dying agonies has been among the mightiest preachers of God's infinite grace.—U.

EXPOSITION.

Vers. 10—13.—THE FIRST SIGN, AND ITS FAILURE TO CONVINCE. Obeying the command given them (vers. 2, 9), Moses and Aaron went to the court a second time, and entering into the royal presence, probably repeated their demand—as from God—that the king would let the Children of Israel go (ch. vi. 11), when Pharaoh objected that they had no authority to speak to him in God's name, and required an evidence of their authority, either in the actual words of verse 9 (" Shew a miracle for you "), or in some equivalent ones. Aaron hereupon cast down on the ground the rod which Moses had brought from Midian, and it became a serpent (ver. 10). Possibly Pharaoh may have been prepared for this. He may have been told that this was one among the signs which had been done in the sight of the elders and people of Israel when the two brothers first came back from Midian (ch. iv. 30). If he knew of it, no doubt the " magicians " knew of it, and had prepared themselves. Pharaoh summoned them, as was natural, to his presence, and consulted them with respect to the portent, whereupon they too cast down the rods which they were carrying in their hands, and they "became serpents; but Aaron's rod swallowed up their rods" (ver. 12). (For the explanation of these facts, see the comment below). Pharaoh was to some extent impressed by the miracle, but not so as to yield. His heart remained hard, and he refused to let the people go.

Ver. 10.—**Aaron cast down his rod.** The rod is called indifferently " Aaron's rod " and " Moses' rod," because, though properly the rod of Moses (ch. iv. 2), yet ordinarily it was placed in the hands of Aaron (vers. 19, 20; ch. viii. 5, 17, etc.) **It became a serpent.** The word for "serpent" is not the same as was used before (ch. iv. 3); but it is not clear that a different species is meant. More probably it is regarded by the writer as a synonym.

Ver. 11.—**Pharaoh also called the wise men and the sorcerers.** That magic was an object of much attention and study in Egypt is abundantly evident from " The tale of Setnau" ('Records of the Past,' vol. iv. pp. 133—148), " The Magic Papyrus" (*ibid.* vol. x. pp. 137–158), and many other writings. It consisted, to a large extent, in charms, which were thought to have power over men and beasts, especially over reptiles. What amount of skill and power the Egyptian magicians possessed may perhaps be doubted. Many commentators believe them to have been in actual communication with the unseen world, and to have worked their wonders by the assistance of evil spirits. Others, who reject this explanation, believe that they themselves were in possession of certain supernatural gifts. But the commonest view at the present day regards them as simply persons who had a knowledge of many secrets of nature which were generally unknown, and who used this

knowledge to impress men with a belief in their supernatural power. The words used to express "magicians" and "enchantments" support this view. The magicians are called *khăkâmim*, "wise men," "men educated in human and divine wisdom" (Keil and Delitzsch); *mĕkashshĕphim*, "charmers," "mutterers of magic words" (Gesenius); and *khartummim*, which is thought to mean either "sacred scribes" or "bearers of sacred words" (Cook). The word translated "enchantments" is *lĕhâtim*, which means "secret" or "hidden arts" (Gesenius). On the whole, we regard it as most probable that the Egyptian "magicians" of this time were jugglers of a high class, well skilled in serpent-charming and other kindred arts, but not possessed of any supernatural powers. **The magicians of Egypt did in like manner with their enchantments.** The magicians, aware of the wonder which would probably be wrought, had prepared themselves; they had brought serpents, charmed and stiffened so as to look like rods (a common trick in Egypt: 'Description de l'Egypte,' vol. i. p. 159) in their hands; and when Aaron's rod became a serpent, they threw their stiffened snakes upon the ground, and disenchanted them, so that they were seen to be what they were—snakes, and not really rods.

Ver. 12.—**But Aaron's rod swallowed up their rods.** Aaron's serpent turned upon its rivals and devoured them, thus exhibiting a marked superiority.

Ver. 13.—**And he hardened Pharaoh's heart.** Rather, "But Pharaoh's heart *was hard.*" The verb employed is not active, but neuter; and "his heart" is not the accusative, but the nominative. Pharaoh's heart was too hard for the sign to make much impression on it. He did not see that Moses had done much more than his own magicians could do. **As the Lord had said.** See ver. 4.

HOMILETICS.

Vers. 10—12.—*False imitations of things Divine not difficult of detection.*—It is Satan's wont, in all ages and on all possible occasions, to set up counterfeits of things Divine, in order to confuse men's minds, and make them mistake the false for the true. Aaron no sooner works a true miracle, a real proof that he is a prophet of God (verse 1), than Satan's instruments, the magicians of Egypt, are ready with an imitation of the miracle, on which they base a claim that Pharaoh is not to listen to Aaron, but to them. "Curious arts" (Acts xix. 19) and "lying wonders" (2 Thess. ii. 9) were employed to discredit the genuine miracles of the Apostles. False Christs rose up in various places, soon after the lifetime of our Lord, claiming to be the Messiah spoken of by the prophets, who "showed great signs and wonders," capable of deceiving, if it had been possible, even "the very elect" (Matt. xxiv. 24). Apocryphal gospels were put out by the side of the true ones. A new and mystic philosophy was set up as the real "knowledge" which the Son of God had come to reveal, and new religions, like Gnosticism and Manichæism, disputed with real Christianity the right to be viewed as the actual religion of Jesus. Fanatics, at the time of the Reformation, parodied the Reformed religion, and established "Churches of the True Saints," which while affecting extreme purity fell practically into fearful excesses. Even at the present day rivals are set up to the revelation of God given us in the Bible—and the religious books of the Egyptians, or the Hindoos, or the Persians, or the Buddhists, or the Mahometans, are declared to be just as good, just as much from God, just as deserving of our attention, as the Old and New Testaments. But, if men are honest and do not wish to be deceived, it is easy, with a little patience, to detect each spurious imitation. Aaron's rod swallowed up the rods of the magicians. It remained, they ceased to exist altogether. The "curious arts" and "lying wonders" of those who opposed the Apostles, if examined into, would have been found either mere tricks, or weak devices of Satan, with none of the power, the dignity, the awfulness, of a true miracle. And time brought them to nought—they built up nothing—effected nothing. So with the "false Christs," and the apocryphal gospels, and the religions of Gnosticism and Manichæism, and the fanatical sects of the Reformation period: they took no hold on the world—the truth "swallowed them up"—they vanished away. With the spurious "revelations," if the case is not the same, it is nearly the same—if they have not, all of them, vanished, they are all of them, vanishing. Brought into contact with the truth—placed side by side with it—they cannot maintain themselves—they are "swallowed up" after a while. The ancient pantheism of Egypt perished in the fourth century; the religion of Zoroaster is almost non-existent; that of the Vedas is now crumbling to decay in the schools of Calcutta and Benares. Mahometanism shows signs of breaking up. When Thibet and China are freely opened to Christian missions, the last day of Buddhism will not be far off. The Divine sweeps away the human—Aaron's rod swallows up its rivals.

HOMILIES BY VARIOUS AUTHORS.

Vers. 8—14.—*The rod turned into a serpent.* On this sign, notice—
I. Its SIGNIFICANCE. 1. *Its distinctness from the similar sign wrought for the conviction of the Israelites.* On the meaning of the latter, see chap. iv. 1—6. There the serpent into which the rod was turned seemed to denote the power of the monarch—the royal and divine power of Egypt—of which the serpent was an Egyptian emblem. However threatening the aspect of this power to Moses and the Israelites, the sign taught them not to fear it, and promised victory over it. Here, on the contrary, the serpent is a *menace* to Pharaoh. It speaks to him in his own language, and tells him of a royal and Divine power opposed to his which he will do well not to provoke. The sign was harmless in itself, but menacing in its import. 2. *Its relation to Egyptian magic.* On this, see the exposition. The magicians produced an imitation of the miracle, but this very circumstance was turned into an occasion of greater humiliation to them. "Aaron's rod swallowed up their rods." The truth taught was the impotence of magic arts as opposed to the power of Jehovah. Royalty, divinity, magic, all are represented as overthrown in this significant marvel. Note—God seldom destroys a sinner without first warning him. The warnings are such that, if taken in time, worse consequences may be escaped. Conscience warns, the Spirit warns, providence warns. Red danger-signals stand at the opening of every path of crime, if the deluded transgressor would but take heed to them.
II. Its EVIDENTIAL VALUE. It was ordered to be wrought in answer to Pharaoh's demand for a miracle (ver. 9). Presumably, Pharaoh made the request, then the wonder was performed. Note here—1. *The human mind naturally craves for miracle as an evidence of revelation.* The evidence of outward miracle is not the highest, but neither should it be disparaged. It is the kind of evidence which minds at an inferior stage of development are most capable of appreciating, while, in connection with other circumstances, it is a powerful confirmation to the faith even of those who might possibly dispense with it. Christ's repeated refusal of a sign was not based upon the principle that signs were unnecessary, but upon the fact that a superabundance of signs had already been given. A faith resting *merely* on miracles (John ii. 23, 24) may be destitute of moral worth, but miracles had their value in certifying the source of the message, as well as in arousing attention, and they were themselves vehicles of moral teaching. 2. *God satisfies this craving of the mind by granting the evidence required.* It does not lessen, but greatly

enhances, the value of this evidence that most of the miracles of Scripture are not merely *credentials* of the revelation, but constitutive parts of it. See this truth wrought out in the chapter on "The Function of Miracle in Revelation" in Dr. Alex. Bruce's book, 'The Chief End of Revelation.' This able writer, however, is unnecessarily vehement in his polemic against the view that miracles are also wrought in *proof* of revelation; especially as in the latter part of his discussion he really admits all that the advocates of the so-called "traditional" view would think worth contending for. "Take away miracle from a revelation of grace, and the revelation can hardly be known for what it is. ... With the miracles retained as an essential part of the story, a gracious purpose towards a chosen people is indubitable; without them, it is very doubtful indeed. ... Retain the miracles, and the gracious purpose is stringently proved, and the contrary opinion excluded as untenable. The miracles and the purpose thus stand or fall together. To certify, beyond all doubt, a gracious purpose, miracle is necessary" (pp. 175—177). In the case before us, the evidential function must be allowed to be the leading one. 3. *Pharaoh's request for the miracle*. It is a significant circumstance that whereas on the previous occasion (chap. v. 1—5) Pharaoh made no request for a sign, he asks for one at this second interview. The unexpected reappearance of these two men, renewing their former demand, and doing so with even more emphasis and decision than at first, must have produced a startling effect upon him. Truth, to a certain extent, carries its own credentials with it. There must have been that in the manner and speech of these grave and aged men (ver. 7) which repelled the hypothesis that they were impostors. Probably Pharaoh had never been quite sure that their mission was mere pretence. A secret fear of the God whose worshippers he knew he was maltreating may have mingled with his thoughts, and kept him in vague uneasiness. He may thus have been more disturbed by the former demand than he cared to allow, and now thought it prudent to satisfy himself further. Professed disbelief in the Bible is in the same way often accompanied by a lurking suspicion that there is more in its teaching than is admitted.

III. Its EFFECT UPON THE MONARCH. 1. *He permitted himself to be imposed on by the counterfeit of the magicians*. Their imitation of the miracle furnished him with a plausible excuse for ascribing the work to magic. It gave him a pretext for unbelief. He *wished* one, and he got it. He ignored the strong points in the evidence, and fixed on the partial resemblance to the miracle in the feats of his tricksters. There were at least *three* circumstances which should have made him pause, and, if not convinced, ask for further proof. (1) The miracle of Moses and Aaron was *not* done by enchantments. (2) The men who did the wonder themselves asserted that it was wrought by Divine power. (3) The superiority of their power to that of the magicians was evinced by Aaron's rod swallowing up the rods of the others. And seeing that the miracle of God's messengers was *real*, while that of the magicians was (so far as we can judge) but a juggler's trick, there were probably numerous other circumstances of difference between them, on which, had Pharaoh been anxious to ascertain the truth, his mind would naturally have rested. But Pharaoh's mind was not honest. He *wished* to disbelieve, and he did it. 2. *He refused the request*. He *hardened* himself, *i.e.* the unwillingness of his heart to look at the truth, now that it had got something to stay itself upon, solidified into a fixed, hard determination to resist the demand made upon him. Note— (1) God tries men's dispositions by furnishing them with evidence which, while abundantly sufficient to convince minds that are honest, leaves numerous loopholes of escape to those indisposed to receive it. (2) It is the easiest thing in the world, if one wants to do it, to find pretexts for unbelief. We are far from asserting that *all* doubt is dishonest, but it is unquestionable that under the cloak of honest intellectual inquiry a great deal that is not honest is frequently concealed. To a mind *unwilling* to be convinced, there is nothing easier than to evade evidence. Specious counter-arguments are never far to seek. Any specious reply to Christian books, any naturalistic hypothesis, any flimsy parallel, will serve the purpose. The text directs attention to the *method of false parallels*—a favourite one with modern sceptics. Parallels are hunted up between Christianity and the ethnic religions. Superficial resemblances in ethics, doctrine and ritual, are laid hold upon and magnified. Christ is compared with Buddha and Confucius, or his miracles are put in comparison with the ecclesiastical miracles of the middle ages. And thus his religion is supposed to be reduced to the naturalistic level. The defeat of all such attempts is shadowed forth in the miracle before us.—J. O.

Vers. 8—13.—*The credentials of God's ambassadors to the froward.* 1. THE DEMANDS OF GOD, THOUGH REJECTED, CANNOT BE BANISHED. The rod which Pharaoh refuses to be shepherded by, cast down before him, springs into life. To those who refuse obedience to God's Word, that Word will cling and become a living thing. Israel thought to have done with God and to be like the heathen: it was a vain dream. Pharaoh would shake off care, and become like one of whom God had asked nothing: the dream was equally vain. We may deny God, but his words will live and pursue us.

II. THE REJECTED GUIDANCE WILL BE THE DESTRUCTION OF THE FROWARD. The rod cast from the hand becomes a *serpent*. The vain demand for righteousness will at last become the sentence of condemnation, and the sin that is clung to, the sting of death.

III. THE WARNING BECOMES THE LOUDER, THE GREATER THE EFFORT TO DEADEN ITS EFFECT. The rods of the magicians were swallowed up and the rod of God left more terrible than it was before. The Divine retribution will swallow up every comfort and stay which the sinful may summon to sustain them.—U.

Vers. 8—13. *The first sign to Pharaoh: the rod becomes a serpent.* I. NOTICE THE REMARKABLE REQUEST WHICH JEHOVAH INDICATES THAT PHARAOH MAY MAKE. Perhaps we might even say, will make. " When Pharaoh shall speak unto you, saying, Shew a miracle for you." This is a great change from his former attitude, that he should be capable of stooping to such a request. But men who have despotic power sometimes do strange and contradictory things. The freaks of tyrants in the way of a seeming liberality and kindliness are among the curiosities of history. Pharaoh may have said to himself, " It will be rare sport to give this monomaniac full scope; let him with his own failure expose the delusion under which he is suffering; it may be the shortest way out of the difficulty." On the other hand, it is not at all improbable that some news of the signs wrought before Israel had percolated through all the barriers which stand between a palace and the life of the common people; and Pharaoh may have wished to discover how far the rumour was founded in reality. Though when we have said all by way of suggesting secondary causes for the request, we must come in the end to this feeling, that the only sufficient way of accounting for it is to treat it as an impulse from Jehovah himself. Certainly his providence must have much to do with gaining access to Pharaoh and keeping up the communications of Moses with him. God can lead Pharaoh, even when he knows not that he is led. Men are walking in the way of God's providence and serving his purposes, even when quite satisfied in the ignorance of their hearts that they are walking in their own way.

II. NOTICE THE MIRACLE ITSELF. Doubtless the rod in question was the same which had been a serpent twice already; so that by this time Moses must have looked upon it with great serenity of confidence. It is now impossible for us to say why the Lord began his manifestations of power to Pharaoh with this rather than with some other sign. Reasons discernible at the time are not discernible now; the light which would have revealed them has long since died away. We can but see that there was much in the miracle which would have taught valuable lessons to Pharaoh, if only he had received it in the simplicity of one who is really looking for truth and guidance. He would have learned not to despise the absence of promise in the external appearance of things. He would have learned that a thing is not ridiculous because it is laughed at. He would have felt, too, that as the innocent and unimposing rod became suddenly a dangerous serpent, so this Moses—humble, unsustained and impotent as he seemed— might also become all at once a destroying force utterly beyond resistance by any Egyptian defence. Nor must we forget that the choice of this particular sign may have been influenced by the fact that *the magicians had a favourite and imposing trick of their art which, to the uninstructed eye, resembled it.* They seemed to do, by their magic, what Moses really did by Divine power, and so their skill, while it had for one result a renewed defiance of Jehovah on the part of Pharaoh, had another result in this, that it led up to a strengthening of the faith of Moses. He might not be able to explain how the magicians did their wonders; but he knew very well that he was no magician himself, and that *his rod had been Divinely changed*, whatever cause had been at work to change the others. And then, at last, whatever perplexity remained in his mind was swept away when he saw the power of God rising supreme over mere trickery, and the serpent from his rod swallowing up the serpents from the other rods.

III. NOTICE THE THOROUGH WICKEDNESS OF THESE MAGICIANS. They know that their wonders are lying wonders. Powers great by nature, trained and increased with the utmost ingenuity, and which were intended to be and might have been for the good of their fellow-men, they turn without any compunction into instruments for the promotion of their selfish glory. They know that, whatever their pretences may be, they are not acting in a straightforward and humble service of supernatural power. They know that when Pharaoh puts confidence in them, he is putting confidence in a lie. Furthermore, they must have known that there was something in the transformation of Moses' rod which wanted accounting for. Magicians understand each other's tricks quite well, and it must have been evident to them that Moses was no magician. They know in their consciences that he is greater than themselves; but what can they say? Committed to lies, they must go on with them. They must pretend to have as much power as Moses, even if they have it not; and thus the induced necessities of their dark and secret arts compel them to hide the truth from Pharaoh. Nor was it any real excuse that Pharaoh was willing to be deceived. His destruction ultimately came from his own perversity; but he also presents the melancholy spectacle of being surrounded by those who, if only they had been truthful, might have interposed some obstacles in his downward way.

IV. NOTICE THE STATE IN WHICH PHARAOH WAS LEFT, EVEN AFTER THE COMPLETION OF THE MIRACLE. When Aaron's rod had swallowed up the others, he still remained unimpressed. It seems as if he had allowed his attention to be fixed on one part of the miracle, while another he regarded but carelessly. When his magicians seemed to produce serpents from rods, this was just according to his inclinations, and he made much of it. Moses could do nothing more than the magicians could do. But when their serpents were swallowed up—well, it was not a very encouraging sight—but still it might be accounted for. And so we are in danger of depreciating the significance of God's works by not looking at them *in every part*. Every part is to be regarded, if we are to get the full impression of the whole. If the magicians did what Moses did, it was equally evident that Moses did what the magicians did. A child could see that his power was at least equal to theirs. If Pharaoh had not been blinded by vanity and by traditional reliance on his magicians, he would have demanded that these magicians should do something more than Moses had done. What an illustration we have here, of how, when a man gets away from right thoughts of God, he soon comes to call evil good and good evil (Isa. v. 20). Pharaoh believes his lying magicians, though he will not believe the truthful servant of a true God. He has no discriminating power to find the difference between things, which, however they may resemble each other outwardly, are yet inwardly quite opposed. He thinks that he has power enough with his gods to meet whatever power has yet been brought against him. It has been already made evident that there is no sense of pity or justice in him; and it is now made plain that he is not to be reached by the exhibition before him of a significant symbol of pain and destruction. *Pharaoh must be touched more closely still*—must be made to suffer, and suffer most dreadfully, before he will consent to let Israel go.—Y.

EXPOSITION.

Vers. 14—21.—THE FIRST PLAGUE. The first miracle had been exhibited, and had failed. It had been a mere " sign," and in no respect a " judgment." Now the " judgments " were to begin. God manifests himself again to Moses, and gives him exact directions what he is to do. He is to meet Pharaoh on the banks of the Nile, and to warn him that a plague is coming upon all Egypt on account of his obstinacy; that the waters of the Nile will be turned to blood, so that the fish will die, and

the river stink, and the Egyptians loathe to drink of the water of the river (vers. 15—18). Pharaoh not yielding, making no sign, the threat is to be immediately followed by the act. In the sight of Pharaoh and his court, or at any rate of his train of attendants (ver. 20), Aaron is to stretch his rod over the Nile, and the water is at once to become blood, the fish to die, and the river in a short time to become offensive, or, in the simple and direct language of the Bible, to stink. The commands given by God are executed, and the result is as declared beforehand by Moses (vers. 20, 21).

Ver. 14. — **Pharaoh's heart is hardened.** Rather, "is hard," "is dull." The adjective used is entirely unconnected with the verb of the preceding verse.

Ver. 15.—**In the morning.** The expression used both here and again in ch. viii. 20 seems rather to imply a daily custom of the Pharaoh. It is conjectured, not without reason, that among the recognised duties of the monarch at this time was the offering of a morning sacrifice to the Nile on the banks of the river (Keil and Delitzsch, Kalisch, etc.). Possibly, however, this may not have been the case, and God may have chosen for certain miracles particular days, on which the king was about to proceed to the river in view of some special ceremony connected with the annual inundation. **Against he come.** Literally, "to meet him." **In their hand.** When the time came for smiting the waters, the rod was transferred to Aaron's hand (ver. 19).

Ver. 16.—**The Lord God ... hath sent me unto thee.** Rather, "*sent* me unto thee." The reference is to the original sending (ch. v. 1). **Thou wouldest not hear.** Literally, "Thou hast not heard," *i.e.* up to this time thou hast not obeyed the command given to thee.

Ver. 17.—**In this thou shalt know that I am the Lord.** Pharaoh had declared on the occasion specially referred to, "*I know not Jehovah*, neither will I let Israel go" (ch. v. 2). He is now told that he shall "know Jehovah" in the coming visitation; he shall know, *i.e.*, that there is a great and truly existent God who controls nature, does as he will even with the Nile, which the Egyptians regarded as a great deity; and can turn, if he see fit, the greatest blessings into curses. **Behold, I will smite.** God here speaks of the acts of Moses and Aaron as his own acts, and of their hands as his hand, because they were mere instruments through which he worked. The Roman law said: "Qui facit per alium, facit per se." **The waters ... shall be turned to blood.** Not simply, "shall be of the colour of blood," as Rosenmüller paraphrases, but shall become and be, to all intents and purposes, blood. It is idle to ask whether the water would have answered to all the modern tests, microscopic and other, by which blood is known. The question cannot be answered. All that we are entitled to conclude from the words of the text is, that the water had all the physical appearance—the look, taste, smell, texture of blood; and hence, that it was certainly not merely discoloured by the red soil of Abyssinia, nor by cryptogamic plants and infusoria. Water thus changed would neither kill fish, nor "stink," nor be utterly undrinkable.

Ver. 18.—**The fish ... shall die.** This would increase the greatness of the calamity, for the Egyptians lived to a very large extent upon fish (Birch, 'Egypt from the Earliest Times,' p. 45), which was taken in the Nile, in the canals, and the Lake Mœris (Herod. ii. 149). **The river shall stink.** As Keil and Delitzsch observe, "this seems to indicate putrefaction." **The Egyptians shall loathe to drink.** The expression is stronger in verse 24, where we find that "they could not drink." We may presume that at first, not supposing that the fluid could really be blood, they tried to drink it, took it into their mouths, and possibly swallowed some, but that very soon they found they could not continue to do so.

Ver. 19.—**Say unto Aaron.** There is an omission here (and generally throughout the account of the plagues) of the performance by Moses of God's behest. The Samaritan Pentateuch in each case supplies the omission. It has been argued (Kennicott) that the Hebrew narrative has been contracted; but most critics agree that the incomplete form is the early one, and that, in the Samar. version, the original narrative has been expanded. **The waters of Egypt ... streams ... rivers ... ponds ... pools of water.** The waters of Lower Egypt, where this miracle was wrought, consisted of (1) the various branches of the Nile, natural and artificial, which were seven when Herodotus wrote (Herod. ii. 17), whence the Nile was called "septemfluus," or "septemgeminus;" (2) the canals derived from each branch to fertilise the lands along its banks; (3) ponds, marshes, and pools, the results of the overflowing of the Nile, or of its percolation through its banks on either side; and (4) artificial reservoirs, wherein water was stored for use after the inundation was over. The four terms of the text seem applicable to this four-fold division, and "show an accurate knowledge of Egypt" (Cook), and of its water system. The "streams" are the Nile branches; the "rivers" correspond to the canals; the "ponds" are the natural accumulations of waters in permanent lakes or in temporary pools and marshes; while the "pools," or "gatherings of waters" (*margin*), are the reservoirs made by art. Aaron was to stretch out his rod over the Nile, but with the intent to smite *all* the Egyptian waters, and all the waters would at once be smitten, the streams and the canals and the natural lakes and the reservoirs. The miracle would even extend to private dwellings, and the change would take place **throughout all the land of Egypt,** not only in respect of the open waters spread over the country, but even in respect of that stored, as was usual, in houses, and contained either in **vessels of wood** or in **vessels of stone.** With respect to these, it is to be observed that the

Nile water was much improved by keeping, since the sediment subsided ; and that tanks, sometimes of wood, sometimes of stone, were usual adjuncts of all the better class of houses.

Ver. 20.—**He lifted up the rod.** "He" must be understood to mean "Aaron" (see ver. 19) ; but the writer is too much engrossed with the general run of his narrative to be careful about *minutiæ.* All that he wants to impress upon us is, that the rod was used as an instrument for the working of the miracle. He is not thinking of who it was that used it. **In the sight of Pharaoh.** See the comment

on ver. 15. **And of his servants.** Either "his courtiers generally," or, at any rate, a large troop of attendants.

Ver. 21.—**The fish that was in the river died.** It is most natural to understand "all the fish." **There was blood,** etc. Literally, "and *the* blood was throughout all the land of Egypt." The exact intention of the phrase is doubtful, since undoubtedly "in numberless instances, the Hebrew terms which imply universality must be understood in a limited sense" (Cook). "All the land" may mean no more than "all the Delta."

HOMILETICS.

Vers. 17—20.—*God's punishments appropriate and terrible* (vers. 17—20). There was something peculiarly appropriate in the first judgment falling upon the Nile. The Nile had been made the instrument of destruction to the Israelites by the first tyrannical Pharaoh (probably Seti I.). It had been defiled with the blood of thousands of innocent victims. Crocodiles had in its waters crushed the tender limbs of those helpless infants, and had stained them with a gore that in God's sight could never be forgotten. The king, and the persons who were his instruments, had in so doing polluted their own holy river, transgressed their own law, offered insults to one of the holiest of their own deities. And all for the destruction of God's people. So, now that destruction was coming upon themselves, now that the firstborn were doomed (ch. iv. 23), and the catastrophe of the Red Sea was impending, the appropriate sign, which threatened carnage, was given—the Nile was made to run with blood. The Egyptians had among their traditions one which said that the Nile had once for eleven days flowed with honey (Manetho ap. Syncell. 'Chronograph.' p. 55 A). As this supposed miracle indicated a time of peace and prosperity, so the present actual one boded war and destruction. Again, Pharaoh's especial crime at this time was, that he despised God. God therefore caused his own chief deity to be despised. There are indications that, about this period, a special Nile-worship had set in. Hâpi, the Nile-god, was identified with Phthah and Ammon—he was declared to stand "alone and self-created"—to be "the Father of all the gods," "the Chief on the waters," "the Creator of all good things," "the Lord of terrors and of choicest joys." "Mortals" were said to "extol him, *and the cycle of Gods*"—he stood above them all as the One Unseen and Inscrutable Being. "He is not graven in marble," it was said; "he is not beheld; he hath neither ministrants nor offerings; he is not adored in sanctuaries; his abode is not known; no shrine of his is found with painted figures ; there is no building that can contain him ;" and again, "unknown is his name in heaven ; he doth not manifest his forms; vain are all representations." ('Records of the Past,' vol. iv. pp. 107—113 ; vol. x. pp. 41—2.) Menephthah was a special devotee of Hâpi (*ib.* vol. x. p. 38). Nothing could have seemed to him more terrible and shocking, than the conversion of his pure, clean, refreshing, life-giving, god-like stream, into a mass of revolting putridity. And on the people the judgment was still more terrible. Under ordinary circumstances, the whole nation depended on the Nile for its water supply. There were no streams in the country other than the Nile branches, no brooks, no rills, no springs or fountains. The sudden conversion of all the readily accessible water—even such as was stored in houses—into blood, was sickening, horrible, tremendous. Scarcely could any severer punishment of the people have been devised. If a partial remedy had not been found (verse 24), it would have been impossible for them to endure through the "seven days" (verse 25). So fearful are the judgments of God upon those who offend him !

HOMILIES BY VARIOUS AUTHORS.

Vers. 14—25.—*The Nile turned into blood.* The first of the series of plagues which fell on Egypt was of a truly terrific character. At the stretching out of the rod of Aaron, the broad, swift-flowing current of the rising Nile suddenly assumed the hue and qualities of blood. The stroke fell also on the reservoirs, canals, and ponds. Whatever connection may be traced between this plague and natural phenomena (see Hengstenberg) it is plain that it stood on an entirely different footing from changes produced under purely natural conditions. 1. The water was rendered *wholly* unfit for use. 2. It became deadly in its properties (ver. 18). 3. The stroke was instantaneous. 4. It was pre-announced. 5. It descended on the river at the summons of Moses and Aaron. 6. It lasted exactly seven days (ver. 25). An event of this kind was palpably of supernatural origin. Contrast Moses with Christ, the one beginning the series of wonders by turning the river into blood; the other, in his first miracle, turning the water into wine (John ii. 1—12). The contrast of judgment and mercy, of law and Gospel. Consider—

I. THE DEMAND RENEWED WITH THE ACCOMPANIMENT OF THREAT (vers. 16—19). 1. *The demand was that which Pharaoh had hitherto resisted.* It was a demand righteous and reasonable in itself—" Let my people go," etc. It had come to him, moreover, as the command of Jehovah, and proof had been given him that such was its character. Still he had resisted it. This, however, did not dispose of the demand, which now confronts him again. 2. *The demand which Pharaoh would not freely grant, he is now to be compelled to grant.* If he will not bow to reason, to persuasion, to evidence, he must bow to power. An unprecedented calamity would overtake his land : " In this shalt thou know that I am the Lord; behold, I will smite with the rod," etc. (ver. 17). Note—(1) Reasonable means are exhausted with the sinner before compulsion is resorted to. God is unwilling to proceed to extremities. (2) Nevertheless, if gentler methods fail, means will be used which will *compel* submission. " As I live, saith the Lord, every knee shall bow to me, and every tongue shall confess to God " (Rom. xiv. 11; Phil. ii. 10, 11). (3) Excuses are not admitted for wilful unbelief. Pharaoh would probably have pleaded as a ground for his refusal, that he did not believe that the command in question proceeded from Jehovah. No such plea will be admitted in the court of heaven. Every allowance will be made for involuntary ignorance, but none for wilful unbelief. What the sinner is asked to do is righteous and reasonable in itself; is made known to him as God's will; and is evidenced to be such by many infallible proofs. Refusal to acknowledge the sufficiency of this evidence does not exculpate from the guilt of disobedience. The question is not—*Does* he, or *will* he, admit its sufficiency, but *is* it sufficient? Not, *Does* it convince him? but, *Ought* it to convince him? Our errors, follies, and mistakes will not hinder the Almighty from executing his purposes. If we stand in the way of them, and will not bend, we must be crushed.

II. THE PLAGUE AS A SIGN TO EGYPT. The smiting of the Nile was—1. *A proof of the power of Jehovah* (ver. 17). It showed him to be an actually existing Being, demonstrated his supremacy in nature, and made manifest his determination to punish resistance to his will. 2. *A blow at Egyptian idolatry.* It turned the river Nile, which itself was worshipped as a divinity, into an object of loathsomeness and source of death to its worshippers. They were the *chief* gods of Egypt, too, who were supposed to be embodied in the river. How clear the proof of the vanity of the idols, and of the unchallengeable superiority of Jehovah ! Yet we do not learn that one idol the less was worshipped in Egypt as the result of it. 3. *A warning of worse evil to come.* The Nile was in a sense symbolical of Egypt, of whose prosperity it was the source. The turning of this river into blood was in fact a prophecy or threat of utter ruin to the state. The succeeding plagues are merely the unfolding of the threat contained in this one. 4. *The removal of the plague at the end of seven days betokened the unwillingness of God to proceed to extremities.* It is very noticeable that the plague was removed unasked, and while Pharaoh was still hardening his heart. So long-suffering is God that he will try all means with sinners before finally giving them up. The lessons for ourselves from this plague are these—(1) The certainty of God's threatenings being executed. (2) The terrible punishments in reserve for disobedience. (3) The ease with which God can smite a nation, and bring it to the point of ruin. The smiting of the Nile meant the immediate paralysis of all industry, commerce, and agriculture throughout the land of Egypt, while, had the plague lasted a few days longer, the result would have been the death of the whole population. We call this "miracle," but miracle is only the coming forth into visibility of the hand which is at all times working in the phenomena of nature, and in the affairs of history. By famine, by pestilence, by blight of crops, by clap of war, turning the river of a nation's life into very literal blood (so France in 1870), by the simplest natural agencies, if so it pleased him—could Jehovah speedily reduce our national pride, and smite at the fountain-heads the sources of our national prosperity. A very sensible proof was given of this—of the readiness with which the trade of a whole country could be paralysed, and great cities reduced in no long period to absolute starvation, by a slight change in natural conditions—in the great snowstorm of January 1881. (See the *Spectator* of 29th January, 1881.) Had the storm lasted but a week or two longer, the effects would have been as serious to cities like London, and to the country as a whole, as this smiting of the Nile in Egypt. (4) God's judgments are anticipative. Judgments in this life forewarn of judgments beyond.

III. THE PUERILE IMITATION OF THE MAGICIANS (ver. 22). 1. The magicians could not remove the plague; they could only with the few drops of water at their command produce a feeble imitation of it. How futile is this as a disproof of God's agency! So it is a pitiable way of disposing of God's judgments to show that something like them can be produced by undivine means. The savant, *e.g.*, may produce in his laboratory an imitation of rain or thunder, and may think that he has thereby disproved God's agency in any infliction he may send upon a land through these instrumentalities; but this is small comfort to the country that is being smitten by them. 2. The attempts of the magicians to refute the pretensions of Moses only resulted in making the supernatural character of the plague more manifest. In the same way, the efforts of sceptics to disprove, *e.g.*, the Divine origin of the religion of the Bible, or of the book itself, only end in making its Divinity more apparent. "The more conclusively you demonstrate to the human reason that that which exists ought not to exist, so much the more do you enhance the miracle of its existence. That must be the most astounding of all facts that still exists notwithstanding the gravest objections to its existence."

IV. THE HARDENING OF PHARAOH (vers. 22, 23). The hardening of Pharaoh here enters on a new phase. It was—1. Hardening against *conviction*. Pharaoh must have felt in this case that he was in presence of a true work of God. The puny efforts of his magicians could not possibly impose upon him. But he would not yield. He would not obey conviction. 2. Hardening under *punishment*. Pharaoh was in the position of one who, being often reproved, hardeneth his neck (Prov. xxix. 1). He had *risked*, even after this last warning, the chances of the threatening turning out to be untrue. Now, to his utter discomfiture, the stroke descends, and his empire is on the point of ruin. Yet he hardened himself in resistance. 3. Hardening which was *deliberate*. "Pharaoh turned and went into his house, neither did he set his heart to this also" (ver. 23). He had reached a point at which he could only stiffen himself in his determination to resist God, by *refusing to think*, by deliberately turning away from the light and resolving *not* to face the question of his duty. The monarch knows his duty, and *knows that he knows it*, yet he will not obey. 4. Hardening *obstinately persevered in*. He held out through all the seven days of the duration of the plague. Hardening of this kind speedily robs the soul of its few remaining sparks of susceptibility to truth.—J. O.

Vers. 14—25.—*The first plague: the water turned to blood.* I. THE PLACE WHERE MOSES WAS TO MEET PHARAOH. Moses was not always to be put to it to find his entrance into the palace. God can arrange things so that Pharaoh shall come to meet him. The instructions given to Moses at once call to our minds how Pharaoh's daughter, eighty years before, had come down to the river to find and protect a helpless babe, and how that same babe—having passed through many chequered years, and many strange experiences at the hands both of God and men—has to meet with another Pharaoh. We are not told why Pharaoh went down to the water; it may have been to worship, for the Egyptians held the Nile in pious regard.   But as the narrative says nothing on this point, we had better not assume it.   It is sufficient to observe that Pharaoh was led down to the stream, to see it, the great benefactor of his land, turned into a curse (that is, if it was down to the Nile that he went.   M. de Lesseps maintains that the city of the Pharaohs was not on the Nile, but on a tributary of it.   See Hunter's ' Life of Lord Mayo,' vol. i. p. 132).

II. The distinct warning given to Pharaoh of what is about to happen. This warning is not peculiar to the first plague.   Warning is mentioned as having been given along with most of the others, and possibly it was given where it is not mentioned. But it is of course a thing to be specially noted that God did not begin this succession of disasters without due and solemn warning.   Not that there was any formal appeal to Pharaoh.   It rather seems to be taken for granted that an appeal will be of no use. But even though Pharaoh disregarded, it was a good thing to say beforehand what was about to happen.   Moses himself, and Aaron, and all devout Israelites who had eyes to perceive, could thus see God's plan opening out more and more.   All information is good that makes us feel how God is working upon an ascertained and settled plan.

III. The plague itself.   Water is changed to blood.   Two of the great elements that belong to life are thus put in sharp contrast.   Water is an element scarcely less distributed than the air itself.   It is one of those common blessings which are so common that we take them with no manner of doubt that we are perfectly sure of them, come what may.   The importance of water is seen by nothing more than by the frequent references to it in Scripture as illustrative of spiritual blessings.   There is water to drink ; water to cleanse ; water to fertilise vegetation.   This element God takes, and all at once, over a wide stretch of territory, turns it to blood.   Thus we see how he can make *mere natural things* a blessing or a curse according to his will.   Water is a blessing, and blood a blessing, according to circumstances of time and place.   There is suffering when blood is where water ought to be ; and equally there is suffering if water is where blood ought to be.   Here there was great suffering because blood was where water was meant to be.   When the people came for water to drink, to cook, to wash, to water plants, they found only blood ; and yet that very blood was the same in its composition with the liquid which flowed incessantly through their own bodies.   Their health depended on its richness, its purity, and the regularity of its flow.   On the other hand, consider the poor man who came to Christ to be cured of the dropsy (Luke xiv. 2). He had to complain, not that blood was where water ought to be, but that water was where blood ought to be.   And here we claim that this miracle is not sufficiently explained by saying that *the water was turned into something like blood.*   We must take it that there was a conversion of the water literally into blood.   We are here just at the beginning of a critical and sublime exhibition of signs and wonders.   Why, then, needlessly make admissions which will diminish the force of these ?   Granting the supernatural at all, let us be ready to grant it to the full where the statements of the text require it.   The Being who changed a rod to a serpent could change, if need were, the waters of the whole globe into blood.   We should be careful not to admit, without sufficient reason, anything to diminish the horrors of this plague.   What a poor picture it presents to the imagination to think of streams stained with red earth or microscopic infusoria !   How much more impressive in every way—how much more consistent with high conceptions of the anger of Jehovah, and of the punitive aspect of his power—to think of blood, real blood everywhere, " vast rolling streams, florid and high-coloured," and becoming after a while, a stagnating, clotting, putrescent mass.   Very fitly does Matthew Henry remark on this plague :—" One of the first miracles Moses wrought was turning water into blood, but one of the first miracles our Lord Jesus wrought was turning water into wine ; for the law was given by Moses, and it was a dispensation of death and terror ; but grace and truth, which, like wine, make glad the heart, came by Jesus Christ."

IV. The apparently successful rivalry of the magicians.   They also were able, or seemed to be able, to turn water into blood.   There are, indeed, some difficulties in understanding the nature of their action here—whether it was mere trickery and deception, or whether God did allow water, as it passed through their hands, to be changed to blood.   An understanding of these points is, however, of secondary importance.   The thing of moment is to mark how unimpressed the magicians themselves seem to have been with the terrible spectacle presented to them. It was not for Pharaoh only to take heed to this river of blood; the intimation was for them also. But they clung, as privileged men almost always do cling, to their position and influence. Not only was Pharaoh's kingdom in danger, but their standing as the professed agents of supernatural powers. They went on, vainly contending against this new manifestation of power, though surely in their hearts they must have felt it was destined to prevail. And their conduct was made worse by the fact that they were pursuing it in the midst of general suffering.

V. THE INTERVAL TO THE NEXT PLAGUE. What was this interval for? Surely to give Pharaoh time—time to consider the miracle in all its bearings, and get over the rashness and pride which prompted his first thoughts of continued resistance. We know not if, during these seven days, the river slowly returned to its natural state. Perhaps there was no sharp dividing line between the plagues; one may have come on as another faded away. Seven days, then, were given to Pharaoh to change his mind; but it is very hard for a man, even in seven days, to say he has been utterly wrong. And then there is the success of these magicians to keep him astray. Yet what was there in them to give satisfaction? It seemed they could do the same thing which Moses was doing, viz. change water into blood. *If only they could have changed blood into water again,* then they might have been of some use and comfort to Pharaoh.—Y.

Ver. 14—25. *The water turned into blood.* I. THE PUNISHMENT. There were two elements in it. 1. The deprivation: water, one of the most essential of all God's gifts, was suddenly made useless. 2. The horror. Had all the water of Egypt suddenly disappeared, the punishment had been infinitely less. Instead of water, there was blood and corruption. 3. It was a judgment on Egypt's idolatry. The things we set in God's stead will be made an abomination and a horror to us. 4. It was the revelation of Egypt's guilt; beneath these waters the babes of Israel had sunk in their hopeless struggle with death. The abused gifts of God will be removed, but the horror of their abuse will abide.

I. THE ATTEMPT TO DISCREDIT GOD'S AGENCY IN THE CALAMITY. The magicians could increase the plague, and therefore it was not from the hand of God! The same argument is used still to prevent misfortune being considered as a chastisement and warning from God. Men can see in it chance only, or man's hand, not the Lord's.

III. PHARAOH'S DOGGED REFUSAL TO OBEY. He "turned and went into his house" (ver. 23). This would prolong his punishment, but could not conquer God. Instead of bowing to God's word, we may shut ourselves in with our sin, but we only bind judgment upon us, and tempt God to inflict a heavier blow.—U.

EXPOSITION.

Vers. 22, 23.—On the occurrence of the second sign and first plague, the magicians were again consulted; and, by means which it is impossible to do more than conjecture, they produced a seeming transformation into blood of a certain quantity of water. The inquiry, whence they procured the water, is answered by ver. 24. That they actually turned water into blood is scarcely asserted in the vague " did so" of ver. 22. Perhaps they had recourse to sleight of hand, and made a substitution, like modern conjurors; perhaps they merely turned the water of a red colour. All that was necessary was to convince Pharaoh that they were able to do what Moses and Aaron had done—there was no one to watch,

and test, and examine their pretended miracle, which consequently passed muster, though it may have been no more than a trick. Pharaoh, however, suffered himself to be convinced, and "turned and went into his house," without paying any attention to the marvel wrought (ver. 23).

Ver. 22.—**The magicians of Egypt did so.** They could not do what Moses and Aaron had done—stretch out, that is, a rod over the Nile, and turn it and all its branches, and ponds, and pools, into blood, for *this was already done.* They could only show their skill upon some small quantity of water in a cup or other vessel. No doubt they produced some apparent change, which was accepted by Pharaoh as an equivalent to what had been effected by the

Israelite chiefs, but which must have fallen far short of it. Pharaoh would not be a severe critic.

Ver. 23.—**Pharaoh turned**—*i.e.* "returned" —quitted the river-bank, satisfied with what the magicians had done, and went back to the palace. **Neither did he set his heart to this also.** A better translation is that of Booth- royd—"Nor did he lay even this to heart." In the expression "even this" there is an allusion to the previous neglect of the first sign (ver. 13).

HOMILETICS.

Vers. 22, 23.—*The power of Satan is with all deceivableness.* Satan himself, and wicked men, his instruments, are especially strong in the power of deception. Satan deceived Eve (1 Tim. ii. 14). The lying spirit deceived Ahab (1 Kings xxii. 22). Rebekah and Jacob together deceived Isaac. Gehazi deceived Naaman. Bad men are clever and plausible, and keensighted, and painstaking, and careful—they lay their plans skilfully, and carry them out boldly, and are usually successful. The magicians had not only their own credit at stake, but also that of the priests, who were in league with them. They would not be very scrupulous what means they used, so that they could persuade the Pharaoh that whatever Moses and Aaron could do, they could do : and they succeeded. The "father of lies" no doubt suggested to them some clever method of seeming to perform the same sort of miracle as the Israelitish leaders had performed— they adopted it, and cheated the eyes of the beholders. When men wished to nip the religion of Christ in the bud, they called its Founder "that deceiver" (Matt. xxvii. 63). Deceit is a device of Satan. In nothing are the powers of light and darkness more contrasted than in the simpleness, the straightforward sincerity that characterises the former, and the crookedness, the tortuousness, the insincerity that goes with the latter. He who is "the Way" and "the Life," is also "the Truth." All who would have fellowship with him must "walk in truth."

EXPOSITION.

Vers. 24—25.—Necessity is the mother of invention. Finding the Nile water continue utterly undrinkable, the Egyptians bethought themselves of a means of obtaining water to which they never had recourse in ordinary times. This was to dig pits or wells at some distance from the river, and so obtain the moisture that lay in the ground, no doubt derived from the river originally, but already there before the change of the water into blood took place. This, it appears, remained water, and was drinkable, though probably not very agreeable, since, owing to the nitrous quality of the soil in Egypt, well-water has always a bitter and brackish taste. It sufficed, however, for drinking and culinary purposes during the " seven days " that the plague con- tinued (ver. 25).

Ver. 24.—**All the Egyptians digged.** Not the Hebrews. The water stored in the houses of the Hebrews in reservoirs, cisterns, and the like, was (it would seem) not vitiated; and this would suffice for the consumption of seven days. **Water to drink.** Blood would not become water by percolation through earth, as Canon Cook appears to think (' Speaker's Commentary,' vol. i. p. 278) ; but there might have been sufficient water in the ground before the plague began, to fill the wells dug, for seven days.

Ver. 25.—**And seven days were fulfilled.** This note of time has been regarded as merely fixing the interval between the first plague and the second. But it is more natural to regard it as marking the duration of the first plague. The intervals between one plague and another are nowhere estimated.

HOMILETICS.

Ver. 24.—*God allows men to seek and obtain alleviations of his judgments.* We are not intended to sit down under the judgments of God, and fold our hands, and do nothing. Whether it be war, or pestilence, or famine, or any other Heaven-sent calamity that comes upon us for our sins and those of our nation, we must beware of sinking into apathy under the infliction, and allowing it simply to run its course. God does not desire that we should show our submission in this way. He gives us thought, and ingenuity, and inventiveness, that, in every difficulty we may devise remedies, and so lessen our own and our neighbours' sufferings. Oriental nations view each calamity that comes upon them as *Kismet*, "fate," and make no exertions to meet it, stem it, minimise it. Christians should act otherwise. They should so far imitate the Egyptians as to set to work actively, to do what can be done in the way of relief and alleviation. God freely allows this. He did not punish the Egyptians for digging, or frustrate their efforts by preventing the water that was in the ground from filling the wells, or by rendering it undrinkable. And so he allows cholera or plague, or even ordinary sickness, which is his judgment on an individual, to be met by care, attention, cleanliness, remedial measures, and is so far from interfering against such exertions, that he blesses them, and for the most part renders them effectual.

HOMILIES BY VARIOUS AUTHORS.

Chaps. vii.—x.—*The great conflict.* "For I will at this time send all my plagues," etc.: Ex. ix. 14. Keeping the last tremendous visitation apart, for it stands out in lone grandeur in the story, it is well to take the other nine plagues together in any homiletic use we make of them; for—1. They have many features in common. 2. And are closely connected with one another. A landscape should not be cut up, when we can see at a sweep the whole panorama. The subject, then, is Jehovah's conflict with this great idolatrous world-power.

I. THE AGENT. What was Moses? What was his Divine legation? 1. He was a *patriot-deliverer*, ranking with Tell, Bruce, etc. etc., as the saviour of his nation—but more! 2. *A statesman*—the creator (under God) of first a polity, and then a nation. He taught free men to govern themselves, under God. But Moses was more! 3. *A prophet of the living God.* Moses was intensely religious. He ranks with the greatest spiritual leaders of the world. His peer is Elijah, though Elijah was not quite equal. So great are they both that they appear on Tabor with the transfigured Lord. God, eternity, the soul, law, salvation, religion are the master motives of this great spirit. All that Moses was besides is to be traced to this deep root. The lesson is obvious: religion first—*then* the things that accompany salvation.

II. HIS DEEDS. 1. *Their historic reality.* Two facts certain—(1) Israel in Egypt. (2) Israel in Canaan. The historic problem is: How was the transition made? (1) Kings are not in the habit of emancipating races (note! apparent exceptions—William III. and Revolution of 1688. Emancipation of serfs by the Russian Czar. Lincoln and the freedom of the four millions of slaves.) (2) Israel never won its own freedom. Nor (3) was Egypt overthrown by a foreign power, and so in the confusion Israel emerged to liberty. (4) The Deliverer was God, and the mode, that described in the book. 2. *Their exact nature.* Exposition here of the miracles seriatim, with a careful note of the specialities of each. This as a foundation for the discussion of the question: Were the plagues natural or supernatural? They were either (1) natural; or (2) supernatural; or (3) natural in kind, but supernatural in degree, in circumstances and in concomitants. See ch. x. 12, 19; xiv. 21. Our view is the last. But that the visitations were direct from the hand of God is clear from—(1) Their colossal proportions. (2) Their concentration upon one epoch. (3) Their relation to the moral controversy. (4) Their gradation. (5) Dependence on the word of Moses. [On the evidential value of the plagues, see 'Speaker's Commentary,' vol. i. 241.] 3. *Their objective.* This word here used in a military sense. What was the Divine object in these visitations? To hurl thunderbolts against the idolatries of Egypt: Ex. xii. 12. For detail, see Dr. Alexander's Kitto's Cyclo., p. 751, vol. i. 4. *Their superiority* to the acts of the magicians. Full discussion of the questions—What the magicians really did, and how they did it, will be found in the Congregational Lectures by Rev. Walter Scott, of Airedale College, on "The Existence of Evil Spirits," 145—156. The conclusion, sustained by argument, is that they were adepts in sleight of hand. But, for homiletic purposes, show the grandeur of the scale on which Moses acted, and the imposing character of his deeds as a moral demonstration to the idolaters of Egypt. 5. *Their climacteric character.* When God deals with sinners, he begins afar off, and only very gradually draws near and close to their deepest life and acutest feeling. So here he touches first the river—then comfort (frogs, lice, flies)—then cattle—then the skin of the people—then food (hail and locusts)—then threatens life by the suffocating effects of the fifty days' sand-storm darkness—at last life itself. "I will sing of *mercy*" as well as "of judgment," etc.

III. His words. Fine homiletic use may be made of the verbal controversy which went on between Moses and Pharaoh all the time of these visitations, and which increased in tragic vehemence as blow after blow descended. Note Pharaoh's waverings, relentings, and anon persistence; and also the occasional passionate entreaties of the hardened sinner on behalf of the awestruck and repentant people. But "whom the gods purpose to destroy they first of all madden."

IV. Effects. 1. *On the Egyptians.* Leading some finally to attach themselves to the redeemed of the Lord. 2. *On Moses.* Called to a stupendous work. Timid. Trained to confidence in God, and obedience to his slightest word. Note!—So God is ever training his servants. 3. *On Israel,* through Moses.

V. Lessons. The main ones of this great controversy. 1. *The object of God in dealing with men.* To beat down the idolatries of the human heart—to reveal himself —his law—his salvation—to reconcile men with himself. 2. *The inevitable conflict,* i.e. until God's purpose be accomplished. Show the reality of this conflict in the case of every sinner. Message after message, mercy after mercy, judgment after judgment. If men will not be reconciled, then there must be antagonism; to that antagonism there can be but one end. It is *in this sense* that Amos challenges Israel—"Prepare to meet thy God, O Israel." This is the word of the Lord as "a man of war." 3. *The futility of the repentance of fear.* Case of Pharaoh. Case of every sinner. Fear, however, has its mission—to awaken to concern. But no repentance is solid, lasting in its effect, but that which takes place in view of the love of our Father as seen in the cross of Jesus Christ our Lord.—R.

Chaps. vii.—x.—"*The Lord, he is the God.*" Egypt was a pleasant land—"the garden of the Lord" (Gen. xiii. 10). The river, the source of its fertility, was fenced off from desert on either side by cliff ranges—canopied from morning to evening by the ever blue, bright sky. No wonder that the inhabitants should think much of such a land, that they should come to say of river, land, sky, "These be thy gods, O Egypt!" The veil of nature, which should reveal—as by shadow cast on sheet—may hide, the unseen God: cf. Rom. i. 20. The struggle with Pharaoh shows us God asserting himself—proving himself "God of gods" as well as "Lord of lords." Regarding the *river* as the source of fertility; the *land* as the sphere for fertility; the *sky* as the guardian of fertility—see how God openly manifests the dependence of each and all on him.

I. The river. "The beneficent Nile, the very life of the state and of the people" (Stanley). (1) Middle of June—season of annual overflow. To all appearance more than ever divine—Pharaoh (ch. vii. 15) probably openly acknowledging its divinity. Suddenly turned into blood—loathsome; no longer a source of fertility, but a source of corruption and death—at the command of Jehovah, the unrecognised invisible Source whence the fertilising power had been derived. (2) Later. Subsidence of the water. The river mud seems to breed frogs. Compelled at the Divine command to fructify not grain but reptiles. (3) Later. Even the dust of the sun-dried mud turned by Jehovah into a tormenting pest. "The river is mine, and the soil which it deposits is mine; even the very dust which it leaves is mine. Have not I, the Lord, made all these things?"

II. The land. So far the river has been made to plague the land; but Jehovah needs no intermediary. He has direct power over the land also. (1) Chap. viii. 21, 22. Swarms of flies (gnats) coming up as it were out of the ground. Yet land severed from land—Goshen spared, "so that thou mayest know that I am Jehovah in the midst of the land." (2) Chap. ix. 3. Murrain in the cattle—the creatures most nearly connected with the land; identified with its prosperity; deified as its representatives—at a set time, within appointed limits. (3) Chap. ix. 9. Pestilence on man and beast. The furnace-ash strewed heavenwards. The land as modified by human agency turned into a plague upon the men who used it. "The land is mine, and the cattle are mine, the very furnace-ash which ye might almost claim as *self*-made is mine. Have not I, the Lord, made all these things?"

III. THE SKY. The previous plague (chap. ix. 8) " toward the heaven," seems to challenge the sky divinities. Now they also are to be proved subject. 1. Chap. ix. 22. At the word of Jehovah the protector becomes the devastator. Clouds gather and pour out water. Pharaoh and Egypt, too, shall know that the earth belongs to no sky divinity, but to Jehovah: chap. v. 29. 2. Chap. x. 13. The winds, compelled into Jehovah's service, become charioteers for his locust armies. 3. Chap. x. 21. The sun, source of light, chief of the gods—even he is draped in darkness at the word of Jehovah. " The sky is mine with its clouds and winds, even the sun in all his glory. Have not I, the Lord, made all these things?"

Application:—People still forget God—still, practically, deify his gifts, and so plant them as to hide the Giver of them. The world, our respectable every-day world, not unlike Egypt. Health (life, ζωή), the river that fertilises it. Circumstances (life, βίος), the land fertilised. Thought, intelligence, wisdom, the sky which seems to canopy and protect both. Deify them and forget the God above them, and God will yet manifest himself by strange plagues on your divinities. Your river shall be turned into blood, and your sun into darkness [cf. Tennyson, " Palace of Art."] These things, too—health, happiness, intelligence—he will surely show that he and no other has made them all.—G.

EXPOSITION.

CHAPTER VIII.

Vers. 1—7.—THE SECOND PLAGUE. After an interval which there are no means of estimating, the second plague followed the first. Again, while the main purpose of the plague was to punish the nation by which Israel had been so long oppressed, the secondary object of throwing contempt upon their religion was maintained. Frogs were among the Egyptian sacred animals. One of their deities, Heka, was a frog-headed goddess; and they seem to have regarded the frog as a sacred emblem of creative power. The great multiplication of frogs, whereby they became an annoyance and a curse, was a trial and strain to the entire Egyptian religious system. The Egyptians might not kill them; yet they destroyed all their comfort, all their happiness. Their animal-worship was thus proved absurd and ridiculous. They were obliged to respect the creatures which they hated—to preserve the animals they would fain have swept from the face of the earth. It is perhaps somewhat difficult for modern Europeans to imagine the plague that frogs might be. The peculiar kind, which has the scientific name of *Rana Mosaica*, resembles our toad, and is a disgusting object, which crawls rather than leaps, and croaks perpetually. To have the whole country filled with these disgusting reptiles, to be unable to walk in the streets without treading on them, to find them not only occupying

one's doorstep but in possession of one's house, in one's bed-chamber, and upon one's bed, to hear their dismal croak perpetually, to see nothing but their loathsome forms whithersoever one looked, to be in perpetual contact with them and feel the repulsion of their cold, rough, clammy skin, would be perhaps as severe a punishment as can well be conceived. Nations are known to have deserted their homes, and fled to a foreign land to escape from it. " In Pæonia and Dardania," says Phœnias, a disciple of Aristotle, " there appeared once suddenly such a number of frogs, that they filled the houses and the streets. Therefore—as killing them, or shutting the doors, was of no avail; as even the vessels were full of them, the water infected, and all food uneatable; as they could scarcely set their foot upon the ground without treading on heaps of them, and as they were vexed by the smell of the great numbers which died—they fled from that region altogether " (Eustath. ad Hom. *Il.* i. p. 35). In Egypt, the young frogs come out of the waters in the month of September, when the inundation is beginning to subside. Even now they sometimes amount to a severe visitation.

Ver. 1.—**Go unto Pharaoh.** The second plague is given simply as a plague, not as a sign. It is first threatened (ver. 2), and then accomplished (ver. 6), an interval being allowed, that Pharaoh might change his mind, and escape the plague, if he chose.

Ver. 2.—**Frogs.** The word used for " frog,"

viz. *tsĕparda*, is thought to be Egyptian, and to remain (abbreviated) in the modern *dofda*, which is in common use, and designates the species known to naturalists as "Rana Mosaica."

Ver. 3.—**The river shall bring forth frogs.** The frogs do not often come directly out of the river. They are bred in the pools and marshes which the Nile leaves as it is retiring. These, however, may be viewed as detached fragments of the river. **Thine house . . . thy bed-chamber . . . thy bed.** The extreme cleanliness of the Egyptians (Herod. ii. 37) rendered this visitation peculiarly disagreeable to them. The frogs under ordinary circumstances do not think of entering houses. **Ovens** in Egypt were probably baking-pans. These were heated from within by a fire of wood, which was withdrawn after a time and the dough attached by pressure to the interior of the vessels. **Kneading-troughs** were vessels in which the dough was prepared. Both these and ovens are represented in the Egyptian tombs. (See Rosellini, 'Mon. Civ.' pl. 84, 85.)

Ver. 5.—**Over the streams . . . rivers . . . ponds.** See the comment on ch. vii. 19.

Ver. 6.—**The frogs came up.** Literally, "The frog came up," the word being used to designate the class or species.

Ver. 7.—**The magicians did so . . . and brought up frogs.** Here again, as in their imitation of the first plague (ch. vii. 22), sleight of hand may have been the means employed by the magicians; or possibly they may have merely claimed that their enchantments "brought up" frogs, which were in reality the consequence of Aaron's act (ver. 2).

HOMILETICS.

Vers. 1—8.—*God can scourge men beyond endurance with a whip of straw.* A frog seems an innocent and harmless reptile enough, not pleasing nor attractive, but scarcely calculated to cause much suffering. When the Egyptians made frogs sacred, they had no notion of one day finding them an intolerable annoyance. But God can make, of the least of his creatures, a weapon to wound, a whip to scourge men. Minute microscopic fungi and entozoa destroy crops and wither up the human frame. Huge ships are utterly ruined by the working of the *Teredo navalis*. White ants bring down houses. And so, on this occasion, poor weak frogs made the lives of the Egyptians a burthen to them. Forced to tread on them as they walked, to feel them crawling upon their naked feet, to see them covering the floors of their chambers and the soft cushions of their beds, finding them in their ovens, their kneading-troughs, the culinary and other vessels, scarcely able to keep them out of their food, always hearing their melancholy croak, the unfortunate wretches had not a moment's comfort or peace. Constant dropping wears out a stone. A trivial annoyance becomes intolerable by repetition and persistence. Thus, even the obdurate Pharaoh, who had borne the first plague till God chose to remove it without a symptom of yielding, is cowed by the second plague, and "calls for Moses and Aaron" (ver. 8).

HOMILIES BY VARIOUS AUTHORS.

Vers. 1—39.—*Three plagues—frogs, lice, flies.* On the precise character of these three plagues, see the exposition. They are to be viewed in their relation to the Egyptians—1. As an intensification of the natural plagues of the land. 2. As a proof of the almightiness of Jehovah (see on ch. vii. 17), and of the folly of further contest with him (vers. 10, 22). 3. As a demonstration of the vanity of the idols. The Egyptian gods were utterly powerless to aid their worshippers. There was not the shadow of help to be derived from them. This was the more remarkable that several of the gods were worshipped as protectors from the very classes of plagues which were here brought upon the country. There were fly-gods, to protect against flies, deities to protect against frogs, etc. And the defeat of the idols was remarkable from this other fact, that several of the agents employed as scourges of Egypt were themselves ranked as deities. This was the case with the river, and with many of the creatures, *e.g.* the beetle, probably included under "flies." 4. The removal of the plagues when Pharaoh showed signs of submission, was a proof of God's mercy, and a token to the monarch of his sincerity in his dealings with him generally. Taken in connection with Pharaoh's behaviour under them, the three plagues read us valuable lessons. They teach—

I. THE SUPREMACY OF GOD IN THE KINGDOM OF NATURE. All creatures, all agencies, are under his control. They come and go, march and countermarch, act in separation or combination, at his pleasure. He sent the hornets before the Israelites to drive out the Amorites from their strong castles (ch. xxii. 28). He frequently punished Israel by sending armies of locusts to devour the produce of the fields (Joel i., ii.; Amos iv.). Jehovah was at the head of these armies (Joel ii. 11), and so was he at the head of the armies of frogs, gnats, flies, and other noxious insects that drove the Egyptians to a state of desperation. This is a striking thought, in as full accordance with a sound philosophy and with the facts presented to us in nature, as with the teaching of Christ, who bids us see the Father's hand even in the fall of a sparrow. What account can be given, *e.g.*, of the migratory instincts of birds, save that suggested by this thought of Jehovah's rule, regulating their motions, and guiding them in their long and perilous journeys (Jer. viii. 7). He rules. He alone rules. " An idol is nothing " (1 Cor. viii. 4).

II. THE IMPOTENCE OF MAN IN THE HANDS OF JEHOVAH. 1. *God's entire control of all things in creation gives him command of exhaustless resources for the punishment of his enemies.* When the river was healed at the end of seven days, Pharaoh may have thought that his trouble had blown past—that the plagues were at an end. But lo ! a new plague is brought upon him, of which he had never dreamed, a plague of " frogs," also from the river. Then in swift successive strokes came the plagues of gnats, of mixed insects, of murrain of beasts, of boils, etc., each breaking out from some new and totally unexpected quarter. If ever the Egyptians thought, Surely the arrows in the quiver of this mighty god are at length all spent, they were speedily undeceived by the breaking forth upon them of some fresh plague. The Almighty's quiver is not thus easily exhausted. There is at every stage in his chastisements an infinite reserve of power to chastise us further, and in new forms. 2. *Natural agents are a frequent means by which God chastises the rebellious.* It is really a truer philosophy which sees God behind all action of natural force, and all movements of the irrational creatures, than that which sees *only* second causes, only laws and instincts, and refuses to recognise the Supreme Orderer in their movements and combinations. There need be no scruple in acknowledging second causes, or even, in a sense, a reign of unvarying law ; but the " laws " of nature are one thing, and the " course " of nature another, and this latter the Theist believes to be no more of chance than the former, while the Christian is taught to trace a Divine purpose and end in its minutest ramifications. Hail, snow, fire, and vapour ; stormy wind ; rain and thunder ; insect and reptile life ; plague and famine ; disease in its myriad forms—all are weapons in the hands of God by which he can fulfil his righteous will to punish. 3. *The minutest forms of life are used by God as his sorest scourges.* Thomas Scott acutely remarks that the plagues would have been easier to bear, and would not have been felt to be so humiliating, had the agents in them been lions and tigers, or other animals of the nobler sort; or perhaps foreign enemies. There would at least have been dignity in succumbing to the attacks of hordes of powerful foes. But how intolerably humiliating to be conquered by shoals of frogs or by insignificant and contemptible creatures like lice and flies ! Yet Pharaoh could more easily have contended with the former classes of enemies than with these latter. One army can charge another with at least some chance of success; and protection is possible against enemies that are of a size which admits of their being shot, hunted, trapped, or kept out by walls and defences ; but nothing of this kind is possible with the minuter creatures. It was impossible to erect defences against locusts ; and to this hour, man is helpless against their ravages. A stray Colorado beetle may be put to death ; but if that form of life were developed to but a small extent among us, it would be impossible to shield ourselves effectually from its destructive operations. Numbers of diseases have now been traced to the presence of germs in the atmosphere and in our food and drink, and it is the very minuteness of these germs—their microscopic and infinitesimal character—which makes them so deadly and so difficult to cope with. When the potato disease appeared in 1846, nothing could be done to check its spread, and little can be done yet to guard against its assaults ! The fungus is of a kind which eludes our efforts to deal with it. Plague and pestilence (Plague of London, Black Death, Cholera, etc.), while depending to a very large extent on material conditions for their development, yet seem connected in their origin with similar organic germs. In this whole wide region, accordingly, God has under his control potent invisible agencies, which ordinarily his providence keeps in check, but which at any hour might be converted into most terrific scourges. He has at command a literally exhaustless array of weapons with which to assail us, if we provoke his chastisements; armies countless in numbers, invisible in form, unseen in their modes of attack, and against which no weapons can be forged likely to secure safety. As knowledge advances, means are discovered for partially protecting ourselves against this or that disorder (sanitary science, vaccination, etc.); but just as, perhaps, we are beginning to think with the Egyptians that the evil day is past, some new plague develops itself (*e.g.* the potato murrain) of which formerly we had no conception. We are still in God's hands and as helpless as ever. The "last days" will probably be marked by a singular intensification of natural plagues (Luke xxi. 25; Rev. xvi. 1—12).

III. The possibilities of resistance to God that lie in human nature. It might have been judged impossible that, after being convinced, as Pharaoh at an early stage in these proceedings must have been, of the reality and power of the Being with whom he was contending—that he was indeed Jehovah, the God of the whole earth— the monarch should still have persevered in his mad resistance. Twice, in the course of this chapter, he is brought to the point of acknowledging the futility of further opposition; yet, immediately on the plague being removed, he reverts to the policy of non-submission. He must have known that he had nothing to gain by it. If he was infatuated enough at first to think that the Almighty, having removed one plague, could not, or would not, send another, he must have been speedily disabused of that impression. It was no longer a question of self-interest with him, for the loss and pain caused by these successive plagues more than counterbalanced any gain he could hope to derive from the retention of the Israelites. Neither had he on his side, in opposition to this command of the Hebrews' God, the least shadow of right or reason, with which to sustain himself. Yet without one conceivable motive save that furnished by his own pride and obstinacy, and by hatred of the Being who was thus coercing him, Pharaoh continued to resist. Conquered for the moment, he returned to his defiant attitude the instant pressure was removed. And this defiant attitude he maintained, with increasing hardness of heart till the very end. Here then we see the possibility of a being finally resisting grace. It appals us to think of the possibilities of resistance to the Almighty thus lying in the constitution of our wills, but the fact is not to be ignored. It is a proof of our original greatness. It reveals to us our immortality. It shows us the possibility of a final loss of the soul. If it be thought that Gospel influences are certain to accomplish that which could not be expected by terrors and judgments, and that changes may be wrought in eternity, which cannot be wrought in time, we have to remember that an even worse hardening is possible under the dispensation of the Son and Spirit than was possible to Pharaoh, and that human nature in the future state is essentially the same as human nature now. No good reason can be shown why a will which resists all that God can do to subdue it here may not from the same motives resist all gracious influences brought to bear on it hereafter. No one, at least, looking to the possibilities of resistance manifested on earth, could guarantee that it will not do so. The tendency to a fixed state of the will in evil as in good, renders the possibility of an ultimate recovery of those who habitually resist light here extremely problematical, even on the grounds of philosophy. If we turn to Scripture, it is difficult to see what warrant we have to expect it. The dream of a future dispensation of grace, and of universal restoration, must find support somewhere else than in its statements. If we accept the plain teaching of Christ and the Apostles, there are those who will finally resist, and their number will not be few. The gift of will is a great, but it is also an infinitely perilous one. Even Dr. Farrar says, "I cannot tell whether some souls may not resist God for ever, and therefore may not be for ever shut out from his presence" (*Mercy and Judgment*, p. 485).

IV. God's readiness to be entreated of the sinner. Though Pharaoh had hardened himself so obstinately, yet, on the first signs of his relenting, mercy was shown to him (ver. 9). There was on God's part, even a *hastening* to be gracious. Pharaoh was taken at his word. He was *trusted*. No guarantees were taken from him that he would fulfil his word, save his simple promise. God might have delayed the removal of the plague till the actual order for Israel's departure from the land had been given. But the plague was removed at once, that Pharaoh might be left to his freedom, and that his heart might be won by the exhibition of the divine goodness to him. And this was done, not merely on the first, but on the second occasion of his entreaty, and after his first promise had been broken (ver. 29). So willing is God to do the sinner every justice, and to grant him every opportunity, which may result in his salvation. He does not wait for complete conversion, but welcomes in man the first signs of a disposition to return to Him. He is as plenteous in mercy as He is severe in judgment, if mercy is despised.

V. THE EFFECT OF CONTINUED IMPENITENCE IN PRODUCING INCREASED HARDNESS OF HEART. It is obvious from this chapter that Pharaoh was making rapid progress in hardening himself. Going back a stage or two, we can trace that progress in very marked degrees. We find him hardening himself—1. Against a miracle which was plainly from God, but which he tried to persuade himself was only a work of magic—the conversion of the rod into a serpent. 2. Against a miracle which he knew to be from God, but against the influence of which his obstinacy enabled him to hold out—the turning of the Nile into blood. 3. Against a miracle which he not only knew to be from God, but which convinced him of the hopelessness of further resistance, and which was removed from him at his own request—the plague of frogs. 4. Against his own promise to release the Israelites. 5. Against a miracle which even his magicians failed to imitate, and declared to be the finger of God, (ver. 19)—the plague of lice. Having broken his promise, Pharaoh now felt, probably, that he must brave it out. 6. Against a miracle which showed yet more distinctly that the work was God's by the difference which was put between the Egyptians and the Israelites dwelling in Goshen—the plague of flies (vers. 22, 23). This seems to have produced a powerful impression upon the king, and he again besought the removal of the plague. 7. Against a second solemn promise, and after being expressly warned against deceitful dealing (ver. 29). As the result of all, Pharaoh was acquiring *facility* in hardening himself, was rapidly losing his susceptibility to truth, was becoming infatuated in his obstinacy, and was strengthening his will in the *habit* of resistance. Thus fatally does hardening make progress!—J. O.

Vers. 1—16.—*The plague of frogs.* Observe on this plague, in addition to what has been said above.

I. PHARAOH'S HARDNESS UNDER THE FIRST PLAGUE WROUGHT NO ESCAPE, EITHER FROM THE DIVINE COMMAND OR FROM THE DIVINE POWER (ver. 1). He probably thought, now that the river was healed, that he had done with Jehovah's demand, and perhaps congratulated himself that he had succeeded in holding out. But divine commands are not thus to be got rid of. They are not to be got rid of by resistance. They are not to be got rid of even by braving out the penalty. They come back and back to us, and always with the old alternative, obey, or incur new punishment. Our most furious opposition cannot rid us of the obligation of rendering to Jesus in the Gospel " the obedience of faith," nor shall we escape judgment if we refuse.

II. THE SECOND PLAGUE INDUCED A SUBMISSION WHICH THE FIRST FAILED TO EXTORT (ver. 8). It was submission under compulsion, but it testified to a remarkable change in the king's views about Moses and Jehovah. It was not long since he had been erecting himself in his pride in supreme defiance of both. Moses and Aaron he had treated as base-born slaves, and had ordered them back to their burdens (ch. v. 4). He had scorned the message of their God, and had shown his contempt for it by heaping new insults on Jehovah's worshippers. So impressed was even Moses by his lordly greatness, that he had shrunk from exposing himself to the proud king's despite. He thought it was useless for *him* to attempt to go to Pharaoh. Very different were Pharaoh's ideas about Moses and Jehovah now he had been smitten by the invisible hand of this God with these two reeling blows, and already he was on his knees asking for deliverance. The vaunting sinner will change his views of the living God when once he falls into His hands.

III. THE SECOND PLAGUE REVERSED THE RELATIONS OF MOSES AND PHARAOH, MAKING PHARAOH THE SUITOR, AND MOSES THE PERSON SUED TO (ver. 8). What a humiliation to this haughty monarch! How much better for himself had he yielded at first, and with a good grace, to the righteous demand made upon him! Nothing is gained by resistance to God, but ultimate pain and humiliation. As Pharaoh was humbled, so Moses was exalted. He began to be "a god" to Pharaoh. Like reversals of the positions of the great ones of the world and despised servants of God have frequently been witnessed. Compare Paul and Felix (Acts xxiv. 25); Paul and the centurion, in the shipwreck at Malta (Acts xxviii.).

IV. The second plague raised Moses to new honours by making his intercession the medium of deliverance (vers. 9—12). God *might* have removed the plague at Pharaoh's simple request, conveyed to him by Moses. In point of fact, he made the intercession of Moses the condition and medium of it. The same thing is seen in the history of Elijah (1 Kings xviii. 41—46). This, 1. Put honour upon Moses. 2. Taught the value of "the effectual fervent prayer of a righteous man" (Gen. xviii. 23—33; Jas. i. 15—18). 3. Gave Moses himself a deeper interest in the event. 4. Trained him for the higher function of mediation on behalf of Israel. It would give him confidence in intercession, would enable him to realise the reality of his power with God, would help in developing the faculty of earnest and sustained prayer. 5. It shadowed forth the higher mediation. Pharaoh was so abandoned in evil, so insincere even in his repentance, that his request, as it were, could only become prevailing when taken up by a holier nature and presented as its own. This is the key to all spiritual intercession, and involves the principle which reaches its full expression in the mediation of our Saviour.

V. The removal of the plague resulted in Pharaoh's breaking of his promise, and in his further hardening. The severity of the plague had for the moment unmanned him. His power of further resistance had broken down. But the *will* to resist was not in the least altered, and when the plague was removed, his obstinate disposition reasserted itself, and produced new rebellion. Rage and pride must at this crisis have overpowered reason, as well as conscience, for Pharaoh could hardly doubt but that his breach of promise would bring new trouble upon him. He *did*, however, return to his contumacy, and by the act cut down another of the bridges which might have conducted him back to peace with God, and to safety and honour in his kingdom. Terror of any kind, the approach, perhaps, of death, or of what seems to threaten death, often produces quakings of soul, and transient repentances. If these are not followed up on recovery—if recovery or escape is granted—they react to induce a very special hardening. A heart seldom gets the better of vows made in a season of deep sorrow, and afterwards, with the return of health and prosperity, renounced.

VI. Minor lessons. 1. God's visitations are not vague and general. They will find us out in every sphere and department of our lives. His stroke will be felt in everything (vers. 3, 4). 2. The power of God's servants (vers. 5, 6 : 12, 13). The stretching out of the rod brought frogs on Egypt. The intercession of Moses removed them. The prayers of a good man are both to be feared and to be desired. Feared, if they are against us; desired, if they are for us. It is lawful to pray, not for the ruin of our enemies' souls, but for the discomfiture of their projects, and the overthrow of their ungodly schemes (Rev. xi. 5, 6). 3. The duty of courtesy, and of returning good for evil (vers. 9, 10). Moses, at the very time of his triumph over Pharaoh, treated him with studious respect, and was ready to pray, at his request, for the removal of the plague. 4. The power of life and death as vested in God (vers. 13, 14). 5. Man's abuse of God's kindness (ver. 15). A respite granted; *therefore* Pharaoh hardened himself (cf. Rom. ii. 4).—J. O.

Vers. 1—15. *The second plague : the frogs.* In intimating the first plague, Moses made no formal demand upon Pharaoh to liberate Israel, though of course the demand was really contained in the intimation. But now as the second plague approaches, the formal demand once again is heard. Pharaoh is left for no long time without a distinct appeal which he must face either with consent or refusal. And so now Moses addresses him in the same words as on his first visit : " Let my people go." It is a challenge to the man who holds by violence and brute force that which is not his own. It is not a mere combat between potentate and potentate. " That they may serve me,"—awful is the wickedness of hindering God's people from serving *him*.

I. Notice the characteristics of this second plague. Hitherto there has been something evidently sublime in God's treatment of Pharaoh. God's treatment is of course always sublime ; but up to this point even Pharaoh must have felt that he was being treated as a king ought to be treated. The messengers of Jehovah were only mean men in appearance, but the first plague itself was certainly an impressive one. We may imagine that Pharaoh would even say to himself with a sort of proud satisfaction, "How great my power must be when all the waters of my land are turned to blood in order to coerce me." He would feel flattered by what we may call the dignity of the attack upon him. But now observe how God changes his mode of working, and proceeds to use little things to humiliate Pharaoh. As he uses those who are reckoned the feeble and contemptible among men, so he uses the feeble and contemptible among the lower creation. He sends out frogs all over the land of Egypt. If only it had been an incursion of lions from the desert, roaring through the streets of the city and tearing down the people, or if it had been a host of mighty beasts trampling down his fields, then Pharaoh would have felt there was dignity in such a mode of attack ;—but frogs! frogs followed by gnats, and gnats by flies! A plague to be made out of frogs seems almost too absurd to think of; and yet we see from the event that these despised little creatures forced Pharaoh to an appeal which not all the evident sublimity of the first plague could extort. More curses could come out of the river than the conversion of it into blood. This plague of the frogs we may judge to have been felt as inconvenient and irritating rather than dangerous. How ridiculous it must have been to have these agile little animals, millions of them, finding their way everywhere. No place safe from them, not even the well-guarded chambers of Pharaoh himself. Here was a plague that did not wait for the people to make acquaintance with it, as when they went to the streams and pools and found them blood. It forced itself upon them by day and by night, as they sat at their meals and as they lay in their beds. The thing that is constantly inconvenient and troublesome, may bring a man to his knees sooner even than a peril which more closely concerns his life.

II. THUS WE COME TO OBSERVE PHARAOH'S FIRST SIGN OF YIELDING. Notice *that as to what will actually have power to produce a certain result, God is a far better judge than we can be.* We should have said, "put the frogs first and the blood afterwards; Pharaoh will yield to the blood what he will not yield to the frogs." But when it comes to a trial, it is quite the contrary. The frogs are so tormenting that they must be got rid of, even at a cost of a humiliating promise. Not even the success of the magicians in bringing up frogs, makes the torment more endurable; and so, perhaps somewhat to the astonishment of Moses, who might hardly expect such a sudden change, Pharaoh makes a promise in the most general terms to let the people forth for sacrifice. But mark, the moment Moses begins *to press him and fix for a day, he procrastinates.* The moment there is any relaxation of pressure upon him, he takes advantage of it. Already he begins to show that he will yield as little as he can. Give him a chance of fixing his time, and he naturally says "to-morrow." Unpleasant things are always put off until to-morrow, either on a supposition that the unpleasantness may be diminished, or on a chance that it may be escaped altogether. And then when to-morrow comes, "to-morrow" is again the cry. Notice that *Moses complies with Pharaoh's wish for this slight delay.* One day is nothing so far as Israel is concerned. They can easily wait, if only the granting of this one day will make Pharaoh's yielding more agreeable to himself. God never humiliates for the sake of humiliating. He chooses the humiliation of his enemies—as when he sends a plague of *frogs,*—because it is the most effectual means to his own ends. But the moment there is a profession of repentance, the humiliation stops, and opportunity is given to make the profession a reality.—Y.

EXPOSITION.

Vers. 8—15.—How long the plague of frogs endured, we are not told. Probably every effort was made, short of intentionally killing them, to get rid of them. Snakes, and chameleons, and ibises would destroy many—others would be crushed beneath wheels, trampled on by animals, squeezed to death by the opening of doors, unintentionally killed by men. But the vacancies made were constantly filled; and there seemed no prospect of the infliction passing away. The influence of his counsellors would under these circumstances be brought to bear upon the mind of the Pharaoh—he would be warned that his subjects were attributing their sufferings to his obstinacy—he would be recommended—perhaps pressed—to yield, and would find in the annoyance which he individually endured a strong motive for compliance. Accordingly, he after a while sent for the two Israelite chiefs, and made the request recorded in the text.

Ver. 8.—**Intreat the Lord**—*i.e.,* "Intreat your God, Jehovah, who has sent this plague, and can doubtless take it away." An acknowledgment of Jehovah's power is now for the first time forced from the reluctant king, who has hitherto boasted that "he knew not Jehovah" (ch. v. 2). **I will let the people go.** The royal word is passed. A positive promise is made. If the Pharaoh does not keep his word, he will outrage even Egyptian morality—he will be without excuse.

Ver. 9.—**Moses said unto Pharaoh, Glory over me.** Probably a phrase of ordinary courtesy, meaning—"I submit to thy will—have the honour of my submission." **When shall I intreat?** Literally "*For* when"—*i.e.,* "for what date shall I make my prayer to God?" And so Pharaoh's answer is not "To-morrow," as in the Authorised Version, but "*For* tomorrow." **Thy houses.** It would seem that the frogs had invaded more than one palace of the Pharaoh. He had perhaps quitted Tanis, and gone to Memphis, when the plague came; but the frogs pursued him there.

Ver. 10.—**To-morrow.** See the comment on ver. 9. **That thou mayest know.** Moses accepts the date fixed by the Pharaoh, and makes an appeal to him to recognise the *unapproachable* power and glory of Jehovah, if

the event corresponds with the time agreed upon.

Ver. 12.—**Moses cried unto the Lord.** The expression used is a strong one, and seems to imply special earnestness in the prayer. Moses had ventured to fix a definite time for the removal of the plague, without (so far as appears) any special command of God. Hence earnest prayer (as Kalisch notes) was doubly necessary. (Compare 1 Kings xviii. 36, 37.)

Ver. 13.—**The villages.** The translation "courts" or "court-yards," is preferred by some. Houses in Egypt had generally a court-yard attached to them.

Ver. 14.—**They gathered them together upon heaps.** Literally "heaps upon heaps." **And the land stank.** Even when the relief came, it was not entire relief. The putrefaction of the dead bodies filled the whole land with a fetid odour.

Ver. 15.—**When Pharaoh saw that there was respite.** Literally, "a taking of breath," *i.e.,* "a breathing-space." **He hardened his heart.** He became hard and merciless once more, believing that the danger was past, and not expecting any fresh visitation. As Isaiah says—"Let favour be shewed to the wicked, yet will he not learn righteousness" (xxvi. 10). Bad men "despise the riches of God's goodness and forbearance, and long-suffering, not knowing that the goodness of God leadeth them to repentance." In this way, they "treasure up to themselves wrath against the day of wrath and revelation of the righteous judgment of God" (Rom. ii. 4, 5), either in this world or in the world to come. **As the Lord had said.** See ch. iii. 19; iv. 21; vii. 4.

HOMILETICS.

Vers. 8—13.—*God's mercy when men repent ever so little.* The object of the judgments, as well as of the goodness of God is "to lead men to repentance" (Rom. ii. 4). He "wouldeth not the death of a sinner, but rather that he should be converted and live" (Ezek. xxxiii. 11). His cry is ever, "Why will ye die, O house of Israel?" And sometimes His judgments have their proper effect on men, partially at any rate. Ahab repented to some extent when woe was denounced upon his house by Elijah—he "rent his clothes, and put sackcloth upon his flesh, and fasted, and lay in sackcloth, and went softly" (1 Kings xxi. 27). The Ninevites "repented at the preaching of Jonah"—the king "proclaimed a fast," and "rose from his throne, and put his robe from him, and covered him with sackcloth, and lay in ashes"—the people moreover, "put on sackcloth from the greatest to the least of them" (Jon. iii. 5—7). And so Pharaoh seems to have repented, in a certain sense, at this time. He abated his pride, and came down from the high position which he had assumed, sent for God's ministers, begged their prayers, and promised compliance with the Divine commands. Probably he was not conscious to himself of insincerity. His spirit was humbled—he was convinced of the power of Jehovah—he believed in the Divine mission of Moses and Aaron—he promised, intending to perform; and God, though knowing well how short-lived his repentance would be, suffered himself to be intreated, took away His heavy hand, and gave to Pharaoh, as He gave to Ahab and to the Ninevites, "a breathing space." We see by this, that such is the mercy of God, such His love for sinners who are not yet wholly hardened, that He looks with favour on the slighest relenting, the least indication of a desire to turn away from sin, forsake it, and turn to righteousness. And this divine pattern must be followed by His ministers. They must not assume that any professed repentance is insincere. They may have their own private belief, as Moses doubtless had; but it is their business to welcome the first show of penitence; to come when the sinner asks their aid, to give him the benefit of their prayers, to seek to obtain for him a remission or alleviation of God's judgments. And further, they will do well to imitate the humility and courtesy of Moses. " A proud look and high stomach" on their part are unsuitable when the sinner abases himself. It is their duty, and their highest wisdom, to be "all things to all men"—to meet repentance half-way—to assist it, forward it, encourage it. No doubt, repentance under the pressure of judgment—such, *e.g.*, as sickness—is in itself suspicious and doubtful; but the wise minister will keep his doubts to himself, and bend his whole mind to the fixing, furthering, and deepening of the repentance, so that (if possible) it may issue in a real conversion of the soul to God.

Ver. 15.—*Double-minded men, unstable in all their ways.* An Egyptian king was not likely, unless exceptionally gifted by nature, to be firm, fixed, and stable in his conduct. Flattered and indulged from infancy, no sooner did he obtain the crown, than he found himself recognised as a divinity by the great mass of his subjects, and regarded as one who "could do no wrong." Occasionally, he may have been so fortunate as to fall under the influence of a wise counsellor, but in general he would have been surrounded by advisers only anxious to please by echoing to him his own wishes and ideas. This Pharaoh—whether he was Menephthah, or any one else—was evidently a weak, impulsive, double-minded monarch. He wavered between good and bad impulses, now inclining one way, now another. He was sure therefore to be unstable in his ways. Similar, though (it may be) less pronounced, instability attaches to all those whose souls are not anchored upon the firm and unchangeable basis of fixed principles. It is fatal to the consistency of a career that a man should be double-minded. No man can serve God and Mammon. There is no fellowship between light and darkness, or between Christ and Belial. A man should make his choice, and not "halt between two opinions." If Jehovah be God, follow Him; but if Baal, then follow him. Shifting, unstable, uncertain, variable souls earn universal contempt, and are powerless to effect anything but their own ruin.

EXPOSITION.

Vers. 16—19.—THE THIRD PLAGUE. The breach of promise on the part of Pharaoh (ver. 15), was punished by the third plague, which was inflicted without being announced. It is disputed among the best critics, whether the plague was really one of " lice " (as given in the Authorised Version) or of mosquitoes. To the present writer the arguments in favour of mosquitoes seem to preponderate ; and he believes the *kinnim* to represent those subtle pests. Such is the view of the LXX. translators, of Philo, Artapanus, Origen, Rosenmüller, Gesenius, Geddes, Boothroyd, Keil, and Kalisch. Mosquitoes are, under ordinary circumstances, a terrible annoyance in Egypt, when the inundation is going off, especially about October. Their power to annoy is witnessed to in ancient times by Herodotus (ii. 95), Philo (*Vit. Mos.* ii. p. 97), and St. Augustine ; in modern by Wilkinson and others. That Aaron was ordered to produce

them out of "the dust of the land," whereas mosquitoes come from larvæ deposited in stagnant waters (Cook), is only a proof that God can transform any kind of matter into any other. He who made man of the dust of the ground (Gen. ii. 7) could with still greater ease have transformed that dust into gnats. It is undoubtedly remarkable that the magicians could not produce the *kinnim;* but this disability does not help us to determine what exactly the *kinnim* were. Conceivably, the magicians were tired of the contest, and feeling that they would ultimately be worsted in it, withdrew before the circumstances compelled them to withdraw.

Ver. 16.—**Lice.** *Kinnim*—the word is only found here and in the Psalms which celebrate the Exodus (Ps. lxxviii. 46; cv. 31). It was understood as "lice" by Josephus, the Talmudical writers, Bochart, Pool, and our translators in the reign of James I. But the great weight of authority is in favour of the render-ing " gnats " or " mosquitoes." See the pre-ceding paragraph. It must also be borne in mind that the nearest Egyptian equivalent, *khennems*, has the signification of " mosquito " (*Speaker's Commentary*, vol. i. p. 490).

Ver. 17.—**And in beast.** Kalisch notes that mosquitoes " molest especially beasts, as oxen and horses, flying into their eyes and nostrils, driving them to madness and fury, and some-times even torturing them to death." He quotes Theodoret, *Hist. Eccles.* viii. 26.

Ver. 18.—**The magicians did so with their enchantments.** The magicians stretched out their rods over certain collections of dust, but no gnats were produced; which would be the natural result, if they had made no secret arrangements. No reason can be assigned why they should not have seemed to produce gnats, as easily as frogs, if they had employed all the arts of which they were masters in so doing. But events had convinced them that they could not cope with Moses and Aaron; and it would seem that they therefore declined further contest.

Ver. 19. — **The magicians said unto Pharaoh, This is the finger of God.** Or " of a God." It is not probable that the magicians believed in a single God, or intended in what they said to express any monotheistic idea. All that they meant to say was—" This is beyond the power of man—it is supernatural —some god must be helping the Israelites." No doubt they had come to this conclusion by a careful scrutiny of all the miracles hitherto wrought by Aaron. **He hearkened not unto them.** The magicians were minded to resist no longer; but Pharaoh was otherwise minded. It is quite possible that the mosquito plague did not greatly annoy him. He would proba-bly possess lofty apartments above the height to which the mosquito ascends (Herod. ii. 95); or he may have guarded himself by mosquito curtains of the finest Egyptian muslin. His subjects would naturally suffer from such a plague far more than he. **As the Lord had said.** See the comment on the same phrase in ver. 11

HOMILETICS.

Ver. 19.—*Moral avalanches not easily arrested when once set in motion.* The magicians had begun by exciting Pharaoh to obstinate unbelief and resistance to the Divine Will. They had, by artifice or otherwise, persuaded him that there was nothing so very marvellous in the wonders wrought by Moses and Aaron, nothing that indicated a Divine author of the wonders. They had thus encouraged and stimulated him to embark upon a fatal course. Now, they would fain have stopped him, but they could not. His pride and self-conceit—his honour, as no doubt he thought it, were concerned in the struggle upon which he had entered—to give way would be to acknowledge himself worsted in a contest with two contemptible Hebrews. In vain did the magicians change their tone, and make the acknowledgment—" This is the finger of God "—their altered spirit had no effect upon him. No—whoever changed or blenched—he would persevere —his heart had become hardened—if now and then he quailed, and seemed on the verge of yielding, yet after a time he drew back—always provoking God more and more by his continual perverseness, until at last all Egypt was involved in destruction (ch. xii. 29, 30 ; xiv. 27–30). The magicians, who had had a large share in causing his entrance upon an evil course, found themselves unable to arrest his steps, and must be regarded as in part responsible for the final catastrophe. So nations are often urged by evil counsellors into wars or rebellions, which they soon bitterly regret; but it is too late to stop the evil. Men in business are recommended to adopt questionable means of pushing or retrieving their fortunes, and embark on courses from which their advisers would fain withdraw them; but it is impossible. Advisers should recognise the great-ness of their responsibility from the first, and set themselves against the very beginning of evil, else they will find the course of affairs soon get beyond their control—they will be utterly powerless to stop the avalanche which they have set in motion.

HOMILIES BY VARIOUS AUTHORS.

Vers. 16—19.—*The plague of lice.* The precise nature of the visitation is matter of dispute. The word " Kinnim " seems to include various kinds of poisonous flies and insects (Geikie ; and see Exposition). Some take it to denote mosquitoes. The plague stands at any rate in immediate relation to the natural troubles of the country. Travel-lers tell how, as the Nile waters spread over the surface of the land, and moisten its fine dust, gnats and flies burst from their pupæ, and spring into perfect existence. They " vivify instantaneously on the dust absorbing moisture enough to discolour it. As the flood advances slowly onwards, a black line of moving insects on the extreme verge moves with it " (Osburn). There is a terrible " tick " described by Sir Samuel Baker, which lives in hot sand and dust, and preys on the blood of animals. " From the size of a grain of sand, in its natural state, it swells to the size of a hazel nut," and is " the greatest enemy to man and beast." Here, then, was a new horror, the intolerableness of the plague being increased by the insignificance of the enemy, and the hopelessness of fighting it down. Note—

I. This plague came from the land, as the two former from the river. Aaron " smote the dust of the earth, and it became lice (Kinnim) in man, and in beast " (ver. 17). This was a new blow at Egyptian idolatry, the earth being worshipped as well as the river. The suddenness, extent, and fearfully aggravated character of the plague, and its appearance in immediate connection with Aaron's act in smiting the earth, proved it to be of supernatural origin, while cognate with the phenomena of the country. 1. At the stroke of God's anger, trouble may be made to break forth upon us from any quarter of our existence. Now, the river; again, the dust. The quarter it comes from is not likely to be that from which we are expecting it. 2. Troubles spring not from the dust (Job v. 6); but they may be made to rise so thickly around us that it may almost seem as if they did spring from it. 3. The most insignificant agencies (and circumstances) may be made the means of severe retribution. It is intensely painful to be made to suffer through things which we despise. 4. God's retributions are often such as strike home to our tenderest points. The Egyptians— especially the priestly classes—were extremely cleanly, and this plague, if it was one of vermin, must have been a grievous infliction to them.

II. The third plague came unannounced. We forfeit our claim to warnings by acting presumptuously (Prov. xxix. 1).

III. It led the magicians to give up the contest (ver. 19). We find them still standing before Pharaoh (ch. ix. 11), but from this point we hear of no more attempts at imitation. They may have abandoned the contest—1. From a *sense of shame.* The paltriness of their attempts at imitating the miracles of Moses and Aaron was so apparent, that the magicians must almost have blushed at them. They would rather give up the attempt than expose themselves to more humiliations. 2. From *astonishment.* As experts in magical arts, they knew very well the difference between false miracles and real ones. They are confounded to find men who can work wonders of so stupendous a character, and this, manifestly, by the real assistance of Deity. 3. From *fear and pain.* They had no interest in courting a continuance of these terrible plagues, which they recognised as true works of God. They were as painful to them as to others, and they dreaded the consequences of perseverance in so unequal a conflict. We see from this (1) That involuntary testimony to the truth is often extracted from those whose inclinations would lead them to oppose it. There are remarkable examples in the life of Christ, *e.g.* " Then gathered the chief priests and the Pharisees a council, and said, What do we? for this man doeth many miracles. If we let him thus alone, all men will believe on him," etc. (John xi. 47, 48); and in the lives of the Apostles, *e.g.* Acts iv. 16; xvi. 17. The confessions of the demons in Christ's history are of the same order. Many testimonies of an extraordinary kind have come from unbelievers. (2) That there are great differences in degree of moral hardihood. Pharaoh held out, but the magicians gave in. They were not converted to the truth, in the sense of becoming servants of Jehovah, but they thought it prudent not to go further in open opposition. Even this degree of submission saved them from being hardened as Pharaoh was subsequently.

IV. The plague had no good effect on Pharaoh (ver. 19). In itself, it was as likely to have produced submission as the previous one, and Pharaoh had now, in addition, the testimony of his own magicians to the reality of the wonder. But to place against this, there was the fact that he had already submitted, and had broken his promise. It was doubly hard to submit again, and stronger means would be required to bring him to the point of a second entreaty. Thus do the influences that work for our good gradually lose their power over us, because so frequently resisted. Every time a vow is made and broken, a good resolution formed, and not kept, it is rendered harder to repeat the act.—J. O.

Vers. 16—19.—*The third plague—the gnats: the finger of God.* I. Consider the plague itself. From the water God comes to the land. He who has power over every drop of water has power over every grain of dust. Everywhere at his touch the inorganic becomes the organic. And he still keeps in the same line of action which has been begun with the frogs. He produces small creatures in immense numbers, rather than larger creatures in fewer numbers; that thus he may the more irritate and humiliate Pharaoh. *Individually*, the gnats are nothing; their delicate little bodies may be crushed out of existence between thumb and finger. *Collectively*, they amount to the dimensions of a plague.

II. Consider the verdict of the magicians upon this plague. The noticeable thing in the plague of the gnats is not so much the new agents of chastisement as the discomfiture of the magicians. Not that they had been really successful before. On any view of their proceedings they were deceivers, for what they did was done either by trickery or by the power of God working through them; whereas they took it all to their own credit and the credit of Egypt's deities. This was not success. No man can be called successful when he has the daily fear that his resources are coming to an end. Much that is reckoned success is only failure after all, ingeniously and impudently delayed. *The verdict of the magicians was worthless so far as it seemed to indicate the real state of affairs.* They say, "This is the finger of God," but we see only too clearly the motive of their admission. When an admission is extorted, as theirs was, it is deprived of all virtue and grace. That the magicians talked of the finger of God was no proof that the finger of God was present. They talked thus because they had no other way of cloaking their own shame, and accounting for their failure. The finger of God was not more evident in the gnats than in the frogs or in the bloody streams, or in the converted rod. He who could really see the finger of God in one of these, could see it in all the rest. That finger had been pointing all the time just as it pointed now. It was a question of hand rather than finger; and the hand was certainly pressing more heavily. Still, though the magicians took up this way of speaking merely for excuse, *we have to thank them for an expressive and appropriate phrase.* They, in their blind selfishness, speak of the finger of God, not knowing all they say; but the finger of God is a great and helpful reality to those who will look for it and be guided by it. It should ever be our business to look for this great finger. In a world of weathercocks, blown about with changing and conflicting opinions, that finger ever points in one direction; and yet while it teaches us to maintain a rigorous adhesion to Christian principles, teaches us at the same time to maintain them in a spirit of wise expediency. He has no true eye for the finger of God who knows not when to bend that he may not break. Pharaoh would not recognise the finger even when his own magicians were compelled to make a show of recognition. When they were defeated he seemed to think they were no longer of any account among his advisers. Thus we have to notice again what poor judges we are of the relative severity of the plagues. Pharaoh was more affected by the frogs than by the gnats. Perhaps he was so disgusted with the failure of the magicians as to be filled with a more rebellious spirit than ever. They said they saw the finger of God; he stubbornly refused to see it. *Whether a man will really see this finger depends on what he is looking for.* Equally pernicious is it to see Divine power where it is not, and to fail in seeing it where it is.—Y.

Vers. 16—19.—I. There is a limit to the Divine mercy. This, like every third plague, came without warning. Opportunity was given twice to avert coming judgment. None is given now. Unannounced it startles them in the midst of their fancied security. 1. When men have baffled the servants of God by unrepentant stubbornness and broken vows the matter is not ended. God who has spoken will also act. 2. God will not always strive. Those who resist mercy pass on to meet sudden destruction. II. The judgment upon the idolatry of Egypt. In the two first plagues God's hand was laid upon the river which the Egyptians worshipped as the giver of life. In this it was laid upon the land—also an Egyptian god and the giver of their food, etc. God proves that these are his servants, and that they will bless or harm according to his word. The works of God's hands—earth, sea, etc.—are still regarded as bestowing good independently of his will. Let us not need Egypt's chastisements to teach us that all are serving him, both in blessing and in judgment.

III. The world's wisdom turned into foolishness. They who have hitherto contended so proudly with God are confounded before the basest of all the miracles. 1. The wisdom that seeks to rob man's heart of God is brought to nothing before the gospel. With all its vaunted power it could not bring peace to a sinner's heart nor change to his life. 2. Atheistic science, that can see God nowhere, will yet be confounded before his judgments.—U.

EXPOSITION.

The Fourth Plague. Vers. 20—24.—It has been noticed that—setting apart the last and most terrible of the plagues, which stands as it were by itself—the remainder divide themselves into three groups of three each—two in each group coming with a warning, and the third without. (See ch. viii. 16; ix. 8; x. 21.) In other respects, no great regularity is observable. There is a general principle of increasing severity in the afflictions, but it does not obtain throughout the entire series. The first three caused annoyance, rather than actual injury, either to persons or property. Of the next three, two were upon property, one upon both property and person (ch. ix. 10). Of the remaining three, two again inflicted injury on property, while one (the plague of darkness) was a mere personal annoyance. The exact character of the fourth plague depends on the proper translation of the word 'arób. The Jewish commentators connected this word with 'Ereb and 'Arab, words meaning "mingled" or "mixed;" and supposed a mixed multitude of animals—beasts, reptiles, and insects—to be meant. But the expression used throughout, which is ha-'arob, "the 'arób," marks very clearly a single definite species. So much was clear to the LXX., who rendered the word by κυνόμυια, "the dog-fly," which is not the common house-fly (Musca domestica), but a distinct species (Musca canina). Flies of this kind are said to constitute a terrible affliction in Egypt (Philo, De vit. Mos. ii. p. 101; Munk, Palestine, p. 120; etc.); but they attack men chiefly, and do no harm to houses or to the fruits of the field, whereas the 'arób is spoken of as a pest in the houses, and as "destroying the land" (verse 24). It has been, therefore, suggested that the Blatta orientalis, or kaker-laque, a kind of beetle, is really intended. These creatures suddenly appear upon the Nile in great numbers; they "inflict very painful bites with their jaws; gnaw and destroy clothes, household furniture, leather, and articles of every kind, and either consume or render unavailable all eatables" (Kalisch).

They sometimes drive persons out of their houses; and they also devastate the fields.

Ver. 20.—Lo, he cometh forth to the water. See ch. vii. 15, and comment. It is suspected that on this occasion Pharaoh "went to the Nile with a procession to open the solemn festival" held in the autumn when the inundation was beginning to abate (Cook). Say unto him. Repeat, i.e., the Divine command so often given (ch. v. 1; vii. 16; viii. 1).

Ver. 21.—Swarms of flies is an unfortunate translation of a single substantive in the singular number, accompanied by the article. A mixture, etc., is nearly as bad. The writer must mean some one definite species of animal, which he called "the 'arób." On the probable identification of the animal, see the Introductory paragraph to this Chapter. And also the ground. The 'arób, like the frogs, was to plague them both inside their houses and outside, but especially inside.

Ver. 22.—I will sever in that day the land of Goshen. On the position of the land of Goshen, see the Excursus on the Geography. The "severance" is a new feature, and one distinguishing the later from the earlier plagues. It was an additional mark of the miraculous character of the visitations, well calculated to impress all thoughtful and honest minds. By all such it would be seen that the God who could make this severance was no local God of the Hebrews only, but one whose power extended over the whole earth.

Ver. 23.—A division. Literally "a redemption," i.e., a sign that they are redeemed from bondage, and are "My people," not thine any longer. To-morrow. Particulars of time and place are fixed beforehand, to mark clearly that the visitation does not take place by chance, or by mere natural law, but by God's positive decree and by his agency.

Ver. 24.—A grievous swarm of flies. Rather "a multitude of beetles." As with the frogs, so with the beetles, it aggravated the infliction, that, being sacred animals, they might not be destroyed or injured. Beetles were sacred to Ra, the sun-god; and one form of Ra, Chepra, was ordinarily represented under the form of a beetle, or as a man with a beetle for his head. The land was corrupted. Rather "destroyed;" i.e. grievously injured, or "devastated" (as Kalisch renders). The beetles seriously damaged the growing crops.

HOMILETICS.

Vers. 22, 23.—*God puts division between the good and bad, both here and hereafter.*—In some respects the good and the bad appear to be treated alike in this life, and no difference to be made between them. "God maketh his sun to rise on the evil and on the good, and sendeth rain on the just and on the unjust" (Matt. v. 45). The Preacher's experience was that "all things come alike to all; there is one event to the righteous and to the wicked; to the clean and to the unclean; to him that sacrificeth and to him that sacrificeth not; as is the good, so is the sinner; and he that sweareth as he that feareth an oath" (Eccles. ix. 2). If God sends a pestilence upon a land, or a drought, or an excess of rain, or any other calamity, the good and the bad seem to suffer equally; no difference to be put between them. This is the first impression of the contemplative philosopher when he looks upon human life; and it is a true impression to a great extent. But there are limitations, which, though easily overlooked at the first glance, become apparent upon more careful examination. God does not treat all nations alike—he favours those which observe his laws; punishes those who disobey them. He seems sometimes especially to bless certain faithful families, as that of David, and to rain plagues upon others, as those of Saul, Herod the Great, and Napoleon. He gives, on the whole, to good men certain temporal advantages over bad men, as those which flow naturally (*i.e.* by his appointment) from industry, honesty, prudence, sobriety, and other virtues. The result is that "godliness" is said in Scripture to "have the promise of *this* life" (1 Tim. iv. 8). And if we take into consideration the satisfaction of a good conscience, the confidence towards God, the calm trust, and the certain hope which sustain the good, and set in the opposite scale the doubts and fears and horrors of an evil conscience which afflict the bad, we shall have little doubt that the balance of happiness, even in this life, *is* with the servants of God. Still, no doubt the *great* "division" is put hereafter. "When the Son of Man shall come in his glory, and all the holy angels with him, before him shall be gathered all nations; and he shall *separate* them one from another, as a shepherd divideth his sheep from the goats—and he shall set the sheep on his right hand, but the goats on the left" (Matt. xxv. 31—3). Awful the separation, where between the two "there is a great gulf fixed" (Luke xvi. 26)—on the one side heavenly joy and perfect felicity—on the other, "the blackness of darkness for ever" (Jude 13).

HOMILIES BY VARIOUS AUTHORS.

Vers. 20—32.—*The plague of flies.* This torment is thought by many to have embraced winged pests of all kinds. In this case, it would include the mosquito, cattle-fly, beetles, dog-flies, and numbers of others. But see the exposition. We have to note regarding it—

I. PHARAOH FINDS AS BEFORE THAT THERE IS NO ESCAPING FROM THE HANDS OF GOD. He is met at the brink of the river, and confronted with the old alternative—"Let my people go . . . else," etc. (vers. 20, 21). The king, when he saw Moses, would have no difficulty in anticipating what was coming. The bitter greeting he would give him would be akin to that of Ahab to Elijah—"Hast thou found me, O mine enemy?" (1 Kings xxi. 20); nor would Moses' reply be very different from that given by the prophet—"I have found thee; because thou hast sold thyself to work evil in the sight of the Lord." What madness in the king to keep up this foolish, this suicidal contest! But the conflict of every sinner with Jehovah is of the same infatuated character. Stroke after stroke descends, yet impenitence is persevered in. Well may God say, "Why should ye be stricken any more?" (Is. i. 5.) *His* demand, through all, abides unchanged.

II. THE FOURTH PLAGUE SPRINGS FROM THE AIR. The sphere of judgment is widening and extending, taking in constantly new regions—water, earth, air. The voices that summon to repentance are heard from every side. A new demonstration of the universality of Jehovah's rule—of the unlimited sweep of his dominion (ver. 22). Flies are agents which God can employ as a scourge of nations still. We read of singular feats in the way of insect-taming; of flies, bees, and even lice being trained to obey orders, and go through wonderful evolutions. Man's power of control over these minute creatures is but a feeble image of the power exercised over them by God. He enrols them among his battalions, and uses them to execute his commissions.

III. A NEW SIGN IS THIS TIME GIVEN—THE SEVERANCE OF THE LAND OF GOSHEN FROM THE REST OF EGYPT (vers. 22, 23). The Israelites had probably been made fellow-sufferers with the Egyptians, at least in part, in the inconvenience experienced from the first three plagues. This was permitted, at once as a chastisement for their unbelief and murmurings, and as a purifying discipline. Nothing has been said as to the effect produced upon their minds by the outbreak of these terrific plagues; but they must have shown the Israelites the folly of their recent conduct, and wrought them up to a high pitch of expectation in the confidence that the day of their redemption was drawing near. With the production of this change of mind in the dwellers in Goshen, the need for further inflictions upon *them* ceased, and a difference was thereafter put between them and the Egyptians. This astonishing separation was as clear a proof as could have been given of Jehovah's absoluteness in the government of the creatures, of the extent of his rule, and of the care he exercised over his chosen people. Possibly, Pharaoh had hitherto been taking encouragement from the fact that Israel was involved in the calamities. He may have been led to question: 1. God's *power*, seeing that he could not protect his own worshippers. It may have suggested itself to him that Jehovah's power was *limited*, and therefore might successfully be braved. 2. God's *love* for Israel. For if he loved them so much, why did he allow them to suffer? And if his interest in them was as weak as facts seemed to show, it was not impossible, if resistance was continued, that he might abandon them altogether. 3. The *likelihood of God's proceeding to extremities*. God, Pharaoh may have thought, must stop somewhere, else his own people will be destroyed together with mine. The need of protecting *them* is a safeguard against his proceeding to extremes with *me*. The severance now effected between Goshen and the rest of Egypt was a cruel blow to all such hopes. Thenceforward it was plain that God *did* care for Israel, that his *power* was as great as his *love*, and that whatever happened to Egypt, Israel was as safe as the pavilion of the Divine protection could make it. The fact is not without significance to ourselves. It teaches us that a deep and broad line of demarcation is really being put in God's thoughts beween his own people and the rest of mankind, and that, whatever be the nature of his *outward* providence, he has their interests and well-being continually at heart. Those who encourage themselves in sin because they see that the righteous suffer with the wicked, and judge that this proves an absence of interest or care on the part of God, must submit to a great undeceiving. The last judgment will make a final separation (Matt. xxv. 31—35).

IV. THE FOURTH PLAGUE BROUGHT PHARAOH A SECOND TIME TO THE POINT OF SUBMISSION TO GOD'S COMMANDS. The separation of the territory of Israel seems greatly to have startled him, and he sent anew for Moses. The unwillingness of his mind to grant the required consent to the departure of the people is apparent from the interview. 1. *Pharaoh proposes a compromise* (v. 25). This is a common expedient with those who are hard pushed with questions of religion. It is, however, only a veil for the spirit of disobedience working underneath. The compromise proposed was unhesitatingly rejected by Moses. He had no authority to accept it. It was in its own nature an untenable one (ver. 26). Nothing was to be gained by accepting it. By standing firm to his demand, he was certain to get the *whole* of what he wanted (ver. 28), why then take a part? Had he accepted the compromise, it would probably only have emboldened Pharaoh to further resistance. God's servants will do well to imitate Moses in this distrust of compromises. Little good ever comes of them. Principle, not expediency, should rule the Christian's conduct. The intrusion of expediency into matters ecclesiastical has been a grievous source of weakness, of scandal, and of loss of spiritual power. 2. *He ultimately yields*. He concedes the whole demand; qualified only by the injunction not to go far away (ver. 28). The interview leaves on one's mind the impression of sincerity—of a real relenting, of however short a duration, on the part of Pharaoh. Just so much the more fatal to his spiritual life was the subsequent hardening.

V. THOUGH WARNED BY MOSES OF THE PERIL OF ACTING DECEITFULLY, PHARAOH ANEW HARDENED HIS HEART (ver. 32). Hardening, after the experience just described, may be regarded as almost settling Pharaoh's doom. He would soon be, if he was not already, irrecoverable. God had trusted him a second time, and this was the result. Obstinacy was passing into obduracy.—J. O.

Vers. 20—32.—*The fourth plague—the flies: the immunities of Goshen.* The mere change from one chastising agent to another is not a matter to be dwelt on in considering this plague. We note that God makes the change from gnats to flies, and that Pharaoh, who was obdurate before the gnats, is so far affected before the flies as to make an offer of submission, but it is obviously impossible for us to see why the flies should be more efficacious than the gnats. The important thing is, not the gradation from gnats to flies, but the way in which Goshen was protected by Jehovah, and thereby proclaimed as under his favour. As in the third plague we are to notice the discomfiture of the magicians, rather than the gnats themselves, so in the fourth plague we are to notice the immunities that were secured to Goshen, rather than the flies. Thus we mark how majestically and how worthily of himself Jehovah moves on from point to point towards the climax of his visitations on Pharaoh. To say that these plagues increased in severity is not to say much. Their succession in this respect is not so traceable as the succession of the events which happened in connection with them. In considering these events in their succession, we see more clearly how far this narrative of the plagues is from being the construction of a mere story-teller. There is a certain Divine art as to what is inserted and what omitted; but of this we may be sure, that nothing is invented. Underneath the condensed and pregnant record there is a tremendous and bitter reality. Consider then—

1. THIS PROTECTION OF GOSHEN. 1. *Note what this protection did for the Israelites.* Had they then up to this time been sharers in the inconveniences and perils of the first three plagues? We must conclude that they had been; and that Jehovah only now deemed it fitting to extend special exemption to them. It was well for them to share somewhat of the sufferings of the Egyptians. (And we must bear in mind that however much they shared of these sufferings, yet afterwards, in the wilderness, the recollection of the comforts and delicacies of Egypt rose above all the recollection of the sufferings. Ch. xvi. 3; Num. xi. 4—6.) But now, with the fourth plague, the time has come to make a perceptible difference between Israelite and Egyptian. True, the contest is advancing, but there is still much to be done; and it is well *to give Israel timely encouragements.* They must wait a while to be liberated from Pharaoh's thraldom, yet surely it must rejoice and comfort their hearts to see themselves, even though in bondage, free from the afflictions which are coming ever more thickly upon Egypt. Though they have not all they want, it is something to have such a clear sign that God has marked them for his own. Even in this world, with all his sufferings, temporal disadvantages, and opportunities of gain missed, because he is a Christian, the Christian has that which makes the world to envy and to fear. For a while we must share in the world's sufferings, but the world cannot share in our joys. Israel has to suffer with Pharaoh in the beginning, but presently it escapes; whereas Pharaoh cannot by any plan extend Goshen among the habitations of his own people. If we would have the comforts of Goshen we must go there, fraternise with them that dwell there, and join ourselves on to them. 2. *Note what this protection may have done for the Egyptians.* It may have done much in the way of revelation as to the cause of their troubles. Up to this point, most of them, even while they experienced great sufferings, had no knowledge of what caused the sufferings. It is very improbable that the demands of Moses had become known to the great bulk of the people. To national troubles they were doubtless used at times—such troubles as had come to their ancestors in the seven years of famine—but these plagues were altogether beyond precedent, and must have provoked much active enquiry as to what possible cause could produce them. And now when this sharp division is made between Egypt and Goshen, this line evidently not of man's making, the Egyptian people cannot but feel at once that there must be some connection between their sufferings and the state of the Israelites. Hence—3. It is possible that *here we have the real reason why Pharaoh is now driven again into a sort of submission.* What if he were more concerned at the absence of the flies from Goshen than at the presence of them among his own people! Might not this extraordinary exemption set his own people thinking too much, and cause his house to be divided against itself?

II. HIS PROPOSITIONS TO MOSES OF COMPROMISE. Pharaoh, on the occasion of his former yielding (ver. 10), proposed to let the people go "*to-morrow*." Now he varies the terms of compromise. The people shall offer their sacrifices *in the land*. This offer he seems to have made in complete ignorance of the difficulties which lay in the way from the feelings of his own people. A fine man this, to be the ruler of a great kingdom! One who had to be taught the feelings of his own people by a stranger. Like most despots, he did not understand how vain it was to contend against the strength of custom and popular sentiment, particularly in matters of religion. Not only were the rites of Israelitish worship different from those of Egyptian worship, but one of the animals most frequently used for Israelitish sacrifice, would if so used before the Egyptians, have been viewed by them with the utmost repugnance. It was no visionary peril which Moses indicated. Whately, in his annotated edition of Bacon's Essays (p. 126), speaking on this very subject of the strength of popular custom, illustrates it, curiously enough, from the conduct of the Alexandrian populace at a much later time. " When the Romans took possession of Egypt, the people submitted without the least resistance to have their *lives and property* at the mercy of a foreign nation : but one of the Roman soldiers happening to kill a cat in the streets of Alexandria, they rose on him and tore him limb from limb , and the excitement was so violent, that the generals overlooked the outrage for fear of insurrection."—In the land of Egypt then, says Moses, the sacrifices of Israel cannot be ; and of course beyond the sufficient reason stated by Moses, there were others which there was no need to state, and which Pharaoh could not have understood, even if they had been stated.—But Pharaoh is driven from one proviso only to seek refuge in another. *If the people go out, they are not to go very far.* And yet this offer, conditional as it seemed, was not conditional in reality. It was enough to serve the purpose of Moses, and he could readily accept it. Once a bird is outside of the cage, a very few minutes will take it clear away from the risk of re-capture. If Pharaoh only lets Israel out of his hands, it matters not how far, the rest will settle itself. This promise was enough to justify Moses, in interceding for a withdrawal of the heavy hand of Jehovah; and Jehovah, in granting the request. Thus a second time was Pharaoh taken at his word. God, we see, takes men at their word *when they make right resolutions.* If they make wrong, selfish resolutions, he would have them alter them. But once they have resolved rightly, he holds them to the resolution, and gives opportunity to carry it out. God withdrew the flies, as he had withdrawn the frogs. There seems even something as miraculous about the withdrawal as about the original infliction. It might have been expected that a few of the flies would remain, just one here and there, but *there remained not one.* Lastly, notice what is now coming to be the *regular result of Pharaoh's temporary yieldings.* He gives way a little to pressure, but as soon as the pressure is removed, he returns to his original position. All these yieldings of his are but as the slight appearance of thaw when the sun is at his best on a keen winter's day. Pharaoh was thawed just a little on the surface of his nature. As soon as the heat of the present plague departed, the frost in his proud heart set in with more severity than ever.—Y.

Vers. 20—32.—*The Fourth Plague.*—I. THE SUPERSTITION OF EGYPT IS MADE ITS SCOURGE. 1. The land was covered with the sacred beetle. It swarmed upon the ground and in their homes. No movement was possible without crushing or treading under foot the insect they adored. When God overthrows idolatries the very reverence with which the idols have been regarded deepens the chastisement. When the covetous sink under the loss of wealth, they themselves have given its weight to the blow whicn crushes them. 2. The land was destroyed by it. No prayer or propitiation served to avert the judgment. A land is ever corrupted by its idolatry. With the knowledge and worship of the true God, purity and righteousness and truth are put far from it. The soul is marred and wasted by covetousness.

II. THE SEPARATION BETWEEN GOSHEN AND EGYPT. 1. Hitherto there had been no separation. Up to a certain point the just and the unjust suffer in common. 2. Beyond this, God shields his loved ones. They are alike visited by sorrow, &c.; but while there is darkness and the ministration of death in the abodes of the unrepentant, there is light and the ministration of life in the dwellings of the righteous.

III. THE REJECTED COMPROMISE. Nothing less than God's demand can be accepted. If we are to go free and to obtain the inheritance, we must make no compromise with the world or with sin; we must offer to God the full unfettered worship he demands.   There must be full and complete separation between Egypt and Israel, the Church and the world, else it will be impossible to present before God the sacrifices he asks for.   A Church unseparated from the world will be a worldly Church.

IV. PHARAOH'S BROKEN FAITH.   We have no reason to doubt that he was sincere when he made the promise (ver. 28).   How many vows sincerely made in trouble are forgotten in the ease they sought to purchase!   Under the pressure of affliction men are ready to sacrifice much to which, when God's hand is removed, they cling as to their life.—U.

EXPOSITION.

Vers. 25—32.—The fourth plague moves the Pharaoh more than any preceding one. He still cannot bring himself to grant the demand of Moses; but he offers a compromise. The Israelites shall have a respite from their toils, and be permitted to hold their festival, and offer the needful sacrifices *in Egypt* (ver. 25). When this offer is for good reasons not accepted, he yields even further—he will let the people go and sacrifice *in the wilderness*—only they must not "go far away" (ver. 28). Having made this promise, he obtains for the second time the intercession of Moses and the discontinuance of the plague in consequence of it. But then, as before, when he saw that there was respite (ver. 15), he retracted his promise, hardened himself, and refused to allow the people to quit Egypt (ver. 32).

Ver. 25.—**In the land**—*i.e.*, in Egypt within the limits of my dominions, so that I may not lose sight of you—far less run the risk of losing you altogether.

Ver. 26.—**It is not meet so to do.** So many animals were held sacred by the Egyptians, some universally, some partially, that, if they held a great festival anywhere in Egypt, the Israelites could not avoid offending the religious feelings of their neighbours. Some animals would be sure to be sacrificed—white cows, or heifers, for instance—by some of the people, which the Egyptians regarded it as sacrilegious to put to death. A bloody conflict, or even a civil war, might be the consequence. By **the abomination of the Egyptians** seems to be meant animals of which the Egyptians would abominate the killing. It has generally been supposed that either cows alone, or "cows, bulls and oxen" are meant; but recent researches seem to show that it was only white cows which it was absolutely unlawful to sacrifice. (See 'Records of the Past,' vol. ii. pp. 90, 96, 99; vol. x. pp. 44, 62, etc.) **Will they not stone us?** Death was the legal penalty for wilfully killing any sacred animal in Egypt (Herod. ii. 65). On one occasion even a Roman ambassador was put to death for accidentally killing a cat (Diod. Sic. i. 83). Stoning does not appear to have been a legal punishment in Egypt, so that we must suppose Moses to have feared the people present taking the law into their own hands, seizing the sacrificers, and killing them by this ready method.

Ver. 27.—**Three days' journey into the wilderness.** This was the demand made from the first (ch. v. 3) by Divine direction (ch. iii. 18). Its object was to secure the absence of Egyptians as witnesses. **As he shall command us.** Compare ch. x. 26, where Moses observes —"We know not with what we must serve the Lord until we come thither." Divine directions were expected as to the number and the selection of the victims.

Ver. 28.—**Only ye shall not go very far away.** Here for the first time Pharaoh shows his real objection to letting the Israelites go— he is afraid that they will escape him. So he suggests the compromise, that they shall just enter the wilderness on his eastern border, remaining near the frontier, and therefore within his reach. Moses seems to have made no objection to this proviso. As Kalisch says, "he committed himself entirely to the guidance and direction of God." The three days' journey which he had requested by Divine command (ch. iii. 18) would not take him far beyond the Egyptian frontier. **Entreat for me.** Compare ver. 8. An abbreviated form is now used, as sufficiently intelligible.

Ver. 29.—**To-morrow.** As Pharaoh had fixed the "morrow" for the departure of the second plague (ver. 10), so Moses now announces a similar date for the departure of the fourth. He adds a remonstrance against any further deceit or tergiversation, which Pharaoh must have felt to be well deserved.

Ver. 31.—**There remained not one.** The hand of God was shewn in the removal no less than in the infliction of the plagues. The complete disappearance was as abnormal as the sudden coming.

Ver. 32.—**At this time also.** Compare ch. vii. 13, 22; ch. viii. 15.

HOMILETICS.

Vers. 25, 26.—*Compromise not allowable in religious matters.* The struggles of political and social life, the conflicting claims of races, nations, states, classes, parties, are usually terminated, and perhaps, under the existing condition of things, are best terminated, by compromise. Let neither side get all it wants—let both yield something to the other—let the prudent and the moderate on each side seek an intermediate course between the two extremes advocated—and the result is often peace and something approaching to contentment. Compromise is the soul of diplomacy—the idol of clever Parliamentary leaders and party managers—the oil, as has been said, whereby the wheels of the world are made to run smoothly. But in religion, compromise is out of place. (1) There must be no compromise on any question of morality. If a thing is wrong, it must be got rid of, not tolerated under certain restrictions; *e.g.*, slavery, prostitution, vivisection, intemperance. A compromise between vice and virtue is an insult to virtue. (2) There must be no compromise with respect to doctrine. Doctrine is either false or true; and between truth and falsity there is no half-way house. Half a truth is a lie. To compromise the truth, is to give place to a lie. (3) There must be no compromise with respect to any Christian duty. The laws of God are plain and must be obeyed. Not to obey them is to disobey them. Moses was ordered to lead his people out of Egypt. To have accepted Pharaoh's offer would have been a flagrant breach of the command given to him. It was not necessary for him to see any ill consequences, in order that he should feel bound to reject it. Ill consequences—even could none have been foreseen—would have been sure to follow. For he would have forfeited God's blessing—he would have entered on the path of disobedience—to curry favour with an earthly monarch he would have offended against the King of Heaven.

Vers. 29.—*The duty of God's servants to rebuke the great of the earth.* "Let not Pharaoh deal deceitfully any more." Deceit is despicable in the meanest of men. How much more in a king! Subterfuge, tricks, lies, are said to be the refuge of the weak, the only resource whereby they can meet and defend themselves against the violence and oppressiveness of the strong. What need has a king of them? A king drags his honour in the dust when he forfeits his word, and does more to lower the dignity of kings in general than fifty rebels or revolutionists. Our own "King Charles the Martyr" has lost half the sympathy which he would otherwise have obtained, by his lamentable want of straightforwardness and steadfastness. And when kings err, in this or any other way, it is the duty of those who have the opportunity, to rebuke them. Elijah rebuked Ahab; Azariah, son of Oded, rebuked Asa; Eliezer, Jehoshaphat; Azariah the high priest, Uzziah; John Baptist, Herod Antipas. Jesus himself spoke of Herod as "that fox." The great are very apt to urge that whoever says a word in their dispraise is "speaking evil of dignities" (Jude 8), and so offending against the law of God. But the examples cited show that "dignities" have no claim to exemption from the rebukes and reproofs of God's servants. Dignities ought to be above needing rebuke. They ought to set an example of virtue and highmindedness, and, above all, of regard for their word, when once they have pledged it. What might be forgiven in inferior men, cannot be pardoned in them. "Be wise, O ye kings; be instructed, ye judges of the earth." "A city set on a hill cannot be hid."

EXPOSITION.

CHAPTER IX.

THE FIFTH PLAGUE. Vers. 1—7.—Hitherto the plagues had been directed rather against the persons of the Egyptians than against their property. Property had perhaps suffered somewhat in the preceding plague, if it was really one of the *Blatta orientalis*; but other-

wise the various afflictions had caused nothing but pain and annoyance to the person. Now this was to be changed. Property was to be made to suffer. It remained to be seen whether the Pharaoh would be impressed more deeply by calamities which impoverished his subjects than by those which merely caused them personal annoyance and suffering. The hand of God was first laid upon the cattle, or rather upon the domesticated animals in general (ver. 3). These were made to suffer from a "murrain" or epidemic pestilence, which carried off vast numbers. Such visitations are not uncommon in Egypt, and generally fall with especial force on the Delta, where the existing Pharaoh and the Hebrew people resided. The miraculous character of the visitation at this time was indicated, 1. By its announcement, and appearance on the day appointed (vers. 3—6); 2. By its severity (ver. 6); and 3. By its attacking the Egyptian cattle only (ver. 7). Pharaoh seems, however, to have been almost less moved by this plague than by any other.

Ver. 1.—Excepting in the designation of Jehovah as "the Lord God of the Hebrews," this verse is an almost exact repetition of the first verse of ch. viii. Such repetitions are very characteristic of the most ancient writings.

Ver. 3.—Thy cattle which is in the field. The word "cattle" here is to be taken generally, as including under it the various kinds particularised. The cattle are mentioned as being at this time "in the field," because during the inundation all of them were brought in and housed, while, after the waters had retired, and the land had dried, most of them were turned out to graze. This is always the time at which epidemics break out. The horses, the asses, etc. Horses, which had been unknown prior to the Hyksos invasion, and which consequently do not appear in the list of animals presented to Abraham (Gen. xii. 16), first became common under the eighteenth dynasty, when they seem to have been employed exclusively in war. Their use for agricultural purposes, which is perhaps here indicated, was not till later. (See Chabas, *Etudes sur l'Antiquité Historique*, p.

421.) The ass was employed in great numbers at all times in Egypt. Women and children rode on them, men sometimes in a sort of litter between two of them. They were chiefly used for carrying burthens, which were sometimes of enormous size (Lepsius, *Denkmäler*, Part ii. pls. 42 *a*, 47, 56, 80 *c*, etc.). The camels. Camels are not represented on any Egyptian monument; but they are occasionally mentioned in the inscriptions (Chabas, *Études*, pp. 400—13). They are called *kauri* or *kamaru*. There is no doubt of their employment by the Egyptians as beasts of burthen in the traffic with Syria and with the Sinaitic peninsula.

Ver. 4.—The Lord shall sever. Compare ch. viii. 22. There shall nothing die, etc The original is more emphatic, and might be rendered literally—"There shall not die of all that is the children's of Israel a thing."

Ver. 5.—To-morrow. God may have interposed the interval in order that such as believed the announcement might save their animals by bringing them in out of the fields. All the cattle died—*i.e.* all that were " in the field " (ver. 3).

Ver. 7.—And Pharaoh sent. This time the king had the curiosity to send out and see whether the Israelites had been spared. Though he found the fact correspond to the announcement, he was not seriously impressed. Perhaps he thought the Israelites took better care of their cattle and were better cattle doctors than his own people. (The doctoring of cattle is represented on the monuments. Rosellini, *Mon. Civ.* pl. 31.) Or he may have attributed the escape of their animals to the more healthy air of Goshen. Pharaoh's heart was hardened. The plague affected him less than others had done, rather than more. He was so rich that an affliction which touched nothing but property seemed a trivial matter What cared he for the sufferings of the poor beasts, or the ruin of those who depended upon the breeding and feeding of cattle?

HOMILETICS.

Vers. 1—7.—*The burthen of man's sin presses on the brute creation, as well as on man himself.* "The whole creation groaneth and travaileth in pain together until now' (Rom. viii. 22). Brutes are to a large extent co-partners with man in his sorrows and his wretchedness. But brute suffering is the product of man's sin. Mostly it is directly caused by man. Man not only kills animals for his food, but he chases them for his diversion, mutilates them for his convenience, vivisects them for his supposed benefit. In chasing them, he wounds more than he kills; in mutilating them, he often removes parts necessary for their comfort; in vivisecting them, he knowingly makes them suffer excruciating pain. His use of them as beasts of draught and burden is a lighter form of evil than any of these; but in the aggregate it causes, perhaps, as much suffering. Again, man makes the horse his companion in war, and exposes him to the most hideous wounds, the most horrid deaths. Nor does the list of his misdoings as respects the animal world end here. To children the wanton torture of insects seems to be a chief delight. For the production of certain delicacies of the table, turkeys and other animals are made to undergo untold agonies. Slow death is inflicted on calves, to make the veal white. Finally, animals are often involved in the Divine judgments by which nations are visited for their sins. "Much cattle" would have perished miserably, if Nineveh had not repented at Jonah's preaching. The beasts endure as much as the men when cities are blockaded. Occasionally, as in this plague, the beasts themselves are the direct sufferers, and God punishes man through them. No doubt there is a mystery in this. The suffering of innocent dumb animals is hard to reconcile with the goodness of God. *His* causing pain to them for man's fault is even more strange. How persons who have a fixed belief that the brute creation enjoys no future life, overcome the difficulty, we know not. But the solution of it may, we think, be found in the Scripture which tells of "the spirit of the beast which goeth downward" (Eccles. iii. 21). If the spirit of a beast survives, it may find compensation in another life for what it has suffered here. Man's coldness and deadness with respect to animal suffering is as marvellous as anything in his nature and history. "Pharaoh's heart" was utterly hard to it. He did not even ask that the plague should be removed. The sufferings and miserable death of thousands of beasts made not the slightest impression upon him. Probably he did not give their sufferings a thought. And even among Christians, is it not much the same? How few protest against even such enormities as promiscuous vivisection! How few, in grieving over the horrors of war, think of the pain which is borne by the animals engaged in it! How few give so much as a sigh to the labour, the weariness, the suffering of millions of poor dumb brute beasts engaged in ministering to their pleasures, amusements, convenience! We grieve bitterly for our own troubles. We have a tear of sympathy, perhaps, for the griefs of humanity generally. But for the rest of creation, "groaning and travailing in pain together until now," we have scarcely a thought. How different from him who was led to spare Nineveh (Jonah iv. 11) because therein were "more than six score thousand persons that could not discern between their right hand and their left hand, *and also much cattle!*"

HOMILIES BY VARIOUS AUTHORS.

Vers. 1—8.—*The plague of murrain of beasts.* I. THE ALTERNATIVE AGAIN (vers. 1, 2). Surely Pharaoh was well warned. The analogy of the third plague would have led us to expect that on this occasion—after a second and glaring breach of faith—there would have been no warning. Yet mercy waits upon him. Faithless though he had been, if even yet he will let the people go, all will be forgiven. If not—then judgments. Mark how sacredly, in all this, the freedom of Pharaoh is respected. "He was not put on the actual rack or held over a slow fire till his cruel hand relaxed, and let the Hebrew bondmen go. The appeal was loud, and each time it was repeated he and his people were shaken more severely than before; but after every demand there was a respite, a pause, an opportunity to ponder, and either yield the point or recall a past concession." (Hamilton.)

II. A MURRAIN OF CATTLE (vers. 3—7). This was the form assumed by the fifth plague. It is to be viewed, 1. As a *new blow at Egyptian idolatry*. The sacredness of the cow and ox are hinted at in ch. viii. 26. It may well have been that the sacred beasts themselves, the bull Apis, the calf Mnevis, and the rest, were smitten by the pestilence. 2. As a *fresh illustration of the manifold resources of Jehovah*. The mortality which came upon the cattle was universal in its sweep, carrying off, not only sheep and oxen, but horses, asses, and camels; destructive in its effects, the greater proportion of the cattle of each class falling victims to it; yet carefully discriminative, attacking the cattle of the Egyptians, but leaving unharmed those of the Israelites (ver. 6). 3. As a *plague of increased severity*. The loss sustained by the Egyptians in this mowing down of their cattle was the greatest they had yet experienced. Cattle constitute a large part of the wealth of every nation. They are of importance for food, for burden, and for the produce of the dairy. What a loss it would be to our own nation were our sheep, cows, oxen, horses, and asses, all suddenly destroyed! In the East the oxen were employed for draught, and in the operations of agriculture. Yet the plague was but the intensification of a natural calamity—one with the effects of which we are not wholly unfamiliar. It may seem "advanced" to scoff at the agency of God in cattle-plague visitations, but the truer philosophy will reverently recognise the fact of such agency, and will not regard it as in the least incompatible with any secondary causes which may be shown to be involved in the production and spread of the disorder. God has this weapon equally with others at his command for chastening a disobedient people. Our wisdom, surely, is to be at peace with him. 4. As a *forewarning of greater judgment.* As yet the *persons* of the Egyptians had escaped. The plagues, however, were coming nearer and nearer them. Their *cattle* had been smitten, and what could the next stroke be, but an infliction upon themselves?

III. This plague also ineffectual (ver. 7). Pharaoh sent to see if any of the cattle of the children of Israel had died. The connection seems to indicate that his hardening was partly the result of the news that they had all escaped. This, instead of softening, maddened and embittered him. Hitherto Pharaoh has been seen hardening himself *in spite of* the influences brought to bear on him. The fact is to be noted that the plagues here begin to produce a positively evil effect. That which ought to have softened and converted, now only enrages, and confirms in the bad resolution.—J. O.

Vers. 1—7.—*The fifth plague—the murrain among the beasts.* I. THE USE WHICH GOD HERE MAKES OF THE LOWER CREATION. In the three plagues immediately preceding God made the lower creation his scourges. He took little creatures, the bare existence of which many, not perceiving the wisdom of God, think to be unnecessary; and these he increased into a vast and most vexatious multitude. The killing of a frog, a gnat, a fly, we are accustomed in our heedlessness to make nothing of; such killing is but sport to thoughtless lads. But we think very differently of such animals as are spoken of in this fifth plague; horses, oxen, asses, sheep, all animals comprehended here under the general term cattle. We should feel it hardly possible to have too many of them. This certainly was the view in ancient times in Scriptural countries, for we read of the wealth of men as being generally measured by the number of animals they possessed. Thus we are led to notice in the course of these plagues, how *God, in his view of the lower creation, rises high above our view.* We look at the lower animals according to their use *to us,* and thus classify them as helpful or hurtful; God looks at them according to their use *to him,* and in his hands they all become abundantly helpful to further his ends. He uses the frogs, gnats, and flies (or beetles) to inconvenience Pharaoh and his people, if thereby a change of mind may be wrought, and when this fails he takes the cattle and causes them to be destroyed in order to bring about, if possible, the same result. Thus creation serves Jehovah; whether living or dying, destroying or destroyed.

II. A MELANCHOLY ILLUSTRATION OF THE UNITY IN WHICH ALL CREATION IS BOUND. A question may be raised as to the goodness of God in thus destroying those creatures because of the wickedness of man. Why should they suffer because of Pharaoh's obduracy? The answer is that the whole creation of God is bound up in a marvellous unity, from the lowest thing that has life, right up to man himself. It is for man himself to help in settling how far the lower creation shall suffer for his sake. It is no more possible for man to do wrong and the rest of sentient creatures to escape the consequences of his wrong-doing, than it is for man to live recklessly in his own person and expect the organs and limbs of his body to escape suffering. Animals are not to be looked at in themselves, but as being created for the comfort and service of man, and especially that in his use of them it may be shown what his own notions of a right use are. Let man do right, and all living creatures within the circle of his influence share in the blessed consequences; let him do wrong, and their lives must also be disarranged.

III. OBSERVE IN THIS PLAGUE HOW FORCIBLE THE ILLUSTRATION IS OF ISRAEL'S EXEMPTION FROM THE MURRAIN. The wealth of Israel was peculiarly pastoral wealth; of the very kind, therefore, which was smitten in this plague. Hence all the more noticeable is the exemption of the Israelites and all the more impressive. If it had been a pestilence coming down upon the country generally, irrespective of territory and of special Divine control, it would have injured Israel a great deal more than Egypt.

IV. WHAT A CLEAR MANIFESTATION THERE IS IN THIS PLAGUE OF HOW REASONLESS AND INFATUATED THE OBDURACY OF PHARAOH IS BECOMING. He is inflexible, not only without reason, but against reason. Not content with dismissing the rumours that come to his ears concerning the exemption of Israel's cattle from the pestilence, he sends to certify himself of the fact, which makes his continued obduracy all the more evidently unreasonable. What excuse was there for a man who asked in the way Pharaoh asked, even after it had been made clear to him that of the cattle of the children of Israel not one had died? It is sad when a man dismisses in this way even the appearance of having reason for what he does, when he says, "I will not, because I will not, and there is an end of it."—Y.

Vers. 1—7.—GOD'S MERCY IN TEMPORAL JUDGMENTS. Hitherto no great loss had been inflicted; now their cattle is taken. In God's mercy the afflictions deepen that Egypt may forsake the path of death. When the Lord's hand falls in heavier blows it is to save from something worse which lies beyond. Israel's calamities preceded her captivity. God's chastisements fall that we may not be condemned with the world (1 Cor. xi. 32).

II. CONVICTION DOES NOT ALWAYS COMPEL OBEDIENCE. Pharaoh had already two proofs that the murrain was from the hand of God. He had foretold it, and it came at the time he said it would come. He himself seeks a third proof; he sends to Goshen, and finds that there was "not one of the cattle of the Israelites dead." Yet he does not bow under the hand of God. Conviction may co-exist with impenitence and stubborn persistence in sin, but, when it does, it is the mark of a soul given over to destruction. The devils believe and tremble.—U.

EXPOSITION.

Vers. 8—12.—THE SIXTH PLAGUE. The sixth plague was sent, like the third, without notice given. It was also, like the third, a plague which inflicted direct injury upon the person. There was a very solemn warning in it; for the same power that could afflict the body with "boils and blains," i.e., with a severe cutaneous disease accompanied by pustulous ulcers—could also (it must have been felt) smite it with death. It is uncertain what exactly the malady was. Some have supposed elephantiasis, some "black leprosy," some merely an eruptive disease such as is even now common in Egypt during the autumn. But it is, at any rate, evident that the malady was exceedingly severe—"the magicians could not stand before Moses" because of it (ver. 11). If it was "the botch of Egypt" (Deut. xxviii. 27), as seems probable, since the name in the Hebrew is the same, it was incurable. Pharaoh and his people were warned by it that God's power would be shown on themselves, not in the way of mere annoyance—as with the earlier plagues—but of serious injury—and if so, why not of death? Thus, the sixth plague heralded the tenth, and, except the tenth, was the most severe of all.

Ver. 8.—Ashes of the furnace. Rather "soot from the furnace." The word commonly used in Hebrew for "ashes" is different. Many recondite reasons have been brought forward for the directions here given. But perhaps the object was simply to show that as water, and earth (ch. viii. 13) and air (ch. x. 13) could be turned into plagues, so fire could be. The "soot of the furnace" might well represent fire, and was peculiarly appropriate for the production of a disease which was in the main an "inflammation." It is not likely that Moses imitated any superstitious practice of the priests of Egypt. Toward the heaven. The act indicated that the plague would come from heaven—i.e. from God. In the sight of Pharaoh. Compare ch. vii. 20 It is probable that the symbolic act which brought the plague was performed "in the sight of Pharaoh" in every case, except where the plague was unannounced, though the fact is not always recorded.

Ver. 9.—It shall become small dust. Rather, "It shall be as dust." No physical change is intended by the expression used, but simply that the "soot" or "ash" should be spread by the air throughout all Egypt, as dust was wont to be spread. And shall be a boil breaking forth with blains. Literally, "an inflammation, begetting pustules." The description would apply to almost any eruptive disease. The attempts definitely to determine what exactly the malady was, seem to be futile—more especially as diseases are continually changing their forms and a malady which belongs to the fourteenth or fifteenth century before our era is almost certain to have been different from any now prevalent. The word "blains"—now obsolete as a separate word—appears in "chilblains."

Ver 10.—**The furnace.** It is perhaps not very important what kind of "furnace" is meant. But the point has been seriously debated. Some suppose a furnace for the consumption of victims, human or other; some a baking oven, or cooking stove; others a furnace for smelting metal; others again a limekiln. The ordinary meaning of the word used, *kibshon*, is a "brick-kiln;" but bricks were not often baked in Egypt. Nor is it at all clear that any victims were ever consumed in furnaces. Probably either a brick-kiln or a furnace for the smelting of metals is meant.

Ver. 11.—**The magicians could not stand.** It is gathered from this that the magicians had, up to this time, been always in attendance when the miracles were wrought, though they had now for some time failed to produce any counterfeits of them. On this occasion their persistency was punished by the sudden falling of the pestilence upon themselves with such severity that they were forced to quit the royal presence and hasten to their homes to be nursed.

Ver 12.—**And the Lord hardened Pharaoh's heart.** Up to this time the hardening of Pharaoh's heart has been ascribed to himself, or expressed indefinitely as a process that was continually going on—now for the first time it is positively stated that God hardened his heart, as he had threatened that he would (ch. iv. 21). On the general law of God's dealings with wicked men, see the comment on the above passage.

HOMILETICS.

Vers. 8—12.—*Sin punished by physical suffering, but such suffering not always a punishment for sin.* God has many weapons in his quiver wherewith to chastise sin. One of them is physical pain. He can cause the limbs to ache, the temples to throb, the blood to be inflamed, the breathing to labour, the head to be racked, the nerves to thrill and tingle—the whole body, from the sole of the foot to the crown of the head, to be nothing but a mass of "wounds and bruises, and putrifying sores." There is no part of our frame, no process, no function, but can be made the seat of an intolerable agony. God, for the most part, spares us, in the hope that his goodness and long-suffering will lead us to repentance. He had long spared Pharaoh and the Egyptians—had shown them his power in ways that annoyed and harassed, but did not seriously hurt. Now he must adopt severer measures. So his hand is laid upon their bodies, which are smitten with disease, disfigured, made loathsome to the eye, and racked with physical suffering. Here we may note three things:—

I. GOD PUNISHES SIN TO A LARGE EXTENT IN THIS WAY. Many sins have physical consequences attached to them by a natural law, which are in the highest degree painful, which injure the health, destroy the tissues, produce disease, madness, idiocy. Men know these consequences, but hope that they may individually escape them. As Moses and Aaron warned in vain, so now vain too often are the uplifted voices of God's ministers. Nine-tenths, probably, of the physical suffering in England at the present day is caused by those sins of intemperance and uncleanness which are the crying evils of our age and country, and which nothing seems able to uproot or even seriously to diminish. Children are born now for the most part with the seeds of disease in them, which are the consequence of their parents' vices. They lack the physical stamina and the moral vigour which they would have possessed, had their parents led good, pious, consistent, religious lives. They have unhealthy appetites, desires, cravings, which they would not have had but for their parents' sins. Too often, to all this is added the force of bad example. Intemperance and uncleanness follow, and the inborn germs of disease are stimulated into activity; pain follows pain, agony follows agony. A wretched life is terminated by an early death. If they leave children behind them, *their* case is even more hopeless. The physical taint is deepened. The moral strength to resist is weaker. Happy is it if God takes the little ones away from the evil to come.

II. GOD DOES NOT EXEMPT FROM THIS PUNISHMENT EITHER THE WEALTHY OR THE HIGHLY EDUCATED. "The boil was on the magicians." The taint of uncleanness, the mental weakness which results from habits of intemperance afflict the great, the rich, the "upper ten thousand," as surely as their humbler fellow-subjects who herd in courts and alleys. There are great families in which it is a well-known fact that intemperance has become hereditary. There are others where the heir never lives to the age of thirty. No rank—not even royal rank—exempts from subjection to hygienic laws. Neither does intellect nor education. It may be that the intellectual and highly educated are less likely than others to plunge into dissipation and sensual vices. But if, in spite of their higher nature, they give the reins to their lower, the same results follow as in the case of the least gifted of their fellow-men. Retribution reaches them. They "receive within themselves the reward of their iniquity." Their physical nature, no less than their moral, is tainted; and pain, suffering, often agony, are their portion.

III. THOSE WHO RECEIVE THE PUNISHMENT OFTEN HARDEN THEMSELVES. The boil was on the magicians; but we do not hear that the magicians submitted themselves, or owned the supremacy of Jehovah. So now, those whose sin draws down upon them suffering rarely repent, rarely forsake their sin, rarely humble themselves beneath the chastening rod of the Almighty. No doubt drunkards are occasionally reformed and profligates reclaimed. But for one lost sheep thus recovered, how many scores perish in their evil courses, and descend the rapid incline which conducts to the gulf of destruction? We are amazed at the obstinacy of Pharaoh; but we are most of us just as obstinate. Nothing will induce us to give up our pet vices. We cling to them, even when the boil is upon us. If we give them up for a time, we recur to them. If we leave them off in act, we dwell fondly upon them in thought and imagination. O hard human hearts, that will not yield to God's discipline of pain, when sent as chastisement! What can ye expect, but that chastisement will give place to vengeance? Physical suffering is sometimes sent, not to punish, but to refine and purify. Job's comforters supposed that one so afflicted must have committed some great crime, or be concealing some habitual vice of a grave character. But it was not so. The sufferings of saints are blessings. They give a fellowship with Christ, which nothing else can give. They make the saint rehearse in thought, over and over again, each step of that grievous, yet blessed *via dolorosa*, along which he went upon his way to the Cross of Calvary. They intensify faith and love—they give assurance of acceptance (Heb. xii. 6)—they elevate, purify, sanctify. Earth has no lovelier sight than that not uncommon one of a crippled sufferer, stretched day after day and year after year upon a bed of pain, yet always cheerful, always thoughtful for others, always helpful by advice, kind word, even (if their strength allows) kind acts. Such blessed ones live with Christ, suffer with Christ, feel themselves to be in Christ; as St. Paul says, they "fill up that which is behind of the afflictions of Christ in their flesh" (Col. i. 24), and "are joyful in their tribulation" (2 Cor. vii. 4).

HOMILIES BY VARIOUS AUTHORS.

Vers. 8—13.—*The plague of boils and blains.* This plague, like the third, was unannounced. God varies his methods. There was need for some token being given of God's severe displeasure at Pharaoh's gross abuse of his goodness and forbearance. This plague is distinguished from the rest by being introduced with a significant *action*. I. THE ACTION INTRODUCING THE PLAGUE (vers. 8—10). Hitherto the only actions employed had been the stretching out of Aaron's rod, and in the case of the third plague, the smiting of the dust with it. Now, Moses is instructed to take handfuls of the ashes from the furnace and sprinkle them towards heaven in the sight of Pharaoh and his servants. The performance of so solemn an act implied that a new stage was being reached in Pharaoh's hardening, as also in God's punitive dealings with him. From this point onwards matters are rapidly developed to a crisis. The act was symbolical, and may be variously interpreted. 1. As *a challenge to the Egyptian Deities*, specially Neit, "who bore the designation of 'The Great Mother of the highest heaven,' and was worshipped as the tutelary goddess of Lower Egypt" (Canon Cook). 2. As *connected with the scattering of the ashes of human victims to avert evil from the land.* This was done, or had been done, in the days of the Shepherds, in the worship of Sutech or Typhon. The victims were usually foreigners, perhaps often Hebrews. "After being burnt alive on a high altar, their ashes were scattered in the air by the priests, in the belief that they would avert evil from all parts whither they were blown" (Geikie). The sprinkling of ashes by Moses, and their descent, not in blessing, but in boils and blains, would thus have a terrible significance. 3. As *symbolical of the laying of a curse upon the people.* It is, at least in some parts of the East, a practice to take ashes and throw them into the air, in token of giving effect to an imprecation. Most probable of all,—4. As *a symbol of retribution for the sufferings of Israel.* The "furnace" is a common Scripture emblem for the bitter slavery of the Hebrews (Gen. xv. 17; Deut. iv. 20; 1 Kings viii. 57; Is. xlviii. 10; Jer. xi. 4). Ashes taken from the furnace and sprinkled towards heaven, whence they descended in a plague, would thus naturally symbolise the return upon Pharaoh and his servants of the cruelties with which they had afflicted Israel. The cry of the sufferers in the furnace had entered into the ears of the Lord of Sabaoth. The evil deeds of the afflicters were now to come back upon them in retribution. It was as though the ashes of the victims sacrificed in the long tyranny were rising in vengeance against the oppressor.

II. THE PECULIARITY OF THE PLAGUE IN THE SMITING OF THE PERSONS (ver. 10). The disease with which the Egyptians were smitten was painful, loathsome, and excruciatingly severe as compared with ordinary inflictions of a similar nature. Tortured in their bodies, they were "receiving *in themselves* that recompense of their error which was meet" (Rom. i. 27). This experience of sore personal suffering ought surely to have arrested their folly. It showed them how absolutely helpless they were in the hands of God. The plague was universal (ver. 11). Not one could boast against another. The plague was peculiarly afflictive to a people which prided itself on its cleanliness. It smote beasts as well as men. What a terrible calamity! The whole head was sick, and the whole heart faint. From the sole of the foot even to the crown of the head there was no soundness in it; but wounds, and bruises, and putrifying sores (Is. i. 6). Yet, instead of repenting, the people appear only to have been stung to further revolt. So it was, at least, with their king. 1. An image of the condition of the sinner. 2. A new proof of the power of God. The hand of God is to be seen in the infliction of diseases. God threatens, in Deuteronomy, to lay the evil diseases of Egypt upon the Israelites if they should prove disobedient (Deut. xxix. 60). 3. An instance of the inefficacy of bodily sufferings to produce repentance. Cf. Rev. xvi. 10, 11, "They gnawed their tongues for pain, and blasphemed the God of heaven because of their pains and their sores, and repented not of their deeds."

III. THE DEFEAT OF THE MAGICIANS (ver. 11). They could not now even *stand* before Moses. Pharaoh is being left more and more alone in his resistance.

IV. PHARAOH STILL HARDENED (ver. 12). Before, one plague was the utmost he could hold out against. He yielded under the *second* and the *fourth*. Now he maintains his attitude of resistance under two plagues in succession.—J. O.

Vers. 8—12.—*The sixth plague—the boils and blains.* Only the barest conjectures are possible as to why these ashes of the furnace were taken as materials whence to draw this sixth plague. If we look at the first two plagues we see that they come out of the water. The next plague, that of the gnats, comes out of the dust of the earth, and the flies may be taken as having the same origin. The murrain probably arose through a vitiating change in the food of the animals; and here again we are directed to look downwards to the earth, out of which comes the food both for man and beast. Next comes this sixth plague, and by the mention of ashes of the furnace it would almost seem as if God meant his people to understand that all the useful elements in nature were to do their part in plaguing Pharaoh. Water has had its share, the earth its share, fire now gets its share; and there only remains the air above and around, and out of this, sure enough, there presently came the hail, the locusts,

Warping on the Eastern wind,

and the thick darkness. Thus, in all visible directions where man looks for blessing, God meets him with a stern intimation that he can turn the blessing into a curse. So much for the origin of this plague; now with regard to its form.—NOTE,

I. THAT GOD'S PUNISHMENTS NOW ADVANCE TO TAKE UP THEIR ABODE IN THE BODIES OF PHARAOH AND HIS PEOPLE. As God can take the lower animals, which he has made for our use, and turn them at his pleasure into a blessing or a curse, so he can come nearer still, and make our bodies, which are agents of the most exquisite pleasures, into agents of pain just as exquisite. Notice that in the very mode of infliction *there was a mixture of severity and mercy*. *Severity*, because undoubtedly there would be terrible pain; *mercy*, because probably the pain was confined to the surface of the body; none the easier to bear, certainly; and yet easier in this, that it did not belong to an affliction of the great vital organs. Severity again, on the other hand, just because it affected the sensitive surface of the body. It is through our sensations that God has caused so much both of pleasure and information to come. Thus God, who had given so much delight to Pharaoh and his people, through making them so sensitive to the outward world, now deranges all the minute nerves and vessels, and by spreading boils and blains over the surface of the body he effectually stops all enjoyment of life. We know that it is possible for a person to be seriously ill—even fatally so, perhaps confined as a hopeless invalid for years— and yet to get considerable enjoyment out of life, as in reading and in light occupations for the mind. But what pleasure can be got when, from head to foot, the body is covered with boils and blains? As long as this sort of pain lasts, little else can be thought of than how to get rid of it.

II. As in the plague of the gnats, so here in the plague of the boils and blains, OUR ATTENTION IS SPECIALLY DIRECTED TO THE MAGICIANS. On the former occasion, with or without sincerity, they had said, "This is the finger of God;" *now* they are in themselves, so to speak, the finger of God. They can neither avert nor dissemble their subjection to the power that works through Moses. At first, doubtless, they had looked upon him with haughtiness, audacity, and scorn, as being hardly worth a moment's attention. Very likely it was counted a great condescension to turn the rods into serpents. But *now*, whatever feeling be in their hearts, the hold that Jehovah has on their bodies is only too evident. Silence and outward serenity are impossible under such suffering as this. The twitchings of the face cannot be concealed, the groan cannot be suppressed, the unquailing attitude cannot be maintained. Who shall tell what individual humiliations and defeats lie behind this brief expression: "The magicians could not stand before Moses because of the boils." *Because of the boils!* It was not a very dignified sort of disaster; not very pleasant to recall in after times. These magicians, we may imagine, had scorned the very name of Jehovah, worse, mayhap, than Pharaoh himself. And now in these boils and blains there is, suppressed as it were, scorn and mockery from Jehovah in return. Opposers of God may not only have to be brought down from their pride, but in such a way as will involve them in ridicule and shame. The exposure of falsehood is only a work of time, and as we see here, it can be accomplished in a comparatively short time. Pain effectually drives away all dissembling, and nature proves too much even for the man to whom art has become second nature.—Y.

Vers. 8—12.—I. *The Sixth Plague.* THE MEANS USED. Ashes were taken from the brick-kiln in which the Israelites toiled, and in Pharaoh's presence sprinkled in mute appeal toward heaven. The memorials of oppression lifted up before God will fall in anguish upon the oppressors (James v. 1—5). The French Revolution and the ages of giant wrong that had gone before. American slavery and its punishment.

II. THE SUDDENNESS OF THE INFLICTION. There was no warning. The dust was cast up, and immediately the plague was upon man and beast. The judgment of wickedness will come as in a moment. Sodom. The flood.

III. THE SHAME OF THE MAGICIANS. 1. Upon them the plague seems to have been more severe than upon others. Upon the abettors of other men's tyranny and wrong, God's judgment will fall heaviest. The deep responsibility of Christian teachers and men of influence and talent. Let them see to it that they are on the side of righteousness, and not of the world's class—selfishness and manifold wrong. 2. They were brought to shame in the presence of those who trusted in them. The falsehood of their pretensions was exposed by their inability to defend themselves. When God visits for the world's sin, there will be everlasting confusion and shame for its apologists and abettors.—U.

EXPOSITION.

Vers. 13—26:—THE SEVENTH PLAGUE. The sixth plague had had no effect at all upon the hard heart of the Pharaoh, who cared nothing for the physical sufferings of his subjects, and apparently was not himself afflicted by the malady. Moses was therefore ordered to appear before him once more, and warn him of further and yet more terrible visitations which were impending. The long message (vers. 13—19) is without any previous parallel, and contains matter calculated to make an impression even upon the most callous of mortals. First there is an announcement that God is about to send "*all* his plagues" upon king and people (ver. 14); then a solemn warning that a pestilence might have been sent which would have swept both king and people from the face of the earth (ver. 15); and finally (ver. 18) an announcement of the actual judgment immediately impending, which is to be a hailstorm of a severity never previously known in Egypt, and but rarely experienced elsewhere. Pharaoh is moreover told that the whole object of his having been allowed by God to continue in existence is the glory about to accrue to his name from the exhibition of his power in the deliverance of his people (ver. 16). A peculiar feature of the plague is the warning (ver. 19) whereby those who believed the words of Moses, were enabled to escape a great part of the ill effects of the storm. It is a remarkable indication of the impression made by the previous plagues, that the warning was taken by a considerable number of the Egyptians, who by this means saved their cattle and their slaves (ver. 20). The injury caused by the plague was very great. The flax and barley crops, which were the most advanced, suffered complete destruction. Men and beasts were wounded by the hail-stones, which might have been—as hail-stones sometimes are—jagged pieces of ice; and some were even killed, either by the hail (see Josh. x. 11), or by the lightning which accompanied it. Even trees were damaged by the force of the storm, which destroyed the foliage and broke the branches.

Ver. 13.—**Rise up early.** Compare ch. vii. 15, and viii. 20. The practice of the Egyptian kings to rise early and proceed at once to the dispatch of business is noted by Herodotus (ii. 173). It is a common practice of oriental monarchs. **And say unto him.** The same message is constantly repeated in the same words as a token of God's unchangingness. See ch. viii. 1—20; ix. 1; x. 3; etc.

Ver. 14.—**I will at this time send all my plagues upon thine heart.** A very emphatic announcement. **At this time** contrasts the immediate future with the past, and tells Pharaoh that the hour of mild warnings and slight plagues is gone by. Now he is to ex-

pect something far more terrible God will send **all his plagues**—every worst form of evil —in rapid succession; and will send them **against his heart.** Each will strike a blow on that perverse and obdurate heart—each will stir his nature to its inmost depths. Conscience will wake up and insist on being heard. All the numerous brood of selfish fears and alarms will bestir themselves. He will tremble, and be amazed and perplexed. He will forego his pride and humble himself, and beg the Israelites to be gone, and even intreat that, ere they depart, the leaders whom he has so long opposed, will give him their blessing (ch. xii. 32). **That thou mayest know.** Pharaoh was himself to be convinced that the Lord God of Israel was, at any rate, the greatest of all gods. He was not likely to desert at once and altogether the religion in which he had been brought up, or to regard its gods as nonexistent. But he might be persuaded of one thing—that Jehovah was far above them. And this he practically acknowledges in vers. 27 and 28.

Ver. 15.—**For now I will stretch out my hand.** It is generally agreed by modern writers that this translation fails to give the true sense of the original God does not here announce what he is going to do, but what he might have done, and would have done, but for certain considerations. Translate, "For now might I have stretched out my hand, and smitten thee and thy people with pestilence; and then thou hadst been cut off from the earth." Scripture shows that pestilence is always in God's power, and may at any time be let loose to scourge his foes, and sweep them into the pit of destruction. (See Lev. xxvi. 25; Num. xi. 33; xiv. 12; xvi. 46; 2 Sam. xxiv. 13—15, etc.) He had not done now what he might have done, and what Pharaoh's obstinacy might well have provoked him to do; and why? On account of the considerations contained in the next verse.

Ver. 16.—**And in very deed,** etc. Rather, "But truly for this cause have I caused thee to stand," *i.e.,* "kept thee alive and sustained thee in the position thou occupiest," **for to shew to thee my power**—*i.e.,* to impress thee, if it is possible that thou canst be impressed, with the greatness of my power, and the foolishness of any attempt to resist it, and also **that my name may be declared throughout all the earth** — *i.e.,* that attention may be called widely among the neighbouring nations to the great truth that there is really but one God, who alone can deliver, and whom it is impossible to resist.

Ver. 17.—**As yet.** Rather "still." And the whole verse should be rendered—"Dost thou still oppose thyself against my people, so as not to let them go." The verb translated "oppose"—("exalt" in the A.V.)—is strictly "to raise a mound, or bank," thence "to obstruct," "oppose."

Ver. 18.—**To-morrow about this time.** As it might have been thought that Moses had done nothing very extraordinary in predicting a storm for the next day, a more exact note of time than usual was here given. Compare ch viii. 23; ix. 5. **I will cause it to rain a very grievous hail.** Rain, and, still more, hail are comparatively rare in Egypt, though not so rare as stated by some ancient authors (Herod. iii. 10; Pomp. Mela, *De Situ Orbis*, i. 9). A good deal of rain falls in the Lower Country, where the north wind brings air loaded with vapour from the Mediterranean; particularly in the winter months from December to March. Snow, and hail, and thunder are during those months not very uncommon, having been witnessed by many modern travellers, as Pococke, Wansleben, Seetzen, Perry, Tooke, and others. They are seldom, however, of any great severity. Such a storm as here described (see especially vers. 23, 24) would be quite strange and abnormal; no Egyptian would have experienced anything approaching to it, and hence the deep impression that it made (ver. 27). **Since the foundation thereof.** Not "since the original formation of the country" at the Creation, or by subsequent alluvial deposits, as Herodotus thought (ii. 5—11), but "since Egypt became a nation" (see ver. 24). Modern Egyptologists, or at any rate a large number of them, carry back this event to a date completely irreconcilable with the Biblical chronology— Böckh to B.C. 5702, Unger to B.C. 5613, Mariette and Lenormant to B.C. 5004, Brugsch to B.C. 4455, Lepsius to B.C. 3852, and Bunsen (in one place) to B.C. 3623. The early Egyptian chronology is, however, altogether uncertain, as the variety in these dates sufficiently intimates. Of the dynasties before the (socalled) eighteenth, only seven are proved to be historical, and the time that the Old and Middle Empires lasted is exceedingly doubtful. All the known facts are sufficiently met by such a date as B.C. 2500—2400 for the Pyramid Kings, before whose time we have nothing authentic. This is a date which comes well within the period allowed for the formation of nations by the chronology of the Septuagint and Samaritan versions.

Ver. 19.—**Thy cattle, and all that thou hast in the field.** During winter and early spring, the Egyptians kept their cattle "in the field," as other nations commonly do. When the inundation began (June or July), they were obliged to bring them into the cities and enclosed villages, and house them. The time of the "Plague of Hail" appears by all the indications to have been the middle of February. **They shall die.** Human life was now for the first time threatened. Any herdsmen that remained with the cattle in the open field and

did not seek the shelter of houses or sheds would be smitten by the huge jagged hailstones with such force that they would be killed outright, or else die of their wounds.

Ver. 20.—**He that feared the word of the Lord among the servants of Pharaoh.** It is a new fact that any of the Egyptians had been brought to "fear the word of Jehovah." Probably, the effect of the plagues had been gradually to convince a considerable number, not so much that Jehovah was *the* one True God as that he was *a* great and powerful god, whose chastisements were to be feared. Consequently there were now a certain number among the "servants of Pharaoh" who profited by the warning given (ver. 19), and housed their cattle and herdsmen, in anticipation of the coming storm.

Ver. 21.—**He that regarded not.** If there were men who believed in the power and truthfulness of Jehovah, there were probably more who did not believe. As Lot "seemed as one that mocked unto his sons-in-law" (Gen. xix 14), so Moses and Aaron appeared to the great mass of the Egyptians. As observed above, a hail-storm that could endanger life, either of man or beast, was beyond all Egyptian experience, and must have seemed almost impossible.

Ver. 22.—**Stretch forth thine hand toward heaven.** The action was appropriate, as the plague was to come from the heaven. Similarly, in the first and second plagues, Aaron's hand had been stretched out upon the waters (ch. vii. 19, 20; viii. 6); and in the third upon "the dust of the ground" (ch. viii. 17). **And upon every herb of the field**—*i.e.*, upon all forms of vegetable life. (Compare Gen. i. 30; ix. 3.)

Ver. 23.—**Moses stretched forth his rod.** In the last set of three plagues, the earthly agent was Moses (ch. ix. 10; ch. x. 13, 22), whose diffidence seems to have worn off as time went on, and he became accustomed to put himself forward. **Thunder and hail.** Thunder had not been predicted; but it is a common accompaniment of a hail-storm, the change of temperature produced by the discharge of electricity no doubt conducing to the formation of hailstones. **The fire ran along upon the ground.** Some very peculiar electrical display seems to be intended—something corresponding to the phenomena called "fireballs," where the electric fluid does not merely flash momentarily, but remains for several seconds, or even minutes, before it disappears.

Ver. 24. — **Fire mingled with the hail.** Rather, "There was hail, and in the midst of the hail a fire infolding itself." The expression used is the same which occurs in Ezek. i. 4. It seems to mean a fire that was not a mere flash, but collected itself into a mass and was seen for some considerable time.

Ver. 25.—**The hail smote.** It is to the hail

and not to the lightning that the great destruction of men and beasts is attributed. Such lightning, however, as is spoken of, would probably kill some. **All that was in the field.** According to the warning given (ver. 19), the herdsmen and cattle left in the open air and not brought into the sheds were killed. **The hail smote every herb of the field.** Even in our own temperate climate, which is free from all atmospheric extremes, hailstorms occasionally do so much damage to crops that it has been found desirable to organise a special insurance against loss from this cause. Such hail as that described in the text would greatly injure every crop that was many inches above the soil, and entirely destroy such as had gone to ear. (See below, ver. 31.) **Broke every tree**— *i.e.*, damaged the smaller branches and twigs, thus destroying the prospect of fruit.

Ver. 26.—**Only in the land of Goshen,** etc. Compare ch. viii. 22; ix. 4; x. 23.

HOMILETICS.

Vers. 13—19.—*The method of the Divine Rule over bad men illustrated by God's message to Pharaoh.* The message illustrates,

I. THE LONG-SUFFERING OF GOD TOWARDS SINNERS. "For now might I have stretched out my hand and smitten thee and thy people with pestilence" (ver. 15). Pharaoh had opposed himself to God so long, had shown himself in various ways so wicked, that he well deserved to have been stricken with plague and made to perish miserably. He had been insolent and blasphemous, when first appealed to in the name of Jehovah (ch. v. 2); cruel and vindictive, when he increased the Israelites' burdens (*ib.* 7—9); hard-hearted, when the taskmasters complained to him (*ib.* 15—18); obdurate and perverse, in resisting so many signs and wonders wrought for the purpose of moving him (ch. vii. 10—13, 20—23; viii. 5, 6, 16—19, 20—24; ix. 6, 7, 10—12); pitiless and false, in twice breaking his promises (ch. viii. 8—15, 28—32). Yet God had spared him. He had "made him to stand" (ver. 16)—*i.e.*, preserved him in being —and had retained him in his high station, when he might readily have caused his overthrow by conspiracy or otherwise. So long-suffering was he, that he even now addressed to him fresh warnings, and gave him fresh signs of his power, thus by his goodness striving to lead him to repentance.

II. THE POWER OF GOD TO BREAK THE WILL EVEN OF THE MOST DETERMINED SINNER. God can so multiply, and vary, and prolong his judgments, that at last the power of endurance, even in the case of the most obdurate sinner, is worn out. First he sends comparatively slight afflictions, then more serious ones; finally, if the stubborn will still refuses to bend, he visits the offender with "all his plagues" (ver. 14). Man cannot triumph over God. Kings may oppose their wills to his, but they cannot make him succumb. He "refrains the spirit of princes," and shows himself "wonderful among the kings of the earth" (Ps. lxxvi. 12). Even the greatest monarchs—this present Pharaoh, Sennacherib, Nebuchadnezzar—are powerless against him. He "refrains" them, breaks them, humbles them, works his will in spite of them. And at what a cost to themselves! Unfortunately kings, and even less exalted sinners, will rarely learn wisdom till too late. He has to send "all his plagues" upon them; whereas, if they had been wise, they might have escaped with a light chastisement.

III. THE FACT THAT ALL RESISTANCE OF GOD'S WILL BY SINNERS TENDS TO INCREASE, AND IS DESIGNED TO INCREASE, HIS GLORY. "The fierceness of man turns to God's praise." He has endowed men with free will, and allows them the free exercise of their free will, because, do as they like, they cannot thwart his purposes. Being, as he is, the God of order, and not of confusion or anarchy, he could not have allowed free will at all to his creatures, if their employment of it prevented the accomplishment of his own designs and intentions. But it does not; it is foreseen, taken into account, provided for. And the only result of men's opposition to his will is the increase of his glory and of his praise. Great kings are seen arraying themselves against God, determining to take Jerusalem, like Sennacherib (2 Kings xviii. 35), or to destroy the infant Church, like Herod Agrippa (Acts xii. 1—3), or to rebuild Jerusalem, like the apostate Julian, or to crush the Reformation, like Philip II. of Spain—and they do their utmost; they levy armies, or man fleets, or collect materials and engage thousands of workmen, or murder and imprison at their pleasure—but nothing comes of it. Their efforts fail utterly. And the sole result of all their exertions is, that men see and recognise God's hand in their overthrow, and that his glory is thereby increased. All this is commonly declared in Scripture, and especially in the Psalms (Ps. ii. 4; v. 10; vii. 11—17; ix. 15—20, &c.). The message sent by God to Pharaoh through Moses *adds*, that the result is designed. "For this cause have I *made thee stand* (marg.), for to show to thee my power; and that my name may be declared throughout all the earth" (ver. 16). Compare ch. xiv. 17, 18; xv. 14—16; Josh. ii. 9—11.

HOMILIES BY VARIOUS AUTHORS.

Vers. 13—35.—*The plague of hail.* This plague was introduced with ampler remonstrance. Moses was commanded to proceed to Pharaoh, and to warn him in stronger and more decisive language than he had yet employed of the folly of this insane resistance. Ver. 15 should probably be translated, "For now indeed *had I* stretched forth my hand, and smitten thee and thy people with the pestilence, thou hadst then been cut off from the earth;" and then ver. 16 will give the reason why God had not cut Pharaoh off, but had "made him stand" (marg.), viz. : that he might show forth in him his power. It does not follow that God would not have preferred to use Pharaoh for his glory in another way than that of destroying him. This strong representation of God's purpose was itself designed to influence the king for good, and had a spark of sense remained to him, it would have wrought an immediate change in his volitions. In that case God's procedure would have undergone a corresponding alteration. For God wills not the death of any sinner (Ez. xviii. 23—32), and threatenings of this kind, as shown by the case of the Ninevites, are always conditional (Jonah iv.). At the same time, God's sovereignty is seen in the way in which he *utilizes* the wicked man whose persistence in his wickedness is foreseen by him. "God might have caused Pharaoh to be born in a cabin, where his proud obstinacy would have been displayed with no less self-will, but without any historical consequence; on the other hand, he might have placed on the throne of Egypt at that time a weak, easy-going man, who would have yielded at the first shock. What would have happened? Pharaoh in his obscure position would not have been less arrogant and perverse, but Israel would have gone forth from Egypt without *éclat*. . . . God did not therefore create the indomitable pride of Pharaoh as it were to gain a point of resistance, and reflect his glory; he was content to use it for this purpose" (Godet on Rom. iv. 17, 18). Notice—

I. THE TERRIBLE RAISING UP (ver. 16). We are taught, 1. That God can find a use even for the wicked (Prov. xvi. 4). 2. That God places wicked men in positions in which their true character is manifested, and his own power and righteousness are glorified in their judgment. 3. That this is not the *primary* desire of God in relation to any wicked man. He would prefer his conversion. If it be urged that the situations in which men are placed are not always those most *favourable* to their conversion, this may be conceded. But they are not placed in these positions arbitrarily, but under a system of administration which regards each individual, not simply as an end in himself, but as a means to a yet higher end, the carrying forward of the world purpose as a whole. God cannot deal with the individual as if there were no such thing as history, or as if that individual constituted the sum-total of humanity, or as if his salvation were the only and the all-ruling consideration in the arrangement of the world. God *disposes* of the evil of the world, decrees the lines and directions of its developments, the persons in whom, and the situations under which, it will be permitted to reveal and concentrate itself; but he neither creates the evil, nor delights in it, and is all the while working for its final and effectual overthrow. No situation in which God places man *necessitates* him to be evil. 4. That the sinner's evil, accordingly, is his own, and his ruin self-wrought. This is shown—and notably in the case of Pharaoh—by the fact that God's dealings with him are fitted to change him if he *will* be changed (Matt. xxiii. 37).

II. A PLAGUE WITH APPALLING ATTENDANT CIRCUMSTANCES (verse xviii. 23—26). This plague, like many of its predecessors, was, 1. Severe in its character (ver. 24). 2. Destructive in its effects (ver. 25). 3. Distinguishing in its range. It spared the land of Goshen (ver. 26). But the peculiar circumstance connected with it—that which marked it as the first of a new order of plagues—was, 4. *Its combination of terror with sublimity*, its power to *appal* as well as to *punish*. A last attempt was to be made to break down the opposition of the monarch by displays of God's majesty and omnipotence which should shake his very heart (ver. 14). Instead of frogs, lice, flies, pestilence, and boils on man and beast, Pharaoh was now to be made to hear "voices of God" in the thunder (ver. 28, Heb.); was to see dreadful lightnings, masses of fire, descending from the sky, and rolling in balls of fire along the ground (ver. 23); was to witness his land smitten with terrific hail "very grievous," the like of which had never been seen in Egypt "since it became a nation" (ver. 24). A thunderstorm is at all times terrible, and when very severe, inspires an awe which few natures can resist. Accompanied by preternatural terrors, its effect would be simply overwhelming. This was the intention here. The strokes of God were to go to the king's heart. They were to convince him that there was "none like Jehovah in all the earth" (ver. 14). They were to be plagues, as Calvin says, "that would not only strike the head and arms, but penetrate the very heart, and inflict a mortal wound." The thunder is introduced as being "the mightiest manifestation of the omnipotence of God, which speaks therein to men (Rev. x. 3, 4), and warns them of the terrors of judgment" (Keil). On the peculiar effect of the thunderstorm in awakening the religious nature, see a paper on "God in Nature and History," Expositor, March, 1881. To the superstitious minds of the heathen these unexampled terrors would seem of awful significance.

III. Twofold effects of warnings (vers. 20, 21). 1. God's judgments, like his overtures of grace, are seldom *wholly* ineffectual. If the king was hardened, there were at least *some* in Egypt who had become alive to the gravity of the situation, "who feared the word of the Lord." Such were to be found even among the servants of Pharaoh, in the palace itself. The preaching of the Gospel, even under the most unpropitious circumstances, will seldom fail of *some* fruit. There were "certain men" which "clave" to Paul, "and believed" at Athens; "among the which was Dionysius, the Areopagite, and a woman named Damaris, and others with them" (Acts xvii. 34). There were "saints"—*mirabile dictu*—even in Nero's palace (Phil. iv. 22). 2. The division of men, in their relation to the Word of God, is a very simple one. There are those who fear and regard it, and there are those who disregard and disobey it. Paul speaks of those to whom Gospel-preaching is a savour of death unto death, and of those to whom it is a savour of life unto life (2 Cor. ii. 16). Between the two classes there is no third. The effects of his own preaching are thus summed up, "And some believed the things which were spoken, and some believed not" (Acts xxviii. 24). 3. Faith reveals itself in obedience. He that feared God's word brought in his cattle; he that disregarded it left them in the fields. 4. The wisdom of regarding God, and the folly of disregarding him, were made manifest by the result.

IV. Pharaoh's capitulation (vers. 27, 28). The supernatural concomitants of this appalling visitation so unnerved the king that he was induced again to send for Moses. He did not yield till the plague was actually on the land, and only then, because he could not help it. The terms in which he makes his submission show, 1. His undisguised terror. 2. His thorough conviction that he was in the hands of the God of the whole earth. Pharaoh had by this time had a course of instruction in the "evidences," which left no room for further doubt. The most striking feature in his submission, however, is, 3. His confession of sin. "I have sinned this time; the Lord is righteous, and I and my people are wicked" (ver. 27). It was good that Pharaoh should be brought to see that it was a righteous demand he was resisting, and that he was inexcusable in resisting it. This much at least the plagues had forced him to acknowledge, and it gave his hardening a yet graver character when subsequently he retracted his word given. But the superficiality of the repentance is very obvious. "I have sinned *this time*;" there is here no adequate sense of the sin he had been guilty of. False repentances have their root in superficial views of sin. They may be produced by terror, under compulsion; but they are accompanied by no real change of heart; and renewed hardening is the only possible outcome of them. "As for thee and thy servants, I know that ye will not yet fear the Lord God" (ver. 30).

V. Judgment tempered with mercy. God's mercy in connection with this plague is conspicuous—1. In giving the warning, so that those who regarded his word had the opportunity of removing their servants and cattle (vers. 20, 21). 2. In sparing the wheat and rye (vers. 31, 32). 3. In removing the plague at the request of Pharaoh, presented through Moses (vers. 28, 29).

VI. HARDENING NOTWITHSTANDING. 1. *Pharaoh* hardened himself (vers. 34, 35). We ask, in surprise, how was such a thing possible? Pride, hate, anger, obstinacy furnish the explanation, though it is truly difficult to conceive how they could so madden a mind as to make it capable of persevering in a course of resistance. *There* is the fact, however, and it is full of terrible warning to us. The hardening was obviously now of the most serious possible kind. Pharaoh's nature had been thoroughly awakened. He was no longer sinning in ignorance, but against clear light and conviction. He had confessed his sin, and promised to obey. Hardening, under these circumstances, was as nearly "sin against the Holy Ghost" as was then possible (John ix. 41). 2. *His servants* hardened themselves (vers. 34). This is a fact which should be well pondered. It might have been thought that only a Pharaoh was capable of such fatuousness. We learn here that there were natures among his servants as susceptible of hardening as his own. We do not need to be Pharaohs to be capable of hardening our hearts against God. Persons in obscure positions can do it as readily as those on the pinnacles of greatness. The king's influence, however, had doubtless much to do with his servants' conduct. They took their cue from their lord. Had he submitted himself, they would have done so also. Because he hardened himself, they must follow suit. What folly! to destroy themselves for the sake of being like a king—of being in the fashion. Learn also the potency of example. Those in high positions have a powerful influence over those dependent upon them. Well for them if they use that influence for God's glory, and not to ruin souls!—J. O.

Ver. 16.—*The road to ruin.* "And in very deed for this cause," &c. (Ex. ix. 16). The character and conduct of Pharaoh as a probationer under the moral government of the Ever Living God is worthy of special and separate consideration. That he was such a probationer should not be simply assumed, but made clearly manifest. All the great light of natural religion shone upon his path (Rom. i. 19—25), like stars in heaven upon the path of every soul. Then there is the inward witness that speaks of the soul, of God, of duty, of immortality (Rom. ii. 14, 15). Within the confines of his empire existed a nation of no less than two millions, to whom had already been confided a part, at least, of the "oracles of God." They were the recipients of such revelations as God had already vouchsafed. Their beliefs ought not to have been unknown to him. Two missionaries, direct from God, Moses and Aaron, were his teachers. They came with full credentials. Providential judgments, not untempered with mercy (for warning after warning came), spake with trumpet tongue. Some of his own people, convinced, probably penitent, pleaded for the right. And yet this soul went from bad to worse. We indicate the stages on the road to ruin. It is only necessary to premise that though the stages are broadly manifest enough, they, in so complicated a character, occasionally overlap, and are blended with each other.

I. UNBELIEF. Pharaoh's of the blankest kind (ver. 2). [Read correctly, "Who is *Jehovah*"?] The man a God unto himself, as all infidels practically are. The representative of the Sun-God. Note the *independent* stand he takes all through this controversy, as against Jehovah. [On this see Kurtz, Hist. of Old Cov. ii. 292.]

II. SUPERSTITION. So does the pendulum ever swing back from the extremes of belief or non-belief. No soul can rest in that infidelity which virtually deifies self. Hence Pharaoh played off against the representatives of Jehovah, the representatives of the polytheism of Egypt—the magicians. So in modern times. There are the credulities of atheism. Men who will not believe in the sublime truths of revelation fall to intellectual drivelling. Notable instance, Comte's "Religion of Humanity." After all, this is a witness that man cannot live without religion. [In this connection note the connection between magic and idolatry, and of that, possibly, with demons, Kurtz, ii. 246—259.]

III. ALARM. In Pharaoh's case this was especially manifest after the second (viii. 8), fourth (viii. 25), seventh (ix. 27), and eighth (x. 16) visitations.

IV. CONFESSION. After the seventh (ix. 27). No wonder, for God had said before this judgment, "I will at this time send all my plagues *upon thy heart.*" Coming calamity was to be of a deeper and more searching kind. The man seems to have had an access of real and honest feeling. Sees the sin of the people as well as his own. Confesses. But the confession was not followed up.

V. PROMISE—VIOLATION. After second (viii. 8—15), fourth (viii. 28—32), and seventh (ix. 28—35) plagues. A very common thing with sinners under Divine discipline—promises of amendment—but the sweep onward of the bias toward iniquity is like that of a mighty river, and carries the most earnest vows into the gulf of oblivion.

VI. DISPOSITION TO COMPROMISE. See viii. 25—28, x. 8—11, x. 24. Such penitence as Pharaoh had was one of conditions and compromise. Israel's festival must be " in the land;" then not "far away;" then only the men should go; then all might go, but the cattle must stay behind. So "We will give up sin, but only part of it. We will yield ninety-nine points, not the hundredth. We will give up what we do not care for so much, but keep what we peculiarly like. We will keep all the commandments, but not give up our money. * * We will gain the credit and reputation of religion, but shun the pain and denial of it." (See on " Pharaoh," in Munro's "Sermons on Characters of the Old Testament," vol. i. ser. xv.)

VII. INDIFFERENCE. Stolidity in matters of such high import as religion is a very dangerous condition. Pharaoh assumed after fifth and sixth visitations an attitude of hardened indifference (ix. 7—12).

VIII. HARDNESS OF HEART. Except in the objective announcement made to Moses at the first, there is no statement that God hardened Pharaoh's heart till after the sixth plague (ix. 12). Up to that time Pharaoh hardened his own heart, or the fact simply is stated, that his heart was hardened. In this matter man acts first sinfully, then God judicially.

IX. RESISTANCE TO APPEAL OF OTHERS. See ix. 20, and x. 7.

X. RUIN.—R.

Vers. 13—16.—*The earth is the Lord's and the fulness of it.* In this comprehensive message from Jehovah, standing as it does about midway in the course of his judgments upon Pharaoh, we have a peculiar and impressive application of the foregoing word of the Psalmist (Ps. xxiv. 1). The word " earth," it will be noticed, stands in a very prominent position in each of the verses 14, 15, 16. Evidently, then, we should give the word an equally prominent position in our thoughts, and connect with it the truths to be drawn out of this message. It will then be seen that Jehovah has many ways of showing that the earth is his and the fulness of it. It is all his; not Pharaoh's, not any other potentate's, not even Israel's—except as Israel is chosen by Jehovah, duly trained and prepared by him, subjected and obedient to him. We have to consider this message, then, under three heads, as suggested by the occurrence of the word " earth " in these three verses. Note, however, first, *the way in which Moses approaches Pharaoh on this occasion.* In ch. vii. 15, he is told to get to Pharaoh in the morning and meet him by the river's brink; thus there is a general indication of time and a particular indication of place. In ch. viii. 20, he is told to go *early* in the morning, as Pharaoh comes forth to the water; thus there is a more particular indication of time. Now, in ch. ix. 13, there is the same particular indication of time, but no reference to place. Thus it seems as if we got a gradation, a sign of increasing pressure and urgency upon Pharaoh. Moses has to be ready for Pharaoh at the very beginning of the day, and then, whenever and wherever he may meet with him, he can deliver his message at once. Pharaoh had the whole day to consider as to the things which were about to happen on the morrow. And now—

I. THERE IS NO ONE LIKE JEHOVAH IN THE WHOLE EARTH, AND PHARAOH IS TO BE MADE TO KNOW THIS. Such is the statement of ver. 14; and of course the whole gist of it lies in the bringing of Pharaoh to a clear and unmistakable knowledge of the supremacy of God over all terrestrial powers. That there is none like God in all the earth may be true, but the thing wanted is to bring that truth *distinctly* and *practically* before our minds, and if *profitably* for us also, then so much the better. This end had to be achieved in the instance of Pharaoh by persistent attacks of Jehovah upon him, attacks ever increasing in effective force, till at last they proved irresistible. It was not enough for others to be assured by Pharaoh's doom that there was none like God in all the earth. Pharaoh must know it for himself, and confess it, not by the ambiguous channel of speech, but by a most decisive act, the committal of which he cannot avoid (ch. xii. 31—33). And that he may be brought to such a knowledge is the reason of the severe plagues that remain. We might, indeed, count it enough to be told that *Jehovah* had sent all his plagues. We might rest upon Jehovah's character, and say that whatever he does is right, even though there be much that at first staggers us, and that continues to perplex. *But the reason for all these plagues is plainly stated,* and if it be looked into 'it will be seen an ample, cheering, and encouraging reason. Though Jehovah is Sovereign of the universe, he does not treat Pharaoh in an arbitrary way; he acts, not as one who says that might makes right, but as using his might in order to secure the attainment of right. Pharaoh's way, on the contrary, is an arbitrary one, without the slightest mitigation or concealment. Everything rests simply on his will; and yet will is too dignified a word—whim would be nearer the mark. And now that proud will is to be subdued and dissolved, so far, at least, as to flow forth in the liberation of Israel, even though immediately they be liberated it hardens again to its former rigidity. The announcement Moses was now to make to Pharaoh we may fairly say would have been inappropriate at an earlier time. It becomes God, in his first approaches to men, to *draw* them, if perchance for their own sakes they may willingly submit; afterwards, when they will not be drawn, then for the sake of others they have to be driven. It is not until Pharaoh fully manifests his selfishness, his malignity, and the reasonless persistency of his refusal, that God indicates the approach of *all his plagues.* The man has been humbled in his circumstances, but his pride of heart remains as erect as ever; and so the full force of Jehovah has to be brought upon it in order to lay it low. He is at last to feel in himself, whatever he may say, that the true question is not "Who is Jehovah, that Pharaoh should let Israel go?" but, "Who is Pharaoh, that he should keep Israel back?" He has gotten some rudiments and beginnings of this knowledge already, even though they have made no difference in his practice. Every time he has opened his eyes he has seen something fresh, which, however quickly he might close his eyes again, he could not unsee. And now he is on the very point of getting more knowledge, and that in a way very disagreeable to a despot. With alarming rapidity, *his people are about to be impressed with the supremacy of Jehovah* (ch. ix. 20; x. 7).

II. Notice the peculiar reference in ver. 15 to THE DESTRUCTION OF PHARAOH. It is spoken of as a being cut off from the earth. It seems that our English version does not give the right tense-rendering in this verse, and that the reference is not to what will happen in the *future*, but to what might have already happened in the *past.* If Pharaoh was not already a dead man, and Israel a free people, there was nothing in this delay for Pharaoh to plume himself upon. Jehovah might have smitten him with pestilence, and slain the strong, proud man on his bed, amid humiliations and pains which would have been aggravated by the vanity of the regal splendours around him. He might have made Egypt one great expanse of the dead, a land which the Israelites could have spoiled at their leisure, and then gone forth at any time most convenient to themselves. And if Jehovah did not thus slay Pharaoh and liberate Israel, it was because he had purposes of his own to accomplish by the lengthened life of the one and the intensified sufferings of the other. But apart from the question of time, what awful significance there is in the expression, "cut off from the earth!" To this separation, made most effectual, Pharaoh came at last. In considering this expression, notice first of all *the suggestion of our connection with the earth.* A thing cannot be cut off from the earth unless first of all it is connected with it. In respect of many things the connection may seem very slight and unimportant; but in the instance of a human being, the connection is evidently intimate and important; and, until our connection with heaven is established, not only important, but all-important. We are connected with the earth by what we get from it. The very limitations of our bodily constitution remind us of our dependence upon the earth. We are not like the birds with wings to soar away from it, nor like fishes who can breathe vital air under water; we are emphatically of the solid earth. To its kindly fruits we look for our sustenance, and out of it also comes our clothing and shelter. And then from the earth in its still larger sense, "the great globe itself," consider what comes to us in the way of occupation, instruction, interest, pleasure, opportunities of getting and giving in all sorts of ways. From all this Pharaoh was at last cut off; and from all this we also must one day be cut off. Cut off from the earth, as the tree, at the roots of which the axe has long lain. When the tree has fallen it is still near the earth, but it gets nothing from it. The question for us to ask is, whether, while the tree of our natural earthly life still stands, we are having the roots of a nobler, richer life, even a Divine one, striking down into the heavenly places? The cutting off from earth will matter little, if the vanished life is found elsewhere, more flourishing and fruitful than ever it was here.

III. Notice from ver. 16 that THE VERY PURPOSE OF PHARAOH'S EMINENCE IS TO MAKE A UNIVERSAL DECLARATION OF THE POWER AND GLORY OF GOD. God did not treat Pharaoh differently from thousands of others, as far as *the essence of his dealing with him is concerned*. All who act as Pharaoh acted will suffer as Pharaoh suffered. He was not a throned puppet, a mere machine in the hands of Divine power; if he had been, no instruction and no warning could be got from him for the guidance of voluntary beings like ourselves. But being a downright selfish, proud, malignant man, God put him in this high position that he might effectually publish both his folly and his doom, and the power and name of that great Being whom he had so pertinaciously defied. He was born a Pharaoh, put in royal prerogative and possessions by no choice of his own, but we may most truly say, by the sovereign disposal of Jehovah. Thousands have been as stubborn against chastisement as he, and have gone down to a destruction as real, even though its circumstances have not been miraculous, imposing and memorable. The difference is that Pharaoh's career was to be known; and not only known, but known as is the course of the sun and the moon, all round the earth. One such career is enough to be recorded in a way so prominent; one capital instance of human folly and weakness and Divine wisdom and power, blazing up like a beacon-fire out of the darkness of that distant past. Little did Pharaoh dream that, by his very perversity and humiliation, he was making a name for himself such as none made who went before or followed him, either in peace or in war. His memory is dragged in a perpetual procession of triumph at Jehovah's chariot-wheels. *And as it is with evil men, so it is with good*. As there have been many of the Pharaoh stubbornness, though only one of the Pharaoh notoriety, so there have been many meek and gentle as Moses, though only Moses has been set for the whole world to gaze upon. It is more important to have Abraham's faith than it is to have Abraham's fame ; more important to have the spiritual susceptibilities, experiences and aspirations of David, than the power which could put them into immortal Psalms. A man is not to be reckoned more wicked because the story of his execrable deeds is borne on every wind. A man is not better because he is better known. A few are taken for examples and located in history, as only God in his wisdom is able to locate them. He is a God who presides not only over *life*, but over *biography* as well.—Y.

Ver. 13.—*Harden not your hearts*. Our position in considering the dealings of God with men, resembles the position of scholars in some school observing and criticizing the conduct of the master. *Certain* inferences cannot be drawn from *partial* knowledge. Moreover, God's dealings with us resemble, to some extent, the dealings of a tutor with his scholars. Where intelligent appreciation is impossible through immaturity of intelligence, then action must *seem* arbitrary, however perfect may be the justification. Consider—

I. GOD'S DEALINGS WITH PHARAOH. We cannot, in this view, separate Pharaoh from the social conditions which shaped his life. Great king as he was, yet, in God's sight, he was but a man with great influence—a man intimately connected with other men whose training and destiny were as important as his own. [*Illustration :* In school —one boy specially influential. The conduct of the master towards him must be regulated by considerations as to what is due to the whole body of scholars. The master must act for the general welfare, without partiality towards any.] Had Pharaoh been the sole occupant of Egypt, he might have been treated differently. As one amongst many, the treatment he received is justified, if it can be shown to have tended to the benefit of the community of which he formed a part. [*Illustration :* Suppose boy in school, bigger and stronger than other scholars, exerting a bad influence, bullying. Teacher will *speak* to him. Knowing, however, his character, may foresee that speech will irritate, make him more obstinate. Still, speech ignored, must go on to enforce it by *punishment*, well knowing, all the while, that punishment will increase the obstinacy of the individual recipient. Finally, may have to *expel*; yet, in justice to the rest, only *finally*, seeing that premature expulsion would but weaken his authority.] So God (1) spoke to Pharaoh by Moses (v. 1), then (2) punished him again and again (ix. 14), only (3) finally expelled him; foreseeing all the while that his treatment would but harden the offender, yet persisting in it for the good of others, to strengthen and maintain his own authority (ix. 16).

II. EFFECT ON PHARAOH OF GOD'S DEALINGS WITH HIM. Keeping to illustration, the effect on Pharaoh was just what might have been, and was, anticipated. 1. *Effect of speech.* Warnings and threats alike disregarded. The man so full of his own importance that he would not listen; would not allow the existence of a superior; only irritated; made more obstinate (cf. chapter v.). 2. *Effect of punishment.* Pain inflicted proves power to inflict pain. Pain felt prompts to any action which may bring relief. Hence we find:—(1) Verbal confession, "I have sinned" [just like boy, *feeling* punishment, ready to say anything which may remit the pain]. (2) A hardened heart. The *disposition* was not altered by the infliction. "I have sinned" only meant "I have suffered." Once remove the suffering, and the sufferer showed himself more obdurate than ever. It would have been easy to remove Pharaoh at once; but he occupied an exemplary position, and must, for the sake of others, be treated in an exemplary manner. Expulsion came at last, but God retained him in his position so long as it was needful thereby to teach others his power (ix. 16). Perfectly just to *all*; for even Pharaoh, though his conduct was foreseen, yet had it in his own power to alter it. Hardened like clay beneath the sun's heat, his own self-determination made him like the clay; it might have made him like the snow, in which case his obduracy would have melted.

Apply. Many like Pharaoh, yet *all* do not act as he did under like treatment. (Cf. Jonah iii.; Daniel iv. 31—34.) The same treatment may soften as well as harden. The heart, the self-will, the seat of the mischief—and there is a remedy for that (cf. Ezek. xxxvi.), but not whether we will or no (Heb. iii. 7, 8). Other ways in which hearts are hardened—Pharaoh's by active resistance, others by persistent inattention. [*Illustration*—the disregarded alarum.] So Israel got used to God's dealing with them; so, too often we do (cf. Rom. ii. 4, 5; Ps. xcv. 8).—G.

Vers. 17—35.—*The seventh plague—the hail mingled with fire.* I. CONSIDER THE PLAGUE ITSELF. 1. *God has his " to-morrow"* (ver. 18) *as well as Pharaoh* (ch. viii. 10). Only when Pharaoh's "to-morrow" comes, there comes with it the evidence that he means not what he says. But when God's "to-morrow" comes there is the evidence of his perfect stability, how he settles everything beforehand, even to the very hour. "To-morrow, about this time." A whole twenty-four hours then Pharaoh gets for considera- tion, although really *he* needs it not, and cannot be expected to profit by it. But as we see presently, it is serviceable to protect the right-minded among his people. Perhaps the very period of consideration would make Pharaoh even to despise the prediction. He would say to himself that a hailstorm, however severe, could be lived through, and the damage from it soon made right again. 2. *This plague comes from a new direction.* The heavens join the earth in serving God against Pharaoh. Our minds are at once directed to the opening of the windows of heaven (Gen. vii. 11), and the raining upon Sodom and Gomorrah of brimstone and fire from the Lord out of heaven. But we see at once the great difference between these two visitations and this one. Terrible as it was, it was not destructive as they, nor was it meant to be. God never acts so that obliteration comes instead of chastisement, or chastisement instead of obliteration. He nicely graduates his agencies so as to attain the desired results. And yet, though this plague was not a Sodom experience, it was a sufficiently dreadful one. There was nothing in Egyptian annals to dwarf it. All the power which God has stored up in the atmosphere, and which, by *its wide and minute diffusion*, he makes such a blessing, is now *concentrated* so as to become correspondingly destructive. When man will not obey, God can show the rest of his creation in remarkable obedience. Man is seen becoming more and more repugnant to Divine control, while over against him other things are seen becoming more and more amenable. What an impressive reminder is thus given to us, concerning our departure from God, and the discord that departure has produced. God sent thunder, and hail, and lightning. Even a slight thunder-storm disturbs the mind, and what a profound commotion of the soul this unequalled storm must have produced. The sound of that thunder, one would think, remained in the ears of those who heard it down to their latest hour. As to the lightning, we know more of its causes than did the Egyptians; but all our science will never rob it of its wonder and terror. Franklin has taken away the mystery of it to our intellects, but God has taken care that its power over our hearts should remain. When flash after flash fills the ░░░░░░, ░░░ ░░░░ ░░░░░ ░░░ ░░░░░░ ░░ ░░░ ░░ ░░░░ ░░░ ░░ ░░░ ░░░░░░ ░░░░░░░░░, ░░ least, for the time.

II. Consider the remarkable discrimination of God in this plague. 1. *The exemption of Goshen from the storm.* " Where the children of Israel were, there was no hail." This exemption now comes almost as a matter of course. (For though Goshen is not mentioned as exempted from the ravages of the locusts, we may fairly conclude that it was exempted.) How clear it thus becomes to those who receive this miracle of the hail in spirit and in truth, that God has complete power over all the order of the sky, sending rain, snow, hail, as it pleases him, gathering the most dreadful of tempests over one district, and leaving another district that skirted it—perhaps even lay inside of it as an inner circle—perfectly secure. In Goshen they heard the thunder, saw the lightning, marked the fall of the bruising hail-stones, but these things touched them not. Here is the oft quoted *suave mari magno* of Lucretius to perfection. God having thus shown here, as elsewhere, his control of the heavens, it is a rational thing enough to supplicate changes of the weather. We are then supplicating for what is quite possible of attainment, even though it might possibly be better in such things to take humbly and trustfully what God may send. 2. But much more notable here than the exemption of Goshen, is *the discriminating way in which God treats the Egyptian people.* More and more have they been getting the opportunity to discover whence and wherefore these visitations have come on their land. A certain preparation was necessary to give them the power fairly and fully to appreciate the appeal of Jehovah in ver. 19. The very exemptions of Goshen already would have done much to lead them to some perception of the real state of affairs, and all along indeed each wonder had said, " He that hath ears to hear, let him hear." There are some who are deaf, even to thunder, and others to whom the still, small voice speaks in the clearest of tones and the plainest of words concerning all truth and duty. Notice with what wisdom God acted in taking a plague of this sort to discriminate among the Egyptians. They had the chance of sheltering themselves from its worst consequences by a timely attention to his warning. The test was effectual as to who feared the word of Jehovah. All that he wanted was that the fear should lead to belief in the prediction, and action corresponding with the belief. When it becomes needful to exempt Goshen, then assuredly it is also just to give right-minded, open-minded, and prudent Egyptians the chance, if not of exemption, at all events, of relief. They are not all Egypt who are of Egypt, as they are not all Israel who are of Israel. Among the nominal believers there are the worst of infidels; and among the nominal infidels there may be, not, of course, the best of believers, but those whose germinant faith may grow up into the most abundant and glorious fruit-bearing. Notice how this was the experience of the Apostles; they constantly found faith and unbelief side by side (Acts xiii. 42—45; xiv. 1—4; xvii. 4, 12, 34; xix. 8, 9). Nowhere is this stated more impressively and antithetically than at the very close of the apostolic story; " Some believed the things which were spoken, and some believed not" (Acts xxviii. 24). Men themselves are continually making preliminary and unconscious separation between the sheep and the goats.

III. Consider the fresh confession and promise which this plague at last extorts from Pharaoh. This confession has a very hopeful appearance upon the surface; but then we suddenly remember how hopeless God himself is of any permanent yielding from Pharaoh, any surrender of his entire nature. Nothing is easier than to say, " I have sinned ; " nothing is harder than to say it with right knowledge of what sin is, and deep contrition and humiliation, because of its all-dominating presence in the life. Pharaoh uses strong words here, and there is a great appearance of spontaneity and sincerity, but God is not deceived; and we only need to look into the words to be very quickly undeceived ourselves. Indeed, as we examine Pharaoh's utterance, we find that by a most effective contrast it shows us how to discern the elements of an adequate and acceptable confession of sin. 1. *Such a confession must have reference to a permanent state of the character.* Sin is not a mere outward act, so that a man may sometimes be sinning, and sometimes not sinning. "I have sinned this time." *This time!* There you have the mark of a mere lip acknowledgment; of one who confounds the mere selfish dangers and discomforts that grow out of sin with sin itself. The right confession therefore, is the word of one who has come to a knowledge of the deep and accursed fountain within, of those reservoirs in the thoughts and intents of the heart whence all particular actions flow. He who rightly confesses knows that it is a life that needs to be cleansed, and not a mere limb that needs to be amputated. 2. *It must be absorbingly personal.* It must occupy in the most imperative fashion all the individual consciousness. If there is any time when, as one may say, it is a man's duty to look on his own things, and not the things of others, it is when he is labouring to get the proper conviction of sin. He is not to lose himself in the crowd; he is to stand out before his own mind's eye—self so unsparingly revealed to self—that nothing less will do to say than, "I am the chief of sinners." For not till a man knows what it is to be the chief of sinners is he in the way of discovering what it is to be the chief of saints. "I and my people are wicked," says Pharaoh. It was a false unity; a claim of unity dictated even by pride, for he had become incapable of thinking of his people apart from himself. He calls them one in wickedness, when they were not one; for some had this possibility of goodness at least, that they feared Jehovah enough to follow his counsels (ver. 20). And later, when the mixed multitude went out with Israel (ch. xii. 38), what then became of the boast, "I and my people"? 3. *It must desire the removal of sin itself;* of the guilty conscience, the depraved imagination, the unbrotherly and unneighbourly feelings, the intellect darkened with ignorance and error. Above all, it will desire to have the life reconciled, filial, and serviceable towards God. What is the avoidance of physical suffering and loss, compared with the sweeping away of far more intimate elements of misery? Only when there are such desires in the heart will the word "I have sinned" operate to secure an immediate reversal of the life. Israel said "we have sinned," when they had rebelled against Jehovah because of the distasteful report of the spies. What their confession was worth is seen in the immediate sequel (Num. xiv. 40—45). Balaam said to the angel in the way, "I have sinned," but for all that he did not turn back; he was only too glad to go forward and work for the wages of unrighteousness (Num. xxii. 34). 4. *It must be a confession to God himself,* and not a mere talk to others about God being righteous. All that Pharaoh wanted was to have Moses entreat for the withdrawal of present suffering. The acknowledgment, such as it was, was to Moses and not to Jehovah. Now confessions of this sort are useless. The thing wanted is, not a supplication to possible intercessors, but to the Holy One on high, seen through and above the mediating agent. It is not enough to be brought to a knowledge of Jesus as saving from sin; indeed we may only be deluding ourselves with mere words, except as we gain that glorious part of the salvation which consists in the knowledge of him whom Jesus himself knew so well, and desired, with such earnest desire, to reveal to his disciples also.—Y.

Vers. 13—21. *Mercy in Judgment.*—I. GOD'S PURPOSE IN DEALING WITH THE WICKED BY CHASTISEMENT AND NOT BY JUDGMENT (13—16). God might have desolated the land, and let Israel pass unquestioned through the midst of it. But in Pharaoh and his people the Lord would, by foretold, continued, deepening chastisements, reveal the terror and resistlessness of his power. He would make the heart of the oppressor quail in every age and nation, and stir up the oppressed to hope and prayer. But for this prolonged contest with Pharaoh we should have lacked much that has gone to deepen holy fear of God and trust in him.

II. HOW GOD LEADS UP THE WEAKEST FAITH INTO STRENGTH (20, 21). 1. Warning was given, and those who had merely faith enough to believe that God's word might be kept, had time to save their servants and their cattle. 2. In the after contrast between themselves and those who had despised the warning, faith would spring up into full assurance. The trust we give to God, like the seed we cast into the soil, is given back to us an hundredfold. How God answers the prayer, "Lord increase our faith."—U.

EXPOSITION.

Vers. 27—35.—The plague of hail impressed the Pharaoh more than any previous one. It was the first which had inflicted death on men. It was a most striking and terrible manifestation. It was quite unlike anything which the Egyptians had ever experienced before (vers. 18, 24). It was, by manifest miracle, made to fall on the Egyptians only (ver. 26). Pharaoh was therefore more humbled than ever previously. He acknowledged that he "had sinned" (ver. 27); he added a confession that "Jehovah [alone] was righteous, he and his people wicked" (*ibid.*). And, as twice before, he expressed his willingness to let the Israelites take their departure if the plague were removed (ver. 28). The ultimate results, however, were not any better than before. No sooner had Moses prayed to God, and procured the cessation of the plague, than the king repented of his repentance, "hardened his heart;" and, once more casting his promise to the winds, refused to permit the Israelites to depart (vers. 33—35). His people joined him in this act of obduracy (ver. 34), perhaps thinking that they had now suffered the worst that could befall them.

Ver. 27.—**And Pharaoh sent.** Compare ch. viii. 8, and 25—28. Pharaoh had been driven to entreat only twice before. **I have sinned this time.** The meaning is, "I acknowledge this time that I have sinned" (Kalisch, Cook). "I do not any longer maintain that my conduct has been right." The confession is made for the first time, and seems to have been extorted by the terrible nature of the plague, which, instead of passing off, like most storms, continued. **The Lord is righteous,** etc. Literally, "Jehovah is *the* Just One; and I and my people are *the* sinners." The confession seems, at first sight, ample and satisfactory; but there is perhaps some shifting of sin, that was all his own, upon the Egyptian "people," which indicates disingenuousness.

Ver. 28.—**Mighty thunderings.** Literally, as in the margin, "voices of God." Thunder was regarded by many nations of antiquity as the actual voice of a god. In the Vedic theology, Indra spoke in thunder. The Egyptian view on the subject has not been ascertained.

Ver. 29.—**As soon as I am gone out of the city.** "The city" is probably Tanis (Zoan). We may gather from the expression of this verse, and again of verse 33, that Moses and Aaron did not live in the city, but in the country with the other Israelites. When it was necessary for them to have an interview with the king, they sought the city: when their interview was over they quitted it. To obtain for Pharaoh a speedy accomplishment of his wish, Moses undertakes to pray for the removal of the plague as soon as he is outside the city walls. **That thou mayest know that the earth is the Lord's.** The phrase used is ambiguous. It may mean either "that the *earth* is Jehovah's," or "that the land (of Egypt) is his." On the whole, perhaps the former rendering is the best. The other plagues sufficiently showed that Egypt was Jehovah's; this, which came from the open heaven that surrounds and embraces the whole world, indicated that the entire earth was his. (Comp. Ps. xxiv. 1: "The earth is the Lord's and the fulness thereof: the world, and they that dwell therein.")

Ver. 30.—**I know that ye will not yet fear the Lord.** True fear of God is shown by obedience to his commands. Pharaoh and his servants had the sort of fear which devils have—"they believed and trembled." But they had not yet that real reverential fear which is joined with love, and has, as its fruit, obedience. So the event showed. (See verses 34, 35.)

Vers. 31, 32.—These verses seem out of place, containing, as they do, an account of the damage done by the hail, and being thus exegetical of verse 25. They are a sort of afterthought, inserted parenthetically, and prepare the way for the understanding of the next plague; since, if the damage done by the hail had extended to all the crops, there would have been nothing left for the locusts to devour.

Ver. 31.—**The flax and the barley was smitten.** Flax was largely cultivated by the Egyptians, who preferred linen garments to any other (Herod. ii. 37), and allowed the priests to wear nothing but linen. Several kinds of flax are mentioned as grown in Egypt (Plin. *H. N.* xix. 1); and the neighbourhood of Tanis is expressly said to have been one of the places where the flax was produced. The flax is **bolled,** *i.e.* blossoms towards the end of January or beginning of February, and the barley comes into ear about the same time, being commonly cut in March. Barley was employed largely as the food of horses, and was used also for the manufacture of beer, which was a common Egyptian beverage. A certain quantity was made by the poorer classes into bread.

Ver. 32.—**The wheat and the rie were not smitten, for they were not grown up.** In Egypt the wheat harvest is at least a month later than the barley harvest, coming in April, whereas the barley harvest is finished by the end of March. Rye was not grown in Egypt; and it is generally agreed that the Hebrew word here translated " rie " means the *Holcus sorghum*, or *doora*, which is the only grain besides wheat and barley represented on the Egyptian monuments. The *doora* is now raised commonly as an after-crop; but, if sown late in the autumn, it would ripen about the same time as the wheat.

Ver. 33.—**The rain was not poured upon the earth.** Rain had not been previously mentioned, as it was no part of the plague, that is, it caused no damage. But Moses, recording the cessation as an eye-witness, recollects that rain was mingled with the hail, and that, at his prayer, the thunder, the hail, and the rain all ceased. The touch is one which no later writer would have introduced.

Ver. 34.—**He sinned yet more, and hardened his heart.** Altogether there are three different Hebrew verbs, which our translators have rendered by "harden," or "hardened"—

kabad, qashah, and *khazaq*. The first of these, which occurs in ch. vii. 14; viii. 15, 32; ix. 7 and 34, is the weakest of the three, and means to be "dull" or "heavy," rather than "to be hard." The second, which appears in ch. vii. 3, and xiii. 15, is a stronger term, and means "to be hard," or, in the Hiphil, "to make hard." But the third has the most intensive sense, implying fixed and stubborn resolution. It occurs in ch. iv. 21; vii. 22; viii. 19; ix. 35; and elsewhere. **He and his servants.** Pharaoh's " servants," *i.e.* the officers of his court, still, it would seem, upheld the king in his impious and mad course, either out of complaisance, or because they were really not yet convinced of the resistless might of Jehovah. After the eighth plague, we shall find their tone change (ch. x. 7).

Ver 35.—**As the Lord had spoken by Moses.** Compare ch. iii. 19; iv. 21; and vii. 3, 4

HOMILETICS.

Vers. 27—30. *The mock repentance of a half-awakened sinner counterfeits the true, but has features by which it may be known.* It is not always easy to distinguish between a true and a mock repentance. Here was the Pharaoh at this time very visibly— it might have seemed deeply—impressed. He was disquieted—he was alarmed—he was ready to humble himself—to make confession—to promise obedience in the future. In what did his repentance differ from true, godly penitence? What points did it possess in common with such penitence? What points did it lack?

I. IT POSSESSED THE FEATURE OF SELF-HUMILIATION. " I have sinned this time—I and my people are wicked." Confession of sin is a very important point in true penitence. There can be no true penitence without it. "I said, I will confess my sin unto the Lord, *and so* thou forgavest the wickedness of my sin " (Ps. xxxii. 5). But it may be made, under a sort of compulsion, as a necessity, without the rightful feeling of contrition, or sorrow for sin, out of which it should spring, and apart from which it is valueless. We may doubt whether Pharaoh's confession sprang from a true, contrite heart. There was a ring of insincerity in it. "I, *and my people*," he said, "are wicked." True penitence leads us to confess our own sins, not those of others. There was no occasion for introducing the mention of his people's sins, and, as it were, merging his own in theirs. The people had not been appealed to, in order that they might say whether the Israelites should be allowed to depart or not. They had no doubt many sins of their own to answer for; but they had had no part in this particular sin. There is a covert self-justification in the introduction of the words "and my people," as if the national sentiment had been too strong for him, and he had only "refused to let Israel go" in consequence of it.

II. IT POSSESSED THE FEATURE OF VINDICATING GOD'S HONOUR. "The Lord is righteous," or "Jehovah is the righteous one," was such a full and frank acknowledgment of the perfect justice and righteousness of God as the heart of man does not very readily make, unless in moments of exaltation. We need not suppose that the monarch was insincere in his utterance. He was temporarily lifted up out of himself—so impressed with the power and greatness of Jehovah, that he had for the time true thoughts and high thoughts concerning him. He had doubtless a very insufficient feeling or appreciation of the awful purity and holiness of God; but he did feel his justice. He knew in his inmost heart that he had deserved the judgments sent upon him, and meant to acknowledge this. He was willing that God should be "justified in his sayings, and overcome when He was judged" (Rom. iii. 4). He may not have had an adequate sense of the full meaning of his own words, but he

had so ning, and did not merely repeat, parrot-like, phrases from a
ritual.

III URES OF SELF-DISTRUST AND OF APPEAL TO THE MINISTERS
of sent and called for Moses and Aaron." Not very long
bef from his presence as impertinent intruders, with the
wo ens" (ch. v. 4). Now he appeals to them for succour.
H for me." Such appeals are constantly made, both
ent Reliance on self disappears. God's ministers
dors for him and stewards of his mysteries. They
ner, to frame a prayer for him, and offer it on his
the circumstances; for lips long unaccustomed to
bly, and intercessory prayer is especially valuable
l soul feels a yearning towards God, to which, if

hey would h
them (vers. 8–
ot consent to t
lague came in fu
red the whole face
land was darkened
all that the hail had
of the wheat and
ed. Then Pharaoh
ent of his sin, and
sion—with the old
removed, and that
as ever (vers. 16—

MAKING PROMISE OF AMENDMENT. "I will let
nted, let but the plague be removed, and the
the will of Jehovah shall cease—the children of
be detained any longer. Amendment of life
is rightly first resolved upon, then professed,
But profession alone is no criterion of the
u criterion is the result. If the resolutions
out in act, then the repentance is proved
e case, then it was spurious. The event,
. Meanwhile, as we must "judge nothing
that in every case a professed repentance
rward, whatever suspicions may be enter-
treating a mock penitent as if he were
mistaken rejection of a true penitent.
OF INTENSE HATRED OF SIN. The sinner
the pardon and removal of his sin. He
of its chastisement. Sin, which separates
bhorrence; and when he asks the prayers
quests them to intercede for him, that he
s past sins forgiven, and strength granted
Pharaoh, instead of such a prayer as this,
temporal evil which had been sent upon
e experienced in the words of man to see
And this Moses seems to have perceived.
he king, "I know that ye will not yet fear
hich now fills your hearts is not the true
but of the pains and sufferings that he can
t reconcilement with God, but exemption
ur course by alarm and terror, not drawn
s removed you will relapse into your former
will be needed to make you really yield.
esses spiritual discernment, may generally
closely it apes the true, may escape being

haraoh, for I have
e word "I" is ex-
is emphatic. It is
as hardened himself
"dulled" or "har-
condescend to see
ear my message to
servants. Compare
oh's determination
uence of the court
the frequent men-
t of the narrative.
m my signs. The
being "turned to
from the obstinacy
nd greater miracles
derful signs shown,
both the Israelites
n nations in contact
deeply impressed.
yest tell in the ears
's son. The Psalms
s dwelt in thought
great deeds done in
ce wrought there.
i. cv. and cvi; but
, 7; lxxvii. 14—
—3; cxxxv. 8, 9;

ilt thou refuse to
nfession recorded in
istinct act of self-
been cancelled by
ib. 34, 35). And,

RIOUS AUTHORS.

's MIGHT. In that awful war of elements
nd Pharaoh trembled. This plague evoked
rto he had reluctantly granted the request of
(27, 28) on God's mercy, and entreats the
his people. There is a point at which the
r be wrung from the lips, "I have sinned."
. 14).
E BORN ONLY OF TERROR. God might thus
would be worth nothing: men's hearts would

not be won. When the terror is gone, Pharaoh's confession fails (30,
no root in any true knowledge of himself. He sees the darkness o
the vileness of his transgressions. God is met with, not in the ten
but in the still small voice which speaks within the breast. Many
of terror to hear this; but till God's voice *is heard* there, speaking of
ness and judgment, there is no true return of the soul to him.
    III. THE FULNESS OF GOD'S MERCY. God knows the worthlessness
yet he is entreated for Pharaoh and the Egyptians. God's pity res
have none upon themselves. Though they believe not, he cannot de

EXPOSITION.

CHAPTER X.

Vers. 1—20.—THE EIGHTH PLAGUE. Notwithstanding his self-condemnation and acknowledgment of the righteousness of God in
all the judgments that had been sent upon
him (ch. ix. 27), Pharaoh no sooner found
that the seventh plague had ceased than he
reverted to his old obstinacy. He both wilfully hardened his own heart (ch. ix. 34);
and God, by the unfailing operation of his
moral laws, further blunted or hardened it
(ch. x. 1). Accordingly, it became necessary
that his stubbornness should be punished by
one other severe infliction. Locusts, God's
" great army," as they are elsewhere called
(Joel ii. 25), were the instrument chosen, so
that once more the judgment should seem to
come from heaven, and that it should be
exactly fitted to complete the destruction
which the hail had left unaccomplished (ver.
5). Locusts, when they come in full force,
are among the most terrible of all the judgments that can befall a country. " A fire
devoureth before them ; and behind them a
flame burneth : the land is as the garden of
Eden before them, and behind them a desolate
wilderness " (Joel ii. 3). They destroy every
atom of foliage—crops, vegetables, shrubs,
trees—even the bark of the fruit-trees suffers
—the stems are injured, the smaller branches
completely peeled and " made white " (*ibid.* i.
7). When Moses threatened this infliction,
his words produced at once a great effect.
The officers of the court—" Pharaoh's servants," as they are called—for the first time
endeavoured to exert an influence over the
king—" Let the men go," they said ; " knowest thou not yet that Egypt is destroyed ?"
(ver. 7). And the king so far yielded that—
also for the first time—he let himself be influenced by the mere threat of a judgment.
He would have let the Israelites depart, before

the locusts came, if only
their " little ones " behind
Moses, however, could
limitation ; and so the
severity—the locusts cov
of the earth, so that the
with them (ver. 15); and
left, including the whole
doora harvests, was destro
made fresh acknowledgm
fresh appeals for interces
result that the plague was
he remained as obdurate
20).

Ver. 1.—**Go in unto P
hardened his heart.** Th
pressed in the original an
not merely that Pharaoh
(ch. ix. 34); but I have
dened " him. Therefore
him once more, and to
him. **The heart of his**
ch. ix. 34.   As Phar
began to waver the inf
officers increased. Hence
tion of them in this pa
That I might shew the
" fierceness of man " was
God's praise." It resulted
of Pharaoh that more a
were wrought, more won
and that by these means
themselves, and the heath
with them, were the more
    Ver. 2.—**That thou ma
of thy son, and of thy son**
show how after generatio
upon the memory of the
Egypt and the delivera
(See especially Ps. lxxvi
compare also Ps. lxviii.
20 ; lxxxi. 5, 6; cxiv.
cxxxvi. 10—15.)
    Ver. 3.—**How long w
humble thyself ?** The co
ch. ix. 27 had been a
humiliation ; but it had
subsequent self-assertion

moreover, humility of speech was not what God had been for months requiring of Pharaoh, but submission in act. He would not really " humble himself " until he gave the oft-demanded permission to the Israelites, that they might depart from Egypt.

Ver. 4.—**To-morrow.** Again a warning is given, and a space of time interposed, during which the king may repent and submit himself, if he chooses. **The locusts.** The species intended is probably either the *Acridium peregrinum* or the *Œdipoda migratoria.* Both are common in Arabia and Syria, and both are known in Egypt. They are said to be equally destructive. The Hebrew name, *arbeh*, points to the " multitudinous " character of the visitation. A traveller in Syria says— " It is difficult to express the effect produced on us by the sight of *the whole atmosphere filled on all sides and to a great height by an innumerable quantity* of these insects, whose flight was slow and uniform, and whose noise resembled that of rain ; the sky was darkened, and the light of the sun considerably weakened. In a moment the terraces of the houses, the streets, and all the fields were covered by these insects." (Ollivier, *Voyage dans l'Empire Ottoman,* vol. ii. p. 424.) **Into thy coast**—*i.e.* " across thy border, into thy territories." The locust is only an occasional visitant in Egypt, and seems always to arrive from some foreign country.

Ver. 5.—**They shall cover the face of the earth, that one cannot be able to see the earth.** This is one of the points most frequently noticed by travellers. " The ground is covered with them for several leagues," says Volney. " The steppes," says Clarke, " were entirely covered by their bodies." " Over an area of 1600 or 1800 square miles," observes Barrow, " the whole surface might literally be said to be covered with them." **They shall eat the residue of that which escaped.** Locusts eat every atom of verdure in the district attacked by them. " In A.D. 1004," says Barhebræus, " a large swarm of locusts appeared in the land of Mosul and Baghdad, and it was very grievous in Shiraz. It left no herb nor even leaf on the trees." " When their swarms appear," writes Volney, " everything green vanishes instantaneously from the fields, as if a curtain were rolled up ; the trees and plants stand leafless, and nothing is seen but naked boughs and stalks." **And shall eat every tree.** The damage done by locusts to trees is very great. " He (the locust) has laid my vine waste, and barked my fig-tree ; he hath made it clean bare and east it away ; the branches thereof are made white " (Joel i. 7). Travellers constantly notice this fact. " When they have devoured all other vegetables," says one, " they attack the trees, consuming first the leaves, then the bark." " After having consumed herbage, fruit, leaves of trees," says

another, "they attacked even their young shoots and their bark." " They are particularly injurious to the palm-trees," writes a third ; " these they strip of every leaf and green particle, the trees remaining like skeletons with bare branches." A fourth notes that " the bushes were eaten quite bare, though the animals could not have been long on the spot. They sat by hundreds on a bush, gnawing the rind and the woody fibres." (See Pusey's *Minor Prophets,* p. 106.)

Ver. 6.—**They shall fill thy houses.** Compare Joel ii. 9. The witness of modern travellers is to the same effect. Morier says— " They entered the inmost recesses of the houses, were found in every corner, stuck to our clothes, and infested our food " (*Second Journey,* p. 100). Burckhardt observes— " They overwhelm the province of Nedjd sometimes to such a degree that, having destroyed the harvest, they penetrate by thousands into the private dwellings, and devour whatsoever they can find, even the leather of the water vessels " (*Notes,* vol. ii. p. 90). An older traveller, Beauplan, writes as follows :—" In June 1646, at Novgorod, it was prodigious to behold them, because they were hatched there that spring, and being as yet scarce able to fly, the ground was all covered, and the air so full of them that I could not eat in my chamber without a candle, all the houses being full of them, even the stables, barns, chambers, garrets, and cellars. I caused cannon-powder and sulphur to be burnt to expel them, but all to no purpose ; for when the door was opened, an infinite number came in, and the others went fluttering about ; and it was a troublesome thing, when a man went abroad, to be hit on the face by those creatures, on the nose, eyes, or cheeks, so that there was no opening one's mouth but some would get in. Yet all this was nothing ; for when we were to eat they gave us no respite ; and when we went to cut a piece of meat, we cut a locust with it, and when a man opened his mouth to put in a morsel, he was sure to chew one of them." Oriental houses, it is to be borne in mind, have no better protection than lattice-work in the windows, so that locusts have free access to the apartments, even when the doors are shut. **Which neither thy fathers, nor thy fathers' fathers have seen.** Inroads of locusts are not common in Egypt. Only one reference has been found to them in the native records. When they occur, they are as destructive as elsewhere. Denon witnessed one in the early part of the present century. Two others were witnessed by Carsten Niebuhr and Forskål in 1761 and 1762 (*Description de l'Arabie,* p. 148) ; and another by Tischendorf comparatively recently. The meaning in the text is probably that no *such* visitation as that now sent had been seen previously, not that Egypt had been hitherto free from the scourge. **He turned himself and went out.** Moses did not wait to learn what effect his announcement would have. He " knew " that Pharaoh would not fear the Lord. (See ch. ix. 30.)

Ver. 7.—**And Pharaoh's servants said unto him.** This marks quite a new phase in the proceedings. Hitherto the courtiers generally had been dumb. Once the magicians had ventured to say—" This is the finger of God " (ch. viii. 19); but otherwise the entire court had been passive, and left the king to himself. They are even said to have " hardened their hearts " like him (ch. ix. 34). But now at last they break their silence and interfere. Having lost most of their cattle, and a large part of the year's crops, the great men became alarmed—they were large landed proprietors, and the destruction of the wheat and *doora* crops would seriously impoverish, if not actually ruin them. Moreover, it is to be noted that they interfere before the plague has begun, when it is simply threatened, which shows that they had come to believe in the power of Moses. Such a belief on the part of some had appeared, when the plague of hail was threatened (ch. ix. 20); now it would seem to have become general. **A snare to us**—*i.e.* " a peril "—" a source of danger," the species being put for the genus.

Ver. 8.—**Moses and Aaron were brought again unto Pharaoh.** Pharaoh did not condescend so far as to send for them, but he allowed his courtiers to bring them to him. And he so far took the advice of his courtiers, that he began by a general permission to the Israelites to take their departure. This concession, however, he almost immediately retracted by a question, which implied that all were not to depart. **Who are they that shall go?** It seems somewhat strange that the king had not yet clearly understood what the demand made of him was. But perhaps he had not cared to know, since he had had no intention of granting it.

Ver. 9.—**And Moses said, We will go with our young, and with our old.** This statement was at any rate unambiguous, and no doubt could henceforth be even pretended as to what the demand was. The whole nation, with its flocks and herds, was to take its departure, since a feast was to be held in which all the nation ought to participate. The Egyptians were accustomed to the attendance of children at national festivals (Herod. ii. 60).

Ver. 10.—**And he said,** etc. Pharaoh's reply to the plain statement of Moses is full of scorn and anger, as if he would say—" When was ever so extravagant and outrageous a demand made? How can it be supposed that I would listen to it? So may Jehovah help you, as I will help you in this—to let you go, with your families." (*Taph* is " family," or

household, not " little ones." See Ex. i. 1.) **Look to it; for evil is before you.** Or, " Look to it; for you have evil in view." Beware, *i.e.*, of what you are about. You entertain the evil design of robbing me of my slaves— a design which I shall not allow you to carry out. There is no direct threat, only an indirect one, implied in " Look to it."

Ver. 11.—**Go now ye that are men.** Or, " ye that are adult males." The word is different from that used in ver. 7, which includes women and children. **And serve the Lord; for that ye did desire.** Pharaoh seems to argue that the request to " serve the Lord " implied the departure of the men only, as if women and children could not offer an acceptable service. But he must have known that women and children attended his own national festivals. (See the comment on ver. 9.) Probably, he knew that his argument was sophistical. **And they were driven out.** Literally, " One drove them out." Pharaoh's manifest displeasure was an indication to the court officials that he wished the interview ended, and as the brothers did not at once voluntarily quit the presence, an officer thrust them out. This was an insult not previously offered them, and shows how Pharaoh's rage increased as he saw more and more clearly that he would have to yield and allow the departure of the entire nation.

Ver. 13.—**The Lord brought an east wind.** Locusts generally come with a wind; and, indeed, cannot fly far without one. An east wind would in this case have brought them from northern Arabia, which is a tract where they are often bred in large numbers. Denon, the French traveller, notes that an enormous cloud of locusts which invaded Egypt during his stay, came from the east. **All that day.** The rest of the day on which Moses and Aaron had had their interview with the Pharaoh.

Ver. 14.—**The locusts went up over all the land of Egypt, and rested in all the coasts of Egypt.** This statement is very emphatic, and seems to imply that the plague was more widely extended than any that had preceded it. Egypt extends about 520 miles from north to south, but except in the Delta is not more than about 20 miles wide. Columns of locusts of the length of 500 miles have been noticed by travellers (Moor in Kirby on *Entomology*, letter vi.), and 20 miles is not an unusual width for them. But such a length and such a breadth are not elsewhere recorded in combination. Thus the visitation was, in its extent as well as in its circumstances, plainly abnormal.

Ver. 15.—**The land was darkened.** It is not quite clear whether the darkness here spoken of was caused by the locusts when they were still on the wing or after they had settled. It is a fact that the insects come in such dense clouds that while on the wing they obscure the light of the sun, and turn noonday into twilight. And it is also a fact that with their dull brownish bodies and wings they darken the ground after they have settled. Perhaps it is most probable that this last is the fact noticed. (Compare ver. 5.) **All the fruit of the trees which the hail had left.** Injury to fruit by the hail had not been expressly mentioned in the account of that plague, though perhaps it may be regarded as implied in the expression—that the hail "brake every tree of the field" (ver. 25). The damage which locusts do to fruit is well known. They devour it with the green crops, the herbage, and the foliage, before setting to work upon the harder materials, as reeds, twigs, and the bark of trees. In Egypt the principal fruits would be figs, pomegranates, mulberries, grapes, olives, peaches, pears, plums, and apples; together with dates, and the produce of the *persea*, and the *nebk* or *sidr*. The fruit of the nebk is ripe in March. **There remained not any green thing.** "It is sufficient," observes one writer, "if these terrible columns stop half an hour on a spot, for everything growing on it, vines, olive-trees, and corn, to be entirely destroyed. After they have passed, nothing remains but the large branches and the roots, which, being underground, have escaped their voracity." "Wherever they settle," says another, "it looks as if fire had burnt up everything." "The country did not seem to be burnt," declares a third, "but to be covered with snow, through the whiteness of the trees and the dryness of the herbs." A fourth sums up his account of the ravages committed by locusts thus—"According to all accounts, wherever the swarms of locusts arrive, the vegetables are entirely consumed and destroyed, appearing as if they had been burnt by fire."

Ver. 16.—**Then Pharaoh called for Moses and Aaron in haste.** Literally, as in the margin, "hasted to call for M. and A." He had made similar appeals before (ch. viii. 8, 25; ix. 27), but never with such haste and urgency. Evidently, the locusts were felt as a severer infliction than any previous one. **I have sinned.** So, after the plague of hail (ix. 27); but here we have the further acknowledgment, **against the Lord your God and against you;** "against the Lord," in disobeying his commands; "against you," in making you promises and then refusing to keep them (ch. viii. 15, 32; ch. ix. 34, 35).

Ver. 17.—**Only this once.** Compare Gen. xviii. 32. Pharaoh kept this promise. He

did not ask any more for the removal of a plague. **This death only**—*i.e.* "this fatal visitation"—this visitation, which, by producing famine, causes numerous deaths in a nation. Pharaoh feels now, as his courtiers had felt when the plague was first threatened, that "Egypt is destroyed" (ver. 7).

Ver. 18. **He . . . intreated the Lord.** Moses complied, though Pharaoh had this time made no distinct promise of releasing the people. He had learnt that no dependence was to be placed on such promises, and that it was idle to exact them. If anything could have touched the dull and hard heart of the king, it would have been the gentleness and magnanimity shown by Moses in uttering no word of reproach, making no conditions, but simply granting his request as soon as it was made, and obtaining the removal of the plague.

Ver. 19.—**And the Lord turned a mighty strong west wind.** Literally, "a very strong *sea*-wind"—*i.e.* one which blew from the Mediterranean, and which might, therefore, so far, be north, north-west, or north-east. As it blew the locusts into the "Sea of Weeds," *i.e.* the Red Sea, it must have been actually a north-west wind, and so passing obliquely over Egypt, have carried the locusts in a south-easterly direction. **Cast them into the Red Sea.** Literally, "the Sea of Weeds." No commentator doubts that the Red Sea is here meant. It seems to have received its Hebrew appellation, *Yam Sûph*, "Sea of Weeds," either from the quantity of sea-weed which it throws up, or, more probably, from the fact that anciently its north-western recess was connected with a marshy tract extending from the present head of the Gulf of Suez nearly to the Bitter Lakes, in which grew abundant weeds and water-plants. **There remained not one locust.** The sudden and entire departure of locusts is as remarkable as their coming. "At the hour of prime," says one writer, "they began to depart, and at midday there was not one remaining." "A wind from the south-west," says another, "which had brought them, so completely drove them forwards that not a vestige of them was to be seen two hours afterwards" (Morier, 'Second Journey,' p. 98).

Ver. 20.—**But the Lord hardened Pharaoh's heart.** The word used here is the intensive one, *khazoq*, instead of the milder *kabod* of ver. 1. Pharaoh's prolonged obstinacy and impenitence was receiving aggravation by the working of the just laws of God. (See the comment on ch. iv. 21.)

HOMILETICS.

Vers. 1, 2.—*God's mercies and wondrous works to be kept in perpetual remembrance.* Man's forgetfulness of God's benefits is one of the saddest features of his existing condition and character. He needs continual urging and exhortation to the duty of remembering them.

I. HE FORGETS ESPECIALLY THOSE BENEFITS WHICH ARE CONSTANT AND CONTINUOUS. (*a*) Temporal benefits. Life, strength, health, intellect, the power to act, the capacity to enjoy, the ability to think, speak, write, are God's gifts, bestowed lavishly on the human race, and in civilised countries possessed in some measure by almost every member of the community. And, for the most part, they are possessed continuously. At any moment any one of them might be withdrawn; but, as it pleases God to make them constant, they are scarcely viewed as gifts at all. The Church would have men thank God, at least twice a day, for their "creation, preservation, and all the blessings of this life." But how few perform this duty! Creation, preservation, daily sustenance, even health, are taken as matters of course, which come to us naturally; not considered to be, as they are, precious gifts bestowed upon us by God. (*b*) Spiritual benefits. Atonement, redemption, reconciliation, effected for us once for all by our Lord's death upon the Cross; and pardon, assisting grace, spiritual strength, given us continually, are equally ignored and forgotten. At any rate, the lively sense of them is wanting. Few say, with David, constantly, "Bless the Lord, O my soul, and all that is within me bless his holy name. Bless the Lord, O my soul, and forget not all his benefits; who forgiveth all thine iniquities; who healeth all thy diseases; who redeemeth thy life from destruction; who crowneth thee with loving-kindness and tender mercies; who satisfieth thy mouth with good things; so that thy youth is renewed like the eagle's" (Ps. ciii. 1—5).

II. HE FORGETS EVEN EXTRAORDINARY MERCIES. A man escapes with life from an accident that might have been fatal; recovers from an illness in which his life was despaired of; is awakened suddenly to a sense of religion when he had long gone on in coldness and utter deadness; and he thinks at first that nothing can ever take the thought of the blessing which he has received out of his remembrance. He is ready to exclaim, ten times a day, "Come and hear, all ye that fear God, and I will tell you what he hath done for my soul!" But soon all fades away and grows dim; the vivid remembrance passes from him; he thinks less and less of what seems now a distant time; he neglects to speak of it, even to his children. Instead of "telling in the ears of his son, and of his son's son, what things God wrought for him in the old time," he does not so much as think of them. Very offensive to God must be this forgetfulness. He works his works of mercy and of power for the very purpose "that men may tell of them and have them in remembrance," may "teach them to their sons and their sons' sons," may keep them "as tokens upon their hands, and as frontlets between their eyes," may "tell them to the following generation."

III. PERPETUAL REMEMBRANCE OF EXTRAORDINARY MERCIES IS BEST SECURED BY THE OBSERVANCE OF ANNIVERSARIES. God instituted the Passover, and other Jewish feasts, that the memory of his great mercies to his people in Egypt and the wilderness should not pass away (Ex. xii. 24—27). So the Christian Church has observed Christmas Day, Good Friday, Ascension Day. Such occasions are properly called "commemorations." And individuals may well follow the Church, by commemorating important events in their own lives, so they do it—(1) Gratefully; (2) Prayerfully; and (3) Unostentatiously.

Vers. 3—6.—*God's long-suffering towards the wicked has a limit.* "How long wilt thou refuse to humble thyself?" (ver. 3). "The goodness of God endureth yet daily." His forbearance and long-suffering are wonderful. Yet they have a limit. God will not proceed to judgment—

I. UNTIL THE SINNER HAS HAD FULL OPPORTUNITY FOR REPENTANCE. Pharaoh had been first warned (ch. v. 3), then shown a sign (ch. vii. 10—12); after this, punished by seven distinct plagues, each of which was well calculated to strike terror into the soul, and thereby to stir it to repentance. He had been told by his own magicians that one of them, at any rate, could be ascribed to nothing but "the finger of God" (ch. viii. 19). He had been impressed, alarmed, humbled so far as to make confession of sin (ch. ix. 27), and to promise three several times that he would let the Israelites depart from Egypt (ch. viii. 8, 28; ch. ix. 28). But all had been of no avail. No sooner was a plague removed at his humble entreaty than he resumed all his old pride and arrogance, retracted his promise, and showed himself as stiff-necked as at the first. The time during which his trial had lasted, and God's patience endured, must have been more than a year—surely ample opportunity!

II. UNTIL IT IS MANIFEST THAT THERE IS NO HOPE THAT HE WILL REPENT. "What could have been done more in my vineyard, that I have not done to it?" God asks in Isaiah (v. 4). And what more could he have done to turn Pharaoh from his evil ways, that he had not done on this occasion? Exhortations, warnings, miracles, light plagues, heavy plagues, had all been tried, and no real, permanent impression made. The worst of all was, that when some kind of impression was made, no good result ensued. Fear—abject, servile, cowardly fear—was the dominant feeling aroused; and even this did not last, but disappeared the moment that the plague was removed. Pharaoh was thus constantly "sinning yet more" (ch. ix. 34). Instead of improving under the chastening hand of God, he was continually growing worse. His heart was becoming harder. His reformation was more hopeless.

III. UNTIL GOD'S PURPOSES IN ALLOWING THE RESISTANCE OF HIS WILL BY THE SINNER ARE ACCOMPLISHED. God intended that through Pharaoh's resistance to his will, and the final failure of his resistance, his own name should be glorified and "declared throughout all the earth" (ch. ix. 16). It required a period of some length—a tolerably prolonged contest—to rivet the attention both of the Egyptians generally, and of the surrounding nations. After somewhat more than a year this result had been attained. There was, consequently, no need of further delay; and the last three plagues, which followed rapidly the one upon the other, were of the nature of judgments.

Ver. 7—11.—*Man's interposition with good advice may come too late.* It is impossible to say what effect the opposition and remonstrances of his nobles and chief officers might not have had upon Pharaoh, if they had been persistently offered from the first. But his magicians had for some time aided and abetted his resistance to God's will, as declared by Moses; and had even used the arts whereof they were masters to make the miracles which Moses wrought seem trifles. And the rest of the Court officials had held their peace, neither actively supporting the monarch, nor opposing him. It was only when the land had been afflicted by seven plagues, and an eighth was impending, that they summoned courage to express disapproval of the king's past conduct, and to recommend a different course. "How long shall this man be a snare unto us? *Let the men go,*" they said. But the advice came too late. Pharaoh had, so to speak, committed himself. He had engaged in a contest from which he could not retire without disgrace. He had become heated and hardened; and, the more the conviction came home to him that he must yield the main demand, the more did it seem to him a point of honour not to grant the whole of what had been asked. But practically, this was the same thing as granting nothing, since Moses would not be content with less than the whole. The interposition of the Court officials was therefore futile. Let those whose position entitles them to offer advice to men in power bear in mind four things—(1) The importance of promptness in bringing their influence to bear; (2) the advantage of taking a consistent line from first to last; (3) the danger of inaction and neutrality; and (4) the necessity of pressing their advice when it has been once given, and of not allowing it to be set aside. If the "servants of Pharaoh" had followed up the interposition recorded in verse 7 by further representations and remonstrances, they would have had some slight chance of producing an effect. But a single isolated remonstrance was valueless.

Vers. 12—15.—*The terribleness of God's severer judgments.* "It is a fearful thing to fall into the hands of the living God." "Our God is a consuming fire." "If the wicked turn not, God will whet his sword; he hath bent his bow and made it ready. He hath also prepared for him the instruments of death; he ordaineth his arrows against the persecutors" (Ps. vii. 11—13). Every calamity which can visit man is at his disposal. God's punishments are terrible—

I. BECAUSE HE IS OMNIPOTENT. He can smite with a thousand weapons—with all the varieties of physical pain—aches, sores, wounds, boils, nerve affections, inflammation, short breath, imperfect heart action, faintings, palpitations, weakness, cramps, chills, shiverings—with mental sufferings, bad spirits, depression, despondency, grief, anguish, fear, want of brain power, loss of self-control, distaste for exertion, &c.; with misfortunes—sickness, mutilation, loss of friends, ill-health, bereavement, death. He can accumulate sorrows, reiterate blows, allow no respite, proceed from bad to worse, utterly crush and destroy those who have offended him and made themselves his enemies.

II. BECAUSE HE IS ABSOLUTELY JUST. God's judgments are the outcome of his justice, and therefore most terrible. What have we not deserved at his hands ? If, after all his gentle teachings, all his mild persuadings, the preaching of his ministers, the promptings of his Holy Spirit, the warnings furnished by the circumstances of life, the special chastisements sent to evoke repentance, men continue obdurate—what remains but a "fearful looking for of judgment and of fiery indignation, which shall devour the adversaries"? (Heb. x. 27.) If each sin committed is to receive its full, due, and appropriate penalty, what suffering can be sufficient? Even in this life, the vengeances that have overtaken the impenitent, have sometimes been most fearful ; what must the full tale be if we take in the consideration of another?

III. BECAUSE HE IS FAITHFUL, AND CANNOT LIE OR REPENT. God in his Word has plainly, clearly, unmistakably, over and over again, declared that the impenitent sinner shall be punished everlastingly. In vain men attempt to escape the manifest force of the words and to turn them to another meaning. As surely as the life of the blessed is never-ending, so is the "death" of the wicked. Vainly says one, that he would willingly give up *his* hope of everlasting life, if so be that by such sacrifice he could end the eternal sufferings of the lost ones. It is not what man feels, what he thinks he would do, or even what he would actually do, were it in his power, that proves anything ; the question is one of fact. God tells us what he is about to do, and he will assuredly do it, whatever we may think or feel. "These (the wicked) shall go into everlasting punishment ; but the righteous into life everlasting" (Matt. xxv. 46). Oh ! terrible voice of most just judgment which shall be pronounced on those to whom it shall be said, "Depart from me, ye cursed, into everlasting fire, prepared for the devil and his angels" (Matt. xxv. 41)! The crowning terror of the judgment of God is the perpetuity which he has declared attaches to it.

Vers. 16—20.—*The agency of nature used by God both in inflicting and removing judgments.* God's footsteps are not known. Since Eden was lost to us it has pleased him, for inscrutable reasons, to withdraw himself behind the screen of nature, and to work out his purposes—in the main, through natural agencies. He punishes idleness and imprudence by poverty and contempt ; intemperance and uncleanness, by disease ; inordinate ambition, by collapse of schemes, loss of battles, deposition, exile, early death. Civil government is one of the agencies which he uses for punishing a whole class of offences ; hygienic laws are another. It is comparatively seldom that he descends visibly to judgment, as when he burnt up the cities of the plains. So, even when he was miraculously punishing Egypt and Pharaoh, he used, as far as was possible, the agency of nature. Frogs, mosquitoes, beetles, thunder, hail, locusts, worked his will—natural agents, suited to the season and the country—only known by faith to have come at his bidding, and departed when he gave the order. And he brought the locusts and took them away, by a wind. So the temporal punishments of the wicked came constantly along the ordinary channels of life, rash speculation producing bankruptcy ; profligacy, disease ; dishonesty, distrust ; ill-temper, general aversion. Men curse their ill-luck when calamity comes on them, and attribute to chance what is really the doing of God's retributive hand. The east wind, they say, brought the locusts on them ; but they do not ask who brought the east wind out of his treasury. God uses natural means also to remove judgments. "A wind takes the locusts away." A severe winter stops a pestilence. An invasion of their own territory recalls devastating hordes to its defence, and frees the land which they were ravaging. Reaction sets in when revolution goes too far, and the guillotine makes short work of the revolutionists. Want stimulates industry, and industry removes the pressure of want. Even when men's prayers are manifestly answered by the cessation of drought, or rain, or the recovery from sickness of one given over by the physicians, the change comes about in a natural way. A little cloud rises up out of the deep, and overspreads the heavens, and the drought is gone. The wind shifts a few points, and the "plague of rain" ceases. The fever abates. little by little, the patient finds that he can take nourishment ; so the crisis is past, and nature, or " the strength of his constitution," as men say, has saved him. The changes are natural ones; but God, who is behind nature, has caused the changes, and, as much as miracles, they are his work.

HOMILIES BY VARIOUS AUTHORS.

Vers. 1—7. *A new Message.* Even yet God had not done with the King of Egypt. He sends Moses again to ply him with reproof and threatening. The final stroke is put off as long as possible. If " by all means " (1 Cor. ix. 22) Pharaoh can be saved, he will not be lost for want of the opportunity. God tells Moses his *design* in dealing with the monarch as he did, and gives him a new message to carry to the royal presence.

I. GOD'S DESIGN (vers. 1, 2). He had hardened Pharaoh's heart and the heart of his servants, that he might show these his signs before him, and that he might secure their being had in remembrance through all succeeding generations in Israel. This bespeaks, on God's part—1. *Definite purpose in the shaping of the events which culminated in the Exodus.* As Jehovah, the all-ruling one, it lay with him to determine *what* shape these events would assume, so as best to accomplish the end he had in view in the deliverance. It was of his ordering that a ruler of Pharaoh's stamp occupied the throne of Egypt at that particular time; that the king was able to hold out as he did against his often reiterated, and powerfully enforced, command; that the monarch's life was spared, when he might have been smitten and destroyed (ch. ix. 15, 16); that the Exodus was of so glorious and memorable a character. 2. *It indicates the nature of the design.* "That ye may know how that I am the Lord" (ver. 2). We have already seen (ch. vi.) that the central motive in this whole series of events was the manifestation of God in his character of Jehovah—the absolute, all-ruling, omnipotent Lord, who works in history, in mercy, and judgment, for the accomplishment of gracious ends. The design was (1) To demonstrate the *fact* that such a Being as is denoted by the name Jehovah, existed; that there *is* an absolute, all-ruling, omnipotent, gracious God; (2) to raise the mind to a proper conception of his greatness, by giving an exhibition, on a scale of impressive magnitude, of his actual working in mercy and judgment for the salvation of his people; and (3) to make thereby a revelation of himself which would lay the foundation of future covenant relations with Israel, and ultimately of an universal religion reposing on the truths of his unity, spirituality, sanctity, omnipotence, and love. Subordinate objects were the making known of his power and greatness to Pharaoh himself (ch. vii. 17; viii. 22; ix. 13, 29), and to the surrounding nations (ch. ix. 16). The design thus indicated required that the facts should be of a kind which admitted of no dispute; that they should palpably and conclusively demonstrate the character of God to be as asserted; and that they should be of so striking and awful a description, as to print themselves indelibly upon the memory of the nation. These conditions were fulfilled in the events of the Exodus. (3) *It shows how God intended his mighty works to be kept in remembrance.* "That thou mayest tell in the ears of thy son, and of thy son's son," &c. (ver. 2). God provided for the handing down of a knowledge of these wonders (1) By giving them a character which *secured* that they should not be forgotten. The memory of these "wonders in the land of Ham" (Ps. cv. 27) rings down in Israel to the latest generations (see Ps. lxxviii.; cv.; cvi.; cxxxv.; cxxvi., &c.); (2) by embodying them in a written record; (3) by enjoining on parents the duty of faithfully narrating them to their children (ch. xiii. 14; Deut. iv. 9; v. 7, 20—23; xi. 19; Ps. lxxviii. 3—7). Bible history will soon get to be forgotten if the story is not taken up and diligently taught by loving parental lips.

II. GOD'S REQUIREMENT—humility. "How long wilt thou refuse to *humble* thyself before me?" (ver. 3.) This lays the finger on the root principle of Pharaoh's opposition, pride. Pride, the undue exaltation of the *ego*, is a hateful quality of character, even as between man and man. How much more, as between man and God! It is described as "the condemnation of the devil" (1 Tim. iv. 6). Pride puffs the soul up in undue conceit of itself, and leads it to spurn at God's dictation and control. It aims at a false independence. It would wish to be *as* God. In the worldly spirit it manifests itself as "the pride of life" (1 John ii. 16). In the self-righteous spirit it manifests itself as spiritual pride. It excludes every quality which ought to exist in a soul rightly exercised towards its Creator. Faith, love, humility, the feeling of dependence, gratitude for benefits, regard for the Creator's glory—it shuts out all. It is incompatible with the sense of sin, with the spirit of contrition, with humble acceptance of salvation through another. It is the great barrier to the submission of the heart to God and Christ, inciting instead to naked and impious rebellion. The degree and persistency of the opposition to God which pride is able to inspire may be well studied in the case of Pharaoh.

III. GOD'S THREAT (vers. 4—7). He would bring upon the land a plague of locusts. The magnitude of the visitation would place it beyond comparison with anything that had ever been known. See below.

IV. MOSES GOING OUT FROM PHARAOH. "And he turned himself, and went out from Pharaoh" (ver. 6). He delivered his message, and did not wait for an answer. This should have told Pharaoh that the bow was now stretched to its utmost, and that to strain it further by continued resistance would be to break it. His courtiers seem to have perceived this (ver. 7). Moses' going out was a prelude to the final breaking off of negotiations (ver. 29). View it also as a studied intimation—1. Of his indignation at the past conduct of the king (cf. ch. xi. 8). 2. Of his conviction of the hopelessness of producing any good impression on his hardened nature. 3. Of the certainty of God's purpose being fulfilled, whether Pharaoh willed it or no. It was for Pharaoh's interest to attend to the warning which had now again been given him, but his refusal to attend to it would only injure himself and his people; it would not prevent God's will from being accomplished.—J. O.

Vers. 7—21.—*The plague of locusts.* Of the two principal terms used to denote "hardening," one means "to strengthen, or make firm," the other, "to make heavy, or obtuse." It is the latter of these (used also in ch. viii. 15, 32 ; ix. 7) which is used in ch. ix. 34, and ch. x. 1. The growing obtuseness of Pharaoh's mind is very apparent from the narrative. He is losing the power of right judgment. He began by hardening himself (making his heart strong and firm) against Jehovah, and he is reaping the penalty in a blinded understanding. This obtuseness shows itself in various ways, notably in the want of unity in his conduct. He is like a man at bay, who feels that he is powerless to resist, but cannot bring himself to yield. His power of self-control is leaving him, and his action, in consequence, consists of a succession of mad rushes, now in one direction, now in another. External influences—the remonstrance of courtiers, the terrors occasioned by the plagues—produce immediate effects upon him; but the recoil of pride and rage, which speedily supervenes, carries him further from reason than ever. Now he is suing in pitiable self-humiliation for forgiveness; again he is furious and unrestrained in his defiance. Passion is usurping the place of reason, and drives him to and fro with ungovernable violence. We are reminded of the heathen saying, "Whom the gods wish to destroy, they first madden;" but it is not God who is destroying Pharaoh; it is Pharaoh who is destroying himself. If God maddens him, it is by plying him with the influences which ought to have had a directly opposite effect. Pharaoh, like every other sinner, must bear the responsibility of his own ruin.

I. THE INTERVENTION OF PHARAOH'S SERVANTS (ver. 7). These may be the same servants who up to this time had hardened themselves (ch. ix. 34). If so, they now see the folly of further contest. More and more Pharaoh is being left to stand alone. First, his magicians gave in (ch. viii. 19), then a portion of his servants (ch. ix. 20); now, apparently, his courtiers are deserting him in a body. It shows the indomitable stubbornness of the king, that under these circumstances he should still hold out. Observe, 1. The subjects of a government have often a truer perception of what is needed for the safety of a country than their rulers and leaders. Pharaoh's servants saw the full gravity of the situation, to which the monarch was so blind. "Knowest thou not yet that Egypt is destroyed?" Rulers are frequently blinded by their pride, passion, prejudices, and private wishes, to the real necessities of a political situation. 2. Hardening against God makes the heart indifferent to the interests of others. The ungodly mind is at bottom selfish. We have seen already (ch. v.) to what lengths in cruelty ungodly men will go in pursuit of their personal ends. We have also seen that hardening at the centre of the nature is bound to spread till it embraces the whole man (on ch. vii. 3). Pharaoh is an illustration of this. He was unboundedly proud; and "pride," says Müller, "is the basest and most glaring form that selfishness can assume." It is an egoistic sin; a sin of the will more than of the affections; a sin rooted in the centre of the personality. But Pharaoh was more than proud; he was God-defying. He had consciously and wilfully hardened himself against the Almighty, under most terrible displays of his omnipotence. Driven to bay in such a contest, it was not to be expected that he would be much influenced by the thought of the suffering he was bringing upon others. Egypt might be destroyed, but Pharaoh recked little of that, or, possibly, still tried to persuade himself that the worst might be averted. The remonstrance of his courtiers produced a momentary wavering, but defiance breaks out again in ver. 10 in stronger terms than ever.

II. A RENEWED ATTEMPT AT COMPROMISE (vers. 8—12). Pharaoh sends for Moses and Aaron, and asks who they are that are to go to sacrifice (ver. 8): the reply was decisive; "we will go with our young and with our old," etc. (ver. 9). At this Pharaoh is transported with ungovernable rage. He accuses the Hebrew brothers of desiring to take an evil advantage of his permission, and practically challenges Jehovah to do his worst against him (ver. 10). He will consent to the *men* going to serve the Lord, but to nothing more (ver. 11). Moses and Aaron were then "driven" from his presence. We are reminded here of the transports of Saul, and his malicious rage at David (1 Sam. xix.). Notice on this, 1. Wicked men *distrust* God. Pharaoh had no reason to question Jehovah's sincerity. God had proved his sincerity by his previous dealings with him. And had God actually demanded—what ultimately *would* have been required—the entire departure of the people from the land, what right had he, their oppressor, to object? 2. Wicked men would fain *compound* with God. They will give up something, if God will let them retain the rest. There is a sweetness to a proud nature in being able to get even *part* of its own way. 3. The thing wicked men will *not* do is to concede the *whole* demand which God makes on them. What God requires supremely is the surrender of the will, and this the recalcitrant heart will not stoop to yield. Part it will surrender, but not the whole. Outward vices, pleasures, worldly possessions, friendships, these, at a pinch, may be given up; but not the heart's love and obedience, which is the thing chiefly asked for; not the "little ones" of the heart's secret sins, or the "flocks and herds" for the pure inward sacrifice (see Pusey on Micah vi. 6—9).

III. THE LOCUST JUDGMENT (ver. 12—16). The predicted plague was accordingly brought upon the land. It was the second of what we may call the greater plagues— the plagues that were to be laid upon the king's "heart" (ch. ix. 14). They were plagues of a character to *appal* and *overwhelm*; to lay hold of the nature on the side on which it is susceptible of impressions from the awful and terrific; to awaken into intense activity its slumbering sense of the infinite; to rouse in the soul the apprehension of present Deity. The first was the plague of hail, thunderings, and lightnings; the second was this plague of locusts. The points on which stress is laid in this second plague are— 1. The supernatural character of the visitation. 2. The appalling numbers of the enemy. 3. The havoc wrought by them. We may compare the language here with the description of the locusts in Joel ii., and it may be concluded that the effects described as following from the latter visitation were more than paralleled by the terror and anguish created by the descent of this scourge on Egypt. "Before their face the people would be much pained; all faces would gather blackness" (Joel ii. 6). It would seem as if the earth quaked before them; as if the heavens trembled; as if sun and moon had become dark, and the stars had withdrawn their shining (ver. 10)! The devastation was rapid and complete. "The land is as the garden of Eden before them, and behind them a desolate wilderness" (ver. 3). Had the plague not speedily been removed Egypt verily *would* have been destroyed. How mighty is Jehovah! How universal his empire! These locusts were brought from afar (ver. 13). All agents in nature serve him; winds (east and west), locusts (cf. Joel ii. 11), as well as hail and thunder. He has but to speak the word, and all we have will be taken from us (ver. 15).

IV. PHARAOH'S PITIABLE PLIGHT AND FURTHER HARDENING (vers. 16—21). What we have here is a specimen of one of those violent contrasts in Pharaoh's later moods to which reference has been made above. Nothing could be more humiliating, more abject, more truly painful, in its self-effacement than this new appeal of the king to Moses.

He had sinned, sinned both against God, and against Moses and Aaron ; would they forgive him this once, only this once, and entreat God that he would take away from him this death only ? (vers. 16, 17.) Contrast this with ver. 10, or with ver. 28, and it can hardly be believed that we are looking on the same man. Pharaoh had never humbled himself so far before. He *beseeches* for mercy ; almost *cringes* before Moses and Aaron in his anxiety to have this dreadful plague removed. Yet there is no real change of heart. The moment the locusts are gone pride reasserts its sway, and he hardens himself as formerly. Learn—1. That *false repentance may be connected with other than superficial states of feeling.* Pharaoh was here in real terror, in mortal anguish of spirit. The pains of hell had truly got hold on him (Ps. cxvi. 3). Yet his repentance was a false one. 2. That *false repentance may ape every outward symptom of real repentance.* Who that saw Pharaoh in that bath of anguish, and heard him pouring out those impassioned entreaties and confessions, but would have supposed that the hard heart had at length been subdued ? The confession of sin is unreserved and unqualified. The submission is absolute. Pharaoh was aware of how little he deserved to be further trusted, and pled to be tried again, " only this once." Yet the repentance was through and through a false one—the product of mere natural terror—the repentance of a heart, not one fibre of which was altered in its moral quality. 3. That *false repentance may not be consciously insincere.* There is no reason to question that Pharaoh was for the time sincere enough in the promises he made. They were wrung from him, but he *meant* to give effect to them. But the momentary willingness he felt to purchase exemption from trouble by granting Jehovah's demand had quite disappeared by the time the plague was removed. The repentance was false. 4. *The test of a repentance being false or true is the fruits yielded by it.* The test is not the depth of our convictions, the anguish of our minds, the profuseness of our confessions, the apparent sincerity of our vows, it is the kind of deeds which follow (Matt. iii. 8). We have need in this matter of repentance to distrust ourselves, to beware of being imposed on by others, and to be careful in public instruction that the real nature of repentance is lucidly expounded.—J. O.

Vers. 1—19.—*The Eighth Plague : the locusts.* I. CONSIDER THE EMPHATIC STATE-MENT WITH RESPECT TO THE HARDENING OF THE HEART. In ch. ix. 34 we are told that when the hail and the thunder ceased, Pharaoh hardened his heart, *he and his servants.* Note here two things : 1. How Pharaoh's heart was hardened just after he had made a confession of sin ; from which we see how little he understood by the word " sin," and how little he meant by the confession. 2. The combination of his servants with him in this hardening ; from which we may judge that just as some among his servants had been taken further away from him by their prudent and believing action when the hail was threatened (ch. ix. 20), so others had been drawn still nearer to their master, and made larger sharers in his obstinacy and pride. The unbelieving, who left their servants and their cattle in the fields, not only lost their property when the hail descended, but afterwards they became worse men. And now in ch. x. 1, not only is there a statement that the hearts of Pharaoh and his servants were hardened, but God in his own person says, " I have hardened his heart," &c. Then after this statement, so emphatic in the expression of it, however difficult to understand in the meaning of it, God goes on to explain why he has thus hardened the heart of Pharaoh and his servants. In the first place, *it gives an opportunity for show-ing God's signs before Pharaoh*—" all my plagues " (ch. ix. 14). Thus God would turn our attention here to the thing of chief importance, namely, *what he was doing himself.* Important it certainly is to notice what *Pharaoh* is doing, but far more important to notice what *Jehovah* is doing. We may easily give too much time to thinking of Pharaoh, and too little to thinking of Jehovah. Thus God would ever direct us into the steps of practical wisdom. We are constantly tempted to ask questions which cannot be answered, while we as constantly neglect to ask questions which both can be answered and ought to be answered. The conduct of Pharaoh is indeed a fascinating problem for those who love to consider the play of motives in the human heart. In considering him there is ample room for the imagination to work out the conception of a very impressive character. Thus, we might come to many conclusions with respect to Pharaoh, some of them right, but in all likelihood most of them wrong, perhaps egregiously wrong. These are matters in which God has not given opportunity for knowledge ; the depths of Pharaoh's personality are concealed from us. *There is true and important knowledge to be gained, but it is in another direction.* The marvellous, exhaustless power of God is to be more prominent in our thoughts than the erratic and violent plunging of Pharaoh from one extreme to another. Amid all that is dark, densely dark, one thing is clear—and clear because God meant it to be clear, and took care to make it so—namely, that all this conduct of Pharaoh was the occasion for unmistakable and multiplied signs of the power of God. One is here reminded of the question of the disciples to Jesus (John ix. 2), "Who did sin, this man, or his parents, that he was born blind ?" To this question more answers than one were possible ; but Jesus gave the answer that was appropriate to the occasion. The man was born blind, that the works of God should be made manifest in him. So not only was Pharaoh's heart hardened, but God himself hardened that heart, in order that these signs might be shown before him. Then, in the second place, *these signs being wrought before Pharaoh, became also matters for consideration, recollection, and tradition to the Israelites themselves.* Moses, taken as the representative of Israel, is to tell to his son, and to his son's son, what things God had done in Egypt. Here is ample occasion given for the observant and devout in Israel to note the doings of Jehovah and communicate them with all earnestness and reverence from age to age. Surely it was worth a little waiting, a little temporal suffering, to have such chapters written as these which record Israel's experiences in Egypt ! What are the sufferings, *merely in body and in circumstances,* of one generation, compared with the ennobling thoughts of God, and the consequent inspiration and comfort which may through these very sufferings be transmitted to many generations following ! Why it is even a great privilege for one generation to be poor, that through its poverty many generations may become rich.

II. Consider how the terrible magnitude of the locust-plague is shown by the effects following on the announcement of it. 1. *There are the expostulations of Pharaoh's servants with him* (ver. 7). *They,* at all events, are not disposed to wait for the coming of the locusts. That the locust-plague was a very dreadful one, we may partly gather from other intimations in the Scriptures with respect to these voracious insects, advancing in their innumerable hosts (Deut. xxviii. 38, 42 ; 1 Kings viii. 37 ; 2 Chron. vii. 13 ; Joel i. 4 ; Nah. iii. 15). The experiences of modern travellers in the East are also such as to assure us that the expectation of a visit from the locust is enough to excite the most alarming thoughts (see in particular Dr. Thomson's observations on the locust in *The Land and the Book*). But in truth we hardly need to go beyond the conduct of Pharaoh's servants themselves. The very name locust was enough to startle them into precautionary activity ; they did not wait for the reality. Some of them, indeed, had anticipated the destructive effect of the hail, and taken suitable precautions ; but others felt there was room for question whether, after all, the hail would be so pernicious. In their presumption they guessed that a hailstorm could inflict only a slight and reparable damage. *But what could escape the locusts ?* Every green thing was well known to perish before their voracity. Even what might be called an ordinary visitation from them would be no trifle ; how much more such a visitation as Pharaoh's servants had now every reason to believe would come upon them ! For the time was long past when they doubted concerning the power of Moses to bring what he threatened. It is no longer a question of the power of Moses, but of the endurance of Egypt. In all likelihood the thought now prevailing in the minds of Pharaoh's servants—possibly in Pharaoh's own mind—was that this run of calamity would presently come to an end, if only it was patiently endured. For in ancient Egypt there was doubtless some such proverb as might be Englished into our common saying, "It is a long lane that has no turning." Egypt has known the long lane of seven plagues ; surely it cannot be much longer. And yet it may easily be long enough to destroy them before they get out of it. Locusts to come, when Moses speaks about them, may be reckoned as good as come, if something be not done promptly to avert their approach ; and once come, then how long will the food of Egypt remain, either for man or beast ! No wonder, then, that Pharaoh's servants turned upon him with such warm—one may almost say threatening—expostulations. The prospect of an immediate and almost instantaneous stoppage of supplies was enough to bring them hastening, as with one consent, to beg a timely submission from their master. 2. *There is the extraordinary yielding of Pharaoh to these expostulations.* Nothing less than extraordinary can it be called. His yieldings hitherto have been under actual chastisement. He has waited for the blow to be struck before he begged for mercy. But now, *upon the mere threatening* of the blow, he is moved to make overtures of submission. We shall have to notice of what a partial and worthless sort this submission was; at present, the main thing to mark is that there was a submission at all. He could not afford to trifle with the warnings of his servants. Hitherto, in all probability, they had been largely flatterers, men who fooled Pharaoh to the top of his bent with compliments as to his absolute power; but now they are turned into speakers of plain and bitter truth; and though Pharaoh may not like it, the very fact that he is thus addressed is enough to show him that he must arrange terms of surrender before another battle has even begun. Thus, by merely studying the conduct of Pharaoh and his servants before the locusts came, we see very clearly what a terrible plague they were. The plague of the locusts was a great deal more than a variation from the plagues of the frogs, the gnats and the flies.

III. Consider how, in spite of all the dread inspired by the thought of these locusts, PHARAOH'S PRIDE STILL HINDERS COMPLETE SUBMISSION. It was in an emergency of his government, and under pressure from his panic-stricken servants, that he consented to treat with Moses. Moses comes, and Pharaoh makes him an offer, which Moses of course cannot accept, seeing that he really has no power to treat; he has but the one unchangeable demand; it is a righteous demand, and therefore the righteous Jehovah cannot permit it to be diminished. But the rejection of Pharaoh's offer gives him a convenient loophole of escape into his former stubbornness. He can turn to his servants and say, " See what an unreasonable man this is. He comes expecting that in the terms of peace I am to yield all, and he is to yield nothing. Better to risk the locusts, and if need be, perish in the midst of our desolated fields, than live dishonoured by yielding up all Israel at his inexorable request." Speaking in some such spirit as this, we may well believe that Pharaoh stirred up his servants, and won them to support him in continuing his dogged resistance. It is a noble principle to die with honour rather than live with shame; it is the very principle that in its holiest illustration has crowded the ranks of Christian martyrdom. But when a principle of this sort gets into the mouth of a Pharaoh, he may so pervert it as to bring about the worst results. There is no manlier way of closing life than to die for truth and Christ; but it is a poor thing to become, as Pharaoh evidently would have his servants become, the victims of a degraded patriotism. It was all very well to talk loud and drive Moses and Aaron from his presence; but what was the good? the locusts were coming none the less. The fact is, that all suggestions of prudent and timely surrender were cast to the winds. The pride of the tyrant is touched, and it makes him blind to everything else. He rushes ahead, reckless of what may come on *the morrow,* if only he can gain the passionate satisfaction of driving Moses out of his presence *to-day.* There is no reasoning with a man in a passion; all arguments are alike to him.

IV. CONSIDER PHARAOH'S ULTIMATE SUBMISSION AND THE CONSEQUENCE OF IT. He drove Moses and Aaron out of his presence, but nevertheless he had to yield, and that in a peculiarly humiliating way. When he saw the locusts actually at work, then he came face to face with reality; and reality sobers a man. He had to send in haste for the men whom he had driven away, for the locusts were in haste. Every minute he delayed brought Egypt nearer and nearer to starvation. Oh, foolish Pharaoh! just for the pleasure, the sweet, momentary pleasure of driving Moses out of your presence, to risk the horrors of this ravaging host. Notice further, for it is a remarkable thing, that *while Pharaoh begs most humbly for mercy, he makes no formal promise of liberation.* The promise, we feel, was really there, all the more emphatic and more evidently unconditional, just because unspoken. Any way, the time had come when formal promises from Pharaoh mattered little, seeing they were never kept. The great thing was that he should be made to feel the pressure of God's hand upon him, so that he could not but cry to escape from it. Every time he thus cried and begged, as he here so piteously does—all his stubbornness for the time melted away into invisibility—he showed in the clearest manner the power of Jehovah. Jehovah's end, in this particular plague of the locusts, was gained when Pharaoh begged that they might be driven away —Y

Ver. 2.—*The tales of a grandfather.*—Jehovah tells Moses, as the representative of Israel, that these glorious Divine actions in Egypt are to be matters of careful instruction in after ages.   Each parent is to speak of them to his children, and each grandparent to his grandchildren.   And is there not something particularly suggestive in this expression, " thy son's son " ?   It brings before us the aged Israelite, his own part in the toil and strife of the world accomplished, his strength exhausted, the scene of his occupations left to a younger generation, and he himself quietly waiting for the close.   How is he to occupy his time ?   Not in utter idleness, for that is good for no man, however long and hard he may have worked.   Some part of his thoughts, it may be hoped, goes out in anticipations of the full and unmixed eternity now so near ; but some part also will go backward into time, not without pensive and painful interest.   He looks from the eminence he has attained, and two generations are behind him, his children and his children's children.   His own children are busy.   The world is with them constantly, and its demands are very pressing.   They hardly see their offspring from Monday morning till Saturday night.   It is only too easy for a man to get so absorbed in seeking the good of strangers, as to have no time for his own household.   The following extract from the biography of Wilberforce bears in a very instructive way on this point.   " It is said that his children seldom got a quiet minute with him during the sitting of Parliament.   So long as they were infants he had not time to seek amusement from them.   Even whilst they were of this age, it made a deep impression on his mind when, one of them beginning to cry as he took him up, the nurse said naturally, by way of explanation, ' He always is afraid of strangers.' " And if this danger of distance between him and his children came to a man like Wilberforce, we may be sure that it comes to thousands who are less sensitive and conscientious than he was.   What a field of usefulness, then, is here indicated for a grandfather !   In his retirement, and out of his long experience, he may speak of principles the soundness of which he has amply established, and errors which he has had painfully to correct ; he may point to a rich harvest gathered from good seed he has been able to sow.   Thus the grandfather finds opportunities for useful instruction which the father, alas !   may not even seek.   Of such it may be truly said, " They shall bring forth fruit in old age " (Ps. xcii. 14).   Notice here two points :—

I. It is well for the younger to look forward with concern to the occupations of a possible old age.   The very fact that life is uncertain dictates the prudence of a consideration like this.   Life may be shorter than we expect it to be, but it may also be longer.   We must not reckon on old age, but that is no reason why we should not prepare for it.   Boys and girls can hardly be expected to look so far ahead ; but those who have come to manhood and womanhood and some exercise of reflective power, may well ask the question, " How shall I occupy old age if it comes ? "   And surely it is much to remember that if each stage in life is occupied as it ought to be, then this very fidelity and carefulness will help to provide congenial occupation for the last stage of all.   Who would wish to spend the closing years of life in such stupor and lethargy as come over only too many, when there are sources of interest and usefulness such as Jehovah indicates to Moses here ?   Old age might be a brighter and more profitable scene than it usually is.   Who can tell, indeed, whether much of the physical prostration, pain, and sensitive decay, which belong to the aged and tend to shut them out from the world, might not be spared, if there were but a wiser life in earlier years, a life spent in obedience to the laws which God has given for life Many of the most important of these laws we either misunderstand or ignore altogether. Old age is a season into which we should not drift, but advance with a calm consideration of what we may be able to do in it, for the glory of God and the good of men.   *If we live to be old, what are our reminiscences to be ?*   You who are on the climbing side of life, ask yourselves what sort of life you are making, what chapters of autobiography you may hereafter be able to write.   Can anything be sadder than some autobiographies and reminiscences ?   There are such books, sad with expressed sadness, where the vanity of life is confessed and bewailed on every page.   But there are other books, far sadder even than the former sort, just because of the very satisfaction with life which they contain.   The men who have written them seem to look back in much the same spirit as once they looked forward.   They looked forward with all the eagerness and enjoying power of youth, and they look back without having discovered how selfish, frivolous and unworthy their lives have been. At eighty they are as well pleased with their notion that man has come into this world to enjoy himself as they were at eighteen. Whether we shall live into old age is not for us to settle, nor what our state of body and circumstances may be if we do so live. But one thing at all events we may seek to avoid, namely, a state of mind in old age such as that in which Wesley tells us he found a certain old man at Okehampton. "Our landlord here informed us that he was upwards of ninety, yet had not lost either his sight, hearing, or teeth. Nor had he found that for which he was born. Indeed he did not seem to have any more thought about it than a child of six years old."

II. Observe, concerning what things in particular God would have the old speak to the young. Not so much concerning what *they* have done, but concerning what *God has done for them.* Every old man, however foolish, blundering and wasted his own career may have been, has this resort—that he can look back on the dealings of God. It may be that he has to think of a late repentance on his own part; it may be that he has to think a great deal more of God's mercy to him after years of utter negligence, than God's help to him through years of struggling obedience. Even so, he can magnify God most abundantly and instructively. Magnifying God is the thing which all Christians should aim at when they look back on the time covered by their own individual life, or over that long, large tract through which authentic history extends. "Tell what things I have wrought in Egypt, and my signs which I have done among them." There will never be lack of voices to celebrate the achievements of men. But what a grand occupation for the aged Christian to turn the thoughts of children to the achievements of God, such works as the overthrow of Pharaoh and the guiding into Canaan, and, above all, the work which he does in the hearts of those who believe in his Son. To look on the works of men, on all their selfishness and rivalry, to see how the success of the few involves the failure of the many—all this is very humiliating. But how glorious to speak of the works of God, to point him out in Creation, in Providence, in Redemption; and then to call on the young, all their life through, to be fellow-labourers together with him—what an occupation is here suggested for old age! The "grey-headed and very aged men" (Job xv. 10) may thus do much for us. When Boaz became the nourisher of Naomi's grey hairs, Naomi took the child of Boaz and Ruth, laid it in her bosom, and became nurse unto it. And surely her nursing would include instruction, the telling of her own personal experiences to the growing Obed, full as these experiences were of things fitted to guide the youth to a good and noble manhood. A friend who called on C. M. Young, the celebrated actor, a few months before his death, reported that he gave a miserable account of himself, and wound up by saying, "Seventy-nine is telling its tale." True! Seventy-nine must tell a tale of exhausted physical energy, but the tale need not therefore be altogether doleful. Serious it must be, and not without touches of shame; but it will be the fault of the teller if it does not contain much to guide, inspire, and invigorate the young. (Job xxxii. 9; Ps. xxxvii. 25; Titus ii. 2—5; 1 Kings xii. 6—8).—Y.

Vers. 1—11.—*God's Judgments on sin and their results for the righteous and the wicked.* I. The fruits for God's people of his judgments upon his enemies. 1. The plagues of Egypt were to be an example to all the generations of Israel (ver. 2). (1) It drew them nearer God. They were his: he gave Egypt for them. (2) It deepened their trust and fear. 2. It was the prophecy of how God will sanctify his people in the latter days. 3. How God sanctifies his people now. Their prolonged waiting and suffering is storing up power for the future. The night of trial makes the day of deliverance brighter and more fruitful.

II. The way of the unrepentant is one of deepening loss. Pharaoh will not retain what God's mercy has left him. The locusts eat what the hail has spared. The path darkens evermore till the night falls to which no day succeeds.

III. God's judgments awaken fear in the hearts of the unrighteous, but no repentance. The advice of Pharaoh's counsellors. 1. Its selfishness. It was inspired not by love of righteousness, but by self interest. If it does not answer to enslave and persecute God's people; the world will desist; and if there is wealth and honour to be got by it, they will even favour them and desire to be numbered with them. 2. Its insufficiency. "Let the men go." They will not yield the whole of what God demands. They will not give up sin or resign the heart. The service of the selfish is as deficient in full obedience, as it is hateful in motive.

Vers. 12—20.—*The plague of locusts.* I. God's judgment. 1. Though restrained for a time, it will surely fall. It is no argument that the threatening is vain, because, while the servants of God try to persuade, there is no token of the coming judgment. 2. When it does come, it is not less than was foretold (14, 15). God's deed is his comment on his Word, and reveals the terror whose shadow lay in it. The flood was not less than Noah's warnings painted it, nor Jerusalem's judgment than the prophecies which predicted it. Nor shall the woes coming upon the nations, nor the end of sin, be less than God's Word has said.

II. Pharaoh's cry. It was sincere, both in confession and entreaty. He saw his folly, he desired relief, he purposed amendment. Good visits him, but it will not abide with him. The self-delusion of repentance born of the visitation of God and the need of heart-searching.

III. Pharaoh's heart hardened through deliverance. With the outward blessing we need inward grace. If we wait upon the Lord he will increase fear, and zeal, and tenderness of heart, but if we still keep far from him we are reserved only for heavier punishment. Instead of forsaking evil we shall build upon God's readiness to forgive, and repentance itself will become impossible through the soul's deep insincerity. Have *we* received no warnings which have been forgotten? Have we made no vows as yet unfulfilled? God's word says, "*Flee* from the wrath to come." Sin cries, "Tarry, there is no danger; wait for a more convenient season."—U.

EXPOSITION

Vers. 21—29—The Ninth Plague. The ninth plague, like the third and the sixth, was inflicted without special warning. God had announced, after the plague of boils, that he was about to "send all his plagues upon the heart" of the king; and so a succession of inflictions was to be expected. The ninth plague probably followed the eighth after a very short interval. It is rightly regarded as an aggravation of a well-known natural phenomenon — the Khamsîn, or "Wind of the Desert," which commonly visits Egypt about the time of the vernal equinox, and is accompanied by an awful and weird darkness. This is caused by the dense clouds of fine sand which the wind brings with it, which intercept the sun's light, and produce a darkness beyond that of our worst fogs, and compared by some travellers to "the most gloomy night." The wind is depressing and annoying to an extreme degree. "While it lasts no man rises from his place; men and beasts hide themselves; the inhabitants of towns and villages shut themselves up in their houses, in underground apartments, or vaults." It usually blows for a space of two, or at most three, days, and sometimes with great violence, though more often with only moderate force. The visitation here recorded was peculiar, 1. In its extent, covering as it did "all the land of Egypt;" 2. In its intensity—"they saw not one another" (ver. 23)—"darkness which may be felt" (ver. 21); 3. In its circumscription, extending, as it did, to all Egypt except only the land of Goshen (ver. 23). These circumstances made Pharaoh at once recognise its heaven-sent character, and request its removal of Moses, whom he sought to persuade by conceding the departure of the Israelites with their families. He marred, however, the whole grace of this concession by a proviso that they should leave behind them their flocks and herds, viewing these as, equally with their families, a security for their return. Moses therefore indignantly rejected his offer—the flocks and the herds should go with them— he would not have a hoof left behind—they did not know what sacrifices would be required at the feast which they were about to keep, or how many (ver. 25, 26)—therefore they must take all. Pharaoh, greatly angered, forthwith broke up the conference (ver. 28), but not, as it would seem, before Moses, equally displeased, had announced the tenth plague, and the results which would follow it (ch. xi. 4—8).

Ver. 21.—**Darkness which may be felt.** Literally, " and one shall feel, or grasp, darkness." The hyperbole is no doubt extreme; but the general sentiment of mankind has approved the phrase, which exactly expresses what men feel in absolute and complete darkness. Kalisch renders, " a darkness in which men grope." But the grammatical construction does not allow of this.

Ver. 22.—**A thick darkness.**— Literally, " An obscurity of darkness." The phrase is intensitive.

Ver. 23.—**They saw not one another.** Or, " Man did not see his brother." The descriptive phrases previously used are poetic, and might imply many different degrees of obscurity. This seems distinctly to shew that pitch darkness is meant. Such absolute obscurity is far beyond anything which the khamsîn produces, even when it is most severe, and indicates the miraculous character of the visitation. **Neither rose any from his place for three days.** It is not meant that no one moved about his house, but that no one quitted it. (Compare ch. xvi. 29, where the phrase used is similar.) No one went out into the unnatural darkness out of doors, which he dreaded. All stayed at home, and did what they had to do by the artificial light of lamps or torches. **All the children of Israel had light in their dwellings.** It is not explained how this was effected. Some suppose that the sand-storm did not extend to the land of Goshen. But in that case, such Egyptians as lived among the Israelites—their neighbours (ch. xi. 2)—would have shared the benefit, which seems not to have been the case. I should rather suppose that the storm was general, and that the Israelites were supplied with a light, not that of the sun, by miracle.

Ver. 24.—**Only let your flocks and your herds be stayed.** The pitch darkness is more than Pharaoh can bear. On the third day of its duration probably, he sends a messenger who succeeds in finding Moses, and conducting him to the monarch's presence. He has made up his mind to yield another point—that on which he insisted so strongly at the last interview (vers. 10, 11)—he will let the Israelites go *with their families*—only, their flocks and herds must remain behind. This will be, he considers, a sufficient security for their return; since without cattle they would be unable to support life for many days in the wilderness. **Your little ones.** Rather, " your families."

Ver. 25, 26.—Moses absolutely refuses the suggested compromise. He had already declared on a former occasion, " With our young and with our old we will go; with our sons and with our daughters, *with our flocks and with our herds* we will go" (ver. 9). He is not inclined to retract now, after two additional plagues, what he had demanded before them. He does not refuse, however, to set forth his reasons. The cattle must go because the feast which they are about to keep requires sacrifices — they must *all* go, because the Israelites do not as yet know what animals, or how many of each, will be required of them. The feast was a new thing, without precedent; its ritual was not yet laid down. No exact directions were to be expected, until the place was reached where God intended that it should be celebrated.

Ver. 27.—**Hardened.** — Again the strong expression, *yekhazak*, is used, as in ver. 20.

Ver. 28.—**And Pharaoh said,** etc. The reply of Pharaoh indicates violent anger. No doubt he thought that now the intention of Moses to deprive him altogether of the services of so many hundred thousand slaves was palpable, and scarcely concealed. Greatly enraged, he gives vent to his rage, with the want of self-control common among Oriental monarchs—rudely bids Moses be gone (**Get thee from me**), threatens him (**take heed to thyself**), and bids hims never more seek his presence, under the penalty of instant death, if he makes his appearance. Considering the degree of civilization, refinement, and politeness to which the Egyptians had attained under the eighteenth and nineteenth dynasties, such an outbreak must be regarded as abnormal, and as implying violent excitement.

Ver. 29.—**And Moses said,** etc. The reply of Moses, so far, is simple and dignified. **Thou hast spoken well,** he says—"thou hast made a right decision—further interviews between me and thee are useless, can lead to no result, only waste time. This shall be our last interview—**I will see thy face no more.**" It is generally agreed however that Moses did not quit the presence with these words; but continued to address Pharaoh for some little time, making his parting speech in the terms which are recorded in vers. 4—8 of the next chapter. Having announced the Tenth Plague, the coming destruction of the first-born, he turned and "went out from Pharaoh in a great anger" (ch. xi. 8).

HOMILETICS.

Vers. 21—23.—*The children of darkness have darkness, and the children of light have light as their portion.* From the beginning of the creation God " divided the light from the darkness " (Gen. i. 4); and ever since the two have been antagonistic the one to the other. Angels as well as men are divided into two classes—bright and glorious spirits, that dwell in the light of God's presence, and are called " angels of light " (2 Cor. xi. 14);

and gloomy spirits of evil, whom God has reserved in everlasting chains under darkness for final judgment (Jude 6). So Scripture speaks of man as divided into those who are "of the night and of darkness," and those who are "children of light and of the day" (1 Thess. v. 5).

I. THE CHILDREN OF DARKNESS, THOSE WHO LOVE DARKNESS RATHER THAN LIGHT, HAVE DARKNESS ASSIGNED TO THEM. 1. *Spiritual darkness.* "Because they do not like to retain God in their knowledge, God gives them over to a reprobate mind" (Rom. i. 28). Their "foolish heart is darkened" (*ib.* ver. 21). They grow continually more blind and more ignorant, more incapable of seeing and understanding the things of the Spirit, since these are "spiritually discerned." Their senses not being "exercised by reason of use to discern both good and evil," they lose the power of discernment, and "put bitter for sweet, and sweet for bitter." "The light that is within them"—*i. e.*, the conscience —having "become darkness, how great is that darkness"! 2. *Mental darkness.* They "grope as the blind in darkness" (Deut. xxviii. 29). They have no clue to the real nature of the universe of which they are a part, or of the world in which they live. They are mentally sightless, unable to perceive the force of arguments and evidences which would convince any one whose mental vision God had not judicially blinded. They sometimes in these days call themselves "Agnostics," implying thereby that they know nothing, see nothing, have no convictions. Not unfrequently they allow themselves to be imposed upon by the most gross illusions, giving that faith to the ravings of Spiritualists which they refuse to the Word of God. Or they accept as certain truth the unverified speculations and hypotheses of so-called scientific men, and consider Revelation to be overruled and set aside by the guesses of a few physiologists. 3. Ultimately, as it would seem, they receive as their portion, *physical darkness.* "Cast ye the unprofitable servant into outer darkness" (Matt. xxv. 30). "The children of the kingdom shall be cast into outer darkness" (*ib.* viii. 12). "Woe unto them! for they have gone in the way of Cain. . . . . to whom is reserved the blackness of darkness for ever" (Jude 13).

II. THE CHILDREN OF LIGHT, THOSE WHO LOVE LIGHT, HAVE LIGHT FOR THEIR PORTION. "Awake, thou that sleepest, and arise from the dead, and Christ shall give thee light." Christ gives his followers, 1. *Spiritual light.* "The commandment is a lamp, the law is light" (Prov. vi. 23). "By doing the will of God, men come to know of the doctrine, whether it is of God" (John vii. 17). Their spiritual discernment is continually increased. Whatever the amount of spiritual darkness around them—in the midst of the clouds of Deism, Pantheism, Agnosticism, scientific materialism, and Atheism, they "have light in their dwellings." Theirs is the true enlightenment. The Lord their God enlightens their darkness (Ps. xviii. 28); opens the eyes of their understanding (Eph. i. 18); fills them with knowledge of his will in all wisdom and spiritual understanding (Col. i. 9). 2. *Mental light.* The true Christian "has a right judgment in all things." God gives to those who are his "the spirit of a sound mind" (2 Tim. i. 7). Not that Christians are always clever—they may be slow, dull, devoid of all quickness or mental brightness. But they will be soberminded, not easily misled; they will see through sophisms, even if they cannot expose them; they will not be imposed upon by charlatans or *soi-disant* "philosophers." They will "try the spirits" that seek to lead them astray, and not very often be deceived by them. 3. *A final reward of heavenly, ineffable, soul-satisfying light.* After the resurrection of the dead, "they that be wise shall shine as the brightness of the firmament" (Dan. xii. 3). They shall dwell where there is light, and "no darkness at all." "The nations of them which are saved shall walk in the light" of that city which shall have "no need of the sun, neither of the moon to shine in it; for the glory of God will lighten it, and the Lamb is the light thereof" (Rev. xxi. 23, 24). "There shall be no night there; and they need no candle, neither light of the sun, for the Lord God giveth them light, and they shall reign for ever and ever" (*ib.* xxii. 5).

Vers. 24—26.—*Compromise the favourite resort of the worldly-minded, the abomination of the spiritually-minded.* Pharaoh had tried compromise more than once and failed (ch. viii. 25—28; x. 8—11); but he must needs try it again. This marks the tenacity with which the worldly-minded cling to what they think the height of policy, but what is, in reality, a weak and unworthy subterfuge. Pharaoh did not wish to grant any part of the request of Moses; but, if he must yield to some extent, he would save his dignity and his interest, he thought, by yielding less than what was demanded. On four occasions he makes four different offers.

I. THEY MAY WORSHIP GOD WHEREVER THEY PLEASE WITHIN THE LIMITS OF EGYPT (ch. viii. 25). A foolish offer, which, if accepted, would certainly have led to a riot and possibly to a civil war (ib. 26). But Pharaoh had only thought of his own dignity, not of the consequences. So civil rulers frequently ask the Church of Christ to concede this or that for the honour of the State, when the concession would do the State the greatest possible injury. In their short-sightedness they do not see that in striking at the Church they will wound themselves. In their zeal for their own honour, they do not care how much the Church, or even how much the State suffers.

II. THEY MAY WORSHIP GOD IN THE WILDERNESS, ONLY THEY MUST NOT GO VERY FAR AWAY (ch. viii. 28). This offer was an improvement; it did not require a plain violation of the express command of God. But it was insidious. It was made with the view of compelling a return. Pharaoh suspected from the first that the message, "Let my people go," meant "let them go altogether." This, until stunned by the dread infliction of the last plague, he was fully resolved not to do. He would let them go as a cat lets a mouse go, so far but not further—not out of his reach. So kings will give their people liberty, or the Church liberty, but only within narrow limits—in seeming rather than in reality—to such an extent as will not interfere with their being the real master, and re-asserting their absolute power at their pleasure. Once more Pharaoh was short-sighted. Had his offer been accepted, and had he then attempted to compel a return, he would only have precipitated some such catastrophe as befel his army at the Red Sea.

III. THEY MAY GO THE THREE DAYS' JOURNEY INTO THE WILDERNESS, ONLY THEY MUST LEAVE THEIR FAMILIES BEHIND (ch. x. 8—11). The rejection of his first and second offers left Pharaoh no choice but to allow of the Israelites departing beyond his reach. So he devises a compromise, by which he thinks to lure them back. They shall leave their families behind. But God had said, "Let my people go," and children are as essential an element in the composition of a nation as either women or men. This offer was therefore more contrary to the Divine message which he had received than his second one. Worldly-minded men will frequently, while pretending to offer a better compromise, offer a worse; and, both in private and public dealings, it behoves prudent persons to be on their guard, and not imagine that every fresh bid that is made must be an advance. The law of auction does not hold good either in private or in parliamentary bargaining.

IV. THEY MAY GO THE THREE DAYS' JOURNEY INTO THE WILDERNESS, AND TAKE THEIR FAMILIES, IF THEY WILL ONLY LEAVE THEIR CATTLE BEHIND (ch. x. 24). This was the most crafty suggestion of all. The cattle had not been mentioned in the Divine message, nor could it be said that they were part of the nation. The king could require the detention of the cattle without infringing the letter of the Divine command. But he secured the return of the nation to Egypt as certainly by this plan as by the retention of the families. A nomadic people could not subsist for many weeks—scarcely for many days, without its flocks and herds. The Israelites would have been starved into surrender. Moses, however, without taking this objection, was able to point out that the terms of the message, rightly weighed with reference to all the circumstances, embraced the cattle, since sacrifice was spoken of, unaccompanied by any limitation. Once more, therefore, he was enabled to decline the compromise suggested as an infraction of the command which he had received, when its terms were rightly understood. Worldly men are continually placing their own construction on the words of God's messages, and saying that this or that should be given up as not plainly contained in them. The example of Moses justifies Christians in scanning narrowly the whole bearing and intention of each message, and insisting on what it implies as much as upon what it expresses. True wisdom will teach them not to be driven to a compromise by worldly men's explanations of the Divine Word. They will study it for themselves, and guide their conduct by their own reading (under God's guidance) of the commands given them. Further, the example of Moses in rejecting all the four offers of Pharaoh, may teach us to suspect, misdoubt, and carefully examine every proposed compromise; the essence of compromise in religion being the surrender of something Divinely ordered or instituted for the sake of some supposed temporal convenience or advantage. It can really never be right to give up the smallest fragment of revealed truth, or to allow the infraction of the least of God's commandments for even the greatest conceivable amount of temporal benefit either to ourselves or others.

Ver. 25.—*Bad men, when unable to overcome good men's scruples, throw off the mask of friendliness, and show themselves in their true colours.* The circumstances of human life are continually bringing good men and bad men into contact and intercourse. Three results may follow :—1. *The bad may corrupt the good.* This is the result too often. "Evil communications corrupt good manners." Few can touch pitch and not be defiled. 2. *The good may convert the bad.* The first Christians converted a world that lay in wickedness. Esther softened the heart of Ahasuerus. St. Ambrose, by long withstanding his will, converted Theodosius. 3. *Neither may make any impression upon the other.* In this case, while the good man merely regrets his inability to turn the bad man to righteousness, the bad man, baffled in his attempts to overcome the scruples of the good man and lead him astray, is apt to be greatly provoked, and to threaten, or even proceed to violence. "Take heed to thyself—in the day thou seest my face thou shalt die." What a spring of bitterness wells up from the evil heart of the sinner who feels himself opposed successfully, thwarted in his schemes, and baffled! While he still hopes to succeed all is smooth speaking. "I have sinned." "Forgive my sin this once only." "Go ye, serve the Lord." When he finds that he cannot prevail, there is a sudden and complete change. Benefits are forgotten; friendliness is a thing of the past; even the prescribed forms of politeness are set aside. The wild beast that lies hid in each unregenerate man shows itself, and the friendly acquaintance of months or years is ready to tear his opposer to pieces.

HOMILIES BY VARIOUS AUTHORS.

Vers. 21—29.—*The plague of darkness.* This was the third of the great plagues, and it came, as in certain previous instances, unannounced.

I. THE LAST OF THE ADMONITORY PLAGUES (vers. 21—24). The plagues, viewed as trials of Pharaoh's character, end with this one. The death of the first-born was a judgment, and gave Pharaoh no further space for repentance. We may view this last of the nine plagues: 1. As *awful in itself.* Whatever its natural basis, the *preter-natural* intensity of the darkness now brought upon the land told plainly enough that it was one of the wonders of Jehovah. For three whole days no one human being in Egypt saw another, even artificial light, it would appear, failing them in their necessity. The fearfulness of the plague was heightened to those stricken by it by the fact that the Israelites "had light in their dwellings"; also by the fact that the sun in his different phases was the chief object of their worship. When one reflects on the terrors which accompany darkness in any case ; on the singular effect it has in working on the imagination, and in intensifying its alarms, it will be felt how truly this was a plague laid upon the *heart* (ch. ix. 14). Darkness suddenly descending on a land invariably awakens superstitious fears, fills multitudes with forebodings of calamity, creates apprehensions of the near approach of the day of judgment; what, then, would be the effect on the Egyptians when they "saw their crystal atmosphere and resplendent heavens suddenly compelled to wear an aspect of indescribable terror and appalling gloom"? We may gather how great was the distress from the fact of the king being compelled, after all that had happened, again to send for Moses (ver. 24). 2. As *symbolic of a spiritual condition.* Egypt was enveloped in the wrath of God. The stroke of that wrath, which might have been averted by timely repentance, was about to descend in the destruction of the first-born. Darkness was in the king's soul. The darkness of doom was weaving itself around his fortunes. Of all this, surely the physical darkness, which, like a dread funeral pall, descended on the land, must be taken as a symbol. When Christ, the sin-bearer, hung on Calvary, a great darkness, in like manner, covered the whole land (Matt. xxvii. 45). The darkness without was but the symbol of a deeper darkness in which Christ's spirit was enveloped. The sinner's condition is one of darkness altogether. He is dark spiritually (2 Cor. iv. 4, 6). He is dark, as under the wrath of God (Eph. ii. 3). God's people are "children of light," but the transgressor's soul is buried in deadliest gloom (Eph. v. 8). The place of woe is described as "the outer darkness" (Matt. xxv. 30).

II. PHARAOH'S LAST ATTEMPT (vers. 24—27). 1. It was *made under dire compulsion.* The darkness had shaken his heart to its foundations. It is noteworthy that *each* of these three last plagues extorted from him a full or partial consent. The lesser plagues, severe though they were, had not had this effect. He could hold out under two, and in one case under three of them. 2. It was, like the former, *an attempt at compromise.* He would let the "little ones" go, but the flocks and herds were to be left; an absurd prohibition, when the object was to sacrifice. It is made painfully evident that Pharaoh's judgment has left him; that he has become absolutely reckless; that he is no longer his own master; that he is being driven by his passions in opposition to all right reason and prudence; that the end, accordingly, is very near. 3. It *testifies to his increasing hardness.* (1) There is on this occasion no confession of sin. (2) Neither does Pharaoh concede the whole demand. (3) He ends the scene with violence, ordering Moses never to appear again before him, under penalty of death.

III. PHARAOH'S REPROBATION (ver. 29). Moses took Pharaoh at his word. "Thou hast spoken well; I will see thy face no more." God's work with this great, bad man was ended, save as the judgment for which he had prepared himself was now to be inflicted upon him. He had not been given up till every conceivable means had been exhausted to bring him to repentance. He had been tried with reason and with threatening; with gentleness and with severity; with mercy and with judgments. He had been reproved, expostulated with, warned, and frequently chastised. His prayers for respite had in every case been heard. He had been trusted in his promises to let Israel go, and when he had broken them was still forborne with and trusted again. Plagues of every kind had been sent upon him. He had suffered incalculable loss, had endured sore bodily pain, had been shaken in his soul with supernatural terrors. His first plea, of ignorance, and his second, of want of evidence, had been completely shattered. He had been made to confess that he had sinned, and that Jehovah was righteous. Yet under all and through all he had gone on hardening himself, till, finally, even God could wring no confession of sin from him, and his mind had become utterly fatuous, and regardless of consequences. What more was to be done with Pharaoh? Even that which must be done with ourselves under like circumstances—he was rejected, reprobated, given over to destruction. "Cut it down; why cumbereth it the ground?" (Luke xiii. 7). It was the same fate which overtook Israel when the nation became finally corrupt and hardened.—J. O.

Vers. 20—29.—*The Ninth Plague—the darkness.* I. CONSIDER THE PLAGUE ITSELF. As with the plagues of the gnats and of the boils and blains, so with this plague— there is no record of any formal intimation of its coming. If such an intimation was absent, we feel that there was good reason for the absence. Though Pharaoh had abased himself in great fear and consternation, so that he might get rid of the locusts, yet the moment they were gone all his stubbornness returned in full force. What use was it, then, any longer to hold threatenings over a man of this sort? Indeed, the proper way of considering this ninth plague seems to be to regard it chiefly as a stepping-stone to the last and decisive visitation. An announcement beforehand would not have been wanting, if at all likely to make any serious difference in Pharaoh's conduct. With respect to the plague itself, four points are noticeable—the kind of it, the degree, the duration, and the customary exemption of the Israelites. 1. *The kind of it.* It was a plague of darkness. God is light, and in him is no darkness at all. He is light, and light continually streams forth from him; and without him the minds of men are in dense darkness as to all that is best in knowledge and most substantial in hope for the time to come. When we consider how much is said about spiritual light and spiritual darkness in the Scriptures, it will be seen how appropriate it was that before Jehovah closed his earthly dealings with Pharaoh he should bring his land under this impenetrable cloud. It was a fitting scourge to come upon a king and people whose minds were so darkened to the perception of God. The light and truth which break forth from God vainly struggled to shine through into Pharaoh's heart. This plague was a sort of approach to the primal chaos, a movement towards dissolving the cosmos into the formless, unillumined mass from which it sprang. God's first great Word in making order was to say, " Let there be light "; now we almost imagine a corresponding word, " Let there be darkness." The sun, though it may pass over Egypt as usual, no longer rules the day; not a ray penetrates to accommodate and cheer the bewildered land. 2. *The degree of this darkness.* Jehovah tells Moses it will be a darkness which may be felt. Not that it was literally palpable, but rather that the darkness was so dense, so utterly beyond all experience, that it could not possibly be described by language taken from the use of the sense of vision. It was not enough to say, as with respect to the hail and the locusts, that there had been no such experience in Egypt since it became a nation. A new sort of darkness required a new mode of expression to indicate it; and thus by a bold figure the darkness is introduced as affecting not only the usual sense of sight, but the sense of touch as well. The privation of light was in the highest conceivable degree. And here it is surely well to dismiss from our minds all attempts, however well intended, to find a natural basis for this plague. That Jehovah might have made a darkness, and a very terrible one, by increasing and intensifying natural elements and causes is quite true; but somehow, such a view of this plague does not satisfy the demands of the strong terms which are used. Far better is it to suppose that in some mysterious way light lost its radiating power when it came into the Egyptian atmosphere. Doubtless even artificial lights proved useless. If the sun could not pierce into Egypt, little lamps and earth-lights were not likely to succeed. 3. *The duration of it.* It lasted for three days. In this duration lay its peculiar severity. Even a darkness that might be felt would not be much if it was a momentary visitation. But when it extended for three days, disarranging and paralyzing all work, then the magnitude of the visitation would fully appear. It was indeed a plague more terrible in reality than in threatening, and in continuance than in its first embrace. In itself it was not a painful thing; it did not irritate like the frogs, the gnats, and the flies; it did not destroy like the murrain, the hail, and the locusts. It simply settled down on the land, and while it lasted made one of the most informing and gladdening of the senses utterly useless. Even those who loved the darkness because their deeds were evil, would feel, after three days of it, that they were having too much of a good thing. It was just the kind of plague that by the very continuance of it would grow in horror, and at last precipitate a panic. Darkness is the time favourable to all terrifying imaginations. 4. *The exemption of the Israelites.* The district where they dwelt had light *in their dwellings.* Here was, indeed, a more impressive and significant separation than any Jehovah had yet made; and that he should thus separate between Israel and Egypt, as between light and the deepest darkness, was a thing to be expected, considering how soon the Israelites were to go out of the land altogether.

II. Consider the consequent proposition by Pharaoh and the reception of it by Moses. After three days of the darkness that might be felt, Pharaoh is again brought to his knees, suing for mercy, and, as usual, he offers something which formerly he had refused. Only a little while ago he had set his face against liberating *the little ones* of Israel. Now he has got so far as to say *all the people may depart*—all the human beings—but the flocks and herds must stay behind; and these, of course, were the very substance of Israel's wealth (Gen. xlvi. 31; xlvii. 6). And not only so, but at present they would look all the more considerable in comparison with the murrain-swept flocks and herds of Egypt. If Pharaoh can only get this request, he thinks he will both serve his dignity and do something to retrieve his fortunes. What a difference between this last interview with Moses and the first! Pharaoh, who began with refusing to yield anything, nay, who by way of answer made the existing bondage even more oppressive, is now, after a course of nine plagues, willing to yield everything—everything *but the property of Israel.* This, indeed, has been a great way to bring him, but it has all been done by a kind of main force. Pharaoh's ignorance of Jehovah's character and demands remains unabated, amid all his experience of Jehovah's power. He cannot yet understand that Jehovah is not to be bargained with. He wants the flocks and herds, as if it were a small matter to keep them back, whereas just one reason why the flocks and herds are so abundant is that there may be enough for sacrifice. Jehovah had a use and place for every Israelite, the oldest and the youngest, and all their belongings. It was an answer of Moses, profoundly suitable to the occasion, when he said, " We know not with what we must serve the Lord, until we come thither." He had been sent to Pharaoh to demand all, and he could take nothing less. Interesting questions arise here, but there is no information by which we can answer them. Pharaoh called to Moses (ver. 24)—but how came they together in this dense darkness ? or was it that Moses waited there in the darkness these three days ? Then when Pharaoh spoke, did the darkness at once begin to pass away ? We must almost assume that it did, the purpose of its coming having been served the moment Pharaoh is got another step onward in his yielding. But on all these points we have no direct information. Jehovah now hastens the readers of the narrative to the final catastrophe. Where we, in our curiosity, desire particulars, he omits, in order that he may be particular and exact in matters of abiding importance. He is presently to speak of the Passover with great minuteness. Details of future and continuous duty are of more moment than mere picturesque embellishments of a passing judgment on Egypt. Thus we are left to infer that the darkness had vanished when for the last time Pharaoh refused to let Israel go. And it must be admitted that there was everything in the inflexible answer of Moses to make Pharaoh, *being such a man as he was*, equally inflexible. " There shall not a hoof be left behind." Israel moves altogether, if it moves at all. This was a very exasperating way for a despot to be spoken to, especially one who felt that he had yielded so much. Indeed, it must have been very astonishing to him to reflect how far he had gone in a path where once it would have seemed ridiculous to suppose that he could take a single step. But now once again he says— in the same reasonless, passionate way that has marked him all along—" Not a step further." After nine plagues he is still the same man at heart. The slightest provocation, and his pride is all aflame, more sensitive than gunpowder to the spark. Nay, most marvellous of all, from the depth of nine successive humiliations he begins to threaten Moses with death. Surely this was the very quintessence of passion and blind rage. The only parallel we can find for it is in the furious, final rush of some great, savage brute, maddened by the shots of the hunter, and making recklessly towards him. What gains he by this advance ? He simply comes within easy reach, and another shot from the same weapon, held with perfect coolness and control, lays him dead in the dust. The saddest part of the reflection on Pharaoh's career is, that it gives the essence of so many human lives beside. The hand with which God would clear our corruption away—were we only willing for it to be cleared—stirs it up into a more self-destroying energy and efficacy, if we in our perversity and ignorance determine that the corruption should remain.—Y.

Ver. 21.—A darkness which might be felt suggests the existence of a darkness which is not felt. Consider :—

I. THE UNFELT DARKNESS. [*Illustration.* Stream in summer on sunny day reflects sun, sky, &c. Contrast with condition in winter, hard, dull, icebound ; it has *hardened* and no longer *reflects*. If it could be conscious, still flowing on, it might not *feel* much difference, scarcely aware of the strange casing shutting it out from warmth and beauty.] Pharaoh and his people, like the stream, once had light (cf. John i. 9 ; Rom. i. 19, 20). Then " hardened their hearts." So self-conditioned them that beneath God's influence they could not but harden (x. 1). The hard heart, like the hard ice-coating, shuts out the light and ensures darkness (Rom. i. 21), none the less such darkness not felt (cf. Eph. iv. 17, 18). A terrible judgment, moral darkness, usually resulting from a man's own fault ; little by little it grows and deepens until it shuts out not merely light, but even the memory of vanished light (cf. John ix. 39—41). The immediate precursor of ruin, that " quenching of the Spirit," which paves the way for " blasphemy."

II. THE DARKNESS THAT WAS FELT. Pharaoh would not recognise Jehovah. He shut out the light from him and gloried in his moral darkness. Again and again did Jehovah flash home the truth of his existence to hearts which seemed almost judgment proof. Each new judgment was but followed by deeper darkness, the crack through which light seemed to pierce being deliberately blocked up when the fright was over. Self-chosen moral darkness is met by God-sent physical darkness ; the darkness of the tempest, the darkness of the locust clouds, lastly, the concentrated darkness of this ninth plague. Through all, the object is to pierce and, if it may be, dispel the moral darkness; a kind of homœopathic treatment, which, if it do not cure, *may* kill. [*Illustration.* The frozen stream. Light fire upon the surface. Clouds and flame shut out the sunlight more than ever, yet heat *may* melt the ice covering, and, if so, then light can enter. If not, when fire is extinguished, the ash-strewn surface more impervious to light than ever.] Pharaoh at first seemed to be thawing (x. 24), but he only felt the *heat*, he did not recognise the *light*. When the heat passed, darker than ever (27—29). The last chance gone, what left? (Jude 13). God still meets this self-chosen moral darkness by similar methods. Judgments which may be felt flash momentary light upon the self-inflicted darkness which is not felt. He *wills* that all men should come to repentance ; if we shut our hearts to the inner voice, he summons us by outer voices, which cannot but attract attention. They *may*, however, be disregarded ; the power of man's self-will in this world seems strong enough to resist anything.

III. LIGHT IN THE DWELLINGS. 1. *Physical.* Egyptians had made a difference between themselves and Israel, a difference which had driven Israel to seek help from God. Now God confirms that difference. The light, perhaps, not perfect. [If darkness caused by sand-storm from S.W. may have been such light as was obtainable at the fringe of the storm cloud.] Still it was sufficient, a sign of God's care and watchfulness for those who were prepared to receive and recognise it. And this the Israelites were prepared to do, for the light in the dwelling was the type of light in the heart. 2. *Moral.* They had been " in darkness," the darkness of slavery and idolatry (cf. Josh. xxiv. 14); but the light had dawned upon them, and, however imperfectly, they had recognised and welcomed it. The cry in the darkness (Ps. cxxx. 6) had been heard and answered. By God's help the inner light had been quickened and fostered ; and to those who have the inner light, however feeble, he gives help that it may grow brighter. He will not quench the smoking flax, but fan it to a flame (cf. Ps. xviii. 27—28).

Application. There is one who is the Light of the World. The great thing for us is to walk in the light (1 John i. 5—7). If we do not, darkness can but deepen till the night come (John ix. 4; cf. Job xviii. 18). Yet even those in darkness of their own making, God, in his love, still tries to lighten (cf. his dealings with the Egyptians ; also our Lord's with the Jews, John ix. 39). If the light is still resisted, then cf. Matt. xxv. 30. If we do walk in the light so far as we know it, then cf. Prov. iv. 18. Even when dark for others, still light for us, Is. lx. 1, 2 ; and if the darkness does, as it sometimes will, overshadow us, even so Ps. cxii. 4 ; Is. l. 10.—G.

EXPOSITION.

CHAPTER XI.

Vers. 1—3.—We have here a parenthetic statement of something that had previously happened. Before Moses was summoned to appear in the presence of Pharaoh as related in ch. x. 24, it had been expressly revealed to him by God, 1. That one more plague, and one only, was impending ; 2. That this infliction would be effectual, and be followed by the departure of the Israelites ; and, 3. That instead of reluctantly allowing them to withdraw from his kingdom, the monarch would be eager for their departure and would actually hasten it. He had also been told that the time was now come when the promise made to him in Mount Horeb, that his people should " spoil the Egyptians " (ch. iii. 22), would receive its accomplishment. The Israelites, before departing, were to ask their Egyptian neighbours for any articles of gold and silver that they possessed, and would receive them (ver. 2). The reasons for this extraordinary generosity on the part of the Egyptians are then mentioned, in prolongation of the parenthesis. 1. God " gave the people favour in the sight of the Egyptians"; and 2. The circumstances of the time had exalted Moses, and made him be looked upon as " very great " (ver. 3), so that there was a general inclination to carry out his wishes.

Ver. 1.—**And the Lord spake unto Moses.** Rather, " Now the Lord had said unto Moses." The Hebrew has no form for the pluperfect tense, and is consequently obliged to make up for the grammatical deficiency by using the simple preterite in a pluperfect sense. We cannot definitely fix the time when Moses had received this revelation ; but the expression, **one plague more,** shows that it was after the commencement of the " **plague of darkness.**"

When he shall let you go, he shall surely thrust you out altogether. The Hebrew will not bear this rendering. It runs distinctly thus—"When he shall let you go altogether, he will assuredly thrust you out hence." As Canon Cook notes, "the meaning is—when at last he lets you depart, with children, flocks, herds, and all your possessions, he will compel you to depart in haste" (*Speaker's Commentary*, vol. i. p. 290). It has been well noticed by the same writer that both this announcement, and the previous relentings of Pharaoh, would have caused Moses to have preparations made, and to hold the Israelites in readiness for a start upon their journey almost at any moment. No doubt a most careful and elaborate organization of the people must have been necessary; but there had been abundant time for such arrangements during the twelvemonth that had elapsed since the return of Moses from Midian.

Ver. 2.—**Every man . . . every woman.** In ch. iii. 22 only women had been mentioned. Now the terms of the direction were enlarged. It is worthy of notice that gold and silver ornaments—ear-rings, collars, armlets, bracelets, and anklets, were worn almost as much by the Egyptian men of the Rameside period as by the women. **Borrow.** On this faulty translation, see the comment on ch. iii. 22. **Jewels.** Literally, "articles." The word is one of a very wide meaning, and might include drinking-cups and other vessels; but from the statement in ch. iii. 22, that they

were to "put them on their sons and on their daughters," it is clear that personal ornaments are especially meant.

Ver. 3.—**And the Lord gave the people favour**—*i.e.* When the time came. See below, ch. xii. 36. **Moreover the man Moses**, etc. It has been supposed that this is an interpolation, and argued that Moses, being so "meek" as he was (Num. xii. 3), would not have spoken of himself in the terms here used. But **very great** here only means "very influential;" and the fact is stated, not to glorify Moses, but to account for the ornaments being so generally given. Moreover, it is highly improbable that any other writer than himself would have so baldly and bluntly designated Moses as **the man Moses**. (Compare Deut. xxxiii. 1; xxxiv. 5; Josh. i. 1, 13, 15; xiv. 6, 7; xxii. 2, 4; etc.) The "greatness" which Moses had now attained was due to the powers which he had shown. First of all, he had confounded the magicians (ch. viii. 18, 19); then he had so far impressed the courtiers that a number of them took advantage of one of his warnings and thereby saved their cattle and slaves (ch. ix. 20). Finally, he had forced the entire Court to acknowledge that it lay in his power to destroy or save Egypt (ch. x. 7). He had after that parleyed with the king very much as an equal (*ib.* 8—11; 16 –18). It is no wonder that the Egyptians, who regarded their king as a "great god," were deeply impressed.

HOMILETICS

Vers. 1—3.—*Crises bring out men's characters, and cause them to be properly appreciated.* It is evident that, as the crisis approached, Pharaoh sank in the estimation of his subjects, while Moses rose. Pharaoh showed himself changeable, faithless, careless of his subjects' good, rude, violent. He was about to show himself ready to rush from one extreme into the other (ver. 1), and to "thrust out" the people whom he had so long detained. The conduct of Moses had been consistent, dignified, patriotic, bold, and courageous. He had come to be regarded by the Egyptians as "very great," and the conduct of the Israelite people had also obtained approval. Their patience, fortitude, submission to their leaders, and quiet endurance of suffering, had won upon the Egyptians, and caused them to be regarded with favour. So it is generally in crises.

I. CRISES BRING OUT THE CHARACTERS OF THE BAD, INTENSIFYING THEIR DEFECTS. Under the pressure of circumstances obstinacy becomes infatuation, indifference to human suffering develops into active cruelty, self-conceit into overbearing presumption, ill-temper into violence. At the near approach of danger the rash grow reckless, the timid cowardly, the hesitating wholly unstable, the selfish utterly egoist. In quiet times defects escape notice, which become palpable when a man is in difficulties. Many a king has reigned with credit till a crisis came, and then lost all his reputation, because his character could not bear the strain put upon it. Such times are like bursts of hot weather, under which "ill weeds grow apace."

II. THE CHARACTERS OF THE BETTER SORT OF MEN ARE ELEVATED AND IMPROVED UNDER CRISES. All the higher powers of the mind, all the nobler elements of the moral character, are brought into play by crises, and through their exercise strengthened and developed. Promptitude, resolution, boldness, trust in God, come with the call for them; and the discipline of a year under such circumstances does the work of twenty.

The Moses of chs. x. xi. is a very different man from the Moses of ch. iii. He is firm, resolute, self-reliant, may we not add, eloquent? No wonder that he was " very great " in the eyes both of the great officers of Pharaoh's court and of the people. He had withstood and baffled the magicians; he had withstood Pharaoh; he had never blenched nor wavered; he had never lost his temper. With a calm, equable, unfailing persistence, he had gone on preferring the same demand, threatening punishments if it were not granted, inflicting them, removing them on the slightest show of repentance and relenting. He had thus won the respect both of the Court and of the common people, as much as Pharaoh had lost it, and was now generally looked up to and regarded with feelings of admiration and approval. So the true character of the Christian minister is often brought out, tested, and recognised in times of severe trial and calamity, in a siege, a famine, a pestilence, a strike; and a respect is won, which twenty years of ordinary quiet work would not have elicited. Let ministers see to it, that they make the most of such occasions, not for their own honour, but for God's.

HOMILIES BY VARIOUS AUTHORS.

Vers. 1—4.—*The beginning of the end.* I. THE STROKE STILL IN RESERVE (ver. 1). God would bring on Pharaoh " one plague more." This would be effectual. It would lead him to let the people go from Egypt. So eager would he be for their departure, that he would even *thrust* them out in haste. The nature of this final stroke is described in vers. 4—7. It would be the death in one night of the first-born of man and beast throughout all the land of Egypt. This stroke might have been delivered earlier, but, 1. It might not at an earlier stage have had the same effect. 2. There was mercy to Pharaoh in giving him the *opportunity* of yielding under less severe inflictions before visiting him with this last and decisive one. 3. The previous plagues gave Pharaoh, moreover, an opportunity of doing *freely* what he now was driven to do under irresistible *compulsion*. 4. The final stroke was delayed that by the succession of plagues which were brought on Egypt, the deliverance might be rendered more imposing, and made more memorable. The object was not simply to get Israel out of Egypt in the easiest way possible, but to bring them forth in the way most glorifying to God's justice, holiness, and power. This has been already shown (ch. vi.; vii. 3, 5; ix. 15, 16; x. 1, 2).

II. THE COMMAND TO ASK FROM THE EGYPTIANS (vers. 2, 3). 1. The *request*. The Israelites were to borrow, or ask, from the Egyptians "jewels of silver, and jewels of gold;" "raiment" also, and whatever else they required (ch. iii. 22; xii. 35, 36). (1) The people were *entitled* to these gifts in repayment for past unrequited services; as compensation for losses and sufferings during the century of slavery. The principle of "compensation" is a prominent one in modern legislation. Governments have been mindful, in decreeing slave-emancipation, of compensation to the *owners*; God bethought himself of compensation to the *slaves*. Which is the more reasonable? (2) God *authorised* the people to *demand* these gifts. A demand, coming under the circumstances from Jehovah, was equivalent to a command. And after what had happened, it was impossible for any reasonable mind to doubt that the demand *had* come from God. This was sanction sufficient. The Lord gives, and the Lord is entitled to take away (Job i. 21). "The Lord hath need of it" is sufficient reason for giving up *anything* (Luke xix. 34). 2. The *response*. The plague would be influential in leading the Egyptians to give of their wealth to the Israelites (cf. ch. xii. 36). God would so incline their hearts. This willingness to part with their valuables arose not so much (1) From gratitude for past benefits, as (2) From a desire to stand well with a people who were so eminently favoured of God, and (3) From *fear* of God, and a desire to get rid of this people, who had proved so terrible a snare to them, as quickly and as peaceably as possible. Suggestions of the passage: (1) The hearts of men are in God's hands (Prov. xxi. 1). He rules in hearts as well as in the midst of worlds. Without interfering with freedom, or employing other than *natural* motives, he can secretly incline the heart in the direction he desires. (2) The time will come when the world will be glad to stand well with the Church. (3.) There is much in the world that the Church may legitimately covet to possess. The " world " is a much abused term. " As the Church in its collective capacity is the region of holiness, so the world is that of sin. But it must be carefully observed, that the view is taken of it in its totality, not of each of the parts. As a whole, moral corruption was (in New Testament times) so interwoven with its entire civilisation that it imparted to it the general aspect of evil. As the teaching of the New Testament by no means asserts that all the various elements which meet in the kingdom of God are good, so it is equally far from intending to affirm that every portion of human civilisation, as it then existed, was the contrary. Many things were only rendered evil by their connection with the prevailing moral corruption." (Rev. C. A. Row.) 4. The Church will ultimately be enriched with the spoils of the world (Rev. xxi. 24—26). 5. Whatever service God requires of his people, he will see that they are suitably equipped for it, and that their needs are, in his providence, abundantly supplied (Phil. iv. 18). 6. The people of God will not ultimately suffer loss from adherence to him. 7. God can make even the enemy a means of benefit to his cause.

III. THE GREATNESS OF MOSES. "Moreover, the man Moses was very great," &c. (ver. 3). The promise was thus fulfilled. "See, I have made thee a god to Pharaoh" (ch. vii. 1). This greatness of Moses was, 1. Got without his *seeking* for it. Like Jesus, he came not doing his own will, but the will of him that sent him (John v. 38). 2. Got without his *expecting* it. Moses looked for anything but honour in the service to which he had been called. Remember his deep despondency at the entrance on his task, and for long after (ch. iii. 11; iv. 10—13; v. 22, 23; vi. 12, 30). 3. Got in *doing God's work.* 4. Got by *God's power resting on him* (cf. Deut. xxxiv. 10—12). The service of God is the path of true greatness, and leads to undying honour (Rom. ii. 7, 10).—J. O.

How God justifies the trust of all who hope in his mercy. I. THE CERTAINTY OF THE DELIVERANCE OF GOD'S PEOPLE. 1. The preceding plagues had terrified for a moment; this will crush resistance. The stroke long delayed was now at length to fall. The last awful pause had come, during which Egypt waited in dread, and Israel in hope mingled with awe. 2. The like moment will come in God's contest with sin. There will be a last awful pause, and then the trump of God shall sound. 3. The last hour of this earthly life of ours will also come, and the soul be freed from the grasp of sorrow, and pass up through the pearly gates into the father's home.

II. ITS COMPLETENESS. "He shall surely thrust you out hence altogether." Every bond will be broken. 1. The churches of God shall no more feel the world's afflicting hand. 2. Sin shall have no more dominion over God's redeemed. God's deliverance comes slowly, but when it does come it is full and lasting.

III. IT WILL BE ATTENDED WITH GREAT ENRICHMENT. It will not be an escape with mere life. To their own shall be added the wealth of their foes. 1. The riches of the nations will yet be the possession of the people of God. 2. This will be only the type of the true riches with which the redeemed shall be endowed.

IV. AND WITH GREAT HONOUR. The despised bondsmen were girt with reverence and awe, such as had never encircled the throne of the Pharaohs. The true kings of the earth for whose manifestation the world waits are the sons of God. They will be, too, the princes of heaven, co-heirs with Christ, sharers of the throne of the Son of God.—U.

EXPOSITION.

Vers. 4—8.—The writer returns here to his account of the last interview between Moses and Pharaoh, repeating the introductory words of ch. x. 29—"and Moses said." Having accepted his dismissal, and declared that he would not see the face of Pharaoh any more (*ibid.*), Moses, before quitting the presence, proceeded to announce the last plague, prefacing the announcement, as usual (ch. vii. 17; viii. 2; ix. 1, 13; x. 3), with the solemn declaration, which showed that he acted in the matter merely as God's instrument—"Thus saith Jehovah." He makes the announcement with the utmost plainness, noting the exact time of the visitation (ver. 4)—its extent (ver. 5)—the terrible "cry" that would follow (ver. 6) — the complete exemption of the Israelites (ver. 7)—the message which Pharaoh would send him by his servants, to depart at once—and his own intention of acting on it (ver. 8). Then, without waiting for a reply, in hot anger at the prolonged obstinacy of the monarch, he went out.

Ver. 4.—**About midnight.**—Compare ch. xii. 29. It would add to the horror of the infliction that it should come in the depth of the night. Probably the night intended was not the next night, but one left purposely indefinite, that terror and suspense might work upon the mind of Pharaoh. **Shall I go out.** The word "I" is repressed in the original, and is emphatic. This crowning plague Jehovah inflicts by no instrumentality, but takes wholly upon himself. (See ch. xii. 12, 13, 23, 27, 29.)

Ver. 5.—**All the first-born.** The law of primogeniture prevailed in Egypt, as among most of the nations of antiquity. The monarchy (under the New Empire, at any rate) was hereditary, and the eldest son was known as *erpa suten sa*, or "hereditary Crown Prince." Estates descended to the eldest son, and in many cases high dignities also. No severer blow could have been sent on the nation, if it were not to be annihilated, than the loss in each house of the hope of the family—the parents' stay, the other children's guardian and protector. **Who sitteth.** "Sitteth" refers to "Pharaoh," not to "first-born." The meaning is, "from the first-born of the king who occupies the throne to the first-born of the humblest slave or servant." This last is represented by **the handmaid who is behind the mill,** since grinding at a mill was regarded as one of the severest and most irksome forms of labour. The work was commonly assigned to captives (Is. xlvii. 1, 2; Judg. xvi. 21). It was done by either one or two persons sitting, and consisted in rotating rapidly the upper millstone upon the lower by means of a handle. **All the first-born of beasts.** Not the first-born of cattle only, but of all *beasts*. The Egyptians had pet animals in most houses, dogs, apes, monkeys, perhaps cats and ichneumons. Most temples had sacred animals, and in most districts of Egypt, some beasts were regarded as sacred, and might not be killed, their death being viewed as a calamity. The loss of so many animals would consequently be felt by the Egyptians as a sensible aggravation of the infliction. It would wound them both in their domestic and in their religious sensibilities.

Ver. 6.—**There shall be a great cry.** The violence of Oriental emotions, and the freedom with which they are vented are well known. Herodotus relates that the Egyptians stript themselves and beat their breasts at funerals (ii. 85) No doubt they also uttered shrill lamentations, as did the Greeks (Lucian, *De Luctu*, § 12) and the Persians (Herod. ix. 24). With bitter mourning in every house, the "cry" might well be one, such as there had been none like before, neither would there be any like again.

Ver. 7.—**Shall not a dog move his tongue.** So far from a sudden destruction coming upon them, there shall not so much as a dog bark at them. They shall incur no hurt—no danger. (Compare Josh. x. 21.) **That ye may know how that the Lord doth put a difference**—*i.e.,* "that both ye courtiers and all Egypt may know how great a difference God puts between us—his peculiar people—and you wretched idolaters."

Ver. 8.—**All these thy servants**—*i.e.,* all these courtiers here present. **Shall come.** Literally, "shall descend." Kalisch observes that by the Hebrew idiom "going from a nobler place to one of less distinction is called descending" (*Comment.* p. 133). **And bow down.** Make obeisance to me, as if I were a king. The last of the plagues would cause the courtiers to look on Moses as the real king of the land, and pay him royal honours. **All the people that follow thee.** Literally, as in the margin, "that is at thy feet;" *i.e.,* that follows and obeys thee." The Egyptians looked on Moses as king, or at any rate prince of his nation. **In a great anger.** Literally, "in heat of anger." The abrupt dismissal (ch. x. 28), the threat against his life (*ibid.*) and the announcement that no more interviews would be granted him moved the indignation of Moses, who was not conscious to himself of having done anything to deserve such treatment. He had answered the king calmly and temperately (ch. x. 29; xi. 4—8); but knew what his feelings had been, and here records them.

HOMILETICS.

Vers. 5—7.—*The issues of life and death are in the hand of God.* For the most part there is, or there seems to be, one event to the righteous and to the wicked (Eccles. ix. 2). Death happens alike to all, and does not appear to choose his victims on any principle of sparing good and punishing ill desert. War, famine, pestilence, sweep away equally the good and the bad. This is the general law of God's providence; but he makes occasional exceptions. The issues of life and death are really his. Not a sparrow falls to the ground without our Father. If he see fit, he can "put a difference" between his own people and others. He can strike with death whomsoever he pleases; he can spare those whom he chooses to spare. We see him here:—

I. Making death an instrument of vengeance, not on those who die, but on those who survive. Pharaoh is punished, and the Egyptians generally are punished, by the sudden death of the first-born. They had deserved this retribution by their cruelty to the Hebrews, and especially by the drowning of the Hebrew male children (ch. i. 22). It afflicted all, however, alike, whether they had taken part in the above-mentioned cruelties or not. This was because it was a *national* chastisement; and the case had been the same with almost all the other plagues.

II. Striking terror into a whole community by visiting with death a certain number. Death is the main fear of worldly men. Anything else may be endured, made up for, made the best of. But for death there is no help, no remedy. The awful phantom is, as far as possible, kept out of sight, unthought of, unprepared for, thrust into the background. Men live as if they had a freehold of life, not a leasehold. When the gaunt spectre draws near; when, in the shape of cholera or fever, he makes his entrance upon the scene and challenges attention, the result is, for the most part, a panic. So it was in Egypt. The Egyptians wrote much of death, reminded each other of death (Herod. ii. 78), prepared tombs for themselves with great care speculated largely upon the condition of souls in another world; but it would seem that they shrank, as much as ordinary men, from near contact with the grisly phantom. It was now about to be suddenly brought home to them how thin a barrier separates between the two worlds. In the presence of death they would wake up to the realities of life. They would be conquered, submissive, ready to do whatever was God's will. Some such results are traceable whenever and wherever imminent death threatens a large number, and are to be watched for by the minister, who will find his opportunity at such seasons, and should take advantage of it.

III. Showing his favour to his own people by exempting them wholly from the visitation. Against the Israelites not even a dog would move his tongue (ver. 7). With mortality all around them, with a corpse in each Egyptian house, with animals lying dead on all sides, in the open country as well as in the towns and houses, they would be completely free from the visitation; a special providence would save and protect them. Such an exemption was, of course, miraculous, and is well nigh unparalleled. But still there have been cases where God's people have suffered marvellously little in a time of pestilence, when it has seemed to strike almost none but reckless and vicious lives, when an arm has appeared to be extended over the righteous. At such times what praise and gratitude are not due to God for " putting a difference between the Egyptians and Israel ! " He spares when we deserve punishment, and in his wrath thinks upon mercy. He gives a token of his approval to men of regular lives and temperate habits, by " passing them over " when he walks through the land dealing out destruction.

Ver. 8.—*Righteous anger.* It seems to be supposed by some that the true Christian ought never to be angry. St. Paul certainly says in one place, " Let *all* bitterness, and wrath, and *anger*, and clamour be put away from you " (Eph. iv. 31); and in another, " Put ye off all these, *anger*, wrath, malice " (Col. iii. 8). But he guards himself from being misunderstood by giving a command in one of these very chapters (Eph. iv. 26), " Be ye angry, and sin not." He was himself angry when he said to the High Priest, " God shall smite thee, thou whited wall " (Acts xxiii. 3), and to the jailer at Philippi, " They have beaten us openly, uncondemned, being Romans, and have cast us into prison; and now do they thrust us out privily? Nay, verily : but let them come themselves and fetch us out " (*ib.* xvi. 37). There is such a thing as " righteous anger ; " and it was righteous anger which Moses felt at this time. He was indignant—

I. Because God was spurned and his commandments made of no account. Pharaoh, after temporising, and professing contrition, and suggesting a variety of compromises, had declared himself finally against God—cast his words behind his back— and resolved on following out his own will, and defying the Almighty. Bold, unblushing wickedness may well make the minister of God angry. It is an insult to God's majesty. It is a contradiction of man's moral nature. It is an open enlisting in the service of Satan.

II. Because his countrymen were wronged, by being disappointed of their

JUST HOPES. Pharaoh's professions, his promises, his attempts at compromise had given the Israelites a right to expect that he would yield in the end. His sudden stiffness was an injury to them, with which Moses did well to sympathise. How should he not be indignant, when the just rights of his nation were wholly ignored, their patience despised, and their legitimate expectations baulked? His anger, so far as it arose out of sympathy for them, was justified—(a) by the bitterness of their feelings; (b) by the heartiness in which he had thrown himself into their cause; (c) by the apparent hopelessness of their case, if the king now drew back.

III. BECAUSE HE HAD BEEN HIMSELF INSULTED AND ILL-USED. The anger which springs from a sense of wrong done to oneself is less noble than that which arises from a sense of wrong done to our fellows, and still less noble than that which has its origin in zeal for the honour of God; but still it is not illegitimate. Wrong done to oneself is nevertheless wrong, and, as wrong, properly stirs up anger within us. Moses had been ill-used by Pharaoh from first to last, derided (ch. v. 4), trifled with (ch. viii. 26—32; x. 16—20), driven from his presence (ch. x. 11); and now at last had been deprived of his right to make personal representations to the monarch, and even threatened with death (ib. ver. 28). And why? What evil had he done? He had simply delivered God's messages to Pharaoh, and inflicted the plagues at God's command. Of his own mere notion he had done nothing but shorten the duration of the plagues by entreating God from time to time at Pharaoh's request. Even, therefore, if his "heat of anger" had been caused solely by the wrong done to himself, it would have been justified.

HOMILIES BY VARIOUS AUTHORS.

Vers. 4—10.—A *finale*. These verses end the story of how God wrought with Pharaoh to subdue him to his will. They prepare us for the catastrophe which brought the long conflict to a termination, and forced a way of egress for two millions of Hebrews through the barred gates of Egypt.

I. LAST WORDS TO PHARAOH (vers. 4—9). Vers. 1—3 of this chapter are obviously parenthetical. They relate to a communication made to Moses prior to the visit to Pharaoh recorded in ch. x. 24—29, and in anticipation of it. The substance of that communication is now conveyed to the king. Having delivered his message as God had directed, Moses finally leaves the royal presence (ver. 9). The present passage is therefore to be read in immediate connection with ch. x. 29. Pharaoh would see the face of Moses no more—*i.e.*, as a commissioner from Jehovah—but before leaving, Moses has words to speak which are to Pharaoh the knell of doom. The judgment he announces is the death of the first-born. On this observe—1. *It was a judgment-stroke more terrible than any which had preceded*. This is plain from the nature of it. What, put one with the other in the balance, was the discomfort, pain, loss, terror, devastation of crops, and darkening of the earth, caused by the previous plagues, to this tremendous horror of finding in one night, in each home throughout the land, a dead first-born? The wound here was truly mortal. The first-born is the special joy of parents. He is loved, fondled, tended, admired, as few of the children are which come after him. The pride of the parents centres in him. Their hopes are largely built up on what he may become. He has drawn to himself, and embodies, a larger share of their thought, interest, sympathy, and affection than perhaps they are well aware of. He is the pillar of their household. They look to him to bear up its honour when their own heads are laid in the dust. To touch him is to touch the apple of their eye, to quench the central illumination of their home. They are proud of him as a babe, the first occupant of the cradle; they are proud of him as a boy, unfolding his mental and physical powers in rivalry with his youthful peers; they are proud of him as a young man, when thought and decision begin to stamp their lines upon his brow, and manly dignity gives a new grace to his deportment. With the help of such considerations, try to estimate the wrench to the heart's tenderest affections, in the million homes of Egypt, by the simultaneous discovery that in each there is a ghastly corpse, and *that* the corpse of the first-born. No wonder there was "a great cry throughout all the land of Egypt, such as there was none like it, nor shall be like it any more" (ver. 6). Natural affection retains a mighty hold of natures often otherwise very depraved. And there is no reason to suppose that, taken in the mass, the people of Egypt were characterised by a greater want of it than others. Even the tiger has a tigerish love of his cubs, and, wicked man though he was, the pride of Pharaoh in his first-born may have been of no ordinary intensity. Note then the following circumstances as indicative of the especial horror of this judgment. (1) It would be *supernatural.* Natural causes were more or less involved in the other plagues, but *this* judgment was to be inflicted by the direct stroke of the Almighty. (2) It would be *sudden.* There would be no preliminary symptoms, no warning of approaching death. (3) It would be at *midnight.* The darkest and " eeriest " hour of the whole twenty-four, the hour specially associated with the gasping out of the spirit in death. (4) It would be *universal.* There would not be a house in which there was not one dead (ch. xii. 30). Not one left to comfort another. All alike swallowed up in indescribable sorrow, in blackest grief and bitterest lamentation—the woe of each intensifying the woe of all the rest. What a horror was this ! Death in a house is always oppressive to the spirit. The muffled steps and woe-disfigured faces tell the melancholy tale to every visitor. When the death is of one high in rank, the mourning is proportionately deep and widely spread. But death in every city, in every street, in every house, among high and low alike, who will unfold the misery which this implied, or do justice to the ghastly sense of mortality with which it would fill the breasts of the survivors ! The nearest image we can form of it is the state of a town or district where a pestilence is raging, and corpses are being hurried to the dead-house in hundreds. And even this falls immeasurably short of the reality. (5) It would *embrace all ranks and ages.* Palace and hovel would have its dead son. The first-born of beasts would be added to the slain. But in the general mourning over dead *men* this would be but little regarded. 2. *It was a judgment-stroke bearing reference to God's relation to Israel.* The key to the form which it assumed is furnished in ch. iv. 22, 23. "Thus saith the Lord, Israel is my son, even my first-born ; and I say unto thee, Let my son go that he may serve me ; and if thou refuse to let him go, behold, I will slay thy son, even thy first-born." See Homily on ch. xii. 29—31. Israel was God's first-born in relation to the "many nations" of the redeemed world, which in its fulness was to embrace "all kindreds, peoples, and tongues" (Gen. xvii. 5; Rom. iv. 16—19; Rev. vii. 9). "As the first-born in God's elect is to be spared and rescued, so the first-born in the house of the enemy, the beginning of his increase and the heir of his substance, must be destroyed—the one a proof that the whole family were appointed to life and blessing, the other, in like manner, a proof that all who were aliens from God's covenant of grace equally deserved, and should certainly in due time inherit, the evils of perdition" (Fairbairn). We may connect the judgment more simply with that law of symmetry which appears in so many of God's judgments, the retribution being modelled after the pattern of the crime to which it is related. Examples : Haman hanged on his own gallows (Esther v. 14); Adoni-bezek mutilated in his thumbs and great toes (Jud. i. 6, 7); David punished for adultery by dishonour done to his own concubines (2 Sam. xvi. 20—23), &c. So Pharaoh, the would-be destroyer of God's first-born, is punished in the destruction of his own first-born. The *jus talionis* has a startling field of operations in the Divine judgments. 3. *It was a judgment involving the whole of Egypt in suffering for the sin of the ruler.* This was the case in all the plagues ; but it is specially noticeable in this, where the judgment strikes a direct blow at every hearth. It may be said, doubtless with truth, that Egypt, in this severe judgment, was punished also for its *own* wickedness, the people, in the matter of the oppression of the Israelites, having been active partners in the guilt of the monarch. It is obvious, however, that the immediate occasion of this terrible blow falling on the land was the continued hardness of heart of Pharaoh. Had *he* relented, the judgment would not have fallen ; it was because he did not relent that it actually fell. We come back here to that principle of solidarity which rules so widely in God's moral administration. The many rise or fall with the one ; the rewards of righteousness and the penalties of transgression alike overflow upon those related to the immediate agent. The widest applications of this principle are those stated in Rom. v. 12—21—the ruin of the race in Adam ; the redemption of the race in Christ. 4. *It was a judgment in which a marked distinction was to be put between the Egyptians and the Hebrews* (ver. 7). Israel, however, was only exempted from like doom by resort to the blood of atonement—a lesson as to their natural state of condemnation, and as to the channel through which alone redeeming grace could flow to them.

II. The withdrawal of Moses. "Moses went out from Pharaoh in a great anger" (ver. 8). 1. *There are occasions on which it is lawful to be angry.* This was one of them. He would have been a man utterly without soul who would not have been roused to indignation by the towering pride and extraordinary ingratitude and faithlessness of Pharaoh, not to speak of the insults he was heaping on Jehovah, and the violence threatened against Moses himself. 2. *The meekest nature is that which, on proper occasions, is capable of the most burning and vehement anger.* On the relation of the anger of Moses to his meekness, see Homily on ch. ii. 12. Another example is found in the apostle John—the apostle of love. The highest example of all is the Son of Man, "meek and lowly in heart," yet capable of terrible and scathing wrath —"the wrath of the Lamb" (Matt. xi. 29 ; Mark iii. 5 ; Rev. vi. 16, 17).

III. A summing up (vers. 9, 10). The conclusion of the series of plagues having been reached, and negotiations with Pharaoh having been finally broken off, Moses sums up the results. The notable point is, that it was all as the Lord had said. It had been foretold that Pharaoh would not hearken, and neither had he hearkened ; but his hardening had been the occasion of God's multiplying his wonders in the land of Egypt. The climax of the hardening was reached under this last warning. Infuriated by his passion, Pharaoh appears to have paid no heed to it. Yet the fact that he did not, illustrates a point already dwelt upon—the tendency of hardening against God to involve the whole moral nature, extending at last to the destruction even of the natural affections. We have seen how reckless Pharaoh had become of the well-being of his subjects (ch. x. 7). See him now perilling the life of his own son, not to speak of the lives of the first-born throughout the whole land, that he may be spared the humiliation of submitting to Jehovah ! Perilling, even, is too weak a word, for experience had taught him that God's threatenings in no case went unfulfilled. "Sacrificing" would be the more proper term. Even to this length was Pharaoh ultimately driven by his enmity against God, and his example remains as a melancholy warning to ourselves.—J. O.

Chap. xi. vers. 4—10 ; chap. xii. vers. 29—36.—*The tenth plague and its decisive result—the destruction of the first-born.* In ch. x. 29, Moses says to Pharaoh, "I will see thy face again no more," while in ch. xi. 4—8, he is represented as making to Pharaoh an announcement of the last plague. Perhaps the best way of clearing this apparent contradiction is to suppose that in the narrative as it originally stood there was really no break between ch. x. 29 and ch. xi. 4, and that the three intervening verses were afterwards introduced in some way which we cannot now explain. So taking the narrative, all is made straightforward and additionally impressive. Moses followed up his intimation that Pharaoh should see his face no more, with a statement which plainly showed the reason why. No more would he come into Pharaoh's presence *uninvited by Pharaoh,* simply because there would be no more be need to do so. Jehovah was about to deal the last blow without any human instrumentality whatever.

I.- Try to estimate somewhat of the combination of forces in this last plague, which made it so effective for its purpose. 1. *There was the hour chosen —midnight.* It was not like the rest of the plagues, which extended over a more or less period of time ; but, *being a momentary blow,* the most impressive moment could be chosen for striking it. This was midnight, the time of security, repose, and deep silence. Each family was gathered together under its own roof ; not separated, as might have been the case during the day, each one at his appointed work. There was no bustle of business, as there might have been at noon, to help in drowning and qualifying the horror of the transaction. 2. *There was an element of peculiar force in the very class of persons who were smitten.* Not only had Jehovah advanced to take away the lives of human beings, but he had directed his destructions, with evident and unerring purpose, upon one particular class. The destruction was not as a mere decimation, the taking of one out of so many, it mattered not who, so long as one was taken. In every household it was the first-born who lay dead. No regard was shown to personal character or special circumstances. All the first-born were stricken, the virtuous as well as the vicious ; the amiable, promising youth from whom much was expected, and the scapegrace who was bringing a father's grey hairs with sorrow to the grave; the young man who might be the only son of his mother and she a widow, alike with him who was the first-born among many brethren. The first-born is the centre of so many hopes and calculations, that when he is stricken there may be the instantaneous reaction of an irretrievable despair. Zechariah speaks very emphatically of those who are in bitterness for their first-born (ch. xii. 10). In many cases the first-born would also be the just-born. 3. *There was an element that helped to bring decision in the very greatness of the cry that was elicited.* How far the announcement made to Pharaoh had travelled we know not; but it must have gone far enough to produce a consentaneous cry of recognition when the blow was struck. Pharaoh would know, and also his courtiers, and many at different points through the city, even before they came out of their houses, that it was by no ordinary death the first-born had died. Each one, thus already informed, would suspect the whole terrible truth with respect to all the first-born of the land. In this way certainty would come that the prediction was fulfilled, even before information on the point was actually obtained. Bad news travels quickly, and all the quicker when special facilities have been prepared by Jehovah himself, as they evidently were in this instance. Remember, also, the demonstrative, vociferous mode of expressing sorrow in bereavement which prevails among Eastern nations. There was hardly an hour of the day or night but from some home in Egypt there went up the wail of the bereaved; but here was a simultaneous wail from every home, and that not over the aged or the sick whose death was expected, but over those the great majority of whom would be young, strong, and vivacious. Thus the very emotions which produced this extraordinary cry, the cry itself served in turn to intensify, and thus to exalt into complete mastery. What wonder, then, that from the king downward the people were swept away by their emotions, and, without thought of past gains or future losses, hurried Israel out of their land in the precipitate way here recorded! Avarice, pride, worldly consequence—all the motives which hold dominion in selfish human breasts—lost their seats for the moment. It was only for a moment, but that moment was time long enough effectually to serve the purposes of God. 4. There was the fact that with all these elements of force and terror in the tenth plague itself, *there had been nine such serious visitations before it.* It was like the last blow of the battering-ram, which, though it may have in itself more force than preceding blows, yet gains not the least part of its efficiency from the shaking which these preceding blows have produced. It is by no means certain that if this destruction of the first-born had come at first it would have had the same effect.

II. Notice, as illustrated by this announcement to Pharaoh, HOW DIFFERENTLY THE SAME FACTS ARE STATED TO DIFFERENT PEOPLE. Pharaoh is plainly told, that amid all this great smiting of Egypt's first-born, Israel will continue perfectly secure. The impression we get is, that not only will there be freedom for Israel from the specific effects of this plague, but even an unusual exemption from ordinary mischances. Not a dog is to move his tongue against any living creature in Israel. The protection would be complete; the favour and discrimination of Jehovah most manifest. But whence all this came, and in what it consisted, Pharaoh cannot be informed. The difference between Israel and Egypt will be plain enough; but the virtue of the slain lamb and the sprinkled blood are hidden from his eyes—all this could not be explained to *him*. If it could have been explained to him, it would never have needed to be explained. In other words, Pharaoh would never have come into such an extremity as that where the death of the first-born landed him. Thus we are helped to see the reason why to some there come revelations producing security and gladness of heart, and to others nothing but tidings of disaster and disappointment. Every great fact of God's dealings has a bright side and a dark side; and if we will not live so that the bright side may be revealed to us, then inevitably we must come face to face with the dark one. Moses told Pharaoh that the death of the first-born was coming, but he only turned away more scornful, stubborn, and infatuated than ever; he told the children of Israel to make the Paschal preparations, and, minute and exact as these preparations were, they at once went away and made them. God might have told Pharaoh all about how Israel was protected, but what would have been the use? If we would discover why great Divine revelations are hidden from us, we must look in our own hearts. A man can never know the comforts and beauties that belong to the temperate zone as long as he stubbornly abides in the frigid one.

III. CONSIDER THIS LAST PLAGUE IN THE ACTUAL EFFECTS OF IT. 1. It produced *immediate action on the part of Pharaoh,* and, what is very noticeable, *on the part of the people also.* Pharaoh called for Moses and Aaron *by night.* He had sent them away with a menace of death, if they ventured again into his presence ; but only a few short hours pass and he has to beg them to hurry and save him. We should never threaten and bluster, for we know not how soon we may have to swallow our words again. He did not wait till morning, even till the early morning. Every moment would bring to him news from a widening circle, and quicken him into the promptest action possible. And yet, immediate as this action appears, we know that it had been led up to very gradually. Jehovah had been for a long time undermining the strength of Pharaoh ; and if it now collapsed in a moment instead of crumbling away, it was because the massive fabric had lost, bit by bit, the foundation on which it had been raised. And in the same way we may be sure that everything in the world which is unjust, ungodly, and tyrannical, is being undermined. There is no proud and stubborn soul but God is working upon it by something substantially the same as the nine plagues ; and the tenth plague will come in due time to produce its immediate and decisive effect. 2. *The action took the shape of complete and eager liberation.* Egypt was filled with panic and terror to the exclusion of every other motive. The full significance of Pharaoh's words in vers. 31, 32, can only be seen by comparing them, *first,* with his contemptuous treatment of Moses in the beginning (ch. v. 2) ; and *next,* with his procrastinating, half-giving, half-grasping attitude during the course of the plagues (ch. viii. 10, 25 ; x. 8—11, 24). Pharaoh began as one whose foot was on the rock— he was sure he could not be shaken ; then he was made to feel himself as more and more in a state of unstable equilibrium ; and now at last he is utterly prostrate at Moses' feet. He who said he would grant nothing, now grants everything. He who, in response to the first request of Moses, added to the severities of the bondage already existing, now, when all requests have ceased, not only undoes the fetters, but hurries the captives out of his realm, as if each of them was a mass of fatal infection.—Y.

EXPOSITION.

Vers. 9—10.—Before proceeding to relate the last and greatest of the plagues, the author allows himself a momentary pause while he casts his eye back on the whole series of miracles hitherto wrought in Egypt, on the circumstances under which they had been wrought, their failure to move the stubborn will of Pharaoh, and the cause of that failure, the hardening of his heart, which hardening the author once more ascribes to Jehovah. With this summary he terminates the second great division of his work, that which began with ch. ii., and which traces the history of Moses from his birth to the close of his direct dealings with Pharaoh.

Ver. 9.—**And the Lord said.** Rather, "had said." God had forewarned Moses that Pharaoh's heart would be hardened (ch. iv. 21 ; vii. 3), and that, in spite of all the miracles which he was empowered to perform before him, he would not let the people go (ch. iii. 19 ; iv. 21). It was not until God took Pharaoh's punishment altogether into his own hands, and himself came down and smote all the first-born, that the king's obstinacy was overcome, and he proceeded to "thrust the people out." **That my wonders may be multiplied.** Compare ch. iii. 20 ; vii. 3. If Pharaoh had yielded at the first, or even after two or three miracles, God's greatness and power would not have been shown forth very remarkably. Neither the Egyptians nor the neighbouring nations would have been much impressed. The circumstances would soon have been forgotten. As it was, the hardness of Pharaoh's heart, while it delayed the departure of the Israelites for a year, and so added to their sufferings, was of advantage to them in various ways :—1. It gave them time to organise themselves, and make all necessary preparations for a sudden departure. 2. It deeply impressed the Egyptians, and led them to abstain from all interference with the Israelites for above three centuries. 3. It impressed the neighbouring nations also to some extent, and either prevented them from offering opposition to the Israelites, or made them contend with less heart, and so with less success against them.

Ver. 10.—**Moses and Aaron did all these plagues before Pharaoh.** Aaron's agency is not always mentioned, and seems to have been less marked in the later than in the earlier miracles, Moses gradually gaining self-reliance. In passing from the subject of the plagues wrought by the two brothers, it may be useful to give a synopsis of them, distinguishing those which came without warning from those which were announced beforehand, and noting, where possible, their actual worker, their duration, their physical source, and the hurt which they did.

Plagues.	Announced or Not.	Actual Worker.	Duration.	Physical Source.	Hurt which they did.
1. River turned into blood	announced	Aaron	7 days	water	annoyance to man and beast.
2. Frogs	do.	do.	unknown	do.	annoyance to man.
3. Mosquitoes	not	do.	do.	{ dust of the earth }	annoyance to man and beast.
4. Beetles	announced	God	do.	air (?)	annoyance and loss to man.
5. Murrain	do.	do.	do.	do.	loss to man.
6. Boils	not	Moses	do.	{ ashes of the furnace }	suffering to man and beast.
7. Hail	announced	do.	do.	air	loss to man.
8. Locusts	do.	do.	do.	east wind	do.
9. Darkness	not	do.	3 days	air (?)	annoyance and horror to man.

HOMILETICS.

Man's ill-doing but causes God's wonders to be multiplied (ver. 9). God's wonders are either such as occur in the general course of his providence, or such as are abnormal and extraordinary. It is these last of which Moses especially speaks to us in the Book of Exodus. But the same law which applies to the abnormal wonders, applies also to those which are constant and ordinary. Men's perverseness leads to their multiplication.

I. PARDON OF SIN IS MULTIPLIED THROUGH HUMAN TRANSGRESSION. Nothing is a greater marvel than God's pardon of sin. How " the High and Holy One who inhabiteth eternity "—he who " is of purer eyes than to behold iniquity "—can pardon sin, is one of those mysteries which must ever remain—in this life, at any rate—unfathomable. Man pardons his fellow-sinner without much difficulty, because he is his fellow-sinner —because he feels that he is himself so much in need of forgiveness. But for a perfect Being to pardon what is utterly alien to his own nature, what he must despise and abhor, what in his eyes is vile, base, mean, wicked, despicable, detestable—is a truth which faith may accept, but which reason is quite incompetent to understand. Yet God does pardon. St. Paul must have been pardoned his persecution of the saints, before he was called to be " a chosen vessel." God bids us ask for pardon, and he would not bid us ask for that which he could not or would not give. And the marvel of pardon is being daily augmented, heaped up, multiplied, by the ever-increasing sum of human transgression.

II. GOD THE SPIRIT'S CONDESCENSION GROWS AND INCREASES THROUGH THE SAME. God the Father declared once upon a time, " My Spirit shall not always strive with man " (Gen. vi. 3). Yet near five thousand years have elapsed, and his Spirit strives still. Man turns away from his Spirit, " grieves " him, vexes him, is deaf to his pleadings, sets at nought his counsel, wills none of his reproof (Prov. i. 25)—yet he does not withdraw himself. He "gives us the comfort of his help again"—he "will not leave us, nor forsake us." We may, no doubt, if we persist in evil courses, and set to work determinedly to drive him from us, in course of time cause him to withdraw, alienate him wholly, "quench" him. But, short of such alienation, our sins do but cause him to multiply the wonders of his love and his long-suffering, to be ever more gracious and more merciful, to plead with us more persuasively, more constantly, and save us, as it were, in spite of ourselves.

III. CHRIST'S PROTECTION OF HIS CHURCH IS SHOWN MORE AND MORE MARVELLOUSLY AS ITS ASSAILANTS INCREASE IN POWER AND BOLDNESS. In prosperous times God seems to do little for his Church; but let danger come, let men rise up against it, let Gebal and Ammon and Amalek be confederate together, and raise the cry, "Down with it, down with it, even to the ground," and the wonders which he proceeds to work on its behalf are simply astounding. Arius would corrupt its doctrine with the Court at his back, and Arius is smitten in the dead of the night by a death as silent, sudden, and inscrutable as that which came in the time of Moses on all the first-born of the Egyptians. Julian would crush it by depriving its ministers of support and its members of education, and Julian is cut off in the flower of his age by the javelin of an unknown enemy. Atheism, Agnosticism, Rationalism, Materialism, and open immorality league themselves against it at the present day, and lo! from without evidences are made to rise up out of crumbling heaps of rubbish in Assyria, Babylonia, and Egypt; while from within is developed a new life, a new zeal, a new vigour and activity, which give sure promise of triumph over the coalition. Man's opposition to God provokes God to arise and show forth his might, to confound and scatter his foes. So men may be led at last to know that he, whose name is Jehovah, is truly "the Most High over all the earth" (Ps. lxxxiii. 18).

SECTION VI.

First Institution of the Passover.

EXPOSITION.

CHAPTER XII.

THE INSTITUTION OF THE PASSOVER AND THE REASONS FOR IT.— In the interval allowed by God, according to the precedent of former announced plagues, between the warning concerning the first-born and the execution, Moses received instructions for the institution of a new religious rite, founded possibly upon some previous national usage, but so re-shaped, re-cast, and remodelled as to have an entirely new and fresh character. In all Eastern nations, the coming in of spring was observed as a jocund and festive time, with offerings, processions, and songs of rejoicings. When the date of the vernal equinox was known, it was naturally made the starting-point for these festivities. Early flowers and fruits, the fresh ears of the most forward kinds of grain, or the grain itself extracted from the ears, were presented as thank-offerings in the temples; hymns were sung, and acknowledgments made of God's goodness. Such a festival was celebrated each year in Egypt; and it is so consonant to man's natural feelings, that, if the family of Jacob did not bring the observance with them from Palestine, they are likely to have adopted it, when they became to some extent agriculturists (Deut. xi. 10) under the Pharaohs. It is, however, a pure conjecture (Ewald) that the name given to this festival was *Pesach*, from the sun's "passing over" at this time into the sign of Aries. The real name is unknown, and there is every reason to believe that the term *Pesach* was now for the first time given a religious sense (upon the ground noticed in verses 11, 12) to what was in reality a new rite. God, being about to smite with death the first-born in each Egyptian house, required the Israelites to save themselves by means of a sacrifice. Each Israelite householder was to select a lamb (or a kid) on the tenth day of the current month (ver. 3), and to keep it separate from the flock until the fourteenth day at even, when he was to kill it, to dip some hyssop in the blood (ver. 22) and to strike with the hyssop on the two posts and lintel of his door-way (ver. 7), so leaving the mark of the blood on it. He was then the same night to roast the lamb whole, and eat it with un-leavened bread and bitter herbs (vers. 8—10). He was to have his dress close girt about him, his sandals on his feet, and his staff in his hand ; to be prepared, that is, for a journey. If he did all this, God, when he went through the land to smite and destroy, would " pass over" the house upon which there was the blood, and spare all that dwelt in it. Other-wise the plague would be upon them to destroy them (vers. 11, 13). Such were the directions given for immediate observance, and such was the Passover proper. The lamb itself was primarily the *Pesach* (ver. 11), the " pass," which secured safety. From this the name spread to the entire festival. Having, by the directions recorded in verses 3—13 instituted the festival, God proceeded, in verses 14—20, to require its continued celebra-tion year after year, and to give additional rules as to the mode of its annual observance. 1. The festival was to last seven days. 2. No leavened bread was to be eaten during that space, and leaven was even to be put away altogether out of all houses. 3. On the first day of the seven and on the last, there was to be " a holy convocation " or gathering for worship. 4. No work not strictly neces-sary was to be done on these days. Other directions were given at a later date. 1. Be-sides the Paschal lamb, with which the festi-val commenced, and which was to be a domestic rite, public sacrifices were appointed for each day of the seven—to consist of two young bullocks, one ram, seven lambs, and one goat, with appropriate " meat-offerings " (Num. xxviii. 19-24). 2. On the second day of the feast, " the morrow after the sabbath," the first fruits of the harvest were to be pre-sented in the shape of a ripe sheaf (of barley) which was to be a wave-offering, and to be accompanied by the sacrifice of a lamb with meat and drink offerings (Lev. xxiii. 10-14). By this regulation the festival was made to embody the old spring feast, and to have thus a double aspect.

Ver. 1.—**The Lord spake.**—According to the Biblical record, neither Moses nor Aaron introduced any legislation of their own, either at this time or later. The whole sys-tem, religious, political, and ecclesiastical,

was received by Divine Revelation, com-manded by God, and merely established by the agency of the two brothers. **In the land of Egypt.** The introduction of these words seems to show that we have here a separate document on the subject of the Passover, written independently of what has preceded, some time after the exodus, and placed here without alteration, when Moses gathered together his various writings into a single work.

Ver. 2.—**This month shall be unto you the beginning of months.** The Israelite year would seem to have hitherto commenced with the autumnal equinox (Ex. xxiii. 16), or at any rate with the month Tisri (or Ethanim), which corresponded to our October. Hence-forth two reckonings were employed, one for sacred, the other for civil purposes, the first month of each year, sacred or civil, being the seventh month of the other. Abib, " the month of ears "—our April, nearly—became now the first month of the ecclesiastical year, while Tisri became its seventh or sabbatical month. It is remarkable that neither the Egyptians nor the Babylonians agreed with the original Israelite practice, the Egyptians commencing their year with Thoth, or July ; and the Babylonians and Assyrians theirs with Nisannu, or April.

Ver. 3.—**Speak ye unto all the congrega-tion.** Under the existing circumstances Moses could only venture to summon the elders of Israel to a meeting. He necessarily left it to them to signify his wishes to the people. (See ver. 21.) **A lamb.** The He-brew word is one of much wider meaning than our " lamb." It is applicable to both sheep and goats, and to either animal without limit of age. In the present case the age was fixed at a year by subsequent enactment (ver. 5) ; but the offerer was left free with respect to the species. It is curious that, such being the case, the lamb alone should, so far as appears, ever have been offered. **Accord-ing to the house of their fathers.** Literally, " for a father's house," *i. e.* for a family.

Ver. 4.—**If the household be too little for the lamb**—*i. e.,* " too few to consume it at a sitting." Usage in course of time fixed the minimum number at ten. (Joseph. *Bell. Jud.* vi. 9, § 3.) The whole family, men, women and children participated. The lamb was generally slain between the ninth hour (3 p.m.) and the eleventh (5 p.m.). **Let him and his neighbour take it according to the number of the souls.** If there were a house-hold of only five, which could not possibly con-sume the lamb, any large neighbouring family was to send five or six of its number, to make up the deficiency. **Every man according to his eating,** etc. It is difficult to see what sense our translators intended. The real direction is that, in providing a proper number of guests, consideration should be had of the amount which they would be likely to eat. Children and the very aged were not to be reckoned as if they were men in the vigour of life. Translate—"Each man according to his eating shall ye count towards the lamb."

Ver. 5.—**Your lamb shall be without blemish.** Natural piety would teach that "the blind, the lame, and the sick" should not be selected for sacrifice (Mal. i. 8). The Law afterwards expressly forbade any blemished animals—"blind, or broken, or maimed, or having a wen, or scurvy, or scabbed"—to be offered for any of the stated sacrifices, though they might be given as free-will offerings (Lev. xxii. 20—25). The absence of blemish was especially important in a victim which was to typify One "holy, harmless, undefiled, separate from sinners." **A male.** As standing in place of and redeeming the first-born of the *males* in each family. **Of the first year.** Perhaps as then more approaching to the ideal of perfect innocence. The requirement was not a usual one. **Or from the goats.** Theodoret says the proviso was made for the relief of the poorer class of persons; but practically it seems not to have taken effect. When people were poor, their richer neighbours supplied them with lambs (Kalisch).

Ver. 6.—**Ye shall keep it up until the fourteenth day.** The interval of four days (see ver. 3) was probably intended to give ample time for the thorough inspection of the lamb, and for obtaining another, if any defect was discovered. The precept is not observed by the modern Jews; and the later Targum (which belongs to the sixth century after Christ) teaches that it was only intended to apply to the first institution; but the text of Exodus is wholly against this. **The whole assembly of the congregation of Israel shall kill it.** One of the main peculiarities of the Paschal sacrifice was this—that the head of each family was entitled—in the early times was required—to offer the sacrifice for himself. In it no one intervened between the individual and God. Thus it was recognised that the whole nation was a nation of priests, as are Christians also, according to St. John (Rev. i. 6) and St. Peter (1 Pet. ii. 5). The intervention of Levites at a late date (2 Chron. xxx. 17; xxxv. 5, &c.) was contrary to the original institution. **In the evening.** Literally, "between the two evenings." This phrase has been explained in two ways. Some regard the first evening as commencing when the sun begins visibly to decline from the zenith, *i.e.* about two or three o'clock; and the second as following the sunset. Others say, that the sunset introduces the first evening, and that the second begins when the twilight ends, which they consider to have been "an hour and twenty minutes later" (Ebn Ezra, quoted

by Kalisch). The use of the phrase in ch. xvi. 12, and the command in Deut. xvi. 6—"Thou shalt sacrifice the passover at even, *at the going down of the sun*," seem to be decisive in favour of the second explanation. The first arose out of the later practice. When the lambs were sacrificed in the temple by a continual succession of offerers, it became impossible to complete the sacrifices in the short time originally allowed. Of necessity the work of killing the victims was commenced pretty early in the afternoon, and continued till after sunset. The interpretation of the direction was then altered, to bring it into accord with the altered practice.

Ver. 7.—**They shall take of the blood.** The blood, which, according to Hebrew ideas, "is the life," and so the very essence of the sacrifice, was always regarded as the special symbol of that expiation and atonement, with a view to which sacrifice was instituted. As by the Paschal sacrifice atonement was made for the *house*, which was therefore to escape unscathed, the sign of atonement was to be conspicuously placed upon it. **And strike.** The "striking" was to be by means of a bunch of hyssop dipped in the blood (ver. 22). The selection of the doorway as the part of the house to receive the stains of blood is probably to be connected with the idea that the secondary agency producing death, whatever it was, would enter by the door—and if the door showed the house to have been atoned for, would not enter. **The upper door-post.** The word used is elsewhere translated "lintel" (ch. xii. 22, 23); but it seems properly to mean the latticed window which was commonly placed over a doorway in Egyptian houses, and which is often represented in the façades of tombs. (See Lepsius, *Denkmäler*, pt. ii. pls. 16, 17, 147, etc.) It is derived from a root signifying "to look out."

Ver. 8.—**Roast with fire.** The meat of sacrificial meals was commonly boiled by the Hebrews (1 Sam. ii. 14, 15). The command to roast the Paschal lamb is accounted for: 1. By its being a simpler and quicker process than boiling; 2. By a special sanctity being regarded as attaching to fire; 3. By the difficulty of cooking the animal *whole* unless it were roasted. Justin Martyr's statement that for roasting two wooden spits were required, placed at right angles the one to the other, and thus extending the victim on a cross, will seem to many a better ground for the direction than any of these. **And unleavened bread.** See below, ver. 18. **With bitter herbs.** Literally, "with bitternesses." That herbs, or vegetables of some kind, are intended, there is no reasonable doubt. The Mishna enumerates endive, chicory, wild lettuce, and nettles among the herbs that might be eaten. It is a strange notion of Kurtz's, that the bitter herbs were a condiment, and "communicated a more agreeable flavour to the food." Undoubtedly they were a disagreeable accompaniment, and represented at once the bitterness of the Egyptian bondage (ch. i. 14) and the need of self-denial, if we would feed on Christ.

Ver. 9.—**Eat not of it raw.** The injunction appears to moderns superfluous; but an ὠμοφαγία, or eating of the raw flesh of victims sacrificed, seems to have been practised by several heathen nations in ancient times, more especially in the worship of Dionysus or Bacchus. **Its head with its legs.** The lamb was to be roasted whole—according to some, as a symbol of the unity of Israel, and especially of the political unit which they were to become so soon as they quitted Egypt; but, as we learn from St. John (xix. 36), still more to prefigure the unbroken body of Him whom the lamb especially represented, the true propitiation and atonement and deliverer of His people from the destroyer, our Lord Jesus Christ. **The purtenance thereof.** Rather, "the intestines thereof." The Jewish commentators say that the intestines were first taken out, washed, and cleansed, after which they were replaced, and the lamb roasted in a sort of oven.

Ver. 10.—**Ye shall let nothing of it remain till the morning.** The whole of the flesh was to be consumed by the guests, and at one sitting, lest there should be any even accidental profanation of the food by man or animal, if part were put away. The English Church, acting on the same principle of careful reverence, declines to allow any reservation of the Eucharistic elements, requiring the whole of the consecrated bread and wine to be consumed by the Priest and communicants in the Church immediately after the service. **That which remaineth**—i.e., the bones, and any small fragments of the flesh necessarily adhering to them. **Ye shall burn with fire.** Thus only could its complete disappearance, and seeming annihilation be secured. It does not appear that this burning was viewed as a sacrificial act.

Ver. 11.—**With your loins girded,** etc. Completely prepared, i.e., to start on your journey—with the loose wrapper (beged), ordinarily worn, collected together and fastened by a girdle about the waist; with sandals on the feet, which were not commonly worn in houses; and with walking-sticks in the hand. There were some Jews who regarded these directions as of perpetual obligation; but the general view was that they applied to the first occasion only, when alone they would have answered any useful purpose. **You shall eat it in haste.** As not knowing at what moment you may be summoned to start on your journey, and as having to see to the burning of the bones after the flesh was eaten, which would take some time.

It is the Lord's Passover. Very emphatic words! "This is no common meal," they seem to say, "it is not even an ordinary sacrificial repast. The lamb is Jehovah's. It is his pass-sign—the mark of his protection, the precious means of your preservation from death. As such view it; and though ye eat it in haste, eat it with reverence."

Ver. 12.—**For I will pass through,** etc. God now proceeds to give the reason for the institution of the new ceremony, and to explain the new term pesach. "I have commanded this rite," He says, "because I am about to go through the whole land of Egypt as a destroyer, executing judgment; I am about to smite and kill every one of the first-born both of man and beast. I shall enter into every house, and slay the first-born in it, unless I see upon the house the token of the blood of the lamb. In that case I shall pass over the house, and you will escape the plague." It would clear the sense if the opening words of verse 12 were translated —"For I shall go through," instead of "pass through." The word translated "pass through" has no connection at all with that rendered "pass over." **Against all the gods of Egypt I will execute judgment.** These words are exegetical of the word "beast," which immediately precedes. Animal worship was an important part of the religion of the Egyptians. At four great cities, Memphis, Heliopolis, Hermonthis, a sort of suburb of Thebes, and Momemphis in the Western Delta, animals were maintained, which were viewed as actual incarnations of deity—the Apis Bull at Memphis, a bull called Mnevis at Heliopolis, one termed Bacis or Pacis at Hermonthis, and at Momemphis a White Cow. If any of these were at the time animals that had "opened the womb," death must have fallen upon them. Thus would judgment have been executed, literally, upon Egyptian "gods." But, besides these, the whole country was filled with sacred animals, regarded as emblematic of certain particular deities, and as belonging to them. Sheep were sacred to Kneph, goats to Khem, cows to Athor, cats to Pasht, dogs and jackals to Anubis, lions to Horus, crocodiles to Set and Sabak, hippopotami to Taouris, cynocephalous apes to Thoth, frogs to Heka. A sudden mortality among the sacred animals would be felt by the Egyptians as a blow struck against the gods to whom they belonged, and as a judgment upon them. It is scarcely necessary to understand literally the expression "all the gods," and to defend it by the assertion that "not a single deity of Egypt but was represented by some beast." Such an assertion cannot be proved; and is probably not correct. It has often been remarked, and is generally allowed, that Scripture uses universal expressions, where most, or even many, of a class are meant. **I am the Lord.** Rather as in ch. vi. 8, "Against all the gods of Egypt I will execute judgment, I, Jehovah."

Ver. 13.—**The blood shall be to you for a token**, etc. The blood was not to be a token *to* the Israelites, but *to* God *for* them. Translate—"and the blood shall be as a token for you upon the houses that you are there." It shall distinguish the houses in which you dwell from the others. **I will pass over you.** This is the emphatic clause. God would pass by, or over the house on which the blood was, spare it, slay none of its inmates; and from this action of His, the lamb itself, and the feast whereof it was the principal part, were to be termed "the Passover." It has been proposed to connect the Hebrew *pesach* with the Egyptian *pesh*, "to stretch, or extend (protection)"; but the name "Tiphsach," borne by the place of passage over the Euphrates (1 Kings iv. 24), would seem to indicate that "crossing," or "passing over" is the primary meaning of the root.

Vers. 14-20.—Hitherto the directions given have had reference, primarily and mainly, if not wholly, to the first celebration of the Passover on the night preceding the Exodus. Now, it is announced, (1) That the observance is to be an annual one; and (2) That it is to be accompanied with certain additional features in the future. These are (*a*) the eating of unleavened bread for seven days after the killing of the Passover; (*b*) the putting away of leaven out of the houses; (*c*) the holding of meetings for worship on the first day and the last; and (*d*) the observance on these days of a sabbatical rest.

Ver. 14.—**This day shall be to you for a memorial.** Annual festivals, in commemoration of events believed to have happened, were common in the religion of Egypt, and probably not wholly strange to the religious ideas of the Hebrews. (See the "Introduction" to this chapter.) They were now required to make the 14th of Abib such a day, and to observe it continually year after year "throughout their generations." There is commendable faithfulness in the obedience still rendered to the command at the present day; and it must be confessed that the strong expression—**throughout your generations** and **as an ordinance for ever**—excuse to a great extent the reluctance of the Jews to accept Christianity. They have already, however, considerably varied from the terms of the original appointment. May they not one day see that the Passover will still be truly kept by participation in the Easter eucharist, wherein Christians feed upon "the Lamb slain from the foundation of the world" —the antitype, of which the Paschal lamb was the type—the true sustenance of souls—

the centre and source of all real unity—the one "perfect and sufficient sacrifice, and oblation, and satisfaction for the sins of the whole world"? The Church *requires* an Easter communion of all her members, proclaims that on that day, Christ our passover being slain, we are to keep the feast; and thus, so far as in her lies, maintains the festival as "an ordinance for ever," to be observed through all her generations.

Ver. 15.—**Seven days** There is no indication that the week of seven days was admitted by the ancient Egyptians, or even known to them. Apparently, the nation which first adopted it was that of the Babylonians. Abraham may have brought it with him from "Ur of the Chaldees;" and from him it may have passed to Jacob, and so to Moses. That the week was known in the family of Abraham before the giving of the law, appears from Gen. xxix. 27, 28. **Unleavened bread** is typical of purity of heart, leaven being an emblem of corruption (Matt. xvi. 6—12; 1 Cor. v. 7). "Leaven," says Plutarch, "comes from corruption, and corrupts the dough with which it is mixed; and every fermentation seems to be a putrefaction." The primary command to celebrate the first passover with unleavened instead of leavened bread (ver. 8), must be attributed wholly to this symbolism. But the permanent institution of a "feast of unleavened bread," to last a week, had a double bearing. Partly, it was designed to deepen and intensify the conviction that corruption and impurity disqualify for religious service; but it was also partly intended as a commemoration of the fact, that in their hasty flight from Egypt the bread which they took with them was unleavened (ver. 34), and that they were forced to subsist on this for several days. (Compare the double meaning of the "bitter herbs," noticed in the comment on verse 8, *ad fin.*) The requirement to "put away leaven out of their houses" is probably intended to teach, that for family worship to be acceptable, the entire household must be pure, and that to effect this result the head of the household must, so far as he can, eject the leaven of sin from his establishment. **Whosoever eateth . . . shall be cut off from Israel.** Expelled, *i.e.*, from the congregation, or excommunicated. If a man wilfully transgresses any plain precept of God, even though it be a positive one, he should be severed from the Church, until he confess his fault, and repent, and do penance for it. Such was the "godly discipline" of the primitive Church; and it were well if the Churches of these modern times had more of it.

Ver. 16.—**On the first day there shall be an holy convocation.** After the Paschal meal on the evening of the 14th of Abib, there was to be a solemn assembly of the people on the next day for religious worship. The name "convocation," applied to these gatherings, seems to show that originally the people were summoned to such meetings, as they still are by the muezzin from the minarets of mosques in Mahommedan countries, and by bells from the steeples of churches in Christian ones. **And on the seventh day.** On the 22nd of Abib—the seventh day after the first holy convocation on the 15th (see Lev. xxiii. 4—8). Only two of the Jewish festivals were of this duration — the feast of unleavened bread, and the feast of tabernacles (ib. 39—42). The Christian Church has adopted the usage for Christmas, Easter, Ascension, and Whitsuntide, where the last day of the week is known technically as "the octave." **No manner of work shall be done in them.** Festivaldays were in all countries days of abstention from the ordinary business of life, which could not conveniently be carried on conjointly with attendance at the services, meetings, processions, etc., wherein the festival consisted. But absolute cessation from all work was nowhere strictly commanded except among the Hebrews, where it appears to have been connected with the belief in God's absolute rest after the six days of creation. The command here given was solemnly repeated in the law (Lev. xxiii. 6–8).

Ver. 17.—**In this self-same day.** The 15th of Abib—the first day of the feast of unleavened bread. **Have I brought your hosts out.** This expression seems to prove that we have in the injunctions of verses 14—20, not the exact words of the revelation on the subject made by God to Moses before the institution of the Passover, but a re-casting of the words after the exodus had taken place. Otherwise, the expression must have been, "I will bring your hosts out." **As an ordinance for ever.** Easter eve, the day on which Satan was despoiled by the preaching of Jesus to the spirits in prison (1 Pet. iii. 19), and on which the Church first realises its deliverance from the bondage of sin by the Atonement of Good Friday, is the Christian continuance of the first day of unleavened bread, and so answers to this text, as Good Friday to the similar command in ver. 14.

Ver. 18.—**In the first month.** The word "month" seems to have accidentally dropt out of the Hebrew text. **In the evening.** The Hebrew day commenced with the evening (Gen. i. 5); but the evening here intended is that at the close of the 14th of Abib, which began the 15th. Similarly, the evening of the 21st is here that which commenced the 22nd.

Ver. 19.—This is not a mere "vain repetition" of verse 15. It adds an important extension of the punitive clause—"that soul shall be cut off from Israel"—from Israelites proper to proselytes. We are thus reminded, at the very time when Israel is about to become a nation and to enter upon its inheritance of exclusive privileges, that no exclusion of the Gentiles by reason of race or descent was ever contemplated by God, either at the giving of the law, or at any other time. In Abraham "all the families of them were to be blessed" (Gen. xii. 3). It was always open to any Gentiles to join themselves to Israel by becoming "proselytes of justice," adopting circumcision and the general observance of the law, and joining the Israelite community. The whole law is full of references to persons of this class (Ex. xx. 10; xxiii. 12; Lev. xvi. 29; xvii. 10; xviii. 26; xx. 2; xxiv. 16; Num. xxxv. 15; Deut. v. 14; xvi. 11—14; xxiv. 17, 19; xxvii. 19; xxix. 11, etc.). It must have been largely recruited in the times immediately following the exodus from the "mixed multitude" which accompanied the Israelites out of Egypt (Ex. xii. 38), and from the Kenites who joined them in the wilderness (Num. x. 29–31; Jud. i. 16). **Born in the land**—i.e., an Israelite by birth—"the land" is, no doubt, Canaan, which is regarded as the true "Land of Israel" from the time when it was assigned by God to the posterity of Abraham (Gen. xv. 18).

Ver. 20.—Here again there is no repetition, but an extension. "Ye shall eat **nothing** leavened," not only no leavened **bread** (ver. 15), but no leavened cake of any kind. And "**in all your habitations** shall ye eat unleavened bread," i.e., wherever ye dwell, whether in Egypt, or in the wilderness, or in Palestine, or in Babylonia, or in Media, this law shall be observed. So the Jews observe it everywhere to this day, though they no longer sacrifice the Paschal lamb.

HOMILETICS.

Vers. 1–2. *The advantages of an ecclesiastical calendar.* With their new position as an independent nation, and their new privileges as God's redeemed people (ch. vi. 6), the Israelites received the gift of a new ecclesiastical calendar. Their civil calendar remaining as before, their civil year commencing with Tisri, about the time of the autumnal equinox, and consisting of twelve months of alternately twenty-nine and thirty days, they were now commanded to adopt a new departure for their sacred year, and to reckon its commencement from Abib or Nisan, which began about the time of the vernal equinox, or March 21. This was advantageous to them in several ways.

I. It secured them a time of religious retrospect and contemplation, not already occupied by worldly cares. The commencement of a civil year naturally brings with it various civil and worldly cares, which occupy the mind, demand the attention, and distract the thoughts. The worldly position has to be reviewed, accounts made up, stock taken, debts claimed and paid, subscriptions renewed or discontinued, agents communicated with, orders given, arrangements made in some instances for the whole of the coming twelvemonth; and the result is, that the mind of most men is then so occupied, not to say harassed, that it cannot turn itself with any vigour or freshness to the contemplation of things heavenly and spiritual. Of great value then, and importance, is it that religion should have a separate time to itself for a review of the spiritual position, for the taking of stock in a religious sense, the balancing of the account with heaven, the forming of plans for the spiritual life beforehand, since that life has as much need to be carefully provided for as the worldly life. The opening of a year being the natural time for such a review, the new arrangement made naturally suggested it, and provided a quiet time for it.

II. It gave the ideas connected with the festival about to be instituted a greater hold on men's thoughts than might otherwise have been the case. Everyone recognises the importance of a new beginning. A religion naturally strikes its key-note at the commencement of its round of services. As the coming of Christ into the world is the very essence of Christianity, the ecclesiastical year of Christendom commences with Advent. Thus Christians are taught that the foundation-stone of their religion, the root out of which it all springs, is the Incarnation. For Mosaism the key-note was deliverance from Egypt, and covenant relationship with God as His people by means of sacrifice. Deliverance from Egypt was redemption from servitude, and the commencement of a free national life. Sacrifice was the appointed means of keeping up and renewing the covenant relationship begun in circumcision. In the Passover these two thoughts were blended together, and Israel had to meditate on both. The one thought was necessary to call forth that loving trust in the favour and goodness of God, which lies at the root of all acceptable service; the other was needed to give ease to the conscience, to reassure the trembling sinner, and remove his sense of a guilt that separated him from God, and made his circumcision unavailing. The prominence given to these ideas by the position of the Paschal Festival, impressed them upon the minds of the Israelites as fundamental and vital truths.

III. It gave the religion generally a status and a position of independence, which increased man's respect for it. In all times and countries the suspicion occurs to some, that religion is but a form of statecraft, a politic invention of governors to render government more easy. Anything that marks the co-ordinate authority of Church and State in their separate spheres, and especially the independence of the Church, is valuable, as an obstacle to Erastianism, and an indication of the Church's inherent right to regulate Church affairs. An ecclesiastical calendar distinct from the civil calendar is no doubt a little matter; but it implies an important principle, and is perhaps not without some influence over the general tone of thought and feeling in a country.

Vers. 3—20.—*The Passover Proper.* The Passover may be viewed :—

I. As a commemorative rite. Instituted with reference to the tenth plague, and as a means by which the first-born of the Israelites might be saved from destruction, but accompanied by ceremonies which were connected with the prospective departure of the whole nation out of Egypt, the Passover feast, as established "by an ordinance for ever," commemorated two distinct and different things. (1) The passing over of the houses of the Israelites by Jehovah, when he went through the land in the character of "destroyer" (ver. 23), to smite the first-born; and (2) the hurried departure of the nation out of Egypt in the night, with bread for their journey, which they had not had time to leaven (ver. 34). It was thus intended to remind them of two great mercies; the lesser one being the escape of their first-born from sudden death, and the greater one the deliverance of the whole people from the bondage and affliction of Egypt, with the consequence of such deliverance, the establishment of them as a nation under the direct government of God, and under laws which were communicated to them by God himself at Sinai. Man is so apt to forget the benefits which God confers upon him, that it has been found necessary, or at least desirable, in almost all countries, to establish, by authority, days of commemoration, when national deliverances, national triumphs, national recoveries, shall be brought prominently before the mind of the nation, and pressed upon its attention. The Passover must be regarded as one of the most effective of such commemorative ceremonies. It has continued to be celebrated for above three thousand years. It brings vividly to the recollection of the Jew that night of trepidation and excitement, when the lamb was first killed, the blood dashed upon the doorposts, and the sequel waited for—that night, when "about midnight" was heard "a great cry," and in every house the Egyptians bewailed one dead—that night, in which, after the cry, a murmur arose, and the Egyptians became "urgent" (ver. 33), and insisted that the Israelites should quit the land forthwith. It has all the political advantage of a great national celebration; and it exalts the political idea by uniting it with religious enthusiasm.

II. As a FEAST OF THANKSGIVING. The sacrifices of the Paschal week, with the exception of the Paschal lamb and the daily goat, must be viewed as thank-offerings. They consisted of fourteen bullocks, seven rams, and forty-nine lambs of the first year, provided by the priests, and offered to God in the name of the nation. They were burnt on the altar as holocausts, accompanied by meat-offerings of flour mingled with oil. At the same time individuals offered their own private thank-offerings. So far, the special object of the thanksgiving was the great deliverance, with which might be conjoined, in thought, God's further mercies in the history of the nation. On the second day of the feast, however, another subject of thankfulness was introduced. The season of the year was that in which the earliest grain ripened in Palestine; according to a conjecture already made, it was the time when the return of spring had been long celebrated among the Semites by a traditional observance. As " each return of the Passover festival was intended to remind the Israelites of their national regeneration" (Kalisch), it was thought appropriate to bring the festival into connection with the regeneration of nature, and the return of vernal vegetation. On the second day, therefore, a sheaf of the first ripe barley was offered as the first-fruits of the coming harvest, and thanks were rendered to God for his bounty in once more bringing to perfection the fruits of the earth. During the remainder of the week, both subjects occupied the thoughts of the worshippers, who passed the time in innocent festivities, as songs, music, and dancing.

III. As a SYMBOLICAL CEREMONY. We have not to guess at the symbolical meaning of the Passover, as of so much that is contained in the Jewish law. Scripture distinctly declares it. "Christ, *our Passover*, is slain," says St. Paul; "therefore let us keep the feast." Christ, who was prefigured and foreshown in every sacrifice, was symbolised especially by the Paschal victim. He was "the Lamb of God" (John i. 29), "without spot or blemish" (1 Peter i. 19), "holy, harmless, undefiled" (Heb. vii. 26); offered to keep off "the destroyer," saving us by His blood from death (Acts xx. 28); slain that we might feed upon His flesh (John vi. 51). The Paschal lamb, when prepared for sacrifice, presented, as Justin Martyr informs us, a lively image of the Saviour upon "the accursed tree," being extended on a cross formed of two wooden spits, one longitudinal, and one transverse, placed at right angles each to the other. "Not a bone of it was to be broken," that it might the better typify Him whom God preserved from this indignity (Ps. xxxiv. 20; John xix. 33). It was to be consumed entirely, as Christ is to be taken entire into the heart of the faithful (Gal. iv. 19). Scripture also distinctly declares the symbolical meaning of the unleavened bread. "Let us keep the feast," says St. Paul, "not with the leaven of malice and wickedness, but with the unleavened bread of sincerity and truth." He who would feed on Christ must first put away from him all corruption and impurity, eject all leaven out of the house wherein his spirit dwells, make himself fit to sit down at that heavenly banquet, by getting rid of all those "evil things which come from within, and defile the man" (Mark vii. 23). There may be some doubt, however, as to the symbolism of the "bitter herbs," which Scripture leaves unexplained. The exegesis, that the bitter herbs symbolised the sufferings of the Israelites in Egypt, if taken as exhausting the meaning, is unsatisfactory. The memory of past sufferings inflicted by others is not a necessary accompaniment of present festal joy, though it may enhance that joy by contrast. The "bitterness" should be something that is always requisite before the soul can find in Christ rest, peace, and enjoyment—something that must ever accompany that rest, peace, and enjoyment, and, so long as we are in the flesh, remain inseparable from it. Two things of this kind suggest themselves—repentance and self-denial. The bitter herbs may perhaps symbolise both, pointing on the one hand to the important truth, that real repentance is a continuous act, never ceasing, while we live below, and on the other to the necessity of men's "taking up their cross *daily*," and striving towards perfectness through suffering.

Ver. 14.—*The Passover continued in the Eucharist.*—It was expressly declared that the Passover was instituted to be observed as a feast "by an ordinance for ever." Jews are justified in remaining Jews, if they cannot otherwise continue to celebrate it. But they can. The Passover is continued in the Eucharist. Hence St. Paul's words at Easter time—"Christ, our Passover, is crucified for us; therefore *let us keep the feast*" (1. Cor. v. 7, 8).

I. The Eucharist is the after commemoration of the event, which the Passover prefigured and foreshadowed. The reality underlying both being the Lord's death upon the cross as a propitiation for the sins of man, this death was set forth in anticipation by the Paschal sacrifice; it is now "shown forth" after the event, in the Eucharist, "until Christ come" (1 Cor. xi. 26). The bread and wine represent the humanity of Christ as truly as the Paschal lamb represented it. The Eucharistic ceremony is "a perpetual memory (ἀνάμνησις) of his precious death," and in some respects a more lively setting forth of that central event of history than ever was the Paschal ceremony.

II. The Eucharist sets forth the Christian's deliverance from bondage, as the Passover did the Jew's. The true bondage is the bondage of sin. This is the "Egypt" from which man requires to be delivered. The death of Christ, which the Eucharist "shews forth," is the one and only remedy for sin, the one and only means whereby it becomes possible for man to shake off the grievous yoke from his shoulders, and become free. By His meritorious sacrifice the guilt of sin is removed; by His assisting grace, given most abundantly through the Eucharist, the power of sin is destroyed, and its taint gradually purged out of our nature.

III. The Eucharist is a feast of thanksgiving to the Christian, as the Passover festival was to the Jew. The very name of Eucharist, which became the usual name of the Holy Communion as early as the second century, indicates how essential a feature of it thanksgiving was felt to be. "We praise thee, we bless thee, we worship thee, we glorify thee, we give thee thanks for thy great glory, O Lord God"—this is the general key-note of Eucharistic services. And naturally. For, if the Jew had much to thank God for, the Christian has more. Redemption, justification, assisting grace, sanctification, union with Christ—clear and distinct promise of everlasting life—are his, and crowd upon his mind in connection with this sacrament.

IV. The Eucharist, like the Passover, is a feast upon a sacrifice. In the Passover, as generally in sacrifices, the victim was first offered on behalf of the sacrificers—in this case the household, and then the flesh of the victim furnished a solemn sacrificial meal to the members of the household. In the Eucharist, where the true victim is Christ himself, whose sacrifice upon the cross is alone propitiatory, a commemoration of the death of Christ is made, and then there follows a feast of the most sacred kind. Whatever benefits may have flowed from participation in the Paschal festival are far exceeded by those attached to the "Supper of the Lord." The Jew felt himself by participation in the Passover festival incorporated anew into the community of Israel; the Christian, by worthy participation in the Eucharist, is engrafted anew into Christ.

HOMILIES BY VARIOUS AUTHORS.

Ver. 2.—*The beginning of months.* The exodus from Egypt was the birthday of the nation of Israel. In commemoration of this great event, the day from which the (religious) year began was changed. The month Abib was thenceforth to be "the beginning of months." The civil year continued to begin with Tisri (cf. ch. xxiii. 16).

I. Redemption, the true starting-point of human existence. The day when salvation comes to a man's house (Luke xix. 9; Acts xvi. 34) is the true "beginning of days" to him. 1. It is *the commencement of a new life.* "Born again" (John iii. 3); "passed from death into life" (John v. 24); "a new creature" (2 Cor. v. 17). "The years we spent before we turned to the Lord are not worth counting; the best that can happen to them is to be buried out of sight" (Dr. J. M. Gibson). 2. It is *the day of separation from the world.* Some think that up to this time the Israelites had used the Egyptian calendar, which began about the time of the summer solstice. "From this time, however, all connection with Egypt was to be broken off, and the commencement of the sacred year was to commemorate the time when Jehovah led them forth to liberty and independence" (Geikie). 3. It is *the day which begins the journey to heaven.* Redemption is the beginning of the new life: it is, however, but the beginning. The wilderness journey follows it. Conversion is not a resting-place, but a starting-point. It begins, but does not complete, salvation.

II. TIME, A MEMORIALIST OF GOD'S MIGHTY WORKS. Even on so immaterial a thing as time, God has inscribed a memorial of His three greatest works. 1. *Creation.* He has built into the structure of the week an imperishable record of the six days' work. 2. The *Exodus.* The order of the year in Israel was made to testify to the deliverance from Egypt. 3. The *Christian redemption.* The advent of Christ has founded an era. The bitterest enemy of the Gospel is compelled to do it, at least, the involuntary homage of dating his years from the Lord's advent. By his use of the Christian calendar, the infidel testifies unwittingly to the power of the religion which he seeks to overthrow.

III. THE SPHERES OF THE SACRED AND THE CIVIL ARE DISTINCT. One indication of this, even in the polity of Israel, is seen in the fact that the sacred year began in one month, and the civil in another.—J. O.

Vers. 1—29.—*The Passover.* God's last and overwhelming blow was about to be struck at Egypt. In anticipation of that blow, and in immediate connection with the exodus, God gave directions for the observance of a Passover.

I. THE PASSOVER IN ITS CONNECTION WITH THE HISTORY. For details of the ritual, see the verses of the chapter. 1. The *design* of the Passover was to make plain to Israel the ground on which its salvation was bestowed—the ground, viz., of Atonement. "The more recent plagues had fallen on Egypt alone. The children of Israel were saved from them. But though the salvation was obvious, the way of salvation had not yet been indicated. But now that the last and heaviest plague is about to fall, not only will Israel be saved from it, but the ground on which (the whole) salvation is bestowed will be made plain." 2. The connection of the Passover *with the exodus.* In this relation it is to be viewed more especially as a *purificatory* sacrifice. Such a sacrifice was peculiarly appropriate on the night of leaving Egypt, and one would probably have been appointed, even had no such special reason existed for it as the judgment on the first-born. 3. The connection of the Passover *with the judgment on the first-born.* Israel was God's Son, His firstborn (ch. x. 22), and is in turn represented by *his* first-born; and so with Egypt. Because Pharaoh would not let Israel (God's first-born) go, God had declared his purpose of smiting "all the first-born in the land of Egypt, both man and beast" (ver. 12); the punishment in this case, as frequently in God's Providence (cf. Is. xxx. 16), taking a form analogous to the sin it is designed to chastise. "The first-born represented the family, so that judgment of the first-born stood for judgment upon all, and redemption of the first-born stood for the redemption of all" (Dr. Gibson). Accordingly, not the firstborn merely, but the entire household, as represented in him, was redeemed by the blood of the Passover, and joined in the subsequent feast upon the lamb (ver. 8). Note, there was a peculiar fitness in the Passover being instituted at this particular crisis. (1) The death of the first-born was a judgment pure and simple; not, like the hail, locusts, etc., an *admonitory* plague. (2) It gave a heightened and impressive character to the salvation that redemption by blood, redemption by power, and the emergence of the people from slavery into distinct existence as a people of God, were thus seen going hand in hand. The analogy with the Christian redemption is obvious. 4. The *teaching* of the Passover. It taught the people (1) that *naturally they were as justly exposed to wrath as the people of Egypt.* "Whether viewed in their individual or in their collective capacity, they were themselves of Egypt—collectively, a part of the nation, without any separate and independent existence of their own, vassals of the enemy, and inhabitants of the doomed territory—individually, also, partakers of the guilt and corruption of Egypt" (Fairbairn). "If the test had been one of character, it is quite certain that the line would not have been run so as to range all Egypt on the one side, and all Israel on the other. No one can suppose that all the real worth and excellence were on the side of the latter, and all the meanness and wickedness on the side of the former. In fact, the children of Israel had shared only too deeply in the sins of Egypt, and, accordingly, if they are to be saved, it must be on some other ground than their own merits" (Gibson). (2) That *the medium of their salvation—the ground on which it was bestowed—was blood of atonement.* It is vain to deny that the Passover victim was truly a propitiatory sacrifice. The use made of its blood is proof sufficient of that. The lamb died in room of the first-born. Sprinkled on the door-posts and lintels, its blood sheltered the inmates of the dwelling from the stroke of the destroyer (vers. 21—24). "A sinless victim, the household might, as it were, hide behind it, and escape the just punishment of their sins" (Köhler in Geikie). The Passover thus emphatically taught the necessity of atonement for the covering of guilt. No thoughtful Israelite but must have deeply realised the truth, "Without shedding of blood is no remission" (Heb. ix. 22). (3) *The solidarity of the nation.* The observance of the Passover was to be an act, not of individuals, but of households and groups of households, and in a wider sense, of the nation as a whole. The Israelites were thus taught to feel their unity as before God—their oneness in guilt as in redemption. (*a*) In guilt. Each was involved in guilt and doom, not only through his own sins, but through the sins of the nation of which he formed a part (cf. Is. vi. 5; Matt. xxiii. 35). (*b*) In redemption. This was beautifully symbolised in the eating of the lamb. The lamb was to be roasted entire, and placed on the table undivided (ver. 9). "By avoiding the breaking of the bones (ver. 46), the animal was preserved in complete integrity, undisturbed and entire (Ps. xxxiv. 20) . . . There was no other reason for this than that all who took part in this one animal, *i.e.* all who ate of it, should look upon themselves as one whole, one community, like those who eat the New Testament Passover, the body of Christ (1 Cor. v. 7), of whom the apostle says (1 Cor. x. 17), 'We being many are one bread, and one body; for we are all partakers of that one bread.'" (Bähr.) (4) It *pointed to an atonement in the future.* For, manifestly, there lay in the blood of the lamb no *real* virtue to take away sin. It declared the necessity of atonement, but could not adequately provide it. The life of a beast was no proper substitute for the life of a first-born son. The Passover, therefore, from its very nature, is to be viewed as a type. It pointed on to Christ, in whom all the types of sacrifices find complete fulfilment. (5) *The various features of the ritual were symbolic.* The unleavened bread was indicative of haste (Deut. xvi. 3); the bitter herbs of the affliction of Egypt, etc. These circumstances, like the blamelessness of the victim, the sprinkling of the blood, etc., had also spiritual significance. See below, Homily on vers. 21—29. It is to be remarked, in general, that "the earthly relations then existing, and the operations of God in connection with them, were framed on purpose to represent and foreshadow corresponding but immensely superior ones, connected with the work and kingdom of Christ." (Fairbairn.)

II. The Passover as an ordinance for later generations (vers. 14, 24—28). In this respect, the Passover is to be viewed—1. As *an historical witness to the reality of the events of the exodus.* See below; also Homily on Deut. xvi. 1—9. The Passover, like the Lord's Supper, was an institution which, in the nature of things, could not have been set up later than the event professedly commemorated. 2. As *a perpetuation of the original sacrifice.* The blood of the lambs was year by year presented to God. This marked that the true sacrifice had not yet been offered (Heb. x. 1—3). Now that Christ has died, and has "put away sin by the sacrifice of himself" (Heb. ix. 26; x. 12), there is no room for further sacrifice, and the Lord's Supper is to be regarded as simply a commemorative ordinance and means of grace. The doctrine of the mass has no foundation in true scriptural analogy. 3. As *a means of grace.* It was a feast, collecting the Israelites in great numbers at the sanctuary, and reviving in their minds the memory of the great deliverance, in which had been laid the foundation of their national existence. The lamb, slain on their behalf, roasted with fire, and set on the table before their eyes, to be handled and eaten by them, in solemn observance of a Divine command, gave them a vivid sense of the reality of the facts they were commemorating.   The Lord's Supper, in like manner, is a powerful means of impressing mind and heart, an act of communion on the part of Christian believers, and a true source of nourishment (through spiritual participation in Christ) to the soul.   4. The observance of the Passover *was connected with oral instruction* (vers. 26, 27).   This was a further guarantee for the handing down of a faithful, ungarbled tradition of the meaning of the ceremony; added to the interest of the service; took advantage of a favourable opportunity to impress the minds of the young; and helped to keep alive in all classes of the community a vivid remembrance of God's mighty works.

III. The feast of unleavened bread (vers. 14—21).   The ordinance for this feast was probably given at Succoth, on the day succeeding the exodus (see ver. 17, and ch. xiii. 5—8).   It is inserted here on account of its internal connection with the Passover.   It is to be viewed—1. *As a memorial of the haste with which the Israelites left Egypt.*   The Israelites had evidently intended to leaven their dough on the night of the exodus, but were prevented by the haste (ver. 34).   "For thou camest out of the land in haste" (Deut. xvi. 3).   This is the historical groundwork of the institution. 2. As *a symbol of spiritual truth.*   (1) The feast lasted seven days, a complete circle of time.   (2) It was rounded off at the beginning and end by an holy convocation. This marked it as a *sacred* period.   (3) Sacrifices were offered during its course (Num. xiii. 16—26; Deut. xv. 2).   (4) The bread eaten was to be unleavened.   So strict was the injunction on this point that the Israelite found eating leaven during these seven days was to be "cut off," *i.e.*, excommunicated.   The general idea of the feast was, therefore, to represent what redeemed life in its entirety ought to be—a life purged from the leaven of "malice and wickedness," and devoted to God's service in "sincerity and truth" (1 Cor. v. 8).   "The exodus formed the groundwork of the feast, because it was by this that Israel had been introduced into a new vital element" (Keil).   The "walk in newness of life" follows on redemption.   We may apply the precept about "cutting off from Israel" to the exclusion of immoral and impure members from the Church.—J. O.

Vers. 1—28.—*The institution of the Passover.*   Moses has now done with requesting and threatening Pharaoh.   He leaves Pharaoh to the terrible smiting hand of Jehovah, and turns, when it is quite time to turn, to his own people.   He who would not listen had to be left for those who would listen.   It is now manifest that Moses is to be profitably occupied with matters which cannot any longer be delayed.   It was needful to give warning concerning the death of the first-born to the Israelites quite as much as to Pharaoh.   For some time they had been the passive, the scarcely conscious objects of Divine mercy and power.   Painfully conscious they were of the physical hardships which Pharaoh inflicted on them, but they had little or no thought of deprivations and hindrances with respect to higher things.   God had been leading them forward by a way they knew not, and now the hour has come for them to know the way and walk in it with understanding, choice, circumspection, and diligence.   All at once, from being passive spectators in the background, they came forward to be prime actors in the very front; and God is here telling them through Moses what to do, and how they are to do it.   More is to be done than simply wait for God's coming at midnight: that coming has to be made ready for with great solemnity and minuteness of preparation.

I. Notice how Jehovah here brings the voluntary element into the deliverance of His people and their connection with Him.   *They are to be delivered, only as they are willing to be delivered.*   They are to signify their willing regard to conform with the will of God.   The matter is made almost a personal one; if not brought before every Israelite, it is brought before every head of a household. Hitherto the immunities of the people during the course of the plagues had been secured in a mere external way.   The protection belonged to a certain territory, and the Israelites had to exert no attention, take no trouble, in order to secure the protection. God kept the flies, the hail, and the darkness out of Goshen without requiring any mark upon the habitations and property of His people.   But now, as the last visitation from God draws nigh, they have to take a part, and a very decided part, in making their exemption effectual.   Jehovah comes, treating all who are in Egypt as belonging fully to Egypt, and it is for the Israelites to show by some significant act the deep difference which separates between them and the Egyptians. There had been, up to this time, certain differences between the Egyptian and the Israelite which did not depend upon the Israelite's choice. The Egyptian was master, and the Israelite slave; assuredly the Israelite had not chosen that. An Egyptian might soon lose all trace of his personal ancestry, but every Israelite could trace his ancestry back to Jacob, to Isaac, to Abraham; and this was a matter he had not chosen. The Egyptian belonged to a nation which had been smitten with nine plagues, but from the later and severer of these the Israelite dwelling in Goshen had been free; yet this freedom had been secured without making it to depend on the Israelite's own action. But now, as the day of redemption draws near, Jehovah reminds every Israelite that underneath all the differences which, in carrying out His purposes, He may make to exist among men, *there is a common humanity.* Before Him who comes smiting at midnight there is neither Israelite nor Egyptian, bond nor free; everything depends on the sprinkled blood; and the sprinkled blood depends on whether the Israelite has put it on his door *of his own accord.* If, that night, the Israelite did not of his own accord make a difference between himself and the Egyptian, then no natural distinction or past immunity was of the slightest avail. Even already it is being shown that circumcision availeth nothing, but a new creature. Israel can only be truly Israel as he is Israel inwardly. The mark upon the door without must come from the perfect heart and willing mind within. The only great abiding differences between man and man are such as we, fully considering our position, concur in making of our own free will. True it is that we cannot establish and complete these differences in our own strength; but it is very certain that God will not do this—indeed, by the very limitations of the thing to be done, he cannot—except as we willingly and with alacrity give him opportunity.

II. In these instructions for the Passover, GOD BRINGS THE FUNDAMENTAL ELEMENT OF PURE FAITH INTO ACTIVE EXERCISE. In Heb. xi. 28 we are told that by faith Moses kept the passover, and the sprinkling of blood, lest he that destroyed the first-born should touch them. And this faith extended from Moses to every head of a household in Israel. The whole instructions imply a trustful, disciplined spirit, on the part of those receiving them. Up to this time nothing had been required of them except to stand still and wait while God dealt with Pharaoh. They are left on one side, treated as helpless captives, whom it is vain to ask for what they cannot give. But now they are asked for something, and they have not only to render it willingly, but *with the obedience of faith* (Rom. xvi. 26). They are asked to slay a number of lambs, the number being determined according to a settled proportion. When the lambs are slain, the blood is to be sprinkled on the doors of each Israelite dwelling, and the flesh, prepared in a peculiar and exact way, is to be eaten by the inhabitants. *Well, what should all this have to do with the protection of Israel?* How should it advance the captives towards deliverance? If God had told them to get ready swords and spears, and discipline themselves for battle there would have been something intelligible in such instructions, something according to the schemes of human wisdom. But God does not deliver as men would deliver. It pleased him, in the fulness of time and by the foolishness of a slain lamb and sprinkled blood to save Israel. And yet it was not the slain lamb and sprinkled blood that saved by themselves. Moses and Aaron might have slain so many lambs and sprinkled their blood, and yet there would have been no efficacy in them. Their efficacy as protectors was not a natural efficacy. The efficacy lay in this: that the lambs were slain and the blood sprinkled *in the obedience of faith.* The thing done and the spirit in which it is done—truth and faith—go together in resistless power. *There must be truth;* faith by itself does nothing; for a man may believe a lie and then where is he? *There must be faith;* truth by itself does nothing; just as food does nothing unless a man takes it into his stomach. Of course it was quite possible for a sceptical Israelite to say, " What can there be in this sprinkled blood?"—and the very fact that such a question was possible shows how God was shutting his people up to pure faith. He asks them *to act simply on the word of Moses.* That word was now to be a sufficient reason for their conduct. Moses had done enough to show from whom he came. It is interesting to notice how faith stands here, asked for, the first thing, by Moses, even as it was afterwards by Jesus. As the Israelites believed because Moses spoke, so we must believe because Jesus speaks. Jesus speaks truth because it is true; but we must receive it and believe it, not because in our natural reason we can see it as true, but because of the ascertained and well-accredited character of him who speaks it. And we must show our faith *by our works*, as these Israelites did. It was not required of them to understand how this sprinkled blood operated. They acted as believing that it would operate, and the indisputable fact is that they were saved. It is a great deal more important to have a thing done, than to be able to understand all the ins and outs by which it is done. A man does not refuse to wind up his watch, because he cannot understand its intricate mechanism. His purposes are served, if he understands enough to turn the key. And so our purposes are served, if we have enough practical faith in Jesus to gain actual salvation through him. Exactly how Jesus saves, is a question which we may ask again and again, and vainly ask. Let us not, in asking it, waste time and risk eternity, when by the prompt and full obedience of faith, we may know in our experience, that however obscure the process may be, the result itself is a real and abiding one.

III. Looking back on this passover lamb in the light of the finished work of Jesus, we see HOW AMPLE A TYPE IT IS OF HIM WHO WAS TO COME AFTER AND STAND BETWEEN THE BELIEVING SINNER AND THE AVENGING GOD. 1. *The lamb was taken so as to bind families and neighbours together.* This reminds us of Him, who gathers round himself, in every place, those who form the true family, the new family; joined together not after the temporary, dissolving order of *nature*, but after the abiding, ever-consolidating order of *grace*. Wheresoever two or three are gathered together in the name of Jesus, there the true Lamb of God is present in all those relations of which the passover lamb gave but a foreshadowing. The true families are made by the coalescence of those who, living in one neighbourhood, have one Lord, one faith, one baptism, one God and Father of all. 2. *The passover lamb was without blemish.* Consider what is said in this respect of Jesus (Matt. iii. 17; Mark i. 11; Luke iii. 22; xxiii. 4—14; John xix. 4—6; 2 Cor. v. 21; Eph. iv. 13; Col. i. 19; Heb. ix. 14; 1 Pet. ii. 22). 3. *It was a male of the first year.* So Jesus was taken in the freshness and strength of his manhood (Luke iii. 23). 4. *The flesh of the lamb was eaten in the company for which it had been slain.* It is only when we bear in mind the first passover in Egypt, that we reach the significance of all that was said and done on the night when Jesus sat down for the last passover feast with his disciples. Jesus took the bread and said: "Take, eat; this is my body." There was to be no more killing of the lamb; the bread, easily made and easily portioned out, took its place. But still the Lord had to say "this is my body." A body had to be thought of as eaten, and not mere bread. Really, when we look into the matter, we find that the sprinkling of the blood was only part of the protection; the eating was protective also. Assuredly the sprinkling by itself would have counted for nothing, if the eating had been omitted. When the blood was sprinkled, it illustrated faith in him who comes between God and the sinner. When the flesh was eaten, it illustrated faith in him whose life becomes our life. Being unblemished, he makes us unblemished, and being acceptable to God, he makes us acceptable also.

IV. We observe that even before the event to be commemorated was accomplished JEHOVAH MADE CAREFUL PROVISION FOR A MEMORIAL OBSERVANCE. Thus another indication is given to us, as to the completeness and order with which his plans were laid. Directions are given for the present need, and along with them are combined directions by which the record of this great liberating event may be transmitted to the remotest generations. Henceforth, the beginning of the year is to date from the month of these dealings with the first-born. Then there was also the appointment of the feast of unleavened bread. So crushing was the blow of Jehovah, and so precipitate the consequent action of Pharaoh and the Egyptians, that the Israelites were hurried out of the land with their dough before it was leavened. Here then in this domestic operation of preparing the daily bread was an opportunity given of setting forth once a year the complete separation which God had effected between the Israelites and the Egyptians. When for seven days no leaven was put in the bread, the great fact to be called up was this: that the Egyptians had hastened the Israelites out of the land. This memorial act called up at once the great change which God had produced, and in a comparatively short time. But a little while before and the Egyptians were spoiling the Israelites, demanding from them bricks without straw; now the Israelites are spoiling the Egyptians, getting gold and silver and raiment from them in profusion, and with the utmost good-will.

V. ALL THE OTHER PREPARATIONS FOR JEHOVAH'S VISIT WERE TO BE CROWNED BY MAKING FULL PREPARATIONS FOR DEPARTURE. Jehovah was coming to open the prison-doors and strike off the fetters; and he would have the captives ready to march on the instant. He is the God who makes all things to work together for good to them who are called according to his purpose. To him who is truly and devoutly obeying God, nothing comes but he is able to meet it. The obedient is never taken at a dis-advantage; he is never defrauded of a great opportunity. The children of Israel were to eat the lamb in full readiness for the journey; even though it might plausibly be said that it was a making ready before the time. The lesson is, obey God in every-thing where as here the terms of his requirement are plain to the understanding and imperative to the conscience. Reasons are not for you, who know only in part, but for him to whom the darkness and the light are both alike.—Y.

I. THE DAY OF DELIVERANCE THE BEGINNING OF A NEW ERA IN THE HISTORY OF GOD'S PEOPLE (vers. 1, 2). I. It was then only that the history of the nation as the people of God began. Before they *had been told* of God's favour towards them; they now *knew* it. "Now we believe, not because of thy saying, for we have heard him ourselves" (John iv. 42). 2. God's final deliverance begins a new era for his people. "Behold I make all things new." 3. This has its correlative type in Christian experience now. The true life of the servant of God dates from the hour of his deliverance from the bondage of sin. "If any man be in Christ Jesus he is a new creature: old things are passed away: behold all things are become new." Before Israel lay the experience of God's care and love, Sinai, the giving of the law, etc. Before us lies the deepening knowledge of his love, and of his will, the priestly service, etc.

II. THE COMMAND TO MAKE IT THE BEGINNING OF MONTHS. 1. The remembrance of God's grace makes the soul the dwelling-place of humbleness and trust. 2. It is joy and strength for service. 3. It is consecration; in the brightness of that unmerited grace the life is claimed for God; the ear is opened, the heart is touched and changed; we forget things that are behind, and reach forth to things that are before.—U.

Vers. 3—6.—*The Passover lamb a prophetic picture of Christ and his salvation.* I. FOR WHOM THE SACRIFICE AVAILS. 1. The families of Israel, the household of faith. There is no other bulwark against the visitation of the angel of death, and it shields these only. 2. Those who feed upon him. Saving faith must be a real, appropriating faith. Mere assent to a form of words avails nothing, neither can a mere intellectual conviction of the truth of Christianity or apprehension of the plan of salvation; it must be the soul's food.

II. THE CHARACTER OF THE SACRIFICE. A lamb without blemish; gentleness and blamelessness. He who dies for us is accepted, *because* he is faultless. The sin-bearer must be sinless. This is redemption's great central mystery. But though the eternal reason of it may not be understood, the wisdom of it is shown in our experience. The power which changes us lies in this, that Christ died for sins of his own, but solely for ours. "He bore *our sins*, in his own body on the tree."

III. HIS STORY. 1. The lamb kept for four days within the house foretold that God's accepted sacrifice should come forth from the homes of Israel. The *four days* may symbolise the nearly four years of our Lord's ministry. 2. The day and hour of the Saviour's death (ver. 6). 3. His death was to be Israel's act; "the whole assembly" were to slay it. (1) Our sins nailed him to the tree. *He was slain* by our iniquities. (2) Israel's act in the murder of the holy and just one was the expression of the sin which is in us all. None are free from this awful blood guiltiness, save the repentant and pardoned.—U.

Vers. 7—13.—*Christ his people's salvation and strength.* I. THE MEANS OF SAFETY (vers. 7—13). 1. They took the blood and struck it on the door posts and the lintel. We must appropriate Christ's atonement. We must say by faith, "he died for *me.*" 2. They passed within the blood-stained portals. Christ's blood must stand between us and condemnation, between us and sin. Our safety lies in setting that between our soul and them. The realising of Christ's death *for our sins* is salvation.

II. THE MEANS OF STRENGTH FOR THE ONWARD WAY. Feeding upon Christ. While Egypt was slumbering Israel was feasting. While the world is busy with its dreams we must feast upon the joy of eternity, and, comprehending with all saints the infinite love of Christ, be filled with all the fulness of God. "Except ye eat the flesh of the Son of Man, and drink his blood, ye have no life in you."

III. HOW CHRIST MUST BE PARTAKEN OF. 1. With unleavened bread and bitter herbs. The old leaven of malice and wickedness must be put away, and the feasting on Christ's love must be accompanied with repentance and self denial. There may be now and again a momentary glimpse of Christ's love where sin is not parted with, but there can be *no communion*, no enduring vision. 2. Christ must be taken as God has set him before us, in the simplicity of the Gospel, with nothing of man's invention, addition, or diminution. The Gospel remedy avails only when taken in the Gospel way (vers. 9, 10). 3. He must be partaken of in the union of love. The Passover is a social, a family feast. Those who refuse to seek church-fellowship are despising God's arrangements for their own salvation, and proving themselves devoid of the spirit which, loving him that begat, loveth him also that is begotten of him. 4. He must be partaken of with the pilgrim spirit and preparedness (ver. 11). They who will be saved by Jesus must take up their cross and follow him.—U.

Vers. 14—20.—*The Passover feast the type of the Christian life.* I. THE CHRISTIAN'S LIFE IS AN UNCEASING FESTIVAL. 1. It is unending, deepening joy. Other joys fade, this brightens. 2. It is a growing appropriation of the Lamb of God. Our union with him grows ever closer, fuller. Is this our experience? A nominal Christianity will never save us. Are we feeding on Jesus? Are we in him and he in us?

II. IT IS THE KEEPING IN REMEMBRANCE OF A PAST DELIVERANCE, AND THE ANTICIPATION OF A GREATER. 1. There was present safety from the destroyer. 2. On the morrow there was to be the passing out from amidst the broken bonds of Egypt to the promised inheritance. The feast pointed backward, the types onward. We have forgiveness through the blood of Jesus, and the expectation of his coming the second time without sin unto salvation. Faith, and love, and hope the threefold glory of Christ's people.

III. IT IS A LIFE OF HOLINESS. From the beginning to the end of the feast the old leaven was not to be found in the dwellings of Israel. The soul that turns back to sin is cut off (vers. 15, 18—20). What was a mere accompaniment in the type, is a fruit of life in Christ.

IV. IT IS A FELLOWSHIP OF ALL BELIEVERS. It was not only a family feast. It began and it closed with an assembly of the whole congregation. There are separate churches still, as there were families then. But the union of all believers must be recognised and rejoiced in.—U.

Vers. 1—28; 43—51.—*The Passover.* "It is the Lord's Passover" (Ex. xii. 11). After Pharaoh's refusal to see Moses again, Jehovah comes more manifestly into the history, in the last judgment and deliverance of his people. Three great events crowd now into a single night, the Passover, the slaying of the first-born, the march out. Consider now the Passover.

I. ITS NECESSITY. 1. Israel must *be separated from Egypt.* This idea of separation runs through all Hebrew history from the time of Abraham to this hour. But to a large extent Israel had now become merged into the Egyptian race, catching the plagues of its idolatry and sins. Great separating acts necessary—*e. g.*, as in some of the earlier visitations, in the tenth, in the passover, in the exodus, in the Red Sea. 2. To this end Israel must *be atoned afresh with God.* The tenth plague was a miracle of pure judgment: for Israel to escape the penalty of *its* sin, an atonement necessary. That atonement was the passover.

II. ITS DESIGNATIONS. They were these: " *A pass-over unto Jehovah:* " " *a sacrificial-slaying* of pass-over unto Jehovah:" " The sacrifice of the *feast* of the passover," xii. 11, 27; xxxiv. 25. Here we have four distinctive ideas. 1. The *Objective* of the pass-over was God. " Unto Jehovah." Like prayer intended to benefit man, but its objective God. Herein lies the distinction between Scriptural and unscriptural ideas of atonement. 2. The pass-over was a *Sacrifice.* [For the argument, see

Kurtz, vol. ii. 297, 298, Eng. ed.] 3. The result was a *Passing-over*. The stained lintel a bridge over which Jehovah was to pass in dread judicial progress through the land. 4. And a more remote result, the ushering in of a *Festal Life* for Israel. The festival of the passover foreshadowed the coming life of liberty.

III. The LAMB. After expository development of the leading incidents, the following truths will emerge in relation to the antitype. 1. *The objective of the death of Christ is God.* The Socinian formula runs: "The death of Christ was not to reconcile God to man, but man to God." The scriptural doctrine is that the atonement does both: but reconciles man to God, by first atoning God with man. 2. Christ is "*without blemish and without spot.*" 3. The atoning Christ was *deliberately selected*, and *fore-appointed*. 4. Kept in *view of the world*, that His worth, beauty and destiny might suitably affect men; as the lamb went in and out, for four days, the homes of Israel. 5. *Slain.* 6. The death was *Sacrificial.* 7. The result a *Passing-over* of judicial wrath. 8. But the sacrifice must be *appropriated.* The blood on the posts of the door a sign of the appropriating faith of the people. Here may be brought out the idea, that the door was the only possible altar at that moment of history. The idea of sacrifice had come down from patriarchal times; but there was no law of sacrifice, for as yet there was no nation to which to give it, and therefore there was no temple, and so no altar. Every family must be atoned for apart; every house was then a temple, and every door an altar. 9. Then, faith in Christ's atonement begins for us *high Festival.*

IV. The MEAL. Show that the meal was much more than a mere supper to prepare for a journey. It had in it spiritual significance, in relation to the Christ. 1. The *Atoning Christ is the Food of the Soul* (John vi. 51). This for the very simple reason, that the truth of the atonement is central, supreme, and comprehensive. 2. An *uncorrupted* Christ. The lamb was roasted, *i.e.*, was pure flesh acted on by fire; not sodden, diluted with water, or any way corrupted. 3. *A perfect* Christ, no bone broken. So on the cross a Christ divided is not sufficient for the nourishment of the soul, *e.g.*, Christ as an "elect spirit of the race;" or as one in whom the "God-consciousness" received high development; or as example; Teacher, etc. Christ in his whole nature, character and office. 4. The enjoyment of Christ and of his salvation will depend on the *memory of the slavery of sin.* "Bitter herbs." 5. The christian life is to be characterised by *simplicity and sincerity.* Note that unleavened bread is simply pure meal, all water parched out by the action of fire. For the significance see the Christian Rabbi, Paul, 1 Cor. i. 6—8. 6. The end of soul nutriment is *the Pilgrim-Life.* Each with staff in hand that night. 7. To the banquet, to the Exodus, to the Pilgrim-Life, *all are welcome*, on conditions, xii. 43—45. In that case, first circumcision; then coming under the sprinkled blood, were needful. The analogy is clear. Note! at the moment, when the distinction between Israel and Egypt was most marked, then did the catholicity of true Judaism most appear. In Abraham all mankind was to be blessed.—R.

Vers. 3—11. *If one died for all then all died.* Pharaoh's heart still hardened. The crowning judgment needs no intermediary; Jehovah will reveal His own right arm. Ex. xi. 4. "Who shall live when God doeth this?" He who obeying His word shelters himself beneath His shadow. See:—

I. The PREPARATION. 1. *A carefully selected victim.* Ver. 5, deliberately set apart four days beforehand. Pure *within*; innocence typified by inexperience, "the first year." Pure without, "no blemish." 2. *A carefully conducted purification.* The partaker of the sacrificial feast must endeavour after a purity resembling that of the victim. Leaven, evil, must be purged out that he may offer and receive worthily.

II. The PASSOVER. *A sacrifice to save from death*, v. 6, 7. Notice (1) Obedience ensured safety. The judgment was to go forth against the first-born; but the lamb slain—his blood duly sprinkled—would be accepted as a substitute. Obedience all that was demanded. (2) The meaning of the command. Few types are arbitrary; almost always some ground of relation between them and the thing typified, even though we may not see it. Here the pure lamb represents the offerer *as he ought to be*; it says in his name "I *would* be pure; I would dedicate myself wholly to thy service; accept me, not for what I am but for what Thou canst make me. Take this lamb for me; make me as this lamb!" Obedience saves, but that which is commanded shadows forth the final result to be achieved by obedience. 2. *Sustenance to nerve for duty.* Lamb not merely to be killed but eaten. The people saved from the destroyer are to be released also from the oppressor; to commence at once the life of liberty. Strength needed for the march. That which saves is that which supports. If the lamb represents the offerer as he *ought to be,* feeding upon the lamb will represent feeding by faith upon the ideal thus figured. To become righteous we must hunger and thirst after righteousness, Matt. v. 6. Dedication is the starting-point, but the road is persistent obedience, and they only can walk that road who feed upon the ideal first set before them (Phil. iii. 12—14).

III. CHRIST OUR PASSOVER. The type leads naturally to the great antitype. 1. *Our sacrifice.* (1) Pure, perfect. Slain *for* us. By faith accepting his work, peace with God ; shelter from the avenging angel. This is what we mean by *substitution*—Christ died for me. Notice however :—(2) Accepting this sacrifice we must still regard it as representative. Pleading its efficacy, we not merely mean " Forgive me for Christ's sake," but also, " I would be like Christ, I would give myself up wholly to Thy will even as he has done—Accept me in him, make me like him!" The doctrine of *substitution* is only explained by this underlying doctrine of *identity*, it could not otherwise be a doctrine of salvation. 2. *Our sustenance.* We too, saved in Christ, have to march on along the road which leads from slavery to freedom. To do this we must *feed* upon our ideal, "inwardly digest" it. What we ought to be; what we hope to be ; what Christ is. Our great advantage over the Jew is that *our* ideal is realised in a person. To feed upon it is to feed upon Christ. To attain it is to be like Christ, to be one with him.

Application. Christ died for us. True, but Christ dying for us implies that we also die with him. Dedication of a substitute not enough unless self is dedicated in the substitute. Very well wishing to be *happy*, and the hope of many is little more than this. God, however, means us to be *holy*, and there is no *easy* road to holiness. Accept the ideal, accept Christ out and out, we shall find him more than an ideal : he will strengthen and sustain us till we attain it. Forget what the ideal is; forget what dedication means ; we may yet find that it is possible for those who are saved from bondage to perish in the wilderness.—G.

EXPOSITION.

Ver. 21—28.—THE FIRST PASSOVER. Having received the Divine directions as to the new rite, if not with all the fulness ultimately given them, yet with sufficient fulness for the immediate purpose, Moses proceeded to communicate the Divine Will to the people under his protection. Having already aroused the jealousy and hatred of Pharaoh, he could not summon a general assembly of the people, but he ventured to call a meeting of the elders, or heads of principal families, and through them communicated the orders which he had received to the entire nation. We find, in the directions which he gave, two small points which are not comprised in the record of God's words to him. 1. The designation of the " hyssop," as the instrument by which the blood was to be placed on the side-posts and lintel (ver. 22) ; and, 2. The injunction not to quit the house " until the morning." These points may have been contained in the original directions, though omitted from the record for

brevity; or they may have been added by Moses of his own authority. On the other hand, several very main points of the original directions are not repeated in the injunctions given to the elders, though there can be no doubt that they were communicated.

Ver. 21.—**Draw out**—*i.e.,* " Withdraw from the flock." (See ver. 3.) **A lamb.** The word used is generic, and would not exclude the offering of a goat.

Ver. 22.—**A bunch of hyssop.** The hyssop was regarded as having purging or purifying qualities, and was used in the cleansing of the leper (Lev. xiv. 4), and of the leprous house (*ibid.* 51—52), and also formed an element in the " water of separation " (Num. xix. 6). It was a species of plant which grew on walls, and was generally low and insignificant (1 Kings iv. 33), yet which could furnish a stick or stalk of some length (John xix. 29). It must also have been a common plant in Egypt, the wilderness, and Palestine. Two suggestions are made with respect to it. One, that it was a species of marjoram (*Origanum*

Ægyptiacum, or O. Syriacum) common in both Egypt and Syria; the other that it was the caper plant (*Capparis spinosa*), which abounds especially in the Desert. (Stanley, *Sinai and Palestine*, p. 21.) It is in favour of this latter identification, that the modern Arabic name for the caper plant is *asaf* or *asuf*, which excellently represents the Hebrew *ezob*, the word uniformly rendered in our version by "hyssop." **The blood that is in the basin.** The Septuagint and Vulgate render—"that is *on the threshold*." *Saph*—the word translated "basin" has the double meaning. **None of you shall go out.** Moses may well have given this advice on his own authority, without any Divine command. (See introductory paragraph.) He would feel that beyond the protection of the blood of the lamb, there was no assurance of safety.

Ver. 23.—Compare verses 12, 13 which are closely followed. The only important difference is, the new expression, "The Lord will not suffer the destroyer to come in," which has generally been regarded as implying, that the actual agent in the killing of the first-born was a "destroying angel." But it is to be noted that elsewhere Jehovah himself is everywhere spoken of as the sole agent; and that in the present passage the word used has the meaning of "destruction" no less than that of "destroyer." Bishop Lowth's idea of an opposition between God and the destroying angel (*Comment on Isaiah* xxxi. 5) is scarcely tenable.

Ver. 24.—**To thee and to thy children.**

The change from the plural to the singular is curious. Perhaps, we are to understand that Moses insisted on the perpetuity of the ordinance to each of the elders severally.

Ver. 25.—**The land which the Lord will give you, according as he hath promised.** See above, ch. iii. 8—17; vi. 4; and compare Gen. xvii. 8; xxviii. 4, etc.

Ver. 26.—**When your children shall say unto you, what mean ye by this service.** Apparently, Moses adds these injunctions by his own sole authority. He assumes that curiosity will be aroused by the strange and peculiar features of the Paschal ceremony, and that each generation in succession will wish to know its meaning and origin.

Ver. 27.—**It is the sacrifice.** It has been denied that the Paschal lamb was, in the true sense of the word, a sacrifice (Carpzov and others). But this passage alone is decisive on the question, and proves that it was. Moreover, it was offered in the holy place (Deut. xvi. 5, 6); the blood of it was sprinkled upon the altar, and the fat was burnt (2 Chr. xxx. 16; xxxv. 11). Compare also Ex. xxiii. 18; Num. ix. 7; Deut. xvi. 2. **The people bowed the head and worshipped.** Rather, "and made obeisance." Compare ch. iv. 31. By "the people" seems to be meant "the elders of the people." (See ver. 21.)

Ver. 28.—**So did they.** The long series of miracles wrought by Moses and Aaron had so impressed the people, that they yielded an undoubting and ready obedience.

HOMILETICS.

Ver. 22.—*No safety for man beyond the limits protected by the Lamb's atoning blood.* No Israelite was to pass beyond the door of his house until the morning, lest he should be destroyed by the destroyer. Within the precincts, protected by the blood of the lamb, he was safe. Let Christians beware of stepping beyond the limits whereto the atoning blood extends. Those step beyond the limits—

I. WHO TEMPT GOD BY DALLYING WITH SIN. Atonement has been made for us, we feel. We have had moments of assurance that atonement and forgiveness are ours. We have had an impression that we were safe. At once the Evil One begins to whisper to our hearts that there is no longer any need of our walking warily, of our being afraid to put ourselves in temptation's way, of our flying all contact with evil; and we are too apt to listen to his suggestions, to regard the danger of falling from grace as past, and to allow ourselves a liberty in which there is too often awful peril. We draw near the confines of sin, confident that we shall sin no more; and lo! we are entangled in the meshes. And why? *Because we have gone beyond the limits protected by the atoning blood.* We have opened the door and stepped out. We have turned our backs upon the redeeming marks and put them behind us. We have been over-trustful in our own strength.

II. WHO ARE PUFFED UP BY THE THOUGHT OF THEIR SPIRITUAL ATTAINMENTS AND PRIVILEGES. "Pride goeth before a fall." Pride was the great temptation of the Jew, who felt himself one of God's peculiar people, to whom pertained "the adoption, and the glory, and the covenants, and the giving of the law, and the service of God, and the promises" (Rom. ix. 4). And pride often tempts the Christian, who has realised the work of Christ on his behalf, and the greatness of the salvation wrought for him. But pride is one of the deadly sins, and at once severs the soul from Christ. The blood of the covenant does not extend its protection over the paths which are trodden by the foot of pride. He who enters on them has wandered beyond the door which bears the redemption-marks, and is open to the assaults of the destroyer.

III. WHO FOLD THEIR HANDS AND CEASE TO BE ZEALOUS OF GOOD WORKS, AS THOUGH THEY HAD ALREADY ATTAINED. Though we cannot, by anything that we can do, merit our own salvation, or redeem ourselves or others (Ps. xlix. 7), yet God will have us " work while it is day," and the atoning blood of Christ atones for those only who are " careful to maintain good works" (Tit. iii. 8). Idleness, apathy, sloth, are contrary to his will and his word; and the man who indulges in them has strayed beyond the prescribed limits and lost the needful protection. Well for him if he discovers his mistake in time to return, and " do again the first works " (Rev. ii. 5), and so regain the lost shelter! It is needless to say that the atoning blood can avail none who (1) reject the atonement; or, (2) despise it, by giving it no thought; or, (3) trample it under foot by leading an immoral and ungodly life. These are as far removed from its protection as were the Egyptians.

Vers. 26, 27.—*The obligation of men to teach the true meaning of rites and cere-monies to their children.* The rites and ceremonies of a religion are liable to be misunderstood in two ways. 1. They may be regarded as unimportant, trifling, nay, even as superstitious—a weight and an encumbrance on true vital religion. Or, 2. They may be assigned more importance than is their due; considered to be that in which religion mainly consists, believed to have an inherent power and efficacy which is far from belonging to them. Men are prone to extremes; and most persons are naturally inclined either unduly to exalt, or unduly to depreciate religious ceremonies. Of the two evils, undue depreciation would seem to be the worse, for the following reason :—

I. UNDUE DEPRECIATION OF CEREMONIES (*a*) tends to make them of little service to men when they actually take part in them, since they neither prepare themselves properly beforehand, so as to derive from them the benefit they might, nor enter into them with much heart at the time of their occurrence, nor help their effect by devout meditation upon them afterwards. (*b*) It causes an infrequent participation in the ceremonies by the depreciators, who, expecting but little benefit in the future, and being conscious of but little benefit in the past, allow small obstacles to prevent their attendance at services which they do not value. (*c*) In extreme cases, it produces either complete abstention from, or sometimes actual abrogation of the rite, whereby advantages are forfeited on the part of whole sections of believers which would other-wise have been enjoyed by them. Thus the Society of Friends loses the benefit of both sacraments, with sad results to the spiritual life of numbers.

II. UNDUE EXALTATION OF CEREMONIES has the advantage of at any rate retaining them in use, so that their benefit is not wholly lost. It often, however, greatly lessens the benefit (*a*) by exaggerated and superstitious views of its nature, and (*b*) by the attribution of the benefit to the mere formal participation in the rite irrespective of the participator's preparation, attention, and devoutness at the time. Further, it is apt to produce such a reliance on the ceremonies as is unfavourable to practical efforts at improving the moral character and making advances towards Christian perfection. Careful instruction in the true nature and value of ceremonial observances is thus of the highest importance; and parents should perhaps scarcely wait till their children " ask the meaning" of public worship, baptism, confirmation, the Lord's supper, etc., before enlightening them on the true nature and value of each. In so doing, it will always be of use to set forth the historical origin of each usage, to show when and how it arose, and to draw attention to what Scripture says on the subject. Men's private views are various, and may be mistaken, but the Scriptures cannot but be true; and a knowledge of what is contained in the Bible with respect to each Christian rite or ceremony will be an excellent basis for the formation of a sound and healthy opinion on the subject when, in the course of time, the different views of different sections of believers come to be known.

HOMILIES BY VARIOUS AUTHORS.

Vers. 21—29.—" *Christ our Passover.*" The Passover was an eminent type of Christ. It was probably to it the Baptist referred when he said, "Behold the Lamb of God, which taketh away the sin of the world" (John i. 29). Paul gives a decisive utterance on the question in the words: "Christ our passover is sacrificed for us" (1 Cor. v. 7).

I. POINTS OF ANALOGY BETWEEN THE TRUE PASSOVER AND ITS TYPE. 1. In both *the death of a blameless victim.* The lamb, physically blameless (ver. 5); Christ, morally faultless. A sinful world needs a sinless Saviour. It has one in Christ. The sinlessness of Christ, a moral miracle. Proofs of this sinlessness. (1) Christ asserts his own freedom from sin (John viii. 29—46; xiv. 30). (2) In no part of his conduct does he betray the least consciousness of guilt. Yet it is admitted that Jesus possessed the finest moral insight of any man who has ever lived. (3) His apostles, one and all, believed him to be sinless (2 Cor. v. 21; Heb. iv. 15; 1 Pet. ii. 22; 1 John iii. 5). (4) His enemies could find no fault in him (Matt. xxvi. 60; xxvii. 23, 24). (5) The very traitor confessed the innocence of Christ (Matt. xxvii. 4). (6) The delineation of his character in the gospels bears out the averment of his moral blamelessness. (7) The captious efforts which have been made, by fixing on a few paltry points in the gospel narratives to impeach Christ's sinlessness, indirectly prove it. "As if sin could ever need to be made out against a real sinner in this small way of special pleading; or as if it were ever the way of sin to err in single particles, or homœopathic quantities of wrong" (Bushnell). 2. In both, *the design is to secure redemption from a dreadful evil.* In the one case, from the wrath of God revealed against Egypt in the smiting of its first-born. In the other, from the yet more terrible wrath of God revealed against all ungodliness and unrighteousness of men (Rom. i. 18). "Jesus, which delivered us from the wrath to come" (1 Thess. i. 10). "Saved from wrath through him" (Rom. v. 9). 3. In both, *the principle of the deliverance is that of vicarious sacrifice.* The lamb was substituted for the first-born. It protected the house, on whose door-posts the blood was sprinkled, from the stroke of the avenger. The substitutionary character of the death of Christ is, in like manner, affirmed in innumerable Scriptures. Jesus "died for the ungodly" (Rom. v. 6). He "suffered for sins, the just for the unjust" (1 Pet. iii. 18). He gave "his life a ransom for many" (Matt. xix. 28). His blood is a propitiation (Rom. iii. 25). There is just ground for the remark of Coleridge (we quote from memory) that a man who would deal with the language of his father's will, as Unitarians on this and other points do with the language of the New Testament, would be liable to an action at law. 4. In both, *there was need for an act of personal, appropriating faith.* "The people bowed the head, and worshipped. And the children of Israel went away, and did as the Lord had commanded" (vers. 27, 28). "Through faith (they) kept the passover, and the sprinkling of blood," etc. (Heb. xi. 28). Their faith showed itself in sprinkling the blood on their door-posts and lintels, and in sheltering themselves under it. Nothing short of this would have availed to save them. So it is not knowledge *about* Christ, but faith *in* him; personal application to his blood, and trust in it as the means of salvation, which secures our safety. Faith is the bunch of hyssop. 5. In both, *the slain lamb becomes the food of the new life.* There was, on the part of the Israelites, a sacrificial feast upon the flesh of the lamb. This denoted, indeed, peace and fellowship with God, but it was also an act of nourishment. Similarly, under the Gospel, the new life is nourished by feeding upon Christ. We make him ours by inward appropriation and assimilation, and so are spiritually nourished for all holy service (cf. John vi.). Minor typical features might be insisted upon (male of the first year, roast with fire, not a bone broken, unleavened bread, bitter herbs of contrition, etc.), but the above are the broad and outstanding ones.

II. THE SURPASSING EXCELLENCE OF THE TRUE PASSOVER. It belongs to the nature of a type that it should be surpassed by the antitype. The type is taken from a lower sphere than the thing which it represents. So completely, in the case of the passover, does the reality rise above the type, that when we begin to reflect on it the sense of likeness is all but swallowed up in the sense of disproportion. How great, 1. The contrast in the *redemptions.* The redemption from Egypt, though spiritual elements were involved in it, was primarily a redemption from the power of Pharaoh, and from a temporal judgment about to fall on Egypt. Underlying it, there was the need for a yet greater redemption—a redemption from the curse of a broken law, and from the tyranny of sin and Satan ; from death spiritual, temporal, and eternal. It is this higher redemption which Christ has achieved, altering, through his death, the whole relation of God to man, and of (believing) man to God. 2. The contrast in the *victims.* That, an irrational lamb; this, the Eternal Son of God in human nature, the Lord's own Christ. 3. The contrast in *the efficacy of the blood.* The blood of the passover lamb had no inherent virtue to take away sin. Whatever virtue it possessed arose from God's appointment, or from its typical relation to the sacrifice of Christ. Its imperfection as a sacrifice was seen (1) In the *multitude* of the victims. (2) In the *repetition* of the service (Heb. x. 1—3). But what the flowing of the blood of millions of lambs, year by year slain in atonement for sin could not achieve, Christ has achieved once for all by the offering up of his holy body and soul. The dignity of his person, the greatness of his love, his holy will, the spirit of perfect self-sacrifice in which he, himself sinless, offered himself up to bear the curse of sin for the unholy, confers upon his oblation an exhaustless meritoriousness. Its worth and sufficiency are infinite (Heb. x. 10—15 ; 1 Pet. i. 19; 1 John ii. 2). 4. The contrast in *the specific blessings obtained.* The difference in these springs from the contrast in the redemptions. Israel obtained (1) Escape from judgment. (2) Outward liberty. (3) Guidance, care, and instruction in the desert. (4) Ultimately, an earthly inheritance. *We* receive, through Christ, (1) Pardon of all sins. (2) A complete justifying righteousness, carrying with it the title to eternal life. (3) Renewal and sanctification by the Spirit. (4) Every needed temporal and spiritual blessing in life. (5) Heaven at the close, with triumph over death, the hope of a resurrection, and of final perfecting in glory.—J. O.

Ver. 26, 27.—" *What mean ye by this service?* " Apply to the Lord's Supper.
I. A QUESTION TO BE PUT BY THE COMMUNICANT TO HIMSELF. Qualification for the Lord's table includes " knowledge to discern the Lord's body," as well as " faith to feed upon him."
II. A QUESTION LIKELY TO BE PUT TO THE COMMUNICANT BY HIS CHILDREN. 1. The children are presumed to be *spectators* of the ordinance. It is well that children should be present during the administration of the sacraments. It awakens their interest. It leads them to inquire. 2. The ordinance is *fitted* to attract attention. An external interest attaches to it. It appeals to the senses. The symbolic acts and movements prompt to inquiry. 3. It furnishes an excellent *opportunity* for imparting instruction. Children will attend to an explanation of the sacraments, who will pay little attention to a book or a sermon. The symbolism of the ordinance aids instruction ; makes it vivid and impressive.
III. A QUESTION WHICH THE CHRISTIAN PARENT SHOULD BE ABLE TO ANSWER TO HIS CHILDREN. It is a sad matter when a parent is incapable of sitting down, and instructing his children in the meaning of the sacramental symbol. It betrays something worse than ignorance ; not improbably, a total want of spiritual religion.
IV. THE ANSWER TO THIS QUESTION INVOLVES A STATEMENT OF THE GREATEST VERITIES OF OUR FAITH. The Jew had to answer to his child—" It is the sacrifice of the Lord's passover," etc. (ver. 27). The Christian has to answer, " It is the memorial of our Lord's death, in atonement for our sins." He has to tell—1. How we were in guilt and danger. 2. How, for the love wherewith he loved us, Christ gave himself up to the death for our redemption. 3. How, for his sake, we are forgiven and accepted. 4. How the ungodly world has still God's wrath resting upon it. It is wonderful to reflect how simply, yet how perfectly, God has provided for the handing down of a testimony to these great truths in the ordinance of the Lord's Supper. The pulpit may fail to preach the doctrine of atonement ; Rationalistic and Unitarian teachers may deny it ; but as often as the Lord's Supper is observed, on the model of the New Testament, the truth is anew proclaimed in unmistakable symbols. To give a child a satisfactory explanation of the Lord's Supper, embodying the words of institution, would be almost of necessity, to preach a sermon on the atonement.—J. O.

Vers. 26—27.—*The children's question in Canaan.* 1. IT WAS A QUESTION TO BE EXPECTED. The service was one to provoke curiosity. It was not some daily action of the household, of which the children learned the meaning and purpose almost unconsciously. The grinding of the corn, the kneading of the dough, in a very short time explained themselves. But when as the beginning of the year drew round, it brought with it these special observances, the slaying and eating of the lamb and the seven days of unleavened bread, there was everything to make a child ask, "What is this being done for?" God makes one thing to fit into another. He institutes services of such a kind, with such elements of novelty and impressiveness in them, that the children make it easier for them to be instructed in the things that belong to his will. And what was true concerning this passover service, is also true, more or less, concerning all that is revealed in the Scriptures. The great facts of Divine revelation are such as to provoke curiosity, even in a child's mind. If it be true that the Scriptures are given to guide us all the way through life, then what is more reasonable to expect than that God will have placed much in them to stir up attention and inquiry from those who are just at the beginning of life?

II. HENCE THIS WAS A QUESTION TO BE ENCOURAGED. Every advantage was to be taken of childish curiosity. Inquisitive children are often reckoned a nuisance, and told to be quiet; yet such a policy as this, though it may save trouble in the present, may lead to a great deal more trouble in the future. A stupid child who never asks questions, is to be reckoned an object of pity and a source of peril. God has always in mind how to make each generation better instructed than the one going before; more obedient to him, and more serviceable for his purposes. The temptation of the grown people in Israel was to undervalue what was going on in the minds of their children. Remember how Mary and Joseph suffered through their want of forethought on this point. The God who watches human beings all the way from the cradle to the grave knows well how children, even very little children, have their own thoughts about things; and he wanted the people to give them every encouragement and information. One question wisely answered leads to the asking of other questions. Thus, by the continuance of an inquiring mood in the mind, and thus only, is profitable information to be given. Information is not to be poured into the mind as into a bucket; it must be taken as food, with appetite, and digestive and assimilating power. Thus if the question were not asked, if, while the passover preparations were being made, a child stood by in stolid unconcern, or ran away heedlessly to play, such conduct would fill a wise parent with solicitude. He would look upon it as being even more serious than a failure of physical health. He would do all he could by timely suggestions to bring the question forth. Ingenuity and patience may do much to bring curiosity into action, and if the question were not *asked* it would have to be *assumed*. The narrative of the passover was a most important one for every Israelite child to hear and remember; and if only the narrative was begun, it might soon excite the requisite and much desired interest.

III. IT WAS A QUESTION WHICH GAVE GREAT SCOPE FOR USEFULNESS TO THE CHILDREN IN THE ANSWERING OF IT. God, indeed, directs how it is to be answered; but of course, it is not meant that there was to be a formal, parrot-like confinement to these words. What, for instance, could be more gratifying to the children, who in after times asked this question, than to begin by pointing out to them, how God himself expected them to ask this question? Then the words he had directed Moses to provide for an answer, might be repeated. But it would have been a poor spiritless answer, unpleasing to God, and profitless to the children, if it had stopped with the bare utterance of the words in ver. 27. There was room for much to be said, that would very peculiarly impress the mind of a thoughtful child. It might be reminded that whereas, *now*, little children were born in the freedom of Canaan, some among their forefathers had been born in the bondage of Egypt. It might be told of that Pharaoh who had threatened the men-children with destruction. In particular, the story of the infant Moses might be told. So now, in those parts of the world where the idols are abolished, and former idolaters are gathered round the throne of grace for Christian worship, an opportunity is given for explaining to the children, in how much better a state, and with how much better surroundings they are brought up. "What mean ye by this service?" was a question which could be answered in form, and yet with such absence of heart, as utterly to chill and thwart the eager inquirer. Whereas, if it were only answered with evident care, with amplitude of detail, with loving desire to interest and satisfy, then the child thus favoured, would be laid under great obligations to be thankful in feeling, and devoted in service. A question of this sort gave great opportunity. Happy those who could seize the opportunity at once, and use it to the full.

IV. IT WAS A QUESTION WHICH CAME TO CALL EVERY ISRAELITE, AT THE ANNUAL OBSERVANCE OF THE PASSOVER, TO A CAREFUL CONSIDERATION OF HIS OWN FEELINGS WITH RESPECT TO IT. It was a question which helped to guard against formality. A little child may render a great service, without knowing it, even to a grown man. God can send the little ones, to test, to rebuke, to warn, to stir out of lethargy. "What mean ye by this service?" How is the Israelite of the grown generation to answer this question? He may tell the child what the service is intended for, the historical facts out of which it arose, and the Divine appointments concerning it; but after all, this is no real answer to the question. It may be an answer to satisfy the inquiring child, and yet leave the person who has to give it, with a barbed arrow in his memory and conscience. Notice the precise terms of the question. *What mean ye* by this service? How should the child ask in any other terms? It looks and sees the parents doing something new and strange; and to them it naturally looks for explanation and guidance. The question is not simply, "Why is this thing being done?" but "Why are *you* doing it, and what do *you mean* by it?" It became only too possible in the lapse of ages, to go through this service in a cold, mechanical, utterly unprofitable way. Not so, we may be sure, was it observed the first time in Egypt, on the night of deliverance. Then all was excitement, novelty, and overflowing emotion. Be it ours, in considering all outward and visible acts in connection with religion, all symbolic and commemorative institutions, to ask ourselves in great closeness and candour of personal self-application, "What mean we by this service?" Do we mean anything at all, and if so, what is it that we mean? To answer this is not easy: it is not meant to be easy. Perhaps one great reason why there are such marked and unabated differences of opinion with respect to Baptism and the Lord's Supper is, that we have never sufficiently considered the question, "What mean *ye* by these services?" It is hard work to be quit of mere superstition, mere clinging to outward observances as matters of custom, tradition, and respectability. It is very certain that to this question of the children, put in all its particular emphasis, only too many fathers in Israel would have been forced to reply, "We do this thing because our fathers did it." Remember that forms are, in themselves, nothing to the invisible, spiritual God. Their value is as containing, protecting and expressing what we have to present. That which pleased Jehovah and profited Israel was not the outward passover service, but the intelligence, the perceptions, the gratitude, the aspirations, and the hopes that lay behind it.—Y.

Vers. 21—28.—*Israel and the sacrifice for sin.* I. CHRIST SLAIN BY US. The lamb's blood was not only shed *for* them, but also *by* them. The crucifying of Jesus by the Jews, the revelation of what lies in every unrenewed heart. "They shall look upon him whom they have pierced."

II. WHAT IS NEEDFUL FOR SALVATION. 1. Appropriating faith. It was the blood applied with their own hands to the door of the dwelling that saved those within. It is not enough that the blood be shed. Is it *upon our gates?* Have we set it by faith between us and destruction? 2. It must be applied as God directs us. It was sprinkled on the lintel and doorposts—not within, but without. It is not enough that we believe. We must make open profession of our faith. 3. We must abide within until the day dawn and salvation come. To put that blood (which should be between us and the world) behind us, no longer to hide within it but to forget it, is to renounce salvation. Are we without or within the blood-stained gateway? We are saved if we hold the beginning of our confidence steadfast unto the end.

III. GOD'S COVENANT GIVES PERFECT SECURITY (ver. 25). The shed blood stands between us and death. The awe and joy of redeemed Israel, a faint emblem of the awe and joy which we shall feel, who shall see the judgment of sin but only from afar.

IV. THE DUTY OF THE REDEEMED. 1. Perpetual remembrance (ver. 23). We must, in the ordinance of Christ's own appointment, shew his death till he come. 2. The handing down the knowledge of salvation (vers. 26, 27). Christians should glory in the story of the Cross.

EXPOSITION.

Vers. 29, 30.—The Tenth Plague. At last the time had come for the dealing of the final blow. Nine plagues had been sent, nine inflictions endured, and no serious effect had been produced. Once or twice Pharaoh had wavered, had made profession of submitting himself, had even acknowledged his sin. But each time he had relapsed into obstinacy. Now at length the fiat had gone forth for that last plague which had been announced the first (ch. iv. 23). Pharaoh's own son, his firstborn, the heir to his throne, was smitten with death, in common with all the other male Egyptians who had "opened the womb." What the effect on the king would have been, had he alone suffered, we cannot certainly say. As it was, the whole population of the country, nobles, tradesmen, peasants, suffered with him; and the feeling aroused was so intense that the popular movement left him no choice. The Egyptians everywhere "rose up in the night" (ver. 30), and raised "a great cry," and insisted that the Israelites should depart at once (ver. 33). Each man feared for himself, and felt his life insecure, so long as a single Israelite remained in the land.

Ver. 29.—At midnight. As prophesied by Moses (ch. xi. 4). The day had not been fixed, and this uncertainty must have added to the horror of the situation. **The first-born of Pharaoh.** We have no proof that the eldest son of Menephthah died before his father, unless we take this passage as proving it. He left a son, called Seti-Menephthah, or Seti II., who either succeeded him, or reigned after a short interval, during which the throne was held by Ammonmes, a usurper. **The first-born of the captive who was in the dungeon.** This phrase takes the place of another expression, viz. "the first-born of the maid-servant that is behind the mill" (ch. xi 5). In both cases, the general meaning is, "all, from the highest to the lowest." This is perhaps the whole that is in the writer's thought; but it is also true that captives in dungeons were in some cases employed in turning hand-mills (Judg. xvi. 21). **And all the first-born of cattle.** Rather, "of beasts." There is no limitation of the plague to domesticated animals.

Ver. 30.—And Pharaoh rose up in the night, and all his servants. This general disturbance differentiates the present visitations from that which came upon the host of Sennacherib (2 Kings xix. 35). Then, the calamity came with such silence and secrecy, that the deaths were not suspected until men rose to go about their various tasks in the morning. Now, every household seems to have been aroused from its sleep in the night. We must suppose sharp and painful illness, terminating after a few hours in death. The disaster itself may have been one from which Egypt often suffers in the spring of the year (Kalisch); but its attacking all the firstborn and no others, and no Israelites, as well as its announcement, plainly showed it to be miraculous. **There was a great cry.** See the comment on ch. xi. 6. **For there was not a house where there was not one dead.** This is perhaps a slight hyperbole. There would be many families in which there was no son; and some houses might contain no male who had opened the womb. It is always to be borne in mind, that the language of Scripture —especially where exciting and tragical events are narrated—is poetical, or at the least highly rhetorical.

HOMILETICS.

Vers. 29, 30.—The death of the first-born. From the death of the first-born we may learn:—

I. The severity of God's long deferred judgments. That punishment will overtake the wicked sooner or later was the conviction of heathendom no less than of the Jewish and Christian worlds. Horace says—"Judgment may halt, but yet it rarely fails to overtake the guilty one at last." Tibullus—"Wretch, though at first thy sin no judgment meet, vengeance will come at length with silent feet." But the greater heaviness of the punishment that is long deferred does not appear to have attracted their notice. Yet experience might have taught it them. Who has not seen the long triumphant career of a thoroughly bad man, crowned with success for years, seeming to turn all he touched to gold, "flourishing," as the Psalmist has it, "like a green bay tree," yet ending in calamities and misfortunes so striking, and so heaped one upon another, as to draw general attention? It is invidious, perhaps, to note instances; but the present generation has seen at least one example among the crowned heads of

Europe. And Scripture is full of examples. How long God's Spirit strove with men in the antediluvian world, as they proceeded from one wickedness to another, heaping up to themselves wrath against the day of wrath, till the flood came and swept away the ungodly! For what a prolonged term of years must the long-suffering of God have borne with the cities of the plain, as they more and more corrupted themselves, till in all Sodom there were not ten godly men left! And then, how signal the punishment! Again, what an instance is Ahab of the operation of the law! Flourishing in every way, in spite of his numerous sins—his idolatries, cruelties, selfishness, meanness, hatred of God's servants—victorious over Benhadad, supported by all the forces of Jehoshaphat, encouraged by his successes to undertake an aggressive war against Syria —and then struck down in a moment, slain by an arrow shot at a venture (1 Kings xxii. 34)—his blood licked up by dogs—his wife and seventy sons murdered! The Pharaohs and the Egyptians had now worked their wicked will on Israel for a century or more, since the king arose "who knew not Joseph"—all this time they had been treasuring up to themselves wrath (Rom. ii. 5)—and now it had fallen upon them in full force. Let sinners beware of trying the forbearance and long-suffering of God too far—let them tremble when all goes well with them, and no punishment comes. Let them be assured that the account of their offences is strictly kept, and that for each they will have to suffer. Delay does but mean accumulation. However long suspended, the bolt will fall at last, and it will be proportioned in its severity to the length of the delay, and the amount of the wrath stored up.

II. THE SUDDENNESS WITH WHICH THEY COME UPON MEN. It was night—it was the hour of repose, of peace, silence, tranquillity. All had gone to rest unsuspectingly. No one anticipated evil. Each said to himself, as he lay down, "To-morrow shall be as this day, and much more abundant," when suddenly, without warning, there was death everywhere. Fathers saw the light of their eyes snatched from them—mothers beheld their darlings struggling in the agonies of dissolution. A shrill, prolonged cry sounded throughout the land. So the flood came upon man unawares (Luke xvii. 27) —and a sudden destruction overthrew the cities of the plain (ib. 28, 29)—and Ahab found himself mortally wounded when he was thinking of nothing but victory—and in the height of his pride Herod Agrippa was seized with a fearful malady—and Uzziah's leprosy smote him in a moment—and in the night of his feast was Belshazzar slain. Wicked men are for the most part thinking of nothing less when the judgments of God fall upon them. They have said to their soul—"Soul, thou hast much goods laid up for many years; take thine ease, eat, drink, and be merry," when the dread sentence goes forth—"Thou fool, this night thy soul shall be required of thee." God's judgments often come in the night. We know not what a day, nor what a night may bring forth. Let us commend our souls to God when we lie down to rest, and repeat the prayer of the Litany against sudden death.

III. THE IMPARTIALITY WITH WHICH THEY ARE DEALT OUT UPON ALL CONDITIONS OF MEN. "Pale death smites equally the poor man's hut and the king's palace," says a heathen moralist. And so it is with all God's judgments. He is no respecter of persons. "Without respect of persons he judgeth according to every man's work" (1 Pet. i. 17). Greatness furnishes no security against him. His messengers can enter the palace, elude the sentinels, pass the locked doors, make their way into the secret chamber, smite the monarch, sleeping or waking, with disease, or death, or frenzy. Nor can obscurity escape him; "All things are naked and open unto the eyes of him with whom we have to do." The lowest dungeon, the most wretched garret, the obscurest cellars are within his ken, their inmates known, the moral condition of each and all of them noted. His judgments find men out as easily in the darkest haunts of vice, or the most wretched abodes of poverty, as in royal mansions. And as greatness will not prevent him from chastising, so neither will meanness. The "woman behind the mill," the "captive in the dungeon" are his creatures and his servants, no less than the great, and must be either his true servants, or rebels against his authority. If they are the latter, their obscurity and insignificance will not save them from his judgments, any more than the great man's greatness will save him. Vice must not look for impunity because it is low-placed, and hides itself in a corner.

HOMILIES BY VARIOUS AUTHORS.

Vers. 29—31.—*The death of the first-born.* On this see ch. xi. 4—7. Observe here—

I. THIS JUDGMENT IS BASED ON THE PRINCIPLE OF REPRESENTATION. Hitherto, the plagues had fallen on the Egyptians indiscriminately. Now, a change is made to the principle of representation. Egypt, Israel also, is represented in its first-born. When a death-penalty was to be inflicted, the lines had to be drawn more sharp and clear. We are reminded that *this principle of representation holds a vitally important place in God's moral government.* The illustrations which more immediately affect ourselves are, first, the representation of the race in Adam, and second, its representation in Christ (Rom. v. 12—21). Hence it is not altogether fanciful to trace a relation to Christ even in this judgment on the first-born. 1. *Christ is the great first-born of the race.* We catch some glimpse of this by looking at the matter from the side of Israel. Israel, as God's son, his first-born, is admitted to have been a type of Christ (cf. Matt. ii. 15). Much more were the first-born *in* Israel—the special representatives of this peculiar feature in the calling of the nation—types of Christ. They resembled him in that they bore the guilt of the rest of the people. But Christ, as the Son of *man,* sustained a relation to more than Israel. He is, we may say, the great First-born of the race. Egypt as well as Israel was represented in him. 2. The *death of Christ is not only God's great means of saving the world, but it is God's great judgment upon the sin of the world.* It is indeed the one, *because* it is the other. There is thus in the death of Christ, both the Israel side and the Egypt side. There is some shadow of vicarious endurance of penalty—of the one suffering for, and bearing the guilt of, the many—even in the destruction of Egypt's first-born. 3. *The death of Christ, which brings salvation to the believing, is the earnest of final doom to the unbelieving portion of the race.* This also is exhibited in principle in the history of the exodus. In strictness, the first-born were viewed as having died, both in Israel and Egypt. The Egyptian first-born died in person; the Israelitish first-born in the substituted lamb. The death of a first-born in person could typify judgment in the room, or in the name, of others; but the first-born being himself one of the guilty, his death could not (even in type) properly redeem. Hence the substitution of the lamb, which held forth in prophecy the coming of the true and sinless first-born, whose death *would* redeem. But Christ's death, to the unbelieving part of mankind—the wilfully and obstinately unbelieving—is a prophecy, not of salvation, but of judgment. God's judgment on sin in the person of Christ, the first-born, is the earnest of the doom which will descend on all who refuse him as a Saviour. And this was the meaning of the death of the first-born in Egypt. That death did not redeem, but forewarned Egypt of yet worse doom in store for it if it continued in its sins. The first-born endured, passed under, God's judgment, for the sin of the nation; and so has Christ passed under, endured God's judgment, for the sin even of the unbelieving. Egypt, not less than Israel, was represented in him; but to the one (Egypt as representative of hostility to the kingdom of God) his death means doom; to the other (Israel as representative of the people of God) it means salvation.

II. THIS JUDGMENT COMPELLED PHARAOH TO RELAX HIS HOLD ON ISRAEL. It was the consummating blow. Imagination fails in the attempt to realise it. As we write, accounts come to hand of the terrific storm of Oct. 14 (1881), attended by a lamentable loss of life on the Berwickshire coast of Scotland. The storm was sudden, and preluded by an awful and ominous darkness. Cf. with remarks on ninth plague the following:—" I noticed a black-looking cloud over by the school, which shortly spread over all the sky out by the Head. Sea, sky and ground all seemed to be turning one universal grey-blue tint, and a horrible sort of stillness fell over everything. The women were all gathering at their doors, feeling that something awful was coming. No fewer than 200 fishermen and others are believed to have perished, the village of Eyemouth alone losing 129. So connected by intermarriage is the population of the villages and hamlets, that there is scarcely a family in any of them which is not called to mourn its dead. The scenes are heart-rending. Business in every shape and form is paralysed." An image this, and yet how faint, of the cry that went up in Egypt that night, when in every house there was found one dead. Yet no stroke less severe would have served the purpose, and this one is to be studied in view of the fact that it *did* prove effectual for its end. Observe, 1. It was a *death-stroke*. Death has a singular power in subduing and melting the heart. It is the most powerful solvent God can apply to a rebellious nature. It is sometimes tried when gentler means have failed. God removes your idol. He lays your dear one in the dust. You have resisted milder influences, will you yield to this? Your heart is for the moment bowed and broken, will the repentance prove lasting, or will it be, like Pharaoh's, only for a time? 2. It is a *death-grip* upon the soul which is needed to make sin relax its hold upon it. "The sorrows of death compassed me, and the pains of hell gat hold upon me; I found trouble and sorrow. *Then* called I upon the name of the Lord: O Lord, I beseech thee, deliver my soul" (Ps. cxvi. 3, 4). God comes in the preaching of his law, and lays his hand, a hand carrying death in it, upon the soul of the trembling transgressor, who then for the first time realises the fatal and unspeakably awful position in which he has placed himself by sin. It is a death-sentence which is written in his conscience. 3. That which completes the liberation of the soul is a view of *the meaning of the death of Christ.* Terror alone will not melt the heart. There is needed to effect this the influence of love. And where is love to be seen in such wonderful manifestation as at the Cross of Christ? What see we there? The first-born of the race expiring in awful agony under the judgment of God for *our* sins. Is not this a spectacle to melt the heart? It is powerful enough, if earnestly contemplated, to make the Pharaoh that is within us all relinquish his grip upon the captive spirit. What read we of the prospective conversion of Israel?—"They shall look on Me whom they have pierced, and they shall mourn for him, as one mourneth for his only son; and shall be in bitterness for him, *as one that is in bitterness for his first-born*" (Zech. xii. 10). See again, Acts ii. 36, 37, "Let all the house of Israel know assuredly, that God hath made that same Jesus whom ye have crucified, both Lord and Christ. Now when they heard this, they were pricked in their hearts," etc. Cf. also Rev. i. 7. The Cross inspires mourning—(1) By the spectacle it presents of holy suffering. (2) By the recollection of who it is that there suffers. (3) By the thought that it is our own sins which are the cause of this suffering. (4) By the thought that it is the judgment of God in the infliction of the curse of sin which the Holy one is thus enduring. (5) By the conviction of sin, and the dread of Divine justice, thus awakened. (6) Above all, by the infinite love shown in this gift of the Son, and in the Son's willingness to endure this awful agony and shame for our salvation.—J. O

EXPOSITION.

Vers. 31—36.—THE DISMISSAL. The first action seems to have been taken by Pharaoh. The "cry" of the people had no doubt been heard in the palace, and he was aware that the blow had not fallen on himself alone, and may have anticipated what the people's feelings would be; but he did not wait for any direct pressure to be put upon him before yielding. He sent his chief officers (ch. xi. 8) while it was still night (ch. xii. 31), to inform Moses and Aaron, not only that they might, but that they *must* take their departure immediately, with all the people, and added that they might take with them their flocks and herds. The surrender was thus complete; and it was accompanied by a request which we should scarcely have expected. Pharaoh craved at the hands of the two brothers a blessing! We are

not told how his request was received; but that it should have been made is a striking indication of how his pride was humbled. The overture from Pharaoh was followed rapidly by a popular movement, which was universal and irresistible. The Egyptians "rose up" everywhere, and "were urgent upon the people," to "send them out of the land in haste" (ver. 33); and to expedite their departure readily supplied them at their request with gold and silver and raiment (ver. 35), thus voluntarily spoiling themselves for the benefit of the foreigners. The Israelites, long previously prepared for the moment which had now arrived, made their final arrangements, and before the day was over a lengthy column was set in motion, and proceeded from Rameses, which seems to have been a suburb of Tanis (Brugsch, *Hist.*

of Egypt, vol. ii. pp. 96—99), to an unknown place called Succoth, which must have lain towards the south-east, and was probably not very remote from the capital.

Ver. 31.—**And he called for Moses and Aaron.** Kalisch understands this as a summons to the King's presence (*Commentary,* p. 130), and even supposes that the two brothers complied, notwithstanding what Moses had said (ch. x. 29). But perhaps no more is meant than at Pharaoh's instance Moses and Aaron were summoned to an interview with some of the Court officials (see ch. xi. 8). **As ye have said.** Literally, "according to your words." The reference is to such passages as ch. viii. 1, 20; ix. 1, 13.

Ver. 32.—**Also take your flocks and your herds.** Pharaoh thus retracted the prohibition of ch. x. 24, and "gave the sacrifices and burnt-offerings" which Moses had required (*ib.* ver. 25). **Bless me also.** Pharaoh was probably accustomed to receive blessings from his own priests, and had thus been led to value them. His desire for a blessing from Moses and Aaron, ere they departed, probably sprang from a conviction—based on the miracles which he had witnessed—that their intercession would avail more with God than that of his own hierarchy.

Ver. 33.—**The Egyptians were urgent upon the people.** The Egyptians feared that, if any further delay took place, the God of the Hebrews might not be content with slaying all the first-born, but might punish with death the whole nation, or at any rate all the males. It is easy to see how their desire to get rid of the Israelites would expedite matters, and enable all to set out upon the journey on the same day.

Ver. 34.—**The people took their dough.**

They probably regarded dough as more convenient for a journey than flour, and so made their flour into dough before starting; but they had no time to add leaven. **Their kneading-troughs.** This rendering is correct, both here and in the two other places where the word occurs (ch. viii. 3, and Deut. xxviii. 5). Kneading-troughs would be a necessity in the desert, and, if like those of the modern Arabs, which are merely small wooden bowls, would be light and portable. The dough and kneading-troughs, with perhaps other necessaries, were carried, as the Arabs still carry many small objects, bound up in their clothes (*i.e.,* in the *beged* or ample shawl) upon their shoulders.

Ver. 35.—**The children of Israel did according to the word of Moses.** See above, ch. xi. 2. **They borrowed.** On this mistranslation, see the comment upon ch. iii. 22. It is plain that the gold and silver articles and the raiment, were free-will gifts, which the Egyptians never expected to see again, and which the Hebrews asked and took, but in no sense "borrowed." Hengstenberg and Kurtz have shown clearly that the primary meaning of the words translated "borrowed" and "lent," is "asked" and "granted," and that the sense of "borrowing" and "lending" is only to be assigned them when it is required by the context.

Ver. 36.—**So that they lent unto them such things as they required.** Rather, "So that they granted them what they asked." **They spoiled the Egyptians.** See the comment on ch. iii. 22, *ad fin.* The result was that the Israelites went forth, not as slaves, but as conquerors, decked with the jewels of the Egyptians, as though they had conquered and despoiled them.

HOMILETICS.

Vers. 31—36.—*Israel's going forth from Egypt a pattern to oppressed Churches.* Churches are sometimes enslaved and oppressed by the civil power. In unsuspecting confidence they have accepted the State's protection, and entered into certain relations with it, supposed to be mutually advantageous. But, as time has gone on, the terms of the original arrangement have been disregarded; the civil power has made encroachments, has narrowed the Church's liberties, has behaved oppressively towards it, has reduced it to actual slavery. A time comes at last when the bondage is felt to be intolerable; and the Church demands its liberty, claims to go out from under the yoke of the oppressor. Under such circumstances the following analogies are noticeable:

I. THE OPPRESSED CHURCH, LONG REFUSED THE LIBERTY WHICH IT HAS BEEN DRIVEN TO CLAIM, IS APT AT LAST TO BE "THRUST OUT" BY ITS OPPRESSOR. The early efforts of a down-trodden church after freedom are strenuously opposed, denounced as at once wrongful, foolish, and futile, sometimes punished by an increase in the oppression. The Church is set to "make bricks without straw." If this process fails, and the demand for freedom continues, the claims made are perhaps at the next stage derided. (See ch. v. 2.) They are then for a long time determinedly and persistently refused. If occasionally a seeming concession is made, it is scarcely made before it is retracted. If still the Church will not give way, but continues the struggle, a crisis arrives. The State finds itself in difficulties. One inconvenience after another befals it in consequence of the prolonged conflict. At length it comes to be felt that the inconveniences of the struggle exceed the benefits of the connection; and a sudden change of policy takes place. The Church is sent adrift; cut away like an encumbering mass of wreck; bidden to shift for itself, and trouble the State no more. The State is glad to be rid of it.

II. THE EMANCIPATED CHURCH FINDS ITSELF, ON EMANCIPATION, SURROUNDED BY DIFFICULTIES AND PERPLEXITIES. In the first place, the attitude of the State towards it is apt to be hostile; and an attempt may even be made to coerce it and force it to resume its old position. Apart from this, it labours under many disadvantages. It has recollections of the "flesh-pots of Egypt," which offer a strong contrast to the fare whereto it is reduced. It has to enter on a dull and wearisome course; to plod forward toilsomely, painfully. It finds its movements hampered by encumbrances. All these things are against it. But if the nerves be braced to bear, if the will be resolute to turn away from all thought of the "flesh-pots," if the fact of freedom be kept before the mind's eye and the old ills of slavery held in recollection, the difficulties of the early journey will pass away, the presence of God will be revealed, and after (it may be) forty years of trial, the wilderness will have been passed through, and there will be a triumphant entrance into Canaan.

III. THE EMANCIPATED CHURCH HAS A RIGHT TO TAKE WITH IT ALL ITS OWN PROPERTY, AND IS ENTITLED, IF OCCASION ARISE, TO " SPOIL THE EGYPTIANS." Moses and Aaron would not stir without their flocks and herds—the main wealth of a pastoral nation. " Not a hoof," they said, " should be left behind " (ch. x. 26). So the emancipated Church should take with her whatever is her own into the wilderness. She must not relinquish her property to the oppressor. It is really not hers, but God's: she is trustee to God for it. She is entitled to say that she "knows not with what she must serve the Lord till she is come out." And she is entitled to ask for parting gifts when she is about to quit a known shelter and to confront the perils and dangers of an unknown future. If God gives her favour in the eyes of those whom she is leaving, she will do well to require of them their silver and their gold and their raiment — all that they have most precious — and take it with her, not as " borrowed " wealth, but as endowment freely " given," intentionally made over for a permanence, out of goodwill and affection, or out of compassion and pity. She will find a proper use for all that is most rich and most rare in the service of the sanctuary.

HOMILIES BY VARIOUS AUTHORS.

Ver. 32.—*Pharaoh's prayer.* It has come then to this, that Pharaoh is glad to beg a blessing from the man whom at first he had so contemptuously spurned. " And bless me also."

I. THE WICKED MAN IS OFTEN MADE PAINFULLY AWARE OF THE MISERABLENESS OF HIS OWN PORTION, AS COMPARED WITH THAT OF THE GODLY. He may be, often is, even when he refuses to acknowledge it, secretly conscious of the superior happiness of the good man. There come times, however, when severe affliction, the sense of a gnawing inward dissatisfaction, or special contact of some kind with a man of genuine piety, extorts the confession from him. He owns that the good man has a standing in the Divine favour; enjoys an invisible Divine protection; and is the possessor of a peace, happiness, and inward support, to which his own wretched life is utterly a stranger.

II. THE WICKED MAN HAS SOMETIMES DESIRES AFTER A SHARE IN THE GOOD OF GOD'S PEOPLE. He envies them. He feels in his heart that he is wretched and miserable beside them, and that it would be happiness to be like them. He says with Balaam, " Let me die the death of the righteous, and let my last end be like his " (Num. xxiii. 10).

III. THE WICKED MAN, IN HIS TIME OF TROUBLE, WILL OFTEN HUMBLE HIMSELF TO BEG THE PRAYERS OF THE GODLY. And this, though but a little before, he has been persecuting them. He feels that the good man has power with God.

IV. THESE FEELINGS OF THE WICKED MAN ARE USUALLY TRANSIENT.—J. O.

Vers. 31—37.—*The dismissal.* The blow had been so measured by infinite wisdom as to produce precisely the desired effect. Pharaoh "called for Moses and Aaron by night," etc. Observe—

I. Pharaoh is now as anxious to get rid of the Israelites as formerly he was to keep them. It had been predicted at the beginning that this would be the issue of God's dealings with him (ch. vi. 1). Note, 1. *Pharaoh's folly in resisting the demand of God so long.* He has to concede everything at last. Had he yielded at the beginning, he could have done so with honour, and with the happiest results to his dynasty and kingdom. As it is, he has gained nothing, and has lost much, nearly all. He has ruined Egypt, suffered severely in his own person, lost his first-born, and irretrievably forfeited his prestige in the eyes of his subjects. Foolish king! and yet the same unequal and profitless contest is being repeated in the history of every sinner! 2. *The dismissal is unconditional.* No more talk of leaving the little ones, or the flocks and herds; or even of returning after the three days' journey. Pharaoh wants no more to do with this fatal people. No one could any longer dream of the Israelites returning, or expect them to do so. They were "thrust out altogether" (ch. xi. 1). 3. *He seeks a blessing* (ver. 32). He wished Moses to leave a blessing behind him. He would be blessed, and still continue in his sins. Beyond letting Israel go, he had no intention of renouncing his idols, and becoming a worshipper of the God he had so long defied. Many would like to be blessed, while cleaving to their sins.

II. The Egyptians are as eager as their monarch to see the Israelites safely out of Egypt. 1. *They were affrighted.* "They said, we be all dead men" (ver. 33). They were perfectly right. Had Israel been detained longer, their nation would have been destroyed. It would be well if every sinner had as clear a perception of the effects of persistence in his evil. 2. *They were urgent to send the people away.* Not simply because this was what Jehovah had commanded, but because they were terrified to have them in their midst any longer. The Israelites were a people of ill-omen to them. They wished to get rid of the nation at once and for ever. This is not without significance. We remember how the Gadarenes besought Jesus that he would depart out of their coasts (Matt. viii. 34). Worldly people have no liking for the company of the converted. Society bustles them out of its midst. Their old companions betray a singular uncomfortableness in their presence. They would rather have done with them. "Therefore they say unto God, Depart from us; for we desire not the knowledge of thy ways" (Job. xxi. 14). Alas! the world that desires to be rid of the society of God's people will one day get its wish. The separation they would fain hasten will take place, *and for ever* (Matt. xxv. 46). 3. They were willing to *buy* the departure of Israel (ver. 35, 36). The Israelites asked, and the Egyptians freely gave, of jewels of gold, of jewels of silver, and of raiment. Thus, singularly did Providence provide for the enriching of the people in the hour of their exodus. They went forth, not in squalor and disorder, but as a triumphant host, laden with the spoils of the enemy. The spoils of the world will yet turn to the enrichment of the Church.

III. The Israelites make no delay in availing themselves of the opportunity of freedom (ver. 34). Pharaoh did not need to tell them twice to leave the land. Their dough was unleavened, but, binding up their kneading-troughs in their clothes upon their shoulders, they prepared at once for departure. There are supreme moments in every man's history, the improvement or non-improvement of which will decide his salvation. Many other things at such a moment may need to be left undone; but the man is insane who does not postpone *everything* to the making sure of his deliverance. Such times are not indolently to be waited for. The Lord is to be sought at once. But God's ways of saving are varied. The seeking, as in Augustine's case, may go on a long time before God is found.—J. O.

EXPOSITION.

Vers. 37—39.—THE DEPARTURE. There are, no doubt, great difficulties in conceiving the departure on one day, from one place, of " six hundred thousand that were men, beside children." The difficulty is increased when we find (from Num. i. 3—43) that by "men" is meant males above twenty years of age. The entire body of Israelites is thus raised from over half a million to over two millions. The whole narrative, however, supposes some such number; and it is accepted by the best critics, as Ewald, Kalisch, Kurtz, Canon Cook, and others. As these two millions must have lived dispersed over a considerable space, and there could have been no advantage in their all assembling at Rameses (Tanis), we are probably to suppose the main body with Moses and Aaron to have started from that place, while the others, obeying orders previously given, started from all parts of Goshen, and converged upon Succoth, which was the first rendezvous. Each body of travellers was accompanied by its flocks and herds, and followed by a number of slaves, dependants, and sympathisers not of Hebrew birth (ver. 38), which still further enlarged their numbers. The extremely open character of the country, and the firmness of the soil at the time of year, would facilitate the journey. There was no marching along roads, which indeed did not exist. Each company could spread itself out at its pleasure, and go its own pace. All knew the point of meeting, and marched towards it, in converging lines, there being no obstacle to hinder them. Arrived in the vicinity of Succoth, they could bivouac without hurt, in that fine climate, in the open air.

Ver. 37.—From Rameses. It has been doubted whether this " Rameses " is the same place as the " Raamses " of ch. i. 11. But the doubt scarcely seems to be reasonable. The two words differ only in the pointing. Brugsch has clearly shown that Rameses (Pa-Ramesu) was a town newly built in the reign of Rameses II., partly erected by himself, in the immediate vicinity of the old city of Tanis or Zoan. It was the favourite capital of both

Rameses II. and Menephthah. (See Brugsch, *Hist. of Egypt*, vol. ii. pp. 96 and 128.) **Succoth.** The meaning of the word " Succoth " is " booths." Mr. Greville Chester tells us that " huts made of reeds " are common at the present day in the tract south-east of Tanis, and suggests that the Succoth here mentioned may have been at Salahiyeh, fifteen miles due south of Tanis. Tel-Defneh, at the same distance to the south-east, is perhaps a more probable site. **Six hundred thousand.** See the Introductory paragraph. At the time of the numbering recorded in Num. i., the males above twenty years of age were 625,550. **Beside children.** Rather, " beside families." The word used includes all the women, and the children under twenty.

Ver. 38.—A mixed multitude went up also with them. Kalisch supposes that these strangers were native Egyptians, anxious to escape the tyranny of the kings. Canon Cook suggests that they were " remains of the old Semitic population " of the Eastern provinces. Perhaps it is more probable that they consisted of fugitives from other subject races (as the Shartana) oppressed by the Pharaohs. We have again mention of this " mixed multitude " in Num. xi. 4, where we find that they were the first to regret the "flesh and the fish, the cucumbers, the melons, the leeks, the onions, and the garlick " which they had eaten in Egypt freely (*ib.* 5). They thus set a bad example, which the Israelites followed. **And flocks, and herds, even very much cattle.** Compare ch. x. 26. It has been noticed that this is important, as lessening the difficulties connected with the sustentation of the Israelites in the wilderness. But it increases, on the other hand, the difficulties connected with the march, and with the possibility of finding pasture for such large flocks and herds in the Sinaitic peninsula.

Ver. 39. Unleavened cakes. Some of the modern Arabs make such cakes by simply mixing flour with water, and attaching flat circular pieces of the dough thus formed to the sides of their ovens after they have heated them. (Niebuhr, *Description de l'Arabie*, p. 45, and pl. 1, F.) Others put a lump of dough into the ashes of a wood fire, and cover it over with the embers for a short time (Layard, *Nineveh and Babylon*, p. 288). All Arab bread is unleavened. **They were thrust out of Egypt.** Compare ver. 33.

HOMILETICS.

Vers. 37—38. In the departure of the Israelites from Egypt, after they had received permission to set out, two things are principally remarkable: 1. All were of one mind— none hung back; 2. A mixed multitude cast in their lot with them, elected to accompany them, and resolved to share their fortunes. The first of these two facts shows—

I. THAT IN TIMES OF EXCITEMENT, UNDER DIVINE GUIDANCE, A WHOLE NATION WILL ACT AS ONE MAN. Critical times are favourable to the formation of a national spirit. Let a powerful invader threaten a people, and differences are at once forgotten, quarrels made up, party spirit held in abeyance. All unite with equal zeal against the common enemy. Or again, let any wave of strong feeling come upon a people, desire of unity, or of freedom, or of taking part in a great enterprise, like the crusades, and much the same unanimity prevails. Such a spirit is found among the Jews who returned from the captivity with Zerubbabel, when in the seventh month they "gathered themselves together to Jerusalem as one man" (Ezr. iii. 1), to set up the altar of burnt offerings. Such a spirit appears again in the time of Nehemiah, when all the people with one accord kept a solemn fast on the 24th of Tisri (Nehem. ix. 1), and then " sealed to the covenant " (ibid x. 1—29). But it was not very frequently exhibited. When proclamation was made by Cyrus the Great that all Israelites who chose might quit his dominions and " go up to Jerusalem and build the house of the Lord " (Ezr. i. 3), it was only a portion of the nation, " whose spirit God had raised," that went forth. But now the whole people was of one mind. Braced by the severe discipline of suffering, their spirits raised—their whole moral tone exalted—by the long series of signs and wonders which they had witnessed, encouraged by the Divine promise of a "land flowing with milk and honey," and confident in the leadership of Moses, they all arose " as one man," left their abodes, their lands, their farming implements, their utensils, their furniture, and started for the rendezvous of Succoth. Such waves of popular feeling have been known from time to time, but scarcely to this extent. When Oubacha started on Jan. 5, 1771, with 70,000 families of Calmucks (420,000 persons) from the banks of the Volga for China, 15,000 families remained behind (De Hell, Travels in the Steppes, p. 227). But God now inspired the whole Israelite nation with one unanimous feeling; and all left Egypt together. The other fact shows—

II. THAT THE ENTHUSIASM OF A UNITED NATION IS CONTAGIOUS, AND EXCITES OTHERS BEYOND ITS LIMITS TO FOLLOW ITS EXAMPLE. The contagious character of a revolutionary spirit has often been noticed. Even the war spirit, when strongly felt, is apt to be contagious, and to overleap national boundaries. Here we see that a righteous enthusiasm will also, on some occasions, catch hold of those seemingly beyond its range, who are in contact with it, and sweep such alien elements into its vortex. The "mixed multitude " who joined the Israelites had none of the reasonable grounds for hoping to better their condition that the Israelites had; but they entertained nevertheless expectations of, somehow or other, sharing in their advantages. They may have contained, 1. Some native Egyptians, connected with the Hebrews by marriage, for the example of Joseph is likely to have been followed; 2. Some slaves anxious for freedom; 3. Some members of oppressed races, held to labour in Egypt, as the Israelites had been. The later facts of the history show—

III. THAT NEITHER OF THESE TWO FORMS OF ENTHUSIASM IS TO BE RELIED UPON AS PERMANENT. The enthusiasm of Israel cooled wonderfully when they found themselves shut in between the host of Pharaoh and the Red Sea (ch. xiv. 10—12). It was revived by the safe passage through the sea, but faded again rapidly under the toils and the monotony of the wilderness. Nor was that of the "mixed multitude " more lasting. They appear to have been the first to grow sick of the continual manna, and to have " lusted" after the rich and varied diet of Egypt (Num. xi. 4). The Israelites were seduced by them into similar misconduct; and the quails, and the plague which followed the quails (ib. 31—33), were the consequence. Enthusiasm is a thing with which we cannot dispense; as a motive force for initiating a great movement, it is invaluable; but we must not trust to it for the accomplishment of anything which requires long and sustained effort. It is an abnormal and excessive stir of feeling, which must be followed by re-action. As it dies away, we must seek to supply its place by the ever increasing force of habit, which may be depended on for continuance.

EXODUS.

HOMILIES BY VARIOUS AUTHORS

Vers. 37—40.— *The exodus as a fact in history.* The exodus from Egypt lay at the foundation of the national life of Israel. It appears in the history as a super-natural work of God. The subsequent legislation assumes it to have possessed this character. The bond of covenant declared to exist between the people and Jehovah had its ground in the same transaction. They were God's people, and were bound to adhere to him, and to obey his laws, because he had so marvellously redeemed them. Every motive and appeal in the later books is drawn from the assumed truth of the events related here, and of those which happened afterwards in the wilderness. Obviously, therefore, the history of Israel presupposes the truth of *this* history ; while if the narrative of the exodus, as here recorded, is admitted to be true, we are in immediate contact with supernatural facts of the most stupendous order. We do not mean to discuss the question in detail, but the following points may be indicated as suitable for popular treatment.

I. OBJECTIONS. We touch only on that which relates to the number of the people (ver. 37). The difficulty here is two-fold. 1. To account for the growth of the nation of Israel from seventy persons to over 2,000,000 in the space of time allowed for that increase. On this see the exposition. The difficulty is not serious (1) if we take the plain wording of the history, and admit that the sojourn in Egypt lasted 430 years (ver. 40); (2) if we do the narrative the justice of allowing it to remain consistent with itself, the increase, on its own showing, being exceptional and marvellous (ch. i. 7, 14, 20). (3) If we admit that the descendants of the households which doubtless accompanied Jacob into Egypt, are included in the numbers. But this supposition, however probable in itself, is really not necessary to vindicate the numbers. The truth is, that granting a highly exceptional rate of increase, with 430 years to increase in, the numbers, as will be seen on calculation, appear small, rather than too great. They certainly could not have been much less than the history makes them. The problem is quite soluble even on the hypothesis of the shorter reckoning, in favour of which there is not a little to be said (see Birk's " Exodus of Israel "). 2. To account for the possibility of so vast a multitude, including women and children, with flocks and herds, effecting an exodus in a single night (and day). The feat in question is certainly unparalleled in history. Even granting what the narrative (as against Colenso) makes perfectly clear, that the Israelites were in a state of tolerably complete organisation, had ample warning to prepare for starting on that particular night, and had for months been on the tip-toe of expectation, as plague after plague descended on Egypt, it is still an event so stupendous as to be difficult of realisation. The narrative itself, however, does not fail to represent it as very extraordinary. And in pronouncing on its possibility, there are several circumstances not always, perhaps, sufficiently taken into account. Justice is not always done (1) to the perfectly superhuman efforts a nation can sometimes make in a great crisis of its history. Even an individual, at a time when feeling is highly strained, is capable of efforts and achievements, which, to read of them in cold blood, we might judge to be impossible. (2) To the order and discipline of which masses of people become capable when called to face an emergency on which they feel that existence itself depends. The picture sometimes drawn of a disorderly rabble pouring out of Egypt has no foundation in the history, and is false to psychology and experience. The narratives of shipwrecks (the Kent, the London, etc.), show us what crowds are capable of in the way of order and discipline, even with certain death staring them in the face. When a people, under the influence of one great over-mastering idea, are called upon to execute difficult movements, or to unite their efforts towards one great end, it is incredible what they can accomplish. The feeling of solidarity takes possession of them. They are of one heart and soul. The mass moves and works as if one mind possessed it, as if it were a machine. Orders are obeyed with promptitude ; movements are executed with rapidity and regularity ; men are lifted for the time out of their littlenesses, and display a spirit of willingness, of helpfulness, and of self-sacrifice truly wonderful. All these conditions were present on the night of the exodus : the result was what might have been anticipated—the people were brought out with wonderful rapidity, and in regular order ; " they went up harnessed "—" five in a rank " (ch. xiii. 18).— (3) We must add to these considerations, the singularly exalted state of the religious consciousness in the companies of the Israelites. Everything in their position combined to awe and solemnize them; to fill them with an over-mastering consciousness of the Divine presence; to inspire them with boundless and grateful joy, yet a joy tempered with the awful sense of death, as forced upon them by the destruction of the first-born, and the lamentations of the bereaved Egyptians. This also would exercise a powerful and steadying influence upon their thoughts and beha viour, and would aid them in taking their measures with decision and speed.

II. PROOFS. Those who pile up the difficulties of the Bible seldom do justice to the difficulties on the other side. We have to ask—1. Is it not absurd to say that so extraordinary an event as, in any case, this exodus of Israel from Egypt must be admitted to have been, happened in the full light of the most powerful civilisation of ancient times, while yet the people who came out did not know, or could not remember, or could ever possibly forget *how* it happened? (Cf. ver. 42.) The Israelites themselves did not believe that they did not know. They had but one story to give of it—the story that rings down in their psalms to latest generations—the same story which, with minute circumstantial detail, is embodied in these chapters. 2. If this is not how the children of Israel got out of Egypt, will the critic show us how they *did* get out? It is admitted on all hands that they were once in; that they were in bondage; that Egypt was at that time ruled by one or other of its most powerful monarchs; that they came out; yet did not come out by war, but peaceably. How then did they make their way out? If the whole history was different from that of which we have a record, how came it that no echo of it was preserved in Israel, and that this sober and matter-of-fact relation has come to take its place? 3. There is the institution of the Passover—a contemporary memorial. We have already expressed our belief that this ordinance was of a kind which could not have been set up at a time later than the events professedly commemorated by it. Glance at the alternative hypothesis. The basis of the institution, we are asked to believe, was an ancient spring festival, on which were grafted by degrees, as the tradition formed, the rites and ideas of a later age. This hypothesis, however, is not only unproved, but violates every law of historical probability. It must in any case be admitted (1) that the exodus took place at the time of the alleged agricultural festival. (2) That the festival thereafter assumed a new character, and was observed, in addition to its agricultural reference, as a memorial of the escape from Egypt. (3) That the use of unleavened bread in connection with it had reference to the haste of the flight. (4) Further, that an essential part of this festival was the offering of a sacrifice. (5) That, being at bottom a spring festival, it must have been observed, with but few interruptions, all down the later history of Israel. But if so much is admitted, we seem driven to admit more. For it is undeniable that the festival, as observed among the Jews, was connected *most especially of all* with the fact of a great judgment, which was believed to have fallen on Egypt on the night of the exodus, and from which the Israelites had been mercifully delivered by the sprinkling of the lamb's blood upon the door-posts; a memorial of which was preserved in the name (Pass-over). "The relation to the natural year expressed in the Passover, was less marked than that in Pentecost or Tabernacles, while its historical import is deeper and more pointed. That part of its ceremonies which has a direct agricultural reference—the offering of the omer—holds a very subordinate place." (Dict. of the Bible.) It is for the sceptic, therefore, to explain how that which enters into the inmost meaning and heart of the observance, could possibly have been engrafted on it as an accident at a later period—yet a period not later than accords with the ritual prescribed in these very ancient written laws: how, moreover, the people could not only be persuaded to accept this new reading of an old familiar ordinance, *but to believe that they had never known any other:* that this had been the meaning and ritual of the ordinance from the beginning. 4. We have not as yet alluded to the Pentateuch, but of course the fact is not to be overlooked that the work before us claims to be historical; that it was probably written wholly or in large part by Moses himself; and that in style, circumstantially, vividness of narration, and minute accuracy of reference, it bears all the marks of a true and contemporary history.—J. O.

Ver. 38.—*The mixed multitude.* The mass of this mixed multitude which left

Egypt with Moses, would consist of foreign settlers in the Delta, victims, like the Hebrews, of the tyranny of the Pharaohs, and, like them, glad to take this opportunity of making their escape (cf. ch. i. 10). The enthusiasm of a great body of people is contagious. When the Israelites left Egypt, numbers would be moved to leave with them. Recent events, too, had doubtless produced a powerful impression on these mixed populations; and knowing that God was with Israel, they naturally expected great benefits from joining the departing nation. They had not calculated on the trials of the desert, and afterwards "fell a-lusting" (Num. xi. 4), provoking Israel to sin, and bringing wrath upon the camp.

I. MULTITUDES JOIN THE RANKS OF THE CHURCH WHO HAVE LITTLE IN COMMON WITH HER SPIRIT AND AIMS. They are like the mixed crowd of hangers-on, which left Egypt with Israel. Their ideas, traditions, customs, maxims of life, habits of thought and feeling generally, are foreign to those of the true Israel of God. Yet they are moved to join the Church—1. From motives of self-interest. 2. Under transient convictions. 3. Caught by a wave of religious enthusiasm. 4. Under partial apprehensions of the importance of religion. 5. Because others are doing it. They hang of necessity on the outskirts of the Church, taking little interest in her work, and acting as a drag upon her progress.

II. THERE ARE MANY BY WHOM THE CHURCH WILL NOT BE BENEFITED, WHOSE ADHERENCE SHE IS YET NOT ENTITLED TO REFUSE. The "mixed multitude" were not forbidden to go with Israel. Because, perhaps, they could not altogether be prevented. It is kindlier, however, to believe that Israel allowed the mixed crowd to accompany it, in the hope of ultimately incorporating them with the people of Jehovah. The Church is certainly not at liberty to encourage nominal adherence. She must do her very utmost to dissuade men from mere empty profession. Neither to swell her numbers, nor to add to her wealth, nor to increase her respectability in the eyes of the world, nor under a mistaken idea of "comprehension," must she open her doors to those who are known to be ungodly, or who give no evidence of serious religious intentions. Yet neither must she draw her lines too stringently. She must not presume to judge the heart, or to deal with men otherwise than on the ground of their professed motives and beliefs. She must teach, exhort, warn, and rigorously exclude all whose lives are openly inconsistent with the Gospel; but she must at the same time exercise great charity, and rather include ten who may possibly prove unworthy, than mistakenly exclude one whom Christ would be willing to receive. The responsibility in the matter of religious profession must, in great measure, be allowed to rest with the individual who professes. The Church is to consider, not only what is best for *her*, but the duty she owes to the world, in laying hold of those who are yet very imperfect, and training them for Christ.

III. NOMINAL ADHERENTS, HOWEVER, ARE NO SOURCE OF STRENGTH, BUT A GREAT WEAKNESS TO THE CHURCH. It may be the Church's duty to bear with them, but she can never derive benefit from them. She may benefit *them*, and in that hope should treat them tenderly, but they will never benefit *her*. They will be a drag upon her activity. In proportion to their numbers they will exert a chilling and detrimental influence. They will stand in the way of good schemes. They will "fall a-lusting," and provoke discontent. The *morale* of a Church can scarcely avoid being lowered by them. What then? Put them out? Not so. We shall work in vain to separate tares and wheat, and we are forbidden to act on this principle (Matt. xiii. 24—31). But, 1. Let us do what we can to keep down their number. Many churches and church office-bearers are greatly to blame for the indiscriminate way in which they receive persons to communion. We are bound to abide by the principles above laid down; but consistently with these principles it should be our care to keep down nominal adherence as far as that is possible. Many of the character of the "mixed multitude" will find their way into the Church without our seeking for them, or giving them any encouragement. 2. Let us do what we can to change their nominal adherence into real adherence. Seek their good. Be not overcome by their evil, but try to overcome *it* by superior goodness. 3. Beware of their influence, and seek to keep it in check.—J. O.

Vers. 29—42.—*Egypt's sorrow: Israel's joy.* I. THE JUDGMENT OF EGYPT THE EMBLEM AND PROMISE OF THE WORLD'S JUDGMENT. 1. The time of visitation; midnight, when all were wrapt in deepest slumber and, notwithstanding the warning which had been given, busy only with dreams. The world will be surprised in the midst of its false security. "As it was in the days of Noe," etc. 2. Its universality. There were none so high that God's hand did not reach them, and none so low that they were over-looked. 3. The after anguish. The whole nation, steeped the one moment in deceitful slumber, the next torn with the most heartrending and hopeless grief. Their sin had slain their dearest and best. 4. It is a hopeless sorrow. Their grief cannot bring back their dead. The anguish of the wicked, like Esau's, will find no place for repentance.

II. THE DELIVERANCE OF ISRAEL THE EMBLEM AND PROMISE OF THE FULL ENFRANCHISE-MENT OF THE PEOPLE OF GOD. 1. All that God had ever asked for them is granted. The demand for freedom to the people of God, and the breaking of the yoke laid upon the poor, will yet be obeyed in fear by the persecutor and the oppressor. 2. It is pressed upon them with all the eagerness of deadly fear. Israel never so desired the boon as the Egyptians that they should now accept it. The persecutors will come and worship at the Church's feet. 3. They go forth laden with the treasures of Egypt (Isaiah lx. 5—17). 4. They go forth awed by the proof of God's faithfulness. To a day had he kept the promise given to the fathers (ver. 41). The prophecies, now dim and misunderstood, will then be read in the light of God's deeds, and like Israel of old, we shall know that God has kept the appointed time.—U.

Vers. 29—42.—*March at midnight.* "This is that night of Jehovah" (Ex. xii. 42). Observe the striking words of the text! "The night of Jehovah," a night in which he specially appeared and acted on behalf of Israel. For a description of the scenery of this eventful night see Dr. W. M. Taylor's "Moses," 99—101. In the treat-ment of this subject considerable exposition will be necessary. For material, see expository section of this commentary. It may, in order to include all important points, be marshalled thus (under each head we give suggestive hints):—

I. THE HAND THAT SMOTE. Most, if not all the nine earlier plagues, had a natural basis, the tenth had none. It was purely supernatural. They blended mercy (first warning and then withdrawal) with judgment. This was pure judgment. In them there was indeed a call to faith, but also room for unbelief. The demonstrations of God are seldom absolute. But the tenth judgment was awfully impressive. There is very little evidence of any secondary instrumentality, angelic, or any other; but see in the Heb. xii. 13, 23. Jehovah this time smote with his own hand.

II. THE VICTIMS. First-borns. Of all beasts. Of men. But here distinguish between the first-borns of fathers and of mothers. In the tenth plague it was so, that the first-borns of mothers were the destroyed (xiii. 2). Now, these were the "sanctified" unto the Lord, first, as "living sacrifices," and as representing the consecration of each family, and then of the entire nation. But failing this consecration, their lives were forfeited. This was the case at that moment with the Israelites and Egyptians alike. In the case of the Egyptians the life of the first-born was taken, in that of the Israelites atoned for. Hence emerges a law of the Kingdom of God, that every soul that will not voluntarily consecrate himself to the Lord, must involuntarily come under the cloud of condemnation.

III. THE OBJECTIVE. The gods of Egypt (Ex. xii. 12). This was so with the nine plagues, it was especially so with the tenth. The heir to the throne was regarded as an incarnation of the Deity; by this plague God pronounced him common clay with the rest. But the first-born of animals also fell. This was a blow against the animal worship of the land.

IV. COMPLETENESS OF THE VICTORY. Here discuss whether Pharaoh's permission was conditioned or unconditioned; and show that with Pharaoh's resistance God's demands increased, and that the king's surrender must have been absolute, in spite of xiv. 8, 9. Note the pathos of the prayer of the now broken-hearted, "*Bless me also,*" xii. 32.

V. THE BATTLE ARRAY. See xiii. 18. Perhaps a good translation, instead of "harnessed," would be "militant," as including the outer armedness, and the inner valorous and jubilant spirit; both which ideas are in the original. Observe; the nine or ten months of preparation, the organisation in which the "elders" and Hebrew "clerks" of the works may have taken part, the arms they surely possessed, as witness the battle at Rephidim—how probably they had become marshalled into detachments—and places of rendezvous been appointed.

VI. The festal raiment. Israel "asked," Egypt "gave," under Divine influence (xii. 36), gold, silver, and raiment; these might be regarded as the "spoils" of Israel's victory, under God. These spoils were such as women might ask of women (see iii. 22—"neighbour" is Feminine in the Hebrew), and such as women value. They were to be put not only on themselves, but on sons and daughters. The contributions of the Egyptian women must have been immense in quantity and value. Now then, *why* this spoiling? That Israel might march, not like a horde of dirty, ragged slaves, but in festal array. Compared with the slavery of Egypt the future might have been one long holiday, one holy day unto the Lord.

VII. Partakers of the joy (xii. 38). Low caste people probably; even as it is at this day in the mission field of India. But the lesson is obvious—the Lord's salvations are for the sinful, the outcast, and the miserable.

VIII. Truths suggested. 1. The moment of salvation is *the beginning of a new time*. Israel's history as a nation dates from that night (xii. 2). So the history of a soul dates from its conversion to God. 2. The new time *is a festal time*. 3. The redeemed should *assume festal attire* (Luke xv. 22), a bright eye, a cheerful countenance, etc. 4. Still he must *don armour*, and *the Church must be militant*. 5. The Church should *welcome all comers*; for the miserable need salvation, and the most rude are capable of some service. Comp. Deut. xxix. 11, with Ex. xii. 38. 6. The salvations of God *are full-orbed in their completeness*. From the months of preparation till Israel went out in festal array, all was complete. 7. The moment of salvation is *to be held in everlasting remembrance* (see Ex. xii. 42). So of the still greater salvation.—R.

EXPOSITION.

Vers. 40—42.—The narrative of the departure from Egypt is followed, not unnaturally, by a notification of the length of the sojourn, which is declared to have been a space of four hundred and thirty years. In the "Introduction" to the Book, we have examined the question, which here arises, 1. As to the soundness; and 2. As to the true meaning, of the Hebrew text, and have arrived at the conclusion that it is sound, and that it means what it says, viz., that 430 years elapsed between the arrival of Jacob in Egypt, with his sons, and sons' sons, and their families, as related in Gen. xlvi. 1—27, and the commencement of the exodus. The time is required by the genealogy of Joshua (1 Chr. vii. 22—27). It is in remarkable accordance with the traditions that Joseph was the minister of Apepi, and that the Jews went out under Menephthah. If not absolutely required for the multiplication of the race from "seventy souls" to above two millions, it is at any rate more in accord with that fact than the alternative number, 215. It is

twice repeated, so that "the mistake of a copyist" is almost impossible.

Ver. 40.—**The sojourning of the children of Israel, which dwelt in Egypt.** Rather, "Which they sojourned in Egypt." (Compare the Septuagint—ἡ κατοίκησις ἣν κατῴκησαν.) **Four hundred and thirty years.** Literally "thirty years and four hundred years."

Ver. 41.—**The self-same day . . . all the hosts went out.** The setting forth upon the journey is regarded as the "going out"—not the actual exit, which was only effected by the passage of the Red Sea.

Ver. 42.—**It is a night to be much observed.** We must suppose that some of the Israelites actually commenced their march before the night was over, being "hastened" by the Egyptians (ver. 33), and having all things in readiness; but the bulk of the people can scarcely have started before daybreak. **This is that night of the Lord**—*i.e.*, the night concerning which directions had been already given (vers. 6—11)—the only "night" for which any observances are appointed. **In their generations.** To all time—so long as they continue to be a people. On the bindingness of this commandment, see the comment on ver. 14 of this chapter.

HOMILETICS.

Vers. 40—42.—*God's discipline of his chosen ones.* I. The trials of God's people are severe, but have a joyful end at last. The sojourn in Egypt was from first to last an affliction (Gen. xv. 13). It was only on account of the famine in Canaan that Jacob consented to change his abode and his condition. In Canaan he and his had been free; had "served" no one; had lived like the sons of the desert. But in Egypt, even during the lifetime of Joseph, they entered on a species of servitude. Not only were they Pharaoh's subjects, but to some extent his servants (Gen. xlvii. 6). They were no longer free to come and go as they chose. They had a certain province assigned to them. They had, it is probable, to pay rent for their lands (Gen. xlvii. 26). After a certain time, during which they suffered only this "light affliction," the severe oppression began. Their lives were "made bitter with hard bondage, in mortar and in brick, and in all manner of service in the field" (Ex. i. 14); then their children were massacred (ib. ver. 22); lastly, they were required to "make bricks without straw" (ch. v. 7—19). So with God's people generally. They are given a time of suffering. They have to learn to "endure hardness." But God afflicts them as a discipline, and makes even their worst afflictions tend to their growth in grace. At last their trial time is over. Sometimes in this world, oftener in another, they find their Canaan, and "enter into rest."

II. THE TRIAL-TIME SEEMS LONG; BUT GOD DETERMINES ITS LENGTH, AND APPORTIONS IT TO THE NEEDS OF THE PARTICULAR CASE. Four hundred and thirty years is a long space, even in the life of a nation. It is about the period of time which separates us from the rebellion of Jack Cade and the commencement of the "Wars of the Roses." The severe oppression of Israel was not, however, nearly so long as this. Perhaps it lasted only about a century. In any case, times and seasons are in God's hands, and as he fixed four centuries for the entire servitude many years before it began (Gen. xv. 13), so, we may be sure, he fixed the term in his own counsels for the severe oppression. And it is doubtless the same with individuals. God knows what kind and length of chastisement they need, and assigns to each of his chosen ones the term of suffering that is needful for him.

III. IF THE TRIAL-TIME ENDS HERE, AND A SEASON OF HAPPINESS SUPERVENES, IT IS WELL TO OBSERVE YEARLY THE DAY OF THE CHANGE AS A DAY OF THANKSGIVING TO GOD. As national mercies are rightfully commemorated by national "days of thanksgiving," so the special blessings vouchsafed to individuals should receive private commemoration. The day, or night, that brought us out of the Egypt of sin, is especially worthy of such honour. Wherever known, it should be "observed unto the Lord."

HOMILIES BY VARIOUS AUTHORS.

Vers. 40—43.—*The Exodus.* View it in three lights.

I. AS AN EMANCIPATION OF SLAVES. God is the sworn foe of the slave-holder. Only in a very modified sense was slavery tolerated in Israel; and the laws were such as gradually to undermine the system. Historically, God's religion has proved itself the great slave-liberator. 1. *In Egypt.* Here were two millions of a slave population set free in a single night. 2. *In Israel.* Consider the effect on the abolition of the slave system of the single precept in ver. 44 of this chapter. The slave sat down with his master on equal terms at the board of the passover. The same thing happened in the Christian Church. When the Lord's Supper was dispensed, the Christian slave remained; the master, if he was only a catechumen or a penitent, retired. 3. In *Christian countries.* Christianity, it is true, did not preach a crusade against slavery— a course which would only have led to a slave-revolt—but it inculcated truths and principles which undermined the system. Slavery was the corner-stone of the ancient civilisations. Philosophers defended it. The pagan religions did nothing to overthrow it. But the Christian Church took up from the very first the cause of the slave. The master who ill-treated his slave was excommunicated. He was compelled to marry the female slave whom he had seduced. He sat with his slave at the Lord's table. The slave might hold office in the church, and thus become, in a spiritual point of view, the superior of his master. The influence of the Church was used to secure the *liberation* of the slave. Under Domitian, a prefect of Rome, named Chromatius, freed one thousand four hundred slaves who had become Christians, saying, "Those who have become the children of God ought to be no longer slaves of men." Says J. S. Mill, "In an age when the weak were prostrate at the feet of the strong, who was there but the Church to plead to the strong for the weak ?" (Dissert. ii. 155). The emancipation of four millions of American slaves—so long a blot on a so-called Christian civilisation—has been accomplished in our sight, a second exodus. "We can say to-day that, with some trifling exceptions, the soil of Christian nations is free from the disgrace of slavery. Under what influences have the efforts been produced which have brought about such a result? We have only to look at recent facts, and we see the whole clearly. What men, in the middle of last century, were the first to advocate and emancipate slaves? The Quakers of America, who held that bondage was contrary to the Gospel. What men have pleaded the cause of the negroes in the English Parliament with the most power and perseverance? Decided Christians—Wilberforce and Buxton. What spirit animated the book called *Uncle Tom*, which acted so powerfully upon opinion in favour of the negroes? A spirit steadfastly Christian. To what sentiment did the Czar of Russia appeal, when he gave liberty to twenty millions of men? Read his proclamation of Feb. 19th, 1864." (Ernest Naville.) Revealed religion—the religion of the Bible, is thus the great liberator of the slave.

II. As A TEMPORAL DELIVERANCE OF THE CHURCH. Many such deliverances has the Church, both in Old and in New Testament times, experienced since. Deliverances under the Judges; destruction of Sennacherib; edict of Cyrus, and return from captivity; Maccabæan Era. Read Christian Church history. See the Church emerging triumphant, laden with the spoils of the foe, from the days of persecution under the Roman Emperors. Later instances in the Albigenses, in the Lollards of England, in the Huguenots of France, in the Covenanters of Scotland, etc.

III. As A TYPE OF A GREATER DELIVERANCE THAN ITSELF. Redemption from sin and wrath through Christ. See previous Homilies.—J. O.

EXPOSITION.

Vers. 43—51. — SUPPLEMENTARY ORDI-NANCE WITH RESPECT TO THE PASSOVER. The position of these verses is curious. We should have expected them to have followed imme-diately on ver. 20, or else to have been reserved for the further consideration of the subject in ch. xxiii. It is suggested, in order to account for their place, that they formed the matter of a special revelation made to Moses at Succoth. They comprise three main points :—1. The absolute exclusion of all uncircumcised per-sons from participation in the passover rite ; 2. The extension of the rite (implied in ver. 19) to all full proselytes; and, 3. The injunction that not a bone of the lamb should be broken. (This last is repeated in Num. ix. 12.)

Vers. 43.—**This is the ordinance of the passover**—*i.e.,* "This is *the* law, in respect of the persons who are to partake of it "—**there shall no stranger eat thereof,** or lite-rally, "No son of a stranger shall eat thereof." By a "stranger" here is meant one of a foreign race who wishes to retain his foreign character and to remain uncircumcised. Com-pare ver. 48.

Ver. 44.—**Every man's servant that is bought for money.** Or "every man's slave." The Mosaic Law found servitude existing, and left it existing, only guarding against its

extreme abuses (ch. xxi. 20—27). It put no check on the traffic in slaves. **When thou hast circumcised him.** The Jewish commentators say, that the desire of the slave to receive the rite and become a Jew is here implied. But it would seem rather, that opposition and refusal is not thought of as possible (see Gen. xvii. 13, 17). The case is like that of baptism among the barbarous nations, where no sooner was the king converted than a general order went forth for the baptism of his subjects, which no one thought of resisting. **Then shall he eat thereof.** It was a principle of the Jewish law that the slaves should be admitted to complete religious equality with the native Israelites. (Compare Lev. xxii. 11.)

Ver. 45.—**A foreigner.** Literally "a so-journer"—*i.e.,* a foreigner who is merely pass-ing through the land, or staying for a time, without intending to become a permanent resi-dent. The Septuagint πάροικος well ex-presses the meaning. **An hired servant.** It is assumed that the "hired servant" will be a foreigner; and intended to guard against any compulsion being put upon him.

Ver. 46.—**In one house shall it be eaten.** Compare the directions in vers. 3—10, which imply this, and see the comment on ver. 10. **Neither shall ye break a bone of it.** Kalisch thinks that the lamb was a symbol of the unity of the nation, and was therefore not to have any of its bones broken. This view may be a true one, without being exhaustive. It may have been to mark the unity of the Church in Christ that his bones were not broken, and in view especially of *that* unity, that the type was made to correspond in this particular with the antitype. (See John xix. 33—36.)

Ver. 47.—**All the congregation . . . shall keep it.** Rather "shall sacrifice it." (Compare ver. 6.)

Vers. 48, 49.—**And when a stranger,** etc. Here we have the positive ordinance corresponding to the implied permission in ver. 19, and modifying in the most important and striking way the prohibitive enactment of ver. 43. The "stranger," even if he only "sojourned" in the land, was to be put on exactly the same spiritual footing as the Israelite ("One law shall be," etc.) if only he and his would be circumcised, and so enter into covenant.

Ver. 50.—**Thus did all the children of Israel** — *i. e.*, the Israelites, at their first passover, acted in accordance with these precepts, especially in admitting to the feast all circumcised persons, whether natives or foreigners, and rejecting all the uncircumcised.

Ver. 51.— This verse should be transferred to the commencement of the next chapter, which should run as follows :—"And it came to pass—on the self-same day that the Lord brought the children of Israel out of the land of Egypt by their armies—that the Lord spake unto Moses, saying," etc. The word " armies," which at first sight may seem inappropriate, occurs also in ch. vi. 26. It is probably intended to mark that the people were thoroughly organised, and marshalled in divisions resembling those of an army.

HOMILETICS.

Vers. 41—50.—*Passover precepts realised in Christian practice.* The precepts were :—

I. THAT NO UNCIRCUMCISED STRANGER, NOT EVEN THOUGH A HIRED SERVANT IN A HEBREW FAMILY, SHOULD EAT OF IT. Formally, baptism corresponds to circumcision, both of them admitting into covenant with God ; and thus the rule of Christian communities generally, that the reception of baptism must precede that of the Lord's Supper, is a carrying out of this precept. But it is also carried out in another way. Spiritually, the correspondent to the circumcision of the flesh is the circumcision of the spirit ; and thus all Churches which warn the wicked from approaching the Lord's table, do their best to enforce the precept, " No uncircumcised person shall eat thereof." Hired servants of the Church, unless circumcised in heart, are as unfit to communicate as those who have no external connection with Divine things. Nay, may we not say more unfit ?

II. THAT ALL THE CONGREGATION OF ISRAEL, FREEMEN AND SLAVES ALIKE, SHOULD EAT OF IT. The frequent exhortation of all Christian Churches to all their members to receive the Communion, especially at Easter-time, and the general allowance of the duty by those who have any real sense of religion constitute a realisation, to a considerable extent, of this precept in Christian practice. It is to be wished that the realisation were complete. The joint participation of freemen with slaves has always characterised the Christian Church ; and though there have been Christian communities which have acted differently, the cases are too exceptional to deserve much notice, and are disappearing as slavery disappears.

III. THAT IT SHOULD BE EATEN IN ONE PLACE, AND NONE OF IT CARRIED FORTH. Churches which allow not only reservation, but the carrying forth of the holy elements to the bedsides of the sick, break at any rate the letter of this precept. But the Reformed Churches, which disallow even reservation, keep close to it.

IV. THAT NOT A BONE OF IT SHOULD BE BROKEN. This precept can only be spiritually observed, for in the Christian passover, the " flesh " to be eaten has no " bones." But it is spiritually kept wherever communicants are warned against dividing Christ in their thoughts, against separating his humanity from his Divinity, or against practising special devotion to any separate portion of his person, as to his " Sacred Heart " or his " Five wounds." It was the essence of one of the early forms of heresy to " divide Christ ;" and on this account the Church of England protests in her second article of religion, that in him " two whole and perfect natures are joined together in one person, *never to be divided,* whereof is *One* Christ."

HOMILIES BY VARIOUS AUTHORS.

Vers. 43—51.—*The spirit of the Passover ordinance.* The features to be specified reappear in the Lord's Supper. The ordinance was—

I. Exclusive. (Vers. 43, 45, 48.) A stranger, an uncircumcised person, and a hired servant, were not to be permitted to eat of it. Their relation to Israel was wholly external. In like manner, the Lord's Supper is exclusive. It excludes the stranger to the death of Christ, the uncircumcised in heart, and those who sustain a merely legal and hireling relation to the Church. These have "neither part nor lot" in the matter.

II. Yet Catholic. (Vers. 48, 49.) The sojourning stranger who wished to keep the passover had only to be circumcised—he and his males—to be admitted to the ordinance. He was then to be as one born in the land. This catholicity of spirit, and kindliness to foreigners, blending with a stern exclusiveness in religion, is characteristic of the whole Mosaic code. Cf. Vinet on the tolerance and intolerance of the Christian religion ("Vital Christianity"). The Lord's Supper is the most catholic of ordinances. It overleaps all barriers of race, nationality, clime, and religion. At the Lord's table there is neither Greek, nor Jew, barbarian, Scythian, bond nor free.

III. Equalising. (Ver. 44.) The master and slave sat down at the same board. See last homily. Christianity is the great social equaliser.

IV. Unifying. (Vers. 46, 47.) It taught the congregation to feel its unity. 1. The lamb was to be eaten in one house. 2. Not a bone of it was to be broken. "Through the unity and integrity of the lamb given them to eat, the participants were to be joined into an undivided unity and fellowship with the Lord, who had provided them with the meal" (Keil). 3. All the congregation were to eat it. The Lord's Supper, in like manner, is a social meal, in which the Church, eating "one bread," and drinking "one cup," declares itself to be "one body" (cf. 1 Cor. x. 16, 17). "The preservation of Christ, so that not a bone was broken, had the same signification; and God ordained this that he might appear as the true Paschal Lamb, that was slain for the sins of the world."—J. O.

Vers. 43—51.—*The Law of the Passover.* I. What God requires in its observance. 1. God demands purity of communion. No stranger is to eat of it. (1) Our holy things are not to be profaned. The life of Christ is lowered and endangered by indiscriminate admission to the Lord's table. (2) They are not to be degraded into superstitious rites. When they are given as if salvation resided in them, we are substituting idols for the unseen Saviour. The only safeguard for purity of worship is purity of communion. 2. It is not to be carried out from the midst of the household of faith. The peace and fellowship of the Gospel are only for the circumcised in heart. 3. Communion with Christ to be characterised by reverence and holy awe: not a bone of him is to be broken. 4. Every wall of partition is removed. All who believe have a right to join in the feast (vers. 41—49); but they must come with the mark of God's people,—a circumcised heart.

II. The obedience of faith is blessed not only with safety but also with deliverance. "Thus did all the children of Israel . . . and on the self-same day" they passed out of Egypt (50, 51). Fellowship with Christ is deliverance from the bondage of evil.—U.

EXPOSITION.

CHAPTER XIII.

Vers. 1–16.—Sanctification of the first-born. In connection with the deliverance from death of the Israelite first-born by the blood of the lamb, and still further to fix the remembrance of the historical facts in the mind of the nation, Moses was commissioned to de-

clare all the firstborn of Israel for all future time, and all the firstborn of their domesticated animals "holy to the Lord." There was, perhaps, already in the minds of men a feeling that peculiar dignity attached to the first-born in each family; and this feeling was now strengthened by the assignment to them of a sacred character. God claimed them, and also the first-born of beasts, as His own. The clean beasts became his by sacrifice; but the unclean ones could not be similarly treated, and therefore had to be "redeemed" (verse 13) by the sacrifice of clean animals in their place. The first-born of men became at the first institution of the new ordinance God's ministers; but as this system was not intended to continue, it was announced that they too would have to be "redeemed" (verses 13, 15). The exact mode of redeeming them was left to be settled afterwards, and will be found in Num. iii. 40–51; xviii. 16.

Ver. 1.—On the true grammatical *nexus* of this verse, see note on ch. xii. 51. The injunctions of verse 2, and probably those of 3–15—were given to Moses on the very day of the setting-forth, most likely, at Succoth in the evening.

Ver. 2.—**Sanctify unto me.** Not by any positive ceremony, but by regarding it as "set apart unto the Lord" (verse 12)—made over to him, that is, as his own. **All the first-born.** The Hebrew word used is masculine, and by its proper force limits the command to the first-born *males*, who alone had been in danger from the tenth plague. **Whatever openeth the womb.** This clause added definiteness, showing that "first-born" did not contain any reference to any later birth, and that it applied to every case where a woman's first child was a male. **It is mine.** Or, "it shall be mine." I claim it.

Ver. 3.—**And Moses said.** Without relating the directions given *to* Moses any further, the author passes to the directions given *by* him. He thus, here and elsewhere, avoids unnecessary repetition. **Remember this day.** The injunction came with great force at the close of the first day's journey, when the good-will of the Egyptians had been shown, and the people had been helped and speeded on their way, and felt that they were actually quitting the house of their bondage, and setting out for Canaan. **By strength of hand the Lord brought you out**—*i.e.*, "by His powerful protection has God brought you on your way thus far." Therefore, "Remember this day, and remember that nothing leavened is to be eaten on it" (see ch. xii. 15–20).

Ver 4.—**In the month Abib.** The name of the month had not been previously mentioned. Some have derived it from the Egyptian Epiphi. As, however, *ab* means "greenness" in Hebrew, and *abib* "green ears of corn," while *ibba* meant "fruit" in Chaldee (Dan. iv. 12, 14), and *abbon* means "green herbs" in Arabic, there is no need of a foreign derivation for the word. The month

of "greenness," or of "green ears of corn," would be both appropriate and intelligible.

Ver. 5.—**The land of the Canaanites,** etc. Compare ch. iii. 8, 17. The six nations of these passages are reduced here to five by the omission of the Perizzites, one of the less important tribes. **Which he sware unto thy fathers to give thee** (see Gen. xv. 18; xxiv. 7; and compare the comment on ch. vi. 8. **That thou shalt keep this service.** This injunction had been already given (ch. xii. 25) almost in the same words; but on the former occasion it was delivered to the elders only; now it is laid upon the whole people.

Ver. 6.—**Seven days.** Compare ch. xii. 15. **In the seventh day shall be a feast to the Lord.** The feast lasted during the whole of the seven days, but the first day and the last were to be kept especially holy. (See ch. xii. 16; Lev. xxiii. 6–8.)

Ver. 7.—Here again the injunctions are mere repetitions of commands already given in ch. xii. (See verses 15 and 19.) Repetition was no doubt had recourse to in order to deepen the impression.

Ver. 8.—**And thou shalt shew thy son.** Repeated from ch. xii. 26, 27.

Ver. 9.—**And it shall be for a sign unto thee upon thy hand, and for a memorial between thine eyes.** There can be no doubt that the Jewish system of *tephillin*, or "phylacteries," grew mainly out of this passage, and was intended as a fulfilment of the commands contained in it. The *tephillin* were strips of parchment with passages of Scripture written upon them and deposited in small boxes, which were fastened by a strap either to the left arm, or across the forehead. The modern Jews argue that they were what Moses here intended, and that their employment began from this time. Some Christian commentators agree with them. But the great majority argue, from supposed probability and from the entire absence of any reference to the actual wearing of *tephillin* in the Old Testament, that the custom must be, comparatively speaking, a modern one. It is generally supposed to have originated, with other superstitious practices, in the time of the Babylonish captivity. Those who take this view regard the words of Moses in the present passage as merely metaphorical, and compare them with Prov. iii. 3; vi. 21; vii. 3. Kalisch, however, observes with reason, that if the injunction to write passages of the Law on the door-posts of their houses (Deut. vi. 9; xi. 20) was intended to be understood literally, and was literally carried out (Is. lvii. 8), the commands with respect to *tephillin*, which are *coupled with them* (Deut. vi. 8; xi. 18) must have been similarly intended. And probability, which is said to be against the Mosaic origin of *tephillin*, may perhaps rather be urged in its favour. The Egyptian practice of wearing as amulets "forms of words written on folds of papyrus tightly rolled up and sewn in linen" (Wilkinson's *Ancient Egyptians*, vol. iii. p. 364) is well attested. Would it not be in harmony with the general character of his legislation, that Moses should adopt and regulate the custom, employing it to do honour to the Law and keep it in remembrance, without perhaps purging it wholly from superstitious ideas? Moses allowed the Israelites in many things "for the hardness of their hearts," content if he could introduce some improvement without insisting at once on an impracticable perfection. **That the law of the Lord may be in thy mouth.** The Israelites are instructed from the first, that the *tephillin* are to be a means to an end; and that the end is to be the retention of God's law in their recollection—"in their mouth," and therefore in their heart, since "out of the abundance of the heart the mouth speaketh."

Ver. 10.—**This ordinance.** The ordinance of unleavened bread. See ch. xii. 14, 24.

Ver. 12.—**Set apart.** The expression is especially appropriate to the case of first-born animals, which would have to be separated off from the rest of the flock, or of the herd, and "put aside" for Jehovah, so as not to be mixed up and confounded with the other lambs, kids, and calves. **The males shall be the Lord's.** This limitation, implied in verse 2, is here brought prominently into notice.

Ver. 13.—**Every firstling of an ass.** The ass was the sole beast of burthen taken by the Israelites out of Egypt. (See Ex. xx. 17.) Neither the horse nor the camel was among their possessions in the wilderness. This is agreeable to the Egyptian monuments, by which the camel appears to have been rare in Egypt at this time, and the horse as yet mainly used for war and by the nobles in their chariots. **With a lamb.** A lamb or a kid. The word used is the generic one. (See the comment on ch. xii. 3.) **If thou wilt not redeem it, then thou shalt break its neck.** This enactment was evidently made to prevent a refusal to redeem. It would not require to be put in force, since by refusing under such a penalty a man would suffer pecuniary loss. **All the first-born of men among thy children.** Rather "among thy sons." **Shalt thou redeem.** Later on, the amount of the redemption money was fixed at five shekels for the sanctuary for each. (Num. iii. 47.)

Ver. 14.—**When thy son asketh thee.** Compare ch. xii. 26, and the comment *ad loc.*

Ver. 15.—**When Pharaoh would hardly let us go.** Rather, "when Pharaoh hardened himself against letting us go." At his last interview with Moses, Pharaoh had absolutely refused to let them go *with their cattle* (ch. x. 24—27), and Moses had absolutely refused to go without them. **I sacrifice all that openeth the womb, being males.** And being clean animals. The common sense of the reader or hearer, is expected to supply the restriction. **Of my children.** Rather, as in verse 13, "of my sons."

Ver. 16.—**A sign . . . frontlets.** See the comment on verse 9. It is the custom among the Jews to write this entire passage—Ex. xiii. 1–16—on two of the four strips of parchment contained in the *tephillin*. The others have inscribed on them Deut. vi. 4–9, and Deut. xi. 13–21.

HOMILETICS.

Vers. 1—16.—*The Dedication and Redemption of the First-born.* In commemoration of the great mercy whereby their first-born sons were spared, when all those of the Egyptians were slain, God required the Israelites to do two things:—(1) To dedicate all their first-born sons, not only of the existing but of all future generations, to himself; and, (2) to redeem them, or buy them back for the purposes of secular life, by a money payment. It is analogous to this—

I. THAT CHRISTIAN PARENTS ARE REQUIRED TO DEDICATE, NOT THEIR FIRST-BORN SONS ONLY, BUT ALL THEIR CHILDREN, TO GOD IN BAPTISM. All have deserved death. All have been in danger of it. All have been spared by the mercy of God, on account of the atoning blood of Christ. All therefore are to be dedicated by their parents to God's service—brought to the font, and presented to him to be his faithful soldiers and servants until their life's end. All are to receive a species of consecration, whereby they become "priests to God" (Rev. i. 6), and may have boldness to approach him without the intervention of a human mediator. But all are not to be ministers. The ministry is for such as have a special call, which cannot be known in infancy, or indeed until persons are well advanced towards manhood.

II. THAT CHRISTIAN PARENTS HAVE, AFTER DEDICATING THEM, TO TAKE THEIR CHILDREN BACK, AS IT WERE, TO SECULAR LIFE. Hannah gave her son up to God from the time that she weaned him, took him to the Temple, and left him with the priests. Christians cannot do this. Though some of their sons may ultimately have a call to the ministry, this will not be the case with all, and they must act as if it would not be the case with any. They must take their children back to their houses, give them a secular education, and prepare them in most instances for secular life. But they have not to buy them back. This arises from the difference between the two dedications, the one having been a dedication to the ministry and the other not. Christians do not need to retract the dedication of their children by any subsequent act. They may and should maintain it. Laymen may lead lives as truly sanctified as clergymen. They may serve God as well, though in a different way. They may be, and should be " holy to the Lord." Who would not desire his children to be such?

Vers. 3—16.—*The rightful use of Church ordinances.* Church ordinances are—(1) Commemorative; (2) Disciplinary; (3) Channels of supernatural grace. The benefits derivable from them depend mainly upon their rightful use. We learn from the instructions here given to the Israelites by Moses, that their rightful use consists especially—

I. In THE REGULAR KEEPING OF THEM. " Thou shalt keep this ordinance in his season from year to year." Spasmodic observance, enthusiastic and frequent at one time, perfunctory and infrequent at another, ten times this year, once the next, will bring no blessing, conduct to no good result. Each ordinance has its own time or times—baptism and confirmation once in a lifetime—the Holy Communion weekly, if opportunity offers; if not, monthly; or, *at the least,* thrice a year—attendance at public worship, each Sunday, twice—fasting, on Fridays and in Lent—commemoration of chief festivals, once a year—and so on. Fitness has in every case been considered, and set times appointed at proper intervals. Let the rule of the Church be *regularly* followed, let there be no needless variation, no will-worship, no caprice, and the greatest benefit may be confidently anticipated. But following one's own fancy in the matter, now observing rules, now breaking them, making ourselves in fact a law to ourselves, is a course that will assuredly obtain no blessing upon it. " Thou shalt keep each ordinance in his season."

II. In THE STRICT KEEPING OF THEM. " There shall no leavened bread be seen with thee, neither shall there be leaven seen with thee, in all thy quarters." Lukewarmness, double-mindedness, half-and-half measures, are everywhere condemned in Scripture. " If the Lord be God, follow Him; if Baal, then follow him." " Because thou art lukewarm, and neither cold nor hot, I will spue thee out of my mouth." If the ordinances of the Church are worth following at all, they are worth following *strictly.* If the Church says—" Put away gaiety and amusement during this or that season," then *all* gaiety and amusement should be put away—none should be seen " in all our quarters." If she appoints two services, or (as some understand it) three for Sundays, then men should not limit their attendance to one. If she urges frequent communions, they should attend frequently, and not be content with the minimum of three times in the year.

III. In THE KEEPING OF SUCH OF THEM AS ARE COMMEMORATIVE WITH REMEMBRANCE. " Remember this day, in the which ye came out from Egypt "—" the Lord slew all the first-born—therefore I sacrifice to the Lord all that openeth the matrix." A large part of the ritual of every church is commemorative. Sunday is a commemoration. The Friday fast, enjoined by the Church of England and others, is a commemoration. Christmas, Easter, Whitsuntide, Ascension Day, are commemorations. And the Holy Communion is in part commemorative. To observe, in a certain sense, these days and seasons and ordinances, without giving serious thought to the historical events with which they are connected, and out of which they have arisen, is to lose half the benefit which their observance was intended to secure to us. It is scarcely, perhaps, to be supposed that any one could receive the Holy Communion without some thought of the death of Christ upon the Cross; but it must greatly conduce to the rite having its due and full operation on our minds and hearts, that we should vividly present to ourselves on the occasion a mental picture of the agonies suffered for us, that we should dwell in thought upon the whole scene of the trial and the crucifixion, and seek to realise its particulars. We cannot have too deeply impressed upon us the recollection of the day on which, and the means by which, God brought the Church of the first-born out of the spiritual bondage of Egypt, saved them from the destroyer, sanctified them, and made them his "peculiar people."

IV. IN THE CONTINUED KEEPING OF THEM THROUGH TIMES OF PROSPERITY. "When the Lord shall bring thee into the land of the Canaanites, thou shalt keep this service." The discipline of adversity is apt to draw men nearer to God than that of prosperity. Many are very careful and regular attendants on Church ordinances when they are afflicted, or in poor circumstances, or suffering from a bereavement; but, if the world smiles upon them, if they grow rich and respected, if men court and flatter them, they grow careless and irregular in such matters. They think that they cease to have the time for them; but in reality they cease to relish them. "The cares of the world and the deceitfulness of riches," choke the good seed that was in them, and "they become unfruitful." They forget God, and the marvellous things that he hath done for them. Hence a warning is required. We must not let the "milk and honey" of Canaan wean our hearts from God, or make us less zealous in his service, or less constant attendants upon his ordinances. The higher we are lifted up the more we need his grace; the greater attraction that the world offers to us, the more helpful to us are those holy rites and usages, which draw our thoughts away from earthly things, and fix them upon things Divine and heavenly.

HOMILIES BY VARIOUS AUTHORS.

Vers. 1—3, 11—17.—*The sanctification of the first-born.* This command has its basis in the fact that on the night when God executed his tremendous judgment against Egypt, the first-born of Israel was spared. Because this great mercy had been shown to Israel, the first-born of man and beast were ever afterwards to be reckoned as specially belonging to Jehovah. The first-born of the generation then living was his by direct purchase; all later first-borns were to be his by grateful dedication. It was required, in addition, that the first-born of man, as well as of unclean beasts, should be "redeemed." This may have been designed to teach that the lives of these later first-borns were as truly forfeited by sin as were those of the original first-born, on the night of the exodus; and that the nearer the relation in which the individual stands to God, the more pressing becomes the need for atonement.

I. REDEMPTION IS BY SUBSTITUTION. This is well illustrated by the law for the redemption of unclean animals (ver. 13; cf. Num. xviii. 15). The firstling of an ass, being unclean, could not be offered on the altar. It was, therefore, to be redeemed by the substitution of a lamb. If not thus redeemed, its neck was to be broken. This teaches the further lesson—*unredeemed life must die.* It was on the same principle that the lamb was substituted for the first-born on the night of the exodus. This law does not specify the manner of the redemption of the first-born of male children, but it was probably originally by a lamb also. The redemption was subsequently effected by a money-payment of five shekels (Num. xviii. 16). This gave prominence to the idea of a *ransom*, already implied in the use of the word "redeem." The principle of the redemption was still the substitution of life for life, the money-payment pointing back to the lamb or other victim of which it was the price. Jesus has fulfilled the type under both its aspects. He has redeemed us by the substitution of his holy life for our sinful ones (Heb. ix. 26—28). His life has been given as a ransom for many (Matt. xx. 28; 1 Tim. ii. 6).

II. REDEEMED LIFE BELONGS TO GOD (vers. 1, 12, 15). As all later generations of Israel were represented in that first one, so all later first-borns were represented in those of the night of the exodus. By redeeming them from death, God purchased the first-born of Israel in a peculiar manner to himself. What held true of the first-born, held true, in a wider sense, of the nation as a whole, and holds true now of all believers. They are God's, because God has redeemed them. We must not seem to lessen the *natural* claim which God has upon our service. All souls are God's; and no moral being has a right to use his powers otherwise than for the glory of him who gave them. But in a special manner Jehovah claims *redeemed* life for himself. "I have redeemed thee, thou art mine " (Is. xliii. 1). " Ye are bought with a price; therefore glorify God in your body, and in your spirit, which are God's " (1 Cor. vi. 20).

III. THE ANIMAL CREATION SHARES IN MAN'S RUIN AND REDEMPTION. First-born of man *and beast.*—J. O.

Vers. 3—11.—"*Remember this day.*" The exhortation in these verses may very well be applied to Christians. They are to remember the *fact* and the *might* of their redemption. They are to commemorate it by observance of appointed ordinances. They are to beware of forgetting it in days of prosperity. They are to show their remembrance of it by a holy walk, and by due instruction of their children.

I. REMEMBER THE FACT AND THE MIGHT OF YOUR REDEMPTION. 1. The *fact* of it (vers. 3—8). How Jesus has brought you up " out of an horrible pit, out of the miry clay " (Ps. xl. 1); has redeemed you from the law's curse, from Satan's tyranny, from a condition of wrath, and from spiritual death ; has introduced you into the liberty of God's children, and started you on your journey to an everlasting and glorious inheritance. Redemption from the thraldom of Pharaoh sinks into insignificance as compared with this " so great salvation." If Israel was summoned to remember the day on which they came out of Egypt, out of the house of bondage, much more is it the duty of Christians to remember what great things God has done for *them.* 2. The *might* of it. " By strength of hand the Lord brought you out of this place " (vers. 3, 9, 14). They were to remember this as enhancing their sense of the greatness of their redemption, and as affording a pledge that God was able to accomplish all else that he had promised (ver. 5). The might expended in the Christian redemption is not less, but greater, than in the exodus from Egypt. It does not detract from its greatness that it is chiefly *moral* strength—power exerted in overcoming evil, in producing moral effects in the minds and consciences of men, and in making them new creatures in Christ Jesus. Redemption has both its objective and its subjective sides, and in both is displayed the power of God. God's might is seen in the upholding of Christ; in the victories which, while on earth, he was enabled to gain over the powers of evil ; in the gigantic triumph of the Cross; and in the spiritual effects produced since, through eighteen centuries, by the preaching of his Gospel ; in the regeneration of souls, in the strength given to his servants to do spiritual work, in the victory whereby they overcome the world.

II. BEWARE OF FORGETTING YOUR REDEMPTION IN THE DAYS OF YOUR PROSPERITY, ver. 15. Prosperity has a subtle influence in leading away the heart from God. When men have eaten, and are full (Deut. viii. 12—18), they are very apt to grow haughty and self-sufficient. This danger is one to be jealously watched against.

III. SHOW THAT YOU REMEMBER YOUR REDEMPTION BY DOING THE THINGS THAT GOD COMMANDS. 1. By *observing his ordinances.* The special ordinance here alluded to is the feast of unleavened bread—a sequel to the passover (vers. 3—10). Christians are to observe the Lord's Supper. 2. By *a holy life.* The observance of the outward ordinance would be valueless if that which it spiritually represented was lost sight of, viz., the need of a walk in " newness of life." We are to " keep the feast, not with old leaven, neither with the leaven of malice and wickedness, but with the unleavened bread of sincerity and truth " (1 Cor. v. 7). To this end has Christ redeemed us, that we may walk in holiness (Rom. vi. 4—7 ; Eph. v. 25—28 ; Titus ii. 14 ; 1 Pet. i. 18). 3. By *instruction of children.* God lays stress on this (vers. 8—14 ; cf. Deut. vi. 6—9 ; xi. 18—22). It is his chief way of perpetuating a holy seed. The responsibility of instruction rests primarily on the parent. No task should be more delightful to him, or should be discharged more faithfully. If the parent is willing, many opportunities will present themselves. A child's curiosity is ever active. The ordinances of the Church will furnish starting-points for conversation. We have in these verses, and elswhere in the book, specimens of the instruction that is to be given.—J. O.

Vers. 1, 2.—*The consecration of the first-born.* I. THE MEANING OF THE TYPE. 1. Man's first-born the type of the first-born of God, in his authority and priestly function among his brethren, and as the object of the father's love and trust. 2. In Egypt's and Israel's first-born we find the two-fold type of Christ and his people. Egypt's die, Israel's are saved. The death of Egypt's first-born bursts the bonds of Israel, the death of God's first-born, the bonds of his people.

II. God's DEMAND. 1. His claim upon the saved life: "It is mine." (1) His right to our service. He has bought us with a great price. (2) His delight in us. We are a treasure and a joy to him. Because he loved us he gave Christ to die for us. 2. The life which Christ has redeemed is to be set apart for God (Rom. xii. 1). (1) With full purpose of heart. (2) Under the power of Christ's love: "the love of Christ constraineth us." (3) With unceasing prayer for the Spirit's indwelling.

Ver. 3—16.—*How to declare God's salvation.* I. BY THE REMEMBRANCE OF HIS MERCIES. 1. "Remember this day in which ye came out from Egypt." (1) The Lord's Supper is an ordinance of remembrance: "Do this in remembrance of me." (2) The remembrance of deliverance extends over the Christian's whole life: "unleavened bread is eaten." 2. The celebration of the Passover awoke inquiry among those who had not witnessed God's deeds (ver. 8).—True gratitude, heartfelt thanksgiving, will make the reality of God's love to be felt by those who have not known him. (1) The place and use of the Lord's Supper in the Christian Church. (2) The power of love in the Christian life. (3) Of true praise and worship in the congregation. To make God something to others, he must first be something to ourselves. II. BY THE DOING OF HIS WILL. The Israelites, in sacrificing or redeeming the first-born, woke again the question, "What is this?" (vers. 14, 15). Our obedience to the good and holy will of God, our consecration to his service will show the reality of his salvation and awaken in many hearts the question whence this consecration flows and the desire to share it. "Let your light so shine" (Matt. v. 16).—U.

Ver. 10. Cf. ch. xii. 42.—*Remember.* Utmost pains taken that the day should be honoured and remembered. (1) The month in which it occurred became the beginning of months. (2) A special ordinance as to the first-born pointed back continually to the event celebrated (vers. 11—13). (3) The annual feast was specially devised to keep it in memory (vers. 14, etc.). Why all this?
I. REASON OF OBSERVANCE. It commemorated: 1. *A great judgment.* Nine plagues had passed; the members of each successive trial following one another at shorter intervals and with increasing severity. [Illustration, siege of town. Besiegers draw parallels closer and closer, each time sounding summons to surrender. Every summons disregarded; at length word given for the assault.] God laying siege to Egypt, now preparing for the assault (cf. generally Amos iv.). "Therefore, prepare to meet thy God" (ch. xi. 4). "*I* will go out;" the representatives stand aside that the arm of Jehovah may be recognised. Fourteenth of month; midnight. God accompanied by the angel of vengeance. Picture result—palace, dungeon, stables, fields, temples, streets. The judgment was upon Egypt and her gods. 2. *A great deliverance.* (1) From death. God the judge is impartial. If Egypt has sinned, so also Israel. Three plagues shared by both, both now threatened by self-same danger. Israel, however, trusting God, may escape by obedience. Lamb chosen four days earlier. Slain that afternoon at sundown. Light of full moon shows blood streaks on lintels and doorposts of houses in Goshen; inside, people prepared for departure, feeding on lamb. Midnight: Is it imagination that rush and quiver of unseen wings? The shadow of the wings of God shelter each blood-stained door, whilst the angel of vengeance passes over, sparing those whom God protects. (2) From slavery. Wailing throughout Egypt. Midnight message, "Go, get ye gone." At once families gather to standards of their tribes. Soon one great army, harnessed and equipped, laden with spoils of Egypt, the Israelites march forth from the land of their captivity. The time fulfilled to the day (xii. 41), when their hour is come their God is ready. 3. *A great exhibition of Divine power.* Not a mere judgment or a mere deliverance, but judgment by a personal judge, deliverance by a personal deliverer. (1) The Egyptians needed to learn who Jehovah was. The Israelites had not done much to make him respected; rather had brought his name into disrepute as the patron of a slavish multitude. Must cause his own name to be hallowed (cf. Ezek. xxxvi. 20—23). (2) Israel needed to learn that Jehovah was the deliverer—a God faithful to his promises, yet who could not endure sin. Moses and Aaron his instruments, but the victory due only to *his* right hand and *his* holy arm.
II. USE OF THE OBSERVANCE. By communicating the judgment and the deliverance,

it was calculated to keep men mindful of the judge and the deliverer, and to prompt respect for his law (xiii. 9). Commemorations are an aid to memory, reminding of past events, and recalling associations connected with them. *Mere* observance as an end in itself, bondage (cf. Gal. iv. 9, 10); as a means to an end, helpful and necessary. The Pharisee *makes* a virtue of observance; the right thing is to *draw* virtue from it. See what this observance taught:—1. God *is* long-suffering, but the day of vengeance comes at length. The help to memory, as to what he *had* done, was a help to conviction as to what he might do. 2. God will not clear the guilty, yet his mercy doth endure for ever. Even with the help, how often were these truths forgotten (cf. Ps. cvi. 7—13, etc.); would any have remembered them without it?

Apply. Life, which forms the memory of the future, grows out of memory of the past. A good memory is a help to good living. What helps do you use to prompt memory? The marked bill, the birthday text-book, the diary—all these helpful; above all, the day, the anniversary, if we use it rightly. Commemorations are but sign-posts pointing to that which is commemorated; use them as such, follow out their indications. So, remembering past mercies, faith will be strengthened and hope sustained.—G.

EXPOSITION.

Ver. 17-20.—The direction of the journey.—The direct road from Tanis to Palestine—a road much frequented under the nineteenth dynasty—lay along the coast of the Mediterranean, and conducted to Philistia. If we look at the map, and observe the position of Tanis (now San) on the old Tanitic branch of the Nile, now nearly dried up, we shall see that the route which would naturally suggest itself to any one wishing to proceed to the Holy Land from Tanis would be one running almost due east, from Tanis to Pelusium, and from Pelusium, south of Lake Serbonis, to Rhinocolura; and thence, following the course of the coast to Gaza, Ascalon, and Ashdod, the chief towns of the Philistine country. It is true that a marsh region intervenes between Tanis and Pelusium which might seem to bar the route; but the Egyptian remains show that, in the times of the eighteenth and nineteenth dynasties, this obstacle was surmounted by means of an embankment which was carried across it, and that a direct road thus connected the two cities.

Moses, at this point of his narrative, being about to trace the onward march of the Israelites from Succoth to Etham, in the direction of the Red Sea, anticipated, it would seem, an objection on the part of his reader, who would naturally ask, Why was not the direct route eastward taken and Canaan entered on the south-west after some half-dozen marches? In verses 17, 18, he gives the reply—1. God led them, they did not determine their own route; and 2, God would not lead them by the direct route, because it would have conducted them to the Philistine country, and the Philistines were strong, and would have resisted the invasion by force of arms. Hence it was that the southern or south-eastern route was taken in preference to the northern one—and that the second stage in the journey was from Succoth to Etham (verse 20).

Ver. 17.—**Although that was near.** Rather "*because* it was near" (ὅτι ἐγγὺς ἦν, LXX.)—*i.e.*, "God did not, because it was near, lead them this way, but a longer one." **Lest peradventure the people repent when they see war.** The Philistines were a powerful and warlike race half a century after this, in the time of Joshua, and were masters of the five important cities of Gaza, Ascalon, Ashdod, Gath, and Ekron, which seem to have formed a confederacy (Josh. xiii. 3). It would appear that their strength was already considerable, and that the Israelites, though perhaps more numerous, were incapable of coping with them, being wholly unaccustomed to war. The Israelites were therefore not allowed to take this route, which would have brought upon them at once a severe trial, and might have led to their voluntary return into Egypt.

Ver. 18.—**God led the people about.** Or "led the people a circuit," *i.e.*, made them take a circuitous route to Canaan, **the way of the wilderness of the Red Sea**—*i.e.*, by the southern wilderness, or what is now called "the wilderness of Sinai." Kalisch shows the wisdom of this course—how it gave time for the nation to be "gradually accustomed to fatigues and hardships by a long **and** tiresome march in the desert "—to learn obedience to their chief—and finally to be "trained to military discipline and martial virtue by occasional expeditions against the weaker tribes of the desert." He errs, however, in ascribing the wisdom of the course taken to Moses, since Moses expressly declares that the conception was not his, but God's. **And the children of Israel went up harnessed.** The word here translated "harnessed," is generally thought to mean either "with their loins girded" (Onkelos, Kimchi, Kalisch) or "in military order" (Gesenius, Lee, Knobel). Ewald, who inclines to the latter of these two senses, suggests that, strictly, it means "in five divisions"—viz., van, centre, two wings, and rearguard. The word is, apparently, a derivative from *khamesh,* "five."

Ver. 19.—**Moses took the bones of Joseph** —*i.e.,* his body, which had been embalmed, and deposited in a mummy case (Gen. l. 26), most probably at Tanis, which was the capital of the Shepherd kings, no less than of Menephthah. **He had straitly sworn the children of Israel.** See Gen. l. 25. Joseph, firmly believing in the promise of God to give Canaan to the descendants of Abraham had made them swear to take his body with them when they left Egypt. The desire to be laid in their native earth was common to most of the nations of antiquity, and, in the case of the Israelites, was intensified by Canaan being the "land of promise." Jacob had had the same feeling as Joseph, and had been buried by Joseph in the cave of Machpelah (Gen. l. 13).

Ver. 20.—**And they took their journey from Succoth and encamped in Etham.** On the probable position of Etham, see the "Introduction" to this book. The word probably means "House of Tum," and implies the existence at the place of a temple of the Sun-God, who was commonly worshipped as Tum or Atum. The name, therefore, is nearly equivalent to Pithom (ch. i. 11), which means "City of Tum;" but it is not likely that Moses designated the same place by two distinct appellations. The site of Etham, moreover, does not agree with that of the Patumos of Herodotus (ii. 158), which is generally allowed to be Pithom.

HOMILETICS.

Vers. 18—21.—*It is the method of the Divine action to accomplish ends by circuitous means.* God "led the Israelites about." Instead of conducting them straight from Tanis to Canaan in the course of six or seven days, he carried them down nearly to the furthest point of the Sinaitic peninsula, at least two hundred miles out of the direct line of route. He afterwards made them occupy in desert wanderings the space of forty years, and brought them into Canaan on the side furthest from Egypt—that which fronted the east. So it is—

I. IN GOD'S NATURAL WORKINGS. To make a planet suitable for the habitation of man, he does not create one fit for him straight off. He prepares an extended mass of matter which gradually condenses, throws off an atmosphere, settles into land and sea, undergoes for many thousands of years a series of aqueous and igneous changes, deposits strata, elevates them into mountains, works out river courses, raises and submerges continents; and only after a number of millennia does he, by this long and tedious process, effect the end aimed at from the first, the construction of a habitation suitable for such a being as man. Again, he will have man live on bread; but he does not make bread. He makes a germ capable of developing into a plant, of throwing out roots and leaves, deriving sustenance from air and earth and showers, increasing gradually for several months, and finally throwing up the tall spike, which after growing, and swelling, and ripening, bears ultimately the golden grain that is suited to be man's food.

II. IN GOD'S SPIRITUAL WORKINGS. If God has a work for a man to do, if for this a certain character is required, God again pursues no compendious method. The man is born in a certain sphere, given certain powers, and then it is left for the circumstances of life to work out in him, under Divine superintendence, the character required. Moses is trained for eighty years in order to qualify him for his position as deliverer of the Israelites from the bondage of Egypt; and is only rendered fit to accomplish the task by what befals him in that long period. All the saints of God, raised up to do any great work, have had some such long training. Even Christ did not enter on his ministry at once, but remained in obscurity for thirty years, before asserting his mission.

III. EVEN IN GOD'S MIRACULOUS WORKINGS. Christ would assuage the pains of hunger of the five thousand. He does not simply, as he might have done, remove them by a word. He obtains such food as there is at hand : he blesses and breaks ; he causes the multitude to sit down ; he distributes the food among the apostles, and bids them distribute to the multitude. If the Red Sea is to be parted, an east wind is made to blow for some hours ; if a blind man is to be cured, clay is taken, and mixed with spittle, and put upon the blind man's eyes, and by a circuitous method his cure is effected. All this seems strange to us because we are so impatient. Our life here endures so short a space, and we so little realise the fact of the life to come, that we are always in a hurry to obtain results, and are annoyed at having to wait for them. But an Eternal Being can afford to be patient. "One day is with the Lord as a thousand years, and a thousand years as one day." The question with God is never as to the quickest, but always as to the best method. Haste is proverbially unsafe. "Most haste, worst speed," says the adage. It would bring much improvement into human life, if there were less of bustle and hurry in it—if men were not in so much haste to be rich—if they did not expect to reap the harvest so soon as they have sown the seed—if they would allow time for plans to take effect, for improvements to be brought to perfection, for institutions to take root and grow.

Ver. 19.—*It is a Christian duty to carry with us on the path of life the bones of our dead.* Joseph had sworn the Israelites to carry his bones with them out of Egypt at their departure; and they were thus in a special way bound to do it. But, apart from any such oath, or any positive wish expressed, it would have been well for them to have taken him with them. We are intimately bound up with the men of the generation before our own, and cannot too carefully carry along with us their memory. Men may be considered to carry their dead with them on their course through life—

I. WHEN THEY BEAR IN MIND AND HAVE RESPECT TO THEIR FATHERS IN THE FAITH, ESPECIALLY THOSE NEAR TO THEM IN TIME. It is almost impossible to measure adequately the amount of our debt to those who have immediately preceded us in life— who have set us an example of a consistent Christian course—and shown us its possibility. What living Christian man does not feel that to some other Christian man, older than himself, still alive or else passed away, he is indebted for the impetus which changed his path in life, turned him from the dumb idols which he was following, and led him to the worship of the living God ? What gratitude is not due in each such case ! Such memories are to be cherished, clung to—not relinquished, because he to whom we owe so much is dead. Being dead, such an one " still speaketh ; " and it is well that our hearts should still hear his voice, and be thankful for it.

II. WHEN THEY CHERISH THE MEMORY OF THE FRIENDS AND RELATIONS WHOM THEY HAVE LOST. It is too common a practice, with men especially, to shut out the memory of the deceased. Bereavement is so terrible a thing, so poignant a grief, that to spare themselves men mostly make a sort of resolve that they will not think upon their dead. And it is quite possible, after a while, so to turn from the thought as to make it both transient and rare. But the better course—the true Christian course—is to retain our dead in our thoughts. The recollection can do us nothing but good. It is sobering, chastening, yet elevating. It is apt to wean us from the world; to soften us; to draw us into communion with the unseen ; to help our higher nature in its struggle with the lower.

III. WHEN THEY BEAR IN REMEMBRANCE THE WORST SINS THAT THEY HAVE COMMITTED. The most terrible death to which we poor human creatures are subject is that " body of death," which we bear about with us in our flesh, and under which we " groan, being burthened "—viz. sin. There are persons who succeed in putting away the memory of their past sins, and who are as gay and light-hearted as if there were nothing against them in God's book. But it is a wiser course to bear about with us always this " death " also, and not seek to hush it up or put it out of sight. The thought of our past sins is well calculated to make us humble, penitent, forgiving; to save us from presumption, and make us throw ourselves absolutely for justification on the merits and atoning blood of Christ.

HOMILIES BY VARIOUS AUTHORS.

Vers. 17—21.—" *The way of the wilderness by the Red Sea.*" The direct road to Canaan lay through the land of the Philistines. God, however, did not lead the people by this way, but round by the Red Sea. " For God said, Lest peradventure the people repent when they see war, and they return to Egypt " (vers. 17). Another reason was that he designed to make his covenant with them, and give them laws, in the solitude of the " mountain of God " (ch. iii. 12).

I. REDEEMED FROM EGYPT, THE PEOPLE ARE NOT PERMITTED TO LINGER ON ITS BORDERS. What snatches of repose are granted, are only meant as a preparation for resumption of the journey on the morrow. Their destination was Canaan. To this they must press forward. A rest of eleven months (at Sinai) will be granted afterwards, meanwhile, on the borders of Egypt, they must pause no longer than is absolutely necessary. At the beginning of the Christian life, delays, pauses, lookings back, are peculiarly dangerous. Egypt is too near. Return to it is too convenient. The pursuer will gain too easy an advantage. There must be no pausing till we are fairly out of the enemy's territory. Succoth to Etham, Etham to Pi-hahiroth (ch. xiv. 2).

II. IT RESTS WITH GOD TO DETERMINE THE WAY BY WHICH HIS PEOPLE SHALL BE LED. " When Pharaoh had let the people go, *God* led them not," etc. (vers. 17). 1. It was the privilege of the Israelites that *they had God as their guide.* His pillar of cloud and fire went before them (vers. 21, 22). What wiser or safer guide could any one desire? 2. *God's guidance was authoritative.* Not only were the Israelites not left to pick out the way for themselves, but whither God directed, thither they were bound to go. They were not permitted to take any route they pleased. They were God's people, and must walk by his law. 3. *God's guidance was frequently mysterious.* They would often be perplexed to understand the reasons of it. A reason seems to have been given here, but otherwise the route chosen must have seemed a very strange one. The believer is often thus led by a way he knows not (Is. xlii. 16).

III. GOD CONSULTS FOR HIS PEOPLE'S GOOD IN THE WAYS BY WHICH HE LEADS THEM. " For God said, peradventure," etc. (ver. 17). Consider here, 1. God's *procedure.* (1) He turned the Israelites aside from the road which naturally they would have followed. The way of the land of the Philistines was no doubt the road by which they *expected* to be led. It was the customary road. It lay straight before them. It was the shortest and most direct. How often does God thus turn us aside in Providence from what might seem to be the natural, as, without a thought to the contrary, it may have been the anticipated course of our lives ? The road that lies straight before us is not the one in which we are permitted to walk. Even in Christian work, by what zigzag ways are we sometimes conducted to our ends ! (2) He led the Israelites by a long detour into the wilderness. If the end was to escape the Philistines, God did not allow the Israelites to suppose that he intended to pamper and indulge them. The wilderness was a worse place to travel in than " the way of the land of the Philistines." They would have to encounter many trials. A heavy strain would be put upon their faith. Though exempted from war at the beginning, they had to fight enemies on the way, and ultimately were marched up to the borders of Canaan, to undertake, at another point, the work of invasion. In like manner, the Christian curriculum is not an easy one. Whoever enters upon the Christian journey, expecting to find it all sunshine and roses, is doomed to sorrowful disappointment. The road, under God's guidance, soon takes a turn, which leads into the wilderness of trial. 2. The *reasons* of God's procedure. (1) The direct way was at that time an *impassable* one. The Israelites, just escaped from Egypt, were not in a condition to force their way through the strongly defended territory of the Philistines. The difficulty, it is true, lay in *them*—in their want of faith, courage, and power of obedience, not in God, whose help was all-sufficient. But practically, the direct road was closed against them. So, in God's merciful guidance of his people, the path is sometimes bent aside, because no other is for the time practicable. Obstacles to their progress, insurmountable by them at that stage of their knowledge and experience, block up the road which seems more direct, and to be allowed to advance in it would be no kindness. (2) The direct road was *fraught with danger* for themselves. Their strength and faith were not equal to the opposition they would encounter. It would have proved too much for them.   They must be allowed time to gather experience, to throw off the habits of their servitude, to be brought under discipline for war, to acquire steadiness and courage in facing an enemy.   Led up against the Philistines in their present undisciplined condition, they would have fled at the first onset, and would have clamoured, even more vehemently than they did in the desert (ch. xiv. 12), to be conducted back to Egypt.   And does not this in large measure explain the mysterious turnings and windings in our own lives?   God, who knows our frame, understands perfectly what degree of severity in temptation we are able to endure, and he mercifully orders our course, so that we may not be tempted above that we are able (1 Cor. x. 13).   We pray, "Lead us not into temptation" (Matt. vi. 13), and this is one way in which the prayer is answered.   Another way is by preventing or restraining the temptation.   But where, as in the present case, it is a temptation which, so to speak, belongs essentially to the situation—which we *must* encounter, if that path is to be travelled at all, then is there no way of avoiding it but by being led in a different road. Especially in the *beginning* of a Christian course may we expect these sudden turnings of our path.   We are not then in a condition to encounter *very* powerful enemies, to endure *very* fierce temptations, and by taking us a little way about God shields us from them.   (3) There was a *discipline* to be gained in the circuitous route by which they were led.   God's design, in sparing his people the battle with the Philistines, was not, as we have seen, to indulge and spoil them.   The place whither he conducted them was the wilderness, and there he purposed to subject them to a severe moral training.   The end of this training was simply to bring them up to the standard which as yet they had not reached, to develop in them the qualities in which they were as yet deficient, to impart to them, in short, that hardihood and strength of character and will which *would* enable them to cope with Philistines, or any other foes.   The end God has in view in our own trials is precisely the same.

IV. OUR WISDOM, UNDER ALL THE CIRCUMSTANCES OF OUR LIVES, IS TO RESIGN OURSELVES TO GOD'S LEADING, BELIEVING IT TO BE ALWAYS THE BEST FOR US.   We cannot err in resigning ourselves to the guidance of one omniscient, wise, loving, and supremely good.—J. O.

Ver. 19.—*Joseph's bones.*   A promise, and most of all a promise to the dead, is to be regarded as sacred.   Amidst the haste of their departure the Israelites did not forget to take with them the bones of Joseph.   They probably carried away also the bones of the other patriarchs (Acts vii. 16).   In this touching incident, see—

I. FAITH'S ANTICIPATIONS VERIFIED.   Joseph had said, "God will surely visit you" (Gen. l. 25).   He had died in faith, not having received the promises, but having seen them afar off (Heb. xi. 13—22).   At the time of Joseph's death the tokens were scant that Israel would grow to be so great a people, and would be led forth, many thousands strong, to go to Canaan.   Joseph's faith rested on God's naked word.   God had said that this time would come, and it did.   We are never wrong in depending on the Divine promise.   Those who trust it, however the world may ridicule them as devout enthusiasts, will prove to be right in the long run.   Events will verify their confidence.   Apply, *e. g.*, to the ultimate triumph of Christianity.

II. FAITH'S CHOICE GIVEN EFFECT TO.   He had strictly sworn the children of Israel, saying, "Ye shall surely carry up my bones away hence with you."   Notwithstanding the splendour of his position in Egypt, Joseph's heart was still with his own people. To his clear moral vision, the godless character of the Egyptian civilisation was sufficiently apparent.   The Hebrews were as yet but a handful of shepherds; but he discerned in them a spiritual greatness which was wanting to Egypt, and he had faith in the magnificent future which God's Word pledged to them.   So he was not ashamed to call the humble settlers in Goshen his brethren, and to declare that he preferred a grave with them to the proudest mausoleum that Egypt could erect for him.   He left a charge that when they departed, they were to take his bones with them, and lay them in Canaan, as subsequently they did (Josh. xxiv. 22).   He thus anticipated Moses in choosing the better part, and in preferring union with God's people to all the treasures and renown of the land of his adoption.   We act in the same spirit when we set the things which are "unseen and eternal" before those which are "seen and temporal," and count it our highest honour to be enrolled among "God's children."

III. A HINT OF THE RESURRECTION. Whence this care of Joseph for the bestowal of his bones? What matters it—it may be asked—where the dust is laid, if only the spirit is secure? In one way it matters very little, though affection naturally inspires the wish to sleep beside one's kindred. There may have been more than this. The care of the body in Egypt was, as we now know, connected with a hope of its revival. And there are good grounds for believing that the same hope had to do with this command of Joseph, and with the loving care shown by the patriarchs generally in the bestowal of their dead. (See the point discussed in Fairbairn's *Typology*, vol. i. p. 355, *et seq.*). The believer's body is a sacred deposit. Destined to share with the soul in the glory yet to be revealed, there is a fitness in treating it with reverence, and in laying it in a place consecrated to the Christian dead.—J. O.

Vers. 17—22.—*Israel's journey the emblem of the Christian's pilgrimage.* I. GOD'S TENDER CARE FOR HIS PEOPLE. 1. Trials and temptations are proportioned to their ability to bear them. "He led them not through the way of the land of the Philistines." The conflict with these was not too much for his strength, but it was too much for Israel's faith. They would have made shipwreck at the very outset. He will not suffer us to be tempted beyond that we are able to bear. 2. It "was near;" but the shortest way to our possession may not be the surest. God's love is more fully displayed in leading us seemingly away from what we desire than it would be in at once leading us to it. 3. His purpose in delay. God leads us by the way of the wilderness where, by the knowledge of ourselves and of him we may be prepared for the earthly and the heavenly portion he designs to give us.

II. THEY BORE WITH THEM A PROOF OF GOD'S FAITHFULNESS (ver. 19). 1. The time might have been when the hope expressed by those unburied bones seemed vanity and folly, but not now. These relics touched a million hearts, and reminded them how gloriously God had redeemed his word. 2. We carry with us mementoes which fill us with strong assurance for the future. The very light we now possess tells how God fulfils his promises. Human hearts believed God of old when he said that the Sun of Righteousness would arise, and human lips declared the hope. The past fulfilments of prophecy lay broad foundations for our trust that every word will in like manner be redeemed.

III. THEY HAD GOD HIMSELF FOR GUIDE. 1. We have the indwelling of the Spirit and of Christ. We cannot mistake the way if we follow him who goes before us. 2. The light of his presence is brighter in the night of trial. When all else is veiled from sight, the light of that gracious presence beams out in fullest splendour. 3. There must be the following by day to have the consolation of the glory by night. Are we following in the footsteps of Jesus? Is he Saviour as well as sacrifice to us?—U.

EXPOSITION.

Vers. 21, 22.—THE PILLAR OF THE CLOUD AND OF FIRE. Having stated, in verse 17, that "God led the Israelites," and determined their route for them, the writer here proceeds to explain how this leading was accomplished. With extreme simplicity and directness he states, that the conduct was effected by means of an appearance, which in the day-time was like a column or pillar of smoke ascending from earth to heaven, and in the night was like a pillar of fire. He considers the presence of God to have been in the pillar, which moved in front of the host, and showed them the way that they were to go. When it halted, they halted when it advanced,

they advanced. Their journeys being made as much in the night-time as in the day, on account of the intense heat, the pillar took in the night the appearance of a column of fire, so as to be equally visible as by day. All attempts to give a rational explanation of the phenomenon are misplaced, since the writer, from whom alone we derive our information on the subject, clearly regarded it as miraculous; and both here and elsewhere (ch. xiv. 19, 20, 24; xxxiii. 9; Num. xii. 5; xiv. 11) speaks of it as a form under which God was pleased to show himself. There is little doubt that fire and smoke signals were already used by commanders of armies for much the same purpose as that which God now accomplished in this way. The Egyptian documents of the period contain indications of the usage; and it is found among the Arabians, the Greeks, and the Persians. (See especially Q. Curt. *Vit. Alex.* v. 2; "Perticam, quæ undique conspici posset, supra prætorium statuit, ex qua signum eminebat pariter omnibus conspicuum: observabatur ignis noctu, fumus interdiu.") The miracle was thus, in a certain sense, founded upon an existing custom, with the difference that God here gave the signals miraculously, which were wont to be given in a natural way by the human leaders of armies. He thus constituted himself the general of the host.

Ver. 21.—**The Lord went before them.** From Succoth at any rate; perhaps even on the journey from Rameses to Succoth. **In a pillar of cloud.** The pillar was seen—the presence of Jehovah, though unseen, was believed to be in it, and to move it. **To go by day and night.** Or, "so that they might march both by day and by night." Night marches are generally preferred by Orientals on account of the great heat of the days. The night-marches of the Israelites are again mentioned in Num. in. 21.

Ver. 22.—**He took not away.** The last distinct mention of the cloud is in Num. xvi. 42, after the destruction of Korah, Dathan, and Abiram. There is perhaps a later allusion to it in Num. xx. 6. In Nehemiah it is said that "the pillar of the cloud departed not from them," so long as they were in the wilderness (Neh. ix. 19); and the same is implied, though not formally stated, in Num. ix. 15-23. There is no mention of the pillar of the cloud as still with the Israelites in the Book of Joshua. Probably it was last seen on the journey from Beth-jesimoth to Abel-Shittim in the rich Jordan valley (Num. xxxiii. 49).

HOMILETICS.

Vers. 21, 22.—*God's guidance of his people.* The Israelites had quitted Egypt, had broken off from their old life, were about to plunge into that wild waste of sand and rock which separates Africa from Asia by an almost impassable barrier. If they took the northern line of march, they would come upon the sandy desert. Before them would stretch " endless sands yielding nothing but small stunted shrubs—broad plains —newly reared hills—valleys dug out by the last week's storm; the hills, and the valleys, and the plains, all sand, sand, sand, still sand, and only sand, and sand, and sand again." (Kinglake, *Eothen*, p. 187.) If they turned southward, they would find themselves in a labyrinth of twisted *wadys*, amid huge mountains, and in a region consisting chiefly of bare granite and sandstone rocks—" the Alps unclothed." (Henneker, *Notes during a Visit to Egypt*, p. 214.) In either case they would sorely need God's guidance; and God's guidance was vouchsafed to them. So it is with Christians.

I. CHRISTIANS HAVE THE GUIDANCE OF GOD'S SPIRIT THROUGH ALL THE INTRICACIES AND DESERT PLAINS OF LIFE. The Lord leads them. God himself, God the Holy Ghost, co-equal Person with the Father and the Son in the Triune Godhead, is their guide and director, "a light to their feet and a lantern to their paths." Most necessary to them such direction. Just escaped from Egypt, just freed from the bondage of sin, how would they wander and go astray, unless his right hand were stretched out to help and guide! On the weary waste, the dry, bare, monotonous plain of an eventless life, where no sign showed the way, where hope would fail and the heart grow faint, what could they do but for him? In the labyrinth of conflicting duties and uncertain devious paths, how could they determine on their course but for him? Alike in both he leads, directs, guides. He "will not leave them nor forsake them."

II. THE GUIDANCE IS PERPETUAL BOTH BY NIGHT AND DAY. "Lo, I am with you *always*, even unto the end of the world" was the promise given us by our Lord. There is no part of life from which he withdraws himself—not the darkest night of earthly misery and disappointment—not the brightest day of worldly success and glory. And in both alike he is needed—perhaps most needed in the day. Then men think they can walk by themselves, choose their own course, direct their own paths. Then consequently they are most apt to go wrong, and "wander out of the way in the wilderness." But he is ever at hand to restrain, correct, recover them. By internal or external checks, by feeling and conscience on the one hand, by his word, his ordinances, his ministers on the other, he interposes to save men from themselves, to keep them in the right way, or lead them back into the right way if they have departed from it.

Darkness does not hide us from him—darkness does not separate us from him—yea, "the darkness is no darkness with him—the night and the day with him are both alike."

III. THE GUIDANCE IS VARIED TO SUIT THE DIFFERENT NEEDS OF THE SOUL. Now by cloud and darkness, an overshadowing of the soul by his felt but unseen presence; now by the flashing in of intolerable light into the secret recesses of the heart and conscience, does the Holy Spirit of God direct and rule our lives. None can limit him as to the means which he shall employ. Now he discomfits our foes, directing his keen gaze upon them "through the pillar of fire and of the cloud" (Ex. xiv. 24); now he simply separates between our foes and us by interposing an insurmountable barrier (*ib.* ver. 19); at one time he shines into our hearts with a mild, gentle, and steady radiance; at another, he gives us rest, as under the shadow of a cloudy canopy. At all times he chooses the means most fit to accomplish his ends, shrinking from none that are potent to effect his gracious purposes. Clouds and darkness would seem to be the things most opposite to the ineffable brightness of his most glorious nature; but even clouds and darkness are pressed into his service, and made his ministers, when they can be ministers of good.

IV. THE GUIDANCE CONTINUES UNTIL THEY REACH THE PROMISED LAND. "The pillar of the cloud departed not" from the Israelites "by day, neither the pillar of fire by night," during the whole time of their long and weary journeying, until they reached Canaan. God's gifts are "without repentance." They are given for the whole period during which we need them. As the Israelites required guidance until they trod the soil of the Jordan vale, and Canaan's hills lay plainly in sight, so do Christians need the Spirit's gentle leading, until the whole wilderness of this life is past, and the true Canaan reached. And what they need, they have. The Spirit's aid is with them to the end.

HOMILIES BY VARIOUS AUTHORS.

Vers. 21, 22.—*The fiery-cloudy pillar.* The visible pillar is no longer beheld, but God's fiery-cloudy presence still attends the Church in her wanderings, and confers upon her benefits analogous to those enjoyed by the ancient people. God's presence, as manifested in the pillar of cloud and fire, was—

I. HOLY.—1. *God is holy.* Holiness is the principle which guards the distinction between the Creator and the creature. It eternally excludes everything evil and impure from the Divine nature (Martensen). It is the "zeal of the Lord of Hosts" for his own honour, and for the maintenance of the interests of truth, purity, and righteousness. The fire in the cloud was a symbol of it. 2. *It is as the Holy One that God dwells in his Church.* "The Holy One of Israel in the midst of thee" (Is. xii. 6). Holiness, accordingly, becomes those who would serve him (Ps. xciii. 5). 3. *The privilege is great, but perilous.* (1) Sin leads to the withdrawal of God's presence. When Israel sinned in the matter of the golden calf, God withdrew beyond the precincts of the camp. The cloudy pillar removed to a distance (ch. xxxiii. 7—10). (2) Rebellion provokes God to anger. On more than one occasion fire came out from the midst of the pillar and destroyed the rebels (Lev. x. 2; Num. xvi. 22; xvii. 10). "Our God is a consuming fire" (Heb. xii. 29). Holiness turned against sin is wrath. God tempers the vision of his holiness, which otherwise would be unendurable to man, by shrouding it in the cloud.

II. ENLIGHTENING. "A pillar of fire to give them light." God's presence in his Church is illuminating. 1. *Whence the light shines.* The light shines in the Word, in Divine providence, and in the teaching of the Spirit which illuminates both. 2. *What the light does.* It shows us spiritual truth. It reveals duty. It guides (see below). It cheers in the night of affliction. 3. *Light with attendant mystery.* The light is in the cloud. At best, we know but "in part" (1 Cor. xiii. 12). Even revealed truth has its side of mystery.

III. SHELTERING. The allusion in Isa. iv. 6 would suggest that the cloud spread itself over the camp in the daytime, and so formed a canopy or shadow from the heat. God's presence is a grateful shelter to his people. They feel the need of it when temptations fiercely assail, or when tribulation and persecution ariseth because of the Word.

"In the time of trouble shall he hide me in his pavilion; in the secret of his tabernacle shall he hide me" (Ps. xxvii. 5).

IV. GUIDING. The pillar went before the camp of Israel "to lead them the way" (cf. Deut. i. 33). The cloud pointed the way in the daytime, the fire by night. The Church and the individual believer are similarly guided. He who seeks to know the will of God will not fail of direction. Providence opens the road. The light that streams from the Word shows the path of duty. "Thine ears shall hear a word behind thee, saying, This is the way: walk ye in it, when ye turn to the right hand and to the left" (Is. xxx. 21).

V. ADAPTIVE. The pillar adapted itself to the circumstances of the people. In the daytime, when the sky was light, it took the form of cloud; in the night season, it shone as bright fire. Now it moved in front as a guiding beacon; again, it was spread as a grateful awning over the camp; at another time, it went behind, intercepting the enemy (ch. xiv. 19). Thus does God vary the aspects of his presence and the modes of his help with unfailing adaptation to the special needs of his people. He is the All-sufficient.

VI. HOSTILE TO THE ENEMY.—He intercepts their pursuit; he hides his people from their fury; he makes their way dark to them; he frowns upon them, and discomfits them (ch. xiv. 19—26).—J. O.

Vers. 17—22. *Fire and cloud.* "And the Lord went before them," etc. (Ex. xiii. 21). Israel might have been in Canaan within ten days. Reason why not is given xiii. 17. This however, not a reason for the forty years wandering: but only for the circuitous route by the desert of Sinai. The line of Israel's march for the first two days is soon given. They start from *Rameses*, capital of Goshen, a store city, recently built by the Hebrews, the king there possibly. The first stage was *Succoth* ("tents") perhaps a caravan station or military camp—a journey of about fifteen miles. Another fifteen miles *to Etham* on the edge of the desert. There roads, canals, now all to be left behind; just there and then appeared the FIRE AND CLOUD.

I. ITS NATURE. Point out the three leading theories, especially as the two earlier mentioned lead up to the third and the true. The phenomenon was: 1. *Common natural fire.* Seen as fire by night, as smoke by day. Perhaps the sacrificial fire of Israel preserved from primitive times. An ordinary caravan fire. Or such as was borne at the head of the Persian armies. 2. The same, but *glorified by association with a religious idea*; viz., that God was in reality the Guide of his people, and that that was well represented by the fire at the head of the hosts. 3. *Altogether supernatural.* God saw the need of Israel at that moment, and met it in his own superb manner. [For full discussion of Ritualistic explanations, see Kurtz, vol. ii. 344—348, Eng. ed.] The phenomenon was a trinity in unity. It was *one*, not two, not one kind of pillar by night and another by day. It consisted of *cloud*, of *fire* (electric?) in the cloud, and of *Jehovah* in both (xiii. 21; xiv. 24). The last doubtless a manifestation of the "Angel-God" of the Old Testament.

II. FORMS AND MOVEMENTS. 1. *Forms.* (1) Usually a *pillar* (xiii. 21). (2) A *wall*, see xiv. 19, 20. Must have been a wall in this case, of perhaps more than a mile in length. A wall of cloud to Egypt, hiding the moon, the sea, and the advanced movements of the armies of Israel. When the cloud lifted, Israel was gone. On the other side, a mile or more of, as it were, electric fire, adding to the moon-illumination by which Israel passed through the sea. (3) *A roof or an awning.* See Num. x. 34; Ps. cv. 39; 1 Cor. x. 1, 2; and the very beautiful passage, Is. iv. 5, 6. 2. *Movements.* (1) Usually *stationary*—on the tabernacle—on the mercy-seat—sometimes filling the tabernacle, so that none could enter to minister. (2) *Lifting*, when Israel advanced. (3) *Descending*, when Israel was to rest.

III. SIGNIFICANCE. Israel could not have seen the fire-cloud for forty years without catching much of the meaning; but we more. The fire-cloud teaches that the Lord Jesus is: 1. *Ever in and with the Church.* The glory of Jehovah appeared in the cloud. 2. *In two-fold glory*; in the fire of holiness; in the cloud of mercy that tempers the blaze. He so appears to the individual soul—to the family—to the Church—to the nation—to the wider world. Note the special outbreakings from the cloud at certain sinful crises in Israel's history. 3. *The leader of our pilgrimage.* See C. Wesley's hymn, in Wesley's *Collection*, 326.   Yet some scope, then as now, seems to have been left for the play of intelligence (Num. x. 31).   4. *Captain in our holy war*.   On Egyptian monuments generals are represented as flames, streaming in darkness, at the head of armies.   See the hymn beginning : " Forward be our watchword."

> " Burns the fiery pillar
>   At our army's head ;
> Who shall dream of shrinking,
>   By our Captain led ? "

5. *Our wall of defence*.   6. *Our canopy for comfort*.   7. Whose interpositions are ever marked by wondrous *timeliness*.   It was on the "edge of the wilderness" that the fire-cloud first appeared ; and after the desert journey, seems to have disappeared, save as it may have been represented by the Shechinah above the mercy seat, which assumed unwonted splendour at the dedication of the first temple.—R.

EXPOSITION.

CHAPTER XIV.

Vers. 1—4.—THE DIRECTION OF THE JOURNEY CHANGED.   Hitherto the march of the Israelites had been to the south-east. Another day's journey in this direction would have taken them beyond the limits of Egypt, into the desert region east of the Bitter Lakes, which was dry, treeless, and waterless.   In this tract there would have been but scant nourishment for their flocks and herds, and absolutely no water for themselves, unless it had been obtained by miracle.   God therefore changed the direction of their route from south-east to due south, and made them take a course by which they placed the Bitter Lakes on their left hand, and so remained within the limits of Egypt, in a district fairly well watered, but shut off from the wilderness by the Bitter Lakes and the northern prolongation of the Gulf of Suez, with which they were connected.   This route suited the immediate convenience of the host ; and, having no suspicion of any hostile movement on the part of the Egyptians, they —not unnaturally—made no objection to it. It had, however, the disadvantage, in case of a hostile movement, of shutting them in between their assailants on the one hand, and the sea upon the other ; and this circumstance seems to have led Pharaoh to make his pursuit.

Ver. 2.—**Speak unto the children of Israel that they turn**.   Kalisch translates " return "—*i. e.*, " retrace their steps," and supposes that Etham lay far south of Pihahiroth, on the west coast of the Gulf of Suez.   But the Hebrew word means either " turn back "

or " turn aside," and is translated here ἀπο-στρέψαντες and not ἀναστρέψαντες by the LXX.   Dr. Brugsch supposes that the turn made was to the north, and the " sea " reached the Mediterranean ; but all other writers, regarding the sea spoken of as the Red Sea (compare ch. xiii. 18), believe the divergence from the previous route to have been towards the south, and place Pihahiroth, Migdol, and Baal-Zephon in this quarter.   **Pihahiroth.** The exact position is unknown.   Neither the Egyptian remains nor the writings of the Greeks or Romans present us with any similar geographic name.   If Semitic, the word should mean " the entrance to the caves," but it is quite possible that it may be Egyptian. **Migdol.**   There was undoubtedly a famous Migdol, or Maktal, on the eastern frontier of Egypt, which was a strong fortified post, and which is often mentioned.   Hecatæus called it Magdolos (Fr. 282).   In the Itinerary of Antonine it is said to be twelve Roman miles from Pelusium (p. 76).   But this is too northern a position for the Migdol of the present passage ; which must represent a " tower " or " fortified post " not very remote from the modern Suez.   **Over against Baal-Zephon.** The accumulation of names, otherwise unknown to the sacred writers, is a strong indication of the familiarity possessed by the author of Exodus with the geography of the country.   No late writer could have ventured on such local details.   A name resembling " Baal-Zephon " is said to occur in the Egyptian monuments.   Dr. Brugsch reads it as " Baal-Zapuna."   He regards it as the designation of a Phœnician god, and compares " Baal-Zebub."   Others have compared the " Zephon " with the Græco-Egyptian form " Typhon," and have supposed " Baal-Zephon " to be equivalent to " Baal-Set " or " Baal-Sutech "—a personification of the principle of evil.

Ver. 3.—**They are entangled in the land.**

Or "they are confused," "perplexed"—*i. e.* "they have lost their way." Pharaoh could not conceive that they would have taken the route to the west of the Bitter Lakes, which conducted to no tolerable territory, unless they were hopelessly at sea with respect to the geography of the country. In this "perplexity" of theirs he thought he saw his own opportunity. **The wilderness hath shut them in.** Pharaoh is thinking of his own "wilderness," the desert country between the Nile valley and the Red Sea. This desert, he says, "blocks their way, and shuts them in"—they cannot escape if he follows in their steps, for they will have the sea on one hand, the desert on the other, and in their front, while he himself presses upon their rear.

Ver. 4.—**I will be honoured** See the comment on ch. ix. 16. **That the Egyptians may know that I am the Lord.** Compare above, ch. vii. 5

HOMILETICS.

Vers. 1—4. *God's trials of His faithful ones.* All hitherto had gone well with the departing Israelites. The Egyptians indeed had "thrust them out"—had hurried their departure—had felt insecure till they were beyond the borders. But they had freely given of their treasures to speed the parting guests, and had in every way facilitated their setting forth. The multitude, vast as it was, had in no respect suffered as yet; it had proceeded in good military order (ch. xiii. 18), had found abundant pasture for its flocks and herds, and was now on the very verge of the desert which alone separated it from Canaan. Egypt was behind them; freedom and safety were in front; no foe forbade their entrance into the vast expanse which met their gaze as they looked eastward, stretching away to the distant horizon of hot haze, behind which lay the Promised Land. The question, how they were to support themselves in the desert had not perhaps occurred to them as yet. They had come out provisioned with bread for a certain number of days, and probably with many sacks of grain laden upon their asses. If the spring rains had been heavy, as is likely to have been the case, since in Egypt there had been both rain and hail (ch. ix. 23—33), the desert itself would have been covered at this season with a thin coat of verdure and "thickly jewelled with bright and fragrant flowers" (*Eothen*, p. 180). The hearts of many were, no doubt, bounding at the thought of quite quitting Egypt at last, and entering on the absolute freedom of the illimitable desert. But at this point God interposed. "Speak unto the children of Israel that they turn, and encamp before Pihahiroth." Egypt is not yet to be quitted; they are still to skirt it—to remain among Egyptian cities—to turn away from Palestine—to interpose a sea between themselves and Asia—to pursue a route which leads into one of the most unproductive portions of the whole African continent. Sore must the trial have been to those who had knowledge of the localities—dark and inscrutable must have seemed the ways of Providence. What was the Almighty intending? How could Canaan ever be reached if they turned their backs on it? Whither was God taking them? Even apart from any pursuit by Pharaoh, the situation must have been perplexing in the extreme, and must have severely exercised the more thoughtful. What then must not the universal feeling have been, when it appeared that the monarch, informed of their movements, had started in pursuit? What but that they were God-forsaken—or, worse, led by God himself into a trap from which there was no escape? Readily intelligible is the bitterness which showed itself in their address to Moses—"Because there were no graves in Egypt hast thou taken us away to die in the wilderness? Wherefore hast thou dealt thus with us?" And so God's people—his faithful and elect children—at all times and under all circumstances, are subject to severe trials. These come upon them either—

I. FOR THEIR MORAL IMPROVEMENT. "The trial of our faith worketh patience," and God wills that "patience should have her perfect work," that his saints may be "perfect and entire, wanting nothing" (James i. 3, 4). "Whom the Lord loveth he chasteneth, and scourgeth every son whom he receiveth." Difficulties, dangers, temptations, perplexities, disappointments, constitute a moral discipline which is to most men absolutely needful for the due training and elevation of their moral characters. By such trials the dross is purged away from them—the pure metal remains. Their love of God and trust in God are tested, and by being tested strengthened. "Tribulation worketh patience; and patience experience; and experience hope; and hope maketh

Don't think it unusual or exceptional that trials come your way.

not ashamed." The man who is perfect in each good word and work has in almost every case passed through a furnace of affliction to attain his perfection.

II. FOR THE GLORY OF GOD. God's glory is often shown forth in the sight of men most conspicuously by the trials of his faithful ones. In Israel's case this was brought about by miracle. But the rule holds good in the ordinary course of human affairs equally. What has so shown forth the glory of God in the past as the endurance of trials, insults, torments, death, by his martyrs? What even now so impresses men with the reality of religion, as suffering on account of the truth? Afflictions, crosses, disappointments, patiently borne, not only strengthen our own spirits, but are a witness for God in a world that for the most part disregards him, and to a considerable extent "get him honour."

III. FROM THE NECESSITY OF THE CASE, BECAUSE GOD'S WAYS ARE NOT AS OUR WAYS. If the children of Israel could have foreseen that God would divide the Red Sea for them and lead them through it, the route southwards to the point of crossing would have been seen to be the fittest and best, securing as it did the continuance of water and of forage, and avoiding one of the worst parts of the wilderness. But it was impossible for them to surmise this; and hence their perplexity, alarm, and anger against Moses. In our ordinary trials it often happens that our inability to understand how we are being dealt with lies at the root of our sufferings. The disappointment which most vexes us may be a necessary preliminary to the success of which we have no thought. The "thorn in the flesh" may bring us to a higher moral condition than we should have reached without it. "God's ways are in the deep, and his paths in the great waters, and his footsteps are not known." He deals with us as he sees to be best, and we cannot see that so it is best. He has surprises in reserve for us, sometimes as little looked for as the division of the Red Sea by the Israelites. Hence, if in cases of this kind we would suffer less, we must trust God more; we must give ourselves wholly up to him, place ourselves in his hands, accept whatever he sends as assuredly, whether we can see it or not, what is fittest for us.

HOMILIES BY VARIOUS AUTHORS.

Vers. 1—5.—*The command to encamp by the sea.* These verses introduce the narrative of what the Lord "did in the Red Sea" (Num. xxi. 14), when his people "passed through . . . as by dry land; which the Egyptians, assaying to do, were drowned" (Heb. xi. 29). This crossing of the Red Sea was no after-thought. God had it in view when he turned aside the path of the children of Israel from the direct route, and ordered them to encamp before Pi-hahiroth, near the northern end of the gulf. His design in this event was to give a new and signal display of his Jehovah attributes, in the destruction of Pharaoh's host (ver. 4), and in working a great salvation for his Church. By the events of the Red Sea, he would be shown to be at once a God of mercy and judgment (Is. xxx. 18); Supreme Ruler in heaven and in earth (Ps. cxxxv. 6); disposing events, great and small, according to his good pleasure, and for the glory of his name; making even the wrath of man instrumental to the accomplishment of his purposes (Ps. lxxvi. 10). Consider—

I. THE MYSTERIOUS TURN IN THE ROUTE. The command was to turn to the south, and encamp between Migdol and the sea, over against Baal-Zephon (ver. 2). This route was—1. Not necessarily an *arbitrary* one. We need not suppose that God brought the Israelites into this perplexity—shutting them up between the sea and the mountains, simply for the purpose of showing how easily he could again extricate them. The choice of routes was not great. (1) The way of the Philistines was blocked (ch. xiii. 17). (2) The way by the north of the Red Sea—between it and the Bitter Lakes—probably did not then exist. The Red Sea seems at that time to have extended much further north than it does at present. (3) To go round by the *upper* end of the Lakes would have been to take the host far out of its way, besides exposing it to the risk of collision with outlying tribes. (4) The remaining alternative was to march southwards, and ford the Red Sea. The route was, nevertheless—2. A *mysterious* and *perplexing* one. Pharaoh at once pronounced it a strategic blunder (ver. 3). Supposing the intention to be to cross the Red Sea, no one could hazard a conjecture as to how this was to be accomplished. Ordinary fords were out of the question for so vast a multitude. Hemmed in by the mountains, with an impassable stretch of water in front, and no way of escape from an enemy bearing down upon them from behind, the Egyptian king might well judge their situation to be a hopeless one. Yet how strangely like the straits of life into which God's people are sometimes led by following faithfully the guiding pillar of their duty; or into which, irrespective of their choice, God's providence sometimes brings them! Observe, further, 3. *No hint was given of how the difficulty was to be solved.* This is God's way. Thus does he test his people's faith, and form them to habits of obedience. He does not show them everything at once. Light is given for present duty, but for nothing beyond. Fain would we know, when difficulties crowd upon us, how our path is to be opened; but this God does not reveal. He would have us leave the future to him, and think only of the duty of the moment. Time enough, when the first command has been obeyed, to say what is to be done next. "We walk by faith, not by sight" (2 Cor. v. 7).

II. GOD'S ENDS IN LEADING THEM BY THIS ROUTE. God *had* ends. He was not guiding the children of Israel blindly. His knowledge, his purpose, no less than his presence, go before his saints, as guiding pillars, to prepare places for them. God had a definite purpose, not only in leading the people by this route, but in planting them down at this particular spot—between Migdol and the sea. His ends embraced—1. *The humiliation of Pharaoh.* That unhappy monarch was still hard in heart. He was torn with vain regrets at having let the people go. He had a disposition to pursue them. God would permit him to gratify that disposition. He would so arrange his providence as even to seem to invite him to do it. He would lure him into the snare he had prepared for him, and so would complete the judgment which the iniquity of Pharaoh and of his servants had moved him to visit upon Egypt. This was God's hardening of Pharaoh's heart (ver. 4). Note (1) If God is not honoured *by* men, he will be honoured *upon* them (Scott). (2) Retributive providence frequently acts by snaring men through the evil of their own hearts. Situations are prepared for them in which they fall a prey to the evil principles or dispositions which, in spite of warnings and of their own better knowledge, they have persisted in cherishing. They wish for something, and the opportunity is presented to them of gratifying their wish. They harbour an evil disposition (say lust, or dishonesty), when suddenly they find themselves in a situation in which, like a wild beast leaping from its covert, their evil nature springs out upon them and devours them. It was in this way that God spread his net for Pharaoh, and brought upon him "swift destruction." 2. *The education of Israel.* The extremity of peril through which Israel was permitted to pass—coupled with the sudden and marvellous deliverance which so unexpectedly turned their "shadow of death into the morning" (Amos v. 8), filling their mouth with laughter and their tongue with singing (Ps. cxxvi. 1)—while their pursuers were overwhelmed in the Red Sea, was fitted to leave a profound and lasting impression on their minds. It taught them (1) That all creatures and agencies are at God's disposal, and that his resources for the help of his Church, and for the discomfiture of his enemies, are absolutely unlimited. As said of Christ, "even the winds and the sea obey him" (Matt. viii. 27). (2) That the Lord knoweth, not only "how to deliver the godly out of temptations," but also how "to reserve the unjust unto the day of judgment to be punished" (2 Pet. ii. 9). It was thus (3) A rebuke to distrust, and a powerful encouragement to faith. 3. *The complete separation of Israel as a people to himself.* Paul says—"all our fathers were under the cloud, and all passed through the sea, and were baptized unto Moses in the cloud and in the sea" (1 Cor. x. 2). Connect this with the spiritual significance of baptism. Baptism, especially as administered by immersion, figures dying to sin, and rising again to righteousness (Rom. vi. 4). It is thus the analogue of the passage through the Red Sea, which was a symbolic death and resurrection of the hosts of Israel. By saving the people from the waves which engulfed their enemies, Jehovah had, as it were, purchased the nation a second time for himself, giving them "life from the dead." The baptism of the sea was thus a sort of "outward and visible sign" of the final termination of the connection with Egypt. Its waters were thereafter "a silver streak" between the Israelites and the land of their former bondage, telling of a pursuer from whom they had been delivered, and of a new life on which they had entered.—J. O.

Vers. 1—12.—*Israel stricken with terror by reason of a deliverance not yet completed.*
It is plain that the Israelites, going out of Egypt in such circumstances as they did,
must have gone out in a state of great exhilaration, almost beside themselves with joy
at such a complete reversal of all their past experiences at the hands of Pharaoh.
Moreover we are assured in ch. xiv. 8 that they went out with a high hand. The
power of God for the deliverance of Israel was manifested in great fulness. What he
had done in the past, and especially in the recent past, if only well considered and
kept in the mind, was sufficient to inspire trust, banish fear, and show the wisdom of
most diligent obedience to every direction that he gave. Nevertheless in verse 10 we
find this humiliating statement, "they were sore afraid"—sore afraid, so soon after
deliverance, and such a deliverance! Whence could their danger have come, and what
could have made them so quickly to forget their God? These are the matters we have
now to consider.

I. CONSIDER WHAT THERE WAS TO EXPLAIN THE LOCAL POSITION WHICH PRODUCED
THEIR FEAR. They were in an awkward and dangerous position from an ordinary point
of view. That position cannot be more forciby indicated than in the words of Pharaoh
himself. "They are entangled in the land, the wilderness hath shut them in." They
were going into a *cul-de-sac*. Before them lay the sea; on either hand, as we imagine,
rose high ground; it only needed that Pharaoh should come in at the rear and close them
up altogether, when they would be compelled to surrender. How then had they come
into this position? It was not through any ignorance or carelessness on the part of
their leader. Any general leading an army into such a trap would have been deservedly
put to death for gross incompetency. It was God who had brought them exactly here,
and if the word "trap" is to be mentioned, it was a trap with regard to Pharaoh and
not with regard to Israel. The God who had led the Israelites *out* with a high hand,
led them *on* with the pillar of cloud, and led them into the very position which,
if they themselves had been consulted, was the last they would have chosen. It
was not the only way God could have taken them, but it was the way in which,
most effectually, speedily, and impressively, he could deliver them from Pharaoh.
For God, of course, well knew that the deliverance of his people was not accomplished,
simply because they had got out of Egypt. The exodus had been a miracle in
many ways, and not least in this, that it had compelled Pharaoh and his servants
to act in contradiction to all the most dominating elements of their character.
Just as afterwards in dealing with the waters of the Red Sea, God made the force
of the wind to overcome the force of gravity; so he had already by another east
wind, in the shape of the death of the first-born, completely set aside for a night
all the most settled habits of Egypt. These habits had stood up on the right hand
and on the left, and made a broad and open way for Israel to go out of the land. But
presently, immediately and according to the natural order, these habits resumed their
former sway. What else was to be expected? It mattered not in what direction Israel
took their flight. Pharaoh and his hosts, smarting with injured pride, panting for
vengeance and recovery of lost treasure, would be after them. There was a void in
Egypt because of the death of the first-born, but after all the mothers would feel that
void the most. There was another void by reason of the loss of all these slaves, these
useful labourers, these accumulators of Egyptian wealth, and this void, we may be sure,
was more operative in the vexation it produced than the loss of the first-born. It is a
humiliating truth, but men, as a rule, can more easily bear the loss of kindred, even
one so dear as the first-born, than the loss of fortune. A failure in business is more
discomposing and fretting than a dozen bereavements, considered simply as bereavements; and thus it is certain that Pharaoh and his generals were very speedily in council
as to the best way of securing the fugitives. While so engaged, the news comes to them
of the direction in which the Israelites had gone. This news was the very thing to
decide Pharaoh and make his preparations large and overwhelming, especially when God
came to harden his heart to a greater pitch of stubbornness than it yet had reached.
Either recapture or destruction seemed now certain. Therefore, seeing Pharaoh was now
bound by the very force of the passions raging in his heart and the hearts of his people
to follow Israel, it was well as soon as possible, to remove all danger to Israel consequent
on this line of action. No good purpose was to be served either towards Israel or
towards Pharaoh himself, by allowing him for any length of time, to harass their rear.

A catastrophe of the Red Sea magnitude had to come, and the sooner it now came, the better. Israel had dangers enough in front and within; from Amalekites, Amorites, Canaanites, and all the rest of their opponents; from their own character, their own depravity, blindness of heart, sensuality, and idolatrous disposition. *God does not allow all possible dangers to come upon us at once.* Do not let us be so occupied, with the dangers that are present and pressing as to forget those which he has utterly swept out of the way, overwhelmed in a Red Sea, whence they will emerge against us no more for ever.

II. Consider what there was to excuse and explain the fear which Israel expressed. In itself this fear was indefensible. There was no ground for it in the nature of things. God had done nothing to produce fear; everything indeed, if only it could be rightly seen, to produce the contrary; everything to call forth the utmost reverence and obedience from every right-minded Israelite. He was *now*, even while the Israelites were entangled in the land, Jehovah as much as ever, the great I Am, leading Israel by a way which, though they knew it not, was the best way. But we must also look at things from Israel's point of view; we must really remember what God really remembers, that men are dust, and that even when they have the greatest reasons for confidence, those reasons get hidden up, or even presented in such forbidding aspects as to make them powerful in producing unbelief. Our great adversary, who can make evil appear good also makes good appear evil. Look then at what there was in the state of things, to excuse the Israelites in being sore afraid. 1. *The magnitude of Pharaoh's preparations.* In spite of all the crippling effects of the plague, he was able to muster a great array. Doubtless he had a big standing army, for chariots are not got ready at a moment's notice. We may infer that he was a man who always had on hand some scheme of ambition and aggrandisement, and because the Israelites had long dwelt in his land, they knew all about the skill, valour and crushing force of the charioteers. Whatever strength there might be in the natural resources of Egypt they knew it well. When the unknown Caanan had to be faced, they gave Moses no rest, till spies were despatched to report on the land; but they needed no report of Egypt. The military strength of Pharaoh was only too deeply impressed on every mind. 2. *There was the exasperation of a great loss.* The people not only knew the strength with which Pharaoh came, but the spirit in which he came. He had lost 600,000 men, with their flocks and herds, and all the choice spoils of Egypt, in the way of gold, silver and raiment. Then there was a further loss of population in the mixed multitude. There was everything to exasperate the despot, and not one thing to soothe his pride or lessen his calamities. If only he had failed in trying to get hold of a new possession, it would not have been so hard. But he had failed in keeping the old; he had gone through ten plagues, and yet lost his treasures after all. We may fear that only too many among the Israelites, had just that spirit of greed and grasping in their own hearts which would enable them to appreciate the spirit of Pharaoh's pursuit. 3. *There was the degrading effect of the long oppression in which the Israelites had been kept.* The spirit of the slave comes out in the way they talk. These are not imaginary words put in their lips; the very "touch of nature" is in them. These are the language and conduct that reveal a real experience. The present generation, and one knows not how many generations before, had been born in servitude. They had not only been in servitude, but they had felt and acknowledged the bitter misery of it. And now the servitude was ended in due course. Freedom was a necessity, a blessing, and a glory to Israel; but they could not be made fit for it all at once. Jehovah could show signs and wonders in many ways; he could by one blow slay the first-born of Egypt and let the oppressed go free; but it required an altogether different power and method to infuse into the liberated the spirit and courage of freemen.—Y.

Vers. 1—9.—*Trial and Judgment.* I. God leads into trial, but assures of victory. 1. The command to turn and shut themselves in between the wilderness and the sea. God leads us where troubles will assail us. Jesus was driven of the spirit into the wilderness to be tempted of the devil. (1) It proves us, and reveals needs which otherwise we might not have suspected. Our weaknesses are manifested. (2) It reveals God. Through experiences of help his glory brightens for us. 2. The circumstances of God's people are taken advantage of by their foes. Pharaoh imagined his time had now come. Earthly foes may strike at such a time; Satan surely will. 3. The result will be God's triumph over the foe, not the foe's over us.

II. THE WICKED CANNOT BE SAVED BY JUDGMENTS. 1. Terrors are soon forgotten. Repression of evil is not conversion. So soon as the repressive force ceases, evil reasserts its sway. 2. Justice done through fear only is regretted, not rejoiced in, by the doer. "Why have we done this," etc.? "As the dog returneth to his vomit." 3. Past lessons are forgotten. Pharaoh might have asked what armies could do against the God of Israel; yet he assembles his forces, never dreaming that they are only marshalled for destruction. Those who have known only the discipline of terror have not found salvation. They have only heard a cry to flee and seek salvation. To linger upon the way is to allow evil to overtake them and lead them again into captivity.—U.

EXPOSITION.

Vers. 5—9.—THE PURSUIT OF ISRAEL BY THE EGYPTIANS. A short respite from suffering was sufficient to enable Pharaoh to recover from his extreme alarm. No further deaths had followed on the destruction of the firstborn; and he might think no further danger was to be apprehended. The worst of Moses' threats had been accomplished — perhaps Jehovah had no more arrows in his quiver. At any rate, as he realised to himself what it would be to lose altogether the services of so vast a body of slaves, many of them highly skilled in different arts, he more and more regretted the permission which he had given. Under these circumstances intelligence was brought him of the change which the Israelites had made in their route, and the dangerous position into which they had brought themselves. Upon this he resolved to start in pursuit, with such troops as he could hastily muster. As his chariots were six hundred, we may presume that his footmen were at least 100,000, all trained and disciplined soldiers, accustomed to warfare. The timid horde of escaped slaves, unused to war, though it might be five or six times as numerous as his host, was not likely to resist it. Pharaoh no doubt expected an unconditional surrender on the part of the Israelites, as soon as they saw his forces.

Ver. 5.—It was told the King of Egypt that the people fled. Pharaoh, when he let the Israelites go, must have felt tolerably certain that they would not voluntarily return. Formally, however, he had only consented to their going a three days' journey into the wilderness (ch. xii. 31). When, being at Etham, on the edge of the wilderness, they did not enter it, but marched southward to Pi-hahiroth, the Egyptians might naturally report that instead of sacrificing, they were flying—hasting forwards—

placing as much distance as they could between themselves and the Egyptian headquarters. But this report alone would scarcely have moved Pharaoh to action. It was in the accompanying circumstances, in the particular line of route, that he thought to find his opportunity. The people "were entangled" (ver. 3). They might be taken at a disadvantage, and might be reduced to choosing between starvation and a return to Egypt. The heart of Pharaoh, and of his servants, was turned against the people. The reaction of feeling was not confined to Pharaoh. His subjects participated in it. The loss of such a large body of labourers would be generally felt as a severe blow to the prosperity of the nation. It would affect all classes. The poor labourers might be benefited; but the employers of labour are the influential classes, and they would be injured. So "Pharaoh's servants" were of one mind with their master, and they "turned against" the Israelites. Why have we done this? In the retrospect, the afflictions which they had suffered did not seem so very great. They at any rate had survived them, and were not perhaps even seriously impoverished. Royal favour will find a way of making up any losses which court minions have suffered, out of the general taxation of the country. But in prospect, the loss of 600,000 (more or less skilled) labourers appeared a terrible thing. The official class was quite ready to make a strenuous effort to avert the loss.

Ver. 6.—He made ready his chariot. The Egyptian monarchs, from the time of the eighteenth dynasty, always went out to war in a chariot. The chariots were, like the Greek and the Assyrian, open behind, and consisted of a semicircular standing-board of wood, from which rose in a graceful curve the antyx or rim to the height of about two feet and a half above the standing-board. The chariot had two wheels and a pole, and was drawn by two horses. It ordinarily contained two men only, the warrior and the charioteer.

Ver. 7.—Six hundred chosen chariots. Diodorus Siculus assigns to one Egyptian king a force of 27,000 chariots (i. 54, § 4), which however is probably beyond the truth. But the 1200 assigned to Shishak (2 Ch. xii. 3) may well be regarded as historical; and the great kings of the nineteenth dynasty would possess at least an equal number. The "six hundred *chosen* chariots" set in motion on this occasion probably constituted a division of the royal body-guard (Herod. ii. 168). The remaining force would be collected from the neighbouring cities of Northern Egypt, as Memphis, Heliopolis, Bubastis, Pithom, and Pelusium. **Captains over every one of them.** Rather, "Captains over the whole of them." So the LXX. the Vulgate and Syriac version. Some, however, understand "warriors in each of them" (Gesenius, Rödiger, Kalisch).

Ver. 8.—**The Children of Israel went out with a high hand**—*i.e.*, boldly and confidently, not as fugitives, but as men in the exercise of their just rights—perhaps with a certain amount of ostentation.

Ver. 9.—**All the horses and chariots of Pharaoh.** Rather, "all the chariot horses."

There is no "and" in the original. **His horsemen.** Rather "his riders," or "mounted men"—*i.e.*, those who rode in the chariots. That the Egyptians had a powerful cavalry at a later date appears from 2 Chron. xii. 3; but the Hebrew text of Exodus, in remarkable accordance with the native monuments of the time, represents the army of this Pharaoh as composed of two descriptions of troops only—a chariot and an infantry force. (See Hengstenberg, *Aegypten und Mose*, pp. 127–9). **Overtook them.** It is uncertain how long the Israelites remained encamped at Pi-hahiroth. They would wait so long as the pillar of the cloud did not move (Num. ix. 18–20). It must have taken Pharaoh a day to hear of their march from Etham, at least another day to collect his troops, and three or four days to effect the march from Tanis to Pi-hahiroth. The Jewish tradition that the Red Sea was crossed on the night of the 21st of Nisan (Abib) is therefore, conceivably, a true one.

HOMILETICS.

Ver. 5.—*The good resolutions of the worldly are short-lived.* By a long series of judgments, culminating in the destruction of all the first-born both of man and beast throughout his whole territory, Pharaoh had been brought down from his original hardness and pride, had acknowledged God's hand, and allowed the Israelites to take their departure. He had even besought them to ask that God would bestow upon him his blessing (ch. xii. 32). But a short time sufficed to change all his good resolutions. The more he reflected on it, the more grievous did it seem to him to lose the services of above half a million of industrious labourers. The further they became removed, the less terrible did God's judgments appear. He had lost one son; but probably he had many others; and time, as it passed, brought consolation. He had quailed before Moses; but now, in Moses' absence, he felt himself a king again, and could not bear to think that he had been made to yield. His state of mind was one ripe for revolt and reaction, when intelligence reached him which brought matters to a crisis. The report that he received seemed to show complete geographical ignorance on the part of the Hebrews, together with "a cessation of the special providence and guidance which their God had hitherto manifested in their favour" (Kalisch). Upon this his "heart was turned," he cast his former good resolutions to the winds, and made up his mind either to detain the Israelites or to destroy them (ch. xv. 9). In all this Pharaoh's conduct is but an example of the general law, that "the good resolutions of the worldly are short-lived." They are so, because :—

I. THEY ARE NOT GROUNDED ON ANY WISH TO DO RIGHT, BUT ON VIEWS OF PRESENT EXPEDIENCY. The immediate effect of the tenth plague was an impression, common no doubt to Pharaoh with the other Egyptians, such as found vent in the words, "We be all dead men" (ch. xii. 33). They were intensely alarmed for their own safety. This and this alone produced the resolution to let Israel go. It was better to lose the services of even six hundred thousand labourers than to lose their own lives. Expediency was their rule and guide. But expediency changes—or at any rate men's views of it change. Were their lives really in danger? Had they not been over-hasty in assuming this? Or, if there had been danger, was it not now over? Might it not be really expedient to arrest the march of the Israelites, to detain them, and once more have them for slaves?

II. THEY ARE THE EFFECT OF IMPULSE RATHER THAN OF PRINCIPLE. Resolutions made upon principle can scarcely change, for they are grounded upon that which is the most fixed and settled thing in human nature. But resolutions based upon impulse are necessarily uncertain and unstable, for there is nothing so variable as impulse. All men have from time to time both good and bad impulses. Impulse exhausts itself from its very vehemence, and can never be counted on as a permanent force. It is here to-day, and gone to-morrow. No reliance can be placed upon it.

III. THEY ARE MADE MERELY BY A MAN TO HIMSELF, NOT MADE TO GOD. When the worldly man says, "I am resolved what to do," he means no more than this : "Under present circumstances, I have come to the conclusion that I will act in this or that way." He does not mean to bind himself, or, if he does, he soon finds that he cannot bind himself. There must be two parties to an obligation or engagement. If we wish our resolutions to be binding, and so lasting, we must make them solemnly, with prayer, in the sight of God, and to God. It is neglecting this which causes so many good resolutions to be broken, so many vows violated, so many pledges taken fruitlessly. Let men be sure, before they make a solemn resolution or a vow, that it is a right one to make, and then let them make the engagement, not to themselves only, or to their erring fellow-mortals, but to the Almighty.

HOMILIES BY VARIOUS AUTHORS.

Vers. 5—10.—*The pursuit* "It was told the King of Egypt that the people fled," etc. Consider :—

I. THE MOTIVES OF THE PURSUIT. The motives were various. 1. *Pharaoh had already repented of having let the people go* (ver. 5). Their departure was a sore humiliation to him. Wounded pride was aggravated by the sense of material loss. "As serfs and bondagers, the Israelites were invaluable, and to let them go was to annihilate the half of Egypt's industry" (Hamilton). Pharaoh and his servants, accordingly, were ready to adopt any plan which promised them revenge. 2. *Pharaoh found an excuse for pursuit, in the allegation that the Israelites had "fled."* Fugitives, in the ordinary sense of the expression, the Israelites were not. Pharaoh having to the last refused to let them go to hold the required feast in the wilderness, God had taken the matter into his own hands, and had given them their freedom. The only sense in which they were "fleeing" was, that, fearing treachery, they were making all the haste they could to get beyond Pharaoh's reach. They had left Egypt, unfettered by any stipulation to return. Return, indeed, after what had happened, was out of the question. When Pharaoh and his people thrust the Hebrews out from their midst (chs. xi. 8; xii. 31—34), they neither desired nor expected to see their faces more. But now that the king had changed his mind, and wished them back again, it suited him to represent their withdrawal into the solitary regions by the Red Sea as a "flight"—a breach of good faith. God had forced him to relax his grasp, and while his hand was open, the nation had escaped, like a bird escaped from the snare of the fowler. As reasonably might the fowler complain that, the bird, thus escaped, does not voluntarily return to its old quarters. 3. *The determining motive of the pursuit was the news that Israel was "entangled in the land."* This decided Pharaoh. Almost would it seem to him as if, by permitting the escaped people to make this huge blunder in their movements, their Deity *designed* to give them back to his hand. As Saul said of David— "God hath delivered him into mine hand, for he is shut up, by entering into a town that hath gates and bars" (1 Sam. xxiii. 7).

II. ITS FORMIDABLE CHARACTER. Probably a pursuit of escaped slaves was never organised with greater chances of success. 1. *The expedition was popular.* "The heart of Pharaoh and of his servants was turned against the people" (ver. 5). Court sentiment is not always a reliable index to the feelings of the commonalty; but it is probable that the movement to pursue Israel commanded a wide measure of popular support. The griefs and humiliations they had sustained would fill the Egyptians with hatred of the Israelitish name, and would make them willing co-partners in any scheme to inflict injury on the fugitives. They also, by this time, would be beginning to realise how great a loss, financially and industrially, they had sustained, by the withdrawal of so vast a body of labourers. 2. *The whole available military force of Egypt was called into requisition.* "All the horses and chariots of Pharaoh, and his horsemen, and his army" (ver. 9). Pharaoh, at the head of this glorious cavalcade, amidst this sheen of weapons, must have felt himself a greater man, and would wonder anew how he could have been so befooled as to let his slaves depart. And little, truly, to all human appearance, would Israel, unpractised in the use of arms, be able to accomplish against this disciplined and splendidly-equipped host. Pharaoh doubtless thought he had the people *this time* securely in his grasp. It was no longer the unarmed Pharaoh of the palace that Moses had to deal with; but Pharaoh, at the head of the thousands of Egypt, with chariots, and horses, and men of war; and who was that God that would be able to deliver him out of his hand? Alas for Pharaoh, and his "pomp and circumstance of war!" It was soon to be seen what short work God can make on the earth of the proudest of his assailants, showing strength with his arm, and scattering the proud in the imagination of their hearts (Luke i. 51; cf. Is. xxxi. 3). 3. *The situation of the Israelites seemed to make them an easy prey.* They were "entangled in the land" (ver. 3). This was the mainstay of Pharaoh's hopes. Israel could do nothing to resist him. Penned up like sheep for the slaughter, they could neither fight nor flee. Success was certain.

III. Its spiritual lesson. It will readily be felt that in this pursuit of Israel by Pharaoh, we have an image—from the typical character of the history, an *intended* image—of a not uncommon experience of the Christian life. 1. *We are liable to be pursued by the evil from which we thought we had escaped.* Whoever thinks to find it otherwise will live to be disappointed. Conversion—even though one has been led into Christian liberty with "an high hand" (ver. 8)—is not the end of spiritual conflicts. We do not escape from the power of evil without many an attempt being made on the part of the enemies of the soul to reassert their dominion over us. We have a Pharaoh in the evil of our own hearts, who, after we have left his service, will not fail to pursue us. Another such Pharaoh we have in the world—old companions, etc. A third is the evil One himself, who lets no soul slip from his grasp, without many an attempt to recover it. This goes on to some extent throughout the whole life. Pharaoh's pursuit may be viewed as gathering up all these separate pursuits into a single picture. 2. *This experience is usually most acute and perilous shortly after conversion.* Naturally, after the first breaking of the soul with sin, there comes, at a little distance, a time of recoil and reaction. Passions formerly indulged, surge back upon the heart with something of the old fury. We thought we had got rid of them; but they return, pursuing us with a vehemence which reminds us of Pharaoh's chariots and horses, and fills us with dismay. Old habits, we thought we had broken with them for ever; but they are back again, struggling for the mastery. The world tries all its arts to regain its former hold. Temptations come in floods. This is the time which tests the reality of conversion, and practically decides whether God is to have us, or Satan. It is the old experience of Israel, entangled in the land, and pursued by Pharaoh: if we gain the victory, we shall probably see our enemies no more, or only in greatly weakened, in semi-ghostlike forms. 3. *The destruction of Pharaoh's host is the pledge of similar victories to the Church and to the individual in like crises of their history.* It involves the promise that what God did for Israel here, he will do for us also, if we rely upon his help, every time we are spiritually tempted. Beyond this, it pledges and foreshadows the ultimate and complete defeat of all the enemies of the Church, and of the individual soul—even to that "last enemy that shall be destroyed," which is death (1 Cor. xv. 26). The victory, like the pursuit, is gathered up typically into a single picture, though in actual spiritual history it is spread over lifetimes and ages. It must, however, be sorrowfully admitted that in individual cases, type and reality too often fall asunder. Who has not to mourn partial victories gained over him by the pursuing Pharaohs of the soul—victories ofttimes almost amounting to the dragging of us back to bondage? And what extensive victories have frequently been gained by evil over sections of the Church—victories which seem the very antithesis of this glorious Red Sea deliverance? These, however, are but ebbings in a tide, which on the whole is on the flow, and they do not touch the lesson of this incident. The pledge given in Pharaoh's destruction, God will not fail to fulfil to those who seek his aid; and as to the final victory, that is secure, beyond all power of man to prevent it.—J. O.

Ver. 8.—*Jehovah hardening Pharaoh's heart.* I. NOTICE THE EMPHASIS WITH WHICH THIS FACT IS STATED. The hardening of Pharaoh's heart is mentioned, not in one place only, but in many. If it were mentioned in one place only, it might be in some doubtful way, such as would excuse us for passing it over without much examination. But being mentioned so many times, we dare not leave it on one side as something to lie in necessary obscurity, meanwhile consoling ourselves that the obscurity is unimportant. The statement meets us in the very midst of the way of Jehovah's judgments on Pharaoh, and we must meet it in return with a resolution to understand it as far as believers in Jehovah may be able to do. *Notice, then, exactly, how often the statement is repeated.* Jehovah says to Moses, or ever he leaves Midian, "I will harden Pharaoh's heart that he shall not let the people go" (ch. iv. 21). Again, just as Jehovah's dealings with Pharaoh were beginning, he says: "I will harden Pharaoh's heart, and multiply my signs and my wonders in the land of Egypt" (ch. vii. 3). After the rod was changed to a serpent his heart was still hardened (ch. vii. 13). Nor was there yet any change after the waters were turned to blood (ch. vii. 22). He yielded a little when the frogs came, but as soon as they vanished and there was respite, he hardened his heart once more (ch. viii. 15). When the magicians confessed the finger of God in the gnats, his heart remained the same (ch. viii. 19). The flies were taken away, and "he hardened his heart at this time also, neither would he let the people go" (ch. viii. 32). In ch. ix. 12 we have an express statement that the Lord hardened the heart of Pharaoh. After the visitation of the hail there seems to have been a complete surrender; but as soon as it ceases the hardening returns (ch. ix. 35); and so the references continue down to the end (ch. x. 1, 20, 27; xi. 10; xiv. 4, 8, 17). Making these references, we are led to notice also *the variety of expressions used.* Sometimes it is simply said that Pharaoh's heart was hardened, sometimes that Pharaoh hardened it, sometimes that God hardened it; and once or twice the expression rises to the emphasis of the first person, and Jehovah himself says "I will harden Pharaoh's heart."

II. NOTICE THE CONSEQUENT OBLIGATION TO MAKE DEVOUT AND REVERENT INQUIRY INTO THIS MATTER.—There is no way to escape from the feeling that Jehovah did actually harden Pharaoh's heart. We must treat the hardening of his heart as a great fact just as Moses did the burning bush; not doubting at all that it did happen, but rather asking how and why it happened. We must turn aside and see this great sign, why Jehovah exercised such a fearful power over Pharaoh that the end of it was the destruction of his host in the waters of the Red Sea. It is a commonplace of speech to say that the expression here is one of the most difficult in all the Scriptures. It is also a commonplace of action to shake the head with what is meant for pious submission to an impenetrable mystery. But what if this be only an indolent and most censurable avoidance of earnest thought on the ways of God towards men? No one will pretend that the mystery of this expression is penetrable to all its depths; but so far as it is penetrable we are bound to explore. How are we really to know that a thing is unfathomable, until we make an attempt to fathom it? A devout Israelite, although excluded from the Holy of Holies, did not make that a reason for neglecting the temple altogether. Our duty then is to inquire what this hardening of the heart may be, in what sense it is reconcilable with the goodness and righteousness of God. One reason why this statement is put so prominently forward in one of the most prominent narratives of Scripture, and therefore one of the most prominent in all history, may be this, that we should be kept from wrong conclusions on man's agency as a responsible being; conclusions dishonouring to God and perilous to ourselves. Is it not a great deal gained if only this narrative sets people thinking, so as to deliver them from the snares of fatalism?

III. Whatever view we take of this statement must evidently be IN THE LIGHT OF ALL WE ARE PERMITTED TO KNOW CONCERNING THE CHARACTER OF JEHOVAH. In considering all difficult statements as to the Divine dealings, we must start with certain postulates as to the Divine character. Before we can say that God does a thing we must know that the thing done is not out of harmony with the rest of his ascertained doings. There may be plenty of evidence as to the thing done, when there is very little evidence as to the doer. That the streams of Egypt were actually turned to blood was a thing that could be certified by the senses of every one who inspected those streams. But that God wrought this strange work could only be made sure by asking, *first*, what evidence there was of God's presence, and *next*, what consistency there was with his acknowledged dealings. It is only too plain that Pharaoh's heart was hardened, that he became ever more settled in his resolution to keep hold of Israel as long as he could. But when we are told that God hardened Pharaoh's heart, then we must at once bring to mind all that we have heard of God in the Scriptures. We must take back into our inspection of those distant times all we know of his character whom Jesus revealed; for the loving Father of our Saviour is the same with the great Jehovah. The same holy personality is at work in the God who so loved the world that he gave his only begotten Son, that whosoever believeth in him should not perish but have eternal life, as in the God who hardened Pharaoh's heart. We must not tolerate any conception of the hardening which contradicts the Divine character. Any view of this expression which does not harmonise with the revelation of God in the New Testament is therefore condemned. There is certainly no word in the Old Testament that more needs to be looked at in the light of the New than this. We must then dismiss from our minds any sort of notion that in hardening Pharaoh's heart, God dulled his moral sensibilities and made him proud, indifferent to pity and justice and the fulfilment of promises. God cannot put even the germs of these feelings into any human heart; much less can he increase them to such portentous magnitude as they attained in Pharaoh. We must start with the conviction and keep to it, that what God does is right, and that it is right not because he does it, but that he does it because it is right. It is not open for us first to fix our own interpretation of what may be meant by hardening the heart, and then call it an outrage on moral sense to say that God should do this. What if we have blundered in our interpretation?

IV. A right view of this statement must evidently also be taken IN THE LIGHT OF ALL THAT WE KNOW BY AN APPEAL TO HUMAN CONSCIOUSNESS. As no word God has ever spoken can contradict the facts of external nature, so neither can it contradict the facts of man's consciousness within. That which is true, independently of the teaching of Scripture, does not become less true, nor does it become false when Scripture begins to speak. Man is a free agent; he acts as one; he resents being treated otherwise by his fellow men. He is degraded and impoverished just in proportion as he sinks to a mere machine. His own decision is required every day, and he finds that wise decisions lead to profit, and foolish ones to loss. The law treats him as a free agent. Nay, more; what can be clearer than that God treated Pharaoh as a free agent? The plain statement that God hardened his heart is not more frequent than the equally plain statement that God demanded from him the liberation of Israel. If the one word is to be taken as simple verity, so is the other. If when God hardened Pharaoh's heart, he really did something in his nature; then also when he asked Pharaoh to liberate Israel, he asked something which he was at liberty to grant or refuse. Moses does not mock us with a mere trick of rhetoric in saying that God hardened Pharaoh's heart; neither did God mock Pharaoh with a useless appeal when he said, "Let my people go." Pharaoh knew well in his heart that it only needed his resolution and the whole of Israel could march forth at very short notice. He himself would have been amazed to hear that God had hardened his heart. True as it was, he would have denied it most strenuously and indignantly; and he would have denied it with justice, if it had been taken to mean the destruction of his own free agency.

V. We may now perhaps consider the ground sufficiently cleared for a positive conjecture as to what is meant by God hardening Pharaoh's heart. It means, we take it, THAT HE WORKED A MIRACULOUS CHANGE IN ONE OF PHARAOH'S NATURAL FACULTIES. There are certain things in every human being we do not hold that being responsible for, *e.g.*, sex, features, temperament, acuteness and activity in senses and intellect. Some persons have good vision, others poor, others are altogether blind. In a similar way, some are naturally of a tenacious, determined will. Whatever they have set their mind upon, they hold to, with bull-dog grip. Others again are easily swayed about. Now clearly just as there are natural differences in sight, or hearing, or intellect, so there must be natural differences in this will-faculty. A man may have it very strong; he may be one who if he sets high and worthy aims before him, will be called resolute, inflexible, tenacious, indomitable, loyal to conscience; whereas if his aims be low, selfish and entirely without ground in reason, he will be called obstinate, stubborn, self-willed in the fullest sense of that word; and is it not plain that God may take this power of volition, this will-energy, and do with it, as we know that Jesus in many of his miracles did with defective or absent faculties? To the blind, Jesus gave vision, and he who could thus call a non-existent faculty into existence, evidently could increase a faculty actually existing to any degree such as man might be able to possess. And was it not something of this kind that God did in hardening Pharaoh's heart? The term has come to have a dreadful meaning to us in connexion with Pharaoh, simply because of Pharaoh's career. But the very miracle which God wrought in Pharaoh's heart would have had good results, *if only Pharaoh had been* a different sort of man. Suppose the instance of a blind man who gets sight from Jesus. He goes into life again with a recovered faculty : and that life, with respect to its opportunities, is vastly larger than it was before. How will he use these opportunities? He may use them selfishly, and Christ's own blessing will thus become a curse; or he may use them as Christ would have him use them, to become his efficient and grateful servant. There is a moral certainty that some who had faith enough in Jesus to have impaired natural faculties put right were yet destitute of that faith which went on to spiritual salvation and spiritual service. It was one thing to believe in Christ for a temporal gain, quite another to believe in him for a spiritual one; and the one faith while meant to lead on to the other, would not always have that effect. It is but a fond imagination to suppose that it would. So Pharaoh, if he had been a humane, compassionate and righteous man, a king with a true king's feelings for his own people, would, through the very process of hardening his heart, have become a more efficient ruler. This is the way God helps men who are struggling with temptation, struggling towards truth and light, towards conquest over appetite, violent temper, evil habits. God does for them and in them exactly what he did in Pharaoh. What he did in Pharaoh happened to hasten him in the way where he was already disposed to go. If Pharaoh had been a blind man as well as a bad one, no one would have had any perplexity as to God's dealings in restoring his sight and giving it the greatest perfection sight can attain. If Pharaoh had used that restored vision for bad, cruel purposes, *he* would have been blamed, and not *Jehovah*, and exactly the same remark applies if we change the name of the faculty. God strengthens the faculty of will, but Pharaoh is responsible for a right use of the strengthened faculty as much as he was for the use of the weaker faculty before. God dealt with a part of his nature where he had no power to resist any more than a blind man would have power to resist, if God were to restore vision to him. It was not against the hardening that Pharaoh struggled, but against the delivering. The hardening worked in a way he was not conscious of, but the delivering was by an appeal to him, and that appeal he was by no means disposed to entertain. It was not an awakened conscience that compelled him to his successive yieldings; these were but as the partial taming of a wild beast. Paul said, " When I would do good, evil is present with me; " but Pharaoh was steadily disposed to do evil. His cry would rather have been, " When I think to get my own way, one of those terrible plagues comes in to relax my resolutions and confuse my plans."

VI. A certain amount of weight must also be allowed for PHARAOH'S TYPICAL POSI-TION AND CHARACTER. We must distinguish between what he was typically and what he was personally. Far be it from us to diminish his guilt or attempt to whitewash his memory. Doubtless he was a bad man, and a very bad man ; but for typical purposes it was needful to represent him as not having one redeeming feature. His name is not linked even with one virtue amid a thousand crimes. He had to be set before the whole world and all ages as the enemy of God's people. He is the type of a permanent adversary far greater than himself. And just as the people of God, typically considered, appeared very much better than they actually were, so Pharaoh, typically considered, is described so as to appear worse. (*E.g.* in Num. xxiii. 21, it is said, " He hath not beheld iniquity in Jacob, neither hath he seen perverseness in Israel.") We do not know all God's dealings with Pharaoh. They are hidden beneath the waters of the Red Sea, and it is no duty of ours to pass judgment on the defeated and baffled opponent. God calls us to the more practical business of going on with the living, struggling people.—Y.

EXPOSITION.

Vers. 10—14.—The terror of Israel and the courage of Moses. It has been argued that the Israelites, if they were so numerous as stated (ch. xii. 37), must have been wretched cowards, if they were afraid to risk an engagement with such an army as that hastily levied one which Pharaoh had brought with him. But the difference between an army of trained soldiers, thoroughly equipped for war, with helmets, shields, breastplates, swords and spears, and an undisciplined multitude, unarmed for the most part, and wholly unaccustomed to warfare, is such, that the latter, whatever its numbers, may be excused if it does not feel able to cope with the former, and declines an engagement. Numbers, without military training and discipline, are of no avail—nay, are even a disadvantage, since the men impede one another. It is not necessary to suppose that the Israelites were debased in character by their long servitude to account for their panic on seeing the army of Pharaoh. They had good grounds for their fear. Humanly speaking, resistance would simply have led to their indiscriminate massacre. The alarm of the Hebrews, and even the reproaches with which they assail Moses, are thus quite natural under the circumstances. What is surprising is, the noble courage and confidence of Moses. Moses, though only vaguely informed, that God would "be honoured upon Pharaoh and all his host" (ver. 4), is perfectly certain that all will go well—how the result will be achieved, he knows not; but he is sure that Israel will be delivered and Egypt discomfited; his people have no reason to fear—they have but to "stand still and see the salvation of God" (ver. 13); "the Lord will fight for them;" they will have simply to "hold their peace" (ver. 14).

Ver. 10.—They were sore afraid. Before the Israelites are taxed with cowardice, let it be considered—1. That they were unarmed. Egypt was so settled a government that civilians generally went unarmed; and slaves, like the Hebrews, would scarcely have been allowed to possess any arms, if the case had been otherwise. 2. They had no military training. Whatever had been done to teach them order and arrangement in connection with their proposed journey, we may be sure there had been no drill or training in the use of arms, since this would have been regarded by the Egyptians as open rebellion. 3. They were quite unaccustomed to warfare. The Pharaohs maintained large garrisons of Egyptian and mercenary troops in the frontier provinces, to resist the invasions to which they were liable. The Hebrews may have had occasionally to defend themselves against a hasty raid: but in real war they had stood aloof, and left the fighting to the regular Egyptian army. **The children of Israel cried out unto the Lord.** The appeal to Jehovah showed that, with all their weaknesses and imperfections, the Israelites were yet true at heart. They knew where alone help was to be obtained, and made their appeal accordingly. No cry is more sure of an answer than the despairing one—"Lord, save us; we perish."

Ver. 11.—And they said to Moses. It was not unnatural that, while flying *to* God as their only refuge, they should be angry with Moses. Moses, they would argue, ought to have known better than to have brought them into a situation of such peril. He, the leader, should have known the geography of the country—he, the courtier, should have known the temper of the court. It is always a satisfaction to men to vent their anger upon some one when they are in a difficulty. **No graves in Egypt.** Egypt, with a necropolis outside every city, was "a land of tombs;" surely they might have found graves there, instead of being led out to such a distance simply to die.

Ver. 12.—Is not this the word that we did tell thee? The reference was probably to that time of depression, after their burdens had been increased, and before the series of miracles began, when the Israelites had addressed reproaches to Moses and Aaron (ch. v. 21), and refused to listen to words of encouragement (ch. vi. 9). It was not true that they had uniformly held the same language, and desired Moses and Aaron to cease their efforts. **It had been better for us to serve the Egyptians than that we should die.** The spirit to prefer death to slavery, where they are the only alternatives, is not a common one; and we must not be surprised that a people which had grown up in servitude and had no traditions of national independence did not rise to the heroic height attained under other circumstances by Greeks, by Switzers, and by Poles. It would have been most extraordinary had they done so.

Ver. 13.—And Moses said ... fear ye not. Moses knew that the pursuit of Israel by the host of the Egyptians was a part of the counsel of God, and was to tend in some way or other to the promotion of God's honour and glory (ver. 4). He had sufficient faith to believe in a deliverance the nature of which it is not likely that he could anyway conjecture. Whether hail would fall from heaven and destroy them (Josh. x. 11); or the earth gape and swallow them up (Num. xvi. 32); or the angel of death smite them all in the night (2 Kings xix. 35); or any other strange form of destruction come upon them, he did not know; but he concluded from what had been revealed to him, that God was about to vindicate his own honour without the aid of man. Hence his words—**Stand still, and see the salvation of the Lord**—which assigned to the Israelites a mere passive attitude of expectation. **For the Egyptians,** etc. The order of the words in the original favours the marginal rendering, which is to be adopted with one slight change. Translate—" For, *as* ye have seen the Egyptians to-day, ye shall see them again no more for ever," *i.e.*, ye shall see them no more alive, vigorous and menacing, but still and lifeless upon the Red Sea shore (ver. 30). There is no reference to any other Egyptians than those with Pharaoh in the camp, nor to any later relations between Egypt and the chosen people.

Ver. 14.—**Ye shall hold your peace**—*i.e.*, "do nothing, remain at rest."

HOMILETICS.

Vers. 10—14.—*Divine trial a touchstone to distinguish faith from unfaithfulness.* The Israelites had almost as much ground as Moses to believe in God, and trust his providential care of them. They had seen the whole series of miracles which Moses had wrought. They had found themselves exempt from visitations which fell with the utmost severity on their near neighbours. They had heard from Moses God's positive promise to bring them into Canaan (ch. xiii. 5, 11). Yet at the first appearance of danger they lost all heart, all hope. They turned upon Moses with reproaches, taxed him with having brought them out of Egypt against their will, and expressed a readiness to return, and resume their old service. Moses, on the other hand, remained firm —did not blench—though, like the people, he felt the need of crying to God for aid (ver. 15), yet he did so in a different spirit from them—he with faith, they, in panic terror, without it; he, sure that God would somehow grant salvation, they expecting nothing less than almost immediate death. Thus the same trial which shows forth one man's faith and trust and confidence in God, reveals other men's want of faith. While things went smoothly, there was no apparent difference—an unprejudiced observer might have thought the people just as trustful as their leader—but it was not so; and God willed that the difference should be made apparent. God will have faith distinguished from unfaithfulness, and each recognised as what it really is.

I. For the honour of his true and faithful servants, which he wills to have set forth in the eyes of men, out of the tender love he bears towards his people. Though they be at the best " unprofitable servants," he deigns to recognise merit in their service, and wishes them to be honoured and held in respect by others, assigning them this as a part of their reward.

II. For the warning of the unfaithful ones, who, unless a severe trial came, might remain self-deceived, imagining themselves to have true faith, though wholly lacking it.

III. For the mere right's sake. Because he is a God of justice and of truth, abhorrent of pretence, semblance, make-believe; and always on the side of sincerity and openness. "There is nothing secret," he tells us, " that shall not be made manifest, nor hid that shall not be known" (Luke viii. 17). And this revelation of the true character of men and actions, which his truthfulness makes an ultimate necessity, his providence works for here. His trials are touchstones, potent to detect shams, and to prove the faithfulness of the faithful.

HOMILIES BY VARIOUS AUTHORS.

Vers. 10—23.—*The deliverance.* Consider on this section :—

I. The critical situation of the Israelites. 1. Their *position*. "Encamping by the sea, beside Pi-hahiroth, before Baal Zephon" (ver. 9). The first view of the sea would probably be attractive to them. Its breeze, after the tedious travel of the desert, would be deliciously refreshing. They would look with a child's wonder and delight on the novel spectacle it presented. They would crowd to the beach to watch its dancing, white-tipped waves, and curiously to listen to its soft, lapping ripple on the shore. Yet this sea, which is to-day their joy and plaything, will have become by the morrow their terror and despair—their impregnable prison barrier. The experience is not uncommon. How often does it happen that the very things which at first we are disposed to hail with delight, to welcome and rejoice in, prove afterwards our greatest causes of sorrow ! The engagements we enter into, the friendships we form, the bargains we make, the society we are introduced to, etc. 2. *The approach of the enemy.* "The children of Israel lifted up their eyes, and behold the Egyptians marched after them" (ver. 10). The mountains are around, the sea is in front, and now—terrible situation !—the Egyptians are pursuing, and close at hand. On they come, in whirling chariots, in ranks upon ranks of footmen ; the long lines are seen defiling in the distance, and Israel knows that in an hour or two more the avalanche will be upon them, sweeping all before it, burying them in destruction. 3. *They were entirely unprepared.* They had been resting and unbending, not preparing for battle. The attack took them by surprise. There was no possibility under the circumstances of presenting an effectual resistance to the enemy. But, indeed, had the circumstances been ever so favourable, these hordes of slaves, accustomed so long to crouch before the rod of the taskmaster, would scarcely have attempted it. How critical, how perilous, therefore, the entire situation ! A picture this of those straits of life formerly referred to, in which having done our utmost, we can do no more, and no alternative remains but prayer, and quiet waiting upon God.

II. Their panic and despair (vers. 10—13). The appearance of the Egyptians naturally threw the Israelites into a state of the most acute terror. Remark : 1. *Great allowance must be made for them.* We do not read that, on this occasion, God dealt severely with them for the wild, ungrateful words they uttered. He made allowance. (1) Their situation was really very serious. Placed in like circumstances, we would perhaps not have shown much more faith than they did. (2) They were unused to the life of freedom. It takes time to teach those who have always been slaves to appreciate the blessings of the opposite condition. They carry their slave habits with them into the state of freedom. The Israelites had not as yet had much comfort in their emancipation. Their painful marches had probably been harder work than even the brick-making of Egypt. They could not as yet feel that it was better to be free, though enduring hardships in their freedom, than to be more comfortably situated and be slaves. Do we blame them ? Then reflect how even Christians sometimes murmur and rebel at the self-denials, the sacrifices, the inconveniences, the persecutions, which their Christian freedom entails upon them. You complain, perhaps, that you have a harder time of it now, than even when you served the flesh. It may be true. But do not forget that the difference between your condition *now* and *then*, is all the difference between slavery and bondage, between salvation and a state of wrath. 2. *Israel's behaviour was nevertheless very unworthy.* (1) It was *faithless.* They did not wait to ask or see what God, who had already done so much for them, was about to do now, but at once concluded that he would leave them to perish. It is, indeed, said that they "cried unto the Lord" (ver. 10), but then, in the next breath, we read of them reproaching his servant and delegate (ver. 11). They are faithless prayers that come from faithless hearts. (2) It was *ungrateful.* How willing they had been to be led out of Egypt ! yet now, at the first approach of danger, they turn on their leader, and taunt him for having given them their liberty. Was Moses to blame for the pursuit of Pharaoh ? Or did he deserve to be thus requited for the noble stand he had taken on their behalf ? Public servants have often much to endure from the fickle humour of the crowd. (3) It was *cowardly.* It showed a servile and ignoble spirit even to breathe so base a regret as that they had not been suffered to continue in Egypt. 3. *The contrast of their conduct with that of Moses.* The bearing of Moses at this crisis was sublime in its calmness and trust. He does not return "railing for railing." No angry word escapes his lips in reply to the reproaches of the people. They murmur ; he betakes himself to prayer (ver. 15). They look to the visible chariots ; he to the invisible power which is mightier than all. They seem bereft of reason, fearing immediate death ; he is calm, undaunted, self-collected, and gives them the best of counsel. Ponder his words— "Fear ye not, stand still, and see the salvation of the Lord, which he will shew to you to-day" (ver. 13). (1) The situation was one in which God alone *could* bring salvation.

They could do nothing for themselves. The salvation must be God's from first to last. (2) God *would* bring them this salvation. The fact that he had brought them into this strait was of itself a pledge that he would find them a way out of it. The believer, who finds himself in situations of difficulty, may cherish the same confidence. (3) Their duty was to *stand still*, and *see* this salvation. So long as means of help are put within our reach, it is our duty to use them. When no such means exist, or when all available means have been exhausted, and still the shadow overhangs us, what remains but to wait patiently on the help of the Most High? " Stand still "—in trust, in prayer, in expectancy, in readiness to advance the instant the word is given. " Stand still "—as opposed to weak murmurings, to passionate regrets, to foolish rebellion against circumstances you cannot alter,—so shall you " see the salvation of the Lord." If nothing else will do, God will cleave a way for you through the waves, or better still, will enable you, like Peter, to walk on them (Matt. xiv. 29).

III. GOD'S COMMAND TO MOSES (vers. 15–19). 1. The command came in answer to prayer. " Wherefore criest thou unto me " (ver. 15). The words contain no reproach, but imply that prayer needed on the instant to be exchanged for action. 2. Moses was to speak to the people that they go forward. See below. 3. He was to stretch his rod over the sea, and divide the waters (ver. 16). The confidence of Moses, that God would show a way of salvation, was thus justified by the result. The light was not given *as early* as the people might have wished, but it was given *in time*. God also announces to Moses his purpose of destroying the Egyptians (vers. 17, 18).

IV. THE ADVANCE THROUGH THE SEA. On this notice—1. *The change in the position of the pillar of cloud and fire* (vers. 19, 20). Moving to the rear, it stood between the Israelites and their pursuers, turning a bright side to the former, and a dark side to the latter. (See below.) By this seasonable change in its position, it (1) Illuminated the passage for the Israelites. The light would stream on in front. (2) Made the way dark and perilous for the pursuers. (3) Hid the pursuers from the pursued, and *vice versâ*. This, besides being an additional *defence* to the Israelites, saved them from the terror which the *sight* of their pursuers would naturally awaken. It is related of a party of the Waldenses, that escaping by night from their cruel persecutors, their path lay through the rugged and perilous defiles of the Alps. At length the day broke, and under the light of the rising sun, they turned to survey the track along which they had trod. By a unanimous and irresistible impulse, they fell on their knees to thank God for their marvellous preservation. " Here, they had walked on the very verge of a tremendous precipice where a false step would have dashed them to atoms; there, they had skirted the banks of a mountain lake, whose black waters seem to indicate unfathomable depths," etc. But the dangers amidst which they had moved had been veiled by the impenetrable darkness. There are some things which it is better for us not to see. Learn (1) That God adapts his manifestations of himself to his people's needs. (2) That God's presence with his Church is an effectual bulwark against attack. He can hide his people from their pursuers. He can darken the path of the latter; can confound their wisdom, divide their counsels, perplex them in their courses, and obstruct their progress by providential obstacles. (3) Spiritually, in times of temptation and trial, we may rely on being illuminated by God's truth, defended by God's power, and ultimately conducted to a place of safety. 2. *The division of the waters* (ver. 21). (1) It was accomplished by natural agencies, supernaturally directed. " The Lord caused the sea to go back by a strong east wind all that night." The recognition of natural agency in no wise detracts from the supernatural character of the transaction; nay, seeing that direct miracles are no longer to be looked for by the Church, it is even more helpful to faith to find that natural means were employed in this instance, than if the result had been wholly miraculous. It heightens our conceptions of what God *can* accomplish by means of the agencies of nature. Instance the defeat of the Spanish Armada (2) It was unexpected and surprising. In considering the ways by which God might conceivably save them, the Israelites probably never dreamt of his opening a path through the sea. So, in those straits of life to which reference has been made, help usually arrives from unexpected quarters, in a way we had not thought of. " God's way is in the sea, and his path in the deep waters, and his footsteps are not known " (Ps. lxxvii. 19). (3) It afforded the passage that was required. The march through the sea, certainly, would not be without its difficulties. The violent gale, the thunderings and lightnings (Ps. lxxvii. 18), the darkness, the boom of the distant waters, the lurid light of the fiery cloud, the uneven passage, the panic and confusion, the strangeness and fearfulness of the entire situation, would make it an experience never to be forgotten. But if the road was difficult, it was practicable. They could pass by it. God promises to make a way for us. He does not promise that the way will always be an easy one. 3. *The safe transit* (ver. 22). The children of Israel got safely across. They were preserved in the very midst of the hostile element. Nay, the sea, which they had so much dreaded, became on either side a protecting wall to them. The same superintending Providence which secured, in the shipwreck of Paul, that "so it came to pass, that they escaped all safe to land" (Acts xxvii. 44), doubtless brought about a like happy result in the case of the Israelites. Their deliverance became, in after days, the type of any great deliverance wrought by God for his saints. See the figure wrought out in Ps. xviii. 1– 20.—J. O.

Ver. 11.—*Cruel words out of cowardly hearts.* There was much, as we have seen, to excuse the terror of Israel; but there is one thing not so easy to excuse, and that is the sarcastic, unjust spirit in which these terrified Israelites treat their visible leader. Formerly (ch. v. 21) they had turned on him with bitter reproaches; but their conduct then was the effect of ignorance and hasty expectations, and their language, however strong, was simply the language of reproach. But now to reproach they add *sarcasm*; they speak so as to set Moses in a ridiculous as well as a painful position. We may suppose that when the question was asked, "Whatever can we have been brought *here* for?" some of the wits of Israel would reply, "There is no room in Egypt to bury us, and so we are brought to be buried here." Then this sharp speech, quickly flying from lip to lip, as clever things usually do, would in no long time become the well-nigh universal thought. We have then here to consider the evils of sarcastic speech. That such speech may do good sometimes, and sometimes be necessary, need not be denied. But inasmuch as the temptation is almost entirely the other way, we may dismiss as needless the work of considering what benefits there may be in sarcastic speech. The ills of sarcasm have so far outweighed the good, that we had better set ourselves earnestly to consider *them.* Is it not to be presumed that fewer such sayings would fall from our lips, if only we habitually considered all the ill effects that may flow from such a way of speaking?

I. CONSIDER THE PAIN INFLICTED BY SARCASTIC SPEECH. There may be a great deal of pain inflicted where no sense of pain is expressed. Moses does not here take any notice of this bitter, clever, far-echoing word about the graves; but thereby, he only gives another illustration of his characteristic natural meekness. He may have felt, and felt deeply, even though he did not speak. If, indeed, we should hardly think so well of him. To be what is called thick-skinned is not good, if it is meant thereby that one has no perception of the insolent, inconsiderate language of others. Lack of sensibility to pain means a corresponding lack of sensibility to pleasure. We can no more avoid feeling pain when a harsh word is spoken, than when we receive a cut or a blow. No doubt it is pleasant to say sharp, clever things; but the pleasure is a momentary one, an entirely selfish one; it will not bear thinking about; and it may inflict a durable pain. Sharp words may be like barbed arrows that not all the lapse of years can work out of the memory. Assuredly we must not shrink from inflicting pain, if duty, affection, and prudence point that way; but we had need to be very sure of the indications. To inflict bodily pain for our own pleasure is admittedly an unchristian thing; and yet what a monstrous inconsistency is revealed in the fact that persons who would not tread on a worm, are constantly found inflicting the intensest pain by the words they speak. Knock a man down, and you might do him less harm than by the few words that pass so lightly, easily, and pleasantly between your lips. Less harm is done by the fist than by the tongue.

II. CONSIDER THE INJUSTICE DONE BY IT. Sarcastic speeches never can be true speeches. If they were true, it would be no justification of them, but in the very nature of things they cannot be true. They must have about them, more or less, elements of the false and exaggerated. If a thing is to be sharp at all, there is an irresistible temptation to make it as sharp and striking as possible; and truth cannot but suffer in the process. Epigrams are always to be distrusted. *How clearly the injustice of sharp sayings comes out in the illustration before us!* The speech about these graves was a witty, clever one, but how unjust! As it happened, Moses was under no responsibility whatever for bringing the Israelites to this particular place. He had not been left to use his own judgment and discretion, but was as much under the guidance of the cloudy pillar as all the rest. Hence from this illustration we receive a slight warning that we may not only be inflicting *pain*, which is *much*, but *injustice*, which is a great deal *more*. You who would not steal the least fragment of a man's property, be equally careful to speak no word which may do hurt to his reputation. Speak that you may inflict no pain; speak also that you may do no injustice.

III. CONSIDER THE PERIL TO THE SPEAKER HIMSELF. Cleverness is a perilous, and not unfrequently a fatal gift. To be sharper than our neighbours may prove in the end a dangerous thing for our own interests. Some who are admired, courted, widely spoken about, for their powers of mimicry, find in the end that it might have been far more for their comfort and permanent well-being, if they had been of only common-place abilities. To be admired is a poor satisfaction, mere dust and ashes, if it has to stand instead of being loved. Make fun of other people, seize without mercy on their weaknesses, their follies and their natural defects, and the chances are that you will find yourself exposed, in turn, to like treatment. Those who attack with sharp speeches are just the men who deserve—if they always got their deserts, and it were expedient to retaliate—equally sharp speeches in return. What about these Israelites here? Did they not by talking in this fashion show clearly what a mean, miserable company they were? They hurt themselves far more than they hurt Moses. There is hardly one who takes pride in what he calls his plain speaking, but might be pilloried himself, and greeted with sarcastic speeches as severe as any he had uttered, and probably more charged with truth. And the worst of all is, that in the end those habituated to evil-speaking may find themselves forsaken in their own great need. We need friends, and, if we would have them, we must show ourselves friendly. If we go through the world constantly replenishing our sarcastic quiver with arrows, and stretching the bow on every slight provocation, then we must expect people to give us a wide berth; and when at last we come to be stricken ourselves, it will be no matter of just complaint if we are left well-nigh alone.

IV. CONSIDER HOW MUCH GOOD IS THWARTED AND NEUTRALISED BY THIS WAY OF SPEAKING. We may flatter ourselves that there is good to be gained in making folly ridiculous, and so there may be; but it can only be when the speaker is one of great wisdom, goodness, and habitual elevation of life. Certainly we find in the Scriptures the language of solemn irony from God himself; but his words are above our criticism, and we are not at liberty to speak as he speaks. We are all upon the same level of sin, ignorance, and partial views, and must speak as remembering this level. To affect authority and superior station will be ruinous to all good effects from any remonstrance of ours. Whatever truth is revealed to us, and put upon our consciences to speak, must be spoken in love, in humility, and in the very best season we can find. If it is really our desire to win others to better, wiser and manlier courses, we had better not begin with sharp speeches. True it may be that the world is mostly made up of fools, and perhaps there is no occasion when we do more to prove our own place in the large company than when, in our contempt and impatience, we call other people fools. We are not then behaving as fishers of men. We are not then becoming all things to all men in order to save some. Many a Christian has had to sorrow for his imperfect control over the gift of intellectual quickness. Before his conversion, he used his gift of wit, repartee, and ludicrous conception with careless freedom and delight, not staying to consider whom he hurt, whom he hindered. Then when such a one submits at last to the true lord of the intellect, he finds it hard, in this matter in particular, to bring his thoughts into captivity to the obedience of Christ.

V. GOD'S PEOPLE MUST THEMSELVES PREPARE TO BE SARCASTICALLY AND BITTERLY SPOKEN OF. Only let each one of us consider his own temptation to say hard things, and then we shall cease to wonder that hard things are said of us. We cannot expect to receive from others, but as we give to them. Anyway we must be ready for hard things, ready in particular for hard speeches. Where Christ went, his people must go;

and he went in a path where he was called a gluttonous man and a winebibber, a friend of publicans and sinners. If he was sneered at on the very Cross, it is babyish on our part to complain because the world sneers at us in the comparatively easy paths we have to tread. Our strength, our joy, and our serenity must not depend on the world's opinion. Moses was getting a hint even thus early that he must not expect consideration from his brethren, with respect to his feelings and difficulties. The joys of Moses were to be got from quite another direction, even from the assiduous tenderness of Jehovah himself.

VI. CULTIVATE A HABIT OF PITIFUL CONSIDERATION TOWARDS THE MEN OF SARCASTIC SPEECH. Remember that they are not happy men. How can a man be happy whose eye is for ever lighting on the blots and loathsome ulcers of human nature; who seems to have a morbid acuteness of vision with respect to them, but to become purblind when noble and Divinely-produced elements of character appear? Such a man is to be pitied with Christ's own gentle pity. Do not meet his sarcasm with sarcasm, but here emphatically return good for evil. Force him to see that there is a great deal more in the world, *if only he will look for it*, than duplicity, selfishness, and stupidity. Show him how to discern, even in the jostling and wrangling crowd, men who have in them the mind which was in Christ.—Y.

The passage of the Red Sea.—"Fear ye not, stand still (firm), and see the salvation of God" (Ex. xiv. 13). Mark, by way of introduction, the critical character of this event, the greatest in Old Testament history. (For valuable suggestions on this point, see Stanley's "Sinai and Palestine," p. 33, and Ewald's "History of Israel," vol. ii. p. 70, Eng. ed. Ewald even is constrained to speak of "this event, *whose historical certainty is well established*.") Lay solid foundations for sermonic treatment by describing first the scene, expounding the history, and then evolving the truths in the history.

I. THE SCENE. In the Gospels, the spiritual significance is almost independent of topography. Only two or three scenes (*e.g.*, Jacob's well: the ridge whence Jesus saw from Olivet the city and wept over it), can be absolutely and certainly identified. But here sermon and story are inextricably blended with sea and shore. Note! twice change of direction: (1) not by way of Philistia: (2) not by caravan road, round by the mouth of the western arm of the Red Sea; but brought into a position of extreme danger, with the sea roaring between Israel and the freedom of the desert. The writer of this section of the commentary believes, that Israel encamped on what is now known as the plain of Suez, the sea reaching then much further north than now. (See maps and interesting article, "Une Splendeur de la Foi," by L'Abbé Moigno,[1] in "Les Mondes" for Aug. 28, 1879.) Any detailed map will show—that there Israel would have the sea on the east, hills to north and south, an open valley to the west, along which the Egyptian forces would charge. Deepen the impression, that these two millions of people, some indeed armed, but not yet organised, with women, children, and the aged, were in a position *utterly hopeless*. It was a situation of despair—but that which is impossible with man is possible with God.

II. THE HISTORY. One of the objects should be to vivify and make very real to the hearers, the histories of the Old Testament, which sometimes seem so very far away from modern thought and life. With this intent, bring out clearly, by aid of exposition elsewhere, points like these:—probably seven days elapsed between the Passover and the song on the eastern shore of the sea, occupied thus:—1. By *Israel*. On the 15th, to Succoth, fifteen miles; on the 16th, to Etham, fifteen miles; on the 17th, to the dangerous position by the sea; on the 18th, 19th, and 20th, encamped there, completing arrangements for the pilgrimage to Sinai and Palestine. 2. By *Egypt*. Every movement watched by the government; night of 15th, report from Succoth; of the 16th, from Etham; morning of the 17th, courier could carry in a few hours, over the thirty miles, intelligence that Israel had taken the wrong (?) road. Sudden determination of the king. Had three days to overtake. Called together six hundred picked chariots, other chariots, infantry, and led in person. On the afternoon of the 20th, the pickets of Israel saw far away the force coming over the sand ridges. Horror of the two millions. The

---

[1] In this article the Abbé proposes to raise £12,000 to search in the sand for the debris of Pharaoh's army. See Is. xi. 15.

splendid cities of tombs in Egypt rose to the memory. But here soon a sort of gigantic anticipation of Isandula. A cry against Moses, and unto Jehovah. The moral attitude of Moses mixed—cheer for the people—a fainting heart before God. His silent prayer. "The upward glancing of an eye." The word of assurance. "Forward." The movement of what must have been, in this instance, *wall* of cloud and fire, to give soft electric light to Israel and over the sea, to be darkness to Egypt, and to cover the greatest military movement in all history. The short time demanded perfect order. Then came the ploughshare of the east wind. In the confusion and darkness, Egypt eagerly followed. The look out of the cloud, shot with thunderbolt—a look which meant ruin. Sea rolls back from the rear of Egypt. Chariot clashes against chariot. Wheels lost. On the night of the 14th Israel became a *nation*. On the morning of the 21st the nation was *free*.

III. TRUTHS. 1. *Neither first nor even second openings in life are always into the way God intends us to take.* A common error to suppose that any opening is "providential." Not *via* Philistia: nor the caravan road to Sinai. God's object to develop moral thoughtfulness, and the scrutiny of apparent leading. *E.g.*, Will this course imperil my principle, lead into temptation, and ruin my soul? 2. *Seemingly hopeless entanglement may have great issues.* Moral firmness developed: dependence upon God. Salvation complete, and anthem of victory. 3. *The temper for crisis is that of calm confidence.* No panic! Had there been panic, Israel had been food for Egyptian sabres! "Stand *firm!*" (see Heb.) Apply this to state of religion; things social, political, at home and abroad; to affairs personal. (See good sermon on this, by Professor Jowett, in "Christian World Pulpit," March 26, 1879.) 4. *Confidence should express itself in prayer.* Note the difference: the cry of Israel, and the evidently silent appeal of Moses. 5. *Action must follow prayer.* "Wherefore criest," etc., an intimation that prayer was already answered; and now Moses to the front, and every man to his post. 6. *When God leads into danger, He will certainly see us safely through it.* If wantonly and wilfully we go into danger, we *may* (through mercy) be delivered; if on Divine leading, we *shall*. *E.g.*, going into some scene of vice, out of curiosity, or worse motive; on the other hand, at the request of a distant friend, to save a soul. Difference between presumption and courage. 7. *Salvations of God are ever timely and complete.* 8. After God's great salvation comes, *the dumbness of amazement, and after the dumbness, song.* "Jehovah shall fight for you, and ye shall be *dumb*." (Heb. xiv. 31; xv. 1; Rev. xv. 2—4.)—R.

EXPOSITION.

Vers. 15—18. — GOD'S ANSWER TO MOSES' PRAYER. To the faithful prayer of Moses, albeit pitched perhaps in too low a key, God made gracious answer. A "cry" had been unnecessary, since his word was already pledged to bring his people safe to Canaan, and to get himself honour upon Pharaoh in connection with the pursuit (ver. 4). But, as the appeal has been made, he responds with a plain statement of what has now to be done:—1. The Israelites are to make themselves ready for a forward movement (ver. 15); 2. Moses is to stretch out his rod over the Red Sea, and it will be divided; 3. The Israelites are then to make the passage on dry ground; 4. The Egyptians are to follow, and then honour is to be gotten upon them; and they are to know by the result that God is indeed Jehovah.

Vers. 15, 16.—**Wherefore criest thou to me?** It is evident that Moses, while boldly encouraging the people, himself needed the support and consolation of prayer. The Syriac translator shows us that he divined the fact aright, when he without authority intruded the words, "Moses then cried to Jehovah." The form of the Divine reply to his prayer seems to indicate a certain amount of reproach, as if Moses himself had become unduly anxious. **Speak unto the children of Israel that they go forward.** The Israelites were not to rest in their encampment, but to form in line of march, and descend to the very shore of the sea, and there hold themselves in readiness. Moses was to **lift up** his **rod**—the rod with which his other miracles had been wrought—and **stretch out his hand over the sea**, and then the drying up was to begin. Thus was most of the night passed.

Ver. 17.—**I will harden the hearts of the Egyptians.** Here, and here only, are the hearts of the Egyptians generally said to have been "hardened." Whatever meaning we attach to the expression, there will be no more difficulty in applying it to them than to Pharaoh. They had made themselves partakers in the monarch's guilt by mustering in hot haste when he summoned them, and had allowed themselves to revel in the anticipation of plunder and carnage (ch. xv. 9). Under such circumstances, the general laws which govern human nature would be quite sufficient to make their hearts grow hard. **They shall follow them.** Upon this act—rash, if the phenomenon had been a mere natural one—presumptuous and infatuated if the drying up were regarded as miraculous—depended altogether the destruction of the Egyptians. They had only to have "stood still" and allowed the escape, which a week previously they had done their best to encourage, in order to have remained safe and unhurt. It was their stupidity and bloodthirstiness which alone brought them into any danger. **Upon his horsemen.** Rather "his chariotmen." See the comment on verse 9.

Ver. 18.—**The Egyptians shall know that I am the Lord.** All Egypt would learn the destruction of the host, and the circumstances under which it occurred, whose miraculous nature could not be concealed. And the consequence would be a wide recognition of the superior might of Jehovah, the God of Israel, over that of any of the Egyptian deities. More than this the Egyptians were not likely to admit under any circumstances.

HOMILETICS.

Vers. 15—18.—*The reward of faith.* God rewarded the faith and trust of Moses by a revelation of the manner of that deliverance which he so confidently expected. Hitherto the manner had been involved in mystery; and it is scarcely likely that any one had even conjectured it as a possible thing. There was no precedent for *such* an interference with the laws of nature; and the thought could scarcely occur to the imagination of any one. But, to reward his faithful servant, to quiet his anxiety, and give definiteness to his expectations of deliverance, God now plainly revealed the mode in which he would save his people. God is ever "a rewarder of them that diligently seek him," and especially rewards faith. The faith of Abraham, which made him trust God's promise to create of him a great nation, when as yet he had no child, obtained for him the gift of Canaan and the covenant of circumcision. The faith of Noah, who believed God's threat of a deluge, which all the rest of the world scorned, saved him and his family from perishing by water. The faith of Enoch, by which he "walked with God"—though he could not see him—caused God to "take him." Faith brings us, to a certainty,—1. The present blessing of an assured trust which nothing can imperil; 2. Quietness and confidence—the feeling that we may "stand still and see the salvation of God;" 3. Freedom from panic fears and unworthy apprehensions; 4. Cheerfulness and hopefulness—a conviction that God will give us what is best for us. Faith may also, by God's mercy, obtain for us further gifts in the future—blessings not naturally arising out of it, but added to it as rewards by God, and signs of his approval. The faith of Moses was ultimately rewarded, 1. By success in the great object of his life—the liberation of his people and their safe-conduct through all the perils of the wilderness to the verge of Canaan; 2. By God's approval of him as "Moses, the servant of the Lord" (Deut. xxxiv. 5); and 3. By the vision of Canaan from Pisgah.

HOMILIES BY VARIOUS AUTHORS.

Ver. 15.—"*Speak unto the children of Israel that they go forward!*" I. FORWARD! —GOD'S CONSTANT INJUNCTION TO HIS CHURCH. The law of Christian life is *advance*. God never brings his Church or people into positions from which retreat is necessary, or in which advance is impossible. We may bring *ourselves* into false positions of this kind, but *God* never leads us into them. In proportion as we surrender ourselves to his guidance, we may depend on being conducted always "forward." There is no instance in the whole history of the Old or New Testament Church in which, while God's guidance was followed, retreat had to be made. Forward! (1) In Christian attainments. (2) In holy living. (3) In labours for the advancement of Christ's kingdom. (4) In missionary enterprise. (5) In doing good to our fellow-men.

II. Forward!—in contrast with vain lamentations, and unbecoming expostulations with Providence. These do no good, but much harm. They betray an unbelieving spirit. If God brings us into situations of trial, the fact that it is he who brings us into them is of itself a pledge that with the trial, he will make also a way of escape (1 Cor. x. 13). When the foe bears hard upon us, we should, instead of losing heart, rather feel that the time has come for getting everything in readiness for aavance—the "great door and effectual" must be on the very point of opening.

III. Forward!—by the way which God makes for us. At the same moment that he is saying—"Speak unto the children of Israel that they go forward," he is doubtless commissioning some Moses to stretch out his rod over the sea, to open up the way for us. God never says "Forward," without at the same time opening the way.

IV. Forward!—with good heart, strong hope, and firm assurance of being protected on the journey. Going forward at God's word, the Israelites were assured of God's protection. They were certain of reaching the further shore in safety. No fear of the waves rushing back, and burying *them*. Pharaoh pursued, but he was not permitted to capture them, and was himself overthrown. We may confront any perils, if duty calls, and God goes with us. Cf. Luther at Worms.—J. O.

Vers. 15—18.—*Obedience necessary to salvation.* I. The duty of those who are leaders among their brethren in times of trial. 1. There is a time for action as well as prayer: "Wherefore criest thou unto me?" (1) The time of the leader must not be spent in prayer only—there are arrangements to make and needs to meet. In times of difficulty God asks for obedience. A path of love, of forgiveness of injuries, of some service, lies right before us as our duty in that hour. True faith will walk in it. This too is an appeal to our Father as well as prayer. (2) Unbelief may hide itself behind a form of devotion. 2. To speak to them that they go forward. 3. To do what God bids them in opening up their brethren's way. "Lift thou up thy rod." The lifting up of the rod seemed a vain thing, but it clove a path for Israel through the heart of the sea. Our service for our brethren in the day of their trouble may cleave a way for them. A people's progress may be hindered by a leader's indolence and selfishness. II. God's unceasing working on his people's behalf (vers. 17, 18). 1. His mercy was veiled, but he was working still. The very pursuit of the foe was from him. 2. Egypt had still to receive one crowning lesson regarding Jehovah's might and unfailing guardianship of his people. When foes pursue, when sins rise up to recover their former sway, it is that God may destroy the one and judge the other.—U.

Vers. 13—31.—*God completes the deliverance of the Israelites from Pharaoh and removes their terror.* I. Note the way in which Moses meets the complaints of the Israelites. They had addressed to him sarcastic, flippant, and in every way unworthy speeches. They were not so filled with fear, not so occupied with the troubles of their own hearts, but that they could find a malignant delight in striving to make him ridiculous. This mingling of feelings on their part, fear mingled with hate, makes the single-heartedness of his reply all the more manifest and beautiful. The time is not one for him to stand on his own dignity, or bandy sharp language with mean men, even were his character such as to incline him that way. There is but a step from the sublime to the ridiculous; in one sense he makes that step, and by his noble, impressive exhortation, he at once sweeps the ridiculous out of the path of the sublime. The subject of the grave surely is never a seemly one for jesting; and the jesting was unseemliest of all at this present hour. One almost sees these little, pert jokers retreating into the background before the great believer. They would not trouble him again for a while. It was not Israel that had come out of Egypt seeking for graves, but Pharaoh and his host. These murmurers did indeed find graves in the wilderness by and by; but it was for a subsequent transgression. It is part of the peculiar pathos of human life that no one can tell where he must die and be buried. So much then with respect to the meek and comely attitude—true attitude of a prophet of God—which Moses here assumed. He rises clear above the little men of the crowd, for God has taken him out, in particular, *with a high hand,* and now what shall the *matter* of his answer be? He does not turn towards God doubtfully. (Contrast his conduct here with his conduct in ch. v. 22—23.) The peril is to the natural eye overwhelming, but it is not peril to him, for God has filled him with the spirit of faith. He himself, unfearing, can tell the people not to fear. He himself, calmly expectant that some great deliverance is on the way, can recommend, his face not belying his tongue, the same calm expectancy to the people. Let them stand still and wait, instead of rushing hither and thither, weakening themselves still more by their disorder. Moses, exactly comprehending that the position is one in which *man can do nothing*, and *God must do everything*, presses this view on his brethren. What is his personal dignity, his *amour propre*, compared with the glorious view to be opened out to them? Here is a lesson then, when people speak to us out of little envies and personal grudges. Reply by directing them to great soul-filling truths. Lead, if you can, mean, grovelling souls to the mountain top. Give them the chance of seeing the wide inheritance of the saints; and if they cannot take it in, then the loss, and the responsibility of the loss, is theirs.

II. Note the instructions which God gives to Moses, vers. 15—18. These instructions, astounding as they must have seemed at the time, were, nevertheless, eminently practical. Those who bear the name of practical among men are those who keep well within what is reckoned possible by the ordinary judgment. Men of the Columbus type, such as great discoverers and great inventors, have to bear for long enough the name of being mere visionaries, day-dreamers, wasters of life. But God's practicality is to set his servants at once to things reckoned impossible. His directions are very simple: "Go forward." He waits till the people are indeed shut up on every hand, and then he says, "Go forward." They were to continue in the same direction, and that led onward to the sea. This was the appointed path to the mountain where they were to serve God. Yes; and if the path had been through the rocky steeps which enclosed them, God could have dissolved those steeps away. Or if it had been through Pharaoh's host, he could have smitten that host utterly, as he afterwards did Sennacherib's. Notice that in this command *there is another proving of faith*. First, with regard to *Moses*. For it will be observed that there is nothing to show that Moses knew anything of what would happen in the Red Sea, until God now made it known. Probably during the whole course of the plagues, the precise nature of each plague was revealed to Moses only just as it was approaching. And so here, in this new imprisonment, he was quietly waiting for light to come from God, well knowing that sufficient would be done to deliver Israel—that God had led his people into this entanglement, not without a perfectly definite purpose, and that the end of all would be the destruction of the Egyptians. But he knew not any more than the least child in Israel, until just beforehand, how all this was to be brought about. There was also *a great proving of the faith of the people*. God has a command for them, and it is one requiring great faith. Notice how appropriately it comes on, as the climax of past treatment. We have seen the Israelites sharing at first in the sufferings of the Egyptian plagues. After a while, the district in which they reside is exempted from the plagues. Then when the first-born are smitten, the Israelites, *by their obedience to Jehovah's instructions*, escape the blow. And now at last their escape is to be completed by again obeying Jehovah's instructions, and *equally in the obedience of a pure faith*. But mark the most important advance and development of faith, which is here illustrated. Two quite different states of mind are brought out by slaying the passover lamb in faith, and by going towards and through the Red Sea in faith. To slay the passover lamb is to do a thing for which no reason is given but the command of God. *But it is a thing which plainly can be done.* It involves no peril; there is no appearance of impossibility about it; the only temptation is to think it useless, a superfluous reasonless form. On the other hand, it is perfectly plain that passage through the Red Sea will provide escape. The question is, can such a passage be gained, and therein the temptation lies. In slaying the passover lamb, the Israelites had to humble their intellects before Divine wisdom; in advancing to the Red Sea, they had to show the utmost confidence in Divine power. We must steadily believe that all God commands is useful and necessary; we must also steadily believe that all which is fit for him to do, he most assuredly can do. It is a matter deserving consideration that Jehovah should have given such a command, *seeing the state of unbelief and carnality in which the Israelites evidently were*. They had not spoken like men ready for such an awful miracle. But we can see certain things which made obedience easier. For one thing, God had shut them up to it. If they had been taken down to the Red Sea, with no Pharaoh behind, with no enclosing mountains on either hand, they might have rebelled. But circumstances lent a strong compulsive aid. We know not what we can do, what triumphs of faith we can achieve till God shuts us up to them. Then there was something also in the sight of the rod. God commanded Moses to exhibit something which had already been associated with wonderful deeds. Thus we see God making plain to Israel the way out of their peril, and so far all is definite. But this being told, the definite immediately shades away into the indefinite. The *indefinite* mark, but not therefore the *uncertain*. All is manifest and straightforward with regard to the Israelites ; they are to be safe. *But what about Pharaoh and his army ?* We remember Peter's question to Jesus concerning John (John xxi. 21). "Lord, what shall this man do ? " So Moses might have questioned Jehovah—" Lord, what is to happen to Pharaoh ? " Something on this matter Jehovah does say, just enough to preserve confidence, attention and expectation ; but for the details Moses and Israel must wait a little longer. Meanwhile an inspiring hint is given of great judgment, great humiliation, and for Jehovah himself, great glory. Here the information stops ; and here we again notice the eminent practicality of God's instructions. For the day's need and for our own need God gives us the amplest guidance ; but what is to happen to our enemies, and exactly how they are to be removed he keeps within his own knowledge, as within his own power. The proper answer to all impious and curious pryings on our part is that which Jesus gave to Peter—" What is that to thee ? follow thou me."

III. NOTE THE CONSEQUENT DEALINGS OF JEHOVAH IN DELIVERING ISRAEL AND DESTROYING THE EGYPTIANS. 1. *The altered position of the cloudy pillar.* The angel of God removed and went behind. By the angel of God is possibly meant the pillar itself. Just as the burning bush is described as a messenger of God (ch. iii. 2), so here there seems an indicating of the cloudy pillar as another messenger. Just at this moment it was not wanted for purposes of guidance. Indeed it would not have proved sufficient for these purposes. Jehovah had found it needful himself to intervene and signify by unmistakable words, the way in which he would have the people go. The cloudy pillar was enough for guidance only as long as the Israelites were in open and ordinary paths. But where it could not be used for *guidance*, it could be used for *defence*. God's messengers can easily change their use. The cloud, by changing its place, hindered Egypt, and thereby helped Israel. Nor did it help Israel in this way alone ; the boon was a positive as much as a negative one. Surely this was a marvellous cloud, for it had in it darkness as well as light. Thus it served a double purpose. Hiding Israel from the Egyptian eyes, it proved the best of fortifications. But at the same time it shone upon the Israelites and gave them the benefits of day with the immunities of night. They could put everything in perfect order for the march, so as to take it the moment the way through the sea was ready. Imagine that miraculous light shining down on that miraculous path, even from end to end ; just like a light shining down a street ; and as it were pointing Israel onward, even though it stood behind them. Thus we are made to think *of all the double aspect of the work of Jesus,* how at the same time he confounds his enemies and guides and cheers his friends. Consider this especially in connection with his resurrection. On the one hand he abolished death ; on the other he brought life and immortality to light. 2. *The obedience of Moses and the Israelites to the Divine command.* As we have noticed, all this had been well prepared for beforehand. Moses had been led up to it, and so had Israel ; and therefore when the moment came, there was no hesitation. After what has been already said there is no need to dwell on this actual obedience. It is enough to note in passing, that God having duly arranged all conspiring causes, the effect followed as a matter of course. But now we come to the point of main interest in the closing section of this chapter, namely, 3. *The conduct, treatment, and ultimate fate of the Egyptians.* There is first, *their infatuated advance.* They go down in the path which Jehovah had made for Israel as if it was to remain a path for them. The Egyptians were too full of their purpose, too full of the spirit of vengeance and greed to notice their danger, even though it was a danger of the most obvious kind. They might have gone into certain positions where a miracle would have been required to put them in danger ; but here the miracle is already wrought, and these enemies of Jehovah and Jehovah's people advance, as if the piled-up waters were thus to remain, their shape settled for ages to come, just like the shape of the solid hills around. The only thing to explain their conduct is the momentum that had been produced in their own breasts. It was with them just as it is with the runner when he has gained a certain speed. Suppose in his headlong career he comes to a chasm, stop he cannot. Either he must clear the chasm or fall into it. The next point to be noticed is *God's treatment of them in their advance.* The whole progress of affairs is exactly arranged so as to produce the deliverance of Israel and the destruction of Pharaoh. The very nearness of Pharaoh and his army to the Israelites, instead of proving ruin to them, only more effectually proves ruin to him. Some of the more timid among the Israelites might be tempted to say, "Oh! that the waters would return, immediately the last Israelite is ashore; let the great barrier be set between us and Pharaoh as soon as possible." But such a course would only have secured a present safety at the expense of a future one. Jehovah has a far better way of working than any which human panic can suggest. He lets the Egyptians go on until the whole army is in the midst of the sea, and then he who has truly proved himself a man of war opens the last decisive battle by making the chariots useless. Nay, not only were they useless; they seem to have become a hindrance and a terror. Jehovah neither hastens nor lingers; he smites at the right time, and therefore he smites effectually; and now we are called to listen to *a resolution made too late.* "Let us flee from the face of Israel." If only they had been wise in time, they would not have had to flee at all. What were *they* doing in the midst of the Red Sea? Nay more, what were they doing out of their own country? They had trifled and-trifled with danger after danger, and now they had trifled beyond escape. It is no time to talk of flight when the door of the trap has fallen. The waters are on the point of returning; the ordinary course of nature is about to assert itself. Why should that course be interrupted one moment longer, simply to preserve a host of proud and dangerous men. The great lesson from Pharaoh's fall is *to be wise in time.* Flee from the wrath to come! there is a possibility of that; but when the wrath has come, who then shall flee? (Rev. vi. 16–17).

IV. NOTE THE IMPRESSION SAID TO HAVE BEEN PRODUCED ON THE MINDS OF THE ISRAELITES. Ver. 31. More desirable words surely could not be spoken of any people than that they fear Jehovah and believe in him and his servants. The fear and the faith, however, must be of the right sort, arising out of a right state of the heart, and cleaving to God through all the vicissitudes of circumstance. Such unfortunately was not the fear and faith of these Israelites. We must have heart knowledge of God's character, and come to understand how necessary it is to pass through a shaking of the things that can be shaken in order that the things which cannot be shaken may remain. Then we shall fear as we ought to fear, and believe as we ought to believe.—Y.

EXPOSITION.

Ver. 19—22.—THE PASSAGE OF THE RED SEA. The Egyptians had arrived in the near neighbourhood of the Israelite camp, at the close of a long day's march, towards evening. Having ascertained that the fugitives were still, as they had expected them to be, shut in between the sea and the wilderness, they were content, and made no immediate attack, but encamped over against them. Hereupon, "the pillar of the cloud," which was at the time in front of the Israelite camp—probably near the point where God intended the passage of the sea to be effected—"removed" from this position, and placed itself directly behind the Israelite encampment, between them and the Egyptians. This movement alone was calculated to alarm the latter, and prevent them from stirring till near daybreak; but, the better to secure their inaction, the pillar was made to overshadow them with a deep and preternatural darkness, so that it became almost impossible for them to advance. Meanwhile, on the side which was turned towards the Israelites, the pillar presented the appearance of a bright flame, lighting up the whole encampment, and rendering it as easy to make ready for the march as it would have been by day. Thus, the beasts were collected and laden—the columns marshalled and prepared to proceed in a certain fixed order—and everything made ready for starting so soon as the bed of the sea should be sufficiently dry. Moses, about nightfall, descending to the water's edge, stretched forth his rod over the waves, and, an east wind at once springing up—accompanied perhaps by a strong ebb of the tide—the waters of the gulf were parted in the vicinity of the modern Suez, and a dry space left between the Bitter Lakes, which were then a prolongation of the Gulf, and the present sea-bed. The space may have been one of considerable width. The Israelites entering upon it, perhaps about midnight, accomplished the distance, which may not have exceeded a mile, with all their belongings, in the course of five or six hours, the pillar of the cloud withdrawing itself, as the last Israelites entered the sea-bed, and retiring after them like a rearguard. Thus protected, they made the transit in safety, and morning saw them encamped upon the shores of Asia.

Ver. 19.—**The angel of God.** The Divine Presence, which manifested itself in the pillar of the cloud, is called indifferently "the Lord" (ch. xiii. 21 ; xiv. 24), and "the Angel of God"—just as the appearance to Moses in the burning bush is termed both "God" and "the angel of the Lord" (ch. iii. 2). **Which went before**—*i.e.*, "which ordinarily, and (so to speak) habitually preceded the camp" (ch. xiii. 21; Ps. lxxviii. 14). **And stood behind them.** Took up a fixed station for the night, or the greater portion of it.

Ver. 20.—**It was a cloud and darkness to them, but it gave light by night to these.** Though there is nothing in the Hebrew correspondent to the expressions "to them," "to these," yet the meaning seems to have been rightly apprehended by our translators. (See the Targums of Onkelos and Jonathan, the Syriac version, and among moderns, Knobel, Maurer, Rosenmüller, and Kalisch.)

Ver. 21.—**Moses stretched out his hand.** As commanded by God (ver. 16). Compare the somewhat similar action of Elijah and Elisha, when they divided the Jordan (2 Kings ii. 8, 14). **The Lord caused the sea to** go back by a strong east wind. The LXX. translate "a strong south wind" (ἐν ἀνέμῳ νότῳ βιαίῳ); but the Hebrew *kadim* is certainly "east" rather than "south." It is not, however, "east" in the sense of due east, but would include all the range of the compass between N.E. and S.E. If we suppose the Bitter Lakes to have been joined to the Red Sea by a narrow and shallow channel, the action of a south-east wind, by driving the water of the Lakes northward, may have easily produced the effect described in the text. A simultaneous ebb of the lower gulf would have further facilitated the passage. **The waters were divided.** Water remained in the upper extremity of the Gulf, now the site of the Bitter Lakes, and also, of course, below Suez. The portion of the sea dried up lay probably between the present southern extremity of the Bitter Lakes and Suez. By the gradual elevation and desiccation of the region, it has passed into permanent dry land.

Ver. 22.—**The waters were a wall**—*i. e.*, a protection, a defence. Pharaoh could not attack them on either flank, on account of the two bodies of water between which their march lay. He could only come at them by following after them. The metaphor has been by some understood literally, especially on account of the expression in ch. xv. 8—"The floods stood upright as an heap;" and again that in Ps. lxxviii. 13—"He made the waters to stand as an heap." But those phrases, occurring in poems, must be taken as poetical; and can scarcely have any weight in determining the meaning of "wall" here. We must ask ourselves—is there not an economy and a restraint in the exertion by God even of miraculous power?—is more used than is needed for the occasion?—and would not all that was needed at this time have been effected by such a division of the sea as we have supposed, without the fluid being converted into a solid, or having otherwise the laws of its being entirely altered. Kalisch's statement, that the word "wall" here is "not intended to convey the idea of protection, but only of hardness and solidity," seems to us the very reverse of the truth. Protection is at any rate the main idea, and any other is secondary and subordinate.

HOMILETICS.

Vers. 19—22.—*God protects his own, but in strange ways.*—The passage of the Red Sea was the crowning miracle by which God effected the deliverance of his people from the bondage of Egypt; and all its circumstances were strange and worthy of notice.

I. THE PRESENCE OF THE LORD, WHICH HAD BEEN WONT TO LEAD THEM, REMOVED AND WENT BEHIND THEM. They had to enter the dark and slimy bed from which the sea had retired without the cheering sight of the Divine presence before their eyes beckoning them on. So there are occasions of trial in the life of every man, when God seems to withdraw his presence, to remove himself, to "go behind us," so that we cannot see him. Sometimes he withdraws himself in grief or in anger; but more often he does it in mercy. The temporary obscuration will advantage the soul under the circumstances. There is perhaps some secular work to be done which requires all its attention, like this passage, where every step had to be taken with care. Short separations are said to intensify affection; and the sense of the Divine presence is more valued after a withdrawal, like the sun's light after an eclipse.

II. THE PILLAR OF THE CLOUD, WHICH HAD BEEN WONT TO BE ALL SMOKE, OR ALL FIRE, WAS NOW BOTH AT ONCE. "It came between the camp of the Egyptians and the camp of Israel; and it was a cloud and darkness to them, but it gave light by night to these." The eye sees that which it has within itself the power of seeing. To the godly the presence of God is a joy and a delight, a brightness and a radiance. To the ungodly it is an awful and alarming thing, a cloud which mars their enjoyment. When Jesus was on earth, there were those among the inhabitants of Palestine who "besought him to depart out of their coasts" (Matt. viii. 34). The ungodly fear to look upon God. He is to them dark, mysterious, terrible. The sense of his presence paralyses them — they cannot stir till it is removed. But to the godly, it is "light in the darkness"—it illuminates mind and soul and spirit—it cheers and brightens the path of life —it irradiates even the obscurest gulf that we have to traverse. Let us bear in mind that when the Divine presence is removed from before our eyes, it is still in no case far from us. If at any time we do not see God, he at all times sees us. We have only to make an effort, and we can in a short time recover our perception of his presence.

III. BY MEANS OF A STRONG EAST WIND THE WATERS WERE DIVIDED, UPON MOSES STRETCHING OUT HIS HAND OVER THE SEA. We may note here, 1. The weakness of the instrument. The rod of Moses, stretched over the sea, or towards the sea, from some vantage-point on the shore—how small a thing was this! How incapable in itself of producing any important effect! Yet in the providence of God, it was made a link in the chain of causation by which was brought about one of the greatest events in the whole course of mundane history. Must we not conclude from this, that, when God appoints means, however weak and trivial they may be in themselves, they become at once by his appointment matters of the highest consequence? Again we may note, 2. The employment of a natural agency, insufficient in itself to accomplish the end, yet having a natural tendency towards its accomplishment. God, the author of nature, uses nature as a help towards accomplishing his ends, even when the help is but small. Our Lord fed the 5000 and the 4000, by means of loaves and fishes already existing, though the material which they furnished could but have gone a short way. He anointed the blind man's eyes with spittle and clay, and bade him "go, wash in the pool of Siloam," using means which were to some extent reputed salutary, but which of themselves could never have restored sight. So with the east wind. We must not suppose that it divided the sea by its own natural force. God used it, as he used the spittle and the clay, and made it accomplish his purpose, not by its own force but by his own power. And so generally with the forces which seem to remove obstacles from the path of God's people in this life—they are potent through his agency, because he sets them to work, and works through them.

IV. THE SEA, ON WHICH PHARAOH COUNTED FOR THEIR DESTRUCTION, BECAME FIRST THEIR DEFENCE AND THEN THEIR AVENGER. "The waters were a wall unto them." But for the two bodies of water, on their right and on their left, Pharaoh's force might have outflanked the host of Israel, and fallen upon it on three sides, or even possibly have surrounded it. God can at any time turn dangers into safeguards. When persecutors threaten the Church, he can turn their swords against each other, and allow the Church to pass on its way in peace. When temptations assault the soul, he can give the soul such strength, that it conquers them and they become aids to its progress. And with equal ease can he make the peril which menaces his faithful ones fall, not upon them, but upon their adversaries. The furnace heated to consume the "three children" destroyed none but those bitter persecutors who had arrested them and cast them into the fire (Dan. iii. 22). The lions of Darius the Mede devoured, not Daniel, but "those men that had accused Daniel" (ib. vi. 24). The Jews, who had sought to destroy the infant Church by prejudicing the Romans against Christ (John xix. 12) and his apostles (Acts xxiv. 1—9), were themselves within forty years of Christ's death, conquered and almost exterminated by these same Romans. The ungodly are ever "falling into their own nets together," while the godly man for whom the nets are set "escapes them."

HOMILIES BY VARIOUS AUTHORS.

Vers. 19, 20.—*Light to the friend, darkness to the foe.* We are told that as the Israelites were about to cross the Red Sea, the fiery-cloudy pillar changed its position, and came between them and the Egyptians. It was the self-same pillar, but it wore a very different aspect to friends and foes respectively. "It was," we read, "a cloud of darkness to them (the Egyptians), but it gave light to these (the camp of Israel)." We should notice that the same double aspect belongs to all God's manifestations of himself, in Law and Gospel, in matter and spirit, in the world, and in the Church.

I. GOD'S ATTRIBUTES have this double aspect. Not one of his attributes but has a bright side turned to the believer, and a dark side to the wicked. This is true even of such attributes as holiness and justice, from which the believer, as a sinner, might seem to have most to fear. "*Faithful* and *just* to forgive us our sins, and to cleanse us from all unrighteousness" (1 John i. 9). So God's omnipotence, which is hostile to the transgressor, is pledged to defend, bless, and save the saint (1 Pet. i. 5; Jude 24). God's eternity, in like manner, is given to the believer for a dwelling-place (Deut. xxxiii. 27; Ps. xc. 1), but how terrible an aspect it has to the evil-doer! The dark side of love is wrath. "If God be for us, who can be against us?" (Rom. viii. 31). But on the other hand, "It is a fearful thing to fall into the hands of the living God" (Heb. x. 31).

II. GOD'S LAWS have this double aspect. 1. *Physical* laws. The constitution of nature is favourable to virtue, hostile to vice (See Butler's *Analogy*). 2. *Moral* law, for this, while awarding life to the obedient, is a ministry of condemnation to the sinner. 3. *Mental* and *spiritual* laws. Take *e.g.* the law of habit. "The law of habit, which applies alike to all our physical, mental, and moral actions, must be regarded in its design as a truly benevolent one. But the law of habit, when the soul yields to sin, works death to the sinner:—like the pillar of cloud which made day to Israel, and was darkness to the Egyptians, so the law, which is bright to the well-doer, sheds night upon the path of the sinner, until he is plunged into the sea of death" (Theodore D. Woolsey).

III. GOD'S WORD has this double aspect. To the prayerful, believing, docile mind, it is a source of unfailing light. It is a lamp to the feet and a light to the path (Ps. cxix. 105). But to the proud, the unbelieving, and the presumptuous, it is only darkness. These can see nothing in it but difficulties, incredibilities, contradictions, moral monstrosities. It is full of stumbling-blocks. The more they read it, the more are they blinded by it. They read only to discover some new fault or error.

IV. GOD'S VERY GOSPEL has this double aspect. "The preaching of the Cross is to them that perish foolishness, but to us who are saved it is the power of God" (1 Cor. i. 18—24). It repels the one class, and attracts the other. To the one, it is a savour of life; to the other, a savour of death (2 Cor. ii. 16).—J. O.

Vers. 19—31.—*The goodness and severity of God.* I. WHAT GOD IS TO HIS OWN IN THE DAY OF TROUBLE. 1. He comes between them and their foes. God's presence is between us and our enemies, and they can do no more against us than his love permits. 2. He is light to them in the time of peril. 3. The waters are divided before them. However much our way may seem hedged in, God's arm will open up a path for us. 4. The way was not only a path of escape, but one of perfect safety; the waters were a wall to them upon the right hand and the left.

II. WHAT GOD IS TO HIS PEOPLE'S FOES. 1. Their path is wrapped in darkness. They cannot lay hold of the weakest of those who but a moment before seemed wholly in their power. They are perplexed and baffled. 2. Daring to follow they are filled with horror by the revelation that their contest is with the mighty God: they are face to face not with the servant, but the master. 3. Their progress is arrested (25). 4. They in vain attempt to flee. Men may flee *to* God; they cannot flee *from* God. 5. They are overwhelmed with destruction.

III. THE RESULT OF THE CONFLICT (31). 1. The people are filled with holy awe. "They feared Jehovah. God's judgments deepen in his people's hearts the sense of his terribleness and majesty." 2. It strengthened their faith; they believed the Lord. 3.

It produced a spirit of obedience: they "believed his servant Moses." They were baptized unto Moses in the cloud and in the sea. The outcome of fear and trust must be full obedience to him who leads us into the promised rest—the Shepherd and Bishop of our souls.—U.

Ver. 22.—*We walk by faith, not by sight.* The great mistake of most people is, that they trust too much to their own eyes. They will not take into consideration anything that lies beyond the field of sensible experience. Now God and his eternity, though manifested in this field, are practically outside it; the spiritual eyesight is more reliable than the physical, because that which it sees is safer to rely upon. Natural sight shows us obstacles, spiritual sight shows us how they may be surmounted. Try to walk by the one and you must stand still; try to walk by the other and nothing can long keep you standing. Notice here:—

I. FAITH'S SECRET. The story illustrates this; it shows us:—1. *What the Israelites saw.* Their position looked bad enough. Behind were the hosts of Pharaoh; before, the sea. They were shut in. Trusting only to their eyes they could hardly do other than despair (xiv. 10—13). Better to have been "let alone" in Egypt, than thus delivered, to be destroyed in the wilderness. A clear head, if the heart be faint, is not much help to any man. 2. *What Moses saw.* He was in the same position as the people whom he led, yet he could see more than they did. He looked not merely before and behind, he looked also up to God. Faith enabled him to ignore sight, and inspired him to encourage his sight-fascinated followers. Soon the word came which justified his faith, obstacles were nothing, let them wait the word of command and then "go forward." Often difficulties seem to surround us—no way of escape anywhere visible. Even so faith can sight the way, for faith can sight God who sees it. Stand still, wait his word; refuse to allow that for those who trust him any difficulties can be insurmountable. Faith would not be of much good were there no obstacles to test it. Faith is not of much good if it cannot learn to ignore obstacles.

II. FAITH'S SUCCESS. The path of faith not merely leads out of danger, it turns dangers into safeguards and transforms them into a protection for those who tread it. When the word came "Go forward," the waters no longer "shut in" the Israelites; instead:—1. They protected them during their passage. The Egyptians could but follow, they could not circumvent. "The waters were a wall unto them" on either side; no wall could have been more impregnable. 2. They secured them against the fury of their pursuers. Israel once across, the waters returned, overwhelming the armies of the enemy. So too faith, facing the flood, found that waters which drowned the world upheld the ark and floated it in safety. So too faith, facing the waters of death, finds that though they overwhelm the unready they float the faithful into a safe harbour. So too with all difficulties, faced in faith, they are our best helpers. "The hand of the diligent" not only "maketh rich," it cleaves a way for him through the sea of difficulty, and leaves his pursuers, sloth, ignorance, all the deadly sins, overwhelmed and swallowed up behind him.

III. FAITH'S STRENGTH. How comes faith to do all this? It is not faith that does it, but the God in whom faith trusts. Nothing is impossible to faith, because nothing is impossible to God. The Egyptians are sure of their prey; the Israelites are sure of destruction; because, whilst reckoning with what sight sees, they fail to reckon with the unseen God. Moses is sure of safety because he is sure of God, and knows that *he* is more than a match for all the seeming tyranny of circumstances.

Application. How many people are shut in, faithless and discouraged before some sea of difficulty! "I cannot do this," "I cannot do that," and yet no progress is possible until I not merely *can* but *do.* "O ye of little faith, wherefore will ye doubt!" "*I* cannot;" no, but *God* can; and what he bids you do that he will strengthen you to do. Don't stand facing the difficulties, but face the God who is above them and beyond them. "Stand still and wait" until the word comes, but when the word does come, "Go forward" (cf. 2 Cor. xii. 9, 10).—G.

EXPOSITION.

Vers. 23—31. THE DESTRUCTION OF THE EGYPTIANS. As the rearguard of the Israelite host having entered the tract from which the waters had retired, proceeded along it, and left the western end of the isthmus vacant, the pillar of the cloud seems to have followed it up and withdrawn with it. The Egyptians immediately advanced. Notwithstanding the preternatural darkness, they had become aware, perhaps by means of their ears, of the movement that was taking place, and with early dawn they were under arms and pressing on the line of the Israelite retreat. They found the channel still dry, and hastily entering it with their chariot force, they hurried forward in pursuit. The first check which they received was wholly supernatural. "The Lord looked unto the host of the Egyptians through the pillar of fire and of the cloud, and troubled the host of the Egyptians" (ver. 24). Details here are wanting; but less cannot be meant, than that some strange phenomena connected with the retiring "pillar" caused a panic and threw the ranks of the army into confusion. Then followed natural impediments. The Lord "took off," or "clogged" their chariot wheels, and made them go heavily—i.e., the chariot wheels, not by miracle, but by the operation of God's natural laws, sank into the soft sand over which the Israelites had passed easily, having no wheeled vehicles, and the chariots were consequently dragged forward slowly and with difficulty. The double hindrance, from the confusion and the stoppage of the chariots, so discouraged the Egyptians, that after a time they resolved on beating a retreat (ver. 25). They had set out on their return, when Moses, at God's instance, stretched forth his hand once more over the sea, and the waters on both sides began at once to return. The Egyptians saw their danger, and "fled against" the advancing tide, racing against it, as it were, and seeking to reach the shore. But in vain. The waves came on rapidly, and (in the language of ver. 28) there was not a man of all those who had entered the dry bed of the sea that was not overwhelmed and drowned in the waters. We should be wrong to press this language to the extreme letter. In graphic narrative the sacred writers uniformly employ universal expressions, where they mean to give the general fact or general result. The true meaning is, that the pursuit altogether failed. Not an Egyptian made his way alive across the strait. All that the Israelites ever saw afterwards of the army that they had so much dreaded (ver. 10) was a ghastly mass of corpses thrown up by the tide on the Asiatic shore (ver. 30).

Ver. 23. — All Pharaoh's horses, his chariots, and his horsemen. Here, as elsewhere, the word translated "horsemen" probably means the men who rode in the chariots. Observe that the Pharaoh himself is not said to have gone in. Menephthah was apt to avoid placing himself in a position of danger (Records of the Past, vol. iv. pp. 44, 45). Nor is any of the infantry said to have entered the bed of the sea.

Ver. 24.—In the morning watch. The "morning watch" of the Hebrews at this period of their history lasted from 2 a.m. to sunrise. Sunrise in Egypt, early in April, would take place about a quarter to six. The Lord looked unto the host of the Egyptians. The description in Ps. lxxvii. 17, 18, is generally regarded as belonging to this point in the narrative of the Exodus, and may be considered as the traditional exposition of it. "The clouds poured out water: the skies sent out a sound; thine arrows also went abroad; the voice of thy thunder was in the heavens; the lightning lightened the world; the earth trembled and shook." As Josephus says— "Showers of rain came down from the sky, and dreadful thunders and lightning, with flashes of fire; thunderbolts also were darted upon them; nor was there anything, wont to be sent by God upon men as indications of his wrath, which did not happen upon this occasion" (Ant. Jud. ii. 16, § 3). And troubled the host. Or "disturbed the host," i.e., "threw it into confusion" (συνετάραξε, LXX.).

Ver. 25. — And took off their chariot wheels. The Sept. has "clogged the axles of their chariots;" but this is from a reading not at present found in the Hebrew MSS. Most modern commentators, however, prefer the reading, which gives a good sense; whereas the existing text is unintelligible. As Kalisch observes, "if the wheels of the chariots had been broken off, the chariots would not have moved at all." That they drove them heavily. The marginal rendering, "and made them go heavily," is preferable. The wheels no doubt sank into the sand up to the axles, and were with difficulty extricated, again to sink a few yards further on. Progress was thus greatly retarded. **So that the Egyptians said, " Let us flee."** Literally, " And Egypt said, 'I will flee.'" **The Lord fighteth for them.** Compare the promise of Moses (ver. 14). The Egyptians were convinced, by the various obstacles which they encountered, that Jehovah was lending his people active aid, and miraculously obstructing their advance. If this were so, it was of no use to persevere, and accordingly they began their retreat.

Vers. 26, 27.—**And the Lord said.** God here interposed a new difficulty. Moses was instructed to stretch out his rod once more, and undo his former work. At the appointed sign, the east wind ceased to blow, and the waters of the Bitter Lakes, no longer driven to the north-west by its force, flowed back with something of a reflux, while at the same time, the tide having turned, the Red Sea waves came rushing on at unwonted speed. In vain the Egyptians fled. They were met by the advancing floods, which poured in on either side, overwhelming and covering up all those who had entered on the dangerous path.

Ver. 28.—**The chariots and the horsemen, and all the host of Pharaoh.** Rather " The chariots, and the chariot men of all the host of Pharaoh." So Knobel correctly. Kalisch thinks—" We are not permitted to suppose that only the Egyptian chariots pursued the Israelites into the sea, while the infantry remained behind, so that the former alone were devoured by the waves." But even he admits that " both in this and in the following chapter, and in most other parts generally, the destruction of the chariots (chariot force?) and its warriors is chiefly alluded to, *so that this particular stress would perhaps justify that conclusion.*" What is clear is, that no force but the chariot force is *said* to have entered the bed of the sea in pursuit of Israel. **There remained not so much as one of them.** On the proper understanding of this statement, see the introductory paragraph to the chapter.

Ver. 29.—**Walked.** Rather, " *had* walked." **The waters were a wall.** Rather, " had been a wall." For the meaning of the expression, see note on ver. 22.

Ver. 30.—**Israel saw the Egyptians dead upon the sea-shore.** Josephus says (*Ant. Jud.* ii. 16, § 6), that, after the passage of the sea by the Israelites, a west wind set in, which (assisted by the current) drove the bodies of the drowned Egyptians to the eastern side of the gulf, where many of them were cast up upon the shore. In this way Moses, according to him, obtained weapons and armour for a considerable number of Israelites.

Ver. 31.—**And Israel saw that great work.** The " work " was, at the least, (1) the (almost) entire destruction of that arm of the service—the chariot force—on which the Egyptian kings mainly relied for success in all their

wars; and (2) the defeat and disgrace of the Egyptian king himself, in an expedition for which he was alone responsible, involving permanent discredit to his military capacity, and naturally tending to shake his authority over his subjects. It secured the Israelites from further persecution, mainly by the reminiscences which it left behind, but partly also by removing them to a distance from the natural course of Egyptian warlike or commercial movement. Though Egypt had mining establishments in the Sinaitic peninsula, at Wady-Magharah and Sarabit-el-Khadim, yet as these were avoided by the Israelites on their way to Sinai, and never afterwards approached, there naturally was no collision between them and the Pharaonic garrisons at those sites. Still more remote were they during their wanderings from the Egyptian military route, which proceeded along the coast from Pelusium to Gaza, and then ran northwards through the Shephelah. Thus the Passage of the Red Sea brought one phase in the life of the people to an end, and was the commencement of another. It separated them from Egypt until the time came when their king would hold communication with its monarch on equal terms (1 Kings iii. 1). It secured their independence, and raised them at once into a nation. It further caused them to exchange the artificial life of a bureaucratical and convention-loving community for the open space and untrammelled freedom of the desert. It thus rejuvenated and reinvigorated the race, and enabled them to enter on that career of conquest which culminated in the Kingdom—may we not say the Empire?—of David. Some writers have supposed that the blow to the Egyptian power was greater than here represented. They believe the entire warrior caste or class to have taken part in the expedition, and to have been destroyed in the Red Sea. Thus they describe the calamity as " the total annihilation of the whole military force of the Egyptians " (Kalisch). They also believe the Pharaoh to have perished with his host. To the present writer it seems that the former opinion is contrary both to the text of Scripture, and to the after course of Egyptian history, for it is agreed on all hands that Egypt continued nearly as powerful as before, while the latter he regards as at least exceedingly doubtful. Ps. lxxxvi. 15, is quoted as asserting it; but it appears to him (1) that " overthrow " is not necessarily " death ; " and (2) that " Pharaoh and his host " may be put for " Pharaoh's host " by *hendiadys.* The absence of any prophecy that God would take the Pharaoh's life, and the entire silence of Moses on the subject in chs. xiv. and xv. seems to be scarcely explicable on any other theory than that he escaped, not having accompanied his chariot force in its rash pursuit of the Israelites.

HOMILETICS.

Vers. 23—30.—*God's dealings with the wicked and impenitent.* If the passage of Israel through the Red Sea shows conspicuously God's protection of his people in the time of trouble, the overthrow of the Egyptians indicates, at least as conspicuously, his execution of wrath upon the wicked.

I. First of all, IT IS NOTICEABLE HOW HIS EYE UPON THEIR HEARTS, LOOKING INTO THEM THROUGH THE CLOUD AND DARKNESS WHEREIN THEY ARE ENVELOPED, TROUBLES THEM. Bad men cannot bear God's eye upon their hearts. It sees through all veils, penetrates all disguises, detects all subterfuges. The bad man is a riddle, even to himself, and would feign continue an enigma, impenetrable, mysterious. But the searching eye of God turned full upon him, so illuminates every dark corner and unexplored cranny of his nature, that all becomes only too patent and clear. "All things are naked and open unto the eyes of him with whom we have to do." Under that steadfast gaze the mystery melts away, like a summer fog, and the bad man sees himself revealed, without disguise as a very ordinary and commonplace offender.

II. IT IS WORTHY OF OBSERVATION THAT HE OFTEN CLOGS THEIR CHARIOT WHEELS, AND MAKES THEM TO GO HEAVILY. The enterprises which the wicked undertake are continually interfered with. God will not let them have the success which their framers anticipate, and which for their cleverness and ingenuity they may be said to deserve. He "clogs the wheels" of their various designs, and makes them drag heavily. One miscarriage follows another. This enterprise will not advance at all; that, by dint of great exertion, moves but slowly. It is as though the chariot wheels sank into quicksands. It is not often that they wake up to the conviction that "the Lord fighteth against the Egyptians;" though this may happen sometimes. Then perhaps they repent them of their vain attempt, and would feign retreat from it. But it is TOO LATE.

III. IT IS MOST NOTICEABLE HOW AT LAST GOD'S JUDGMENTS COME IN WITH AN OVERWHELMING FLOOD, WHICH THERE IS NO ESCAPING. "It is a fearful thing to fall into the hands of the living God." Upon the ungodly God at the last rains down "snares, fire and brimstone, storm and tempest—this is their portion to drink." "Sudden destruction comes upon them unawares." Now it is in financial ruin, now in utter failure of health, now in complete prostration of the spirit, and an intolerable sense of remorse and despair that the judgment descends—blow follows blow, failure succeeds to failure, all the old refuges and supports prove unavailing—angry floods pour in on every side— there is no reaching the shore—all is tossing surf, slippery rock, and entangling seaweed—not a hand is stretched out to save. So they go down to the pit—the devouring waves swallow them up—the water-floods go up over their heads—they disappear, and their place knows them no more. The wages of sin is death; and the end of sin is death. The ultimate end of impenitent sin is eternal death. Let men, *while there is time,* turn away from sin, give up their wicked enterprises, retrace their steps—taking warning from the awful Red Sea calamity, and the terrible destruction there wrought.

HOMILIES BY VARIOUS AUTHORS.

Vers. 23—31.—*The overthrow of the Egyptians.* "The Egyptians pursued, and went in after them to the midst of the sea," etc. On this observe:—

I. THE INFATUATION OF THE PURSUERS (ver. 23). We do not speak of the lessons they had *already* received as to the folly of contending with Jehovah. The plagues were past. The memory of them had been cast behind their backs. What we do wonder at is, that when the Egyptians reached the shore, and saw there what they *did* see, they were not deterred from proceeding further. What did they see? 1. *They saw the sea divided.* They could hardly mistake this for a merely natural phenomenon. The place where the Israelites crossed may have been, under special conditions, and to a limited extent, fordable. But it is safe to say that the division now effected was one the like of which had never been heard of before, and such as, occurring at this particular juncture, ought to have convinced the Egyptians that it was a result of God's special Providence, and intended for the protection of the Israelites. Special interpositions, on behalf of the Church, ought to arrest the attention of her enemies. 2. *They saw the cloud that went with Israel move to the rear,* obviously with the design of intercepting their pursuit (vers. 19, 20). This, with the ominous darkness which enveloped them, was a second circumstance which ought to have warned them that Jehovah was fighting for his people. 3. *There was the danger, which could not but present itself to them, of being overwhelmed by the returning sea.* In whatever way the division of the waters was conceived of, whether as a natural phenomenon, or as a fact of supernatural origin, it was plainly a perilous experiment to attempt the pursuit. Viewing it as the result of an ebb-tide, aided by a strong east wind, there was the risk of being caught by the returning tide; or if the wind abated, or changed its direction, of being immediately submerged. In the other case there was the danger, almost the certainty, of the supernatural power which restrained the waters permitting them to flow back on the pursuers. What infatuation, then, possessed the Egyptians, prompting them to enter the sea? (1) *A false sense of honour.* Having engaged in the pursuit, it would be deemed a point of honour not to desist from it, so long as the faintest chance of success remained. They had gone too far to retreat now at the water's edge. (2) *Rage.* Fury and disappointment would possess them, as, in the very hour of their fancied triumph, they saw their prey thus elude them. Was Pharaoh and his mighty host to be thus mocked and set at nought—thus suddenly reined up and baffled? What would Egypt think of her warriors, if, setting out on such an expedition, they returned humiliated and empty-handed? At all hazards Israel must be pursued. (3) There was the *chance* of getting through. The distance was short; the way lay open; if Israel had got across, so might the Egyptians. On this chance, in the spirit of the gambler, they would stake everything. What havoc have these same motives—a false sense of honour (cf. Matt. xiv. 9), a spirit of uncalculating rage, the headstrong *gambling* disposition,—played in the history of the world! Together, or apart, they account for much of its infatuation. See specially in this conduct of Pharaoh, a picture of the infatuation to which the enemies of Christ's Church have so frequently been given over, and which will linger among them till the end. Compare *e.g.* the Apocalyptic gathering of the antichristian powers, to do battle with the Lamb (Rev. xvi. 14—17; xix. 11—21).

II. THE RECEPTION WHICH THEY RECEIVED FROM GOD. 1. In "the morning watch," and when the Egyptians were in "the midst of the sea," *God looked forth upon them from the pillar of cloud* (ver. 23). The expression is a pregnant one. The look was a "fire-look"—some fire-appearance of a startling kind which issued from the cloud, and shed terror over the pursuers. It was accompanied with thunderings and lightnings (Ps. lxxvii. 18, 19). God's looks are potent. When God "looked" on Israel (ch. ii. 25), it meant that he was about to bring salvation to them. When he "looked" on the Egyptians, it was the prelude to their destruction. Through that pillar glares forth an eye which sends a separate dismay into each Egyptian heast and all is felt to be lost. We find two imitations of this in modern poetry—one by Coleridge, in his 'Ode on the Departing Year,' where he prays God to—

"Open his eye of fire from some uncertain cloud,"

and another (by Southey) in the 'Curse of Kehama,' where, after the 'Man Almighty,' holding his Amreeta Cup, had exclaimed—

"Now, Seeva, look to thine abode!"

it is added, when the cup is drunk—

"Then Seeva open'd on the accursed one
His *eye of anger*—upon him alone
The wrath beam fell. He shudders, *but too late.*" (Gilfillan.)

2. *God troubled their hosts* (vers. 24, 25). There is meant by this some supernatural exertion of power. It was not due to natural causes alone that the chariot wheels were "taken off," and that they drave heavily. It was God who, by his heavy hand upon them, was thus obstructing their progress. The invisible powers were fighting against the Egyptians, as "the stars in their courses fought against Sisera" (Jud. v. 20).

Those are sure to drive heavily, who drive in the face of God's inhibition, and under his ban.   3. *God brought the sea back upon them* (ver. 26).   Swiftly, fatally, at the stretching forth of Moses' rod, the sea returned in its strength, and utterly overwhelmed them.   And such, in its main outline, is the reception which Jehovah must give to all his enemies.   His wrath already rests upon them.   His fiery look will one day scare them.   Even now they are troubled and impeded by it, and by the resistance which he opposes to their plans.   Finally, he will overwhelm them in the sea of his wrath.   He will visit them with "everlasting destruction from the presence of the Lord, and from the glory of his power" (1 Thess. i. 9).   Hence—

III. THEIR COMPLETE DESTRUCTION (vers. 27, 28).   They perished suddenly, miserably, and all together.   Type of the overthrow of God's enemies in the end (2 Thess. ii. 8; Rev. xvi. 16, 17; xix. 17—21; xx. 9).   The blow was a crushing one to Egypt. It filled up the measure of her punishment for the evil she had done to Israel.   After the death of the first-born, there could remain nothing to Pharaoh and his servants, in the event of their still hardening themselves, but "a certain fearful looking for of judgment, and fiery indignation" (Heb. x. 27).   Does some one say, what a waste of human life—how unlike a God of mercy!   Rather, surely, how striking a testimony to the reality of retribution—how sure a token of the righteous doom which in the end will infallibly overtake every obdurate transgressor!   God will not permit sinners always to defy him.   His wrath and power are resistless.   The "ungodly and sinner" must expect to feel the weight of them (1 Pet. 17, 18).

IV. RESULT (vers. 30, 31).   1. Israel was saved.   2. The Egyptian dead were found strewn upon the shore.   This—(1) A memorial of God's vengeance.   (2) An awful satire on so-called human greatness.   (3) A pledge of security to Israel.   3. The people were filled with gratitude and fear.   They "believed the Lord."   The wonder is that after so marvellous a deliverance they could ever again doubt him.—J. O.

THE

BOOK OF EXODUS

VOL. II

EXPOSITION.

CHAPTER XV.

Vers. 1—21.—THE SONG OF MOSES. Full of
gratitude, joy, and happiness—burning with a
desire to vent in devotional utterance of the
most fitting kind, his intense and almost
ecstatic feelings, Moses, who to his other
extraordinary powers, added the sublime gift
of poesy, composed, shortly after the passage,
a hymn of praise, and sang it with a chorus
of the people as a thanksgiving to the
Almighty. The hymn itself is generally
allowed to be one of transcendent beauty.
Deriving probably the general outline of its
form and character of its rhythm from the
Egyptian poetry of the time, with which
Moses had been familiar from his youth, it
embodies ideas purely Hebrew, and remarkable for grandeur, simplicity, and depth.
Naturally, as being the first outburst of the
poetical genius of the nation, and also connected with the very commencement of the
national life, it exerted the most important
formative influence upon the later Hebrew
poetic style, furnishing a pattern to the later
lyric poets, from which they but rarely

deviated. The "parallelism of the members,"
which from the middle of the last century has
been acknowledged to be the only real
rhythmical law of Hebrew poetry, with its
three forms of "synonymous, antithetic, and
synthetic (or verbal) parallelism" is here
found almost as distinctly marked as in any of
the later compositions. At the same time, a
greater lyrical freedom is observable than was
afterwards practised. The song divides itself
primarily into two parts:—the first (vers.
1—12) *retrospective*, celebrating the recent
deliverance; the second (vers. 13—18) *prospective*, describing the effects that would flow
from the deliverance in future time. The
verbs indeed of the second part are at first
grammatical preterites; but (as Kalisch observes) they are "according to the sense,
futures"—their past form denoting only that
the prophet sees the events revealed to him
as though they were already accomplished.
Hence, after a time, he slides into the future
(ver. 16). The second part is continuous, and
has no marked break: the first sub-divides
into three unequal portions, each commencing
with an address to Jehovah, and each termi-

nating with a statement of the great fact, that the Egyptians were swallowed up. These three portions are: 1. vers. 2—5, "The Lord is my strength," to "They sank into the bottom as a stone." 2. vers. 6—10, "Thy right hand, O Lord," to "They sank like lead in the mighty waters." 3. vers. 11—12, "Who is like unto Thee, O Lord," to "The earth swallowed them." The first verse stands separate from the whole, as an introduction, and at the same time as the refrain. Moses and a chorus of men commenced their chant with it, and probably proceeded to the end of ver. 5, when Miriam, with the Hebrew women, interposed with a repetition of the refrain (see ver. 21). The chant of the males was resumed and carried to the close of ver. 10, when again the refrain came in. It was further repeated after ver. 12; and once more at the close of the whole "song." Similar refrains, or burdens, are found in Egyptian melodies

PART I.

Ver. 1.—**Then sang Moses and the children of Israel.** It is in accordance with the general modesty of Moses, that he says nothing of the composition of the "song." No serious doubt of his authorship has ever been entertained; but the general belief rests on the improbability of there having been among the Israelites a second literary genius of the highest order, without any mention being made of him. The joint-singing by Moses and "the children of Israel" implies the previous training of a choir, and would seem to show that the Israelites remained for some days encamped at the point which they had occupied on quitting the bed of the sea. **He hath triumphed gloriously.** Literally, "He is gloriously glorious." (ἐνδόξως δεδόξασται, LXX.) **The horse and his rider.** Rather, "The horse and his *driver*." Chariots, not cavalry, are in the mind of the writer.

Ver. 2.—**The Lord is my strength and song.** Literally, "My strength and song is Jah." The name *Jah* had not previously been used. It is commonly regarded as an abbreviated form of Jehovah, and was the form generally used in the termination of names, as Abijah, Ahaziah, Hezekiah, Zedekiah, Mount Moriah, etc. It takes the place of "Jehovah" here, probably on account of the rhythm. **He is become my salvation.** Literally, "He has been to me for salvation," *i.e.*, "He has delivered me out of the hand of Pharaoh and his host, and so saved me from destruction." **I will prepare him a habitation.** This translation seems to have come originally from the Targum of Onkelos, who paraphrases the

single word of the text by the phrase "I will build him a sanctuary." The meaning is a possible one: but most modern commentators prefer to connect the verb used with a root meaning "beautiful," and translate "I will glorify him." (So Gesenius, Rosenmüller, Knobel, Kalisch, Cook. The LXX have δοξάσω. The Vulgate has *glorificabo*. The Syrian and Coptic versions agree, as do also the Targums of Jonathan and of Jerusalem.) **The God of my father.** See the comment on ch. iii. 6.

Ver. 3.—**A man of war.** A strong anthropomorphism, but one that could scarcely be misunderstood—"a man of war," meaning commonly "a warrior," or "one mighty in battle" (Ps. xxiv. 8). God's might had just been proved, in that he alone had discomfited and destroyed the most potent armed force in the whole world. **The Lord is his name.** Jehovah—the alone-existing One "truly describes him," before whom all other existence fades and falls into nothingness. On the full meaning of the name, see the comment on ch. iii. 14.

Ver. 4.—**Pharaoh's chariots and his host.** The "host" of this passage is not the "army" of ch. xiv. 9, though in the original the same word is used, but the whole multitude of those who rode in the chariots, and were drowned in the sea. **Hath he cast.** Or "hurled." The verb commonly expresses the hurling of a javelin or the shooting of an arrow. **His chosen captains.** Compare ch. xiv. 7. **Are drowned.** Literally, "were submerged." The word describes the act of drowning, not the state of lying drowned in the depths of the sea.

Ver. 5.—**The depths have covered them.** Rather "covered them." **Into the bottom.** Literally, "into the abyss." **Like a stone.** The warriors who fought in chariots commonly wore coats of mail, composed of bronze plates sewn on to a linen base, and overlapping one another. The coats covered the arms to the elbow, and descended nearly to the knee. They must have been exceedingly heavy: and the warrior who wore one must have sunk at once, without a struggle, like a stone or a lump of lead (verse 10).

Vers. 6—18.—Between verses 5 and 6, Miriam's chorus was probably interposed— "Sing ye unto the Lord," etc. Then began the second strophe or stanza of the ode. It is, in the main, expansive and exegetical of the preceding stanza, going into greater detail, and drawing a contrast between the antecedent pride and arrogance of the Egyptians and their subsequent miserable fall.

Ver. 6.—**Thy right hand, O Lord.** Another anthropomorphism, here used for the first time. Compare ver. 12; Deut. xxxiii. 2; and the

Psalms, *passim*. **Is become glorious.** Or "is glorious." Kalisch rightly regards verses 6 and 7 as containing "a general description of God's omnipotence and justice," and notes that the poet only returns to the subject of the Egyptians in verse 8. So also Knobel. **Hath dashed in pieces.** Rather, "Will dash in pieces," or "dashes in pieces" a general statement.

Ver. 7.—**Thou hast overthrown,** etc. Here again the verbs are future. Translate—"thou wilt overthrow," or "thou overthrowest them that rise up against thee; thou (wilt send) sendest forth thy wrath, which consumes them as stubble." The metaphor in the last clause was one known to the Egyptians.

Ver. 8.—**With the blast of thy nostrils the waters were gathered together.** Poetically, Moses describes the east wind which God set in motion as "the blast" or "breath of his nostrils." By means of it, he says, the waters were "gathered together," or "piled up;" then, growing bolder in his imagery, he represents the floods as "standing in a heap" on either side, and the depths as "congealed." No doubt, if these terms are meant to be taken literally, the miracle must have been one in which "the sea" (as Kalisch says) "giving up its nature, formed with its waves a firm wall, and instead of streaming like a fluid, congealed into a hard substance." But the question is, are we justified in taking literally the strong expressions of a highly wrought poetical description?

Ver. 9.—**The enemy said.** This verse is important as giving the *animus* of the pursuit, showing what was in the thoughts of the soldiers who flocked to Pharaoh's standard at his call—a point which had not been previously touched. It is remarkable as a departure from the general stately order of Hebrew poesy, and for what has been called its "abrupt, gasping" style. The broken speech imitates the utterance of one at once eager and out of breath. **I will divide the spoil.** The Israelites, it must be remembered, had gone out of Egypt laden with ornaments of silver and of gold, and accompanied by flocks and herds of great value. Pharaoh's soldiers regarded this wealth as legitimate plunder, and intended to appropriate it. **My lust.** Literally, "my soul." Rage and hate were the passions to be satiated, rather than lust. **My hand shall destroy them.** So the Vulgate, Onkelos, Rosenmüller, Knobel, Kalisch, and others. The LXX. have κυριεύσει, "acquire the lordship over them" (whence our marginal rendering) But the drawn sword points to death rather than recapture.

Ver. 10.—**Thou didst blow with thy wind.** Here we have another fact not mentioned in the direct narrative, but entirely harmonising with it. The immediate cause of the return of the waters, as of their retirement, was a wind. This wind must have come from a new quarter, or its effects would not have been to bring the water back. We may reasonably suppose a wind to have arisen contrary to the former one, blowing from the north-west or the north, which would have driven the water of the Bitter Lakes southward, and thus produced the effect spoken of. The effect may, or may not, have been increased by the flow of the tide in the Red Sea. **They sank as lead.** See the comment on verse 5.

Vers. 11, 12 contain the third stanza of the first division of the ode. It is short compared to the other two, containing merely a fresh ascription of praise to God, cast in a new form; and a repetition of the great fact which the poem commemorates — the Egyptian overthrow. We conceive that Miriam's chorus (ver. 21) was again interposed between verses 10 and 11.

Ver. 11.—**Who is like unto thee, O Lord, among the gods?** It was one great object of the whole series of miraculous visitations whereof Egypt had been the scene, that the true God, Jehovah, should be exalted far above all the gods of the heathen. (See ch. vii. 5; xiv. 4, 18.) Moses therefore makes this one of his topics of praise; and at the same time notes three points in which God has no rival—1. Holiness; 2. Awfulness; and 3. Miraculous power. Compare Ps. lxxxvi. 8; "Among the gods there is none like unto thee, O Lord; neither are there any works like thy works." **Fearful in praises**—*i.e.*, "to be viewed with awe even when we praise Him."

Ver. 12.—**Thou stretchedst out thy right hand.** Thou hadst only to stretch out an arm, and at once thy enemies perished. **The earth swallowed them up**—*i.e.*, the sea, which is a part of the earth.

PART II.

Ver. 13.—**Thou in thy mercy hast led forth.** Or "leadest forth." See the Introduction to the chapter. **Which thou hast redeemed.** See the comment on ch. vi. 6. **Thou hast guided.** Or "thou guidest." **Thy holy habitation.** By "God's holy habitation" some understand Mount Sinai, others Canaan, others Mount Moriah, or even the temple there to be built ultimately. That Sinai is not intended seems clear from verses 14, 15, where the nations mentioned are such as were untouched by the occupation of that mountain. Canaan might sufficiently answer the requirements of the present verse, but scarcely comes up to those of verse 17. Altogether, it is clear that Moses knew there would be a place in the land of Canaan where God would "put his name" (Deut. xii. 5,

11, 14 ; xiv. 23, 24 ; xvi. 6, 11 ; xxvi. 2 ; etc.) ; and it would seem to be not unlikely that he may have known where the place would be by special revelation.

Ver. 14.—**The people shall hear.**—Rather, "the peoples"—*i.e.*, the tribes, or nations, of these parts—Philistines, Amalekites, Edomites, Moabites, etc.—will hear of the wonders done in Egypt, especially of the crowning wonder of all—Israel's passage through the Red Sea and Egypt's destruction in it—and will in consequence tremble with fear when the Israelites approach them, and offer them no effectual opposition. **Palestina.** This is a Greek form. The Hebrew is *Phĕlāsheth*, which would perhaps be best translated "Philistia." (Compare Ps. lx. 8 ; lxxxvii. 4 ; cviii. 9.) The Philistine country was a strip of territory extending along the coast of the Mediterranean from a little below Gaza on the south, nearly to Mount Carmel on the north. It is curious that the Philistines are not mentioned under that name on any of the early Egyptian monuments. They may perhaps be the *Purusata* of the time of Rameses III., whom some however identify with the Pelasgi.

Ver. 15.—**The Dukes of Edom.** Compare Gen. xxxvi. 15. By the time that the Israelites approached the borders of Edom, the dukes had given place to kings (Num. xx. 14), and everything like abject fear of Israel had passed away. The Edomites " came out against Moses with much people and with a strong hand," and refused to allow the Israelites passage through their borders (*ib.* vers. 20, 21). **The mighty men of Moab.** The alarm of the Moabites was indicated by Balak's efforts to induce Balaam to curse the Israelites (Num. xxii.–xxiv.). By their "mighty men" some understood men of unusual strength and stature (Cook) ; but the expression, which is very frequent both in the prophetical and the historical books, seems to be a mere periphrasis for " warriors." **All the inhabitants of Canaan shall melt away.** This prophecy received a remarkable accomplishment when " it came to pass that all the kings of the Canaanites heard that the Lord had dried up the waters of Jordan from before the children of Israel, and *their heart melted*, neither was their spirit in them any more " (Josh. v. 1).

Ver. 16.—**Fear and dread shall fall upon them.** Compare Deut. ii. 25 ; xi. 25. The Edomites of Mount Seir and the Moabites gave Israel a free passage through their borders (Deut. ii. 4–8, 18, 29), being afraid to oppose them. **Till thy people pass over, O Lord.** Some see in this an anticipation of the crossing of Jordan ; but perhaps Moses meant no more than the crossing of the Canaanite frontier, in some place or other, which must take place if the land was to be

occupied. The event made the expression used peculiarly appropriate. **When thou hast purchased.** By bringing his people out of Egypt, their ownership had passed to him from the Egyptians, just as if he had bought them. (See ch. vi. 6, 7 ; xix. 5.)

Ver. 17. **Thou shalt bring them in**—*i.e.*, give them possession of the land. **And plant them**—*i.e.*, fix them firmly in it—enable them to take root there. **The mountain of thine inheritance.** The land of Canaan, which is almost wholly mountainous, and which God had given as an inheritance to his people (Gen. xv. 7 ; Heb. xi. 8). **The sanctuary.** See the comment on verse 13. **Which thy hands have established.** Moses sees in idea the sanctuary already set up, and God dwelling in it ; and emphasises his conviction by using the past tense.

Ver. 18.—In terms most simple yet most grand, often imitated (Ps. x. 16 ; xxix. 10 ; cxlvi. 10, etc.), but never surpassed, the poet gives the final result of all God's providential and temporary arrangements, to wit, the eternal establishment of his most glorious kingdom. And here reaching the final consummation of all things (1 Cor. xv. 28), he will not weaken the impression made by adding another word, but ends his ode.

Vers. 19—21.—*Sequel to the Song.* The " sequel " treats of two quite separate matters. 1. It asserts, in verse 19, the historic groundwork of the song, reiterating in a condensed form the three principal facts of the passage—already recorded in ch. xiv.—(*a*) Israel's safe transit across the sea-bed ; (*b*) the pursuit attempted by the Egyptian chariot-force ; and (*c*) the return of the waters upon the pursuers by God's providential action. 2. It relates, in verses 20 and 21, the part taken by Miriam in the recitation of the ode, which has been noticed in the " introduction " to the chapter.

Ver. 19.—**The horse of Pharaoh, with his chariots, and with his horsemen.** Rather, " with his chariots, and with his chariot men." Compare ch. xiv. 23. **The Lord brought again the waters of the sea upon them.** See ch. xiv. 26, 27 ; and xv. 10. The waters did not merely return to their natural place when the east wind ceased to blow, but were " brought back " by miraculous power, and with abnormal rapidity.

Ver. 20.—**Miriam, the prophetess.** Miriam is regarded by the prophet Micah (vi. 4), as having had a share in the deliverance of Israel, and claims the prophetic gift in Num. xii. 2. Her claim appears to be allowed both in the present passage, and in Num. xii. 6–8. where the degree of her inspiration is placed below that of Moses. She is the first woman whom the Bible honours with the title of "prophetess." Prophetesses were common in Egypt at a much earlier date; and thus, that a woman should have the gift would have seemed no strange thing to the Hebrews. For examples of other prophetesses, see Judg. iv. 4; 2 Kings xxii. 14; Is. viii. 3; Luke ii. 36. **The sister of Aaron.** Compare Num. xxvi. 59. Miriam is generally regarded as the sister of Moses mentioned in Ex. ii. 4—8, whose name is not there given. If so, she was considerably older than either Moses or Aaron. **Took a timbrel.** By "a timbrel" our translators meant what is now called "a tambourine." Such instruments were common in Egypt (Wilkinson, *Ancient Egyptians*, vol. i. p. 93), and in the representations are generally played by women. The separation of the men and women into distinct bands was an Egyptian custom; as likewise was the execution of dances by performers who accompanied their steps with music (*ibid.* vol. ii. pp. 235, 301).

Ver. 21.—**Miriam answered them.** Miriam, with her chorus of women, answered the chorus of men, responding at the termination of each stanza or separate part of the ode with the refrain, "Sing ye to the Lord," etc. (See the "Introduction" to this chapter.) While responding, the female chorus both danced and struck their tambourines. This use of dancing in a religious ceremonial, so contrary to Western ideas of decorum, is quite consonant with Oriental practice, both ancient and modern. Other examples of it in Scripture are David's dancing before the ark (2 Sam. vi. 16), the dancing of Jephthah's daughter (Judg. xi. 34), and that of the virgins of Shiloh (*ib.* xxi. 21). It is also mentioned with approval in the Psalms (cxlix. 3; cl. 4). Dancing was practised as a religious ceremony in Egypt, in Phrygia, in Thrace, by the Phœnicians, by the Syrians, by the Romans, and others. In the nature of things there is clearly nothing unfitting or indecorous in a dedication to religion of what has been called "the poetry of gesture." But human infirmity has connected such terrible abuses with the practice that the purer religions have either discarded it or else denied it admission into their ceremonial. It still however lingers in Mohammedanism among those who are called "dancing dervishes," whose extraordinary performances are regarded as acts of devotion.

HOMILETICS.

Vers. 1—18.—*The song of Moses a pattern thanksgiving.* There is nothing in the whole range of sacred or profane literature more fresh, more vigorous, more teeming with devotional thought than this wonderful poem. In rhythm it is grand and sonorous, in construction skilful and varied, in the quality of the thoughts lofty, in the mode of expression at once simple and sublime. Partly historic, partly prophetic, it describes the past with marvellous power, and gives with a few touches a glorious picture of the future. Throughout it breathes the warmest love of God, the deepest thankfulness to him, the strongest regard for his honour. We may well take it for our model when we have to thank God :—

I. FOR A TEMPORAL DELIVERANCE; and observe (1) its matter; (2) its manner; (3) its form. (1) *Its matter* comprises (*a*) distinct and repeated enunciation of the deliverance itself, with expatiation on its circumstances; (*b*) anticipation of further advantages to flow from the deliverance in the future; (*c*) transition from the particular mercy to the consideration of God's power, greatness and goodness in the abstract; and (*d*) glorification of God on all three accounts. (2) Its manner comprises, among other points, (*a*) beginning and ending with praise; (*b*) intermixture of the praise with the grounds of praise; (*c*) persistence and repetition, but with the introduction of new touches. (3) Its form is (*a*) poetic; (*b*) discontinuous, or broken into stanzas; (*c*) irregular. Our thanksgivings for great national or even great personal deliverances may well, if our powers suffice, take a poetic shape. Poetry is more expressive than prose, more heart-stirring, more enthusiastic. It is also better remembered, and it is less diffuse.

II. FOR SPIRITUAL DELIVERANCE FROM THE EGYPT OF SIN. Each man's deliverance will have its own peculiar features, which he will do well to note and make special subjects of thankfulness, not sparing repetition, that he may present the matter to himself in various lights, and see *all* God's goodness in respect of it. Each deliverance will also lead naturally to prospective thoughts, extending beyond the wilderness of this life to the Canaan which is our inheritance. Each will profitably lead us to go beyond ourselves, and dwell for a while on the general attributes of God, whence proceed the mercies that we individually experience; and we shall do well to praise God on all these accounts. Manner and form are of less importance than matter, and admit of more variety without sensible loss; but even here "the song" furnishes a pattern on which it would be hard to improve. The grounds for preferring poetry to prose for such an outpouring of the heart as a thanksgiving have been already stated. The propriety of beginning and ending with praise is unquestionable. Repetition has a value as deepening impressions, and affording opportunity for remedying accidental coldness or inattention. In private devotion the actual repetition of the very same words has an occasional place, as we see by our Lord's example in the garden of Gethsemane (Matt. xxvi. 44); but in a composition, phrases should be varied. Moses's song may well guide us as to the extent and character of such variation (e.g., vers. 5, 10, and 12).

Vers. 20, 21.—*The aid which devout women can render to the Church.* There are religions which exclude women from consideration altogether, express a doubt whether they have souls, and assign them no special Church work. But Judaism did not make this mistake. It utilised the services of women—

I. As PROPHETESSES. Miriam was a prophetess. So was Deborah, whose song is one of the most beautiful compositions in the Bible (Judges v. 2—31). So was Huldah, who delivered God's message to Hezekiah (2 Kings xxii. 14—20). So was Anna (Luke ii. 36), whom the tradition makes the virgin's mother. God did not disdain to hold spiritual converse with women and enlighten them supernaturally; nor did the Israelites omit to take cognizance of the fact and give such persons their due honour.

II. As NATIONAL DELIVERERS. Deborah "judged Israel" (Judges iv. 4), and it was she, rather than Barak, who delivered the Israelites from Jabin (*ib.* vers. 8, 14). Esther saved her people from the malice of Haman. Judith is said to have delivered them from Holofernes. Sex was no disqualification for high place among the Jews, any more than among their neighbours, the Arabs. The queens of Judah obtain constant mention in Kings and Chronicles.

III. As PARTICIPATORS IN RELIGIOUS CEREMONIALS. In the instance of Miriam we see how an important part of the thanksgiving service which Moses celebrated on the passage of the Red Sea was assigned to females. Apparently, on this occasion, half the chanting, and the whole of the instrumental music, was placed in their hands. Miriam acted as Choragus, or conductor, of the female chorus. Music is one of woman's commonest gifts; and, though not eminent as composers, as renderers of the music of others, they have a fame exceeding that of men. They can do much for the glory of God in contributing to, and even sometimes superintending, the musical services of the sanctuary. In the Christian Church, there has been, equally from the first, a recognition of the services that may be rendered to religion by women. The apostles, after the ascension of our Lord, "continued with one accord in prayer and supplication *with the women, and Mary, the mother of Jesus*" (Acts i. 14). Phœbe, who conveyed to Rome St. Paul's Epistle to the Romans, was "a deaconess of the church that was at Cenchrea" (Rom. xvi. 1); and an Order of deaconesses was generally recognised in the primitive Church, and believed to have been instituted by the apostles (*Apost. Const.* vi. 17). In all periods some church work, in many very important church work, has been assigned to women, with great advantage both to themselves and to the community. Though St. Paul forbade their speaking in the Church (1 Cor. xiv. 35), and they thus cannot be ministers, subordinate employments of various kinds, suited to the nature of women, are everywhere open to them. The work of Sisters of Charity in various parts of the world is above all praise. That of district visitors, teachers in Sunday schools, Scripture readers, etc., though less attracting the praise of men, is most valuable. Devout women, working under their ministers, can be the instruments of incalculable good, and do as much for the promotion of true religion as if they were men.

HOMILIES BY VARIOUS AUTHORS.

Vers. 1—19. *Moses' Song.* The sublimity of this noble ode is universally admitted. It brings Moses before us in the new character of "poet." Moses does not seem to have devoted himself largely to this species of composition; but the three specimens of his work which remain to us—this ode, his "Song" and "Blessing" in Deuteronomy, and Ps. xc.—show him to have possessed a poetical genius of the very highest order; to have been as great as poet, as we know him to have been as warrior, leader, statesman, legislator, historian, patriot, and saint. The grandest features of poetry belong to the thrilling piece before us. It is the magnificent outburst of the feeling of uncontrollable triumph, awakened by the sight of the overthrow of the Egyptians in the Red Sea, and by the sense of deliverance and safety thence resulting. The language quakes and thunders in keeping with the grandeur of the theme. The presentation of the ideas is in the highest degree picturesque. The strokes of imagery are masterpieces—the whole scene of defeat and disaster being repeatedly revealed, as by lurid lightning-flashes, in single sentences, and even single words. The movement is rapid, rhythmical, inspiring. The art displayed in the minutiæ of literary construction is very great, while in all, and through all, pervading, as its energising soul, every syllable and stanza of the composition, is the spirit of adoring awe 'and wonder, blending with gratitude, which ascribes all the greatness, and honour, and renown, of the victory to Jehovah. We have to touch at present, however, less on the literary beauties than on the religious teaching of the ode ; and the nature of this, after what has been said on ch. xiv., admits of being briefly indicated.

I. THE TRIUMPH CELEBRATED (vers. 1, 2). This celebration of the deliverance at the Red Sea was—1. *Natural.* Adoring and exultant feeling naturally passes into song. It seeks expression. It tends to become rhythmical. It unites itself with music. Like mountain torrents, tearing down to the plain, and cutting their channels as they flow, pent-up emotion of this kind will not be denied utterance, and if suitable channels of rhythmical expression are not provided for it, will cut out channels for itself. 2. *Appropriate.* It was *right* that, having experienced this great deliverance, the children of Israel should give utterance, in strains of praise, to the feelings of wonder, gratitude, and adoration with which it inspired them. It was due to God, and it would be beneficial in its reactive effects upon themselves. The duty of praise for benefits received is one to which no religious mind can be indifferent. If God has gifted us with the faculty of song, it is right that the first use we make of it should be to extol his goodness. See the Psalms (Ps. xcii. 1 ; xcviii. 1 ; cv. 1, 2 ; cxi. 1 ; etc.). 3. *Elevating.* The faculty of song is not merely *one* of the faculties of our nature. It is connected with that which is deepest in us. When the Psalmist bids his faculty of song awake, he speaks of it as his "glory."—"Awake up, my glory" (Ps. lvii. 8 ; cf. Ps. xvi. 9 ; xxx. 12). It is Carlyle who says—"All *deep* things are musical." Song, in its higher reaches, unites all the faculties of the soul in consentaneous exercise— heart, intellect, conscience, the religious nature, imagination, the artistic and tuneful sentiments, the social feelings. It arouses, elevates, fructifies, enkindles. It awakens the spirit to the sense of its own infinitude ; fills it with scorn of what is base ; attunes and harmonises it to what is noble. We do well, therefore, to cultivate the faculty of song ; to exercise it in public and in private worship ; to make it the daily vehicle of the expression of our religious feelings. "Speaking to yourselves in psalms and hymns," etc. (Eph. v. 19). See that the melody is from the heart, yet with the understanding also (1 Cor. xiv. 15).

II. THE TRIUMPH DESCRIBED (vers. 3—13). The quick, abrupt, vivid language of the ode brings the whole scene of Pharaoh's pursuit and destruction before us, almost as if it were transacting in our sight. The hot, breathless, intensely eager *pursuit* is depicted in ver. 9, but it is chiefly the *destruction* that is dwelt on, and dwelt on in such terms, with the use of such similes, and in such relations of contrast to the proud monarch's insolence and boasting, as limns it with photographic distinctness on the mental vision. The design in the description being to exalt and glorify God's power in the overthrow, the points chiefly exhibited are these—1. The *ease* of this destruction. It is done in an instant, and without effort. In striking contrast with Pharaoh's para- phernalia of war, with his savage exertions in pursuit, and with his elaborate drawing out of his purposes in ver. 9—"I will pursue, I will overtake, I will divide the spoil," etc.—God simply blows with his wind, and the enemy is annihilated. "Thou didst blow with thy wind ; the sea covered them ; they sank as lead in the mighty waters" (ver. 10). A movement of his hand, a blast of his nostrils, a solitary waft from the heat of his anger, suffices to destroy them. 2. The *swiftness* of it. This, which was a most impressive feature of the overthrow, is brought out in various images. "The depths have covered them ; *they sank to the bottom as a stone . . . they sank as lead* in the mighty waters" (vers. 5—10). 3. The *fatality* of it. The destruction was complete. There was no recovery from it. Horse and chariot and charioteer; the chosen captains; the whole array of Pharaoh's military strength—all went down in one swift, fell swoop, to the sea-bottom. "Thy right hand, O Lord, hath *dashed in pieces* the enemy" (ver. 6). Pondering these images, we cannot but be impressed by the folly, the insanity, as well as the futility, of all attempts at contending with the Almighty.

III. THE ATTRIBUTES OF GOD AS REVEALED IN THE TRIUMPH. These, naturally, are made conspicuous in the ode. It was Jehovah, not Israel, who had achieved the triumph; and to Jehovah, accordingly, was all the praise due. Further, the design in the transaction had been precisely this: to display the character of God as Jehovah, and give a new demonstration of his possession of the attributes denoted by the name Jah (vers. 2, 3). The attributes of Jehovah specially extolled are—1. *Power.* "Thy right hand, O Lord, is become glorious in power" (ver. 6). The greatness of this power is seen by its being measured against the military might of Pharaoh, which thereby becomes a foil to it: another measure being found in the might and fury of the elements which it controls—winds, mighty waters, etc. Its resistlessness is seen in the suddenness and decisiveness of the overthrow. 2. *Supremacy* (vers. 11—18). This attribute, which is of the very essence of the Jehovah conception, was signally illustrated in the Red Sea catastrophe (Ps. cxxxv. 6). Not only was God therein revealed as absolute Ruler in the domain of nature, but it was shown how Pharaoh himself, pursuing his own end, was yet *bent* to be an instrument in accomplishing God's; how, when he thought he was freest, and most certain of victory, God had the hook in his jaws, and was leading all his host straight into the grave prepared for him; how, accordingly, God is Supreme Ruler in the moral as well as in the natural world, in the region of human wills as well as in that of natural causation. 3. *Holiness.* The holiness of God, burning like fire among stubble, and utterly consuming the hosts of the enemy, is justly celebrated in these verses (ver. 7). God was revealed as "glorious in holiness" (ver. 13); and because he was so, Israel was filled with awe in his presence (ver. 13), and his habitation is spoken of as an "holy habitation" (ver. 13), a sanctuary (ver. 17). 4. *Mercy.* This is the other side of the transaction of the Red Sea—the side of deliverance, as the former was of judgment, and mention is made of it in vers. 2, 13. Here, then, is a wonderful constellation of Divine attributes—exhibited, too, not in word, but in suitable action, in deeds which gave them embodiment, and impressive manifestation. They are the same attributes which have been at work all down history, operating for the good of the Church, and for the overthrow of evil.

IV. THE EFFECTS OF THE TRIUMPH (vers. 13—18). It is viewed—1. As inspiring fear in the surrounding nations, in Edom, in Moab, among the Philistines, and other inhabitants of Canaan. Every powerful manifestation of God's attributes is fitted to awaken terror among his enemies, and actually does so. Results similar to those here described will follow the great predicted judgments on the last representatives of Antichristianism (Rev. xi. 13). The nations who heard of Israel's deliverance would have *reason* to fear, for their position exposed them to risk of attack, and Canaan was actually the destination of the tribes. This may suggest to us that if Israel had gone up to conquer these tribes, at the time when God wished them, they would not have found the conquest so hard as their fears represented. The Philistines and Canaanites were "melted" with terror: they were paralysed by their fears, and "still as a stone" (vers. 15, 16). Yet, through the unbelief and cowardice of the attacking force, this great opportunity was missed. 2. As a pledge that God would complete the work he had begun, and would ultimately "plant them in the mountain of his inheritance" (vers. 13—17). In several of the expressions, the tenses are past, as though the thing prophesied were already as good as done. This also is an apostle's mode of arguing—God who has done the greater, will not now fail to do the less, and perfect the work he has begun (Rom. v. 9, 10; viii. 32; Phil. i. 6). Mark in this ode the designation of Israel as a redeemed, a purchased people (ver. 13)—the Red Sea deliverance being viewed as a second purchasing of Israel by God to himself.—J. O.

Vers. 1—20, 21.—*The song of Moses and of the Lamb.* We cannot fail to connect in our thoughts the circumstances of this magnificent triumph-celebration with that other scene, described in the Apocalypse, where they who have "gotten the victory over the beast, and over his image, and over the number of his name, stand on—*i.e.*, on the margin of—the sea of glass, having the harps of God," and "sing the song of Moses, the servant of God, and the song of the Lamb" (Rev. xv. 2). We do not enter into any elaborate explication of the Apocalyptic symbols. The beast and his followers obviously represent the Antichristian foes of the Church—the worldly secular powers that resist, oppose, and persecute the true servants of Christ. God's judgment on these hostile world-powers, already summarily depicted in ch. xiv. 19, 20, is to be afterwards more fully described under the imagery of the seven last plagues. This vision of the multitudes on the sea of glass is anticipative, and represents the celebration by the Church of her own deliverance, and of the completion of judgment upon her enemies. The "sea of glass" has obvious reference to the Red Sea, made to roll back, and stand up like a sea of crystal (ver. 8), yet illuminated and filled with lurid radiance, by the fiery glow of the pillar which shone on Israel. The "sea" is the symbol (in this instance) of deliverance achieved, of victory won, of enemies judged and overwhelmed—the fire in the crystal pointing to the burning wrath which consumed them. But what we have immediately to do with is the fact that the saved multitudes sing the "song of Moses, and of the Lamb." This plainly does not mean that they sing *two* songs; nor yet that the song which they sing is the song recorded here; for the terms of what they sing are subsequently given (Rev. xv. 3, 4). The meaning is that the Church, having experienced a deliverance similar to that experienced by Israel at the Red Sea, but as much *greater* than that old deliverance, as Christ is greater than Moses, and his salvation greater than the salvation from Egypt,—the old song is re-cast, and its terms re-adapted, to express both victories at once, the lower and the higher. The old is taken up into the new and is celebrated along with it. No victory of God for his Church will ever pass out of remembrance. Each will be the theme of grateful celebration to all eternity. But type must merge in antitype, and be celebrated with it in a single strain. The song of the redeemed over the defeat of the Antichristian powers at the end—over the defeat of *all* their enemies—is the true counterpart of this song of Moses, and the one (the latter) remains for ever the background of the other (the former), and is blended with it in the united celebration. Glancing at the two songs, this in Exodus, and that in the Revelation, we note—1. That the *scope* of both is the same—the defeat of hostile, pursuing, persecuting powers. And as the defeat of Pharaoh was the natural sequel to the exodus, and confirmed to Israel that redemption then achieved, so will the defeat of Christ's enemies in the end appear as the appropriate sequel to his work upon the Cross, and will complete the deliverance of his Church from those that trouble her (2 Thess. i. 6). 2. That the *attributes of God* extolled in both are the same. This of necessity, for the work being similar, so must be the attributes revealed in it—holiness, power, unchallengeable supremacy, justice and truth, which here include mercy. "Great and marvellous are thy works, Lord God Almighty," etc. (Rev. xv. 3). The effects produced on the nations by this display of God's attributes are also similar— "who shall not fear thee, O Lord, and glorify thy name . . . for all nations shall come and worship before thee." A higher result this, however, than in the case of the type. 3. The *singers* in both cases are the same—those viz. who have experienced the deliverance which they celebrate. Would we join them? We, too, must be in Christ, and partakers with those who, in the strength which he gives, are overcoming the world (1 John iv. 4).—J. O.

Vers. 1—19.—*The song of triumph—God exalted in the lips of the people.* This song we may take as being in some measure the result and expression of the state of feeling mentioned in ch. xiv. 31. People who feared Jehovah and believed in him were very likely, in such a rush of feeling, to sing as did the Israelites here : at the same time we must be careful not to rest content with attributing this song *merely to natural causes.* There is no need to deny the presence of genius; if only we bear in mind at the same time, that it is genius elevated and sanctified by the inspiration which Jehovah alone can give. Who else than God himself can lead into a true acquaintance with him? and if they who thus know him would speak of him and sing of him, it must be with such an arrangement of thoughts and choice of expressions as he alone can supply. The history of hymnology makes it very evident that genius is not enough for distinction in this sacred service. Poems full of genius, and almost faultless in form, are yet worthless for praise. For in this as other matters God has taken the weak things of the world to confound the things that are mighty. He puts the holy and eternal fire on lips that the world despises. They who have made the praises of the Church have not been the writers of epics; they are not found among the poets-laureate; and so here we must look for the power of God as much in the construction of this song, as in the production of the events it celebrates. We are called on to observe him who somehow makes men to utter even more than they know. It may be needful at the proper time to consider this as a contribution to Hebrew poetry; it is better still ever to remember it as a contribution to the worthy praise of God, that praise which while it celebrates him, instructs and ennobles the man who renders it. The question of authorship here, bear in mind, is not to be settled right off by saying that Moses composed it. He and the people sang it, but who composed it is quite another question. And that this point is left undetermined only throws us back more on the thought of God as the great agent in bringing this song into existence. *As to the topics treated of in the song*, the very fact that there have been so many different ways of dividing it, makes one more disposed to consider it in its unity, without any attempt to divide it into sections at all. Thus then let us notice in succession the dominant truths and convictions which run through the song. The first point is the exaltation of God amongst his people. This is the word with which the song begins. "I will sing unto Jehovah, for he is highly exalted."

I. NOTICE THE FACT THAT THERE IS EXALTATION OF GOD. God, in ruling the composition of this song, takes care of this most important point. It was the very point that needed to be brought out in all its prominence, so that no man should be exalted instead of God. Men exalt one another. They are constituted so as to admire that which is great and powerful, and when they are not men of faith, able to comprehend the greatness of the invisible God, their admiration must needs expend itself on the visible man. All temptation of this kind is here kept out of the way. The feeling that Jehovah is exalted runs all through the song. Everything is ascribed to him. Moses himself makes no claim, expects no praise. The people do not gather round him and hail him as deliverer. The tone of the praise is thus in perfect harmony with the deed that has been done. God becomes practically everything and man nothing. *For what had Israel done here?* They had indeed walked down to the Red Sea, through it, and on to the other side, but no one who regards the proprieties of language would speak of this as contributing to their salvation. We do not praise a man for availing himself of the conditions of safety. Thus we have a type of the way in which God is exalted and glorified in spiritual salvation. When we consider what has to be done in saving a man from his sins; and when we consider also the manifestations, so abundant, so transcendent, of God's power in doing so, then how plainly incongruous it is to begin praising man for that simple act of faith by which he avails himself of God's goodness in Christ. The more we consider, the more we shall feel that whatever praise man may deserve is better left to God to express. By all means let us have brotherly appreciation for brotherly kindness; brotherly gratitude encouraging brotherly love. But God only can praise rightly. Though nothing is said of Moses in this song, God took ample care of the fame and reward of his faithful servant. We had better keep to that which God requires from us, namely, praise to himself. As he requires it, so we may be sure he will fit us to render it.

II. THE EXALTATION OF JEHOVAH IS AN EXALTATION TO SUPREMACY. He is supreme over physical force in one of its most imposing forms. "The horse and his rider hath he thrown into the sea." Perhaps those who have had to meet a charge of cavalry in the battle-field can best appreciate this expression. Jehovah is a man of war, and he goes out with strange weapons against great kings and their chosen captains; weapons which they cannot understand and cannot meet. He does not meet sword with sword, and chariot with chariot; the elements of nature are at his instant and entire command. In his hand *the mightiest* are as nothing. What is the excellency of Pharaoh, even though he be king of Egypt, before the greatness of the excellency of Jehovah? The answer is that as stubble before the fire, so is opposing man before Almighty God. "What a wind that must be, that strong east wind which raises waters, even from the deep, and keeps them when they are raised!" So we imagine *man* speaking in his inevitable submission to the powers of nature when they are roused. But when God has to speak of the east wind, it is as of something which comes as easily as a blast from the nostrils. True, this expression is chiefly used to indicate his wrath; but it also indicates the ease—if ease be a fitting word to use of Jehovah—with which his work is done. In ver. 9, man is represented as resolving and rushing forth in the utmost confidence; anticipating the end from the beginning; certain of his resources and certain of the result, and then as he advances in all his pride and ostentation, God meets him in equal simplicity and sublimity. "*Thou didst blow with thy breath*, the sea covered them; they sank as lead in the mighty waters." One breath from God, and the mightiest fabric goes down like a house of cards! Man accumulates his resources, he strains with prodigious efforts, he gathers his forces without mercy and without scruple; and then when all is in array, God calmly lifts his right hand, and the earth swallows the preparation and the pride of years.

III. THERE IS THE EXALTATION OF GOD ABOVE ALL OTHER DEITIES WORSHIPPED BY MEN. "Who is like unto thee, O Jehovah, among the gods?" This, of course, is also an illustration of Jehovah's exaltation to supremacy. Moses and the Israelites had not attained the feeling that all other deities than Jehovah were but empty and delusive names. That discovery was reserved in the wisdom of God for later and prepared generations. The feeling that the gods of the nations were real beings with terrible power, was very potent in the breasts of the Israelites, as was evidenced by their frequent and facile lapses into idolatry. Therefore this uplifting of Jehovah above the gods was most appropriate praise to put into the lips of Israel at this time. The gods of Egypt represented the strength of Egypt; the gods of Philistia the strength of Philistia; the gods of every country the strength of every country where they were worshipped. When the strength of a land was broken, it was like writing Ichabod on the statue of its presiding deity.

IV. THIS WAS AN EXALTATION IN SUPREMACY WHICH EXTENDED TO THE FUTURE. God, shown supreme in the midst of his people and over their enemies, will maintain and manifest that supremacy in all the time to come. The calamities of Egypt travelling, as it had done, in the path of ten humiliations, and now utterly overthrown, are to be made known in Philistia, in Edom, in Moab, and all through Canaan. Here we find some explanation of the apprehension with which the progress of Israel was afterwards viewed, as by the Edomites and Balak. The Israelites came to be looked on to some extent as a peculiar foe. The utter destruction of a whole army in the Red Sea was not an event which could be kept in a corner. God had now done something for Israel which enemies might notice as a measure and an index of what would yet be done. Then from the mention of these typical enemies, Philistia, Moab, etc., we are led to consider *the abiding enemies of God's abiding people*, those invisible ones who are fully known only to God himself. They have some sense that what has been done by Jesus against them is the measure of what will yet be done. Just as the Philistines felt the sound of Pharaoh's destruction echoing against their fastnesses, and even in the very echo, shaking them, so we may be sure the principalities and powers of evil felt the greatness of what had been achieved when Christ was raised from the dead. That great act of Jehovah has been far more appreciated in the invisible world, among the powers of evil, than it is among us. They cannot but feel what the end will be. What forgetting fools the Israelites were in after ages, to act in contradiction to this exultant song of praise, trembling and fleeing before the nations that were round about.—Y.

Vers. 1—19.—*The song of triumph. The sense of Israel's obligation to Jehovah fully expressed.* God, we have noticed, is lifted up in this song. We now proceed to observe how he is lifted up in the midst of his people, whom he encompasses with his protection, whom he cheers and illuminates with his favour. His destruction is not mere destruction; his supremacy is not only over his enemies, but also as the guide, the comforter, and the portion of his own. Hence we discover almost immediately on breaking into the song, how Israel is found expressing complete dependence on Jehovah.

I. THERE IS THE EXPRESSION OF INDEBTEDNESS. God has come to Israel in its suffering, need, and helplessness. Israel is weak, and God gives the strength it needs. Israel is sad-hearted, and God enables it to burst forth in songs of gladness. Israel is in peril, and God has interposed with effectual and abiding salvation. He has not only supplied some needs, but all needs wherein Israel was able to receive his aid. More needs would have been supplied, if more had been felt; more causes of gratitude given, if more could have been brought into operation. God is now felt to be a guide (ver. 13), and the land that was thought to fasten the people in, now takes its right place in the memory of the devout as an evident part of the highway of God's holy ones. What expressions of indebtedness could be more complete? It was impossible to exaggerate the debt, and God took care that the words of the song should not fall short in acknowledging it. Thus let it ever be our aim to thank God for his goodness to us, in such words as he supplies, and fill his forms full with the devotion of meditative and observant hearts.

II. This expression is a personal one. The word "I" stands out prominently. The song was not only for a delivered nation, but for a nation in whose deliverance every individual was blessed. It was emphatically a song for every Israelite. God had done all this for Israel, not that he might have a nation for his own to be looked at in the mass, averaged over the whole, the good along with the bad; it was to be a nation made up of holy, obedient, and grateful individuals. Even already, God is indicating that his true people must be bound to him *by personal attachment and service*. Pharaoh had said in his haste and thoughtlessness, "I and my people are wicked" (ch. ix. 27). Here Jehovah gives something for each one of his own people to say; and if each of them labours to say it with a feeling corresponding to the words, then indeed there will come an outburst from the nation such as could not in any other way be produced.

III. This expression being personal, is also an expression as to the source of personal ability. "The Lord is my strength." The strength of a believer just amounts to that which God puts into him according to his need and according to his faith. Bring to God as many vessels as you will, and if it be wise to fill them, then God can fill them all. Learn that the natural strength of man, even at its best, is inadequate for some purposes and uncertain for any. It breaks down, often without warning and without recovery. Therefore it is a great matter for me to feel that "the Lord is my strength." He himself comes in, not to supplement human efforts, nor to fill up human defects, but rather to make his presence felt with men in *the choosing of right purposes*, and the carrying of them out to a full and satisfying attainment. The Israelite had been nothing in himself; nothing as against the tyranny of Pharaoh in Egypt; nothing as against the pursuing chariots by the Red Sea. And now all at once he is able to sing as if he were a portion and a factor of Omnipotence.

IV. This expression being personal is also an expression as to the source of personal gladness. "The Lord is my song." From him comes real and abiding gladness, such gladness as becomes man at his best estate. The world has its great singers, and what it reckons imperishable songs. Each nation has its own patriotic effusions, and excited and often half-drunken crowds will roar themselves hoarse over national anthems. There are love songs, drinking songs, war songs, and all that great number besides which elude classification. It would be foolish indeed of the Christian, in his haste, to despise these productions, for many of them are very beautiful, and they have an unquestionable and not astonishing hold on the general heart. But after all, we must escape into higher and holier associations, and dwell in them, if we would have gladness, such as will satisfy. *The Lord must be our song.* He, in his attributes, his actions, and the history of his dealings with the children of men, must be the topic of our praise. The great thing to make each of us glad must be that our minds are kept in perfect peace because they are stayed upon him. All other gladness, sweet as it may be in the beginning, will prove bitter, perhaps very bitter, in the end. Nor was Jehovah any less the song of every true Israelite here, because he was shown acting in such a stern, uncompromising way. The people had to praise God for an actual, present, and overwhelming mercy; and if they had to sing of destruction, that was a necessity not to be escaped. True, there is no word of pity all the way through this song for the destroyed host of Pharaoh, simply because it was not the place for such an expression. The thing to be here expressed and dwelt upon is praise to Jehovah, because of the greatness and completeness of the Divine action. And what an impressive contrast there is between the conduct of these Israelites when delivered and the conduct in the hour of victory, which only too many pages of history record· indeed, such conduct is not absent from the pages of the Old Testament itself. It was, of course, impossible, that any scene of butchery, pillage, and violation, could be presented to us here; but there is not even any tone of savage, revengeful exultation over the destroyed. Israel stands by the mighty waters, looks on the corpses of the Egyptians, and sends up this volume of undiluted, unqualified praise to Jehovah. Let us, for the moment, forget the personal unworthiness of the singers, their past unbelief, their future lapses into idolatry, rebellion, and self will. The words of praise here were the right words to speak; and at the time, we may be sure, many of them felt them. The words were true, the feeling real; the fault was that the singers did not continue to live so as to root the feeling more deeply in their breasts.

V. THIS EXPRESSION BEING PERSONAL, IS ALSO AN EXPRESSION AS TO THE SOURCE OF PERSONAL SAFETY. "He has become my salvation." There is thus an experience to dwell on that peculiarly inspires grateful acknowledgment. We are grateful to those who provide for us, who instruct us, who supply us with comforts and pleasures; but there is a peculiar tie to him who saves us in any hour of peril. God himself cannot but look with peculiar interest to those whom he has delivered; and the delivered should look with peculiar devotion to him. If it is much to create men and to provide for them in their natural existence, it is more still to save them from death and to give them eternal life in Christ; and thus God must look in a special way on those who believe and are being saved. And so also, if it is much to be created and much to be provided for, it is even more to be saved; to have the sure feeling that beyond this changing, corruptible scene, there is the house of God, not made with hands, eternal in the heavens. There are untold millions who owe existence and all their power of enjoyment to God, yet *not one syllable of real thankfulness* has ever passed their lips. But as to those who are saved, *if they be truly in process of salvation, thankfulness is part of their life.* Of this be perfectly sure, no salvation is going on if thankfulness for it be not in the heart and some sort of praise on the lip and in the life.

VI. In view of all that has thus been considered, it will be seen as a fitting consequence that JEHOVAH SHOULD BE DISTINCTLY SET FORTH AS WORTHY OF ADORATION AND HONOUR. "He is my God and I will glorify him, my father's God and I will exalt him." *My father's God.* Here is the response, more or less appreciative, to all declarations in which Jehovah speaks of himself as the God of Abraham, Isaac, and Jacob. True praise of God takes in the great historic past, yes, and also the past which is not historic; a past none the less real, none the less contributory to the present, even though there be no record of it such as we can read. Jehovah was deliverer to Israel that day by the Red Sea, because of what he had been to Abraham, Isaac, and Jacob centuries before. What God is to each of us to-day, is possible because of what he was to our fathers long ago. Explore then and discover how present blessings are rooted in the past. This will not only be an interesting study, but will increase gratitude, and fix it more surely in the regions of the understanding.—Y.

Ver. 11.—*Jehovah among the gods.* As long as these deities—the deities, say, of Egypt, Philistia, Edom, Moab, Canaan—were simply to be compared among themselves, there might be room for rivalries among them; there might be reasons for asserting superiority because of a more splendid worship and a larger host of worshippers. But, when Jehovah steps in upon the scene, all discussions as to the comparative excellences of other deities cease to have interest. The most renowned of them becomes of no more account than the most obscure. Even the temple of the great goddess Diana is then despised, and her magnificence destroyed, whom all Asia and the world worshippeth. At Ephesus, under the very shadow of the far famous building, Paul persuades and turns away much people, saying that they be no gods which are made with hands. Whether stars be of the first magnitude or not ceases to be a question of interest when the sun rises; for then they all vanish alike. "Who is like unto thee, Jehovah, among the gods?" Nor is this question left as a mere vague vociferation. It is pursued into instructive detail, and illustrated by the mention of three particular features of pre-eminence. These words are spoken with the signs of Jehovah's glory right before the eyes of those who speak. Not mere symbolic signs, such as the burning bush, the rod changed to a serpent, and the leprous hand; but signs that were also great benefits and judgments. Fresh from the miraculous passage, and with the destruction of Pharaoh's host scarcely faded from their eyes, these singers of praise very fitly ask, Who is like to Jehovah, glorious in holiness, fearful in praises doing wonders?

I. GLORIOUS IN HOLINESS. Some word is needed to indicate the distinction between deity and all lesser existence, and that word we find in "holiness." Hence holiness and even some sort of glory in their holiness might be attributed to all the gods. All places and symbols associated with them would be approached with scrupulous veneration and only too often with abject terror. But who had such holiness as Jehovah possessed? We may take the question as running—"Whose glory in holiness is like unto thine?" Then, standing in our position as Christians, with the light we thus enjoy, and considering all the conceptions of Deity which our present knowledge of the world, in all lands and through past ages, supplies, we can put this question with a richness of meaning which was not possible to Moses or to his brother Israelites. Consider the deities of the Grecian and Roman mythology—for with that we are perhaps best acquainted—or any deities the wide world over, either among barbarous peoples or civilised; and then consider the Jehovah of the Hebrew Scriptures, the God who revealed himself more fully and in due time by his Son. Look how the worship of an idolater drags him down. Think of the unutterable prostitution and sensualities connected with certain idolatries. Think of those miserable parents in whom idolatry had so destroyed natural affection that they could cause their sons and daughters to pass through the fire to Moloch. Many are rigorous, fanatical and even furious in their religion, who yet show by their lives that they care nothing for great duties; their religion, alas! seems to make them worse instead of better. How great, then, is the privilege of him who has indeed come to perceive that Jehovah is *glorious* in holiness! He is light, and in him is no darkness at all. He is love—such love as is set forth in John iii. 16. His wrath is revealed against *all* unrighteousness of men. The very nation that he chose, sanctified and cherished, he made to be "scattered and peeled," because it would not do righteousness according to his will. What a cheering and inspiring thing to turn from the inspection of our own hearts with its dismal results, and from our observation of the seething selfishness of the world, to think of the God and Father of the Lord Jesus Christ! For Christ moves before us in the beauty of holiness, a great, attractive, rebuking *reality* ; and we know that as is the Son, so is the Father; as is the visible and Incarnate One, so is the invisible and purely spiritual Jehovah above. It is through the Son we know the Father; and it is everything to feel that he is not a mere imagination. He is drawing us to himself; so that as he is glorious in the holiness of the Uncreated and Pure, so we, even though sadly fallen, may become glorious in the holiness of the restored and the perfected. We have yet to sing the new song from those who are glorious in the holiness of matured sonship to him who is glorious in the holiness of our Father in heaven.

II. FEARFUL IN PRAISES. Though this expression is beyond exact definition, yet it is obvious that a certain way of understanding it is appropriate to the present occasion. Jehovah is a God to be praised for his terrible doings. It is part of his very holiness that he makes that holiness to be respected by his treatment of those who presumptuously despise it. If he be not approached with reverence and obeyed with promptitude, and from the heart, he can make the irreverent ones to feel the evil consequences. He is not one to make claims which he cannot authenticate and enforce. It was not as the priest of some foreign deity, with empty pomp, that Moses came forth before Pharaoh, trusting by a great show to terrify him into acquiescence. There is *manifested power* ; power so widespread and various in its manifestations, so overwhelming in its concluding operations, that even the most ignorant can appreciate it. If God is not loved, he must be feared; if his good and perfect gifts are not accepted, then his visitations of perfect and holy wrath must take their place. The mercies for which Israel had now to praise Jehovah were such as could not be sung without recounting an awful story. Nor must we ever shrink from dwelling on such scenes when needed. We must praise God for his severity to the wicked, as much as for anything else. We could not truly praise him for his love, unless we were also able to praise him for his wrath.

III. DOING WONDERS. Here is another peculiar Divine prerogative. Jehovah does wonders such as none among the gods can do. One has almost forgotten the magicians, it is so long since they retreated into obscurity and shame. This is praise to Jehovah, which at once pushed aside all magicians and pretenders to the supernatural. The wonders they do would cease to be wonders, if they would only allow us to become a little better acquainted with them; and not only would they cease to be wonders, they would even become despicable, as we consider the lying with which they are supported, and the knavish ends for which they are produced. A conjuror's tricks are only like common things hidden away; show us where they are hidden, and the mystery ceases. *The mystery is in the concealment and nothing else.* But Jehovah's dealings, as in Egypt, are true wonders. They are brought out to the light so that all men can gaze on them and examine them, and the more they are examined the more mysterious they prove. It would not be good for us—it would, indeed, be very bad, as starving a thing as could happen to our imagination and our highest capacities of enjoyment— were we to cease from wondering in the presence of God. Wonder must ever arise within us when we consider his operations, alike in nature and in grace.—Y.

Vers. 20, 21.—*Woman's part in the song of triumph.* In the history of Israel, we are called on to observe woman coming forward, not continuously, but every now and then, to show how real is her share in the lot of Israel. She has had that share in *suffering*, being consumed with anxiety as to the fate of her offspring. (Ch. i.) She has had it in *ministration*,—Jochebed, Miriam and Pharaoh's daughter, being combined in the work—unconscious ministration towards the fitting of Moses for his great work. Whatever may be said of women speaking in the Church, we here behold them joining, *in the most demonstrative way*, in the public praises of Jehovah. The blessing by the Red Sea was one which went down to that common humanity which underlies the great distinction of sex. But it was also *a very special blessing to women.* Trials, such as had come to Jochebed when Moses was born, were to cease. Woman would have her own trials in the time to come—the pangs of childbirth, the cares of offspring, and all a mother's peculiar solicitudes; but it was a great deal to have the special curse of bondage in Egypt removed. Then there would be deep thankfulness for the escape of the first-born; a feeling, too, of self-congratulation that they had been obedient in slaying the lamb and sprinkling the blood, and had thus escaped the blow which had fallen heavily on so many homes in Egypt. All these considerations would lead up to and prepare for the final outburst of praise and triumph. And so, if women consider still, they will be both astonished and profoundly grateful because of all that God in Christ Jesus has done for *them.* They have gained not only according to their simple share in humanity, but according to their peculiar relation towards man. If it be true, that Eve fell first, dreadfully have all her daughters suffered since. As belonging to this fallen world, woman is now in a double subjection. In her creation she was to be subordinate to man, and if she had stood, and he had stood, then what glory and blessedness would have come to both! But when man became the slave of sin, she became doubly slave, as being now linked to one who had himself the servile spirit. What had been *subordination* in Eden became *servitude* outside of it. He who is himself the abject slave of passion and selfishness makes woman his slave, so that in addition to all that comes through her own sin as a human being there is the misery that comes through her having got into a wrong relation to man. Hence the peculiar hideousness of a bad woman, a Jezebel or a Herodias. Hence, too, through the work of redemption we get the peculiar beauty of the good woman. Whence should we have got those types of saintly women which beam from the pages of Scripture and Christian biography, save for that great work one stage of which is celebrated in this song?—Y.

Vers. 1—21.—*Song of Moses and the Lamb.* "And they sing the song of Moses," etc. (Rev. xv. 3). It is quite impossible to sever in thought the song by the sea, and the reference in the Book of the Revelation. We therefore take for our text the words chosen, and in our homily keep ever in view—the passage of the sea.

I. THE SINGERS. "They that have gotten the victory." But conquerors must first have been soldiers. Here they are Christians who have become part of the Church militant by faith in our Lord Jesus Christ. Over what victorious? As a matter of fact Christians are brought off more than conquerors over " the world, the flesh, and the devil." But in Rev. xv. 2, only " the world" is referred to ; and of it only two constituents are mentioned : " the beast " and " the image " or likeness " of the beast." [On these and that " other beast " see Rev. xiii. ; and for such exposition as is calculated to place the symbols in a reasonable light, see Porter's " Christian Prophecy :" Maclehose, Glasgow ; and " The Apocalypse " by Prof. Godwin : Hodder and Stoughton.] The enemies overcome were, and ever are :—1. *Force :* as directed against the Kingdom of God. The " beast " of Rev. xiii. is anti-theistic, or anti-Christian civil despotism, wherever found. Read Rev. xiii. 1—10, with this idea in the mind, and the description is seen to be vividly true. Illustrations of battle and victory may be found in Egypt tyrannising over Israel, in early persecutions of the Christian Church. As soon as ever Christianity became a spiritual power conspicuous enough to attract attention, force set itself against it. So ever since down to martyr history in Madagascar. Note : there are instances now in which force, in varied forms, will set itself against the conscience. [The " mark " and " number " of the image are the signs, open or secret, of being iden- tified with anti-theistic despotism.]   2. *Opinion.* That which resembles godless government, viz. godless opinion, the tone of society, etc. This power of society against the Divine Kingdom, this pressure of opinion must have been terrible in Egypt. Felt to-day, not only at the " club," but in every workshop. One may add to this, not mentioned in Rev. xv., but in Rev. xiii., " another beast," viz. :—3. *Fraud.* Specially as associated with " Priestcraft," whether of false religions, or of corrupted forms of Christianity. [For illustration of the despotism of Egyptian priestcraft, see Ebers' " Uarda."] This power seems mild as a lamb, with the speech of a dragon ; rises out of the earth (does not descend from heaven) ; wields civil power for its own purpose (as in the case of Rome) ; pretends to miracle ; gives power to anti-Christian public opinion ; inflicts social wrong. How strong their enemies are, viz., anti-Christian government, anti-Christian public opinion, anti-Christian religion, every Christian comes sooner or later to know.

II. THEIR POSITION. " And I saw as it were a sea of glass," etc. Here note :—1. *The sea.* A sea of crystal flaked with fire. Such as we may sometimes see under light of setting sun. The symbol of the experience of life, *i.e.*, of mingled mercy and judg- ment (Ps. ci. 1). 2. *The shore, i.e.,* the position of the victorious—ἐπὶ τὴν θάλασσαν— not in the sense of standing on the wave, but of an army encamped " upon the sea," *i. e.,* upon the shore. 3. *The allusion.* To Israel on the eastern shore of the Red Sea. 4. *The reality* in this symbol. The victorious redeemed Church, on the further side of the experience of life, singing the new and everlasting song.

III. THE SONG. It is " of Moses . . . and of the Lamb." A song like that of old, springing out of similar circumstances, celebrating a like deliverance. Here observe :— 1. *The place of Moses* in relation to Christ. Moses is " the servant," etc. Incidental evidence of Christ's superiority and Deity. Christ is not a servant, save as he volun- tarily took that position (Phil. ii. 7). 2. *The central place of the Lamb* throughout the Book of the Revelation. Argument for the transcendent import of the Atonement. The song is—1. *One.* Not two. 2. *Thankful.* Some of the songs of earth are penitential, prayerful, plaintive. 3. Of the *Saved.* From guilt, sin, darkness, sorrow. [Go into detail.] What a song it will be ! 4. Of the *Free.* The three despotisms of force, opinion, fraud, were left by Israel behind. So with the redeemed Church of God. 5. Of the *New-born.* A new departure for Israel ; the unending life before the Church triumphant. 6. Of the *Seers*, who now see past all subordinate and second causes— past Moses—past even the Mediator Jesus, to the First Origin of all, " great and marvellous . . . *Lord God Almighty.*" 7. A song of *review.* This is the final verdict, " Just and true," etc.

IV. LESSONS. 1. *To Christians.* Do not wait for the final song. Sing in the passage of the sea. Poetry and music the natural expression of praise. Some can pour forth their own song, *e.g.*, Keble and Watts, Wesley and Lyte. Others must adopt praise furnished to their lips. But for all there is the poetry and the music—the sweet psalm—of a pure and holy life. 2. *To those not Christians.* To sing the song of the saved, we must *be* saved.

> " No lips untuned can sing that song
> Or join the music there."—R.

Vers. 1—21.—One of the first songs in the Bible—*the* first Jewish song—we may almost call it the tap-root whence springs the main stem of Jewish psalmody. The art of poetry and instruments of music were no doubt brought from Egypt; the land of slavery was yet the land of science. Such "spoils" were made all the more valuable, and appropriated all the more firmly by consecration (cf. Keble, Christian Year, 3rd Sunday in Lent). All the wealth of the world is at the disposal of God's children—for the earth is the Lord's, and the fulness thereof—the problem which they have to solve is how to use it without abusing it (of. 1 Cor. x. 23—29). Turn to the song itself, and see what lessons it has to teach. Three stanzas (vers. 1—5, 6—10, 11—18)—each begins with ascription of praise to Jehovah; each ends with a reference to Jehovah's treatment of his foes. Notice:—

I. PRESENT GRATITUDE. Vers. 1—5.—In the excitement of the great deliverance, words almost fail to express the praise. The name of the deliverer is repeated four times in eight lines. Yet not once is it a "vain repetition." All the difference in the world between using God's name to disguise an empty heart and using it to express the feelings of a full one. Here, "out of the fulness of the heart the mouth speaketh." God loves such praise, the praise of a heart which cannot help praising. Some try to praise because they think God expects it of them; their hearts are like dry wells whilst yet, out of supposed respect to God, they keep on working the pump-handle! Fill the heart first and all such artificial efforts will be needless; the full heart is a springing well. "*How* fill?" By letting the thought of God's great mercies pierce through to the heart's deeps. If the thought of God and of his deeds comes home to us, our praise will soon flow forth freely.

II. PAST MERCIES THE CAUSE OF PRESENT GRATITUDE. Vers. 6—10.—This is what called forth the praise. All real, all genuine. Moses is not sending up his song to a "*possible*" God, but to one whom he believes in utterly as a living, present, powerful ruler. Notice—1. *The reality of the enemy.* No doubt about the tyranny in Egypt. Brickfields and scourges had left their mark upon the memory. No doubt either as to the late danger (ver. 9). The exasperated pursuers determined to repossess their prey. 2. *The reality of the deliverance.* Where were the pursuers now? The wreckage drifting within sight marked the spot where they had sunk for ever! 3. *The reality of the deliverer.* No doubt as to his existence—no doubt as to his goodness—in face of such overwhelming evidence. We also, if we would but realise it, have been as truly delivered from dangers just as real. If we but half believe in God, and offer him only a make-shift praise, it is not because he has done less for us; it is because we think less on the meaning of his mercies.

III. PAST MERCIES THE PLEDGE OF FUTURE TRIUMPHS. Vers. 11—18.—Moses was confident about the future because he had no doubt about the past. He was prepared to go "from strength to strength," because he could start from a strong position. From what God *has* done, we may rightly infer what he *will* do. If he has made a way for his people through the sea of waters, he will also make a way for them through yet stormier and more perilous seas (ver. 16). The first deliverance is a pledge and prophecy of all future deliverances. Thus the song of Moses, strong in a present confidence, firmly based upon past mercies, finds its outcome in a good hope, inspiring men along the path of progress. If we would sing the song as it should be sung, we must learn from memory to praise truly; and true praise will soon quicken hope. To live for the future we must live upon the past. The song of the Lamb, the song which specially expresses the full satisfaction of all our hopes, can only be sung by those who have sung first this other song; the song which still feeds hope at the same time that it expresses gratitude.—G.

Vers. 1, 2.—*The sacrifice of praise.* I. THE PLACE OF PRAISE. The first provision for God's ransomed is a song. God's hand must be recognised in the mercy, otherwise its blessing is missed. The place bright with God's goodness is meant to be a meeting-place between the soul and himself.

II. THE REASONS FOR PRAISE. 1. The greatness of God's deed. The chariots and the horses had been the reliance of Egypt and the terror of Israel; and "the horse and his rider" had God cast in the sea. 2. He who had been their strength and their song had become their salvation. Their confidence had not been misplaced: he had not failed them in their need. 3. The individualising love of God: he is "my God." God had appeared for each: not one had been lost. 4. The glory of God's past deeds—he was their fathers' God. This was but one of many like judgments and deliverances, and their song was only swelling the mighty chorus of God's unending praise.

III. The resolves of praise. 1. They will prepare a habitation for God. It is the work of God's people in every age to prepare a dwelling-place for him where his character is made known, his voice heard, and his love and fear shed abroad. 2. To exalt God's fame. He was their fathers' God, and that was a call to make him known. He had given a fuller revelation of himself than even this great mercy contained. There were purposes and promises in that record which outran this mercy and themselves. Our praise must ever add, "these are but part of his ways," and exalt God as the world's refuge and help.—U.

Vers. 3—21.—*The results of deliverance to God's people.* I. The knowledge of the marvellousness of God's power (3—12). 1. The might of Egypt, when measured with the strength of God, was utter vanity (4, 5). The Lord's right hand had *dashed in pieces* the enemy. What can make the heart afraid which knows the power of God? 2. The deadly malice of Egypt was extinguished in a moment like a spark beneath the heel. The picture of the foe's deadly purpose (9) set side by side with God's deed: "Thou didst blow with thy wind—they sank as lead in the mighty waters."

II. Confidence for the onward way. 1. In his mercy and strength God will lead them to the rest he has promised (13). 2. This deliverance will fight for them (14—16). The heart of their foes will die within them. And when led into their land this fear of the Lord will be a wall between them and the nations round about. They shall not only be led in, but planted there in undisturbed security (17). 3. God will, as now, triumph through all the ages, and accomplish, no matter how his people may fear and his enemies may vaunt themselves. all his righteous will (18).—U

EXPOSITION.

Vers. 22—27.—The journey from the Red Sea to Elim. After a stay, which cannot be exactly measured, but which was probably one of some days, near the point of the Eastern coast of the Gulf of Suez, at which they had emerged from the sea-bed, the Israelites, under the guidance of the pillar of the cloud, resumed their journey, and were conducted southwards, or south-eastwards, through the arid tract, called indifferently "the wilderness of Shur" (verse 22), and "the wilderness of Etham" (Num. xxxiii. 8), to a place called Marah. It is generally supposed that the first halt must have been at Ayun Musa, or "the springs of Moses." This is "the only green spot near the passage over the Red Sea" (Cook). It possesses at present seventeen wells, and is an oasis of grass and tamarisk in the midst of a sandy desert. When Wellsted visited it in 1836, there were abundant palm-trees. It does not lie on the shore, but at the distance of about a mile and a half from the beach, with which it was at one time connected by an aqueduct, built for the convenience of the ships, which here took in their water. The water is regarded as good and wholesome,

though dark-coloured and somewhat brackish. From Ayun Musa the Israelites pursued their way in a direction a little east of south through a barren plain where sand-storms are frequent—part of the wilderness of Shur—for three days without finding water. Here their flocks and herds must have suffered greatly, and many of the animals probably died on the journey. On the last of the three days water was found at a spot called thenceforth "Marah," "bitterness," because the liquid was undrinkable. After the miracle related in ver. 25, and an encampment by the side of the sweetened spring (Num. xxxiii. 8), they proceeded onward without much change of direction to Elim, where was abundance of good water and a grove of seventy palm-trees. Here "they encamped by the waters," and were allowed a rest, which probably exceeded a fortnight (See the comment on ch. xvi. 1.)

Ver. 22.—So Moses brought Israel from the Red Sea. There is no such connection between this verse and the preceding narrative as the word "so" expresses. Translate "*And* Moses brought." The wilderness of Shur, called also that of Etham (Num. xxxiii.

8) appears to have extended from Lake Serbonis on the north, across the isthmus, to the Red Sea, and along its eastern shores as far as the Wady Ghurundel. It is almost wholly waterless; and towards the south, such wells as exist yield a water that is bitter in the extreme. **Three days.** The distance from Ayun Musa to Ain Howarah, the supposed representative of Marah, is not more than about 36 miles; but the day's march of so large a multitude through the desert may not have averaged more than twelve miles. **And found no water.** No doubt the Israelites carried with them upon the backs of their asses water in skins, sufficient for their own wants during such an interval; but they can scarcely have carried enough for their cattle. These must have suffered greatly.

Ver. 23.—**And when they came to Marah.** It is not clear whether the place already bore the name on the arrival of the Israelites, or only received it from them. *Marah* would mean "bitter" in Arabic no less than in Hebrew. The identification of Marah with the present Ain Howarah, in which most modern writers acquiesce, is uncertain from the fact that there are several bitter springs in the vicinity—one of them even bitterer than Howarah. (See Winer, *Realwörterbuch*, ad voc. MARAH.) We may, however, feel confident that the bitter waters of which the Israelites "would not drink" were in this neighbourhood, a little north of the Wady Ghurundel.

Ver. 24. — **And the people murmured against Moses.** As they had already done on the western shores of the Red Sea (ch. xiv. 11, 12), and as they were about to do so often before their wanderings were over. (See below, ch. xvi. 2; xvii. 3; Num. xiv. 2; xvi. 41; Deut. i. 27, etc.) "Murmuring" was the common mode in which they vented their spleen, when anything went ill with them; and as Moses had persuaded them to quit Egypt, the murmuring was chiefly against him. The men who serve a nation best are during their lifetime least appreciated. **What shall we drink?** Few disappointments are harder to bear than that of the man, who after long hours of thirst thinks that he has obtained wherewith to quench his intolerable longing, and on raising the cup to his lips, finds the draught so nauseous that he cannot swallow it. Very unpalatable water *is* swallowed when the thirst is great (*Eothen*, p. 197). But there is a limit beyond which nature will not go. There "may be water, water everywhere, yet not a drop to drink."

Vers. 25, 26.—**The Lord shewed him a tree.** —Several trees or plants belonging to different parts of the world, are said to possess the quality of rendering bitter water sweet and agreeable; as the *nellimaram* of Coromandel, the *sassafras* of Florida, the *yerva Caniani* of Peru, and the *perru nelli* (Phy-

lanthus emblica) of India. But none of them is found in the Sinaitic peninsula. Burckhardt suggested (*Travels in Syria*, p. 474) that the berries of the *ghurkud* (Peganum retusum), a low thorny shrub which grows abundantly round the Ain Howarah, may have been used by Moses to sweeten the drink; but there are three objections to this. 1. Moses is not said to have used the berries, but the entire plant; 2. The berries would not have been procurable in April, since they do not ripen till June; and 3. They would not have produced any such effect on the water as Burckhardt imagined. In fact there is no tree or shrub now growing in the Sinaitic peninsula, which would have any sensible effect on such water as that of Ain Howarah; and the Bedouins of the neighbourhood know of no means by which it can be made drinkable. Many of the Fathers believed that the "tree" had no natural effect, and was commanded to be thrown in merely to symbolise the purifying power of the Cross of Christ. But to moderns such a view appears to savour of mysticism. It is perhaps most probable that there was some tree or shrub in the vicinity of the bitter fountain in Moses' time which had a natural purifying and sweetening power, but that it has now become extinct. If this be the case, the miracle consisted in God's pointing out the tree to Moses, who had no previous knowledge of it. **The waters were made sweet.** Compare the miracle of Elisha (2 Kings ii. 19—22). **There he made for them a statute and an ordinance.** See the next verse. God, it appears, after healing the water, and satisfying the physical thirst of his people, gave them an ordinance, which he connected by a promise with the miracle. If they would henceforth render strict obedience to all his commandments, then he would "heal" them as he had healed the water, would keep them free at once from physical and from moral evil, from the diseases of Egypt, and the diseases of their own hearts. **And there he proved them.** From the moment of their quitting Egypt to that of their entering Canaan, God was ever "proving" his people—trying them, that is—exercising their faith, and patience and obedience and power of self-denial, in order to fit them for the position which they were to occupy in Canaan. He had proved them at the Red Sea, when he let them be shut in between the water and the host of the Egyptians—he proved them now at Marah by a bitter disappointment—he proved them again at Meribah (ch. xvii. 1—7); at Sinai (ch. xx. 20); at Taborah (Num. xi. 1—3); at Kibroth-hattaavah (*ib.* verse 34); at Kadesh (*ib.* xiii. 26—33), and elsewhere. For forty years he led them through the wilderness "to prove them, to know what was in their heart" (Deut. viii.), to fit them for their glorious and conquering career in the land of promise **All those diseases.** See Deut. vii 15; xxviii. 27. Kalisch correctly observes that, though the Egyptians had the character in antiquity of being among the healthiest and most robust of nations (Herod. ii. 77), yet a certain small number of diseases have always raged among them with extreme severity He understands the present passage of the plagues, which, however, are certainly nowhere else called "diseases." There is no reason why the word should not be taken literally, as all take it in the passages of Deuteronomy above cited.

Ver. 27.—**They came to Elim.** Elim was undoubtedly some spot in the comparatively fertile tract which lies south of the "wilderness of Shur," intervening between it and the "wilderness of Sin"—now El Murkha. This tract contains the three fertile wadys of Ghurundel, Useit, and Tayibeh, each of which is regarded by some writers as the true Elim. It has many springs of water, abundant tamarisks, and a certain number of palm-trees. On the whole, Ghurundel seems to be accepted by the majority of well-informed writers as having the best claim to be considered the Elim of this passage **Twelve wells.** Rather

"springs." The "twelve springs" have not been identified; but the Arabs are apt to conceal the sources of their water supplies (Niebuhr, *Arabie*, p. 347). A large stream flows down the Wady Ghurundel in the winter-time (*ibid.*), which later becomes a small brook (Burckhardt, *Syria*, p. 778), and dries up altogether in the autumn. The pasture is good at most seasons, sometimes rich and luxuriant; there are abundant tamarisks, a considerable number of acacias, and some palms. **Three score and ten palm trees.** The palm-trees of this part of Arabia are "not like those of Egypt or of pictures, but either dwarf—that is, trunkless—or else with savage hairy trunks, and branches all dishevelled" (Stanley, *Sinai and Palestine*, p. 68). There are a considerable number in the Wady Ghurundel, and others in the Wady Tayibeh (*ib.* p. 69). **They encamped there.** It has been observed that the vast numbers of the host would more than fill the Wady Ghurundel, and that while the main body encamped there, others, with their cattle, probably occupied the adjacent wadys—Useit, Ethal, and even Tayibeh or Shuweikah—which all offer good pasturage

HOMILETICS.

Vers. 23—27.—*The trials and vicissitudes of life.* Israel in the wilderness is a type of our pilgrimage through life.

I. MONOTONY. The long weary sameness of days each exactly resembling the last (ver. 22)—the desert all around us—and no water! No refreshing draughts from that living spring, which becomes in them that drink it "a well of water springing up into everlasting life" (John iv. 14). Israel was afflicted by want of earthly water for three days. Many poor pilgrims through the wilderness of life are debarred the spiritual draughts of which Jesus spoke to the Samaritan woman for twenty, thirty, forty years! Debarred, it may be, by no fault of their own, born in heathenism, bred up in heathenism, uneducated in what it most concerns a man to know. How sad their condition! How thankful those should be who may draw of the water of life freely (*a*) from the written word; (*b*) from the Living and Eternal Word who has said—"If any man thirst, let him come unto me and drink!"

II. DISAPPOINTMENT. Hopes long cherished seem about, at last, to be satisfied. The long sought for treasure—of whatever kind it may be—is announced as found. Now we are about to enjoy ourselves, to take our fill of the delight long denied us. Alas! the dainty morsel as we taste it proves to be—

> "As Dead Sea fruit, which, fair to view,
> Yet turns to ashes on the lips."

The delicious draught, as we expected it to be, is "Marah," "bitterness." Most of life is to most men made up of such disappointments. Men crave happiness, and expect it here, and seek it through some earthly, some temporal means—wealth, or power, or fame, or a peaceful domestic life, or social success, or literary eminence—and no sooner do they obtain their desire, and hold it in their grasp, than they find its savour gone— its taste so bitter that they do not care to drink. Then, how often do they turn to vent the anguish of their heart on some quite innocent person, who, they say, has led them wrong! Their disappointment should take them with humbled spirits to God.

It actually takes them with furious words to the presence of some man, whom it is a relief to them to load with abuse and obloquy. They imitate the Israelites, not Moses —they murmur, instead of crying to the Almighty.

III. UNEXPECTED RELIEF. God can turn bitter to sweet. Often, out of the bitter agony of disappointment God makes gladness to arise. Sometimes, as in the miracle of Marah, he reverses the disappointment itself, turning defeat into victory, giving us the gratification of the desire which had been baulked of fruition. But more often he relieves by compensating. He gives something unexpected instead of the expected joy which he has withheld. He makes a temporal evil work for our spiritual good. He takes away the sting from worldly loss, by pouring into our hearts the spirit of contentment. He causes ill-success to wean us from the world and fix our thoughts on him.

IV. A TIME OF REFRESHMENT. Marah led to Elim. If there are times of severe trial in life, there are also "times of refreshing from the Lord" (Acts iii. 19)—times of enjoyment—even times of mirth (Eccles. iii. 4; Ps. cxxvi. 2). But lately toiling wearily through an arid wilderness, only to reach waters of bitterness, on a sudden the Israelites found themselves amid groves of palms, stretched themselves at length on the soft herbage under the shadow of tall trees, and listened to the breeze sighing through the acacias, or to the murmur of the babbling rill which flowed from the "twelve springs" adown the dale. 'Encamped there by the waters" (ver. 27) they were allowed to rest for a while, secure from foes, screened from the heat, their eyes charmed by the verdure, their ears soothed by gentle sounds, their every sense lapped in soft enjoyment by the charms of a scene which, after the wilderness, must have appeared "altogether lovely." And so it is in our lives. God does give us, even here in this world, seasons of repose, of satisfaction, of calm content. It were ingratitude in us not to accept with thankfulness such occasions when they arise. He knows what is best for us; and if he appoints us an Elim, we were churlish to withdraw ourselves from it. The Church has its festivals. Christ attended more than one banquet. "Times of refreshing" are to be received joyously, gratefully, as "coming from the Lord," and designed by him to support, strengthen, comfort us. They are, as it were, glimpses into the future life.

HOMILIES BY VARIOUS AUTHORS.

Vers. 22—27.—*Marah and Elim.* "So Moses brought Israel from the Red Sea, and they went out into the wilderness of Shur," etc. The main topics here are—

I. THE SWEET FOLLOWED BY THE BITTER. Singing these songs of triumph, and praising God with timbrel and dance, on the further shores of the Red Sea, the Israelites may have felt as if nothing remained to them but to sing and dance the rest of their way to Canaan. They would regard their trials as practically at an end. It would be with regret that they broke up their pleasant encampment at the Red Sea at all. Their thought would be, "It is good for us to be here, let us make here tabernacles" (cf. Matt. xvii. 4). But this was not to be permitted. The old call comes—"Speak to the children of Israel that they go forward" (ch. xiv. 15), and the halcyon days of their first great exuberant joy are over. Their celebration of triumph is soon to be followed by sharp experience of privation. 1. *The Israelites were conducted by the wilderness of Shur.* There they went three days without water. God might, as afterwards at Rephidim (ch. xvii. 6), have given them water; but it was his will that they should taste the painfulness of the way. This is not an uncommon experience. Every life has its arid, waterless stretches, which may be compared to this "wilderness of Shur." "There are moments when the poet, the orator, the thinker, possessed, inspired with lofty and burning thoughts, needs nothing added to the riches of his existence; finds life glorious and sublime. But these are but moments, even in the life of genius; and after them, and around them, stretches the weary waste of uninspired, inglorious, untimeful days and years" (Dr. J. Service). It is the same in the life of religion. Seasons of spiritual enjoyment are frequently followed by sharp experience of trial. We are led by the wilderness of Shur. Spiritual comforts fail us, and our soul, like Israel's at a later period, is "much discouraged because of the way" (Num. xxi. 4). We are brought into "a dry and thirsty land, where no water is" (Ps. lxiii. 1). A certain sovereignty is to be recognised in the dispensation of Divine comforts. God leaves us to taste the sharpness of privation, that we may be led to cry after him (Ps. cxix. 81, 82). 2. *They came to Marah, where the waters were bitter.* This was a keen and poignant disappointment to them—"sorrow upon sorrow." As usual, it drove the people to murmuring, and Moses to prayer. Bear gently with their infirmity. Do them the justice of remembering that there is no record of their murmuring during the three past days of their great privation in the wilderness. It was this disappointment at the well of Marah which fairly broke them down. Would many of us have borne the trial better? It is easy to sing when the heart is full of a great fresh joy. But let trial succeed trial, and disappointment follow on disappointment, and how soon do the accents of praise die away, to be replaced by moaning and complaint! The "Song of Moses," which was so natural on the banks of the Red Sea, would have had a strange sound coming from these dust-parched throats, and fainting, discouraged hearts. The note of triumph is not easily sustained when the body is sinking with fatigue, and when the wells to which we had looked for refreshment are discovered to be bitter. Take Marah as an emblem (1) of life's *disappointments.* Our life-journey is studded with disappointments. Hard to bear in any case, these are doubly bitter to us, when they come on the back of other trials, and cheat us of an expected solace. When friends, *e.g.*, turn their backs on us in time of need, or come with cold comfort when we expected ready help, or give chiding instead of sympathy; when trusted projects fail, or fond anticipations are not realised; most of all, when God himself seems to desert us, and grants no answer to our prayers; the waters given us to drink are bitter indeed. (2) Of life's *bitter experiences generally.* "Call me not Naomi," said the mother-in-law of Ruth, "call me Mara: for the Almighty hath dealt very bitterly with me" (Ruth i. 20). The only wells that never become bitter are the "wells of salvation" (Is. xii. 3)—the waters of Divine consolations (cf. John iv. 14). The waters of our creature-comforts admit of being very easily embittered. Relationships, friendships, possessions, business, social position—sweet to-day, any or all of these may be made bitter to us to-morrow. The life of Israel was made "bitter" by bondage (ch. i. 14). God dealt "bitterly" with Naomi in taking husband and sons from her, and reducing her to poverty (Ruth i. 21). Hannah was "in bitterness of soul" because she had no child, and "her adversary provoked her sore, for to make her fret" (1 Sam. i. 6—10). Job was embittered by his afflictions (Job vii. 11; ix. 18; x. 1). The tears of the Psalmist were his meat day and night, while they continually said unto him, where is thy God? (Ps. xlii. 3). Mordecai cried, when the decree went forth against his nation, "with a loud and bitter cry" (Esther iv. 1). Bitter waters there are, too, in our own hearts, and in society, engendered by sin—by the presence of envy, jealousy, strife, hatred, malignity, and revengefulness. No scarcity, then, of Marah experiences, no want of wells that stand in need of the healing tree being cast in to sweeten them. 3. *God's ends in permitting Israel to suffer these severe privations.* We do not ask why God led the Israelites by this particular way, since probably there was no other way open by which they *could* have been led. But we may very well ask why, leading them by this way, God, who had it in his power to supply their wants, permitted them to suffer these extreme hardships? (1) We may glean one hint in reply from Paul's experience in 2 Cor. xii., "Lest," he says, "I should be exalted above measure through the abundance of the revelation, there was given to me a thorn in the flesh, the messenger of Satan to buffet me, lest I should be exalted above measure" (ver. 7). (2) A second hint is to be drawn from ver. 25—"There he proved them" Cf. Deut. viii. 2 —"To humble thee, and prove thee to know what was in thine heart, whether thou wouldest keep his commandments, or no." We do not know what unbelief, what rebellion, what impatience there is in our hearts, till trial comes to draw it out.

II. THE BITTER CHANGED INTO THE SWEET. Moses, we read, "cried unto the Lord, and he showed him a tree, which when he had cast into the waters, the waters were made sweet" (ver. 25). Observe, 1. *The agency employed.* The tree had probably some peculiar properties which *tended* in the direction of the result which was produced, though, of itself, it was incompetent to produce it. The supernatural does not, as a rule, contravene the natural, but works along the existing lines, utilising the natural so far as it goes. 2. *The spiritual meaning.* That God intended the healing of these bitter waters to be a "sign" to Israel—a proof of his ability and willingness to heal them of *all* their natural and spiritual diseases, is abundantly plain from vers. 25, 26.

The lesson God would have them learn from the incident was—"I am Jehovah that healeth thee." His Jehovah character guaranteed that what he had shown himself to be in this one instance, he would be *always*, viz., a Healer. As Jehovah, God is the Being of exhaustless resource. As Jehovah, he is the Being eternally identical with himself—self-consistent in all his ways of acting; so that from any one of his actions, if the principle of it can but be clearly apprehended, we are safe in inferring what he always will do. God sweetens, or heals, the bitter waters of life—(1) By altering the outward conditions—*e.g.*, by removing sickness, sending aid in poverty, taking away the *cause* of bitterness, whatever that may be. He healed Naomi's bitterness by the happy marriage of Ruth (Ruth iv. 14, 15); Hannah's by giving her a son (1 Sam. i. 20); Job's by restoring his health and prosperity (Job xlvii. 10), etc. The tree here is whatever agency God employs to accomplish his purpose. (2) And this is the diviner art, by infusing sweetness into the trial itself. He makes that which is bitter sweet to us, by adding himself to it. This Divine change in our experiences is accomplished by means of a very simple but potent secret—as simple as the casting of the tree into the waters, as potent in its efficacy. Would we know it? It is simply this—denying our own natural will, and taking God's instead. "Not my will but thine be done" (Luke xxii. 42). This it is which will make even the bitterest of trials sweet. Call it, if you will, the taking up of the cross; it is, at all events, the *spirit* of the cross which is the sweetening, heavenly element in all affliction—the tree that heals. It is invaluable to bear this in mind, that be our trial, our grief, what it may, half its pain has departed the moment we can bring ourselves to embrace God's will in it. Heavenly consolations will sweeten what remains. Mediæval mystics, like Tauler, dwelt much on this thought, and it is the true and all-important element in their teaching. With God at hand to bless, "Ills have no weight, and *tears no bitterness;*" or as another "sweet singer" expresses it—

> "Just to let thy Father do
>   What he will.
> Just to know that he is true,
>   And be still.
> Just to let him take the care,
>   Sorely pressing,
> *Finding all we let him bear*
>   *Changed to blessing.*
> This is all! and yet the way,
>   Marked by him who loves thee best!
> Secret of a happy day,
>   Secret of his promised rest."
>
> FRANCES RIDLEY HAVERGAL.

(3) By removing the cause of all evil and bitterness—sin itself. It is as the God of Redemption that Jehovah reveals himself pre-eminently as the Healer. His Gospel goes to the root of the matter, and strikes at the *malum originale* of the bitterness in us, and around us. From this point of view, it is not fanciful to trace an analogy—we need not allege a direct typical relation—between this tree cast in to sweeten the bitter waters, and the Cross of the Redeemer. God through Christ; Christ through what he has accomplished by this Cross; the Cross, by being made the object of faith, and again, by being set up in men's hearts, effects this sweetening of the waters. We have but to compare ancient with modern civilization, to see how much the Cross of Christ, cast into the bitter waters of society, has already done to sweeten them. Trusted in for salvation, it renews the heart in its inmost springs, and so heals the bitter waters there; while, as the power of God unto salvation, it will ultimately heal the world of all its woes, abolishing even death, from which already it extracts the sting and bitterness.

III. THE RIGHT IMPROVEMENT OF MARAH EXPERIENCES (ver. 26). We should accept them, 1. As a *motive to obedience*. If God has healed us that is a new reason for loving, trusting, and obeying him (Ps. cxvi.). Accordingly, consequent on this healing of the bitter waters, God made "a statute and an ordinance" for Israel, taking them bound to serve him, and promising them new blessings, if they should prove obedient.

This "statute and ordinance" is the comprehensive germ of the subsequent covenant (ch. xxiv. 3—9). 2. As a *pledge*. The sweetening of the waters, as already seen, was a revelation of Jehovah in his character as Healer. It pledged to Israel that he would, if only they obeyed his statutes, exempt them from such plagues as he had brought upon the Egyptians, and, by implication, that he would heal them of whatever diseases were already upon them. He would be a God of health to them. The healthy condition of body is one which not only throws off existing disease, but which fortifies the body against attacks of disease from without. Natural healing, as we see in the New Testament, and especially in the miracles of Christ, is a symbol of spiritual healing, and also a pledge of it. In the gospels, "to be saved," and "to be made whole," are represented by the same Greek word. We may state the relation thus :— (1) Natural healing is the symbol of spiritual healing. (2) Spiritual healing, in turn, is a pledge of the ultimate removal of all natural evils (Rev. xxi. 4). (3) Each separate experience of healing is a pledge of the whole. It is a fresh testimony to the truth that God is a healer (cf. Ps. ciii. 1—4). Every recovery from sickness is thus, in a way, the preaching of a gospel. It pledges a complete and perfect healing—entire deliverance from natural and spiritual evils—if only we will believe, obey, and use God's method.

IV. ELIM (ver. 27). 1. An illustration of the chequered experiences of life. The alternation of gladness and sorrow; of smiles and tears; followed again by new comforts and seasons of joy. 2. There are Elim spots—places of cool shade, of abundant waters, of rest and refreshment provided for us all along our way through life. In the times of hottest persecution, there were intervals of respite. The Covenanters used to speak of these as "the *blinks*." 3. These Elim-spots should not lead us to forget that we are still in the wilderness. The prevailing aspect of life, especially to one in earnest, is figured by the wilderness, rather than by Elim. Our state here is one of trial, of discipline, of probation—no passing snatches of enjoyment should cause us to forget this.—J. O.

Vers. 22—27.—*The want of water and the want of faith—Marah and Elim.*—It will be noticed at once how the interest of this passage is gathered round that great natural necessity, water. It is a necessity to man in so many ways. He needs it for drinking, for cleansing, for cooking, and for helping to renew the face of the earth. We may note also that Israel was soon to discover the necessity of water in ceremonial duties. A great deal of water had to be used in the tabernacle service. (Ex. xxix. 4; xxx. 18—21; Lev. vi. 27, 28; chaps. xiii.—xvii.) Hence it is no wonder that the very first thing Jehovah does after delivering the Israelites finally from Pharaoh, is to bring them face to face with this great want of water. We see them passing in a short time through a great variety of experiences with regard to it. First, they go three days in the wilderness and find no water; next they come to the waters of Marah and find them undrinkable; then these waters are suddenly made sweet; and lastly, they journey on to the abundant supplies, and therefore inviting neighbourhood of Elim.

I. THE ISRAELITES EXPERIENCE THE WANT OF WATER. There is here a curious contrast between the *fate* of the Egyptians and the *want* of the Israelites. Water proved the ruin of Pharaoh and his host, while the want of water led Israel rapidly into murmuring and unbelief. Thus we have another illustration of how temporal things— even the very necessities of life from a natural point of view—are only blessings as God makes them so. He can turn them very rapidly and easily into curses. We call to mind the grotesque words of Laertes over his drowned sister :—" Too much of water hast thou, poor Ophelia." So the Egyptians had too much of water, and the Israelites could not get any at all. God was immediately beginning to teach and test his own people according to the explanation of Moses in vers. 25, 26. They were to learn faith in Jehovah for *support* as well as *deliverance*; and the first lesson was to be taught by a three days' deprivation of water. If they had had the believing spirit in them this was an opportunity to say, "Assuredly such an awful deliverance has not been wrought that we may straightway perish of thirst." Notice also how *the reality of the wilderness life is at once brought before us* by these three days of waterless wandering. So short a time had they been out of Egypt, and so little distance had they got away; and yet they are as it were in the very worst of wilderness experiences. Thus even the moment they became effectually clear of the external bondage of Egypt, the truth was impressed upon them that they were without a home. There was no swift exchange from one storehouse of temporal comforts to another. For remember, Egypt with all its misery was a sort of home; there the Israelites had been born and trained; there they had got into a bondage of habits and traditions which was not to be removed in a day. And now Jehovah would have them understand that to be free and able to serve him meant that they must endure with these privileges the privations of the wilderness. We cannot have everything good all at once. If we would be clear of the bondage of this world's carnal ways, we must be ready for certain consequent and immediate privations. We cannot get away from Egypt and yet take with us the pleasant waters of Egypt. Unless our springs be in God, and heaven begun in the heart, the needful change of external associations may bring little but pain. External circumstances, and to some extent external companionships, may remain the same; the new home feeling must be produced by the change within.

II. When the Israelites find water it is bitter. Imagine, when they see the water after three days privation, how they run to it. But taste does not confirm sight. The water is not drinkable. Possibly this was a just complaint; although it may rather be suspected that the water, even if bitter, was not so bitter but that it could have been drunk by thirsty people. The Israelites, however, were thinking of the sweet waters of Egypt. A little longer privation and they might have found sweetness even in bitter waters. Still one cannot but consider how it is there should be this difference between the bitter waters and the sweet, between Marah and Elim. And then we are at once reminded that bitterness is no essential part of water, but comes from foreign and separable matters. So the comforts and resources flowing from God get mixed on the way with human and embittering elements, and these elements are so strong and disturbing that we utterly forget the sweet Divine part because of the discomforts of the bitter human one. We are ready to cast all away as if the nauseous could not be expelled. When Jesus told his disciples certain things which required a changed mind, and the creation of spiritual perceptivity in order to lay them to heart, they called these things hard sayings; not considering that hardness might be made easiness. In our early experiences of religion there is sure to be something of the bitter. The exhortation, "Taste and see that the Lord is good," is a serious and experimental one, yet many on their tasting find bitterness. The water of life has flowed through nauseating channels. Moses had his Marah: he got a taste of it even here, and he had full draughts afterwards. (Ch. xxxii. 19; Num. xi. 10—15; xii. 1; xiv. 5; xvi. 3.) David also had his Marah. (Ps. xlii. 3; lxxx. 5; cii. 9.) One can see a good deal of Marah even in the letters of the Christian Paul to his brethren in Corinth and Galatia. He had expected great things from the gifts of the Spirit, and correspondingly bitter would be his disappointment. We must have our Marah water to drink. Water may fail altogether for a while, and then when it does come it may seem worse than none at all.

III. God quickly makes the water palatable. *Note the request of the people.* They do not stop to consider even for a moment whether this water, bitter as it is, may be made palatable. They turn from the whole thing in disgust and despair. "What shall we drink?" If Moses had straightway replied, "Ye shall drink of Marah," they would have counted him a mocker; yet his reply would have been correct. In the very things from which we turn as obviously useless, we may be destined to find an ample and satisfying supply. Moses himself knew not at the moment what they were to drink, but he takes the wise course and cries to Jehovah. More and more does his now habitual faith come out in contrast with the unbelief of the people. With regard to *the casting in of the tree,* it may have been that the tree had in itself some salutary effect; but the probability rather is that Moses was asked for another *pure act of faith.* This is more in harmony with the miraculous progression observed hitherto. When we remember the multitude that had to be supplied from these waters, there is something ludicrously inadequate in the supposition that the branches gathered to themselves the saline incrustations. The casting in of the tree was rather a symbolic channel for the sweetening than the actual cause of it.

IV. God seizes the opportunity to show Israel wherein their safety lies. "He proved them" (ver. 25). He points out, as it were, that they have been subjected to a test and have failed. At Marah they are shown forth as inattentive to past experiences, forgetful as to how God had remembered them and delivered them. Being now free from the bondage of Egypt, they must no longer blame outward constraints, but look earnestly on inward defects, for these are about to prove their greatest hindrance and danger. Yet this was not a time to speak sternly, even though unbelief had put forth its baleful front; they were but at the beginning of the journey, and gentle admonition was more proper than stern reproach. Therefore he counsels them—1. To listen steadily to his voice; 2. To make his will, as expressing most clearly that which is right, the rule of their conduct; 3. To carry out all his commandments and statutes, some of the most important of which had already been laid before them in connection with their departure from Egypt. Let them attend to all this, and they will be free from Egypt's calamities. *Notice the negative aspect of this promise.* God promises exemption from suffering rather than attainment of good. It was well thus to make Israel give a backward look, not only towards the Red Sea, but across it, and into Egypt, where so many troubles had come on their recent oppressors. It would almost seem as if already the hearts of many were filling with the expectation of carnal comforts. They were thinking, eagerly and greedily, of what they were to get. But God speaks out very plainly. He demands obedience; and the most he has to say is that if obedience is given, there will be exemption from suffering. The positive element is left out, and doubtless there is wisdom in the omission. That element will come in due time. Yet of course it is there even now, for the devout and discerning, who can penetrate below the surface. The keeping of Jehovah's commandments is, infallibly, the attaining of the highest and purest blessedness.

V. AFTER MARAH HAS DONE ITS WORK, THE ISRAELITES COME TO ELIM. The pillar of cloud doubtless led them to Marah purposely before Elim, and to Elim purposely after Marah. Thus the people got a rest before coming to another trial of their faith and submissiveness; God did not take them straight from the difficulty with regard to the water to the next difficulty with regard to the bread. It is easy to understand that there were many attractions at Elim which would make them wish to linger there; but at Elim they could not stay. It had water in abundance; but water, great blessing as it is, is not enough. Pleasant it was to rest for awhile at these wells and seventy palm-trees; but before them lay a still better land where they would have, not only brooks of water and fountains and depths that spring out of valleys and hills, but also wheat and barley and vines and fig-trees and pomegranates; and all the rest of the good things mentioned in Deut. viii. 7—9. The great lesson of Elim is that we must not make a resting-place, however attractive, into a home.—Y.

Vers. 22—27.—*I will hear what God, the Lord, will say.* There is no reason why a powerful sermon should not be preached from a seemingly strange text. All depends on how the text is treated. God himself is the greatest of all preachers. See what sort of a sermon he preached from a text which most would have thought unpromising. I. THE TEXT (ver. 22—25). 1. *What it was.* Israel three days without water; at length " a large mound, a whitish petrifaction," from which flowed a fountain. Eagerness followed by disgust. The water bitter, loathsome, undrinkable. " Marah." The people murmured against their leader. A bitter fountain and an embittered murmuring people. Such the text. 2. *How treated.* The text was improved by applying to it the context. Many other texts might be best improved in like manner. " The Lord showed him a tree," etc. (ver. 25). Clearly somewhere close at hand. The bitter waters made sweet. Discontent changed to satisfaction. II. THE SERMON (vers. 25, 26). Israelites too much like the bitter water. When God looked to refresh himself by their confidence and gratitude, he was met by murmuring and distrust. They, too, must learn not to fix attention wholly on disagreeables, but to take the bitter out of them by considering the never-absent context. God himself is the context to every incident which could befall them, but they must apply his help by obedience and simple trust. Obey him and no bitter, in the heart or out of it, but his presence would sweeten. " I am the Lord that healeth *thee*," even as I have healed the waters. Notice :—1. The sermon does not dwell upon the text, though it springs out of it quite naturally. Exceedingly plain and simple, so that a child can understand it. 2. The text (the ordinance) illustrates the sermon (the statute). Yet the illustration is not forced; not even strongly emphasized; just allowed to speak for itself. Some preachers make so much of an illustration, that that which it illustrates is forgotten. [You may drive a brass-headed nail so " home," that while *it* is fixed nothing will hang upon it.]

III. A RETREAT FOR MEDITATION AFTERWARDS (ver. 27). Some excellent sermons are forgotten directly in the hurry and bustle that succeeds them. To gain by sermons we must recollect them; and to recollect them we must have time and place for recollectedness. This God gave to the Israelites at Elim; yet, even so, they failed to profit by it. Had they used their time for meditation better, much after trouble, caused by forgetfulness, would have been saved.

Application. " A sermon for preachers ! " Yes, but a sermon for people also. If God's sermons can be so soon forgotten, even when he gives time for pondering them, how much sooner those *we* preach ! Everything does not rest with the preacher. If the people will not *take pains* to remember—to ponder, meditate, inwardly digest— the best of preachers, even God himself, may preach home to them, and the result be *nil.*—G.

Vers. 22—27.—*Trial and Blessing.* I. THE CLOUD AND SUNSHINE OF THE PILGRIM LIFE. The weariness of the wilderness journey, the disappointment of Marah, and the comforts of Elim, all lie along the appointed way.

II. A HEAVY TRIAL BADLY BORNE. The wilderness thirst had been endured without a murmur; but when in addition they were mocked by the bitter springs of Marah their spirit broke. 1. The end of a prayerless faith is soon reached. If we have not learned to cast burdens upon God and to wait upon him, but expect him to fill our life with ease and pleasure, we shall soon be offended. 2. A spirit with such a faith speedily turns away from God and breaks into complaint against man.

III. FAITH'S TRIUMPH IN DIFFICULTY (25). 1. Moses " cried unto the Lord." The need of the time was rightly read. It was a call to prayer. In times of difficulty and reproach our first recourse should be to God. 2. In answer to believing prayer the bitter waters are sweetened, and the soul finds God in the gift as without the previous disappointment he could not be manifested.

IV. GOD'S COVENANT TIME. 1. In the full experience of his mercy. We must know God's love in Christ before his covenant of service and blessing can be made with us. 2. In the midst of self-knowledge and repentance. At the sweetened waters the faithless ones knew themselves and were ashamed. 3. The nature of the covenant. If they cleave to and serve him, there may be affliction, but there shall be no judgment. 4. How God will be known in Israel. " I am the Lord that healeth thee." Note:—When God's goodness has rebuked our unbelief, he means us to listen to the assurance of his love and to renew our vows.—U.

Vers. 22—26.—*The well of bitterness.* " For I am Jehovah that healeth thee " (Ex. xv. 26). A new chapter of history now opens, that of the wandering; it comprises the following passages. 1. Two months to Sinai. 2. Eleven months at Sinai. 3. Thirty-eight years of virtual settling down in the wilderness of Paran. 4. March upon Canaan in the last year. Introductory to this sermon give description of the journey from the sea to Marah, keeping prominent these points, the first camp probably at " The Wells of Moses," the road thence varying from ten to twenty miles wide, the sea on the right, the wall-looking line of mountain on the left for nearly all the way—this the wilderness of " Shur," *i.e.*, of " the wall." There may indeed have been a city called " Shur," but the wall of mountain may have given name both to city and desert. (On the line of the Roman wall in Northumberland is a village " Wall.") The route here quite unmistakable. More than forty miles. No water. The modern caravan road marked by bleached camel bones. Num. xxxiii. 8, gives the impression of a forced march. At length Marah, to-day a solitary spring of bitter water with stunted palm-tree beside it. Here too is the place to point out, that Israel's wanderings are not so much allegorical, but tautegorical. The phenomena of spiritual life and those of Israel's desert history are not so much two sets of things—one pictorial the other real, but one and the same. This truth lies at the base of all successful practical homiletic treatment.

I. MAN MAY NOT LIVE IN THE PAST. " And Moses brought [forced away] Israel from the Red Sea." Note:—1. *Henceforth Moses is supreme leader.* Aaron and Miriam sink to subordinate places. Besides these, the entourage of Moses consists of Hur, Miriam's husband; Jethro for guide; and Joshua, a sort of body servant. All over the desert are names witnessing to this hour to the sole supremacy of Moses. 2. *Divine Guidance did not impair his individuality.* Inspiration and the "Cloud and Fire" did not so lead as to leave no room for the exercise of judgment or the spontaneity of consecrated genius. Lesson:—*God does not crush individuality, but develops it into fulness and power.* 3. *Moses brought Israel quickly from proximity to Egypt, and even from the scene of victory.* [See Heb. verb, to cause the camp to remove.] The last cadences of the song, the last sound of dancing had hardly died away; Miriam's timbrel was scarcely out of her hand, before "Forward!" Out of this, two lessons. Leave behind: —1. *The memory of Egypt*; of old sins, of old sorrows. 2. *The memory of victory.* As in common life, so in spiritual, *e.g.*, the schoolboy. (John Singleton Copley, a painter's son, had for motto "Ultra pergere," and became Lord Lyndhurst.) Graduate at University. Young tradesman. So with things spiritual, each victory the point of a new departure, even with the aged. "Christian progress by oblivion of the past." Phil. iii. 13, 14.

II. FIRST STAGES IN NEW CHAPTERS OF LIFE'S HISTORY ARE TEDIOUS. Look here at: — 1. *The experience of Israel.* They had left behind many sights, they, even though slaves, would greatly miss; the Nile and its green line of fertility; cities in all their splendour; life in all its rich variety. Now, the hardship and silence of the desert, only trumpet-broken at morn and eve. And this first stage was terrible. (For accurate idea of this road, see "Forty days in the desert," pp. 30, 31.) Nothing so bad as this further on—further on oases, wells, filmy streams, tamarisk, palm, mountain shadows, and even cultivated regions. Excitement perhaps of the first day, the experience novel, the sea in view; but on the second and third, plodding, fainting, and disgust. 2. *The present reality.* So is it with all new chapters in life; the first steps are tedious, *e.g.*, child going to school; boy to college; first steps in business; so with every serious break-up and change in life's pilgrimage. The first steps are arduous. And so too is spiritual life—to break with sin, to stand ridicule, to keep advancing in spite of comparative ignorance, etc. 3. *The temptation.* Many fail to stand it. Young men yield and go back to the fleshpots of Egypt—loneliness with duty and God does not suit them. If we can march from the sea to Marah, all may be well. 4. *The encouragement.* To say nothing of truths like these, that the way was right, the guidance sufficient, the land of Promise was before them; there was a nearer benediction. "The far horizon in front was bounded, not by a line of level sand, but by sharp mountain summits, tossing their peaks into the sky in wild disorder, and suggesting irresistibly the thought of torrents and glens, the shadow of great rocks, and groves of palms." The view was of the range of Sinai, and there Israel was to have nearly a year of high communion with God.

III. DISAPPOINTMENT WAITS US ON OUR WAY. The high-wrought expectation of the people: and lo! the spring is bitter. So with life. So much is this the case, that men of genius have described life as one long illusion. Things are never what they seemed. Neither school nor college, courtship nor marriage, home nor church, business nor pleasure. So much the worse for those who have ideality large.

IV. INTO DISAPPOINTMENT COMES HEALING. All through nature, it is probable, that every poison has its antidote, every evil its corrective, every disappointment its compensation. "Dr. Johnston, in his 'Chemistry of Common Things,' explains at length how the bark of a certain tree has power to precipitate the mineral particles, which embitter the waters, and to make them sweet and clear." Did God "show" this secret thing to Moses? Let every man examine his own life, and he will find by the side of every disappointment a compensating mercy; and more, that out of every such has come a lesson to sweeten life. It is as when (to take the most striking illustration of all) the Saviour came down into human nature, turned to bitterness by sin, and made the bitter sweet.

V. LIFE IS ONE LONG PROBATION. This is a truth illustrated by the journey to, and by the incidents at Marah. There God laid down a *Fixed Principle* [חֹק], and one that was absolutely *Righteous.* [מִשְׁפָּט]. 1. Israel was to hear (*i.e.* believe) and do. 2. And then Jehovah would be to Israel, what the "wood" had been to the water, their Healer.—R.

Ver. 27.—*Elim.* "And they came to Elim, where were twelve wells of water," etc. (Ex. xv. 27). Describe locality, and point out the great change from Marah, and the miserable preceding three days in the desert. And then note the following suggestions as to the pilgrim path of a human soul.

I. OUR PILGRIMAGE LIES THROUGH EVER-VARIED SCENERY. The changes here are so great that they cannot fail to suggest the corresponding truth, *e.g.*, fear on the west of the Red Sea, deliverance, triumph, three days' march, disappointment and healing at Marah, Elim.

II. THE SCENERY WILL INCLUDE "ELIMS." In dark days we believe no bright will dawn, and *vice versâ.* So the sorrowful must be reminded of Elims to come. Many oases for Israel; so to-day even in Sahara. Our Elims.—1. *Lift the mind to their Giver.* 2. *Are earnests of the Better Land.*

III. "ELIMS" ARE THE CREATIONS OF TRUTH. Imagine all the beauty of Elim, and ask, what made it? It was the *water* that made the Paradise. Now, note the place of water in the economy of nature; as a constituent of the human body, in vegetation; as the chief element in all food, medicine, drink; as the universal solvent and purifier; as an agent in all dyes, gorgeous and homely; as "the eye" in every landscape, etc. It is no wonder then that water in Scripture is so often the emblem of truth, for which the soul thirsts, which is given as "water of life" from the throne of God and the Lamb. Doctrine "distils as the dew." God "pours clean water upon us that we may be clean." Note the analogy between truth and water implied in Matt. xxviii. 19. (See illustrations further in Bayley's "Egypt to Canaan," pp. 110—112). And is it not new discovery of truth at crises in our lives, that make our "Elims"? Not at all anything external to the soul; but internal uncoverings of the goodness, grace and glory of our Heavenly Father, etc., etc. [Develop and illustrate.] Will it be considered fanciful to add, that :—

IV. OUR "ELIMS" HAVE AN INDIVIDUAL IMPRESS. "*Twelve* wells," as many as tribes of Israel. "*Seventy* palms," for the tent of each elder a palm. There is any way a speciality in our Father's mercies, which marks them as for us, and reveals to us his personal love.

V. THE "ELIMS" OF OUR PILGRIMAGE ARE NOT FAR FROM OUR "MARAHS." Only some eight or ten miles is that journey of Israel. Then :—1. *At Marah let us hope for Elim.* 2. *From Marah push on for Elim.* Never good to lie down and nurse sorrows and disappointments. Push "forward" along the pilgrim path of duty. 3. *Marah prepares for the delight of Elim.*

VI. "ELIM" IS ONLY FOR ENCAMPMENT. "They encamped there by the waters;" did not dwell, or build a city there.

VII. THE CHANGING SCENERY LEADS TO CANAAN. All the succeeding transformations of life are intended to prepare for the heavenly stability and rest.—R.

EXPOSITION.

CHAPTER XVI

Vers. 1—3.—THE FIRST MURMURING FOR FOOD. From Elim, or the fertile tract extending from Wady Ghurundel to Wady Tayibeh, the Israelites, after a time, removed, and encamped (as we learn from Num. xxxiii 10) by the Red Sea, probably along the narrow coast tract extending from the mouth of Tayibeh to the entrance upon the broad plain of El Markha. Hence they entered upon "the wilderness of Sin," which is between Elim and Sinai "—a tract identified by some with the coast plain, El Markha, by others with the inland undulating region known at the present day as the Debbet-er-Ramleh It is difficult to decide between these two views. In favour of El Markha are: 1. The fact that the Egyptian settlements in the Sinaitic peninsula would thus be avoided, as they seem to have been, since no contest with Egyptians is recorded; 2. The descent of the quails, who, wearied with a long flight over the Red Sea, would naturally settle as soon as they reached the shore; 3. The greater openness and facility of the El Markha and Wady Feiran route, which is admitted by all; and 4. The suitability of the latter to the particulars of the narrative in ch. xviii. In favour of the route by the Debbet-er-Ramleh are, 1 The fact that it is better watered at present than the other; 2. Its being somewhat less removed from the direct line between Wady Ghurundel and Sinai than El Markha; and 3. A certain correspondency of sound or meaning between some of the present geographical names along this route and those of the Mosaic narrative. In "the wilderness of Sin" the Israelites for the first time found themselves in want of sufficient nourishment. They had consumed the grain which they had brought with them out of Egypt; and though no doubt they had still considerable flocks and herds, yet they were unaccustomed to a mere milk and flesh diet, having in Egypt lived principally upon bread (ver. 3), fish (Num. xi. 5), and vegetables (*ibid.*). They therefore "murmured," and accused Moses and Aaron of an intention to starve them. It is quite possible that many of the poorer sort, having brought with them no cattle, or lost their cattle by the way, and not being helped by their brethren, were in actual danger of starvation. Hence God was not angry, but "heard their murmurings" (ver. 9) patiently, and relieved them.

Ver. 1.—**They journeyed from Elim, and all the congregation came.** It has been noted (Cook) that the form of expression "seems to imply that the Israelites proceeded in detachments from Elim, and were first assembled as a complete host when they reached the wilderness of Sin." This accords well with their numbers and with the character of the localities. They could only assemble all together when they reached some considerable plain. **Between Elim and Sinai.** This expression must be regarded as vague to some extent. On the direct line, as the crow flies, there is no "wilderness" (*midbar*) between Wady Ghurundel and Sinai. All is mountain and valley. All that the writer means is that "the wilderness of Sin" lay upon the ordinary, or at any rate an ordinary route between Elim and the great mountain. This is equally true of El Markha and the Debbet-er-Ramleh. **On the fifteenth day of the second month**—*i.e.*, on the 15th of Zif, exactly one month after their departure from Egypt. As only seven camping places are mentioned (Num. xxxiii. 5—11), and one journey of three days through a wilderness (ch. xv. 22), it is evident that there must either have been long stays in several places, or that they must have often encamped in places which had no name. Viewed as an itinerary, the record is manifestly incomplete.

Ver. 2.—**The whole congregation ... murmured,** It has been observed above, that only the poorer sort could have been as yet in any peril of actual starvation; but it may well have been that the rest, once launched into the wilderness, and becoming practically acquainted with its unproductiveness, foresaw that ultimately starvation must come upon them too, when all the cattle were eaten up, or had died through insufficient nourishment Nothing is more clear than that, without the miracle of the manna, it would have been impossible for a population of two millions to have supported themselves for forty years, or even for two years, in such a region as the Sinaitic peninsula, even though it had been in ancient times three or four times as productive as at present. The cattle brought out of Egypt must have rapidly diminished (ch. xvii. 3); and though the Israelites had brought with them also great wealth in the precious metals, yet it must have been some time before they could establish commercial relations with the neighbouring nations so as to obtain such supplies as they needed. Thus we can well understand that at the expiration of a month the people generally should have recognized that their situation was one of great danger, and should have vented their discontent upon their leaders.

Ver. 3.—**Would to God we had died by the hand of the Lord in the land of Egypt**— *i.e.*, "Would that God had smitten us with a painless death, as he did the first-born of the Egyptians! Then we should have avoided the painful and lingering death from starvation which we now see before us." The cry puts on the garb of piety, and names the name of Jehovah, but indicates a want of faith in him, his power, and his promises (ch. iv. 8, 17; vi. 8; xii. 25; xiii. 5, 11), which was sinful, and, after the miracles that they had seen, barely excusable. **When we sat by the flesh-pots of Egypt.** Compare Num. xi. 5. Both passages make it clear that, whatever the sufferings of the Israelites in Egypt from the cruelty of the taskmasters and the hard tasks set them, at any rate their sustenance was well cared for—they had abundance of agreeable food. **Did eat bread.** It has been said that "bread" here means "food in general" (Kalisch); and no doubt the word has sometimes that sense. But it was probably actual bread, rather than anything else, for which the Israelites were longing. See the Introduction to the chapter.

HOMILETICS.

Vers. 1—3.—*The unreasonableness of discontent*. The people of Israel experience now the second trial that has come upon them since the passage of the Red Sea. First, they had nothing which they could drink (ch. xv. 24); now they are afraid that they will soon have nothing to eat. They have consumed their dough (ch. xii. 39), their grain, their flour; many of them have consumed, or lost, their beasts. The land around them produces little or nothing that is edible; no settled inhabitants show themselves from whom they may purchase food. If there are Egyptian storehouses in the district, they are shut against the enemies of Egypt. So the Israelites, one and all, begin to despair and murmur. How irrational their conduct! The unreasonableness of discontent is shown—

I. IN DISTRUSTING GOD'S POWER OF DELIVERANCE, WHEN WE HAVE SEEN FREQUENT INSTANCES OF IT. The Israelites had been brought out of Egypt "by a mighty hand"—delivered through means of a series of wonderful miracles. They had escaped the pursuit of Pharaoh by having a path made for them through the waters of the Red Sea. They had witnessed the destruction of Pharaoh's choicest warriors by the return of the waves on either side. They had very recently thought themselves on the point of perishing with thirst; and then by the simplest possible means God had made the bitter water sweet and agreeable. Now, they had found themselves fallen into a new difficulty. They had no bread, and foresaw a time when all their food would be exhausted. They were not really, if the rich imparted of their superfluous cattle to the poor, in any immediate danger. Yet, instead of bearing the trial, and doing the best they could under the circumstances, they began to murmur and wish themselves dead. They did not reflect upon the past; they did not use it as a standard by which to estimate the future. They acted exactly as they might naturally have done, had they had no previous evidence of God's power to deliver. And so it is to this day in human life frequently. We do not witness miracles, but we witness signal deliverances of various kinds—an enemy defeated at the moment that he seemed about to carry all before him—the independence of a nation saved when it appeared to be lost—drought succeeded by copious rains—overmuch rain followed by a glorious month for harvest. Yet, each time that a calamity threatens, we despond; we forget all the past; we distrust God's mercy; we murmur; we wish, or say we wish, that we had died before the trial came.

II. IN CONTRASTING ALL THE DISADVANTAGES OF OUR PRESENT POSITION, WITHOUT ITS COMPENSATING ADVANTAGES, WITH ALL THE ADVANTAGES, AND NONE OF THE DISADVANTAGES, OF SOME PREVIOUS ONE. The Israelites, fearing starvation, thought of nothing but the delight of sitting by the flesh-pots of Egypt, and eating bread to the full. They omitted to reflect on their severe toils day after day, on the misery of feeling they were slaves, on the murder of their children by one tyrant, and the requirement of impossible tasks by another, on the rudeness to which they were daily exposed, and the blows which were hourly showered on them. They omitted equally to consider what they had gained by quitting Egypt—the consciousness of freedom, the full liberty of worshipping God after their conscience, the constant society of their families, the bracing air of the Desert, the perpetual evidence of God's presence and providential care in the sight of the pillar of the cloud and of fire, which accompanied them. And men still act much the same. Oh! for the delights of boyhood, they exclaim, forgetting all its drawbacks. Oh! for the time when I occupied *that* position, which I unwisely gave up (because I hated it). The present situation is always the worst conceivable—its ills are magnified, its good points overlooked, thought nothing of. Again, how unreasonable! The allegorical tale which tells of a pilgrim who wished to change his cross, and after trying a hundred others, found that the original one alone fitted him, is applicable to such cases, and should teach us a lesson of content.

III. IN ITS VENTING ITSELF TOO OFTEN ON THE WRONG PERSON. Moses and Aaron were not to blame for the situation in which the Israelites found themselves. They had done nothing but obey God from first to last. God had commanded the exodus—God had led the way—God had forbidden the short route along the shore to the country of the Philistines, and had brought them into the "wilderness of the Red

Sea," and that desolate part of it called "the wilderness of Sin." Moses and Aaron were but his mouthpieces. Yet the Israelites murmured against *them*. Truly did Moses respond—"What are we? Your murmurings are not against us, but against the LORD." And so are all murmurings. Men are but God's instruments; and, in whatsoever difficulty we find ourselves, it is God who has placed us there. Murmuring against men is altogether foolish and vain. We should take our grief straight to God; we should address him, not with murmuring, but with prayer. We should entreat him to remove our burthen, or to give us strength to bear it. We should place all in his hands.

HOMILIES BY VARIOUS AUTHORS.

Vers. 1—4.—*Murmurings.* In the "Wilderness of Sin," between Elim and Sinai, on the 15th day of the second month after the departing of Israel out of Egypt (ver. 1). One short month, but how much can be forgotten even in so brief a space of time! (cf. ch. xxxii. 1). Egypt now lay at a little distance. The supplies of the Israelites were failing them. God lets the barrel of meal and the cruse of oil run out (1 Kings xvii. 12), before interposing with his help. Thus he tries what manner of spirit we are of. Our extremity is his opportunity. Consider here—

I. THE PEOPLE'S MURMURINGS (ver. 2). These are brought into strong relief in the course of the narrative. "The whole congregation of the children of Israel murmured" (ver. 2). "He heareth your murmurings against the Lord, and what are we that ye murmur against us?" (ver. 7). "The Lord heareth your murmurings which ye murmur against him, and what are we? Your murmurings are not against us, but against the Lord" (ver. 8). "He hath heard your murmurings" (ver. 9). "I have heard the murmurings of the children of Israel" (ver. 12). 1. *They murmured, and did not pray.* They seem to have left that to Moses (cf. ch. xiv. 15). Remembering what Jehovah had already done for them—the proofs he had already given them of his goodness and faithfulness—we might have thought that prayer would have been their first resource. But they do not avail themselves of it. They do not even raise the empty cries of ch. xiv. 10. It is a wholly unsubmissive and distrustful spirit which wreaks its unreasonableness on Moses and Aaron in the words, "Ye have brought us forth into the wilderness to kill this whole assembly with hunger" (ver. 3). We who blame them, however, have only to observe our own hearts to see how often we are in the same condemnation. (See Hamilton's "Moses," Lect. xiv.—"Murmurs.") It is ever easier, in times of difficulty, to murmur than to pray. Yet how much better for ourselves, as well as more dutiful to God, could we learn the lesson of coming with every trouble to the throne of grace.

> " But with my God I leave my cause;
>   From Him I seek relief;
> To Him in confidence of prayer
>   Unbosom all my grief "

Had Israel prayed more, relief might have come sooner. 2. Their behaviour affords some interesting illustrations of *what the murmuring spirit is.* Distinguish this spirit from states of mind which bear a superficial resemblance to it. (1) From the cry of natural distress. When distress comes upon us, we cannot but acutely feel the pain of our situation, and with this is connected the tendency to lament and bewail it. The dictates of the highest piety, indeed, would lead us to imitate David in studying to be *still* before God. "I was dumb, I opened not my mouth because *thou* didst it" (Ps. xxxix. 9). Yet listen to this same David's lamentations over Absalom (2 Sam. xviii. 19). There are few in whom the spirit of resignation is so perfectly formed—in whom religious motives so uniformly and entirely predominate—that a wail of grief *never* escapes their lips. It would, however, be cruel to describe these purely natural expressions of feeling as "murmurings," though it is to be admitted that an element of murmuring frequently mingles with them. (2) From the expostulations of good men with God, caused by the perplexity and mystery of his dealings with them. Such expostulations, *e.g.*, as those of Moses in ch. v. 22, 23; or of Job, in several of his speeches (Job vii. 11—21; x. 1—22, etc.); or of Jeremiah (Jer. iv. 10; xx. 7). As Augustine says of Moses, "These are not words of contumacy or indignation, but of inquiry and prayer." 3. Even from the desperate speeches of good men, temporarily carried beyond bounds by their sorrow. Job enters this plea for himself—"Do ye imagine to reprove words, and the speeches of one that is desperate, which are as wind" (Job vi. 26); and we feel at once the justice of it. This was not murmuring. These wild speeches—though not blameless—were but a degree removed from raving. What elements, then, do enter into the murmuring spirit—how is it to be described? (1) At the basis of it there lies *distrust* and *unsubmissiveness*. There is distrust of God's goodness and power, and want of submission to his will in the situation in which he has placed us. The opposite spirit is exemplified in Christ, in his first temptation in the wilderness (Matt. iv. 1—4; cf. Deut. viii. 3). (2) Connected with this, there is *forgetfulness of, and ingratitude for, benefits formerly received*. This is very conspicuous in the case of these Israelites (ver. 3). (3) The characteristic feature of this spirit is *the entertaining of injurious thoughts of God*—the attempt to put God in the wrong by fastening on him the imputation of dealing harshly and injuriously with us. The murmuring spirit keeps the eye bent on self, and on self's fancied wrongs, and labours hard to make out a case of ill treatment. Its tone is complaining. It would arraign the Eternal at its puny bar, and convict him of injustice. It is narrow, self-pitying, egoistic. (4) It expresses itself in *accusations* and *reproaches*. The mental point of view already indicated prepares the way for these, and leads to them being passed off as righteous charges. God is charged foolishly (Job i. 22). (5) It is prone to *exaggeration*. The Israelites can hardly have been as well off in Egypt as they here pretend, though their words (ver. 3) show that their rations in bondage must have been fairly liberal. But the wish to make their present situation look as dark as possible, leads them to magnify the advantages of their former one. They did not think so much of it when they had it. (6) Murmuring against God *may not venture to express itself directly, and yet may do so indirectly*. The murmuring of the Israelites was of this veiled character. They masked their rebellion against God, and their impeaching of his goodness, by directing their accusations against his servants. It was God against whom they murmured (ver. 7, 8), but they slightly veiled the fact by not mentioning God, but by speaking only of Moses and Aaron. We should remember this, in our contendings with Providence. The persons on whom our murmuring spirit wreaks itself may be secondary agents—the voluntary or involuntary causes of our misfortunes—or even persons in no way directly concerned with our trouble—but be they who they may, if the spirit be bitter and rebellious, it is God, not they, whom we are contending against (cf. Gen. l. 19, 20; 2 Sam. xvii. 10).

II. GOD'S SURPRISING TREATMENT OF THESE MURMURINGS (ver. 4). It is a most astonishing fact that on this occasion there is not, on God's part, a single severe word of reproof of the people's murmurings, far less any punishment of them for it. It could not at this time be said—"Some of them also murmured, and were destroyed by the destroyer" (1 Cor. x. 10). The appearance of the glory in the cloud warned and abashed, but did not injure them (ver. 10). The reason was not that God did not hear their murmuring, nor yet that he mistook its import, as directed ostensibly, not against him, but against Moses and Aaron. The Searcher of Hearts knows well when our murmurings are against *Him* (vers. 7, 8). But, 1. He *pitied* them. They were really in great need. He looked to their need, more than to their murmurings. In his great compassion, knowing their dire distress, he treated their murmurings almost as if they were prayers—gave them what they should have *asked*. The Father in this way anticipated the Son (Matt. xv. 32). 2. He was *forbearing with them in the beginning of their way*. God was not weakly indulgent. At a later time, when the people had been longer under training, they were severely punished for similar offences (cf. Num. xxi. 5); but in the preliminary stages of this wilderness education, God made large and merciful allowances for them. Neither here, nor at the Red Sea, nor later, at Rephidim, when they openly "tempted" him (ch. xvii. 1—8), do we read of God so much as chiding them for their wayward doings: he bore with them, like a father bearing with his children. He knew how ignorant they were; how much infirmity there was about them; how novel and trying were the situations in which he was placing them; and he mercifully gave them *time* to improve by his teaching. Surely a God who acts in this way is not to be called " an hard master." Instead of sternly punishing their murmurings, he took their need as a starting-point, and sought to educate them out of the murmuring disposition. 3. He purposed to *prove them.* He would fully supply their wants, and so give them an opportunity of showing whether their murmuring was a result of mere infirmity—or was connected with a deeply ingrained spirit of disobedience. When perversity began to show itself, he did not spare reproof (ver. 28).—J. O.

EXPOSITION.

Vers. 4—8.—THE PROMISE OF BREAD FROM HEAVEN. When men who are in real distress make complaint, even though the tone of their complaint be not such as it ought to be, God in his mercy is wont to have compassion upon them, to " hear their murmurings," &c., and grant them some relief. But the relief is seldom of the kind which they expect, or pray for. The Israelites wished for actual bread, made of wheaten or barley flour. God gave them, not such bread, but a substitute for it. And first, before giving it, he promised that it should be given. Thus expectation was aroused ; faith was exercised ; the supernatural character of the relief was indicated ; the power and the goodness of God, were, both of them, shown forth. And with the promise was given a law. They were on each occasion to gather no more than would suffice for the day. Thus they would continually " live by faith," taking no thought for the morrow, but trusting all to God.

Ver. 4.—Bread from heaven. Compare Ps. lxxviii. 24 ; Neh. ix. 15 ; John vi. 31—51. The expression is of course not to be understood literally. The substance was not actual bread, neither was it locally transferred from the distant region called " heaven " to the soil of the Sinaitic peninsula. But it was called " bread," because it was intended to serve instead of bread, as the main support of life during the sojourn of Israel in the wilderness ; and it was said to be " from heaven," first, as descending on the ground out of the circumambient air ; and secondly, as miraculously sent by him, whose seat is in heaven. **The people shall gather a certain rate every day.** Rather " a *day's supply* every day," such a quantity as shall seem to each man reasonably sufficient for himself and his family. **That I may prove them.** As in Paradise God coupled with his free gift of " every tree of the garden " the positive precept, " But of the tree of the knowledge of good and evil thou shalt not eat,"—that he might prove our first parents, whether they would obey him or not—so now he

" proved " the obedience of the Israelites by a definite, positive command—they were not to gather on ordinary days more than was sufficient for the day. All life is intended as a probation.

Ver. 5.—On the sixth day. That a period of seven days was known to the Hebrews as a week appears from the story of Jacob and Laban (Gen. xxix. 27). But there is no distinct evidence that the year was as yet divided into weeks, much less that the several days of the week were as yet distinguished as the first, second, third day, etc. " The sixth day," here probably means (as Kalisch says), " the sixth day after the first supply of the manna." **They shall prepare.** The preparation would be, first, by measurement (ver. 18), and then by pounding and grinding (Num. xi. 8). **It shall be double.** Some commentators suppose that in these words is implied an order that on the sixth day they should set themselves to gather a double quantity. But the natural meaning of the words is, that, having gathered the usual quantity, they should find, when they measured it, that, by miracle, the supply sufficient for one day was multiplied, so as to suffice for two. (So Kalisch, Knobel, Kurtz, and others.) This view is in harmony with verse 18, which tells of a miraculous expansion and diminution of the manna after it had been gathered, and with verse 22, which shows us " the rulers " surprised by the miracle of the sixth day.

Ver. 6.—At even, then ye shall know. See verses 12 and 13. The first evidence which the Israelites would have, that God had heard and considered their complaints, would be the descent of the quails at even of the day on which Moses and Aaron addressed them. **That the Lord hath brought you out**—*i.e.,* " that it is not we who, to gratify our own personal ambition, have induced you to quit Egypt under our guidance ; but that all which we have done has been to act as God's instruments, and to carry out his designs."

Ver. 7.—And in the morning then ye shall see the glory of the Lord. This has been supposed to refer to the manifestation of God's presence recorded in verse 10 ; but the balance of the two clauses in verses 6 and 7 implies two *similar* manifestations, and their arrangement shows the priority of the evening one.

Now the manifestation of verse 10 preceded the coming of the quails. The manifestation which followed it, which was similar, and in the morning, was the fall of the manna. **For that he heareth your murmurings.** The connection of this clause with the preceding furnishes an additional argument in favour of the exposition that " the glory of God," spoken of in this verse is the manna. **Against the Lord.** Professedly and directly against *us*, but indirectly and really against God, whose instruments we have been in the whole matter of the exodus. **What are we ?**—*i.e.*, " What power have we of our own? We have no hereditary rank, no fixed definite position. We are simply the leaders whom you have chosen to follow, because you believed us to have a commission from God. Apart from this, we are nobodies. But, if our commission is conceded, we are to you in the place of God ;

and to murmur against us is to murmur against Jehovah."

Ver. 8.—**When the Lord shall give you in the evening flesh to eat.** Moses must have received a distinct intimation of the coming arrival of the quails, though he has not recorded it, his desire of brevity causing him to retrench all that is not absolutely necessary for the right understanding of the narrative. It is, comparatively, seldom that he records both the Divine message and his delivery of it. In general, he places upon record either the message only, or its delivery only. **Bread to the full.** Compare above, verse 4 ; and *infra*, verses 12 and 18. **The Lord heareth your murmurings.** The latter part of this verse is, in the main, a repetition of verse 7 ; but it emphasises the statements of that verse, and prepares the way for what follows.

HOMILETICS.

Vers. 4—8. *The mercy of God in hearing and helping even an ungrateful and discontented people.*—God is very merciful to those who are in covenant with him, whom he has chosen for his own, and made " the sheep of his pasture." Very often, and very far may they go astray, turn from the right way, rebel against him, refuse to hearken to his voice, murmur, misuse his ministers and slander them, yet not alienate him wholly. Indefectible grace must not indeed be claimed by any man as his own portion ; for none can know that he possesses it ; yet the way of God, on the whole, appears to be to reclaim his wandering sheep ; recall them to a sense of what is their duty ; and restore them to the fold whence they have strayed. All that can be done with this object he does for the Church now, as for the congregation of the children of Israel in the wilderness.

I. He PARDONS THEIR OFFENCES. Distrust, discontent, ingratitude, even when openly expressed in speech, he forgives in his mercy, not seven times only, but " seventy times seven." How many murmur at their lot ; complain of their worldly condition, or their lack of spiritual gifts, or their unhappy position under ministers of whom they do not approve ; or the coldness and unsympathetic temper of their friends, or the want of any due appreciation by others of their merits ! It is, comparatively speaking, rarely that we meet with a contented person. Yet God is so merciful, that he bears with the murmurers—yea, even " hears their murmurings," and devises means for their relief.

II. He GIVES THEM BREAD FROM HEAVEN. " Every good gift and every perfect gift " is from him, and " cometh down from the Father of Lights." The material sustenance of daily life is one form of " bread from heaven," wherewith he daily provides the millions who look to him. His holy word is another form, a heavenly gift, the sustenance of many souls. But, as he tells us, he himself is " the *true* bread from heaven " (John vi. 32—51). In and through the Eucharist, he gives us himself to be our spiritual food and sustenance, the bread of life, the true manna, meat indeed. If we worthily receive the blessed sacrament of his body and blood, then we " spiritually eat the flesh of Christ and drink his blood ; then we dwell in Christ, and Christ in us ; we are one with Christ, and Christ with us "—" our sinful bodies are made clean by his body, and our souls washed through his most precious blood." Thus, he gives us, in the highest, most perfect, and most spiritual way, that which is the great need of our souls, " bread from heaven."

III. He GIVES THEM LAWS TO PROVE THEM. With blessing duty goes ever hand in hand. To every gift God attaches some law of direction for its use. The gift of the manna had its own laws—its law of gathering, and its law of reserving or not reserving. The holy Eucharist has also its one great law—a law fixing the mental attitude—" Do this *in remembrance of me*." To make it a mere supper, as the Corinthians did (1 Cor.

xi. 20—34), albeit a love-feast, symbolical of Christian fellowship and unity, is to break this law. The Eucharist is "for the continual remembrance of the sacrifice of the death of Christ"—for the calling to mind his sufferings for our sins, his atonement for our guilt, his deliverance of us from Satan, death, and hell, by his one oblation of himself once offered upon the Cross. It is by this remembrance that our penitence is made acute, our gratitude called forth, our hearts enabled to "lift themselves up," our spirits stirred to love, and joy, and thankfulness; and obedience to this law on our part is a necessary condition to our receiving the benefits of the Eucharist. Thus we too, when "bread from heaven" is rained upon us, have a law given to us to prove us, whether we will walk in God's law or not.

HOMILIES BY VARIOUS AUTHORS.

Vers. 4—16.—*The gift of Manna.* Quails also were given, on this occasion in mercy, and on a later occasion in wrath (Num. xi. 31—34); but it was the manna which was the principal gift, both as providing Israel with a continuous supply of food, and as having a permanent significance in the history of God's dealings with his Church (vers. 32—35).

I. THE MANNA PROMISED (vers. 4—9). 1. *God would rain bread from heaven for them* (ver. 4). He would spread a table for them, even in the wilderness, a thing they had deemed impossible (Ps. lxxviii. 19). He would give them to eat of "the corn of heaven" (Ps. lxviii. 24). He would thus display himself as Jehovah,—the God of exhaustless resources,—able and willing to supply all their need (cf. Phil. iv. 19). He would remove from himself the reproach wherewith they had reproached him, that he had brought them into the wilderness, "to kill this whole assembly with hunger" (ver. 3). He would testify of his loving care for them (cf. Deut. i. 31). 2. *The supply would be continuous*—"Every day" (ver. 4). The regularity of the supply would be a daily proof of God's faithfulness—another of the Jehovah attributes. We have a similar proof of the Divine faithfulness in the constancy of the laws of nature on which our own supplies of food depend; in particular, in the regular succession of seed-time and harvest, and cold and heat, and summer and winter, which God has promised to maintain (Gen. viii. 22; cf. Ps. cxix. 89—92). 3. *The gift of quails and manna would be a manifestation of his glory as Jehovah* (vers. 6, 7; also ver. 12—"and ye shall know that I am Jehovah your God"). His Jehovah character would be revealed in it. Note, in addition to what is said above, the following illustrations of this. (1) The gift of manna was an act of free origination. Compare with Christ's multiplication of the loaves, brought in John vi. into close association with this miracle. (2) So far as natural materials were utilised in the production of the manna (dew, etc.), it was shown how absolutely plastic nature was in the hands of its Creator. (3) The gift of quails was a further testimony to God's supreme rule in nature. (4) It was a special feature in this transaction that God was seen in it acting solely *from himself*—finding the law and reason of what he did in himself alone. He interposes with a simple "I will" (ver. 4). It was neither the people's merits nor the people's prayers, which moved him to give the manna. Merits they had none; prayers they did not offer. But God, who brought them out of Egypt, and had bound himself by covenant with their fathers, found a reason in himself for helping them, when he could find none in *them* (cf. Deut. ix. 4, 5). He showed them this kindness for his own name's sake (cf. Ps. cvi. 8); because he was Jehovah, who changed not (Mal. iii. 6). 4. *The gift of manna would prove a trial of obedience* (ver. 4). God bound himself to send the manna day by day, and this would be a test of *his* faithfulness. But rules would be prescribed to the people for gathering the manna, and this would be a test of *their* obedience. God's design in giving the manna was thus not merely to supply the people's natural wants. He would also train them to dependence. He would test their characters. He would endeavour to form them to habits of obedience. A like educative and disciplinary purpose is to be recognised as bound up with all God's leading of us. Gifts are at the same time trusts. They impose duties upon us, and lay us under responsibilities. There are rules to be observed in the use of them which test our inner dispositions. There is a law of temperance in the use of food. There is a law of modesty in dress. There are the laws relating to the acquisition and expenditure of money—honesty in acquisition, economy in use, liberality in giving (cf. Deut. xv. 7—12), devotion of the first fruits of income to God. There is the supreme law, which includes all others—" Whether, therefore, ye eat or drink, or whatsoever ye do, do all to the glory of God" (1 Cor. x. 31). There is no action, no occupation, however seemingly trivial, which has not important relations to the formation of character. "The daily round, the common task," etc.

II. THE PREPARATORY THEOPHANY (vers. 9—13). Moses summoned the people to draw near before the Lord. Then, as they came together, and looked toward the wilderness, lo! "the glory of the Lord appeared in the cloud." It is a suggestive circumstance that it is Aaron, who by command of Moses, collects the congregation (ver. 10). Moses, according to his wont, had probably withdrawn to pray (cf. ch. xiv. 15). In this, as in other instances, Moses might be taken as an example of *secrecy* in prayer. His prayers are never paraded. They are even studiously kept in the background—a proof surely of the Mosaic authorship of the book. When they come to light, it is often incidentally (ch. xiv. 15). On one notable occasion an intercessory prayer of his was not made known till near the end of his life (Deut. ix. 25). We know of his prayers mostly by their results. This appearance of the glory of God to Israel may be viewed :—1. *As a rebuke of the people's murmurings.* Unlike the "look" from the pillar of fire with which the Lord discomfited the Egyptians (ch. xiv. 24), it was a look with as much mercy as anger in it. Yet it conveyed reproof. It may be compared with the theophany which terminated the dispute between Job and his friends, and caused the patriarch to abhor himself, and to repent in dust and ashes (Job xxxviii. 1; xlii. 6); or to the look of sorrow and reproof which the Lord cast on Peter, which caused him to go out, and weep bitterly (Matt. xxvi. 75). How abashed, humbled, and full of fear, those murmurers would now be, as with mouths stopped (Rom. iii. 19), they beheld that terrible glory forming itself in the cloud, and looking down full upon them! 2. *As a fitting introduction to the miracle that was to follow.* It gave impressiveness to the announcement—showed indubitably the source of the miraculous supply—roused the minds of the people to a high pitch of expectation —prepared them for something grand and exceptional in the Divine procedure. It thus checked their murmurings, convinced them of their sin in distrusting God, warned them of the danger of further rebellion, and brought them back to their obedience. God's words—" I have heard the murmurings of the children of Israel"—at the same time reminded them that he was fully aware of all their "hard speeches" which they had spoken against him. 3. *As an anticipation of the revelation of Sinai.* These chapters are full of anticipations. In ch. xv. 25, 26, we have "statute and an ordinance," anticipatory of the later Sinaitic covenant; in this chapter, we have an anticipation of Sinai glory and also of the sabbath law (ver. 23); in ch. xviii. 16, we have an anticipation of the *civil* code of Sinai; for Moses makes the people "know the statutes of God, and his laws."

III. THE MANNA GIVEN (vers. 13—16). Quails came in the evening, and next morning the manna fell with the dew. We observe concerning it—1. *That it came in a not unfamiliar form.* The "angel's food" (Ps. lxxviii. 25), wore the dress, and had the taste of the ordinary manna of the desert. We miss in the miracles of the Bible the grotesque and bizarre features which mark the supernatural stories of other books. They testify to the existence, as well as respect the laws, of an established natural order. The plagues of Egypt, *e.g.*, were thoroughly true to the natural phenomena of that country, and made the largest possible use of existing agencies. The crossing of the Red Sea was accomplished by the supernatural employment of natural conditions and agencies. There is in all these miracles the constant observance of the two laws: (1) Of economy—utilising the natural so far as it will go; and (2) of congruity—keeping as closely as possible to the type of the natural, even when originating supernatural phenomena. 2. *That it was a direct production of the power of God.* It was in the truest sense bread from heaven, and is thus a type of Christ, the Bread of Life (see below). Yet the power exerted in the creation of the manna—and it is important to remember this—is but the same power, only more visibly put forth, which operates still in nature, giving us our yearly supplies of the good things of the earth. The annual harvest is only not a miracle, because it comes regularly, season after season, and because numerous secondary agencies are employed in its production. You plough, that is, break up the ground to receive the seed; but whence came the seed? From last year's gift. You sow it in the fields, cover it up again and leave it—to whose care? To God's. It is he who now takes the matter into his own hands, and in what remains you can but wait upon his will. It rests with him to send his rains or to withhold them; to order the sunshine and heat; to bless or blast your harvest. What man does is but to put matters in train for God's working—God himself does the rest; in the swelling and germination of the seed, in all the stages of its growth, in the formation of the blade, in the modelling of the ear, in the filling of it with the rich ripe grain, his power is absolutely, and all throughout, the only power at work. And how great the gift is when it comes! It is literally God opening his hand and putting into ours the food necessary for our sustenance. But for that gift, year by year renewed, man and beast would utterly perish. It is calculated that a year's produce in Great Britain alone amounts in money value to over £160,000,000. The corn crop alone was valued in 1880 at £90,000,000. It is as if God had made a direct gift of that sum of money to our nation in the year named, only it was given in a better than money form—in food. How little we think of it! Men are proud and self-sufficient, and speak sometimes as if they would almost disdain to accept or acknowledge a favour even from the Almighty. While yet, in truth, they are, like others, the veriest pensioners on his bounty, sustained by his power, seeing by his light, warmed by his sun, and fed year by year by the crumbs that fall from his table. Were God for a single year to break the staff of bread over the whole earth, where would either it or they be? 3. *That it was given day by day, and with regularity.* Thus the manna taught a daily lesson of dependence on God, and so played an important part in the spiritual education of Israel. Yet familiarity must have done much then, as it does still, to deaden the impression of God's hand in the daily gift. Because the manna came to them, not by fits and starts, but regularly; because there was a "law" in its coming—they would get to look on it as quite a common occurrence, no more to be wondered at than the rising and setting of the sun, or any other sequence in nature. "Laws of nature" tend, in precisely the same way, to blind us to the agency of God working behind and in them, as well as to hide from us his agency in the *origination* of the sequences that now flow so uniformly. We have spoken of God's agency in the production of the harvest. But there is good ground for speaking of our cereal crops as in yet another sense—"bread from heaven." These cereal plants, it is affirmed, are never found in a wild state; cannot by any known process be developed from plants in a wild state; and if once allowed to degenerate, can never again be reclaimed for human food. Not inaptly, therefore, have they been represented as even now a kind of *standing miracle*—a proof of direct creative interposition for the good of man. (See "The Cerealia: a Standing Miracle," by Professor Harvey, in "Good Words," vol. ii.) Yet how entirely is this veiled from us by the fact that "all things continue as they were from the beginning of the creation" (2 Pet. iii. 4). 4. *That it was a food entirely suitable to the circumstances of the Israelites.* It was light, nutritious, palatable; comprised variety by admitting of being prepared in different ways (baked, seethed, ver. 23; cf. Num. xi. 8); was abundant in quantity, readily distinguishable by the eye, and being of a granulated nature, and strewn thickly throughout all the camp, could be collected with a very moderate expenditure of labour. It was thus, like so much in our own surroundings, and in the provision which God makes for our wants, a constant witness to the care, goodness, wisdom, and forethought of the great Giver.—J. O.

EXPOSITION.

Vers. 9—21.—THE PROMISE FULFILLED. Moses had made a double promise to the Israelites in God's name. "The Lord shall give you," he had said, "in the evening flesh to eat, and in the morning bread to the full" (ver. 8). And now the time for the fulfilment of the double promise approached. First, however, before they received the blessings, he required them to present themselves before the Lord. As they had rebelled in murmuring, an act of homage was proper; and as they had called in question the conduct of Moses and Aaron.

some token that God approved the action of these his faithful servants, and would support them, was needed. Hence the appearance of the Lord to the congregation in the cloud (ver. 10). After this, when evening approached, the quails fell. A vast flight of this migratory bird, which often arrives in Arabia Petræa from the sea (Diod. Sic. i. 60), fell to the earth about the Hebrew camp, and, being quite exhausted, lay on the ground in a state which allowed of their being taken by the hand. The Israelites had thus abundant " flesh to eat" (ver. 8), for God "sent them meat enough" (Ps. lxxviii. 26). The next morning, the remainder of the promise was fulfilled. When they awoke, they found that the vegetation about the camp was covered with a sort of dew, resembling hoar-frost, which was capable of easy detachment from the leaves, and which proved to be an edible substance. While they were in doubt about the phenomenon, Moses informed them that this was the " bread from heaven" which they had been promised (ver. 15). At the same time he instructed them as to the quantity which they should gather, which he fixed at an omer for each member of their family (ver. 16). In attempting to carry out these instructions, mistakes were not unnaturally made; some exceeded the set quantity, others fell short of it. But the result was found to be the same. Whatever the quantity gathered, when it was brought home and measured, the amount was by miracle made to be exactly an omer for each (ver. 18). Afterwards, Moses gave another order. The whole of the manna was to be consumed (ordinarily) on the day on which it was gathered. When some wilfully disobeyed this command, the reserved manna was found on the next day to have become bad—it had bred worms, and gave out an offensive odour. This circumstance put a stop to the malpractice.

Ver. 12.—**At even.** Literally, " between the two evenings." For the meaning of the phrase, see the comment on ch. xii. 6. **Ye shall eat flesh.** The quails, as appears by the subsequent narrative, were supplied, not regularly, but only on rare occasions; in fact (so far as appears), only here in the wilderness of Sin, and at Kibroth-hattaavah in the wilderness of Paran (Num. xi. 31—34). They were not a necessary, but an indulgence. **Ye shall know that I am the Lord.** The miracle of the manna, and the timely appearance of the

quails at the hour announced, will sufficiently show that it is God himself who has you under his charge and watches over you.

Ver. 13.—**The quails came up.** The word here translated, " quails" has been supposed to designate the flying-fish (*Trigla Israelitarum* of Ehrenberg), or a species of locust (Ludolf). But Ps. lxxviii. 28, makes it clear that " feathered fowls" are intended; and moderns generally, are agreed that the rendering " quails" is right. It has the authority of the Septuagint, of Josephus, and of the Vulgate. Diodorus says that " the inhabitants of Arabia Petræa prepared long nets, spread them near the coast for many stadia, and thus caught a great number of quails which are in the habit of coming in from the sea" (ii. 60). The quail regularly migrates from Syria and Arabia in the autumn, and winters in the interior of Africa, whence it returns northwards in immense masses in the spring (Schubert, *Reise*, vol. ii. p. 361). Kalisch thinks that the particular species of quail intended is the *kata* of the Arabs (*Tetrao Alchata* of Linnæus); but the common quail (*Tetrao coturnix*) is preferred by most commentators. When these birds approach the coast after a long flight over the Red Sea, they are often so exhausted that they rather fall to the ground than settle, and are then easily taken by the hand or killed with sticks. Their flesh is regarded by the natives as a delicacy. **Covered the camp**—*i.e.*, covered all the ground between the tents in which the Israelites lived in the wilderness. **The dew lay.** Literally, " there was a layer of dew"—something, *i.e.*, lay on the ground outside the camp which looked like dew, and was in part dew, but not wholly so.

Ver. 14.—**When the dew that lay was gone up.** The moisture which lay upon the herbage soon evaporated, drawn up by the sun; and then the miracle revealed itself. There remained upon each leaf and each blade of grass a delicate small substance, compared here to **hoar frost**, and elsewhere (Num. xi. 7) to " coriander seed," which was easily detached and collected in bags or baskets. The thing was altogether a novelty to the Israelites, though analogous in some degree to natural processes still occurring in the country. These processes are of two kinds. At certain times of the year there is a deposit of a glutinous substance from the air upon leaves and even upon stones, which may be scraped off, and which resembles thick honey. There is also an exudation from various trees and shrubs, especially the tamarisk, which is moderately hard, and is found both on the growing plant and on the fallen leaves beneath it, in the shape of small, round, white or greyish grains. It is this last which is the manna of commerce. The Biblical manna cannot be identified with either of these two substances.

In some points it resembled the one, in other points the other; in some, it differed from both. It came out of the air like the "air-honey," and did not exude from shrubs; but it was hard, like the manna of commerce, and could be "ground in mills" and "beaten in mortars," which the "air-honey" cannot. It was not a medicament, like the one, nor a condiment, like the other, but a substance suited to be a substitute for bread, and to become the main sustenance of the Israelitish people. It was produced in quantities far exceeding anything that is recorded of either manna proper, or air honey. It accompanied the Israelites wherever they went during the space of forty years, whereas the natural substances, which in certain points resemble it, are confined to certain districts, and to certain seasons of the year. During the whole space of forty years it fell regularly during six consecutive days, and then ceased on the seventh. It "bred worms" if kept till the morrow on all days of the week except one: on that one—the Sabbath—it bred no worms, but was sweet and good. Thus, it must be regarded as a peculiar substance, miraculously created for a special purpose, but similar in certain respects to certain known substances which are still produced in the Sinaitic region.

Ver. 15.—**They said one to another, this is manna.** Rather, "this is a gift." To suppose that they recognised the substance as one known to them in Egypt under the name of *menu* or *mennu*, is to make this clause contradict the next. To translate "what is this?" gives good sense, but is against grammar, since the Hebrew for "what" is not *man* but *mah*. The Septuagint translators (who render τί ἐστι τοῦτο) were probably deceived by their familiarity with the Chaldee, in which *man* corresponds to "what." Not knowing what to call the substance, the Israelites said one to another, "it is a gift"—meaning a gift from heaven, God's gift (compare verse 8); and afterwards, in consequence of this, the word *man* (properly "gift") became the accepted name of the thing.

Ver. 16.—**An omer for every man.** Ac-cording to Kalisch, the omer is about two quarts (English): but this estimate is probably in excess. Josephus makes the measure one equal to six cotyles, which would be about a quart and a half, or three pints. **In his tents.** Rather, "in his *tent*."

Ver. 17.—**The children of Israel did so** The Israelites set themselves to obey Moses, and gathered what they supposed to be about an omer; but, as a matter of course, some of them exceeded the amount, while others fell short of it. There was no wilful disobedience thus far.

Ver. 18.—**When they did mete it with an omer.** On returning to their tents, with the manna which they had collected, the Israelites proceeded to measure it with their own, or a neighbour's, omer measure, when the wonderful result appeared, that, whatever the quantity actually gathered by any one, the result of the measurement showed, exactly as many omers as there were persons in the family. Thus, he that had gathered much found that he had nothing over, and he that had gathered little found that he had no lack.

Ver. 19.—**Let no man leave of it till the morning.** Moses, divinely instructed, warned the people that they were not to lay up in store any of their manna to be eaten the next day. God would have them trust their future wants to him, and "take no thought for the morrow." Some of them, however, were disobedient, with the result stated in the next verse.

Ver. 20.—**It bred worms.** This was a supernatural, not a natural result. It served as a sort of punishment of the disobedient, and effectually checked the practice of laying up in store.

Ver. 21.—**When the sun waxed hot it melted.** The manna had to be gathered early. What had not been collected before the sun grew hot, melted away and disappeared from sight. In this respect the miraculous manna resembled both the manna of commerce and the "air-honey."

HOMILETICS.

Vers. 9—21.—*God and Nature.* I. GOD IS THE MASTER OF NATURE, NOT NATURE'S SERVANT. A school of modern thought places nature above God, or at any rate on a par with God. It is an absolute impossibility, we are told, that a law of nature should be broken or suspended. Miracles are incredible. But all this, it must be borne in mind, is mere assertion, and assertion without a tittle of proof. All that we can *know* is, that we ourselves have never witnessed a miracle. We may further *believe*, that none of our contemporaries have witnessed any. But that miracles have never taken place, we cannot know. There is abundant testimony in the records of humanity that they have. To say that they are impossible, is to assume that we know the exact relation of God to nature, and that that relation is such as to preclude any infraction or suspension of a natural law. This would only be the case, 1. If nature were entirely independent of God; or, 2. If God had bound himself never under any circumstances to interfere with the course of nature. But neither of these positions is true. So far from nature being independent of God, nature wholly proceeds from God, is his creation, and momentarily depends on him both for its existence and its laws. Its laws are simply the laws which he imposes on it; the rules which he sees fit under ordinary circumstances to lay down and maintain. And he has nowhere bound himself to maintain all his laws perpetually without change. He will not, we may be sure, capriciously or without grave cause, change or suspend a law, because he is himself immutable, and "without shadow of turning." But, like a wise monarch, or a wise master of a household, he will make exceptions under exceptional circumstances. And thus it was at this time. Israel was brought out of Egypt—was promised Canaan —but required a prolonged course of training to be rendered fit for its promised inheritance. Geographically, Canaan could only be reached through the wilderness; and so the wilderness was the necessary scene of Israel's education. How then was the nation to be supported during the interval? Naturally the wilderness produced only a scanty subsistence for a few thousand nomads. How was it to support two millions of souls? There was no way but by miracle. Here then was a "dignus vindice nodus,"—a fitting occasion for the exertion of supernatural power—and God gave by miracle the supply of which his people had need.

II. God, EVEN WHEN PRODUCING EFFECTS THAT ARE BEYOND NATURE, WORKS TO A LARGE EXTENT THROUGH NATURE. The Israelites needed, or at any rate craved for flesh. God did not create for them new animals, as he might have done (Gen. i. 25), or even give them meat by any strange and unknown phenomenon. He brought a timely flight of quails—a migratory bird, in the habit of visiting Arabia at the time of year—and made them alight exactly where the camp was fixed, in too exhausted a condition to fly further—a phenomenon not at all unusual at the particular season and in the particular country. The Israelites needed bread, or some substitute for it. God gave them manna—not a wholly new and unknown substance, but a modification of a known substance. He made previously existing nature his basis, altering and adding qualities, greatly augmenting the quantity, but not exerting more supernatural power than was necessary, or departing further from the established course of nature than the occasion required. The same "economy" is seen in the sweetening of the waters of Marah by the wood of a particular tree (ch. xv. 21), etc. The method of God's supernatural working is to supplement, not contradict, nature.

Verses 14—18.—*Bread from heaven.* Our Lord tells us that the manna was a type of him, and that he was the "true bread from heaven" (John vi. 32). We may profitably consider, in what respects the type held good.

I. IT WAS THE NOURISHMENT OF THE BODY, AS CHRIST IS OF THE SOUL. The manna constituted almost the sole nourishment of the Israelites from this time forth until they entered Canaan (Josh. v. 12). So Christ is the food of the soul during its entire pilgrimage through the wilderness of this world, until it reaches the true Canaan, heaven. The Israelites were in danger of perishing for lack of food—they murmured— and God gave them the manna. The world was perishing for lack of spiritual nourishment—it made a continual dumb complaint—and God heard, and gave his own Son from heaven. Christ came into the world, not only to teach it, and redeem it, but to be its "spiritual food and sustenance." He feeds us with the bread of life. He gives us his own self for nourishment. Nothing else can truly sustain and support the soul— not creeds, not sacraments, not even his own Word without him.

II. IT WAS GIVEN FREELY FOR ALL THE PEOPLE OF ISRAEL, AS CHRIST IS GIVEN TO BE THE SAVIOUR OF THE WHOLE WORLD. The manna fell all around the camp of Israel, close to them, so that they had but to stretch out the hand and take it. None could lack sufficient sustenance except by his own fault. If he refused to gather, he might starve; but not otherwise. So Christ gave himself for all men, "not willing that any should perish, but that all should come to repentance." His was "a full, perfect, and sufficient sacrifice for the sins of the *whole world.*" Even they who know him not may be saved by him, "if they will do the works of the law written in their hearts," or, in other words, act up to the light that has been vouchsafed them. Thus, his salvation is free, and open to all. In Christian lands it is close to all, made palpable to all, shown them openly, daily pressed upon them.   He who starves here in England can scarcely starve save by his own fault—because he will not stretch out his hand to gather of the bread of life, will not take it when it is offered to him, rejects it, despises it, "loathes" it.

III. IT WAS WHITE, AND SWEET TO THE TASTE, AS CHRIST IS PURE AND SPOTLESS, AND SWEET TO THE SOUL.   A master mind of these modern times has made his hero, a well-disposed heathen, see in Christ, even before he could bring himself to believe in him, "the WHITE Christ."   "Holy, harmless, undefiled, separate from sinners," he presents himself to all who will read his life, and contemplate his character, as pure, stainless, innocent.   The Lamb is his fitting emblem.   Driven snow is not purer or more speckless.   "Thou art all fair, my love ; there is no spot in thee" (Cant. iv. 7). And he is sweet also.   "Thy lips, O my spouse, drop as the honeycomb ; honey and milk are under thy tongue" (ib. 11).   "How sweet are thy words unto my taste ! yea, sweeter than honey unto my mouth !" (Ps. cxix. 103).   His words, his life, his promises, his influence, his presence, are all sweet, especially the last.   Let those who know him not, once "taste and see how gracious the Lord is," and they will desire no other nourishment.

IV. IT DESCENDED NOISELESSLY IN THE NIGHT.   So Christ comes to us, not "with observation"—not in the wind, or in the fire, or in the earthquake, but in silence and in quietude, when other voices are hushed within us and about us, when we sit and watch, in patience possessing our souls.   His doctrine drops as the rain, and his peace distils as the dew.   It comes down "like the rain into a fleece of wool, even as the drops that water the earth."   In the whirl of passion, in the giddy excitement of pleasure, in the active bustle of business, there is no room for Christ, no fit place for his presence. Christ comes to the soul when it is calm and tranquil, when it waits for him, and believing in his promise that he will come, is at rest.

V. IT REQUIRED TO BE GATHERED EARLY, AND IF NOT GATHERED MELTED AWAY. "Remember thy Creator in the days of thy youth."   Unless we will seek Christ early, we have no warrant to expect that he will condescend to be found of us.   If we slight him, if we dally with the world, if we put off seeking him till a "more convenient season," we may find, when we wake up from our foolish negligence, that he has withdrawn himself, has (as it were) melted away.   If an Israelite put off his gathering of the manna until the sun was hot, he obtained nothing—the manna no longer lay ready to his hand.   So with the Christian who is slothful, self-indulgent, careless—when, after long neglect, he at length seeks spiritual food, he may find it too late, the opportunity may be irrevocably gone.

Vers. 19, 20.—*God's curse upon ill-gotten gains.*—In order to try the Israelites, whether they would be obedient to him or no (ver. 4), God gave them, by the mouth of Moses, a positive law—"Let no man leave of the manna till the morning."   By some the law was disobeyed.   Disregarding the Divine command—perhaps distrusting the Divine promise (ver. 4), to give them food day by day, a certain number of the Israelites, kept some of the manna till the morning.   They wished to have a store laid up, on which they might subsist, should the daily supply fail.   But God would not be disobeyed with impunity.   His curse was on the ill-gotten gain—it bred worms and stank, becoming a source of annoyance both to themselves and their neighbours.   So, God's curse is ever on ill-gotten gains—*e.g.* :—

I. WHEN MEN SET THEIR HEARTS ON HOARDING ALL THEY CAN.   Some provision for the future is required of us.   "Go to the ant, thou sluggard," says the wise man, "consider her ways, and be wise."   "He that doth not provide for them of his own household," St. Paul declares, "is worse than an infidel."   Prudence is a Christian, no less than a heathen virtue.   But to hoard everything, to give nothing away, to make the accumulation of wealth our main object, is to fly in the face of a hundred plain precepts, and necessarily brings God's curse upon us.   The wealth rots—the concerns wherein it is invested fail—it disappears and is brought to nought—and all our careful saving advantages us nothing.   God vindicates his own honour ; and disperses or destroys the hoard accumulated contrary to his will.

II. WHEN, TO AUGMENT THEIR HOARDS, MEN BREAK A DIVINE COMMAND.   There are some who, in their haste to be rich, disregard the Divine injunction to keep holy one day in seven, and pursue their secular calling without any intermission. Conveyancers draw out their deeds, barristers study their briefs, business men balance their books, authors ply their pens, as busily on the Sunday as on week days. What blessing can be expected on the gains thus made? Is it not likely that they will breed corruption? Still more wholly under a curse are gains made by unlawful trades or dishonest practices—by the false weight or the scant measure, or the adulterated article—or again by usurious lending, by gaming, by brothel-keeping.

III. When the motive for the hoarding is distrust of God's promise. God bids us not to be anxious for the morrow, what we shall eat, or what we shall drink, or what we shall put on (Matt. vi. 31)—and promises that, if we will "seek first the kingdom of God and his righteousness, all these things shall be added unto us" (ib. 33). He caused holy David to declare—"I have been young and now am old, yet saw I never the righteous forsaken, nor his seed begging their bread." If men hoard in distrust of these gracious words, not believing that God will make them good, and thinking to assure the future of wife or child, or both, by their own accumulations, they provoke God to bring their accumulations to nothing. Riches, however invested, can make themselves wings and disappear, if God's blessing does not rest on their possessor.

HOMILIES BY VARIOUS AUTHORS.

Chap. xvi.—*The manna of the body.*—*A homily on providence.* "They said one to another, what is this? (marg.) for they wist not what it was" (Ex. xvi. 15). Introduction:—Trace the journey from Elim to the sea (Num. xxxiii. 10); and thence to the wilderness of Sin; and give a thoroughly good exegetical exposition of the facts of the manna story. It would be well also to show the supernatural character of the manna; and, at the same time, that the manna supernatural was not unlike (and yet unlike also) the manna natural of the desert of to-day; that God, in a word, did not give the food of either Greenland or Australia in the Arabian wilderness. The spiritual lessons of the miracle move on two levels, one higher than the other. There is a body, and a soul: food for the one, and for the other. There are then in the manna story truths concerning Divine providence, and also touching Divine grace. Hence two homilies on the manna. This on the manna of providence.

I. Bodily need is an appeal to God. Before Israel articulately prayed, its need cried: so now with twelve hundred millions of men. No man "gets his own living," but God gives it. Imagine one famine round the world, and every living thing would become dumb and dead. The world's need is one majestic monotone of prayer.

II. The answer is full and free. No stint in that desert—no stint now. A picture of the fulness with which God ever gives bread. There has never been such an event as *universal* famine. Ps. civ. 21—28.

III. There is mystery in the answer. Note the question of the text, and the wonder of the people, which was never relieved through all the forty years. So with bread to-day. A great mystery! A common thing to common minds; and perhaps to uncommon minds, that would like, as scientists, to bow all mystery out of the universe. But as there was mystery in the manna, so is there in every grain of corn. No scientist could produce one, were he to try for fifty years. Why? Because the secret of life is a secret of God; and the creation of organization lies in his own power alone.

IV. The blame of want is not with God. The question arises: if God hears the moaning of the world's need, and gives answer, why is there so much want? Murmuring against Moses and Aaron, Israel murmured against the Lord; so we, grumbling against secondary causes, may be arraigning the First Cause. But the blame lies not there. Political economy might give answer to the question:—Why want? But behind its answers lie deeper causes—all summed up in the one word *sin*—not only the folly and sin (improvidence, drunkenness, etc. etc.) of the individual, but of all the ages, that is to say, self-centredness (the root principle of sin), forming and solidifying customs and institutions, which have for their effect the oppression and privation of millions. The instances are numberless.

V. But if all the heritage of sin were to disappear, man must work. Israel must gather manna. Here enforce, not only the dignity of work, but the Christian duty thereof. The idle, whether in high life or low, are the dangerous classes. If exempted from toil for bread, all the more obligation to labour for the good of man to the glory of God.

VI. YET—THERE MUST BE SABBATH.

VII. A HINT AGAINST MERE HOARDING. Distinguish between extravagance, a due providence, and hoarding after a miserly fashion. The *via media* here, as elsewhere, the right ethical path.

VIII. The manna story gives us THE TRUE THEORY OF LIFE. See the view of Moses as to the purpose of the manna, in the light of experience, after the lapse of forty years, in Deut. viii. 3. (comp. Matt. iv. 4). Man is to live, not for that which is lowest in him, but for that which is highest. Life is to be DEPENDENCE UPON GOD; 1:—*For leading.* 2:—*For support.* This was *the* object of the giving of the manna.—R.

Ch. xvi.—*Manna for the soul; a homily on grace.* " I am the living bread . . . he shall live for ever." John vi. 51. Having given the manna story, discussed the miracle, and given the lessons bearing on our providential path, we now go up to the higher level, and listen to the truths taught in relation to the kingdom of God's grace. These gather round the central truth—that the Lord Jesus Christ is the nutriment of the soul. For that truth we have his own supreme authority. [See the full discourse from his own lips on the manna, in John vi.] Avoid small typologies— small every way—*e.g.*, that the roundness of the manna stands for Christ's eternity ; its whiteness for his purity ; its sweetness for the preciousness of Christ. When men would estimate the majesty of a mountain they play not with the pebbles at its feet.

I. THE OBJECT OF GOD IN THE GIFT OF THE HEAVENLY MANNA. Why Christ? Long before Israel cried, the Father saw the coming distress ; and resolved to give the manna to meet it. So with Christ. Christ *was* given for atonement, and to bring from under the cloud of condemnation ; but also for other reasons beyond, to give life and strength to the moral and spiritual man. There is a rich provision in the world for the body and for the mind [describe] ; but there is something higher in man—the spiritual—not only a ψυχή, but a πνεῦμα—for which provision must be made.

II. THE FAMINE OF THE SOUL WITHOUT CHRIST. Very difficult to imagine a world without bread ; more to suppose a world without Christ. His name, his history, his death, his reign, his presence, power, and love are implied, and involved always, everywhere, in all the phenomena of life. But endeavour to imagine Christ annihilated— no name of Christ to entwine in the lullaby at the cradle, and so on through every stage and circumstance of life, till the dying moment—no Christ for the guilty, sinning, sorrowing, tempted, etc. etc. What a famine of the soul!

III. THE SUPPLY OF THE SOUL WITH CHRIST. Having seen what the world would be without Christ, see positively what Christ is to the world. The understanding cannot live without objective truth (mere opinion will not suffice) ; Christ is that truth : nor the heart without a supreme object of love ; Christ that object : nor the conscience without authority behind its moral imperative ; Christ is that authority : nor the will without a living inward abiding power ; and Christ is that power. In very real and intelligible sense, Christ is the manna, bread, nutriment, sustenance, vitality, and power of the believing soul.

IV. THE FULNESS OF THE SUPPLY. *All* we need certainly in bread, probably in the manna, assuredly in Christ.

V. ITS FREENESS. Men may confuse themselves, and imagine they "get" their own bread. But manna was manifestly the free gift of heaven. So Christ. This the one truth, which it is so difficult for men to receive. See 1 John v. 11, 12 ; Rom. vi. 23.

VI. ITS MYSTERY. The name of the desert provision was " Man-Hu ? "—" What is it ? " Men did not solve the mystery ere they ate. Why should men wait to solve the mystery of Christ's person, office, etc. etc., ere they eat "the living bread"?

VII. ITS NEARNESS. Both the manna and Christ at every man's tent-door.

VIII. ITS APPROPRIATION. Vain that manna for the two millions, if no man went out to gather ; so vain the all-sufficiency of Christ, if no man "comes," "believes," appropriates. John vi. 35, 37, 40, 47, 57.

IX. ITS EVERY-DAYNESS. No man can live upon a past experience of the sufficiency of Christ.

X. ITS ORDER. Full and free as the supply of manna was, its appropriation and use were under Divine direction, were according to a certain order. So are there now channels, means, ordinances of grace, which no man can safely neglect.

XI. THE AIM IN MAN'S APPROPRIATION. Not self-indulgence; not merely his own growth. No man an end unto himself. The final end of food is strength, work, good for others. The danger of middle-class evangelicalism is that of making personal salvation the ultimate aim of God's grace. We are saved, that we may save. The end of bread is labour.

XII. The subject carries our thoughts on to THE HIDDEN MANNA. Rev. ii. 17.— Christ will be the soul's nutriment in heaven. "Hidden," for there will be in heaven as yet undiscovered glories of Christ the Lord. For the final lesson see John vi. 27.—R.

Vers. 1—15.—*The provision of the manna.* This chapter contains an account of the first provision of miraculous bread for Israel in the wilderness. We are told very fully the circumstances in which it was given and the regulations for obtaining and using it. This provision of bread comes very appropriately after the visits to Marah and Elim. The waters had been made sure, and were soon to be made sure again (ch. xvii.); and now the bread is given (Is. xxxiii. 16). Before God takes the people to Sinai, he does everything to show that they may confidently depend on him for necessities, however vainly they look for superfluities. Consider—

I. THE STATE OF MIND AMONG THE ISRAELITES WHICH PRECEDED THIS GIFT. It is important to notice that such an ample, gracious and miraculous gift as Jehovah here bestowed was bestowed on the unthankful and the evil. With many reasons for faith, they were unbelieving; instead of being patient and submissive, considerate towards their leader, and thankful for liberty, they broke out into selfish and unjust complaints. Things were going far otherwise than as they wanted them to go. They have now been a month or more out of Egypt and it is wilderness, wilderness, wilderness still! They have got water, but what is water without bread; and what is bread, unless it be the bread along with the flesh of Egypt? And, letting their minds dwell on these lost delicacies, their discontent breaks out in *the most expressive way.* Discontent is assuredly at a high pitch in a man's mind, when he begins to talk of death as a thing to be desired. It shows that he has got so reckless and peevish as not to care what he says, what others may think, or who may be hurt by his random talk. The low ideal of life on the part of Israel is here revealed. God has delivered a whole nation, and this is their idea of why he has delivered them. They think a life, from which the flesh pots and the fulness of bread are absent, is not worth living; and such is indeed a very excusable conception of life, if hunger and thirst after righteousness have not become vigorous desires within us. If one is to become a freeman simply to die, then it seems as if one might just as well live a little longer as a slave. Note further how the people try to throw *the responsibility of their present position on Moses.* It was a consequence of their carnal-mindedness that they could not think of the Jehovah who was behind and above the visible leader. They are where they are because Moses has brought them. Thus they utter an unconscious but weighty and significant testimony to the fact, that they had not come there of their own accord or wandered there in an aimless fashion. But for the mighty power that held them fast together, they might have straggled back to Egypt with its comforts and delights. Strange that with such a rebellious spirit, there should yet be such a measure of outward obedience. Evidently they had invisible constraints all around them, so that they could not help but follow the cloud.

II. THE MANNER IN WHICH GOD TREATS THIS STATE OF MIND. As he dealt in supplying the water so he deals in supplying the bread. There was a real and pressing want, and though the people made it the occasion for foolish talk, it was also to be the occasion for immediate Divine supply. God does not let the existence of the unthankful and evil fail, for presently, at Sinai, they will have the chance of learning such things as may lead them into a thankful, trustful and noble spirit; and so he hastens to meet Moses with the cheering promise—cheering in the *substance* of it, and cheering none the less in the expression—"I will rain bread from heaven." **1.** *They shall have bread.* He does not yet tell Moses what shape the bread will take; but the people shall have something to sustain them, and that something in sufficient quantity. **2.** *The bread shall be rained from heaven.* We do not read that Moses repeated this expression to the Israelites; but it must have been very cheering to himself. The words "rain" and "heaven" were enough to put fresh courage into the man. Then we find too that when the promise came to be fulfilled, these words were not taken in a figurative way. The manna came with the dew, and when the dew disappeared there the manna lay, waiting to be gathered. Hence for the supply of bread the people were to look heavenward; and doubtless Moses himself did so look. In whatsoever part of the wilderness they might be, however sterile and unpromising the earth was below, the same heavens stretched out above them, distilling from their treasuries the daily manna. The contrast is thus very striking between the varying earth and the un-changing, exhaustless heaven; and as to the rain, we may be very sure that when God says, "I will rain," he means a copious and adequate shower. But even in this imme-diate promise of copious giving *Jehovah combines demands with gifts.* If there is great grace, there are great expectations. He gives and at the same time he asks. He points out to Moses the manner in which the food was to be gathered. Though given copiously, it was not therefore given carelessly; nor was it to be used carelessly. It was given on certain principles and with certain restrictions, so as to be not only the means of staying hunger but of disciplining Israel at the same time. In eating bread, they were to learn habitual faith and habitual and exact obedience. God is ever showing men how he can make one thing to serve more purposes than one.

III. THE EXPOSTULATIONS OF MOSES AND AARON WITH THE PEOPLE (vers. 6—10). Though it is not expressly said that he spoke thus by Jehovah's instructions, yet these remonstrances evidently accorded with his will. For the people to complain as they did was not only an unjust thing to Moses; it was also a perilous thing for themselves. They could not thus vent their spleen on the visible Moses without despising the invisible God. Their insult to their brother man on earth was as nothing compared with their insult to Jehovah on high. And, indeed, we cannot too much consider that *all murmuring, when it is brought to its ultimate ground and effects, is a reproach against God.* For it is either a complaint because we cannot get our own way, or it is an impeachment of God's way as not being a loving and a wise one. What a different scene life would become, how much more equable, serene and joyous, if we could only take the invisible as well as the visible into all our thoughts. The people felt the lack of bread, the loss of Egypt, the hardships of a life unfamiliar and unprepared for; and Moses could sympathise with all these feelings; although of course, after forty years of shepherd life in Midian, the hardships his brethren complained of were as nothing to him. But at the same time, Moses felt very keenly what many of his brethren did not feel at all, the mysterious presence of God. More and more distinctly would the words now be rising to his mind, "Ye shall serve God upon this mountain" (ch. iii. 12); for the cloud was taking the multitude nearer and nearer to Sinai. It is very significant of the feeling in Moses' mind that he dwells on this charge of murmuring, returning to the word again and again. He wanted these people who so felt the pangs of hunger to be equally sensitive to the perils of impiety. Jehovah had heard their reckless speeches as well as Moses; and now, in recognition, he was about to make manifest his glorious presence. The connection of the cloud with himself was to be proved by the appearing of his glory in it. What the people found fault with was that they had been guided wrong: and now the nature of the guidance stands out, distinct, impressive, and full of warning. He who found fault with Moses really found fault with Jehovah. Remember the words of Jesus: "He that despiseth you despiseth me; and he that despiseth me despiseth him that sent me." (Luke x. 16.) If we presumptuously neglect the apostle-ship of any one, we have to do with the Being who made him an apostle. Wherefore we should show all diligence to keep murmuring off our lips; and the only effectual way is to keep it out of our hearts by filling them with a continual sense of the presence of God. Instead of murmuring, let there be honest shame because of the selfishness that runs riot in our hearts. God can do everything to make our lives joyous, and banish causes of complaint for ever, if only we will take right and sufficient views of his purposes toward us and his claims upon us.

IV. THE ACTUAL GIVING. Here again we notice the tender and gentle dealings of God. The necessary and permanent supply of bread is preceded by a special and occasional supply of quails. By this gift he, as it were, runs towards Israel to soothe their murmurings. The flesh of Egypt was the thing they missed the most, and it comes first, in the evening; whereas the manna did not come till the next morning. By this supply of the quails God showed an attentiveness to the feelings of the people which should have had the best effect on their minds. They murmured against Moses, forgot Jehovah, and yet Jehovah gave them in reply a delightful feast of quails. So to speak, he was heaping coals of fire on their heads: and we should take special note of this Divine conduct, *just in this particular place.* It is very natural that as we consider Israel in the wilderness, we should think of God's severity rather than any other feature of his character. The whole tenor of the New Testament—the contrast between the law and the gospel—makes this view inevitable. But as we read the whole of this chapter, and ponder it carefully, how shall we do other than confess " Verily, Jehovah is love"? It is love that leads to Sinai. And assuredly there is not less of love in the thunders, lightnings and terrors of Sinai than in the gift of the quails. The expression is different—that is all. The quails were but a slight, passing thing, bestowed upon Israel much as a toy is bestowed on a child. There is love in the gift of a toy; but there is love also in the discipline and chastisement which soon may follow from the same hand. So there was love in the quails; but there was equal love, stretching out to far deeper results, in the demonstrations of Sinai and the commandments which accompanied them.—Y.

Vers. 11—12. *He nurtured them in the wilderness.* Continual mention of murmurings; yet all such murmurings do not meet the same treatment (cf. Num. xi. 31—33). Much alike to outward seeming, but not so in the sight of God. (Illustration—the ruddy hue of health; the hot flush of passion; the hectic of consumption. All much alike in appearance, yet how different to those who know what they betoken!) Comparing the history of one murmuring with that of another, we can see by God's treatment of each how different must have been the states from which they resulted. Here it is the impatience of ill-instructed children; later on, it has become hostility and rebellion. Consider in this case:—

I. THE SYMPTOMS. Cf. vers. 3. The monotony of the wilderness had had time to tell upon the people; so different from the varied routine of Egypt. Slavery, too, had become, from long use, almost a second nature with many; they had chafed under it, yet, in some sort, they had relied upon its restraint as a support. After the first novelty has passed, unaccustomed freedom is felt to be a weariness. (Illustration: The cripple rejoices to be quit of his supporting irons and crutches, but without them, at first, he soon tires.) Present privation, contrasted with past sufficiency, intensified the misgivings which were sure to come when the new life was fairly entered upon. Freedom wedded to starvation seemed to be but a poor exchange for tyranny. " The people murmured." It was the murmuring of the half-weaned child, the yet weak though enfranchised cripple; it expressed itself in strong language; but the language was stronger than the offence. Under the circumstances murmuring was so natural that it did not call for severe censure; it was rather a symptom of imperfect health, suggesting the need of strengthening medicine.

II. THE TREATMENT. God knew what was the matter; His action shows His knowledge. No rebuke, only a promise, which is to be, and is, fulfilled immediately. (Illustration: The doctor does not take offence at the irritability of the convalescent; says, " I will send some strengthening medicine," sends it, and relies on the effect.) A table spread in the wilderness; the love of freedom revived and strengthened, *nurtured* by the longed-for food. What should be the effect of such treatment? It stays murmuring, of course; but, further, it should strengthen against further murmuring. On the other hand, whilst it may, as it ought to do, lead to reliance upon the provider, it may also lead to reliance upon the food provided. (Illustration: One patient, strengthened by medicine, will have more confidence in the doctor. Another, strengthened in like manner, will be always grumbling, whatever the circumstances, if he do not experience like treatment.)

Practical lessons.—1. *God treats us all according to our real character and position.*

" How unjust," says one, " that that man should have so much easier a time than I. That my comparatively slight offence should be punished so much more heavily than his, which is far more heinous!" Nay! By what standard do you measure the relative enormity of the offences? God's standard is character and experience; the child's open defiance is less heinous than the man's half-veiled impatience. 2. *God's treatment should inspire confidence in Himself.* All God's gifts are index fingers saying, " Look off from us to God." Our tendency is to rest upon them and credit them as the *causes* of the satisfaction they *occasion.* The same *medicine* may not be appropriate next time, but the same *doctor* may be trusted. If we forget the doctor and think only of the medicine, we shall be as irritable and dissatisfied as ever; only by confidence in the Physician himself can we hope to go on "from strength to strength."—G.

Ver. 15.—*Christ the bread from heaven.* The manna, which is described in ver. 4 as " bread from heaven," was typical of Christ, who is " the true bread from heaven "— " the bread of God which cometh down from heaven and giveth life unto the world " (John vi. 31–34). The connection in John vi. is with the Jews' demand for a sign. The interrogators reminded Christ of how their fathers did eat manna in the desert; as it was written, He gave them bread from heaven to eat! (Ps. cv. 40). The design of Jesus in his reply was, *first,* to wean their hearts away from merely carnal expectations in connection with his appearing, and, *secondly,* to lead them to see in the gift of manna, as well as in the miracle he had just performed—the feeding of the multitudes—something more than the mere supplying of bodily necessities;—to see in them " signs " (John vi. 26—" Ye seek me, not because ye saw *signs,*" etc. Rev. Ver.) *i.e.* types, allegories, suggestive earthly symbols, of spiritual realities—of what he was in himself, of the work he came to do, of the relations in which he stood to perishing men. The manna is thus figured as " spiritual meat " (1 Cor. x. 3), a type of Christ as the living bread for the souls of men. Consider in illustration of this analogy—

I. THE NEED WHICH EXISTED FOR THIS PROVISION. The Israelites were in the desert, where nature, if left to itself, would inevitably perish. Their supplies of food were exhausted. The whole multitude would have died of hunger, had not Divine mercy interposed for their relief. The manna which God gave them literally stood between them and death. In this circumstance we see one feature imaged in which Christ clearly appears as the bread of life. When he uses this language of himself he means to tell us, that just as these Israelites under Moses absolutely hung for any hope of life they had on that food which was miraculously supplied to them; so does the world hang—hang absolutely—for its life, its salvation, its eternal well-being on *him.* It needs eternal life. Its heart craves for it. It is perishing for want of it. But if it is ever to get it, Christ says, it must get it through him, through receiving him, through appropriating what he is, and what he has done for it as Saviour.

II. THE SUPERNATURAL CHARACTER OF THE PROVISION. There could be no question as to the supernatural character of the supply in the case of the manna. The Israelites needed to be saved, and God saved them by a miracle. There was, as it were, a distinct opening of heaven for their benefit. The hand that fed them came from the unseen. In like manner, Christ lays emphasis on the fact that he—the bread of life for men—is " bread from heaven." The salvation that embodies itself in him is no salvation of man's devising, nor one which, even had the thought of it entered his mind, man could ever from his own resources have achieved. If the world is to be saved at all, if it is to be delivered from its woes, if it is to have eternal life, Saviour and salvation must come from heaven. Our hope, as of old, is in God, and in God only. It is not for us to provide, but only thankfully to receive, and earnestly to appropriate the salvation. God *gives* us the bread from heaven; gives it freely; gives it as bread which no efforts of our own, however laborious, could have enabled us to procure; gives it, that is, as a Divine, supernatural bread, the boon of sovereign grace.

III. THE AMPLE ABUNDANCE OF THE PROVISION. The manna was given in abundance. There was neither lack nor stint. The table that was spread in the wilderness was one of royal bounty; as in the later miracle of the loaves, " they did all eat, and were filled " (Matt. xiv. 20). There was, as in the father's house in the parable, " Enough and to spare " (Luke xv. 17), overflowing provision. How significant a fact when the heart is putting to itself the question, Will Christ's death avail for *me?* He calls himself " tho *true* bread which cometh down from heaven;" and it cannot be but that this feature in the type will be reflected in the antitype. There is provision in Christ for *all*. He gives his flesh for the life of the *world* (ver. 51). He is come that men "might have life, and that they might have it more abundantly" (John x. 10). No stint, no lack no scarcity in the salvation of Christ.

IV. THE PROVISION NOW, AS THEN, NEEDS TO BE APPROPRIATED. It was nothing to the Israelites that the manna, sparkling like pearls in the morning sunshine, lay all around them; they must gather, they must eat, they must make the "bread from heaven" food for their own life. So with Christ and his salvation. He calls himself "bread," to bring out strongly, not only what he *is* in himself in relation to human wants, but what men must *do* with him, if they would partake in the life he comes to give. He must be received, "eaten," inwardly appropriated, fed upon, made part, so to speak, of our very selves; only thus will the new life be begotten in us. This "eating" of Christ is parallel with the "believing" of other verses (vers. 29, 40, 47). Some, remembering this, may be disposed to say, it is *only* believing. But the use of such a metaphor should rather teach us how real, and inward, and appropriating a principle, this believing on Jesus is. It is clearly no slight, transitory act of mind or heart which is denoted by it, but a most spiritual, most inward, most vital and personal energy of appropriation; a process of reception, digestion, and transformation into spiritual substance, and new powers of spiritual life, of what we have in the Saviour. How great Christ must be, who thus declares himself to be the bread of life for the whole world—the support and food (consciously or unconsciously) of all the spiritual life there is in it! No wonder that the work of works which God requires of us is that we believe on him whom he has sent (John vi. 29).

V. WHAT THERE IS IN CHRIST WHICH CONSTITUTES HIM THE WORLD'S BREAD OF LIFE. We set aside as unsupported the analogies which some have sought between the roundness, sweetness, whiteness, etc., of the manna, and qualities in the person and work of the Redeemer. It is, however, clear that if Christ is the antitype of the manna, and the true bread which cometh down from heaven, it must be in virtue of certain qualities in him which admit of being specified. And what these are, it is not difficult to show. He is the bread of life to men—1. *As incarnate God.* In the humanity of Jesus Christ, the Divine is brought near to us, and made apprehensible, and provision is also made for the communication of the Divine life in its fullest, richest form to our souls. In him dwells the fulness of the Godhead bodily (Col. ii. 9). He is the medium of the communication of that Divine fulness to us (1 John i. 16). In him, the Divine life is embodied in a holy, perfect humanity; and in that form—a form which brings it within our reach, which makes apprehension and assimilation possible—it is presented to us to be partaken of. 2. *As an atoning Saviour.* Did Christ not bear this character of Atoner, he would not be truly bread of life to the guilty. Our guilt, our sin, our whole moral condition, stands between us and God, an insuperable barrier to the peace and fellowship for which we crave. But Christ has taken away that barrier. He has made a sacrifice of himself for sin (John vi. 51). To appropriate what I have in Christ, is, accordingly, to appropriate to myself the certainty of forgiveness through his death, the assurance of peace with God, the knowledge of reconciliation. And to have done this is already to have begun to live. It is to feel the awakening within me of new-born powers of love, and trust, and service; to feel the dread and despair that before possessed me vanishing like a dark nightmare from my spirit, to be replaced by the joy of pardon, and the sense of the Divine favour. It is to realise the accomplishment of that spiritual change which the Scriptures describe as a "passing from death unto life" (John v. 24). "Old things have passed away; behold, all things have become new" (2 Cor. v. 17). 3. *As a life-giving Spirit.* Jesus is what he is to man, in virtue of his possession of the holy, life-giving Spirit—the personal Holy Ghost—by whom he dwells in the hearts of his people, and through whom he communicates to them all the fulness of his own life. This operation of the Spirit is already implied in what we have said of the results of faith in him. He is the effectual agent in converting, quickening, enlightening, sanctifying, comforting, strengthening, beautifying, and spiritually edifying the souls of such as attain to salvation. The influences of this Spirit in the soul are but another name for eternal life. And Christ is the giver of this Spirit. It is from him the Spirit comes. His work on earth has opened the way for the free communication of the Spirit's influences. He dwells by this Spirit in each of his members, nourishing, strengthening, and purifying them. To nourish ourselves upon Christ is to take more of this Spirit into our hearts and lives. Thus is Christ the bread of life.—J. O.

Vers. 16—22.—*The law of the manna.* God had said (ver. 4) that rules would be given in connection with the manna by which the people would be proved, whether they would walk in his law, or no. One rule is given in ver. 5, and the rest are given here. Consider—

I. THE LAW AS TO QUANTITY (vers. 16—18). "According to his eating," in this passage, means, according to the quantity allowed to each person for consumption. This was fixed at an omer a head (ver. 16). The simplest way of explaining what follows is to suppose that each individual, when he went out to gather, aimed, as nearly as possible, at bringing in his exact omer; but, necessarily, on measuring what had been gathered, it would be found that some had brought in a little more, some a little less, than the exact quantity; excess was then to go to balance defect, and the result would be that, on the whole, each person would receive his omer. It may be supposed, also, that owing to differences of age, strength, agility, etc., there would be great room left for one helping another, some gathering more, to eke out the deficiencies of the less active. If the work were conscientiously done, the result, even on natural principles, would be pretty much what is here indicated. The law of averages would lead, over a large number of cases, to a mean result, midway between excess and defect, *i.e.*, to the net omer. But a special superintendence of providence—such, *e.g.*, as that which secures in births, amidst all the inequalities of families, a right proportion of the sexes in society as a whole—is evidently pointed to as *securing* the result. We cannot suppose, however, that an intentionally indolent or unconscientious person was permitted to participate in this equal dividend, or to reap, in the way indicated, the benefit of the labours of others. The law here must have been, as with St. Paul, " if any would not work, neither should he eat" (2 Thess. iii. 10). There is nothing said as to the share to be allotted to juveniles: these may be supposed to have received some recognised proportion of an omer. The lessons of all this and its importance as a part of the spiritual education of Israel, are very obvious. It taught—1. *That what is of Divine gift is meant for common benefit.* The individual is entitled to his share in it; but he is not entitled selfishly to enrich himself, while others are in need. He gets that he may give. There was to be a heavenly communism practised in respect of the manna, in the same way as a common property is recognised in light and air, and the other free gifts of nature. This applies to intellectual and spiritual wealth. We are not to rest till all have shared in it according to their God-given capacity. 2. *That in the Church of Christ it is the duty of the stronger to help the weaker, and of the richer to help the poorer.* This is the lesson drawn from the passage by St. Paul in 2 Cor. viii. 12—16. It is presumed in his teaching, *first,* that there is the "willing mind," in which case a gift " is accepted according to that a man hath, and not according to that he hath not" (ver. 12). Each gatherer of the manna was honestly to do his part, and put what he could into the common stock. The end is not, *secondly,* that other men be eased, and the Corinthians burdened (ver. 13). But, each doing what he can, the design is, *thirdly,* that the abundance of one may be a supply for the deficiency of another, that so there may be equality (ver. 14). This is a principle of wide application in Church finance, and also in the aiding of the poor. Strong congregations should not be slow to aid weak ones, that the work of the latter may go on more smoothly, and their ministers may at least be able to subsist comfortably. The Scottish Free Church has given a praiseworthy illustration of this principle in her noble "Sustentation Fund." 3. *That where a helpful spirit is shown by each towards all, there will be found no lack of what is needful for any.* God will see that all are provided for. The tendency of the rule is to encourage a friendly, helpful, unselfish spirit generally, and in all relations. The gatherer of manna was *forbidden* to act selfishly. A Nemesis would attend an attempt on the part of any to appropriate more than his proper share.

II. THE LAW AS TO TIME. 1. The manna was to be gathered *in early morning.* The people had to be up betimes, and had to bestir themselves diligently, that their manna might be collected before "the sun waxed hot" (ver. 21). If not collected then, the substance melted away, and could not be had at all. A lesson, surely, in the first instance, of diligence in business; and secondly, of the advantage of improving morning hours. The most successful gatherer of manna, whether in the material, intellectual, or spiritual fields, is he who is up and at his work early. Albert Barnes tells us that all his commentaries were due to this habit of rising early in the morning, the whole of them having been written before nine o'clock in the day, and without encroaching on his proper ministerial duties. 2. On six days of the week only (ver. 5). God teaches here the lesson of *putting forward* our work on week days, that we may be able to enjoy a Sabbath free from distraction. He puts honour on the ordinance of the Sabbath itself, by requiring that no work be done upon it.

III. THE LAW AS TO USE (ver. 19). None of the manna was to be left till the morning. We have here again a double lesson. 1. A lesson against *hoarding*. God gave to each person his quantity of manna; and the individual had no right to more. What excess he had in his gathering ought to have gone to supplement some other person's deficiency. But greed led some of the Israelites to disobey. It would save them trouble to lay by what they did not need, and use it again next day. They might make profit out of it by barter. All such attempts God defeated by ordaining that the manna thus hoarded should breed worms, and grow corrupt. A significant emblem of the suicidal effects of hoarding generally. Hoarded treasure is never an ultimate benefit to its possessor. It corrupts alike in his heart and his hands. It breeds worms of care to him, and speedily becomes a nuisance (cf. Matt. vi. 19, 20). 2. A lesson against *distrust*. Another motive for laying up the manna would be to provide for the morrow in case of any failure in the supply. But this was in direct contradiction to God's end in giving the people their manna day by day, viz., to foster trust, and keep alive their sense of dependence on him. Christ warns us against the spirit of distrust, and of anxiety for the morrow, and teaches us to pray for "daily bread" (Matt. vi. 11, 31). We should not even *desire* to be independent of God.

IV. THE FAILURE OF THE PEOPLE TO OBSERVE THESE LAWS. They failed at each point. They tried to hoard (ver. 20). They went out to gather on the Sabbath (ver. 27). This showed both disobedience and unbelief, for it had been distinctly said of the seventh day, "in it there shall be none" (ver. 26). What a lesson!—1. Of the sottish insensibility of human nature to God's great acts of goodness. God had miraculously supplied their wants, yet so little sensible were they of his goodness—so little did it influence them—that they declined to obey even the few simple rules he had laid down for the reception and use of his benefits. 2. Of its ineradicable contumacy and self-will (cf. Deut. ix.; and Psalms lxxviii. and cvi.).—J. O.

Vers. 13—31.—*Divine provision for daily need.* I. THE LORD'S FAITHFULNESS. 1. Their varied need was met. Flesh as well as bread was given. God gives us richly all things to enjoy. 2. They came in the order and at the time God said they would come. The evening brought the quails—the morning the manna. Nothing failed of all that he had promised. 3. They were given in abundance. The quails "covered the camp;" of the manna they "had no lack." There is princely bounty with God for all who trust in him. He gives richly, even where he has made no covenant: he fills "men's hearts with food and gladness." How much more then will he bless those whom he has pledged himself to sustain!

II. THE SPIRIT OF THOSE WHO ARE THUS FED FROM GOD'S TABLE. 1. They wait on him. The supply he sends is only for the day, and he is trusted for the days that are to follow. They do not refuse to pass on further upon the wilderness path, because they do not see at the beginning all the needed provision for the way. 2. They obey God's call to toil. (1) They "gathered" of it every man according to his eating." (2) They did not miss the opportunity God gave them. "When the sun waxed hot it melted;" and they therefore gathered it "in the morning." Be "not slothful in business."

III. ISRAEL'S FAITHLESSNESS. 1. In attempting to save themselves from the toil which God commanded, they kept the manna for next day's use in defiance of the command to preserve none of it till the morning (ver. 27). 2. In refusing to rest on the Sabbath. The contradiction and wilfulness of unbelief: it hoards to be able to abstain from toil, and refuses to obey God's command to rest. 3. Public indifference to the existence of sin. These things were done by a few only; but they called forth no public condemnation or holy fear of God's anger. The Christian community which does not mourn the sin abounding in its midst has itself no living trust in God.—U.

EXPOSITION.

Vers. 22—30.—THE GATHERING OF THE SIXTH DAY. When the Israelites, having collected what seemed to them the usual quantity of manna on the sixth day, brought it home and measured it, they found the yield to be, not an omer a head for each member of the family, but two omers. The result was a surprise and a difficulty. They could not consume more than an omer a-piece. What was to be done with the remainder? Was it to be destroyed, or kept? If kept, would it not "breed worms"? To resolve their doubts, the elders brought the matter before Moses, who replied—"This is that which the Lord hath said." It is to be supposed that, in his original announcement to the elders of God's purposes as to the manna, Moses had informed them that the quantity would be double on the sixth day (ver. 5); but his statement had not made any deep impression at the time, and now they had forgotten it. So he recalls it to their recollection. "This is no strange thing—nothing that should have surprised you—it is only what God said would happen. And the reason of it is, that to-morrow, the seventh day is, by God's ordinance, the rest of the Holy Sabbath,"—or rather "*a* rest of *a* holy Sabbath to the Lord." Whether or no the Sabbath was a primeval institution, given to our first parents in Paradise (Gen. ii. 3), may be doubted: at any rate, it had not been maintained as an institution by the Hebrews during their sojourn in Egypt; and this was, practically, to them, the first promulgation of it. (See Hessey's *Bampton Lectures*, p. 149.) Hence, in the original, it is not called "*the* sabbath," as if already known, but "*a* sabbath,"—*i.e.*, a rest—until verse 29.

Ver. 22.—This is that which the Lord hath said. Rather, "said," *i.e.*, declared to me when he announced the manna. See verse 5. It has been supposed that Moses had not communicated the declaration to the elders; but this seems unlikely. **The rest of the holy sabbath.** If this translation were correct, the previous institution of the sabbath, and the knowledge of its obligation by the Hebrews, would follow; but the absence of the article

is a strong indication that the whole idea was new, at any rate to those whom Moses was addressing. **Bake that which ye will bake,** etc. "Do," *i.e.*, "as you have done on other days—bake some and seethe some—but also reserve a portion to be your food and sustenance to-morrow."

Ver. 24.—They laid it up. The great bulk of the Israelites obeyed Moses, and laid by a portion (half?) of the manna gathered on the sixth day. On the morning of the seventh, this was found to be perfectly good, and not to have "bred worms" in the night. Either this was a miracle, or the corruption previously noticed (ver. 20) was miraculous.

Vers. 25, 26.—And Moses said. The Sabbath being come, Moses explained fully the reason for the order which he had given, and generalized it. God required the Sabbath to be "a day of holy rest"—no manna would fall on it, and therefore none could be gathered — the produce of the sixth day's gathering would be found to suffice both for the sixth day and the seventh.

Ver. 27.—There went out some of the people on the seventh day for to gather. There will always be some persons in a nation, or in a Church, who will refuse to believe God's ministers, and even God himself. They persuade themselves that they "know better" —it will not be as announced—it will be as they wish it to be. More especially is this so where the idea of continuance comes in— where some interruption of the ordinary course of things is announced, which they deem unlikely or impossible. Compare Gen. xix. 14.

Ver. 28.—How long refuse ye to keep my commandments? Though Moses is addressed, it is the people who are blamed. Hence the plural verb, "refuse *ye*." Already there had been one act of disobedience in connection with the manna (see ver. 20)—now there was another—when would such sinful folly come to an end? When would the people learn that they could gain nothing by disobedience? It was "long" indeed before they were taught the lesson.

Ver. 29.—See, for that, etc. Rather, "See, that." Consider that God has given you the Sabbath, or the holy rest: and therefore it is that he gives you on the sixth day the food for two days—that the rest may not be interfered with. **Abide ye every man in his place.** One Jewish sect, the Masbothei, took this command absolutely literally, and held that in whatsoever position a man was at the commencement of the Sabbath day, he was bound to retain it to the close. But generally it was held that the " place " intended was the camp, which the Israelites were forbidden to quit; and hence was derived the idea of the " sabbath day's journey," which was reckoned at six stadia—the supposed distance of the furthest bounds of the camp from its centre.

Ver. 30.—**So the people rested.** Having found by experience that nothing was to be gained by seeking manna on the sabbath, and received the severe rebuke of verse 28, the people henceforth obeyed the new commandment, and " rested on the sabbath day." Of the nature of the " rest " intended more will be said in the comment on Ex. xx. 8—11.

HOMILETICS.

Vers. 23—30.—*The institution of the Sabbath.* That, in some sense, the Sabbath was instituted in Paradise seems to follow from Gen. ii. 3. It was at any rate then set apart by Divine counsel and decree. And it is quite possible that a revelation of its sanctity was made to Adam. The week of seven days may, however, have arisen simply out of the lunar month, the four weeks corresponding to the moon's four phases. In any case, as the early Egyptians had no such institution as a weekly sabbath, and certainly would not have tolerated abstinence from work on the part of their Hebrew slaves one day in seven, we must suppose that the sabbatical rest, if ever known to the Hebrews, had fallen into desuetude during their Egyptian sojourn. God now formally either instituted or re-instituted it. He seized the occasion of giving the manna, to mark in the strongest way, and impress upon the people, the strict observance of a sabbatical rest, which forty years' experience would engrain into the habits of the nation. The chief practical points of interest connected with Sabbath observance in the present condition of the Christian world are—1. The relation of the Christian Sunday to the Jewish Sabbath; 2. The authority upon which the change of day has been made; and 3. The proper mode of keeping the Lord's day at the present time. A few words will be said on each of these points.

I. The relation of the Christian Sunday to the Jewish Sabbath. Both the Christian Sunday and the Jewish Sabbath have for their basis the expediency of assigning to the worship and contemplation of God some definite and regularly recurring portions of human life, instead of leaving individuals free to choose their own times and seasons. Temporal concerns so much occupy men, that, if there were no definite rule, they would be apt to push religious observance into the odd corners of human life, if not even to oust it altogether. This evil is prevented, or at any rate checked, by the appointment of a recurrent day, which is also almost a necessity for the practice of *common* worship. In both the Christian and the Jewish religion the same proportion of time is fixed upon, the appointment being that of one day out of seven, or one-seventh part of life, which certainly cannot be said to be an undue requirement. Thus far then the two institutions resemble one the other; but in the primary characteristics of the observance there is a remarkable contrast. The Jewish Sabbath was emphatically a day of holy rest—the Christian Sunday is a day of holy activity. The key-note of our Lord's teaching on the subject is to be found in the words—" It is lawful to *do good* on the Sabbath day." The Jews thought they " hallowed the Sabbath " by mere inaction—some, as we have seen, would not move all day from the place and attitude in which their waking moments found them. Christ taught that there was no virtue in idleness. " My Father worketh hitherto " (on the Sabbath), he said, " and I work." On the Sabbath day he did his miracles, he taught the people, he walked through the cornfields, he journeyed to Emmaus. And the Christian Church has, in the main, continued true to her Founder's teaching. The Christian Sunday has been, and is, a day of holy joy and holy activity. Ministers are of necessity more active on it than on any other. Lay people have felt it to be the special day for imitating their Lord in " going about and doing good "—in teaching the ignorant, visiting the poor and the afflicted—reading to them, praying with them, ministering to their necessities. Cessation from worldly business has come to be the rule on the Lord's day, not from any superstitious regard for mere rest, but in order that the active duties peculiarly belonging to the day shall not be neglected.

II. Although exception may be taken to the expression—used in a tract attributed to

Athanasius—that "our Lord changed the Jewish Sabbath into the Lord's day," yet, practically speaking, it cannot be denied that such a change has been made ; the Christian Sunday has taken the place of the Jewish Sabbath, and occupies in the Christian system the position which the Sabbath occupied in the Jewish. By what authority, then, has the change been made ? How are Christians justified in keeping holy the first day instead of the seventh ? Not, certainly, by any direct command of our Lord, for none such is recorded. Not even by any formal decision of the Apostolic college, for the question was untouched at the only council which they are known to have held (Acts xv. 6—29). But, as it would seem, by consentient apostolic practice. The apostles appear, both by Scripture and by the records of primitive Christian antiquity, to have practically made the change—*i.e.*, they sanctioned the discontinuance of seventh-day observance (Col. ii. 16 ; Gal. iv. 9, 10), and they introduced first-day observance in its stead (John xx. 19, 26 ; Acts ii. 1, xx. 7 ; 1 Cor. xvi. 2). They regarded the Jewish sabbath as abrogated with the rest of the ceremonial law ; and they established by their own authority, and doubtless by the direction of the Holy Ghost, the keeping holy of the "Lord's Day," by meetings for Holy Communion, worship, and instruction on that, the first day of the week, instead.

III. With respect to the proper mode of keeping the Lord's Day at the present time, there would seem to be different degrees of obligation as to different parts of the customary observance. Attendance at Holy Communion, and by analogy at other services, has distinct apostolic sanction (Acts xx. 7 ; Heb. x. 25), and is obligatory in the highest sense. Cessation from worldly business is a matter of ecclesiastical arrangement, in which individual Christians should follow the regulations or traditions of their own ecclesiastical community. Mere inaction should not be regarded as in any sense a "keeping" of the day—the time abstracted from worldly affairs should be given to prayer, reading of the Scriptures, and works of mercy. Gentle and healthful exercise should not be interrupted, being needful to make the body a useful instrument of the soul. Relaxations, not required by adults or by those who are rich, should be allowed to children and to the poor, every care being taken that Sunday be not made to them a day of gloom, restraint, and discomfort. Sunday was intended to be the Christian's weekly festival, a day of cheerfulness and holy joy, a foretaste of the joys of Heaven.

> "The Sundays of man's life,
>   Threaded together on Time's string,
>   Make bracelets for the wife
>   Of the Eternal King.
>   On Sunday, heaven's gate stands ope,
> Blessings are plentiful and ripe—
>   More plentiful than hope."

HOMILIES BY VARIOUS AUTHORS.

Vers. 22—30.—*The Manna and the Sabbath.*—I. THE FACT OF MANNA BEING GIVEN ON SIX DAYS, AND NOT ON THE SEVENTH, IS A PROOF OF THE EXISTENCE OF THE SABBATH. It would certainly seem from this passage that the Israelites had not up to this time been very good Sabbath keepers; that if they knew of any special distinction attaching to the seventh day, they had no very strict ideas as to its observance; that its sanctity was but little recognised by them. It could scarcely have been otherwise with a people just escaped from a long and degrading bondage. It does not follow, however, that this was the first institution of the Sabbath. There is every reason for believing the contrary. That God had the Sabbath in view in the arrangements made, and the laws laid down, about the manna, every one admits. The only question which arises is, whether these arrangements were modelled on the basis of a division of time already existing, or whether this was absolutely the first indication to mankind of a weekly day of rest. 1. *Presumptively*—this latter alternative seems improbable. It is incredible that so important an institution as the Sabbath should be introduced in this casual, unannounced way—should be taken for granted in certain outward arrangements relating to a different matter, and then, when curiosity has been excited by these arrangements, should be first made known by the side-door of an explanation of the novel injunctions. Such a case of the existence of an important institution being assumed before the law which gives it existence has been either promulgated or heard of, is without precedent or parallel in history. It seems plain that whether Israel knew of the existing Sabbath or not, God did, and framed his arrangements in view of it. The inference is that the religious observance of the seventh day had been sanctioned by old tradition, but had fallen largely into desuetude. 2. *On Biblical grounds—* it seems certain that the Sabbath is of older date than the sojourn in the wilderness. We need not review all the evidence which points in the direction of a primeval institution of the Sabbath. It is sufficient to instance the primary text upon the subject (Gen. ii. 1—4), which speaks with a voice as plain as could well be wished to those who are willing to hear. 3. *Historically—*it has been recently proved that the Sabbath was known in ancient Assyria and Babylonia, long before the days of Moses. No Orientalist will any longer question, in face of the evidence furnished by the recently deciphered cuneiform tablets, that a Sabbath was observed in Assyria in the days of Sardanapalus, and for ages previously. But the ancient Accadian records, which go as far back as 2000 B.C., and many of which have been deciphered by the aid of competent Assyrian translators, show that a Sabbath was observed in the very earliest time. The very name "Sabattu," with the meaning "a day of rest for the heart," has been found in the old Accadian tongue (see "Records of the Past," vol. iii. p. 143; "Assyrian Discoveries," by George Smith; the *Academy,* Nov. 1875). Special points in these researches will need confirmation, but on the whole, the early and wide-spread observance of the Sabbath must be held as established. In the light of Oriental discovery, it will soon be regarded as an anachronism to speak of prolepsis in connection with Gen. ii. 1—4; or to urge the view that the Sabbath is a purely Judaic institution, and originated with Moses.

II. The rule for gathering a double supply of manna on the sixth day, and laying by for the seventh, taught the lesson of a proper respect for the Sabbath. It taught—1. That the Sabbath was to be kept free from unnecessary work. 2. That in order to leave the Sabbath clear, as a day of rest, work was to be *forwarded* on week days. 3. That God has a respect for his own ordinance.

III. By granting this double supply on the sixth day, and securing its preservation on the seventh, God taught that his blessing rests upon the Sabbath, and that his people will be no losers by keeping it.

IV. God's care thus early to re-establish the ordinance of the Sabbath in Israel, shows the importance of the institution as bearing on health, morals, and religion. It must be reckoned a noteworthy circumstance that, in arranging the affairs of Israel, with a view to the recovery of his people from the low and demoralised condition, physically, morally, and spiritually, into which they had fallen, and with a view to their elevation to a state of prosperous national existence, God's first step, even before the law was given from Sinai, was to put on a proper foundation, the observance of the Sabbath.

V. God's displeasure at the breach of this law by the people who went out to gather on the Sabbath, shows his zeal for the honour of the commandment (vers. 27—29). The thing chiefly condemned, no doubt, was the *spirit* of disobedience, which showed itself in more ways than one (cf. ver. 20). But is it not plainly reckoned a special aggravation of the offence of these would-be gatherers, that they so defiantly set at nought God's ordinance of a day of rest? Does God show a like zeal for the observance of any purely ceremonial precept?—J. O.

Vers. 16—36.—*The manna—regulations for the gathering and using of it.* I. The effective distribution of it is provided for. The responsibilities and opportunities of the family relation, which had been touched upon in the institution of the Passover, are here touched upon again. Each head of a household had to see that the daily supply was gathered for his family. Thus God shows that he is not only attentive for that great nation which now, as a whole, is so clearly dependent on his providing, so visibly cut off from secondary grounds of confidence, but also has his eye on the under-providers. What he is to all the children of men, he expects earthly parents to be in their measure and opportunity. Earthly parents, even though evil, are yet able to give some good gifts; and God will hold them responsible thus to give what they can. The peculiar and transcendent gifts of grace they are not able to bestow; but seeing God has constituted them the channels of certain blessings, woe be to them if they block up the channels, or in any way diminish the flow of blessings through them.

II. A SUFFICIENT SUPPLY IS PROVIDED FOR. Some gathered more and some less; but the gathering amounted to the same thing in the end. There was neither defect nor superfluity. We may take it that *those who gathered more* did it in a spirit of unbelief and worldly wisdom, a spirit of anxious questioning with regard to the morrow. They wanted to make sure, lest the morrow's manna did not come. God disappointed their plans, and doubtless soon altered their conduct, by reducing the quantity gathered to the stipulated omer. Thus unbelief's labour was lost. And *those who gathered less* did so through straitened opportunity. It may be they had less time; it may be they were feeble or aged. But we are sure that, whatever the cause of their deficiency, they must have been those who did their best; and God honoured their honest endeavours by making up the deficiency. If they had been careless, it is pretty certain they would have had to go starving. God has ever taken care of the principle that, if a man will not work, neither shall he eat. All that is required is, that we should do our best according to our opportunities; but so much, at least, assuredly is required. Remember the teaching of the parable (Matt. xx. 1—16). The lord of the vineyard gave the same amount to those coming in at the eleventh hour as to those who began early in the morning. He considered pressing need to be as important a thing as actual exertion. But at the same time he had his eye on what had really been done. Those who entered at the eleventh hour had to do their best even though it was but for a short time. Thus the lord of the vineyard respected need on the one hand and disposition and embraced opportunities on the other. And so with the manna in the wilderness: every Israelite had to do his best, with a believing mind and an industrious hand. Then God took care that he should have enough; and "enough is as good as a feast."

III. GOD MADE PLAIN THAT IT WAS TO BE A DAILY SUPPLY. He did this, first of all, by diminishing the quantity gathered to the stipulated omer. Then, when the omer was secured, he made the daily character of the supply still more evident by commanding that none should be left till morning. This was but carrying the former provision—that of gathering an omer full—out to its logical conclusion. Nor must we take this to mean, of necessity, that *all the manna was to be eaten up.* "Leave it not till the morning" can only mean "leave it not as food." There could hardly have been an obligation on the Israelites to eat more than nature demanded or appetite desired. Let no fond, economising parent quote this regulation to a child by way of enforcing the request to eat up its food. How much harm is done by forcing children to empty the plate, lest anything be wasted! Surely it is more waste to cram a recalcitrant stomach than to throw undemanded food away, if that be the only alternative. Evidently what God meant here is, that Israel should not keep its manna for to-morrow's supply. There is more likelihood of imperilling the spirit of faith than the habit of economy. Note, too, that *the efficacy of this regulation was soon exemplified when the people broke it.* Indeed, it is curious to notice how, all through the passage, the regulations and the exemplification of them are mixed up. They were regulations which came into operation at once; for there was a present need, and the people learnt to meet it by paying at first the penalties of disobedience or imperfect obedience. They could put away the manna; but they could not therefore preserve it. Putting it away was only turning it into one of the treasures which moth and rust corrupt. Even if we could imagine that it had been possible to seal the manna hermetically, and keep it from the germs of corruption in the air, the result would have been the same. Whatever the precautions adopted, it would have bred worms and stunk by morning. God is ever turning our boasted prudence into ridiculous folly; faith and obedience are the only real prudence.

IV. Not only was it a daily supply, but A MORNING SUPPLY. An early morning supply, for when the sun waxed hot the manna was melted. They were to go out and gather the manna the first thing, and then, whatever else might be lacking that day, the great temporal necessity of food was provided for. God demanded of his people that they should be trustful and satisfied in the reception of a daily supply; but that supply was brought at the very beginning of the day. It was not at their option to gather it at any time of the day they chose. The supply was at the beginning of the day, because day is the time for eating as night is for sleeping. Then, with minds free from anxiety and bodies duly supported, they could each one set about his appointed business.

V. IN HIS METHOD OF SUPPLY GOD MADE SPECIAL PROVISION FOR THE SABBATH. On the sixth day of the week, a double portion was provided, and was to be gathered in correspondence with the provision. Certainly it must be admitted that the regulation here gives no means of judging how far the Sabbath was a recognised institution in Israel, if indeed it was an institution at all. This is a matter on which we are not able to affirm; nor are we able to deny. To whatever extent there may have been a weekly Sabbath among the patriarchs, it could not have been kept up through the hardships of Egypt! Anyway, this remarkable increase of an extra omer on the sixth day—when the reason of it was explained—was the very thing to prepare the people for the exact commandment which so soon followed. Jehovah had thus more ways than one of impressing upon them the sanctity and peculiarity of the Sabbath. In Egypt they had doubtless been required to toil every day, knowing little rest, save the inevitable rest of sleep, and it would be hard to break them away from this expectation of daily drudgery. Early association and training are wanted to make one day different from others; and we may conclude that it was only the generation growing up in the wilderness and becoming habituated to the Sabbath rest that really took to it in a natural and easy way. But this regulation of the manna must have been a great help *even to the elder generation.* As each sixth day came round they were reminded that God himself was remembering the Sabbath day to keep it holy, and therefore they should do the same. And as we think of this special provision for the weekly interval of rest, continued through forty years, we may well ask ourselves what feelings God entertains as he looks down on the world and sees the incessant, driving, suicidal toil in which many men engage, *on the plea that it is necessary.* They say they have no choice. Toil all day, and when evening comes utter exhaustion! and thus life is wasted in the struggle to maintain it. When we consider such struggling in the light of this sixth day's double provision, a strong suspicion rises in our minds that this plea of necessity is a delusion. Is it not probable that if men would only throw off, boldly and trustfully, many of what are reckoned social necessities, they would have a healthier piety and a happier life? At present, with only too many, when they are asked for a little more attention to the things of God and a little more interest in them, the plea comes in reply, easily urged and not easily met, that there is no time. See then what God did for his own people. He made time for them, and jealously hedged it about; a time for needed rest, holy rest and holy service. When they went out food-seeking on the morning of his day, he manifestly cursed their disobedience and unbelief. May we not be perfectly sure that if in a spirit of faith, we give all the time and effort that are necessary to cultivate personal religion and diffuse gospel truth, God will see to it that we get the manna? and if we have the manna, we need nothing more. Whatever else be left unsought and unenjoyed, seek first the kingdom of God and his righteousness. Seek these, for they bring in their train everything a Christian can lawfully enjoy.—Y.

Vers. 19—36. *The law of the manna.* I. THERE MUST BE INDIVIDUAL EFFORT FOR INDIVIDUAL NEED. 1. The manna lay around their tents, but it had to be gathered. To feed on Christ each must lay hold of him for his own soul by meditation and prayer and trust. 2. If we do not "taste and see that the Lord is gracious," his nearness to us will only deepen our condemnation. How shall we escape if we neglect so great salvation? II. CHRIST MUST BE LAID HOLD OF DAILY DURING THE WEEK'S TOIL. 1. The sabbath has its provision without labour. This law is sometimes inverted—sabbath day's toil, six days' negligence—but in this way Christ will be fed upon neither in labour nor in rest. They who come from daily walking with Christ, find the sabbath feast spread for them. 2. The life of labour in striving to lay hold of and feed upon him, is followed by the rest that remaineth and the feast which his own hand will spread. III. GRACE WILL NOT CONSORT WITH DISOBEDIENCE. The manna stored up to save from toiling, when God commands to toil, was unfit for use. We cannot live on the memories of past experiences of Christ's graciousness. He must be daily sought for.

IV. CHRIST THE SOUL'S FOOD DURING THE ENTIRE EARTHLY PILGRIMAGE (ver. 35). During the whole forty years Israel fed upon the manna. We must feed daily upon Christ till we reach the inheritance. They who will be sustained in their journey must determine to know nothing save Christ and him crucified.—U.

EXPOSITION.

Vers. 31—36.—THE APPEARANCE OF THE MANNA, ITS CONTINUANCE, AND ITS DEPOSITION IN THE TABERNACLE.—In bringing the subject of the manna to a conclusion, the writer adds a few words. 1. On its appearance; 2. On its deposition by divine command in the Ark of the Covenant; and 3. On its continuance during the forty years of the wanderings. It is evident that verses 32—34 cannot have been written until after the sojourn in Sinai, and the command to make a tabernacle (ch. xxvi.): as also that verse 35 cannot have been written till the arrival of the Israelites at the verge of the land of Canaan. But there is nothing in the passage that militates against the Mosaic authorship of the whole.

Ver. 31.—**The house of Israel.** This expression is unusual, and is not admitted by the Septuagint, the Syriac, or the Arabic versions, which all have "the *children* of Israel." Several Hebrew MSS. have *beni*, "sons," instead of *beyth* "house." **Manna.** Literally, as in the Septuagint, *man*—the word used when they first beheld the substance (verse 15), and probably meaning "a gift." The elongated form *manna*, first appears in the Sept. rendering of Num. xi. 6, 7. **It was like coriander seed.** This is "a small round grain of a whitish or yellowish grey." The comparison is made again in Num. xi. 7, where it is added that the colour was that of *bdellium*—either the gum so called, or possibly the pearl. **The taste of it was like wafers made with honey.** Such wafers or cakes were constantly used as offerings by the Egyptians, Greeks, and other nations. They were ordinarily compounded of meal, *oil*, and honey. Hence we can reconcile with the present passage the statement in Num. xi. 8, that "the taste of it was as the taste of fresh oil."

Ver. 32.—**And Moses said.** Not at the moment, but some time subsequently. See the introductory paragraph. **Fill an omer.** In the original it is "the omer," and so the LXX.; but the reason for the introduction of the article is obscure. **For your generations—** *i.e.*, "for your descendants."

Ver. 33.—**Take a pot.** The word here translated "pot" does not occur elsewhere in Scripture, and is believed to be of Egyptian origin Gesenius translates it "basket;" but

the author of the Epistle to the Hebrews (ix. 4) follows the LXX. in representing the word used by στάμνος, which certainly means "a jar" or "pot." **Lay it up before the Lord.** The "pot of manna" was laid up before the Lord with the "tables of the covenant," and "Aaron's rod that budded" as symbolical that God's mercy was as eternal and essential, and as much to be remembered as his justice, and perhaps also as especially symbolising the "true bread of life."

Ver. 34.—**Aaron laid it up before the testimony.** "The testimony" is not the Ark of the Covenant, which is never so called, but the Covenant itself, or the two tables of stone engraved by the finger of God, which are termed "the testimony" in ch. xxv. 16—21; xl. 20; etc. The pot of manna was laid up inside the ark (Heb. ix. 4) in front of the two tables.

Ver. 35.—**The children of Israel did eat manna forty years.** Kalisch observes that the actual time was not forty full years, but about one month short of that period, since the manna began after the fifteenth day of the second month of the first year (verse 1) and terminated just after Passover of the forty-first year (Josh. v. 10—12). It may be added that Moses cannot have written the present passage later than about the eleventh month of the fortieth year (Deut. i. 3; xxxiv. 10; Josh. iv. 19); when the manna had continued thirty-nine years and nine months. **Until they came to a land inhabited.** Kalisch translates "the land of their habitation," or "which they were to inhabit," remarking that they had reached inhabited countries, *e.g.*, those of Sihon and Og, much earlier. But the words will not bear this rendering. What the writer intends to note is, that the manna continued all the time they were in the wilderness, until they reached inhabited territory, and then further (in the next clause), that it lasted after that, until they came to the borders of Canaan. He does not say that it even then left off. He writes exactly as Moses might be expected to have written towards the close of his life. A later writer would, as Canon Cook observes, have been more specific.

Ver. 36.—**An omer.** The "omer" must be distinguished from the "homer" of later times. It was an Egyptian measure, as also was the "ephah." It is not improbable that the verse is an addition by a later writer, as Joshua, or Ezra.

HOMILETICS.

Vers. 32—34.—*Memorials of mercies.* It is indicative of the weakness and imperfection of human nature, that memorials of mercies should be needed. But frail humanity cannot do without them; and God in his goodness, knowing this, sanctions them. As he had the rod of Aaron, which budded (Num. xvii. 10), and the pot of manna, made permanent portions of the furniture of the tabernacle for memorials, so he had memorial days established, Sabbath, and Passover, and Pentecost, and memorial seasons, as the feasts of unleavened bread and tabernacles, that the children of Israel might keep his mercies in perpetual remembrance. We Christians have no such material memorials as the tables of stone, the rod, and the manna; for the "True Cross" is historically untrustworthy, and the "Holy Coat" *could* not have been a Jewish garment. We have, however, memorials of mercies.—

I. IN OUR HOLY DAYS. Our Sunday is a perpetual memorial and reminder of the great mercy of Christ's Resurrection, the earnest, and efficient cause, of our own. Christmas-day, Good Friday, Ascension-day, are memorials of the same kind; not so universally acknowledged, but useful memorials, where they are established and observed. Christianity commands that no man shall judge another in respect of such observances; but it would be an ill day for Christendom, if they were universally given up. Thousands find them great helps to devotion, great stimulants to gratitude and love.

II. IN OUR HOLY EMBLEMS. The Cross, the Lamb, the Eagle, the Crown of Thorns, the Vine, the Rose, the Lily of the Valley, wherever we behold them, are memorials of divine mercies, never sufficiently remembered, most useful in recalling to our minds the acts, events, persons, wherewith they are scripturally connected. Some minds are so constituted as not to require such reminders. But to the mass of men they are of inexpressible value, waking up (as they do) twenty times a day holy thoughts that might otherwise have slumbered, and stirring the heart to devotions that might otherwise have been unthought of.

III. IN OUR HOLY BUILDINGS. What the entire tabernacle was to the Israelites in the wilderness, what the temple, so long as it stood, was to the Israelite nation, such to Christians are their cathedrals, abbeys, churches, chapels, oratories, perpetual reminders of holy things, memorials pointing heavenwards, and bringing to mind all that God has done for us. That they are also intended for practical use as places where we may worship in common, and be taught in common, does not prevent their being at the same time memorials. It is as memorials that they lift themselves up so high, ascending in tier over tier of useless pinnacle, and high-pitched roof, and spire-crowned tower. They aim at catching our attention, forcing us to look at them, and making us think of God's mercies.

HOMILIES BY VARIOUS AUTHORS.

Vers. 32—34.—*The pot of manna.* Aaron was ordered to take a pot, and put an omer full of manna therein, and lay it up before the Lord, to be kept for future generations. The pot of manna is alluded to in Hebrews, where it is described as "golden," and as laid up in the ark (Heb. ix. 4). It may be questioned how so corruptible a substance admitted of preservation. But it is not so plain that the manna had in itself any tendency to corrupt, so that the miracle is perhaps to be looked for, not in the keeping fresh of the portion laid up in the ark, but in the smiting with corruption of any portions sinfully hoarded by the Israelites (ver. 20). We are taught—

I. THAT THE GREATER MERCIES OF GOD OUGHT SPECIALLY TO BE REMEMBERED BY US. It is fitting, even in the Church, to appoint memorials of them.

II. THAT THE PECULIAR LESSONS OF THE MANNA OUGHT SPECIALLY TO BE KEPT IN REMEMBRANCE. Among these note the following:—1. "Man doth not live by bread alone," etc. (cf. Deut. viii. 4; Matt. iv. 4). 2. The lesson of dependence on God for supply of daily wants (Matt. vi. 2). 3. Typical lessons. The manna reminds us of Christ, our Bread of Life, in heaven. "Your life is hid with Christ in God" (Col. iii. 3). The "hidden manna" in Rev. ii. 17, would seem to indicate the spiritual nourishment in communion with God and Christ which will maintain soul and body for ever in the possession of an incorruptible life—life undecaying, self-renewing, everlasting.

III. The indissoluble union of law and grace in God's dealings with his Church. The pot of manna was laid up (after the ark was made) "before the testimony, to be kept" (ver. 34). The law is the stern background, but near it is the golden pot, filled with the manna which told of God's goodness and grace to a people whom mere law would have condemned. God can be thus gracious to his Church, not because his law has been set aside, but because it has been magnified and made honourable by Christ, whose blood pleads at the mercy-seat for the transgressor.—J. O.

EXPOSITION.

CHAPTER XVII.

Vers. 1—7.—The second murmuring for water. When the Israelites had come to Rephidim which was probably in the Wady Feiran, near its junction with the Wady Esh-Sheikh, complaint arose, not, as at Marah (ch. xv. 23), that there was no drinkable water, but that there was no water at all. Water had been expected, and consequently no supply had been brought; but none was found. Violent murmurs arose, and the people were ready to stone their leader (ver. 4), who had, they considered, brought them into the difficulty. As usual, Moses took his grief to God, and laid it before him, with the result that God gave miraculous relief. Moses was bidden to take his rod, and go with the elders to a particular rock known as "the rock in Horeb" (ver. 6), and there strike the rock, and water would flow forth. This he did, and a copious stream welled out, which furnished abundant drink to the whole multitude. In remembrance of the murmuring, he called the place Massah (trial) and Meribah (quarrel).

Ver. 1.—**From the wilderness of Sin.** See the comment on ch. xvi. 1. The sandy coast tract (El Murka) was probably quitted in lat. 28° 42' nearly, and the Wady Feiran entered on at its south-western extremity. Two stations, Dophkah and Alush, lay between the Sin wilderness and Rephidim, as we learn from Num. xxxiii. 12, 13. It is impossible to locate these places with exactness. **After their journeys.** The three stages—from Sin to Dophkah, from Dophkah to Alush, and from Alush to Rephidim—seem to be alluded to. **According to the commandment of the Lord.** Literally, "at the mouth of Jehovah," i.e. as God ordered them. The command was signified by the movement of the "pillar of the cloud." **And pitched in Rephidim.** The word Rephidim signifies "resting places," and "is the natural name for the paradise of the Bedouins in the palm-grove where the church

and palace of the bishops of Paran formerly stood" (Stanley, *Sinai and Palestine*, p. 41). **There was no water.** The Wady Feiran is watered ordinarily by a copious stream; but at times the brook is dry (*ibid.* p. 40, note 3).

Ver. 2.—**The people did chide.** I.e. "quarrelled," made open murmurs and complaint—as before frequently (ch. xiv. 11, 12; xv. 24; xvi. 2, 3). **Give us water.** As Moses had already given them flesh (the quails) and bread (the manna), so it perhaps seemed to the people easy that he should give them such a common thing as water. Stanley notices (p. 70) that the wadys suggest the idea of water, and make its absence the more intolerable—they are "exactly like rivers," with "torrent bed, and banks, and clefts in the rock for tributary streams, and at times even rushes and shrubs fringing their course" —signs of "water, water everywhere, yet not a drop to drink." **Wherefore do ye tempt the Lord?** To "tempt the Lord" is to try his patience by want of faith, to arouse his anger, to provoke him to punish us. It was the special sin of the Israelites during the whole period of their sojourn in the wilderness. They "tempted and provoked the most high God" (Ps. lxxviii. 56); "provoked him to anger with their inventions" (*ib.* cvi. 29), "murmured in their tents" (*ib.* 25), "provoked him at the sea" (*ib.* 7), "tempted him in the desert" (*ib.* 14). God's long-suffering, notwithstanding all, is simply amazing!

Ver. 3.—**The people thirsted there for water.** There is probably no physical affliction comparable to intense thirst. His thirst was the only agony which drew from the Son of Man an acknowledgment of physical suffering, in the words "I thirst." Descriptions of thirst in open boats at sea are among the most painful of the records of afflicted humanity. Thirst in the desert can scarcely be less horrible. **The people murmured and said.** When the worst comes on men, if they are alone, they bear it silently; but if they can find a scapegoat, they murmur. To lay the blame of the situation on another is a huge satisfaction to the ordinary human mind, which shrinks from responsibility, and would fain shift the burthen on some one else. **To kill us.** Compare ch. xiv. 11,

xvi. 3. The circumstances of their life in the wilderness were such, that, until accustomed to them, the people thought that, at each step, they must perish. It may be freely admitted, that without continual miraculous aid this would have been the natural *dénouement.* **And our cattle.** It is interesting to see that the " cattle " still survived, and were regarded as of great importance. How far they served as a secondary head of subsistance to the people during the 40 years, is a point not yet sufficiently elaborated.

Ver. 4.—**And Moses cried unto the Lord.** It is one of the most prominent traits of the character of Moses, that, at the occurrence of a difficulty, he always carries it straight to God. (See ch. xv. 25; xxiv. 15; xxxii. 30; xxxiii. 8; Num. xi. 2, 11; xii. 11; xiv. 13—19, etc.) **They be almost ready to stone me.** This is the first which we hear of *stoning* as a punishment. It is *naturally* one of the easiest modes of wreaking popular vengeance on an obnoxious individual, and was known to the Greeks as early as the time of the Persian war (Herod. ix. 5), to the Macedonians (Q. Curt. *Vit. Alex.* vi. 11, 38), and others. There is, however, no trace of it among the Egyptians.

Ver. 5.—**Go on before the people.** " Leave the people," *i.e.,* "where they are, in Rephidim, and go on in front of them, with some of the elders as witnesses, that the miracle may be sufficiently attested." On the other occasion, when water was brought forth out of the rock (Num. xx. 8—11), it was done in the presence of the people. Perhaps now there was a real danger of their stoning Moses, had he not quitted them. **Thy rod with which thou smotest the river.** See above, ch. vii. 20.

Ver. 6.—**Behold, I will stand before thee there.** A visible Divine appearance seems to be intended, which would guide Moses to the exact place where he should strike. **The rock in Horeb** must have been a remarkable object, already known to Moses during the time that he dwelt in the Sinai-Horeb region; but its exact locality cannot be pointed out. It cannot, however, have been very far distant from Rephidim. (See ver. 8.)

Ver. 7.—**He called the name of the place Massah.** *Massah* is from the root *nasah,* " to try," or " tempt," and means " trial " or " temptation." **Meribah** is from *rûb,* " to chide, quarrel," and means " contention, chiding, strife." Moses gave the same name to the place near Kadesh, where water was once more brought out of the rock, near the end of the wanderings. (See Num. xx. 13; Deut. xxxii. 51; Ps. cvi. 32.)

HOMILETICS.

Vers. 1—7.—*Water out of the rock.* " They did all drink the same spiritual drink; for they drank of that spiritual rock that followed them, and that rock was Christ " (1 Cor. x. 4). When man is at his last gasp, perishing for lack of what he sorely needs, then God lavishes his mercies. All previous trials were as nothing compared with that which befel Israel at Rephidim. Lips parched, throats dry, bodies fevered with heat, hearts expectant and buoyed up with hope till the close of the day, then suddenly despairing—they lay on the arid soil around the ill-named " resting-places," maddened, furious, desperate. Without water, they must perish in the course of a few hours— they, " and their children " (ver. 3)—the little tender innocents, a while ago so gay and sprightly and joyous, now drooping, listless, voiceless. What wonder that some hearts were stirred with fury against Moses, that some hands clutched stones, and were ready to launch them at their leader's head? Men in such straits are often not masters of themselves, and scarcely answerable for the thoughts they think or the acts they do. But the greater the need, the richer the manifestation of God's mercy. At God's word, Moses strikes the rock; and the outcome is an abundant copious stream—aye, " rivers of living water! " All were free to drink at once—men, women, little children, cattle, asses—all could take without stint, satiate themselves, drink of the water of life freely. And the water " followed them." From Rephidim, in the second year, to Kadesh, in the thirty-eighth year of the wanderings, there is no more complaint of want of water at any time, no need apparently of any new and distinct miracle.

And we too have WATER OUT OF THE ROCK, which is—1. *Miraculous;* 2. *Abounding;* 3. *Life-giving.* 1. *Miraculous.* For our Rock is Christ himself—not the type, not the shadow, but the reality. Christ himself, the true and only-begotten Son of God, makes himself to us a perpetual, abiding, exhaustless source of a constant living stream, from which we may drink continually. " If any man thirst," he says, " let him come unto ME and drink " (John vii. 37); and again—" Ho, every man that thirsteth, come ye to the waters " (Is. lv. 1). He " opens rivers in high places, and fountains in the midst of the valleys "—he " makes the wilderness a pool of water, and the dry land springs of water" (*ib.* xli. 18). As from his riven side, upon the Cross, blood and water flowed down in a mingled stream, so ever does he give us by a standing miracle his atoning blood to expiate our guilt, and his pure spiritual influences to cleanse our hearts and purify our souls. And the supply is—2. *Abounding.* The water that he gives, is in each man "a well of water, springing up into everlasting life" (John iv. 14). It is given without let or stint—freely to "every one that thirsteth." This is his promise—"I will pour water upon him that is thirsty, and floods upon the dry ground; I will pour my spirit upon thy seed, and my blessing upon thy offspring" (Is. xliv. 3). Men have but to thirst for the living stream, to desire it, long for it, and he pours it forth. As in heaven, "a pure water of life, clear as crystal, proceeds out of the throne of God and of the Lamb" (Rev. xxii. 2), so even here there is a fountain opened for sin and for uncleanness, abundant, copious, never-failing—of which all may drink freely. And the draught is—3. *Life-giving.* However weak we are, however drooping, however near to death, once let us drink of the precious water that he gives, and we are saved. Death is foiled, the destroyer forced to release his prey, life springs up again within the heart; every nerve is invigorated; every fibre of our frame recovers its tone. True "water of life" is that stream which wells forth from the riven side of the Lamb. Christ is "our Life;" and in him, and through him we have life. The water that he gives us is "living water"—for it is in truth the Spirit of him who is "the true God and the eternal life" (1 John v. 20)—who "hath life in himself." Lord, evermore give us this "life!"

HOMILIES BY VARIOUS AUTHORS.

Vers. 1—7.—*The water from the rock.* The Israelites pursued their journey to the mount of God. It was— 1. By stages—"after their journeys." It is well to discipline the mind to look at life as a succession of stages. "Most people can bear one day's evil; the thing that breaks one down is the trying to bear on one day the evil of two days, twenty days, a hundred days." 2. According to God's commandment—following still the guiding cloud. 3. It brought them in due course to Rephidim, the scene of a new trial, and of a new theocratic mercy.

I. THE SITUATION. Its horrors can be better imagined than described. 1. *The want of water.* "There was no water for the people to drink" (ver. 1). Even where water was comparatively abundant, it would be a task of no small difficulty to supply the wants of so immense a multitude. Now they are conducted into a region where water absolutely fails them. The last drop in their water-skins is exhausted. There is a famine of the needful element. Scouts bring in the intelligence that the place is one of utter drought, without streams, wells, rivulets, oozing rocks, or any other means of renewing the supplies. Consternation sits on every face. Dismay is in every heart. 2. *The consequent thirst.* "And the people thirsted there for water" (ver. 3). The pangs of unallayed thirst constitute an intolerable torture. Hunger is attended by gnawings and tearings in one organ of the body—that concerned in the reception of food. But thirst possesses the whole being. It mounts to the brain. It burns and rages like fever in the blood. Draining the body of its juices, it causes every nerve to throb with acute suffering. "Heart and flesh" cry out for the boon of water. It has been remarked that "I thirst" was the only expression of bodily suffering wrung from our Lord upon the cross. 3. *The spiritual analogue.* God brought the people into a situation in which they not only experienced acute thirst, but were made to feel that in their sore strait, nature could do nothing for them. If left to the resources of nature, they must inevitably perish. They cried for water, but it was not to be had. The depth said, It is not in me. The thirsty sand said, It is not in me. The sky that was as brass above them said, It is not in me. The dry, dead rocks around said, It is not in us. From no quarter could they extract so much as a drop of the precious liquid. The analogue to this is the condition of the spirit which has become awakened to the emptiness and unsatisfyingness of the world around it, of the finite generally; which feels the need of a higher life than the world can give it. In the renewed nature, it becomes definitively the thirst for God, for the living God, for his love, his favour, for knowledge of him, for participation in his life (Ps. xlii. 1, 2; lxiii. 1—3). Under conviction of sin, it is specially the thirst for pardon and holiness (Ps. li.; cxix. 41, 81, 123, 166, 174). By bestowing on the Israelites supernatural water to quench their thirst, God declared at the same time his ability and willingness to supply these higher wants of the soul; nay, held out in type the promise of this gift. This is not a far-fetched application of the incident. The word spoken to the Israelites at Marah, "I am Jehovah that healeth thee" (ch. xv. 26), gave them a key to the interpretation of this whole series of miraculous facts. We cannot say to what extent they used it; but the key was there. Just as at Marah, the healing of the waters was a symbol of the truth that Jehovah would be their healer in every sphere of their existence; as the gift of manna was the type and pledge of the gift of "that meat which endureth unto everlasting life" (John vi. 27); so, in the case before us, was the water from the rock, this supernatural water, an emblem and token of a supply in God for the satisfaction of spiritual thirst, and a pledge to his people that this supply would actually be made available for their wants.

II. THE CHIDING (vers. 1—5). The behaviour of the people (making all allowance for their sore necessity) showed how little they had profited by past experiences of God's kindness. 1. They *chided with Moses*. This is, they blamed, rebuked, reproved, reproached him for having brought them into this unhappy situation. How unreasonable was this, to chide with Moses, when they knew that in every step by which he had led them, Moses had only done God's bidding. It was God's arrangements they were quarrelling with, not the arrangements of Moses. But it is usually in this indirect way that murmuring against God, and rebellion against his will are carried on. Because of this chiding of the people, the place was called Meribah (ver. 7). 2. They *asked Moses for the impossible*. They said, "Give us water to drink" (ver. 2). Here was further unreasonableness. They knew very well that Moses could not give them water. There was none to give. Probably they meant that he should supply their wants by miracle. If so, the spirit of their demand was wholly unbecoming. (1) They addressed themselves to Moses, not to God. They *ought* to have addressed themselves to God, but they did not. (2) They did not in a becoming manner *ask* for the water, but violently *demanded* it. (3) The demand was made in a spirit of unbelief. This is evident from verse 7—"they tempted the Lord, saying, Is the Lord among us, or not?" They did not believe that water could be provided for them. 3. They *taunted Moses with a design to kill them*. This was a further disclosure of their unbelief. Twice, on previous occasions, they had made the same complaint, ostensibly against Moses, but really against God (ch. xiv. 11; xvi. 3), and twice had God shown them how unfounded were their ungenerous suspicions. He had saved them from the Egyptians. He had supplied them with bread. Could they not now trust him to supply them with water? Perhaps, as a writer has remarked, had the combination of circumstances been exactly the same as before, their hearts would not have failed them. "But when are combinations of circumstances exactly the same? and when the new combination arises, the old faith is apt to fail" (Gibson on the miracle at Marah, "the Mosaic Era"). This, however, was part of the design, to reveal the Israelites to themselves, and show them the strength of this "evil heart of unbelief" within them, which was ever prompting them anew to depart from the living God (Heb. iii. 12). We have equal need to beware of its operations in ourselves. 4. They *were like to stone Moses*. Moses speaks, in verse 5, as one driven to his wits' end by the unreasonableness and violence of the mob. He did, however, the right thing—betook himself in his strait to God. There is perhaps no prayer, which in the discharge of public duties, servants of God are more frequently tempted to offer, or do offer with greater heartiness than this, that they "may be delivered from unreasonable and wicked men; for all men have not faith" (2 Thess. iii. 2).

III. THE DELIVERANCE (vers. 5, 6). God, as before, grants a supply for the people's wants. By bringing streams out of the rock for them, and causing waters to run down like rivers (Ps. lxxviii. 15, 16; Is. xlviii. 21), he showed how wanton and ungrateful had been their suspicions of him, and how foolishly they had limited his power. Notice—1. *God's loving-kindness in this gift*. This was very marked, when we remember how soon the people had forgotten previous mighty works. (1) The water was given without chiding and rebuke. Save, indeed, as it was itself the most pointed of all rebukes of the unbelief of the murmurers. They had chided with Moses; but God, in return, does not chide with them. He is merciful to their unrighteousness, and seeks to overcome it by showering on them his undeserved benefits. He does not return them evil for evil, but seeks to overcome their evil with his good. It is the same loving-kindness which we see in the Gospel. God seeks to conquer us by love. (2) The gift was plentiful. All scripture allusions to the miracle confirm this idea (Ps. lxxviii. 20; cv. 41; Is. xlviii. 21). The tradition was, that the waters continued to flow, and followed the Israelites wherever they went. The Rabbins had a fable that the rock itself, in some way, accompanied the people in their journeys. In a figure, or parabolically even this was true, for the real rock was God himself, whose presence and agency in the miracle is denoted by the words, " Behold, I will stand before thee there upon the rock in Horeb " (ver. 6). It was probably in the parabolic sense that the Rabbins used the expression. 2. The *manner of the gift*. This is to be carefully noted. (1) Elders were to be taken as witnesses of the transaction (ver. 5). This denoted that in what he did, God was looking beyond the immediate supply of the people's bodily wants. The design was, of course, to secure for posterity a properly authenticated account of the miracle. The importance attached to evidence in this whole series of transactions is very marked (cf. chs. iv. 1—10; vii. 9). A similar importance is attached to evidence in the law (Deut. xvii. 6, 7; xix. 15—21). This suggests to us how far we are, in believing scripture, from relying on " cunningly-devised fables " (2 Pet. i. 16). God took pains that his mighty works should not lack contemporary authentication. Christ, in like manner, took security for the transmission to posterity of a faithful account of his words and works, by appointing twelve apostles (Luke xxiv. 48; Acts i. 21, 22). What additional confidence all this inspires in the historic ground-work of our religion! The direction for the appointment of formal witnesses had no doubt in view the character of the miracle as a pledge and type of spiritual blessings. As myths, these miracles might still suggest to us certain spiritual ideas; but their value would be gone as Divine acts, positively pledging the Divine fulness for the supply of " all the need " of the children of faith. (2) Moses was to work the miracle by means of the rod (ver. 5). The rod appears here as the symbol of the authority with which Moses was invested, and also as the vehicle of the Divine power. The personal character of Moses sinks in this miracle as nearly out of sight as possible. God stands before him on the rock, and is all in all in the cleaving of it, and giving of the water. God is everything, Moses nothing. (3) The rock was to be smitten (ver. 6). The distinction made between this miracle and that at Kadesh in the 40th year (Num. xx. 7—12), where the rock was only to be *spoken to*, shows conclusively that the act of smiting was meant to be significant. The smiting was, first, a cleaving of the way for the passage of the waters, which otherwise would not have flowed, as contrasted, in the later miracle, with a renewal of what was practically the same supply. God would plainly have the people recognise a *continuity* in the supply of water at different stages of the journey, the outward rock merging in the spiritual and invisible one from which the supply really came, and which was with them at all times and places (cf. 1 Cor. x. 4). But this is not the whole. The singular fact remains that the rock was to be *smitten*, and smitten with the rod wherewith " thou *smotest* the river." In other words, the way was to be opened for the waters by an act of violence, the smiting here, as in the case of the river, almost necessarily suggesting judgment. If there were indeed in this any typical allusion to the actual mode in which living waters were to be given to the world, viz. by the smiting of the rock Christ, it must have remained an enigma till later prophecies, and ultimately the event itself, threw light upon it. There is, how-ever, nothing extravagant in believing that this form was given of design to the transaction, that, when the truth *was* known, believing minds, reverting to this smitten rock, might find in it all the more apt and suggestive an emblem of the great facts of their redemption. 3. *Its spiritual teaching.* The rock points to Christ (1 Cor. x. 4). The waters which flowed from it, accordingly, are to be taken, not simply as streams of literal refreshment for the Israelites, but spiritually, typically, symbolically—may we not almost say sacramentally?—as representative of spiritual blessings. So, in the above-cited passage, the apostle calls the water " spiritual drink," even as the manna was " spiritual meat " (1 Cor. x. 3, 4). See below. We may extend the figure, and think of Christ, in turn, smiting with his cross the hard rock of the human heart, and causing living waters to flow forth from *it* (cf. John vii. 38). While this obvious lesson is taught in addition, that in providing and ministering spiritual refreshment to his people,

God can, and will, break through the greatest outward hindrances and impediments (cf. Is. xxxv. 6).

IV. TEMPTING GOD. "They tempted the Lord, saying, Is the Lord among us or not?" (ver. 7). The peculiarity of this sin of Rephidim deserves to be carefully noted. Rephidim, it is true, is not the only instance of it; but it is the outstanding and typical one, and, as such, is frequently alluded to in Scripture (cf. Deut. vi. 16; Ps. xcv. 8, 9; Heb. iii. 8, 9). The allusion in Ps. lxxviii. 18, 19—"They tempted God in their heart by asking meat for their lust. Yea, they spake against God; they said, Can God furnish a table in the wilderness?" is to the incident in Num. xi. Comparing the different scripture references to this sin of "tempting," it will be found that both in the Old and New Testaments, it is invariably connected with the idea of *proposing tests* to God, of putting him in some way *to the proof*, of prescribing to him conditions of action, compliance or non-compliance with which is to settle the question of his continued right to our trust and obedience. It is the spirit which *challenges* God, and is even peremptory in its demand that he shall do as it requires, if, forsooth, he is not to fall in its esteem. It is, as in the gospels (Matt. xvi. 1, etc.), the *sign-seeking* spirit, which, not satisfied with the ordinary evidences, demands exceptional ones, and lays down conditions on which belief in the revealed word is to be made to depend. Cf. Renan's demand for "a commission, composed of physiologists, physicists, chemists, and persons accustomed to historical criticism," to sit in judgment on the miracles ("Life of Jesus," Introduction). It is, in short, the spirit which requires from God *proofs* of his faithfulness and love other than those which he has been pleased to give us, and which even presumes to dictate to him what these proofs shall be. It is, therefore, a spirit which carries distrust on the face of it, and is, besides, daringly presumptuous and irreverent. This furnishes the key to Christ's second temptation in the wilderness. It was a temptation to put his father's care and faithfulness to the test by casting himself down from the pinnacle of the temple (Matt. iv. 5—8). And he repelled it by quoting the passage in Deuteronomy which alludes to this sin of Massah, "Ye shall not tempt the Lord your God" (Deut. vi. 16). It is forgotten by those who are guilty of this sin, that God brings us into situations of trial, not that we may test *him*, but that he may test *us*. Professor Tyndall's proposal of a prayer-test may be cited as a not irrelevant illustration of the type of transgression referred to.—J. O.

Ver. 6.—"*That rock was Christ.*" In the statement of Paul—"They drank of that spiritual Rock that followed them, and that Rock was Christ" (1 Cor. x. 4)—we have a clear assertion of the typical character of this transaction at Rephidim. We may either suppose the term "Rock" in the first clause to be used by metonymy for the water which flowed from the rock, or we may understand the allusion to be to him of whom the rock was but a symbol, and who *did* accompany the Israelites in their wanderings, abundantly supplying their wants. The latter view, which conserves the grain of truth in the Rabbinical traditions above referred to, to which the apostle seems to make allusion, is most in keeping with the further statement, "that Rock was Christ." An interesting comparison is with the words of Christ himself, when, on "the last day, that great day of the feast," he "stood and cried, saying, If any man thirst, let him come unto me and drink" (John vii. 37). The libation of water from the pool of Siloam, which was a ceremony connected with the feast of tabernacles, and which most commentators take to be the subject of Christ's allusion in these memorable words, was commemorative of this miraculous supply of water in the desert. Dr. Godet goes further, and takes this passage in Exodus to be itself the "scripture" (John vii. 38), and the bringing of the water from the rock the event, which Jesus had in view when he gave his invitation. "Why," he says, "should not Jesus, instead of stopping at the emblem, go back to the Divine fact which this rite commemorated. . . . . He had in ch. ii. (of John's Gospel) represented himself as the true temple, in ch. iii. as the true brazen serpent, in ch. vi. as the bread of heaven; in ch. vii. he is the true rock: in ch. viii. he will be the true light-giving cloud, and so on till ch. xix., when he will at length realise the type of the Paschal Lamb" (Godet on John vii. 37). The points to be noted here are these:—

I. HUMAN NATURE IS IN A CONDITION OF THIRST. Its state is figured by that of the Israelites in the desert. It thirsts for a satisfaction which the world cannot give it.

Give man all of the world he asks for, and still his soul is deeply athirst. His increasing cry is, who will show us any good? (Ps. iv. 6). *Learning* does not satisfy this thirst (Ecclesiastes, Goethe's "Faust"). *Pleasures* do not satisfy it (Byron's "Childe Harold"). Colonel Gardiner told Dr. Doddridge how, on one occasion, when his companions were congratulating him on his distinguished felicity, a dog happening to come into the room, he could not help groaning inwardly, and saying to himself, "Oh, that I were that dog." *Riches* do not satisfy it. It is, however, when spiritual awakening comes, and the sinner is brought to realise his true condition as alienated from the life of God, that his thirst enters on the phase which makes satisfaction of it possible. It is now *spiritual* thirst—thirst for pardon, for holiness, for salvation. Note, in passing, how this deep-seated thirst of man testifies to his spiritual dignity. If man is merely a *natural* being—the highest of the animals—why does not nature satisfy him? Why are all things thus full of labour—the eye not satisfied with seeing, nor the ear filled with hearing (Eccles. i. 8)? The mere animal is easily satisfied, and returns into its rest. How different with man! His bodily comforts may be every one attended to; his senses filled with grateful pleasures; his imagination fed with the most gorgeous images of beauty; his intellect stored with the facts and laws of every department of finite science, but all does not slake the thirst of his spirit. His soul still cries, "Give, give; I want not *this*, nor *this*; give me *living water*, of which, if a man drink he will never thirst again."

II. CHRIST IS THE SATISFACTION OF THIS THIRST. He says—"If any man thirst, let him come unto me and drink" (John vii. 37). He understands better than any one else the nature, causes, and intensity of our thirst, yet he promises to gratify it. And who that puts his word to the test is ever sent disappointed away? His salvation is found by every one that tries it, to have really this property of quenching spiritual thirst. He meets the special thirst of the *sinful* soul, by satisfying its desires for pardon and holiness. He meets the more fundamental thirst of our nature—the thirst for blessed *life*—by admitting us to fellowship with himself, the perfect embodiment of truth, purity, and goodness; by giving us a true end in our existence; by furnishing the soul, in the living God (1) with a *spiritual* object, congruous to its own nature; (2) with an *adequate* object, capable of filling and occupying all its powers; (3) with a *living* object, in communion with whom it specially attains to the blessedness of life eternal: finally, by imparting to us, in fullest measure, the influences of the Spirit, source of all light, joy, strength, and powers of holy obedience.

III. CHRIST SATISFIES THIS THIRST IN VIRTUE OF HIS HAVING BEEN SMITTEN. It was only as a rock "smitten" that Jesus could yield waters of salvation to mankind. Atonement must be made for sins. The Christ must be smitten for the transgressions of the world. He came to save. He must appear as the Lamb of God, that taketh away the sin of the world (John i. 29). Jesus was thus smitten in the garden and on Calvary. John notes how from his wounded side there came forth the water and the blood (John xix. 34, 35). "Rock of Ages," etc.

IV. THE WATERS OF CHRIST'S SALVATION ARE FREE AND PLENTIFUL. 1. Free. "Ho, every one that thirsteth" etc. (Is. lv. 1), "Whosoever will" (Rev. xxii. 17). 2. Plentiful. "Preach the Gospel to every creature" (Mark xvi. 15).—J. O.

Vers. 1—7.—*Christ our Spring.* "They drank of that spiritual rock," etc. (1 Cor. x. 4). Introduction may deal with the following important items, as all leading up to the theme of the homily—the journey from Sin to Rephidim (Num. xxxiii. 12—14), the incidents connected with furnishing water out of the rock—the fact that the water may have followed Israel for at least a few stations—and on that fact (not on the Rabbinical legend) found the New Testament application of the Apostle Paul—which justifies us in speaking here of Christ as *The Eternal Spring of Refreshment to all believers*. Expound the connection of 1 Cor. x. 4; thus:—By passing under the cloud and through the sea "our fathers" were baptised unto Moses, committed to him as to a leader, they being his disciples. Thereupon two necessities—bread and water—both in a spiritual sense found in Christ. Even in the desert the water came not so much from the rock, as from the Lord of the rock: *i.e.* Christ.

I. THE SOUL NEEDS REFRESHMENT—*i.e.*, not only food for strength, but spiritual influences for refreshment. Show from Christian experience how many and powerful are the causes of depression, weariness, and fainting.

II. OUT OF THE ROCK—CHRIST—REFRESHMENT SPRINGS. Refreshment does come from time to time to the faint. (See Dr. Raleigh on refreshing influences of "The Dew," in "Quiet Resting Places," p. 34—37.) But the cause is Christ, the living and the ever near. As to the way in which the ministration comes, it does not concern us much to point out; enough to know the fact. Still there are many channels of this grace, e.g., a gleam of morning sunshine, the song of a bird, the pleasant letter of a friend, etc. etc. Channels of the grace, mark! But what is the water itself? See John vii. 37, 38, 39. "This spake he of the Spirit," etc. The water is the consolation of the Spirit; and the rock (from whom proceeds the Spirit) is Christ.

III. THE REFRESHMENT SPRINGS IN UNLIKELY PLACES. As out of the very desolations of Rephidim came the water; so out of our very sorrows come our deepest consolations.

IV. THE ROCK—CHRIST—EVER FOLLOWS US. Here give the fable of the Rabbis; and show that in it there was a deeper truth than the Rabbis knew. Paul saw it. The refreshments of the Spirit are not like angels' visits; for the Dispenser of the grace is never far away.

V. WE ARE REFRESHED THAT WE MAY REFRESH. See John vii. 38. "Out of his belly," etc.—R.

Vers. 1—7. *The giving of water in Rephidim.* I. OBSERVE HOW THE PEOPLE CAME TO REPHIDIM. There is a distinct intimation that it was according to the commandment of Jehovah. He it was who led them where there was no water to drink, and equally he must have given them the intimation to pitch their tents. And we who read the narrative are not at all discomposed on learning that there was no water in this place of encampment. We remember how God has already shown that his ways are not as men's ways, by taking his people where they were entangled in the land, and the wilderness shut them in (ch. xiv. 3). And we are sure that as he then showed what men count folly to be the highest wisdom, so it would prove again. Water is a necessity, and when Jehovah takes his people where there is no water to drink, it must be under the compulsion of a still higher necessity. If water had been one of the chief things to consider, the people would never have gone to Rephidim at all. But at present the great matter for consideration was Sinai, the mountain where the people were to serve God. Everything else was in subordination to the sojourn at Sinai. God could bring Rephidim to Sinai, and he did so when he caused Moses to smite the rock; but it was not possible to bring Sinai to Rephidim.

II. OBSERVE THEIR FIRST REQUEST, AND THE ANSWER OF MOSES. "Give us water that we may drink." The mere words, of course, tell us nothing as to the spirit of the request. In certain circumstances such a request would be innocent and natural enough. Jesus began his conversation with the woman at the well by asking her for a drink of water. The request here, however, was evidently expressed in a complaining, chiding tone; and we can only understand it as we come to study the rejoinder of Moses. That rejoinder shows how he is becoming more and more alarmed at the perils into which the unbelief of the people is taking them. They are still looking towards Moses; they cannot be got to understand that he is as much dependent on the cloudy pillar as are the rest of them. Him who had been given to help and encourage their faith, they treat in such a way that he becomes a stumbling-block. Hence he tries his best to move away their thoughts from himself to Jehovah, with whose long-suffering he warns them that they are making very presumptuous and perilous experiments. They are on dangerous ground, and none the less dangerous because they tread it with such profane unconcern. There had now been several trials of the Divine long-suffering in the short time since they had left Egypt (ch. xiv. 11, xv. 24, xvi. 3, 20, 27); and through all these God had moved gently, providing and protecting, even in the midst of their unbelief. But this gentleness of dealing could not go on for ever; and Moses felt it was quite time to warn them, so that none in Israel might delude themselves with the notion that whatever they said and however they complained Jehovah would not smite them.

III. IN DUE COURSE, THERE IS A SECOND APPEAL TO MOSES. Their first request seems to have come immediately on encamping. They look round with an instinctive feeling for the water supply; and, missing it, they ask for it. Then they wait awhile; and, of course, the longer they wait the more thirst begins to assert itself. Their children cry; and all the cattle signify, in an equally impressive way, their want of water. (Remember what a terrible calamity the want of water is in eastern countries.) No wonder then that increasing thirst drove the Israelites to the bitter complainings of ver. 3. It was not without a profound reason in the plans of God that waterless Rephidim lay so near Sinai. He will make his people to know the *utter privations* that belong to Rephidim as well as the *bitterness* of Marah and the *abundance* of Elim. Thus they passed in a very remarkable way, and in a very short time, through three great representative experiences with regard to the resources of nature. They found those resources existent but impaired at Marah; well-nigh perfect at Elim; and at Rephidim altogether absent. Then, to add further to the significance of Rephidim, God made the people to wait there till their want of water became little short of agony. Not that he delights in inflicting pain; but pain is often needful to teach great lessons. He seems to have made them wait longer at Rephidim where there was no water, than at Marah where the water was only bitter. Hence the exasperation, defiance, almost despair which find utterance in their second cry. For all they can see, they are on the point of death; they, their children and their cattle. And yet this very reference—excusable as it might be in their half-maddened state—suggested at once its own confutation. God had worked by special interventions to bring those very children and cattle out of Egypt intact. Those first-born especially, for whom the lamb had been slain and the blood sprinkled, was it likely they would perish from a thing so entirely within Divine control as lack of water? The truth seems to be that one more great discovery had to be made by Israel before they came to Sinai. They had known Jehovah appearing to them in bondage and more and more manifesting his power; giving them at last an exceeding abundant deliverance from bondage and overwhelming their great enemy in all his strength. These were all completed experiences. There remained one thing more, namely that they should be made to feel their dependence on Jehovah for bread and water. That dependence must be taught in the most practical way, before he proceeded formally to ask as he did at Sinai, for the unreserved regard and obedience of his people.

IV. This occasion evidently became the means of drawing Moses himself nearer to God. We feel that he was coming into peril from the exasperated people. They were, indeed, past all argument and expostulation—suffering themselves, and made more frantic still by the cries of their children and the threatened damage to their property. So here again we see how Moses' own path was the path of faith. Jehovah has ever some fresh revelation of power to deepen the impression already made on the mind of his servant with regard to his omnipotence. Moses must be brought to feel by all sorts of illustrations that God can do everything which is not by its very nature impossible and which does not contradict his own character.

V. Observe the method of supply. 1. *God has the elders called out from among the people.* Thus, for his own purposes, he still further extends the period of waiting. Possibly it was through these very elders, chosen and responsible men among the people, that the complaints and threats had come. The Israelites, even in their unbelief and worldliness, did not degenerate into a rabble. They had *their leaders*, whom they chose, recognised from the human point of view, as well as *that leader whom God* had sent, and whom they so often had despised and rejected. The time had come to make these elders feel their responsibility. Many who made light of Moses looked to them; and according to the way they spoke and acted, they would do much either to produce faith throughout the people, or, on the other hand, to produce unbelief. 2. *God brings the rod once more into requisition,* and as he does, makes a special connection of it with one accomplished work in particular. With that rod Moses had been the means of smiting the river and turning it to blood; the import of the reference evidently being that water everywhere is under the Divine control. By this time there must surely have been great virtue in the sight of the rod to call forth faith and expectation. Hitherto it had been used to destroy—it delivered, indeed, at the same time that it destroyed—but now it is called to a work of unmixed beneficence. All that had been done so far was right and necessary; but it is well that there should now be one work of the rod which, in blessing Israel, does not inflict harm on a single human being. 3. *The source whence the water comes.* From a rock. The smiting, of course, was simply a symbolic action, just as the smiting of the water was. It was not as if some blow had been struck, suddenly opening up a hidden reservoir. What God did here by smiting he commanded, at a later date, to be done by speaking. (Num. xx. 8.) The water came, and was to be understood as coming, from a most unlikely place. Did we know more of the details, more as to the kind of rock that was smitten and the way in which the water gushed forth, we might be even more deeply impressed with the miracle. It may not be going too far to say that no amount of excavating or tunnelling would have got water from that rock. He who turned the water to blood made water to flow from an arid rock in some altogether mysterious way. Doubtless many of the Israelites were beginning to think that it was with a rocky God they had to deal; a hard, unsympathising Deity; that, in short, they had exchanged a human Pharaoh for a Divine one. And so God shows them that even the rock holds unexpected, abundant, and exactly appropriate blessings. The rock at Meribah was a good symbol of Jehovah for the time. He had already presented to the people much that was in aspect stern and unyielding; and he would have to do this still more in the future. And yet in the midst of all necessary hardness, he took care to refresh his people with gracious comforts and promises. He who demands that everything shall be done in righteousness, truth, and profound reverence for his will, is by no means one of those tyrants who seek to reap where they have not sown. Rather does he take his people into circumstances seemingly the most unfavourable, seeking there to teach them how, if they only sow a spirit of faith, obedience, and expectation, they shall reap a sufficient and steady supply for all their daily wants.

VI. OBSERVE THE NAME THAT WAS GIVEN TO THE PLACE. Massah and Meribah. These words did not so much mark the power and providence of God as the unbelieving, self-regarding spirit of the people. This they constantly needed to be reminded of. It might well happen that some of the more sanguine would say, " We shall never be unbelievers again; we shall go with confidence into any place whatever, whither the Lord may lead us." And so these warning names are fixed for them to look back upon. The unbelief of the people was not to be lost in the glory of the Divine action, as if it were a thing of no consequence. We cannot dispense with any recollection of the past, however disagreeable it may be, which keeps before us our own deficiencies, and impresses upon us the need of constant humility.—Y.

Ver. 7.—*They tempted God in the desert. Illustration.* Child cries; parent sends for doctor; pleasant medicine is prescribed. Later the child cries again; cry is apparently addressed to parent, but real aim is to see if the doctor will give more pleasant medicine. Chiding with the parent is a cover for experimenting upon the doctor. Here—previous murmuring against Moses had resulted (xvi. 2—5) in food from God. The people would see whether like conduct might not lead to a like result; they chode with Moses, but, in reality, they were tempting—trying experiments upon—God. Notice:—

I. THE CHIDING (ver. 2). An outward manifestation of displeasure against the visible leader. Why should Moses have brought them, thirsting, to this barren and inhospitable spot? The fact that their journeys were "according to the commandment of Jehovah" (ver. 1) is altogether forgotten or ignored. Not a rare offence: the people, displeased, blame the minister, quite forgetting that he has a master other than themselves. Churches are called Eben-ezers and the like; they might often as truly be called Meribahs. The question which must be put in such cases is one not easy to answer: " Why strive ye with *me* ? " The answer is involved in that other question which few grumblers care to face—" Why do ye tempt Jehovah ? " Chiding can only be passed on with the motive which inspires it to its true object; he who tries to answer it otherwise does but stand in God's light, doing that which Joash declined to do for Baal (Judges vi. 31), and which, with yet more reason, God's servants had best abstain from in his cause.

II. THE TEMPTATION. The inner motive for the outward manifestation was to see whether God was really among them, and would indicate his presence by supporting his servant. He had given quails and bread, would he now shield Moses by supplying the demand for water? Observe—1. *The favourable side of the offence.* The people remembered that God had helped, whence they inferred that he might help again.

Memory fed hope. So far it was well. Memory, however, was but half instructed. The remembered gift was more thought of than the giver. Hope was not faith; it could not prompt the prayer of faith. God was not regarded as he should have been, and consequently men could not state their needs with confidence, "nothing doubting." 2. *The unfavourable side of the offence.* Jehovah, they thought, was the friend, if of any one, of Moses. They regarded him as a being apart, quite as likely to be *their* enemy as the enemy of the Egyptians. Perhaps, however, if they put his friend in difficulties, to help his friend he might appease them. Is not the same thought latent still in like cases? "If the minister is a good man, God will help him, and we shall be the gainers. If not, we shall get quit of him, and possibly his successor may remedy his defects." A kind of witches' ordeal from which the accusers hope to profit any way. Trouble should strengthen trust, and when it does, trust will be rewarded. Beware, however, lest imperfect trust take the form of temptation. God will justify his own elect, but experiments made on him are apt to recoil on the experimenters.

III. THE RESULT (vers. 5, 6). The people spoke *at* God instead of *to* him. Moses, instead of being the channel for their prayers, was the rock whence might echo their complaints. God, in answer, draws himself yet further off from the complainers. They get their water; but they lose that which they might have had as well, the sense of the presence of their God. The experiment was successful, physical thirst was slaked; it was also a disastrous failure: instead of gaining a strong assurance that God was indeed among them, they gained rather a confirmation of their suspicion that he was not among them, but at a distance.

Conclusion.—Beware how you tempt God. Whether is it better to endure discomfort and have a nearer sense of his presence, or to escape discomfort and endure his absence? Thirst endured trustfully must have brought the Israelites such a realisation of the Divine presence as would have quenched, what was worse than thirst, the irrepressible desire to murmur. Temporary satisfaction then, as ever, thus obtained, led on to yet deeper doubt.—G.

Vers. 1—7.—*Trial and failure.* I. THE PURPOSE OF RECURRING TRIALS. Israel, tried before at Marah, is now led from the comforts of Elim to the thirsty land of Rephidim. They might have learned something of their own heart and of God's unfailing goodness, and now they are led hither that he may prove whether they will serve him or no. Trial comes that the teachings of truth may be changed into the convictions of trust.

II. ISRAEL'S CRIME. 1. It was not unbelief, but *impious presumption.* They demand water, believing that it can be produced. They regard themselves as having a right to the choicest of God's blessings. This presumptuous claim lies in the heart of all unbelief. 2. Their accusation of Moses and of God (ver. 3). They have belief but no prayer, no trust, only strife and bitterness. (1) Their base ingratitude. All past mercies are blotted out because of a little present suffering. (2) Their blindness. They might have asked themselves whether there was cause for this rebuke. (3) Their stubbornness. They refused to bow themselves in prayer, or even to ask Moses to intercede for them. (4) Their readiness to entertain the grossest suggestions of doubt.

III. GOD'S LONG-SUFFERING. 1. Their murmuring is met with help. He might have proved himself to be among them by his judgments; but he gives them water from the flinty rock. Not till mercy has done her utmost is judgment let loose against his people. 2. He labours to establish their faith in himself. The elders are taken as witnesses, and the rock is smitten with the rod of God.

(*Second sketch.*) I. A PICTURE OF THE SEEKERS AFTER MORAL IMPROVEMENT WHO DO NOT FOLLOW THE PATHWAY OF FAITH. 1. Their unquenched thirst. 2. Their despair. It had been better for them, they say, that the desire to go forth had never been awakened; that the quest after a better country had never been entered upon. 3. Their cry, "Is the Lord among us or not?" Does God take thought of us? Is there a God? How often has youthful earnestness come to rest at last in the blankest unbelief!

II. A PICTURE OF CHRIST, THE ANSWER TO THE SEEKER'S NEED. 1. The living rock, the changeless one, the sure foundation. 2. How he is made to us the fountain of living waters: he is smitten by the rod of God on behalf of the sinful. 3. The water "followed them." Christ's consolations the one perennial stream for refreshment and strength. 4. How he may be found: by following the guidance of those who testify of him.—U.

EXPOSITION.

Vers. 8—16.—The war with Amalek. The Amalekites seem to have been descendants of Amalek, the grandson of Esau (Gen. xxxvi. 12). They separated themselves off from the other Edomites at an early date, and became the predominant tribe in the more northern parts of the Sinaitic peninsula, claiming and exercising a sovereignty over the whole of the desert country between the borders of Palestine and Egypt. We do not find the name Amalek in the Egyptian records; but the people are probably represented by the Mentu, with whom so many of the early Egyptian kings contended. The Pharaohs dispossessed them of the north-western portion of the mountain region; but they probably claimed the suzerainty of the central hills and valleys, which the Egyptians never occupied; and on these they no doubt set a high value as affording water and pasture for their flocks during the height of summer. When the Israelites pressed forward into these parts, the Amalekites, in spite of the fact that they were a kindred race, determined on giving them battle. They began by "insidiously attacking the rear of the Hebrew army, when it was exhausted and weary"(Deut. xxv. 18). Having cut off many stragglers, they attacked the main body at Rephidim, in the Wady-Feiran, and fought the long battle which the text describes (vers. 10—13). The result was the complete discomfiture of the assailants, who thenceforth avoided all contact with Israel until attacked in their turn at the southern frontier of Canaan, when, in conjunction with the Canaanites, they were victorious (Num. xiv. 45). A bitter and long continued enmity followed. Amalek, "the first of the nations" to attack Israel (ib. xxiv. 20), was pursued with unrelenting hostility (Deut. xxv. 17—19), defeated repeatedly by Saul and David (1 Sam. xiv. 48; xv. 7; xxvii. 8; xxx. 17; 2 Sam. viii. 12); the last remnant of the nation being finally destroyed by the Simeonites in the reign of king Hezekiah, as related by the author of Chronicles (1 Chr. iv. 41—43).

Ver. 8—Then came Amalek. The bulk of the Amalekites would have been passing the spring in the lower plains, where herbage is abundant after the early rains, while later in the year it dries up. They would hear of the threatened occupation of their precious summer pastures by the vast host of the Hebrews, and would seek to prevent it by blocking the way. Hence they are said to have "come"— i.e., to have marched into a position where they were not previously, though it was one situated within their country. We must remember that they were nomads. **And fought with Israel.** For the nature of the fighting on the first day, see Deut. xxv. 18; by which it appears that the original attack was made on the rear of the long column, and was successful. The Amalekites "smote the hindmost" of the Israelites, "even all that were feeble behind them, when they were faint and weary."

Ver. 9.—And Moses said to Joshua. On hearing what had happened, Moses summoned to his presence an Ephraimite in the prime of life—about 45 years old—and devolved on him the military command. The man's name at the time was Hoshea or Oshea (Num. xiii. 8). He was the son of a certain Nun (ibid.) or Non (1 Chr. vii. 27), and the tenth in descent from Ephraim, the son of Joseph (ib. 23—27). Some forty years later Moses changed his name from Hoshea to Jehoshua, which became contracted into Joshua. The occurrence of this form in the present passage may be accounted for. 1. By Moses having written (or reviewed) Exodus late in his life; or 2. By a later authorised reviser (Ezra ?) having altered the text. **Choose out for us men**—i.e. "Select from the congregation such a number of fit men as appear to thee sufficient, and with them fight Amalek." **To-morrow.** It was probably evening, when Moses heard of the attack on his rear, and there was consequently no possibility of retrieving the disaster till the next day. He could but make his arrangements for retrieving it. **I will stand on the top of the hill.** It is implied that there was a conspicuous hill (gibeah), not a rock (tsur) in the near vicinity of Rephidim, whence Moses could see the fight, and be seen by those engaged in it. Dean Stanley finds all the conditions answered by an eminence on the south side of the Wady Feiran (Sinai and Palestine, p. 41). Others suggest the Jebel Tahuneh north of the same wady. **With the rod of God in my hand.** Moses meant to indicate by this, that he looked for victory to God alone, and did not trust in an "arm of flesh," while, nevertheless, he sent his soldiers to the combat.

Ver. 10.—**Hur.** Hur has not been mentioned hitherto. According to one Jewish tradition, he was the son, according to another, the husband of Miriam. Scripture only tells us of him, that he was descended from Judah, through Caleb the son of Hezron (1 Chr. ii. 18—20), and that his grandson, Bezaleel, was the artificer of the tabernacle (Ex. xxxi. 2). He is again associated with Aaron in ch. xxiv. 14.

Ver. 11.—**When Moses held up his hand, . . . Israel prevailed.** The elevation of Moses' hand, with the rod held in it, was an appeal to God for aid, and must be supposed to have been accompanied by fervent prayer to God, that he would help his people and give them victory over their enemies. So long as the hand was upraised, the Israelites prevailed; not because they saw it, and took it as directing them to continue the fight (Kalisch), but because God gave them strength, and vigour and courage, while Moses interceded, and left them to themselves when the intercession ceased. It may be said, that Moses might have continued to pray, though his hands were weary; but only those who have tried, know how difficult a thing it is to pray with any intensity for a continuance. Probably Moses' spiritual and physical powers collapsed together; and when he dropped his hand through physical fatigue, he rested also from his mental effort. To impress upon Israel the importance of intercessory prayer, God made success and failure alternate with its continuance and discontinuance, thus teaching his people a lesson of inestimable value.

Ver. 12.—**But Moses' hands were heavy.** Moses, no doubt, held the rod alternately with one hand and the other, until both were so tired that he could hold them up no longer. It is this natural weariness which is expressed by the words—"his hands were heavy." When Aaron and Hur perceived this, they brought a stone for him to sit on, and then, standing one on either side of him, alternately supported his hands until the sun set and the battle was over. To reward the faith and perseverance of the three, God gave Israel in the end a complete victory.

Ver. 13.—**Amalek and his people**—*i.e.* "the Amalekites proper, and the tribes subject to them, who fought on their side."

Ver. 14.—**Write this . . . in a book.** The original has, "Write this in *the* book." It is clear that a book already existed, in which Moses entered events of interest, and that now he was divinely commanded to record in it the great victory over Amalek, and the threat uttered against them. The record was to be **for a memorial**—1. that the victory itself might be held in remembrance through all future ages, as a very signal instance of God's mercy; and 2, that when the fulfilment of the threat came (1 Chr. iv. 43), God might have his due honour, and his name be glorified. **Rehearse it in the ears of Joshua.** "Hand down," *i.e.*, to thy successor, Joshua, the tradition of perpetual hostility with Amalek, and the memory of the promise now made, that the whole nation shall be utterly blotted out from under heaven. (Compare Deut. xxv. 19.) The special sin of Amalek was, 1. That he attacked God's people, not fearing God (*ib.* verse 18); 2. That he had no compassion on his own kindred : and 3. That he fell on them when they were already suffering affliction, and were "feeble, and faint and weary" (*ib.*)

Ver. 15.—**Moses built an altar.** An altar naturally implies a sacrifice, and Moses may well have thought that the signal victory obtained required to be acknowledged, and as it were requited, by offerings. In giving his altar a name, he followed the example of Jacob, who called an altar which he built, El-Elohe-Israel (Gen. xxxiii. 20). Moses' name for his altar, **Jehovah-nissi,** meant "the Lord is my banner," and was intended to mark his ascription of the entire honour of the victory to Jehovah but had probably no reference to the particular mode in which the victory was gained.

Ver. 16.—**Because the Lord hath sworn.** Rather, as in the margin, "Because the hand of Amalek was against the throne of the Lord"—"because," *i.e.*, "in attacking Israel, Amalek had as it were lifted up his hand against God on his throne," therefore should there be war against Amalek from generation to generation.

HOMILETICS.

Vers. 8—13.—*The uselessness of fighting against God.* Amalek was "the first of the nations" in audacity, in venturesomeness, perhaps in military qualities, but scarcely in prudence or longsightedness. Amalek must precipitate its quarrel with Israel, must "come to Rephidim" and offer battle, instead of letting Israel go· on its own way unmolested, and shunning a contest. They might have known that they were about to fight against God, and that to do so is useless. None can contend with him successfully. It is curious that sinners do not see this. Some of them seem to hope to escape the notice of God; others appear to doubt his power; a few seem to disbelieve in his existence. The uselessness of contending against him would be generally recognised, if men would bear in mind, as most sure—

I. THAT THERE IS A GOD, DESERVING OF THE NAME, THE MAKER AND RULER OF THE UNIVERSE. The disbelief in a Personal God underlies much of the resistance which men offer to his will on earth. They admit an impersonal something external to themselves, which they call "Nature," and speak of as having immutable "laws." These they profess to respect. But the law of righteousness, decreed by a God who is a Person, and written by him in the hearts of his human creatures, is not among these "laws of nature," they think, since in many people it is not found to exist. Neither to this law, nor to the God who made it, do they profess any allegiance. They claim the liberty to do that which is right in their own eyes. But, as surely as they are confounded, if they set themselves in opposition to a law of physical nature—walk on the sea, or handle fire, or seek to fly without wings—so surely does a Nemesis attend their efforts, if they transgress a moral law, be it the law of chastity, or of truth, or of general kindliness, or of special regard for God's day, God's house, God's ministers, God's people. The Amalekites attacked the last, and were overthrown. Final discomfiture will assuredly overtake all who attack anything that is God's or in any way set themselves in opposition to his will.

II. THAT GOD IS REALLY OMNIPOTENT. It often pleases God to allow for a time the contradiction of sinners against himself, and even to let the ungodly enjoy a long term of worldly prosperity. Some of the worst men have prospered during their whole lives, and have died at the height of earthly greatness, self-satisfied, so far as men could see, happy. Men have questioned whether God, if really omnipotent, could have allowed this, and have doubted his ability to carry on a real moral government of the entire universe. But omnipotence is included in the very idea of God; and it is quite inconceivable that any of his creatures should be really able to thwart or resist him further than he himself permits. Their very existence depends on him, and unless he sustained them in being, they would perish at each moment. He temporarily allows the opposition of other wills to his, not through any defect of power, but for his own wise purposes. Some time or other he will vindicate himself, and show forth his Almighty power, to the utter confusion of his enemies.

III. THAT GOD IS ALSO OMNISCIENT. The Psalmist tells us (Ps. lxxiii. 11) of those who said—"Tush, how should God perceive? Is there knowledge in the Most High?" and, again, "God hath forgotten; he hideth away his face, and he will never see it" (Ps. x. 11). These are bold utterances, such as men scarcely make nowadays; but still there are many who in their inmost heart seem to cherish the Epicurean notion, "Deos securum agere ævum," that the Divinity does not care for what men do, or that, at any rate, words or thoughts are beyond his cognisance. He, however, himself declares the contrary. "For every idle word that men shall speak they shall give account." "Thou knowest the very secrets of the heart." "All things are open and revealed unto him with whom we have to do." We cannot resist him secretly or without his knowledge. He knows all our words, and all our thoughts, as well as all our acts, "long before." We cannot take him by surprise and gain an advantage over him. There is not a word in our mouth, or a thought in our heart, but he "knows it altogether"—has always known it, and has provided accordingly. If we were "wise," if we were even moderately prudent, we should give up the idea of resisting God. Instead of "raging" and "imagining vain things"—instead of "taking counsel together against the Lord and against his Anointed"—instead of seeking to "break their bands asunder and cast away their cords from us" (Ps. ii. 1—3), we should submit ourselves—we should be content to "serve the Lord with fear and rejoice unto Him with reverence"—we should "kiss the Son, lest he be angry, and so we perish from the right way, if his wrath be kindled, yea, but a little"—we should "take his yoke upon us, and learn of him"—satisfied that in no other way can we prosper, in no other way can we obtain rest, or peace, or happiness.

Vers. 9—13.—Diversities of gifts, but the same spirit. DIVERSITIES OF GIFTS. The needs of life are various, and the gifts which God imparts to his saints are correspondingly diversified. In Moses, at the age of eighty (ch. vii. 7), the qualities required for the successful conduct of military matters were not present. It may be doubted whether he would at any period of his life have been a good general. But his age, his temperament, and his training made him emphatically a man of prayer. Joshua, on the other hand, in the full vigour of middle life, active, energetic, bold, intrepid, indefatigable, was a born soldier, and a man well suited for military command. To Moses belongs the credit of having recognised the needs of the occasion, and the "diversity of gifts" in himself and his "minister." He took the duties, for which he felt himself fit, upon himself; he delegated those, for which he knew that he was unfit, to the individual who, among the thousands of Israel, appeared to him, and no doubt was, the most perfectly fitted for them. In a minor way, it may be noticed that Aaron and Hur, unsuited for either military command or the leading part in sustained intercessory prayer, had yet gifts which enabled them to play a useful secondary part in support of Moses, and were selected by him for their fitness. The recognition of DIVERSITIES OF GIFTS is required—1. *For the best utilisation of all the powers possessed by God's people at any given time.* Unless diversity be recognised, all aspirants naturally seek the same posts. All are rivals. Jealousies, sure to arise, are intensified. Discontents multiply. Rulers find the difficulty of government augmented. Again, special talents are wasted. The man most suited to one post occupies another. The gifts which he needs he often does not possess; those which he possesses he cannot exercise. 2. *For the satisfaction of individuals.* It is a sore grief to feel unfit for the work which we have to do; but it is a still sorer grief to be conscious of powers which have no field of exercise, while we see others in possession of the field without the powers. Individuals perhaps ought to be content if they can perform satisfactorily the work that is set them. But minds of superior capacity are not, and never will be, thus satisfied. They want a congenial sphere, an occupation which would put their powers to the proof, a task which they would feel that they, and they alone, could perform properly. Hence, it is of great importance, for the contentation of those under their charge, that such as have the rule over men should both recognise the fact of "diversity of gifts," and seek to obtain a full knowledge of the special gifts of those to whose services they have to give employment. 3. *For the general advance of God's kingdom.* It is only by utilising to the utmost all the gifts possessed by members of the Church at any given time, that the Church can be brought into the highest possible state of efficiency. "Diversities of gifts" are a fact (1 Cor. xii. 4). "To one is given the word of wisdom; to another, the word of knowledge; to another, faith; to another, the gifts of healing; to another, the working of miracles; to another, prophecy; to another, discerning of spirits; to another, divers kinds of tongues; to another, the interpretation of tongues" (*ib.* 8—11). Unless this be recognised, unless each gifted one is put to his proper use, there is a waste of power—an absolute loss to the Church—a stoppage of possibilities which might have occurred, had things been better ordered.

The SAME SPIRIT. Different as are the duties of life, various as are the calls made upon the individuals who compose the Christian community—now for courage, now for counsel, now for governmental capacity, now for military skill, anon for earnest and prolonged prayer—there is, after all, but one spirit in which all have to act, as there is also but One Spirit from whom the power to act aright in all cases comes. The merchant in his trade, the soldier on the battle field, the minister in his parish, the man of learning in his study, all may and all ought to act in one and the same spirit, diligently, manfully, earnestly, striving to do their duty, under their various circumstances, in singleness of heart, as unto the Lord and not unto man. The true Christian temper is one and the same, whatever a man's occupation may be; and it is not very difficult to recognise in a Havelock or a Lawrence the identical tone and temper which we have admired in a Channing and a Wesley, a Pascal and a Fénelon. From One Spirit flow all the graces that adorn the Christian character; and the unity of the source is traceable in the graces themselves, which, amid all their diversity, have an element of likeness.

Vers. 14—16.—*God's mercies need memorial, and obtain it in several ways.* Deliverance from Amalek was a great and noticeable mercy. It was. 1. UNDESERVED, as the people had just been murmuring against God, and threatening to stone his prophet (vers. 3—4). 2. TIMELY. Defeat, or even an indecisive success, would have brought upon the Israelites a host of enemies, under whose combined or continuous attacks they must have succumbed. The complete discomfiture of the powerful Amalek struck terror into the hearts of the neighbouring peoples, and induced them to leave Israel for nearly forty years unmolested. 3. WONDERFUL. Amalek was warlike, accustomed to contend with the great nation of the Egyptians; Israel had had all warlike aspirations checked and kept down by above 400 years of servitude and peace. Amalek was no doubt well armed; Israel can have possessed few weapons. Amalek knew the country, could seize the passes, and select a fitting moment for attack; to all Israel, except Moses and Aaron (ch. iv. 27), the country was strange, the passes unknown, and perhaps the very idea of their being attacked unforeseen and unexpected. The attack actually came close upon the great suffering from thirst, when Israel was "feeble" and "faint and weary" (Deut. xxv. 18). So signal a mercy deserved special remembrance. Men soon forget the favours they receive at God's hands. That this favour might not be forgotten, God required two things: 1. *That a record of it should be inserted in his book.* There is no other memorial comparable with this, whether we consider the honour of it, since to obtain record there, an event must be indeed an important one; or the enduringness, since God's book will continue to the world's end; or the celebrity, since it is read by all nations. And God's special command for the insertion, stamps the event with an extra mark of dignity. 2. *That it should be handed on traditionally to Joshua,* and through him to others. Tradition is one of the modes by which God maintains the knowledge of his truth in the world, and is at no time wholly superseded by the written Word, since there are at all times persons in the world too young or too illiterate to have direct access to the Word, who must receive their religious instruction orally from teachers. Tradition alone would be a very unsafe guide; but tradition, checked by a book, is of no little value in enlarging the sphere of religious knowledge, and amplifying and rendering more intelligible the written record. To the two modes of securing continued remembrance of the defeat of Amalek required by God, Moses added a third—the erection of a material monument, to which he gave a commemorative name. Many victories have been thus commemorated, as those of Marathon, Blenheim, Trafalgar, Waterloo, etc.; but no erector of such a memorial has ever given to his work so noble and heart-stirring a name as Moses gave. "The Lord is my banner"—under no other standard will I serve or fight—no other leader will I acknowledge—no other lord shall have dominion over me. "The Lord is my banner"—under this banner I engaged Amalek—he, and he alone, gave me the victory—through him, and him alone, do I look to discomfit my other enemies. Be the enemies material or spiritual, external or internal, to him only do I trust to sustain me against them. None other name is there under heaven, through whom salvation is to be obtained, the adversary baffled, Amalek put to confusion.

HOMILIES BY VARIOUS AUTHORS.

Vers. 8—16. *Christ our Banner.*—"Jehovah-Nissi." Ex. xvii. 15. Historical introduction: The Amalekites—their territory—reasons why they barred Israel's way. 1. Fear. 2. Religious animosity—incidents of the engagement—the two memorials, book and altar—judgment pronounced on Amalek, and why—the slow execution through the centuries, ending in the final blotting out of the nation. "The counsel of the Lord standeth for ever, the thoughts of his heart to all generations." Show further that the rod of Moses was in reality the *banner* of Israel; the pole of a banner without drapery, affording a rallying-point for Israel's armies, a memorial of past achievement, a force therefore, a guide, an appeal to heaven, an earnest of victory. By that banner Israel conquered. But again, as with the water and the rock we ascended to the First Cause of all refreshments, so here we ascend beyond the rod-banner to the Real Cause and Giver of all victory, *i.e.,* to Jehovah, *i.e.,* to Christ.

I. ALL IN THE WILDERNESS MUST FIGHT.—In the moral wilderness there are only two great hosts (on this division into two only, see most valuable and suggestive paper in Dr. James Martineau's "Hours of Thought" on "The Soul's Forecast of Retribution.") Amalek and Israel, pilgrims going to the heavenly country, and children of the desert that withstand their way. 1. Amalek *cannot* let Israel alone—if of the world we must fight—for there seems a certain constraint that will not permit us to leave the truth,

Christ and God, without antagonism. 2. Israel *will* fight—dutifully—and inspired thereto.

II. PILGRIM WARRIORS MAY BE TAKEN AT A DISADVANTAGE. See Deut. xxv. 18. The attack of Amalek was—1. *Sudden.* 2. On an *undefended rear.* 3. On *the faint.* 4. On *the demoralised by sin.* Trace the analogies in moral conflict.

III. OUR BANNER COMPENSATES FOR ALL DISADVANTAGE. Jehovah-Nissi—Christ our banner. See Is. xi. 10—12; ·Rom. viii. 37; Rev. xii. 11; Constantine's "In hoc signo." The banner Christ:—1. *Rallies to decision.* Christ lifted up in the realms of thought, domestic life, business, social life, political life, men must take sides; must answer the question, What think ye of Christ? A Christ-side to every moral question. Reason why Christian men not always on the same side in reference to particular questions (*e.g.*, abstinence) may be, because in actual conflict issues get confused. But wilful trimming not permissible. Nothing like the conduct of the Frenchman, who at the outbreak of the revolution wore both cockade and tricolour, one under one coat lappel, the other under the other. Rather should we be like Hedley Vicars, who, the morning after the great decision for God, unfurled his banner by laying an open Bible on his table for all his comrades to see. 2. *Is a memorial of victories achieved.* It was so with the rod of Moses (go over instances). So is it with regimental ensigns, inscribed oft with glorious names, *e.g.* Salamanca, Vittoria, etc. Picture the shot-rent, tattered banners, hung under vaulted roof, for a memorial. So Christ—he shines before us in the light of ten thousand victories—on "his head many crowns." Recall the history of the Church, public and more private, its confessors and martyrs. 3. *Is a force therefore* (ver. 11). The moral power for a regiment in the possession of its colours; its demoralisation when lost. Christ seen in the host. Illustration: Castor and Pollux at the battle of Lake Regillus. 4. *Is direction in the fray.* No man *in* a battle can see it, understand it. Leadership necessary by trumpet, by signal, by aide-de-camp, by banner. So was it here. Moses directed the battle by the standard in his hand. So Christ to every soldier-saint. We may not fight for our own hand, nor according to our own whims; but take direction from him. 5. *Is appeal for heavenly help.* That banner-pole of Moses was not only for encouragement and lead to Israel, but also was an appeal to God for that aid which ensures victory. So, wherever Christ is, the intercessor is. 6. *Is earnest of victory.* Christ is a force that cannot fail (Rom. viii. 37).—R.

Vers. 8—16.—*Amalek.* Various circumstances are to be noted in connection with this attack of Amalek on Israel. 1. It was *unprovoked.* "Then *came* Amalek" (ver. 8). 2. It was *unfriendly.* The Amalekites were descended from a grandson of Esau, and so were related to the Israelites (Gen. xxxvi. 12). 3. It was *bitterly hostile.* This fierce and warlike tribe attacked Israel in the rear, and with great cruelty smote those who had fallen behind, whether from natural infirmity or from weariness and faintness in the march (Deut. xxv. 18). This was a peculiarly malignant and vindictive act, and as perpetrated upon the people with whose well-being God had specially identified himself, was never to be forgotten. It was in truth one of those wrongs which burn themselves into the memory of a nation, and never *can* be forgotten. A special Nemesis waits on acts of flagrant inhumanity. 4. *It was not without knowledge of the mighty works which God had wrought for Israel.* We may be certain of that from what was said in ch. xv. of the effects produced on the surrounding peoples by the deliverance of the Red Sea. The Amalekites knew that the children of Israel were the people of Jehovah. They knew what great things Jehovah had done for his nation. They probably shared in the fear which these wonders of Jehovah had inspired. Their hostility to Israel, indeed, may partly have sprung from this cause. The opportunity seemed given them of making a successful raid upon a people whom they both dreaded and despised, and they hastened to avail themselves of it. Knowing that the Israelites were inexperienced in war, and being themselves numerous and powerful, they may have counted on an easy victory, especially as the people were fatigued with marching and encumbered with baggage, with women and children, and with the aged and infirm. It was a time well chosen for delivering an attack, and for inflicting a mortal injury on the advancing host. 5. It was *the first attack of its kind.* And this circumstance gives it a very special significance. It makes it typical. In the issue of the conflict with Amalek is to be seen the result of the whole conflict, prolonged down the ages, between the friends and the enemies of God, between the Church of living believers and the world that hates and seeks to destroy it, waging against it an incessant warfare. Consider—

I. THE BATTLE. 1. How *fought*. Observe (1) Fighting was in this case called for. It was not a case, like that at the Red Sea, where the Israelites could do nothing to help themselves. The command, accordingly, is not, "Stand still, and see the salvation of the Lord" (ch. xiv. 13), but, "Go out, *fight* with Amalek" (ver. 9). When means of help are put within our reach, God expects us to use them. He would have us exercise our own powers, still, however, in the spirit of due dependence upon him. "Work out your own salvation with fear and trembling, for it is God which worketh in you," etc. (Phil. ii. 12, 13). (2) The conflict was entered upon with a full appreciation of the gravity of the crisis. The leaders did not commit the error of despising their enemy. They knew how ill-prepared they were for entering upon a contest of the kind. There was no disguising the fact that the men of Israel were raw, undisciplined, wanting in courage, and prone to panic, while those of Amalek were men of the desert, bold, warlike, fierce, able to hold their own with the stoutest foe. This was the first battle of the former; it was but an episode in the life of continual warfare of the latter. Judged by appearances, the chances of war were, therefore, greatly against the Israelites, and it was felt that the most strenuous efforts, aided by earnest intercessions, would be needed to gain a victory. The Church, in like manner, will do well not to take too poor an estimate of her spiritual enemies. They are not to be made light of. They are not to be fought with sham weapons, or in the indolent, half-in-earnest spirit, with which so many are content to attempt the conquest. "We wrestle not against flesh and blood," etc. (Eph. vi. 12). The Church need not count on *cheap* victories. (3) The dispositions for the fight were made with skill and judgment. The men sent into the battle were *picked* men, and over them was appointed a brave general —Joshua (ver. 9). This is the first appearance of Joshua in the history, but he must have been already known to Israel as a man possessed of the strategical and other qualifications needful in a military commander. Another lesson as to the use of means, and as to the adaptation of means to ends in God's service. The battle was God's, but it was to be fought through human instrumentalities. The strongest, bravest, most valorous men in the camp were, accordingly, selected for the service. No measure was omitted which was likely to ensure success. It is the old law of the economy of miracles. What man can do for himself, God will not work miracles to do for him. Doubtless, but for Moses' intercession on the hill, the battle would still have been lost; on the other hand, had the military arrangements been less perfect, even Moses' prayers might not have turned the tide of conflict so decisively in favour of the Israelites. Cf. Cromwell's advice to his men—"Trust in Providence, and *keep your powder dry*." Note, further, how the same God who gave the Israelites a Moses, gave them also a Joshua, when a man of Joshua's gifts was specially required. Cf. with the promise as to Christ, Is. lv. 4. It is for our own benefit that God thus summons our gifts into exercise, and furnishes occasions for their trial and development. 2. How *won*. First, as seen above, by dint of hard fighting, but second, and more specially, by Moses' intercessions. This portion of the narrative (vers. 10—12) is full of richest instruction. Observe—(1) Moses took with him Aaron and Hur, and ascended to the hill summit, to watch the battle, and to pray (ver. 10). Advanced in years, he could not personally take part in the *mêlée*; but he could pray for those who *were* in it. His prayer was as essential to success as their fighting. It was fighting of its own kind (cf. Col. iv. 12). Real prayer is hard, exhausting *work*. Even had Moses been physically capable of taking part in the conflict, he was better employed where he was, in this work of earnest intercession. Gifts differ. Joshua's right place was on the field; that of Moses, on the hill. Many can pray who are debarred from fighting, *e.g.*, invalids—Moses sitting on the stone (ver. 12), they, perhaps, lying on their couches—and it is well for them to realise the value of their work, how *much* they can still do, how *useful* they are. Note, also, it was *in view of* the battle that this intercession of Moses was carried on. Prayer needs to be fed by knowledge, by watchful interest in events as they shape themselves around us, by study of the special needs of circumstances of the time. Of what essential service would it be in the warfare of the Church were praying men and women to act more on this principle—seeking, as far as possible, to keep themselves informed of the progress and vicissitudes of the Lord's work at home and abroad, and endeavouring to order their prayers with constant reference to the fluctuations in the battle! Moses praying on the hill may remind us of Christ in heaven, interceding for his Church militant on earth. (2) Moses interceded, while holding up in his hands the rod of God (vers. 9, 11). The rod was the symbol of God's power as pledged for the defence of Israel. Faith holds up the rod in laying hold on God's word and promise, and pleading the same before him. (3) Moses had able coadjutors. Aaron and Hur stayed up his hands when they grew heavy through fatigue (ver. 12). It is a happy circumstance when those who bear the principal burden of responsibility in spiritual work can rely on being aided by the sympathy and co-operation of others, "like-minded" (Phil. ii. 20), with themselves in their desire to see God's kingdom making progress. God's people hold up the hands of ministers by praying for them (1 Thess. v. 25). (4) The intercession of Moses had a decisive influence upon the tide of battle. When Moses held up his hands, Israel prevailed; when he let down his hands, Amalek prevailed (ver. 11). His hands being steadily supported till the going down of the sun, Amalek was completely discomfited (ver. 13). The letting down of Moses' hands may have been accompanied by a corresponding flagging in the earnestness of his supplications; or it may have been that the outward act, as indicative of the need of sustained and persevering entreaty of God, was itself made essential to the victory. In either case, we have a testimony to the power of prayer. Would that the Church were more alive to this secret of gaining victories by earnest supplication! The influence of prayer cannot be overrated. It decides battles. It sways the tides of history. It opens and shuts the windows of heaven (Jas. v. 17, 18). It puts to the rout spiritual enemies. Paul made use of this mighty power (Rom. i. 9, 10; Phil. i. 4, 9, etc.). But even Paul did not pray so much as Christ (Matt. xiv. 23; Mark i. 35; Luke vi. 12, etc.). 3. *Connection with previous miracle.* Is it fanciful to trace in the boldness, valour, and spiritual confidence of the Israelites in this battle, some relation to the wonderful deliverance they have just experienced? It was "at Rephidim," the scene of the miraculous supply of water, that the attack of Amalek took place (ver. 8). This water, in the first place, refreshed the Israelites *physically,* and so enabled them to fight; but we may believe that it had also a powerful, if temporary, effect upon their minds. It would banish doubt, restore trust, inspire enthusiasm. They drank of the brook by the way, and now lifted up the head (Ps. cx. 7). Thus does God time *his* mercies to *our* trials, and make the one a preparation for the other.

II. THE RECORD IN THE BOOK (ver. 14). This command to insert in "the book" an account of the battle with Amalek was connected: 1. With *God's design to give his Church a Bible.* A "book" is presupposed, in which, apparently, a journal was kept of the transactions of the march. Such a contemporary record was plainly necessary, if exact accounts of these mighty acts of God in the desert were to be preserved. In no other way could the knowledge of them have been handed down to posterity without distortion, mutilation and adulteration. And God was not giving these mighty revelations of himself, to waste them on the air of the wilderness, or to leave them to the risk of being mixed up with legendary matter of man's adding. This part of Israel's history was being shaped and guided with a view to the instruction of the Church to the end of time (1 Cor. x. 6, 11); and it was requisite that a proper account should be kept of its memorable events. Hence the existence of "the book," out of the contents of which, we may believe, these narratives in the book of Exodus are principally compiled. 2. With a *special significance attaching to this particular event.* Amalek's attack on Israel was, as already observed, the first of its kind. "In Amalek the heathen world commenced that conflict with the people of God, which, while it aims at their destruction, can only be terminated by the complete annihilation of the ungodly powers of the world" (Keil). This explains the severe sentence pronounced upon the tribe, as also the weighty significance attached to this first defeat. It takes many types to set forth completely the many-sided enmity of the world to God and to his Church. Pharaoh was one type, Amalek is another. Pharaoh was more especially the type of the enmity of the world against the church, viewed as having escaped from its power. Amalek, as Edom afterwards, is peculiarly the type of vindictive hostility to the kingdom of God as such—of implacable *hate.* Between Amalek (spiritually) and the church, therefore, there can never be aught but warfare. "Because his hand is against the throne of the Lord" (marg.), *therefore* "the Lord will

have war with Amalek from generation to generation" (ver. 16).   In this first defeat
we have the type of all.

III. JEHOVAH-NISSI.   Moses reared an altar in commemoration of the victory, and
inscribed upon it the name—"Jehovah-Nissi"—"Jehovah, my banner" (ver. 15).
This name inscribed upon the altar is at the same time a name of God.   It extracts
and generalises the principle involved in the victory over Amalek, as a former name,
"Jehovah-jireh" (Gen. xxii. 14) extracted and generalised the principle involved in
the interposition on Moriah; and as the words, "I am Jehovah that healeth them"
(ch. xv. 26), extracted and generalised the principle involved in the miracle at Marah.
The truth taught by the name is precious and consolatory.   Jehovah is the Church's
banner.   His invisible presence goes with her in her conflicts.   His help is certain.
With him on her side, she is assured of victory.   His name is her sure and all-sufficient
trust.   Learn 1. God's deeds reveal His name.   The revelation of the Bible is a fact-
revelation. 2. It is the Church's duty gratefully to remember the interpositions of God
on her behalf.   3. It is her duty to seek to apprehend the *principle* of God's dealings
with her, and to treasure up the knowledge for further use.—J. O.

Vers. 15, 16.—*Jehovah-Nissi.*   The use of this name by the Church bespeaks—1. Her
militant condition.   "The Lord will have war with Amalek from generation to generation." 2. The side on which she fights—"*My* banner." 3. The name round which she
rallies—"Jehovah." "One Lord, one faith, one baptism" (Eph. vi. 5). 4. The confidence by which she is inspired.   The inscription on a banner frequently sets forth the
ground of confidence. "God and my right." 5. The certainty she has of victory.—J.O.

Ver. 9.—*"Thou hast given a banner unto them that fear thee.* 1. THE ATTACK BY
AMALEK.   It was cowardly, malicious, merciless (cf. Deut. xxv. 17; 1 Sam. xv. 2);
not open, straightforward enmity; cutting off the feeble and the stragglers; a vulture-
like hostility; a type and sample of *diabolical* hatred.   Notice the parallel between
Israel's position with regard to Amalek and our position with regard to Satan and his
emissaries. 1. Israel was passing through the wilderness.   So God's people are passing
through this world (Heb. xi. 14).   The country through which the route lies is not
claimed by those who use it. 2. Amalek considered the wilderness as their own.   So
Satan claims to be the prince of this world.   In either case the authority is usurped.
3. Amalek took Israel at a disadvantage.   No cause of enmity assigned, only apparently
the right assumed for the stronger to prey upon the weaker.   Satan, too, always
endeavours to take us at a disadvantage.   He did not attack Christ until "he was
an hungered;" he attacks us, also, when we are weakest.

II. THE DEFENCE AND CONFLICT.—1. *A chosen captain.*   Joshua—"Jehovah is
help." Perhaps name changed from Hoshea at this time; shows, at any rate, whence
the leader derived his ability to lead.   Our captain, "manifested to destroy the works
of the devil." Had it not been for Satan's enmity, how should we have known the power
of Christ? 2. *Selected soldiers.* Not all the people, but chosen from the people.   All
share the danger, but the defence may best be undertaken by a few, though, no doubt,
these few are supported and encouraged by the general sympathy.   In the war with
Satan the brunt of the battle must fall on the selected soldiers—Christ chose apostles,
and in every age the majority has been protected by representative champions.   Satan
must make more headway than he does, were it not that the weaker and more ignorant
are sheltered from direct attack behind the bulwarks raised by the stronger and the
wiser. 3. *An uplifted banner.*   Usually the colours go before the army; here the
banner—God's rod—is upheld upon the mountain—(1) in full sight of all; (2) in a
position of comparative security.   Notice—1. This banner was a sign of God's helpful
presence. 2. It was in full view of the fighters, and the fortune of the battle varied
according as it was raised or lowered.   Two things were necessary to ensure victory—
(1) that the banner should be held up; (2) that the fighters should keep looking at it.
In the fight with Satan the same principle applies.   God's law, God's righteous purpose,
must be upheld by the Prophet, supported on one hand by the priest, on the other by
the noble; but, further, the fighters must keep it well in view, nothing less than the
assurance of its fixedness can nerve them so as to ensure victory.

III. THE MEMORIAL. 1. A book.   This victory a pledge of Amalek's final extermination. 2. An altar. "Jehovah our Banner," sign of a continuous war to be ended only with the fulfilment of God's purpose. In the fight with Satan our Lord's victory in the wilderness and on the cross, a pledge of final victory for all. 1. It is written in a book. Who has not read of it? 2. It is commemorated by a memorial, which all may see. "This do as a memorial of me." So long as there is evil in the world, so long there must be war. God's soldiers must fight from generation to generation until the final victory be achieved. What is the secret of their strength? The banner uplifted upon the mountain. The rod of God. "It is written." The prophet uprears it. Priest and noble, in so far as they fulfil their office, unite to support the prophet. The fighters look up to the banner, and, encouraged by its steadfast maintenance, fight on till victory be secured.—G.

Vers. 8—16.—*The discomfiture of Amalek in Rephidim.* I. AMALEK'S IGNORANCE OF THE RESOURCES OF ISRAEL. Amalek attacked Israel in *Rephidim.* Rephidim stands very well as the type of all places and positions where human resources appear utterly wanting. It was a place where no water could be found, and where of course there must also have been little growth. Everything therefore would lead Amalek to say, "We shall easily conquer these people, being but an undisciplined, unmanageable crowd." How should outsiders understand anything of the way in which the Lord had led Israel? To Israel itself, the way had been one which it knew not; and to Amalek, able to judge only by first appearances it would seem the way of folly, rashness, and certain ruin. The Amalekites could very well see that there was no ordinary source of supplies open, and extraordinary sources were beyond their ken, beyond their powers of imagination. We shall do well to consider, before we oppose anything, what its resources are; apparent weakness may not only hide real strength, but may be almost the condition of it. We shall do well also to consider whether under erroneous notions of self-preservation, we may not often be found fighting against God. These Amalekites went out to war against Israel upon motives of self-interest. It seemed to them if they did not destroy Israel, Israel would destroy them. Yet if they had only inquired, if they had only asked the question how this great company had managed to get so far, they might have been spared all anxiety and the great destruction which came upon them. The wisest plan would have been to leave Israel alone and wait; then it would have been seen that Israel was not going to stop in that district.

II. THE WAY IN WHICH ISRAEL MEETS AMALEK.—1. *The spirit and conduct of Moses are to be considered.* Hitherto in his difficulties he has cried to the Lord, not of course despairingly, but feeling deeply his need of Divine direction. Here however he is ready for action at once. No mention is made of recourse to God, from which we assume that the line of action was at once apparent to Moses. The promptitude of his action is indeed remarkable; and yet it is clear from the result that there was nothing presumptuous in it. Everything evidently accorded with the will and purpose of God. This was an occasion when Israel could do something, and they were bound to make the attempt. Moses was a man who appreciated the principle that God helps those who help themselves. When the people were entangled in the land by the Red Sea they could do nothing; when they came into the wilderness with its scarcity of food and drink, they could do nothing; they had simply to wait on God's provisions. But here where fighting men appear against them, and there is space and time for resistance, Moses rightly takes means to bring the strength of his people into operation. 2. *The spirit and conduct of the people are also to be considered.* Their faith, promptitude and composure are also very remarkable, more remarkable even than the like conduct on the part of Moses. Those who had been so long, and only so lately, unbelieving and unmanageable, all at once manifest a surprising readiness to meet the foe. Considering the way in which they had recently behaved, it is a marvellous thing that all was not thrown into panic and confusion, immediately on the appearance of Amalek. To what then can this composure and readiness be attributed? Evidently it was the effect—a temporary effect certainly, yet not insufficient for its purpose—of the gift of the manna and of the water in a dry and thirsty land. God took care that all troubles should not come on them at once. They were strong with a strength Amalek knew nothing of; and it was in *the fresh consciousness* of that strength that they made ready for the battle. We imagine that on this occasion, Joshua found abundance of volunteers, and that those who went out against Amalek were the very pick and pride of Israel's warriors.

III. THE WAY IN WHICH GOD SIGNIFIES HIMSELF TO BE THE CONTROLLER OF VICTORY. Moses knows right well that after all preparations, the victory must come from Jehovah. He sets the discriminating Joshua to lead a chosen and competent army against Amalek, as if everything depended upon them, and yet at the same time he remembers that God must be glorified in the very best of human preparations. God will have us to honour him by our very best, and yet our very best must be considered as no more than the humble channel of his power. We must not suppose, because it pleases God in his wisdom, to put the excellency of his treasure into earthen vessels, that we are at liberty to offer him anything which first comes to hand. And then Moses, having done his best in the choice of means, takes his conspicuous position on the hill, to cheer his fighting friends with the sight of the lifted rod. Through the lifting of that rod the energies of victory were to flow into the bodies of Israel's warriors. To Amalek the sight of Moses told nothing. They knew nothing of the significance of the rod, and may rather have wondered why he should stand so long in this position of constraint. But Israel, we cannot doubt, quickly discerned the significance of their leader's attitude and the close connection between the lifted hand and the progress towards victory. The lesson for us is the oft taught one, that while God would have us to labour strenuously and bear the heat and burden of the day in all the inevitable conflicts of life, we must do it with the remembrance that victory really comes from him. We are only strong, as Paul felt he was, by the strength which Christ puts into us.—Y.

Vers. 8—16.—*Victory through faith.*—I. IN THE WARFARE OF FAITH, PRAYER AND EFFORT MUST BE JOINED TOGETHER. 1. Arrangements are carefully made for both. (1) Men are picked out for a battle, and Joshua descends with them into the valley. (2) Moses, with Aaron and Hur, climbs to the hill-top with the rod of God in his hand. 2. Joshua discomfited Amalek with the edge of the sword; but the battle was for or against Israel, as Moses' hands were lifted up in strong supplication or hung down in weariness. (1) To pray without using means is to mock God. (2) To use means without prayer is to depise God. II. AIDS TO PREVAILING PRAYER. 1. The remembrance of past deliverances and services. Moses takes the rod of God in his hand. 2. The union of many hearts: he sat on the hill-top in sight of Israel. 3. Friendly help in weakness. Aaron and Hur hold up the wearied hands. III. IN THE VICTORY OF THE RIGHTEOUS, A YET FURTHER TRIUMPH IS PROMISED. The promise is recorded in the book that that against which they war shall be swept from under heaven. IV. THE GRATITUDE OF THE REDEEMED IN THE HOUR OF TRIUMPH. The monument of victory is an altar and its name Jehovah-Nissi.—U.

SECTION XII.—CHAPTER XVIII.

JETHRO'S VISIT TO MOSES.

EXPOSITION.

CHAPTER XVIII.

Ver. 1—12.—JETHRO'S VISIT TO MOSES. It has been noticed, in the comment on ch. iv., that shortly after the circumcision of Eliezer, Moses' second son, he sent back his wife, Zipporah, to her own kinsfolk, the Midianites, together with her two sons, Eliezer and Gershom. Reuel, Zipporah's father, was then dead (ch. iii. 1), and had been succeeded in his priesthood and headship of the tribe by Jethro, probably his son, and therefore the brother-in-law, and not the father-in-law, of

Moses. (The Hebrew word used, as already observed, has both meanings.) Jethro gave protection to his sister and her children until he heard of the passage of the Red Sea, when he set forth to meet and congratulate his kinsman, and to convey back to him his wife and his sons. The meeting took place "at the mount of God" (verse 5), or in the near vicinity of Sinai, probably in some part of the plain Er-Rahah, which extends for five miles, or more, to the north-west of the Sinaitic mountain-group

Ver. 1.—**Jethro, the priest of Midian, Moses' father-in-law.** Rather, " Jethro, priest of Midian, Moses' brother-in-law." See the comment on ch. iii. 1 ; and note that the Seventy use the ambiguous word γαμβρός, while the Vulgate has *cognatus.* **And that.** Rather " *in* that." The clause is exegetical of the preceding one.

Ver. 2.—**After he had sent her back.** Literally " after her dismissal." It is curious that the fact of the dismissal had not been previously mentioned, yet is here assumed as known. Some commentators (as Knobel) find, in what is said of Zipporah, the trace of two distinct writers who give two contradictory narratives ; but the difficulties and obscurities of the history are sufficiently intelligible, if we bear in mind—1. That Moses was addressing immediately those who knew the facts ; and 2. That he was studious of brevity.

Ver. 3.—**And her two sons.** That Zipporah had borne Moses at least two sons before his return to Egypt from Midian, had appeared from ch. iv. 20. **The name of the one, Gershom,** and the ground of it, had been declared in ch. ii. 22. The repetition here may be accounted for by the present chapter having been originally a distinct and separate composition, written on a distinct roll, and subsequently incorporated by Moses into his great work.

Ver. 4.—**Eliezer.** Eliezer had not been previously mentioned by name ; but he was probably the son circumcised by Zipporah, as related in ch. iv. 25. We learn from 1 Chr. xxiii. 15—17, that he grew to manhood, and had an only son, Rehabiah, whose descendants were in the time of Solomon very numerous. **For the God of my father, said he, was my help.** Eliezer means literally, " My God (is my) help." It would seem that Zipporah, when she circumcised her infant son, omitted to name him ; but Moses, before dismissing her, supplied the omission, calling him Eliezer, because God had been his help against the Pharaoh who had sought his life (ch. ii. 15), and of whose death he had recently had intelligence (ch. iv. 19). Thus the names of the two sons expressed respectively, the despondency natural to an exile, and the exultant gratitude of one who had just learned that by God's goodness, the term of his banishment was over.

Ver. 5. — **The wilderness.** This term, which has the article, seems to be here used in that wide sense with which we are familiar from ch. iii. 18 ; iv. 27 ; v. 3 ; vii. 16 ; etc. It is not " the wilderness of Sin," or " the wilderness of Sinai," that is intended, but generally the tract between Egypt and Palestine. Jethro, having entered this tract from Midian, had no difficulty in discovering from the inhabitants that Moses was **encamped at the mount of God,**—*i.e.,* Sinai, and there sought

and found him. There is no trace of any previous " engagement " to meet at a particular spot.

Ver. 6.—**And he said.** It is suspected that the true reading here is, " and *they* said,"—*i.e.,* some one said—" to Moses, behold thy father-in-law " (or " brother-in-law "), " Jethro, is come unto thee." So the LXX., and many moderns, as Kennicott, Geddes, Boothroyd, Canon Cook, and others. But the explanation, that Jethro, on arriving in the vicinity of Moses, sent a messenger to him, who spoke in his name (Rosenmüller, Patrick, Pool, Kalisch, Keil, etc.) is at any rate plausible, and removes all necessity of altering the text.

Ver. 7.—**Moses went out to meet his father-in-law.** Oriental ideas of politeness require such a movement in case of an honoured or even of a welcome visitor (see Gen. xviii. 2 ; xix. 1 ; xxxii. 6 ; xxxiii. 1 ; Luke xv. 20 ; etc.). It was evidently the intention of Moses to receive Jethro with all possible marks of honour and respect. He not only went out to meet him, but **did obeisance** to him, as to a superior. **They asked each other of their welfare.** Rather " exchanged salutations ; " addressed each other mutually with the customary phrase " Peace be unto you." **Came into the tent**—*i.e.,* went together into the tent of Moses, which had been already glanced at in the word " encamped " (verse 5).

Ver. 8.—**Moses told his father-in-law.** Jethro had heard in Midian the general outline of what had happened (verse 1). Moses now gave him a full and complete narrative (*misphar*) of the transactions. Compare Gen. xxiv. 66 ; Josh. ii. 23 ; where the same verb is used. **All the travail.** Literally, " the weariness." Compare Malachi i. 13, where the same word is used. **The Lord delivered them.** The Septuagint adds " from the hand of Pharaoh and from the hand of the Egyptians."

Ver. 10.—**Blessed be the Lord.** Compare Gen. xiv. 20 ; xxiv. 27. The heathen blessed *God* no less than the Israelites ; but Jethro's blessing *the Lord* (*i.e.* Jehovah) is unusual As, however, Moses had attributed his own deliverance, and that of Israel, entirely to Jehovah (verse 8), Jethro, accepting the facts to be as stated, blessed *the Lord.* **Who hath delivered you.** Kalisch takes the plural pronoun to refer to Moses *and Aaron* ; but Aaron seems not to have been present, since he afterwards " came " (**verse 12**). It is better to regard Jethro as addressing all those who were in the tent with Moses. From them he goes on in the last clause to " the people." **And out of the hand of Pharaoh.**—*i.e., especially* out of the hand of Pharaoh, who had especially sought their destruction (ch. xiv. 6, 8, etc.).

Ver. 11.—**Now know I that the Lord is**

greater than all gods. It would seem that Jethro, like the generality of the heathen, believed in a plurality of gods, and had hitherto regarded the God of the Israelites as merely one among many equals. *Now,* he renounces this creed, and emphatically declares his belief that Jehovah is above all other gods, greater, higher, more powerful. Compare the confessions of Nebuchadnezzar (Dan. ii. 47; iii, 26, 27) and Darius the Mede (*ib.* vi. 26). **For in the thing wherein they dealt wickedly he was above them.** There is no "he was above them" in the original, nor is the clause a distinct sentence from the preceding one. It is merely a prolongation of that clause, without any new verb; and should be translated, "Even in the very matter that they (the Egyptians) dealt proudly against them" (the Israelites). The superiority of Jehovah to other gods was shown forth even in the very matter of the proud dealing of the Egyptians, which was brought to shame and triumphed over by the might of Jehovah. The allusion is especially to the passage of the Red Sea.

Ver. 12.—**Jethro took a burnt offering.** Or "*brought* a burnt offering;" as the same verb is rendered in ch. xxv. 2. It is not distinctly related that he offered the victim; but as no other offerer is mentioned, and as he was a priest (ch. iii. 1; xviii. 1), we may assume that he did so. Moses, Aaron, and the elders, partook of the sacrificial meal, regarding the whole rite as one legitimately performed by a duly qualified person, and so as one in which they could properly participate. Jethro, like Melchisedek (Gen. xiv. 18), was recognised as a priest of the true God, though it would seem that the Midianites generally were, a generation later, idolaters (Num. xxv. 18; xxxi. 16). **To eat bread . . . before God.** This expression designates the feast upon a sacrifice, which was the universal custom of ancient nations, whether Egyptians, Assyrians, Phenicians, Persians, Greeks, or Romans. Except in the case of the "whole burnt offering" (ὁλοκαύτωμα), parts only of the animals were burnt, the greater portion of the meat being consumed, with bread, at a meal, by the offerer and his friends and relatives

HOMILETICS.

Vers. 1—12.—*The blessedness of family reunions, when rightly ordered.* The family is God's ordinance, and among the most sacred and blessed of his ordinances. All fatherhood is based upon his (Eph. iii. 15); and human family ties reproduce those of the celestial region. Upon earth partings must and will occur, the family bond being thereby not broken, but strained and impaired. Sometimes necessity breaks up the household. Wife and children may not go whither the husband and father is ordered to proceed, as in the naval and military services. Sometimes prudential considerations assert themselves, and the children must quit the domestic hearth to get their own living, or even the wife and husband must seek separate employments with the same object. Occasionally, the husband, having to go on a difficult or dangerous mission, where wife and children would be encumbrances, has to part from them temporarily, and to provide for their support and sustenance during his absence. This last was the case of Moses. In returning to Egypt, and coming forward as the champion of his nation, he confronted great dangers. The presence of wife and children would have hampered him, and, therefore, he resolved to return alone. Zipporah and his infant sons were left with her nearest male relative. But now the time had come for re-union. We may note as blissful elements in the re-union—

I. THAT IT WAS COMPLETE, NO DEATHS HAVING OCCURRED SINCE THE PARTING. The bitterness of parting is especially in the uncertainty whether we shall ever see again in this life the individuals from whom we part. Death comes suddenly, and without warning; infants are especially subject to his attack; and when Moses, having recently parted from Jethro (ch. iv. 8), sent back his wife and two young sons to be under his charge, he must have felt that it was exceedingly doubtful whether there would ever again be a meeting of the five near relations. But God brought it to pass. Jethro, with a promptitude which indicates a warm heart, no sooner heard of his kinsman's safe arrival in the region of the "wilderness," than he put himself to the trouble of a long journey, partly to congratulate him, but mainly to restore to him the wife and children, whom he had received as a sacred trust. He could not be content unless he himself delivered them safe into the hands of Moses, and thus "gave a good account of his stewardship." And he was fortunate in being able to deliver them all safe and sound, and apparently in good health. No insidious disease had nipped the life of either child in the bud; no unlucky accident had removed either from the land of the living. Moses was able to greet, at one and the same moment, his wife, his two sons, and his brother-in-law. Doubtless, he felt that God had been specially good and gracious to him in restoring to him all his treasures.

II. THAT IT WAS CHARACTERISED BY COURTESY AND GOOD FEELING, AND FREE FROM ANY REPROACH ON EITHER SIDE. Jethro sent a message to announce his arrival, which was a courteous act, not strictly necessary. He relieved at once any anxiety which Moses might naturally feel, by letting him know that he had brought with him his wife and both his sons. That they had been able to make the long journey implied that they were well. Moses, on his part, responded by going out to meet his brother-in-law, thus requiting courtesy with courtesy; when he met him, he "did obeisance," not standing upon his own present dignity; having done obeisance, he rose and "kissed him," thus showing tender affection. Greetings by word of mouth followed, and then friendly conversation. The great leader had much to relate, and gave a full account, both of his perils and hair-breadth escapes, and of his divinely-wrought deliverances. Hereat Jethro "rejoiced." No word of reproach or blame seems to have been uttered on either side. No discord marred the perfect harmony. Over the still tenderer meeting of the husband and father with his wife and children, the sacred historian, with a wise reticence, draws the veil. There are scenes which are at once too private and too sacred for description; and this was one of them.

III. THAT IT WAS CROWNED BY AN ACT OF RELIGIOUS THANKFULNESS AND ACKNOW-LEDGMENT OF THE GOODNESS OF GOD. The sense that God has been good to us should lead in all cases to an act of acknowledgment. Jethro was not content with mere words of joy and gratitude—not even with a solemn ascription of praise and blessing to Jehovah (ver. 10). He must shew his feelings by an act; so, in accordance with the ritual of the time, he "took a burnt-offering and sacrifices." Christians should similarly signalise their own re-unions, and other important events in their lives, by joining together in the highest act of Christian worship—the Holy Communion. Joint participation in the "bread of life" and "cup of the Lord" brings home to us the sense of family oneness, as nothing else has the power to do. Prayers uttered side by side bind men's hearts together in indissoluble union; participation in the same precious gifts gives the sense of unity in him who is the source of unity to all who are his. Aaron and the elders do well to join; their presence does not mar the family concord; it does but enlarge the family circle, and add new links to the chain that binds Heaven to earth. Some day the whole Church will be one family, of which all the members will worship God perpetually in the Father's house. The nearest approach to happiness on earth is that anticipation of the final bliss which Holy Communion furnishes.

HOMILIES BY VARIOUS AUTHORS.

Vers. 1—13.—*The visit of Jethro.* When Jethro "*heard* of all that God had done for Moses,"—a hint that the news of the great events of the past few weeks had spread far and wide through the Sinaitic peninsula,—and when he learned that the Israelites were encamped at the Mount of God, within reachable distance of the Midianitish settlement (cf. ch. iii. 1), he at once resolved on paying his former friend, who had so suddenly blazed into an unexpected greatness, a personal visit. He came, accordingly, accompanied by Moses' wife and two sons.

I. JETHRO'S COMING (vers. 1—7). This visit of Jethro to Moses may be considered with reference to the following particulars. He came—1. *Cordially recognising the honour which God had put on Moses* (ver. 1). Moses had stood to Jethro for years in a relation of dependence. He had kept the priest's flocks (ch. iii. 1). Yet Jethro was not offended or made envious by this sudden greatness which had fallen to the lot of his old associate. The proverb was for once falsified that "a prophet is not without honour, save in his own country, and in his own house" (Matt. xiii. 5—7), for Jethro heartily acknowledged and rejoiced in all that the Lord had done for Moses and for Israel. It might have been otherwise. He might, like the Nazarenes in their slighting of Christ, have asked—"Was not this my shepherd? Is not his wife called Zipporah? and his sons, Gershom and Eliezer, are they not with us? Whence then hath this man all these things?" But a far different spirit possessed him. In this, Jethro showed his freedom from a very common littleness of nature. 2. *As an act of personal friendship.* A large part of the joy of life springs from friendship. We see friendship at its best in the case of those who are thrown much into each other's society, and who cherish for each other, under the conditions which most of all reveal and test character, a cordial respect and esteem. " Friendship," says Cicero, "is nothing else than a perfect concurrence on all subjects Divine and human, accompanied by a feeling of kindness and attachment, and I am not sure that any better boon than this, with the exception of wisdom, could be conferred on man by the immortal Gods." The bond of attachment thus created between good men makes association a pleasure, and, of necessity, causes pain at parting. While separation lasts, longings do not cease to be felt for a renewal of the prized intercourse, and when, after years of severance, an opening for such renewal of intercourse is presented, the opportunity is eagerly and joyfully embraced. Such friendship may be presumed· to have existed between Jethro and Moses. The two had lived in close intimacy for the space of forty years. According to the text, Moses was Jethro's son-in-law; according to the more probable view, his brother-in-law. Jethro, with his stores of practical wisdom, his desert courtesy, and his evidently sincere piety, was a man whom Moses would early learn to respect, and with whom he would find it pleasant and profitable to associate; and the Midianitish priest, in turn, would never be weary of the companionship of Moses, whose learning was so ripe, whose spirit was so excellent, whose early life had been spent under such different conditions from his own, and who had consequently so much to tell, which he (Jethro) would delight to hear. This intercourse had been suddenly broken up by Moses' determination to return to Egypt (ch. iv. 18); but an opportunity now presented itself of renewing it, and of this Jethro gladly availed himself. 3. *Desirous of hearing more perfectly of the wonderful works of God.* This, as is apparent from the sequel (ver. 8), was another motive of Jethro's visit. He had come to be more fully and exactly instructed in the wonders which God had wrought " for Moses, and for Israel, his people" (ver. 1). Something of these "mighty acts" he had heard from current report, but what he had heard only whetted his appetite to hear more. It is the mark of the good man that he earnestly desires to grow in the knowledge of God and of his ways. 4. *With the intention of restoring to Moses his wife and two sons* (vers. 2—6). In taking this earliest opportunity of bringing Zipporah and her two sons to Moses, Jethro acted rightly. A wife's proper place is with her husband. Sons, again, in view of the special responsibility resting on the father in connection with their proper up-bringing, should be as much as possible under direct paternal influence. The kingdom of God, doubtless, is to be more to us than father, or mother, or wife, or child; and should *its* interests imperatively demand separation, this must be submitted to (Matt. viii. 21, 22): but relationships are not thereby dissolved, and the active discharge of the duties connected with them should be resumed at the earliest opportunity. For the sake of Moses himself, reunion was desirable. He was not a man who spurned the joys of domestic existence, but, like Peter, led about a wife (cf. Num. xii. 1; 1 Cor. ix. 5). It would contribute to his happiness to have his family beside him. Attention is anew called to the significant names of his sons (vers. 3, 4). These noteworthy names would be perpetual reminders to Moses of the lessons of his stay in Midian. The one spoke of human weakness, the other of Divine aid. If the one embalmed the memory of his heart-loneliness in a strange land, the other told of how God had been his help even there. The one recalled trials, the other mercies. While in both was embodied a memorial of the heart-discipline, of the solitary communion with God, of the lonely days and nights of prayer, watching, and spiritual meditation, which had helped so largely during the forty years of that weary but precious exile, to make him the man he was.

II. JETHRO AND MOSES (vers. 7—13). The visit here described is a model of brotherly and religious intercourse. Christians would do well to study and imitate it. Observe— 1. *The courtesy of their greeting* (ver. 7). The two men stood on a very different moral and intellectual level, but, in their exchanges of civility, Jethro is treated as the superior, and is received by Moses with every outward demonstration of respect. As on Jethro's side there is no trace of mortification or jealousy at finding Moses, once the keeper of his sheep, in so exalted a position, so, on the side of Moses now Israel's deliverer and leader, there is an utter absence of pride and hauteur, and a painstaking desire to put Jethro—a plain wilderness priest—as fully as possible at his ease. Everything is real. The greetings of the friends are unaffectedly cordial—their behaviour towards each other studiously polite. Lesson—the duty of courtesy. Courtesy is an essential part of what has been defined as the outward grace of life. " By the grace of life is meant all that embellishes, softens, and brightens our present existence. It is that which is to human life what the shape and bloom and odour are to the plant. The flower is not simply useful. It is pleasing. There is grace about it. . . . The grace of life has its simplest manifestation in our external behaviour—in our manners. There is a joy to observed and observer in graceful motion and pleasant phrase. . . . Politeness is the science and art of the outward grace of life. It enunciates that strange code of salutations and farewells—those buffers which soften approach, and with a last gentle touch make parting easy. Under the fiction of giving information as to the weather, one spirit expresses to its fellow respect and continued friendship. That spirit, in turn, under the form of confirming the afore-said meteorological intelligence, reciprocates the kindly feeling. In such queer fashion is human kindliness flashed from heart to heart." (Rev. David Burns.)   2. *Their affectionate interest in each other's welfare.* " They asked each other of their welfare " (ver. 7). Burdened as he was, almost beyond endurance, with "the cumbrance, and burden, and strife " (Deut. x. 12) of the congregation, Moses could unbend to show his kindly interest in what was taking place in the quiet tents at Midian. This is a point of greatness. The greatest man is not he who occupies so serene an elevation of spirit, or whose mind is so engrossed with the duties of an exalted station, that he cannot stoop to share in, and, as occasion offers, to testify his sympathy with, the joys and sorrows of humbler people. No deficiency of this kind is seen in Moses—or in Jesus. It is well to cultivate the habit of putting ourselves in the place of others, however remote in station from ourselves, and of trying to feel a kindly interest in all that concerns them. This will prevent us from becoming self-absorbed and egoistic. *Their* lives, we should remember, are of as much importance to *them* as ours are to us, and the interest we show in them will be proportionately valued. A minister once wrote in his note-book : " Don't *pretend* an interest in the members of your congregation, but try to *feel* it." " Be kindly affectioned one to another with brotherly love" (Rom. xii. 10).   3. *The theme of their converse.* " Moses told his father-in-law (brother-in-law) all that the Lord had done to Pharaoh," etc. (ver. 8). As under a former head we had a model meeting, so here we have a model conversation. Jethro and Moses conversed on the affairs of God's kingdom. No greater subject could have occupied their thoughts. It is the subject of deepest and most central interest in history—the grandest in its essential nature, the widest in its relations, the most momentous in its issues. All other movements in time are side issues as compared with this one. In considering it *man* passes out of sight, and the only question is, What hath God wrought! (Num. xxiii. 23). We renew this conversation of Jethro and Moses every time we " speak of the glory of (God's) kingdom and talk of (his) power" (Ps. cxlv. 11). Cf. the conversation of Christian with Prudence, Piety, and Charity in the House Beautiful :—" Now the table was furnished with fat things, and wine that was well refined; and all their talk at the table was about the Lord of the Hill; as, namely, about what he had done, and wherefore he did what he did," etc. (Pilgrim's Progress.) Converse in heaven will turn on the same themes. Note—(1) It is profit-able for Christians to exchange experiences as to the manner of the Lord's dealings with them. Few but can tell something of " the travail that has come upon them by the way, and how the Lord delivered them." (2) It is a mark of grace to feel an interest in what relates to God's work, and to the progress of his kingdom at home and abroad. This will show itself in a desire to read, hear, and converse on such subjects, and in the interest discovered, and zeal shown, in the general work of the Church, in special spiritual movements, in the success of missions, in spiritual operations in our own town and neighbourhood. (3) Some are called to more active service in God's work than others. There are those that fight the battle, and there are those who tarry at home and divide the spoil (Ps. lxviii. 12). And those who have been personally engaged in God's work—especially those who have returned from the high places of the field (missionaries, etc.)—have always much to tell which it is of interest to hear, and which will enkindle our hearts with new ardour in the cause of the Gospel. We should seek the society of such, and take the opportunity of hearing them when they are to be heard, that we may be instructed and profited. What a thrilling history, *e.g.*, is that of Christian missions, but what an additional interest it gives to its narrations when we hear the story from the lips of the men who have actually fought the battles! (4) Christian workers cannot converse together on the plans, methods, difficulties, conflicts, and successes of their work without being mutually helped and edified. 4. *Jethro's joy in the relation* (vers. 9—11). We are reminded of Barnabas, who, "when he came" to Antioch, "and had seen the grace of God, was glad. . . . For he was a good man, and full of the Holy Ghost and of faith" (Acts xi. 23). The history which Moses gave to Jethro—(1) Filled Jethro with joy; (2) Strengthened his faith in God—"Now I know that the Lord is greater than all gods" (ver. 11); (3) Incited him to praise—"And Jethro said, Blessed be the Lord," etc. (ver. 10). It will be observed how distinctly in ver. 11 Jethro seizes the point in the contest between Jehovah and Pharaoh, and draws the proper inference from it. God had chosen as a field for the display of his perfections a case in which all the pride and power of man were arrayed against him in a determined effort to resist, oppose, and make void his will, and he had demonstrated his supremacy by completely annihilating that opposition, and overwhelming the Egyptians, who embodied it, in the Red Sea. The army of Egypt was in some sense the country's pride and boast, so that (though the translation in ver. 11 is apparently incorrect) it was literally true that "in the thing wherein they dealt proudly" Jehovah was "above them." God exalts himself by discomfiting his enemies in what they deem their points of special strength. "Poor perfection which one sees an end of! yet such are all those things in this world which pass for perfections. David, in his time, had seen Goliath, the strongest, overcome; Asahel, the swiftest, overtaken; Ahithophel, the wisest, befooled; Absalom, the fairest, deformed" (M. Henry on Ps. cxix. 96). "It is written, I will destroy the wisdom of the wise, and will bring to nothing the understanding of the prudent" (1 Cor. i. 19). 5. *The sacrificial feast* (ver. 16). We have here—(1) Friendship cemented by an act of worship; (2) Religious converse culminating in devotion; (3) A feast sanctified by the enjoyment of the Divine presence—"before God;" (4) A foreshadowing of the union of Jews and Gentiles in the fellowship of the church; (5) An instance of catholicity in worship. Moses did not scruple to join in sacrifice or to sit down at the same festival board with the Midianitish Jethro. The lesson is thus enunciated by Peter: "Of a truth I perceive that God is no respecter of persons; but in every nation he that feareth him, and worketh righteousness, is accepted with him" (Acts x. 34, 35).—J. O.

Vers. 1—5.— *The claims of home.* "And Jethro, Moses' kinsman (not father-in-law) came with his sons and his wife unto Moses into the wilderness, where he encamped at the mount of God" (Ex. xviii. 5).

I. Circumstances may justify the temporary remission of home responsibilities upon others (ver. 2). For example—and the history of Moses will illustrate each point—we may be justified by—1. *The nature of external duty.* We may be providentially called away from home; or the discharge of public responsibilities may for the time be incompatible with our usual attention to the interests of the domestic circle, *e.g.*, Moses going to Egypt (Ex. iv. compare with Ex. xviii. 2). 2. *The probability of danger.* 3. *Defective sympathy.* It is clear that Zipporah was not in sympathy with the religious object of Moses, nor yet with his specific mission. Need, however, to be on our guard against making this a reason for withdrawal permanently from home responsibility. Want of perfect compatibility in domestic life makes marriage to be an occasion for self-discipline, and is thus converted into a means of grace. (Eph. v. 25—27.)

II. Circumstances scarcely ever justify the permanent remission. There are a few cases, perhaps, in which this responsibility may be devolved: *e.g.*, the case of the missionary who must, for various reasons, send home from his station his children to be educated; and not seldom the wife with them. Other cases there are, no doubt. But generally the father may not devolve this obligation. It is one—1. *Of necessity.* No one else *can* meet the responsibility as the natural head of the family—this is true in all cases—even in that of the missionary named above—for the children suffer. 2. *Of duty*:—(1) To *ourselves.* We owe it to our own convictions of truth, as to thought, life, and work, to perpetuate them. (2) To *dependents*. Whether wife, children, or servants. [On this point some valuable suggestions in Dr. Taylor's "Moses the Lawgiver," pp. 173—176.] (3) To our *generation*; and (4) to the *Great Father* in heaven.

III. IF TEMPTED TO THIS REMISSION GOD WILL BRING HOME TO US OUR DUTY. Probably by some providence, may be painful or otherwise. At such a *time*, on such an *occasion* (Moses face to face with Sinai and the giving of the law) in such a *place*, Jethro re-introduced to Moses wife and children. Even such duties as his could not exempt him from domestic responsibility.—R.

Vers. 1—12.—*The Consolations of those who suffer loss for the Kingdom of God.* I. THE REUNION OF THE SEPARATED. To Moses, who had to leave behind him wife and children because God's errand would brook no delay, these are now restored. 1. There is no loss to those who suffer for the kingdom of God's sake. 2. God fills the cup of his servants with consolations. God's care had been exercised not only over him in Egypt, but also over wife and children in Midian.

II. THE THEME OF THOSE WHO FEAR GOD. God's marvellous works (vers. 8, 9). It was not the subject of public discourse or formal greeting, but of private converse within "the tent." This is a mark of the true servant of God; to *him* God and his goodness are the most real and wondrous of all things.

III. THE RESULT OF THE TESTIMONY. 1. Jethro's confession of Jehovah. 2. His sacrifice to him. The stranger makes a feast before Israel's God for the princes of Israel. Those whom we bring to God make a feast, in their faith and love, for our soul before the Lord.—U.

Vers. 6—12.—*Friendship in its loftiest form.* "They asked each other of their welfare." Ex. xviii. 7. The visit of Jethro comes between the agony of Rephidim and the solemnities of "Sinai," like the insertion of a sweet pastoral poem between two tragedies. Something may be learnt from it as to what should characterise friendship in its highest form, that is, between two devout souls, as consecrated and elevated by religion.

I. CONSTANCY. Moses and Jethro met as in the earlier years; no assumption with Moses, no sycophancy with Jethro.

II. COURTESY. Ver. 7. The nearer our relations to each other, the more indispensable this grace.

III. MUTUAL SOLICITUDE. Ver. 7.

IV. INTERCHANGE OF EXPERIENCE. Vers. 8—11. Happy time, when the deeper experiences (religious) can be exchanged to mutual advantage.

V. COMMUNION IN WORSHIP. Ver. 12. It is clear that Jethro and Moses were one as to Monotheism, in their common possession of the great Divine traditions of the race. Jethro spiritually was in the descent of Abel, Enoch, Noah, and Melchisedek. For him but one God, the God of heaven and earth, and *therefore* the God of Israel. Contrast with Amalek! Hence the sacrifice and the sacrificial feast.

VI. FIDELITY IN GIVING COUNCIL. Vers. 14, 17—23. Great courage required.

VII. HUMILITY IN RECEIVING IT. This the moral attitude of Moses.

VIII. AN ULTIMATE REFERENCE IN ALL INTERCOURSE TO THE DIVINE FRIEND. Ver. 23. "And God commanded thee so."

IX. SYMPATHY AS TO GREAT OBJECT. Jethro knew the destiny of Israel, and was concerned for the realisation.

X. PEACEFUL PARTING AT LIFE'S DIVERGING PATHS. Ver. 27. Apply this to moral and intellectual cross-roads; and to that which is so difficult—agreeing to differ—and that with mutual respect and affection. All in view and hope of the perfect and immortal amity that is beyond the sky.—R.

Vers. 1—12.—*Jethro's visit—Moses in his domestic relations.* In this visit of Jethro three persons are brought prominently before us—Moses, Jethro, his father-in-law, and Zipporah, his wife. Let us consider the details of the visit in their bearing on all these three persons.

I. ON MOSES. Moses is usually seen either in the presence of God or in the presence of the people; but here we get a peep at his private and domestic life, and nothing is revealed but what adds dignity and beauty to his character. A servant of God must have the same character, in all circumstances. It is not every public man that could afford to have his private life laid open; and only too often an earnest plea for pity has to be based on the remembrance of how frail and infirm a thing human nature is. But in the instance of Moses neither veil nor plea are needed. This meeting with Jethro has to take place, and there was no reason to evade it; it had also to be mentioned, and there was no reason to conceal it. Moses had done nothing in his past residence in Midian to make him ashamed or afraid of returning to it. He had been a faithful shepherd to Jethro; a loving husband to Zipporah; an equally loving father to Gershom and Eliezer. It was Zipporah who had forsaken him, and not he Zipporah. He returned as a prophet into what, in a certain sense, was his own country, and, if not exactly honoured neither could he be dishonoured. Again we behold Moses showing, in the most practical way, *his respect for the family relation and the ties of kinship generally.* The importance of the family relation we have seen already brought out in the institution of the Passover and the provision of the manna. Here Moses puts emphasis on the relation by his own example. He showed himself one who regarded domestic obligations as of the first importance Zipporah has failed him once, and that in circumstances of great perplexity; but he does not make this a plea for getting rid of her. He knows his duties towards her, and by undertaking them in a manful and conscientious way, he may bring her to a full recognition of her duty towards him. A truly great nation, having a strong and beneficial society, is only possible by an aggregation of households where household claims are respected by all. And evidently he who must lead the way in acknowledging the claim is he who stands at the head. *So Moses did here.* Lastly, Moses makes clear by his reception of Jethro and Zipporah that he was *the same kind of man as in the old shepherd days.* Altered circumstances with all their temptations had not made alterations for the worse in character. How many there are who while lifted in one way are lowered in another! They become bigger men; but, alas! not better. Everything that reminds them of former and humbler scenes is as wormwood to the taste. To all such Moses, by his conduct here, teaches a most powerful lesson. His strength among the thousands of Israel was not that of a human ruler who was to be girt about with all the paraphernalia of government, in order to overawe the populace. Moses can step out of his tent, as if he were one of the humblest of Israel, not only in character, but also in position. He can go out and welcome his kindred, show to Jethro the outward signs of filial respect, talk to them all in the old familiar way, and do it without the slightest fear that his authority as leader is in any way affected. And this conduct would be all the more beautiful if, as we may easily imagine, Zipporah came back to him rather lifted up because of her husband's new position, and disposed with feminine vanity to make the most of it for her own satisfaction.

II. ON JETHRO. This chapter, full as it is of Jethro, is another forcible illustration as to how much revelation of character the Scripture record can put into a small space. Jethro, hitherto known only as the near connection of Moses, stands before us here as a noble, pious, and truly affectionate and considerate man. Much, indeed, he has had to try and perplex him. Moses, who had made his first acquaintance with him under prepossessing circumstances, who had become his brother-in-law and faithful shepherd, all at once comes to him, without any previous notice, and asks his permission to return to Egypt. Moses, we know, had been sternly shut up to this course by Jehovah, and to Jethro it must have seemed entirely inexplicable. He had to part with his near relations; and a great void must thus have been left in his heart. Then presently Zipporah returns, with her sons, in a very sore and rebellious frame of mind. All Jethro can yet see is that this departure of Moses has brought nothing but domestic discord. And yet it is impossible for him to say that Moses has not done right. He can only wait for the unfoldings of time, listening meanwhile with what patience he can muster to reproaches from neighbours and daughter and perhaps grandsons, with respect to the unaccountable vagaries of Moses. And at last relief comes, and not only relief, but abundant justification. The information is such as to make Moses stand out in the esteem of his father-in-law more highly than ever. All suspense as to Zipporah's duty is removed; she must rejoin her husband. It was Moses and not Jethro who was responsible for her; and, besides, Moses and Zipporah had a joint responsi-bility for their offspring. Jethro is commonly set before us, in contrast to Amalek, as the illustration of heathenism, looking favourably and amicably upon Israel. But even more let us look upon him as the great illustration of those noble souls who strive to unite what sin divides. Jesus in his teaching had occasion to lay emphasis on the dividing effect of discipleship to himself. He intimated that the acceptance of himself would only too often rupture, or at least strain, natural ties. But this of course was not presented as a thing to cause satisfaction. It was only another sad evidence of how sin turns to evil what God meant for good. And yet here we see the other side, reunion as well as separation. The liberation of Israel, glorious in its total result, and lifting Moses to high eminence in respect of personal character, has yet involved at the same time the wreck of his domestic peace. Whatever the comforts of wife and children in this world may be, he has lost them. But now these comforts are coming again, and coming in the most satisfactory of all ways, by the voluntary entrance of his old friend Jethro on the scene. Blessed are the peacemakers; and surely of all peace-making, that is not the least fruitful of good which reunites and reconstitutes a sepa-rated family. Moses acting with a single eye to what is right has to part from his wife, and let her go back to her own family. Jethro acting in the same spirit, brings the wife to her husband again. Often we may have to become agents and helpers in division; but if we only go on, union and harmony will return. What Zipporah's future was we know not; but Jethro had done his utmost to put matters right.

III. On Zipporah. Her name occurs but little, and her appearance hitherto has not been such as to make us think she would prove a helpful companion to Moses (ch. iv. 25, 26). Still we must not judge too hastily from silence. It is not for Zipporah's sake she happens to be mentioned here. It is sufficient to learn, by the way, that an opportunity for repentance and for devotion to him who had such a burden to bear, was now given her.—Y.

Ver. 5.—"*Ye are come unto Mount Zion.*" The way in which we view facts depends a great deal on the eyes through which we look at them. Here, as regards Moses and the Israelites in the wilderness, we may look on them through the eyes of Jethro, or of Zipporah, or of the children; for a change let us use the children's eyes, and enquire how they transmit the facts to us. Sketch previous history of the children, their stay in Midian, and journey to the camp. Notice:—

I. What the children saw and heard. As they came they would notice, first, the mountains, then the camp in the plain, then, perhaps, people moving about and cloudy pillar suspended over all. At last, one man comes to meet them; their father is the leader of the host. 1. *A new flock.* In the old days Gershom must often have looked out for his coming home; then (cf. iii. 1) he had sheep to care for, now his flock is of another kind (Ps. lxxvii. 20). No longer Jethro's shepherd, but the shepherd of Jehovah. Not really changed his profession—still the same kind of work—only, having served his apprenticeship with Jethro, he has been called to a higher grade of service. 2. *A memorable spot.* How had he come to change his service? The very place would remind them of the answer. There is the rough hill-side—there, perhaps, the very bush where the angel appeared. The whole scene a fulfilment of God's pro-mise and a pledge of his faithfulness (cf. iii. 12). 3. *New-found relatives.* A new uncle and aunt, never seen before—could tell them about the old life in Egypt, their father's birth and escape—the cruel slavery of their kindred—all the past would seem more real now that they were confronted by these witnesses to its reality. Comparing the past with the present, a suggestive commentary on Eliezer's name; Moses had good reason for saying, "my God is a help."

II. Parallel with ourselves. (Cf. Heb. xii. 22—24.) We, too, like the sons of Moses, have been brought into new relations with our Father. As we approach him, what may we see and hear? 1. *We find him in a holy place.* Not a camp of wanderers in the wilderness, but a holy city, one which hath foundations, the settled home of its redeemed inhabitants. Pleasant for Gershom and his brother to find their father, but they still had to look on to the day when they should find their home; for us home is our Father's house in the holy city upon the holy mountain. 2. *He introduces us to holy fellowships.* As Moses' children found new relatives, so do we: "an innumerable company, the general assembly of the angels, and the Church of the first-born, and the spirits of the justified." We may picture the interest with which Gershom and Eliezer must have viewed the camp and listened to the story of deliverance; but the company to which they had come was very different to that to which we have come; the deliverance of which they heard was but a first step to freedom. They, no doubt, learnt to sing, perhaps from Miriam, the song of Moses; from those with whom *we* have communion we may learn the song of the Lamb.

Conclusion. After all, the children, amid all the new sights, would rejoice most at meeting their father—at seeing *him*, and remaining with him. As Jethro led them towards the mount, their father was, doubtless, the subject of their talk; all else derived its interest only from its relation to him. Just so, too, with us. Heaven is our Father's house; it is our Father's presence that makes it *home* to us. As our Lord leads us thitherward, it is still of the Father whom he speaks. Those whom the Father has given into his care he will bring to their journey's end in safety.—G.

EXPOSITION.

Vers. 13—26.—Jethro's advice to Moses, and its adoption. The office of ruler in ancient times, whether exercised by a king, a prince, or a mere chieftain, was always understood to include within it the office of judge. In the Greek ideal of the origin of kingly government (Herod. i. 96), the able discharge of judicial functions marks the individual out for sovereignty. The successors of Moses, like the chief rulers of Carthage, bore the title of "Judges" (*shophetim, suffetes*). Moses, it appears, had from the time when he was accepted as leader by the people (ch. iv. 29—31), regarded himself as bound to hear and decide all the causes and complaints which arose among the entire Israelite people. He had not delegated his authority to any one. This can scarcely have been because the idea had not occurred to him, for the Egyptian kings ordinarily decided causes by judges nominated *ad hoc.* Perhaps he had distrusted the ability of his countrymen—so recently slaves—to discharge such delicate functions. At any rate, he had reserved the duty wholly to himself (ver. 18). This course appeared to Jethro unwise. No man could, he thought, in the case of so great a nation, singly discharge such an office with satisfaction to himself and others. Moses would "wear himself away" with the fatigue; and he would exhaust the patience of the people through inability to keep pace with the number of cases that necessarily arose. Jethro therefore recommended the appointment of subordinate judges, and the reservation by Moses of nothing but the right to decide such cases as these judges should, on account of their difficulty, refer to him (ver. 22)   On

reflection, Moses accepted this course as the best open to him under the circumstances, and established a multiplicity of judges, under a system which will be discussed in the comment on verse 25.

Ver. 13.—On the morrow. The day after Jethro's arrival. **Moses sat to judge the people.** Moses, *i. e.,* took his seat in an accustomed place, probably at the door of his tent, and was understood to be ready to hear and decide causes. **The people stood by Moses.** A crowd of complainants soon collected, and kept Moses employed incessantly from the morning, when he had taken his seat, until the evening, *i.e.,* until nightfall. It is conjectured that many complaints may have arisen out of the division of the spoil of the Amalekites.

Ver. 14.—Why sittest thou thyself alone, etc. A perverse ingenuity has discovered that the emphatic words in this passage are "sittest" and "stand," Jethro having blamed Moses for humiliating the people by requiring them to stand up while he himself sat! But the context makes it abundantly clear that what Jethro really blames, is Moses sitting *alone* and judging the whole people single-handed.

Ver. 15.—And Moses said . . . . Because the people come unto me, to inquire of God. To inquire of God is certainly not a mere "juridical phrase," meaning to consult a judge (Kalisch), nor, on the other hand, is it necessarily "to consult God through an oracle." It cannot, however, mean less than to seek a decision from some one regarded as entitled to speak for God; and it is certainly assigned by Moses as the reason why he judged all the causes himself, and did not devolve the duty upon others. They could not be supposed to know the mind of God as he knew it. Jethro, however, points out, that it is one thing to lay down principles, and another to apply them. Moses might reserve the legislative function—the inculcation of principles—to himself, and

so still, " be for the people to Godward " (ver.
19); but he might find "able men" among
the congregation, quite capable of applying
the principles, and delegate to them the judicial
function (vers. 21, 22).

Ver. 16.—I judge . . . and I do make them
know the statutes of God. As the Israelites
were, up to this time, without any code of
written laws, Moses took the opportunity furnished by such cases as came before him, to
lay down principles of law, and enjoin them
upon the people; thus making them to know
the statutes of God and his eternal unwritten
laws. Such a practice would not have been
necessary after the giving of the law on Mount
Sinai; and its existence at the time of Jethro's
visit helps to fix that visit as occurring *before*
the giving of the law.

Ver. 18.—The thing . . . is not good—*i.e.*,
not expedient, and so not the right thing to
do. It is a man's duty to have regard to his
health, and not unnecessarily overtask his
strength.

Ver. 18.—Thou wilt surely wear away.
Literally, " Wasting thou wilt waste away,"
Thy strength, *i.e.*, will not long hold out, if
thou continuest this practice. Both thou, and
this people. The people's strength and patience
will also fail, if, owing to the number of the
complaints, they have—some of them—to wait
all day at the tribunal before they can obtain
a decision.

Ver. 19.—I will give thee counsel, and God
shall be with thee. Rather—" And may God
be with thee!" May God incline thine
heart to accept my counsel and act upon it.
Be thou for the people to God-ward, etc.
" Continue," *i.e.*, as at present, to be the intermediary between God and the people—still be
the whole and sole source of legislative power
(ver. 20), and still be the fount and origin of
judicial authority; but commit the actual
decision of the lighter causes to others chosen
by thyself for the office (vers. 21, 22). The
separation of the legislative and judicial functions was well known in Egypt, where the
kings alone made new laws (Herod. ii. 109,
136, 177, etc.), but causes were ordinarily
determined by a body of judges. Bring the
causes unto God. In difficult cases, Moses
actually laid the cause before God, and obtained directions from God as to the manner
in which he was to decide it. See Num.
xxvii. 5—11.

Ver. 20.—Thou shalt teach them ordinances
and laws. Or, "statutes and laws," as in
ver. 16. It is not quite clear how these differ.
Some regard "statutes" as connected with
religion, and laws as regulations with respect
to civil and social matters. Others explain
the first as "specific" and the second as
"general enactments." The way wherein
they must walk. The general line of conduct
which all are bound to pursue. The work that

they must do. The special task which each
has to perform individually.

Ver. 21.—Able men. Literally, "men of
might"—*i.e.*, of capacity or ability—men competent for the office of judge; who are further
defined to be, such as possess the three qualities
of piety, veracity, and strict honesty, or incor-
ruptness. Jethro's conception of the true judicial character leaves little to be desired. If
among every ten Israelites there was one such
person, the moral condition of the nation cannot have been so much depressed by the
Egyptian servitude as is sometimes represented. Place such over them to be rulers of
thousands, etc. A decimal organisation naturally presents itself to men's minds as the
simplest in a simple state of society, and was
probably already in use among the Arab tribes
with whom Jethro was familiar. The graduated series—rulers of tens, of fifties, of hundreds, and of thousands, implies a power of
three-fold appeal, from the "ruler of ten" to
the "ruler of fifty"—from him to the "ruler
of a hundred"—and from him to the "ruler of
a thousand." Whether there was an appeal
from the last-named to Moses, is doubtful.
Probably there was not; Moses deciding those
cases only which the "rulers of thousands"
reserved for him as being specially difficult or
important.

Ver. 22.—Let them judge the people at all
seasons. Instead of occasional court-days, on
which Moses sat from morning to evening
hearing causes, judgments were to be given
continually by the rulers of tens, fifties, etc.,
the accumulation of untried causes being thus
avoided, and punishment following promptly
on the committal of an offence. The elaborately minute organisation was only suited for
the period of the wanderings, and was of a
semi-military character, such as might have
suited an army on the march When the
Israelites became settled dwellers in Palestine,
such a multiplicity of judges was unnecessary,
and was discontinued. So shall it be easier.
Literally, "So make it easier." Compare
ver. 18.

Ver. 23.—And God command thee so.
Jethro does not suppose that Moses will take
his advice without further consultation. He
assumes that the matter will be laid by Moses
before God, and God's will learnt concerning
it. The entire narrative supposes that there
was some established means by which the
Israelite leader could refer a matter to Jehovah
and obtain a decision upon it. This can
scarcely have been as yet the Urim and
Thummim. Probably Moses held frequent
communication with Jehovah by means of
waking visions. Thou shalt be able to endure—*i.e.*, "the work will not be too much
for thee—thou wilt be able to bear it." This
people shall also go to their place in peace.
The "place" intended would seem to be

Palestine. Keil supposes that the word "peace" is to be taken literally, and concludes from it that breaches of the peace had previously been frequent, the people having "often taken the law into their own hands on account of the delay in the judicial decision;" but this is to extract from the words more than they naturally signify. "In peace" means "cheerfully, contentedly." If the changes which he recommends are carried out, Jethro thinks that the people will make the rest of the journey to Canaan quietly and contentedly, without complaint or dissatisfaction.

Ver. 24.—**So Moses hearkened.** Moses took the advice tendered him, not immediately, but after the law had been given at Sinai, and the journeying was about to be resumed. See Deut. i. 9–15.

Ver. 25.—**Moses chose able men.** It appears from Deut. i. 13, that instead of selecting the men himself, which would have been an invidious task, Moses directed their nomination by the people, and only reserved to himself the investing them with their authority. **Heads over the people.** From the time of their appointment, the "rulers" were not merely judges, but "heads" of their respective companies, with authority over them on the march, and command in the battle-field (Num. xxxi. 14). Thus the organisation was at once civil and military.

Ver. 26.—**At all seasons.** See the comment on verse 22. **The hard causes they brought unto Moses.** It must have been left to the discretion of the judges to determine whether a cause was hard or easy, a great or a little matter. Probably only those causes which seemed "hard" to the "rulers of thousands" were brought before Moses for decision.

HOMILETICS.

Vers. 14—23.—*The unwisdom of a monopoly of power.* The principle of the division of labour, which is essential to progress in the arts, was well known in Egypt, and was applied there, not to the arts only, but also to government and administration. Moses, who had resided forty years at the court of a Pharaoh (Acts vii. 23), must have been thoroughly acquainted with the fact that, in a well-ordered community, judicial functions were separated from legislative and administrative, and entrusted to a large number of persons, not monopolised by a single individual. But it had appeared to him that the condition of his own people was exceptional. Just released from the cruel bondage of a hard and pitiless slavery, without education, without habits of command or self-control, without any knowledge of the principles of law or experience in the practice of courts, they seemed to him unfit for the exercise of the judicial office—especially as he understood it. For his view was, that each particular decision should be made an occasion of educating the people in the principles of law and justice (ver. 16), and upon these it was his habit to descant in connection with each judgment that he delivered. As he felt that he alone among all the Israelites was equal to this task, he had undertaken to discharge singly the office of judge in a community consisting of above two millions of persons. Jethro, on visiting him, was struck with the unwisdom of such an attempt, and honestly gave expression to his feelings. Jethro saw—

I. THAT TO MONOPOLISE THE JUDICIAL FUNCTION IN SO LARGE A COMMUNITY WAS UNWISE, AS AN UNDUE STRAIN UPON THE MENTAL AND PHYSICAL POWERS OF THE MONOPOLISER. So numerous were the causes brought before him that Moses had to sit "from morning to evening"—probably from early dawn until the dusk of the evening twilight—hearing them. At eighty years of age, or more (ch. vii. 7), his physical strength was not equal to this exertion. Our physical powers have to be considered. No one is justified in overtaxing them unnecessarily. The body needs change of attitude and employment, air, gentle exercise, freedom from restraint, confinement, tension. No one could habitually sit at any one task for twelve hours continuously without its telling on his bodily frame and injuring his constitution. Again, the mental strain must have been injurious to him, and if not actually impairing his faculties, must have interfered with their due exercise and rendered him unfit to perform the delicate duties of a judge late in the day. Had necessity been laid upon him, had God appointed him to be the sole judge of the people, or had there actually been no one else among the Israelites competent to the performance of any part of the work, he would have been right in acting as he did, for health is not the first consideration; but this was not so. God had not spoken upon the point; and there was an abundance of men in the congregation, quite competent to perform minor judicial functions, as Jethro clearly perceived, and as he himself also saw when it was pointed out to him. Thus he was exhausting himself unnecessarily, a proceeding which cannot be justified.

II. THAT IT WAS ALSO UNWISE, AS UNDULY TAXING THE PATIENCE OF THE PEOPLE. One man could not keep pace with the number of constantly arising causes, which must have tended to accumulate, whence would arise a delay of justice. It was inconvenient enough to have to wait from the morning until the evening before obtaining a hearing ; but probably the case was not uncommon of a cause being put off to the next court-day, which, if the people were on the march, might be several days distant. The convenience of suitors is an important consideration in the administration of justice, which should be prompt as well as sure, to content men's natural sense of what is fitting.

III. THAT, FURTHER, IT TENDED TO CRAMP THE EXERCISE BY THE PEOPLE OF POWERS WHICH THEY POSSESSED, AND THE EMPLOYMENT OF WHICH WOULD HAVE ELEVATED THEM. There were in Israel and will always be in every community, "able men," well fitted to take part in the decision of causes. Such men will commonly be very numerous; and if they have no part in the administration of justice, a large section of the community will at once be dissatisfied with the slight passed upon them, and debarred from an employment which would have tended to their moral education and elevation. The jury system of modern states is a recognition of the fact, that judicial capacity is widely spread, and that society ought to provide a field for its exercise. It is important to utilise the powers possessed by all members of the community, both for their own contentation and for the general welfare of the community itself. The world is over-full of despots and monopolists, persons who desire to grasp as much power as possible, and are unwilling to share their office with others. We may acquit Moses of such selfishness; but we cannot acquit all those who follow in his footsteps. It would be well if persons in positions of authority nowadays sought generally to associate others in their work—to call out latent talent, exercise it, and so educate its possessors.

Ver. 21.—*The necessary qualifications of such as are to exercise the office of judges.*— Few positions in life are more important than that of the judge. Not only are the lives and liberties of individual citizens at his disposal, but the very existence of the State depends on him, since unless justice is in the main administered states fly to pieces. It has been said that the whole elaborate machinery of the British Constitution has been designed and arranged with the ultimate object of putting twelve honest men together into a jury box. Where the functions to be discharged are so important, it is of the utmost moment that qualifications should be laid down in theory, and strictly adhered to in practice. Jethro saw that judges ought to be—

I. MEN OF ABILITY. Ordinary, common-place powers are not enough.. " Non ex quovis ligno Mercurius fit." Something above the average is necessary. Jethro thought one man in ten among the Israelites might possess sufficient intelligence and discrimination to judge the lowest class of causes, those of the least account. This was a somewhat sanguine estimate. In modern communities, which boast of their general enlightenment, considerably less than one-tenth of the citizens have their names inscribed upon the jury lists. The standard of intelligence however varies in different ages and countries, so that no hard-and-fast line can be laid down on the subject. All that can be insisted upon is this—the judge should be a person recognised to possess ability for his office, *i.e.*, sagacity and practical discernment. If he has not these gifts, it is no use his possessing others, as learning, scholarship, artistic or scientific attainments. He will not be respected; no confidence will be felt in him; his decisions will carry no weight, and will injure rather than benefit the community.

2. MEN OF PIETY. " Provide out of all the people such as fear God," said Jethro. It is greatly to be feared that this qualification is in modern times but slightly regarded. How seldom do we hear it asked of any newly-appointed judge—Is he a religious man ? And yet unless God is feared, there can be no security that justice will be done even by the judge of the greatest possible intelligence. If a man be not God-fearing, he may allow prejudice, passion, even caprice to sway his judgments. He may gradually become like the "unjust judge," who "feared not God neither regarded man." Or, again, he may have to pronounce judgment in matters concerning religion, for such will often come before courts, and then what weight can he expect his decisions to

have? It is a wise and venerable custom which makes it incumbent on our "judges of assize" to preface the opening of their commission in each assize town by attendance at Divine service and hearing of God's word preached by a minister of the Gospel. It would be still better if those who nominate judges would follow Jethro's counsel, and take care in each instance to select for the office "such as fear God"—*i.e.*, sincerely religious persons. The reality of religion is preferable to the show of it; and the only security for righteous judgments is that the judge be himself a righteous man.

3. MEN OF TRUTH. There can be no real piety without truthfulness, so that this qualification is, in fact, included in the last. But there is a semblance of piety which is not over-scrupulous with regard to truth, or "pious frauds" would not have passed into a bye-word. Truth, the love of it, the honest desire to search it out, and make it manifest, is so essential a quality in a judge, that it deserves separate mention, and can never be dispensed with, whatever other qualifications a man may have. Let there be any suspicion of a man's truthfulness, and then, whatever reputation for piety may attach to him, he is not fitted to be a judge, and ought not to be selected for the judge's office.

4. MEN OF PROBITY, who would scorn to take a bribe. The "corrupt judge" is the opprobrium of debased nations, the disgrace of his calling, the destroyer of the state to which he belongs. In many ancient kingdoms corruption, when detected in a judge, was punished by instant execution. Where it has been regarded as venial and punished inadequately, as at Rome, society has rapidly deteriorated and a revolution has shortly supervened. We may congratulate ourselves that judges in our own country are not only incorrupt, but beyond suspicion, so far above taking a bribe that no one would dare to offer them one. In the East, on the contrary, according to the universal testimony of travellers, it is scarcely possible to find the office of judge exercised by any one who is not notoriously open to corrupt influence, who does not expect, and is not anxious to receive, bribes. Among the Jews, judicial corruption is first noticed among the sons of Samuel, who "turned aside after lucre, and *took bribes*, and perverted judgment" (1 Sam. viii. 3). In the decline of the nation, the evil grew and increased, and is frequently denounced by the prophets (Is. i. 23; Jer. v. 28; Ezek. xxii. 27; Micah iii. 11; vii. 3, etc.).

HOMILIES BY VARIOUS AUTHORS.

Vers. 13—27.—*The appointment of judges.* During the few days that Jethro was with Moses, he did the latter an essential service, and initiated nothing short of a revolution in the manner of conducting judicial business. Besides its immediate lessons (noted below), this incident of the appointment of judges is valuable as illustrating—1. The scope left in the arrangements of Israel for the independent action of the human mind. Various examples of this occur in the history—*e.g.*, the retention of Hobab as a guide in the wanderings (Num. x. 31), and the suggestion of the spies (Deut. i. 22). 2. The truth that in God's ways of dealing with Israel, existing capabilities were utilised to the utmost. We have seen this in regard to the miracles, and again in the conflict with Amalek; it is now to be noted in the formation of a polity. The same principle probably applies to what is said in ver. 16 of Moses making the people to "know the statutes of God and his laws." That Moses, in giving forth these statutes, acted under supernatural direction, and frequently by express instruction of God, is not to be denied; but it is equally certain that existing usages, embodying principles of right, were taken advantage of as far as they went. We cannot err in supposing that it is this same case-made law which, in its completed form, and under special Divine sanction, is embodied in the code of chs. xxi-xxiii. But neither in substance nor in form is this code, so various in its details, a direct Divine product. It grew up under Moses' hand in these decisions in the wilderness. Traditional materials were freely incorporated into it. 3. The assistance which a man of moderate gifts is often capable of rendering to another, greatly his superior. Jethro's was certainly a mind of no ordinary capacity; but we do this excellent man no injustice in speaking of his gifts as moderate in comparison with the splendid abilities of Moses. Yet his natural shrewdness and plain common-sense enabled him to detect a blunder in Moses' system of administration of which the lawgiver himself was apparently oblivious, and furnished him, moreover, with the suggestion of a remedy. The greatest minds are in this way often dependent on the humblest, and are, by the dependence, taught humility and respect for the gifts of others. There is no one who is not his neighbour's superior in *some* matter—none from whom his neighbour may not learn *something*. The college-bred man may learn from the rustic or mechanic, the merchant from his clerk, the statesman from the humblest official in his department, the doctor of divinity from the country minister, studious men generally, from those engaged in practical callings. Let no man, therefore, despise another. Jethro could teach Moses; and the plainest man, drawing on the stores with which experience has furnished him, need not despair of being of like service to those above him. It is for our own good that God binds us together in these relations of dependence, and we should be thankful that he does so. "The eye cannot say to the hand, I have no need of thee : nor, again, the head to the feet, I have no need of thee," etc. (1 Cor. xii. 14-31). Observe—

I. MOSES' ERROR (ver. 13). He took upon himself the whole burden of the congregation. He sat from morning till evening to hear their causes. We naturally wonder that the suggestion of appointing judges was left to come from Jethro—that so obvious an expedient for getting rid of the difficulty did not occur to Moses himself. It is astonishing, however, how wise a man may be in *great* things, and yet miss some little bit of sense which is right before his vision, and which is picked up at once by another and possibly a more ordinary mind. It is of Sir Isaac Newton the story is told, that being troubled by the visits of a cat and kitten, he fell on the expedient of making two holes in his study door to admit of their entrance and exit—a large hole for the cat, *and a small hole for the kitten !* Moses' error, we may be sure, did not arise from that which is a snare to so many in responsible positions—an exaggerated idea of his own importance. He would not fancy that everything must be managed by himself, because no one else was able to do it so well. But :—1. The burden which now pressed upon him had probably grown from small beginnings. It is proverbially easier to set a system in operation, than to get rid of it again, when it presses and becomes inconvenient. 2. Moses probably accepted the position of judge and arbiter, as inseparable from the peculiar relation in which he stood to the people. They naturally looked to him, God's delegate, and in some sense their spiritual father, as the proper person to hear their causes, and settle their disputes. He felt the burden, but submitted to it as inevitable. 3. It was a further difficulty in the situation that no code of laws had as yet been formed; he was *making the law* as well as deciding cases. This may have seemed a bar in the way of the appointment of deputies. 4. The method by which the reform could be accomplished was not obvious. Jethro's scheme exactly met the case; but it had not as yet been suggested. Even had it occurred to Moses, he might have shrunk from entertaining it. There is always a hesitancy felt in entering on reforms which necessitate a large recasting of the frame-work of society, which involve new and untried arrangements. Difficulties might have been anticipated in finding the requisite number of men, in imparting to them the requisite amount of instruction, in making the scheme popular among the people, etc. It is useful to observe that when the scheme was actually set on foot, these difficulties did not prove to be insuperable. Nor, when Jethro made his proposal, do the difficulties seem to have been much thought of. Moses saw the wisdom of the plan, and readily adopted it. We are often thus kept back from useful undertakings by the ghosts of our own fears.

II. JETHRO'S EXPOSTULATION (vers. 14—19). If Moses did not see the mistake he was committing, Jethro did. To his clearer vision, the evils of the system in vogue were abundantly apparent. He saw :—1. That Moses was taking upon himself a task to which his strength was quite unequal (ver. 18). 2. That, notwithstanding his exertions, the work was not being done. 3. That the time and energy which Moses was expending in these labours could be bestowed to infinitely better purpose (ver. 20). 4. Above all, that this expenditure of strength on subordinate tasks was unnecessary, seeing that there were men in the camp as capable as Moses himself of doing a large part of the work (ver. 21). On these grounds he based his expostulation. The lessons taught are of great importance. (1) The neglect of division of labour in Christian work leads to serious evils. The work is not overtaken, the strength of those engaged in it is greatly overtaxed, while energy is bestowed on inferior tasks which might be applied to better purpose. (2) The adoption of division of labour in Christian work secures obvious advantages. It relieves the responsible heads, expedites business and promotes order, secures that the work is better done, and utilises a great variety of talent which would otherwise remain unemployed. These are important considerations, and the application of them to hard wrought clergymen, and to others in responsible positions, is sufficiently obvious (see an essay by Dr. Caird, on "The co-operation of the laity in the government and work of the Church," in *Good Words* for 1863). Not a little work is heaped by congregations on ministers which could be far better done by persons among themselves, and the doing of which by laymen would leave the minister free in mind and heart for the discharge of his higher and proper duties.

III. THE PROPOSAL OF THE APPOINTMENT OF JUDGES (vers. 19—27). Jethro's scheme had every merit which a scheme of the kind could have. It relieved Moses, provided for the overtaking of the work, and secured that, while being overtaken, the work would be done with greater efficiency. It was a bold, comprehensive measure, yet withal perfectly workable. It would also have an important effect in welding the nation together. It is to be noted concerning it:—1. That it reserved to Moses various important duties (vers. 19, 20). He was still to be the teacher of the people in the ordinances and laws of God, and had the duty of trying and of deciding upon causes of special difficulty. This would fully occupy his powers, while his relation to the people, as God's vicegerent, would be better preserved by his retaining a position apart, and keeping himself from their petty strifes. 2. That special stress is laid upon the *character* of the men to be selected as judges (ver. 21). Ability is not overlooked, but peculiar importance is attached to their being men that fear God, love truth, and hate covetousness. Happy the country which has such judges! Jethro's insistance on these particulars shows him to have been a man of true piety, and one who had an eye to the true interests of the people, as well as to the good of Moses. 3. The scheme, before being adopted, was to be submitted for God's approval (ver. 23). This should be done with all our schemes. Jethro, having accomplished this useful bit of work, returned to his home in peace (ver. 27).—J. O.

Vers. 13—16.—*The Christian in Public Paths.* "Moses sat to judge the people: and the people," etc. (Ex. xviii. 13). Explain with accuracy the work of Moses. On such a text might be based a homily on the functions, work and bearing of a civil magistrate or judge. But it is better to give the subject a wider application, and to treat it under Christian lights.

I. THE FUNCTIONS OF A CHRISTIAN. Moses sat as a *prophet*, expounding the Divine will, as revealed to his exalted soul by the Spirit of God; and as a *judge*, deciding controversies. Indeed the two functions were blended; in giving legal decisions, he treated the suitors as intelligent and moral beings, assigning the principles on which they were based. These functions of Moses may suggest what should be those of a Christian in the public paths of life. 1. *To expound the mind and will of God:* i.e., his truth and his law. 2. *To promote peace:* i.e., in all the relations of life (Matt. v. 9).

II. THE MANNER OF THEIR DISCHARGE. 1. *With patience.* "From the morning unto the evening." 2. *In the spirit of brotherhood.* "The people stood by Moses." No airs of superiority. 3. *With diligence.* Moses went on with his work, though (1) *He had distinguished visitors.* Jethro might have been an excuse for a vacation or a short session. No! "on the morrow" he went on with duty, and worked as long as it was light. "Necessary business must always take the place of ceremonious attention. It is too great a compliment to our friends to prefer the enjoyment of their company before our duty to God." (2) *He had come to great honour.* Moses did not take his ease and throw the burdens upon others. "Noblesse oblige." It is the honour of angels to minister (Heb. i. 14; Matt. xx. 28). (3) *He had received great provocation.* (4) *Advancing in years.* To life's last hour Moses worked for the public good.—R.

Vers. 17—27.—*The Economy of Force.* "The thing that thou doest is not good," etc. Ex. xviii. 17, 18. In the error of Moses, and the amendment suggested by Jethro, are to be discovered most valuable lessons. This day in the life of Moses was a microcosm of all his days. His whole life was service. So with all true life. But in such a life mistakes are possible.   We inquire then what are the Divine conditions of a life of true ministry ?

I. CHARACTER.   The elements were laid down by Jethro as qualifications of the new judges.   Certain that Moses possessed them.   So must all who aim at usefulness (ver. 21).   1. *Ability.*   Strange that ability comes first ; but so it must be.   Piety without ability can adorn only obscurity.   Service and responsibility demand the man of power.   Ability may be natural ; but is also to be acquired.   Hence duty of hard work, especially in morning of life.   2. *Piety.*   Ability is the engine of the soul, the fear of God the helm.   Richard Cobden was wont to say :—" You have no security for a man who has no religious principle."   Said his colonel to Hedley Vicars, offering him in 1852 the adjutancy of his regiment :—" Vicars, you are the man I can best trust with responsibility."   3. *Truth.*   4. *Disinterestedness.*

II. ECONOMY, *i.e.,* of force and of resource (vers. 17, 18).   Remark :—1. *That the most earnest are likely to neglect it.*   It is not the hack but the thoroughbred that needs to be held in.   The energy of Moses led him into error.   So earnestness kills itself with excess of work.   2. *That there is necessity for economy.*   As with money, one must not spend 25s. a week, if one has only 20s. ; so there is a limitation as to *strength* (of every kind), *time,* and *opportunity.*   3. *That the economy is easy.*   The Christian worker should not attempt that which is *above, beside,* or *beneath* his power or vocation.   Nor *all* that is *on the level* of his ability.   4. *That the consequences will be abundant and rich.*   The result of division of labour in a factory ; so with spiritual enterprise, the effects will be the enrichment of the Church, and the largest service for the world.

III. CONCENTRATION.   The more we withdraw effort from that which is not within our own province, the more must we accumulate and concentrate energy upon that which is.—R.

Vers. 13—27.—*Good counsel well taken.*   I. ZEAL MAY OUTRUN DISCRETION. 1. Moses' strength was overtaxed, his spirit needlessly burdened.   2. There was delay for the people with its vexation and loss.   The most self-sacrificing love will not of itself make our methods the best and wisest.

II. WHAT IS NEEDFUL FOR THE GIVING OF ADVICE.   1. Affectionate interest and care.   The people's need and Moses' burden both weigh upon Jethro's spirit.   2. Wisdom.   A better way is clearly conceived, all the requirements of the case are grasped and met.   3. Honest plainness.   4. Piety.   He asked Moses to take his advice only so far as God will command him.

III. WHAT IS NEEDFUL FOR PROFITING BY GOOD COUNSEL.   1. Readiness to listen. There is on Moses' part no proud resenting of a stranger's interference.   The voice was heard as if it rose up within his own bosom.   2. Obedience to conviction.   He not only heard and assented, he went and did it.—U.

Vers. 13—26.—*Jethro's advice.*   In considering this passage it is desirable to form some distinct opinion as to the time of Jethro's visit to Moses.   *How comes this episode to be mentioned at all,* and what is its point of attachment to the main course of the history ?   Evidently it would not have been inserted unless as explaining how these rulers of thousands, hundreds, fifties and tens, had first been appointed.   The origin of this appointment is then seen to be traceable to Jethro's prudent and sagacious suggestions.   It has then to be further explained how Jethro happens to be in the camp at all. And so we have another illustration of how things which seem utterly disconnected from one another yet have a very real connection.   See Zipporah on the way from Midian to Egypt rebelling against the ordinance of the Lord ; and then look on all this orderly and careful provision for the administration of justice through the tribes of Israel.   What connection should there be between these ?   Yet one leads to the other.   As to the time of the visit, any exact determination is of course out of the question, but this much at least may be guessed that the visit was after the giving of the law.   What if it happened just about the time of Miriam's jealousy against Moses, and was in some measure the cause of it ? (Num. xii.)   Such a supposition too would better harmonise with the reference in ver. 16, when Moses represents himself as explaining the statutes of God and his laws.   May we not almost say that if this chapter were inserted somewhere in the earlier part of the book of Numbers, and from it we looked back on all the mass of legislation in Exodus and Leviticus, it would read with far greater force?

I. WE HAVE GOD'S PEOPLE PRESENTED TO US AS ABOUNDING IN OCCASIONS OF DISPUTE AMONG THEMSELVES. This appears as a certain consequence of that spirit of self-seeking so manifest and strong among them. The law from Sinai of course conflicted with many old and honoured traditions. That law had been given to secure in the first place a nation devoted to the service of God; and in the second place the mutual prosperity of all the members of that nation. If only every Israelite had obeyed these laws from the heart, and entered into the spirit of them, then the prosperity of all would have been ensured. But as a matter of fact most part of the Israelites wanted to conform to the laws just so far as suited their convenience and no further. Laws were to be interpreted very strictly when such interpretations were for their advantage, and very loosely when the contrary. The disputes, misunderstandings, and lawsuits of society are a great reproach, and ought to be a great humiliation. Think of all the machinery which is in daily operation through such a land as England to secure, as far as may be, the doing of right between man and man. And yet this machinery, expensive and elaborate as it is, works in a very unsatisfactory way; indeed that which is meant to work justice very often works injustice, and certainly very seldom ensures the exact attainment of right. Hence, however pleased we are to look on Jethro's suggestions here, and see them carried out with a measure of success, we feel that they must not be suffered to hide an end more desirable still. Law reformers cry out, and with ample cause, for the adoption of such means as will secure a cheap and speedy settlement of all disputes. But how much more would be gained if only there was a universal acceptance of the Gospel, with all its powers and principles! That Gospel puts into man a loving and unselfish heart and a spirit of brotherliness, which, if allowed fair play, would soon do away with litigation and all that leads to it. A world of Christians would be a simple-hearted, plain-living people, ever acting towards one another in truth, kindness, and goodwill. Cheap justice is good; but the new heavens and the new earth, wherein dwelleth righteousness, are much better.

II. WE SEE MOSES DOING HIS BEST, BY INDIVIDUAL EFFORT, TO RECONCILE AND SATISFY THESE DISPUTANTS. We get the impression of a man whose hands are full with his judicial work. When his own dear kinsfolk come in such affecting and pressing circumstances, he can only spare for them a brief interval; and a large part of that interval seems to have been occupied with religious exercises. With the morning light Moses settles down to what he must have found a weary and discouraging work. Many a perjury, many an impudent claim, many a reckless slander, many a pitiful story of oppression and extortion he would have to listen to. It is the daily work of judges and magistrates to deal with the seamy side of human nature, but then this is their business; they look for it, they get used to it, above all they are paid for it. Perhaps they would say, most of them, that it is no affair of theirs to ask too curiously whence all this disputing comes and how it is to be cured. They are there to administer laws and not to make them. But Moses was more than a judge. He had not only to settle these disputes by the way, but also to guide the disputers towards Canaan. We are perfectly certain, too, that the great bulk of those against whom justice compelled him to decide would become his enemies. Yet he struggled on, accepting the responsibility, and trying to get the laws of God for Israel more and more accepted among the people. He indeed sets us, in this matter, a noble example. The pressure which was upon him will never rest upon us, for all men sought him; but we also have our limited opportunity, larger alas! than we seek to use, of advancing the things that make for peace. There is so much to promote discord, so much to excite partisan spirit; there are so many to tear every rent wider, instead of putting in the little stitch in time that saves nine, that we may well ask for grace, gentleness, fidelity, and impartiality, in order to put in our intervening word when such a word may be possible and acceptable. The more we think of all that there is in this world acting, often alas! consciously and deliberately, to spite, separate, and irritate, the more let us determine to form part of a reuniting and cementing force.

III. NOTICE THE TIMELY PRESENCE AND COUNSEL OF JETHRO. Truly there is appearance here of something unaccountable in the dealings of God. Such a seemingly important matter as the judicial system of Israel owes its existence to the suggestion of an outsider. And yet it might have been thought that this was exactly one of the things which Jehovah would provide for by express enactments. When it is a matter of making the tabernacle, he is very particular as to measurements and materials, but when it is a matter of judging causes, he leaves it to be determined by the advice of an apparently casual visitant to the camp. There is nothing really strange in all this, if we remember that God only instructs us where we cannot make discoveries for ourselves. Revelation does not supersede, it rather assumes and requires the exercise of common sense and natural judgment. We find a somewhat parallel case to this in the New Testament when the deacons were appointed. Common sense told the apostles they were becoming burdened with work which did not properly belong to them, and only hindered them in the doing of work for which they were specially responsible; and so here the common sense of Jethro steps in to suggest to Moses a more excellent way. Why did not Moses think of it himself? The very fact that he did not shed a great deal of light on his character. His strength lay not in personal initiation, but in complete waiting and dependence on God. If God had commanded the institution of these rulers, he would very quickly have had the command in operation; but he never thought of proposing the plan himself. But when another proposes it, he can see at once that it is a wise, practicable, and necessary one. Moses is not to be blamed as wanting in sagacity in that he failed to see this remedy before. Great discoveries are simple enough when once they are made; and then everyone wonders they were not made long before.

IV. OBSERVE THE DETAILS OF JETHRO'S ADVICE. Not only does he suggest the obtaining of help from somewhere, but taking in the whole situation at a glance, he can suggest exactly the best thing to be done. Probably as a priest in Midian he had seen a great many disputings and helped to some extent in the settlement of them. We cannot but feel as we read through the details of the counsel, that whatever may be lacking in Jethro's formal standing, he acquits himself as one who is really and opportunely the messenger of God. He speaks as a good and true man ought to speak both for the relief of his kinsman and for the abiding good of the whole people. He judges that in Israel itself there are resources enough to meet the emergency, if only properly searched out and arranged. Given 600,000 men, surely among them there will be a fair proportion who have the qualities required. Notice that Jethro aims at a high standard (ver. 21); able men are wanted, and wherein does the ability consist? No doubt a certain acuteness and general power of mind was required, but the chief elements of the ability lay in those qualities which Jethro went on to specify. An efficient judge between man and man must be also one who fears God. The fear of man that bringeth a snare must not be allowed to enter his mind. He must measure things by Divine standards, ever asking what God would wish his judgments to be. He must be a man of truth, sparing no effort and avoiding no danger; in order to get at it he must try to keep his mind clear from prejudices. If he has fallen into any error he will promptly confess it, feeling that the interests of truth are more important than a reputation for consistency. And he must be free from covetousness. No suspicion of a bribe will cling to his judgments, nor will he be infected with that worldliness of spirit which looks to the property of men a great deal more than to the interest and comfort of their persons. But now the half-incredulous question cannot be kept out of the mind, "where shall such judges be found?" At all events let them be sought for. We cannot find perfect men; but we know the direction in which to seek. Probably, in the course of a long life, Jethro has discovered that men are both better and worse than he thought at first; and he is perfectly certain that men can be found to do all that is indispensably requisite for the present need. Moses was wearing himself out with duties which many in Israel were quite competent to perform; but who of them all could do the work which had been put specially into his hands?—Y.

Vers. 19.—"*The eye cannot say unto the hand, I have no need of thee.*" Men may make a channel for the stream, but they cannot make the stream. Water-power is a grand *natural* agency; but it is by means of *human* agency that it may be applied to the best advantage. So also in other matters; *power* comes from God; the way to use and economise power it is left for man to discover and to act upon. Consider here:—

I. THE DIVINE POWER. "God shall be with thee," said Jethro. The history shows how

God had been with him already, how he was with him all through his life. Especially we may notice—1. *His relation to Pharaoh.* The shepherd facing the king. Whence his boldness? He had shrunk beforehand at the mere prospect; when the hour came Pharaoh quailed before him. It was not Moses, it was the power which manifested itself through Moses, that humbled Pharaoh. Moses was but the visible rod in the outstretched hand of the invisible Jehovah. 2. *His relation to the people.* Harder to face a fickle multitude than to face an obstinate and powerful monarch. Here too the Divine power was manifested; the glory of Jehovah was, as it were, reflected from the face of his servant. It was the radiancy of the reflected glory which again and again cowed the rebels to submission. As with Jeremiah (Jer. i. 4—8), Zerubbabel (Zed. iv. 6), St. Paul (2 Cor. xii. 9, 10), so also with Moses; human weakness the more evidently testified to Divine power.

II. THE HUMAN COUNSEL. Notice:—1 *The need of it.* Men are so weak that they are soon unhinged by a great trust reposed in them. Their attention is so fixed upon the one thing, that other things are seen out of perspective. Moses was so filled with the consciousness of a Divine power working through him, that he failed at first to realise the fact that he was unequal to the friction necessitated by such a power. He realised the effect of the power in prospect more accurately than he could do after it possessed him (cf. ch. iv.). As the mediator between God and Israel, had it not been for Jethro's counsel, he must soon have been worn out through forgetting the necessities of his own nature. Lives are still wasted and shortened through a like oversight. The man who feels that he is the channel of Divine power is, for the time, so God-intoxicated, that it does not occur to him to share his responsibilities. He must be both head and hands in everything, and the head in consequence soon grows heavy, and the hands hang down. Under the force of inspiration, common-sense is in abeyance; all the more need for wise counsel from those who occupy a neutral stand-point. 2. *The wisdom of it.* Jethro saw that the great thing was not that Moses should do all the work, but that all the work should be done. The power to do it, was no doubt lodged with Moses (cf. water-power lodged with keeper of sluice gates). The work, however, might be best done by a distribution of the power through selected agents. Moses need not to be head *and* hands; he might choose other hands, making them responsible to himself as head. Moses showed his wisdom by accepting the wise counsels of Jethro; many men would have shown their folly by setting them aside as the suggestions of ignorance.

Concluding considerations. Inspiration is a grand thing; but it may be best utilised by common-sense. God's power enables for action; but that power is best applied when the counsels of Jethro are attended to. All men have not the same gifts; and those who have what seem to be the higher gifts, are apt to set too small a value upon advice given by those less gifted. Even the gift of faith, however, needs the gift of wisdom to direct it. Moses was able to do more than he otherwise could have done because he was wise enough to hearken to the voice of Jethro, his father-in-law.

G.

EXPOSITION.

Ver. 27.—DEPARTURE OF JETHRO. The time of Jethro's departure, and indeed of his entire visit, has been matter of controversy. Kurtz is of opinion that Jethro waited till the news of Israel's victory over Amalek reached him, before setting out from his own country. Hence he concludes, that " a whole month or more may easily have intervened between the victory over Amalek and the arrival of Jethro," whose arrival in that case " would not even fall into the very earliest period of the sojourn at Sinai, but after the promulgation of the first Sinaitic law." Those who identify Hobab

with Jethro find in Num. x. 29—32 a proof that at any rate Jethro prolonged his visit until after the law was given, and did not " depart to his own land " before the removal of the people from the wilderness of Sinai to that of Paran, " in the 20th day of the second month of the second year " (ib. ver. 11). The position, however, of ch. xviii., together with its contents—both what it says and what it omits—are conclusive against this view. Jethro started on his journey when he heard " that the Lord had brought Israel out of Egypt " (ver. 1), not when he heard that Israel

had been victorious over Amalek. His conversation with Moses (vers. 7—11) ranged
over the entire series of deliverances from the
night of the departure out of Egypt to the
Amalekite defeat, but contained no allusion to
the giving of the law. The occupation of
Moses on the day after his arrival (ver. 13)
is suitable to the quiet period which followed
the Amalekite defeat, but not to the exciting
time of the Sinaitic manifestations. It may
be added that the practice of inculcating
general principles on occasion of his particular
judgments, of which Moses speaks (ver. 16),
is suitable to the period anterior to the promulgation of the law, but not to that following it.

The argument from Num. x 29—32 fails
altogether, so soon as it is seen that Jethro and
Hobab are distinct persons, probably brothers,
sons of Reuel (or Raguel), and brothers-in-law
of Moses.

Ver. 27.—**Moses let his father-in-law
depart.** Literally, " dismissed him," " sent
him away." This single expression is quite
enough to prove that the Hobab, whom Moses
made strenuous efforts to keep with him after
Sinai was left, is not the Jethro whom he was
quite content to let go. **He went his way into
his own land.** He returned to Midian, probably
crossing the Elanitic gulf, which divided Midian
from the Sinaitic region. The exact time of
the departure is uncertain; but it was probably
before the main events related in ch. xix.

HOMILETICS.

Ver. 27.—*Jethro the model of a friendly adviser.* A man's friends often hesitate to
offer advice, from the fear of its being ill received. Jethro showed himself superior to
this weakness, and risked being rebuffed for officiousness, confident in his singleness
of purpose and honest intentions. He had all the qualities of a good adviser. He
was—1. SAGACIOUS. There can be no doubt that he rightly forecast the results, if
Moses had continued his unwise monopoly of the judicial office, or that he suggested a
prudent course in place of that whereof he disapproved. His reservation of a certain
judicial power to Moses (vers. 20—22) was especially wise, since had he not done so, it
is highly probable that his counsel would not have been followed;—2. SYMPATHETIC.
Kindness and warm feeling breathed in his warning words:—" Thou wilt surely wear
away, both thou and this people . . . for this thing is too heavy for thee; thou art
not able to perform it thyself alone." He feels for Moses; he feels for the people;
he has no thought for himself; he is solely anxious, and deeply anxious, to save others
from unnecessary suffering;—3. STRAIGHTFORWARD. He does not use periphrases, or
beat about the bush, but goes straight to his point, making his purpose clearly intelligible, and indeed unmistakable—" The thing that thou doest is not good "—" provide
out of the people able men." 4. WHOLLY DISINTERESTED. The advice which he
tenders can do him no good. He asks no employment, no place for himself. He
will not even participate in the general prosperity of Israel if good results follow the
adoption of his counsel; for he is not about to cast in his lot with the Israelites.
On the contrary, he is bent on withdrawing at once into his own country. Moses
will not find him that keen annoyance, an ever-present friend, who because his advice
has been taken once, regards himself as entitled to obtrude it whenever he pleases,
and to feel aggrieved if it is not in every case followed. If advisers generally acted
in the spirit of Jethro, there would be far less unwillingness than there is to ask
advice, and far more gratitude felt towards those who volunteer it.

HOMILIES BY VARIOUS AUTHORS.

Ver. 27. *Jethro's departure.* I. JETHRO DEPARTS AFTER A MOST SATISFACTORY VISIT.
That visit was made not perhaps without some anxiety and doubt as to the results, but
still under the clear dictation of duty. Therefore, it would have been satisfactory even
if less successful. Moses might, conceivably, have looked on Zipporah coldly and
received her reluctantly; but there would have remained to Jethro the priceless satisfaction that he had done the right thing. But Jethro, we have seen, had more even than
the satisfaction of a good conscience; he had been successful, and successful beyond all
that he could have anticipated when he set out. To a man of Jethro's disposition, that
would indeed be a joyous visit, which had proved so useful to Moses, to Zipporah, to
their children, to Israel, and may we not add, towards the glorifying of Jethro himself?
Keep ever in the path that is clearly right, and you have Jethro's experience to

encourage you in the expectation that it may also be the path of noble and joyous opportunities.

II. JETHRO DEPARTS, AND MOSES IS MADE TO FEEL, MORE THAN EVER, THAT JEHOVAH REMAINS. Very helpful are human counsel and sympathy, and especially when they come from old friends. There are no friends like old friends, and Jethro was a very old friend to Moses. But Jethro's abilities and opportunities as adviser extended only a little way. Like Moses we may all have our Jethros whom we may love, cherish and venerate ; for God distributes such men everywhere about the world to be, as it were, fellow-workers with him in giving stability and illumination to the perplexed. But we cannot keep them ; we may lose them at any moment ; and while it is great wisdom to listen to them, it would be great folly to put them in the place of God. Though Jethro was very decided in the counsels he gave, he knew equally when to stop. We may look at him as coming in here to teach us that what we can expect from the most competent and loving of human friends is but a trifle compared with the great tota of our needs. We are allowed to have but small expectations from the brother sinner, the brother mortal, the brother who is liable to ignorance and error, just as much as we are ourselves. When Jethro went away, Moses would feel himself all the more shut up to Jehovah. When the earthly is dumb, misleading, estranged, or dead, then the heavenly will speak in clear and loving accents to all who have ears to hear.

III. Jethro departs into his own land, for HE HAD DOUBTLESS PRESSING CLAIMS UPON HIM THERE. He was just the kind of man to make his presence, as long as he lived, a kind of necessity to his neighbours. He had come on a matter of urgency, not for his own pleasure or ease ; and we may imagine he went back as soon as he conveniently could to finish such affairs at home as had been left unfinished. Note, however, that in going back to his own land, and away from Moses, he did not therefore retire from the service of God and the reach of God's blessings. Jethro and Moses seemed to be going different ways ; but they only differed in external circumstances. Moses does not seem even to have asked Jethro to stay with him ; whereas we know that he pressed and urged Hobab. Perhaps he felt that he had no sufficient reason for asking Jethro, or that it would be of no use.—Y.

SECTION XIII.

ISRAEL AT SINAI.—PREPARATIONS FOR THE GIVING OF THE LAND.

EXPOSITION.

CHAPTER XIX.

Vers. 1—2. — THE JOURNEY TO MOUNT SINAI. From Rephidim in the Wady Feiran, where they had discomfited Amalek (ch. xvii. 8—13), the Israelites moved towards Sinai, probably by the two passes known as Wady Solaf and Wady-esh-Sheikh, which gradually converge and meet at the entrance to the plain of Er-Rahah. This plain is generally allowed to be "the Desert of Sinai." It is "two miles long, and half-a-mile broad" (Our Work in Palestine, p. 268), nearly flat, and dotted with tamarisk bushes. The mountains which enclose it have for the most part sloping sides, and form a sort of natural amphitheatre. The plain abuts at its south-eastern extremity on abrupt cliffs of granite rock rising from it nearly perpendicularly, and known as the Ras Sufsafeh. " That such a plain should exist at

all in front of such a cliff is," as Dean Stanley well remarks, " so remarkable a coincidence with the sacred narrative, as to furnish a strong internal argument, not merely of its identity with the scene, but of the scene itself having been described by an eye-witness " (Sinai and Palestine, pp. 42-3). All the surroundings are such as exactly suit the narrative. " The awful and lengthened approach, as to some natural sanctuary, would have been the fittest preparation for the coming scene. The low line of alluvial mounds at the foot of the cliff exactly answers to the ' bounds ' which were to keep the people off from ' touching the mount.' The plain itself is not broken and uneven and narrowly shut in, like almost all others in the range, but presents a long retiring sweep, against which the people could ' remove and stand afar off ' The cliff, rising like a huge altar, in front of the whole congregation, and visible against the sky in lonely grandeur from end to end of the whole plain, is the very image of the mount that might be touched,' and from which the voice of God might be heard far and wide over the plain below, widened at that point to its utmost extent by the confluence of all the contiguous valleys. Here, beyond all other parts of the peninsula, is the *adytum*, withdrawn as if in the end 'of the world,' from all the stir and confusion of earthly things" (*ib.* p. 43). As an eminent engineer has observed—"No spot in the world can be pointed out which combines in a more remarkable manner the conditions of a commanding height and of a plain in every part of which the sights and sounds described in Exodus would reach an assembled multitude of more than two million souls." Here then, we may well say, in the words used by the most recent of scientific explorers, "was the scene of the giving of the law. From Ras Sufsâfeh the law was proclaimed to the children of Israel, assembled in the plains of Er Rahah" (*Our Work in Palestine*, p. 268).

Ver. 1.—**In the third month.** The month Sivan, corresponding nearly with our June. **When the children of Israel were gone forth.** Rather, "after the children of Israel had gone forth," or "after the departure of the children of Israel out of the land of Egypt." Compare ch. xvi. 1, where the expression used is the same. **The same day.** Literally, "on that day"—which can only mean "on the day that the month began"—on the 1st of Sivan. **The wilderness of Sinai.** The plain Er-Rahah; as is now generally allowed, since the true character of the Wady Sebaiyeh has been shown by Dean Stanley (*Sinai and Palestine*, p. 76) and others.

Ver. 2.—**They were departed from Rephidim.** See the comment on ch. xvii. 1, and compare Num. xxxiii. 15. **There Israel encamped before the mountain.** The bulk of the tents were no doubt pitched in the plain, Er-Rahah; but this may not have sufficed, and some may have been located in the Wadyed-Deir, north-east of the Ras Sufsâfeh, and others in the Seil-Leja to the west. The Ras Sufsâfeh is visible from both these valleys.

HOMILETICS.

Vers. 1—2.—*Localities shaped to suit God's moral purposes.* It is scarcely possible to read the descriptions of the Sinaitic localities by modern travellers, who pointedly note their exact adaptation to the scenes transacted among them, without the feeling stealing upon us, that God, in the countless ages during which he was shaping and ordering the earth to be a fitting habitation for man was also arranging it in such sort as would best conduce to the exhibition upon it of those supernatural occurrences, which in his counsels were to constitute turning-points in the moral history of man. Take for instance Jerusalem: are we to suppose that the valleys were furrowed and the rocky platform upraised by the elements acting mechanically, as chance might direct, or not rather that God lovingly shaped, age after age, the mountain where he was about to set his name, and which was to be "the joy of the whole earth"? (Ps. xlviii. 2.) Rome again, with its seven hills: was not this remarkable formation brought into existence to constitute the site for that capital which was to be, first and last, the pivot of the world's secular history; for five hundred years the seat of an almost universal empire; for a thousand the western ecclesiastical centre; and having in the future possibilities which the wisest forecast can only dimly indicate, but which transcend those of any other existing city. And, if in these cases Providence contrived and shaped the geographic features with a view to the future history, must it not have been the same at Sinai? Must not that vast granite cluster have been upreared in the place it holds by a series of throes which shook all the regions of the east, *in order that* from it the law might be given in such a way as to impress men deeply? Must not the plain Er-Rahah have been washed by floods into its present level surface to furnish a convenient place from which the multitudinous host of Israel might at once see and hear? Must not the entire Sinaitic region have been so modelled, that here should be the *adytum*—here and here alone in the entire district, should be the natural "inmost sanctuary"—*penetrale*—"holy of holies"—the centre of attraction—the fit spot for supernatural events, on which the future of mankind was to hinge for fourteen centuries? To us it seems, that God did not so much select for his supernatural communications with man the fittest of existing localities, as design the localities themselves with a view to the communications, shaping them to suit his moral purposes.

HOMILIES BY VARIOUS AUTHORS.

Vers. 1, 2. *Arrival and encampment at Sinai.*—We come now to the consideration of what, next to the exodus, is the greatest event in Israel's history—the ratification at Sinai of the nation's covenant with God, preceded by the giving of the law. We cannot attach too great importance to these Divine acts. The covenant at Sinai placed Israel in a totally unique relation to Jehovah. It conferred on that people an honour the like of which no nation on earth ever had, or ever has since, enjoyed. It gave rise to an economy, the express design of which was to prepare the way for Christ—to shut men up under a conviction of the hopelessness of attaining righteousness by the law, to the faith that should afterwards be revealed (Gal. iii. 23). This covenant, as befitted the majesty of God, dealing with a sinful people, was to be ordained "in the hand of a mediator" (Gal. iii. 19). Moses, accordingly, is seen in these verses entering on his mediatorial functions. Once, a second, and a third time, in the course of this single chapter, he is seen ascending the mount, to meet with God (vers. 3, 8, 20); and once, a second, and a third time, he is sent back from its awful recesses with a message to the people. Vers. 1, 2 relate the arrival at Sinai.

I. THE NOTE OF TIME.—"In the third month," etc. (ver. 1). That is, about six weeks—forty or fifty days—after leaving Egypt. This was close on the date of Pentecost, afterwards traditionally observed as the anniversary of the giving of the law. It was probably with allusion to this fact that, in the new economy, the day of Pentecost was chosen for the gift of the Spirit to the Church (Acts ii.). Thus was fulfilled the prophecy—"Behold the days come, saith the Lord, that I will make a new covenant with the house of Israel, and with the house of Judah . . . I will put my law in their inward parts, and write it in their hearts" (Jer. xxxi. 31—33). "Sinai, then, was the Pentecost of the old dispensation. And, conversely, Pentecost is the Sinai of the new." (Gibson.)

II. THE PLACE OF ENCAMPMENT.—"The wilderness of Sinai . . . before the mount" (vers. 1, 2). A fitter theatre for the awful revelation about to be given could scarcely be imagined. The heart of the desert, it was—1. A place of *absolute solitude*. The people were absolutely alone with God—withdrawn from everything which could distract their thoughts from him and from his message. Owen observes—"When God deals with men by the law, he will let them see nothing but himself and their own consciences . . . For the most part, when the law is preached to sinners, they have innumerable diversions and reliefs at hand to shield them from its terror and efficacy. . . . They have other things to do than to attend to the voice of the law; at least, it is not yet necessary that they should so do. But when God will bring them to the mount, as he will here or hereafter, all these pretexts will vanish and disappear" (on Heb. xii. 18). For the thorough awakening of conscience, we must get a man *alone*—must, in some way or other, sever him from his ordinary surroundings. 2. A place of *great sublimity*. Travellers dwell with awe on its bare, desolate grandeur—on "the lengthened approach" to the mount, "as to some natural sanctuary." The mind, amidst such grandeur, is irresistibly drawn upwards. It is brought into the condition most fit for the reception of thoughts of the everlasting and sublime. How suitable was such a place for the promulgation of that moral law which Kant said affected him with such indescribable awe every time he thought of it! Every circumstance was present which could lend body, vastness, volume, impressiveness, and reduplicated sublimity to the terrors of the revelation. The "sound of the trumpet and the voice of words" would reverberate with strange power amid those rocky heights, and along the echoing valleys. The sternness of the environment was itself a commentary on the law's sanctities. 3. A place of *barrenness*. "It was a barren and fruitless desert, where there was little water or food, and, answerably thereunto, the law in a state of sin, would bring forth no fruit, nothing acceptable to God, nor useful to the souls of men." (Owen.) So entirely has the spirit of this scene—of this awful desert solitude—passed into the revelation connected with it, that the two can no longer be dissociated. Sinai, unconsciously to ourselves, acts upon us to this hour, in every contact of our minds with the truths of the law.

III. THE DESIGN OF THE STAY. Israel abode at Sinai for eleven months. During this period the nation enjoyed a season of rest, received the law, ratified its covenant with God, constructed a sanctuary, and was otherwise equipped and organised. It was a time of repose, of retired communion with God, of receptivity. Such times are very needful in the spiritual life. 1. *Needful for all.* The Christian toiler needs seasons of rest (Mark vi. 31). His truest rest will be found in communion with God and study of his will. By-and-by the call will come, summoning him to renewed activity— " Ye have dwelt long enough in this mount," etc. (Deut. i. 6). 2. *Specially needful in the stage of spiritual history immediately succeeding conversion.* Young converts will do well to ponder the example of Paul, who, after God had revealed his Son in him, and before entering on his work as an apostle, " went into Arabia," perhaps revisiting this very spot (Gal. i. 17). They are all the better for some such season of solitary communion with God as is represented by Israel's stay at Sinai. They need repose of mind. Like the Israelites, they have a covenant to ratify with God. Like the Israelites, they stand greatly in need of instruction. They need time for lengthened study of the Divine will. They need equipment and preparation for the trials they are afterwards to encounter. Their coming, it is true, is rather figured as a coming to Mount Sion, than as a coming to Mount Sinai (Heb. xii. 22); but none the less has Sinai important lessons which it will be for their interest not to overlook. The Christian who does not frequently in spirit visit Sinai will not readily understand his privileges at Sion. The following words of Dr. Candlish express important truth :—" Individually, by a separate process in each mind, a distinct spiritual change in every soul, God effects the rescue of his people. There cannot, therefore, be any general gathering together, in a literal sense, such as there was at Sinai. But practically, in a real though spiritual sense, every converted soul has to pass through an analogous spiritual crisis. It is a momentous crisis, as regards both the exodus and the pilgrimage ; the escape he has made and the way he has to go. It is, in fact, the settlement, once for all, of the terms upon which he is henceforth to be with his God as his Sovereign Lord. It is his being confronted and brought face to face with God, in a new state and character, as redeemed by his grace, and ready for his work." (" Fatherhood of God.")—J. O.

EXPOSITION.

Ver. 3—9.—The First Covenant between God and Israel. As Moses, having reached the foot of Sinai, was proceeding to ascend the mountain, where he looked to have special revelations from God, God called to him out of the mountain, and required a positive engagement on the part of the people, before he would condescend to enter into further direct relations with them. If, through gratitude for what had been done for them in the deliverance from Egypt, and since, they would solemnly engage to obey God and keep the covenant that he should make with them (verse 5), then a fresh revelation should be made, and fresh engagements entered into; but not otherwise. Moses communicated the message to the people through the elders, and received the solemn promise, which he carried back to God. " All that the Lord hath spoken we will do."

Ver. 3.—Moses went up unto God. From the time of his call Moses had known that Israel was to serve God upon Sinai (ch. iii. 12), and had regarded either one special peak, or the whole range as " the mount of God"—a

place dedicated and set apart to Jehovah. It was natural, therefore, that, so soon as he reached the near vicinity of the mount, he should ascend it. The Lord called to him out of the Mount. God often accepts the will for the deed, and spares his saints a needless toil. Here, as Moses was on his way, God anticipated him, and calling to him out of the mountain sent him back to the people with a message. The house of Jacob. This rare expression, familiar to no sacred writer but Isaiah, recalls the promises made to Jacob of a numerous seed, which should grow from a house to a nation (Gen. xxviii. 14; xxxv 11).

Ver. 4.—Ye have seen what I did unto the Egyptians. God prefaces his appeal to Israel with respect to the future, by reminding them of what he had done for them in the past. In the fewest possible words he recalls to their recollection the whole series of signs and wonders wrought in Egypt, from the turning of the water into blood to the destruction of Pharaoh's host in the Red Sea. These, he implies, ought to have taught them to trust him. I bare you on eagle's wings (compare Deut. xxxii. 11), where the metaphor is expanded at considerable length The strength and might of God's sustaining care, and its loving tenderness, are especially glanced at in the comparison. **Brought you unto myself.** "Brought you," *i.e.*, "to Sinai, the mount of God, where it pleases me especially to reveal myself to you."

Ver. 5.—**Now therefore.** Instead of asking the simple question—"Will ye promise to obey me and keep my covenant?"—God graciously entices the Israelites to their own advantage by a most loving promise. If they will agree to obey his voice, and accept and keep his covenant, then they shall be to him **a peculiar treasure** (*segullah*)—a precious possession to be esteemed highly and carefully guarded from all that might injure it. (Compare Ps. cxxxv. 4; and see also Is. xliii. 1—4.) And this preciousness they shall not share with others on equal terms, but enjoy exclusively — it shall be theirs **above all people.** No other nation on the earth shall hold the position which they shall hold, or be equally precious in God's sight. All the earth is his: and so all nations are his in a certain sense. But this shall not interfere with the special Israelite prerogative—they alone shall be his "peculiar people" (Deut. xiv. 2).

Ver. 6.—**Ye shall be unto me a kingdom of priests.** Or "a royalty of priests"—at once a royal and a priestly race—all of you at once both priests and kings. (So the LXX. render, βασίλειον ἱεράτευμα; the Targums of Onkelos and Jerusalem, "kings and priests;" that of Jonathan, "crowned kings and ministering priests.") They would be "kings," not only as "lords over death, the devil, hell, and all evil" (Luther), but also partly as having no earthly king set over them, but designed to live under a theocracy (1 Sam. xii. 12), and partly as intended to exercise lordship over the heathen. Their unfaithfulness and disobedience soon forfeited both privileges. They would be "priests," as entitled—each one of them—to draw near to God directly in prayer and praise, though not in sacrifice, and also as intermediaries between God and the heathen world, to whom they were to be examples, instructors, prophets. **And an holy nation.** A nation unlike other nations—a nation consecrated to God's service, outwardly marked as his by the symbol of circumcision, his (if they chose) inwardly by the purity and holiness whereto they could attain. **These are the words.** Much speaking was not needed. The question was a very simple one. Would they accept the covenant or no, upon the conditions offered? It was not likely that they would reject such gracious proposals.

Ver. 7.—**And Moses came.** Moses descended from the point of the mountain which he had reached, and summoned a meeting of the elders of the people. When they were come together, he reported to them *totidem verbis* the message which he had received from God. He is said to have laid the words "be-

fore *their faces*"—a Hebraism, meaning simply "before them."

Ver. 8.—**And all the people answered together.** It would seem that the elders submitted to the whole congregation the question propounded by Moses; or at any rate submitted it to a popular meeting, fairly representing the congregation. No doubt the exact purport of the question was made known by the usual means beforehand, and the assembly was summoned to declare, by acclamation, its assent or dissent. The result was a unanimous shout of approval:—"**All that the Lord hath spoken we will do**"—*i.e.*, "we will obey his voice indeed, and keep his covenant" (see ver. 5). In this way they accepted the covenant beforehand, not knowing what its exact provisions would be, but assured in their hearts that all would be right, just, and good; and anxious to secure the promised blessings (vers. 5, 6) for themselves and their posterity **Moses returned the words of the people unto the Lord**—*i.e.*, Moses was the mouthpiece both ways. He took the messages of God to the people, and carried back ("returned") their answer.

Vers. 9.—**I came unto thee in a thick cloud.** Literally, "in the thickness of a cloud." God must always veil himself when he speaks with man, for man could not bear "the brightness of his presence." If he takes a human form that form is a veil; if he appears in a burning bush, the very fire is a shroud. On the present occasion it was the more needful that he should cover himself up, as he was about to draw near to the whole congregation, among whom were many who were impure and impenitent. It was necessary, in order that all might be convinced of the Divine mission of Moses, for all to be so near as to hear him speak out of the cloud; but sinners cannot abide the near presence of God, unless he is carefully hidden away from them. Probably, the cloud out of which he now spoke was that which had accompanied the Israelites out of Egypt, and directed their march (ch. xiii. 21, 22), though this is not distinctly stated. **That the people may believe thee for ever.** In "the people" are included their descendants; and they are to "believe Moses *for ever*, because the law is in some sense of eternal obligation on all men" (Matt. v. 18). **And Moses told the words of the people unto the Lord.** It is not easy to assign a reason for the repetition of this clause from vers. 8, in almost identical terms. There were no fresh "words of the people" to report. We can only say that such seemingly needless repetitions are *in the manner* of archaic writers, who seem to intend in this way to emphasise a fact. The acceptance of the covenant by the people beforehand, completed by Moses reporting it to God, is the necessary basis of all that follows—the required preliminary to the giving of any covenant at all.

HOMILETICS.

Vers. 5, 6.—*God's promises to such as keep his covenant.* Three things are here specially worthy of consideration:—1. The nature of the promises; 2. The grounds on which they may be believed and trusted; and 3. The conditions attached to them.

I. THE NATURE OF THE PROMISES. God's promises to Israel are threefold—they shall be kings; they shall be priests; they shall be his peculiar treasure.—(*a*) *Kings.* Most men are slaves—servants of Satan, servants of sin, slaves to their evil passions, slaves to opinion, abject slaves to those among their fellow-men on whom they depend for daily bread, or for favour and advancement. The glorious liberty of the children of God shakes off all these yokes. Man, awakened to his true relations with God, at once asserts himself, realises his dignity, feels that he need "call no man, master." He himself is supreme over himself; his conscience is his law, not the will of another. His life, his acts, his words, are under his own control. Within this sphere he is "king," directing and ruling his conduct according to his own views of what is right and fitting; and this kingship is mostly followed by another. Let a man once show himself a true, brave, upright, independent person, and he will soon have subjects enough. The weak place themselves under his protection, the timid under his guidance. He will have a *clientèle*, which will continually grow so long as he remains on earth, and in Heaven he will be a "king" too. The "faithful and true servant" has "authority over ten cities." He "reigns with Christ for ever and ever" (Rev. xx. 6; xxii. 5). (*b*) *Priests.* A priest is one who is consecrated to God, who has free and ready access to him without an intermediary at all times and seasons, and who acts as an intermediary between God and others. As circumcision consecrated the Israelite, so baptism consecrates the Christian. He receives "an unction from the Holy One" (1 John i. 20), and is thenceforth a "priest to God," bound to his service, brought near to him, entitled to "go boldly to the throne of grace," to offer up his own prayers and intercessions, nay—even to "enter into the holiest" (Heb. x. 19). He is further not only entitled, but bound to act as intermediary between God and those who do not know God; to teach them; convert them, if he can; intercede for them; under certain circumstances, to baptise them. (*c*) *His peculiar treasure.* The world despises God's servants, sets little store by them, regards them as poor weak creatures, whom it may ill-use at its pleasure. But God holds each servant dear, sets a high value on him, regards him as precious. "They shall be mine, saith the Lord of hosts, in that day when I make up my *jewels*" (Mal. iii. 17). Each saint is a jewel in the crown of the Lord Christ, and is estimated accordingly. A king would as soon lose one of his crown jewels as Christ one of those for whom he shed his precious blood. He has "bought them at a price;" they are his; and the value which he sets on them no man can know. They are to him "more precious than rubies."

II. THE GROUNDS ON WHICH THE PROMISES MAY BE BELIEVED AND TRUSTED. As we have found of men in the past, so we look to find of them in the future. God bade the Israelites look back, and consider what he had already done for them—whether in the past he had proved himself faithful and true—whether he had supported and sustained them, "borne them up on eagle's wings," protected them, delivered them from dangers. If this were so, could they not trust him for the future? Would they not believe the promises which he now held out to them? Would they not regard them as certain of accomplishment? The Israelites appear to have believed; and shall not Christians do the like? Have not above three thousand years tested God's faithfulness, since he thus spoke to Israel? In the whole long course of these millennia has he ever been proved unfaithful? Assuredly not. All that he promises, and more than all he promises, does he perform for the sons of men. Never does he disappoint them; never does he fail to make good his word. Each promise of God therefore may be trusted implicitly. "God is not a man that he should lie, or the son of man that he should repent." He is true, and therefore must will to do as he has said; he is omnipotent, and therefore must be able to do as he wills.

III. THE CONDITIONS ON WHICH THE PROMISES ARE GIVEN. "If ye will obey my voice indeed, and keep my covenant." The precious promises of God to man are conditional upon (*a*) his general obedience; (*b*) his observance of a certain formal covenant. The obedience must be "an obedience *indeed*"—*i.e.*, an obedience from the heart, sincere, loving, complete, so far as human frailty permits—not partial, not grudging, not outward only. The covenant must be kept in all its essentials. To the Jew, circumcision was necessary, after which he had to make offerings, to attend certain festivals year by year, to pay tithes, and to observe numerous minute regulations with regard to "cleanness" and "uncleanness." The Christian covenant has but two essential rites, Baptism and the Lord's Supper. Even these are only "*generally* necessary to salvation." Still, if we look for covenanted mercies and claim them, we must take care to be within the covenant. We must inquire dispassionately, what the terms are upon which Christ receives us into covenant with him, and not take upon ourselves a dispensing power, absolving us from all such obligations. Christ rejected from the marriage-feast the man who had not on a wedding-garment. No one who neglects either of the two solemn and simple ordinances which alone Christ has ordained in his Church can be sure that he will not in the last day be rejected.

HOMILIES BY VARIOUS AUTHORS.

Vers. 3—10.—*The covenant proposed.* A characteristic difference is to be observed between the covenant made at Sinai and that formerly established with Abraham. In both, there is a wonderful act of Divine condescension. In both, God as well as man comes under engagements, ratified by outward formalities. But there is a difference in the design. In Abraham's case, the covenant was obviously intended as an aid to faith, an expedient for strengthening confidence in the Divine word. It is God who, in condescension to man's weakness, binds *himself* to be faithful to his word. At Sinai, on the other hand, it is the people who bind themselves to be faithful to God. They take the oath of allegiance to their invisible king. They pledge themselves to be obedient. God, on his side, appears as the promiser. He will make this nation a peculiar treasure unto himself, a kingdom of priests, etc. The present passage deals with preliminaries.

I. The Divine proposals (vers. 3—7). A covenant, from its nature, is an act of freedom. Prior to the formation of *this* covenant, it was obviously necessary that Jehovah should approach the people, should state his terms to them, and should require them to declare whether they approved of these terms, and were willing to assent to them. This is what is here done. Observe:—1. *The initiative in the covenant was taken by Jehovah.* This was inevitable. "The characteristic thing about such 'covenants' with God lies here, that the engagement must originate on the side of God himself, springing out of his free favour with a view to ratify some spontaneous promise on his part. Man can exact no terms from Heaven. No creature dare stipulate for conditions with his Creator. It is when the Most High, out of his own mere mercy, volunteers to bind himself by a promise for the future, and having done so, stoops still further to give a pledge for the execution of that promise, that what may fairly be deemed a 'covenant' is established" (Dr. Dykes). 2. *The people are reminded of past gracious dealings of God with them* (ver. 4). God reminds them, to begin with, of how he had taken them from Egypt, and had borne them on eagle's wings, and had brought them to this desert place unto himself. "Eagle's wings" signify that his help had been strong, sustaining, protecting. In Egypt, at the Red Sea, in the wilderness, they had experienced this help, and had found it all sufficient. The resources of the infinite had been placed at their disposal. The special point, however, is, that all this which had been done for them was the fruit of free, unmerited favour; of a grace which imposed no conditions, and had as yet asked for no return. This was an important point to be reminded of on the eve of a revelation of law. These past actings of God testified that his relation to Israel was fundamentally a gracious one. Law might veil grace, but it could not cancel or annul it. Like primitive rock, underlying whatever strata might subsequently be reared upon it, this gracious relation must abide. With a relation of this kind to fall back upon, the Israelite need not despair, even when he felt that his law condemned him. It was a pledge to him that, not only amidst daily error and shortcoming, but even after grievous falls—falls like David's—mercy would receive the man of contrite spirit (Ps. li.). Thus far, we are quite in the element of the Gospel. Salvation precedes obedience. Obedience follows, a result of the free acceptance of the obligations which redemption imposes on us. 3. *The condition of the fulfilment of promise is that the people obey God's voice, and keep his covenant* (ver. 5). On no other terms could God consent to be *their* God, and on no other terms would he consent to have them for *his* people. Grace *precedes* law, grace *accompanies* law, grace *passes beyond* law; nevertheless, grace must *conserve* law (Rom. iii. 31). God can propose to man no terms of favour, which do not include the need for an obedient will. He does not do so under the Gospel any more than he did under the law (cf. Matt. vii. 21; Rom. ii. 6, 7; vi.; 1 Cor. vii. 19; 1 John ii. 4, etc.). "It is exclusively Christ's righteousness which is of grace imputed to us. Yet this has to be *appropriated in an upright heart*" (Martensen). When God took Israel out of Egypt, it was implied and intended that the redeemed people should "obey his voice." The covenant but made explicit an *implicit* obligation. 4. *The promises themselves are of the grandest possible description* (vers. 5, 6). (1) Israel would be to God "a peculiar treasure." Out of all the nations of the earth—for all the earth was his—Jehovah had chosen this one, to reveal himself to it, to give it laws and judgments, and to dwell in its midst as its king, benefactor, and defender (cf. Deut. iv. 33—37). What an honour was this! And yet how inferior to the spiritual privileges of believers in Christ, who enjoy a nearness to God, an interest in his love, a special place in his regard, of which, not the earth only, but the universe, affords no other example. (2) Israel would be to God "a kingdom of priests." There is implied in this, on the one hand, royalty, dignity, rule; on the other, special consecration to God's service, the privilege of acceptable approach to him, and an intercessory and mediatorial function in relation to other nations. This promise also, has its higher counterpart in the privileges of Christians, who are "a chosen generation, a royal priesthood, an holy nation, a peculiar people" (1 Pet. ii. 9). Grace in the soul is a kingly, a dignifying, an ennobling principle. It confers true royalty of character. And in the future form of his kingdom, God, we may be sure, has royal places for all his royal children (Luke xix. 17, 19; Rev. i. 6; ii. 26; iii. 21). And believers are a "priesthood." Not, indeed, in the old sense of having to offer atoning sacrifices, but priests in virtue of special consecration, of right of near approach to God, and of their calling "to offer up spiritual sacrifices, acceptable to God by Jesus Christ" (1 Pet. ii. 5), and to intercede for the world (1 Tim. ii. 1). (3) Israel would be to God "an holy nation." This is involved in their calling to be priests. God being holy, those who are about him—who serve him—who worship him, or who stand in any near relation to him—must be holy also. "Be ye holy, for I am holy" (1 Pet. i. 16). This requirement of holiness is unchangeable. Believers have in them the *principle* of holiness, and are engaged in "perfecting holiness in the fear of God" (2 Cor. vii. 1). Holiness is that essential qualification, "without which no man shall see the Lord" (Heb. xii. 14). 5. *The promise contains a hint of the catholicity of God's design in the calling of Israel.* "For all the earth is mine" (ver. 5). Israel was called with a view to the ultimate benefit of the world. It was but the "first-born" of many sons whom God would lead to glory.

II. THE PEOPLE'S RESPONSE (vers. 7—10). They willingly took upon themselves the obligations indicated in the words, "Now, therefore, if ye will obey my voice indeed, and keep my covenant;" etc. (verse 5). They said at once "all that the Lord hath spoken we will do." There is a certain nobleness in this reply—a temporary rising of these long-enslaved minds to something like the dignity of their high calling as sons of God. Yet—1. It was a reply given *without much knowledge of the law*. They apprehended but little of its breadth, and of the spirituality of its requirements, else they would not have engaged so readily to do all that it enjoined. One design in placing Israel under law was just that they might *grow* in this knowledge of the breadth of the commandment, and so might have developed in them the consciousness of sin (Rom. vii. 7—25). 2. It was a reply given *without much knowledge of themselves.* The people do not seem to have doubted their ability to keep God's word. They thought, like many more, that they had but to *try*, in order to do. Accordingly, a second design in placing them under law was to convince them of their mistake—to discover to them their spiritual inability. There is no way of convincing men of their inability to keep the law of God like setting them to try (Rom. vii.). 3. It was a reply given, as respects the mass of the people, *without heart-conversion*. It was the outcome of a burst of enthusiasm, of an excited state of feeling. There was not the true "heart" in them to do what God commanded (Deut. v. 29). Hence their speedy apostasy (ch. xxxii.) The test of true conversion is perseverance (Heb. iii. 14; I John ii. 19). Moses, having received the reply of the people, returned it to God, who, on hearing it, declared his purpose of coming in a thick cloud, and of speaking with Moses in the audience of all the people (cf. verse 19). The design was "that the people may hear when I speak with thee, and believe thee for ever" (verse 9).—J. O.

Ver. 5.—"*My covenant.*" It may be proper at this stage to indicate briefly the nature of the constitution under which Israel was placed at Sinai, directing attention to some of the resemblances and contrasts between it and the new and better covenant which has since superseded it. The nature of the old covenant, though set in a very clear light in the writings of St. Paul, does not seem to be well understood. Sometimes it is too much assimilated to the New Testament covenant: sometimes it is viewed as totally diverse from it. The truth is, the covenant may be looked at from a number of very different points of view, and according as it is thus regarded, it will present itself under very different aspects. It was a covenant of law; yet under it Israel enjoyed many privileges which more properly belong to a state of grace. We should, *e.g.*, greatly misconceive its nature, if, looking only to the tender, almost caressing words of this text, we did not also take into account the manifestations of terror amidst which the law was given from Sinai (verses 16—20), with such other facts as the planting of the stones on Mount Ebal (Deut. xxvii. 1—9; Josh. viii. 30—35), and the recital of the blessings and curses (Deut. xxvii. 11—26). But we should do the covenant equal injustice if we looked only to the *latter* class of facts, and did not observe the *former*. That Israel's standing under the law was modified by grace is shown: 1. From the fact of grace preceding law; 2. From the employment of a mediator; 3. From the "blood of sprinkling" at the ratification of the covenant (ch. xxiv.); 4. From the propitiatory arrangements subsequently introduced; 5. From the revealed scope and design of the economy; 6. From the actual facts of Israel's history. Keeping in view this double aspect of the covenant of Sinai—that on its inner side it was one of grace, on its outer side one of law—we have to consider its relations to the covenant of the Gospel.

I. THE COVENANTS ARE, IN CERTAIN OBVIOUS RESPECTS, STRIKINGLY CONTRASTED. The contrasts in question arise from the particularistic character, the defective spirituality, and the pædagogic design, of the older covenant. That which has succeeded it is more inward and spiritual in its nature; is universal in its scope; and is made primarily with individuals. Special contrasts are these: 1. The older covenant is more *preceptive* in its character than the later one. "Tutors and governors" (Gal. iv. 2). 2. It is more concerned with *outward rites and ceremonies* (Heb. ix. 10). 3. It relies more on *penalty and reward* as motives. 4. The blessings promised are largely *temporal*. In the new covenant, temporal promises hold a very subordinate place. They are overshadowed by spiritual ones.

II. THERE ARE ELEMENTS OF CONTRAST EVEN IN THE RESEMBLANCES BETWEEN THE TWO COVENANTS. The covenants of the law and of the Gospel are alike—1. In *requiring that the people of God shall be "an holy people."* But the holiness of Israel was made to consist largely in the observance of outward distinctions. It was largely ceremonial. The holiness of the new covenant is purely spiritual. 2. In *requiring obedience as the condition of fulfilment of promise.* But (1) under the law, life and blessing were attached to obedience in the way of *legal reward.* The rubric was: "Do this, and thou shalt live" (Rom. x. 5). Under the Gospel, this element is wholly eliminated. The law having done its work in showing that "by the deeds of the law there shall no flesh be justified in (God's) sight" (Rom. iii. 20), the bestowal of reward is taken from this ground, and placed explicitly on that of grace. All we receive is for the sake of Christ—a fruit of *his* righteousness. (2) The law, while requiring obedience, did not raise the point of man's ability to render that obedience. But power to render obedience is itself one of the blessings of the new covenant, which thus goes deeper, and includes vastly more than the older one. (3) In general, the Gospel, while agreeing with the law in aiming at forming a people unto righteousness, takes up the individual at a riper stage in his religious development. It assumes that the law has done its work in him—has convinced him of sin, and of his inability to attain to life through legal efforts. It supposes him to be aware of his guilt and danger as a sinner. In this condition—broken and humbled by the action of the law upon his conscience—it meets him with the tidings of redemption, and of life and blessing (including spiritual renewal) coming to him on the ground of "the righteousness of faith" (cf. Acts xiii. 38, 39); 3. *The privileges of the older covenant foreshadowed those of the new* (1 Pet. ii. 9). But the contrast is great here also. See above.

III. These contrasts all depend upon a fundamental contrast. The deepest contrast between the two covenants is to be sought for in the view which each takes of the direction in which the individual (formerly the nation) is to look for acceptance and happiness—for "life." 1. The *law*. The law appears in the covenant with Sinai in its original, unqualified severity, as, on the one hand, awarding life to the obedient, and on the other, denouncing penalties against the breakers of even the least of its commandments (Gal. iii. 10—13). Doubtless, but for daily pardon of daily offences, the Israelite, under so strict a constitution, would have been totally unable to maintain his footing. These offences, however, appear as so many breaches of the covenant bond, which, in strictness, was the keeping of the whole law. A right apprehension of God's design in placing Israel under this constitution will do away with any appearance of harshness in the arrangement, as if God were purposely mocking the weakness of the people by setting them to work out a problem—the attainment of righteousness—in that way incapable of solution. The moral task given to Israel among the nations was, indeed, to aim at the realisation of righteousness, of righteousness as prescribed by the law. But God's design in this was not, certainly, to make the salvation of any Israelite depend on the fulfilment of impossible conditions, but, primarily, to conduct the seeker after righteousness by the path of honest moral endeavour, to a consciousness of his *inability* to keep the law, and so to awaken in him the feeling of the need of a better righteousness than the law could give him—to drive him back, in short, from law to faith, from a state of satisfaction with himself to a feeling of his need of redemption—of redemption at once from the guilt of past transgressions, and from the discord in his own nature. The law had thus an end beyond itself. It was a schoolmaster to lead to Christ. The later Jews totally misconceived its nature when they clung to it with unbending tenacity as the sole instrument of justification (Rom. x. 1—4). 2. The *Gospel*. In this is revealed "the righteousness of faith"—the righteousness which is "unto all and upon all them that believe." This is the only righteousness which can make the sinner truly just before God" (Rom. iii. 21—27). But the law is not thereby made void. It remains, as before, the standard of duty—the norm of holy practice. The design of the Gospel is not to abolish it, but to establish it more firmly than ever (Rom. iii. 31). Faith includes the obedient will. The end of redemption is holiness.

IV. The Israelite, while bound to God by a covenant of law, yet enjoyed many benefits of the state of grace. The better part of the Israelites were perfectly aware that had God been strict to mark iniquities, they could not stand before him (Ps. cxxx. 3); that their own law would have condemned them. But they knew, too, that there was forgiveness with God, that he might be feared (ver. 4). Piously availing himself of the expiatory rites provided for the covering of his sin, the godly Jew had confidence towards God. Many in the nation grasped the truth that an obedient will is, in God's sight, the matter of chief importance, and that, where this is found, much else will be forgiven—that he that feareth God, and worketh righteousness, is accepted with him (Acts x. 35), notwithstanding the special imperfections which may mark his daily life. This was practically to rise from the standpoint of the law, to that of the righteousness of faith. It enabled those who had attained to it, though under the law, to cherish a delight in spiritual righteousness, and even to find joy in the law itself, as the outward expression of that righteousness. It was not, however, the complete joy of salvation. The law still hovered above the consciousness of the Israelite with its unfulfilled demand; and he had not the means of perfectly pacifying his conscience in relation to it. While in those in whom the law had wrought its work most effectually, there was a deep feeling of sin, a painful consciousness of frustration in efforts after the highest goodness, which day by day wrung from them such cries as that of St. Paul—"O wretched man," etc. (Rom. vii. 24). Here, again, the Gospel reveals itself as the termination of the law of Moses (Rom. x. 4).—J. O.

Ver. 3—6.—*God's first message to the people at Sinai.* The cloud going on before the people from Rephidim, brings them at last to what by pre-eminence is called the mount. *The* mount, not because it was higher, but because there the burning bush appeared, and there the people were to serve God. Moses goes up to the mount, probably to the very spot where a while ago he had seen the burning bush and received his great commission to Pharaoh. From this scene he had been travelling in a circle, and had now come whence he had started, but not as many travellers in a circle do, returning poor and profitless as they went. Here he is, treading once again the hallowed mountain side; the people whom he has brought are below; God, he knows, is near, for he has just had most gracious experience of him in Rephidim; and now he waits for further revelations and commands. A great deal Moses has to listen to in Sinai from Jehovah; and therefore it is very interesting to notice the words with which Jehovah begins. Consider—

I. THE TERMS BY WHICH GOD INDICATES HIS PEOPLE. "The house of Jacob"—"the children of Israel." Thus Jehovah was ever sending the thoughts of his people far back into the past, and making them feel its important and glorious connection with the present. The house of Jacob was the house of him who had known many changes of circumstances, many disappointments and trials. It was the house of one who, born in Canaan, spent some of the best of his time at a distance with Laban, and died at last in Egypt. If he, the great ancestor, had thus been a man of change, what wonder that trying changes came upon the posterity! Then they were also the children of Israel. This was the name Divinely given; and if Israel forgets its purport and the privilege involved, Jehovah himself assuredly did not. Significant names, that would otherwise get hidden in the past, God takes special care to preserve.

II. THE WAY IN WHICH GOD DESCRIBES HIS RECENT DEALINGS. To the Israelites all had been very confused, tedious, and trying, in spite of all the miraculous exemptions, escapes, and provisions they had enjoyed. They had not very well known what was being done with them. But now, in the compass of a sweeping verse, the whole course of affairs is presented as one rapid and decisive action. As a bird might snatch its offspring out of captivity and bear it far on high to some safe shelter, so Jehovah has done with Israel. He puts before them, as in a vision, these three things to be considered—1. The liberation. 2. The consequent journey. 3. The destination. And these three things he describes in a peculiar way. 1. *The liberation* he indicates by this signification, "what I did unto the Egyptians." He wished the people here to ponder the extent and significance of his terrible dealings in Egypt. The Israelites had gazed on a succession of varied and penetrating calamities coming on the Egyptians. But Jehovah wishes the observers to mark that these things were of his doing. Jehovah's actions are not to be buried in oblivion when once they are past, because they are terrible actions. It is just because they are the terrible acts of a holy and just God that they are to be remembered. There was in them nothing of a tyrant's caprice; they were not wild gusts of power to be ashamed of in calmer moments. There had been due prediction and preparation; there was an orderly, gradual, impressive, instructive mounting to a climax: and if any of the people were inclined to forget the doer in the deeds, the liberator in the liberation, here is a warning that things must not be so thought on. God is ever devising to make us look at events in their connection and continuity. The plagues of Egypt were only the preliminary overturning to carry on the greater plan of God. Egypt had fast hold of Israel; wherefore Israel's God smote Egypt so that he might free his own people and bring them to himself. 2. *The journey* Jehovah indicates by a peculiarly beautiful and inspiring figure. "I bare you on eagles' wings." This was an appropriate figure for people dwelling in the wilderness. Moses had, doubtless, seen many eagles in his shepherd experiences; and the Israelites would become familiar with them during their wanderings. Thus the eagle's ways would be known; and after this word of Jehovah Moses would study them more and more, and one result of such observation we find in Deut. xxxii. 11. When men exalt themselves as the eagle, and set their nests among the stars, God can bring them down; but when *he* puts on the eagle's wings, it is to exalt himself into a place which shall be one of perfect safety for his people. One imagines the eaglet thus lying on the parent's wing. It may wriggle about uneasily, wondering at the speed with which it is taken, the shaking it has to undergo and the unfamiliar scenes through which it is passing. But these struggles count for little; they are natural enough, but they do not hinder the eagle in its progress. Patiently, calmly, strongly, it rises towards its secure destination. These unfamiliar scenes are by-and-by to be the frequent path of the now struggling, bewildered eaglet; in due time its own wings will appear in them—

> Sailing with supreme dominion
> Through the azure deep of air

Paul himself, dazed and shaken to the very depths of his being on his first dealings with Jesus, had known what it was to be borne on eagle's wings, and he lived to render a little of the same sort of ministry to the perplexed and desponding Timothy. The Israelites had been struggling and unbelieving, as at the Red Sea, at Marah, at the time when the manna was given, and at Rephidim; but in spite of all these, the strong eagle wings of God had borne them onward. Our struggles are but a trifle, if only God has us really in charge. Let us think ever of the eagle wings rather than the ignorant offspring carried thereon. 3. *The destination.* "I brought you unto myself." Just as the eagle brings its young to a place where without distraction or fear of interruption it can attend to their nourishment and growth. How beautifully God thus turns away the thoughts of his people from the desolation of the visible scene! True it was a wilderness; emphasis is laid upon this in vers. 1, 2; but if we are brought to God, this is more than all that may be barren and cheerless in mere circumstances. The place which men do not care about and where they would not come of their own accord, is the place where God reveals himself gloriously and graciously to his own. Israel will now do well to consider, not what carnal comforts they lack, but what dangers they have escaped, and what Divine possessions they are in the way to acquire. To be brought to God in the fullest sense of the word, and to lie comfortably under his protection and nurture, what a great matter! (Rom. viii. 38, 39).

III. So much, then, for what Jehovah has done in the past, and now he turns to the future, making A LARGE PROMISE DEPENDENT ON THE FULFILLING OF STRICT CONDITIONS. He had to bring the people to himself on eagle's wings, because they themselves were helpless to achieve the deliverance and security they needed. And now the time has come for *response from them.* He has brought them to himself, that being with him they may become his, fully and acceptably. They are put into external conditions such as make it possible for them to obey; therefore Jehovah has a right, and does right, to ask them for obedience. He who speaks about Jacob and Israel, cannot but also speak of the ancient covenant, with respect to which the children of Israel must labour earnestly to fulfil their part. God has already made certain requirements from the people, such as the passover regulations and those concerning the manna. But now his requirements are to flow forth in a great continuing stream. He will go on asking, as if asking were never to be at an end; and therefore it is well to start with a solemn preparatory word. As to *the promise itself,* we notice that it is a promise to a nation—to a whole people. As we see in the next chapter, the conditions are to be achieved by individual obedience: God comes to the individual with his commandments, and says, "Thou." But the promise is for the nation. It is a promise, too, which seems worded for appreciation in the future rather than in the present, or if in the present, only by a few who had been prepared to understand it. Perhaps it may be most fittingly described as a promise to be the stimulus and stay of truly patriotic hearts. Wherever there is a man who glories in the race from which he sprang and the land where he was born, there is one who may be expected to understand the force of an appeal like this. No nation could really be more to God than another nation, unless it were a better one. Israel had been made free from Egypt that it might then rise into all the fulness of what a nation ought to be; and therefore God sets these great possibilities before the people. All the earth, he said, was his. He had proved his complete control over one much esteemed tract of territory by the confusions and calamities he had brought into Pharaoh's domains; and there was no nation among men that he could not treat in the same fashion. But, if only men will submit, he can make to himself a peculiar people, testifying to his power, not from among humiliations consequent on despising him, but from the heights of glory and blessedness to which ne lifts those who obey him. He mingles in one glorious expression the thought of all those blessings which come from the union of true religion and right government. A kingdom of priests is one where harmony and right dealing will be found running through all relations, because each member is continually serving God with the great, loving, acceptable sacrifice of his own life. God is not really king in any society of men, unless each member of that society is fully a priest towards him.—Y.

Vers. 1—6.—*The Lord and his people.* I. WHO THE PEOPLE OF GOD ARE. 1. The children of the promise, "the house of Jacob," etc., the household of faith. 2. They who have experienced deliverance and known God's love: "Ye have seen what I did," etc. The law the picture of the Gospel: those only can enter into the covenant of obedience who have known that God has chosen and blessed them. "We love him because he first loved us."
II. WHAT THE LORD ASKS OF THEM. 1. True obedience: not a profession, but a life. 2. To keep his covenant: to understand his will, and make that will their law. The whole end of both law and gospel is missed if the life is not laid hold of, if the man is not brought to wear again the image of him who created him.
III. THE GLORY GOD WILL GIVE THEM IN THE EARTH. 1. They will be God's best beloved—a peculiar treasure unto him "above all people." Note the true position of God's people. It is not that God cares for them only. He cares for all: "all the earth is mine." They are the choicest of his earthly treasures. 2. They are to be "a kingdom of priests." They will minister to the nations in the things of God—leading them into his presence, teaching them his will. 3. They will be "a holy nation," a consecrated people. The Spirit's anointing will rest upon them. 4. This threefold glory the portion of God's people to-day: the knowledge that God has chosen us; our priestly service among our brethren; the unction from on high.—U.

Vers. 1—15.—*Covenant before law.* "Now, therefore, if ye will obey," etc.—Ex. xix. 5, 6. This subject might well be introduced by:—1. Showing how exactly the topography of Sinai (*i.e.*, the plain of Er Rahah, Ras Sufsâfeh, and Jebel Musa) agrees with the sacred history. [For material of description see "The Desert of the Exodus."] 2. How suitable mountains were to constitute the scenery of Divine manifestation. 3. An analysis of this section—(1) God and Moses; (2) Moses with the people; (3) God and Moses again; (4) Once more Moses with the people. In this preparation for the law, we shall see the Gospel. The Gospel antedated law (see Gal. iii.). Here we have several evangelical principles:—
I. NO COVENANT, NO LIVING OBEDIENCE. Here may be discussed and illustrated the whole question whether God's grace precedes our obedient living unto him, or *vice versâ*.
II. NO OVERTURE FROM GOD, NO COVENANT. The initiative is ever with God (vers. 3, 4). To illustrate:—Suppose the words had run this way: "Ye know what *ye* did in Egypt, how ye sought me, if haply ye might find me; how all the way through the desert ye have followed hard after me, if peradventure ye might see my face, and hear my voice in this mountain." Not one word would have been true. God ever first seeks man, not man God.
III. NO REDEMPTIVE ACTION, NO OVERTURE POSSIBLE. God's appeal is ever strengthened by his deeds. In the case of Israel, there had been the paschal lamb, the passing over, the passage of the Red Sea, and the constitution of a Church. Thereafter covenant, and anon law! Show the analogies in Christian times—the atonement, pardon, adoption, inclusion in the Church, the establishment of covenantal relations, the coming under the Christian rule of life.
IV. NO CONCURRENCE, NO RESULT (ver. 5). "*If*," etc. 1. In all God's dealing with us *he has respect to our liberty.* 2. The condition here is a *believing obedience.* The Hebrew word for "obey" seems to carry pregnantly within it all these meanings— hearing, listening, heeding, trusting, acting according to what we hear and believe. It might be well to show that practically in Christian life the believing man is the obedient, and *vice versâ*. 3. *And keeping the covenant.* Bring out the sentinel idea in the "keeping," and then show that we keep the covenant: (1) By complying with the conditions on our side. (2) By jealously guarding the conditions on God's side against the tamperings of error.

V. WITH CONCURRENCE, THE MOST BLESSED RESULTS. They who believe and keep the covenant become:—1. *The private and peculiar treasure of the King of kings.* Amongst earthly potentates there is a distinction between the treasures which they hold in their public capacity and those which are their own private property. When a king abdicates, he leaves behind him the public treasure, but carries with him his own. In an analogous sense we become the priceless jewels of the King of kings, though "all the earth is his" (same Hebrew word in Mal. iii. 17). 2. *A kingly priesthood* (ver. 6). "A royalty of priests," *i.e.*, every king a priest, and every priest a king. Here we have —(1) The royalty of religion. Religion the most powerful factor in life. Illustrate the monarchy of religion—*e.g.*, St. Paul on board the ship. (2) The priesthood of religion. Priestcraft is vile; priesthood a benediction. The priest receives from God for man; offers for man to God, *e.g.*, the priesthood Aaronic, that of the Lord Jesus, that of Israel for the nations, that of the Christian believer. 3. *Separate.* Negatively, from the world, but also positively unto God. "A holy nation."—R.

EXPOSITION.

Vers. 10—15.—THE PREPARATION OF THE PEOPLE AND OF THE MOUNTAIN FOR THE MANIFESTATION OF GOD UPON IT. The people having accepted God's terms, the time had come for the revelation in all its fulness of the covenant which God designed to make with them. This, it was essential, they should perceive and know to come from God, and not to be the invention of Moses. God, therefore, was about to manifest himself. But ere he could do this with safety, it was requisite that certain preparations should be made. Before man can be fit to approach God, he needs to be sanctified. The essential sanctification is internal; but, as internal purity and holiness cannot be produced at a given moment, Moses was ordered to require its outward symbol, external bodily cleanliness, by ablution and the washing of clothes, as a preliminary to God's descent upon the mountain (vers. 10, 13). It would be generally understood that this external purity was symbolical only, and needed to be accompanied by internal cleanliness. Further, since even the purest of men is impure in God's sight, and since there would be many in the congregation who had attempted no internal cleansing, it was necessary to provide that they should not draw too near, so as to intrude on the holy ground or on God's presence. Moses was therefore required to have a fence erected round the mountain, between it and the people, and to proclaim the penalty of death against all who should pass it and touch the mount (vers. 12, 13). In executing these orders, Moses gave an additional charge to the heads of families, that they should purify themselves by an act of abstinence which he specified (ver. 15)

Ver. 10.—**Go unto the people.** Moses had withdrawn himself from the people to report their words to God (vers. 8, 9). He was now commanded to return to them. **Sanctify them.** Or "purify them." Purification in Egypt was partly by washing, partly by shaving the hair, either from the head only, or from the entire body (Herod. ii. 37), partly perhaps by other rites. The Israelites seem ordinarily to have purified themselves by washing only. **To-day and to-morrow.** The fourth and fifth of Sivan, according to the Jewish tradition, the Decalogue having been given upon the sixth. The requirement of a two-days' preparation marked the extreme sanctity of the occasion. **Let them wash their clothes.** Compare Lev. xv. 5. Rich people could "change their garments" on a sacred occasion (Gen. xxxv. 2); the poorer sort, having no change, could only wash them.

Ver. 11.—**The Lord will come down.** Jehovah is regarded as dwelling in the heaven above, not exclusively (Ps. cxxxix. 7–10), but especially; and therefore, when he appears on earth, he "comes down" (Gen. xi. 5—7; xviii. 21; Ex. iii. 8; etc.). **In the sight of all the people.** That a visible manifestation of the Divine presence is intended appears, unmistakably, from verses 16 and 18.

Ver. 12.—**Thou shalt set bounds.** The erection of a fence or barrier, between the camp and the mountain—not necessarily all round the mountain—seems to be meant. This barrier may have run along the line of low alluvial mounds at the foot of the cliff of Ras Sufsâfeh, mentioned by Dean Stanley (*Sinai and Palestine*, p. 43), but cannot have been identical with them, since it was an artificial fence. **That ye go not up into the mount.** Curiosity might have tempted some to ascend the mount, if it had not been positively forbidden under the penalty of death; carelessness might have brought many into contact with it, since the cliff rises abruptly from the plain. Unless the fence had been made, cattle would, naturally, have grazed along its base. To impress the Israelites with a due sense of the awful majesty of God, and the sacredness of everything material that it brought into close relations with him, the mount itself was declared holy—none but Moses and Aaron might go up into it; none might touch it; even the stray beast that approached it must suffer death for its unwitting offence (ver. 13). **Whosoever toucheth the mount.** The mountain may be "touched" from the plain—it rises so abruptly. **Shall be surely put to death.** A terrible punishment, and one which, to modern ideas, seems excessive. But it was only by terrible threats, and in some cases by terrible punishments (2 Sam. vi. 7), that the Israelites could be taught reverence. A profound reverence lies at the root of all true religious feeling; and for the education of the world, it was requisite, in the early ages, to inculcate the necessity of this frame of mind in some very marked and striking way.

Ver. 13.—**There shall not an hand touch it.** Rather, "there shall not an hand touch *him*." The transgressor shall not be seized and apprehended, for that would involve the repetition of the offence by his arrester, who must overpass the "bounds" set by Moses, in order to make the arrest. Instead of seizing him, they were to kill him with stones or arrows from within the "bounds," and the same was to be done, if any stray beast approached the mountain. **When the trumpet soundeth long, they shall come up to the mount.** By translating the same Hebrew phrase differently here and in verse 12, the A. V. avoids the difficulty which most commentators see in this passage. According to the apparent construction, the people are first told that they may, on no account, ascend the mountain (ver. 12), and

then that they may do so, so soon as the trumpet sounds long (ver. 13). But they do not ascend at that time (ver. 19), nor are they allowed to do so—on the contrary, Moses is charged anew to prevent it (ver. 21-25); nor indeed do *the people* ever ascend, but only Moses, Aaron, Nadab, Abihu, and the seventy elders (ch. xxiv. 1, 9). What, then, is the permission here given? When we scrutinise the passage closely, we observe that the pronoun "they" is in the Hebrew, *emphatic*, and, therefore, unlikely to refer to "the people" of ver. 12. To whom then does it refer? Not, certainly, to "the Elders" of ver. 7, which would be too remote an antecedent, but to those chosen persons who are in the writer's mind, whom God was about to allow to ascend. Even these were not allowed to go up until summoned by the prolonged blast of the trumpet.

Ver. 14.—In obedience to the commands which he had received (ver. 10), Moses returned to the camp at the foot of Sinai, and issued the order that the people were to purify themselves and wash their garments during that day and the next, and be ready for a great solemnity on the third day. He must also, at the same time, have given directions for the construction of the fence, which was to hedge in the people (ver. 12), and which he speaks of as constructed in ver. 23.

Ver. 15.—**Come not at your wives.** Compare 1 Sam. xxi. 4, 5; 1 Cor. vii. 5. A similar obligation lay on the Egyptian priests (Porphyr. *De Abstin.* iv. 7); and the idea which underlies it was widespread in the ancient world (See Herod. i. 198; Hesiod. *Op. et Di.* 733-4; Tibul. *Carm.* ii. 1; ll. 11, 12.) The subject is well treated, from a Christian point of view, by Pope Gregory the First, in his answers to S. Augustine's questions (Bede, *Hist. Eccl.* ii.).

HOMILETICS.

Vers. 10—15. *The awfulness of God's presence, and the preparation needed ere we approach him.* I. THE AWFULNESS OF GOD'S PRESENCE. The presence of God is awful, even to those holy angels who are without spot or stain of sin, having done the holy will of their Maker from their creation. But to sinful man it is far more awful. No man "can see God's face, and live" (Ex. xxxiii. 20). Jacob was mistaken when he said, "I have seen God face to face, and my life is preserved" (Gen. xxxii. 30). He had really wrestled with an angel (Hos. xii. 4). When Moses requested to see the Almighty's glory, he was told, "Thou shalt see my back parts; but my face shall not be seen" (Ex. xxxiii. 23). "No man has seen God at any time," says St. John the Evangelist (John i. 18). But, even apart from sight, there is in the very sense of the presence of God an awful terribleness. "I am troubled at his presence," said Job; "when I consider, I am afraid of him" (ch. xxiii. 15). "Truly the Lord is in this place," said Jacob, "and I knew it not. *How dreadful* is this place!" (Gen. xxviii. 16, 17). God is at all times everywhere; but he veils himself, he practically withdraws himself; and, though he is where we are, we do not see him, or perceive him (Job xxiii. 8, 9). But, let him reveal his presence, and at once all tremble before it. "Mine eye seeth him," says Job again, "wherefore I abhor myself, and repent in dust and ashes" (ch. xlii. 5, 6) "When I heard," says Habakkuk, "my belly trembled, my lips quivered at the voice;

rottenness entered into my bones, and I trembled in myself" (ch. iii. 16). In part, no doubt, weakness trembles before strength, littleness before greatness, finiteness before infinity; but, mainly, it is sinfulness that quakes and shrinks before perfect holiness, corruption that shivers before incorruption, rottenness before absolute purity.

II. THE PREPARATION NEEDED ERE WE APPROACH HIM. Only the "pure in heart" can "see God." In all our approaches to him, we must seek first to be made fit for propinquity by separation from sin. Moses was bidden to "sanctify the people" (ver. 10), which he could only do outwardly. This true sanctification, the true purification, was heart-felt repentance, deep contrition, and the earnest resolve to forsake sin, and henceforth live righteously. This preparation each man had to make for himself. It was in vain that he should wash himself seven times, or seven times seven, in vain that he should purify his garments, and keep himself free from material pollutions of every sort and kind—something more was needed—he required to be purified in heart and soul. And so it is with Christians—with all men universally. God must be approached with humility—not in the spirit of the Pharisee; with reverence—head bowed down, and voice hushed to a low tone, and heart full of the fear of his holiness; with a pure mind—that is, with a mind averse from sin, and resolved henceforth to do righteously. The publican's approach was better than the pharisee's. Let men "smite upon their breast," let them be deeply convinced of sin, and own themselves sinners; let them implore the blotting out of their sins, and the cleansing of their entire nature; let them heartily resolve to sin no more, but walk in newness of life, and there is no contact which they need dread, no nearness of approach from which they need shrink. We are not, indeed, to hope in this life for that vision of God, or for that degree of communion, which our souls desire. "Now we see through a glass darkly—now we know in part." The full vision of God, full access to him, complete communion, is reserved for the next world, where it will form our perfect bliss and consummation.

HOMILIES BY VARIOUS AUTHORS.

Vers. 10—25.—" *The mount that might be touched, and that burned with fire* " (Heb. xii. 18). It is interesting to observe that, with the latter part of this chapter, we enter on an entirely new phase in the history of God's revelation of himself to Israel. Terror enough there has been in the previous portions of the book—terror and " a mighty hand "—awful manifestations of God's power and holiness; but towards Israel there has been displayed only benignity and fatherly affection. Their wants have been ungrudgingly supplied; even their murmurings, as we have seen, did not elicit from God more than a passing reproof. But now that Jehovah takes his awful seat on Sinai, and proceeds to give forth his law, he clothes himself, even towards Israel, with a majesty and terror which strike the people with dismay. The fact is obviously one of deep significance, requiring, as it will repay, our close attention. What, meanwhile, we have to note is, that God did not reveal himself in law and terror till he had given the people many practical evidences of his love for them, and so had won their confidence. Without this, the terrors of Sinai could scarcely have been borne by them.

I. THE PREPARATION (vers. 10—16). The revelation at Sinai was distinctively a revelation of the Divine holiness. From this fact, rightly apprehended, we may deduce the necessity for the preparations and precautions referred to in the text. The design of the lawgiving was to bring to light, and impress on men's minds, that holiness and justice which are essential parts of God's character, and which underlie all his dealings with them, even when most veiled by tenderness and grace. The time had come which God judged best for such a revelation being made. Made it *had* to be at *some* point or other in the history of the Divine dealings with men; and no time was so suitable for it as this of the constitution of the covenant with Israel. The instructions issued to the people accord with this design, and have as their end the impressing of their minds with a deep sense of the holiness of the Being into whose presence they are approaching, and of their own *unholiness* and unfitness to draw near to him. Holiness is—1. *Absolute moral purity and perfection.* It is sanctity of character. It implies, whether in God or man, the steadfast bent of the will towards all that is good and true and just and pure. In God, it is an inflexible determination to uphold at all costs the interests

EXODUS.

of righteousness and truth.   It is an intensity of nature, a *fire* of zeal or jealousy, directed to the maintenance of these interests.   Hence the requirement that in preparation for their meeting with him at the mount, the people should " sanctify " themselves for two whole days (ver. 10).   The sanctification enjoined was mainly external —the washing of clothes, etc.; but this, in itself a symbol of the need of heart purity, was doubtless to be attended with mental and spiritual preparations. Holiness is to be studied by us in all our approaches to God.   The unholy will not be spurned by God, if they come to him in penitence, relying on his grace in Christ; but his end in receiving them is that he may make them holy, and holiness is the condition of subsequent fellowship (Rom. vi. ; 2 Cor. v. 15 ; Eph. i. 4; vi. 25—27; 1 Thess. iv. 3 ; Titus ii. 11—15; Heb. xii. 14; 1 John i. 6, 7). 2. *The principle which guards the Divine honour.*   Thus Martensen defines it— " Holiness is the principle that guards the eternal distinction between Creator and creature, between God and man, in the union effected between them : it preserves the Divine dignity and majesty from being infringed upon."   Hence the command to Moses to set bounds to the mountain, that the people might be kept back (vers. 12, 13).   So stringently was this to be enforced, that if a man, or even a beast, should touch the mountain, the trespasser was to be put to death.   The statement—"When the trumpet soundeth long, they shall come up to the mount " (ver. 13), is probably to be read in the light of ver. 17.   The lesson taught is that of reverential awe of God.   Even when we have the fullest confidence in approaching God as a Father, we ought not to allow ourselves to forget the infinite distance which still exists between him and us.   Our service is to be " with reverence and godly fear " (Heb. xii. 28).

II. GOD'S DESCENT ON SINAI (vers. 16—19).   God's descent on Mount Sinai was in fire (ver. 18), and with great terribleness.   The scene, as described in these verses, is sufficiently awful.   The adjuncts of the descent were—1. A thick cloud upon the mount. 2. Thunders and lightnings.   3. The voice of a trumpet exceeding loud.   4. A fire " burning unto the midst of heaven " (Deut. iv. 11).   5. Smoke as of a furnace—the result of the action of the fire.   6. The mountain quaking.   This awfulness and terror are the more remarkable when we remember—(1) That what we have here is not God the Judge, arraigning before him trembling and convicted sinners, to pronounce on them sentence of doom ; but a God of grace, summoning to his presence a people whom he loves, and has redeemed, and has just declared to be to him a peculiar treasure, above all people.   (2) That the design of this manifestation is to give to Israel a law which shall be the bond of a covenant between him and them, and by which it is intended that they shall order their lives.   The facts to be explained are—(1) That the phenomena alluded to are all of an alarming nature, and (2) That most of them have a symbolical significance, which enhances the impression of terror.   The fire, *e.g.*, is the symbol of holiness.   The thick cloud suggests mystery.   It tells also of how God must veil his glory from man, if man is not to be consumed by it.   The smoke speaks of wrath (Deut. xxix. 20).   To the question thus raised, Why all this awfulness and terror ? the following answers may be made :—1. *Law is the revelation of God's holiness.*   It is the expression of the demand of holiness.   This is the one thing it has to do, to declare what *are* the requirements of holiness, and to enunciate these requirements in the form of commands to be obeyed.   But in order that law may serve its ends, it must be given in its proper character *as* law with all the adjuncts of authority and majesty which rightfully belong to it, and without dilution or weakening of any kind.   Time enough, after the law has been given, and the constitution is firmly settled on its bases, to say how grace is to deal with such as fall short of the standard of its requirements.   And, as formerly remarked, a revelation of law, at some period or other in the history of God's dealings with mankind, was plainly necessary—(1) That the full requirements of God's holiness should be made known.   Nothing was to be gained by the establishment of a constitution in which the requirements of holiness should be glozed over, veiled, treated as non-existent, kept out of view.   Sooner or later they must be brought to light. The relations of God with men could never be placed upon a satisfactory footing, till the fullest recognition had been accorded to them.   If the breach between heaven and earth is to be healed—healed thoroughly—it is not to be by ignoring the claims of holiness, but by recognising them to the utmost, and then " devising means " whereby, in consistency with these claims, God's " banished " may still not be " expelled from

him" (2 Sam. xiv. 14). The choice of *this* time for making the revelation was connected with God's whole design in the calling of Israel. (2) That men might have the
knowledge of sin. The law must be made known that men may understand the
number and extent of their transgressions. The lawgiving at Sinai, therefore, marks a
distinct stage in the progress of God's revelations. The design was to give Israel just
impressions of what the law really was—this law which they were binding themselves
to keep—to force upon them the conviction of its great awfulness and sanctity. Fitly,
therefore, was it promulgated with every circumstance which could arouse the torpid
conscience, and give impressiveness and force to the revelation. 2. *Most of those to
whom the law was given, while outwardly the people of God, and about to take on them
the obligations of a solemn covenant, were really unregenerate.* This circumstance,
which lay in *the truth* of their relation to God as distinguished from mere profession,
was fitly signified by the manner in which the law was given. The law shows by its
form that it was not made for a righteous man (1 Tim. i. 9). 3. *For the sin which the
law brought to light, no proper expiation was as yet provided.* Typical atonements might
indeed be offered; but not till the great propitiator came could the guilt be actually
removed. God's forgivenesses, under this first covenant, were not remission proper, but
*praeter*mission (Rom. iii. 25). Christ came "for the redemption of the transgressions
that were under the first testament" (Heb. ix. 15), which, therefore, were standing over
unexpiated. This fact, that the law had claims against the sinner, no proper means of
discharging which as yet existed, had also its recognition in the manner in which the
law was promulgated. 4. *The law, in the peculiar way in which it entered into
the Sinaitic covenant, was not a saving and blessing power, but, on the contrary, could
only condemn.* The law, as it entered into the covenant with Israel, could neither
justify nor sanctify. It concluded all under sin, and left them there. It proved itself
unequal even to the lower task of restraining outward corruptions. Its curb was ineffectual to keep sin in check. It could give commandments written on stone, but had
no power to write them on the fleshly tables of the heart (cf. 2 Cor. iii.).

III. THE RENEWED WARNING (vers. 19—25). God, probably by a voice audible to
the whole congregation (cf. ver. 6), called Moses to the top of the mount. No sooner,
however, had he ascended than he was sent back again to renew the warning to the
people to keep strictly within their bounds. The reason given was—" Lest they break
through unto the Lord to gaze, and many of them perish . . . . lest the Lord
break forth upon them" (vers. 21, 22). The passage teaches, 1. That the heart is
naturally disobedient. Even under these most solemn circumstances the Israelites could
hardly be restrained. The very prohibition was a provocative to their self-will to
transgress the boundary. To gratify this impulse they were disposed to risk the consequences. Had the danger not been very real, Moses would not have been sent back
so promptly as he was. Cf. what Paul says on the law—" I had not known sin but by the
law," etc. (Rom. vii. 7—14). 2. That temerity in Divine things exposes the transgressor to
severe punishment. Cf. the men of Bethshemesh and the ark (1 Sam. vi. 19), Uzzah,
Uzziah, etc. 3. That it is hard even for good men to credit the extent of the rebellious-
ness of the human heart. Moses thought it extremely unlikely that the people would do
what God told him they were just on the point of doing. He relied upon his " bounds,"
and on the strict charges he had given them to keep them back (ver. 23). Alas! it was
soon to be discovered that even stronger bounds than his would not restrain them. One
design of the economy of law was to demonstrate the futility of every attempt to restrain
wickedness by the system of mere " bounds." What is needed is not " bounds," but
renewal. 4. God's near presence is perilous to the sinner.—J. O.

Vers. 9—25.—*The manifestation of God's glory at Sinai.* I. THE PURPOSE OF THIS
MANIFESTATION. God made this purpose known beforehand; and it was that the people
who saw and heard these dreadful phenomena might believe Moses for ever, might permanently acknowledge his authority as a messenger and representative of God. When
Moses was at Sinai before and then entrusted with a Divine message to Israel, he urged
it as one of his difficulties that Israel would not believe him. " They will say, the Lord
hath not appeared unto thee" (ch. iv. 1). Now without appeal in any way from Moses,
Jehovah provides a sublime demonstration of his presence, which he expressly mentions
as being intended to establish the position of Moses. Testimony must always be chosen

corresponding with the character and circumstances of those to whom it is presented. There is a time when it will do to change the rod into a serpent; and so there is a time when the same people before whom this was done must be confronted with all the terrors of Sinai. It was a great defect on the part of the people that they had no adequate sense—it may almost be said they had no sense at all—of the holiness of God. Upon the slightest interference with their self-indulgent desires, they broke out into reproach, almost into rebellion. Therefore, in the very midst of gracious and unfailing providences, they must be made to feel that it is a fearful thing as well as a happy thing to fall into the hands of the living God. He is ever loving and desires our good; but he is also supreme in holiness, and in all our thoughts he must be hallowed as one who, when the need appears, can make most terrible manifestations of his power. We must be alive to God's presence in the terrible and destructive phenomena of the natural world as much as in those which are gentle, attractive, and pleasing. By the terrors of Sinai he intimated to his people, once for all, that he was a God not to be trifled with, but one who demanded careful and humble attention at all times when he expressed his will.

II. The preparation for it which had to be made by the people. The manifestation was not to come at once; the people had to wait for it; but waiting was not all. The waiting indeed was necessary that they might have sufficient opportunity to prepare. Even already it was being signified to them that in external things, and even in such a slight matter as the washing of the clothes, they were to be a holy people. All the defilements gathered by the way, all the dust of the conflict with Amalek had to be washed off; and short of water as they had lately been, God, we may be sure, provided an abundant supply before giving this command. He required his people through certain symbolic actions to enter into a special state of readiness for himself. Then when they were so far ready by what they did to themselves, they must take further special precautions not to enter on the holy ground. As God took from the dwellers of the earth the house of Jacob to be his holy nation, so he took these steeps of Sinai to be a holy place for himself. Evidently all these preparations being of the character they were, must have produced a state of mind full of expectation and suspense. God fixed the very day of this appearing. This is a thing he can do, sure that the reality will not fall short of the popular notion formed beforehand. But there is another great day of the Lord; and the precise point of this in time no man knoweth. It was in mercy that the date of the visitation on Sinai was made known to Israel; it is in equal mercy that the great day of the Lord yet remaining is veiled, as to its date, from us. Those who live as they ought to live, trusting in Christ and knowing the indwelling of the Spirit, are doing that which secures present profit and blessedness, makes meet for the inheritance of the saints in light, and at the same time adequate preparation for the trials of the last great day. There is no way of being ready for them except to live near to God in prayer and faith and faithfulness in little things. Believe in Christ, and show your faith by your works, and then you are ready whatever comes.

III. The manifestation itself and its effects. Precisely how the manifestation was to take place does not seem to have been indicated beforehand; and even as it stands described by all those terrible terms, thunder, lightning, the smoking and the quaking mount, we feel that the reality must far have transcended the power of human speech to describe. It was truly an unspeakable visitation. The word telling us most is that which says that before this visitation all the people trembled. Evidently it had an overwhelming effect upon them. It is made perfectly plain that when God cannot draw men by love, he can hold them fast by fear. If they will not go like invited children in his way, they are shaken *nolentes volentes* out of their own. Whatever else men may refuse to God, love, worship, service,—this at all events is ensured, that they shall be terrified before him. They have no choice. The earth cannot but quake when he sets to work the mighty hidden powers underneath. And so the most atheistic life must acknowledge by its disturbed emotions that there is a power it cannot resist. The boasted discipline and sovereignty of human reason count for nothing then. The earthquake without gets its due result from the quaking heart within. Man may set up his will against God's will; but that only means that he refuses obedience; he cannot keep God from shaking him to the very foundations of his being. Though the people in a few months left Sinai, yet Sinai in a very important sense followed them. The fire that went out from the Lord and devoured Nadab and Abihu—the fire that burned at

Taberah among the complaining people (Num. xi. 1)—the opening earth and the devouring fire at the time of the conspiracy of Korah (Num. xvi.)—what are all these but proofs of the God of Sinai travelling in all his terror and glory along with Israel and making sharp visitations in the hour of worldliness, unbelief, and negligence? Those trained in idolatry may well become sceptical and end in utter unbelief, for they never see anything in the way of subduing power save the power of knavish priests over superstitious devotees. There are great pretensions and professions, but never anything done corresponding with them. But here as Jehovah begins to specify his requirements, he first of all shows his power in the most impressive way. As an Israelite looked back on Sinai, whatever other feelings he might have, he could not deny the terrible reality that was there. And one very remarkable thing is, that through all this thunder and lightning, smoking and quaking, there was no actual destruction. If there had been such, it would certainly have been recorded. But so far from this being the case, there were special and very earnest directions in order to avert it (ver. 12, 13, 21, 24.) So long as they kept outside the Divinely appointed barrier and observed the cleansing regulations, neither life nor property was lost. Sinai, with all its undescribed terrors, was not Vesuvius: the people beneath were not gathered in a doomed Herculaneum or Pompeii. The purpose of Jehovah was simply to manifest the reality, extent, and proximity of his destroying power. Men were made to feel what it could do, if they were so presumptuous or negligent as to come within its rightful exercise.—Y.

Vers. 7—25. *The revelation of Jehovah.* I. WHAT IS DEMANDED ERE THE REVELATION CAN BE IMPARTED. 1. The will must be surrendered to God, " All that the Lord hath spoken we will do" (ver. 8). 2. The filthiness of the past must be put away; "Sanctify them" (ver. 10). There must be loathing of, and separation from, sin. 3. There must be a sense of the distance sin has put between the soul and God; "Take heed to yourselves that ye go not up into the mount, or touch the border of it" (vers. 12, 13).
II. HOW THE REVELATION IS IMPARTED. 1. In the awful manifestation of his majesty (vers. 16—19). The first step is the recognition of the livingness and greatness and holiness of God. Hitherto he has been to the soul a name only; now the Creator, the Holy One, against whom and in whose sight all sin has been wrought, the Righteous Judge from whom there is no escape, from whose face death itself affords no covering. 2. In the glorifying of a Mediator, to whom he speaks, and who shall declare him to us. This is reflected in the Christian's experience—(1) Sinai, the knowledge of sin; (2) Calvary, peace through the blood of Jesus, acceptance in the Beloved.—U.

EXPOSITION.

Vers. 16—20.—THE MANIFESTATION OF GOD UPON SINAI. All was ready. The fence had been made (ver. 23); the people had purified themselves—at least so far as externals went. The third day was come—there was a breathless hush of expectation. Then suddenly, in the morning, the presence manifested itself. " There were thunders and lightnings, and a thick cloud upon the mount, and the voice of the trumpet exceeding loud " (ver. 16); " and Mount Sinai was altogether on a smoke, because the Lord descended upon it in fire; and the smoke thereof ascended as the smoke of a furnace; and the whole mount quaked greatly" (ver. 18) Or, as the scene is elsewhere (Deut. iv. 11, 12) described by Moses—" Ye came near and stood under the mountain, and the mountain burned with fire *unto the midst*

of heaven, with darkness, clouds, and *thick darkness.* And the Lord spoke unto you *out of the midst of the fire:* ye heard the voice of the words, but saw no similitude; only ye heard a voice." The phenomena were not a mere " storm of thunder and lightning, whereof Moses took advantage to persuade the people that they had heard God's voice "— not " an earthquake with volcanic eruptions " —not even these two combined—but a real theophany, in which amid the phenomena of storm and tempest, and fire and smoke, and thick darkness, and heavings of the ground as by an earthquake shock, first the loud blast of a trumpet sounded long commanding attention, and then a clear penetrating voice, like that of a man, made itself heard in distinctly articulated words, audible to the whole multitude, and recognised by them as superhuman—as "the voice of God" (Deut. iv. 33). It is in vain to seek to minimise, and to rationalise the scene, and tone it down into something not supernatural. The only honest course is either to accept it as a plain record of plain (albeit miraculous) facts, or to reject it altogether as the fiction of a romancer.

Ver. 16.—**There were thunders.** Literally, "voices," as in ch. ix. 23; but there can be no doubt that "thunder" is meant. **A thick cloud.** Compare above, ver. 9, and the comment *ad loc*. **The voice of the trumpet.** Literally, "a trumpet's voice." The word used for "trumpet" is not the same as in ver. 13; but the variation does not seem to have any importance.

Ver. 17.—**Moses brought forth the people out of the camp.** The camp itself must have been withdrawn to some little distance from the foot of the mount, so that a vacant space intervened between the first tents and the "fence" which Moses had caused to be erected almost close to the mount. Into this vacant space Moses now led "the people"—*i.e.*, the chief of the people—so bringing them as near as they might come to God.

Ver. 18.—**Mount Sinai was altogether on a smoke.** Literally, "smoked, all of it." Kalisch suggests that "the dense clouds from which the thunders broke forth had *the appearance* of smoke." But the reason assigned —"because the Lord descended on it *in fire*," seems to imply real smoke; and the same results from the comparison of it to "the smoke of a furnace." **The whole mount quaked greatly.** Scarcely "through the vehemence

of the thunder" (Kalisch), for thunder does not shake the earth, though it shakes the air —but rather by an actual earthquake. Compare Ps. xviii. 7; Matt. xxvii. 51—54; Acts iv. 31; xvi. 26.

Ver. 19.—**When the voice of the trumpet sounded long, and waxed louder and louder.** This is a somewhat free translation; but it gives well the real meaning of the Hebrew. We may conclude that the trumpet's blast was not continuous. It sounded when the manifestation began (ver. 16). It sounded again, much louder and with a much more prolonged note, to herald the actual descent of God upon the mount. This time the sound was so piercing, so terrible, so intolerable, that Moses could no longer endure to keep silence, but burst out in speech. Were his words those recorded in Heb. xii. 21—"I exceedingly fear and quake" —words not found now in the Old Testament —or were they others which have been wholly lost to us? It is impossible to say. His speech, however, had the effect of bringing the awful preparations to a close—"Moses spake, and God answered him by a voice, and the Lord came down upon Mount Sinai."

Ver. 20.—**On the top of the mount.** Not, probably, on the highest point of the Sinaitic group, the Jebel Musa, which is out of sight from the plain Er-Rahah, where the Israelites must have been assembled; but on the highest part of the face of Sinai fronting that plain, the Ras Sufsâfeh, which would be to the Israelites at the base "the top of the mount." **The Lord called Moses up.** Perhaps with Aaron, who certainly accompanied him when he next ascended (ver. 24), and who seems to be glanced at in the phrase used at the end of ver. 23

HOMILETICS.

Vers. 16—20.—*God's various modes of manifesting himself.* It has been well said that "when God reveals himself it is in a manner suitable to the occasion." No revelation that he has made of himself has ever been so terrible in its material accompaniments as that at Sinai; and no occasion can ever be conceived of as more needing the employment of solemn, startling, and impressive circumstances. Here was a people gross of heart, delighting in flesh-pots, debased by slavery, careless of freedom, immoral, inclined to idolatry, which had to be elevated into God's living witness among the nations, the depositary of his truth, the teacher of the rest of mankind for ages. Given the object of impressing such a nation permanently with the conviction that it had received a Divine revelation, and that very dreadful consequences would follow the neglect of it, and the need of the thunders and other terrors of Sinai becomes manifest. At other times and in other places God has pursued quite different methods. To Elijah he revealed himself in the "still small voice;" to Isaiah and St. John in visions; to the apostles generally in the solemn teaching of his Son; to St. Paul in ecstasies, wherein he heard unspeakable words. The contrast between the day of the giving of the law on Sinai and the day of Pentecost has often been noticed.

> "When God of old came down from Heaven,
> In power and wrath he came;
> Before his feet the clouds were riven,
> Half darkness and half flame."

"But when he came the second time,
He came in power and love :
Softer than gale at morning prime,
Hovered his holy Dove."

The coming of the Spirit at Pentecost and the coming of Jesus were, both of them, gentle and peaceful Epiphanies, suited to the time, when God, having educated the world for four thousand years or more, was about to seek to win men to himself by the preaching of "good tidings"—of the gospel of love. The clouds and terrors of Sinai would here have been out of place—unsuitable anachronisms. In complete harmony with the two occasions were—at Bethlehem, the retired village, the humble stable, the angels singing of peace on earth, the lone shepherds watching their flocks at night—in Jerusalem the voiceless wind, "mighty" yet subdued, the lambent light playing round the heads of holy men, the unseen inward influence shed into their hearts at the same time, impalpable to sense, but with power to revolutionise the world. And as God reveals himself to his Church in manifold ways, each fitting the occasion, so does he reveal himself to individuals. Now he comes clothed in his terrors. He visits with calamity or with sickness, or with that awful dread which from time to time comes over the soul, that it is lost, hopelessly lost, alienated from God for ever. Anon, he shows himself in gentler guise—he whispers hope, he instils faith, he awakens love. In every case he studies the needs of the individual, and adapts his revelation of himself to them. Now he calls by his preachers, now he warns by the "still small voice" of conscience; now he wakes men out of sleep by a sudden danger or a sudden deliverance; anon, he startles them out of a self-complacency worse than sleep by withdrawing himself and allowing them to fall. It is for man to take advantage of every Divine manifestation, to listen when God speaks, to obey when he calls, to make the use of each occasion which it was intended to have, to "receive God's revelations of himself in his own way."

HOMILIES BY VARIOUS AUTHORS.

Vers. 16—19.—*Sinai and Sion.* In studying these verses we cannot but be reminded of the picture drawn by the writer of the Epistle to the Hebrews of the contrast in respect of Church state and privilege between believers of the Old and believers of the New Testament dispensations. "Ye are not come," he says, "unto the mount that might be touched, and that burned with fire, nor unto blackness, and darkness, and tempest. . . . But ye are come unto Mount Sion, and unto the city of the living God, the heavenly Jerusalem," etc. (Hebrews xii. 18—25). Briefly stated, what is set forth here is the contrast of legal with Gospel privilege. The writer is addressing Jews, who were in danger of apostatising from Christ. He seeks to dissuade them from going back to Judaism by showing them the vast superiority of the privileges which they enjoyed as Christians to those enjoyed under the law. *We,* who are Christians, and are in no temptation to return to Judaism, approach the subject from a different side. But the verses are still of use as showing us, by contrast, the greatness of our privilege. We have, 1. the *negative* side of Christian privilege—what we are delivered from, "Ye are *not* come," etc.; 2. The *positive* side of Christian privilege—what we have come *to,* "Ye are come unto Mount Sion," etc. It will better suit our present purpose to view the contrast along different lines.
I. THE CONTRAST IN THE MOUNTAINS. Sinai and Sion. 1. *Sinai.* Sinai, the mountain of law, stands as the proper representative of the old economy. The Israelites, as seen above, were under a peculiar constitution. Bound to God by a covenant of law, they yet enjoyed many of the benefits of a state of grace. Sinai, however, was the proper representation of their economy. Divest that economy of all that it derived from the new and better covenant which has since superseded it, and it would have been a Sinai economy pure and simple. The law said, Do this and thou shalt live; and if the Israelite did not do it, *it* could award no blessing to him, could only condemn. This was the formal constitution. As placed under law, the people, in their approaches to God, were constantly coming anew to the mount that might be touched, and that burned with fire. 2. *Sion.* The first thing which strikes us here is—(1) That *there*

was this contrast between Sinai and Sion within Israel itself. Sinai and Sion were, so to speak, the two poles round which the whole national and religious life of Israel revolved. As Sinai, the mountain of the law, represents their position *under* law, so the grace element in their economy comes to light in Mount Sion. As on Sinai, God descended in awful smoke and flame, so on Sion he dwelt in peace in the midst of Israel, giving forth his oracles, receiving his people's worship, and dispensing mercy and favour from between the cherubim, above the blood-sprinkled mercy-seat. God came down for a season only on Sinai; on Sion, he was said to dwell (Ps. cxxxii. 10, 11). He appeared in terror on Mount Sinai; but Sion displayed the milder glories of his character. Sion was the place of salvation (Ps. xiv. 7 ; Is. xlvi. 13, etc.). In Sion God ruled ; from it he sent forth strength and help ; from it was to go forth the Gospel law (Ps. xx. 2 ; cx. 2 ; Is. ii. 2, 3). Yet Sion, under that economy, was only the type of something better. Grace at that time was only very imperfectly revealed ; it was hidden under types and forms of law ; it has now been made fully manifest, and the old covenant has been superseded by a better and enduring one. (2) *Sinai and Sion as representing the contrast between the two dispensations.* Sion has not ceased to exist, it has only, so to speak, gone up higher. Its special seat is now in heaven. *There* is the throne of God ; *there*, the capital or head-quarters of that great spiritual commonwealth, here denominated "the city of the living God, the heavenly Jerusalem," and elsewhere, "the Jerusalem that is above," "New Jerusalem," in plain terms, the Church or kingdom of God on earth and in heaven. This heavenly Sion alone perfectly realises and fulfils the idea embodied in the earthly one. Do we ask why the Church or kingdom of God, as respects its state of privilege, is in this text figured as on a mountain —as a city set on Mount Sion ? The answer is—1. Because the special seat of God's holy abode in the midst of his Church is now literally in heaven, *i.e.*, spiritually removed from, and exalted above the earth. 2. Because the kingdom of God is spiritually the highest thing on earth—founded on the highest order of ideas, on those principles of righteousness and justice which dominate all others. 3. Because it is, in point of fact, the central, commanding, controlling power in history. 4. Because entrance into it, and growth in its spirit and power, involves a spiritual rise—is a true moral ascent. These facts evince the propriety of this figurative representation.

II. THE CONTRAST IN THE ACCESSORIES. Each mountain, in the passage in Hebrews, is made the centre of a scene. We have, accordingly, two groups of attendant circumstances, the details of which are placed studiously in contrast. The series of manifestations at Sinai has already engaged our attention, and we need not dwell upon them further. In contrast to Sinai is placed the picture of the convocation at Mount Sion. The picture is ideal; but the features in it are severally real, and the whole are needed to set forth Christian privilege in its completeness. 1. The mount is represented as crowned by "the city of the living God, the heavenly Jerusalem"—the city denoting that great spiritual polity into which believers are admitted, and in which they have rights of citizenship, but which, like every other polity, has an existence of its own, irrespective of the individuals who at any time compose its membership. The *civitas* endures, though the *cives* come and go. The ideas suggested are order, beauty, symmetry. God has founded this city. God defends it. It has salvation for walls and bulwarks. The capital of this great "City of God" is heaven; but believers, even on earth, are enfranchised members of it, and, spiritually, have come to it (Eph. ii. 19; Phil. iii. 20). 2. Crowding the mount, thronging its sides, and hovering above, behind, around, is "an innumerable company of angels." Cf. 2 Kings vi. 17, where the servant of Elisha saw the mountain "full" of horses and chariots of fire round about Elisha; or Dan. vii. 10, where thousand thousands minister to the Ancient of Days, and ten thousand times ten thousand stand before him ; or Rev. v. 11, where the number of the angels round about the throne was "ten thousand times ten thousand, and thousands of thousands." The truths figured are these two—(1) That the angelic hosts stand in a relation of ministry to the Church and kingdom of God (Heb. i. 14); and (2) That they take a deep interest in its fortunes (Eph. iii. 10; 1 Pet. i. 12). Their bright forms, crowding the mount, add augustness, splendour, and beauty to the scene. 3. The mount is further occupied by "the general assembly and Church of the first-born, which are written in heaven"—this designation including the whole body of Christian believers both those on earth and those in heaven;

the Church catholic, spiritual, invisible. "The whole family in heaven and earth"—
"one Church, above, below." But why called "first-born"? "They are partakers with
Christ in all the privileges of that right of primogeniture, which properly and essentially
belongs to him alone." (Candlish.) The truth figured here is, that in Christ we are
admitted to the "communion of saints." "I believe in the holy Catholic Church. . . . I
believe in the communion of saints." Yet how little, sometimes, does this great privilege
mean to us! 4. Another part of the assembly on the mount is denoted by the words
—"the spirits of just men made perfect." These are the holy and good of the former
dispensation, now admitted to equality of privilege and blessedness with Christians
(cf. Heb. xi. 40). 5. God himself sits enthroned in the midst—"Judge of all." The
expression reminds us of the writer's design, which is not consolatory, but admonitory.
It is still the holy God with whom we have to do, the Judge (cf. Rom. ii. 6; 1 Pet. i. 17)
as well as Father; one who will punish disobedience to his voice now with even greater
severity than he did of old (Heb. xii. 25, 29). The God of Sinai and the God of Sion
are after all the *same* God. What, then, makes the difference between Sinai and Sion?
The answer is—6. "Jesus, the mediator of the new covenant, and the blood of sprinkling."
It is Christ's presence in the scene which has changed all the surroundings. To all
these things, if we are indeed in Christ, we *come*. How? (1) By coming to Jesus
himself. To come to Jesus, as has been well said, is to come to all else that is here
described. We may or may not realise our privileges; but they are there. We are
members of the spiritual commonwealth, enjoy the ministry of angels, are part of the
invisible Church, have rights of the first-born, etc. (2) In the realisation of spiritual
privilege (cf. 1 Cor. ii. 12). (3) In the use of our rights. (4) We shall "come" more
perfectly at death. Hence—

III. THE CONTRAST IN PRIVILEGE. 1. In the *character* of the privilege. In Israel's
case, the privilege was of so awful a kind, that the sense of privilege was well-nigh
swallowed up in the terror which the scene inspired. How different with believers!
Their approach to this spiritual mount is solemnising indeed, yet joyful. They have
boldness in drawing nigh by the blood of Christ. 2. In the *degree* of the privilege. The
Israelites were not permitted to ascend, or even to come near the mount. Bounds were
erected to keep them back. Did they so much as touch it, they would perish. How
different the privilege of Christians, who not only ascend this spiritual Mount Sion, but
are enrolled as citizens in its heavenly city, and have boldness to enter the holiest of all
in their approaches to the throne of grace (Heb. iv. 14—16; x. 19—23).—J. O.

Ver. 17.—*Prepare to meet thy God.* God's revelation of himself to man is gradual, as
man can bear it. [Cf. the way in which a parent reveals himself to his child, Is. xxviii.
11, with stammering lips and a feigned tongue.] Israel had learnt to know God as a
deliverer; must learn to know him further as a lawgiver and ruler.

I. THE SCENE. A long, broad valley. Rocks on each side widening out into a natural
amphitheatre. Facing down the valley is a steep, precipitous mountain; grey, streaked
with red. The whole scene, not unlike, on a huge scale, that presented by the avenues
leading up to the Egyptian temples. It is a place where those accustomed to Egypt
might expect to meet with God. "Now" probably the people may have thought, "we
shall see for ourselves this mysterious Jehovah; he has brought us to his temple; he
will introduce us to his shrine."

II. THE MEDIATOR AND HIS MESSAGE. Israel is encamped. Moses ascends the mountain (ver. 3). Again God meets with him and sends a message by him to the people.
Notice:—1. Reminder of what he has done for them already (ver. 4). 2. Obedience the
condition of future favour (ver. 5). Fulfil the condition and the promise is secure. The
earth itself is God's temple; if Israel will obey and keep his covenant they shall be "a
kingdom of priests, and a holy nation." 3. The answer given (ver. 8). No hesitation,
no expression of doubt. The promised blessing so attractive that they are ready to promise anything, never doubting their ability to fulfil their promise. It is easy enough
to say "I will"—the hard thing is to translate it into "I do."

III. THE PROMISED INTERVIEW. The people shall be conscious of the presence of their
God. Jehovah will publicly attest the authority of his servant. Notice:—1. *The preparation.* God requires it. It is easy for familiarity to breed irreverence; and irreverence
soon leads on to low views of the Divine character. Love is degraded into mere kindli-

ness; an easy-going people believe in an easy-going God.   See here:—(1) The people have to prepare *themselves* for the meeting (ver. 10).   (2) The *place* has to be prepared. God reveals himself to prepared people in a prepared place.   Why do so few have revelations nowadays?   Some come to the prepared place, but they omit the personal preparation; others, even after personal preparation, lose much through neglecting the prepared place.   We need to remember Eccles. v. 1, and Heb. x. 25.   2. *The revelation.* The third day comes (ver. 16).   Storm, sound of trumpet, assembly of people without the camp, trembling, earthquake, intense suspense.   "Now surely God will show himself.   Can we endure the sight and live?"   At length (ver. 19) "a voice"—cf. Deut. iv. 12; "no similitude, only a voice."   For the present it is enough; reverence is the first lesson those whom God has delivered have to learn; "Hallowed be thy Name" is the first petition they are taught to offer.   For effect (cf. xx. 18—22) which also teaches the object of the revelation.   "That his fear may be before your faces that ye sin not."

Conclusion.   We have learnt many more lessons about God than the Israelites could then learn.   Have we not too often slurred over or half-forgotten that first lesson?

> "Let knowledge grow from more to more,
>   But more of reverence in us dwell;
>   That mind and soul, according well,
> May make our music as before,
>   But vaster. We are fools and slight;
>   We mock thee when we do not fear;
>   But help thy foolish ones to bear;
> Help thy vain worlds to bear thy light."—G.

Ver. 19.—*Only a voice.*   The people were expecting a revelation—a vision of the hitherto unseen Jehovah—it came, but not as they expected; no *vision*, only a *voice* (cf. Deut. iv. 12).   The fact was the law was not a *final*, only a *preparatory* revelation; it is related to the Gospel as John Baptist was related to Christ.   "A voice crying in the wilderness, prepare ye the way of the Lord.   Consider in this view:—

I. THE STRENGTH OF THE LAW.   1. *It was a voice—a Divine voice.*   In spite of the confusion not unmixed with disappointment, none doubted whence it came.   It gave a Divine authority to the commandment even when given through a mediator.   2. *It was adapted to the condition of those who heard it.*   A revelation must be fitted for those to whom it is addressed.   (*Illust.* a highly-finished picture is of small value to the half-blind; they can better appreciate a rough sketch in coarse, bold outline.)   The animal, or natural man, as exemplified in the character of Israel in the wilderness, could not have understood anything more spiritual; its religion is obedience.   The natural man can only be reached by such sensual methods as his nature can respond to.   Through them the spiritual nature, which is cradled in the natural, may be educated and fostered, prepared to receive in due course that higher revelation which befits it.

II. THE WEAKNESS OF THE LAW.   1. *It was only a voice.*   As the spiritual nature grows (cf. infants attaining consciousness) it craves for something more than this.   It needs not a voice only, but a *presence.*   From the first we find Israel longing after a "similitude."   Even Moses (xxxiii. 18) beseeches that God will show him his glory.   Later the cry grows ever more distinct through psalmists and prophets, itself a continuous preparation for the fulfilment ultimately reserved for it.   2. *Evidence in the law itself* (cf. second commandment).   A fence to guard an empty shrine, but a shrine kept empty only in preparation for some coming inmate.   A preparation for the Incarnation.   The Pharisee comes to worship the fence; the idolater ignores it; both illustrate the weakness of the merely "vocal" revelation.

III. CONTRAST WITH THE GOSPEL.   Christ is "the *Word* made *Flesh*;" the express *image* of God.   Not a voice only, but a *person.*   The more perfect revelation indicates a fuller development in those to whom it is addressed, but we must remember that a fuller development implies also a greater responsibility.   [The offence which we condone in the child, is unpardonable in the man.   Mistakes made by the half-blind are no longer excusable when a man can see.]   If Israel fell and was rejected, must not our far greater privileges be followed, if profaned, with deeper ruin?   (Cf. Heb. xii. 25, 26; 1 Cor. x. 1—12.)—G.

EXPOSITION.

Vers. 21—25.—*The further warning to the people and the priests.* It is very remarkable that, after all the directions given (vers. 10—13), and all the pains taken by Moses and the Israelites themselves (vers. 14, 15, 23), God should still have thought it necessary to interpose with a fresh warning, and to send Moses back from the top of the mount to the bottom, in order to communicate the renewed warning to the people. We can only suppose that, in spite of the instructions previously given and the precautions taken, there were those among the people who were prepared to "break through" the fence, and invade the mount, and who would have done so, to their own destruction (ver. 21), but for this second warning. The special mention of the "priests" (vers. 22, 24) raises the suspicion, that this proud and rebellious spirit was particularly developed among them. Accustomed to the exercise of sacred functions, they may have been inclined to regard their own purity as equal to that of Moses and Aaron; and they may even have resented their exclusion from a sacred spot to which the two sons of Amram were admitted. Apparently, they had conceived that the injunction to go through the recognised ceremonies of purification (ver. 10) did not apply to them, and had neglected to do so, on which account a special command had to be issued, addressed to them only (ver. 22).

Ver. 21.—**Charge the people lest they break through**—*i.e.*, "lest they force a passage through the barrier made by Moses" in accordance with the command given in ver. 12. **And many of them perish.** Irreverent gazing on holy things was forbidden by the law (Num. iv. 20), and on one occasion (1 Sam. vi. 19) was actually punished with death. It did not, however, require a law to make it an offence, natural reason being quite sufficient to teach the duty of reverence.

Ver. 22.—**Let the priests also.** It has been objected, that no priests had been as yet appointed, and that we have here therefore an anachronism. But every nation in ancient times had priests, appointed on one principle or another: and the Levitical priesthood must be regarded as having superseded one previously existent, not as the first priesthood known to Israel. We have a second mention of priests, previous to the appointment of Aaron's sons to the office (in ch. xxiv. 5), which confirms the present passage. **Sanctify themselves.** The verb used is identical with that which occurs in ver. 10; and there is no reason to believe that any different sanctification was intended. The natural inference is that the priests had neglected to sanctify themselves. (See the introductory paragraph.) **Lest the Lord break forth.** Compare 2 Sam. vi. 8, where we have an instance of such a "breaking forth" upon Uzzah.

Ver. 23.—**The people cannot come up.** Moses can only have meant, that the people could not approach the mount unwittingly, since the fence commanded (ver. 12) was made. But to scale the fence, or break through it, was of course possible. (See ver. 13.)

Ver. 24.—**And the Lord said ... Away, Get thee down.** God wholly rejected the plea of Moses, that there was no need to give an additional warning. *He knew best,* and would not have issued the order to "go down and charge the people" (ver. 21), unless there had been a need for it. In the abrupt words "Away, get thee down," we may see a rebuke, addressed to Moses, for his folly in thinking that he could change the purposes of God. **Thou and Aaron with thee.** This is the first express mention of Aaron as called to ascend with Moses. But it is quite possible that he may have accompanied his brother in either or both the previous ascents (vers. 3, 20. Compare ch. x. 1, 3; xii. 21, 28; etc.) **But let not the priests and the people break through.** Both the *priests* and the people were to be again solemnly warned that it would be death to break through the fence. This warning seems to have been sufficient.

Ver. 25.—**So Moses went down.** After the sharp rebuke addressed to him in ver. 24, Moses made no further resistance, but returned to the camp, delivered the warning to priests and people, and having so done re-ascended the mount with Aaron.

HOMILETICS.

Vers. 22—24.—*The priestly office does not dispense a man from personal purity, but obliges him the more to it.* Holiness of office, of profession, of function is too often regarded as if it secured, by some occult power, the personal holiness of the individual, or even of the class, exercising it. The priest castes of Egypt, India, and other countries, assumed to stand on a completely different footing from the rest of the community in respect of nearness, and acceptability to God. And both under the Jewish and the Christian dispensation, there has been in different times and countries a vast amount of sacerdotal pretension, a wide-spread disposition to assume that official covers and includes personal holiness. But Holy Scripture abounds in warnings against any such assumption. "Let the priests sanctify themselves." Nadab and Abihu, the sons of Aaron, were chosen among the first of the Levitical priests (ch. xxviii. 1), yet their priestly office did not prevent them from sinning grievously by offering "strange fire before the Lord," and perishing for their impiety (Num. x. 1, 2). Eli's sons were "sons of Belial" (1 Sam. ii. 12), whose "sin was very great before the Lord" (*ib.* verse 17). Even among the apostles there was a "son of perdition." Priests have to remember—

I. THAT THE PRIESTLY OFFICE DOES NOT SECURE THEM AGAINST BEING TEMPTED. Even Christ, our great High Priest—the only true priest that the world has ever seen, was "in all points tempted like as we are" (Heb. iv. 15). Eli's sons were tempted by greed and fleshly lusts (1 Sam. ii. 16, 22); Nadab and Abihu by pride; Judas by covetousness. All men have the same nature, like passions, similar appetites. The priest, after all, is a man. Satan watches for him no less—or rather much more—than for others. It is a greater triumph for him to lead astray the shepherd than the sheep. And the relations of a priest towards his flock are of such a nature—so close, so private sometimes—as to lay him open to special temptations.

II. THAT THE PRIESTLY OFFICE DOES NOT SECURE THEM AGAINST YIELDING TO TEMPTATION. Jesus alone was "in all points tempted, *yet without sin*" (Heb. iv. 15). "ALL we the rest, although baptised and born again in Christ, yet offend in many things," yield to the temptations which surround us, transgress the Divine law. Nadab, Abihu, Eli's sons, Judas, were not only tempted, but fell. The priests of Judah, towards the close of the independent kingdom, were among those who provoked God the most (Jer. xxxii. 32; Zeph. iii. 4). Christian ministers, even at the present day, too often disgrace their profession, bring shame upon their church, and even upon religion itself, by acts of sin or sometimes by scandalous lives, no better than those of the sons of Eli. These terrible examples should be a warning to all of their danger, and should render the minister distrustful of himself, circumspect, vigilant, and above all prayerful. Only by God's help can he hope to stand upright.

III. THAT SIN IS WORSE IN THE PRIEST THAN IN OTHERS, AND WILL ENTAIL A SORER PUNISHMENT. Ministers of Christ pledge themselves by special vows, over and above their baptismal vows, to lead godly lives. They are bound to be examples to the flock. They have greater opportunities of grace than others. Their offences cause greater scandal than the offences of others, and do greater damage to the cause of religion. There is something shocking, even to the worldly man, in the immorality of one whose business in life is to minister in holy things. The impure minister is a hypocrite; and hypocrisy is hateful to God, and even in the sight of man contemptible.

IV. THAT THE PRIESTLY PROFESSION BINDS TO HOLINESS. Priests are they whose office it is to "come near the Lord" (Ex. xix. 22)—to draw closer to him than others —to lead others on to him, by exhortation, by example, by intercessory prayer. Without holiness they are impotent to perform their work—they are of no service either to God or man—they do but help forward the work of the devil. Ministering in a holy place, in holy things, with holy words continually in their mouths, if they have not holiness in their hearts, their lives must be a perpetual contradiction, a continual profanity. Again, as already observed, they take special vows: they profess before God and the congregation to have an inward call; they spontaneously promise to live as examples to others; they enter on their position in life on these conditions: they bind themselves. Not to live holy lives is to fly in the face of these obligations—to break the promises made to man and the vows offered to God—to violate faith—to destroy, so far as lies in their power, the great bond of human society. And what must not the offence be to God which they commit, by continually drawing near to him with their lips, when their hearts are far from him? He is "of purer eyes than to behold iniquity." "Without holiness no one shall see him." "*Let the priests sanctify themselves.*"

EXPOSITION.

CHAPTER XX.

Vers. 1—17.—THE DELIVERY OF THE MORAL LAW. Every necessary preparation had now been made. The priests, as well as the people, had "sanctified themselves." A wholesome dread of "breaking" through the fence, and "touching" the mount, had spread itself among the people. Moses had returned from the camp to the summit of the mount; and both he and the people were attent to hear the words of the "covenant," which had been announced to them (ch. xix. 5). Then, amid the thunderings, and the lightnings, and the noise of the trumpet, and the smoke, and the earthquake throbs which shook the ground, a voice like that of a man, distinctly articulate, pronounced the words of that "moral law," which has been from that day to this the guide of life to thousands upon thousands, the only guide to some, a very valuable and helpful guide to all who have known of it. It is well said by Kalisch, that the delivery of the Decalogue on Sinai "formed a decisive epoch in the history of the human race," and was even perhaps "the greatest and most important event in human history," up to the time of its occurrence. Considering the weakness, imperfection, and moral obliquity of man, it was to the last degree important that an authoritative code should be put forth, laying down with unmistakable clearness the chief heads of duty, and denouncing the chief classes of sins. It may be true that the educated moral sense of mankind in civilised communities is sufficient to teach them all, or nearly all, of what the Decalogue forbids and enjoins; but this is the effect produced upon the internal constitution of our nature by long centuries of moral training; and nothing like it existed in primitive times. Then the moral sense was much duller; men's perceptions of right and wrong were confused, uncertain, and not unfrequently perverted and depraved. Even in Egypt, where a priest class, established as the spiritual guides of the nation for a thousand years or more, had elaborated a moral system of considerable merit, such a code as that of the Decalogue would have been a marked improvement upon anything that they had worked out for themselves. And the authoritative sanction by the "voice" and the "finger of God" was an enormous advantage, being imperatively needed to satisfy doubt, and silence that perverse casuistry which is always ready to question the off-hand decisions of the moral consciousness, and to invent a more refined system, wherein "bitter is put for sweet, and sweet for bitter." Altogether the Decalogue stands on a moral eminence, elevated above and beyond all other moral systems—Egyptian, Indian, Chinese, or Greek, unequalled for simplicity, for comprehensiveness, for solemnity. Its precepts were, according to the Jewish tradition, "the pillars of the law and its roots." They formed to the nation to which they were given "fons omnis publici privatique juris." They constitute for all time a condensed summary of human duty which bears divinity upon its face, which is suited for every form of human society, and which, so long as the world endures, cannot become antiquated. The retention of the Decalogue as the best summary of the moral law by Christian communities is justified on these grounds, and itself furnishes emphatic testimony to the excellency of the compendium.

Ver. 1.—**God spake all these words.** It has been suggested that Moses derived the Decalogue from Egypt, by summarising the chief points of the Egyptian teaching as to the duty of man. But neither the second, nor the fourth, nor the tenth commandment came within the Egyptian ideas of moral duty; nor was any such compendious form as the Decalogue known in Egypt. Moreover, Egyptian morality was minute and complex, rather than grand and simple. *Forty-two* kinds of sin were denied by the departed soul before Osiris and his assessors. The noble utterances of Sinai are wholly unlike anything to be found in the entire range of Egyptian literature.

Ver. 2.—**I am the Lord thy God.** The ten precepts were prefaced by this distinct announcement of who it was that uttered them. God would have the Israelites clearly understand, that he himself gave them the commandments. It is only possible to reconcile the declarations of the New Testament, that the law was given by the ministration of angels (Acts vii. 53; Gal. iii. 19; Heb. ii. 2) with this and other plain statements, by regarding God the Son as the actual speaker. As *sent* by his father, he too was, in a certain sense, an angel (*i.e.*, a messenger). **Which**

brought thee out of the land of Egypt. God does not appeal to his authority as creator, but to his mercy and kindness as protector and deliverer. He would be obeyed by his people from a sentiment of love, not by fear. **Out of the house of bondage.** Compare ch. xiii. 3, 14; and for the ground of the expression, see ch. i. 14; vi. 9.

Ver. 3.—**Thou shalt have.** The use of the second person *singular* is remarkable when a covenant was being made with the *people* (ch. xix. 5). The form indicated that each individual of the nation was addressed severally, and was required himself to obey the law, a mere general national obedience being insufficient. No one can fail to see how much the commands gain in force, through all time, by being thus addressed to the individual conscience. **No other gods before me.** "Before me"—literally, "before my face," is a Hebrew idiom, and equivalent to "beside me," "in addition to me." The commandment requires the worship of one God alone, Jehovah—the God who had in so many ways manifested himself to the Israelites, and implies that there is, in point of fact, no other God. A belief in the unity of God is said to lie at the root of the esoteric Egyptian religion; but Moses can scarcely have derived his belief from this source, since the Egyptian notions on the subject were tinged with pantheism and materialism, from which the religion of Moses is entirely free. Outwardly the Egyptian religion, like that of the nations of Western Asia generally, was a gross polytheism; and it is against polytheistic notions that the first commandment raises a protest.

Ver. 4. As the first commandment asserts the unity of God, and is a protest against polytheism, so the second asserts his spirituality, and is a protest against idolatry and materialism. Verses 4 and 5 are to be taken together, the prohibition being intended, not to forbid the arts of sculpture and painting, or even to condemn the religious use of them, but to disallow the worship of God under material forms. When the later Jews condemned all representations of natural objects (Philo, *De Orac.* 29; Joseph. *Ant. Jud.* viii. 7, § 5), they not only enslaved themselves to a literalism, which is alien from the spirit of *both* covenants, but departed from the practice of more primitive times—representations of such objects having had their place both in the tabernacle (ch. xxv. 31—34; xxviii. 33, 34) and in the first temple (1 Kings vi. 18, 29, 32, &c.). Indeed, Moses himself, when he erected the "brazen serpent" (Num. xxi. 9) made it clear that representations of natural objects were not disallowed by the law. To moderns in civilized countries it seems almost incredible that there should ever have been anywhere a real worship of images. But acquaint-

ance with ancient history or even with the present condition of man in savage or backward countries, renders it apparent that there *is* a subtle fascination in such material forms, and that imperfectly developed minds will rest in them not as mere emblems of divinity, but as actually possessed of Divine powers. The protest raised by the second commandment is still as necessary as ever, not only in the world, but in the very Christian Church itself, where there exists even at the present day a superstitious regard for images and pictures, which is not only irrational, but which absorbs the religious feelings that should have been directed to higher objects. **Any graven image.** Perhaps it would be better to translate "any image," for the term used (*pesel*) is applied, not only to "graven" but also to "molten images" (Is. xl. 19; xliv. 10; Jer. x. 14; etc.), since these last were in almost every instance *finished* by the graving tool. **Or any likeness of anything that is in heaven above**—*i.e.*, "any likeness of any winged fowl that flieth in the air." Compare Deut. iv. 17. **The water under the earth.** See Gen. i. 6, 7. The triple division here and elsewhere made, is intended to embrace the whole material universe. Much of the Egyptian religion consisted in the worship of animals and their images.

Ver. 5.—**Thou shalt not bow down thyself to them.** Every outward sign of honour was shown to images in the ancient world. They were not regarded as emblems, but as actual embodiments of deity. There was a special rite in Greece (Theopœa) by means of which the gods were inducted into their statues, and made to take up their abodes in them. Seneca says of the Romans of his own day—"They pray to these images of the gods, implore them *on bended knee*, sit or stand long days before them, throw them money, and sacrifice beasts to them, so treating them with deep respect, though they despise the man who made them" (Ap. Lact. ii. 2). **I, the Lord thy God am a jealous God.** God "will not give his glory to another" (Is. xlii. 8; xlviii. 11), will not suffer a rival near his throne. He is not "jealous," as the Greeks thought (Herod. vii. 10, § 5), of mere success, or greatness; but he is very jealous of his own honour, and will not have the respect and reverence, which is his due, bestowed on other beings or on inanimate objects. Compare with the present passage ch. xxxiv. 14; Deut. iv. 24; v. 9; vi. 15; Josh. xxiv. 19; etc. **Visiting the iniquity of the fathers upon the children.** Exception has been taken to the plain meaning of this passage by a multitude of writers, who dread the reproach of the sceptic, that the God of the Old Testament is a God careless of justice and bent upon revenge. But neither does society, **nor** does civil justice itself, regard the visiting **of** parents' sins upon their children as in all cases unjust. Society by its scorn punishes for their parents' transgressions the illegitimate, the children of criminals, the children—especially the daughters—of adulteresses. Civil justice condemns to forfeiture of their titles and their estates, the innocent children of those executed for treason. God again manifestly does by the laws which obtain in his moral universe, entail on children many consequences of their parents' ill-doing—as the diseases which arise from profligacy or intemperance, the poverty which is the result of idleness or extravagance, the ignorance and evil habits which are the fruit of a neglected education. It is this sort of visitation which is intended here. The children and grandchildren of idolaters would start in life under disadvantages. The vicious lives of their parents would have sown in them the seeds both of physical and moral evil. They would commonly be brought up in wrong courses, have their moral sense early perverted, and so suffer for their parents' faults. It would be difficult for them to rise out of their unhappy condition. Still, "each would bear his own iniquity." Each would "be judged by that he had, not by that he had not." An all-wise God would, in the final award, make allowance for the disadvantages of birth and inherited disposition, and would assign to each that position to which his own conduct—his struggles, efforts, endeavours after right—entitled him.

To say that the threat "applies only to such children as follow the sins of their fathers" (Kalisch) is to empty the passage of all force. It applies to all; but the visitation intended consists in temporal disadvantages, not in the final award of happiness or misery.

Ver. 6.—**Shewing mercy unto thousands.** Or, "*to the thousandth generation.*" (Compare Deut. vii. 9.) In neither case are the numbers to be taken as exact and definite. The object of them is to contrast the long duration of the Divine love and favour towards the descendants of those who love him, with the comparatively short duration of his chastening wrath in the case of those who are his adversaries. **And keep my commandments.** Thus only is love shown. Compare John xiv. 15—21; 1 John ii. 5; 2 John 6.

Ver. 7.—**Thou shalt not take the name of the Lord thy God in vain.** It is disputed whether this is a right rendering. *Shâv* in Hebrew means both "vanity" and "falsehood;" so that the Third Commandment may forbid either "vain-swearing" or simply "false-swearing." It is in favour of the latter interpretation, that our Lord seems to contrast his own prohibition of unnecessary oaths with the ancient prohibition of false oaths in the words—"Ye have heard that it hath been said by" (or "to") "them of old time—Thou shalt

not forswear thyself, but shalt perform unto the Lord thine oaths. *But I say unto you*—Swear not at all" (Matt. v. 33—34). It is also in favour of the command being levelled against false-swearing, that perjury should naturally, as a great sin, have a special prohibition directed against it in the Decalogue, while vain-swearing, as a little sin, would scarcely seem entitled to such notice. Perjury has always been felt to be one of the greatest both of moral and of social offences. It implies an absolute want of any reverence at all for God; and it destroys civil society by rendering the administration of justice impossible. There has been a general horror of it among all civilised nations. The Egyptians punished perjury with death. The Greeks thought that a divine Nemesis pursued the perjured man, and brought destruction both upon himself and upon his offspring (Herod. vi. 86). The Romans regarded the perjurer as infamous, and the object of Divine vengeance in the other world (Cic. *De Leg.* ii. 9). The threat contained in the words—"The Lord will not hold him guiltless"—may be taken as an argument on either side. If viewed as equivalent to "the Lord will punish severely" (Kalisch), it accords best with the view that perjury was intended; if taken literally, it would suit best a lesser sin, of which men ordinarily think little.

Ver. 8.—**Remember the sabbath day.** The institution of the sabbath dates, at any rate, from the giving of the manna (ch. xvi. 23). Its primeval institution, which has been thought to be implied in Gen. ii. 3, is uncertain. The word "remember" here may be simply a reference to what passed in the "wilderness of Sin" as related in ch. xvi. 22—30. On the sabbath itself, both Jewish and Christian, see the comment upon that chapter.

Ver. 9.—**Six days shalt thou labour.** This is not so much a command as a prohibition—"Thou shalt *not* labour more than six (consecutive) days." In them thou shalt do all thy necessary work, so as to have the Sabbath free for the worship and service of God.

Ver. 10.—**The seventh day is the sabbath of the Lord thy God.** Rather—"The seventh day shall be a sabbath to the Lord thy God;" *i.e.*, the seventh day shall be a day of holy rest dedicated to religion. All unnecessary labour shall be suspended and put aside—the law of rest and ease, so far as bodily toil is concerned, which was the law of man's existence before the fall, shall supersede for the time that law of heavy toil and continual unrest, which was laid on man as the penalty of his transgression (Gen. iii. 17—19). Eden shall be, as it were, restored—man shall not "go out to his toil and his labour"—even the very beasts, pressed into man's service since the fall, shall rest. **In it thou shalt not do any work.** On the exceptions to this rule, which even Judaism, with its extreme formality and literalism, saw to be necessary, see Matt. xii. 5, 11. Still in many respects, a superstitious adherence to the precept was maintained by religious Jews, who would not even defend themselves on the sabbath, if attacked by an enemy (1 Mac. ii. 32—38; 2 Mac. v. 25, 26; vi. 11; xv. 1). Experience, however, taught them that the law had not been intended to extend so far, and after a time they determined, not to seek battle, but to accept it, and do their best, on the sabbath day (1 Mac. ii. 41). **Thou, nor thy son, nor thy daughter.** The rest is to extend to the whole family. Work is not to be merely devolved by the parents upon the children. **Thy manservant, nor thy maidservant.** It is to extend beyond the family proper, to the domestics of the household, who are to enjoy the respite from toil and to have the advantage of the religious refreshment, no less than their masters. **Nor thy cattle.** God's care for cattle is a remarkable feature of the Old Testament dispensation. God, at the time of the flood, " remembered *Noah and the cattle which were with him in the ark*" (Gen. viii. 1). Soon after, his covenant, not to drown the earth any more, was established " with the fowl, and with the cattle, and with every beast of the earth," no less than with man (*ib.* ix. 9—11). In the Psalms he declares that " the cattle upon a thousand hills " are *his* (Ps. l. 10). In Jonah, we find that Nineveh was spared, in part because there was in it " much cattle " (Jon. iv. 11). The precept, " Thou shalt not muzzle the ox when he treadeth out the corn" is characteristic of the Mosaic dispensation, and had no parallel in the written codes or in the actual customs of other ancient nations. Animal suffering was generally regarded as of small account in the ancient world; and the idea of protecting animals from ill usage was wholly unknown. On the contrary, as Dr. Döllinger well observes (*Jew and Gentile*, vol. ii. pp. 346—7): " The law was specially careful about the welfare of animals ; they were to be treated with compassion and kindness. Domestic animals were to be well fed, and to enjoy the rest of the sabbath. The Israelites were to help to lift up the ass which had fallen beneath its burden, and to bring back the beast that had gone astray (Ex. xxiii. 5, 12 ; Deut. xxv. 4) . . . . The young was not to be taken from its mother before the seventh day . . . . From these and similar ordinances—such, for instance, as about the least painful method of killing animals—it is plain that the law tried to subdue that coarse turn of mind and unfeeling cruelty, which are engendered by the maltreatment of animals." **Nor the stranger that is within thy gates.** The " strangers within the gates " of Israel are those foreigners who voluntarily sojourned with them in their camps or (afterwards) in their towns. A mixed multitude " had gone up out of Egypt

with them (ch. xii. 38), and accompanied them in their wilderness wanderings. The command that these too should rest, was at once a restriction upon their liberty, requiring them to conform to the habits of those among whom they dwelt, and an admission of them into participation in some portion of the privileges of Israel. The sacred rest of the sabbath prefigured the final peace and happiness of the blest in heaven ; and they who were commanded to share in the first, were encouraged to hope that they might also participate in the second.

Ver. 11.—**For in six days the Lord made heaven and earth.** Two reasons are assigned for the sanctification of the seventh day in the Pentateuch :—1. The fact that the work of creation took six days, and that on the seventh God rested ; and 2. The further fact, that God brought the Israelites out of Egypt, and gave them a time of rest after a time of labour and toil (Deut. v. 15). It is not expressly said that the deliverance took place on the Sabbath, but such is the Jewish tradition on the subject. The reason here assigned must be regarded as the main reason, man's rest being purposely assimilated to God's rest, in order to show the resemblance between man's nature and God's (Gen. i. 27), and to point towards that eternal rest wherein man, united with God, will find his highest bliss and the true end of his being. " There remaineth a rest for the people of God."

Ver. 12.—**Honour thy father and thy mother.** The obligation of filial respect, love, and reverence is so instinctively felt by all, that the duty has naturally found a place in every moral code. In the maxims of Ptahhotep, an Egyptian author who lived probably before Abraham, " the duty of filial piety is strictly inculcated" (Birch, *Egypt from the Earliest Times*, p. 49). Confucius, in China, based his moral system wholly upon the principle of parental authority ; and in Rome it may be regarded as the main foundation of the political edifice. In the Decalogue, the position of this duty, at the head of our duties towards our neighbour, marks its importance; which is further shown by this being " the first commandment with promise" (Eph. vi. 2). It is curious that the long life here specially attached to the observance of this obligation, was also believed to accompany it by the Egyptians. " The son," says Ptah-hotep, " who accepts the words of his father, will grow old in consequence of so doing ; " and again—" The obedient son will be happy by reason of his obedience ; he will grow old; he will come to favour." Modern commentators generally assume that the promise was not personal, but national—the nation's days were to be " long upon the land," if the citizens generally were obedient children. But this explanation cannot apply to Eph. vi

1—3. And if obedience to parents is to be rewarded with long life under the new covenant, there can be no reason why it should not have been so rewarded under the old. The objection that good sons are not *always* long-lived is futile. God governs the universe by general, not by universal laws.

Ver. 13.—**Thou shalt not kill.** Here again is a moral precept included in all codes, and placed by all in a prominent position. Our first duty towards our neighbour is to respect his life. When Cain slew Abel, he could scarcely have known what he was doing; yet a terrible punishment was awarded him for his transgression (Gen. iv. 11—14). After the flood, the solemn declaration was made, which thenceforward became a universal law among mankind—" Whoso sheddeth man's blood, by man shall his blood be shed : for in the image of God made he man " (*ib.* ix. 6). In the world that followed the flood, all races of men had the tradition that only blood could expiate blood. In the few places where there was an organised government, and a systematic administration of justice, the State acted on the principle, and punished the murderer capitally. Elsewhere, among tribes and races which had not yet coalesced into states, the law of blood-revenge obtained, and the inquisition for blood became a private affair. The next of kin was the recognised " avenger," upon whom it devolved to hunt out the murderer and punish him. Here the sin is simply and emphatically denounced, the brevity of the precept increasing its force. The Israelites are told that to take life is a crime. God forbids it. As usual, no exceptions are made. Exceptions appear later on (Num. xxxv. 22—25; Deut. iv. 42 ; etc.); but the first thing is to establish the principle. Human life is sacred. Man is not to shed the blood of his fellow-man. If he does, of his hand will the life taken surely be required. The casuistic question whether suicide is forbidden under this precept, probably did not occur to the legislator or to the Hebrews of his time. Neither the Hebrews, nor the Egyptians, among whom they had so long lived, were addicted to suicide; and it is a general rule that laws are not made excepting against tolerably well-known crimes. It has been argued that angry thoughts and insulting words were forbidden by it on the strength of our Lord's comment in the Sermon on the Mount (Matt. v. 21, 22). But it seems to the present writer that in Matt. v. 21—47 our Lord is not so much explaining the Jewish law as amplifying it on his own authority—note the repetition of the phrase, " But *I* say unto you "—and making it mean to Christians what it had not meant to Jews.

Ver. 14.—**Thou shalt not commit adultery.** Our second duty towards our neighbour is to respect the bond on which the family is based, and that conjugal honour which to the true man is dearer than life. Marriage, according to the original institution, made the husband and wife " one flesh " (Gen. ii. 24) ; and to break in upon this sacramental union was at once a crime and a profanity. Adulteresses and their paramours were in most ancient nations liable to be punished with death by the injured party; but the adultery of a married man with an unmarried woman was thought lightly of. The precept of the Decalogue binds both man and woman equally. Our Lord's expansion of this commandment (Matt. v. 27—32) is parallel to his expansion of the preceding one (*ib.* 21—26). He shows that there are adulterous marriages in countries where the law gives a facility of divorce, and that without any overt act adultery may be committed *in the heart.*

Ver. 15.—**Thou shalt not steal.** By these words the right of property received formal acknowledgment, and a protest was made by anticipation against the maxim of modern socialists—" La propriété, c'est le vol." Instinctively man feels that some things become his, especially by toil expended on them, and that, by parity of reasoning, some things become his neighbour's. Our third duty towards our neighbour is to respect his rights in these. Society, in every community that has hitherto existed, has recognised private property ; and social order may be said to be built upon it. Government exists mainly for the security of men's lives and properties ; and anarchy would supervene if either could be with impunity attacked. Theft has always been punished in every state ; and even the Spartan youth was not acquitted of blame unless he could plead that the State had stopped his supplies of food, and bid him forage for himself.

Ver. 16.—**Thou shalt not bear false witness against thy neighbour.** False witness is of two kinds, public and private. We may either seek to damage our neighbour by giving false evidence against him in a court of justice, or simply calumniate him to others in our social intercourse with them. The form of the expression here used points especially to false witness of the former kind, but does not exclude the latter, which is expressly forbidden in ch. xxiii. 1. The wrong done to a man by false evidence in a court may be a wrong of the very extremest kind—may be actual murder (1 Kings xxi. 13) More often, however, it results in an injury to his property or his character. As fatal to the administration of justice, false witness in courts has been severely visited by penalties in all well-regulated states. At Athens the false witness was liable to a heavy fine, and if thrice convicted lost all his civil rights. At Rome, by a law of the Twelve Tables, he was hurled headlong from the Tarpeian rock. In Egypt, false witness was punished by amputation of the nose and ears (*Records of the Past*, vol. viii. p. 65). Private calumny may sometimes involve as serious consequences to individuals as false witness in a court. It may ruin a man ; it may madden him ; it may drive him to suicide. But it does not disorganise the whole framework of society, like perjured evidence before a tribunal ; and states generally are content to leave the injured party to the remedy of an action-at-law. The Mosaic legislation was probably the first wherein it was positively forbidden to circulate reports to the prejudice of another, and where consequently this was a criminal offence.

Ver. 17.—**Thou shalt not covet.** Here the Mosaic law takes a step enormously in advance of any other ancient code. Most codes stopped short at the deed ; a few went on to words ; not one attempted to control thoughts. "Thou shalt not covet" teaches men that there is One who sees the heart ; to whose eyes "all things are naked and open ; " and who cares far less for the outward act than the inward thought or motive from which the act proceeds. "Thou shalt not covet" lays it down again that we are not mere slaves of our natural desires and passions, but have a controlling power implanted within us, by means of which we can keep down passion, check desire, resist impulse. Man is lord of himself, capable, by the exercise of his free-will, of moulding his feelings, weakening or intensifying his passions, shaping his character. God, who "requires truth in the inward parts," looks that we should in all cases go to the root of the matter, and not be content with restraining ourselves from evil acts and evil words, but eradicate the evil feeling from which the acts and words proceed. **Thy neighbour's house,** etc. The "house" is mentioned first as being of primary necessity, and as in some sort containing all the rest. A man does not take a wife until he has a home to bring her to, or engage domestic servants, or buy slaves, except to form part of a household. The other objects mentioned are placed in the order in which they are usually valued. The multiplication of objects is by way of emphasis.

HOMILETICS.

Vers. 1—17.—*The ten commandments collectively.* The ten commandments form a summary of our main duties towards God, and towards man. They stand out from the rest of the Old Testament in a remarkable way. 1. They were uttered audibly by a voice which thousands heard—a voice which is called that of God himself (Deut. v. 26) and which filled those who heard it with a terrible fear (verse 19). 2. They were the only direct utterance ever made by God to man under the Old Covenant. 3. They were not merely uttered by God but written by him, inscribed in some marvellous way *by the finger of God* on the two tables of testimony (ch. xxxi. 18 ; Deut. iv. 13). 4. They have the additional testimony to their primary importance, that our Lord himself appealed to them as laying down that which men must do to inherit eternal life (Matt. xix. 18, 19). We may observe of them collectively—

I. THAT THEY ARE ALL-EMBRACING. They include our obligations to both God and man ; they are both prohibitive and directive ; they reach to the heart as well as to the outward life ; they comprise both moral and positive precepts. According to the division adopted by the English Church, and by the reformed churches generally, the first four lay down our duty to our Maker, the last six our duty to our fellow men. Mostly they are prohibitive ; but this is not the case with the fourth and fifth. The generality are concerned with acts, but words form the subject matter of the third ; and both the tenth and the fifth deal with thoughts. As the moral is much more important than the positive, they are naturally in the main moral ; but, to show that the positive is an essential element in religion, they are also partly positive—no moral ground being assignable for the consecration of one day in seven, rather than one in eight or six, much less for the definite selection of "*the seventh* day" as the one to be kept holy.

II. THAT THEY ARE SYSTEMATIC, BOTH IN MATTER AND ARRANGEMENT. The Decalogue takes as its basis the fact that all our duties are owed either to God or man. It regards our duties to God as the more important, and therefore places them first. The duties consist : 1. In acknowledging his existence and unity, and in "having him" for our God and none other (first commandment) ; 2. In conceiving aright of his incorporeity and spirituality, and worshipping him as a Spirit, in spirit and in truth (second commandment) ; 3. In reverencing his holy Name, and avoiding the profane use of it (third commandment) ; and, 4. In setting apart for his worship some stated portion of our time, since otherwise we shall be sure to neglect it (fourth commandment). Our duties towards our fellow men are more complicated. First, there is a special relation in which we stand towards those who bring us into the world and support us during our early years, involving peculiar duties to them, analogous in part to those which we owe to God, and so rightly following upon the summary of our Divine duties (fifth commandment). Next, with respect to men in general, we owe it them to abstain from injuring them in deed, word, or thought. In deed we may injure their person, their honour, and their property, which we are consequently forbidden to do in the sixth, the seventh, and the eighth commandments. In word, we injure our neighbour especially by false witness, public or private, both of which are forbidden in the ninth commandment. We injure him in thought, finally, when we covet what is his; hence the tenth commandment.

III. THAT THEY ARE THE FIRST GERMS OUT OF WHICH THE WHOLE OF THE MORAL LAW MAY BE EVOLVED. The Decalogue is a collection of *elementary* moral truths. Its predominantly negative form is indicative of this, since abstaining from evil is the first step on the road to virtue. Each command asserts a principle; and the principle is in every case capable of being worked out to a thousand remote consequences. The letter may be narrow; but the spirit of the commandment is in every case "exceeding broad." This will appear, more clearly, in the ensuing section, in which the ten commandments will be considered severally.

Vers. 1—17.—*The ten commandments severally.* THE FIRST COMMANDMENT. To the Christian the First Commandment takes the form which our Lord gave it—"Thou shalt love the Lord thy God with all thy heart, and with all thy soul, and with all thy mind. This is the first and great commandment" (Matt. xxii. 37, 38). Not merely abstract belief, not merely humble acknowledgment of one God is necessary, but heartfelt devotion to the One Object worthy of our devotion, the One Being in all the universe on whom we may rest and stay ourselves without fear of his failing us. He is the Lord *our* God—not an Epicurean deity, infinitely remote from man, who has created the world and left it to its own devices—not a Pantheistic essence spread through all nature, omnipresent, but intangible, impersonal, deaf to our cries, and indifferent to our actions—not an inscrutable "something external to us making for righteousness," in the words of the religious Agnostic—but a Being very near us, "in whom we live, and move, and have our being," who is "about our path and about our bed, and spieth out all our ways," a Being whom we may know, and love, and trust, and feel to be with us, warning us, and cheering us, and consoling us, and pleading with us, and ready to receive us, and most willing to pardon us—a Being who is never absent from us, who continually sustains our life, upholds our faculties, gives us all we enjoy and our power to enjoy it, and who is therefore the natural object of our warmest, tenderest, truest, and most constant love. The first commandment should not be difficult to keep. We have only to open our eyes to the facts, and let them make their natural impression upon our minds, in order to love One who has done and still does so much for us.

THE SECOND COMMANDMENT. On its prohibitive side, this Commandment forbids us to have unworthy thoughts of God, to liken him to an idol, or regard him as "even such an one as ourselves." Considered as directive, it requires us to form in our minds a just and true idea of the Divine nature, and especially of its spirituality, its lofty majesty, and its transcendent holiness. All materialistic ideas, and consequently all Pantheistic notions, are degrading to the dignity of God, who "is a Spirit," without body, parts, or passions, not mixed with matter, but wholly separate from it, yet everywhere present after a supersensuous manner. Again, anthropomorphic notions of God are degrading to him, though it is scarcely possible to speak of him without anthropomorphic expressions. When we use such terms—as when we call God just, or merciful, or long-suffering—we should remember that those qualities in him are not identical with the human ones, but only analogous to them; and altogether we should be conscious of a deep mysteriousness lying behind all that we know of God, and rendering him a Being awful, inscrutable—whom we must not suppose that we can fathom or comprehend.

THE THIRD COMMANDMENT. Primarily, the Third Commandment forbids perjury or false swearing; secondarily, it forbids all unnecessary oaths, all needless mention of the holy name of God, and all irreverence towards anything which is God's—his name, house, day, book, laws, ministers. Whatever in any sense belongs to God is sacred, and, if it has to be mentioned, should be mentioned reverently. The true main object of the Third Commandment is to inculcate reverence, to point out to us that the only proper frame of mind in which we can approach God is one of self-abasement and deeply reverential fear. "Keep thy foot, when thou goest to the house of God," says the Preacher, "and be more ready to hear than to offer the sacrifice of fools, for they consider not that they do evil. Be not rash with thy mouth, and let not thine heart be hasty to utter anything before God: for God is in heaven, and thou upon earth; therefore let thy words be few" (Eccles. v. 1, 2).

THE FOURTH COMMANDMENT. In the Fourth Commandment we have the basis for all that is external in religion. The dedication of one entire day out of seven to God, and the command to abstain on that day from the ordinary labours of life, led on naturally to the institution of sacred services, holy convocations, meetings for united worship and prayer. Man is an active being, and a social being. If the ordinary business of life is stopped, some other occupation must be found for him: he will not sit still from morning to night with folded hands wrapped in pious contemplation. The institution of the Sabbath stands in close relation to the appointment of a priesthood, the construction of a holy place, and the establishment of a ceremonial. On the Christian the Fourth Commandment is not binding in respect of the letter—he is not to remember the *Seventh* day to keep it holy, but the *First*; he is not tied to hallow it by an abstinence from all labour, but encouraged to devote it to the performance of good works; but in the spirit of it, the commandment is as binding as any. Men need, under Christianity as much as under Judaism, positive religious institutions, places of worship, hours of prayer, a liturgy, a ritual, ceremonies. The value of the Lord's Day as a Christian institution is incalculable; it witnesses for religion to the world; it constitutes a distinct call on men to take into consideration the aim and intent of the day; and its rightful use is of inestimable benefit to all truly religious persons, deepening in them, as it does, the sense of religion, and giving them time and opportunity for the training of their spiritual nature, and the contemplation of heavenly things, which would otherwise to most men have been unattainable. It has been well called "a bridge thrown across life's troubled waters, over which we may pass to reach the opposite shore—a link between earth and heaven—a type of the eternal day, when the freed spirit, if true to itself and to God, shall put on for ever the robe of immortal holiness and joy."

THE FIFTH COMMANDMENT. The honour which this commandment exacts from us is irrespective of our parents' personal merits or demerits. We are to honour them as being our parents. Difficulties may be raised easily enough in theory; but they are readily solvable in practice. Let us defer to our parents' commands in all things lawful—let us do everything for them that we can—let us anticipate their wishes in things indifferent—let us take trouble on their behalf—let us be ever on the watch to spare them vexatious annoyance—let us study their comfort, ease, peace—and without any sacrifice of principle, even if they are bad parents, we may sufficiently show that we feel the obligation of the relationship, and are anxious to discharge the duties which it involves. Comparatively few men are, however, severely tried. We are not often much better than our parents; and it is seldom difficult to honour them. 1. For their age and experience. 2. For the benefits which they have conferred on us. 3. For the disinterested affection which they bear to us, and which they evince in their conduct. As a rule, parents have very much more love for their children than these have for them, and make sacrifices on their children's behalf, which their children neither appreciate nor reciprocate. The honour which, according to this commandment, has to be shown to parents, must *of course* be extended, with certain modifications, to those who stand to us *in loco parentis*—to guardians, tutors, schoolmasters, and the like. It is not perhaps quite clear that the commandment extends also to those who are set over us in Church and State, though it is usual so to interpret it. There are certain relations of parents to their offspring which are altogether peculiar; and these are absolutely incommunicable. There are others, which are common to parents with rulers; but these, unless in very primitive communities, can scarcely be said to rest upon the domestic relation as their basis. The ordinary relation of the governed to their governors is rather one parallel to that of children to their parents, than one which grows out of it; and though either may be used to illustrate the other, we must view the two as separate and independent of each other.

THE SIXTH COMMANDMENT. How wide is the scope of this commandment to Christians, our Lord has shown. Not only are murder and violence prohibited by it, but even provoking words, and angry thoughts (Matt. v. 21—26). The "root of bitterness" whence murder springs, is either some fierce passion, or some inordinate desire. To be secure from murderous impulses, we must be free from such emotions as these,—we must have tender and loving feelings towards all our fellow-men. "Love is the fulfilling of the law;" and unless a man really "love the brethren," he has no security against being surprised into violence towards them, which may issue in death. Nor is there one species of murder only. The sixth commandment prohibits, not only violence to the body, but—what is of far greater consequence—injury to the soul. Men break it most flagrantly when they lead another into deadly sin, thereby—so far as in them lies— destroying his soul. The corrupter of innocence, the seducer, the persuader to evil, are "murderers" in a far worse sense than the cut-throat, the bandit, or the bravo. Death on the scaffold may expiate the crimes of these latter; eternal punishment alone would seem to be an adequate penalty for the guilt of the former. He that has eternally ruined a soul should surely be himself eternally unhappy.

THE SEVENTH COMMANDMENT. Here again we have the inestimable advantage of our Lord's comment on the commandment, to help us to understand what it ought to mean to us. Not only adultery, but fornication—not only fornication, but impurity of any and every kind—in act, in word, in thought—is forbidden to the Christian. He that looketh on a woman with the object of lusting after her, has already committed adultery with her in his heart (Matt. v. 28). He that dallies with temptation, he that knowingly goes into the company of the impure, he that in his solitary chamber defiles himself, he that hears without rebuking them obscene words, transgresses against this law, and, unless he repents, cuts himself off from God. And observe—the law is one both for men and women. We are ready enough to speak with scorn of "fallen women,"— to regard them as ruined for ever, and treat their sin as the one unpardonable offence; but what of "fallen men"? Is not their sin as irreversible? Is it not the same sin? Is it not spoken of in Scripture in the same way? "Whoremongers and adulterers God will judge" (Heb. xiii. 4). "Murderers, and whoremongers, and sorcerers, and idolaters, and all liars shall have their part in the lake which burneth with fire and brimstone; which is the second death" (Rev. xxi. 8). And is it not as debasing, as deadening to the soul, as destructive of all true manliness, of all true chivalry, of all self-respect? *Principiis obsta.* Let the young keep that precious gift of purity which is theirs, and not be induced by the ridicule of unclean men to part with it. Once gone it can never return. Let them be pure, as Christ was pure. Blessed are the pure in heart!

THE EIGHTH COMMANDMENT. Simple direct stealing, being severely punished by the law in most countries, is seldom practised, unless it be by children and slaves. But indirect stealing of various kinds is common. It should be clearly understood that the Christian precept forbids any act by which we fraudulently obtain the property of another. Adulteration, concealment of defects, misrepresentation of quality, employment of false weights or measures, are the acts of a thief, as much as pocket-picking or shop-lifting. Servants steal when they take "commission" from tradesmen unknown to their masters, or appropriate as "perquisites" what their masters have not expressly agreed to allow, or neglect to do the work which they undertook, or do it in a slovenly manner, or damage their master's property by carelessness or diminish it by waste. Masters steal when they do not permit their servants the indulgences they promised, or allow their wages to fall into arrear, or force them to work overtime without proper remuneration, or deprive them of such "rest" as they had a reasonable right to expect upon the Sunday. Those steal who cheat the revenue by smuggling, or false returns to tax-collectors; or who cheat tradesmen by incurring debts which they can never pay, or who in view of coming bankruptcy pass over their property to a friend, with the understanding that it is to be restored to them, or who have recourse of any of the "tricks of trade," as they are called. All men are sure to steal in one way or another, who are not possessed by the spirit of honesty, who do not love justice and equity and fair-dealing, who do not make it the law of their life to be ever doing to others as they would that others should do unto them.

THE NINTH COMMANDMENT. False witness in a court is but rarely given. We most of us pass our lives without having once to appear in a court, either as prosecutor, witness, or accused. The false witness against which the generality have especially to be on their guard, is that evil speaking which is continually taking place in society, whereby men's characters are blackened, their motives misrepresented, their reputations eaten away. It is dull and tame to praise a man. We get a character for wit and shrewdness if we point out flaws in his conduct, show that he may have acted from a selfish motive, "just hint a fault and hesitate dislike." It is not even necessary in all cases to establish our character for shrewd insight that we should say anything. Silence when we hear a friend maligned, a shrug of the shoulders, a movement of the eyebrows, will do. Again, false witness may be given in writing as well as in speech. The reviewer who says of a book worse than he thinks of it, bears false witness. The writer for the Press who abuses in a leading article a public man whom he inwardly respects, bears false witness. The person who vents his spite against a servant by giving him a worse character than he deserves, bears false witness. We can only be secure against daily breaches of this commandment by joining the spirit of love with a deep-seated regard for truth, and aiming always at saying of others, when we have occasion to speak of them, the best that we can conscientiously say.

THE TENTH COMMANDMENT. The tenth commandment is supplementary to the eighth. Rightly understood, the eighth implies it, covetousness being the root from which theft springs. The command seems added to the Decalogue in order to lay down the principle that the thoughts of the heart come under God's law, and that we are as responsible for them as for our actions. Otherwise, it would not be needed, being implied in the eighth and in the seventh. Since, however, it was of the greatest importance for men to know and understand that God regards the heart, and " requires truth in the inward parts;" and since covetousness was the cause of the greater portion of the evil that is in the world, the precept, although already implied, was given expressly. Men were forbidden to covet the house, wife, slaves, cattle, property of their neighbour—in fact, " anything that is his." They were not forbidden to desire houses, or wives, or cattle, or property generally—which are all, within limits, objects of desire and things which men may rightfully wish for—but they were forbidden to desire for themselves such as were already appropriated by their fellows, and of which, therefore, they could not become possessed without their fellows suffering loss. A moderate desire for earthly goods is not forbidden to the Christian (Matt. xix. 29; 1 Tim. iv. 8); though his special covetousness should be for " the best gifts "—the virtues and graces which make up the perfect Christian character (1 Cor. xii. 31; xiv. 1).

HOMILIES BY VARIOUS AUTHORS.

Ver. 1.—*The moral law—Preliminary.* The law given from Sinai is the moral law *by pre-eminence.* The principles which it embodies are of permanent obligation. It is a brief summary of the whole compass of our duty to God and man. It is a law of supreme excellence—" holy, just, and good " (Rom. vii. 12). God's own character is expressed in it; it bears witness to his unity, spirituality, holiness, sovereignty, mercy, and equity; truth and righteousness are visible in its every precept. Listening to its "thou shalts" and "thou shalt nots," we cannot but recognise the same stern voice which speaks to us in our own breasts, addressing to us calls to duty, approving us in what is right, condemning us for what is wrong. These ten precepts, accordingly, are distinguished from the judicial and ceremonial statutes subsequently given—(1) As the moral is distinguished from the merely positive; (2) As the universally obligatory is distinguished from what is local and temporary; (3) As the fundamental is distinguished from the derivative and secondary. The judicial law, *e.g.*, not only draws its spirit, and derives its highest authority, from the law of the ten commandments, but is, in its own nature, simply an application of the maxims of this law to the problems of actual government. Its binding force was confined to Israel. The ceremonial law, again, with its meats and drinks, its sacrifices, etc. bore throughout the character of a positive institution, and had no independent moral worth. It stood to the moral law in a triple relation of subordination—(1) As inferior to it in its own nature. (2) As designed to aid the mind in rising to the apprehension of the holiness which the law enjoined. (3) As providing (typically) for the removal of guilt contracted by the breaking of the law. This distinctness of the "ten words" from the other parts of the law is evinced—

I. IN THE MANNER OF THEIR PROMULGATION. 1. They alone were spoken by the voice of God from Sinai. 2. They were uttered amidst circumstances of the greatest magnificence and terror. 3. They alone were written on tables of stone. 4. They were written by God's own finger (ch. xxxi. 18). The rest of the law was communicated *privately* to Moses, and through him delivered to the people.

II. IN THE NAMES GIVEN TO THEM, AND THE USE MADE OF THEM. 1. They are "the words of the Lord," as distinguished from the "judgments" or "rights" derived from them, and embraced with them in "the book of the covenant," as forming the statutory law of Israel (ch. xxiv. 3). 2. The tables on which they were written are—to the exclusion of the other parts of the law—called "the testimony" (ch. xxv. 16), "the covenant" (Deut. iv. 13), "the words of the covenant" (ch. xxxiv. 28), "the tables of testimony" (Ex. xxxi. 18; xxxii. 15), "the tables of the covenant" (Deut. ix. 9—11). 3. The tables of stone, and they only, were placed in the ark of the covenant (ch. xxv. 21). They were thus regarded as in a special sense the bond of the covenant. The deposition of the tables in the ark, underneath the mercy seat, throws light on the *nature* of the covenant with Israel. The law written on the tables is the *substratum* of the covenant—its obligatory document—the bond; yet over the law is the mercy-seat, sprinkled with blood of propitiation—a testimony that there is forgiveness with God, that he may be feared (Ps. cxxx. 4), that God will deal *mercifully* with Israel under this covenant. It is obvious, from these considerations, how fallacious is the statement that the Old Testament makes no distinction between the moral, juristic, and ceremonial parts of the law, but regards all as of equal dignity.—J. O.

Vers. 1—18.—*The moral law—General survey.* View this law of the ten commandments as—

I. AUTHORITATIVELY DELIVERED. "God spake all these words, saying," etc. (ver. 1). An authoritative revelation of moral law was necessary—1. *That man might be made distinctly aware of the compass of his obligations.* The moral knowledge originally possessed by man had gradually been parted with. What remained was distorted and confused. He had little right knowledge of his duty to God, and very inadequate conceptions even of his duties to his fellow-men. This lost knowledge was recovered to him by positive revelation. Consider, in proof of the need of such a revelation, the ignorance of God which prevails still, men's imperfect apprehensions of his holiness, their defective views of duty, etc. And this though the revelation has so long been given. 2. That a *basis of certainty* might be obtained for the *inculcation* of moral truth. This also was necessary. Man has ever shown himself ingenious in explaining away the obligations which the law imposes on him. He may deny that they exist. He may make light of holiness. He may take up utilitarian ground, and ride off on disputes as to the nature of conscience, the origin of moral ideas, the diversities of human opinion, etc. The law stops all such cavilling by interposing with its authoritative "Thus saith the Lord." See on this point a valuable paper on "Secularism," by R. H. Hutton, in "Expositor," January, 1881. 3. *That the authority of conscience may be strengthened.* Conscience testifies, in however dim and broken a way, to the existence of a law above us. It speaks with authority. "Had it might as it has right, it would rule the world." In order, however, that we may be made to feel that it is a living *will*, and no mere impersonal law, which thus imposes its commands upon us, there is a clear need for the voice within being reinforced by the voice without—for historical revelation. Sinai teaches us to recognise the authority which binds us in our consciences as *God's* authority. 4. For *economic* purposes. See previous chapter.

II. GRACIOUSLY PREFACED. "I am the Lord, thy God," etc. (ver. 2). This preface to the law is of great importance. 1. *It testified to the fact that God's relation to Israel was fundamentally a gracious one.* "The law was introduced with the words, 'I am the *Lord thy God*,' and speaks with the majestic authority of the Eternal, dispensing blessings and cursings on the fulfilment and transgression of the law. But although this is given amidst the thunder and lightning of Sinai, whose roll seems to be heard constantly in its mighty imperatives—'Thou shalt not!' or 'Thou shalt!' yet still it points back to grace; for the God who speaks in the law is he who led the people out of Egypt, freed them from the yoke of bondage—the God who gave the promise to Abraham, and who has prepared a highest good, the Messianic kingdom, for his people" (Martensen). 2. *It furnished a motive for obedience to the law.* Mark the order the same as in the Gospel, God first saves Israel, then gives them his *law* to keep. *Because* God had redeemed them from Egypt, and had given them, of his free mercy, this glorious privilege of being his people, *therefore* were they to keep his commandments. This was the return they were to make to him for the so great love wherewith he had loved them. Their relation to the law was not to be a servile one. Obedience was not to be a price paid for favour, but a return of grateful hearts for favours already received. From this motive of gratitude, and that they might retain the privileges he had given them, and inherit further blessing, they were to walk in the prescribed way. If, notwithstanding, a pronouncedly legal element entered into that economy, a curse even being pronounced against those who failed to keep the whole law, while the good promised to obedience appears more as legal award than as a gift of grace—we know now the reason for the covenant being cast into this legal form, and can rejoice that in Christ our justification is placed on so much better a footing. Obedience, however, is still required of us as a condition of continuance in God's favour, and of ultimate inheritance of blessing. 3. *It furnished to the pious Israelite a pledge of merciful treatment when he transgressed or fell short of the requirements of his law.* What, *e.g.*, had David to fall back upon in the hour of his remorse for his great transgression (Ps. li.), but just such a word as this, confirmed as it was by *acts* of God, which showed that it was a word always to be depended on. This one saying, prefacing the law, altered the whole complexion of Israel's standing *under* law. It gave to the Israelite the assurance that he most needed, namely— that, notwithstanding the strictness of the commandment, God would yet accept him in his *sincere endeavours after* obedience, though these fell manifoldly short of the full requirement, *i.e.*, virtually on the ground of *faith*—in connection, however, with propitiation.

III. MORAL IN ITS SUBSTANCE. This has been adverted to above. Though imposed on man by Divine authority, moral law is no arbitrary creation of the Divine will. It is an emanation from the Divine nature. (Cf. Hooker—"Of law there can be no less acknowledged than that her seat is the bosom of God; her voice the harmony of the world.") Herbert Spencer was never guilty of a greater misrepresentation than when he affirmed—"Religious creeds, established and dissenting, all embody the belief that right and wrong are right and wrong simply in virtue of Divine enactment" ("Data of Ethics," p. 50). We may reply with Stahl—"The primary idea of goodness is the essential, not the creative, will of God. The Divine will, in its essence, is infinite love, mercy, patience, truth, faithfulness, rectitude, spirituality, and all that is included in the idea of holiness, which constitutes the inmost nature of God. The holiness of God, therefore, neither precedes his will ('*sanctitas antecedens voluntatem*' of the schoolmen) nor follows it, but is his will itself. The good is not a law for the Divine will (so that God wills it because it is good); neither is it a creation of his will (so that it becomes good because he wills it); but it is the nature of God from everlasting to everlasting." (See also Martensen's "Christian Ethics," on "God the only Good," and on "The Law's Content.") The law, in a word, expresses immutable demands of holiness. What these are is determined in any given case by the abstract nature of holiness and by the constitution and circumstances of the being to whom the law is given. Man, *e.g.*, is a free, immortal spirit; but he is at the same time an inhabitant of the earth, bound by natural conditions, and standing to his fellow-men in relations, some of which at least belong only to his present state of existence. Hence we find in the Decalogue precepts relating to the weekly Sabbath, to marriage, to the institution of private property, etc. These precepts are founded on our nature, and are universally obligatory. They show what duty immutably requires of us as possessing such a nature; but obviously their application will cease under different conditions of existence (Matt. xxii. 30). Only in its fundamental principles of love to God and to our fellow-beings, and in its *spiritual* demands for truth, purity, uprightness, reverence, and fidelity, is the law *absolutely* unchangeable.

IV. COMPLETE IN ITS PARTS. Observe—1. Its *two divisions*, turning, the one on the principle of love to God, the other, on the principle of love to man. 2. *The relative position of the two divisions*—duty to God standing first, and laying the needful foundation for the right discharge of our duties to mankind. True love to man has its fountain head in love to God. Neglect of the duties of piety will speedily be followed by the neglect of duty to our neighbour. The Scripture does not ignore the distinction between religion (duties done directly to God) and morality (duties arising from earthly relations), but it unites the two in the deeper idea that all duty is to be done to God, whose authority is supreme in the one sphere as in the other. 3. *The scope of its precepts.* These cover the entire range of human obligation. The precepts of the first table (including here the Fifth Commandment) require that God be honoured in his being, his worship, his name, his day, his human representatives. The precepts of the second table require that our neighbour be not injured in deed, in word, in thought; and in respect neither of his person, his wife, his property, nor his reputation. So complete and concise a summary of duty—religious and ethical—based on true ideas of the character of God, and taking holiness, not bare morality, as its standard, is without parallel in ancient legislation.

V. SPIRITUAL IN ITS PURPORT. "The law is spiritual" (Rom. vii. 14). 1. *The law to be studied in its principles.* Taken in its bare letter, it might appear narrow. Here, however, as everywhere in Scripture, the letter is only the vehicle of the spirit. The whole law of Moses being founded on this part of it—being viewed simply as an expansion or amplification in different relations of the principles embodied in the ten words— it is plain, and common sense supports us in the view, that the *principles* are the main things, the true roots of obligation. Thus, the Third Commandment, in the letter of it, forbids false swearing, or generally, any vain use of the name of God. But underlying this, and obviously forming the ground of the command, is the *principle* that God's name, *i.e.*, everything whereby he manifests himself, is to be treated with deepest reverence. This principle, in its various applications, carries us far beyond the letter of the precept. Read in the same way, the Sixth Commandment forbids killing, but not less the murderous motive than the murderous act; while the principle involved, viz., reverence for, and care of, human life (cf. Gen. ix. 6), branches out into a multiplicity of duties, of which the other parts of the law of Moses furnish numerous illustrations. The true key to the spiritual interpretation of the law is that given by Christ in the sermon on the Mount (Matt. v.—vii.). 2. *Summed up in love.* "Love is the fulfilling of the law" (Rom. xiii. 8—10). (1) It is the *central* requirement. "Them that love me" (ver. 6). Implied in the first and all later precepts. Whatever in the way of outward service we render to God, or man, if *love* is withheld, the law is not fulfilled. (2) It is needed to fill up the *meaning* of the special precepts. These receive their fulness of interpretation only through love. And, in the spiritual reading of them, they cannot be kept without love. It is impossible, *e.g.*, to keep the heart free from all envy, malice, hate, covetousness, save as it is possessed by the opposite principle of love. Love is the root of fidelity to God, of spirituality in his worship, of reverence for his name, of delight in his day, etc. The more deeply we penetrate into the meaning of the law, the more clearly do we perceive that love to God and love to man are indispensable for the fulfilling of it. (3) Love *secures* the fulfilling of the law. For "love worketh no ill to his neighbour" (Rom. xiii. 10). It will not voluntarily injure another. It will not kill, rob, defraud, slander a fellow-man, or covet his possessions. On the contrary, it will seek in every way it can to do him good. It is the great *impelling* motive to obedience. "The love of Christ constraineth us" (2 Cor. v. 14). "Faith, which worketh by love" (Gal. v. 6).

VI. POWERFULLY ENFORCED,—1. By Divine threatenings (vers. 5—7). 2. By Divine example (ver. 11). 3. By Divine promises (vers. 6—12). See below. Behold, then, the beauty and perfection of the law. "Thy commandment is exceeding broad" (Ps. cxix. 96). We are not to be misled, 1. By the studied *brevity* of the law, which is part of its excellency; or, 2. By its prevailing *negative* form—a testimony, not to the unspirituality of the law, but to the existence of strong evil tendencies in the heart, needing to be repressed (Rom. vii. 7, 8; 1 Tim. i. 9 10). Yet perfect as it is of its kind, it is not to be compared, as a mirror of holiness, with the perfect human life of Jesus Christ. No accumulation of separate precepts can exhaust all that is contained in holiness. Precepts convey also a defective idea of the good by breaking up that which is in its own nature one—an ideal—into a number of separate parts. What, however, the law could not do for us, is done in the perfect example of our Lord. In him, law is translated into life. The ideal is no longer presented to us, as even in the Decalogue, in detached precepts, "broken lights," "words," which just because holiness is so vast a thing—are left to hint more than they express, but in its true unbroken unity, in the sphered whole of a perfect human character. *Our* law is Christ.—J. O.

Vers. 1, 2.—*The Ten Commandments—an introductory reminder.* Before the speaker of these commandments proceeded to the utterance of them, it was necessary that he should call special and reverent attention to himself. Not one of the words he was about to say could either be understood or obeyed without a constant reference in thought to him who had delivered and arranged them. He did not bring them before Israel as a far seeing legislator might bring such rules as were best adapted to the limitations and infirmities of those whom he sought to guide. They were the laws of that kingdom where the King himself is a real and immutable lawgiver, he whose reign never comes to an end. Some of the commandments had a direct reference to himself; and all had to do with his service. Should it not, then, be ever a helpful and sobering truth to us that the great laws for human life thus come as expressions through a Divine will? We cannot overrate the importance of requirements which God himself solemnly declares. And just as we Christians in repeating the Lord's prayer must think constantly of the invocation to our Father in heaven, in order to enforce and enrich the plea of each petition, so in carrying out these ten commandments, each Israelite was bound to think of each commandment in connection with that Jehovah who had spoken it. The thought that he had brought them out of the land of Egypt and out of the house of bondage was meant to give special force to everything he required from the hands of his people.

I. JEHOVAH SPEAKS OF HIMSELF IN THE LIGHT OF WHAT HE HAS DONE FOR THEM TO WHOM HE SPEAKS. He solemnly charges them to look back on *their own experience*, to consider their past suffering and helplessness, and how they had come to the present hour entirely because of what he had done for them. Note that he does not, as on former occasions, speak of himself as the God of Abraham, Isaac, and Jacob; that was a necessary mode of description when he made his first approach to them, but now they have their own rich and crowded experiences to constitute a claim for their attention and obedience. God bases his expectations on services rendered to the present generation; and the claim he makes is founded on the greatest boon that could be conferred, liberty. When from this very mountain he sent Moses to them, they were in bitter servitude; now Moses finds himself at this mountain again, with a nation of freemen around him. Jehovah is not afraid of referring to the land of Egypt, even though the people had allowed the agreeable associations of the name to override the disagreeable ones. They delighted in thinking of it as a land where they sat by the fleshpots and ate bread to the full (ch. xvi. 3 ; Num. xi. 4, 5). But now in this reference to himself which would henceforth be so conspicuous, Jehovah fixes together in a permanent association the land of Egypt and the house of bondage. When the people disparaged the wilderness and glorified Egypt, he made them hear again the sound of the clanking chain; and if that sound, heard only in memory, was not dreadful as in the old reality, yet God, who is not influenced by the lapses of time, knew how dreadful that reality was. It is a good thing that he remembers what men forget. Even though we be Christians, and should have better aims and better joys, we too often catch our thoughts turned longingly towards a forsaken world. And so God comes in to speak plainly and burst the bubble of this world's attractions by the emphasised truth that spiritual Egypt is the house of bondage. He that committeth sin is the slave of sin. While the people were in Egypt they had not talked of these things as pleasant; the life there, in the actual experience of it, was intolerable. And so with perfect confidence God could appeal to their past consciousness.

II. There was also an indication that GOD HAD TAKEN AWAY ALL EXTERNAL HINDRANCES TO OBEDIENCE. He had taken them clean out of the house of bondage. They were now free to carry out all the observances which Jehovah was about to appoint. They had no Pharaoh to struggle with, grudging them time to serve their God (ch. v. 4); they had no danger to fear from sacrificing the abominations of Egypt within its borders. If God asks us for service, we may be sure that in the very first place, he will provide all the conditions of rendering it effectually and comfortably. As we read our New Testament, we are made to feel that God expects very large things from us. He is most exacting in his claims for self-denial and completeness of devotion to his cause, but what of that? Has he not given us his own Spirit, which is a spirit of liberty, working for the express purpose of lifting us above the crippling restraints of natural life? The very largeness of God's demands helps us to measure the largeness of God's spiritual gifts; and the very largeness of the gifts should prepare us for large demands. God's expectations are from the free. He asked nothing from Israel, save silent and submissive waiting, until the verge of the last plague, which was also the verge of liberty; and from the free *because he has freed them*, he entertains large expectations. It was to those who believed in Jesus, risen from the dead, and making his people to live in newness of life, that he gave a spirit of such power in producing obedience and conformity as never had been known before.—Y.

Vers. 3—6.—*The first and second commandments: against polytheism and image-worship*. These two commandments seem to be bound together naturally by the reason given in ver. 5. There Jehovah says, "I am a jealous God;" obviously such a feeling of jealousy applies with as much force to the worship of other gods as to the making of graven images. Consider—

I. THE POSSIBLE TRANSGRESSION HERE INDICATED. The having of other gods than Jehovah, and the representation of them by images of created things. The declaration here is not against more gods than one. Such a declaration would have been incomprehensible to the Israelite at this time, even to Moses himself. The utter emptiness of all idolatry, the non-existence, except as the imagination of a superstitious and darkened mind, of any other Deity than Jehovah was a truth not yet appreciable by those to whom Jehovah spoke. He had to take his people as they stood, believers in the existence and power of other gods, and proclaim to them with all the impressiveness that came from the demonstrations of Sinai, that none of these gods was to be in the smallest degree recognised. An idolater in the midst of his idolatries, and not yet laid hold of by Jehovah's hand, might as well have a thousand gods as one. Jehovah speaks here to those who are already bound to himself. Have they not made their promise? Did not the people answer and say, "All that the Lord hath spoken we will do"? It was the right and dutiful course of every Israelite to worship him, serve him, and depend upon him. The great and pressing peril was that, side by side with Jehovah, the people should try to put other gods. And to have other gods meant, practically, to have images of them. How necessary and appropriate these two commandments were to come at this particular time and in this particular order, is seen when we consider the image-making into which Israel fell during the seclusion of Moses in the mount. This seems to have been the accordant act of the whole people; Aaron, who was soon to be the chief official in Jehovah's ritual, being the eager instrument to gratify their desires. Nor was this a mere passing danger to the Israelites, a something which in due time they would outgrow. The peril lies deep in the infirmities of human nature. Those whom Jehovah has brought in any measure to himself, need to be reminded that he is master. Jesus has put the thing as plain as it can be put, "No man can serve two masters." We cannot serve God and Mammon. Dependence on something else than God, even though there be nothing of religious form in the dependence, is a peril into which we are all liable to come. It is hard to fight—harder than we imagine till we are fairly put to the struggle —against the allurements of the seen and temporal. Even when we admit that there is an invisible God whose claims are supreme, and whose gifts, present and future, are beyond anything that the seen in its pride and beauty can afford—even then we have the utmost difficulty in carrying our admission into practice.

II. CONSIDER IN PARTICULAR HOW THE COMMANDMENT AGAINST IMAGE-WORSHIP MAY APPLY TO US. Those who go in the way of right worship are in the way to a profitable knowledge of God. They come to be recognised by him, accepted by him, and blessed by him. Having graven images inevitably led away from Jehovah. There was no possibility of keeping the first commandment, even in the least degree, if the second even in the least degree was broken. Certainly we are under no temptation to make images, but it comes to the same thing if we have images ready made. It is conceivable that the day may come when not an image shall be left in the world, except on museum shelves, and the trade of Demetrius thus come to an end. But what of that? The change may simply be one of form. Why men should first have made images and called them gods is an impenetrable mystery. We cannot but wonder who was the first man to make an image and why he made it. But that image-making, once established, should continue and return into practice again and again in spite of all attempts to destroy it, is easy enough to understand. Habit, tradition, training, will account for everything in this way. Yet the practice of image-worship, at all events in its grossest forms, can only exist together with dense intellectual darkness. When men begin to think and question as to the foundation of things, when they get away from their mother's knee, then the simple faith in what they have been taught deserts them. There is a frequent and natural enough lamentation that those who have been taught concerning Christ in childhood, oftentimes in manhood depart from him by the way of scepticism, into utter disbelief and denial. Yet we must remember that it is exactly by this kind of process thousands in still image-worshipping lands have broken away from their image-worship. It has not satisfied the awakened and expanding intellect. There is this difference, however, that whereas the awakened intellect forsaking Christ may come back to him, and indeed actually does so oftener than we think, the awakened intellect forsaking image-worship cannot go back to it. But to something as a dependent creature he must go. A man leaving his old idolatries and not finding Christ, must needs turn to some new idolatry, none the less real as an idolatry, none the less injurious to his best interests because the image-form is absent. We must not make to ourselves anything whatever to take the place of God, intercept the sight of him, or deaden his voice. We may contradict the spirit of the second commandment, in doing things which we think profitable to the religious life and glorifying to God. A great deal that is reckoned beneficial and even indispensable in the Church of Christ, that has grown with its growth and strengthened with its strength, might come to look very questionable, if only the spirit of this commandment were exactly appreciated. How many splendid buildings, how many triumphs of the architect, how many combined results of many arts would then be utterly swept away! Men delude themselves with the notion that these things bring them nearer to God, whereas they simply take his place. In worshipping him we should regard with the utmost jealousy all mere indulgence of the senses and even of the intellect.

III. The Divine reason given for attending to these commandments. Many reasons might have been given, as for instance, the vanity of graven images, their uselessness in the hour of need, the degradation in which they involved the worshippers. But God brings forward a reason which needed to be brought forward, and put in the very front place, where human thought might continually be directed to it. Polytheism and image-worship are indeed degrading and mischievous to man—but what is of far greater moment, they are also dishonouring to the glory of Deity. Those who were sliding away into the service of other gods were showing that they had no truly reverent appreciation of Jehovah; and in order to intimate the severity of his requirements with respect to exclusive and devoted service, Jehovah speaks of himself as possessing a feeling which, when found among men is like a devouring and unquenchable fire. A jealous man does well to be jealous, if he has sufficient ground for the feeling at all, if the affection, service, and sympathies that should be reserved for him are turned elsewhere. Think then of such a feeling, exalted into the pure intensity of a holy anger and bursting into action from God himself, and then you have the measure of his wrath with those who think that the glory of the incorruptible God can be changed into an image made like to corruptible man. He makes his jealousy apparent in unquestionable, deeply penetrating action. It is the action of the great I AM, who controls thousands of generations. God does, as a matter of fact, visit the iniquities of the fathers on the children, and the magnitude of what he does is accounted for by the intensity of his feelings with respect to those who give his glory to another. His almighty hand comes down with a blow the afflictive energies of which cannot be exhausted in one or even two generations. Say not that there is something unjust about this. That each generation must take something in the way of suffering from preceding generations is a fact only too plain, altogether apart from the Scriptures. The mercy of God is that he here gives us something in explanation of the fact, and of how to distinguish its working and at last destroy it. To serve idols, to depend upon anything else than God, anything less than him, anything more easily reached and more easily satisfied—this, when stripped of all disguise, *amounts to hating God*. And a man living in this way is preparing, not only punishments for himself, but miseries for those who come after him. Many times we have advice given us to think of posterity. Depend upon it, he thinks most of posterity who serves the will of God most humbly and lovingly, with the utmost concentration and assiduity, in his own generation. Note here also the unmistakable revelation of God's merciful disposition. He visits iniquity to the third and fourth generation of them that hate him. But those who love him are blessed to thousands of generations. Not that the blessing will be actually operative, for, alas, there may come in many things to hinder. But the expressed disposition of God remains. If the posterity of the faithful to God are unblessed, it is because they themselves are utterly careless as to the peculiar privileges into which they have been introduced.—Y.

Ver. 7.—*The Third Commandment. Profanity forbidden.* This Commandment clearly comes as an appropriate sequel to the two preceding ones. Those who are Jehovah's, and who are therefore bound to glorify and serve him alone, depend on him alone, and keep themselves from all the degradations and obscuring influences of image worship, are now directed to the further duty of avoiding all irreverent and empty use of the sacred name. With respect to this, there must have been a very real danger in Israel. We have only to observe the licence of modern colloquial speech in this respect, we have only to call to mind some of the most common expletives in English, French, and German, and we shall then better understand that there may have been a great deal of the same sad and careless licence among the ancient Hebrews. Not that we are to suppose Jehovah directed this command exclusively or even chiefly against profane swearers in the ordinary sense of the term. They are included, but after all they are only a small part of those to whom the commandment is directed. It is quite possible for a man to keep above all coarseness and vulgarity of speech, and yet in God's sight be far worse than an habitual swearer. Many are concerned to avoid profane swearing, not because it is offensive to God, but because it is ungentlemanly. It needs no devoutness or religious awe to understand the couplet :—

> "Immodest words admit of no defence, .
> For want of decency is want of sense."

And there is as much want of decency in profane words as in immodest ones. The thing to be considered is not only the words we avoid, but the words we use. Out of the abundance of the heart the mouth will speak. This commandment, like the rest, must be kept positively, or it cannot be kept negatively. If we are found making a serious and habitual use of God's name in a right way, then, and only then, shall we be kept effectually from using it in a wrong one.

I. Evidently the first thing to keep us from empty words with respect to God is TO KEEP FROM ALL EMPTINESS AND SHALLOWNESS OF THOUGHT WITH RESPECT TO HIM. Thinking is but speaking to oneself; and God's commandment really means that we must labour at all times to have right and sufficient thoughts concerning him. We might almost say, take care of the thought and the speech will take care of itself. All our thinking about God, as about every topic of thought, should be in the direction of what is practical and profitable. Blessed is he who has made the great discovery, that of the unseen cause and guide, behind all things that are seen, he can only get profitable knowledge as that Great Unseen is pleased to give it. We who live amid the great declarations of the Gospel are really thinking of God in a vain and displeasing way as long as we suppose it possible to get any true knowledge of him except in Christ. Right knowledge of God, and therefore profitable thoughts of him must be gained by experimental personal search into the riches of God in Christ Jesus. Thinking of this sort will not be vain, shallow, fugitive thinking, seeing that it springs out of apprehended, personal necessities, has an immutable basis of fact, a rewarding element of hope, and is continually freshened by a feeling of gratitude towards one who has conferred on us unspeakable benefits. Surely it is a dreadful sin to think little, to think seldom, and to think wrongly of that profoundly compassionate God, who so loved the world that he gave his only begotten Son, to save it from perishing by the gift of eternal life. No thoughts of ours indeed can measure the fulness of that sublime love, and we shall even fall short of what the holiest and devoutest of men can reach; but there is all the more need why we should labour in constant meditation on the saving ways of God, according to our abilities. Put the word "God" on a sheet of paper, and then try to write underneath all that the name suggests, particularly all that it suggests in the way of individual benefit. Perhaps the writing may come to an end very soon, and even what is written be so vague and valueless as to make you feel that this commandment of God here is not a vain one so far as concerns you.

II. THEN WE MUST NOT TAKE THE NAME OF GOD IN VAIN, IN OUR INTERCOURSE WITH OUR FELLOW-MEN. God, our God, with all his claims and all his benefits, cannot be spoken about too much in the circles of men, if only he is spoken about in a right way: but that right way—*how hard it is to attain*. Much speaking concerning him, even by those who do it officially, is very dishonouring to his name and hindering to his rule in the hearts of men. Preachers of the word of life and duty, the word concerning divine gifts and requirements, need to take great heed in this respect, for whenever they speak without proper impressions as to the solemnity of their message, they are assuredly taking God's name in vain. There has also to be a consideration of the audience. The words of God's truth and salvation must be as far as possible words in season, not wasted, as pearls before swine. It needs that we should strive and watch incessantly to have all attainable fitness as the witnesses of God. Jesus would not have the testimony of demons to his Messiahship, but chose, prepared, and sanctified such men as he saw to be suitable; and then when he had found fit witnesses, even though few, he sent them forth to bear their testimony, sure that it would be sufficient for all who had the right mind to receive it. It is awful, when one only considers it, in how many instances God's name is taken in vain, by the use of it to sanctify unholy ends, justify unrighteousness, and give to error what dignity and force can be gained from an appeal to divine authority. When the Scriptures were quoted to justify slavery, what was this but taking the name of God in vain? How much of it there must have been in theological controversy, where disputants have got so embittered by partisan spirit that they would twist Scripture in any way so as to get God on their side, instead of labouring as honest men to be on the side of God. Look at the glutton sitting down to pamper his stomach from the loaded table; but first of all he must go through the customary grace and make a show of eating and drinking to the glory of God in heaven, when in truth the god he really worships is his greedy, insatiable belly. We may do many things in the name of the Lord, but that does not make them the Lord's things. "Lord, Lord" may ever be on our lips, we may even get a very general reputation for our devotedness to God and goodness; but all this may not prevent us from hearing at the last, "Depart from me, ye that work iniquity."

III. Most particularly we must guard against profanity IN OUR APPROACHES TO GOD. If we are his at all, there must be constant approaches to him, and his name therefore must be constantly on our lips. 1. We must guard against *formality*. We must not take a name on our lips that expresses no felt reality. To confess sins and needs and supplicate pardon and supply when the heart is far away from the throne of grace, is certainly taking God's name in vain. 2. We must guard against coming *in other than the appointed way*. A very elaborate and comprehensive prayer may be constructed to the God of nature and providence, but even though it may seem to be of use for a while, it will show its emptiness in the end if God's own appointment of mediation through Christ Jesus be neglected. Do not let us deceive ourselves with words and aspirations that are only dissipated into the air. For a suppliant to know of Christ and yet ignore his mediation, is assuredly to take God's name in vain, however honest the ignoring may be. 3. Then surely there is an empty use of God's name in prayer, if we ask *in other than the appointed order*. The order of thought in all right approach to God is such as our Great Teacher has himself presented to us. Is it the sinner who is coming, wretched and burdened? Jesus approves the prayer, "God be merciful to me a sinner." Sinners never take the name of God in vain, if they come to him with two feelings blended in one irrepressible cry, the feeling of God's anger with all sin and the feeling of his unfailing compassion for the sinner. Or if it be the disciple and servant who is coming to God, then the order of thought for his approach Jesus has also given. We must ever think of him as our Father in heaven, and first of all of such things as will sanctify his name, advance his kingdom and procure the perfect doing of his will on earth. We must make all our approaches to God with our hearts entirely submitted to him, otherwise we shall only find that we are taking his name in vain.—Y.

Vers. 8—11.—*The Fourth Commandment: the sacred Sabbath.* I. THE GROUND OF THIS COMMANDMENT. God, who had spoken to Israel as to those whom he had brought out of the house of bondage, and who had bidden Moses speak of him to the captives as the God of Abraham, Isaac, and Jacob, now takes the thoughts of his people as far back as it is possible for them to go. They are directed to think of the great work of him who in six days made heaven and earth, the sea, and all that in them is. "All the earth is mine," he had bidden Moses say in ch. xix. 5; and of course the Israelites, whatever their other difficulties in the way of understanding God's commandments, had no question such as modern science has thrown down for us to ponder with respect to these alleged days of creation. Though indeed, as is now generally agreed, no difficulty is found in this question when we approach it rightly. God's thoughts are not as our thoughts; his ways are not as our ways; and so we may add his days are not as our days, seeing that with him one day is as a thousand years and a thousand years as one day. The great matter to be borne in mind by ancient Israelites—and for every Christian the consideration remains whether he also should not very strictly bear it in mind—was that by this seventh day of rest after creation, God gave the great rule for the consecration of his people's time. It is to a certain extent correct to say that this precept is a positive one; but it is not therefore arbitrary. God may have seen well to give the precept in such emphatic way, just because the need of setting apart one day out of seven is in some way fixed in the nature of things. It is a question worth while asking, why creation is set before us as having occupied six successive periods. Why not some other number? May not the periods of creation have been so arranged with a view to the use of them as a ground for this commandment? God sanctified the seventh day because it was the best day—best for human welfare and Divine glory; and it seems to have been at Sinai that he first distinctly made this sanctification. Israel knew already that God rested on the seventh day from all his work which he had made (Gen. ii. 2); now it is known—at least it is known in part—why this resting was not till the seventh day, and also not later. May it not be that the expression "God blessed the seventh day, and sanctified it, because that in it he had rested from all his work which God created and made," (Gen. ii. 3) was inserted by Moses after the transactions at Sinai, as a suitable addition to the statement that God rested from his work? If this verse was not inserted in the Genesis record until after the instructions from Sinai, then we have some sort of explanation why no clear, indubitable sign of the Sabbath is found in patriarchal times.

II. THE MODE OF KEEPING THIS COMMANDMENT. Let us distinctly bear in mind the object to be attained. The seventh day was to be *sanctified,* and in order that it might be properly sanctified, a scrupulous rest from ordinary work was necessary. The *rest* was but the means to the *sanctification;* and the sanctification is the thing to be kept prominently in view. The mere resting from work on the seventh day did an Israelite no good, unless he remembered what the rest implied. The commandment began, "Remember the Sabbath day, to *keep it holy*," not "Remember to do no work therein." Certainly it was only too easy to forget the requirement of rest; but it was easier still to forget the requirement of holiness. A man might rest without hallowing, and so it had to be enjoined on him to shape his rest that hallowing might be secured by it. Certain of the animals required for holy purposes by God, were to be such as had not borne the yoke. The animal could not be given to God and at the same time used for self. And in like manner the Sabbath could not both be given to God and used for self. Therefore the Israelite is charged to do no work and let no work be done, even by the humblest of his slaves. He himself must get no temporal benefit from this day. God has so arranged, in his loving providence and holy requirements, that six days' work shall supply seven days' need. This lesson the manna distinctly teaches if it teaches anything at all. And now that the Jewish Sabbath has gone, the Christian has to ask himself how far the mode of Sabbath-keeping in Israel furnishes any guide for him in his use of the Lord's day. He is a miserable Christian who begins to plead that there is no distinct and express commandment in the New Testament for the keeping of a sacred day of rest. To say that the Sabbath is gone with the outward ordinances of Judaism is only making an excuse for self-indulgence. True, the sacrifices of the law are done away with, but only that imperfections may give place to perfections. In the very doing away, a solemn claim is made that the Christian should present his body as a living sacrifice; and one cannot be a living sacrifice without feeling that all one's time is for doing God's will. When in the inscrutable arrangements of Providence, we find that one day in seven has actually come to be so largely a day of cessation from toil, surely the part of Christian wisdom is to make the very best of the opportunity. There is, and there always will be, room for much improvement as to the mode of keeping the day of rest; but in proportion as we become filled with the spirit of Christ and the desire for perfection, in that proportion we shall be delivered from the inclination to make Sunday a day for *self*, and led forward in resolution, diligence and love, to make it a day for God. The more we can make our time holy time, the more we shall make ourselves holy persons. If in God's mercy we find Sunday a day of larger opportunities, let it be *according to our individual opportunity*, a day of larger achievements. Each one of us should say, " I am bound to discover how God would have *me* use this day." My neighbour Christian may feel constrained to use it in a way that, if I were to imitate him, might not promote my own spiritual advantage, or the glory of God. Let every man be fully persuaded in his own mind, only let him take care that he has a persuasion and acts conscientiously and lovingly up to it.

III. THE PECULIAR EMPHASIS LAID ON THIS COMMANDMENT. "Remember." Not of course that this commandment is more important than the rest. He who breaks one breaks all, for each is a member of the whole as of a living unity. But there must have been a special reason in the mind of God for calling attention to this commandment. We are told to remember what we are likely to forget. Also, certain things we are exhorted to remember, because if we only remember them we shall come in due course to other things which cannot be so constantly in the mind, and which indeed the mind may not yet be able properly to grasp. He who remembers the right way will assuredly come to the right end, even though he may not be constantly thinking of it. We may be sure that keeping the Sabbath day *really* holy, had a very salutary effect towards keeping all the rest of the commandments. It gave time for reflection on all those affairs of daily life in which there are so many opportunities and temptations to set at nought the righteous claims both of God and of our fellow-men. And so the Christian may ever say to himself, "Soul, *remember* the day of rest which God has so graciously secured to thee." God, though he has condescendingly done so much to come near to needy men with his supplies of grace, gets soon hidden by the cloud and dust of this world's business. It is only too easy to forget the spirit of these commandments, and be unfair, unkind, malicious and revengeful toward our fellow-men in the jostlings and rivalries of life. *Remember* then. Let us but attend to this and the rest of *God's remembers*, and we may be sure they will do a great deal to neutralise that forgetting which is inevitably incident to the infirmities of fallen human nature.—Y.

Ver. 12.—*The Fifth Commandment: the commandment for children.* I. LOOK AT THIS COMMANDMENT AS IT CONCERNED THE PARENTS. 1. *This commandment gave the parents an opportunity for telling the children how it originated.* Not only an opportunity, but we may say a necessity. It was a commandment to children, through their parents. All the commandments, statutes, and judgments, were to be taught diligently to the children (Deut. vi. 7), and this one here would require very earnest and special explanation in the family. It will be seen that it was a commandment which could not be isolated; a self-willed parent could not quote it with any advantage for the sake of upholding arbitrary authority. The Israelite parent had to explain how these commandments were given; he had to narrate the events in Sinai, and these in turn compelled a reference to the exodus and the bitter experiences of Egypt. Parents had well to consider how much depended on themselves in making their children duly acquainted with all the glorious doings and strict requirements of Jehovah. If a parent had to deal with a disobedient and despising child, he was able to point out that this requirement of honouring father and mother was God's most strict requirement, and God was he who had rule and authority over parent and child alike. 2. *Thus father and mother were evidently required to honour themselves.* No special verbal utterance was here required, telling father and mother to remember the obligations to offspring, and anyway this was not the proper place for it. The commandments here are *universal* commandments, such as all men incur the temptation of breaking. Thus it was eminently fitting to have a word for children, enjoining upon them the proper feeling towards parents; as all know the filial relation, but all do not know the parental one. One of the merits of the Decalogue is its brevity and sententiousness. No father could expect his children to honour the parental relation unless he did so himself; and in measure as he more and more comprehended the import of the relation, in that measure might his children be expected to respond to his treatment of them. "Honour all men," says the apostle Peter; and to do this we must begin at home in our own life, and put the proper value on ourselves. God has put immense honour on father and mother; and it is the curse, loss, and fearful reservation of penalty for many parents that they do not see what momentous interests have been put in their stewardship. 3. *God thus showed his earnest desire to help parents in their arduous, anxious work.* The work of a parent in Israel who had weighed all his responsibilities was no light matter. Great opportunities were given him, and great things might be done by him; things not to be done by any other teacher or guide, and he had thus a very comforting assurance that God was his helper. Helper to the father, and, bear in mind, to the mother also. It is worthy of note that father *and mother* are specially mentioned. She is not left in the obscurity of a more general term. God would give to both of them according to their peculiar opportunities all understanding, wisdom, forbearance, steadfastness, discrimination of character, that might be necessary for their work.

II. As IT CONCERNED THE CHILDREN. A commandment was not needed to teach children as to the making of some sort of distinction between their father and mother and other men and women. But, in order that the distinction might be a right one, and evermore real and deepening in its presence and influence, such a commandment as this was imperatively needed. As we have said, it was a commandment universal in its scope, because all are or have been in the filial relation, but as a matter of fact it would address itself directly to the young. They were laid hold of as soon as anything like intelligence, power to obey, and power to understand the difference between right and wrong manifested themselves. God came and made his claim upon them, in a way as suitable as any to their childish consciousness. They were to honour father and mother, not because father and mother said so, but because God said so. Plainly the honouring included both deep inward feeling and clear outward expression. The outward expression, important as it was, could only come from real and habitual feeling within. Outward expression by itself counted for nothing. Honouring with the lips while the heart was far removed from the parent would be reckoned a grievous sin against God. The child had to grow up esteeming and venerating the parental relation everywhere. It could not honour its own father and mother and at the same time despise the parents of other children. *The promise here given* obviously a suitable one for children. To them the prospect of a long life, in the land already promised, was itself a promise agreeable to the limitations of the old covenant, when there could be no pointing in clear terms to the land beyond death; and we may be very sure that, according to this promise, filial obedience had a corresponding temporal reward.—Y.

Vers. 13—17.—*The individual Israelite considered in his duties towards his neighbour.* Of these five commandments—namely, against murder, adultery, theft, slander and covetousness, it almost goes without saying that their very negativeness in form constitutes the strongest way of stating a positive duty. From a proper consideration of these commandments all possible manifestations of brotherliness will flow. They show the spirit we should cherish towards our neighbours; those who equally with ourselves are the objects of Divine providence and mercy. They show what we are bound to give and what we have equally a right to expect.   Pondering the serious and injurious actions here indicated we note—

I. THE GREAT HARM WHICH MEN CAN DO TO ONE ANOTHER.   A man maliciously disposed, sensual, reckless, unscrupulously selfish, has thus the extent of his power set before him.   That life which man has no power to give, he can take away at a single blow.   A man in the gratification of his sensual passions is able to destroy domestic peace, gladness and purity.   Property, which may be the fruit and reward of long industry, is swept away by those who will not work for themselves as long as they can get others to work for them.   Reputation may be taken away by adroit and plausible slander.   A man's whole position may be made uncertain by those who on the right hand and the left look enviously on that position and wish to make it their own.   It is when these possibilities are borne in mind that we feel how true it is that even the best guarded of earthly store-houses is nevertheless the one where the thief can break through and steal.   Industry, temperance, caution, vigilance, will guard many points of human life, but what avails, if even a single one is left that cannot be called invulnerable ?   If, then, our fellow men are so much in our power, how it becomes us to quell the very first outbreaks of all that is malicious, envious, selfish and sensual !   If we allow the evil in us to grow, we know not what evil it may inflict on the innocent and happy.

II. But if these commandments show a dark and menacing side in our relations to others, they equally show a bright one.   THERE IS GREAT GOOD WHICH WE CAN DO TO ONE ANOTHER.   The man who has power to kill, has, on the other hand, power to do much in the way of preserving, cherishing and invigorating the lives of others. Instead of pulling down others by a degrading companionship to the level of his own impure heart, he can do something by seeking purity himself to draw others toward a like quest.   Instead of stealing, he will work not only to sustain himself, but that from his superfluity, if possible, he may give to those who have not.   He who has spoken ill of men will find it just as easy to speak well, if only he is so disposed.   That tongue with which the renewed heart blesses God will also be constrained to say what is kind, commendatory and helpful to others.   Covetousness will give place to a gracious and generous disposition that constantly takes for its motto, " It is more blessed to give than to receive."   It is only when we are doing our neighbours all the good we can, that we may be really sure we are carrying out the commandments of God.   There are only the two ways, the forbidden and the commanded one ; and if we are not treading heartily and resolutely in the commanded one, it follows as a matter of course that we are in the forbidden one.

III. It is something to remember that THE GOOD WE CAN DO BY KEEPING THESE COMMANDMENTS IS GREATER THAN THE ILL WE CAN DO BY BREAKING THEM.   God has put us largely in the power of one another, that thereby we might have the happiness coming from loving service and mutual association in giving and receiving; but, at the same time, he has made us so that while we are very powerful as co-workers with him, yet even our greatest efforts are comparatively powerless against those who put themselves under his protection.   Those injuring others do indeed inflict a great injury from a certain point of view ; but they terribly deceive themselves in thinking that the injury is such as can never be compensated for.   Christ has given to his people the word of comfort against all assault and spoliation from evil men :—" Fear not them that kill the body."   The priceless treasures, constituting the essence of every human life, are not without a storehouse because the earthly storehouse proves insufficient.   The truth seems to be that man has it in his power to do more good than he can conceive, more good certainly than he ever attempts.   He has not the faith to believe that incessant and plenteous sowing will bring good results, to be manifested in that day when all secrets are brought fully to light.   And so on the other hand, the malicious man exaggerates his power.   He thinks he has done more than he possibly can do.   Good is left undone for want of faith, and evil is done through too much faith.   Many an evil act would never have been committed if the doer had only known how his evil, in the wondrous reach of God's providence, would be turned to good.   And so the evil-doer, the man of many crimes, if perchance the hour comes to him when he reflects in self-condemnation in the past, and says in his heart that all repentance is vain, should yet find hope and illumination as he considers how the evil done to others is an evil which

God can neutralise, which he can even transmute into good. He who hurts his neighbour and rejoices over the mischief, may find, when it is too late, that the only real evil has been to himself, because he has persisted in an impenitent heart.—Y.

Vers. 16—21.—*The ten words.* "And God spake all these words." "And the people stood afar off: and Moses drew near unto the thick darkness where God was." (Ex. xx. 1, 21). Our subject is the law of the ten commandments, and—

I. The NAMES of the code, for names are oft the keys to things. There are five chief names; four in the Old Testament and one in the New. 1. "*The ten words.*" ["The ten commandments" is an unscriptural phrase.] (Ex. xxxiv. 28; Deut. iv. 13; x. 4 See Heb.) This name implies that the code was in a very special sense the distinct *utterance* of God. The utterance touched that which was central in human life, viz., duty. 2. "*The law,*" *i.e.*, the heart and core of the Mosaic legislation. All the rest was as the fringe to the robe of righteousness. 3. "*The testimony.*" God's attestation of his mind as to our moral carriage through life. 4. "*The covenant.*" But care should be exercised as to the putting of this. Israel was not to keep the ten words in order to salvation, but because Israel *had been* saved. Spiritual obedience springs from gratitude—cannot be given as *the price of salvation.* 5. "*The commandments*" (Matt. xviii. 17). The names of the code stamp it as unique. The Mosaic legislation stands out like a mountain range from all other codes historic in the world; but the "ten words" are the ten peaks of that mighty range.

II. The MOMENT when God gave the "ten" was critical and significant. 1. *Subsequent to salvation* (Ex. xx. 1). Trace the evangelical parallel, show that this is the order of the divine love, first deliverance, and then direction for life. 2. *Before ritual.* Hence the subordination, even for the Jew, of ritual to morals. For us the symbolic ritual is no more. Our prerogative is that of unveiled gaze upon the spiritual.

III. The DELIVERY of the "ten words." [The object here should be so to describe the incidents of the delivery, on the basis of the sacred narrative, aided by topographical illustration, as to exhibit the unique character of this code. The following hints may be of service]:—The great plain north of Sinai; Sinai to the south; the barren character of this huge natural temple [Stanley's "J. C." i. 128]; on the third day every eye turned to the mountain; mists rising like smoke; lightning; thunder like ten thousand trumpets; reverberation; earth-trembling. The people would have drawn away, but Moses led them near the base. He ascended; but returned, that he, as *one of the people,* and with them, might hear the code. God alone. Then the very voice of very God, possibly pronouncing the "ten" in their shortest form. [Ewald: "Israel," ii. 163, Eng. tr.] The cry of the people for a mediator. If we had to-day a phonogram even of that awful voice, some would still say, "It is the voice of a man, and not of a god."

IV. The PRESERVATION. The "ten" were—1. *Graven by God.* The record supernatural, like the delivery. On granite; not too large for a man to carry; graven on both sides; symbol of the completeness, inviolability, and perpetuity of the Divine law. Note the seven or eight weeks' delay ere the tables were given, and the intervening incidents. 2. *Kept in the ark.* In that which was a memorial of the desert life; the wood, acacia of the wilderness. In that which was central to the life of Israel. In Israel a sanctuary, a holiest of all, the ark, and in the deep recesses of that the idea of duty enshrined. The tables last seen at Solomon's dedication. Are they now lying with the wreck of Babylon in the valley of the Euphrates?

V. The ORDER AND THE ARRANGEMENT. 1. *There were five words on each table.* So we think. Great diversity of opinion as to the division and the throwing of the "ten words" on the two tables. According to the division we adopt, the first table concerned itself with God—his *existence, worship, name, day,* and *representative.* But if the parent is the representative of God, then there are suggestions for the character and the administration of the parent; as well as for the intelligent obedience of the child. 2. The five words *concerning duty to God come first.* Religion ever comes before morality, and morality without that foundation must be partial and imperfect. Man must first be in right relation with the Father in heaven, then he will come to be right with all the children.

VI. The COMPREHENSIVENESS. Passages like Josh. i. 7, 8; Ps. cxix. 18, 72, imply a great depth and breadth in these " ten." Are they really so comprehensive as is implied ? 1. *Glance at the " ten."* We have seen how comprehensive are the first five. [See above, v. 1.] Note the comprehensiveness of the second. We are not to assault the *life*, the *family*, the *property*, the *reputation*, the *peace* (by coveting and threatening what they have), of our fellow-men. 2. *Pierce into the spirit of the " ten,"* and note !— (1) *The negative must include the positive ;* e.g., we are bound to conserve life, lest by neglect we kill. (2) *The absolute form covers all cases ;* e.g., the sixth commandment stands absolute, unless dispensed with by the supervention of a higher law. There may be things more sacred even than life. (3) *The external includes the internal.* (Matt. v. 27, 28.) Given the lust, its gratification does not depend upon the man, but upon circumstances out of his control ; therefore he is guilty. Besides, what we *are* is of more moment than what we *do*. (4) *The principle of obedience in all is love.*

VIII. THE PRESENT USE AND OFFICE OF " THE TEN." [For detailed exposition of each of " the ten," in relation to our own time and circumstances, see " The Ten Commandments," by R. W. Dale, M.A.] On the use and office the following positions may be firmly laid down :—1. *The law of " the ten words " was, and is, something absolutely unique.* Of the unique character all that has been previously said is illustration. It may, then, be reasonably inferred that " the ten " will have some special bearing on our moral life. 2. It implies that *God claims authority over the moral life of man.* [On this see valuable observations on the decay of the sense of authority, its evil effects, etc., Dale's " Ten Commandments," pp. 6—13.] 3. It was not intended *to afford man an opportunity for winning salvation.* That is God's free gift. 4. Salvation given, *God means the law to be obeyed.* [On this see also Dale, pp. 13—16.] 5. The effort to obey will *deepen man's sense of the need of God's delivering mercy.* The effort brings a deeper acquaintance with the law, and so we come to know more of—(1) the righteousness of God—(2) the depravity of man. 6. *A growing conformity is, however, blessedly possible.* 7. *There comes* with growing conformity *freedom from law.* Love dispenses with the literal precept. This is the ideal of the New Testament. Still." the ten words " have ever their use for those on the low planes of spiritual life. 8. And even with those free from the law, *it will still have the following offices :*—(1) To keep the Christian under grace as the source of all his serenity and bliss. (2) To restrain from sin in the presence of temptation. (3) To keep before the aspiring saint the fair ideal of righteousness.—R.

Vers. 3—11.—*The soul for God only.* I. GOD'S DEMAND. " Thou shalt have no other," &c. All else is emptiness and falsehood. There must be nothing even of our holy things put between the soul and 'God. His presence must be the soul's life, the very air it breathes.

II. HOW THE DEMAND MAY BE FULFILLED. 1. By keeping ourselves from idols. Our daily avocations, our interests, affections, pleasures, may lead to our esteeming something our chief good and making it to be instead of God to us. God must be seen behind his gifts, and be more to us than all besides. 2. By watchful fear and hope. We bring evil not upon ourselves only, and the blessings which rest upon obedience are an everlasting heritage. We sow seeds of evil or of blessing which yield many harvests (vers. 5, 6). 3. By reverence (ver. 7). God's name must not be emptied of its power to touch the heart by our lightness or hypocrisy. 4. By keeping sacred the sabbath rest (vers. 8—11). (1) It will be a day of self-revelation, of rebuke for the evil in us, of strengthening to the good. (2) It will be a day for the remembrance of God ; and (3) of participation in his rest.—U.

Ver. 12.—*The commandment with promise.* I. THE DUTY IMPOSED. 1. Its reasonableness. Reverent, loving subjection to parents is obedience to the deepest instincts of the heart. 2. Its pleasantness. This subjection is rest and joy : it is ceasing from doubt and inner conflict ; it lets into the spirit the sunshine of a parent's loving approbation.

II. THE PROMISE : " That thy days," &c. Obedience to parents is the condition of national prosperity. 1. It is respect for law and loyal acceptance of the teachings of the past. 2. It is denial of the spirit of self will and self pleasing. 3. It guards youth from excess and vice. 4. It prepares for the understanding of and submission to the will of God.   5. It lays broad and deep in the nation's life the foundations of industry and strength and of moral, as well as material, greatness.—U.

Vers. 13—17.—*Our threefold duty to our neighbour.*   I. HE IS NOT TO BE INJURED IN ACT.   1. *His life is to be held sacred.*   It is God's great gift to him and it is God's only to take it away, by express command, or by his own judgment.   This is a law for nations as well as individuals.   In every unjust war this command is trampled under foot.   2. *His home is sacred.*   The wreck of homes which lust has made !   The holy, loving refuge of childhood and youth desolated, and its very memory made a horror and anguish !   3. *His property is sacred.*   It is the man's special stewardship from God.   God can bless us also, for all things are his, but this stands between our neighbour and the Master, to whom he must render his account.

II. HE IS NOT TO BE INJURED BY WORD.   We may lay no hand upon his life, his home, his goods, and yet our tongue may wound and rob him.   We may cause respect and love to fall away from him wrongfully.   Our dimininishing aught of these, save as the servants of truth, is a crime before God.

III. HE IS NOT TO BE WRONGED IN THOUGHT.   God asks not only for a blameless life but also for a pure heart, in which lust and hate and envy and greed have no place.   Sin is to be slain in its root.—U.

Vers. 1—2.—*Utility of a course of teaching on the commandments,* that Divine law which can never be destroyed.   Let those who object to the preaching of morality remember John Wesley's words : " I find more profit in sermons on either good tempers or good works than in what are vulgarly called ' gospel sermons.' "   Consider—

I. THE DIVISION AND GROUPING OF THE COMMANDMENTS.   1. *Division.*   We know that there are *ten*—the ten words—but how are the ten words made up ?   The modern Jewish method makes the introductory announcement, a " first word," and combines our first and second as the " second word."   By others the first and second are combined as the first, and then the tenth divided to complete the number.   Our own ordinary division is most likely to be correct ; but various usage shows that the importance attaches not to the *number* but the *sense.*   2. *Grouping.*   Two tables, but how many on each ?   Augustine held that the first table contained three, the second seven, whence he drew some mystical conclusions with regard to the Trinity.   The popular view includes four in the first table, and six in the second.   Most likely, however, there should be five in each table [perhaps connected with the hand as the symbol of action].   On this view we shall see that in each table the four first commandments are rooted in the fifth.

II. THE SPEAKER AND THE MOTIVE.   1. *The speaker* (cf. Deut. v. 22).—God, Jehovah, a personal Deity, and one whose nature is changeless (Mal. iii. 6 ; Jas. i. 17).   Moses did not evolve the law out of his own head ; he *heard* it, he *received* it, he *enunciated* it, but " God spake all these words."   2. *The motive.*—The motive appealed to for obedience is too often *fear* ; the motive too which Israel was most inclined to act upon.   God, however, makes his appeal not to fear, but to the sense of gratitude :— " Remember what I have done for you, then hear what I expect you to do for me."   The deliverer has a right to lay down rules of conduct for those whom he has delivered ; whilst at the same time gratitude to him inspires them with a motive for obedience.   Apply to ourselves : God has redeemed *us* ; we should obey him not from fear, but from love— not that we *may* get something out of him, but because we have got so much already.

III. GENERAL CONSIDERATIONS.   1. There is an *order* in the arrangement.   " Order is heaven's first law," and it shows itself in the code from heaven.   *First* God, our *filial* relations ; then man, our *fraternal* relations ; the upward-looking and the outward-looking aspects of life.   Under each, too, the order is maintained ; first we are shown the blossom, then the stem, then the root.   The flower of worship is rooted in the home, and the flower of love is rooted in the heart.   2. The commandments are indications of the Divine will from which they spring.   Our duty is to study what God has *said* in order that we may discover what he *wishes.*   The *old* covenant was on stone-tables, easily intelligible and very definite ; the *new* covenant is on hearts of flesh, it contains *promptings* to duty, rather than directions.   We need both ; we must use the old that we may give effect to the new, and the new that we may fulfil the old. [*Illustration.*—For engine to fulfil its work, *steam* needed inside to propel, *lines* outside to direct.] The new covenant cannot render the old nugatory; it is well to have motive power, but we still need the lines laid down by which to guide ourselves when we have it.—G.

Vers. 3—6. These two commandments are complementary: one God only to be worshipped, one way only in which to worship him. Consider:—

I. THE FIRST COMMANDMENT. 1. *How Israel would understand it.* "No foreign god in opposition to me." The natural idea would be that Jehovah was one amongst many deities; that possibly, away from Egypt, some other god might have higher authority (cf. 2 Kings xviii. 33—35). In any case it would be hard to realise that he was more than God of gods; others might be inferior to him, but surely they might claim an inferior worship. All such notions are set aside at once. Whether there are other gods or no, all such must be Jehovah's enemies; to offer them worship of any kind was to be disloyal to Jehovah, and to break the covenant. 2. *How it applies to ourselves.* Polytheism, a thing of the past! In theory perhaps, but how about our practice? Obedience is the best evidence of worship; our God is he by reference to whom we govern our conduct, and regulate our actions. Illustrate from the case of the man whose life is given to the pursuit of wealth—wealth is practically his deity; or the case of one whose conduct is regulated by constant reference to public opinion; wealth, public opinion, and the like may be nothing more than personified abstractions, none the less we may serve them far more consistently than we serve God. Such service is worship, worship of an alien deity; it involves disloyalty to Jehovah, and enrols us amongst the forces of his foes. Quite as easy for *us* to break this commandment as it was for Israel; it needs to be reiterated in *our* ears no less persistently than it was in their ears.

II. THE SECOND COMMANDMENT. As the first has to do with the *object* of worship, so this has to do with the *manner* of worship. An image degrades the ideal, it can only present God, and that imperfectly, under one out of many aspects. One image of God alone is adequate (Col. i. 15). To the Jew, this second commandment was a fence to guard the empty shrine, which shrine could only receive its occupant when "the Word was made flesh" at the incarnation of our Lord. Notice:—1. *The effect of breaking the commandment.* Degrading the God worshipped, it led on naturally to the degradation of the worshipper, and through the worshipper his posterity was affected, so as to become yet more degraded. Who could have a better excuse than Jeroboam, the son of Nebat, for breaking the commandment? Who could have broken it more carefully? Considerations of utility seemed to justify him. He might have argued that the first commandment was all-important, and that to ensure respect for it he must tamper with the second. None the less the effect was manifest (2 Kings xvii. 22, 23). The sin of Jeroboam was the ruin of his people. 2. *The bearing of the commandment on ourselves.* Christ has come. The empty shrine is filled. We possess the true image, and can worship God in Christ. "But Christ, you say, is 'unseen; thoughts wander in prayer, I need some object by which to fix them, some symbol upon which they may stay themselves and rest." The excuse is plausible; but it is the same excuse as a Jew in old times might have offered. A man may use, as good men have used, the crucifix, *e.g.*, as an aid to devotion. But the crucifix, or any other symbol, is utterly inadequate; it shows Christ only under one aspect: we must worship him in all his fulness if we take him as the image of the invisible Jehovah. To confine our thoughts to Calvary is to limit, and by limiting to degrade the ideal. The crucifix has much to answer for in narrowing men's views, and making their religion one-sided and incomplete. For a Christian to obey the second commandment, he must worship Christ in all his fulness. Only so can he worship God with that pure worship which is alone acceptable.

> "Show me not only Jesus dying,
>   As on the cross he bled,
> Nor in the tomb a captive lying,
>   For he has left the dead.
> Not only in that form suspended,
>   My Saviour bid me see;
> For to the highest heavens ascended,
>   He reigns in majesty!"—G.

Vers. 7, 8.—The first commandment deals with the *object* of worship; the second, with the *manner* of worship; in the third and fourth we have the *method* of worship, true reverence and genuine devotion.

I. THE THIRD COMMANDMENT. 1. *Obedience to the letter insufficient.* None ever obeyed it thus more strictly than the Jews did. The Sacred Name, called the shuddering name; only pronounced once annually by the High Priest on the Great Day of Atonement. So strictly was the command kept that the true pronunciation of the name is lost to us. Even in our own Bibles we have evidence of the ancient practice, "The LORD" being used as a substitute for Jehovah. Yet, with all this, cf. Ezek. xxxvi. 20. The name, which was never uttered by the lips, was yet profaned by the conduct of the worshippers. We, too, may never perjure ourselves, or speak profanely, yet the tenor of our whole life may bring God's name into contempt. The commonest excuse made by those who never enter a place of worship is based upon the inconsistent conduct of those who frequent such places regularly. They may not go themselves, but they know well enough who do go, and they know also the kind of lives which they who do go are leading. 2. *The true obedience.* They who worship God must worship him in spirit and in truth. True reverence is a thing of the heart, which shines through and illuminates the conduct. This leads us to:—

II. THE FOURTH COMMANDMENT. True reverence will best show itself in copying the example of the person reverenced. The fourth commandment shows us God's example made plain for a man to copy. 1. *The rest-day to be kept holy.* (1) Nature teaches us that a rest-day, a Sabbath, is a necessity. He who works seven days a week is a bad economist of his time. He simply shortens life. The body must be laid aside the sooner to keep its disregarded Sabbaths in the grave. (2) The Holy-day is no less necessary than the holiday. Man's nature is complex, and his spirit needs rest and refreshment, quite as surely as his body needs them. [*Illust.:* You may shut up a man's piano, but that only rests the instrument, it does not necessarily rest the instrumentalist.] The rest for a man's spirit is only to be obtained by sharing the spiritual rest of God; if the holiday be not a holy-day this spiritual rest will still be lacking. 2. *The days of labour to be modelled on God's pattern.* Labour as much commanded as rest; but labour, as rest, after the Divine model. All that God does, he does earnestly and thoroughly. To work as God works is to work with the *heart* as well as with the hands (Col. iii. 23). One cannot wonder that the rest-day is profaned, when the days of toil are profaned no less, when a man's chief object seems to be not to *do* his work, but to have done with it. If God had worked as we work, he could scarcely have called his work "very good." The world by now would have been a dilapidated chaos, more appalling than the waste from which it sprang. The commandment is not "Six days shalt thou *loiter*," but "Six days shalt thou *labour*."

CONCLUDING REFLECTIONS.—Mere literal keeping of the commandments may bring them and their author into contempt. We can only "magnify the law and make it honourable" by keeping it from the heart outwards. The Jews kept the third and fourth commandments literally enough. Our own Sunday legislation dates from the time of Charles II., when, of all times, God's law was, perhaps, the most fearfully profaned. "My son, give me thine heart," that is the invitation which first requires to be accepted. If we would really keep the commandments, let our prayer be: "Lord have mercy upon us, and incline *our hearts* to keep thy law."—G.

Ver. 12.—Previous commandments have dealt with the *object and manner* of worship; this deals with the nursery and school of worship. Consider:—

I. THE INJUNCTION IN ITSELF. 1. *Absolute;* parents to be *honoured*, whether living or departed, known or unknown, good or evil. 2. *Hard to obey in some cases;* yet always *possible*, for remember the *father* and *mother* may be honoured, even though the individuals fall short of the ideal they should exemplify. One can honour from the standpoint of the *child*, even those who from any other standpoint may be despicable. [*Illust.:* Dr. Macdonald's story of "Robert Falconer;" the father is a reprobate scamp, yet the son, persistently honouring his fatherhood, at length wins him back to respectability.] 3. *Mischief of thoughtless disrespect.* No honourable shame to be ashamed of one's own parentage, especially when, if rightly looked at, there is nothing to be ashamed of in it. No doubt apparent disrespect may sometimes grow out of a wholesome familiarity;

still, even so, painful to the parent, whilst it injures the child in the opinion of right-minded people. [Common shame of doing, or refusing to do things out of respect to a parent's wishes. At most, if the wish is respected, it is merely a "humouring of the old people," as though the command were "humour," instead of "honour" "thy father and mother."] Why chafe at such simple duties as those which spring from the most sacred of relations. There is a far worse bondage than that of "a mother's apron strings;" it is not well to rupture needlessly those cords of a man which are the bonds of love. If you want a reason for the command:—

II. Home reverence is the root of worship. That ladder which Jacob saw is always reared within the shadow of the home. Even with him, an exile, it was the God of *his father* who stood above it. The parents, or those who stand in the place of parents, are the only God a child knows at first. Worship, like other things, comes by practice and experience: the first lessons are learnt in the home. Practically, God is revealed through the parent; other things equal, no reverence for parents, there will be no reverence for God. No doubt there are homes and homes; some where you can almost catch the rustle of the angel wings; others, withered husks of home, blasted before the breath of hell. Still, even in the worst homes the ladder is planted, could one but see it. Take away home and its associations, and you leave it with no ground to stand on. Notice in this light the great responsibility of parents. Further:—

III. Home reverence is the source of individual and national permanence. The *position* of the commandment teaches its connection with worship, the *promise* attached to it its connection with prosperity. It ensures:—1. *The prosperity of the individual.* The man who does not honour and respect his parents has not gained the *habit* of reverence; he does not honour God, he does not honour all men. What follows?—(1) Not honouring God, there is no power but self to restrain self. Impulses, desires, etc., are likely, unreined, to run away with him. A man so run away with is rushing post haste to death. (2) Not honouring men, he will hold aloof from men. They may hinder, they are not likely to help him. The friction of life intensified; all that is done—done with twice the effort. Such a man may be successful, not likely to be long-lived. The needless friction must wear out the life. Could the test be applied, an insurance company would be justified in charging a lower premium on one who kept this commandment, than on one who habitually disregarded it. 2. *The prosperity of the nation.* For (1) That nation is most stable which founds itself in reverence for the past. The "Land of settled government" is the land—

> "Where Freedom broadens slowly down
> From precedent to precedent."

(2) That nation is most stable which adopts the principle of the fourth commandment and respects authority above numbers. The commandment does not say, "Honour the family vote," it says, "Honour thy father and thy mother."

Conclusion.—Home is linked with heaven; the earthly parent with the Father of eternity. Would you reach heaven, then reverence home; would you worship God, then honour your parents.—G.

Ver. 13.—The second table. Fraternal relations; the outward-looking aspect of life. May classify them either (1) as they affect us personally, or (2) as they affect man generally. According to (1) they deal with our *actions*, our *words*, and our *thoughts*. According to (2) they teach us:—The sanctity of life, of home, of property, of character; whilst the tenth commandment shows further that the heart is the source whence springs reverence for these sanctities. Notice as regards this sixth commandment:—

I. Its bearing on actions. Murder, the criminal taking of life, varies in character; according to the nature of the life destroyed and according to the nature of the action of the destroyer. Life is threefold, of the *body*, of the *mind*, and of the *spirit*: and murder, as against each, may be *deliberate* or *careless*, resulting from *action* or from *inaction*. Illustrate from cases affecting the bodily life:—1. *Deliberate murder.* Life taken of malice aforethought. 2. *Careless murder*, resulting from negligence or culpable ignorance; *e.g.*, the house builder who so builds his house as to injure the health of a tenant, neglecting drains, etc.; or the parent who spreads some infectious disorder through sending his children to school whilst tainted with it. 3. *Inactive murder.* Paraphrasing James iv. 17, " He that knoweth to save life and doeth it not, to him it is murder;" *e.g.*, a man who allows his neighbour to murder others deliberately or through carelessness. Like kinds of murder apply to the cases of the mind and spirit. The slave-owner who forbade his slaves to be educated, and who debarred them from religious privileges; the parent who stifles the spiritual development of his child through indifference. These and like cases might be instanced. " Thou shalt do *no* murder," such is the command. To the question, " Am I my brother's keeper ? " the answer is, " Undoubtedly you are." If you can save life of any kind, and fail to do so, you must be classed with Cain.

II. ITS BEARING ON THOUGHTS (Matt. v. 21 ; 1 John iii. 15). Really a special case of the tenth commandment ; or rather, this commandment is viewed in the light of the tenth. The unkind thought, fostered, soon becomes the malicious thought, and a malicious thought acts like leaven, resulting in a murderous heart. [*Illustration :* cotton wool, pure, soft, innoxious. Treat it with certain chemicals. It *looks* just the same ; but its character is completely altered, it is transformed into an explosive, gun cotton. So, too, treat the human heart with the chemistry of envy, hatred, and malice, and it too will become an explosive—murderous, and ready for murder.] From the murderous heart proceeds murder of the worst kind ; but saturate the heart with indifference or carelessness, and you still make it an explosive. " Keep," *i.e.*, guard " thy heart with all diligence, for out of it are the issues of life," or death !

III. A SPECIAL CASE. SUICIDE. Self murder does not imply hatred or malice, Still it is unlawful killing, and may be classed with extreme forms of manslaughter. It is however to be condemned on more general principles as against the spirit of the whole table of the law. It is cowardly. It is selfish. If a brother commit suicide, what are your feelings ? What then your brother's feelings if you destroy your life ? Juries should give in such cases more stringent verdicts. A verdict of temporary insanity results from misplaced charity ; it cannot do much to alleviate the distress of friends ; it helps to facilitate suicide, which would be far less frequent if the verdict on it were usually more severe.

Conclusion.—The justification of this commandment is to be found in the sanctity of the life which it protects. Bear in mind that life is God's gift, an emanation from the Deity. Keep the eyes open and keep the heart open, so will you soon find opportunities to preserve life and ward off death.—G.

Ver. 14.—A correspondence between the two tables : to worship a false god is to aim at the life of the true God. Idolatry is spiritual adultery. Besides this the sixth and seventh commandments are clearly related ; the one guards the life of the individual, the other the life of the family, the sanctity of the home. Consider :—

I. THE SIN ITSELF. When a man by anticipation, or after marriage, breaks the marriage vow ; when a woman acquiesces in the crime thus perpetrated, it is murder aimed at the collective life of the family. Madness for society to make light of such a crime, which, if permitted, must destroy society. For notice, the family, not the individual, is the ultimate social unit. [*Illustration.* Tree covered with foliage : individual leaves and blossoms are connected with twigs and boughs ; you may kill a leaf without injury to the bough, but kill the bough, and what about the leaves ?] Individuals are leaves and blossoms on the tree of life ; it is through the family that they belong to the tree at all. Adultery poisons the bough, and through that withers the leaves and blossoms. Further, the sin involves a spreading plague. It spreads not merely far and wide, but on and on through future generations. You may keep it hid, you cannot keep it inactive. [Illustrate from case of David and Bathsheba ; may we not trace his mother's influence in Solomon's sin? He goes after strange women, and then after strange gods. On David's side we have Amnon's sin directly connected with Absolom's rebellion, which again is connected indirectly with the successful rebellion of Jeroboam and resulting idolatry of the northern kingdom. It is still the one sin which spreads ; outwards and onwards.] A pure home is a sound spot in the social organism ; corrupt its purity, and it becomes a centre of corruption. May notice also, in this connection, that all sins of this class, fornication, uncleanness, etc., do and must manifest themselves in spite of concealment. Other sins (1 Cor. vi. 18) are " outside the body." These are

" against the body," and through the body they declare themselves. The pure may not know why they shun the impure, but instinctively they discern the signs of his impurity. His sin shows through him, as a lurid light shows through a lantern.

II. CAUSES WHICH OCCASION THE SIN. 1. *A low ideal of womanhood.* According to the Divine ideal, " man " is " male and female ; " it is in the union of the sexes that the " image of God " is reflected. According to the human ideal, woman is rather man's play-mate than his help-mate ; he chooses her as he would a picture, because he likes the *look* of her. She is in thought his toy, his doll. In unchristian countries this low ideal of woman is universally prevalent, but even in Christian countries it is too often tacitly if not verbally accepted. Such an ideal cannot but be mischievous. [*Illustration:* Take lantern from summit of light-house and place it at the foot. It will still guide the ships, though no longer *off* the rocks but *on* to them.] Woman must exert influence ; place her high and it will be ennobling, set her low and it will become degrading. 2. *A low ideal of manhood.* If woman is a toy, then that part of a man's nature which can require such a costly toy, will be the most important. The animal nature will be uppermost. The desires will rule. 3. *A low level of life.* This results naturally from 1 and 2. A man cannot live above the level of his own ideals. If man is a mere animal, woman a mere toy, then marriage is a mere convention. All its sanctity has evaporated. A man will marry if he can afford a wife, if not he will take some cheaper substitute. In the light of the Divine ideal, marriage becomes a duty and a privilege ; the completion of that Divine idea of which man unmarried is a mere *torso.* Guard, of course, against improvident marriages ; at the same time it is not improvidence to share, in common, sacrifice and self-denial. One man has two hundred pounds per annum and cannot marry under four hundred pounds ; another has four hundred pounds and requires one thousand pounds. If a man divides himself into his income and finds he goes once and nothing over, he may set to work and make his income larger, or he may try to make *self* smaller ; many a man could so reduce his divisor, that, without any increase in his income, the quotient should be two, with a fair remainder.

Conclusion.—All such evils spring no doubt from a corrupt heart ; but a high ideal will guard the heart and tend to purify it if impure. By the help of God's grace, let man reverence woman, and woman reverence man, and each reverence in himself and in the other that ideal which is their common glory. Before the splendour of the Divine image as thus mirrored in their union, adultery and sins of uncleanness must be driven afar off.—G.

Ver. 15.—The eighth commandment guards the sanctity of property. Consider :—

I. PROPERTY AND THE RIGHTS OF PROPERTY. Property is that which gives expression to individual and family life. In some sort it is an extension of the bodily organism, an added possibility of self-revelation in the sphere of sense. Social usage allows a man's right, or the right of a corporation, to absolute possession of certain things. Primarily, probably, such right is founded on the right of the labourer to the product of his labour ; a man's own is what he has made his own. Such limit, however, has come to be enlarged on grounds of general utility ; we may say generally that a man's property is that which social usage allows him to consider such.

II. OFFENCES AGAINST PROPERTY. 1. *Stealing.* Appropriating a man's property against the will of the owner. All condemn the thief, he is condemned even by his own conscience ; however much he may steal from others he can never think it right for them to steal from him! There are, however, various kinds of diluted theft which are equally offences against the eighth commandment, though not so strongly stigmatised by society. 2. *Cognate offences.* Property in the old times consisted mainly of land, crops, and cattle. The principle involved in the eighth commandment illustrated, as applied to them, by a number of cases in Ex. xxi., xxii., all such acts as result in loss to one's neighbours, provided that loss was not inevitable, are condemned by it. Circumstances, nowadays, are somewhat different, but the principle of honesty still applies. Take a few instances :—(1) *Acts of petty dishonesty.* (*a*) When in a bargain one party takes advantage of the ignorance of the other ; *e.g.,* a collector finds some rarity in the possession of a man who does not know its value, and secures it far below its proper price. (*b*) Borrowing without definite intention to return ; *e.g.,* books, money, or other property. (*c*) Leaving bills unpaid for a needlessly long time. In such case, even though paid eventually, the creditor is defrauded of the profit which he might have made by the use of his money. (2) *Mischievous actions*; *e.g.*, marking books or scribbling in them. Cutting initials in trees and buildings. No man has any right to depreciate by his actions the value of another man's property. (3) *Culpable negligence.* Must be as careful with the property of others as with our own property. A pure accident is not a pure accident if it would not have happened had the property been our own.

III. COMPENSATION FOR OFFENCES AGAINST PROPERTY. Cf. Ex. xxii. 9. Not enough to make good the original value, the law of restitution requires double and, in some cases, fivefold or fourfold. Such a law:—1. *Emphasises the importance of strict honesty.* In view of it possible offenders will be more cautious as to how they offend. Should it be enforced now-a-days; how many struggling tradesmen and mechanics might find themselves rescued from the verge of bankruptcy! How might charity in a thousand places spring up to banish and destroy suspicion! 2. *Secures something like adequate atonement.* Defraud a man of anything, and you defraud him of more than the value of that thing. His loss occasions further loss; loss of time, loss of temper, anxiety, inconvenience, for all which the sufferer is entitled to a recompense. Fourfold restitution may sound generous, yet even that may be less than just.

Conclusion.—Honesty is by no means such a common virtue as some suppose. It behoves us to examine ourselves as to how far our conduct may bear strict scrutiny. Are there none to whom *we* should make restitution? If so, let us be thankful if we can make it. There are losses which we occasion others, dues which we owe to God and man, yet which now, it may be, we can never make good—no remedy now exists for the lasting evil they have occasioned. There are debts we can still pay, there are others which we can never pay; who has not need to join in the petition in the Lord's Prayer, " Forgive us our debts"?—G.

Ver. 16.—Connect with the preceding commandment. That guards the property, what belongs to a man outside himself. This guards the character, what belongs to a man inside himself. To steal the purse may be only to steal trash, but to defraud a man of his good name is to do him an irreparable injury.

I. COMMONEST FORM OF THE OFFENCE. Most often committed against comparative strangers. We calculate the effect of our words when speaking of people whom we know— the consequences may be unpleasant to ourselves if we fail to use due care. As regards others, we are far too ready to catch up and publish some prejudicial opinion; it is so much easier to speak evil than to keep silence and say nothing. Take, *e.g.*, the language current with regard to politicians of an opposite party; what disgraceful imputation of unworthy motives is constantly permitted without a protest! We have a right to our own opinion, if we have taken due pains to form it, as to the public acts of public men; we have no right to go beneath those acts and assume that the actors are less honourable than we are. Partisans of the platform and the correspondence column would seem to care nothing for the sanctity of truth, their one aim is to blacken the character of their opponents, so as to emphasise by contrast their own purity.

II. HOW HABIT STRENGTHENS BY PRACTICE. Bear false witness against a stranger and it will be easier to bear false witness against a friend; the use of unmeasured language in the one case will lead to less measured language in the other. As a fact this is the case. People who express themselves so strongly when speaking of political opponents, are just the people who behind your back will speak of you with inaccurate unkindness. They misrepresent and misinterpret from the mere pleasure of lowering a man in the eyes of others:—

> " Low desire
> Not to feel lowest makes them level all;
> Yea they would pare the mountain to the plain,
> To leave an equal baseness."

We are all mirrors in which our neighbours' characters must be in some sort reflected; let us take care lest we reflect falsely, distorting, through flaws in our own character,

the character which is reflected through us. Two special cases should be noted:—
1. *False witness embodied in accurate speech.* We may use true words and yet create a
false impression; *e.g.*, a remark made and repeated verbatim. The way, however, in
which it is repeated, the special setting, the peculiar intonation; these things give it a
very different meaning to that intended by the original speaker. The words are
accurate, the testimony is false. (New music alters the character of a song.) 2. *False
witness may be borne by silence.* In discussing a man's character, silence, with or without significant looks, is eloquent. "He could have spoken," it is argued, "had he been
able to say anything favourable." Silent acquiescence in the charges made is quite
sufficient confirmation of their truth!
    Conclusion.—The character of our neighbour, whatever his rank or position, whether
the neighbour be a Prime Minister or only a domestic servant, ought to be as precious to
us as our own character. It is easy enough to injure a man's good name by thoughtless
speech or cowardly silence. We cannot rid ourselves of the responsibility which
attaches to our carelessness or cowardice. By speech or silence we give our testimony,
whether the testimony be true or false.—G.

    Ver. 17.—The last commandment of the second table. Murder, adultery, theft,
slander, all these spring from a corrupt heart. The wrong thought admitted nourishes
the wrong desire, which in time gives birth to the wrong action. Out of the heart are
the issues of life, therefore keep thy heart with all diligence.
    I. THE SOURCE OF COVETOUSNESS. There are two ideals by which men mould their
lives. One makes God the centre of all things, the other makes self the centre. One
says "Thy will be done," the other says "My will be done." It is in the heart that
accepts this latter ideal that covetousness has its home. Everything is regarded in its
relation to self—the neighbour's life and home, and property, and character, are only so
many possible instruments which may thwart or assist the gratification of selfishness.
The thought of something which may give pleasure, leads us to the desire for the
possession of that thing, and the desire will only be restrained from fulfilment by
external checks which may make fulfilment difficult. A man may refrain from
adultery or theft, because of the social penalties which attach to such transgressions; all
the same in his inmost heart he may be a thief and an adulterer. Selfishness is the
parent of all sins; its offspring is only dwarfed in growth when selfishness is restrained
by society. (Cf. Matt. v. 22, 28.)
    II. THE CURE FOR COVETOUSNESS. The only radical remedy is that which starts by
cutting at the root of selfishness. God, not the individual man, is the centre of the
universe. Man is related directly to him, and to all other things through him. It is
God's will, not our own will, by reference to which we may live righteously. What
then is God's will? It is that which corresponds with his character, which is love. To
live as in his sight is to live in the light of love. Love in us is kindled and developed
by contemplation and experience of the love which is in him. Love is that Divine
affection which alone has power to expel all selfishness. Love alone can purify the
heart, guard the thoughts, and discipline the desires. And what is love in practice?
It is nothing more nor less than doing to others as we would they should do unto us.
All men as related to God are on an equality, all, as in his sight, have equal rights.
Here, however much we may differ, we are yet all on common ground. They who
acknowledge one God, who accept redemption through one Saviour, who yield to the
influence of one sanctifying Spirit, are in the way to the attainment of that love which
is the fulfilling of the law. (Rom. xiii. 10.)
    Conclusion.—Notice how the last commandment links itself on to the fulfilment of
the first. The ten precepts of the two tables are ten golden links in a perfect circle.
Thus regarded, that circle is none other than the perfect bond of charity (Col. iii. 14),
a girdle wherewith whoso girds himself ensures a twofold peace, "Peace on earth
towards men of good will," and the peace of God to keep his heart.—G.

EXPOSITION.

Vers. 18—21.—WITHDRAWAL OF THE PEO-
PLE, AND NEARER APPROACH OF MOSES TO
GOD. The effect produced upon the people
by the accumulated terrors of Sinai—" the
thunderings and the lightnings, the noise of
the trumpet, and the mountain smoking"—
the cloud, and the voice out of the cloud—was
an awful and terrible fear. They could not
bear the manifestation of the near presence of
God; and therefore " they removed and stood
afar off." It seemed to them as if, on hearing
the voice of God, speaking out of the thick
darkness, they must die (ver. 19). Moses,
upon their expressing these feelings, comforted
them with an assurance that God had shown
his terrors, not for their injury, but to put his
fear in their hearts (ver. 20), and allowed
them to retire to a distance from the mount,
while he himself "drew near unto the thick
darkness where God was " (ver. 21).

Ver. 18.—The people saw the thunderings.
The use of a specific verb for a generic one,
with terms to all of which it is not, strictly
speaking, applicable, is common to many
writers, and is known to grammarians as
zeugma. " Saw " here means " perceived,
witnessed." The mountain smoking. Compare ch. xix. 18. In Deut. v. 23 it is said
that " the mountain did burn with fire."
When the people saw it, they removed. It
appears, from Deut. v. 23, that, before retiring,
the people sent a deputation of heads of tribes
and elders up to Moses in the mount, to convey to him their wishes, and suggest that *he*
should be their intermediary with God. Moses
laid their wishes before God, and was directed
to give them his sanction, whereupon they
withdrew *to their tents* (*ib.* 30).

Ver. 19.—And they said unto Moses. Their
whole speech, as delivered in Deuteronomy,
was as follows:—" Behold, the Lord our God
hath shewed us his glory and his greatness,
and we have heard his voice out of the midst
of the fire : we have seen this day, that God

doth talk with man, and he liveth. Now,
therefore, why should we die ? for this great
fire will consume us : if we hear the voice of
the Lord our God any more, then we shall die.
For who is there of all flesh, that hath heard
the voice of the living God, speaking out of
the midst of the fire, as we have, and lived ?
Go then near, and hear all that the Lord our
God shall say ; and speak thou unto us all that
the Lord our God shall speak unto thee ; and
we will hear it, and do it " (Deut. v. 24—27).
The speech is here abbreviated greatly ; but
its essential points are preserved — " Speak
thou with us "—be thou our intermediary—
" Let not God speak with us, lest we die."

Ver. 20.—And Moses said unto the people.
Not immediately—Moses first held colloquy
with God. God declared that the people had
" spoken well" (Deut. v. 28) ; and authorised
Moses to allow of their withdrawal (*ib.* 30).
Fear not. Here Exodus is more full in its
details than Deuteronomy. Moses, finding the
people in a state of extreme alarm, pacified
them—assured them that there was no cause
for immediate fear—God had not now come
in vengeance—the object of the terrors of
Sinai was to " prove " them—*i.e.*, to test them,
whether they were inclined to submit themselves to God, or not—and to impress upon
their minds permanently an awful fear of God,
that they might be kept back from sin by
dread of his almighty power. The motive of
fear is, no doubt, a low one ; but where we
can appeal to nothing else, we must appeal to
it. Israel was still a child, only fit for childish
discipline ; and had to be directed by the harsh
voice of fear, until it had learnt to be guided
by the tender accents of love.

Ver. 21.—The people stood afar off. They
retired from the base of Sinai to their tents,
where they " stood," probably in their tent
doors. And Moses drew near unto the thick
darkness. As the people drew back, Moses
drew near. The display which drove them
off, attracted him. He did not even fear the
" thick darkness"—a thing from which human
nature commonly shrinks. Where God was,
he would be.

HOMILETICS.

Vers. 18—21.—*The Divine presence at once attractive and repellent.* When Christ
was upon the earth, so winning was his graciousness that crowds flocked to him, and
one man at least exclaimed, " Lord, I will follow thee whithersoever thou goest." But
at the same time so terrible was the manifestation of his power, that there were those
who " besought him that he would depart out of their coasts." God is love, and God is
power, and wherever he is, he exhibits both qualities ; but there are some who see
mainly the love, and there are others who see only the power. Hence the Divine
presence at once attracts and repels, charms men and affrights them. The Israelites
invited to draw near to God, and hold with him direct communication, after brief trial,

decline the offer, and will have an intermediary. Moses, given the same invitation, and a witness of the same sights and sounds, not only stands his ground, but at the end draws more near. The reasons for the difference would seem to be these—

I. FEAR, WHERE IT IS EXCESSIVE, EXPELS LOVE. The devils, who have no love, " believe and tremble." Men, who have greatly sinned, and who therefore cannot help seeing in God mainly a " consuming fire," and " an avenger to execute wrath," lose sight of all his gentler attributes, cease to feel that he is their Father, no longer look upon him as " merciful and gracious," and consequently no longer have any feeling of love towards him. We cannot love one from whom we expect nothing but punishment.

II. LOVE, WHERE IT IS STRONG, COUNTERACTS FEAR AND MASTERS IT. " The fear of the Lord endureth for ever "—no love of which a creature is capable can altogether cast it out. The very angels veil their faces before the Lord of Hosts, and feel themselves unworthy to gaze upon the Divine perfections. But where love increases, fear diminishes. Let love grow, and become strong, and glow within the heart like a flame of fire—by degrees fear changes its character, ceases to be a timorous dread, and becomes awe. Awe and love can very well co-exist; and love draws us towards God more than awe keeps us back. Love is glad to have no intermediary—rejoices that it may " go boldly to the throne of grace "—seeks to draw as near as possible to the beloved one—so constrains fear, that fear ceases to act any longer as a deterrent, is mastered, and held under restraint. " Moses drew near into the thick darkness where God was." The loving soul presses towards God—would " see him face to face "—and " know even as it also is known."

HOMILIES BY VARIOUS AUTHORS.

Vers. 18—22.—*The terrors of Sinai—their design and their effects.* I. THEIR DESIGN. 1. *Not to slay the people.* The people dreaded that if God spoke to them again, they would die (ver. 19). But Moses said—No; this was not the design of the manifestation. " Fear not " (ver. 20). The voice of the law in Scripture, though it is felt in the conscience to be a voice of death (Rom. vii. 9—11), is not intended to be really so. It is meant to lead to Christ. 2. *To prove the people* (ver. 20). God gave this awful manifestation, that his fear might ever after be before their faces. They had heard with their own ears the proclamation of the law, and they had seen these terrors. If anything could awaken fear in them—a salutary fear—and keep them from apostasy, these things should. But, alas! terror is a very ineffective instrument of conversion. These Israelites soon forgot their terrors, and within forty days were dancing in mad glee round their golden calf (ch. xxxii.). II. THEIR EFFECTS. 1. *They inspired the keenest alarm.* This is the invariable result in the sinful breast of any near approach of God. A fear akin to that of the Israelites has often been manifested—(1) In presence of unusual appearances of nature (comets, eclipses, etc.). (2) Under the powerful preaching of the realities of judgment. (3) In prospect of death. 2. *They awakened the cry for a mediator* (ver. 19). However much, under ordinary circumstances, the unbeliever may scout the idea of being indebted to a mediator, it will be strange if there do not come times in his life when he feels that he needs one. Three principles in our nature give birth to this feeling—(1) The sense of *weakness* and *finitude*. (2) The sense of *sin*. (3) The feeling of *need*. The longing for fellowship with God gives rise to the desire for one to mediate that fellowship, to bring it about by making peace. 3. *They impelled the self-convicted Israelites to flee from God's presence* (vers. 18, 21). This is what will take place at the last judgment. How different with Moses, who had " boldness " to enter even into the thick darkness! The good man need not fear to be *anywhere* with God—J. O.

EXPOSITION.

Vers. 22—26.—THE BOOK OF THE COVE-NANT, (chap. xx. ver. 22, to chap. xxii. ver. 23). The Decalogue is followed by a series of laws, civil, social, and religious, which occupy the remainder of ch. xx. and the whole of the three following chapters (ch. xxi., xxii. and xxiii.). It appears from ch. xxiv. that these laws, received by Moses on Sinai, immediately after the delivery of the ten commandments, were at once committed to writing and collected into a book, which was known as "the Book of the Covenant" (ch. xxiv. 7), and was regarded as a specially sacred volume. The document, as it has come down to us, "cannot be regarded as a strictly systematic whole" (Canon Cook) : yet still, it is not wholly unsystematic, but aims in some degree at an orderly arrangement. First and foremost are placed the laws which concern the worship of God, which are two in number :—1. Against idols ; 2. Concerning altars (ch. xx. 23—26). Then follow the laws respecting what our legal writers call "the rights of persons"—which occupy thirty-two verses of ch. xxi. and fall under some twenty different heads, beginning with the rights of slaves, and terminating with the compensation to be made for injuries to the person caused by cattle. The third section is upon "the rights of property," and extends from ch. xxi. 33, to ch. xxii. 15, including some ten or twelve enactments. After this we can only say that the laws are mixed, some being concerned with Divine things (as ch. xxii. 20, 29, 30 ; and ch. xxiii. 10—19) : others with human, and these last being of various kinds, all, however, more or less "connected with the civil organization of the state" (Kalisch). In the fourth section the enactments seem to fall under about twenty-five heads. The result is that the "Book of the Covenant" contains, in little more than three chapters, about seventy distinct laws.

Ver. 22.—**Ye have seen that I have talked with you from heaven.** The book opened with this reminder, which at once recalled its author and declared its authority. "I, who give these laws, am the same who spake the ten commandments amid the thunders of Sinai. Reverence the laws accordingly."

Ver. 23.—**Ye shall not make with me gods of silver,** etc. This is a repetition, in part, of the second commandment, and can only be accounted for by the prohibition being specially needed. The first idea of the Israelites, when they considered that Moses had deserted them, was to make a golden calf for a god.

Ver. 24.—**An altar of earth.** Among the nations of antiquity altars were indispensable to Divine worship, which everywhere included sacrifice. They were often provided on the spur of the occasion, and were then "constructed of earth, sods, or stones, collected upon the spot." The patriarchal altars had probably been of this character, and it was now provided that the same usage should continue : at any rate, elaborate structures of hewn and highly ornamented stone should not be allowed, lest thus idolatry should creep in, the images engraved upon the altars becoming the objects of worship. **Thy burnt offerings and thy peace offerings.** The mode in which these are introduced implies that sacrifice was already a long-standing practice. The patriarchal sacrifices are well known (Gen. viii. 20 ; xii. 7 ; xxii. 9 ; xxxv. 1). Jethro had recently offered sacrifice in the camp of Israel (ch. xviii. 12). If the Israelites had not sacrificed to God during the sojourn in Egypt, at any rate they had kept up the idea of sacrifice ; and it was for the purpose of offering sacrifices that Moses had demanded permission to go with all his nation into the wilderness. **I will come unto thee and I will bless thee.** The promise is conditional on the observance of the command. If the altars are rightly constructed, and proper victims offered, then, in all places where he allows the erection of an altar, God will accept the sacrifices offered upon it and bless the worshippers.

Ver. 25.—**And if thou wilt make me an altar of stone**—i.e., if, notwithstanding my preference expressed for an altar of earth, thou wilt insist on making me one of stone, as more permanent, and so more honourable, then I require that the stones shall be rough stones shaped by nature, not stones chiselled into shape by the art of man. **For if thou lift up thy tool upon it thou hast polluted it.** It is conjectured with reason that we have here an old traditional idea, which God thought fit under the existing circumstances to sanction. The real object was that altars should not be elaborately carved with objects that might superinduce idolatry. The widely prevalent notion, that nature is sacred, and that all man's interference with nature is a defilement, was made use of economically, to produce the desired result. No tool being allowed to be used, no forms of living creatures could be engraved, and so no idolatry of them could grow up.

Ver. 26.—**Neither shalt thou go up by steps unto mine altar.** Here the reason of decency, added in the text, is obvious ; and the law would necessarily continue until sacerdotal vestments of a very different character from the clothes commonly worn by Orientals were introduced (xxviii. 3—43). After their introduction, the reason for the law, and with it the law itself, would drop. The supposed "slope of earth" by which the priests are thought to have ascended to the "ledge" on the altar of burnt offerings, and the "inclined plane," said by Josephus to have given access to the great altar of Solomon, rest on no sufficient authority, and are probably pure fictions. As soon as an ascent was needed, owing to the height of the altar, it was probably an ascent by steps (See Ezek. xliii. 17.)

HOMILIES BY VARIOUS AUTHORS.

Vers. 22—26.—*The law of the altar.* I. THE OBJECT OF WORSHIP. The true God, not gods of silver, or gods of gold (ver. 23). The God who had talked with them from heaven had appeared in no visible form. " Ye heard the voice of the words, but saw no similitude; only ye heard a voice " (Deut. iv. 12). Let the sole object of our worship be the invisible, spiritual, infinite, yet *revealed* God. God's revelations of himself lay the basis of right worship. God has spoken. How reverently should we hear!

II. THE PLACE OF WORSHIP. " In all places where I record my name" (ver. 24). God records his name by making a revelation of himself, as at Bethel, Peniel, etc. Whatever places he chose for the building of his altar, till the time came for the erection of a permanent sanctuary, there would he meet with them. Religion is now set free from places (John iv. 23). Wherever two or three are met in Christ's name, there will he be in the midst of them (Matt. xviii. 20).

III. THE ALTAR OF WORSHIP. To be built of unhewn stone—*i.e.*, of natural materials (ver. 25). It was the altar of propitiation. Man is viewed as one whose sins are yet unexpiated. His art, in *that* state, would have polluted the altar. Art came in afterwards (ch. xxv. etc.). Nothing of man's own avails for propitiation.

IV. THE MATERIALS OF WORSHIP. Animal sacrifices (ver. 24). For purposes of atonement—as symbols of personal consecration (burnt offerings)—as pledges of peace and renewed fellowship (peace offerings). Not in the first, but in the other meanings of sacrifice, we are still summoned to bring them in our worship—" spiritual sacrifices " of self-surrender (Rom. xii. 1), of the broken spirit (Ps. li. 17), of praise and thanksgiving (1 Peter i. 5).

V. THE MANNER OF WORSHIP (ver. 26). Reverence and decency.—J. O.

Ver. 22—26.—*I will go unto the altar of God.* The directions given shadow forth the essentials of genuine worship. Amongst the heathen the idol is the central figure, the human symbol of the unseen God. The true God will admit no such symbol; it is a barrier against, not a step towards, the worship he desires. In true worship there must be utter self-suppression. " Obedience is better than sacrifice;" it is only through obedience that the sacrifice becomes acceptable. In this light consider—

I. THE ALTAR. To be made of earth or unhewn stones. The simple unadorned material as provided by God himself. Anything beyond this, any touch of human handicraft, pollutes it. The principle which underlies this fact:—sacrifices offered in the appointed way are acceptable; if we try to better the appointed way—to put something of our own into the sacrifice as a ground for acceptance—we spoil all. Self-obtrusion, however well-intended, is pollution. The altar is the expression of God's will: try to improve it, and it becomes instead an expression of the will of the would-be improver. " I give thee this, O God; it is not worth much, but I give it thee in this self-chosen manner, and surely that adds to its value." Not a bit: it deprives it of all value. The altar of self is not the altar of God; sacrifices offered upon it may perhaps soothe the worshipper, they cannot propitiate the Deity. The pillar, *e.g.*, of a St. Simeon Stylites does not add to the value of his prayers; they have a better chance of reaching heaven from the contrite heart at the foot of the pillar. (Cf. Col. ii. 22, 23.)

II. THE APPROACHES. If the offering be made with a pure motive, it must also be offered in a pure and reverent manner. The special direction, no doubt, aimed against the enthusiastic indecencies associated with idolatry. Still, it illustrates a principle: " All things," in the worship of God, should be done " decently and in order." God looks first at character, but he requires also that character be matched by conduct. The Corinthian Christians (1 Cor. xi., xiv.) infringed the principle, if not the precept. Many amongst modern worshippers infringe it also, *e.g.*, by indecencies of *dress, behaviour,* etc., in a place of worship or when engaged in prayer.

Conclusion.—Two things required of us, *humility* and *reverence;* inward and outward self-suppression. Do we want a motive? " *Mine* altar " (ver. 26). Remember who it is whom we worship. What place left for self when the heart is fixed on God?—G.

EXPOSITION.

CHAPTER XXI.

THE BOOK OF THE COVENANT.—*Continued.*

I. *Laws connected with the rights of persons* (vers. 1—32). The regulations of this section concern—1. Slavery (vers. 2—6); 2. Murder and other kinds of homicide (vers. 12—15 and 20, 21); 3. Man-stealing (ver. 16); 4. Striking or cursing of parents (vers. 15, 17); 5. Assaults and injuries to the person not resulting in death (vers. 18, 19, and 22—27), both in the case of free men and of slaves; and 6. Injuries done by cattle both to free men and to slaves (vers. 28—32). The chief bodily injury whereto women are liable is not mentioned. A later enactment (Deut. xxii. 25—29) made it expiable by marriage, or else a capital offence. There are no other remarkable omissions.

Ver. 1. **These are the judgments.** The term "judgment" applies most properly to the decisions of courts and the laws founded upon them. No doubt the laws contained in the "Book of the Covenant" were to a large extent old laws, which had been often acted on; but we should do wrong to suppose that there was nothing new in the legislation. The Hebrew *mishphat* is used with some vagueness.

Vers 2—11.—*Slavery.* Ver. 2. **If thou buy an Hebrew servant.** Slavery, it is clear, was an existing institution. The law of Moses did not make it, but found it, and by not forbidding, allowed it. The Divine legislator was content under the circumstances to introduce mitigations and alleviations into the slave condition. Hebrews commonly became slaves through poverty (Lev. xxv. 35, 39), but sometimes through crime (ch. xxii. 3).

In the seventh he shall go out. Not in the Sabbatical year, but at the commencement of the seventh year after he became a slave. If the jubilee year happened to occur, he might be released sooner (Lev. xxv. 40); but in any case his servitude must end when the sixth year of it was completed. This was an enormous boon, and had nothing, so far as is known, correspondent to it in the legislation of any other country. Nor was this all. When he went out free, his late master was bound to furnish him with provisions out of his flock, and out of his threshing floor, and out of his winepress (Deut. xv. 12—14), so that he might have something wherewith to begin the world afresh. The humane spirit of the legislation is strikingly marked in its very first enactment.

Ver. 3.—**If he came in by himself,** etc. The first clause of this verse is further explained in the next; the second secured to the wife who went into slavery with her husband a participation in his privilege of release at the end of the sixth year.

Ver. 4.—**If his master have given him a wife.** If the slave was unmarried when he went into servitude, or if his wife died, and his master then gave him a wife from among his female slaves, the master was not to lose his property in his female slave by reason of having permitted the marriage. When the man claimed his freedom at the end of the sixth year, he was to "go out" alone. Should children have been born, they were also to be the property of the master and to remain members of his household. No doubt these provisos, which cannot be regarded as unjust, had the effect of inducing many Hebrew slaves not to claim their release (vers. 5, 6).

Vers. 5, 6.—**I love my master,** etc. Affection might grow up between the slave and the master, if he were well treated. The Hebrew form of slavery was altogether of a mild kind. Masters are admonished to treat their slaves "not as bond-servants, but as hired servants or sojourners," and again "not to rule over them with rigour" (Lev. xxv. 39, 40, 43). Even among the heathen, slaves often bore a true affection to their masters. Or, the slave might be so attached to his wife and children as to be unwilling to separate from them, and might prefer slavery with the solace of their society to freedom without it. For such cases the provision was made, which is contained in ver. 6. On the slave declaring to his master his unwillingness to go free, the master might take him before the judges, or magistrates (literally "gods") as witnesses, and perhaps registrars of the man's declaration, and might then reconduct him to his house, and by a significant ceremony mark him as his slave "for ever." The ceremony consisted in boring through one of his ears with an awl, and driving the awl into the door or doorpost of the house, thereby attaching him physically to the dwelling of which he became thenceforth a permanent inmate. Almost all commentators assert that some such custom was common in the East in connection with slavery, and refer to Xen. *Anab.* iii. 1, § 31; Plaut. *Pœnul.* v. 2, 21; Juv. *Sat.* i. 104; Plutarch. *Vit. Cic.* § 26, etc. But these passages merely show that the Orientals generally—not slaves in particular—had their ears bored for the purpose of wearing earrings, and indicate no usage at all comparable to the Hebrew practice. The Hebrew custom — probably a very ancient one — seems to have had two objects—1. The declaring by a significant act, that the man belonged to the house ; and 2. The permanent marking of him as a slave, disentitled to the rights of freemen. **He shall serve him for ever.** Josephus (*Ant. Jud.* iv. 8, § 20) and the Jewish commentators generally maintain that the law of the jubilee release overruled this enactment ; but this must be regarded as very doubtful.

Ver. 7.—**If a man sell his daughter to be a maid-servant.** Among ancient nations the father's rights over his children were generally regarded as including the right to sell them for slaves. In civilised nations the right was seldom exercised ; but what restrained men was rather a sentiment of pride than any doubt of such sales being proper. Many barbarous nations, like the Thracians (Herod. v. 6), made a regular practice of selling their daughters. Even at Athens there was a time when sales of children had been common (Plut. *Vit. Solon.* § 13). Existing custom, it is clear, sanctioned such sales among the Hebrews, and what the law now did was to step in and mitigate the evil consequences. (Compare the comment on verse 2.) These were greatest in the case of females. Usually they were bought to be made the concubines, or secondary wives of their masters. If this intention were carried out, then they were to be entitled to their status and maintenance as wives during their lifetime, even though their husband took another (legitimate) wife (ver. 10). If the intention was not carried out, either the man was to marry her to one of his sons (ver. 9), or he was to sell his rights over her altogether with his obligations to another Hebrew ; or he was to send her back at once *intact* to her father's house, without making any claim on him to refund the purchase-money. These provisos may not have furnished a remedy against all the wrongs of a weak, and, no doubt, an oppressed class ; but they were important mitigations of the existing usages, and protected the slave-concubine to a considerable extent.

Ver. 8.—**If she please not her master.** If he decline, *i.e.*, to carry out the contract, and take her for his wife. **Then let her be redeemed.** Rather, " Then let him cause her to be redeemed." Let him, *i.e.*, look out for some one who will buy her of him and take his obligation of marriage off his hands **To sell her to a strange nation he shall not have power.** Only, this purchaser must be a Hebrew, like himself, and not a foreigner, since her father consented to her becoming a slave only on the condition of her being wedded to a Hebrew. **Seeing he hath dealt deceitfully with her.** By professing to take

her as a secondary wife, and not carrying out the contract.

Ver. 9.—**And if he hath betrothed her unto his son.** A man might have bought the maiden for this object, or finding himself not pleased with her (ver. 8), might have made his son take her place as her husband. In this case but one course was allowed—he must give her the status of a daughter thenceforth in his family.

Ver. 10.—**If he take him another wife**—*i.e.*, If he marry her himself, and then take another, even a legitimate, wife—**her food, her raiment, and her duty of marriage shall he not diminish**—she shall retain during her life all the privileges of a married woman—he shall not diminish aught from them. The word translated " duty of marriage " seems to mean " right of cohabitation."

Ver. 11.—**If he do not these three unto her.** Not the " three " points of the latter part of ver. 10 ; but one of the three courses laid down in vers. 8, 9, and 10. **She shall go out free**—*i.e.*, she shall not be retained as a drudge, a mere maidservant, but shall return to her father at once, a free woman, capable of contracting another marriage ; **and without money**—*i.e.*, without the father being called upon to refund any portion of the sum for which he had sold her.

Vers. 12—14.—*Homicide.* Ver. 12 reiterates the Sixth Commandment, and adds to it a temporal penalty—"he shall surely be put to death." The substance of this law had already been given to Noah in the words, " Whoso sheddeth man's blood, *by man shall his blood be shed* " (Gen. ix. 6). Real murder, with deliberate intent, was under no circumstances to be pardoned. The murderer was even to be torn from the altar, if he took refuge there, and relentlessly punished (ver. 14). See the case of Joab (1 Kings ii. 28—34). But, if a man happened suddenly upon his enemy, without having sought the opportunity, and slew him (ver. 13), then the case was one not of murder, but at most of manslaughter, or possibly of justifiable homicide. No legal penalty was assigned to such offences. They were left to the rude justice of established custom, which required " the avenger of blood " to visit them with due retribution. According to the general practice of the Eastern nations, he might either insist on life for life or take a money compensation. With this custom, deeply ingrained into the minds of the Oriental people, the law did not meddle. It was content to interpose between the avenger of blood and his victim the chance of reaching an asylum. Places were appointed, whither the shedder of blood might flee, and where he might be safe until his cause was tried before the men of his own city (Num. xxxv. 22—25), and afterwards, if the judgment were in his favour. Some particular part of the camp was probably made an asylum in the wilderness.

Ver. 13.—**God deliver him into his hand.** This does not seem to mean more than, " if he chance upon him without seeking him." God's providence does in fact bring about the meetings which men call accidental. **I will appoint thee a place.** When we first hear of the actual appointment, the number of the places was six—three on either side of Jordan. (See Josh. xx. 7, 8; and compare Num. xxxv. 10—15, and Deut. xix. 2.) Thus there was always a city of refuge at a reasonable distance.

Ver. 14.—**Presumptuously.** Or " proudly," "arrogantly." **Thou shalt take him from mine altar.** See the comment on ver. 12.

Vers. 15—17.—*Other capital offences.* The unsystematic character of the arrangement in this chapter is remarkably shown by this interruption of the consideration of different sorts of homicide, in order to introduce offences of quite a different character, and those not very closely allied to each other—*e.g.*, 1. Striking a parent; 2. Kidnapping; 3. Cursing a parent.

Ver. 15.—**He that smiteth his father,** etc. To " smite " here is simply to " strike "—to offer the indignity of a blow—not to kill, which had already been made capital (ver. 12), not in the case of parents only, but in every case. The severity of the law is very remarkable, and strongly emphasises the dignity and authority of parents. There is no parallel to it in any other known code, though of course the *patria potestas* of the Roman father gave him the power of punishing a son who had struck him, capitally.

Ver. 16.—**He that stealeth a man.** Kidnapping, or stealing men to make them slaves, was a very early and very wide-spread crime. Joseph's brothers must be regarded as having committed it (Gen. xxxvii. 28); and there are many traces of it in the remains of antiquity. (See Herod. iv 183; Strab. vii. p. 467; Sueton. *Octav.* § 32; etc.) Most kidnapping was of foreigners; and this was a practice of which the laws of states took no cognizance, though a certain disrepute may have attached to it. But the kidnapping of a fellow-countryman was generally punished with severity. At Athens it was a capital offence. At Rome it made a man infamous. We may gather from Deut. xxiv. 7, that the Mosaic law was

especially levelled against this form of the crime, though the words of the present passage are general, and forbid the crime altogether. Man-stealing, in the general sense, is now regarded as an offence by the chief civilised states of Europe and America, and is punished by confiscation of the stolen goods, and sometimes by imprisonment of the man-stealers.

Ver. 17.—**He that curseth his father,** etc. Blasphemy against God, and imprecations upon parents, were the only two sins of the tongue which the law expressly required to be punished with death (Lev. xxiv. 16). In later times analogy was held to require that " cursing the ruler of the people " (Ex. xxii. 28) should be visited with the same penalty (2 Sam. xix. 22; 1 Kings ii. 8, 9, 46). The severity of the sentence indicates that in God's sight such sins are of the deepest dye.

Vers. 18, 19 —*Severe assault.* Assault was punishable by the law in two ways. Ordinarily, the rule was that of strict retaliation— " Eye for eye, tooth for tooth, hand for hand, foot for foot, burning for burning, wound for wound, stripe for stripe " (vers. 24, 25; compare Lev. xxiv. 20, and Deut. xix. 21). But where the assault was severe, causing a man to take to his bed, and call in the physician's aid, something more was needed. The Rabbinical commentators tell us that in this case he was arrested, and sent to prison until it was ascertained whether the person hurt would die or no. If he died, the man was tried for murder; if he recovered, a fine was imposed. This was fixed at such a sum as would at once compensate the injured man for his loss of time and defray the expense of his cure. A similar principle is adopted under our own law in many cases of *civil* action.

Ver. 18.—**If men strive together.** If there is a quarrel and a personal encounter. In our own law this would reduce this offence, if death ensued, to manslaughter. **With a stone, or with his fist.** The use of either would show absence of premeditation, and of any design to kill. A weapon would have to be prepared beforehand: a stone might be readily caught up.

Ver. 19.—**If he rise again and walk upon his staff.** If he recovered sufficiently to leave his bed, and get about with a stick to lean on, his hurt was not to be brought up against the injurer, though he died soon afterwards. Compensation was to be received, and the score regarded as wiped off.

Vers. 20, 21.—*Homicide of slaves.* In most ancient states the slave was the absolute property of his master, and might be ill-used to any extent, even killed, without the law in any way interfering. It is said that the state of things was different in Egypt (Kalisch); but we have scarcely sufficient evidence on the point to be certain that the slave enjoyed there any real and efficient protection. At Athens, beyond a doubt, the law protected the life of the slave; and a very moderate amount of ill-treatment entitled a slave to bring an action. At Rome, on the contrary, "the master could treat the slave as he pleased, could sell him, punish him, and put him to death" (*Dict. of Greek & Rom. Antiq.* p. 1036). And this was the ordinary state of the law, particularly in Oriental countries. The Mosaic legislation must be regarded as having greatly ameliorated the condition of the native slave population. Hebrew bondmen it placed nearly upon a par with hired servants (Lev. xxv. 40); foreign slaves, whether prisoners taken in war, or persons bought in the market, it protected to a very great extent. By the law given in verses 26, 27, it largely controlled the brutality of masters, who had to emancipate their slaves if they did them any serious injury. By the law laid down in verse 20, it gave their lives the same protection, or nearly the same, as the lives of freemen. "Smiting" was allowed as a discipline, without which slavery cannot exist; but such smiting as resulted in death was, as a general rule, punishable like any other homicide. The only exception was, if the slave did not die for some days (ver. 21). In that case the master was considered not to have intended the slave's death, and to be sufficiently punished by the loss of his property.

Ver. 20.—**If a man smite his servant, or his maid.** "Maids" would commonly be chastised by their mistress, or by an upper servant acting under the mistress's authority. "A man" here means "any one." **With a rod.** The rods wherewith Egyptian slaves were chastised appear upon the monuments. They were long canes, like those used by our schoolmasters. **Under his hand.** Criminals in the East are said often to die under the bastinado; and even in our own country there have been cases of soldiers dying under the lash. A special delicacy of the nervous system will make a punishment of the kind fatal to some, which would have been easily borne by others.

Ver. 21.—**If he continue a day or two—**

i.e., "If the slave does not die till a day or two afterwards." Compare the provision in ver. 19, with respect to persons who were not slaves. No special callousness to the sufferings of slaves is implied. **He is his money.** The slave had been purchased for a sum of money, or was at any rate money's worth; and the master would suffer a pecuniary loss by his death.

Ver. 22 — 25. — *Assault producing miscarriage. Retaliation.* Women in all countries are apt to interfere in the quarrels of men, and run the risk of suffering injuries which proceed from accident rather than design, one such injury being of a peculiar character, to which there is nothing correspondent among the injuries which may be done to man. This is abortion, or miscarriage. The Mosaic legislation sought to protect pregnant women from suffering this injury by providing, first, that if death resulted the offender should suffer death (ver. 23); and, secondly, that if there were no further ill-result than the miscarriage itself, still a fine should be paid, to be assessed by the husband of the injured woman with the consent of the judges (ver. 22). The mention of "life for life," in ver. 23, is followed by an enunciation of the general "law of retaliation," applied here (it would seem) to the special case in hand, but elsewhere (Lev. xxiv. 19, 20) extended so as to be a fundamental law, applicable to all cases of personal injury.

Ver. 22.—**If men strive and hurt a woman.** A chance hurt is clearly intended, not one done on purpose. **So that her fruit depart from her.** So that she be prematurely delivered of a dead child. **And no mischief follow.** "Mischief" here means "death," as in Gen. xlii. 4, 38; xlv. 29. **He shall pay as the judges determine.** He was not to be wholly at the mercy of the injured father. If he thought the sum demanded was excessive, there was to be an appeal to a tribunal.

Ver. 23.—**Then thou shalt give life for life.** "Life for life" seems an excessive penalty, where the injury was in a great measure accidental, and when there was certainly no design to take life. Probably the law was not now enacted for the first time, but was an old tribal institution, like the law of the "avenger of blood." There are many things in the Mosaic institutions which Moses tolerated, like "bills of divorce"—on account of "the hardness of their hearts."

Vers. 23, 24.—**Eye for eye, tooth for tooth,** etc. Aristotle says in the Nicomachean Ethics, that this was the rule of justice which Rhadamanthus was supposed to act on in the judgment after death (book 5, sec. 3), and that it had the approval of the Pythagoreans. Solon admitted it to a certain extent into the laws of Athens, and at Rome it found its way into the Twelve Tables. There is a *primâ facie* appearance of exact equality in it, which would captivate rude minds and cause the principle to be widely adopted in a rude state of society. But in practice objections would soon be felt to it. There is no exact measure of the hardness of a blow, or the severity of a wound; and "wound for wound, stripe for stripe," would open a door for very unequal inflictions "Eye for eye" would be flagrantly unjust in the case of a one-eyed man. Moreover, it is against public policy to augment unnecessarily the number of mutilated and maimed citizens, whose power to serve the state is lessened by their mutilation. Consequently in every society retaliation has at an early date given way to pecuniary compensation; and this was the case even among the Hebrews, as Kalisch has shown satisfactorily. If the literal sense was insisted on in our Lord's day (Matt. v. 38), it was only by the Sadducees, who declined to give the law a spiritual interpretation.

Vers. 26, 27.—*Assaults on Slaves.* The general law of retaliation was not made to extend to slaves. For ordinary blows the slave was not thought entitled to compensation, any more than the child. They were natural incidents of his condition. In extremer cases, where he was permanently injured in an organ or a member, he was, however, considered to have ground of complaint and to deserve a recompense. But for him to revenge himself upon his master by inflicting the same on him was not to be thought of. It would have put the slave into a false position, have led to his prolonged illtreatment, and have been an undue degradation of the master. Therefore, compulsory emancipation was made the penalty of all such aggravated assaults, even the slightest (ver. 27).

Vers. 26, 27.—**If a man smite the eye**, etc. The "eye" seems to be selected as the most precious of our organs, the "tooth" as that the loss of which is of least consequence. The principle was that any permanent loss of any part of his frame entitled the slave to his liberty. A very considerable check must have been put on the brutality of masters by this enactment.

Vers. 28—32.—*Injuries done by cattle to slaves and freemen.* For the purpose of in-

culcating as strongly as possible the principle of the sanctity of human life, the legislator notices the case where mortal injury is done to a person by a domesticated animal. The ox is taken as the example, being the animal most likely to inflict such an injury. In accordance with the declaration already made to Noah (Gen. ix. 6), it is laid down that the destructive beast must be killed. Further, to mark the abhorrence in which murder ought to be held, the provision is made, that none of the creature's flesh must be eaten. The question then arises, is the owner to suffer any punishment? This is answered in the way that natural equity points out—"If he had reason to know the savage temper of the animal, he is to be held responsible; if otherwise, he is to go free." In the former case, the Hebrew law assigned a higher degree of responsibility than accords with modern notions; but practically the result was not very different. The neglectful Hebrew owner was held to have been guilty of a capital offence, but was allowed to "redeem his life" by a fine. His modern counterpart would be held to have been guilty simply of *lâches* or neglect of duty, and would be punished by fine or imprisonment

Ver. 28.—**The ox shall be surely stoned.** He shall suffer the same death that would have been the portion of a human murderer. **His flesh shall not be eaten.** The animal was regarded as accursed, and therefore, as a matter of course, no Hebrew might eat of it. According to the Rabbinical commentators, it was not even lawful to sell the carcase to Gentiles. **The owner shall be quit**—*i.e.*, "shall be liable to no punishment."

Ver. 29.—**If the ox were wont to push with his horns.** If he were notoriously, and to his owner's knowledge, a dangerous animal, which required watching, and no watch was kept on him, then the owner became blameable, and having by his neglect contributed to a homicide, was "guilty of death."

Ver. 30.—**If there be a fine laid upon him.** There can scarcely have been any circumstances under which the penalty of death would have been enforced. No neglect could bring the crime into the category of murder. It is assumed, therefore, that practically the penalty would be a fine, proportioned no doubt to the value of the life taken.

Ver. 31.—**Whether he have gored a son or a daughter.** If the sufferer were a child, the value of the life, and therefore the amount of the fine, would be less.

Ver. 32.—**If the ox shall push a man-servant or a maidservant.** Hitherto, the case of free persons only has been considered. But the accident might have happened to a slave. Where this was the case, the death of the ox was still made indispensable, and thus far the same sacredness was made to attach to the life of the slave and of the free-man. But, in lieu of a varying fine, the average price of a slave, thirty shekels of silver, was appointed to be paid in all cases, as a compensation to the master

HOMILETICS.

Vers. 2—11 ; 20, 21 ; 26, 27 ; 32. *The slave laws.* Slave laws belong to all communities, and not to some only, slavery being really a universal and not a partial institution. In the most civilised communities of modern Europe, there are two large classes of slaves—lunatics and criminals. The law openly condemns these last to penal *servitude*, which may be for life; and this " servitude," as Lord Chief Justice Coleridge has repeatedly pointed out, is simply a form of slavery. Ancient communities differed from modern—1. In the extent to which slavery prevailed ; 2. In the grounds upon which men were bound to it ; and 3. In the treatment whereto those bound to it were subjected.

I. EXTENT OF ANCIENT SLAVERY. The slaves in ancient states were almost always more numerous than the freemen. At Athens they amounted to more than four-fifths of the community. Every free person was a slave owner, and some owned hundreds of their fellow-creatures. Perpetual insecurity was felt in consequence of the danger of revolt ; and this fear reacted on the treatment of slaves, since it was thought necessary to break their spirit by severities. The evil effects of the institution pervaded all classes of the community, fostering pride and selfishness in the masters, dissimulation, servility, and meanness in the slaves.

II. GROUNDS ON WHICH ANCIENT SLAVERY RESTED. Ancient slavery did not necessarily imply any mental or moral fault in the slave. Some reached it through mental defect, as our lunatics ; some through crime, as our convicts (see Ex. xxii. 3). But the great majority were either born in the condition, or became slaves through the fortune of war. Thus slavery was not commonly a deserved punishment, but an undeserved misfortune. Men found themselves, without any fault of their own, the goods and chattels of another, with no political and few social rights, bound to one who might be in all respects inferior to themselves, but who was their lord and master. A sense of injustice consequently rankled in the bosom of the slave, and made him in most cases dangerous. Slave revolts were of frequent occurrence.

III. TREATMENT OF SLAVES IN ANCIENT STATES. Some considerable differences may be observed between the treatment of slaves in different communities ; but there are certain features which seem to have been universal. 1. Slaves were for the most part the property of individuals, and depended largely on the caprice of individuals, who might be harsh or mild, brutally tyrannical, or foolishly indulgent. 2. Slave families might at any time be broken up, the different members being sold to different masters. 3. Slaves might everywhere be beaten, and unless in case of serious injury, there was no inquiry. 4. Very severe labour might be required of them ; they might be confined in workshops, which were little better than prisons, made to toil in mines, or chained to the oar as galley slaves. 5. They might be badly lodged, badly clothed, and badly fed, without the law taking any notice. 6. In most places there was no redress for any injury that a slave might suffer short of death ; and in some the law took no cognisance even of his murder. The Mosaic legislation, finding slavery established under these conditions, set itself to introduce ameliorations, without condemning the institution altogether. Compare St. Paul's conduct when he sent Onesimus back to Philemon (Phil. 12, 16). It divided slaves into two classes, Hebrew and foreign, changing the slavery of the former into a species of apprenticeship for six years, and guarding, not merely the life, but the members and organs of the latter. It acknowledged the family tie in the case of the slave, and laid down rules tending to check the separation of wives from husbands. It protected slave concubines from the caprice of a sated husband. It absolutely forbade the practice of kidnapping, whereby the slave-market was largely recruited in most countries, putting men-stealers on a par with murderers, and requiring that they should suffer death. We may gather from the Mosaic legislation on the subject—

I. THAT THERE ARE CIRCUMSTANCES UNDER WHICH SLAVERY SHOULD BE TEMPORARILY MAINTAINED. Where a whole community is uncivilised, or half-civilised, where slavery is an old-established institution, engrained not only into the laws, but into the habits and manners of the people—where there are no prisons or means of building them, and where the alternative for slavery would be the massacre of prisoners taken in war, and of criminals, it may be well that even Christian legislators should for a time tolerate the institution. The Europeans who obtain political influence in Central Africa, and other similar regions are bound to bear this in mind; and while doing their utmost to put down man-stealing, should carefully consider in each case that comes before them, whether slavery can in the particular community be dispensed with or no. To tolerate it for a while is simply to act on the lines laid down by Moses and St. Paul.

II. THAT IF UNDER ANY CIRCUMSTANCES SLAVERY HAS TO BE MAINTAINED, ALL POSSIBLE AMELIORATIONS OF IT SHOULD BE INTRODUCED WITHOUT DELAY. The slave is entitled to be protected in life and limb, to be decently lodged, fed, and clothed, to have the enjoyment of the Sunday rest, to be undisturbed in his family relations, to have the honour of his wife and daughters respected, to have an appeal from his master if he regards himself as in any way wronged. The efforts of missionaries and other humane men in uncivilised communities, should be directed primarily to the introduction of such reforms as these into the systems which they find established there.

III. THAT, WHERE DOMESTIC SERVICE HAS SUPERSEDED SLAVERY, THERE IS STILL ROOM FOR AMELIORATIONS IN THE CONDITIONS OF SERVICE. It is not the masters of slaves only who are hard and tyrannical. In all service there is room for the exhibition on the part of the master, of indulgence on the one hand, or strictness and severity on the other. We at the present day may either oppress our servants, or deal kindly with them. True, they may leave us if we oppress them; but a good servant will not readily leave a respectable place, and a good deal of tyranny is often borne before warning is given. It is the duty of masters, not only to "give to their servants that which is just and equal" (Col. iv. 1), but to show them sympathy and kindness, to treat them with consideration, and avoid hurting their feelings. More warmth and friendliness than are at all usual in the present treatment of servants, seem to be required by the fact that they are our brethren in the Lord, joint-heirs of salvation with us, and perhaps to be preferred above us in another world.

Vers. 12—14 and 20, 21.   *Laws on homicide.*   Here again, in the time of Moses, a custom, regarded as of absolute obligation upon all, held possession of the ground; and nothing was practicable but some modification of it. The next-of-kin was "avenger of blood," and was bound to pursue every homicide to the bitter end, whether it was intentional and premeditated (*i.e.*, murder), or done hastily in a quarrel (*i.e.*, manslaughter), or wholly unintentional (*i.e.*, death by misadventure). Moses distinguished between deliberate murder, which the State was to punish capitally (vers. 12—14) and any other sort of homicide, which was left to the avenger of blood. In mitigation of the blood-feud, he interposed the city of refuge, whereto the man who had slain another might flee and be safe until his cause was tried. And in the trial of such persons he introduced the distinction between manslaughter and death by misadventure, allowing the avenger of blood to put the offender to death in the former case, but not in the latter. (Num. xxxv. 16—25.) Mercy and truth thus went together in the legislation.

I. TRUTH. The primary truth is the sacredness of man's life. In rude times, where it is everywhere "a word and a blow," very severe laws were necessary, if human life was not to be continually sacrificed; and so manslaughter was placed on a par with murder, made a capital offence; the sudden angry blow which caused death, though death might not have been intended, was to receive as its due punishment death at the hands of the "avenger of blood."

II. MERCY. The "avenger of blood" was not allowed to be judge in his own cause. Cases of unpremeditated homicide were to go before the judges, who were to decide whether the death was intentional or by mischance. Mercy was to be shown to the man who had blood on his hands through accident. He was to be safe within the walls of the "city of refuge." Cities of refuge were multiplied, that one might be always within easy reach. Legislation should always seek to combine mercy with justice. Draconian enactments defeat their own purpose, since over-severe laws are sure not to be carried out. The moral sense revolts against them. Thus, when in our own country forgery was a capital offence, juries could not be got to convict of forgery. Laws should be in accordance with the conscience of the community, or they will cease to command respect. Good men will infringe them; and even courts will be slow to enforce obedience when they are infringed. Wise legislators will ever aim at embodying in the law the judgments of the more advanced conscience, and making it thus an instrument for elevating the moral sentiments of the community.

Verses 15—17.—*Injuries to parents.* The command to honour father and mother (ch. xx. 12), which is enough for the conscience, and which, if obeyed, would render all further laws upon the subject unnecessary, is here reinforced by two important enactments, intended to restrain those who do not scruple to disobey mere moral laws. The penalty of death is affixed to two crimes: 1. Smiting a parent; 2. Cursing a parent.

I. SMITING A PARENT. When it is considered that our parents represent God to us, that they are in a real sense authors of our being, that they protect and sustain us for years during which we could do nothing for ourselves, and that nature has implanted in our minds an instinctive reverence for them, the punishment of parent-strikers by death will not seem strange or excessive. A son must have become very hardened in guilt, very reckless, very heartless, very brutal, who can bring himself to lift a hand against a father, not to say a mother. There is as much moral guilt in a light blow dealt to one whom we are bound to love, honour, and protect from hurt, as in the utmost violence done to a stranger. However, according to the Talmud, it was not every light blow that was actually punished with death, but only a blow which caused a wound; and, of course, the punishment was only inflicted upon the complaint of the party aggrieved, who would be unlikely to take proceedings, unless the assault was of grave character. Probably the law had very seldom to be enforced. What it did was to invest parents with a sacred and awful character in their children's eyes, and to induce them to submit to chastisement without resistance.

II. CURSING A PARENT. To curse a parent is almost as unnatural as to strike one. ALL cursing is unsuitable to such a being as man—so full of faults himself, so liable to misjudge the character and conduct of others; but to curse those to whom we owe our existence is simply horrible. The sin is akin to blasphemy, and is awarded the same punishment. At the present day, when the Mosaic law is no longer in force, and when on this point no echoes of the Mosaic legislation are to be traced in existing codes, it is specially incumbent on conscientious persons to observe the *spirit* of the Mosaic enactments, and (as it were) make a Christian use of them. (1) "Smite not a parent," said the law, "or die the death." "Grieve not a parent" is the Christian paraphrase. "Grieve him not by disobedience, by idleness, by extravagance, by misconduct of any kind. Do not discredit his bringing up by misbehaviour. Do not stab his heart by ingratitude. Do not wither up his nature by unkindness." A child may easily, without lifting a finger, "bring down the grey hairs" of his father "with sorrow to the grave." He may "smite" him in half-a-dozen ways without touching him. Let Christian men beware of such "smiting" of their parents, and dread the "eternal death" which may follow in the place of Moses' temporal death. (2) "Curse not a parent," said the law again. We do not now, unless we part with religion altogether, curse any one. But we too often break the spirit of this law, notwithstanding. We speak slightingly of our parents; we join in disrespectful comments on their manners or behaviour; we use language to them, face to face, which is wanting in reverence and unsuitable. If we would act in the spirit of the law, "curse not a parent," we must avoid all disrespectful words, all disrespectful thoughts towards them or concerning them; we must give them the honour due to parents; we must seriously consider their counsels, and as a general rule follow their advice. As temporal death was awarded to those who "cursed" parents by the Jewish law (Ex. xxi. 17), so eternal death will be the portion of such as are determinately "disobedient to parents" under the Christian dispensation.

Ver. 16.—*The crime of man-stealing.* To steal the purse of a man is a trivial crime; to filch his good name is a serious one; but the worst robbery of all is to steal his person. Civilised, refined, polished, intellectual men, happy in the enjoyment of freedom, wealth, honour, domestic happiness, have gone to sleep in comfort, peace, and fancied security, to wake up in the grip of lawless man-stealers, who have bound them and carried them into a hopeless captivity, far from any relative or friend, to become familiar with every sort of ill-usage and indignity. Cilician and other pirates did this in the olden time; Norman sea-kings in the middle ages; Algerine corsairs so late as the last century. The blood boils when we think of the sufferings inflicted on thousands of our species by these fiends in human shape, without pity, without conscience, without remorse. Death was certainly a punishment not one whit too severe for this atrocious crime, by which the happiest of the human race might become suddenly one of the most wretched. In modern times, the conscience of mankind, enlightened by eighteen centuries of Christianity, has revolted against the enormity long committed with impunity on the negro races of Western Africa, and the slave-trade has been proclaimed a form of piracy. Yet the accursed traffic still continues in the centre and in the east of the " Dark Continent ; " still quiet villagers are awakened in the dead of night by the news that the kidnapper is upon them; harmless, peaceable men, together with their wives and children, are carried off in hundreds by Arab and sometimes by so-called Christian traders, driven to the coast in gangs, shipped in crowded dhows, and sold to the best bidder in the marts of Arabia and Persia. It is a subject well worthy the consideration of Christian governments, whether a revival of the Mosaic enactment is not required, to stop a trade the profits of which are so enormous, that nothing short of death is likely to deter avaricious men from engaging in it.

Vers. 23—25.—*The rule of retaliation.* " To suffer that a man has done is strictest, straightest right," was a line which passed into a proverb in ancient Greece. The administration of justice is rendered very simple and easy by the adoption of the principle, which approves itself to simple minds, and might work well in a simple state of society. The law of " life for life " (ver. 23) remains, and must always remain, the basis on which society justifies the execution of the murderer. If " eye for eye, hand for hand, foot for foot " (ver. 24), were enforced, the criminal could not complain; but the State would suffer by the mutilation and consequent debilitation of its members. In the administration of " burning for burning, wound for wound, stripe for stripe " (ver. 25), there would be difficulties, it being almost impossible for the public executioner to inflict a burn, wound, or blow exactly similar to the burn, wound, or blow given by the criminal. These difficulties lead naturally to the substitution of " compensation " for " retaliation," which we find sanctioned in vers. 19, 22, 30, and 32. If the damage caused by a wound, burn, blow, or even by the loss of a slave or wife, can be estimated, and the injurer be made to pay that amount to the injured party, then the original loss is in a certain sense retaliated, and the wrongdoer " suffers what he has done." In the administration of justice the rule of retaliation has thus still a place. Retaliation is made unlawful by Christianity (Matt. v. 38—42), not in the administration of justice, but in the private dealings of man with man. We must not ourselves give blow for blow, " wound for wound, burning for burning; " no, nor gibe for gibe, slight for slight, insult for insult. Firstly, because we are not fair judges in our own case, and should be almost sure to overestimate our own injury; and, secondly, because we should provoke a continuance of strife. We should not even be eager to prosecute those who have injured us, if there be a chance that by patience and forbearance we may bring them to a better mind. We should be content to " suffer wrong," if by so doing we may win souls to Christ. The Christian law is, " Love your enemies; bless them that curse you; do good to them that hate you; and pray for them which despitefully use you and persecute you ; " and the ground of the law is, that by so doing we may " overcome evil with good " (Rom. xii. 21).

HOMILIES BY VARIOUS AUTHORS.

Ver. 1.—*The " judgments."* The " rights " or " judgments " contained in this and the two following chapters show the manner in which the spirit and principles of the preceding moral legislation were intended to be applied to the regulation of the outward life of the Jewish state. (1) As respects their *origin*, not a few of these laws have obviously their root in old customs, while others may have been derived from the decisions of Moses in the wilderness (ch. xviii. 16). The code, therefore, in its present shape, cannot be supposed to have been verbally dictated by Jehovah to Moses; yet God may have instructed Moses as to the particular laws which were to be embraced in it, and may have revealed his will on special points which were as yet undetermined. The " judgments " were, in any case, given to Israel under express Divine sanction (ver. 1). (2) As respects their *nature*, the laws relate to the determination of legal rights, and to the ordering of the course of justice; in part, also, to the behaviour of the members of the community to each other in various outward relations, and to fundamental religious ordinances. The spirit of the code is throughout that of the moral law; the principles embodied in it are those of the commandments. The point of view from which its statutes are to be regarded is, however, a different one from that which was occupied in considering the moral law as such. Moral law speaks with the voice of "the categorical imperative." It sets up the perfect ethical standard. What falls short of this is wrong, involves sin, and is condemned. It knows nothing of a morality which is merely relative. The practical legislator, on the other hand—much as he might wish to do so—cannot so mould external institutions as to make them all at once, and at every point, correspond with the requirements of ideal morality. He must, to a large extent, take things as they are—must start with existing conditions and usages, and try to make the best of them. Absolute morality, *e.g.*, would refuse to recognise such a state as that of war; yet, so long as wars exist—and to this hour they are of frequent occurrence—*some* code must be devised, representing such application of ethical maxims as is possible to military life, and to that extent stamping a moral character on the profession of the soldier. The cases of deviation from ideal morality in the laws of Moses are, however, remarkably few, relating chiefly to war, slavery, and marriage. In regard to these subjects, the legislation necessarily partakes of the backward character of the times. The statutes given are not the *absolutely* best, but the best which the people, at that stage of their moral and social development, could receive; that is, the *relatively* best—the best for them. This leads to a third point—(3) The *incompleteness* of the law. The statutes here given, so far as they partook of the imperfection of the time, were not intended to be final. Within the law itself, as will be readily perceived, there was large room for development; but even the letter of the law was not so fixed, but that, in course of time, large parts of it might, and did, become obsolete; new institutions, adapted to new needs, and introduced by proper authority, taking the place of the old ones. Mr. Robertson Smith is therefore not fair in his representation of what he calls the "traditional view," when he affirms—" The Divine laws given beyond Jordan were to remain unmodified through all the long centuries of development in Canaan, an absolute and immutable code" ("Old Testament," p. 333). On such a theory, if anyone held it, his criticism would be quite just—"I say, with all reverence, that this is impossible. God, no doubt, could have given by Moses' mouth a law fit for the age of Solomon or Hezekiah, but such a law could not be fit for immediate application in the days of Moses and Joshua. . . . God can do all things, but he cannot contradict himself; and he who shaped the eventful development of Israel's history must have framed this law to correspond with it." The reply to this is, that the most conservative defenders of the Mosaic authorship of the Pentateuch do not deny the necessity for, and admissibility of, great developments of the principles of the law. It may suffice to quote Hengstenberg—" *First*, it is a gross error, though often repeated, that the Pentateuch embraces the whole civil law of the Israelites. In that portion of the Scriptures *there is shown the greatest aversion from all untimely interference with the course of historical development*. Only those points are determined which must be so, and in no other way, according to the fundamental maxims of the theocracy," etc. ("Authenticity," vol. ii. p. 498, Eng. trans.).—J. O.

Vers. 2—12.—*Hebrew bond-service.* The laws relating to this subject are to be found, in addition to those in the present chapter, in chs. xii. 43—45; xxii. 3; Lev. xxv. 39—55; xxvi. 13; Deut. xii. 12, 18; xv. 15—19; xvi. 11, 14; xxi. 10—15; xxiii. 15; xxiv. 7. An impartial examination of these laws will show how fallacious must be every argument attempted to be deduced from them in favour of modern slave-holding. (On the fallacy of *all* such arguments, based on the state of matters in primitive society, see Maine's "Ancient Law," pp. 162—166.) The Mosaic law did not establish slavery—at most it accorded to it a very modified toleration. It accepted it as an existing usage, labouring to the utmost to reduce, and as far as that was practicable, to abolish, the evils connected with it. It could not well do more, for slavery, under the then existing conditions of society, was in some form or other almost inevitable, and was often the only alternative to a worse evil. Yet the law in its entire spirit and fundamental doctrines was opposed to slavery. Its doctrines of the dignity of man as made in God's image, and of the descent of all mankind from one pair, contained in principle the recognition of every human right. As a member of the theocracy, redeemed by Jehovah for himself, every Israelite was free by constitutional right (see the emphatic annunciation of this principle in Lev. xxv. 42, 55; xxvi. 13). If from temporary causes, the Hebrew lost the use of his freedom, the right to it was not thereby destroyed. It returned to him at the beginning of the seventh year. A law can hardly be regarded as favourable to slavery which makes man-stealing a crime punishable by death (ver. 18), and which enacts that a fugitive slave, taking refuge in Israel from his heathen master, is not to be delivered back to him, but is to be permitted to reside where he will in the land (Deut. xxiii. 15, 16). Bondsmen (both Hebrew and non-Israelite) were incorporated as part of the nation, had legal rights, sat with the other members of the family at the board of the passover, took part in all religious festivals, and had secured to them the privilege of the Sabbath rest. The master was responsible for the treatment of his slave; and if he injured him, even to the extent of smiting out a tooth, the slave thereby regained his freedom (vers. 26, 27). A female slave was to be treated with strictest honour (vers. 7—11), and with due consideration for her womanly feelings (Deut. xxi. 10—15). Humanity and kindness are constantly inculcated. When the Hebrew bondsman went out in the seventh year he was to go forth loaded with presents (Deut. xv. 13—16). The legislation of Moses is thus seen to be studiously directed to the protection of the slave's interests and rights. If there is a seeming exception, it is the one precept in ver. 20, on which see below. The law as a whole must be admitted to be framed in the spirit of the greatest tenderness and consideration, recognising the servant's rights as a man, his privileges as a member of the theocracy, his feelings as a husband and father. As respects the Hebrew bondsman, indeed, his position did not greatly differ from that of one now who sells his labour to a particular person, or engages to work to him on definite terms for a stated period (Fairbairn). He could be reduced to servitude only by debt, or as the penalty for theft. In this latter case (ch. xxii. 3), liberty was justly forfeited—is forfeited still in the case of those convicted of felony, and doomed to compulsory labours, or to transportation, or lengthened terms of imprisonment. The laws in the present section embrace three cases—1. That of the Hebrew servant who is *unmarried* (ver. 2). He goes out at the beginning of the seventh year. 2. That of the Hebrew servant who is *married*. In this case, if the wife came in with her husband, she goes out with him in the year of release (ver. 3); but if his master has given him a wife—presumably a non-Israelite—he has not the privilege of taking her with him when he leaves. He may, however, elect to remain in his master's service, in which case his servitude becomes perpetual (vers. 5, 6). The retention of the wife may appear oppressive, but it was, as Keil points out, "an equitable consequence of the possession of property of slaves at all." 3. The third case is that of a Hebrew daughter, sold by her father to be a maid-servant, *i.e.*, as the sequel shows, as a housekeeper and *concubine* (vers. 7—12). The master may betroth her to himself, or may give her to his son, but in either case the law strictly guards her honour and her rights. If her full rights are not accorded her, she is entitled to her freedom (ver. 11). *Lessons.* (1) Ver. 2.—The natural right of man to his freedom. (2) Ver. 5.—Recognition of the slave's personality. "In modern systems, the man is a mere chattel, but in the Mosaic system, the slave's manhood is declared. He is sovereign over himself, and is allowed the power of choice. The Southern slaveholder would not permit his slave to say, 'I will not'; but the Hebrew slave is permitted to say, 'I love my master, my wife, and my children; I will not go out free'" (Burrows). (3) Vers. 5, 6.—Love, the true reconciler between servitude and freedom. Paul the "slave" of Christ, yet the truest freeman. (4) Jehovah's care for the unfriended. This comes beautifully out in the law for the protection of the woman.—J. O.

Vers. 12—18.—*Murder and related capital offences.* It is characteristic of the law of Moses that its first care, in the practical ordering of the Hebrew theocracy, is for the rights of the slave. These are dealt with in the opening paragraphs. The next laws relate to murder, to man-stealing, and to smiting and cursing of parents.

I. MURDER (vers. 12—15). The same spirit of justice which attaches severe penalties to proved crimes, leads to the drawing of a sound line of distinction between voluntary and involuntary actions. Only for actions of the former class is the individual held responsible. Homicide which is purely accidental is not treated as a crime (ver. 13). Not only is the man who kills his neighbour inadvertently not punished with death, but the law interposes to protect him from the fury of such as might unjustly seek his life, by appointing for him a place of refuge. (Cf. Num. xxxv.; Deut. xix.) The deliberate murderer, on the other hand, was to be taken even from God's altar, and put to death (ver. 14). Deliberate murder implies " malice aforethought "—" intent to kill "—but it was sufficient to expose a man to the penalty attaching to this crime, that he had been guilty of an act of violence, resulting in another's death (ver. 12; cf. vers. 19, 23). Note on this law—1. The recognition of Divine Providence in the so-called accidents of life (ver. 13). 2. The sacredness attached to the human person. The religious ground of the enactment is given in Gen. ix. 6—" Whoso sheddeth man's blood, by man shall his blood be shed: for *in the image of God made he man.*" " The true Shechinah is man " (Chrysostom). 3. The ethical character of the Hebrew religion. The altar is to afford no sanctuary to the murderer. The Bible knows nothing of a religion which is in divorce from morality. This law condemns by implication all connivance at, or sheltering of, immorality, under religious sanctions (Romish huckstering of pardons, etc.).

II. MAN-STEALING (ver. 16). The statute is perfectly general. There is no evidence that it applied *only* to Hebrews, though these are specially mentioned in Deut. xxiv. 7. The stealing and selling of a Hebrew was a direct offence against Jehovah. (Cf. Lev. xxv. 42.) " For they are my servants, which I brought forth out of the land of Egypt: they shall not be sold as bondsmen." The passage is a direct condemnation of the modern slave trade.

III. SMITING AND CURSING OF PARENTS (vers. 15—17). These offences also were to be punished with death. The fact that they were bracketed in the law with murder and manstealing, gives a peculiar impression of their enormity. As if the statute book had said, after laying down the law for murder—" And for the purposes of this law, the smiting or cursing of a father or a mother shall be regarded as equivalent to the taking of a life." And this view of the matter is, in a moral respect, hardly too strong. It would be difficult to say what crime a man is not capable of, who could deliberately smite or curse father or mother. As special reasons for the severity of the law, observe —1. Hebrew society rested largely on a patriarchal basis, and the due maintenance of parental authority was a necessity of its existence. Just as it is found still that, whatever the form of social order, the spread of a spirit of insubordination to parents is the invariable prelude to a universal loosening of ties and obligations. 2. Parents are regarded as standing to their children in the relation of visible representatives of Jehovah (see fifth commandment). This, in the Hebrew theocracy, gave to the crime of cursing or smiting a parent the character of a treasonable act. It was an offence against the majesty of Jehovah, and as such, required to be promptly avenged. On the same ground it was forbidden to revile magistrates, or curse the ruler of the people (ch. xxii. 28). The law is a standing testimony to the heinousness attaching in the sight of God to the sin of filial disobedience.—J. O.

Vers. 18—36.—*Bodily injuries.* The laws in this section may be thus classified:—

I. INJURIES BY MAN. 1. *Strivers* (vers. 18, 19). The man who injured another in strife was required to pay for the loss of his time, and to cause him to be thoroughly healed. Had the man died, the case would have come under the law of ver. 12. As it was, blame attached to both parties, and the law waived the right to further satisfaction. Note—(1) One way of atoning for wrong is to seek in every way in our power to *undo* the mischief we have caused. This, alas! cannot always be accomplished. Not always is "thorough healing"—whether bodily, mental, or moral—possible. So far as it *is* possible we are bound to attempt it. (2) Justice obtains her highest satisfaction when the wrongdoer can be made to contribute to the undoing of his own wrong. This principle might be more acted on than it is. 2. *Servants* (vers. 20, 21; 26, 27). A master was not to be allowed to injure with impunity even a slave purchased with his "money." If the slave was wantonly murdered, the case would come under the law of murder. If he died under chastisement, the master was punished at discretion of the judges. If the slave was in any way maimed, he obtained his freedom. It has been remarked that this is the earliest certain trace of legislation for the protection of the slave. See below. 3. *A woman with child* (vers. 22—26). The injury here is indirect. The woman is hurt in interfering in the strife between two men. Yet the law holds the man who has injured her responsible for his fault, and decrees that he shall pay heavy damages. If evil effects follow, he is to be punished under the *jus talionis*.

II. INJURIES BY BEASTS. The distinction formerly observed as made by the law between voluntary and involuntary actions (vers. 13, 14) meets here with fresh illustrations. 1. If an ox gore a man or a woman, and the gored person dies, the ox is to be stoned—a testimony to the sacredness of human life (cf. Gen. ix. 5), but the owner shall be quit (ver. 28). 2. If, however, the owner had been previously warned of the dangerous habits of the animal, and had not kept it in, there devolved on *him* the entire responsibility of the fatal occurrence. (1) If the person gored was a free Israelite (male or female), the life of the owner of the ox was forfeited; but an opportunity was given him of redeeming it by payment of a ransom (vers. 29—32). (2) If the person gored was a slave, the owner of the ox had to compensate the owner of the slave for the loss of his servant. The price fixed was thirty shekels of silver (ver. 32). In either case the ox was to be stoned.

III. INJURIES TO BEASTS. The same principles of equity apply here. 1. If an ox or an ass fall into a pit which has been carelessly left uncovered, the owner of the pit is required to pay in full (vers. 33, 34). 2. If one man's ox kill another's, the loss is to fall equally on both owners (ver. 35). 3. If the owner of the ox was aware of its propensity to gore, and had not kept it in, he must, as before, bear the whole loss (ver. 36). The equity of this series of precepts is not more conspicuous than their humanity. The important lesson taught by these enactments is, that *we cannot evade responsibility for our actions*. Our actions abide with us. They cleave to us. We cannot shake ourselves rid of them. We are responsible, not only for the actions themselves, but for the consequences which flow from them—for the influences they set in motion. And we are responsible, not only for direct, but for indirect consequences (ver. 22). Involuntary acts are not imputed to us, but all voluntary ones are. We are responsible, as well for what we do *not* do (having the power to do it), as for what we actually perform. We are responsible for the effects of negligence and carelessness. These principles have wide application. They cover the whole range of conduct. They apply to the moral sphere as well as to the physical. They apply, not simply to definite acts, but to the entire influence exerted by our lives. What a responsibility is this! Only grace will enable us to bear its burden.—J. O.

Ver. 20.—*The servant dying under chastisement.* This law has frequently been seized on as a blot on the Mosaic legislation—as inculcating the odious doctrine which lies at the root of modern slave-systems, viz. that the slave is a mere "chattel," and as such, has no personal rights—is entitled to no protection of life or limb. The interpretation put on this particular clause is the more unfair, that it must be admitted to be opposed to the spirit and enactments of the law as a whole, taking, as this does, so exceptionally humane a view of the slave's position (see above); and is, moreover, directly in the teeth of such clauses as those in the immediate context—"If a man smite the eye of a servant," etc. (vers. 26, 27). The enactment will appear in its right light if we view it with regard to the following considerations:—1. The law deals with slavery, not from the point of view of abstract right—from which point of view it could only be condemned—but as a recognised part of the then existing constitution of society. It takes its existence for granted. It deals with it as statesmen have constantly to deal with institutions and customs which they do not wholly approve of, but which they cannot summarily abolish without entailing on society worse evils than those from which escape is sought. But if the right to hold property in slaves—to however limited an extent—be granted, the corollaries of this possession must be granted also. A slave cannot be treated in the eye of the law quite as a free man. His position is relatively a degraded one. The owner of slaves has pecuniary and proprietary rights in his bond-servants, which the law must take account of. The slave *is* the owner's "money." 2. The *aim* of the law is not to place the slave at the master's mercy, but to restrict the master's power over him. Ancient law recognised *no* restriction. The Mosaic law does. It goes at least thus far, that if the slave dies under the rod, the master shall be punished. The drift and bent of the law is for the slave's benefit. 3. It is important to remember that the case is treated here, not in its *moral* aspects, but solely as a question *in criminal jurisprudence*. The moral law has its own say in the matter, and pronounces its own judgment, irrespectively of whether the individual is proceeded against under criminal law or not. The master who, by the undue exercise of the large right of chastisement which the usage of the time allowed him, occasioned his slave's death, was responsible to God for the excess of passion which led to this catastrophe. The law of Moses gave no sanction to the master to endanger his servant's life with the rod. But moral offences do not always admit of being dealt with as crimes. To convict of murder, *e.g.*, there is proof required of *malice prepense*, and this, in the case before us, was precisely what was not forthcoming. The legal tribunals had authority to punish the master, if the slave died under his hand; if immediate death did not take place, the master was to have the benefit of the doubt, and in view of the heavy money loss sustained in the death of the slave (on the average, " thirty shekels of silver," ver. 32), was not to be further pro-ceeded against. 4. The law in this verse—taken in conjunction with others—was really a powerful deterrent from the misuse of authority on the part of the master. (1) It relates only to chastisement with the rod. If the master assaulted his slave with any lethal weapon, the case came under other laws, and might involve his being tried for murder. (2) The case supposed is that of a slave dying under *bonâ fide* chastisement. If murderous intent could be proved against the master—whether the slave lingered a day or two or not—there is no reason to doubt but that the law of ver. 14 would have been applied, and the master would have been put to death. (3) Involving, as the death of the slave did, criminal proceedings, and, on conviction, severe punishment, the mere *danger* of a fatal result ensuing would be a powerful deterrent from exceptional violence. The punishment appears to have been left to the discretion of the judges, and probably ranged from the death penalty (if deliberate murder could be proved), to a simple money fine. The mere *risk* of incurring such a penalty would inspire salutary caution. (4) The master also knew that if, by his temporary violence, the slave should suffer serious bodily injury, he would be entitled, if he did not die, to claim his freedom (vers. 26, 27). The fear of losing a valuable property, whether by death, or, if the slave did not die, in the way last mentioned, would infallibly co-operate with other motives in the direction of restraint. The case, therefore, stood thus, that failing proof of direct intent to murder, the probabilities were in favour of the theory that the death of the slave to whom severe chastisement had been administered, was a result not *designed* ; and the money loss involved in the death of the slave being regarded as equivalent to a heavy fine, the law, in ordinary cases, did not see it necessary to go further. But if the case was so serious that the slave had actually died under his master's hand, or within a short space of time, then, whether the death was designed or not, the law took the matter up, and inflicted punishment according to discretion. *Criminal* law could scarcely have done more. The amelioration of the condition of the slave was to be looked for mainly from *moral* influences, which, under the Mosaic system, were assuredly not wanting.—J. O.

Vers. 23—26.—*"An eye for an eye,"* etc. (cf. Matt. v. 38—43). The principle here enunciated is that of the *jus talionis*. Stripped of its concrete form, it is simply the assertion of the dictate of justice, that when a wrong has been done to anyone, and through him to society, an adequate compensation ought to be rendered. So rendered, it is the principle underlying every system of criminal jurisprudence. We need not suppose that (in Jewish society) it was ever literally acted upon. Commutations of various kinds would be admitted (cf. ver. 30). As a rule for courts of justice, therefore, this principle must remain. But error arises when this rule, intended for the regulation of public justice, is transferred into private life, and is applied there to sanction the spirit of revenge. This is to pervert it from its proper purpose. So far from sanctioning private retaliation, the object of this law is to set *limits* to the passion for revenge, by taking the right to avenge out of the hands of private individuals altogether, and committing it to public officers. In contrast with the retaliatory disposition, our Lord inculcates on his disciples a forbearing and forgiving spirit; a spirit which seeks to overcome by love; a spirit, even, which is willing to forego legal rights, whenever by doing so, it can promote the good of a fellow man.—J. O.

Vers. 1—11.—*Regulations for the treatment of slaves.* I. THE CONDITIONAL ELEMENT RUNNING THROUGH THESE REGULATIONS. What a difference there is here from the strong, uncompromising imperatives of chapter xx.! There we feel that we have to do with man, not only as he is at the time, a Hebrew in the wilderness, but with every man, in every age, and in all sorts of social circumstances. The ten commandments simply assume humanity and society. But the regulations now to be considered abound in the word "if." If certain things are done, then certain other things must be done. But then these things need not to be done at all. A man need not buy a servant; a man need not take a woman to be his companion in servitude, knowing that thereby he runs the risk of being separated from her and his offspring afterwards. These regulations have to be made for free agents, acting often thoughtlessly, or in a matter-of-fact compliance with the customs of their country. There was no real need for any of these "ifs" to pass into action. Consider how ludicrous such regulations would appear if propounded as possibilities in modern English society. The actions which they assume would be scouted as scarcely conceivable. Our notions of property, of service, and of the position of woman are quite different. And yet how many things there are even now, commonly accepted indeed as right and proper, which are no more defensible on the highest grounds than these practices of Israel in the wilderness. There are practices among Christians now, considered proper enough according to the present notions of society, and yet the day is assuredly coming when they too will seem as strange and abhorrent as the practice of a man selling his daughter to be a maid-servant. Things done without scruple, even by enlightened Christians, are far enough from what Christ would have them be. And all that can be reached is to regulate and mitigate what there is not sufficient enlightenment of conscience to abolish.

II. THE EVIDENT DESIRE TO BE JUST TO ALL THE INDIVIDUALS CONCERNED IN THESE REGULATIONS. The purchased individual must have his benefit by liberation in the seventh year; and yet the master is to be treated justly too by the recognition of the woman whom, as it were, he had lent to be a companion to the slave. So also if the slave has a notion of staying, he is compelled to treat it as a serious matter, and not play fast or loose either with master or companion. She who had been, as it were, a concubine, becomes by his desire to stay, lifted to the full privileges of a wife; and to leave then would be a wrong to her as well as the master. The principle holds good all through human society—whatsoever we want in the way of temporal advantages we must take with certain limitations. Whatever benefit there might be in buying a slave must be taken along with the limitation of the seventh year. If the slave chose to have a companion, he must make up his mind how to treat her at the six years' end; either to have liberty and lose her or keep her with life-long bondage. We should choose our position in this world, looking steadily for the guidance of infinite wisdom in our choice. If we be sure of that, then all advantages will be golden to us, and we shall not for a moment think of grumbling because of the disadvantages that must inevitably accompany them.

III. Still though there is a desire here to be just to all, IT IS EVIDENTLY THE WEAK AND UNFORTUNATE WHO ARE CHIEFLY THOUGHT OF. It is for the sake of the slave and the despised woman that these regulations are here specified. The strong in such circumstances are as a rule well able—only too well able—to look after themselves. It is the glorious mark, again and again appearing in God's dealings, that he loves to bring the enslaved nearer to liberty, the degraded nearer to the normal elevation of humanity.—Y.

Vers. 12—17.—*Capital offences.* As we look through the penalties specified for wrong-doing in chaps. xxi., xxii., we notice that they are divisible into two great classes. Some offences are punished by death, and others by some sort of compensation for the injury done. The graduated terms of imprisonment with which we are familiar, were not of course possible to the Israelites, and if possible, perhaps would not have seemed desirable. We notice that in this chapter five capital offences are specified; there were doubtless many besides; but these are enough to show the principles on which Jehovah acted in taking away the life of the offender.

I. THE MURDERER PROPER. In chap. xx. we find the general command not to kill; and here is the instruction for the Israelites what to do with the man who deliberately and maliciously took away the life of a fellow-man. This, it is plain, was done under special authority and for special reasons. It was Jehovah's regulation for his people in their then circumstances; but we must not quote it as applicable to the punishment of the murderer generally. If on the authority of this passage we are bound to punish the murderer by death, obviously we are bound to punish him who reviles his parents, in the same way. There were reasons then for putting the murderer to death which do not now apply. The principle underlying the enactment seems to be that murder is one of the crimes which must be followed by the severest penalty man is *disposed to inflict*. So long as the infliction of a death penalty at all harmonises with the general consciousness of men, it is plain that any lesser penalty for murder is inadequate. But if once we get to the position—and it is to be hoped we are ever getting nearer to it—that only the sternest necessity justifies taking human life away, we shall then substitute perpetual imprisonment as the extreme penalty. We shall all feel then that murder is assuredly a crime which should condemn the perpetrator to life-long seclusion from the society of his fellow-men.

II. THE SMITER OF FATHER OR MOTHER. Here we see how different are the principles underlying Divine law from those underlying human law. In a modern English court of justice the smiting of a parent might perhaps receive the highest penalty incurred for the commission of an assault; but it would never be exalted into a special offence. But God in his government of Israel makes an offence against a parent to be one of the first magnitude. The severe penalty specified here corresponds with the position occupied in the Decalogue by the commandment to honour parents. God we see is ever saying and doing things to set great honour on the family, and indicate great expectations from it. It has been a boldly proclaimed principle in all ages, never more proclaimed than now, and often with great arrogance and intolerance, that individuals and families exist for the State. But here in the state that is under God's special governance provision is made that, in its punishments, that state shall honour parental authority and dignity. And of course when once *smiting* a parent was made into such a serious offence, it was but carrying the principle out to a logical and necessary conclusion to make the *curse* as great an offence. Generally, indeed, the rebellious reviling word of the lips would do more injury, inflict more pain, and be more promotive of insubordination than the blow of the hand. In the light of this enactment we see how much God expects from the parental relation. One, who in the Divine order of things, stood so high that smiting or cursing him was made a capital offence, must have been a man to whom Jehovah looked for great services, great contributions to the Divine glory, and to the prosperity of Israel.

III. THE MAN-STEALER. Within the compass of the same chapter we find provision made for recognised and openly practised customs of servitude, and also for a kind of slavery which by the penalty attached to the procuring of it is indicated as one of the worst of crimes. There was slavery and slavery. There was the buying of men in such sort as is indicated in verse 2; there was also such stealing and selling as we find an actual instance of in Gen. xxxvii. 28. Such crimes were evidently only too possible, and once committed, it might be very hard to discover the criminal or restore the captive to liberty. There was perhaps many a Joseph—and when we consider his sufferings, and the sufferings of his father, we shall not wonder at the penalty attached to the crime. Then suppose an Israelite were to sell a brother Israelite to some band of Midian merchantmen, who would take him into a far country, what would the upshot be? Not only would he be lost to loving kindred, and shut out from the sight of his dear native land, but excluded from religious privileges. God had brought out Israel *from the house of bondage*, that in freedom, *necessary freedom*, they might find him their God, and become, in many privileges, his people. What a monstrous thing then for an Israelite, through cupidity or revenge, to sell away his brother from peculiar, from unique possibilities! He would not find in any other land the things which God intended him to have at home.

IV. THE KNOWING OWNER OF A DANGEROUS BEAST. (Ver. 29.) Here is the sound principle—a principle which goes deep in its application—that a man is responsible for all foreseen consequences of an act which it is in his power to prevent. Examine the illustrative instances mentioned. A man is the owner of a pushing ox, well known to be a brute of vicious and uncertain temper. The owner indeed has been made specially acquainted with the fact. He can then take one of the two courses, either put sufficient watch over the beast, as not knowing when it may be dangerous to human life and limb, or else in sheer recklessness determine to take the chance of all keeping right. How plain it is that a man of such a heedless spirit is not fit to have free course among his fellow-men! A human life, be it that of the veriest stranger, a mere waif and stray, or say that of an old man on the very verge of the grave, is of much more account than the life of an ox, though it be in the very prime of its strength and usefulness. The property even of a millionaire must perish sooner than the life of the poorest be imperilled. The owner of the ox is looked to here, just because the brute itself cannot be looked to. The master would not be held responsible for the action of a human servant as for that of a brute beast. And is it not plain that the announcement of this penalty here has a very stringent application to all self indulgence? When a man is told that his course of action, however profitable, however pleasant to himself, has been actually injurious to some and is likely to be injurious to others, what is he to do? If he would do as Christ wishes him—the Christ who came to fulfil the law and the prophets—he would straightway refrain from that course of action. Commercial profits and temporal pleasures will be dearly purchased by us, if one day we have to stand before the throne of him who judges righteous judgment, to answer for selfish, reckless trifling with the best interests of our neighbours The owner of the ox may say, "Let people keep out of my animal's way and guard themselves." God, we see, did not admit that principle with regard to the pushing ox; nor will he with regard to our pushing business habits or our pushing pleasures—our reckless resolution to get all we can for ourselves, at whatever risk of loss to those who may come in our way.

V. From the instances given, we may easily infer WHAT OTHER OFFENCES OF THE SAME KIND WOULD BE PUNISHED IN THE SAME WAY. Wherever there was anything peculiarly presumptuous or daring, there the occasion for death seems to have been found. That which most deeply affects the constitution of society is to be treated with the greatest severity. One man might kill another; but because it was misadventure, he would escape with temporary inconvenience. Another man, for no more than the utterance of the tongue, has to die the death. Thus, even in a scheme of government which had so much to do with outward acts as had God's government of Israel, we have regulations which got their severity almost entirely from the evidenced state of heart on the part of the transgressor. In purely human laws the magnitude of the actual offence is always taken into account; there must be some tangible injury to person or property. But it is the very glory of these illustrative penalties here, that cursing father or mother is punished with as much severity as the actual taking away of life. How true it is from these five instances that God's thoughts are not as our thoughts, nor his ways as our ways!—Y.

Vers. 22—25.—*The requirement of strict equivalents in making compensation for injuries.* The particular illustration here is confessedly obscure; but there can hardly be a mistake as to the principle illustrated, viz., that when injury is inflicted on the person, the very best should be done that can be done to make an adequate compensation. When property is taken it can often be restored or things put practically as they were before; but when the person is seriously injured, there is then no possibility of exact restoration. Hence the injurer might be inclined to say that because he could not do everything by way of compensation he was at liberty to do nothing. But the requirement comes in to stop him from such easy-going reflections. Eye for eye is wanted. You must do your best to restore what you have destroyed. Obviously the purpose of the regulation is, not to justify or aid in anything like revenge, but to make men be contented with the best they can get in substitution for the injury that has been done. The regulation of course was never meant to be interpreted literally, any more than our Lord's counsel that he who had been smitten on the right cheek, should turn the other to the smiter. What good would it do literally to render an eye for an eye? That would be great loss to the person injuring and not the slightest gain to the person injured. Persistent requirement of compensation is to be distinguished from a passionate seeking for revenge. And be it noted that this requirement of compensation is not to be omitted under any erroneous notions of what weakness and self-denial may compel from us as Christians. We must keep to the principle underlying the regulation here, as well as to that other glorious and beautiful principle which our Lord laid down in quoting this regulation (Matt. v. 39). He spoke to stop revenge. But surely he would have been the first to say, on needful occasion, that reckless men must not be suffered to inflict injury on the supposition that Christians would not resent it. Certainly we are not to seek compensation for injuries or punishment of those who injure simply to gratify private feelings, or get a private advantage. But if conscience is clear as to its being for the public good, we must be very urgent and pertinacious in demanding compensation. We may be sure our Master would ever have us contend with all meekness and gentleness, but also with all bravery and stedfastness for all that is right. But the thing of most importance to be learnt from this regulation is, that the most precious things attainable by us are beyond human malice or carelessness to spoil in the slightest degree. The treasures God loves to make the peculiar possession of his children are such as eye has not seen. The eye may be lost, and yet the enjoyment of these treasures remain—nay more, the very loss of the natural may increase the susceptibility of the spiritual in us. The very crippling of the body may help us to make wonderful advances towards the perfect man in Christ Jesus.—Y.

Vers. 5, 6.—" *Mine ears hast thou opened.*"—Slavery not usually considered a desirable condition. The Israelites as a people were just casting the slough of it, and God helps them in their social ordinances by emphasising the value of freedom. None the less, even here, a higher state than *mere* freedom is suggested; voluntary servitude may be preferred to liberty, and is very near akin to sonship. Consider:—

I. The preference. Naturally, to a slave freedom is an object. Slavery was a misfortune or a punishment resulting from debt or misconduct (cf. Lev. xxv. 39; Ex. xxii. 3). Thus viewed God only permitted it to continue at most for six years. Every Hebrew had been redeemed by him; and therefore permanent slavery to man would have been an infringement of his rights of ownership. Temporary serfdom under the conditions which he imposed secured his rights and the privileges of those whom he had redeemed [cf. the right of a tenant to sublet a house by arrangement with the actual owner]. The relation between a serf and his employer was thus carefully defined and limited; in so far as they were linked together by a purely external bond, that bond ceased to exist at the close of six years' servitude. During six years, however, a firmer bond might have been formed and strengthened. Possession of the slave's body does not carry with it the possession of his affections; they cannot be bought and sold, but they may be won. If the owner during six years could find bands to bind the heart (Hos. xi. 4); in such case, the serf desiring it, a permanent relation might be established. It is not the abnegation of freedom, it is the exercise of freedom to choose for oneself; if a man was so bound to his employer that he preferred continuing in his service, God was willing to endorse such a preference with his consent. Nowadays, the relation of servant and employer is still more temporary than of old. At the same time, now as ever, love can prevail to win the affections and so weave by means of them a permanent and enduring bond. Love transmutes the conditions of servitude. It changes them into something which is preferable to freedom. The cords of a man bind more firmly than any other cords; but they do not confine or fetter.

II. The sign of the preference. The servant who wished to remain a servant was to be brought before the judges (Elohim), the representatives of God. As God's ministers they were empowered to permit the satisfaction of his desire. The ear pierced against the door post was the outward sign of this sacrament of servitude. Henceforth the man by his own desire was permanently united to the family of his employer. The pierced ear testified to the pierced heart. The sign of slavery was the badge of love.

III. SERVANTS OF GOD. The relation of the slave to his employer is analogous to the relation between the natural man and God. All men are his servants—debtors who cannot pay their debts. The relation however may be of a temporary character; God seeks to make it permanent by winning our hearts and our affections. Work for him in this world we must, willingly or unwillingly. He would have us willing servants; compulsory service has no moral value. "The ears opened" (Ps. xl. 6), in token of the heart won, are of more value than sacrifice and offering. Are we such willing servants? (Is. l. 5). He is willing to "open our ears," to take us as his own for ever, but we must also ourselves be willing:—"He hath opened mine ears and I was not rebellious." Slavery is a state of imperfection; but so also is the miscalled liberty of independence; the only perfect state for man is that "service which is perfect freedom."—G.

EXPOSITION.

II. LAWS CONNECTED WITH RIGHTS OF PROPERTY (vers. 33—36). From the consideration of injuries to the person, the legislator proceeds to treat of injuries to property, and, as he has been speaking of cattle under the one head, places cattle in the fore-front of the other. In this chapter two enactments only are made—one providing compensation in the case of a man's cattle being killed by falling into the pit, or well, of a neighbour (vers. 33, 34); and the other making provision for the case of one man's cattle killing the cattle of another (vers. 35, 36)

Ver. 33.—**If a man shall open a pit.** Rather, "If a man shall uncover a cistern." Cisterns, very necessary in Palestine, were usually closed by a flat-stone, or a number of planks. To obtain water from them, they had to be uncovered; but it was the duty of the man who uncovered them, to replace the covering when his wants were satisfied. **Or dig a pit and not cover it.** A man who was making a cistern might neglect to cover it while it was in course of construction, or even afterwards, if he thought his own cattle would take no hurt. But in the unfenced fields of

Palestine it was always possible that a neighbour's cattle might go astray and suffer injury through such a piece of negligence. An ox, or an ass, falling into a cistern, would be unable to extricate itself, and might be drowned.

Ver. 34.—**The owner of the pit shall make it good**—*i.e.*, "shall duly compensate the owner of the cattle for its loss." **And the dead beast shall be his.** Having paid the full price of the slain beast, the owner of the cistern was entitled to its carcase.

Vers. 35, 36.—**If one man's ox hurt another's,** etc. The hurt might be purely accidental, and imply no neglect. In that case the two parties were to divide the value of the living, and also of the dead ox—*i.e.*, they were to share between them the loss caused by the accident equally. If, however, there was neglect, if the aggressive animal was known to be of a vicious disposition, then the man who had suffered the loss was to receive the full value of the slain animal, but to lose his share of the carcase. This explanation, which the words of the text not only admit, but invite, seems better than the Rabbinical one, "that the dead ox should also be the property of the injured party."

HOMILETICS.

Vers. 33—36.—*The guilt of neglect.* Sins of omission are thought lightly of by most men; but God holds us answerable for them, as much as for sins of commission. The Psalmist defines the wicked man as one who neglects to "set himself in any good way." The neglect of the Israelites to cover their wells, or keep their cattle from goring others was to be heavily punished. Neglect and carelessness are culpable—

I. BECAUSE THEIR EFFECTS ARE AS RUINOUS AS THOSE OF MALICE AND EVIL INTENT. Carelessness and neglect of precautions may set a town on fire and burn hundreds in their beds. Or it may spread a loathsome and dangerous disease through a whole district. Or it may destroy the cattle of a whole county. Or it may allow moral evil to have free course, until an entire nation is sunk in corruption. Or, again, it may endanger our own lives, or destroy our souls. It is a question whether more evil does not actually result from carelessness than from deliberate intent. Youth is naturally careless. Desultory habits intensify carelessness. A deficient sense of the seriousness of life encourages and fosters it.   Advanced civilisation, with its foppishness and super-ciliousness, developes its growth.   The present age asks, "Is anything worth caring about?"—and is deaf to the Prophet's words, "Tremble and be troubled, ye careless ones" (Isaiah xxxii. 11).

II. BECAUSE GOD HAS IMPLANTED IN US FACULTIES OF PREVISION AND CALCULATION OF CONSEQUENCES, WHICH WERE INTENDED TO PREVENT OUR BEING CARELESS AND NEGLIGENT. Man differs from the lower animals chiefly in the possession of reason; and it is an essential part of human reason to look to the future, to forecast results, and calculate the balance of ultimate advantage and disadvantage.   We know instinctively that our happiness depends on our actions; and it is therefore wholly unreasonable to be careless about how we act.   If we have faculties which we might use and refuse to use them, God will be righteous to punish us for despising his gifts.

III. BECAUSE GOD HAS EXPRESSLY WARNED US AGAINST BEING CARELESS, AND EX-HORTED US TO PRUDENCE AND FORETHOUGHT.   "I will send a fire among them that dwell *carelessly*," said the Lord by Ezekiel.   "Rise up, ye women that are at ease; hear my voice, ye *careless* daughters; give ear unto my speech; many days and years shall ye be troubled, ye *careless* women," are God's words by Isaiah.   "Go to the ant, thou sluggard," exclaims the wise man, "consider her ways and be wise."· And again— "Ponder the path of thy feet, and let all thy ways be established—keep thy heart with diligence—remove thy feet from evil."   A careful cautious walk through the dangers and difficulties of life is everywhere enjoined upon us in the Scriptures; and we are plainly disobedient if we are careless.

EXPOSITION.

CHAPTER XXII.

THE BOOK OF THE COVENANT, *continued.*

Laws connected with rights of property, continued (vers. 1—15).   The first section— vers. 1—6—is upon theft.   The general principle laid down is, that theft shall be punished if possible, by a fine.   There is a moral fitness in this, since a man's desire to get what was his neighbour's would lead to the loss of what was his own.   In ordinary cases the thief was to restore to the man robbed double of what he had stolen (ver. 4)   but, if he had shewn persistence in wrong doing by selling the property, or (if it were an animal) killing it, he was to pay more—fourfold in the case of a sheep, fivefold in that of an ox.   If the criminal could not pay the fine, then he was to be sold as a slave (ver. 3).   Burglary, or breaking into a house at night, might be resisted by force, and if the burglar were killed, the man who killed him incurred no legal guilt (ver. 2); but, if the house were entered by day, the proviso did not hold (ver. 3).

Vers. 1—4.—*Laws about theft.* Ver. 1.— **If a man shall steal an ox.**   The principal property possessed by the Israelites in the wilderness was their cattle; whence this occurs to the legislator as the thing most likely to be stolen.   It required more boldness

in a thief to carry off an ox than a sheep or goat; and so the crime was visited with a heavier penalty.

Ver. 2.—**If a thief be found breaking up.** Rather, "Breaking in"—*i.e.*, making forcible entry into a house.   The ordinary mode of "breaking in" seems to have been by a breach in the wall.   Hence the word here used, which is derived from *khâthar*, "to dig."   **There shall no blood be shed for him.** Rather, "the blood-feud shall not lie upon him"—*i.e.*, the avenger of blood shall not be entitled to proceed against his slayer.   The principle here laid down has had the sanction of Solon, of the Roman law, and of the law of England.   It rests upon the probability that those who break into a house by night have a murderous intent, or at least have the design, if occasion arise, to commit murder.

Ver. 3.—**If the sun be risen upon him.**   If the entry is attempted after daybreak.   In this case it is charitably assumed that the thief does not contemplate murder.   **There shall be blood shed for him.**   Or, "the blood-feud shall hold good in his case"—*i.e.*, his slayer shall be liable to be put to death by the next of kin.   **For he should make full resti-tution.**   Rather, "He shall make full restitu-tion."   The punishment of the housebreaker, who enters a house by day, shall be like that of other thieves—to restore *double*. **If he have nothing.**   Rather, "if he have not enough"— *i.e.*, if he cannot make the restitution required, **then he shall be sold for his theft.**   It is somewhat fanciful to suppose, that this pun-ishment aimed at enforcing labour on those who preferred stealing to working for their own living (Kalisch). Probably the idea was simply the compensation of the injured party, who no doubt received the proceeds of the man's sale.

Ver. 4.—**If the theft be certainly found in his hand.** If he be caught *in flagrante delicto*, with the thing stolen in his possession,

" whether it be ox, or ass, or small cattle," he shall restore double. The law of theft in the Mosaic legislation is altogether of a mild character, as compared with the Roman, or even with the English law, until the present century. Double restitution was a sort of " retaliation "—it involved a man losing the exact amount which he had expected to gain

HOMILETICS.

Vers. 1—4. *Punishment, even for one and the same offence, should be graduated.* Some codes treat a crime which can be given a single definite name, *e.g.*, theft, as if it were in all cases uniform, and prescribe a single penalty—death, the bastinado, a month's imprisonment. The Mosaic Law, with greater refinement and greater propriety, graduated the punishment according to the special character of the offence. The worst form of theft proper is burglary. Burglary destroys the repose of the household, introduces a feeling of insecurity, trenches upon the sacredness of the hearth, endangers life, affrights tender women and children. By permitting the destruction of the burglar, the law pronounced him worthy of death. Other forms of thieving were punished in proportion to the audacity and persistence of the thief. A man who had stolen without converting the property, was to pay back double. If he had converted it to his own use, or sold it, the penalty was heavier—fourfold for a sheep or goat, fivefold for an ox. There was especial audacity in stealing an ox—an animal so large that it could not readily be converted; so powerful that it could not easily be carried off. The graduation of punishment for all crimes is desirable—

I. BECAUSE THE SAME OUTWARD OFFENCE INVOLVES VARIOUS DEGREES OF INWARD WICKEDNESS; *e.g.*, homicide varies between absolute blamelessness (ver. 2) and the highest degree of culpability (ch. xxi. 14). Assault may be the lightest possible matter, or approach closely to murder. False witness may arise from imperfect memory, or from a deliberate design to effect a man's ruin. Lies may be " white," or the blackest falsehoods which it is possible for the soul of man to invent. Punishment is, and ought to be, in the main retributive; and as the moral guilt varies, so should the penalty.

II. BECAUSE THE OUTWARD OFFENCE ITSELF IS MORE OR LESS INJURIOUS. By an act of stealing we may rob a man of a trifle, or reduce him to beggary. By a blow of a certain force we may inflict on him a slight pain, or render him a cripple for life. By a false statement in a court of justice we may do him no harm at all, or we may ruin his character. All crimes short of homicide vary in the extent to which they injure a man; and it is reasonable that the amount of injury received should be taken into consideration when punishment is apportioned. Therefore, a rigid unbending law, assigning to each head of crime a uniform penalty would be unsuitable to the conditions of human life and the varying motives of criminals. A wise legislator will leave a wide discretion to those who administer justice, trusting them to apportion to each offence the punishment which under the circumstances it deserves.

EXPOSITION.

Vers. 5, 6.—LAW OF TRESPASS.—Next to theft, and not much behind it, is the wanton damage of what belongs to another—as when a person injures his neighbour's crops, either by turning beasts into his field, or by causing a conflagration in it. To turn beasts in was the more determinedly malicious act, and therefore the damage done was to be compensated by making over to the injured party a like quantity of produce out of the *best* that a man

was possessed of; whereas simple restitution was sufficient when fire had spread accidentally from a man's own land to his neighbour's. We may conclude that if the trespass of the cattle were accidental, simple restitution sufficed; and if the fire were kindled of set purpose, the heavier rate of penalty was exacted.

Ver. 5.—**If a man shall cause a field or vineyard to be eaten.**—Rather " to be eaten *of*," or "to be browsed *upon*." **And shall feed.**—Rather, "and *it* shall feed." **Of the best,** etc.—This means that, without reference to the quality of the crop damaged, the injurer should forfeit an equal amount of his own *best* produce.

Ver. 6.—**If fire break out.**—It is usual in the East (as in England) to burn the weeds on a farm at certain seasons of the year.

When this is done, there is always a danger, in the dry parched-up Eastern lands, of the fire spreading, and careful watch has to be kept. If this watch were neglected, a neighbour's sheaves or standing corn might be seriously damaged or even destroyed. The law punished such carelessness, by requiring the man who had kindled the fire to make restitution.

HOMILETICS.

Vers. 5, 6.—*The law of love forbids all injury to a neighbour*. There are many who would scorn to steal the property of a neighbour, who yet make light of injuring it in other ways, as by trespass, or by negligence. But if we love our neighbour we shall be anxious not to injure him in any way. "Love worketh no ill to his neighbour." He that allows his cattle to pasture in a neighbour's field, or his hares and rabbits to spoil a neighbour's crops, or his poultry to break bounds and damage a neighbour's garden, cannot feel towards him as a Christian should feel. Love would hinder any injuries, nay, even any intrusive or obnoxious act. Love would also be a strong check upon neglect and carelessness. Men are careful enough not to damage their own property; did they really love them, they would be as careful not to damage the property of their neighbours. And what is true of property is true of other things also. We are bound—

I. NOT TO INJURE OUR NEIGHBOUR'S CHARACTER, either by direct attacks upon it, or by carelessly suffering it to be maligned by others.

II. NOT TO INJURE HIS DOMESTIC PEACE. 1. By impertinent intrusion; 2. By spying and tale-bearing; 3. By scattering suspicions.

III. NOT TO INJURE HIS INTERESTS. 1. By divulging without necessity what may hurt him; 2. By pushing our own interests at his expense; 3. By knowingly advising him ill; 4. By setting pitfalls that he may fall into them. If we offend in any of these respects, it is our duty, so far as possible, to "make restitution"—(1) By compensating to him any loss he may have sustained; (2) By disabusing those whose minds we may have poisoned; (3) By ample and humble apology. Too often this last will be all that is in our power; for "the tongue is a fire" (Jas. iii. 6), which scatters its brands far and wide, and creates conflagrations that it is impossible to extinguish. Let each and all seek to control that "unruly member" which "setteth on fire the course of nature," and is itself "set on fire of hell."

EXPOSITION.

Vers. 7—13.—LAW OF DEPOSITS.—Deposition of property in the hands of a friend, to keep and guard, was a marked feature in the life of primitive societies, where investments were difficult, and bankers unknown. Persons about to travel, especially merchants, were wont to make such a disposition of the greater part of their movable property, which required some one to guard it in their absence. Refusals to return such deposits were rare; since ancient morality regarded such refusal as a crime of deep dye (Herod. vii. 86). Sometimes, however, they took place; and at Athens there was a special form of action which might be brought in such cases called

παρακαταθήκης δίκη. The penalty, if a man were cast in the suit, was simple restitution, which is less satisfactory than the Mosaic enactment—"He shall pay double" (ver. 9).

Ver. 7.—**Stuff.**—Literally "vessels"—but the word is used in a very wide sense, of almost any inanimate movables.

Ver. 8.—**If the thief be not found.**—It is not clear what was to be done in this case. Kalisch supposes that it came under the law of the oath (ver. 10), and that if the man entrusted with the deposit swore that he had not embezzled it, he was let go free. But as stolen cattle were to be compensated for to the owner (ver. 12), it would seem to be more consistent that stolen money or chattels should also have been made good.

Ver. 9.—**For all manner of trespass.**—It has been supposed that this refers to "every case of *theft* ;" but Kalisch is probably right in restricting it to cases where a person was accused of having embezzled property committed to his care. He was in that case to appear before the judges (ch. xviii. 23), together with his accuser, and to clear himself if he could. When he failed to do so, and was "condemned," he was bound to restore double. **Which another challenges to be his.** —Rather, "which a man challenges to be the very thing" (that he deposited). The case is supposed of the depositor being able to point out that the person to whom he entrusted the deposit has it still in his keeping.

Vers. 10, 11.—**If a man deliver unto his neighbour an ass or an ox**, etc.—The deposit of cattle is unheard of in classical antiquity ; but it might well be the usage of a pastoral race (Gen. xlvii. 3). The parallelism of the

verse with verse 6 indicates that a deposit of the same kind is intended. **If it die, or be hurt, or driven away.**—The deposited beast might "die" naturally ; or "be hurt" by a wild beast or a fall ; or be "driven away" by thieves, without anyone seeing what had happened.. In that case, if the man to whom the animal was entrusted would swear that he was no party to its disappearance, the owner had to put up with the loss.

Ver. 12.—**If it be stolen.**—If, however, the case was not an ambiguous one, but certainly known to be one of theft, restitution had to be made, since it was supposed that with proper care the theft might have been prevented.

Ver. 13.—**If it be torn in pieces.**—If again there was evidence that the creature had been killed by a wild beast, this evidence had to be produced, before the owner or the judges, for the trustee to be exonerated from blame. A similar proviso is found in the laws of the Gentoos (Rosenmüller, *Orient.* vol. i. p. 148).

HOMILETICS.

Ver. 7, 8.—*The sacred character of trusts.* The main teaching of this third paragraph of ch. xxii. is the sacred character of human trusts. Men are taught that they must carefully guard the property of others when committed to their charge, and religiously restore it upon demand to its rightful owner. No conversion of such property to the use of the trustee, under any circumstances whatever, is to be tolerated. The principle laid down with respect to ancient, will apply equally to modern, trusts :—

I. If the thing entrusted be stolen, without the trustee being justly chargeable with having contributed to the theft by negligence, the loss must fall on the owner.

II. If it be lost by non-preventible accident, as when a lion carries off a lamb, or when a ship goes down at sea, the case is the same—the trustee is not liable.

III. If, on the other hand, the trustee neglect to take sufficient care, and damage occurs, he is bound to make good the injury caused by his own *laches*.

IV. If he actually embezzle the trust, simple restitution will not meet the full claims of justice. He ought to be made to refund, and to be punished besides.

V. In doubtful cases the oath, or solemn assurance, of the trustee, that he has conveyed no part of the trust to his own use, ought to be accepted.

Trusts are among the most important of the contracts and obligations, whereby human society is carried on. Strict honesty and much thought and care are requisite on the one hand, confidence, gratitude and tender consideration on the other. Trustees, it is to be remembered, do, for the most part, unpaid work. No one can be compelled to be a trustee. And unless a generous confidence is put in them, and their good intentions are presumed, alike by the law and by those for whom they act, trusteeship will be declined by prudent men, and great inconveniences will follow.

EXPOSITION.

Vers. 14, 15 LAW OF BORROWING.—The act of borrowing is connected with that of depositing, since in both cases, the property of one man is committed to the hands of another ; only, in the one case, it is at the instance and for the benefit of the man into whose hands the property passes ; in the other case, it is at

the instance and for the benefit of the other party. This difference causes a difference of obligation. The borrower, having borrowed solely for his own advantage, must take all the risks, and in any case return the thing borrowed, or its value, unless the owner was still, in some sort, in charge of his own property.

Things hired are not, however, to be regarded as borrowed. If harm come to them, the owner must suffer the loss.

Ver. 14. **And it be hurt or die.**—The thing borrowed might be animate or inanimate; either might be "hurt;" the former might not only be hurt, but "die." Whatever the damage, and whatever the cause, unless in the single rare case of the owner being in charge, the law required the borrower to make good the loss to the owner. This law must have acted as a considerable check upon borrowing.

Ver. 15. **If the owner thereof be with it.**

—By "with it," we must understand, not merely present, but in charge of it, or at any rate so near it that he might have prevented the damage, had prevention been possible. **If it be an hired thing.**—If anything were paid for the use of the thing, then it was not borrowed, but hired; and the owner was considered to have counted in the risk of loss or damage in fixing the amount of the hire. He was entitled therefore to no compensation Our own law does not rule this absolutely, but takes into consideration the proportion of the sum paid for hire to the value of the thing hired, and the general tacit understanding.

HOMILETICS.

Ver. 14.—*The duty of borrowers.* The duty of borrowers is very simple. It is to take care that that which they borrow suffers as little hurt as possible while it remains in their possession, and to return it unhurt, or else make compensation to the lender. People will not often be found to question the propriety of these rules; but in action there are not very many who conform to them. It is a common thing to take but little care of what we have borrowed; to keep it an unconscionable time; to neglect returning it until the lender has asked for it repeatedly; to keep it without scruple, if he does not happen to ask for it. Curiously enough, there are particular things—*e.g.*, umbrellas and books, which it is supposed not to be necessary to return, and which borrowers are in the habit of withholding. Many go further, and feel under no obligation to repay even money which they have borrowed. All such conduct is, however, culpable, since it is tainted with dishonesty. Borrowers should remember—

I. That they fail in their duty to themselves if they do not restore what they have borrowed. Self-respect should prevent them from a line of conduct which assimilates them to thieves, and is wanting in the boldness and straightforwardness that characterise ordinary thieves.

II. That they fail egregiously in their duty to the lender, who has put them under a special obligation to him.

III. That they fail in their duty to mankind at large, since they do their best to deter men from ever lending, and so place difficulties in the way of borrowers. We all need to borrow at times.

IV. That they fail in their duty to God, who has declared in his word, that it is "the wicked" who "borroweth and payeth not again" (Ps. xxxvii. 21).

HOMILIES BY VARIOUS AUTHORS.

Vers. 1—16.—*Restitution.* We have to mark again in this chapter with how even a hand the law of Moses holds the scales of justice. The cases ruled by the principle of restitution are the following:—

I. Theft (vers. 1—5). The illustrations in the law relate to thefts of cattle. But the principles embodied apply to thefts generally (cf. ver. 7). Note—1. The law which punishes the theft, protects the thief's life. It refuses, indeed, to be responsible for him in the event of his being smitten in the night-time, while engaged in the act of house-breaking (ver. 2)—large rights of self-defence being in this case necessary for the protection of the community. The thief might be killed under a misapprehension of his purpose; or by a blow struck at random in the darkness, and under the influence of panic; or in justifiable self-defence, in a scuffle arising from the attempt to detain him. In other circumstances, the law will not allow the thief's life to be taken (ver. 3). All the ends of justice are served by his being compelled to make restitution. Blood is not to be spilt needlessly. The killing of a thief after sunrise is to be dealt with as murder. We infer from this that theft ought not to be made a capital offence. English law, at the beginning of this century, was, in this respect, far behind the law of Moses. 2. Theft is to be dealt with on the principle of restitution. (1) It calls for more than *simple* restitution. At most the restitution of the simple equivalent brings matters back to the position in which they were before the criminal act was committed. That position ought never to have been disturbed; and punishment is still due to the wrong-doer for having disturbed it. Hence the law that if the stolen animal is found in the thief's hand alive, he shall restore double (ver. 4); if he has gone the length of killing or selling it, he shall restore five oxen for an ox, and four sheep for a sheep (ver. 1). (2) Penalty is proportioned to offence. Both as respects the value of the things stolen, and as respects the lengths to which criminality has proceeded. 3. If direct restitution is impossible, the thief shall be compelled to make restitution by his labour—" He shall be sold for his theft" (ver. 3). It would be an improvement in the administration of justice if this principle were more frequently acted on. The imprisoned thief might be made to *work out* an equivalent for his theft; and this, in addition to the hardships of his imprisonment, might be accepted as legal restitution.

II. DAMAGE (vers. 5, 6). The damage done, in the one case to a field or vineyard, by allowing a beast to stray into it, and feed upon the produce; in the other, by setting fire to thorn hedges, and injuring the corn-stacks, or standing corn, is supposed to be unintentional. Yet, as arising from preventible causes—from carelessness and neglect —the owner of the beast, or the person who kindled the fire, is held responsible. He must make good the damage from the *best* of his own possessions. We are held fully responsible for the consequences of neglect (cf. Heb. ii. 3).

III. DISHONEST RETENTION OF PROPERTY (vers. 7—14). Cases of this kind involved judicial investigation. 1. If the charge of dishonest retention was made out, the fraudu-lent party was to restore double (ver. 9). 2. If an ox, ass, sheep, or any beast, entrusted to another to keep, died, was hurt, or was driven away, "no man seeing it," the person responsible for its safety could clear himself by an oath from the suspicion of having unlawfully "put his hand" to it (ver. 11). In this case, he was not required to make good the loss. 3. If, however, the animal was stolen from his premises, under circum-stances which implied a want of proper care, he was required to make restitution (ver. 12). 4. If the animal was alleged to have been torn to pieces, the trustee was required to prove this by producing the mangled remains (ver. 13).

IV. LOSS OF WHAT IS BORROWED (vers. 14, 15). 1. If the owner is not with his pro-perty, the borrower is bound to make good loss by injury or death. 2. If the owner *is* with it, the borrower is not held responsible. 3. If the article or beast be lent on hire, the hire is regarded as covering the risk.—J. O.

EXPOSITION.

MISCELLANEOUS LAWS (vers. 16—31)

Vers. 16, 17.—*Laws against seduction.* It has been already observed that in the remainder of the Book of the Covenant there is a want of method, or logical sequence. Seduction, witchcraft, bestiality, worship of false gods, oppression, are sins as different from each other as can well be named, and seem to have no connecting link. Possibly, Moses simply follows the order in which God actually delivered the laws to him. Possibly, he wrote them down as they occurred to his memory. It is remarkable in his "law of seduction," that he makes the penalty fall with most weight on the man, who must either marry the damsel whom he has seduced, or provide her with a dowry, or, if she is a betrothed

maiden, suffer with her the penalty of death (Deut. xxii. 23, 24).

Ver. 16.—**If a man entice.** Rather "seduce." **He shall surely endow her to be his wife.** In the East a man commonly pays money, or money's worth, to the parents in order to obtain a wife. The seducer was to comply with this custom, and make over to the dam-sel's father the sum of fifty shekels of silver (Deut. xxii. 29), for his sanction of the marriage. If the father consented, he was compelled to marry the girl, and he was for-bidden to repudiate her afterwards (*ibid.*).

Ver. 17.—**If her father utterly refuse,** etc There might be such a disparity between the parties, or such an ineligibility of the man for a son-in-law, that the father might refuse to re-establish his daughter's status by the alliance. In that case the offender was to pay such a sum as would form a handsome dowry for the injured female, and enable her to enter with proper dignity the house of whatever man might be selected for her husband.

Ver. 18.—*Law against witchcraft.* Witchcraft was professedly a league with powers in rebellion against God. How far it was delusion, how far imposture, how far a real conspiracy with the powers of evil, cannot now be known. Let the most rationalistic view be taken, and still there was in the practice an absolute renunciation of religion, and of the authority of Jehovah. Wizards (Lev. xix. 31) and witches were, therefore, under the Jewish theocracy, like idolaters and blasphemers, to be put to death.

Ver. 19.—*Law against unnatural crime.* The abomination here mentioned is said to have prevailed in Egypt, and even to have formed part of the Egyptian religion (Herod. ii. 46; Strab. xvii. p. 802; Clem. Al. *Cohort. ad Gentes*, p. 9; etc.). Though regarded by the Greeks and Romans as disgusting and contemptible, it does not seem to have been made a crime by any of their legislators. It was, however, condemned by the Gentoo laws and by the laws of Menu (xi. 17).

Ver. 20.—*Law against sacrificing to false gods.* Sacrifice was the chief act of worship; and to sacrifice to a false god was to renounce the true God. Under a theocracy this was rebellion, and rightly punished with temporal death. In ordinary states it would be no civil offence, and would be left to the final judgment of the Almighty. **Utterly destroyed.** Literally, " devoted ; " but with the meaning of " devoted to destruction."

Ver. 21. — *Law against oppression of foreigners.* It may be doubted whether such a law as this was ever made in any other country. Foreigners are generally looked upon as " fair game," whom the natives of a country may ridicule and annoy at their pleasure. Native politeness gives them an exceptional position in France; but elsewhere it is the general rule to " vex " them. The Mosaic legislation protested strongly against this practice (ch. xxiii. 9; Lev. xix. 33), and even required the Israelites to "love the stranger who dwelt with them *as themselves*" (Lev. xix. 34). **For ye were strangers.** Compare Lev. xix. 34, and Deut. x. 19. In Ex. xxiii. 9 the addition is made—" For ye know the heart of a stranger "—ye know ; *i.e.*, the feelings which strangers have when they are vexed and oppressed—ye know this by your own sad experience, and should therefore have a tenderness for strangers.

Vers. 22—24. — *Law against oppressing widows and orphans.* With the stranger are naturally placed the widow and orphan; like him, weak and defenceless; like him, special objects of God's care. The negative precept here given was followed up by numerous posi-

tive enactments in favour of the widow and the orphan, which much ameliorated their sad lot. (See ch. xxiii. 11; Lev. xix. 9, 10; Deut. xiv. 29; xvi. 11, 14; xxiv. 19—21; xxvi. 12, 13.) On the whole, these laws appear to have been fairly well observed by the Israelites; but there were times when, in spite of them, poor widows suffered much oppression. (See Ps. xciv. 6; Is. i. 23; x. 2; Jer. vii. 3—6; xxii. 3; Zech. vii. 10; Mal. iii. 5; Matt. xxiii. 14.) The prophets denounce this backsliding in the strongest terms.

Ver. 22.—**Ye shall not afflict.** The word translated " afflict " is of wide signification, including ill-usage of all kinds. " Oppress," and even " vex," are stronger terms.

Ver. 23.—**And they cry at all unto me.** Rather, " *Surely*, if they cry unto me." Compare Gen. xxxi. 42.

Ver. 24.—**I will kill you with the sword.** It was, in large measure, on account of the neglect of this precept, that the capture of Jerusalem by Nebuchadnezzar, and destruction of its inhabitants, was allowed to take place (Jer. xxii. 3—5). **Your wives shall be widows,** etc. A *quasi*-retaliation. They shall be exposed to the same sort of ill-usage as you have dealt out to other widows.

Vers. 25—27.—*The law of lending money and borrowing.* It is peculiar to the Jewish law to forbid the lending of money at interest by citizen to citizen. In the present passage, and in some others (Lev. xxv. 35; Deut. xv 7), it might seem that interest was only forbidden in the case of a loan to one who was poor; but the general execration of usury (Job xxiv. 9; Prov. xxviii. 8; Ezek. xviii. 13; xxii. 12), and the description of the righteous man as "he that hath not given his money upon usury" (Ps. xv. 5; Ezek. xviii. 8), seem rather to imply that the practice, so far as Israelites were concerned, was forbidden altogether. On the other hand, it was distinctly declared (Deut. xxiii. 20) that interest might be taken from strangers. There does not seem to have been any rate of interest which was regarded as excessive, and " usurious," in the modern sense. In Scripture usury means simply interest.

Ver. 26.—**If thou take at all thy neighbour's raiment to pledge.** Lending upon pledge, the business of our modern pawnbrokers, was not forbidden by the Jewish law; only certain articles of primary necessity were forbidden to be taken, as the handmill for grinding flour, or either of its mill-stones (Deut. **xxiv.**

6). Borrowing upon pledge was practised
largely in the time of Nehemiah, and led to
very ill results. See Neh. ch. v. **Thou shalt
deliver it unto him by that the sun goeth
down.** The reason is given in the next verse.
As it could not have been worth while to take
the pledge at all, if it was immediately to
have been given back for good, we must suppose a practice of depositing the garment
during the day, and being allowed to have it
out at night.

Ver. 27.—**Wherein shall he sleep?** The
outer garment worn by the ancient Hebrews
was like that of the modern Bedouins—a sort
of large woollen shawl or blanket, in which
they enveloped the greater part of their
persons. It serves the Bedouins, to the present time, as robe by day, and as coverlet by
night. **When he crieth unto me.** Compare ver. 23. If the law is broken, and the
man cry unto the Lord, he will hear, and
avenge him.

Ver. 28. — *Law against reviling God, or
rulers.* It has been proposed to render
Elohim here either 1. "God;" or 2. "The
gods;" or 3. "Judges." The last of these
renderings is impossible, since *Elohim* in the
sense of "judges" always has the article.
The second, which is adopted by the Septuagint and the Authorised Version, seems precluded by the constant practice of the most
religious Jews, prophets and others, to speak
with contempt and contumely of the false
gods of the heathen. The passage must therefore be understood as forbidding men to speak
evil of God. (Compare Lev. xxiv. 15, 16.)
Nor curse the ruler of thy people. Rather,
" one exalted among thy people." The term
is generally used of the heads of families
(Num. iii. 24, 30, 35, etc.) and tribes (*ibid.* vii.
10, 18, 24, etc.) in the Pentateuch. Later, it
is applied to kings (1 Kings xi. 34; Ezek.
xii. 10; xlv. 7, etc.). Our translators generally render it by " prince."

Vers. 29, 30.—*Law concerning first-fruits.*
God required as first-fruits from his people, 1.
The first-born of their children ; 2. The first-
born of all their cattle ; and 3. The first of all
the produce of their lands, whether wet or dry ;
wine, oil, grain of all kinds, and fruits. The

first-born of their children were to be redeemed
by a money payment (ch. xiii. 13; Num. iii.
46—48); but the rest was to be offered in
sacrifice. The phrase, " thou shalt not *delay*,"
implies that there would be reluctance to
comply with this obligation, and that the
offering would be continually put off. In
Nehemiah's time the entire custom had at one
period fallen into disuse. (Neh. x. 35, 36.)
The first of thy ripe fruits. Literally, "thy
fulness." The paraphrase of the A. V. no
doubt gives the true meaning. **The first-born
of thy sons.** Compare above, ch. xiii. 2, 12.

Ver. 30.—**Seven days it shall be with its
dam.** See Lev. xxii. 27. The main object is
that the dam may have during that time the
natural relief derivable from suckling its offspring. **On the eighth day thou shalt give it
me.** Some analogy may be traced between
this proviso and the law of circumcision. Birth
was viewed as an unclean process, and nothing
was fit for presentation to God excepting after
an interval.

Ver. 31.—**And ye shall be holy men unto
me.** Ye shall not be as other men, but " an
holy nation, a peculiar people; " and therefore
your separateness shall be marked by all
manner of laws and regulations with respect
to meats and drinks, designed to keep you free
from every uncleanness. One such law then
follows—

*Law against eating the flesh of an animal
killed by another.* The blood of such an
animal would not be properly drained from it.
Some would remain in the tissues, and thence
the animal would be unclean ; again, the carnivorous beast which " tore " it would also be
unclean, and by contact would impart of its
uncleanness to the other. **Ye shall cast it to
the dogs,** is probably not intended to exclude
the giving or selling of it to an alien, if one
were at hand, according to the permission
accorded in Deut. xiv. 21; but points simply
to the mode whereby the flesh was to be got
rid of, if aliens were not at hand, or if they
declined to eat the animals. Dogs were so
unclean that they might be fed on anything.
Their chief use was to be scavengers (2 K.
ix. 35, 36).

HOMILETICS.

Vers. 16—28.—*The severity and the tenderness of God.* The miscellaneous laws
thrown together, without any clear logical sequence or indeed any manifest connection,
in the latter part of this chapter, may, generally speaking, be grouped under the two
heads of instances of the Divine severity, and instances of the Divine tenderness. Here, as
in so many places, " mercy and truth meet together—righteousness and peace kiss each
other." God is as merciful to the weak and helpless as severe towards the bold and
stubborn evil-doer. If his justice is an inalienable attribute, so is his kindness and

compassion. The twofold aspect of the Divine Nature is steadily kept before us by an arrangement in which its opposite sides are presented to our contemplation alternately.

I. INSTANCES OF THE DIVINE SEVERITY. 1. "Thou shalt not suffer a witch to live" (verse 18). 2. "Whoso lieth with a beast shall surely be put to death" (verse 19). 3. "He that sacrifices to any god, save unto the Lord only, he shall be utterly destroyed ' (verse 20). 4. "Thou shalt not revile the gods (God) nor curse the ruler of thy people" (verse 28). In these utterances it is Justice that makes itself heard, wrath that manifests itself, severity that gives strict rules for human conduct, and threatens tremendous penalties in case of their infringement. (1) *Witchcraft is made a capital offence.* Moderns constantly speak of witchcraft as founded on mere illusion, and regard witches and wizards as unfortunate persons, labouring under a certain amount of self-deception, and hounded to their death by persecutors far more to blame than their victims. It is generally assumed at the present day that to hold actual communication with evil spirits, and thus obtain supernatural power, is impossible. We are told that "it is absolutely impossible to acknowledge sorcerers or witches," and that "those who pretend to be such must be considered as impious and nefarious impostors" (Kalisch). The whole round of natural phenomena is presumed to be known, and no mystery to remain anywhere. Witches and wizards are tricksters ; demonology and magic, delusions ; evil spirits themselves either non-existent, or relegated to another sphere, and so entirely beyond human cognisance. But the language and ideas of Scripture are different. There evil spirits are regarded as really existing, and the witch is considered to have access to them. Death would scarcely be assigned as the penalty for mere trickery and imposture. It is well deserved by those who renounce God, and place their trust in spirits of darkness altogether. While the subject must be allowed to be one about which much obscurity still lingers, it would seem necessary for those who accept Scripture as an infallible guide, to put aside the shallow theories of modern sciolists, and hold, with the wisest of all ages, that "there are more things in heaven and earth, than are dreamt of in our philosophy." (2) *Unnatural crime is made capital.* All that is contrary to nature, all that tends to produce "confusion" in his universe, is absolutely hateful to God. Human legislators cared little about a sin which a natural repulsion caused to be rare, and which had no very obvious ill effects upon society. Some religions consecrated it and made it a portion of their ceremonial. Some, and they were the greater number, viewed it with complete indifference. The Mosaic legislation, differing from almost all others, placed upon the offence the brand of heinous guilt, and required that both the man and the beast should die (Lev. xx. 15, 16). (3) *The acknowledgment of false gods in an open and public way is forbidden under the same penalty.* Thought is left free—no inquisitorship is established—but if men parade their misbelief by offering sacrifices to the gods of other nations, the insult to Jehovah is to be punished capitally. It was flagrant rebellion against God, and a transgression of the fundamental law on which the community was built (ch. xx. 3). It was a pollution to the land, and might draw down Divine judgment on the nation. It was offensive to the consciences of all God-fearing men in the community. No punishment under the death-penalty could be adequate for a crime, which was against God, against the State, and against society. The severity was, however, without parallel in other codes. (4) *Reviling God, and reviling rulers are both sternly forbidden ; but the penalty is not as yet affixed.* Reviling God was, like sacrificing to false gods, an overt act of insult, challenging notice, and if allowed, destructive of the theocracy. The penalty afterwards affixed to it was death (Lev. xxiv. 16). In the Book of the Covenant it was thought enough to forbid it, the temptation to such an act not being great. Reviling rulers seems to have been coupled with reviling God in order to introduce the idea that "the powers that be are ordained of God," and consequently that those who resist them "resist the ordinance of God." The death-penalty, though not positively enacted in this case, is the natural consequence of resisting one who "beareth not the sword in vain." Thus far, therefore, the legislation here placed before us is severe—almost Draconic. Expressly or impliedly the death-penalty is threatened in every case. God is shown forth as an inexorable judge, who "will by no means absolve the wicked"—and man can but tremble before him. On the other hand, in the remainder of the passage we have—

II. INSTANCES OF THE DIVINE TENDERNESS. 1. "Thou shalt neither vex a stranger nor oppress him" (ver. 21). 2. "Ye shall not afflict any widow or fatherless child" (ver. 22). 3. "Thou shalt not lend thy money unto any of my people that is poor upon usury" (ver. 25). 4. "Thou shalt not take thy neighbour's raiment to pledge" (ver. 26). The Divine protection is extended especially over four classes of persons. (1) *The stranger*—the sojourner in a foreign land—alien in blood, in language, in religion probably—cut off from the protection of his own government, or kinsfolk, or fellow-tribesmen, and therefore all the more appealing for protection to the pity and the providence of God. To him the Sabbath rest had been already extended by a special provision (ch. xx. 10); if he would be circumcised, he might eat the passover (ch. xii. 48, 49); he might make his offerings at the door of the tabernacle (Lev. xvii. 8, 9); he was to have access to the cities of refuge (*ib.* xxxv. 15). It was now enjoined that he should not be oppressed in any way; that he should not even be "vexed." Kindness, consideration, courtesy, were made the stranger's due. In the final summary of the law (Deut. x. 18, 19) it was declared that God "loved" him, and the general command was given to all Israelites—"Love ye the stranger; for ye were strangers in the land of Egypt." (2) *The widow.* His *widowed* mother was especially dear to our Lord; and it is perhaps with secret reference to the boundless tenderness called forth in him by her condition that throughout Scripture there is so deep a sympathy with the widow's lot. From the sad Naomi, with her piteous outbreak—"Call me not Naomi, but Mara"—to the blessed Anna and the pious Dorcas, the widows of the Revealed Word have the testimony of the Spirit in their favour. For the widow of Sarepta the great law of there being no return from the grave is first broken through, and the mother is comforted by receiving back her dead child (1 Kings xvii. 9—24). For the widow of Nain Christ wrought one of his three similar miracles. In the early Church special care was taken of widows (Acts vi. 1; 1 Tim. v. 3—9 and 16); and St. James was inspired to declare to the Church of all ages that "Pure religion and undefiled before God is this—to visit the fatherless and widows in their affliction, and to keep himself unspotted from the world" (Jas. i. 27). (3) *The fatherless.* The orphan is generally coupled with the widow in Scripture, and God's protection is equally extended over both. In the present passage the oppression of both is alike forbidden; and in other parts of the law both are secured certain advantages (Deut. xiv. 29; xxiv. 17, 19, 21; xxvi. 12, 13, etc.). God proclaims himself in an especial sense "the father of the fatherless" (Ps. lxviii. 5), and "the helper of the fatherless" (*ib.* x. 14); in him the fatherless "find mercy" (Hos. xiv. 2). That tender compassion of the Most High, wherewith he looks on affliction generally, is poured without stint upon those who have so much need of his support and guidance, being left without their natural earthly protector. (4) *The poor.* Poverty is a far milder affliction than bereavement, since by nature all are poor, no man bringing with him into the world any property. Still, in states where there has been an accumulation of wealth, it is a disadvantage to be born poor, and a still greater disadvantage to have known riches and to have lost them. Poverty will ever be the lot of large numbers; of the greater portion through their own fault, but of many without fault of their own. "The poor shall never cease out of the land," we are told (Deut. xv. 11); and, again, "The poor ye have always with you" (John xii. 8). God's pity embraces this large class also; and he seeks to attract to them the regards of their more fortunate brethren. Not only were the Israelites forbidden to lend money to them upon usury; but they were expressly commanded to be ready to lend to them without (Deut. xv. 7—10). Such as fell into servitude for debt, and completed their time, were not to be cast adrift or sent away empty, but to be furnished liberally out of their master's flock and granary and winepress (*ib.* vers. 13, 14), that they might begin the world again with a little capital, and be saved from destitution. In modern times, owing to change of circumstances, laws such as this do not admit of a literal obedience; but we may act in the spirit of them, by never pressing hard on the poor, by sharing with them our superfluity, by pleading for them with others, and "seeing that such as are in need and necessity have right." There is still much oppression of poor men even in Christian countries—much need of improvement in their cottages, in the sanitary condition of their surroundings, in the medical provision made for them, and in the administration of the laws for their relief when old and infirm. A wide field is open for those who would obtain the blessing promised to such as "consider the poor" (Ps. xli. 1).

HOMILIES BY VARIOUS AUTHORS.

Vers. 16—21.—*Abominations.* This series of precepts deals with seduction, witch-craft, bestiality, and the sin of sacrificing to other gods than Jehovah. The case of the seducer might have been brought under the laws embodying the principle of resti-tution. It forms a transition to the others, in which we pass from the sphere of judicial right to what is negatively and positively due from Israel as "an holy people" to Jehovah. 1. *Seduction.* Lewdness in every form is sternly reprobated by the law of Moses (cf. Deut. xxii. 13—30). The man who seduced an unbetrothed maid was to be compelled to marry her; or, if her parents refused, was to pay her a dowry. 2. *Witchcraft.* With equal strictness was forbidden all trafficking, whether in pretence or in reality, with unholy powers. The crime—a violation of the first principles of the theocracy—was to be punished with death. There cannot be perfect love to God, and communion with him, and trafficking with the devil at the same time. The witch-craft condemned by the law was evil in itself, and was connected with foolish and wicked rites (cf. Deut. xviii. 9—15). 3. *Bestiality.* This, as an inversion of the order of nature, and in itself an act of the grossest abominableness, was "surely" to be punished with death. 4. *Sacrificing to other gods.* Possibly this crime is mentioned here as, in a sense, the spiritual counterpart of the vices above noted, *i.e.*, as involving (1) Spiritual adultery, (2) The worshipping of "devils" (Lev. xviii. 7; Deut. xxxii. 17), (3) Filthy and impure rites (cf. Deut. xxiii. 17, 18).—J. O.

Vers. 21—29.—*Jehovah's protégés and representatives.* I. JEHOVAH'S PROTÉGÉS (vers. 21—28). These are the stranger, the fatherless, the widow, and the poor gene-rally—all of whom the Israelites are forbidden to "afflict." The ground of Jehovah's interest in them is his own character—"for I am gracious" (ver. 27). In him, how-ever little they may sometimes think of it or feel it, they have a constant Friend, a great invisible Protector. They are (in the sense of Roman law) Jehovah's "clients." He is their great Patron; he identifies himself with their interests; he will uphold their cause. Injuries done to them he will resent as if done to himself, and will call the wrong-doer to strict account. If earthly law fails, let them cry to him, and he will put the *jus talionis* in operation with his own hands (vers. 23, 24, 27). Vers. 25—28 specially forbid exacting treatment of the poor. Liberal help is to be afforded them. A neighbour is not to be harshly dealt with when driven to a strait. His garment, if given as a pledge, is not to be kept beyond nightfall, which is practically equivalent to saying that it is not to be taken from him at all (ver. 27). What kindness breathes in these precepts! How justly does the law which embodies them claim to be a law of love! And how far, even yet, is our Christian society from having risen to the height of the standard they set up! Let us seek ourselves to translate them more uniformly into practice. Learn also, from these precepts, inculcating love to the stranger, how little ground there is for accusing the religion of Moses of fanatical hatred of foreign peoples. II. JEHOVAH'S REPRESENTATIVES (ver. 28). Magistrates and rulers are to be treated with respect. They are invested with a portion of God's authority (Rom. xiv. 1). —J. O.

Vers. 29—31.—*Jehovah's dues.* These, as part of the law's righteousness, are to be faithfully rendered. Let us not forget, when reflecting on what is due from man to man, to reflect also on what is due from man to God. When inwardly boasting of conscientiousness in rendering to every man his own, let us ask if we have been equally scrupulous in the discharge of our obligations to our Maker. In all spheres of life God claims of our first and best (see on ch. xiii. 2, 12). God's highest due is that we be "holy." The precept in ver. 31 is connected with the prohibition to eat flesh with the blood in it.—J. O.

Ver. 21.—*The treatment of the stranger.* I. NOTE THE FACT THAT STRANGERS WOULD COME INTO SUCH CONTACT WITH ISRAEL AS TO PROVIDE OPPORTUNITY FOR THIS TREAT-MENT. Jehovah had done a great deal in Israel to make them a separated people—

separated in many ways as by the land of their dwelling, their national institutions, their worship, their personal rite of circumcision; but separation, with all its rigours and all the penalties for neglecting it, could never become isolation.   Solemnly indeed were the people enjoined to drive out the Canaanites, and trample down all idolatry; but there still remained the fact, that by a certain Divine and glorious necessity, strangers were to come into considerable intercourse with them.   That strangers should have been drawn to them when they settled in their fertile home was only likely; but this must have happened to some extent even before.   We may be perfectly certain, considering the analogies of after generations and what we read of proselytism in the New Testament, that from the very first there must have been some with the proselyte disposition in them.   Few perhaps of this sort were to be found in the mixed multitude coming out of Egypt—but still there were some.   The Lord knoweth them that are his.   If there are those of whom John might say, " They went out from us because they were not of us," so there are those of whom the Church may ever say, " They come to us because they are of us."   For such God lovingly and amply provided from the first, even when they came with all the disadvantages and difficulties of strangers to contend against. There is in this very injunction, a foreshadowing of the power and attractiveness to which Israel in due time would rise, though as yet it was but a fugitive people without discipline and without coherence.   Strangers in their need were even now drawn to Israel and would be drawn still more, just as years ago their needy ancestor and his children were drawn to Egypt because of the corn that was there.

II. THE STRONG TEMPTATION TO TREAT THESE FOREIGNERS BADLY.   There is a very melancholy picture of human inconsistency here presented.   Liberated slaves, forgetting the horrors of their own servitude, treat with like cruelty those exposed to the opportunity of that cruelty.   Men soon forget their past condition.   Israel, we see, forgot the horror of their own Egyptian experiences in two ways.   1. They lusted after the flesh-pots of Egypt.   2. They failed in sympathy for the foreigners among themselves. When we have possessions and power and thus get the chance of domination, we are only too ready to treat foreigners either as interlopers wishing to spoil us, or tools fitted to increase our possessions.   The world, alas! is always abounding in a great number of the feeble and unfortunate, of whom it is only too easy to take advantage.   More than one class of these are mentioned in this chapter, and among them we see that the foreigner occupies a conspicuous place.   The stranger is the man without friends; he comes into a place where the very things that profit the knowing are traps and snares for the ignorant.   Consider the difficulties of a foreigner planted down in the midst of a huge city like London, a place of dangers and difficulties even for an Englishman who is thrown into it for the first time, and how much more for one whom ignorance of the language makes doubly strange!   Blanco White, who it will be remembered was an exile from his native land of Spain, gives as an instance of Shakespeare's surprising knowledge of the human mind and heart " the passage in which he describes the magnitude of the loss which a man banished from his country has to endure by living among those who do not understand his native language."   The words are those put into the mouth of Mowbray Duke of Norfolk, on his banishment by Richard II.

> " The language I have learn'd these forty years,
> My native English, now I must forego.
> And now my tongue's use is to me no more
> Than an unstringed viol or a harp,
> Or like a cunning instrument cased up
> Or, being open, put into his hands
> That knows no touch to tune the harmony:
> Within my mouth you have engaoled my tongue,
> Doubly portcullis'd with my teeth and lips;
> And dull unfeeling barren ignorance
> Is made my gaoler to attend on me."

If this be so, the stranger's feelings are some index to the temptations of those among whom he is cast.   There may not be downright robbery, but there are tricks of trade, extortionate charges on pretence of making hay while the sun shines; in short there are all sorts of human foxes ever on the watch to catch the ignorant, the innocent, and the confiding. But are God's people amenable to charges of this kind? It is evident that the Israelites were, from this warning to them. It was so easy to turn Jehovah's denunciations of the idolater into excuses for maltreating the stranger because he had the look of an idolater. Nay more, how easy it was both to yield to the idolatry and maltreat the stranger!

III. THE GREAT CONSIDERATION WHICH IS TO LEAD TO PROPER TREATMENT OF THE STRANGER. "Ye were strangers in the land of Egypt." Great as the temptation was to treat strangers badly, such treatment if only looked at in a certain light would be scarcely excusable at all. This possible treatment of the stranger is to be looked at in the clear light of our Lord's parable concerning the forgiven yet unforgiving debtor. Israel had been strangers in Egypt, not only foreigners among the Egyptians, but to some extent exiles from God, who had put on the appearance of having forgotten them. But now he had brought them to himself, they were to be his people, a holy nation; and it was want of loyalty to God, it was behaviour unworthy of a holy nation for them to treat strangers as the Egyptians had treated Israel. God hates the oppressor everywhere and pities the oppressed. The people of God never dishonour their name more than when they trample on the alien from the commonwealth of Israel and the stranger from the covenant of promise. The alien may become as the home-born. The stranger may become familiar with Divine covenants and promises as if he were an Israelite from the womb. Even already the Israelites were being warned against counting too much on outward signs and natural descent. We should ever be looking for the minimum of living faith rather than the maximum of formal orthodoxy. A tiny seed is more to be cherished than a huge log of timber; for the one has whole living forests in it, and the other is dead and dead it must remain. We must labour to get the insight whereby we may penetrate through strange outward aspects and discern the spiritual life and sympathies underneath. God will give us the eye to discover, the honest and good eye, whether the stranger who comes is a wandering sheep seeking the true flock or a wolf in sheep's clothing. To mistake the sheep for the wolf is equally lamentable with mistaking the wolf for the sheep. The Pharisaic spirit so easily finds entrance, welcome and dominion in our breasts. It is so natural to play the censor towards those who sin the sins which we have no temptation to fall into. He without mercy for him that seems a stranger to God, may suspect that he is still a stranger himself. Many even of the Israelites at Mount Sinai had not been brought to God in the full sense of the term. Theirs was but a local contiguity to the awful demonstrations, not an attachment of the whole heart to the pure and glorious God who was behind the demonstrations.—Y.

Vers. 22—24.—*The treatment of the widow and the fatherless.* This injunction is even more humiliating to receive than the preceding one. It was bad enough to find those who had been foreigners in Egypt oppressing foreigners among themselves, and forgetting their own sufferings and deliverances. Still the slight excuse was available that as God's mercy to Israel receded into the past, and became a mercy to a former generation rather than a present one (at least, so it might be plausibly put), it was only too likely to be forgotten. Men are unable to make the past stand with any power against the influences of the present. But here are those, the widow and the fatherless, whom Nature in her ever fresh and living power, marks out herself as irresistible objects for pity and succour. What a disgrace to human nature that an injunction not to afflict the widow and fatherless should be necessary! And yet common observation only too often and sadly tells us that the widow and fatherless children may easily become the victims of an inconsiderate and unscrupulous self-seeking, which in its practical results is as afflicting as the most deliberate cruelty. *It is a very beautiful element of God's revelation of himself in the Scriptures, that he is so often set before us as caring for the fatherless and the widow, and denouncing those who do not care for them.* Widows in their needs, and his supply for their needs, appear in some of the most prominent scenes of the sacred page. Observe the provision that was made for the fatherless and the widow, along with the Levite and the stranger, to eat of the tithe of the yearly produce (Deut. xiv. 29), and also to get their share in the rejoicings at the feast of weeks and the feast of tabernacles (Deut. xvi. 11—14). The neighbour's raiment might be taken to pledge under certain conditions, but a widow's raiment was not to be taken in pledge at all (Deut. xxiv. 17). The forgotten sheaf in the field, and the gleanings of the olive boughs and of the vineyards, were to be left for the stranger, the fatherless, and the widow (Deut. xxiv. 19—21); and cursed was he to be who perverted the judgment of the same (Deut. xxvii. 19). When God sustained Elijah, at the time of judicial drought and famine in the land, he sustained the widow and the fatherless at the same time; and who knows how many widows and fatherless besides? It is part of the praise which is due to God in song, that he relieves the fatherless and the widow. A Father of the fatherless, and a Judge of the widows is God, in his holy habitation (Ps. lxviii. 5; cxlvi. 9). There can thus be no mistake about God's interest in those who are left without their natural provider and protector. But then on the other hand, these very same Scriptures *which assure us of God's concern, remind us of man's cruelty, unrighteousness, and oppression.* Job tells us of those who drive away the ass of the fatherless, and take the widow's ox for a pledge (xxiv. 3); and it was part of memory's brightening, as he thought upon his happier past, that he had delivered the fatherless and caused the widow's heart to sing for joy. God sent Isaiah to the hypocrites, the formal religionists who satiated God with ceremonial observances, to bid them turn to the realities of righteousness; and one of the foremost things among these was to judge the fatherless and plead for the widow. The faithful city had fallen, until those whose duty it was to judge the fatherless, and have the cause of the widow come to them, had sunk into companions of thieves and seekers of bribes. In the parable of the judge who feared not God, neither regarded man, we may be sure there is great significance beyond the purpose for which it was spoken. While first of all it teaches the need of importunity in prayer, it reminds us also how hard it is for the feeble woman, whose sphere has been the seclusion of home, to come out in the world and make her way against the oppressor and against the judge, who would be quick enough to listen to her if she was only rich, and could bribe him. By sheer carelessness and thoughtlessness, *by the sin of omission even more than the sin of commission*, we may fall into the wickedness of afflicting the widow and the fatherless; and to be on the alert to succour them is the only way in which we can effectually guard against this wickedness. We see that even in the Church of Christ, and in those first days when all that believed were together, and had all things in common—when all seemed so beautiful and promising, heaven fairly begun on earth—even then, and only too soon, the widows began to complain that they were neglected in the daily ministrations. Some of this perhaps was mere mendicant grumbling, but much of it would have a real cause. The only way we can keep the oppressor's heart out of us is to have the heart living and acting under the power of a Divinely-inspired love. It is a first principle of Christian ethics that if we are not doing good, we are doing ill; and we may be parties to the worst oppression, even when we are not thinking of oppression at all. In what a light does this Mosaic injunction bring out the teaching of James as to that practical element in pure religion of visiting the fatherless and the widow. If the Christian— his opportunities, his motives, his consolations, his resources to help and advise being what they are—does not visit the fatherless and the widow, depend upon it others will with very different designs. The greatest promptitude and decision are needed to anticipate the action of the rapacious and selfish.—Y.

Vers. 25—27.—*The treatment of the poor.* Here are two regulations, commanding not to be usurious in the lending of money to the poor, and not to retain the pledged garment over night. How forcibly they bring out the one crowning ill connected with poverty in the eyes of the world! The poor man is the man without money; and lack of money bars his way in only too many directions. Let him be ever so noble in character, ever so heroic, wise, and self-denying in action, it avails nothing. The poor wise man delivered the little city that was besieged by a great king; yet no man remembered that same poor man. These Israelites had gone out of Egypt with immense wealth, but probably even then it was very unequally distributed; and the tendency would be, as the tendency always is, for the inequality to become greater still. Hence in this regulation God was addressing those who from the inordinate feeling of desire which wealth inspires, would be peculiarly tempted to take advantage of the poor. God never shows any mercy to the rich man so far as his riches are concerned. Those riches are full of peril, and fuller of peril to their owner than to any one else.

He who counselled, by his Son, to pluck out the right eye and cut off the right hand, is not likely to pay respect to a thing like wealth, even more external still. The chief matter in these regulations is how the poor and needy may be most advantaged, and whatever will do *that* most effectually is the thing to be done. Whether *mere money* be lost or gained is a matter of no consequence whatever.

I. These provisions with respect to lending obviously do not exclude giving. "*If* thou lend money," etc. But God, in many instances, would be better pleased with giving than with lending. If only men were seeking with all their hearts to do his will, all these minute regulations would be unnecessary. *The advantage of the poor*, as we have just seen, was the main thing to be considered here. And it might be for the advantage of the receiver, and still more for the advantage of the giver in the highest sense of the word advantage, to give, hoping to receive nothing again. Just as money does untold harm when foolishly and wickedly spent, so when wisely spent it may do untold good. Lending may serve well, but giving may serve much better; and that is the wisest course which is judged to do the most good. Some would find it easier to give than to lend, being naturally generous, disposed to lavishness, shrinking from the risk of being thought stingy. And yet sometimes in giving they would be doing a very hurtful thing, for lending would be better.

II. Nor is there anything like a forbidding of the loan of money for commercial purposes. If one man lends to another a certain sum of money with which to trade, it is plain that he acts lawfully in getting interest for the use of it. For if he were not lending money to another, he would be using it himself, and the interest represents his profit, which is the same whoever uses the money. The trade of the world, and therefore the good of the world would be greatly limited and hampered but for the use of borrowed capital. It may be that the man who has the capital has neither the disposition nor ability to use it. Let him then, upon a fair consideration, lend the capital to the man who can use it.

III. Chiefly we must strive to avoid the taking selfish advantage of our neighbour's necessities. Rather we should rejoice to take advantage of these necessities to show beyond all dispute, that the love of God is indeed the ruling principle of our hearts. Man's extremity, it has often been said, is God's opportunity, and so it should be the Christian's opportunity. By timely aid, if we have it to bestow, let us strive to deliver the poor from the clutches of the usurer, and especially let us give our aid to what may be devised for the curing of poverty's disease altogether. Every alteration either in laws or customs which will tend to diminish poverty—let it have our strenuous support. Bear in mind that whatever each man has beyond a certain moderate share of this world's goods can only come to him because others have less than reasonable comfort demands. We should ever be aiming by all methods that are reasonable, just, and practicable, to secure to each one neither poverty nor riches, but just that food which is convenient for him. God wishes every man to have his daily bread; and it is an awful thing that we by our selfishness do so much to make the question of daily bread the only one that many of our fellow-creatures have time or inclination to ask. It seems to take every hour and every energy to keep the wolf from the door.—Y.

EXPOSITION.

CHAPTER XXIII.

The Book of the Covenant.—*Continued.*

Vers. 1—19.—Miscellaneous Laws—*continued.* The same want of logical arrangement appears in this chapter as in the preceding one. The first nine verses contain some twelve laws, of which not more than two that are consecutive can be said to be on the same subject. There is perhaps in the section a predominant idea of warning against sins and

errors connected with the trial of causes before a court, but verses 4 and 5, at any rate, lie quite outside this idea. From verse 10 to verse 19 the laws are connected with ceremonial observance and include (1) The law of the Sabbath, (2) of the Sabbatical year, (3) of the Great Festivals, (4) of sacrifice, and (5) of first-fruits.

Ver. 1.—The ninth commandment is here expanded and developed. **Thou shalt not raise a false report,** forbids the origination of a calumny; the other clause prohibits the joining with others in spreading one. Both clauses have a special reference to bearing witness in a court, but neither would seem to be confined to it.

Ver. 2.—**Thou shalt not follow a multitude to do evil.** Rather, "Thou shalt not follow a multitude *to evil.*" A law alike for deed, for word, and for thought. The example of the many is to be shunned. "Wide is the gate and broad is the way that leadeth to destruction, and many there be which go in thereat." But "strait is the gate and narrow is the way, which leadeth unto life; and few there be that find it" (Matt. vii. 13, 14). It is extraordinary that so many, even of professing Christians, are content to go with the many, notwithstanding the warnings against so doing, both of the law and of the Gospel. **Neither shalt thou speak,** etc. Rather, "Neither shalt thou bear witness in a cause to go aside after a multitude to put aside justice." The general precept is followed by a particular application of it. In judging a cause, if thou art one of the judges, thou shalt not simply go with the majority, if it be bent on injustice, but form thine own opinion and adhere to it.

Ver. 3.—**Neither shalt thou countenance a poor man in his cause.** After the many precepts in favour of the poor, this injunction produces a sort of shock. But it is to be understood as simply forbidding any undue favouring of the poor because they are poor, and so as equivalent to the precept in Lev. xix. 15, "Thou shalt not respect the person of the poor." In courts of justice, strict justice is to be rendered, without any leaning either towards the rich, or towards the poor. To lean either way is to pervert judgment.

Ver. 4.—**Thine enemy's ox.** A private enemy is here spoken of, not a public one, as in Deut. xxiii. 6. It is remarkable that the law should have so far anticipated Christianity as to have laid it down that men have duties of friendliness even towards their enemies, and are bound under certain circumstances to render them a service. "Hate thine enemies" (Matt. v. 43) was no injunction of the Mosaic law, but a conclusion which Rabbinical teachers unwarrantably drew from it. Christianity, however, goes far beyond Mosaism in laying down the broad precept—"Love your enemies."

Ver. 5.—**If thou see the ass of him that hateth thee,** etc. The general meaning of the passage is clear—assistance is to be given to the fallen ass of an enemy—but the *exact* sense of both the second and third clauses is doubtful. Many renderings have been suggested; but it is not clear that any one of them is an improvement on the Authorised Version. **Thou shalt surely help with him.** The joint participation in an act of mercy towards a fallen beast would bring the enemies into friendly contact, and soften their feelings towards each other.

Ver. 6.—As in verse 3 men were warned not to favour the poor unduly in courts of justice out of compassion for them, so here there is a warning against the opposite, and far more usual error, of leaning against the poor man in our evidence or in our decisions. The scales of justice are to be held even; strict right is to be done; our feelings are not to be allowed to influence us, much less our class prejudices.

Ver. 7.—**Keep thee far from a false matter.** Hold aloof, *i.e.*, from anything like a false accusation. Neither bring one, nor countenance one, else those mayest cause the death of an innocent and righteous man, and bring down on thyself the vengeance of him, who **will not justify the wicked.**

Ver. 8.—**And thou shalt take no gift.** The worst sin of a judge, and the commonest in the East, is to accept a bribe from one of the parties to a suit, and give sentence accordingly. As such a practice defeats the whole end for which the administration of justice exists, it is, when detected, for the most part, punished capitally. Josephus tells us that it was so among the Jews (*Contr. Apion.* ii. 27); but the Mosaic code, as it has come down to us, omits to fix the penalty. Whatever it was, it was practically set at nought. Eli's sons "turned aside after lucre, and took bribes, and perverted judgment" (1 Sam. viii. 3). In David's time, men's hands were "full of bribes" (Ps. xxvi. 10). Solomon complains of wicked men "taking gifts out of their bosoms to pervert the ways of judgment" (Prov. xvii. 23). Isaiah is never weary of bearing witness against the princes of his day, who "love gifts and follow after rewards" (Is. i. 23); who "justify the wicked for reward, and take away the righteousness of the righteous from him" (*ib.* v. 23). Micah adds his testimony —"Hear this, I pray you, ye heads of the house of Jacob and princes of the house of Israel, that *abhor judgment and pervert all equity.* They build up Zion with blood, and Jerusalem with iniquity. The heads thereof *judge for reward*" (ch. iii. 9—11). **The gift blindeth the wise.** See Deut. xvi. 19.

Ver. 9.—**Thou shalt not oppress a stranger.** This is a repetition of ch. xxii. 21, with perhaps a special reference to oppression through courts of justice. **For thou knowest the heart of a stranger.** Literally, "the *mind* of a stranger," or, in other words, his thoughts and feelings. Thou shouldest therefore be able to sympathise with him.

CEREMONIAL LAWS (vers. 10—19).

Vers. 10, 11.—*Law of the Sabbatical year.* Days of rest, at regular or irregular intervals, were well known to the ancients · and some regulations of the kind existed in most countries But entire years of rest were wholly unknown to any nation except the Israelites, and exposed them to the reproach of idleness. (See Tacit. *Hist.* v. 4 :—" Septimo die otium placuisse ferunt, quia is finem laborum dedit; dein, *blandiente inertia*, septimum quoque annum ignaviæ datum ") In a primitive condition of agriculture, when rotation of crops was unknown, artificial manure unemployed, and the need of letting even the best land sometimes lie fallow unrecognised, it may not have been an uneconomical arrangement to require an entire suspension of cultivation once in seven years. But great difficulty was probably experienced in enforcing the law. Just as there were persons who wished to gather manna on the seventh day (ch. xvi. 27), so there would be many anxious to obtain in the seventh year something more from their fields than Nature would give them if left to herself. If the " seventy years " of the captivity were intended exactly to make up for omissions of the due observance of the sabbatical year, we must suppose that between the time of the exodus and the destruction of Jerusalem by Nebuchadnezzar, the ordinance had been as often neglected as observed. (See 2 Chron. xxxvi. 21.) The primary object of the requirement was, as stated in ver. 11, **that the poor of thy people may eat,** what the land brought forth of its own accord in the Sabbatical year being shared by them (Lev. xxv. vi.). But no doubt it was also intended that the Sabbatical year should be one of increased religious observance, whereof the solemn reading of the law in the ears of the people at the Feast of Tabernacles " in the year of release " (Deut. xxxi. 10) was an indication and a part. That reading was properly preceded by a time of religious preparation (Neh. viii. 1—15), and would naturally lead on to further acts of a religious character, which might occupy a considerable period (*ibid.* chs. ix. and x.). Altogether, the year was a most solemn period, calling men to religious self-examination, to repentance, to the formation of holy habits, and tending to a general elevation among the people of the standard of holiness. **What they leave the beasts of the field shall eat.** There was to be no regular ingathering. The proprietor, his servants, the poor, and the stranger were to take what they needed; and the residue was to be for the cattle and for the beasts that were in the land (Deut. xxv. 6, 7). **Thy vineyard—thy oliveyard.** Corn, wine, and oil were the only important products of Palestine; and this mention of the vineyard and the oliveyard shows that one and the same law was to hold good of all the lands in the country, however they might be cultivated. The whole land was to rest.

Ver. 12.—*Law of the Sabbath, repeated.* Nothing is here added to the teaching of the Fourth Commandment; but its *merciful* character is especially brought out. Men are called on to observe it, *in order that* their cattle may obtain rest, and their servants, together with the stranger that is within their gates, may find refreshment. It is to be borne in mind that the foreign population of Palestine was mostly held to hard service. (See 2 Chron. ii. 17, 18.)

Verse 13 contains two injunctions—one general, one special :—1. " Be circumspect " (or cautious, careful) " in respect of *all* that I command you." 2. "Do not so much as utter the name of any false god." Not even to mention their names, was to show them the greatest contempt possible; and, if followed out universally, would soon have produced an absolute oblivion of them. Moses, it may be observed, scarcely ever does mention their names. Later historians and prophets had to do so, either to deliver the true history of the Israelites, or to denounce idolatries to which they were given. There are many words one would wish never to utter; but while wicked men do the things of which they are the names, preachers are obliged to use the words in their sermons and other warnings.

Vers. 14—17.—*Law of Festivals.* " The sanctification of days and times," says Richard Hooker, " is a token of that thankfulness and a part of that public honour which we owe to God for admirable benefits, whereof it doth not suffice that we keep a secret calendar, taking thereby our private occasions as we list ourselves to think how much God hath done for all men ; but the days which are chosen out to serve as public memorials of such his mercies ought to be clothed with those outward robes of holiness whereby their difference from other days may be made sensible " (*Eccles. Pol.* v. 70, § 1). All ancient religions had solemn festival seasons, when particular mercies of God were specially commemorated, and when men, meeting together in large numbers, mutually cheered and excited each other to a warmer devotion and a more hearty pouring forth of thanks than human weakness made possible at other times. In Egypt such festivals were frequent, and held a high place in the religion (Herod. ii. 58—64). Abraham's family had probably had observances of the kind in their Mesopotamian home. God's providence saw good now to give supernatural sanction to the natural piety which had been accustomed thus to express itself. Three great feasts were appointed, of which the most remarkable features were—1. That they were at once agricultural and historical—connected with the regularly recurrent course of the seasons, and connected also with great events in the life of the nation; 2. That they could be kept only at one spot, that namely where the tabernacle was at the time located; 3. That they were to be attended by the whole male population. The three festivals are here called—1. *The Feast of Unleavened Bread* (ver. 15), the early spring festival, at the beginning of barley harvest in the month Abib (Nisan), commemorative of the going forth from Egypt; 2. *The Feast of Harvest* (elsewhere called "of weeks") at the beginning of summer, when the wheat crop had been reaped, commemorative of the giving of the law; and 3. *The Feast of Ingathering* (ver 16) in Tisri, at the close of the vintage, when all the crops of every kind had been gathered in, commemorative of the sojourn in the wilderness. The first of the three, the feast of unleavened bread, had been already instituted (ch. xiii. 3—10); the two others are now for the first time sketched out, their details being kept back to be filled in subsequently (Lev. xxiii. 15—21, and 34—36). Here the legislator is content to lay it down that the great feasts will be three, and that all the males are to attend them.

Ver. 15.—**The feast of unleavened bread.** This commenced with the Passover, and continued for the seven days following, with a "holy convocation" on the first of the seven and on the last (Lev. xxiii. 5—8). Unleavened bread was eaten in commemoration of the hasty exodus from Egypt (ch. xii. 34). A sheaf of new barley—the first-fruits of the harvest—was offered as a wave-offering before the Lord (Lev. xxiii. 10—14). Every male Israelite of full age was bound to attend, and to bring with him a free-will offering. **In the time appointed of the month**—*i.e.*, on the fourteenth day (ch. xii. 18). **None shall appear before me empty.** This rule applies, not to the Passover only, but to all the feasts.

Ver. 16.—**The feast of harvest.** Fifty days were to be numbered from the day of offering the barley sheaf, and on the *fiftieth* the feast of harvest, thence called "Pentecost," was to be celebrated. Different Jewish sects make different calculations; but the majority celebrate Pentecost on the sixth of Sivan (May 25). The main ceremony was the offering to God of two leavened loaves of the finest flour

made out of the wheat just gathered in, and called the first-fruits of the harvest. The festival lasted only a single day; but it was one of a peculiarly social and joyful character (Deut. xvi. 9—11). Jewish tradition connects the feast further with the giving of the law, which must certainly have taken place *about* the time (see ch. xix. 1—16). **The first-fruits.** Rather, "*Of* the first-fruits." The word is in apposition with "harvest," not with "feast." **Which thou hast sown.** The *sown* harvest was gathered in by Pentecost; what remained to collect afterwards was the produce of plantations.

The feast of ingathering. Called elsewhere, and more commonly, "the feast of tabernacles" (Lev. xxiii. 34; Deut. xvi. 13; xxxi. 10; John vii. 2), from the circumstance that the people were commanded to make themselves booths, and dwell in them during the time of the feast. The festival began on the 15th of Tisri, or in the early part of our October, when the olives had been gathered in and the vintage was completed. It lasted seven, or (according to some) eight days, and comprised two holy convocations. In one point of view it was a festival of thanksgiving for the final getting in of the crops; in another, a commemoration of the safe passage through the desert from Egypt to Palestine. The feast seems to have been neglected during the captivity, but was celebrated with much glee in the time of Nehemiah (Neh. viii. 17). **In the end of the year**—*i.e.*, the end of the agricultural year—when the harvest was over —as explained in the following clause.

Ver. 17.—**Three times in the year all thy males shall appear before the Lord God.** This seems to moderns a very burthensome enactment. But we must remember that Palestine is not bigger than Wales, and that great gatherings had great attractions for many in the ancient world, when they were the only means by which information was spread, and almost the only occasions on which friends and relations who lived far apart could expect to see each other. The European Greeks had, in their Olympian and other games, similar great gatherings, which occurred once or twice in each year, and, though under no obligation to do so, attended them in enormous numbers. It may be doubted if the religious Hebrews *felt* the obligation of attendance to be a burthen. It was assuredly a matter of great importance, as tending to unity, and to the quickening of the national life, that they should be drawn so continually to one centre, and be so frequently united in one common worship. Most students of antiquity regard the Greek games as having exerted a strong unifying influence over the scattered members of the Grecian family. The Hebrew festivals, occurring so much more frequently, and required to be attended by *all*, must have had a similar, but much greater, effect of the same kind.

Ver. 18.—*Law of the Paschal sacrifice.* That the Paschal lamb is here intended by "my sacrifice," seems to be certain, since the two injunctions to put away leavened bread, and to allow none of the victim's flesh to remain till the morning (see ch. xii. 10), are combined in the Paschal sacrifice only. Of all the offerings commanded in the law the Paschal lamb was the most important, since it typified Christ. It may therefore well be termed, in an especial way, "God's sacrifice." By **the fat of my feast** some understand the fat of the lamb, others the best part of the feast (Keil)—*i.e.*, the lamb itself. In ch. xxxiv. 25, which is closely parallel to the present place, we read, for "the fat of my feast," "the sacrifice of the feast of the passover."

Ver. 19.—*Law of first-fruits.* **The first of the first-fruits** may mean either "the best of the first-fruits" (see Num. xviii. 12), or "the *very* first of each kind that is ripe" (*ib.* verse 13). On the tendency to delay, and not bring the very first, see the comment on ch. xxii. 29. **The house of the Lord.** Generally, in the Pentateuch we have the periphrasis—"the place which the Lord thy God shall choose to put his name there" (Deut. xii. 5, 11, 14; xvi. 16; xxvi. 2, etc.); but here, and in ch. xxxiv. 26, and again in Deut. xxiii. 18, this "place" is plainly declared to be a "house" or "temple."

Law against seething a kid in the mother's milk. The outline of law put before the Israelites in the "Book of the Covenant" terminated with this remarkable prohibition. Its importance is shown—1. By its place here; and 2. By its being thrice repeated in the law of Moses (see ch. xxxiv. 16; and Deut. xiv. 21). Various explanations have been given of it; but none is satisfactory, except that which views it as "a protest against cruelty, and outraging the order of nature," more especially that peculiarly sacred portion of nature's order, the tender relation between parent and child, mother and suckling. No doubt the practice existed. Kids were thought to be most palatable when boiled in milk; and the mother's milk was frequently the readiest to obtain. But in this way the mother was made a sort of accomplice in the death of her child, which men were induced to kill on account of the flavour that her milk gave it. Reason has nothing to say against such a mode of preparing food, but feeling revolts from it; and the general sense of civilised mankind re-echoes the precept, which is capable of a wide application—**Thou shalt not seethe a kid in his mother's milk.**

HOMILETICS.

Vers. 1—3; 6—9.—*God's care for the administration of justice.* The well-being of a community depends largely on the right administration of justice within its limits. It has been said that the entire constitution of England with all its artifices, complications, balances, and other delicate arrangements, exists mainly for the purpose of putting twelve honest men into a jury-box. *Fiat justitia, ruat cœlum.* Anything is preferable to the triumphant rule of injustice. The present passage clearly shows that God recognises very decidedly the importance of judicial proceedings. By direct communication with Moses, he lays down rules which affect—1. The accuser; 2. The witnesses; and 3. The judge.

I. WITH RESPECT TO THE ACCUSER. False accusation is to be avoided, and especially capital charges against the innocent (ver. 7).

II. WITH RESPECT TO WITNESSES. Men are to beware of either inventing an untrue tale or giving any support to it when it has been invented by others (ver. 1).

III. WITH RESPECT TO JUDGES. 1. They are not to act like Pilate and "follow a multitude to do evil" (ver. 2). 2. They are not either unduly to favour the poor (ver. 3); or 3. To wrest justice against them (ver. 6). 4. They are not to oppress strangers (ver. 9). And 5. They are, above all things, not to take a bribe.

Accusers, beware! Be sure that your charge is true, or do not make it. A false charge, even though proved false, may injure a man for life—he may never be able to recover from it. Particularly, be careful, if your charge is a serious one, involving risk to life. You may, if successful, "slay the innocent and the righteous" (ver. 7). Nay, you may slay a man by a false charge which does not directly affect his life—you may so harass and annoy him as to drive him to suicide, or "break his heart," and so shorten his days. Even if you have a true charge to bring, it is not always wise or Christian to bring it. St. Paul would have us in some cases "take wrong" and "suffer ourselves to be defrauded" (1 Cor. vi. 7).

Witnesses, beware! Do not give untrue evidence, either in the way of raising false reports yourselves, or of supporting by your evidence the false reports of others. The witnesses who cause an innocent person to be condemned are as much to blame as the false accuser. Be very careful in giving evidence to speak "the truth, the whole truth, and nothing but the truth." Depose to nothing of which you are not sure. If you are uncertain, say that you are uncertain, however much the adverse counsel may browbeat you. In cases of personal identity, be specially careful. It is exceedingly easy to be mistaken about a man whom you have seen only once or twice.

Judges, beware! On you the final issue depends. Be not swayed by popularity. Yield not to the outcries either of an excited mob, or a partisan press, when they shout, "away with him!" Hold the scales of justice even between the rich man and the poor, neither suffering your prejudice of class to incline you in favour of the former, nor a weak sentimentality to make you lean unduly towards the latter. Be sure not to oppress foreigners, who must plead to disadvantage in a country, and amid proceedings, that are strange to them. Above all, do not condescend to take a bribe from either side. A gift is a weight in the scales of justice; and "a false balance is an abomination to the Lord" (Prov. xi. 1).

Vers. 5, 6.—*The duties which men owe to their enemies.* These duties may be considered as they were revealed to men. 1. Under the law: and 2. Under the gospel.

I. UNDER THE LAW. Men were required to protect the interests of their enemies, when they could do so without loss to themselves. For instance—1. They were not to cut down fruit trees in an enemy's country (Deut. xx. 19, 20). 2. They were not to remove a neighbour's landmark, even though he might be an enemy. 3. They were to hasten after an enemy's ox or ass if they saw it going astray, to catch it, and bring it back to him. 4. They were to approach him, if they saw his ass fallen under the weight of its load, and to help him to raise it up. 5. If he were suffering from hunger or thirst, they were to give him bread to eat and water to drink (Prov. xxv. 21). 6. They were to refrain from rejoicing over his misadventures (*ib.* ch. xxiv. 17).

II. UNDER THE GOSPEL. Men are required under the Gospel to do all this, and *much more.* 1. They are to "love their enemies" (Matt. v. 44). 2. To do good to them in every way—feed them (Rom. xii. 20), bless them (Matt. l.s.c.), pray for them (*ib.*), be patient towards them (1 Thess. v. 14), seek to convert them from the error of their ways (Jas. v. 20), save them (*ib.*). Christ set the example of praying for his enemies upon the cross—God set the example of loving his enemies when he gave his Son to suffer death for them—the Holy Spirit sets the example of patience towards his enemies, when he strives with them. We have to forgive our enemies day by day their trespasses against us—to pray and work for their conversion—to seek to overcome their evil with our good. In temporal matters, it is our business to be most careful that we do them no injury, by misrepresentation, by disparagement, by unfair criticism, by lies, even by "faint praise." We are to "love" them; or, if poor human nature finds this too hard, we are to act as if we loved them, and then ultimately love will come.

Vers. 10, 11.—*The Sabbatical year.* The Sabbatical year—an institution peculiar to the Israelites, and quite contrary to anything of which they had had experience in Egypt—is a remarkable proof,

I. OF THE DIVINE WISDOM. Under the ordinary circumstances of tillage, land from time to time requires rest. In Egypt it was otherwise. There, under the exceptional circumstances of a soil continually recruited by the spread over it of a rich alluvium from the great river, not only was the whole arable area capable of producing good crops year after year, without ever lying fallow, but from the same soil several crops were ordinarily taken, in the course of the twelvemonth. The Israelites had had no experience of any other agriculture than this for above four centuries. Yet now, suddenly, a new system is adopted by them. God knew that the system of Egyptian tillage was not suitable for Palestine—that there the soil would not recruit itself—that, cultivated on the Egyptian system, it would rapidly become exhausted; and therefore he devised, in the interests of his people, a new system for Palestine. The whole land should have rest one year in seven. Thus only, in the then existing condition of agriculture, could exhaustion be prevented, productiveness secured, and the land enabled to retain its character of "a good land," "a land flowing with milk and honey," "a land of corn and wine, of bread and vineyards, and oil olive," "a land of wheat, and barley, and vines, and fig-trees, and pomegranates —a land of oil olive, and honey—a land wherein thou shalt eat bread without scarceness, thou shalt not lack anything in it" (Deut. viii. 8, 9).

II. Of the Divine beneficence. Under the system thus Divinely imposed upon the Israelites, three beneficent purposes were accomplished. 1. *The proprietor was benefited.* Not only was he prevented from exhausting his farm by over-cropping, and so sinking into poverty, but he was forced to form habits of forethought and providence. He necessarily laid by something for the seventh year, and hence learnt to calculate his needs, to store his grain, and to keep something in hand against the future. In this way his reason and reflective powers were developed, and he was advanced from a mere labouring hind to a thoughtful cultivator. 2. *The poor were benefited.* As whatever grew in the seventh year grew spontaneously, without expense or trouble on the part of the owner, it could not be rightfully considered to belong exclusively to him. The Mosaic law placed it on a par with ordinary wild fruits, and granted it to the first comer (Lev. xxv. 5, 6). By this arrangement the poor were enabled to profit, since it was they especially who gathered the store that Nature's bounty provided. In the dry climate of Palestine, where much grain is sure to be shed during the gathering in of the harvest, the spontaneous growth would probably be considerable, and would amply suffice for the sustenance of those who had no other resource. 3. *The beasts were benefited.* God "careth for cattle." He appoints the Sabbatical year, in part, that "the beasts of the field" may have abundance to eat. When men dole out their food, they have often a scanty allowance. God would have them, for one year in seven at least, eat their fill.

Ver. 12.—*The rest of the Sabbath.* In the fourth commandment it is the *main* object of the Sabbath that is put prominently forward. It is a day to be "kept holy"—a day which God has "blessed and hallowed." Here, on the contrary, our attention is called to its secondary object—it is for "*rest*" and "*refreshment.*" Perhaps men of the classes who are in easy circumstances do not sufficiently realise the intense relief that is furnished by the Sunday rest to the classes below them, to the over-taxed artisan, the household drudge, the wearied and stupefied farm-labourer—nay, even to the clerk, the accountant, the shopkeeper, the salesman. Continuous mechanical work of one and the same kind is required of most of those who labour, from morning till night, and from one end of the week to the other. The monotony of their occupations is terrible— is deadening—is sometimes maddening. For them, the treat that the Sunday affords is the single gleam of light in their uniformly murky sky, the single ray of hope that gilds their else miserable existence, the single link that connects them with the living world of thought, and sentiment, and feeling, for which they were born, and in which their spirits long to expatiate. *Rest!* To the tired brute, forced to slave for his owner up to the full measure of his powers, and beyond them—ready to sink to the earth the moment he is not artificially sustained—who goes through his daily round in a state that is half-sleep, half-waking—what a blessed change is the quietude of the Sunday, when for four-and-twenty hours at least he enjoys absolute and entire repose, recruits his strength, rests all his muscles, is called on to make no exertion! *Refreshment!* How thrice blessed to the overwrought man, and still more to the overwrought woman, is the relaxation of the dreadful tension of their lives which Sunday brings! "No rest, no pause, no peace," for six long days—days beginning early and ending late— days without change or variety—without relaxation or amusement—wretched, miserable days, during which they wish a hundred times that they had never been born. On such the Sunday rest falls as a refreshing dew. Their drooping spirits rise to it. They inhale at every pore its beneficent influences. They feel it to be "a refuge from the storms of life, a bourne of peace after six days of care and toil, a goal to which they may look with glad hearts, and towards which they may work with hopeful spirits amid the intense struggles, and fervid contests, and fierce strifes of existence." Without the Sunday rest, *modern* life, at any rate, would be intolerable; and the mass of those who are actively engaged in its various phases would drift into idiocy, or be driven to madness!

Vers. 14—17.—*Festival times.* I. Festivals are commemorations. The joyful occurrences of our own lives we by a natural instinct commemorate yearly, as the day comes round when they happened to us. Our birth-day, our wedding-day, are thus made domestic festivals. Similarly, a nation commemorates the Day of its Independence, or the three glorious days of its Revolution, or the day on which its armies gained a great and crowning victory. It is reasonable that the practice thus established should be followed also in the Church of God, and the days on which great spiritual blessings or deliverances were granted to it kept in remembrance by some appropriate and peculiar observance. The Jews kept three great festivals, to which afterwards two others were added, all of them more or less commemorative. The Passover commemorated the *passing over* of the houses of the Israelites by the destroying angel and the hasty flight out of Egypt; the feast of Pentecost commemorated, according to Jewish tradition, the giving of the law; tabernacles recalled and perpetuated the dwelling in tents in the wilderness; Purim, the deliverance from the malice of Haman; the Dedication, that from Antiochus Epiphanes. And Christian festivals are of a similar character. Advent commemorates the approach, and Christmas the birth, of Christ, Epiphany his manifestation to the Gentiles, Easter his resurrection from the dead, Ascension-day his ascent into heaven, Whitsuntide the coming of the Holy Ghost. "Saints' days," as they are called, commemorate the entrance into final bliss of those whose names they bear. All the greater, and almost all the lesser, festivals of the Christian Church are commemorations, days appointed for perpetuating the remembrance of events dear to the Christian heart and deeply interwoven with the Christian life. It follows that—

II. FESTIVALS ARE TIMES OF SPIRITUAL JOY. There are some to whom religion seems altogether a melancholy thing. Religious persons they suppose to be dwellers in perpetual sadness, gloomy, ascetic, dull, cheerless, miserable. But this is altogether a mistake. Holy joy is continually required of men as a duty in the Bible. "Rejoice evermore," says the great apostle of the Gentiles (1 Thess. v. 16); and again, "Rejoice with them that do rejoice" (Rom. xii. 15). "O be joyful in the Lord," is a constant cry of the Psalmist. Our Lord bade us "rejoice and be exceeding glad," even when we are persecuted, and assured us that "our joy no man taketh from us." There may be a sobriety in Christian joy which distinguishes it from the fitful, feverish, and excited joy of the world; but it is joy—true joy—nevertheless. And for this joy no times are so fitting as festival times. "This is the day which the Lord hath made," said holy David; "*let us rejoice and be glad in it.*" "Offices and duties of religious joy," as Hooker notes, "are that wherein the hallowing of festival times consisteth" (Eccl. Pol. v. 70, § 2). The set services of religion on festival days take a tone of gladness beyond the common; and the "psalms and hymns and spiritual songs" suited for such occasions are of a still more jubilant type. Then especially do the precepts hold—"Rejoice in the Lord," "Serve the Lord with gladness," "Show yourselves joyful unto the Lord —sing, rejoice, and give thanks."

III. FESTIVALS SHOULD BE TIMES OF THANKSGIVING. Nothing is more remarkable in man than his deadness, and dulness, and apathy in respect to all that God has done for him. Warm gratitude, lively thankfulness, real heartfelt devotion, are rare, even in the best of us. Festivals are designed to stir and quicken our feelings, to rouse us from our deadness, to induce us to shake off our apathy, and both with *heart* and voice glorify God, who hath done so great things for us. Festivals bring before us vividly the special Divine mercy which they commemorate, and at the same time present to our view the beneficent side, so to speak, of the Divine nature, and lead us to contemplate it. God is *essentially* love; "he declares his Almighty power *most chiefly* in showing mercy and pity" (Collect for Eleventh Sunday after Trinity). Festivals remind us of this. We lose the advantage of them wholly if we do not stir ourselves, on occasion of them, to some real outpouring of love and thanks to him who granted us the blessing of the time, as well as every other blessing, and every "good and perfect gift" of which we have the enjoyment.

IV. FESTIVALS SHOULD BE TIMES OF BOUNTY. When the soul of a man is glad, and penetrated with the sense of God's goodness and mercy towards it, the heart naturally opens itself to a consideration of other men's needs and necessities. Being glad itself, it would fain make others glad. Hence, in the old world, great occasions of joy were always occasions of largess. The Israelites were commanded to remember the stranger, the fatherless, and the widow at the time of their festivals (Deut. xvi. 14); and the practice was to "send portions" to them (Neh. viii. 10; Esth. ix. 22). We shall do well to imitate their liberality, and to make, not Christmas only, but each festival season a time of "sending portions" to the poor and needy.

HOMILIES BY VARIOUS AUTHORS.

Vers. 1—10.—*Doing justice and loving mercy.* In pursuance of its great requirement of love to one's neighbour, the law next prohibits the raising of a false report, the bearing of false witness in a court of justice, and the wresting of judgment. Recognising however, that "out of the *heart* proceed *evil thoughts*, murders, adulteries, fornications, thefts, *false witness*, blasphemies" (Matt. xv. 19), the law, in addition to forbidding the outward acts, is at pains to warn against the motives and influences which most commonly lead to these acts. This section naturally follows the catalogue of "rights" in previous chapters, as dealing with cases of litigation arising on the basis of these "rights." Notice:—

I. THE SINS PROHIBITED. 1. *The raising of a false report.* This also is a species of false witness, though of a less formal character than the bearing of false witness in a court of justice. The forms it may assume are innumerable. The three principal are: —(1) Deliberate invention and circulation of falsehoods. (2) Innuendo, or malicious suggestion. (3) Distortion or deceitful colouring of actual facts. In God's sight slander ranks as one of the worst of offences. It indicates great malevolence. It is grievously unjust and injurious to the person traduced. It is certain to be taken up, and industriously propagated. For a calumny is never wholly wiped out. There are always some evil-speaking persons disposed to believe and repeat it. It affixes a mark on the injured party which may remain on him through life. Everyone is interested in the suppression of such an offence—the parties immediately concerned, the Church, society at large, the magistracy, God himself—of one of whose commandments (the 9th) it is a daring violation. It is a form of vice which should incur the emphatic reprobation of society, and which, where possible, should be visited with heavy legal penalties. 2. *False witness in court.* This, as a deliberate attempt to poison the stream of public justice, is a crime which admits of no palliation. It is a form of vice which, so far as we know, has never found a defender. All ages and all societies have united in condemning it as an offence deserving of severe punishment. Yet many a privately-circulated slander may do more harm than a falsehood uttered in the witness-box. God judges of these matters, not by their legal but by their moral turpitude. 3. *Wresting of judgment.* The corruption of public justice here reaches the fountain head. The judge who gives dishonest decisions betrays the cause of righteousness. He misrepresents the mind of God. He inflicts irremediable injury on the innocent. He opens a floodgate to iniquity. Few men, therefore, are guiltier than he. God will not spare him in the day of his judgment. Even in private life, however, we need to beware of judging rashly, of judging with bias and prejudice, of judging so as to do wrong to individuals, of judging so as to injure truth and retard progress and improvement. This also is "wresting judgment."

II. MOTIVES LEADING TO THESE SINS. 1. *The influence of the crowd* (ver. 2). There is an infectiousness in the example of a crowd which only a firm back-bone of principle, and some independence of mind, will enable us to resist. The *tendency* is to follow the multitude, even when it is to do evil. (1) Men like to be on the side that is popular. They dread the reproach of singularity. There are those who would almost rather die than be out of the fashion. (2) A crowd can ridicule, and a crowd can intimidate. It may put pressure upon us which we have not the moral courage to resist. (3) A thing, besides, does not look so evil, when many are engaged in doing it. They do not, of course, call it evil. They put new names upon it, and laugh at us for our scruples. This may lead us to think that the course in which we are asked to join is not so very bad after all. So we belie or dissemble our real convictions, and do what the crowd bids us. To such influences we are certain to fall a prey, if we are governed by the fear of man more than by the fear of God (Acts iv. 19, 20), or if we seek the praise of man more than the honour which comes from God (John v. 44; xii. 43). As counteractives to the influence of the crowd we do well to remember that the "vox populi" is not always "vox Dei;" that the fashion of the day can never make that right which the law of God declares to be wrong; that the voice of the multitude is one thing to-day, and another thing to-morrow, while truth and duty remain one and the same; that whatever others think, it can never be lawful for us to act contrary to our *own* convictions; that if the multitude are bent on doing evil, it is our duty, not to go with them, but to be witnesses for the truth in opposition to their courses; that great guilt attaches to us if we do wrong simply in deference to popular sentiment; finally, that there is one who judges us, that is, God, and that he will surely call us to account for all such unfaithfulness to conviction (ver. 7). 2. *False sympathy.* Judgment was not to be wrested, nor false witness given, out of any quasi-benevolent wish to do a good turn to the poor (ver. 3). The poor man is not to be unjustly dealt with (ver. 6), but neither is he to receive favour. A court of law is not the place for sentiment. Equal measure is to be meted out to all. Judgment is to be given impartially as between brother and brother; rich and poor; citizen and foreigner (ver. 9); applying the same principles to each case, and keeping in view the essential merits as the sole thing to be regarded. 3. *Enmity.* Enmity to another, or the consideration of another's enmity to us, is not to be allowed to sway us in giving judgment in his cause, or in any other matter in which his rights are affected. This seems to be the connection of vers. 4, 5, with what precedes and follows; but the duty is taught somewhat indirectly by laying down the principle that enmity is not to be allowed to influence us *at all*, in *any* of our dealings with our neighbours. The illustrations taken are very striking, and fairly anticipate the gospel inculcation of love to enemies (cf. Deut. xxii. 1, 4). If an enemy's ox or ass was seen going astray, the Israelite was not to hide himself, and let it go, but was "surely" to take it back again. Or if his enemy's ass fell under a burden, he was not to yield to the temptation to forbear help, but was "surely" to help him to lift it up. *A fortiori,* he was not to allow himself to be in any way influenced by enmity in giving evidence before the judges, or in pronouncing judgment on a cause brought before him. 4. *Covetousness.* (Ver. 8.) This forbids bribery. It is impossible for a judge to take a bribe, whether given directly or indirectly, and yet retain his integrity. Despite of himself, the gift will blind his eyes, and pervert his words. For the same reason a man can never be an impartial judge in his own cause.—J. O.

Vers. 10—20.—*Sabbaths and feasts.* I. SABBATHS. 1. *The Sabbatic year* (vers. 10, 11). Every seventh year the land was to lie fallow, and what it spontaneously produced was to be a provision for the poor, and for the beasts of the field. There was connected with the ordinance a special promise of unusual fertility in the sixth year—of such plenty as would make the nation independent of a harvest in the seventh (Lev. xxv. 21, 22). The Sabbatic year was (1) A period of rest for the land. Even nature requires her seasons of rest. Only thus will she yield to man the best of her produce. The seventh year's rest was an agricultural benefit. (2) A period of rest for the labourer. It gave him time for higher employment. Moses enjoined that the whole law should be read on this year at the feast of Tabernacles (Deut. xxxi. 10, 14). This may have been designed to teach, "that the year, as a whole, should be much devoted to the meditation of the law, and engaging in services of devotion" (Fairbairn). (3) A merciful provision for the poor. It laid an arrest on man's natural selfishness, and taught beneficence and consideration for the needy. It showed that if *man* cared not for the poor, *God* did. (4) It was a test of obedience. It would test conclusively whether the people were disposed to obey God, or would be ruled only by their own wills. In point of fact, the ordinance was not kept. It proved to be too high and Divine a thing for covetous and selfish dispositions. The neglect of it commenced very early, and lasted till the period of the captivity (2 Chron. xxxvi. 21). (5) A periodical reminder that the land, and everything that grew upon it, belonged to God. Had the Israelites observed the ordinance, the recurrent plenty of the sixth year would, like the double supply of manna on the sixth day in the wilderness, have been a visible witness to them of the supernatural presence of Jehovah in their midst. 2. *The weekly Sabbath* (ver. 12). The invaluable seventh day's rest was also to be sacredly observed by the nation. Well-kept Sabbaths have much to do with national prosperity.

II. FEASTS. The stated festivals were three (vers. 14—17). The design in their appointment was to commemorate mercies, to keep alive the memory of national events, to foster a sense of unity in the people, to quicken religious life, to furnish opportunities of public worship. They afforded a means of strengthening the bond between the people and Jehovah, promoted brotherly intercourse, infused warmth and gladness into religious service, and were connected with a ritual which taught the worshippers solemn and impressive lessons. The feasts were :—1. The *Passover*—here called "the feast of unleavened bread" (vers. 15—18). It commemorated the great National Deliverance (see on Ex. xii.). The use of unleavened bread was a call to spiritual purity (1 Cor. v. 8). The blood was offered (ver. 18) as an ever-renewed atonement for sin. The "fat" of the sacrifice betokened the consecration of the best. 2. *Pentecost*—here called "the feast of harvest, the first-fruits of thy labours" (ver. 16). Its primary reference was agricultural. It was a recognition of God in the gift of the harvest. It besought his blessing upon the labours of the field. It consecrated to him the first-fruits (ver. 19) of what he had given (two wave-loaves, Lev. xxiii. 17). In the dedication of the wave-loaves, as in the weekly presentation of the shewbread in the tabernacle (ch. xxv. 30), there was further symbolised the dedication to God of the life which the bread nourished. Fitly, therefore, was this day chosen for the presentation to God of the first-fruits of his Church (Acts ii.). 3. *The feast of Tabernacles*—"the feast of ingathering" (ver. 16). This was the feast of the completed harvest, when the corn, the wine, and the oil, had all been gathered in. During the seven days of the feast the people dwelt in booths, in commemoration of their wanderings in the wilderness. The dwelling in booths was a symbol also of their present pilgrim condition on earth, as "strangers and sojourners" (Ps. xxxix. 12). The precept in ver. 19, which seems related to this feast,—"Thou shalt not seethe a kid in his mother's milk," had probably reference to some harvest superstition. On its moral lessons, see Deut. xiv. 21.—J. O.

Vers. 1—9.—*Seeking the things which make for justice.* The illustrations adduced in these nine verses show the various ways in which men may be tempted to injustice in judicial procedure. Those who believe themselves wronged have to appeal to their fellow men to settle the matter so far as human capacity can settle it. Hence the positions indicated in this passage. We see plaintiffs, defendants, witnesses, judges, and supporters and sympathisers, and the great aim set before all of them is the attainment of just conclusions. Men feel nothing more bitterly than unjust treatment; and yet just treatment is one of the most difficult of all things to get. Even he who himself has been unjustly treated cannot be induced to treat others justly. Thus there are put before the individual Israelite here illustrations of all the ways in which it is possible for him either to help or to hinder justice.

I. THE ISRAELITE IS CAUTIONED LEST BY YIELDING TO UNWORTHY MOTIVES, HE SHOULD HELP OTHERS TO GAIN VICTORIES OF UNRIGHTEOUSNESS. It is only too easy to send abroad an empty story which may end in the ruin of an innocent man. We may become afflicted with a spirit of partisanship which, even if it lead not to downright lying, may prompt to exaggerations and distortions, just as valuable for the attainment of malicious purposes. He who would not deliberately fabricate a lie will nevertheless be well disposed to believe it when fabricated by another, and will then utter it for truth. We easily believe what we want to believe. It is so pleasant to be with the multitude; to go against it requires a great deal of courage, and a deep devotion to what is just, as the paramount thing to be considered in all judicial enquiries. Let us feel that justice is not a matter of majorities, but of great principles honestly and ably applied to particular cases, the nature of these cases being determined by evidence which has been carefully sifted and arranged so as to get at the truth. He who comes into a court of justice comes there in the simple and sufficient claims of his humanity; all considerations of popular applause, all sympathy with a poor man, *merely as a poor man*, are entirely out of place. We must guard against all cheap sentiment; we must be just before we are generous. Adroit appeals to the feelings of a jury are part of the stock-in-trade of a practised advocate; and witnesses themselves understand how to profit by the prejudices and weaknesses of sensitive minds. The poor, the sick, the maimed, only too often think that they may gain by their poverty, their feebleness, their mutilation, what is not to be gained by the righteousness of their cause. Everyone, therefore, who has to do with a court of justice needs great circumspection to keep himself clear of all words and actions such as might lend themselves to injustice. The effort of one may not secure a just judgment, but each individual must do his part. Then the stain of injustice is not on his garments.

II. AN INJURED PERSON MUST KEEP CLEAR OF PERSONAL ANIMOSITY IN THE PURSUIT OF HIS RIGHTS. An illustration is given from the misfortune which may happen to his enemy's ox or ass (vers. 4, 5). We must never forget that our enemy is also our neighbour. If a man wrongs us, it does not cancel that wrong to do him wrong in return. There is a certain appointed way of getting all such wrong put right, and if it cannot be put right in that way there is no other to be found,—no other at least so far as human aid avails. For a man to see his enemy in this position, with ox or ass gone astray or in any way needing help, is a capital chance for showing that no petty grudge actuates him in legal proceedings. He who is treated wrongly must seek for justice, but he will gladly hail the opportunity of showing that it is justice only that he seeks. It is often those who are most unyielding in the matter of right who are also most tender and assiduous in the matter of compassion. It is an easier thing through sentimental weakness to countenance a poor man in his cause than to take the trouble of driving home a lost ox or ass to its owner. The very same considerations of right which make a man feel that he cannot sit down tamely under injustice, should also make him feel that he cannot allow the property of others to go to ruin, when his timely intervention will save it.

III. THERE ARE DIRECTIONS IN PARTICULAR FOR THOSE WHO HAVE TO JUDGE. The instructions in vers. 6—9 seem specially to concern the judge. Plaintiffs, defendants and witnesses are only occasionally in courts of justice, but the judge is always there. It is his daily work to settle right as between man and man. Those who have to come before him are instructed and cautioned to come in a just spirit; but inasmuch as many of them will not attend to the instructions, it is the business of the judge to neutralise as far as he can their unrighteous approaches; and it seems to be particularly implied that he must keep himself from all temptations such as come so fascinatingly through the rich and the powerful. He with whom judicial decisions rest will have many to tempt him if he shows himself at all open to temptation. Let the judge remember that his judgment, though it may gain a cause, does not effect a final settlement. Through prejudice or bribery he may justify the wicked; but that does not hold them justified. He must not say of anyone who comes before him, that he is only a poor man or a foreigner and therefore his interests cannot matter. It should be his joy to feel and his pride to say that no one went away from him with wrongs unredressed, so far as any searching of his could discover the doer of the wrong. A judge has great opportunities. Every upright, discerning and scrupulous judge does much in the circle of his own influence to keep a high standard of right and wrong before the minds of his fellow men.—Y.

Vers. 14—17.—*A threefold cord is not quickly broken.* To forget is far easier than to remember. Festivals are like posts to which we can fasten the cords of memory, so that, securely fastened, we may not drift down the stream of Lethe. To forget facts is to ignore the duties to which facts prompt us. We must leave undone what we ought to do, unless we take measures to keep us in remembrance. The great fact which the Israelites needed to remember was the relation of dependence in which they stood to God. He had freed them from slavery, he had provided them with food, he had given them, besides, the means of enjoyment—wine and oil—above all that they could ask or think. By means of the three great annual festivals threefold security was given against forgetfulness of this fact. To keep the festivals was to realise the relation, and to strengthen it by practical acknowledgment. Consider—

I. THE FEAST OF FREEDOM. In this connection (ver. 15) the unleavened bread is the point emphasised—to be eaten for seven days, a full week, at the commencement of the sacred year. As a reminder it suggested—1. *Past slavery.* The tyrannous oppression of Egypt; hopeless condition ere God looked upon them; life but a synonym for bare existence; even sustenance depending upon the caprice of others. 2. *Past deliverance.* The paschal night; unleavened bread the accompaniment of the first paschal feast; food a very secondary consideration when freedom was in question. 3. *Present duties.* God had delivered them from slavery that they might serve him as his free people; an inner slavery worse than the outer; a purification needed in the heart even more important than that in the home. The leaven of malice and wickedness must be sought out and put away; so long as they retained *that*, freedom was but a nominal privilege.

II. THE FEAST OF FIRST-FRUITS. Linked on to the second day of unleavened bread. God would have his children look forward; and so he makes the first blessing a seed in which are enwrapped others. Freed by God, the people could appropriate, as his children, the promise made to children (Gen. i. 29, as modified by the fall, Gen. iii. 19). The gift of food was God's gift, but their cooperation was needed for its fruition; it was to be the *fruit*, not the *creation* of their labours. Familiarity breeds forgetfulness as often as it breeds contempt. A reminder needed that human labour can, at most, work up God's raw material. [The *cerealia*, or corn plants, well called " a standing miracle." Apparently a cultivated grass, yet no known grass can be improved into corn by cultivation. Corn can be degraded by artificial means into a worthless perennial; as it is, it is an annual, exhausting itself in seeding, needing man's labour to its perfection and preservation.] To get his food, man is constantly reminded that he must be a fellow-worker with God.

III. THE FEAST OF INGATHERING. As the year rolls on, it exhibits more and more of God's goodness and bounty. It calls for ever fresh acknowledgment of that love which gives " liberally and upbraideth not." Freedom a great gift, the capacity to work for one's own livelihood; so, too, food, the means through which that capacity may find exercise; further, God gives all the fruits of the earth in their season, so that man through his labour may find not merely health but happiness. Naturally this was the most joyful of all the festivals—the blossoms which glorified the stem springing from the root of freedom. To rejoice in the Lord is the final outcome of that faith which enables us to realise our sonship.

Conclusion.—These festivals have more than an historical interest. They teach the same truths as of old, but for Christians their meaning is intensified. Unleavened bread is associated with Calvary, freedom from the tyranny of sin (1 Cor. v. 7, 8). Linked to this is our first-fruits festival; Christ, the first-fruits (1 Cor. xv. 20), made our food through the gift of the Spirit at Pentecost. The feast of ingathering is not yet, but we may rejoice in it by anticipation (1 Peter i. 6). The final festival is described for us by St. John in the Revelation (vii. 9—17). Blessed are they who, with robes washed white, shall share the joy of that feast of Ingathering.—G.

EXPOSITION.

Vers. 20—31.—THE REWARDS OF OBEDI-ENCE. God always places before men " the recompense of the reward." He does not require of them that they should serve him for nought. The " Book of the Covenant " appropriately ends with a number of promises, which God undertakes to perform, if Israel keeps the terms of the covenant. The promises are:— 1. That he will send an angel before them to be their guide, director, and helper (vers. 20 —23). 2. That he will be the enemy of their enemies (ver. 22), striking terror into them miraculously (ver. 27), and subjecting them to other scourges also (ver. 28). 3. That he will drive out their enemies " by little and little " (ver. 30), not ceasing until he has destroyed them (ver. 23). 4. That he will give them the entire country between the Red Sea and the Mediterranean on the one hand, the Desert and the Euphrates on the

other (ver. 31). And 5. That he will bless their sustenance, avert sickness from them, cause them to multiply, and prolong their days upon earth (vers. 25, 26). At the same time, all these promises—except the first—are made conditional. If they will " beware " of the angel and " obey his voice," then he will drive their enemies out (vers. 22, 23): if they will serve Jehovah, and destroy the idols of the nations, then he will multiply them, and give them health and long life (vers. 24—26), and " set their bounds from the Red Sea even unto the Sea of the Philistines, and from the desert unto the river" (ver. 31). So far as they fall short of their duties, is he entitled to fall short of his promises. A reciprocity is established. Unless they keep their engagements, he is not bound to keep his. Though the negative side is not entered upon, this is sufficiently clear. None of the promises, except the promise to send the angel, is absolute. Their realisation depends on a strict and hearty obedience.

Ver. 20.—**Behold, I send a messenger before thee.** Jewish commentators regard the messenger as Moses, who, no doubt, was a specially commissioned ambassador for God, and who might, therefore, well be termed God's messenger. But the expressions—"He will not pardon your transgressions," and "My name is in him," are too high for Moses. An angel must be intended—probably "the Angel of the Covenant,"—whom the best expositors identify with the Second Person of the Trinity, the Ever-Blessed Son of God. **To keep thee in the way** is not simply "to guide thee through the wilderness, and prevent thee from geographical error," but to keep thee altogether in the right paths, to guard thy going out and thy coming in, to prevent thee from falling into any kind of wrong conduct. **The place which I have prepared** is not merely Palestine, but that place of which Palestine is the type—viz., Heaven. Compare John xiv. 2:—"I go to prepare a place for you."

Ver. 21.—**Provoke him not.** On the disobedience of the Israelites to this precept, see Num. xiv. 11; Ps. lxxviii. 17, 40, 56, etc. **My name is in him.** God's honour he will not give to another. He does not set His Name in a man. The angel, in whom was God's Name, must have been co-equal with God—one of the Persons of the Blessed Trinity.

Ver. 22.—**If thou shalt indeed obey his voice, and do all that I speak.** The change of persons in the latter clause—"all that I speak," instead of "all that he speaks"—implies the doctrine of the *perienchoresis* or *circuminsessio*, that God the Father is in the Son and the Spirit, as they are in him. **An adversary to thy adversaries.** Rather "an afflictor of thy afflictors."

Ver. 23.—**The Amorites, and the Hittites,** etc. The nations of Canaan proper, to whom the Gergashites are sometimes added. See the comment on ch. iii. 8. **I will cut them off.** Or "cut them down," *i.e.*, destroy them from being any longer nations, but not exterminate them, as is generally supposed. David had a "Hittite" among his "mighty men" (2 Sam. xxiii. 39), and was on friendly terms with Araunah the "Jebusite" (*ibid.* ch. xxiv. 18—24).

Ver. 24.—**Thou shalt not bow down to their gods, nor serve them, nor do after their works.** It is always to be borne in mind that with the idolatries of the heathen were connected "works of darkness," which it is shameful even to speak of. The rites of Baal and Ashtoreth, of Chemosh, Molech, Rimmon, and the other Canaanite and Syrian deities were at once defiled by the abomination of human sacrifices, and polluted with the still more debasing evil of religious impurity. "The sacrifice offered to Ashtoreth," says Dr. Döllinger, "consisted in the prostitution of women: the women submitted themselves to the visitors of the feast, in the temple of the goddess or the adjoining precinct. A legend told of Astarte (Ashtoreth) having prostituted herself in Tyre for ten years: and in many places matrons, as well as maidens, consecrated themselves for a length of time, or on the festivals of the goddess, with a view of propitiating her, or earning her favour as *hieroduli* of unchastity. . . . In this way they went so far at last as to contemplate the abominations of unnatural lust as a homage rendered to the deity, and to exalt it into a regular cultus. The worship of the goddess at Aphaca in Lebanon was specially notorious in this respect. The temple in a solitary situation was, as Eusebius tells us, a place of evil-doing for such as chose to ruin their bodies in scandalous ways. . . . . Criminal intercourse with women, impurity, shameful and degrading deeds, were practised in the temple, where there was no custom and no law, and no honourable or decent human being could be found." (*Jew and Gentile*, vol. i. pp. 428, 429; Darnell's translation.) **Thou shalt utterly overthrow them.** The heathen gods are identified with their images. These were to be torn from their bases, overthrown, and rolled in the dust for greater contempt and ignominy. They were then to be broken up and burnt, till the gold and the silver with which they were overlaid was calcined and could be stamped to powder. Nothing was to be spared that had been degraded by idolatry, either for its beauty or its elaborate workmanship, or its value. All was hateful to God, and was to be destroyed.

Ver. 25.—**He shall bless thy bread and thy water.** If the Israelites were exact in their obedience, and destroyed the idols, and served God only, then he promised to bless "their bread and their water"—the food, *i.e.*, whether meat or drink, on which they subsisted, and to give them vigorous health, free from **sickness** of any kind, which he pledged himself to **take away from the midst** of them. Though Christians have no such special pledge, there is, no doubt, that virtuous and godly living would greatly conduce to health, and take away half the sicknesses from which men suffer, even at the present day.

Ver. 26.—**There shall nothing cast their young, nor be barren in thy land.** This blessing could not have followed upon godly living in the way of natural sequence, but only by Divine favour and providential care. It would have rendered them rich in flocks and herds beyond any other nation. **The number of thy days I will fulfil.** There shall be no premature deaths. All, both men and women, shall reach the term allotted to man, and die in a good old age, having fulfilled their time. Godly living, persisted in for several generations, might, perhaps, produce this result.

Ver. 27.—I will send my fear before thee. The fear which fell upon the nations is seen first in the case of Balak and the Moabites. " Moab was sore afraid of the people, because they were many " (Num. xxii. 3). Later it is spoken of by Rahab as general (Josh. ii. 9, 11). A very signal indication of the alarm felt is given in the history of the Gibeonites (*ib*. ix. 3, 27). **I will make all thine enemies turn their backs unto thee.** For the fulfilment of this promise see Num. xxi. 3, 24, 35 ; xxxi. 7 ; Josh. viii. 20—24 ; x. 10, etc. Had their obedience been more complete, the power of the Canaanitish nations would have been more thoroughly broken, and the sufferings and servitudes related in the Book of Judges would not have had to be endured.

Ver. 28.—And I will send hornets before thee. This is scarcely to be taken literally, since no actual plague of hornets is mentioned in the historical narrative. " Hornets " here, and in Deut. vii. 20 ; Josh. xxiv. 12, are probably plagues or troubles of any kind, divinely sent to break the power of the heathen nations, and render them an easier prey to the Israelites, when they made their invasion. Possibly, the main " hornets " were the Egyptians, who, under Rameses III., successfully invaded Palestine about the time of Israel's sojourn in the wilderness, and weakened the power of the Hittites (Khita). **The Hivite, the Canaanite, and the Hittite.** By a common figure of speech, a part is put for the whole—three nations for seven. The three names seem to be taken at random, but include the two nations of most power—the Canaanites and the Hittites.

Ver. 29.—I will not drive them out from before thee in one year. The Divine action is for the most part " slack, as men count slackness "—it is not hasty, spasmodic, precipitate, as human action is too often. Men are impatient ; God is strangely, wonderfully patient. He would not drive out the Canaanitish nations all at once—1. **Lest the land should become desolate,** there being an insufficient population to keep down the weeds and maintain the tillage ; and 2. **Lest the beast of the field should multiply** so as to become a danger to the new-comers. It is

related that when the kingdom of Samaria was depopulated by the removal of the Ten Tribes, there was a great increase of lions, which preyed upon the scanty remnant left (2 Kings xvii. 25). Even in France, after the Franco-German war, it was found that in many districts wolves increased. A third reason why the nations were not subdued all at once, not mentioned here, is touched in Judg. ii. 21 —23—" The Lord left those nations, without driving them out hastily, that through them he might prove Israel, whether they would keep the way of the Lord to walk therein, or not."

Ver. 31. And I will set thy bounds from the Red Sea even unto the sea of the Philistines. This passage by itself would be sufficient to confute Dr. Brugsch's notion, that the *Yam Suph* (or " Red Sea " of our translators) is the Lake Serbônis, which is a part of the Mediterranean or "Sea of the Philistines," and cannot stand in contrast with it. The " Sea of the Philistines " and the " Red Sea " mark the boundaries of the Holy Land East and West, as the " Desert " and the " River " (Euphrates) do its boundaries North and South. That Moses here lays down those wide limits which were only reached 400 years later, in the time of David and Solomon, and were then speedily lost, can surprise no one who believes in the prophetic gift, and regards Moses as one of the greatest of the Prophets. The tract marked out by these limits had been already promised to Abraham (Gen. xv. 18). Its possession by Solomon is distinctly recorded in 1 Kings iv. 21, 24 ; 2 Chr. ix. 26. As Solomon was " a man of peace," we must ascribe the acquisition of this wide empire to David. (Compare 2 Sam. viii. 3—14 ; x. 6— 19.) **The river** (*han-nahar*) is in the Pentateuch always the Euphrates. The Nile is *ha-y'or*. A powerful kingdom established in Syria is almost sure to extend its influence to the Euphrates. **I will deliver the inhabitants of the land into your hand.** Compare Josh. xxi. 44, for the first fulfilment of this prophecy. Its *complete* fulfilment was reserved for the time of David. **Thou shalt drive them out.** The mass of the Canaanites were no doubt " driven out " rather than exterminated. They retired northwards, and gave strength to the great Hittite kingdom which was for many centuries a formidable antagonist of the Egyptian and Assyrian empires.

HOMILETICS.

Vers. 20—31.—*God's promises sometimes absolute, but for the most part contingent on obedience.* " Behold, I send an angel before thee." Here was a positive promise. An angel, a guide, a protector, would go before them throughout their wanderings in the wilderness, and lead them into the promised land—lead, at any rate, some remnant of them, out of which God would make a great nation. Thus much was certain. God's word to give his descendants the land of Canaan was pledged to Abraham, and he would not go back from it. They should reach Canaan, and an angel should lead them; but the rest was all more or less uncertain. If they *indeed* obeyed God, and did as he commanded, then he would be an enemy to their enemies, and give them full possession of the land of promise. If they truly served Jehovah, and not idols, then he would grant them health and long life, and other temporal blessings. And so it is with Christians. God gives absolutely certain blessings to all whom he accepts into covenant with him; but the greater part of the blessings which he has promised are contingent on their behaviour.

I. BLESSINGS PROMISED TO CHRISTIANS ABSOLUTELY. 1. A Divine guide is promised to all. The Holy Spirit, speaking in men's hearts, directing and enlightening their conscience, tells them continually how they ought to walk, points cut the way, offers his guidance, nay, presses it on them, and seeks to lead them to heaven. The guide is more than an angel—God's holy name is in him. Nor does he guide only. He supports the footsteps, strengthens, sustains, comforts men. 2. Membership in Christ is promised. "I am the vine; ye are the branches." "Abide in me." We are as branches cut out of a wild olive, which have been grafted, contrary to nature, into a good olive-tree, to partake of its root and fatness (Rom. xi. 17—24). We are "made members of Christ," for the most part, in our infancy, without effort or merit of our own, by God's great mercy.

II. BLESSINGS WHICH ARE CONTINGENT ON OUR OBEDIENCE. 1. The answer of a good conscience towards God—a great blessing—can only, by the very nature of the case, belong to those who have striven always to be obedient, and have served the Lord from their youth. 2. Growth in grace is granted only to such as cherish and follow the grace already vouchsafed them. 3. Spiritual wisdom and understanding are attained by none but those who, having "done the will of God, know of the doctrine" (John vii. 17). 4. Assistance against spiritual enemies is contingent on our doing our best to resist them. 5. Length of days is attached as a special blessing to obedience to parents (Eph. vi. 2, 3). Finally, and above all—6. The eternal bliss which is promised us in another world is conditional upon our "patient continuance in well-doing" in this. We must "so run that we may obtain." Most of those to whom the promises of Ex. xxiii. were addressed, forfeited them by their misconduct, and did not enter Canaan. They "lusted," they became "idolaters," they "tempted God," they "committed fornication," they "murmured"—and the result was that they "were overthrown in the wilderness." And "all these things happened unto them for ensamples, and they are written for our admonition, upon whom the ends of the world are come. Wherefore let him that thinketh he standeth take heed lest he fall" (1 Cor. x. 11, 12).

HOMILIES BY VARIOUS AUTHORS.

Vers. 20—33.—*Promises and warnings.* These conclude the Book of the Covenant. I. PROMISES. 1. *An angel guide* (vers. 20—23). But this angel was no ordinary or created angel. He is repeatedly identified with Jehovah himself. God's "name"—his essential nature—was in him. He is one with Jehovah, yet distinct from him—no mere personification, but a real hypostasis. See the careful treatment of "the doctrine of the Angel of the Lord," in Oehler's "Old Testament Theology," vol. i. pp. 188—196 (Eng. trans.). We view the "angel" as the pre-incarnate Logos—Christ in the Old Testament. Israel's guide was the Son of God—the same Divine Person who is now conducting "many sons unto glory," and who is become "the author of eternal salvation to all them that obey him" (Heb. ii. 10; v. 9). 2. *Defence against enemies* (ver. 22). If Israel obeyed God's voice, and did all that God spake, their enemies would be reckoned *his* enemies, and their adversaries *his* adversaries. And "if God be for us, who can be against us?" (Rom. viii. 31). 3. *Aid in the conquest of Canaan* (vers. 23, 27—31). Apply throughout to the spiritual warfare of the individual and of the Church. (1) The way for the conquest would be prepared. God would send his *fear* before the Israelites (ver. 27)—would, as stated in Deuteronomy, put the dread of them, and the fear of them, upon the nations that were under the whole heaven (Deut. ii. 25; xi. 25; cf. ch. xv. 15, 16). There is a presentiment of defeat in the hearts of the enemies of God, especially when the Church is energetic and fearless in her work, which goes far to secure the victory for the latter. Something whispers to them that their "time is short" (1 Cor. vii. 29; Rev. xii. 12; cf. Matt. viii. 29). Moral forces are all on the side of the kingdom of God. They assist its friends, and operate to enervate and discourage its enemies. The Christian worker may rely on numerous invisible allies in men's own hearts. Workings of conscience, stings of fear, dread of God, etc. God would also send *hornets* before the Israelites, to drive out the Canaanites from their strong castles (ver. 28). To us there seems no good reason for taking this declaration otherwise than literally. If taken symbolically, the "hornets" are equivalent to the stings of fear, etc., above referred to. A veritable hornet warfare this, and one of great value to the Gospel cause. Taken literally, the "hornets" may be regarded as types of secret *providential* allies—of the co-operation of God in his providence, often by means of things insignificant in themselves, but working, under his secret direction, for the furtherance of his kingdom, and the defeat of those opposed to it. In a million unseen ways—how encouraging the reflection!—Providence is thus aiding the work of those who fight under Christ's captaincy. (2) They would be prospered in battle (ver. 27). The individual, in his warfare with the evil of his own heart—the Church, in her conflict with the evil of the world—enjoy a similar promise. If Christ inspires, if he, the captain of the Lord's host, gives the signal to advance, victories are certain. However numerous and powerful our spiritual enemies, greater is he that is with us than they that are against us (1 John iv. 4). (3) The conquest would be given by degrees. God would drive out their enemies before them, "little by little" (ver. 30). The reason given is, "lest the land become desolate, and the beast of the field multiply against thee" (ver. 27). The method was a wise one. It doubtless had its dangers. Remaining idolatry would tend to become a snare. The delay in the extirpation of the Canaanites had thus its side of trial—it would act as a moral test. In other respects it was attended with advantage. It would make the conquest more thorough. It would enable the Israelites to consolidate, organise, and secure their possessions as they went along. It would prevent the multiplying of the beasts of the field. And quite analogous to this is God's method of conducting us unto our *spiritual* inheritance. The law of "little by little" obtains here also. "Little by little" the believer gains the victory over evil in self, and the heart is sanctified. "Little by little" the world is conquered for Christ. In no other way is thorough conquest possible. Suppose, *e.g.*, that, as the result of extraordinary shakings of the nations, a multitude of uninstructed tribes, peoples, communities, were suddenly thrown into the arms of Christendom—even supposing the conversions real, how difficult would it be to prevent mischiefs from arising! Compare the troubles of the Reformation Churches. Make the yet more extravagant supposition that by some supreme moral effort—the evil of our own hearts being suddenly aroused to intense activity—it pleased God to give us the victory over the whole of this evil at once. How little could we do with such a victory when we had it! Thrown at once upon our own hands, how difficult it would be to know what to do with ourselves! Would not new foes—fantastic conceits —speedily arise from the ground of our yet undisciplined natures, to give us new troubles? The surest method is "little by little." It is not good for any man to have more than he needs—to have a greater victory than he can rightly use; *e.g.*, a man who reads more books than he can mentally digest and assimilate; who has a larger estate than he can manage; who has more money than he can make a good use of. And yet the fact of evil still lurking in our hearts, and continuing in the world around us, exposes us to many perils. It acts as a moral test, and so indirectly conduces to the growth of holiness. 4. *Material blessings* (vers. 25, 26). In the land to which he was conducting them, God would give the people of Israel abundance of food and water; would take away all sickness from their midst (cf. "I am the Lord that healeth thee." ch. xv. 26); would greatly bless their flocks and herds; and would lengthen out their days to the full term (cf. Deut. xxviii. 1—14). The blessings of the new covenant are predominantly spiritual (Eph. i. 3). Yet even under it, "godliness is profitable unto all things, having promise of the life that now is, and of that which is to come" (1 Tim. iv. 8). Godliness has a natural tendency to promote temporal well-being. So ample a measure of prosperity as that promised in the text could, however, only accrue from direct Divine blessing. The absolute form of the expression answers to the absoluteness of the requirement—"Obey my voice, and do *all* that I speak" (ver. 31). Falling short of the ideal obedience, Israel fell short also of the ideal fulness of the blessing. 5.

Expansion of bounds (ver. 31). Only once or twice was this maximum of possession *touched* by Israel. Failure in the fulfilment of the condition kept back fulfilment of the promise. The Church's destiny is to possess the whole earth (Ps. ii. 8).

II. WARNINGS. If these glorious promises are to be fulfilled to Israel, they must obey the voice of God and of his angel. Let them beware, therefore,—1. Of *provoking the angel* (ver. 21). God's name was in him, and he would not pardon their transgressions. That is, he would not take a light view of their sins, but would strictly mark them, and severely punish them. He was not a Being to be trifled with. If his wrath against them were kindled but a little, they would perish from the way (Ps. ii. 12). He was one with Jehovah in his burning zeal for holiness, and in his determination not to clear the guilty. See below. The Gospel is not wanting in its similar side of sternness. There is a "wrath of the Lamb" (Rev. vi. 17). There is a "judgment" which "begins at the house of God" (1 Pet. iv. 17). There is the stern word—"It shall come to pass, that every soul, which will not hear that prophet, shall be destroyed from among the people" (Acts iii. 23). Cf. also Heb. ii. 2, 3; x. 26—39; xii. 25. 2. They *must not serve other gods* (ver. 24). Conversely, they were utterly to overthrow the idol gods, and to break down their images. "Where Jesus comes, he comes to reign." No rival will be tolerated alongside of him. We cannot serve (1) God and Mammon (Matt. vi. 24). (2) God and fashion (1 John ii. 15—18). (3) God and our own lusts (2 Pet. i. 4; ii. 20, 21). (4) God and human glory (John v. 44). The worship of Jehovah and that of *any* of the world's idols will not amalgamate. See reflected in these commands the principles which are to regulate the relation of God's servants at this hour to the world and to its evil—(1) No toleration of it (Matt. v. 29, 30). (2) No communion with it (2 Cor. vi. 14—18; Eph. v. 3, 11). (3) Unceasing war against it (2 Cor. x. 4; Col. iii. 5). 3. They *must make no league with the Canaanites* (ver. 32). The lesson taught is, that believers are to seek their friendships, their alliances, their consorts, etc., elsewhere than among the ungodly. We are not only to keep out of harm's way, and avoid occasions of sin, but we are to labour to remove from our midst *entirely* what experience proves to be an incurable snare.—J. O.

Ver. 21.—*The angel provoked.* The language in this passage is very strong, and may occasion difficulty. "Provoke him not, for he will not pardon your transgressions; for my name is in him." If this angel is the Son of God, he who afterwards became incarnate for man's salvation, and who died to procure forgiveness for us, it startles us to hear of him—"he will not pardon your transgressions." When we think, too, on what God's name imports—on the revelation subsequently made of it,—"The Lord, the Lord God, merciful and gracious, long-suffering, and abundant in goodness and truth, keeping mercy for thousands, *forgiving iniquity and transgression and sin,*" etc., it astonishes us to learn that this angel, in whom the name is, will not pardon Israel's sin. The history, also, may be thought to create difficulties. For, undeniably, the Israelites were often pardoned. They were, in truth, continually being pardoned; for, "stiff-necked" as they were, they could not have stood for a day in their covenant, had not God's mercy been constantly extended to them. It is plain, therefore, from the nature of the case, that the expression is not to be taken absolutely; the sense in which it *is* to be understood well deserves investigation.

I. IN WHAT SENSE TRUE OF ISRAEL. The general meaning is, as stated above, that the angel would not look lightly on their offences, would not pass them over, but would severely punish them. This accorded with the constitution under which they were placed, to which it belonged, that "every transgression and disobedience" should "receive a just recompense of reward" (Heb. ii. 2). The context suggests, or admits of, the following qualifications—1. The statement refers, it will be observed, to what the angel will do when "provoked"—to what will happen when his wrath is "kindled" against Israel (cf. Ps. lxxviii. 21, 49, 50, 59, etc.). But how long did this Divine conductor *bear* with Israel before permitting his wrath to be thus kindled against them! He was "slow to anger." What pardon was implied in his very long-suffering! 2. The transgressions alluded to are not ordinary offences—not the sins of infirmity and short-coming which mark the lives even of the best—but such outstanding acts of transgression as are mentioned in the context—fundamental breaches of the covenant. These were the sins which would specially provoke the angel (cf.

Deut. xxxii. 5, 15—28). They would be "surely" punished. 3. The general assertion that transgressions will not be pardoned does not imply that there is *no* room left
for intercession and repentance; that, *e.g.*, an alteration in the spiritual conditions
might not procure, if not remission, at least a sensible *alleviation* of the penalty; that
prayer, proceeding from a contrite heart, might not obtain the *removal* of affliction, or
the restoration of the penitent to Divine favour. Great severity, nevertheless, attaches
to this announcement. The history is the best commentary upon it. It is literally
true that, after the ratification of the covenant at Sinai, no serious transgression of
Israel was allowed to go unpunished. In no case did even repentance avail *wholly* to
avert chastisement. At most, the penalty was lightened, or shortened in duration.
Thus, on the occasion of the sin of the golden calf, the earnest intercession of Moses
availed to save the people from destruction, and obtained from God the promise that he
would still go with them; but it did not save the idolaters from being smitten with the
sword of Levi (ch. xxxii. 28), or prevent the Lord from still "plaguing" the people
"because they made the calf, which Aaron made" (ch. xxxii. 35). Cf. later instances,
e.g., Nadab and Abihu (Lev. x. 1—8); the murmuring at Taberah (Num. xi. 1—3);
the lusting at Kibroth-hattaavah (Num. xi. 4—35); the rebellion at Kadesh, punished
by the rejection of that whole generation (Num. xiii., xiv.); the revolt of Korah (Num.
xvi., xvii.); the sin at Meribah, when even Moses forfeited his right to enter the land
of promise (Num. xx. 1—13); the later murmuring, when the people were punished
by fiery serpents (Num. xxi. 7—9); the idolatry and fornication of Baal-peor (Num.
xxv.). This severity is the more remarkable when we remember how leniently God
dealt with the people *before* the ratification of the covenant with Sinai. "All murmurings before they came to Sinai were passed over, or merely rebuked; all murmurings and rebellions after Sinai bring down punishment and death" (Kitto). We trace
the same principle of dealing through the whole history of the Old Testament. David,
e.g., is personally forgiven for his sin of adultery; but the temporal penalty is not
remitted (2 Sam. xii.). He is punished on a later occasion for numbering the people,
and has the choice given him of three evils; and this, notwithstanding his sincere
repentance (2 Sam. xxiv.). So Manasseh is said to have "filled Jerusalem with
innocent blood, which the Lord would not pardon" (2 Kings xxiv. 5). The congruity of this strict dealing with a dispensation of law is sufficiently obvious; and, in
the light of the examples quoted, the language of the text will not be felt to be too
strong.

II. HOW FAR TRUE UNDER THE GOSPEL. The Gospel, as befits its nature, places
in the forefront, not the declaration that God will *not* pardon sin, but the announcement
of the terms on which he *will* pardon. It is a declaration of mercy to those who are
viewed as already under wrath—the law having accomplished its design of convincing
men of sin. The terms, however, on which the Gospel proposes to grant forgiveness are
of such a nature as fully to establish the truth underlying this text; viz., that God, as
a God of holiness, will not clear the guilty (cf. Ex. xxxiv. 7). 1. This truth is the
presupposition of the Gospel. Else whence its demand for atonement? Why is sin
not simply condoned—not simply waived aside as something admitting of unconditional
pardon? In view of the fact that the Gospel absolutely refuses pardon save on the
ground of "the shedding of blood," it certainly cannot be accused of making light of
guilt, or of ignoring its relations to justice. God remains the just God, even while he
is the Saviour (Rom. iii. 26). Stated otherwise, it is on the ground of the principle in
the text, that a Gospel is needed. "The wrath of God is revealed from heaven against
all ungodliness and unrighteousness of men" (Rom. i. 18). No clearing of the guilty
here. The principle in question is the general principle of God's moral administration
(Rom. ii. 6—12). 2. This truth still applies in its rigour to those who "disobey" the
Gospel. For these there is no pardon. There remains for them only judgment and
fiery indignation (Heb. x. 27). So solemn is the truth that "there is none other name
under heaven given among men whereby we must be saved" (Acts iv. 12). 3. Even
believers, notwithstanding that they receive spiritual pardon, must not expect to escape
temporal chastisements, appropriate to their offences. So far as sin's penalties are
bound up with natural law it is certain that they will *not* escape them. They may be
spiritually pardoned, yet, as respects the temporal penalty, may, like Esau, find no
place for repentance, though they seek it carefully with tears (Heb. xii. 17). God

alone is judge of how far, and with what measure of benefit to the individual, and of glory to himself, he can remit temporal chastisements (Ex. xxxiii. 19). Respect will doubtless be had to the circumstances under which the sin was committed, to the depth and sincerity of the repentance, to the publicity of the scandal (cf. 2 Sam. xii. 14), to the moral benefit likely to accrue, etc. 4. Hypocritical professors of Christ's name will be dealt with according to this rule. They will be punished with special severity (Matt. xxiv. 51).

III. How RECONCILABLE WITH GOD'S REVEALED ATTRIBUTE OF MERCY. Our thoughts revert to the revelation of God's name in ch. xxxiv. 6, 7. The attributes of mercy occupy the foreground, yet not to the denial of the sternness of holiness, which, in the latter clauses, finds distinct expression. "Forgiving iniquity and transgression and sin, and *that will by no means clear the guilty, visiting the iniquity of the fathers*," etc. God's mercy to Israel was exhibited compatibly with what has been seen to be the meaning of the text—(1) In his great long-suffering in *bearing* with their provocations. (2) In his turning aside the fierceness of his anger, in answer to earnest intercession, or when signs were shown of repentance. (3) In limiting the *measure* of his wrath— either by exchanging a severer penalty for a lighter one, or by shortening the time of infliction. Cf. Ps. lxxviii. 38—"But he, being full of compassion, forgave their iniquity, and destroyed them not, yea, many a time turned he his anger away and did not stir up all his wrath. For he remembered that they were but flesh," etc. (4) In granting spiritual pardons, even when temporal penalties were not revoked. (5) In restoring the penitent to favour, after punishment had taken effect in inducing con- trition. (6) In keeping covenant with the children, even when rejecting the fathers. (7) The full reconciliation is seen in the Gospel, in the fact of the atonement.—J. O.

Vers. 20—23.—*The angel of the covenant.* Certain of the matters on which Jehovah had been speaking immediately before the promise of the angel, assumed that the people would assuredly come to dwell in a land very different from that in which they were now sojourning. God had done so much to call forth faith that, in spite of all ugly symptoms of unbelief and murmuring, he could only go on speaking as if the faith would become a regular habit steadily finding deeper root in the Israelite heart. Thus we find him giving rules for the cultivation of cornlands, vineyards and oliveyards into which they had not yet come ; rules for the harvest feast and a feast of ingathering of all the fruits, when as yet there was no indication of such an ingathering being possible. It was fitting, therefore, that Jehovah should follow up his statement of regulations by speaking confidently of the people's entrance into the land where the regulations were to be observed. That land was not yet in sight. So far, indeed, they had been travelling away from it rather than towards it, and the district in which they now were was suggestive of anything but cornlands, oliveyards and vineyards.

I. THERE IS THE DISTINCT ASSURANCE OF SUFFICIENT GUIDANCE. The reference here is presumably to that glory-cloud in which God was to manifest his presence right onward till Canaan was reached. That cloud was to be unintermitting and unmis- takable in its guiding efficiency. Whatever perplexities might come to a devout and attentive Israelite because of other things, no perplexities were possible as to the way in which he should go. He might wonder why God led him in such a way; but that it was really God's way he need not have any doubt whatever. Thus we see how lovingly God ever deals with the ignorance of his people. What is necessary for them to know is made as plain as the necessity demands. They did not need any discussions and counsels among themselves, any balancing of the pros and cons which might determine them to one path rather than another. God perfectly knew the way and the needs and dangers of the way. He himself is never in doubt as to what his people should do. He is no blind leader of the blind. He was taking Israel into the land which he had prepared, and the way was prepared as much as the destination. Whatever uncertainty and vacillation there may be about the Christian life comes not from him who leads, but from those who follow. Indeed, our very vacillation becomes more conspicuous as we contrast it with the steady undeviating path marked out by our leader. Compare the announcement that is made concerning the angel here with the demand of Jesus upon his disciples—' Follow me."

II. THERE IS THE INDICATED PERIL OF NEGLECTING THAT GUIDANCE. Not to follow the true guide, of course, means all the loss, pain and destruction that come from getting into false ways. But such consequences are not dwelt upon here. The thoughts of the people are rather directed to the sin they would commit by neglecting the intimations of the angel. " My name is in him." It was not a mere creature of Jehovah, which he used for an index. There was in the guiding-cloud a peculiar manifestation of Jehovah himself, whom the people would neglect if in a fit of self-will they were to turn away and follow the superficial intimations of their earthly surroundings. The great peril was that of coming under the wrath of God because of disobedience. It was only too easy to become used even to the presence of a miraculous cloud. The after conduct of the people shows that the tone of warning here adopted was a wise tone. They were likely to forget how much the presence of the angel demanded from them. That angel was there not only in mercy but in authority. To neglect him was to offend him. And because the cloud, in the ordinary circumstances of it, had nothing to terrify, because the penal consequences of neglecting it did not lie on the surface, it was needful to remind the people how much of holy wrath with unbelief and self-reliance lay within this messenger from God. The negligent Israelite needed to be solemnly assured that there was something even worse than mere failure to attain the earthly Canaan. The foreshadowing is here given of that dreadful doom which fell upon Israel shortly after and kept them in the wilderness for forty years. God can turn all the wanderings of the disobedient into a species of imprisonment and punishment from himself.

III. There is a most instructive intimation as to the results of accepting that guidance. The very results show how indispensable the guidance is. Enemies and adversaries are in front, and God makes no concealment of the fact. If Israel has had already to deal with Amalekites in the comparative barrenness of the Sinaitic peninsula, what may not be expected when the confines of the fertile promised land are reached? That which is to be a good land to Israel, has long been a good land to the nations at present dwelling in it. But though these enemies lie in front,—enemies fighting with all the valour of desperation for their homes and their property,—yet all will prove victorious for Israel, if only Israel acts obediently towards God's angel. The enemies of God's people are not great or little in themselves. That which is great at one time may become little at another, and that which is little, great; and all because of the fluctuations in the spirit of faith. In Ex. xvii. we read of Amalekites discomfited and Jehovah threatening utterly to put out the remembrance of Amalek from under heaven. But turn to Num. xiv. and a very different story has to be told of how the Amalekites smote and discomfited the children of Israel. If we would be strong for every conflict and assured of every victory, it must be by a calm looking towards the will of God. The will of God tells the way of God; and when we meet our enemies in that way all their preparations avail them nothing.—Y.

Vers. 24—33.—*The prospect in the promised land.* I. The treatment of its former occupants. 1. *The avoidance of their idolatries.* God cautions us against those dangers which we are most likely to overlook. When once the Israelites entered the promised land and were fairly settled there, they would show no lack of energy and discrimination in doing their best to guard their temporal possessions. But the most serious dangers are those against which walled cities and great armies are no defence. God could easily cut off the idolaters and put Israel in their place; but what about the idolatries? Whether these should also be expelled would depend upon the guard which God's people kept over their own hearts. It is very noticeable that as God takes the thoughts of his people forward to their future habitation, he begins with a solemn caution against idolatry and closes with the same. There is thus a kind of correspondence with the order occupied in the Ten Commandments by those against polytheism and image-worship. It was not possible to make mention too often of the subtle perils which lay in the Canaanitish gods. 2. *Jehovah's complete defeat and expulsion of the former inhabitants.* This is indicated in a variety of impressive ways. Only let his people be faithful to him, and Jehovah will go before them as a dread to all who come in contact with them. Evidently God would have his people understand that nothing was to be feared from the very greatest external resources available against them. Let enemies threaten and unite and seek allies far and wide. The greater their efforts, the more signal will be their defeat. We must ever believe that our true strength is in God. It was never intended that Israel should be looked on as a mighty military power. Rather it should be a cause of astonishment among the nations that it was able to stand against all the resources gathered against it. Whenever the Israelites began to trust in themselves and think they were able to awe their enemies, then they were lost. God only can terrify with the terror that lasts. We may confidently leave him to scatter con-·· fusion among those whom we, with all our demonstrations, are unable to impress. 3. *The injunction to enter into no covenant with the former inhabitants.* He who had been expelled by nothing less than an awful Divine force was not to be allowed to return under pretence of a peaceful submission. Peace, concord, mutual help—we may say God would ever have these between man and man, nation and nation—but at the same time we constantly get the warning against crying, peace! peace! when there is no peace. If a foreigner came forsaking his idolatries, there was an appointed way for him into Israel, and a welcome to be cordially given. But by no stretching of charity could it be made attainable for the idolater to settle down side by side with the worshipper and servant of Jehovah.

II. THE LARGE POSITIVE BLESSINGS TO COME UPON ISRAEL. The expulsion and permanent exclusion of the former inhabitants, much as they are insisted on, were but the negative condition, the clearing of the ground, so as to bless Israel with something positive. Very fittingly does God blend together the mention of these positive blessings with cautions and warnings as to the treatment of the former occupants. As the blessings were considered, the wisdom of the cautions would appear; and as the cautions were considered, so earnest and express, the greatness of the blessings would appear. God presents himself here as one very solicitous to make the land not only a good land for his people, but one cherished so as to make the best of its advantages. For this purpose he begins with a kind of graduated expulsion of the former inhabitants. Instead of expelling them by a sudden overwhelming blow, he rather does it little by little. The enemies of Israel were not to be multiplied needlessly by exposing their land to wild beasts; and the human enemies, contrary to their own designs and desires, were to leave for Israel the fruit of their own industries. If the Israelites had been asked which would be better,—to cast out their enemies at once or by a gradual process, they would probably have replied, "at once." God will ever adopt the right plan to secure the most of blessing for his people. Thus we may learn a lesson with regard to the expulsion of evil still. God is still driving out evil little by little, and in so doing he is building up good little by little. Thus the Israelites were to get a gradual and secure settlement in the land; and then that settlement was to prove eminently profitable. Four great elements of prosperity are mentioned. 1. The *blessing of the bread and the water.* All that was connected with the obtaining of food and drink would be under God's watchful providence. What are the bread and the water unless he blesses them? God can turn the most fertile of lands into a very proverb of barrenness. Why, this very Canaan had been afflicted with famine. It was because for some reason the blessing of God had been withheld from the bread and the water that the fathers of Israel had found their way into Egypt. 2. *The maintenance of health.* This is put in the most expressive way by indicating it in the aspect of banished sickness. Disease is such a common sight to us, and presents itself in such varied forms, that in no way can God's blessing of health be more emphatically revealed than by describing him as the one who healeth all our diseases. To a large extent this health was to be the consequence of blessing the bread and the water, giving by them, thus blessed, abundant and nutritious food. 3. *The productiveness of animal life.* In a perfectly obedient Israel there were to be no abortions, no barren wombs. It was just because there was disobedience in Israel that such cries as those of Hannah were heard (1 Sam. i. 11). Evidently all this normal generative efficacy largely depended on the blessing of the bread and water and the blessing of health. That any animal whatever, either human, or lower than human, should cast its young or be barren, was in itself a sort of disease. 4. *The fulfilling of the days.* The hoary head with its crown of glory is the appointed possession of God's people. That so few obtained it only showed how much there was of imperfection in Israelite national life. These purposed blessings did not find their way into reality. The people were disobedient, unbelieving, self-regarding; and hence the seeds of blessing which assuredly God sowed among them either remained dead or struggled forth into a very imperfect life.—Y.

Ver. 20.—*Mine angel shall go before thee.* A prepared people have to be led into a prepared place (ver. 20). To lead them a guide is necessary, and God provides a guide. I. THE GUIDE AND HIS OFFICE. 1. *His nature and character.* (1) *An angel, i.e.,* a Divine messenger; not merely a messenger of God's appointment, but a messenger from God's presence. Men may be empowered to act as angels; but naturally during his time of probation man is made "lower than the angels." The angel guide is superhuman; he helps to direct affairs in this world, but his home is in another. The history certainly implies so much as this; and no theory save that which assumes the fact of such superhuman guidance can adequately account for the marvellous coincidences through which progress was ensured. The enthusiasm of Moses might fire a people, but it is not enough to fire them; they must be fired at the right moment, and with a definite aim. Some superhuman agent, who could view time from the standpoint of eternity and direct men's actions in accordance with the real necessities of the position, there must have been. [Cf. a game of chess played, as sometimes in India, with living pieces. Success does not depend so much on the strength of the armies *on* the board as on the skill of the players *off* the board, who view the whole position from above.] History cannot be explained if we ignore the unseen hand which directs and controls the movements of the actors. (2) "*My name is in him.*" The Divine guide must share the Divine character. God's deputy must be God-like. As viewing things from the standpoint of eternity, he is able to guide through the maze of time; but to view things from the standpoint of eternity he must be a sharer in the life of eternity, the eternal name must be so written on his heart that his guidance may be free from all suspicion of caprice. 2. *His office.* (1) *To keep in the way.* The guide must be a guardian as well. Guides who forget the dangers of the way, intent only on reaching their destination, may push on to the goal themselves, yet lose their charge before they reach it. God-commissioned guides are empowered also to keep and guard those who are given into their care (John xvii. 12). (2) *To bring to the prepared place.* If the guide must be a guardian, the guardian must also be a guide. He must protect during the advance, but he must not protect at the expense of progress; his charge has to be brought through the wilderness, not to be maintained there behind barricades and bulwarks. The people of Jehovah are led by the minister of Jehovah, who secures their entrance into the place prepared, if only they will accept his guidance. A place is prepared for us, as for Israel (John xiv. 2). A guide also is given us (John xiv. 16—18). We must not forget his twofold office, to keep in the way and to insist upon our moving forward. II. THOSE GUIDED AND THEIR DUTIES. The angel guide has to direct men; that he may direct them, they must acknowledge his authority. Two things necessary:—1. *Reverence.* The disposition of the heart which cannot but show itself in the conduct. Assured that the angel bore the Divine name, men must beware of him, assured that he had the right to speak with authority. A command from such a guide needed no reasons to enforce it. 2. *Obedience.* (1) *Positive.* His commands must be obeyed. There must be no delay, no shrinking back. (2) *Negative.* There must be no attempt to evade their real fulfilment by a merely apparent and formal compliance. True obedience is obedience of the spirit as well as of the letter; mere literal obedience may consist with actual provocation. Remembering who our guide is, we must remember also that the like duties are required of us in relation to him. To resist the Spirit is to grieve him, and grieving may eventually quench his power with us; one more step seals our destruction—"He that blasphemeth the Spirit of God" sins the unpardonable sin. III. BLESSINGS CONSEQUENT ON FULFILMENT OF DUTIES. We may call them temporal and eternal; blessings of the pilgrimage and blessings of the home. By the way, guarded by our guide, no enemy has power to hurt us; at the last we reach our home, to find there eternal health and happiness.

Concluding question.—What is our relation towards the guide whom God has given us? (Heb. ii. 2—3.)—G.

Vers. 20—33.—*The Mediatorial Guide.* "Behold I send an angel before thee," etc. (Exodus xxiii. 20). [We omit from homiletic treatment Exodus xx. 22—xxiii. 19, containing a large amount of minute legislation; but if any one for special reason wishes to deal with any of these laws, he will find a careful and exhaustive analysis in Lange on "Exodus." Most of them have strict and sole reference to the Hebrew Commonwealth, and are obsolete for the Christian.] This passage contains a series of promises, which all centre in an august personage, called here an "angel." That this is so will determine the character of our exposition, and the Christian uses of it.

I. THE ANGEL. None other than the "Angel of Jehovah," the Angel-God of the Old Testament, i.e., the Lord Jesus Christ. Reference is here made to those many epiphanies, which preceded the Great Epiphany of the incarnation. That these were appearances of the Lord Jesus may be argued :—1. *It seems reasonable that there should be anticipations of the incarnation.* True, we could not prophesy them beforehand ; but when they do take place, they commend themselves to our reason. It seems in a sense natural, that He, who was coming to dwell here, should once and again "come down to deliver." 2. *The history of the appearance of the angel shows:*—(1) *That he was Divine.* (i.) Perfection implied in the authority he wields, and the promises he gives. (ii.) Swears by himself. (iii.) The object of worship. (iv.) Subject of Divine names and attributes. (2) And yet there is *that which differentiates Him from the Eternal Father.* All this accords with the doctrine of the Trinity ; and that the angel was Christ the Lord.

II. HIS OFFICE. We assume now that the angel was the Lord Jesus ; that what he was to the ancient Church he is now. He is ever present—sometimes unseen—often recognised. His office as here set forth is that of:—1. *A Leader.* He led Israel, mainly by the pillar of cloud ; but not in such a way as to dispense with Israel's action. The Lord acts, but never so as to swamp our individuality. It was for Israel : (1) To watch the cloud : (2) To exercise their own judgment on minor matters. See Num. x. 31. Our danger is to rely exclusively on our own judgment, and not to look for the waving of *That Hand.* 2. *A Sentinel.* "To keep in the way" in the double sense ;—(1) To hold us in the path, and (2) to defend us on that path. The practical truth here is, that Christ's keeping is not absolute or independent of our will and action. He watches, that we may watch. This vital practical truth seems to us to be well illustrated by Swedenborg's doctrine of the "Proprium ;" which is well exhibited in "Outlines of the Religion and Philosophy of Swedenborg" by Dr. Parsons. Ch. viii. 3. *Moral magistracy.* "He will not pardon your transgressions, for my name is in Him"—what can this mean ? There is reference here to the moral magistracy exercised over us, on our pilgrim way, noting transgression, visiting for it, chastising, chastening, with a view to ultimate removal. Appeal to life for evidence of the reality of that corrective jurisdiction.

III. OUR DUTY. 1. *Loyalty to God,* ver. 25. 2. *Recognition of his representative;* i.e., the angel ; i.e., the Lord Jesus. 3. *Obedience; i.e.,* to the leader, etc. (vers. 21, 22.) N.B. "If thou shalt indeed obey *His* voice, and do all *that I speak.*" Mark how God identifies himself with the angel. 4. *Avoidance of fellowship and complicity with evil* (vers. 32, 33). *Any* intercourse for the Jew with the heathen was full of peril. It seems now to be assumed that *no* companionship for the Christian has any danger. This assumption false, as the tendency to worldliness and open sin shows. 5. *Active antagonism to all Anti-theisms* (v. 24). It will not do to be content with standing on the defensive. Has not the time now come to carry the war into the enemy's camp ?

IV. THE PROMISES. These cover really all the blessings consequent on a life of practical godliness. Thinking rather of our own position than of the literal meaning of the promises in relation to the life of Israel, they may be classified as follow :—1. *God on our side* (vers. 22, 23). 2. *Our daily provision blessed* (ver. 25). There shall be enough ; but whatever there is shall have gladness with it. 3. *Health* (ver. 25). 4. *Wealth* (ver. 26). 5. *Long life* (ver. 26). 6. *Influence,* before which even adversaries shall bend (ver. 27). 7. *Enlargement* of power and of room for its exercise (v. 31). 8. In the bestowal of these blessings, our Father in heaven will show to us great *considerateness* (vers. 29, 30). 9. *Safe conduct to the promised rest* (ver. 20). Those who know the argument of Binney :—"Is it possible to make the best of Both Worlds ?" will well understand how, under what conditions, and with what limitations, blessings of this sort—mainly secular in character—fall to the lot of the Lord's redeemed.—R

EXPOSITION.

Vers. 32, 33.—FINAL WARNING AGAINST IDOLATRY. The "Book of the Covenant" ends as it began, with a solemn warning against idolatry. (See ch. xx. 23.) "Thou shalt make no covenant with them *nor with their gods.*" Thou shalt not even suffer them to dwell side by side with thee in the land, on peaceable terms, with their own laws and religion, lest thou be ensnared thereby, and led to worship their idols and join in their unhallowed rites (ver. 33). The after history of the people of Israel shows the need of the warning. From the exodus to the captivity, every idolatry with which they came into close contact proved a sore temptation to them. As the author of Kings observes of the Ten Tribes— "The children of Israel did secretly those things which were not right against the Lord their God, and they built them high places in all their cities. .... And they set them up images and groves in every high hill, and under every green tree; and there they burnt incense in all the high places, as did the heathen whom the Lord carried away before them; and wrought wicked things to provoke the Lord to anger; for they served idols, whereof the Lord had said unto them, "Ye shall not do this thing" (2 Kings xvii. 9—12).

Ver. 32.—**Thou shalt make no covenant with them.** See below, ch. xxxiv. 12—15. According to the forms usual at the time, a treaty of peace would have contained an acknowledgment of the gods of either nation, and words in honour of them. (See the "Treaty of Rameses II. with the Hittites," given in the *Records of the Past*, vol. iv. pp. 27—32.) This would have been equivalent to "making a covenant with their gods."

Ver. 33.—**They shall not dwell in the land.** This law did not, of course, affect proselytes; nor was it considered to preclude the continuance in the land of the enslaved Gibeonites. It forbade any Canaanite communities being suffered to remain within the limits of Palestine on friendly terms with the Hebrews. The precaution was undoubtedly a wise one.

HOMILETICS.

Vers. 32, 33.—*The Peril of Idolatry.* Idolatry is the interposition of any object between man and God, in such sort that the object takes the place of God in the heart and the affections, occupying them to his exclusion, or to his disparagement. Idolatry proper, the interposition between God and the soul of idols or images, seems to have possessed a peculiar fascination for the Israelites, either because their materialistic tendencies made them shrink from approaching in thought a mere pure Spirit, or perhaps from their addiction to the sensual pleasures which accompanied idolatry, as practised by the greater part of the heathen. (See the comment on ver. 24.) In modern times, and in countries where Protestantism is professed by the generality, there is little or no danger of this gross form of the sin. But there is great danger of other forms of it. In order to make any practical use of those large portions of the Old Testament which warn against idolatry, we have to remember—

I. THAT COVETOUSNESS IS IDOLATRY. Wealth is made an idol by thousands in these latter days. All hasten to be rich. Nothing is greatly accounted of which does not lead to opulence. God is shut out from the heart by desires, and plans, and calculations which have money for their object and which so occupy it that there is no room for anything else. The danger has existed at all times, but it has to be specially guarded against at the present day, when Mammon has become the most potent of all the spirits of evil, and men bow down before, not an image of gold, but gold itself, whatever shape it may take.

II. THAT SELFISHNESS IS IDOLATRY. Men make idols of themselves—of their own happiness, quiet, comfort—allowing nothing to interfere with these, and infinitely preferring them to any intrusive thoughts of God, his glory, or his claims upon them. Persons thus wrapped up in themselves are idolaters of a very gross type, since the object of their worship is wholly bad and contemptible.

III. THAT PROFLIGACY IS IDOLATRY. Men idolise a wretched creature,—a girl, or woman, possessed of some transient beauty and personal attractions, but entirely devoid of a single estimable quality. For such a creature they peril all their prospects, both in this life and the next. They make her the queen of their souls, the object of their adoration, the star by which they direct their course. The ordinary consequence is shipwreck, both here and hereafter. When so poor an idol as a weak wanton has stepped in between the soul and God, there is little chance of a real repentance and return of the soul to its Maker.

IV. THAT AMUSEMENT MAY BE IDOLATRY. It is quite possible so to devote oneself to amusement as to make it shut out God from us. Those who live in a whirl of gaiety, with no time set apart for serious duties, for instructing the ignorant, consoling the afflicted, visiting the poor and needy—nay, with scant time for private or family prayer —are idolaters, and will have to give account to a "jealous God," who wills that his creatures should worship him and not make it their highest end to amuse themselves.

V. THAT LOVE OF FASHION MAY BE IDOLATRY. Vast numbers of persons who find no amusement in the pursuit, think it necessary to do whatever it is the fashion to do. Their life is a perpetual round of employments in which they have no pleasure, and which they have not chosen for themselves, but which the voice of fashion forces upon them. They drag themselves through exhibitions which do not interest them; lounge at clubs of which they are utterly weary; dine out when they would much rather be at home; and pass the evening and half the night in showing themselves at balls and assemblies which fatigue and disgust them. And all because Fashion says it is the correct thing. The idol, Fashion, has as many votaries in modern Europe as ever the Dea Syra had in Western Asia, or Isis in Egypt; and her votaries pass through life as real idolaters as the worshippers of the ancient goddesses, albeit unconscious ones.

SECTION XIV.—CHAPTER XXIV.

COMPLETION OF THE COVENANT, AND ASCENT OF MOSES INTO THE CLOUD ON SINAI.

EXPOSITION.

CHAPTER XXIV.

Vers. 1—8.—THE RATIFICATION OF THE COVENANT. The giving of the Book of the Covenant being now completed, Moses, having received directions with respect to another ascent into the mount (vers. 1, 2), descended to the people, and in the first instance declared to them the main heads of the Covenant, which they received with favour, and expressed their willingness to obey (ver. 3). Not, however, regarding this as a sufficiently formal ratification, the Prophet proceeded to write out in a "Book" the whole of the commands which he had received. He then built an altar, erected twelve pillars, offered sacrifice, and having collected half the blood of the victims in basins, summoned the people to an assembly. At this, he read over solemnly all the words of the Book to them, and received their solemn adherence to it (ver. 7); whereupon, to complete the ceremony, and mark their entrance into covenant, he sprinkled the blood from the basins on the twelve tribes, represented by their leaders, and declared the acceptance complete (ver. 8). The ceremony was probably modelled on some customary proceedings, whereby important contracts between man and man were ratified among the Hebrews and Syrians.

Vers. 1, 2.—It has been supposed that these verses are out of place, and suggested to remove them to the end of verse 8. But no change is necessary. It is quite natural that God should have given the directions before Moses descended from the mount, and that he should have deferred executing them until the people had accepted the covenant. **Nadab and Abihu** were the two eldest of Aaron's sons, and so his natural successors in the priesthood, had they not sinned by offering "strange fire" (Lev. x. 1, 2). They had been mentioned previously, in ch. vi. 23. **Seventy of the elders.** On the elders of Israel, see ch. iii. 16, and xviii. 21. The "seventy" elders may, together with Nadab and Abihu, have represented the twelve tribes, six from each. **Worship ye afar off.** Though all were to ascend the mount to a certain height, only Moses was to go to the top. The others, being less holy than Moses, had to worship at a distance.

Ver. 3.—**And Moses came.** Moses descended from the mount, and reported to the people **all the words of the Lord**—all the legislation contained in the last three chapters and a half (ch. xx. 19, to ch. xxiii. 33), not perhaps *in extenso*, but as to its main provisions. **And all the people answered with one voice**, promising obedience. In times of excitement, a common impulse constantly animates an entire multitude, and an exaltation of feeling leads them to make pledges, which they are very unwilling to stand by afterwards. Hence Moses requires something more than a verbal assent.

Ver. 4.—**Moses wrote all the words of the Lord.** We may presume that they were miraculously brought to his remembrance by that Spirit of Truth which guided all the Prophets (2 Pet. i. 21 ; John xiv. 26). Having written the words, he waited till the next day, and then **rose up early and builded an altar**, in preparation for the sacrifice without which no covenant was regarded as binding. **And twelve pillars.** Symbolical of the twelve tribes. Compare Josh. iv. 3, 9, 20.

Ver. 5.—**And he sent young men.** The Levitical priesthood not being as yet instituted, either all the people were regarded as holy, and so any one might offer sacrifice, or the " young men" selected may have been of the number of the first-born, who were priests in their respective families until the appointment of Aaron and his sons to be priests of the nation (ch. xxviii. 1). No doubt young men were selected as most competent to deal with struggling animals.

Ver. 6.—**Moses took half of the blood.** The blood, which symbolised the life of the victim, was the essential part of every sacrifice, and was usually poured over the altar, or at any rate sprinkled upon it, as the very crowning act of offering. (See Lev. i. 5 ; iii. 8 ; etc.) On this occasion Moses retained half of the blood, **and put it in basins,** for the purpose of so uniting all the people in the sacrifice, and thereby the more solemnly pledging them to the covenant, which the sacrifice at once consecrated and consummated. (See Heb. ix. 18—20.) The other **half of the blood** was, according to the usual practice, **sprinkled upon the altar.**

Ver. 7.—**And he took the Book of the Covenant.** In this book we have the germ of the Holy Scriptures—the first " book " actually mentioned as written in the narrative of the Bible. Genesis may contain other older documents, inserted by Moses, under the sanction of the Holy Spirit, in his compilation. But his own composition, if we except the burst of poesy called forth by the passage of the Red Sea (ch. xv. 1—18), would seem to have commenced with " the Book of the Covenant." Upon this nucleus the rest of the law was based ; and it was to explain and enforce the law that Moses composed the Pentateuch. **In the audience of the people.** Literally, " in the ears of the people," which is equally intelligible, and more graphic. **And they said,** etc The people made the same answer as before (ver. 3), adding a general promise of obedience to all that God might command in future.

Ver. 8.—Moses then proceeded to the final act—He took the blood from the basins, **and sprinkled it**—not certainly upon all the people, who numbered above two millions—but upon their leaders and representatives, the " elders " and other chief men, drawn up at the head of each tribe, and thus brought within his reach. It has been supposed by some that he merely sprinkled the blood on the twelve pillars, as representing the twelve tribes ; but, had this been the case, the expression in the text would probably have been different. We read, in the Epistle to the Hebrews, that he " sprinkled both the book, and *all the people* " (Heb. ix. 19). As he sprinkled, he said, **Behold the blood of the covenant,** etc. It was a common practice among the nations of antiquity to seal covenants with blood. Sometimes the blood was that of a victim, and the two parties to the covenant prayed, that, if they broke it, his fate might be theirs (Hom. *Il.* iii. 298 ; xix. 252 ; Lev. i. 24 ; xxi. 45 ; etc.). Sometimes it was the blood of the two parties themselves, who each drank of the other's blood, and thereby contracted a blood-relationship, which would have made their breaking the covenant more unpardonable (Herod. i. 74 ; iv. 70 ; Tacit. *Ann.* xii. 47). Moses seems to have followed neither practice at all closely, but, adopting simply the principle that a covenant required to be sealed with blood, to have arranged the details as he thought best. By the sprinkling of both the altar and the people the two parties to the covenant were made partakers of one and the same blood, and so brought into a sort of sacramental union.

HOMILETICS.

Vers. 3—8.—*Man's readiness to enter into covenant with God, and promise unlimited obedience.* In any covenant which God proposes to man, the advantages offered to him are so great, and the requirements made of him so manifestly " holy, just, and good," that it is almost impossible that he should calmly consider the terms and reject them. It is his natural instinct to exclaim—" All that the Lord hath said I will do, and be obedient." There are many reasons for this feeling, of which the following are some :—

I. THE CREATURE IS MORALLY BOUND TO OBEY ITS CREATOR. That which an intelligent agent has made belongs to him absolutely, and cannot resist his will without rebellion. Now, " it is God that has made us, and not we ourselves." We are his, whether we choose to obey him or no—his to punish or reward—to kill or make alive—to exalt to happiness or condemn to misery. We cannot resist his will without being self-condemned. The reasons which make disobedience to a father morally wrong tell with increased force if applied to God, who is far more truly than our father,—1. The author of our existence; 2, The preserver of our life; and 3, The bestower upon us of favours and benefits which we cannot possibly repay.

II. MAN'S BEST INTERESTS ARE PROMOTED BY A PERFECT OBEDIENCE. Every law ever imposed by God on man has been imposed for man's sake, and tends to his advantage. If a man were truly wise, he would lay down for himself as rules of conduct exactly those laws which are laid down for his guidance in Holy Scripture. The man whose obedience approaches nearest to perfection is the happiest. For every act of disobedience there is a natural penalty.

III. THE HIGHEST ASPIRATION OF MAN'S NATURE IS TO DO GOD'S WILL. Angels have no other desire but this. Man has a thousand desires, but, together with them, has an inward conviction that it is better for him to resist than to gratify the greater number. His passions draw him one way, his reason another, his affections, perhaps, a third. He has no unmixed satisfaction but in following the lead of the highest principle within him; and this principle is the love of God, which prompts him to make it the sole object of his life to please God by so acting as God would have him. Man, therefore, readily promises obedience—as of old at Sinai, so now at baptism and confirmation, or, again, after a sudden conversion; and, under the excitation of stirred feelings and an awakened conscience, imagines that he will keep to his brave resolve; but when the excitement is past, and the feelings have calmed down, and the tame, dull course of ordinary life is entered upon, then it is found not so easy to observe the promises made, and "do all that the Lord has said, and be obedient." The flagrant contrast between the conduct of the Israelites and their words is known to all. The contrast is, perhaps, less, but it is still great, between the pledges given by Christians and their acts. Performance ever lags far behind promise. "The spirit, indeed, is willing, but the flesh is weak." Temptations assail—Satan spreads his wiles—the lower nature turns traitor, and men fall away. Happy, if, while there is still time, they "return and repent, and do the first works," and casting themselves upon Christ obtain pardon for their disobedience from the ever-merciful God.

HOMILIES BY VARIOUS AUTHORS.

Vers. 1—2, 9—11.—*The vision of God for the selected few.* I. THOSE SELECTED FOR THIS VISION. That Moses himself went up was a matter of course. It was good for him to be there for the strengthening of his own faith. He himself would rejoice in the assurance thus given that the promise of the people was accepted. As to those who went up with him, it is clear that in the revelation something was being done to prepare them for official positions afterwards. They got this glorious sight not because they deserved it more than others, but because they needed it more. Moses required helps in order that he might be a mediator between God and the whole nation, and so these men, the seventy elders in particular, needed help in acting as mediators between Moses and the people. Doubtless it was intended that they should go down again among the people and be witnesses as to what they had seen. Would it not give an elder greater influence in after days if the people took knowledge of him that he had been with Moses in the mount? Notice, that in spite of this great revelation, Aaron soon fell away into the great transgression of the golden calf, and a little later Nadab and Abihu perished before the Lord for their disobedience. And may we not say that their sin was all the greater, just because they had been favoured with a privilege which they had failed to profit by?

II. THE VISION ITSELF. "They saw the God of Israel." There is a mysterious yet most instructive reticence as to exactly what it was that they saw. As to what shape and form were seen nothing is said; and even concerning the circumstances nothing more is ventured than an indication of the sapphire work on which he stood. And since we find this reticence of description it behoves us to put corresponding restraint on our conjectures: we may infer that the purpose of this vision was to give a plain and encouraging contrast between what was now seen and what had been seen before. When God's people are at peace with him—and there was a symbolic peace at this time—then there is a cessation of such terrorising manifestations as we read of in ch. xix. When we see all that strange mingling of terrible darkness, light, and sound, which make up the thunderstorm, we know that Nature is striving to recover her balance. That balance recovered, the body of heaven resumes its clearness; nay it often appears in even more than its accustomed beauty. All the dark and frowning appearances of God, all things that shake and confuse the soul, are meant to lead on to a calming and attracting revelation of God such as this revelation to Aaron and his companions but feebly typifies. First, the presence of God is made known amid thunder, lightning and smoke, and everything trembles to its centre at but the touch of his feet: then there is the change to where he is lifted clean above the polluting earth. Instead of disturbance there is unruffled peace, the beauty and profundity of the cloudless heaven. Thus by this outward symbol should we think of the quiet, untroubled heart where dwells the reconciled God. The more complete that reconciliation, the more settled the peace which we have with God, the more may the state of our hearts be indicated by the language which is here employed.

III. THE EXPERIENCES OF THIS CHOSEN COMPANY DURING THE VISION. 1. *They were made to feel unmistakably God's benignity towards them.* He did not lay his hand upon them. That they were not swiftly stretched in death upon the mountain side is spoken of as if in itself a subject of congratulation. The negative must come before the positive. The thought of complete salvation from danger must precede the thought of positive growth and enrichment. It was scarcely credible that men should see God and live. How dependent we are for our conclusions on narrow experiences, sometimes on most superstitious fears! The day is coming when, if we only accept all purifying ministrations, we shall not only see God and live, but also wonder that so long we should have been able to live without seeing him. 2. *This benignity is particularly experienced in their being allowed to eat and drink before God.* It is in the companionship of the table that social intercourse is commonly supposed to reach its perfection. This eating and drinking before God indicated that a certain composure of mind had been attained, and that the company had some real enjoyment of the position in which it was placed. There is a setting forth of the Divine blessing which ever rests on true fellowship of the saints. As many as are right with God personally are drawn together for united enjoyment as well as for united service. There is no place where the hearts of men are really one but when they are gathered before him who has the sapphire work under his feet. There, and there only, do we find the secret of that penetrating harmony which dissolves and utterly destroys all discords.—Y.

Vers. 3—8.—*The terms of the covenant accepted.* I. OBSERVE HOW CLEARLY THESE TERMS HAD BEEN STATED. Moses came and told the people all the words of the Lord and all the judgments. All the way to Sinai the people had the opportunity of seeing the *power* of Jehovah; at Sinai something of his *glory* had been manifested; and now in these words and judgments the *character* and will of Jehovah were made known. It is observable that at their first approach to Sinai the people had expressed their willingness to be obedient to God (ch. xix. 8). But he does not seek to bind them down by a formal contract until he has made clear the laws under which he would have them to live. It is well for us to bear in mind that God distinctly and emphatically states all things of practical and present importance. We indeed may have a very imperfect understanding of his statements; but the statements in themselves are perfectly plain, only requiring that our minds should be brought into a right state of humility, and concentrated upon the study of God's holy commandments with the requisite degree of attention.

II. OBSERVE ALSO THE WAY IN WHICH THESE TERMS HAD BEEN ACCEPTED. The people answered with one voice. There was a remarkable unanimity. Are we to take it that there was a complete, universal, cordial shout of acceptance? There is no reason to suppose otherwise, no reason to suppose but that a profound impression had been made on every mind. Not the slightest word appears to indicate discord. But of course, although there was no discord in the expression, there was great diversity in the state of mind which underlay the shout of acceptance. The emotion finding vent in this unanimous acceptance could be traced back in a few instances to a thoroughly awakened conscience, desiring to live a thoroughly righteous life, and be in true and complete conformity to the will of God; for there were men of David's spirit long before David's time. But in how many was there nothing more than the inconsiderate shout of those who, after all God had said, had yet not the slightest knowledge of his will! And yet with all these profound differences the superficial enthusiastic agreement evidently served a purpose. For not only was there a word, but also a highly significant and impressive deed. Notice that all the preparations in the way of altar, pillars, offerings, etc., made so carefully by Moses, are not said to have been made by God's commandment. The most we can say is, that they were not out of harmony with his will. They were a visible representation, a kind of writing out of the great contract into which the people thus entered. There stood the altar signifying the presence of God, and there the pillars signifying the twelve tribes, and there was the blood with its principle of life joining together, in a glorious unity, Jehovah and his people. The great and lamentable differences underneath are neither forgotten nor underrated; but for the time they are not regarded. The unity of feeling thus secured was made to serve a great symbolic purpose. These people, by word and deed, by the erection of these pillars, and by the acceptance of the sprinkled blood, took part in a great historic act, and declared that they were the people of God in a way the consequences of which they could not afterwards escape.

iII. Observe this very remarkable thing—THAT GOD SHOULD HAVE ACCEPTED THEIR ACCEPTANCE. He knew how much and how little it meant, and yet he did not point out the rashness of the utterance, he did not interfere with the symbolic actions by which Moses more deliberately set forth the adhesion of the people. We are bound, therefore, to conclude that in whatever ignorance and sudden enthusiasm the people might subscribe to this covenant, yet that subscription was right. The laws that God gave from Sinai are the laws for men to live by. The constitution of God's kingdom was by this great symbolic act solemnly introduced into Israel, and made the constitution of Israel also. Every nation, if it is to be anything more than a mere crowd, must have a constitution. Some constitutions grow, and like all things that grow, they occasionally branch out in unexpected directions. Other constitutions, men meet together to determine and formulate, like that of the American republic. But here is a constitution which comes down out of heaven from God; and in a great historic act, the nation into which it comes accepts it. Hence those born under that constitution were bound to accept it also. There was no nation on the face of the earth that had such securities, privileges, and prospects as Israel had under these laws from Sinai. The government was neither a despotism nor a democracy. The people were neither under an arbitrary will which might capriciously change, nor did they depend upon their own fluctuating opinions. God, if we might use such an expression, was bound by these laws, even as the people were themselves.—Y.

Vers. 4.—"*If any man will do the will he shall know of the doctrine.*" What a man receives must depend upon what he is able to receive. [Illustration. The sponge absorbs more water than the wood, because its pores are more open.] To receive the light of revelation the spiritual pores must be well opened; and this depends upon inward conditions—the will to obey, followed by obedience. Here a revelation is impending. Notice—

I. READINESS OF THE WOULD-BE RECIPIENTS. Moses had declared the Divine will. The hearers might have been indifferent, or they might have been disheartened by the stringency of the injunctions. In either case, through their imperfect condition, more perfect light must have been delayed. For a little, however, they were rapt out of self; and though, it may be, the momentary enthusiasm did not pierce clouds which years only could disperse, yet they were ready for the moment to gain a glimpse, at any rate, of the Divine glory. "All the words which the Lord hath said will we do:" such was the utterance of the people's disposition at the moment. Temporary inclination, however, is not everything; at best it only marks out the way along which effort may compel habit. For a nation to speak with "one voice" is something; but it needs discipline and training to secure the "one heart" as well. The first step towards securing this has next to be taken:—

II. READINESS CONFIRMED AND ACCEPTED. A record needed to impress the memory; a sacramental symbol to impress the imagination. 1. *The record.* "Moses wrote all the words of the Lord," and, when he had read what he had written, the people confirmed their previous promise (ver. 7). A written reminder of the covenant as accepted by them was all-important; a dying enthusiasm goes hand in hand with a waning memory; only a record which will revive the memory can avail to rekindle the enthusiasm. Our own experience illustrates this. The diary, the marked Bible—what a suggestive eloquence they have, not only to remind of old times, but to re-awaken old feelings! 2. *The sacramental symbol.* Burnt-offerings, the outward sign of dedication and obedience; peace offerings, the outward sign of gratitude and thanksgiving. Half the blood sprinkled on the people and half on the altar, symbol of the union between man and God so long as his commands were thankfully obeyed. So long as man is in the flesh he needs such sensible and visible emblems. His senses are a function of himself; to lay hold of them is to lay hold of him through them. The Bible is our record of what God requires of us; but baptism and the Lord's Supper give outward expression to the teaching of the Bible. Each confirms the influence of the other; we need both to support our resolutions.

III. THE PARTIAL REVELATION. The people had expressed their willingness to obey; and, further, they had openly confirmed that expression. Time, however, was needed to test and strengthen their resolution: they could not be admitted to the full blaze of light merely because, in partial darkness, they had for a little gazed towards its dawning. A few are selected to represent the multitude (vers. 1, 9—11); and even of these few, not all are admitted to equal nearness. Enough is revealed to help faith, more would probably have only injured its growth. [Illustration: Plants are kept from too much light until they are firmly rooted.] Faith, here, needed *rooting:* until that was accomplished an economy of reserve was necessary.

Concluding considerations.—1. The honest promise of obedience is accepted by God as of moral value. He encourages sincerity by glimpses of the reward in store. 2. Only obedience tested by difficulty can win the realisation of the beatific vision. The people must share the life-long training of Moses before they can enjoy with the like freedom his privilege of intimacy with God. Willingness to obey brings knowledge; but full knowledge comes with full obedience.—G.

Vers. 3—9.—*The ratification of the covenant.* These verses contain the account of the formal ratification of the covenant between Israel and Jehovah—an event, the most momentous in the history of the nation, big, for weal or woe, with unimaginable issues, and a shadow of the better covenant which God now makes with Christians. Observe—

I. THE RATIONALITY OF THE COVENANT. God desires from his people "reasonable service" (Rom. xii. 1). He would not have them enter it in haste. Vows made under the influence of sudden impressions are not to be trusted. Once committed to his service, God will deal with us with strictness (ch. xxiii. 21). But he does not wish us to commit ourselves till we have carefully considered the nature of the step we are taking, and the magnitude of the issues involved (cf. Luke xiv. 26—34). See this illustrated in the history of the covenant with Israel. The covenant was entered into— 1. *With great deliberation.* It was not forced on Israel. The negotiations connected with it were intentionally drawn out and prolonged, just that the people might have the opportunity of pondering well the character of the proposed engagement. Alike in the events of the exodus, and in the miracles of the desert, they had had abundant experience of the character of the Being with whom they were allying themselves. Arrived at Sinai, preliminary proposals were made to them, and an opportunity given them at the outset of saying Yea or Nay (ch. xix. 3—9). Their acceptance of these proposals was followed by the giving of the law, which drew from them a new promise to do whatever God should speak to them (ch. xx. 19; Deut. v. 27). An interval ensued, during which Moses was in the mountain (ch. xx. 21). On descending, he recites to them "All the words of the Lord, and all the judgments" (ver. 3); and once again they promise full obedience. Even then the matter is allowed to stand over till the morrow, when Moses appears with the written book in his hand, and they are asked, finally, if they adhere to what they have said (ver. 7). Greater precautions against rash committal could scarcely have been taken. 2. *After careful instruction.* Pains were taken fully to inform the people of the terms of the covenant, before asking them to enter into it. The law was uttered by God's own voice. The "judgments" were recited to them by Moses. They were read a second time from the "book." Their assent to the covenant was thus sought to be made an intelligent one. If we engage ourselves to God, he would have us do it with "understanding." 3. *Amidst impressive solemnities.* These—the reading of the words from the book, the sprinkling of the blood, etc.—were of a nature adapted to arouse the minds of the people to a just sense of the momentousness of the transaction. From the whole we learn that if dedication is the result of an act, it should be of a calm, sober, thoughtful act; it cannot be done too solemnly or too intelligently. Our religious life should have a rational basis.

II. THE BOND OF THE COVENANT. The nucleus of the transaction is the people's promise—"All the words which the Lord hath said will we do" (ver. 3)—"All that the Lord hath said will we do, and be obedient" (ver. 7). There is a tone of rashness—of self-confidence—in this promise, as given by Israel, which forewarns of subsequent defection. The people evidently had but little knowledge of their own hearts. They had little perception of the spiritual requirements of this law. They had not learned to distrust themselves. Their surrender to the Divine will was not thorough or heart-whole. (See on ch. xix. 8.) It remains true, however, that surrender of the will to God, in the spirit of obedience, is an indispensable condition of being received into covenant with him. "The idea of the servant of God is complete only when he who is bound to God also binds himself to God's will, following God perfectly." (Oehler.) This is as true of the Gospel as of the law. The obedient will is implicit in faith. The end contemplated in salvation is obedience. We are made free from sin that we may become servants of righteousness (Rom. vi. 18). The recognition of this—the acceptance of the obligation—is involved in conversion, in saving faith, in the new birth, in the coming to Christ, or however else we may express the change from death to life. If we no longer speak of the promise of obedience as the "bond" of the covenant, it is only because that which the Gospel primarily demands of us, viz. faith, goes deeper than such a promise, while implicitly containing it. The object of spiritual trust is, ulti-mately, God himself, and in the Gospel, Christ, as the sent of God to be the Saviour of the world; but such trust invariably involves the yielding up of the will to God, and is on its practical side, an energy of holiness. The true believer is, of necessity, a doer of the will of the Father. "Faith, without works, is dead" (James ii. 17—26). (See further, on ch. xix. 5.) It is, however, well that this *implicit* element in faith should also be allowed to become *explicit* in distinct acts of consecration or of self-dedication to God. This brings us very near to what we have in this covenant with Israel. See below.

III. THE CEREMONIAL OF RATIFICATION. (1) Moses "builded an altar under the hill, and twelve pillars, according to the twelve tribes of Israel" (ver. 4). (2) Young men of his appointment sacrificed burnt-offerings and peace-offerings unto the Lord (ver. 5). (3) The blood of the sacrificed animals was divided: half was put in basins, and half sprinkled on the altar (ver. 6). (4) The words of the book of the Covenant were next solemnly read in the audience of the people; and the latter renewed their assent to them (ver. 7). (5) The blood was then cast upon the people out of the basins, and the Covenant was declared to be concluded (ver. 8). Two points here claim our attention. 1. The ratifying of the Covenant with sacrifice; and 2. The action with the blood. Both were significant. 1. *The sacrifices.* The burnt-offering was primarily a symbol of self-surrender (cf. Ps. li. 16—19). The idea embodied here, therefore, was, that in the institution of the Covenant, what was required was the unconditional sur-render of the offerer, with all that belonged to him, to God. The peace-offering sym-bolises reconciliation and fellowship. But the offering of the sacrifices had also a propitiatory reference. This is plain from the sprinkling of the blood on the altar. It is sprinkled there as atoning for the people's sins. It was through the blood of propi-tiation that peace was made, that reconciliation was brought about. This teaches several things. It shows (1) That Israel was viewed by God as sinful. (2) That it was not on legal grounds, but as an act of grace, that they were being admitted into covenant. (3) That the covenant embodied grace as well as law. (4) That God would deal graciously with Israel, if they sincerely *endeavoured* to keep his law, not-withstanding many defects and failures. (5) That their attitude under the law, in seeking to fulfil its righteousness, ought to be an evangelical, not a legal one, *i.e.*, they ought to draw their motives, their encouragement, and their hope, not from the thought of their self-sufficiency to keep the law, or from the idea that they were actually keeping it in such a way as legally to entitle them to the blessing, but from the conviction of God's mercy to them, which, as it was the *foundation* of their national existence, so was it the real ground of their standing all along. 2. *The sprinkling of the blood on the people.* It is, as Keil remarks, the *one* blood which is sprinkled on the altar and on the people; and it is not sprinkled on the people, till it has been presented and accepted on the altar. Applied to the people, the blood had the effect of formally cleansing them from sin, and of consecrating them to God's service. God thereafter claimed them as his special property. Redeemed life is his. Made free from sin, we become servants of God (Rom. vi. 22).—J. O.

Vers. 7, 8.—*Consecration.* By the sprinkling of the blood of sacrifice, and by their voluntary acceptance of obligations to obedience, the children of Israel became, formally, the people of Jehovah. They had avouched themselves to be the Lord's. They had taken on them the vows of his service. They were now consecrated to be doers of his will. The same idea of consecration is embodied in the New Testament word "saint." The believer is one of a sanctified, a consecrated, a priestly people, set specially apart "to offer up spiritual sacrifices acceptable to God by Jesus Christ" (1 Pet. ii. 5). Consider—

I. THE NATURE OF CONSECRATION. Consecration, as a Christian duty, involves three ideas—separation from evil, devotement to God, and ceaseless pursuit of holiness in heart and life. It has its ground in the fact of redemption, and in the sense of God's mercies. The consecrated heart then becomes a sanctuary in which God dwells by his Holy Spirit; while this sacred indwelling in turn becomes a new source of obligations to holiness. The holiness we are to aim at is a holiness like God's own—nothing lower (1 Pet. i. 15, 16). Consecration, if never so complete as the Christian could wish, may always be perfect, at least in aim, in spirit, in intention, in desire. We are expected, like Caleb, to follow the Lord *fully*. The Divine ideal is the absolute consecration of him who said—" Lo, I come to do thy will, O God." "My meat is to do the will of him that sent me, and to finish his work" (Heb. x. 9; John iv. 34). "I would rather," says Spurgeon, "my child had a perfect copy to write by, though he might never equal it, than that he should have an imperfect copy set before him, because then he would never make a good writer at all." The Scriptural idea of consecration comes out in the light of the usage of the cognate word—"sanctify." God himself is the fountain of sanctity or holiness. The whole Mosaic ritual was a grand apparatus for impressing this thought of God's holiness upon the minds of his worshippers. Everything to be used in his service, as contaminated by sin, required to be purged with blood (Heb. ix. 21). To this, in special cases, succeeded an anointing with oil (ch. xxx. 25—32). Thus purged and anointed, the sanctuary, person, sacred vessel, or whatever it might be, was regarded as completely sanctified; in other words, as separated from common uses to the service of a holy God. The High Priests and Levites of the Old Covenant were all thus specially sanctified to God. But these things were only shadows; we have the realities corresponding to them under the New Covenant. If a man is really in Christ, he is already, by God's act, through the sprinkling of the blood of Jesus Christ, and the holy anointing of the Spirit, a consecrated person, and ought to regard himself as such. This is the Divine side of the matter. There is clearly, however, a vast difference between the consecration of a mere utensil, say the golden candlestick, or the pots and vessels of the sanctuary, and the consecration of a living, moral, intelligent being. A material thing is sanctified simply by the act of setting it apart to sacred uses; its nature admits of nothing more. But the consecration of a moral being implies an act on his own part, as well as on God's, else the consecration has no reality; it is such only in name and form. The essence of it lies in a free, cheerful, *self*-dedication of the person (cf. Rom. xii. 1). Here, then, are two sides of this subject, the Divine and human—the ideal and the real—which two sides are constantly reappearing in Scripture, sometimes apart, sometimes blending together, sometimes standing side by side, almost with the force of contradictions, *e.g.,* "Purge out therefore the old leaven, that ye may be a new lump, *even as ye are unleavened*" (1 Cor. v. 7). In short, God's consecration gives us a standing and an ideal; but it is only as we consciously accept this standing and ideal as our own, and seek to give them reality by *self*-dedication, and the strenuous pursuit of holiness, that our consecration becomes truly effectual.   God's consecration of us becomes, so to speak, the ground of our own consecration of ourselves, and of constant striving after that perfection which is implied in the ideal he sets before us. Hence all those manifold Scripture images which imply sanctification as a *process*, and a work of God's grace constantly going on within us.

II. ADVANTAGES OF CONSECRATION. We come back to the old point that consecration, regarded as a duty, is a personal act whereby, out of a sense of God's mercies, and specially his grace in redemption, a believer solemnly dedicates himself and all that he has to the service and glory of God.   Such consecration, with the surrender of the obedient will, is already, as seen in the previous homily, implicit in every exercise of saving faith.   Great moral advantages, however, accrue from making one's consecration to Christ a distinct solemn act, again and again to be repeated, each time, we shall hope, with more perfect self-surrender;   and the remembrance of which is to go along with us in the discharge of every duty.   This corresponds pretty nearly to the meaning of the Israelitish covenant.

Consecration is *the basis of acceptable service*.   (1) Consecration of self *precedes* all other consecrations; as of time, substance, talents, service, etc.   It is only where self is consecrated, that the consecration of anything else is acceptable.   What St. Paul says of charity, that without it all special gifts and acts, even feeding the poor, or giving his body to be burned, are valueless, we may say with equal truth of self-dedication. It is *self* God wants—the love, reverence, devotion, service of self; not a mere share of self's possessions.   On the other hand (2), the consecration of self *includes* all other consecrations.   If we are God's, then all is God's that is ours.   Our time is God's; so is our money, our talents, our influence, everything we have.   Let Christians ask, whether, in this view of the matter, consecration is in their case being carried out into all its legitimate results.   Not that God desires "a gift;" but he desires "fruit that may abound to our account" (Phil. iv. 17).

Consecration secures nobler service; it is likewise *a source of immense strength in the active pursuit of holiness*.   In any course of conduct, we know the value of a definite purpose and aim.   Most of all is it important to have as the clear, definite motto of our lives—"To me to live is Christ."   We know then exactly what we are living for. Consecration invests a man's whole being with a sanctity from which evil shrinks back repelled.   The same sanctity spreads itself over all he has and does.   He feels that he must be holy " in *all* manner of conversation."   Even on the bells of his horses he sees something written, "holiness to the Lord."   He has " holy garments;" and his great business is to watch and keep his garments, lest he walk naked, and they see his shame (Rev. xvi. 15).   His body is the temple of the Holy Ghost; and he dare not desecrate with worldly pollutions the place where God dwells.   He has definitely separated himself from evil; and he must not return to it.

Consecration *resolves questions of casuistry*.   How often do we find good people, or people who wish to be good, puzzling and perplexing themselves with questions of this kind—Dare I read this book?   Should I go to this party?   May I engage in this amusement?   Can I take this profit?   Unless we greatly mistake, most of these difficulties would disappear with more perfect consecration.   A truly consecrated man carries in his breast a principle which easily guides him through all such cases, and makes many things right and pure to him which others would stumble at, while it leads him to discountenance and condemn much that they would pass unnoticed.

Finally, consecration is *absolutely essential to success in prayer*.   The heart that has not said—" All for Christ," is in no fit state to approach God's throne to supplicate blessings for Christ's sake.   There must be iniquity hidden away in that heart somewhere; and "if I regard iniquity in my heart, the Lord will not hear me" (Ps. lxvi. 18).   But the consecrated man, as a true priest of God, has free access to the holiest of all.   He asks what he will, and it is given him.   Prayer, indeed, is no prayer, unless it is the outcome of a heart which is the seat of deep consecration, and where the Lord is *habitually* sanctified.   Only to such prayer are the promises yea and amen.

From all this, it is manifest that consecration pertains to the deepest essence of religion.   Yet many feel as if sometimes they could almost close with Christ, were it not for this very matter of consecration.   Their hearts are still clinging to something which God requires them to forego; and clinging to this, they rightly judge that they cannot be Christ's disciples.   Let them reflect that for this something they sacrifice eternal life.—J. O.

Vers. 1, 2, 9—11.—*The Covenant made.*   1. THE VISION OF GOD (1, 2, 9, 11).—1. It is for the called alone.   God manifests himself only to the repentant and the believing. 2. These are commanded to approach.   This is our warrant for confident boldness of access: he has called us.   3. The vision is bestowed upon those from whose midst the mediator has gone into God's immediate presence and who wait his return (ver. 2). 4. It is given as they go upwards into the mount where the Lord's will is declared (9). The heart which seeks after holiness admits the light in which God will by-and-by be manifested.   5. The vision is sure: "they saw the God of Israel."   6. For the called the vision of God is not destruction, but safety and joy.   We meet the unveiling, not only of infinite holiness, but also of infinite love.   The vision of the Divine glory was a wonder and delight; and the place of vision became a place of feasting.

II. THE RATIFYING OF THE COVENANT.—1. It was made with a willing people: "all the words which the Lord hath said will we do."   2. It was made with a people who were in possession of God's testimonies: he "told them all the words of the law," he "wrote all the words of the Lord."   God's light must reveal sin and need before it may manifest his salvation.   3. God and his people are bound together by the blood of accepted sacrifice.   The blood of sprinkling is peace and power to the saved.—U.

EXPOSITION.

Vers. 9—11.—THE SACRIFICIAL FEAST AND THE VISION OF GOD.   After the covenant had been ratified by the unanimous voice of the people, Moses proceeded to carry out the injunctions with respect to Aaron, Nadab, Abihu, and the elders, which he had received while still in the mount (see the comment on vers. 1, 2). Taking them with him, he ascended Sinai once more to a certain height, but clearly not to the summit, which he alone was privileged to visit (vers. 2 and 12).   The object of the ascent was twofold.   1. A sacrificial meal always followed upon a sacrifice; and the elders might naturally desire to partake of it as near the Divine presence as should be permitted them.   This was their purpose in ascending.   2. God desired to impress them with a sense of his awful majesty and beauty, and was prepared for this end to manifest himself to them in some strange and wonderful way as they were engaged in the solemn meal (ver. 11).   This was his purpose in inviting their presence.   The manifestation is described in ver. 10.   It was a "vision of God," but of what exact nature it is impossible to say.   Having recorded it, the author parenthetically notes that the Divine vision did not destroy any of those who beheld it, or cause them any injury, as might have been expected.

Ver. 9.—**Then went up.**   Compare ver. 1.

The mountain was to be partially ascended, but not to any great height.   Nadab, Abihu, and the elders were to "worship God *afar off.*"

Ver. 10.—**They saw the God of Israel.** These words can scarcely mean less than that they saw with their bodily eyes some appearance of the Divine being who had summoned them to his presence for the purpose.   Moses, we know, saw a "similitude of God" (Num. xii. 8).   Isaiah "saw the Lord sitting upon his throne " (Is. vi. 1).   Ezekiel saw upon the throne "the appearance of a man " (Ezek. i. 26).   It does not follow from Deut. iv. 12, 15, that *the elders* saw no similitude, since in that passage Moses is speaking, not to the elders, but to the people, and referring, not to what occurred at the sacrificial feast after the ratification of the covenant, but to the scene at the giving of the Ten Commandments previously (ch. xx. 1—18).   What the form was which the elders saw, we are not told; but as it had "feet," it was probably a human form.   It may have been hazy, indefinite, "too dazzling bright for mortal eye" to rest upon.   But it was a true "vision of God " —and, as Keil says, "a foretaste of the blessedness of the sight of God in eternity." **There was under his feet, as it were, a paved work of a sapphire stone.**   Rather, "and under his feet was, as it were, a work of clear sapphire."   Nothing is said concerning a pavement, but only that below the feet of the figure which they saw was something, which looked as if it were made of bright blue sapphire stone, something as clear and as blue as the blue of heaven.   Canon Cook supposes the actual sky to be meant; but the expression, " *as it were*, the body of heaven," or " *like* the very heaven," makes this impossible. A thing is not like itself.

Ver. 11.—**The nobles**—*i.e.*, the notables—the seventy elders, and other persons, already mentioned (vers. 1, 9). **He laid not his hand.** God did not smite them with death, or pestilence, or even blindness. It was thought to be impossible to see God and live. (See above, Gen. xxxii. 30; Ex. xxxii. 20; Judg. vi. 22, 23, etc.) Man was unworthy to draw near to God in any way; and to look on him

was viewed as a kind of profanity. Yet sometimes he chose to show himself, in vision or otherwise, to his people, and then, as there could be no guilt on their part, there was no punishment on his. It is generally supposed that, in all such cases, it was the Second Person of the Blessed Trinity who condescended to show himself. **Also they saw God.** Rather, " they both saw God, and did eat and drink." The two were simultaneous. As they were engaged in the sacrificial meal, God revealed himself to them.

HOMILETICS.

Vers. 9—11. *The Covenant Meal on Sinai.*—The Old Testament contains no mention of any other meal so wonderful as this. Newly entered into covenant with God, fresh from the blood of sprinkling, which was representative of the blood of Christ, Moses, Aaron with his two sons, and the seventy elders, half-way up Sinai, engaged in the sacrificial feast upon the peace-offerings (ver. 5), when lo! the heaven was opened to them, and there burst upon their astonished sight a vision of Jehovah in his glory and his beauty, standing on pellucid sapphire, dazzling in its brilliance. As the meat and drink entered their mouths, God shone in upon their souls. It was indeed a " wondrous festivity," and certainly not without a spiritual meaning, extending to all time, and even beyond time into eternity. Surely, we may say, without over-great boldness, or any undue prying into holy things :—

I. THAT THE MEAL WAS A TYPE OF THAT DIVINE FEAST WHICH THE LORD INSTITUTED ON THE NIGHT OF HIS BETRAYAL, FOR THE SUSTENTATION OF HIS PEOPLE. The Holy Communion is a feast upon a sacrifice—the sacrifice of Christ—partaken of by Christians as the most solemn rite of their religion, in the wilderness of this life, for their better sustentation and support through its trials. It brings them very near to him, as it were into his presence. As they partake of the bread and wine, they partake of him; his light shines into their souls; his beauty and glory are revealed to their spirits; they obtain a foretaste of heaven. Blessed is the man who thus eats and drinks in his kingdom—eating and drinking *and seeing God*.

II. THAT THE MEAL WAS, FURTHER, A TYPE OF THAT MARRIAGE-SUPPER OF THE LAMB, WHEREOF ALL THE FAITHFUL SHALL ONE DAY PARTAKE IN HEAVEN (Rev. xix. 7—9). There the saints shall eat and drink in the Divine presence, their meat the heavenly manna, angels' food, their drink the wine which they " drink new " in their Father's kingdom. The glory of God shall shine on them. For the place of their dwelling " has no need of the sun, neither of the moon to shine in it ; " for it is " the glory of God that lightens it, and the Lamb that is the light thereof " (*ib.* xxi. 23). The sapphire of Sinai has there its counterpart; for " the first foundation " of the city wherein they dwell " is jasper, and the second sapphire " (*ib.* 19). The Divine presence is with them perpetually ; for the " throne " of God is there, and they " see his face," and " his Name is in their foreheads " (*ib.* xxii. 4). Thrice blessed they who attain to this heavenly feast, and are counted worthy of that beatific vision !

HOMILIES BY VARIOUS AUTHORS.

Vers. 1, 2, 9—12. *A vision of God.*—Prior to the ratification of the covenant, God had given Moses instructions that, immediately on the conclusion of the ceremonies, he, together with Aaron, Nadab, and Abihu (representatives of the future priesthood), and seventy of the elders of Israel (representatives of the body of the people), should again ascend the mountain (vers. 1, 2). The design was to partake of a sacrificial feast, perhaps held on the flesh of the peace-offerings of ver. 5, by way of solemn conclusion to the proceedings of the day. Another part of the design was that the elders might receive a new revelation of Jehovah, setting forth the milder glories of his character as a God reconciled with Israel, in contradistinction to the manifestations on Sinai, which revealed him solely as the God of law and terror. The later revelation was the counterbalance of the earlier. It does that justice to the character of God, as standing in friendly relations to his people, which was not possible in harmony with the special design, and within the special limits, of the revelation from the summit of the mount. It showed him as the God of grace. It taught Israel to think of him, to love him, to trust him, and to worship him as such. It kept them from being overwhelmed by the remembrance of the former terrors. It forestalled that view of the graciousness of God which was afterwards peculiarly associated with the mercy-seat and with Mount Zion, and is now the aspect of his character predominant in the Gospel (see on Sinai and Zion, ch. xix. 16—19). We are told, accordingly, that when the company ascended the mount, "they saw the God of Israel" (ver. 10). What they did see is not further described than that "there was under his feet as it were a paved work of a sapphire stone, and as it were the body of heaven in his clearness" (ver. 10). The vision, however, was plainly one addressed to the outer or inner sense, an "appearance" of God in some recognisable way. So mild and beneficent was the spectacle, nevertheless, that it seems to have disarmed all terror; and Aaron and his sons, with the "nobles," ate and drank while still witnessing it. We may regard the vision, in its relation to the situation of Israel, as—1. *Declarative.* It gave a view of the character of God. (1) To some extent of his *essential* character. The blue of the sapphire symbolised his holiness, while in the deep, clear ether was mirrored his untroubled purity, his superiority to earthly passion and disturbance, his perfect blessedness, his transcendency over creation, etc. (2) More especially of his *gracious* character. The idea suggested was that of a God *at peace* with Israel—reconciled. The vision would be read in its contrast with the previous revelation. The terrors of the law-giving were now laid aside; all is sweetness, beauty, mildness, serenity, love. This vision of God as a God *at peace* with Israel, is mediated by the offering of sacrifice. It is so also under the Gospel. "God was *in Christ* reconciling the world unto himself" (2 Cor. v. 19). 2. *Symbolic of privilege.* (1) The "nobles," though in God's presence, suffered no harm. "Upon the nobles of the children of Israel he laid not his hand" (ver. 11). He *might* have done so, for they were by nature sinners. But they were safe, as sprinkled with blood of atonement, and as in presence of a God of mercy. Though sinners, we are permitted in Christ to draw nigh to God. He will not harm us; he will welcome, accept of, and bless us. (2) Though in God's presence, they "did eat and drink" (ver. 11). They had this freedom before him; this feeling of confidence. It is only the revelation of God as a God of grace which can inspire this confidence. Their eating and drinking was symbolical of the privilege of every pious Israelite, sheltered from his sin in God's mercy, and taking confidence from his word of grace. Much more is it symbolic of the privilege of Christians, in whom perfect love casts out fear (1 John iv. 18). 3. *Prefigurative of future blessedness.* The goal of the kingdom of God is the feast of perfected bliss in glory, where the saints shall eat and drink and see God with no intervening veils, and in the full beauty of his love and holiness. 4. A *warning.* These seventy elders ate and drank in God's presence, yet at last perished in the desert. Nadab and Abihu were consumed by fire. Cf. the warning (Luke xiii. 26, 27).

Lessons—1. The vision of God in Christ disarms fear. 2. Let us try to see God, even in our eating and drinking (1 Cor. x. 31). 3. Those sheltered by Christ's blood are safe. Note the following—"(1) There are those who eat and drink, and do not see God. (2) There are those who see God, and cannot eat and drink. (3) There are those who eat and drink, *and* see God" (Rev. W. B. Robertson, D.D.).—J. O.

EXPOSITION.

Vers. 12—18.—Moses' entry into the cloud, and forty days' commune with God. It was necessary now that Moses should receive full directions for the external worship of God, the sanctuary, and the priesthood. Every religion has something tangible and material about it—holy places, holy things, rites, ceremonies, rules, forms, regulations. If man sets himself to devise these things of his own head, he may very easily go wrong, and find his elaborate inventions "an offence" to God. To avoid this—to secure the result that all should be pleasing and acceptable to " the High and Holy One which inhabiteth eternity," it was thought fitting that " patterns " should be shown to Moses of all that was to be made for the worship (Heb. viii. 5), and exact details given him with respect to the material, size, shape, and construction of each. The results are put before us in seven chapters (chs. xxv.—xxxi.). For the purpose of allowing ample time for the communications which had to be made and of securing that un-divided attention which was requisite in order that all should remain fixed in the memory, God summoned his servant to a long and solitary colloquy, on the mountain summit whereon the cloud rested (ch. xix. 18), apart from all his people. Moses, of course, obeyed; but before ascending, arranged with the elders that in his absence Aaron and Hur should have the direction of affairs, and decide all doubtful questions (ver. 14). He then went up the mountain, accompanied for part of the way by Joshua, who is now spoken of as his "minister," or "attendant" (ver. 13). Joshua probably remained with him for six days, while Moses waited for a summons to enter the cloud. On the seventh day the summons came: and Moses, leaving Joshua, entered the cloud, and was hid from the sight of all men.

Ver. 12.—**Come up to me**. Moses, appa-rently, had descended again into the plain, with Aaron and the seventy elders, after the festival was over. (See ver. 14, and compare ch. xxxii. 1.) He is now commanded to reascend, **and be there**—i.e., "And continue there" —foreshadowing the length of the stay. **Tables of stone, and a law, and commandments**, etc. Literally, "Tables of stone, and the law and the commandments which I have written." The three expressions alike refer to the De-calogue, which alone God wrote. **That thou mayest teach them**. Rather, " to teach them." God wrote the commandments on stone, in order to inculcate them with the greater force upon his people.

Ver. 13.—**Moses went up**. Prompt to obey, Moses, though he had only just descended from the mount, immediately made ready to set forth and again ascend it. This time he was attended by **his minister, Joshua**, whose arm he had employed on a former occasion against the Amalekites (ch. xvii. 9—13). The name, Joshua, is, however, still given him by anticipation, since he did not receive it until he was sent by Moses to explore the land of Canaan (Num. xiii. 8, 16).

Ver 14.—**And he said unto the elders**.

Before taking his departure for the long sojourn implied in God's address to him, " Come up to me into the mount, and be there" (ver. 12), Moses thought it necessary to give certain directions to the elders as to what they should do in his absence—1. They were to remain where they were—i.e., in the plain at the foot of Sinai, until his return, however long it should be delayed. 2. They were to regard Aaron and Hur as their leaders, and his (Moses') representatives. In case of any difficulty arising, they were to refer the matter to them. On Hur see the comment upon ch. xvii. 12.

Ver. 15.—**Moses went up into the mount**. Having made the necessary arrangements for the government of the people during his absence, Moses ascended, in company with Joshua, to the upper part of the mountain, and there waited for some further summons. **A cloud**, or, rather, the cloud previously men-tioned (ch. xix. 16), stood gathered upon the highest eminence, and marked the special presence of God there. Moses, though called up into the mount, would not intrude into this inner sanctuary, until specially bidden to enter it.

Ver. 16. — Now occurred a remarkable pause. The summons had been given to Moses, and he had obeyed it. He was there on the platform a little below the summit, ready, but waiting for a further call. The call was not made for six days. A holy calm reigned upon Sinai—the cloud rested upon the summit, and in the cloud was **the glory of the Lord**. Moses and Joshua waited near—but for six days there was no sign. God thus taught Moses, and through him the world, that near approach to him requires long and careful preparation. Moses, no doubt, was occupied during the **six days** in continual prayer. At last, on **the seventh day**, the call, which Moses had expected, came. **God called unto Moses out of the midst of the cloud**. God summoned him to a closer approach—bade him enter the cloud— and draw as nigh to him as possible.

Ver. 17—Meanwhile, to those below in the plain, " the glory of the Lord " on the summit above them, was **like devouring fire on the top of the mount**. They had but to lift their eyes thither, and they saw his wonderful glory—showing like a huge fire—on the spot from which he had spoken to them (ch. xx. 18). This manifestation continued certainly for the first six days; whether it lasted longer or not is open to question.

Ver. 18.—**And Moses went into the midst of the cloud**. Quitting Joshua, Moses at last, in obedience to the call out of the midst of the cloud, entered within its shadow and dis-appeared from human vision In this ab-normal condition, alone with God, he con-tinued for thirty-four days, making, together with the six days before he entered the cloud, the **forty days and forty nights** of the text before us. It is noted in Deut. ix. 9, that during the whole of this time he was without food. Compare Elijah's fast (1 Kings xix. 8), and our blessed Lord's (Matt. iii. 2).

HOMILETICS.

Vers. 12—18.—*Prolonged commune with God.* Prolonged commune with God is the soul's truest strengthening, and sweetest refreshment. Without it our spirits languish— we grow weary and faint—worldliness creeps upon us—our thoughts and discourse become "of the earth, earthy"—we have no life or liveliness in ourselves, and can impart none to others. Moses' commune was abnormal, extraordinary, inimitable by us in its main features—its duration, locality, nearness of access, and completeness of isolation. But it may serve as a pattern to us in many respects, nevertheless.

I. IN THE PREPARATION FOR IT. Here we note (1) a ready heart. " Moses rose up"—did not delay, did not offer objections, did not say, " Suffer me first " to do this or that, but responded to the call of God *at once.* (2) A thoughtful regard for others. Moses instructed the elders how to act while he was away. "Tarry ye here "—" Seek ye to Aaron and Hur, if ye have matters to do." (3) A willingness to help others towards the higher life, to carry them on with him, as far as he might. "Moses rose up, *and his minister, Joshua.* (4) A patient and reverential waiting. Summoned, called up, bidden to draw near, he yet rested for six days outside the cloud, longing to enter in, but withheld by a sense of unworthiness and a fear of intrusion, fasting all the while, and seeking to prepare himself for the nearer approach by supplication and meditation.

II. IN THE PLACE OF IT. A holy place—"the mount of God"—a place sacred from common uses—into which worldly thoughts could scarcely penetrate. We, who have no Sinai, have at any rate our churches, and other sacred buildings—some of them always open, not merely for public worship, but for private prayer and meditation— inviting us to enter in and draw nigh to God. In our houses we have, or may easily have, our oratories—spots reserved for prayer and praise, and sacred thought—sanctuaries in the desert of life—places in which all that we see will remind us of heavenly things.

III. IN THE SECLUSION OF IT. The world was shut out. Relations, elders, people, left below in the plain—left with strict injunctions to remain—" Tarry ye here." Even the faithful Joshua parted from—and " the cloud " entered. The cloud—the awful cloud —" thick darkness" (ch. xx. 21); yet within the darkness a marvellous light. *Such* seclusion we cannot obtain—but we may obtain an approach to it. We may "enter our closet, and *shut to the door*" (Matt. vi. 6), and let it be known that we would be undisturbed; or we may seek the solitude of a church at an hour when there is no public service, and no one present who will meddle with us; or we may, even at the present day, find solitudes in nature, deep woods, or lone mountain tops, or unfrequented glens, where we may feel ourselves secure from intrusion, and stand face to face with God, and know him near, and pour out our hearts before him. A modern poet, in one of his better moments, says —

> " My altars are the mountains, and the ocean,
> Earth, air, sea—all that springs from the Great Whole,
> Who hath produced, and will receive the soul "—

and truly on any lone spot an altar may be raised, and worship offered, as acceptable to God as any that is addressed to him " in pillared fanes, 'neath fretted roofs, 'mid storied glass or sculptured monuments." Even in the whirl and bustle of a great city, solitude is not very far from us. Half an hour's journey by steamer or rail, and ten minutes' walk, may take us into still woods, or shady lanes, or on to open heaths, where we shall not see a fellow creature or hear a sound reminding us of man.

IV. IN THE CONTINUANCE OF IT. " Forty days and forty nights ! " As we cannot have the *complete* seclusion which Moses enjoyed, so neither can we look for such sustained commune as his. *We* must eat and drink—*we* can rarely leave our worldly work to others—family claims, correspondence, business imperatively require our attention—six weeks' interruption of communication between ourselves and the outer world would, in most cases, break or tangle all the threads of which our life is composed. But still some prolonged periods of religious contemplation and commune between the soul and God are needed, if the soul is to retain the vigour of its life, or its ability to be of service to others. With this view religious "retreats" have been devised, lasting sometimes a week or ten days. Where men's duties allow of it, they may be well worth a trial. The weary spirit may derive more refreshment from them than from the ordinary "holiday." The heart may be purified, the aspirations raised, the insight into doctrinal truth augmented, above all, the love of God so intensified in the soul, by the suspension of all secular thought and the devotion of the whole mind to religion and worship, during the three, or five, or seven, or ten days of a "retreat," as would scarcely be possible, under the present conditions of our life, in any other way.

HOMILIES BY VARIOUS AUTHORS.

Vers. 12—18.—*Moses ascends the mount.* Observe, 1. He *alone* ascends (ver. 12). Aaron and his sons, with the seventy elders, were left behind. *Their* privilege was great as compared with that of the body of the people. Yet even they are not permitted to enter the cloud—to draw nigh into God's immediate presence. The limitations and imperfections of the legal economy are stamped on these arrangements. How superior the standing of Christians, who are *all* permitted to draw nigh; who have now the privilege, formerly possessed only by Moses, of beholding with unveiled face the Divine glory in the ecstasy of immediate vision (2 Cor. iii. 18). 2. The design of this ascending *was primarily to receive the stone tables* (ver. 12). These were to be written by God's own finger. God took every pains to impress upon the minds of the people that the law they had to deal with was *his* law. Its perpetuity was symbolised by the rock tablets. 3. Moses *made arrangements for the conduct of business in his absence* (ver. 14). His absence would be a trial of the faith and disposition of all parties. 4. *The fire still burned on the summit of the mount* (vers. 16, 17). This, notwithstanding the vision of ver. 10. The economy was outwardly and characteristically one of law; interiorly, one of grace. Even Moses had to wait seven days for the summons (ver. 16).—J. O.

Moses' sojourn with God the type of Christ's. I. The MEDIATOR: MOSES THE TYPE OF JESUS. He must needs pass up into God's presence: "Come up to me . . . and be there." It is there, in communion with God, that gifts are received for men. The power and blessing we now receive there, are prophecies of the power and glory with which Jesus will come again. 2. He must pass up to receive the law and commandments which God had written. Jesus will return with the perfected will of the Father. 3. The days of seclusion are numbered. Moses was in the mount forty days and forty nights. We know not how many or few they be; but each hour the coming of the Lord draws nearer. II. THE ATTITUDE OF GOD'S PEOPLE MEANWHILE. They tarry for the Mediator: "tarry ye here for us until we come again unto you." The attitude of the Churches to-day should be confident, joyous expectation: "this same Jesus will in like manner come again." 2. They are ministered unto by those who tarry with them (ver. 14). (1) The blessing bestowed in these temporary leaders. (2) Their responsibility: let them not be leaders or helpers to the people in their idolatry, as Aaron. III. THE VISION GRANTED THEM. The mountain is covered with clouds; but from the mountain top flames out the glory of the Lord. The eye cannot follow him who has entered within the veil; but we can behold the glory of the Lord, and know that every word of God will be fulfilled.—U.

SECTION XV.—CHAPTERS XXV.—XXXI.

INSTRUCTIONS CONCERNING THE TABERNACLE AND ITS FURNITURE, INCLUDING THE
PRIESTLY ATTIRE.

EXPOSITION.

CHAPTER XXV

Vers. 1—7.—THE TABERNACLE AND THE GIFTS FOR IT. The great principles of the moral law had been given in the Ten Commandments uttered by God amid the thunders of Sinai. The "Book of the Covenant," or short summary of the main laws, civil, political, and social, had been communicated to Moses, and by him reduced to a written form (ch. xxiv. 4). A solemn league and covenant had been entered into between God and his people, the people undertaking to keep all the words of the Lord, and God to be their Protector, Guide, and King. But no form of worship had been set up. Abstract monotheism had been inculcated; and worship had been so far touched upon that an "altar" had been mentioned, and certain directions, chiefly negative, had been given with respect to it (ch. xx. 24—26). It remained that the abstract monotheism should be enshrined in forms, obtain a local habitation, and be set forth before the eyes, and so fixed in the heart and affections of the people. God was now about to declare to Moses what the character of the habitation should be, its size, form, and materials. But before doing this, as a first and fitting, if not necessary, preliminary, he required of the people to bring of the best of their possessions for the service which he was about to institute, enumerating the substances which he would condescend to receive at their hands, and especially enjoining upon them that all should be offered willingly and from the heart (ver. 2).

Ver. 2.—**Speak unto the children of Israel that they bring me an offering.** The word translated "offering" is that commonly rendered "heave-offering;" but it seems to be used here (as in ch. xxx. 13; xxxv. 5, etc.) in a generic sense. The propriety of the people, when God was about establishing his habitation among them, presenting to God all the materials needed, is self-evident and requires no comment. **Of every man that giveth it willingly.** Literally, "of every man whose heart drives him." God will have no gifts but such as are freely offered. He "loveth a cheerful giver." If a man gives "grudgingly or of necessity," God rejects the gift. On the

noble spirit which the people showed when the appeal was made to them, see ch. xxxv. 21—29; and ch. xxxvi. 3—7.

Ver. 3.—**This is the offering—gold and silver and brass.** Gold was needed for the overlaying of the boards, whereof the ark was composed (ver. 11); for the "crown of gold," which surmounted it (ibid.); for the "rings" (ver. 12); the "mercy-seat" (ver. 17); the cherubim (ver. 18); the dishes, the spoons, the covers, the bowls (ver. 29); the candlestick (ver. 31); the tongs and snuff dishes (ver. 28); the hooks and taches (xxvi. 6, 32); for the covering of the table of shew bread (ch. xxv. 24); and of the staves and pillars (ib. 28: ch. xxvi. 32, 37); and also for many parts of the dress of the High Priest (ch. xxviii. 6, 8, 11, 14, etc.). Silver was required for the sockets which supported the boards of the Tabernacle (ch. xxvi. 19); and for the "hooks" and "fillets" of the pillars of the court (ch. xxvii. 10) Brass, or rather bronze, was wanted for the "taches" which coupled together the curtains of the tent (ch. xxvi. 11); for the "sockets" which received the pillars or tent-poles (ib. 37); for the external coating of the altar (ch. xxvii. 2); for the vessels and utensils of the altar (ib. 3); for the covering of its staves (ib. 6); for the sockets of the pillars of the Court (ch. xxvii. 10); for the "pins" of the Court (ib. 19); and generally for the vessels of the Tabernacle (ibid.). To understand how the Israelites could supply all that was wanted, we must remember, 1. That they had a certain amount of ancestral wealth, as that which Joseph had accumulated, and what Jacob and his sons had brought with them into Egypt. 2. That they had received large presents of gold and silver from the Egyptians just before their departure (ch. xii. 35); and 3. That they had recently defeated, and no doubt despoiled, the Amalekites (ch. xvi. 8—13). Whether they had further made money by trade since they entered the Sinaitic peninsula, may be doubted. The supposition is not at all needed in order to account for their wealth.

Ver. 4.—**And blue, and purple, and scarlet.** Cloths of these three colours seem to be meant. The material was probably wool; the blue dye probably indigo, which was the ordinary blue dye of Egypt; the purple was no doubt derived from one or other of the shell-fish so well-known to the Syrians (of which the one most used was the *Murex trunculus*), and was of a warm reddish hue, not far from crimson; the scarlet (literally, "scarlet *worm*" or "*worm* scarlet,") was the produce of the

Coccus ilicis, or cochineal insect of the holm oak, which has now been superseded by the *Coccus cacti*, or cochineal insect of the prickly pear, introduced into Europe from Mexico. **And fine linen.** The word used is Egyptian. It seems to have designated properly the fine linen spun from flax in Egypt, which was seldom dyed, and was of a beautiful soft white hue. The fineness of the material is extraordinary, equalling that of the best Indian muslins (Wilkinson's *Ancient Egyptians*, vol. iii. p. 121). It would seem that the Israelite women spun the thread from the flax (ch. xxxv. 25), and that the skilled workmen employed by Moses wove the thread into linen (*ib.* 35). **And goat's hair.** The soft inner wool of the Angora goat was also spun by the women into a fine worsted (*ib.* 26), which was woven into cloths, used especially as coverings for tents.

Ver. 5.—**And rams' skins dyed red.** The manufacture of leather was well-known in Egypt from an early date, and the Libyan tribes of North Africa were celebrated for their skill in preparing and dyeing the material (Herod. iv. 189). Scarlet was one of the colours which they peculiarly affected (*ibid.*). We must suppose that the skins spoken of had been brought with them by the Israelites out of Egypt. **And badgers' skins.** It is generally agreed among moderns that this is a wrong translation. Badgers are found in Palestine, but not either in Egypt or in the wilderness. The Hebrew *takhash* is evidently the same word as the Arabic *tukhash* or *dukhash*, which is applied to marine animals only, as to seals, dolphins, dugongs, and perhaps sharks and dog-fish. "Seals' skins" would perhaps be the best translation. (Compare Plin. *H. N.* ii. 55; Sueton. *Octav* § 90.) **Shittim wood.** It is generally agreed that the *Shittah* (plural *Shittim*) was an acacia, whether the seyal (*Acacia seyal*) which now grows so abundantly in the Sinaitic peninsula, or the *Acacia Nilotica*, or the *Serissa*, is uncertain. The seyal wood is "hard and close-grained" of an orange colour with a darker heart, well-adapted for cabinet work;" but the tree, as it exists nowadays, could certainly not furnish the planks, ten cubits long by one and a half wide, which were needed for the Tabernacle (ch. xxxv. 21). The *Serissa* might do so, but it is not now found in the wilderness. We are reduced to supposing either that the seyal grew to a larger size anciently than at present, or that the serissa was more widely spread than at the present day.

Ver. 6.—**Oil for the light.** That the sanctuary to be erected would require to be artificially lighted is assumed. Later, a "candlestick" is ordered (vers. 31—37). The people were to provide the oil which was to be burnt in the "candlestick." In ch. xxvii. 20, we are told that the oil was to be "pure oil olive beaten." **Spices for anointing oil.** Anointing oil would be needed for the sanctification of the Tabernacle, the ark, and all the holy vessels, as also for the consecration of Aaron and his sons to the priesthood. The spices required are enumerated in ch. xxx. 23, 24. They consisted of pure myrrh, sweet cinnamon, sweet calamus, and cassia. **And for sweet incense.** The spices needed for the incense were, according to our translators, stacte, onycha, galbanum and frankincense (*ib.* 34).

Ver. 7.—**Onyx stones.** On the need of onyx stones, see ch. xxviii. 9, 20. **Stones to be set in the ephod**, etc. Rather, "stones for setting, for the ephod and for the breastplate." The only stones required for the ephod were two large onyx stones; for the breastplate twelve jewels were needed (*ibid.* 17—20), one of them being an onyx. It has been proposed to translate the Hebrew *shoham* by "beryl" instead of "onyx;" but onyx, which is more suitable for engraving, is probably right.

HOMILETICS.

Vers. 1—7.—*The law of acceptable offerings.*—For offerings to be acceptable to God, it is necessary—

I. THAT THEY BE FREELY OFFERED BY A WILLING HEART. Offerings were to be taken of those "whose heart *drove* them to it" (compare Tennyson—"His own heart *drove* him, like a goad"), not of others. There was to be no tax—no church rate. The entire tent-temple was (with one unimportant exception) to be the produce of a free offertory. Thus was generosity stirred in the hearts of the people, and emulation excited. They gave so liberally that they had to be "restrained from bringing" (ch. xxxvi. 6). This is noble and acceptable service, when no exhortation is required, no persuasion, no "pressing".—but each man stirs himself up, and resolves to do the utmost that he can, not seeking to obtain the praise of men, but desirous of the approval of God. A like spirit animated those who lived in David's time (1 Chr. xxix. 6—9); and again those who returned from the Babylonian captivity with Zerubbabel (Ezr. ii. 68, 69; Neh. vii. 70—72).

II. THAT THEY BE OF THINGS EXCELLENT IN THEIR KIND, AND THE BEST THAT WE POSSESS OF EACH. All that is rich and rare, all that is lovely and beautiful, all that is expensive and magnificent, is suitable for an offering to God. We must not "give to him of that which costs us nothing." We must not offer "the blind, and the lame, and the sick" (Mal. i. 8) to him. Things excellent in their kind befit *his* service. Gold and silver, of metals; of fabrics, silk, and velvet, and fine linen; of woods, cedar, and acacia, and olive, and sandal-wood; of stones, ruby and diamond, and emerald; of spices, myrrh, and cinnamon, and cassia, and frankincense. Each, however, can only give what he has. Cedar, and olive, and sandal-wood were unattainable in the desert, and so acacia sufficed; silk and velvet were unknown, wherefore God accepted linen and woollen fabrics, and goat's hair; rubies and diamonds were uncut, so God was content with emeralds and sapphire, and onyx. The widow's mite pleases him, as much as the alabaster box of spikenard very precious, or the price of an estate brought and laid at the apostles' feet. If men "have little," he is content when they "give gladly of that little," provided still that they give him of their best. And this is true of other offerings besides material ones. The best of our time should be his—the fair promise of youth—the strength of manhood—not the weakness of decrepitude. The best of our powers should be his—our warmest affections, our intensest thoughts, our highest aspirations—not the dull tame musings of an exhausted and jaded spirit. Each man should seek to consecrate to God's service the best that he possesses in intellect, in knowledge, in fortune.

III. THAT THEY BE SUCH IN KIND AS HE HAS DECLARED HIS WILLINGNESS TO ACCEPT. There were "unclean animals" which were an abomination if offered to God. There are gifts of intellect, valuable in their way, which are unsuitable for the service of the sanctuary. Many a picture of the highest power, and exhibiting the greatest genius, would be out of place in a church. God points out with sufficient clearness in his holy word, the kinds of gifts with which he is pleased. It will be well for man to "do all things after the pattern showed him in the mount"—to avoid "will-worship"—and even in his offerings, to follow in the line of precedent, and see that he has a warrant for what he proposes doing in God's honour.

HOMILIES BY VARIOUS AUTHORS.

Vers. 1—7.—*The materials for the sanctuary.* I. GOD REQUIRED THESE FROM THE PEOPLE. It might have been thought that in order to make this holy habitation, this tent for God travelling along with his people, God himself would have in some way supplied the material. Even as he gave Moses the stones on which the law was written (in the first instance at all events), so he might have made a sanctuary to descend in marvellous manner into the midst of Israel. But it pleased him, who we may be sure always does the wise and fitting thing, to act differently. He required the materials for this sanctuary from the people. They could not provide food for themselves—but they could provide such a dwelling-place for Jehovah as he would approve and accept. These people who had required so many interventions of God to deliver and secure them had yet been carrying with them in the midst of all their helplessness the great store of wealth indicated in this passage. It is somewhat perplexing to consider the revelation thus afforded of the Israelite condition. In their hearts these people were sinful, idolatrous, unbelieving, unstable—it is humiliating to gaze on the sad exhibition of human nature they present—and yet they had managed to surround themselves with these treasures. They were those who had been laying up treasures on earth; and so far these treasures had been of little use; for what will it profit a man to have all this store of gold and silver, and brass and fine linen, and what not, if he lack the daily bread?—all the efforts of the people, all their scraping, had ended in the bringing of these things into the wilderness where they seemed of no use. Even gold and silver would not buy bread in the wilderness. But now, behold how God can take this gold and silver and show how to make a profitable and acceptable use of it. When we begin to look regretfully on the results of our natural efforts as if those efforts had been wasted, he comes in to overrule our ignorance and folly. By his consecrating and re-arranging touch, the treasures upon earth can be transmuted into treasures in heaven.

II. THE WILLINGNESS THAT MARKED THESE GIFTS. These materials, valuable as they were, yet yielded in respect of worth to an element more valuable still. These rare and beautiful materials, workable into such beautiful forms, could have been gotten without human intervention at all, if that had been the whole of the necessity. As not even Solomon in all his glory was arrayed like one of the lilies, so nothing man can make with his utmost art is so beautiful as the handiwork of God. Nor is the question altogether one as to what is beautiful to the outward eye. The value of beautiful forms is a thing only too easily exaggerated. But no one can exaggerate the beauty of a spiritual action, the beauty of a gift where the willingness and devotion of the whole heart are manifest. This tabernacle might be a very inferior structure, when measured by such principles as dictated Grecian art; but this was a thing of no consequence when compared with the higher consideration that its materials were freely brought. There was none of that extortion and slavish toil, such as we read of in connection with some of the huge fabrics of ancient civilisations. What blood and tears, what reckless expenditure of human life, for instance, in the construction of buildings like the pyramids! When we look at the great buildings—aqueducts, roads, of ancient times—we must not look at the outward appearance only. These Israelites doubtless had helped in the building of splendid structures; but the foundation of these structures was laid in oppression, and therefore on their topstone rested a destroying curse. There was nothing about all the tabernacle more beautiful than the willingness that marked the gift of the materials. There was no specific demand on any particular person. Let everyone consider for himself whether he will give, and how much. A free-will offering of the inferior brass would be of ever so much more value than an extorted one of gold or silver, or precious stones.

III. The materials of the gifts. Evidently such things were taken as the people had by them; but *of these things the very best were taken.* Being already in the possession of the people, and valued by them, they were exactly the things to test the willingness of their disposition. When God asks us to give, he asks us to give of our best. All this gold and silver symbolised what was most precious in the heart within. One is reminded of Paul's words with respect to the materials that might be laid upon the foundation given in Christ (1 Cor. iii. 12). We must not bring to God just what we do not want ourselves. The *value* of the gifts constituted a most searching test of willingness, and willingness was the particular quality that needed to be tested at this time. Men willing to give gold and silver, might be reasonably supposed as willing to give anything else within their power. Then there was a test also in the *variety* of the gifts. The man without gold and silver would not escape the responsibility of considering what he could do in the way of another gift. For the needs of the tabernacle God required a large diversity of materials; and probably there were few in Israel but could do something towards the supply if only they were so disposed.—Y.

Vers. 1, 2.—*God loveth a cheerful giver.* A message to the people. Like messages are often sent, but seldom welcomed. Even when God demands an offering, many people grudge to give it; they yield, as to a kind of heavenly highwayman, of necessity if at all. Consider here :—

I. The offering required. 1. *Purpose.* Jehovah will give the people a visible sign of his presence in their midst. He will have a home amid their homes, a tent dwelling like in character to their dwellings. More than this—he will be their guest. They shall provide for him the sacred tent. If we count it an honour for a town to receive and entertain a member of our royal family, how much greater an honour to be permitted to entertain the head of the royal family of heaven! 2. *Materials.* All manner of things required (vers. 3—7), so that all can share the privilege of providing them. Some may give a few gold ornaments; even a poor man may yet find some goat's hair for cloth. Not a member of the nation but can do his part in helping to rear the tabernacle for God. All gifts can be used, so that each may have a share in the work. 3. *A precedent for ourselves.* God treats us as he treated Israel. He asks our help in building for him a spiritual temple, a dwelling-place in which men are the living stones. Some can give personal effort; some can give money to assist the actual workers; no one so poor but that he can give something. Surely the opportunity of helping God is one which ought not to be undervalued.

II. The condition of acceptance. All may help, but on one condition—they must help " willingly," with the " heart." The offering is valued not on its own account, but as a symbol of that which is more valuable. Gifts to God are a kind of human sacrament, which God deigns to receive at the hands of man: they are acceptable as outward and visible signs of an inward and spiritual grace. If the grace be wanting, the gifts are worthless. God is good enough to make needs for himself that his creatures may have the privilege of satisfying them; if they degrade the privilege into a tax, he would rather be without their assistance. How often is this forgotten! We give to God, when asked, for many reasons. It is the proper thing to do, and respectability requires it; or it will get our name into some subscription list; or we may have an uneasy feeling that we ought to give, and to soothe our uneasiness we must do something. "Grudgingly and of necessity" is the epitaph which must be written above such wasted offerings. God cannot accept as gifts offerings which are never truly given. He may use them, for they are his in any case to do as he wills with them; he cannot, however, enter them in his inventory as received from the giver who nominally presents them. Only he who gives with his heart has his name set down in the inventory of God. The two mites of the widow are remembered; the talents of the ostentatious tax-payer are forgotten.

III. THE RESPONSE MADE. The people of Israel realised their privileges. They remembered what God had done for them, and were eager to manifest their gratitude. They gave even more than enough (xxxvi. 6, 7). Their hearts stirred them up, and their spirits made them willing (xxxv. 21); so that they even had to be restrained. What an example for us! Church debts, fettered missionary enterprise, ministers of the Gospel converted into persistent yet unsuccessful beggars; what are the Lord's people doing when such phenomena abound? Do we not need to be reminded of the privilege offered us, which is so fearfully profaned? Do we not need to stir up *our* hearts, and to take active measures to make our spirits willing? The roused heart loosens the purse-strings; only the willing spirit can offer the willing and generous gift.—G.

Vers. 1—9.—*The rearing of the Lord's sanctuary.* I. FROM WHAT IT IS FORMED. 1. Of material supplied by his redeemed. To them only request and direction come— "Let *them* make me a sanctuary that I may dwell among them." This is still our high calling, to make God a dwelling-place in the earth. Are we obeying? Is God being glorified by us? 2. Of their free-will offerings. There is no constraint; everything is free and spontaneous—the loving gifts of children, not the forced labour of slaves. 3. Of their choicest and best, and yet, 4, of things named by God himself. Even here we are not left to impose burdens upon ourselves. God's word and the Spirit's voice in the heart will direct us.

II. GOD IS THE ARCHITECT OF HIS OWN SANCTUARY. The building and furniture are to be in every particular according *to his own plan* (ver. 9). We may not bring into God's worship or service our own devices. The stepping aside from the simplicity of God's ordinances is disservice. It is contempt of God or open rebellion to his authority.—U.

Vers. 1—10.—*The command to build a sanctuary.* The covenant being now ratified, everything was prepared for Jehovah taking up his abode with the people. He would dwell among them as their King. In keeping with the genius of the dispensation, commands are given for the erection of a visible sanctuary. It is here called "mikdash," or sanctuary (ver. 8), and "mishkân," or dwelling-place (tabernacle, ver. 9), the latter being the name most commonly applied to it. Considering the purpose which the sanctuary was to serve, and the "plenitude of meaning" designed to be conveyed by its symbolism, it was necessary that the whole should be constructed under immediate Divine direction. A plan of the tabernacle, embracing minute details, was accordingly placed before the mind of Moses on the mount (ver. 9). It was presented in its completeness to his inner eye, before any part of it was set up on earth. The ark of Noah, the tabernacle of Moses, and the temple of Solomon (cf. 1 Chron. xxviii. 11, 12, 19), are probably the only buildings ever erected from plans furnished by direct revelation. In the building of the spiritual temple—the Church—God is himself not merely the architect, but the builder; and the beauty and symmetry of the structure will be found in the end to be perfect (cf. Rev. xxi.). Consider—

I. THE MATERIALS OF THE TABERNACLE. These were ordered to be collected before the work began. They were to be—1. *Costly* and *various*—representing (1) every department of nature (mineral, vegetable, animal); (2) the richest products of each, so far as accessible in the desert (gold, silver, fine linen, dyed skins, precious stones, etc.);

(3) all varieties of human skill. The design was to make a *palace* for Jehovah: a beautiful and glorious house. 2. *Abundant.* There was to be no stint in the gifts. Profuse liberality befitted the occasion. Grudging in our gifts to God betrays an unworthy spirit. 3. *Free-will offerings* (ver. 2). This point is put in the foreground. The people were to bring an offering—" Of every man that giveth it willingly with his heart ye shall take my offering." Observe in this—(1) The people first offered *themselves* to God (ch. xxiv. 7), then their gifts. This is the true order. Compare what is said of the Macedonian believers (2 Cor. viii. 1—6). (2) The giving of *themselves* to God was followed by the devotion to his service of the best of their *possessions.* The consecration of self, as formerly remarked, includes all other consecrations. If we are God's, then all is God's that is ours. He has the first claim on everything we have. Our best ought cheerfully to be dedicated to him. (3) God values only such gifts as come from a *willing* heart. He loves the cheerful giver (2 Cor. ix. 7). He puts no value on givings which are *not* cheerful. (4) Free-will offerings are necessarily various in kind and amount. Not all could give gold, or silver, or precious stones. Some, whose means were small, could probably give only their labour in working up the gifts of the wealthier. Each gave as he was able, and according to the *kind* of material in his possession. So far, however, as the gifts were offered willingly, they met with God's acceptance. The giver was accepted in his gift, not according to its absolute amount, but according to his ability, and to the spirit in which he gave. (Cf. 2 Cor. viii. 12.) And all the gifts were needed. The variety which they exhibited was part of their appropriateness. What one could not furnish another could. Many kinds of gifts are required in Christ's service, and there is none so poor but he can furnish something which others have not at command. The Lord accepts, and will use, all. (5) God's dwelling with his people must rest on a voluntary basis. They must *wish* him to dwell among them, and must *prove* their wish by voluntarily providing the materials for his sanctuary. A living Church will show its desire for God's presence, and will evince its gratitude, and its sense of obligation to him, by large and willing gifts in his service. These, indeed, are not conclusive as proofs of genuine spiritual interest; but the absence of them speaks with sufficient plainness of spiritual coldness. (6) The ideal state in the Church is that in which " ordinances of Divine service " are freely supported by the gifts of the people. This principle found distinct expression, not simply in the free-will offerings for the making of the tabernacle, but in the general arrangements of the Jewish economy. The law prescribed amounts—commanded tithes, etc., but the fulfilment of the obligation was left to the individual conscience. It was not enforced by legal means. What was given had to be given freely.

II. THE IDEA OF THE TABERNACLE. Some remarks on this subject seem called for before entering on the study of details. A firm grasp of the central idea is essential to a right understanding of the parts. The tabernacle may be considered—(1) *Actually*, as the literal dwelling-place of Jehovah with his people; (2) *symbolically*, as in its different parts and arrangements symbolical of spiritual ideas; and (3) *typically*, as prophetic of better things to come. The typical treatment, however, will best be connected with what is to be said under the two former heads. 1. *Actually*, the tabernacle was the place of Jehovah's dwelling with his people (ver. 8). This is to be viewed as, on the one side, a privilege of the Church of Israel; but, on the other, as a step towards the realisation of the great end contemplated by God from the first, as the goal of all his gracious dealings with our race, namely, the taking up of his abode among them. God *seeks* an abode with men. He cannot rest with perfect satisfaction in his love to them till he has obtained this abode (Ps. cxxxii. 13, 14). He *wishes* to dwell with them. The history of revelation may be viewed as but a series of steps towards the realisation of this idea. The steps are the following—(1) God dwelling with men *in the visible sanctuary of the Jews*—the tabernacle and temple. This served important ends. It brought God near to men. It enabled them to grasp the reality of his presence. It was, however, but a very imperfect stage in the realisation of the truth. It would not have suited a universal religion. There was, besides, no congruity between the nature of the spiritual Deity and a building "made with hands." It was but an outward, local presence which this visible sanctuary embodied. The union between the dwelling and the Dweller was not inherent or essential; it could at any moment be dissolved. Higher realisations of the idea were possible. (2) God dwelling with men *in Christ.*

Christ pointed to himself as the antitype of the temple (Matt. xii. 6 ; John ii. 19—22).
He was Immanuel, God with us (Matt. i. 23). The fulness of the Godhead dwelt in
him (John i. 14; Col. i. 15; ii. 9). The temple in this case is not a mere material
structure, but a holy, and now perfected, humanity. The union is personal and indissoluble. The revelation of God, through the medium of humanity, cannot rise higher
than it has done in Christ. The life of God in the individual and in the Church is but
the unfolding of the fulness already contained in him (John i. 16). This unfolding,
however, is necessary, that the temple-idea may reach its complete fulfilment. A third
stage, accordingly, is (3) God dwelling *in the soul of the believer.* Rather, we should
say, in the *humanity* of the believer—body, soul, and spirit forming, unitedly, a habitation for God through the Holy Ghost (1 Cor. vi. 19). In this tabernacle, as in the
former, there is the innermost shrine—the holy of holies of the spirit, the " inner
man " in which is deposited the law of the Lord (Eph. iii. 16); a holy place—the soul or
mind, with its lamps of understanding, etc.; and an outer court—the body—the external
side of the being, open and visible to all. The individual, however, taken by himself,
is but a fragment. The full idea is realised (4) *in the Church as a whole*—the whole
body of believers, in heaven and on earth, with Christ as Head. This is the true and
the living temple (Eph. ii. 21, 22). Realised in part on earth, and wherever a portion of
the Church of Christ exists, the perfection of the manifestation of the idea is reserved
for the future and for glory. Cf. Rev. xxi. 3—" The tabernacle of God is with men," etc.
The idea of the Jewish tabernacle thus finds its fulfilment (1) in the body of Christ;
(2) in the body of the believer; (3) in the body of the Church. 2. *Symbolically*—the
tabernacle figured out, in its structure, its contents, and its arrangements, various
spiritual truths. (1) On the ark and its symbolism, see next homily. (2) The separation into two apartments had as its basis the twofold aspect of God's fellowship with
man. The holy of holies was *God's* part of the structure. Its arrangements exhibited
God in relation to his people. The outer apartment—the holy place—exhibited in
symbol the calling of the people in relation to God. The shew-bread and the lighted
lamps, with the incense from the golden altar, emblematised aspects of that calling.
See next homily. (3) The arrangements of the tabernacle had further in view the
symbolising of the imperfect condition of privilege in the Church under the old economy.
A veil hung between the holy place and the holy of holies. Into this latter the high
priest only was permitted to enter, and that but once a year, and not without blood of
atonement. The mass of the people were not allowed to come nearer than the outer
court. They could enter the holy place only in the persons of their representatives, the
priests. All this spoke of distance, of barriers as yet unremoved, of drawbacks to
perfected communion. The arrangements were of such a nature as studiously to impress
this idea upon the mind. Accordingly, at the death of Christ, the removal of these
barriers, and the opening of the way for perfected fellowship between God and man,
was signified by the striking circumstance of the rending of the veil (Matt. xxvii. 51).
It is implied in the teaching of Scripture that a like imperfection of privilege marked
the condition of the departed just, and that this also was removed by Christ, who,
passing into the highest heavens, made manifest, both for them and for us, the way
into the holiest of all. (Cf. Heb. ix. 6—13; x. 19, 20; xi. 39, 40; xii. 23.)—J. O.

EXPOSITION.

Vers. 8, 9.—GENERAL DIRECTIONS. After
the gifts which God will accept have been specified, and the spirit in which they are to be
offered noted (ver. 2), God proceeds to unfold
his purpose, and declare the object for which
the gifts are needed. He will have a " sanctuary" constructed for him, an habitation in
which he may " dwell." Now, it is certainly
possible to conceive of a religion which should
admit nothing in the nature of a temple or
sanctuary ; and there are even writers who tell
us that a religion has actually existed without
one (Herod. i. 131, Strab. xv. pp. 1039—41)
That God should " dwell" in a house, as a man
does, is of course impossible ; and the Hebrews
were as deeply impressed with this truth as
any other nation (1 Kings viii. 27; 2 Chr. ii.
6 ; Is. lvi. 1 ; Jer. xxiii. 24, etc.). But a religion
without a temple was probably unknown in
the days of Moses ; and, with such a people as

the Hebrews, it is inconceivable that religion could have maintained its ground for long without something of the kind. " It was," as Kalisch says, " above all things necessary to create a firm and visible centre of monotheism, to keep perpetually the idea of the one omnipotent God alive in the minds of the people, and so to exclude for ever a relapse into the pagan and idolatrous aberrations" (*Comment on Exodus,* p. 365). A sanctuary was therefore to be constructed ; but, as the nation was in the peculiar position of being nomadic, without fixed abode, that is, and constantly on the move, the usual form of a permanent building was unsuitable under the circumstances. To meet the difficulty, a tent-temple was designed, which is called *mishkân,* " the dwelling," or *'ôhel,* " the tent," which was simply an Oriental tent on a large scale, made of the best obtainable materials, and guarded by an enclosure. The details of the work are reserved for later mention. In the present passage two directions only are given :—1. A sanctuary is to be constructed ; and 2. Both it, and all its vessels, are to be made after patterns which God was about to show to Moses.

Ver. 8.—**A sanctuary** well expresses the Hebrew *micdash,* which is derived from *câdash*—" to be holy." It is a name never given to the temples of the heathen deities. **That I may dwell among them.** Compare

•ch. xxix. 45 ; Num. xxxv. 34. There is a sense in which " God dwelleth not in temples made with hands"(Acts vii. 48; xvii. 24)—*i.e.,* he is not comprehended in them, or confined to them ; but there is another sense in which he may be truly said to dwell in them, viz., as manifesting himself in them either to the senses, or to the spirit. In the tabernacle he manifested himself sensibly (ch. xl. 34, 35, 38).

Ver. 9.—**The patterns.** Many of the old Jewish commentators supposed, that Moses was shown by God a real material structure, which actually existed in the heavens, far grander than its earthly copy, after which he was to have the tabernacle fashioned. Some recent Christian writers, without going these lengths, suggest that " an actual picture or model of the earthly tabernacle and its furniture was shown to him" (Keil). But the words of the text, as well as those of Acts vii. 44, and Heb. viii. 5, are sufficiently justified, if we take a view less material than either of these—*i.e.,* if we suppose Moses to have had impressed on his mind, in vision, the exact appearance of the tabernacle and its adjuncts, in such sort that he could both fully understand, and also, when necessary, supplement, the verbal descriptions subsequently given to him. It is unnecessary to inquire how the impression was produced. God who in vision communicated to Ezekiel the entire plan of that magnificent temple which he describes in ch. xl.—xlii., could certainly have made known to Moses, in the same way, the far simpler structure of the primitive Tabernacle.

HOMILETICS.

Ver. 8.—*Earthly sanctuaries typical of the heavenly dwelling-place.* Such habitations as God condescends to acknowledge for his in this earthly sphere, are, all of them, more or less types of the New Jerusalem, the eternal heavenly home. " The temple of God was opened in heaven," says St. John the Divine, " and there was seen in his temple the ark of his testament" (Rev. xi. 19); and again, " After that I looked, and, behold, the temple of the tabernacle of the testimony in heaven was opened" (ch. xv. 5). Note the following common features :—

I. THE CENTRAL CARDINAL FACT IN EACH AND ALL IS, THE MANIFEST PRESENCE OF GOD. Of the Tabernacle we are told—" Then a cloud covered the tent of the congregation, and the glory of the Lord filled the tabernacle. And Moses was not able to enter into the tent of the congregation, because the cloud abode thereon, and the glory of the Lord filled the tabernacle " (Ex. xl. 34, 35). Christian churches have the promise, " Lo, I am with you always, even unto the end of the world "—and again, " Where two or three are gathered together in my name, there am I in the midst of you." In the New Jerusalem " the city has no need of the sun, neither of the moon, to shine in it ; for the glory of God doth lighten it, and the Lamb is the Light thereof " (Rev. xxi. 23). And the saints " see his face " (*ib.* xxii. 4).

II. THE SECOND LEADING FACT IS THE EXISTENCE IN EACH OF " MANY MANSIONS." An outer court, a porch, a holy place, and a holy of holies, are features manifestly common to the Hebrew tabernacle and temple with Christian churches. These give different degrees of access to God, and imply different degrees of fitness to contemplate him. In heaven there is a throne—the throne of God and of the Lamb—and round about the throne four and twenty seats for four and twenty elders to sit on (Rev. iv. 4); and beyond these angels (*ib.* v. 11), and martyrs (*ib.* vii. 14); and, last of all, "the nations of them that are saved" (*ib.* xxi. 24). And each individual of the "nations" finds his fitting place.

III. IN ALL, THE OCCUPATION OF THOSE WHO HAVE FOUND ENTRANCE IS THE PRAISE AND WORSHIP OF GOD, "Enter into his courts with praise," says holy David, of the tabernacle (Ps. c. 4)—"be thankful unto him, and bless his name." "When ye come together, every one of you has a psalm," says St. Paul of a Christian Church. In heaven there is "a great voice of much people, saying, Alleluia: Salvation and glory, and honour, and power, unto the Lord our God, for true and righteous are his judgments . . . and again they say, Alleluia: for the Lord God omnipotent reigneth; let us be glad and rejoice, and give honour to him" (Rev. xix. 1—7).

IV. IN ALL, THE WORSHIPPERS ENJOY A SACRED FEAST. Of the worship of the tabernacle sacrifice was an essential part; and a sacrificial feast, of which the offerer partook, always followed the sacrifice. In Christian worship upon earth, the crowning act is a heavenly banquet, to which the minister in Jesus' name invites all the faithful.

> " Hail sacred feast, which Jesus makes
> Rich banquet of his flesh and blood!
> Thrice happy he, who here partakes
> That sacred stream, that heavenly food."

In the New Jerusalem there is a "tree of life," which bears "twelve manner of fruits;" and they who enter in "have right to the tree of life" (Rev. xxii. 2, 14), and are "given to eat of the tree of life, which is in the midst of the paradise of God" (*ib.* ii. 7). How far this is literal, how far allegorical, we shall scarcely know till we are translated to that celestial sphere, and become dwellers in that glorious city.

HOMILIES BY VARIOUS AUTHORS.

Vers. 8, 9.—*God's dwelling-place among his people.* God announces to Israel that he is about to take up his abode in their midst, and that various offerings are to be used in the construction of a suitable dwelling-place. Observe here—

I. JEHOVAH'S CONDESCENDING REGARD FOR THE WANTS OF ISRAEL. This tabernacle with all its belongings was not constructed for any real need that Jehovah had of it. The people had to construct tents for themselves because they needed them, and the making of a tent for Jehovah was also in condescending compliance with *their need*. This thought is brought out still more clearly by the parallel reference to the incarnation in John i. 14, where it is said that the Word tabernacled among us. Something in the shape of an ever visible dwelling-place of God was given to the people, that thus they might comfort their hearts with the assurance that he was constantly near them, sympathising with them in their changing circumstances and requirements. The people had been compelled to go to Sinai, there to be impressed with the majesty of God and receive his commandments; but at Sinai they could not stay. With all its glories and revelations, it was but a halting place on the way to Canaan. God had indeed already given an assurance of his daily providence in the manna; but he now added a further sign than which none could be more expressive, none more illustrative of the desire of God to adapt himself to the spiritual blindness and infirmity of men. He took for himself a tent like the rest of the travellers through the wilderness. Where a dwelling place is we look for an inhabitant, and especially where it is manifestly kept in order and regularly attended to. If at any moment an Israelite was in doubt whether God was indeed with the people, here through the sight of the tabernacle was his readiest resource to expel all doubt. God's own house with its services and attendants was continually before him to rebuke and remove his unbelief.

II. THOUGH JEHOVAH CONDESCENDED TO DWELL IN A TENT, YET THAT TENT HAD TO BE A HOLY PLACE. The condescension was simply a condescension in circumstances. God himself remained the same. He who was holy and jealous, when removed to a distance from the people, amid the clouds and sounds of Sinai, was not the least altered as to his vigilant holiness by coming down to the apparent limitations of a tent. Coarse and humble though the tent appears, there is an unspeakably glorious inhabitant within whose presence exalts and sanctifies the tent. God himself thus furnishes an illustration of the truth that those who humble themselves shall be exalted. He needs not to preserve his glory by extraneous and vulgar pomps. And just because this dwelling-place of God was a tent, the people needed to remember its function with peculiar carefulness. Though it was only a tent, it was God's tent. A very mean tent, that in ordinary circumstances would excite no attention, would be carefully guarded if the king happened for a night to make his abode therein.

III. This holiness was made conspicuous by the character and form of the tabernacle and its furniture. Just imagine if, instead of prescribing an exact pattern for everything, God had left the people to make any sort of structure they liked. In the first place there would hardly have been unanimity. Those who might have been very willing and united in the bestowal of raw material would at once have split asunder in attempting to settle how the material was to be used. Then, even if a majority had proceeded to action, they would probably have introduced something idolatrous, assuredly something that savoured rather of human error than Divine truth; and the error would have been none the less because those who committed it, committed it in a spirit of cordial devotion to what they believed was best. What an exposure is thus made of the plausible notion that if only men are in earnest, God will accept the will for the deed! As to the supply of the raw material, God stipulated for free will there—perfect liberty either in giving or withholding. But the raw material once gathered, the freedom of the givers was at an end. God himself supplied the moulds in which the gifts were to flow. A dwelling-place for God must supply all his wants for the time being. He must have just exactly those ordinances of worship and those channels of Divine distribution which he deems best. God's wants, as we see more and more from a careful study of the Scriptures, are not as man's wants; and therefore we must wait humbly for him to reveal what it is impossible for man to conjecture. The materials for the tabernacle and the instruments thereof were human and earthly, but the patterns are Divine and heavenly. We know not into what beautiful, glorious, and serviceable forms man and his belongings may be wrought, if only he will humbly and attentively wait for directions from God above. These Israelites, when all was finished according to the pattern in the mount, had then something to show which would make an impression on men of the right sort in the outside world. Here was an answer to the question, "Where is now your God?" Visible he himself is not; but here is a dwelling-place not in anything constructed after art and man's device, but entirely of Divine direction. All our institutions are nothing unless we can trace them to the inspiration and control of God.—Y.

EXPOSITION.

Vers. 10—22.—The pattern of the ark. —Moses is first shown, not the pattern of the tabernacle, but the patterns of those things which it was to contain—the ark, the table of shew-bread, and the seven-branched candle-stick, or lamp-stand, with its appurtenances. The ark, as the very most essential part of the entire construction, is described first.

Ver. 10.—Thou shalt make an ark of shittim wood. Arks were an ordinary part of the religious furniture of temples in Egypt, and were greatly venerated. They usually contained a figure or emblem, of some deity. Occasionally they were in the shape of boats; but the most ordinary form was that of a cup-board or chest. They were especially con-structed for the purpose of being carried about

in a procession, and had commonly rings at the side, through which poles were passed on such occasions. It must be freely admitted, that the general idea of the "Ark," as well as certain points in its ornamentation, was adopted from the Egyptian religion. Egyptian arks were commonly of sycamore wood. Two cubits and a half, etc. As there is no reason to believe that the Hebrew cubit differed seriously from the cubits of Greece and Rome, we may safely regard the Ark of the Covenant as a chest or box, three feet nine inches long, two feet three inches wide, and two feet three inches deep.

Ver. 11.—Thou shalt overlay it with pure gold. Or, "cover it with pure gold." As gilding was well known in Egypt long before the time of the exodus, it is quite possible that the chest was simply gilt without and within. It may, however, have been overlaid with thin plates of gold (a practice also known in Egypt, and common elsewhere)—which is the view taken by the Jewish commentators. The **crown of gold** was probably an ornamental moulding or edging round the top of the chest.

Ver. 12.—**Four rings of gold.** These rings were to be fixed, not at the upper, but at the lower **corners** of the chest, which are called *pa'amoth*, literally "feet" or "bases." The object was, no doubt, that no part of the chest should come in contact with the persons of the priests when carrying it (see ver. 14). As Kalisch notes, "the smallness of the dimensions of the ark rendered its safe transportation, even with the rings at its feet, not impossible."

Ver. 13.—**Staves of shittim wood.** Similar staves, or poles, are to be seen in the Egyptian sculptures, attached to arks, thrones, and litters, and resting on the shoulders of the men who carry such objects.

Ver. 14.—**That the ark may be borne with them.** The Hebrew ark was not made, like the Egyptian arks, for processions, and was never exhibited in the way of display, as they were. The need of carrying it arose from the fact, that the Israelites had not yet obtained a permanent abode. As soon as Canaan was reached, the ark had a fixed locality assigned to it, though the locality was changed from time to time (Josh. xviii. 1; 1 Sam. iv. 3; vii. 1; 2 Sam. vi. 10, etc.); but in the desert it required to be moved each time that the congregation changed its camping-ground.

Ver. 15.—The staves, when once inserted into the rings of the ark, were never to be taken from them. The object probably was that there might be no need of touching even the rings, when the ark was set down or taken up. The bearers took hold of the staves only, which were no part of the ark. On the danger of touching the ark itself, see 2 Sam. vi. 6, 7.

Ver. 16.—**The testimony which I will give thee**, is undoubtedly the Decalogue, or in other words, the two tables of stone, written with the finger of God, and forming his testimony against sin. (Compare Deut. xxxi. 26, 27.) The main intention of the ark was to be a repository in which the two tables should be laid up.

Ver. 17.—**Thou shalt make a mercy seat.** Modern exegesis has endeavoured to empty the word *kapporeth* of its true meaning, witnessed to by the Septuagint, as well as by the Epistle to the Hebrews (ix. 5). It tells us that a *kapporeth* is simply a cover," being derived from *kâphar*, to cover,"—used in Gen. v. 14, with respect to covering the ark with pitch. But the truth is that *kapporeth* is not derived from *kâphar*, but from *kipper*, the Piel form of the same verb, which has never

any other sense than that of covering, or forgiving sins. In this sense it is used in the Old Testament some seventy times. Whether the mercy seat was the real cover of the ark of the covenant, or whether that had its own lid of acacia wood, as Kalisch supposes, is uncertain. At any rate, it was not called *kipporeth* because it was a cover, but because it was a seat of propitiation. On the importance of the mercy seat, as in some sort transcending the ark itself, see Lev. xvi. 2, and 1 Chr xxviii. 11. Atonement was made by sprinkling the blood of expiation upon it (Lev. xvi. 14, 15). **Of pure gold.** Not of wood, plated with metal, or richly gilt, but of solid gold—an oblong slab, three feet nine inches long, two feet three inches wide, and probably not less than an inch thick. The weight of such a slab would be above 750 lbs. troy, and its value above 25,000*l.* of our money. The length and breadth were exactly those of the ark itself, which the mercy seat thus exactly covered (ver. 10).

Ver. 18.—**Two cherubims.** The form "cherubims," which our translators affect, is abnormal and indefensible. They should have said either "cherubim," or "cherubs." The exact shape of the Temple cherubim was kept a profound secret among the Jews, so that Josephus declares—"No one is able to state, or conjecture of what form the cherubim were" (*Ant. Jud.* viii. 3, § 3). That they were winged figures appears from verse 28 of this chapter, while from other parts of Scripture we learn that cherubim might be of either human or animal forms, or of the two combined (Ezek. i. 5—14; x. 1—22). These last have been with some reason compared to the symbolical composite figures of other nations, the andro-sphinxes and crio-sphinxes of the Egyptians, the Assyrian winged bulls and lions, the Greek chimæræ, and the griffins of the northern nations. But it is doubtful whether the cherubim of Moses were of this character. The most sober of recent inquirers (Bp. Harold Browne, Canon Cook, Kalisch, Keil), while admitting the point to be doubtful, come to the conclusion that they were in all probability, "winged human figures, with human face too." In this case their prototype would seem to have been the winged figures of Ma, the Goddess of Truth, frequently seen inside Egyptian arks, sheltering with their wings the scarabæus or other emblem of the deity. (See Lepsius, *Denkmäler*, pt. iii. pl. 14; Wilkinson in Rawlinson's *Herodotus*, vol. ii. p. 85, 2nd edition; Smith's *Dictionary of the Bible*, vol. i. p. 304.) **Of beaten work shalt thou make them.** Not cast, *i.e.*, but hammered into shape (LXX. τορευτά. The word "cherub" is thought to be derived from an Egyptian root, *karabu*, signifying "to hammer" (*Speaker's Commentary*, vol. iv. p. 207). **In the two ends.** Rather, "From the two ends"—*i.e.*, "rising," or, "standing up from the two ends."

Ver. 19.—**On the one end . on the other end . . . on the two ends.** The preposition used is in every case the same as that of the last clause of ver. 18—viz., *min,* "from." The idea is that the figures rose from the two ends.

Ver. 20.—**The cherubims shall stretch forth their wings on high.** Compare ch. xxxvii, 9. It would seem that the two wings of both cherubs were advanced in front of them, and elevated, so as to overshadow the mercy seat. This was a departure from the patterns furnished by the figures of Ma (see the comment on ver. 18), since in them one wing only was elevated, and the other depressed. It is clear that in no case was any part of the Hebrew sacred furniture a mere reproduction of Egyptian models. Whatever was made use of was so transformed or modified as to acquire a new and independent character. **Their faces,** etc. The words are not without difficulty ; but the generally received meaning appears to be correct—that the faces were bent one towards the other, but that both looked downwards, towards the mercy seat. Thus the figures, whether they were standing or kneeling, which is uncertain, presented the appearance of guardian angels, who watched over the precious deposit below—to wit, the two tables.

Ver. 21.—**Thou shalt put the mercy seat above the ark.** Rather, "upon the ark"— " thou shalt cover the ark with it." This had not been expressed previously, though the dimensions (ver. 17), compared with those of the ark (ver. 10), would naturally have suggested the idea. **In the ark thou shalt put the testimony.** This is a mere repetition of verse 16, marking the special importance which attached to the provision.

Ver. 22.—**And there I will meet with thee.** The whole of the foregoing description has been subordinate to this. In all the arrangements for the tabernacle God was, primarily and mainly, providing a fit place where he might manifest himself to Moses and his successors. The theocracy was to be a government by God in reality, and not in name only. There was to be constant "communing" between God and the earthly ruler of the nation, and therefore a place of communing. Compare ch. xxix. 42—45. The special seat of the Divine presence was to be the empty space above the mercy seat, between the two cherubim, and above the ark of the covenant.

HOMILETICS.

Vers. 10—22.—*The symbolism of the ark of the covenant.* The symbolical meaning of the ark of the covenant may be considered, either (1) separately, as to its parts ; or (2) collectively, as to the bearing of its several parts one upon the other.

I. SEPARATELY, AS TO ITS PARTS. These were (1) The ark itself, or chest ; (2) The mercy seat ; and (3) The cherubim. (1) The ark, or coffer of acacia wood, coated within and without with pure gold, and intended as a receptacle for the law written by the finger of God, would seem to have represented Divine law as enshrined in the pure nature of God. Acacia is said to be one of the most incorruptible of woods, and gold is undoubtedly the most incorruptible, as well as the most precious, of metals. The law of God—"holy, just, and good" (Rom. vii. 12)—needs such a receptacle. It dwells fitly in God himself—in the incorruptible hearts of the sinless angels—and in the undefiled hearts of godly men. It is in itself pure and incorrupt, an emanation from him who is essential purity. It is a "golden" rule, perfect, lovely, beautiful. It is no cruel code of a tyrant, but the only rule of action by which the well-being of man can be secured. At the same time there is severity and sternness in it. It was written on *stone,* and shrined in gold. It was fixed, unbending, unchangeable. (2) The mercy seat represented God's attribute of mercy. It covered up the law, as he "covers up" the sins and offences of his people (Ps. xxxii. 1 ; lxxxv. 2 ; Rom. iv. 7). It was prepared to receive the expiatory blood wherewith the high-priest was to sprinkle it, the blood that typified the propitiatory sacrifice of Christ (Lev. xvi. 14). It was of gold because mercy is the most precious of God's attributes. It was placed *over* the law, because mercy transcends justice. (3) The cherubim represented at once guardianship and worship. Doubtless holy angels at all times guarded invisibly the ark, and especially the "testimony" which it contained. The presence of the two golden figures signified this holy watchfulness to the Israelites, and spoke to them of the intense holiness of the place. The shadowing wings represented protecting care ; and the cherubic form showed that the most exalted of creatures were fitly employed in watching and guarding the revelation of the will of the Almighty. By their attitude, standing or kneeling with bent heads and faces turned down toward the mercy seat, they further spoke of worship. On the Divine presence, which was manifested "from between them," they dared not gaze—their eyes were lowered, and fixed for ever on the mercy seat—the embodiment of the Divine attribute of mercy. As under the new covenant angels desired to look into the mystery of redemption (1 Pet. i. 12), so, under the old, angels doubtless saw with admiring wonder God commencing the recovery of a lost world; they looked on his attribute of mercy with rapture but with amaze; it was a new thing to them; the angels who lost their first estate had not elicited it; man alone had been thought worthy of the "afterthought," whereby sin was condoned, and the salvation of sinners made possible.

II. COLLECTIVELY, AS TO THE BEARING OF THE SEVERAL PARTS ONE UPON ANOTHER. The teaching of the ark in this respect was, primarily, that of David in the eighty-fifth psalm: "Mercy and truth are met together; righteousness and peace have kissed each other." Mercy without justice is a weak sentimentality, subversive of moral order. Justice without mercy is a moral severity—theoretically without a flaw, but revolting to man's instinctive feelings. The synthesis of the two is required. The law, enshrined in the holiest place of the sanctuary, vindicated the awful purity and perfection of God. The mercy seat, extended above the law, assigned to mercy its superior directive position. The cherubic figures showed the gaze of angels riveted in astonishment and admiration on God's mode of uniting mercy with justice, by means of vicarious suffering, which he can accept as atonement. Finally, the Divine presence, promised as a permanent thing, gave God's sanction to the expiatory scheme, whereby alone man can be reconciled to him, and the claims both of justice and of mercy satisfied.

HOMILIES BY VARIOUS AUTHORS.

Chap. xxv., vers. 10—16; chap. xxxvii., vers. 1—5.—*The ark of the testimony.* When Jehovah provided for Israel an abiding record of his holy will, it was needful that Israel should also provide an appropriate receptacle. Nor was it left to Moses and the people to determine what might be most appropriate. Jehovah arranged things so that all the religious service of the people gathered around the two tables of stone. An Israelite gazing upon the great holy place of another nation and inquiring what might be its innermost treasure hidden and guarded from all presumptuous approach, would get for answer that it was some image graven by art and man's device; and he would further learn that the supposed will of this deity found its expression in all licentious and abominable rites. But, on the other hand, a gentile, looking towards Israel's holy place and inquiring what might be behind the curtains of the tabernacle, and expecting perhaps to hear of some magnificent image, would be astounded with a very different reply. No image there! and not only no image, but words graven by God's desire which forbade fabrication of everything in the shape of an image. Within that gilded box of shittim wood there lie written the leading requirements for those who would obey the will of Jehovah. *Litera scripta manet.* The spot where that ark had a resting-place was a sacred spot, not approachable by the common multitude: but this was not because there was anything to conceal. The recesses of heathenism will not bear inspection. The character of the deity worshipped corresponds with the degradation of the worshippers. But here is the great distinction of that Divine service found in Israel, that however vile the people might be, and even the officiating priests, an exposure of the hidden things of their sacred place would have been an exposure of their apostasy. No Israelite needed to be ashamed of what lay within the ark on which he was bound to look with such veneration, which he was bound to guard with such assiduity; and if it be true that every human heart ought to be a sanctuary of God, then the very heart of hearts should be as the ark of the testimony in the sanctuary of old. Our hearts should be better than our outward services. We should have the consciousness that God's will has a real, an abiding, a cherished, a predominating place in our affections. All the actions of life should flow from the fountain formed by the ever living force of a Divine will within us. Let us ever consider the internal more than the external. If the internal be right, the external will come right in due time. If God's commandments—the full scheme of Christian virtues—are indeed written in our hearts, then all superficial hindrances and roughness can only last for a little time. The Divine life ruling within must subdue all things to itself.—Y.

Chap. xxv., vers. 17—22; chap. xxxvii., vers. 6—9.—*The mercy seat and the cherubim.* The ark already indicated as the repository of the two tables, is now further indicated as the resting-place of the mercy seat and the cherubim. Thus there was presented to the thoughts of the people a Divinely constituted whole, a great symbolic unity which set forth the glory and the mystery of God's presence as no unaided human conception could have done, however sublime, however sincere. The ark, the mercy seat, and the cherubim once made and placed in position, were hidden away from the general gaze. Bezaleel looked no more upon his handiwork. But though the things behind the veil were themselves hidden, yet their general character and relations were known. Hidden in one sense, in another sense they were all the more manifest just because they were hidden. It was perfectly well known that behind the veil God made himself known as the God of the commandments, the God of the mercy seat, the God shining forth between the cherubim. The proximity of the mercy seat to the tables of the law was an excellent way of showing that the requirements inscribed on these tables were to be no dead letter. If they could not be honoured by a heartfelt and properly corresponding obedience, then they must be honoured by a heartfelt repentance for transgression, an adequate propitiation, and an honourable forgiveness. There was a place for profound and permanent repentance, and a place for real and signal mercy to the transgressor: but for a slurring over of disobedience there was no place at all. Very close indeed are the law and the gospel. The law, when its comprehensiveness and severity are considered, magnifies the gospel; and the gospel, when we consider how emphatically it is proclaimed as being a gospel, magnifies the law. Then we have also to consider *what may be signified by the presence of the cherubim*; and surely we shall not go far wrong in connecting these golden figures here with the presence of those awful guardians who prevented the return of Adam and Eve to the scene of earthly bliss which they had forfeited. The presence of these cherubim suggested a solemn consideration of all that man had actually lost; God looking from between the cherubim, was looking as it were from the scene of the ideal human life on earth; that life which might have been the real, if man had only persisted according to the original injunction of his Maker. Thus the cherubim are associated, first with the barrier against return, and then with the working out of a plan for glorious and complete restoration. There is here no word of the flaming sword. The cherubim seem to be regarded as contemplative rather than active, somewhat as St. Peter phrases it when he speaks of things which the angels desire to look into. Over against the delight of those faithful ones who guarded Eden, we must set the thought of those in whose presence there is such inexpressible joy over the repenting sinner. God looked forth from between these symbols of the unsullied creatures who serve him day and night continually, and towards those people whom, though at present they were disobedient, carnalised, and unsusceptible, he nevertheless called his own. Sinners may be so changed, renewed, and energised as to be joined in the most complete harmony of service even with the cherubim.—Y.

Vers. 10—40. What must be found with every soul that is God's dwelling-place:—
I. THE ARK (vers. 10—22). *The place where the Lord meets and communes with us.* 1. It contained the testimony. The light of the meeting-place with God is the word concerning righteousness and sin. There is no communion with God if that be left out. The law which searches and condemns us must be honoured as God's testimony. 2. Between God and the law we have broken is the mercy seat, sin's glorious covering, on which the cherubim—emblems of the highest intelligence and purity of creation—look, and before which we also bow, with adoring awe. 3. Over the mercy seat rests the cloud of God's glory. We shall meet God only as we seek him here. His glory can be fully revealed and the might of his salvation proved here alone.
II. THE TABLE OF SHEW-BREAD, THE SOUL'S ENTIRE CONSECRATION. 1. The bread was the emblem of God's people. The twelve cakes represented the twelve tribes. The fruit of the great Husbandman's toil is to be found in us. 2. God's joy is to be found in us. The Lord's portion is his people. 3. We are to be prepared and perfected for his presence, and to be for ever before him (ver. 30).
III. THE CANDLESTICK, THE EMBLEM OF THE LORD'S PEOPLE, AND THEIR WORLD-SERVICE. 1. It is made of pure gold, the only metal that loses nothing, though passed through the fire and whose lustre is never tarnished. 2. It was the only light of the

holy place. The true Christian Church the only light which in the world's darkness reveals the things of God and the pathway to his presence.—U.

Vers. 10—40.—*The ark, the table, and the candlestick.* The instructions for the making of these essential parts of the tabernacle furniture occupy the remainder of the chapter. The directions for making the altar of incense are postponed to ch. xxx. 1—10. The reason seems to be that the uses of this altar could not be described without reference to commands which were to be given respecting the altar of burnt-offering—to which the altar of incense stood in a certain relation of dependence—and to the ordinance for the institution of the priesthood. The instructions have respect to the internal relation of the parts.

I. THE ARK AND MERCY SEAT (vers. 10—23). This was the heart of the sanctuary —the throne of Jehovah. As the nucleus of the whole structure, it is described first. 1. *The ark proper* (vers. 10—17). For details, consult the exposition. A plain wooden box or chest, overlaid within and without with pure gold, and borne upon staves, for the insertion of which rings were provided in its feet or corners, its structure could not well have been simpler. On the resemblances and differences between this ark and the religious arks of the Egyptians, see the interesting article in " Kitto's Cyclopædia." The ark, in the religion of Israel, was simply a depository for the two tables of stone—the tables of the covenant. In its freedom from idolatrous symbols (in this respect a contrast to the Egyptian arks), it was a testimony to monotheism ; in the character of its contents, it testified to the ethical foundation of the religion—to the severe and stern morality which formed its basis. If ever doubt is cast on the pure moral character of the Hebrew faith, it should suffice to refute it, to point to the ark of the testimony. What a witness to the ruling power of the moral in this religion that, when the sacred chest is opened, the sole contents are found to be the two stone tables of the moral law (ver. 16) ! The deposition of these tables in the ark, underneath the mercy seat, had three ends. (1) They testified to the fact that God's kingdom in Israel was founded on immutable justice and righteousness (Ps. lxxxix. 15 ; xcvii. 2). Even grace, in its actings, must respect law. Favour cannot be dispensed on terms which make the law "void" (Rom. iii. 31). If sin is pardoned, it must be with full recognition of the law's claims against the sinner. The ultimate end must be to " establish the law" (Rom. iii. 31). Only in the Gospel have we the clear revelation of how, on these terms, mercy and truth can meet together, and righteousness and peace can kiss each other (Ps. lxxxv. 10 ; Rom. iii. 21—27). (2) They testified to the covenant obligation. The tables were, as Oehler calls them, " the obligatory document of the covenant." As such they were laid up in the heart of the sanctuary. (3) They testified against Israel's sins and backslidings. They testified against *all* sin in Israel, but especially against rebellion and deliberate apostasy. This appears to be the special force of the expression—" the testimony," " tables of testimony," etc. (Cf. Deut. xxxi. 26, 27—" Take this book of the law, and put it in the side of the ark of the covenant of the Lord your God, *that it may be there for a witness against thee.* For I know thy rebellion," etc.) 2. *The mercy seat* (ver. 17). The mercy seat, or propitiatory, made of pure gold, served as a lid or covering to the sacred chest. The name, however, as the Piel form implies, had more especial reference to the covering of sins. Sprinkled with blood of atonement, the mercy seat cancelled, as it were, the condemnatory witness of the underlying tables—covered sin from God's sight (ver. 21). From above this mercy seat, and from between the two cherubim that were upon it, God promised to meet with Moses, and to commune with him (ver. 22). The gracious element in the covenant with Israel here reaches its distinct expression. Jehovah could " by no means clear the guilty ; " *i.e.*, he could not call sin anything else than what it was, or tamper in the least degree with the condemnatory testimony of the law against it ; but he could admit atonements, and on the ground of expiatory rites, could *forgive* sin, and receive the sinner anew to his favour. The mercy seat thus foreshadowed Christ, as, in his sacred Person, the great Propitiatory for man (Rom. iii. 25)—priest, sacrifice, and mercy seat in one. On the basis of mere law, there can be no communion between God and man. The blood-sprinkled mercy seat must intervene. Only on the ground of Christ's mediation and intercession, can God transact with sinners. 3. *The cherubim* (vers. 18—23). The cherubic figures were formed from the same piece of gold which constituted the mercy seat, and rose at either end of it, with wings over-spreading the place of propitiation, and faces turned inward. On the various interpre-tations, see the exposition. The view which finds most favour is that which regards the cherubim, not as real and actual, but only as symbolic and imaginary beings—hieroglyphs of creation in its highest grade of perfection. Egyptian and Assyrian art abound in similar ideal forms, most of them representative, not of qualities of the creature, as distinct from its Creator, but of attributes of God revealed *in* creation. This view, also, has been taken of the cherubim of Scripture, but it must be rejected as untenable. We confess that, after all that has been written of the purely ideal signifi-cance of these figures—" the representative and quintessence of creation, placed in subordination to the great Creator "—we do not feel the theory to be satisfactory. We incline very much to agree with Delitzsch : " The Biblical conception considers the cherub as a *real heavenly being*, but the form which is given to it changes; it is sym-bolical and visionary." (*Hist. of Redemption*, p. 29.) It seems fair to connect the cherubim with the seraphs of the temple-vision in Isaiah (vi. 2); and this, taken with Gen. iii. 24, points strongly in the direction of an angelic interpretation. The concep-tion, however, unquestionably underwent development, and in the highly complex form in which it appears in Ezekiel may quite possibly take on much more of the ideal character than it had at first ; may, in short, closely approximate to what is commonly given as the meaning of the symbol. Confining ourselves to the figures of the taber-nacle, we prefer to view them, with the older writers, and with Keil and others among the moderns, as symbolic of the angel hosts which attend and guard the throne of Jehovah, zealous, like himself, for the honour of his law, and deeply interested in the counsels of his love (1 Pet. i. 12). The angel-idea is so prominent in the theology of Israel that we should expect it to find *some* embodiment in this symbolism. And what finer picture could be given of angels than in these cherubic figures, who, with wings outspread and faces lowered, represent at once humility, devotion, adoration, intelligence, service, and zeal ? On the angels at the giving of the law, see Deut. xxxiii. 2. On the assembly or council of holy ones, see Ps. lxxxix. 6—9. The wings of the cherubs con-stituted, as it were, a protecting shade for those who took refuge under them in the Divine mercy (Ps. xci. 1). Jehovah's guards, they appear in the symbol as ready to defend his Majesty against profane invasion; as avengers of disobedience to his will; as sheltering and aiding those who are his friends. They are, when otherwise unemployed, rapt in adoration of his perfections, and deeply attent on the study of his secrets. So interpreted, the cherubs are hieroglyphs of the heavenly spiritual world.

II. THE TABLE OF SHEW-BREAD (vers. 23—31). The table was part of the belongings of the holy place. This shows it to have been primarily connected, not with the relation of God to Israel, but conversely, with the works and services of the people, in their relation to Jehovah. Like other articles in the sanctuary, the table was to present a golden exterior, and on it were to be placed twelve cakes of shew-bread (ver. 30; Lev. xxiv. 5—9), with flagons for purposes of libation (ver. 29). The shew-bread had thus the significance of a meat-offering. The sense may be thus exhibited. Bread is the means of nourishment of the natural life. The twelve cakes represented the twelve tribes. The presentation of the bread on the table was, accordingly, 1. A recognition of Jehovah's agency in the bestowal of what is necessary for the support of life. Natural life is supported by his bounty. The cakes on the table were a grateful acknowledgment of this dependence. Spiritually, they pointed to the higher bread with which God nourishes the soul. They remind us of our duty to give thanks for this, not less than for the other. The true bread is Christ (John vi. 32). 2. A dedication of the life so nourished to him whose goodness constantly sustained it. We take this to be the essential feature in the offering. The life-sustaining food and drink is placed upon the table of Jehovah. In the act of placing it there, the tribes offer, as it were, to God, the life which it sustains, and which is derived from his bounty. The meaning could not be better expressed than in words borrowed from St. Paul—" Unto which promise, our twelve tribes, *instantly serving God day and night*, hope to come " (Acts xxvi. 7). Perpetual consecration—a life fruitful in good works, and acts of holy service to God. This is the conception which is embodied in the shew-bread. Here, also, the symbolism points to a life higher than that nourished on material bread, and might almost be said to pledge to Israel the gift of the higher bread needed for it. Fed on this bread from heaven—*i.e.*, on Christ, who gave himself for us (John vi. 51), we are to live, not to ourselves, but to him who died for us, and rose again (2 Cor. v. 15).

III. THE GOLDEN CANDLESTICK (vers. 31—40). This sacred ornament was, like the mercy seat, to be made of pure gold. Art was to be allowed to do its best to make it massive, shapely, beautiful. Stem and branches were to be wrought with great artistic skill. The lamps, seven in number, fed with beaten olive oil (ch. xxvii. 20, 21), were to burn all night in the sanctuary. The immediate design of its introduction was, of course, to illuminate the holy place. Symbolically, the candlestick represented the calling of Israel to be a people of light. Compare, as regards Christians, Matt. v. 14, 16; Phil. ii. 15. The church is the abode of light. It has no affinity with darkness. The light with which it is lighted is the light of truth and holiness. The lamps are the gifts of wisdom and holiness, which Christ bestows upon his people. Their own souls being filled with light, they become, in turn, the lights of the world. The oil which feeds the light is the oil of God's Holy Spirit. Note—we cannot make a higher use even of natural gifts, say of knowledge or wisdom, than to let their light burn in the sanctuary—in the service of God.—J. O.

Vers. 18—21.—*He maketh the winds his messengers, and his ministers a flame of fire.* The cherubim were to be of one piece with the mercy seat, the whole a lid, or guard above the lid, to the ark or chest which contained the tables of the law.

I. THE CHERUBIM AND THEIR MEANING. 1. *The symbol.* They are not described here; but by comparing the various passages in which they are referred to we may get a general notion as to their appearance. Ezekiel, who must have been familiar with their appearance, describes them as seen in his vision (Ezek. i.), four wings, four faces, etc. In Rev. iv. the same idea is seen in a developed form, four creatures having each a different face, and each having six wings. This latter feature suggests identity with the seraphim in Isaiah's vision (ch. vi.), and the name "seraphim," which seems connected with fire or burning, reminds us of the "flaming sword" with which the cherubim are associated in Gen. iii. 24. In any case wings, fire, and a mixture of the human and the animal in their appearance are characteristic features. 2. *That which is symbolised.* Wings in Scripture almost always represent *the wind.* The appearance of the cherubim is as *fire.* Their faces are those of the chief beasts—the lion, the bull-calf, the man, the eagle. Their form tends towards the human. On the whole, we may say they represent nature under her manifold aspects, nature as interpreted chiefly through the natural man in his perfection regarded as a part of nature. The cherubim shadow forth the natural creation according to the Divine ideal. The clause in the Te Deum—"To thee, cherubim and seraphim continually do cry," is the Benedicite condensed into a sentence!

II. POSITION AND OFFICE OF THE CHERUBIM. 1. *Position.* One piece with the mercy seat. Nature, in spite of appearances, is a manifestation of God's mercy to man. His voice may not be in the tempest or the fire, yet the tempest and the fire form a canopy to that throne whence issues the "still, small voice." If we regard the mercy seat as typical of Christ (cf. Rom. iii. 25), then we are reminded of the mysterious relation which exists between Christ and nature (Col. i. 17; John i. 1, etc.). 2. *Office.* Here they protect the ark and its contents, as in 'Gen. iii. 24, they "keep the way of the tree of life." The way of the tree of life is the way of righteousness, the way of the law of God. Thus the cherubim above the ark declare that nature, a manifestation of God's mercy, is also the guardian of God's law.

III. PRACTICAL CONCLUSIONS. 1. Nature *does* guard the way of the tree of life, the law of God. There is a tendency implanted in the very constitution of nature which "makes for righteousness." Break a law, and, by God's merciful ordinance, you are compelled to reap the penalty. Sin in secret, yet you cannot escape the cognisance of this vigilant, sleepless, unconscious sentinel [cf. Eugene Aram's dream]. It is "full of eyes within and without." 2. Nature is a manifestation of mercy. Undiscoverable transgression would be irretrievable damnation. Christ, too, is one with the mercy seat; nature is rooted in the Divine Word. If we go to that throne of grace we may still obtain mercy, and win, through Christ, peace with the avengers.—G.

EXPOSITION.

Vers. 23—30.—THE TABLE OF SHEW-BREAD. From the description of the ark, which constituted the sole furniture of the *most* holy place, God proceeded to describe the furniture of the holy place, or body of the tabernacle, which was to consist of three objects—1. A table, called the table of shew-bread (" bread of presence " or " bread of setting-forth "). 2. A candelabrum, or lamp-stand ; and 3. An altar for the offering of incense. Of these the table seems to have been regarded as of primary importance ; and its description is therefore made to follow immediately on that of the ark. It was of acacia wood, overlaid with pure gold, and was of the most ordinary shape—oblong-square, *i.e.*, with four legs, one at each corner. The only peculiar features of the table, besides its material, were the border, or edging, which surrounded it at the top, the framework which strengthened the legs (ver. 25), and the rings by which it was to be carried from place to place.

Ver. 23.—**Two cubits shall be the length thereof**, etc. The table was to be three feet long, one foot six inches broad, and two feet three inches high. It was thus quite a small table, narrow for its length, and about two inches below the ordinary height.

Ver. 24.—**Thou shalt overlay it with pure gold.** Again, gilding may be meant ; but a covering with thin plates of gold is perhaps more probable. **A crown of gold round about.** A border, or edging round the top, which would prevent anything that was placed on the table from readily falling off. (Compare ver. 11.)

Ver. 25.—**A border of a hand-breadth.** Rather " a band " or " framing." This seems to have been a broad flat bar, placed about half-way down the legs, uniting them and holding them together. It was represented in the sculpture of the table which adorned the Arch of Titus. (See the *Speaker's Commentary*, vol. i. p. 363.) **A golden crown to the border**—*i.e.*, an edging at the top of the bar, which could be only for ornament.

Ver. 26.—**The four corners that are on the four feet**, is scarcely an intelligible expression. *Pe'oth*, the word translated " corners," means properly " ends ; " and the direction seems to be, that the four rings should be affixed to the four " ends " of the table ; those ends, namely, which are " at the four feet." It is a periphrasis, meaning no more than that they should

be affixed to the feet, as Josephus tells us that they were. (*Ant. Jud.* iii. 6, § 6.)

Ver. 27.—**Over against the border.** Rather " opposite the band " or " framing " — *i.e.*, opposite the points at which the " band " or " framing " was inserted into the legs. Bishop Patrick supposes that the table " was not carried up as high as the ark was, but hung down between the priests, on whose shoulders the staves rested." But it is carried upright in the bas-relief on the Arch of Titus, and might have been as easily so carried as the ark. (See the comment on ver. 12.) **Of the staves.** Rather, " for staves." Staves for the table had not yet been mentioned ; and naturally the word has no article.

Ver. 29.—**The dishes thereof.** Literally " its dishes," or rather perhaps, " its bowls " (LXX. τρύβλια). They were probably the vessels in which the loaves were brought to the table. Loaves are often seen arranged in bowls in the Egyptian tomb decorations (Lepsius, *Denkmäler*, pt. ii., pls. 5, 19, 84, 129, &c.). **Spoons thereof.** Rather, " its incense cups "—small jars or pots in which the incense, offered with the loaves (Lev. xxiv. 5), was to be burnt. Two such were represented in the bas-relief of the table on the Arch of Titus. **Covers thereof and bowls thereof.** Rather, " its flagons and its chalices " (LXX. σπονδεῖα καὶ κύαθοι)—vessels required for the libations or " drink offerings " which accompanied every meat-offering. **To cover withal.** Rather, as in the margin, " to pour out withal." So the Septuagint, Vulgate, Syriac, and most of the Targums.

Ver. 30.—**Thou shalt set upon the table shew-bread before me alway.** Here we have at once the object of the table, and its name, explained. The table was to have set upon it continually twelve loaves, or cakes, of bread (Lev. xxiv. 5), which were to be renewed weekly on the sabbath-day (*ibid.* ver. 8), the stale loaves being at the same time consumed by the priests in the holy place. These twelve loaves or cakes were to constitute a continual thank-offering to God from the twelve tribes of Israel in return for the blessings of life and sustenance which they received from him. The bread was called " bread of face," or " bread of presence," because it was set before the " face " or " presence " of God, which dwelt in the holy of holies. The Septuagint renders the phrase by ἄρτοι ἐνώπιοι " loaves that are face to face "—St. Matthew by ἄρτοι τῆς προθέσεως, " loaves of setting-forth "—whence the *Schaubrode* of Luther, and our " shew-bread," which is a paraphrase rather than a translation

HOMILETICS.

Vers. 23—30.—*The symbolism of the table of shew-bread.* Before the holy of holies, within which was the Divine Presence, dwelling in thick darkness behind the veil, was to be not perpetually this golden table, bearing bread and wine and frankincense. The bread and wine and frankincense constituted a perpetual thank-offering, offered by Israel as a nation to the high and holy God. The idea was that of a constant memorial (Lev. xxiv. 8), a continual acknowledgment of the Divine goodness on the part of the nation. The essence of the offering was the bread—we know of the wine only by implication; the frankincense is distinctly mentioned (*ib.* ver. 7), but is altogether subordinate. Israel, grateful to God for maintaining and supporting its life, physical and spiritual, expressed its gratitude by this one and only *never ceasing* offering. It was intended to teach—

I. THAT GRATITUDE WAS DUE TO GOD FROM HIS PEOPLE PERPETUALLY. Men are so cold by nature, so selfish, so little inclined to real thankfulness, that it was well they should be reminded, as they were by the shew-bread, of thankfulness being a continuous, unending duty, a duty moreover owed by all. No tribe was ever exempt, however reduced in numbers, however little esteemed, however weak and powerless. The *twelve* loaves were perpetually before the Lord.

II. THAT GRATITUDE MUST BE SHOWN BY OFFERINGS. The best offering is that of a " pure heart ; " but no man of a pure heart, who possessed aught, was ever yet content to offer merely " the calves of his lips "—men instinctively give of their best to God. Bread, the staff of life—wine, that maketh glad the heart of man—frankincense, the most precious of spices, are fitting gifts to him. The offering of bread signifies the devotion of our strength—of wine, the devotion of our feelings—of frankincense, the devotion of our most sublimised spiritual aspirations to the eternal. Israel, as a nation, perpetually offered these offerings, and thereby inculcated on each individual of the nation the duty of doing the same, separately and individually, for private, as the nation did for public, benefits.

III. THAT NO OFFERING COULD BE ACCEPTABLE TO GOD, UNLESS ALL ITS SURROUND-INGS WERE PURE AND HOLY. The loaves were to be of the finest flour (Lev. xxiv. 5). The frankincense was to be " pure frankincense" (*ib.* ver. 7). The table was to be overlaid with " pure gold" (Ex. xxvi. 24). All the utensils of the table were to be of the same (*ib.* ver. 29). Nothing " common or unclean" was to come into contact with the offering, which was " the most holy unto the Lord" of all the offerings made to him (Lev. xxiv. 8). The purity and perfection of all the material surroundings of the offering suggested the need of equal purity in those who offered it.

HOMILIES BY VARIOUS AUTHORS.

Chap. xxv., vers. 23—30; chap. xxxvii., vers. 10—16.—*The table of shew-bread.* Between the ark of the testimony and the table of the shew-bread we see this great correspondence—that they were of the same material of shittim wood and had the same adornment of gold. But along with this correspondence there was a great difference, in that the ark of the testimony stood within the veil, while the table of shew-bread stood without. The ark of the testimony had the mercy seat above it, while the table of the shew-bread had the lighted candlestick over against it. There must be some significance in having the table on the people's side of the veil rather than God's side ; and may it not be that the table with its bread and the candlestick with its light were meant to set forth God's providential support and illumination of all his people ? The shew-bread was not so much an offering presented to God as something placed on the table by his command, regularly and unfailingly, to symbolise the unfailing regularity with which he supplies his people in their ordinary wants. The daily meat offering with its fine flour was the representation of the labour of the people : and so we may take the shew-bread as representing that blessing of God without which the most diligent toil in sowing and watering avail nothing. The God of the shew-bread is the God in whom we live and move and have our being ; we cannot do without him for the necessities and comforts of natural life. Were he to cease the operations of his energy in nature, it would soon be seen how utterly fruitless is all our working just by itself. A great and efficient providing power cannot be denied by whatsoever name we choose to call him. Would we know him and more of him than we can ever know in nature— we must think of what lies within the veil. He gives us the things belonging to the outer holy place, the bread and the light, the natural strength and the natural wisdom, in order that we may come to know him in his spiritual demands and his ability to satisfy the deepest demands of our hearts. The God who gives that bread to his people, of which the shew-bread was an ever renewed sample, gives it that we whose lives are continued by the bread may spend them to his glory. God feeds us that we may be in *all things his servants*, and not *in anything* our own masters.—Y.

EXPOSITION.

THE GOLDEN CANDLESTICK (vers. 31—40). Though the holy of holies was always dark, unless when lighted by the glory of God (ch. xl. 34, 35), the holy place, in which many of the priests' functions were to be performed, was to be always kept light. In the day-time sufficient light entered from the porch in front; but, as evening drew on, some artificial illumination was required. In connection with this object, the golden candlestick, or rather lamp-stand, was designed, which, together with its appurtenances, is described in the remainder of the chapter.

Ver. 31.— **A candlestick.** The golden candlestick is figured upon the Arch of Titus, and appears by that representation to have consisted of an upright shaft, from which three curved branches were carried out on either side, all of them in the same plane. It stands there on an octagonal pedestal, in two stages, ornamented with figures of birds and sea-monsters. This pedestal is, however, clearly Roman work, and no part of the original. **Of beaten work.** Not cast, but fashioned by the hand, like the cherubim (ver. 18). **His shaft.** Rather, "its base" (literally "flank"). **His branches.** Our version follows the Septuagint; but the Hebrew noun is in the singular number, and seems to designate the upright stem, or shaft. The "branches are not mentioned till ver. 32, where the same noun is used in the plural. **His bowls, his knops, and his flowers.** Rather, "its cups, its pomegranates, and its lilies." The "cups" are afterwards likened to almond flowers (ver. 33); they formed the first ornament on each branch; above them was a representation of the pomegranate fruit; above this a lily blossom. The lily-blossoms supported the lamps, which were separate (ver. 37). The remainder were of one piece with the candlestick.

Ver. 32.—**Six branches.** The representation on the Arch of Titus exactly agrees with this description. It was a peculiarity of the "candlestick," as compared with other cande-

labra, that all the branches were in the same plane.

Ver. 33.—**Three bowls made like unto almonds.** Cups shaped like almond blossoms seem to be intended. Each branch had three of these in succession, then a pomegranate and a lily-flower. The lily probably represented the Egyptian lotus, or water-lily. **In the other branch.** Rather, "on *another* branch." There were six branches, not two only. The ornamentation of two is described; then we are told that the remainder were similar.

Ver. 34.—**In the candlestick:** *i.e.*, in the central shaft or stem, which is viewed as "the candlestick" *par excellence.* Here were to be twelve ornaments, the series of cup, pomegranate, and lily being repeated four times, once in connection with each pair of branches, and a fourth time at the summit.

Ver. 35.—**A knop under two branches of the same.** The branches were to quit the stem at the point of junction between the pomegranate (knop) and the lily.

Ver. 36.— **All it.** Rather, "all of it." **Shall be one beaten work.** Compare ver. 31

Ver. 37.—**The seven lamps.** The lamps are not described. They appear by the representation on the Arch of Titus to have been hemispherical bowls on a stand, which fitted into the lily-blossom wherewith each of the seven branches terminated. **They shall light the lamps.** The lamps were lighted every evening at sunset (ch. xxvii. 21; xxx. 8; Lev. xxiv. 3, etc.), and burnt till morning, when the High Priest extinguished them and "dressed" them (ch. xxx. 7). **That they may give light over against it.** The candlestick was placed on the southern side of the holy place, parallel to the wall, the seven lamps forming a row. The light was consequently shed strongly on the opposite, or northern wall, where the table of shew-bread stood.

Ver. 38.—**The tongs thereof.** Tongs or pincers were required for trimming the wicks of the lamps. Compare 1 Kings vii. 49; 2 Chr. iv. 21. **Snuff-dishes** were also needed for the reception of the fragments removed from the wicks by the tongs. "Snuffers," though the word is used in Ex. xxvii. 23, in the place of tongs, had not been invented, and were indeed unknown to the ancients.

Ver. 39.—**Of a talent of pure gold shall he make it.** The candlestick, with all its appurtenances, was to weigh exactly a talent of gold. The value of the Hebrew gold talent is supposed to have been between 10,000*l.* and 11,000*l.* of our money.

Ver. 40.—**Their pattern, which was shewed thee in the mount.** Compare ver. 9, and the comment *ad loc.* It would seem from this passage that the "patterns" were shown to Moses first, and the directions as to the making given afterwards.

HOMILETICS.

Vers, 31—40.—*The symbolism of the candlestick.* The light which illuminated the darkness of the tabernacle can represent nothing but the Holy Spirit of God, which illuminates the dark places of the earth and the recesses of the heart of man. That the light was sevenfold is closely analogous to the representation of the Holy Spirit in the Revelation of St. John, where there are said to be " seven lamps of fire burning before the throne, which are the seven Spirits of God" (Rev. iv. 5). It is generally allowed that these " seven spirits " represent the one indivisible but sevenfold Spirit, who imparts of his sevenfold gifts to men. Seven is, in fact, one of the numbers which express perfection and completeness; and a sevenfold light is merely a light which is full and ample, which irradiates sufficiently all that it is designed to throw light upon. The light from the golden candlestick especially irradiated the opposite wall of the tabernacle where the table of shew-bread was set, showing how the offerings of the natural man require to be steeped in the radiance of the Spirit of God in order to be an acceptable gift to the Almighty. We may see—

I. In the pure gold of the candlestick the spotless perfection of him, whose emblem is the innocent dove—who is " the spirit of purity." The pure light of the refined olive oil, and the pure gold of the candlestick were in harmony. Both indicated alike the Spirit's awful holiness. Both taught the presence of One, who was " of purer eyes then to behold iniquity."

II. In the simple yet beautiful ornamentation of almond buds, and pomegranates, and lilies, we may see the delight of the Spirit in all things lovely, sweet, and innocent. The Spirit of God, which, when the earth was first made, " brooded upon the face of the waters" (Gen. i. 2), still tenderly watches over creation, and rejoices in the loveliness spread over it by his own influences. Flowers and fruits are among the most beautiful of created things, and well befit the interior of the sanctuary where God's presence is manifested, whether cunningly carved in stone, or fashioned in metal-work, or, best of all, in their own simple natural freshness.

III. In the soft radiance shed around by the candlestick, we must see the illuminating power of the Spirit, which gives light to the world. Spiritual gifts, however diverse, are his gifts. " To one is given by the Spirit the word of wisdom; to another the word of knowledge by the same Spirit; to another gifts of healing; to another faith; to another prophecy; to another miracles; to another tongues; to another the interpretation of tongues; but all these worketh that one and the self-same Spirit, dividing to every man severally as he will" (1 Cor. xii. 8—11). It is he who " doth our souls inspire, and lighten with celestial fire." It is he from whom all wisdom and knowledge, and spiritual illumination are derived. He informs the conscience, guides the reason, quickens the spiritual insight, gives us discernment between good and evil. Christ is " the light of the world," but Christ diffuses his light by his Spirit. Man's contact is closest with the Third Person of the Trinity, who communicates to the soul every good and perfect gift which has come down to it from the Father of lights. Illumination is especially his gift; and it is therefore that light and fire are made the especial symbols of his presence (Matt. iii. 11; Acts ii. 3, 4; Rev. iv. 5).

IV. In the sevenfold light of the seven lamps we may see the fulness and completeness of the illumination which the Spirit vouchsafes to man. Fulness and completeness in respect to man's needs—not absolute completeness or fulness; for " Now, we see through a glass darkly," " we know in part only—not as we are known." But "his grace is sufficient for us." We know all that we need to know —we see all that we need to see. "*Full* light" and "*true* knowledge" are for another sphere; but still, even here, we are privileged to see and know as much as would be of advantage to us. Inspired messengers have declared to us what they have felt justified in calling "the whole counsel of God" (Acts xx. 27). We are familiarly acquainted with mysteries, which the very "angels desire to look into" (1 Pet. i. 12).

V. IN THE PROVISION OF TONGS AND SNUFF-DISHES WE MAY SEE THAT THE CO-OPERA-TION OF MAN IS REQUIRED, IF THE BRIGHTNESS OF THE SPIRITUAL LIGHT VOUCHSAFED TO HIM IS TO REMAIN UNDIMMED. The lamps of the golden candlestick had to be "dressed" each morning. Perpetual vigilance is necessary. Phrases once instinct with power lose their force; and new phrases, adapted to each new generation, have to be coined and circulated. The translation of the word of God in each country has from time to time to be revised, or an accretion of usage will dim the light of the pure word, and overshadow it with traditional glosses. Teachers must be watchful, that they do not suffer the light of their teaching to grow dim; hearers must be watchful, that they do not by their obstinacy refuse to give the light passage into their souls.

HOMILIES BY VARIOUS AUTHORS.

Chap. xxv., vers. 31—40; chap. xxvii., vers. 17—24.—*The candlestick.* As the shew-bread was a symbol of what Jehovah gave to his people in one way, so the lighted candlestick in all the preciousness of its material and elaboration of its workmanship was a symbol in another way. And even as the shew-bread was in magnitude only as a crumb of all the great supply which God gives in the way of food, so the candlestick even in full blaze was but as a glimmer compared with all the light which God had gathered and arranged in various ways to guide and cheer his people. But glimmer though the light of the candlestick might be, it was quite enough to act as an inspiring and encouraging symbol for all who, seeing, were able to understand. From that place between the cherubim, shrouded as it was in awful sanctity, there radiated forth abundance of light for every one in Israel who was disposed to profit by it. In heathendom the perplexed went long distances to consult renowned oracles, only to find that for all practical purposes they might just as well have stayed at home. There was a great boast of illumination; but the reality turned out ambiguous and delusive. But here is the seven-branched candlestick (seven being the perfect number) to indicate that God would assuredly give all needed light to his people. On one side stood the shew-bread, and over against it the light. So we need God's guidance to show us how to use what materials he puts in our hands for our support. It is only too easy for man, following the light of a corrupted nature, to waste, abuse, and degrade the choice gifts of God. Consider the vast quantities of grain that instead of passing through the hands of the baker to become food, pass through the hands of the brewer and distiller to become alcohol. In all our use of the resources which God has placed in our hands, we must seek with simplicity of purpose and becoming humility for God's light, that we may be assured of God's will. God has placed us in the midst of such profusion that we may use it for him and not for self. And is not a lesson taught us in this respect by the very candlestick itself? It was made of gold. The Israelites at this time seem to have had great store of gold; and left to their own inclinations, they gave it for shaping into an image to be worshipped. Now, by causing this candlestick to be made of gold, Jehovah seemed to summon his people to give their gold to aid in supporting and diffusing his light. What God gives may be a curse or a blessing, just according to the spirit in which we receive and use it. We can desire no nobler office than to be ourselves as lamps, doing something to shed abroad that great, true light of the world, which radiates from the person of Christ. He who is living so as to make Christ better known amid the spiritual darkness of the world has surely learnt the great lesson that God would teach to all ages by this golden candlestick in his sanctuary of old.—Y.

EXPOSITION.

CHAPTER XXVI.

Vers. 1—37.—THE TABERNACLE. The sacred furniture which the tabernacle was to contain having been described, with the exception of the "altar of incense"—the description of which is reserved for ch xxx. (vers. 1—10)—directions were next given for the sacred structure itself. This was to consist of three main things—1. A quadrangular enclosure thirty cubits long by ten broad, open at one end, and on the other three sides enclosed by boards of acacia-wood overlaid with gold—called the *mishkân*, or "the dwelling-place," in our version usually translated "tabernacle." 2. A tent of goat's hair, supported upon poles, and stretched by means of ropes and tent-pegs in the ordinary manner over the *mishkân*. This is called the *'ôhel*—which is the usual word for a "tent" in Hebrew, and is so translated generally (Gen. iv. 20; ix. 21; xiii. 31; xviii. 1, etc.), though in this chapter, unfortunately, "covering" (ver. 7); and 3. A "covering"—*mikseh*, to be placed over the *'ôhel*, composed of rams' skins dyed red, and seals' skins (ver. 14). Subordinate parts of the structure were—(*a*) The sockets, or bases, which were to receive and support the upright boards (vers. 19—25); (*b*) The bars which were to hold the boards together (vers. 26—29); (*c*) The veil, stretched on pillars, which was to be hung across the "dwelling-house," and to separate it into two parts, the "holy place" and the "holy of holies" (vers. 31—33); and (*d*) The curtain or "hanging" at the open end of the "dwelling-place," where there were no boards, which was intended to close that side of the structure when necessary (vers. 36, 37).

The fine linen covering (vers. 1—6).

Ver. 1.—**Thou shalt make the tabernacle with ten curtains.** These "ten curtains" are explained in the verses which follow to be ten "breadths," so fastened together as to form practically a single curtain or awning, which constituted the cieling or inner covering of the tabernacle. The mode of its arrangement is not quite certain. Some suppose that it was really a part of the "tent," being laid over the same framework as the goats' hair curtain (Fergusson, Cook); others believe it to have been strained across the *mishkân* and fastened to the top of the boards on either

side, thence depending, either inside or outside (Bähr, Keil). The former supposition appears the more probable. **Fine twined linen** is linen the threads of which are formed of several fine strands twisted together. This is often the case with Egyptian linen. On **blue and purple and scarlet,** see the comment upon ch. xxv. 4. **Cherubims of cunning work.** Rather, "cherubim, the work of a skilled weaver." Figures of cherubs were to be woven into the hangings in the loom itself, not embroidered upon them afterwards.

Ver. 2.—**Eight and twenty cubits.** This is the exact length required for a rectangular tented roof over such a space, which should descend (as tent roofs usually do) within about seven feet of the ground. The comparison made in vers. 12, 13, between the fine linen covering of the *mishkân* and the goats' hair covering of the "tent," implies that the one was directly under the other, and that both were arranged in the same way. **The breadth of four cubits.** This gives for the entire length of the curtain (4 by 10), 40 cubits, or ten cubits more than the length of the boarded space. The roof must thus have been advanced some distance in front of the tabernacle proper, or rectangular boarded space. **Every one of the curtains shall have one measure.** They shall all, *i.e.*, have the same measure.

Ver. 3.—When the ten "breadths" had been woven, five were to be sewn together to form one portion of the awning, and the other five to form another portion, the reason for this being, probably, that if all the ten breadths had been sewn together, the awning would have been too cumbrous to have been readily folded together, or easily conveyed when the people journeyed.

Ver. 6.—The Authorised Version gives the sense fairly. The two curtains, each composed of five "breadths," were to be united by means of one hundred loops, fifty on each curtain, which were to be coupled together by fifty "taches" or clasps. The loops were to be of the "blue" material used generally in the textile fabrics of the tabernacle (ch. xxv. 4; xxvi. 1, 31, 36), and the "taches" or clasps were to be of gold. In this way the covering of the *mishkân* was to be completed.

The goat's skin tent-cloth (vers. 7—13).

Ver. 7.—From the inner covering of the tabernacle the directions proceed to the external covering, or rather coverings, which constituted the real strength of the structure, and its protection from wet or stormy weather. Curtains of goats' hair, such as the Arabs still use, as the ordinary covering of their tents (Layard, *Nin. and Bab.*, p. 171), were to form a true "tent" (*'ôhel*) above the tabernacle, being supported by tent-poles, and kept taut by means of cords and pegs (ch. xxvii. 19 ; xxxv 18). See the representation in Dr. W. Smith's *Dictionary of the Bible*, vol. iii. p. 1454, which is reproduced in the *Speaker's Commentary*, vol. i. p. 376. **To be a covering.** In ch. xxxvi. 14, we have—"he made curtains of goats' hair *for the tent* over the tabernacle," which is far better. The word used in both places is the same (*'ôhel*). **Eleven curtains**—*i.e.*, "eleven *breadths*." Compare ver. 1.

Ver. 8.—**The length . . . shall be thirty cubits.** A tent with a rectangular roof, over such a chamber as the *mishkân*, brought down, as tents usually are, within six or seven feet of the ground, would have required a covering of this length. If the slope of the roof had been greater, the covering must have been longer. **The breadth . . . four cubits.** This gives for the entire covering, when made up, a width of forty-four cubits, or sixty-six feet. As the entire length of the *mishkân* was only thirty cubits, or forty-five feet, it is evident that the tent projected considerably beyond the tabernacle, either at both ends, or, at any rate, at one end. Probably the projection was at one end only—*viz.*, in front ; where it constituted a porch, eighteen or twenty feet deep. The temple, which was modelled after the tabernacle, had a porch fifteen feet deep.

Ver. 9.—**Thou shalt couple,** etc. As with the inner awning of linen, so with the goats' hair tent-cloth. The whole when made up was to be in two pieces, for convenience of transport. (See the comment on ver. 3.) The number of breadths in the tent-cloth being uneven, the two pieces were to be of different sizes, one containing five, and the other six, "breadths." **Thou shalt double the sixth curtain in the forefront of the tabernacle.** "Tabernacle" here is a mistranslation ; since the Hebrew word is *'ôhel*, "tent." The meaning may be, either that the sixth breadth was to be doubled back upon the fifth, or that half of it was to be doubled back upon the other half. The latter view is to be preferred, since otherwise the extra breadth would have been superfluous.

Ver. 10.—**Fifty loops in the edge of the curtain that coupleth the second.** Rather, "fifty loops at the edge of the second curtain of coupling." The two portions of the goats' hair covering were to be united in exactly the same way as those of the inner awning of linen. Fifty loops were to be sewn on to the edge of the extreme, or outermost, breadth of each portion, and these loops were to be connected by clasps or links. The outermost breadth on which the loops are sewn, is called the curtain of coupling."

Ver. 11.—**Fifty taches of brass.** Rather

"of bronze." The links of the inner curtain were of gold (ver. 6).

Ver. 12.—**The remnant which remaineth,** etc. Both this and the next verse presume a very close connection between the fine linen covering of the *mishkân* and the goats hair tent-cloth which protected it. "The remnant that remaineth" is the half-breadth by which the tent-cloth would overlap the linen covering at the back of the tent, when at the front half of the eleventh breadth had been turned back upon the other half (see comment on ver. 9). This "remnant" was to be allowed to hang down over the back part of the tabernacle.

Ver. 13.—**And a cubit.** Rather, "And *the* cubit." *The* cubit by which the goats' hair tent-cloth, which was thirty cubits across (ver. 8), would exceed the linen covering, which was twenty-eight cubits (ver. 2), on either side of the tabernacle, was to be allowed to hang down, like a valance, hiding so far the golden boards of the tabernacle.

The outer protection (ver. 14).

Ver. 14.—**And thou shalt make a covering for the tent.** Nothing is said of the size of this covering ; but, as its object was clearly to protect the roof of the tent from penetration by wet, it seems reasonable to suppose that it extended at least as far as the boards of the tabernacle. To do this, it must have been thirty cubits long, and fourteen broad.

The boarding of the tabernacle (vers. 15—30).

Ver. 15.—**Boards . . . of shittim wood.** These boards were to be fifteen feet long by two feet three inches broad, and, if they were each of a single plank, can scarcely have been furnished by any of the acacias which now grow in the Sinaitic peninsula. It is possible, however, that they were made up of two or more planks, since the name by which they are designated, *kereth*, is thought to be applied in Ezek. xxvii. 6, to the "deck of a ship." **Standing up.** The way in which they were to be made to "stand up" is explained in vers. 17 and 19. They were not to have one end sunk in the ground, but to be fitted by means of "tenons" into silver "sockets."

Ver. 17.—**Two tenons.** Literally, "hands." Projecting rods, such as those common in our dinner tables, seem to be meant. They may have been of metal, let into the boards to a certain depth, and projecting several inches beyond them. Or, possibly, they may have been of acacia wood. **In one board**—*i.e.* "In each board"—no doubt, at the bottom of each. **Set in order one against the other.** Arranged, *i.e.*, at regular intervals, the position of each corresponding to the position of its fellow.

Ver. 18.—**Twenty boards.** Each board being a cubit and a half in width (ver. 16), the length of the chamber was, necessarily, thirty cubits. **On the south side southward.** Literally, " On the south side, to the right." The Orientals regarded it as natural to look to the east, and spoke of the east as " in front," the west as " behind," the north as " on the left," and the south as " on the right hand."

Ver. 19 —**Forty sockets of silver.** Nothing is said of the shape of these " sockets." They were certainly very massive, as each contained a silver talent (ch. xxxviii. 27), and thus weighed from eighty to ninety pounds. It has been supposed that they stood on the ground, and formed a sort of continuous base, out of which the planks rose. But this would have constituted a very unsafe structure. Kalisch is probably right in his view, that the sockets were let into the ground—resembling those at the bottom of a gate, into which the bolt is pressed down. Each socket received one of the " tenons."

Ver. 20.—**The second side . . . the north side.** The north side, or left hand, was always regarded as less honourable than the south side or right hand (see Gen. xlviii. 13—20), probably because in the northern hemisphere the sun illumines the south side. It showed the superior dignity of the south side that the golden candlestick was set against it (ch. xl. 24).

Vers. 22, 23.—**For the sides of the tabernacle westward.** Rather, " for the back " (τὰ ὀπίσω—LXX.). Here there were to be **six boards** only, which would give the abnormal and improbable width of nine cubits. The additional cubit required was no doubt obtained from the corner boards, or posts, each of which added to the (internal) width half a cubit (see ver. 23).

Ver. 24.—**They shall be coupled together beneath . . . unto one ring.** This is very obscure, and might be explained in several ways. Perhaps it is best to suppose that the coupling was by the " bars," cf. vers. 26—29, the ends of which fitted into a sort of double ring, like the figure 8, attached to the corner posts. **Above the head.** Rather " *at* " or *near* the head."

Ver. 25.—**And they shall be eight boards.** Counting in the two corner boards, or posts, the boards of the back would be eight. Each of them was to have two " tenons," like the boards of the sides, and every " tenon " was to have its own silver " socket." Thus the " sockets" would be sixteen, two under each board.

Vers. 26—28.—**Bars of shittim wood.** To give greater stability to the structure, to keep the boards in their places, and to prevent there being any aperture between them, five bars were to be made for each side, and the same number for the end, of the *mishkân*, which were to be passed through rings attached to the boards—one at least to each—and thus to hold the boards firmly together. The middle bar in each case was to extend the whole length of the enclosure (ver. 28), and thus in two cases to be thirty cubits, or forty-five feet long. The exact length, and the disposition of the other bars is not indicated ; but it is with reason conjectured that two were above and two below the " middle bar"—that all were horizontal—and that each coupled together one half of the boards of each side. The length of each was probably fifteen cubits ; and the ends which reached the two corner posts at the back ran into the corner rings, which were shaped so as to receive the two bars (see ver. 24). It is not said whether the bars were inside or outside the *mishkân* ; but the best authorities suppose them to have been outside.

Ver. 29.—The rings were to be of solid gold ; the boards and the bars of acacia wood overlaid with gold.

Ver. 30.—**According to the fashion.** Where the description was incomplete (and it could not but be incomplete in many points), Moses was to follow his recollection of the " pattern," which either in vision, or otherwise—he had seen in the mount This would be his best guide, for

" Segnius irritant animum demissa per aures,
  Quam quæ sunt oculis subjecta fidelibus."

Vers. 31—35.—*The veil and the ordering of the holy places.*

Ver. 31.—**A vail.** The veil was to be of the same material and workmanship as the inner covering extended over the *mishkân*, and like that, was to have figures of cherubim woven into its texture by a skilled weaver.

Ver. 32.—**Four pillars.** The contrast between these *four* pillars of the interior, and the " *five* pillars " at " the door of the tent " (vers. 36, 37), is striking, and justifies the supposition that the veil in the tabernacle did not completely divide the holy of holies from the holy place, but formed a screen, above which the space was open. If the veil had been hung from the top of the tented roof, so as completely to separate the two places, there must have been *five* pillars, or at any rate an odd number, in the interior. **Their hooks shall be of gold.** These are hooks attached to the pillars, for the purpose of their having the curtains hung upon them. **Upon the four sockets.** The word " sockets" has no article. Translate—" Thou shalt hang it upon four pillars of shittim wood overlaid with gold, *with their hooks of gold, and standing upon four sockets of silver*." The pillars probably had " tenons," like the boards (ver. 17), which were inserted into silver sockets, let into the ground.

Ver. 33.—**Thou shalt hang up the veil**

under the taches. If the "taches" of ver. 6, or even of ver. 11, are intended, and "under" is to be taken strictly as "immediately under," the *mishkân* must have been divided by the veil into two equal, or very nearly equal parts ; and the tabernacle must in an important particular have completely differed from the temple. In the temple the holy place was twice the length of the holy of holies (1 Kings vi. 16, 17). It is possible that "under" may be used vaguely, or that the "taches" of this verse are the "hooks" of ver. 32. **That thou mayest bring in.** Rather, "And thou shalt bring in." The clause is directive. **The most holy.** Literally, "the holy of holies"—the inner chamber, that within the veil, which constituted the adytum, or innermost recess of the tabernacle. The ark and the mercy-seat were the special furniture of this inner sanctuary. To these is added later (ch. xxx. 1—10) the altar of incense.

Ver. 35.—**The table** here is, of course, "the table of shew-bread" described in the preceding chapter (vers. 23—30), immediately after the mercy-seat. It was to be set "without the veil," in the holy place or outer chamber, against the north wall. **The candlestick** is the seven-branched lamp-stand described in ch. xxv. 31—39. It was to be placed **over against the table**, and consequently on the south side (ch. xl. 24).

Vers. 36, 37.—*The entrance to the tent.*

Ver. 36.—**Thou shalt make a hanging.** A curtain which could draw up and down, seems to be intended. When let down, it probably covered the entire eastern side, or front of the tabernacle. When raised, it allowed the eye to penetrate into the holy place.

Ver. 37.—**Five pillars.** The central pillar was, no doubt, as Mr. Fergusson long ago pointed out, one of two tent-poles, which supported between them a ridge-pole, over which were thrown the coverings that formed the roof of the tent. Its height was probably fifteen cubits, so as to give a due slope to the roof. The two pillars nearest to the central one probably measured ten cubits, and stood in line with the two walls of the *mishkân*. The outer pair would then have a height of five cubits, and support the two extremities of the goats' hair covering. **Their hooks.** The hooks whereby the "hanging" was attached to the pillars. Compare ver. 32. **Sockets of brass**—*i.e.*, of bronze. These were probably let into the ground, like the other sockets.

HOMILETICS.

Vers. 1—37.—*The symbolism of the tabernacle structure.* I. That the HOLY OF HOLIES typified heaven itself is declared in the Epistle to the Hebrews (ch. ix. 7—12). In it were the forms of cherubim, representing the angelic choir, and between them was the manifestation of the presence of God himself. It was cut off from the rest of the sanctuary by the veil, which none was to lift save the High Priest once a year: "the Holy Ghost thus signifying, that the way into the holiest of all"—*i.e.*, into heaven—"was not made manifest, while as the first tabernacle was yet standing" (*ib.* ver. 8).

II. THE VEIL thus typified and represented the separation between man and God—the awful barrier which shuts out from the Divine presence all, even the holiest, unless they have with them the blood of expiation, "that speaketh better things than that of Abel." The veil was covered with cherubic forms, reminding men of those watchers at the gate of Eden, who with "a flaming sword that turned every way, kept the way of the tree of life" (Gen. iii. 24). Men saw in the thick curtain that hid the holiest from view, that heaven was shut to them, unless a "new and living way" could be found, whereby they might enter. They had impressed upon them the awful holiness and inaccessibility of the Supreme Being, and their own unworthiness to approach him. They learnt that God had hidden himself from them, until some "better time," when the veil would be rent, and in and through their true High Priest, and through faith in his blood, they might "have boldness to enter into the holiest."

III. The tabernacle outside the veil—THE HOLY PLACE, as it was called—represented the church militant. Here was perpetual worship offered to the God behind the veil. Hither were all who had received the holy anointing, and so been made "priests to God" (Rev. i. 6) privileged to enter. Here was a perpetual thank-offering presented to God in the shew-bread that lay always upon the table. Here was illumination from the sevenfold lamp which typified the Holy Spirit (see above on "the symbolism of the candlestick"). The place was "all glorious within" (Ps. xlv. 13)—on the walls "clothing of wrought gold,"—above, a canopy of "fine twined linen, and blue and purple and scarlet, with cherubim of cunning work" interwoven into it—at either end a curtain of nearly similar materials. Those who looked on the tabernacle from without saw the goats' hair, and the rams' skins, and seals' skins, and perceived in it no beauty that they should desire it. The beauty was revealed to those only who were within. So now, the Church is despised and vilified by those without, valued as it deserves only by those who dwell in it. Again, the structure seems weak, as does the structure of the Church to worldlings. A few boards, an awning, a curtain or two—what more frail and perishable! But, when all is "fitly joined together, and compacted by that which every joint supplieth" (Eph. iv. 16), when by a machinery of rings and bars, and tenons and solid sockets, and pillars and hooks, the whole is welded into one, under Divine direction and contrivance, the fragility disappears. "God's strength is made perfect in weakness." A structure is produced which continues, which withstands decay, which defies assaults from without, which outlasts others seemingly far stronger, and bids fair to remain when all else is shattered and destroyed. "Behold! I am with you alway, even unto the end of the world." The tabernacle, frail as it was, lasted from the exodus until the time when Solomon expanded it into the temple. Our tabernacle, the Church, will endure until it shall please God to merge it in a new and wonderful creation—"the new Jerusalem" (Rev. xxi. 2, 10—27; xxii. 1—5).

IV. THE CURTAIN AT THE ENTRANCE symbolises the fact, that there is a division between the Church and the world. The curtain may be lifted at times; but the world has only glimpses of the real inner life of the Church, does not fully see it, does not comprehend it. The life consists in worship—in contemplation, prayer, and praise. The world "cares for none of these things." It may glance curiously at the external fabric, and scoff a little at the contrast between the homely goats' hair that shows itself in one part, and the "blue and purple and scarlet, and fine twined linen wrought with needlework" that is seen in another; it may be angered at the sight of "pillars overlaid with gold," and ask scornfully, "Wherefore this waste?" But it does not care to consider seriously the fitness of these things, or to weigh the reasons for them. The only interest which it feels is one arising from cupidity: the Church, it thinks, would be worth plundering; and it looks forward hopefully to the time when it will "divide the spoil."

V. The support of the entire fabric upon TENONS and SOCKETS indicates that the Church is detached from earth, has here no resting-place, no continuing abode, awaits removal to heaven. What is of the earth, is earthy. If the Church were of the earth, if it were a human institution, if it rested on human wisdom, or power, or affection, it would be swayed by human emotions; it would seek those things which are the main objects of human desire; it would cease to witness for God; it would be powerless to raise man above himself and fit him for the life which is to come. But the Church is not of man's building. Christ built it. It is his. He is its "chief corner-stone;" and therefore, "while it touches earth, it belongs altogether to heaven."

HOMILIES BY VARIOUS AUTHORS.

Vers. 1—37.—*Jehovah's dwelling.* Instructions are now given for the making of the "dwelling-place," of that sacred house or tent which was to be the special abode of Jehovah, and within which, when reared according to the fashion shown to Moses in the mount (ver. 30), the sacred articles described in the previous chapter were to be deposited. We need not encumber our homily with the minutiæ of construction. It will suffice to direct attention to the general arrangement of parts, and to the costly and beautiful character of the erection as a whole. 1. *General arrangement.* The tabernacle may be described as a quadrangular enclosure of boards, sumptuously overlaid with gold, and fitted beneath into sockets of silver (vers. 15—30). Over this were placed (1) the tabernacle-cloth proper—a finely-woven double curtain of byssus, glowing all over with figures of cherubim, in blue, and purple, and scarlet (ver. 1). (2) A tent cloth of goats' hair (ver. 7). (3) Exterior coverings. These consisted of rams' skins dyed red, and of skins of seals (ver. 14). Loops and taches united the two divisions of the tabernacle and tent-cloths. The clasps in the one case were of gold (ver. 6), in the other of brass (ver. 11). Internally, four pillars supported a magnificent veil, also wrought in blue, and purple, and scarlet with figures of cherubim (vers. 31, 32). This divided the sacred enclosure into two apartments, the outer, the holy place, and the inner, the holy of holies, the true dwelling of Jehovah. The division, as already seen, " corresponded to the design of the tabernacle, where Jehovah desired not to dwell alone by himself, but to come and meet with his people" (Keil). The holy of holies, accordingly, contained the ark; the holy place, the symbols of the vocation of the people. It was the place of the people's approach to God. Another curtain, "wrought with needlework," and, like the veil, suspended from pillars by hooks of gold, hung before the entrance in front. The pillars, in this case, were *five* in number (vers. 36, 37). For details, dimensions, and theories of arrangement, consult the exposition. No scheme yet propounded is entirely free from difficulties. The general measurements, and the mention of "pins" in ch. xxvii. 19, point strongly in the direction of a tent form such as that suggested by Mr. Fergusson (*Dict. of Bible, art. Temple*). A difficulty, on this theory, arises from the statement that the veil was to be hung " under the taches" (ver. 33). But the expression, " under the taches," may be used of a high-roofed structure with some degree of latitude, otherwise we must suppose that the veil originally divided the sanctuary into two apartments of equal size. 2. *Glory and beauty of the dwelling-place.* Within the limits of its dimensions, the tabernacle was really a place of great splendour—a costly and magnificent erection. We should err, however, in going much beyond the general effect to be produced in seeking for symbolical meanings. The shittim wood, the precious metals, the colours, the finely-embroidered linen fabrics, have significance only as adding to the beauty and richness of the place designed for Jehovah's abode. The end was, as far as possible, to rear a residence worthy of " the King of glory," or, from another point of view, to set forth, by the external splendour of the dwelling, the surpassing glory and magnificence of him who dwelt in it. Thus also was enhanced the idea of the singular honour enjoyed by those who were permitted to minister before him (see Fairbairn). The cherubic figures woven into the tabernacle drapery, point, if our interpretation of these figures is correct—to the host of angels who continually attend Jehovah, who are his willing servants in all that relates to his kingdom, who take so deep an interest in its progress, who furnish to his people a constant model of obedience (Matt. vi. 10), and who may be viewed as joining with them, in all their services, in the worship of their King. They are part of the heavenly community, to which, as citizens in God's kingdom, we belong (Heb. xii. 22). The chapter suggests the following general reflections:— 1. Whatever glory or beauty the tabernacle possessed was derived ultimately from God. Man could but work up materials furnished to him by the Maker of all. So with the " beauties of holiness" in the Church. It is God who gives us of his grace, and who works in us to will and to do of his good pleasure (Phil. ii. 13). 2. The tabernacle, in another aspect of it, was a product of human art and skill. The plan was Divine; the materials were from God; but the workmanship was man's. It is a characteristic of the " spiritual house" which God is now building on earth, that it also is being reared by human agency, and that each individual has it in his power to contribute something to its beauty. Every holy life that is being lived is the weaving of a beautiful fabric for the adornment of this house. 3. God's condescension is seen in his *willingness* to dwell with Israel in this wilderness-made abode. Magnificent as it was, it was but a paltry abode to offer to the maker of heaven and earth—to the possessor of all things. Yet Jehovah did not spurn it. He sought an abode with men. His dwelling in the tabernacle was, in some aspects of it, a grander thing than his inhabitation of the infinities of space. It told of a God who does not spurn to enter into personal relations with his creatures. He will stoop as far as holiness permits, in his endeavour to reach them, and to lift them up to communion with himself. 4. The tabernacle, glorious as it was, was but the type of dwelling-places more glorious than itself. We have found the antitypes in the once abased, but now glorified, humanity of Christ; in the renewed heart of the believer; in the redeemed Church as a whole. God prefers the temple of the humble and contrite heart to the grandest building ever reared by hands of man (Is. lvii. 15).—J. O.

Vers. 1—37.—*The tabernacle itself.* Consider here—
I. GOD'S COMMANDMENT THAT A DWELLING-PLACE SHOULD BE PROVIDED FOR HIM. Against even the least degree of image-making there was a stern edict; and we might also

have expected that there would be equal sternness in forbidding the creation of aught in the shape of a holy house. For what on the face of it would seem more probable than this, that the erection of a holy house would be a strong inducement towards the fashioning of some visible representation of Deity? Thus we might conjecture; but our conjectures soon get swept away as we are made clearly to understand that it was a good thing for Israel that Jehovah their God, their guide, and their unfailing support, should have a dwelling-place in the midst of their dwelling-places. Such a dwelling-place was no necessity for him, but to the people it was a help so great, that it became a necessity; and so we see they were more than permitted, they were even commanded, to construct an enclosure which should be reckoned the house of God. When we want to find one of our fellow-men, we reckon that it is at his house we shall find him easiest; and just as it is possible, by going and making proper request at the palace-gates, to get a great favour from a king without even a momentary vision of his face, so an Israelite was to be taught that by going to the holy dwelling of Jehovah—whom no man had seen or could see—he might unquestionably secure Divine benefits. As there was a condescension in the new dispensation, so there was in the old. He who became to a certain extent circumscribed in the limits of a human body, only carried out into a more abiding and far-reaching mystery, the circumscribing which first became a fact at Sinai. He who has the heaven for his throne and the earth for his footstool, chose to make the narrow limits of the tabernacle his peculiar dwelling-place. He meant Israel to understand that he was there, as he was nowhere else.

II. THE PECULIAR FORM WHICH THIS DWELLING-PLACE ASSUMED. Even as the people dwelt in tents, easily set up and easily taken down, so God, in the midst of them, likewise dwelt in a tent. There was of course an elaboration and costliness about the tent of Jehovah, such as could not be found in the tents of even the noblest and wealthiest of the people; but still it was essentially a tent. A correspondence obtained between this tabernacle with all its splendid adornments which could not have obtained, if even the plainest of true buildings had taken its place. It is most needful for us to remember that the house of God in the midst of his people was not a building that had foundations. It was strictly suited to their wants. It was more suited to their immediate future than they themselves had any apprehension of; and we cannot but feel that for one thing, God had in view their forty years' wandering. They had not yet sinned the sin which led to this penalty; but that sin was before the mind of him who knew their expectations and their instability. Then it would appear also that God had nothing else than a tabernacle in view, even after his people secured each one their place in the lot of their temporal inheritance. It is not perhaps too much to say that the erection of the splendid temple which glorified Solomon's reign was no part of the Divine intent. God made the erection of that imposing mass to work in with his intent; but in the end it proved to have no more stability than the tabernacle which preceded it. Bear in mind what Jesus said of the temple which was standing in his time. His disciples in admiration pointed to the great stones which went to compose it; but Jesus in the discernment of his heart nevertheless was able to point out that not one stone should be left on another. The temple seemed more stable than the tabernacle; but it was only a seeming. Well-meaning men, not able to escape from carnal notions, may make God's house to take the temple-form, but God himself will take care that it has the tabernacle-reality. It is not in what we can make with our hands, be we ever so liberal, be we ever so diligent, that God can find a real abode. His real abode is in ourselves, in each of us who are holy and perfected individuals through our believing connection with Christ, and still more in the midst of his perfected people, joined together in the inexpressible, indestructible harmony of heaven.—Y.

Ver. 30.—" *God dwelleth not in temples made with hands.*" An idea, to be realised, must be embodied; *e.g.*, thoughts must be expressed in words; the vision of the artist must take form on canvas or in marble. So, too, with the Divine ideas; they also must be embodied, and as presented for man's instruction, they must be so embodied that man may apprehend them. The unseen must be made visible; the pattern on the mount must be modelled and reared up upon the plain. Notice—

I. THE DIVINE IDEAL. Moses was shown the original Divine embodiment, not a mere toy model which he was to enlarge, but the actual God-fashioned tabernacle, in all the perfection of its related parts. So far as man was concerned, it might be a purely ideal structure; but the ideals of earth are the realities of heaven. The holy of holies, and the holy place, and the outer court—all these must exist, or Moses could not have been shown them. May we not also discern dimly that reality which Moses saw? The holy of holies, where God's throne is set—heaven in its innermost recesses, screened off from earth by the blue sky-curtain, which no unaided eye can pierce. The holy place and the outer court, God's earthly sanctuary, his Church in this world, related on the one side to heaven, and on the other to the world around it; the visible heavens are, in some sort, an expression of this Divine idea, illuminated by the sun (cf. Ps. xix.), and with the earth—from man's standpoint—forming a kind of outer court. Even this true tabernacle (cf. Heb. viii. 2) is only an embodiment of the Divine idea; but then it is the Divine embodiment, the expression found for it by God himself.

II. THE HUMAN COPY. The divine ideal as divinely embodied is still beyond man's understanding; it needs to be translated for men into language with which they are familiar. The child must be spoken to as a child (Is. xxviii. 11), "with stammering lips and a feigned tongue." The tabernacle of nature expresses God's idea in polysyllables; the tabernacle which Moses reared translates it into easier language. Notice —1. *The holy of holies.* (1) The sanctity of the Divine dwelling-place emphasises the sanctity of its Divine inmate. "Clouds and darkness are round about him." "Holiness becometh his house for ever." (2) "Righteousness and judgment are the establishment of his throne;" it is founded upon a guarded law. (3) Mercy rejoiceth over judgment. God is just, or righteous, but also the justifier who makes righteous. "Mercy and truth are met together; righteousness and peace have kissed each other." 2. *The holy place.* God has made it possible for man to approach him. They who may not bear the presence may yet be admitted to the ante-chamber. The Church is the link between heaven and earth, as the high priest is the link between the Divine and human. Notice—(1) *The golden altar.* The fumes of the incense may penetrate the veil, which shuts out the priest who offers it. Prayer can go where the worshipper cannot go. (2) *The golden candlestick.* No lamp needed in the holiest place (cf. Rev. xxi. 23). Here, when man meets with God, for man's sake the lamp is needed. The light derived from God must be guarded by man, so only is the required illumination to be secured. (3) *The golden table.* Furnished week by week with food satisfying alike to God and man. Such the Church—a heaven on earth. Prayer ascending towards the unseen holy; light from God carefully guarded; offerings wherein God and man both find satisfaction —such are the notes of a true Church, one wherein man may have communion with his Maker, holy as preluding to the holy of holies. (4) *The outer court.* Here we have the first stage in man's progress from the world God-wards. The altar and the laver, sacrifice and purification, must come before communion. Consecration and cleansing precede intercourse and fellowship, and these again prepare for the beatific vision.

Conclusion.—What is the central thought thus shadowed forth? Is it not this:— God's holiness can only be approached step by step, whilst the road by which we must approach it is that which will ensure for us growth in holiness. "The pure in heart shall see God;" the beatific vision is for those only whose spiritual eyesight has been prepared for its reception. We cannot come up to the throne of God save through the outer court and through the sanctuary; sacrifice and cleansing, illumination and communion; then, for those who can receive it, the open vision and the presence of God.—G.

EXPOSITION.

CHAPTER XXVII

Vers. 1—8.—THE ALTAR OF BURNT OFFERING. From the description of the tabernacle, or sacred tent in which worship was to be offered by the priests, it followed in natural sequence, that directions should be given concerning the court, or precinct, within which the taber-

nacle was to stand Ancient temples were almost universally surrounded by precincts, which the Greeks called τεμένη, whereto a sacred character attached; and this was particularly the case in Egypt, where the *temenos* seems to have been a regular adjunct to the temple (Wilkinson in Rawlinson's *Herodotus*, vol. ii. p. 202, 2nd edition). Among the chief uses of such an open space, was the offering of victims on altars, as these could not be conveniently consumed elsewhere than in the open air, on account of the clouds of smoke and the fumes of the sacrifices. As in the description of the tabernacle, the furniture was first described, then the structure, so now the altar takes precedence of the court which was to contain it.

Ver. 1. — **Thou shalt make an altar.** Rather, " *the* altar." God had already declared that he would have an altar made to him in the place where he should " record his name " (ch. xx. 24). And, even apart from this, an altar would be regarded as so essential an element in Divine worship, that no place of worship could be without one. **Of shittim wood.** God had required (l. s. c.) that his altar should be " of earth," or else of unhewn stones (ch. xx. 25). The command now given was to make, not so much an altar, as an altar-case (see ver. 8). There can be no doubt that Jarchi is right in supposing that, whenever the tabernacle for a time became stationary, the hollow case of the altar was filled up with earth, and that the victims were burnt upon this. **Four-square.** Altars were commonly either square or round. An Assyrian triangular one was found by Mr. Layard at Nineveh ; but even this had a round top. The square shape is the most usual, and was preserved, probably in all the Temple altars, certainly in those of Solomon (2 Chr. iv. 1) and Herod (Joseph. *Bell. Jud.* v. 5, § 6).

Ver. 2.—**The horns of it.** Literally, " its horns." Horns were not usual adjuncts of altars ; indeed they seem to have been peculiar to those of the Israelites. They were projections at the four top corners, probably not unlike the horns of bulls, whence their name. Criminals clung to them when they took sanctuary (1 K. i. 50 ; ii. 28) ; and the blood of sin-offerings was smeared upon them (ch. xxix. 12 ; Lev. viii. 15 ; ix. 9 ; xvi. 18, etc.). Victims also were sometimes, when about to be sacrificed, bound to them (Ps. cxviii. 27). According to Kalisch, " The horns were symbolical of power, of protection and help ; and at the same time of glory and salvation." **His horns shall be of the same.** Part and parcel of the altar, that is, not extraneous additions. **Thou shalt overlay it with brass.** A solid plating of bronze is no doubt intended, such as would protect the shittim wood and prevent it from being burnt.

Ver. 3.—**His pans to receive his ashes.** Literally, " to cleanse it from fat "—*i.e.*, to receive what remained after burning the victims, which would be ashes mixed with a good deal of fat. **His shovels.** These would be used in removing the ashes from the altar, and depositing them in the pans. **His basins.**

Vessels for receiving the blood of the victims and from which it was poured on the altar. Compare ch. xxiv. 6. **His flesh hooks.** So the Septuagint, and our translators again in 1 Sam. ii. 13. They would seem by the latter passage to have been three-pronged forks, the proper use of which was, no doubt, to arrange the various pieces, into which the victim was cut, upon the altar. **His fire-pans.** The word used is generally translated " censers " (Lev. x. i. ; xvi. 12 ; Num. iv. 14 : xvi. 6, 17, etc.), but sometimes " snuff-dishes " (ch. xxv 38 ; xxxvii. 23). It here perhaps designates the vessels used for carrying burning embers from the altar of burnt-offering, to the altar of incense on certain occasions (Lev. xvi. 12). Etymologically, it means simply " a receptacle." **All the vessels thereof thou shalt make of brass.** Rather, " of bronze." Bronze was the usual material of utensils and implements in Egypt (Birch, *Guide to British Museum*, pp. 13—21 ; 28, 29 ; 35—41 ; etc.). Copper was scarcely used without the alloy of tin which converts it into bronze ; and brass was wholly unknown. A trace of iron is sometimes found in Egyptian bronze.

Ver. 4.—**Thou shalt make for it a grate.** Rather, " a grating." This was probably a protection for the lower part of the altar, and prevented it from being touched by the feet of the ministrant priests. It was outside the altar, and had the rings attached to it, by which the altar was carried when the Israelites journeyed.

Ver. 5.—**Thou shalt put it under the compass.** The " compass " (*karkôb*) is spoken of as if it were something well-known ; yet it had not been previously mentioned. Etymologically the word should mean " a cincture " or " band " round the altar ; and thus far critics are generally agreed. But its position, size, and object, are greatly disputed. Some hold that it was a broad bench, or step, on which the officiating priests stood at the time of a sacrifice, and that its position was about the middle of the altar. Others think that it was a mere border round the top, from which the net-work depended, and that the object of both was to catch anything that might fall from the altar. Others again, while placing it mid-way in the altar, regard it as a mere ornament, only projecting slightly, and forming a sort of finish to the net-work. This, which is the view of Knobel, seems to be, on the whole, the most probable one. **That the net may be even to the midst of the altar.** If the " compass " was at the top, the net must have extended thence to the middle. If it was mid-way in the altar, the net must have covered the lower half. To us this latter seems the more probable view. But the point is uncertain.

Vers. 6, 7.—**Staves**, or poles, were needed for the carriage of the altar from place to place, as for the ark (ch. xxv. 13) and the table of shew-bread (*ib.* ver. 28). They were to be inserted into **the rings** mentioned in ver. 4. As the altar was of bronze, so the rings were to be of bronze, and the staves overlaid with bronze. There is a gradual descent in the preciousness of the materials from the holy of holies to the holy place, and from that to the court.

Ver. 8.—**Hollow with boards shalt thou make it.** See the comment on ver. 1. The term here used for "boards," (which is different from that in ch. xxvi. 15—29) implies strength and solidity. **As it was showed thee in the mount.** Compare ch xxvi. 30, with the comment *ad loc.*

HOMILETICS.

Vers. 1—8.—*The symbolism of the brazen altar.* The noticeable points of this altar are its position, material, ornaments, and purpose or use.

I. ITS POSITION. (1) It was without the sanctuary, in the open court beyond; (2) under the canopy of heaven; (3) directly in front of the sanctuary, and so of the ark and the mercy-seat. (1) It was without the sanctuary, that none might venture inside the holy structure, and so draw nigh to God without passing it, and obtaining from it the purification which it could confer. Even if the priests on the way to the tabernacle did not always stop at the altar to offer a victim as a sacrifice, they would have the thought of the need of expiation brought home to them by the sight of it, and might as they passed propitiate the Most High by the offering of a prayer. The position of the altar taught that man's *first* need is to have his sins and impurities purged away; and that until this is done, he must not presume to worship God, or enter into his presence, or offer the sacrifice of praise, or mingle in the company of those who form "the general assembly and church of the first-born, which are written in heaven." (2) It was under the open canopy of heaven, visible to all, accessible to all, for all Israel might enter the court; thereby teaching, that the necessary purification was intended by God to be open to all, and that his eye looked down from heaven with favour upon all who desired to be purged from their impurities, and were willing to accept the appointed mode of purging. (3) It was directly in front of the sanctuary, and so of the ark and the mercy-seat. By this position it pointed to them, led the eye towards them, reminded men of them. With God, in the holy of holies, was at once justice, and also mercy—the law and the mercy-seat. Here, at the altar, was the place where the two could be reconciled, where "mercy and truth might meet together, righteousness and peace kiss each other." Here was to be begun that purging, both of the nation and of individuals, which was only complete when once in the year the high priest entered into the holiest, with the blood of the sin-offerings, and sprinkled it on the horns of the altar that was within the veil (ch. xxx. 10), and "on the mercy-seat eastward" (Lev. xvi. 14), so atoning both for himself and for the sins of the people (Heb. ix. 7).

II. ITS MATERIAL. The material was (1) shittim or acacia wood; (2) bronze; and (3) earth; the earth alone constituting the true altar (ch. xx. 24), and the wood and metal a casing, by means of which the earth was kept together. (1) Shittim, or acacia, the most incorruptible of woods, typified the purity required in all that is set apart for God. (2) Bronze, the metal most common in the use of the time, indicated that the altar was for every-day employment by the mass of the people (Lev. i.—vii.). (3) Earth, pure fragrant mould, that of which man was formed at the first (Gen. ii. 7), and into which he is resolved at the last (Gen. iii. 19), may well have represented Humanity; so that in the altar, which God had required to be made of earth (Ex. xx. 24), he saw Humanity making its offerings to him,—peace-offerings in thankfulness for his mercies, sin-offerings in deprecation of his anger, burnt-offerings in complete dedication of the whole being to his service. Or the mould may primarily have represented this earth, on which we live, whereof it is the essence as being the life-sustaining portion, and only secondarily man, for whom the earth was brought into existence, and of which he is the master.

III. ITS ORNAMENTS. These were, (1) perhaps, its cincture; (2) certainly, its horns. (1) The cincture, or "compass" (ver. 5), if it was wholly for ornament, may simply have indicated the propriety of adorning and beautifying everything which is brought into the service of the sanctuary. Without some wreath, or moulding, where the grating began, the altar would have had a bare and unfinished look. It would have been wanting in elegance and beauty. The pattern shown to Moses in the mount did not allow of this. It left nothing bare, unsightly, inelegant, out of taste. God chose to be worshipped "in the *beauty* of holiness." It is easy to disparage beauty; and certainly beauty alone, not accompanied by purity and goodness, is worthless, vain, trivial. But, as men desire beauty in their own houses, furniture, utensils, vessels, implements, so natural piety leads them to desire even greater beauty for the houses, vessels, etc., used in the service of God. "The house," said David, "that is to be builded for the Lord, *must be* exceedingly magnifical" (1 Chron. xxii. 5). And congruity requires that, if a house be magnifical, all its contents, down to the meanest vessel, should possess some beauty; otherwise, the law of harmony is broken—a discord manifests itself. (2) The horns at the four corners, uprearing themselves to heaven, and showing conspicuously, as symbols of power and strength, spoke of the God to whom the altar was reared, and indicated his ability to help, protect, and succour his worshippers. But there was also a human side to their symbolism. They further indicated the victory which man gains over death and Satan by means of expiation, the height to which he is exalted when the atonement made for him cleanses him from all sin. "O death, where is thy sting? O grave, where is thy victory? The sting of death is sin; and the strength of sin is the law; but thanks be to God, who giveth us the victory through Jesus Christ our Lord!"

IV. ITS PURPOSE. We have assumed throughout that the purpose of the altar—its main purpose—was expiation. Its proper title was "the altar of burnt-offering." *All* offerings, except those which the high priest offered at the altar of incense in the holy of holies, were to be made at this brazen altar before the door of the tabernacle. Hither were the Israelites to bring alike their peace or thank-offerings, their burnt-offerings, and their sin-offerings. Expiation was the sole idea of the last of these, and a main idea of the second; it was absent only from the first. Thus it was the predominant idea of sacrifice. The altar witnessed to the guilt of man in God's sight, and the need of an atonement being made for him before he could be reconciled to "the High and Holy One." It witnessed also to God's eternal purpose, that a way of reconciliation should be devised, and made known to man, and that thus it should be put into his power to make his peace with God. The true victim was not indeed as yet offered. Bulls and goats, lambs and rams, could never of themselves, or of their own proper force, sanctify the unclean or take away sin. It was only by virtue of the death which their sacrifice prefigured, that they had any atoning force, or could be accepted by God as expiatory. Each victim represented Christ—the one and only sacrifice for sin which could propitiate the Father. And the altar therefore represented and typified the cross on which Christ died, offering himself thereon to the Father as both priest and victim. Shape and material were different, and the mode of death was different; but each was the material substance on which the atoning victim died, each was stained with the atoning blood; and each was unspeakably precious to the trembling penitent who felt his need of pardon, and, if possible, even more precious to him who knew that atonement had thereon been made for him, and felt his pardon sealed. No true Israelite would sacrifice on any altar but that of the sanctuary. No true Christian will look for pardon and atonement anywhere but to the cross of Christ, and to him who on that altar gave his life for man.

HOMILIES BY VARIOUS AUTHORS.

Vers. 1—21.—*The tabernacle and its teachings.* I. THE ALTAR OF SACRIFICE. 1. The situation of the altar. (1) It faced the worshipper as he entered. The cross of Christ must be held up before men, if they are to be brought nigh to God. (2) It stood before the holy place, and had to be passed by all who entered there. The realisation of Christ's atonement for sin is the only path to God's presence. 2. The altar, on which the sacrifice for sin is laid, is the place of power. The horns, the symbol of Divine power. The gospel of Christ is the power of God unto salvation. 3. In Christ God gives us a place for accepted offerings. The altar was Israel's as well as God's: upon it were laid their offerings as well as those prescribed for the daily service and the great day of atonement. In Christ we are able to offer sacrifices that are well pleasing to God.

II. THE COURT OF THE TABERNACLE. 1. Its limits were appointed by God himself. The Church must be made no broader than his commandment makes it. In his own time he will make it conterminous with the world; but meanwhile we must obey his commandment and fulfil his purpose by making it conterminous with living faith. 2. It was for all Israel. Living faith in Christ should be a passport to all his churches. 3. How the court was formed—(1) Its walls were made of fine linen. The distinction between the world and the Church is righteousness. (2) The gate was formed of blue and purple and scarlet. Entrance is had not by man's righteousness, but by bowing beneath the manifested grace of God in Christ.

III. THE OIL FOR THE LAMPS. 1. It was the free-will offering of the people. The light of the world springs from the consecration of believers. 2. It was to be pure. Believers must keep themselves unspotted from the world. 3. It was to be beaten, not pressed, and thus be the finest which the olive could yield. The highest outcome of humanity is the Christ-like life. 4. The lamps were to burn always. Our light, the flame of love, must burn constantly before God, and its radiance be shed always before men. 5. The lamps were to be tended by the ministers of God. The aim of those who labour in word and doctrine should be the development of Christ-like life, love to God and man.—U.

EXPOSITION.

Ver. 9—18.—THE COURT BEFORE THE TABERNACLE. The description of the altar is (as already observed) naturally followed by that of the court which was to contain it, and in which it was to be the most conspicuous object. This is given with great clearness in ten verses, and presents scarcely any problem for solution. The court was an oblong square, three hundred feet in length and seventy-five in breadth. It was enclosed by curtains, hung on sixty pillars, placed at intervals of seven feet and a half apart. The pillars were connected by rods, and each of them fitted into a socket. There was but one entrance, which was at the eastern side, midway in it. It was thirty feet wide, and had its own curtains and its own pillars. These curtains were of similar material with those at the entrance to the tabernacle, but the hangings round the rest of the court were merely of fine white linen.

Ver. 9.—**Thou shalt make the court.** Rather, "a court." **For the south side southward.** Rather, "For the south side, upon the right." Compare the comment on ch. xxvi. 18. **Hangings.** The word used is a rare one in this sense, quite different from those which have been employed for "curtains" or "hangings" previously (ch. xxvi. 1, 7, 36). The LXX. translate by ἱστία "sails;" and the Jewish commentators believe a loosely woven sail-cloth to be intended. **Fine twined linen.** See the comment on ch. xxvi. 1.

Ver. 10.—**And the twenty pillars thereof, etc.** Literally, "And its pillars, twenty (in

number), and their sockets, twenty (in number, shall be) of bronze." **The hooks of the pillars** are loops whereto the curtains were to be attached. See ch. xxvi. 32. **Their fillets.** It is now generally agreed that the word used designates "connecting rods," which joined the pillars at the top, and probably helped to support the "hangings." These, and the "hooks," were of solid silver.

Ver. 11.—The north side of the court is to be exactly similar to the south in all respects.

Ver. 12.—The west side is also to be similar, except that it is to be half the length, fifty cubits—and, therefore, requires only half the number of pillars and sockets.

Ver. 13.—**The breadth of the court on the east side eastward.** Rather, "in front toward the east." The Rabbinical tradition was that Adam found himself on his creation fronting towards the east, and had consequently the south on his right, the north on his left, and the west behind him. Hence, they said, the four cardinal points received the names of kedem, "in front" (the east); yâmin, "the right hand" (the south); 'akhôr, "behind" (the west); and shemôl, "the left hand" (the north). For this use of all four words, see Job xxiii. 8, 9.

Ver. 14. — **The hangings of one side.** Literally, "of one shoulder." The two extreme parts of the east side, between the entrance (ver. 16) and the corners are thus named. They were to extend on either side a distance of fifteen cubits, and to have their curtains suspended to four pillars, one of them being the corner pillar, which is not counted. Hence the pillars are said to be three

Ver. 16.—**For the gate.** The word used is

the common one for "gate;" but here it rather signifies "entrance." Strictly speaking, there was no "gate;" the worshippers entered by drawing aside the curtain. This was a **hanging** of similar material, colours, and workmanship to that which hung in front of the tabernacle (ch. xxvi. 36). By its contrast with the white linen screen which surrounded the rest of the court, it would show very clearly where men were to enter.

Ver. 17.—**Filleted with silver.** Rather, "joined by silver rods." See the comment on ver. 10. They were also to have their capitals overlaid with silver (ch. xxxviii. 17).

Ver. 18.—**The length and the breadth** of the court had been already implied in what had been said of the external screen-work, or "hangings" (vers. 9 and 12). What this verse adds is the height of the pillars, which was five cubits, or seven feet six inches.

HOMILETICS.

Vers. 9—18.—*The Court of the Tabernacle.* I. The use of the court. The court was primarily a precinct inclosing the sacred structure, and preserving it from contact with the roughnesses of the rude world without. It formed a sort of vestibule to the tent-temple, which awoke solemn thoughts, and gave men time to put away secular considerations, and attune their minds to the Divine harmonies, before entering the house itself, which contained the manifestation of the Divine presence. God must be approached with preparation, humbly, reverently, tremblingly. The court at once preserved the sacred structure from accidental or intentional profanation, and helped to prepare the priests for the duties of their office. Secondly, the court was the place of sacrifice. It contained the brazen altar, whither all Israel was to bring their gifts. Here were offered, at once all the stated sacrifices, daily, or weekly, or monthly, or yearly, and all the irregular and voluntary offerings which the piety of the Israelites induced them to bring in. The smoke of victims continually ascended from it to heaven. Here was the place for expiation—for thankfulness—for self-dedication to the service of God.

II. The persons entitled to have the use of it. These were all Israel—young and old, rich and poor, great and small, priests and laymen. Into the holy of holies none but the high priest, into the holy place none but the priests might enter. But the court was common to the priesthood with the laity. Hither came, to "the door of the tabernacle of the congregation," every pious Israelite who was minded to offer a sacrifice of any kind—whose heart swelled with gratitude for mercies received, and who therefore brought a "thank-offering"—whose soul was weighed down with the sense of sin, and who sought relief by the sacrifice of a "sin-offering"—whose awakened spirit told him that unless the soul wholly rests on God there is no peace for it, and who, as a sign of absolute self-dedication, came to offer a "burnt-offering." Hither came many a man, and many a woman, like Hannah (1 Sam. i. 7—11), in sore trouble, and offered to the Lord Almighty their vows. Whatever may have been the practice with respect to the temple, while the tabernacle endured, the whole congregation had free access to it. Here they felt themselves to be that "kingdom of priests"—that "holy nation"—which God had declared that they should be (ch. xix. 6). Here they realised, at any rate to some extent, that blessing which is among the greatest of the Christian's privileges—the right to "come boldly to the throne of grace" (Heb. iv. 16)—to "draw near to God," without an earthly mediator, "in full assurance of faith" (*ib.* x. 22)—to "cast all our care upon him"—to have direct communion with him—to speak with him, "as a man speaks with his friend."

III. The position of the court with respect to the rest of the tabernacle. There was clearly a gradation in holiness. The inner shrine had a sanctity peculiar to itself, expressed by the very name, "holy of holies." Here was the greatest beauty and the greatest magnificence. Walls entirely of gold, curtains of cunning work, interwoven with the graceful forms of cherubim, furniture all covered with gold, golden cherubs of beaten work upon the mercy-seat—above all, the glory of God showing in the space between these figures. A lesser degree of sanctity belonged to the outer chamber—"the holy place;" and this was indicated by inferior richness and magnificence. Though gold was still the metal chiefly used, silver, and even bronze (ch. xxvi. 37), were introduced. The outer curtain was not wrought with cherubim (ver. 36). The change was even greater between the "holy place" and the court. In the court was no gold, but only silver and bronze. The "hangings" were for the most part plain. Only at the entrance did the eye rest upon the mingled glory of blue and purple and scarlet, and upon the cunning work of embroidery. The furniture and utensils were of bronze only. Again, the gradation was marked by the law of admission: into the court, all the congregation; into the "holy place," the priests only; into the "holy of holies," none but the high priest. And thus it will be always, as we are nearer to God or further from him. If we dwell only in his courts, on the outer verge of his kingdom, we must be content with the bronze and plain linen of bare acceptance; we must not expect favour, glory, beauty. If, on the other hand, we press forward from his courts into his sanctuary; if we strive ever to advance in holiness, then he has better things in store for us. "For brass he will give gold" (Is. lx. 17), for acceptance, approval—for mere pardon, communion and fellowship; and to such as press into the inner shrine, with the "boldness" that is now legitimate (Heb. x. 19), he will reveal himself in the full splendour of his majesty, and in the perfect glow of his love.

EXPOSITION.

Ver 19.—THE VESSELS OF THE TABERNACLE. There were many "vessels of the tabernacle" which have not hitherto been mentioned, as the great laver in the court (ch. xxx. 18; xl. 30) with the basins for washing which must have belonged to it; the pins or pegs whereby the various curtains were extended and supported; and probably much sacrificial apparatus besides what is enumerated in ver. 3. All these were to be of bronze, the commonest metal of the time, but one very suitable for the various purposes, being, as the Egyptians manufactured it, of great hardness, yet exceedingly ductile and ready to take all shapes. Its usefulness and convenience caused it to retain its place, even in the gorgeous and "magnificent" temple of Solomon (1 Chron. xxix. 2, 7), where it was employed for the two great pillars, Jachin and Boaz, for the great laver or "brazen sea," for the smaller lavers upon wheels, for the pots, the shovels, the basins, the snuffers, the spoons, and many other sacred vessels (1 Kings vii. 15—45; 2 Kings xxv. 13, 14). Though "common," it was never reckoned "unclean," or less fitted for the service of the sanctuary than silver or gold. It had, however, its own proper place, an inferior place to that held by the more precious metals.

Ver. 19.—**All the pins thereof.** The "pins" of the tabernacle are undoubtedly the pegs or tent-pins, whereby the tent-cloth wherewith it was covered was extended and kept taut. There were also probably similar pegs or pins for cords used to keep the "pillars" (ch. xxvi. 37) or tent-poles in place. **The pins of the court** supported in the same way the pillars of the court (vers. 10—15).

HOMILETICS.

Ver. 19.—*The value in God's sight of what is common and homely.* God does not despise anything that he has made. "His mercy is over all his works" (Ps. cxlv. 9). Each of them has its fit and proper place. Each one of them is needed in his universe. Much less does he despise any of his human creatures. He has seen fit to gift them variously, to make some of gold, some of silver, and some of brass, some to honour, and some to comparative dishonour; but for all he has a use. No intellect is too homely, no nature too rude and unrefined to find a place *somewhere* in his Church where it can do him service, and even perhaps do it better than a more refined and more highly gifted nature. Difference, gradation, variety, is the law of his universe. "There is one glory of the sun, and another glory of the moon, and another glory of the stars; for one star differeth from another star in glory" (1 Cor. xv. 41). In the angelic hierarchy there are angels and archangels, principalities, and powers; in the Church triumphant there are grades—princes who sit on thrones, judges of tribes, rulers over ten cities, rulers over five cities, and a "great multitude" who have no authority, but are simply "saints." And so it is, and must ever be, in the Church militant. "There are diversities of gifts," higher and lower natures, minds of extraordinary power, and dull, homely intellects. But all have their use; for all there is room; and God values each. God will have none despised. The brazen vessels of the outer court—ash-pans and basins, and flesh-hooks, and fire-pans, and tent-pins—were as much needed for the tabernacle and its service, as the silver sockets and rods, or the golden taches, and rings, and snuff-dishes. Bronze is more suitable for many purposes than gold; and ordinary human nature can do God's work better in many positions than great gifts or extraordinary intellect.

EXPOSITION.

Vers. 20, 21.—THE OIL FOR THE LAMP. It has been observed that this paragraph is somewhat out of place. It would more appropriately, according to human ideas, have terminated ch. xxv. But "God's ways are not as man's ways, nor his thoughts as man's thoughts." It is frequently difficult—sometimes impossible—for the keenest human intellect to trace the connecting links between one portion of God's word and the next. In such cases it is best not to speculate on the nature of the connection, but to content ourselves with laying to heart the lesson which each portion teaches separately.

Ver. 20.—**Thou shalt command.** Compare ch. xxv. 6, where the general command had been given. Here certain additions are made as to the quality of the oil which was to be brought. The oil was to be **pure olive oil beaten**—that is to say, it was to be olive oil purified from any admixture of that watery juice which the Romans called *amurca;* and it was to be of the kind which is obtained by mere beating or pounding in a mortar, and not by crushing in a mill. Oil of this kind, which is usually made from the unripe fruit, is reckoned much the best; it is clear and colourless, and gives a bright pure light with little smoke. **To cause the lamp to burn always.** It has been supposed from this expression that the lamp must have been kept constantly burning both day and night; and Josephus declares that this was actually so, at least with three out of the seven lights (*Ant. Jud.* iii. 7, § 7). But there are several places in Scripture which state, or imply, the contrary. (See especially Ex. xxx. 8 ; and 1 Sam. iii. 3.) It seems to have been the duty of the high-priest to light the lamps every evening, and to give them a sufficient supply of oil to last till daybreak, at which time "the lamp of God went out" (1 Sam. l. s. c.) The supposition that "one light at least was always burning" (Kalisch), because no daylight could penetrate into the structure through the *fourfold* covering, ignores the fact that light would enter through the *single* curtain at the entrance, as well as the probability that some portion of that curtain may generally have been looped up. If we regard the lamp as extinguished during the daytime, we must understand "always" here to mean "regularly every night."

Ver. 21.—**The tabernacle of the congregation.** Rather, "the tent of meeting"—the tent where God would meet the earthly ruler of the people (ch. xxv. 22), and give him commands and directions—not the place of meeting for the people themselves, who might in no case go beyond the entrance to the structure. **The testimony**—*i.e.,* the ark which contained the "testimony," or two tables of stone written with the finger of God. **Aaron and his sons.** Compare ch. xxiv. 1. The intention to confer the priesthood on the descendants of Aaron, first openly revealed in the next chapter (vers. 1—43), is tacitly assumed from time to time in the earlier narrative. **Shall order it from evening to morning.** See the comment on ver. 20. It is difficult to assign these words any distinct meaning unless we accept the view, that the lamp burnt during the night only. **It shall be a statute for ever.** This expression is not at all common. In Exodus it occurs only here and in four other places. In Leviticus it is met with some six or seven times. The portions of the law thus characterised must be regarded as of special importance. (See the homiletics on this verse.)

HOMILETICS.

Vers. 20, 21.—*Oil for the lamp.* I. THE PEOPLE'S DUTY. (1) The people were to bring the oil regularly—to attend to what may have seemed to them a little matter, but what was in God's sight of such importance that he made it "a statute for ever"—and to attend to it with such regularity that oil should never be lacking. (2) They were to bring of their best. The oil was to be from the olive—not from the sesamé plant, or the castor-oil plant, or the *Raphanus ol ifer,* or from any vegetable which furnished oil of a coarse kind. It was to be "pure," not adulterated, as oils often were in Egypt (Plin. *H. N.* xiii. 1), and not mixed with the *amurca,* or watery juice of the olive, which made it unfit for burning. Next, it was to be " beaten oil "—oil made with extra trouble by careful pounding with the hand, instead of rough mechanical crushing in mills.

II. THE PRIESTS' DUTY. The priests were perpetually to trim and tend the lamps. Daily, at even, they were to light them; daily, in the morning, they were to extinguish them, if any were still alight; to trim the wicks; to cleanse the bowls which held the oil; and to replenish them with a proper supply. They were to take every care that a pure light was constantly maintained night after night, so that the house of God should never be dark, or even obscure, but be ever ready for worship, ever illumined, ever prepared for any visitation of its Lord, who might come at the third, or the sixth, or the ninth, or the twelfth hour. It does not appear that there were any night services in the tabernacle; but the lighted lamp was a testimony that the Church continued ever on the watch, strove ever to be " the light of the world " (Matt. v. 14)—like the wise virgins, " kept its lamp burning." And this is the duty of ministers at all times. The Christian ministry must take care that the light of the Church shines pure and bright continually —that nothing dims it—that it glows ever as a beacon light, a guide and a help amid the storms and tempests of the world. If the people do not bring a due supply of oil—*i.e.*, of loving, faithful service—the Church must suffer, its light be dimmed. If the people do their duty, and the ministers fail, if they are careless, or slothful, or self-seeking, or worldly, or wanting in faith, the result is the same—the flame flickers; the light sinks and threatens to go out; gross darkness settles down upon the people. A Church in this condition must expect to have its candlestick removed, unless it repents, and bestirs itself, and turns to God, and " does the first works " (Rev. ii. 5), and " strengthens the things that remain and are ready to die " (*ib.* iii. 2).

III. THE TRUE LIGHT. After all, let ministers and people be as faithful as they will, let them " keep their lamps burning," and cause " their light to shine before men " ever so brightly, still they are not, they will never be, " the true light." Christ is " the true light "—" the light that shineth in darkness and the darkness comprehendeth it not "—" the light which lighteth every man that cometh into the world " (John i. 4—9). In him are hid " all the treasures of wisdom and knowledge "—nothing needful for man to know but he has taught it—nothing expedient for man to see but he has revealed it. " His word is a lantern unto our feet, and a light unto our paths." He is both an outward and an inward light. His gospel illumines the world without—penetrates its dark places, exposes its unholy doings, throws a flood of light upon the past, makes plain to us the ways of God with man. And his Spirit illumines the soul within, quickens and guides the conscience, makes our own way plain before our face, " enables with perpetual light the dulness of our blinded sight." He is the only true " light of the world "—the light which will endure throughout all time—the one Teacher who cannot deceive—the one Guide who cannot lead astray! And he is the light of the world to come. " In him is the well of life; and in his light shall we see light " (Ps. xxvi. 9). The " holy city, New Jerusalem," has therefore " no need of the sun, neither of the moon, to shine in it," because " the glory of God doth lighten it, and the Lamb is the light thereof."

HOMILIES BY VARIOUS AUTHORS.

Vers. 1—20.—*The brazen altar and court of the tabernacle.* From the sanctuary, we pass in this chapter to the outer court, the principal object in which was the brazen altar, or altar of burnt offering.

I. THE BRAZEN ALTAR (vers. 1—9). 1. *Form of the altar.* The altar was a four-square case of shittim wood, five cubits long and five broad, made with four horns, and overlaid with plates of bronze. Round it, at some distance from the ground, was apparently a ledge, on which the priests stood when engaged with the sacrifices. We must suppose that the central part was filled with earth, or with the unhewn stones commanded in ch. xx. 24, 25. The " grate of network " of ver. 4, seems to us to have supported the ledge, or compass of ver. 5. Some take a different view of it. 2. *Its horns.* These are rightly understood as the points in which the force or virtue of the altar concentrated itself. 3. *Its uses.* It was—(1) the place to which the people brought their offerings to God; (2) the place at which reconciliation was made for sin; (3) the place on which the parts of the sacrifices which belonged to God were consumed by fire. Here, at the altar, were the victims slain ; around the altar the atoning blood was poured or sprinkled ; in the case of the sin offering, the blood was smeared upon the horns : with live coals from the altar did the priest replenish his censer when he went in to burn incense before the Lord. On this altar was laid the daily burnt-offering, together with the " sacrifices of righteousness," " the burnt-offering, and whole burnt-offering " (Ps. li. 19), by which the people expressed their consecration to God. Here were consumed the fat and choice parts of the peace-offerings, etc. 4. *Its typical significance.* (1) The altar, as the place of atonement, reminded the worshipper of sin, and of his need of cleansing from sin's guilt. In this way, it pointed forward to Christ, in whom the whole ritual of sacrifice reaches its consummation. (2) As the altar of burnt-offering, it taught the duty of unconditional and entire surrender to the will of God. This offering up of the whole being to God in inward consecration underlies the special acts of consecration symbolised in the shew-bread, in the lighted candlestick, and in the ascent of incense from the golden altar. (3) As God's altar, it was a witness to the Divine readiness to pardon ; yet a testimony to the stern truth that without shedding of blood there is no remission (Heb. ix. 22).

II. THE COURT OF THE TABERNACLE (vers. 9—20). On the general construction of the court, see the exposition. We have to view it as a spacious enclosure of a hundred cubits by fifty, its sides formed by linen hangings, five cubits in height, and supported by pillars of brass (bronze) five cubits apart, to which the hangings were attached by hooks and fillets of silver. The brazen altar stood in the forepart of the court; the tabernacle towards the rear. Between the brazen altar and the tabernacle was the laver. The design of this court was to furnish the people, who were precluded from entering the sanctuary, with a place in which they might still, though at some distance, personally appear before Jehovah. The court conferred a privilege, yet taught a lesson. The fact that he could approach no further than its precincts painfully reminded the Israelite that, as yet, the work of atonement was incomplete—that he still stood, because of his unholiness, at a great distance from God. In the gospel of Christ, these barriers are all done away with.—J. O.

Vers. 20, 21.—*The burning lamp.* God's care for his sanctuary descends even to so small a matter as the replenishing and trimming of its lamps. Note—1. The *end* of the ordinance. God desires that the light obtained from the lamps in his sanctuary be —(1) pure, (2) bright, (3) constant. The best light possible. Such should be the light of the Christian life. 2. The *means* to this end. (1) The lamps were to be fed with the *best* and *purest* oil. The Holy Spirit. (2) The lamps were to be duly trimmed and ordered. Watchfulness, care. The light needs to be attended to.—J. O.

Vers. 20, 21.—*The oil for the lamp.* A special commandment was given that the oil should be pure and rich :—

I. THAT THERE MIGHT BE A DUE CORRESPONDENCE BETWEEN THE LIGHT AND THE GLORY OF THE CANDLESTICK. The candlestick was composed of the most precious of all metals, and it had been fashioned by the hands of an artist Divinely chosen and inspired. Great, therefore, would have been the incongruity, if any but the steadiest and most brilliant light had shone forth from this candlestick. Indeed the provision of the very best material might seem to have been self-suggested and to require no commandment at all, did we not know how forgetful, how inconsiderate human nature is. Man needs to be kept up to the mark by sharp and frequent admonitions ; else he will keep the best for himself, and let anything be put forward for such a mere formality as too often he reckons the service of God to be. Still it surely would not require much thought to perceive how disgraceful a dim light would be in connection with such a glorious fabric as the candlestick presented. But there is a more glorious fabric far than this candlestick, if we only consider each human life that comes into this world ; if we only consider the riches and strength that are in each one of us by natural constitution. There is something very glorious about the natural life of man, in spite of its depravity, its miseries and its mortality ; and God has given us the opportunity of still further glorifying our natural life in this world by offering to make us supports such as may aid in sustaining and diffusing the light he would shed abroad amongst men. When God puts his gospel into the charge of human beings he calls attention to the peculiar glory and eminence of our nature. The more faithful his servants have been to the gospel charge put into their hands, the more they have revealed how vile a thing humanity is. God wishes us in all our connection with him to be worthy of our humanity, and to keep ever in our thoughts the gulf that divides us from even the highest of the brutes. Man is never more truly human, never more fully an exponent of the peculiarities of his nature than when he is doing his best to reveal the saving light of God to men. The Christian, no matter what he may lack in such endowments as the world values, is the best kind of man; and the better Christian he becomes, the higher he stands in that best kind wherein he is already numbered.

II. THAT THERE MIGHT BE A DUE CORRESPONDENCE BETWEEN THE LIGHT AND THE GLORY OF THE MOST HOLY PLACE. From between the cherubim within the veil God shone forth when it was so required with a glory and impressiveness which no light of human invention could rival. But outside the veil the seven-branched candlestick was ever to be lighted in the night-time to symbolise the glorious illumination which came from Jehovah himself. How important, therefore, that the light should be the very best which man could afford! Nowhere in all the tents of Israel was there to be a brighter light than that which shone in the holy place. A symbol was needed of such light, instruction and wisdom, as are not to be found in the most sagacious and experienced of men, advising simply upon the grounds of human sagacity and experience. When we look at a Christian we must be able to look at one whose light, while it does not fail in a certain sense to glorify himself, glorifies still more his Father who is in heaven. Every Christian is meant to live so as to arrest the attention of men, and make them ask whence comes the power to inspire him with such remarkable motives and make him the agent of such remarkable effects. Whereas the humiliating confession is to be made that most Christian lives are lived on such a low level that one is led to ask "Is this all?" We read of remarkable manifestations and approaches of the Divine in the way of an incarnate Son of God, a resurrection of the dead, a descent into the Church of a life-giving and transforming Spirit, so that all believers may become new creatures in Christ Jesus; and then, when we look at these professed new creatures, and see how much remains unchanged, inveterate as ever, we ask "Is this all the product of Christ's appearance on the earthly scene?" It is a dreadful reproach that we should let our inconsistency and infirmity be made an excuse for unbelievers to mock at God. We ought to be so under Divine influences, as to combine in one the bright candlestick and the pure, rich oil; and then from us there might shine forth in a pure inviting radiance, a light such as would guide, and cheer while it guided, many a wanderer to God.—Y.

EXPOSITION.

CHAPTER XXVIII.

Vers. 1—12.—THE HOLY GARMENTS. The special object of the present chapter is to prescribe the form, materials, colour, etc., of the holy garments—or the attire of those who were to minister in the tabernacle at the time of their ministration. As the service of the tabernacle was about to be committed to Aaron and his sons, their selection for this office is mentioned in verse 1, and their investiture and consecration briefly touched in verse 41. Otherwise the whole chapter is concerned with the attire That of Aaron is first prescribed (vers. 4—39). It consists of an ephod (vers. 6—12); a breastplate (vers. 13—30); a robe (vers. 31—35); a mitre (vers 36—38); a coat, or tunic; and a

girdle (ver. 39). The dress of his sons follows. It comprises drawers (ver. 42), tunics, girdles, and caps or turbans (ver. 40). Incidentally it is mentioned in verse 43, that drawers are also to be worn by Aaron; and, in conclusion, the neglect of this ordinance in the case of either Aaron or his sons is forbidden under penalty of death

Ver. 1.—**Take thou unto thee.** Literally, "Make to draw near to thee." Moses had hitherto been of all the people the one nearest to God, *the* medium of communication. He was now to abdicate a portion of his functions, transferring them to his brother and his brother's sons. By this act he would draw them nearer to him than they were before. It is worthy of remark that he makes no remonstrance or opposition, but carries out God's will in this matter as readily and willingly as in all others. (See Lev. viii. 4—30.) **From among the children of Israel.** The LXX. read "*And* from among the children of Israel," as if others besides the family of Aaron had been admitted to the priesthood. But this is contrary to the entire tenor of the later narrative. The existing Hebrew text is correct. **Nadab and Abihu,** and again, **Eleazar and Ithamar,** are always coupled together in the Pentateuch (ch. vi. 23; xxiv. 1; Lev. x. 1, 12; etc.), while a marked division is made between the two pairs of brothers. It is probably the sin and early death of the two elder (Lev. x. 1—2) that causes the separation. Of Ithamar after the death of his brothers, nothing is known. Eleazar became high priest (Num. xxxiv. 17; Josh. xiv. 1; xvi. 4; etc.).

Ver. 2.—**Holy garments** have provoked an extreme aversion and an extreme affection at different periods of the world's history. In Moses' time probably no one thought of raising any objection to them. Priestly dresses of many different kinds were worn in Egypt, and some costume other than that of ordinary life, was probably affected by the priest class of every nation. Without entering into any elaborate "philosophy of clothes," we may say that the *rationale* of the matter would seem to be that expressed with great moderation by Richard Hooker—"To solemn actions of royalty and justice their suitable ornaments are a beauty. Are they in religion only a stain?" (See *Eccl. Pol.* v. 29, § 1.) The garments ordered to be made for Aaron and his sons (ver. 41), are said to have been **for glory and for beauty. 1.** "For glory." To exalt the priestly office in the eyes of the people—to make them look with greater reverence on the priests themselves and the priestly functions—to place the priests in a class by themselves, in a certain sense, above the rest of the nation. **2.** "For beauty." As fit and comely in themselves—suitable to the functions which the priests exercised—in harmony with the richness and beauty of the sanctuary wherein they were to minister. God, himself, it would seem, is not indifferent to beauty. He has spread beauty over the earth. He will have beauty in his earthly dwelling-place. He requires men to worship him "in the beauty of holiness" (Ps. xxix. 2; xcvi. 9; 1 Chron. xvi. 29). He ordains for his priests rich and splendid dresses "for glory and for beauty."

Ver. 3.—**Wise-hearted.** In modern parlance the heart is made the seat of the affections and emotions, the brain of the intellect. But the Hebrew idiom was different. There the heart was constantly spoken of as the seat of wisdom. (See below, ch. xxxi. 6; xxxv. 10, 25; xxxvi. 1, 2; Job ix. 4; Prov. xi. 29, etc.) **The spirit of wisdom** might seem to be scarcely necessary for the work of con-

structing a set of priestly garments; but where "glory and beauty" are required, high artistic power is needed; and this power is regarded by the sacred writers, as indeed it is by most of those who have written on the human understanding—notably Plato and Aristotle—as a very important part of the intellect. *Techné,* says Aristotle, involves *theoria,* as well as *æsthesis* and *genesis,* requires, *i.e.,* a knowledge of high abstract truths, as well as the perceptive faculty which we commonly call "taste," and the constructive one known as "power of execution." (See *Eth. Nic.* vi. 4, § 4.) It is, with him, one of the five chief intellectual excellences. **To consecrate him.** Investiture in the holy garments was made a part of the ceremony of consecration (ch. xxix. 5—9; Lev. viii. 7—9, 13), as it is in the English Ordinal in the consecration of a bishop.

Ver. 4.—**These are the garments.** The enumeration does not follow the same order exactly as the description. The two agree, however, in giving the precedence to the same three articles of apparel out of the six—viz., the breast-plate, the ephod, and the robe. **His sons**—*i.e.,* his successors in the office of high priest.

The materials of the priestly garments.

Ver. 5.—The materials for the priestly garments were to be limited to six——precious stones, which are not here mentioned, as being ornamental, rather than essential, parts of the apparel; a blue thread, known as "blue" (compare ch. xxv. 4); a purple or crimson one, known as "purple;" a scarlet one, known as "scarlet;" and a white one, which is called "fine linen." These were the same materials as those used for the veil (ch. xxvi. 31), and curtains (*ib.* 1, 36) of the sanctuary; but probably the fabric was of a more delicate quality. **They shall take**—*i.e.,* "They," the wise-hearted men to whom the work was to be entrusted—"shall take," or receive from Moses—"*the* (necessary) gold, blue, purple," etc. In the original all these words have the definite article prefixed.

The Ephod.

Ver. 6.—**They shall make the ephod** The word *ephod* signifies etymologically any "vestment" or "garment;" but in its use it is confined to the special vestment here described, the great object of which was to be a receptacle for the "breast-plate." The ephod was a sort of jerkin or waistcoat, consisting of two pieces, one to cover the chest and the other the back, joined together probably by a seam, above the shoulders, and united at the waist by a band called "the curious girdle of the ephod." This band was of one piece with the ephod, being woven on either to the front or the back part; it held the other part in place, and was passed round the body and fastened either with a clasp, or with buttons, or strings. **Of gold, of blue, of purple**, etc.—*i.e.*, " of the same materials as the curtains and veil of the sanctuary, with the addition of gold." The gold was probably in the shape of gold thread, or wire of extreme tenuity, and was introduced by the needle after the fabric had been woven, as was commonly done in Egypt (Herod. iii. 47 ; Wilkinson's *Ancient Egyptians*, vol. iii. p. 128: compare below, ch. xxxix. 3). The white, blue, purple, and scarlet threads were doubtless woven into a pattern of some kind ; but it is impossible to say what the pattern was. In Egypt patterns were not much affected, the dress worn being commonly white, with a stripe sometimes at the edge ; but the Semitic tribes, who bordered Egypt on the East, affected gay colours and varied designs, if we may trust the Egyptian wall-paintings. **With cunning work.** Literally, " work of the skilled (workman)." Some of the Hebrews had evidently carried on the trade of weaving in Egypt, and had brought their looms with them. The Egyptian looms were hand-looms, and of no great size ; they admitted of easy transport.

Ver. 7.—**The two shoulder-pieces thereof.** Literally, " Two shoulder-pieces." There is no article, and no possessive pronoun. **At the two edges thereof.** Literally, " at its two ends." A union of the back and front flaps of the dress by a seam at the top of the shoulder seems to be intended. Female dresses were made in this way among the Greeks, but fastened with a brooch or buckle.

Ver. 8.—**The curious girdle.** Josephus says of the ephod, ζώνη περισφίγγεται βάμμασι διαπεποικιλμένη, χρυσοῦ συνυφασμένου, " it is fastened with a girdle dyed of many hues, with gold interwoven in it." Hence its name, *khêsheb*, which means properly " device " or " cunning work." **Of the ephod.** Rather " of its girding "—*i.e.* " wherewith it (the ephod) was to be girded." **Shall be of the same.** Compare above, ch. xxv. 19. The girdle was to be " of one piece " with the ephod, woven on to it as part of it, not a separate piece attached by sewing. **According to the work thereof.** Rather, " of like workmanship with it."

Ver. 9.—**Two onyx stones.** The correctness of this rendering has been much disputed. The LXX. give σμάραγδος, " eme-

rald," as the Greek equivalent in the present passage, while many argue for the beryl (Winer, Rosenmüller, Bollermann), and others for the sardonyx. This last rendering has the support of Josephus and Aquila. The sardonyx is, in fact, nothing but the best kind of onyx, differing from the onyx by having three layers—black, white, and red—instead of two —black and white—only. When large, it fetches a high price, as much as a thousand pounds having been asked for one by a dealer recently. The probability is, that it is the stone here intended. It is an excellent material for engraving. With respect to the possibility of Moses having in the congregation persons who could engrave the sardonyx, we may remark that the Egyptians cut stones quite as hard, from a date long anterior to the exodus. **Grave on them the names of the children of Israel.** Egyptian names are frequently found engraved on rings and amulets in hard stone ; these rings and amulets date from the time of the twelfth dynasty. The names here intended are evidently the Israelite tribe names, which are reckoned as twelve, the double tribe of Joseph counting as one only. (Compare Num. i. 10 ; Deut. xxxiii. 13—17.)

Ver. 10.—**The other six names of the rest.** Literally, " The remaining six names." **According to their birth**—*i.e.*, in the order of seniority—or perhaps, in the order observed in ch. i. 2—4, where the children of the two legitimate wives are given the precedence.

Ver. 11.—**With the work of an engraver.** Rather, " an artificer." **The engravings of a signet.** Signets in Egypt were ordinarily rings, on the bezel of which the name of the owner was inscribed Some were of solid gold ; others with cylindrical bezels of glass or hard stone. On the early use of such signet rings in Egypt see Gen. xli. 42. Cylinders, strung round the wrist and engraved with a name and titles, were common in Mesopotamia from B.C. 2000. **Ouches of gold.** Settings in open-work or filagree seem to be intended—a kind of setting which is very common in Egyptian ornaments.

Ver. 12.—**Stones of memorial unto the children of Israel.** Rather *" for* the children of Israel "—stones, *i.e.* which should serve to remind God that the high priest represented the twelve tribes, officiated in their name, and pleaded on their behalf.

HOMILETICS.

Vers. 1—5.—*The glory of holy garments.* " Holy garments"—garments appropriated to the service of God in his sanctuary—will always be " glorious," however simple they are :—1. As the dress of office for those whose office is of an exalted and glorious charatcer, who are "ambassadors for God," and " stewards of his mysteries." 2. As associated with rites, which show forth, and help forward, the glorious work of redemption : and 3. As typical of the glorious robes which will be worn by the saints in heaven. The garments assigned by the will of God to the Levitical priesthood were, further, glorious in themselves, *i.e.*, splendid, magnificent, of rich and beautiful materials. They thus harmonised with the richness and magnificence of the tabernacle, and afterwards of the temple, and taught the people, by the eye, that whatever is rich and rare should be devoted to the service of God. But the highest glory of holy garments is to be found in those "robes of righteousness," which the set apparel of priests is intended to suggest and signify (Ps. cxxxii. 9; Is. lxi. 10). The white linen of priestly robes tells of purity and innocence—gold and jewels, of precious gifts and graces—azure, the hue of heaven, speaks of heavenly thoughts and aspirations—the scarlet and the purple are signs of the martyr spirit, which is willing to "resist unto blood" (Heb. xii. 4). If the priest or the Levite have no other adorning but that of the outward apparel, if they are not "clothed with the garments of salvation" (Is. l. s. c.), and robed with righteousness, "holy garments" will little avail either themselves, or those to whom they minister. The "marriage garment" required of each Christian in Holy Scripture is purity of life and conduct; and certainly without this, "holy garments" are vain, and lose both their "glory" and their "beauty."

Vers. 6—12.—*The symbolism of the ephod and its onyx stones.* The ephod was, *par excellence*, the priestly garment. When idolatrous rites grew up in Palestine, which sheltered themselves under the pretence of being modifications, or adaptations, of the Sinaitic religion, an ephod was always retained, and made a prominent feature in the new form of worship (Jud. viii. 27; xvii. 5; xviii. 14; etc.). The ephod came to be worn by *all* Israelitish priests (1 Sam. xxii. 18; Hos. iii. 4), and even by laymen when engaged in sacred functions (2 Sam. vi. 14; 1 Chron. xv. 27). Its materials and workmanship united it pointedly with the tabernacle (ch. xxvi. 1), and especially with the holy of holies (*ib.* ver. 31). It may be considered—

I. As TYPIFYING THE UNITY OF THE CHURCH. The shoulder pieces of the ephod were to be "joined together" (ver. 7). The "curious girdle" was to be of one piece with it (ver. 8). Though formed of various parts, it was to be one single indivisible garment, united both above and below, and always worn in its entirety. The seamless robe of our Blessed Saviour is generally allowed to prefigure his one Church. The ephod as worn, was, perhaps, not seamless; but still it was "woven of one piece," and so far resembled the Lord's garment.

II. As REPRESENTING THE VARIETY OF GIFTS AND GRACES WITHIN THE CHURCH. The blue, and purple, and scarlet, and fine linen, and gold, and gems of the ephod gave it a variety and a beauty which made it the most glorious of all the priestly vestments. Variety has a charm of its own, and is a mark of the Church, in which there is such vast "diversity of gifts," though there is but one spirit. Gold is especially appropriate for the dignity of those whom God has made "both priests and kings." "The king's daughter is all glorious within; her clothing is of wrought gold" (Ps. xlv. 13). Purple, too, is an imperial colour, and suits those who shall "reign with Christ for ever" (Rev. xxii. 5).

III. As CONSTITUTING, WHEN WORN BY THE HIGH-PRIEST, A PRESENTATION OF THE CHURCH TO GOD IN PERFECT BEAUTY. The onyx, or sardonyx stones, with the twelve names engraved upon them, completed the representative character of the ephod, and showed clearly that the high priest, when, thus attired, he entered the sanctuary, presented before God the Church whereof he was the head, as freed from sin by the expiation which he had made at the altar before entering, and made meet for the presence of the Most High. And this presentation was, we are distinctly told (Heb. ix. 9—12; x. 19—22), a type or figure of that far more precious one, which Christ is ever making before his Father's throne in heaven, where he presents to him his Church, "a glorious Church, not having spot, or wrinkle, or any such thing, but holy and without blemish" (Eph. v. 27), washed in his blood, redeemed by his death, sanctified by his in-dwelling. Christ can and will purge his elect from all sin (1 John i. 7); Christ can and will present them pure before God. He has his "sealed" ones of all the twelve tribes (Rev. vii. 4—8); and, besides these, he has others who are equally his—"a great multitude, which no man could number, of all nations, and kindreds, and peoples, and tongues" (*ib.* 9)— who "have washed their robes and made them white in the blood of the Lamb" (*ib.* 14), and whom he will "present faultless" to his Father.

HOMILIES BY VARIOUS AUTHORS.

Vers. 1—4.—*The priests' garments.* I. OBSERVE HOW THE INDIVIDUAL IS HERE SUBORDINATED TO THE OFFICE. Jehovah tells Moses here, amid the solemnities of the mount, that his brother Aaron and Aaron's sons are to be taken for service in the priest's office; but no word is said concerning the characters of any of these men, not even Aaron himself. There is a demand that those who made the priestly garments should be wise-hearted, men with a spirit of wisdom which Jehovah himself would put into them; but nothing is said as to Aaron himself being wise-hearted. Nor is there any indication given beforehand of any personal fitness that he had for the office. We gather much as to the way in which God had been training Moses; but Aaron so far as we can see, seems to have been led by a way that he knew not. All the commandment to Moses is, "take to thee Aaron thy brother." He is indicated by a natural relation, and not by anything that suggests spiritual fitness. It is interesting to compare the utter absence of any reference here to personal character with the minute details of what constitutes fitness for bishop and deacon, as we find these details in the epistles to Timothy and Titus. In the old dispensation where there was but the shadow of good things to come, the trappings of the official and the ceremonies of the office were of more importance than the character of any individual holder. The purpose of Jehovah was best served, in proportion as the people, beholding Aaron, forgot that it was Aaron, and were chiefly impressed by the fact that they were looking on the appointed priest of the Most High.

II. OBSERVE WHAT WAS AIMED AT IN THE CONSTRUCTION OF THE PRIESTLY GARMENTS. They were to be for glory and for beauty. Not only different from the garments of the common people, but much more splendid. Gold was worked into the very substance of these garments; precious stones glittered upon them; and everything was done to make them beautiful and impressive. Nor was the splendour of these garments for a mere occasional revelation. Though not worn constantly, yet they had to be assumed for some part of every day; and thus all eyes were continually directed to symbols of the glory, beauty, and perfection which God was aiming to produce in the character of his people. There was as yet no finding of these things in human nature. The gold of human nature could not yet be purified from its debasing dross; but here for a symbol of the refined and perfected man, was gold, pure and bright, we may imagine, as ever came out of the furnace; and here were these precious stones, inestimably more precious since the tribal names were graven on them, and with the preciousness crowned when they took their place on the shoulders and breasts of the priest. Thus, whenever these stones flashed in the light, they spoke forth afresh the great truth, that this priest so gloriously attired, was the representative of the people before God; not a representative whom they had elected for themselves, and who would therefore go to God on a peradventure, but one who, because God himself had chosen him, could not fail to be acceptable. The principle underlying the direction to make these splendid garments is that which underlies the use of all trappings by government and authority. The outward shows of kingly state, the crown, the sceptre, the throne, the royal robes—these may not be impressive now as once they were; but they have been very serviceable once, and may still serve an important purpose, even though it be not easily perceived. It might make a difference in the administration of justice, if the garb of those who are the chief administrators were to differ nothing in public from what it is in private.

III. OBSERVE THAT TO SHOW FURTHER THE IMPORTANCE ATTACHED TO THESE GARMENTS, GOD HIMSELF PROVIDED SKILL FOR THE MAKING OF THEM. Much skill might be needed, far more than could be guessed by the observer, to make these garments graceful and impressive. What was all the richness of the material unless there was also dextrous, tasteful, and sympathetic workmanship? The gold, and the blue, and the purple, and all the rest of the promising materials would have availed nothing in some hands to avert a clumsy and cumbrous result. The people provided all they could, and it was a great deal; but God had to provide the craftsmen in order to make full use of the people's gift.—Y.

Vers. 1, 2.—" *Who shall ascend into the hill of the Lord?* " The tabernacle (cf. outline on xxvi. 30) shows through what steps a man must pass who would approach God. The high priest shows what the man must be like who would attempt to take those steps. The dress of the high priest is usually said to have consisted of eight pieces, viz.: breast-plate, ephod with its girdle, robe of the ephod, mitre, gold plate or holy crown, broidered robe, drawers, girdle. Such a dress is meant to be *characteristic*, to shadow forth what ought to be the character of the man who wears it. As the high priest represents the people in their relation to God, the character required in him must be the character required in all would-be worshippers. Take a few points:—

I. THE WORSHIPPER MUST BE IN HARMONY WITH HIS SURROUNDINGS. The colours and materials of the garments are the same as those of the tabernacle with its veil and entrance curtain—gold, blue, purple, scarlet, fine linen. So, too, the character of the worshipper must match with the character of the sanctuary. What can a man do in heaven if he be not heavenly-minded? Every one, in the end, like Judas, must go to his own place; the character of the individual must decide the character of his surroundings (cf. Matt. xxii. 11—13).

II. HE MUST BE CAPABLE OF REFLECTING THE LIGHT AMID WHICH HE WALKS AND THE GLORY WHICH HE IS APPROACHING. The breast-plate is, amongst the garments of the high priest, what the mercy seat is amongst the furniture of the sanctuary. In some sort, also, the two are related; the mercy seat is the throne of glory, the resting-place of the shechinah, whilst the breast-plate reflects the same glory, and glorifies the wearer by reflecting it. 1. *Man is glorified by reflecting the glory of God.* The more he can reflect, the more manifold the ways in which he can reflect it, the more perfect is the glory which is revealed on him. We may note, however, that the high priest representing the nation, the breast-plate which he wears suggests rather the *national* than the *individual* reflecting power. The one grows out of the other, but amongst individuals some may reflect as the sardius, some as the topaz, etc. The great thing is that they *do* reflect, though each may reflect differently to others. Remember, too, that the glory of each helps to make and to intensify the glory of the whole. 2. *The reflector is the breast-plate.* The breast-plate covers and symbolises the heart or the affections. " God is love," and the glory of God is the glory of love made manifest. Only love can reflect love; the loving heart is the enlightened and the enlightening heart.

III. PROGRESS MUST NOT BE SILENT BUT MUSICAL. The robe of the ephod with its border of embroidered pomegranates, blue, red, and crimson; bells of gold alternating with the pomegranates. The music of the priest's movement is associated with fruitfulness; look whence the sound comes and you see the varicoloured pomegranates. So, too, the melody of a holy life rings out from amongst good deeds; deeds which like the varicoloured pomegranates are all one fruit, " the fruit of the Spirit" (cf. Gal. v. 22). Such fruit advertises to his fellows a man's progress along the way of holiness (cf. Ecclesiasticus xlv. 9, " a memorial to the children of his people "); yet specially is it required by God for his own pleasure and satisfaction (cf. xxviii. 35): whether men hear or no, the golden bells must not be silent.

IV. THE WORSHIPPER MUST BE HELMETED AND CROWNED WITH HOLINESS. (Cf. xxviii. 36.) The golden plate with its inscription. 1. Generally, it may be said, that they who approach a holy place must approach it as a holy people. We have safeguards against unseemliness and impurity (xxviii. 42). 2. Specially does the head, associated with the intellect, need consecration. Unless the head be protected the heart must soon cease to reflect. He who lays aside the helmet of holiness cannot retain the breast-plate of glory.

Conclusion.—We want to draw nigh to God. The tabernacle shows us by what successive stages we must approach him; the high priest shows us how in character and conduct we must be prepared for those successive stages. As we should put it now-a-days,—to get to heaven a man must be like Christ; the journey thither can only be achieved by those who are in communion with the great High Priest. In and through him we may draw nigh; growing daily more heavenly-minded, and therefore more fit for heaven; reflecting more and more of the light and glory which shines out upon us; making life musical with the melody of good works, a sweet sound in God's ears and a sign to direct men's attention God-wards; consecrated wholly to God's service, hallowed now by outward dedication; at length like the great High Priest himself, to be not merely *hallowed* but altogether holy.—G.

Vers. 1—43.—*The priests and their garments.* From instructions about inanimate things, we come now to *persons.* Aaron and his four sons were to be set apart for the office of the priesthood, and garments were to be made for them, "for glory and for beauty." Aaron was to be high priest ("the priest who is higher than his brethren, upon whose head the anointing oil was poured," Lev. xxi. 16); his sons were to be ordinary priests. The high priest was a very especial type of Christ.

I. THE INSTITUTION OF THE PRIESTHOOD (ver. 1). Hitherto there had been no distinct class invested with the office of the priesthood. The need for a separate priesthood arose with the giving of the law, with the entrance of Israel into covenant relationship with God, and with the founding of a sanctuary. 1. *With the giving of the law.* A distinct revelation had been made of God's holiness. But God's holiness had as its correlative the unholiness of the people. By the law came the knowledge of sin. A priesthood, specially sanctified to God's service, became necessary to mediate between an unholy people and a holy God. 2. *With the establishment of a covenant relationship between Israel and Jehovah.* In virtue of the covenant, Israel became to God "a kingdom of priests and an holy nation" (ch. xix. 5). It was this priestly calling of the nation which found official expression in the priesthood of the house of Aaron. The priests were "vicars," in the sense of the following passage—"A truly vicarious act does not supersede the principal's duty of performance, but rather implies and acknowledges it. . . . . In the old monastic times, when the revenues of a cathedral or cure fell to the lot of a monastery, it became the duty of that monastery to perform the religious services of the cure. But inasmuch as the monastery was a corporate body, they appointed one of their number, whom they denominated their vicar, to discharge those duties for them. His service did not supersede theirs, but was a perpetual and standing acknowledgment that they, as a whole and individually, were under the obligation to perform it" (Robertson of Brighton, Sermons, vol. ii. p. 92). That is to say, the priests stood in a representative relation to the body of the people. They acted in the name of the community. 3. *With the founding of a sanctuary.* "The groundwork of this new form of religion stood in the erection of the tabernacle, which God chose for his peculiar dwelling-place, and through which he meant to keep up a close and lively intercourse with his people. But this intercourse would inevitably have grown on their part into too great familiarity, and would thus have failed to produce proper and salutary impressions upon the minds of the worshippers, unless something of a counteracting tendency had been introduced, fitted to beget feelings of profound and reverential awe toward the God who condescended to come so near to them. This could no otherwise be effectually done than by the institution of a separate priesthood, whose prerogative alone it should be to enter within the sacred precincts of God's house, and perform the ministrations of his worship" (Fairbairn). The Aaronic priesthood had thus a twofold function to discharge in relation to the people. 1. *Representative.* It represented the nation in its priestly standing and vocation. It performed sacerdotal acts in the name of the tribes. The representative character culminated in the person of the high priest. 2. *Mediatory.* The priesthood mediated between the people and Jehovah. It was the link of communion between the holy and the unholy. Gifts and offerings, which otherwise, on account of the unholiness of the people, would not have been accepted, were accepted at the hands of the priests. The high priest transacted with God *on behalf of* his constituents as well as in their name. It pertained to him, and to the other priests, "to make reconciliation for the sins of the people" (Heb. ii. 17). The priesthood, and especially the high priest, thus typifies Christ—(1) in his Divine appointment to his office (Heb. v. 5, 6); (2) in his personal and official holiness (Heb. iv. 15; vii. 26); (3) in his representative relations to his people (Heb. vi. 20); (4) in his work of mediation and intercession (Heb. ix. 11, 12, 24); (5) in his heavenly glory (Heb. ii. 9). Note, however, the following point of difference (one among many) between the high priest and Christ. The Jewish high priest embodied priestly rights *already existing in the nation.* Believers, on the contrary, derive their priestly rights *from* Christ. They are admitted to a share in *his* priestly standing. Their priesthood, unlike that of the old covenant, is purely spiritual. It includes privileges formerly possessed only by the official classes, *e.g.,* the right of direct access to God (Eph. ii. 18; iii. 12; Heb. x. 19).

II. THE PRIESTLY GARMENTS (vers. 2—43). Having chosen his priests, God next proceeds to clothe them. As the office was of his appointment, so must the garments be which are to be the *insignia* of it. Nothing is left to individual taste. The articles of attire; their shape, material, colour, workmanship; the manner of their ornamentation; everything is fixed after a Divine pattern. The garments are to be "for glory and for beauty" (vers. 2, 40), indicative of the official dignity, of the sacred character, and of the honourable prerogatives of the wearers of them. Men are even to be inspired with "the spirit of wisdom" (ver. 3), for the purpose of making them, so entirely are they to be garments of Divine origin. Look (1) at what these garments were, and (2) at the functions and privileges of the priesthood as shadowed forth in them. 1. *The parts of the priestly dress.* The dress of the ordinary priests, with the exception of the girdle of needlework (cf. ch. xxxix. 29), was to be of fine white linen. It consisted of an embroidered coat, a cap, and plain white linen drawers. The high priest's garments were of a much richer order. They embraced (1) the ephod, with its curious girdle (vers. 6—15). (2) The breast-plate, in which were to be placed "the Urim and Thummim" (vers. 15—31). (3) The robe of the ephod, "all of blue," and embroidered along the hem with pomegranates. Alternating with the pomegranates were to be little golden bells, which should give a sound when the priest went into the holy place, and when he came out (vers. 31—36). (4) The mitre, on which was to be a plate of gold, fastened with blue lace, and engraved with the words—"Holiness to the Lord" (vers. 36—39). (5) A broidered coat, girdle, and drawers, similar to those of the ordinary priests (ver. 39). 2. *The symbolism of the dress.* The blue of the robe of the ephod denoted the heavenly origin of the priest's office; the shining whiteness of the ordinary garments, the purity required in those who served before Jehovah; the gold, the diversified colours, the rich embroidery and gems, in the other articles of attire, the exalted honour of those whom Jehovah had chosen, and caused to approach to him, that they might dwell in his courts (Ps. lxv. 4). More specifically, the garments bore testimony (1) to the fundamental requirement of holiness in the priesthood. This requirement found its most distinct expression in the engraved plate on the high priest's mitre. Holiness was to be the characteristic of the people as a whole. Most of all was it required in those who stood in so peculiarly near a relation to Jehovah, and on whom it devolved to make atonement for the others. The requirement is perfectly fulfilled in Christ, whose people, in turn, are called to holy living. (2) To the representative character of the priesthood. This was beautifully imaged by the fact that, both on his shoulders and on his breast, the high priest bore precious stones engraved with the names of the twelve tribes of Israel (vers. 9—13; 17—23). Another indication of this representative character is found in the order to place bells upon the hem of the robe of the ephod, that the people might hear the sound of his movements as he went in and out of the holy place (ver. 35). Conscious that he was transacting in God's presence in their name, they were to follow him with their thoughts and prayers in the different parts of his sacerdotal task. It was, however, the wearing of "the breast-plate of judgment" (ver. 29), which most specially declared that the high priest appeared before God as the people's representative. His function, as clothed with the breast-plate, was to sustain the "right" of the children of Israel before Jehovah (ver. 30). The "right" included whatever claims were given them on the justice and mercy of Jehovah by the stipulations of the covenant. It was a "right" derived, not from unfailing obedience to the law, but from Jehovah's goodness. It was connected with atonement. Our "right," in like manner, is embodied in Christ, who bears us on his heart continually in presence of his Father. (3) To the priestly function of mediation. The onyx stones on the shoulders of the high priest, each having engraved on it six of the names of the tribes of Israel (ver. 12), indicated that on him rested the burden or responsibility of the entire congregation. A more distinct expression of this idea is given in ver. 38, in connection with the gold plate of the mitre, engraved with HOLINESS TO THE LORD—"It shall be upon Aaron's forehead, that Aaron may bear the iniquity of the holy things, which the children of Israel shall hallow in all their holy gifts; and it shall be always upon his forehead, that they may be accepted before the Lord." A shadow of the higher mediation. Our persons, gifts, and works find acceptance only in Christ. (4) To the need of sympathy in the priest, as a qualification for his office. The high priest was to bear the names of the children of Israel *upon his heart,* graven on the stones of the breast-plate (ver. 29). Christ has perfect sympathy

(Heb. ii. 14—18 ; iv. 14—16). The people also, as is hinted in ver. 35, were to have sympathy with their priest. (5) To the function of the priest, as revealer of God's will (ver. 30). Urim and Thummim—whatever these were—are now superseded by the external word, and the inward illumination of Christ's Spirit. Christ gives forth unerring revelations of the will of the Father. "Lights and perfections" is not too high a name to bestow upon the Scriptures (Ps. xix. 7—12; 2 Tim. iii. 15, 16).—J. O.

EXPOSITION.

Vers. 13—30.—The breast-plate. It has been noticed that the ephod had for its main object or purpose to be a receptacle for the breast-plate which was attached to it after it had been put on, and formed its principal ornament. The Hebrew word khoshen, which is translated "breast-plate," means "ornament;" and the khoshen must certainly have been the most striking and brilliant object in the whole attire of the high priest. Externally, it did but repeat the symbolism of the ephod, exhibiting the high priest as the representative of the twelve tribes, whose names were engraved upon its twelve stones, as well as upon the onyxes of the ephod. Internally, it had, however, another, and a deeper import. It contained within it the Urim and the Thummim (ver. 30), by means of which God was consulted, and signified his will to his people. This must be regarded as its main end and use. It was from the decisions thus given that it received the name of "the breast-plate (or ornament) of judgment."

Ver. 13.— Ouches of gold. "Buttons" according to one view (Cook): "sockets," according to another (Kalisch): "rosettes," according to a third (Keil). Some small ornament of open-work (see the comment on ver. 11), which could be sewn on to the ephod, and whereto a chain might be attached, seems to be intended. The object was to fasten the "breast-plate" firmly to the ephod.

Ver. 14.—At the ends. The meaning of the Hebrew word migbâlôth is very doubtful. Jarchi and Rosenmüller approve of the rendering of our translators. Geddes, Boothroyd, and Dathe render "chains of equal length." Gesenius, Kalisch, Canon Cook, and others, believe the true meaning to be "wreathed," or "of wreathen work," so that the next clause, "after the manner of a rope," would be simply exegetic. Of wreathen work. Literally, "after the manner of a rope." Cords of twisted gold wire were frequently used, instead of chains, by the Egyptians.

Ver. 15.—The breast-plate. As the khoshen was to be worn upon the breast (ver. 29), this name is appropriate; but it is not a translation of khoshen. Of judgment. See the

introductory paragraph to this section. Kalisch translates "the breast-plate of decision." It was to be made, so far as its main fabric was concerned, of exactly the same materials as the ephod. See ver. 6.

Ver. 16.—Four square . . . being doubled. It has been generally supposed that the doubling was merely for the purpose of giving additional strength to the work, which was to receive twelve heavy gems; but Gesenius and others are of opinion that the object was to form a bag, in which the Urim and Thummim, which they regard as material objects, might be kept. A span. Half a cubit, or about nine inches.

Ver. 17.—Settings of stones. These were similar to those of the two shoulder stones—i.e. of filagree or cloisonné work—as appears from ch. xxxix. 13. The first row of the stones is said to have been composed of a sardius, or sard, a topaz, and a carbuncle. Of these names the first only would seem to be tolerably certain. The second cannot be right, since the topaz was too hard a stone to be engraved by the ancient engravers. We may conjecture that the chrysolite, a pale stone not unlike the topaz, but far less hard, was the gem intended. The "carbuncle" is also thought to be wrong; and the "beryl" is suggested by some ; by others "a sort of precious corundum." Emerald, to which the "smaragdus" of the LXX. and Josephus would seem to point, cannot be right, since that stone is fully as hard as the topaz.

Ver. 18.— The second row an emerald, a sapphire, and a diamond. Here all the names must be wrong, for none of these three stones could be cut by the ancient engravers. Probably, carbuncle (or garnet), lapis lazuli, and onyx are intended.

Ver. 19.—The third row a ligure, an agate, and an amethyst. The term "ligure" is unknown in modern mineralogy ; and it is to the last degree uncertain what stone the ancients intended by their lingurium or lapis ligurius Some think that "jacinth," others that "tourmaline," is the stone here meant. A few suggest amber, but amber cannot receive an engraving. "Agate" and "amethyst" are generally allowed to be right translations.

Ver. 20.— The fourth row a beryl, and an onyx, and a jasper. If the identifications above suggested are allowed, two at least of these translations must be rejected. We have supposed the third stone in the first row to have been the "beryl," and the third in the second the "onyx." Perhaps we should translate, "a turquoise, a sardonyx, and a jasper." (See the comment on ver. 9.) **Their inclosings.** Rather, "their settings," as in ver. 17.

Ver. 21.—**The stones shall be with the names.** Rather, "according to the names;" the number of the stones shall agree with that of the names, viz., twelve. **Everyone with his name shall they be according to the twelve tribes.** Rather, "every one according to its name, they shall be for the twelve tribes," *i.e.*, each, according to the name that is on it, shall stand for one of the twelve tribes.

Ver. 22.—**Chains at the ends.** Compare the comment on ver. 14. Kalisch translates, "chains of wreathen work, twisted in the manner of ropes."

Vers. 23—28. — These verses present no difficulty. They describe very minutely, and with some tautology, the mode in which the breast-plate was to be fastened to the ephod. It was to have four rings, two at its two upper corners (ver. 23), and two just behind its two lower corners (ver. 26); a gold twist or cord was to be passed through each of the two upper rings, and then attached to the "ouches" or settings of the shoulder stones (ver. 25; compare vers. 11—14). A blue lace or ribbon was to be passed through each of the two lower rings, and these laces were to be tied to two rings, sewn for the purpose on to the front of the ephod a little above the "curious girdle" (vers. 26, 27). By these four fastenings at its four corners, the breast-plate was securely attached to the ephod, and could not readily get loose from it.

Ver. 27.—**Over against the other coupling thereof.** Rather, "near its joining." The "joining" of the ephod is perhaps the place where the "curious girdle" was woven on to it.

Ver. 29.—**And Aaron shall bear,** etc. "Aaron," *i.e.*, "shall not only bear the names of the twelve tribes upon his shoulders (ver. 12), but also upon his heart." He shall thus make a double presentation of them to God continually. The explanation is somewhat fanciful, that the names on the shoulder-stones indicated that the people were a burthen to him, while those on the stones of the breast-plate, being upon his breast, indicated that he bore them affection. The breast and the shoulder were probably chosen as being conspicuous and honourable positions.

Ver. 30.—**Thou shalt put in the breast-plate of judgment the Urim and the Thummim.** The words *Urim* and *Thummim* mean respectively "Lights" and "Perfections," or perhaps "Light" and "Perfection—the plural form being merely a plural of honour. They were well translated by Aquila and Symmachus, φωτισμοὶ καὶ τελειότητες: less well by the

LXX. ἡ δήλωσις καὶ ἡ ἀλήθεια: still worse by the Vulgate, *Doctrina et Veritas*. What exactly the two words represented is doubtful in the extreme. It has been supposed by some that they were not material objects, but a method by which God communicated his will; *e.g.*, a miraculous light, or a miraculous voice. But such things as these could not have been put by Moses either "in," or "on the breast-plate of judgment." Modern critics are generally agreed that the Urim and Thummim must have been material objects of one kind or another. The objects suggested are 1. The engraved stones of the breast-plate. 2. Two small images, like the teraphim. 3. A gold plate, engraved with the name of Jehovah. 4. Three plates or slips; one blank, one engraved with "yes," and one with "no." 5. Diamonds, cut and uncut, with marks engraved on them. Against the first of these views it is urged with very great force that the present passage shows the Urim and Thummim to be something quite distinct from the breast-plate—something which was to be added to the breast-plate after all the stones had been set in it; and which Aaron was to bear upon his breast in addition to the breast-plate and its jewels (compare ver. 29 with ver. 30). Against the fourth and fifth, it is sufficient to observe that they are pure conjectures, without any basis of authority, either in Scripture or tradition. The second and the third remain. The third has important Jewish names in its favour, but is open to the objection that it makes a single object correspond to both words. The second alone seems to have any basis in Scripture, which certainly connects the use of *teraphim* with the use of an ephod (Judg. xvii. 5; xviii. 14, 17, 20; Hosea iii 4). On the whole, while admitting that there is no sufficient evidence to determine the question, we incline to regard the Urim and Thummim as small images, kept in the bag of the "breast-plate" (ver. 16), by means of which the high priest gave a decision when he was consulted. How the decision was arrived at, is an even more difficult problem than the one which we have attempted to solve. Some suppose the two images to have been used as lots, one giving an affirmative and the other a negative answer. Others imagine, that by gazing attentively upon them, and fixing his thoughts on the qualities which they symbolised — illumination and perfection — the high priest was thrown into an ecstatic state which enabled him to prophesy aright. The notion has even been started, that an angel spoke by their lips, and answered any question that was put to them. The truth seems to be that no theory on the subject can be more than a theory—quite arbitrary and conjectural—neither Scripture nor tradition furnishing any hint on the matter. If we knew how men divined from teraphim (2 Kings xxiii. 24;

Ezek. xxi. 21; Zech. x. 2), we might thence obtain some inkling of the truth, since there is much probability in the view, that the teraphim were employed as an unauthorised substitute for the Urim and Thummim. (See Judg. xvii. 5; xviii. 5, 6, 14—20.) But the method of this divination is wholly unknown. It is not however likely to have been a mere casting of lots, which is a very simple process, and requires no images; nor can this explanation of the decision by Urim and Thummim be regarded as having probability in its favour. Perhaps, of all the theories, that which supposes the Urim and Thummim to have been objects gazed at by the high priest until he entered the ecstatic state, is the least objectionable. It must not, however, be considered an essential part of this

theory, that the material objects were derived from the religion of Egypt (Plumptre). The objects must have been well known to Moses and to those for whom he wrote; otherwise, they could not have been introduced, without any account of their nature, as, " *The* Urim " and " *The* Thummim." They had probably been long possessed and consulted by the nation, which was accustomed to believe that it received enlightenment from them. Perhaps they were a sort of teraphim, but unconnected with any idolatrous worship. It is quite conceivable that an old usage, hitherto unauthorised, but not debased by any flagrant corruption, should have been adopted by Divine command into the Mosaic ritual, purified of any evil that attached to it, and consecrated to an important purpose.

HOMILETICS.

Vers. 13—30.—*The Teachings of the Breast-plate.* The breast-plate of judgment has many aspects, and teaches us several important truths—*e.g.* :—

I. THE PRECIOUSNESS OF SOULS IN GOD'S SIGHT. The tribes of Israel are represented by gems—gems of the most precious kinds known to, and workable by the engravers of the day—sard, and onyx, and carbuncle, and lapis lazuli, and chrysolite, and perhaps turquoise. We are reminded by this of the saying of the Lord recorded by the prophet Malachi—" They (that fear me) shall be mine in that day *when I make up my jewels* " (Mal. iii. 17). His own elect are the "jewels" of Christ, wherewith he decks himself as a bridegroom with his ornaments (Is. lxi. 10). As Israel was of old, not only his "special people," but his "peculiar treasure" (Ex. xix. 5), so are Christians now—each one of them dear to him; each one of them purchased with his blood; each one of them a stone in that glorious temple whereof he is the chief corner stone—a " white stone," having on it " a new name written " (Rev. ii. 17; iii. 12).

II. THE VARIETY IN THEIR GIFTS. Each stone in the breast-plate was different from all the rest—each had its own peculiar beauty. One was more brilliant, one more lovely in its hue, one more curious from its complexity. Yet the breast-plate needed all, would not have been perfect without all. None could say to its neighbour—" I have no need of thee." Contrast with its neighbours heightened the effect of each and so added to its beauty. It is the same with Christ's " jewels"—no two are alike—each has his own peculiar characteristics, his idiosyncrasy. And the crown in which the jewels are set is rendered more beautiful than it would otherwise have been by this diversity and variety. An endless repetition of even that which is most lovely palls. Of the thousands upon thousands whom Christ has saved and will save, no two but will be different; no one but will add somewhat to the majesty and beauty of the Church in heaven by its peculiar and distinctive character.

III. THE HIGH VALUE OF HIDDEN GIFTS OF WISDOM AND KNOWLEDGE. It was not from its external beauty—from the gold and purple, and scarlet, and blue, and fine linen of its main fabric, or from its ouches and its golden chains of wreathed work; or even from the dazzling brilliancy and varied hues of its twelve gems—that the breast-plate of the high priest drew either its main value or its honourable title. It was " the breast-plate of judgment;" and this "judgment" was wholly unconnected with the external beauty and gorgeous appearance of the breast-plate. Hidden away in the treasury of its innermost folds lay the mysterious objects, known as "light" and "perfection," by means of which the priest pronounced his "judgments," and declared the will of God to the people. These constituted the true glory of the breast-plate. While the twelve stones symbolised the twelve tribes, with their varied gifts and faculties (Gen. xlix. 3—27; Deut. xxxiii. 6—25), the Urim and the Thummim symbolised light and perfection—intellectual and moral excellence—those best gifts of wisdom and moral knowledge which are the crowning graces of the regenerate human being (Eph. i. 8, 17; Phil. i. 9; Col. i. 9, 10; etc.).

IV. THE PROPRIETY OF REFERRING ALL OUR DOUBTS TO GOD FOR DECISION. Though the Christian Church does not enjoy, any more than did the post-captivity Jewish Church (Ezra ii. 63), the advantage of oracular responses from on high, though our High Priest is gone before us into the holiest, and has taken with him the light and perfection, which are his alone, yet it is still possible to refer doubts to God, and so obtain light enough to serve as a guide to conduct. If we take our difficulties to God on our knees, and ask his counsel upon them in a faithful spirit, we have full reason to trust that we shall receive illumination from him. What after prayerful communion with God appears to us the best course to take, we may accept as his decision, his voice speaking to us. How consoling and encouraging the thought that we can, each one for himself, in the solitude of our chambers cast the burthen of our cares upon One who is perfectly good and perfectly wise, and who has promised to be our guide unto death!

HOMILIES BY VARIOUS AUTHORS.

Vers. 1—38.—*Aaron in his priesthood the type of Jesus.*

I. IN HIS APPOINTMENT (ver. 1). 1. He is chosen of God (Heb. v. 4), and therefore our accepted intercessor. 2. He is taken from among his brethren; "from among the children of Israel, that he may minister unto me." The priest who ministers before God for us must go up with a brother's heart and with experience of human infirmity (Heb. iv. 15).

II. IN HIS ARRAY. The holy garments were "for glory and for beauty," the symbol of the perfect humanity of Jesus; "holy, harmless, undefiled and separate from sinners."

III. IN HIS SYMPATHY. 1. The names of the tribes were engraved upon and identified with the choicest jewels. Christ not only remembers us; we are loved, honoured, treasured by him. 2. The name of each tribe was engraved upon a separate, and different kind of jewel. We are not grasped by our high priest in a mass; we are individually known, loved, cared for. 3. The names were borne upon Aaron's heart whenever he went into the holy place (ver. 29), for a memorial before the Lord continually. We are held in perpetual remembrance before God.

IV. IN HIS VICARIOUSNESS. 1. That remembrance was burden-bearing; he went in *for them*, his heart was bowed before God in the consciousness of *their* sin and need. For us in our sin and need Christ's entreaties ascend day and night. 2. In his zeal for holiness (vers. 36—38). Christ, sin's sacrifice, shall also be sin's destruction.—U.

EXPOSITION.

Vers. 31—35.—THE ROBE OF THE EPHOD. Underneath the ephod and breast-plate the high priest was to wear a robe, or frock, wholly of blue. This robe was to have a hole for the head at the top, and was to be woven without seam (ch. xxxix. 22). It was put on over the head, like a habergeon or coat of mail, and probably reached below the knee. Josephus says that it had no sleeves.

Ver. 31.—**All of blue.** This plainness and uniformity offered a strong contrast to the variegated hues of the breast-plate and ephod, and threw those portions of the attire into greater prominence. If the blue used was indigo, the effect of the contrast must have been heightened

Ver. 32.—**An hole in the top of it.** A mere circular hole for the head to go through, unaccompanied by a slit or longitudinal opening. **In the midst of it.** Midway between the two arm-holes. **A binding of woven work round about the hole of it.** This would strengthen the edge of the opening, and prevent it from tearing or fraying. The binding was probably sewn on after the frock was woven. **As it were the hole of an habergeon.** Linen corselets or habergeons have been found in Egypt. They were sometimes covered with metal scales, and were of the make here indicated. (See the author's *History of Egypt*, vol. i. p. 446.) The word here used for "habergeon" (*takhărâh*) is Egyptian.

Ver. 33.—**Upon the hem of it.** Literally "at its edge" **Pomegranates.** Tassels in the shape of pomegranates, of three colours, seem to be intended. An ornament of the kind is common in Assyria, but not in Egypt. **Bells of gold between them.** The bell is not often found in Egypt, and seems certainly not to have been in common use there. It was, however, often hung round the necks of horses in Assyria (*Ancient Monarchies*, vol. ii. pp. 8, 14, 15, 27), and is so simple an object that its invention was probably very early. The Assyrian bells are shaped almost exactly like our own, as are the classical ones.

Vers. 34, 35.—**A golden bell and a pomegranate.** Hebrew tradition gives a most uncertain sound with respect to the number of the bells. According to some, they were 12 only; according to others, 72; according to a third school, 365! Equally conflicting are the explanations given of their symbolism—(1) that they typified the proclamation and expounding of the law by the high-priest—(2) that they were a musical offering of praise—(3) that they marked kingly dignity, since Oriental kings sometimes wore bells—and (4) that

they were a call to vigilance and attention. This last view is supported by the words of verse 35—**it shall be upon Aaron to minister, and his sound shall be heard,** or "that its sound may be heard." The bells were a means of uniting priest and people in one common service—they enabled the people to enter into and second what the priest was doing for them, and so to render his mediation efficacious—they made the people's worship in the court of the sanctuary a "reasonable service." And hence the threat, which certainly does not extend to *all* the priestly garments, implied in the words, "that he die not." If the high priest neglected to wear the robe with the bells, he separated himself off from the people; made himself their substitute and not their mouthpiece; reduced their worship to a drear formality; deprived it of all heartiness and life and vigour. For thus abusing his office, he would deserve death, especially as he could not do it unwittingly, for his ears would tell him whether he was wearing the bells or not.

HOMILETICS.

Ver. 31.—*The Teachings of the Robe.* I. THE NEED OF HEAVENLY CALM AND PURITY. The robe was to be of one hue—uniform, peaceful; without glitter; something on which the eye could rest itself with a quiet satisfaction. And it was to be "blue"— the colour of heaven, the hue which God has spread over "that spacious firmament on high," which in his word represents to us his dwelling. "The blue sky is an image of purity." Nothing purer, nothing calmer, nothing more restful, than the deep soft azure of the eternal unchanging sky. The high priest's robe was to mirror it. He was to present himself before God in a robe "all of blue." So let us present ourselves before him arrayed in purity and peacefulness.

II. THE NEED OF UNITY. If the ephod was to some extent emblematic of the oneness of the Church, so, and much more, was "the robe of the ephod." It was of woven work (ch. xxxix. 22), absolutely seamless—one, emphatically, in material, in hue, in texture. So Christ prayed that his Church might be one—"as thou, Father, art in me, and I in thee, that they also may be one in us—one, even as we are one; I in them, and thou in me, that they may be made perfect in one" (John xvii. 21—23). Visible unity is broken up; but something of invisible unity there may still be, if all true lovers of Christ will cultivate the spirit of unity; judge charitably; think the best they can of all branches of the Church; look to the good points of each; pray for their advance in holiness and in the knowledge of Christ; work with them so far as they can —*e.g.*, for charitable and moral objects, amicably. If we thus act, if we be thus minded, we shall, in a true sense, put on "the robe of the ephod"—we shall be promoters, and not hinderers, of unity.

III. THE NEED OF KEEPING OUR ATTENTION FIXED ON THE ACTIONS OF OUR TRUE HIGH PRIEST, AND JOINING IN THEM. The bells of the robe were to advertise the people of every movement made by the high priest, and enable them to take their part in his actions. To profit by the contrivance, they had to keep their ears attent to the sound, and their minds fixed on the service which was in progress within the sanctuary. We Christians have equal need to mount up in thought continually to that holy place, whither Christ has taken our nature, and set it down at the right hand of God—to join with him as he pleads his meritorious sacrifice on our behalf; to "have boldness" with him "to enter into the holiest;" with him to ask the Father to pardon our sins; with him to intercede for the whole Church; with him to pray that strength may be given us to persevere. We do not, indeed, need bells to tell us how he is employed at each successive moment, because he is always doing all these things for us—always interceding, always pleading his sacrifice, always beseeching his Father to forgive us and sustain us. We may join him in these acts at any moment. Thus, bells are not necessary for us; but still they may sometimes help us. Many an Israelite, whose thoughts wandered and became fixed on worldly things, when no sound issued from the sanctuary, was recalled to a sense of religion, and the recollection of his soul's needs, by the tinkling of the priest's golden bells. So Christians, who ought in heart and mind ever to ascend to where Christ sits at the right hand of God (Col. iii. 1—3; Eph. ii. 6, etc.), but whose attention will wander to earth and earthly objects, may sometimes by the chime of bells, or by their solemn toll, be woke up to higher thoughts,—recalled, as it were, from earth to heaven, taken back from the vain distractions of the world to that holy place where their High Priest is ever interceding for them.

EXPOSITION.

Vers. 36—38.—THE MITRE. Josephus tells us that the head-dress of the high priest was "not a conical cap, but a sort of crown, made of thick linen swathes" (*Ant. Jud.* iii. 7, § 3). It was thus really a species of turban. The colour was white; and the only ornament on it was the gold plate, with its blue ribbon or fillet.

Ver. 36.—**Thou shalt make a plate of pure gold.** The plate, though a mere ornament of the mitre, was, at once, its most conspicuous and its most significant feature. Placed directly in front, right over the forehead, and probably of burnished gold, it would attract universal attention, and catch the eye even more than the breast-plate. Its position made it "the culminating point of the whole priestly attire" (Kalisch)—and its inscription gave to that position extraordinary force and significance. For it taught that "**holiness to the Lord**" is the very highest crown and truest excellence of religion—that to which all ceremonial is meant to conduce—that without which all the paraphernalia of worship must ever be in God's sight a mockery. It set this truth conspicuously before the eyes, and was apt to impress it upon the hearts of all. It

taught the high priest himself not to rest upon outward forms, but to aim in his own person, and teach the people to aim continually, at internal holiness. The extreme importance of this, causes the putting forward at once of the plate and its inscription before any account of the "mitre" is given.

Ver. 37.—**Thou shalt put it on a blue lace.** In ch. xxxix. 31, it is explained that the blue lace, or ribbon, was "tied to it," probably at either end. **That it may be upon the mitre**—*i.e.*, "that it may be kept in place, and not slip from its position on the mitre."

Ver. 38.—**It shall be upon his forehead, that Aaron may bear the iniquity of the sacred things.** Imperfection attaches to everything that man does; and even the sacrifices that the people offered to God required to be atoned for and purified. It was granted to the high priest in his official capacity to make the necessary atonement, and so render the people's gifts acceptable. For this purpose he was invested with an official holiness, proclaimed by the inscription upon the plate, which exhibited him as the type and representative of that perfectly Holy One, through whom alone can any real atonement be made to the Father. **It shall be always upon his forehead**—*i.e.*, whenever he ministers.

HOMILETICS.

Vers. 36—38.—*The Teachings of the Mitre.* The main lesson taught by all the priestly garments is intensified in the mitre, namely, the need of holiness. "Without holiness no one shall see God;" "Holiness becometh thine house for ever." The high priest was to be—

I. HOLY, OFFICIALLY. By his birth, of Levi and Aaron—by his bringing up—by his consecration—by his investiture—by his representative position as priestly head of his nation and type of Christ—he was set apart from all others, dedicated to holy employments, assigned a holy character. Of these things he could not dispossess himself. Even a Caiaphas "prophesied, being high priest that same year."

II. HOLY, PERSONALLY. To wear holy garments, to be employed about holy things, and yet to be impure in heart and life, is to be a "whited sepulchre," beautiful outwardly, but "within full of dead men's bones and of all uncleanness" (Matt. xxiii. 27). Nothing can be a greater offence to God. A high priest, with "holiness to the Lord" written upon his brow, and unholiness working in his brain and nestling in his heart, was a moral contradiction, a paradox, a monstrosity. Such there may have been, and their official acts for the benefit of others God may have accepted and allowed, since otherwise the innocent would have suffered for the guilty; but their hatefulness in his sight must have been great, and their punishment will be proportionate. We may believe that such cases were few. Not many men can bear to be hypocrites. The holy attire, the holy offices, the profession of holiness upon the brow, must have helped to make the great majority holy, or at least harmless, in life—true "examples to the flock" (1 Pet. v. 3)—holy, not merely officially, but personally.

III. A CAUSE OF HOLINESS IN OTHERS. The high priest, as the religious leader of the nation, had to help forward holiness in every possible way—(1) Ceremonially, by his official actions; (2) Ministerially, by teachings and exhortations; (3) Individually, by the force of example. It was his mission to make the people "accepted before the Lord." The mediation which he offered not only purified from legal defilements, but, by virtue of his typical character, purged the conscience and cleansed the soul from sin. His exhortations and example had the natural force of one in authority, and must have been potent at all times. It was at his peril if he took life too easily, and rebuked sin too mildly, and was not "a faithful priest," as appears from the history of Eli (1 Sam. ii. 22—36; iii. 13; iv. 11—18). Unfaithful priests are, in truth, an abomination, and have need to tremble at the "terrors of the Lord." Those who have undertaken a holy office are doubly bound to holiness. If men "corrupt the covenant of Levi," God will "send a curse upon them, and curse their blessings" (Mal. ii. 2, 8).

EXPOSITION

Ver. 39.—THE TUNIC AND GIRDLE. From the outer garments, which were the most important and distinctive, a transition is now made to the inner ones, in which there was nothing very remarkable. The linen drawers are for the present omitted, as not peculiar to the high priest. Directions are given for the tunic and the girdle. The former is to be woven in some peculiar way—so as to be diapered, as some think—and the latter is to be "the work of the embroiderer."

Ver. 39.—**Thou shalt embroider.** This is certainly not the meaning of the Hebrew. Some peculiar mode of weaving the coat is intended. **The coat.** Rather, "the tunic" or "shirt." The *kĕtôneth* was a long linen gown or cassock, worn immediately over the drawers. It reached to the feet, and had tightly-fitting sleeves (Joseph. *Ant. Jud.* iii. 7, § 2). Whether it showed beneath the "robe of the ephod," or not, is uncertain; but the sleeves must certainly have been visible. The *kĕtôneth* was white. **Thou shalt make the mitre of fine linen.** This direction had not been previously given. It is a little out of place. **Thou shalt make the girdle of needlework.** Literally, "of the work of the embroiderer." The girdle was worn directly over the linen shirt, and under "the robe of the ephod." It would seem that it was not seen at all, unless its ends hung down below "the robe of the ephod." It was however to be artistically embroidered (See ch. xxxix. 29.)

HOMILETICS.

Ver. 39.—*The Lesson of the Tunic.* The tunic, or inner vest, was to be of fine linen, and of spotless white. Both the material and the hue denoted purity. God's priests must be clothed in purity from top to toe. Purity must wrap them round on every side. This purity may be hidden—unseen of man, or nearly unseen. But God sees it and honours it. The tunic, though it must be all of white, shall not lack its ornamentation. It is to be diapered with a pattern, like the best damask cloths, and so to be rich and costly.

The Lessons of the Girdle. (1) Girdles were less for beauty than for use. Men girded themselves for battle, for a race, for active exertion of any kind. The high priest was to have his loins continually girded, that he might be ready at all times for God's service. But he was not to make a parade of this readiness. The girdle was to be hidden under the robe of the ephod. (2) Hidden as it was, the girdle was to be costly and beautiful—of many colours, the work of the skilled embroiderer. The Israelites were taught by this, that things devoted to God's service, *whether they be seen or not*, should be of the best. The intention is not to please men's eyes by beauty of colour or form, or richness of material, but to do honour to God. Scamped work in places where it is not seen has been thought allowable by many a church architect; dust and untidiness in hidden corners are tolerated by many who have the care of sacred buildings. True piety will make no difference between the seen and the unseen, the hidden and that which is open to sight, but aim at comeliness, fitness, beauty, in *all* that appertains to the worship of God.

EXPOSITION.

Vers. 40—43.—THE APPAREL OF THE ORDINARY PRIESTS. The chapter concludes with brief directions concerning the official attire of the ordinary priests. This was to consist of linen drawers like those of the high priest; of a tunic, also of linen (ch xxxix. 27), shaped like his, but not diapered; of a linen girdle, the exact character of which is not stated; and of a close-fitting cap. The entire dress, with perhaps the exception of the girdle, was white. The linen drawers were regarded as of primary necessity, and the priest who did not wear them was threatened with death.

Ver. 40.—For Aaron's sons. His actual sons at this time—his descendants afterwards, to whom the priesthood was rigidly confined. **Thou shalt make coats.** The verb is different from that used in ver 39, and seems to imply that the priests' tunics were not to be patterned. **Girdles.** It has generally been supposed that these were of the same material and workmanship as the high priest's; but this is nowhere stated. In ch. xxxix. 29, the high priest's girdle alone is spoken of. **Bonnets.** Certainly not "bonnets" in the modern sense. Plain, close-fitting caps, shaped like a cup, or rather basin, seem to be meant. Such caps were often worn in Egypt, but not by the priests. **For glory and for beauty.** See above, ver. 2. It is very noticeable, that the extremely simple attire of the ordinary priests—a dress of pure white, without anything ornamental about it, unless it were the girdle—is still regarded as sufficient "for glory and for beauty." White robes have certainly a vast amount of scriptural testimony

in their favour (Lev. xvi. 4; Mark ix. 3; John xx. 12; Acts i. 10; Rev. iv. 4 · vi. 11 ; vii. 9, 14, etc.).

Ver. 41. — Thou shalt put them upon Aaron thy brother, etc. These words serve to connect the present chapter with the following one. They contain the first intimation that Moses is not only to cause the holy garments to be made, but to invest the priests in them, and further to consecrate both Aaron and his sons by anointing. On this point, see the comment on ch. xxix. 7—9.

Ver. 42.—Linen breeches. Rather, "linen *drawers*" (Kalisch), such as we see worn by the Egyptians generally, reaching from the waist to a little above the knee. (See Wilkinson in Rawlinson's *Herodotus*, vol. ii. p. 113, 2nd ed.) This also was of linen (Herod. ii. 83). **Unto the thighs**—*i.e.*, to the bottom of the thighs where they adjoin on the knee.

Ver. 43.—When they go into the tabernacle of the congregation. Literally, "when they go into the *tent of meeting*—*i.e.*, the place where God and the high priest were to meet. **The holy place.** The "holy place" seems in this passage to include the court of the tabernacle, wherein the altar was situated. **That they bear not iniquity.** To "bear iniquity" is to incur guilt, or have sin imputed to one. If even through forgetfulness a priest entered the sanctuary without this necessary article of clothing, and so risked an unseemly exposure of his person, he was to be accounted guilty, and punished by death. This was to be a "statute for ever," and to apply both to the high priest and the ordinary priests. Compare ch. xx. 26.

HOMILETICS.

Vers. 40—42.—*The priests' attire.* The dress of the ordinary priests teaches us—

I. THAT NOT ONLY THE CHIEF, BUT THE SUBORDINATE, MINISTERS OF THE SANCTUARY MUST BE CLAD IN HOLINESS. The priests' garments are called "holy," no less than the high priest's (ver. 4). They are almost entirely of fine white linen. The linen drawers denote the need of holiness with respect to sins of the flesh. The linen cap implies purity of thought and imagination. The linen tunic is symbolical of the complete sanctification in which the whole man should be wrapped. The girdle, also of linen, marks the need of purity in respect of all the active part of life. In every one of these respects the ordinary priests were on a par with the high priest. The same holiness was required of both.

II. That in extreme simplicity there may be a high degree of beauty. The priests' garments were, like the high priest's (ver. 2), "for glory and for beauty" (ver. 40). And, being designed by God for those ends, they doubtless attained them. Yet, unless the girdle was an exception, they were all white. So, when Jesus was transfigured, "his raiment became shining, exceeding white as snow; so as no fuller on earth can white them" (Mark ix. 3). There is a wondrous beauty in pure, spotless, snow-white raiment. Still more is there beauty in the simplicity of a spotless life. A pure mind— a pure heart—pure conduct—simple, uniform performance of every-day duty—what is more lovely, more glorious? To such the Divine Bridegroom will address the words— "Thou art all fair, my love; there is no spot in thee" (Cant. iv. 7).

EXPOSITION.

CHAPTER XXIX.

Vers. 1—37.—The Consecration of the Priests. From the description of the priestly attire, the Divine Law-giver passed to the form of priestly consecration, whereof investiture in the "holy garments" was a part. The ceremony of consecration was to consist of four things:—1. Ablution; 2. Investiture; 3. Chrism or Anointing with oil; and 4. Sacrifice. In the directions given, we have, first, the preparation of the offerings (vers. 1—3); secondly, directions for the ablutions (ver. 4); thirdly, directions for the investiture of Aaron (vers. 5, 6), of his sons (vers. 8, 9); fourthly, directions for the anointing (ver. 7); and fifthly, directions as to the mode in which the sacrifices should be offered and disposed of (vers. 10—34). A command is then given that the ceremonies should be repeated every day for a week (ver. 35); and another, that the altar should receive consecration at the same time as the priests (vers. 36, 37). Additional light is thrown on most of these matters by the account contained in Leviticus (ch. viii.), of the manner in which Moses carried out the directions here given to him.

Ver. 1.—**This is the thing that thou shalt do to them**—*i.e.*, " This is the ceremonial that thou shalt use on the occasion." There is a tacit reference to verse 41 of ch. xxviii., which had announced that the priests were to be consecrated. **Take one young bullock.** The offerings were to be provided beforehand, so as to be in readiness when the investiture and anointing were over. Hence they are mentioned first. **Rams without blemish.** Literally " perfect." On the offence to God of offering him blemished offerings, see Mal. i. 6—14.

Ver. 2.—**Unleavened bread** was regarded as purer than leavened, since fermentation is a

sort of corruption. See the comment on ch. xii. 15. **Cakes tempered with oil.** Literally, " mixed with oil," *i.e.*, having oil as one of their ingredients, in contrast with the **wafers,** which had oil poured over them.

Ver. 3.—**Thou shalt bring them in the basket.** Rather, " Thou shalt *offer* them." A preliminary offering of the animals and of the " meat-offerings," in the lump seems to be intended. This, apparently, preceded the ablution.

Ver. 4.—*The Ablution.*

Ver. 4.—**Unto the door of the tabernacle.** The great laver was to be placed between the entrance to the tabernacle and the altar of burnt-offering (ch. xxx. 18). It was to this probably that Aaron and his sons were to be brought. Its main purpose was to be a lustral vessel, placed ready for the various ablutions which the law required (*ib.* 19—21). **Thou . . . . shalt wash them with water.** Ablutions were an important part of the ceremonial of almost all ancient religions. In Egypt, the priests were compelled to wash themselves from head to foot in cold water twice every day, and twice every night (Herod. ii. 37). In the religion of Zoroaster frequent washing with water was prescribed for many kinds of impurity (Zendavesta, viii. p. 271, et seq.). The Greeks were particularly addicted to ceremonies of which ablution formed a part; and it is to Rome that we are indebted both for the word and for the idea of " lustration." It is a true instinct which has taught men the analogy between physical and moral purity, and led them to typify the removal of spiritual, by the cleansing from physical, defilement. The religion given at Sinai set a stamp of approval in many points on what may be called " the religion of nature ;" and among them on this. Ablutions were required of the priests, not only at consecration, but every time that they entered the tabernacle, or sacrificed on the altar of burnt-offering (ch. xxx. 20). Washing was a main feature in the cleansing of leprosy (Lev. xiii. 54, 58) and of the leper (*ib.* xiv. 8). It was also employed for the purification of many minor defilements (*ib.* xi. 25; xv. 5; xvii. 15, etc.). At what date it first came into use in the admission of proselytes is uncertain. Whether the washing of consecration extended to the whole body, or was limited to the hands and feet, is also a point on which critics have disagreed, but one of no great importance. (See John xiii. 9, 10.)

Vers. 5, 6.—*The Investiture of Aaron.*

Ver. 5.—**Thou shalt take the garments.** The directions, as here given, are incomplete, and not quite in the right order. In the LXX. they are still more incomplete. For the full process of investiture, we must look to Lev. viii. 7—9. There we find that the process included nine acts.—1. The putting on of the linen tunic. 2. The girding with the under-girdle. 3. The putting on of the robe of the ephod. 4. The putting on of the ephod. 5. The girding with the curious girdle of the ephod. 6. The putting on of the breast-plate. 7. The putting into the breast-plate of the Urim and Thummim. 8. The putting on of the mitre. 9. The affixing to the mitre of the golden plate.

The second and seventh are omitted here; and the order of the fifth and sixth is inverted. Ver. 6.—**The holy crown.** The plate of gold with its blue ribbon, or lace, formed a species of diadem, such as in the East seems to have been always regarded as the special emblem of royalty. An ornament of the kind seems to have been introduced into Egypt by Khuenaten or Amenôphis IV. It marked the royal character of the high priest, who, as the main type of Christ in the Mosaic law, was bound to be "Prophet, Priest, and King." (Compare Lev. viii. 9.)

Ver. 7.—*The Chrism or Anointing.*

Ver. 7.—**The anointing oil** had been mentioned previously in ch. xxv. 6, when "spices" had been required from the congregation to form a portion of it. Its composition is given in ch. xxx. 23—25; a passage from which we gather that it was exceedingly rich and costly. **And pour it upon his head.** Compare Ps. cxxxiii. 2. While ablution is a rite common to many religions, the religious use of unction is peculiar to the Mosaic and the Christian. In the Mosaic it was applied to initiate into their office the prophet, the priest, and the king. In Christianity it was originally a rite by which sick persons were miraculously cured (Jas. v. 14, 15), from which use it was afterwards extended by ecclesiastical authority to other important ceremonies. The typical meaning under Christianity is clear; the oil represents the Holy Spirit, and the anointing the outpouring of that Spirit on those who are the objects of it. Christ himself obtained his title of Christ (or Messiah), because he was "anointed with the Holy Ghost and with power" (Acts x. 38). Under Mosaism this idea was, at most, latent. Unction was understood to mark (1) Dignity, because the olive was the first of trees (Judg. ix. 9); and (2) Continuance, because oil preserves things for a long time from corruption. Unction with the holy oil of the sanctuary no doubt further signified consecration to God's service. It was applied not only to the priests, but to the tabernacle, the ark, the table of shew-bread with its vessels, the seven branched candlestick, the altar of incense, the altar of burnt offering, and the laver, all of which thereupon became "most holy" (ch. xxx. 26—29).

Vers. 8, 9.—*The Investiture of Aaron's sons.*

Ver. 8.—**Thou shalt bring his sons.** See verse 4. They were to be brought to the door of the tabernacle. **Put coats upon them.** The investiture of the high priest consisted of nine acts (see the comment on ver. 5); that of the ordinary priests of three only. 1. The putting on of the linen tunics. 2. The girding with the girdles. 3. The putting on of the cap. They do not seem to have been anointed, as Aaron was, by having the holy oil poured upon their heads, but only by having some of it sprinkled upon their garments (ver. 21; Lev. viii. 30).

Ver. 9.—**The bonnets.** Rather "caps." There is no article. **Thou shalt consecrate Aaron and his sons.** Literally, "Thou shalt fill the hand of Aaron and the hand of his sons." Installation in an office was usually effected among the Eastern nations by putting into the hand of the official the insignia which marked his functions. In this particular case certain portions of the offerings were used as the insignia. See ver. 24.

Vers. 10—34.—*The Consecration Offerings.*

Ver. 10.—**Thou shalt cause a bullock to be brought.** Rather, "*the* bullock,"—*i.e.,* "the bullock mentioned in ver. 1, which was to be made ready before the ceremonies commenced." Aaron and his sons were to **put their hands upon the head of the bullock,** in order to identify themselves with it, and transfer to it the guilt of their own sins and imperfections, since it was to be a "sin-offering" (ver. 14; compare Lev. iv. 4).

Ver. 12.—**Thou shalt take of the blood, and put it upon the horns of the altar.** The virtue of the altar was regarded as residing especially in its horns. Here expiation was obtained by the blood—"which is the life"— of the victim being first smeared upon the four horns, and then the remainder poured out at the altar's base. Such was the usual practice with "sin-offerings" (Lev. iv. 7) whereof this was to be the first example.

Ver. 13.—**Thou shalt take all the fat**, etc. Among all nations who have offered sacrifices, it has been very usual to select certain parts of the victim only for burning upon the altar, and to dispose otherwise of the remainder. The Greeks commonly burnt on the altar the thighs and the fat only. The Romans burnt certain parts of the intestines only, and called them *prosecta, prosiciæ*, or *ablegmina*. In Egypt, according to Herodotus, the greater part of the body was burnt; but the head, the neck, the shoulders, and the lower part of the legs, as well as the paunch, were reserved and not burnt (Herod. ii. 40). The fat was generally regarded as the best part of the offering, and most acceptable to the gods. This was probably on account of its burning with a bright flame and helping to consume the rest of the offering. **The caul that is above the liver.** Probably the membrane which covers the upper part of the liver, sometimes called "the small omentum." (*reticulum jecoris*, Vulg.)

Ver. 14.—**The flesh . . . shalt thou burn with fire without the camp.** Such was the rule with sin-offerings generally (Lev. iv. 11, 12). The curse of sin which was on them, made them unfit for food and even unworthy of burial within the camp. On the symbolism of the burial, see Heb. xiii. 11—13. **His dung.** That which the bowels contained at the time of death.

Ver. 15.—**One ram.** Literally "*the* one ram"—*i.e.*, "one of the two rams mentioned in verse 1." **Put their hands.** Here, again, the object was to identify themselves with the victim, and make it their representative; though now, as the ram was to be a *burnt* offering, self-sacrifice, rather than expiation, was the leading thought.

Ver. 16.—**Thou shalt take his blood and sprinkle it.** Rather, "and *cast* it." The blood was to be thrown from a basin, not sprinkled with the hand or with hyssop. Rabbinical tradition says that it was so cast at two of the corners, and thus moistened all the four sides. This was regarded as casting it "on the altar round about."

Ver. 17.—**Thou shalt cut the ram in pieces.** Literally, "into *its* pieces," which Kalisch supposes to mean "into its natural limbs." Egyptian sculptures show us animals thus cut up, and offered at sacrificial feasts to ancestors. **Wash its inwards**—*i.e.*, its "intestines"—probably the stomach and bowels only. **Its legs.** The lower joints of the leg, with the foot, to which it was likely that dust might attach. **Put them unto his pieces** — *i.e.*, "replace them after washing with the other pieces," or joints, into which the animal had been cut.

Ver. 18.—**Thou shalt burn the whole ram upon the altar.** This became the general law of the burnt-offering (Lev. i. 9, 13, 17). It

indicated that self-sacrifice was wholly acceptable to God; whereas in sin-offerings there was a taint of evil which rendered all but certain parts of the victim unacceptable (ver. 14). **A sweet savour.** This is not to be understood in the coarse sense in which heathen writers used similar expressions, meaning by them (as it would seem) that the gods were really pleased with the *odour* of sacrifices. No candid mind can ascribe to the Hebrews such anthropomorphism. Evidently no more is meant than that the offering would be pleasing to God. See Gen. viii. 21; Lev. i. 9, 13, 17, etc.

Ver. 19.—**The other ram.** Compare ver. 15; and see also vers. 1 and 3, where two rams had been mentioned. This second ram is called, "the ram of consecration" in ver. 22, and again in Lev. viii. 22. It was "by far the most peculiar part of the whole ceremony" (S. Clark). It must be viewed as a "peace-offering" (Lev. iii. 1—17), but one of a peculiar character. The application of the blood to the persons of the priests was altogether unique, and most significant. It was the crowning act of consecration, and implied the complete dedication of their life and of all their powers to the service of the Almighty.

Ver. 20.—The victim having been offered and accepted, its blood had a sanctifying power. Placed **upon the tip of the right ear of Aaron and his sons**, it sanctified that organ, which was to be ever open to the Divine voice; placed **upon the thumb of their right hand**, it sanctified their ministerial actions; placed **upon the great toe of their right foot**, it sanctified their whole walk in life, their "going out," and their "coming in." The consecrated life of the victim which they had offered "was given back to them, in order that it might be devoted to the service of the Lord."

Ver. 21.—**Thou shalt take of the blood . . . . and of the anointing oil.** Apparently, this is the only unction that the ordinary priests were to receive. (Compare Lev. viii. 30.) The mixture of the blood with the oil is unusual, and presents some difficulties; but perhaps it is best to view it as symbolising the intimate union which exists between justification and sanctification—the atoning blood, and the sanctifying grace of the Holy Spirit. **And sprinkle it.** The verb is different from that used in ver. 16, and is rightly rendered, "sprinkle." **He shall be hallowed and his garments.** As the garments shared in the sprinkling, they shared also, so far as was possible, in the consecration. It was hence especially that they became "holy garments."

Ver. 22.—**The rump.** Rather, "the tail." Oriental sheep have very commonly a broad fat tail, which weighs from six to twenty pounds, and is sometimes laid upon a little cart with two wheels, which the sheep drags after it (Herod. iii. 113; Leo African. ix. p. 293 A; Fellows, *Asia Minor*, p. 10; Gesenius ad voc. אַלְיָה). There is no doubt that a "tail" of this kind is here meant. **The caul.** Rather, " the membrane." See the comment on ver 13. **The right shoulder.** Or " leg," according to some. The difference is not important.

Ver. 23.—**One cake of oiled bread**—*i.e.*, one of the " unleavened cakes tempered with oil," mentioned in ver. 2. **Out of the basket of the unleavened bread.** See ver. 3.

Ver. 24.—**Thou shalt put all in the hands**, or " *on* the hands." The offerings were to be laid first, on the hands of Aaron, and then on those of his sons, which were to support them; while Moses, putting his hands under theirs, made a waving motion with them towards the four corners of the heavens, to indicate that the gifts were offered to the omnipresent God. This process was that " filling of the hand," by which the actual installation in office took place. Moses, by the act, transferred the priestly functions, which he had hitherto exercised, to his brother and his brother's descendants. He made them by his muscular energy perform their first priestly act.

Ver. 25.—**Thou shalt receive them at their hands and burn them.** Moses was still to continue the priestly acts, and to complete the peace-offering by burning the selected parts (ver. 22) on the brazen altar. (See Lev. iii. 3—5.)

Ver. 26.—**Thou shalt take the breast.** Henceforth Aaron and his sons were to have the breast of all wave-offerings (Lev. vii. 31—34); but on this occasion, as Moses officiated, the breast was to be his.

Vers. 27, 28.—A short digression is here made, from this particular offering, to all future offerings for consecration. For the future both the breast and the right shoulder are to belong to the priests. The shoulder, moreover, is to be " heaved," and only the breast " waved;" " heaving " being a single lifting up of the offering towards heaven, while " waving " was a repeated movement in a horizontal direction. Wave and heave offerings are always connected with the portions of the priests, or with things dedicated to God's service. (See ch. xxv. 2; xxxv. 22, 24; xxxviii. 24, 29; Lev. vii. 30—34; Num. xviii. 11, 19, 24, etc.)

Vers. 29, 30.— Here we have a second digression, also concerning future consecrations. **The holy garments** made for Aaron were to be preserved after his death, and used at the consecration of each successive high priest, who was to be **anointed and consecrated in them**, and to wear them for seven days from the time that he entered upon his office. Eleazar's investment in them is mentioned (Num. xx. 28); but not that of any later high priest.

Ver. 31.— **The ram of consecration**—*i.e.*, the part of the ram that was left and had not been burnt (ver. 25). **Seethe his flesh in the holy place.** This was understood to mean boiling *at the door* of the tabernacle (Lev. viii. 31). A sacrificial meal followed on every peace-offering, in which the offerers participated. (See above, ch. xviii. 12.)

Ver. 32.—**The bread that is in the basket** —*i.e.*, the loaf, cake, and wafer which still remained in the basket after one of each had been subtracted (see ver. 23, and compare vers. 2, 3).

Ver. 33.— **They shall eat those things wherewith the atonement was made.** An atoning force pervaded all sacrifice. Sin-offerings were wholly expiatory; burnt-offerings and peace-offerings partially so (Lev i. 4). **A stranger shall not eat thereof.** " A stranger " in this place does not mean a foreigner, but anyone who is not a priest.

Ver. 34.—**Thou shalt burn the remainder with fire.** Compare above, ch. xii. 10.

Vers. 35—37.—*The repetition of the ceremonial, and the consecration of the altar.*

Ver. 35.—**Seven days shalt thou consecrate them.** The repetition of the ceremony seven times on seven separate days seems to be intended. Thus was an ideal completeness given to it. Compare the seven days' compassing around of Jericho (Josh. vi. 3, 4,), the seven washings in Jordan by Naaman (2 Kings v. 14), the seven ascents to the top of Carmel by the servant of Elijah (1 Kings xviii. 43, 44), etc.

Ver. 36.—**Thou shalt cleanse the altar, when thou hast made an atonement for it.** Rather, " thou shalt purify the altar by making an atonement for it." The sin-offering for the altar was the same bullock which served for Aaron and his sons. Its virtue was applied to the altar by smearing the blood upon its horns and pouring the remainder at its base (ver. 12). See Lev. viii. 15:—" And Moses took the blood, and put it upon the horns of the altar round about with his finger, *and purified the altar*, and poured the blood at the bottom of the altar, *and sanctified it.*" **And thou shalt anoint it.** In his execution of these directions, Moses separated the anointing of the altar from the cleansing, placing it even before the anointing of Aaron. He anointed it by sprinkling the holy oil upon it seven times (Lev. viii. 11).

Ver. 37.—**Seven days shalt thou make an atonement.** *All* the ceremonial was to be repeated seven times, not only the atonement for the altar (Lev. viii. 33). **An altar most holy.** Literally, " holiness of holinesses," as in ch. xl. 10. **Whatever toucheth the altar shall be holy.** Rather, " must be holy." Nothing that is not holy must touch it (Kalisch).

HOMILETICS.

Vers. 1—37.—*The Consecration of the first High Priest.* Aaron may be viewed as either (1) a type of Christ, or (2) a pattern to all ministers who shall come after him.

I. As a type of Christ, he typifies especially Christ's priestly character. (1) Christ "glorified not himself to be made an high priest" (Heb. v. 5), but was appointed by his Father, when he sware to him, "Thou art a priest for ever after the order of Melchizedek" (Ps. cx. 4). So Aaron took not the honour of the high priesthood to himself (Heb. v. 4), but was chosen by God (Ex. xxviii. 1—38), and invested with his office by Moses (Lev. viii. 6—36). (2) Christ was "*the* Messiah"—*the* anointed one—anointed with that profusion and abundance, with which none other ever was or will be—for "God gave not the Spirit unto him by measure" (John iii. 34). Aaron received the holy oil in profusion, by pouring. "The precious ointment ran down upon his beard" —nay, "went down to the skirts of his clothing" (Ps. cxxxiii. 2). (3) Christ was at once priest and king—"born king of the Jews" (Matt. ii. 2); crucified as "king of the Jews" (*ib.* xxvii. 37); crowned by the soldiers in mockery (*ib.* 29); founder of an imperishable "kingdom" in reality. Aaron, in his capacity of priest, wore a diadem, a "holy crown" (Ex. xxix. 6; Lev. viii. 9), and may thus be regarded as having had committed to him "a royal priesthood." (4) Christ has "all the treasures of wisdom and knowledge hid away (ἀπόκρυφοι) in him" (Col. ii. 3), and could freely declare the will of God to man. Aaron had the precious Urim and Thummim hid away in the folds of his breast-plate, and by their means could obtain a knowledge of God's will in any practical matter. Lastly, (5) Christ is the great mediator between God and man, the one and only man who can intercede for his brethren effectually, who can make real atonement for their sins, and reconcile them to his Father. Aaron's special office was to make continual atonement for all the sins of the people by such sacrifices as were appointed by the law, to intercede for his brethren with God continually, and to be a mediator between them and him, representative of the true mediator.

II. As a pattern to ministers, Aaron is (1) solemnly called by God and set apart for his high office. (2) Prepared for it by an ablution, which typifies the removal of all impurity. (3) Invested with it by a human authority, viz., Moses. (4) Required on all occasions of its exercise to wear robes of office. (5) Anointed with a holy oil, typical of the graces of the Holy Spirit. (6) Appointed to minister *continually* before God in the tabernacle of the congregation. (7) Appointed to resolve doubts by declaring God's will in difficult cases which should be brought before him. (8) Required to bear upon his brow, in the sight of all men, a profession of "Holiness to the Lord." The official Aaron is thus, in numerous respects, a pattern and example to all—even Christian ministers; but the personal Aaron is, on the contrary, rather a warning. The weakness which allowed the worship of the golden calf, and the presumption which led to "murmuring against Moses" (Num. xx. 10—12) indicate a character which, if it had some virtues, had many and very serious defects.

HOMILIES BY VARIOUS AUTHORS.

Vers. 1—38.—*The rites of consecration for the priesthood.* The next portion of the Divine directions relates to the formal investiture of Aaron and his sons with the priests' office. This was to be made the occasion of a solemn and imposing ceremonial. "The rites of consecration proclaimed the necessity of holiness—a holiness not their own, but imputed to them by the grace of God; and following upon this, and flowing from the same source, a plentiful endowment of gifts for their sacred office, with the manifest seal of heaven's fellowship and approval" (Fairbairn). We may view the inaugurative ceremonies as having reference—

I. To the priesthood, in the simplest idea of it (vers. 4—10). Aaron and his sons were to be—1. Washed with water—symbol of purification from all uncleanness (ver. 4). 2. Clothed with the holy garments—which robing was the real installation. Aaron was to be first robed (vers. 6, 7), afterwards his sons (vers. 8, 9). 3. Anointed —symbol of the abundant communication of Divine influences (ver. 7). The anointing took place immediately after investiture. See exposition. Nothing could be simpler than these introductory ceremonies, which yet, in connection with the symbolism of the dress, meant a great deal. They "filled the hand" of the priest with his office (ver. 9), declared the need of holiness in the discharge of his duties, and conveyed to him the gifts of heavenly grace necessary for their right performance. So Christ "glorified not himself to be made an high priest" (Heb. v. 5), but was formally installed in his office by the Father; was "holy, harmless, undefiled, separate from sinners" (Heb. vii. 26); and is endued above measure with the Spirit (John iii. 34).

II. To THE PRIESTHOOD, AS HELD BY SINFUL MEN (vers. 10—15). The direct installation to the priesthood is followed by ceremonies having reference to the personal sinfulness of the holders of the office. The fact could not be overlooked that the law was making men priests that had infirmity (Heb. vii. 28). Themselves sinful, Aaron and his sons were not as yet fit to transact with God as mediators for others. The true High Priest, having no sin, laboured under no disqualification of this kind (Heb. vii. 27); but it was different with priests "taken from among men" (Heb. v. 1). They needed to have sacrifices offered for themselves. "This, therefore, was what was next provided; and through an entire series of sacrifices and offerings they were conducted as from the depths of guilt and condemnation to what indicated their possession of a state of blessed peace and most friendly intercourse with God" (Fairbairn). The sacrifices were three— a sin-offering (vers. 10—15); a burnt-offering (vers. 15—19); and a peace-offering (vers. 19—22); and these sacrifices, with the accompanying ceremonies, were to be repeated on seven successive days (ver. 35). The altar, as defiled by the sin of those officiating at it, was likewise to be cleansed by the blood of the sin-offering (vers. 36, 37). This is the first appearance of the sin-offering in the law.

III. To QUALIFICATIONS, DUTIES, AND EMOLUMENTS (vers. 15—38). The sin-offering had especially to do with the removal of guilt. The second sacrifice—the burnt-offering— denoted the duty of unconditional and entire surrender to Jehovah. The third—"the ram of consecration" (ver. 22)—was that by which the newly-made priests were wholly put into the functions and rights of their office. 1. The ram's blood was significantly applied to different members of the person (ver. 20). It was put upon the tip of the right ear, upon the thumb of the right hand, and upon the great toe of the right foot, of Aaron and of his sons. This denoted, of course, entire dedication of the person to God's service, in hearing, in acting, and in the daily walk. It beautifully symbolises, not only the perfect consecration of him whose meat it was to do his Father's will (John iv. 34), but the completeness of devotion which ought to characterise each of his disciples, who also are priests to God. 2. The priests were sprinkled with the ram's blood and oil mingled (ver. 21). This symbolised the new life of God, in which the priest was "henceforth to move and have his being, in conjunction with the Spirit, on whose softening, penetrating, invigorating influence all powers and movements of that Divine life depend" (Fairbairn). 3. The portions of the sacrifice which belonged to God, with a loaf, cake, and wafer, of the meat offering—symbolic of fruitfulness in good works—were next to be placed on the priests' hands, and waved before the Lord (ver. 24). This signified, (1) "The conveyal of the function which belongs to the priest to offer the fat pieces of God's altar; and (2) the infeoffment of the priests with the gift, which they receive in future for their service, but which they must now give over to Jehovah, because they are not yet fully dedicated, and therefore cannot yet themselves act as priests" (Oehler). The conclusion of the ceremony was a sacrificial meal, indicative of restored fellowship, and happy communion with God (vers. 31—35). Vers. 29, 30, provide for the handing down of the high priest's office to Aaron's sons. The priesthood continued till superseded by that of the greater Priest "after the order of Melchizedek" (Heb. vii.).—J. O.

EXPOSITION.

Vers. 38—42.—THE DAILY SACRIFICE. The consecration of the altar, which is made a part of the consecration of the priests, is to be followed immediately by the establishment of the daily sacrifice. Two lambs are to be offered day by day to the Lord, one in the morning and the other in the evening, as "a continual burnt-offering" (ver. 42), in acknowledgment that the life of the people belonged to Jehovah (Cook), and that they were bound to offer perpetually "themselves, their souls and bodies, to be a reasonable holy, and lively sacrifice " to him. The burnt-offerings were to be accompanied by appropriate " meat and drink-offerings "—i.e., by a certain quantity of flour mingled with olive oil for the one, and a certain quantity of wine for the other — indications of the debt of gratitude which the nation owed to God for his continual benefits

Ver. 38.—**Lambs of the first year.** Compare ch. xii. 5. The LXX. add "without blemish." But this is unnecessary, as all victims were to be without blemish (Lev. xxii. 20 ; Deut. xv. 21, etc.)

Ver. 39.—**At even.** Literally, " between the two evenings." (See the comment on ch. xii. 6.) Josephus says (*Ant. Jud.* xiv. 4, § 3) that the hour in ordinary use was three.

Ver. 40. — **A tenth deal**—i.e., a "tenth part." The tenth part of an ephah is no doubt meant. This was sometimes called " an omer" (ch. xvi. 36), and would be about three pounds weight of flour, or a little more. **One fourth part of an hin of beaten oil.** The word *hin* is said to be Egyptian. It occurs here for the first time. The *hin* was the sixth part of a *bath*, and probably contained about one pint and a half English. **The fourth part of an hin of wine for a drink-offering.** The application of the " drink-offerings " is uncertain. Josephus says (*Ant. Jud.* iii. 9, § 4) that they were poured out round the brazen altar. But the analogy of the " meat offering " makes it probable that a portion only was thus treated, while the greater part belonged to the priests. In the entire provision by which burnt and peace-offering were to be necessarily accompanied with meat-offerings and drink-offerings, we can scarcely be wrong in seeing an arrangement made especially for the convenience of the priests.

Ver. 41.—**Thou shalt do thereto according to the meat - offering,** etc. " Thou shalt offer "—i.e., " the same meat-offering and drink-offering with the evening as with the morning sacrifice." **For a sweet savour.** See the comment on ver. 18.

Ver. 42.—**Throughout your generations.** Rather, " *for* your generations." **The tabernacle of the congregation.** Rather, " of meeting "—" the tabernacle of *meeting*, where I will *meet* you." The verb and substantive are modifications of the same word, וְעַד. It is this passage which definitely fixes the meaning of the phrase incorrectly rendered " the tabernacle of the congregation" by our translators.

HOMILETICS.

Vers. 38—42.—*The value of a daily service.* Perpetual remembrance of God is one of the greatest needs for the maintenance and furtherance of religion. " Pray *without ceasing.*" "*In everything* by prayer and supplication with thanksgiving let your requests be made known unto God" (Phil. iv. 6). " I have set the Lord *alway* before my face " (Ps. xvi. 8). These and numerous other texts lay down the perfect law—constant worship of the Almighty. But human weakness, and the pressing concerns of life, make literal compliance with the perfect law impossible. And in his mercy God relaxes the law. " At evening and morning, and at noonday, will I pray," says the man after his own heart (Ps. lv. 17); "and he shall hear my voice." Daniel prayed "three times a day, with his window open towards Jerusalem" (Dan. vi. 10). Coldness and worldliness have in the Christian Church reduced, for the most part, the "three times" to twice; but still the obligation is acknowledged under all circumstances at morn and even to lift the heart to God, and "look up." Now, it is a great help towards maintaining this minimum that there should be, twice a day, a public service. The daily morning and evening sacrifice were a perpetual reminder to the Israelites of their duty in respect of prayer—they felt the "lifting up of their hands" to be—according to the time of it—a morning or "an evening sacrifice" (Ps. cxli. 2). And so, in the Christian Church, public service twice a day, which prevails widely, is of great value.

I. As REMINDING MEN OF THE DUTY OF SUCH CONSTANT SUPPLICATION—as keeping it before them, by the sight of open church doors, and the sound of chiming bells, that God is, at the least, to be addressed twice a day, at morn and even, in earnest, heartfelt prayer; to be praised and thanked for his mercies, intreated for his forgiveness, besought for his support, and help, and blessing. What is done by public authority rouses attention, provokes inquiry, raises a general feeling that it would not be done unless it were right. Many a man, who has long neglected private prayer, has been led to acknowledge himself wrong, and to revert to the practice of it by the witness borne—the protest made —by those churches which persistently keep up the substitute for the morning and evening sacrifice of the tabernacle and temple, to wit—that daily morning and evening service in the sanctuary, which the Church of England, among others, enjoins upon her ministers.

II. AS ENABLING THEM TO PERFORM THE DUTY IN QUIETNESS, WITHOUT DISTRACTION. In many homes there is no quietness, no retired spot to which husband, or wife, or child can go for silent communion with the Almighty Father, or the Saviour. All is noise, tumult, bustle, hurry—nay, sometimes, all is quarrel, angry words, cruel blows, threats, curses. Private prayer in such households, if it was ever known, drops out of use. Frequently, it is not allowed—it provokes an outbreak—if done at all, it has to be done secretly, hastily, in fear and trembling. In such cases, how great a blessing is it to those who feel the need of prayer, that there should be somewhere near them a sacred spot, whither they can, occasionally at any rate, betake themselves to pray their own prayers, or join in the prayers of others as may seem best to them, and feel the near presence of the Almighty! "How amiable are thy tabernacles, O Lord of Hosts! My soul longeth, yea, even fainteth for the courts of the Lord!" "One day in thy courts is better than a thousand" elsewhere.

HOMILIES BY VARIOUS AUTHORS.

Vers. 38—43.—*The daily burnt-offering.* Symbol of consecration of life of the nation. 1. Offered at morn and even. 2. Continually. 3. With meat-offering—dedication of life in its practical activities.—J. O.

EXPOSITION.

Vers. 43—46.—GOD'S PROMISES. The chapter terminates with a parenthetic insertion of various promises, intended to cheer the Israelites under the hard circumstances of their wanderings in the wilderness, and growing out of the mention of the tabernacle as "the tabernacle of meeting" (ver. 42). "There," says God, "He will meet, not only Moses, to speak to him, but also the children of Israel, to receive their offerings, hear their prayers, and grant their requests. There will he meet them, and there his glory shall be; and the tabernacle shall be thereby sanctified. He will sanctify both the tabernacle and the altar; he will sanctify, moreover, both Aaron and his sons; and he will dwell among the children of Israel, and be their God; and they shall know him." Very precious and gracious promises, made absolutely; though, as the result showed (2 Chr. xxxvi. 14—18), contingent on their obedience; and faithfully performed, as long as even a remnant was obedient, during a space of above seven hundred years from the Exodus to the Captivity!

Ver. 43.—**There will I meet the children of Israel.** Lay Israelites might not enter the tabernacle, and could only "meet God" at its entrance, when they brought their sacrifices to the altar. He promises, however, to meet them on these occasions with favour and acceptance. **The tabernacle shall be sanctified by my glory.** Compare ch. xl. 34. The presence of the Shechinah was the true sanctification of the tabernacle—all the rest was mere type and figure. God not only "put his name there," but put his presence there visibly.

Ver. 44.—**I will sanctify . . . the altar.** See Lev. ix. 24, where we learn that on the first occasion of Aaron's offering sacrifice upon the brazen altar, "there came a fire out from before the Lord, and consumed upon the altar the burnt offering and the fat." Thus the altar had its miraculous sanctification, as well as the tabernacle, and was not merely consecrated by human instrumentality. **I will sanctify also both Aaron and his sons.** It would seem to follow, by parity of reasoning, that here also something more is intended than had been accomplished by the rites of consecration. The verb is in the future—" I *will* sanctify "—and must allude to something which has not yet taken place. Probably, sanctification of the spirit is intended—that Divine influence upon the heart which alone makes men really and truly "holy." (Compare Lev. xxi. 8, 15; xxii. 9, 16.) But in this case the promise must have been conditional. God would sanctify them so far as they would allow him.

Ver. 45.—**I will dwell among the children of Israel.** Compare ch. xxv. 8. Primarily, the indwelling of the Shechinah in the holy of holies is, no doubt, meant; but the expression need not be limited to this. God would be present with his people in manifold ways

—to direct, sustain, enlighten, defend, and save them. **And will be their God.** Compare ch. vi. 7. What treasures of love, protection, bounty, tenderness, and pardon, are there in this phrase!

Ver. 46.—**And they shall know**, etc. When they experience my protection, bounty, love, tenderness, pardon· they shall truly feel and know in their inmost hearts, that I am the same God who delivered them out of the bondage of Egypt, and brought them forth, for the very purpose of "dwelling among them." **I am Jehovah, their God.** No other God could deliver after this sort. No other God could be so long-suffering to a "stiffnecked people."

HOMILETICS.

Vers. 43—46.—*God's promises to Israel.* Here we may note—I. The Divine goodness as shown in the making of promises. Man has no claim upon his Maker. Our "goodness extendeth not to him." So far forth as we "do him true and laudable service," we are "unprofitable servants—we have done that which was our duty to do" (Luke xvii. 10). But how little of such service is rendered! How great are our short-comings! How many our "sins, negligences, and ignorances!" How little do we deserve anything but evil at God's hand! And yet, he not only bears with us, but makes us gracious promises. He binds himself to us beforehand by express engagements—he pledges his own sacred word to bestow upon us divers blessings. Here he promised Israel five things—1. The sanctification of the tabernacle by the Shechinah; 2. The sanctification of the altar; 3. Holiness in Aaron and his sons; 4. His own permanent abiding presence with them as their God; and 5. Their own recognition of him as their Lord God—the deliverer who brought them out of Egypt—the eternal—*Jehovah Eloheyhem.* And to Christians he has promised far more—pardon, redemption, acceptance, sanctification by the Holy Spirit, eternal life! Utterly unworthy as we are, these promises have been made to us. God's infinite goodness has caused him to condescend to enter into covenant with his creatures; and the promises which he has made to us, "he for his part will most surely keep and perform."

II. The Divine faithfulness, as shown in the fulfilment of the promises made. (1) The sanctification of the tabernacle was effected by the entrance into it of the Shechinah (ch. xl. 34); (2) That of the altar by the fire which "came out from before the Lord" (Lev. ix. 24); (3) Aaron and his sons were sanctified to the effectual performance of all their ministerial acts, and were further personally sanctified, so far as their own wills would permit; (4) God did abide with his people Israel, notwithstanding all their short-comings, for at least seven centuries; defended them from their enemies; taught them by his prophets; made them a praise and a wonder among the nations. And, on the whole, (5) notwithstanding occasional defections, Israel did recognise Jehovah as their God, did maintain his worship, did observe his laws, did believe that he dwelt among them, and was "the Lord their God." Shall we think that to us he will be less faithful? Shall we doubt that he will give to us the covenanted blessings—pardon, and redemption, and acceptance, and sanctification, and eternal life? Surely, "God is not a man that he should lie, or the son of man that he should repent." He is "the faithful and the true" (Rev. xix. 11). He never broke a promise. All to which he is pledged he will most assuredly perform, if we only are not wanting on our part.

HOMILIES BY VARIOUS AUTHORS.

Vers. 43—46.—*Israel sanctified by God's presence.* 1. Three grades of sanctification. (1) By blood. (2) Unction of the Spirit. (3) Personal Divine indwelling. 2. God's dwelling with Israel sanctifies (1) the tabernacle; (2) his servants; (3) the whole people.—J. O.

EXPOSITION.

CHAPTER XXX.

Vers. 1—10.—The altar of incense. This chapter has the appearance of being one in which accidental omissions are supplied. The natural place for a description of the altar of incense—part of the furniture of the holy place (ver. 6) — would seem to have been ch. xxv. 10—40, where we have the descriptions of the ark, the mercy-seat, the table of shew-bread, and the candlestick; the natural place for "the ransom of souls," the earlier part of the same chapter (ver. 3), where the silver is required which was to be collected in this way; the natural place for an account of the bronze laver, ch. xxvii., where the bronze altar, near which it stood, is described; the natural place for the composition of the holy oil, ch. xxix., where its use is commanded (vers. 7, 21); and the natural place for a description of the perfume the same as for the altar on which it was to be offered. Whether Moses made the omissions in writing his record, and afterwards supplied them in the present chapter, or whether Divine wisdom saw fit to give the directions in the order in which we now have them, cannot be determined. Hitherto certainly no sufficient reason has been shown for the existing order, which hence *appears* accidental. The altar of incense was to be in many respects similar to the altar of burnt-offering, but of smaller size and richer material. Both were to be " four-square," and both of shittim wood cased with metal; but the former was to be taller, the latter shorter, than it was broad; and while the latter was to be cased with bronze, the former was to have a covering of gold. The place for the altar of incense was the main chamber of the tabernacle, a little in front of the veil; and its purpose was, as the name implied, the offering of incense to Almighty God. This was to be done by the officiating priest, twice a day, morning and evening, and in practice was performed before the morning, and after the evening sacrifice.

Ver. 1.—**An altar to burn incense upon.** The offering of incense was an element in the religious worship of most ancient nations. In Egypt frankincense was especially used in the festivals of the god Ammon (*Records*

of the Past, vol. x. pp. 18, 19); and on one occasion an Egyptian sovereign sent a naval expedition to Arabia for the express purpose of bringing frankincense and frankincense trees to Egypt, in connection with the Ammon feasts (Brugsch, *History of Egypt,* vol. i. pp. 305—311). The Babylonians burnt a thousand talents' weight of frankincense every year at the great festival of Bel (Herod. i. 183). The Greeks and Romans offered frankincense, as a rule, with every offering; and in the early ages of Christianity it was made the test of a Christian whether he would do this or no. What exactly the religious notion was which underlay these acts, or whether it was the same everywhere, may be questioned. In the Mosaic religion, however, there can be little doubt that, in the main, incense symbolised prayer. (See Ps. cxli. 2; Luke i. 10.) **Of shittim wood.** Compare above, ch. xxvii. 1.

Ver. 2.—**Four square shall it be.** Like the altar of burnt-offering. See the comment on ch. xxvii. 1. **Two cubits shall be the height thereof.** Altars of this small size are often represented on ancient vases and other remains. (See Dr. Smith's *Dictionary of Greek and Roman Antiquities,* pp. 117 and 1174.) **The horns thereof.** It seems to be assumed that an altar must have horns. Those of the altar of incense were to have the blood of certain sin-offerings smeared upon them (Lev. iv. 7, 18). **Shall be of the same**—*i.e.,* " shall be of one piece with the top of the table"—not projections added to it. Compare ch. xxvii. 2.

Ver. 3.—**Thou shalt make unto it a crown of gold**—*i.e.,* a border, or moulding, all round the top, to prevent anything from falling off. Compare what is said of the table of shew-bread, ch. xxv. 24.

Ver. 4.—**By the two corners.** Rather, " on its two sides." The ensuing clause is redundant. All that is meant is, that the altar should have two rings only—not four—one at each side, directly below the moulding. As it was so small, two rings were enough. **For the staves.** Rather, " for staves."

Ver. 5.—The staves were to be of acacia wood, overlaid with gold, like those used for carrying the ark (ch. xxv. 13) and the table of shew-bread (*ib.* 28).

Ver. 6.—**Thou shalt put it before the vail.** It might have been doubtful from what is said here, which side of the veil the altar was to be placed. The doubt is precluded by the narrative of what Moses actually did in ch. xl. 21—29, which makes it clear that the altar was placed with the golden candlestick and the table of shew-bread, outside the veil, in the "holy place," and not within the "holy of holies." **Where I will meet with thee.** See above, ch. xxv. 22.

Ver. 7.—**Sweet incense.** Literally, "incense of perfumes." For the composition of the incense, see vers. 34—38. **When he dresseth the lamps.** The lamps of the golden candlestick were to be trimmed and cleaned, their wicks looked to, and fresh oil added, if necessary, every morning, immediately after daybreak. See the comment on ch. xxvii. 21. The duty devolved on the priests.

Ver. 8.—**At even.** Literally, "between the two evenings." (See the comment on ch. xii. 6.) The offering of incense by the high priest twice a day, at the time of the morning and evening sacrifice, indicated that prayer was needed as constantly as expiation, and that neither might for a single day be intermitted. **A perpetual incense.** "Perpetual," in the sense that it was to be burnt twice a day, as long as the religion lasted—not in the sense that it was to be kept burning constantly.

Ver. 9.—By **strange incense** is meant any which was not prepared according to the directions given in vers. 34—38. None such was ever to be offered. Nor was the altar to be used for **burnt-offering, meat-offering,** or **drink-offering.** For burnt-offering it was manifestly unfit; but the prohibition of the others seems to show a determination to keep its use markedly distinct from that of the brazen altar in the court, which was to receive all that was offered either for expiation, or for self-dedication, or in gratitude. On the sole

exception made to this general law, see the comment on the next verse.

Ver. 10.—**Aaron shall make an atonement upon the horns of it once in the year.** Once in the year, on the great day of atonement—the tenth day of the seventh month—the high priest, after burning incense within the veil, and sprinkling the blood of a bullock and a ram towards the mercy seat, was to take of the blood, and put it on the horns of the altar of incense "to make an atonement for it—to cleanse it and hallow it from the uncleanness of the children of Israel" (Lev. xvi. 18, 19). This was not making it an altar of expiation, but merely expiating it. There was, however, another use for the altar, where it seems to have served for an altar of expiation. When the high priest had sinned in his official character, and offered a sin-offering for his cleansing (Lev. iv. 3—12), or when the whole congregation had committed an offence through inadvertence, and did the same (*ib.* 13—21), the high priest was to put of the blood of the sacrifice on the horns of the altar of incense, "for the expiation of his own sin and the sin of the people" (Keil). In these two cases, the altar of incense served purpose of the altar of burnt-offering, on which was put the blood of private sin-offerings (*ib.* 22—35). **It is most holy.** There seems to be sufficient reason for considering the altar of incense as, next to the ark and mercy seat, the most sacred object in the furniture of the tabernacle. This precedence indicates the *extreme* value which God sets upon prayer.

HOMILETICS.

Vers. 1—10.—*The symbolism of the Altar of Incense.* We have seen that the ascent of incense signifies the mounting up to heaven of the grateful odour of man's earnest and heart-felt prayers. The altar, therefore, symbolises the heart which offers such prayers,—

I. IN ITS MATERIALS. The altar is of acacia wood and gold—the one a symbol of soundness and strength, the other of purity. Prayer, to be acceptable, must proceed out of a true heart—a sound, honest, sincere, strong heart—not one that is weak and unstable, one thing to-day and another to-morrow; but one that is consistent, steady, firm, brave, resolute. And it must also proceed out of a pure heart. The gold of the altar was to be "pure gold," refined till every atom of the native dross was purged away. And the heart of the worshipper should be refined similarly. There is much native dross in the hearts of all men. The discipline of life, the furnace of affliction, under God's blessing, does much to purge the dross. But something of it always remains. One only was absolutely pure. We must approach God through the intercession of Christ, and then our incense will mount up from a golden altar heavenwards.

II. IN ITS SITUATION. The altar was "by the ark of the testimony"—directly in front of the mercy seat—very close to the Divine presence, therefore. Prayer brings us into the presence of God. The heart that is drawn upward, and fixed in worship and adoration in its Creator and Redeemer, feels itself near to him. Near, very near; yet still separated by a veil. The eyes of the body cannot pierce that impenetrable curtain, which shrouds the invisible world from our eager, curious gaze. The heart itself cannot so lift itself up as to rise out of the present conditions of its mortal, finite nature, and really enter the empyrean. There is still a veil between man and the spiritual world. Through death only can he pass beyond it.

III. IN ITS HORNS, WHICH WERE SYMBOLS OF POWER. Great is the might of prayer. By means of it the heart has power with God, can wrestle with him, as Jacob did; and as it were, force him to bless it (Gen. xxxii. 26). The parable of the importunate widow illustrates this power. Let us follow her example; let us persist, let us besiege God with our prayers, for ourselves, for others, and we shall prevail with him; at length he will hear us. It has been questioned in these "last days" whether prayer is ever answered; and tests have been proposed, by which men have hoped to demonstrate its inefficiency. But God will not be tested. "Thou shalt not tempt" (*i.e.* "try" or "test") "the Lord thy God." He does not undertake to answer faithless, or even doubting, wavering prayers. The promise is—"Whoever shall say to this mountain, Be thou removed, and be thou cast into the sea; and *shall not doubt in his heart, but shall believe* that those things which he saith shall come to pass, he shall have whatsoever he saith" (Mark xi. 23).

HOMILIES BY VARIOUS AUTHORS.

Vers. 1—11.—*The Altar of Incense.* See below, vers. 34—38.—J. O.

EXPOSITION.

Vers. 11—16.—THE RANSOM OF SOULS. The various commands given with respect to the tabernacle and its furniture would necessarily involve a very considerable outlay; and it was important that Moses should receive directions as to the source, or sources, whence this expenditure was to come. In ch. xxv. 2—7, one source had been indicated, viz., the voluntary contributions of the people. To this is now added a second source. On occasion of the numbering of the people—an event which is spoken of as impending (ver. 12)—Moses was told to exact from each of them, as atonement money, the sum of half a shekel of silver. The produce of this tax was to be applied to the work of the sanctuary (ver. 16), and it is found to have formed an important element in the provision for the cost, since the total amount was above a hundred talents, or, more exactly, 301,775 shekels (ch. xxxviii. 25). The requirement of atonement money seems to have been based on the idea, that formal enrolment in the number of God's faithful people necessarily brought home to every man his unworthiness to belong to that holy company, and so made him feel the need of making atonement in some way or other. The payment of the half-shekel was appointed as the legal mode under those circumstances. It was an acknowledgment of sin, equally binding upon all, and so made equal for all; and it saved from God's vengeance those who,

if they had been too proud to make it, would have been punished by some "plague" or other (ver. 12).

Ver. 12.—**When thou takest the sum.** The sum had been taken roughly at the time of the exodus (ch. xii. 37). Moses was now, it would seem, about to take it again, more accurately. No command had ever been given that the people should not be numbered; and the Egyptian habit of compiling exact statistics naturally clung to one who had had an Egyptian training. (See the "Statistical Tables of Karnak," in the "*Records of the Past,*" vol. ii. pp. 19—28.) **A ransom.** Rather "an expiation," "an atonement"—(as in ch. xxix. 33, 36)—something to show that he was conscious of sin, and of his not deserving to be numbered among God's people. **That there be no plague.** "That they be not punished for undue pride and presumption." There is no thought of such a "plague" as was provoked by David's numbering (2 Sam. xxiv. 15).

Ver. 13.—**Half a shekel.** The shekel of later times was a silver coin, about the size round of our shilling, but considerably thicker, and worth about one shilling and eightpence. But at the date of the exodus coins were unknown, and the "shekel" meant a certain weight. The burthen imposed by the tax was evidently a light one. **The shekel of the sanctuary.** A standard weight in the possession of the priests, equal probably to about 220 grains troy. **Twenty gerahs.** The word "gerah" means "a bean;" and the *gerah* must have been a weight equal to about eleven grains troy. It remained in use to the time of the captivity (Ezek. xlv. 12).

Ver. 14.—**From twenty years old and upward.** Twenty was the age at which an Israelite was reckoned a man ; at twenty he became liable to serve in the wars (2 Chron. xxv. 5), and entered otherwise on the duties of citizenship. At twenty the Levites began their service in the temple (1 Chron. xxiii. 24, 27 ; 2 Chron. xxxi. 17 ; Ezra iii. 8).

Ver. 15.—**The rich shall not give more, and the poor shall not give less.** This is very emphatic testimony to the equal value of souls in God's sight. The payment was " the ransom of a soul " (ver. 12)—an acknowledgment of God's mercy in sparing those whose

life was justly forfeit. As each soul that he has created is equally precious in his sight, and as he designs equally the salvation of all —it was fitting that the same exact sum should be paid in every case.

Ver. 16.—The application of the " atonement money " is stated more distinctly in ch. xxxviii. 27, 28. It was employed for the silver sockets that supported the boards of the tabernacle, and for the hooks, capitals, and connecting rods of the pillars which surrounded the court. Thus employed, it was a continual " memorial " in the eyes of the people, reminding each man of his privileges and duties

HOMILETICS.

Vers. 12—16.—*The atonement money.* Remark three things :—

I. THE ATONEMENT MONEY WAS REQUIRED OF ALL. " All have sinned, and come short of the glory of God " (Rom. iii. 23). " If we say that we have no sin, we deceive ourselves, and the truth is not in us " (1 John i. 8). There was to be no exemption. Moses and Aaron were to bring their half-shekel no less than the others ; the priests had to make the offering, just the same as the laity ; the rulers, as much as the common people. The lesson taught was, that every soul was guilty before God—all unclean in his sight, who " is of purer eyes than to behold iniquity "—all in need of pardon and cleansing. So far there was certainly " no difference " (Rom. iii. 22). " Every mouth was stopped " (*ib.* 19). Boasting was excluded—the right attitude of the soul towards God shown to be one of humility, deprecation, penitence.

II. THE SAME ATONEMENT MONEY WAS REQUIRED OF EACH. It is true to say, that all men equally are guilty in God's sight ; but it would not be true to say that all are equally guilty. Yet the same atonement was required of all. " The rich shall not give more, and the poor shall not give less." This marks that one and the same atonement is required, whatever be the degree of a man's guilt, whether he be (so far as is possible) " a just man needing no repentance," or " the chief of sinners." On the man's part is required in every case " repentance and faith ;" these, however, cannot atone. The true " atonement money," the true " redemption," the real " ransom of souls," is the death of Christ—one and the same for all—necessary for all—not too much for the least, not too little for the most guilty ; but " a full, perfect, and sufficient sacrifice for the sins of the whole world." It saves all that trust in it—saves them from wrath and death—saves them from sin—atones for them—puts them " at one " with the Father.

III. THE ATONEMENT WAS TO BE KEPT IN MIND, TO BE FOR A PERPETUAL MEMORIAL. There are those who are content to acknowledge that Christ has died for them, and has saved them, who yet object to giving the fact, what they call, undue prominency. They would acknowledge it once for all, and then have done with it. But this is not the general teaching of the Bible, nor is it that of the present passage. The " atonement money " was to be so employed as to be " a memorial unto the children of Israel before the Lord " perpetually. They were to have the shapes of silver, into which it had been cast, ever before their eyes. And assuredly there is nothing in the whole range of spiritual facts which deserves such continual remembrance, such constant dwelling upon in thought, as the atonement made for us by Christ. Herein alone have we hope, trust, confidence. Hereby alone are we saved. The cross of Christ should be ever before the Christian's eye, mind, heart. He should not for a moment forget it, much less be ashamed of it.

HOMILIES BY VARIOUS AUTHORS.

Vers. 11—16.—*The numbering of Israel and their ransom.* I. THE NUMBERING OF THE PEOPLE, AN EMBLEM OF THE JUDGMENT God's claims were brought home to them; their unworthiness was contrasted with the place assigned to them as the people whom God had visited with his light and salvation. When we remember that we are the Lord's, and the light of that just claim is shed upon our life, it is to our shame and confusion. But life will be read at last in this very light!

II. THE ATONEMENT WHICH SHIELDS US. 1. It is a ransom for the life: "that there be no plague among them when thou numberest them." God's wrath will not smite if this be provided. 2. It must be given from one's own in that judgment day. Christ to avail us then must have been made ours by faith. It must be Christ in us. 3. It is required from all. None are guiltless. 4. The same is demanded from each. All alike are in themselves lost and under God's wrath. 5. The atonement is for the service of the tabernacle. The changed life of God's people through the indwelling of Christ is for God's service now, and the manifestation of his glory hereafter.—U.

Vers. 11—17.—*The atonement money.* It pertained to the full admission of Israel to theocratic privilege, that, the nation as a whole having been admitted into covenant, a formal registration should be made of at least the grown part of the community. Directions were accordingly issued for the taking of a census, which had also in view a more complete military organisation of the nation than as yet existed. The males of the tribes from twenty years old and upwards were to be made to pass before Jehovah, and were to be regularly counted and enrolled as members of the holy commonwealth. This act, however, which involved a near approach to Jehovah, and was on the part of the individual an entrance into the full rights of his citizenship, called for some new recognition of the principle of atonement on which the covenant was built. Hence the ordinance that each individual of those who were numbered should make an offering of half a shekel of silver, as a ransom or atonement for his soul (ver. 15). The silver thus obtained was to go for the service of the tabernacle (ver. 16). On which observe—1. *The money was money of atonement.* It was paid in ransom for life. If we seek the principle on which the ransoming proceeds, we must view the half shekel in the light of the practice of commutation. In strictness, atonement could be made only by blood. Here, as in other cases, the animal sacrifice is commuted for money, and the money, in virtue of that for which it is commuted, is admitted as atonement. The purpose to which the silver was to be applied required that the ransom should take this form. 2. *All were to be taxed alike.* "The rich shall not give more, nor the poor less" (ver. 15). This intimates that, as respects his need of atonement, no man has any advantage over his neighbours. "There is no difference" (Rom. iii. 22). It intimates, too, the essential equality of men in the eyes of God. 3. *The money was to be applied to the work of the tabernacle.* The greater part of it was used in making the silver sockets for the dwelling-place (ch. xxxviii. 27). Thus (1) the tabernacle—symbol of God's kingdom in Israel—was founded on the silver of atonement. This, surely, was a profound testimony to the fact that only on the basis of atonement can communion exist between heaven and earth. (2) Each Israelite was individually represented in Jehovah's sanctuary. His tribute money formed part of it. He had a stake and interest in it. The honour was great: not less so the responsibility.—J. O.

EXPOSITION.

Vers. 17—21.—THE BRAZEN LAVER. That the tabernacle was to have an ample supply of water had been implied in the directions given for the washing of Aaron and his sons at its outer door (ch. xxix. 4). That it would contain some provision of the kind is further indicated by the command to "wash the inwards" of victims (*ib.* 17). We have now, in this place, the special directions given to Moses on the subject. He was to provide a brazen, or rather a bronze laver, which was to stand on a separate "foot," or base, of bronze, in the court of the tabernacle, between the entrance to the tabernacle and the "brazen altar." This was to be kept constantly supplied with water, and was to furnish whatever might be needed for the various ceremonies. Among its other uses, it was to supply liquid for the constant ablution of the priests, who were to wash both their hands and their feet on every occasion of their entering the sacred tent, and even on every occasion of their ministering at the brazen altar (ver. 20). This law was to be "a statute for ever" (ver. 21), and its violation was to be punished by death.

Ver. 18.—**A laver.** It is remarkable that nothing is said respecting either the shape or the size of the laver. In 1 Kings we have an elaborate description of the "molten sea," which replaced it in Solomon's temple, as well as an almost equally elaborate one of ten other lavers made by Hiram, Solomon's artist, at the same time. We may perhaps assume from these examples that the brazen laver of the tabernacle was a large bronze vase or basin, standing upon a stem, which was fixed into a base. It was probably fitted up with an apparatus of taps and cocks. **Between the tabernacle . . . . and the altar.** The Rabbinical commentators say that it was not exactly in the middle, but a little towards the south side.

Ver. 19. **Aaron and his sons shall wash their hands and their feet.** Ablution by clear fresh water is so plain and simple a type of purity as to have been used in almost all religions. The hands and the feet would designate symbolically all a man's active doings, and even his whole walk in life—his "goings out" and his "comings in," in the phraseology of the Hebrews. There would also be a special practical need for such ablutions in the case of persons who were employed about bloody sacrifices, who slew the victims, sprinkled the blood, and even dashed it against the base of the altar. On some rare occasions the priests were required to bathe their whole persons, and not their hands and feet only (see above, ch. xxix. 4; and below, Lev. xvi. 4).

Ver. 20.—**That they die not.** Compare ch. xxviii. 35 and 43. Contempt of the simple and easy regulation to wash at the laver would imply contempt of purity itself; and so an entire hypocrisy of life and character, than which nothing could be a greater offence to God.

Ver. 21.—**It shall be a statute for ever.** Compare ch. xxvii. 21; xxviii. 43; xxix. 9, etc. **Even to him**—i.e., to Aaron.

HOMILETICS.

Vers. 18—21.—*The Brazen Laver.*—Primarily, the brazen altar has its antitype in THE CHRISTIAN FONT. "Baptism *saves* us," says St. Peter (1 Pet. iii. 21). "Arise and be baptised, and wash away thy sins," said Ananias (Acts xxii. 16). "There is one baptism for the remission of sins," said the Nicene Fathers. As the priests had to wash at the laver ere they might enter the sanctuary, so entrance into the Church, by the institution of Christ (Matt. xxviii. 19; Mark xvi. 16; John iii. 5), is by baptism. To wash, of course, is by itself not enough—each of us must "lead the rest of his life according to this beginning." So the priests, besides washing, had to observe *all* God's other ordinances.

Ultimately, both the laver and the font, both the priestly ablutions and the Christian sacrament of baptism, are types of the true washing, which is WASHING IN THE BLOOD OF CHRIST. This washing is—

I. ABSOLUTELY, AND IN ALL CASES, NEEDFUL. Only "the blood of Jesus Christ cleanseth us from all sin" (1 John i. 7). "If Christ wash us not, we have no part in him" (John xiii. 8). The saved in heaven are those who have "washed their robes and made them white in the blood of the Lamb" (Rev. vii. 14). Baptism is "generally necessary" since Christ came and instituted it; yet no one doubts that many unbaptized persons have entered heaven. But not one has entered, or will ever enter, whom the blood of Christ has not cleansed. "Wash me, Saviour, or I die," is the constantly repeated cry of every Christian heart.

II. A SOVEREIGN REMEDY THAT NEVER FAILS TO SAVE. Thus "washed," we are at once both "justified and sanctified" (1 Cor. vi. 11); both pardoned and made pure. Thus washed, we have access to the Father; we are made fit to enter his courts; our robes are made white, and not only our robes, but our souls. God will never reject one who comes to him in the wedding garment of a robe that Christ has cleansed. Only we must be sure to keep our robes clean—we must not "defile our garments" (Rev. iii. 4) —we must wash them again and again in the purifying blood; we must look nowhere else for salvation, but only to the Cross, and we must look to that perpetually.

HOMILIES BY VARIOUS AUTHORS.

Vers. 17—34.—*The laver and the anointing oil.*

I. THE LAVER (vers. 17—22). This was to be made of brass (bronze), and was to be placed near the door of the tabernacle between it and the altar. It was to be used by Aaron and his sons for purposes of ablution. A new symbol of the purity required in those who serve before Jehovah. The Christian contracts daily defilements in his walk, for which also daily cleansing is required (cf. John xiii. 10; 1 John i. 7).

II. THE ANOINTING OIL (vers. 22—34). Precious, fragrant, holy. To be applied not only to Aaron and his sons, but to the tabernacle and all its vessels. See Homily on Consecration (ch. xxiv. 6, 7). The oil is the symbol of the Spirit. The holiness imparted to Aaron and his sons by this anointing, and by the rites of consecration generally, was indeed no more than a ceremonial or official holiness. It pertained to the office rather than to the man. Yet the holders of the office were, in virtue of their consecration, laid under obligations to personal holiness as well. The private character of the priest might not avail to nullify his official acts; but the absence in the public representative of the spiritual qualifications for his office would not be allowed to go unpunished. Iniquity in the priest would be visited both on priest and people.—J. O.

EXPOSITION.

Vers. 22—33.—THE HOLY OIL. The composition of the oil required for anointing the priests (ch. xxix. 7), the altar (*ib.* 36), the tabernacle itself (ver. 26), and its furniture (vers. 27, 28), was a necessary matter for Moses to know, and is now declared with much minuteness; the exact weight of each spice, and the exact quantity of the olive oil being given (vers. 23, 24). Directions are added for its use (vers. 26—30): and finally, a warning is given against its application to any persons except the priests, or its composition for any other purpose besides the use of the sanctuary (vers. 31—33).

Ver. 23.—**Principal spices.** The ancients recognised a vast variety of spices. Pliny notices an ointment which was composed of twenty-six ingredients, chiefly spices (*H. N.* xiii. 2, § 18). Herodotus mentions five " principal spices " as furnished by Arabia (iii. 107), of which four seem to be identical with those employed in the holy oil. **Pure myrrh.** Literally, " myrrh of freedom," or " freely flowing myrrh." The shrub which yields myrrh (*Balsamodendron myrrha*) produces two kinds—one, which exudes spontaneously, and is regarded as the best (Plin. *H. N.* xii. 35; Theophrast. *De Odoribus,* § 29); and another, of inferior quality, which flows from incisions made in the bark. It is the former kind which is here intended. Myrrh was among the ancients in high request as a spice. It was used by the Egyptians for embalming (Herod ii. 86), in Persia as an odour (Athen. *Deipn.* xii. p. 514, A); by the Greeks for incense (Soph. Fr. 340) and in unguents (Aristoph. *Eq* l. 1332); by the later Jews in funerals (John xix. 39); and was largely exported from Arabia and Ethiopia into various parts of Asia and Europe. **Sweet cinnamon.** Cinnamon was a far rarer spice than myrrh. It is only mentioned three times in the Old Testament (cf. Prov. vii. 16; Cant. iv. 14). I am not aware of any trace of it in Egypt; but Herodotus says that it was obtained by the Greeks from Arabia in his day (iii. 111). It is the inner bark or rind of a tree allied to the laurel, and called by some *Laurus cinnamomum,* by others *Cinnamomum zeylanicum.* The tree now grows only in India on the Malabar coast, in Ceylon, Borneo, Sumatra, Cochin China, and China. If its habitat has not suffered contraction, we must regard the mention of it here as indicative of a very early commerce of a very extensive character. **Sweet calamus.** Aromatic reeds, probably of several distinct kinds, seem to have been the produce anciently of Palestine, Arabia, Mesopotamia, and India. It is impossible to say what exactly was the species here intended. Calamus is mentioned as a spice in Is. xliii. 24; Jer. vi. 20; Ezek. xxvii. 17; and Cant. iv. 14; but the term used (*kâneh,* " cane ") is vague; and it is not at all clear that one species only is alluded to.

Ver. 24.—**Cassia.** The modern cassia is the inner bark of a tree distinct from the cinnamon tree, known to botanists as *Cinnamomum cassia,* which is a native of India, Java, and the Malay peninsula. In taste and scent, it " bears a strong resemblance to cinnamon, but is more pungent and of coarser texture " (Cook). It is uncertain, however, if this is the spice here indicated. The Hebrew word used is *kiddâh,* not *kĕtsiôth* (as in Ps. xlv. 8); and it is very doubtful whether the two are identical. On the **shekel of the sanctuary.**

see the comment on ver. 13; and on the **hin**, see ch. xxix. 40.

Ver 25.—**An oil of holy ointment.** Literally, "an oil of holy anointing," or "a holy anointing oil," as our translators render in ver. 31, and also in the last clause of the present verse. **An ointment compound after the art of the apothecary.** Not a simple mixture of the ingredients mentioned, but the product of trained skill and knowledge applied to the materials. Jewish tradition says that the essence of each spice was extracted from it, and only these essences mingled with the olive oil. We are told later (ch. xxxvii. 29) that the task of preparing the holy oil was committed to Bezaleel.

Vers 26—29.—**Thou shalt anoint the tabernacle.** The first application of the holy oil was to be to the inanimate objects constituting the paraphernalia of worship—viz., 1. The tabernacle itself as a whole; 2. The furniture of the holy of holies—the ark and mercy seat; 3. The furniture of the holy place—the shewbread table, the candlestick, and the altar of incense; and 4. The furniture of the court—the altar of burnt-offering, and the laver. After applying the oil to these, Moses was to proceed to the anointing of the priests. (Compare Lev. viii. 10—12.)

Ver. 27.—**The table and all his vessels.** See above, ch. xxv. 29. **The candlestick and his vessels.** See ch. xxv. 37, 38.

Ver. 28.—**The altar of burnt-offering with all his vessels.** See ch. xxvii. 3.

Ver. 30.—**And thou shalt anoint Aaron,** etc. Not till all his surroundings had received sanctification was Aaron to be consecrated. The tent, the ark, the table, the candlestick, the altar of incense, the brazen altar, the laver, and its base, each and all were to be touched with the holy oil, and thereby formally dedicated to God's service (Lev. viii. 10, 11), and then at last was Moses to "pour of the anointing oil upon Aaron's head, and anoint him, to sanctify him" (*ib.* 12). So God constantly prepares men's spheres for them before he inducts them into their spheres. Even in the next world our Blessed Lord "prepares places for us."

Ver. 32.—**Upon man's flesh shall it not be poured**—*i.e.*, "it shall not be used by any privately as a mere unguent, but shall be reserved wholly for sacred purposes." **Neither shall ye make any other like it, after the composition of it.** Rather, "after its *proportion.*" The Israelites were not forbidden the use of the different materials in their unguents, or even the combination of the same materials, provided they varied the proportions. The object is simply that the holy oil should remain a thing separate and apart, never applied to any but a holy use.

Ver. 33.—**Upon a stranger.** A "stranger" here means any one not of the family of Aaron. Compare ch. xxix. 33.

HOMILETICS.

Vers. 23—25.—*The sweetness of the Holy anointing Oil.* The holy oil had infused into it the essence of four "principal spices"—myrrh, that scents the garments of the great king (Ps. xlv. 8; Cant. iii. 6); cinnamon, the choicest of the spices of distant Ind; sweet calamus, that exhales its best fragrance when bruised; cassia, which, together with sweet calamus, formed one of the glories of the market of Tyre (Ezek. xxvii. 19). How passing sweet must have been the odour of these blended perfumes—each delicious alone—all enhanced by the combination, which had taxed the best skill of the "apothecary" (ver. 25)! But the sweetness of our anointing oil is greater. "We have an unction from the Holy One." Our "anointing oil" is the Blessed Spirit of God. What is there in all the experiences of this world so sweet to the weary soul as he? How sweet and dear is he—

I. IN THE SOFT GENTLENESS OF HIS DESCENT UPON US. Silently, unperceivedly, without sight, or sound, or stir, the gentle influence comes—steals into the heart—only by degrees makes its presence known to us. A crisis—a manifest change—"tongues of fire," or the rush of a "mighty wind" would cause the weak believer to tremble with fear, and perhaps draw back to his undoing. Our "anointing oil" descends upon us soft as "the dew of Hermon, which fell upon the hill of Sion."

> "He comes, sweet influence to impart,
> A gracious willing guest,
> While he can find one humble heart
> Wherein to rest."

II. IN THE METHOD OF HIS ORDINARY WORKING. Not by rude shocks, or sudden terrible alarms; but by the mild coercion of little checks and scarcely-felt restraints—

by whispers softly breathed into the ear of the soul—by the suggestion of good thoughts —by the presentation of holy memories—does he effect his ends. Wise as any serpent, harmless as his own emblem, the dove, he feeds us as we are able to receive of him. He has " milk " for such as stand in need of milk. He has " strong meat" for such as can bear it. Manifold and diverse are his gifts, but given to every man " to profit withal " (1 Cor. xii. 7).

> " His is that gentle voice we hear,
> Soft as the breath of even,
> That checks each fault, that calms each fear,
> And speaks of Heaven.

> " And every virtue we possess,
> And every conquest won,
> And every thought of holiness,
> Are his alone."

III. In his patience with us when we are wayward. God once declared, " My spirit shall not always strive with man" (Gen. vi. 3); and Scripture warns us that the Holy Ghost may be "resisted" (Acts vii. 51) and even "quenched" (1 Thess. v. 19). But how wonderful is his patience and forbearance towards those who thwart and oppose him! How unwilling is he to give them up! How loth to quit their souls, and leave them to their own guidance! Assuredly he is "provoked every day" by each one of us. But he is not even angry—he simply " grieves " (Eph. iv. 30)—is "vexed" (Is. lxiii. 10)—made sorrowful. No sooner do we show any signs of relenting than he forgives—encourages us, cheers, comforts, consoles. "There is a friend that sticketh closer than a brother." Such a friend to man is "the Comforter."

IV. In his kindness towards us when we turn to him. It is the Christian's privilege to speak with God "as a man to his friend" (Ex. xxxiii. 11). With the in-dwelling Spirit we may ever have this "mystic sweet communion." Would we speak to him at any moment, his ear is attent to hear. Unworthy as we are, unclean as we are, rebellious as we are, and self-willed, and self-seeking, he will commune with us, if we will commune with him—he will tell us of the things of heaven, "guide us into all truth" (John xvi. 13), "receive of Christ's and show it unto us" (ib. 14). The sweetness of such commune is inexpressible—it may well "ravish our heart" (Cant. iv. 9) and make us "sick of love" (ib. v. 8).

EXPOSITION.

Vers. 34—38.—The holy incense. It remained to give directions concerning the composition of the incense, which, according to verse 7, was to be burnt upon the altar of gold. That it was to be of one and one only peculiar kind had been already implied in the prohibition to burn "strange incense" (ver. 9). Moses is now told exactly how it was to be composed. As the oil was to contain four spices, so was the incense to be made of a like number—stacte, onycha, galbanum, and frankincense—of each the same quantity (ver. 34). The art of the apothecary was to be called in for making it up (ver. 35). A portion of it was to be "beaten very small," and placed in front of the ark of the covenant, probably on the golden altar outside the vail (ver. 36). A prohibition is added, similar to that given with respect to the holy oil: no one is to make any like it for private use, under pain of being "cut off from his people" (vers. 37, 38).

Ver. 34.—Take unto thee sweet spices. Rather, "Take unto thee spices," or "perfumes." The word has no epithet. Stacte. The Hebrew word used means simply "a drop" (Job xxxii. 27), and might be applied to any gum or resin which exuded from a tree. We have no clue to the gum here intended but that which is furnished by the rendering of the LXX., στακτή, which our translators have followed. Now the Greeks seem to have called two gums by this name—one, the natural exudation from the myrrh tree, called above (ver. 23) "pure myrrh," or "the myrrh that flows freely; " and the other gum storax. As it is not likely that the same substance has been given two names within the space of ten verses, we must suppose the latter to be meant. Gum storax is the produce of a tree allied to the poplar, and known as *Styrax officinalis*, which grows abundantly in Syria and Palestine. It was frequently used as a perfume by the ancients (Herod. iii. 107; Plin. *H. N.* xii. 17, §40). **Onycha.** The Hebrew word, *shĕ-khĕleth*, seems to mean a "shell" of some kind or other. The Greek ὄνυξ, Lat. *onycha*, was applied to the *operculum*—the "nail" or "claw"—of certain shell-fish of the genus Strombidæ, which were common in the Red Sea, and elsewhere. The particular *strombus* which furnishes the onycha of the ancients is thought to have been the *Unguis odoratus* or *Blatta Byzantina.* The *opercula* of these shell-fish have, when burnt, a strong odour, "something like castoreum." The onycha is, again coupled with galbanum and gum storax in Eccl. xxiv. 15. **Galbanum.** The Hebrew word *khelb'nah*, is so near the Greek χαλβάνη and the Latin *galbanum* that it has with good reason been assumed to designate the same substance. Galbanum is a gum well known both to ancients and moderns. It is admitted into the pharmacopeia. Several plants seem to produce it, as the *Opoidia galbanifera*, the *Galbanum Persicum*, and a plant which grows in Northern Persia, very like the *Ferula erubescens.* When burnt, galbanum has a strong pungent odour, which is said to be disagreeable by itself, but to improve and preserve other odours (Plin. *H. N.* xii. 54). **Frankincense.** On the wide use of frankincense, see the comment on ver. 1. It was the produce of a tree which anciently flourished in Arabia, but which appears to have degenerated, and now produces only an inferior quality. The best frankincense comes now from the high lands of India. It exudes from a tree called *salai* (the *Boswellia serrata* or *thurifera* of botanists). Some think that the frankincense exported largely from Arabia to the neighbouring nations was in part the produce of this tree imported by the Arab merchants from Hindustan.

Ver. 35.—**A confection after the art of the apothecary.** Like the holy oil, the incense was to be artistically compounded by one accustomed to deal with such ingredients. It was actually, in the first instance, the work of Bezaleel (ch. xxvii. 29). **Tempered together.** This translation is supported by the authority of the Septuagint and the Vulgate, and is defended by Canon Cook. But the mass of modern critics is in favour of the translation "salted," or "with salt." (So Buxtorf, Gesenius, De Wette, Kalisch, Keil, etc.) Knobel suggests "comminuted," identifying *málakh* with *márakh.* The point is not one of much importance.

Ver. 36.—**Thou shalt beat some of it very small.** This is against Knobel's rendering of *málakh*, which would imply that *all* was broken into small pieces. A certain portion only was to be thus prepared from time to time and placed ready for offering. It was to be **put before the testimony**—*i.e.*, opposite the ark, but outside the vail. This near vicinity to the Divine Presence rendered it **most holy.**

Vers. 37, 38.—**Ye shall not make unto yourselves,** etc. None shall be made by any man for private use according to the same recipe, since the compound, as described, is "holy unto the Lord." If any man does so, he shall be "cut off from among his people" —*i.e.*, "put to death by the civil authority." (See ch. xxxi. 14.)

HOMILETICS.

Vers. 34—38.—*The Holy Incense.* Let us note here—

I. THE COMPOSITION OF THE INCENSE (vers. 34, 35). The utmost care was taken in the law that the incense should be properly composed, of the right materials, in the right proportion. Equal care is to be taken by Christians with their incense. Prayer is not to be adventured on rashly, carelessly, unpreparedly. The matter, even the very words, of prayer should be carefully weighed beforehand. To approach God with unworthy thoughts, to beseech him for those temporal advantages which we ought to regard as of no moment at all, is to "pray amiss"—to approach him with "strange incense." Equally unbecoming is it to use homely or over-familiar expressions in prayer. What we have to aim at is to reflect "the mind of Christ." Christ has given us three pattern prayers—1. The Lord's prayer; 2. The intercessory prayer after the last supper (John xvii.), and 3. The prayer in the garden of Gethsemane (Matt. xxvi. 39). Let these be our frankincense, and stacte, and onycha. For a fourth material, we may use the Psalms of David—especially the penitential Psalms. We need not then to fear lest our incense should be "strange."

II. THE CONTINUAL PRESENTATION OF THE INCENSE (ver. 30).—A portion of the incense was to be "beaten very small, and put before the testimony"—*i.e.*, before the ark and the presence of God, where it was to remain continually. It was not to be lighted, but to be in constant readiness for lighting. So there is in the Christian heart a prayerful temper, ever present before God, which God accepts and values, in the intervals between actual prayer. Our incense cannot always be mounting in cloud after cloud to the courts of heaven. But the temper may be in us, ready to kindle, at all times.

III. THE VALUE OF THE INCENSE. The incense was among the things that were "*most holy*" (ver. 36). God set special store by it. He would have it near him—in front of the tabernacle—only just outside the vail—and he would have it there constantly. So it pleases him to value the prayers of his saints. Angels offer them (Rev. viii. 3). They ascend before his throne (*ib*. 4). They are acceptable to him. They have power with him. "The effectual fervent prayer of a righteous man availeth much" (Jam. v. 16). One humble prayer, breathed by the publican, gained him forgiveness—"justified" him. One earnest prayer, uttered by the penitent thief, obtained him Paradise. There is no limit to the value of faithful prayer, whereby we draw upon the bank of omnipotence.

HOMILIES BY VARIOUS AUTHORS.

Vers. 1—11, 34—38.—*The golden altar and the perfume.* The golden altar was of small dimensions, a cubit in length, a cubit in breadth, and two cubits high. It was a true altar, as shown by its square shape, and by its horns. Its place was immediately in front of the vail dividing the two portions of the sanctuary, with the innermost of which—the holy of holies—it was regarded as having the more intimate connection (1 Kings vi. 22; Heb. ix. 4). The command was that Aaron should burn upon it sweet incense morning and evening—in the morning when he trimmed, and in the evening when he lighted, the lamps. This was done, in the one case, at the offering of morning, in the other, at the offering of evening sacrifice, the synchronism of the acts deserving our attention. Once a year the horns of the altar were to be smeared with the blood of the sin-offering. Minute directions are given for the making of the incense (vers. 34—38). It was to be "salted, pure, and holy" (ver. 35). The burning of this incense on the altar was at once a symbol of prayer and devotion, and a call to the congregation to engage in these spiritual exercises (Ps. cxli. 2; Luke i. 10; Rev. v. 8; viii. 3, 4). As an act of the priest, it may be viewed as a type of the intercession of Christ. The service of this altar suggests the following ideas—1. *Prayer*—taking the word in its widest sense, as denoting the exercise of all devout feeling and spiritual desire towards God—*is the holiest act of the spiritual life.* It is figured as incense. And the altar of incense stood in immediate relation with the holy of holies. The altar and the incense offered upon it, are declared to be "most holy" (vers. 10, 36). The reason is not difficult to find. The very essence of the devotional life expresses itself in prayer. Its love, its awe, its thankfulness, its aspirations, its unutterable yearnings after God—its breathings after holiness, its very contrition and sorrow for its sins—all ascend to Jehovah in this supreme act of the nature. Words bear but a small part in prayer. The province of words is to define. Hence the soul, in the intensity of its aspirations, in its reachings out towards the infinite, often feels the need of escaping from words, of leaving them behind. Prayer becomes "the burden of a sigh"—"the falling of a tear"—perhaps a purely inward act of the mind realising union with Jehovah. Or its uncontrollable desires may express themselves in "groanings which cannot be uttered" (Rom. viii. 26). And it is precisely these unutterable parts of our prayers which are the sweetest to God. The appropriate symbol of them is the incense, rising in its unconfined wreaths from the priest's censer, or from the golden altar. 2. *Prayer is an act of sacrifice.* "In prayer," says Martensen, "the profoundest act of conscience and obedience is inwardly accomplished, for prayer is only in so far a laying hold and appropriation of God, as it is likewise a *sacrifice*; and we can only receive God into us when we likewise give ourselves to him. He who offers no sacrifice in his prayer, who does not sacrifice his selfwill, does not really pray." 3. *The connection with the sacrifice of burnt-offering.* The coals for the altar of incense were brought from the altar of burnt-offering (cf. Lev. xvi. 12, 13). This teaches that the worshipper needs reconciling before he can acceptably offer the sacrifices of his devotion. But there is a further connection, arising from the significance of the burnt-offering as a symbol of dedication. Keil says truly—"The incense-offering was not only a spiritualising and transfiguring of the burnt-offering, but a completion of it also." The connection may be stated thus. The yielding up of the life to God, symbolised in the continual burnt-offering, transforms itself in practice into the three following modes of self-surrender. 1. Holy practical activity, of which the fruit, good works, is represented in the *shew-bread*. 2. Public witness-bearing for God, by manifestation of the truth, and by holiness of walk—represented by the *candlestick*. 3. Devotion—"the soul's going forth to unite itself in appropriate actings with the great centre of Being, and to devote its own inmost being to him" (Fairbairn)—symbolised by the *burning of the incense*. This is the culminating act of self-devotion, and crowns the sanctuary-worship, raises it to its consummation. 4. *Connection with light.* The incense was to be burned at the time of the trimming, and again of the lighting of the lamps. The brighter the light, the purer the devotion. In Christianity no countenance is given to the maxim that devotion is connected with ignorance. Christ and his apostles attach the utmost importance to the possession of right knowledge, and to growth in it. Growth in knowledge is the condition of sanctification, of spiritual fruitfulness, of enlargement of nature, of being filled with all the fulness of God. 5. *Prayer a daily duty.* The "perpetual incense before the Lord" reminds us of the apostolic injunction, "Pray without ceasing" (1 Thess. v. 17). Prayer, devotion, is to be the element we live in. And prayer, "with thanksgiving," is to sanctify everything we do (Eph. v. 20; Phil. iv. 6; Col. iii. 17; 1 Tim. iv. 4, 5).—J. O.

EXPOSITION.

CHAPTER XXXI

Vers. 1—11.—THE CALL OF BEZALEEL AND AHOLIAB. The directions for the construction of the tabernacle and its furniture being now complete, and the composition of the holy oil and the holy incense having been laid down minutely, it only remained to designate the persons to whom the oversight of the work was to be especially entrusted. These were to be two—Bezaleel, of the tribe of Judah, as head and chief; Aholiab, of the tribe of Dan, as his assistant. There can be no doubt that they were selected, primarily, as already possessing superior artistic powers and acquirements; but in appointing them God promised an infusion of special wisdom and knowledge, so that they were at once naturally and supernaturally fitted for their task. It is important to note that artistic ability is thus distinctly recognised as being quite as much a gift of God as any other, and indeed as coming to man through the Spirit of God (ver. 3). Artistic excellence is not a thing to be despised. It is very capable of abuse; but in itself it is a high gift, bestowed by God on a few only, with the special intent that it should be used to his honour and glory—not indeed in his direct service only—but always so as to improve, elevate, refine mankind, and thus help towards the advancement of God's kingdom

Ver. 2.—I have called by name. God "calls by name" only those whom he appoints to some high office, as Moses (ch. iii. 4; xxxiii. 12), Cyrus (Is. xlv. 3, 4), and here Bezaleel and Aholiab. He honours us highly in even condescending to "know us by name," still more in "calling" us. Bezaleel is traced to Judah in Chronicles through five ancestors—Uri, Hur, Caleb, Hezron, and Pharez, Judah's son by Tamar. The genealogy, though less contracted than most of those in Exodus, probably contains two or three omissions. The son of Hur. Hur, the grandfather of Bezaleel, is thought to be the person mentioned in ch. xvii. 10, and ch. xxiv. 14.

Ver. 3.—The Spirit of God. There is no article in the Hebrew, any more than in Gen. i. 1; and some would therefore translate "a Divine Spirit"; but no change is needed. *Ruakh elohim* contains in itself the idea of singularity, since God has but one Spirit. The Holy Spirit is the medium of communication whereby God the Father bestows *all* gifts upon us. In wisdom, and in understanding, and in knowledge. By the first of these terms is meant the power to invent and originate; by the second ability to receive and appreciate directions and suggestions; by the third, such information as is acquired by experience and acquaintance with facts. Bezaleel was to have all these, and, in addition, was to be wise in all manner of workmanship; *i.e.*—to possess manual dexterity, the power of artistic execution.

Vers. 4, 5.—The result of these gifts would be to enable him—1. To devise cunning works—*i.e.*, to design everything excellently; and 2. To work in all manner of workmanship—*i.e.*, to carry out his designs with success. It has been said that "as everything that had to be done was prescribed in strict and precise detail, there was to be no exercise of original powers of invention nor of taste" (Cook); but this was scarcely so. The forms of the cherubim, the patterns to be woven into the stuffs, or embroidered on them, the shapes of the vessels, of the capitals of the pillars, and of the laver were not prescribed in the directions. Bezaleel and Aholiab would have had to design them after such a description as Moses could give of the " pattern" which he had seen in the mount. In doing this, there would be much room for the exercise of inventive power and taste.

Ver. 5.—**In cutting of stones**—*i.e.*, "in gem-cutting." The fabric of the tabernacle was entirely of metal, cloth, and wood. **In carving of timber.** Rather "cutting." The word is the same as that used of the stones. And no ornamental "carving" of the woodwork was prescribed.

Ver. 6.—**Aholiab** appears to have had the entire charge of the textile fabrics, both woven and embroidered (ch. xxxviii. 23). **Of the tribe of Dan.** It is remarkable that Hiram, the chief artist employed by Solomon for the ornamental work of the temple, was also a descendant of Dan (2 Chron. ii. 14).

Yet the Danites were in general rather warlike and rude than artistic (Gen. xlix. 17 ; Deut. xxxiii. 22 ; Judg. xiii. 2 ; xviii. 11, 27). **In the hearts of all that are wise hearted have I put wisdom.** "Unto him that hath shall be given." Those who were already "wise hearted"—possessed, that is, of artistic power—were selected by God to receive extraordinary gifts of the same kind.

Ver. 7—11 contain an enumeration of the various works already commanded to be made The same order is observed, except that here the tabernacle itself is placed first, and the altar of incense takes its natural position next to the candlestick.

Ver. 10. **The cloths of service.** Rather " the vestments of office"—*i.e.*, the distinguishing vestments of the High Priest, which he alone was allowed to wear. These were the blue robe, the ephod, the girdle of the ephod, and the breast-plate (ch. xxviii. 6—35). **The holy garments.** The rest of the High Priest's dress—*i.e.*, the linen drawers, the diapered tunic, the inner girdle and the mitre (*ib.* 39, 43 ; Lev. xvi. 4), which constituted his whole apparel on the great day of atonement. **The garments of his sons**—*i.e,* the linen drawers, tunics, girdles, and caps, mentioned in ch. xxviii. 40, 42.

HOMILETICS.

Vers. 3—6.—*Artistic excellence.* I. ITS FOUNDATION A NATURAL GIFT. God singled out from the mass of the people such as were "wise hearted." A natural foundation was necessary for his spirit to work upon. It is generally allowed, in the case of a poet, that "*nascitur, non fit.*" But the same is true of all art-genius. Every artist, be he poet, painter, sculptor, musician, or mere designer of furniture, requires to have a something implanted within him from the first, out of which his artistic power is to grow, and without which he could never attain to excellence. Bezaleel and Aholiab were such persons. They were men of natural genius, with a special aptitude for the task to which they were set.

II. THE NATURAL GIFT MAY BE LARGELY INCREASED AND IMPROVED BY GRACE. There is a natural affinity between artistic excellence and spirituality. God, who gives artistic power originally for wise and good purposes, will, if men use the power worthily, augment it by the direct action of his Spirit on their intellects. Those poets, painters, etc., who have been good men, have found that their artistic ability improve with time. Those who have lived evil lives have found it deteriorate. The spirit of devotion gave to the school of Angelico, Francia, and Perugino, its wonderful power and intensity. Milton's religious ardour sublimised his poetry. The best art has always had a religious purpose, and derived much of its excellence from its association with religion. Men who regard their gifts as a trust, and exercise them in the fear of God, find constantly that their conceptions grow in grandeur and dignity, while their execution becomes more and more happy. The spirit of God fills them with wisdom, and understanding, and knowledge, and even with "all manner of workmanship."

III. ON THE OTHER HAND, THE NATURAL GIFT MAY BE PERVERTED TO EVIL, AND BECOME A CURSE BOTH TO ITS POSSESSOR AND OTHERS. There is no intellectual power which is not liable to misuse. Artistic excellence is perhaps more liable to it than most others. If it is divorced from moral goodness, and made a mere instrument of self-glorification, it becomes debased at once. And the decline is easy from bad to worse. "*Facilis descensus Averni.*" There are few things which have worked greater evil in the world than high artistic genius combined with moral depravity. A whole generation may be utterly corrupted by a single sensualistic poet. Sculpture and painting have less influence; yet still a sensualistic school of either may have a most deleterious effect upon the morals of an age. It is of the greatest importance that such a perversion of artistic genius should not take place. It should be impressed on all that their artistic powers are the gift of God, to be accounted for just as much as other gifts; to be used, as *all* gifts are to be used, to his honour; to be made to subserve the ends for which his kingdom has been established upon earth—the advance of holiness, the general elevation, refinement and spiritualisation of mankind, and the special purifying to himself of a peculiar people, zealous of good works.

HOMILIES BY VARIOUS AUTHORS.

Vers. 1—12.—*Bezaleel and Aholiab.* The calling of these two craftsmen for the work of the sanctuary, and the statement concerning Bezaleel that Jehovah had "filled him with the spirit of God, in wisdom, and in understanding, and in knowledge, and in all manner of workmanship" (ver. 3), suggest various important lessons. On the distinction of the terms—"wisdom," "understanding," "knowledge," see the exposition, and consult the valuable notes on Eph. i. 8, Col. i. 9, in the Bishop of Durham's Commentaries. The general moral is, that when God has any important work to be done, whether in Church or State, he will not fail to raise up, and in due time to "call by name," the individuals needed for the doing of it. The preparatory training school of these individuals may be far removed from the scene of their future labours. Bezaleel and Aholiab were trained in Egypt. Cf. what is said in "From Log Cabin to White House" of Presidents Lincoln and Garfield, of the United States—"Both of these statesmen were born in log-cabins, built by their fathers, in the wilderness, for family homes. Both were poor as mortals can well be. Both were born with talents of the highest order; but neither enjoyed early advantages of schools and teachers . . . Both worked on a farm, chopped wood, and did whatever else was needful for a livelihood, when eight years of age," etc. Thus God gifts, trains, prepares men, without a hint of the use to which he means afterwards to put them. Till the event discloses it, the honour in reserve for them is kept a secret, even from themselves. The gem is polished in obscurity by the master's hand. Ultimately it is brought to light, and astonishes the beholders by the rare finish of its beauty. The tabernacle was built with the spoils of the Egyptians in more senses than one. More special lessons are the following—

I. ALL GIFTS ARE FROM GOD. Not simply gifts of intellect, of oratory, of holiness, of spiritual understanding, but gifts of every kind, from the highest to the lowest. Grace, in the case of Bezaleel, Aholiab, and their fellow-craftsmen, proceeded on a basis of natural endowment. Cf. ver. 6—"into the hearts of *all that are wise hearted* I have put wisdom." Skill in handicraft is a species of mental excellence, and deserves the name "wisdom." It, also, is from God. So with *all* natural talents; with, *e.g.*, the poetic gift; gifts of music, painting, sculpture, architecture; business faculty; the gift of statesmanship; the power to "think out inventions"; the skill of the artificer. This truth lies at the basis of the demand for a religious use of gifts.

II. NATURAL GIFTS ADMIT OF INDEFINITE EXPANSION AND ENLARGEMENT UNDER THE INFLUENCE OF GOD'S SPIRIT. The workers in the tabernacle were supernaturally assisted in their work. Nothing less than this is implied in the words—"And I have filled him with the spirit of God" (ver. 3); "into the hearts of all that are wise hearted I have put wisdom" (ver. 6). Grace aids nature. Regeneration is often accompanied by a mysterious and almost miraculous improvement in the powers of knowledge, so much so that, from a state of stolid imbecility, a person may be seen rising up and standing forth an acute argumentative pleader for the truth. (Cf. Dr. Wm. Anderson on "Regeneration," p. 37.) What holds good of the general invigoration of the powers, may be expected to apply in the particular. Dedication of self carries with it dedication of gifts. And if an individual dedicates to God any special gift which he possesses, seeking, whether in the Church or in pursuit of an ordinary calling, to use the same for God's glory, it will be his privilege to have it aided, strengthened, purified, and largely enhanced in its operations by the influences of Divine grace. The commonest work will thus be better done, if done in the spirit of prayer. And so with the noblest. Milton speaks of his great epic as a work " not to be raised from the heat of youth, or the vapours of wine, like that which flows at waste from the pen of some vulgar amourist or the trencher-fury of a rhyming parasite—nor to be obtained by invocation of Dame Memory and her siren daughter, but by devout prayer to that Eternal Spirit who can enrich with all utterance and knowledge, and sends out his seraphim, with the hallowed fire of his altar, to touch and purify the lips of whom he pleases."

III. RELIGION SANCTIFIES LABOUR. The Bible is a text-book of instruction on the dignity of labour. It has no sympathy with the contemptible foppishness which looks on labour as degrading. It includes labour in religion. It sees in the occupation of the humblest handicraftsman the exercise of a Divine gift. The good man who, whether he eats or drinks, or whatsoever he does, does all to the glory of God (1 Cor. x. 31) does not demean himself by an honest calling, but transfigures his calling into part of his service to his Maker. In his case, *laborare est orare.* The shewbread on the table in the sanctuary was a recognition of the sacredness of labour. It had as one of its meanings the dedication to God of the exercise of the calling by which Israel won its daily bread. So *manual* labour was sanctified to God in the making of the tabernacle. But it was reserved for Christianity to give the crowning proof of the dignity of labour by showing it ennobled and glorified in the person of its Founder. The fathers of the Christian Church, in contrast with the Greeks and Romans, who looked on artisans and barbarians with contemptuous disgust, preached in their noblest tones the duty and dignity of honourable toil. "The proudest bishops were not ashamed to dig; a Benedict worked six hours a day with hoe and spade; a Becket helped regularly to reap the fields. The monks at once practised labour, and ennobled and protected it. The towns and the middle classes grew up under their shelter. *Laborare est orare* became the motto of Christian life" (Farrar; cf. Lecky, "History of Rationalism," vol. ii. p. 261).

IV. THE HIGHEST USE OF GIFTS IS TO DEDICATE THEM TO THE SERVICE OF GOD IN THE WORK OF HIS CHURCH. Transformed by grace, and employed in the service of religion, gifts become graces—" Charismata." All labour, all gifts, admit of being thus devoted. The handicrafts can still bring their tribute to God, if in no higher way, in the erection of places for his worship. Art can labour in the adornment of the sanctuary (cf. Is. lx. 13). The service of praise affords scope for the utilisation of gifts of music, vocal and instrumental. There is need for care lest art, ministering to the worship of God, should overpower devotion; but, considered in itself, there need be no jealousy of the introduction of the tasteful and beautiful into God's service. It is meet that the Giver of gifts should be served with the best our gifts can yield. Earthly callings may minister to God's kingdom in another way, by bringing of their lawful gains and laying them at Christ's feet. There is, besides, the private consecration of gifts to God, as in the case of Dorcas, making coats and garments for the poor (Acts ix. 39), or as in the case of a Miss Havergal, or an Ira D. Sankey, consecrating to God a gift of song. Minor lessons taught are—(1) Gifts are not all alike, yet God can use all. (2) Some are made to lead, others to serve and follow, in the work of God's kingdom. We glorify God most when unambitiously content to fill our *own* place; when not envious of the greater gifts of others. The humblest is needed. Bezaleel could ill have dispensed with the artificers; Aholiab, with the needle-workers. They in turn needed the master minds to direct *them.* There should be no jealousy among those engaged in the same work (cf. 1 Cor. xii.). (3) Diversity of gifts gives rise to division of labour. (4) Bezaleel and Aholiab, though of different tribes (Judah and Dan), wrought together as friends, were not opposed as rivals. What kept out the spirit of rivalry was the consciousness that both were working in a sacred cause, and for God's glory, not their own. The feeling that we are working for Christ should keep down dissensions among Christians.—J. O.

EXPOSITION.

Vers. 12—17.—THE PENALTY FOR NOT OBSERVING THE SABBATH. Various reasons have been given for this recurrence to the sanctity of the sabbath. Kurtz connects it with the giving of the two tables, in which " the law of the sabbath held a particularly prominent place." Kalisch and others view it rather as the sequel to the directions concerning the tabernacle, and as designed to teach "that the holy service in the tabernacle could not supersede the observance of the sabbath, but derived from that observance its true value." A third set of critics regard the recurrence to the subject as purely practical—being intended to meet an immediate danger—that of the people, in their zeal to erect the tabernacle, setting sabbath observance at nought. (So Jarchi, Aben-Ezra, Clark, Rosenmüller, Canon Cook, and others.) It is to be observed, however, that the present passage is not a mere repetition. It adds to former notices (ch. xx. 8—11; xxiii. 12) two new points :—1. That the sabbath was to be a sign between God and Israel, a "distinguishing badge," a "sacramental bond" (Cook); and 2. That its desecration was to be punished with death (ver. 15). These were supplementary points of so much importance as to furnish ample reason against their announcement being delayed.

Ver. 13.—**Verily.** Rosenmüller suggests, "Nevertheless." But there is no need for any change. **It is a sign.** Hitherto circumcision had been the only visible "sign" that the Israelites were under a special covenant with God—his people, bound to him by special ties (Gen. xvii. 9—14; Acts vii. 8). The adoption of circumcision by the Egyptians and other nations (Herod. ii. 104) had produced the effect that this "sign" was no longer distinguishing. It might be still "a sign of profession"; but it had ceased to be "a mark of difference"; and some other mark was therefore needed. Such the observance of the sabbath by entire abstinence from servile work became. No other nation adopted it. It continued to Roman times the mark and badge of a Jew (Juv. *Sat.* vi. 159; xiv. 96). **That ye may know,** etc. By keeping the sabbath day as a day of holy rest the Israelites would know—

i.e., would realise severally in their own persons, that God was their sanctifier. Sanctification would be the fruit of their obedience.

Ver. 14.—**Every one that defileth it shall surely be put to death.** To defile the sabbath was to do any unnecessary servile work upon it. Works of mercy, works of necessity, and works connected with religious observance were not prohibited. (See Matt. xii. 1—7; 10—12.) The penalty of death for breaking the sabbath seems to moderns over-severe; but the erection of sabbath-observance into *the* special sacramental sign that Israel was in covenant with God made non-observance an offence of the gravest character. The man who broke the sabbath destroyed, so far as in him lay, the entire covenant between God and his people—not only broke it, but annulled it, and threw Israel out of covenant. Hence, when the sin was committed, no hesitation was felt in carrying out the law. (See Numb xv. 32—36.)

Ver. 15.—**The sabbath of rest.** Rather, "*a* sabbath." There were other sabbaths besides that of the seventh day (ch. xxiii. 11; Lev. xxv. 2—12; &c.). By the expression, "a sabbath of rest"—literally, "a rest of resting"—the idea of completeness is given. Perhaps the best translation would be—" in the seventh is complete rest."

Ver. 16.—**For a perpetual covenant.** The sabbath is itself a covenant—*i.e.*, a part of the covenant between God and Israel (ch. xxiv. 4)—and it is, also, a sign of covenant—*i.e.*, a perceptible indication that the nation has entered into a special agreement with God, and undertaken the observance of special laws.

Ver. 17.—**It is a sign.** See above, ver. 13. **For in six days the Lord made heaven and earth.** See the comment on ch. xx. 11. **And was refreshed.** Literally, "and took breath." The metaphor is a bold one, but not bolder than others which occur in holy scripture (Ps. xliv. 23; lxxviii. 65). It does but carry out a little further the idea implied in God's "resting." We cannot speak of any of God's acts or attributes without anthropomorphisms.

HOMILETICS.

Vers. 13—17.—*Covenant signs.* To each covenant which he has made with man, God has attached some special sign or signs. And each sign has been significant, has set before the mind of those to whom it was given some great religious truth.

I. THE FIRST COVENANT SIGN WAS THE RAINBOW. God had destroyed by a deluge the whole human race, except eight persons. It pleased him, after this, to enter into a covenant with Noah and his sons (Gen. ix. 8, 9), and through them with the human race, that he would never bring such a destruction upon the world again (*ib.* 11). Of this covenant he appointed the rainbow to be the sign, symbolising by its brightness and beauty his own mercy (*ib.* 14—17). Here the religious truth taught and impressed by the sign was that precious one, that God is not only a just, but also a merciful God.

II. The second covenant sign was circumcision. When God selected Abraham out of the entire mass of mankind to be the progenitor of the chosen race and of him especially in whom all the families of the earth should be blessed, and entered into a covenant with him, it was in these words—"Thou shalt keep my covenant, thou and thy seed after thee in their generations—this is my covenant which ye shall keep between me and you, and thy seed after thee, every man child among you shall be circumcised" (Gen. xvii. 9, 10). Hence the covenant itself was called "the covenant of circumcision" (Acts vii. 8). This rite of initiation, the covenant sign of the Abrahamic dispensation, shadowed forth the great truth that man has an impurity of nature, which must be put away before he can be brought near to God and received into his full favour.

III. The third covenant sign was the sabbath. Its institution to be a covenant sign is set forth in the words, "Verily, my sabbaths ye shall keep, for it is a sign between me and you throughout your generations" (Ex. xxxi. 13). It witnessed to the truth that God requires distinct and open acknowledgment at the hands of men, and not only so, but material worship at stated times, the least that will content him being one day in seven. The nations, when they served him at all (Acts x. 35), served him irregularly. They knew nothing of a definite day, or a formal apportionment of time, for his service. By the institution of the Sabbath the Israelites were taught, and through them the world, that God is interested in man, claims his thoughts, sets a value on his worship, and will not be satisfied with mere occasional acknowledgment, but demands that a fixed proportion of our time shall be dedicated to his worship exclusively.

IV. Other covenant signs. No further covenant signs were given until our Lord came upon earth. Then two were instituted in the Sacraments. Baptism taught the same truth as circumcision—the need of putting away impurity; but taught it by a simpler rite, and one to which no exception could be taken. The Lord's Supper taught a new truth, the necessity of reconciliation through the death and atoning blood of Christ. It witnessed to the certain fact that man cannot save himself, cannot atone for his own sins, but needs a mediator, a redeemer, an atoner, to make satisfaction for him.

HOMILIES BY VARIOUS AUTHORS.

Vers. 12—18.—*The Sabbath.* If this prohibition to work upon the Sabbath is introduced, as probably it is, lest the people, in their zeal for the service of the sanctuary, should be tempted to infringe upon the holy day, it has certain obvious sides of instruction turned towards ourselves. We cannot but see in it *the high honour which God puts upon his Sabbath.* 1. It is the one command of the Decalogue to which reference is made in the conclusion of this series of instructions. This implies its great importance. It shows that, in God's esteem, the observance of the Sabbath was intimately bound up with the best interests of Israel. 2. The Sabbath is declared to be a *sign* between God and the Israelites. It was to be a memorial to future generations that Jehovah had made a covenant with the nation, and had sanctified them to himself. But its very selection for this purpose was a tribute to its importance. The reason of the selection could only be that the Sabbath was in itself a boon of the highest kind to Israel, and had important bearings on the state of morals and religion. A well- or ill-spent Sabbath, as all history shows, has much to do with the character both of the individual and of the community. The Sabbath, further, is a "sign" in this respect, that it is at once a means for the promotion of true religion, and a *test* or *indication* of its presence. A disregard of Divine authority shows itself in nothing more readily than in a disposition to break in upon the day of rest—to take from it its sacred character. 3. The Sabbath is not to be infringed upon, even for the work of the tabernacle. There was no such excessive haste, no such imperative call, for the sanctuary being finished, that the Sabbath needed to be broken by the plying of handicrafts, in order to get it done. We are taught that even our zeal for God's work is not to be allowed to betray us into unnecessary infractions of the day of rest. , This is not, of course, to be applied to spiritual work, to afford an opportunity for which is one end of the giving of the Sabbath. 4. The breaker of the Sabbath was to be put to death. This was not too severe a punishment for the deliberate breaking of a law so repeatedly enforced, and the observance of which had been made by Jehovah a "sign" of the covenant between himself and Israel. Slight as the act seems, it was, in this case, a crime of a very flagrant order. It was punished as an act of treason. At the conclusion of these commands, God gave to Moses the two tables of testimony, "tables of stone, written with the finger of God." A symbol (1) of the perpetuity of the law, (2) of its want of power to regenerate (2 Cor. iii. 7).—J. O.

EXPOSITION.

Ver. 18.—THE TABLES OF TESTIMONY. It had been assumed, in the directions given for the construction of the ark, that God would give, in some material form, a document to be called "the testimony," which was to be laid up inside it (ch. xxv. 16). It is not too much to say that the tabernacle, with its various appurtenances, was constructed for this purpose; the rest of the tabernacle was designed with a view to the holy of holies—the holy of holies was designed as a receptacle for the ark—and the ark was designed as a receptacle for the tables of testimony. This section could, therefore, scarcely be concluded without some definite account of the document which was to give the ark and the tabernacle itself, its main significance.

Ver. 18.—**When he had made an end of communing.** Literally, "when he had finished speaking." **Two tables.** Rather, "*the* two tables"—*i.e.*, *the* tables promised when he went up into the mount (ch. xxiv. 12). **Of stone.** Stone was the ordinary material on which Egyptian documents were engraved, both at the time of the Exodus, and before and after. They were, however, for the most part, either inscribed upon the natural rock, or engraved on the walls of temples or tombs. Inscriptions upon slabs of stone are rare, more especially in the early times, and would scarcely have occurred to Moses himself. **Written with the finger of God**—*i.e.*, "inscribed supernaturally"—not cut by any human hand. Compare ch. xxxii. 16. It is idle to speculate on the exact mode of the Divine operation.

HOMILETICS.

Ver. 18.—*The Tables of Testimony* were in many respects like the document impressed upon them. For instance, they were—

I. OF STONE, AND THEREFORE ENDURING AND WELL NIGH IMPERISHABLE. Few things are more enduring than some kinds of stone. Inscriptions exist, engraved on stone, which are certainly anterior to Abraham. No remains in metal go back so far. Gold and silver are, comparatively speaking, soft. Iron corrodes. Steel was unknown at the period. The material selected to receive the moral law was as nearly indestructible as possible. The tables may still exist, and may one day be discovered under the mounds of Babylon, or in the bed of the Euphrates. The character of the material was thus in harmony with the contents of the tables, consisting, as they did, of laws whereof no jot or tittle shall pass away till the fulfilment of all things (Matt. v. 18).

II. WRITTEN WITH THE FINGER OF GOD. The stones had the laws engraved upon them by a Divine agency which is called "the finger of God." The laws themselves had been long previously written with the finger of God in the fleshly tables of men's hearts. The Divine power, which was competent to do the one, could no doubt with ease accomplish the other. The human heart is the most stubborn of all materials, and the most difficult to impress permanently.

III. TWO-FOLD. Twin tables, alike in the main, but inscribed differently. So was the law of the tables two-fold—containing (1) man's duty to God, and (2) his duty to his neighbour. It is uncertain how the Ten Commandments were divided between the two tables, but quite possible that the first four were written on one table, and the last six on the other. In that case the material division would have exactly corresponded to the spiritual.

IV. WRITTEN ON BOTH THEIR SIDES (ch. xxxii. 15). So the moral law—the law of the Decalogue—is written both within and without the human heart—presses externally upon men as a rule of right which they are constrained to obey, and approves itself to them from within, as one which the voice of conscience declares to be binding, apart from external sanction. The book seen in vision by Ezekiel (Ezek. ii. 9) was "written within and without" (*ib.* 10), like the tables; but its entire contents were "lamentation, and mourning, and woe." The moral law, as convincing us of sin, has a painful side; but it sustains as much as it alarms, and produces as much effort as mourning.

EXPOSITION.

CHAPTER XXXII.

Vers. 1—6.—THE IDOLATRY OF THE GOLDEN CALF. During the absence of Moses in Mount Sinai, an absence of nearly six weeks, the Israelites grew impatient, and regarding their leader as lost to them, and the Divine Presence which they had hitherto enjoyed as lost with him, insisted on having a symbol of that presence made for them, which should henceforth go in front of the host and so lead them on in their journeyings. It would seem that the pillar of the cloud, which had gone before them from Succoth to Sinai, was now removed from the camp, and resting upon the "mount" where Moses was (ch. xxiv. 15). Under these circumstances they wanted a visible tangible something, in which they could regard the Divine Presence as resting, and whereto they might offer worship and sacrifice (ver. 8). They therefore went to Aaron, whom Moses had bid them consult in any difficulty (ch. xxiv. 14), and requested him to "make them a god." Aaron had not the courage to meet this request with a plain negative. As Augustine and Theodoret conjecture with much probability, he sought to turn them from their purpose by asking them to give up those possessions which he conceived that they most valued—viz. the personal ornaments of their wives and children. But he had miscalculated the strength of their fanaticism. The people immediately complied — the ornaments were brought in—and Aaron was compelled, either to fly from his word, or to lend himself to the people's wishes. He did the latter. Either looking to Egypt for a pattern, or falling back on some old form of Syrian or Chaldæan idolatry (see the comment on ver. 4), he melted down the gold and cast it into the form of a calf. The "god" being thus made, an altar was built to it (ver. 5) and sacrifice offered (ver 6). Such was the condition of affairs when Moses, having just received the two tables of stone, was warned by God of what had occurred, and bidden to descend from Sinai.

Ver. 1.—**The people saw that Moses delayed to come down.** He had been absent, probably, above a month. It was the first day of their worship when he descended; and a week would suffice for the collection of the ornaments, the formation of the mould, and the casting of the idol. **Unto Aaron.** It is not clear why no mention is made of Hur, who had been made co-regent with Aaron (ch. xxiv. 14); but perhaps Aaron was known to be the weaker of the two. **Up, make us gods.** Most moderns translate " a god." But the word is vague, and the speakers did not themselves perhaps care whether one idol was made or more. **Which shall go before us.** The Israelites were apparently tired of their long delay at Sinai, and were anxious to proceed upon their journey. They wanted a visible god at their head, to give them confidence and courage. Compare 1 Sam. iv. 3—8. **We wot not what is become of him.** He might, they thought, be dead—he might have returned to Egypt—he might be going to stay always with God in the mount which they did not dare to approach. At any rate, he was lost to them, and they might never see him again.

Ver. 2.—**Break off.** " Take off " would perhaps be a better translation. The ear-rings would not require any breaking. They were *penannular*, and could be removed by a smart pull. **Your wives, your sons, and your daughters.** See the comment on ch. iii. 22. It is implied that the men did not wear ear-rings. At an earlier date the household of Jacob, chiefly men, had worn them (Gen. xxxv. 4).

Ver. 3.—**All the people broke off the golden ear-rings.** Thus, as is supposed, disappointing Aaron, who had counted on the refusal of the women to part with their finery, and the reluctance of the men to compel them. Had ear-rings been still regarded as amulets (Gen. l. s. c.) it is not likely that they would have been so readily given up.

Ver. 4.—**And fashioned it with a graving tool.** Rather, "and bound it (the gold) in a bag." Compare 2 Kings v. 23, where the same two Hebrew words occur in the same sense. It is impossible to extract from the original the sense given in the Authorised Version, since the simple copula *vau* cannot mean " after." When two verbs in the same tense are conjoined by *vau* " and," the two actions must be simultaneous, or the latter follow the former. But the calf cannot have been graven first, and then molten. It is objected to the rendering, " he bound it in a bag," that that action is so trivial that it would be superfluous to mention it (Keil). But it is quite consonant with the simplicity of Scripture to mention very trivial circumstances. The act of putting up in bags is mentioned both here and also in 2 Kings v. 23, and 2 Kings xii. 9. **They said.** The fashioners of the image said this. **These be thy gods.** Rather, " This is thy God." Why Aaron selected the form of the calf as that which he would present to the Israelites to receive their worship, has been generally explained by supposing that his thoughts reverted to Egypt, and found in the Apis of Memphis or the Mnevis of Heliopolis the pattern which he thought it best to follow. But there are several objections to this view. 1. The Egyptian gods had just been discredited by their powerlessness being manifested—it was an odd time at which to fly to them. 2. Apis and Mnevis were not molten calves, but live bulls. If the design had been to revert to Egypt, would not a living animal have been selected? 3. The calf when made was not viewed as an image of any Egyptian god, but as a representation of Jehovah (ver. 5). 4. The Israelites are never taxed with having worshipped the idols of Egypt anywhere else than in Egypt (Josh. xxiv. 14; Ezek. xx. 8; xxiii. 3). To us it seems probable that Aaron reverted to an earlier period than the time of the sojourn in Egypt, that he went back to those " gods on the other side of the flood," which Joshua warned the Israelites some sixty years later, to " put away " (Josh. l. s. c.). The subject is one too large for discussion here; but may not the winged and human-headed bull, which was the emblem of divine power from a very early date in Babylon, have retained a place in the recollections of the people in all their wanderings, and have formed a portion of their religious symbolism? May it not have been this conception which lay at the root of the cherubic forms, and the revival of which now seemed to Aaron the smallest departure from pure monotheism with which the people would be contented?

Ver. 5.—**He built an altar before it.** Aaron thus proceeded to " follow a multitude to evil" (ch. xxiii. 2), and encouraged the idolatry which he felt himself powerless to restrain. Still, he did not intend that the people should drift away from the worship of Jehovah, or view the calf as anything but a symbol of him. He therefore **made proclamation and said, Tomorrow is a feast to the Lord** (literally, " to Jehovah").

Ver. 6.—**They rose up early on the morrow.** The people were like a child with a new toy. They could scarcely sleep for thinking of it. So, as soon as it was day, they left their beds, and hastened to begin the new worship **Burnt offerings and peace offerings.** It is evident that both of these were customary forms of sacrifice—neither of them first introduced by the Law, which had not—except so far as the " Book of the Covenant " was concerned—been promulgated. Compare Jethro's offerings (ch. xviii. 12). **The people sat down to eat and drink.** A feast almost always followed upon a sacrifice, only certain portions of the victim being commonly burnt, while the rest was consumed by the offerers. See the comment on ch. xviii. 12. **And rose up to play.** This " play " was scarcely of a harmless kind. The sensualism of idol-worship constantly led on to sensuality; and the feasts upon idol-sacrifices terminated in profligate orgies of a nature which cannot be described. See the application of the passage by St. Paul in the First Epistle to the Corinthians (x 7), and compare verse 25

HOMILETICS.

Vers. 1—6.—*The hankering after idols, and its consequences.* There is a war ever going on in human nature between the flesh and the spirit (Rom. vii. 23; viii. 1—13). The two are " contrary the one to the other." From the time of their leaving Egypt, the Israelites had been leading a spiritual life, depending upon an unseen God—following his mandates—reposing under the sense of his protection. But the strain was too much for them. So long as they had Moses with them, to encourage them by his exhortations and support them by his good example, they managed to maintain this higher life, to " walk in the spirit," to " live by faith and not by sight." When he was gone, when he seemed to them lost, when they had no hope of seeing him again, the reaction set in. The flesh asserted itself. They had given way to idolatry in Egypt, and worshipped, in part, Egyptian gods, in part, " the gods which their fathers served on the other side of the flood " (Josh. xxiv. 14, 15); they had, no doubt, accompanied this worship with the licentiousness which both the Egyptians (Herod. ii. 60) and the Babylonians (*ib.* i. 199) made a part of their religion. Now the recollection of these things recurred to them, their desires became inflamed—the flesh triumphed. The consequences were—

I. THAT THEY BROKE A PLAIN COMMAND OF GOD, AND ONE TO WHICH THEY HAD RECENTLY PLEDGED THEMSELVES. "All the words which the Lord hath said," they had declared "we will do" (ch. xxiv. 3); and among these "words" was the plain one—"Thou shalt not make to thyself any graven image, nor the likeness of anything that is in heaven above, or in the earth beneath, or in the water under the earth; thou shalt not bow down thyself to them, nor serve them." Nevertheless they required Aaron to make them a material god, and it was no sooner made than they hastened to worship it with burnt-offerings and other sacrifices.

II. THAT THEY PROCEEDED TO BREAK THE MORAL LAW WRITTEN IN THEIR HEARTS, AND LATELY REINFORCED BY THE PLAIN PROHIBITION OF THE SEVENTH COMMANDMENT. "They sat down to eat and drink, and *rose up to play*." They engaged in licentious dancing (ver. 19), and perhaps laid aside some of their usual garments (ver. 25). They turned a worship, which they still pretended to render to Jehovah (ver. 5) into an orgy. If they did not proceed to the lengths of completed sin, they entered upon the slippery path which, almost of necessity, leads to it. By this conduct they so provoked God—

III. THAT THEY RAN THE RISK OF BEING SWEPT AWAY FROM THE EARTH. A sentence of death was at first pronounced against the whole people (ver. 10), and would infallibly have taken effect, had not Moses interceded, and by his intercession prevailed. Universal apostasy deserved universal destruction. There is no reason to believe that the execution of the sentence pronounced would have been stayed, but for the expostulation and the prayer recorded in verses 11—13.

IV. THAT THEY ACTUALLY BROUGHT UPON THEMSELVES A HEAVY PUNISHMENT. The immediate slaughter of three thousand was required to purge the offence (ver. 28). The sin was further visited upon the offenders subsequently (see comment on ver. 34). Some were, on account of it, "blotted out of God's book" (ver. 33). Christians should take warning, and not, when they have once begun "living after the Spirit," fall back and "live after the flesh" (Rom. viii. 13). There are still in the world numerous tempting idolatries. We may hanker after the "lusts of the flesh," or "of the eye"—we may weary of the strain upon our nature which the spiritual life imposes—we may long to exchange the high and rare atmosphere in which we have for a while with difficulty sustained ourselves, for the lower region where we shall breathe more easily. But we must control our inclinations. To draw back is to incur a terrible danger—no less a one than "the perdition of our souls." It were better "not to have known the way of righteousness," or walked in it for a time, "than, after we have known it," and walked in it, "to turn from the holy commandment delivered unto us" (1 Pet. ii. 21).

HOMILIES BY VARIOUS AUTHORS.

Vers. 1—6.—*The Golden Calf.* I. THE PEOPLE'S REQUEST TO AARON. 1. *The cause of the request.* There are really two causes to be considered here, first, a cause of which they were conscious, and then, secondly, a deeper cause of which they were not conscious. The delay of Moses to return was the reason they put forward. We must do them the justice of noticing that they seem to have waited till the forty days were well-nigh expired before preferring their request; and an absence of forty days was inexplicable to minds as yet so spiritually darkened and benumbed as those of the majority of the people. What he could have to do, and how he could live so long, away up on a barren mountain, was beyond their power of imagination. Moses was given up just as a ship is given up when it has not been heard of for many days after the reasonable period of the voyage. It was not a case of being out of sight, out of mind; he had been a great deal in mind, and the general conclusion was that in some mysterious way he had vanished altogether. But there is also the deeper reason of the request to be found in the people's continued ignorance of the real hold which Jehovah had upon them, and the sort of future towards which he would have them look. Their action here was founded not on what they knew, but emphatically on what they did not know. They could not say, "Moses is dead," or "he has forsaken us." They could only say, "We wot not what is become of him." So far as outward circumstances were concerned, the people seem to have been in a state of comparative security and comfort. When

Moses went up into the mountain, he knew not how long he would have to wait; that was not for him or Aaron or any man to know. But however long he was to be away, all due provision had been made for the people's welfare. The daily morning manna was there; and Aaron and Hur were appointed to settle any disputes that might arise. There is no word of any external enemy approaching; there is no threatening of civil strife; there is not even a recurrence of murmuring after the fleshpots of Egypt. All that was needed was quiet waiting on the part of the people; if they had waited forty months instead of forty days, there would have been nothing to cause reasonable astonishment; for Jehovah and not man is the lord of times and seasons. 2. *The request itself.* There is a certain unexpectedness in this request. Who is it that is missing? Moses, the visible leader, "the man that brought us up out of the land of Egypt." Hence we might suppose the first feeling of the people would be to put some one in Moses' place; even as later they said, "Let us make a captain, and let us return into Egypt" (Num. xiv. 4). But instead of this their cry to Aaron is, "Make us gods." How little did Moses expect, when he put Aaron to be counsellor of the people in his absence, that it was for image-worship they would seek his help! And yet the more we ponder, the more we shall be led to feel that this was just the kind of request that might be expected from the people. Their ancestors, Abraham, Isaac and Jacob believed in the invisible Jehovah; but faith in the invisible will not go down from generation to generation, as if it were a blood quality. The God of Abraham was one whom, though Abraham could not see, he could hear as speaking with most miraculous organ. But these people at Sinai wanted above all things a god whom they could see, even though it was but a lifeless, sightless, voiceless image. Great is the mystery of idolatry. How men have come to bow down to stocks and stones is not a question to be dismissed with a few contemptuous words. These idolatrous Israelites were seeking satisfaction for a desire of the heart as imperious in its own way as bodily hunger and thirst. They wanted something to be a centre of worship and religious observances in general, and the quickest way seemed to fabricate such a centre by the making of gods. Whereas, if they had only been patient and trustful and waited for Moses, they would have found that, even by the very absence of Moses, God himself was providing for the worship of the people. We have here another illustration of the frequent follies of popular decisions. The greatest thing that required to be done for these Israelites was the thing that needed to be done *in them.*

II. AARON'S COMPLIANCE WITH THE REQUEST. He shewed great readiness in falling in with the request; and it has been suggested that his readiness was only in appearance, and that he hoped the women would refuse to surrender their cherished ornaments, thus making the construction of a suitable image impossible. It may have been so; but why should we not think that Aaron may have been as deeply infected with the idolatrous spirit as any of his brother Israelites? There is everything to indicate that he went about the execution of the request with cordiality and gratification. And it must not be forgotten that in the midst of all his forgetfulness of the command against image-worship, he evidently did not think of himself as forsaking Jehovah. When the image and the altar were ready, it was to Jehovah he proclaimed the feast. What Aaron and the people along with him had yet to learn was that Jehovah was not to be served by will-worship or by a copy of the rites observed in honouring the gods of other nations. Thus all unconsciously, Israel demonstrated how needful were the patterns given in the mount. The feast to Jehovah, indicated in ver. 6, was nothing but an excuse for the most reckless and degrading self-indulgence. How different from the ideal of those solemn seasons which Jehovah himself in due time prescribed; seasons which were meant to lift the people above their common life into a more hearty appreciation of the Divine presence, goodness and favour, and thus lead them into joys worthy of the true people of God.—Y.

Vers. 1—7.—*The sin of the golden calf.* Disastrous effects followed in the camp of Israel on the withdrawal of Moses to the mount. Moved as by a common impulse, the people "gathered themselves together," and demanded of Aaron that he should make them "a god," *i.e.* an idol, that it might go—be carried in procession—before them (cf. Amos v. 26). It was a case of "hand joined in hand" to do iniquity (Prov. xi. 21). Many, doubtless, looked on the movement with dismay and horror (cf. ver. 26); but their voices were drowned in the general clamour. The "lewd fellows of the baser sort" (Acts xvii. 5) had, for the moment, the upper hand in the host, and swept all before them. Intimidated by the show of violence, Aaron weakly acceded to the people's request. The whole incident strikingly illustrates the commanding space which must have been filled in the camp of Israel by the personality of Moses, and affords some measure of the turbulent and refractory dispositions of the multitude whom ordinarily he had to deal with. It sheds light, also, on the greatness of Moses' character, set as that is in contrast with the weakness and irresolution exhibited by Aaron. Consider—

I. THE PEOPLE'S TRIAL (ver. 1). Every situation in which we can be placed has its elements of trial. These are purposely mingled with our lot (1) that dispositions may be tested, and (2) that life may be to us in fact, what it is needful that it should be for the proper development of character, viz. a succession of probations. The trial of the Israelites consisted: 1. In *the delay in the return of Moses.* Moses had disappeared in the mountain. Weeks had passed without his return. It had not been told the people how long his absence was to last. This constituted a trial of faith and patience. It gave colour to the allegation that Moses had perished—that he had gone from them for ever. Cf. what is said in Luke xii. 37—49 of the uncertainty left to rest upon the time of the Lord's second advent. Faith has its trial here also. Because Christ's coming is delayed, there are those who would fain persuade themselves that he will not return at all (2 Pet. iii. 4). 2. In *the scope given by his absence for the manifestation of character.* On this, again, compare Luke xii. 37—49. It was the first time since the departure from Egypt that the people had been left much to themselves. Hitherto, Moses had always been with them. His presence had been a check on their wayward and licentious tendencies. His firm rule repressed disorders. Whatever inclinations some of them may have felt for a revival of the religious orgies, to which, perhaps, they had been accustomed in Egypt, they had not ventured, with Moses in the camp, to give their desires publicity. The withdrawal of the lawgiver's presence, accordingly, so soon after the conclusion of the covenant, was plainly of the nature of a trial. It removed the curb. It left room for the display of character. It tested the sincerity of recent professions. It showed how the people were disposed to conduct themselves when the tight rein, which had hitherto kept them in, had been a little slackened. It tested, in short, whether there were really a heart in them to keep all God's commandments always (Deut. v. 29). Alas! that in the hour of their trial, when so splendid an opportunity was given them of testifying their allegiance, their failure should have been so humiliating and complete.

II. THE PEOPLE'S SIN. Note—1. *The sin itself.* They had made for them "a molten calf" (ver. 4), which, forthwith, they proceeded to worship with every species of disgraceful revelry (ver. 6). The steps in the sin are noted in the narrative. (1) They approached Aaron with a demand to make them "a god." The light, irreverent way in which, in connection with this demand, they speak of their former leader—"As for this Moses, the man that brought us up out of the land of Egypt, we wot not what is become of him" (ver. 1)—betrays an extraordinary levity, ingratitude, and callousness of nature. (2) They stripped themselves of their ornaments of gold for the making of the "god" (ver. 3). They did this gladly. People, as a rule, spend freely on their vices. They are not so ready to part with their valuables for the service of Jehovah. (3) They mixed up their calf worship with the service of the true God. On the supposed connection with the ox- and calf-worship of Egypt, see the exposition. The calf made by Aaron was evidently intended as a symbol of Jehovah (ver. 4). The result was an extraordinary piece of syncretism. An altar was built before the calf, and due honours were paid to it as the god which had brought Israel out of Egypt (vers. 4, 5). A feast was proclaimed to Jehovah (ver. 5). When the morrow came, the people "offered burnt offerings, and brought peace offerings," only, however, to engraft on the sacrificial festivities the rites of the filthiest heathen worships (ver. 6; cf. ver. 25). It was their own passions which they sought to gratify; but, in gratifying them, they still endeavoured to keep up the semblance of service of the revealed God. Strange that the wicked should like, if possible, to get the cloak of religion even for their vices. But light and darkness will not mingle. The first requirement in worship is obedience. "To obey is better than sacrifice, and to hearken than the fat of rams" (1 Sam. xv. 22). "The sacrifice of the wicked is an abomination to the Lord" (Prov. xv. 8). It was monstrous to propose to worship the spiritual Jehovah, who had expressly forbidden the use of graven images in his service, under the symbol of a *calf*, albeit the idol was of gold. It was worse than monstrous, it was hideous, to employ the name of the Holy One to cover the shameless and revolting orgies with which their calf-worship was associated. (4) They were *eager* in this worship. They rose up early in the morning to engage in it (ver. 6). Would that God's people were as eager in *his* service as these servants of Belial were in the service of their idol! 2. *The sin in its generic character.* The sin at Sinai was a case (1) of sense reasserting its supremacy over faith. "As for this Moses, we wot not what has become of him" (ver. 1). (2) Of carnal tendencies regaining the ascendancy over temporary religious impressions. (3) Of engrained evil habits resuming their sway after having been for a time forcibly kept in check. The incident shows that nothing short of a thorough regeneration, of a radical change of heart, can be relied on to keep men in the way of good. It is the *heart* that needs renewal. David seized the matter at the root when he was led to pray, "Create in me a clean heart" etc. (Ps. li. 10). It was the want of this thorough renewal which was the bane of Israel (Deut. xxxi. 27—30). 3. *Aggravations of the sin.* The circumstances under which the sin was committed added greatly to its enormity. (1) It was a sin committed immediately after solemn covenant with God. The transactions recorded in ch. xxiv. were not yet forty days old. The people had literally heard God speaking to them. They had acknowledged the solemnity of the situation by entreating Moses to act as mediator. They had formally, and under awful impressions of God's majesty, pledged themselves to life-long obedience. Yet within this brief space of time, they had thrown off all restraints, and violated one of the main stipulations of their agreement. A more flagrant act of impiety it would be difficult to imagine. (2) It was a sin committed while Moses was still in the mount transacting for them. He had gone to receive the tables of the law. He had been detained to receive instructions for the making of the sanctuary—that God might dwell among them. A solemn time, truly! While it lasted, the people might surely have been depended on to conduct themselves with at least ordinary propriety. Instead of this, witness their mad gambols round their calf. The very time when, of all others, their frame of mind ought to have been devout, sober, prayerful, was the time chosen for the perpetration of this great iniquity.

III. Aaron's share in the transgression. This, it is to be noted, the narrative makes no attempt to conceal. It tells the story with perfect impartiality. The Bible, like its author, is without respect of persons. If Aaron leads the people astray, he must, like others, submit to have the truth told about him. This is not the way of ordinary biographies, but it is the way of Scripture. It is one mark of its inspiration. It is a guarantee of its historic truthfulness. The conduct of Aaron cannot be justified; but suggestions may be offered which help to render intelligible. 1. *Aaron was placed in a situation in which it was very difficult to know exactly what to do.* A mob confronted him, evidently bent on gratifying its dangerous humour. Its demand was peremptory. To resist its will was to run the risk of being stoned. The temptation which, in these circumstances, naturally presented itself to a timid mind, and to which Aaron yielded, was to put the people off, and endeavour to gain time by some show of concession. In the interval, Moses might return, and the difficulty would be solved. See the mistake of this policy. It was (1) wrong. It involved a sacrifice of principle. It was temporising. (2) Weak. Had Aaron been brave enough to take a firm stand, even at the risk of losing his life for it, not improbably he might have crushed the movement in its bud. As it was, his sanction and example gave it an impetus which carried it beyond the possibility of being subsequently controlled. (3) Self-defeating. A temporising policy usually is. The favourable chance on which everything has been staked, does not turn up. Moses did *not* return, and Aaron, having yielded the preliminary point, found himself hopelessly committed to a bad cause. 2. *Aaron may have thought that by requiring the women of the camp to part with their personal ornaments, he was taking an effectual plan to prevent the movement from going further* (ver. 2). They might, he may have reasoned, be very willing to get gods, and yet not be willing to make this personal sacrifice to obtain them. If this was his idea, he was speedily undeceived. The gold ornaments came pouring in (ver. 3), and Aaron, committed by this act also, had no alternative but to proceed further. " He received them at their hands," etc. (ver. 4). 3. *Aaron may have thought that, of the two evils, it would be better to put himself at the head of the movement, and try to keep it within bounds, than to allow it to drift away, without any control whatever.* He may have argued that to allow himself to be stoned would not make matters better, but would make them greatly worse. On the other hand, by yielding a little, and placing himself at the head of the movement, he might at least succeed in checking its grosser abuses. This is a not uncommon opiate to conscience, in matters involving compromise of principle. It is the idea of the physician who humours a mad patient, in the hope of being able to retain some control over him. The step was a false one. Even with madmen, as wiser doctors tell us, the humouring policy is not the most judicious. With a mob, it is about the worst that could be adopted.

IV. GENERAL LESSONS. 1. The strength of evil propensities in human nature. 2. The fleetingness of religious impressions, if not accompanied by a true change of heart. 3. The degrading character of idolatry. Sin bestialises, and the bestial nature seeks a god in bestial form (cf. Rom. i. 21—32). " Men," says Xenophanes, " imagine that the gods are born, are clothed in our garments, and endowed with our form and figure. But if oxen or lions had hands, and could paint and fashion things as men do, they too would form the gods after their own similitude, horses making them like horses, and oxen like oxen." But we have seen that men also can fashion their gods in the similitude of oxen. " They that make them are like unto them" (Ps. cxv. 8). 4. Mammon-worship is a worship of the golden calf. Cf. Carlyle on " Hudson's Statue' (" Latter-Day Pamphlets ").—J. O.

EXPOSITION.

Vers. 7—14.—THE INTERCESSION OF MOSES. Moses, in Sinai, was so far removed from the camp, and the cloud so shut out his vision of it, that he had neither seen nor heard anything unusual, and was wholly ignorant of what had happened, until God declared it to him (vers. 7, 8). After declaring it, God announced his intention of destroying the people for their apostasy, and fulfilling his promise to Abraham by raising up a " great nation " out of the seed of Moses (ver. 10). No doubt this constituted a great trial of the prophet's character. He might, without sin, have acquiesced in the punishment of the people as deserved, and have accepted the promise made to himself as a fresh instance of God's goodness to him. There would have been nothing wrong in this; but it would have shown that he fell short of the heroic type, belonged to the ordinary run of mortals, was of the common " delf," not of " the precious porcelain of human clay." God's trial of him gave him an opportunity of rising above this ; and he responded to it. From the time that he reached full manhood (ch. ii. 11) he had cast in his lot with his nation ; he had been appointed their leader (ch. iii. 10); they had accepted him as such (ch. iv. 31) ; he had led them out of Egypt and brought them to Sinai; if he had looked coldly on them now, and readily separated his fate from theirs, he would have

been false to his past, and wanting in tenderness towards those who were at once his wards and his countrymen. His own glory naturally drew him one way, his affection for Israel the other. It is to his eternal honour that he chose the better part; declined to be put in Abraham's place, and generously interceded for his nation (vers. 11—13). He thereby placed himself among the heroes of humanity, and gave additional strength and dignity to his own character.

Ver. 7.—**Go, descend**—*i.e.*, " make haste to descend—do not tarry—there is need of thy immediate presence." **Thy people, which thou broughtest,** etc. Words calculated to awaken the tenderness between which and self-love the coming struggle was to be.

Ver. 8.—**They have turned aside quickly.** A few weeks have sufficed to make them forget their solemn pledges (ch. xix. 8 ; xxiv. 3), and fly in the face of a plain unmistakable commandment. **A molten calf.** In the contemptuous language of Holy Scripture when speaking of idols, such an emblematic figure as the Babylonion man-bull would be a mere " calf." That the figure made by Aaron is called always " a *molten* calf "—literally, " a calf of fusion "—disposes of the theory of Keil, that it was of carved wood covered with gold plates hammered on to it. **These be thy gods, which have brought thee.** Rather, " This is thy god, which has brought thee." The plural must be regarded as merely one of dignity.

Ver. 9. — **A stiffnecked people.** This

epithet, which becomes *epitheton usitatum*, is here used for the first time. It does not so much mean "obstinate" as "perverse"—like a horse that stiffens the neck when the driver pulls the right or left rein, and will not go the way he is wanted to go. (Compare ch. xxxiii. 3, 5; xxxiv. 9; Deut. ix. 6, 13; xxxi. 27; etc.)

Ver. 10.—**Now, therefore, let me alone.** This was not a command, but rather a suggestion; or, at any rate, it was a command not intended to compel obedience—like that of the angel to Jacob—"Let me go, for the day breaketh" (Gen. xxxii. 26). Moses was not intended to take the command as absolute. He did not do so—he "wrestled with God," like Jacob, and prevailed. **That my wrath may wax hot.** Literally, "and my wrath will wax hot." **I will make of thee a great nation.** (Compare Num. xiv. 12.) God could, of course, have multiplied the seed of Moses, as he had that of Abraham; but in that case all that had been as yet done would have gone for nought, and his purposes with respect to his "peculiar people" would have been put back six hundred years and more.

Vers. 11—13.—Moses has three pleas where-with he "wrestles with God:"—1. Israel is God's people, for whom he has done so much that surely he will not now destroy them, and so undo his own work. 2. Egypt will be triumphant if Israel is swept away, and will misapprehend the Divine action. 3. The promises made to Abraham (Gen. xv. 5; xvii. 2—6; etc.), Isaac (*ib.* xxvi. 4), and Jacob (*ib.* xxviii. 14; xxxv. 11), which had received a partial fulfilment, would seem to be revoked and withdrawn if the nation already formed were destroyed and a fresh start made.

Ver. 14.—**The Lord repented of the evil.** Changes of purpose are, of course, attributed to God by an "economy," or accommodation of the truth to human modes of speech and conception. "God is not a man that he should repent." He "knows the end from the beginning." When he threatened to destroy Israel, he knew that he would spare; but, as he communicated to Moses, first, his anger, and then, at a later period, his intention to spare, he is said to have "repented." The expression is an anthropomorphic one, like so many others, on which we have already commented. (See the comment on ch. ii. 24, 25; iii. 7, 8; xxxi. 17; etc.)

HOMILETICS.

Vers. 7—10.—*The anger of God.* God may well be angry when his people apostatise; and having recently professed entire submission to his will (ch. xix. 8; xxiv. 3), rebel suddenly, and cast his words behind their backs. God's anger against Israel was at this time intensified—

I. BY THEIR EXTREME INGRATITUDE. He had just delivered them by a series of stupendous miracles from a cruel bondage. He had brought them out of Egypt—he had divided the Red Sea before them, and led them through it—he had given them a complete victory over the Amalekites. He was supporting them day after day by a miraculous supply of food. He had condescended to enter into covenant with them, and to make them his "peculiar treasure"—"a kingdom of priests, and an holy nation" (ch. xix. 5, 6). He was further engaged in giving them a law which would place them far in advance of other nations, and render them the main source of life and light in a world of moral darkness and deadness. There had been no moment in their history when they were more bound by every consideration of duty, honour, and thankfulness to cling to Jehovah—yet, spite of all, they had rebelled and rushed into idolatry.

II. BY THE SUDDENNESS OF THEIR APOSTASY. "They have turned aside *quickly* out of the way," said the Almighty to Moses (ver. 8). A few weeks only had gone by since they had declared themselves God's willing servants—had entered into covenant with him, and promised to keep all his commandments. What had caused the sudden and complete change? There was nothing to account for it but the absence of Moses. But surely it might have been expected that their convictions would have had sufficient root to outlive the disappearance of Moses for as long as six weeks. The fact, however, was otherwise. They were of those who had "no root in themselves"—and as soon as temptation came, they fell away. The remembrance of their old idolatries came upon them with a force that they had not strength to resist—and it happened unto them according to the true proverb: "The dog is turned to his own vomit again, and the sow that was washed to her wallowing in the mire" (2 Pet. ii. 22).

III. BY THEIR SINNING AGAINST ABUNDANT LIGHT. Until the delivery of the second commandment at Sinai, it might perhaps have been a doubtful point whether the worship of God under a material form was, or was not, offensive to him. But after that delivery, all doubt was removed. The bowing down to an image had been then and there declared an "iniquity," an offence to a "jealous God," which he would visit unto the third and fourth generation. Nor was this all. An express prohibition of the very act that Israel had now committed, had been put in the forefront of the "Book of the Covenant" which opens thus—"Ye have seen that I have talked with you from heaven—ye shall not make with me gods of silver, *neither shall ye make unto you gods of gold*" (ch. xx. 22, 23). It was impossible therefore that they should plead ignorance. Knowingly and wilfully they had transgressed a plain command of the Great God, whose power and glory had so lately been revealed to them. They had sinned in the full light of day. Christians in their manifold idolatries—of covetousness, lust, fashion-worship, etc.—are more ungrateful than even the Israelites, since they sin against One who has died to redeem them, and they sin against a still clearer light - the double light of a full revelation of God's will, and of a conscience enlightened by the Holy Ghost. God's wrath may well "wax hot against them, to consume them from the face of the earth."

Ver. 11—15.—*The intercession of Moses.* This intercession should be studied and laid to heart by all Christians, especially by Christian ministers, whose duty it is to "watch for the souls" of others, as "they that must give account." It was—

I. EARNEST AND IMPASSIONED. No feeble voice, no lukewarm, timid utterance, was heard in the words whereby the leader sought to save his people. Prayer, expostulation, almost reproach, sound in them. God is besought, urged, importuned, to grant the boon begged of him. The tone of Jacob's answer rings in them,—"I will not let thee go, except thou bless me" (Gen. xxxii. 26).

II. UNSELFISH, OR RATHER SELF-RENOUNCING. The promise, "I will make *of thee* a great nation," has evidently taken no hold of the unselfish nature of the prophet. He declines to give it a thought. God must keep his promises to Abraham, Isaac, and Jacob—not make a new promise, as if everything was now to begin afresh. The offer, which might have tempted any man, is simply set aside, as if it had not been made, or at any rate could not have been seriously meant; and the whole energy of the speaker concentrated on inducing God to spare his people.

III. WELL-REASONED. Three arguments are used, and each of them has real weight. (1) Israel is God's people—has been chosen, called, taken into covenant, protected and defended after a marvellous fashion. All this Divine effort would have been simply thrown away, if the announced purpose were carried out and Israel destroyed. God does not usually allow his plans to be baulked, his designs to remain unaccomplished. If he "has begun a good work," he (commonly) wills to "bring it to good effect." Will he not do so in this case? (2) Are the enemies of God to be allowed a triumph? Israel's destruction would afford to the Egyptians an ample field for scoffs, ridicule, self-glorification. Would God suffer this? (3) Promises had been made, with great solemnity ("Thou swarest by thine own self," ver. 13), to the patriarchs, Abraham, Isaac, and Jacob, that the "peculiar people" should spring from them. These might be kept in the letter, but would they be kept in the spirit, if all their descendants were now destroyed, except some three, and a new nation was created out of the descendants of Moses?

IV. EFFECTUAL. "The Lord repented of the evil, which he thought to do unto his people" (ver. 14). The intercession of Moses prevailed—the announced purpose was given up. God spared his people, though his anger against them continued; and they were punished in a different way (vers. 33—35).

HOMILIES BY VARIOUS AUTHORS.

Vers. 7—14.—*The wrath of Jehovah and the intercession of Moses.* I. JEHOVAH DESCRIBES TO MOSES THE APOSTASY OF ISRAEL. Jehovah is omniscient; even while spreading before Moses, with all elaboration, the patterns in the mount, his all-observant eye is equally on the doings of the people below. And now, just when Moses is expecting to be dismissed with his instructions for the people, he is fated to learn that they have proved themselves utterly unworthy of Jehovah's great designs. The thing described is an utter, shameless, and precipitate apostasy from Jehovah. Previous outbreaks of the sinful heart were as nothing compared to this. If it had only been the sin of a few, some half-secret departure from Jehovah confined to a corner of the camp; if there had been a prompt repudiation of it and punishment of it on the part of the great majority: then, indeed, Jehovah might have found cause even for rejoicing that the apostasy of the few had been occasion to prove the fidelity of the many. But alas! the transgression is general; there is a public adoption of the golden calf with worship and sacrifice. The idolatrous spirit has been shown in the completest and most demonstrative way. Idolatry, with its awful degradations and its fatal influences, must always be an abomination to God; but how peculiarly abominable when it rose in the midst of a people with whom God had been dealing with the tenderest compassion and the sublimest power! It is to be noticed that God calls special attention to the *quickness* of this apostasy. "They have turned aside *quickly* out of the way." The fact of course was that they had also been turned quickly *into that way*, and kept in it by a kind of external force. They might promise, and while they promised mean to keep the promise, but nature was too much for them; and as soon as the Divine constraint was in any way relaxed they returned to the old path. The impression Jehovah would make on the mind of his servant is that nothing can be expected from them.

II. Jehovah indicates to Moses THE RIGHTEOUS SEVERITY WITH WHICH HE PROPOSES TO TREAT ISRAEL (vers. 9, 10). We have to think here not only of the words of Jehovah, but also of the attitude of Moses, which seems to be indicated by these words. Even before Moses puts in his earnest intercession, we have a hint of what is in his heart. Jehovah says, "Let me alone;" as one man, about to strike another, might speak to some third person stepping between to intercept the blow. In the speaking of Jehovah's words there must have been an indication of wrath, such as of course cannot be conveyed by the mere words themselves. And what, indeed, could Jehovah do, but give an unmistakable expression of his wrath with such an outbreak of human unrighteousness as is found in idolatry? No doubt there is great difficulty in understanding such expressions as those of Jehovah here. When we remember the low estate of the Israelites spiritually, and the infecting circumstances in which they had grown up, it seems hardly just to reproach them for their lapse into idolatry. But then we must bear in mind that the great object of the narrative here is to show how Jehovah cannot bear sin. The thing to be considered first of all is, not *how* these Israelites became idolaters, but the sad and stubborn fact that they seemed inveterate idolaters. Such a decided manifestation of idolatry as the one here revealed, when it came to the knowledge of Jehovah, was like a spark falling into the midst of gunpowder. It matters not how such a spark may be kindled; it produces an explosion the moment it touches the powder. The wrath of God must be revealed against all ungodliness and unrighteousness of men. Yet doubt not that the God who spoke here in such wrath and threatening *loved these Israelites in the midst of their apostasy*. But it was not possible in one and the same moment, and from one and the same voice, to make equally evident love for the benighted apostate himself, and wrath because of the evil that was so intimately mixed with his nature. On such an occasion it became God to give a direct and emphatic expression of wrath from his own lips, leaving his love and pity to be known indirectly through the intercession of his servant Moses. When Jehovah is angry, it is then we need most of all to remember that love is the great power in his nature.

III. Jehovah further indicates A CERTAIN TEMPTING POSSIBILITY TO MOSES. "I will make of thee a great nation." Thus we see how the word of Jehovah is made to serve two purposes. It both expresses the fulness of wrath with an apostate people, and at the same time puts a cherished servant upon a most effectual trial of his magnanimity and mediatorial unselfishness. Thus this proposition of Jehovah comes in most beautifully to emphasise the simplicity and purity of the feeling of Moses in his subsequent mediation. And though Moses makes no reference to this proposition, it is well to be enabled to see how little hold any self-seeking thoughts took of his mind.

IV. THE REPLY OF MOSES HAS NOW TO BE CONSIDERED. Not that we need stay to investigate the merits of the considerations which Moses here puts forward. He could only speak of things according as they appeared to him. We know, looking at these same things in the light of the New Testament, that even if God had destroyed these people as at first he hinted, his promises would not therefore have been nullified. The temporal destruction of a single generation of men, however perplexing it might have seemed at the time, would afterwards have been seen as neither any hindrance in the fulfilment of God's purposes, nor any dimming of the brightness of his glory. Be it remembered that these same people whom God brought out with great power and a mighty hand, yet nevertheless perished in the wilderness. Spared this time, they were in due season cut down as cumberers of the ground. And as to any scornful words the Egyptians might speak, God's glory was not at the mercy of their tongues; for it had been manifested beyond all cavil in a sufficiently terrible chapter of their own history. Then as to the words spoken to Abraham, Isaac, and Jacob, even if all but Moses had been swept away, yet in him the seed of Abraham would have been continued, just as in the days of the flood. God did not utterly destroy the human race, but narrowed it down to one family. And more than all we should bear in mind that the true fulfilment of God's promises was to Abraham's spiritual seed; they who being of faith are blessed with faithful Abraham. Hence we must not too readily conclude that *what Moses said* was the thing which here influenced Jehovah in what is called his repentance. The influential power was, that here was a man *to say something*, to act as a mediator, one deeply concerned to secure escape for these people, even while they, revelling in the plain below, are all unconscious of their danger. Notice that Moses says nothing by way of excuse for the people. Indeed, the full magnitude of their offence had not yet been comprehended by him; and it is interesting to contrast his pleadings here with an angry God, and his own wrath when he came actually in sight of the golden calf. The one thing Moses fixes on, in his appeal to God, is the great Divine purpose for Israel. He recalls how great that purpose is; he is profoundly concerned that it should not be interfered with; and so we are led to think of Jesus the true Mediator, with a knowledge of Divine purposes and human needs, such as it was not for Moses to attain. Consider how Jesus dwells and caused his apostles to dwell on God's great purposes for the children of men. Thus both from Moses the type, and Jesus the antitype, we should learn to think of men not as they are only, but as they ought to be, and as God proposes they should be. Evidently Moses kept constantly in mind God's purposes for Israel, even though he knew not how profound and comprehensive those purposes were. So let us, knowing more than Moses of God's purposes for men in Christ Jesus, keep constantly in mind that which will come to all who by a deep patient, and abiding faith approve themselves true children of Abraham.—Y.

Ver. 14.—*Some powers restrain, some compel.* Here we see a restraining power, and one which can even restrain God. Notice—

I. Evil threatened. 1. *Justly merited.* Remember all that had gone before: deliverance after a series of awe-inspiring judgments on the oppressors; warnings after previous murmurings; now, with a fuller revelation of God's majesty, this act of impatient apostasy: all compelled to the conclusion that the people were utterly stiff-necked (ver. 9). 2. *Complete and final.* As a moulder in clay, when he finds his material getting hard and intractable, throws it down, casts it away, and takes up with something more pliable, so God determines with regard to Israel (ver. 10). Let the children of Israel go, and let the children of Moses inherit the promises.

II. The intercession. Only one thing held back the judgment (ver. 10). As though God could not act without the consent of Moses. [Cf. Hot sun would melt snow but for shadow of protecting wall.] The heat of God's wrath cannot consume so long as Moses stands in the way and screens those against whom it burns. What a power! See how it was exercised:—1. *Unselfishly.* He might have thought, "A disgrace to *me* if these people are lost when I have led them;" this fear, however, provided against by the promise that he shall be made "a great nation." The intercession is prompted by pure unselfishness; Moses identifies himself with those for whom he pleads; and this gives the power. To come between the sun and any object, you must be in the line of the sun's rays; and to come, as Moses did, between God and a people, you must be in the line of God's will. 2. *With perfect freedom.* Moses talks with Jehovah as a trusted steward might with his employer: (1) Why so angry when he has exercised such power on their behalf? (ver. 11). (2) Why should the Egyptians be permitted to taunt him with caprice and cruelty? (ver. 12). (3) Let him remember his oath to Abraham, Isaac, and Jacob (ver. 13). The unselfish man need not fear to speak thus openly with God. Unselfishness is so God-like that it permits familiarity whilst it guards against irreverence.

III. Evil repented of. Notice:—1. The repentance was in direct answer to the intercession (cf. vers. 12, 14). God did as Moses begged that he would do. Had Moses been less firm, God's wrath would certainly have consumed the people. Yet—2. God cannot change! No: but Moses kept his place [cf. the wall screening the snow]; and therefore the conditions were never such as they must have been for judgment to be executed. God's repentance was one with Moses' persistence. The evil threatened was against *the people*, but the people *apart from Moses*. Moses identifying himself with them altered the character of the total.

Conclusion.—What Moses did for his people that our Lord does for his Church (Rom. viii. 34; Heb. vii. 25). That also we may do, each in his measure in behalf of others. It is the Pharisee who thanks God that he is not as other men are! True men love rather to identify themselves with their race, thus, salt-like, saving it from corruption; giving it shelter by the intercession of their lives.—G.

Vers. 7—15.—*The first intercession.* If Israel has been forgetting God, God has not been forgetting Israel. His eye has been on all their doings. There has not been a thought in their heart, or a word on their tongue, but, lo! it has altogether been well known to him (Ps. cxxxix. 4). It is God's way, however, to permit matters to reach a crisis before he interposes. For a time he keeps silence. During the inception and early stages of the movement in Israel, he makes no discovery of it to Moses. He allows it to ripen to its full proportions. Then he tells his servant all that has happened, and orders him to repair at once to the scene of the apostasy (vers. 7—11). Mark the expression:—" *Thy* people, which thou broughtest out of the land of Egypt, have corrupted themselves"—indicating that they are no longer God's, that the covenant is broken. Moses intercedes for Israel, urging various pleas why God should not destroy them (vers. 11—14). Consider—

I. The Divine wrath. " Let me alone," says God, " that my wrath may wax hot against them, and that I may consume them " (ver. 10). This wrath of God against the sin of Israel was—1. *Real.* What we have in these verses is no mere drama, *acted* between God and Moses, but a most real wrath, averted by most real and earnest intercession. But for Moses' intercession, Israel would actually have been destroyed. 2. *Holy.* Wrath against sin is a necessary part of God's character. Not that we are to conceive of the thrice Holy One as swayed by human passions, or as needing to be soothed by human entreaty. But sin does awaken God's displeasure. He would not be God if it did not. " Resentment against sin is an element in the very life of God. It can no more be separated from God than heat from fire. . . . God is merciful. What does this mean? It means a willingness to lay aside resentment against those who have sinned. But it follows that the greater the resentment, the greater is the mercy; if there is very little resentment, there can be very little mercy; if there is no resentment at all, mercy is impossible. The difference between our religion, and the religion of other times, is this—that we do not believe that God has any very strong resentment against sin, or against those who are guilty of sin; and since his resentment has gone, his mercy has gone with it. We have not a God who is more merciful than the God of our fathers, but a God who is less righteous; and a God who is not righteous, a God who does not glow with fiery indignation against sin is no God at all." Put otherwise,— a God who cannot be angry with my sin, is one from whom it would be meaningless in me to sue for pardon. His pardon, could I obtain it, would have no moral value. Yet, 3. *Restrained.* The expression is peculiar—" Now, therefore, *let me alone, that my wrath may wax hot,*" etc. · The meaning is, that God is self-determined in his wrath, even as in his love (cf. ch. xxxiii. 19). He determines himself in the exercise of it. It does not carry him away. In the present instance he restrained it, that room might be left for intercession. The words were a direct encouragement to Moses to entreat for his erring charge.

II. Moses' intercession (vers. 11—15). The last occasion on which we met with Moses as an intercessor was at the court of Egypt. We have now to listen to him in his pleadings for his own people. Four separate acts of intercession are recorded in three chapters (cf. vers. 31—35; chs. xxxiii. 12—18; xxxiv. 9). Taken together, they constitute a Herculean effort of prayer. Each intercession gains a point not granted to the previous one. First, the reversal of the sentence of destruction (ver. 14); next, the consent of God to the people going up to Canaan, only, however, under the conduct of an angel (ch. xxxiii. 1—4); third, the promise that his own presence would go with them (ch. xxxiii. 14); finally, the perfect re-establishment of friendly relations, in the renewal of the covenant (ch. xxxiv. 10). Like Jacob, Moses, as a prince, had power with God, and prevailed (Gen. xxxii. 28). It is to be noted, also, that this advance in power of prayer is connected with an advance in Moses' own experience. In the first intercession, the thought which chiefly fills his mind is the thought of the people's *danger*. He does not attempt to excuse or palliate their *sin*, but neither does he make direct confession of it. He sees only the nation's impending destruction, and is agonisingly earnest in his efforts to avert it. At this stage in his entreaty, Moses might almost seem to us more merciful than God. A higher stage is reached when Moses, having actually witnessed the transgression of the people, is brought to take sides with God in his wrath against it. His second intercession, accordingly, is pervaded by a much deeper realisation of the *enormity* of the sin for which forgiveness is sought. His sense of this is so awful, that it is now a moot question with him whether God possibly *can* forgive it (ver. 32). The third intercession, in like manner, is connected with a special mark of Jehovah's condescending favour to himself (ch. xxxiii. 9), emboldening him to ask that God will restore his presence to the nation (ver. 15); while the fourth follows on the sight which is given him of Jehovah's glory, and on the revelation of the name (ch. xxxiv. 5—8). Observe more particularly in regard to the intercession in the text—1. *The boon sought*. It is that God will spare the people, that he will turn aside his fierce anger from them, and not consume them (ver. 12). Thus far, as above hinted, it might almost seem as if Moses were more merciful than God. God seeks to destroy; Moses pleads with him to spare. The wrath is in God; the pity in his servant. (Contrast with this the counter scene in Jonah iv.) The affinity of spirit between Jehovah and Moses, however, is evinced later, in the hot anger which Moses feels on actually witnessing the sin. God's mercy, on the other hand, is shown in giving Moses the opportunity to intercede. It was he who put the pity into his servant's heart, and there was that in his own heart which responded to it. 2. *The spirit of the supplication*. (1) How absolutely *disinterested*. Moses sets aside, without even taking notice of it, the most glorious offer ever made to mortal man—"I will make of thee a great nation" (ver. 10). This was *Moses'* trial. It tested "whether he loved his own glory better than he loved the brethren who were under his charge." He endured it nobly. (2) How intensely *earnest*. He seems to clasp the feet of God as one who could not, would not, leave, till he had obtained what he sought. (3) How supremely *concerned about God's glory*. That is with Moses the consideration above all others. 3. *The pleas urged*. Moses in these pleas appeals to three principles in the Divine character, which really govern the Divine action— (1) To God's regard for his own work (ver. 11). The finishing of work he has begun (Phil. i. 6). (2) To God's regard for his own honour (ver. 12). Moses cannot bear to think of God's action being compromised. (3) To God's regard for his own servants (ver. 13). The love he bears to the fathers (cf. Deut. iv. 31; x. 15). These are points in God's heart on which all intercession may lay hold. 4. *The effect produced*. God repented him of the evil he thought to do to Israel (ver. 14). Repented, *i.e.*, turned back from a course which his displeasure moved him to pursue, and which, but for Moses' intercession, he would have pursued. It does not appear, however, that Moses was at this time informed of the acceptance of his intercession. Notice, also, that the *actual* remission was bestowed gradually. In this first act of intercession God sees, as it were, the point to which the whole series of intercessions tends, and in anticipation thereof, lays aside his anger.—J. O.

EXPOSITION.

Ver. 15—19.—MOSES BREAKS THE TWO TABLES. The entire conference between God and Moses being now ended, Moses hastened to descend from the mount, and interpose in the crisis that had arisen. He took carefully the two tables of stone, which he had received, in his two hands (Deut. ix. 15), and set out on his return to the camp. On the way, he fell in with Joshua, who must have been on the watch for his descent, and the two proceeded together. When a certain portion of the distance had been traversed, the sounds of the festivity which was going on in the camp reached their ears; and Joshua, mistaking the nature of the shouts, suggested that fighting was in progress (ver. 17). Moses, however, better instructed in the actual nature of the proceedings (vers. 7, 8), caught their character more correctly, and declared that what he heard was nothing but shouting (ver. 18). Soon afterwards, the camp came into sight—a disorderly crowd, half stripped of their garments (ver. 25), was singing choruses and dancing round the figure which Aaron had cast—the sights and sounds were those of a dissolute orgy—Moses was struck with horror and in the frenzy of his indignation, dashed the two tables to the ground and broke them into fragments (ver. 19). The people, he felt, were utterly unworthy of the holy laws which he had brought them—they had "altogether gone out of the way"—they had become "abominable"—at the moment he perhaps despaired of obtaining mercy for them, and expected their entire destruction. God had not as yet told him whether he would "turn from his fierce wrath," or not.

Ver. 15.—**The two tables . . . were in his hand.** In Deut. ix. 15, using greater particularity, Moses says that they were "in his *two hands.*" One was in each hand probably. **Written on both their sides.** This is the case generally with Assyrian and Babylonian tablets, but not with Egyptian ones, which are moreover scarcely found at this early date. Here we seem to have again an indication that some of the Israelitic civilisation had come to them from "Ur of the Chaldees."

Ver. 16.—**The tables were the work of God.** Shaped, *i.e.*, by the same power by which the commandments were inscribed upon them; not, necessarily, of matter newly created for the purpose.

Ver. 17.—**When Joshua heard.** This abrupt introduction of Joshua, who has not been mentioned for seven entire chapters, is curious. Probably he had considered himself bound, as Moses' minister (ch. xxiv. 13), to await his return, and had remained in the middle portion of the mount, where he may have fed upon manna, until Moses came down from the top. **The noise of the people.** It is noted by travellers, that in all the latter part of the descent from Sinai, the plain at its base is

shut out from sight; and that sounds would be heard from it a long time before the plain itself would open on the view (Stanley, *Sinai and Palestine*, p. 44). Sounds, however, which come circuitously, are always indistinct; and it is not surprising that Joshua, knowing nothing of the proceedings in the camp, should have fancied he heard **a sound of war.**

Ver. 18. This verse is difficult to translate, being markedly antithetical and at the same time idiomatic. Perhaps it would be best to render—"It is not the voice of them who raise the cry of victory, nor is it the voice of them who raise the cry of defeat—the voice of them who raise a cry do I hear." The verb is the same in all the three clauses; and it would seem that Moses simply denied that there was any sound of war without making any clear suggestion as to the real character of the disturbance.

Ver. 19.—**The dancing.** Rather "dancing." There is no article; and as the subject had not been mentioned before, the use of the article would have been unmeaning. Dances were a part of the religious ceremonial in most ancient nations. Sometimes they were solemn and grave, like the choric dances of the ancient Dorians, and (probably) that of David in front of the Ark (2 Sam. vi. 5—22); sometimes festive and joyous, yet not immodest, like the Pyrrhic and other dances at Sparta, and the dancing of the Salii at Rome; but more often, and especially among the Oriental nations, they were of a loose and lascivious character. In Egypt, the dancers appear to have been professionals of a degraded class, and the dancing itself to have been always sensual and indecent; while in Syria, Asia Minor, and Babylon, dancing was a wild orgy, at once licentious and productive of a species of phrenzy. We must suspect that it was this sort of dancing in which the Israelites were engaged—whence the terrible anger of Moses. He saw idolatry before his eyes, and idolatry with its worst accompaniments. In the extremity of his anger, **he cast the tables out of his hands,** dashed them violently against the ground, **and brake them.** For this act he is never reprehended. It is viewed as the natural outcome of a righteous indignation, provoked by the extreme wickedness of the people. We must bear this in mind when we come to consider the justice or injustice of the punishment which he proceeded to inflict on them for their sin (vers. 26—29).

HOMILETICS.

Vers. 15—19.—*The act of Moses in breaking the tables.* At first sight the act seems impious, and wholly inexcusable. Here was a marvel—the greatest marvel existing in all the world—transcending the finest statue, the most glorious picture—more wonderful than the pyramids themselves or the great temple of Karnak—here was a monument shaped by the hand of God, and inscribed with his finger in characters that would have possessed through all ages an undying interest for man. Here, moreover, was a precious deposit of truth—God's *great* revelation to his people—put in a written form, and so rendered unalterable; no more liable to be corrupted by the uncertainty of human memory, or the glosses of tradition—pure, changeless, perfect truth; the greatest blessing that man can receive. All this, committed by God to his servant's care, and knowingly, wilfully destroyed in a moment of time! The thing seems, at first, incredible; yet we have the witness of God that it is true. Then we ask, How could Moses have so acted, and was not his action inexcusable? We look to Scripture, and we find that he is never blamed for it. He relates it of himself without any sign of self-condemnation—nay! he, at a later date, reminds the people of it in a tone which is evidently one of self-approval (Deut. ix. 17). What is the explanation of all this? It may help us to find a satisfactory answer, if we consider—

I. THE PROVOCATION TO THE ACT. Moses had left the people devoted apparently to God's service. When he reported to them the entire contents of the "Book of the Covenant," they had answered *with one voice,* "All the words which the Lord hath said, we will do" (ch. xxiv. 3). He had given them in charge to Aaron and Hur, on whose faithfulness he might well imagine himself justified in placing complete reliance. He had been absent less than six weeks—it might seem to him that he had been absent but a few days. And now—now that on rounding a corner of the gorge through which he was descending—he comes in sight of them once more and has them fully presented to his view, what is it he beholds? He sees the entire people—Levites and priests as well as laymen—dancing around a golden idol in a lewd and indecent way! Was not this enough to move him? Was it not enough to transport him out of himself, and render him no longer master of his actions? The wickedness of the people stood revealed to him, and made him feel how utterly unworthy they were of the treasure which he was bringing them. Yielding to an irresistible impulse, in a paroxysm of indignation, to shew his horror at what he witnessed, he cast the tables to the ground. God seems to have regarded the provocation as sufficient, and therefore Moses receives no blame for what he did.

II. THE ACT ITSELF. The act was the destruction of a record which the people were at the moment setting at nought. It was akin to the action of God in withdrawing light from them who sin against light. It was a deserved punishment. It was a way of declaring to the people that they were unworthy to receive the truth and should not receive it. Those who saw Moses descend saw that he was bringing them something, carefully, in his two hands, and must have felt that, as he had gone up to the summit to God, it must be something from God. When he lifted up his two hands, and with a gesture of abhorrence, cast the "something" to the ground, there must have gone through them a sudden thrill of fear, a sudden sense of loss. They must have felt that their "sin had found them out"—that their punishment had begun. Casting the tables down and breaking them, was saying to the multitude in the most significant way— "God has cast you off from being his people."

III. THE SEQUEL OF THE ACT. If anything could have brought the Israelites generally to a sense of their guilt and shame, it would have been the act of Moses which they had witnessed. As it was, a deep impression seems to have been made; but only on the men of his own tribe. When Moses, shortly afterwards, demanded to know, "Who was on the Lord's side?" (verse 26), "all the men of Levi"—*i.e.*, the great mass of the tribe—rallied to him, and were ready to become the executioners of his wrath upon the most determined of the idolaters. This revulsion of feeling on their part was probably brought about, in a great measure, by the exhibition of indignation on the part of Moses, which culminated in his dashing the tables to the earth.

HOMILIES BY VARIOUS AUTHORS.

Vers. 15—25.—*The return of Moses to the camp.* It may well be believed that it was with deeply agitated heart that Moses, stunned by the tidings he had just received, rejoined his faithful attendant, and as speedily as possible descended the rocky sides of the mountain. Great was the contrast between the things heavenly on which for forty days and forty nights his eyes had been uninterruptedly feasting, and the scenes he was now to witness. Even the light of common day could hardly seem otherwise than strange to him, emerging from his ecstasy. His bodily aspect, too, would be considerably altered. But in his spirit there is a stored-up energy, the product of his long rapture, which it only needs the sight of Israel's sin to kindle into awful heat of wrath.

I. THE BREAKING OF THE TABLES (vers. 15—19). The downward journey was a silent one. Moses refrains from communicating to Joshua the news he has received. He is absorbed in his own thoughts. And while he muses, the fire burns (Ps. xxxix. 3). So soon as they approach the camp, sounds of revelry are heard. Joshua, with his soldier's instinct, thinks at once of war, but Moses can tell him that it is "not the voice of them that shout for mastery," nor yet "the voice of them that cry for being overcome" that he hears, but "the voice of them that cry" (ver. 8). Even Moses, however, is unprepared for the spectacle which presents itself, as, pursuing the descent, some turn in the road at length puts before his eyes the whole scene of folly. The tables of testimony are in his hands, but these, in his hot anger, he now dashes from him, breaking them in pieces on the rocks (ver. 19). It was an act of righteous indignation, but symbolic also of the breaking of the covenant. Of that covenant the tables of stone were all that still remained, and the dashing of them to pieces was the final act in its rupture. Learn, 1. The actual sight of wickedness is necessary to give us full sympathy with God in the hot displeasure with which he regards it. 2. The deepest and most loving natures are those most capable of being affected with holy indignation. Who shall compete with Moses in the boundlessness of his love for Israel? But the honour of Jehovah touches him yet more deeply. 3. It is right, on suitable occasions, to give emphatic expression to the horror with which the sight of great wickedness inspires us.

II. THE DESTRUCTION OF THE CALF (ver. 20). Returning to the camp, Moses brought the orgies of the people to a speedy termination. He had little difficulty in restoring order. His countenance, blazing with anger, and exhibiting every sign of grief, surprise, and horror, struck immediate dismay into the evil-doers. No one, apparently, had the courage to resist him. The idolaters slunk in guilty haste to their tents, or stood paralysed with fear, rooted to the spot at which he had discovered them. He, on his part, took immediate steps for ridding the camp of the visible abomination. "He took the calf which they had made and burnt it in the fire, and ground it to powder, and strewed it upon the water, and made the children of Israel drink of it." View this— 1. As a *bitter humiliation*. What could be more humiliating to these idolaters than to see their god ground to powder, and its dust made into a nauseous mixture, which afterwards they were compelled to drink? But is not this the end of all sin? The instruments of our sin become the instruments of our punishment. Our sin turns to bitterness. The golden sheen by which it at first allured us disappears from it. It ends in humiliation and degradation. 2. As a *righteous retribution*. Why was the calf thus ground to powder, and given to the Israelites to drink? It was no mere act of revenge on Moses' part. It was no hasty doing of his anger. It was a just retribution for a great sin. It was a method deliberately adopted of branding idol and idolaters alike with the print of the Almighty's judgment. It suggests to us the *correspondence* between sin and its punishment; the certainty of our sins coming home to roost; the fact that sin will be paid back to us in its own coin. Sin and retribution hang together. We "receive the things done in the body" (2 Cor. v. 10). 3. *As a prophecy of worse evil to come*. Bitter as this humiliation was, it was not the whole. It was but the mark put upon the deed by God, which told those who had committed it that they must abide by it, and be prepared to eat the fruit of their doings. The drinking of the dust had its sequel in the slaughter and the plagues (vers. 27, 35). Even so, the bitterness and humiliation following from sins in this life do not exhaust their punishment. They warn of worse punishment in the world to come.

III. AARON'S EXCUSES (vers. 21—25). The first duty was to destroy the calf. This accomplished, or while the work was proceeding, Moses addresses himself to Aaron. His words are cuttingly severe,—"What did this people unto thee?" etc. (ver. 21). Aaron, on his side, is deprecating and humble. He is afraid of Moses' anger. He addresses Moses as "my lord," and proceeds to make excuses. His excuses are typical, and deserve consideration. 1. He falls back upon the old, old plea—as old as Eden—

that the blame of his sin rested on some one else than himself. "Let not the anger of my lord wax hot: thou knowest the people, that they are bent on mischief. For they said to me," etc. (vers. 22—24). It is, as we say, the old, old story of all evil-doers— "It wasn't me, indeed it wasn't; it was those wicked people who made me do it." It is the weak, childish excuse of all who, having been tempted into sin, or having through their own irresolution fallen into it, have not the honesty or manliness to make at once a frank avowal of their fault. An easy way this, were the excuse admissible, of getting rid of our responsibility; but transgressors were early taught that they will not be allowed to avail themselves of it (Gen. iii. 12—20). It is not a plea which will be held valid on the day of judgment. All, more or less, are conscious of pressure exerted on them by their circumstances. There is, however, no fatality binding us to yield to that pressure, if yielding means sin. The pressure is our *trial.* Aaron's sin lay in his unmanly fear, in his not having the resolution to say at the critical time, No. Probably Aaron would have urged that if he had not yielded, the people would have killed him. "Then," Moses would have answered, "let them kill you. Better a thousand times that they had killed you than that you should have been the means of leading Israel into this great sin." Yet how often is the same species of excuse met with! "I couldn't help it;" "The necessity of my situation;" "Compelled by circumstances;" "Customs of the trade;" "If I hadn't done it, I would have offended all my friends;" "I should have lost my situation," etc. It may be all true: but the point is, Was the thing wrong? If it was, the case of Aaron teaches us that we cannot shield ourselves by transferring the blame of what we have done to circumstances. 2. If Aaron's first excuse was bad, the second was worse—*it just happened.* He put the gold, poor man, into the fire, and "*there came out* this calf!" It came out. He did not make it; it just *came out.* This was a kind of explaining which explained nothing. Yet it is precisely paralleled by people attributing, say, to their "luck," to "chance," to "fate," to "destiny," what is really their own doing. Thomas Scott says—"No wise man ever made a more unmeaning or foolish excuse than Aaron did. We should never have supposed 'that he could speak well,' were we to judge of his eloquence by this specimen." Note —(1) The right way of dealing with a fault is frankly to acknowledge it. (2) Though Moses so severely rebuked Aaron, he could yet intercede for him (Deut. ix. 20). The future high priest, who truly had "infirmity" (Heb. v. 2), needed, on this occasion, an intercessor for himself. The severity of Moses was the severity of aggrieved love.—J. O.

Vers. 15—35.—*Judgment and mercy.* I. THE DESCENT OF MOSES THE EMBLEM OF THE LAW'S ENTRANCE INTO A WORLD OF SIN (vers. 15—29). 1. He came with tables written by God's own finger. The Divine origin and claims of the law are still attested by its own nature and by man's conscience. 2. He was met by the exhibition of gross and defiant sin. The law does not come to a people waiting to receive the knowledge of God's will, but busy with their idolatry and breaking what they already know to be his will. 3. The law's advent, therefore, is in wrath (ver. 19). (1) The broken tables declare that God's covenant is broken. This is still shown in the taking away of God's word from the sinful: it is not understood. Though held in the hand, a veil is drawn between the soul and it. Spiritual death, rationalism, and infidelity, are tokens to-day of God's broken covenant. (2) The burning of the idol, etc. The broken law is a prophecy and foretaste of wrath. (3) The slaughter of the persistent idolaters. The place of feasting becomes the place of death.
II. THE INTERCESSOR. 1. His deep consciousness of the evil of their sin (vers. 30, 31). The intercessor cannot make light of man's iniquity. He who bore our burdens felt their weight and terribleness as we have never yet done. 2. His love. Though he hates their iniquity, his life is bound up with theirs (ver. 32).
III. THE TERRIBLENESS OF SIN AS SEEN IN THE MIRROR OF THE DIVINE ANGER. 1. The impossibility of ransom. "Whosoever hath sinned against me him will I blot out of my book." There is but one sacrifice which avails, and that reaches the heart of the sinful and changes it. 2. Mercy to the unrenewed only means a delayed judgment: "Nevertheless, in the day when I visit I will visit their sins upon them."—U.

EXPOSITION.

Ver. 20.—MOSES DESTROYS THE GOLDEN CALF. The first vengeance which Moses took was upon the idol. It was probably hollow, and possibly of no great size. He might easily break it to pieces and subject the pieces to the action of fire, whereby they would be calcined, and might then be easily reduced to powder. This powder he caused to be mixed with the stream of the brook that flowed from Sinai, so that the Israelites were obliged to swallow with their drink particles of their own idol. Compare the action of Josiah with respect to the "grove" set up in the temple precincts by Manasseh (2 Kings xxiii. 6), which was not identical, but still was similar. It has been suggested that this portion of the narrative is out of proper chronological order ; and this may be so far true that the calcining and mixing with the water were at this point commanded rather than executed; but the destruction of the idol would naturally be the first thing which Moses would take in hand, and provide for, before proceeding to anything else. Only when the "abomination" was removed and its destruction commenced, would he turn his attention to other points.

Ver. 20.—**Burnt it and ground it to powder.** Silver and gold subjected for a short time to a white heat, which may be easily produced by bellows, readily calcine, and are then easily crushed to a fine powder. Silver becomes detonating. I am not aware whether the case is the same with gold also. **Strawed it**—*i.e.*, "sprinkled it." We need not suppose Moses to have done the whole—or even any part—himself. It was enough that he directed it to be done. **The water.** The article shows some particular water to be meant. We learn from Deuteronomy that it was the water of "the brook that descended out of the mount." **Made the children of Israel drink of it.** The brook being the only water readily accessible, the Israelites, if they drank at all, were compelled to risk swallowing particles of their "god."

HOMILETICS.

Ver. 20.—*Idolatry condemned by the idol's weakness and nothingness.* An idol is "nothing in the world" (1 Cor. viii. 4)—has no power—cannot even save itself. Nothing convinces men of the vanity of idolatry so much as to see their idol destroyed. We read in Bede that Northumbria was converted chiefly through the priest Coifi running a tilt at the great idol of the day, and throwing it to the ground (*Eccles. Hist.* ii. 13). Hence the command given "utterly to abolish idols" (Is. ii. 18). And what is true of idols proper, is true also, in its measure, of all those substitutes for God which the bulk of men idolise. Riches readily make themselves wings, and vanish, leaving their worshipper a beggar. Wife, mistress, favourite child, lover, erected into an idol, is laid low by death, decays, and crumbles in the grave. Reputation, glory, sought and striven for throughout long years as the one sole good, fades suddenly away before the breath of slander or the caprice of fortune. And when they are gone —when the bubble is burst—men feel how foolish was their adoration. Their idolatry stands self-condemned by their idol's weakness and nothingness.

EXPOSITION.

Vers. 21—24.—AARON TRIES TO EXCUSE HIMSELF. Having taken the needful steps for the destruction of the idol, Moses naturally turned upon Aaron. He had been left in charge of the people, to guide them, instruct them, counsel them in difficulties (ch. xxiv. 14). How had he acquitted himself of his task ? He had led the people into a great sin—had at any rate connived at it—assisted in it. Moses therefore asks, "What had the people done to him, that he should so act ? How had they injured him, that he should so greatly injure them ?" To this he has no direct reply. But he will not acknowledge himself in fault — he must excuse himself. And his excuse is twofold:—1. It was the people's fault, not his; they were "set on mischief." 2. It was a fatality—he threw the gold into the fire, and "it came out this calf." We are not surprised, after this, to read in

Deuteronomy, that " the Lord was very angry with Aaron to have destroyed him," and was only hindered from his purpose by the intercession of Moses

Ver. 21.—**What did this people unto thee?** Moses does not suppose that the people had really done anything to Aaron. He asks the question as a reproach—they had done nothing to thee—*had* in no way injured thee—and yet thou broughtest this evil upon them. **So great a sin.** Literally, "a great sin"—the sin of idolatry. If Aaron had offered a strenuous opposition from the first, the idolatry might not have taken place—the people might have been brought to a better mind.

Ver. 22.—**Let not the anger of my lord wax hot.** Aaron's humility is extreme, and the result of a consciousness of guilt. He nowhere else addresses Moses as "my lord." **Set on mischief.** Or "inclined to evil" (Kalisch).

Ver. 23.—**Make us gods.** Rather "Make us *a god*."

Ver. 24.—**There came out this calf.** Aaron speaks as if he had prepared no mould, but simply thrown the gold into the hot furnace, from which there issued forth, to his surprise, the golden calf. This was not only a *suppressio veri*, but a *suggestio falsi*. Having no even plausible defence to make, he is driven to the weakest of subterfuges.

HOMILETICS.

Vers. 22—24.—*Aaron's excuses.* We are all ready enough to condemn Aaron for his insincere and shifty answer; but do not the apostle's words occur to any of us?— " Therefore, thou art inexcusable, O man, whosoever thou art that judgest, for wherein thou judgest another, thou condemnest thyself; for thou that judgest doest the same things " (Rom. ii. 1). Do not we all, when we are taxed with faults, seek to shift the blame of them elsewhere? *e.g.* :—

I. ON THE PEOPLE WITH WHOM WE LIVE. Society, we say, is corrupt—is "set on mischief." Its customs are wrong, we know; but it is too strong for us. We must conform to its ways. There is no use in resisting them. Public men say—" Such and such changes in the law would be bad—we know it—we admit it—but the people ask for them, so we must lend ourselves to their wishes, and take steps to get the changes made." Or again—" This or that war would be unjust, iniquitous, a flying in the face of Christian principle. To engage in it would be a crime—a disgrace to the age we live in." But let the popular voice call for the war a little loudly—and the public man yields, silences the remonstrances of his conscience, and becomes an active agent in bringing the war about. And the case is the same in private life. Ask a man why he spends on entertainments twice as much as he spends in charity, and he will immediately lay the blame on others—" every one does it." Ask him why he wastes his whole time in frivolous pursuits, newspaper-reading, club-gossiping, card-playing, party-going, and his reply is the same. Descend a little in the social scale, and ask the manufacturer why he scamps his goods; the shopkeeper why he adulterates; the ship-owner why he insures ships that he knows to be unseaworthy and sends out to be wrecked—and his answer is parallel—" every one in his line of business does the same." They compel him to follow their bad example. Descend again, ask the confidential servant why he takes " commission" from tradesmen; the cook, why she hides fresh joints among the broken victuals; the footman, why he purloins wine and cigars; they defend themselves with the same plea—" It is wrong, they know: but their class has established the practice." " We are all the victims of our social surroundings; it is not we who are in fault, but the crowd that pushes us on."

II. ON THE NATURE THAT GOD HAS GIVEN US, ON THE CIRCUMSTANCES IN WHICH WE ARE PLACED. Sins of temper and sins of impurity are constantly set down by those who commit them to their *nature*. Their tempers are naturally so bad, their passions naturally so strong. As if they had no power over their nature; as if again, they did not voluntarily excite their passions, work themselves up into rages; " make provision for the flesh, to fulfil the lusts thereof." In thus doing they construct the mould into which the sins run. Sins of dishonesty are commonly attributed to *circumstances:* the temptation came in their way, men say, without their seeking it, and was too much for them, was not to be resisted. So with drunkenness, idleness, and the other sins connected with evil companionship; men's plea is they were brought into contact with persons who dragged them, almost forced them into evil courses. Had they been more happily circumstanced it would have been different. As if a man did not to a large extent make his own circumstances, choose his companions, construct his own way of life. We are not forced to company with any men, much less any women, out of business hours. We are not compelled to go to places of public amusement where we are tempted. The "circumstances" which lead to sin are usually circumstances which we might easily have avoided, if we had chosen, as Aaron might have avoided making the mould, or even asking for the ornaments.

EXPOSITION.

Vers. 25—29.—Moses punishes the ring-leaders. The presence of Moses in the camp —his impressive act in breaking the tables— even his seizure of the idol and consignment of it to destruction—did not arrest the licentious orgy in which the people had engaged before his coming. The "play" that had followed on the feasting still continued; though we may suppose that many had been impressed and had desisted. Moses felt that an example must be made, and a stop put to conduct which was more and more provoking the Almighty, and might at any moment bring down the judgment of complete destruction upon the whole people. He therefore took his station at the main gate of the camp (ver. 26), and shouted the words— "Who is on Jehovah's side? Here, to me!" The sound of the words could not, of course, have reached very far—but they rallied to him those of his own tribe who stood near, and thus placed a strong force at his disposal. Moses bade them get their swords, and proceed through the camp from end to end, slaying the idolaters—not, we may be sure, indiscriminately, but executing God's judgment on those who were most conspicuous and persistent. They were especially bidden not to spare their own nearest and dearest, which implies that many Levites were among the ringleaders. The result was the destruction by the sword of three thousand men—and the suppression of the festival. It is not to be doubted that Moses had Divine sanction for what he did in this matter (ver. 27).

Ver. 25.—The people were naked. It has been suggested that "licentious" or "unruly" would be a better rendering (Gesenius, Dathe, Rosenmüller, Kalisch, Cook), but the primary sense of *phârua* is "naked," "stript;" and of the licentious orgies of the East, stripping or uncovering the person was a feature (Herod. ii. 60), so that there is no reason for changing the expression used in the Authorised Version. Moses saw that most of the people were still without the garments that they had laid aside when they began to dance, and were probably still engaged in dancing and shouting. **Aaron had made them naked.** Aaron is said to have done that to which his actions had led. He had made the calf and proclaimed a festival. The "nakedness" had naturally followed. **Unto their shame among their enemies.** Amalekites were no doubt still hovering about the camp; indeed, the tribe probably still held most of the surrounding mountains. They would witness the orgy, and see the indecent and shameful exposure.

Ver. 26.—Moses stood in the gate of the camp. We must understand "the principal gate," since the camp had several (ver. 27) **Who is on the Lord's side? Let him come to me.** Literally, "Who for Jehovah? To me"—but expressed, as the Hebrew idiom allows, in three words, forming an excellent rallying cry. **All the sons of Levi**—*i.e.*, all who heard the cry. It is evident that there were Levites among the idolaters (vers. 27, 29).

Ver. 27.—Go in and out from gate to gate, etc.,—*i.e.*, "pass through the whole camp—visit every part of it—and, where you see the licentious rites continuing, use your swords—do not spare, though the man be a brother, or a companion, or a neighbour— strike nevertheless, and bring the revel to an end."

Ver. 28.—About three thousand. We cannot gather from this, as some have done, that the Levites who rallied to Moses were only 3,000—for every Levite was not obliged to kill a man—but only that, when this number was slain, the idolaters desisted from their orgy

Ver. 29.—For Moses had said. Moses, on giving them their commission (ver. 27), had told them, that their zeal in the matter would be a consecration, and would secure them God's blessing. They earned by it the semi-priestly position, which was soon afterwards assigned to them (Num. iii. 6—13).

HOMILETICS.

The punishment of idolatry. God did not long allow the sin against ... unpunished. He declared his will to Moses (ver. 27)—"Thus ... of Israel"—and Moses, with his usual dutifulness, was prompt to ... having obtained the necessary force, he lost no time in inflicting the ... punishment itself, we shall do well to note—

Men talk and think very slightingly in these days of sins against ... profess scepticism, agnosticism, atheism, "with a light heart." ... to them that their conduct is likely to bring upon them any ... thoughts are not as man's thoughts"—God visits such sins ... and are slain with the sword on one day because of a few ... is God's award. And the record of it has been "written ... the ends of the world are come." It is intended to teach us ... things; and, if not in this world, then assuredly in the next. ... apostasy. It is a "casting of God behind the back"— ... deliberate preference to him of something which is not ... but be infinitely inferior. The heart witnesses against ... bound, being God's creatures, to devote our whole ... well be punished with death, if it had never been ... raelites had heard it forbidden amid the thunders of ... a law against it in "the Book of the Covenant" ... themselves to obey this law (ch. xxiv. 3). They ... If all who had taken part in the calf-worship had ... been done. But God tempers justice with mercy. ... thousand sinners; but the lives of three thousand

... S ESCAPED. Those escaped who put away their sin ... repent, and placed themselves on the Lord's side at ... This was the best course, and the only safe one. ... all the heart;" and, though no atonement for past ... e (coming) atonement of his Son, and obtained from ... lessing (ver. 29). 2. Those escaped who desisted ... eal, or even when they saw the swords drawn, and ... aw back from sin is the only way to escape its ... its consequences are not escaped. Their iniquity ... ere now allowed to escape with their lives—"the ... made the calf" (ver. 35) at a later date.

BY VARIOUS AUTHORS.

... Panic was in the camp. The idolaters stood as ... revels. Their sin had been of too heinous a nature ... without severe punishment. Law must be vindicated. ... injury offered to the majesty of Jehovah. Stern as ... t shrink from immediately addressing himself to the

... in the gate of the camp and said, "Who is on the ... into me" (ver. 26). This must be taken to mean, not, ... Lord's side now?" but "Who has shown himself on the ... apostasy?" Note—the Lord's side, though for a time the ... end to be the side of honour, of safety, and of comfort. ... rd. Wisdom is justified of her children. (Matt. xi. 19.) ... the sons of Levi gathered themselves together unto him" ... tribe, would thus appear to have been less implicated in ... the people.

"Faithful found ... mong the faithless, faithful only he"

This now turns to their honour. The text, however, does not forbid the
that *individuals* from the other tribes also came out, and separated thems
call of Moses.

III. THE COMMISSION. This was sufficiently sanguinary. It put the fide
to a terrible test. "Thus saith the Lord God of Israel, Put every man his s
side, and go in and out," etc. (ver. 27). 1. In the work of executin
vengeance, *the Levites were to "consecrate" themselves* (ver. 29). They wer
themselves. They were to be actuated in what they did by pure zeal for
They were to obey to the letter the command he had given them. 2. In t
this work, *they were sternly to repress all natural impulses:* "every man u
and upon his brother" (ver. 29; cf. Deut. xxxiii. 9). So earthly ties a
permitted to stand between us and duty to Christ (Matt. viii. 21, 22; x. 27

IV. THE EXECUTION OF THE MANDATE. 1. *The Levites showed unflin*
the work entrusted to them. By their zeal on this, and on other occasions (
8), they reversed the curse which lay upon their tribe, and won for them
honour and blessing. In particular, they won the privilege of ser
sanctuary. 2. *They slew three thousand of the people* (ver. 28). "Ter
this," as Carlyle says of the storming of Drogheda; "but *is* it surgery, and
atrocious murder merely?" The number of the slain was after all small
with the whole body of the people. Probably only the ringleaders and chi
of the revolt were put to death, with those who still showed the disposit
Note, that notwithstanding their great zeal on this occasion, the Levites
those afterwards excluded from Canaan for unbelief. This is a striking
It shows how those that think they stand need to take heed lest they fall
It reminds us that one heroic act of service is not enough to win for us th
God. "We are made partakers of Christ, if we hold the beginning of
fast *unto the end*" (Heb. iii. 14). It may suggest to us also, that many o
who failed under the later trial, and so were excluded from Canaan, thus
earthly inheritance, may yet have had the root of the matter in
spiritually, were saved.—J. O.

Ver. 26.—" *Who is on the Lord's side? Let him come unto me.*"
points suggest a practical treatment of the passage—

I. IN THE WARFARE BETWEEN GOOD AND EVIL, THERE IS NEED FOR
Some side we *must* take. We cannot remain neutral. Not to be on the
to be on the side of his enemies. It is our duty to choose the Lord's
has a claim on our allegiance. (2) It is the side of honour and of duty.
side we will ultimately wish we *had* chosen.

II. THE EXAMPLE OF ONE GOOD MAN, IN DECLARING HIMSELF ON TH
AFFORDS A RALLYING-POINT FOR OTHERS. He gathers others around him.
decides and emboldens them.

III. THE TEST OF BEING ON THE LORD'S SIDE IS, THAT, WHEN OTHERS
ING AROUND US, WE REMAIN FAITHFUL. Weak natures will always go wit
Decided piety shows itself in being able to resist the contagion of num
courage to be singular.

IV. BEING ON THE LORD'S SIDE CARRIES WITH IT CERTAIN OBLIGA
obligation of personal consecration. (2) The obligation of renouncing
far as inconsistent with the higher allegiance. (3) The obligation of
work.

V. FIDELITY ON THE LORD'S SIDE WILL MEET WITH AN ULTIMATE REW

EXPOSITION.

Vers. 30—35.—MOSES ONCE MORE INTER-
CEDES WITH GOD FOR THE PEOPLE— GOD
ANSWERS HIM. No distinct reply seems to
have been given to the previous intercession
of Moses (vers. 11—13). He only knew that

the people were not as ye
therefore that God's wrath
held in suspense. It mi
punishment inflicted on t
peased God's wrath: or

might be needed. In the latter case, Moses was ready to sacrifice himself for his nation (ver. 32). Like St. Paul, he elects to be "accursed from God, for his brethren, his kinsfolk after the flesh" (Rom. ix. 3). But God will not have this sacrifice. "The soul that sinneth, it shall die" (Ezek. xviii. 4). He declares, "Whosoever hath sinned against me, him will I blot out of my book" (Ex. xxxii. 33). Moses shall not make himself a victim. Without any such sacrifice, God will so far spare them, that they shall still go on their way towards the promised land, with Moses as their earthly, and an Angel as their heavenly leader. Only, their sin shall still be visited in God's own good time and in his own way. How, is left in obscurity; but the decree is issued—"In the day that I visit, I will visit their sin upon them" (ver. 34). And, writing long years after the event, the author observes —"And God did plague the people because they made the calf which Aaron made" (ver. 35).

Ver. 30.—**On the morrow.** The day must have been well-nigh over when the slaughter of the 3000 was completed: and after that the corpses had to be buried, the signs of carnage to be effaced, and the wounded, of whom there must have been many, cared for. Moses would have had to direct, if not even to superintend, everything, and therefore could not reascend Sinai until the next day. **Moses said unto the people.** Not now to the elders only, as in ch. xxiv. 14, but to all the people, since all had sinned, and each man is held by God individually responsible for his own sin. **Ye have sinned a great sin.** One which combined ingratitude and falseness with impiety. **Peradventure I shall make an atonement.** Moses has formed the design, which he executes (ver. 32); but will not reveal it to the people, from modesty probably.

Ver. 31.—**Gods of gold.** Rather "a god of gold."

Ver. 32.—**If thou wilt forgive their sin.** The ellipsis which follows, is to be supplied by some such words, as "well and good"—"I am content"—"I have no more to say." Similar cases of ellipses will be found in Dan. iii. 5; Luke xiii. 9; xix. 42; John vi. 62; Rom. ix. 22. **And if not, blot me, I pray thee, out of thy book.** Some interpret this as merely equivalent to, "Blot me out of the book of the living," and explain that phrase as meaning simply—"Take my life—kill me instead of them"—but something more seems to be meant. "The book of the living"— "the book of life"—the book of God's writing —is not merely a register of those who happen to be alive at any given time. It "contains

the list of the righteous, and ensures to those whose names are written therein, life before God, first in the earthly kingdom of God, and then eternal life also" (Keil). Thus Moses declared his willingness—nay, his wish—that God would visit on him the guilt of his people, both in this world *and the next*, so that he would thereupon forgive them. St. Paul has a similar burst of feeling (Rom. ix. 1—3); but it does not involve a formal offer—it is simply the expression of a willingness. Ordinary men are scarcely competent to judge these sayings of great saints. As Bengel says—"It is not easy to estimate the measure of love in a Moses and a Paul; for the narrow boundary of our reasoning powers does not comprehend it, as the little child is unable to comprehend the courage of heroes." Both were willing—*felt* willing, at any rate—to sacrifice their own future for their countrymen—and Moses made the offer. Of all the noble acts in Moses' life it is perhaps the noblest; and no correct estimate of his character can be formed which does not base itself to a large extent on his conduct at this crisis.

Ver. 33.—**Whosoever hath sinned against me, him will I blot out of my book.** Beyond a doubt, it is the general teaching of Scripture that vicarious punishment will not be accepted. "The son shall not bear the iniquity of the father, neither shall the father bear the iniquity of the son—the righteousness of the righteous shall be upon him, and the wickedness of the wicked shall be upon him" (Ezek. xviii. 20). Man "cannot deliver his brother, or make agreement with God for him; for it cost more to redeem their souls, so that he must let that alone for ever" (Ps. xlix. 7, 8). One only atonement is accepted—that of him who is at once man and God—who has, himself, no sin —and can therefore take the punishment of others.

Ver. 34.—**Lead the people unto the place,** etc. This was a revocation of the sentence of death passed in verse 10. The people was to be spared, and Moses was to conduct them to Palestine. **Mine Angel shall go before thee.** Mine Angel—not I myself (compare ch. xxxiii. 2, 3). Another threatened punishment, which was revoked upon the repentance of the people (*ib.* 4, 6), and the earnest prayer of Moses (*ib.* 14—16). **I will visit their sin upon them.** Kalisch thinks that a plague was at once sent, and so understands verse 35. But most commentators regard the day of visitation as that on which it was declared that none of those who had quitted Egypt should enter Canaan (Num. xiv. 35), and regard that sentence as, in fact, provoked by the golden calf idolatry (*ib.* 22).

Ver. 35.—**The Lord plagued,** or "struck"— *i.e.*, "punished" the people. There is nothing in the expression which requires us to understand the sending of a pestilence.

HOMILETICS.

Vers. 30—34.—*Moses as the forerunner of Christ.* " A prophet shall the Lord your God raise up unto you *like unto me*," said the great lawgiver, ere he left the earth (Deut. xvii. 15, 18); and the parallelism between Christ and Moses is in many respects most striking. 1. Both were of obscure birth—"the son of a carpenter"—the son of "a man of the house of Levi." 2. Both were in great peril in infancy—their life sought by the civil ruler—Herod—Pharaoh. 3. Both passed their youth and early manhood in obscurity—Christ for thirty, Moses for forty years. 4. Both felt they had a mission, but on coming forward were rejected by their brethren. " He came unto his own, and his own received him not" (John i. 11). " He supposed his brethren would have understood how that God by his hand would deliver them : but they understood not" (Acts vii. 25). 5. Both showed " signs and wonders," such as have rarely been seen upon earth, and thus made it manifest that their missions were from God. 6. Both were law-givers—promulgators of a new moral code—Moses of an imperfect, Christ of a perfect law—(" the perfect law of love"). 7. Both were founders of a new community—Moses of the Hebrew state, Christ of the Christian Church. 8. Both were great deliverers and great teachers—Moses delivered his people from Egypt and Pharaoh, and led them through the wilderness to Canaan; Christ delivers his from sin and Satan, and leads them through the wilderness of this life to heaven. 9. Both willed to be a sacrifice for their brethren—God could not accept the one sacrifice (ver. 33), but could and did accept the other.

HOMILIES BY VARIOUS AUTHORS.

Vers. 31, 32.—*The confession and intercession of Moses.* Notice here—

I. THE AMPLITUDE OF THIS CONFESSION. It is very necessary to contrast the words of Moses in vers. 31 and 32 with his previous words in vers. 11—13. What a difference there is in the ground, elements, and tone of the two appeals! and this difference is fully explained by the experience through which he had been in the interval. It was a bitter and humiliating experience—we may almost say an unexpected one. For, although, before he had gone down from the mount, Jehovah had given him a clear forewarning of what awaited him, somehow he seems not to have taken in the full drift of Jehovah's words. It is not till he gets down into the camp and sees the golden image, and the revelry and riot, and the implication of his own brother in a broken covenant, that he discerns the full extent of the calamity, and the difficulty, almost the impossibility of bringing together again Jehovah and his revolted people. Vain is it to seek for anything like sure conclusions in the details of Moses' conduct on this occasion. The things he did were almost as the expressions of a heart beside itself with holy grief. There is a good deal of obscurity in this portion of the narrative; and our wisest course is to turn to what is clear and certain and most instructive, namely, the great result which came out of this experience. It was truly a result, beyond all estimation, to have been led to the conclusion—"This people have sinned a great sin." That was just the light in which Jehovah looked upon their conduct; and though Moses could not see all that Jehovah saw, we may well believe that he saw all that a brother man could see, one whose own heart's vision was not yet perfectly clear. Blessed is that man who, for himself and for others, can see the reality and magnitude of the human heart's departure from God. It would not, indeed, be hard, from a certain point of view, to frame a very plausible story on behalf of these Israelites; but it is far better to bear in mind that just at this particular juncture this very Moses who at first had expostulated with Jehovah, making not the slightest reference to the people's sin, is now found on account of that sin bending himself in the utmost submission before God. Aaron came to Moses with an excuse (vers. 22—24); he spoke in the spirit of Adam, laying the blame elsewhere. But Moses attempts neither excuse nor extenuation. Nor was any enlargement needed. The brief sentence he spoke, standing in all its naked severity, was quite enough.

II. HOW UNCERTAIN MOSES IS IN HIS EXPECTATIONS. The confession is as full and emphatic as it can be, but the heart is of necessity very doubtful as to what may come out of the confession. The words of Moses here are very consistent with the quick fluctuations of human nature. From extreme to extreme the pendulum swings. Previously he spoke as almost rebuking Jehovah for thinking to destroy his people; now even when the insulting image is ground to powder, and the ringleaders in transgression destroyed, he makes his way into the Divine presence as one who is fully prepared for the worst. "If thou wilt forgive them." One can imagine the stammering, half-ashamed tones in which these words would issue from the lips of Moses. The man who was so fruitful of reasons before is silent now. Jehovah's past promises and past dealings he cannot urge; for the more he thinks of them, the more by an inevitable consequence, he thinks of the broken covenant. The light of these glorious promises shines for the present, upon a scene of ruin and shame. Then it is noteworthy that Moses had to go up, from the impulse of his own heart. We do not hear as yet of any general confession; it is not the weeping and wailing of a nation returning in penitence that he bears before God. If only the people had sent him to say, "We have sinned a great sin;" if only they had made him feel that he was their chosen spokesman; if only their continued cry of contrition, softened by distance, had reached his ears, as he ventured before God, there might have been something to embolden him. But as yet there was no sign of anything of this sort. He seems to have gone up as a kind of last resort, unencouraged by any indication that the people comprehended the near and dreadful peril. Learn from this that there can be no availing plea and service from our great advocate, except as we look to him for the plea and service, in full consciousness that we cannot do without them. We get no practical good from the advocacy of Jesus, unless as in faith and earnestness, we make him our advocate.

III. How COMPLETELY MOSES ASSOCIATES HIMSELF WITH THE FATE OF HIS BRETHREN. He could not but feel the difference there was between his position and theirs; but at the moment there was a feeling which swallowed all others up, and that was the unity of brotherhood. The suggestion to make out of him a new and better covenant people came back to him now, with a startling significance which it lacked before. Israel, *as the people of God*, seemed shut up to destruction now. If God said the covenant could not be renewed; if he said the people must return and be merged and lost in the general mass of human-kind, Moses knew he had no countervailing plea; only this he could pray that he also might be included in their doom. He had no heart to go unless where his people went; and surely it must have a most inspiring and kindling influence to meditate on this great illustration of unselfishness. Moses, we know, had been brought very near to God; what glimpses must have been opened up to him of a glorious future. But then he had only thought of it as being his future along with his people. In the threatenings that God was about to forsake those who had forsaken him, there seemed no longer any brightness even in the favour of God to him as an individual. Apostate in heart and deed as his brethren were, he felt himself a member of the body still; and to be separated from them would be as if the member were torn away. He who had preferred affliction with the people of God rather than the pleasures of sin for a season, now prefers obliteration along with his own people rather than to keep his name on God's great book. It can hardly be said that in this he spurns or depreciates the favour of God; and it is noticeable that God does not rebuke him as if he were preferring human ties to Divine. Jehovah simply responds by stating the general law of what is inevitable in all sinning. He who sins must be blotted out of God's book. God will not in so many words rebuke the pitying heart of his servant; but yet we clearly see that there was no way out by that course which Moses so very deferentially suggests. When first Moses heard of the apostasy of Israel he spoke as if the remedy depended upon Jehovah; now he speaks as if it might be found in his own submission and self-sacrifice; but God would have him understand that whatever chance there may be depends on a much needed change in the hearts of the people, a change of which all sign so far was lacking.—Y.

Vers. 30—35.—*The second intercession.* This second intercession of Moses is even more wonderful than the first. The question raised on that former occasion—Is Moses more merciful than God?—will, indeed, no longer occur. Those who might have been disposed to press that question then will probably not be disposed to press it now. They have since had sufficient evidence of Moses' severity. They have found that, whatever elements of character are lacking to him, he is not wanting in energy of indignation at patent wickedness. The temptation, on the contrary, may now be to accuse the law-giver of unjustifiable and unholy anger—of reckless disregard of human life. The charge is groundless; but if, for a moment, it should appear natural, the reply to it is found in the study of this second scene upon the mount. Surely, if ever human heart laid bare its intense and yearning love for those whose sin fidelity to duty yet compelled it to reprobate and loathe, it is the heart of Moses in this new, and altogether marvel-lous, juncture in his history. Consider—

I. THE CONFESSION MADE (vers. 30, 31). Moses makes a full confession of the sin of the people. This confession was—1. *Holy.* He has just views of the demerit of the sin for which he seeks forgiveness. His impressions of its enormity are even stronger than at the time of his first intercession. So heinous does it now appear to him that he is mentally in doubt whether God possibly *can* forgive it. 2. *Perfectly truthful.* Moses fully admits the people's sin. He does not make light of it. He does not seek to minimise it. Not even to secure the salvation of the people over whom he yearns with so intense an affection will he unduly palliate their offence, or feign an excuse where he knows that there is none to offer. Mark how, in both of these respects, Moses answers to the true idea of a mediator. "A mediator is not a mediator of one" (Gal. iii. 20). It is his function, in conducting his mediation, to uphold impartially the interests of *both* of the parties between whom he mediates. Both are represented in his work. He stands for both equally. He must do justice by both. His sympathy with both must be alike perfect. He must favour neither at the expense, or to the disadvantage, of the other. These acts of intercession show in how supreme a degree this qualification of the mediator is found in Moses. He has sympathy with the people, for whose sin he is willing, if need be, even to die; he has also the fullest sympathy with God. He looks at the sin from God's standpoint. He has sympathy with God's wrath against it. He is as jealous for God's honour as he is anxious for the forgiveness of the people. He is thus the true daysman, able to lay his hand upon both. 3. *Vicarious.* He confesses the people's sin *for* them. On the depth to which this element enters into the idea of atonement, and on the place which it holds in the atonement of Jesus, see J. McLeod Campbell's work on *The Nature of the Atonement.*

II. THE ATONEMENT OFFERED (ver. 32). The new and awful impressions Moses had received of the enormity of the people's conduct gave rise in his mind to the feeling of the need of atonement. "Now I will go up to the Lord," he says to them, "peradven-ture I shall make an atonement for your sin" (ver. 30). That the intercessory element entered into Moses' idea of "making an atonement" is not to be denied. But it is not the only one. So intensely evil does the sin of the people now appear to him that he is plainly in doubt whether it can be pardoned without some awful expression of God's punitive justice against it; whether, indeed, it can be pardoned at all. This sense of what is due to justice resolves itself into the proposal in the text—a proposal, probably, in which Moses comes as near anticipating Christ, in his great sacrifice on Calvary, as it is possible for any one, bearing the limitations of humanity, to do (cf. Rom. ix. 3). Observe—1. *The proposal submitted.* It amounts to this, that Moses, filled with an immense love for his people, offers himself as a sacrifice for their sin. If God cannot otherwise pardon their transgression, and if this will avail, or can be accepted, as an atonement for their guilt, let him—Moses—perish instead of them. The precise meaning attached in Moses' mind to the words, "If not, blot me, I pray thee, out of the book which thou hast written," must always be a difficulty. Precision, probably, is not to be looked for. Moses' idea of what was involved in the blotting out from God's book could only be that afforded him by the light of his own dispensation, and by his sense of the exceeding greatness of God's wrath. His language is the language of love, not that of dogmatic theology. Infinite things were to be hoped for from God's love; infinite things were to be dreaded from his anger. The general sense of the utterance is, that Moses was willing to die; to be cut off from covenant hope and privilege; to undergo whatever awful doom subjection to God's wrath might imply; if only thereby his people could be saved. It was a stupendous proposal to make; an extraordinary act of self-devotion; a wondrous exponent of his patriotic love for his people; a not less wondrous recognition of what was due to the justice of God ere sin could be forgiven—a glimpse even, struck out from the passionate yearning of his own heart, of the actual method of redemption. A type of Christ has been seen in the youthful Isaac ascending the hill to be offered on the altar by Abraham his father. A much nearer type is Moses, "setting his face" (cf. Luke ix. 51) to ascend the mount, and bearing in his heart this sublime purpose of devoting himself for the sins of the nation. "Greater love hath no man than this, that a man lay down his life for his friends" (John xv. 13). 2. *The alternative desired.* If the people must perish—this meaning also seems to be conveyed in the words—Moses would wish to perish with them. Not only has the proposal to make of him "a great nation" (Ex. xxxii. 10) no allurement for his mind, but, if the people are to be destroyed, he would prefer to die with them. He desires no life outside of theirs. Patriotic devotion could no further go. Noble Moses! Yet only the type of the nobler than himself, who, devoting himself in the same spirit, has actually achieved the redemption of the world. See in this incident (1) The connection of a feeling of the need of atonement with just views of sin's demerit. (2) The certainty, when just views of sin are entertained, of this feeling of the need of atonement arising. In declining the proposal of Moses, God does not say that atonement is not needed. He does not say that his servant has exaggerated the enormity of the sin, or the difficulties which stand in the way of its forgiveness. He does not say that it is not by means of atonement that these difficulties connected with the forgiveness of sins are ultimately to be removed. On the contrary, the spirit of Moses in this transaction is evidently in the very highest degree pleasing to Jehovah, and so far as atonement *is* made for the people's sins, it is by Jehovah accepting the *spirit* of his sacrifice, even when rejecting the proposal in its letter. (3) The *naturalness* of this method of salvation. The proposal sprang naturally from the love of Moses. It expressed everything that was grandest in his character. It shadowed forth a way in which, conceivably, a very true satisfaction might be offered to Divine justice, while yet mercy was extended to the sinner. The fulfilment of the prophecy is the Cross.

III. THE REPLY GIVEN. 1. *The atonement is declined in its letter.* God declares that so far as there is to be any blotting from the book of life, it will be confined to those who have sinned. It may be noted, in respect to this declinature of the proposal of Moses that, as above remarked, it does not proceed on the idea that atonement is not needed, but (1) Moses could not, even by his immolation, have made the atonement required. (2) God, in his secret counsel, had the true sacrifice provided. (3) Atonement is inadmissible on the basis proposed, viz. that the innocent should be "blotted out from the book of life." Had no means of salvation presented itself but this, the world must have perished. Even to redeem sinners, God could not have consented to the "blotting from his book" of the sinless. The difficulty is solved in the atonement of the Son, who dies, yet rises again, having made an end of sin. No other could have offered this atonement but himself. 2. *While declining the atonement in its letter, God accepts the spirit of it.* In this sense Moses, by the energy of his self-devotion, *does* make atonement for the sins of Israel. He procures for them a reversal of the sentence. Further intercession is required to make the reconciliation complete. 3. *God makes known his purpose of visiting the people for their sin* (ver. 34). The meaning is— (1) That the sin of the people, though for the present condoned, would be kept in mind in reckoning with them for future transgressions. (2) That such a day of reckoning would come. God, in the certainty of his foreknowledge, sees its approach.—J. O.

EXPOSITION.

CHAPTER XXXIII.

Vers. 1—6.—THE THREAT OF GOD'S WITHDRAWAL, AND THE HUMILIATION OF THE PEOPLE. The intercession of Moses, and his offer to sacrifice himself for his people had obtained from God some great concessions, viz. —1. That the people's lives should be spared (ch. xxxii. 14); 2. And that they should be led into Palestine (*ibid.* ver. 34) But a change

had been introduced into the conditions under which the future journeys were to be made, somewhat obscurely indicated in the words —"Behold, mine angel shall go before thee" (*ibid.*)—which was now to be more distinctly set forth. "God's angel" may mean his Presence in the Person of his Son—as it appears to mean in ch. xxiii. 20—23—or it may mean simply one of the created angelic host, which seems to be its sense in ch. xxxii.

34, and in ver 2 of this chapter. By vers. 2 and 3 taken in combination it was rendered manifest, both to Moses and to the people (ver. 4), that they were threatened with the loss of God's actual presence and personal protection during the remainder of their wanderings, and would have, instead of it, the mere guidance and help of an angel in the inferior sense of the word. This was felt to be " evil tidings "—and the people consequently "mourned" and "stripped themselves of their ornaments" (ver. 6). Real penitence at last entered their hearts, and led to self-abasement.

Ver. 1.—**The Lord said unto Moses.** In continuation of what he had said in ch. xxxii. 33, 34, but possibly at another time; and with the object of fully explaining what had been meant in ver. 34. **The land which I sware unto Abraham.** See Gen. xii. 7; xiii. 15; xv. 18, etc.

Ver. 2. — **I will send an angel before thee.** Note the change from " *my* angel " (ch. xxxii. 34) to " *an* angel;" which, however, would still have been ambiguous, but for what follows in ver. 3. The angel of God's presence is " an angel" in ch. xxiii. 20. **I will drive out.** The whole covenant had fallen with Israel's infraction of it, and it was for God to retract or renew his part of it as it pleased him. He here of his free grace renews the promise to drive out the Canaanitish nations. Compare ch. xxiii. 23—31.

Ver. 3.—**Unto a land.** Ver. 2 is parenthetic, and ver. 3 coheres with ver. 1—"Go up hence, thou and the people, unto the land which I sware unto Abraham—unto a land flowing," etc. On the **milk and honey** of Canaan, see the comment upon ch. iii. 8. **For I will not go up in the midst of thee.** At length there was an end of ambiguity—God's purpose was made plain — the people had shown themselves unfit for his near presence, and he would withdraw himself. So it would be best even for them ; since, if they were about to show themselves as perverse in the future as they had in the past, his near presence could only lead to their entire destruc-

tion. Some day they would so provoke him, that he would **consume** them **in the way.**

Ver. 4.—**When the people heard.** Moses had communicated to the people what God had said to him. They felt it to be **evil tidings**—they woke up at last to a feeling of the ineffable value of the privileges which they had hitherto enjoyed—his guidance by the pillar of the cloud (ch. xiii. 21)—his counsel, if there were need to ask anything (ch. xv. 25)—his aid in the day of battle (ch. xvii. 8—13)—his near presence, by day and by night, constantly (ch. xiii. 22)—and they dreaded a change, which they felt must involve a loss, and one the extent of which they could not measure. " An angel" is a poor consolation when we are craving for Jehovah! So the people **mourned**—felt true sorrow—were really troubled in their hearts— and, to show their penitence, ceased to wear their customary **ornaments.** These may have consisted of armlets, bracelets, and even, perhaps, anklets, all of which were worn by men in Egypt at this period.

Ver. 5. — **For the Lord had said unto Moses,** etc. Rather, " And the Lord said unto M." (so most recent commentators, as Keil, Kalisch, etc.) The message was sent to the people after their repentance, and in reply to it. It was not, however, as our version makes it, a threat of destruction, but only a repetition of the statement made in ver. 2, that, *if* God went up with them, the probable result would be their destruction. Translate— " Ye are a stiff-necked people ; were I for one moment to go up in the midst of thee, I should destroy thee." **Put off thy ornaments.** The command seems strange, when we had just been told that "no man did put on him his ornaments" (ver 4); but the word translated " put off " probably means " lay aside altogether." The intention was to make their *continued* disuse of the ornaments a test of their penitence.

Ver. 6.—The people accepted the test and **stripped themselves of their ornaments**—*i.e.*, ceased to wear them henceforward. **By the Mount Horeb.** Rather, " *from* Mount Horeb." From and after this occurrence at Horeb (=Sinai), the Israelites wore no ornaments, in token of their continued contrition for their apostasy

HOMILETICS.

Vers. 1—6.—*The hiding of God's face from man.* When God hides away his face from his people, it may be—

I. As a JUDGMENT. It was as a judgment that God separated between himself and man after the Fall, and " drove man forth " from the Garden of Eden (Gen. iii. 24). It was as a judgment that he withdrew from Saul, and "answered him not, neither by dreams, by Urim, nor by prophets " (1 Sam. xxviii. 6). When he " hid his face" from David, and forgot all his misery and trouble, it was because David had offended him by the grievous sin into which he had fallen. This, again, was a judgment. Of a similar character was his "removal of Israel out of his sight" (2 Kings xvii. 23) in the reign of Hoshea, and his "casting of Jerusalem and Judah out of his sight" (2 Kings xxiv. 20), in the reign of Zedekiah. And so, when, at the present day, he ceases to make his light shine upon us, withdrawing, as it were, behind a cloud, and no longer shedding the brightness of his radiance upon our souls—it may be, it sometimes is, in judgment. Our sins separate between us and him. They raise the barrier which conceals him from us. They constitute the cloud which shuts him out from our sight. And he judges us for them. Or, the withdrawal may be made—

II. As an act of mercy. When Jesus "did not many miracles" at Capernaum "because of their unbelief," it was in mercy. When he retired to Galilee, and "walked no more in Jewry," it was in mercy. When he spake in parables, "that hearing they might not understand," it was in mercy. Our responsibilities are co-ordinate with the light vouchsafed us; and the more God reveals himself to us, the more he makes his presence manifest, the greater the peril which we incur. Unless his near presence purifies us and spiritualises us, it deadens us. Two disciples were the nearest to Jesus —one "lay upon his breast," the other habitually "dipped with him in the dish"— one was "the beloved disciple," the other was "the traitor." In either case, the withdrawal is properly regarded—

III. As a ground for sadness. "The people mourned when they heard the evil tidings." Justly, for, if it was in mercy, how sad that they should need such a mercy! How sad that to be removed further from God should be a mercy to them! And, if it was in judgment, how much more sad that their conduct should have brought upon them such a judgment—have caused God to withdraw himself—have led him to punish them by banishment from his near presence! What real satisfaction is there in existence except his presence? Whom have we in heaven but him, or who is there upon earth that we can desire in comparison with him? In him is life; "in his presence is fulness of joy, and at his right hand are pleasures for evermore." If we lose him, we lose all; if we are shut out, even for a time, from him, we lose more than we can express. He is to our spirits more than the sun to all material things. "In him we live, and move, and have our being." Happily for us, while we live, we may recover his favour; we may prevail on him once more to "lift up the light of his countenance upon us." Mourning, self-abasement, real heart-felt sorrow for sin will in every case find acceptance with him for his Son's sake, and obtain for us a restoration of the light of his presence.

EXPOSITION.

Vers. 7—11.—The first erection of a tabernacle. The decision of the matter still hung in suspense. God had not revoked his threat to withdraw himself and leave the host to the conduct of an angel. He had merely reserved his final decision (ver. 5). Moses was anxious to wrestle with him in prayer until he obtained the reversal of this sentence; but he could not be always ascending Sinai, when the camp needed his superintending care, and the camp as yet contained no place of worship, where a man could pray and be secure against disturbance. Moses, under these circumstances, with the tabernacle in his mind, but without leisure to construct it, contrived "for the present distress" a temporary tabernacle or tent. He took, apparently, the tent that had hitherto been his own, and removed it to a position outside the camp, erecting it there, and at the same time giving it the name of "the tent of meeting" (ver. 7). Hither he decreed that all persons should come who desired communion with God (ver. 7), and hither he resorted himself for the same purpose (ver. 8). It pleased God to approve these arrangements; and to show his approval by a visible token. Whenever Moses entered the "tent of meeting," the pillar of the cloud descended from the top of Sinai, and took up its station at the door of the tent (ver. 9), thus securing Moses from interruption. At the sight the people "worshipped," each at his tent's door, while Moses was privileged to speak with God "face to face, as a man speaketh unto his friend" (ver. 11). Joshua accompanied him on the first occasion, and remained behind, to guard the tent, when Moses left it (ibid.).

Ver. 7 —**Moses took the tabernacle.** The "tabernacle" proper was not yet constructed. (See chs. xxxv.—xl.) And the word used is not that properly rendered "tabernacle"— viz., *mishkân* (ch. xxvi. 1) ; but the far more common word *'ôhel*, which means "tent." The proper translation would be, "Moses took the tent." But the question at once arises—What tent ? It is suggested that the article may have the force of the possessive pronoun, and indicate that he took "his tent." (Compare Matt. ix. 10, where "*the* house" undoubtedly means "*his* house.") Moses took his own tent, probably as the best in the encampment, and converted it to a sacred use, transferring his own abode to another. **Afar off from the camp.** The sacred and the profane must not approach each other too closely—an interval must be set between them. But the distance, evidently, was not great (ver. 10). **The tabernacle of the congregation.** Rather, "the tent of meeting" or "of conference"—*i.e.*, the tent in which he expected to meet and converse with God. See the comment on ch. xxvii. 21. **Every one which sought the Lord went out.** Moses must have commanded this. The "tent" was not to be a mere oratory for himself, but open to all Israelites.

Ver. 8.—**When Moses went out . . . . all the people rose up.** Probably Moses "went out" at a set time, or at set times, each day ; and the people watched for his going, and "rose up," as a mark of respect and reverence. They felt that he went to the tent mainly to pray for *them.*

Ver. 9.—**As Moses entered into the tabernacle.** Rather, "When Moses was gone into the tent." **The cloudy pillar descended.** It is not quite clear whether this was done once only, or whether the pillar, during the continuance of this "tent of meeting," alternated between the top of Sinai and the door of the tent, descending when Moses entered the tent and reascending when he quitted it. The latter supposition is most consonant with the previous statement (ver. 7) that "every one which sought the Lord went out unto the tabernacle" (tent), for the people were at no time allowed to approach the cloud. **And the Lord talked with Moses.** Literally, "And talked with Moses." The cloudy pillar, in and through which God made his presence felt, is here identified with God, and said to have conversed with Moses.

Ver. 10.—**And all the people saw . . . and all the people rose up.** This is a literal translation ; but it would make the sense clearer to the ordinary reader if the passage were rendered—"And when all the people saw the cloudy pillar stand at the door of the tent, then all the people rose up," etc. **Worshipped.** Literally, "bowed themselves down"—"made an obeisance," in token that they recognised the presence of God.

Ver. 11.—**The Lord spake unto Moses face to face.** As one present—not as one at a distance—"mouth to mouth," as we read in Num. xii. 8—but not under any visible form (see vers. 20, 23, and compare Deut. iv. 12, 15). **He turned again.** After each conference, Moses returned to the camp, where, no doubt, he had put up for himself another tent, and where his presence was needed He left, however, his personal attendant ("minister"), Joshua, to watch and guard the sacred structure during his absence. It is remarkable that the trust was committed to Joshua, rather than to Aaron, or any of the Levites. Probably the reason of this was, that Joshua alone had had no part in the idolatry of the calf. (See ch. xxxii. 17.)

HOMILETICS.

Vers. 9—11.—*The mode of recovering God's presence.* Moses felt that he could not rest till he had obtained for the people the complete return of God's favour, and the assurance of his perpetual presence. But this was no easy task. The offence given was so grievous that it could not be condoned at once. Even the penitence of the people had produced no more than a promise that God would take the matter into his consideration, and determine later what he would do to the people (ver. 5). Moses sought to hasten a favourable decision. It is well worth noting the means whereto he had recourse. These were—

I. THE ERECTION OF A HOUSE OF PRAYER. Moses called it "the tent of meeting"; because he hoped that there God would be met with or would suffer himself to be addressed—would let his people draw nigh to him. He erected it "without the camp," afar off—partly on account of the recent pollution of the camp—partly to separate and sunder it from secular sights and sounds. Intolerant of delay, he thought it better to take the best of existing structures, rather than wait till he could erect a new one. As his own tent was the best in the camp, he gave it, not without some self-sacrifice.

II. THE RESORT OF THE PEOPLE TO THE HOUSE. "Every one which sought the Lord went out unto the tent" (ver. 7). Doubtless Moses urged the need of all the people's seeking the Lord, turning to him, besieging him with their prayers, importuning him. There had been, so far as appears, no set times of prayer hitherto, and no set place of

HOMILETICS.

Vers. 26—28.—*The punishment of idolatry.* God did not long allow the sin against his majesty to remain unpunished. He declared his will to Moses (ver. 27)—"Thus saith the Lord God of Israel"—and Moses, with his usual dutifulness, was prompt to execute his will. Having obtained the necessary force, he lost no time in inflicting the punishment. Of the punishment itself, we shall do well to note—

I. Its SEVERITY. Men talk and think very slightingly in these days of sins against God's majesty. They profess scepticism, agnosticism, atheism, "with a light heart." The idea does not occur to them that their conduct is likely to bring upon them any punishment. But "God's thoughts are not as man's thoughts"—God visits such sins with death. Three thousand are slain with the sword on one day because of a few hours of idol-worship. Such is God's award. And the record of it has been "written for our learning, upon whom the ends of the world are come." It is intended to teach us that God will visit for these things; and, if not in this world, then assuredly in the next.

II. Its JUSTICE. Idolatry is apostasy. It is a "casting of God behind the back"—a turning away from him, and a deliberate preference to him of something which is not he, and which cannot therefore but be infinitely inferior. The heart witnesses against idolatry; it tells us that we are bound, being God's creatures, to devote our whole existence to him. Idolatry might well be punished with death, if it had never been positively forbidden. But the Israelites had heard it forbidden amid the thunders of Sinai (ch. xx. 4, 5). They had a law against it in "the Book of the Covenant" (ch. xx. 23). They had pledged themselves to obey this law (ch. xxiv. 3). They could not therefore now complain. If all who had taken part in the calf-worship had perished, no injustice would have been done. But God tempers justice with mercy. There were well-nigh six hundred thousand sinners; but the lives of three thousand only were taken.

III. THE METHOD WHEREBY IT WAS ESCAPED. Those escaped who put away their sin as, 1. The Levites, who hastened to repent, and placed themselves on the Lord's side at the first summons made by Moses. This was the best course, and the only safe one. This was "turning to the Lord with all the heart;" and, though no atonement for past sin, was accepted by God through the (coming) atonement of his Son, and obtained from him, not only forgiveness, but a blessing (ver. 29). 2. Those escaped who desisted either when Moses made his first appeal, or even when they saw the swords drawn, and vengeance about to be taken. To draw back from sin is the only way to escape its worst consequences. Even then, all its consequences are not escaped. Their iniquity was still "visited" on those who were now allowed to escape with their lives—"the Lord plagued the people because they made the calf" (ver. 35) at a later date.

HOMILIES BY VARIOUS AUTHORS.

Vers. 25—30.—*The zeal of Levi.* Panic was in the camp. The idolaters stood as they had been taken in their guilty revels. Their sin had been of too heinous a nature to admit of its being passed over without severe punishment. Law must be vindicated. Vengeance must be taken for the injury offered to the majesty of Jehovah. Stern as the duty is, the mediator does not shrink from immediately addressing himself to the execution of judgment.

I. THE SUMMONS. He stood in the gate of the camp and said, "Who is on the Lord's side? Let him come unto me" (ver. 26). This must be taken to mean, not, "Who is willing to be on the Lord's side now?" but "Who has shown himself on the Lord's side during the recent apostasy?" Note—the Lord's side, though for a time the unpopular one, proves in the end to be the side of honour, of safety, and of comfort. Fidelity has its ultimate reward. Wisdom is justified of her children. (Matt. xi. 19.)

II. THE RESPONSE. "All the sons of Levi gathered themselves together unto him" (ver. 26). The Levites, as a tribe, would thus appear to have been less implicated in the idolatry than the rest of the people.

"Faithful found

Among the faithless, faithful only he"

This now turns to their honour. The text, however, does not forbid the supposition that *individuals* from the other tribes also came out, and separated themselves at the call of Moses.

III. THE COMMISSION. This was sufficiently sanguinary. It put the fidelity of Levi to a terrible test. "Thus saith the Lord God of Israel, Put every man his sword by his side, and go in and out," etc. (ver. 27). 1. In the work of executing Jehovah's vengeance, *the Levites were to "consecrate" themselves* (ver. 29). They were to devote themselves. They were to be actuated in what they did by pure zeal for God's glory. They were to obey to the letter the command he had given them. 2. In the doing of this work, *they were sternly to repress all natural impulses:* "every man upon his son, and upon his brother" (ver. 29; cf. Deut. xxxiii. 9). So earthly ties are not to be permitted to stand between us and duty to Christ (Matt. viii. 21, 22; x. 27).

IV. THE EXECUTION OF THE MANDATE. 1. *The Levites showed unflinching zeal in the work entrusted to them.* By their zeal on this, and on other occasions (Deut. xxxiii. 8), they reversed the curse which lay upon their tribe, and won for themselves great honour and blessing. In particular, they won the privilege of serving in the sanctuary. 2. *They slew three thousand of the people* (ver. 28). "Terrible surgery this," as Carlyle says of the storming of Drogheda; "but *is* it surgery, and judgment, or atrocious murder merely?" The number of the slain was after all small as compared with the whole body of the people. Probably only the ringleaders and chief instigators of the revolt were put to death, with those who still showed the disposition to resist. Note, that notwithstanding their great zeal on this occasion, the Levites were among those afterwards excluded from Canaan for unbelief. This is a striking circumstance. It shows how those that think they stand need to take heed lest they fall (1 Cor. x. 12). It reminds us that one heroic act of service is not enough to win for us the kingdom of God. "We are made partakers of Christ, if we hold the beginning of our confidence fast *unto the end*" (Heb. iii. 14). It may suggest to us also, that many of the Israelites who failed under the later trial, and so were excluded from Canaan, thus forfeiting the earthly inheritance, may yet have had the root of the matter in them, and so, spiritually, were saved.—J. O.

Ver. 26.—"*Who is on the Lord's side? Let him come unto me.*" The following points suggest a practical treatment of the passage—

I. IN THE WARFARE BETWEEN GOOD AND EVIL, THERE IS NEED FOR TAKING SIDES. Some side we *must* take. We cannot remain neutral. Not to be on the Lord's side, is to be on the side of his enemies. It is our duty to choose the Lord's side. (1) He has a claim on our allegiance. (2) It is the side of honour and of duty. (3) It is the side we will ultimately wish we *had* chosen.

II. THE EXAMPLE OF ONE GOOD MAN, IN DECLARING HIMSELF ON THE LORD'S SIDE, AFFORDS A RALLYING-POINT FOR OTHERS. He gathers others around him. His influence decides and emboldens them.

III. THE TEST OF BEING ON THE LORD'S SIDE IS, THAT, WHEN OTHERS ARE APOSTATISING AROUND US, WE REMAIN FAITHFUL. Weak natures will always go with the multitude. Decided piety shows itself in being able to resist the contagion of numbers. It needs courage to be singular.

IV. BEING ON THE LORD'S SIDE CARRIES WITH IT CERTAIN OBLIGATIONS. (1) The obligation of personal consecration. (2) The obligation of renouncing earthly ties, so far as inconsistent with the higher allegiance. (3) The obligation of doing the Lord's work.

V. FIDELITY ON THE LORD'S SIDE WILL MEET WITH AN ULTIMATE REWARD.—J. O.

EXPOSITION.

Vers. 30—35.—MOSES ONCE MORE INTERCEDES WITH GOD FOR THE PEOPLE — GOD ANSWERS HIM. No distinct reply seems to have been given to the previous intercession of Moses (vers. 11—13). He only knew that the people were not as yet consumed, and therefore that God's wrath was at any rate held in suspense. It might be that the punishment inflicted on the 3000 had appeased God's wrath: or something more might be needed. In the latter case, Moses was ready to sacrifice himself for his nation (ver. 32). Like St. Paul, he elects to be "accursed from God, for his brethren, his kinsfolk after the flesh" (Rom. ix. 3). But God will not have this sacrifice. "The soul that sinneth, it shall die" (Ezek. xviii. 4). He declares, "Whosoever hath sinned against me, him will I blot out of my book" (Ex. xxxii. 33). Moses shall not make himself a victim. Without any such sacrifice, God will so far spare them, that they shall still go on their way towards the promised land, with Moses as their earthly, and an Angel as their heavenly leader. Only, their sin shall still be visited in God's own good time and in his own way. How, is left in obscurity; but the decree is issued—"In the day that I visit, I will visit their sin upon them" (ver. 34). And, writing long years after the event, the author observes —"And God did plague the people because they made the calf which Aaron made" (ver. 35).

Ver. 30.—**On the morrow.** The day must have been well-nigh over when the slaughter of the 3000 was completed: and after that the corpses had to be buried, the signs of carnage to be effaced, and the wounded, of whom there must have been many, cared for. Moses would have had to direct, if not even to superintend, everything, and therefore could not reascend Sinai until the next day. **Moses said unto the people.** Not now to the elders only, as in ch. xxiv. 14, but to all the people, since all had sinned, and each man is held by God individually responsible for his own sin. **Ye have sinned a great sin.** One which combined ingratitude and falseness with impiety. **Peradventure I shall make an atonement.** Moses has formed the design, which he executes (ver. 32); but will not reveal it to the people, from modesty probably.

Ver. 31.—**Gods of gold.** Rather "a god of gold."

Ver. 32.—**If thou wilt forgive their sin.** The ellipsis which follows, is to be supplied by some such words, as "well and good"—"I am content"—"I have no more to say." Similar cases of ellipses will be found in Dan. iii. 5; Luke xiii. 9; xix. 42; John vi. 62; Rom. ix. 22. **And if not, blot me, I pray thee, out of thy book.** Some interpret this as merely equivalent to, "Blot me out of the book of the living," and explain that phrase as meaning simply—"Take my life—kill me instead of them"—but something more seems to be meant. "The book of the living"— "the book of life"—the book of God's writing —is not merely a register of those who happen to be alive at any given time. It "contains

the list of the righteous, and ensures to those whose names are written therein, life before God, first in the earthly kingdom of God, and then eternal life also" (Keil). Thus Moses declared his willingness—nay, his wish—that God would visit on him the guilt of his people, both in this world *and the next*, so that he would thereupon forgive them. St. Paul has a similar burst of feeling (Rom. ix. 1—3); but it does not involve a formal offer—it is simply the expression of a willingness. Ordinary men are scarcely competent to judge these sayings of great saints. As Bengel says—"It is not easy to estimate the measure of love in a Moses and a Paul; for the narrow boundary of our reasoning powers does not comprehend it, as the little child is unable to comprehend the courage of heroes." Both were willing—*felt* willing, at any rate—to sacrifice their own future for their countrymen—and Moses made the offer. Of all the noble acts in Moses' life it is perhaps the noblest; and no correct estimate of his character can be formed which does not base itself to a large extent on his conduct at this crisis.

Ver. 33.—**Whosoever hath sinned against me, him will I blot out of my book.** Beyond a doubt, it is the general teaching of Scripture that vicarious punishment will not be accepted. "The son shall not bear the iniquity of the father, neither shall the father bear the iniquity of the son—the righteousness of the righteous shall be upon him, and the wickedness of the wicked shall be upon him" (Ezek. xviii. 20). Man "cannot deliver his brother, or make agreement with God for him; for it cost more to redeem their souls, so that he must let that alone for ever" (Ps. xlix. 7, 8). One only atonement is accepted—that of him who is at once man and God—who has, himself, no sin —and can therefore take the punishment of others.

Ver. 34.—**Lead the people unto the place,** etc. This was a revocation of the sentence of death passed in verse 10. The people was to be spared, and Moses was to conduct them to Palestine. **Mine Angel shall go before thee.** Mine Angel—not I myself (compare ch. xxxiii. 2, 3). Another threatened punishment, which was revoked upon the repentance of the people (*ib.* 4, 6), and the earnest prayer of Moses (*ib.* 14—16). **I will visit their sin upon them.** Kalisch thinks that a plague was at once sent, and so understands verse 35. But most commentators regard the day of visitation as that on which it was declared that none of those who had quitted Egypt should enter Canaan (Num. xiv. 35), and regard that sentence as, in fact, provoked by the golden calf idolatry (*ib.* 22).

Ver. 35.—**The Lord plagued,** or "struck"— *i.e.,* "punished" the people. There is nothing in the expression which requires us to understand the sending of a pestilence.

HOMILETICS.

Vers. 30—34.—*Moses as the forerunner of Christ.* "A prophet shall the Lord your God raise up unto you *like unto me*," said the great lawgiver, ere he left the earth (Deut. xvii. 15, 18); and the parallelism between Christ and Moses is in many respects most striking. 1. Both were of obscure birth—"the son of a carpenter"—the son of "a man of the house of Levi." 2. Both were in great peril in infancy—their life sought by the civil ruler—Herod—Pharaoh. 3. Both passed their youth and early manhood in obscurity—Christ for thirty, Moses for forty years. 4. Both felt they had a mission, but on coming forward were rejected by their brethren. "He came unto his own, and his own received him not" (John i. 11). "He supposed his brethren would have understood how that God by his hand would deliver them: but they understood not" (Acts vii. 25). 5. Both showed "signs and wonders," such as have rarely been seen upon earth, and thus made it manifest that their missions were from God. 6. Both were law-givers—promulgators of a new moral code—Moses of an imperfect, Christ of a perfect law—("the perfect law of love"). 7. Both were founders of a new community—Moses of the Hebrew state, Christ of the Christian Church. 8. Both were great deliverers and great teachers—Moses delivered his people from Egypt and Pharaoh, and led them through the wilderness to Canaan; Christ delivers his from sin and Satan, and leads them through the wilderness of this life to heaven. 9. Both willed to be a sacrifice for their brethren—God could not accept the one sacrifice (ver. 33), but could and did accept the other.

HOMILIES BY VARIOUS AUTHORS.

Vers. 31, 32.—*The confession and intercession of Moses.* Notice here—
I. THE AMPLITUDE OF THIS CONFESSION. It is very necessary to contrast the words of Moses in vers. 31 and 32 with his previous words in vers. 11—13. What a difference there is in the ground, elements, and tone of the two appeals! and this difference is fully explained by the experience through which he had been in the interval. It was a bitter and humiliating experience—we may almost say an unexpected one. For, although, before he had gone down from the mount, Jehovah had given him a clear forewarning of what awaited him, somehow he seems not to have taken in the full drift of Jehovah's words. It is not till he gets down into the camp and sees the golden image, and the revelry and riot, and the implication of his own brother in a broken covenant, that he discerns the full extent of the calamity, and the difficulty, almost the impossibility of bringing together again Jehovah and his revolted people. Vain is it to seek for anything like sure conclusions in the details of Moses' conduct on this occasion. The things he did were almost as the expressions of a heart beside itself with holy grief. There is a good deal of obscurity in this portion of the narrative; and our wisest course is to turn to what is clear and certain and most instructive, namely, the great result which came out of this experience. It was truly a result, beyond all estimation, to have been led to the conclusion—"This people have sinned a great sin." That was just the light in which Jehovah looked upon their conduct; and though Moses could not see all that Jehovah saw, we may well believe that he saw all that a brother man could see, one whose own heart's vision was not yet perfectly clear. Blessed is that man who, for himself and for others, can see the reality and magnitude of the human heart's departure from God. It would not, indeed, be hard, from a certain point of view, to frame a very plausible story on behalf of these Israelites; but it is far better to bear in mind that just at this particular juncture this very Moses who at first had expostulated with Jehovah, making not the slightest reference to the people's sin, is now found on account of that sin bending himself in the utmost submission before God. Aaron came to Moses with an excuse (vers. 22—24); he spoke in the spirit of Adam, laying the blame elsewhere. But Moses attempts neither excuse nor extenuation. Nor was any enlargement needed. The brief sentence he spoke, standing in all its naked severity, was quite enough.
II. HOW UNCERTAIN MOSES IS IN HIS EXPECTATIONS. The confession is as full and emphatic as it can be, but the heart is of necessity very doubtful as to what may come out of the confession. The words of Moses here are very consistent with the quick

fluctuations of human nature. From extreme to extreme the pendulum swings. Previously he spoke as almost rebuking Jehovah for thinking to destroy his people; now even when the insulting image is ground to powder, and the singledom in measureisation destroyed, he makes his way into the Divine presence as one who is fully prepared for the worst. "If thou wilt forgive them." One can imagine the stammering, half-ashamed tones in which these words would issue from the lips of Moses. The man who was so fruitful of reasons before is silent now. Jehovah's past promises and past dealings he cannot urge; for the more he thinks of them, the more by an inevitable consequence, he thinks of the broken covenant. The light of these glorious promises shines for the present, upon a scene of ruin and shame. Then it is noteworthy that Moses had to go up, from the impulse of his own heart. We do not hear as yet of any general confession; it is not the weeping and wailing of a nation returning in penitence that he bears before God. If only the people had sent him to say, "We have sinned a great sin;" if only they had made him feel that he was their chosen spokesman; if only their continued cry of contrition, softened by distance, had reached his ears, as he ventured before God, there might have been something to embolden him. But as yet there was no sign of anything of this sort. He seems to have gone up as a kind of last resort, unencouraged by any indication that the people comprehended the near and dreadful peril. Learn from this that there can be no availing plea and service from our great advocate, except as we look to him for the plea and service, in full consciousness that we cannot do without them. We get no practical good from the advocacy of Jesus, unless as in faith and earnestness, we make him our advocate.

III. HOW COMPLETELY MOSES ASSOCIATES HIMSELF WITH THE FATE OF HIS BRETHREN. He could not but feel the difference there was between his position and theirs; but at the moment there was a feeling which swallowed all others up, and that was the unity of brotherhood. The suggestion to make out of him a new and better covenant people came back to him now, with a startling significance which it lacked before. Israel, *as the people of God*, seemed shut up to destruction now. If God said the covenant could not be renewed; if he said the people must return and be merged and lost in the general mass of human-kind, Moses knew he had no countervailing plea; only this he could pray that he also might be included in their doom. He had no heart to go unless where his people went; and surely it must have a most inspiring and kindling influence to meditate on this great illustration of unselfishness. Moses, we know, had been brought very near to God; what glimpses must have been opened up to him of a glorious future. But then he had only thought of it as being his future along with his people. In the threatenings that God was about to forsake those who had forsaken him, there seemed no longer any brightness even in the favour of God to him as an individual. Apostate in heart and deed as his brethren were, he felt himself a member of the body still; and to be separated from them would be as if the member were torn away. He who had preferred affliction with the people of God rather than the pleasures of sin for a season, now prefers obliteration along with his own people rather than to keep his name on God's great book. It can hardly be said that in this he spurns or depreciates the favour of God; and it is noticeable that God does not rebuke him as if he were preferring human ties to Divine. Jehovah simply responds by stating the general law of what is inevitable in all sinning. He who sins must be blotted out of God's book. God will not in so many words rebuke the pitying heart of his servant; but yet we clearly see that there was no way out by that course which Moses so very deferentially suggests. When first Moses heard of the apostasy of Israel he spoke as if the remedy depended upon Jehovah; now he speaks as if it might be found in his own submission and self-sacrifice; but God would have him understand that whatever chance there may be depends on a much needed change in the hearts of the people, a change of which all sign so far was lacking.—Y.

Vers. 30—35.—*The second intercession.* This second intercession of Moses is even more wonderful than the first. The question raised on that former occasion—Is Moses more merciful than God?—will, indeed, no longer occur. Those who might have been disposed to press that question then will probably not be disposed to press it now. They have since had sufficient evidence of Moses' severity. They have found that, whatever elements of character are lacking to him, he is not wanting in energy of indignation at patent wickedness. The temptation, on the contrary, may now be to accuse the law-giver of unjustifiable and unholy anger—of reckless disregard of human life. The charge is groundless; but if, for a moment, it should appear natural, the reply to it is found in the study of this second scene upon the mount. Surely, if ever human heart laid bare its intense and yearning love for those whose sin fidelity to duty yet compelled it to reprobate and loathe, it is the heart of Moses in this new, and altogether marvel-lous, juncture in his history. Consider—

I. The CONFESSION MADE (vers. 30, 31). Moses makes a full confession of the sin of the people. This confession was—1. *Holy.* He has just views of the demerit of the sin for which he seeks forgiveness. His impressions of its enormity are even stronger than at the time of his first intercession. So heinous does it now appear to him that he is mentally in doubt whether God possibly *can* forgive it. 2. *Perfectly truthful.* Moses fully admits the people's sin. He does not make light of it. He does not seek to minimise it. Not even to secure the salvation of the people over whom he yearns with so intense an affection will he unduly palliate their offence, or feign an excuse where he knows that there is none to offer. Mark how, in both of these respects, Moses answers to the true idea of a mediator. "A mediator is not a mediator of one" (Gal. iii. 20). It is his function, in conducting his mediation, to uphold impartially the interests of *both* of the parties between whom he mediates. Both are represented in his work. He stands for both equally. He must do justice by both. His sympathy with both must be alike perfect. He must favour neither at the expense, or to the disadvantage, of the other. These acts of intercession show in how supreme a degree this qualification of the mediator is found in Moses. He has sympathy with the people, for whose sin he is willing, if need be, even to die; he has also the fullest sympathy with God. He looks at the sin from God's standpoint. He has sympathy with God's wrath against it. He is as jealous for God's honour as he is anxious for the forgiveness of the people. He is thus the true daysman, able to lay his hand upon both. 3. *Vicarious.* He confesses the people's sin *for* them. On the depth to which this element enters into the idea of atonement, and on the place which it holds in the atonement of Jesus, see J. McLeod Campbell's work on *The Nature of the Atonement.*

II. The ATONEMENT OFFERED (ver. 32). The new and awful impressions Moses had received of the enormity of the people's conduct gave rise in his mind to the feeling of the need of atonement. "Now I will go up to the Lord," he says to them, "peradven-ture I shall make an atonement for your sin" (ver. 30). That the intercessory element entered into Moses' idea of "making an atonement" is not to be denied. But it is not the only one. So intensely evil does the sin of the people now appear to him that he is plainly in doubt whether it can be pardoned without some awful expression of God's punitive justice against it; whether, indeed, it can be pardoned at all. This sense of what is due to justice resolves itself into the proposal in the text—a proposal, probably, in which Moses comes as near anticipating Christ, in his great sacrifice on Calvary, as it is possible for any one, bearing the limitations of humanity, to do (cf. Rom. ix. 3). Observe—1. *The proposal submitted.* It amounts to this, that Moses, filled with an immense love for his people, offers himself as a sacrifice for their sin. If God cannot otherwise pardon their transgression, and if this will avail, or can be accepted, as an atonement for their guilt, let him—Moses—perish instead of them. The precise meaning attached in Moses' mind to the words, "If not, blot me, I pray thee, out of the book which thou hast written," must always be a difficulty. Precision, probably, is not to be looked for. Moses' idea of what was involved in the blotting out from God's book could only be that afforded him by the light of his own dispensation, and by his sense of the exceeding greatness of God's wrath. His language is the language of love, not that of dogmatic theology. Infinite things were to be hoped for from God's love; infinite things were to be dreaded from his anger. The general sense of the utterance is, that Moses was willing to die; to be cut off from covenant hope and privilege; to undergo whatever awful doom subjection to God's wrath might imply; if only thereby his people could be saved. It was a stupendous proposal to make; an extraordinary act of self-devotion; a wondrous exponent of his patriotic love for his people; a not less wondrous recognition of what was due to the justice of God ere sin could be forgiven—a glimpse even, struck out from the passionate yearning of his own heart, of the actual method of redemption. A type of Christ has been seen in the youthful Isaac ascending the hill to be offered on the altar by Abraham his father. A much nearer type is Moses, " setting his face " (cf. Luke ix. 51) to ascend the mount, and bearing in his heart this sublime purpose of devoting himself for the sins of the nation. "Greater love hath no man than this, that a man lay down his life for his friends" (John xv. 10). 2. *The alternative desired.* If the people must perish—this meaning also seems to be conveyed in the words—Moses would wish to perish with them. Not only has the proposal to make of him "a great nation" (Ex. xxxii. 10) no allurement for his mind, but, if the people are to be destroyed, he would prefer to die with them. He desires no life outside of theirs. Patriotic devotion could no further go. Noble Moses! Yet only the type of the nobler than himself, who, devoting himself in the same spirit, has actually achieved the redemption of the world. See in this incident (1) The connection of a feeling of the need of atonement with just views of sin's demerit. (2) The certainty, when just views of sin are entertained, of this feeling of the need of atonement arising. In declining the proposal of Moses, God does not say that atonement is not needed. He does not say that his servant has exaggerated the enormity of the sin, or the difficulties which stand in the way of its forgiveness. He does not say that it is not by means of atonement that these difficulties connected with the forgiveness of sins are ultimately to be removed. On the contrary, the spirit of Moses in this transaction is evidently in the very highest degree pleasing to Jehovah, and so far as atonement *is* made for the people's sins, it is by Jehovah accepting the *spirit* of his sacrifice, even when rejecting the proposal in its letter. (3) The *naturalness* of this method of salvation. The proposal sprang naturally from the love of Moses. It expressed everything that was grandest in his character. It shadowed forth a way in which, conceivably, a very true satisfaction might be offered to Divine justice, while yet mercy was extended to the sinner. The fulfilment of the prophecy is the Cross.

III. The reply given. 1. *The atonement is declined in its letter.* God declares that so far as there is to be any blotting from the book of life, it will be confined to those who have sinned. It may be noted, in respect to this declinature of the proposal of Moses that, as above remarked, it does not proceed on the idea that atonement is not needed, but (1) Moses could not, even by his immolation, have made the atonement required. (2) God, in his secret counsel, had the true sacrifice provided. (3) Atonement is inadmissible on the basis proposed, viz. that the innocent should be " blotted out from the book of life." Had no means of salvation presented itself but this, the world must have perished. Even to redeem sinners, God could not have consented to the " blotting from his book " of the sinless. The difficulty is solved in the atonement of the Son, who dies, yet rises again, having made an end of sin. No other could have offered this atonement but himself. 2. *While declining the atonement in its letter, God accepts the spirit of it.* In this sense Moses, by the energy of his self-devotion, *does* make atonement for the sins of Israel. He procures for them a reversal of the sentence. Further intercession is required to make the reconciliation complete. 3. *God makes known his purpose of visiting the people for their sin* (ver. 34). The meaning is— (1) That the sin of the people, though for the present condoned, would be kept in mind in reckoning with them for future transgressions. (2) That such a day of reckoning would come. God, in the certainty of his foreknowledge, sees its approach.—J. O.

EXPOSITION.

CHAPTER XXXIII.

Vers. 1—6.—The threat of God's with-drawal, and the humiliation of the people. The intercession of Moses, and his offer to sacrifice himself for his people had obtained from God some great concessions, viz. —1. That the people's lives should be spared (ch. xxxii. 14); 2. And that they should be led into Palestine (*ibid.* ver. 34) But a change

had been introduced into the conditions under which the future journeys were to be made, somewhat obscurely indicated in the words —" Behold, mine angel shall go before thee " (*ibid.*)—which was now to be more distinctly set forth. "God's angel" may mean his Presence in the Person of his Son—as it appears to mean in ch. xxiii. 20—23—or it may mean simply one of the created angelic host, which seems to be its sense in ch. xxxii.

34, and in ver 2 of this chapter. By vers. 2 and 3 taken in combination it was rendered manifest, both to Moses and to the people (ver. 4), that they were threatened with the loss of God's actual presence and personal protection during the remainder of their wanderings, and would have, instead of it, the mere guidance and help of an angel in the inferior sense of the word. This was felt to be " evil tidings "—and the people consequently "mourned" and "stripped themselves of their ornaments " (ver. 6). Real penitence at last entered their hearts, and led to self-abasement.

Ver. 1.—**The Lord said unto Moses.** In continuation of what he had said in ch. xxxii. 33, 34, but possibly at another time; and with the object of fully explaining what had been meant in ver. 34. **The land which I sware unto Abraham.** See Gen. xii. 7; xiii. 15; xv. 18, etc.

Ver. 2. — **I will send an angel before thee.** Note the change from " *my* angel " (ch. xxxii. 34) to "*an* angel ;" which, however, would still have been ambiguous, but for what follows in ver. 3. The angel of God's presence is " an angel " in ch. xxiii. 20. **I will drive out.** The whole covenant had fallen with Israel's infraction of it, and it was for God to retract or renew his part of it as it pleased him. He here of his free grace renews the promise to drive out the Canaanitish nations. Compare ch. xxiii. 23—31.

Ver. 3.—**Unto a land.** Ver. 2 is parenthetic, and ver. 3 coheres with ver. 1—" Go up hence, thou and the people, unto the land which I sware unto Abraham—unto a land flowing," etc. On the **milk and honey** of Canaan, see the comment upon ch. iii. 8. **For I will not go up in the midst of thee.** At length there was an end of ambiguity—God's purpose was made plain — the people had shown themselves unfit for his near presence, and he would withdraw himself. So it would be best even for them ; since, if they were about to show themselves as perverse in the future as they had in the past, his near presence could only lead to their entire destruc-

tion. Some day they would so provoke him, that he would **consume** them **in the way.**

Ver. 4.—**When the people heard.** Moses had communicated to the people what God had said to him. They felt it to be **evil tidings**—they woke up at last to a feeling of the ineffable value of the privileges which they had hitherto enjoyed—his guidance by the pillar of the cloud (ch. xiii. 21)—his counsel, if there were need to ask anything (ch. xv. 25)—his aid in the day of battle (ch. xvii. 8—13)—his near presence, by day and by night, constantly (ch. xiii. 22)—and they dreaded a change, which they felt must involve a loss, and one the extent of which they could not measure. " An angel " is a poor consolation when we are craving for Jehovah ! So the people **mourned**—felt true sorrow—were really troubled in their hearts—and, to show their penitence, ceased to wear their customary **ornaments.** These may have consisted of armlets, bracelets, and even, perhaps, anklets, all of which were worn by men in Egypt at this period.

Ver. 5. — **For the Lord had said unto Moses,** etc. Rather, "And the Lord said unto M." (so most recent commentators, as Keil, Kalisch, etc.) The message was sent to the people after their repentance, and in reply to it. It was not, however, as our version makes it, a threat of destruction, but only a repetition of the statement made in ver. 2, that, *if* God went up with them, the probable result would be their destruction. Translate— " Ye are a stiff-necked people ; were I for one moment to go up in the midst of thee, I should destroy thee." **Put off thy ornaments.** The command seems strange, when we had just been told that " no man did put on him his ornaments " (ver 4); but the word translated " put off " probably means " lay aside altogether." The intention was to make their *continued* disuse of the ornaments a test of their penitence.

Ver. 6.—The people accepted the test and **stripped themselves of their ornaments**—*i.e.,* ceased to wear them henceforward. **By the Mount Horeb.** Rather, "*from* Mount Horeb." From and after this occurrence at Horeb (=Sinai), the Israelites wore no ornaments, in token of their continued contrition for their apostasy

HOMILETICS.

Vers. 1—6.—*The hiding of God's face from man.* When God hides away his face from his people, it may be—

I. As a JUDGMENT. It was as a judgment that God separated between himself and man after the Fall, and " drove man forth " from the Garden of Eden (Gen. iii. 24). It was as a judgment that he withdrew from Saul, and " answered him not, neither by dreams, by Urim, nor by prophets " (1 Sam. xxviii. 6). When he " hid his face " from David, and forgot all his misery and trouble, it was because David had offended him by the grievous sin into which he had fallen. This, again, was a judgment. Of a similar character was his "removal of Israel out of his sight" (2 Kings xvii. 23) in the reign of Hoshea, and his "casting of Jerusalem and Judah out of his sight" (2 Kings xxiv. 20), in the reign of Zedekiah. And so, when, at the present day, he ceases to make his light shine upon us, withdrawing, as it were, behind a cloud, and no longer shedding the brightness of his radiance upon our souls it may be it sometimes in, in judgment. Our sins separate between us and him. They raise the barrier which conceals him from us. They constitute the cloud which shuts him out from our sight. And he judges us for them. Or, the withdrawal may be made—

II. As AN ACT OF MERCY. When Jesus "did not many miracles" at Capernaum "because of their unbelief," it was in mercy. When he retired to Galilee, and "walked no more in Jewry," it was in mercy. When he spake in parables, "that hearing they might not understand," it was in mercy. Our responsibilities are co-ordinate with the light vouchsafed us; and the more God reveals himself to us, the more he makes his presence manifest, the greater the peril which we incur. Unless his near presence purifies us and spiritualises us, it deadens us. Two disciples were the nearest to Jesus —one "lay upon his breast," the other habitually "dipped with him in the dish"— one was "the beloved disciple," the other was "the traitor." In either case, the withdrawal is properly regarded—

III. As A GROUND FOR SADNESS. "The people mourned when they heard the evil tidings." Justly, for, if it was in mercy, how sad that they should need such a mercy! How sad that to be removed further from God should be a mercy to them! And, if it was in judgment, how much more sad that their conduct should have brought upon them such a judgment—have caused God to withdraw himself—have led him to punish them by banishment from his near presence! What real satisfaction is there in existence except his presence? Whom have we in heaven but him, or who is there upon earth that we can desire in comparison with him? In him is life; "in his presence is fulness of joy, and at his right hand are pleasures for evermore." If we lose him, we lose all; if we are shut out, even for a time, from him, we lose more than we can express. He is to our spirits more than the sun to all material things. "In him we live, and move, and have our being." Happily for us, while we live, we may recover his favour; we may prevail on him once more to "lift up the light of his countenance upon us." Mourning, self-abasement, real heart-felt sorrow for sin will in every case find acceptance with him for his Son's sake, and obtain for us a restoration of the light of his presence.

EXPOSITION.

Vers. 7—11.—THE FIRST ERECTION OF A TABERNACLE. The decision of the matter still hung in suspense. God had not revoked his threat to withdraw himself and leave the host to the conduct of an angel. He had merely reserved his final decision (ver. 5). Moses was anxious to wrestle with him in prayer until he obtained the reversal of this sentence; but he could not be always ascending Sinai, when the camp needed his superintending care, and the camp as yet contained no place of worship, where a man could pray and be secure against disturbance. Moses, under these circumstances, with the tabernacle in his mind, but without leisure to construct it, contrived "for the present distress" a temporary tabernacle or tent. He took, apparently, the tent that had hitherto been his own, and removed it to a position outside the camp, erecting it there, and at the same time giving it the name of "the tent of meeting" (ver. 7). Hither he decreed that all persons should come who desired communion with God (ver. 7), and hither he resorted himself for the same purpose (ver. 8). It pleased God to approve these arrangements; and to show his approval by a visible token. Whenever Moses entered the "tent of meeting," the pillar of the cloud descended from the top of Sinai, and took up its station at the door of the tent (ver. 9), thus securing Moses from interruption. At the sight the people "worshipped," each at his tent's door, while Moses was privileged to speak with God "face to face, as a man speaketh unto his friend" (ver. 11). Joshua accompanied him on the first occasion, and remained behind, to guard the tent, when Moses left it (ibid.).

Ver. 7 —**Moses took the tabernacle.** The "tabernacle" proper was not yet constructed. (See chs. xxxv.—xl.) And the word used is not that properly rendered "tabernacle"— viz., *mishkân* (ch. xxvi. 1) ; but the far more common word *'ôhel*, which means "tent." The proper translation would be, "Moses took the tent." But the question at once arises—What tent ? It is suggested that the article may have the force of the possessive pronoun, and indicate that he took "his tent." (Compare Matt. ix. 10, where "*the* house" undoubtedly means "*his* house.") Moses took his own tent, probably as the best in the encampment, and converted it to a sacred use, transferring his own abode to another. **Afar off from the camp.** The sacred and the profane must not approach each other too closely—an interval must be set between them. But the distance, evidently, was not great (ver. 10). **The tabernacle of the congregation.** Rather, "the tent of meeting" or "of conference"—*i.e.*, the tent in which he expected to meet and converse with God. See the comment on ch. xxvii. 21. **Every one which sought the Lord went out.** Moses must have commanded this. The "tent" was not to be a mere oratory for himself, but open to all Israelites.

Ver. 8.—**When Moses went out .... all the people rose up.** Probably Moses "went out" at a set time, or at set times, each day ; and the people watched for his going, and "rose up," as a mark of respect and reverence. They felt that he went to the tent mainly to pray for *them*.

Ver. 9.—**As Moses entered into the tabernacle.** Rather, "When Moses was gone into the tent." **The cloudy pillar descended.** It is not quite clear whether this was done once only, or whether the pillar, during the con-

tinuance of this "tent of meeting," alternated between the top of Sinai and the door of the tent, descending when Moses entered the tent and reascending when he quitted it. The latter supposition is most consonant with the previous statement (ver. 7) that "every one which sought the Lord went out unto the tabernacle" (tent), for the people were at no time allowed to approach the cloud. **And the Lord talked with Moses.** Literally, "And talked with Moses." The cloudy pillar, in and through which God made his presence felt, is here identified with God, and said to have conversed with Moses.

Ver. 10.—**And all the people saw . . . and all the people rose up.** This is a literal translation ; but it would make the sense clearer to the ordinary reader if the passage were rendered—"And when all the people saw the cloudy pillar stand at the door of the tent, then all the people rose up," etc. **Worshipped.** Literally, "bowed themselves down"—"made an obeisance," in token that they recognised the presence of God.

Ver. 11.—**The Lord spake unto Moses face to face.** As one present—not as one at a distance—"mouth to mouth," as we read in Num. xii. 8—but not under any visible form (see vers. 20, 23, and compare Deut. iv. 12, 15). **He turned again.** After each conference, Moses returned to the camp, where, no doubt, he had put up for himself another tent, and where his presence was needed He left, however, his personal attendant ("minister"), Joshua, to watch and guard the sacred structure during his absence. It is remarkable that the trust was committed to Joshua, rather than to Aaron, or any of the Levites. Probably the reason of this was, that Joshua alone had had no part in the idolatry of the calf. (See ch. xxxii. 17.)

HOMILETICS.

Vers. 9—11.—*The mode of recovering God's presence.* Moses felt that he could not rest till he had obtained for the people the complete return of God's favour, and the assurance of his perpetual presence. But this was no easy task. The offence given was so grievous that it could not be condoned at once. Even the penitence of the people had produced no more than a promise that God would take the matter into his consideration, and determine later what he would do to the people (ver. 5). Moses sought to hasten a favourable decision. It is well worth noting the means whereto he had recourse. These were—

I. THE ERECTION OF A HOUSE OF PRAYER. Moses called it "the tent of meeting"; because he hoped that there God would be met with or would suffer himself to be addressed—would let his people draw nigh to him. He erected it "without the camp," afar off—partly on account of the recent pollution of the camp—partly to separate and sunder it from secular sights and sounds. Intolerant of delay, he thought it better to take the best of existing structures, rather than wait till he could erect a new one. As his own tent was the best in the camp, he gave it, not without some self-sacrifice.

II. THE RESORT OF THE PEOPLE TO THE HOUSE. "Every one which sought the Lord went out unto the tent" (ver. 7). Doubtless Moses urged the need of all the people's seeking the Lord, turning to him, besieging him with their prayers, importuning him. There had been, so far as appears, no set times of prayer hitherto, and no set place of prayer. All had been left to individual feeling or conviction. And the people, we may be sure, had for the most part neglected prayer. In their difficulties they had been content that Moses should pray for them (ch. xiv. 15; xv. 25; xvii. 4, 11, 12, etc.). Now at length they had awoke to the need of personal religion; they had "mourned" and "put off their ornaments"; they—some of them, at any rate—"sought the Lord," and resorted to the "tent of meeting," in the hope of finding him there.

III. HIS OWN FREQUENT RESORT TO IT, AND CONSTANT, EARNEST INTERCESSION. The narrative of verses 8—11 describes a continual practice. Moses made it his habit to go forth from the camp to the "tent of meeting" at a fixed hour each day—possibly more than once a day; and, when there, no doubt prayed to the Lord with all the fervour that we observe in the recorded prayer of the next section (vers. 12—16). "The effectual fervent prayer of a righteous man availeth much" (Jam. v. 16). The daily intercession, recorded in verses 8—11, culminated in the "wrestle with God," which obtained the gracious promise—"I will do this thing that thou hast spoken" (ver. 17). The general lesson taught is the might of prayer (1) for oneself; (2) for others. There is a further particular lesson upon the value of a "house of prayer"—most appreciated, through the perversity of human nature, where least readily obtainable, least regarded where closest to men's doors and most accessible.

HOMILIES BY VARIOUS AUTHORS.

Vers. 1—12. *A nation in garb of penitence.* On this section consider—

I. THE CONDITIONED PROMISE (vers. 1—4). God has consented to spare the nation. They are to set out forthwith on the journey to Canaan. But his presence is no longer to go with them. He would send an angel. Notice—1. *Everything, in one sense, remains the same.* The people are to be conducted to Canaan. They are to inherit the promises. God will drive out their enemies before them. The land will still flow with milk and honey. It will still be able to be said of them, that there is no nation on earth so favoured as they are. Yet, 2. *Everything, in another sense, is different.* Blessings without God in them are not the same blessings. They want that which gives them their chief value. See below, on ver. 15.

II. THE SUMMONS TO REPENTANCE (vers. 4—7). A command is next given to the people to strip off their ornaments. They are to humble themselves before Jehovah that Jehovah may know what to do with them. This command they obeyed. From this time forward they ceased to wear ornaments. On this observe, 1. *Repentance for sin is an indispensable condition of restoration to God's favour.* It was required of Israel. It is required of us. There can be no salvation without it (Luke xvii. 5). "Cease to do evil; learn to do well" (Is. i. 16, 17). Had Israel not repented, Moses would have interceded in vain. 2. *Repentance, if sincere, must approve itself by appropriate deeds.* —"Bring forth therefore fruits meet for repentance" (Matt. iii. 8). The people put off their ornaments. Ornaments do not become those with whom God is displeased. This act of the people was a first step in obedience. 3. *A very imperfect repentance is sometimes accepted by God as a reason for forbearance with the sinner.* The people mourned; but their repentance, as events showed, did not amount to a real change of heart. They mourned for "the evil tidings." It was the *consequences* of their sin which distressed them, more than the sin itself. Yet do them justice. The "evil tidings" was not the loss of any *material* blessings, but, solely, the loss of God's presence. There is still good in a heart which feels the withdrawal of God's presence to be a loss to it. 4. *It is well that the remembrance of great sins should go with us all our days.* Those who have committed them should go softly ever after.

III. THE WITHDRAWAL OF JEHOVAH'S PRESENCE FROM THE CAMP (vers. 7—9). Moses, we are next informed, took a tent, possibly his own, possibly one which had hitherto served as a sanctuary, pitched it "without the camp, afar off from the camp," and called it "the tent of meeting." Thither came out every one that sought the Lord. The act was, 1. A symbol of Jehovah's formal withdrawal from the midst of the people. 2. A token that a final decision had not yet been come to as to how God meant to deal with them. Communications were not wholly broken off. Space was left for repentance. God might still be entreated of them. Learn (1) iniquities separate between man and

God (cf. Is. lix. 2); (2) the withdrawal of God's presence is not necessarily the end of the day of grace. There is an "accepted time" during which, if the sinner repents, he will be forgiven, and God's presence will be restored to him (2 Cor. vi. 2). Meanwhile, even God's keeping back from him has its side of mercy. God's near presence would consume (cf. ver. 5). (3) The day of grace which sinners enjoy is won for them by the intercession of another. Israel's "accepted time" was based on the intercession of Moses. Ours, as the passage above referred to implies, rests on the intercession of Christ. "I have heard thee (Christ) in a time accepted" (cf. Is. xlix. 8)—"Behold, now is the accepted time"—for men (2 Cor. vi. 2). (4) it is our duty to seek the Lord while he may be found, and to call on him while he is near (Is. lv. 6).

IV. THE TOKEN OF FAVOUR TO MOSES (vers. 9—12). The cloudy pillar descended, and stood at the door of the tabernacle. There the Lord talked with Moses, as a man talketh with his friend. This was (1) a mark of favour to Moses himself; (2) an honour put upon him before the people; (3) an encouragement to further intercession.—J. O.

EXPOSITION.

Vers. 12—17.—THE REVOCATION OF THE THREAT OF WITHDRAWAL. After some days' "wrestling with God" in the "tent of meeting," Moses prayed to know definitely what God had determined on. "Show me thy way," he said (ver. 13)—"Whom wilt thou send with me?" To this demand, God made the gracious reply—"My presence shall go with thee, and I will give thee rest" (ver. 14). This was satisfactory, except that it did not distinctly include the conduct of the people—it might be merely a promise to himself. So Moses (vers. 15, 16) requires a more explicit assurance, and, closely associating the people with himself, declares that he will not move a step further, unless God allows the people to find grace in his sight, and consents to "distinguish" them by "going up" with them. Then at length God yields and gives the assurance—"I will do this thing also that thou hast spoken" (ver. 17)—i.e. "I will go up visibly with the people and distinguish them." (See the comment on ver. 16.)

Vers. 12, 13.—See, thou sayest. Moses takes advantage of his privilege of speaking as friend with friend, and uses familiar terms —"See," he says, "thou hast told me to conduct the people to Canaan, yet thou hast not made it clear whom thou wilt send with me. If it is to be an angel, what angel? Why not the angel of the original promise (ch. xxiii. 20 —23)? Thou hast distinguished me with thy favour — Consider that this nation is thy people, and extend thy favour to them. At any rate shew me thy way—tell me plainly what thou wilt do."

Ver. 14.—My presence shall go with thee. Literally, "My presence shall go up"—my own presence, not that of an angel. That for which Moses had been so earnestly pleading is, seemingly, granted. God will go up. I will give thee rest.—i.e. "bring thee to Canaan." (Compare Deut. iii. 20 ; Heb. iv. 8.)

Vers. 15, 16.—And he said. Still Moses is not quite satisfied. God had said—"I will give thee rest"—not "I will give you rest." Moses must see distinctly that the people are associated with him before he desists. So he replies—"If thy presence go not up, carry us not up hence. For wherein shall it be known that I and thy people have found grace in thy sight? Is it not in that thou goest with us?" The reply in ver. 17 sets his doubt finally at rest.

Ver. 16.—So shall we be separated. Rather, "So shall we be distinguished." God's presence with them would distinguish them from all the other nations of the earth—place them in a category alone and apart from all others. Angelic guidance would not have done this; for even heathen nations had their protecting angels (Dan. x. 13, 20 ; xi. 1).

Ver. 17.—I will do this thing also. "I will extend my favour to thy people also, and distinguish them, as well as thee, by going up with them. I will do this for thy sake, because thou hast found grace in my sight." Moses' petition is at last fully granted—the threat of withdrawal cancelled—the promise of Divine guidance and protection renewed. I know thee by name. It is a supreme favour for God to know us by name. It marks "a specifically personal relation to God" (Keil). The expression is perhaps taken from the phraseology of Oriental Courts, where not one in a hundred of the courtiers is known to the monarch by name.

HOMILETICS.

Vers. 12—17.—*Effectual importunity.* Our Lord Jesus Christ spoke a parable to show " that men ought always to pray and not to faint" (Luke xviii. 1). The present record is, we may be sure, inserted in the Old Testament for the same purpose. God wills to be importuned. Not, however, for his own sake, but for ours. He would have us fervent and persistent in prayer, for the improvement of our characters, the increase of our faith by exercise, the intensifying of our sense of dependence upon him. Especially he would have us persistent in intercessory prayer, because we are then exercising, not only faith, but love; and by increasing in love, we advance in resemblance to himself. For "God is Love." Note, that, to be importuned effectively, God must be importuned—

I. WITH FERVOUR. Mere repetition will not do. Cold prayers, repeated day after day for blessings on ourselves or others, are a mere *battologia*, no more effectual than the involuntary repetitions of a stammering tongue. God grants nothing to coldness, nothing to mere words, nothing unless it be earnestly desired by a fervid heart. The Buddhists, in many parts of Asia, erect praying-machines, which are turned by a small windmill, believing that in every revolution of the machine a prayer is offered, and that, after so many turns, Buddha is bound to grant it. As well expect God to respect the requests of a praying-machine, as the utterances of many who languidly repeat the prayers of the Church after the clergyman, or say a set form, with small thought and no heart, morning and evening. It is "the fervent prayer of a righteous man"—nay, even of a sinner —that is "effectual."

II. UNSELFISHLY. Moses postponed his now earnest desire to behold for his own satisfaction God's glory, until he had obtained the restitution of the people to favour. His importunity was for them. Let us importune God for the conversion of our relatives and friends, the forgiveness of their sins, the awakening of their consciences, their perseverance in well-doing, and their final entrance into his glory, and we may feel confident of prevailing with him. But, if we importune him for our own worldly advancement, or even if we ask increase of grace for our own sakes solely or mainly, we must not be surprised if our prayers remain unanswered. "Ye ask and obtain not, because ye ask amiss." The spirit of sacrifice is required to sanctify prayer. Those who in a spirit of self-seeking asked to sit on the right hand and left hand of Christ in his kingdom obtained no promise. Our prayers even for our spiritual advancement will scarcely be answered, unless we desire it to promote God's glory, or to help forward the salvation of our fellow-men.

HOMILIES BY VARIOUS AUTHORS.

Vers. 12—18.—*The third intercession.* Moses on this occasion pleads with God to restore his presence to the people. Very noteworthy are the steps in his entreaty. 1. He veils his request under the form of a desire to know the divine intentions (ver. 12). Will God go up with them or not? God has not yet told him—will he tell him now? What, underneath this form of expression, the heart of Moses really presses for, is, of course, the assurance that God *will* go with them. 2. He urges the friendship God has shown him as a reason for granting his request—"Thou hast said, I know thee by name," etc. (ver. 12). 3. He entreats God to consider that Israel is his own people (ver. 13). He has chosen them; he has redeemed them; he has declared his love for them; can he bring himself now to cast them off? 4. When God at length—reading in his servant's heart the thought which he has not as yet dared openly to express— says, "My presence shall go with thee, and I will give thee rest" (ver. 14); Moses eagerly seizes on the promise thus given him, and pleads with God to make it good. "If thy presence go not with me, carry us not up hence" (ver. 15). This, in Moses' view, is the greatest distinction of Israel, that it has God in its midst, and if this distinction is withdrawn, he cares not what else remains (ver. 16). The earnestness of his entreaty secures for him a confirmation of the promise, this time given without reserve. For in the utterance of ver. 14, perhaps, a certain tone of distance is still to be detected. This disappears in ver. 17. View the passage as illustrating—

I. THE PRIVILEGES OF FRIENDSHIP WITH GOD (vers. 12, 13). 1. Friendship with God *gives boldness of approach to him.* It casts out fear (1 John iv. 18). 2. Friendship with God *admits to intimacy with his secrets* (ver. 13). "The secret of the Lord is with them that fear him" (Ps. xxv. 14). Cf. God's words concerning Abraham—" Shall I hide from Abraham that thing which I do, seeing that Abraham shall surely become a great and mighty nation," etc. (Gen. xviii. 17); and Christ's words to his disciples—" I call you not servants; for the servant knoweth not what his Lord doeth: but I have called you friends; for all things that I have heard of my Father I have made known unto you" (John xv. 15). 3. The best use we can make of friendship with God *is to intercede for others.* So Abraham for Sodom (Gen. xviii. 23—33). So Moses here. So Daniel (Dan. ix.). So Christ for his disciples (John xvii.).

II. THE BLESSING OF GOD'S PRESENCE (vers. 14, 15). 1. God's presence is the *highest* blessing. Nought else can be compared with it (Ps. lxxiii. 25, 26). 2. It is the blessing which enriches all *other* blessings. It is that which makes earthly blessings truly worth having. They are not the same to us without it as with it. 3. God's presence, going with us, invariably *conducts to rest.*

III. THE POWER OF PERSEVERING PRAYER (vers. 16, 17).—J. O.

EXPOSITION.

Vers. 18—23.—THE REQUEST TO SEE GOD'S GLORY, AND THE REPLY TO IT. Having obtained the full restoration of the people to God's favour, Moses felt emboldened to ask a boon for himself. He had already been admitted to closer communion with God than any one of the race of man since Adam in Paradise. But what had been granted him, instead of satisfying, only made him desirous of something further, something closer, something than which nothing more close could be imagined. So he asks to see the unveiled glory of God (ver. 18). He asks, that is, to see exactly that which man in the flesh cannot see, or at any rate cannot see and live. But, of course, he does not know this. God, in reply, tells him he shall see all that can be seen of him—more than anything which he has seen before. He shall see "all his goodness"—he shall have another revelation of the name of God (ver. 18); and, further, he shall be so placed as to see as much as mortal man can behold of "his glory"—God will pass by him, and when he has passed, Moses shall be allowed to look *after* him, and see what is here called "his back." This was probably some after-glow or reflection from the Divine glory, which language must have been as inadequate to describe as it was to embody the "unspeakable words" heard by St. Paul in the "third heaven," and declared by him "impossible for a man to utter" (2 Cor. xii. 4).

Ver. 18.—**Shew me thy glory.** The glory of God had been seen by Moses to a certain extent, when God "descended in fire" upon Mount Sinai (ch. xix. 18). It had been seen with more distinctness when he was called up and "went into the midst of the cloud" (ch. xxiv. 18). But he felt, nevertheless, that he had not as yet really beheld it. He longed for that ineffable blessing of the full "beatific vision," which is promised to us after death, if we die in the faith and fear of Christ (1 Cor. xiii. 12). "Increase of appetite doth grow by what it feeds on"—and the veiled splendours that he had been allowed to see only made him hunger the more for the unveiled radiance that he had not seen as yet.

Ver. 19.—**I will make all my goodness pass before thee.** It is not quite clear what this means, or how it was fulfilled—whether the reference is to the revelation of God's goodness in ch. xxxiv. 7, or to the entire experience that Moses would have of God in his later life. It is against the former view, that, if we take it, we can assign to the ensuing clause no distinct and separate sense. **I will proclaim the name of the Lord before thee.** See ch. xxxiv. 5, 6. **And I will be gracious to whom I will be gracious**—*i.e.,* I am not bound to do all this for thee. It is of my free grace that I do it. I intend, however, to be gracious, and **show mercy** to thee, because thou hast found favour in my eyes.

Ver. 20.—**No man can see me and live.** The inability proclaimed in these words is not an absolute inability to see God, but an inability to see and survive the sight. Jacob, when he wrestled with the angel, marvelled that he could see God, even in that intermediate way, and live (Gen. xxxii. 30). It may well be that actually to see God, while we are in the flesh, would kill us.

Ver. 21.—**Behold, there is a place by me.** No sufficient indication is given by these words, or by any other words in Scripture, of the exact locality of the manifestation to

Moses. The so-called " traditions " are worthless; and we can only say that the scene was probably some portion of the upper part of the Ras Sufsafeh.

Ver. 22.—**I will put thee in a clift of the rock.** The " clift " has been identified with the " cave of Elijah " (1 Kings xix. 9); but the words used are different; and even were they the same, no identity could be established. It is rather in the broader lines of their missions and characters that resemblance is to be sought between Moses and Elijah than in the minuter details of their careers. **Cover thee with my hand**—*i.e.*, " at once conceal thee and protect thee." Without these precautions, it is implied, the nearness of the Divine Presence might have had injurious effects.

Ver. 23.—**Thou shalt see my back parts.** Literally, " my back." The anthropomorphisms of the passage are numerous and strong —they must, of course, be regarded as accommodations to human ideas. After the Divine Presence had passed by, Moses was to be permitted to look out, and would see so much of the Divine glory as he would be able to bear; but still something far short of that which he had desired to see. The explanation that " the back of God " means " his works—the consequences of his activity " (Kalisch) is fanciful, and not borne out by the context. **My face cannot be seen.** See above, ver. 20; and compare John i. 18; vi. 46; 1 Tim. i. 17; 1 John iv. 12.

HOMILETICS.

Ver. 18.—*The craving for close communion with God,* may be considered—

I. As BASED ON A NATURAL INSTINCT. Man without God—without the consciousness of being sustained and upheld by an eternal omnipotent being—can have no strength or confidence in the present, no hope in the future. He is a feeble part of the vast mechanism of a great incomprehensible universe—a form which matter has assumed for a time—powerless to shape his future—the sport of circumstance. From this his better nature revolts, and, like some marine organism, throws out tentacles to seek a hold on some firm solid object without him. God is the only such object truly firm and stable; and hence man may be said to have a natural desire for God. As soon as the idea of God is in any way brought before him, he feels that it exactly answers an instinctive craving of his nature. His soul goes out to it—seizes it—appropriates it—rests on it as a sure prop and stay. Intellectually, the idea clears up the riddle of the universe; morally, gives a firm foundation to right and wrong, explains the authority of conscience, and supplies a motive for virtue; even physically it has a value, reducing the infinitude of nature within limits, and furnishing a reasonable origin to nature's laws.

II. As A TEST OF SPIRITUALITY. Man needs the idea of God, and cannot be satisfied without it; but whether, having got it, he shall thrust it into the background, or ever more and more cling to it, and seek to realise it, depends on his spiritual condition. Adam and Eve, after they had sinned, " hid themselves from the presence of God amongst the trees of the garden" (Gen. iii. 8). The Gergesenes " besought Christ that he would depart out of their coasts" (Matt. viii. 34). The guilty conscience cannot bear the near presence of the Most High, shrinks from the keen inspection of the all-seeing Eye, would fain skulk and hide among the bushes. The worldly heart is indifferent to the thought of God—turns away from it in the present—reserves it for a more convenient season. Only the spiritually minded delight in dwelling on the thought of God —seek him constantly—crave for communion with him. Only they can say with sincerity—" As the hart panteth after the water brooks, so panteth my soul after thee, O God. My soul thirsteth for God, for the living God" (Ps. xlii. 1, 2). They, however, can, and do say this continually. And the more communion they obtain, the more they desire. It is after Moses had entered into the cloud, and " spoken with God face to face, as a man speaketh unto his friend " (ver. 11), that he beseeches him to " show him his glory." We cannot while on earth obtain the *full* communion for which our spiritual nature craves. We cannot therefore while on earth be satisfied, but must ever be craving for something more, ever crying—" Nearer, my God, to thee, nearer to thee !" Only in heaven, if we be found worthy, shall we " see face to face, and know as we are known" (1 Cor. xiii. 12).

Ver. 22.—*Clifts in the rock.* God has many places of safety—" clifts in the rock"— where he puts us when trials approach. " As our day is, so is our strength." Bereavement comes upon us, and he elevates us on a pinnacle of faith to which we had never before mounted. Poverty and disgrace fall on us, and he gives us insensibility to them. Pain comes, and he enables us to see that pain is exactly the chastening we want, and to thank him for it. We do not cry out, with the Stoic, " How sweet !" for " no chastening for the present seemeth to be joyous, but grievous" (Heb. xii. 11); yet we have the spiritual strength to cry out to him—" How kind! How gracious !" The best " clift in the rock," is that cleft in the " Rock of Ages,"·which the soldier's spear made, wherein, if we please, we may lie hidden from every danger that can assail us.

" Rock of Ages, cleft for me,
Let me hide myself in thee ! "

HOMILIES BY VARIOUS AUTHORS.

Vers. 18—23.—" *Shew me thy glory.*" On this incident, remark—

I. THE GOOD MAN THIRSTS FOR EVER FULLER MANIFESTATIONS OF THE DIVINE GLORY. The more he knows of God, the more he would know. The nearer he gets, he presses nearer still. He " longs" to see God's power and glory" (Ps. lxiii. 2). He prays to see as much of it as may be possible to him on earth. He will only be satisfied when admitted to the full vision of it in heaven (Ps. xvi. 11; xvii. 15; 1 John iii. 2).

II. GOD'S GLORY IS TWOFOLD—ESSENTIAL AND ETHICAL. 1. God's *essential* glory. This is the glory which pertains to his *existence*. It is compared in Scripture to the white dazzling light—" light which no man can approach unto" (1 Tim. vi. 16). 2. God's *ethical* glory. This is the glory of his *character*. It was revealed when God proclaimed his " name" to Moses (ver. 19; ch. xxxiv. 5—8).

III. MAN, IN HIS PRESENT STATE OF EXISTENCE, CAN RECEIVE THE VISION OF GOD'S ESSENTIAL GLORY ONLY UNDER GREAT LIMITATIONS. The full discovery of it would slay him (ver. 20). Moses beheld it but *partially*, hid in a clift of the rock—saw but its reflection (vers. 21—23). Even thus to perceive it implied an exaltation of the consciousness—an opening of the spiritual eyes—not vouchsafed to ordinary men. A *mediate* revelation is at present all that is possible to us. We have this in the reflection of the Creator's glory in creation (Ps. xix. 1, 2).

IV. GOD'S ETHICAL GLORY ADMITS OF BEING REVEALED WITH MUCH GREATER FULNESS. 1. No barrier, either to the revelation or the perception of it, exists in physical conditions. It is glory of *character*. It is discerned by the same faculties by which we discern spiritual beauty and goodness in the characters of our fellow-men. 2. God *has* revealed it. We are not straitened in him. *He* has kept nothing back. He has made his goodness pass before us. He has revealed his name. The Divine Son is a *perfect* embodiment of the moral glory of the Father (John i. 14). 3. The sole barrier to the perception of it is the limitation of moral capacity in ourselves. It is in ourselves we are straitened. We lack the purity of heart necessary to give right spiritual discernment. Our perception of the glory of truth, righteousness, holiness, love, and mercy in God, will be in precise proportion to the degree in which these qualities are formed in our own natures.—J. O.

Ver. 19.—*Divine sovereignty.* On this note—

I. GOD IS SOVEREIGN IN THE EXERCISE OF HIS MERCY. He dispenses it to whom he will. He is free and unconstrained in its bestowal. The sinner cannot claim it as a right. He is not entitled to reckon upon it, save as the free promise of God gives him a warrant to do so. He dare not dictate to God what he *shall* do. God is sovereign as respects (1) The objects, (2) The time, (3) The manner, (4) The measure of his mercy. He gives no account of his matters to any one. He allows none to challenge him.

II. GOD'S SOVEREIGNTY IS BEST STUDIED ON ITS SIDE OF MERCY. This is the easier and more approachable side. It is the least disputable. It does not raise the same dark and knotty problems as the other side —" Whom he will he hardeneth " (Rom. ix. 18). The contemplation of it is purely delightful and consolatory. It is, besides, the side to which the other—the side of judgment—is subordinate. See this sovereignty of God illustrated in the history of Israel—(1) In the initial choice of the nation in Abraham. (2) In the deliverance from Egypt, with its attendant circumstances. (3) In the forming of the covenant at Sinai. (4) In the restoration of the people to favour after the covenant had been broken.

III. God's sovereignty in the exercise of mercy is not arbitrariness. (See on ch. vi. 14—28.) It has, as there shown, its self-imposed limitations and inherent laws of operation. It is holy, wise, and good. It aims, we may believe, at the ultimate salvation of the largest number possible, consistently with all the interests involved. J. O.

Vers. 1—32.—*The restoration to Divine favour completed.* This is a chapter which, beginning very gloomily, ends very gloriously. In the beginning Jehovah seems as if bidding farewell to the people for whom he had done so much; but at the close he is seen giving a revelation to Moses their leader, which must have sent him forth to resume his arduous work with greater encouragements than he ever had before. It is therefore very interesting to trace how this change was brought about.

I. We see the people are brought to a measure of penitence. We cannot assume that this penitence went very deep, so far as the general apprehension of unworthiness of conduct was concerned. But there was this depth in it, that the people perceived they had done something wrong, something insulting to Jehovah, something very dangerous to their own prospects. And how had this been brought about? Simply by the statement of Jehovah that he would not go up with those who had hitherto been his people. He would not go—the real truth was that he could not go. The sin of the people, their reckless, thoughtless trifling with holy things made his presence among them a peril. Something, indeed, had to be done to get these people from Horeb to Canaan, and settle them in possession; but that could be done by a sort of exercise of physical force. So much Jehovah could do for these Israelites, howsoever idolatrous they became. But his great blessing for them was not in the mere possession of Canaan, with its temporal riches and comforts. The temporal riches of Canaan were no more than those of any other land, save as God himself was in the midst of those who possessed the riches. What a humiliating thing to consider that God had to threaten withdrawal from his people in a sort of exercise of mercy. Suppose for a moment that the people had continued obdurate, what would the end have been? They would, indeed, have gone forward and got Canaan, and then sunk back, so that Israelite would have had no more importance in the history of the world and the development of God's purposes than Amorite, Hittite, or any of the other tribes mentioned in ver. 2.

II. Consider the significance of the separated tabernacle. In all probability this was the tent of Moses, and if so, we see at once a beautiful mingling of grace with necessary severity. Moses was prompted to *separate* from the people, but not to *depart* from them. Jehovah could not come down in the pillar of cloud into the midst of the camp; and for this no reason needs be sought other than the peril to the people flowing from his holiness. Thus there was everything to fill the minds of the people with a suitable mingling of humility and hope. Moses, true type of the greater Mediator yet to come, gave a point where God and the people could meet together. Jehovah will not depart, unless, so to speak, he is driven away. These people could not bear his presence; and yet—apparent contradiction—they could not do without him. Individual Israelites made it plain by their seeking Jehovah that they could not do without him; and he in his never-failing loving-kindness and pity, provided for such. The fate of the nation was trembling in the balance; but ample access and counsel were secured to the individual believer. There was a definite and favoured place for every individual who in his need sought the Lord. National trouble did not eclipse, it rather intensified and aggravated, individual trouble and need.

III. Note the points of interest in the conversation between Moses and Jehovah with which this chapter concludes. 1. There is what we may call *the holy boldness of Moses.* There is an illustration here of the importunity and great confidence with which God's people should persist in their approaches to the throne of the heavenly grace. Only just before God had spoken in great anger; and Moses, when he became aware from his own observation of the extent of the people's transgression, approached Jehovah with the utmost deference. But as time went on, and he was able to take all the elements of the position more and more into consideration, he felt himself shut up to persistent waiting upon God. A return to God's favour and guidance is the only way out of the difficulty; and therefore Moses cannot but be bold and pertinacious in doing his best to secure that way. 2. *He makes the most out of God's favour to him as an individual.* Not only have the people been apostate and reckless, but their very apostasy and recklessness bring out into stronger relief the clinging obedience of Moses. He has done well, and, more than that, Jehovah has approved him; and now, therefore, he pleads that the approval may not be in word only, but in deed; not in the promise of some future and distant recompense, but in deliverance from a present difficulty near at hand. Moses is not slow to avail himself of every legitimate consideration which he may plead with God. There were times when he would have been the first to allow and indeed affirm his unworthiness before God; but God had counted him worthy, and in his present need he avails himself of God's gracious regard to gain as much as he can for his needy brethren. Thus some slight hint is given to us of the way in which, for Christ's sake, God regards men. God had made it plain to Moses that he regarded him; and in effect Moses says, " If this regard be real, I will try it by large requests for my people." So let us feel that from the undisputed regard of God for the person, obedience, and everything belonging to his well-beloved Son, there will also come a regard to all the intercessions of that Son on behalf of a world so much alienated from God; and yet the more it is alienated, only the more in need of his mercy and deliverance. 3. *The determined manner in which Moses associates himself with his people.* He and Israel were as one. He may not in so many words speak of them as his people; on the contrary, he very emphatically alludes to them, in addressing Jehovah, as " thy people;" but we feel that underneath mere expressions there lies this natural and beautiful resolution, not to be separated from those who were one with him in blood. He felt that if Israel was to be frowned upon, he could not, so far as his consciousness was concerned, be favoured; and so we are led to think of the intimate association of Jesus with the children of men. Human nature is his nature; and however unworthy and polluted human nature often shows itself, however low it may sink in forgetfulness of its original constitution and purpose, the fact remains that the Word of God became flesh, and the consequent kinship and claim must ever be recognised. 4. *The cry to God for a revelation of his glory.* Much intercourse Moses had enjoyed with Jehovah, and often had he heard the voice that gave commandment and guidance. Indeed, as our minds go back over the past experience of Moses, and we consider how much he had been through, this strikes us at first as a somewhat puzzling request :—" I beseech thee show me thy glory." But the puzzle rises rather from unspirituality in our minds than from anything in the circumstances of Moses himself. Consider well the point to which he had attained, the distance which there was between him and his brethren, heart-infected as they still were with image-worship, and there will seem little wonder that in the heart of this lonely servant of God there should rise desires for what strength and satisfaction might come to him from the vision of God. He had asked much for his people, and it was fitting that he should ask something for himself. And he asked something worthy, something pleasing to God, something of highest profit to himself, even as Solomon did later on. He asked that he might no longer have to deal with a voice as behind a vail, but might see the face from which that voice came. The request was right and acceptable; but it could not be fully granted. What a fact to ponder over ! What a humbling and yet hope-inspiring fact that sinful man cannot look upon the glory of the Lord and live ! What of Divine glory is manifested to us has to be manifested in a way that is safe; and surely this is part of the salvation wherewith we are saved, that by-and-bye, when all pollution is cleansed away, we may be able to bear visions and revelations which, if they were to be attempted now, would only destroy us.—Y.

Vers. 1—11.—*Mercy vailed in judgment.* I. GOD'S SEPARATION FROM THE PEOPLE AND ITS EFFECTS. 1. The separation. (1) In wrath he remembers mercy. They will receive the land, but for the fathers' sake and his oath's sake, not because he has delight in *them.* God's goodness is not always a proof of his being pleased with us, any more than his chastisements prove his anger. The former may be a loud call to repentance. (2) The reason for God's absence; his presence would be judgment, not mercy :—" Lest I consume thee in the way." If God's face be hidden, and the sense of his presence and guiding gone from us, his next revelation may be judgment. 2. Its effects. (1) The people mourned. It was no satisfaction that God and they were no longer to walk together. (2) Other delights lost their attractiveness :—" No man did put on his ornaments." (3) They were troubled by fear of judgment, for the Lord had said, " I will come up into the midst of thee in a moment and consume thee." These are the effects of the Spirit's work to-day. The same cry is lifted :—" Flee from the wrath to come."

II. THE SEPARATION OF GOD'S PEOPLE FROM THE MIDST OF SURROUNDING SIN AND ITS RESULTS. 1. Its necessity as a testimony to God's separation from sin. This is the duty of the Church to-day :—" Come ye out from among them and be ye separate." The tabernacle of the congregation, meant though it be for all, must be pitched " without the camp." 2. The results. (1) Moses' example led others to declare themselves on God's side (ver. 7). (2) The people " looked after Moses." Yearning for the light of God's face is stirred up in the hearts of men by those who go forth to meet with him. (3) God manifests himself to the separated (ver. 9). A living Church is ever the means of revealing God's reality. (4) The people worshipped " every man in his tent-door." A true Church will send forth a cry for mercy from the homes of the sinful.—U.

Vers. 12—23.—*Intercession and its reward.* I. THE INTERCESSOR'S POWER. 1. God, who had disowned Israel, and refused to go with them, consents to go with *him* :— " My presence shall go with *thee*, and I will give *thee* rest." The first step in successful intercession for others is the receiving of power to serve God among them. This is the dropping which foretells the shower. 2. God is brought back by persistent asking into the midst of Israel :—" I will do this thing also that thou hast spoken " (ver. 17). We must not be content till our whole desire is given us. He can make not only our words a power to others, but also his own presence felt by them.

II. THE INTERCESSOR'S PLEAS. 1. God's love to himself :—" Thou hast said I know thee by name," etc. The realisation of our personal interest in God's love is the basis of intercession for others. It gives confidence that God will hear us. It gives hope. He who has blessed us can also bless them. 2. God's relation to them for whom he entreats :—" Consider that this nation is *thy people*." We can urge on behalf of the vilest that God created them, and gave Christ to die for them. 3. That God's presence and favour are needful to make himself and the people what God desires them to become :—" So shall we be separated." They can be consecrated only by the might of God's revealed love.

III. THE INTERCESSOR'S REWARD : THE VISION OF GOD'S GLORY. 1. " And he said, Show me thy glory." The lifting up of availing prayer for others quickens our desire to know more of him with whom we speak. 2. The full vision of God is for the sinless life. The splendour of the Divine purity would slay us. John fell at Christ's feet as one dead. 3. How the fuller vision granted in the present may be had. (1) By listening to the proclamation of the Lord's name in his word. (2) We can see the glory which has passed us. God's deeds reveal him. 4. The place of vision :—" A rock," " by me." Taking our stand upon Christ, the glory of God's words and deeds breaks upon us. 5. The place of safety, " in a clift of the rock." Only in the riven side of Jesus the vision of God is not to condemnation and death, but to justification and life.—U.

SECTION XVI.—CHAPTER XXXIV.

THE RESTORATION OF THE TWO TABLES, AND RENEWAL OF THE COVENANT.

EXPOSITION.

CHAPTER XXXIV.

Vers. 1—4.—THE TWO TABLES RENEWED. The fervent and prolonged intercession of Moses had brought about the pardon of the people ; and that, together with their repentance and their prayers (ch. xxxiii. 7), had been accepted as a renewal of the covenant on their part ; but it remained for God to renew the covenant on his part. The first step to this was the restoration of the tables, which were essential to the covenant, as being at once the basis of the law and of the ordained worship. To mark, however, that something is always forfeited by sin, even when forgiven, the new tables were made to lose one glory of the first —they were not shaped by God, as the first were (ch. xxxii. 16), but by Moses.

Ver. 1.—**Hew thee two tables of stone.** Literally, " of *stones* "—two separate tables, *i.e.*, made of two separate stones. Moses is required to do this with strict justice, since it was by his act that the former tables were broken (ch. xxxii. 19). **Upon these tables.** Literally, " upon *the* tables," which has exactly the same force. **The words that were in the first tables.** It is quite true that we have not yet been explicitly told what these words were. (See ch. xxxi. 18 ; xxxii. 15, 16, 19.) It has been left to our natural intelligence to understand that they must have been the " ten words" uttered in the ears of all the people amid the thunders of Sinai, as recorded in ch. xx. 1—19, which are the evident basis of all the later legislation. We have, however, in ver. 28, and still more plainly in Deut. x. 4, and v. 22, the desired statement. The fiction of a double decalogue, invented by Goethe and supported by Hitzig, and even Ewald, is absolutely without foundation in fact.

Ver. 2.—**Be ready in the morning.** An interval was required for the hewing of the tables. It was made as short as possible. **In the top of the mount.** Where he had been with God previously (ch. xix. 20 ; xxiv. 12, 18).

Ver. 3.—**No man shall come up with thee.** This time, no one, not even Joshua, was to accompany Moses. The new manifestation of the glory of God was to be made to him alone. **Neither let any man be seen throughout all the mount**, etc. Compare the injunctions given in ch. xix. 12, 13. The present orders are even more stringent.

Ver. 4.—Moses obeys all the directions given him to the letter—hews, or causes to be hewn, the two tables, making them as like as he can to the former ones—rises early, and ascends the mountain to the appointed spot— and takes with him the tables, for God to perform his promise (ver. 1) of writing the commandments upon them. It has been questioned whether God did actually write the words upon the second tables ; but Kurtz's arguments upon the point are unanswerable. (*History of the Old Covenant*, vol. iii. p. 186, E. T.)

HOMILETICS.

Vers. 1—4.—*The second promulgation of the moral law, by the renewal of the two tables*, may teach us—

I. THAT ALL COVENANT WITH GOD MUST REST ON THE BASIS OF THE MORAL LAW. Moses had not asked for a renewal of the tables. He had requested the return of God's favour and the renewal of God's share of the covenant. It was God who made the restoration of the tables a condition. God, that is, will not divorce favour from obedience, privilege from the keeping of his law. Man desires the rewards that God has to bestow, but is not anxious to have the rewards tied to a certain course of action. God insists on the combination. He can only enter into covenant with those who accept his law as their rule of life. This is not for his own sake, but for theirs. They can only be fitted to enjoy his favour, and the rewards which he has to bestow on them, by leading a life in accordance with his law and acquiring the character which such a life forms in them.

II. THAT THE MORAL LAW IS ETERNAL AND UNALTERABLE. The broken tables must be restored. In restoring them no change must be made. Their very form must resemble as nearly as may be the form of the preceding ones. This, of course, was typical. It foreshadowed the further—not mere resemblance, but—identity of the words that were to be written on the tables. From first to last, " the words were those that were in the first table " (ver. 1). There is no hint of any alteration. Even Christianity changes nothing in the law that is moral. " Think not that I am come to destroy the law and the prophets," says our Lord ; " I am not come to destroy but to fulfil " (Matt. v. 17). No " jot or tittle " of the moral law is to pass away. Even with respect to the Sabbath, which verges upon positive law, nothing is changed but the day of the week, and to a small extent the method of observance. Apostolic writings show us the Decalogue as still binding (Rom. xiii. 9 ; Eph. vi. 2 ; James ii. 11 ; etc.).

III. THAT BREAKING THE MORAL LAW IMPOSES ON US FRESH OBLIGATIONS. " Hew thee "—literally, " hew *for thyself* "—" two tables of stone," said the Lord to Moses ; repair the loss caused by thine own action. Repentance is no part of man's original duty to God ; but if he once break the moral law, it becomes obligatory on him. Every infraction involves this new duty ; some infractions involve more. Fraud involves the duty of restitution ; calumny, that of retractation ; insult, that of apology ; and the like. Each of our sins lays upon us as a new burthen, not only of guilt, but also of labour, to efface it. We had best refrain from evil, even in our own interest, or we may increase our burthen till we sink under it.

HOMILIES BY VARIOUS AUTHORS.

Vers. 1—4. *The renewal of God's covenant.* I. THE FIRST EFFECT OF RECONCILIA-
TION IS THE RE-WRITING OF THE LAW. Moses ascends that God may again inscribe his
commandments upon the tables of stone; Jesus, that God may write them upon the
fleshly tables of the heart. The sprinkling of the blood is "unto obedience." We are
to be "zealous of good works."

II. THE AWFULNESS OF GOD'S HOLINESS MORE EVIDENT IN THE RESTORATION THAN
IN THE FIRST GIVING OF THE LAW. Formerly Moses had been accompanied so far by
the elders, and further still by Joshua. Now he must go up alone. No man is to be
seen throughout the mount. Neither flocks nor herds are to feed before it. The
terrors of Sinai awe the heart less than the cross of him who treads the wine-press
alone.

III. THE REDEEMER'S ZEAL. "And Moses rose up early in the morning." He
cannot loiter; for man's life hangs upon the issue; the world's cry rings in his ears.
"For Zion's sake I will not hold my peace," etc. (Isaiah lxii. 1).

IV. THE MEDIATOR MUST MOULD THE HEART TO RECEIVE GOD'S LAW. "He hewed
two tables of stone, like unto the first." The power of Christ's love must cut between
us and sin, and give again the form man wore when he came from the hands of God.
We must experience the circumcision of Christ. Christ's work may be measured by the
heart's tender receptivity for the re-writing of God's law.

V. THERE MUST BE UNION BY FAITH WITH CHRIST IN HIS RISEN LIFE. He "took
in his hand the two tables of stone." We pass up with Jesus into the presence of God.
That the law may be written upon the heart, our life must be hid with Christ in God.
—U.

Vers. 1—4.—*The second set of tables.* Jehovah graciously answered the supplications
of Moses (xxxiii. 12—23) so far as it was possible to answer them. Supplications may
be very importunate, and, therefore, so far well pleasing to God, and yet at the same time
they may be faulty in two respects: first, they may ask for things which it is impossible altogether to grant; and, secondly, they may omit from the field of view, certain
other things which form a necessary accompaniment of every Divine gift. In all his
supplications, Moses said nothing about these broken tables; it would be too much to
say that they were never in his thoughts. But whether in his thoughts or not, they
assuredly had to be considered and provided for. Moses had asked for the presence of
God to go with Israel; and the presence of God meant for one thing the commandments
of God. Furthermore, all the elaborate furniture of the tabernacle had for the centre
around which it was gathered, these very tables of stone. When Moses broke them, he
broke the holiest thing in all Israel's belongings; these tables, appointed to rest within
the ark, and underneath the cherubim. No word of censure indeed is uttered against
Moses for having broken them; but it does not therefore follow that he is to be praised
for having broken them. The action, so to speak, was one to be regarded neither with
praise nor blame, but simply as an inevitable result of Moses' sudden and violent wrath.
When Moses broke the tables, he was not in a mood of mind for considering anything
but the monstrous transgression before his eyes. What had happened to the fragments
we are not told; except this much, that they were no longer available. All that Jehovah
does is simply to command from Moses the preparation of new tablets. As Moses prepares them, he may safely be left to his own thoughts. Whatever lesson he needed in
respect of self-control, the opportunity was given him to learn. Opportunity was also
given to learn the need of being continually on the watch for manifestations of human
weakness and instability. If Moses was in so many things the type of Christ in respect
of mediatorial office, it was, alas! also true that he was unlike Christ in respect of penetrating insight into human nature. Moses was not like Christ; it could not be said of
him that he knew what was in man.—Y.

Vers. 1—10, 28.—*Renewal of the tables, and fourth intercession.* One more mighty
effort of intercession, and Moses will bear away the blessing which he seeks. It needs,
however, that it *be* a mighty one. The covenant is not yet restored in its integrity.

The people's sin is not yet perfectly forgiven. God, indeed, has promised to go with them, but he has not said, as of old, " I will take you to me for a people, and I will be to you a God" (Ex. vi. 7). The new relations are not those of perfected friendship. They are moreover, unstable. New transgressions of the people may at any moment upset them. Moses, accordingly, would not only have the covenant renewed—restored in its old completeness and integrity—the last trace of the Divine displeasure wiped away—but would have God give him a pledge of grace beyond anything he has yet received—a pledge that he will show great *forbearance* with the people : that he will not deal summarily with them, or cast them off, on account of backslidings which he now perceives to be inevitable (ver. 9). It was a high thing to ask : too high, Moses may have thought, for him to be able to attain to it. If he did, it could only be as the result of an earnestness, a perseverance, and a sublimity in intercesssion beyond everything of which he had yet felt himself capable. The strength he needed, however, was not to be withheld from him. He had already, though, probably, without this being present to his mind as a motive, put himself in the way of getting it, by asking for a vision of the Divine glory. From this would flow into his soul a spiritual might which would make " all things possible" to him (cf. Mark ix. 23). By sheer power of prayer, he would obtain what he desired. Jehovah, on his side, was too well pleased with his servant's zeal and devotion, too willing to be entreated of him, too entirely in accord with the object of his supplication, not readily to grant him the opportunity of pressing his request.

I. JEHOVAH'S " COME UP HITHER" (vers. 1—4). 1. *The command to hew out tables* (ver. 1). Formerly, it was God himself who furnished the tables on which the law was written (ch. xxxii. 16). Now, the tables are to be provided by Moses. This may have had reference to the facts (1) that it was Moses who had destroyed the former tables (ch. xxxii. 19); and (2), that it was by the mediation of Moses that the covenant was being renewed. It was a suitable reward for his intercession, that God should give him this honour of supplying the tables on which the covenant terms were to be inscribed. View the command to hew out tables as (1) Retrospective. God had already promised that his presence should go with Israel (ch. xxxiii. 14). This implied, on the part of the people, return to their obedience. The law is unalterable. God can walk with men only as they are willing to walk with him in the way of his commands. The tables testified to the unchangingness of the obligation. (2) Anticipative. It had in view the fact that, through Moses' intercession, the covenant was about to be restored. (3) Promissory. It gave Moses encouragement to entreat for its restoration. 2. *The command to ascend the mount* (ver. 2). The summons to ascend the mount was, (1) An answer to prayer—"Shew me thy glory" (ch. xxxiii. 18). (2) A preparation for vision. (3) An opportunity for intercession. 3. *The command to preserve the sanctity of the mount* (ver. 3). This was to be done by keeping man and beast from approaching it. Moses was to ascend alone. The command—a parallel to that in Ex. xix. 12—13—has for its end the warning back of intruders from what, for the time being, is " holy ground" (cf. ch. iii. 5). Other reasons are, that there might be (1) No interruption of communion. (2) No distraction in intercession. (3) No injury done by the manifestation of the Divine glory. " The manifested glory of the Lord would so surely be followed by the destruction of man that even Moses needed to be protected before it" (ch. xxxiii. 21, 22).

II. THE NAME REVEALED (vers. 4—8). (1) Jehovah " passed by before him" (ver. 5), *i.e.*, gave him the glimpse of his glory promised in ch. xxxiii. 22, 23. (2) He " proclaimed his name"—*i.e.*, made known to Moses the essence of his *character*. This was the higher revelation. The other is only alluded to ; this is dwelt on and expanded (vers. 6, 7). 1. *The name itself.* Note here in regard to it—(1) It unites mercy and justice. (2) The merciful attributes preponderate. (3) The word which syllables it is " Love." Love is the union of goodness and holiness. The history of revelation has been but the spelling out of this name. Christ is the perfect embodiment of it. 2. *The effects on Moses.* (1) It awed him (ver. 8). (2) It encouraged him. It gave him a new ground of confidence in entreaty (ver. 9). (3) It strengthened him. Cf. the chorus of the archangels in Goethe's " Faust " —

" Though none may fathom thee—thy sight
Upon the angels power bestows," etc

III. THE COVENANT RESTORED (vers. 9, 27, 28). 1. *The intercession.* This fourth and last intercession presents us with several noteworthy features. (1) It was very prolonged. The account here is summary; but Moses tells us in Deuteronomy (ch. ix. 25), that he "fell down before the Lord forty days and forty nights as at the first," and prayed earnestly that the people might not be destroyed (cf. ver. 28). (2) It included intercession for Aaron (Deut. ix. 20). (3) It is marked by a deep perception of the root of depravity in the people's nature. Moses has no longer the same optimistic views regarding them as when he disputed with God the necessity of giving them further warning about not approaching the mount (ch. xix. 23). Note how, in the first intercession, it is the people's *danger*; in the second, the people's *guilt*; and in the last, the people's *depravity*, which is chiefly before the intercessor's mind. He here pleads the innate tendency as a reason why God should deal mercifully with them (ver. 9). Human nature does not improve on closer inspection. But there is weakness as well as sin in its condition. The Divine ruler may be trusted to make the requisite allowances (cf. Gen. viii. 21). (4) It is marked—and this is the outstanding circumstance in connection with it—by the degree in which Moses is now able to identify himself with the people for whom he intercedes. "Let my Lord, I pray thee, go among us . . . . And pardon *our* iniquity and *our* sin, and take us for thine inheritance" (ver. 9). More than ever he feels himself one with his nation. Intercession has perfected sympathy. But not intercession alone. It may be inferred that no act had more to do with this result than the supreme act of self-devotion, already considered, in which he expressed his willingness to die, and, if need be, to be blotted out of God's book, for the salvation of the people. In that amazing act, the last traces of selfishness must have perished. He has given himself for Israel, and is thenceforth one with it. Subsequent intercessions can but develop, and give clearer and fuller expression to the sense of unity with his people born within him in that supreme hour in his experience. Sinful as the people are, accordingly, Moses, in his present entreaty does not shrink from including himself among them. "Our iniquity"—"our sin." The just takes part with the unjust. He makes their sin his, and pleads for its forgiveness. The worse they show themselves, the more earnestly he holds by them, and endeavours to sustain them by his prayers. If sympathy is a qualification for the task of mediation, Moses thus possesses it. His intercession, in this respect, throws striking lights on Christ's. 2. *The success.* The prolonged, fervent, and sympathetic intercession of Moses did not fail of its reward. "The Lord," he tells afterward, "hearkened unto me at that time also" (Deut. ix. 19). Nothing was wanting to the completeness of his success. The last frown had disappeared from the countenance of Jehovah. Covenant relations were perfectly restored. The people were reinstated in privilege. No wonder that the mediator's face "shone" as he descended from the mount! We, too, have an intercessor whom the Father "heareth always" (John xi. 42).—J. O.

EXPOSITION.

Vers. 5—8.—THE FULFILMENT BY GOD OF HIS PROMISE TO MOSES. This section coheres closely with the last section of the preceding chapter, and must be regarded as the historical account of how God fulfilled the promises there made by him to Moses (ch. xxxiii. 19—23). The promises were mainly two—1. That he would proclaim his name to him afresh; and 2. That he would pass by him, and let him see, after he had passed, what man might see of his glory. The fulfilment of the first promise appears in the long enumeration of attributes contained in vers. 6, 7; the fulfilment of the second is expressed with extreme brevity in the words—" And the Lord passed by before him " (ver. 6). Probably no further description could be given of that marvellous manifestation beyond those words in which it was promised (ch. xxxiii. 21—23). Its effects were seen in that permanent reflection of God's glory on the face of Moses, which thenceforth compelled him to wear a veil mostly when he showed himself to the people (vers. 33—35).

Ver. 5.—**The Lord descended in the cloud.** The cloudy pillar, which had stood at the door of the Tent of Meeting (ch. xxxiii. 10), was withdrawn while Moses ascended Sinai, and probably disappeared from men's sight. When Moses reached the top, it **descended** once more from the sky, and **stood with him there.** Then a voice from the cloud proclaimed the name of the Lord in the manner more fully stated in the ensuing verses.

Vers. 6, 7.—**The Lord passed by before him.** God did as he had promised in ch. xxxiii. 22, 23. He made his glory pass by,Moses, as he stood in a " clift of the rock," and " covered him with his hand as he passed by," and, when he had passed, " took away his hand," and allowed Moses to look after him, and see a glorious and transcendent vision—a vision so bright and radiant, *and so real,* that the light which streamed from it settled on Moses' face, and remained there (ver..30). **And proclaimed.** In his passage God proclaimed his name; not however, as in the burning bush, an actual name contained in a single word—but a description in many words of his essential nature —a description setting forth especially his three qualities of mercy, truth, and justice, but dwelling most upon the first of the three —perhaps, as most essential, for " God is love " (1 John iv. 8)—certainly, as most needing to be prominently set forth at the time, when his favour had been justly forfeited, and but for his mercy could not have been restored. Note the accumulation of terms that are nearly synonymous—1. Merciful (or pitiful); 2. Gracious; 3. Long-suffering; 4. Abundant in goodness; 5. Keeping mercy for thousands;

and 6. Forgiving iniquity and transgression and sin—an accumulation for the purpose of emphasis—to assure Moses, and through him mankind at large, of the reality of this attribute, on which the possibility of our salvation depends, and which had never hitherto been set forth with anything like such fulness. **That will by no means clear the guilty.** Some critics take this clause in an entirely different sense, translating " who in destroying will not wholly destroy" (Maimonides, Pool, De Dieu, Patrick), or, " who acquits even him who is not innocent " (Geddes); but the rendering of our translators (which agrees with the LXX.), is approved by Rosenmüller, Gesenius, Kalisch, Keil, and others. It seems to have been also the meaning assigned to the passage by the prophet Nahum, who quotes it (i. 3) when he is threatening Nineveh. **Visiting the iniquity.** See above, ch. xx. 5. While setting forth his attribute of mercy in all its fulness, God will not have his attribute of justice forgotten (ver. 8).

Ver. 8.—**Moses made haste and bowed his head.** Worshipping the glory that had passed by, and accepting the gracious words addressed to him.

HOMILETICS.

Vers. 6, 7.—*The second proclamation of God's name.*—God had proclaimed his name to Moses, when he spoke with him out of the burning bush. He had declared it to be JEHOVAH, " the Self-Existent One." Under this name the people of Israel had known him from the time of Moses' return to Egypt from Midian, until that of which he is here speaking. Hitherto it had sufficed for them. It had marked him as, 1. eternal; 2. uncaused; 3. unconditioned; 4. self-sufficient; 5. all-powerful. But it had not revealed his moral nature. Something of that had always been known to man. Something more had become known to Israel through the law already given from Sinai. But in their present state of sorrow and depression (ch. xxxiii. 4—6) something further was needed. God accordingly " proclaimed his name " afresh. Of this second proclamation we may note—

I. THAT IT CANCELS NOTHING, BUT ADDS. The first words of the name are " *Jehovah, Jehovah El,*" or " the Self-Existent, the Self-Existent God." What had been revealed before is confirmed; nay, is still put in the fore-front, as the proper foundation of all the rest. For a true knowledge of God, we must, *first and foremost,* have the conviction that there is a self-existent being, eternal, uncaused, the cause of all things, and therefore of our own existence, on whom we are absolutely dependent. It follows, after this, to inquire and learn the moral character of this Eternal One.

II. THAT IT SETS FORTH GOD AS, ABOVE ALL THINGS, MERCIFUL. The Jewish commentators make out thirteen epithets of God in these two verses, and say that all but one are epithets of mercy. This seems to be an overstatement of the actual fact, that the epithets of mercy form a large numerical majority. They are 1. *Rakhum,* " the tender or pitiful one," who is full of kindness and compassion; 2. *Khannun,* " the gracious one," who bestows his benefits out of mere favour, without obligation; 3. *Erek appayim,* " the long-suffering one," who is not easily provoked, but " suffers long and is kind "; 4. *Rab-khesed,* " the great in mercy " which needs no explanation ; 5. *Notser-khesed,* " the keeper of mercy," he who does not desert those he loves, but is merciful to them, *and their children,* from generation to generation; 6. *Nose 'avon vapesha vekhattaah,* " the forgiver of iniquity and transgression and sin "—the being who alone can forgive sin and give peace to the guilty soul. Moses did well to make appeal to this description of himself by God himself, when Israel had a second time provoked God to destroy them (Num. xiv. 17, 18). We shall do well to make our appeal to the same, whenever we have offended our Lord and Master by our faults and shortcomings, our "sins, negligences, and ignorances." Conjured by this "name," God can scarcely refuse to reply, as he replied to Moses, "I have pardoned according to thy word" (Num. xiv. 20).

III. That it further sets him forth as just and true. God gives it as part of his name, that he "will by no means clear the guilty," or rather perhaps that he will not "always" do so (Kalisch). There is some guilt that he will not, cannot pardon. "There is a sin unto death—I do not say that a man shall pray for it" (1 John v. 16). Unrepented sin cannot be forgiven. "Blasphemy against the Holy Ghost" cannot be forgiven. God's justice is an essential part of his nature, no less than his mercy; and is perhaps, as has been argued, a necessary consequence of his love.* Again, God is true—"abundant in truth" (ver. 6). There can be no trust in any being who is not true. Truth lies at the root of all moral goodness; and the truth of God is pre-supposed in any revealed religion, since without it revelation could have no force or value. Further, both in the Old and the New Testament, God reveals himself as "true," or sometimes as "the truth." "Thy truth reacheth unto the clouds" (Ps. cviii. 4). "The truth of the Lord endureth for ever" (ib. cxvii. 2). "God is true." "I am the truth." It is essential to a right conception of him that we should believe in his absolute veracity. If we "make him a liar," we ruin our whole idea of him. We might as well make him non-existent.

HOMILIES BY VARIOUS AUTHORS.

Vers. 5—8.—*The "name."* Consider on this

I. The connection with the name Jehovah. "Proclaimed the name of *Jehovah*" (ver. 5). Observe—1. The name Jehovah *connotes* moral attributes. The absolute being is, at the same time, the most perfect being. His excellence includes all possible perfection. This implies the possession of moral attributes. "That character," says Dean Graves, "from which the acutest reasoners have endeavoured demonstratively to deduce as from their source all the Divine attributes, is self-existence. Is it not then highly remarkable that it is under this character the divinity is described, on his first manifestation to the Jewish lawgiver?" 2. Former revelations *implied* moral attributes. The attributes on which, in former revelations, the main stress needed to be laid, were those to be illustrated in the events of the exodus—power, freedom, supremacy, changelessness (cf. on ch. iii. 14; vi. 2, 3). But that moral attributes—the attributes of truth, mercy, goodness, justice, also belonged to Jehovah was shown—(1) From the nature of his purpose. (2) From the character of his actings. (3) From the simple fact of his revealing himself. 3. The new revelation *declares* moral attributes. Formerly, the revelation was in deeds, now it is in words. Formerly, God told Moses what, as Jehovah, he would *do*. Now he declares what, as Jehovah, he *is*. The name was first *spelt*, then *pronounced*. Cf. with law of ordinary historical progress—(1) action; (2) reflection on what has been done, with generalisation of principles. Or of scientific progress—(1) accumulation of facts; (2) generalisation of law. For this announcement of the name, the renewal of the covenant furnished an appropriate historical occasion.

II. Teaching of the name. The name exhibits the Divine character. It lays bare to us God's very heart. It reveals his essence. Learn—1. *There is justice in God.* "That will by no means clear the guilty," etc. (ver. 7). (1) This attribute is essential. Without it, God would not be God. Says the poet, "A God all mercy is a God unjust." We go further, and affirm that without justice, there would be no mercy left to exercise. See Homily on ch. xxxii. 10. We have defined love in God as the perfect union of goodness and holiness. Mercy we would define as a mixed feeling of pity and resentment. See this point well illustrated in the chapters on "the Law of

* Dante makes Hell in part the creation of the Primal Love, *Inferno*, Canto iii ll 5, 6

Mercy " in " *Ecce Homo*." (2) Justice cannot be laid aside. God " will by no means clear the guilty." See Homily on ch. xxiii. 21. But if God cannot *clear* the guilty, cannot, *i.e.* call guilt other than what it is, or refuse to punish it, he can, on the ground of his Son's atonement, which fulfils every condition of a perfect satisfaction to justice, *forgive* the guilty. (3) Manifestation of justice. In his personal dealings with individuals—not clearing the guilty. In his general government of the world—" visiting the iniquity of the fathers," etc. (cf. on ch. xx. 5 ; Deut. v. 9). 2. *There is mercy in God.* This side of the Divine character is exhibited with much greater fulness than the other. " Merciful and gracious, long-suffering, and abundant in goodness and truth, keeping mercy, forgiving iniquity, and transgression, and sin " (vers. 6, 7). (1) God delights in mercy ; he does not delight in judgment. Judgment is " his work, his strange work " (Is. xxviii. 21). The visitation of sin is viewed as extending only " unto the third and fourth generation " ; mercy is kept for " thousands " (cf. Ps. ciii. 17). (2) Mercy is " abundant." Cf. Is. lv. 7—" will abundantly pardon." A wonderful utterance this from the standpoint of the Old Testament. Anticipates Paul—" where sin abounded, grace did much more abound " (Rom. v. 20). (3) Mercy qualifies judgment. It leads to *forbearance* with the sinner—" long-suffering " (cf. Rom. ii. 4). It secures *pardon* on repentance—" forgiving iniquity," etc. (4) It is yet exercised in strictest harmony with the requirements of justice. The *mode* of the reconciliation of these two sides of the Divine character, however, remains in the Old Testament a partially unsolved problem. 3. Mercy *rules* in the character of God. This is a fair inference (1) from the preponderating place assigned to the attributes of mercy, and (2) from the fact that the attributes of mercy stand *before* the attributes of justice. It is but an earlier expression of the truth which the Gospel has now made a great spiritual certainty to us—" God is love " (1 John iv. 16). Not simply *loves*, but *is* love. But if God is love, and love constitutes his essence, then must love dominate, wield, work through his other perfections, using all for its own purposes, transmuting all into its own nature. There cannot be discord or division in the breast of the Eternal. What God is, he must ever ·have been, must be at all times, through all ages, in all his works, under all forms of his manifestation. This is a conception so deep and far-reaching as to pass in its length and breadth beyond our grasp. Its lines prolong themselves to infinity. There lie in it possibilities which it is not given to man to fathom.

III. THE NAME AS REVEALED. 1. We *need* a revelation. It is but a dumb, inarticulate revelation of this name which we have in nature. What *is* revealed relates more to God's justice than to God's love. If there is much in nature which supports, there is also much which seems to discredit, belief in the entire goodness of God. Nature in particular, has no answer to give to the questions—Can God forgive and restore sinners? Can he undo their evil? Can he turn back from its avenging course that terrible law of retribution which holds us in its grasp? 2. We may *expect* a revelation. If God loves men, we may expect him in some way personally to attest his love to them. " Gracious thoughts never revealed are not gracious thoughts at all. It is essential to the being of grace or love that it manifest itself. Love unrevealed is love unreal " (Dr. A. B. Bruce). 3. The revelation has been *given*. (1) In deeds. (2) In words. (3) In the Son.—J. O.

Vers. 5—9.—*The Manifestation of God.* I. GOD'S GLORY VEILED THAT IT MAY BE REVEALED. " The Lord descended in the cloud." The glory of Jesus was veiled by his humanity. There is but one avenue through which the knowledge of God can come —the spirit; it cannot come by the senses. God reveals himself by a word, by one in whom he has put his name, and by the Spirit's unveiling of the word in the heart.

II. GOD'S NAME. 1. Faithfulness: he proclaimed " JEHOVAH." He changes not, his purpose abides, his word is fulfilled. 2. Faithfulness and might. " Jehovah, Elohim." God's power waits upon his unchanging purpose. 3. " Merciful." He will not spurn need. He is moved by, and drawn to, it. 4. " Gracious." God is not merely a just master, bestowing rewards which have been earned. There is favour to be found with him, unmerited and free. 5. " Long-suffering." He is patient with blindness and weakness and sin. He *waits* to be gracious. The great husbandman waiteth for the precious fruit of the earth and " hath long patience for it." 6. " Abundant in goodness and truth." The ages have been unveiling their fulness; but the story is not yet told.

Eternity will never know all the length and breadth and depth and height. 7. The largeness of God's mercy (1) toward persons. "Keeping mercy for thousands," (2) toward sins, "forgiving iniquity and transgression and sin." 8. The severity of God. (1) He will not always leave sin unpunished. (2) His mercy may save men from sin, but will not acquit them in sin. "Be not deceived." (3) The father's sins are visited upon the children. The inheritance of wrong is accompanied by an inheritance of wrath. What is punishment for the fathers may be mercy for the children.

III. THE FRUITS OF THE KNOWLEDGE OF GOD. 1. Adoration. For deep and true worship the soul must know God in the reality of his existence and the glory of his nature. 2. Prayer for himself and his people. To Jesus the vision of God is intercession for his Church and the world. (1) Prayer for God's presence. "Let my Lord, I pray thee, go among us." (2) That God may come in mercy, not in judgment. "Pardon our iniquity." (3) The transforming power of the presence of God. "And (so) take us for thine inheritance."—U.

Vers. 6, 7.—*The name of the Lord.* Moses had asked to see the glory of Jehovah, a request which it was possible to grant only in a very modified way. As much as Moses could bear to see he was allowed to see; and for what he was not able to see he received a most abundant and timely compensation in the revelation made to him of the Divine character. For this of course is what the proclamation of the name of Jehovah amounts to. The name of Jehovah is what we should call the character of Jehovah. It is always a great comfort and stay to know that the character of one with whom we have to deal is satisfactory through and through. Nay more, it is well to know character, whether it be good or bad; not to go to a man, uncertain of his disposition and altogether in doubt as to what we may expect. From the proclamation here made we may judge Moses to have been up to this point ignorant of certain fundamental qualities in the character of God. He might have certain guesses, certain inward promptings, which led him into supplication and conduct accordant with the Divine character; but now he is lifted above all guess-work. From God's own lips he gets an account of all that is deepest in the disposition and relations of God toward man. He is made to see that God's recent action towards apostate Israel was based, not on incessant importunity in supplication, but on what was a constant source of the Divine action. God was pleased to see Moses so importunate; importunity we may even say was needful to the occasion; but God had not in him the spirit of the unjust judge, that he should be moved by importunity alone. The character here revealed doubtless gave Moses confidence in all future necessary intercession. Henceforth he knew, and knew from as solemn and authoritative a communication as could be made, what there was in the great Disposer of his movements upon which he could at all times rely. The aspect of Jehovah's character here presented is of course one which it is important for his sinful creature man to know. God does not tell us here all that may be known of him; he singles out that, the knowledge of which we cannot do without in our hours of deepest need, and although there is thus revealed to us only a part of the Divine nature, it is a part which has the harmony of a whole. God is here made known as indescribably considerate of all the needs of men, and yet at the same time inexorably just. His mercy and love are not as human mercy and love too often are. There is a mercy which, while it may soothe present agonies and smooth present difficulties, is yet essentially nothing more than an opiate; it does not go to the root of the trouble and show how it may be entirely swept away. The tender mercies of the wicked, it is said, are cruel; and so in another sense the tender mercies of the thoughtless and the ignorant may be called cruel. Stopping suffering for the immediate present, they may be sowing the seed of suffering a hundred times greater in the future. But God's mercy is so offered and exercised that it needs never to be regretted. It is mercy gloriously allied with great considerations of righteousness. It is mercy for the repentant; for those who confess and forsake their sins; and although from a superficial glance this visitation of suffering upon children and children's children may seem to contradict the mercy of God, we find on further reflection that it is a great warning against human selfishness. What a rebuke to the man who, knowing that his sin will involve posterity in suffering, yet goes on with the sin! Who are we, to indulge in aspersions on the mercy of God, when perhaps at the very moment we are sowing in self-indulgence what others must reap in pangs which our self-denial and regard for God's wise will might have utterly prevented?—Y.

Vers. 6, 7.—*God is love.* A previous revelation, cf. iii. 14. Then the emphasis was on the *name*, now it is on the *character* of him who bears the name. Moses, in common with the people, longed after some visible manifestation of the glory of the unseen God who spoke to him (xxxiii. 18). His desire is granted; but at the same time God turns his thoughts from the visible to the invisible. "It is not," he seems to say, "what I *appear* to be that man has to trust to; it is what I *am*." Consider—

I. THE CHARACTER REVEALED. 1. *It implies intelligence in the Being who is characterised.* The name Jehovah might, conceivably, be given to "a stream of tendency." Law, irresistible and impersonal, might be described as "the eternal." You cannot, however, speak of law as "merciful and gracious," etc. There must be some one who works through law. A divine heart is the mainspring whence flow all "streams of tendency," the issues of the universal life. 2. *It is not such as man could have imagined.* Men do create their own gods; deifying the exaggerated and distorted shadows cast by their own characters—so the mountaineer is at first awe-struck when confronted by his own gigantic shadow. Here, however, is a character which cannot be traced to such an origin; it is not man's thought about God, it is God's revelation of himself to man. Contrast the character of the shadow, man-created, god, with that of Jehovah. The one is revengeful, arbitrary, cruel, etc.; the other is merciful and gracious, etc. The man-made god is at best kindly with a weak and sentimental kindliness; with Jehovah, love is the heart-root of his nature, a love which will by no means clear the guilty. Nature "red in tooth and claw" scarcely suggests such a god as this; man could never have conceived him. The character is a revelation of himself, made here to Moses; made, yet more clearly, later, in the life of "the Word made Flesh."

II. THE CHARACTER AS EXPRESSED IN ACTION. Men *are* treated by some *one* or some *thing* as God says he treats them. The "stream of tendency" makes for righteousness; it is not purposeless, it must be purposed. Though experience was insufficient to suggest the character, it yet helps us to verify the revelation. Notice, specially, the stern side of love. The latter part of the revelation seems at first inconsistent with the first part; they give, however, two aspects of the same homogeneous character. True love is quite distinct from kindliness; its brain is wisdom, and justice nerves its right hand. 1. *The action which love will take, must depend upon the circumstances which call for action.* Our own experience shows sufficiently that love does not shrink from giving pain. The parent will *forgive* his child, and yet, at the same time, not "clear" him; he cannot pass over without notice conduct of which he disapproves. Love may wield the surgeon's knife; or the scourge, with a view to *moral* surgery. So long as the child keeps sound and well, physically and morally, love is all sunshine; with illness or danger, physical or moral, love—seeking the good of the beloved object—may strike and pierce like lightning. Apply the general principle and it explains:— 2. *A special case.* Can love visit upon children the sins of their parents? Yes, for children inherit the sinful tendencies of their parents; and it is just this visitation which may best secure them against falling into sin. Sad that the drunkard's child should be an epileptic; yet epilepsy may be a loving visitation if it guard against the confirmed drunkenness which might otherwise have ruined body and soul. A warning for parents; yet consolation for the victims of *their* sins, when it is seen that love has inspired severity (cf. Heb. xii. 11).

Conclusion. Such the God revealed to Moses, and such the God revealed in Christ. Before such a Being what attitude so fitting as that of Moses? (ver. 8; cf. Job xlii. 1—6).—G.

EXPOSITION.

Vers. 9—26.—THE RENEWAL OF THE COVENANT. Dazed, as it would seem, by the splendour of the vision which he had beheld, Moses forgot that God had already pledged himself to renew the covenant, and lead the people in person to Canaan. In his forgetfulness, he once more set himself to intercede with God on their behalf, and besought him—1. That he would go up with them; 2. That he would pardon them; and 3. That he would once more take them as his inheritance (ver. 9). Without replying separately to these requests, God formally renews the covenant; promises not only to go up with the people, but to work miracles for them (ver. 10), and to drive out the nations before them when they have arrived (ver. 11); and makes a brief summary of the chief points of positive observance, which he requires of them in addition to the moral law. These points may be reduced to twelve:—1. That no treaty of peace should be made with the Canaanite nations (ver. 12). 2. That all their images, altars, and groves should be destroyed (ver. 13). 3. That no molten image should be made to represent God (ver. 17). 4. That the Passover festival should be observed as previously commanded (ver. 18). 5. That the first-born should be dedicated, or redeemed (vers. 19, 20). 6. That the Sabbath rest should be observed at all times of the year (ver. 21). 7. That the feast of Pentecost (weeks) should be observed regularly (ver. 22). 8. That the feast of tabernacles should also be observed (ib.). 9. That at all the three great festivals all the males should appear before God (ver. 23). 10. That no leaven should be used with any sacrifice (ver. 25). 11. That first-fruits of all things should be offered to God (ver. 26). 12. That no kid should be seethed in her mother's milk (ver. 26).

Ver. 9.—**If now I have found grace in thy sight.** The vision vouchsafed him makes Moses feel that he has indeed been received into favour with God. The first use which it occurs to him to make of his position is to intercede anew for his people. He, apparently, forgets that God has already promised to go with them (ch. xxxiii. 17), and prefers exactly the same request which he had made on the preceding day, and which had been granted. To this he adds a prayer for **pardon**, and a request that God would take Israel **for his inheritance.** The last phrase is a new one, but expresses perhaps no more than has been implied in such phrases as " thy people, which thou hast purchased" (ch. xv. 16)—" ye shall be a peculiar treasure unto me" (ch. xix. 5).

Ver. 10.—**I make a covenant**—i.e., " I lay down afresh the terms of the covenant between me and Israel." On my part, I will go with them (implied, not expressed), and do miracles for them, and drive out the nations before them (vers. 10, 11), and enlarge their borders, and not allow their land to be invaded at the festival seasons (ver. 24) : on their part, they must "observe that which I command them" (ver. 11). **Marvels such as have not been done in all the earth.** As the drying up of the Jordan (Josh. iii. 16, 17) ; the falling down of the walls of Jericho (ib. vi. 20), the slaughter of the army of the five kings by hailstones (ib. x. 11), and the like. **It is a terrible thing that I will do with thee.** Terrible, not to Israel, but to Israel's enemies. Compare Deut. x. 21 ; Ps. cvi. 22 ; cxlv. 6, etc.

Ver. 11.—**Observe thou that which I command thee this day.** The precepts expressly given (vers. 12—26) are, as observed above, almost wholly positive. The moral law did not require recapitulation, because it was enjoined on the people afresh by the writing on the two tables (ver. 28). **I drive out before thee.** Compare iii. 8, 17; vi. 4, 8; xiii. 5, 11; xxxiii. 2.

Ver. 12.—**Take heed to thyself lest thou make a covenant.** See above, ch. xxiii. 32 **A snare.** See ch. xxiii. 33.

Ver. 13.—**Ye shall destroy their altars,** etc. This command is more sweeping than the corresponding one in the "Book of the Covenant" (ch. xxiii. 24), which expressly mentions only the "images." Here the destruction of idol-altars and idol-groves is further commanded. On idol-altars, see Num. xxiii. 1, 29 ; Judg. ii. 2 ; 1 Kings xvi. 32 ; xviii. 26, etc. **Groves** are here for the first time mentioned. They appear to have been artificial constructions, either of wood or metal, or both, more or less imitative of trees, and regarded as emblems of the Oriental naturedeities, especially Baal and Astarte or Ashtoreth. The word translated "grove" (ashêrah) is a modification of the name Ashtoreth. The well-known "sacred tree" of the Assyrians is probably an ashêrah.

Ver. 14.—**For thou shalt worship no other God.** This is a reference to the Second Commandment (ch. xx. 5). The meaning is— "Thou shalt not spare the idolatrous emblems of the Canaanite nations, for thou couldst only do so to worship them, and thou art already forbidden to worship any other god beside me." The existence of the Decalogue and its binding nature, is assumed throughout this chapter

Vers. 15, 16.—The probable consequences of making treaties with the Canaanite nations, alluded to in ver. 12, and in ch. xxiii. 33, are here fully set forth. They include—1. Joining in their idol-feasts ; 2. Intermarriages ; 3. The actual apostasy of those who married idolatrous wives. The event fully justified the warning here given. See Judg. ii. 2, 11—13, 17; vi. 25; x. 6, etc. **They go a whoring.** This expression, so common in the later books, is here used for the first time   It implies that the relation between man and God is analogous to that of the marriage-bond, so that deserting him for other gods is a species of adultery. Compare the frequent representations in the New Testament of Christ as the "Bridegroom" and the Church as his "Bride."

Ver. 17.—**Thou shalt make thee no molten gods.** An express allusion to the recent sin of the golden calf.

Ver. 18.—**The feast of unleavened bread shalt thou keep.** See ch. xxiii. 15, and compare chs. xii. 14—20, and xiii. 3—10. **The month Abib.** See the comment on ch. xiii. 4.

Vers. 19, 20.—**All that openeth the matrix is mine,** etc. This is a repetition of the command given in ch. xiii. 12, 13, which had not been inserted in the "Book of the Covenant." It is again enjoined in Lev. xxvii. 26, 27. **None shall appear before me empty.** Repeated from ch. xxiii. 15.

Ver. 21.—**Six days,** etc. This is repeated from the "Book of the Covenant" (ch. xxiii. 12), but with a remarkable addition—**in earing time and in harvest thou shalt rest.** "Earing time" is "ploughing time"—to "ear" being to "plough" in Old English, a word cognate with the Greek ἄρω and the Latin *aro;* and the command to rest both then and at harvest time is a command not to break the Sabbath rest at the seasons when it might seem most necessary so to do The temptation to "save the harvest" is readily intelligible to Englishmen. To appreciate the other temptation, we require to know the peculiar circumstances of the East. It is necessary there to complete the ploughing before the spring rains are over. These last but a short time; and when they are once

past no rain can be looked for till the autumn.

Ver. 22.—**Of the first-fruits.** There is here an unfortunate ambiguity. The English reader naturally supposes that three festivals are mentioned—1. That of weeks; 2. That of the first-fruits of wheat harvest; and 3. That of in-gathering. But in reality the feast of weeks is that of the first-fruits of wheat harvest. See Lev. xxiii. 17; Num. xxviii. 26. The observance of this feast, as well as that of the feast of in-gathering, was commanded in the "Book of the Covenant" (ch. xxiii. 16).

Ver. 23.—**Thrice in the year.** Repeated from ch. xxiii. 17.

Ver. 24.—**I will .... enlarge thy borders.** The original promise to Abraham was to give to his seed "the land of Canaan" (Gen. xii. 5—7). Afterwards this promise was enlarged, and he was told that the land assigned them was the entire tract between the Nile and the Euphrates (*ib.* xv. 18). And practically, they took possession first of the one, while at a later date their border was enlarged, and they became masters of the other. See 1 Kings iv 21, 24; 2 Chron. ix. 26. **Neither shall any man desire thy land,** etc. This promise is nowhere else made. It would serve as a great encouragement to the proper observance of the festivals.

Ver. 25.—Repeated from ch. xxiii. 18.

Ver. 26.—Repeated from ch. xxiii. 19. It is remarkable that both legislations terminate with the same, somewhat strange, proviso. There must have been an intention of impressing strongly upon the people the principle of tenderness involved in it. (See the comment on ch. xxiii. 19.)

HOMILETICS.

Vers. 9—26.—*The covenant renewed.* That God should have consented to renew the covenant with Israel after it had been violated so flagrantly is evidence of two things : 1. His faithfulness towards his true followers, which makes him "merciful unto thousands of those that love him," and renders him tender to the children for the sake of the fathers ; 2. The value that he sets on intercessory prayer, when offered earnestly by a believer. In the renewal itself we may notice :—

I. THAT THE PROMISES NOW MADE EXCEED ALL THOSE WHICH HAD BEEN MADE TO THE PEOPLE PREVIOUSLY. Leadership had been promised ; help in driving out the nation had been promised ; the possession of Canaan had been promised. But not "marvels such as had not been done in all the earth, nor in any nation" (ver. 10)—not an enlargement of the nation's boundaries beyond the limits of Canaan (ver. 24)—not security against their land being invaded when they went up to the three great festivals (*ibid.*). These, so far as the people were concerned, were new and additional pledges. God is apt "to do exceeding abundantly beyond all that we ask or think." He ties himself down to perform certain promises ; but he does not tie himself down not to do more than he has promised. He will give to man ultimately, not only more than he is bound to give, but more than "it has entered into the heart of man to conceive."

II. THAT THE PROHIBITIONS ARE IN SOME CASES MORE STRINGENT THAN BEFORE. According to the former covenant, idolatrous images were not to be spared; according to this neither images, nor altars, nor groves (ver. 13); according to that, the Sabbath was not to be infringed, as a general rule—according to this, not even on account of the most necessary operations of husbandry (ver. 21); according to that, treaties were not to be made with the Canaanitish nations—according to this, neither treaties nor matrimonial alliances. To balance the greater favours, there were imposed greater obligations, whereby was inculcated the lesson that the two are correlative.

III. THE PRECEPTS REIMPOSED WERE, IN ADDITION TO THE DECALOGUE, CHIEFLY THOSE CONNECTED WITH WORSHIP. It was the attraction of a corrupt worship which had caused Israel to fall away. Their best security against a second similar fall would be careful and constant observance of the pure worship prescribed to them. If they kept properly the Sabbath, the great festivals, the laws of sacrifice, of redemption, of first fruits, and whatever was similar to these, it might well content their religious aspirations, and leave no such vacuum in their lives as they had hoped to fill with their calf-worship. True, that many of the precepts could not be observed until they reached Canaan; but, as a compensation, they would have in the wilderness the daily worship—morning and evening—of the tabernacle, and the near presence of God in the pillar of the cloud, not henceforth to be withdrawn from them. The true spiritual life could be amply sustained on these—it was only a pseudo-spiritualism that the calf-worship would have exercised.

HOMILIES BY VARIOUS AUTHORS.

Ver. 10.—"*I make a covenant.*" I. A COVENANT RENEWED. Mark how in connection with this there is—(1) A new command to ascend the mount. (2) A new command that the mount shall not be touched. (3) A new manifestation of the Divine glory. Yet how different! (4) A new giving of the law. (5) A new rehearsal (in summary) of the "rights." (6) A new fast of forty days and forty nights.

II. A COVENANT RENEWED ON THE BASIS OF INTERCESSION. We have even more than this—we have a "shadow of the Cross" (ch. xxxii. 32). Peace made by (1) mediation, (2) atonement, (3) intercession. The bestowal of the blessing on this ground—1. Prevented the people from looking lightly on sin, or from imagining that God looked lightly on it. 2. Conserved the Divine honour. 3. Gave a higher value to the gift. 4. Put honour upon Moses. 5. Taught that blessings can be won from God by intercession.—J. O.

Vers. 10—29.—*Revived obligations.* Former instructions are renewed; only, however, so far as relates to the duties of religion. Renewal of the civil code was not required. Subject to this limit, the new book of the covenant (ver. 27) revives, supplements, expands, and endorses the teachings and precepts of the old one. We have in it—

I. PROMISE (vers. 10, 11). God, as on the former occasion (ch. xxiii. 23—30), pledges himself to drive out all their enemies. The work would be—1. *Wonderful*—"Before all the people will I do marvels," etc. 2. *Terrible*—"For it is a terrible thing which I will do with thee." Men have passed the same judgment upon it. God however, called it terrible before they did. They should remember this when they build on it an objection to the Bible. God *can* do terrible things. 3. *Thorough.* The extirpation would be complete.

II. CAUTION (vers. 12—18). The Israelites were to beware of being snared into idolatry. To this end they were—1. *To make no league with the Canaanites.* "Evil communications corrupt good manners" (1 Cor. xv. 33). 2. *To destroy all signs of their idolatrous worship.* No good comes of retaining in our midst that which can only be a snare to us. 3. *To avoid intermarriages.* "Be ye not unequally yoked together with unbelievers" (2 Cor. vi. 14).

III. COMMAND (vers. 18—27). The command relates to the three feasts. See former Homilies.—J. O.

EXPOSITION.

Vers. 27—35.—FINAL DESCENT OF MOSES FROM SINAI. The covenant having been renewed, Moses prepared to descend, having first however received a command to commit to writing the words of this second covenant (ver. 27). He received back the tables from God, inscribed with the Ten Commandments, and after a stay in Sinai of equal duration with the former one (ver. 28), descended, having the tables in his hands. He was not aware that the skin of his face had become radiant (ver. 29), and first learnt the fact by the rulers being afraid to come near him (ver. 30). After conversing with them and with the people he resolved to "put a vail on his face" ordinarily, only taking it off when he "went in before the Lord" into the "tent of meeting," and when, having received a message from the Lord to the people, he came out to deliver it.

Ver. 27.—Write thou these words. Literally, "write *thee* these words"—*i.e.*, "write them for thyself and for thy people." **According to the tenor of these words have I made a covenant.** That is, "the covenant on my part is conditional on the observance of **these words** on the part of Israel." The "words" intended are those of vers. 10—26.

Ver. 28.—He was there with the Lord forty days and forty nights. As on the former occasion (ch. xxiv. 18). The patience and faith of the people was tested by this second long delay. Happily, they stood the test; and on Moses' final descent from Sinai the Israelites were found expectant and obedient (vers. 30—32). **He did neither eat bread nor drink water.** This was so also on the former occasion (Deut. ix. 9), though it is not mentioned in Exodus. The near presence of God sustained the vital powers and made food unnecessary. Moses, Elijah (1 Kings xix. 8), and our Lord have alone accomplished a fast of this duration. Modern parodies are not held by scientific men to belong to the category of established facts. **He wrote upon the tables.** It has been argued from this expression that Moses wrote the words on the second tables; and it would be natural so to understand the passage, had nothing else been said on the subject. But in ver. 1 we are told that "God said, I will write upon these tables;" and the same is repeated in Deut. x. 2. Moreover in Deut. x. 4, it is distinctly declared "He" (*i.e.* God) "wrote on the tables according to the first writing." We must therefore regard "he" in this passage as meaning "the Lord," which is quite possible according to the Hebrew idiom.

Ver. 29 —The skin of his face shone while he talked with him. Rather, "through his talking with him." The glory of God, as revealed to Moses on this occasion, caused his face to become henceforth radiant. Compare the effect of the transfiguration (Matt. xvii. 2). The Vulgate wrongly translates *kâran*, "to shine," as if it were derived from *keren*, "a horn"—whence the painters of mediæval times commonly represent Moses as horned. St. Paul's words (2 Cor. iii. 7) are conclusive as to the true meaning.

Ver. 30.—They were afraid. They shrank from Moses, as if he were more than man. (Compare Ezek. i. 28; Rev. i. 17.) Perhaps they thought that what they saw was his spirit.

Ver. 31.—Moses called unto them. Moses bade them approach—no doubt assured them that there was no cause for fear (cf. Luke xxiv. 38, 39)—and by his manner and familiar voice dispelled their fears and re-assured them. **Aaron and all the rulers . . . returned unto him.** Apparently, in their alarm they had drawn back. Being re-assured, they "returned."

Ver. 32.—All that the Lord had spoken. "All," *i.e.*, "that the Lord had commanded him to enjoin upon them"—especially the precepts in vers. 10—26—not all that he had heard from God in the space of forty days and forty nights.

Vers. 33—36.—Till Moses had done speaking with them. The Hebrew text will not bear this rendering. All the ancient versions (LXX. Vulg. Syr. etc.) and the Targums agree that the meaning is—"when Moses had done speaking, he put a veil on his face." And this agrees with the plain meaning of vers. 34 and 35, which are to be taken connectedly. Moses first delivered his message with face unveiled, then he veiled himself, and thenceforth he wore a veil at all times except when he sought the Divine presence in the "tent of meeting" or the tabernacle, and when he delivered to the people any message sent them from God by him. He wore the veil ordinarily to prevent them from being dazzled. He took it off when he entered the tabernacle, that the Divine presence might shine fully on him and renew his strength. He kept it off when he returned, if he had any message to the people, until he had delivered it, in order the more fully to authenticate the message and shew to the people that it was from God. Then **the children of Israel saw the face of Moses, that the skin of Moses' face shone** (ver. 35). Having discharged himself of the message intrusted to him, he once more covered himself, and continued veiled until he again entered the tabernacle. The only objection that can be taken to this exegesis is derived from 2 Cor. iii. 7—16, which has been thought to imply that Moses wore the veil whenever he was in the sight of the people.

But the passage does not really assert any such thing. It is quite enough for the argument, that under the old covenant a veil had been worn to conceal some of its glory. This concealment St. Paul contrasts with the openness of Christianity (vers. 13, 18); while at the same time he argues that it may be viewed as typical of that blindness and darkness which was characteristic of the Jewish nation of his day.

HOMILETICS.

Vers. 29, 30, 35.—*The shining of Moses' face.* This strange phenomenon, one of the distinctive marks which most closely assimilate the Jewish with the Christian law-giver, is well worthy of our attentive consideration.

I. As to its origin. Admission to the Divine presence within the cloud had not, on the former occasion, left any such visible trace. It cannot, therefore, be ascribed simply to communion with God for a period of a certain duration. We must endeavour to see how the second sojourn in Sinai was differentiated from the first, if we would discover the real cause of the wonder. Now the difference was mainly this: that Moses in the interval had been severely tried, and had emerged from the trial better, purer, fitter for close intercourse with the Supreme. He had shown zeal, fervour, promptness, in checking the revolt against Jehovah; he had shown a spirit of extraordinary self-sacrifice in refusing to become the sole male progenitor of a people whom God would substitute for the existing Israel (ch. xxxii. 10), and in offering himself as an atonement for the people's sins (*ib.* 32); and he had shown that persistent importunity in kindly intercession for others (ch. xxxiii. 12—16) with which God is especially pleased. Under these circumstances—thus elevated above his former self—he had been admitted, not only to a second conference of forty days' duration, but also to a special vision—never vouchsafed to any but him—of the Divine glory (*ib.* 8—28; ch. xxxiv. 5, 6). The radiance that rested on his face is ascribed especially to his long "talk" with God (ver. 29); but we can scarcely doubt that a portion of it was due to the transcendent vision which passed before him prior to the forty days' conference. The brightness then shed upon his face increased from day to day during the long and close com-munion—closer now than before, from his greater fitness; and he, "with open face beholding the glory of the Lord, was changed into the same image from glory to glory" (2 Cor. iii. 18), until his countenance was such that it could not be steadfastly beheld for long; and he, in mercy to his people, veiled it.

II. As to its effect. 1. Its immediate effect was to alarm. "Aaron and the elders were afraid to come nigh him." The unknown and unexpected is always fearful to man; and this was a novelty which might well startle. What did the sight portend? Certainly, an increase of supernatural power. Would this power be used to punish and avenge? Would the radiance burn like fire, or scathe like the thunder-bolt? They could not tell. Knowing their own sinfulness, they trembled, conscience making cowards of them, as it does of us all. And they feared to approach—nay, they drew back—perhaps fled. 2. Its after effect was to increase Moses' authority. The glow was a perpetual credential of his Divine mission. Like the moon, it witnessed, whenever seen, to the absent sun. Always beheld, whenever Moses had any new orders to give, it was a sanction to his entire legislation, and caused the laws which were least palatable to be accepted without resistance. Though it did not prevent partial revolts, it kept the bulk of the nation faithful to their leader for forty years. Even when they did not see the brightness, the veil that hid it showed that it was there. Its presence could never be forgotten. Moses was exalted by it into a condition half-Divine, half-human; and was felt to be marked out by Heaven as the supreme chief of the nation.

III. As to its intent. Its intent would seem to have been—1. To strengthen and support Moses in his difficult position as leader of a wayward and "stiff-necked" people. 2. To impress the people, and render them more submissive and obedient. (See the preceding section.) 3. To symbolise the great truth, that by drawing near to God, by communion with him, we become like him—like him and ever more like; changing "from glory to glory;" reflecting his attributes, as snow-summits reflect the sunset; receiving from him a real effluence, which shows itself in our lives, in our acts, in our very features. There is in the countenances of God's most advanced servants a bright-ness, a gladness, a beaming radiance, which can come only of long communion with him, and which is a sensible evidence, to those who "have eyes to see," that they are indeed his friends, his favoured ones. The best artists—Perugino, Francia, Rafaelle sometimes, Fra Angelico, Fra Bartolomeo, Bellini, Luini, Basaiti—express this in their pictures. But it is not a grace that has passed away. The eye that has true spiritual vision may still see among those who walk the earth faces with such an unmistakable glow of true piety upon them as marks their owners for God's friends, Christ's loved ones, souls constant in their communion with him who is " the Light of the world," and " in whose light we shall see light."

Vers. 33—35.—*The symbolism of the veil.* The veil upon Moses' face shrouded the glory of his countenance from Israel, except at such times as he spake to them the commands of God. So God himself shrouds his glory from us ordinarily, and only at rare intervals, when he would impress us most deeply, lifts the veil and lets the brightness flash forth. So Christ, when he came on earth, emptied himself of the glory which he had with the Father, hid it away, and seldom let it be seen. Tenderness and compassion for man's weakness is the cause of the concealment in such case. Human nature, while we are in the flesh, cannot bear the blinding light of Divine glory, any more than the eye can bear to gaze upon the noonday sun. The veil was thus, primarily, a token of Moses' love for Israel; but it was also a token of many other things besides; *e.g.*—

I. OF THE DARKNESS AND MYSTERY IN WHICH DIVINE TRUTH WAS SHROUDED UNDER THE MOSAICAL DISPENSATION. The Trinity, the Incarnation, the Atonement, Justification, Sanctification, even Immortality—all the great doctrines which constitute the heart and kernel of true religion, though in a certain sense contained in Mosaism, were concealed, hidden away, wrapt in a veil. Men " saw through a glass darkly" fewer or more of these truths—had, that is, some dim conception of them, but saw none of them clearly till they were " brought to light" by the Gospel. " Lord, *now* lettest thou thy servant depart in peace, according to thy word, for *mine eyes have seen thy salvation,*" said holy Simeon, when he looked upon the Lord, then first having made plain to him what had been darkness and cloud previously. Much of the Divine scheme of man's salvation had been a mystery even to angels until it was revealed to them by and through the Church (Eph. iii. 4—10). When Christ came, and lived, and preached, " the people which sat in darkness saw great light, and to them which sat in the region and shadow of death light sprang up" (Matt. iv. 16). A solemn thought to Christians that this is so; for responsibility is in proportion to the light vouchsafed. " He that despised Moses' law died without mercy under two or three witnesses. Of how much sorer punishment shall he be thought worthy who hath trodden under foot the Son of God?" (Heb. x. 28, 29).

II. OF THE BLINDNESS WHICH LIES PERMANENTLY UPON THE HEARTS AND MINDS OF THE JEWS. The veil of obstinate unbelief has so shrouded, and still so shrouds, the intelligence of the race, that, though Moses is read to them every Sabbath day, and the words of the prophets are continually sounded in their ears, they cannot see or understand. Still they remain " fools and slow of heart to believe all that the prophets have spoken" (Luke xxiv. 25). Like the Ethiopian eunuch, they " understand not what they read" (Acts viii. 31); but, unlike him, they will not accept guidance. " The veil is upon their heart" (2 Cor. iii. 15). Christians should ever pray that the time may come, and come speedily, when " the veil shall be taken away" (*ib.* 16), and so " all Israel be saved" (Rom. xi. 26). Hopeless as the task seems, Christians should still labour for the conversion of the eight millions of Jews dispersed throughout the world. Christians should beware lest they themselves, by their sinful lives, intensify and prolong the blindness of Israel, pressing the veil down upon the brows that otherwise might have cast it off, and dimming the brightness of the Gospel of Christ that otherwise might have pierced through the veil's folds, and have given sight to the shrouded eyes.

HOMILIES BY VARIOUS AUTHORS.

Vers. 29—35.—*The shining face.* Consider—
I. THE SHINING OF MOSES' FACE (vers. 29, 30). (1) A result of personal communion. (2) A symbol of the glory of his dispensation (2 Cor. iii. 7). (3) A foreshadowing of the

transfiguration (Matt. xvii. 1—8). (4) Partly a consequence of inward mental exaltation (cf. Acts vi. 15). Communion with God, vision of Jesus, the joy of salvation,
fulness of spiritual life, make both face and character to shine (cf. 2 Cor. iii. 18).

II. The fear of this shine (ver. 30). The beauty of the glory had something of
terror in it. Symbol of the dispensation—" a ministration of death" (2 Cor. iii. 7). See
sermon by Dr. John Ker on Moses and Stephen—" The Old Testament and the New"
("Sermons," p. 170).

III. The veil (vers. 31—33). The notable fact is that Moses did not veil his face
during the time when veiling might seem to be most required, viz., while speaking to
the people. The commandments were delivered with the face unveiled. When he
had " done" speaking, Moses put this screen before it. The act, therefore, must be taken
as symbolic. A symbol—1. *Of the veiled character of the dispensation*—types,
carnal ordinances, " broken lights," etc. Its " end" was not manifest. 2. *Of the veiled
hearts of the people.* This kept them from perceiving even what might have been seen
(cf. 2 Cor. iii. 12—18). The Gospel, in contrast with the law, is an unveiled system
(2 Cor. iii. 14). Preachers of the gospel, bearing this in mind, should use " great plainness of speech" (vers. 11, 12). The later system provides further for the removal of
the veil from the heart (vers. 16, 17). It ministers " the Spirit."

IV. The veil taken off on entering the sanctuary (vers. 34, 35). " When
Moses went in before the Lord," etc. Again symbolic—1. *Of what is necessary for the
removal of the veil from the heart.* It must " turn to the Lord" (2 Cor. iii. 16). The
instant it does so the veil will be taken away (ver. 16). 2. *Of the privilege of Christian
believers.* They are admitted to gaze " with unveiled face " on the " glory of the Lord "
(ver. 18).

V. Resemblances and contrasts. Compare and contrast the privilege of Moses with
that now enjoyed by believers in Christ (2 Cor. iii. 18). 1. *Resemblances.* (1) Both
have a vision of the divine glory. (2) Both are admitted to gaze upon it with face
" unveiled." (3) On both the vision exercises a transforming influence. (4) Both
must " go in" to the divine presence in order to obtain it. 2. *Contrasts.* (1) It is a
higher glory which is revealed in Christ. (2) That, the privilege of *one* man; *this,* the
privilege of *all*—" we all." (3) That, an external transfiguration; this, spiritual.
(4) That, a transitory glory; this, permanent and progressive. " From glory to
glory."—J. O.

Vers. 29—35.—*The shining of Moses' face.* I. The phenomenon itself. The skin
of Moses' face shone. As to the precise manner of this shining, it is of course vain to
speculate; but we may be tolerably certain it was not anything in the way of a mere
reflection from a mirror. It must surely have been the shining out for a little while of
some glorious gift which had entered, if one may say so, into the bodily constitution of
Moses. There may be some connection of this glory with the miraculous sustaining of
his life without the eating of bread, or the drinking of water. Thus we are led
to consider what wondrous capabilities there may be in matter, capabilities beyond our
present knowledge to conceive. Even with unorganised matter, man himself has been
able to do much. And the God of the physical universe has shown us how many
wonders, beauties, and enjoyments rise out of matter under the power of vital action.
Think of all that is exquisite in form, colour, and fragrance in plant-life. Think of the
refinement which distinguishes the face of a cultivated man from that of some embruted
savage. Think of that best of all charms visible in the face of one who is truly good.
Then think, on the other side, of the degradations of matter. Think of the physical
results of sottishness and sensuality. Think of the putrescence and corruption which
seem to dominate a body when its principle of life has passed away. We shall then feel
how, beyond anything we can at present conceive, there may be on the one hand an
exaltation of matter, and on the other a degradation of it.

II. The unconsciousness of Moses. He wist not that the skin of his face shone in
this way. Of some change within him during the time when he was with God in the
mount, he was doubtless conscious. He may have felt himself getting a clearer view of
Jehovah's purposes, and a heartier fellow-feeling with respect to them. He may have
felt himself conscious of a remarkable approach to inward holiness and purity; but of
this outward and visible expression of it he knew nothing at all. That which was

intolerable to his deeply-polluted brethren, so much alienated in heart from God, was utterly unperceived by him. Thus effectually separated from his brethren, the separation came from no pretension of his own, but from an inevitable confession made by those who once and again tried to repudiate him. He who is filled with the spirit of God becomes more glorious than he can imagine. And from those who live near to God, we may be sure there goes out an influence, which, though they themselves be utterly unconscious of it, is yet most mighty in its effect on others. As Moses came down from the mountain, he would be anxiously thinking how he could convey to the people some sense of that which he himself had been privileged to see. He may have despaired of putting into words the impression made on his mind; but now behold God has taken the matter into his own hands. When we take care to keep right *Godwards*, God will take care that we are kept right and powerful *manwards*. Our greatest impression upon men is to be made, not by that which we are labouring to achieve, but by that which we achieve unconsciously, when we become as much as possible mere instruments of the wisdom and power coming from above.

III. THE CONDUCT OF THE PEOPLE. It is not made clear as to whether the people were unable to gaze upon the splendour of Moses' face through the excess of light which radiated thence, or whether they were filled with superstitious terror because one who hitherto had looked but as themselves had become so changed in appearance. Probably the latter way of accounting for their conduct comes nearest to the truth. They were afraid of Moses, much as the disciples were of Jesus when they saw him walking on the lake and thought it was an apparition. Hence we have another instance of how men, whom God made to be so near to him, yet through their alienation from him, and constant immersion in earthly concerns, start back when there is some overwhelming manifestation of the unearthly and the divine. Presence of mind is lost just when presence of mind would be most helpful. Moses put on the veil in necessary toleration of human weakness; but we should always read of such necessities with a feeling of humiliation. In only too many things these ungodly Israelites are our representatives. God, who is our benefactor, cannot reveal himself in all his glory, because of our weakness. When God honoured and enriched the mediator Moses by putting a divine splendour into his countenance, as he came down among men with the laws of a holy and a happy life, this very splendour became a cause of abject terror rather than of confidence and gladness. Yet when the final Mediator came, full of grace and truth, men rushed to the other extreme. They could see no divinity and authority, and in their contempt and presumption, put the Mediator to death. It is very difficult for men to make a right estimate of the outward shows of things.—Y.

Vers. 28—35.—*Fellowship with God and its fruits.* I. COMMUNION WITH GOD. 1. The length of his sojourn—forty days and forty nights. Time sped unmarked in the presence and fellowship of God. The future glory an untiring joy. The redeemed serve him day and night in his temple. 2. Lower wants were forgotten: "he did neither eat bread nor drink water." The need of the body was unfelt in the satisfying of the desires of the spirit. "In thy presence is fulness of joy." To escape from temptation we have only to enter into the presence of God and to let the eye rest upon his glory.

II. MAN GLORIFIED THROUGH COMMUNION. 1. The descent of Moses, radiant with the glory of God, the type of Jesus in his coming again the second time without sin unto salvation. 2. A prophecy of the after glory of them who believe. "They that be wise shall shine as the brightness of the firmament, and they that turn many to righteousness as the stars for ever and ever." "We shall be like him, for we shall see him as he is." 3. An example of the present glory of those who have fellowship with him who is light. We are "light in the Lord." 4. Its effect upon the worldly and the sinful. They were afraid to come nigh. It awakens conscience. It proves the reality of the Unseen. It reveals the distance between the soul and God.

III. THE VEILING OF MOSES' FACE. He was unconscious of the glory: "he wist not that his face shone." The vision of God is ever accompanied with lowly self-judgment. 2. It was not worn ostentatiously. We may not boast of our nearness to God. Vanity in the Divine life is an impossibility. 3. The glory was veiled in accordance with the dispensation which alone these men were able to receive. The whole law with its types and shadows was a veiling of the sun of righteousness, and the redemption glory. We must meet men where they are that they may be led to God. The Apostle who spoke "wisdom among them that were perfect" knew how to give milk also to babes in Christ and to speak to the carnal.—H.

Ver. 29.—*Moses wist not that the skin of his face shone while he talked with him.*— His face "shone"—literally, "shot out rays"—as we say, was *irradiated*, became *radiant*. Notice: I. THE CAUSE OF THE PHENOMENON. "Talked with him." Self had been forgotten in communion with Jehovah, in hearing him and attending to his utterances. It is from such communion as this that the radiant countenance results. 1. *What the communion is.* God a Spirit. Communion must be spiritual. The fleshly face cannot directly reflect spiritual light, that light "which never was on sea or land." Spirit is kindled by spirit, the human by the Divine, when spirit meets with spirit and realizes the sympathy which exists between them. 2. *What the communion does.* The illuminated spirit, reflecting God, kindled into brilliancy by his light, cannot but shine out through the fleshly envelope which shrouds it. [Illustration: As opaque porcelain shade to lamp, so is the body to the spirit; light the lamp, illuminate the spirit, and the shade, in either case, becomes radiant.] If you would have a happy face, a radiant countenance, you must first have an illuminated spirit. That can only be gained from the Fount of light in and through communion with God.
II. UNCONSCIOUSNESS OF THE SUBJECT OF THE PHENOMENON. "Wist not." His face was radiant, but Moses knew nothing of it. His mind was so full of God that his attention was drawn off from all thought of his appearance. Notice: 1. *All sincerity forgets egotism* (F. W. Robertson). Attention is a fixed quantity; to fix it on God is to draw it off from self [cf. a lock on a river; open the flood-gates of communion and the level of self-love is soon lowered]. 2. *Radiancy cannot be obtained by trying for it.* If aim in prayer is to increase self-glory, it cannot succeed. God first; God all in all; then comes the illumination, and the light flows forth. Self lost in God [cf. wick saturated with oil] before we can ray out the light of God. How many selfish prayers are offered, and the countenances of those who offer them are often anything but radiant! The puritanical cast of countenance repels by its gloom rather than by its brilliancy. The best prayer is that which rises from communion; which seeks first, as in Christ's model prayer, that God's name may be hallowed, and his kingdom come, and his will be done, before going on further to seek satisfaction for personal needs.
Conclusion.—Do you want to have a radiant face? The best way is not to think about it. Lose self, as Moses did, in communion with God; then your face will be radiant, though you know it not.—G.

SECTION XVII.—CHAPTERS XXXV.—XL.

THE CONSTRUCTION AND UPREARING OF THE TABERNACLE.

EXPOSITION.

CHAPTER XXXV.

Vers. 1—3.—ITERATION OF THE LAW CONCERNING THE SABBATH. The work commanded during the time of Moses' first stay upon Sinai (ch. xxv.—xxxi.), and hindered first by the infraction (ch. xxxii.), and then by the renewal (chs. xxxiii., xxxiv.) of the covenant, was now about to commence under the direction of Moses, who alone knew what was to be constructed. Before giving his orders upon the matter, he assembled the people (ver. 1) and once more recited to them in a solemn manner the law of the sabbath (ver. 2), adding to the general law a special injunction concerning the kindling of fire (ver. 3), which may have been required by some recent breach of the law in this respect. The iteration of a command, already so often enjoined upon the people (ch. xvi. 23—30; xx. 8—11; xxiii. 12; xxxi. 13—17), is best accounted for by the consideration, that a caution was needed, lest the people, in their zeal to hurry on the work of the tabernacle, and regarding that work as a sacred one, and so exceptional, might be tempted to infractions of the law, or even to an entire neglect of it, while the work was in progress.

Ver. 1.—**All the congregation.** All the Israelites were to be allowed the privilege of making offerings for the tabernacle (ch. xxv. 2—7), and all who were competent might take part in the spinning and the weaving of the materials for the curtains and the holy vestments (chs. xxviii. 3; xxxv. 10, 25; xxxvi. 4, etc.). All therefore had to be summoned, to learn what was required. **These are the words,** etc.—*i.e.,* " These are the injunctions especially' laid' upon you at this time."

Ver. 2 is almost a repetition of ch. xxxi. 15.

Ver. 3.—**Ye shall kindle no fire.** The kindling of fire in early times involved con-siderable labour. It was ordinarily affected by rubbing two sticks together, or twisting one round rapidly between the two palms in a depression upon a board. Fire only came after a long time. Moreover, as in the warm climate of Arabia and Palestine artificial warmth was not needed, fire could only have been kindled there for cooking purposes, which involved further unnecessary work, and had already been forbidden (ch. xvi. 23). The Karaite Jews still maintain the observance of this precept to the letter, even in cold climates, as in that of the Crimea, and allow neither fire nor light in their houses on the sabbath day; but the Jews generally view the precept as having had only a temporary force, and have lights and fires, like other persons, even in Palestine. Strict Jews, however, still cook no food on the sabbath day.

HOMILETICS.

Vers. 1, 2.--*The sabbath rest not to be broken even for sacred work.* Note here a difference. Some work is rendered necessary by the very nature of that public worship which is especially commanded on the sabbath. " On the sabbath days the priests in the temple," says our Lord, " profane the sabbath day *and are blameless* " (Matt. xii. 5). Offering sacrifice was a heavy work—cleansing the altar and its precincts after sacrifice was perhaps a heavier one—reading aloud, teaching, preaching are works, the last-named to many a most exhausting work. Against such kinds of work there is no law. But physical toil, not needed for Divine worship, and so not necessary to be undergone on the sabbath day, stands on a different footing, and was forbidden, at any rate to the Jews. The spinning, weaving, dying, embroidering, carpentering, metallurgy, which occupied hundreds during the rest of the week, were to cease upon the sabbath. Men were not to consider that the fact of the purpose whereto the fabrics were about to be applied so sanctified the making of them as to render that a fit occupation for the " day of holy rest "—of " rest to the Lord."

Application.—Christians will do well to apply the lesson to themselves, and not allow themselves in occupations, on their " day of holy rest," which are really secular, because it may be argued that they have, in some respects, a sacred aspect. To play sacred music, for the excitation of devotional feelings in themselves and others, is a fitting Sunday occupation; but to practise Handel as an exercise, for the acquirement of skill in execution, would be no better than to practise Rossini or Auber. To write articles for the press on Sundays, if otherwise wrong, is not justified by the fact that they are written for a " religious " newspaper. To cast up accounts does not become a right act because they are the accounts of a charity. Whatever our rule of Sunday observance, let us beware of evading it under the excuse that our employment has a connection with religion when it is essentially secular in its character.

HOMILIES BY VARIOUS AUTHORS.

Vers. 1—4.—*The new start.* Moses' second absence, though, like the first, it lasted forty days and forty nights (ch. xxxiv. 28), was not followed by the same disastrous effects as the former one. The people had meantime had enough of " gods of gold." They were too frightened at what had happened to think of seeking out any more " inventions " (Eccles. vii. 29). They were penitent and well disposed. When at length the news came that God had forgiven them, no bounds could be set to their zeal for service. Learn—1. How God brings good out of evil. The Divine physician so treated the distemper of the people that it ended, not simply in restored health, but in increased vitality and energy. The lapse into sin was made the means of imparting to the people the stimulus necessary for the erection of the tabernacle. 2. That revival of religion evinces its reality by the effects which it produces. (1) Willingness to *hear*. "I will hear what God the Lord will speak " (Ps. lxxxv. 8). Happy would it have been for Israel had it not " turned again to folly " (8) Willingness to *give*. Liberality in the Lord's service. (3) Willingness to *work*. The joy of salvation cannot better spend itself than in the doing of the work of the Lord's kingdom. Willing hearts, ready hands. On the injunction to keep the sabbath, see Homily on ch. xxxi. 12—18. —J. O.

EXPOSITION.

Vers. 4—20.—THE PEOPLE INVITED TO BRING GIFTS, AND ASSIST IN THE WORK OF THE TABERNACLE. Having warned the Israelites against breaches of the sabbath, Moses proceeded to enumerate the offerings which God had said that they might bring (vers. 4—9), and the works which he had required to be constructed (vers. 10—19). In the former enumeration, he follows exactly the order and wording of the Divine command to himself, as recorded in ch. xxv. 3—7; in the latter, he changes the order, mentioning first the building, with its component parts (ver. 11), then the contents of the building (vers. 12—15), then the court with its contents (vers. 16, 17) together with some details which had been omitted in the former account (ver. 18), and finally the holy garments (ver. 19). After hearing him, the people returned to their several tents (ver. 20).

Vers. 5—10 correspond to vers. 2—7 of ch. xxv., the correspondence in the list of offerings being exact.

Ver. 11.—On **the tabernacle**, see ch. xxvi. 1—6; on **the tent**, *ib.* 7—13; on the cover-

ing, *ib.* 14; the **boards**, *ib.* 15—25; the **bars**, *ib.* 26—29; the **pillars**, *ib.* 32—37; and the **sockets**, *ib.* 19, 21, 25, 32, and 37. The enumeration comprises all the main parts of which the tabernacle consisted.

Ver. 12.—On **the ark and the staves thereof**, see ch. xxv. 10—15; on **the mercy-seat**, *ib.* 17—22; on **the vail of the covering**, see ch. xxvi. 31.

Ver. 13.—On **the table** and its appurtenances, see ch. xxv. 23—30.

Ver. 14.—For **the candlestick**, its **furniture**, and its lamps, compare ch. xxv. 31—39.

Ver. 15.—**The incense altar.** See ch. xxx. 1—10. **His staves.** See ch. xxx. 5. **The anointing oil** is described in the same chapter, vers. 23—25; the **sweet incense** in vers. 34, 35; the **hangings for the door** in ch. xxvi. 36.

Ver. 16 is a reference to ch. xxvii. 1—8, ch. xxx. 18—21. Ver. 17 to ch. xxvii. 9—18.

Ver. 18.—**The pins of the tabernacle and the court** had not been previously mentioned. They must be regarded as tent-pegs, whereto were attached the **cords** which kept taut the covering of the tent over the tabernacle, and which steadied the pillars whereto the hangings of the court were fastened.

Ver. 19.—**The cloths of service.** See the comment on ch. xxxi. 10.

HOMILETICS.

On the symbolism of the Tabernacle and its parts, see the Homiletics on ch. xxv. 10—39; ch. xxvi.; ch. xxvii. 1—8; and ch. xxx. 1—10. On the symbolism of the anointing oil and the holy incense, see the Homiletics on ch. xxx. 23—28.

Vers. 5—19.—*The duty and privilege of making offerings to God.* That God allows us to offer to him of his own, and accepts such offerings as free gifts, is one of his many gracious condescensions. It is the part of all ministers to give opportunity for such offerings—to encourage them, suggest them, elicit them. Moses now summoned "all the congregation of the children of Israel," that he might give to all, without partiality or favouritism, the opportunity for a good action, which would obtain its due reward. Doubtless he pointed out that the object was one for the glory of God and the edification of his people—no less an object than the substitution for that poor "tent of meeting," which he had extemporised on the morrow of his first descent from Sinai (ch. xxxiii. 7), of a glorious structure, of the richest materials, designed by God himself, worthy of him, and suited to intensify and spiritualise the devotions of all worshippers. It was fit that the structure should, if possible, be raised by means of the free gifts of the faithful. For this Moses now, like a faithful minister of Christ, made appeal to all. In doing so, he pointed out the two modes in which such offerings may be made.

I. OFFERINGS MAY BE MADE BY THE ASSIGNMENT TO A SACRED USE OF A PORTION OF OUR SUBSTANCE. All who had gold, silver, brass, blue, purple, scarlet, fine linen, goat's hair, etc., were invited to contribute out of their abundance to the erection of the new sanctuary. It was especially urged that, if they did so, it should be with "a willing heart" (ver. 1)—"not grudgingly, or of necessity; for God loveth a cheerful giver" (2 Cor. ix. 7). Such a mode of offering is open to those only who have property of some kind or other, and is especially suited to the rich and well-to-do classes; and it was no doubt the wealthy who at this time chiefly contributed in this way. But, as God is "no respecter of persons," and regards the poor and needy fully as much as those who are of high estate, some further mode of making him an offering is necessary. Note, in this connection, that—

II. OFFERINGS MAY BE MADE BY THE DEVOTION TO A SACRED USE OF SOME PORTION OF OUR TIME AND LABOUR. "Every wise-hearted among you shall come, and make all that the Lord hath commanded" (ver. 10). All who had sufficient skill were invited to join in the actual work of preparing and making the various fabrics. Carpenters, weavers, dyers, smiths, embroiderers, metallurgists, might contribute their time and work, and so make an offering to God as acceptable as that of the gold or jewels of the wealthy. Even poor women, whose only skill was to spin thread with their hands (ver. 25), might "bring that which they had spun," and were accepted as offering worthily. In this way there were few families that might not have their part in the work, for spinning was a wide-spread accomplishment. And so, in our own day, whenever any good work is taken in hand, it will always be found that every one who wills can have some part in it—can help, by headwork or by handiwork, to effect the end desired. And the value of such participation is quite equal to that rendered by rich contributors, at any rate, in the sight of God. For observe, the women who spun goat's hair are placed side by side with the "rulers" who "brought onyx stones," and costly spices, and jewels to be set in the high-priest's breastplate (vers. 26—28).

HOMILIES BY VARIOUS AUTHORS.

Ver. 4—ch. xxxvi. 8.—*Gifts and workers.* Learn from this section that the Lord's work requires—

I. LIBERAL GIVERS. Almost everything needed for the sanctuary was provided by the free gifts of the people. What was required was readily forthcoming. The only exception to the voluntariness of the givings was the half-shekel of atonement money (chs. xxx. 11—17; xxxviii. 25, 26). These givings, which may well be made the model of our own, were: 1. Willing—"Every one whose heart stirred him up, and whom his spirit made willing" (ver. 21). The Lord "loveth a *cheerful* giver" (2 Cor. ix. 7). 2. According to ability. Each gave as he was able (vers. 23—29). The princes gave costly gifts. Others brought silver and brass. Others gave wood. Those who could not give anything else gave work (vers. 25, 26). 3. Universal. *All* classes gave. The princes, the people, young and old, men and women. 4. Overflowing. So zealous was the spirit of the people, and so abundant were their gifts, that they had in the end to be restrained (ch. xxxvi. 5—7). When will a like liberality be manifested in the cause of Christ? Liberal givings are *needed.* There is still much land to be possessed at home. Heathen lands are opening to the Gospel. 5. It sufficed for the work (ch. xxxvi. 7). Thus would God teach us that it is his will that his work should be supported by the voluntary contributions of his people. 6. The giving was made an act of worship— "Every man that offered, offered an offering (*lit.* a *wave-*offering) of gold unto the Lord" (ver. 22). "Every one that did offer an offering of silver and brass brought the Lord's offering" (ver. 24). This is the true spirit of religious giving. The humblest offering, thus presented, will not fail of acceptance. Cf. the widow with her two mites (Mark xii. 41—44).

II. WILLING WORKERS (ch. xxxvi. 1, 2). The work, like the giving, was *hearty.* Those only were asked to engage in this work whose hearts stirred them up to do it. God desires no other kind of workers.

III. DIVERSE GIFTS. These were needed for the different parts of the work. The man who made the "pin" (ver. 18) was as truly a worker in God's service, as Bezaleel, who drew the plans. He had his own gift and use.

IV. THE WISDOM OF THE SPIRIT. "He hath filled him with the spirit of God" (ver. 31). "Them hath he filled with wisdom of heart," etc. (ver. 35).—J. O.

EXPOSITION.

Vers. 21—29.—The zeal of the people in offering. Moses dismissed the people; but they soon began to return, bringing their offerings with them. There was a general, if not a universal, willingness Men and women alike "brought bracelets (brooches?), and earrings, and rings, and armlets—all articles of gold," and offered them to the Lord (ver. 22). Others brought blue and purple and scarlet and fine linen, and goats' hair and rams' skins dyed red, and badger (or rather, seal) skins (ver. 23). Silver and bronze and shittimwood were contributed by others (ver. 24). The women, who were the only spinners, brought their spun yarn of blue and purple and scarlet and fine linen, and their yarn of goats' hair (vers. 25, 26); while the richest class of all—"the rulers"—gave, as their contribution, the onyx stones for the ephod, the jewels for the high-priest's breast-plate, and the oil needed for the light, together with rare spices for the anointing ointment and the incense (vers. 27, 28). Subsequently, we are told that what was contributed was "much more than enough" (ch. xxxvi. 5), and that the people had to be "restrained from bringing" (*ibid.* 6).

Ver. 21.—**The Lord's offering**—*i.e.*, "their offering to Jehovah." **For all his service.** The use of "his" for "its" causes an unfortunate ambiguity here. The antecedent to the pronoun is not the Lord, but the tabernacle.

Ver. 22. — **They came, both men and women.** That among the Hebrews gold ornaments were worn by men, as well as by women, is indicated by ch. iii. 22, and ch. xxxii. 2. The Egyptian men at the time of the Exodus wore armlets, bracelets, and sometimes anklets, but not often earrings Earrings, however, had been worn by the household of

Jacob (Gen. xxxv. 2). **Bracelets.** Rather, "bangles" or "bracelets." Kalisch gave "nose-rings," and so Gesenius and Rosenmüller. **Tablets.** Rather, "armlets" (Furst, Cook), or perhaps "necklaces" (Gesenius Kalisch, Knobel). **Every man that offered, offered an offering of gold.** It is not meant that every man who offered anything gave with it an offering of gold, but simply that, besides those who brought the articles named there were others who brought gold offerings of some different kind.

Ver. 23.—**Red skins of rams.** The words are the same as those translated "rams' skins dyed red" in ch. xxv. 5. The earlier rendering is the better one. **Badger skins.** Rather, "seal skins." See the comment on ch. xxv. 5.

Ver. 24.—**Every one that did offer an offering of silver.** It would seem that silver was offered by some in the way of a free-will offering, in addition to the compulsory half-shekel (ch. xxx. 12—16). Curiously, however, the amount obtained in this way is not given in ch. xxxviii. 24—29.

Ver. 25.—**All the women that were wise-hearted**—*i.e.*, "skilful." See the comment on ch. xxviii. 3. **Brought that which they had spun, both of blue,** etc. The flax itself was dyed, so that the thread produced was already coloured. **Of fine linen**—*i.e.* "white." All the threads were flaxen.

Ver. 26.—**All the women whose heart stirred them up in wisdom.** This strong expression seems to imply that *peculiar* skill was required for spinning goats' hair.

Vers. 27, 28.—**The rulers** are, no doubt, the "elders" of ch. iii. 16; iv. 29; xxiv. 9, etc. Moses had made them "rulers," or rather, "princes" (*sárey*), according to the advice of Jethro (ch. xviii. 25). They brought **onyx stones** for the ephod (ch. xxviii. 9—12) and **stones to be set,**—*i.e.*, gems for the breastplate (*ibid.* 17—20); **oil** of olive for the lamp (ch. xxvii. 20) and the holy ointment (ch. xxix. 24), and **spice** for the same (*ibid.* 23, 24) and for the incense (*ibid.* 34).

HOMILETICS.

Vers. 21—29.—*Zeal in offering.* Appeals are made to men, in all parts of the world, and in all ages, for material contributions towards the erection of structures in which God is to be worshipped. The spirit in which such appeals are met varies. (1) Occasionally, they are met in a scoffing spirit. "What, your God needs a house, and cannot build one for himself! He must beg contributions, put out a subscription list! And for what? To make a huge building, which will be of no practical use—not a school, not a hospital, not a corn-exchange, but a Church! Catch us giving anything!" Or (2) it is met in a grudging spirit. "Why is so much required? What need is there for so large a building, or for such rich ornament, or for such architectural display?" And the general inclination is to give as little as it is decent to give. Or (3) it is met in a fussy spirit. "Let the matter be well considered—let meetings be held—let a committee be formed—let our advice be taken. If we give, we must be consulted—we must have a voice in the arrangements—we must examine the plans and express our opinion upon them. Then perhaps we may head the subscription-list with something handsome." Very different was the spirit which now animated the Israelites, and which is here held up for our imitation. Their response to the appeal made to them by Moses was—

I. DEVOUT. None objected. None asked why a tabernacle was wanted, or why the tent which Moses had made a place of worship would not suffice. None scoffed at the idea of a "House of God." All seemed to see the propriety of it. All felt that what they brought was "the Lord's offering" (vers. 21, 24)—a real gift to Jehovah. All longed to have a place of worship of a worthy character.

II. UNGRUDGING AND SPONTANEOUS. Their "hearts stirred them up," their "spirits made them willing" (ver. 21). They "brought a willing offering unto the Lord" (ver. 29). The rich brought jewels and precious spices; the men and women of the middle class brought their personal ornaments; the poor men gave brass, or silver, or a ram's skin, or a piece of acacia wood; the poor women gave the labour of their hands, and spun thread for the hangings. There was no murmuring, no complaining, no fabrication of excuses—so far as appears, no open refusing to give, though there was some abstention.

III. IMMEDIATE. In one verse we read "they departed" (ver. 20), in the next (ver. 21) "they came." There was no delay, no considering, no discussing one with another, no asking "How much do you intend to give?" Each man seemed to be well persuaded of the truth of the adage—"Bis dat qui cito dat," and brought his offering at once.

IV. UNSELFISH AND UNCONDITIONAL. No one wanted to have a *quid pro quo* as the condition of his giving. No one asked to "see the plans." All were willing to leave the ordering of the work to Moses, and put their contributions absolutely in his hands. A spirit of enthusiasm was stirred up, and none thought of anything but how much he could possibly spare for the grand work which they understood Moses to contemplate. The wealth of Easterns is stored chiefly in the form of ornaments, and to denude themselves of these was a great effort of self-sacrifice.

EXPOSITION.

Vers. 30—35.—THE APPOINTMENT OF BEZALEEL AND AHOLIAB TO SUPERINTEND THE WORK. Though, in some real sense, "learned in all the wisdom of the Egyptians," still Moses was probably devoid of the technical knowledge requisite for a "superintendent of the works" on the present occasion. At any rate, his other duties imperatively required that he should decline to undertake, in addition to them, so onerous an office. And God had told him whom it would be best for him to set over the work (ch. xxxi. 1—6). Accordingly, he now made known to the people that the construction of the tabernacle and its appurtenances would be committed to two men—Bezaleel, the son of Uri, as principal, and Aholiab, the son of Ahisamach, as his assistant—who would "teach" those under them what they were to do (ver. 34).

Ver. 30.—**The Lord hath called.** etc See

cn. xxxi. 2:—"I have called by name Bezaleel," etc. **Of the tribe of Judah.** The descent of Bezaleel from Judah has been already traced. (See the comment on ch. xxxi. 2.)

Vers. 31—33—Correspond almost word for word with vers. 3—5 of ch. xxxi., *q. vide.*

Ver. 34.—**And he hath put in his heart that he may teach.** Rather, "And he hath put it into his heart to teach." He (God) has given him the gift of being able to teach others, and so has enabled him to form a body of workmen competent to carry out his conceptions. **Both he and Aholiab.** God has given the same gift to Aholiab. On the special talent of Aholiab, see the comment upon ch. xxxi. 6.

Ver. 35.—**Them hath he filled with wisdom of heart**—*i.e.,* "with talent or genius." **Of the engraver.** Rather, "of the *artificer*," a general term, under which working in metal, gem-engraving, and wood-carving are included. **And of the cunning workman.** Rather, "and of the *skilful weaver.*" This clause seems to apply to Aholiab (ch. xxxviii

23), the preceding one to Bezaleel. **And of the embroiderer.** This also applies to Aholiab (l.s.c.). **And of the weaver**—*i.e.,* "the ordinary weaver," who wove a cloth all of one colour. The "skilful weaver" produced a patterned fabric. (See ch. xxvi. 1.) The methods of working here spoken of are, all of them, such as were well known in Egypt at the time, and which, consequently, it would

have been quite natural for some of the Israelites to have learnt. We are not to suppose that God supernaturally communicated to Bezaleel and Aholiab the technical knowledge required in their occupations, but only that he gave them genius and artistic skill, so that both their designs, and their execution of them, were of unusual excellence.

HOMILETICS.

Vers. 30—35.—MASTER-CRAFTSMEN. The qualities needed for a master-craftsman are fourfold. These are here enumerated (ver. 31) as—

I. WISDOM (Heb. *khâkam* ; LXX. σοφία; Vulg. *sapientia*), the highest gift of all— the power of original conception, which, if he combines with it the other necessary qualities, makes the true artist, the master-workman, in whatsoever branch of art his work may lie. This is appropriately placed first as the most necessary quality for those who are to direct a great construction of an artistic character.

II. UNDERSTANDING (Heb. *tâban* ; LXX. σύνεσις; Vulg. *intelligentia*), a desirable, but very inferior quality, consisting in the power of appreciating the work of others, and estimating it aright. This power is needed in master-craftsmen, to qualify them for passing judgment on the work produced by those under their direction.

III. KNOWLEDGE (Heb. *yâda'* ; LXX. ἐπιστήμη; Vulg. *scientia*), or acquaintance with the laws and facts of science bearing on their art. In the present case, acquaintance with such things as elementary mechanics, the method of cutting hard stones, the process of dyeing, the best mode of working different metals, and the like. An inferior quality this, which the master-craftsman should not lack, but which will avail him little without the higher excellences.

IV. WORKMANSHIP (Heb. *m'lâkah* ; LXX. ἀρχιτεκτονία; Vulg. *doctrina*), or power of execution, next to genius the most necessary quality of the artist, and accepted to a large extent in lieu of genius, as placing a man high in the artistic scale. This excellence does not consist in mere dexterity of hand, but in a happy way of working out designed effects, producing the feeling of complete mastery over the materials. It is by their wonderful execution that the genuine works of great masters are known from copies. Note, that all these qualities were possessed by both of the master-craftsmen in an eminent degree, and that all of them were the gift of "the Spirit of God" (ver. 31), from whom comes down "every good gift and every perfect gift" (Jam. i. 17). Artists should bear this in mind, and sanctify their art by directing it to holy, or at any rate to good ends. What a sad spectacle is genius prostituted to the service of Satan !

HOMILIES BY VARIOUS AUTHORS.

Vers. 30—35.—*Bezaleel and Aholiab.* Note—I. THE FACT THAT THE LORD CHOSE MEN TO DO THE WORK. It might have been otherwise. As the people were requested of their free-will to provide the materials, so they might have been requested to provide the necessary artificers. But it is easy to see what differences and jealousies might have resulted, all to end in some unsatisfactory compromise. There was no difficulty as long as each one gave of his own decision ; and what further difficulty then threatened to come, God immediately removed by himself selecting the men who were to carry out his designs. It is very likely that Bezaleel and Aholiab were not the men whom the people themselves would have chosen. So far as pure artistic originality was concerned they may have been excelled ; for the possession in Israel of so much material for artistic and precious work seems to show that there must have been many with the ability requisite for such work. But God had his own principles of choice, his own purposes to serve ; and it would appear in due time how wise God was in indicating certain men and not others for what needed to be done.

II. THE QUALIFICATIONS WITH WHICH GOD ENDOWED THEM. God, we may be sure, to some extent took them for what they were by nature. He always looks at the natural basis on which he proposes to build up some Divine work. But he did not leave them to their natural strength to carry out his designs. He did not leave them to toil onward to impressive results through many attempts which had to be forsaken as failures. Great works of art, which only too many spectators regard with but a glance, are to the artist memorials of weary and tantalising hours. Sir Joshua Reynolds said of one of his completed paintings, " there are ten under it, some better, some worse." Bezaleel and Aholiab were spared all such disappointments, all vain hunts after the unattainable ideal. A variety of words are used with respect to them, as if to signify how eminently and abundantly God had endowed them with all that was necessary for the task. Thus it was to be made plain to the then living generation and their successors that the tabernacle and its contents were in a very important sense the work of God. These things were to be sacred in every way : they were not to be criticised and compared, as if they were the outcome of art and man's device. Perhaps criticism did come, for fault-finders are numerous in every age ; but the two chosen artificers needed not to trouble themselves about any complaining. And should we not all find it better if, instead of straining to do work for God in our own strength and wisdom—which must ever be a saddening failure as to spiritual results—we sought to be as tools directed by the wisdom of God? We have no right to complain if keen eyes discover the weak points in what is fashioned by our own skill; but if we are sure that God's Spirit is ruling in all we do for him, then we may meet complaints with a meek indifference.—Y.

Vers. 30—35.—*Bezaleel and Aholiab.* See Homily on chap. xxxi. vers. 1—12.—J. O.

EXPOSITION.

CHAPTER XXXVI.

Vers. 1—3 and 8—38.—THE PROGRESS OF THE WORK, AND THE SUPERFLUOUS LIBERALITY OF THE PEOPLE—THE LATTER HAS TO BE RESTRAINED (vers. 3—7). Bezaleel and Aholiab felt that the time for action was now come. They at once addressed themselves to their task. Moses delivered into their hands all the various offerings which the people, rich and poor, had brought in (ch. xxxv. 21—29); and skilled workmen were immediately called upon to shape it for the designed uses. The fact of the work being commenced did not stop the inflow of gifts. More and yet more continued to be brought " every morning " (ver. 3). At last it became clear that the supply had exceeded the demand ; and the workmen reported so to Moses (vers. 4, 5), who thereupon commanded that the offerings should cease (ver. 6). The progress of the work is then reported in detail, and in the following order :—1. The covering for the tabernacle (vers. 8—13) ; 2. The goats' hair covering for the tent above the tabernacle (vers. 14—18) ; 3. The outer coverings of rams' skins and seals' skins (ver. 19) ; 4. The boards for the walls of the tabernacle (vers. 20—30) ; 5. The bars for the boards (vers. 31—34) ; 6. The

veil of the most holy place (vers. 35, 36) ; 7. The hanging for the entrance to the tabernacle (vers. 37, 38). The chapter, from ver 8, runs parallel with ch. xxvi., differing from it mainly in describing as made that which in ch. xxvi. is ordered to be made.

Ver. 1.—**Then wrought Bezaleel**, etc. This is introductory to the entire sub-section, which extends to the end of ch. xxxix. It means— " Then, under the direction of Bezaleel and Aholiab, began the work of constructing that place of meeting for which commandment had been given to Moses in the mount." The master-craftsmen, and those under them, " wrought," and took care that all was done **according to all that the Lord had commanded.** It is to mark the exactitude of the obedience that chs. xxxvi.—xxxix. follow so closely, and with such minuteness, the wording of chs. xxvi.—xxviii.

Vers. 2, 3.—**Moses called Bezaleel,** etc. Having received sufficient materials for a beginning, Moses summoned Bezaleel, Aholiab, and their chief assistants, to his presence, and delivered into their hands the various offerings —the wood, the metal, the precious stones, the thread, the goats' hair, the rams' skins, the seals' skins, etc. Upon these materials they proceeded at once to work. **They brought yet unto him free offerings every morning.** The people still continued to give. Freewill offerings kept continually flowing in. Morn-

(torn overlapping fragment, partially legible)

mportance of the
y the symbolical
To us it ...
n... and we are
ts of exactitude
from the strict
be such an one
vice summoned
el that he is so
se with verse,
e lesson that
point. Cer-
s the extreme
he directions
vere ordered
" were com-
e four were
s to have a.
l with em-
n them as
y in one or
given, a
ement o
e rarity o
om men
lience
the wi
vest n

1.

v

be ... de ...es, to came, cry— enough by the be put to proclama- nd so put a der of this since it goes The passage responds exactly from ver. 19—34 hat consisting of

vers. 35, 36, with ch. xxvi. 33, 34; and the two concluding vers. with ch. xxvi. 36, 37. Under these circumstances a few mistranslations will alone be noticed.

Ver. 22.—Two tenons, equally distant one from another. Rather, as in ch. xxvi. 17, "two tenons, set in order one against another."

Ver. 27.—For the sides of the tabernacle westward. Literally correct; but it would be more intelligible to render "for the side," or "for the back."

Ver. 32.—For the sides westward. The same alteration should be made.

Ver. 33.—He made the middle bar to shoot through the boards. Rather, as in ch. xxvi. 28, "to reach from end to end of the boards."

Ver. 37.—For the tabernacle door. Rather, as in ch. xxvi. 36, "for the door of the tent." Their chapiters and their fillets. Rather "their capitals and their rods." These had not been previously mentioned.

HOMILETICS.

...abundant giving.—Too much is far better than too little. Let a ... in hand, and it is impossible to anticipate the exact quantity of the ...ill require, or the exact cost of work and material together. Care ... taken to have a margin beyond the supposed necessity. Unless this

... IS APT TO BE SCAMPED AND STINTED TOWARDS THE CLOSE. Fear ... lest the material or the money should not hold out; and economies are ...h detract from the beauty, the finish, the perfection of the construction. ...worse) desirable, even necessary, adjuncts are omitted, given up as im-...nder the circumstances.

...WORK MAY ACTUALLY HAVE TO BE LEFT UNFINISHED. All calculations of ...ncertain. Prices rise while a work is in progress; material purchased, or ..., turns out to be defective, and has to be replaced by something better. ...s occur. The actual cost of a work almost always exceeds the estimate—some-...reatly exceeds it. How often do we hear of there being a debt upon a building! ...ould occur far less frequently, if gifts and offerings kept flowing in until the ...ity entrusted with the work cried "Stop."

...perabundant giving shows a truly liberal spirit in those who give. It is not a ...common thing. Cases are rare of its needing to be "restrained." The example of ...Israelites should stir Christians to emulate them. While these poor wanderers ...he desert were so generous, how is it that we are, for the most part, so niggardly? ...Superabundant giving is a trial to those who receive the gifts. How easy to appro-...riate what is not required to our own advantage! Moses withstood this temptation. Bezaleel and Aholiab withstood it. It may be doubted whether all Christians have always done so. The gifts that flowed in at the shrine of Becket, at the exhibition of the holy coat of Treves, at the altar of St. Januarius, were intended as offerings for the service of the sanctuary. Were they always used for sacred purposes? Was there not often a superfluity, which men converted to their own benefit? There have certainly been those in modern times who have enriched themselves out of moneys subscribed for charitable purposes, as the records of our assize courts sufficiently show.

Vers. 8—38.—Exactitude in obedience. Kalisch observes on this passage, that, "though even literal repetitions of the same occurrence, or the same command, are not unusual in the Biblical style, yet the lengthened and accurate reiteration" which here occurs, is unusual and must have some special meaning. He himself considers that he

has sufficiently accounted for it as intended to draw attention to the
tabernacle in the Mosaic system, and the significance, and especiall
character of the descriptions ('Commentary on Exodus,' pp. 449, 450)
that there must have been some further reason for the phenomen
inclined to find it in the importance of the example which Moses here
in obedience. If any one might ever be supposed entitled to depart
letter of observance, where the commands of God are concerned, it woul
as Moses, who had conversed as friend to friend with God, and had been t
to a conference of forty days' duration. But Moses does not seem to f
privileged. The exact correspondency of paragraph with paragraph, ve
clause with clause, word with word, seems intended to teach and enforce t
what God commands is to be observed to the letter, down to its minutes
tainly, what these five concluding chapters of Exodus especially set forth,
exactitude which Moses and those under him showed in carrying out all
that God had given with regard to the tabernacle. If "fifty taches"
(ch. xxvi. 6), "fifty taches" were made (ch. xxxvi. 13); if "five pillars
manded here (ch. xxvi. 37), and "four pillars" there (*ib.* 32), the five and t
constructed and set up accordingly (ch. xxxvi. 36, 38); if this curtain wa
pattern woven into it (ch. xxvi. 31), and that curtain was to be adorne
broidery (*ib.* 36), the embroiderer's and the weaver's art were employed upo
ordered (*ib.* xxxvi. 35, 37). Nothing commanded was ever neglected; onl
two cases (notably in verse 38) small additions were made, if not to the orders
any rate to the orders recorded. Generally, however, there was an entire effa
self, a complete restraint of private fancy and private preference. Note—1. Th
exact obedience; 2. The difficulty of it; 3. The scant praise which it obtains fr
4. The certainty that it is approved in God's sight. Examples—1. The obe
Moses as here set out; 2. The perfect obedience of Christ. "My meat is to do
of him that sent me" (John iv. 34). "I have finished the work which thou ga
to do" (*ib.* xvii. 4).

Vers. 8—37.—On Tabernacle symbolism see the Homiletics on ch. xxvi. 1—

HOMILIES BY VARIOUS AUTHORS.

Ver. 8; ch. xxxix. 43.—*The Tabernacle made.* These chapters recount ho
tabernacle, etc., was actually made. On the several sections, see the Homiletics
Homilies on chs. xxvi.—xxviii. We have in them—

I. WORK DONE. The point to be observed here is that everything was done
cisely according to the Divine directions. The makers turned not aside, either to
right hand or to the left, from what had been commanded them. They attempted
alteration on the plans. They did not try improvements; they added no orname
This was their wisdom, and secured for their work the Divine approval. Work
Christ should be done in the same way. We cannot improve upon his Gospel. We
not entitled to add to, or take from, his commands.

II. WORK INSPECTED (ch. xxxix. 33—43). When the work was finished the make
brought it to Moses, who looked upon it and pronounced that all had been done accord
ing "as the Lord had commanded" (ver. 43). The day of inspection will come for ou
work also (1 Cor. iii. 14, 15). Happy for us if the same verdict can be passe
upon it!

III. WORK BLESSED. "And Moses blessed them" (ver. 43). "If any man's work
abide which he has built thereupon, he shall receive a reward" (1 Cor. iii. 14).—J. O.

Vers. 8—38.—*Jehovah's dwelling-place.* See homily on chap. xxvi.—J. O.

Vers. 1—38.—*The work fails not either for gifts or skill.*

I. MOSES GOES FORWARD IN FAITH. 1. He makes an immediate beginning. He
might have doubted the people's liberality (so much was required) or the workmen's
ability, and have waited; but it was enough that God had commanded the work. If
Christ has commanded us to rear up a tabernacle for God in every land nothing should
stay us. He will give offerings and men. 2. He followed the Lord's guiding. He

called the men whom he had named and prepared. There must be obedience as well as faith, not calling those we would choose, but hailing gladly, and honouring, the men whom God has prepared. 2. The materials are committed to them. If we are to be built into God's temple we must obey them who have the rule over us.

II. THE PEOPLE HAVE TO BE RESTRAINED FROM GIVING. 1. The glory of a liberal spirit. There was no need of a second appeal. Though they knew that much had been contributed they still gave. 2. It consecrated the work. (1) It was a joy for the work-men to labour amid that generous liberality. (2) It was a joy to Israel and their children to remember the story of the tabernacle. To labourers in the Lord's vineyard it is a mighty consecration when hearts are yielded on every side and more is thrust upon them than they can well use for the Master ; and the remembrance of such times is power and refreshing in after days.

III. THE WORK PROCEEDS; THE SKILL AND LABOUR FAILED NOT. First the frame-work of the tabernacle is reared and the inner curtains made and placed; then the outer curtains, and lastly the boards, and bars, and veils are set up. The heart is first gained for God, then more and more of light and power is poured upon the outer life till the whole " grows unto an holy temple in the Lord."—U.

EXPOSITION.

CHAPTER XXXVII.

Vers. 1—29.—THE FURTHER PROGRESS OF THE WORK—THE CONSTRUCTION OF THE FUR-NITURE FOR THE HOLY OF HOLIES (vers. 1, 9)—AND FOR THE HOLY PLACE (vers. 10—28)—THE MAKING OF THE HOLY OIL AND OF THE INCENSE (ver. 29). On the history of the con-struction of the tabernacle follows naturally that of the construction of its furniture. The order of dignity is followed, as in ch. xxv., and the furniture of the holy of holies taken first. Vers. 1—9 correspond to vers. 10—20 of ch. xxv.; vers. 10—16 to vers. 23—29 ; vers. 17—24 to vers. 31—39 of the same; and vers. 25—28 to vers. 1—5 of ch. xxx. Ver. 29 is an abbreviation of ch. xxx. 23—25, and 34, 35.

Ver. 1.—**Bezaleel made the ark.** The particular maker of the various parts and con-tents of the tabernacle is not elsewhere pointed out. Thus this mention of Bezaleel is em-phatic, and seems intended to mark the em-ployment of the highest artistic skill on that which was the most precious of all objects connected with the new construction.

Ver. 7.—**Beaten out of one piece.** Rather, " of beaten work," as the same word is trans-lated in the corresponding passage, ch. xxv. 18.

Ver. 23.—**His snuffers.** Or, "tongs," as in ch. xxv. 38.

Ver. 25.—**The incense altar** here occurs in its right place, among the furniture of the outer chamber of the tabernacle—not, as in ch. xxx. 1—6, out of place.

Ver. 29.—**The holy anointing oil.** For the composition of the oil, see ch. xxx. 23—25 ; for the uses whereto it was to be applied, ib. 26—30. **The pure incense of sweet spices.** The composition of the incense is given in ch. xxx. 34, 35. It is there said to have been " a confection after the art of the apothecary—tempered together, pure and holy." The com-bination of artistic power with practical knowledge in Bezaleel and Aholiab calls to mind cinque-cento Italy, and the wonderful grasp of art and science possessed by Michael Angelo and Benvenuto Cellini

HOMILETICS.

Ver. 1. _Art's highest efforts should be concentrated on what is most essential to the work in hand._ " Bezaleel made the ark." Bezaleel, " filled with the spirit of God, in wisdom, in understanding, and in knowledge, and in all manner of workmanship " (ch. xxxv. 31), while he entrusted most of the rest of the work to others, reserved to himself the construction of the ark, with the cherubim and mercy seat. The ark was clearly the central object of the newly devised structure, that towards which the eyes of all would be directed, on which the thoughts of all would rest, which, itself unseen, dominated the entire edifice and formed its material basis and _raison d'être_. Shrined in the holy of holies, shrouded from sight by the veil, never seen but by the high-priest once a-year, yet known to occupy the innermost _penetrale_ of the sanctuary, and to lie there in the light of the Divine presence constantly, it challenged the attention of all, and occupied a unique position among the sacred objects which the sanctuary was to contain.

Bezaleel, the master-artist, felt that there was a call on him to construct it. What wealth of loving work he lavished on the construction, with what rich and delicate tracery of fanciful ornament he adorned it, no one can say. The ark never returned from Babylon; and the master-work of the master-artist of these times has been lost to humanity. But his choice asserted some important principles, and deserves imitation through all ages. It pointed out—

I. THAT THE LAW OF ORNAMENT IS NOT ONE OF GENERAL UNIFORM ELABORATION UP TO A CERTAIN HEIGHT, BUT ONE OF SPECIAL CONCENTRATION UPON A POINT OR POINTS. Compare Magdalen Tower with the Houses of Parliament, the western front of the Parthenon with the ordinary porch of a church of the Jesuits, the façade of St. Zeno at Verona with even the front of St. Mark's at Venice, and it will at once be seen how superior is ornament concentrated to ornament dispersed, elaboration of certain parts, set off by the comparative plainness of others, to diffusion generally of equal elaboration everywhere. A sense of heaviness, of over-loading, of weariness, is produced by the one plan, a feeling of unmixed pleasure by the other.

II. THAT THE CONCENTRATION SHOULD BE ON SUCH PARTS OF THE WORK AS ARE MOST ESSENTIAL TO IT. If a *campanile* or bell-tower be the work in hand, the concentration should be towards the chamber in which the bells are hung, as in the great *campanile* of St. Mark's, Venice. If a college, towards the parts common to all, the chapel, hall, library; if a sepulchral monument, towards the tomb; if a palace, towards the state-rooms; and the like. Here, in this case of the tabernacle, the concentration was towards the holy of holies. Most properly. And on the ark: since, of the holy of holies, the ark was the glory.

In Christian churches, according as preaching, or the administration of the sacraments, or the elevation of the thoughts to heaven, are regarded as the main object of sacred buildings, the concentration of artistic effort will naturally be towards the pulpit, or towards font and altar, or towards the roof. Examples of the first are common in Germany and Switzerland, of the second in Roman Catholic churches generally, of the third in English churches of the Tudor period, *e.g.* Henry the Seventh's Chapel in Westminster Abbey, and the like.

For further Homiletics, see those on chs. xxv. and xxx.

HOMILIES BY VARIOUS AUTHORS.

Vers. 1—28—*The furnishing of the tabernacle.* I. ALL WAS ACCOMPLISHED AS GOD HAD COMMANDED. 1. Successfully. It might have been feared that though the tabernacle was erected there would be some failure in this more delicate and ornate work; but all is perfectly executed even to the smallest details. In the work of him whom God has called by name there will be no failure. His work will be presented faultless, and every word which God has spoken will be fulfilled. 2. Faithfully: as they failed in nothing, so they added nothing. In God's work there must be no alloy of human devices. In worship, ordinances, life, our sole guide must be God's commandment.

II. THE CONTENTS OF THE TABERNACLE: THE FOURFOLD ADORNMENT OF THE BELIEVER'S LIFE. 1. The ark, the meeting-place of righteousness and peace. The heart in which God's law is set, on which the atonement rests, and which is bathed in the glory of the Divine love. There is, in a word, *living faith.* 2. The table of shew-bread: a yielded life, the sacrifice presented before God of body, soul, and spirit. 3. The candlestick: "ye are the light of the world." (1) There is life, which in the measure it exists is, like Christ's, the light of men. It shows the reality and power of God's grace. (2) There is labour in word and doctrine. God's mind and will are understood. 4. The incense altar, the uplifting of holy desire and intercession for all men. Are these things found in us? They may be. It is the work to which Christ has been called, and he is waiting to accomplish it in us.—U.

Vers. 1—25.—*The ark, the table, and the candlestick.* See Homily on ch. xxv. 10—40.—J. O.

Vers. 25—29.—*The altar of incense.* See Homily on ch. xxx. 1—11; 34—38.—J. O.

EXPOSITION.

CHAPTER XXXVIII.

Vers. 1—8.—THE FURTHER PROGRESS OF THE WORK—THE CONSTRUCTION OF THE FURNITURE FOR THE COURT.—Vers. 9—20.—AND OF THE COURT ITSELF. On the completion of the tabernacle, Bezaleel and his assistants turned their attention to the court and its furniture; and constructed, first, the altar of burnt offering (vers. 1—7); secondly, the bronze laver (ver. 8); and thirdly, the hangings, pillars, connecting-rods, hooks and pins for the circuit of the court (vers. 9—20). Vers. 1—7 correspond to vers. 1—8 of ch. xxvii.; ver. 8 corresponds to ver. 18 of ch. xxx.; and vers. 9—20 correspond to vers. 9—19 of ch. xxvii.

Ver. 3.—**The pots.** This translation is better than that of ch. xxvii. 3, which is "pans." Buckets or scuttles to convey the ashes from the altar to the ash-heap (Lev. i. 16) are intended.

Ver. 8.—**Of the looking-glasses of the women.** This interesting fact has not been previously mentioned. Bronze plates, circular or oval, admitting of a high polish, were used by the Egyptian women as mirrors from a very early date, and may be seen in the Egyptian collection of the British Museum. They have handles like those of our fire-screens, generally also of bronze. It was natural that the Hebrew women should possess similar articles, and should have taken care to bring them with them out of Egypt. The avulsion of them for a sacred purpose is rather to be ascribed to their own self-denying piety than to any command issued by Moses (Spencer). **Which assembled.** Literally, "who came by troops." Women assembled themselves by troops at the entrance of the "tent of meeting" set up by Moses (ch. xxxiii. 7), as at a later date we find Hannah (1 Sam. i. 9—12) and other women who were less worthy (*ib.* ii. 22) doing. The women who showed this zeal were those that made the sacrifice of their mirrors for God's service. There is no reason to suppose (with Hengstenberg and others) that they constituted a regular "order."

Ver. 10.—**Their fillets.** Rather, "their *connecting-rods,*" as in ch. xxvii. 10.

Ver. 17.—**The overlaying of their chapiters of silver.** This is additional to what is recorded in ch. xxvii., and is parallel to what we find related of the tabernacle pillars in ch. xxxvi. 38. **Filleted with silver.** Rather, "connected with silver rods." Compare ch. xxvii. 17.

Ver. 18.—**The height in the breadth was five cubits.** The height of the hangings all round the court was required to be five cubits, or seven and a-half feet (ch. xxvii. 18). It appears by the expression here used—" in the breadth "—that the material was woven of exactly this width.

Ver. 19.—**Their chapiters.** This again is additional to the directions given. Compare the comment on ver. 17.

HOMILETICS.

Ver. 8.—*The triumph of female piety over female vanity.* Hebrew women were, it must be presumed, much like other women in their natural dispositions, and therefore not without their share of personal vanity. The fact, that in all the haste of their sudden departure from Egypt they had not omitted to carry with them their metal mirrors, is indicative of this. The mirror was the most valued of toilet articles, and the most indispensable for effecting that end, at which almost all women aim—the making the best of those advantages of personal appearance which nature has vouchsafed to them. It is difficult to imagine any material sacrifice to which a woman would not more readily have consented than the loss of her mirror. Yet we know that the sacrifice was made by large numbers; for the laver was a vessel of considerable size. Let us consider then, 1. The motive of the act; 2. the antecedent conduct which led up to it; 3. the reward which it obtained.

I. THE MOTIVE OF THE ACT. No other motive can be conceived of than true piety. Piety loves to make offerings to God. Piety does not count the cost. Piety, the gift of grace, can triumph over nature; transform a poor vain worldling into a saint; make no sacrifice seem a hard one. It must have been piety which made these women give their mirrors, either, 1. In addition to their personal ornaments (ch. xxxv. 22), or 2. In default of them. Some after offering their ear-rings, rings, necklaces, bracelets, and the like, may have desired, from pure love of God, to give more, and casting about to consider what more they could give, may have bethought them of their mirrors. Others may have had no personal ornaments to give; and if unable to spin, may have had nothing else but their mirrors which they could contribute. In either case, piety was at the root of their giving.

II. THE ANTECEDENT CONDUCT WHICH LED UP TO IT. They who contributed their mirrors were women wont to "assemble at the door of the tabernacle of the congregation." In other words, they were such as had previously made all the use they could of their religious opportunities. We see that God does not shower down his precious gifts of grace at random—but "helps such as help themselves." He granted the priceless grace of self-denying love to those who were constant in serving him at the place where he had "set his name," and was to be found of them that sought him. Much prayer, much waiting upon God, had gone to form the character of those who now found themselves able to make a willing sacrifice of their vanity.

III. THE REWARD WHICH THEIR ACT OF SACRIFICE OBTAINED FOR THEM. It obtained for them the high reward of special mention in God's holy word—a place in his "Valhalla"—a record in his "Roll of worthies." Of the other offerings we know not, for the most part, whether they were made by men or women—much less by what class of men, or what class of women. Only here, and in ch. xxxv. 25, 26, is the sex specified, and only here the class. Let women take this to heart. Let them be ready to sacrifice to him all their adornments—"braided hair and gold and pearls, and costly array" (1 Tim. ii. 9)—let them be ready to sacrifice even, if need be, their personal charms (as many do in fever or small-pox hospitals), and they will not be forgotten by him—they will not go without a recompense. If their act be not recorded in any other book it will be written in that heavenly record, out of which all will be judged at the last day (Rev. xx. 12).

For other Homiletics on the subjects of this chapter, see those on ch. xxvii.

HOMILIES BY VARIOUS AUTHORS.

Vers. 1—21.—*The brazen altar, the laver, and the court.* See Homilies on chs. xxvii. 1—20; xxx. 17—22.—J. O.

Ver. 8.—*The mirrors of the women.* The women assembling at the door of the tabernacle (see Hengstenberg's "Egypt and the Books of Moses,"—"The Institution of Holy Women") gave up their mirrors for the making of the laver. Learn—1. Peculiar devotion to God expresses itself in acts of sacrifice (cf. Mary of Bethany, Matt. xxvi. 6—14). 2. Religion gives power to *make* sacrifices. 3. It weans the affections from the world. 4. It gives superiority to the motives of personal vanity. The mirror is peculiarly a woman's instrument of self-pleasing. It is her means of pleasing the world. 5. Religion teaches godly women to study simplicity in personal adornment (1 Pet. iii. 1—5). 6. Self-denial in outward adornment is valueless, unless "in the hidden man of the heart," there be the positive inward adornment of holiness (1 Pet. iii. 4). This was taught by the use to which Moses put the offerings—the making of the "laver." Regeneration is the true beautifier.—J. O.

Vers. 1—31.—*The Court and its lessons.* I. THE FURNISHING AND CONSTRUCTION OF THE COURT (1) The altar on which the sacrifice for Israel's sin was laid, and their own offerings accepted. Christ is the foundation and the power of all our service. (2) The laver. It was fashioned from the mirrors of the women, The adornment of the outward was exchanged for inward purity, the ornament of a meek and quiet spirit. It stood there for the daily use of God's priests. They could pass into God's presence only as their defilement had been washed away. "Without holiness no man shall see the Lord." Are we being washed ere that hour comes when we must appear before him? 2. *The construction of the court.* (1) God's grace makes a separation between the Church and the world. To break down this is to undo God's work. (2) The wall of separation was fine twined linen. It is a separation not only between faith and unbelief, but between righteousness and unrighteousness. (3) The world sees the results only, the means by which they are attained are hid from its view; but the results are a call to come and see. 3. *The order in which they were made.* The altar first, then the laver, and, last of all, the enclosing of the court. First, Christ and his sacrifice; next, the washing of regeneration by him through the Spirit; and, last of all, the gathering together of the Church. This is the Divine order. The true Church has ever this history. None have a right to be there on whom the work of altar and laver has not first been done.

II. THE MATERIAL. 1. *The record of it is kept.* There is nothing of all that is given for God's service, the history or place of which is forgotten. 2. *The use to which it is applied.* The gold is put to the highest use; the silver—the redemption money— is the foundation of the sanctuary; the brass is used for the altar, the laver, and the court. Each is put to its proper use, and a place is found for all. No gift can be brought to God which he will not employ.—U.

EXPOSITION.

Vers. 21—31.—THE SUM OF THE TABERNACLE, OR WEIGHT OF THE METALS EMPLOYED IN IT. Before dismissing the subject of the construction of the tabernacle, Moses places on record the sum of the gold, silver and bronze contributed and consumed in the work. At the same time he informs us who was the accountant by whom the sum was made up (ver. 21), and what were the portions of the work formed of each metal (vers. 24, 27, 28, 30, 31). Incidentally he mentions the number of the congregation at this period (ver. 26), and the weight of the " sockets " or " bases " (ver. 27).

Ver. 21.—**This is the sum.** Or "numbering " (as in Num. xxvi. 63). **The tabernacle of testimony.** The tabernacle, *i.e.*, of which the great glory was that it contained "the testimony " or "Two Tables." Compare ch. xxv. 16. **For the service of the Levites.** Literally "a service of the Levites by the hand of Ithamar," etc.—*i.e.* "a service which was performed by the Levites at the command of Ithamar." It is somewhat remarkable that the direction of the Levites should be assigned to Ithamar, rather than to Nadab or Abihu.

Ver. 22.—**Bezaleel made all.** The direction of the *whole* work by Bezaleel is here asserted more definitely and decidedly than elsewhere. Compare ch. xxxi. 2—6; xxxvi. 1, 2.

Ver. 23.—Aholiab's special gifts are here pointed out. He was 1. An artificer (a general term with no special application); 2. A skilled weaver; and 3. An embroiderer. Altogether, his business was with the textile fabrics—not with the wood-work or the metal-work—of the sanctuary.

Ver. 24.—**The gold.** The value of the gold has been estimated by Canon Cook at £175,075 13s. 0d. of our money; by Thenius at 877,300 Prussian thalers, or about £131,595. It was certainly under £200,000. De Wette and others have argued that the possession of so large a sum in gold at this time by the Hebrew nation is inconceivable. But most critics are of a different opinion. Gold was very abundant in Egypt at the period, being imported from Ethiopia, a rich gold-producing country (Herod. iii. 23; Diod. Sic. iii. 11), as well as taken in tribute from the nations of Asia. The wealth of Rhampsinitus (Rameses III.), a little later than the exodus, was enormous (Herod. ii. 121; Rawlinson, *History of Egypt*, vol. ii. pp. 368, 378). According to the preceding narrative (ch. xii. 35, 36) much of the wealth of Egypt had, at the moment of their quitting the country, passed from the Egyptians to the Hebrews. If they numbered two millions of souls, their gold ornaments are likely to have been worth very much more than £200,000 of our money. On **the shekel of the sanctuary,** see the comment upon ch. xxx. 13.

Ver. 25.—**The silver.** The silver seems to have amounted to about four times the weight of the gold; but the value of it was very much less, not exceeding £40,000 of our money (Cook). It may seem surprising that this should have been so; but there are grounds for believing that both in Africa and in Asia gold was more plentiful than silver in the early ages. And it is certainly much more suitable for ornaments. **Of them that were numbered.** See above, ch. xxx. 12—16. The silver for the sanctuary was collected by a compulsory tax, of the nature of a church-rate. This produced the amount here given, No estimate is made of the weight of the silver freewill offerings (ch. xxxv. 24), nor is any account given of their application. It has been suggested that they were returned to the donors as superfluous, which is certainly possible,

Ver. 26.—**A bekah for every man.** Literally, " for every *head.*" **From twenty years old and upward.** Compare Num. i. 3, 22, etc. **Six hundred thousand,** etc. It is remarkable that this number agrees *exactly* with the sum total of the numbering in Num. ii. 32, which took place about six months later, and was exclusive of 22,000 Levites. Perhaps the number was lost in this place, and restored from **Num.**

ii. 32, without its being recollected that the Levites were not included in that reckoning.

Ver. 27.—**The sockets of the sanctuary and of the veil.** See above, ch. xxxvi. 24, 26, 30, and 36. The numbers given are 40, 40, 16, and 4, making exactly the hundred.

Ver. 28.—**Hooks for the pillars.** See above, vers. 10, 12, 17, and 19. **Chapiters.** See ver. 19. **Filleted them.** Rather, "connected them with rods "

Ver. 29.—**The brass of the offering**—*i e*, the bronze which had been brought by the people in answer to the invitation of Moses (ch. xxxv. 24).

Vers. 30, 31.—**The sockets.** See ch. xxxvi. 38. **The brazen altar and the brazen grate.** See vers. 1 and 4. **The vessels.** See ver. 3. **The sockets of the court.** See above, vers. 11, 14, 15, 17, and 19. **The pins of the tabernacle and of the court.** See above, ver. 20.

HOMILETICS.

Vers. 24—31.—*Great wealth worthily employed.* I. THE AMOUNT EXPENDED BY THE ISRAELITES WAS GREAT ABSOLUTELY. Although the materials contributed for the construction of the tabernacle are quite within the estimate which would reasonably be formed of the wealth of the Israelites from the general tenor of the narrative, yet they certainly reach altogether to such an amount of value as would constitute a very serious call on the resources of such a people. The worth of the metals alone was not far short of a quarter of a million of our money. (Gold, £175,000; silver, £40,000; bronze (say) £15,000—total, £230,000.) The precious stones, the spices, the wood-work, the raw material for the cloths, the dyed rams' skins and seals' skins, have to be added, and would raise the sum total to at least £250,000. This was contributed by a population of about two millions; which may be regarded as equivalent to 10*s.* a family, or half-a-crown a head. Now the entire taxation for imperial purposes of each British subject is about £2 a head, of which the amount paid in direct taxation is not more than 5*s.* a head. So that the Israelite of the 13th or 14th century, B.C., paid at one time for church purposes of his own free will, half as much as the British subject of the present day pays directly for State purposes in the whole course of the year. Thus *the amount was great absolutely*, and showed a noble spirit in those who contributed.

II. THE AMOUNT EXPENDED WAS ALSO GREAT RELATIVELY TO THE PURPOSE OF THE EXPENDITURE. What was required was a structure sixty feet long by thirty, with a skirting for a court or precinct 150 feet long by seventy-five. The main structure, or tabernacle, would be about the size of a small college chapel. The precinct would be smaller than most churchyards. Yet upon these two objects, without making any estimate for labour, a quarter of a million of money was spent. On the first blush, one asks, how was it possible for so enormous an outlay to be made? The answer is, by the lavish use of the precious metals, especially gold. That the structure might be rich, splendid, magnificent, gold and silver were lavished upon it, both externally and internally—scarcely any wood was seen—nothing caught the eye but costly fabrics of rich colour, and masses of silver or gold. A warm, harmonious, rich result was no doubt produced ; and nomadic Israel, unable to compete with the settled nations in the size and grandeur of its "holy place," erected for itself a sanctuary, which in its own way was unequalled and unique.

III. THE OBJECT OF THE EXPENDITURE WAS A WORTHY ONE. If a people have temples at all, men will always judge their religious views, more or less, by them. If Israel was to have a place of worship—and it may be doubted whether any race of men will ever be able to do without one—it would certainly be subjected to rough criticism and comparison. The Egyptian temples were magnificent—of vast size, of the most solid construction, of handsome material, elaborately painted and adorned ; they delighted those who worshipped in them, and challenged the admiration of extraneous beholders. Israel, in the desert, could not possibly vie with these. But it might construct a work perfect in its kind, of a different class, which would compensate for smallness of size by richness of material and artistic elaboration. It could show in this way its sense that men should give to God of their best. It could secure an extraordinary degree of beauty, finish, and elegance. The nations among which the tabernacle passed—even those who heard an account of it—must have been impressed with the feeling that here was a people which thoroughly believed in its God ; which thought nothing too good for him ; which was ready for his sake to submit to much self-sacrifice. And the people itself must also have been impressed by its own work. No such apostasy as the worship of the calf ever took place after the tabernacle had been constructed. It was no longer faith, but sight, which told them, that " God was in the midst of them." The sense of this begat a courage and a confidence, which supported the nation under many trials, and many temptations. They had never to regret the outlay which they had made upon their " tent-temple."

Application.—There has been much church-building in modern times, but in no instance such a lavish outlay as that here held up to our imitation. Germany, indeed, has completed the Dom of Cologne; but not much of the money was subscribed; for the most part, it came out of the general taxation of the country. Glasgow, Edinburgh, Calcutta, have raised cathedrals; but the cost has not been very considerable. The spirit of munificence has been shown rather by individuals than by any nation; and, in England at any rate, the nineteenth century will not, it is to be feared, be signalised among others by the completion of any really first-rate ecclesiastical edifice. New dioceses are formed; but new cathedrals, worthy of taking rank with the masterpieces of former times, do not arise. The prevailing practice is to convert a parish church into a cathedral. May it not be hoped that ere long some new diocese, where wealth abounds, will devote to its cathedral some such amount as the Israelites in the desert contributed towards their tabernacle, and raise an edifice which will prove to the world that Post-Reformation England does not yield to the England of the Middle Ages in the virtue of Christian munificence ?

HOMILIES BY VARIOUS AUTHORS.

Vers. 21—31.—*The enumeration of the metals used.* This served a useful purpose— 1. As an account rendered to the people of what had been done with their gifts. 2. As gratifying a very laudable wish of the contributors to know how much the sum-total of their contributions amounted to. 3. As giving a just idea of the splendour and costliness of the building. 4. As a testimony to the liberality, willingness, and unstinting self-sacrifice of all classes in the congregation. 5. As specially indicating the destination of the atonement-money—the making of the " sockets" on which the tabernacle was reared (ver. 27). 6. As a lesson of exactitude in church finance. A church is not at liberty to deal in a slovenly manner with its receipts and disbursements. Careful accounts should be kept and published. This (1) Gives confidence in the management; (2) is an encouragement to giving; (3) prevents charges of maladministration; (4) is a prevention against waste.—J. O.

EXPOSITION.

CHAPTER XXXIX.

Vers. 1—31.—THE FURTHER PROGRESS OF THE WORK — THE MAKING OF THE PRIESTS' DRESSES. Vers. 32—43.—THE GENERAL AP-PROVAL OF THE WORK BY MOSES. The entire work for the structure of the tabernacle being completed, it only remained for Bezaleel and Aholiab to take in hand the priestly vestments, which had been prescribed with the greatest elaboration in ch. xxviii. 4—40. The present chapter is mainly occupied in relating how the vestments were made, and follows, very nearly, the order of the directions. Vers. 1—7 correspond to vers. 5—14 of ch. xxviii.; vers. 8—21 to vers. 15—38; vers. 22—26 to vers. 31—34; vers. 27—29 to vers. 39, 40;

and vers. 30, 31 to vers. 36, 37. The re-mainder of the chapter (vers. 32—43) contains a recapitulation of the work done, and a statement that it was all submitted to Moses and approved by him.

Ver. 1.—**Of the blue, and purple, and scar-let**—*i.e.*, of the blue, purple, and scarlet *thread* which had been spun by the women, and brought to Moses. See ch. xxxv. 25. The omission of " fine linen " seems to be accidental. **Cloths of service.** See the com-ment on ch. xxxi. 10.

Ver. 3.—**They did beat the gold into thin plates and cut it into wires.** This mode of producing gold thread is remarkable, and had not been previously mentioned.

Ver. 9.—**For a memorial.** Compare ch. xxviii. 12.

Vers. 10—13.—On the probable stones in-

tended, see the comment upon ch. xxviii.
17—20.

Ver. 16.—**Two ouches of gold.** Compare
ch. xxviii. 13 and 25.

Ver. 24.—**And twined linen.** Rather
"twined," *i.e.*, twisted together. There was
no direction to use "fine twined linen" in
making the pomegranates. See ch. xxviii. 33.

Ver. 27.—**Coats of fine linen of woven
work for Aaron and for his sons.** Compare
ch. xxvii. 29 and 30.

Ver. 28.—**A mitre . . . and goodly bonnets.** The "mitre" for Aaron (ch. xxviii.
37—39), the "goodly bonnets," or rather
"caps" for his sons (*ib.* 40). The linen
breeches, or "drawers," were for both (*ib.*
42, 43).

Ver. 29.—**A girdle of fine twined linen,**
etc. In the directions of ch. xxviii. 39, this
is called simply, "A girdle of needlework."

Vers. 30, 31.—**The plate of the holy crown.**
See ch. xxix. 6, and compare ch. xxviii. 36.

To fasten it on high. This was not mentioned in the directions, which only ordered
that it should be placed in front (ch. xxviii.
37).

Vers. 32—43.—Everything was brought to
Moses for his approval—not perhaps all things
at once, but each as it was finished—and was
judged by him "according to the pattern
which he had seen upon the mount"
(ch. xxv. 40; xxvi. 30, etc.). The order
observed in the enumeration is nearly, but
not quite, the order in which it has been
stated that the various things were made.
We must suppose that if Moses disapproved
of anything, it was rejected; but no disapproval is mentioned. **Moses did look upon
all the work, and behold, they had done it
as the Lord commanded.** Accordingly Moses
concluded all by "blessing" them; thereby
signifying, not his own approval only, but
the Divine approval, of their diligence and
obedience.

HOMILETICS.

Ver. 43.—*A blessing upon obedience.* It is not every kind of obedience that brings
down a blessing upon it. To deserve the Divine approval, and obtain the Divine
benediction, obedience must be, as was that here recorded—

I. EXACT. "According to all that the Lord commanded, so the children of Israel
made the work" (ver. 42). "As the Lord had commanded, even so had they done
it" (ver. 43).

II. PROMPT. The work could not have commenced before the sixth or the seventh
month, since Sinai was not reached till the third month (ch. xix. 1), and Moses
passed in conference with God nearly three months. Yet the whole was finished before
the year was out (see ch. xl. 1). Thus it appears that six months sufficed for the
completion of everything.

III. INTELLIGENT. There was little misunderstanding—few, if any, mistakes. All
comprehended the orders given to them, and each carried out his assigned portion. Unless this had been the case very generally, it is impossible that all would have been
ready by the end of the year. The rapid completion of the work proves the intelligence
of the workmen. Note what is said of their being "wise-hearted" (ch. xxxvi. 1, 2, 8).
Men, for the most part, think to obtain the supreme blessing of eternal life, though
their obedience has been 1. Partial and inexact; 2. tardy; 3. marred by misapprehension
of the commands given them. They do not seem to imagine that there will be any real
inspection of their work, such as that which is here ascribed to Moses. "Moses did look
upon *all* the work" (ver. 43). Yet surely at the last day, man's work will be tested in
some real, searching way. Whatever may be meant by the expression—"The fire shall
try every man's work" (1 Cor. iii. 13), at any rate, *some* trial there will be. Faithful
service to Christ will be rewarded by a blessing exceeding all that we can ask or think;
but there will be minute inquiry, whether the service has been indeed faithful.

For further Homiletics on the subjects of this chapter, see those upon ch. xxviii.

HOMILIES BY VARIOUS AUTHORS.

Vers. 1—32.—*The garments of the priests.* See Homily on ch. xxviii.—J. O.

Vers. 1—41.—*The Clothes of Service; the work perfected.* I. THE PRIESTS' GARMENTS.
1. Their splendour. They were fashioned of gold and jewels, and blue, and purple, and
scarlet. God gives glory to his servants. He makes us kings and priests unto himself.

Tho spiritual nobleness and beauty given now are but the earnest of the glory which will be hereafter. 4. Their purpose; they were clothes of service. The honour and comeliness which God bestows are for serving to him in the midst of our brethren, not to minister to our own spiritual pride and unbrotherly judgment. II. ALL THE WORK WAS DONE IN STRICT OBEDIENCE TO THE LORD'S COMMANDMENT. "As the Lord commanded Moses" (5, 7, 21, 26, 29, 31). "The children of Israel did according to all that the Lord commanded Moses, so did they" (32). "And Moses did look upon all the work; and behold, they had done it as the Lord had commanded, even so had they done it" (43). 1. There was no deficiency: no part of the work was slighted. We may not abate anything of all the Lord has commanded. The ordinances must be observed as they have been delivered to us. The cross which Jesus has called us to take up in his service must not be laid aside. 2. There was no excess. No room was given for the exercise of fancy, or taste, or judgment, as to what might better impress, or improve, the vulgar. There was only one solicitude—to do what the Lord had commanded. He alone is master here. We are merely servants. The things which God had not commanded were as carefully kept out of the worship as the things he had commanded were kept in it. 3. "And Moses blessed them." Serving God thus, the blessing of a greater than Moses will rest upon us. And there awaits us in the eternal light the "Well done! good and faithful servant!"—U.

Vers. 42, 43.—*The commanded work completed and commended.* I. THERE IS A PROFESSED COMPLETION. We know not exactly how long this work took to do. That it could not be done in a few days or even a few weeks is plain; but it is equally plain that however long the time was, the work was done with steadiness and devotion. There is no mention of any hitch or unseemly dispute; all seems to have gone on with holy industry and patience to the end. Looking, then, on this work, for which a special endowment of the Spirit's help was given, and *which was completed*, we are bound also to feel that the work for which God in Christ has given his Spirit to his Church in these latter days will also be accomplished. Hindered and fragmentary is the appearance that it now presents; but it is going on. The wonderful manifestations of Pentecost are the pledge of a work that some day will have *finis* written upon it. Amid all the uncertainties of prophecy; amid all the hapless guesses with respect to the time of events, one thing is clear, that the prophecies point to a consummation. There is a συντέλεια to the work of the Church even as to this typical work of Bezaleel and Aholiab. II. THERE IS A RIGOROUS INSPECTION. Many human observers, we may be sure, had also inspected the work of Bezaleel and Aholiab; some to praise, some also to carp. But it is not those whom men commend who are really praiseworthy, nor those whom men censure who are censurable. Moses looks, and ever as he looks there is the remembrance of his solemn sojourn in the mount. He has in his instructed mind the standard of success and excellence. Let us also, as being invited to become temples of the living God—temple and sacrifice comprised in the varied faculties of one living organism—consider the rigorous demand which is made on us. These sacred articles, fashioned from perishable materials, and by human hands, were yet such that they could be stamped with Divine approval; and thus they are meant to direct us, that we may fashion all our life, in affections, in aims, and in service, according to the pattern given in the mount—that mount in Galilee, where Jesus talked with all who were willing to admit his authority. III. THERE IS A HEARTY COMMENDATION. "Moses blessed them." There had been so much disobedience and pursuit of selfish aims before, that when an obedience comes like the one mentioned here, it is important to note the way in which God smiles upon it. For the blessing of Moses is as the smile of God. God is as quick to show approval of all compliance with his wishes as he is to frown upon all disregard of them; only, as men will have it, there is more occasion for the frowning than for the favour. This commendation is more fully expressed in ch. xl. 34, where the wrapping of the tabernacle with the glory-cloud signifies that what God did through Moses in the well-understood formula of blessing, he could also do himself by his own miraculous manifestations. The successful work here and the immediate recognition of it serve to show, in a more condemnatory aspect, the subsequent transgression of the people. In the making of the tabernacle-furniture, they had recognised the claims of God, and God had recognized their ability to meet his claims. He knew that they could not yet be obedient in all things; he only asked that they should be obedient as far as they were able to be obedient. They had shown their ability once; and it was their great blame that they did not show it again and again.—Y.

EXPOSITION.

CHAPTER XL.

Vers. 1—33.—THE COMMAND TO SET UP THE TABERNACLE, AND ITS PERFORMANCE. All was now ready. Bezaleel and Aholiab had completed their task. The work for the tabernacle had been given in, and had been approved Moses did not however at once set it up. He waited for a command from God. After a short interval, the command came. He was ordered to select the first day of the ensuing year—the first day of the first year of freedom—for the operation. Directions were given him, which fixed the order in which the various parts were to be set up, and assigned to the various articles of furniture their proper places (vers. 1—8). When he had arranged the whole as directed, he was to anoint the various parts (vers. 9—11). He was then to wash and dress Aaron, and his sons; to invest them with their robes of office (vers. 12—14), and to anoint them to be priests (ver. 15). The orders given were executed, except (as it would seem) those concerning the investiture of the priests and the anointing, which were deferred. (See Lev. viii. 6—30.) In one day the sanctuary was completely set up (vers. 18—33).

Vers. 1—8.—*The directions to set up the tabernacle.*

Ver. 2.—**On the first day of the first month.** The first of Abib, or Nisan, the "New Year's Day" of Israel, coinciding nearly with the opening of the vernal equinox, a very suitable day for the inauguration of a place of worship. **The tabernacle** was to be set up first of all; then the **tent** was to be placed over it. See vers. 18, 19.

Ver. 3.—The first thing to be placed within the tabernacle was **the ark of the testimony**, as containing the foundation of the covenant between God and Israel, and being the special token of God's presence with his people. See the comment on ch. xxv. 10. The "two tables" were placed within the ark before it was brought into the tabernacle (vers. 20, 21). **Cover the ark with the veil**—*i.e.,* "hang up the veil in front of the ark, so as to cover or conceal it."

Ver. 4.—**Thou shalt bring in the table**—*i.e.,* "the table of shew-bread" (ch. xxv. 23—30; xxxvii. 10—16). **And set in order the things,** etc. It has been observed with reason that the directions of Lev. xxiv. 5—7 must have been already given, though not recorded till so much later. Bread and frankincense were to be "set in order" on the table in a particular way. **The candlestick.** The seven-branched candelabrum (ch. xxv. 31—39; ch. xxxvii. 17—24). **And thou shalt light the lamps.** The lamps would have to be lighted on the first day *at even* (ch. xxvii. 21; xxx. 8).

Ver. 5.—**The altar of gold.** See ch. xxx. 1—10; ch. xxxvii. 25—28. **Before the ark of the testimony**—*i.e.,* "before the veil, opposite the ark of the testimony," not within the veil. See the comment on ch. xxx. 6. **The hanging of the door**—*i.e.,* "the curtain which closed the front or eastern end of the tabernacle." (See ch. xxvi. 36; ch. xxxvi. 37.)

Ver. 6.—**The altar of burnt-offering.** See ch. xxvii. 1—8; ch. xxxviii. 1—7. **Before the door of the tabernacle.** In the court, directly in front of the entrance, but not close to it, since the place of the laver was between the entrance and the altar. See the next verse.

Ver. 7.—**The laver.** See ch. xxx. 18; ch. xxxviii. 8. **Put water therein.** The water was required:—1. For the ablution of the priests (ch. xxx. 19—21; xl. 12, 31; Lev. viii. 6), and 2. For washing the victims (Lev. viii. 21).

Ver. 8.—**The court.** See ch. xxvii. 9—18; ch. xxxviii. 9—20. **The hanging at the court gate**—*i.e.,* the curtain at the entrance of the court (ch. xxvii. 16; ch. xxxviii. 18).

Vers. 9—16.—*The directions to anoint, etc.*

Vers. 9—16.—It does not appear that these directions were carried out at this time. Probably, there would not have been time to go through all the ceremonies enjoined (ch. xxix. 1—34) on the same day with the erection of the sanctuary. They were consequently deferred, either till the next day, or possibly to a later date. (See Lev. viii.) The anointing of the tabernacle is recorded in ver. 10; of the vessels in ver. 11; of the altar and laver in the same. The washing of Aaron and his sons in ver. 6; their investiture in vers. 7—9; the anointing of Aaron in ver. 12; and a further anointing of Aaron together with his sons in ver. 30.

Ver. 10.—**An altar most holy.** Not really more holy than the rest of the tabernacle and its contents, which are all pronounced "most holy" in ch. xxx. 29 ; but requiring more to have its holiness continually borne in mind, since "it was more exposed to contact with the people" than the tabernacle and its vessels (Keil).

Ver. 12.—**Unto the door of the tabernacle** —*i.e.*, to the place where the laver was situated (ver. 7).

Ver. 14.—**Coats.** Rather, "tunics." They were to be "of fine linen, woven work" (ch. xxxix. 27).

Ver. 15.—**Thou shalt anoint them as thou didst anoint their father.** The mode of anointing does not seem to have been identical in the two cases. The oil was first poured upon Aaron's head (Lev. viii. 12 ; Ps. cxxxiii. 2), and afterwards sprinkled upon him (Lev. viii. 30). It was, apparently, only sprinkled upon the priests (*ib.*). This was a lower form of anointing ; and hence the high priest was sometimes called "*the* anointed priest" (Lev. iv. 5, 16 ; vi. 22 ; xvi. 32, etc.). **Their anointing shall surely be an everlasting priesthood.** The Rabbinical commentators maintain that these words apply to the ordinary priests only, and on the strength of them establish a difference between the ordinary priests and the high priests. The latter were in every case to be anointed to their office. A single anointing sufficed for the former. It is scarcely necessary to say that there is no Scriptural ground for this distinction. The natural sense of the words is, rather, that as long as the anointing continued, the priesthood should continue.

Vers. 17—33.—*The actual setting up of the tabernacle.*

Ver. 17.—**On the first day the tabernacle was reared up.** Being constructed after the fashion of a tent, it was quite possible to rear up and also to take down, the tabernacle in less than a day.

Ver. 18.—**Fastened his sockets.** Rather, "placed its sockets." The "sockets" or "bases" appear to have been simply laid on the flat sand of the desert, not "fastened" to it in any way. They were heavy masses of metal and would remain where they were placed. **His pillars.** The pillars that supported the "veil," and also those at the east end, where the entrance was.

Ver. 19.—**He spread abroad the tent over the tabernacle.** The entire distinctness of the tent (*'ôhel*) from the tabernacle (*mishkân*) is here very strongly marked. The "tent" was the goats' hair covering, with the framework of wood that supported it. **The covering.** The outer covering of rams' skins and seals' skins. (See ch. xxvi. 14.)

Ver. 20.—**The testimony**—*i.e.*, the two tables of stone containing the Ten Commandments (ch. xxv. 16 ; xxxi. 18). **Set the staves on the ark.** "Put the staves," that is, "into the rings, and left them there" (ch. xxv. 14). **Put the mercy seat above upon the ark.** See ch. xxv. 21.

Ver. 21.—**Set up the veil of the covering**— *i.e.*, hung the veil on the four pillars between the holy place and the holy of holies, and thus **covered**—*i.e.*, concealed from sight, the ark of the testimony. (See the comment on ver. 3.)

Ver. 22.—**Upon the side of the tabernacle northward.** Upon the right hand, as one faced the veil. No direction had been given upon this point, but Moses probably knew the right position from the pattern which he had seen upon the mount.

Ver. 23.—**He set the bread in order upon it.** Upon the subject of this "order," see Lev. xxiv. 6—8, and compare the comment on ver. 4.

Ver. 24.—**Over against the table**—*i.e.*, exactly opposite to the table, on the left as one faced the veil.

Ver. 25.—When evening came, **he lighted the lamps.** (See the comment on ver. 4.) Whatever the priests ordinarily had to do was on this occasion done by Moses.

Ver. 26.—**The golden altar,** or "altar of incense," was placed **before the veil**—*i.e.*, outside it, in the holy place, midway between the table of shew-bread and the golden candlestick.

Ver. 28.—**He set up the hanging at the door.** He hung on the five pillars at the entrance to the tabernacle the "hanging" or "curtain," which had been made for the purpose (ch. xxxvi. 37).

Ver. 29.—**He put the altar of burnt-offering by the door of the tabernacle.** See the comment on ver. 6. **And offered upon it the burnt-offering and the meat-offering**—*i.e.*, in his priestly character inaugurated the altar by offering upon it the first evening sacrifice. (See ch. xxix. 38—41.)

Ver. 30.—**He set the laver.** As directed in ver. 7. For the position of the laver, see ch. xxx. 18.

Vers. 31, 32.—**Moses and Aaron and his sons washed their hands.** This is not a part of the narrative of what was done at this time, but a parenthetic statement of the purpose to which the laver was subsequently applied. On the importance attached to these ablutions, see ch. xxx. 20, 21.

Ver. 33.—**He reared up the court,** etc., as directed in ver. 8. **So Moses finished the work.** With the hanging of the curtain at the entrance to the court, the erection of the tabernacle was complete. It was probably not till after this that Moses performed the acts of worship mentioned in the course of the narrative—put water in the laver (ver. 30), offered sacrifice (ver. 29), lighted the lamps (ver. 25), and burnt incense on the golden altar (ver. 26).

HOMILETICS.

Vers. 1—33.—*The erection of the tabernacle.* At last the work of preparation was over. The work for which God had begun to give instructions more than nine months previously (ch. xxv. 1) was completed. All the parts of the structure, pillars, curtains, boards, sockets, bars, taches, hooks, pins; and all the furniture, ark, altars, table, candlestick, laver, vessels, censers, tongs, ash-pans—were finished and ready. All had been inspected by Moses, and approved (ch. xxxix. 43); they answered to the pattern which had been shown him in the mount (ch. xxv. 40). Still, however, Moses waited until he received from God:—1. The order for erection. 2. Instructions as to details.

I. THE ORDER FOR ERECTION. "On the first day of the first month shalt thou set up the tabernacle of the tent of the congregation" (ver. 2). The order included:—1. *The act.* "Set up the tabernacle." 2. *The agent.* "Thou"—*i.e.*, Moses. 3. *The time.* "The first day of the first month." Concerning the *act* there is nothing to be said. It was implied in the first order given, and lay at the root of every subsequent direction. The tabernacle could only have been devised in order to be set up. But concerning the agent and the time there was room for doubt. As to the *agent:* Bezaleel, the master craftsman, might have been chosen to erect what he had constructed; or Aaron might have been deputed to arrange the temple of which he was to be chief minister; or Moses and Aaron and Bezaleel might have been constituted a commission to carry out the work conjointly. But it pleased God to appoint Moses alone. For every enterprise it is best to have one directing mind, one ultimate authority. Otherwise there will be conflicting views, waste of time and energy, and commonly an inharmonious result. And Moses, who had alone seen "the pattern on the mount," was beyond all doubt the fittest director that could have been selected. As to the *time:* any day that was not a Sabbath would have been fairly suitable; but there seems an especial appropriateness in the selection of the first day of a new year. "To everything there is a season, and a time to every purpose under the heaven" (Eccles. vii. 1). A new year should begin with a good work. What better work for such a day than the opening of a Bethel—a house of God—a "tent of meeting," where God himself was to be met? God, who is the first, should have the first. First fruits of all things should be given to him. Thus, New Year's-day is a natural holy day. It opens the year. It is thus the most appropriate for openings.

II. INSTRUCTIONS AS TO DETAILS. A certain order had to be observed. God determined the order. First, the tabernacle itself was to be erected (ver. 2); then the ark was to be brought in and placed in the holy of holies (ver. 3); then the veil was to be hung up (*ib.*). After this the furniture of the holy place was to be brought in—the table of shewbread (ver. 4), the candlestick (*ib.*), and the altar of incense (ver. 5). Next, the hanging at the entrance to the tabernacle was to be put up (*ib.*) Lastly, the outer court and its furniture were to be taken in hand. The laver and altar of burnt offering were to be set in their places (vers. 6, 7); the pillars and hangings which enclosed the court were to be arranged, and the curtain hung at the entrance to it (ver. 8). The general law which pervades the whole is the precedence of the more important over the less important. We do not know what time intervened between the delivery of these instructions to Moses and "the first day of the second year"; but probably the interval was not long. Moses would employ it in selecting a site, and in preparing the artificers and others for the day's proceedings. When the appointed day arrived, he applied himself to the work (ver. 17). First, he stretched, by means of cords and tent-pins, probably on a light wooden framework, the tabernacle cloth of blue and purple and scarlet and fine twined linen (ch. xxvi. 1—6). Then he laid down the "sockets" of silver in their places, fitted the boards into them by means of their "tenons," put in the bars which kept the boards together, and reared up the pillars for the veil (ch. xl. 18). After this he stretched the goats'-hair covering, which constituted the tent, outside and above the tabernacle cloth, and placed over the goats'-hair covering the rams' skins and the seals' skins (ver. 19). So much constituted the erection of the tabernacle proper. Next he proceeded to the furniture; he brought in the ark and mercy seat, and, having placed them in the holy of holies (ver. 21), set up the vail; thus completing it, and isolating it from the holy place. After this, he brought in the furniture of the holy place—the table, the candlestick, and the golden altar—and arranged it (vers. 22 26). He then, and not till then, according to the direction given to him (ver. 5), put up the hanging which separated the tabernacle from the court (ver. 28). Finally, he proceeded to set in order the court. He put the altar of burnt offering and the laver into their places (vers. 29, 30), carried the hangings alongside the court's four sides, and arranged the curtain at the entrance (ver. 33). So, with a minute observance of the directions given, "Moses finished the work." Note the exactitude with which Moses followed all the directions given him, together with the liberty which he claimed and exercised:—1. To determine the time of their execution.　2. To fill up particulars with respect to which no directions had been given. 1. Of the first, the deferring of the consecration by anointment of the tabernacle and its furniture, and of the consecration of Aaron and his sons (vers. 9—15), is the crucial instance. It has been said that these may have taken place on the same day as the erection of the tabernacle; but the mode in which the narrative of the consecration is introduced in Lev. viii. 1—5, no less than the separation of the narrative from that of the present chapter, implies an interval between the two events. Probably, by the time of the completion of the court, the day was far advanced, and it would have been impossible to perform all the ceremonies commanded (ch. xxix. 1—36) in the remaining space.　2. Of the second, the emplacement of the table and the candlestick (vers. 22, 24), the burning of incense (ver. 27), and the offering upon the altar of burnt offering (ver. 29) are specimens. Evidently Moses considered that "God's instructions were not always to be carried out with literal exactness, but sometimes with an enlightened spiritual freedom."

Vers. 18—33.—*The sanctification of material things.* Objections are raised to the entire idea of a holiness in things. Holiness, it is said, being a personal quality, cannot reside in things, or be communicated to them, or be rightly predicated of them. God is holy; angels are holy; some men are holy; but nothing else. To imagine a holiness in things is superstition. This is to effect a complete severance of matter from spirit—to dig an abyss between them—to regard them as asymptotes, which cannot ever touch one the other. But if God became incarnate, if "the Word was made flesh" (John i. 14), then that matter which constituted the body of Christ, most certainly became holy. And if that matter, why not other matter? Why not the food which he "blessed and brake, and gave to his disciples"? Why not the drink which he called "his blood"? If there is a contact between matter and spirit, and some spirits are holy, then it is readily intelligible that the matter which comes into contact with them may be, in a certain sense, holy also. And this is, beyond all doubt, the language of the Scriptures. We hear of "holy ground" (ch. iii. 5), "holy places" (ch. xxvi. 33), "holy garments" (ch. xxviii. 2), "holy oil" (ch. xxx. 31), "a holy perfume" (*ib.* 35), etc. Things material may become holy in various ways, *e.g.*—

I. BY BEING TAKEN INTO GOD. Christ took our nature upon him, joined for ever the Manhood to the Eternal Godhead, and so gave to his own body an eternal sanctification of the highest possible kind, which renders it *most* holy.

II. BY BEING BROUGHT INTO CONTACT WITH HIM. The Cross of Christ, the crown of thorns, the nails, the soldier's spear, the raiment, the vesture, the napkin which was about his head when in the grave, became hallowed by association with him, and must ever be regarded by all Christians as holy. If the garment shown at Trèves were indeed what it professes to be—a garment once worn by Christ—it would well deserve the name, by which it is commonly called, of the "holy coat." As it is, we have no sufficient evidence of any existing piece of matter, that it ever came into contact with our Lord's blessed body; but, if we had, any such piece of matter would be "holy."

III. BY DESIGNATION FOR A HOLY PURPOSE. It is in this way especially that buildings, garments, vessels, cloths, and the like, are "holy." They are intended for and serve a holy purpose—are employed in the worship or service of Almighty God. It is felt on all hands that such things ought to be set apart from secular uses, reserved for the sacred end to which they have been designated, and applied to that only. Now, in cases of this kind, it does not appear to be inappropriate that the designation should be by a material act; and certainly no more significant act than anointing with oil is possible. For oil is symbolical of the Holy Spirit; and as it is by the Holy Spirit that individuals are sanctified, not only personally but officially, so as to be media of grace to others, so it may well be conceived that even inanimate things may become channels of grace and blessing to men, through an effluence from the same Spirit. The Holy Spirit does not disdain all contact with matter. At the beginning of creation he "moved," or rather brooded, "upon the face of the waters" (Gen. i. 2). At the baptism of Jesus, the Spirit was seen "descending like a dove, and lighting on him" (Matt. iv. 16). At Pentecost he showed himself in the form of "tongues of fire" (Acts ii. 3). In every consecration it is quite possible that he may bear a part, though in general he shrouds himself, and does not let his presence be perceived.

HOMILIES BY VARIOUS AUTHORS.

Vers. 1—33.—*The erection of the tabernacle.* I. THE TIME. 1. It reminded them of their deliverance from Egyptian bondage; "this month shall be unto you the beginning of months" (ch. xii. 2). God's dwelling-place is ever erected amid the adoring remembrance of his redemption. "The love of Christ constraineth us." 2. It was a consecration of the year upon which they were entering. It struck the key-note of the after time. The joy of the new year was to rise into the greater joy of the new life. The joy which hallows all time is that of reconciliation to, and union with, God.

II. THE ORDER OF CONSTRUCTION. 1. The tabernacle was first erected in which God was to be served. The duty to serve God is confessed before the power is attained or the way understood. (1) The emblem of the law in its strength and weakness. (2) The story of all the saved. 2. The tabernacle is next furnished, and the altar and laver and outer court set up. The means are given of reconciliation and service. It is not enough to be convinced of duty. God must be waited upon for power. His way must be taken. "No other foundation can any man lay." 3. All things are anointed with the holy oil. The spirit hallows and energizes all the means of grace which God has given. 4. The priests also are anointed; we, too, must be so in order to serve, and we shall be if we come, as they did, into the midst of what God has provided and sanctified for man's redemption.

III. THE ERECTION OF THE TABERNACLE WAS FOLLOWED BY ITS IMMEDIATE USE. So soon as the shew-bread table was placed, the bread was set in order upon it. The lamps were immediately lighted. He burnt sweet incense upon the altar before the veil. On the altar of sacrifice he offered burnt offering and meat offering. At the laver "Moses and Aaron and his sons washed their feet." Belief should follow fast upon the heels of knowledge. God has sent forth his salvation, not to be the subject of intellectual interest and theological speculation, but to touch and change the heart. The bread of life has been given to feed the perishing, not merely to be examined, weighed, analysed.—U.

Ver. 10.—*The altar most holy.* There is a difference at once perceptible between the words of sanctifying in ver. 9, and the words of sanctifying in ver. 10. Whereas the tabernacle and all therein are declared as *holy*, a special sanctity is somehow attached to the altar of burnt offering. "It shall be an altar most holy." The reasonable explanation of this is, not that there was any special sanctity in the altar of burnt offering itself, but that from its exterior position it was in great danger of being treated thoughtlessly, and therefore needed special attention to be called to it. Hence we are led to note the existence of a similar distinction among such things as we are bound to treat in a reverent and careful manner. Certain persons, things, and places are of such a kind as to be their own protection. Perhaps it is still true to some extent, though doubtless it was much more felt in former times, that there is a divinity which doth hedge a king. Men of coarse and scandalous tongues manage to put a check on themselves in the presence of women and children. Some are still alive who remember the horror and indignation excited by the resurrection-men of fifty or sixty years ago, and how little watch-houses were built in some churchyards, and men took it in turns to guard by night the resting-places of their beloved dead. But those who would shrink with loathing from the bare possibility that they could be guilty of such desecration are nevertheless found treating great realities of holiness with indifference, if not with contempt. Remember with what profaning hands the Holy One of God was abused; he who spake concerning the temple of his body; he who was holy, not by any mere association, not for the purposes of some temporary economy, but essentially holy. Are there not those who, thoughtless enough of all the evil they are doing, crucify the Son of God afresh, and put him to an open shame? (Heb. vi. 6.) What a fearful outlook is indicated for those who tread underfoot the Son of God, and count the blood of the covenant, wherewith they are sanctified, an unholy thing, and do despite unto the spirit of grace! (Heb. x. 29.) The very same thing may in one way be hallowed, and in another be desecrated. There is a great semblance of hallowing in the huge family Bibles so often seen in English houses, rich, and not unfrequently tawdry, in their binding and gilding; but after all they may only be there as part of a reputation for respectability. The true hallowing is in the dog's-eared, well-worn book, poorly printed it may be, and on common paper, and with that indefinable appearance about it which tells of constant use. It is only too easy a thing to put superstition in the place of an intelligent, diligent, profound, and practical reverence. Even Christians are strangely negligent concerning the holiness inherent in them if they are really born again. Very unobservant are they of the persistent references in the New Testament to the holiness of a Christian's personality. How much is done, as a matter of course, that is inconsistent, yea, scarcely compatible with being, indeed, a living sacrifice!—Y.

Vers. 1—33.—*The tabernacle set up.* The sanctuary did not take long in making. When hearts are willing, gifts liberal, and hands active, work is soon accomplished. Everything was ready by the first day of the new year after leaving Egypt. The new year was inaugurated by the setting up of the finished dwelling. How suitable an employment for the new year, to consecrate our *hearts* anew as dwelling-places for Jehovah! The section conveys lessons as to—

I. ORDER IN THE SANCTUARY. Every thing was done with order and deliberation. "Set the bread *in order*" (vers. 4, 23). "Let all things be done decently and in order" (1 Cor. xv. 40).

II. BEAUTY IN THE SANCTUARY. God's house, when completed, was a *beautiful* house. Cf. Is. lx. 13.

III. HOLINESS IN THE SANCTUARY. The place was holy. Moses consecrated it by anointing (vers. 9—12). Those who served in it were to be holy. This is signified by the wearing of "holy garments" (ver. 13), and by washing in the laver (ver. 31). Holiness becomes God's house (Ps. xciii. 5). His servants are to serve him in "beauties of holiness" (Ps. cx. 3).

IV. WORSHIP IN THE SANCTUARY. Moses set the bread in order on the table, lighted the lamps, burnt incense, etc. He offered burnt offerings and meat offerings on the altar (ver. 39). The tabernacle was a picture Gospel.—J. O.

Ver. 33.—*The two finishings.* "So Moses finished the work." Cf. ch. xxxix. 32—"Thus was all the work of the tabernacle finished." View the tabernacle as a type of the spiritual house—the Church. This tabernacle is being *made.* A time is coming when, in a more special sense, it will be *reared*,—the "day of Christ"—the day of "the manifestation of the sons of God" (Rom. viii. 19. Cf. Rev. xxi. 2, 3).

I. THE TABERNACLE WAS NOT REARED TILL ALL THE LABOURS IN CONNECTION WITH THE MAKING OF IT HAD BEEN FINISHED. 1. The tabernacle was made *with a view to* its being reared. This was the *end.* So the calling, saving, and perfecting of individuals for the kingdom of God has always reference to their ultimate manifestation with Christ in glory (Rom. viii. 17—26; 2 Cor. iv. 15—18; v. 1—11; Eph. v. 25—28; Phil. i. 6, 10; Col. iii. 1—4, etc.). 2. The labours of making were entirely *finished*, before the rearing was begun. The rearing was but the bringing into visibility of an already finished work. (1) All the *parts* of the tabernacle were made. (2) All the *furniture* of the tabernacle was made. (3) The *dress* of the *servants* of the tabernacle was made. Not till all this was done was the command given to rear. So the day of the manifestation of believers will not arrive till all labours preparatory to the setting up of the kingdom of God in glory have been concluded. The Gospel preached through all the world

(Matt. xxiv. 14), the "elect" (ver. 31) gathered in, the last soul saved, believers sanctified, every "living stone" (1 Pet. ii. 4) shaped and fashioned for the place it is ultimately to occupy in the heavenly building, etc. 3. These labours having been concluded, the rearing was proceeded with *without delay*. The rearing included (1) the putting of the parts of the tabernacle together. (2) The arrangement of its furniture. (3) The ordering of its service. So, when once the preparatory labours in connection with the kingdom of God have been finished, no time will be lost in setting it up in its final glory. Christ will appear, and his people will appear with him (Col. iii. 4). He and they will be glorified together (Rom. viii. 17). 4. The rearing of the tabernacle was the setting of it *in visible glory* before the eyes of the Israelites. So will Christ come to be "glorified in his saints, and admired in all them that believe" (2 Thess. i. 10). 5. The rearing of the tabernacle completed the preparation of it *as a sanctuary for Jehovah*. The same will be true of the glorification of the Church (Rev. xxi. 3, 4).

II. The tabernacle, made by the people, was reared by Moses. 1. Christ admits us to be fellow-workers with himself in the *labours* of his Church. These are carried on by human agency (2 Cor. vi. 1). 2. He alone has to do with the *glorification* of his Church.

III. When the tabernacle was reared, it was found that nothing was wanting to its perfection as a sanctuary. So will the glorification of the Church make manifest the beauty, symmetry, completeness, and perfection of the spiritual structure. It will be found to be "a glorious Church, not having spot, or wrinkle, or any such thing" (Eph. v. 27); complete as a place of habitation for Jehovah; a unity, and a perfect one.—J. O.

EXPOSITION.

Vers. 34—38.—The descent of the glory of God on the completed work. The work was finished—the first incense burnt (ver. 27)—the first sacrifice offered (ver. 29). Those who had watched the proceedings, and those who had been engaged in them, were probably about to retire to rest. Even Moses had withdrawn, and left the tabernacle to itself—when suddenly, there was a manifestation of Divine Power. The cloud, which had gone before the Israelites from Succoth onward (ch. xiii. 20—22), and which had recently settled upon the extemporised "Tent of Meeting" (ch. xxxiii. 9), left its place, and "covered" the newly-erected structure externally (ver. 34), while an intensely brilliant light—here called 'the glory of God"—filled the whole interior of the tabernacle (*ib.*). Moses, it appears, would fain have re-entered the tabernacle—to see the great sight" (ch. iii. 3); but he could not—the "glory" was too dazzling (ver. 35). Thus a distinct approval was given to all that had been done. God accepted his house, and entered it. The people saw that he had foregone his wrath, and would be content henceforth to dwell among them and journey with them. Henceforth, throughout the wanderings, the cloud and tabernacle were inseparable. If the cloud was lifted a little

off it and moved in front, the tabernacle had to follow (ver. 36)—if it settled down on the roof, the people stopped and remained until it moved again (ver. 37). The appearance was as of a cloud by day, and as of fire by night, so that all could always see where the tabernacle was, and whether it was stationary or in motion (ver. 38). After the first descent, it would seem that "the glory" withdrew into the Holy of Holies, so that both Moses and the priests could enter the holy place, and minister there (Lev. viii. 10 ; x. 13, etc.).

Ver. 34.—**Then a cloud.** In the original "*the* cloud," *i.e.* the cloud so often spoken of (ch. xiii. 21, 22 ; xiv. 19, 20, 24 ; xix. 9 ; xxiv. 15—18 ; xxxiii. 9, 10). **Covered the tent.** Descended on the outer covering and rested there. **Filled the tabernacle.** Entered inside, and filled both holy place and Holy of Holies.

Ver. 35.—**Moses was not able to enter.** It is implied that he wished—nay, tried—to enter —but the "glory" prevented him. (Compare 1 Kings viii. 11 ; 2 Chr. v. 14 ; vii. 2.) **Because the cloud abode thereon.** It was not the external "cloud" which prevented Moses from entering, but the internal "glory." But the two are regarded as inseparable.

Vers. 36—38.—**And when**—*i.e.* "whensoever." The last three verses describe the manner in which the cloud henceforth served the Israelites as guide—not only directing their course, but determining when they were to move, and how long they were to rest at each encampment. For a further account of the same, see Num. ix. 15—23.

Ver. 38.—The cloud ... was upon the taber-nacle by day and fire was on it by night. Compare ch. xiii. 21, 22 ; and ch. xiv. 20, 24 ; Num. ix. 15, 16. The cloud had two aspects —one obscure, the other radiant. It was a dark column by day—a pillar of fire by night. Thus it was always visible.

HOMILETICS.

Vers. 34—38.—*The symbols of God's presence.* I. GOD IS SEEN BY THOSE WHO UNFEIGNEDLY LOVE HIM AS PURE LIGHT. "I am the light of the world" (John viii. 12; ix. 5). "In him was life, and the life was the light of men" (*ib.* i. 4). "In him is no darkness at all" (1 John ii. 5). With clear unclouded radiance he shines on those who tread his heavenly courts, which need no other light besides him. "The city hath no need of the sun, neither of the moon, to shine in it; for the glory of God doth lighten it, and the Lamb is the light thereof" (Rev. xxi. 23). With a radiance not much less bright, he looks upon his saints on earth, cheering them, illumining their paths, making them glad with the light of his countenance. He may veil himself in condescension to their infirmity; but the veil is translucent; it covers without concealing; it tempers the brightness, but only as a thin haze tempers the splendours of the lord of day.

II. GOD SHOWS HIMSELF TO THE GENERALITY OF MEN AS MINGLED LIGHT AND CLOUD. To Abraham he appeared as "a smoking furnace and a burning lamp" (Gen. xv. 17); to the Israelites at Sinai as combined smoke and fire (Ex. xix. 18); to Solomon, dazzled by his glory, he was still one who "dwelt in the thick darkness" (1 Kings viii. 12). When Isaiah beheld him sitting in his temple "the house was filled with smoke" (Is. vi. 1—4); when Ezekiel "saw visions of God," he "looked and behold, a great cloud, and a fire infolding itself." Wherever the glory of the Lord is seen, wherever he looks upon men with mercy and compassion, there his proper symbolism is light, though it may be a light partially obscured and mingled with darkness. For darkness symbolises his anger; and in the case of his wayward children, he cannot but be at once compassionate and angry; displeased, yet anxious to forgive. Or the darkness may be the dense cloud of human ignorance which the Divine light can only partially pierce through. Any way, the bulk of men see God as a light amid smoke. "Clouds and darkness are round about him" (Ps. xcvii. 2)—"he makes darkness his secret place, his pavilion round about him with dark waters, and thick clouds to cover him" (*ib.* xviii. 11). Fire flashes out of the clouds occasionally; gleams of light stream forth; "at the brightness of his presence, his clouds remove" (*ib.* 12), and he is seen to be man's "true light."

III. GOD IS TO SOME MERE DARKNESS, A DENSE OPAQUE CLOUD. This he is:—1. To agnostics—to them who know him not, and refuse to believe that he can be known; 2. To them who have never heard of him, but have a dim unconscious feeling that some infinite unknown being exists; 3. To them that have been taught to view him as a remorseless, revengeful being, without pity or mercy; 4. To them that, having known him aright, have cast his words behind their back, thrown off his authority, and placed themselves in determined antagonism to his will and commandments. All is dark in the future to such persons ; and in the thought of God is "the blackness of darkness for ever." Because they have not chosen to retain God in their knowledge, God has given them over to a reprobate mind (Rom. i. 28). They "put bitter for sweet, and sweet for bitter." He, in whom is no darkness at all, is to them mere darkness. The God of this world has "blinded their eyes" that they cannot see ; and, like a blind man, looking at the sun, the darkness which is in their own vision they ascribe to the object which their dim sight fails to distinguish. God is "the true light, which lighteth every man that cometh into the world" (John i. 9). But "if the light that is within thee be darkness, how great is that darkness!" (Matt. vi. 23.)

HOMILIES BY VARIOUS AUTHORS.

Vers. 34—38.—*Indwelling and guidance.* I. GOD OWNS THE DWELLING-PLACE SET UP ACCORDING TO HIS COMMANDMENTS. "Then the cloud," etc. "And Moses was not able to enter in," etc.; it was claimed as his own and taken possession of by the Lord. 1. The soul which comes by God's way will be filled with God's glory. 2. The Church which honours God he will glorify. 3. The full glory of the perfected Church, the bride of Christ.

II. WHERE THE LORD DWELLS HE GUIDES. When the cloud was taken up they went onward; when it rested they rested. 1. He is our guide in our onward journey. (1) In providence. We must make sure that we follow him. It will not avail to choose our own way and then ask God to be with us. We are to follow his leading, not he ours. (2) In grace. We may be mourning departed joy. There may be no longer the freshness and power we once felt in the ministration of the word, or in prayer. We have been slumbering and loitering. We have not striven to press through our sins and into fuller light. The cloud has lifted and gone onward, and we must follow after. "This one thing I do." 2. He is our guide into patience. (1) He teaches us to bear and so to overcome. (2) By the resting of faith to possess and to grow.—U.

Vers. 34—38.—*The house filled with glory.* The close of the book of Exodus is worthy of the greatness of its subject. It ends where the history of the world will end, with the descent of Jehovah's glory to dwell with men (Rev. xxi. 3). We have seen Israel in bondage; have beheld its redemption; have followed it through the wilderness; have heard the thunders of the law at Sinai; have been witnesses of the nation's covenant with God; have seen its shameful apostasy; have traced the steps of its reconciliation; have heard the instructions given for the building of this tabernacle; have viewed the tabernacle itself. We see now the symbol of Jehovah's glorious presence in the midst of the people whom he has thus in so many ways made his own. What a wondrous succession of subjects we have thus had before us in the course of our review. The intolerable anguish of oppressed Israel; the birth of the deliverer; the singular providence of his early life; his great choice; the call in Midian; the revelation of the name; the return to Egypt; first failures; the long and tragic contest with Pharaoh; the hardening of Pharaoh's heart; the exodus; the Red Sea; the miracles of the desert; the law; the covenant; the "patterns" shown to Moses in the mount; the sin of the calf; the great intercession; the name of mercy; the preparation of the sanctuary. There remains to complete the series only this final scene of the entrance of Jehovah's glory into the house prepared for his habitation. This was the true consecration of the sanctuary, and the true consecration of the nation. "A cloud covered the tent of the congregation, and the glory of the Lord filled the tabernacle" (ver. 14). In what is related in these verses we have:—

I. A THREEFOLD PRIVILEGE. 1. *Indwelling.* The filling of the tabernacle with the glory was the symbol of Jehovah's taking up his abode in it, and so in Israel (cf. ch. xxv. 8). It testified (1) to the completeness of his reconciliation with the people. Cf. Is. xii. 1—"O Lord, I will praise thee, though thou wast angry with me, thine anger is turned away, and thou comfortedst me." (2) To his complacency in the beautiful house they had reared for him. Cf. Ps. cxxxii. 14—"This is my rest for ever, here will I dwell; for I have desired it." (3) To his desire to dwell among them. Note—1. The true glory of the Church is God's residence in her midst. This was Israel's highest distinction (ch. xxxiii. 16). 2. We should pray that the time may come when the Church shall be, not only dwelt in by her Lord, but "filled" with the "glory" of his presence (Is. lx.). 2. *Protection.* The glory filled the tabernacle within, while the cloud spread itself above the tent as a protective covering without. So is Jehovah the protection of his Church (Is. iv. 5, 6; Zech. ii. 5). 3. *Guidance* (vers. 36—38). See Homily on ch. xiii. 21, 22.

II. A HINT OF IMPERFECTION. "Moses was not able to enter into the tent of the congregation," etc. (ver. 35). Thus are we reminded that, amidst all these glorious circumstances, that which is perfect is not yet come. 1. Law, not gospel. 2. A material building, not a spiritual house. 3. Earth, not heaven. It was a glory (1) too great for man to see.   Even Moses, who had seen so much of the Divine glory, was not able to look upon it.   (2) Too great for such a building—a mere material structure —to contain.   Man longs for nearer communion.   So great a glory needs a better house to contain it—a spiritual (1 Pet. ii. 5).

III. A FORECAST OF WHAT SHALL BE.   That which is perfect is not yet come, but it will come by-and-by.   1. The tabernacle of God will be with men, and he will dwell among them (Rev. xxi. 3, 4).   His glory will fill it.   "The glory of God did lighten it, and the Lamb is the light thereof" (Rev. xxi. 23).   2. This glory will be no longer unapproachable.   We shall be able to endure the sight.   "His servants shall serve him, and they shall see his face" (Rev. xxii. 3, 4).   We shall receive the Vision.   3. This, however, will only be when earthly conditions have been exchanged for heavenly. "This corruptible must put on incorruption, and this mortal must put on immortality" (1 Cor. xv. 53).   Till that hour arrives, we must be content to "walk by faith, not by sight" (2 Cor. v. 7), seeing only "as through a glass darkly" (1 Cor. xiii. 12).—J. O.

THE END.

HOMILETICAL INDEX

TO

THE BOOK OF EXODUS

——◆◆——

VOLUME II.